How To Use This Book

GUIDE TO CORRECT GRAMMAR

For simple, practical information on punctuation, grammar, and letter-writing, as well as guidance to the correct use of English today, consult *The Guide to Correct Grammar* beginning on page 551.

RAPID VOCABULARY BUILDER

For a concise guide on how to increase the range and effectiveness of your vocabulary, consult *The Rapid Vocabulary Builder* beginning on page 563.

DICTIONARY OF THE ENGLISH LANGUAGE

All material in this dictionary is included in a single alphabetical list for quick and easy reference.

Common meanings of words are given first and all definitions are individually numbered.

The pronunciation system is simple, accurate, and easily understood. It is the same system used in training radio announcers to speak naturally and distinctly.

Words are defined under their commonest spelling, and alternative spellings are shown whenever necessary.

The syllables of words are separated by a small dot, as an aid to those wishing to know how to divide a word at the end of a line.

Plurals of nouns, past tenses and participles of verbs, and comparatives and superlatives of adjectives and adverbs are given when they are irregular or difficult.

Wherever helpful, words or meanings are labeled regionally as *U.S.*, *Scot.*, etc.; technically as *Chem.*, *Naut.*, *Theat.*, *Elect.*, etc.; or functionally as *Slang*, *Poetic*, etc.

Pictorial illustrations and spot maps have been included wherever they will help to make the meaning clearer.

Signs and symbols and tables of weights and measures will be found on the end pages at the back of the book.

The American Everyday Dictionary

THE
AMERICAN
EVERYDAY
DICTIONARY

Edited by Jess Stein

Managing Editor of

The American College Dictionary

RANDOM HOUSE · NEW YORK

78

PREFACE

MORE THAN 300,000,000 people in the world speak English today. Yet it is highly doubtful that any two people have completely identical vocabularies. Our vocabularies overlap but never coincide exactly. To understand one another more perfectly, we turn to the dictionary, for the dictionary is an instrument by which exact understanding in language is achieved.

In this dictionary we have included all the everyday words and meanings, together with the less common words that the average person might occasionally use. Special attention has been given to new words and meanings, many of which have never before appeared in dictionaries of comparable scope and size. The text is based on *The American College Dictionary*, edited by Clarence L. Barnhart with the assistance of more than 350 recognized authorities in over 70 universities. The ACD has been widely hailed as the best desk dictionary ever published, and we believe that this abridgment will be favorably received as a compact version of the ACD.

The value of this book has been enhanced by the special sections at the back, one by Harrison Platt on English usage and one by S. Stephenson Smith on vocabulary building.

This dictionary has been prepared by the permanent lexicographic staff of Random House, Inc., the major burden of assistance being borne by Nancy Rayfiel, Elizabeth Gedney Christensen, Leonore Crary, and John Wasley.

JESS STEIN

A

A, a (ā), *n.*, *pl.* **A's** or **As, a's** or **as.** **1.** the first letter of the English alphabet. **2.** *U.S.* the highest mark for school or college work. **3.** *Music.* the sixth tone in the scale of C major.

a[1] (ā; *unstressed* ə), *adj. or indef. article (before words beginning with consonant sounds).* **1.** some (referring to one individual of a class). **2.** another. **3.** one. **4.** any (a single). **5.** indefinite plural: *a few.*

a[2] (ā; *unstressed* ə), *adj. or indef. article.* each.

A, 1. *Chem.* argon. **2.** *Physics.* angstrom unit.

a., 1. about. **2.** acre; acres. **3.** adjective.

Aa·chen (ä'kən), *n.* a city in western Germany. 162,164.

aard·vark (ärd'värk'), *n.* a large, nocturnal, burrowing mammal of Africa, subsisting largely on termites, and having a long tongue and long ears.

Aar·on (âr'ən), *n.* the first high priest of the Hebrews and the brother of Moses.

Ab, *Chem.* alabamine.

ab., 1. about. **2.** *Baseball.* (times) at bat.

Aardvark
(overall length 5 to 6 ft.)

A.B., 1. (L *Artium Baccalaureus*) Bachelor of Arts. **2.** able-bodied (seaman).

a·ba·cá (ä'bä kä'), *n.* **1.** a Philippine plant. **2.** the fiber of this plant, used in making hemp.

a·back (ə băk'), *adv.* **1.** taken aback, suddenly disconcerted. **2.** with the wind blowing against the forward side of a sail or sails.

ab·a·cus (ăb'ə kəs), *n.*, *pl.* **-cuses, -ci** (-sī'). **1.** a contrivance for calculating, consisting of beads on wires in a frame. **2.** *Archit.* a slab forming the top of the capital of a column.

a·baft (ə băft', ə bäft'), *Naut.* —*prep.* **1.** in the rear of. —*adv.* **2.** at or toward the stern; aft.

ab·a·lo·ne (ăb'ə lō'nē), *n.* a large snail having a bowllike shell. The flesh is used for food.

a·ban·don[1] (ə băn'dən), *v.t.* **1.** to leave completely and finally; forsake utterly. **2.** to give up all concern in. **3.** to give up the control of. **4.** to yield unrestrainedly. —**a·ban'don·ment,** *n.*

a·ban·don[2] (ə băn'dən), *n.* freedom from constraint or conventionality.

a·ban·doned (ə băn'dənd), *adj.* **1.** forsaken. **2.** unrestrained. **3.** shamelessly wicked.

a·base (ə bās'), *v.t.*, **abased, abasing.** to reduce or lower, as in rank. —**a·base'ment,** *n.*

a·bash (ə băsh'), *v.t.* to make ashamed or embarrassed. —**a·bash'ment,** *n.*

a·bate (ə bāt'), *v.t.*, *v.i.*, **abated, abating. 1.** to reduce in amount, etc.; lessen. **2.** *Law.* to put an end to; suspend; annul. —**a·bate'ment,** *n.*

ab·at·toir (ăb'ə twär'), *n.* a slaughterhouse.

ab·ba·cy (ăb'ə sī'), *n.*, *pl.* **-cies.** an abbot's office, rights, privileges, or jurisdiction.

ab·bé (ăb'ā), *n.* an abbot or priest.

ab·bess (ăb'ĭs), *n.* the superior of a convent.

ab·bey (ăb'ĭ), *n.*, *pl.* **-beys. 1.** a monastery or convent. **2.** the monastic buildings. **3.** the church of an abbey.

ab·bot (ăb'ət), *n.* the head of a monastery.

abbr., abbreviation. Also, **abbrev.**

ab·bre·vi·ate (ə brē'vĭ āt'), *v.t.*, **-ated, -ating.** to make shorter by contraction or omission.

ab·bre·vi·a·tion (ə brē'vĭ ā'shən), *n.* **1.** a shortened or contracted form of a word or phrase. **2.** reduction in length; abridgment.

Ab·di·as (ăb dī'əs), *n.* Obadiah (Douay).

ab·di·cate (ăb'də kāt'), *v.t.*, **-cated, -cating.** —*v.i.* **1.** to renounce or relinquish a throne, a right, etc. —*v.t.* **2.** to renounce (office, duties, etc.). —**ab'di·ca'tion,** *n.*

ab·do·men (ăb'də mən, ăb dō'-), *n.* **1.** that part of the body of a mammal between the thorax and the pelvis, containing most of the digestive organs. **2.** (in animals below mammals) any region of the body corresponding to the human abdomen. —**ab·dom·i·nal** (ăb dŏm'ə nəl), *adj.*

ab·duct (ăb dŭkt'), *v.t.* to carry off surreptitiously or by force, esp. to kidnap. —**ab·duc'tion,** *n.* —**ab·duc'tor,** *n.*

a·beam (ə bēm'), *adv. Naut.* at right angles to the keel of a ship.

a·bed (ə bĕd'), *adv.* in bed.

A·bel (ā'bəl), *n. Bible.* the second son of Adam and Eve, slain by his brother, Cain.

Ab·é·lard (ăb'ə lärd'), *n.* **Pierre,** 1079–1142, French scholastic philosopher.

Ab·er·deen (ăb'ər dēn'), *n.* a seaport in NE Scotland. 178,200.

ab·er·rant (ăb ĕr'ənt), *adj.* **1.** straying from the right course. **2.** deviating from normal.

ab·er·ra·tion (ăb'ə rā'shən), *n.* **1.** act of wandering from the normal course. **2.** deviation from truth or rectitude. **3.** lapse from a sound mental state. **4.** *Optics.* any disturbance of the rays of a pencil of light so that they cannot be focused.

a·bet (ə bĕt'), *v.t.*, **abetted, abetting.** to encourage or countenance by aid or approval. —**a·bet'ment,** *n.* —**a·bet'tor, a·bet'ter,** *n.*

a·bey·ance (ə bā'əns), *n.* temporary inactivity.

ab·hor (ăb hôr'), *v.t.*, **-horred, -horring.** to regard with repugnance; loathe. —**ab·hor'rer,** *n.*

ab·hor·rence (ăb hôr'əns, -hŏr'-), *n.* **1.** extreme repugnance. **2.** something detested.

ab·hor·rent (ăb hôr'ənt, -hŏr'-), *adj.* extremely repugnant. —**ab·hor'rent·ly,** *adv.*

a·bide (ə bīd'), *v.*, **abode** or **abided, abiding.** —*v.i.* **1.** to remain; stay. **2.** to dwell; reside. **3.** to continue in a certain condition. **4. abide by, a.** to stand by. **b.** to await the consequences of. —*v.t.* **5.** to wait for. **6.** *Colloq.* to tolerate.

a·bid·ing (ə bī'dĭng), *adj.* steadfast.

a·bil·i·ty (ə bĭl'ə tĭ), *n.*, *pl.* **-ties. 1.** power or capacity to do or act in any relation. **2.** competence in any field of action. **3.** (*pl.*) talents.

ab·ject (ăb'jĕkt, ăb jĕkt'), *adj.* **1.** utterly humiliating. **2.** despicable. —**ab'ject·ly,** *adv.*

ab·jure (ăb jōōr'), *v.t.*, **-jured, -juring. 1.** to renounce or repudiate; retract. **2.** to renounce upon oath; forswear. —**ab·ju·ra·tion** (ăb'jōō rā'shən), *n.* —**ab·jur'er,** *n.*

abl., ablative.

ab·la·tive (ăb'lə tĭv), *Gram.* —*adj.* **1.** (in some inflected languages) denoting a case which has among its functions the indication of place from which, means, etc. —*n.* **2.** the ablative case.

a·blaze (ə blāz'), *adv.* **1.** on fire. —*adj.* **2.** gleaming. **3.** excited. **4.** very angry.

a·ble (ā'bəl), *adj.*, **abler, ablest. 1.** having sufficient power, strength, or qualifications; qualified. **2.** having unusual intellectual qualifications. **3.** showing talent or knowledge. —**a·bly** (ā'blĭ), *adv.*

-able, a suffix used to form adjectives, esp. from verbs, to denote ability, liability, tendency, worthiness, or likelihood, as in *teachable.*

a·ble-bod·ied (ā'bəl bŏd'ĭd), *adj.* physically competent.

able-bodied seaman, an experienced seaman who has passed certain tests.

ab·lu·tion (ăb lōō'shən), *n.* **1.** a cleansing with water or other liquid, as in ceremonial purification. **2.** the liquid used.

ab·ne·gate (ăb'nə gāt'), *v.t.*, **-gated, -gating.** to deny to oneself; reject. —**ab'ne·ga'tion,** *n.*

ab·nor·mal (ăb nôr'məl), *adj.* not typical, usual, or average. —**ab·nor'mal·ly,** *adv.*

ab·nor·mal·i·ty (ăb'nôr măl'ə tĭ), *n.*, *pl.* **-ties. 1.** an abnormal thing or event. **2.** deviation from the standard, rule, or type.

a·board (ə bōrd'), *adv.* **1.** on board; on or in a ship, etc. **2.** alongside. —*prep.* **3.** on board of.

a·bode (ə bōd'), *n.* **1.** a dwelling place. **2.** sojourn; stay. —*v.* **3.** pt. and pp. of **abide.**

a·bol·ish (ə bŏl'ĭsh), *v.t.* to put an end to; annul or make void. —**a·bol'ish·ment,** *n.*

ab·o·li·tion (ăb/ə lĭsh/ən), n. 1. annulment; abrogation. 2. the legal extinction of slavery. —ab/o·li/tion·ist, n.

A-bomb (ā/bŏm/), n. atomic bomb.

a·bom·i·na·ble (ə bŏm/ə nə bəl), adj. detestable; loathsome. —a·bom/i·na·ble·ness, n. —a·bom/i·na·bly, adv.

a·bom·i·nate (ə bŏm/ə nāt/), v.t., -nated, -nating. 1. to regard with intense aversion; abhor. 2. to dislike strongly. —a·bom/i·na/tor, n.

a·bom·i·na·tion (ə bŏm/ə nā/shən), n. 1. an object greatly disliked or abhorred. 2. intense aversion. 3. a detestable action.

ab·o·rig·i·nal (ăb/ə rĭj/ə nəl), adj. 1. pertaining to aborigines. 2. original; indigenous. —n. 3. an aborigine. —ab/o·rig/i·nal·ly, adv.

ab·o·rig·i·nes (ăb/ə rĭj/ə nēz/), n., pl. of aborigine. original inhabitants of a country.

a·bor·tion (ə bôr/shən), n. 1. the expulsion of a human fetus before it is viable. 2. any premature failure.

a·bor·tion·ist (ə bôr/shən ĭst), n. one who produces a criminal abortion.

a·bor·tive (ə bôr/tĭv), adj. 1. failing to succeed. 2. born prematurely. 3. imperfectly developed. 4. Med. producing abortion.

a·bound (ə bound/), v.i. 1. to be in great plenty. 2. to be rich. 3. to be filled; teem.

a·bout (ə bout/), prep. 1. of; concerning. 2. connected with. 3. somewhere near or in. 4. close to. 5. on every side of. 6. on or near (one's person). 7. on the point of (fol. by an infinitive). 8. here and there in or on. —adv. 9. approximately. 10. Colloq. nearly; almost. 11. nearby. 12. on every side; in every direction. 13. half round. 14. to and fro; here and there. 15. in rotation or succession. 16. on the move.

a·bout-face (n. ə bout/fās/; v. ə bout/fās/), n., v., -faced, -facing. —n. 1. a sudden reversal in principle, etc. —v.i. 2. to turn in the opposite direction.

a·bove (ə bŭv/), adv. 1. in or to a higher place; overhead. 2. higher in rank or power. 3. before in order, esp. in a book. 4. in heaven. —prep. 5. in or to a higher place than. 6. more in quantity or number than. 7. superior to. —adj. 8. foregoing. —n. 9. the above, the aforesaid part.

a·bove·board (ə bŭv/bôrd/), adv., adj. in open sight; without tricks or disguise.

ab·ra·ca·dab·ra (ăb/rə kə dăb/rə), n. 1. a mystical word used in incantations, etc. 2. any word charm. 3. gibberish.

a·brade (ə brād/), v.t., v.i. abraded, abrading. to wear off or down by friction; scrape off.

A·bra·ham (ā/brə hăm/, -həm), n. Bible. the first patriarch: founder of Hebrew people.

a·bra·sion (ə brā/zhən), n. 1. an abraded spot or place. 2. act or process of abrading.

a·bra·sive (ə brā/sĭv, -zĭv), n. 1. any material used for grinding, polishing, etc., as emery or sand. —adj. 2. tending to produce abrasion.

a·breast (ə brĕst/), adv., adj. 1. side by side. 2. alongside in progress or attainment.

a·bridge (ə brĭj/), v.t., abridged, abridging. 1. to shorten, as by condensation. 2. to lessen.

a·bridg·ment (ə brĭj/mənt), n. 1. a condensation, as of a book; a reproduction in reduced form. 2. act of abridging. Also, esp. Brit., a·bridge/ment.

a·broad (ə brôd/), adv. 1. in a foreign country or countries. 2. outdoors. 3. astir; in circulation. 4. broadly; widely. 5. wide of the truth.

ab·ro·gate (ăb/rə gāt/), v.t., -gated, -gating. to abolish; annul; repeal. —ab/ro·ga/tion, n.

a·brupt (ə brŭpt/), adj. 1. terminating or changing suddenly. 2. sudden; unceremonious. 3. having sudden transitions. 4. steep; precipitous. —ab·rupt/ly, adv. —ab·rupt/ness, n.

ab·scess (ăb/sĕs), n. a localized collection of pus in the tissues of the body. —ab/scessed, adj.

ab·scis·sa (ăb sĭs/ə), n., pl. -scissas, -scissae (-sĭs/ē). Math. the x-coördinate of a point, i.e., its horizontal distance from the y-axis measured parallel to the x-axis.

Abscissa: P, any point; AP or OB, abscissa of P; XX, axis of abscissa; YY, axis of the ordinate

ab·scond (ăb skŏnd/), v.i. to depart in a sudden and secret manner, esp. to avoid legal process.

ab·sence (ăb/səns), n. 1. state or period of being away. 2. lack.

ab·sent (adj. ăb/sənt; v. ăb sĕnt/), adj. 1. not present; away. 2. lacking. 3. absent-minded. —v.t. 4. to take or keep (oneself) away.

ab·sen·tee (ăb/sən tē/), n. 1. one who is absent. 2. one who is away from his property, post, etc. —ab/sen·tee/ism, n.

ab·sent-mind·ed (ăb/sənt mīn/dĭd), adj. forgetful; preoccupied. —ab/sent-mind/ed·ly, adv. —ab/sent-mind/ed·ness, n.

ab·sinthe (ăb/sĭnth), n. 1. a strong, bitter, green-colored, aromatic liqueur. 2. wormwood (def. 1). Also, ab/sinth.

ab·so·lute (ăb/sə lōōt/), adj. 1. complete; perfect. 2. not mixed; pure. 3. free from restriction; unqualified. 4. arbitrary or despotic. 5. viewed independently. 6. positive. 7. Gram. a. syntactically independent. b. (of a transitive verb) used with no object expressed. —n. 8. the absolute, the ultimate ground of all things. —ab·so·lute·ly (ăb/sə lōōt/lĭ; emphatic ăb/sə lōōt/lĭ), adv. —ab/so·lute/ness, n.

absolute zero, the lowest possible temperature which the nature of matter admits.

ab·so·lu·tion (ăb/sə lōō/shən), n. 1. act of absolving; release from consequences. 2. state of being absolved. 3. Rom. Cath. Theol. a remission of sin or of the punishment due to sin. 4. Prot. Theol. a declaration of divine forgiveness to penitent believers.

ab·so·lut·ism (ăb/sə lōō tĭz/əm), n. the principle or the exercise of absolute power in government. —ab/so·lut/ist, n.

ab·solve (ăb sŏlv/, -zŏlv/), v.t., -solved, -solving. 1. to free from the consequences attaching to actions. 2. to set free or release. 3. to grant pardon for. 4. to grant remission of sins to.

ab·sorb (ăb sôrb/, -zôrb/), v.t. 1. to swallow up the identity or individuality of. 2. to engross wholly. 3. to suck up or drink in (liquids). 4. to take in without echo or recoil.

ab·sorbed (ăb sôrbd/, -zôrbd/), adj. engrossed.

ab·sorb·ent (ăb sôr/bənt, -zôr/-), adj. 1. capable of absorbing. —n. 2. a thing that absorbs. —ab·sorb/en·cy, n.

ab·sorb·ing (ăb sôr/bĭng, -zôr/-), adj. engrossing. —ab·sorb/ing·ly, adv.

ab·sorp·tion (ăb sôrp/shən, -zôrp/-), n. 1. assimilation. 2. passage of substances to the blood, lymph, and cells, as from the alimentary canal. 3. preoccupation. —ab·sorp/tive, adj.

ab·stain (ăb stān/), v.i. to refrain voluntarily. —ab·stain/er, n.

ab·ste·mi·ous (ăb stē/mĭ əs), adj. 1. moderate in the use of food and drink; temperate. 2. characterized by abstinence. 3. sparing. —ab·ste/mi·ous·ly, adv. —ab·ste/mi·ous·ness, n.

ab·sten·tion (ăb stĕn/shən), n. a refraining; abstinence from action. —ab·sten/tious, adj.

ab·sti·nence (ăb/stə nəns), n. 1. forbearance from any indulgence of appetite, esp. from alcoholic liquors. 2. restraint. —ab/sti·nent, adj.

ab·stract (adj. ăb/străkt, ăb străkt/; n. ăb/străkt; v. ăb străkt/ for 8-11, ăb/străkt for 12), adj. 1. conceived apart from matter and from special cases. 2. theoretical; not applied. 3. difficult to understand. 4. of or pertaining to nonrepresentational art. —n. 5. a summary of a statement, etc. 6. the essence. 7. in the abstract, without reference to particular applications. —v.t. 8. to draw or take away; remove. 9. to withdraw or divert (the attention). 10. to steal. 11. to consider as a general object apart from special circumstances. 12. to summarize. —ab/stract·ly, adv. —ab/stract·ness, n.

ab·stract·ed (ăb străk/tĭd), adj. lost in thought; preoccupied. —ab·stract/ed·ly, adv.

ab·strac·tion (ăb străk/shən), n. 1. an abstract idea or term. 2. a visionary idea. 3. act of considering something as a general object apart from special circumstances. 4. act of taking away or separating. 5. absent-mindedness.

ab·struse (ăb strōōs/), adj. difficult; esoteric. —ab·struse/ly, adv. —ab·struse/ness, n.

ab·surd (ăb sûrd/, -zûrd/), adj. ridiculous. —ab·surd/ly, adv. —ab·surd/ness, n.

ab·surd·i·ty (ăb sûr/də tĭ, -zûr/-), n., pl. -ties. 1. absurd state or quality. 2. something absurd.

a·bun·dance (ə bŭn/dəns), n. 1. an overflowing quantity or supply. 2. overflowing fullness.

a·bun·dant (ə bŭn/dənt), adj. 1. present in great quantity. 2. full. —a·bun/dant·ly, adv.

a·buse (v. ə būz/; n. ə būs/), v., abused, abus-

ing, *n.* —*v.t.* **1.** to use wrongly or improperly. **2.** to do wrong to. **3.** to revile; malign. —*n.* **4.** wrong or improper use. **5.** insulting language. **6.** ill-treatment of a person. **7.** corrupt practice.

a·bu·sive (ə bū/sĭv), *adj.* **1.** using harsh words or ill-treatment. **2.** characterized by or containing abuse. **3.** corrupt. —**a·bu/sive·ly,** *adv.*

a·but (ə bŭt/), *v.i.*, **abutted, abutting.** to be adjacent to (often fol. by *on, upon,* or *against*).

a·but·ment (ə bŭt/mənt), *n.* **1.** that part of a structure which receives, sustains, or resists pressure. **2.** the place where projecting parts meet.

a·byss (ə bĭs/), *n.* **1.** a bottomless or deep, immeasurable space. **2.** anything profound and unfathomable. **3.** hell. Also, **a·bysm** (ə bĭz/əm). —**a·bys/mal,** *adj.* —**a·bys/mal·ly,** *adv.*

Ab·ys·sin·i·a (ăb/ə sĭn/ĭ ə), *n.* Ethiopia.

Ac, *Chem.* actinium.

A.C., *Elect.* alternating current. Also, **a.c.**

a·ca·cia (ə kā/shə), *n.* **1.** any of certain trees or shrubs of the mimosa family, native in warm regions. **2.** the locust tree. **3.** gum arabic.

ac·a·dem·ic (ăk/ə dĕm/ĭk), *adj.* **1.** pertaining to an advanced institution of learning, as a college. **2.** *U.S.* pertaining to the classical, mathematical, and general literary departments of a college. **3.** theoretical. **4.** conventional. Also, **ac/a·dem/i·cal.** —**ac/a·dem/i·cal·ly,** *adv.*

academic freedom, freedom of a teacher to discuss social, economic, or political problems.

a·cad·e·my (ə kăd/ə mǐ), *n.,* *pl.* **-mies. 1.** a secondary school, esp. a private one. **2.** a school for instruction in a particular art or science. **3.** an association or institution for the promotion of literature, science, or art. **4.** **the Academy,** the public grove in Athens, in which Plato taught.

A·ca·di·a (ə kā/dĭ ə), *n.* a former French colony in SE Canada: ceded to Great Britain, 1713.

a·can·thus (ə kăn/thəs), *n.,* *pl.* **-thuses, -thi** (-thī). **1.** a Mediterranean plant with large spiny or toothed leaves. **2.** an architectural ornament resembling the leaves of this plant.

a cap·pel·la (ä/ kə pĕl/ə), *Music.* without instrumental accompaniment.

acc., **1.** account. **2.** accusative.

ac·cede (ăk sēd/), *v.i.,* **-ceded, -ceding. 1.** to give consent; agree; yield. **2.** to attain.

accel., accelerando.

ac·cel·er·an·do (ăk sĕl/ə răn/dō), *adv.,* *adj.* *Music.* gradually increasing in speed.

ac·cel·er·ate (ăk sĕl/ə rāt/), *v.,* **-ated, -ating.** —*v.t.* **1.** to cause to move or advance faster. **2.** to bring about more speedily. **3.** to increase or change the velocity of (a body) or the rate of (motion). —*v.i.* **4.** to increase in speed.

ac·cel·er·a·tion (ăk sĕl/ə rā/shən), *n.* **1.** act of accelerating. **2.** a change in velocity.

ac·cel·er·a·tor (ăk sĕl/ə rā/tər), *n.* **1.** one that accelerates. **2.** *Auto.* a device for opening and closing the throttle, esp. by the foot.

ac·cent (*n.* ăk/sĕnt; *v.* ăk/sĕnt, ăk sĕnt/), *n.* **1.** the distinctive character of a vowel or syllable determined by its degree or pattern of stress or musical tone. **2.** any one of the degrees or patterns of stress used as essential features of vowels, syllables, or words. **3.** a mark indicating stress, musical tone, or vowel quality. **4.** *Pros.* **a.** regularly recurring stress. **b.** a mark indicating stress. **5.** characteristic style of pronunciation. **6.** *Music.* **a.** stress or emphasis given to certain notes. **b.** a mark denoting this. **c.** stress or emphasis regularly recurring as a feature of rhythm. **7.** words or tones expressive of some emotion. **8.** (*pl.*) *Poetic.* words; language. **9.** distinctive character or tone. —*v.t.* **10.** to pronounce or mark (a vowel, syllable, or word) with one of the distinctive accents. **11.** to emphasize.

ac·cen·tu·al (ăk sĕn/chŏŏ əl), *adj.* pertaining to accent; rhythmical. —**ac·cen/tu·al·ly,** *adv.*

ac·cen·tu·ate (ăk sĕn/chŏŏ āt/), *v.t.,* **-ated, -ating. 1.** to emphasize. **2.** to mark or pronounce with an accent. —**ac·cen/tu·a/tion,** *n.*

ac·cept (ăk sĕpt/), *v.t.* **1.** to take or receive with approval or favor. **2.** to agree to; assent to. **3.** to take with formal acknowledgment of responsibility. **4.** to accommodate oneself to. **5.** to believe. —*v.i.* **6.** to accept an invitation, gift, position, etc. —**ac·cept/er, ac·cep/tor,** *n.*

ac·cept·a·ble (ăk sĕp/tə bəl), *adj.* **1.** capable or worthy of being accepted. **2.** pleasing to the receiver; agreeable. —**ac·cept/a·bil/i·ty, ac·cept/a·ble·ness,** *n.* —**ac·cept/a·bly,** *adv.*

ac·cept·ance (ăk sĕp/təns), *n.* **1.** act of taking or receiving something offered. **2.** favorable reception. **3.** act of assenting or believing. **4.** fact or state of being accepted. **5.** *Com.* an order, etc., which a person has accepted for payment.

ac·cep·ta·tion (ăk/sĕp tā/shən), *n.* **1.** favorable regard. **2.** belief. **3.** usual meaning.

ac·cess (ăk/sĕs), *n.* **1.** act or privilege of coming to; admittance; approach. **2.** approachability; accessibility. **3.** way or eans of approach. **4.** an attack, as of disease. **5.** outburst of passion.

ac·ces·sa·ry (ăk sĕs/ə rĭ), *n.,* *pl.* **-ries,** *adj.* *Chiefly Law.* accessory. —**ac·ces/sa·ri·ly,** *adv.*

ac·ces·si·ble (ăk sĕs/ə bəl), *adj.* **1.** easy to reach; approachable. **2.** obtainable; available. **3.** open to the influence of (fol. by *to*). —**ac·ces/si·bil/i·ty,** *n.* —**ac·ces/si·bly,** *adv.*

ac·ces·sion (ăk sĕsh/ən), *n.* **1.** act of coming into the possession of a right, office, etc. **2.** an increase by something added. **3.** thing added.

ac·ces·so·ry (ăk sĕs/ə rĭ), *n., pl.* **-ries,** *adj.* —*n.* **1.** a subordinate part or object added for convenience, attractiveness, etc. **2.** *Law.* one who, without being present at its commission, is guilty of aiding or abetting another who commits a felony. —*adj.* **3.** contributing to a general effect.

ac·ci·dence (ăk/sə dəns), *n.* **1.** the rudiments of any subject. **2.** *Gram.* that part of morphology dealing with inflection.

ac·ci·dent (ăk/sə dənt), *n.* **1.** an undesirable or unfortunate happening; mishap. **2.** anything that happens unexpectedly, without design, or by chance. **3.** the operation of chance. **4.** a nonessential circumstance.

ac·ci·den·tal (ăk/sə dĕn/təl), *adj.* **1.** happening by chance or accident, or unexpectedly. **2.** nonessential; subsidiary. **3.** *Music.* relating to or indicating sharps, flats, or naturals. —*n.* **4.** a nonessential or subsidiary circumstance or feature. **5.** *Music.* a sign before a note indicating a change of its pitch. —**ac/ci·den/tal·ly,** *adv.*

ac·claim (ə klām/), *v.t.* **1.** to salute with words or sounds of joy or approval; applaud. **2.** to announce or proclaim by acclamation. —*v.i.* **3.** to make acclamation. —*n.* **4.** act of acclaiming.

ac·cla·ma·tion (ăk/lə mā/shən), *n.* **1.** a shout or other demonstration of welcome, applause, etc. **2.** acclaim. **3.** an oral vote, often unanimous.

ac·cli·mate (ə klī/mĭt, ăk/lə māt/), *v.t.,* *v.i.,* **-mated, -mating.** *Chiefly U.S.* to habituate or become habituated to a new climate or environment. —**ac·cli·ma·tion** (ăk/lə mā/shən), *n.*

ac·cli·ma·tize (ə klī/mə tīz/), *v.t.,* *v.i.,* **-tized, -tizing.** *Chiefly Brit.* to acclimate. —**ac·cli/ma·ti·za/tion,** *n.*

ac·cliv·i·ty (ə klĭv/ə tĭ), *n.,* *pl.* **-ties.** an upward slope, as of ground.

ac·co·lade (ăk/ə lād/, -lād/), *n.* **1.** a ceremony used in conferring knighthood. **2.** any honor.

ac·com·mo·date (ə kŏm/ə dāt/), *v.t.,* **-dated, -dating. 1.** to do a kindness or favor to; oblige. **2.** to provide suitably; supply (fol. by *with*). **3.** to provide with room and sometimes with food, etc. **4.** to make suitable; adapt. **5.** to reconcile. **6.** to furnish with accommodations.

ac·com·mo·dat·ing (ə kŏm/ə dā/tĭng), *adj.* obliging. —**ac·com/mo·dat/ing·ly,** *adv.*

ac·com·mo·da·tion (ə kŏm/ə dā/shən), *n.* **1.** act of accommodating; state or process of being accommodated; adaptation. **2.** adjustment of differences; reconciliation. **3.** anything which supplies a want; a convenience. **4.** (*chiefly pl.*) lodging, or food and lodging. **5.** readiness to aid others. **6.** *U.S.* a loan.

ac·com·pa·ni·ment (ə kŭm/pə nĭ mənt), *n.* **1.** something incidental or added for ornament, etc. **2.** *Music.* subsidiary music to enhance or aid the main voice or instrument parts.

ac·com·pa·nist (ə kŭm/pə nĭst), *n.* *Music.* one who plays an accompaniment.

ac·com·pa·ny (ə kŭm/pə nĭ), *v.t.,* **-nied, -nying. 1.** to go along with. **2.** to exist in company with. **3.** to put in company with; associate. **4.** *Music.* to play or sing an accompaniment to.

ac·com·plice (ə kŏm/plĭs), *n.* an associate in a crime; partner in wrongdoing.

ac·com·plish (ə kŏm/plĭsh), *v.t.* to bring to pass; perform; finish. —**ac·com/plish·ment,** *n.*

ac·com·plished (ə kŏm/plĭsht), *adj.* **1.** completed; effected. **2.** perfected; expert.

ac·cord (ə kôrd/), *v.i.* **1.** to be in harmony; agree. —*v.t.* **2.** to make to agree; adapt. **3.** to grant; concede. —*n.* **4.** harmony. **5.** agreement.

ac·cord·ance (ə kôr/dəns), *n.* agreement; conformity. —**ac·cord/ant,** *adj.*

ac·cord·ing (ə kôr/dĭng), *adv.* **1.** according **to, a.** in accordance with. **b.** proportionately.

c. on the authority of; as stated by. **2.** according as, proportionally as. —*adj.* **3.** agreeing.

ac·cord·ing·ly (ə kôr′dĭng lĭ′), *adv.* **1.** in accordance. **2.** in due course; therefore; so.

ac·cor·di·on (ə kôr′dĭ ən), *n.* **1.** a portable, keyed, bellowslike wind instrument sounded by means of metallic reeds. —*adj.* **2.** having folds like the bellows of an accordion. —**ac·cor′di·on·ist,** *n.*

ac·cost (ə kôst′, ə kŏst′), *v.t.* to approach, esp. with a greeting or remark.

ac·count (ə kount′), *n.* **1.** a verbal or written recital of events; narrative. **2.** an explanatory statement of conduct, as to a superior. **3.** a statement of reasons, causes, etc., explaining some event. **4.** reason; consideration (prec. by *on*). **5.** consequence; importance. **6.** estimation; judgment. **7.** profit; advantage. **8.** on account of, **a.** because of. **b.** for the sake of. **9.** a statement of pecuniary transactions. **10.** *Bookkeeping.* **a.** a formal record of the debits and credits relating to the person named (or caption placed) at the head of the ledger account. **b.** a balance of a specified period's receipts and expenditures. —*v.i.* **11.** to give an explanation. **12.** to answer concerning one's conduct, duties, etc. **13.** to render an account, esp. of money. **14.** to cause death, capture, etc. —*v.t.* **15.** to consider as.

ac·count·a·ble (ə koun′tə bəl), *adj.* **1.** liable; responsible. **2.** that can be explained. —**ac·count′a·bil′i·ty,** *n.* —**ac·count′a·bly,** *adv.*

ac·count·an·cy (ə koun′tən sĭ′), *n.* the art or practice of an accountant.

ac·count·ant (ə koun′tənt), *n.* a person whose profession is inspecting business accounts.

ac·count·ing (ə koun′tĭng), *n.* the theory and system of setting up, maintaining, and auditing the books of a firm.

ac·cou·ter (ə kōō′tər), *v.t.* to equip or array.

ac·cou·ter·ments (ə kōō′tər mənts), *n.pl.* **1.** equipage; trappings. **2.** the equipment of a soldier except arms and clothing.

ac·cred·it (ə krĕd′ĭt), *v.t.* **1.** to ascribe or attribute to (fol. by *with*). **2.** to attribute. **3.** to send with credentials. **4.** to certify as meeting official requirements. **5.** to invest with credit or authority. **6.** to believe.

ac·cre·tion (ə krē′shən), *n.* **1.** an increase by natural growth or gradual external addition. **2.** the result of this process. **3.** an extraneous addition. **4.** the growing together of separate parts.

ac·cru·al (ə krōō′əl), *n.* **1.** act or process of accruing. **2.** something accrued; accretion.

ac·crue (ə krōō′), *v.i.*, **-crued, -cruing.** to happen or result as a natural growth.

acct., account.

ac·cu·mu·late (ə kū′myə lāt′), *v.*, **-lated, -lating.** —*v.t.* **1.** to heap up; gather as into a mass; collect. —*v.i.* **2.** to grow, as into a heap.

ac·cu·mu·la·tion (ə kū′myə lā′shən), *n.* **1.** a collecting together. **2.** that which is accumulated. **3.** growth by continuous additions.

ac·cu·mu·la·tive (ə kū′myə lā′tĭv), *adj.* tending to or arising from accumulation. —**ac·cu′mu·la·tive·ly,** *adv.*

ac·cu·mu·la·tor (ə kū′myə lā′tər), *n.* **1.** one that accumulates. **2.** *Brit.* a storage battery.

ac·cu·ra·cy (ăk′yə rə sĭ′), *n.* condition or quality of being accurate; precision; correctness.

ac·cu·rate (ăk′yə rĭt), *adj.* free from error or defect. —**ac′cu·rate·ly,** *adv.* —**ac′cu·rate·ness,** *n.*

ac·curs·ed (ə kûr′sĭd, ə kûrst′), *adj.* **1.** subject to a curse. **2.** detestable. Also, **ac·curst′.**

ac·cu·sa·tion (ăk′yŏŏ zā′shən), *n.* **1.** a charge of guilt or blame. **2.** the specific offense charged.

ac·cu·sa·tive (ə kū′zə tĭv), *adj.* **1.** (in Greek, Latin, and English grammar) denoting a case which has as one of its chief functions the indication of the direct object of a finite verb. —*n.* **2.** the accusative case. **3.** a word in that case.

ac·cu·sa·to·ry (ə kū′zə tōr′ĭ), *adj.* accusing.

ac·cuse (ə kūz′), *v.t.*, **-cused, -cusing.** to charge with the fault or crime. —**ac·cus′er,** *n.*

ac·cus·tom (ə kŭs′təm), *v.t.* to habituate.

ac·cus·tomed (ə kŭs′təmd), *adj.* **1.** customary; habitual. **2.** in the habit of.

ace (ās), *n.* **1.** a single spot or mark on a card or die. **2.** a card or die marked with a single spot. **3.** (in tennis, badminton, etc.) **a.** a serve which the opponent fails to touch. **b.** the point thus scored. **4.** a very small amount or degree; particle. **5.** a highly skilled person; an expert. **6.** a fighter pilot officially credited with shooting down five or more enemy airplanes. —*adj.* **7.** excellent.

a·cer·bi·ty (ə sûr′bə tĭ′), *n., pl.* **-ties. 1.** sourness, with roughness or astringency of taste. **2.** harshness or severity, as of expression.

ac·et·an·i·lide (ăs′ə tăn′ə lĭd′, -lĭd), *n.* an organic compound, C_8H_9ON, used as a remedy for fever, etc. Also, **ac·et·an·i·lid** (ăs′ə tăn′ə lĭd).

ac·e·tate (ăs′ə tāt′), *n.* *Chem.* a salt or ester of acetic acid.

acetate rayon, a rayon made from the acetic ester of cellulose, differing from viscose rayon in having a greater strength when wet.

a·ce·tic (ə sē′tĭk, ə sĕt′ĭk), *adj.* pertaining to, derived from, or producing vinegar or acetic acid.

acetic acid, a colorless liquid, CH_3COOH, the essential constituent of vinegar, used in the production of solvents and flavoring agents.

a·cet·y·lene (ə sĕt′ə lēn′), *n.* a colorless gas, C_2H_2, prepared by the action of water on calcium carbide, used in metal welding, etc.

ace·tyl·sal·i·cyl·ic acid (ăs′ə tĭl săl′ə sĭl′ĭk, ə sē′təl-), aspirin.

ace·y·deuc·y (ā′sĭ dū′sĭ, -dōō′-), *n.* a form of backgammon.

ache (āk), *v.*, **ached, aching,** *n.* —*v.i.* **1.** to suffer pain, esp. continued pain. **2.** *Colloq.* to yearn; long. —*n.* **3.** continued pain.

a·chene (ā kēn′), *n.* *Bot.* a small, dry, hard, one-seeded, indehiscent fruit.

Ach·er·on (ăk′ə rŏn′), *n.* **1.** *Gk. and Rom. Myth.* a river in Hades, over which Charon ferried the souls of the dead. **2.** the lower world; hell.

a·chieve (ə chēv′), *v.*, **achieved, achieving.** —*v.t.* **1.** to bring to a successful end; accomplish. **2.** to bring about, as by effort; obtain. —*v.i.* **3.** to bring about a result. —**a·chiev′a·ble,** *adj.*

a·chieve·ment (ə chēv′mənt), *n.* **1.** something accomplished. **2.** act of achieving.

A·chil·les (ə kĭl′ēz), *n.* *Gk. Legend.* the hero of Homer's *Iliad,* the greatest Greek warrior in the Trojan war.

Achilles heel, a vulnerable spot.

Achilles' tendon, *Anat.* the tendon joining the calf muscles to the heelbone.

ach·ro·mat·ic (ăk′rə măt′ĭk), *adj.* *Optics.* free from color due to the decomposition of light in chromatic aberration.

ac·id (ăs′ĭd), *n.* **1.** *Chem.* a compound containing hydrogen which can be replaced by a metal or an electropositive radical to form a salt. **2.** a sour substance. —*adj.* **3.** *Chem.* **a.** belonging or pertaining to acids or the anhydrides of acids. **b.** having only a part of the hydrogen of an acid replaced by a metal or its equivalent. **4.** tasting like vinegar. **5.** sour; sharp. —**ac′id·ly,** *adv.*

a·cid·ic (ə sĭd′ĭk), *adj.* **1.** *Petrog.* containing a large amount of silica. **2.** *Chem.* acid-forming.

a·cid·i·fy (ə sĭd′ə fī′), *v.t., v.i.,* **-fied, -fying.** to make or become acid. —**a·cid′i·fi·ca′tion,** *n.*

a·cid·i·ty (ə sĭd′ə tĭ′), *n., pl.* **-ties.** **1.** quality of being acid. **2.** excessive acid quality.

ac·i·do·sis (ăs′ə dō′sĭs), *n.* *Pathol.* poisoning by acids forming under morbid conditions.

acid test, a critical test; final analysis.

a·cid·u·late (ə sĭj′ə lāt′), *v.t.,* **-lated, -lating.** **1.** to make somewhat acid. **2.** to sour; embitter.

a·cid·u·lous (ə sĭj′ə ləs), *adj.* **1.** slightly sour. **2.** sharp; caustic.

-acious, an adjective suffix made by adding **-ous** to nouns ending in **-acity** (the **-ty** being dropped), as *audacious.*

-acity, a suffix for nouns denoting quality, etc.

ack-ack (ăk′ăk′), *n.* *Slang.* anti-aircraft fire.

ac·knowl·edge (ăk nŏl′ĭj), *v.t.,* **-edged, -edging.** **1.** to admit the existence, truth, or fact of. **2.** to express recognition or realization of. **3.** to recognize the authority or claims of. **4.** to indicate appreciation for. **5.** to admit the receipt of. —**ac·knowl′edg·ment,** *n.*

ac·me (ăk′mĭ), *n.* the highest point.

ac·ne (ăk′nĭ), *n.* an inflammatory disease of the sebaceous glands, characterized by eruptions.

ac·o·lyte (ăk′ə līt′), *n.* **1.** an altar attendant of minor rank. **2.** *Rom. Cath. Ch.* a member of the highest of the minor orders. **3.** an attendant.

A·con·ca·gua (ä′kŏn kä′gwä), *n.* a mountain in W Argentina, in the Andes: the highest peak in the Western Hemisphere. 23,003 ft.

ac·o·nite (ăk′ə nīt′), *n.* **1.** any plant of the genus *Aconitum,* including plants with poisonous and medicinal properties, as monkshood or wolfsbane. **2.** an extract or tincture from the root of any of these plants.

a·corn (ā′kôrn, ā′kərn), *n.* the fruit of the oak, a nut in a hardened scaly cup.

a·cous·tic (ə kōōs′tĭk *or, esp. Brit.,* ə kous′-), *adj.* pertaining to the sense or organs of hearing, or to the science of sound. Also, **a·cous′ti·cal.** —**a·cous′ti·cal·ly,** *adv.*

a·cous·tics (ə kōōs′tĭks *or, esp. Brit.,* ə kous′-), *n.* **1.** *Physics.* the science of sound. **2.** (*construed as pl.*) acoustic properties, as of an auditorium.

ac·quaint (ə kwānt′), *v.t.* **1.** to make familiar or conversant (fol. by *with*). **2.** to inform.

ac·quaint·ance (ə kwän′təns), *n.* **1.** a person known to one, usually only slightly. **2.** state of being acquainted. —**ac·quaint′ance·ship′,** *n.*

ac·quaint·ed (ə kwān′tĭd), *adj.* having personal knowledge (fol. by *with*).

ac·qui·esce (ăk′wĭ ĕs′), *v.i.,* **-esced, -escing.** to assent tacitly; comply quietly; agree.

ac·qui·es·cence (ăk′wĭ ĕs′əns), *n.* act or condition of acquiescing. —**ac′qui·es′cent,** *adj.*

ac·quire (ə kwīr′), *v.t.,* **-quired, -quiring.** to come into possession of; get as one's own.

ac·quire·ment (ə kwīr′mənt), *n.* **1.** act of acquiring. **2.** (*often pl.*) that which is acquired.

ac·qui·si·tion (ăk′wə zĭsh′ən), *n.* **1.** act of acquiring. **2.** something acquired.

ac·quis·i·tive (ə kwĭz′ə tĭv), *adj.* tending to make acquisitions. —**ac·quis′i·tive·ness,** *n.*

ac·quit (ə kwĭt′), *v.t.,* **-quitted, -quitting. 1.** to relieve from a charge of fault or crime. **2. acquit oneself,** to behave oneself.

ac·quit·tal (ə kwĭt′əl), *n.* **1.** act of acquitting. **2.** state of being acquitted.

ac·quit·tance (ə kwĭt′əns), *n.* **1.** act of acquitting. **2.** discharge of or from debt, etc.

a·cre (ā′kər), *n.* **1.** a unit of land measure, now equal to ¹/₆₄₀ sq. mile. **2.** (*pl.*) fields.

A·cre (ā′kər, ä′kər), *n.* a seaport in NW Palestine: captured during the Third Crusade. 12,360.

a·cre·age (ā′kər ĭj), *n.* acres collectively.

ac·rid (ăk′rĭd), *adj.* **1.** sharp or biting to the taste. **2.** violent; stinging. —**ac′rid·ly,** *adv.*

ac·ri·mo·ni·ous (ăk′rə mō′nĭ əs), *adj.* caustic; stinging; bitter. —**ac′ri·mo′ni·ous·ly,** *adv.*

ac·ri·mo·ny (ăk′rə mō′nĭ), *n., pl.* **-nies.** sharpness or severity of temper or expression.

ac·ro·bat (ăk′rə băt′), *n.* a skilled performer on a tightrope, trapeze, etc. —**ac′ro·bat′ic,** *adj.*

ac·ro·bat·ics (ăk′rə băt′ĭks), *n.pl.* the feats of an acrobat; gymnastics.

ac·ro·meg·a·ly (ăk′rō mĕg′ə lĭ), *n. Pathol.* a chronic nervous disease characterized by enlargement of the head, feet, hands, etc.

ac·ro·nym (ăk′rə nĭm), *n.* a word formed from the initial letters of other words.

a·crop·o·lis (ə krŏp′ə lĭs), *n.* **1.** the citadel of an ancient Greek city. **2. the Acropolis,** the citadel of Athens.

a·cross (ə krôs′, ə krŏs′), *prep.* **1.** from side to side of. **2.** on the other side of. **3.** so as to meet with. —*adv.* **4.** *U.S.* from one side to another. **5.** *U.S.* on the other side. **6.** crosswise. **7.** *U.S. Colloq.* so as to pay or own up.

a·cros·tic (ə krôs′tĭk, ə krŏs′-), *n.* a series of lines or verses in which the first, last, or other particular letters form a word, phrase, etc.

act (ăkt), *n.* **1.** anything done; deed. **2.** the process of doing. **3.** a decree, edict, law, statute, judgment, resolve, or award. **4.** a deed or instrument recording a transaction. **5.** one of the main divisions of a play or opera. **6.** an individual part in a variety show, radio program, etc. —*v.i.* **7.** to do something; exert energy or force. **8.** to perform specific duties or functions. **9.** to produce effect. **10.** to behave. **11.** to pretend. **12.** to perform as an actor. **13.** to serve or substitute (fol. by *for*). **14. act on** or **upon, a.** to follow. **b.** to affect. —*v.t.* **15.** to represent (a character). **16.** to feign. **17.** to behave as.

act·ing (ăk′tĭng), *adj.* serving temporarily.

ac·tin·ic (ăk tĭn′ĭk), *adj.* **1.** pertaining to actinism. **2.** (of radiation) chemically active.

ac·tin·ism (ăk′tə nĭz′əm), *n.* the action or the property of radiant energy of producing chemical change, as in photography.

ac·tin·i·um (ăk tĭn′ĭ əm), *n. Chem.* a radioactive chemical element, occurring in pitchblende. Symbol: Ac; at. no.: 89; at. wt.: 227.

ac·ti·noid (ăk′tə noid′), *adj.* raylike; radiate, as a starfish.

ac·tion (ăk′shən), *n.* **1.** process or state of acting or of being active. **2.** something done; deed. **3.** (*pl.*) conduct. **4.** energetic activity. **5.** an exertion of power or force. **6.** way or manner of moving. **7.** the mechanism by which something is operated. **8.** a small battle. **9.** military and naval combat. **10.** the main subject or story. **11.** *Law.* a proceeding instituted against another.

ac·tion·a·ble (ăk′shən ə bəl), *adj.* **1.** furnishing ground for a law suit. **2.** liable to a law suit. —**ac′tion·a·bly,** *adv.*

ac·ti·vate (ăk′tə vāt′), *v.t.,* **-vated, -vating. 1.** to make active. **2.** *Physics.* to render radioactive. **3.** to aerate (sewage) as a purification measure. **4.** *Chem.* **a.** to make more active. **b.** to hasten. —**ac′ti·va′tion,** *n.* —**ac′ti·va′tor,** *n.*

ac·tive (ăk′tĭv), *adj.* **1.** in actual progress or motion. **2.** constantly engaged in action; busy. **3.** nimble. **4.** brisk; lively. **5.** causing change; exerting influence. **6.** *Gram.* denoting a voice of verb inflection, in which the subject is represented as performing the action expressed by the verb. **7.** requiring action; practical. **8.** (of a volcano) in eruption. **9.** *Accounting.* profitable; busy. —*n.* **10.** *Gram.* the active voice. —**ac′tive·ly,** *adv.* —**ac′tive·ness,** *n.*

ac·tiv·i·ty (ăk tĭv′ə tĭ), *n., pl.* **-ties. 1.** state of action; doing. **2.** quality of acting promptly; energy. **3.** a specific deed or action. **4.** an active force, movement, or operation. **5.** liveliness.

ac·tor (ăk′tər), *n.* **1.** one who represents fictitious or historical characters in a play, motion picture, broadcast, etc. **2.** one who acts; doer.

ac·tress (ăk′trĭs), *n.* a female actor.

Acts of the Apostles, the fifth book in the New Testament. Also, **Acts.**

ac·tu·al (ăk′chŏō əl), *adj.* **1.** existing in act or fact; real. **2.** present. —**ac′tu·al·ness,** *n.*

ac·tu·al·i·ty (ăk′chŏō ăl′ə tĭ), *n., pl.* **-ties. 1.** actual existence; reality. **2.** (*pl.*) actual conditions or circumstances; facts.

ac·tu·al·ize (ăk′chŏō ə līz′), *v.t.,* **-ized, -izing.** to make actual; realize in action or fact.

ac·tu·al·ly (ăk′chŏō ə lĭ), *adv.* really.

ac·tu·ar·y (ăk′chŏō ĕr′ĭ), *n., pl.* **-aries.** *Insurance.* an officer who computes risks, rates, and the like. —**ac·tu·ar·i·al** (ăk′chŏō âr′ĭ əl), *adj.*

ac·tu·ate (ăk′chŏō āt′), *v.t.,* **-ated, -ating. 1.** to incite to action. **2.** to put into action. —**ac′tu·a′tion,** *n.*

a·cu·men (ə kū′mən), *n.* quickness of perception; mental acuteness; keenness of insight.

a·cute (ə kūt′), *adj.* **1.** sharp at the end; ending in a point. **2.** sharp in effect; intense. **3.** severe; crucial. **4.** brief and severe, as disease. **5.** sharp or penetrating in intellect. **6.** having quick sensibility. **7.** high in pitch, as sound. **8.** *Geom., etc.* (of an angle) less than 90°. **9.** *Gram.* designating or having a particular accent (′) indicating stress, quality of sound, etc. —*n.* **10.** the acute accent. —**a·cute′ly,** *adv.* —**a·cute′ness,** *n.*

-acy, a suffix of nouns of quality, state, office, etc., as in *efficacy, advocacy, accuracy,* etc.

ad (ăd), *n. Colloq.* advertisement.

A.D., (L *anno Domini*) since Christ was born.

ad·age (ăd′ĭj), *n.* a proverb.

a·da·gio (ə dä′jō, -zhĭ ō′), *adv., adj., n., pl.* **-gios.** *Music, etc.* —*adv.* **1.** in a leisurely manner. —*adj.* **2.** slow. —*n.* **3.** an adagio piece.

Ad·am (ăd′əm), *n. Bible.* the name of the first man, the progenitor of the human race.

ad·a·mant (ăd′ə mănt′ *or, esp. Brit.,* -mənt), *n.* **1.** (in ancient times) an imaginary impenetrably hard substance. **2.** any impenetrably hard substance. —*adj.* **3.** hard as adamant.

ad·a·man·tine (ăd′ə măn′tĭn, -tēn, -tīn), *adj.* **1.** impenetrable. **2.** like a diamond in luster.

Ad·ams (ăd′əmz), *n.* **1. Charles Francis,** 1807–86, U.S. statesman (son of John Quincy Adams). **2. Henry** (**Brooks**), 1838–1918, U.S. historian, writer, and teacher (son of Charles Francis Adams). **3. John,** 1735–1826, second president of the U.S., 1797–1801. **4. John Quincy** (kwĭn′sĭ), 1767–1848, sixth president of the U.S., 1825–1829 (son of John Adams). **5. Samuel,** 1722–1803, leader in the American Revolution.

Adam's apple, a projection of the thyroid cartilage at the front of the (male) throat.

a·dapt (ə dăpt′), *v.t.* to make suitable to requirements; adjust. —**a·dapt′er,** *n.*

a·dapt·a·ble (ə dăp′tə bəl), *adj.* **1.** capable of being adapted. **2.** able to adapt oneself easily. —**a·dapt′a·bil′i·ty, a·dapt′a·ble·ness,** *n.*

ad·ap·ta·tion (ăd′əp tā′shən), *n.* **1.** act of adapting. **2.** state of being adapted; adjustment. **3.** something produced by adapting. **4.** *Biol.* alteration in the structure or function of organisms which fits them to survive and multiply in a changed environment.

a·dap·tive (ə dăp′tĭv), *adj.* serving to adapt.

A.D.C., aide-de-camp.

add (ăd), *v.t.* **1.** to unite or join, so as to increase the number, size, etc. **2.** to find the sum of (often fol. by *up*). **3.** to say or write further. **4.** to include (fol. by *in*). —*v.i.* **5.** to find sums arithmetically. **6.** to be or serve as an addition (fol. by *to*). **7.** to make the desired or expected total. —**add/a·ble,** *adj.* —**add/er,** *n.*

ad·dax (ăd/ăks), *n.* a large, pale-colored antelope of North Africa, with loosely spiral horns.

ad·dend (ăd/ĕnd, ə dĕnd/), *n.* a part of a sum.

ad·den·dum (ə dĕn/dəm), *n., pl.* **-da** (-də). **1.** a thing to be added. **2.** an appendix to a book.

ad·der (ăd/ər), *n.* the common European viper, a small venomous snake.

ad·dict (*n.* ăd/ĭkt; *v.* ə dĭkt/), *n.* **1.** one who is addicted to a practice or habit. —*v.t.* **2.** to give (oneself) over, as to a habit. —**ad·dict/ed,** *adj.* —**ad·dic·tion** (ə dĭk/shən), *n.*

Ad·dis A·ba·ba (ăd/ĭs ä/bə bä/), the capital of Ethiopia, in the central part. 300,000.

Ad·di·son (ăd/ə sən), *n.* **Joseph,** 1672–1719, British essayist and poet.

ad·di·tion (ə dĭsh/ən), *n.* **1.** act or process of adding. **2.** the process of uniting two or more numbers into one sum, denoted by the symbol +. **3.** anything added. **4. in addition to,** besides. —**ad·di/tion·al,** *adj.* —**ad·di/tion·al·ly,** *adv.*

ad·dle (ăd/əl), *v.,* **-dled, -dling,** —*v.t., v.i.* **1.** to make or become confused. **2.** to spoil, as eggs. —*adj.* **3.** confused; muddled. **4.** rotten.

ad·dress (*n.* ə drĕs/, ăd/rĕs; *v.* ə drĕs/), *n., v.,* **-dressed** or **-drest, -dressing.** —*n.* **1.** a formal speech or writing directed to someone. **2.** a direction as to name and residence inscribed on a letter, etc. **3.** a place where a person lives or may be reached. **4.** manner of speaking to persons. **5.** skillful management; ready skill. **6.** (*usually pl.*) courtship. —*v.t.* **7.** to direct speech or writing to. **8.** to direct to the attention. **9.** to apply in speech. **10.** to direct for delivery. **11.** to apply (oneself). **12.** *Golf.* to adjust the club to (the ball) in preparing for a stroke.

ad·dress·ee (ə drĕ sē/, ăd/rĕ-), *n.* *U.S.* one to whom anything is addressed.

ad·duce (ə dūs/, ə dōōs/), *v.t.,* **-duced, -ducing.** to offer in argument; cite as conclusive.

Ad·e·laide (ăd/ə lād/), *n.* a city in S Australia. 350,000.

A·den (ä/dən, ā/-), *n.* **1.** a British protectorate in SW Arabia. ab. 600,-000 pop.; ab. 112,000 sq. mi. **2.** a British colony adjoining this protectorate. 45;992 pop.; 77 sq. mi. **3.** the capital of this protectorate and colony. ab. 33,000. **4. Gulf of,** an arm of the Arabian Sea S of the Arabian peninsula.

Aden (defs. 1, 2)

ad·e·noid (ăd/ə noid/), *n.* **1.** (*usually pl.*) an enlarged mass of tissue in the upper pharynx, often preventing nasal breathing. —*adj.* **2.** Also, **ad/e·noi/dal.** pertaining to the lymphatic glands.

ad·ept (*n.* ăd/ĕpt, ə dĕpt/; *adj.* ə dĕpt/), *n.* **1.** one fully skilled in anything. —*adj.* **2.** well-skilled. —**a·dept/ly,** *adv.* —**a·dept/ness,** *n.*

ad·e·qua·cy (ăd/ə kwə sĭ), *n.* sufficiency.

ad·e·quate (ăd/ə kwĭt), *adj.* fully sufficient, suitable, or fit. —**ad/e·quate·ly,** *adv.*

ad·here (ăd hĭr/), *v.i.,* **-hered, -hering. 1.** to stick fast; cling. **2.** to be attached as a follower or upholder. **3.** to hold closely or firmly.

ad·her·ence (ăd hĭr/əns), *n.* **1.** quality of adhering; fidelity. **2.** act or state of adhering.

ad·her·ent (ăd hĭr/ənt), *n.* **1.** one who follows or upholds a leader, etc. —*adj.* **2.** adhering.

ad·he·sion (ăd hē/zhən), *n.* **1.** act or state of adhering. **2.** steady attachment of the mind or feelings. **3.** assent. **4.** *Physics.* the molecular force exerted across the surface of contact between unlike liquids and solids which resist their separation.

ad·he·sive (ăd hē/sĭv), *adj.* **1.** clinging; sticking fast. **2.** gummed. —*n.* **3.** an adhesive plaster, bandage, etc. —**ad·he/sive·ness,** *n.*

a·dieu (ə dū/, ə dōō/), *interj., n., pl.* **adieus, adieux** (ə dūz/, ə dōōz/). —*interj.* **1.** good-by; farewell. —*n.* **2.** a farewell.

a·dios (ä dyôs/), *interj.* *Spanish.* good-by.

ad·i·pose (ăd/ə pōs/), *adj.* fatty; consisting of, resembling, or having relation to fat. —**ad/i·pose/ness, ad·i·pos·i·ty** (ăd/ə pŏs/ə tĭ), *n.*

Ad·i·ron·dack Mountains (ăd/ə rŏn/dăk), a mountain range in NE New York. Highest peak, Mt. Marcy, 5344 ft. Also, **Adirondacks.**

adj., 1. adjective. **2.** adjourned. **3.** adjutant.

ad·ja·cen·cy (ə jā/sən sĭ), *n.* adjacent state.

ad·ja·cent (ə jā/sənt), *adj.* lying near, close, or contiguous; adjoining. —**ad·ja/cent·ly,** *adv.*

ad·jec·tive (ăj/ĭk tĭv), *n.* **1.** *Gram.* **a.** one of the major form classes, or parts of speech, of many languages, comprising words used to qualify or limit a noun. **b.** such a word, as *wise* in *a wise ruler.* —*adj.* **2.** *Gram.* pertaining to or functioning as an adjective. —**ad·jec·ti·val** (ăj/ĭk-tī/vəl), *adj.* —**ad/jec·ti/val·ly,** *adv.*

ad·join (ə join/), *v.t., v.i.* to be in connection or contact (with). —**ad·join/ing,** *adj.*

ad·journ (ə jûrn/), *v.t.* **1.** to suspend the meeting of (a court, club, etc.) to a future day or to another place. **2.** to postpone. —*v.i.* **3.** to postpone proceedings. —**ad·journ/ment,** *n.*

adjt., adjutant.

ad·judge (ə jŭj/), *v.t.,* **-judged, -judging. 1.** to pronounce formally; decree. **2.** to award judicially; assign. **3.** to decide by a judicial opinion or sentence. **4.** to sentence. **5.** to deem.

ad·ju·di·cate (ə jōō/də kāt/), *v.t.,* **-cated, -cating.** to pronounce or decree by judicial sentence. —**ad·ju/di·ca/tion,** *n.* —**ad·ju/di·ca/tor,** *n.*

ad·junct (ăj/ŭngkt), *n.* something added to another thing but not essentially a part of it.

ad·jure (ə jōōr/), *v.t.,* **-jured, -juring. 1.** to charge or command, earnestly and solemnly, often under oath or the threat of a curse. **2.** to entreat or request earnestly.

ad·just (ə jŭst/), *v.t.* **1.** to fit, as one thing to another; adapt. **2.** to put in working order; regulate. **3.** to settle or bring to a satisfactory state or agreement. **4.** to settle (a claim). —**ad·just/-a·ble,** *adj.* —**ad·just/er, ad·jus/tor,** *n.*

ad·just·ment (ə jŭst/mənt), *n.* **1.** act of adjusting. **2.** state of being adjusted. **3.** a means of adjusting. **4.** a settlement of a claim.

ad·ju·tant (ăj/ə tənt), *n.* **1.** *Mil.* a staff officer who assists the commanding officer to issue orders. **2.** an assistant. **3.** Also, **adjutant bird.** a large East Indian stork. —**ad/ju·tan·cy,** *n.*

ad·lib (ăd lĭb/), *v.i., v.t.,* **-libbed, -libbing.** *Colloq.* to improvise during rehearsal or performance.

ad lib·i·tum (ăd lĭb/ə təm), *Latin.* at pleasure; without restriction. Abbr.: **ad lib.**

Adm., 1. Admiral. **2.** Admiralty.

ad·min·is·ter (ăd mĭn/əs tər), *v.t.* **1.** to manage or have executive charge of. **2.** to bring into use or operation; dispense. **3.** to make application of; give. **4.** to tender or impose. **5.** *Law.* to manage or dispose of (an estate, etc.). —*v.i.* **6.** to give aid or supplies (fol. by *to*). **7.** to perform the duties of an administrator. —**ad·min·is·tra·tive** (ăd mĭn/ə strā/tĭv), *adj.*

ad·min·is·tra·tion (ăd mĭn/ə strā/shən), *n.* **1.** the conducting of any office or work; management. **2.** the function of a political state in exercising its governmental duties. **3.** the duty of an administrator. **4.** the administrative officers. **5.** *U.S.* their period of service. **6.** *U.S.* any body of men entrusted with executive powers. **7.** *Law.* management of a decedent or trust estate. **8.** act of dispensing, esp. formally. **9.** act of tendering.

ad·min·is·tra·tor (ăd mĭn/ə strā/tər), *n.* **1.** one who directs or manages. **2.** *Law.* a person in charge of a decedent or trust estate.

ad·mi·ra·ble (ăd/mə rə bəl), *adj.* worthy of admiration; exciting approval. —**ad/mi·ra·bly,** *adv.*

ad·mi·ral (ăd/mə rəl), *n.* **1.** the commander in chief of a fleet. **2.** a naval officer of high rank.

Admiral of the Fleet, *U.S. Navy.* the highest ranking naval officer.

ad·mi·ral·ty (ăd/mə rəl tĭ), *n., pl.* **-ties,** *adj.* —*n.* **1.** the office or jurisdiction of an admiral. **2.** the governmental department in charge of naval affairs. **3.** maritime law. **4.** a tribunal administering it. —*adj.* **5.** pertaining to the sea.

ad·mi·ra·tion (ăd/mə rā/shən), *n.* **1.** a feeling of wonder, pleasure, and approbation. **2.** act of admiring. **3.** an object of wonder or approbation.

ad·mire (ăd mīr/), *v.t.,* **-mired, -miring.** to regard with wonder, pleasure, and approbation. —**ad·mir/er,** *n.* —**ad·mir/ing·ly,** *adv.*

ad·mis·si·ble (ăd mĭs/ə bəl), *adj.* **1.** that may be allowed or conceded; allowable. **2.** capable or worthy of being admitted. —**ad·mis/si·bly,** *adv.*

ad·mis·sion (ăd mĭsh/ən), *n.* **1.** act of allowing to enter; entrance. **2.** power or permission to enter. **3.** the price paid for entrance, as to a theater, etc. **4.** acceptance into a position or office; appointment. **5.** confession of a charge, error, or crime. **6.** an acknowledgment of the truth of something. **7.** a point admitted.

ad·mit (ăd mĭt′), *v.t.*, **-mitted, -mitting. 1.** to allow to enter. **2.** to give the right or means of entrance to. **3.** *U.S.* to permit to exercise a certain function or privilege. **4.** to permit; allow. **5.** to concede as valid. **6.** to have capacity for the admission of at one time. **7.** to acknowledge; confess. **—ad·mit′ted·ly,** *adv.*

ad·mit·tance (ăd mĭt′əns), *n.* **1.** permission to enter. **2.** act of admitting. **3.** actual entrance.

ad·mix (ăd mĭks′), *v.t.* to mingle with or add to.

ad·mix·ture (ăd mĭks′chər), *n.* **1.** act of mixing. **2.** state of being mixed. **3.** anything added.

ad·mon·ish (ăd mŏn′ĭsh), *v.t.* **1.** to caution or advise. **2.** to notify of or reprove for a fault, esp. mildly. **—ad·mon′ish·ment, ad·mo·ni·tion** (ăd′mə nĭsh′ən), *n.* **—ad·mon·i·to·ry** (ăd mŏn′ə tōr′ĭ), *adj.*

a·do (ə dōō′), *n.* activity; bustle; fuss.

a·do·be (ə dō′bĭ), *n.* **1.** the sun-dried brick in common use in countries having little rainfall. **2.** a building constructed of adobe.

ad·o·les·cence (ăd′ə lĕs′əns), *n.* the transition period between puberty and adulthood.

ad·o·les·cent (ăd′ə lĕs′ənt), *adj.* **1.** growing to manhood or womanhood; youthful. **—n. 2.** an adolescent person.

A·do·nis (ə dō′nĭs *or, esp. for* 2, ə dŏn′ĭs), *n.* **1.** *Gk. Myth.* a favorite of Aphrodite. **2.** a very handsome young man.

a·dopt (ə dŏpt′), *v.t.* **1.** to choose for or take to oneself. **2.** to take as one's own child. **3.** to vote to accept. **4.** to take or receive into relationship. **—a·dop′tion,** *n.* **—a·dop′tive,** *adj.*

a·dor·a·ble (ə dōr′ə bəl), *adj.* **1.** worthy of being adored. **2.** *Colloq.* very likable. **—a·dor′·a·bly,** *adv.*

ad·o·ra·tion (ăd′ə rā′shən), *n.* **1.** act of paying honor, as to a divine being; worship. **2.** reverent homage. **3.** fervent and devoted love.

a·dore (ə dōr′), *v.t.,* **adored, adoring. 1.** to regard with the utmost esteem or love. **2.** to worship. **3.** *Colloq.* to like dearly. **—a·dor′er,** *n.*

a·dorn (ə dôrn′), *v.t.* to make pleasing or more attractive; embellish; decorate.

a·dorn·ment (ə dôrn′mənt), *n.* **1.** ornament. **2.** an adorning; ornamentation.

a·down (ə doun′), *adv., prep. Poetic.* down.

ad·re·nal glands (ə drē′nəl), *Anat., Zool.* a pair of ductless glands, located above the kidneys, which secrete at least two hormones.

ad·ren·al·in (ə drĕn′əl ĭn), *n.* **1.** a white crystalline drug, purified from the adrenal secretion of animals and used to speed heart action, etc. **2.** (*cap.*) a trademark for this drug.

A·dri·at·ic Sea (ā′drĭ ăt′ĭk), an arm of the Mediterranean between Italy and Yugoslavia.

a·drift (ə drĭft′), *adv., adj.* **1.** not fastened by moorings. **2.** moving helplessly or aimlessly.

a·droit (ə droit′), *adj.* expert; skillful; deft; ingenious. **—a·droit′ly,** *adv.* **—a·droit′ness,** *n.*

ad·sorb (ăd sôrb′), *v.t.* to gather (a gas, liquid, or dissolved substance) on a surface in a condensed layer. **—ad·sorp′tion** (ăd sôrp′shən), *n.* **—ad·sorp′tive,** *adj., n.*

ad·u·late (ăj′ə lāt′), *v.t.,* **-lated, -lating.** to flatter servilely. **—ad·u·la′tion,** *n.* **—ad·u·la·to·ry** (ăj′ə lə tōr′ĭ), *adj.*

a·dult (ə dŭlt′, ăd′ŭlt), *adj.* **1.** having attained full size and strength; grown-up; mature. **2.** pertaining to or designed for adults. **—n. 3.** a person who is grown-up or of age. **—a·dult′hood,** *n.*

a·dul·ter·ant (ə dŭl′tər ənt), *n.* **1.** a substance used for adulterating. **—adj. 2.** adulterating.

a·dul·ter·ate (ə dŭl′tə rāt′), *v.t.,* **-ated, -ating.** to debase by adding inferior materials or elements; make impure. **—a·dul·ter·a′tion,** *n.*

a·dul·ter·er (ə dŭl′tər ər), *n.* a person, esp. a man, guilty of adultery. **—a·dul·ter·ess,** *n. fem.*

a·dul·ter·y (ə dŭl′tə rĭ), *n., pl.* **-teries.** voluntary sexual intercourse between a married person and any other than the lawful spouse. **—a·dul′·ter·ous,** *adj.* **—a·dul′ter·ous·ly,** *adv.*

ad·um·brate (ăd ŭm′brāt, ăd′əm brāt′), *v.t.,* **-brated, -brating. 1.** to give a faint shadow of. **2.** to overshadow. **—ad′um·bra′tion,** *n.*

adv., 1. adverb. **2.** advertisement. **3.** Also, **ad val.** ad valorem.

ad va·lo·rem (ăd′ və lōr′ĕm), (of a duty on imported goods, etc.) based on a percentage of the customs value as stated on the invoice.

ad·vance (ăd văns′, -väns′), *v., -vanced, -vanc·ing, n., adj.* **—v.t. 1.** to move or bring forward in place. **2.** to bring to view or notice; propose. **3.** to improve; further. **4.** to raise in rank; promote. **5.** to raise in rate. **6.** to accelerate. **7.** to supply beforehand. **8.** to supply or pay in expectation of reimbursement. **—v.i. 9.** to move or go forward; proceed. **10.** to improve or make progress; grow. **11.** to increase in quantity, value, price, etc. **—n. 12.** a moving forward; progress. **13.** promotion. **14.** (*usually pl.*) an effort to bring about acquaintance, etc. **15.** rise in price. **16.** money or goods furnished before due. **17. in advance, a.** in front. **b.** ahead of time. **—adj. 18.** going before. **19.** made or issued ahead of time.

ad·vanced (ăd vănst′, -vänst′), *adj.* **1.** placed ahead or in front. **2.** far on in progress; beyond the average. **3.** far on in time.

ad·vance·ment (ăd văns′mənt, -väns′-), *n.* **1.** act of moving forward. **2.** promotion.

ad·van·tage (ăd văn′tĭj, -vän′-), *n., v.,* **-taged, -taging. —n. 1.** anything specially favorable to success, interest, or any desired end. **2.** benefit; gain; profit. **3.** superiority. **4.** *Tennis.* the first point scored after deuce. **5. take advantage of, a.** to make use of. **b.** to impose upon. **6. to advantage,** with good effect. **—v.t. 7.** to benefit.

ad·van·ta·geous (ăd′vən tā′jəs), *adj.* giving an advantage. **—ad′van·ta′geous·ly,** *adv.*

ad·vent (ăd′vĕnt), *n.* **1.** a coming into place, view, or being; arrival. **2.** (*cap. or l.c.*) the coming of Christ into the world. **3.** (*cap.*) a season (including four Sundays) preceding Christmas, commemorative of Christ's coming.

ad·ven·ti·tious (ăd′vən tĭsh′əs), *adj.* **1.** accidentally or casually acquired; added extrinsically. **2.** *Bot., Zool.* appearing in an abnormal or unusual position or place. **—ad′ven·ti′tious·ly,** *adv.*

ad·ven·ture (ăd vĕn′chər), *n., v.,* **-tured, -turing. —n. 1.** a bold, hazardous undertaking. **2.** an exciting experience. **3.** participation in exciting undertakings. **—v.t. 4.** to risk or hazard. **5.** to take the chance of; dare. **6.** to venture to say or utter. **—v.i. 7.** to take the risk involved.

ad·ven·tur·er (ăd vĕn′chər ər), *n.* **1.** one who adventures. **2.** a soldier of fortune. **3.** a speculator. **4.** a seeker of fortune by underhand or equivocal means. **—ad·ven′tur·ess,** *n. fem.*

ad·ven·tur·ous (ăd vĕn′chər əs), *adj.* **1.** inclined or willing to engage in adventures. **2.** attended with risk. **—ad·ven′tur·ous·ly,** *adv.*

ad·verb (ăd′vûrb), *n.* **1.** one of the major form classes, or parts of speech, comprising words used to qualify or limit a verb, a verbal noun, an adjective or another adverb, or an adverbial phrase or clause. **2.** such a word. **—ad·ver·bi·al** (ăd vûr′bĭ əl), *adj.* **—ad·ver′bi·al·ly,** *adv.*

ad·ver·sar·y (ăd′vər sĕr′ĭ), *n., pl.* **-saries. 1.** an unfriendly opponent. **2.** an opponent in a contest. **3. the Adversary,** the Devil.

ad·verse (ăd vûrs′, ăd′vûrs), *adj.* **1.** antagonistic in purpose or effect. **2.** opposing one's interests or desire. **3.** opposite. **—ad·verse′ly,** *adv.*

ad·ver·si·ty (ăd vûr′sə tĭ), *n., pl.* **-ties. 1.** adverse fortune or fate. **2.** an unfortunate event.

ad·vert (ăd vûrt′), *v.i.* **1.** to remark about or refer. **2.** to turn the attention.

ad·ver·tise (ăd′vər tīz′, ăd′vər tīz′), *v., -tised, -tising. —v.t. 1.** to make public announcement of, by publication in periodicals, by printed bills, by broadcasting over the radio, etc. **2.** to praise the good qualities of, in order to induce the public to buy or invest in. **3.** to inform. **—v.i. 4.** to ask (*for*) by placing an advertisement in a newspaper, magazine, etc. Also, **ad′ver·tize′. —ad′ver·tis′er, ad′ver·tiz′er,** *n.*

ad·ver·tise·ment (ăd′vər tīz′mənt, ăd vûr′tĭs mənt, -tĭz-), *n.* **1.** a printed announcement, as of goods for sale, in a newspaper, etc. **2.** a public notice. Also, **ad′ver·tize′ment.**

ad·ver·tis·ing (ăd′vər tī′zĭng), *n.* **1.** act or practice of bringing anything into public notice, esp. by paid announcements in periodicals, on billboards, etc., or on the radio. **2.** paid announcements; advertisements. **3.** the profession of writing advertisements. Also, **ad′ver·tiz·ing.**

ad·vice (ăd vīs′), *n.* **1.** an opinion recommended, or offered, as worthy to be followed. **2.** a communication, esp. from a distance.

ad·vis·a·ble (ăd vī′zə bəl), *adj.* proper to be advised or to be recommended. **—ad·vis′a·bil′·i·ty, ad·vis′a·ble·ness,** *n.* **—ad·vis′a·bly,** *adv.*

ad·vise (ăd vīz′), *v., -vised, -vising. —v.t. 1.** to offer an opinion to, as worthy to be followed. **2.** to recommend as wise, prudent, etc. **3.** to give information or notice. **—v.i. 4.** to take counsel. **5.** to offer counsel. **—ad·vis′er, ad·vis′or,** *n.*

ad·vis·ed·ly (ăd vī′zĭd lĭ), *adv.* deliberately.

ad·vise·ment (ăd vīz′mənt), *n.* deliberation.

ad·vi·so·ry (ăd vī′zə rĭ), *adj.* giving advice.

ad·vo·ca·cy (ăd′və kə sĭ), *n.* act of pleading for or supporting; active espousal.

ad·vo·cate (*v.* ăd′və kāt′; *n.* ăd′və kĭt, -kāt′), *v.*, **-cated, -cating,** *n.* —*v.t.* 1. to plead in favor of; recommend publicly. —*n.* 2. one who defends or espouses a cause. 3. a lawyer.

advt., advertisement.

adz (ădz), *n.* a heavy chisellike steel tool fastened at right angles to a wooden handle, used to remove surplus material, etc. Also, **adze.**

A.E.F., American Expeditionary Forces.

Ae·ge·an Sea (ē jē′ən), an arm of the Mediterranean between Greece and Asia Minor. ab. 350 mi. long.

A B
Adz
A, Cooper's adz;
B, Carpenter's adz

ae·gis (ē′jĭs), *n.* 1. protection; sponsorship. 2. *Gk. Myth.* the shield of Zeus.

Ae·ne·as (ĭ nē′əs), *n.* *Class. Myth.* the son of Anchises and Aphrodite: a Trojan hero, who founded Rome.

Ae·ne·id (ĭ nē′ĭd), *n.* a Latin epic poem by Vergil, reciting the adventures of Aeneas.

ae·o·li·an harp (ē ō′lĭ ən), a box over which are stretched a number of strings of equal length, sounded by the wind. Also, **aeolian lyre.**

Ae·o·lus (ē′ə ləs), *n.* *Gk. Myth.* ruler of winds.

ae·on (ē′ən, ē′ŏn), *n.* an indefinitely long period.

aer·ate (âr′āt, ā′ə rāt′), *v.t.*, **-ated, -ating.** 1. to expose to the free action of the air. 2. to charge or treat with air or a gas. —**aer·a′tion,** *n.* —**aer·a·tor** (âr′ā tər, ā′ə rā′tər), *n.*

aer·i·al (*adj.* âr′ĭ əl, ā ĭr′ĭ əl; *n.* âr′ĭ əl), *adj.* 1. of, in, or produced by the air. 2. inhabiting or frequenting the air. 3. high; lofty. 4. partaking of the nature of air; airy. 5. unsubstantial; visionary. 6. having a light and graceful beauty; ethereal. 7. used for, against, or in aircraft. —*n.* 8. *Radio.* an antenna. —**aer′i·al·ly,** *adv.*

aer·i·al·ist (âr′ĭ əl ĭst, ā ĭr′ĭ əl-), *n.* a trapeze artist.

aer·ie (âr′ĭ, ĭr′ĭ), *n.* 1. the nest of a bird, esp. a bird of prey. 2. the brood in the nest.

aer·obe (âr′ōb), *n.* a bacterium or other microörganism whose existence requires, or is not destroyed by, free oxygen. —**aer·o′bic,** *adj.*

aer·o·dy·nam·ics (âr′ō dī năm′ĭks, -dĭ′-), *n.* the science that treats of the motion of the air and other gases. —**aer′o·dy·nam′ic,** *adj.*

aeron., aeronautics.

aer·o·naut (âr′ə nôt′), *n.* the pilot of a balloon or other lighter-than-air craft.

aer·o·nau·tics (âr′ə nô′tĭks), *n.* the science or art of flight in aircraft. —**aer′o·nau′tic, aer′o·nau′ti·cal,** *adj.*

aer·o·plane (âr′ə plān′), *n.* *Brit.* airplane.

aer·o·sol bomb (âr′ə sōl′, -sŏl′), a small metal container that sprays insecticide in a mist.

aer·o·stat (âr′ə stăt′), *n.* 1. a balloon, airship, or any lighter-than-air craft. 2. an aviator.

Aes·chy·lus (ĕs′kə ləs *or, esp. Brit.,* ēs′-), *n.* 525–456 B.C., Greek tragic poet and dramatist.

Aes·cu·la·pi·us (ĕs′kyə lā′pĭ əs *or, esp. Brit.,* ēs′-), *n.* *Rom. Myth.* the god of medicine and healing. —**Aes′cu·la′pi·an,** *adj.*

Ae·sir (ā′sĭr, ē′-), *n.pl.* the gods of the Scandinavian mythology, dwelling in Asgard.

Ae·sop (ē′səp, ē′sŏp), *n.* 620?–560? B.C., Greek writer of fables.

aes·thete (ĕs′thēt *or, esp. Brit.,* ēs′-), *n.* one who is sensitive to beauties of art or nature.

aes·thet·ic (ĕs thĕt′ĭk *or, esp. Brit.,* ēs-), *adj.* 1. pertaining to the sense of the beautiful or the science of aesthetics. 2. having a sense of the beautiful; characterized by a love of beauty. Also, **aes·thet′i·cal.** —**aes·thet′i·cal·ly,** *adv.*

aes·thet·ics (ĕs thĕt′ĭks *or, esp. Brit.,* ēs-), *n.* *Philos.* the science which deduces from nature and taste the rules and principles of art.

A.F., audio frequency. Also, **a.f.**

a·far (ə fär′), *adv.* 1. from a distance (usually prec. by *from*). 2. at or to a distance.

a·feard (ə fĭrd′), *adj.* *Archaic or Dial.* afraid.

af·fa·ble (ăf′ə bəl), *adj.* 1. easy to talk to or to approach; friendly. 2. mild; benign. —**af·fa·bil′i·ty, af′fa·ble·ness,** *n.* —**af′fa·bly,** *adv.*

af·fair (ə fâr′), *n.* 1. anything done or to be done; business; concern. 2. (*pl.*) particular doings

or interests. 3. an event or performance. 4. a vaguely understood thing. 5. a love interest.

af·fect¹ (ə fĕkt′), *v.t.* 1. to produce an effect or a change in. 2. to impress; move (in mind or feelings). —*n.* 3. *Psychol.* feeling or emotion.

af·fect² (ə fĕkt′), *v.t.* 1. to make a show of; pretend; feign. 2. to make a show of liking or imitating. 3. to use or adopt by preference.

af·fec·ta·tion (ăf′ĭk tā′shən, -ĕk-), *n.* 1. a striving for the appearance of (a quality not really or fully possessed); pretense (fol. by *of*). 2. artificiality of manner or conduct.

af·fect·ed¹ (ə fĕk′tĭd), *adj.* 1. acted upon; influenced. 2. impaired; attacked. 3. moved.

af·fect·ed² (ə fĕk′tĭd), *adj.* 1. assumed artificially. 2. assuming or pretending to possess characteristics which are not natural. —**af·fect′ed·ly,** *adv.* —**af·fect′ed·ness,** *n.*

af·fect·ing (ə fĕk′tĭng), *adj.* having power to excite or move the feelings. —**af·fect′ing·ly,** *adv.*

af·fec·tion (ə fĕk′shən), *n.* 1. a settled good will, love, or zealous attachment. 2. emotion or feeling. 3. *Pathol.* a disease.

af·fec·tion·ate (ə fĕk′shən ĭt), *adj.* 1. characterized by or manifesting affection; tender. 2. having great love or affection; warmly attached. —**af·fec′tion·ate·ly,** *adv.*

af·fec·tive (ə fĕk′tĭv), *adj.* emotional.

af·fer·ent (ăf′ər ənt), *adj.* *Physiol.* bringing to or leading toward a central organ or point.

af·fi·ance (ə fī′əns), *v.*, **-anced, -ancing,** *n.* —*v.t.* 1. to bind by promise of marriage; betroth. —*n.* 2. a marriage contract. 3. trust.

af·fi·da·vit (ăf′ə dā′vĭt), *n.* *Law.* a written declaration upon oath, esp. one made before an authorized official.

af·fil·i·ate (*v.* ə fĭl′ĭ āt′; *n.* ə fĭl′ĭ ĭt, -āt′), *v.*, **-ated, -ating,** *n.* —*v.t.* 1. to bring into association or close connection. 2. to connect in the way of descent or derivation (fol. by *upon*). 3. to adopt. —*v.i.* 4. to be intimately united in action or interest. —*n.* 5. *U.S.* a branch organization. —**af·fil·i·a·tion** (ə fĭl′ĭ ā′shən), *n.*

af·fin·i·ty (ə fĭn′ə tĭ), *n., pl.* **-ties.** 1. a natural liking for, or attraction to, a person or thing. 2. inherent likeness or agreement between things. 3. *Biol.* the relationship between two organisms resulting in a close resemblance.

af·firm (ə fûrm′), *v.t.* 1. to state or assert positively; maintain as true. 2. to establish, confirm, or ratify. —*v.i.* 3. to declare positively; assert solemnly. —**af·firm′a·ble,** *adj.*

af·fir·ma·tion (ăf′ər mā′shən), *n.* 1. the assertion that something exists or is true. 2. that which is affirmed. 3. confirmation; ratification. 4. *Law.* a solemn declaration accepted instead of a statement under oath.

af·firm·a·tive (ə fûr′mə tĭv), *adj.* 1. giving affirmation or assent; not negative. —*n.* 2. that which affirms or asserts. 3. an affirmative word or phrase, as *yes* or *I do.* 4. **the affirmative,** the concurring side. —**af·firm′a·tive·ly,** *adv.*

af·fix (*v.* ə fĭks′; *n.* ăf′ĭks), *v.t.* 1. to fix; fasten; join, or attach (fol. by *to*). 2. to impress (a seal or stamp). 3. to attach (blame, ridicule, etc.). —*n.* 4. that which is attached. 5. *Gram.* a prefix, infix, or suffix.

af·fla·tus (ə flā′təs), *n.* inspiration.

af·flict (ə flĭkt′), *v.t.* to distress with mental or bodily pain; trouble greatly. —**af·flict′er,** *n.*

af·flic·tion (ə flĭk′shən), *n.* 1. a state of pain, distress, or grief. 2. a cause of continued pain.

af·flu·ence (ăf′lŏŏ əns), *n.* 1. abundance of material goods; wealth. 2. an abundant supply.

af·flu·ent (ăf′lŏŏ ənt), *adj.* 1. abounding in means; rich. 2. abundant. 3. flowing freely. —*n.* 4. a tributary stream. —**af′flu·ent·ly,** *adv.*

af·ford (ə fōrd′), *v.t.* 1. to be able, or have the means. 2. to be able to meet the expense or price of. 3. to be able to give or spare. 4. to supply; furnish. 5. to give or confer upon.

af·fray (ə frā′), *n.* a public fight; noisy quarrel.

af·front (ə frŭnt′), *n.* 1. a personally offensive act or word; an insult. 2. an offense to one's dignity or self-respect. —*v.t.* 3. to offend by an open disrespect or insolence. 4. to confront.

Af·ghan (ăf′găn, -gən), *n.* 1. a native of Afghanistan. 2. (*l.c.*) a kind of woolen blanket. 3. (*l.c.*) a breed of hound with a long narrow head and a long silky coat.

Af·ghan·i·stan (ăf găn′ə stăn′), *n.* a kingdom in S Asia, NW of India, E of Iran, and SW of the Soviet Union. 7,000,000 pop.; 250,000 sq. mi.

a·field (ə fēld′), *adv.* 1. away from home. 2. off the beaten path; far and wide. 3. in the fields.

a·fire (ə fīr′), *adv., adj.* on fire.

A.F.L., American Federation of Labor. Also, **A.F. of L.**

a·flame (ə flām′), *adv., adj.* on fire.

a·float (ə flōt′), *adv., adj.* **1.** borne on the water; in a floating condition. **2.** on board ship. **3.** moving without control. **4.** in circulation.

a·foot (ə fŏŏt′), *adv., adj.* **1.** on foot. **2.** astir.

a·fore (ə fōr′), *adv., prep., conj.* *Archaic or Dial.* before.

a·fore·men·tioned (ə fōr′měn′shənd), *adj.* mentioned earlier or previously.

a·fore·said (ə fōr′sĕd′), *adj.* said or mentioned previously.

a·fore·thought (ə fōr′thôt′), *adj.* **1.** thought of beforehand. —*n.* **2.** premeditation.

a·fore·time (ə fōr′tīm′), *adv.* **1.** in time past; previously. —*adj.* **2.** former; previous.

a·foul (ə foul′), *adv., adj.* **1.** *U.S.* in a state of collision or entanglement. **2.** **run afoul of,** to become entangled with.

Afr., **1.** Africa. **2.** African.

a·fraid (ə frād′), *adj.* feeling fear; apprehensive.

a·fresh (ə frĕsh′), *adv.* anew; again.

Af·ri·ca (ăf′rə kə), *n.* the second largest continent, S of Europe and between the Atlantic and Indian Oceans. 158,000,000 pop.; ab. 11,700,000 sq. mi. —**Af′ri·can,** *adj., n.*

African violet, a plant with violet, pink, or white flowers, popular in cultivation.

Af·ri·kan·der (ăf′rə kăn′dər), *n.* a descendant of European settlers in southern Africa.

aft (ăft, äft), *adv.* *Naut.* at, in, or toward the stern.

af·ter (ăf′tər, äf′-), *prep.* **1.** behind in place; following behind. **2.** in pursuit or search of; with desire for. **3.** concerning. **4.** later than; at the close of. **5.** subsequent to and in consequence of. **6.** below in rank; next to. **7.** in imitation of. **8.** with the name of; for. **9.** in proportion to; in accordance with. **10.** in agreement with; in conformity to. —*adv.* **11.** behind; in the rear. **12.** later in time. —*adj.* **13.** later; next; subsequent. **14.** *Naut.* farther aft. —*conj.* **15.** subsequent to the time that.

af·ter·birth (ăf′tər bûrth′, äf′-), *n.* the placenta and fetal membranes expelled from the uterus after parturition.

af·ter·damp (ăf′tər dămp′, äf′-), *n.* a mixture of gases, chiefly carbon dioxide and nitrogen, left in a mine after an explosion or fire.

af·ter·ef·fect (ăf′tər ə fĕkt′, äf′-), *n.* a delayed effect; effect that follows later.

af·ter·glow (ăf′tər glō′, äf′-), *n.* the glow frequently seen in the sky after sunset.

af·ter·math (ăf′tər măth′, äf′-), *n.* **1.** results, esp. of a catastrophe. **2.** a second mowing or crop of grass from land in the same season.

af·ter·most (ăf′tər mōst′, -məst, äf′-), *adj.* **1.** *Naut.* farthest aft. **2.** hindmost.

af·ter·noon (ăf′tər nōōn′, äf′-), *n.* **1.** the time from noon until evening. **2.** the latter part. —*adj.* **3.** pertaining to the after part of the day.

af·ter·thought (ăf′tər thôt′, äf′-), *n.* **1.** reflection, answer, or the like, that occurs to one's mind afterward. **2.** a second thought.

af·ter·ward (ăf′tər wərd, äf′-), *adv.* in later or subsequent time. Also, **af′ter·wards.**

Ag, *Chem.* (L *argentum*) silver.

Ag., August.

a·gain (ə gĕn′ *or, esp. Brit.,* ə gān′), *adv.* **1.** once more; in addition; anew. **2.** moreover; besides; furthermore. **3.** on the other hand. **4.** back; in return; in reply. **5.** in the opposite direction.

a·gainst (ə gĕnst′ *or, esp. Brit.,* ə gānst′), *prep.* **1.** in an opposite direction to, so as to meet; toward; upon. **2.** in contact with. **3.** in opposition to; adverse to. **4.** in resistance to or defense from. **5.** in preparation or provision for. **6.** having as background. **7.** in exchange for.

Ag·a·mem·non (ăg′ə mĕm′nŏn, -nən), *n.* *Gk. Legend.* a king of Mycenae, who led the Greeks against Troy, later slain by Clytemnestra.

A·ga·ña (ä gä′nyä), *n.* capital of Guam. 10,004.

a·gape (ə gāp′, ə găp′), *adv., adj.* with the mouth wide open, as in wonder or eagerness.

a·gar-a·gar (ä′gär ä′gär, ăg′ər ăg′ər), *n.* a gelatinlike product of certain seaweeds, used to solidify culture media and in cookery, etc.

Ag·as·siz (ăg′ə sĭ), *n.* **(Jean) Louis (Rodolphe),** 1807–73, Swiss-born zoölogist in U.S.

ag·ate (ăg′ĭt), *n.* **1.** a variegated variety of quartz (chalcedony) showing colored bands or

other markings. **2.** a child's playing marble made of this substance, or of glass in imitation of it.

a·ga·ve (ə gä′vĭ), *n.* an American (chiefly Mexican) plant, species of which yield useful fibers, are used in making a fermented beverage, or are cultivated for ornament.

age (āj), *n., v.,* **aged, aging** or **ageing.** —*n.* **1.** the length of time during which a being or thing has existed. **2.** the lifetime of an individual, or of the individuals of a class or species on an average. **3.** a period of human life usually marked by a certain stage of development, which involves legal responsibility and capacity. **4.** one of the stages of human life. **5.** old age. **6.** a particular period of history, as distinguished from others. **7.** a generation or a succession of generations. **8.** *Colloq.* a great length of time. **9.** *Psychol.* the comparative mental, emotional, etc., development of a person, expressed by equating performance in various tests to the average age at which the same result is attained. **10.** *Geol.* a part of earth history distinguished by special features. —*v.i.* **11.** to grow old. —*v.t.* **12.** to cause to grow or to seem old.

a·ged (ā′jĭd for 1, 2; ājd for 3), *adj.* **1.** having lived or existed long. **2.** pertaining to or typical of old age. **3.** of the age of. —**a′ged·ness,** *n.*

age·less (āj′lĭs), *adj.* never growing old.

age·long (āj′lông′, -lŏng′), *adj.* lasting an age.

a·gen·cy (ā′jən sĭ), *n., pl.* **-cies.** **1.** a commercial or other bureau furnishing some form of service for the public. **2.** the place of business of an agent. **3.** the office or business of an agent. **4.** state of being in action or of exerting power; action; operation. **5.** a mode of exerting power.

a·gen·da (ə jĕn′də), *n.pl., sing.* **-dum** (-dəm). **1.** things to be done. **2.** matters to be brought before a committee, council, board, etc.

a·gent (ā′jənt), *n.* **1.** a person acting on behalf of another. **2.** one who or that which acts or has the power to act. **3.** a natural force or object producing or used for obtaining specific results. **4.** an active cause; an efficient cause. **5.** an official. **6.** *Colloq.* a representative of a business. **7.** *Chem.* a substance which causes a reaction.

Ag·ge·us (ə gē′əs), *n.* Haggai (Douay).

ag·glom·er·ate (*v.* ə glŏm′ə rāt′; *adj., n.* ə glŏm′ər ĭt, -ə rāt′), *v.,* **-ated, -ating,** *adj., n.* —*v.t., v.i.* **1.** to collect or gather into a mass. —*adj.* **2.** gathered together into a ball or mass; clustered. —*n.* **3.** a clustered mass of things. —**ag·glom·er·a·tion** (ə glŏm′ə rā′shən), *n.*

ag·glu·ti·nate (*v.* ə glōō′tə nāt′; *adj.* ə glōō′tə nĭt, -nāt′), *v.,* **-nated, -nating,** *adj.* —*v.t., v.i.* **1.** to unite or cause to adhere, as with glue. —*adj.* **2.** united by or as by glue. —**ag·glu·ti·na·tion** (ə glōō′tə nā′shən), *n.*

ag·gran·dize (ăg′rən dīz′, ə grăn′dĭz), *v.t.,* **-dized, -dizing.** **1.** to increase in size or intensity; enlarge; extend. **2.** to make great or greater in power, wealth, rank, or honor. —**ag·gran·dize·ment** (ə grăn′dĭz mənt), *n.*

ag·gra·vate (ăg′rə vāt′), *v.t.,* **-vated, -vating. 1.** to make worse or more severe. **2.** *Colloq.* to provoke; irritate. —**ag′gra·va′tion,** *n.* —**ag′gra·va′tor,** *n.*

ag·gre·gate (*adj., n.* ăg′rə gĭt, -gāt′; *v.* ăg′rə gāt′), *adj., n., v.,* **-gated, -gating.** —*adj.* **1.** formed by the collection of particulars into a whole mass or sum; total; combined. —*n.* **2.** a sum, mass, or assemblage of particulars. **3.** **in the aggregate,** collectively. —*v.t.* **4.** to collect into one sum, mass, or body. **5.** to amount to. —**ag′gre·gate·ly,** *adv.*

ag·gre·ga·tion (ăg′rə gā′shən), *n.* **1.** a combined whole; an aggregate. **2.** collection into an unorganized whole.

ag·gres·sion (ə grĕsh′ən), *n.* **1.** the action of a state in violating by force the rights of another state, particularly its territorial rights. **2.** any offensive action or procedure.

ag·gres·sive (ə grĕs′ĭv), *adj.* **1.** characterized by aggression. **2.** energetic; vigorous. —**ag·gres′sive·ly,** *adv.* —**ag·gres′sive·ness,** *n.*

ag·gres·sor (ə grĕs′ər), *n.* a person who attacks first; one who begins hostilities; an invader.

ag·grieve (ə grēv′), *v.t.,* **-grieved, -grieving.** to oppress or wrong grievously; injure unjustly.

a·ghast (ə găst′, ə gäst′), *adj.* struck with amazement; filled with sudden fright or horror.

ag·ile (ăj′əl *or, esp. Brit.,* ăj′īl), *adj.* **1.** quick and light in movement. **2.** active; lively. —**ag′ile·ly,** *adv.* —**a·gil·i·ty** (ə jĭl′ə tĭ), *n.*

ag·i·tate (ăj′ə tāt′), *v.,* **-tated, -tating.** —*v.t.* **1.** to move or force into violent irregular action; shake or move briskly. **2.** to disturb, or excite

into tumult; perturb. 3. to discuss; debate; plan.
—*v.i.* 4. to arouse public interest.

ag·i·ta·tion (ăj/ə tā/shən), *n.* 1. act of agitating. 2. state of being agitated. 3. persistent public urging of a political or social question.

ag·i·ta·tor (ăj/ə tā/tər), *n.* 1. one who stirs up others, as to political action. 2. a machine for agitating and mixing.

a·glow (ə glō/), *adv., adj.* glowing.

ag·nos·tic (ăg nŏs/tĭk), *n.* 1. one who holds that the ultimate cause (God) and the essential nature of things are unknown or unknowable. —*adj.* 2. pertaining to the agnostics or their doctrines. —**ag·nos·ti·cism** (ăg nŏs/tə sĭz/əm), *n.*

a·go (ə gō/), *adj.* 1. gone; gone by; past (now follows noun). —*adv.* 2. in past time.

a·gog (ə gŏg/), *adj.* 1. highly excited by eagerness or curiosity. —*adv.* 2. eagerly; excitedly.

ag·o·nize (ăg/ə nīz/), *v.* **-nized, -nizing.** —*v.i.* 1. to writhe with extreme pain or anguish. —*v.t.* 2. to torture. —**ag/o·niz/ing·ly,** *adv.*

ag·o·ny (ăg/ə nĭ), *n., pl.* **-nies.** 1. extreme, and generally prolonged, pain; intense suffering. 2. intense mental excitement of any kind.

a·gou·ti (ə gōō/tĭ), *n., pl.* **-tis, -ties.** any of several short-haired, short-eared, rabbitlike rodents of South and Central America and the West Indies, destructive to sugar cane.

a·grar·i·an (ə grâr/ĭ an), *adj.* 1. relating to land, land tenure, or the division of landed property. 2. pertaining to the advancement of agricultural groups. —*n.* 3. one who favors the equal division of land. —**a·grar/i·an·ism,** *n.*

a·gree (ə grē/), *v.,* **agreed, agreeing.** —*v.i.* 1. to yield assent; consent (often fol. by *to*). 2. to be of one mind; harmonize in opinion or feeling (often fol. by *with*). 3. to live in concord or without contention. 4. to come to an arrangement, understanding, or settlement. 5. to be consistent. 6. to be similar. 7. to suit. 8. *Gram.* to correspond in inflectional form, as in number. —*v.t.* 9. to concede; grant.

a·gree·a·ble (ə grē/ə bəl), *adj.* 1. to one's liking; pleasing. 2. *Colloq.* willing or ready to agree. 3. suitable; comformable. —**a·gree/a·bly,** *adv.*

a·gree·ment (ə grē/mənt), *n.* 1. act of coming to a mutual arrangement. 2. the arrangement itself. 3. unanimity of opinion or feeling. 4. state of being in accord; conformity. 5. *Gram.* correspondence in number, case, gender, person, etc., between syntactically connected words.

agric., 1. agricultural. 2. agriculture. Also, **agr.**

A·gric·o·la (ə grĭk/ə lə), *n.* **Gnaeus Julius,** A.D. 37–93, Roman general: governor of Britain.

ag·ri·cul·ture (ăg/rə kŭl/chər), *n.* the cultivation of land, as in the raising of crops; husbandry; tillage; farming. —**ag/ri·cul/tur·al,** *adj.* —**ag/·ri·cul/tur·al·ly,** *adv.*

ag·ri·cul·tur·ist (ăg/rə kŭl/chər ĭst), *n.* a farmer. Also, *Now U.S.,* **ag/ri·cul/tur·al·ist.**

A·grip·pa (ə grĭp/ə), *n.* **Marcus Vipsanius,** 63–12 B.C., Roman statesman, general, engineer.

ag·ro·nom·ics (ăg/rə nŏm/ĭks), *n.* the art and science of managing land and crops.

a·gron·o·my (ə grŏn/ə mĭ), *n.* 1. the applied phases of both soil science and the several plant sciences, often limited to applied sciences of crops. 2. agriculture. —**a·gron/o·mist,** *n.*

a·ground (ə ground/), *adv., adj.* on the ground.

Agt., agent. Also, **agt.**

a·gue (ā/gū), *n. Pathol.* a malarial fever characterized by regularly returning paroxysms, marked by successive cold, hot, and sweating fits.

A·gui·nal·do (ä/gē näl/dō), *n.* **Emilio** (ĕ mē/lyō), born 1870?, Filipino patriot.

A·hab (ā/hăb), *n. Bible.* king of Israel of the ninth century B.C.: husband of Jezebel.

a·head (ə hĕd/), *adv.* 1. in or to the front; in advance; before. 2. forward. 3. *U.S.* winning.

Ah·med·a·bad (ä/məd ä bäd/), *n.* a city in W India. 591,267. Also, **Ah/mad·a·bad/.**

a·hoy (ə hoi/), *interj. Naut.* a call used in hailing.

ai (ä/ĭ), *n., pl.* **ais** (ä/ĭz). a large three-toed sloth of Central and South America.

aid (ād), *v.t.* 1. to afford support or assistance to; help. 2. to promote the course or accomplishment of; facilitate. —*v.i.* 3. to give help. —*n.* 4. help. 5. one that helps. 6. *U.S.* an aide-de-camp.

aide (ād), *n.* an aide-de-camp.

aide-de-camp (ād/də kămp/), *n., pl.* **aides-de-camp.** *Mil.* a confidential assistant to a superior officer.

ai·grette (ā/grĕt, ä grĕt/), *n.* 1. a plume or tuft of feathers arranged as a head ornament. 2. a copy in jewelry of such a plume.

ail (āl), *v.t.* 1. to affect with pain or uneasiness; trouble. —*v.i.* 2. to feel pain; be unwell.

ai·lan·thus (ā lăn/thəs), *n.* a tree with pinnate leaves and ill-scented greenish flowers.

ai·ler·on (ā/lə rŏn/), *n. Aeron.* a hinged, movable part of an airplane wing, usually part of the trailing edge, used to bank, roll, etc.

ail·ment (āl/mənt), *n.* a slight illness.

aim (ām), *v.t.* 1. to give a certain direction and elevation to (a gun, etc.), for the purpose of causing the projectile to hit the object. 2. to direct or point at something. —*v.i.* 3. to strive. 4. *U.S.* to intend. 5. to direct efforts toward an object. —*n.* 6. act of directing anything at or toward a particular object. 7. the direction in which a missile is pointed. 8. the thing or person aimed at. 9. the object of one's efforts; purpose.

aim·less (ām/lĭs), *adj.* without aim; purposeless. —**aim/less·ly,** *adv.* —**aim/less·ness,** *n.*

ain't (ānt), *Now Illiterate or Dial.* 1. a contraction of *am not,* extended in use as contraction of *are not* and *is not.* 2. a contraction of *have not.*

air (âr), *n.* 1. a mixture of oxygen, nitrogen, and other gases, which surrounds the earth and forms its atmosphere. 2. a movement of the atmosphere; a light breeze. 3. circulation; publication; publicity. 4. the general character of anything; appearance. 5. the peculiar look, appearance, and bearing of a person. 6. (*pl.*) affected manner. 7. *Music.* a tune; a melody. 8. *Radio.* the atmosphere through which radio waves are sent. 9. **in the air, a.** without foundation. **b.** in circulation. **c.** undecided or unsettled (often prec. by *up*). 10. **on the air,** in the act of broadcasting; being broadcast. —*v.t.* 11. to expose to the air; ventilate. 12. to expose to public notice.

air base, operating center for air force units.

air bladder, a vesicle or sac containing air.

air-borne (âr/bôrn/), *adj. Mil.* (of ground forces) carried in airplanes or gliders.

air brake, *U.S.* a brake, or system of brakes, operated by compressed air.

air brush, *Orig. U.S.* a kind of atomizer for spraying liquid paint upon a surface.

air castle, a daydream; a visionary scheme.

air chamber, a chamber containing air, as in a pump or a lifeboat or in an organic body.

air-con·di·tion (âr/kən dĭsh/ən), *v.t. Orig. U.S.* 1. to furnish with an air-conditioning system. 2. to treat (air) with such a system. —**air/-con·di/tioned,** *adj.*

air conditioning, *Orig. U.S.* a system of treating air in buildings to assure a desirable temperature, humidity, dustlessness, etc.

air-cool (âr/kool/), *v.t.* 1. *Mach.* to remove the heat of combustion, friction, etc., from by air. 2. to air-condition. —**air/-cooled/,** *adj.*

air·craft (âr/krăft/, -kräft/), *n., pl.* **-craft.** any machine supported for flight in the air by buoyancy (such as balloons) or by dynamic action of air on its surfaces (such as airplanes).

aircraft carrier, a warship with a deck for the taking off and landing of aircraft.

air·drome (âr/drōm/), *n.* an airport.

Aire·dale (âr/dāl/), *n.* a large, heavy kind of terrier with a rough brown or tan coat.

air·field (âr/fēld/), *n.* a level area, usually equipped with hard-surfaced runways, on which airplanes take off and land.

air·foil (âr/foil/), *n. Aeron.* any surface, such as a wing, aileron, or stabilizer, designed to help in lifting or controlling the aircraft by making use of the current of air through which it moves.

Air Force, *U.S.* the department consisting of practically all military and naval aviation forces.

air gun, a gun operated by compressed air.

air hole, 1. an opening to admit or discharge air. 2. *U.S.* a natural opening in the frozen surface of a river or pond. 3. *Aeron.* air pocket.

air·i·ly (âr/ə lĭ), *adv.* 1. in a gay manner; jauntily. 2. lightly. —**air·i·ness** (âr/ĭ nĭs), *n.*

air·ing (âr/ĭng), *n.* 1. an exposure to the air, as for drying. 2. a walk, drive, etc., in the open air.

air lane, a route regularly used by airplanes.

air·less (âr/lĭs), *adj.* lacking air, esp. fresh air.

air lift, a system of transportation by aircraft, esp. that established in 1948 by the Western powers to supply Berlin during the Soviet blockade. Also, **air/lift.**

air line, 1. a system furnishing (usually) scheduled air transport between specified points. 2. a company that operates such a system.

air liner, a passenger aircraft of an air line.

air lock, *Civ. Eng.* an airtight transition compartment at the entrance of a pressure chamber in which men work, such as a submerged caisson.

air mail, *Orig. U.S.* **1.** the system of transmitting mail by aircraft. **2.** mail so transmitted. —**air′-mail′,** *adj.*

air·man (âr′mən), *n.*, *pl.* **-men.** **1.** an aviator. **2.** an enlisted man in the U.S. Air Force.

air-mind·ed (âr′mīn′dĭd), *adj.* **1.** interested in aviation. **2.** favoring increased use of aircraft.

air·plane (âr′plān′), *n.* an aircraft, heavier than air, kept aloft by the upward thrust exerted by the passing air on its fixed wings, and driven by propellers, jet propulsion, etc.

air pocket, *Aeron.* a downward current of air, usually causing a sudden loss of altitude.

air·port (âr′pōrt′), *n.* a tract of land or water with facilities for aircraft.

air pressure, the pressure of the atmosphere.

air raid, a raid or incursion by hostile aircraft.

air sac, *Orig. U.S.* **1.** a sac containing air. **2.** any of certain cavities and cells in a bird's body connected with the lungs.

air·screw (âr′skrŏō′), *n.* *Brit.* an airplane propeller.

air·ship (âr′shĭp′), *n.* a self-propelled, lighter-than-air craft that can be steered.

air·sick (âr′sĭk′), *adj.* ill as the result of traveling in the air. —**air′sick′ness,** *n.*

air·strip (âr′strĭp′), *n.* *Aeron.* runway.

air·tight (âr′tīt′), *adj.* **1.** so tight or close as to be impermeable to air. **2.** invulnerable.

air·way (âr′wā′), *n.* **1.** an air route fully equipped with emergency landing fields, beacon lights, radio beams, etc. **2.** a ventilation shaft.

air·wor·thy (âr′wûr′thĭ), *adj.* *Aeron.* meeting accepted standards for safe flight. —**air′wor′-thi·ness,** *n.*

air·y (âr′ĭ), *adj.*, **airier, airiest. 1.** consisting of or having the character of air; immaterial. **2.** light in appearance; thin. **3.** light in manner; gay; lively. **4.** light in movement; graceful; delicate. **5.** unsubstantial; unreal. **6.** visionary. **7.** performed in the air. **8.** lofty. **9.** well ventilated.

aisle (īl), *n.* **1.** a passageway between seats in a church, hall, etc. **2.** *Archit.* a lateral division of a church or other building, esp. one separated from the nave by piers or columns. —**aisled** (īld), *adj.*

A·jac·cio (ä yät′chō), *n.* a seaport in and the capital of Corsica: birthplace of Napoleon. 33,060.

a·jar[1] (ə jär′), *adj.*, *adv.* partly opened.

a·jar[2] (ə jär′), *adv.*, *adj.* out of harmony; jarring.

A·jax (ā′jăks), *n.* *Gk. Legend.* a mighty warrior of the Greeks before Troy.

a·kim·bo (ə kĭm′bō), *adj.*, *adv.* with hand on hip and elbow bent outward.

a·kin (ə kĭn′), *adj.* **1.** of kin; related by blood. **2.** allied by nature; having the same properties.

Ak·ron (ăk′rən), *n.* a city in NE Ohio. 244,791.

-al[1], a suffix meaning "of or pertaining to," "like," "befitting," etc., as in *annual, choral.*

-al[2], a suffix forming nouns of action from verbs, as in *refusal, denial, recital, trial.*

Al, *Chem.* aluminum.

Al·a·ba·ma (ăl′ə băm′ə), *n.* **1.** a State in the SE United States. 2,807,817 pop.; 51,609 sq. mi. *Cap.:* Montgomery. *Abbr.:* **Ala. 2.** a river flowing from central Alabama SW to the Mobile river. 315 mi. —**Al′a·bam′an,** *adj.*, *n.*

al·a·bam·ine (ăl′ə băm′ēn, -ĭn), *n.* *Chem.* a rare element claimed to have been found in monazite sands (1931). *Symbol:* Ab; *at. no.:* 85.

al·a·bas·ter (ăl′ə băs′tər, -bäs′-), *n.* **1.** a finely granular variety of gypsum, often white and translucent, used for lamp bases, figurines, etc. **2.** a variety of calcite, often with a banded structure. —*adj.* **3.** of or like alabaster.

à la carte (ä′ lə kärt′), with a stated price for each dish.

a·lack (ə lăk′), *interj.* *Archaic.* an exclamation of sorrow, regret, or dismay. Also, **a·lack·a·day** (ə lăk′ə dā′).

a·lac·ri·ty (ə lăk′rə tĭ), *n.* **1.** liveliness; briskness. **2.** readiness. —**a·lac′ri·tous,** *adj.*

à la king (ä′ lə kĭng′), creamed with pimiento, etc.

Al·a·me·da (ăl′ə mē′də, -mä′-), *n.* a city in W California, SE of San Francisco. 89,906.

Al·a·mo (ăl′ə mō′), *n.* a mission building in San Antonio, Texas: heroic defense, 1836.

à la mode (ä′ lə mōd′, ăl′ə-), *adv.* **1.** in the fashion. **2.** served with ice cream. Also, **a la mode, a′la-mode′.**

Al·a·ric (ăl′ə rĭk), *n.* A.D. c370–410, king of the Visigoths: captured Rome, A.D. 410.

a·larm (ə lärm′), *n.* **1.** a sudden fear of some danger; apprehension; fright. **2.** a warning of approaching danger. **3.** a self-acting device to rouse from sleep, warn of danger, etc. **4.** a call to arms. —*v.t.* **5.** to surprise with apprehension of danger. **6.** to warn of danger. —**a·larm′ing·ly,** *adv.*

a·larm·ist (ə lär′mĭst), *n.* one given to raising alarms, esp. without sufficient reason.

a·lar·um (ə lăr′əm, ə lär′-), *n.* *Archaic.* alarm.

a·las (ə lăs′, ə läs′), *interj.* an exclamation expressing sorrow, grief, pity, concern, etc.

Alas., Alaska.

A·las·ka (ə lăs′kə), *n.* **1.** a territory of the United States, in NW North America. 81,441 pop.; 586,400 sq. mi. *Cap.:* Juneau. **2.** Gulf of, a large gulf of the Pacific, on the S coast of Alaska. —**A·las′kan,** *adj.*, *n.*

Alaska Highway, a highway extending from E British Columbia, Canada, to Fairbanks, Alaska. 1671 mi.

alb (ălb), *n.* *Eccles.* a white linen robe with close sleeves, worn by an officiating priest.

Al·ba·ni·a (ăl bā′nĭ ə, -bān′yə), *n.* a republic in S Europe, N of Greece. 1,115,350 pop.; 10,632 sq. mi. *Cap.:* Tirana. —**Al·ba′ni·an,** *adj.*, *n.*

Al·ba·ny (ôl′bə nĭ), *n.* the capital of New York, in the E part, on the Hudson. 130,577.

al·ba·tross (ăl′bə trôs′, -trŏs′), *n.* any of various large web-footed sea birds related to the petrels.

al·be·it (ôl bē′ĭt), *conj.* although; notwithstanding.

Alb worn by a priest

Al·bert (ăl′bərt), *n.* **Prince,** 1819–61, a German prince, husband of Queen Victoria of Great Britain.

Al·ber·ta (ăl bûr′tə), *n.* a province in W Canada. 796,169 pop.; 255,285 sq. mi. *Cap.:* Edmonton.

al·bi·no (ăl bī′nō *or, esp. Frit.,* -bē′-), *n.*, *pl.* **-nos. 1.** a person with a pale, milky skin, light hair, and pink eyes. **2.** an animal or plant with a marked deficiency in pigmentation. —**al·bi·nism** (ăl′bə nĭz′əm), *n.*

Al·bi·on (ăl′bĭ ən), *n.* *Poetic.* Britain.

al·bum (ăl′bəm), *n.* a book consisting of blank leaves for photographs, stamps, autographs, etc.

al·bu·men (ăl bū′mən), *n.* **1.** the white of an egg. **2.** *Chem.* albumin.

al·bu·min (ăl bū′mən), *n.* *Chem.* any of a class of water-soluble proteins composed of nitrogen, carbon, hydrogen, oxygen, and sulfur, occurring in animal and vegetable juices and tissues.

al·bu·mi·nous (ăl bū′mə nəs), *adj.* **1.** of albumin. **2.** containing albumin. **3.** resembling albumin. Also, **al·bu·mi·nose** (ăl bū′mə nōs′).

Al·bu·quer·que (ăl′bə kûr′kĭ), *n.* a city in central New Mexico. 35,449.

Al·can Highway (ăl′kăn), unofficial name of Alaska Highway.

Al·ca·traz (ăl′kə trăz′), *n.* **1.** an island in San Francisco Bay. **2.** the U.S. penitentiary there.

al·che·my (ăl′kə mĭ), *n.* *Medieval Chem.* an art which sought to transmute baser metals into gold, and to find a universal solvent and an elixir of life. —**al·chem·ic** (ăl kĕm′ĭk), **al·chem′i·cal,** *adj.* —**al·chem′i·cal·ly,** *adv.* —**al′che·mist,** *n.*

al·co·hol (ăl′kə hôl′, -hŏl′), *n.* **1.** a colorless, inflammable liquid (**ethyl alcohol**), the intoxicating principle of fermented liquors, formed from certain sugars by fermentation, now usually prepared by treating grain with malt and adding yeast. **2.** any intoxicating liquor containing this spirit. **3.** *Chem.* any of a class of chemical compounds having the general formula, ROH, where R represents a group derived from an aliphatic hydrocarbon.

al·co·hol·ic (ăl′kə hôl′ĭk, -hŏl′ĭk), *adj.* **1.** pertaining to or of the nature of alcohol. **2.** containing or using alcohol. —*n.* **3.** a person suffering from alcoholism.

al·co·hol·ism (ăl′kə hôl ĭz′əm, -hŏl′-), *n.* a diseased condition due to the excessive use of alcoholic beverages.

al·cove (ăl′kōv), *n.* **1.** a recess opening out of a room. **2.** any recessed space, as in a garden.

Al·den (ôl′dən), *n.* **John,** 1599?–1687, Pilgrim settler (1620) in Plymouth, Mass.

al·der (ôl′dər), *n.* a shrub or tree of the birch

family, growing in moist places in northern temperate or colder regions.

al·der·man (ôl´dər mən), *n., pl.* -men. **1.** *U.S.* one of a body of municipal officers with powers varying according to locality, often representing a municipal ward. **2.** *Eng.* one of the members of a borough or county council. —**al·der·man·ic** (ôl´dər măn´ĭk), *adj.*

Al·der·ney (ôl´dər nĭ), *n.* one of the Channel Islands. 1521 pop.; 3 sq. mi.

ale (āl), *n.* a fermented malt beverage, darker, heavier, and more bitter than beer.

A·le·mán (ä´lĕ män´), *n.* **Miguel** (mē gĕl´), born 1902, president of Mexico since 1946.

a·lem·bic (ə lĕm´bĭk), *n.* **1.** a vessel with a beaked cap or head, formerly used in distilling. **2.** anything that transforms, purifies, or refines.

A·lep·po (ə lĕp´ō), *n.* a city in NW Syria. 257,-300.

a·lert (ə lûrt´), *adj.* **1.** vigilantly attentive. **2.** nimble. —*n.* **3.** an attitude of vigilance. **4.** an air-raid alarm. **5.** the period during which an air-raid alarm is in effect. —*v.t.* **6.** to prepare (troops, etc.) for action. **7.** to warn of an impending attack. —**a·lert´ly**, *adv.* —**a·lert´ness**, *n.*

A·leu·tian Islands (ə lōō´shən), an archipelago extending W from the Alaska peninsula for ab. 1200 mi.: a part of the Territory of Alaska. Also, **Aleutians.** —**A·leu´tian**, *adj., n.*

Al·ex·an·der (ăl´ĭg zăn´dər, -zän´-), *n.* **1.** Sir Harold R.L.F., born 1891, British general: governor general of Canada since 1946. **2. the Great**, 356–323 B.C., king of Macedonia, 336–323 B.C.: conqueror of Greek city-states and Persian Empire from Asia Minor and Egypt to India.

Al·ex·an·dri·a (ăl´ĭg zăn´drĭ ə, -zän´-), *n.* **1.** a seaport in N Egypt, on the Nile delta: ancient center of learning. 729,900. **2.** a city in NE Virginia, opposite the District of Columbia. 33,523.

Al·ex·an·drine (ăl´ĭg zăn´drĭn, -drēn´, -zän´-), *Pros.* —*n.* **1.** a verse or line of poetry of six iambic feet. —*adj.* **2.** designating such verse.

al·fal·fa (ăl făl´fə), *n.* a European forage plant with bluish-purple flowers, now much cultivated in the U.S.; lucerne.

Al·fon·so XIII (ăl fŏn´sō), 1886–1941, king of Spain from 1886 until deposed in 1931.

Al·fred the Great (ăl´frĭd), A.D. 849–899, king of England, A.D. 871–899.

alg., algebra.

al·ga (ăl´gə), *n., pl.* -gae (-jē). any chlorophyll-containing plant of the phylum comprising seaweeds and various fresh-water forms. —**al´gal**, *adj.*

al·ge·bra (ăl´jə brə), *n.* the mathematical art of reasoning about (quantitative) relations by means of a systematized notation including letters and other symbols. —**al·ge·bra·ic** (ăl´jə brā´ĭk), **al´ge·bra´i·cal**, *adj.* —**al´ge·bra´i·cal·ly**, *adv.*

Al·ger (ăl´jər), *n.* **Horatio**, 1834–99, U.S. author of novels, esp. for boys.

Al·ge·ri·a (ăl jĭr´ĭ ə), *n.* a French possession in N Africa, near the W end of the Mediterranean. 7,234,684 pop.; 851,298 sq. mi. *Cap.:* Algiers. —**Al·ge´ri·an, Al·ge·rine** (ăl´jə rēn´), *adj., n.*

Al·giers (ăl jîrz´), *n.* a seaport in and the capital of Algeria, in the N part. 264,232.

Al·gon·kin (ăl gŏng´kĭn), *n.* Algonquin.

Al·gon·qui·an (ăl gŏng´kĭ ən, -kwĭ ən), *n.* **1.** one of the principal linguistic stocks of North America, including languages spoken by the Micmac, Ojibwa, Cree, Blackfoot, Cheyenne, Arapaho, etc. **2.** an Algonquian tribe member. —*adj.* **3.** belonging to or constituting this stock.

Al·gon·quin (ăl gŏng´kĭn, -kwĭn), *n.* **1.** a member of a group of Indian tribes formerly along the Ottawa river and north of the St. Lawrence. **2.** their language. **3.** any Algonquian Indian.

Al·ham·bra (ăl hăm´brə), *n.* **1.** the palace of the Moorish kings at Granada, Spain. **2.** a city in SW California, near Los Angeles. 38,935.

a·li·as (ā´lĭ əs), *adv., n., pl.* aliases. —*adv.* **1.** wise. —*n.* **2.** an assumed name.
‹ al·i·bi (ăl´ə bī´), *n., pl.* -bis. **1.** *Law.* the defense accused person that he was elsewhere at the of an offense. **2.** *U.S. Colloq.* an excuse.

al·ien (āl´yən, ā´lĭ ən), *n.* **1.** one born in or belonging to another country who has not yet acquired citizenship. **2.** a foreigner. —*adj.* **3.** residing under a government of which one is not a citizen. **4.** belonging or relating to aliens. **5.** foreign; strange. **6.** adverse; hostile; opposed.

al·ien·ate (āl´yə nāt´, ā´lĭ ə-), *v.t.*, -ated, -ating. **1.** to make indifferent or averse. **2.** to turn away. **3.** *Law.* to transfer or convey title, property, etc. —**al´ien·a´tion**, *n.* —**al´ien·a´tor**, *n.*

al·ien·ist (āl´yən ĭst, ā´lĭ ən-), *n.* a psychiatrist who specializes in giving legal evidence.

a·light[1] (ə līt´), *v.i.* alighted or (*Rare*) alit, alighting. **1.** to get down from a horse or out of a vehicle; dismount. **2.** to settle or stay after descending. **3.** to come accidentally.

a·light[2] (ə līt´), *adv., adj.* lighted up; burning.

a·lign (ə līn´), *v.t.* **1.** to adjust to a line; form in line. **2.** to bring into line. —*v.i.* **3.** to be or come into line. **4.** to join with others in a cause. Also, **a·line´.** —**a·lign´er**, *n.* —**a·lign´ment**, *n.*

a·like (ə līk´), *adv.* **1.** in the same manner, form, or degree. —*adj.* **2.** having similarity.

al·i·ment (ăl´ə mənt), *n.* food.

al·i·men·ta·ry (ăl´ə mĕn´tə rĭ), *adj.* **1.** concerned with nutrition. **2.** nutritious.

alimentary canal, the food passage in any animal from mouth to anus.

al·i·mo·ny (ăl´ə mō´nĭ), *n.* an allowance paid to a woman by her husband or former husband for her maintenance, granted by a court, upon a legal separation or a divorce, or pending action.

al·i·phat·ic (ăl´ə făt´ĭk), *adj. Chem.* pertaining to or concerned with those organic compounds which are open chains, as the paraffins or olefins.

al·i·quant (ăl´ə kwənt), *adj. Math.* contained in a quantity, but not dividing it evenly.

al·i·quot (ăl´ə kwət), *adj. Math.* forming an exact proper divisor.

a·live (ə līv´), *adj.* **1.** in life or existence; living. **2.** of all living. **3.** in action, force, or operation. **4.** full of life; lively. **5.** **alive to**, attentive or sensitive to. **6.** swarming; thronged.

al·ka·li (ăl´kə lī´), *n., pl.* -lis, -lies. *Chem.* **1.** any of various bases, the hydroxides of the alkali metals, and of ammonium, which neutralize acids to form salts and turn red litmus paper blue. **2.** any of various other more or less active bases.

al·ka·line (ăl´kə lĭn´, -lĭn), *adj.* of or like an alkali; having the properties of an alkali. —**al·ka·lin·i·ty** (ăl´kə lĭn´ə tĭ), *n.*

al·ka·lize (ăl´kə līz´), *v.t.*, -lized, -lizing. to make alkaline. —**al´ka·li·za´tion**, *n.*

al·ka·loid (ăl´kə loid´), *n.* one of a class of basic nitrogenous organic compounds occurring in plants, such as nicotine, morphine, or quinine.

all (ôl), *adj.* **1.** the whole of. **2.** the whole number of. **3.** the greatest possible. **4.** every (chiefly with *kinds, sorts, manner*). **5.** any; any whatever. —*pron.* **6.** the whole quantity or amount. **7.** the whole number. **8.** everything. —*n.* **9.** a whole; a totality of things or qualities. **10.** one's whole interest or property. **11. above all**, before everything else. **12. after all**, a. notwithstanding. b. in spite of all that was done, said, etc. **13. all in all**, everything together. **14. at all**, a. in any degree. b. for any reason. c. in any way. **15. for all (that)**, notwithstanding; in spite of. **16. in all**, all included. **17. once and for all**, for the final time. —*adv.* **18.** wholly; entirely. **19.** exclusively. **20.** each.

Al·lah (ăl´ə, ä´lə), *n.* the Mohammedan name of the Supreme Being.

all-a·round (ôl´ə round´), *adj. U.S.* all-round.

al·lay (ə lā´), *v.t.*, -layed, -laying. **1.** to quiet (fear, etc.). **2.** to relieve. —**al·lay´er**, *n.*

al·le·ga·tion (ăl´ə gā´shən), *n.* **1.** act of alleging. **2.** a statement offered as a plea, excuse, or justification. **3.** an assertion without proof.

al·lege (ə lĕj´), *v.t.*, -leged, -leging. **1.** to declare with positiveness; assert. **2.** to declare before a court or upon oath. **3.** to assert without proof. **4.** to plead in support of; urge as a reason. —**al·leg·ed·ly** (ə lĕj´ĭd lĭ), *adv.* —**al·leg´er**, *n.*

Al·le·ghe·ny (ăl´ə gā´nĭ), *n.* a river flowing from SW New York through W Pennsylvania into the Ohio river at Pittsburgh. 325 mi.

Allegheny Mountains, a mountain range in Pennsylvania, Maryland, West Virginia, and Virginia. Also, **Alleghenies.**

al·le·giance (ə lē´jəns), *n.* **1.** the obligation or duty owed to a sovereign or state. **2.** observance of obligation.

al·le·gor·i·cal (ăl´ə gôr´ə kəl, -gŏr´-), *adj.* consisting of or pertaining to allegory; figurative. Also, **al'le·gor'ic.** —**al'le·gor'i·cal·ly,** adv.

al·le·go·rize (ăl'ə gə rīz'), v., **-rized, -rizing.** —v.t. 1. to turn into allegory. 2. to interpret allegorically. —v.i. 3. to use allegory.

al·le·go·ry (ăl'ə gōr'Y), n., pl. **-ries.** 1. figurative treatment of one subject under the guise of another. 2. a symbolical narrative.

al·le·gro (ə lā'grō, ə lĕg'-), adj., n., pl. **-gros.** Music. —adj. 1. brisk; rapid. —n. 2. an allegro movement.

al·le·lu·ia (ăl'ə lōō'yə), interj. 1. praise ye the Lord; hallelujah. —n. 2. a song of praise to God.

Al·len·town (ăl'ən toun'), n. a city in E Pennsylvania. 96,904.

al·ler·gic (ə lûr'jYk), adj. 1. of or pertaining to allergy. 2. affected with allergy.

al·ler·gy (ăl'ər jY), n., pl. **-gies.** a state of hypersensitiveness to certain things, as pollens, food, etc.

al·le·vi·ate (ə lē'vY āt'), v.t., **-ated, -ating.** to make easier to be endured; lessen; mitigate. —**al·le'vi·a'tion,** n. —**al·le'vi·a'tive,** adj.

al·ley (ăl'Y), n., pl. **-leys.** 1. a narrow, back street. 2. a walk, enclosed with hedges or shrubbery, in a garden. 3. a long narrow enclosure with a smooth wooden floor for bowling, etc.

All·hal·lows (ôl'hăl'ōz), n. All Saints' Day.

al·li·ance (ə lī'əns), n. 1. state of being allied or connected. 2. marriage, or the relation between families through marriage. 3. formal agreement by two or more nations to coöperate for specific purposes. 4. any joining of efforts or interests by persons, states, or organizations. 5. the persons or parties allied.

al·lied (ə līd', ăl'īd), adj. 1. joined by treaty. 2. related.

al·li·ga·tor (ăl'ə gā'tər), n. 1. the broad-snouted representative of the crocodile group found in the SE U.S. 2. any crocodilian.

alligator pear, an avocado (fruit).

al·lit·er·ate (ə lYt'ə rāt'), v.t., **-ated, -ating.** to show alliteration (with).

al·lit·er·a·tion (ə lYt'ə rā'shən), n. the commencement of two or more stressed syllables of a word group with the same sound or sound group (as in from stern to stern). —**al·lit'er·a'tive,** adj. —**al·lit'er·a'tive·ly,** adv.

al·lo·cate (ăl'ə kāt'), v.t., **-cated, -cating.** to assign or allot. —**al'lo·ca'tion,** n.

al·lo·path (ăl'ə păth'), n. one who practices allopathy. Also, **al·lop·a·thist** (ə lŏp'ə thYst).

al·lop·a·thy (ə lŏp'ə thY), n. the method of treating disease by the use of agents, producing effects different from those of the disease treated (opposed to homeopathy). —**al·lo·path·ic** (ăl'ə-păth'Yk), adj. —**al'lo·path'i·cal·ly,** adv.

al·lot (ə lŏt'), v.t., **-lotted, -lotting.** 1. to divide or distribute as by lot. 2. to appropriate to a special purpose. 3. to assign as a portion (to).

al·lot·ment (ə lŏt'mənt), n. 1. distribution as by lot. 2. a portion or thing allotted.

al·lo·trope (ăl'ə trōp'), n. one of two or more existing forms of a chemical element.

al·lot·ro·py (ə lŏt'rə pY), n. a property that certain chemical elements have of existing in two or more distinct forms. Also, **al·lot'ro·pism.** —**al·lo·trop·ic** (ăl'ə trŏp'Yk), adj.

all-out (ôl'out'), adj. complete; total.

al·low (ə lou'), v.t. 1. to grant permission to or for; permit. 2. to grant or give; assign as one's right. 3. to permit by neglect or oversight. 4. to admit; concede. 5. to take into account; deduct. 6. U.S. Dial. to say; think. —v.i. 7. allow of, to permit; admit. 8. allow for, to make concession, allowance, or provision for. —**al·low'a·ble,** adj.

al·low·ance (ə lou'əns), n., v., **-anced, -ancing.** —n. 1. a definite amount or share allotted. 2. a definite sum of money allotted for expenses. 3. a deduction. 4. admission. 5. tolerance.

al·loy (n. ăl'oi, ə loi'; v. ə loi'), n. 1. a substance composed of two or more metals intimately mixed by fusion or the like. 2. a metal mixed with a more valuable one. 3. standard; quality. 4. admixture, as of good with evil. —v.t. 5. to mix (metals) so as to form an alloy. 6. to reduce in value; debase, impair, or reduce by admixture.

all right, 1. safe and sound. 2. yes. 3. satisfactory. 4. correctly. 5. certainly.

all-round (ôl'round'), adj. 1. U.S. extending all about. 2. versatile; general.

All Saints' Day, a church festival celebrated Nov. 1 in honor of all the saints.

all·spice (ôl'spīs'), n. 1. the berry of a tropical American tree of the myrtle family. 2. a mildly sharp and fragrant spice made from it; pimento.

al·lude (ə lōōd'), v.i., **-luded, -luding.** to refer casually or indirectly (fol. by to).

al·lure (ə lōōr'), v., **-lured, -luring,** n. —v.t. 1. to attract or tempt by something flattering or desirable. —n. 2. charm. —**al·lure'ment,** n.

al·lu·sion (ə lōō'zhən), n. a passing or casual reference. —**al·lu·sive** (ə lōō'sYv), adj.

al·lu·vi·um (ə lōō'vY əm), n., pl. **-viums, -via** (-vY ə). a deposit of sand, mud, etc., formed by flowing water. —**al·lu'vi·al,** adj.

al·ly (v. ə lī'; n. ăl'ī, ə lī'), v., **-lied, -lying,** n., pl. **-lies.** —v.t. 1. to unite by marriage, treaty, league, etc. (fol. by to or with). 2. to connect by some relation, as by resemblance or friendship; associate. —v.i. 3. to join or unite. —n. 4. a person, nation, sovereign, etc., associated with another, esp. by treaty. 5. an associate.

al·ma ma·ter (ăl'mə mä'tər, ăl'-, ăl'mə mā'-tər), (also cap.) one's school, college, or university.

al·ma·nac (ôl'mə năk'), n. a calendar of the days of the year, indicating the various events or phenomena during the period, etc.

al·might·y (ôl mī'tY), adj. 1. possessing all power. —n. 2. the Almighty, God.

al·mond (ä'mənd, ăm'ənd), n. 1. the stone (nut) or kernel of the fruit of a tree in the peach family, which grows in warm temperate regions. 2. the tree itself. —**al'mond-like',** adj.

al·mon·er (ăl'mən ər, ä'mən-), n. a dispenser of alms or charity, esp. for a religious house.

al·most (ôl'mōst, ôl mōst'), adv. very nearly.

alms (ämz), n. sing. or pl. that which is given to the poor or needy; anything given as charity.

al·oe (ăl'ō), n., pl. **-oes.** 1. a liliaceous plant, chiefly African, various species of which yield a drug and a fiber. 2. (often pl. construed as sing.) a bitter purgative drug derived from this plant.

a·loft (ə lôft', ə lŏft'), adv., adj. 1. high up; in or into the air. 2. Naut. at or toward the masthead.

a·lo·ha (ə lō'ə, ä lō'hä), n., interj. Hawaiian. 1. greetings. 2. farewell.

a·lone (ə lōn'), adj. 1. apart from another or others. 2. to the exclusion of all others or all else. 3. by oneself. —adv. 4. solitarily. 5. only.

a·long (ə lông', ə lŏng'), prep. 1. through or by the length of; from one end to the other of. —adv. 2. in a line with the length. 3. onward. 4. U.S. Colloq. (of time) some way on. 5. together (fol. by with). 6. U.S. as a companion; with one.

a·long·side (ə lông'sīd', ə lŏng'-), adv. 1. along or by the side. —prep. 2. beside; by the side of.

a·loof (ə lōōf'), adv. 1. at a distance, but within view. —adj. 2. reserved; disinterested. —**a·loof'-ly,** adv. —**a·loof'ness,** n.

a·loud (ə loud'), adv. 1. with the natural tone of the voice, as distinguished from whispering. 2. with a loud voice; loudly.

al·pac·a (ăl păk'ə), n. 1. a domesticated sheep-like South American ruminant allied to the llama, having long, soft, silky hair or wool. 2. the hair. 3. a fabric made of it.

al·pen·stock (ăl'pən stŏk'), n. a strong staff pointed with iron, used by mountain climbers.

al·pha (ăl'fə), n. 1. the first letter in the Greek alphabet (A, α). 2. the first; beginning.

al·pha·bet (ăl'fə bĕt'), n. the letters of a language in their customary order.

al·pha·bet·i·cal (ăl'fə bĕt'ə kəl), adj. 1. in the order of the alphabet. 2. pertaining to or expressed by an alphabet. Also, **al'pha·bet'ic.** —**al'pha·bet'i·cal·ly,** adv.

al·pha·bet·ize (ăl'fə bə tīz'), v.t., **-ized, -izing.** to arrange in the order of the alphabet.

alpha particle, Physics. a positively charged particle composed of two protons and two neutrons, and spontaneously emitted by some radioactive material such as radium.

alpha ray, Physics. a stream of alpha particles.

al·pine (ăl'pīn, -pYn), adj. 1. of or pertaining to a lofty mountain. 2. (cap.) of the Alps.

Alps (ălps), n. a mountain system in S Europe from France through Switzerland and Italy into Austria and Yugoslavia. Highest peak, Mt. Blanc.

al·read·y (ôl rĕd'Y), adv. by this (or that) time; previously to or at some specified time.

al·so (ôl'sō), adv. in addition; too; further.

alt., 1. alternate. 2. altitude. 3. alto.

al·tar (ôl'tər), n. 1. an elevated place or structure, on which sacrifices are offered or at which religious rites are performed. 2. (in most Christian churches) the communion table.

al·ter (ôl′tər), *v.t., v.i.* to make or become different. —**al′ter·a·ble,** *adj.*

al·ter·a·tion (ôl′tə rā′shən), *n.* **1.** act of altering. **2.** condition of being altered. **3.** a change. —**al′ter·a′tive,** *adj.*

al·ter·ca·tion (ôl′tər kā′shən, ăl′-), *n.* a heated or angry dispute; a noisy wrangle.

al·ter·nate (*v.* ôl′tər nāt′, ăl′-; *adj., n.* ôl′tərnĭt, ăl′-), *v.,* -nated, -nating, *adj., n.* —*v.i.* **1.** to follow one another in time or place reciprocally. **2.** *Elect.* to reverse direction or sign periodically. —*v.t.* **3.** to perform by turns, or one after another. **4.** to interchange successively. —*adj.* **5.** being by turns. **6.** reciprocal. **7.** every other one of a series. —*n.* **8.** *U.S.* an authorized substitute. —**al′ter·nate·ly,** *adv.*

alternating current, *Elect.* a current that reverses direction in regular cycles.

al·ter·na·tion (ôl′tər nā′shən, ăl′-), *n.* alternate succession, appearance, or change.

al·ter·na·tive (ôl tûr′nə tĭv, ăl-), *n.* **1.** a possibility of one out of two (or, less strictly, more) things. **2.** one of the things thus possible. **3.** a remaining course or choice. —*adj.* **4.** affording a choice between two things. **5.** (of two things) mutually exclusive. —**al·ter′na·tive·ly,** *adv.*

al·ter·na·tor (ôl′tər nā′tər, ăl′-), *n. Elect.* a generator of alternating current.

alt·horn (ălt′hôrn′), *n.* a valved, brass-wind horn, a fourth or fifth below the ordinary cornet. Also, **alto horn.**

al·though (ôl thō′), *conj.* even though. Also, **al·tho′.**

al·tim·e·ter (ăl tĭm′ə tər, ăl′təmē′tər), *n.* **1.** a sensitive aneroid barometer used in aviation, etc., to measure altitudes by means of air pressure. **2.** any device for the same purpose which operates by other means, as by radio waves, etc.

al·ti·tude (ăl′tə tūd′, -tōōd′), *n.* **1.** height above sea level. **2.** extent or distance upward. **3.** *Astron.* the angular distance of a star, planet, etc., above the horizon. **4.** *Geom.* the perpendicular distance from the base of a figure to its highest point.

Althorn

al·to (ăl′tō), *n., pl.* -tos, *adj. Music.* —*n.* **1.** the lowest female voice. **2.** a singer with such a voice. **3.** a musical part for such a voice. **4.** the viola. —*adj.* **5.** of the alto; having the alto compass.

al·to·geth·er (ôl′tə gĕth′ər), *adv.* **1.** wholly; entirely. **2.** in all. **3.** on the whole.

Al·ton (ôl′tən), *n.* a city in SW Illinois. 31,255.

Al·too·na (ăl tōō′nə), *n.* a city in central Pennsylvania. 80,214.

al·tru·ism (ăl′trōō ĭz′əm), *n.* the principle or practice of seeking the welfare of others. —**al′tru·ist,** *n.* —**al′tru·is′tic,** *adj.*

al·um (ăl′əm), *n.* **1.** an astringent crystalline substance, a double sulfate of aluminum and potassium, used in medicine, dyeing, and many technical processes. **2.** one of a class of double sulfates analogous to the potassium alum.

al·u·min·i·um (ăl′yə mĭn′ĭ əm), *n. Brit.* aluminum.

a·lu·mi·num (ə lōō′mə nəm), *n.* a silver-white metallic element, light in weight, ductile, and malleable. *Symbol:* Al; *at. wt.:* 26.97; *at. no.:* 13; *sp. gr.:* 2.70 at 20°C. —**a·lu′mi·nous** (ə lōō′mənəs), *adj.*

a·lum·na (ə lŭm′nə), *n., pl.* -nae (-nē) *Chiefly U.S.* fem. of alumnus.

a·lum·nus (ə lŭm′nəs), *n., pl.* -ni (-nī) a graduate or former student of a school, college, etc.

al·way (ôl′wā), *adv. Archaic or Poetic.* always.

al·ways (ôl′wāz, -wĭz), *adv.* **1.** all the time; uninterruptedly. **2.** every time; on every occasion.

a·lys·sum (ə lĭs′əm), *n.* **1.** any of the herbs of the mustard family, characterized by small yellow or white racemose flowers. **2.** sweet alyssum.

am (ăm; *unstressed* əm, m), *v.* 1st pers. sing. pres. indic. of be.

Am, *Chem.* americium.

Am., **1.** America. **2.** American.

A.M., **1.** (L *ante meridiem*) before noon. **2.** the period from 12 midnight to 12 noon. Also, **a.m.**

A.M., amplitude modulation. Also, **AM**

A.M., (L *Artium Magister*) Master of Arts.

a·main (ə mān′), *adv. Archaic and Poetic.* **1.** with full force. **2.** at full speed. **3.** suddenly.

a·mal·gam (ə măl′gəm), *n.* **1.** an alloy of mercury with another metal or metals. **2.** a rare mineral, an alloy of silver and mercury. **3.** a mixture.

a·mal·gam·ate (ə măl′gə māt′), *v.,* -ated, -ating. —*v.t.* **1.** to blend; unite; combine. **2.** *Metall.* to mix or alloy (a metal) with mercury. —*v.i.* **3.** to combine or coalesce. **4.** to blend with another metal. —**a·mal′gam·a′tion,** *n.*

a·man·u·en·sis (ə măn′yōō ĕn′sĭs), *n., pl.* -ses (-sēz) a person employed to take dictation or copy what has been written by another; secretary.

am·a·ranth (ăm′ə rănth′), *n.* **1.** *Poetic.* a flower that never fades. **2.** any plant, chiefly herbaceous or shrubby, of a genus which includes species cultivated for their showy flowers.

am·a·ran·thine (ăm′ə răn′thĭn, -thīn), *adj.* **1.** of the amaranth. **2.** unfading. **3.** purplish.

Am·a·ril·lo (ăm′ə rĭl′ō), *n.* a city in NW Texas. 51,686.

am·a·ryl·lis (ăm′ə rĭl′ĭs), *n.* **1.** a bulbous plant with large, lilylike, normally rose-colored flowers. **2.** any of several related plants.

a·mass (ə măs′), *v.t.* **1.** to gather or collect for oneself. **2.** to collect into a mass or pile. —**a·mass′ment,** *n.*

am·a·teur (ăm′ə chōōr′, -tyōōr′; ăm′ə tûr′), *n.* **1.** one who cultivates any study, art, etc., for personal pleasure instead of professionally or for gain **2.** a superficial or unskillful worker. —**am′a·teur′ish,** *adj.* —**am′a·teur′ish·ly,** *adv.* —**am′a·teur′ish·ness,** *n.* —**am′a·teur·ism,** *n.*

Amaryllis

am·a·to·ry (ăm′ə tōr′ĭ), *adj.* pertaining to lovers or lovemaking; expressive of love.

a·maze (ə māz′), *v.t.,* amazed, amazing. to overwhelm with surprise; astonish greatly.

a·maze·ment (ə māz′mənt), *n.* overwhelming surprise or astonishment.

a·maz·ing (ə mā′zĭng), *adj.* causing great surprise; wonderful. —**a·maz′ing·ly,** *adv.*

Am·a·zon (ăm′ə zŏn′, -zən), *n.* **1.** a river in N South America, flowing from the Peruvian Andes E through N Brazil to the Atlantic: the largest river in the world. ab. 3500 mi. **2.** *Gk. Legend.* one of a race of female warriors said to dwell near the Black Sea. **3.** (*often l.c.*) a tall, powerful, aggressive woman. —**Am·a·zo·ni·an** (ăm′ə zō′nĭən), *adj.*

am·bas·sa·dor (ăm băs′ə dər), *n.* **1.** a diplomatic agent of the highest rank, sent by one sovereign or state to another. **2.** an authorized messenger. —**am·bas·sa·do·ri·al** (ăm băs′ə dōr′ĭ əl), *adj.* —**am·bas′sa·dor·ship′,** *n.*

am·ber (ăm′bər), *n.* **1.** a pale-yellow, sometimes reddish or brownish, fossil resin of vegetable origin. **2.** yellowish brown. —*adj.* **3.** of or like amber.

am·ber·gris (ăm′bər grēs′, -grĭs′), *n.* an opaque, ash-colored substance, a morbid secretion of the sperm whale, usually found floating on the ocean or cast ashore, used in perfumery.

am·bi·dex·trous (ăm′bə dĕk′strəs), *adj.* **1.** able to use both hands equally well. **2.** unusually skillful. —**am′bi·dex′trous·ly,** *adv.*

am·bi·ent (ăm′bĭ ənt), *adj.* **1.** completely surrounding. **2.** circulating.

am·bi·gu·i·ty (ăm′bə gū′ə tĭ), *n., pl.* -ties. **1.** doubtfulness or uncertainty of meaning. **2.** an equivocal or ambiguous word or expression.

am·big·u·ous (ăm bĭg′yōō əs), *adj.* **1.** open to various interpretations; having a double meaning. **2.** of doubtful nature. **3.** indistinct. —**am·big′u·ous·ly,** *adv.* —**am·big′u·ous·ness,** *n.*

am·bi·tion (ăm bĭsh′ən), *n.* **1.** an eager desire for distinction, preferment, power, or fame. **2.** the object desired or sought after. **3.** energy.

am·bi·tious (ăm bĭsh′əs), *adj.* **1.** eagerly desirous of obtaining power, superiority, or distinction. **2.** showing ambition. **3.** pretentious. —**am·bi′tious·ly,** *adv.* —**am·bi′tious·ness,** *n.*

am·bi·ver·sion (ăm′bə vûr′zhən, -shən), *n. Psychol.* the condition between extrovert and introvert personality types. —**am′bi·vert′,** *n.*

am·ble (ăm′bəl), *v.,* -bled, -bling, *n.* —*v.i.* **1.** to move with the gait of a horse when it lifts first the two legs on one side and then the two on the other. **2.** to go at an easy pace. —*n.* **3.** an ambling gait. **4.** an easy pace. —**am′bler,** *n.*

am·bro·sia (ăm brō′zhə), *n.* the food of the gods of classical mythology, imparting immortality. —**am·bro′sial, am·bro′sian,** *adj.*

am·bu·lance (ăm′byə ləns), *n.* a vehicle, boat, or aircraft, equipped for carrying sick or wounded.

am·bu·late (ăm/byə lāt/), v.i., -lated, -lating. to walk or move about, or from place to place.

am·bu·la·to·ry (ăm/byə lə tōr/ĭ), adj., n., pl. -ries. —adj. 1. pertaining to or capable of walking. 2. adapted for walking. 3. moving about. 4. Med. not confined to bed. —n. 5. Archit. a place for walking.

am·bus·cade (ăm/bəs kād/), n., v., -caded, -cading. —n. 1. an ambush. —v.i. 2. to lie in ambush. —v.t. 3. to attack from ambush.

am·bush (ăm/bŏŏsh), n. Also, **am/bush·ment.** 1. act of lying concealed so as to attack by surprise. 2. act of attacking unexpectedly from a concealed position. 3. a concealed station where troops wait to attack unawares. —v.t. 4. to attack from ambush. —**am/bush·er**, n.

a·me·ba (ə mē/bə), n. amoeba.

a·mel·io·rate (ə mēl/yə rāt/), v.t., v.i. -rated, -rating. to improve. —**a·mel/io·ra·ble**, adj. —**a·mel/io·ra/tion**, n. —**a·mel/io·ra/tive**, adj.

a·men (ā/mĕn/, ä/-), interj. it is so; so be it (used after a prayer, creed, etc.).

a·me·na·ble (ə mē/nə bəl, ə mĕn/ə-), adj. disposed or ready to answer, yield, or submit. —**a·me/na·bil/i·ty**, n. —**a·me/na·bly**, adv.

a·mend (ə mĕnd/), v.t. 1. to alter (a motion, bill, constitution, etc.) by due formal procedure. 2. to improve. 3. to rectify. —v.i. 4. to become better by reforming oneself. —**a·mend/a·ble**, adj.

a·mend·ment (ə mĕnd/mənt), n. 1. act of amending; improvement. 2. alteration of a motion, constitution, etc. 3. a change so made.

a·mends (ə mĕndz/), n. sing. or pl. reparation or compensation for a loss, damage, or injury.

a·men·i·ty (ə mĕn/ə tĭ, -mē/nə-), n., pl. -ties. 1. (pl.) agreeable features, ways, etc.; civilities. 2. pleasantness or agreeableness.

am·ent (ăm/ənt, ā/mənt), n. Bot. a spike of unisexual apetalous flowers with scaly bracts.

Amer., 1. America. 2. American.

A·mer·i·ca (ə mĕr/ə kə), n. 1. the United States of America. 2. North America. 3. South America. 4. North America and South America. —**A·mer/i·can**, adj., n.

A·mer·i·ca·na (ə mĕr/ə kä/nə, -kăn/ə, -kä/nə), n.pl. books, papers, etc., relating to America, esp. to its history and geography.

American cheese, a smooth white or yellow hard cheese with a slightly acid flavor; cheddar.

A·mer·i·can·ism (ə mĕr/ə kə nĭz/əm), n. 1. devotion to or preference for the United States and its institutions. 2. a custom, trait, expression, or thing peculiar to the United States.

A·mer·i·can·ize (ə mĕr/ə kə nīz/), v.t., v.i., -ized, -izing. to make or become American in character. —**A·mer/i·can·i·za/tion**, n.

American plan, (in hotels) a system of paying a fixed sum that includes both room and meals.

American Revolution, the war between Great Britain and her American colonies, 1775–83, by which the colonies won their independence.

am·er·i·ci·um (ăm/ə rĭsh/ĭ əm), n. a radioactive element, one of the products of the bombardment of uranium and plutonium by very energetic helium ions. Symbol: Am; at. no.: 95.

am·e·thyst (ăm/ə thĭst), n. 1. Mineral. a coarsely crystallized purple or violet quartz used in jewelry. 2. the violet sapphire.

a·mi·a·ble (ā/mĭ ə bəl), adj. 1. having or showing agreeable personal qualities, as kindheartedness, etc. 2. friendly; kindly. —**a/mi·a·bil/i·ty, a/mi·a·ble·ness**, n. —**a/mi·a·bly**, adv.

am·i·ca·ble (ăm/ə kə bəl), adj. friendly; peaceable. —**am/i·ca·bil/i·ty**, n. —**am/i·ca·bly**, adv.

a·mid (ə mĭd/), prep. in the midst of; among.

am·ide (ăm/īd, -ĭd), n. Chem. a metallic derivative of ammonia in which the NH_2 grouping is retained.

a·mid·ships (ə mĭd/shĭps), adv. in or toward the middle of a ship. Also, **a·mid/ship.**

a·midst (ə mĭdst/), prep. amid.

a·mine (ə mēn/, ăm/ĭn), n. Chem. any of a class of compounds prepared from ammonia by replacing one, two, or all hydrogen atoms with organic radicals.

am·i·no acids (ăm/ə nō, ə mē/nō), Chem. a group of organic acids containing the NH_2 radical: the basic constituents of proteins.

a·miss (ə mĭs/), adv. 1. out of the proper course or order; wrongly. 2. **take amiss**, to be offended at; resent. —adj. 3. improper; wrong.

am·i·ty (ăm/ə tĭ), n., pl. -ties. friendship; harmony; good understanding, esp. between nations.

am·me·ter (ăm/mē/tər), n. Elect. an instrument for measuring electric currents in amperes.

am·mo·nia (ə mōn/yə, ə mō/nĭ ə), n. 1. a colorless, pungent, suffocating gas, NH_3, a compound of nitrogen and hydrogen, very soluble in water. 2. Also, **ammonia water** or **aqueous ammonia.** this gas dissolved in water, the common commercial form. —**am·mo·ni·ac** (ə mō/nĭ ăk/), **am·mo·ni·a·cal** (ăm/ə nī/ə kəl), adj.

am·mo·ni·um (ə mō/nĭ əm), n. Chem. a radical, NH_4, which plays the part of a metal in compounds formed when ammonia reacts with acids.

am·mu·ni·tion (ăm/yə nĭsh/ən), n. the material used in discharging firearms or other weapons that throw projectiles, as powder, shot, shrapnel, bullets, etc.

am·ne·sia (ăm nē/zhə), n. Psychiatry. loss of a large block of interrelated memories.

am·nes·ty (ăm/nəs tĭ), n., pl. -ties, v., -tied, -tying. —n. 1. a general pardon for offenses against a government. —v.t. 2. to grant amnesty to.

a·moe·ba (ə mē/bə), n., pl. -bae (-bē), bas. Zool. a microscopic, one-celled animal consisting of a naked mass of protoplasm constantly changing in shape as it moves and engulfs food. —**a·moe/bic**, adj.

a·mok (ə mŭk/, ə mŏk/), n. 1. (among Malays) a psychic disturbance characterized by depression followed by overwhelming desire to murder. —adv. 2. **run amok.** See **amuck.**

a·mong (ə mŭng/), prep. 1. in or into the midst of; in association with. 2. to each of. 3. in the number, class, or group of. 4. with or by all of. 5. by the joint action of. 6. mutually.

a·mongst (ə mŭngst/), prep. Literary or Brit. among.

a·mon·til·la·do (ə mŏn/tə lä/dō), n. a pale-colored, quite dry, Spanish sherry.

a·mor·al (ā môr/əl, ā mŏr/-, ă-), adj. without moral quality; neither moral nor immoral.

am·o·rous (ăm/ə rəs), adj. 1. inclined or disposed to love. 2. in love; enamored. 3. showing love. —**am/o·rous·ly**, adv. —**am/o·rous·ness**, n.

a·mor·phism (ə môr/fĭz əm), n. 1. state or quality of being amorphous. 2. nihilism.

a·mor·phous (ə môr/fəs), adj. 1. lacking definite form. 2. of no particular kind or character; indeterminate. 3. Geol. occurring in a mass, as without stratification. 4. Chem. non-crystalline. —**a·mor/phous·ly**, adv.

am·or·tize (ăm/ər tīz/, ə môr/tĭz), v.t., -tized, -tizing. to liquidate (an indebtedness). —**am/or·tiz/a·ble**, adj. —**am·or·ti·za·tion** (ăm/ər tə zā/-shən, ə môr/-), **a·mor·tize·ment** (ə môr/tĭz mənt), n.

A·mos (ā/məs), n. 1. a Hebrew prophet of the eighth century B.C., author of the Old Testament book bearing his name. 2. this book.

a·mount (ə mount/), n. 1. the sum total of two or more quantities; the aggregate. 2. quantity. 3. the full effect, value, or import. —v.i. 4. to reach, extend, or be equal in quantity, effect, etc.

a·mour (ə mŏŏr/), n. 1. a love affair. 2. an illicit love affair.

am·per·age (ăm pĭr/ĭj, ăm/pər-), n. Elect. the strength of an electric current, in amperes.

am·pere (ăm/pĭr, ăm pĭr/), n. Elect. the usual unit of current strength: the current produced by an electromotive force of one volt acting through a resistance of one ohm. Also, **am·père** (äN pĕr/).

am·per·sand (ăm/pər sănd/, ăm/pər sănd/), n. the name of the character (&) meaning and.

am·phet·a·mine (ăm fĕt/ə mēn/, -mĭn), n. Pharm. a drug which is commonly used as a spray or inhaled to relieve nasal congestion.

Am·phib·i·a (ăm fĭb/ĭ ə), n.pl. Zool. the class of vertebrates that includes the frogs, salamanders, etc. Typically they lay eggs that hatch in water, and the young go through a fishlike larval, or tadpole, stage, later metamorphosing into lung-breathing quadrupeds.

am·phib·i·an (ăm fĭb/ĭ ən), n. 1. any animal of the class Amphibia. 2. an amphibious plant. 3. an airplane that can take off from and land on either land or water. —adj. 4. belonging to the class Amphibia. 5. capable of operating on land or water.

am·phib·i·ous (ăm fĭb/ĭ əs), adj. 1. living both on land and in water. 2. capable of operating on both land and water. 3. of a twofold nature. —**am·phib/i·ous·ly**, adv.

am·phi·the·a·ter (ăm/fə thē/ə tər), n. a building with tiers of seats around a central area, as those used in ancient Rome for gladiatorial contests.

am·ple (ăm'pəl), *adj.*, **-pler, -plest. 1.** of great extent, size, or amount. **2.** copious. **3.** sufficient. —**am'ple·ness,** *n.* —**am·ply** (ăm'plĭ), *adv.*

am·pli·fi·ca·tion (ăm'plə fə kā'shən), *n.* **1.** act of amplifying; expansion. **2.** *Elect.* increase in the strength of current, voltage, or power.

am·pli·fy (ăm'plə fī'), *v.,* **-fied, -fying.** —*v.t.* **1.** to make larger or greater; enlarge. **2.** to expand in stating or describing, as by details, etc. **3.** *Elect.* to increase the amplitude of (impulses or waves). —*v.i.* **4.** to discourse at length. —**am'pli·fi'er,** *n.*

am·pli·tude (ăm'plə tūd', -tōōd'), *n.* **1.** extension in space, esp. width. **2.** abundance. **3.** *Physics.* the distance or range from one extremity of an oscillation to the middle point or neutral value. **4.** *Elect.* the maximum strength of an alternating current during its cycle.

amplitude modulation, *Electronics.* a system of radio transmission in which the carrier wave is modulated by changing its amplitude.

am·pu·tate (ăm'pyŏŏ tāt'), *v.t.,* **-tated, -tating.** to cut off (a limb, arm, etc.) by a surgical operation. —**am'pu·ta'tion,** *n.* —**am'pu·ta'tor,** *n.*

am·pu·tee (ăm'pyŏŏ tē'), *n.* one who has lost an arm, hand, leg, etc., by amputation.

Am·ster·dam (ăm'stər dăm'), *n.* a seaport in and the parliamentary capital of the Netherlands, in the W part. 780,070.

amt., amount.

a·muck (ə mŭk'), *adv.* (*orig. adj.*) **1. run amuck, a.** to rush about in a murderous frenzy. **b.** to rush about wildly. —*n.* **2.** amok.

am·u·let (ăm'yə lĭt), *n.* an object superstitiously worn to ward off evil; a protecting charm.

a·muse (ə mūz'), *v.t.,* **amused, amusing. 1.** to hold the attention of agreeably; entertain. **2.** to excite mirth in. —**a·mus'a·ble,** *adj.* —**a·mus'er,** *n.* —**a·mus'ing,** *adj.* —**a·mus'ing·ly,** *adv.*

a·muse·ment (ə mūz'mənt), *n.* **1.** state of being amused; enjoyment. **2.** that which amuses.

am·y·tal (ăm'ə tôl', -tăl'), *n.* *Pharm.* a colorless crystalline substance, used esp. as a sedative.

an[1] (ăn; *unstressed* ən), the form of the indefinite article before an initial vowel sound. See **a**[1].

an[2] (ăn; *unstressed* ən), *conj.* **1.** *Dial. and Colloq.* and. **2.** *Archaic and Dial.* if. Also, **an'.**

-an, a suffix meaning "belonging to," "pertaining to," "adhering to," etc., serving to form adjectives (as *American* and *republican*) and some nouns (as *historian* and *theologian*).

a·nab·o·lism (ə năb'ə lĭz'əm), *n.* *Biol.* constructive metabolism. —**an·a·bol·ic** (ăn'ə bŏl'ĭk), *adj.*

a·nach·ro·nism (ə năk'rə nĭz'əm), *n.* **1.** a crediting of a person or thing to a time other, esp. earlier, than the actual period. **2.** something placed out of its proper time. —**a·nach·ro·nis·tic** (ə năk'rə nĭs'tĭk), *adj.*

an·a·co·lu·thon (ăn'ə kə lōō'thŏn), *n., pl.* **-tha** (-thə). *Rhet.* a break in grammatical sequence.

an·a·con·da (ăn'ə kŏn'də), *n.* a large South American snake of the boa family.

A·nac·re·on (ə năk'rĭ ən), *n.* c563–c478 B.C., Greek poet: wrote love poems and drinking songs.

a·nae·mia (ə nē'mĭ ə), *n.* anemia.

an·aer·o·bic (ăn'â rō'bĭk), *adj.* *Biol., Physiol.* (of organisms or tissues) requiring the absence of free oxygen or not destroyed by its absence.

an·aes·the·sia (ăn'əs thē'zhə), *n.* anesthesia.

an·a·gram (ăn'ə grăm'), *n.* **1.** a transposition of the letters of a word or sentence to form a new word or sentence. **2.** (*pl.* construed as *sing.*) a game in which the players build words by transposing or adding letters.

a·nal (ā'nəl), *adj.* of or near the anus.

an·al·ge·si·a (ăn'əl jē'zĭ ə, -sĭ ə), *n.* *Med.* absence of sense of pain.

an·al·ge·sic (ăn'əl jē'zĭk, -sĭk), *Med.* —*n.* **1.** a remedy that relieves or removes pain. —*adj.* **2.** pertaining to or causing analgesia.

a·nal·o·gous (ə năl'ə gəs), *adj.* **1.** having analogy; corresponding. **2.** *Biol.* corresponding in function, but not evolved from corresponding organs. —**a·nal'o·gous·ly,** *adv.*

a·nal·o·gy (ə năl'ə jĭ), *n., pl.* **-gies. 1.** a partial similarity in particular circumstances on which a comparison may be based. **2.** agreement; similarity. **3.** *Biol.* an analogous relationship.

a·nal·y·sis (ə năl'ə sĭs), *n., pl.* **-ses** (-sēz'). **1.** separation of a whole into its constituent ele-

ments. **2.** this process as a method of studying the nature or essential features of a thing. **3.** an outline or summary, as of a book; synopsis. **4.** *Chem.* the ascertainment of the kind or amount of one or more of the constituents of a substance. **5.** psychoanalysis.

an·a·lyst (ăn'ə lĭst), *n.* **1.** one who analyzes or who is skilled in analysis. **2.** a psychoanalyst.

an·a·lyt·ic (ăn'ə lĭt'ĭk), *adj.* pertaining to or proceeding by analysis. Also, **an'a·lyt'i·cal.** —**an'a·lyt'i·cal·ly,** *adv.*

an·a·lyze (ăn'ə līz'), *v.t.,* **-lyzed, -lyzing. 1.** to determine the elements or essential features of. **2.** to subject to chemical, etc., analysis. Also, *esp. Brit.,* **an'a·lyse'.** —**an'a·lyz'a·ble,** *adj.* —**an'a·lyz'er,** *n.*

an·a·pest (ăn'ə pĕst'), *n.* *Pros.* a foot of three syllables, two short followed by one long (quantitative meter), or two unstressed followed by one stressed (accentual meter). Also, **an'a·paest'.**

an·ar·chism (ăn'ər kĭz'əm), *n.* the doctrine urging the abolition of government and governmental restraint as the indispensable condition of political and social liberty. —**an'ar·chist,** *n.* —**an'ar·chis'tic,** *adj.*

an·ar·chy (ăn'ər kĭ), *n.* **1.** a state of society without government or law. **2.** confusion; disorder. —**an·ar·chic** (ăn är'kĭk), **an·ar'chi·cal,** *adj.* —**an·ar'chi·cal·ly,** *adv.*

anat., **1.** anatomical. **2.** anatomy.

a·nath·e·ma (ə năth'ə mə), *n., pl.* **-mas. 1.** a formal ecclesiastical curse involving excommunication. **2.** any imprecation of divine punishment. **3.** a curse. **4.** a person or thing detested.

a·nath·e·ma·tize (ə năth'ə mə tīz'), *v.t., v.i.,* **-tized, -tizing.** to curse.

an·a·tom·i·cal (ăn'ə tŏm'ə kəl), *adj.* pertaining to anatomy. Also, **an'a·tom'ic.** —**an'a·tom'i·cal·ly,** *adv.*

a·nat·o·mist (ə năt'ə mĭst), *n.* an expert in anatomy.

a·nat·o·mize (ə năt'ə mīz'), *v.t.,* **-mized, -mizing. 1.** to dissect, as an animal, to show the position, structure, and relation of the parts. **2.** to examine minutely. —**a·nat'o·mi·za'tion,** *n.*

a·nat·o·my (ə năt'ə mĭ), *n., pl.* **-mies. 1.** the structure of an animal or plant, or any of its parts. **2.** the science of the structure of animals and plants.

anc., ancient.

-ance, a suffix of nouns denoting action, state, or quality, or something exemplifying one of these, as in *brilliance, distance,* or *defiance.*

an·ces·tor (ăn'sĕs tər), *n.* one from whom a person is descended, usually distantly.

an·ces·tral (ăn sĕs'trəl), *adj.* pertaining to ancestors; descending or claimed from ancestors.

an·ces·try (ăn'sĕs trĭ), *n., pl.* **-tries. 1.** ancestral descent. **2.** honorable descent. **3.** a series of ancestors.

an·chor (ăng'kər), *n.* **1.** a device for holding boats, floating bridges, etc., in place. **2.** any similar device for holding fast or checking motion. **3.** a means of stability. **4. at anchor,** anchored. —*v.t.* **5.** to hold fast by an anchor. **6.** to fasten. —*v.i.* **7.** to lie or ride at anchor.

an·chor·age (ăng'kər ĭj), *n.* **1.** a place for anchoring. **2.** a charge for anchoring.

an·cho·ress (ăng'kə rĭs), *n.* a female anchorite.

an·cho·rite (ăng'kə rīt'), *n.* one who has retired to a solitary place for a life of religious seclusion. Also, **an·cho·ret** (ăng'kə rĭt, -rĕt').

an·cho·vy (ăn'chō vĭ, -chə vĭ, ăn chō'vĭ), *n., pl.* **-vies. 1.** a small herringlike marine fish, abundant in South Europe, much used pickled and in the form of a paste. **2.** *U.S.* any smelt.

an·cient (ān'shənt), *adj.* **1.** of or in time long past, esp. before the end of the Western Roman Empire, A.D. 476. **2.** of great age. **3.** very old. —*n.* **4.** a person who lived in ancient times, esp. one of the Greeks, Romans, etc.

an·cient·ly (ān'shənt lĭ), *adv.* in ancient times.

-ancy, an equivalent of **-ance,** used chiefly in nouns denoting state or quality, as in *buoyancy.*

and (ănd; *unstressed* ənd, ən), *conj.* **1.** with; along with; besides; also (used to connect grammatically coördinate words, phrases, or clauses). **2.** as well as. **3.** *Colloq.* to (used between verbs). **4.** *Archaic or Literary.* also; then.

An·da·lu·sia (ăn'də lōō'zhə, -shĭ ə), *n.* a region in S Spain, bordering on the Atlantic and the Mediterranean. —**An'da·lu'sian,** *adj., n.*

an·dan·te (ăn dăn'tĭ), *Music.* —*adj., adv.* **1.**

moderately slow and even. —*n.* 2. an andante movement or piece.

An·der·sen (ăn'dər sən), *n.* **Hans Christian**, 1805–75, Danish author, esp. of fairy tales.

An·der·son (ăn'dər sən), *n.* a city in central Indiana. 41,572.

An·des (ăn'dēz), *n.pl.* a lofty mountain system in W South America, extending ab. 4500 mi. from N Colombia and Venezuela S to Cape Horn. Highest peak, Aconcagua, 23,003 ft. —**An·de·an** (ăn dē'ən, ăn'dĬ-), *adj.*

and·i·ron (ănd'ī'ərn), *n.* one of a pair of metallic stands, usually of iron, used to support wood burned in an open fireplace.

An·dor·ra (ăn dôr'ə, -dôr'ə), *n.* a small republic in the E Pyrenees between France and Spain. ab. 6000 pop.; 191 sq. mi. *Cap.:* Andorra.

An·drew (ăn'drōō), *n. Bible.* one of the twelve apostles of Jesus.

an·dro·gen (ăn'drə jən), *n. Biochem.* any substance, natural or synthetic, which promotes masculine characteristics.

An·drom·e·da (ăn drŏm'ə də), *n. Astron.* a northern constellation.

an·ec·dote (ăn'Ĭk dōt'), *n.* a short narrative of a particular incident or occurrence of an interesting nature. —**an·ec·do·tal** (ăn'Ĭk dō'təl, ăn'Ĭk·dō'təl), *adj.*

a·ne·mi·a (ə nē'mĬ ə), *n. Pathol.* a quantitative deficiency of the hemoglobin, often accompanied by a reduced number of red blood cells, and causing pallor, weakness, and breathlessness. —**a·ne·mic** (ə nē'mĬk), *adj.*

an·e·mom·e·ter (ăn'ə mŏm'ə tər), *n. Meteorol.* an instrument for indicating wind velocity.

a·nem·o·ne (ə něm'ə nē'), *n.* any plant of the crowfoot family, esp. a spring wild flower with slender stem and delicate whitish blossoms.

an·er·oid (ăn'ə roid'), *adj.* 1. using no fluid. —*n.* 2. an aneroid barometer.

aneroid barometer, an instrument for measuring atmospheric pressure and, indirectly, altitude, by registering the pressure exerted on the elastic top of a chamber exhausted of air.

an·es·the·sia (ăn'əs thē'zhə), *n.* general or local insensibility, as to pain and other sensation, induced by certain drugs, caused by disease, etc.

an·es·thet·ic (ăn'əs thĕt'Ĭk), *n.* 1. a substance such as ether, cocaine, etc., that produces anesthesia. —*adj.* 2. pertaining to or causing physical insensibility. 3. insensitive.

an·es·the·tist (ə nĕs'thə tĬst), *n.* a person who administers anesthetics.

an·es·the·tize (ə nĕs'thə tīz'), *v.t.*, **-tized, -tizing.** to render physically insensible, as by an anesthetic. —**a·nes'the·ti·za'tion,** *n.*

a·new (ə nū', ə nōō'), *adv.* again; once more.

an·gel (ān'jəl), *n.* 1. *Theol.* one of a class of spiritual beings, attendants or messengers of God. 2. a person who resembles an angel in beauty, kindliness, etc. 3. *Colloq.* a financial backer of a play, campaign, etc. —**an·gel·ic** (ăn jĕl'Ĭk), **an·gel'i·cal,** *adj.*

angel food cake, a delicate white cake made without shortening. Also, **angel cake.**

An·ge·lus (ăn'jə ləs), *n. Rom. Cath. Ch.* 1. a devotion in memory of the Annunciation. 2. the bell (**Angelus bell**) tolled morning, noon, and evening, to indicate the Angelus is to be said.

an·ger (ăng'gər), *n.* 1. a revengeful passion or emotion directed against one who inflicts a real or supposed wrong; wrath; ire. —*v.t.* 2. to excite to anger or wrath.

an·gi·na (ăn jī'nə; *in Med. often* ăn'jə-), *n. Pathol.* 1. any inflammatory affection of the throat or fauces, as mumps. 2. angina pectoris.

angina pec·to·ris (pĕk'tə rĬs), *Pathol.* a syndrome characterized by paroxysmal, constricting pain below the sternum, usually due to a coronary artery disease.

an·gi·o·sperm (ăn'jĬ ə spûrm'), *n.* a plant having its seeds enclosed in an ovary.

an·gle¹ (ăng'gəl), *n., v.,* **-gled, -gling.** —*n.* 1. *Geom.* **a.** the space within two lines or three planes diverging from a common point, or within two planes diverging from a common line. **b.** the figure so formed. **c.** the amount of rotation needed to bring one line or plane into coincidence with another. 2. an angular projection; a projecting corner. 3. a point of view; standpoint. 4. an aspect; side. —*v.t., v.i.* 5. to move or bend in angles. —**an'gled,** *adj.*

an·gle² (ăng'gəl), *v.i.,* **-gled, -gling.** 1. to fish with hook and line. 2. to try by artful means to get. —**an'gler,** *n.*

An·gles (ăng'gəlz), *n.* a West Germanic people that migrated to Britain in the fifth century A.D. —**An·gli·an** (ăng'glĬ ən), *adj., n.*

an·gle·worm (ăng'gəl wûrm'), *n.* an earthworm used for bait in angling.

An·gli·can (ăng'glə kən), *adj.* 1. of or pertaining to the Church of England. 2. related in origin to and in communion with the Church of England, as various episcopal churches in other parts of the world. 3. *Chiefly U.S. English.* —*n.* 4. a member of the Church of England or of a church in communion with it. —**An'gli·can·ism,** *n.*

Anglican Church, the Church of England and the churches in other countries in full accord with it as to doctrine and church order.

An·gli·cism (ăng'glə sĬz'əm), *n.* 1. an English idiom. 2. *U.S.* a Briticism.

An·gli·cize (ăng'glə sīz'), *v.t., v.i.,* **-cized, -cizing.** to make or become English in form or character. —**An'gli·ci·za'tion,** *n.*

an·gling (ăng'glĬng), *n.* act or art of fishing with a hook and line, usually attached to a rod.

An·glo·ma·ni·a (ăng'glō mā'nĬ ə), *n.* an excessive attachment to or imitation of English manners, customs, etc. —**An'glo·ma'ni·ac,** *n.*

An·glo·Nor·man (ăng'glō nôr'mən), *adj.* 1. pertaining to that period, 1066–1154, when England was ruled by Normans. 2. pertaining to the Normans who settled in England, or their descendants, or their dialect of French. —*n.* 3. a Norman who settled in England after 1066, or one of his descendants.

An·glo·phile (ăng'glə fĬl', -fĬl), *n.* one who admires England or English customs, etc.

An·glo·phobe (ăng'glə fōb'), *n.* one who hates or fears England or the English.

An·glo·Sax·on (ăng'glō săk'sən), *n.* 1. one who belongs to the English-speaking world, irrespective of historical periods, political boundaries, etc. 2. an Englishman of the period before the Norman Conquest. 3. a person of English stock and traditions. 4. Old English. —*adj.* 5. of, pertaining to, or characteristic of the Anglo-Saxons. 6. pertaining to Anglo-Saxon.

An·go·la (ăng gō'lə), *n.* a Portuguese colony in SW Africa. 3,738,010 pop.; 481,226 sq. mi. *Cap.:* Nova Lisbon. Also, **Portuguese West Africa.**

An·go·ra (ăng gôr'ə, ăn- *for 1;* ăng gôr'ə, ăng'gə rə *for 2*), *n.* 1. an Angora cat. 2. Ankara.

Angora cat, a long-haired variety of the domestic cat, orig. from Angora.

an·gry (ăng'grĬ), *adj.,* **-grier, -griest.** 1. feeling or showing anger (*with* or *at* a person, *at* or *about* a thing). 2. characterized by anger; wrathful. 3. *Med.* inflamed, as a sore. —**an'gri·ly,** *adv.* —**an'gri·ness,** *n.*

ang·strom unit (ăng'strəm), a unit (a ten millionth of a millimeter) used to express the length of very short waves.

an·guish (ăng'gwĬsh), *n.* 1. excruciating pain of either body or mind; acute suffering. —*v.t., v.i.* 2. to affect with or suffer anguish.

an·gu·lar (ăng'gyə lər), *adj.* 1. having an angle or angles. 2. measured by an angle. 3. bony; gaunt. —**an·gu·lar·i·ty** (ăng'gyə lăr'ə tĬ), **an'gu·lar·ness,** *n.* —**an'gu·lar·ly,** *adv.*

an·hy·drous (ăn hī'drəs), *adj. Chem.* indicating loss of all water, esp. water of crystallization.

an·i·line (ăn'ə lĬn, -lĬn'), *n.* 1. an oily liquid, $C_6H_5NH_2$, obtained first from indigo but now prepared from benzene: used in making dyes, plastics, resins, etc. —*adj.* 2. pertaining to or derived from aniline. Also, **an·i·lin** (ăn'ə lĬn).

an·i·mad·ver·sion (ăn'ə măd vûr'zhən, -shən), *n.* 1. a remark, usually implying censure. 2. act or fact of criticizing.

an·i·mad·vert (ăn'ə măd vûrt'), *v.i.* to comment critically (fol. by *on* or *upon*).

an·i·mal (ăn'ə məl), *n.* 1. any living thing that is not a plant, generally capable of voluntary motion, sensation, etc. 2. any animal other than man. 3. a beastlike person. —*adj.* 4. of, pertaining to, or derived from animals. 5. pertaining to the physical or carnal nature of man.

an·i·mal·cule (ăn'ə măl'kūl), *n.* a minute or microscopic animal. —**an·i·mal'cu·lar,** *adj.*

an·i·mal·ism (ăn'ə mə lĬz'əm), *n.* animal state; sensuality. Also, **an·i·mal·i·ty** (ăn'ə măl'ə tĬ).

an·i·mate (*v.* ăn'ə māt'; *adj.* ăn'ə mĬt), *v.,* **-mated, -mating,** *adj.* —*v.t.* 1. to give life to; make alive. 2. to make lively, vivacious, or vigorous. **3.** to encourage. **4.** to move to action. —*adj.* **5.** alive. —**an/i·mate·ly,** *adv.* —**an/i-mat/er, an/i·mat/or,** *n.*

an·i·mat·ed (ăn/ə mā/tĭd), *adj.* full of life, action, or spirit; lively. —**an/i·mat/ed·ly,** *adv.*

animated cartoon, a motion picture consisting of a series of drawings, each slightly different from the ones before and after it.

an·i·ma·tion (ăn/ə mā/shən), *n.* **1.** animated quality; liveliness; vivacity. **2.** act of animating. **3.** the process of preparing animated cartoons.

an·i·mism (ăn/ə mĭz/əm), *n.* **1.** the belief that all natural objects and the universe itself possess a soul. **2.** the belief that natural objects have souls. —**an/i·mist,** *n., adj.* —**an/i·mis/tic,** *adj.*

an·i·mos·i·ty (ăn/ə mŏs/ə tĭ), *n., pl.* **-ties.** a feeling of ill will or enmity tending to display itself in action or conduct (fol. by *between* or *against*).

an·i·mus (ăn/ə məs), *n.* **1.** hostile spirit; animosity. **2.** purpose; intention; animating spirit.

an·i·on (ăn/ī/ən), *n.* **1.** a negatively charged ion attracted to the anode in electrolysis. **2.** any negatively charged atom, radical, or molecule.

an·ise (ăn/ĭs), *n.* an herbaceous plant of Mediterranean regions, yielding aniseed.

an·i·seed (ăn/ə sēd/, ăn/ĭs sēd/), *n.* the aromatic seed of the anise, used in cookery, etc.

An·ka·ra (ăng/kä rä, -kə rə), *n.* the capital of Turkey, in the central part. 157,242.

an·kle (ăng/kəl), *n.* **1.** the aggregate joint connecting the foot with the leg. **2.** the slender part of the leg above the foot.

an·klet (ăng/klĭt), *n.* **1.** a sock which reaches just above the ankle. **2.** an ornament for the ankle, corresponding to a bracelet.

ann., **1.** annual. **2.** annuity. **3.** (L *anni*) years.

an·na (ăn/ə), *n.* **1.** a money of account in India: sixteenth part of a rupee. **2.** a coin of this value.

an·nal·ist (ăn/əl ĭst), *n.* a chronicler of annals.

an·nals (ăn/əlz), *n.pl.* **1.** history of events recorded year by year. **2.** historical records.

An·nam (ə năm/), *n.* a kingdom along the E coast of French Indo-China: a French protectorate. 5,656,000 pop.; 56,988 sq. mi. *Cap.:* Hué. —**An·na·mese** (ăn/ə mēz/, -mēs/), *adj., n.*

An·nap·o·lis (ə năp/ə lĭs), *n.* the capital of Maryland: U.S. Naval Academy. 13,069.

Ann Ar·bor (ăn är/bər), city in SE Mich. 29,815.

Anne (ăn), *n.* 1665–1714, queen of England, 1702–14. (daughter of James II of England).

an·neal (ə nēl/), *v.t.* **1.** to heat (glass, metals, etc.) to remove or prevent internal stress. **2.** to toughen or temper.

an·ne·lid (ăn/ə lĭd), *n.* *Zool.* a member of the phylum of worms comprising earthworms, leeches, etc., characterized by segmented bodies.

Anne of Cleves (klēvz), 1515–57, the fourth wife of Henry VIII of England.

an·nex (*v.* ə nĕks/; *n.* ăn/ĕks), *v.t.* **1.** to attach, join, or add. —*n.* **2.** something annexed. **3.** a subsidiary building. —**an·nex/a·ble,** *adj.*

an·nex·a·tion (ăn/ĭk sā/shan, -ĕk-), *n.* **1.** act of annexing. **2.** something annexed.

an·ni·hi·late (ə nī/ə lāt/), *v.t.,* **-lated, -lating.** **1.** to wipe out utterly. **2.** to destroy. **3.** to annul. —**an·ni/hi·la/tion,** *n.* —**an·ni/hi·la/tor,** *n.*

An·nis·ton (ăn/ĭs tən), *n.* city in E Alabama. 25,523.

an·ni·ver·sa·ry (ăn/ə vûr/sə rĭ), *n., pl.* **-ries,** *adj.* —*n.* **1.** the yearly recurrence of the date of a past event. **2.** the celebration of such a date. —*adj.* **3.** yearly. **4.** of an anniversary.

an·no Dom·i·ni (ăn/ō dŏm/ə nī/), *Latin.* in the year of our Lord. *Abbr.:* A.D., as A.D. 597.

an·no·tate (ăn/ō tāt/), *v.,* **-tated, -tating.** —*v.t.* **1.** to supply with notes. —*v.i.* **2.** to make notes. —**an/no·ta/tion,** *n.* —**an/no·ta/tor,** *n.*

an·nounce (ə nouns/), *v.t.,* **-nounced, -nouncing.** **1.** to make known publicly. **2.** to state the approach or presence of.

an·nounce·ment (ə nouns/mənt), *n.* **1.** public or formal notice. **2.** act of announcing.

an·nounc·er (ə noun/sər), *n.* one who announces, esp. over the radio.

an·noy (ə noi/), *v.t.* **1.** to disturb in a way that displeases or troubles. **2.** *Mil.* to molest. —**an·noy/er,** *n.* —**an·noy/ing,** *adj.* —**an·noy/ing·ly,** *adv.*

an·noy·ance (ə noi/əns), *n.* **1.** that which annoys; a nuisance. **2.** act of annoying.

an·nu·al (ăn/yōō əl), *adj.* **1.** of, for, or pertaining to a year; yearly. **2.** occurring once a year.

3. *Bot.* living but one growing season. **4.** performed during a year. —*n.* **5.** a plant living but one year. **6.** an annual literary publication. —**an/nu·al·ly,** *adv.*

an·nu·i·ty (ə nū/ə tĭ, ə nōō/-), *n., pl.* **-ties.** **1.** a specified income payable at stated intervals for an agreed period in consideration of a premium paid in advance. **2.** the right to receive such an income.

an·nul (ə nŭl/), *v.t.,* **-nulled, -nulling.** to make void; abolish. —**an·nul/la·ble,** *adj.* —**an·nul/ment,** *n.*

an·nu·lar (ăn/yə lər), *adj.* ring-shaped. —**an·nu·lar·i·ty** (ăn/yə lăr/ə tĭ), *n.* —**an/nu·lar·ly,** *adv.*

annular eclipse, *Astron.* an eclipse in which the sun is visible as a ring around the moon.

an·nun·ci·ate (ə nŭn/shĭ āt/, -sĭ-), *v.t.,* **-ated, -ating.** to announce. —**an·nun/ci·a/tor,** *n.*

an·nun·ci·a·tion (ə nŭn/sĭ ā/shən, -shĭ-), *n.* **1.** (*often cap.*) the announcement by the angel Gabriel to the Virgin Mary of the incarnation of Christ. **2.** (*cap.*) the festival (March 25) in memory of this.

An·nun·zi·o (dän nōōn/tsyô), *n.* **Gabriele d'** (gä/brē ĕ/lĕ), 1863–1938, Italian writer and soldier.

an·ode (ăn/ōd), *n.* **1.** the electrode which gives off positive ions, or toward which negative ions collect, in a voltaic cell or other device. **2.** the positive pole, as of a battery. **3.** the plate of an electron tube. —**an·od·ic** (ăn ŏd/ĭk). *adj.*

an·o·dyne (ăn/ə dīn/), *n.* **1.** a medicine that relieves pain. —*adj.* **2.** relieving pain.

a·noint (ə noint/), *v.t.* **1.** to apply oil, an unguent, or the like, to. **2.** to consecrate by applying oil. —**a·noint/er,** *n.* —**a·noint/ment,** *n.*

a·nom·a·lous (ə nŏm/ə ləs), *adj.* deviating; irregular. —**a·nom/a·lous·ly,** *adv.* —**a·nom/a·lous·ness,** *n.*

a·nom·a·ly (ə nŏm/ə lĭ), *n., pl.* **-lies.** **1.** deviation from the common rule, type, or form. **2.** something anomalous.

a·non (ə nŏn/), *adv.* *Archaic.* **1.** soon. **2.** at once.

anon., anonymous.

a·non·y·mous (ə nŏn/ə məs), *adj.* **1.** without any acknowledged name, as of author. **2.** of unknown name. —**an·o·nym·i·ty** (ăn/ə nĭm/ə tĭ), **a·non/y·mous·ness,** *n.* —**a·non/y·mous·ly,** *adv.*

a·noph·e·les (ə nŏf/ə lēz/), *n., pl.* **-les.** a mosquito which, when infested with the organisms causing malaria, may transmit the disease to human beings.

an·oth·er (ə nŭth/ər), *adj.* **1.** a second; additional. **2.** a different. —*pron.* **3.** one more. **4.** a different one. **5.** one just like. **6.** one another, each other.

ans., answer.

an·swer (ăn/sər, än/-), *n.* **1.** a reply to a question, request, letter, etc. **2.** a reply in act. **3.** a reply to a charge or accusation. **4.** a solution to a problem. —*v.i.* **5.** to make a reply. **6.** to respond by an act. **7.** to act or suffer in consequence of. **8.** to be or declare oneself responsible. **9.** to be satisfactory. **10.** to correspond. —*v.t.* **11.** to reply to. **12.** to act in reply to. **13.** to suit. **14.** to discharge (a debt, etc.). **15.** to correspond to.

an·swer·a·ble (ăn/sər ə bəl, än/-), *adj.* **1.** responsible. **2.** capable of being answered. —**an/swer·a·bly,** *adv.*

ant (ănt), *n.* any of a family of small hymenopterous insects that are widely distributed in thousands of species, all of which have some social organization. —**ant/like/,** *adj.*

-ant, **1.** an adjective suffix, as in *pleasant.* **2.** a noun suffix denoting agency, as in *servant.*

ant., antonym.

ant·ac·id (ănt ăs/ĭd), *adj.* **1.** neutralizing acidity, as of the stomach. —*n.* **2.** an antacid remedy.

an·tag·o·nism (ăn tăg/ə nĭz/əm), *n.* **1.** activity or relation of conflicting forces. **2.** opposing force.

an·tag·o·nist (ăn tăg/ə nĭst), *n.* opponent.

an·tag·o·nis·tic (ăn tăg/ə nĭs/tĭk), *adj.* opposing. —**an·tag/o·nis/ti·cal·ly,** *adv.*

an·tag·o·nize (ăn tăg/ə nīz/), *v.t.,* **-nized, -nizing.** **1.** to make hostile; provoke. **2.** to oppose.

ant·arc·tic (ănt ärk/tĭk, -är/-), *adj.* **1.** of, at, or near the South Pole. —*n.* **2. the Antarctic,** the Antarctic Ocean and Antarctica.

Ant·arc·ti·ca (ănt ärk/tə kə, -är/-), *n.* an uninhabited continent around the South Pole, almost wholly covered by a vast continental ice sheet. ab. 5,000,000 sq. mi. Also, **Antarctic Continent.**

Antarctic Circle, the northern boundary of the South Frigid Zone, 23° 28' from the South Pole.

Antarctic Ocean, the ocean S of the Antarctic Circle.

An·tar·es (ăn tār′ēz), *n.* a red giant star of the first magnitude in Scorpio.

ant bear, a large terrestrial tropical American edentate, subsisting on termites, ants, and other insects, and having a long, tapering snout and a shaggy gray coat with a black band.

an·te (ăn′tĭ), *n., v.,* **-ted** or **-teed, -teing.** —*n.* **1.** *Poker.* a stake put into the pool by each player. —*v.i., v.t.* **2.** *Poker.* to put (one's stake) into the pool. **3.** to pay (one's share).

ant·eat·er (ănt′ē′tər), *n.* **1.** any of several related edentates of tropical America, feeding chiefly on termites, and including the ant bear.

an·te·bel·lum (ăn′tĭ bĕl′əm), *adj.* **1.** before the war. **2.** *U.S.* before the American Civil War.

an·te·ced·ent (ăn′tə sē′dənt), *adj.* **1.** preceding; prior. —*n.* **2.** (*pl.*) **a.** ancestry. **b.** one's past history. **3.** a preceding event, etc. **4.** *Gram.* the word or phrase replaced by a pronoun or other substitute later. **5.** *Math.* the first or third term of a proportion. —**an′te·ced′ence,** *n.*

an·te·cham·ber (ăn′tĭ chām′bər), *n.* a room which leads into a principal room.

an·te·date (*v.* ăn′tĭ dāt′, ăn′tĭ dāt′; *n.* ăn′tĭ-dāt′), *v.,* **-dated, -dating,** *n.* —*v.t.* **1.** to precede in time. **2.** to date before the true time. —*n.* **3.** a prior date.

an·te·di·lu·vi·an (ăn′tĭ dĭ lōō′vĭ ən), *adj.* **1.** belonging to the period before the Flood. **2.** antiquated. —*n.* **3.** one who is very old or old-fashioned.

an·te·lope (ăn′tə lōp′), *n., pl.* **-lope, -lopes. 1.** a slenderly built ruminant allied to the sheep, found chiefly in Africa and Asia. **2.** leather from its hide. **3.** *U.S.* pronghorn.

an·te me·rid·i·em (ăn′tĭ mə rĭd′Ĭ ĕm′, -əm), *Latin.* before noon. *Abbr.:* A.M. *or* a.m.

an·ten·na (ăn tĕn′ə), *n., pl.* **-tennas** for 1; **-tennae** (-tĕn′ē) for 2. **1.** *Radio.* the conductor by which the electromagnetic waves are sent out or received. **2.** *Zool.* one of the jointed appendages occurring in pairs on the heads of insects, etc.

an·ten·nule (ăn tĕn′ūl), *n.* a small antenna.

an·te·pe·nult (ăn′tĭ pē′nŭlt, -pĭ nŭlt′), *n.* the last syllable but two in a word.

an·te·ri·or (ăn tĭr′Ĭ ər), *adj.* **1.** situated more to the front. **2.** earlier. —**an·te′ri·or·ly,** *adv.*

an·te·room (ăn′tĭ rōōm′, -rŏŏm′), *n.* a room through which access is had to a main room.

an·thel·min·tic (ăn′thĕl mĭn′tĭk), *Med.* —*adj.* **1.** destroying or expelling intestinal worms. —*n.* **2.** an anthelmintic remedy.

an·them (ăn′thəm), *n.* **1.** a hymn, as of patriotism. **2.** a piece of sacred vocal music.

an·ther (ăn′thər), *n.* *Bot.* the pollen-bearing part of a stamen.

an·ther·id·i·um (ăn′thə rĭd′Ĭ əm), *n., pl.* **-theridia** (-thə rĭd′Ĭ ə). *Bot.* a male sex organ containing motile male gametes. —**an′ther·id′-i·al,** *adj.*

an·thol·o·gy (ăn thŏl′ə jĭ), *n., pl.* **-gies. 1.** any collection of varied authorship. **2.** a collection of poems, especially epigrams, of varied authorship. —**an·tho·log·i·cal** (ăn′thə lŏj′ə kəl), *adj.* —**an·thol′o·gist,** *n.*

An·tho·ny (ăn′tə nĭ, -thə- for 1; ăn′thə nĭ for 2), *n.* **1.** *Saint,* A.D. 251?–356?, Egyptian founder of monasticism. **2. Susan Brownell,** 1820–1906, U.S. suffragist.

an·thra·cene (ăn′thrə sēn′), *n.* a hydrocarbon, C₁₄H₁₀, found in coal tar: important source of alizarin.

an·thra·cite (ăn′thrə sīt′), *n.* a mineral coal containing little of the volatile hydrocarbons.

an·thrax (ăn′thrăks), *n., pl.* **-thraces** (-thrə-sēz′). a malignant infectious disease of cattle, sheep, and other animals and of man.

anthrop., anthropology. Also, **anthropol.**

an·thro·poid (ăn′thrə poid′), *adj.* **1.** resembling man. —*n.* **2.** an anthropoid ape.

anthropoid ape, any ape of the family comprising the gorilla, chimpanzee, orang-utan, and gibbon, without cheek pouches or developed tail.

an·thro·pol·o·gy (ăn′thrə pŏl′ə jĭ), *n.* the science of the origin, development, and varieties of mankind. —**an·thro·po·log·i·cal** (ăn′thrə pə-

lŏj′ə kəl), **an′thro·po·log′ic,** *adj.* —**an′thro·po·log′i·cal·ly,** *adv.* —**an′thro·pol′o·gist,** *n.*

an·thro·pom·e·try (ăn′thrə pŏm′ə trĭ), *n.* the measurement of the human body. —**an·thro·po·met·ric** (ăn′thrə pō mĕt′rĭk), **an′thro·po·met′-ri·cal,** *adj.*

an·thro·po·mor·phic (ăn′thrə pō môr′fĭk), *adj.* ascribing human form or attributes to beings or things not human, esp. to a deity. —**an′thro·po·mor′phism,** *n.* —**an′thro·po·mor′phist,** *n.*

an·thro·poph·a·gi (ăn′thrə pŏf′ə jī′), *n.pl., sing.* **-agus** (-ə gəs). man-eaters; cannibals.

an·ti (ăn′tī, ăn′tĭ), *n., pl.* **-tis.** *Colloq.* one who is opposed to a particular party, policy, etc.

anti-, a prefix meaning: **1.** opposed. **2.** spurious. **3.** the opposite of. **4.** not. **5.** placed opposite. **6.** moving in the opposite direction. **7.** *Med.* corrective.

an·ti-air·craft (ăn′tĭ âr′krăft′, -kräft′), *adj.* designed for or used in defense against enemy aircraft.

an·ti·bod·y (ăn′tĭ bŏd′Ĭ), *n., pl.* **-bodies.** any of various substances in the blood which counteract or destroy bacteria.

an·tic (ăn′tĭk), *n., adj., v.,* **-ticked, -ticking.** —*n.* **1.** (*often pl.*) a fantastic or ludicrous gesture or posture. —*adj.* **2.** *Archaic.* fantastic; odd. —*v.i.* **3.** to caper.

an·ti·cath·ode (ăn′tĭ kăth′ōd), *n.* the plate, often of platinum, on which cathode rays impinge in an x-ray tube, thus producing x-rays.

An·ti·christ (ăn′tĭ krīst′), *n.* **1.** a particular power conceived as a mighty antagonist of Christ. **2.** (*sometimes l.c.*) an opponent of Christ.

an·tic·i·pate (ăn tĭs′ə pāt′), *v.t.,* **-pated, -pating. 1.** to realize beforehand. **2.** to expect. **3.** to perform (an action) before another has had time to act. **4.** to be before (another) in doing something. **5.** to consider or mention before the proper time. **6.** to accelerate.

an·tic·i·pa·tion (ăn tĭs′ə pā′shən), *n.* **1.** act of anticipating. **2.** realization in advance; hope. **3.** previous notion; intuition. —**an·tic′i·pa′tive,** *adj.* —**an·tic′i·pa·to·ry** (ăn tĭs′ə pə tôr′Ĭ), *adj.*

an·ti·cler·i·cal (ăn′tĭ klĕr′ə kəl), *adj.* opposed to the political influence of the clergy.

an·ti·cli·max (ăn′tĭ klī′măks), *n.* **1.** a noticeable or ludicrous descent from lofty ideas or expressions. **2.** an inglorious conclusion. —**an·ti·cli·mac·tic** (ăn′tĭ klī măk′tĭk), *adj.*

an·ti·cli·nal (ăn′tĭ klī′nəl), *adj.* inclining in opposite directions from a central axis.

an·ti·cline (ăn′tĭ klīn′), *n.* *Geol.* an anticlinal rock structure.

an·ti·cy·clone (ăn′tĭ sī′klōn), *n.* *Meteorol.* an extensive horizontal movement of the atmosphere spirally around and away from a gradually descending central region of high barometric pressure. —**an·ti·cy·clon·ic** (ăn′tĭ sī klŏn′Ĭk), *adj.*

an·ti·dote (ăn′tĭ dōt′), *n.* a medicine for counteracting poison, disease, etc. —**an′ti·dot′al,** *adj.*

An·tie·tam (ăn tē′təm), *n.* a creek flowing from S Pennsylvania through NW Maryland into the Potomac: battle, 1862.

an·ti·fe·brile (ăn′tĭ fē′brəl, -fĕb′rəl), *Med.* —*adj.* **1.** efficacious against fever. —*n.* **2.** an antifebrile agent.

An·ti·fed·er·al Party (ăn′tĭ fĕd′ər əl, -fĕd′-rəl), the party which, before 1789, opposed the adoption of the Constitution. —**An′ti·fed′er·al·ist,** *n.*

an·ti·freeze (ăn′tĭ frēz′), *n.* a liquid used in the radiator of an internal-combustion engine to lower the freezing point of the cooling medium.

An·tig·o·ne (ăn tĭg′ə nē′), *n.* *Gk. Legend.* a daughter of Oedipus by his mother, Jocasta.

An·ti·gua (ăn tē′gwə, -gə), *n.* one of the Leeward Islands. 40,122 pop.; 108 sq. mi.

an·ti·his·ta·mine (ăn′tĭ hĭs′tə mēn′, -mĭn′), *n.* any of certain medicines or drugs, used mainly in the treatment of allergy.

an·ti·knock (ăn′tĭ nŏk′), *n.* a material, usually a lead compound, added to fuel to lessen detonation in an internal-combustion engine.

An·til·les (ăn tĭl′ēz), *n.pl.* a chain of islands in the West Indies, divided into the **Greater Antilles** (Cuba, Hispaniola, Jamaica, Puerto Rico), and **Lesser Antilles** (a group of smaller islands to the SE).

an·ti·log·a·rithm (ăn′tĭ lôg′ə rĭth′əm, -lŏg′-ə-), *n.* *Math.* the number corresponding to a logarithm.

an·ti·ma·cas·sar (ăn′tĭ mə kăs′ər) *n.* an ornamental covering for the backs and arms of chairs, etc., to keep them from being soiled by hair oil.

an·ti·mo·ny (ăn′tə mō′nĭ), n. a brittle, lustrous, white metallic element used chiefly in alloys and in medicine. *Symbol:* Sb; *at. no.:* 51; *at. wt.:* 121.76. —**an′ti·mo′ni·al**, *adj.*, *n.*

An·ti·och (ăn′tĭ ŏk′), n. a city in S Turkey: capital of the ancient kingdom of Syria, 300–64 B.C. 26,939.

An·ti·o·chus III (ăn tī′ə kəs), 241?–187 B.C., king of Syria, 223–187 B.C.: fought against the Romans.

an·ti·pas·to (ăn′tē päs′tô), n. *Italian.* an appetizer course of relishes, smoked meat, fish, etc.

An·tip·a·ter (ăn tĭp′ə tər), n. 398?–319 B.C., general under Alexander the Great.

an·tip·a·thy (ăn tĭp′ə thĭ), n., *pl.* **-thies. 1.** a natural dislike; aversion. **2.** an instinctive opposition in feeling. **3.** an object of natural aversion or dislike. —**an·tip·a·thet·ic** (ăn tĭp′ə thĕt′ĭk, ăn′tĭ pə-), **an·tip′a·thet′i·cal**, *adj.* —**an·tip′a·thet′i·cal·ly**, *adv.*

an·ti·phlo·gis·tic (ăn′tĭ flō jĭs′tĭk), *adj.* **1.** checking inflammation. —n. **2.** antiphlogistic remedy.

an·ti·phon (ăn′tə fŏn′), n. **1.** a verse sung in response. **2.** *Eccles.* a psalm, hymn, or prayer sung in alternate parts. —**an·tiph·o·nal** (ăn tĭf′ə nəl), *adj.* —**an·tiph′o·nal·ly**, *adv.*

an·tip·o·dal (ăn tĭp′ə dəl), *adj.* **1.** *Geog.* on the opposite side of the globe. **2.** opposite.

an·ti·pode (ăn′tə pōd′), n. a direct opposite.

an·tip·o·des (ăn tĭp′ə dēz′), *n.pl.* **1.** diametrically opposite places on the globe. **2.** those who dwell there. —**an·tip·o·de·an** (ăn tĭp′ə dē′ən), *adj.*, *n.*

an·ti·pope (ăn′tĭ pōp′), n. one who is elected pope in opposition to one canonically chosen.

an·ti·py·ret·ic (ăn′tĭ pī rĕt′ĭk), *Med.* —*adj.* **1.** checking fever. —n. **2.** an antipyretic agent.

an·ti·quar·i·an (ăn′tə kwâr′Y ən), *adj.* **1.** pertaining to the study of antiquities or to antiquaries. —n. **2.** antiquary. —**an′ti·quar′i·an·ism**, n.

an·ti·quar·y (ăn′tə kwĕr′Y), n., *pl.* **-quaries.** a student or collector of antiquities.

an·ti·quate (ăn′tə kwāt′), *v.t.*, **-quated, -quating. 1.** to make old and useless. **2.** to make antique.

an·ti·quat·ed (ăn′tə kwā′tĭd), *adj.* **1.** grown old; obsolete. **2.** old-fashioned. **3.** aged.

an·tique (ăn tēk′), *adj.*, *n.*, *v.*, **-tiqued, -tiquing.** —*adj.* **1.** belonging to former times. **2.** old-fashioned. —n. **3.** an object of art or a furniture piece of a former period. —*v.t.* **4.** to make appear antique.

an·tiq·ui·ty (ăn tĭk′wə tĭ), n., *pl.* **-ties. 1.** the quality of being ancient. **2.** ancient times. **3.** the people of ancient times. **4.** (*usually pl.*) something belonging to or remaining from ancient times.

an·ti·ra·chit·ic (ăn′tĭ rə kĭt′ĭk), *adj.* pertaining to the prevention or cure of rickets.

an·ti·scor·bu·tic (ăn′tĭ skôr bū′tĭk), *adj. Med.* efficacious against scurvy.

an·ti-Sem·ite (ăn′tĭ sĕm′īt, -sē′mīt), n. one hostile to the Jews. —**an·ti-Sem·it·ic** (-sə mĭt′-Yk), *adj.* —**an·ti-Sem·i·tism** (-sĕm′ə tĭz′əm), n.

an·ti·sep·sis (ăn′tə sĕp′sĭs), n. destruction of the organisms that produce sepsis or septic disease.

an·ti·sep·tic (ăn′tə sĕp′tĭk), *adj.* **1.** of or affecting antisepsis. —n. **2.** an antiseptic agent. —**an′ti·sep′ti·cal·ly**, *adv.*

an·ti·slav·er·y (ăn′tĭ slā′və rĭ), *adj.* opposed to slavery, esp. Negro slavery.

an·ti·so·cial (ăn′tĭ sō′shəl), *adj.* **1.** averse to social relations. **2.** opposed to social order.

an·ti·spas·mod·ic (ăn′tĭ spăz mŏd′Yk), *adj.* **1.** checking spasms. —n. **2.** antispasmodic agent.

an·tis·tro·phe (ăn tĭs′trə fĭ), n. the part of an ancient Greek ode answering to a previous strophe.

an·tith·e·sis (ăn tĭth′ə sĭs), n., *pl.* **-ses** (-sēz′). **1.** opposition. **2.** the direct opposite. **3.** *Rhet.* the setting of a member of a sentence against another. —**an·ti·thet·ic** (ăn′tə thĕt′Yk), **an·ti·thet′i·cal**, *adj.*

an·ti·tox·in (ăn′tĭ tŏk′sĭn), n. **1.** a substance formed in the body, which counteracts a specific toxin. **2.** the antibody formed in immunization with a given toxin. Also, **an′ti·tox′ine** (-sĭn, -sēn).

an·ti·trust (ăn′tĭ trŭst′), *adj.* opposed to trusts or large combinations of capital.

ant·ler (ănt′lər), n. one of the solid deciduous horns, usually branched, of an animal of the deer family. —**ant′lered**, *adj.*

ant lion, a larval neuropterous insect, the larva of which (doodlebug) digs a pit in sand, where it lies in wait for ants, etc.

An·to·fa·gas·ta (än′tô fä gäs′tä), n. a seaport in N Chile. 49,106.

An·toi·nette (ăn′twə nĕt′), n. **Marie,** 1755–93, wife of Louis XVI: executed during Revolution.

An·to·ni·nus (ăn′tə nī′nəs), n. **Marcus Aurelius,** A.D. 121–180, emperor of Rome, A.D. 161–180: Stoic philosopher and writer.

An·to·ny (ăn′tə nĭ), n. **Mark,** (*Marcus Antonius*) 83?–30 B.C., Roman general: friend of Caesar.

an·to·nym (ăn′tə nĭm), n. a word opposed in meaning to another (opposed to *synonym*).

Ant·werp (ănt′wərp), n. a seaport in N Belgium, on the Scheldt river. 257,897.

a·nus (ā′nəs), n. *Anat.* the opening at the lower end of the alimentary canal for excretion.

an·vil (ăn′vĭl), n. **1.** a heavy iron block on which heated metals are hammered into shape. **2.** *Anat.* the incus.

anx·i·e·ty (ăng zī′ə tĭ), n., *pl.* **-ties. 1.** distress caused by apprehension of misfortune. **2.** eagerness.

anx·ious (ăngk′shəs, ăng′-), *adj.* **1.** full of anxiety or solicitude. **2.** earnestly desirous. **3.** attended with or showing anxiety. —**anx′ious·ly**, *adv.* —**anx′ious·ness**, n.

an·y (ĕn′Y), *adj.* **1.** one, a, an, or (as *pl.*) some. **2.** in whatever quantity, great or small. **3.** every. **4.** (with a negative) none at all. **5.** any one, any single (person or thing). —*pron.* **6.** (*sing.*) anybody, or (*as pl.*) any persons. **7.** any single one or any ones. —*adv.* **8.** in any degree.

an·y·bod·y (ĕn′Y bŏd′Y, -bə dĭ), *pron.*, *n.*, *pl.* **-bodies. 1.** any person. **2.** an important person.

an·y·how (ĕn′Y hou′), *adv.* **1.** in any way whatever. **2.** in any case. **3.** in a careless manner.

an·y·one (ĕn′Y wŭn′, -wən), *pron.* any person.

an·y·thing (ĕn′Y thĭng′), *pron.*, n. **1.** any thing whatever. —*adv.* **2.** in any degree.

an·y·way (ĕn′Y wā′), *adv.* **1.** in any manner. **2.** in any case. **3.** carelessly; haphazard.

an·y·where (ĕn′Y hwâr′), *adv.* in, at, or to any place.

an·y·wise (ĕn′Y wīz′), *adv.* in any way.

A one (ā′ wŭn′), **1.** (of a ship) of the highest quality. **2.** *Colloq.* first-class; excellent.

A·o·ran·gi (ä′ō räng′gĭ), n. See **Cook,** Mount.

a·o·rist (ā′ə rĭst), n. *Gram.* a tense expressing action without further limitation.

a·or·ta (ā ôr′tə), n., *pl.* **-tas, -tae** (-tē). *Anat.* the main trunk of the arterial system, conveying blood from the left ventricle of the heart to all of the body except the lungs. —**a·or′tic, a·or′tal**, *adj.*

a·ou·dad (ä′ŏŏ dăd′), n. a wild sheep of northern Africa.

Ap., **1.** Apostle. **2.** April.

a·pace (ə pās′), *adv.* with speed; quickly; swiftly.

A·pach·e (ə păch′Y), n., *pl.* **Apaches, Apache.** one of a group of Indian tribes in southwest U.S.

a·pache (ə päsh′, ə păsh′), n. a Parisian gangster or tough.

ap·a·nage (ăp′ə nĭj), n. appanage.

a·part (ə pärt′), *adv.* **1.** in or to pieces. **2.** separately in motion, place, or position. **3.** to or at one side. **4.** separately in consideration. **5.** aside. —*adj.* **6.** separate.

a·part·ment (ə pärt′mənt), n. *U.S.* **1.** a set of rooms, among other sets in one building (**apartment house or building**), for use as a dwelling. **2.** a single room in a building.

ap·a·thet·ic (ăp′ə thĕt′Yk), *adj.* **1.** having or exhibiting little or no emotion. **2.** indifferent. Also, **ap′a·thet′i·cal.** —**ap′a·thet′i·cal·ly**, *adv.*

ap·a·thy (ăp′ə thĭ), n., *pl.* **-thies. 1.** lack of emotion, etc. **2.** indifference.

ape (āp), n., *v.*, **aped, aping.** —n. **1.** a tailless monkey. **2.** an anthropoid ape. **3.** an imitator. **4.** any monkey. —*v.t.* **5.** to imitate. —**ape′like′**, *adj.*

Ap·en·nines (ăp′ə nīnz′), *n.pl.* a mountain range traversing Italy from NW to SW.

a·pe·ri·ent (ə pĭr′Y ənt), *Med.* —*adj.* **1.** laxative. —n. **2.** a laxative medicine or food.

a·pé·ri·tif (á pĕ rē tēf′), *n.* *French.* a small drink of liquor to whet the appetite before a meal.

ap·er·ture (ăp′ər chər), *n.* a hole, slit, crack, gap, or other opening.

a·pet·al·ous (ā pĕt′əl əs), *adj.* *Bot.* having no petals.

a·pex (ā′pĕks), *n.*, *pl.* **apexes, apices** (ăp′ə sēz′, ā′pə-). **1.** the tip, point, or vertex of anything; the summit. **2.** climax; acme.

a·pha·sia (ə fā′zhə), *n.* *Pathol.* impairment or loss of the faculty of using or understanding spoken or written language. —**a·pha·sic** (ə fā′zĭk, -sĭk), *adj.*, *n.*

a·phe·li·on (ə fē′lĭ ən), *n.*, *pl.* **-lia** (-lĭ ə). *Astron.* the point of a planet's or comet's orbit most distant from the sun (opposed to *perihelion*).

a·phid (ā′fĭd, ăf′ĭd), *n.* any of certain plant-sucking insects; plant louse. —**a·phid·i·an** (ə fĭd′Y ən), *adj.*, *n.*

a·phis (ā′fĭs, ăf′ĭs), *n.*, *pl.* **aphides** (ăf′ə dēz′). an aphid.

aph·o·rism (ăf′ə rĭz′əm), *n.* a terse saying embodying a general truth. —**aph′o·ris′tic**, *adj.*

aph·ro·dis·i·ac (ăf′rə dĭz′Y ăk′), *adj.* **1.** arousing sexual desire. —*n.* **2.** such a drug or food.

Aph·ro·di·te (ăf′rə dī′tY), *n.* Greek goddess of love and beauty, identified by Romans with Venus.

a·pi·ar·y (ā′pĭ ĕr′Y), *n.*, *pl.* **-aries.** a place in which bees are kept. —**a′pi·a·rist**, *n.*

ap·i·cal (ăp′ə kəl, ā′pə-), *adj.* of, at, or forming the apex. —**ap′i·cal·ly**, *adv.*

ap·i·ces (ăp′ə sēz′, ā′pə-), *n.* pl. of **apex.**

a·pic·u·late (ə pĭk′yə lĭt, -lāt′), *adj.* *Bot.* tipped with a short, abrupt point, as a leaf.

a·pi·cul·ture (ā′pə kŭl′chər), *n.* the rearing of bees. —**a′pi·cul′tur·al**, *adj.*

a·piece (ə pēs′), *adv.* for each piece, thing, or person; for each one; each.

ap·ish (ā′pĭsh), *adj.* **1.** like an ape. **2.** imitative. **3.** foolishly affected. —**ap′ish·ly**, *adv.*

Apl., April.

a·plomb (ə plŏm′), *n.* imperturbable self-possession, poise, or assurance.

Apoc., **1.** Apocalypse. **2.** Apocrypha.

a·poc·a·lypse (ə pŏk′ə lĭps), *n.* **1.** (*cap.*) the Revelation of the apostle John. **2.** revelation. —**a·poc′a·lyp′tic, a·poc′a·lyp′ti·cal,** *adj.*

a·poc·o·pe (ə pŏk′ə pY), *n.* the cutting off of the last sound of a word.

A·poc·ry·pha (ə pŏk′rə fə), *n.pl.* **1.** fourteen books included in the Septuagint and Vulgate as an appendix to the Old Testament, but usually omitted from Protestant editions of the Bible. **2.** (*l.c.*) works of doubtful authenticity. —**a·poc′-ry·phal,** *adj.*

ap·o·gee (ăp′ə jē′), *n.* **1.** *Astron.* the point in the orbit of a heavenly body most distant from the earth (opposed to *perigee*). **2.** the apex or climax.

Apogee · Earth · Perigee

A·pol·lo (ə pŏl′ō), *n.*, *pl.* **-los.** a Greek (and Roman) deity, the god of light, healing, music, poetry, prophecy, youthful manly beauty, etc.

a·pol·o·get·ic (ə pŏl′ə jĕt′Yk), *adj.* **1.** making excuse for fault, etc. **2.** defending. Also, **a·pol′o·get′i·cal.** —**a·pol′o·get′i·cal·ly,** *adv.*

a·pol·o·get·ics (ə pŏl′ə jĕt′Yks), *n.* branch of theology concerned with defense of Christianity.

ap·o·lo·gi·a (ăp′ə lō′jY ə), *n.* an apology.

a·pol·o·gist (ə pŏl′ə jYst), *n.* one who makes an apology or defense in speech or writing.

a·pol·o·gize (ə pŏl′ə jīz′), *v.i.,* **-gized, -gizing.** to offer or make an apology. —**a·pol′o·giz′er,** *n.*

ap·o·logue (ăp′ə lôg′, -lŏg′), *n.* a moral fable.

a·pol·o·gy (ə pŏl′ə jY), *n.*, *pl.* **-gies. 1.** an expression of regret offered for some fault, failure, insult, or injury. **2.** a formal defense in speech or writing. **3.** a poor specimen or substitute.

ap·o·plec·tic (ăp′ə plĕk′tYk), *adj.* Also, **ap·o·plec′ti·cal. 1.** of, having, or inclined to apoplexy. —*n.* **2.** an apoplectic person.

ap·o·plex·y (ăp′ə plĕk′sY), *n.* *Pathol.* a sudden, usually marked, loss of bodily function due to rupture or occlusion of a blood vessel.

a·port (ə pōrt′), *adv.* on or toward the port side.

a·pos·ta·sy (ə pŏs′tə sY), *n.*, *pl.* **-sies.** a total desertion of one's principles, party, cause, etc.

a·pos·tate (ə pŏs′tāt, -tYt), *n.* **1.** one who forsakes his church, etc. —*adj.* **2.** guilty of apostasy.

a pos·te·ri·o·ri (ā pŏs tĭr′Y ōr′Y), based upon actual observation or upon experimental data.

a·pos·tle (ə pŏs′əl), *n.* **1.** one of the twelve disciples sent forth by Jesus Christ to preach the gospel. **2.** a pioneer of any great moral reform. —**a·pos′tle·ship′,** *n.*

Apostles' Creed, a creed of virtually universal acceptance in the Christian church.

ap·os·tol·ic (ăp′ə stŏl′Yk), *adj.* **1.** of or pertaining to an apostle, esp. of the twelve apostles. **2.** papal. Also, **ap′os·tol′i·cal.**

Apostolic See, the Church of Rome.

a·pos·tro·phe¹ (ə pŏs′trə fY), *n.* the sign (') indicating the omission of one or more letters in a word, the possessive case, and certain plurals.

a·pos·tro·phe² (ə pŏs′trə fY), *n.* a digression, esp. a personal address to someone not present.

a·pos·tro·phize (ə pŏs′trə fīz′), *v.t., v.i.,* **-phized, -phizing.** *Rhet.* to address by apostrophe.

apothecaries' measure, a system of units used in compounding and dispensing liquid drugs. In the United States 60 minims = 1 fluid dram; 8 fluid drams = 1 fluid ounce; 16 fluid ounces = 1 pint; 8 pints = 1 gallon.

apothecaries' weight, a system of weights used in compounding and dispensing drugs: 20 grains = 1 scruple; 3 scruples = 1 dram; 8 drams = 1 ounce; 12 ounces = 1 pound.

a·poth·e·car·y (ə pŏth′ə kĕr′Y), *n.*, *pl.* **-caries.** a druggist; a pharmacist.

ap·o·thegm (ăp′ə thĕm′), *n.* a short, pithy, instructive saying; aphorism.

a·poth·e·o·sis (ə pŏth′Y ō′sYs, ăp′ə thē′ə sYs), *n.*, *pl.* **-ses** (-sēz, -sēz′). **1.** exaltation to the rank of a god. **2.** the glorification of any person. **3.** a deified or glorified ideal.

a·poth·e·o·size (ə pŏth′Y ə sīz′, ăp′ə thē′ə-sīz′), *v.t.,* **-sized, -sizing.** to deify; glorify.

app., 1. apparent. **2.** appendix. **3.** appointed.

Ap·pa·lach·i·an Mountains (ăp′ə lăch′Y ən, -lā′chY ən, -chən), a mountain system of E North America, from Quebec province to N Alabama. Highest peak, 6711 ft. Also, **Appalachians.**

ap·pall (ə pôl′), *v.t.* to overcome with fear; fill with consternation and horror. Also, **ap·pal′.** —**ap·pall′ing,** *adj.* —**ap·pall′ing·ly,** *adv.*

ap·pa·nage (ăp′ə nYj), *n.* **1.** land or revenue for the maintenance of a member of the royal family. **2.** a natural attribute or accompaniment.

appar., 1. apparent. **2.** apparently.

ap·pa·ra·tus (ăp′ə rā′təs, -răt′əs), *n.*, *pl.* **-tus, -tuses. 1.** an assemblage of instruments, materials, etc., for a particular use. **2.** *Physiol.* a collection of organs for the same function.

ap·par·el (ə păr′əl), *n., v.,* **-eled, -eling** or (*esp. Brit.*) **-elled, -elling.** —*v.* **1.** a person's outer clothing. **2.** guise. —*v.t.* **3.** to dress or adorn.

ap·par·ent (ə păr′ənt, ə pâr′-), *adj.* **1.** plain or clear. **2.** seeming; ostensible. **3.** open to view. **4.** absolutely entitled to an inherited throne, title, or other estate, by right of birth. —**ap·par′ent·ly,** *adv.*

ap·pa·ri·tion (ăp′ə rYsh′ən), *n.* **1.** a specter. **2.** anything that appears, esp. something remarkable. **3.** act of appearing. —**ap′pa·ri′tion·al,** *adj.*

ap·peal (ə pēl′), *n.* **1.** a call for aid, mercy, etc. **2.** reference to some authority for corroboration, decision, etc. **3.** *Law.* an application or proceeding for review by a higher tribunal. **4.** power to move the feelings. —*v.i.* **5.** to call for aid, mercy, or the like. **6.** *Law.* to apply for review of a case to a higher tribunal. **7.** to resort for proof or settlement. **8.** to offer a peculiar attraction, etc. —*v.t.* **9.** *Law.* to apply for review of (a case) to a higher tribunal. —**ap·peal′a·ble,** *adj.* —**ap·peal′er,** *n.* —**ap·peal′ing·ly,** *adv.*

ap·pear (ə pYr′), *v.i.* **1.** to come into sight. **2.** to seem or look. **3.** to be clear or made clear by evidence. **4.** to come before the public. **5.** *Law.* to come formally before a tribunal, authority, etc.

ap·pear·ance (ə pYr′əns), *n.* **1.** act or fact of appearing. **2.** *Law.* the coming into court of a party to a suit. **3.** outward look; mien. **4.** outward seeming; semblance. **5.** (*pl.*) indications. **6.** an apparition.

ap·pease (ə pēz′), *v.t.,* **-peased, -peasing. 1.** to bring to a state of peace, quiet, ease, or content. **2.** to satisfy. **3.** to accede to the belligerent demands of (a country, etc.). —**ap·peas′a·ble,** *adj.* —**ap·pease′ment,** *n.* —**ap·peas′er,** *n.*

ap·pel·lant (ə pĕl′ənt), *n.* **1.** one who appeals, as to a higher tribunal. —*adj.* **2.** appellate.

ap·pel·late (ə pĕl′ĭt), *adj. Law.* **1.** pertaining to appeals. **2.** having power to review appeals.

ap·pel·la·tion (ăp′ə lā′shən), *n.* **1.** a name, title, or designation. **2.** act of naming.

ap·pel·la·tive (ə pĕl′ə tĭv), *n.* **1.** a common noun. **2.** a descriptive name. —*adj.* **3.** pertaining to a common noun. **4.** descriptive.

ap·pel·lee (ăp′ə lē′), *n. Law.* the defendant or respondent in an appellate proceeding.

ap·pend (ə pĕnd′), *v.t.* to add, as an accessory.

ap·pend·age (ə pĕn′dĭj), *n.* **1.** a subordinate attached part of anything. **2.** *Biol.* any member of the body diverging from the axial trunk.

ap·pen·dec·to·my (ăp′ən dĕk′tə mĭ), *n.*, *pl.* -mies. *Surg.* excision of the vermiform appendix.

ap·pen·di·ci·tis (ə pĕn′də sī′tĭs), *n. Pathol.* inflammation of the vermiform appendix.

ap·pen·dix (ə pĕn′dĭks), *n.*, *pl.* -dixes, -dices (-də sēz′). **1.** matter which supplements the main text, as of a book. **2.** *Anat.* **a.** a process or projection. **b.** the vermiform appendix.

ap·per·cep·tion (ăp′ər sĕp′shən), *n. Psychol.* **1.** conscious perception. **2.** act of apperceiving. —ap′per·cep′tive, *adj.*

ap·per·tain (ăp′ər tān′), *v.i.* to belong as a part, possession, attribute, etc.; pertain.

ap·pe·tite (ăp′ə tīt′), *n.* **1.** a desire for food or drink. **2.** a desire to supply any demand or bodily want.

ap·pe·tiz·er (ăp′ə tī′zər), *n.* a food or drink that stimulates the desire for food.

ap·pe·tiz·ing (ăp′ə tī′zĭng), *adj.* exciting or appealing to the appetite. —ap′pe·tiz′ing·ly, *adv.*

ap·plaud (ə plôd′), *v.i., v.t.* **1.** to express approval (of) by clapping, shouting, etc. **2.** to praise.

ap·plause (ə plôz′), *n.* hand clapping, shouting, or other expressions of approval.

ap·ple (ăp′əl), *n.* **1.** the common edible fruit, usually round and red, of a tree of the rose family. **2.** the tree, cultivated in most temperate regions.

apple butter, a thick, spiced applesauce.

ap·ple·jack (ăp′əl jăk′), *n. U.S.* **1.** a brandy distilled from fermented cider. **2.** See cider.

ap·ple·sauce (ăp′əl sôs′), *n.* **1.** apples stewed to a soft pulp. **2.** *U.S. Slang.* nonsense; bunk.

Ap·ple·ton (ăp′əl tən), *n.* a city in E Wisconsin. 28,436.

ap·pli·ance (ə plī′əns), *n.* **1.** an instrument or device for a particular use. **2.** application.

ap·pli·ca·ble (ăp′lə kə bəl, ə plĭk′ə-), *adj.* capable of being applied; relevant. —ap′pli·ca·bil′i·ty, ap′pli·ca·ble·ness, *n.* —ap′pli·ca·bly, *adv.*

ap·pli·cant (ăp′lə kənt), *n.* one who applies.

ap·pli·ca·tion (ăp′lə kā′shən), *n.* **1.** act of putting to a special use or purpose. **2.** relevance; suitability. **3.** act of applying. **4.** the thing applied. **5.** act of requesting. **6.** a request or appeal. **7.** persistent effort.

ap·plied (ə plīd′), *adj.* put to practical use.

ap·pli·qué (ăp′lə kā′), *adj., n., v.*, -quéd, -qué-ing. —*adj.* **1.** formed with ornamentation of one material applied to another. —*n.* **2.** the ornamentation used. —*v.t.* **3.** to apply or form as in appliqué work.

ap·ply (ə plī′), *v.*, -plied, -plying. —*v.t.* **1.** to lay on; bring into contact. **2.** to put into practical operation, as a rule. **3.** to employ. **4.** to devote to some specific purpose. **5.** to employ with close, diligent attention. —*v.i.* **6.** to be pertinent. **7.** to make application; ask. —ap·pli′er, *n.*

ap·pog·gia·tu·ra (ə pŏj′ə tyŏŏr′ə, -tŏŏr′ə), *n. Music.* a note of embellishment (short or long) preceding another note and taking a portion of its time.

ap·point (ə point′), *v.t.* **1.** to nominate or designate. **2.** to ordain by decree. **3.** to determine by authority or agreement. **4.** to furnish or equip. —ap·point·ee′, *n.* —ap·point′er, *n.*

ap·poin·tive (ə poin′tĭv), *adj.* pertaining to or dependent on appointment.

ap·point·ment (ə point′mənt), *n.* **1.** act of appointing. **2.** an office held by a person appointed. **3.** engagement. **4.** (*usually pl.*) equipment. **5.** decree.

Ap·po·mat·tox (ăp′ə măt′əks), *n.* a town in central Virginia: Lee surrendered here, 1865.

ap·por·tion (ə pōr′shən), *v.t.* to divide proportionally. —ap·por′tion·ment, *n.*

ap·pose (ə pōz′), *v.t.*, -posed, -posing. to put (one thing) near or next to another.

ap·po·site (ăp′ə zĭt), *adj.* suitable; pertinent. —ap′po·site·ly, *adj.* —ap′po·site·ness, *n.*

ap·po·si·tion (ăp′ə zĭsh′ən), *n.* **1.** act of adding to or together. **2.** *Gram.* a syntactic relation between expressions with the same function in the sentence, the second expression identifying or supplementing the first.

ap·pos·i·tive (ə pŏz′ə tĭv), *n.* **1.** a word or phrase in apposition. —*adj.* **2.** placed in apposition.

ap·prais·al (ə prā′zəl), *n.* an estimate of value. Also, **ap·praise′ment**.

ap·praise (ə prāz′), *v.t.*, -praised, -praising. to estimate generally, as to quality, size, weight, value, etc. —ap·prais′a·ble, *adj.* —ap·prais′er, *n.* —ap·prais′ing·ly, *adv.*

ap·pre·ci·a·ble (ə prē′shĭ ə bəl, -shə bəl), *adj.* capable of being perceived. —ap·pre′ci·a·bly, *adv.*

ap·pre·ci·ate (ə prē′shĭ āt′), *v.*, -ated, -ating. —*v.t.* **1.** to place a sufficiently high estimate on. **2.** to be fully aware of. **3.** to raise in value. —*v.i.* **4.** to increase in value. —ap·pre·ci·a·tive (ə prē′shĭ ā′tĭv, -shə tĭv), *adj.* —ap·pre′ci·a′tive·ly, *adv.* —ap·pre′ci·a′tor, *n.*

ap·pre·ci·a·tion (ə prē′shĭ ā′shən), *n.* **1.** estimate, perception, or recognition, esp. of aesthetic quality. **2.** increase in value of property.

ap·pre·hend (ăp′rĭ hĕnd′), *v.t., v.i.* **1.** to take into custody; arrest. **2.** to understand. **3.** to fear or anticipate.

ap·pre·hen·sion (ăp′rĭ hĕn′shən), *n.* **1.** dread of coming evil. **2.** understanding. **3.** a view on any subject. **4.** seizure.

ap·pre·hen·sive (ăp′rĭ hĕn′sĭv), *adj.* **1.** uneasy or fearful about something that may happen. **2.** quick to learn or understand. **3.** perceptive. —ap′pre·hen′sive·ly, *adv.* —ap′pre·hen′sive·ness, *n.*

ap·pren·tice (ə prĕn′tĭs), *n., v.*, -ticed, -ticing. —*n.* **1.** one who works for another with obligations to learn a trade. **2.** a novice. —*v.t.* **3.** to bind as an apprentice. —ap·pren′tice·ship′, *n.*

ap·prise (ə prīz′), *v.t.*, -prised, -prising. to give notice to; inform; advise. Also, **ap·prize′**.

ap·proach (ə prōch′), *v.t., v.i.* **1.** to come nearer or near to. **2.** to come near to in quality, time, or condition. **3.** to bring near to something. **4.** to make a proposal to. **5.** to begin work on. —*n.* **6.** act of drawing near. **7.** nearness. **8.** any means of access. **9.** the method used in setting about a task, problem, etc. **10.** (*sing. or pl.*) advances made to a person. **11.** *Golf.* a stroke after teeing off, by which a player endeavors to get his ball on the putting green. —ap·proach′a·ble, *adj.*

ap·pro·ba·tion (ăp′rə bā′shən), *n.* **1.** approval; commendation. **2.** sanction.

ap·pro·pri·ate (*adj.* ə prō′prĭ ĭt; *v.* ə prō′prĭ āt′), *adj., v.*, -ated, -ating. —*adj.* **1.** suitable for a particular purpose, person, etc. **2.** belonging or peculiar to one. —*v.t.* **3.** to set apart for some specific purpose. **4.** to take possession of. —ap·pro′pri·ate·ly, *adv.* —ap·pro′pri·ate·ness, *n.* —ap·pro′pri·a′tion, *n.*

ap·prov·al (ə prōō′vəl), *n.* **1.** act of approving. **2.** sanction. **3. on approval**, for examination.

ap·prove (ə prōōv′), *v.*, -proved, -proving. —*v.t.* **1.** to pronounce or consider good. **2.** to confirm or ratify. —*v.i.* **3.** to speak or think favorably. —ap·prov′er, *n.* —ap·prov′ing·ly, *adv.*

approx., approximately.

ap·prox·i·mate (*adj.* ə prŏk′sə mĭt; *v.* ə prŏk′sə māt′), *adj., v.*, -mated, -mating. —*adj.* **1.** nearly exact, equal, or perfect. **2.** near. **3.** very similar. —*v.t.* **4.** to come near to. **5.** to bring near. —*v.i.* **6.** to come near in character, amount, etc. —ap·prox′i·mate·ly, *adv.*

ap·prox·i·ma·tion (ə prŏk′sə mā′shən), *n.* **1.** an approach in position, degree, etc. **2.** a result which is sufficiently exact for a given purpose.

ap·pur·te·nance (ə pûr′tə nəns), *n.* something accessory to a more important thing.

ap·pur·te·nant (ə pûr′tə nənt), *adj.* **1.** belonging; pertaining. —*n.* **2.** an appurtenance.

Apr., April.

a·pri·cot (ā′prə kŏt′, ăp′rə-), *n.* **1.** a downy yellow fruit, somewhat resembling a small peach. **2.** the tree it grows on. **3.** a pinkish yellow or yellowish pink.

A·pril (ā'prəl), *n.* the fourth month of the year, containing 30 days.

April Fools' Day, April 1, a day observed by playing jokes on people (**April fools**).

a pri·o·ri (ā prī ōr'ī, ä prī ōr'Ī), 1. from cause to effect; from a general law to a particular instance. 2. not based on or supported by factual study.

a·pron (ā'prən), *n.* 1. a piece of apparel for covering, and usually also protecting, the front of a person's clothes. 2. anything resembling or suggesting such an apron. 3. a flat continuous conveyor belt. 4. *Civ. Eng.* **a.** any device for protecting a surface of earth from the action of moving water. **b.** a platform to receive the water falling over a dam. —*v.t.* 5. to put an apron on.

ap·ro·pos (ăp'rə pō'), *adv.* 1. opportunely. 2. with reference (fol. by *of*). —*adj.* 3. opportune; pertinent.

apse (ăps), *n.* *Archit.* a vaulted recess in a building, esp. at the end of the choir of a church.

apt (ăpt), *adj.* 1. inclined; prone. 2. likely. 3. unusually intelligent. 4. suited to the occasion. —**apt'ly,** *adv.* —**apt'ness,** *n.*

apt., *pl.* **apts.** apartment.

ap·ter·ous (ăp'tər əs), *adj.* *Zool.* wingless.

ap·ter·yx (ăp'tər Ĭks), *n., pl.* **-teryxes** (-tər Ĭk-sĭz). any of several flightless ratite birds of New Zealand, allied to the extinct moas; kiwi.

ap·ti·tude (ăp'tə tūd', -tōod'), *n.* 1. a natural or acquired inclination. 2. readiness in learning; talent. 3. special fitness.

A·pu·le·ius (ăp'yə lē'əs), *n.* **Lucius** (lōō'shəs), born A.D. 125?, Roman philosopher and satirist.

Apteryx. (27 in. long)

Aq., (L *aqua*) water. Also, **aq.**

aq·ua (ăk'wə, ä'kwə), *n., pl.* **aquae** (ăk'wē, ä'-kwē). *Chiefly Pharm.* water; a liquid; a solution.

aqua for·tis (fōr'tĬs), nitric acid.

aq·ua·ma·rine (ăk'wə mə rēn'), *n.* 1. a transparent light greenish-blue variety of beryl, used as a gem. 2. Also, **aqua.** light greenish blue.

aq·ua·plane (ăk'wə plān'), *n., v.,* **-planed, -planing.** —*n.* 1. a board which carries a rider behind a towing speedboat. —*v.i.* 2. to ride an aquaplane.

a·quar·i·um (ə kwâr'Ī əm), *n., pl.* **aquariums, aquaria** (ə kwâr'Ī ə). a pond, tank, or building in which aquatic animals or plants are exhibited.

A·quar·i·us (ə kwâr'Ī əs), *n., gen.* **Aquarii** (ə-kwâr'Ī ī'). 1. *Astron.* a zodiacal constellation; the water bearer. 2. the eleventh sign of the zodiac.

a·quat·ic (ə kwăt'Ĭk, ə kwŏt'-), *adj.* 1. of, living in, or growing in water. 2. practiced on or in water. *n.* 4. *(pl.)* aquatic sports.

aq·ua·tint (ăk'wə tĬnt'), *n.* 1. a process imitating ink or wash drawings by etching a microscopic crackle on the copperplate intended for printing. 2. an etching made by this process.

aqua vi·tae (vī'tē), 1. alcohol. 2. brandy.

aq·ue·duct (ăk'wə dŭkt'), *n.* 1. *Civ. Eng.* a conduit or channel for carrying water from a distance. 2. *Anat.* a canal or passage.

a·que·ous (ā'kwĬ əs, ăk'wĬ-), *adj.* of, like, containing, or formed by water; watery.

Aq·ui·la (ăk'wə lə), *n., gen.* **-lae** (-lē'). *Astron.* a northern constellation lying south of Cygnus.

aq·ui·line (ăk'wə lĭn', -lĬn), *adj.* 1. of or like the eagle. 2. (of the nose) curved; hooked.

A·qui·nas (ə kwī'nəs), *n.* **Thomas,** 1225?–1274, Italian scholastic philosopher and theologian.

-ar, an adjective suffix meaning "of, pertaining to, or like."

Ar, *Chem.* argon.

ar., 1. arrival. 2. arrive; arrives.

Ar·ab (ăr'əb), *n.* 1. a native of Arabia, or a member of the Arabic race (now widely spread in Asia and Africa). 2. a horse of a graceful, intelligent breed, native to Arabia. 3. a street Arab. —*adj.* 4. Arabian.

Arab., 1. Arabia. 2. Arabic.

ar·a·besque (ăr'ə bĕsk'), *n.* a kind of ornament in which flowers, foliage, fruits, vases, etc., are represented in a fanciful pattern.

A·ra·bi·a (ə rā'bĬ ə), *n.* a peninsula in SW Asia, including Saudi Arabia, Yemen, Oman, Aden, etc.: divided in ancient times into **Arabia De·ser·ta** (dĬ zûr'tə), the N part, **Arabia Fe·lix** (fē'lĬks), the S part, and **Arabia Pe·trae·a** (pə-trē'ə), the NW part. 7,000,000 pop.; ab. 1,000,-

000 sq. mi. Also, *Poetic,* **Ar·a·by** (ăr'ə bĬ). —**A·ra'bi·an,** *adj., n.*

Arabian Sea, the NW part of the Indian Ocean, between India and Arabia.

Ar·a·bic (ăr'ə bĬk), *adj.* 1. belonging to or derived from Arabia or the Arabians. —*n.* 2. any of the related languages of the Arabians.

Arabic numerals, the characters 0, 1, 2, 3, 4, 5, 6, 7, 8, 9. Also, **Arabic figures.**

ar·a·ble (ăr'ə bəl), *adj.* capable, without much modification, of producing crops by tillage.

a·rach·nid (ə răk'nĬd), *n.* any arthropod of a class which includes the spiders, scorpions, mites, etc. —**a·rach·ni·dan** (ə răk'nə dən), *adj., n.*

Ar·al Sea (ăr'əl), an inland sea in the SW Soviet Union in Asia, E of the Caspian Sea. 26,166 sq. mi. Also, **Lake Aral.**

Ar·a·ma·ic (ăr'ə mā'Ĭk), *n.* 1. any of a group of Semitic languages which became the speech of Syria, Palestine, and Mesopotamia after c300 B.C., including the language of Christ. —*adj.* 2. pertaining to these languages.

A·rap·a·ho (ə răp'ə hō'), *n., pl.* **-ho.** a member of a tribe of Indians once dwelling in the Colorado plains.

ar·ba·lest (är'bə lĬst), *n.* a powerful medieval crossbow. Also, **ar'ba·list.** —**ar'ba·lest·er,** *n.*

Ar·be·la (är bē'lə), *n.* an ancient city of Assyria: Alexander defeated Darius near here, 331 B.C.

ar·bi·ter (är'bə tər), *n.* a person chosen to decide points at issue, usually with absolute power.

ar·bit·ra·ment (är bĬt'rə mənt), *n.* 1. arbitration. 2. the decision pronounced by an arbiter. 3. the power of absolute and final decision.

ar·bi·trar·y (är'bə trĕr'Ĭ), *adj.* 1. subject to individual will or judgment. 2. capricious; unreasonable. 3. uncontrolled by law; despotic. —**ar'bi·trar·i·ly,** *adv.* —**ar'bi·trar·i·ness,** *n.*

ar·bi·trate (är'bə trāt'), *v.t., v.i.,* **-trated, -trating.** 1. to decide as arbiter; determine. 2. to submit to or settle by arbitration.

ar·bi·tra·tion (är'bə trā'shən), *n.* the hearing and determining of a dispute between parties by a person or persons chosen or agreed to by them.

ar·bi·tra·tor (är'bə trā'tər), *n.* a person chosen to decide a dispute.

Ar·blay (där'blā), *n.* **Madame d',** *(Frances or Fanny Burney)* 1752–1840, British novelist.

ar·bor[1] (är'bər), *n.* a bower formed by trees, shrubs, or vines. Also, *esp. Brit.,* **ar'bour.**

ar·bor[2] (är'bər), *n.* *Mach.* 1. a beam, shaft, axis, or spindle. 2. a bar or shaft to support the work or the cutting tools.

ar·bor[3] (är'bər), *n., pl.* **arbores** (är'bə rēz'). a tree.

Arbor Day, a day, varying in date, observed in individual States for planting trees.

ar·bo·re·al (är bōr'Ī əl), *adj.* 1. pertaining to trees; treelike. 2. living in or among trees.

ar·bo·res·cent (är'bə rĕs'ənt), *adj.* treelike.

ar·bo·re·tum (är'bə rē'təm), *n., pl.* **-tums, -ta** (-tə). a plot of land where different trees or shrubs are grown for study or popular interest.

ar·bor vi·tae (är'bər vī'tē), an evergreen tree of the pine family, planted for hedges, etc. Also, **ar'bor·vi'tae.**

ar·bu·tus (är bū'təs), *n.* 1. any of certain evergreen shrubs or trees of the heath family, esp. one of southern Europe with scarlet berries, cultivated for ornament and food. 2. a creeping plant of the heath family, of the U.S., with fragrant white and pink flowers (**trailing arbutus**).

arc (ärk), *n., v.,* **arced** (ärkt), **arcing** (är'kĬng) or **arcked, arcking.** —*n.* 1. *Geom.* any part of a circle or other curved line. 2. *Elect.* the luminous bridge formed by the passage of a current across a gap between two conductors or terminals. 3. *Astron.* the part of the apparent course of a heavenly body. 4. anything bow-shaped. —*v.i.* 5. to form an electric arc.

ARC, American Red Cross. Also, **A.R.C.**

ar·cade (är kād'), *n.* 1. *Archit.* **a.** a series of arches supported on columns. **b.** an arched, roofed-in gallery. 2. an arched or covered passageway, usually with shops on either side.

Ar·ca·di·a (är kā'dĬ ə), *n.* a district in ancient Greece, proverbial for pastoral simplicity of its people. Also, *Poetic,* **Ar·ca·dy** (är'kə dĬ). —**Ar·ca'di·an,** *adj., n.*

ar·ca·num (är kā'nəm), *n., pl.* **-na** (-nə). *(often pl.)* a secret; mystery.

arch[1] (ärch), *n.* 1. a curved structure resting on supports at both extremities, used to bridge an

open space, etc. 2. something curved. —*v.t.*
3. to cover or span with an arch. 4. to curve.
—*v.i.* 5. to form an arch.

arch² (ärch), *adj.* 1. chief; principal. 2. cunning;
roguish. —**arch'ly**, *adv.* —**arch'ness**, *n.*

arch., 1. archaic. 2. (*cap.*) archbishop.

ar·chae·ol·o·gy (är'kĭ ŏl'ə jĭ), *n.* the scientific study of any prehistoric culture by excavation and description of its remains. —**ar·chae·o·**
log·i·cal (är'kĭ ə lŏj'ə kəl), **ar'chae·o·log'ic**,
adj. —**ar'chae·o·log'i·cal·ly**, *adv.* —**ar'chae·**
ol'o·gist, *n.*

ar·cha·ic (är kā'ĭk), *adj.* 1. ancient; antiquated. 2. no longer used in ordinary speech or
writing.

ar·cha·ism (är'kĭ ĭz'əm, -kā-), *n.* 1. something
archaic, as a word. 2. the use of what is archaic.
3. archaic quality or style.

arch·an·gel (ärk'ān'jəl), *n.* a chief or principal angel; one of a particular order of angels.

Arch·an·gel (ärk'ān'jəl), *n.* a seaport in the
NW Soviet Union. 281,091.

arch·bish·op (ärch'bĭsh'əp), *n.* a bishop of
the highest rank.

arch·bish·op·ric (ärch'bĭsh'əp rĭk), *n.* the
see, diocese, or office of an archbishop.

arch·dea·con (ärch'dē'kən), *n.* an ecclesiastic
who has charge of the temporal administration of
a diocese. —**arch·dea·con·ate** (ärch'dē'kən ĭt),
n.

arch·dea·con·ry (ärch'dē'kən rĭ), *n., pl.* -**ries.**
jurisdiction, residence, or office of an archdeacon.

arch·di·o·cese (ärch'dī'ə sēs', -sĭs), *n.* the diocese of an archbishop.

arch·duch·ess (ärch'dŭch'ĭs), *n.* the wife of
an archduke.

arch·duch·y (ärch'dŭch'ĭ), *n., pl.* -**duchies.**
the territory of an archduke.

arch·duke (ärch'dūk', -dŏŏk'), *n.* a prince of
certain European ruling houses. —**arch'du'cal**,
adj.

ar·che·go·ni·um (är'kə gō'nĭ əm), *n., pl.* -**nia**
(-nĭ ə). *Bot.* the female reproductive organ in
ferns, mosses, etc. —**ar'che·go'ni·al**, *adj.*

arch·en·e·my (ärch'ĕn'ə mĭ), *n., pl.* -**mies.** 1.
a chief enemy. 2. Satan; the Devil.

ar·che·ol·o·gy (är'kĭ ŏl'ə jĭ), *n.* archaeology.
—**ar'che·o·log'i·cal**, **ar'che·o·log'ic**, *adj.* —**ar'-**
che·o·log'i·cal·ly, *adv.* —**ar'che·ol'o·gist**, *n.*

Ar·che·o·zo·ic (är'kĭ ə zō'ĭk), *adj.* 1. pertaining to the oldest part of earth history. —*n.* 2. the
Archeozoic era or series of rocks.

arch·er (är'chər), *n.* 1. one who shoots with a
bow and arrow. 2. (*cap.*) *Astron.* the zodiacal
constellation Sagittarius.

arch·er·y (är'chə rĭ), *n.* 1. the art of an archer.
2. an archer's weapons.

ar·che·type (är'kə tīp'), *n.* a model or pattern. —**ar'che·typ'al**, **ar·che·typ·i·cal** (är'kə-
tĭp'ə kəl), *adj.*

arch·fiend (ärch'fēnd'), *n.* a chief fiend.

ar·chi·di·ac·o·nal (är'kĭ dī ăk'ə nəl), *adj.* of
or pertaining to an archdeacon or his office.
—**ar·chi·di·ac·o·nate** (är'kĭ dī ăk'ə nĭt), *n.*

ar·chi·e·pis·co·pal (är'kĭ ĭ pĭs'kə pəl), *adj.* of
or pertaining to an archbishop or his office. —**ar-**
chi·e·pis·co·pate (är'kĭ ĭ pĭs'kə pĭt, -pāt'), *n.*

Ar·chi·me·des (är'kə mē'dēz), *n.* 287?–212
B.C., a Greek mathematician and physicist.

ar·chi·pel·a·go (är'kə pĕl'ə gō'), *n., pl.* -**gos,**
-**goes.** 1. any large body of water with many
islands. 2. the island groups in such a body of
water.

archit., architecture.

ar·chi·tect (är'kə tĕkt'), *n.* 1. one whose profession it is to design buildings and superintend
their construction. 2. the deviser or maker of
anything.

ar·chi·tec·ture (är'kə tĕk'chər), *n.* 1. the art
or science of building. 2. the style of building.
3. the process of building. 4. buildings collectively. —**ar'chi·tec'tur·al**, *adj.* —**ar'chi·tec'-**
tur·al·ly, *adv.*

ar·chi·trave (är'kə trāv'), *n. Archit.* 1. the
lowest division of an entablature, resting immediately on the columns. 2. a band of ornament
about a door, other opening, or a panel.

ar·chives (är'kīvz), *n.pl.* 1. a place where public records or other historical documents are kept.
2. public or historical documents, records, etc.

ar·chon (är'kŏn), *n.* 1. a higher magistrate in
ancient Athens. 2. any ruler. —**ar'chon·ship'**,
n.

arch·priest (ärch'prēst'), *n.* a senior priest,
as among the members of a cathedral chapter.

arch·way (ärch'wā'), *n. Archit.* 1. a passage
under an arch. 2. a covering or enclosing arch.

arc light, Also, **arc lamp.** a lamp in which the
light source of high intensity is an electric arc.

arc·tic (ärk'tĭk *or, esp. for 3,* är'tĭk), *adj.* 1. of,
at, or near the North Pole. —*n.* 2. the arctic
regions. 3. (*pl.*) waterproof overshoes.

Arctic Circle, the southern boundary of the
North Frigid Zone, 23°28' from the North Pole.

Arctic Ocean, an ocean N of North America,
Asia, and the Arctic Circle. ab. 5,400,000 sq. mi.

Arc·tu·rus (ärk tyŏŏr'əs, -tŏŏr'-), *n. Astron.* a
bright star in the constellation Boötes.

ar·dent (är'dənt), *adj.* 1. glowing with feeling,
earnestness, or zeal. 2. glowing; flashing. 3.
burning, fiery, or hot. —**ar'den·cy**, *n.* —**ar'-**
dent·ly, *adv.*

ar·dor (är'dər), *n.* 1. fervor; zeal. 2. burning
heat. Also, *esp. Brit.*, **ar'dour.**

ar·du·ous (är'jŏŏ əs), *adj.* 1. requiring great
exertion; difficult. 2. energetic; strenuous. 3.
hard to climb; steep. 4. hard to endure; severe.
—**ar'du·ous·ly**, *adv.* —**ar'du·ous·ness**, *n.*

are¹ (är; *unstressed* ər), *v.* pres. indic. pl. of **be.**

are² (âr, är), *n. Metric System.* a surface measure
equal to 100 square meters, or 119.6 square yards.

ar·e·a (âr'ĭ ə), *n.* 1. any particular extent of
surface; region. 2. extent, range, or scope. 3.
Brit. areaway (def. 1). 4. *Math.* amount of surface. —**ar'e·al**, *adj.*

ar·e·a·way (âr'ĭ ə wā'), *n.* 1. a sunken area
leading to a basement entrance. 2. *U.S.* a passageway.

a·re·na (ə rē'nə), *n.* 1. oval space in a Roman
amphitheater for combats, etc. 2. any field of
conflict.

aren't (ärnt), contraction of *are not.*

A·re·qui·pa (ä'rĕ kē'pä), *n.* a city in S Peru.
79,185.

Ar·es (âr'ēz), *n.* the Greek god of war, identified
by the Romans with Mars.

ar·e·thu·sa (är'ə thŏŏ'zə), *n.* a small bog orchid
of North America with a pink, or occasionally
white, flower.

ar·gent (är'jənt), *n.* 1. *Archaic or Poetic.* silver.
—*adj.* 2. like silver; silvery-white.

ar·gen·tic (är jĕn'tĭk), *adj. Chem.* of or containing silver, esp. with a higher valence.

Ar·gen·ti·na (är'jən tē'nə; *Sp.* är'hĕn tē'nä), *n.*
a republic in S South America. 13,909,950 pop.;
1,073,698 sq. mi. *Cap.:* Buenos Aires. —**Ar·gen·**
tine (är'jən tēn', -tīn'), **Ar·gen·tin·e·an** (är'jən-
tĭn'ĭ ən), *n., adj.*

ar·gen·tous (är jĕn'təs), *adj. Chem.* containing monovalent silver.

ar·gen·tum (är jĕn'təm), *n. Chem.* silver.

Ar·go (är'gō), *n. Astron.* a very large southern
constellation, south of Canis Major.

ar·gon (är'gŏn), *n.* a colorless, odorless gaseous
element. *Symbol:* A; *at. no.:* 18; *at. wt.:* 39.94.

Ar·go·naut (är'gə nôt'), *n.* 1. *Gk. Legend.* a
member of the band that sailed with Jason in
search of the golden fleece. 2. a person who emi-
grated to California during the gold rush of 1848.
—**Ar'go·nau'tic**, *adj.*

ar·go·sy (är'gə sĭ), *n., pl.* -**sies.** 1. a large merchant ship, esp. one with a rich cargo. 2. a fleet
of such ships.

ar·got (är'gō, -gət), *n.* the peculiar language or
jargon of any class or group.

ar·gue (är'gū), *v.,* -**gued,** -**guing.** —*v.i.* 1. to
present reasons for or against a thing. 2. to dispute. —*v.t.* 3. to state the reasons for or against.
4. to reason. 5. to persuade, etc., by reasoning.
6. to show, imply.

ar·gu·ment (är'gyə mənt), *n.* 1. a debate. 2.
a process of reasoning. 3. a statement or fact to
prove a point. 4. a summary, as of a book.

ar·gu·men·ta·tion (är'gyə mĕn tā'shən), *n.* 1.
reasoning; discussion. 2. a debate.

ar·gu·men·ta·tive (är'gyə mĕn'tə tĭv), *adj.* 1.
addicted to argument. 2. controversial. —**ar'-**
gu·men'ta·tive·ly, *adv.* —**ar'gu·men'ta·tive-**
ness, *n.*

Ar·gus (är'gəs), *n. Gk. Legend.* a giant with a
hundred eyes, set to guard the heifer Io.

Ar·gy·rol (är'jə rōl', -rŏl'), *n.* a trademark for
an antiseptic compound of silver and a protein.

a·ri·a (ä'rĭ ə, âr'ĭ ə), *n.* 1. a melody. 2. an
elaborate melody for a single voice in an opera,
etc.

Ar·i·an (âr′Y ən), *adj.* **1.** pertaining to Arius. **—n. 2.** an adherent of Arius. **—Ar′i·an·ism,** *n.*

ar·id (âr′Yd), *adj.* **1.** dry; parched. **2.** dull. **—a·rid·i·ty** (ə rĭd′ə tЎ), **ar′id·ness,** *n.* **—ar′-id·ly,** *adv.*

Ar·ies (âr′ēz, -Y̆ ēz′), *n., gen.* **Arietis** (ə rī′ə tY̆s). **1.** the Ram, a zodiacal constellation between Pisces and Taurus. **2.** the first sign of the zodiac.

a·right (ə rīt′), *adv.* rightly; correctly; properly.

ar·il (âr′Yl), *n. Bot.* an accessory covering or appendage of certain seeds. **—ar·il·late** (âr′ə lāt′), *adj.*

a·rise (ə rīz′), *v.i.,* **arose, arisen, arising. 1.** to come into being or action. **2.** to result. **3.** to move upward. **4.** to get up.

ar·is·toc·ra·cy (âr′ə stŏk′rə sЎ), *n., pl.* **-cies. 1.** a state characterized by the rule of a nobility, elite, or privileged upper class. **2.** a body of persons holding exceptional rank or privileges. **3.** government by the best men. **4.** a governing body composed of the best men. **5.** any superior class.

a·ris·to·crat (ə rĭs′tə krăt′, âr′Y̆s tə-), *n.* **1.** one who has the tastes, manners, etc., of a superior class. **2.** a member of an aristocracy. **3.** an advocate of aristocratic government. **—a·ris′to·crat′ic, a·ris′to·crat′i·cal,** *adj.* **—a·ris′to·crat′i·cal·ly,** *adv.*

Ar·is·toph·a·nes (âr′ə stŏf′ə nēz′), *n.* 448?-385? B.C., Athenian poet and writer of comedy.

Ar·is·tot·le (âr′ə stŏt′əl), *n.* 384–322 B.C., Greek philosopher; pupil of Plato. **—Ar·is·to·te·lian** (âr′Y̆s tə tēl′yən, -tĕ′lY̆ ən), *adj., n.* **—Ar′is·to·te′lian·ism,** *n.*

arith., 1. arithmetic. **2.** arithmetical.

a·rith·me·tic (*n.* ə rĭth′mə tЎk; *adj.* âr′Y̆th-mĕt′Y̆k), *n.* **1.** the art of computation with figures. **—adj. 2.** Also, **ar′ith·met′i·cal.** of or pertaining to arithmetic. **—ar′ith·met′i·cal·ly,** *adv.* **—a·rith·me·ti·cian** (ə rĭth′mə tĭsh′ən, âr′-Y̆th-), *n.*

A·ri·us (ə rī′əs, âr′Y-), *n.* died A.D. 336, Christian priest at Alexandria, who held that Christ the Son was not consubstantial with God the Father.

Ar·i·zo·na (âr′ə zō′nə), *n.* a State in the SW United States. 622,804 pop.; 113,909 sq. mi. *Cap.:* Phoenix. *Abbr.:* **Ariz. —Ar′i·zo′nan,** *adj., n.*

ark (ârk), *n.* **1.** the vessel built by Noah for safety during the Flood. **2.** Also, **ark of the covenant.** a chest containing the Tables of the Law.

Ar·kan·sas (ärk′ən sô′; *also for 2* är kăn′zəs), *n.* **1.** a State in the S central U.S. 1,884,659 pop.; 53,103 sq. mi. *Cap.:* Little Rock. *Abbr.:* **Ark. 2.** a river from central Colorado to SE Arkansas. 1450 mi. **—Ar·kan·san** (är kăn′zən), *n., adj.*

Ark·wright (ärk′rĭt), *n.* **Sir Richard,** 1732–92, British inventor of the spinning jenny.

Ar·ling·ton (är′lĭng tən), *n.* **1.** a national cemetery in NE Virginia. **2.** a town in E Mass. 40,013.

arm¹ (ärm), *n.* **1.** the upper limb of the human body from the shoulder to the hand. **2.** the forelimb of any vertebrate. **3.** any armlike part, as of a lever. **4.** a support for the forearm at the side of a chair, etc. **5.** an inlet or cove. **6.** power; authority.

arm² (ärm), *n.* **1.** (*usually pl.*) a weapon. **2.** *Mil.* a combat branch. **—v.i. 3.** to become ready for war. **—v.t. 4.** to equip with arms. **5.** to provide with whatever will add strength, force, or security.

Ar·ma·da (är mä′də, -mä′-), *n.* **1.** Also, **the Spanish** or **Invincible Armada.** a fleet sent by Spain against England in 1588, but shattered and dispersed by storms. **2.** (*l.c.*) any fleet of warships.

ar·ma·dil·lo (är′mə dЎl′ō), *n., pl.* **-los.** any of a great variety of omnivorous burrowing mammals, having a jointed, protective covering of bony plates. They are found throughout South America and north to Texas.

Ar·ma·ged·don (är′mə gĕd′ən), *n.* **1.** *Bible.* the place where the final battle will be fought between the forces of good and evil. **2.** any crucial conflict.

ar·ma·ment (är′mə mənt), *n.* **1.** the weapons with which a military unit, as a warship, is equipped. **2.** a land, sea, or air force. **3.** the process of arming for war.

ar·ma·ture (är′mə chər), *n.* **1.** armor. **2.** *Biol.* the protective covering of an animal or plant, or any part serving for defense or offense. **3.** *Elect.* **a.** the iron or steel applied across the poles of a permanent magnet to close it. **b.** the part of an electrical machine which includes the main current-carrying winding. **c.** a pivoted part of an electrical device activated by a magnetic field.

arm·chair (ärm′châr′), *n.* a chair with arms to support the forearms or elbows.

armed forces, all of the principal naval or military forces of a nation.

Ar·me·ni·a (är mē′nĭ ə, -mĕn′yə), *n.* an ancient country in W Asia: now a region in the SW Soviet Union, E Turkey, and NW Iran. **—Ar·me′ni·an,** *adj., n.*

Ar·men·tières (âr măn tyĕr′), *n.* a city in extreme N France: battles, 1914, 1918. 22,667.

arm·ful (ärm′fŏŏl′), *n., pl.* **-fuls.** as much as the arm, or both arms, can hold.

arm·hole (ärm′hōl′), *n.* a hole for the arm.

ar·mi·stice (är′mə stЎs), *n.* an agreed temporary suspension of hostilities; truce.

Armistice Day, November 11: anniversary of cessation of hostilities of World War I in 1918.

arm·let (ärm′lЎt), *n.* **1.** *Chiefly Brit.* an ornamental band worn on the arm. **2.** a little arm.

ar·mor (är′mər), *n.* **1.** any covering worn as a protection against offensive weapons. **2.** a metallic protective covering, used on warships, fortifications, etc. **3.** any protective covering. **—v.t. 4.** to cover with armor. Also, *esp. Brit.,* **ar′mour.**

ar·mor·er (är′mər ər), *n.* a maker or repairer of armor or arms.

ar·mo·ri·al (är mōr′Y əl), *adj.* belonging to heraldry or to heraldic bearing.

ar·mor·y (är′mə rY̆), *n., pl.* **-mories. 1.** a storage place for war equipment. **2.** a building which is the headquarters and drill center of a military unit. **3.** *U.S.* an arsenal.

arm·pit (ärm′pY̆t′), *n. Anat.* the hollow under the arm at the shoulder; the axilla.

arms (ärmz), *n.pl.* **1.** arms² (def. 1). **2.** small arms, all weapons of small caliber carried by hand, as rifles, pistols, etc. **3.** heraldic bearings.

ar·my (är′mY̆), *n., pl.* **-mies. 1.** (*cap. or l.c.*) the military land forces of a nation. **2.** (in land forces) the second largest unit, consisting of two or more corps. **3.** a large body of soldiers. **4.** any body of persons organized for any cause. **5.** a multitude.

army worm, a caterpillar which often travels in destructive hosts.

Arn·hem (ärn′hĕm), *n.* a city in central Netherlands, on the Rhine: battle, 1944. 91,828.

ar·ni·ca (är′nə kə), *n.* **1.** any plant of the aster family from which is obtained a tincture much used as an external application in sprains and bruises. **2.** the tincture itself.

Ar·nold (är′nəld), *n.* **1. Benedict,** 1741–1801, American general who turned traitor. **2. Matthew,** 1822–88, British essayist, poet, and literary critic. **3. Thomas,** 1795–1842, British clergyman (father of Matthew).

a·ro·ma (ə rō′mə), *n.* a fragrant odor.

ar·o·mat·ic (âr′ə măt′Y̆k), *adj.* **1.** fragrant. **—n. 2.** a fragrant plant, drug, or medicine. **—ar′o·mat′i·cal·ly,** *adv.*

a·rose (ə rōz′), *v.* pt. of **arise.**

a·round (ə round′), *adv.* **1.** in a circle; on every side. **2.** *U.S.* here and there. **3.** *U.S. Colloq.* somewhere near. **—prep. 4.** on all sides. **5.** *U.S. Colloq.* here and there in. **6.** *U.S. Colloq.* somewhere in or near. **7.** *U.S. Colloq.* approximately.

a·rouse (ə rouz′), *v.t.,* **aroused, arousing.** to stir; awaken. **—a·rous·al** (ə rou′zəl), *n.* **—a·rous′er,** *n.*

ar·peg·gi·o (är pĕj′Y ō′, -pĕj′ō), *n., pl.* **-gios.** *Music.* **1.** the sounding of the notes of a chord in rapid succession. **2.** a chord thus sounded.

arr., 1. arranged. **2.** arrival. **3.** arrive; arrived.

ar·raign (ə rān′), *v.t.* **1.** *Law.* to call before a court to answer to a charge. **2.** to accuse. **—ar·raign′ment,** *n.*

ar·range (ə rānj′), *v.t.,* **-ranged, -ranging. 1.** to place in proper, desired, or convenient order. **2.** to come to an understanding regarding. **3.** to prepare or plan. **4.** *Music.* to adapt for a particular rendering. **—ar·rang′er,** *n.*

ar·range·ment (ə rānj′mənt), *n.* **1.** act of arranging. **2.** state of being arranged. **3.** the manner in which things are arranged. **4.** a final settlement. **5.** (*usually pl.*) previous plan; preparation. **6.** something arranged in a particular way. **7.** *Music.* **a.** the adaptation of a composition. **b.** a piece so adapted.

ar·rant (âr′ənt), *adj.* downright; thorough.

ar·ras (ăr′əs), *n.* a rich tapestry.
Ar·ras (ăr′əs; *Fr.* à räs′), *n.* a city in N France: battles in World War I. 33,345.
ar·ray (ə rā′), *v.t.* **1.** to place in proper or desired order. **2.** to clothe; deck. —*n.* **3.** order, as of troops for battle. **4.** an impressive group of things on exhibition. **5.** regular order. **6.** attire. —**ar·ray′al,** *n.*
ar·rear (ə rĭr′), *n.* **1.** state of being behind. **2.** (*usually pl.*) an overdue debt. **3. in arrears,** behind in payments.
ar·rest (ə rĕst′), *v.t.* **1.** to seize (a person), esp. by legal authority. **2.** to stop. —*n.* **3.** taking a person into custody for a legal proceeding. **4.** any seizure. **5.** act of stopping. **6.** state of being stopped. —**ar·rest′er,** *n.* —**ar·rest′ment,** *n.*
ar·riv·al (ə rī′vəl), *n.* **1.** act of arriving. **2.** the reaching of any object or condition. **3.** the person or thing that arrives, or has arrived.
ar·rive (ə rīv′), *v.i.,* **-rived, -riving. 1.** to come to a certain point or to one's destination. **2.** to reach. **3.** to come.
ar·ro·gance (ăr′ə gəns), *n.* quality of being arrogant; offensive pride. Also, **ar′ro·gan·cy.**
ar·ro·gant (ăr′ə gənt), *adj.* **1.** insolently proud. **2.** characterized by or proceeding from arrogance. —**ar′ro·gant·ly,** *adv.*
ar·ro·gate (ăr′ə gāt′), *v.t.,* **-gated, -gating.** to claim presumptuously. —**ar′ro·ga′tion,** *n.*
ar·row (ăr′ō), *n.* **1.** a slender, straight, pointed weapon shot by a bow. **2.** anything resembling an arrow. **3.** a figure used to indicate direction. **4.** (*cap.*) *Astron.* Sagitta.
ar·row·head (ăr′ō hĕd′), *n.* **1.** the head of an arrow. **2.** an aquatic plant with arrowheaded leaves.
ar·row·root (ăr′ō rōōt′, -rŏŏt′), *n.* **1.** a tropical American plant whose rhizomes yield a nutritious starch. **2.** the starch itself.
ar·roy·o (ə roi′ō), *n., pl.* **-os** (-ōz). a small, steep-sided watercourse or gulch, usually dry.
ar·se·nal (ăr′sə nəl), *n.* **1.** a respository of arms and military stores. **2.** a public establishment where military supplies are manufactured.
ar·se·nic (*n.* ăr′sə nĭk, ärs′nĭk; *adj.* är sĕn′ĭk), *n.* **1.** a grayish-white element having a metallic luster, forming poisonous compounds. *Symbol:* As; *at. wt.:* 74.91; *at. no.:* 33. **2.** arsenic trioxide, used in poisons for vermin. —*adj.* **3.** Also, **ar·sen′i·cal.** of or containing arsenic.
ar·son (ăr′sən), *n. Law.* the malicious burning of a building.
ars·phen·a·mine (ärs′fĕn ə mēn′, -fĕn ăm′ĭn), *n. Pharm.* a yellow crystalline powder used esp. to treat syphilis and trench mouth.
art[1] (ärt), *n.* **1.** the production or expression of what is beautiful, appealing, or of more than ordinary significance. **2.** any illustration. **3.** a department of skilled performance. **4.** (*pl.*) liberal arts. **5.** skilled workmanship. **6.** cunning. **7.** artificiality in behavior. **8.** (*usually pl.*) an artifice.
art[2] (ärt), *v. Archaic or Poetic.* 2nd pers. sing. pres. indic. of **be.**
art., *pl.* **arts. 1.** article. **2.** artificial.
Ar·te·mis (är′tə mĭs), *n. Gk. Myth.* a goddess of the moon: identified by Romans with Diana.
ar·te·ri·al (är tĭr′ĭ əl), *adj.* **1.** *Physiol.* pertaining to the blood in the arteries which has been charged with oxygen during its passage through the lungs. **2.** *Anat.* of, pertaining to, or resembling the arteries. **3.** having a main channel and many branches.
ar·te·ri·o·scle·ro·sis (är tĭr′ĭ ō sklə rō′sĭs), *n. Pathol.* a disease characterized by inelasticity and thickening of the artery walls.
ar·ter·y (är′tə rĭ), *n., pl.* **-teries. 1.** *Anat.* a blood vessel which conveys blood from the heart to any part of the body. **2.** any main channel.
ar·te·sian well (är tē′zhən), a well whose shaft penetrates through an impervious layer into a water-bearing stratum from which the water rises under pressure.
art·ful (ärt′fəl), *adj.* **1.** crafty; tricky. **2.** ingenious. **3.** done with skill. —**art′ful·ly,** *adv.* —**art′ful·ness,** *n.*
ar·thri·tis (är thrī′tĭs), *n. Pathol.* inflammation of a joint. —**ar·thrit·ic** (är thrĭt′ĭk), *adj.*
ar·thro·pod (är′thrə pŏd′), *n.* any of a phylum of segmented invertebrates, having jointed legs, as the insects, arachnids, and crustaceans.
Ar·thur (är′thər), *n.* **1.** legendary king in ancient Britain: head of Round Table. **2. Chester**

Alan, 1830–86, 21st president of the U.S., 1881–85.
Ar·thu·ri·an (är thŏŏr′ĭ ən), *adj.* of or pertaining to King Arthur and his knights.
ar·ti·choke (är′tə chōk′), *n.* **1.** a herbaceous, thistlelike plant with an edible flower head. **2.** the edible portion, used as a table vegetable. **3.** Jerusalem artichoke.
ar·ti·cle (är′tə kəl), *n., v.,* **-cled, -cling.** —*n.* **1.** a literary composition on a specific topic, forming part of a publication. **2.** an individual piece or thing of a class. **3.** a thing, indefinitely. **4.** (in some languages) either of the two words *a* or *an* (**indefinite article**) and *the* (**definite article**), whose main function is to precede common nouns. **5.** a particular in a contract or other formal agreement. —*v.t.* **6.** accuse specifically. **7.** to bind by articles of covenant or agreement. —*v.i.* **8.** to make specific charges.
ar·tic·u·lar (är tĭk′yə lər), *adj.* of the joints.
ar·tic·u·late (*adj., n.* är tĭk′yə lĭt; *v.* är tĭk′yə lāt′), *adj., v.,* **-lated, -lating.** —*adj.* **1.** clear; distinct. **2.** uttered clearly in distinct syllables. **3.** capable of speech. **4.** having joints or segments. —*v.t.* **5.** to utter, esp. to utter distinctly. **6.** to unite by a joint or joints. —*v.i.* **7.** to utter distinct syllables or words. **8.** to form a joint. —*n.* **9.** a segmented invertebrate. —**ar·tic′u·late·ly,** *adv.* —**ar·tic′u·late·ness,** *n.*
ar·tic·u·la·tion (är tĭk′yə lā′shən), *n.* **1.** act or process of articulating speech. **2.** any speech sound. **3.** act of jointing. **4.** a jointed state or formation. **5.** *Bot.* **a.** a joint between two separable parts. **b.** a node in a stem.
ar·ti·fact (är′tə făkt′), *n.* any object made by man with a view to subsequent use.
ar·ti·fice (är′tə fĭs), *n.* **1.** a clever trick or stratagem. **2.** trickery.
ar·tif·i·cer (är tĭf′ə sər), *n.* a craftsman.
ar·ti·fi·cial (är′tə fĭsh′əl), *adj.* **1.** made by human skill and labor. **2.** made in imitation of or as a substitute. **3.** assumed. **4.** affected. —**ar′ti·fi′cial·ly,** *adv.*
ar·ti·fi·ci·al·i·ty (är′tə fĭsh′ĭ ăl′ə tĭ′), *n., pl.* **-ties. 1.** artificial quality. **2.** an artificial thing.
ar·til·ler·y (är tĭl′ə rĭ), *n.* **1.** mounted guns, as disting. from small arms. **2.** the branch of an army concerned with such guns. —**ar·til′ler·y·man, ar·til′ler·ist,** *n.*
ar·ti·san (är′tə zən), *n.* a skilled craftsman.
art·ist (är′tĭst), *n.* **1.** a person who practices one of the fine arts. **2.** an actor or singer.
ar·tis·tic (är tĭs′tĭk), *adj.* **1.** aesthetically excellent. **2.** of an artist. Also, **ar·tis′ti·cal.** —**ar·tis′ti·cal·ly,** *adv.*
art·ist·ry (är′tĭs trĭ′), *n., pl.* **-ries.** artistic workmanship, effect, or quality.
art·less (ärt′lĭs), *adj.* **1.** free from deceit or cunning. **2.** natural. **3.** lacking art. —**art′less·ly,** *adv.* —**art′less·ness,** *n.*
ar·um (âr′əm), *n.* any of a genus of plants having an inflorescence consisting of a spadix enclosed in a large sheath.
A.R.V., American Revised Version (of the Bible).
-ary, an adjective suffix meaning "pertaining to," etc.
Ar·y·an (âr′ĭ ən, -yən, är′-; är′yən), *n.* **1.** *Ethnol.* a member or descendant of the prehistoric people who spoke Indo-European. **2.** a non-Semitic person. —*adj.* **3.** of or pertaining to an Aryan or the Aryans.
as[1] (ăz; *unstressed* əz), *adv.* **1.** to such an extent. **2. as well as,** as much as. **3. as well,** equally; also. —*conj.* **4.** the consequent in the correlations *as . . . as, same . . . as,* etc., or *so as, such as.* **5.** (without antecedent) in the degree, manner, etc., of or that. **6.** while. **7.** because. **8.** for instance. **9.** even or just. **10.** *Colloq.* that. —*rel. pron.* **11.** that.
as[2] (ăs), *n., pl.* **asses** (ăs′ĭz). a copper coin, the unit of the early monetary system of Rome.
As, *Chem.* arsenic.
AS., Anglo-Saxon. Also, **A.-S., A.S.**
as·a·fet·i·da (ăs′ə fĕt′ə də), *n.* a gum resin with a garliclike odor, obtained from the roots of several species of Asiatic plants and used in medicine. Also, **as′a·foet·i·da.**
as·bes·tos (ăs bĕs′təs, ăz-), *n.* **1.** *Mineral.* a fibrous amphibole, used for making fireproof articles. **2.** a fabric of asbestos fibers. Also, **as·bes′tus.**
as·cend (ə sĕnd′), *v.i.* **1.** to climb or go upward. —*v.t.* **2.** to climb. —**as·cend′a·ble, as·cend′i·ble,** *adj.*

as·cend·an·cy (ə sĕn'dən sĭ), *n.* domination. Also, **as·cend'en·cy, as·cend'ance, as·cend'-ence.**

as·cend·ant (ə sĕn'dənt), *n.* **1.** the position of dominance or controlling influence. —*adj.* **2.** predominant. Also, **as·cend'ent.**

as·cen·sion (ə sĕn'shən), *n.* **1.** act of ascending. **2.** (*often cap.*) the bodily passing of Christ to heaven. **3.** (*cap.*) Ascension Day.

As·cen·sion (ə sĕn'shən), *n.* a British island in the S Atlantic. 159 pop.; 34 sq. mi.

Ascension Day, the fortieth day after Easter, commemorating the ascension of Christ.

as·cent (ə sĕnt'), *n.* **1.** act of ascending; rise or advancement. **2.** upward slope.

as·cer·tain (ăs'ər tān'), *v.t.* to determine by trial or examination. —**as'cer·tain'a·ble,** *adj.* —**as'-cer·tain'a·bly,** *adv.* —**as'cer·tain'ment,** *n.*

as·cet·ic (ə sĕt'ĭk), *n.* **1.** a person who leads an abstemious life. **2.** one who practices religious austerities. —*adj.* **3.** pertaining to asceticism or ascetics. **4.** rigorously abstinent. —**as·cet'i·cal·ly,** *adv.*

as·cet·i·cism (ə sĕt'ə sĭz'əm), *n.* **1.** the life or practice of an ascetic. **2.** *Theol.* the theory of the means by which conformity with the divine will may be attained.

as·cid·i·an (ə sĭd'ĭ ən), *n.* *Zool.* a tunicate.

as·cid·i·um (ə sĭd'ĭ əm), *n., pl.* **-cidia** (-sĭd'ĭ ə). *Bot.* a baglike or pitcherlike part.

as·co·my·cete (ăs'kə mī sēt'), *n.* *Bot.* a fungus of a class including yeasts, mildews, etc., characterized by bearing sexual spores in a sac.

a·scor·bic acid (ā skôr'bĭk), *Biochem.* the antiscorbutic Vitamin C in citrus fruits, etc.

as·cot (ăs'kət), *n.* a type of necktie.

as·cribe (ə skrīb'), *v.t.,* **-cribed, -cribing. 1.** to attribute; assign. **2.** to consider or allege to belong. —**as·crib'a·ble,** *adj.* —**as·crip·tion** (ə skrĭp'shən), *n.*

a·sep·sis (ə sĕp'sĭs, ā-), *n.* **1.** absence of the microörganisms that produce sepsis or septic disease. **2.** *Med.* methods characterized by the use of instruments, etc., that are free from such microörganisms. —**a·sep'tic,** *adj.* —**a·sep'ti·cal·ly,** *adv.*

a·sex·u·al (ā sĕk'shoŏ əl), *adj.* **1.** not sexual. **2.** having no sexual organs. —**a·sex'u·al·ly,** *adv.*

ash¹ (ăsh), *n.* the powdery residue of matter that remains after burning. See **ashes.**

ash² (ăsh), *n.* a tree of the olive family, esp. one of North America (**white ash**) that yields a tough, straight-grained, and elastic wood.

a·shamed (ə shāmd'), *adj.* **1.** feeling shame. **2.** restrained through fear of shame.

ash·en¹ (ăsh'ən), *adj.* **1.** gray. **2.** of ashes.

ash·en² (ăsh'ən), *adj.* of or from the ash tree.

ash·es (ăsh'ĭz), *n.pl.* **1.** ruins or remains, as from burning. **2.** a dead body.

Ashe·ville (ăsh'vĭl), *n.* a city in W North Carolina. 51,310.

Ash·land (ăsh'lənd), *n.* a city in NE Kentucky, on the Ohio river. 29,537.

ash·lar (ăsh'lər), *n.* **1.** a squared block of building stone. **2.** such stones collectively. **3.** masonry made of them. Also, **ash'ler.**

a·shore (ə shôr'), *adv., adj. Naut.* to shore.

Ash Wednesday, the first day of Lent.

ash·y (ăsh'ĭ), *adj.,* **ashier, ashiest. 1.** ash-colored. **2.** consisting of ashes. **3.** covered with ashes.

A·sia (ā'zhə, ā'shə), *n.* the largest continent, bounded by Europe and the Pacific, Arctic, and Indian Oceans. ab. 1,250,000,000 pop.; ab. 16,-000,000 sq. mi. —**A·si·at·ic** (ā'zhĭ ăt'ĭk, ā'shĭ-), **A'sian,** *adj., n.*

Asia Minor, a peninsula in W Asia between the Black and the Mediterranean Seas.

a·side (ə sīd'), *adv.* **1.** on or to one side; apart. **2.** away from one's thoughts. **3. aside from,** *U.S.* excluding. —*n.* **4.** *Theat.* a part not supposed to be heard by others on the stage.

as·i·nine (ăs'ə nīn'), *adj.* stupid; obstinate. —**as'i·nine'ly,** *adv.* —**as·i·nin·i·ty** (ăs'ə nĭn'ə tĭ), *n.*

ask (ăsk, äsk), *v.t.* **1.** to put a question to. **2.** to seek to be informed about. **3.** to request. **4.** to request of. **5.** to demand. **6.** to require. **7.** to invite. **8.** to publish the (banns) of (persons). —*v.i.* **9.** to inquire. **10.** to request. —**ask'er,** *n.*

a·skance (ə skăns'), *adv.* **1.** with suspicion, mistrust, or disapproval. **2.** sidewise. Also, **a·skant'.**

a·skew (ə skū'), *adv.* **1.** awry. —*adj.* **2.** oblique.

a·slant (ə slănt', ə slänt'), *adv.* **1.** at a slant. —*adj.* **2.** slanting. —*prep.* **3.** athwart.

a·sleep (ə slēp'), *adv.* **1.** in or into a state of sleep. —*adj.* **2.** sleeping. **3.** inactive. **4.** numb.

asp (ăsp), *n.* **1.** any of several poisonous snakes, esp. the Egyptian cobra. **2.** the European viper.

as·par·a·gus (ə spăr'ə gəs), *n.* **1.** a plant of the lily family cultivated for its edible shoots. **2.** the shoots.

as·pect (ăs'pĕkt), *n.* **1.** appearance; look. **2.** facial expression. **3.** a way in which a thing may be regarded. **4.** view or exposure.

as·pen (ăs'pən), *n.* **1.** any of various species of poplar having leaves that tremble in the slightest breeze. —*adj.* **2.** of the aspen. **3.** trembling.

as·per·i·ty (ăs pĕr'ə tĭ), *n., pl.* **-ties. 1.** roughness or sharpness, as of temper. **2.** hardship.

as·perse (ə spûrs'), *v.t.,* **-persed, -persing. 1.** to slander. **2.** to sprinkle. —**as·pers'er,** *n.*

as·per·sion (ə spûr'zhən, -shən), *n.* **1.** a damaging imputation; a derogatory criticism. **2.** a sprinkling.

as·phalt (ăs'fôlt, -fălt), *n.* Also, **as·phal·tum** (ăs fôl'təm). **1.** any of various dark-colored, solid bituminous substances, occurring native and as a by-product of petroleum refinement. **2.** a mixture of such a substance with rock, etc., for pavements, etc. —*v.t.* **3.** to cover with asphalt. —**as·phal'tic,** *adj.*

as·pho·del (ăs'fə dĕl'), *n.* **1.** any of various plants of the lily family, with white, pink, or yellow flowers. **2.** the daffodil.

as·phyx·i·a (ăs fĭk'sĭ ə), *n.* the serious condition caused by lack of oxygen and excess of carbon dioxide in the blood.

as·phyx·i·ate (ăs fĭk'sĭ āt'), *v.t.,* **-ated, -ating.** to produce asphyxia in. —**as·phyx'i·a'tion,** *n.* —**as·phyx'i·a'tor,** *n.*

as·pic¹ (ăs'pĭk), *n.* an appetizing jelly used as a garnish or as a base for meat, vegetables, etc.

as·pic² (ăs'pĭk), *n.* *Poetic.* an asp.

as·pir·ant (ə spĭr'ənt, ăs'pə rənt), *n.* **1.** a person who aspires to honor, etc. —*adj.* **2.** aspiring.

as·pi·rate (*v.* ăs'pə rāt'; *n., adj.* ăs'pə rĭt), *v.,* **-rated, -rating,** *n., adj. Phonet.* —*v.t.* **1.** to release (a stop) in such a way that the breath escapes with audible friction. **2.** to begin (a word or syllable) with an *h* sound. —*n.* **3.** a puff of unvoiced air, represented in many languages by *h.* —*adj.* **4.** aspirated.

as·pi·ra·tion (ăs'pə rā'shən), *n.* **1.** lofty or ambitious desire. **2.** act of aspirating (a stop, word, etc.). **3.** *Med.* act of removing a fluid, as pus, by a suction syringe.

as·pi·ra·tor (ăs'pə rā'tər), *n.* an apparatus employing suction, as for medical use.

as·pire (ə spĭr'), *v.i.,* **-pired, -piring. 1.** to long, aim, or seek ambitiously. **2.** *Archaic or Poetic.* to soar.

as·pi·rin (ăs'pə rĭn), *n.* a white crystalline derivative of salicylic acid, $C_9H_8O_4$, used to relieve the pain of headache, gout, neuralgia, etc.

ass (ăs), *n.* **1.** a long-eared mammal, related to the horse, serving as a beast of burden. **2.** a fool.

as·sa·fet·i·da (ăs'ə fĕt'ə də), *n.* asafetida. Also, **as'sa·foet'i·da.**

as·sa·gai (ăs'ə gī'), *n., pl.* **-gais,** *v.t.,* **-gaied, -gaiing.** assegai.

as·sail (ə sāl'), *v.t.* to set upon with violence, arguments, entreaties, etc. —**as·sail'a·ble,** *adj.* —**as·sail'ant,** *n., adj.* —**as·sail'er,** *n.*

as·sas·sin (ə săs'ĭn), *n.* one who undertakes to murder, esp. from fanaticism or for a reward.

as·sas·si·nate (ə săs'ə nāt'), *v.t.,* **-nated, -nating.** to kill by premeditated assault. —**as·sas'-si·na'tion,** *n.* —**as·sas'si·na'tor,** *n.*

as·sault (ə sôlt'), *n.* **1.** act of assailing. **2.** *Mil.* close combat. **3.** rape¹. —*v.t.* **4.** to make an assault upon. —**as·sault'er,** *n.*

as·say (*v.* ə sā'; *n.* ə sā', ăs'ā), *v.t.* **1.** to examine by trial; test. **2.** to analyze (an ore, drug, etc.) in order to determine its contents. **3.** to evaluate. —*v.i.* **4.** *U.S.* to contain, as shown by analysis, certain ingredients. —*n.* **5.** determination of the nature, quantity, strength, etc., of the ingredients of an ore, drug, etc. **6.** a listing of the findings in assaying a substance. —**as·say'er,** *n.*

as·se·gai (ăs'ə gī'), *n., pl.* **-gais,** *v.t.,* **-gaied, -gaing.** —*n.* **1.** the slender throwing spear of the Kaffirs. —*v.t.* **2.** to pierce with an assegai.

as·sem·blage (ə sĕm'blĭj), *n.* **1.** an assembly. **2.** act of assembling. **3.** state of being assembled as·sem·ble (ə sĕm′bəl), v.t., v.i., -bled, -bling. 1. to gather into one place, body, etc. 2. to put or fit together. —as·sem′bler, n.

as·sem·bly (ə sĕm′blĭ), n., pl. -blies. 1. a company of persons gathered together. 2. (cap.) *Govt.* a legislative body. 3. act of assembling. 4. state of being assembled. 5. *Mil.* a signal for troops to assemble. 6. the putting together of complex machinery from parts of standard dimensions. 7. such parts.

as·sem·bly·man (ə sĕm′blĭ mən), n., pl. -men. U.S. a member of a legislative assembly.

as·sent (ə sĕnt′), v.i. 1. to agree by expressing acquiescence or admitting truth. —n. 2. agreement.

as·sert (ə sûrt′), v.t. 1. to state as true; declare. 2. to maintain (claims, etc.). 3. to put (oneself) forward boldly and insistently. —as·sert′er, n.

as·ser·tion (ə sûr′shən), n. 1. a positive or unsupported declaration. 2. act of asserting.

as·ser·tive (ə sûr′tĭv), adj. positive, dogmatic. —as·ser′tive·ly, adv. —as·ser′tive·ness, n.

as·sess (ə sĕs′), v.t. 1. to estimate (property, etc.) for taxation. 2. to determine the (damages, etc.). 3. to tax. —as·sess′a·ble, adj. —as·sess′ment, n. —as·ses′sor, n.

as·set (ăs′ĕt), n. 1. a useful thing or quality. 2. a single item of property.

as·sets (ăs′ĕts), n.pl. 1. resources such as real property, securities, cash, etc. 2. *Accounting.* the list of property owned by a firm and money owing to it.

as·sev·er·ate (ə sĕv′ə rāt′), v.t., -ated, -ating. to affirm positively. —as·sev′er·a′tion, n.

as·si·du·i·ty (ăs′ə dū′ə tĭ, -dōō′-), n. constant or close application; diligence.

as·sid·u·ous (ə sĭj′ōō əs), adj. 1. constant. 2. devoted. —as·sid′u·ous·ly, adv. —as·sid′u·ous·ness, n.

as·sign (ə sīn′), v.t. 1. to give or allot. 2. to appoint, as to a post. 3. to designate. 4. to ascribe; refer. 5. *Law.* to transfer. —n. 6. (usually pl.) *Law.* a person to whom something is or may be transferred. —as·sign′a·ble, adj. —as·sign·ee′, n. —as·sign′er; *Chiefly Law,* as·sign·or (ə sī nôr′, ăs′ə nôr′), n.

as·sig·na·tion (ăs′ĭg nā′shən), n. 1. an appointment for a meeting. 2. assignment.

as·sign·ment (ə sīn′mənt), n. 1. something assigned, as a task. 2. act of assigning. 3. *Law.* the transference of a right, interest, or title, or the instrument of transfer.

as·sim·i·la·ble (ə sĭm′ə lə bəl), adj. capable of being assimilated. —as·sim′i·la·bil′i·ty, n.

as·sim·i·late (ə sĭm′ə lāt′), v., -lated, -lating. —v.t. 1. to take in and incorporate as one's own. 2. *Physiol.* to convert for absorption into the system. —v.i. 3. to be or become absorbed.

as·sim·i·la·tion (ə sĭm′ə lā′shən), n. 1. act of assimilating. 2. state of being assimilated. 3. the merging of cultural traits from previously distinct cultural groups. —as·sim′i·la′tive, adj.

as·sist (ə sĭst′), v.t. 1. to give support or aid to. —v.i. 2. to give aid. 3. to be present. —n. 4. *Baseball.* a play which helps to put a runner out.

as·sist·ance (ə sĭs′təns), n. help; aid.

as·sist·ant (ə sĭs′tənt), n. 1. one who assists another; helper. —adj. 2. assisting; helpful. 3. associated with a superior in work.

as·size (ə sīz′), n. 1. a session of a legislative or administrative agency. 2. an enactment issued by such an agency. 3. (usually pl.) a trial session held periodically in specific locations in England by a judge of a superior court. 4. judgment.

assn., association. Also, **Assn.**

assoc., 1. associate. 2. association.

as·so·ci·ate (v. ə sō′shĭ āt′; n., adj. ə sō′shĭ ĭt, -āt′), v., -ated, -ating, n., adj. —v.t. 1. to connect by some relation, as in thought. 2. to join. 3. to combine. —v.i. 4. to unite. 5. to keep company. —n. 6. a partner, as in business. 7. a comrade. 8. a confederate. 9. an accompaniment. 10. one with a limited membership in an organization. —adj. 11. associated. 12. having limited rights and privileges of membership. 13. allied.

as·so·ci·a·tion (ə sō′sĭ ā′shən, -shĭ-), n. 1. a formal organization of people with a common purpose. 2. act of associating. 3. state of being associated. 4. companionship. 5. combination. 6. the connection of ideas in thought. —as·so·ci·a·tive (ə sō′shĭ ā′tĭv), adj.

association football, *Chiefly Brit.* soccer.

as·so·nance (ăs′ə nəns), n. 1. resemblance of sounds. 2. *Pros.* a substitute for rhyme, in which the same vowel sounds are used. —as′so·nant, adj., n.

as·sort (ə sôrt′), v.t. 1. to classify. 2. to furnish with a suitable variety of goods. —v.i. 3. to be suited. 4. to associate.

as·sort·ed (ə sôr′tĭd), adj. 1. arranged in varieties. 2. miscellaneous.

as·sort·ment (ə sôrt′mənt), n. 1. act of assorting; classification. 2. an assorted collection.

asst., assistant.

as·suage (ə swāj′), v.t., -suaged, -suaging. 1. to make milder; ease. 2. to appease; satisfy. 3. to mollify; pacify. —as·suage′ment, n.

as·sume (ə sōōm′), v.t., -sumed, -suming. 1. to take without proof. 2. to undertake. 3. to put on oneself. 4. to pretend. 5. to appropriate. —as·sum′a·ble, adj. —as·sum′er, n.

as·sum·ing (ə sōō′mĭng), adj. arrogant.

as·sump·tion (ə sŭmp′shən), n. 1. act of taking for granted. 2. something taken for granted. 3. act of taking to or upon oneself. 4. arrogance. 5. *Eccles.* a. (often cap.) the bodily taking up into heaven of the Virgin Mary after her death. b. (cap.) a feast commemorating it, August 15.

as·sur·ance (ə shŏŏr′əns), n. 1. a declaration intended to give confidence. 2. pledge. 3. full trust. 4. self-reliance. 5. impudence. 6. *Brit.* insurance.

as·sure (ə shŏŏr′), v.t., -sured, -suring. 1. to declare earnestly or positively to. 2. to make (one) sure; convince. 3. to make (a future event) sure. 4. to render safe or stable. 5. to encourage. 6. to insure. —as·sur′er, n.

as·sured (ə shŏŏrd′), adj. 1. certain. 2. confident. —n. 3. *Insurance.* the person covered by a policy. —as·sur·ed·ly (ə shŏŏr′ĭd lĭ), adv. —as·sur′ed·ness, n.

As·syr·i·a (ə sĭr′ĭ ə), n. an ancient empire in SW Asia: greatest extent from ab. 750–612 B.C. *Cap.:* Nineveh. —As·syr′i·an, adj., n.

as·ter (ăs′tər), n. 1. *Bot.* any plant of a large composite genus, having rays varying from white or pink to blue around a yellow disk. 2. a plant of some allied genus, as the China aster.

as·ter·isk (ăs′tər ĭsk), n. the figure (*), used in writing and printing as a reference mark.

a·stern (ə stûrn′), adv., adj. *Naut.* 1. in a backward direction. 2. in the rear.

as·ter·oid (ăs′tə roid′), n. 1. *Zool.* a starfish. 2. *Astron.* one of several hundred planetoids with orbits lying mostly between those of Mars and Jupiter. —adj. 3. starlike. —as′ter·oi′dal, adj.

asth·ma (ăz′mə, ăs′-), n. a paroxysmal disorder of respiration, with labored breathing, a feeling of constriction in the chest, and coughing. —asth·mat·ic (ăz măt′ĭk, ăs-), adj., n.

a·stig·ma·tism (ə stĭg′mə tĭz′əm), n. a defect of the eye or of a lens whereby rays of light converge unequally, causing imperfect images. —as·tig·mat·ic (ăs′tĭg măt′ĭk), adj.

a·stir (ə stûr′), adj., adv. in motion or activity.

as·ton·ish (ə stŏn′ĭsh), v.t. to strike with sudden and overpowering wonder; surprise greatly; amaze. —as·ton′ish·ing, adj. —as·ton′ish·ing·ly, adv.

as·ton·ish·ment (ə stŏn′ĭsh mənt), n. 1. amazement. 2. cause of amazement.

As·to·ri·a (ăs tōr′ĭ ə), n. a seaport in NW Oregon, near the mouth of the Columbia river. 10,389.

as·tound (ə stound′), v.t. to overwhelm with amazement; astonish greatly. —as·tound′ing·ly, adv.

a·strad·dle (ə străd′əl), adv., adj., prep. astride.

as·trag·a·lus (ăs trăg′ə ləs), n., pl. -li (-lī′). *Anat.* the uppermost bone of the tarsus; anklebone.

as·tra·khan (ăs′trə kən), n. a fur of young lambs, with lustrous closely curled wool, from Astrakhan. Also, **as′tra·chan.**

As·tra·khan (ăs′trə kän′), n. a city in the SE Soviet Union. 253,655.

as·tral (ăs′trəl), adj. 1. of, from, or resembling stars; starry. 2. *Biol.* star-shaped.

a·stray (ə strā′), adv., adj. straying; wandering.

a·stride (ə strīd′), adv., adj. 1. in the posture of straddling. —prep. 2. with one leg on each side of.

as·trin·gent (ə strĭn′jənt), adj. 1. *Med.* contracting; styptic. 2. austere. —n. 3. *Med.* an astringent substance. —as·trin′gen·cy, n. —as·trin′gent·ly, adv.

astrol., 1. astrologer. 2. astrology.

as·tro·labe (ăs/trə lāb/), *n.* an astronomical instrument for taking the altitude of the sun or stars, etc.

as·trol·o·gy (ə strŏl/ə jĭ), *n.* a study which assumes, and professes to interpret, the influence of the heavenly bodies on human affairs. —**as·trol/o·ger,** *n.* —**as·tro·log·i·cal** (ăs/trə lŏj/ə·kəl), **as/tro·log/ic,** *adj.* —**as/tro·log/i·cal·ly,** *adv.*

astron., astronomy.

as·tron·o·mer (ə strŏn/ə mər), *n.* an expert in astronomy.

as·tron·o·my (ə strŏn/ə mĭ), *n.* the science of the celestial bodies, their motions, positions, distances, magnitudes, etc. —**as·tro·nom·i·cal** (ăs/trə nŏm/ə kəl), **as/tro·nom/ic,** *adj.* —**as/tro·nom/i·cal·ly,** *adv.*

as·tro·phys·ics (ăs/trō fĭz/ĭks), *n.* astronomical physics, treating of the physical properties of celestial bodies. —**as/tro·phys/i·cal,** *adj.*

as·tute (ə stūt/, ə stōōt/), *adj.* of keen discernment; shrewd. —**as·tute/ly,** *adv.* —**as·tute/ness,** *n.*

A·sun·ción (ä/sōōn syôn/, -thyôn/), *n.* the capital of Paraguay, on the Paraguay river. 177,001.

a·sun·der (ə sŭn/dər), *adv., adj.* 1. in or into pieces. 2. apart.

a·sy·lum (ə sī/ləm), *n.* 1. an institution for the maintenance and care of the insane, orphans, etc. 2. an inviolable refuge.

a·sym·me·try (ā sĭm/ə trĭ), *n.* lack of symmetry or proportion. —**a·sym·met·ric** (ā/sə mĕt/-rĭk, ăs/ə-), **a/sym·met/ri·cal,** *adj.* —**a/sym·met/ri·cal·ly,** *adv.*

at (ăt; *unstressed* ət, ĭt), *prep.* a particle specifying a point occupied, attained, sought, or otherwise concerned, as in place, time, order, experience, etc., as in *at home, at noon, at last,* etc.

at·a·brine (ăt/ə brĭn, -brēn/), *n. Pharm.* 1. a synthetic antimalarial substance. 2. (*cap.*) a trademark for this substance.

at·a·vism (ăt/ə vĭz/əm), *n. Biol.* the reappearance in an individual of remote ancestral characteristics. —**a/a·vis/tic,** *adj.*

a·tax·i·a (ə tăk/sĭ ə), *n. Pathol.* loss of coördination of the muscles. —**a·tax/ic,** *adj.*

ate (āt; *Brit.* ĕt), *v.* pt. of **eat.**

-ate, a suffix forming adjectives equivalent to -ed, as in *accumulate.*

at·el·ier (ăt/əl yā/), *n.* an artist's studio.

Ath·a·bas·can (ăth/ə băs/kən), *n.* an American Indian linguistic stock, including languages of northwest Canada and Alaska, the Pacific coast, and Arizona and the Rio Grande basin.

Ath·a·na·sius (ăth/ə nā/shəs), *n. Saint,* A.D. 296?-373, bishop of Alexandria: opponent of Arianism. —**Ath·a·na·sian** (ăth/ə nā/zhən), *adj., n.*

a·the·ism (ā/thĭ ĭz/əm), *n.* the doctrine that there is no God. —**a/the·ist,** *n.* —**a·the·is/tic,** **a/the·is/ti·cal,** *adj.* —**a/the·is/ti·cal·ly,** *adv.*

A·the·na (ə thē/nə), *n.* the Greek goddess of wisdom, arts, industries, and prudent warfare.

ath·e·nae·um (ăth/ə nē/əm), *n.* 1. an institution for the promotion of literary or scientific learning. 2. a library or reading room. Also, **ath/-e·ne/um.**

Ath·ens (ăth/ĭnz), *n.* 1. the capital of Greece, in the SE part. 481,225. 2. a city in N Georgia. 20,650. —**A·the·ni·an** (ə thē/nĭ ən), *adj., n.*

a·thirst (ə thûrst/), *adj.* eager.

ath·lete (ăth/lēt), *n.* any one trained to exercises of physical agility and strength.

athlete's foot, a contagious disease of the feet, caused by a fungus that thrives on moist surfaces.

ath·let·ic (ăth lĕt/ĭk), *adj.* 1. physically active and strong. 2. of or pertaining to athletics or athletes. —**ath·let/i·cal·ly,** *adv.*

ath·let·ics (ăth lĕt/ĭks), *n.* (*usually construed as pl.*) athletic sports, as running, boxing, etc.

a·thwart (ə thwôrt/), *adv.* 1. from side to side. —*prep.* 2. from side to side of. 3. *Naut.* across the line or course of.

a·tilt (ə tĭlt/), *adj., adv.* at a tilt; tilted.

-ation, a suffix forming nouns denoting action, process, state, result, or something producing a result, usually accompanying verbs or adjectives of Latin origin ending in -*ate,* as in *agitation* and *decoration.* Also, **-ion, -tion.**

-ative, an adjective suffix expressing tendency,

function, bearing, connection, etc., as in *affirmative, demonstrative, talkative.* See **-ive.**

At·lan·ta (ăt lăn/tə), *n.* the capital of Georgia, in the N part. 302,288.

At·lan·tic (ăt lăn/tĭk), *n.* 1. the Atlantic Ocean. —*adj.* 2. of or pertaining to the Atlantic Ocean.

Atlantic Charter, the joint declaration of Roosevelt and Churchill (August 14, 1941) after a meeting at sea, setting forth a program of peace purposes.

Atlantic City, city in SE New Jersey. 64,094.

Atlantic Ocean, an ocean bordered by North and South America and Europe and Africa. ab. 31,530,000 sq. mi.

At·lan·tis (ăt lăn/tĭs), *n.* a mythical sunken island in the Atlantic Ocean.

at·las (ăt/ləs), *n.* 1. a bound collection of maps. 2. *Class Myth.* (*cap.*) a demigod condemned to support the sky on his shoulders.

Atlas Mountains, a mountain range in NW Africa, through Morocco, Algeria, and Tunisia.

at·mos·phere (ăt/məs fĭr/), *n.* 1. the gaseous fluid surrounding the earth; the air. 2. any gaseous envelope. 3. a conventional unit of pressure, the normal pressure of the air at sea level, about 15 pounds per square inch. 4. pervading influence or mood.

at·mos·pher·ic (ăt/məs fĕr/ĭk), *adj.* Also, **at/-mos·pher/i·cal.** 1. pertaining to or existing in the atmosphere. 2. caused or operated on by the atmosphere. —*n.* 3. (*pl.*) *Radio.* static. —**at/-mos·pher/i·cal·ly,** *adv.*

at. no., atomic number.

at·oll (ăt/ŏl, ə tŏl/), *n.* a ringlike coral island enclosing a lagoon.

at·om (ăt/əm), *n.* 1. *Physics, Chem.* the smallest unitary constituent of a chemical element, composed of a more or less complex aggregate of protons, neutrons, and electrons, whose number and arrangement determine the element. 2. anything extremely small.

a·tom·ic (ə tŏm/ĭk), *adj.* 1. pertaining to atoms. 2. driven by atomic energy. 3. *Chem.* existing as free uncombined atoms. 4. minute. Also, **a·tom/-i·cal.** —**a·tom/i·cal·ly,** *adv.*

atomic bomb, a bomb whose potency is derived from atomic fission of atoms of fissionable material, with consequent conversion of part of their mass into energy. Also, **atom bomb.**

atomic energy, energy from changes within the atomic nucleus, chiefly from nuclear fission.

atomic number, the number of positive charges on the nucleus of an atom of a given element.

atomic theory, the modern theory of the atom as having a complex internal structure and electrical properties. Also, **atomic hypothesis.**

atomic warfare, warfare by atomic bombs, etc.

atomic weight, *Chem.* the average weight of an atom of an element measured in units each of which corresponds to one sixteenth of the average weight of the oxygen atom. *Abbr.:* at. wt.

at·om·ize (ăt/ə mīz/), *v.t.,* -ized, -izing. to reduce to atoms or to fine particles or spray. —**at/-om·iz/er,** *n.*

a·ton·al (ā tō/nəl), *adj. Music.* having no key. —**a·ton/al·ism,** *n.* —**a·ton/al·is/tic,** *adj.* —**a·ton/al·ly,** *adv.*

a·to·nal·i·ty (ā/tō năl/ə tĭ), *n. Music.* the absence of key or tonal center.

a·tone (ə tōn/), *v.i., v.t.,* atoned, atoning. to make amends or reparation (for). —**a·ton/er,** *n.*

a·tone·ment (ə tōn/mənt), *n.* 1. reparation; amends. 2. *Theol.* the reconciliation of God and man by Christ.

a·top (ə tŏp/), *adj., adv.* 1. on or at the top. —*prep.* 2. on the top of.

a·tri·um (ā/trĭ əm), *n., pl.* atria (ā/trĭ ə). 1. *Archit.* the central main room of an ancient Roman private house. 2. *Anat.* an auricle of the heart.

a·tro·cious (ə trō/shəs), *adj.* 1. extremely wicked or cruel. 2. shockingly bad. —**a·tro/cious·ly,** *adv.* —**a·tro/cious·ness,** *n.*

a·troc·i·ty (ə trŏs/ə tĭ), *n., pl.* -ties. 1. quality of being atrocious. 2. an atrocious deed.

at·ro·phy (ăt/rə fĭ), *n., v.,* -phied, -phying. —*n.* 1. *Pathol.* a wasting away of the body or of a part. —*v.t., v.i.* 2. to affect with or undergo atrophy. —**a·troph·ic** (ə trŏf/ĭk), *adj.* —**at/ro·phied,** *adj.*

at·ro·pine (ăt/rə pēn/, -pĭn), *n.* a poisonous crystalline alkaloid, obtained chiefly from belladonna, used as a sedative. Also, **at·ro·pin** (ăt′rə-pĭn).

att., attorney.

at·tach (ə tăch′), *v.t.* **1.** to fasten to; connect. **2.** to join in action. **3.** *Mil.* to place on duty with. **4.** to associate. **5.** to attribute. **6.** to bind by ties of regard. **7.** *Law.* to take by legal authority. —*v.i.* **8.** to adhere; belong. —**at·tach′a·ble,** *adj.*

at·ta·ché (ăt′ə shā′), *n.* one attached to an official staff, esp. that of an embassy or legation.

at·tach·ment (ə tăch′mənt), *n.* **1.** act of attaching. **2.** state of being attached. **3.** affection; regard. **4.** a fastening. **5.** supplementary device. **6.** *Law.* seizure of property or person by legal authority.

at·tack (ə tăk′), *v.t.* **1.** to set upon with force or weapons. **2.** to direct unfavorable criticism, etc., against. **3.** to set about (a task) vigorously. **4.** (of disease, etc.) to begin to affect. —*v.i.* **5.** to begin hostilities. —*n.* **6.** assault. **7.** an offensive military operation. **8.** *Pathol.* seizure by disease. **9.** the onset. —**at·tack′er,** *n.*

at·tain (ə tān′), *v.t.* **1.** to reach or accomplish by continued effort. **2.** to arrive at in due course. —*v.i.* **3. attain to,** to succeed in reaching or obtaining. —**at·tain′a·ble,** *adj.* —**at·tain′a·bil′i·ty, at·tain′a·ble·ness,** *n.*

at·tain·der (ə tān′dər), *n.* the legal consequence of judgment of death or outlawry for treason or felony, involving the loss of all civil rights.

at·tain·ment (ə tān′mənt), *n.* **1.** act of attaining. **2.** something attained.

at·taint (ə tānt′), *v.t.* **1.** to disgrace. —*n.* **2.** a disgrace; taint.

at·tar (ăt′ər), *n.* a perfume or essential oil from flowers or petals, esp. of damask roses.

at·tempt (ə tĕmpt′), *v.t.* **1.** to make an effort at; try. **2.** to attack. —*n.* **3.** effort put forth. **4.** an attack. —**at·tempt′er,** *n.*

at·tend (ə tĕnd′), *v.t.* **1.** to be present at. **2.** to go with as a concomitant or result. **3.** to minister to. **4.** to wait upon as a servant. **5.** to tend. **6.** to give heed to. —*v.i.* **7.** to be present. **8.** to give attention. **9.** to apply oneself. **10.** to take care of.

at·tend·ance (ə tĕn′dəns), *n.* **1.** act of attending. **2.** the persons present.

at·tend·ant (ə tĕn′dənt), *n.* **1.** one who attends another, as for service. **2.** *Chiefly Brit.* an usher or clerk. —*adj.* **3.** being present; accompanying. **4.** concomitant; consequent.

at·ten·tion (ə tĕn′shən), *n.* **1.** act or faculty of attending. **2.** *Psychol.* concentration of the mind upon an object. **3.** consideration; notice. **4.** civility or courtesy.

at·ten·tive (ə tĕn′tĭv), *adj.* **1.** giving attention. **2.** courteous. —**at·ten′tive·ly,** *adv.* —**at·ten′-tive·ness,** *n.*

at·ten·u·ate (*v.* ə tĕn′yŏŏ āt′; *adj.* ə tĕn′yŏŏ ĭt, -āt′), *v.*, **-ated, -ating.** —*v.t.* **1.** to make thin or slender. **2.** to weaken or reduce in intensity, effect, quantity, or value. —*v.i.* **3.** to become thin or fine. —*adj.* **4.** thin. —**at·ten′u·a′tion,** *n.*

at·test (ə tĕst′), *v.t.* **1.** to declare to be correct, true, or genuine. **2.** to give proof of. —*v.i.* **3.** to certify by signing as witness. —**at·tes·ta·tion** (ăt′ĕs tā′shən), *n.* —**at·test′er, at·tes′tor,** *n.*

at·tic (ăt′ĭk), *n.* **1.** that part of a building directly under a roof. **2.** a room or rooms in that part.

At·tic (ăt′ĭk), *adj.* **1.** pertaining to Athens. **2.** (*often l.c.*) displaying simple elegance and delicacy.

At·ti·la (ăt′ə lə), *n.* ("*Scourge of God*") died A.D. 453, king of Huns who invaded Europe.

at·tire (ə tīr′), *v.*, **-tired, -tiring,** *n.* —*v.t.* **1.** to dress or adorn. —*n.* **2.** clothes.

at·ti·tude (ăt′ə tūd′, -tōōd′), *n.* **1.** position, disposition, or manner. **2.** position of the body appropriate to an action, emotion, etc.

At·tle·bor·o (ăt′əl bûr′ō), *n.* a city in SE Massachusetts. 22,071.

Att·lee (ăt′lĭ), *n.* **Clement Richard,** born 1883, British statesman: prime minister since 1945.

at·tor·ney (ə tûr′nĭ), *n., pl.* **-neys.** **1.** a lawyer. **2.** one empowered to transact business for another (**attorney in fact**). —**at·tor′ney·ship′,** *n.*

attorney general, *pl.* **attorneys general, attorney generals.** the chief law officer of a nation.

at·tract (ə trăkt′), *v.t.* **1.** to act upon by a physical force causing approach or union. **2.** to

invite or allure. —*v.i.* **3.** to possess the power of attraction. —**at·tract′a·ble,** *adj.*

at·trac·tion (ə trăk′shən), *n.* **1.** act, power, or property of attracting. **2.** allurement. **3.** *Physics.* a situation in which bodies tend to draw together and particles of matter tend to unite or cohere. **4.** *Theat.* entertainment.

at·trac·tive (ə trăk′tĭv), *adj.* **1.** alluring; pleasing. **2.** attracting. —**at·trac′tive·ly,** *adv.* —**at·trac′tive·ness,** *n.*

attrib., **1.** attribute. **2.** attributive.

at·trib·ute (*v.* ə trĭb′ūt; *n.* ăt′rə būt′), *v.*, **-uted, -uting,** *n.* —*v.t.* **1.** to consider as belonging. —*n.* **2.** something attributed as belonging. **3.** *Gram.* a word or phrase grammatically subordinate to another, serving to limit the meaning of the form to which it is attached. **4.** office, character, or personality. —**at·trib′ut·a·ble,** *adj.* —**at·trib′-ut·er, at·trib′u·tor,** *n.*

at·tri·bu·tion (ăt′rə bū′shən), *n.* **1.** act of attributing. **2.** that which is ascribed; an attribute.

at·trib·u·tive (ə trĭb′yə tĭv), *adj.* **1.** pertaining to or having the character of attribution. **2.** *Gram.* expressing an attribute. —*n.* **3.** an attributive word, phrase, or clause. —**at·trib′u·tive·ly,** *adv.*

at·tri·tion (ə trĭsh′ən), *n.* **1.** friction. **2.** a wearing down or away by friction.

at·tune (ə tūn′, ə tōōn′), *v.t.*, **-tuned, -tuning.** to adjust to harmony or accord.

atty., attorney.

at. wt., atomic weight.

a·typ·i·cal (ā tĭp′ə kəl), *adj.* not typical.

Au, *Chem.* (L *aurum*) gold.

A.u., angstrom unit. Also, **a.u., A.U.**

au·burn (ô′bərn), *n., adj.* reddish brown.

Au·burn (ô′bərn), *n.* **1.** a city in central New York. 35,753. **2.** a city in SW Maine. 19,817.

Auck·land (ôk′lənd), *n.* the principal seaport of New Zealand. 106,800.

auc·tion (ôk′shən), *n.* **1.** a public sale at which property or goods are sold to the highest bidder. **2.** *Cards.* auction bridge. —*v.t.* **3.** to sell by auction.

auction bridge, a variety of bridge in which players bid to declare the trump or no-trump.

auc·tion·eer (ôk′shə nĭr′), *n.* **1.** one who conducts sales by auction. —*v.t.* **2.** to auction.

au·da·cious (ô dā′shəs), *adj.* **1.** bold or daring. **2.** reckless in wrongdoing. —**au·da′cious·ly,** *adv.* —**au·da′cious·ness,** *n.*

au·dac·i·ty (ô dăs′ə tĭ), *n.* **1.** boldness or daring, esp. reckless boldness. **2.** insolence.

au·di·ble (ô′də bəl), *adj.* that can be heard. —**au·di·bil′i·ty, au·di·ble·ness,** *n.* —**au′di·bly,** *adv.*

au·di·ence (ô′dĭ əns), *n.* **1.** an assembly of hearers or spectators. **2.** opportunity of being heard. **3.** admission of a diplomatic representative to a sovereign or high officer of government.

audio frequency, *Physics, etc.* a frequency of the order of audible frequencies of sound waves.

au·dit (ô′dĭt), *n.* **1.** an official verification of records. —*v.t.* **2.** to examine (accounts, etc.) officially. —*v.i.* **3.** to verify accounts by reference to vouchers.

au·di·tion (ô dĭsh′ən), *n.* **1.** act, sense, or power of hearing. **2.** a hearing given to a musician, speaker, etc. —*v.t., v.i.* **3.** to give an audition (to).

au·di·tor (ô′də tər), *n.* **1.** a hearer; listener. **2.** a person authorized to verify records.

au·di·to·ri·um (ô′də tôr′ĭ əm), *n., pl.* **-tori·ums, -toria** (-tôr′ĭ ə). the space for the audience in a church, theater, school, or other building.

au·di·to·ry (ô′də tôr′ĭ), *adj., n., pl.* **-ries.** —*adj.* **1.** *Anat., Physiol.* pertaining to hearing, the sense of hearing, or the organs of hearing. —*n.* **2.** an audience.

Au·du·bon (ô′də bŏn′), *n.* **John James,** 1785?–1851, U.S. naturalist.

Aug., August.

au·ger (ô′gər), *n.* a carpenter's tool larger than a gimlet, with a spiral groove for boring holes in wood.

aught[1] (ôt), *n.* **1.** anything whatever. —*adv.* **2.** at all.

aught[2] (ôt), *n.* a cipher (0).

Augers

aug·ment (ôg mĕnt′), *v.t.* **1.** to make larger; increase. —*v.i.* **2.** to become larger. —**aug·ment′a·ble,** *adj.* —**aug′men·ta′tion,** *n.*

—aug·ment/a·tive, *adj., n.* —aug·ment/-er, *n.*

au gra·tin (ō grä/tən), *French.* made with browned crumbs or cheese, or both.

Augs·burg (ôgz/bûrg), *n.* a city in S Germany, in Bavaria. 185,374.

au·gur (ô/gər), *n.* **1.** a soothsayer. —*v.t.* **2.** to predict, as from omens. —*v.i.* **3.** to conjecture from omens. **4.** to bode.

au·gu·ry (ô/gyə rĭ), *n., pl.* **-ries. 1.** divination. **2.** an omen, token, or indication.

Au·gust (ô/gəst), *n.* the eighth month of the year, containing 31 days.

au·gust (ô gŭst/), *adj.* **1.** inspiring reverence; majestic. **2.** venerable. —**au·gust/ly,** *adv.* —**au·gust/ness,** *n.*

Au·gus·ta (ô gŭs/tə), *n.* **1.** a city in E Georgia, on the Savannah. 65,919. **2.** the capital of Maine, in the SW part, on the Kennebec. 19,360.

Au·gus·tan (ô gŭs/tən), *adj.* **1.** pertaining to Augustus Caesar or to his reign (the **Augustan Age**). **2.** pertaining to the highest point in the literature of any country. **3.** having characteristics of Augustan literature, as classicism, correctness, etc. —*n.* **4.** an author in an Augustan age.

Au·gus·tine (ô/gə stēn/, ô gŭs/tĭn), *n.* **1. Saint,** (*Austin*) A.D. 354–430, leader of the early Christian Church. **2. Saint,** died A.D. 604, Roman monk and missionary to England. —**Au·gus·tin·i·an** (ô/gə stĭn/ĭ ən), *adj., n.*

Au·gus·tus (ô gŭs/təs), *n.* 63 B.C.–A.D. 14, first Roman emperor.

auk (ôk), *n.* any of certain short-winged, three-toed diving birds of northern seas, esp. the **razor-billed auk** and the extinct, flightless **great auk.**

auld lang syne (ōld/ lăng sīn/), *Scot.* old times, esp. times fondly remembered.

aunt (ănt, änt), *n.* **1.** the sister of one's father or mother. **2.** the wife of one's uncle.

au·ra (ôr/ə), *n., pl.* **auras, aurae** (ôr/ē). **1.** a distinctive air, atmosphere, character, etc. **2.** a subtle and surrounding emanation from a body.

au·ral (ôr/əl), *adj.* of, or perceived by, the organs of hearing. —**au/ral·ly,** *adv.*

au·re·ate (ôr/ĭ ĭt, -āt/), *adj.* **1.** golden. **2.** brilliant; splendid.

au·re·ole (ôr/ĭ ōl/), *n.* **1.** a halo. **2.** *Astron.* corona. Also, **au·re·o·la** (ô rē/ə lə).

au·re·o·my·cin (ô/rĭ ō mī/sĭn), *n.* a recently developed drug that is effective against certain virus-caused diseases.

au re·voir (ō rə vwär/), *French.* good-by for the present.

au·ri·cle (ôr/ə kəl), *n.* *Anat.* **1.** the projecting outer portion of the ear. **2.** one of two chambers of the heart through which blood passes into the ventricles. —**au/ri·cled,** *adj.*

au·ric·u·lar (ô rĭk/yə lər), *adj.* **1.** of or pertaining to the organs of hearing. **2.** perceived by or addressed to the ear. **3.** dependent on hearing.

au·rif·er·ous (ô rĭf/ər əs), *adj.* yielding or containing gold. —**au·rif/er·ous·ly,** *adv.*

au·rochs (ôr/ŏks), *n., pl.* **-rochs.** a European wild ox, now extinct.

Au·ro·ra (ô rôr/ə), *n.* **1.** *Class. Myth.* dawn, often personified by the Romans as a goddess. **2.** (*l.c.*) the rise or dawn of something. **3.** (*l.c.*) *Meteorol.* an electrical atmospheric phenomenon, consisting of streamers, arcs, etc., of light. **4.** a city in NE Illinois. 47,170. —**au·ro/ral,** *adj.*

aurora bo·re·al·is (bôr/ĭ ăl/ĭs, -ā/lĭs), *Meteorol.* the aurora of the northern hemisphere.

au·rum (ôr/əm), *n.* *Chem.* gold.

aus·pice (ô/spĭs), *n., pl.* **auspices** (ô/spə sĭz). **1.** (*usually pl.*) patronage. **2.** a propitious circumstance. **3.** a divination, originally from the flight of birds.

aus·pi·cious (ô spĭsh/əs), *adj.* **1.** favorable. **2.** prosperous; fortunate. —**aus·pi/cious·ly,** *adv.* —**aus·pi/cious·ness,** *n.*

Aus·ten (ô/stən), *n.* **Jane,** 1775–1817, British novelist.

aus·tere (ô stēr/), *adj.* **1.** harsh in manner; stern in appearance. **2.** severe in self-discipline. **3.** grave. **4.** severely simple. —**aus·tere/ly,** *adv.* —**aus·tere/ness,** *n.* —**aus·ter·i·ty** (ô stĕr/ə tĭ), *n.*

Aus·tin (ô/stən), *n.* **1.** the capital of Texas, in the central part. 87,930. **2.** Saint Augustine (def. 1).

Austral., 1. Australasia. **2.** Australia.

Aus·tral·a·sia (ô/strə lā/zhə, -shə), *n.* Aus-

tralia, New Zealand, and neighboring islands of the S Pacific Ocean. —**Aus/tral·a/sian,** *adj., n.*

Aus·tral·ia (ô strāl/yə), *n.* **1.** the continent SE of Asia. 7,197,538 pop.; 2,948,366 sq. mi. **2. Commonwealth of,** a dominion of the British Commonwealth, consisting mainly of Australia and Tasmania. 7,448,601 pop.; 2,974,581 sq. mi. *Cap.:* Canberra. —**Aus·tral/ian,** *adj., n.*

Aus·t′i·a (ô/strĭ ə), *n.* a country in central Europe. 7,000,000 pop.; 32,381 sq. mi. *Cap.:* Vienna. —**Aus/tri·an,** *adj., n.*

au·tar·chy (ô/tär kĭ), *n., pl.* **-chies. 1.** absolute sovereignty. **2.** self-government. **3.** autarky. —**au·tar/chic,** *adj.*

au·tar·ky (ô/tär kĭ), *n., pl.* **-kies.** national self-sufficiency. —**au·tar/ki·cal,** *adj.* —**au/tar·kist,** *n., adj.*

auth., 1. author. **2.** authorized.

au·then·tic (ô thĕn/tĭk), *adj.* **1.** entitled to acceptance or belief; reliable. **2.** of genuine origin. Also, **h au·ten/ti·cal.** —**au·then/ti·cal·ly,** *adv.* —**au·then·tic·i·ty** (ô/thən tĭs/ə tĭ, -thĕn-), *n.*

au·then·ti·cate (ô thĕn/tə kāt/), *v.t.,* **-cated, -cating. 1.** to make valid. **2.** to establish as genuine. —**au·then/ti·ca/tion,** *n.* —**au·then/ti·ca/tor,** *n.*

au·thor (ô thər), *n.* **1.** a person who writes a novel, poem, essay, etc. **2.** the originator or creator of anything. —**au·thor·ess** (ô/thər ĭs), *n. fem.* —**au·tho·ri·al** (ô thôr/ĭ əl), *adj.* —**au/thor·less,** *adj.*

au·thor·i·tar·i·an (ə thôr/ə târ/ĭ ən, ə thŏr/-), *adj.* **1.** favoring subjection to authority rather than individual freedom. —*n.* **2.** one who favors such subjection. —**au·thor/i·tar/i·an·ism,** *n.*

au·thor·i·ta·tive (ə thôr/ə tā/tĭv, ə thŏr/-), *adj.* **1.** having due authority. **2.** having an air of authority; dictatorial. —**au·thor/i·ta/tive·ly** *adv.* —**au·thor/i·ta/tive·ness,** *n.*

au·thor·i·ty (ə thôr/ə tĭ, ə thŏr/-), *n., pl.* **-ties. 1.** the right to control, command, judge, or determine. **2.** a person or body with such rights. **3.** an accepted source of information, advice, etc. **4.** an expert. **5.** commanding influence.

au·thor·ize (ô/thə rīz/), *v.t.,* **-ized, -izing. 1.** to give authority to. **2.** to sanction (an act). **3.** to establish by authority or usage. **4.** to justify. —**au/thor·i·za/tion,** *n.* —**au/thor·iz/er,** *n.*

Authorized Version, an English revision (1611) of the Bible prepared under James I.

au·thor·ship (ô/thər shĭp/), *n.* **1.** the occupation or career of writing books, articles, etc. **2.** origin as to author, composer, or compiler.

Auth. Ver., Authorized Version (of the Bible).

au·to (ô/tō), *n., pl.* **-tos.** automobile.

au·to·bi·og·ra·phy (ô/tə bī ŏg/rə fĭ, -bī-), *n., pl.* **-phies.** an account of a person's life written by himself. —**au/to·bi·og/ra·pher,** *n.* —**au·to·bi·o·graph·ic** (ô/tə bī/ə grăf/ĭk), **au/to·bi/o·graph/-i·cal,** *adj.* —**au/to·bi/o·graph/i·cal·ly,** *adv.*

au·to·clave (ô/tə klāv/), *n.* a strong closed vessel in which steam under pressure is used to sterilize, cook, cause chemical reactions, etc.

au·toc·ra·cy (ô tŏk/rə sĭ), *n., pl.* **-cies.** uncontrolled or unlimited authority over others, invested in a single person. —**au·to·crat·ic** (ô/tə krăt/ĭk), **au/to·crat/i·cal,** *adj.* —**au/to·crat/i·cal·ly,** *adv.*

au·to·crat (ô/tə krăt/), *n.* a person with absolute and unlimited authority.

au·to·da·fé (ô/tō də fā/), *n., pl.* **autos-da-fé.** the public declaration of the judgment on persons tried in the courts of the Spanish Inquisition.

au·to·gi·ro (ô/tə jī/rō), *n., pl.* **-ros. 1.** an aircraft with supplementary horizontal revolving wings which allow it to move vertically. **2.** (*cap.*) a trademark for this aircraft. Also, **au/to·gy/ro.**

au·to·graph (ô/tə grăf/, -gräf/), *n.* **1.** a person's own signature. **2.** a manuscript in the author's handwriting. —*adj.* **3.** written by a person's own hand. **4.** containing autographs. —*v.t.* **5.** to write one's name on or in. —**au/to·graph/ic, au/to·graph/i·cal,** *adj.* —**au/to·graph/i·cal·ly,** *adv.*

au·to·mat (ô/tə măt/), *n.* a restaurant using automatic apparatus for serving food to customers upon dropping the proper coins into a slot.

au·to·mat·ic (ô/tə măt/ĭk), *adj.* **1.** self-acting; mechanical. **2.** *Physiol.* occurring independently of volition. **3.** (of a firearm, etc.) utilizing the recoil to eject the spent shell, introduce a new cartridge, and fire repeatedly. **4.** done unconsciously or from force of habit. —*n.* **5.** a machine which operates automatically. **6.** automatic rifle or pistol. —**au/to·mat/i·cal·ly,** *adv.*

au·tom·a·ton (ô tŏm′ə tŏn′, -tən), n., pl. **-tons, -ta** (-tə). **1.** a mechanical figure or contrivance constructed to act as if spontaneously. **2.** a person who acts in a monotonous routine manner.

au·to·mo·bile (ô′tə mə bēl′, ô′tə mō′bēl, -məbēl′), n. Chiefly U.S. a land vehicle carrying its own propelling mechanism. —**au·to·mo·bil·ist** (ô′tə mə bē′lĭst, -mō′bĭl ĭst), n.

au·to·mo·tive (ô′tə mō′tĭv), adj. **1.** pertaining to automobiles. **2.** self-propelled.

au·to·nom·ic (ô′tə nŏm′ĭk), adj. **1.** autonomous. **2.** Physiol. pertaining to a system of nerves and ganglia controlling the involuntary functions of certain glands, etc. **3.** Bot. spontaneous. —**au′to·nom′i·cal·ly**, adv.

au·ton·o·my (ô tŏn′ə mĭ), n., pl. **-mies. 1.** the condition of being independent. **2.** a self-governing community. —**au·ton′o·mist**, n. —**au·ton′o·mous**, adj. —**au·ton′o·mous·ly**, adv.

au·top·sy (ô′tŏp sĭ, ô′təp-), n., pl. **-sies.** inspection and dissection of a body after death.

au·to·sug·ges·tion (ô′tō səg jĕs′chən), n. Psychol. suggestion arising from within oneself.

au·tumn (ô′təm), n. the third season of the year, between summer and winter; fall. —**au·tum·nal** (ô tŭm′nəl), adj.

aux., auxiliary. Also, **auxil.**

aux·il·ia·ry (ôg zĭl′yə rĭ, -zĭl′ə-), adj., n., pl. **-ries.** —adj. **1.** assisting. **2.** subsidiary; additional. **3.** used as a reserve. —n. **4.** person or thing that aids. **5.** auxiliary verb. **6.** (pl.) foreign troops in the service of a nation at war. **7.** Naval. a noncombat naval vessel.

auxiliary verb, a verb preceding others to express distinctions of time, etc., as am.

av., **1.** avenue. **2.** average. **3.** avoirdupois.

A/V, ad valorem. Also, **a.v.**

A.V., Authorized Version (of the Bible).

a·vail (ə vāl′), v.i. **1.** to have force; serve. **2.** to be of value or profit. —v.t. **3.** to be of use or value to. **4.** avail oneself of, to give oneself the advantage of. —n. **5.** efficacy or advantage. —**a·vail′ing·ly**, adv.

a·vail·a·ble (ə vā′lə bəl), adj. **1.** suitable or ready for use. **2.** valid. —**a·vail·a·bil·i·ty** (ə vā′lə bĭl′ə tĭ), **a·vail′a·ble·ness**, n. —**a·vail′a·bly**, adv.

av·a·lanche (ăv′ə lănch′, -länch′), n., v., **-lanched, -lanching.** —n. **1.** a large mass of snow, ice, etc., falling down a mountain slope. —v.i. **2.** to come down in, or like, an avalanche.

av·a·rice (ăv′ə rĭs), n. greed for riches. —**av·a·ri·cious** (ăv′ə rĭsh′əs), adj. —**av′a·ri′cious·ly**, adv. —**av′a·ri′cious·ness**, n.

a·vast (ə văst′, ə väst′), interj. Naut. stop!

a·vaunt (ə vônt′, ə vänt′), adv. Archaic. away!

avdp., avoirdupois.

a·ve (ä′vĭ, ä′vā), interj. **1.** hail! **2.** farewell! —n. **3.** the salutation "ave." **4.** (cap.) Ave Maria.

Ave., avenue. Also, **ave.**

A·vel·la·ne·da (ä vě′yä ně′dä), n. a city in E Argentina, near Buenos Aires. 399,021.

A·ve Ma·ri·a (ä′vĭ mə rē′ə, ä′vä), Rom. Cath. Ch. a prayer based on the salutation of the angel Gabriel to the Virgin Mary and the words of Elizabeth to her. Also, **A·ve Mar·y** (ä′vĭ mâr′ĭ).

a·venge (ə vĕnj′), v.t., v.i., avenged, avenging. to take vengeance (for on behalf of). —**a·veng′er**, n. —**a·veng′ing·ly**, adv.

av·e·nue (ăv′ə nū′, -nōō′), n. **1.** a wide street. **2.** the main way of approach, usually lined with trees, to a building. **3.** a way for entrance. **4.** means of access or attainment.

a·ver (ə vûr′), v.t., averred, averring. **1.** to affirm in a positive manner. **2.** Law. to allege as a fact. —**a·ver′ment**, n.

av·er·age (ăv′ər ĭj, ăv′rĭj), n., adj., v., -aged, -aging. —n. **1.** the mean obtained by adding several quantities together and dividing the sum by the number of quantities. **2.** Math. a quantity intermediate to a set of quantities. **3.** the ordinary amount, rate, kind, etc. —adj. **4.** of, forming, or estimated by an average. **5.** intermediate or typical in amount, degree, quality, etc. —v.t. **6.** to find an average value for. **7.** to result in or amount to, as an arithmetical mean. —v.i. **8.** U.S. to have or show an average.

a·verse (ə vûrs′), adj. disinclined, reluctant, or opposed. —**a·verse′ly**, adv. —**a·verse′ness**, n.

a·ver·sion (ə vûr′zhən, -shən), n. **1.** repugnance or dislike. **2.** a cause or object of dislike.

a·vert (ə vûrt′), v.t. **1.** to turn away or aside. **2.** to ward off; prevent. —**a·vert′er**, n.

A·ves (ā′vēz), n.pl. Zool. the class of vertebrates comprising the birds.

A·ves·ta (ə vĕs′tə), n. the sacred scriptures of Zoroastrianism. —**A·ves′tan**, adj.

a·vi·ar·y (ā′vĭ ĕr′ĭ), n., pl. **-aries.** a large cage or enclosure in which birds are kept.

a·vi·a·tion (ā′vĭ ā′shən, ăv′ĭ-), n. **1.** science of flying aircraft. **2.** the aircraft of an air force.

a·vi·a·tor (ā′vĭ ā′tər, ăv′ĭ-), n. a pilot of an airplane. —**a·vi·a·trix** (ā′vĭ ā′trĭks, ăv′ĭ-), **a·vi·a·tress** (ā′vĭ ā′trĭs, ăv′ĭ-), n. fem.

av·id (ăv′ĭd), adj. **1.** keenly desirous; eager. **2.** keen. —**a·vid·i·ty** (ə vĭd′ə tĭ), n. —**av′id·ly**, adv.

A·vi·gnon (à vē nyôN′), n. a city in SE France, on the Rhone: papal residence, 1309–77. 59,982.

av·o·ca·do (ăv′ə kä′dō, ä′və-), n., pl. **-dos. 1.** a tropical American fruit, green to black in color and commonly pear-shaped, borne by a tree of the laurel family, eaten raw, esp. as a salad fruit; alligator pear. **2.** the tree.

av·o·ca·tion (ăv′ə kā′shən), n. **1.** a hobby. **2.** Colloq. one's regular occupation.

a·void (ə void′), v.t. **1.** to keep away from; shun; evade. **2.** Law. to invalidate. —**a·void′a·ble**, adj. —**a·void′a·bly**, adv. —**a·void′ance**, n. —**a·void′er**, n.

av·oir·du·pois (ăv′ər də poiz′), n. **1.** avoirdupois weight. **2.** U.S. Colloq. weight.

avoirdupois weight, the system of weights in British and U.S. use for goods other than gems, precious metals, and drugs.

A·von (ā′vən, ăv′ən), n. a river in central England, flowing SE past Stratford. 80 mi.

a·vouch (ə vouch′), v.t. **1.** to declare or assert with positiveness. **2.** to guarantee. **3.** to confess.

a·vow (ə vou′), v.t. to declare frankly; confess. —**a·vow′a·ble**, adj. —**a·vow′al**, n. —**a·vowed′**, adj. —**a·vow′ed·ly**, adv. —**a·vow′ed·ness**, n. —**a·vow′er**, n.

a·vun·cu·lar (ə vŭng′kyə lər), adj. of an uncle.

a·wait (ə wāt′), v.t., v.i. **1.** to wait for; expect. **2.** to be in store for; be ready for.

a·wake (ə wāk′), v., awoke or awaked, awaking, adj. —v.t., v.i. **1.** to rouse from sleep. **2.** to rouse to action, awareness, etc. —adj. **3.** not sleeping. **4.** alert.

a·wak·en (ə wā′kən), v.t., v.i. to awake; waken.

a·wak·en·ing (ə wā′kən ĭng), adj. **1.** rousing. —n. **2.** act of awaking. **3.** a revival.

a·ward (ə wôrd′), v.t. **1.** to adjudge to be merited; bestow. **2.** to bestow by judicial decree. —n. **3.** something awarded. **4.** a judicial decision.

a·ware (ə wâr′), adj. cognizant or conscious (usually fol. by of). —**a·ware′ness**, n.

a·wash (ə wŏsh′, ə wôsh′), adv., adj. covered or tossed about by waves.

a·way (ə wā′), adv. **1.** from this or that place. **2.** far; apart. **3.** aside. **4.** out of possession, notice, use, or existence. **5.** continuously; on. **6.** without hesitation. —adj. **7.** absent. **8.** distant.

awe (ô), n., v., awed, awing. —n. **1.** respectful or reverential fear. —v.t. **2.** to inspire with awe. **3.** to influence by awe. —**aw′less, awe′less**, adj.

a·weigh (ə wā′), adj. Naut. (of an anchor) raised just enough to be clear of the bottom.

awe·some (ô′səm), adj. inspiring or full of awe. —**awe′some·ly**, adv. —**awe′some·ness**, n.

awe·struck (ô′strŭk′), adj. filled with awe. Also, **awe·strick·en** (ô′strĭk′ən).

aw·ful (ô′fəl), adj. **1.** inspiring fear; dreadful. **2.** Colloq. extremely bad. **3.** Colloq. very. **4.** full of awe. **5.** solemnly impressive. —**aw′ful·ly**, adv. —**aw′ful·ness**, n.

a·while (ə hwīl′), adv. for a short time or period.

awk·ward (ôk′wərd), adj. **1.** lacking dexterity; clumsy. **2.** ungraceful. **3.** unhandy. **4.** requiring caution. **5.** difficult to handle. **6.** embarrassing or trying. —**awk′ward·ly**, adv. —**awk′ward·ness**, n.

awl (ôl), n. Carp., etc. a pointed instrument for piercing small holes in leather, wood, etc.

awn (ôn), n. Bot. a bristlelike appendage of a plant. —**awned**, adj. —**awn′less**, adj.

awn·ing (ô′nĭng), n. a rooflike shelter of canvas, etc., before a window, over a deck, etc.

A.W.O.L., *Mil.* absent without leave.

a·wry (ə rī′), *adv., adj.* **1.** with a twist to one side; askew. **2.** wrong.

ax (ăks), *n., pl.* **axes,** *v.,* **axed, axing.** —*n.* **1.** an instrument with a bladed head on a handle, used for chopping, etc. —*v.t.* **2.** to shape or trim with an ax. Also, **axe.** —**ax′like′,** *adj.*

ax·i·al (ăk′sĭ əl), *adj.* of, forming, or on an axis. Also, **ax·ile** (ăk′sĭl, -sīl). —**ax′i·al·ly,** *adv.*

ax·il (ăk′sĭl), *n. Bot.* the angle between the upper side of a leaf and the supporting stem, etc.

ax·il·la (ăk sĭl′ə), *n., pl.* **axillae** (ăk sĭl′ē). the armpit.

ax·il·lar (ăk′sə lər), *n. Ornith.* a feather growing under the wing.

ax·il·lar·y (ăk′sə lĕr′ĭ), *adj., n., pl.* **-laries.** —*adj.* **1.** pertaining to the axilla. **2.** *Bot.* of or growing from the axil. —*n.* **3.** *Ornith.* axillar.

ax·i·om (ăk′sĭ əm), *n.* a recognized or accepted principle or truth. —**ax′i·o·mat′ic, ax′i·o·mat′i·cal,** *adj.* —**ax′i·o·mat′i·cal·ly,** *adv.*

ax·is (ăk′sĭs), *n., pl.* **axes** (ăk′sēz). **1.** the line about which a rotating body turns. **2.** the central line of any body. **3.** *Bot.* the longitudinal support on which parts are arranged. **4. the Axis,** the alliance of Germany, Italy, and Japan prior to and during World War II.

ax·le (ăk′səl), *n.* the pin, bar, shaft, or the like, on which or with which a wheel rotates.

ay¹ (ā), *adv. Poetic or Dial.* always. Also, **aye.**

ay² (ī), *adv., n.* aye¹.

aye¹ (ī), *adv.* **1.** yes. —*n.* **2.** an affirmative vote or voter. Also, **ay.**

aye² (ā), *adv.* ay¹.

Ayr (âr), *n.* a seaport in SW Scotland. 42,500.

a·zal·ea (ə zāl′yə), *n.* any of certain plants of the heath family, having handsome, variously colored flowers.

az·i·muth (ăz′ə məth), *n.* the arc of the horizon from the celestial meridian to the foot of the great circle passing through the zenith, the nadir, and the point of the celestial sphere in question.

A·zores (ə zōrz′, ā′zōrz), *n.* a group of islands in the N Atlantic, W of and belonging to Portugal. 287,091 pop.; 890 sq. mi.

A·zov (ā zôf′), *n.* **Sea of,** a sea NE of the Black Sea. ab. 14,500 sq. mi. Also, **A·zof′.**

Az·tec (ăz′tĕk), *n.* a member of an Indian people dominant in Central Mexico before the Spanish invasion (1519). —**Az′tec·an,** *adj.*

az·ure (ăzh′ər, ā′zhər), *adj.* **1.** of a sky-blue color. —*n.* **2.** blue of unclouded sky. **3.** the sky.

az·u·rite (ăzh′ə rīt′), *n.* a blue mineral, a hydrous copper carbonate: an ore of copper.

B

B, b (bē), *n., pl.* **B's** or **Bs, b's** or **bs.** **1.** the second letter of the English alphabet. **2.** the second in any series. **3.** *Music.* the seventh tone in the scale of C major.

B, *Chem.* boron.

B., **1.** bay. **2.** Bible. **3.** British. **4.** (*l.c.*) born.

Ba, *Chem.* barium.

B.A., Bachelor of Arts.

baa (bä, bā), *v.i.* **baaed, baaing,** *n.* bleat.

Ba·al (bā′əl, bāl), *n., pl.* **Baalim** (bā′ əl ĭm). any of numerous deities among the ancient Semitic peoples. —**Ba′al·ism,** *n.*

Bab·bitt metal (băb′ĭt), an antifriction alloy of tin, antimony, lead, and copper.

bab·ble (băb′əl), *v.,* **-bled, -bling,** *n.* —*v.i.* **1.** to talk indistinctly or foolishly. **2.** to make a continuous murmuring sound. —*v.t.* **3.** to utter incoherently or foolishly. —*n.* **4.** inarticulate or foolish speech. **5.** a murmuring sound. —**bab′ble·ment,** —**bab′bler,** *n.*

babe (bāb), *n.* **1.** baby. **2.** an innocent person.

Ba·bel (bā′bəl), *n.* **1.** *Bible.* an ancient city where a tower to heaven was unfinished because of a confounding of the language of the people. **2.** (*usually l.c.*) a confused mixture of sounds.

ba·bies′-breath (bā′bĭz brĕth′), *n.* a tall herb of the pink family, bearing numerous small, fragrant, white or pink flowers.

bab·i·ru·sa (băb′ə rōō′sə, bä′bə-), *n.* an East Indian swine. Also, **bab′i·rous′sa, bab′i·rus′sa.**

ba·boon (bă bōōn′), *n.* any of various large, terrestrial monkeys of Africa and Arabia, with a doglike muzzle, large cheek pouches, and a short tail.

ba·by (bā′bĭ), *n., pl.* **-bies,** *adj., v.,* **-bied, -by-ing.** —*n.* **1.** an infant. **2.** the youngest member of a family, etc. **3.** a childish person. —*adj.* **4.** of, like, or for a baby. **5.** *Colloq.* small. —*v.t.* **6.** to pamper. —**ba′by·hood′,** *n.* —**ba′by·ish,** *adj.* —**ba′by·ish·ly,** *adv.* —**ba′by·like′,** *adj.*

Bab·y·lon (băb′ə lən, -lŏn′), *n.* an ancient city of SW Asia, famed for its magnificence and culture: capital of Babylonia.

Bab·y·lo·ni·a (băb′ə lō′nĭ ə), *n.* an ancient empire in SW Asia. —**Bab′y·lo′ni·an,** *adj., n.*

baby sitter, a person hired to take charge of a child while the parents are temporarily away.

bac·ca·lau·re·ate (băk′ə lôr′ĭ ĭt), *n.* **1.** the bachelor's degree. **2.** Also, **baccalaureate sermon.** a farewell sermon to a graduating class.

bac·ca·rat (băk′ə rä′, băk′ə rä′), *n.* a gambling game at cards. Also, **bac′ca·ra′.**

bac·cate (băk′āt), *adj. Bot.* **1.** berrylike. **2.** bearing berries.

bac·cha·nal (băk′ə nəl), *n.* **1.** a follower of Bacchus. **2.** a drunken reveler. **3.** a drunken orgy. —*adj.* **4.** pertaining to Bacchus.

Bac·cha·na·li·a (băk′ə nā′lĭ ə, -nāl′yə), *n.pl.* **1.** a Roman festival in honor of Bacchus. **2.** (*l.c.*) drunken orgies. —**bac′cha·na′li·an,** *adj.*

bac·chant (băk′ənt), *n., pl.* **bacchants, bacchantes** (bə kăn′tēz). a priest, priestess, or votary of Bacchus. —**bac·chan·tic** (bə kăn′tĭk), *adj.*

bac·chan·te (bə kăn′tĭ), *n.* female bacchant.

Bac·chic (băk′ĭk), *adj.* **1.** relating to or in honor of Bacchus. **2.** (*l.c.*) jovial; drunken.

Bac·chus (băk′əs), *n.* Roman god of wine.

Bach (bäĸĦ), *n.* **Johann Sebastian,** 1685–1750, German organist and composer.

bach·e·lor (băch′ə lər, băch′lər), *n.* **1.** an unmarried man of any age. **2.** a person who has taken the first degree at a college. **3.** a young knight who followed the banner of another. —**bach′e·lor·hood′,** *n.* —**bach′e·lor·ship′,** *n.*

bach·e·lor's-but·ton (băch′ə lərz bŭt′ən), *n.* any of various plants with round flower heads.

ba·cil·lus (bə sĭl′əs), *n., pl.* **-cilli** (-sĭl′ī). any of the group of rod-shaped bacteria which produce spores in the presence of free oxygen.

back¹ (băk), *n.* **1.** the hinder part of the human body, from the neck to the end of the spine. **2.** the corresponding part of the body of animals. **3.** the rear part. **4.** the spine. **5.** the strength to carry a burden. **6.** *Football, etc.* a player behind the forward line. —*v.t.* **7.** to support, as with authority or money. **8.** to cause to move backward. **9.** to bet in favor of. **10.** to mount. **11.** to furnish with a back. **12.** to form a back or background for. —*v.i.* **13.** to go backward. **14.** (of wind) to change direction counterclockwise. **15. back down,** to abandon an opinion, claim, etc. **16. back out** or **out of,** to withdraw from (a promise, etc.). —*adj.* **17.** being behind. **18.** (in) **back of,** *U.S. Colloq.* behind. **19.** remote. **20.** belonging to the past. **21.** overdue. **22.** *Phonet.* pronounced with the tongue drawn back in the mouth, as the vowels of *bought, boat,* and *boot.*

back² (băk), *adv.* **1.** at, to, or toward the rear. **2.** toward the past. **3.** toward the original starting point or condition. **4.** in return. **5.** in reversal of the usual course.

back·bite (băk′bīt′), *v.t., v.i.,* **-bit, -bitten** or (*Colloq.*) **-bit, -biting.** to speak evil of (the absent). —**back′bit′er,** *n.* —**back′bit′ing,** *n.*

back·bone (băk′bōn′), *n.* **1.** *Anat.* the spine. **2.** something resembling a backbone. **3.** strength of character. —**back′boned′,** *adj.*

back·er (băk′ər), *n.* sponsor or supporter.

back·field (băk′fēld′), n. Football. the quarter-back, the two halfbacks, and the fullback.

back·fire (băk′fīr′), v., -fired, -firing, n. —v.i. 1. (of an internal-combustion engine) to have a premature explosion. 2. to check a forest or prairie fire by burning off an area in advance of it. 3. to bring results opposite to those planned. —n. 4. (in an internal-combustion engine) premature ignition. 5. a fire started to check a forest fire.

back·gam·mon (băk′găm′ən), n. a game played by two persons on a board, with pieces moved in accordance with throws of dice.

back·ground (băk′ground′), n. 1. the parts situated in the rear. 2. the portions of a picture represented as more distant. 3. the historical and other antecedents which explain an event or condition. 4. a person's origin, education, etc.

back·hand (băk′hănd′), n. 1. the hand turned backward in making a stroke, as in tennis. 2. such a stroke. 3. writing which slopes to the left. —adj. 4. backhanded.

back·hand·ed (băk′hăn′dĭd), adj. 1. per-formed with the hand turned backward, cross-wise, or in any oblique direction. 2. sloping to the left. 3. oblique or opposite in meaning. —back′hand′ed·ly, adv.

back·ing (băk′ĭng), n. 1. aid or support of any kind. 2. supporters or backers collectively.

back·log (băk′lôg′, -lŏg′), n. U.S. 1. a reserve supply. 2. a large log at the back of the hearth.

back·sheesh (băk′shēsh), n., v.t., v.i. bak-sheesh. Also, **back′shish.**

back·side (băk′sīd′), n. 1. back part. 2. rump.

back·slide (băk′slīd′), v.i., -slid, -slidden or -slid, -sliding. to relapse into sin. —back′-slid′er, n.

back·stage (băk′stāj′), adv. 1. behind the curtain in a theater. 2. toward the rear of the stage.

back·stay (băk′stā′), n. 1. Mach. a support-ing or checking piece. 2. Naut. a stay from a masthead to the ship's side or stern.

back·stroke (băk′strōk′), n. a stroke in swim-ming on one's back.

back talk, impertinent talk; answering back.

back·ward (băk′wərd), adv. Also, **back′-wards. 1.** toward the rear. 2. with the back fore-most. 3. in the reverse of the usual or right way. 4. toward the past. 5. in time past. —adj. 6. directed toward the back or past. 7. returning. 8. behind in time or progress. 9. reluctant; bash-ful. —back′ward·ly, adv. —back′ward·ness, n.

back·wa·ter (băk′wô′tər, -wŏt′ər), n. 1. water held or forced back. 2. a backward place.

back·woods (băk′wŏŏdz′), n.pl. 1. wooded or unsettled districts. —adj. Also, **back′wood′.** 2. of or pertaining to the backwoods. 3. uncouth. —back′woods′man, n.

ba·con (bā′kən), n. the back and sides of the hog, salted and dried or smoked.

Ba·con (bā′kən), n. 1. **Francis,** 1561–1626, British essayist and philosopher. 2. **Roger,** 1214?–1294?, British philosopher and scientist. —Ba·co·ni·an (bā kō′nĭ ən), adj., n.

bac·te·ri·a (băk tĭr′Y ə), n., pl. of **bacterium.** the morphologically simplest group of nongreen vegetable organisms, various species of which are concerned in fermentation and putrefaction, the production of disease, etc. —bac·te′ri·al, adj. —bac·te′ri·al·ly, adv.

bac·te·ri·cide (băk tĭr′ə sīd′), n. an agent for destroying bacteria. —bac·te′ri·cid′al, adj.

bac·te·ri·ol·o·gy (băk tĭr′Y ŏl′ə jY), n. the science that deals with bacteria. —bac·te′ri·o·log′i·cal, adj. —bac·te′ri·ol′o·gist, n.

Bac·tri·an camel (băk′trĭ ən), the two-humped camel.

bad[1] (băd), adj., **worse, worst,** n., adv. —adj. 1. not good. 2. defective; worthless. 3. inade-quate. 4. incorrect; faulty. 5. not valid or sound. 6. having an injurious or unfavorable effect. 7. sick. 8. sorry. 9. unfavorable; unfor-tunate. 10. offensive; painful. 11. severe. 12. decayed. —n. 13. that whir h is bad. 14. a bad condition or quality. —adv. 15. badly. —bad′-ness, n.

bad[2] (băd), v. pt. of bid. Also, **bade.**

bad blood, hate; dislike.

badge (băj), n., v., **badged, badging.** —n. 1. a mark, token, or device worn as a sign of member-ship, authority, etc. —v.t. 2. to furnish with a badge.

badg·er (băj′ər), n. 1. a burrowing carnivorous

mammal, about two feet long, with short legs. 2. the fur of this mammal. —v.t. 3. to harass.

bad·i·nage (băd′ə näzh′, băd′ə nĭj), n., v., -naged, -naging. —n. 1. light playful banter. —v.t. 2. to force by badinage.

bad·ly (băd′lY), adv. 1. in a bad manner. 2. very much.

bad·min·ton (băd′mĭn tən), n. a game, similar to lawn tennis, played with a shuttlecock.

baf·fle (băf′əl), v., -fled, -fling, n. —v.t. 1. to thwart or disconcertingly confuse. —v.i. 2. to struggle ineffectually. —n. 3. a balk; perplexity. 4. an obstruction for checking or deflecting the flow of gases, sounds, etc. —baf′fle·ment, n. —baf′fler, n. —baf′fling·ly, adv.

bag (băg), n., v., **bagged, bagging.** —n. 1. a receptacle of leather, cloth, paper, etc. 2. Chiefly Brit. a suitcase. 3. a purse. 4. Hunting. a sports-man's take of game, etc. —v.i. 5. to bulge. —v.t. 6. to bulge. 7. to put into a bag. 8. to kill or catch.

bag·a·telle (băg′ə těl′), n. a trifle.

Bag·dad (băg′dăd, băg däd′), n. the capital of Iraq. 449,881. Also, **Bagh·dad′.**

bag·gage (băg′Yj), n. 1. trunks, suitcases, etc., used in traveling. 2. portable army equipment.

bag·ging (băg′ĭng), n. woven material for bags.

bag·gy (băg′Y), adj., -gier, -giest. baglike; hanging loosely. —bag′gi·ly, adv. —bag′gi·ness, n.

bagn·io (băn′yō, bän′-), n., pl. **bagnios. 1.** a prison for slaves, as in the Orient. 2. a brothel.

bag·pipe (băg′pīp′), n. (often pl.) a reed instru-ment consisting of a melody pipe and accompany-ing drone pipes protruding from a windbag. —bag′pip′er, n.

ba·guette (bă gět′), n. a gem cut in a long, rectangular shape. Also, **ba·guet′.**

Ba·gui·o (băg′Y ō′), n. a city in the Philippine Islands, on Luzon: summer capital. 24,117.

Ba·ha·ma Islands (bə hä′mə; esp. Brit. and locally bə hä′mə), a group of islands in the British West Indies: a British colony. 73,000 pop.; 4375 sq. mi. Cap.: Nassau. Also, **Bahamas.**

Ba·hi·a Blan·ca (bä ē′ä bläng′kä), a seaport in E Argentina. 121,055.

bail[1] (bāl), n. Law. —n. 1. property given as surety that a person released from custody will return at an appointed time. 2. the person or persons giving it. 3. release from prison on bond. —v.t. 4. to grant or to obtain the liberty of on bail. —bail′a·ble, adj. —bail′ment, n.

bail[2] (bāl), n. the handle of a kettle or pail.

bail[3] (bāl), v.t. 1. to dip out of a boat, as with a bucket. —v.i. 2. to bail water. 3. to make a parachute jump. —n. 4. a bucket, etc., used for bailing. —bail′er, n.

bail[4] (bāl), n. Cricket. either of two bars across the tops of stumps which form the wicket.

bail·iff (bā′lYf), n. 1. an officer similar to a sheriff or his deputy. 2. an overseer of a landed estate.

bail·i·wick (bā′lə wĭk), n. 1. the district with-in which a bailiff has jurisdiction. 2. a person's area of skill, work, etc.

bails·man (bālz′mən), n., pl. -men. Law. one who gives bail or security.

bairn (bârn), n. Scot. and N. Eng. a child.

bait (bāt), n. 1. food, or some substitute, used as a lure in angling, etc. 2. an allurement. —v.t., v.i. 3. to prepare (a hook or trap) with bait. 4. to lure. 5. to set dogs upon (an animal) for sport. 6. to torment. —bait′er, n.

baize (bāz), n. a soft, usually green, woolen fabric, used chiefly for tops of billiard tables.

bake (bāk), v., **baked, baking.** —v.t. 1. to cook by dry heat, as in an oven, under coals, etc. 2. to harden by heat. —v.i. 3. to bake bread etc. 4. to become baked. —n. 5. U.S. a social occa-sion, at which the chief food is baked.

bak·er (bā′kər), n. 1. one who bakes; one who makes and sells bread, cake, etc. 2. a portable oven.

baker's dozen, thirteen, reckoned as a dozen.

Bak·ers·field (bā′kərz fēld′), n. a city in S California, N of Los Angeles. 29,252.

bak·er·y (bā′kə rY), n., pl. -eries. a baker's shop.

bak·ing (bā′kĭng), n. 1. act of one who or that which bakes. 2. the quantity baked at one time.

baking powder, a powder used as a substi-tute for yeast in baking, composed chiefly of so-dium bicarbonate.

baking soda, sodium bicarbonate, $NaHCO_3$.

bak·sheesh (băk′shēsh), (in India, etc.) —*n.*
1. a tip or present. —*v.t., v.i.* 2. to tip. Also,
bak′shish.

Ba·ku (bä kōō′), *n.* a seaport in the Soviet Union
on the Caspian Sea. 809,347.

bal., balance.

Ba·laam (bā′ləm), *n.* a Mesopotamian diviner,
who was rebuked by the ass he rode.

bal·a·lai·ka (băl′ə lī′kə), *n.* a Russian musical
instrument with a triangular body and a guitar
neck.

bal·ance (băl′əns), *n., v.,* **-anced, -ancing.** —*n.*
1. an instrument for weighing, typically a bar
poised on a central support according to the
weights in pans at the ends. 2. power to decide,
as by a balance. 3. state of equilibrium. 4.
mental steadiness, calm, etc. 5. harmonious arrangement, esp. in design. 6. something used to
produce equilibrium. 7. act of balancing. 8.
U.S. the remainder. 9. *Com.* equality or difference between the totals of the two sides of an account. 10. *Horol.* a wheel regulating the beats of
a watch or clock. 11. (*cap.*) the zodiacal constellation Libra or the sign named for it. —*v.t.*
12. to weigh in a balance. 13. to estimate the
relative importance of. 14. to offset. 15. to hold
in equilibrium. 16. to arrange the parts of symmetrically. 17. to be equal or proportionate to.
18. *Com.* to make necessary entries in (an account) so that the two sides will be equal. —*v.i.*
19. to have an equality in weight, parts, etc.
20. *Com.* to reckon or adjust accounts. 21. to
waver; hesitate. —**bal′anc·er,** *n.*

balance sheet, a statement of the financial
position of a business on a specified date.

Bal·bo·a (băl bō′ə), *n.* **Vasco Núñez de,** 1475?–
1517, Spanish explorer.

bal·brig·gan (băl brĭg′ən), *n.* a kind of un-
bleached cotton, used esp. in hosiery and underwear.

bal·co·ny (băl′kə nĭ), *n., pl.* **-nies.** 1. a balus-
traded platform projecting from the wall of a
building. 2. a gallery in a theater. —**bal′co-
nied,** *adj.*

bald (bôld), *adj.* 1. lacking hair on some part of
the scalp. 2. destitute of some natural growth or
covering. 3. plain. 4. undisguised. —**bald′ly,**
adv. —**bald′ness,** *n.*

bal·der·dash (bôl′dər dăsh′), *n.* nonsense.

bal·dric (bôl′drĭk), *n.* a belt worn diagonally
from shoulder to hip, supporting a sword, horn,
etc.

Bald·win (bôld′wĭn), *n.* **Stanley,** 1867–1947,
British statesman.

bale[1] (bāl), *n., v.,* **baled, baling.** —*n.* 1. a large
bundle or package. —*v.t.* 2. to make into bales.
—**bal′er,** *n.*

bale[2] (bāl), *n.* *Archaic.* 1. evil. 2. woe.

ba·leen (bə lēn′), *n.* *Zool.* whalebone (def. 1).

bale·ful (bāl′fəl), *adj.* evil; malign. —**bale′-
ful·ly,** *adv.* —**bale′ful·ness,** *n.*

Bal·four (băl′fŏŏr), *n.* **Arthur James,** 1848–
1930, British statesman.

Ba·li (bä′lē), *n.* an island in the Dutch East
Indies, E of Java. 1,101,393 pop.; 2147 sq. mi.
Cap.: Singaraja. —**Ba·li·nese** (bä′lə nēz′, -nēs′),
adj., n.

balk (bôk), *v.i.* 1. to stop, as at an obstacle.
2. (of horses) to stop short and refuse to go on.
—*v.t.* 3. to hinder; thwart. 4. to let slip; fail to
use. —*n.* 5. a check or hindrance. 6. a miss,
slip, or failure. 7. a strip of land left unplowed.
8. a tie beam. 9. *Baseball.* an illegal deceptive
motion of a pitcher. —**balk′er,** *n.*

Bal·kan (bôl′kən), *adj.* pertaining to the Balkan Peninsula or the inhabitants.

Balkan Mountains, a mountain range extending from W Bulgaria to the Black Sea.

Balkan Peninsula, a peninsula in S Europe,
containing the **Balkan States** (Yugoslavia, Rumania, Bulgaria, Albania, Greece, and European
Turkey).

balk·y (bô′kĭ), *adj.,* **balkier, balkiest.** *U.S.*
given to balking.

ball[1] (bôl), *n.* 1. a round or roundish body, as
one for use in various games. 2. a game played
with a ball. 3. *Baseball.* **a.** a ball in play, as
tossed, struck, etc. **b.** a ball pitched too high or
low or not over the plate, and not struck at by
the batter. 4. *Mil.* a solid projectile for a cannon,
rifle, etc., usually spherical. 5. any part that is
rounded or protuberant. 6. *Astron.* a celestial
body, esp. the earth. —*v.t.* 7. to make into a
ball. 8. *U.S. Slang.* to confuse hopelessly (fol. by
up). —*v.i.* 9. to form into a ball.

ball[2] (bôl), *n.* a social assembly for dancing.

bal·lad (băl′əd), *n.* a simple narrative poem or
song, esp. one of popular origin.

bal·last (băl′əst), *n.* 1. any heavy material carried by a ship for insuring proper stability. 2.
something heavy, as bags of sand, placed in the
car of a balloon for control of altitude. 3. anything that gives stability. 4. gravel, etc., between and under railroad ties to give stability,
etc. —*v.t.* 5. to furnish with ballast. 6. to give
steadiness to.

ball bearing, *Mach.* 1. a bearing in which the
shaft or journal turns upon steel balls in a track.
2. any of the steel balls so used.

bal·le·ri·na (băl′ə rē′nə), *n., pl.* **-nas.** the
principal female dancer in a ballet company.

bal·let (băl′ā, bă lā′), *n.* 1. a spectacular entertainment rendered by professional dancers. 2. a
dance interlude in an operatic performance. 3.
the style of dancing used in such a performance.
4. the company of dancers.

bal·lis·ta (bə lĭs′tə), *n., pl.* **-tae** (-tē). an ancient military engine for throwing stones or other
missiles.

bal·lis·tics (bə lĭs′tĭks), *n.* the science or
study of the motion of projectiles, such as bullets,
shells, bombs, etc. —**bal·lis′tic,** *adj.*

bal·loon (bə lōōn′), *n.* 1. a bag filled with some
gas lighter than ordinary air, designed to rise and
float in the atmosphere, in large forms having a
cabin for passengers. 2. an inflatable rubber bag,
used as a child's toy. —*v.i.* 3. to go up in a balloon. 4. to swell. —*v.t.* 5. to fill with air.
—*adj.* 6. puffed out like a balloon. —**bal·loon′-
ist,** *n.*

bal·lot (băl′ət), *n., v.,* **-loted, -loting.** —*n.* 1. a
ticket, paper, etc., used in voting. 2. the whole
number of votes cast. 3. the method of secret
voting. 4. voting in general, or a round of voting.
—*v.i.* 5. to vote by ballot. —*v.t.* 6. to vote on by
ballot.

ball point pen, a fountain pen in which the
point is a fine ball bearing, depositing a film of
ink.

ball·room (bôl′rōōm′, -rōōm′), *n.* a large room
with a polished floor for balls or dancing.

bal·ly·hoo (băl′ĭ hōō′), *n., pl.* **-hoos,** *v.,* **-hooed,
-hooing.** *U.S. Slang.* —*n.* 1. blatant advertising
or publicity. 2. clamor or outcry. —*v.t., v.i.*
3. to advertise or push by ballyhoo.

balm (bäm), *n.* 1. any of various oily, fragrant,
resinous substances, often of medicinal value, exuding from certain tropical trees. 2. a tree yielding such a substance. 3. any aromatic ointment.
4. aromatic fragrance. 5. any of various aromatic
plants of the mint family. 6. anything which
heals or mitigates pain.

balm·y (bä′mĭ), *adj.,* **balmier, balmiest.** 1.
mild and refreshing. 2. aromatic; fragrant. 3.
Eng. Slang. silly. —**balm′i·ly,** *adv.* —**balm′i-
ness,** *n.*

ba·lo·ney (bə lō′nĭ), *n.* *Slang.* nonsense.

bal·sa (bôl′sə, băl′-), *n.* 1. a tree of tropical
America with an exceedingly light wood used for
life preservers, rafts, etc. 2. a life raft.

bal·sam (bôl′səm), *n.* 1. any of various fragrant
exudations from certain trees, used in medicine,
etc. 2. oleoresin. 3. any of certain transparent
turpentines. 4. a plant or tree yielding a balsam.
5. any aromatic ointment. —**bal·sam′ic,** *adj.*

balsam fir, a North American species of fir
which yields a turpentine.

Bal·tic (bôl′tĭk), *adj.* 1. of, near, or on the Baltic Sea. 2. of or pertaining to the **Baltic States**
(Estonia, Latvia, Lithuania).

Baltic Sea, a sea in N Europe, bounded by
Sweden, Finland, the Soviet Union, Poland, Germany, and Denmark. ab. 160,000 sq. mi.

Bal·ti·more (bôl′tə mōr′), *n.* a seaport in N
Maryland, on an estuary near Chesapeake Bay.
859,100.

Baltimore oriole, an American oriole, the
male of which has black and orange feathers.

bal·us·ter (băl′ə stər), *n.* *Archit.* 1. one of a
series of short, pillarlike supports for a railing, as
of a staircase. 2. (*pl.*) balustrade.

bal·us·trade (băl′ə strād′), *n.* *Archit.* a series
of balusters supporting a railing.

Bal·zac (băl′zăk, bôl′-), *n.* **Honoré de,** 1799–
1850, French novelist.

bam·bi·no (băm bē′nō), *n., pl.* **-ni** (-nē). 1. a
baby. 2. an image of the infant Jesus.

bam·boo (băm bōō′), *n., pl.* **-boos.** any of certain woody or treelike tropical and semitropical

grasses whose hollow woody stem is used for building purposes and for making furniture, poles, etc.

bam·boo·zle (băm bōō′zəl), v., -zled, -zling. —v.t. 1. to deceive by trickery. 2. to mystify. —v.i. 3. to practice trickery. —**bam·boo′zler**, n.

ban[1] (băn), v., banned, banning, n. —v.t. 1. to prohibit. 2. Archaic. to curse. —n. 3. a denunciation or prohibition, as by public opinion. 4. Law. a sentence of outlawry. 5. Eccles. excommunication. 6. a curse.

ban[2] (băn), n. 1. a proclamation. 2. (pl.) banns.

ba·nal (bā′nəl, bə năl′, -năl′, băn′əl), adj. hackneyed; trite. —**ba·nal·i·ty** (bə năl′ə tĭ, bā-), n.

ba·nan·a (bə năn′ə), n. 1. a tropical plant cultivated for its nutritious fruit. 2. the fruit, long and slender with a yellow or red rind and growing in large clusters.

band[1] (bănd), n. 1. a company of persons joined or acting together. 2. a company of musicians. —v.i., v.t. 3. to unite.

band[2] (bănd), n. 1. a thin, flat strip of some material for binding, trimming, etc. 2. a fillet, belt, or strap. 3. a stripe, as of color. 4. a collar with two pendent strips in front, sometimes worn by clergymen (**Geneva bands**). 5. Radio. a group of frequencies which can be tuned in closely together. —v.t. 6. to mark with bands.

band[3] (bănd), n. 1. (usually pl.) a shackle, manacle, or fetter. 2. an obligation; bond.

band·age (băn′dĭj), n., v., -aged, -aging. —n. 1. a strip of cloth or other material used to bind up a wound, etc. —v.t. 2. to bind with a bandage. —**band′ag·er**, n.

ban·dan·na (băn dăn′ə), n. a large colored handkerchief with spots or figures, usually white on a red or blue background. Also, **ban·dan′a**.

band·box (bănd′bŏks′), n. a light box of pasteboard, thin wood, etc., for a hat, collars, etc.

ban·deau (băn dō′, băn′dō), n., pl. -deaux (-dōz′, -dōz). a band worn about or on the head.

ban·de·role (băn′də rōl′), n. a small pennant.

ban·dit (băn′dĭt), n., pl. -dits, banditti (băn-dĭt′ĭ). 1. a robber. 2. an outlaw. —**ban′dit·ry**, n.

band·mas·ter (bănd′măs′tər, -mäs′tər), n. the conductor of a band.

ban·do·leer (băn′də lĭr′), n. a belt worn over the shoulder by soldiers, having loops or pockets for cartridges. Also, **ban′do·lier′**.

bands·man (băndz′mən), n., pl. -men. a musician who plays in a band.

band·stand (bănd′stănd′), n. a platform, often roofed, for outdoor band performances.

band wagon, 1. a wagon carrying a band of music, as in a parade. 2. **climb aboard the band wagon,** U.S. Colloq. to shift one's vote or aid to an apparently successful candidate or cause.

ban·dy (băn′dĭ), v., -died, -dying, adj., n., pl. -dies. —v.t. 1. to throw or strike to and fro. 2. to pass (words, remarks, etc.) back and forth. —adj. 3. (of legs) having a bend outward. —n. 4. Chiefly Brit. hockey. —**ban′dy-leg′ged**, adj.

bane (bān), n. 1. that which causes death. 2. a deadly poison. 3. a thing that ruins or spoils.

bane·ful (bān′fəl), adj. destructive; poisonous. —**bane′ful·ly**, adv. —**bane′ful·ness**, n.

bang[1] (băng), n. 1. a loud, sudden, explosive noise. 2. a resounding stroke or blow. 3. U.S. Slang. thrill. —v.t. 4. to strike resoundingly; slam. —v.i. 5. to strike violently or noisily. 6. to make a loud noise. —adv. 7. suddenly and loudly.

bang[2] (băng), n. 1. (often pl.) a fringe of hair over the forehead. —v.t. 2. to cut (the hair) so as to form a bang. 3. to dock (the tail of a horse, etc.).

Bang·kok (băng′kŏk), n. the capital of Siam: the principal port of Siam. 685,000.

ban·gle (băng′gəl), n. 1. a bracelet in the form of a ring, without a clasp. 2. an anklet.

Ban·gor (băng′gôr, -gər), n. a city in S Maine: a port on the Penobscot river. 29,822.

ban·ian (băn′yən), n. 1. a loose shirt, jacket, or gown worn in India. 2. banyan.

ban·ish (băn′ĭsh), v.t. 1. to condemn to exile. 2. to send, drive, or put away. —**ban′ish·ment**, n.

ban·is·ter (băn′ĭs tər), n. 1. baluster. 2. (pl.) the balustrade of a staircase.

ban·jo (băn′jō), n., pl. -jos. a musical instrument of the guitar family, having a circular body. —**ban′jo·ist**, n.

bank[1] (băngk), n. 1. a long pile or heap. 2. a slope or acclivity. 3. the slope immediately bordering a stream, river, etc. 4. a broad, shallow, submarine elevation near the coast. 5. the lateral inclination of an airplane. 6. Billiards, Pool. the cushion of the table. —v.t. 7. to border with a bank. 8. to form into a heap. 9. Aeron. to tip (an airplane) laterally. 10. to cover (a fire) with ashes or fuel to make it burn slowly. —v.i. 11. to form banks, as clouds. 12. Aeron. to tip an airplane laterally.

bank[2] (băngk), n. 1. an institution for receiving and lending money, etc. 2. the office of such an institution. 3. (in games) a. the stock of pieces from which players draw. b. the fund of the dealer. 4. any reserve. —v.i. 5. to exercise the functions of a bank or banker. 6. to keep money in a bank. 7. Colloq. to rely. —v.t. 8. to deposit in a bank.

bank[3] (băngk), n. 1. an arrangement of objects in line. 2. a row of keys in an organ. 3. a bench for rowers in a galley. 4. a row of oars. —v.t. 5. to arrange in a bank.

bank·book (băngk′bŏŏk′), n. a depositor's book in which a bank records his account.

bank·er (băngk′ər), n. a bank officer.

bank·ing (băngk′ĭng), n. business of a bank.

bank note, a promissory note issued by a bank and circulated as money.

bank·rupt (băngk′rŭpt, -rəpt), n. 1. a person who is adjudged insolvent by a court and whose property is divided among his creditors. —adj. 2. subject to, or under, legal process because of insolvency. 3. lacking. —v.t. 4. to make bankrupt.

bank·rupt·cy (băngk′rŭpt sĭ, -rəp sĭ), n., pl. -cies. 1. bankrupt state. 2. utter ruin.

ban·ner (băn′ər), n. 1. the flag of a country, troop, etc. 2. an ensign or the like borne in processions. —adj. 3. leading.

banns (bănz), n.pl. notice of an intended marriage, given three times in the parish church.

ban·quet (băng′kwĭt), n., v., -queted, -queting. —n. 1. a feast. 2. a ceremonious public dinner. —v.t., v.i. 3. to entertain at a banquet. —**ban′quet·er**, n.

ban·quette (băng kĕt′), n. Fort. a platform or step along the inside of a parapet.

ban·shee (băn′shē, băn shē′), n. Irish and Scot. a supernatural being supposed to warn by its wails of approaching death in the family.

ban·tam (băn′təm), n. 1. (often cap.) a domestic fowl of any of certain breeds of very small size. 2. a small, quarrelsome person. —adj. 3. tiny.

ban·ter (băn′tər), n. 1. playful teasing; good-humored raillery. —v.t. 2. to address with banter. —v.i. 3. to use banter. —**ban′ter·er**, n. —**ban′ter·ing·ly**, adv.

Ban·tu (băn′tōō), n., pl. -tu, -tus, adj. —n. 1. (pl.) a large family of Negro tribes in central and southern Africa. 2. a member of any of these tribes. —adj. 3. of the Bantu tribes or their languages.

ban·yan (băn′yən), n. an East Indian fig tree whose branches send out adventitious roots to the ground.

ban·zai (băn′zä ē′, -zī′), interj. a Japanese salutation or patriotic shout, as in honor of the emperor, meaning "long life."

Bap., Baptist. Also, **Bapt.**

bap·tism (băp′tĭz əm), n. 1. a ceremonial immersion in water, or application of water, as an initiatory rite of the Christian church. 2. any similar ceremony. —**bap·tis′mal**, adj. —**bap·tis′mal·ly**, adv.

Bap·tist (băp′tĭst), n. 1. a member of a Christian denomination which maintains that baptism should only follow personal profession of faith. 2. **the Baptist.** See **John the Baptist.**

bap·tis·ter·y (băp′tĭs tə rĭ, -tĭs trĭ), n., pl. -teries. a building, or a part of a church, in which baptism is administered. Also, **bap′tist·ry.**

bap·tize (băp tīz′, băp′tīz), v., -tized, -tizing. —v.t. 1. to immerse in water, or sprinkle water on, in baptism. 2. to cleanse spiritually. 3. to christen. —v.i. 4. to administer baptism. —**bap·tiz′er**, n.

bar (bär), n., v., barred, barring, prep. —n. 1. a relatively long and evenly shaped piece of wood or metal used as a guard or for some mechanical purpose. 2. crowbar. 3. an oblong piece of any solid material. 4. a band or stripe. 5. a long ridge in coastal waters, near or slightly above the surface. 6. anything which obstructs, hinders, or impedes. 7. Music. the line marking the division between two measures of music. **8.** a counter or a place where liquors, etc., are served to customers. **9.** the legal profession. **10.** the members of the legal profession. **11.** a railing in a courtroom separating the public from the part occupied by the judges, jury, attorneys, etc. **12.** the place in court where prisoners are stationed. **13.** (in a bridle) the mouthpiece connecting the checks. —*v.t.* **14.** to provide or fasten with a bar. **15.** to shut in or out by bars. **16.** to block. **17.** to debar, as a person. —*prep.* **18.** except; but.

bar., **1.** barometer. **2.** barrel. **3.** barrister.

barb (bärb), *n.* **1.** a point projecting backward from a main point, as of a fishhook. **2.** *Bot., Zool.* a beardlike part. —*v.t.* **3.** to furnish with a barb or barbs. —**barbed,** *adj.*

Bar·ba·dos (bär bā′dōz, bär′bə dōz′), *n.* an island in the West Indies: a British colony. 202,-588 pop.; 166 sq. mi. *Cap.:* Bridgetown.

bar·bar·i·an (bär bâr′ī ən), *n.* **1.** a man in a rude, savage state. **2.** an uncultured person. **3.** a foreigner (orig. a non-Greek). —*adj.* **4.** uncivilized. **5.** foreign. —**bar·bar′i·an·ism,** *n.*

bar·bar·ic (bär bâr′ĭk), *adj.* **1.** uncivilized. **2.** of, like, or befitting barbarians. **3.** crudely rich or splendid. —**bar·bar′i·cal·ly,** *adv.*

bar·ba·rism (bär′bə rĭz′əm), *n.* **1.** uncivilized condition. **2.** a barbarous act. **3.** the use in a language of undesirably alien forms. **4.** such a form.

bar·bar·i·ty (bär bâr′ə tĭ), *n., pl.* **-ties.** **1.** cruelty. **2.** act of cruelty. **3.** crudity of style, taste, etc.

bar·ba·rize (bär′bə rīz′), *v.i., v.t.,* **-rized, -riz·ing.** to make or become barbarous.

bar·ba·rous (bär′bə rəs), *adj.* **1.** uncivilized. **2.** excessively harsh. **3.** harsh-sounding. **4.** not conforming to classical standards or accepted usage. **5.** foreign (orig. non-Greek). —**bar′ba·rous·ly,** *adv.* —**bar′ba·rous·ness,** *n.*

Bar·ba·ry (bär′bə rĭ), *n.* a region in N Africa, extending from W of Egypt to the Atlantic.

Barbary States, Morocco, Algiers, Tunis, and Tripoli.

bar·bate (bär′bāt), *adj. Zool., Bot.* bearded.

bar·be·cue (bär′bə kū′), *n., v.,* **-cued, -cuing.** —*n.* **1.** *U.S.* a large open-air gathering at which animals are roasted whole. **2.** a dressed ox or other animal roasted whole. —*v.t.* **3.** to broil or roast whole before an open fire, on a spit. **4.** to cook in a highly seasoned sauce.

bar·bel (bär′bəl), *n.* a slender cylindrical tactile process at the mouth of certain fishes.

bar·ber (bär′bər), *n.* **1.** one whose occupation it is to give haircuts, shaves, etc. —*v.t.* **2.** to shave or cut the hair of.

bar·ber·ry (bär′bĕr′ĭ), *n., pl.* **-ries.** an Asiatic shrub bearing red, elongated, acid fruit.

Bar·ber·ton (bär′bər tən), *n.* a city in NE Ohio, near Akron. 24,028.

bar·bi·tal (bär′bə tăl′, -tôl′), *n. Pharm.* a drug, containing barbituric acid, sold as sleeping pills.

bar·bi·tu·rate (bär bĭch′ə rāt′, -rĭt; bär′bə tyōōr′āt, -ĭt), *n. Chem.* a derivative of barbituric acid.

bar·bi·tu·ric acid (bär′bə tyōōr′ĭk, -tōōr′-), *Chem.* an acid, $C_4H_4N_2O_3$, a crystalline powder from which several hypnotic and sedative drugs are derived.

bar·ca·role (bär′kə rōl′), *n.* **1.** a boating song of the Venetian gondoliers. **2.** a piece of music in the style of such songs. Also, **bar′ca·rolle′.**

Bar·ce·lo·na (bär′sə lō′nə), *n.* a seaport in NE Spain. 1,109,000.

bard (bärd), *n.* **1.** one of an ancient Celtic order of poets. **2.** a poet. —**bard′ic,** *adj.*

bare (bâr), *adj., barer, barest, v.,* **bared, baring.** —*adj.* **1.** without covering or clothing. **2.** with the head uncovered. **3.** without the usual furnishings, etc. **4.** open to view; unconcealed. **5.** plain. **6.** threadbare. **7.** mere. —*v.t.* **8.** to make bare. —**bare′ness,** *n.*

bare·back (bâr′băk′), *adv., adj.* with the back (of a horse, etc.) bare; without saddle.

bare·faced (bâr′fāst′), *adj.* **1.** with the face uncovered. **2.** undisguised. **3.** impudent. —**bare′fac′ed·ly,** *adv.* —**bare′fac′ed·ness,** *n.*

bare·foot (bâr′fŏŏt′), *adj., adv.* with the feet bare. —**bare′foot′ed,** *adj.*

bare·hand·ed (bâr′hăn′dĭd), *adj.* **1.** with hands uncovered. **2.** without means.

bare·ly (bâr′lĭ), *adv.* **1.** only; no more than. **2.** without disguise or concealment. **3.** nakedly.

bar·gain (bär′gĭn), *n.* **1.** an agreement between parties in a transaction. **2.** such an agreement as affecting one of the parties. **3.** that which is acquired by bargaining. **4.** an advantageous purchase. —*v.i.* **5.** *Colloq.* to discuss the terms of a bargain. **6.** to come to an agreement. —**bar′gain·er,** *n.*

barge (bärj), *n., v.,* **barged, barging.** —*n.* **1.** an unpowered vessel for transporting freight. **2.** a vessel of state used in pageants. **3.** a ship's boat used in visits of courtesy. —*v.t.* **4.** to carry by barge. —*v.i.* **5.** to move in a slow, heavy manner. **6.** *Colloq.* to force oneself rudely. **7.** *Colloq.* to collide. —**barge′man,** *n.*

Ba·ri (bä′rĭ), *n.* a seaport in SE Italy. 244,522.

bar·ite (bâr′īt, băr′-), *n.* a mineral, barium sulfate, $BaSO_4$, occurring in tabular crystals.

bar·i·tone (băr′ə tōn′), *Music.* —*n.* **1.** a male voice between tenor and bass. **2.** a singer with such a voice. **3.** a large, valved brass instrument. —*adj.* **4.** of or pertaining to the baritone.

bar·i·um (bâr′ĭ əm, băr′-), *n.* a whitish malleable, active, metallic element. *Symbol:* Ba; *at. wt.:* 137.36; *at. no.:* 56; *sp. gr.:* 3.5 at 20°C.

bark[1] (bärk), *n.* **1.** the abrupt, explosive cry of a dog. **2.** any similar sound. —*v.i.* **3.** to utter an abrupt, explosive cry. **4.** to speak or cry out sharply or gruffly. —*v.t.* **5.** to utter with a bark. —**bark′er,** *n.*

bark[2] (bärk), *n.* **1.** *Bot.* the external covering of the woody stems, branches, and roots of plants. —*v.t.* **2.** to strip off the bark of. **3.** to cover with bark. **4.** to rub off the skin of.

bark[3] (bärk), *n.* a type of three-masted vessel.

bar·keep·er (bär′kē′pər), *n.* a bartender. Also, *U.S.,* **bar′keep′.**

bark·en·tine (bär′kən tēn′), *n.* a type of three-masted vessel. Also, **bark′an·tine′.**

Bark·ley (bärk′lĭ), *n.* **Alben William,** born 1877, vice-president of the U.S., 1949–53.

bar·ley (bär′lĭ), *n.* an edible cereal plant whose awned flowers grow in tightly bunched spikes.

Bar·ley·corn (bär′lĭ kôrn′), *n.* **John,** a humorous personification of malt liquor.

barm (bärm), *n.* yeast formed on malt liquors while fermenting.

barm·y (bär′mĭ), *adj.* **barmier, barmiest.** containing or resembling barm; frothy.

barn (bärn), *n.* a building for storing hay, grain, etc., and often for stabling livestock.

bar·na·cle (bär′nə kəl), *n.* any of certain crustaceans which cling to ship bottoms, floating timber, etc. —**bar′na·cled,** *adj.*

barn·storm (bärn′stôrm′), *v.i. U.S. Colloq.* to tour rural areas, giving speeches, plays, etc. —**barn′storm′er,** *n.* —**barn′storm′ing,** *n., adj.*

Bar·num (bär′nəm), *n.* **Phineas Taylor,** 1810–91, U.S. showman: established circus.

barn·yard (bärn′yärd′), *n.* a yard next to a barn.

bar·o·graph (bär′ə grăf′, -gräf′), *n.* an automatic recording barometer. —**bar′o·graph′ic,** *adj.*

ba·rom·e·ter (bə rŏm′ə tər), *n.* an instrument for measuring atmospheric pressure, thus determining height, weather changes, etc. —**bar′o·met′ric, bar′o·met′ri·cal,** *adj.* —**bar′o·met′ri·cal·ly,** *adv.*

bar·on (bär′ən), *n.* **1.** a member of the lowest nobility. **2.** *U.S.* a powerful industrialist. —**ba·ro·ni·al** (bə rō′nĭ əl), *adj.*

bar·on·age (bär′ən ĭj), *n.* **1.** the whole body of British barons. **2.** the dignity or rank of a baron.

bar·on·ess (bär′ən ĭs), *n.* **1.** the wife of a baron. **2.** a lady holding a baronial title in her own right.

bar·on·et (bär′ən ĭt, -ə nĕt′), *n.* a member of a British hereditary order of honor, ranking below the barons and made up of commoners. —**bar′on·et·cy,** *n.*

bar·o·ny (bär′ə nĭ), *n., pl.* **-nies.** **1.** the rank or dignity of a baron. **2.** the domain of a baron.

ba·roque (bə rōk′), *n.* **1.** *Art.* a style characterized by grotesque or odd effects. **2.** anything in this style. —*adj.* **3.** of or like the baroque.

bar·o·scope (bär′ə skōp′), *n.* an instrument showing roughly the variations in atmospheric pressure.

ba·rouche (bə rōōsh′), *n.* a four-wheeled carriage with a seat outside for the driver and with a calash top.

bar·rack[1] (bär′ək), *n.* (*usually pl.*) **1.** a building or range of buildings for lodging soldiers, esp. in

garrison. **2.** any large, plain building. —*v.t.,
v.i.* **3.** to lodge in barracks.

bar·rack² (băr′ək), *Austral. and Brit.* —*v.i.*
1. to root. —*v.t.* **2.** to shout for or against.

bar·ra·cu·da (băr′ə kōō′də), *n., pl.* **-da, -das.**
any of several species of elongate, predacious,
tropical and subtropical marine fishes.

bar·rage (bə räzh′), *n.* **1.** *Mil.* a barrier of artillery fire used to prevent the enemy from advancing, etc. **2.** any overwhelming quantity.

Bar·ran·quil·la (băr′rän kē′yä), *n.* a port in
N Colombia, on the Magdalena river. 197,830.

bar·ra·try (băr′ə trĭ), *n.* fraud by a master or
crew at the expense of the owners. —**bar′ra-
trous,** *adj.* —**bar′ra·trous·ly,** *adv.*

barred (bärd), *adj.* having bars or stripes.

bar·rel (băr′əl), *n., v.,* **-reled, -reling** or (*esp.
Brit.*) **-relled, -relling.** —*n.* **1.** a wooden cylindrical vessel, with slightly bulging sides and with
flat ends. **2.** the quantity which such a vessel
can hold. **3.** any similar vessel, case, or part.
—*v.t.* **4.** to put or pack in a barrel or barrels.

barrel organ, a hand organ.

bar·ren (băr′ən), *adj.* **1.** not producing offspring; sterile. **2.** unfruitful. **3.** destitute of interest. **4.** dull; stupid. —*n.* **5.** (*usually pl.*) level,
relatively infertile land. —**bar′ren·ly,** *adv.*
—**bar′ren·ness,** *n.*

bar·rette (bə rĕt′), *n.* a hair clasp.

bar·ri·cade (băr′ə kād′, băr′ə kād′), *n., v.,*
-caded, -cading. —*n.* **1.** a defensive barrier
hastily constructed. **2.** any barrier. —*v.t.* **3.** to
block with a barricade. **4.** to defend with a barricade. —**bar′ri·cad′er,** *n.*

Bar·rie (băr′ĭ), *n.* **Sir James Matthew,** 1860–
1937, Scottish writer.

bar·ri·er (băr′ĭ ər), *n.* **1.** anything that bars
passage, as a railing. **2.** any natural obstacle.
3. anything that obstructs progress, etc. **4.** a
limit of any kind.

bar·ring (băr′ĭng), *prep.* except for.

bar·ris·ter (băr′ĭs tər), *n.* *Eng.* a counselor admitted to plead at the bar in any court.

bar·room (băr′rōōm′, -rŏŏm′), *n.* *U.S.* a room
containing a bar for the sale of liquors.

bar·row¹ (băr′ō), *n.* a flat rectangular frame
used for carrying a load, esp. one with handles.

bar·row² (băr′ō), *n.* **1.** a burial mound of prehistoric Britain. **2.** a hill.

Bart., Baronet.

bar·tend·er (băr′tĕn′dər), *n.* *U.S.* a man who
mixes and serves drinks in a bar.

bar·ter (băr′tər), *v.i.* **1.** to trade by exchange of
commodities. —*v.t.* **2.** to exchange in trade.
—*n.* **3.** act of bartering. **4.** the thing bartered.
—**bar′ter·er,** *n.*

Bar·ton (băr′tən), *n.* **Clara,** 1821–1912, U.S.
woman who organized the American Red Cross
in 1881.

ba·ry·tes (bə rī′tēz), *n.* barite.

bar·y·tone (băr′ə tōn′), *adj., n.* *Music.* baritone.

bas·al (bā′səl), *adj.* **1.** of, at, or forming the
base. **2.** fundamental. **3.** *Physiol.* indicating a
standard low level of activity of an organism.
—**bas′al·ly,** *adv.*

ba·salt (bə sôlt′, băs′ôlt), *n.* the dark, dense
igneous rock of a lava flow or minor intrusion.
—**ba·sal′tic,** *adj.*

bas·cule bridge (băs′kūl), a bridge in which
the rising floor or section is counterbalanced by
a weight.

base¹ (bās), *n., adj., v.,* **based, basing.** —*n.* **1.**
the bottom of anything, considered as its support.
2. a fundamental principle; basis. **3.** the principal element. **4.** that from which a commencement is made. **5.** *Baseball.* one of the four corners
of the diamond. **6.** *Mil.* **a.** a protected place
from which operations proceed. **b.** a supply installation. **7.** *Geom.* the line or surface forming
that part of a figure on which it is supposed to
stand. **8.** *Chem.* a compound which reacts with
an acid to form a salt. —*adj.* **9.** serving as a base.
—*v.t.* **10.** to make foundation for. **11.** to establish, as a fact.

base² (bās), *adj.,* **baser, basest. 1.** morally low;
cowardly. **2.** characteristic of an inferior person
or thing. **3.** of little value. **4.** debased or counterfeit. **5.** of illegitimate birth. **6.** deep in sound;
bass. —**base′ly,** *adv.* —**base′ness,** *n.*

base·ball (bās′bôl′), *n.* **1.** a game of ball
played by two sides of nine players each, on a
diamond connecting four bases. **2.** the ball used
in this game.

base·board (bās′bōrd′), *n.* a board around
the walls of a room, next to the floor.

Ba·sel (bä′zəl), *n.* a city in NW Switzerland,
on the Rhine. 167,000.

base·less (bās′lĭs), *adj.* groundless.

base·ment (bās′mənt), *n.* a story of a building
partly or wholly underground.

bash (băsh), *Dial. or Slang.* —*v.t.* **1.** to strike
with a smashing blow. —*n.* **2.** a crushing blow.

bash·ful (băsh′fəl), *adj.* uncomfortably shy;
timid. —**bash′ful·ly,** *adv.* —**bash′ful·ness,** *n.*

bas·ic (bā′sĭk), *adj.* **1.** of, pertaining to, or
forming a base; fundamental. **2.** *Chem.* **a.** pertaining to, of the nature of, or containing a base.
b. alkaline. —**bas′i·cal·ly,** *adv.*

Basic English, a simplified English for use as
an international auxiliary language.

bas·il (băz′əl), *n.* a plant of the mint family,
the leaves of some species being used in cooking.

ba·sil·i·ca (bə sĭl′ə kə), *n.* an oblong building
with a nave higher than its aisles.

ba·sin (bā′sən), *n.* **1.** a circular container, used
chiefly to hold water or other liquid. **2.** any similar container. **3.** the quantity held by such a
container. **4.** a hollow place containing water.
5. *Phys. Geog.* **a.** an area surrounded by higher
land. **b.** the area drained by a river. —**ba′-
sined,** *adj.*

ba·sis (bā′sĭs), *n., pl.* **-ses** (-sēz). **1.** the bottom
or base of anything. **2.** a fundamental principle.
3. the principal ingredient.

bask (băsk, bäsk), *v.i.* **1.** to lie in a pleasant
warmth. —*v.t.* **2.** to expose to warmth, etc.

bas·ket (băs′kĭt, bäs′-), *n.* **1.** a receptacle
woven of twigs, thin strips of wood, or the like. **2.**
the contents of a basket. **3.** anything like a
basket. **4.** *Basketball.* **a.** a short open net, suspended before a board, through which the ball
must pass to score points. **b.** a score.

bas·ket·ball (băs′kĭt bôl′, bäs′-), *n.* **1.** an indoor game played by two teams of five players
each. Points are scored by throwing the ball
through the baskets at the ends of the oblong
court. **2.** the round leather ball used.

Basque (băsk), *n.* **1.** one of a people inhabiting
the western Pyrenees regions in France and Spain.
2. their language. **3.** (*l.c.*) a woman's bodice extending over the hips. —*adj.* **4.** of the Basques
or their language.

bass¹ (bās), *adj.* *Music.* **1.** of the lowest pitch or
range. —*n.* **2.** the bass part. **3.** a bass voice,
singer, or instrument.

bass² (băs), *n., pl.* **basses,** (*esp. collectively*) **bass.**
any of various edible spiny-finned fishes, some
species of which (as the **black bass**) are prized as
game fish.

bass drum (băs), *Music.* the largest of the
drum family, having two membranes.

bas·set (băs′ĭt), *n.* a long-bodied, short-legged
dog resembling a dachshund but larger. Also, **bas-
set hound.**

bass horn (bās), *Music.* a tuba.

bas·si·net (băs′ə nĕt′, băs′ə nĕt′), *n.* a basket
with a hood over one end, used as a cradle.

bas·so (băs′ō, bäs′ō), *n., pl.* **-sos, -si** (-sē). one
who sings bass; a bass.

bas·soon (bă sōōn′, bə-), *n.* *Music.* a wood-
wind instrument in baritone range.

bass viol (bās), *Music.* viola da gamba (def.
1).

bass·wood (băs′wŏŏd′), *n.* a linden.

bast (băst), *n.* **1.** *Bot.* phloem. **2.** the inner bark
of the linden and other trees.

bas·tard (băs′tərd), *n.* **1.** an illegitimate child.
2. something irregular, inferior, spurious, etc.
—*adj.* **3.** illegitimate in birth. **4.** spurious; false.
5. of abnormal shape or size. —**bas′tar·dy,** *n.*

baste¹ (bāst), *v.t.,* **basted, basting.** to sew with
temporary stitches. —**bast′ing,** *n.*

baste² (bāst), *v.t.,* **basted, basting.** to moisten
(meat, etc.) while cooking, with drippings, etc.

baste³ (bāst), *v.t.,* **basted, basting. 1.** to beat
with a stick. **2.** to denounce vigorously.

Bas·tille (băs tēl′), *n.* a fortress in Paris, used
as a prison until destroyed July 14, 1789.

bas·tion (băs′chən, -tĭ ən), *n.* **1.** a projecting
portion of a fortification. **2.** a fortified place.
—**bas′tioned,** *adj.*

bat¹ (băt), *n., v.,* **batted, batting.** —*n.* **1.** *Sports.*
a. the club or racket used in certain games to
strike the ball. **b.** the right or turn to bat. **2.** a
club or cudgel. **3.** *Colloq.* a blow as with a bat.
4. *Slang.* a spree. —*v.t.* **5.** to strike with a bat.
—*v.i.* **6.** *Baseball, etc.* **a.** to strike at the ball with

the bat. **b.** to take one's turn as a batter. **7.** *Slang.* to rush.

bat² (băt), *n.* any of the nocturnal flying mammals, characterized by modified forelimbs which serve as wings.

bat³ (băt), *v.t.*, **batted, batting.** *Colloq.* to wink.

Ba·ta·an (ba tän'), *n.* a peninsula on W Luzon, in the Philippine Islands: U.S. troops surrendered to Japanese, 1942.

Ba·ta·vi·a (ba tā'vĭ a), *n.* a seaport in and the capital of the Dutch East Indies, on the NW coast of Java. 533,015.

batch (băch), *n.* **1.** the quantity of bread made at one baking. **2.** a single quantity. **3.** the quantity of material prepared or required for one operation.

bate (bāt), *v.t.*, **bated, bating.** **1.** to moderate or restrain (the breath). **2.** to lessen.

bath (băth, bäth), *n.*, *pl.* **baths** (băthz, bäthz), *v.* —*n.* **1.** a washing of the body in water, vapor, etc. **2.** the water or other agent used. **3.** a bathtub. **4.** a bathroom. **5.** a building containing rooms for bathing. **6.** a preparation, as an acid solution, in which something is immersed. —*v.t.* **7.** to put in a bath.

bathe (bāth), *v.*, **bathed, bathing,** *n.* —*v.t.* **1.** to immerse in water or other liquid for cleansing, etc. **2.** to moisten with any liquid. **3.** to apply liquid to. **4.** to cover with anything like water. —*v.i.* **5.** to take a bath. **6.** to swim for pleasure. **7.** to be covered as if with water. —*n.* **8.** *Brit.* act of bathing. —**bath'er,** *n.*

ba·thos (bā'thŏs), *n.* **1.** a ludicrous descent from the elevated. **2.** insincere pathos. —**ba·thet·ic** (ba thĕt'ĭk), *adj.*

bath·robe (băth'rōb', băth'-), *n.* a long, loose garment for wear in going to and from a bath.

bath·room (băth'rōōm', -rŏŏm', băth'-), *n.* **1.** a room fitted up for taking a bath. **2.** toilet.

bath·tub (băth'tŭb', băth'-), *n.* a tub to bathe in, in a bathroom.

ba·tik (ba tēk', băt'ĭk), *n.* **1.** a method of printing cloth using a wax deposit in the desired pattern. **2.** the fabric so decorated.

ba·tiste (ba tēst'), *n.* a delicate cotton fabric.

ba·ton (bă tŏn', băt'an), *n.* **1.** *Music.* the wand used by a conductor. **2.** a staff, etc., as a mark of office.

Bat·on Rouge (băt'an rōōzh'), the capital of Louisiana, in the SE part. 34,719.

ba·tra·chi·an (ba trā'kĭ an), *Zool.* —*adj.* **1.** of or pertaining to the genus including frogs, toads, etc. —*n.* **2.** a member of this genus.

bat·tal·ion (ba tăl'yan), *n.* **1.** *Mil.* a ground force unit composed of three or more companies. **2.** an army in battle array.

bat·ten¹ (băt'an), *v.i.*, *v.t.* to fatten or grow fat.

bat·ten² (băt'an), *n.* **1.** a light strip of wood used to fasten main members of a structure together. **2.** *Naut.* a strip of wood, as one to secure a tarpaulin over a hatchway. —*v.t.* **3.** to fasten (*down*) or furnish with battens.

bat·ter¹ (băt'ar), *v.t.* **1.** to beat persistently or hard. **2.** to damage by hard usage. —*v.i.* **3.** to deal heavy, repeated blows.

bat·ter² (băt'ar), *n.* a mixture of flour, milk or water, eggs, etc., beaten together in cookery.

bat·ter³ (băt'ar), *n.* *U.S.* one whose turn it is to bat. Also, *Brit.*, **bats'man.**

battering ram, an ancient military device with a heavy beam for battering down walls, etc.

bat·ter·y (băt'a rĭ), *n.*, *pl.* **-teries. 1.** *Elect.* a combination of two or more galvanic cells electrically connected to work together to produce electric energy. **2.** a set of similar machines, parts, or the like. **3.** *Mil.* **a.** a fortification equipped with artillery. **b.** two or more pieces of artillery for combined action. **4.** *Naval.* a group of guns on, or all the guns of, a vessel of war. **5.** *Baseball.* the pitcher and catcher together. **6.** act of beating. **7.** *Law.* an unlawful attack upon another by beating or wounding.

bat·ting (băt'ĭng), *n.* **1.** act of using a bat. **2.** cotton or wool in sheets, used in quilts.

bat·tle (băt'al), *n.*, *v.*, **-tled, -tling.** —*n.* **1.** a hostile encounter; fight. —*v.i.*, *v.t.* **2.** to engage in battle. **3.** to struggle. —**bat'tler,** *n.*

bat·tle-ax (băt'al ăks'), *n.* an ax for use in war. Also, **bat'tle-axe'.**

Battle Creek, a city in S Michigan. 43,453.

bat·tle·dore (băt'al dōr'), *n.*, *v.*, **-dored, -doring.** —*n.* **1.** a racket used in striking a shuttlecock in play. **2.** Also, **battledore and shuttlecock,** the game played with this racket and a shuttlecock. —*v.t.*, *v.i.* **3.** to toss to and fro.

bat·tle·field (băt'al fēld'), *n.* the field on which a battle is fought. Also, **bat'tle·ground'.**

bat·tle·ment (băt'al mant), *n.* (*often pl.*) *Archit.* an indented parapet, having a series of openings, orig. for shooting through.

bat·tle·ship (băt'al shĭp'), *n.* a warship of the most heavily armored and armed type.

bat·ty (băt'ĭ), *adj.*, **-tier, -tiest.** *Slang.* crazy.

bau·ble (bô'bal), *n.* a trinket; gewgaw.

baulk (bôk), *v.i.*, *v.t.*, *n.* balk.

baux·ite (bôk'sīt, bō'zīt), *n.* a rock consisting chiefly of aluminum oxide or hydroxide with various impurities: the principal ore of aluminum.

Ba·var·i·a (ba vâr'ĭ a), *n.* a state in S Germany. 8,222,982 pop.; 29,378 sq. mi. *Cap.*: Munich. —**Ba·var'i·an,** *adj.*, *n.*

bawd (bôd), *n.* a procuress or procurer.

bawd·y (bô'dĭ), *adj.*, **bawdier, bawdiest.** obscene. —**bawd'i·ly,** *adv.* —**bawd'i·ness,** *n.*

bawl (bôl), *v.t.*, *v.i.* **1.** to shout out. **2.** *U.S. Colloq.* to scold. —*n.* **3.** a loud shout. —**bawl'er,** *n.*

bay¹ (bā), *n.* an inlet of a sea or lake between two capes or headlands.

bay² (bā), *n.* **1.** *Archit.* **a.** the part of a window included between two mullions. **b.** a bay window. **2.** a compartment, as in a barn for storing hay, or in an airplane.

bay³ (bā), *n.* **1.** a deep, prolonged bark, as of a hound in hunting. **2.** a stand made by a hunted animal or person to face or repel pursuers. **3.** the position of the pursuers thus kept off. —*v.i.* **4.** to bark, esp. with a deep, prolonged sound. —*v.t.* **5.** to beset with deep, prolonged barking. **6.** to express by barking. **7.** to bring to bay.

bay⁴ (bā), *n.* **1.** the European laurel tree. **2.** a bayberry (def. 3).

bay⁵ (bā), *n.* **1.** reddish-brown. **2.** a bay horse. —*adj.* **3.** of the color bay.

bay·ber·ry (bā'bĕr'ĭ), *n.*, *pl.* **-ries. 1.** any of certain shrubs or trees of the myrtle family. **2.** the berry of such a plant. **3.** a West Indian tree whose leaves are used in making bay rum.

Bay City, a city in E Michigan. 47,956.

bay·o·net (bā'a nĭt), *n.*, *v.*, **-neted, -neting.** —*n.* **1.** a daggerlike instrument, attached at the muzzle of a rifle. —*v.t.* **2.** to kill or wound with the bayonet.

Ba·yonne (bā yōn'), *n.* a city in NE New Jersey. 79,198.

bay·ou (bī'ōō). *n.*, *pl.* **-ous.** *Southern U.S.* an arm or outlet of a lake, river, etc.

bay rum, a fragrant liquid used as a cosmetic, etc., esp. after shaving.

bay window, a window projecting outward from the wall of a building.

ba·zaar (ba zär'), *n.* **1.** a market place. **2.** any place for the sale of miscellaneous goods. **3.** a sale for some worthy purpose. Also, **ba·zar'.**

ba·zoo·ka (ba zōō'ka), *n.* *Mil.* a cylindrical rocket launcher, used esp. by infantry against tanks.

bbl., *pl.* **bbls.** barrel.

B.C., **1.** before Christ. **2.** British Columbia.

bd., *pl.* **bds. 1.** board. **2.** bond. **3.** bundle.

be (bē; *unstressed* bĭ), *v.*, *pres. indic. sing.* **am, are, is,** *pl.* **are;** *pt. indic.* **was, were, was,** *pl.* **were;** *pp.* **been;** *ppr.* **being.** —*substantive.* **1.** to exist; live; occur. —*copula.* **2.** (a link connecting a subject with predicate or qualifying words, or serving to form infinitive and participial phrases). —*auxiliary.* **3.** (used with the present participle of a principal verb to form the progressive tense, or with a past participle in passive forms, regularly of transitive verbs).

Be, *Chem.* beryllium.

B/E, bill of exchange. Also, **b.e.**

beach (bēch), *n.* **1.** the sand or pebbles of the seashore. **2.** that part of the shore washed by the waves. —*v.t.*, *v.i.* **3.** *Naut.* to run or haul up (a ship) on the beach. —**beach'less,** *adj.*

beach·comb·er (bēch'kō'mar), *n.* **1.** a vagrant around the beaches and wharves. **2.** a long, rolling wave.

beach·head (bēch'hĕd'), *n.* the first area seized by a military force landing on an enemy shore.

bea·con (bē'kan), *n.* **1.** a signal, such as a fire.

esp. one on a pole, tower, etc. **2.** a lighthouse, signal buoy, etc. **3.** a radio beacon. —*v.t., v.i.* **4.** to serve as a beacon (to).

bead (bēd), *n.* **1.** one of a string of small balls of glass, pearl, etc., used as an ornament or in a rosary. **2.** (*pl.*) a necklace. **3.** (*pl.*) a rosary. **4.** any small globular body or drop. **5.** a bubble rising through effervescent liquid. **6.** a mass of such bubbles on the surface of a liquid. **7.** the front sight of a gun. **8.** aim. **9.** *Archit., etc.* a narrow convex molding. —*v.t.* **10.** to ornament with beads. —*v.i.* **11.** to form beads.

bead·ing (bē′dĭng), *n.* material composed of or adorned with beads.

bea·dle (bē′dəl), *n. Eccles.* a parish officer having various subordinate duties.

bead·y (bē′dĭ), *adj.,* **beadier, beadiest. 1.** beadlike. **2.** covered with or full of beads.

bea·gle (bē′gəl), *n.* one of a breed of small hounds with short legs and drooping ears.

beak (bēk), *n.* **1.** the horny bill of a bird. **2.** a similar horny head part in animals, as in turtles, etc. **3.** anything pointed or like a beak. —**beaked** (bēkt, bē′kĭd), *adj.*

beak·er (bē′kər), *n.* a large glass.

beam (bēm), *n.* **1.** a thick and relatively long piece of timber, metal, stone, etc., shaped for use. **2.** one of the principal horizontal supporting members in a building, ship, or the like. **3.** *Naut.* the greatest breadth of a ship. **4.** the transverse bar of a balance. **5.** a ray, or bundle of parallel rays, of light or other radiation. **6.** a gleam. **7.** *Radio, Aeron.* a signal transmitted along a narrow course, used to guide pilots. —*v.t.* **8.** to emit in beams or rays. —*v.i.* **9.** to emit beams, as of light. **10.** to look or smile radiantly. —**beamed,** *adj.* —**beam′ing,** *adj.* —**beam′·less,** *adj.* —**beam′like′,** *adj.*

bean (bēn), *n.* **1.** the edible nutritious seed of various species of leguminous plants. **2.** a plant producing such seeds. **3.** any of various beanlike seeds or plants. **4.** *Slang.* head. —*v.t.* **5.** *Slang.* to hit on the head.

bear[1] (bâr), *v.,* **bore** or (*Archaic*) **bare, borne** or **born, bearing.** —*v.t.* **1.** to hold up; support. **2.** to carry. **3.** to guide; take. **4.** to press against. **5.** to render; give. **6.** to spread (gossip, etc.). **7.** to sustain without yielding or suffering injury. **8.** to undergo. **9.** to have as an obligation. **10.** to hold up under. **11.** to be worthy of. **12.** to have and be entitled to. **13.** to possess as a quality, etc. **14.** to stand in (a relation). **15.** to carry in the mind. **16.** to show. **17.** to have and use. **18.** to manage (oneself, etc.). **19.** to give birth to or produce by growth. **20.** to prove. —*v.i.* **21.** to remain firm, as under pressure. **22.** to be patient. **23.** to press. **24.** to have an effect or relation. **25.** to move; go. **26.** to bring forth young, fruit, etc.

bear[2] (bâr), *n., v.,* **beared, bearing.** —*n.* **1.** any of a family of mammals having massive bodies, coarse heavy fur, relatively short limbs, and almost rudimentary tails. **2.** any of various animals resembling the bear. **3.** a clumsy or rude person. **4.** *Stock Exchange.* one who sells short with the expectation of covering at a lower price. **5.** *Astron.* either of two constellations in the northern hemisphere, the **Great Bear** and the **Little Bear.** —*v.t.* **6.** *Stock Exchange, etc.* to operate in for a decline in price.

bear·a·ble (bâr′ə bəl), *adj.* capable of being borne. —**bear′a·bly,** *adv.*

beard (bîrd), *n.* **1.** the growth of hair on the face of an adult man. **2.** a tuft, growth, or part resembling a human beard. —*v.t.* **3.** to seize or pluck the beard of. **4.** to defy. —**beard′ed,** *adj.* —**beard′less,** *adj.* —**beard′like′,** *adj.*

bear·er (bâr′ər), *n.* **1.** a person or thing that carries, upholds, or brings. **2.** one who presents an order. **3.** a plant that yields fruit or flowers. **4.** the holder of rank.

bear·ing (bâr′ĭng), *n.* **1.** the manner in which a person carries himself. **2.** act, capability, or period of producing. **3.** a crop. **4.** act of enduring or capacity to endure. **5.** reference or relation. **6.** *Archit.* a supporting part. **7.** *Mach.* a part in which a journal, pivot, or the like, moves. **8.** (*often pl.*) direction or relative position. **9.** *Her.* any single device on a coat of arms.

bear·ish (bâr′ĭsh), *adj.* **1.** like a bear. **2.** causing a decline in price. —**bear′ish·ly,** *adv.*

bear·skin (bâr′skĭn′), *n.* **1.** the skin or pelt of a bear. **2.** a tall black fur cap worn esp. by soldiers.

beast (bēst), *n.* **1.** any animal except man. **2.** a coarse, filthy, or inhuman person. —**beast′like′,** *adj.*

beast·ly (bēst′lĭ), *adj.,* **-lier, -liest. 1.** bestial. **2.** *Brit. Colloq.* nasty. —**beast′li·ness,** *n.*

beat (bēt), *v.,* **beat, beaten** or **beat, beating,** *n.* —*v.t.* **1.** to strike repeatedly, as in chastising, etc. **2.** to dash against. **3.** to sound, as on a drum. **4.** to break, forge, or make, esp. by blows. **5.** *Music.* to mark (time) by strokes. **6.** *Hunting.* to scour (the forest, etc.) for game. **7.** to defeat. **8.** to be superior to. **9.** to be too difficult for. —*v.i.* **10.** to strike repeated blows. **11.** to throb. **12.** to dash. **13.** to resound under blows. **14.** to win. **15.** to play, as on a drum. **16.** to scour cover for game. —*n.* **17.** a blow. **18.** the sound made by it. **19.** a throb. **20.** one's habitual course. **21.** *Music.* **a.** the audible, visual, or mental marking of the metrical divisions of music. **b.** a stroke of the hand, baton, etc., marking time division or accent. —*adj.* **22.** *U.S. Colloq.* exhausted. —**beat′er,** *n.*

beat·en (bē′tən), *adj.* **1.** having undergone blows. **2.** much used. **3.** defeated. **4.** exhausted.

be·a·tif·ic (bē′ə tĭf′ĭk), *adj.* **1.** rendering blessed. **2.** blissful. —**be′a·tif′i·cal·ly,** *adv.*

be·at·i·fy (bĭ ăt′ə fī′), *v.t.,* **-fied, -fying. 1.** to make blissfully happy. **2.** *Rom. Cath. Ch.* to declare (a deceased person) to be among the blessed. —**be·at′i·fi·ca′tion,** *n.*

be·at·i·tude (bĭ ăt′ə tūd′, -tōōd′), *n.* **1.** supreme blessedness. **2.** (*often cap.*) any one of the declarations of blessedness by Christ in the Sermon on the Mount.

beau (bō), *n., pl.* **beaus, beaux** (bōz). **1.** a lover; swain. **2.** an escort. **3.** a fop.

Beau·mont (bō′mŏnt), *n.* a city in SE Texas. 77,335.

beau·te·ous (bū′tĭ əs), *adj. Chiefly Poetic.* beautiful. —**beau′te·ous·ly,** *adv.* —**beau′te·ous·ness,** *n.*

beau·ti·ful (bū′tə fəl), *adj.* having beauty; delighting the eye; admirable to the taste or the mind. —**beau′ti·ful·ly,** *adv.* —**beau′ti·ful·ness,** *n.*

beau·ti·fy (bū′tə fī′), *v.t., v.i.,* **-fied, -fying.** to make or become beautiful. —**beau′ti·fi·ca′tion,** *n.* —**beau′ti·fi′er,** *n.*

beau·ty (bū′tĭ), *n., pl.* **-ties. 1.** that quality of any object of thought whereby it excites an admiring pleasure. **2.** something beautiful, esp. a woman. **3.** a pleasing excellence.

bea·ver (bē′vər), *n.* **1.** an amphibious rodent, valued for its fur, noted for its ingenuity in damming streams with branches, stones, mud, etc. **2.** its fur. **3.** a hat made of beaver fur.

be·calm (bĭ käm′), *v.t.* **1.** (*usually in pp.*) to halt (a ship, etc.) by a lack of wind. **2.** to calm.

be·cause (bĭ kôz′, -kŏz′), *conj.* **1.** for the reason that. —*adv.* **2.** by reason; on account.

be·chance (bĭ chăns′, -chäns′), *v.i., v.t.,* **-chanced, -chancing.** to befall.

beck (bĕk), *n.* a beckoning gesture.

Beck·et (bĕk′ĭt), *n.* **Saint Thomas,** 1118?–70, Archbishop of Canterbury.

beck·on (bĕk′ən), *v.t., v.i.* **1.** to signal, summon, or direct by a gesture. **2.** to lure. —*n.* **3.** a beckoning. —**beck′on·er,** *n.*

be·cloud (bĭ kloud′), *v.t.* to obscure.

be·come (bĭ kŭm′), *v.,* **became, become, becoming.** —*v.i.* **1.** to come or grow to be. **2.** to be the fate (of). —*v.t.* **3.** to suit.

be·com·ing (bĭ kŭm′ĭng), *adj.* **1.** attractive. **2.** suitable. —**be·com′ing·ly,** *adv.*

bed (bĕd), *n., v.,* **bedded, bedding.** —*n.* **1.** a piece of furniture upon which a person sleeps. **2.** the mattress and bedclothes together with the bedstead. **3.** a piece of ground in which plants are grown. **4.** the bottom of a body of water. **5.** a piece or part forming a base. **6.** a rock layer. —*v.t.* **7.** to provide with a bed. **8.** to put to bed. **9.** *Hort.* to plant in a bed. **10.** to lay flat or in a layer. —*v.i.* **11.** to go to bed.

be·daub (bĭ dôb′), *v.t.* to besmear; soil.

be·daz·zle (bĭ dăz′əl), *v.t.,* **-zled, -zling.** to blind or confuse by dazzling.

bed·bug (bĕd′bŭg′), *n.* a small flat, wingless, hemipterous, bloodsucking insect that infests houses and esp. beds.

bed·clothes (bĕd′klōz′, -klōᵺz′), *n.pl.* coverings for a bed; sheets, blankets, etc.

bed·ding (bĕd′ĭng), *n.* **1.** blankets, sheets, etc., for a bed. **2.** straw, etc., as a bed for animals.

be·deck (bĭ dĕk′), *v.t.* to adorn showily.

be·dev·il (bĭ dĕv′əl), *v.t.,* **-iled, -iling** or (*Brit.*) **-illed, -illing. 1.** to torment. **2.** to bewitch. **3.** to confound. —**be·dev′il·ment,** *n.*

be·dew (bǐ dū′, -dōō′), v.t. to wet with dew.

bed·fel·low (bĕd′fĕl′ō), n. 1. a sharer of one's bed. 2. close companion.

be·dight (bǐ dīt′), v.t., -dight, -dight or -dighted, -dighting. Archaic. to deck out; array.

be·dim (bǐ dǐm′), v.t., -dimmed, -dimming. to make dim.

be·di·zen (bǐ dī′zən, -dǐz′ən), v.t. to dress or adorn gaudily. —be·di′zen·ment, n.

bed·lam (bĕd′ləm), n. 1. a scene of wild uproar and confusion. 2. a lunatic asylum.

Bed·ou·in (bĕd′ŏŏ ǐn), n. 1. an Arab of the desert, in Asia or Africa. 2. a nomad.

bed·pan (bĕd′păn′), n. 1. a toilet pan for persons confined to bed. 2. a warming pan.

be·drag·gle (bǐ drăg′əl), v.t., -gled, -gling. to make limp and soiled, as with wet or dirt.

bed·rid·den (bĕd′rǐd′ən), adj. confined to bed. Also, **bed′rid′**.

bed·rock (bĕd′rŏk′), n. 1. unbroken solid rock, overlaid by soil or rock fragments. 2. bottom layer. 3. any firm foundation.

bed·room (bĕd′rōōm′, -rŏŏm′), n. a sleeping room.

bed·side (bĕd′sīd′), n. 1. the side of a bed. —adj. 2. attending a sick person.

bed·sore (bĕd′sōr′), n. a sore due to prolonged contact with a bed, as in a long illness.

bed·spread (bĕd′sprĕd′), n. an outer covering, usually decorative, for a bed.

bed·stead (bĕd′stĕd′, -stǐd), n. the framework of a bed supporting the springs and a mattress.

bed·time (bĕd′tīm′), n. time to go to bed.

bee (bē), n. 1. any of various hymenopterous insects of the family which includes many social and solitary bees. 2. U.S. a local gathering for work, entertainment, etc.

bee·bread (bē′brĕd′), n. a protein food mixture, containing pollen, stored up by bees.

beech (bēch), n. 1. a tree of temperate regions having a smooth gray bark and bearing small edible triangular nuts (**beech′nuts′**). 2. its wood. —beech/en, adj.

beef (bēf), n., pl. **beeves** (bēvz) for 1; **beefs** for 5, -n. 1. a bull, cow, or steer, esp. one intended for meat. 2. the flesh of such an animal, used for food. 3. Colloq. brawn. 4. Colloq. weight. 5. U.S. Slang. a complaint. —v.i. 6. U.S. Slang. to complain.

beef·steak (bēf′stāk′), n. a slice of beef.

beef·y (bē′fǐ), adj. beefier, beefiest. fleshy; brawny; solid; heavy. —beef′i·ness, n.

bee·hive (bē′hīv′), n. a hive, conventionally dome-shaped, serving as a habitation for bees.

bee·line (bē′līn′), n. a direct line.

Be·el·ze·bub (bē ĕl′zə bŭb′), n. the devil.

beer (bǐr), n. 1. an alcoholic beverage made by brewing and fermentation from cereals, usually malted barley, and flavored with hops, etc. 2. any of various beverages, whether alcoholic or not.

Beer·she·ba (bǐr shē′bə, bǐr′shǐ-), n. a town near the southern tip of Biblical Palestine.

bees·wax (bēz′wăks′), n. wax secreted by bees, of which they construct their honeycomb.

beet (bēt), n. any of various biennial plants of a genus including the edible **red beet** and the **sugar beet**, which yields sugar. —beet′like′, adj.

Bee·tho·ven (bā′tō vən; Ger. bāt′hō fən), n. Ludwig van (lōōd′vĬKHn fän), 1770–1827, German composer.

bee·tle¹ (bē′təl), n. an insect characterized by having forewings modified as hard, horny structures, useless in flight.

bee·tle² (bē′təl), n., v., -tled, -tling. —n. 1. a heavy wooden mallet. —v.t. 2. to use a beetle on.

bee·tle³ (bē′təl), adj., v., -tled, -tling. —adj. 1. projecting. —v.i. 2. to project.

be·fall (bǐ fôl′), v., -fell, -fallen, -falling. —v.i. 1. to happen. —v.t. 2. to happen to.

be·fit (bǐ fǐt′), v.t., -fitted, -fitting. to be fitting or appropriate for; be suited to. —be·fit′ting, adj. —be·fit′ting·ly, adv.

be·fog (bǐ fŏg′, -fôg′), v.t., -fogged, -fogging. to involve in fog or obscurity; confuse.

be·fore (bǐ fōr′), adv. 1. in front; ahead. 2. in time preceding. 3. earlier. —prep. 4. in front of. 5. previously to. 6. in the future of. 7. in preference to. 8. in precedence of, as in rank. 9. in the presence of. 10. under the jurisdiction of.

—conj. 11. previously to the time when. 12. sooner than.

be·fore·hand (bǐ fōr′hănd′), adv., adj. in anticipation; in advance; ahead of time.

be·foul (bǐ foul′), v.t. to make foul; defile.

be·friend (bǐ frĕnd′), v.t. to act as a friend to.

be·fud·dle (bǐ fŭd′əl), v.t., -dled, -dling. 1. to make stupidly drunk. 2. to confuse.

beg (bĕg), v.t., v.i., begged, begging. 1. to ask for in charity. 2. to ask humbly or earnestly. 3. to take for granted without warrant.

be·get (bǐ gĕt′), v.t., begot or (Archaic) begat, begotten or begot, begetting. 1. to procreate. 2. to cause. —be·get′ter, n.

beg·gar (bĕg′ər), n. 1. one who begs alms. 2. a penniless person. 3. (in playful use) a rogue. —v.t. 4. to reduce to beggary. 5. to exhaust the resources of. —beg′gar·dom, beg′gar·hood′, n.

beg·gar·ly (bĕg′ər lǐ), adj. wretchedly poor.

beg·gar·y (bĕg′ə rǐ), n. utter poverty.

be·gin (bǐ gǐn′), v.i., v.t., began, begun, beginning. 1. to start. 2. to originate. —be·gin′ner, n.

be·gin·ning (bǐ gǐn′ǐng), n. 1. act or fact of starting. 2. the point at which anything begins. 3. the first part. 4. origin; source.

be·gird (bǐ gûrd′), v.t., -girt or -girded, -girding. to gird about; encompass; surround.

be·gone (bǐ gôn′, -gŏn′), v.i. to depart.

be·gon·ia (bǐ gōn′yə, -gō′nǐ ə), n. any plant of a tropical genus including species cultivated for their handsome leaves and waxy flowers.

be·grime (bǐ grīm′), v.t., -grimed, -griming. to make grimy.

be·grudge (bǐ grŭj′), v.t., -grudged, -grudging. 1. to be discontented at seeing (a person) have (something). 2. to be reluctant to give or allow.

be·guile (bǐ gīl′), v.t., -guiled, -guiling. 1. to delude. 2. to charm or divert. 3. to while away (time) pleasantly. —be·guile′ment, n. —be·guil′er, n.

be·guine (bǐ gēn′), n. 1. a South American dance in bolero rhythm. 2. music for this dance.

be·half (bǐ hăf′, -häf′), n. 1. side or part. 2. interest, favor, or aid.

be·have (bǐ hāv′), v., -haved, -having. —v.i. 1. to conduct oneself or itself. 2. to act properly. —v.t. 3. **behave oneself**, to conduct oneself in a specified way or properly.

be·hav·ior (bǐ hāv′yər), n. 1. manner of behaving. 2. the action of material. Also, Brit., be·hav′iour.

be·hav·ior·ism (bǐ hāv′yə rǐz′əm), n. Psychol. a theory that regards objective and accessible facts of behavior as the only proper subject for psychological study. —be·hav′ior·ist, n., adj. —be·hav′ior·is′tic, adj.

be·head (bǐ hĕd′), v.t. to cut off the head of.

be·hest (bǐ hĕst′), n. bidding or injunction.

be·hind (bǐ hīnd′), prep. 1. at the back of. 2. later than. 3. less advanced than. 4. on the farther side of. 5. supporting; promoting. 6. hidden or unrevealed by. —adv. 7. at or toward the back. 8. in a place, state, or stage already passed. 9. remaining; in reserve. 10. in arrears. 11. slow, as a watch.

be·hind·hand (bǐ hīnd′hănd′), adv., adj. 1. late. 2. in arrears.

be·hold (bǐ hōld′), v., beheld, beholding, interj. —v.t. 1. to look at; see. —interj. 2. look! see! —be·hold′er, n.

be·hold·en (bǐ hōl′dən), adj. obliged.

be·hoove (bǐ hōōv′), v.t., -hooved, -hooving. to be needful or proper for.

beige (bāzh), n. very light brown.

be·ing (bē′ǐng), n. 1. existence. 2. life. 3. lifetime. 4. substance or nature. 5. something that exists. 6. a human being. 7. (cap.) God.

Bei·rut (bā′rōōt, bā rōōt′), n. a seaport in and capital of Lebanon. 233,700.

be·jew·el (bǐ jōō′əl), v.t., -eled, -eling or (esp. Brit.) -elled, -elling. to adorn with jewels.

be·la·bor (bǐ lā′bər), v.t. 1. to beat vigorously. 2. to assail persistently.

be·lat·ed (bǐ lā′tǐd), adj. late; tardy. —be·lat′ed·ly, adv. —be·lat′ed·ness, n.

be·lay (bǐ lā′), v.t., v.i., -layed, -laying. 1. Naut. to fasten (a rope) by winding around a pin (belaying pin) or the like. 2. to stop.

belch (bĕlch), v.i. 1. to eject wind from the stomach through the mouth. 2. to emit contents violently. —*v.t.* **3.** to eject. —*n.* **4.** a belching. **5.** a burst of flame, gas, etc.

bel·dam (bĕl/dəm), *n.* hag. Also, **bel/dame.**

be·lea·guer (bĭ lē/gər), *v.t.* to surround, as with an army. —**be·lea/guer·er,** *n.*

Be·lém (bĕ lĕN/), *n.* a seaport in N Brazil, on the Pará river. 227,460.

Bel·fast (bĕl/făst, -făst), *n.* a seaport in and capital of Northern Ireland. 441,700.

bel·fry (bĕl/frĭ), *n., pl.* **-fries.** a bell tower, esp. one attached to a church.

Belg., 1. Belgian. **2.** Belgium.

Belgian Congo, a Belgian colony in central Africa. 10,600,000 pop.; 902,274 sq. mi. *Cap.:* Leopoldville.

Bel·gium (bĕl/jəm, -jĭ əm), *n.* a kingdom in W Europe, N of France. 8,344,534 pop.; 11,779 sq. mi. *Cap.:* Brussels. —**Bel·gian** (bĕl/jən, -jĭ ən), *n., adj.*

Bel·grade (bĕl grăd/, bĕl/grăd), *n.* the capital of Yugoslavia, in the E part. 238,775.

Be·li·al (bē/lĭ əl, bēl/yəl), *n.* the devil; Satan.

be·lie (bĭ lī/), *v.t.,* **-lied, -lying. 1.** to misrepresent. **2.** to show to be false. **3.** to fail to justify. **4.** to lie about. —**be·li/er,** *n.*

be·lief (bĭ lēf/), *n.* **1.** that which is believed. **2.** conviction of the truth or reality of a thing. **3.** faith; trust. **4.** a religious tenet.

be·lieve (bĭ lēv/), *v.,* **-lieved, -lieving.** —*v.i.* **1.** to trust. **2.** to accept a doctrine, system, etc. (fol. by *in*). —*v.t.* **3.** to accept as true. **4.** to think. —**be·liev/a·ble,** *adj.* —**be·liev/er,** *n.* —**be·liev/ing·ly,** *adv.*

be·lit·tle (bĭ lĭt/əl), *v.t.,* **-littled, -littling.** to make little or less important; disparage.

bell (bĕl), *n.* **1.** a metal instrument, typically cup-shaped with flaring mouth, struck to produce a metallic ringing sound. **2.** the sound of such an instrument. **3.** anything of the form of a bell. —*v.t.* **4.** to put a bell on. —*v.i.* **5.** to shape like a bell. —**bell/-like/,** *adj.*

Bell (bĕl), *n.* **Alexander Graham,** 1847–1922, U.S. scientist: invented telephone.

bel·la·don·na (bĕl/ə dŏn/ə), *n.* **1.** a poisonous plant of the nightshade family. **2.** a poisonous drug from this plant.

bell·boy (bĕl/boi/), *n.* U.S. an employee in a hotel who attends to the needs of guests.

bell buoy, *Naut.* a buoy having a bell hung on it to ring from the action of the waves.

belle (bĕl), *n.* a beautiful woman or girl.

belles-let·tres (bĕl lĕt/r), *n.pl.* the finer or higher forms of literature. —**bel·let·rist** (bĕl-lĕt/rĭst), *n.* —**bel·le·tris·tic** (bĕl/lĕ trĭs/tĭk), *adj.*

bell·hop (bĕl/hŏp/), *n.* U.S. Colloq. bellboy.

bel·li·cose (bĕl/ə kōs/), *adj.* warlike; pugnacious. —**bel/li·cose/ly,** *adv.*

bel·lig·er·ent (bə lĭj/ər ənt), *adj.* **1.** warlike; pugnacious. **2.** engaged in war. **3.** pertaining to war or those engaged in war. —*n.* **4.** a state or nation at war. —**bel·lig/er·ence, bel·lig/er·en·cy,** *n.* —**bel·lig/er·ent·ly,** *adv.*

bel·low (bĕl/ō), *v.i.* **1.** to make a hollow, loud cry, as a bull. **2.** to roar. —*v.t.* **3.** to utter in a loud deep voice. —*n.* **4.** act or sound of bellowing.

bel·lows (bĕl/ōz, -əs), *n. sing. and pl.* **1.** a device for producing a strong current of air, as for a draft for a fire, consisting essentially of a compressible air chamber. **2.** anything resembling a bellows.

bell·weth·er (bĕl/wĕth/ər), *n.* a male sheep which leads the flock, usually wearing a bell.

bel·ly (bĕl/ĭ), *n., pl.* **-lies,** *v.,* **-lied, -lying.** —*n.* **1.** the front or under part of a vertebrate body from the breastbone to the pelvis; the abdomen. **2.** the stomach. **3.** the inside of anything. **4.** a protuberant surface of anything. —*v.t., v.i.* **5.** to swell out.

be·long (bĭ lŏng/, -lŏng/), *v.i.* **1.** to have relation as a member, etc. **2. belong to, a.** to be the property of. **b.** to be a part of. **3.** to have the proper qualifications.

be·long·ing (bĭ lŏng/ĭng, -lŏng/-), *n.* **1.** something that belongs. **2.** (*pl.*) possessions.

be·lov·ed (bĭ lŭv/ĭd, -lŭvd/), *adj.* **1.** greatly loved. —*n.* **2.** one who is greatly loved.

be·low (bĭ lō/), *adv.* **1.** in or to a lower place; beneath. **2.** on or to a lower floor. **3.** on earth. **4.** in hell. **5.** at a later point. **6.** in a lower rank or grade. —*prep.* **7.** lower down than. **8.** lower in rank, rate, etc., than. **9.** too base to be worthy of.

belt (bĕlt), *n.* **1.** a band of flexible material for encircling the waist. **2.** any encircling band, strip, or stripe. **3.** *Ecol.* a region having distinctive characteristics. **4.** *Mach.* a flexible band connecting two or more wheels, or the like, to transmit motion or transport objects. —*v.t.* **5.** to gird or furnish with a belt. **6.** *Colloq.* to give a blow to. —**belt/less,** *adj.*

belt·ing (bĕl/tĭng), *n.* material for belts.

be·mire (bĭ mīr/), *v.t.,* **-mired, -miring. 1.** to soil with mire. **2.** to sink in mire.

be·moan (bĭ mōn/), *v.t., v.i.* to lament.

be·mused (bĭ mūzd/), *adj.* confused; muddled.

ben·a·dryl (bĕn/ə drĭl), *n.* *Pharm.* **1.** a synthetic drug used esp. to relieve hay fever and hives. **2.** (*cap.*) a trademark for this drug.

Be·na·res (bə nä/rĭz), *n.* a city in N India, on Ganges: holy city of Hinduism. 263,100.

bench (bĕnch), *n.* **1.** a long seat for several people. **2.** the seat on which judges sit in court. **3.** the position or office of a judge. **4.** the body of persons sitting as judges. **5.** the strong work table of a carpenter or mechanic. **6.** a flat, terracelike tract of land, as on a valley slope. —*v.t.* **7.** to furnish with benches. **8.** to seat on a bench.

bench warrant, *Law.* a warrant issued by a judge or court for the apprehension of an offender.

bend (bĕnd), *v.,* **bent** or (*Archaic*) **bended, bending,** *n.* —*v.t.* **1.** to bring (a bow, etc.) into a state of tension by curving it. **2.** to force into a curved shape. **3.** to cause to submit. **4.** to turn in a particular direction. **5.** to incline mentally. **6.** *Naut.* to fasten. —*v.i.* **7.** to become curved or crooked. **8.** to stoop. **9.** to bow in submission or reverence. **10.** to turn or incline in a particular direction. —*n.* **11.** act of bending. **12.** state of being bent. **13.** a bent thing or part. **14.** *Naut.* **a.** (*pl.*) the wales of a ship. **b.** a knot by which a rope is fastened. —**bend/a·ble,** *adj.*

bend·er (bĕn/dər), *n.* **1.** one who or that which bends. **2.** U.S. Slang. a drinking spree.

be·neath (bĭ nēth/, -nĕth/), *adv.* **1.** in a lower place, state, etc. **2.** underneath. —*prep.* **3.** below; under. **4.** further down than. **5.** lower down on a slope than. **6.** inferior in position, power, etc., to. **7.** unworthy of.

Ben·e·dic·i·te (bĕn/ə dĭs/ə tĭ), *n.* **1.** *Eccles.* the canticle beginning in Latin "Benedicite, omnia opera Domini." —*interj.* **2.** (*l.c.*) bless you!

ben·e·dict (bĕn/ə dĭkt), *n.* a newly married man, esp. one who has long been a bachelor.

Ben·e·dict (bĕn/ə dĭkt), *n.* **Saint,** A.D. 480?–543?, Italian monk: founded Benedictine order.

Ben·e·dic·tine (bĕn/ə dĭk/tĭn, -tēn, -tĭn *for 1;* bĕn/ə dĭk/tēn *for 2, 3*), *n.* **1.** *Rom. Cath. Ch.* a member of an order of monks founded by St. Benedict or of nuns following his rule (**Benedictine rule**). **2.** (*usually l.c.*) a French liqueur. —*adj.* **3.** pertaining to St. Benedict or an order following his rule.

ben·e·dic·tion (bĕn/ə dĭk/shən), *n.* **1.** act of uttering a blessing. **2.** the blessing by a minister. —**ben/e·dic/tion·al,** *adj.*

ben·e·fac·tion (bĕn/ə făk/shən), *n.* **1.** act of doing good. **2.** the benefit conferred.

ben·e·fac·tor (bĕn/ə făk/tər, bĕn/ə făk/-), *n.* one who confers a benefit. —**ben·e·fac·tress** (bĕn/ə făk/trĭs, bĕn/ə făk/-), *n. fem.*

ben·e·fice (bĕn/ə fĭs), *n., v.,* **-ficed, -ficing.** —*n.* **1.** an ecclesiastical living. **2.** the revenue itself. —*v.t.* **3.** to invest with a benefice or ecclesiastical living.

be·nef·i·cent (bə nĕf/ə sənt), *adj.* doing good or causing good to be done. —**be·nef/i·cence,** *n.* —**be·nef/i·cent·ly,** *adv.*

ben·e·fi·cial (bĕn/ə fĭsh/əl), *adj.* conferring benefit; helpful. —**ben/e·fi/cial·ly,** *adv.*

ben·e·fi·ci·ar·y (bĕn/ə fĭsh/ĭ ĕr/ĭ, -fĭsh/ə rĭ), *n., pl.* **-aries.** one who receives benefits, profits, or advantages.

ben·e·fit (bĕn/ə fĭt), *n., v.,* **-fited, -fiting.** —*n.* **1.** act of kindness. **2.** anything that is for the good of a person or thing. **3.** a performance or entertainment to raise money for a worthy purpose. —*v.t.* **4.** to do good to. —*v.i.* **5.** to gain advantage. —**ben/e·fit·er,** *n.*

Ben·e·lux (bĕn/ə lŭks), *n.* a customs union (since Jan. 1, 1948) of Belgium, the Netherlands, and Luxemburg.

Be·nes (bĕn/ĕsh), *n.* **Eduard,** 1884–1948, Czechoslovakian patriot and statesman.

be·nev·o·lent (bə nĕv/ə lənt), *adj.* **1.** desiring to do good for others. **2.** intended for benefits rather than profit. —**be·nev/o·lence,** *n.* —**be·nev/o·lent·ly,** *adv.*

be·night·ed (bĭ nī'tĭd), *adj.* unenlightened.

be·nign (bĭ nīn'), *adj.* **1.** kind. **2.** showing or caused by kindness. **3.** favorable; propitious. **4.** (of weather) salubrious. **5.** *Pathol.* not malignant. **—be·nign'ly,** *adv.*

be·nig·nant (bĭ nĭg'nənt), *adj.* **1.** kind, esp. to inferiors. **2.** beneficial. **3.** *Pathol.* benign. **—be·nig'nan·cy,** *n.* **—be·nig'nant·ly,** *adv.*

be·nig·ni·ty (bĭ nĭg'nə tĭ'), *n., pl.* **-ties. 1.** benign state or quality. **2.** a good deed.

Ben·ja·min (běn'jə mən), *n. Bible.* **1.** the youngest son of Jacob. **2.** a tribe of Israel.

Ben·nett (běn'ĭt), *n.* **(Enoch) Arnold,** 1867–1931, British novelist.

bent (běnt), *adj.* **1.** curved; crooked. **2.** determined; set (fol. by *on*). **—n. 3.** curved state or form. **4.** inclination. **5.** capacity of endurance.

Ben·tham (běn'thəm, -təm), *n.* **Jeremy,** 1748–1832, British jurist and philosopher.

Ben·ton (běn'tən), *n.* **Thomas Hart,** born 1889, U.S. painter.

be·numb (bĭ nŭm'), *v.t.* **1.** to make numb. **2.** to render inactive; stupefy.

Ben·ze·drine (běn'zə drēn', -drĭn), *n.* a trademark for amphetamine.

ben·zene (běn'zēn, běn zēn'), *n.* a colorless, volatile, inflammable, liquid aromatic hydrocarbon, C_6H_6, obtained chiefly from coal tar: used as a solvent and in the manufacture of dyes, etc.

ben·zine (běn'zēn, běn zēn'), *n.* a colorless, volatile, inflammable liquid, a mixture of various hydrocarbons, obtained in the distillation of petroleum: used in cleaning, dyeing, etc.

ben·zo·ate (běn'zō āt', -ĭt), *n.* a salt or ester of benzoic acid.

ben·zo·ic acid (běn zō'ĭk), a white, crystalline acid, C_6H_5COOH, obtained from benzoin, toluene, etc.: used in medicine, aniline dye manufacture, as a food preservative, etc.

ben·zoin (běn'zoin, -zō ĭn, běn zō'ĭn), *n.* a balsamic resin obtained from certain species of trees of Java, Sumatra, etc., and used in perfumery, medicine, etc.

Be·o·wulf (bā'ə wŏolf'), *n.* **1.** an English alliterative epic poem of the 8th century. **2.** its hero.

be·queath (bĭ kwēth', -kwēth'), *v.t.* **1.** to dispose by last will of. **2.** to hand down. **—be·queath·al** (bĭ kwē'thəl), *n.*

be·quest (bĭ kwěst'), *n.* **1.** a disposition in a will concerning property. **2.** a legacy.

be·rate (bĭ rāt'), *v.t.,* **-rat·ed, -rat·ing.** to scold.

Ber·ber (bûr'bər), *n.* a member of the North African tribes living mainly in Barbary.

be·reave (bĭ rēv'), *v.t.,* **-reaved** or **-reft, -reav·ing. 1.** to deprive (*of*) ruthlessly. **2.** to make desolate through loss (*of*), esp. by death. **—be·reave'ment,** *n.*

berg (bûrg), *n. Oceanog.* iceberg.

ber·ga·mot (bûr'gə mŏt'), *n.* **1.** a small tree of the citrus family, the rind of whose fruit yields a fragrant essential oil (**essence of bergamot**). **2.** the oil itself.

Ber·gen (bûr'gən), *n.* a seaport in SW Norway, on the Atlantic. 106,662.

Berg·son (bûrg'sən, běrg'-), *n.* **Henri,** 1859–1941, French philosopher.

ber·i·ber·i (běr'ĭ běr'ĭ), *n.* a disease of the peripheral nerves caused by deficiency in vitamin B_1: marked by pain in and paralysis of the extremities, and severe emaciation or swelling.

Ber·ing Sea (bĭr'ĭng, bâr'-), a part of the N Pacific, N of the Aleutian Islands.

Bering Strait, the strait between Alaska and the Soviet Union in Asia. 36 mi. wide.

Berke·ley (bûrk'lĭ), *n.* a city in W California, on San Francisco Bay. 100,024.

Ber·lin (bər lĭn'), *n.* the capital of Germany, in the NE part. 4,339,756.

Ber·li·oz (běr'lĭ ōz'), *n.* **Louis Hector,** 1803–69, French composer.

Ber·mu·da (bər mū'də), *n.* a group of islands in the Atlantic, 580 miles E of North Carolina: a British colony; resort. 33,925 pop.; 19 sq. mi. *Cap.:* Hamilton. Also, **Bermudas. —Ber·mu·di·an** or **Ber·mu'dĭ'ən),** *adj., n.*

Bern (bûrn), *n.* the capital of Switzerland, in the W part. 133,700. Also, **Berne.**

Bern·hardt (bûrn'härt), *n.* **Sarah,** (*Rosine Bernard*) 1845–1923, French actress.

ber·ry (běr'ĭ), *n., pl.* **-ries,** *v.,* **-ried, -ry·ing. —n. 1.** any small, (usually) stoneless, juicy fruit, as the strawberry, etc. **2.** a dry seed or kernel, as of wheat. **3.** *Bot.* a simple fruit having a pulpy

pericarp in which the seeds are embedded, as the tomato, etc. **—v.i. 4.** to produce berries. **5.** to gather berries.

ber·serk (bûr'sûrk), *adj.* violently and destructively frenzied.

berth (bûrth), *n.* **1.** a shelflike sleeping space allotted to a passenger in a vessel or railroad car. **2.** room for a vessel to moor at a dock or to ride at anchor. **3.** *Brit.* job. **—v.t. 4.** *Naut.* to assign anchoring ground to. **—v.i. 5.** *Naut.* to come to a dock or anchorage.

Ber·wyn (bûr'wĭn), *n.* a city in NE Illinois, near Chicago. 48,451.

ber·yl (běr'əl), *n.* a mineral, beryllium aluminum silicate, usually green and either opaque or transparent, the latter including emeralds and aquamarines.

be·ryl·li·um (bĭ rĭl'ĭ əm), *n. Chem.* a steelgray, divalent, hard, light, metallic element: used in copper alloys for springs and contacts. *Symbol:* Be; *at. wt.:* 9.02; *at. no.:* 4; *sp. gr.:* 1.8 at 20°C.

be·seech (bĭ sēch'), *v.t.,* **-sought, -seech·ing. 1.** to implore urgently. **2.** to beg eagerly for. **—be·seech'er,** *n.* **—be·seech'ing·ly,** *adv.*

be·seem (bĭ sēm'), *v.t.* **1.** to be fit for or worthy of. **—v.i. 2.** to be seemly or fitting.

be·set (bĭ sět'), *v.t.,* **-set, -set·ting. 1.** to attack on all sides. **2.** to surround. **3.** to place upon.

be·side (bĭ sīd'), *prep.* **1.** by or at the side of. **2.** compared with. **3.** in addition to. **4.** not connected with. **5. beside oneself,** out of one's senses through strong emotion. **—adv. 6.** in addition.

be·sides (bĭ sīdz'), *adv.* **1.** moreover. **2.** in addition. **3.** otherwise; else. **—prep. 4.** in addition to. **5.** other than; except.

be·siege (bĭ sēj'), *v.t.,* **-sieged, -sieg·ing.** to lay siege to. **—be·sieg'er,** *n.*

be·smear (bĭ smĭr'), *v.t.* to smear over; soil.

be·smirch (bĭ smûrch'), *v.t.* to soil; defile.

be·som (bē'zəm), *n.* **1.** brush or twigs bound together as a broom. **2.** a broom of any kind.

be·sot (bĭ sŏt'), *v.t.,* **-sot·ted, -sot·ting. 1.** to make a drunkard of. **2.** to make stupid.

be·span·gle (bĭ spăng'gəl), *v.t.,* **-gled, -gling.** to adorn with or as with spangles.

be·spat·ter (bĭ spăt'ər), *v.t.* **1.** to soil with spattered dirt, water, etc. **2.** to slander.

be·speak (bĭ spēk'), *v.t.,* **-spoke** or (*Archaic*) **-spake, -spoken** or **-spoke, -speak·ing. 1.** to ask for in advance. **2.** *Brit.* to reserve beforehand. **3.** *Poetic.* to speak to. **4.** to indicate.

Bes·se·mer process (běs'ə mər), a process of producing steel, in which impurities are removed by a blast of air through molten iron.

best (běst), *adj.* (*superlative of* **good**). **1.** of the highest quality or standing. **2.** most suitable or desirable. **3.** largest. **—adv.** (*superlative of* **well**). **4.** most excellently or suitably. **5.** most fully. **6. had best,** would be wiser, etc. **—n. 7.** the best thing, state, or part. **8.** one's finest clothing. **9.** utmost quality. **—v.t. 10.** to defeat. **11.** to surpass.

bes·tial (běs'chəl, běst'yəl), *adj.* **1.** of or belonging to a beast. **2.** brutal; inhuman. **3.** carnal. **—bes·ti·al·i·ty** (běs'chĭ' ăl'ə tĭ, -tĭ' ăl'-), *n.* **—bes'tial·ly,** *adv.*

be·stir (bĭ stûr'), *v.t.,* **-stirred, -stir·ring.** to stir up; rouse to action.

best man, the chief attendant of the bridegroom at a wedding.

be·stow (bĭ stō'), *v.t.* **1.** to present; confer. **2.** to apply. **3.** to put; store. **—be·stow'al,** *n.* **—be·stow'ment,** *n.*

be·strew (bĭ strōō'), *v.t.,* **-strewed, -strewed** or **-strewn, -strew·ing. 1.** to cover (a surface). **2.** to scatter about. **3.** to lie scattered over.

be·stride (bĭ strīd'), *v.t.,* **-strode** or **-strid, -stridden** or **-strid, -strid·ing. 1.** to get or be astride of. **2.** to step across.

best seller, 1. a book that has a very large sale in a given period. **2.** the author of such a book.

bet (bět), *v.,* **bet** or **betted, betting,** *n.* **—v.t., v.i. 1.** to pledge as a forfeit in support of an opinion; wager. **—n. 2.** that which is pledged. **—bet'ter, bet'tor,** *n.*

bet., between.

be·ta (bā'tə, bē'-), *n.* the 2nd letter of the Greek alphabet (B, β), often used to designate the second in a series.

be·take (bĭ tāk'), *v.t.,* **-took, -taken, -taking. —betake oneself, 1.** to go. **2.** to resort to.

beta particle, *Physics.* an electron in a beta ray.

beta ray, *Physics.* a ray emitted by radium and other radioactive substances, resembling the cathode ray and consisting of electrons.

be·ta·tron (bā′tə trŏn′, bē′-), *n.* a device which accelerates electrons to high energy by a magnetic field varying with time.

Be·tel·geuse (bē′təl jōōz′, bĕt′əl jœz′), *n.* a giant star in the constellation Orion.

be·tel nut (bē′təl), the nut of the **betel palm** (a tall Asiatic tree), chewed extensively with lime by East Indian natives.

Beth·a·ny (bĕth′ə nĭ), *n.* a village in central Israel, near Jerusalem.

beth·el (bĕth′əl), *n.* a church for seamen.

Be·thes·da (bə thĕz′də), *n. Bible.* a pool with healing powers in Jerusalem.

be·think (bĭ thĭngk′), *v.t.,* **-thought, -thinking.** (generally reflexive) **1.** to think. **2.** to remember.

Beth·le·hem (bĕth′lĭ əm, -hĕm′), *n.* **1.** a town in central Palestine, near Jerusalem: birthplace of Jesus and David. 8820. **2.** a city in E Pennsylvania. 58,490.

be·tide (bĭ tīd′), *v.,* **-tided, -tiding.** *—v.t.* **1.** to happen. *—v.i.* **2.** to come to pass.

be·times (bĭ tīmz′), *adv.* **1.** early. **2.** soon.

be·to·ken (bĭ tō′kən), *v.t.* to indicate.

be·tray (bĭ trā′), *v.t.* **1.** to deliver or expose to an enemy by treachery. **2.** to be unfaithful in keeping. **3.** to be disloyal to. **4.** to reveal unintentionally. **5.** to show. **6.** to deceive. **7.** to seduce and desert. **—be·tray′al,** *n.* **—be·tray′er,** *n.*

be·troth (bĭ trōth′, -trôth′), *v.t.* **1.** to promise to marry. **2.** to arrange the marriage of.

be·troth·al (bĭ trō′thəl, -trô′thəl), *n.* act of betrothing. Also, **be·troth′ment.**

bet·ter (bĕt′ər), *adj.* (*comparative of* **good**). **1.** of superior quality. **2.** of superior value, use, etc. **3.** larger; greater. **4.** healthier. *—adv.* (*comparative of* **well**). **5.** in a more excellent way. **6.** in a superior degree. **7.** more. **8. had better,** would be wiser, etc., to. *—v.t.* **9.** to improve. *—n.* **10.** that which has superior excellence, etc. **11.** (*usually pl.*) one's superior in wisdom, etc. **12.** superiority; mastery. **—bet′ter·ment,** *n.*

be·tween (bĭ twēn′), *prep.* **1.** in the space separating (two objects, etc.). **2.** intermediate to, as in time, quantity, or degree. **3.** connecting. **4.** involving. **5.** by joint action or possession of. *—adv.* **6.** in the intervening space or time.

be·twixt (bĭ twĭkst′), *prep., adv. Archaic and Poetic.* between.

bev·el (bĕv′əl), *n., v.,* **-eled, -eling** or (*esp. Brit.*) **-elled, -elling,** *adj.* *—n.* **1.** the inclination that one line or surface makes with another when not at right angles. **2.** an adjustable instrument for drawing angles, etc. *—v.t., v.i.* **3.** to cut or slant at a bevel. *—adj.* **4.** oblique.

bev·er·age (bĕv′ər ĭj, bĕv′rĭj), *n.* a drink of any kind.

bev·y (bĕv′ĭ), *n., pl.* **bevies. 1.** a flock of birds. **2.** a group, esp. of girls.

be·wail (bĭ wāl′), *v.t., v.i.* to lament.

be·ware (bĭ wâr′), *v.i., v.t.,* **-wared, -waring.** to be wary, cautious, or careful (*of*).

be·wil·der (bĭ wĭl′dər), *v.t.* to confuse or puzzle completely. **—be·wil′dered,** *adj.* **—be·wil′dered·ly,** *adv.* **—be·wil′der·ing,** *adj.* **—be·wil′der·ing·ly,** *adv.* **—be·wil′der·ment,** *n.*

be·witch (bĭ wĭch′), *v.t.* **1.** to affect by witchcraft or magic. **2.** to enchant. **—be·witch′er,** *n.* **—be·witch′er·y,** *n.* **—be·witch′ing,** *adj.* **—be·witch′ing·ly,** *adv.* **—be·witch′ment,** *n.*

be·yond (bĭ yŏnd′), *prep.* **1.** on or to the farther side of. **2.** farther on than. **3.** later than. **4.** outside the understanding, limits, or reach of. **5.** superior to; above. **6.** more than. *—adv.* **7.** farther on or away. *—n.* **8.** the life after the present one.

b.f., *Printing.* boldface. Also, **bf.**

Bi, *Chem.* bismuth.

bi·an·nu·al (bī ăn′yōō əl), *adj.* occurring twice a year. **—bi·an′nu·al·ly,** *adv.*

bi·as (bī′əs), *n., adj., adv., v.,* **biased, biasing** or (*esp. Brit.*) **biassed, biassing.** *—n.* **1.** an oblique line of direction, esp. across a woven fabric. **2.** prejudice. *—adj.* **3.** cut, set, etc., diagonally. *—adv.* **4.** slantingly. *—v.t.* **5.** to prejudice.

bib (bĭb), *n.* article of clothing worn by a child, esp. while eating, to protect the dress.

Bib., 1. Bible. **2.** Biblical.

Bibl., Biblical. Also, **bibl.**

Bi·ble (bī′bəl), *n.* **1.** the collection of sacred writings of Christianity, comprising the Old and New Testaments. **2.** the Old Testament only.

Bib·li·cal (bĭb′lə kəl), *adj.* of, in, or in accord with the Bible. **—Bib′li·cal·ly,** *adv.*

bibliog., bibliography.

bib·li·og·ra·phy (bĭb′lĭ ŏg′rə fĭ), *n., pl.* **-phies. 1.** a compilation of a list of books, etc., on a particular subject. **2.** the art of describing books with respect to authorship, format, etc. **—bib′li·og′ra·pher,** *n.* **—bib·li·o·graph·ic** (bĭb′lĭ ə grăf′ĭk), **bib′li·o·graph′i·cal,** *adj.*

bib·li·o·phile (bĭb′lĭ ə fīl′, -fĭl), *n.* a lover of books. Also, **bib·li·o·phil** (bĭb′lĭ ə fĭl).

bib·u·lous (bĭb′yə ləs), *adj.* **1.** addicted to alcoholic drinking. **2.** absorbent; spongy. **—bib′u·lous·ly,** *adv.* **—bib′u·lous·ness,** *n.*

bi·cam·er·al (bī kăm′ər əl), *adj.* having two branches or houses, as a legislative body.

bi·car·bo·nate (bī kär′bə nĭt, -nāt′), *n.* a salt of carbonic acid, containing the HCO_3^{-1} radical.

bi·cen·te·nar·y (bī sĕn′tə nĕr′ĭ, bī′sĕn tĕn′ə-rĭ), *adj., n., pl.* **-naries.** *Chiefly Brit.* bicentennial.

bi·cen·ten·ni·al (bī′sĕn tĕn′ĭ əl), *adj.* **1.** consisting of or lasting 200 years. **2.** occurring every 200 years. *—n.* **3.** a 200th anniversary. **4.** its celebration.

bi·ceps (bī′sĕps), *n.* a muscle having two heads of origin, as (in man) the muscle on the front of the upper arm, which bends the forearm.

bi·chlo·ride (bī klōr′īd, -ĭd), *n. Chem.* **1.** a compound in which two atoms of chlorine are combined with another element or radical. **2.** corrosive sublimate.

bick·er (bĭk′ər), *v.i., n.* squabble.

bi·cus·pid (bī kŭs′pĭd), *adj.* **1.** Also, **bi·cus·pi·date** (bī kŭs′pĭ dāt′). having two points. *—n.* **2.** one of eight such teeth in man.

bi·cy·cle (bī′sə kəl, -sĭk′əl), *n., v.,* **-cled, -cling.** *—n.* **1.** a vehicle with two wheels, one in front of the other, and a saddlelike seat. *—v.i.* **2.** to ride a bicycle. **—bi′cy·cler, bi′cy·clist,** *n.*

bid (bĭd), *v.,* **bade** or **bad** (for 1, 2) or **bid** (for 3–6), **bidden** or **bid, bidding,** *n.* *—v.t.* **1.** to command; direct. **2.** to say, as a greeting. **3.** to offer, as a price at an auction. **4.** *Cards.* to enter (a bid) of a given quantity or suit. *—v.i.* **5.** to make an offer to purchase at a price. **6. bid fair,** to seem likely. *—n.* **7.** act of one who bids. **8.** *Cards.* **a.** the number of points or tricks a player offers to make. **b.** the turn of a person to bid. **9.** *Colloq.* an invitation. **10.** an attempt to attain some goal. **—bid′da·ble,** *adj.* **—bid′der,** *n.*

bid·ding (bĭd′ĭng), *n.* invitation or order.

bide (bīd), *v.t.,* **bided, biding.** **—bide one's time,** to wait for an opportunity.

bi·en·ni·al (bī ĕn′ĭ əl), *adj.* **1.** happening every two years. **2.** *Bot.* completing its normal term of life in two years. *—n.* **3.** any biennial event. **4.** *Bot.* a biennial plant. **—bi·en′ni·al·ly,** *adv.*

bier (bĭr), *n.* a stand on which a corpse or coffin is laid before burial.

biff (bĭf), *U.S. Slang. n., v.t.* punch.

bi·fo·cal (bī fō′kəl), *adj.* **1.** having two foci. **2.** (of eyeglass lenses) having two portions, one for near and one for far vision. *—n.* **3.** (*pl.*) eyeglasses with bifocal lenses.

bi·fur·cate (bī′fər kāt′, bī fûr′kāt), *v.,* **-cated, -cating,** *adj.* *—v.t., v.i.* **1.** to divide into two branches. *—adj.* **2.** divided into two branches. **—bi·fur·ca′tion,** *n.*

big (bĭg), *adj.,* **bigger, biggest,** *adv.* *—adj.* **1.** large in size, amount, etc. **2.** pregnant. **3.** filled. **4.** important in influence, wealth, etc. **5.** haughty; boastful. **6.** generous; kindly. **7.** loud. *—adv.* **8.** *Colloq.* boastfully. **—big′gish,** *adj.* **—big′ly,** *adv.* **—big′ness,** *n.*

big·a·my (bĭg′ə mĭ), *n. Law.* the crime of marrying while one has a wife or husband still living, from whom no valid divorce has been effected. **—big′a·mist,** *n.* **—big′a·mous,** *adj.* **—big′a·mous·ly,** *adv.*

Big Dipper, *Astron.* the Dipper.

big game, 1. large animals, esp. when hunted for sport. **2.** an important prize.

big·horn (bĭg′hôrn′), *n., pl.* **-horn, -horns.** a wild sheep of the Rocky Mountains, with large, curving horns.

bight (bīt), *n.* **1.** the part of a rope between the ends. **2.** the loop of a rope. **3.** a bend in the shore of a sea or a river. **4.** a bay. *—v.t.* **5.** to fasten with a bight of rope.

big·ot (bĭg′ət), *n.* a bigoted person.

big·ot·ed (bĭg′ə tĭd), *adj.* intolerantly convinced of a particular creed, etc. —**big′ot·ed·ly**, *adv.*

big·ot·ry (bĭg′ə trĭ), *n.*, *pl.* **-ries.** bigoted conduct, action, or attitude.

big·wig (bĭg′wĭg′), *n. Colloq.* an important person.

bi·jou (bē′zhōō), *n.*, *pl.* **-joux** (-zhōōz). **1.** a jewel. **2.** something small and choice.

bike (bīk), *n.*, *v.*, **biked, biking.** *Colloq.* bicycle.

Bi·ki·ni (bē kē′nē), *n.* an atoll in the N Pacific, in Marshall Islands: atomic bomb tests.

bi·la·bi·al (bī lā′bĭ əl), *Phonet.* —*adj.* **1.** pronounced with the two lips brought close together or touching. —*n.* **2.** a bilabial speech sound, as *p, b, m,* and *w.*

bi·lat·er·al (bī lăt′ər əl), *adj.* **1.** pertaining to, affecting, or arranged by two or both sides. **2.** disposed on opposite sides of an axis; two-sided. —**bi·lat′er·al·ism, bi·lat′er·al·ness,** *n.* —**bi·lat′er·al·ly,** *adv.*

Bil·ba·o (bēl bä′ō), *n.* a seaport in N Spain, near the Bay of Biscay. 208,000.

bil·ber·ry (bĭl′bĕr′ĭ), *n.*, *pl.* **-ries.** the edible fruit of the shrub of several species of the heath family.

bile (bīl), *n.* **1.** a bitter yellow liquid secreted by the liver to aid digestion. **2.** ill nature.

bilge (bĭlj), *n.*, *v.*, **bilged, bilging.** —*n.* **1.** *Naut.* **a.** the approximately flat under portion of a ship's hull. **b.** the lowest portion of a ship's interior. **c.** Also, **bilge water.** foul water that collects in a ship's bilge. **2.** the wider part of a cask. —*v.i.* **3.** *Naut.* to spring a leak in the bilge. —*v.t.* **4.** to break in the bilge of. —**bilg′y,** *adj.*

bil·i·ar·y (bĭl′ĭ ĕr′ĭ), *adj.* **1.** *Physiol.* **a.** of bile. **b.** conveying bile. **2.** *Pathol.* bilious.

bi·lin·gual (bī lĭng′gwəl), *adj.* **1.** able to speak one's native language and another with equal facility. **2.** expressed or contained in two languages. —*n.* **3.** a bilingual person. —**bi·lin′·gual·ly,** *adv.*

bil·ious (bĭl′yəs), *adj.* **1.** *Physiol., Pathol.* pertaining to bile or to an excess secretion of bile. **2.** *Pathol.* suffering from, caused by, or attended by trouble with the bile or liver. **3.** peevish. —**bil′ious·ly,** *adv.* —**bil′ious·ness,** *n.*

-bility, a suffix forming nouns from adjectives in *-ble,* as in *nobility.*

bilk (bĭlk), *v.t.* **1.** to evade payment of (a debt). **2.** to frustrate. **3.** to elude. —*n.* **4.** a trick; fraud. **5.** a cheater; swindler. —**bilk′er,** *n.*

bill¹ (bĭl), *n.* **1.** an account of money owed for goods or services supplied. **2.** a bill of exchange. **3.** *U.S.* a piece of paper money. **4.** a draft of a proposed statute presented to a legislature. **5.** a written or printed public notice or advertisement. **6.** any written paper containing a statement of particulars. **7.** *Law.* a written statement, usually of complaint, presented to a court. **8.** a printed theater program or the like. **9.** entertainment. —*v.t.* **10.** to make a bill or list of. **11.** to charge for by bill. **12.** to announce by public notice. **13.** to schedule on a program.

bill² (bĭl), *n.* **1.** that part of the jaws of a bird covered with a horny sheath; a beak. —*v.i.* **2.** to join bills or beaks, as doves.

bill³ (bĭl), *n.* a medieval shafted weapon with a broad hook-shaped blade.

bill·board (bĭl′bōrd′), *n. U.S.* a board on which advertisements are posted.

bil·let¹ (bĭl′ĭt), *n.*, *v.*, **-leted, -leting.** —*n.* **1.** lodging for a soldier, esp. in private buildings. **2.** *Mil.* an official order directing a person to provide lodging for a soldier. **3.** job; appointment. —*v.t.* **4.** to provide lodging for; quarter.

bil·let² (bĭl′ĭt), *n.* **1.** a small thick stick of wood, esp. one cut for fuel. **2.** a bar or slab of iron or steel, esp. when obtained from an ingot by forging, etc.

bil·let-doux (bĭl′ĭ dōō′, bĭl′ā-), *n.*, *pl.* **billets-doux** (-dōōz′). a love letter.

bill·fold (bĭl′fōld′), *n. U.S.* a wallet.

bill·head (bĭl′hĕd′), *n.* a printed heading on paper for making out bills.

bil·liards (bĭl′yərdz), *n.* a game played on a rectangular table enclosed by a ledge, with balls (**billiard balls**) of ivory or other hard material, driven by cues. —**bil′liard,** *adj.* —**bil′liard·ist,** *n.*

bil·lings·gate (bĭl′ĭngz gāt′; *esp. Brit.* -gĭt), *n.* coarse language or abuse.

bil·lion (bĭl′yən), *n.* **1.** *U.S.* a thousand millions. **2.** *Brit.* a million millions. —**bil′lionth,** *adj., n.*

bill of exchange, a written order to pay a specified sum to a specified person.

bill of fare, a menu.

bill of health, a certificate as to the health of a ship's company.

bill of lading, a written receipt given by a carrier for goods accepted for transportation.

bill of rights, 1. a formal statement of the fundamental rights of the people. **2.** (*cap.*) such a statement incorporated in the Constitution as Amendments 1–10.

bill of sale, a document transferring title in personal property from seller to buyer.

bil·low (bĭl′ō), *n.* **1.** a great wave or surge of the sea. **2.** any surging mass. —*v.i.* **3.** to rise or roll in billows; surge.

bil·low·y (bĭl′ō ĭ), *adj.,* **-lowier, -lowiest.** full of billows; surging. —**bil′low·i·ness,** *n.*

bil·ly (bĭl′ĭ), *n.*, *pl.* **-lies. 1.** *Colloq.* a policeman's club. **2.** a small cudgel.

billy goat, a male goat.

bi·me·tal·lic (bī′mə tăl′ĭk), *adj.* **1.** of or pertaining to two metals. **2.** pertaining to bimetallism.

bi·met·al·lism (bī mĕt′ə lĭz′əm), *n.* the use of gold and silver at a fixed relative value, as the monetary standard. —**bi·met′al·list,** *n.*

bi·month·ly (bī mŭnth′lĭ), *adj., n., pl.* **-lies,** *adv.* —*adj.* **1.** occurring every two months. **2.** semimonthly. —*n.* **3.** a bimonthly publication. —*adv.* **4.** every two months. **5.** semimonthly.

bin (bĭn), *n.*, *v.*, **binned, binning.** —*n.* **1.** a box or enclosed place used for storing grain, coal, and the like. —*v.t.* **2.** to store in a bin.

bi·na·ry (bī′nə rĭ), *adj., n., pl.* **-ries.** —*adj.* **1.** consisting of, indicating, or involving two. —*n.* **2.** a whole composed of two.

binary star, *Astron.* a system of two stars revolving round a common center of gravity.

bind (bīnd), *v.*, **bound, binding,** *n.* —*v.t.* **1.** to make fast with a band. **2.** to encircle with a band. **3.** to bandage. **4.** to cause to cohere. **5.** to unite by any legal or moral tie. **6.** to hold to a particular state, place, obligation, etc. **7.** *Law.* to put under legal obligation. **8.** *Pathol.* to constipate. **9.** to fasten within a cover, as a book. —*v.i.* **10.** to become compact or solid. **11.** to be obligatory. **12.** to tie up anything. —*n.* **13.** something that binds.

bind·er (bīn′dər), *n.* **1.** person or thing that binds. **2.** a detachable cover for loose papers. **3.** a bookbinder. **4.** *Agric.* an attachment to a harvester or reaper for binding the cut grain.

bind·er·y (bīn′də rĭ), *n.*, *pl.* **-eries.** an establishment for binding books.

bind·ing (bīn′dĭng), *n.* **1.** act of fastening or uniting. **2.** anything that binds. **3.** the covering within which the leaves of a book are bound. **4.** a strip that protects or adorns the edge of cloth, etc. —*adj.* **5.** obligatory. —**bind′ing·ly,** *adv.*

Bing·ham·ton (bĭng′əm tən), *n.* a city in S New York, on the Susquehanna river. 78,309.

bin·go (bĭng′gō), *n.* a game similar to lotto.

bin·na·cle (bĭn′ə kəl), *n. Naut.* a special stand built in the hull for the compass and fitted with lights by which the compass can be read at night.

bin·oc·u·lar (bə nŏk′yə lər, bī-), *adj.* **1.** involving two eyes. —*n.* **2.** (*often pl.*) a field glass. —**bin·oc′u·lar·i·ty,** *n.* —**bin·oc′u·lar·ly,** *adv.*

bi·no·mi·al (bī nō′mĭ əl), *Alg.* —*n.* **1.** an expression which is a sum or difference of two terms. —*adj.* **2.** consisting of or pertaining to a binomial. —**bi·no′mi·al·ly,** *adv.*

biochem., biochemistry.

bi·o·chem·is·try (bī′ō kĕm′ĭs trĭ), *n.* the chemistry of living matter. —**bi′o·chem′i·cal**, *adj.* —**bi′o·chem′i·cal·ly,** *adv.*

biog., **1.** biographical. **2.** biography.

bi·og·ra·phy (bī ŏg′rə fĭ), *n.*, *pl.* **-phies. 1.** a written account of a person's life. **2.** such writings collectively. —**bi·og′ra·pher,** *n.* —**bi·o·graph·i·cal** (bī′ə grăf′ə kəl), **bi′o·graph′ic,** *adj.* —**bi′o·graph′i·cal·ly,** *adv.*

biol., **1.** biological. **2.** biology.

bi·o·log·i·cal (bī′ə lŏj′ə kəl), *adj.* **1.** Also, **bi′o·log′ic.** pertaining to biology or to the products and operations of applied biology. —*n.* **2.** any biochemical product. —**bi′o·log′i·cal·ly,** *adv.*

bi·ol·o·gy (bī ŏl′ə jĭ), *n.* the science of life or living matter in all its forms and phenomena. —**bi·ol′o·gist,** *n.*

bi·par·ti·san (bī pär′tə zən), *adj.* representing two parties. —**bi·par′ti·san·ship′,** *n.*

bi·par·tite (bī pär′tīt), *adj.* divided into two parts. —**bi·par′tite·ly**, *adv.* —**bi·par·ti·tion** (bī′pär tĭsh′ən), *n.*

bi·ped (bī′pĕd), *Zool.* —*n.* 1. a two-footed animal. —*adj.* 2. having two feet.

bi·plane (bī′plān′), *n.* an airplane with two wings, one above and usually slightly forward of the other.

birch (bûrch), *n.* 1. any tree of a genus comprising species with a smooth, laminated outer bark and close-grained wood. 2. the wood itself. 3. a birch rod, or a bundle of birch twigs, used as a whip. —*adj.* 4. of birch. —*v.t.* 5. to beat with a birch. —**birch·en** (bûr′chən), *adj.*

bird (bûrd), *n.* 1. any of a class of warm-blooded vertebrates having a feathered body and forelimbs modified to form wings. 2. *Slang.* a person, esp. one having some peculiarity. 3. *Slang.* a sound of derision. —**bird′like′**, *adj.*

bird·lime (bûrd′līm′), *n.*, *v.*, **-limed, -liming.** —*n.* 1. a sticky material, generally prepared from holly, smeared on twigs to catch small birds that light on it. —*v.t.* 2. to smear or catch with birdlime.

bird of paradise, any bird of a family found in New Guinea, etc., noted for magnificent plumage.

bird of passage, a bird that migrates seasonally.

bird of prey, any of numerous predacious, flesh-eating birds such as the eagles.

bird′s-eye (bûrdz′ī′), *adj.* 1. seen from above. 2. general. 3. having spots resembling birds' eyes. —*n.* 4. a fabric, either cotton or linen, used for diapers or toweling.

bi·ret·ta (bə rĕt′ə), *n.* a stiff, square cap worn by Roman Catholic ecclesiastics.

Bir·ken·head (bûr′kən hĕd′, bûr′kən hĕd′), *n.* a seaport in W England, opposite Liverpool. 131,900.

Bir·ming·ham (bûr′mĭng əm *for 1*; -hăm′ *for 2*), *n.* 1. a city in central England. 1,063,000. 2. a city in central Alabama. 267,583.

birth (bûrth), *n.* 1. fact of being born. 2. act of bearing; parturition. 3. lineage; descent. 4. high or noble lineage. 5. supposedly natural heritage. 6. that which is born. 7. any coming into existence; origin.

birth·day (bûrth′dā′), *n.* 1. (of persons) the day of one's birth. 2. (of things) beginning. 3. the anniversary of one's birth.

birth·mark (bûrth′märk′), *n.* a congenital mark on the body.

birth·place (bûrth′plās′), *n.* place of birth.

birth rate, the proportion of births in a place in a given time to the total population.

birth·right (bûrth′rīt′), *n.* any right or privilege to which a person is entitled by birth.

Bis·cay (bĭs′kā, -kĭ), *n.* **Bay of,** a large bay of the Atlantic between W France and N Spain.

bis·cuit (bĭs′kĭt), *n.* 1. *U.S.* a kind of bread in small, soft cakes, raised with baking powder or the like. 2. *Brit.* a cracker. —**bis′cuit-like′**, *adj.*

bi·sect (bī sĕkt′), *v.t.* 1. to cut or divide into two parts. 2. *Geom.* to divide into two equal parts. —*v.i.* 3. to split into two. —**bi·sec′tion,** *n.* —**bi·sec′tion·al,** *adj.* —**bi·sec′tion·al·ly,** *adv.* —**bi·sec′tor,** *n.*

bish·op (bĭsh′əp), *n.* 1. an overseer over a number of local churches or a diocese. 2. *Chess.* a piece which moves obliquely on squares of the same color. —**bish′op·less,** *adj.*

bish·op·ric (bĭsh′əp rĭk), *n.* the see, diocese, or office of a bishop.

Bis·marck (bĭz′märk), *Ger.* bĭs′-), *n.* 1. **Otto von** (ō′tō fən), 1815–98, German statesman. 2. the capital of North Dakota, in the central part. 15,496.

bis·muth (bĭz′məth), *n.* *Chem.* a brittle, metallic element, used in medicine. *Symbol:* Bi; *at. no.:* 83; *at. wt.:* 209.00; *sp. gr.:* 9.8 at 20° C. —**bis′muth·al,** *adj.*

bi·son (bī′sən, -zən), *n.*, *pl.* **-son.** a large North American bovine ruminant (American bison, or buffalo), with high, well-haired shoulders.

American bison
(10 to 12 ft. long
ab. 6 ft. high at the shoulder)

bisque (bĭsk), *n.* any smooth and creamy soup.

bis·tro (bĭs′trō), *n.* *Colloq.* 1. a small, unpretentious tavern or café. 2. a bartender.

bit¹ (bĭt), *n.*, *v.*, **bitted, bitting.** —*n.* 1. the metallic mouthpiece of a bridle. 2. anything that curbs or restrains. 3. the movable drilling part in a carpenter's brace. —*v.t.* 4. to put a bit in the mouth of. 5. to restrain.

bit² (bĭt), *n.* 1. a small piece or quantity. 2. a short time. 3. *U.S. Colloq.* 12½ cents.

bitch (bĭch), *n.* 1. a female dog. 2. *Vulgar.* a woman, esp. a disagreeable or lewd one. —*v.i.* 3. *Slang.* to complain. —*v.t.* 4. *Slang.* to bungle.

bite (bīt), *v.*, **bit, bitten,** or **bit, biting.** —*v.t.* 1. to cut (*into, off, out,* etc.) with the teeth. 2. to grip with the teeth. 3. to pierce. 4. to sting. 5. to cause to smart. 6. to corrode, as an acid. —*v.i.* 7. to press the teeth (*into, on,* etc.). 8. (of fish) to take the bait. 9. to accept a deceptive offer or suggestion. —*n.* 10. act of biting. 11. a wound made by biting. 12. a cutting, stinging, or nipping effect. 13. a piece bitten off. 14. food. 15. a small meal. —**bit′er,** *n.*

bit·ing (bī′tĭng), *adj.* 1. nipping. 2. sarcastic. —**bit′ing·ly,** *adv.* —**bit′ing·ness,** *n.*

bitt (bĭt), *Naut.* —*n.* 1. a strong post projecting (usually in pairs) above the deck of a ship, and used for securing cables, etc. —*v.t.* 2. to put round the bitts.

bit·ter (bĭt′ər), *adj.* 1. having a harsh, disagreeable taste. 2. hard to receive. 3. hard to bear. 4. causing pain. 5. characterized by intense animosity. 6. harsh; sarcastic. —*n.* 7. that which is bitter. —*v.t.* 8. to make bitter. —**bit′ter·ish,** *adj.* —**bit′ter·ly,** *adv.* —**bit′ter·ness,** *n.*

bit·tern (bĭt′ərn), *n.* any of several herons of North America and Europe.

bit·ters (bĭt′ərz), *n.pl.* a liquor in which bitter herbs or roots are steeped.

bit·ter·sweet (*n.* bĭt′ər swēt′; *adj.* bĭt′ər-swēt′), *n.* 1. the woody nightshade, a climbing or trailing poisonous plant with scarlet berries. 2. a climbing plant of a genus with orange capsules opening to expose red-coated seeds. —*adj.* 3. both bitter and sweet to the taste. 4. both pleasant and painful.

bi·tu·men (bī′ tū′mən, -tōō′-, bĭch′ōō-), *n.* any of various natural substances, as asphalt, etc., consisting mainly of hydrocarbons. —**bi·tu′mi·nous,** *adj.*

bi·va·lent (bī vā′lənt, bĭv′ə-), *adj.* *Chem.* 1. having a valence of two. 2. having two valences. —**bi·va′lence, bi·va′len·cy,** *n.*

bi·valve (bī′vălv′), *Zool.* —*n.* 1. a mollusk having two shells hinged together, as the oyster, clam, or mussel. —*adj.* 2. having two shells, usually united by a hinge. —**bi·val·vu·lar** (bī-văl′vyə lər), *adj.*

biv·ou·ac (bĭv′ōō ăk′, bĭv′wăk), *n.*, *v.*, **-acked, -acking.** —*n.* 1. an area in the field where troops rest or assemble, usually in tents or temporary housing. —*v.i.* 2. to rest or assemble in such an area.

bi·week·ly (bī wēk′lĭ), *adj.*, *n.*, *pl.* **-lies,** *adv.* —*adj.* 1. occurring every two weeks. 2. semiweekly. —*n.* 3. a periodical issued every other week. —*adv.* 4. every two weeks. 5. twice a week.

bi·zarre (bĭ zär′), *adj.* strange; odd. —**bi·zarre′ly,** *adv.* —**bi·zarre′ness,** *n.*

Bi·zet (bē zā′), *n.* **Georges,** 1838–75, French composer.

Bi·zo·ni·a (bī zō′nĭ ə, bī-), *n.* the combined U.S. and British zones of occupation in Germany after World War II.

bk., 1. bank. 2. book.

blab (blăb), *v.*, **blabbed, blabbing.** —*v.t., v.i.* 1. to reveal or talk indiscreetly and thoughtlessly. —*n.* 2. idle, indiscreet chattering. 3. a person who blabs. —**blab′ber,** *n.*

black (blăk), *adj.* 1. without brightness or color. 2. wearing black or dark clothing, etc. 3. *Anthropol.* pertaining or belonging to an ethnic group characterized by dark skin pigmentation. 4. soiled with dirt. 5. characterized by absence of light. 6. gloomy. 7. boding ill. 8. wicked. 9. without milk or cream. —*n.* 10. a member of a dark-skinned people, as a Negro. 11. black clothing. 12. *Chess, Checkers.* the dark-colored pieces. 13. black pigment. 14. **in the black,** financially solvent. —*v.t.* 15. to make black. 16. to polish with blacking. 17. *Mil.* to obscure by concealing all light in defense against air raids (fol. by *out*). —*v.i.* 18. to become black. 19. to lose consciousness. —**black′ish,** *adj.* —**black′ish·ly,** *adv.* —**black′ness,** *n.*

black·a·moor (blăk/ə mŏŏr/), *n.* **1.** a Negro. **2.** any dark-skinned person.

black art, witchcraft; magic.

black·ball (blăk/bôl/), *n.* **1.** an adverse vote. —*v.t.* **2.** to vote against. **3.** to ostracize.

black bass, an American fresh-water fish.

black·ber·ry (blăk/bĕr/ĭ), *n., pl.* **-ries. 1.** the fruit, dark purple when ripe, of certain species of the rose family. **2.** the plant.

black·bird (blăk/bûrd/), *n.* one of various black-feathered birds of the American family which includes the **crow blackbird.**

black·board (blăk/bôrd/), *n.* a smooth dark board for writing or drawing with chalk.

Black Death, bubonic plague.

black·en (blăk/ən), *v.,* **-ened, -ening.** —*v.t.* **1.** to make black; darken. **2.** to defame. —*v.i.* **3.** to grow or become black. —**black/en·er,** *n.*

black eye, discoloration of the skin around the eye, resulting from a blow, etc.

black-eyed Su·san (blăk/īd/ sŏŏ/zən), any of a number of plants having flowers with a dark center against a lighter, usually yellow, background.

black·guard (blăg/ärd, -ərd), *n.* **1.** a coarse, despicable person. —*v.t.* **2.** to revile in scurrilous language. —*v.i.* **3.** to behave like a blackguard. —**black/guard·ism,** *n.* —**black/guard·ly,** *adj., adv.*

Black Hand, a criminal secret society.

black·head (blăk/hĕd/), *n.* a small black-tipped, fatty mass in a follicle of the face.

black·ing (blăk/ĭng), *n.* any preparation for a black finish on shoes, stoves, etc.

black·jack (blăk/jăk/), *n.* **1.** a short club, usually leather-covered, consisting of a heavy head on an elastic shaft. **2.** the black flag of a pirate. **3.** a small oak of the eastern U.S., with a nearly black bark. —*v.t.* **4.** to strike or beat with a blackjack.

black·leg (blăk/lĕg/), *n.* **1.** an infectious, generally fatal disease of cattle and sheep characterized by painful, gaseous swellings in the muscles. **2.** a swindler.

black list, a list of persons under suspicion, disfavor, censure, etc.

black-list (blăk/lĭst/), *v.t.* to put on a black list.

black·ly (blăk/lĭ), *adv.* with a black or dark appearance; darkly; gloomily; wickedly.

black magic, magic used for evil purposes.

black·mail (blăk/māl/), *n.* **1.** any payment extorted by intimidation. **2.** the extortion of such payment. —*v.t.* **3.** to extort blackmail from. —**black/mail/er,** *n.*

black market, an illegal market violating price controls, rationing, etc.

black·out (blăk/out/), *n.* **1.** the extinguishing of all visible lights in a city, etc., as a war protection. **2.** unconsciousness.

Black Sea, a sea of S of E Europe, bounded by the Soviet Union, Turkey, Rumania, and Bulgaria. ab. 164,000 sq. mi.

Black Shirt, a member of a fascist organization in Europe.

black·smith (blăk/smĭth/), *n.* **1.** a person who shoes horses. **2.** an artisan who works in iron.

black·snake (blăk/snāk/), *n.* **1.** a strong, agile, nonvenomous snake of the U.S. **2.** *U.S.* a heavy whip of braided cowhide. Also, **black snake.**

black widow, a poisonous female spider, common in the U.S., that eats its mate.

blad·der (blăd/ər), *n.* **1.** a pelvic sac for urine secreted by the kidneys. **2.** any similar sac. —**blad/der·like/,** *adj.* —**blad/der·y,** *adj.*

blade (blād), *n.* **1.** the flat cutting part of a sword, knife, etc. **2.** the leaf of a plant. **3.** a thin, flat part, as of an oar. **4.** a dashing young fellow. —**blad/ed,** *adj.* —**blade/like/,** *adj.*

Blake (blāk), *n.* **William,** 1757–1827, British poet and artist.

blam·a·ble (blā/mə bəl), *adj.* deserving blame. —**blam/a·ble·ness,** *n.* —**blam/a·bly,** *adv.*

blame (blām), *v.,* **blamed, blaming,** *n.* —*v.t.* **1.** to lay the responsibility of (a fault, etc.) on a person. **2.** to find fault with. —*n.* **3.** censure. **4.** responsibility for censure. —**blame/ful,** *adj.* —**blame/ful·ly,** *adv.* —**blame/ful·ness,** *n.* —**blame/less,** *adj.* —**blame/less·ly,** *adv.* —**blame/less·ness,** *n.*

blame·wor·thy (blām/wûr/thĭ), *adj.* deserving blame. —**blame/wor/thi·ness,** *n.*

blanch (blănch, blänch), *v.t.* **1.** to whiten. **2.** to make pale. —*v.i.* **3.** to become white; turn pale. —**blanch/er,** *n.*

blanc·mange (blə mänzh/, -mäNzh/), *n.* a pudding made with cornstarch, gelatin, or the like.

bland (blănd), *adj.* **1.** gentle or agreeable. **2.** balmy. **3.** nonirritating. —**bland/ly,** *adv.* —**bland/ness,** *n.*

blan·dish (blăn/dĭsh), *v.t.* to coax; flatter. —**blan/dish·er,** *n.* —**blan/dish·ment,** *n.*

blank (blăngk), *adj.* **1.** (of paper, etc.) not written or printed on. **2.** not filled out. **3.** unrelieved by ornament or opening. **4.** lacking some usual feature. **5.** void of interest, results, etc. **6.** showing no attention or emotion. **7.** disconcerted. **8.** complete. **9.** white or pale. —*n.* **10.** a place where something is lacking. **11.** a space in a printed form to be filled in. **12.** a printed form containing such spaces. **13.** *Mach.* a piece of metal to be stamped or cut into a finished object. —*v.t.* **14.** to make blank or void. **15.** *Colloq.* to keep from scoring in a game. —**blank/ly,** *adv.* —**blank/ness,** *n.*

blan·ket (blăng/kĭt), *n.* **1.** a large rectangular fabric, used esp. as a bedcovering. **2.** any thin, extended covering. —*v.t.* **3.** to cover with or as with a blanket. —*adj.* **4.** covering a group of things, conditions, etc.

blank verse, 1. unrhymed verse. **2.** unrhymed iambic pentameter verse.

blare (blâr), *v.,* **blared, blaring,** *n.* —*v.i.* **1.** to emit a loud raucous sound. —*v.t.* **2.** to sound loudly. —*n.* **3.** a loud raucous noise.

blar·ney (blär/nĭ), *n., v.,* **-neyed, -neying.** —*n.* **1.** flattering talk. —*v.t., v.i.* **2.** to ply with blarney; wheedle.

bla·sé (blä zā/, blä/zā), *adj.* indifferent to and bored by pleasures or life.

blas·pheme (blăs fēm/), *v.,* **-phemed, -pheming.** —*v.t.* **1.** to speak irreverently of (God or sacred things). **2.** to speak evil of. —*v.i.* **3.** to utter impious words. —**blas·phem/er,** *n.*

blas·phe·my (blăs/fə mĭ), *n., pl.* **-mies.** impious utterance or action concerning God or sacred things. —**blas/phe·mous,** *adj.* —**blas/phe·mous·ly,** *adv.*

blast (blăst, bläst), *n.* **1.** a sudden gust of wind. **2.** the blowing of a trumpet, etc. **3.** the sound produced by this. **4.** a forcible stream of air from bellows or the like. **5.** *Metall.* air under pressure directed into a furnace, etc., to support combustion. **6.** the charge of explosive used at one firing. **7.** explosion. **8.** any destructive influence. —*v.t.* **9.** to blow (a trumpet, etc.). **10.** to blight. **11.** to destroy. **12.** to tear (rock, etc.) to pieces with an explosive. —*v.i.* **13.** to be blighted. —**blast/er,** *n.*

bla·tant (blā/tənt), *adj.* **1.** loud-mouthed; offensively noisy. **2.** obtrusive. **3.** bleating. —**bla/tan·cy,** *n.* —**bla/tant·ly,** *adv.*

blaze[1] (blāz), *n., v.,* **blazed, blazing.** —*n.* **1.** a bright flame or fire. **2.** a bright, hot gleam or glow. **3.** a sparkling brightness. **4.** a sudden, intense outburst, as of fury. **5.** (*pl.*) *Slang.* hell. —*v.i.* **6.** to burn or shine brightly. —*v.t.* **7.** to exhibit vividly.

blaze[2] (blāz), *n., v.,* **blazed, blazing.** —*n.* **1.** a mark made on a tree, as to indicate a boundary. **2.** a white spot on the face of a horse, cow, etc. —*v.t.* **3.** to mark with blazes.

blaze[3] (blāz), *v.t.,* **blazed, blazing.** to make known; proclaim; publish.

blaz·er (blā/zər), *n.* a bright-colored jacket worn by tennis players and others.

bla·zon (blā/zən), *v.t.* **1.** to display; proclaim. **2.** to describe or depict in heraldic terminology. —*n.* **3.** armorial bearings. —**bla/zon·er,** *n.* —**bla/zon·ment, bla/zon·ry,** *n.*

bldg., building.

-ble, var. of **-able,** as in *noble.*

bleach (blēch), *v.t., v.i.* **1.** to make or become white. —*n.* **2.** a bleaching agent.

bleach·ers (blē/chərz), *n.pl.* a roofless stand for spectators at games.

bleak (blēk), *adj.* **1.** bare, desolate, and wind-swept. **2.** cold and piercing. **3.** dreary. —**bleak/ly,** *adv.* —**bleak/ness,** *n.*

blear (blĭr), *v.t.* **1.** to make (the eyes or sight) dim, as with tears. —*adj.* **2.** (of the eyes) dim from a watery discharge. —*n.* **3.** a bleared state. —**blear/y,** *adj.* —**blear/i·ness,** *n.*

bleat (blēt), *v.i.* **1.** to cry as a sheep, goat, or calf. —*n.* **2.** such a cry. —**bleat/er,** *n.*

bleed (blēd), *v.,* **bled** (blĕd), **bleeding.** —*v.i.* **1.** a to lose blood. **2.** to cause blood to flow. **3.** to feel pity, sorrow, or anguish. —*v.t.* **4.** to cause to lose blood. **5.** to lose (blood). **6.** *Colloq.* to extort money from.

bleed·er (blē′dər), *n.* a hemophiliac.

blem·ish (blĕm′ĭsh), *v.t.* **1.** to destroy the perfection of. —*n.* **2.** a defect; stain. —**blem′ish·er,** *n.*

blench[1] (blĕnch), *v.i.* to shrink; flinch.

blench[2] (blĕnch), *v.i., v.t.* to blanch.

blend (blĕnd), *v.,* **blended** or **blent, blending,** *n.* —*v.t., v.i.* **1.** to mix smoothly and inseparably together. —*n.* **2.** act or manner of blending. **3.** a mixture produced by blending.

bless (blĕs), *v.t.,* **blessed** or **blest, blessing. 1.** to consecrate. **2.** to request divine favor on. **3.** to bestow good upon. **4.** to extol as holy.

bless·ed (blĕs′ĭd, blĕst), *adj.* **1.** consecrated. **2.** supremely fortunate; happy. **3.** beatified. **4.** bringing happiness. —**bless′ed·ly,** *adv.* —**bless′ed·ness,** *n.*

bless·ing (blĕs′ĭng), *n.* **1.** act or words of one who blesses. **2.** a special favor, mercy, or benefit, esp. one bestowed by God.

blight (blīt), *n.* **1.** a widespread and destructive plant disease. **2.** any cause of ruin or frustration. —*v.t.* **3.** to cause to wither or decay. **4.** to ruin. —*v.i.* **5.** to suffer blight.

blimp (blĭmp), *n.* a small, nonrigid airship or dirigible, used chiefly for observation.

blind (blīnd), *adj.* **1.** lacking sight. **2.** unwilling or unable to understand. **3.** not controlled by reason. **4.** not possessing or proceeding from intelligence. **5.** lacking all awareness. **6.** drunk. **7.** hard to see or understand. **8.** hidden from view. **9.** having no outlet. **10.** done without seeing. **11.** made without knowledge in advance. **12.** of or pertaining to blind persons. —*v.t.* **13.** to make blind. **14.** to make obscure or dark. —*n.* **15.** something that obstructs vision or keeps out light. **16.** a cover for masking action or purpose. —**blind′ing,** *adj.* —**blind′ing·ly,** *adv.* —**blind′ly,** *adv.* —**blind′ness,** *n.*

blind·er (blīn′dər), *n.* a blinker for a horse.

blind·fold (blīnd′fōld′), *v.t.* **1.** to cover the eyes of. —*n.* **2.** a bandage over the eyes. —*adj.* **3.** with eyes covered.

blink (blĭngk), *v.i.* **1.** to wink, esp. rapidly and repeatedly. **2.** to ignore. **3.** to twinkle. —*v.t.* **4.** to cause to blink. —*n.* **5.** a blinking. **6.** a gleam.

blink·er (blĭngk′ər), *n.* **1.** a device for flashing light signals. **2.** either of two flaps on a bridle, to prevent a horse from seeing sidewise or backward.

bliss (blĭs), *n.* **1.** lightness of heart; gladness. **2.** supreme happiness. —**bliss′ful,** *adj.* —**bliss′ful·ly,** *adv.* —**bliss′ful·ness,** *n.*

blis·ter (blĭs′tər), *n.* **1.** a thin vesicle on the skin, containing watery matter, as from a burn. **2.** any similar swelling, as on paint. —*v.t., v.i.* **3.** to raise a blister or blisters (on). —**blis′ter·y,** *adj.*

blithe (blīth, blīth), *adj.* joyous, merry, or gay in disposition; cheerful. —**blithe′ly,** *adv.* —**blithe′some,** *adj.*

blitz (blĭts), *n.* **1.** war waged by surprise, swiftly and violently, as by aircraft, tanks, etc. —*v.t.* **2.** to attack with a blitz. Also, **blitz·krieg** (blĭts′krēg′).

bliz·zard (blĭz′ərd), *n.* a violent windstorm with dry, driving snow and intense cold.

bloat (blōt), *v.t., v.i.* **1.** to swell, as with air, water, etc. **2.** to make conceited.

blob (blŏb), *n.* a small lump, drop, or daub.

bloc (blŏk), *n.* a coalition of factions or parties for a particular purpose.

block (blŏk), *n.* **1.** a solid mass of wood, stone, etc. **2.** a mold on which something is shaped. **3.** a piece of wood for engraving. **4.** a platform on which a person is beheaded. **5.** a platform from which an auctioneer sells. **6.** a device consisting of grooved pulleys in a casing or shell, to which a hook or the like is attached, used for transmitting power, etc. **7.** an obstacle. **8.** *Sports.* a hindering of an opponent's actions. **9.** a quantity or portion taken as a unit. **10.** *U.S.* a portion of a city, etc., enclosed by neighboring and intersecting streets. **11.** *U.S.* the length of one side of this. —*v.t.* **12.** to mount on a block. **13.** to prepare on or with a block. **14.** to outline roughly. **15.** to obstruct. **16.** *Football.* to bump (an opponent) out of the play. —*v.i.* **17.** to obstruct an opponent, as in football, etc. —**block′·er,** *n.*

block·ade (blŏ kād′), *n., v.,* **-aded, -ading.** —*n.* **1.** the shutting up of a place by hostile ships

or troops to prevent entrance or exit. **2.** any obstruction of passage. —*v.t.* **3.** to subject to a blockade. —**block·ad′er,** *n.*

block·bust·er (blŏk′bŭs′tər), *n.* *Colloq.* an aerial bomb weighing 4 to 8 tons.

block·head (blŏk′hĕd′), *n.* a stupid fellow.

block·house (blŏk′hous′), *n.* a fortified structure with ports or loopholes for gunfire.

block·y (blŏk′ĭ), *adj.,* **blockier, blockiest. 1.** stocky. **2.** marked by patches.

blond (blŏnd), *adj.* **1.** (of hair, skin, etc.) light-colored. **2.** having light-colored hair and skin. —*n.* **3.** a blond person. —**blonde,** *adj., n. fem.* —**blond′ness,** *n.*

blood (blŭd), *n.* **1.** the red fluid that circulates in the arteries and veins. **2.** life. **3.** bloodshed; murder. **4.** the juice or sap of plants. **5.** temper or state of mind. **6.** extraction. —**blood′like′,** *adj.*

blood·ed (blŭd′ĭd), *adj.* **1.** having blood. **2.** (of horses, etc.) having a good pedigree.

blood·hound (blŭd′hound′), *n.* one of a breed of large, powerful dogs with a very acute sense of smell, used for tracking fugitives, etc.

blood·less (blŭd′lĭs), *adj.* **1.** pale. **2.** free from bloodshed. —**blood′less·ly,** *adv.*

blood money, 1. a fee to a murderer. **2.** money paid to survivors of a slain man.

blood plasma, the liquid part of human blood, often stored in hospitals, etc., (**blood banks)** for transfusions.

blood poisoning, a morbid condition of the blood due to the presence of toxic matter, etc.

blood pressure, the pressure of the blood against the inner walls of the blood vessels.

blood·root (blŭd′rōōt′, -rŏŏt′), *n.* a North American plant of the poppy family with red root and root sap.

blood·shed (blŭd′shĕd′), *n.* slaughter.

blood·shot (blŭd′shŏt′), *adj.* (of the eyes) red from dilated blood vessels.

blood·suck·er (blŭd′sŭk′ər), *n.* **1.** any animal that sucks blood; a leech. **2.** extortioner.

blood·thirst·y (blŭd′thûrs′tĭ), *adj.* murderous. —**blood′thirst′i·ly,** *adv.* —**blood′thirst′-i·ness,** *n.*

blood vessel, any of the vessels (arteries, veins, capillaries) through which blood circulates.

blood·y (blŭd′ĭ), *adj.,* **bloodier, bloodiest,** *v.,* **bloodied, bloodying.** —*adj.* **1.** stained with blood. **2.** attended with bloodshed. **3.** inclined to bloodshed. —*v.t.* **4.** to stain with blood. —**blood′i·ly,** *adv.* —**blood′i·ness,** *n.*

bloom (blōōm), *n.* **1.** the flower of a plant. **2.** flowers collectively. **3.** state of having the buds opened. **4.** a flourishing, healthy condition. **5.** a healthy glow on the cheek. —*v.i.* **6.** to produce blossoms. **7.** to flourish. **8.** to be in a state of healthful beauty and vigor. **9.** to glow with a warm color. —*v.t.* **10.** to cause to yield blossoms. —**bloom′ing,** *adj.* —**bloom′ing·ly,** *adv.* —**bloom′-less,** *adj.*

bloom·ers (blōō′mərz), *n.pl.* loose trousers gathered at the knee, worn by women as an undergarment, etc.

Bloom·field (blōōm′fēld′), *n.* a city in NE New Jersey. 41,623.

Bloom·ing·ton (blōō′mĭng tən), *n.* a city in central Illinois. 32,868.

blos·som (blŏs′əm), *n.* **1.** the flower of a plant. **2.** the state of flowering. —*v.i.* **3.** to produce blossoms. **4.** to develop. —**blos′som·less,** *adj.* —**blos′som·y,** *adj.*

blot (blŏt), *n., v.,* **blotted, blotting.** —*n.* **1.** a spot or stain, esp. of ink on paper. **2.** a blemish on reputation. **3.** an erasure. —*v.t.* **4.** to spot, stain, or bespatter. **5.** to darken. **6.** to make indistinguishable. **7.** to dry with absorbent paper or the like. **8.** to destroy. —*v.i.* **9.** (of ink, etc.) to spread in a stain. **10.** to become stained. —**blot′less,** *adj.*

blotch (blŏch), *n.* **1.** a large irregular spot. —*v.t.* **2.** to blot, spot, or blur. —**blotch′y,** *adj.*

blot·ter (blŏt′ər), *n.* **1.** a piece of blotting paper used to absorb excess ink, etc. **2.** a book in which sales, arrests, etc., are recorded.

blotting paper, a soft, absorbent, unsized paper.

blouse (blous, blouz), *n.* **1.** a loosely fitting waist worn by women or children. **2.** a single-breasted, semifitting jacket worn as part of some army uniforms. **3.** a smock. —**blouse′like′,** *adj.*

blow[1] (blō), *n.* **1.** a sudden stroke with hand,

fist, or weapon. **2.** a sudden shock, calamity, or reverse. **3.** a sudden attack or drastic action.

blow² (blō), v., **blew, blown, blowing,** n. —v.i. **1.** (of the wind or air) to be in motion. **2.** to move along, carried by the wind. **3.** to produce or emit a current of air. **4.** *Music.* (of horn, etc.) to give out sound. **5.** to whistle. **6.** to pant. **7.** *Colloq.* to brag. **8.** (of a fuse, tire, etc.) to go bad. —v.t. **9.** to drive by means of a current of air. **10.** to drive a current of air upon. **11.** to clear or shape with a current of air. **12.** to cause to sound. **13.** to cause to explode. **14.** *Photog.* to enlarge. **15.** to expel noisily. **16.** *U.S. Slang.* to spend money on. —n. **17.** a blast of air or wind. **18.** act of producing a blast of air. —**blow′er,** n.

blow³ (blō), v., **blew, blown, blowing,** n. —v.i., v.t. **1.** to blossom. —n. **2.** state of blossoming.

blow·hole (blō′hōl′), n. **1.** an air or gas vent. **2.** a nostril at the top of the head in whales. **3.** a defect.

blow·out (blō′out′), n. **1.** a rupture of an automobile tire. **2.** a sudden escape of air, steam, or the like. **3.** *Colloq.* a big entertainment.

blow·pipe (blō′pīp′), n. a tube through which air or gas is forced into a flame to concentrate and increase its heating action.

blow·torch (blō′tôrch′), n. a small portable apparatus which gives an extremely hot flame.

blow·up (blō′ŭp′), n. an explosion.

blowz·y (blou′zĭ), adj., **blowzier, blowziest.** **1.** disheveled. **2.** red-faced.

blub·ber (blŭb′ər), n. **1.** *Zool.* the fat of whales and other cetaceans. **2.** act of blubbering. —v.i., v.t. **3.** to weep, usually noisily. —**blub′ber·er,** n. —**blub′ber·ing·ly,** adv. —**blub′ber·y,** adj.

bludg·eon (blŭj′ən), n. **1.** a short, heavy club. —v.t. **2.** to strike or fell with a bludgeon. **3.** to bully. —**bludg′eon·er, bludg·eon·eer** (blŭj′ə-nĭr′), n.

blue (blōō), n., adj., **bluer, bluest,** v., **blued, bluing** or **blueing.** —n. **1.** the pure hue of clear sky. **2. the blue,** *Poetic.* **a.** the sky. **b.** the sea. **3.** bluing. **4.** (pl.) See **blues.** —adj. **5.** (of the skin) discolored by cold, fear, etc. **6.** depressed in spirits. **7.** characterized by or stemming from rigid morals. —v.t. **8.** to make blue. —**blue′ly,** adv. —**blue′ness,** n.

Blue·beard (blōō′bĭrd′), n. (in folklore) a man whose seventh wife found in a forbidden room the bodies of the other six.

blue·bell (blōō′bĕl′), n. any of various plants with blue bell-shaped flowers.

blue·ber·ry (blōō′bĕr′ĭ), n., pl. **-ries.** **1.** the edible berry, usually bluish, of any of various shrubs of the heath family. **2.** any of these shrubs.

blue·bird (blōō′bûrd′), n. any bird of a genus comprising small North American passerine songbirds whose prevailing color is blue.

blue book, *U.S. Colloq.* a directory of socially prominent persons. Also, **blue′book′.**

blue·bot·tle (blōō′bŏt′əl), n. the cornflower.

blue·fish (blōō′fĭsh′), n., pl. **-fishes,** (esp. collectively) **-fish.** a predacious marine food fish, bluish in color, of the Atlantic coast.

blue·grass (blōō′grăs′, -gräs′), n. a grass with bluish stems, esp. **Kentucky bluegrass.**

blue·jack·et (blōō′jăk′ĭt), n. a sailor.

blue·jay (blōō′jā′), n. a well-known crested jay of the Eastern U.S. and Canada.

blue·pen·cil (blōō′pĕn′səl), v.t., **-ciled, -ciling** or (esp. *Brit.*) **-cilled, -cilling.** to edit.

blue·print (blōō′prĭnt′), n. **1.** a photograph in which the prints are white on a blue ground. **2.** a detailed plan. —v.t. **3.** to make a blueprint of.

blues (blōōz), n. pl. **1.** melancholy. **2.** *Jazz.* a melancholy type of song.

blue·stock·ing (blōō′stŏk′ĭng), n. a woman who affects intellectual tastes.

blu·et (blōō′ĭt), n. any of various plants with blue flowers, as the cornflower.

bluff¹ (blŭf), adj. **1.** abrupt and unconventional in manner; hearty. **2.** presenting a bold, steep front, as a coastline. —n. **3.** a bold, steep cliff or hill. —**bluff′ly,** adv. —**bluff′ness,** n.

bluff² (blŭf), v.t., v.i. **1.** to mislead by presenting a bold front. **2.** to gain by bluffing. —n. **3.** act of bluffing. **4.** one who bluffs. —**bluff′er,** n.

blu·ing (blōō′ĭng), n. a substance used to whiten laundered clothes.

blu·ish (blōō′ĭsh), adj. somewhat blue.

blun·der (blŭn′dər), n. **1.** a gross or stupid mistake. —v.i. **2.** to move or act blindly or

stupidly. —v.t. **3.** to bungle. —**blun′der·er,** n. —**blun′der·ing·ly,** adv.

blun·der·buss (blŭn′dər bŭs′), n. a short musket of wide bore with expanded muzzle.

Blunderbuss

blunt (blŭnt), adj. **1.** having a thick or dull edge or point. **2.** abrupt in manner. **3.** slow in understanding. —v.t. **4.** to make blunt. —**blunt′ly,** adv. —**blunt′ness,** n.

blur (blûr), v., **blurred, blurring,** n. —v.t. **1.** to obscure, as by smearing. **2.** to make indistinct or insensible. —v.i. **3.** to become indistinct. —n. **4.** a smudge or smear. **5.** a blurred condition. —**blur′ry,** adj.

blurb (blûrb), n. an announcement or advertisement, esp. an effusively laudatory one.

blurt (blûrt), v.t. **1.** to utter suddenly or inadvertently. —n. **2.** an abrupt utterance.

blush (blŭsh), v.i. **1.** to redden, as from shame. **2.** to feel shame. —v.t. **3.** to make red. —n. **4.** a reddening, as of the face. **5.** rosy tinge. —**blush′ful,** adj. —**blush′ing·ly,** adv.

blus·ter (blŭs′tər), v.i. **1.** to be tumultuous, as wind. **2.** to be loud, noisy, or swaggering. —n. **3.** boisterous noise and violence. **4.** noisy, boastful talk. —**blus′ter·er,** n. —**blus′ter·ing·ly,** adv. —**blus′ter·y, blus′ter·ous,** adj.

blvd., boulevard.

bo·a (bō′ə), n., pl. **boas.** **1.** any of various nonvenomous snakes, as the **boa constrictor** of the American tropics. **2.** a long scarf of silk, feathers, or other material, worn by women.

boar (bōr), n. **1.** the uncastrated male of swine. **2.** the wild boar.

board (bōrd), n. **1.** a piece of timber sawed thin. **2.** a flat slab of wood for some specific purpose. **3.** a sheet of wood, paper, etc., for some special use. **4.** a table, esp. to serve food on. **5.** daily meals, esp. as provided for pay. **6.** an official body of persons who direct or supervise some activity. **7.** (pl.) the stage. **8. on board,** on or in a ship, plane, or vehicle. —v.t. **9.** to cover or close with boards. **10.** to furnish with food, esp. for pay. **11.** to enter (a ship, train, etc.). —v.i. **12.** to take one's meals.

board·er (bōr′dər), n. one who is supplied with meals, and, often, with lodgings.

board·ing (bōr′dĭng), n. **1.** wooden boards collectively. **2.** a structure of boards. —adj. **3.** providing meals and lodging.

board·walk (bōrd′wôk′), n. *U.S.* a promenade made of boards, usually along a beach.

boast (bōst), v.i. **1.** to speak exaggeratedly about oneself. **2.** to speak with pride. —v.t. **3.** to speak of with excessive pride. **4.** to be proud of. —n. **5.** a thing boasted of. **6.** exaggerated speech. —**boast′er,** n. —**boast′ful,** adj. —**boast′ful·ly,** adv. —**boast′ful·ness,** n. —**boast′ing·ly,** adv.

boat (bōt), n. **1.** a vessel for transport by water. **2.** a small ship. **3.** an open dish resembling a boat. —v.i. **4.** to go in a boat. —v.t. **5.** to transport in a boat.

boat·house (bōt′hous′), n. a shed for boats.

boat·man (bōt′mən), n., pl. **-men.** an expert in the use of boats. —**boat′man·ship′,** n.

boat·swain (bō′sən), n. an officer in charge of rigging, anchors, cables, etc.

bob¹ (bŏb), n., v., **bobbed, bobbing.** —n. **1.** a short jerky motion. —v.t., v.i. **2.** to move quickly or jerkily. —**bob′ber,** n.

bob² (bŏb), n., v., **bobbed, bobbing.** —n. **1.** a style of short haircut for women. **2.** a horse's tail cut short. **3.** a small dangling object, as the weight on a plumb line. **4.** a float for a fishing line. —v.t. **5.** to cut short.

bob·bin (bŏb′ĭn), n. a reel or spool on which thread is wound.

bob·by (bŏb′ĭ), n., pl. **-bies.** *Brit. Colloq.* a policeman.

bobby pin, a metal hairpin with close prongs.

bob·by·socks (bŏb′ĭ sŏks′), n.pl. *Colloq.* ankle-length socks, esp. as worn by young girls.

bob·by·sox·er (bŏb′ĭ sŏks′ər), n. *Colloq.* a girl who enthusiastically follows adolescent fads. Also, **bob′by sox′er.**

bob·cat (bŏb′kăt′), n. an American wildcat.

bob·o·link (bŏb′ə lĭngk′), n. a common North American passerine songbird.

bob·sled (bŏb′slĕd′), n., v., **-sledded, -sledding.**

U.S. —*n.* 1. a type of high-speed sled. —*v.i.* 2. to ride on a bobsled.

bob·tail (bŏb/tāl/), *n.* 1. a short or docked tail. 2. a bobtailed animal. —*adj.* 3. cut short. —*v.t.* 4. to cut short the tail of.

bob·white (bŏb/hwīt/), *n.* a common North American quail.

Boc·cac·ci·o (bō kä/chĭ ō/), *n.* Giovanni, 1313–75, Italian writer.

bock beer (bŏk), a strong, dark beer.

bode (bōd), *v.t., v.i.,* **boded, boding.** to portend. —**bode/ment,** *n.*

bod·ice (bŏd/ĭs), *n.* the fitted waist of a dress.

bod·i·less (bŏd/ĭ lĭs), *adj.* having no body.

bod·i·ly (bŏd/ə lĭ), *adj.* 1. of or pertaining to the body. 2. corporeal or material. —*adv.* 3. as a whole.

bod·kin (bŏd/kĭn), *n.* a small pointed instrument for making holes in cloth, etc.

bod·y (bŏd/ĭ), *n., pl.* **bodies,** *v.,* **bodied, bodying.** —*n.* 1. the physical structure of an animal. 2. a corpse. 3. the trunk or main mass of a thing. 4. *Colloq. and Dial.* a person. 5. a collective group. 6. consistency or density. —*v.t.* 7. to invest with or as with a body. 8. to represent in bodily form (usually fol. by *forth*). —**bod/ied,** *adj.*

bod·y·guard (bŏd/ĭ gärd/), *n.* 1. a private guard, as for a high official. 2. a retinue; escort.

Boer (bōr), *n.* 1. a South African of Dutch extraction. —*adj.* 2. of or pertaining to Boers.

bog (bŏg, bôg), *n., v.,* **bogged, bogging.** —*n.* 1. wet, spongy ground. —*v.t., v.i.* 2. to sink in a bog. —**bog/gish,** *adj.* —**bog/gy,** *adj.*

bo·gey (bō/gĭ), *n., pl.* **-geys.** 1. a bogy. 2. *Golf.* a. par. b. one stroke above par on a hole.

bog·gle (bŏg/əl), *v.,* **-gled, -gling,** *n.* —*v.i.* 1. to take alarm. 2. to hesitate; waver. 3. to bungle. —*n.* 4. act of shying or taking alarm. 5. *Colloq.* bungle. —**bog/gler,** *n.*

Bo·go·tá (bō/gō tä/), *n.* the capital of Colombia, in the central part. 416,107.

bo·gus (bō/gəs), *adj. U.S.* counterfeit; sham.

bo·gy (bō/gĭ), *n., pl.* **-gies.** a hobgoblin; evil spirit. Also, **bo/gie.**

Bo·he·mi·an (bō hē/mĭ ən, -hēm/yən), *n.* 1. (*often l.c.*) a person with artistic or intellectual tendencies who disregards conventional rules of behavior. —*adj.* 2. pertaining to Bohemians. —**Bo·he/mi·an·ism,** *n.*

boil[1] (boil), *v.i.* 1. to be heated to the point of bubbling agitatedly. 2. to be agitated by angry feeling. —*v.t.* 3. to cause to boil. 4. to cook by boiling. —*n.* 5. act of boiling. 6. state or condition of boiling.

boil[2] (boil), *n. Pathol.* a painful suppurating inflammatory sore forming a central core.

boil·er (boi/lər), *n.* 1. a tank and furnace in which steam is generated for heating, etc. 2. a vessel for boiling. 3. a tank for hot water.

Boi·se (boi/zĭ, -sĭ), *n.* the capital of Idaho, in the SW part. 26,130.

bois·ter·ous (boi/stər əs), *adj.* 1. rough and noisy. 2. stormy. —**bois/ter·ous·ly,** *adv.* —**bois/ter·ous·ness,** *n.*

bold (bōld), *adj.* 1. fearless; brave. 2. impudent; brazen. 3. calling for daring action. 4. conspicuous; vigorous. 5. steep; abrupt. —**bold/ly,** *adv.* —**bold/ness,** *n.*

bold·face (bōld/fās/), *n. Print.* type that has thick, heavy lines, used for emphasis, etc.

bole (bōl), *n.* the stem or trunk of a tree.

bo·le·ro (bō lâr/ō), *n., pl.* **-ros.** 1. a lively Spanish dance in three-four time. 2. a short jacket ending at the waistline.

Bol·í·var (bŏl/ə vər), *n.* Simón, 1783–1830, Venezuelan statesman and hero.

Bo·liv·i·a (bō lĭv/ĭ ə, bə-), *n.* a republic in W South America. 3,533,900 pop.; 416,040 sq. mi. *Caps.:* La Paz and Sucre. —**Bo·liv/i·an,** *adj., n.*

boll (bōl), *n. Bot.* a rounded seed vessel or pod of a plant, as of flax or cotton.

boll weevil (bōl), a snout beetle that attacks the bolls of cotton.

bo·lo (bō/lō), *n., pl.* **-los** (-lōz). a large, heavy single-edged knife for hacking used esp. in the Philippines.

Bo·lo·gna (bə lōn/yə), *n.* a city in N Italy. 320,787.

bologna sausage, a large-sized kind of sausage. Also, **bo·lo·gna** (bə lō/nə, -lōn/yə, -lō/nĭ).

bo·lo·ney (bə lō/nĭ), *n. U.S.* baloney.

Bol·she·vik (bŏl/shə vĭk, bōl/-), *n., pl.* **-viks,**

-viki (-vē/kē). 1. (in Russia) a. (1903–1917) a member of the radical majority of the Social Democratic Party. b. (since 1918) a member of the Russian Communist Party. 2. (in derisive use) any radical. Also, **bolshevik.**

Bol·she·vism (bŏl/shə vĭz/əm, bōl/-), *n.* the doctrines or methods of the Bolsheviks. —**Bol/she·vist,** *n., adj.* —**Bol/she·vis/tic,** *adj.*

bol·ster (bōl/stər), *n.* 1. a long pillow for a bed. —*v.t.* 2. to support with a pillow. 3. to prop or support. —**bol/ster·er,** *n.*

bolt[1] (bōlt), *n.* 1. a movable bar which when slid into a socket fastens a door, etc. 2. the part of a lock protruded and drawn back by the key. 3. a strong threaded metal pin. 4. a sudden swift motion, flight, escape, etc. 5. sudden desertion of a meeting, political party, etc. 6. a roll of cloth or wall paper. 7. an arrow, esp. one for a crossbow. 8. a thunderbolt. —*v.t.* 9. to fasten with bolts. 10. *U.S. Pol.* to refuse to support. 11. to shoot. 12. to blurt. 13. to swallow (one's food) hurriedly. —*v.i.* 14. to make a sudden, swift movement. 15. *U.S. Pol.* to refuse to support one's party. —*adv.* 16. suddenly. 17. stiffly. —**bolt/er,** *n.*

bolt[2] (bōlt), *v.t.* 1. to sift through a cloth or sieve. 2. to examine, as if by sifting. —**bolt/er,** *n.*

bomb (bŏm), *n.* 1. projectile filled with a bursting charge, exploded by a fuse, by impact, or otherwise. —*v.t., v.i.* 2. to hurl bombs (at).

bom·bard (bŏm bärd/), *v.t.* 1. to attack with artillery or bombs. 2. to assail vigorously. —**bom·bard/er,** *n.* —**bom·bard/ment,** *n.*

bom·bar·dier (bŏm/bər dĭr/), *n.* member of plane crew who aims the bomb.

bom·bast (bŏm/băst), *n.* high-sounding words. —**bom·bas/tic, bom·bas/ti·cal,** *adj.*

Bom·bay (bŏm bā/), *n.* a city in W India. 1,489,883.

bomb·er (bŏm/ər), *n. Mil.* an airplane employed to drop bombs.

bomb·proof (bŏm/prōof/), *adj.* strong enough to resist bombs or shells.

bomb·shell (bŏm/shĕl/), *n.* a bomb.

bomb·sight (bŏm/sīt/), *n.* an instrument used in aiming bombs from an aircraft.

bo·na fi·de (bō/nə fī/dĭ), genuine.

bo·nan·za (bō năn/zə), *n. U.S.* 1. a rich mass of ore, as found in mining. 2. good luck.

Bo·na·parte (bō/nə pärt/), *n.* Napoléon, Corsican-born French general: emperor of France as Napoleon I, 1804–1815.

Bo·na·part·ist (bō/nə pär/tĭst), *n.* an adherent of the Bonapartes. —**Bo/na·part/ism,** *n.*

bon·bon (bŏn/bŏn/), *n.* a candy.

bond (bŏnd), *n.* 1. something that binds, fastens, confines, or holds together. 2. something that unites people into a group. 3. a bondsman. 4. a sealed instrument which guarantees to pay a stated sum by a specified day. 5. any written obligation. 6. the government-held state of dutiable goods on which the duties are unpaid. 7. a certificate indicating ownership of a portion of a debt due by government, a railroad, etc. —*v.t.* 8. to put (goods, an employee, etc.) on or under bond. 9. to mortgage. —**bond/ed,** *adj.* —**bond/er,** *n.*

bond·age (bŏn/dĭj), *n.* slavery.

bond·man (bŏnd/mən), *n., pl.* **-men.** 1. a male slave. 2. a man bound to service without wages. —**bond/maid/,** *n.fem.* —**bond/wom/an,** *n.fem.*

bonds·man (bŏndz/mən), *n., pl.* **-men.** one who by bond becomes surety for another.

bone (bōn), *n., v.,* **boned, boning.** —*n.* 1. any of the discrete pieces of which the skeleton is composed. 2. the hard tissue which composes skeleton. 3. (*pl.*) the skeleton. 4. any of various similar substances, such as ivory. 5. something made of bone. 6. (*pl.*) *U.S. Slang.* dice. —*v.t.* 7. to take out the bones of. —*v.i.* 8. *Slang.* to study hard. —**bone/less,** *adj.* —**bone/like/,** *adj.*

bon·er (bō/nər), *n. Colloq.* a foolish blunder.

bon·fire (bŏn/fīr/), *n.* a large outdoor fire.

bo·ni·to (bə nē/tō), *n., pl.* **-tos, -toes.** any of various large mackerellike fishes.

bon·net (bŏn/ĭt), *n.* 1. a woman's or child's outdoor head covering, often tied on with strings. 2. *Chiefly Scot.* a man's or boy's cap.

bon·ny (bŏn/ĭ), *adj.* **-nier, -niest.** handsome; pretty. Also, **bon/nie.**

bo·nus (bō/nəs), *n.* something given or paid over and above what is due or regularly paid.

bon·y (bō′nĭ), *adj.*, **bonier, boniest. 1.** of or like bone. **2.** full of bones. **3.** gaunt. —**bon′i-ness,** *n.*

boo (bōō), *interj., n., pl.* **boos,** *v.,* **booed, booing.** —*interj.* **1.** an exclamation used to express contempt, etc., or to frighten. —*n.* **2.** this exclamation. —*v.i., v.t.* **3.** to cry "boo" (at).

boob (bōōb), *n. U.S. Slang.* a fool; dunce.

boo·by (bōō′bĭ), *n., pl.* **-bies. 1.** a stupid person. **2.** the worst student, player, etc.

booby trap, *Mil.* a bomb hidden so that it is set off by an unsuspecting person.

boo·dle (bōō′dəl), *n., v.,* **-dled, -dling.** *U.S. Slang.* —*n.* **1.** (often contemptuous) the lot, pack, or crowd. **2.** a bribe. —*v.i.* **3.** to obtain money dishonestly. —**boo′dler,** *n.*

boog·ie-woog·ie (bŏŏg′ĭ wŏŏg′ĭ), *n. Jazz.* a form of instrumental blues using melodic variations over a constantly repeated bass figure.

book (bŏŏk), *n.* **1.** a printed work on sheets bound together. **2.** a ledger. **3.** a division of a literary work. **4.** the Book, the Bible. **5.** libretto. **6.** a record of bets, as on a horserace. **7.** *Cards.* the number of tricks taken before any trick scores. —*v.t.* **8.** to enter in a book or list. **9.** to engage (a place, etc.) beforehand. —*v.i.* **10.** to register one's name.

book·bind·er·y (bŏŏk′bīn′də rĭ), *n., pl.* **-eries.** an establishment for binding books. —**book′-bind′er,** *n.* —**book′bind′ing,** *n.*

book·case (bŏŏk′kās′), *n.* a set of shelves for books.

book end, a support for a row of books.

book·ie (bŏŏk′ĭ), *n. Colloq.* bookmaker (def. 2).

book·ish (bŏŏk′ĭsh), *adj.* **1.** fond of reading. **2.** more acquainted with books than with real life. **3.** literary. **4.** stilted; pedantic. —**book′ish·ly,** *adv.* —**book′ish·ness,** *n.*

book·keep·ing (bŏŏk′kē′pĭng), *n.* the work or art of keeping systematic records of money transactions. —**book′keep′er,** *n.*

book·let (bŏŏk′lĭt), *n.* a pamphlet.

book·mak·er (bŏŏk′mā′kər), *n.* **1.** a maker of books. **2.** a professional betting man who accepts the bets of others, as on horses in racing.

book·mark (bŏŏk′märk′), *n.* something put in a book to mark a place.

book·plate (bŏŏk′plāt′), *n.* a label, bearing the owner's name, etc., pasted in a book.

book·sell·er (bŏŏk′sĕl′ər), *n.* a person whose occupation or business is selling books.

book·store (bŏŏk′stōr′), *n. U.S.* a store where books are sold. Also, **book′shop′.**

book·worm (bŏŏk′wûrm′), *n.* **1.** an insect that feeds on books. **2.** an avid reader.

boom[1] (bōōm), *v.i.* **1.** to make a deep, resonant sound. **2.** to flourish vigorously. —*v.t.* **3.** to give forth with a booming sound. **4.** to push (a cause, etc.) vigorously. —*n.* **5.** a deep, hollow, continued sound. **6.** a rapid increase in price, numbers, popularity, etc. —*adj.* **7.** *U.S.* caused by a boom.

boom[2] (bōōm), *n.* **1.** *Naut.* a long spar to extend the foot of certain sails. **2.** a chain of connected floating timbers, etc., serving to obstruct navigation, to confine floating timber, etc. **3.** a beam projecting from the mast of a derrick.

boom·er·ang (bōō′mə răng′), *n.* **1.** a curved piece of wood used as a missile by the native Australians, one form of which can be so thrown as to return to the thrower. **2.** a scheme, etc., which recoils upon the user.

boon[1] (bōōn), *n.* a benefit or favor.

B, Boom; G, Gaff

boon[2] (bōōn), *adj.* jolly; convivial; congenial.

boon·dog·gle (bōōn′dŏg′əl), *v.i.,* **-gled, -gling.** *U.S. Slang.* to do work of little or no practical value. —**boon′dog′gler,** *n.* —**boon′dog′gling,** *n.*

Boone (bōōn), *n.* **Daniel,** 1735–1820, American pioneer in Kentucky.

boor (bŏŏr), *n.* **1.** a clownish or unmannerly person. **2.** a peasant; rustic. —**boor′ish,** *adj.* —**boor′ish·ly,** *adv.* —**boor′ish·ness,** *n.*

boost (bōōst), *U.S.* —*v.t.* **1.** to lift by pushing from behind or below. **2.** to aid by speaking well of. **3.** to increase. —*n.* **4.** an upward push. **5.** an aid to success. —**boost′er,** *n.*

boot[1] (bōōt), *n.* **1.** a covering, usually of leather, for the foot and leg. **2.** any sheathlike protective covering. **3.** a kick. —*v.t.* **4.** to put boots on. **5.** *Slang.* to kick. **6.** *Slang.* to discharge.

boot[2] (bōōt), *n.* **to boot,** in addition.

boot·black (bōōt′blăk′), *n.* a person whose occupation it is to shine shoes, boots, etc.

booth (bōōth, bōōth), *n., pl.* **booths** (bōōthz). **1.** a light structure for shelter, exhibition of wares, etc. **2.** a small compartment for a telephone, for voters at elections, etc.

Booth (bōōth), *n.* **John Wilkes,** 1838–65, U.S. actor: assassin of Abraham Lincoln.

boot·leg (bōōt′lĕg′), *n., v.,* **-legged, -legging,** *adj. U.S.* —*n.* **1.** illicit alcoholic liquor. —*v.t.* **2.** to deal illicitly in. —*v.i.* **3.** to deal in illicit goods. —*adj.* **4.** illicit. —**boot′leg′ger,** *n.*

boot·less (bōōt′lĭs), *adj.* unavailing; useless. —**boot′less·ly,** *adv.* —**boot′less·ness,** *n.*

boot·lick (bōōt′lĭk′), *v.t., v.i. U.S. Slang.* to curry favor (with). —**boot′lick′er,** *n.* —**boot′-lick′ing,** *n., adj.*

boo·ty (bōō′tĭ), *n., pl.* **-ties.** plunder.

booze (bōōz), *n. Colloq.* alcoholic liquor.

bo·rac·ic (bə răs′ĭk, bō-), *adj. Chem.* boric.

bo·rate (*n.* bōr′āt, -ĭt; *v.* bōr′āt), *n., v.,* **-rated, -rating.** *Chem.* —*n.* **1.** a salt of any boric acid. —*v.t.* **2.** to treat with borate, boric acid, or borax.

bo·rax (bōr′əks, -ăks), *n.* a white, crystalline sodium borate, used as a flux, cleansing agent, etc.

Bor·deaux (bôr dō′), *n.* **1.** a seaport in SW France. 253,751. **2.** wine produced in the region surrounding Bordeaux.

bor·der (bôr′dər), *n.* **1.** a side, edge, or margin. **2.** the frontier line. **3.** an ornamental strip or design around the edge of a printed page, a garment, etc. —*v.t.* **4.** to make a border about. **5.** to adjoin. —**bor′dered,** *adj.*

bor·der·land (bôr′dər lănd′), *n.* land forming a border or frontier.

bor·der·line (bôr′dər līn′), *adj.* **1.** on or near a boundary. **2.** uncertain; debatable.

bore[1] (bôr), *v.,* **bored, boring,** *n.* —*v.t.* **1.** to pierce (a substance) or make (a hole, etc.) with a drill. **2.** to force by persistent forward thrusting. —*v.i.* **3.** to make a hole, as with a drill. —*n.* **4.** a hole made by boring. **5.** the inside diameter of a hollow cylindrical object. —**bor′er,** *n.*

bore[2] (bôr), *v.,* **bored, boring,** *n.* —*v.t.* **1.** to weary by dullness. —*n.* **2.** a dull person or thing. —**bore′dom,** *n.*

Bo·re·as (bōr′ĭ əs), *n.* the north wind.

bo·ric (bōr′ĭk), *adj.* containing boron.

boric acid, *Chem.* **1.** a white crystalline acid, H_3BO_3, used as a mild antiseptic. **2.** any of a group of acids containing boron.

born (bôrn), *adj.* **1.** brought forth by birth. **2.** possessing from birth.

Bor·ne·o (bôr′nĭ ō′), *n.* an island in the Malay Archipelago. ab. 3,000,000 pop.; ab. 290,000 sq. mi.

bo·ron (bōr′ŏn), *n.* a nonmetallic element present in borax, etc. *Symbol:* B; *at. wt.:* 10.82; *at. no.:* 5.

bor·ough (bûr′ō), *n.* **1.** *U.S.* an incorporated municipality smaller than a city. **2.** one of the five divisions of New York City. **3.** *Brit.* an urban community incorporated by royal charter.

bor·row (bôr′ō, bŏr′ō), *v.t.* **1.** to take or obtain (a thing) on the promise to return it. **2.** to appropriate or adopt. —*v.i.* **3.** to borrow something. —**bor′row·er,** *n.*

borsch (bôrsh), *n.* a Russian stock soup containing beets. Also, **borscht** (bôrsht).

bosh (bŏsh), *n. Colloq.* complete nonsense.

bosk·y (bŏs′kĭ), *adj.* **1.** woody. **2.** shady.

bo's'n (bō′sən), *n. Naut.* boatswain.

bos·om (bŏŏz′əm, bōō′zəm), *n.* **1.** the breast. **2.** that part of a garment which covers the breast. **3.** the breast, conceived of as the seat of thought or emotion. **4.** something likened to the human bosom. —*adj.* **5.** of or pertaining to the bosom. **6.** intimate. —*v.t.* **7.** to cherish. **8.** to conceal.

Bos·po·rus (bŏs′pə rəs), *n.* a strait connecting the Black Sea and Sea of Marmara. 18 mi. long.

boss[1] (bôs, bŏs), *n.* **1.** *Chiefly U.S. Colloq.* one who employs or superintends workmen. **2.** *U.S.* a politician who controls his party organization. —*v.t.* **3.** to manage; control. —*v.i.* **4.** to be boss. **5.** to be too domineering. —*adj.* **6.** chief.

boss[2] (bôs, bŏs), *n.* **1.** a protuberance or roundish knoblike projection. **2.** an ornamental protuberance of metal, ivory, etc., or knoblike projection. —*v.t.* **3.** to ornament with bosses.

boss·y (bôs′ĭ, bŏs′ĭ), *adj.,* **bossier, bossiest.** *Colloq.* domineering.

Bos·ton (bôs′tən, bŏs′tən), *n.* the capital of Massachusetts, in the E part. 770,816. —**Bos·to·ni·an** (bôs tō′nĭ ən, bŏs tō′-), *adj., n.*

Boston terrier, any of a breed of small, smooth-coated dogs with brindle coat. Also, **Boston bull.**

bo·sun (bō′sən), *n. Naut.* boatswain.

Bos·well (bŏz′wĕl, -wəl), *n.* **James,** 1740–95, Scottish biographer of Samuel Johnson.

bot·a·nize (bŏt′ə nīz′), *v.i.,* -nized, -nizing. to study plants botanically. —**bot′a·niz′er,** *n.*

bot·a·ny (bŏt′ə nĭ), *n., pl.* -nies. the branch of biology that deals with plant life. —**bo·tan·i·cal** (bə tăn′ə kəl), **bo·tan′ic,** *adj.* —**bo·tan′i·cal·ly,** *adv.* —**bot·a·nist** (bŏt′ə nĭst), *n.*

botch (bŏch), *v.t.* **1.** to bungle. **2.** to mend in a clumsy manner. —*n.* **3.** a clumsy piece of work. —**botch′er,** *n.* —**botch′er·y,** *n.* —**botch′y,** *adj.*

both (bōth), *adj., pron.* **1.** the two together. —*conj., adv.* **2.** alike; equally.

both·er (bŏth′ər), *v.t.* **1.** to give trouble to; annoy. **2.** to bewilder. —*v.i.* **3.** to trouble oneself. **4.** to cause annoyance. —*n.* **5.** something annoying or disturbing.

both·er·some (bŏth′ər səm), *adj.* troublesome.

Bot·ti·cel·li (bŏt′ə chĕl′ĭ), *n.* **Sandro,** 1447–1510, Italian painter.

bot·tle (bŏt′əl), *n., v.,* -tled, -tling. —*n.* **1.** a container, usually glass, with a neck or mouth, used for holding liquids. —*v.t.* **2.** to put into a bottle. **3. bottle up,** to shut in or restrain closely. —**bot′tler,** *n.*

bot·tle·neck (bŏt′əl nĕk′), *n.* **1.** a narrow place. **2.** a stage in a process where progress is retarded.

bot·tom (bŏt′əm), *n.* **1.** the lowest or deepest part of anything. **2.** the under side. **3.** the ground under any body of water. **4.** (*usually pl.*) *Phys. Geog.* low-lying alluvial land adjacent to a river. **5.** a ship. —*v.t.* **6.** to furnish with a bottom. **7.** to base. —*v.i.* **8.** to reach the bottom. —*adj.* **9.** lowest; undermost. **10.** fundamental. —**bot′tom·less,** *adj.*

bot·u·lism (bŏch′ə lĭz′əm), *n.* a disease caused by a toxin developed in spoiling foods.

bou·doir (bōō′dwär, -dwôr), *n.* a lady's bedroom or private sitting room.

bough (bou), *n.* a branch of a tree, esp. one of the main branches. —**bough′less,** *adj.*

bouil·lon (bōōl′yŏn, -yən), *n.* a clear, thin soup made by boiling meat, etc.

boul·der (bōl′dər), *n.* a detached and rounded or worn rock, esp. one of some size.

Boul·der (bōl′dər), *n.* a city in N Colorado. 12,958.

Boulder Dam, a large dam on the Colorado river, in SE Nevada and NW Arizona.

boul·e·vard (bōōl′ə värd′, bōō′lə-), *n.* a broad avenue of a city, often lined with trees.

bounce (bouns), *v.,* bounced, bouncing, *n., adv.* —*v.i.* **1.** to rebound, as a ball. **2.** to burst noisily or angrily. —*v.t.* **3.** to cause to bound or rebound. **4.** *Slang.* to eject or discharge summarily. —*n.* **5.** a rebound or bound. **6.** a sudden leap. **7.** resilience. **8.** *Slang.* expulsion; dismissal. —*adv.* **9.** suddenly. —**bounc′er,** *n.*

bounc·ing (boun′sĭng), *adj.* **1.** stout, strong, or vigorous. **2.** big; hearty; noisy.

bound[1] (bound), *adj.* **1.** tied; in bonds. **2.** made fast, as by a bond. **3.** secured within a cover, as a book. **4.** under obligation. **5.** sure. **6.** determined. **7.** *Pathol.* constipated.

bound[2] (bound), *v.i., v.t.* **1.** to jump. **2.** to rebound. —*n.* **3.** a jump. **4.** a rebound.

bound[3] (bound), *n.* **1.** (*usually pl.*) a boundary or limit. **2.** (*pl.*) an area within boundary lines. —*v.t.* **3.** to limit as by bounds. **4.** to form the boundary of. **5.** to name the boundaries of. —*v.i.* **6.** to abut. —**bound′less,** *adj.* —**bound′-less·ly,** *adv.*

bound[4] (bound), *adj.* on the way (*to*).

bound·a·ry (boun′də rĭ, -drĭ), *n., pl.* -ries. something that indicates bounds or limits.

boun·te·ous (boun′tĭ əs), *adj.* **1.** generously liberal. **2.** plentiful; abundant. Also, **boun′ti·ful.** —**boun′te·ous·ly,** *adv.* —**boun′te·ous·ness,** *n.*

boun·ty (boun′tĭ), *n., pl.* -ties. **1.** generosity in giving. **2.** a benevolent or generous gift. **3.** a reward.

bou·quet (bō kā′, bōō-), *n.* **1.** a bunch of flowers. **2.** the characteristic aroma of wines, liqueurs, etc.

Bour·bon (bōōr′bən; bûr′bən *for 3, occas. for 2*), *n.* **1.** a member of the last house of the royal family of France or any of its branches. **2.** an extreme conservative. **3.** (*l.c.*) Also, **bourbon whiskey.** a straight corn whiskey.

bour·geois (bōōr zhwä′, bōōr′zhwä), *n., pl.* -geois, *adj.* —*n.* **1.** a member of the middle class. —*adj.* **2.** of or belonging to the middle class. **3.** lacking elegance.

bour·geoi·sie (bōōr′zhwä zē′), *n.* **1.** the bourgeois class. **2.** the antithesis of the proletariat.

bourn (bôrn, bōōrn), *n.* **1.** a bound; limit. **2.** destination; goal. Also, **bourne.**

bout (bout), *n.* **1.** a contest. **2.** period.

bo·vine (bō′vīn, -vĭn), *adj.* **1.** of the ox kind. **2.** oxlike. —*n.* **3.** a bovine animal.

bow[1] (bou), *v.i.* **1.** to bend downward. **2.** to submit. **3.** to bend the body or head in worship, respect, or submission. —*v.t.* **4.** to bend in worship, submission, respect, etc. **5.** to subdue. **6.** to cause to stoop. —*n.* **7.** an inclination of the head or body in salutation, assent, reverence, etc. —**bow′er,** *n.*

bow[2] (bō), *n.* **1.** a strip of elastic wood or other material bent by a string stretched between its ends, used for shooting arrows. **2.** a curve. **3.** a looped knot, as of ribbon. **4.** *Music.* a rod with horsehairs stretched upon it, for playing the violin, etc. **5.** something curved. —*adj.* **6.** curved. —*v.t., v.i.* **7.** to curve.

bow[3] (bou), *n.* the forward end of a ship, airship, etc.

bowd·ler·ize (boud′lə rīz′), *v.t.,* -ized, -izing. to expurgate prudishly. —**bowd′ler·ism,** *n.* —**bowd′ler·i·za′tion,** *n.*

bow·el (bou′əl, boul), *n., v.,* -eled, -eling or (*esp. Brit.*) -elled, -elling. —*n.* **1.** (*usually pl.*) an intestine. **2.** the interior parts. —*v.t.* **3.** to disembowel.

bow·er (bou′ər), *n.* a leafy shelter.

Bow·er·y (bou′ə rĭ, bou′rĭ), *n.* **the,** a street in New York City, notorious for its saloons, rundown hotels, etc.

bow·ie knife (bō′ĭ, bōō′ĭ), a heavy sheath knife having a long, single-edged blade.

bowl[1] (bōl), *n.* **1.** a deep, round dish or basin. **2.** the contents of a bowl. **3.** a rounded, hollow part. **4.** an arena, as for athletic contests, etc. —**bowl′like′,** *adj.*

bowl[2] (bōl), *n.* **1.** one of the balls used in playing ninepins, tenpins, or bowls. —*v.i.* **2.** to play at bowling. **3.** to roll a bowl. **4.** to move along smoothly and rapidly. **5.** *Cricket.* to deliver the ball to the batsman. —*v.t.* **6.** to knock. **7.** to disconcert. —**bowl′er,** *n.*

bowl·der (bōl′dər), *n.* boulder.

bow·leg (bō′lĕg′), *n. Pathol.* outward curvature of the legs. —**bow′leg′ged,** *adj.*

bow·line (bō′lĭn, -līn′), *n.* **1.** Also, **bowline knot.** a knot which forms a nonslipping loop. **2.** *Naut.* a rope to steady the weather leech of the sail.

bowl·ing (bō′lĭng), *n.* **1.** act of playing bowls. **2.** the game of bowls. **3.** *U.S.* tenpins.

bowls (bōlz), *n.* **1.** a game in which the players roll balls as near as possible to a stationary ball. **2.** ninepins or (*U.S.*) tenpins.

bow·man (bō′mən), *n., pl.* -men. an archer.

bow·shot (bō′shŏt′), *n.* the distance a bow sends an arrow.

bow·sprit (bou′sprĭt, bō′-), *n. Naut.* a large spar projecting forward from the stem of a vessel.

box[1] (bŏks), *n.* **1.** a receptacle of wood, metal, cardboard, etc., with a lid. **2.** the quantity contained in a box. **3.** a compartment, esp. in theaters. **4.** a small shelter. **5.** the driver's seat on a coach. —*v.t.* **6.** to put into a box. **7.** *Naut.* to name consecutively the points of (the compass). —**box′like′,** *adj.*

box[2] (bŏks), *n.* **1.** a blow, as with the hand or fist. —*v.t., v.i.* **2.** to strike with the hand or fist, esp. on the ear. **3.** to fight in a boxing match. —**box′er,** *n.* —**box′ing,** *n.*

box[3] (bŏks), *n.* an evergreen shrub or small tree much used for ornamental borders, hedges, etc.

box·car (bŏks′kär′), *n. Railroads.* an enclosed and covered freight car.

box office, *Theat.* **1.** the office in which tickets are sold. **2.** receipts from a play, etc.

box·wood (bŏks′wŏŏd′), *n.* box[3].

boy (boi), *n.* **1.** a male child. **2.** a grown man. **3.** a young servant. —**boy′hood,** *n.* —**boy′ish,** *adj.* —**boy′ish·ly,** *adv.* —**boy′ish·ness,** *n.*

boy·cott (boi'kŏt), *v.t.* **1.** to abstain from dealings with, as a means of coercion. **2.** to abstain from buying or using. —*n.* **3.** the practice of boycotting. **4.** an instance of boycotting.

boy scout, a member of an organization of boys (**Boy Scouts**), founded to develop manly character, etc.

boy·sen·ber·ry (boi'zən bĕr'Y), *n.*, *pl.* **-ries.** a blackberrylike fruit with a flavor similar to that of raspberries.

Br, *Chem.* bromine.

bra (brä), *n. Colloq.* brassière.

brace (brās), *n.*, *v.*, **braced, bracing.** —*n.* **1.** something that holds parts in place; clamp. **2.** *Mach.* a device for holding and turning tools for boring or drilling. **3.** (*often pl.*) *Dentistry.* a metal wire placed to straighten irregular teeth. **4.** *Med.* an appliance for supporting a weak joint or joints. **5.** (*pl.*) *Chiefly Brit.* suspenders. **6.** a pair; a couple. **7.** one of two characters { or } for connecting lines. —*v.t.* **8.** to furnish, fasten, or strengthen with a brace. **9.** to make steady. **10.** to make tight. **11.** to act as a stimulant to. —*v.i.* **12. brace up,** *Colloq.* to rouse one's vigor.

brace·let (brās'lYt), *n.* an ornamental band for the wrist or arm.

brac·er (brā'sər), *n.* **1.** one that braces. **2.** *U.S. Colloq.* a stimulating drink.

bra·chi·o·pod (brā'kY ə pŏd', brăk'Y-), *n. Zool.* any of a phylum (mostly extinct) of mollusklike animals having dorsal and ventral shells.

bra·chi·um (brā'kY əm, brăk'Y-), *n.*, *pl.* **brachia** (brā'kY ə, brăk'Y ə). *Anat.*, *Zool.* the upper arm. —**bra'chi·al,** *adj.*

brac·ing (brā'sĭng), *adj.* **1.** invigorating. —*n.* **2.** a brace. —**brac'ing·ly,** *adv.*

brack·et (brăk'Yt), *n.* **1.** a triangular support under a shelf or the like. **2.** one of two marks, [], used to enclose parenthetical matter, etc. **3.** a grouping of taxpayers based on income. —*v.t.* **4.** to furnish with a bracket. **5.** to place within brackets. **6.** to associate or mention together.

brack·ish (brăk'Ysh), *adj.* **1.** salty. **2.** distasteful. —**brack'ish·ness,** *n.*

bract (brăkt), *n. Bot.* a specialized leaf or leaflike part, usually at the base of a flower. —**brac·te·al** (brăk'tY əl), *adj.*

brad (brăd), *n.* a small wire nail with a head like a finishing nail.

Brad·ley (brăd'lY), *n.* **Omar Nelson,** born 1893, U.S. general: Chief of Staff since 1948.

brae (brā, brē), *n. Scot.* a hillside.

brag (brăg), *v.*, **bragged, bragging,** *n.*, *adj.* —*v.i.*, *v.t.* **1.** to use boastful language (about). —*n.* **2.** a boast or vaunt. **3.** a thing to boast of. **4.** a boaster. —*adj.* **5.** first-rate. —**brag'ger,** *n.*

brag·gart (brăg'ərt), *n.* **1.** one given to bragging. —*adj.* **2.** boastful. —**brag'gart·ism,** *n.*

Brah·ma (brä'mə), *n.* **1.** (in philosophic Hinduism) the impersonal Supreme Being. **2.** (in later Hinduism) a trinity of the personal Creator along with Vishnu the Preserver and Siva the Destroyer.

Brah·man (brä'mən), *n.*, *pl.* **-mans.** a member of the highest, or priestly, caste among the Hindus. —**Brah·man·ic** (brä măn'Yk), **Brah·man'i·cal,** *adj.* —**Brah'man·ism,** *n.*

Brah·min (brä'mYn), *n.*, *pl.* **-min.** **1.** Brahman. **2.** a person of great intellect.

Brahms (brämz), *n.* **Johannes,** 1833–97, German composer.

braid (brād), *v.t.* **1.** to weave together. **2.** to bind (the hair) with a ribbon, etc. —*n.* **3.** a braided length of hair, etc. —**braid'er,** *n.*

Braille (brāl), *n.* a system of writing or printing for the blind, in which combinations of tangible dots or points are used to represent letters, etc. Also, **braille.**

brain (brān), *n.* **1.** (*sometimes pl.*) the soft mass of nerve substance which fills the cranium of man and other vertebrates. **2.** (*usually pl.*) intelligence. —*v.t.* **3.** to dash out the brains of.

brain·less (brān'lYs), *adj.* stupid.

brain·pan (brān'păn'), *n.* the skull or cranium.

brain·sick (brān'sYk'), *adj.* crazy; mad.

brain storm, *Colloq.* a sudden inspiration, idea, etc.

brain trust, a group of experts who give counsel, help shape policy, etc. —**brain truster.**

brain·y (brā'nY), *adj.*, **brainier, brainiest.** intelligent; clever. —**brain'i·ness,** *n.*

braise (brāz), *v.t.*, **braised, braising.** to cook (meat, etc.) slowly in little moisture.

brake[1] (brāk), *n.*, *v.*, **braked, braking.** —*n.* **1.** any device for arresting motion. **2.** a tool for breaking up flax or hemp, to separate the fiber. —*v.t.* **3.** to slow or stop the motion of (a wheel, etc.). **4.** to process (flax or hemp) by crushing it in a brake. —*v.i.* **5.** to use or run a brake.

brake[2] (brāk), *n.* a thicket.

brake[3] (brāk), *n.* any large or coarse fern.

brake·man (brāk'mən), *n.*, *pl.* **-men.** a member of a train crew, assisting the conductor. Also, *Brit.*, **brakes'man.**

bram·ble (brăm'bəl), *n.* **1.** any plant of the rose family. **2.** any rough prickly shrub. —**bram'bly,** *adj.*

bran (brăn), *n.* the ground husk of grain, separated from flour or meal by bolting.

branch (brănch, bränch), *n.* **1.** *Bot.* a division or subdivision of the stem or axis of a tree, shrub, or other plant. **2.** a limb, offshoot, or ramification. **3.** any part of a system. **4.** a local operating division of a business, library, or the like. **5.** a particular line of family descent. —*v.i.* **6.** to put forth branches. **7.** to divide into separate parts or subdivisions. —*v.t.* **8.** to divide as into branches. —**branch'less,** *adj.* —**branch'like',** *adj.*

brand (brănd), *n.* **1.** a trademark to identify a product. **2.** kind, grade, or make. **3.** a mark to indicate ownership, etc. **4.** an iron for branding. **5.** a burning or partly burned piece of wood. **6.** *Archaic or Poetic.* a sword. —*v.t.* **7.** to mark with a brand. —**brand'er,** *n.*

bran·dish (brăn'dYsh), *v.t.* **1.** to shake or wave, as a weapon. —*n.* **2.** a wave, as of a weapon.

brand-new (brănd'nū', -nōō'), *adj.* quite new.

bran·dy (brăn'dY), *n.*, *pl.* **-dies,** *v.*, **-died, -dying.** —*n.* **1.** the spirit distilled from the fermented juice of grapes, etc. —*v.t.* **2.** to mix, flavor, or preserve with brandy. —**bran'died,** *adj.*

brant (brănt), *n.*, *pl.* **brants, brant.** any of several species of small, dark-colored geese.

brash (brăsh), *adj.* **1.** headlong; rash. **2.** impertinent.

brass (brăs, bräs), *n.* **1.** a durable, malleable, and ductile yellow alloy, consisting essentially of copper and zinc. **2.** a utensil, ornament, etc., made of brass. **3.** a musical instrument of the trumpet or horn families. **4.** such instruments (**brass winds**) collectively in a band or orchestra. **5.** *U.S. Slang.* high-ranking officials, esp. of the army and navy. **6.** *Colloq.* impudence. —*adj.* **7.** made of brass. **8.** using musical instruments made of brass.

brass hat, *Slang.* a high-ranking officer.

brass·ie (brăs'Y, bräs'Y), *n.* a golf club with a wooden head soled with a brass plate.

bras·sière (brə zYr'), *n.* a woman's undergarment which supports the breasts.

brass·y (brăs'Y, bräs'Y), *adj.*, **brassier, brassiest. 1.** made of or resembling brass. **2.** metallic. **3.** *Colloq.* brazen. —**brass'i·ly,** *adv.* —**brass'i·ness,** *n.*

brat (brăt), *n.* a child (used usually in contempt).

bra·va·do (brə vä'dō), *n.*, *pl.* **-does, -dos.** boasting; swaggering; pretense.

brave (brāv), *adj.*, **braver, bravest,** *n.*, *v.*, **braved, braving.** —*adj.* **1.** possessing or exhibiting courage. **2.** making a fine appearance. —*n.* **3.** a brave person. **4.** a North American Indian or other savage warrior. —*v.t.* **5.** to meet courageously. **6.** to defy. —**brave'ly,** *adv.* —**brave'ness,** *n.*

brav·er·y (brā'və rY), *n.*, *pl.* **-eries. 1.** brave spirit or conduct; valor. **2.** splendor.

bra·vo[1] (brä'vō), *interj.*, *n.*, *pl.* **-vos.** —*interj.* **1.** well done! —*n.* **2.** a shout of "bravo!"

bra·vo[2] (brä'vō, brä'-), *n.*, *pl.* **-voes, -vos.** a daring bandit, assassin, or murderer.

brawl (brôl), *n.* **1.** a noisy quarrel. **2.** a clamor. —*v.i.* **3.** to quarrel angrily or noisily. —**brawl'er,** *n.*

brawn (brôn), *n.* **1.** well-developed muscles. **2.** muscular strength. —**brawn'y,** *adj.*

bray (brā), *n.* **1.** a harsh cry, as of the donkey. **2.** any similar sound. —*v.i.*, *v.t.* **3.** to utter (with) a loud, harsh sound. —**bray'er,** *n.*

Braz., 1. Brazil. **2.** Brazilian.

braze (brāz), *v.t.*, **brazed, brazing.** to make of or ornament with brass.

bra·zen (brā'zən), *adj.* **1.** made of brass. **2.** like brass. **3.** shameless or impudent. —*v.t.* **4.** to face with boldness, etc. **5.** to make bold. —**bra'zen·ly,** *adv.* —**bra'zen·ness,** *n.*

bra·zier[1] (brā'zhər), *n.* a worker in brass.

bra·zier[2] (brā'zhər), *n.* a receptacle for burning charcoal or other fuel, as for heating a room.

Bra·zil (brə zĭl'), *n.* a republic in South America. 45,300,000 pop.; 3,286,170 sq. mi. *Cap.:* Rio de Janeiro. —**Bra·zil'ian,** *adj., n.*

Brazil nut, the triangular edible seed (nut) of certain species of trees growing in Brazil, etc.

breach (brēch), *n.* 1. act or result of breaking. 2. a gap made in a wall, dike, fortification, etc. 3. an infraction or violation, as of law, promise, etc. 4. a severance of friendly relations. —*v.t.* 5. to make an opening in.

bread (brĕd), *n.* 1. a food made of flour or meal, milk or water, etc., made into a dough, and baked. 2. livelihood. 3. *Eccles.* the wafer or bread used in the Eucharist. —*v.t.* 4. to cover with bread crumbs or meal.

bread·fruit (brĕd'frōōt'), *n.* 1. a large, round, starchy fruit yielded by a tree of the Pacific islands, etc., much used, baked or roasted, for food. 2. the tree bearing this fruit.

bread·stuff (brĕd'stŭf'), *n.* 1. grain, flour, or meal for making bread. 2. bread.

breadth (brĕdth, brĕtth), *n.* 1. the measure of the distance from one side of a surface or solid to another; width. 2. an extent or piece of something as measured by its width. 3. freedom from narrowness or restraint. 4. extent.

break (brāk), *v.,* **broke** or (*Archaic*) **brake; broken,** or (*Archaic*) **broke; breaking,** *n.* —*v.t.* 1. to reduce to pieces. 2. to violate. 3. to dissolve. 4. to fracture a bone of. 5. to lacerate; wound. 6. to interrupt. 7. to destroy the regularity of. 8. to put an end to. 9. to destroy the unity, continuity, or arrangement of. 10. to exchange for a smaller amount or smaller units. 11. to make one's way through. 12. *Law.* a. to open or force one's way into (a dwelling, etc.). b. to contest successfully (a will) by judicial action. 13. to make one's way out of. 14. to exceed. 15. to disclose, with caution or delicacy. 16. to disable or destroy. 17. (pp. **broke**) to ruin financially. 18. to reduce in rank. 19. to weaken in strength, spirit, etc. 20. to tame. 21. to train away from a habit. 22. *Elect.* to render (a circuit) incomplete. —*v.i.* 23. to separate into parts. 24. to leave off abruptly. 25. to become detached. 26. to dissolve and separate. 27. to sever relations. 28. to escape suddenly. 29. to force a way. 30. to burst. 31. to dawn, as the day. 32. to give way or fail as under strain. 33. (of the heart) to be overwhelmed. 34. (of prices) to drop sharply. 35. *Music.* a. to change or go from one register to another. b. to change or be interrupted unmusically. —*n.* 36. a forcible disruption or separation of parts. 37. a gap. 38. an attempt to escape. 39. an interruption of continuity. 40. an abrupt or marked change. 41. *Colloq.* an opportunity. 42. *Colloq.* a social error. 43. a brief rest. 44. *Pros.* a pause or caesura. 45. *Jazz.* a solo passage, usually of about two bars, during which the accompaniment rests. 46. *Music.* the point in the scale where the quality of voice of one register changes to that of another. 47. a sudden drop in prices. 48. *Elect.* an opening or discontinuity in a circuit. —**break/a·ble,** *adj.*

break·age (brā'kĭj), *n.* 1. act of breaking. 2. the amount of things broken. 3. *Com.* an allowance for articles broken in transit or in use.

break·down (brāk'doun'), *n.* 1. a breaking down; collapse. 2. decomposition. 3. analysis. 4. *U.S.* a noisy, lively folk dance.

break·er (brā'kər), *n.* 1. one that breaks. 2. a wave that dashes into foam.

break·fast (brĕk'fəst), *n.* 1. the first meal of the day; a morning meal. 2. the food eaten at the first meal. —*v.i.* 3. to take breakfast. —*v.t.* 4. to supply with breakfast. —**break/fast·er,** *n.*

break·neck (brāk'nĕk'), *adj.* hazardous.

break·up (brāk'ŭp'), *n.* disintegration.

break·wa·ter (brāk'wô'tər, -wŏt'ər), *n.* a barrier which breaks the force of waves.

bream (brēm), *n., pl.* **breams,** (*esp. collectively*) **bream.** 1. any of various fresh-water cyprinoid fishes with a compressed, deep body. 2. any of certain fresh-water sunfishes.

breast (brĕst), *n.* 1. the chest. 2. the milk gland. 3. the bosom regarded as the seat of thoughts and feelings. 4. thoughts; feelings. —*v.t.* 5. to meet boldly or advance against.

breast·bone (brĕst'bōn'), *n.* sternum.

breast·pin (brĕst'pĭn'), *n.* a brooch.

breast·plate (brĕst'plāt'), *n.* armor for the front of the torso.

breast·work (brĕst'wûrk'), *n.* *Fort.* a defensive work usually breast high, hastily thrown up.

breath (brĕth), *n.* 1. *Physiol.* the air inhaled and exhaled in respiration. 2. respiration. 3. ability to breathe, esp. freely. 4. pause. 5. a light current of air.

breathe (brēth), *v.,* **breathed** (brēthd), **breathing.** —*v.i.* 1. to inhale and exhale air. 2. to pause, as for breath. 3. to blow lightly, as air. 4. to live; exist. —*v.t.* 5. to inhale and exhale in respiration. 6. to allow to rest. 7. to put out of breath; exhaust. 8. to utter; whisper. 9. to inject or infuse. —**breath/a·ble,** *adj.*

breath·er (brē'thər), *n.* a pause.

breath·ing (brē'thĭng), *n.* 1. respiration. 2. a single breath. 3. the short time required for it. 4. a pause. 5. utterance. 6. aspiration. 7. gentle blowing. 8. *Gram.* aspiration.

breath·less (brĕth'lĭs), *adj.* 1. out of breath. 2. with the breath held, as in suspense. 3. that takes away the breath. 4. dead. 5. motionless, as the air. —**breath/less·ly,** *adv.* —**breath/-less·ness,** *n.*

breech (brēch), *n.* 1. the buttocks. 2. the hinder part of anything. 3. *Ordn.* the mass of metal behind the bore of a cannon.

breech·es (brĭch'ĭz), *n.pl.* 1. trousers covering the hips and thighs. 2. trousers.

breeches buoy, *Naut.* a lifesaving apparatus, like a short pair of breeches, moving on a rope stretched from a wreck to the shore or another ship.

breed (brēd), *v.,* **bred, breeding,** *n.* —*v.t., v.i.* 1. to produce (offspring). 2. to procure by the mating of parents. 3. to raise (livestock, etc.). 4. to cause; produce. 5. to be the native place or the source of. —*n.* 6. a relatively homogenous group of animals within a species. 7. lineage. 8. sort; kind. —**breed/er,** *n.*

breed·ing (brē'dĭng), *n.* 1. act of one who or that which breeds. 2. nurture; training. 3. manners.

breeze (brēz), *n.* a current of air, esp. a light one.

breez·y (brē'zĭ), *adj.,* **breezier, breeziest.** 1. abounding in breezes; windy. 2. sprightly. —**breez/i·ly,** *adv.* —**breez/i·ness,** *n.*

Brem·en (brĕm'ən), *n.* a city in NW Germany. 424,137.

Bren gun (brĕn), *Brit.* a kind of machine gun.

Bren·ner Pass (brĕn'ər), a pass in the Alps, on the Italian-Austrian border.

breth·ren (brĕth'rĭn), *n.* a pl. of brother.

Bret·on (brĕt'ən), *n.* 1. a native of Brittany. —*adj.* 2. pertaining to Brittany, the Bretons, or their language.

breve (brēv), *n.* a mark (˘) placed over a vowel to show that it is short.

bre·vet (brə vĕt' *or, esp. Brit.,* brĕv'ĭt), *n., v.,* **-vetted, -vetting** *or* **-veted, -veting.** —*n.* 1. a commission promoting a military officer without increase of pay. —*v.t.* 2. to appoint by brevet.

bre·vi·ar·y (brē'vĭ ĕr'ĭ, brĕv'ĭ-), *n., pl.* **-aries.** *Rom. Cath. Ch.* a book of daily prayers and readings to be read by those in major orders.

brev·i·ty (brĕv'ə tĭ), *n., pl.* **-ties.** 1. shortness of time; briefness. 2. conciseness.

brew (brōō), *v.t., v.i.* 1. to make (beer, ale, etc.) from malt, etc., by steeping, boiling, and fermentation. 2. to prepare (any beverage) by a similar process. 3. to concoct or contrive. —*n.* 4. a quantity brewed in a single process. 5. a particular brewing. —**brew/er,** *n.* —**brew/ing,** *n.*

brew·er·y (brōō'ə rĭ, brōō'rĭ), *n., pl.* **-eries.** an establishment for brewing malt liquors.

bri·ar (brī'ər), *n.* brier. —**bri'ar·y,** *adj.*

bribe (brīb), *n., v.,* **bribed, bribing.** —*n.* 1. a gift, sum of money, or the like, given or promised for corrupt performance of duty. 2. anything given or serving to induce. —*v.t.* 3. to give or promise a bribe to. 4. to influence by a bribe. —*v.i.* 5. to give bribes. —**brib/a·ble,** *adj.* —**brib/er,** *n.*

brib·er·y (brī'bə rĭ), *n., pl.* **-eries.** act or practice of giving or accepting bribes.

bric-a-brac (brĭk'ə brăk'), *n.* miscellaneous articles of curiosity or interest.

brick (brĭk), *n.* 1. a block of clay, hardened by heating, and used for building, etc. 2. any similar block. 3. *Colloq.* a good fellow. —*v.t.* 4. to lay,

line, or build with brick. —**brick′like′**, *adj.*
—**brick′y**, *adj.*

brick·bat (brĭk′băt′), *n.* **1.** a piece of broken brick. **2.** *Colloq.* a caustic criticism.

brick·lay·ing (brĭk′lā′ĭng), *n.* the art or occupation of building with bricks. —**brick′-lay′er**, *n.*

brid·al (brī′dəl), *adj.* **1.** of or pertaining to a bride or a wedding. —*n.* **2.** a wedding.

bride (brīd), *n.* a woman newly married, or about to be married.

bride·groom (brīd′grōōm′, -grŏŏm′), *n.* a man newly married, or about to be married.

brides·maid (brīdz′mād′), *n.* a young unmarried woman who attends the bride at a wedding.

bridge[1] (brĭj), *n., v.,* **bridged, bridging.** —*n.* **1.** a structure spanning a river, road, or the like. **2.** a platform from side to side of a ship above the rail, for the officer in charge. **3.** *Anat.* the ridge line of the nose. **4.** *Dentistry.* an artificial replacement of a missing tooth or teeth. **5.** a piece raising the strings of a musical instrument above the sounding board. —*v.t.* **6.** to make a bridge over; span. —**bridge′a·ble**, *adj.*

bridge[2] (brĭj), *n.* *Cards.* a game in which one partnership plays to fulfill a certain declaration against opponents.

bridge·head (brĭj′hĕd′), *n.* a position held on the enemy side of a river, to cover the crossing of friendly troops.

Bridge·port (brĭj′pōrt′), *n.* a seaport in SW Connecticut. 147,121.

bridge·work (brĭj′wûrk′), *n.* *Dentistry.* **1.** bridges collectively. **2.** any of various bridges.

bri·dle (brī′dəl), *n., v.,* **-dled, -dling.** —*n.* **1.** the part of the harness of a horse, etc., about the head, used to guide the animal. **2.** anything that restrains. —*v.t.* **3.** to put a bridle on. **4.** to restrain.

brief (brēf), *adj.* **1.** of little duration. **2.** concise. **3.** curt. —*n.* **4.** a concise statement. **5.** an outline of the arguments and information on one side of a controversy. **6.** *Law.* a memorandum of points of fact or law for use in conducting a case. —*v.t.* **7.** to make a summary of. **8.** to instruct by a brief or summary. —**brief′ly**, *adv.* —**brief′ness**, *n.*

brief case, a flat, rectangular leather case used for carrying documents, books, etc.

bri·er[1] (brī′ər), *n.* a prickly plant or shrub, esp. the sweetbrier. —**bri′er·y**, *adj.*

bri·er[2] (brī′ər), *n.* the white heath of France and Corsica, whose woody root is used for making tobacco pipes.

brig (brĭg), *n.* **1.** a two-masted vessel square-rigged on both masts. **2.** the compartment of a ship where prisoners are confined.

bri·gade (brĭ gād′), *n., v.,* **-gaded, -gading.** —*n.* **1.** a unit consisting of several regiments, squadrons, or battalions. **2.** a large body of troops. **3.** a group organized for a special purpose. —*v.t.* **4.** to form into a brigade.

brig·a·dier (brĭg′ə dĭr′), *n.* an officer ranking between colonel and major general.

brigadier general, *pl.* **brigadier generals.** *U.S. Army.* an officer between colonel and major general.

brig·and (brĭg′ənd), *n.* a bandit. —**brig′and·age,** *n.*

brig·an·tine (brĭg′ən tēn′, -tĭn′), *n.* *Naut.* a type of two-masted vessel.

bright (brīt), *adj.* **1.** radiating or reflecting light; shining. **2.** filled with light. **3.** brilliant, as color. **4.** clear, as liquids. **5.** glorious, as a period. **6.** intelligent. **7.** clever or witty. **8.** lively; cheerful. **9.** characterized by gladness. **10.** favorable or auspicious. —*adv.* **11.** in a bright manner. —**bright′ly**, *adv.* —**bright′ness**, *n.*

bright·en (brī′tən), *v.i., v.t.* to become or make bright or brighter.

Brigh·ton (brī′tən), *n.* a city in SE England, on the English Channel: seaside resort. 146,190.

bril·liant (brĭl′yənt), *adj.* **1.** shining brightly; sparkling. **2.** illustrious. **3.** having or showing great intelligence. —*n.* **4.** a diamond (or other gem) with many facets. —**bril′liant·ly**, *adv.* —**bril′liance, bril′lian·cy, bril′liant·ness**, *n.*

bril·lian·tine (brĭl′yən tēn′), *n.* a preparation for the hair.

brim (brĭm), *n., v.,* **brimmed, brimming.** —*n.* **1.** the upper edge of anything hollow; rim. **2.** a projecting edge. —*v.i.* **3.** to be full to the brim. —*v.t.* **4.** to fill to the brim. —**brim′ful′**, *adj.*

brim·stone (brĭm′stōn′), *n.* sulfur.

brin·dle (brĭn′dəl), *n.* **1.** a brindled coloring. **2.** a brindled animal.

brin·dled (brĭn′dəld), *adj.* gray or tawny with darker streaks or spots.

brine (brīn), *n., v.,* **brined, brining.** —*n.* **1.** salt water. **2.** water strongly salted for pickling. **3.** the sea. —*v.t.* **4.** to treat with or steep in brine.

bring (brĭng), *v.t.,* **brought, bringing.** **1.** to cause to come with oneself. **2.** to cause to come, as to a particular state, opinion, action, etc. **3.** to lead or induce. **4.** *Law.* to put forward before a tribunal. **5.** bring about, to cause; accomplish.

brink (brĭngk), *n.* the edge of a steep place or of land bordering water.

brin·y (brī′nĭ), *adj.,* **brinier, briniest.** of or like brine; salty. —**brin′i·ness**, *n.*

bri·oche (brē′ōsh, -ŏsh), *n.* a light, sweet bun or roll, raised with eggs and yeast.

bri·quette (brĭ kĕt′), *n.* a molded block of coal dust for fuel. Also, **bri·quet′.**

Bris·bane (brĭz′bān, -bən), *n.* a seaport in E Australia. 344,200.

brisk (brĭsk), *adj.* **1.** quick and active; lively. **2.** sharp and stimulating. —*v.t., v.i.* **3.** to liven (*up*). —**brisk′ly**, *adv.* —**brisk′ness**, *n.*

bris·ket (brĭs′kĭt), *n.* the breast of an animal, or the part of the breast lying next to the ribs.

bris·tle (brĭs′əl), *n., v.,* **-tled, -tling.** —*n.* **1.** one of the short, stiff, coarse hairs of certain animals, esp. hogs. —*v.i.* **2.** to stand or rise stiffly, like bristles. **3.** to erect the bristles, as an irritated animal. **4.** to be full of something suggestive of bristles. **5.** to be visibly roused or stirred. —*v.t.* **6.** to erect like bristles. —**bris′tly**, *adj.*

Bris·tol (brĭs′təl), *n.* **1.** a seaport in SW England. 444,000. **2.** a city in central Connecticut. 30,167.

Brit., **1.** Britain. **2.** British.

Brit·ain (brĭt′ən), *n.* Great Britain.

Bri·tan·ni·a (brĭ tăn′ĭ ə, -tăn′yə), *n.* **1.** British Empire. **2.** Great Britain.

Bri·tan·nic (brĭ tăn′ĭk), *adj.* British.

Brit·i·cism (brĭt′ə sĭz′əm), *n.* an English language usage peculiar to British people.

Brit·ish (brĭt′ĭsh), *adj.* **1.** of or pertaining to Great Britain, the British Empire, or its inhabitants. —*n.* **2.** the British people, collectively.

British Columbia, a province in W Canada, on the Pacific coast. 817,861 pop.; 366,255 sq. mi. *Cap.:* Victoria.

British Commonwealth of Nations, the United Kingdom of Great Britain and Northern Ireland, the Dominions (Canada, Australia, New Zealand, Union of South Africa), and Eire.

British Empire, the territories under the leadership or control of the British crown, including those in the British Commonwealth and their colonies, protectorates, dependencies, and mandates. 481,100,000 pop.; ab. 11,460,000 sq. mi.

Brit·ish·er (brĭt′ĭsh ər), *n.* a native or inhabitant of Britain.

British Guiana, a British crown colony on the NE coast of South America. 364,000 pop.; 89,480 sq. mi. *Cap.:* Georgetown.

British Honduras, a British crown colony in N Central America. 62,000 pop.; 8598 sq. mi. *Cap.:* Belize.

British Isles, Great Britain, Ireland, the Isle of Man, and adjacent islands. 50,231,000 pop.; 120,592 sq. mi.

British West Indies, the British islands in the West Indies, including the Bahama Islands, Jamaica, Barbados, Trinidad, Tobago, and islands of the Leeward and Windward groups. 2,230,200 pop.; ab. 12,500 sq. mi.

Brit·on (brĭt′ən), *n.* **1.** a native or inhabitant of Great Britain. **2.** one of the Celts of early Britain.

Brit·ta·ny (brĭt′ə nĭ), *n.* a peninsula in NW France between the English Channel and the Bay of Biscay.

brit·tle (brĭt′əl), *adj.* **1.** breaking readily, as glass. —*n.* **2.** a confection of melted sugar, usually with nuts. —**brit′tle·ness**, *n.*

Br·no (bûr′nô), *n.* a city in central Czechoslovakia: the capital of Moravia. 295,400.

bro., *pl.* **bros.** brother. Also, **Bro.**

broach (brōch), *n.* **1.** a tapered tool with serrations which enlarges a given hole as the tool is pulled through. —*v.t.* **2.** to enlarge with a broach. **3.** to pierce. **4.** to draw as by tapping. **5.** to mention or suggest for the first time. —broach′er, n.

broad (brôd), adj. **1.** of great breadth. **2.** large. **3.** open; full. **4.** not limited; liberal. **5.** of extensive scope. **6.** main or general. **7.** clear. **8.** bold; plain-spoken. **9.** indecent. **10.** unrestrained. —adv. **11.** fully. —broad′ly, adv.

broad·ax (brôd′ăks′), n. **1.** an ax for hewing timber. **2.** a battle-ax. Also, **broad′axe′**.

broad·cast (brôd′kăst′, -käst′), v., -cast or -casted, -casting, n., adj. —v.t. **1.** to send by radio. **2.** to scatter or disseminate widely. —v.i. **3.** to send radio messages, etc. **4.** to scatter or disseminate something widely. —n. **5.** that which is broadcast. **6.** a radio program. **7.** the method of sowing by scattering seed. —adj. **8.** sent out by broadcasting, as radio messages, etc. **9.** cast all over an area. —broad′cast′er, n.

broad·cloth (brôd′klôth′, -klŏth′), n. **1.** cotton material, usually mercerized, resembling fine poplin. **2.** woolen dress goods with nap laid parallel with selvage.

broad·en (brô′dən), v.i., v.t. to widen.

broad-mind·ed (brôd′mīn′dĭd), adj. free from prejudice; tolerant. —broad′-mind′ed·ly, adv. —broad′-mind′ed·ness, n.

broad·side (brôd′sīd′), n. **1.** a simultaneous discharge of all the guns on one side of a vessel of war. **2.** a sheet of paper, esp. of large size, printed on one side only, as for posting.

broad·sword (brôd′sôrd′), n. a straight, broad, flat sword, usually with a basket hilt.

Broad·way (brôd′wā′), n. a street in New York City, famous for its theaters.

bro·cade (brō kād′), n., v., -caded, -cading. —n. **1.** a fabric woven with an elaborate design. —v.t. **2.** to weave with a design or figure. —brocad′ed, adj.

broc·co·li (brŏk′ə lĭ), n. a plant of the mustard family resembling the cauliflower, the green saps and the stalk of which are a common vegetable.

bro·chure (brō shŏŏr′), n. a pamphlet.

Brock·ton (brŏk′tən), n. a city in E Massachusetts. 62,343.

bro·gan (brō′gən), n. a coarse, stout shoe.

brogue (brōg), n. an Irish accent in English.

broil[1] (broil), v.t., v.i. **1.** to cook by direct heat, as on a gridiron. —n. **2.** a broiling. **3.** something broiled.

broil[2] (broil), n., v.i. quarrel.

broil·er (broi′lər), n. **1.** any device for broiling. **2.** a young chicken suitable for broiling.

broke (brōk), v. **1.** pt. of **break**. —adj. **2.** Slang. out of money; bankrupt.

bro·ken (brō′kən), v. **1.** pp. of **break**. —adj. **2.** reduced to fragments. **3.** torn; fractured. **4.** changing direction abruptly. **5.** incomplete. **6.** violated. **7.** interrupted. **8.** weakened in strength, spirit, etc. **9.** tamed. **10.** imperfectly spoken. **11.** ruined; bankrupt. —bro′ken·ly, adv. —bro′ken·ness, n.

bro·ken-heart·ed (brō′kən här′tĭd), adj. crushed by grief.

bro·ker (brō′kər), n. an agent, as one who buys or sells for a principal on a commission basis.

bro·ker·age (brō′kər ĭj), n. **1.** the business of a broker. **2.** the commission of a broker.

bro·mide (brō′mīd, -mĭd), n. **1.** Also, **bro·mid** (brō′mĭd). Chem. a compound usually containing two elements only, one of which is bromine. **2.** a tiresome platitude. —bro·mid·ic (brō mĭd′ĭk), adj.

bro·mine (brō′mēn, -mĭn), n. Chem. an element, a dark-reddish fuming liquid. Symbol: Br; at. wt.: 79.92; at. no: 35; sp. gr. (liquid): 3.119 at 20°C. Also, **bro·min** (brō′mĭn).

bron·chi·a (brŏng′kĭ ə), n.pl. Anat. the ramifications of the bronchi or tubes.

bron·chi·al (brŏng′kĭ əl), adj. Anat. pertaining to the bronchia or bronchi.

bron·chi·tis (brŏng kī′tĭs), n. Pathol. inflammation of the windpipe and bronchial tubes. —bron·chit·ic (brŏng kĭt′ĭk), adj.

bron·chus (brŏng′kəs), n., pl. **-chi** (-kī). Anat. either of the two main branches of the trachea.

bron·co (brŏng′kō), n., pl. **-cos**. a pony or mustang of the western U.S., esp. one that is not broken. Also, **bron′cho**.

bron·co-bust·er (brŏng′kō bŭs′tər), n. Western U.S. one who breaks broncos to the saddle.

Bron·të (brŏn′tĭ), n. **1.** Anne, (Acton Bell) 1820–49, British novelist. **2.** her sister, Char-

lotte, (Currer Bell) 1816–55, British novelist. **3.** her sister, **Emily Jane**, (Ellis Bell) 1818–48, British novelist.

bron·to·sau·rus (brŏn′tə sôr′əs), n. a large, extinct, amphibious, herbivorous dinosaur.

Brontosaurus
(66 ft. long, 12 ft. high)

Bronx (brŏngks), n. The, a N borough of New York City. 1,-394,711; 54 sq. mi.

bronze (brŏnz), n., v., bronzed, bronzing. —n. **1.** Metall. a. a durable brown alloy, consisting essentially of copper and tin. b. any of various other copper-base alloys. **2.** a metallic brownish color. **3.** a statue or medal made of bronze. —v.t. **4.** to give the appearance of bronze to.

brooch (brōch, brōŏch), n. a clasp or ornament for the dress, fastened by a pin and catch.

brood (brōōd), n. **1.** a number of young creatures produced at one time. **2.** breed or kind. —v.t., v.i. **3.** to sit as a bird over (eggs or young); hatch. **4.** to think persistently or moodily about. —adj. **5.** kept for breeding purposes. —brood′y, adj.

brood·er (brōō′dər), n. **1.** a device or structure for the artificial rearing of young chickens or other birds. **2.** one that broods.

brook[1] (brŏŏk), n. a small, natural stream of fresh water. —brook′let, n.

brook[2] (brŏŏk), v.t. to bear; tolerate.

Brook·line (brŏŏk′lĭn), n. a town in E Massachusetts, near Boston. 49,786.

Brook·lyn (brŏŏk′lĭn), n. a borough of New York City, on W Long Island. 2,698,285 pop.; 89 sq. mi.

brook trout, the common speckled trout of eastern North America.

broom (brōōm, brŏŏm), n. **1.** a sweeping implement consisting of a brush of twigs or plant stems on a handle. **2.** a shrubby plant of the bean family bearing yellow flowers. —v.t. **3.** to sweep.

broom·stick (brōōm′stĭk′, brŏŏm′-), n. the long stick forming the handle of a broom.

bros., brothers. Also, **Bros.**

broth (brôth, brŏth), n. thin soup of concentrated meat or fish stock.

broth·el (brŏth′əl, brŏth′-, brôth′əl), n. a house of prostitution.

broth·er (brŭth′ər), n., pl. **brothers, brethren,** v. —n. **1.** a male child of the same parents. **2.** a male member of the same kinship group, nationality, profession, etc. **3.** Eccles. a male lay member of a religious organization which has a priesthood.

broth·er·hood (brŭth′ər hŏŏd′), n. **1.** condition of being a brother or brothers. **2.** a fraternal or trade organization.

broth·er-in-law (brŭth′ər ĭn lô′), n., pl. **brothers-in-law. 1.** one's husband's or wife's brother. **2.** one's sister's husband. **3.** the husband of one's wife's or husband's sister.

broth·er·ly (brŭth′ər lĭ), adj. **1.** of, like, or befitting a brother; fraternal. —adv. **2.** as a brother. —broth′er·li·ness, n.

brough·am (brōō′əm, brōōm, brō′əm), n. **1.** a four-wheeled carriage with the driver's perch outside. **2.** a limousine having an open driver's compartment.

brow (brou), n. **1.** the ridge over the eye. **2.** the eyebrow. **3.** (sing. or pl.) the forehead. **4.** the edge of a steep place.

brow·beat (brou′bēt′), v.t., -beat, -beaten, -beating. to intimidate or bully.

brown (broun), n. **1.** a dark shade with yellowish or reddish hue. —adj. **2.** having skin of that color. **3.** sunburned. —v.t., v.i. **4.** to make or become brown. —brown′ish, adj. —brown′ness, n.

brown·ie (brou′nĭ), n. **1.** (in folklore) a little brown goblin who helps secretly in household work. **2.** U.S. a small chocolate cake, often containing nuts.

Brown·ing (brou′nĭng), n. **1.** Elizabeth Barrett, 1806–61, British poetess. **2.** her husband, Robert, 1812–89, British poet.

brown·stone (broun′stōn′), n. a reddish-brown sandstone, used as a building material.

browse (brouz), v., browsed, browsing, n. —v.t. **1.** (of cattle, etc.) to nibble or feed on.

—*v.i.* 2. (of cattle, etc.) to graze. 3. to glance at random through a book or books. —*n.* 4. tender shoots or twigs as food for cattle, etc. —**brows'-er,** *n.*

Bruce (brōōs), *n.* **Robert the,** 1274–1329, king of Scotland, 1306–29: defeated English in 1314.

bru·in (brōō'ĭn), *n.* a bear.

bruise (brōōz), *v.,* **bruised, bruising.** *n.* —*v.t.* 1. to injure without breaking the skin. 2. to injure superficially. 3. to crush by pounding. —*v.i.* 4. to be bruised. —*n.* 5. an injury due to bruising.

bruis·er (brōō'zər), *n.* a boxer.

bruit (brōōt), *v.t.* to rumor widely.

brunch (brŭnch), *n.* a mid-morning meal that serves both as breakfast and lunch.

bru·net (brōō nĕt'), *adj.* 1. (of skin, eyes, or hair) dark; brown. 2. having dark or brown hair, eyes, or skin. —*n.* 3. a brunet man or boy.

bru·nette (brōō nĕt'), *adj.* 1. brunet. —*n.* 2. a brunette woman or girl.

brunt (brŭnt), *n.* the main stress, force, or violence.

brush¹ (brŭsh), *n.* 1. an instrument consisting of bristles, hair, or the like, set in a handle, used for painting, etc. 2. act of brushing. 3. the bushy tail of an animal. 4. a brief encounter. 5. a quick ride across country. 6. *Elect.* a conductor serving to maintain electric contact between stationary and moving parts. —*v.t.* 7. to sweep, rub, remove, etc., with a brush. 8. to touch lightly in passing. —*v.i.* 9. to move with a slight contact. 10. to rush. —**brush'y,** *adj.*

brush² (brŭsh), *n.* 1. a dense growth of bushes, shrubs, etc. 2. *U.S.* brushwood (def. 1). 3. *U.S.* backwoods. —**brush'y,** *adj.*

brush·off (brŭsh'ôf', -ŏf'), *n.* *U.S. Slang.* an abrupt or final dismissal or refusal.

brush·wood (brŭsh'wŏŏd'), *n.* 1. branches of trees cut or broken off. 2. brush² (def. 1).

brusque (brŭsk), *adj.* abrupt; blunt. Also, **brusk.** —**brusque'ly,** *adv.* —**brusque'ness,** *n.*

Brus·sels (brŭs'əlz), *n.* the capital of Belgium, in the central part. 185,514.

Brussels sprouts, small edible cabbagelike heads on the stalk of a common garden plant.

bru·tal (brōō'təl), *adj.* 1. savage; cruel. 2. crude; coarse. 3. irrational. 4. of or pertaining to lower animals. —**bru·tal·i·ty** (brōō tăl'ə tĭ), *n.* —**bru'tal·ly,** *adv.*

bru·tal·ize (brōō'tə līz'), *v.t., v.i.,* **-ized, -izing.** to make or become brutal.

brute (brōōt), *n.* 1. a nonhuman animal; beast. 2. a brutal person. —*adj.* 3. animal; not human. 4. irrational. 5. characteristic of animals. 6. savage; cruel. 7. carnal.

brut·ish (brōō'tĭsh), *adj.* 1. brutal. 2. gross; carnal. 3. lacking civilized sensibilities. —**brut'ish·ly,** *adv.* —**brut'ish·ness,** *n.*

Bru·tus (brōō'təs), *n.* **Marcus Junius,** 85?–42 B.C., Roman provincial administrator: one of the assassins of Julius Caesar.

Bry·an (brī'ən), *n.* **William Jennings,** 1860–1925, U.S. political leader.

Bry·ant (brī'ənt), *n.* **William Cullen,** 1794–1878, U.S. poet.

B.S., Bachelor of Science.

bu., bushel; bushels.

bub·ble (bŭb'əl), *n., v.,* **-bled, -bling.** —*n.* 1. a small globule of gas in or rising through a liquid, or in a solid substance. 2. anything that lacks firmness, substance, or permanence. 3. an inflated speculation. —*v.i.* 4. to effervesce. 5. to flow with a gurgling noise. —*v.t.* 6. to cause to bubble. —**bub'bly,** *adj.*

bu·bon·ic plague (bū bŏn'ĭk), a contagious epidemic disease in which the victims suffer chills, fevers, and swellings, and which often has rat fleas as its carrier.

buc·ca·neer (bŭk'ə nĭr'), *n.* a pirate.

Bu·chan·an (bū kăn'ən, bə-), *n.* **James,** 1791–1868, 15th president of the U.S., 1857–61.

Bu·cha·rest (bū'kə rĕst', bōō'-), *n.* the capital of Rumania, in the S part. 990,983.

buck¹ (bŭk), *n.* 1. the male of the deer, antelope, rabbit, hare, sheep, goat, etc. 2. a fop. 3. *U.S. Slang.* a dollar. —*adj.* 4. *Mil. Slang.* of the lowest of several ranks involving the same principal designation.

buck² (bŭk), *v.i.* 1. (of a saddle or pack animal) to leap with arched back and come down with head low and forelegs stiff, in order to dislodge rider or pack. 2. *U.S. Colloq.* to resist obstinately. 3. *Colloq.* to become more cheerful, vigorous, etc. —*v.t.* 4. to throw or attempt to throw (a rider) by

bucking. 5. *U.S.* to butt. 6. *U.S. Colloq.* to resist obstinately. 7. *Colloq.* to make more cheerful, etc. 8. *Football.* to charge into with the ball. —*n.* 9. act of bucking. —**buck'er,** *n.*

buck³ (bŭk), *n.* *U.S. Colloq.* responsibility or blame.

buck·a·roo (bŭk'ə rōō', bŭk'ə rōō'), *n., pl.* **-roos.** *Western U.S.* a cowboy.

buck·et (bŭk'ĭt), *n., v.,* **-eted, -eting.** —*n.* 1. a container, usually round with flat bottom and a semicircular handle, for carrying water, etc. 2. anything resembling this. —*v.t.* 3. to lift, carry, or handle in a bucket. —**buck'et·ful',** *n.*

buck·eye (bŭk'ī'), *n.* any of various trees or shrubs allied to the true horse chestnut.

buck fever, *U.S. Colloq.* nervous excitement of an inexperienced hunter upon sighting game.

buck·le (bŭk'əl), *n., v.,* **-led, -ling.** —*n.* 1. a clasp used for fastening together two loose ends, as of a belt. 2. an ornament of metal, beads, etc., of similar appearance. —*v.t.* 3. to fasten with a buckle or buckles. 4. to shrivel, by applying heat or pressure. 5. to prepare for action. —*v.i.* 6. to set to work with vigor. 7. to bend or give way suddenly, as with pressure.

buck·ler (bŭk'lər), *n.* 1. a round shield, with grip for holding. 2. any means of defense. —*v.t.* 3. to support; defend.

buck·ram (bŭk'rəm), *n., v.,* **-ramed, -raming.** —*n.* 1. a stiff cotton fabric for interlining, binding books, etc. —*v.t.* 2. to strengthen with buckram.

buck·saw (bŭk'sô'), *n.* a saw consisting of a blade set across an upright frame, used with both hands in cutting wood on a sawhorse.

buck·shot (bŭk'shŏt'), *n.* a large size of lead shot used on big game.

buck·skin (bŭk'skĭn'), *n.* the skin of a deer or sheep.

buck·tooth (bŭk'tōōth'), *n., pl.* **-teeth** (-tēth'). a projecting tooth.

Bucksaw

buck·wheat (bŭk'hwēt'), *n.* 1. a herbaceous plant whose triangular seeds are used as a food for animals, made into flour, etc. 2. the seeds.

bu·col·ic (bū kŏl'ĭk), *adj.* Also, **bu·col'i·cal.** 1. of or pertaining to shepherds. 2. rustic; rural. —*n.* 3. *Humorous.* a rustic. 4. a pastoral poem. —**bu·col'i·cal·ly,** *adv.*

bud (bŭd), *n., v.,* **budded, budding.** —*n.* 1. *Bot.* a small protuberance on a plant, containing a rudimentary leaf, flower, or stem. 2. *Anat.* any small rounded part, as a taste bud. 3. an immature person or thing. —*v.i.* 4. to produce buds, as a plant. 5. to begin to grow and develop. —*v.t.* 6. to cause to bud. 7. *Hort.* to graft by inserting a single bud into the stock.

Bu·da·pest (bōō'də pĕst', bōō'də pĕst'), *n.* the capital of Hungary, on the Danube. 1,035,000.

Bud·dha (bōŏd'ə), *n.* a great religious teacher who flourished in India about the 6th century B.C.

Bud·dhism (bōŏd'ĭz əm), *n.* the cult, founded by Buddha, which teaches that the supreme felicity is to be striven for by psychological and ethical self-culture. —**Bud'dhist,** *n., adj.*

bud·dy (bŭd'ĭ), *n., pl.* **-dies.** *U.S. Colloq.* a comrade or mate.

budge (bŭj), *v.i., v.t.,* **budged, budging.** to move slightly.

budg·et (bŭj'ĭt), *n., v.,* **-eted, -eting.** —*n.* 1. an estimate of expected income and expense for a given period. 2. a plan of operations based on such an estimate. 3. an itemized allotment of funds for a given period. 4. a stock; collection. —*v.t.* 5. to plan allotment of (funds, time, etc.). 6. to deal with (specific funds) in a budget. —**budg·et·ar·y** (bŭj'ə tĕr'ĭ), *adj.*

Bue·nos Ai·res (bwā'nəs ī'rĭz, bō'nəs âr'ēz), a seaport in and the capital of Argentina, in the E part. 2,567,763.

buff (bŭf), *n.* 1. a kind of thick leather, orig. of buffalo skin, light-yellow with napped surface, used for making belts, etc. 2. a thick coat of buff leather, worn esp. by soldiers. 3. yellowish brown. —*adj.* 4. made of buff. 5. having the color of buff. —*v.t.* 6. to polish or give a high luster to.

buf·fa·lo (bŭf'ə lō'), *n., pl.* **-loes, -los,** (*esp. collectively*) **-lo,** *v.,* **-loed, -loing.** —*n.* 1. any of several mammals of the ox kind, as the **water buffalo** of the Old World, valued as a draft animal, the **Cape buffalo** of South Africa, and the **American buffalo** or **bison.** —*v.t.* *U.S. Slang.* 2. to baffle. 3. to impress by a display of power, importance, etc.

Buf·fa·lo (bŭf′ə lō′), *n.* a city in W New York: a port on Lake Erie. 575,901.

buff·er[1] (bŭf′ər), *n.* 1. a shock-absorbing apparatus.

buff·er[2] (bŭf′ər), *n.* a device for polishing.

buffer state, a smaller state lying between potentially hostile larger states.

buf·fet[1] (bŭf′ĭt), *n., v.,* **-feted, -feting.** —*n.* 1. a blow, as with the hand or fist. —*v.t.* 2. to strike. 3. to battle. —*v.i.* 4. to struggle with blows. 5. to force one's way by a struggle, etc. —**buf′fet·er,** *n.*

buf·fet[2] (bə fā′, bŏŏ-), *n.* 1. a cabinet for china, etc. 2. a counter for lunch or refreshments. —*adj.* 3. (of a meal) spread on tables or buffets from which the guests serve themselves.

buf·foon (bə fōōn′), *n.* a clown; joker.

bug (bŭg), *n.* 1. any of a group of insects characterized by having the forewings thickened at base and membranous at tip, and the hindwings membranous. 2. any insect. 3. *Chiefly Brit.* a bedbug. 4. (*often pl.*) *U.S. Colloq.* defect or difficulty.

bug·a·boo (bŭg′ə bōō′), *n., pl.* **-boos.** some imaginary cause of fear or worry. Also, **bug-bear** (bŭg′bâr′).

bug·gy[1] (bŭg′ĭ), *n., pl.* **-gies.** *U.S.* a light four-wheeled carriage.

bug·gy[2] (bŭg′ĭ), *adj.,* **-gier, -giest.** infested with bugs.

bu·gle (bū′gəl), *n., v.,* **-gled, -gling.** —*n.* 1. a cornetlike military wind instrument. —*v.i.* 2. to sound a bugle. —*v.t.* 3. to call by bugle. —**bu′gler,** *n.*

build (bĭld), *v.,* **built** or (*Archaic*) **builded, building,** *n.* —*v.t.* 1. to construct by assembling parts. 2. to establish, increase, and strengthen. 3. to base; form. —*v.i.* 4. to engage in the art or business of building. 5. to form a plan, etc. —*n.* 6. manner or form of construction. —**build′er,** *n.*

build·ing (bĭl′dĭng), *n.* 1. anything constructed. 2. act or business of constructing.

bulb (bŭlb), *n.* 1. *Bot.* **a.** a bud, having fleshy leaves and usually subterranean, as in the onion, lily, etc. **b.** a plant growing from a bulb. 2. any round, enlarged part. 3. an incandescent electric lamp. 4. an electron tube. —**bulb·ar** (bŭl′bər), **bulb·ous** (bŭl′bəs), *adj.*

Bul·gar·i·a (bŭl gâr′ĭ ə, bŏŏl-), *n.* a republic in SE Europe. 7,022,206 pop.; 42,800 sq. mi. *Cap.:* Sofia. —**Bul·gar′i·an,** *n., adj.*

bulge (bŭlj), *n., v.,* **bulged, bulging.** —*n.* 1. a rounded projecting part. —*v.i., v.t.* 2. to swell out. —**bulg′y,** *adj.*

bulk (bŭlk), *n.* 1. magnitude. 2. the main mass or body. 3. goods or cargo not in packages, bags, etc. —*v.i., v.t.* 4. to be of size, weight, or importance. 5. to increase in size.

bulk·head (bŭlk′hĕd′), *n.* one of the upright partitions dividing a ship into compartments.

bulk·y (bŭl′kĭ), *adj.,* **bulkier, bulkiest.** of great and usually cumbersome bulk or size. —**bulk′i·ly,** *adv.* —**bulk′i·ness,** *n.*

bull[1] (bŏŏl), *n.* 1. the male of a bovine animal. 2. the male of certain other animals. 3. a bull-like person. 4. one who buys in the hope of profit from a rise in prices. 5. (*cap.*) *Astron.* the zodiacal constellation Taurus. 6. bulldog. —*adj.* 7. male. 8. bull-like; large. 9. (in the stock exchange, etc.) marked by a rise in price. —**bull′-ish,** *adj.*

bull[2] (bŏŏl), *n.* *Rom. Cath. Ch.* a formal papal document.

bull·dog (bŏŏl′dôg′, -dŏg′), *n.* 1. a large-headed, short-haired, heavily built variety of dog, very muscular and courageous. —*adj.* 2. like or characteristic of a bulldog. —*v.t.* 3. *Western U.S.* to throw (a calf, etc.) by seizing it by the horns.

bull·doze (bŏŏl′dōz′), *v.t.,* **-dozed, -dozing.** *U.S. Slang.* to bully or intimidate.

bull·doz·er (bŏŏl′dō′zər), *n.* 1. *U.S. Slang.* a person who intimidates. 2. a powerful caterpillar tractor for moving earth, rocks, etc.

bul·let (bŏŏl′ĭt), *n.* a small metal projectile for firing from small arms.

bul·le·tin (bŏŏl′ə tən, -tĭn), *n.* 1. a brief account, as of news, issued for the information of the public. 2. a periodical publication. —*v.t.* 3. to make known by a bulletin.

bul·let·proof (bŏŏl′ĭt prōōf′), *adj.* capable of resisting the impact of a bullet.

bull·fight (bŏŏl′fīt′), *n.* a combat between men and a bull or bulls in an enclosed arena. —**bull′fight′er,** *n.* —**bull′fight′ing,** *n.*

bull·finch (bŏŏl′fĭnch′), *n.* a rosy-breasted European bird, with a short, stout bill, valued as a cage bird.

bull·frog (bŏŏl′frŏg′, -frôg′), *n.* a large frog with an exceptionally deep bass voice.

bull·head (bŏŏl′hĕd′), *n.* 1. any of various fishes with a large or broad head. 2. an obstinate person.

bull·head·ed (bŏŏl′hĕd′ĭd), *adj.* obstinate.

bul·lion (bŏŏl′yən), *n.* 1. gold or silver in the mass. 2. gold or silver in the form of bars or ingots.

bull·ock (bŏŏl′ək), *n.* a castrated bull.

Bull Run, a small river in NE Virginia: two important defeats of Union forces, 1861, 1862.

bull's-eye (bŏŏlz′ī′), *n.* 1. the central spot of a target. 2. a shot that strikes the bull's-eye. 3. a thick disk of glass inserted in a deck or the like to admit light.

bull terrier, one of a breed of dogs produced by crossing the bulldog and the terrier.

bul·ly[1] (bŏŏl′ĭ), *n., pl.* **-lies,** *v.,* **-lied, -lying,** *adj., interj.* —*n.* 1. a blustering, quarrelsome, overbearing person who browbeats weaker people. —*v.t.* 2. to act the bully toward. —*v.i.* 3. to be loudly arrogant and overbearing. —*adj.* 4. *Colloq.* fine. —*interj.* 5. *Colloq.* good!

bul·ly[2] (bŏŏl′ĭ), *n.* bully beef.

bully beef, canned or pickled beef.

bul·rush (bŏŏl′rŭsh′), *n.* 1. (in Biblical use) the papyrus. 2. any of various large rushes or rushlike plants, esp. those from which mats, etc., are made.

bul·wark (bŏŏl′wərk), *n.* 1. *Fort.* a defensive mound of earth or other material; rampart. 2. any protection. 3. (*usually pl.*) *Naut.* a solid part of a ship's side extending above the level of the deck. —*v.t.* 4. to fortify with a bulwark.

bum (bŭm), *n., v.,* **bummed, bumming,** *adj.* *U.S. Colloq.* —*n.* 1. a dissolute person. 2. a habitual loafer. —*v.t.* 3. to borrow without expectation of returning. —*v.i.* 4. to sponge on others. 5. to lead a dissolute life. —*adj.* 6. bad. —**bum′mer,** *n.*

bum·ble·bee (bŭm′bəl bē′), *n.* any of various large, hairy, social bees.

bump (bŭmp), *v.t.* 1. to come violently in contact with; strike. 2. to cause to strike or collide. —*v.i.* 3. to collide. —*n.* 4. act of bumping. 5. the shock of a blow or collision. 6. a swelling from a blow.

bump·er (bŭm′pər), *n.* 1. a horizontal bar at the front or rear of a car to give protection in collisions. 2. a glass filled to the brim. —*adj.* 3. unusually abundant.

bump·kin (bŭmp′kĭn), *n.* a clumsy yokel.

bump·tious (bŭmp′shəs), *adj.* offensively self-assertive. —**bump′tious·ly,** *adv.* —**bump′tious·ness,** *n.*

bump·y (bŭm′pĭ), *adj.,* **bumpier, bumpiest.** 1. of uneven surface. 2. full of jolts. —**bump′i·ly,** *adv.* —**bump′i·ness,** *n.*

bun (bŭn), *n.* a kind of bread roll.

bu·na (bōō′nə, bū′-), *n.* a synthetic rubber.

bunch (bŭnch), *n.* 1. a cluster. 2. any group; lot. 3. a knob; lump. —*v.t.* 4. to group together. —*v.i.* 5. to gather together.

bun·combe (bŭng′kəm), *n.* 1. insincere political speechmaking. 2. insincere talk; humbug.

bun·dle (bŭn′dəl), *n., v.,* **-dled, -dling.** —*n.* 1. a group bound together. 2. a package. 3. a number of things considered together. —*v.t.* 4. to tie or wrap in a bundle. 5. to dress snugly. 6. to send away hurriedly. —*v.i.* 7. to leave hurriedly. 8. to dress warmly. —**bun′dler,** *n.*

bung (bŭng), *n.* 1. a stopper for the hole of a cask. 2. a bunghole. —*v.t.* 3. to close with a bung.

bun·ga·low (bŭng′gə lō′), *n.* a cottage, commonly of one story.

bung·hole (bŭng′hōl′), *n.* a hole in a cask.

bun·gle (bŭng′gəl), *v.,* **-gled, -gling,** *n.* —*v.i., v.t.* 1. to do (something) clumsily. —*n.* 2. a bungling performance. 3. a bungled job. —**bun′gler,** *n.* —**bun′gling·ly,** *adv.*

bun·ion (bŭn′yən), *n.* a swelling on the foot caused by inflammation, esp. of the great toe.

bunk[1] (bŭngk), *n.* 1. a built-in platform bed, as

on a ship. **2.** *Colloq.* any bed. —*v.i.* **3.** *Colloq.* to sleep, esp. in rough quarters.

bunk² (bŭngk), *n.* *U.S. Slang.* nonsense.

bunk·er (bŭng′kər), *n.* **1.** a large bin or receptacle. **2.** *Golf.* an obstacle on a course, as a sandy hollow. —*v.t.* **3.** *Golf.* to drive (a ball) into a bunker.

Bunker Hill, a hill in Charlestown, Mass.: first major battle of American Revolution fought June 17, 1775.

bun·kum (bŭng′kəm), *n.* buncombe.

bun·ny (bŭn′ĭ), *n., pl.* **-nies.** *Colloq.* a rabbit.

Bun·sen burner (bŭn′sən), a type of gas burner with which a very hot flame is obtained by allowing air to enter at the base and mix with the gas.

bunt¹ (bŭnt), *v.t., v.i.* **1.** to push with the horns or head. **2.** *Baseball.* to bat (the ball) lightly. —*n.* **3.** a push with the head or horns. **4.** *Baseball.* act of bunting.

bunt² (bŭnt), *n.* the middle part of a square sail.

bun·ting¹ (bŭn′tĭng), *n.* **1.** coarse fabric of worsted or cotton used for flags, etc. **2.** flags.

bun·ting² (bŭn′tĭng), *n.* any of numerous small birds of the finch family, as the **snow bunting** of arctic regions.

Bun·yan (bŭn′yən), *n.* **John,** 1628–88, British preacher: author of *Pilgrim's Progress.*

buoy (boi, boo′ĭ), *n.* **1.** an anchored float, sometimes carrying a light, whistle, or bell, marking a channel or obstruction. —*v.t.* **2.** to support by or as by a buoy. **3.** to furnish or mark with a buoy or buoys. **4.** to sustain, as hope does. —*v.i.* **5.** to float.

buoy·ant (boi′ənt), *adj.* **1.** tending to float. **2.** capable of keeping a body afloat. **3.** not easily depressed; cheerful. **4.** invigorating. —**buoy·an·cy** (boi′ən sĭ), *n.* —**buoy′ant·ly,** *adv.*

bur (bûr), *n., v.,* **burred, burring.** —*n.* **1.** the rough, prickly case around the seeds of certain plants, as of the chestnut. —*v.t.* **2.** to remove burs from.

bur·den¹ (bûr′dən), *n.* **1.** a load. **2.** *Naut.* **a.** the weight of a ship's cargo. **b.** the carrying capacity of a ship. —*v.t.* **3.** to load heavily.

bur·den² (bûr′dən), *n.* **1.** the principal idea. **2.** *Music.* the refrain or recurring chorus of a song.

bur·den·some (bûr′dən səm), *adj.* oppressively heavy. —**bur′den·some·ly,** *adv.*

bur·dock (bûr′dŏk), *n.* a coarse, broad-leaved weed of the aster family, with prickly heads or burs.

bu·reau (byoͦor′ō), *n., pl.* **-eaus, -eaux** (-ōz). **1.** a chest of drawers for clothing, etc. **2.** *Brit.* a desk. **3.** a government department or unit. **4.** an office for giving out information, etc.

bu·reauc·ra·cy (byoͦo rŏk′rə sĭ), *n., pl.* **-cies.** **1.** government by bureaus. **2.** the officials administering bureaus. **3.** excessive governmental power, red tape, and routine.

bu·reau·crat (byoͦor′ə krăt′), *n.* **1.** an official of a bureaucracy. **2.** an official who works by fixed routine without exercising intelligent judgment. —**bu′reau·crat′ic,** *adj.*

burg (bûrg), *n.* *Colloq.* a city or town.

bur·geon (bûr′jən), *n.* **1.** a bud; sprout. —*v.i., v.t.* **2.** to put forth (buds, etc.).

bur·gess (bûr′jĭs), *n.* **1.** an inhabitant, esp. a citizen or freeman, of an English borough. **2.** *U.S. Hist.* a representative in the popular branch of the colonial legislature of Virginia or Maryland.

burgh (bûrg; *Scot.* bŭr′ō, -ə), *n.* a borough.

burgh·er (bûr′gər), *n.* an inhabitant of a borough.

bur·glar (bûr′glər), *n.* one who commits burglary.

bur·glar·ize (bûr′glə rīz′), *v.t.,* **-ized, -izing.** *Colloq.* to commit burglary upon.

bur·gla·ry (bûr′glə rĭ), *n., pl.* **-ries.** breaking into and entering the house of another with intent to commit a felony.

bur·go·mas·ter (bûr′gə măs′tər, -mäs′tər), *n.* the chief magistrate of a town of Holland, Flanders, Germany, or Austria.

Bur·gun·dy (bûr′gən dĭ), *n., pl.* **-dies.** **1.** a region in SE France. **2.** (*often l.c.*) wine produced in the Burgundy region. —**Bur·gun·di·an** (bər·gŭn′dĭ ən), *adj., n.*

bur·i·al (bĕr′ĭ əl), *n.* act of burying.

Burke (bûrk), *n.* **Edmund,** 1729–97, British statesman, orator, and writer.

burl (bûrl), *n.* **1.** a small knot or lump in wool,

thread, or cloth. **2.** a wartlike growth on the trunk of a tree. —**burled,** *adj.*

bur·lap (bûr′lăp), *n.* coarse fabric made of jute, hemp, or the like; gunny.

bur·lesque (bər lĕsk′), *n., adj., v.,* **-lesqued, -lesquing.** —*n.* **1.** an artistic composition which, for the sake of laughter, vulgarizes lofty material or treats ordinary material with mock dignity. **2.** *U.S.* a theatrical entertainment featuring coarse comedy and dancing. —*adj.* **3.** of or pertaining to risqué burlesque. —*v.t.* **4.** to make ridiculous by mocking representation. —*v.i.* **5.** to use caricature. —**bur·les′quer,** *n.*

bur·ley (bûr′lĭ), *n., pl.* **-leys.** (*often cap.*) a tobacco grown esp. in Kentucky and Ohio.

bur·ly (bûr′lĭ), *adj.,* **-lier, -liest.** **1.** great in bodily size. **2.** bluff; brusque. —**bur′li·ness,** *n.*

Bur·ma (bûr′mə), *n.* a British dependency in SE Asia, on the Bay of Bengal. 14,667,000 pop.; 233,492 sq. mi. *Cap.:* Rangoon. —**Bur·mese** (bər mēz′, -mēs′), *n., adj.*

Burma Road, a strategic highway from Burma to China, used during World War II for supplying Allied military forces in China.

burn (bûrn), *v.,* **burned** or **burnt, burning,** *n.* —*v.i.* **1.** to be on fire. **2.** to contain fire. **3.** to feel heat. **4.** to give light. **5.** to glow like fire. **6.** to feel strong passion. **7.** *Chem.* to undergo combustion. **8.** to become discolored, tanned, or charred through heat. —*v.t.* **9.** to consume with fire. **10.** to cause to feel the sensation of heat. **11.** to injure, discolor, char, or treat with heat. **12.** to produce with fire. **13.** *Chem.* to cause to undergo combustion. —*n.* **14.** a burned place. **15.** an injury, produced by heat, or by abnormal cold, chemicals, electricity, etc.

burn·er (bûr′nər), *n.* **1.** one that burns. **2.** that part of a gas fixture, etc., from which flame issues.

burn·ing (bûr′nĭng), *adj.* intense; serious.

bur·nish (bûr′nĭsh), *v.t.* **1.** to polish by friction. **2.** to make smooth and bright. —*n.* **3.** gloss; brightness. —**bur′nish·er,** *n.*

bur·noose (bər noos′, bûr′noos), *n.* a hooded cloak, such as that worn by Arabs, etc.

Burns (bûrnz), *n.* **Robert,** 1759–96, Scottish poet.

burr¹ (bûr), *n.* **1.** any of various tools for cutting or drilling. **2.** a rough ridge left on metal after cutting with an engraver's tool, etc. **3.** any rough or irregular protuberance. **4.** bur. —*v.t.* **5.** to form a rough point or edge on.

burr² (bûr), *n.* **1.** a guttural pronunciation of the letter *r.* **2.** any rough pronunciation. **3.** a whirring sound. —*v.i.* **4.** to speak with a burr. **5.** to make a whirring sound. —*v.t.* **6.** to pronounce with a burr.

bur·ro (bûr′ō, boͦor′ō), *n., pl.* **-ros.** *Southwestern U.S.* **1.** a pack donkey. **2.** any donkey.

bur·row (bûr′ō), *n.* **1.** a hole in the ground made by a small animal for refuge and habitation. —*v.i.* **2.** to make a hole or passage. **3.** to lodge in a burrow. **4.** to hide. —*v.t.* **5.** to put a burrow or burrows into (a hill, etc.). —**bur′row·er,** *n.*

bur·sa (bûr′sə), *n., pl.* **-sae** (-sē), **-sas.** *Anat., Zool.* a sac to facilitate motion, as between a tendon and a bone. —**bur′sal,** *adj.*

bur·sar (bûr′sər), *n.* a treasurer.

burst (bûrst), *v.,* **burst, bursting,** *n.* —*v.i.* **1.** to break open with sudden violence. **2.** to issue forth suddenly and forcibly. **3.** to give way from violent pain or emotion. **4.** to be extremely full, as if ready to break open. **5.** to become visible, evident, etc., suddenly. —*v.t.* **6.** to break suddenly and violently. **7.** to cause or suffer the rupture of. —*n.* **8.** act of bursting. **9.** a sudden display of activity. **10.** a sudden expression of emotion, etc. **11.** a sudden and violent issuing forth. **12.** *Mil.* **a.** the explosion of a projectile. **b.** the series of shots fired by one pressure on the trigger of an automatic weapon. **13.** the result of bursting. **14.** a sudden opening to view.

bur·then (bûr′thən), *n., v.t.* *Archaic.* burden¹.

bur·y (bĕr′ĭ), *v.t.,* **buried, burying.** **1.** to put in the ground and cover with earth. **2.** to cause to sink in. **3.** to conceal. **4.** to involve (oneself) deeply. —**bur′i·er,** *n.*

bus (bŭs), *n., pl.* **buses** or **busses.** a large motor vehicle with seats for passengers, usually operating as part of a scheduled service line.

bus boy, a waiter's helper in a restaurant.

bush (boͦosh), *n.* **1.** a plant, esp. a low one with many branches, which usually arise from or near the ground. **2.** something resembling this. **3.** a stretch of land covered with bushy vegetation or trees. —*v.i.* 4. to be or become bushy. —*v.t.* 5. to cover or protect with bushes.

bush·el (bŏŏsh′əl), *n.* 1. a unit of dry measure containing 4 pecks. 2. a container of this capacity.

bush·ing (bŏŏsh′ĭng), *n.* a protective or insulating lining for a hole.

bush·y (bŏŏsh′ĭ), *adj.*, **bushier, bushiest.** 1. resembling a bush. 2. full of bushes. —**bush′i·ness,** *n.*

bus·i·ly (bĭz′ə lĭ), *adv.* in a busy manner.

busi·ness (bĭz′nĭs), *n.* 1. one's occupation, profession, or trade. 2. the purchase and sale of goods in an attempt to make a profit. 3. a person, partnership, or corporation engaged in commerce or manufacture. 4. volume of trade. 5. one's place of work. 6. that with which one is principally, seriously, or rightfully concerned. 7. affair; matter. —**busi′ness·man′, busi′ness·wom′an,** *n.*

busi·ness·like (bĭz′nĭs līk′), *adj.* efficient.

bus·kin (bŭs′kĭn), *n.* 1. a half boot. 2. the high shoe of ancient Greek and Roman tragic actors. 3. tragic drama.

buss (bŭs), *n., v.t., v.i. Colloq.* kiss.

bust[1] (bŭst), *n.* 1. the head and shoulders of a person done in sculpture. 2. the bosom.

bust[2] (bŭst), *Colloq. or Slang.* —*v.i.* 1. to burst. 2. to go bankrupt. —*v.t.* 3. to burst. 4. to bankrupt. 5. to reduce in rank or grade. 6. to hit. —*n.* 7. a complete failure. 8. a drunken party.

bus·tle[1] (bŭs′əl), *v.*, **-tled, -tling,** *n.* —*v.i., v.t.* 1. to move or act with a great show of energy. —*n.* 2. energetic activity. —**bus′tling·ly,** *adv.*

bus·tle[2] (bŭs′əl), *n.* a pad or wire framework worn by women on the back below the waist to expand and support the skirt.

bus·y (bĭz′ĭ), *adj.*, **busier, busiest,** *v.*, **busied, busying.** —*adj.* 1. actively and attentively engaged. 2. not at leisure. 3. full of or characterized by activity. 4. officious; meddlesome. —*v.t.* 5. to keep occupied; make or keep busy. —**bus′y·ness,** *n.*

bus·y·bod·y (bĭz′ĭ bŏd′ĭ), *n., pl.* **-bodies.** a prying or meddlesome person.

but (bŭt; *unstressed* bət), *conj.* 1. on the contrary; yet. 2. except or save. 3. except that. 4. without the circumstance that. 5. other than. 6. that (esp. after *doubt,* etc., with a negative). 7. that not (after a negative or question). 8. who or which not. —*prep.* 9. except; save. —*adv.* 10. only; just. 11. all but, almost. —*n.* 12. a restriction or objection.

bu·ta·di·ene (bū′tə dī′ēn, -dī ēn′), *n. Chem.* an inflammable, colorless, hydrocarbon gas, C_4H_6, used in making synthetic rubber.

butch·er (bŏŏch′ər), *n.* 1. a retail dealer in meat. 2. one who slaughters large domesticated animals, or dresses their flesh for food. —*v.t.* 3. to kill for food. 4. to bungle; botch.

butch·er·y (bŏŏch′ə rĭ), *n., pl.* **-eries.** 1. a slaughterhouse. 2. slaughter; carnage.

but·ler (bŭt′lər), *n.* the head male servant of a household. —**but′ler·ship′,** *n.*

But·ler (bŭt′lər), *n.* 1. **Samuel,** 1612–80, British poet. 2. **Samuel,** 1835–1902, British writer.

butt[1] (bŭt), *n.* 1. the end of anything, esp. the thicker, larger, or blunt end, as of a musket. 2. an end which is not used up.

butt[2] (bŭt), *n.* 1. a person or thing that is an object of wit, ridicule, etc. 2. (in rifle practice) a wall of earth behind the targets of a target range. —*v.i.* 3. to be adjacent (*to*). —*v.t.* 4. to join the ends of (two things) together.

butt[3] (bŭt), *v.t., v.i.* 1. to strike (something) with the head or horns. 2. to project. 3. *Colloq.* to interrupt or intrude. —*n.* 4. a push with head or horns.

butt[4] (bŭt), *n.* a large cask.

butte (būt), *n. Western U.S. and Canada.* an isolated hill or mountain rising steeply.

Butte (būt), *n.* a city in SW Montana. 37,081.

but·ter (bŭt′ər), *n.* 1. the solid fatty portion of milk, separated by churning. 2. any of various soft spreads for breads. —*v.t.* 3. to put butter on or in. 4. *Colloq.* to flatter grossly.

but·ter·cup (bŭt′ər kŭp′), *n.* a plant of the crowfoot family with yellow cup-shaped flowers.

but·ter·fat (bŭt′ər făt′), *n.* milk fat; butter.

but·ter·fish (bŭt′ər fĭsh′), *n., pl.* **-fishes,** (*esp. collectively*) **-fish.** a small, flattened, marine food fish, of the Atlantic coast of the U.S.

but·ter·fly (bŭt′ər flī′), *n., pl.* **-flies.** any of a group of lepidopterous insects characterized by clubbed antennae, broad colorful wings, and diurnal habits.

but·ter·milk (bŭt′ər mĭlk′), *n.* the liquid remaining after butter has been separated from milk.

but·ter·nut (bŭt′ər nŭt′), *n.* 1. the edible oily nut of an American tree of the walnut family. 2. the tree itself. 3. dark brown.

but·ter·scotch (bŭt′ər skŏch′), *n.* a kind of taffy made with butter, brown sugar, etc.

but·ter·y[1] (bŭt′ə rĭ), *adj.* 1. like, containing, or spread with butter. 2. *Colloq.* flattering.

but·ter·y[2] (bŭt′ə rĭ, bŭt′rĭ), *n., pl.* **-teries.** a pantry.

but·tock (bŭt′ək), *n.* 1. either of the two protuberances which form the rump. 2. (*pl.*) the rump.

but·ton (bŭt′ən), *n.* 1. a disk or knob on a piece of cloth which, when passed through a slit or loop in the same piece or another, serves as a fastening. 2. anything resembling a button. 3. a disk pressed to close an electric circuit, as in ringing a bell. —*v.t.* 4. to fasten with a button or buttons. —*v.i.* 5. to be capable of being buttoned.

but·ton·hole (bŭt′ən hōl′), *n., v.,* **-holed, -holing.** —*n.* 1. the slit or loop through which a button is passed. —*v.t.* 2. to make buttonholes in. 3. to seize by or as by the buttonhole and detain in conversation.

but·ton·wood (bŭt′ən wŏŏd′), *n.* a tall, North American plane tree, yielding a useful timber.

but·tress (bŭt′rĭs), *n.* 1. *Archit.* a structure against a wall or building to give it stability. 2. any prop or support. —*v.t.* 3. *Archit.* to support by a buttress. 4. to prop up; support.

bux·om (bŭk′səm), *adj.* 1. (of a woman) attractively plump and healthy. 2. cheerful and lively. —**bux′om·ness,** *n.*

buy (bī), *v.*, **bought, buying,** *n.* —*v.t.* 1. to acquire by paying money. 2. to hire; bribe. 3. to get rid of (a claim, opposition, etc.) by payment. —*v.i.* 4. to be or become a purchaser. —*n.* 5. act of buying. 6. *U.S.* a purchase. 7. *U.S. Colloq.* a bargain. —**buy′er,** *n.*

buyer's strike, a boycott by consumers against high prices.

buzz (bŭz), *n.* 1. a low, humming sound, as of bees. 2. a rumor. —*v.i.* 3. to make a low, humming sound. 4. to speak with such a sound. —*v.t.* 5. to make a buzzing sound with. 6. to spread (a rumor) secretively. 7. to communicate with buzzes. 8. *Aeron.* to fly a plane very low over.

buz·zard (bŭz′ərd), *n.* 1. any of various heavily built, slow-flying hawks. 2. any of various carrion-eating birds, as the **turkey buzzard.**

buzz bomb, *Mil.* a type of self-steering aerial bomb, launched from rocket platforms.

buzz·er (bŭz′ər), *n.* 1. one that buzzes. 2. a signaling apparatus producing a buzz.

buzz saw, a small, circular, motor-driven saw.

by (bī), *prep.* 1. near to. 2. using as a route. 3. through or on as a means of conveyance. 4. to and past a point near. 5. within the compass or period of. 6. not later than. 7. to the extent of. 8. by evidence or authority of. 9. with the participation of. 10. in the presence of. 11. through the agency of. 12. in serial order. 13. combined with in multiplication or relative dimension. 14. involving as unit of measure. —*adv.* 15. near to something. 16. to and past a point near something. 17. aside. 18. over; past. 19. by and by, before long. 20. by and large, in general. —*adj.* 21. situated to one side. 22. secondary; incidental. —*n.* 23. bye.

by-and-by (bī′ən bī′), *n.* the (near) future.

bye (bī), *n.* 1. *Sports.* state of having no competitor in a contest where other competitors are already paired. 2. something subsidiary or out of the way. 3. by the bye, incidentally. —*adj.* 4. by.

by·gone (bī′gôn′, -gŏn′), *adj.* 1. past; out-of-date. —*n.* 2. that which is past.

by·law (bī′lô′), *n.* a standing rule, as of a society, not in its constitution.

by·line (bī′līn′), *n. U.S.* a line at the head of a newspaper article giving the writer's name.

by-pass (bī′păs′, -päs′), *n.* 1. a road enabling motorists to avoid heavy traffic areas or obstructions. 2. *Elect.* a shunt. —*v.t.* 3. to avoid (obstructions, etc.) by following a by-pass. 4. to go over the head of (one's supervisor, etc.)

by-path (bī′păth′, -päth′), *n.* a byway.

by·prod·uct (bī/prŏd/əkt), *n.* a secondary or incidental product.

by·road (bī/rōd/), *n.* a side road.

By·ron (bī/rən), *n.* George Gordon, Lord, 1788–1824, British poet.

by·stand·er (bī/stăn/dər), *n.* a person present but not involved; a chance looker-on.

by·way (bī/wā/), *n.* 1. a secluded or private road. 2. a subsidiary field of research, etc.

by·word (bī/wûrd/), *n.* 1. a catchword. 2. a proverb. 3. an object of general reproach, scorn, etc.

Byz·an·tine (bĭz/ən tēn/, -tīn/, bĭ zăn/tīn), *adj.* 1. of or pertaining to Byzantium. 2. of, pertaining to, or resembling architecture of Byzantium, characterized esp. by domes over square areas, elaborate mosaics, etc. —*n.* 3. a native or inhabitant of Byzantium.

By·zan·ti·um (bĭ zăn/shĭ əm, -tĭ əm), *n.* an ancient Greek city on the Bosporus: present site of Istanbul.

C

C, c (sē), *n., pl.* **C's** or **Cs, c's** or **cs.** 1. the third letter of the English alphabet. 2. *Music.* the first, or keynote, of the C major scale. 3. (as a mark at school or college) fair.

C, 1. *Chem.* carbon. 2. 100. See **Roman numerals.**

C., 1. Catholic. 2. Centigrade.

c., 1. Also, **ca.** (L *circa, circiter, circum*) about. 2. cent; cents. 3. centimeter. 4. century. 5. copyright. 6. cubic.

Ca, *Chem.* calcium.

cab (kăb), *n.* 1. taxicab. 2. any of various one-horse vehicles for public hire. 3. the covered part of a locomotive or truck, where the engineer or driver sits.

ca·bal (kə băl/), *n., v.,* **-balled, -balling.** —*n.* 1. intrigue. 2. a small group of plotters. —*v.i.* 3. to plot.

cab·a·la (kăb/ə lə, kə bä/-), *n.* 1. a system of esoteric theosophy, based on the Scriptures. 2. any occult doctrine or science. —**cab/a·lism,** *n.* —**cab·a·lis·tic** (kăb/ə lĭs/tĭk), *adj.*

ca·bal·le·ro (kăb/əl yâr/ō), *n., pl.* **-ros.** a Spanish gentleman.

cab·a·ret (kăb/ə rā/), *n.* a restaurant that provides entertainment and space for dancing by patrons.

cab·bage (kăb/ĭj), *n., v.,* **-baged, -baging.** —*n.* 1. any of various cultivated varieties of a plant with short stem and leaves formed into a compact, edible head. —*v.i.* 2. to form a head like a cabbage.

cab·by (kăb/ĭ), *n., pl.* **-bies.** *Colloq.* a cab driver.

cab·in (kăb/ĭn), *n.* 1. a small house. 2. a room in a ship, as for passengers, or (in a warship) the commanding officer. 3. *Aeron.* the enclosed place for the pilot, passengers, or cargo. —*v.i.* 4. to live in a cabin. —*v.t.* 5. to confine.

cab·i·net (kăb/ə nĭt), *n.* 1. (*also cap.*) a council advising a sovereign or government head. 2. a piece of furniture with shelves, drawers, etc., for dishes, etc. 3. a case with compartments for precious objects, etc. 4. a private room. —*adj.* 5. pertaining to a political cabinet. 6. secret. 7. of suitable value, beauty, or size for a private room, small case, etc.

cab·i·net-mak·er (kăb/ə nĭt mā/kər), *n.* a workman who builds fine furniture, etc. (**cabinetwork**).

ca·ble (kā/bəl), *n., v.,* **-bled, -bling.** —*n.* 1. a thick, strong rope, wire, etc. 2. *Elect.* a stranded conductor. 3. cablegram. —*v.t.* 4. to send (a message) by submarine cable. 5. to send a cablegram to. 6. to fasten or furnish with a cable. —*v.i.* 7. to send a message by submarine cable.

ca·ble·gram (kā/bəl grăm/), *n.* a telegram sent by a submarine cable.

cable's length, *Naut.* a unit of length (720 ft. in the U.S. Navy).

cab·man (kăb/mən), *n., pl.* **-men.** a cab driver.

ca·boo·dle (kə bōō/dəl), *n.* *Colloq.* the lot.

ca·boose (kə bōōs/), *n.* *U.S.* a car (usually last) on a freight train, used by the crew.

Cab·ot (kăb/ət), *n.* John, c1450–1498?, Italian navigator who discovered North America in 1497.

cab·ri·o·let (kăb/rĭ ə lā/), *n.* 1. a type of automobile resembling a coupé, with a folding top. 2. a light, hooded one-horse carriage with two seats.

ca·ca·o (kə kā/ō, -kä/ō), *n., pl.* **-caos.** 1. a small, tropical American evergreen tree, cultivated for its seeds, the source of cocoa, chocolate, etc. 2. the seeds of this tree.

cach·a·lot (kăsh/ə lŏt/, -lō/), *n.* the sperm whale.

cache (kăsh), *n., v.,* **cached, caching.** —*n.* 1. a hiding place for provisions, treasure, etc. 2. the provisions, etc., so hidden. —*v.t.* 3. to put in a cache; hide.

ca·chet (kă shā/, kăsh/ā), *n.* 1. a seal, as on a letter. 2. a distinguishing mark.

cack·le (kăk/əl), *v.,* **-led, -ling,** *n.* —*v.i.* 1. to utter a shrill, broken cry, as a hen after laying an egg. 2. to laugh brokenly. 3. to chatter noisily. —*v.t.* 4. to utter with cackles. —*n.* 5. act or sound of cackling. 6. idle talk. —**cack/ler,** *n.*

ca·coph·o·ny (kə kŏf/ə nĭ), *n., pl.* **-nies.** 1. the quality of having a harsh sound. 2. *Music.* frequent use of discords. —**ca·coph/o·nous,** *adj.*

cac·tus (kăk/təs), *n., pl.* **-tuses, -ti** (-tī). any of a family of fleshy-stemmed plants that are usually leafless and spiny, chiefly natives of the hot, dry regions of America.

cad (kăd), *n.* a contemptible, ungentlemanly person. —**cad/dish,** *adj.* —**cad/dish·ly,** *adv.*

ca·dav·er (kə dăv/ər, -dā/vər), *n.* a corpse.

ca·dav·er·ous (kə dăv/ər əs), *adj.* 1. of or like a corpse. 2. pale. 3. haggard. —**ca·dav/er·ous·ly,** *adv.* —**ca·dav/er·ous·ness,** *n.*

cad·die (kăd/ĭ), *n., v.,* **-died, -dying.** *Golf.* —*n.* 1. an attendant, hired to carry the player's clubs, find the ball, etc. —*v.i.* 2. to work as a caddie. Also, **cad/dy.**

ca·dence (kā/dəns), *n.* 1. rhythmic flow, as of verses. 2. the beat of any rhythmical movement. 3. a fall of the voice. 4. *Music.* a sequence of notes or chords which indicates the end of a composition, section, etc. Also, **ca/den·cy.** —**ca/denced,** *adj.*

ca·den·za (kə dĕn/zə), *n.* *Music.* an elaborate passage in an aria or concerto.

ca·det (kə dĕt/), *n.* 1. a student training for service as an officer in the army or air force. 2. a younger son or brother. 3. the youngest son. —**ca·det/ship, ca·det·cy** (kə dĕt/sĭ), *n.*

ca·di (kä/dĭ, kā/-), *n., pl.* **-dis.** a judge in a Moslem community.

Cá·diz (kā/dĭz, kə dĭz/), *n.* a seaport in SE Spain. 87,767.

cad·mi·um (kăd/mĭ əm), *n.* *Chem.* a white, ductile divalent metallic element resembling tin. *Symbol:* Cd; *at. wt.:* 112.41; *at. no.:* 48; *sp. gr.:* 8.6, at 20°C. —**cad/mic,** *adj.*

ca·dre (kä/dər; *Mil. usually* kăd/rĭ), *n.* 1. *Mil.* the key group of officers and men necessary to establish and train a new unit. 2. a framework.

ca·du·ce·us (kə dū/sĭ əs, -dōō/-), *n., pl.* **-cei** (-sĭ ī/). 1. the staff carried by Mercury as herald or messenger of the gods. 2. a similar staff used as an emblem of the medical profession.

cae·cum (sē/kəm), *n., pl.* **-ca** (-kə). *Anat., Zool.* a cul-de-sac, esp. the one at the beginning of the human large intestine, bearing the vermiform appendix. —**cae/cal,** *adj.*

Cae·sar (sē/zər), *n.* 1. Gaius Julius (gā/əs jōōl/yəs), 102 or 100–44 B.C., Roman general, statesman, and historian. 2. a title of the Roman emperors from Augustus to Hadrian. 3. any emperor. 4. a tyrant. —**Cae·sar·e·an** (sĭ zâr/ĭ ən), **Cae·sar/i·an,** *adj.*

Caesarean operation, *Surg.* the operation by which a fetus is taken from the uterus by cutting through the walls of the abdomen and uterus. Also, **Caesarean section.**

cae·su·ra (sĭ zhŏŏr′ə, -zyŏŏr′ə), *n., pl.* **-suras,** **-surae** (-zhŏŏr′ē, -zyŏŏr′ē). a break, esp. a sense pause, usually near the middle of a verse. —**cae-su′ral,** *adj.*

ca·fé (kǎ fā′, kə-), *n.* 1. a restaurant. 2. a barroom. 3. coffee.

caf·e·te·ri·a (kǎf′ə tĭr′Y ə), *n.* a restaurant in which the patrons carry the food from a serving counter to their tables.

caf·feine (kǎf′ēn, kǎf′Y Yn), *n.* a bitter crystalline alkaloid in coffee, tea, etc., used in medicine as a stimulant, diuretic, etc. Also, **caf′fein.**

caf·tan (kǎf′tən, kǎf tän′), *n.* a garment having long sleeves and tied at the waist by a girdle, worn under a coat in the Near East. —**caf′taned,** *adj.*

cage (kāj), *n., v.,* **caged, caging.** —*n.* 1. a boxlike enclosure for birds or other animals, made with openwork of wires, bars, etc. 2. anything that confines or imprisons. 3. the car of an elevator. —*v.t.* 4. to put in a cage.

cag·ey (kā′jǐ), *adj.,* **cagier, cagiest.** *Colloq.* shrewd. Also, **cag′y.** —**cag′i·ly,** *adv.* —**cag′i·ness,** *n.*

ca·hoot (kə hŏŏt′), *n.* *U.S. Slang. (often pl.* prec. by *in)* partnership.

Cain (kān), *n.* 1. the first son of Adam and Eve: murdered his brother Abel. 2. a murderer.

cairn (kârn), *n.* a heap of stones set up as a landmark, tombstone, etc. —**cairned** (kârnd), *adj.*

Cai·ro (kī′rō), *n.* the capital of Egypt, in the N part, on the Nile. 1,396,500.

cais·son (kā′sən, -sŏn), *n.* 1. a watertight structure in which men can work on river bottoms, etc. 2. a pontoon (def. 3). 3. an ammunition chest. 4. an ammunition wagon.

cai·tiff (kā′tYf), *Archaic and Poetic.* —*n.* 1. a base, despicable person. —*adj.* 2. base; despicable.

ca·jole (kə jōl′), *v.t., v.i.,* **-joled, -joling.** to persuade by flattery or promises; wheedle; coax. —**ca·jole′ment,** *n.* —**ca·jol′er,** *n.* —**ca·jol′er·y,** *n.*

cake (kāk), *n., v.,* **caked, caking.** —*n.* 1. a sweet baked food in loaf or layer form, usually made with flour, sugar, eggs, flavoring, baking powder, and a liquid. 2. a flat, thin mass of dough, batter, etc., usually fried or baked. 3. a shaped or molded mass of other food. 4. a shaped or compressed mass. —*v.t., v.i.* 5. to form into a compact mass.

cake·walk (kāk′wôk′), *n.* a promenade, of American Negro origin, in which the couples with the most intricate steps receive cakes as prizes.

Cal., 1. California. 2. *Physics.* large calorie.

cal., 1. *Physics.* small calorie. 2. caliber.

cal·a·bash (kǎl′ə bǎsh′), *n.* 1. any of various gourds, esp. the fruit of a certain tropical American tree. 2. the dried hollow shell of the fruit, used as a vessel or otherwise. 3. a bottle, tobacco-pipe bowl, etc., made from it.

cal·a·boose (kǎl′ə bŏŏs′, kǎl′ə bŏŏs′), *n.* *U.S. Colloq.* lockup; jail.

Cal·ais (kǎl′ā, -Ys), *n.* a seaport in N France, on the Strait of Dover: the nearest French port to England. 50,048.

ca·lam·i·tous (kə lǎm′ə təs), *adj.* causing or involving calamity; disastrous. —**ca·lam′i·tous·ly,** *adv.*

ca·lam·i·ty (kə lǎm′ə tĭ), *n., pl.* **-ties.** 1. grievous affliction; misery. 2. a disaster.

ca·lash (kə lǎsh′), *n.* a light, low-wheeled carriage, usually with a folding top.

cal·car·e·ous (kǎl kâr′ə əs), *adj.* of, containing, or like calcium carbonate; chalky.

cal·cif·er·ous (kǎl sĭf′ər əs), *adj.* 1. forming salts of calcium. 2. containing calcium carbonate.

cal·ci·fy (kǎl′sə fī′), *v.t., v.i.,* **-fied, -fying.** *Physiol.* to make or become calcareous or bony. —**cal′ci·fi·ca′tion,** *n.*

cal·ci·mine (kǎl′sə mīn′, -mYn), *n., v.,* **-mined, -mining.** —*n.* 1. a white or tinted wash for walls, ceilings, etc. —*v.t., v.i.* 2. to cover with calcimine.

cal·cine (kǎl′sīn, -sYn), *v.t., v.i.,* **-cined, -cining.** 1. to convert or be converted into an ash by heat. 2. to roast. 3. to oxidize by heating.

cal·cite (kǎl′sīt), *n.* one of the commonest minerals, calcium carbonate, $CaCO_3$. Limestone, marble, and chalk consist largely of calcite.

cal·ci·um (kǎl′sǐ əm), *n.* *Chem.* a silver-white

divalent metal. *Symbol:* Ca; *at. wt.:* 40.08; *at. no.:* 20; *sp. gr.:* 1.52 at 20°C.

calcium carbide, *Chem.* a crystalline compound of calcium and carbon, CaC_2, which reacts with water to form acetylene.

calcium carbonate, *Chem.* a crystalline compound, $CaCO_3$, occurring in nature as calcite, etc.

calcium chloride, *Chem.* a white, deliquescent powder, $CaCl_2$, used as a drying agent, etc.

cal·cu·la·ble (kǎl′kyə lə bəl), *adj.* 1. that can be calculated. 2. reliable. —**cal′cu·la·bly,** *adv.*

cal·cu·late (kǎl′kyə lāt′), *v.,* **-lated, -lating.** —*v.t.* 1. to ascertain by mathematics; compute. 2. to make suitable, adapt, or plan. —*v.i.* 3. to make a computation; form an estimate. 4. to rely. —**cal′cu·la′tor,** *n.*

cal·cu·lat·ing (kǎl′kyə lā′tYng), *adj.* 1. that performs calculations. 2. shrewd. 3. scheming.

cal·cu·la·tion (kǎl′kyə lā′shən), *n.* 1. act, process, or result of calculating. 2. a forecast. 3. forethought. —**cal′cu·la′tive,** *adj.*

cal·cu·lus (kǎl′kyə ləs), *n., pl.* **-li** (-lī′), **-luses.** 1. a method of calculation, esp. one using a special system of algebraic notation. 2. *Pathol.* a stone or concretion found in the gall bladder or other part of the body.

Cal·cut·ta (kǎl kŭt′ə), *n.* a seaport in NE India, in W Bengal. 2,108,891.

cal·dron (kôl′drən), *n.* a large kettle or boiler.

Cal·e·do·ni·a (kǎl′ə dō′nY ə), *n.* *Chiefly Poetic.* Scotland. —**Cal′e·do/ni·an,** *adj., n.*

cal·en·dar (kǎl′ən dər), *n.* 1. any of various systems of reckoning time, esp. by divisions of the year. 2. a tabular arrangement of the days of each month and week in a year. 3. a list or register, as of cases to be tried in court. —*v.t.* 4. to register.

cal·en·der (kǎl′ən dər), *n.* 1. a machine in which cloth, paper, or the like is smoothed, glazed, etc., by pressing between revolving cylinders. —*v.t.* 2. to press in a calender. —**cal′en·der·er,** *n.*

cal·ends (kǎl′əndz), *n.pl.* (in the Roman calendar) the first day of the month.

ca·len·du·la (kə lěn′jə lə), *n.* a plant in the aster family, having yellow or orange flower heads.

calf¹ (kǎf, käf), *n., pl.* **calves.** 1. the young of the cow or other bovine mammals. 2. the young of certain other animals, as the elephant, seal, and whale. 3. calfskin leather.

calf² (kǎf, käf), *n., pl.* **calves.** the fleshy part of the back of the human leg below the knee.

calf·skin (kǎf′skYn′, käf′-), *n.* 1. the skin or hide of a calf. 2. leather made from it.

Cal·ga·ry (kǎl′gə rY), *n.* a city in SW Canada, in Alberta. 88,904.

cal·i·ber (kǎl′ə bər), *n.* 1. the diameter of something of circular section, as a bullet, or esp. that of the inside of a tube, as the bore of a gun. 2. degree of capacity or ability. 3. degree of merit; quality. Also, *esp. Brit.,* **cal′i·bre.**

cal·i·brate (kǎl′ə brāt′), *v.t.,* **-brated, -brating.** to determine, check, or rectify the graduation of (any instrument giving quantitative measurements). —**cal′i·bra′tion,** *n.* —**cal′i·bra′tor,** *n.*

cal·i·co (kǎl′ə kō′), *n., pl.* **-coes, -cos,** *adj.* —*n.* 1. *U.S.* a printed cotton cloth. 2. *Brit.* white cotton cloth. —*adj.* 3. made of calico. 4. spotted; piebald.

Cal·i·cut (kǎl′ə kŭt′), *n.* a seaport in SW India. 126,352.

Calif., official abbreviation for California.

Cal·i·for·nia (kǎl′ə fôrn′yə, -fôr′nY ə), *n.* 1. a State in the W United States, on the Pacific coast. 9,550,727 pop.; 158,693 sq. mi. *Cap.:* Sacramento. 2. Gulf of, an arm of the Pacific, between Mexico and the peninsula of Lower California. ab. 750 mi. long. —**Cal′i·for′nian,** *adj., n.*

cal·i·per (kǎl′ə pər), *n.* 1. *(usually pl.)* a tool, resembling a draftsman's compass, used for obtaining inside and outside measurements. —*v.t.* 2. to measure with calipers.

ca·liph (kā′lYf, kǎl′Yf), *n.* the head of a Moslem state. —**cal·iph·ate** (kǎl′ə fāt′, -fĭt), *n.*

cal·is·then·ics (kǎl′əs thěn′Yks), *n.* 1. (*construed as sing.*) the practice or art of physical exercise for health, strength, and grace. 2. (*construed as pl.*) such gymnastic exercises. —**cal′is·then′ic,** *adj.*

calk¹ (kôk), *v.t.* 1. to fill or close (a seam, etc.), as in a boat. 2. to make (a vessel) watertight by filling the seams between its planks with oakum or other material driven snug. —**calk′er,** *n.*

calk² (kôk), *n.* **1.** a projection on a shoe or horseshoe to prevent slipping. —*v.t.* **2.** to provide with calks.

call (kôl), *v.t.* **1.** to cry out in a loud voice. **2.** (of a bird or animal) to utter its characteristic cry. **3.** to announce; proclaim. **4.** to read over (a list) in a loud tone. **5.** to attract the attention of by shouting. **6.** to rouse from sleep as by a call. **7.** to summon or convoke. **8.** to bring under consideration. **9.** to telephone to. **10.** *Baseball.* to terminate (a game) because of rain, etc. **11.** to demand payment or fulfillment of (a loan, etc.). **12.** to demand (bonds, etc.) for payment. **13.** to give a name to; name. **14.** to designate or consider. **15.** *Poker.* to require (a player) to show his hand, after equaling his bet. —*v.i.* **16.** to speak loudly; shout. **17.** to make a short visit. **18.** to telephone a person. **19.** *Poker.* to demand a showing of hands. **20. call down,** to scold. **21. call for,** a. to go and get. b. to need. **22. call on,** a. to appeal to. b. to make a short visit to. **23. call up,** a. to communicate (with) by telephone. b. to recollect. —*n.* **24.** a cry or shout. **25.** the cry of a bird or other animal. **26.** an instrument for imitating this cry and luring the animal. **27.** a summons or signal sounded by a bugle, etc. **28.** a short visit. **29.** a summons; invitation. **30.** a need or occasion. **31.** a demand or claim. **32.** *Poker.* a demand for the showing of hands. **33.** a demand for payment of an obligation, esp. where payment is at the option of the creditor. —**call′er,** *n.*

cal·la (kăl′ə), *n.* a plant of a genus that is native in Africa, esp. one variety (**calla lily**), which has a large white spathe enclosing a yellow spadix, and is familiar in cultivation.

cal·lig·ra·phy (kə lĭg′rə fĭ), *n.* **1.** beautiful handwriting. **2.** handwriting; penmanship. —**cal·lig′ra·pher, cal·lig′ra·phist,** *n.* —**cal·li·graph·ic** (kăl′ə grăf′ĭk), *adj.*

call·ing (kô′lĭng), *n.* **1.** vocation, profession, or trade. **2.** summons. **3.** invitation.

calling card, a small card bearing one's name, used on various social or business occasions.

cal·li·o·pe (kə lī′ə pē′; *for 1, also* kăl′ĭ ōp′), *n.* **1.** a harsh musical instrument consisting of a set of steam whistles, played from a keyboard. **2.** (*cap.*) *Gk. Myth.* the Muse of heroic poetry.

cal·lis·then·ics (kăl′ĭs thĕn′ĭks), *n.* calisthenics. —**cal′lis·then′ic,** *adj.*

cal·los·i·ty (kə lŏs′ə tĭ), *n., pl.* **-ties. 1.** a callous condition. **2.** *Bot.* a hardened or thickened part of a plant. **3.** callus (def. 1a).

cal·lous (kăl′əs), *adj.* **1.** hardened. **2.** hardened in mind, feelings, etc. **3.** having a callus. —*v.i., v.t.* **4.** to become or make callous. —**cal′lous·ly,** *adv.* —**cal′lous·ness,** *n.*

cal·low (kăl′ō), *adj.* **1.** immature or inexperienced. **2.** (of a young bird) featherless. —**cal′low·ness,** *n.*

cal·lus (kăl′əs), *n., pl.* **-luses,** *v.* —*n.* **1.** *Pathol., Physiol.* a hardened or thickened part of the skin. b. a new growth at the ends of a fractured bone, serving to unite them. —*v.i.* **2.** to make a callus.

calm (käm), *adj.* **1.** without motion; still. **2.** not windy. **3.** free from excitement; tranquil. —*n.* **4.** freedom from motion; stillness. **5.** absence of wind. **6.** freedom from excitement; tranquillity. —*v.t.* **7.** to make calm. —*v.i.* **8.** to become calm. —**calm′ly,** *adv.* —**calm′ness,** *n.*

cal·o·mel (kăl′ə mĕl′, -məl), *n.* *Pharm.* mercurous chloride, Hg_2Cl_2, a white, tasteless solid, used in medicine as a purgative, etc.

ca·lor·ic (kə lôr′ĭk, -lŏr′-), *n.* **1.** heat. —*adj.* **2.** pertaining or relating to heat.

cal·o·rie (kăl′ə rĭ), *n.* **1.** *Physics.* **a. gram calorie** or **small calorie,** the quantity of heat required to raise the temperature of one gram of water one degree centigrade. **b. kilogram calorie** or **large calorie,** a quantity of heat, equal to 1000 gram calories. **2.** *Physiol.* a unit equal to the large calorie, used to express the heat output of an organism and the fuel or energy value of food. Also, **cal′o·ry.**

cal·o·rif·ic (kăl′ə rĭf′ĭk), *adj.* pertaining to conversion into heat.

cal·o·rim·e·ter (kăl′ə rĭm′ə tər), *n.* *Physics, etc.* an apparatus for measuring heat.

cal·u·met (kăl′yə mĕt′, kăl′yə mĕt′), *n.* a tobacco pipe used by North American Indians on ceremonial occasions, esp. in token of peace.

ca·lum·ni·ate (kə lŭm′nĭ āt′), *v.t.,* **-ated, -ating.** to make false and malicious statements about; slander. —**ca·lum′ni·a′tion,** *n.* —**ca·lum′ni·a′tor,** *n.*

ca·lum·ny (kăl′əm nĭ), *n., pl.* **-nies.** a false and malicious statement designed to injure someone's reputation; slander. —**ca·lum·ni·ous** (kə lŭm′nĭ əs), *adj.* —**ca·lum′ni·ous·ly,** *adv.*

Cal·va·ry (kăl′və rĭ), *n.* Golgotha, the place where Jesus was crucified.

calve (kăv, käv), *v.i.,* **calved, calving.** to give birth to a calf.

Cal·vin (kăl′vĭn), *n.* **John,** 1509–64, religious reformer and theologian, born in France.

Cal·vin·ism (kăl′və nĭz′əm), *n.* *Theol.* the doctrines and church practices taught by John Calvin, who emphasized predestination, the authority of Scriptures, etc. —**Cal′vin·ist,** *n., adj.* —**Cal′vin·is′tic, Cal′vin·is′ti·cal,** *adj.*

Ca·lyp·so (kə lĭp′sō), *n.* **1.** *Gk. Legend.* a sea nymph who detained Odysseus for seven years. —*adj.* **2.** (*l.c.*) pertaining to a musical style of West Indian Negro origin, influenced by jazz.

ca·lyx (kā′lĭks, kăl′ĭks), *n., pl.* **calyxes, calyces** (kăl′ə sēz′, kā′lə-). *Bot.* the outermost group of floral parts, usually green; the sepals.

cam (kăm), *n.* *Mach.* a device for converting regular rotary motion into irregular rotary or reciprocating motion, etc.

ca·ma·ra·de·rie (kä′mə rä′də rĭ), *n.* comradeship.

cam·ber (kăm′bər), *v.t., v.i.* **1.** to arch slightly. —*n.* **2.** a slight arching or convexity above. **3.** a slightly arching piece of timber. **4.** *Aeron.* the rise of the curve of an airfoil.

Cams
A. Elliptical cam; B. Cam wheel; C. Heart cam

cam·bi·um (kăm′bĭ əm), *n.* *Bot.* a layer of soft cellular tissue between the bark and wood in plants, from which new bark and new wood originate.

Cam·bri·a (kăm′brĭ ə), *n.* medieval name of Wales. —**Cam′bri·an,** *adj., n.*

cam·bric (kām′brĭk), *n.* a cotton or linen fabric of fine close weave, usually white.

Cam·bridge (kām′brĭj), *n.* **1.** a city in E England. 78,370. **2.** a city in E Massachusetts, near Boston. 110,879.

Cam·den (kăm′dən), *n.* a city in SW New Jersey. 117,536.

cam·el (kăm′əl), *n.* either of two large Old World ruminant quadrupeds, used as beasts of burden: **a.** the **arabian camel,** or dromedary, with one hump. **b.** the **Bactrian camel,** with two humps.

ca·mel·lia (kə mēl′yə, -mĕl′lĭ ə), *n.* a plant, native in Asia, with glossy evergreen leaves and waxy roselike flowers.

Cam·e·lot (kăm′ə lŏt′), *n.* the legendary site of King Arthur's palace and court.

camel's hair, 1. the hair of the camel, used for cloth, painters' brushes, etc. **2.** cloth made of this hair, usually tan.

Cam·em·bert (kăm′əm bâr′), *n.* a rich, yellowish variety of soft cheese.

cam·e·o (kăm′ĭ ō′), *n., pl.* **cameos. 1.** an engraving in relief upon a gem, stone, etc. **2.** a gem, etc., so engraved.

cam·er·a (kăm′ər ə, kăm′rə), *n., pl.* **-eras** *for 1,* **-erae** (-ə rē′) *for 2.* **1.** a photographic apparatus in which sensitive plates or film are exposed, the image being formed by means of a lens. **2.** a judge's private room. **3. in camera, a.** *Law.* in the privacy of a judge's chambers. **b.** privately.

Cam·e·roons (kăm′ə rōōnz′), *n.* **1.** a region in W Africa, now two trusteeships of Gt. Britain and France. **2.** British trusteeship in the NW part of this region. 886,000 pop.; 34,081 sq. mi.

Ca·me·roun (kăm rōōn′), *n.* a territory in W Africa, under the trusteeship of France. 2,341,000 pop.; 162,900 sq. mi. *Cap.:* Yaoundé.

cam·i·sole (kăm′ə sōl′), *n.* **1.** *Chiefly Brit.* an ornamental underbodice, worn under a thin outer bodice. **2.** a woman's dressing jacket.

cam·o·mile (kăm′ə mīl′), *n.* any of certain plants of the aster family, esp. one variety with strongly scented foliage and flowers which are used medicinally.

cam·ou·flage (kăm′ə fläzh′), *n., v.,* **-flaged, -flaging.** —*n.* **1.** act, art, means, or result of disguising things to deceive the enemy, as by painting or screening objects, etc. **2.** disguise; deception. —*v.t.* **3.** to disguise, hide, or deceive by means of camouflage.

camp (kămp), *n.* **1.** a place where an army or other group is lodged in tents or other temporary shelter. **2.** the tents, etc., collectively. **3.** the persons sheltered. **4.** a camping out. **5.** a body of troops, etc., camping and moving together. **6.** army life. **7.** a group of people favoring the same ideals, etc. **8.** any position in which ideals, etc., are strongly entrenched. —*v.i.* **9.** to establish or pitch a camp. **10.** to live temporarily in a tent. —*v.t.* **11.** to put or station (troops, etc.) in a camp. —**camp′er,** *n.*

cam·paign (kăm pān′), *n.* **1.** the military operations during one season or enterprise. **2.** any course of aggressive activities for some special purpose. **3.** the competition by rival political candidates and organizations. —*v.i.* **4.** to serve in, or go on, a campaign. —**cam·paign′er,** *n.*

cam·pa·ni·le (kăm′pə nē′lĭ), *n.,* *pl.* **-niles,** **-nili** (-nē′lē). a bell tower.

camp·fire (kămp′fīr′), *n.* **1.** a fire in a camp for warmth or cooking. **2.** a reunion of soldiers, scouts, etc.

cam·phor (kăm′fər), *n.* a whitish, translucent, crystalline, pleasant-odored substance, $C_{10}H_{16}O$, obtained chiefly from an Asiatic laurel tree (**camphor tree**) and used in medicine, etc. —**cam·phor·ic** (kăm fôr′ĭk, -fŏr′-), *adj.*

cam·phor·ate (kăm′fə rāt′), *v.t.,* **-ated, -ating.** to impregnate with camphor.

camphor ball, a moth ball, usually consisting of naphthalene.

cam·pus (kăm′pəs), *n.* *U.S.* the grounds of a college or other school.

can¹ (kăn; *unstressed* kən), *v.,* *pres. sing.* **1 can; 2 can** or (*Archaic*) **canst; 3 can;** *pt.* **could.** —*aux.* **1.** to have the ability, right, qualifications, or means to. **2.** *Colloq.* to have permission. —*v.t., v.i.* **3.** *Obs.* to know.

can² (kăn), *n.,* *v.,* **canned, canning.** —*n.* **1.** a container for food, milk, etc., usually of metal. **2.** a receptacle for garbage, ashes, etc. **3.** a tankard. **4.** *U.S. Colloq.* a jail; a dungeon. **5.** *U.S. Slang.* a sealed bomb. —*v.t.* **5.** to put in a can, esp. a sealed one. **6.** *U.S. Slang.* to dismiss.

Can., **1.** Canada. **2.** Canadian.

Ca·naan (kā′nən), *n.* the ancient region between the Jordan, the Dead Sea, and the Mediterranean: the land promised by God to Abraham. —**Ca′naan·ite′,** *n.*

Can·a·da (kăn′ə də), *n.* a dominion of the British Commonwealth, in N North America. 11,506,655 pop.; 3,690,410 sq. mi. *Cap.:* Ottawa. —**Ca·na·di·an** (kə nā′dĭ ən), *adj., n.*

Canada goose, the common wild goose of North America.

ca·naille (kə nāl′), *n.* the rabble.

ca·nal (kə năl′), *n.,* *v.,* **-nalled** **-nalling** or **-naled, -naling.** —*n.* **1.** an artificial waterway for navigation, irrigation, etc. **2.** a tubular passage, esp. in an animal or plant, for food, air, etc. —*v.t.* **3.** to make a canal through.

ca·nal·ize (kə năl′īz, kăn′ə līz′), *v.t.,* **-ized, -izing.** **1.** to make a canal or canals through. **2.** to divert into certain channels. —**ca·nal′i·za′tion,** *n.*

Canal Zone, a strip of territory 10 mi. wide across the Isthmus of Panama, on both sides of the Panama Canal, excluding the cities of Panama and Colón: perpetually leased to and governed by the U.S. 51,827 pop.; 553 sq. mi.

can·a·pé (kăn′ə pĭ, -pā′), *n.* a thin piece of bread, etc., topped with cheese, caviar, anchovies, or other appetizing foods.

ca·nard (kə närd′), *n.* a false story, report, or rumor; hoax.

ca·nar·y (kə nâr′ĭ), *n.,* *pl.* **-naries. 1.** Also, **canary bird.** a well-known yellow cage bird, a kind of finch, native of the Canary Islands. **2.** Also, **canary yellow.** a light, clear yellow color.

Canary Islands, a group of mountainous islands in the Atlantic, near the NW coast of Africa, forming two provinces of Spain. 680,294 pop.; 2894 sq. mi. Also, **Canaries.**

ca·nas·ta (kə năs′tə), *n.* a card game of the rummy family in which the main object is to meld sets of seven or more cards.

Can·ber·ra (kăn′bĕr ə, -bə rə), *n.* the capital of Australia, in the SE part. 7325.

can·can (kăn′kăn), *n.* a disorderly form of quadrille marked by much high kicking.

can·cel (kăn′səl), *v.,* **-celed, -celing** or (*esp. Brit.*) **-celled, -celling,** *n.* —*v.t.* **1.** to cross out (writing, etc.) by drawing a line or lines over. **2.** to make void or invalid. **3.** to counterbalance. **4.** *Math.* to eliminate by striking out (equivalent quantities on opposite sides of an equation, etc.). —*n.* **5.** act of canceling. —**can′cel·la′tion,** *n.* —**can′cel·er;** *esp. Brit.,* **can′cel·ler,** *n.*

can·cer (kăn′sər), *n.* **1.** *Pathol.* a malignant growth or tumor, tending to recur after excision and to spread. **2.** any evil condition or thing that spreads destructively. **3.** (*cap.*) *Astron.* a constellation and a sign of the zodiac, represented by a crab. —**can′cer·ous,** *adj.*

can·de·la·brum (kăn′də lä′brəm, -lā′-), *n.,* *pl.* **-bra** (-brə), **-brums.** a branched candlestick.

can·did (kăn′dĭd), *adj.* **1.** frank; outspoken. **2.** honest; impartial. **3.** white. **4.** clear; pure. —**can′did·ly,** *adv.* —**can′did·ness,** *n.*

can·di·date (kăn′də dāt′, -dĭt), *n.* one who seeks an office, an honor, etc. —**can·di·da·cy** (kăn′də də sĭ), **can′di·date·ship′,** *n.*

candid camera, a small camera, usually having a fast lens for unposed, informal pictures.

can·died (kăn′dĭd), *adj.* **1.** impregnated or incrusted with sugar. **2.** crystallized, as sugar.

can·dle (kăn′dəl), *n.,* *v.,* **-dled, -dling.** —*n.* **1.** a slender piece of tallow, wax, etc., with an embedded wick, burned to give light. **2.** *Physics.* the luminous intensity of a **standard candle** (a candle of specified size, composition, character of wick, and rate of burning, whose flame is taken as a unit of luminous intensity). —*v.t.* **3.** to examine (esp. eggs for freshness) by holding in front of a light. —**can′dler,** *n.*

can·dle·stick (kăn′dəl stĭk′), *n.* a holder for a candle.

can·dor (kăn′dər), *n.* **1.** frankness; sincerity. **2.** fairness. Also, *Brit.,* **can′dour.**

can·dy (kăn′dĭ), *n.,* *pl.* **-dies,** *v.,* **-died, -dying.** —*n.* **1.** a confection made with sugar, syrup, etc., combined with other ingredients. —*v.t.* **2.** to cook in sugar or syrup, as sweet potatoes. **3.** to cook in heavy syrup until transparent, as fruit peel. **4.** to reduce (sugar, etc.) to a crystalline form, usually by boiling down. **5.** to make sweet or palatable. —*v.i.* **6.** to become covered with sugar. **7.** to crystallize.

can·dy·tuft (kăn′dĭ tŭft′), *n.* a cultivated annual plant with tufted flowers.

cane (kān), *n.,* *v.,* **caned, caning.** —*n.* **1.** a stick used in walking. **2.** a long, jointed woody stem, as that of bamboo. **3.** a plant having such a stem. **4.** sugar cane. **5.** a rod for flogging. —*v.t.* **6.** to beat with a cane. **7.** to furnish or make with cane. —**can′er,** *n.*

cane·brake (kān′brāk′), *n.* a thicket of canes.

ca·nine (kā′nīn, kə nīn′), *adj.* **1.** of or like a dog. **2.** *Anat., Zool.* of or pertaining to the four pointed teeth, situated one on each side of each jaw, next to the incisors. —*n.* **3.** *Zool.* any animal of the dog family, including the wolves, coyotes, and foxes. **4.** a dog. **5.** a canine tooth.

can·is·ter (kăn′ĭs tər), *n.* a small box, usually of metal, for holding tea, coffee, etc.

can·ker (kăng′kər), *n.* **1.** *Pathol.* a gangrenous or ulcerous sore, esp. in the mouth. **2.** anything that corrodes, corrupts, destroys, or irritates. —*v.t., v.i.* **3.** to infect or become infected with canker. —**can′ker·ous,** *adj.*

can·ker·worm (kăng′kər wûrm′), *n.* a striped green caterpillar injurious esp. to fruit trees.

can·na (kăn′ə), *n.* any of certain tropical plants, some of which are cultivated for their large, handsome leaves and showy flowers.

canned (kănd), *adj.* **1.** preserved in a can or jar. **2.** *Slang.* recorded.

can·nel coal (kăn′əl), a compact coal burning readily and brightly. Also, **cannel.**

can·ner (kăn′ər), *n.* one who cans fruit, etc.

can·ner·y (kăn′ə rĭ), *n.,* *pl.* **-neries.** a place where meat, fish, fruit, etc., are canned.

can·ni·bal (kăn′ə bəl), *n.* **1.** a human being that eats human flesh. **2.** any animal that eats its own kind. —*adj.* **3.** of or like cannibals. —**can′ni·bal·ism′,** *n.* —**can′ni·bal·is′tic,** *adj.* —**can′ni·bal·is′ti·cal·ly,** *adv.*

can·ning (kăn′ĭng), *n.* act, process, or business of preserving fruits, etc., in sealed cans or jars.

can·non (kăn′ən), *n.,* *pl.* **-nons,** (*esp. collectively*) **-non,** *v.* —*n.* **1.** a mounted gun for firing heavy projectiles. **2.** the part of a bit that is in the horse's mouth. **3.** *Zool.* the cannon bone. —*v.i.* **4.** to discharge cannon.

can·non·ade (kăn′ə nād′), *n.,* *v.,* **-aded, -ading.** —*n.* **1.** a continued discharge of cannon. —*v.t., v.i.* **2.** to attack with or discharge cannon.

cannon bone, *Zool.* the greatly developed bone of hoofed quadrupeds from the wrist or ankle to the first joint of the digit.

can·non·eer (kăn′ə nĭr′), *n.* an artilleryman.

can·non·ry (kăn′ən rĭ), *n.,* *pl.* **-ries. 1.** a discharge of artillery. **2.** artillery (def. 1).

can·not (kăn′ŏt, kă nŏt′, kə-), *v.* a form of can not.

can·ny (kăn′Y), *adj.*, **-nier, -niest.** *Scot.* **1.** careful; wary. **2.** shrewd. **3.** thrifty. **4.** expert. **—can′ni·ly,** *adv.* **—can′ni·ness,** *n.*

ca·noe (kə nōō′), *n., v.,* **-noed, -noeing. —***n.* **1.** any light and narrow boat, often canvas-covered, that is propelled by paddles in place of oars. **—***v.i.* **2.** to paddle a canoe. **3.** to go in a canoe. **—ca·noe′ing,** *n.* **—ca·noe′ist,** *n.*

can·on[1] (kăn′ən), *n.* **1.** an ecclesiastical rule or law. **2.** any rule or law. **3.** a criterion. **4.** the books of the Bible recognized by the Christian Church as genuine and inspired. **5.** any officially recognized set of sacred books. **6.** a catalogue or list.

can·on[2] (kăn′ən), *n.* **1.** *Chiefly Brit.* a member of the chapter of a cathedral or a collegiate church. **2.** *Rom. Cath. Ch.* one of the members (**canons regular**) of certain religious orders.

ca·non·i·cal (kə nŏn′ə kəl), *adj.* Also, **ca·non′·ic.** **1.** conforming to a canon or canons. **2.** included in the canon of the Bible. **—***n.* **3.** (*pl.*) the dress prescribed by canon for the clergy when officiating. **—ca·non′i·cal·ly,** *adv.*

can·on·ize (kăn′ə nīz′), *v.t.,* **-ized, -izing. 1.** *Eccles.* to place in the canon of saints. **2.** to glorify. **3.** to make canonical. **—can′on·i·za′tion,** *n.*

canon law, the body of ecclesiastical law.

can·o·py (kăn′ə pY), *n., pl.* **-pies,** *v.,* **-pied, -pying. —***n.* **1.** a covering suspended over a throne, entrance, etc., or held over a person, etc. **—***v.t.* **2.** to cover with or as with a canopy.

canst (kănst), *v. Archaic or Poetic.* 2nd pers. sing. pres. of **can.**

cant[1] (kănt), *n.* **1.** insincere expressions of goodness or piety. **2.** the special language or jargon spoken by thieves, gypsies, etc. **—***v.i.* **3.** to speak with pretended goodness or piety.

cant[2] (kănt), *n.* **1.** a salient angle. **—***v.t.* **2.** *Mech.* to bevel. **3.** to tilt; tip. **—***v.i.* **4.** to tilt; turn.

can't (kănt, känt), contraction of *cannot.*

can·ta·bi·le (kän tä′bē lĕ), *adj. Music.* song-like and flowing in style.

can·ta·loupe (kăn′tə lōp′), *n.* a variety of melons with hard, scaly, or warty rinds. Also, **can′ta·loup′.**

can·tan·ker·ous (kăn tăng′kər əs), *adj.* ill-natured; quarrelsome; contrary. **—can·tan′·ker·ous·ly,** *adv.* **—can·tan′ker·ous·ness,** *n.*

can·ta·ta (kən tä′tə), *n. Music.* a choral composition in dramatic form but not to be acted.

can·teen (kăn tēn′), *n.* **1.** *U.S.* a small container used by soldiers and others for water or other liquids. **2.** a place in a military camp, etc., for the sale of personal necessities and supplies to members of the army. **3.** a place where free entertainment is provided for enlisted men.

can·ter (kăn′tər), *n.* **1.** an easy gallop. **—***v.i., v.t.* **2.** to go or ride at a canter.

Can·ter·bur·y (kăn′tər bĕr′Y), *n.* a city in SE England: famous cathedral. 23,780.

Canterbury bell, a plant cultivated for its showy violet-blue, pink, or white flowers.

cant hook, a wooden lever with a movable iron hook near the lower end, used for grasping and canting or turning over logs, etc.

can·ti·cle (kăn′tə kəl), *n.* **1.** one of the nonmetrical hymns or chants used in church services. **2.** (*cap., pl.*) a book of the Old Testament, also known as the *Song of Solomon.*

can·ti·lev·er (kăn′tə lĕv′ər, -lē′vər), *n.* **1.** a free part of any horizontal member projecting beyond a support. **2.** either of two bracketlike arms projecting toward each other to form the span of a bridge (**cantilever bridge**) when united.

can·tle (kăn′təl), *n.* **1.** the hind part of a saddle, usually cuved upward. **2.** a portion.

can·to (kăn′tō), *n., pl.* **-tos.** one of the main or larger divisions of a long poem.

can·ton (kăn′tən, -tŏn, kăn tŏn′ for 1, 2; kăn-tŏn′, -tōn′, *esp. Brit.* -tōōn′ for 3), *n.* **1.** a small territorial district, esp. one of the states of the Swiss confederation. **—***v.t.* **2.** to divide into territorial districts. **3.** to allot quarters to (soldiers, etc.). **—can·ton·al** (kăn′tən əl), *adj.*

Can·ton (kăn tŏn′ *for 1;* kăn′tən *for 2*), *n.* **1.** a seaport in SE China. 852,000. **2.** a city in NE Ohio. 108,401.

can·ton·ment (kăn tŏn′mənt, -tōn′-; *esp. Brit.* -tōōn′-), *n.* a camp where men are trained for military service.

can·tor (kăn′tər, -tôr), *n. Eccles.* **1.** an officer who leads the singing in a cathedral or church. **2.** the Jewish religious official singing the liturgy.

can·vas (kăn′vəs), *n.* **1.** a closely woven, heavy cloth used for tents, sails, etc. **2.** a piece of this material on which an oil painting is made. **3.** an oil painting.

can·vas·back (kăn′vəs băk′), *n.* a North American wild duck with a whitish back.

can·vass (kăn′vəs), *v.t.* **1.** to examine carefully; discuss. **2.** to solicit votes, subscriptions, opinions, etc., from. **—***v.i.* **3.** to solicit votes, opinions, etc. **—***n.* **4.** examination. **5.** a soliciting of votes, orders, etc. **—can′vass·er,** *n.*

can·yon (kăn′yən), *n. U.S.* a deep valley with steep sides, often with a stream through it.

caou·tchouc (kōō′chŏŏk, kou chōŏk′), *n.* **1.** India rubber. **2.** pure rubber.

cap (kăp), *n., v.,* **capped, capping. —***n.* **1.** a covering for the head, esp. one fitting closely and having little or no brim. **2.** a special headdress denoting rank, occupation, etc. **3.** anything resembling or suggestive of a covering for the head in shape, use, or position. **—***v.t.* **4.** to provide or cover with a cap. **5.** to complete. **6.** to surpass.

cap., **1.** capital. **2.** (*pl.* **caps.**) capital letter.

ca·pa·bil·i·ty (kā′pə bYl′ə tY), *n., pl.* **-ties.** ability or capacity.

ca·pa·ble (kā′pə bəl), *adj.* **1.** able; competent. **2.** capable of, **a.** qualified for. **b.** susceptible to. **c.** wicked enough for. **—ca′pa·ble·ness,** *n.* **—ca′pa·bly,** *adv.*

ca·pa·cious (kə pā′shəs), *adj.* capable of holding much. **—ca·pa′cious·ly,** *adv.*

ca·pac·i·ty (kə păs′ə tY), *n., pl.* **-ties.** **1.** the power of receiving or containing. **2.** volume. **3.** ability. **4.** position; function.

ca·par·i·son (kə păr′ə sən), *n.* **1.** a covering, usually ornamented, over a horse, etc. **2.** dress; outfit. **—***v.t.* **3.** to cover with a caparison. **4.** to deck.

cape[1] (kāp), *n.* a sleeveless garment fastened at the neck and falling loosely over the shoulders.

cape[2] (kāp), *n.* a piece of land jutting into the sea or some other body of water.

Cape of Good Hope, a cape near the S extremity of Africa.

ca·per[1] (kā′pər), *v.i.* **1.** to leap or skip playfully. **—***n.* **2.** a playful leap or skip. **—ca′per·er,** *n.*

ca·per[2] (kā′pər), *n.* a shrub of Mediterranean regions whose flower bud is pickled and used for garnish or seasoning.

Cape Town, a seaport in the Union of South Africa, near the Cape of Good Hope. With suburbs, 454,052. Also, **Cape′town′.**

cap·il·lar·i·ty (kăp′ə lăr′ə tY), *n.* **1.** state of being capillary. **2.** *Physics.* capillary action.

cap·il·lar·y (kăp′ə lĕr′Y), *adj., n., pl.* **-laries. —***adj.* **1.** pertaining to or occurring in a thin tube. **2.** *Physics.* pertaining to the property of surface tension. **3.** *Bot.* resembling hair. **—***n.* **4.** *Anat.* one of the minute blood vessels between the terminations of the arteries and the beginnings of the veins. **5.** Also, **capillary tube.** a tube with a small bore.

cap·i·tal[1] (kăp′ə təl), *n.* **1.** the city which is the official seat of government in a state, etc. **2.** a capital letter. **3.** the wealth owned or employed by an individual, firm, etc. **4.** an accumulated stock of such wealth. **5.** any source of profit, advantage, etc. **6.** capitalists as a group or class. **—***adj.* **7.** pertaining to capital. **8.** important. **9.** chief. **10.** excellent. **11.** (of letters) of the large size used at the beginning of a sentence, etc. **12.** punishable by death. **13.** fatal; serious. **14.** of the largest, most heavily armed, etc., type.

cap·i·tal[2] (kăp′ə təl), *n. Archit.* the head, or uppermost part, of a column, pillar, etc.

cap·i·tal·ism (kăp′ə tə lYz′əm), *n.* a system under which the means of production, distribution, and exchange are in large measure privately owned and directed. **—cap′i·tal·is′tic,** *adj.*

Capitals
A. Doric; B. Ionic; C. Corinthian

cap·i·tal·ist (kăp′ə təl Yst), *n.* one who has extensive capital in business enterprises.

cap·i·tal·i·za·tion (kăp′ə təl ə zā′shən), *n.* **1.** act of capitalizing. **2.** the authorized stocks and bonds of a corporation. 3. *Accounting.* the total investment in a business enterprise.

cap·i·tal·ize (kăp/ə tə līz/), *v.t.*, **-ized, -izing.** 1. to write or print in capital letters, or with an initial capital. 2. to authorize a certain amount of stocks and bonds in the corporate charter. 3. to supply with capital. 4. to take advantage of (often fol. by *on*).

cap·i·tal·ly (kăp/ə tə lǐ), *adv.* excellently.

cap·i·ta·tion (kăp/ə tā/shən), *n.* a poll tax.

Cap·i·tol (kăp/ə təl), *n.* 1. the building at Washington, D.C., used by Congress. 2. (*often l.c.*) a building occupied by a State legislature. 3. the ancient temple of Jupiter at Rome.

ca·pit·u·late (kə pǐch/ə lāt/), *v.i.*, **-lated, -lating.** to surrender unconditionally or on agreed terms.

ca·pit·u·la·tion (kə pǐch/ə lā/shən), *n.* 1. a surrender unconditionally or on agreed terms. 2. the instrument containing a surrender. 3. a summary.

ca·pon (kā/pŏn, -pən), *n.* a rooster castrated to improve the flesh for use as food.

Ca·pri (kä/prē), *n.* a rocky island in the Bay of Naples, in W Italy. 7984 pop.; 5½ sq. mi.

ca·price (kə prēs/), *n.* 1. a sudden change of mind without apparent or adequate motive; whim. 2. whimsicality.

ca·pri·cious (kə prǐsh/əs), *adj.* subject to, led by, or indicative of caprice or whim. —**ca·pri/cious·ly,** *adv.* —**ca·pri/cious·ness,** *n.*

Cap·ri·corn (kăp/rə kôrn/), *n.* *Astron.* 1. a zodiacal constellation between Sagittarius and Aquarius. 2. the tenth sign of the zodiac.

cap·si·cum (kăp/sǐ kəm), *n.* 1. a common garden plant, in many varieties, with mild to hot, pungent seeds enclosed in a bell-shaped pericarp. 2. the fruit of these plants, or some preparation of it, used as a condiment and in medicine.

cap·size (kăp sīz/), *v.*, **-sized, -sizing.** —*v.i.* 1. to overturn. —*v.t.* 2. to upset.

cap·stan (kăp/stən), *n.* a device resembling a windlass but with a vertical axis, commonly turned by a bar (**capstan bar**), and winding a cable, for raising weights (as an anchor).

cap·sule (kăp/səl), *n.* 1. a gelatinous case enclosing a dose of medicine. 2. *Bot.* a dry dehiscent fruit, composed of two or more carpels. 3. *Anat., Zool.* a membranous sac or integument. —**cap/su·lar,** *adj.*

Capt., Captain.

cap·tain (kăp/tən, -tǐn), *n.* 1. one who is in authority over others; leader. 2. an officer in most armies, just below a major. 3. the commander or master of a merchant ship or other vessel. 4. an officer in the navy, just below a rear admiral. —*v.t.* 5. to lead as a captain. —**cap/tain·cy,** *n.* —**cap/tain·ship/,** *n.*

cap·tion (kăp/shən), *n.* 1. a heading, as of a chapter, article, or page. 2. *Print.* a text under a picture or illustration.

cap·tious (kăp/shəs), *adj.* 1. apt to make much of trivial defects; faultfinding. 2. proceeding from a faultfinding disposition. —**cap/tious·ly,** *adv.* —**cap/tious·ness,** *n.*

cap·ti·vate (kăp/tə vāt/), *v.t.*, **-vated, -vating.** to enthrall; charm. —**cap/ti·va/tion,** *n.* —**cap/ti·va/tor,** *n.*

cap·tive (kăp/tǐv), *n.* 1. a prisoner. 2. one who is enslaved by love, beauty, etc. —*adj.* 3. made or held prisoner, esp. in war. 4. captivated. 5. of or pertaining to a captive. —**cap·tiv/i·ty,** *n.*

cap·tor (kăp/tər), *n.* a person who captures.

cap·ture (kăp/chər), *v.*, **-tured, -turing,** *n.* —*v.t.* 1. to take prisoner; seize. —*n.* 2. act of capturing. 3. the thing or person captured. —**cap/tur·er,** *n.*

cap·u·chin (kăp/yŏŏ chǐn, -shǐn), *n.* 1. a prehensile-tailed, Central and South American monkey, whose head hair presents a cowllike appearance. 2. (*cap.*) *Rom. Cath. Ch.* one of an order of Franciscan friars, wearing a long cowl.

car (kär), *n.* 1. an automobile. 2. a vehicle running on rails, as a streetcar. 3. the part of a balloon, elevator, etc., for carrying the passengers, etc. 4. *Poetic.* a chariot.

ca·ra·ba·o (kär/ə bä/ō), *n., pl.* **-baos.** (in the Philippine Islands) the water buffalo.

Ca·ra·cas (kə rä/kəs), *n.* the capital of Venezuela, in the N part. 269,030.

car·a·cul (kăr/ə kəl), *n.* 1. the fur of the very young of certain Asiatic or Russian sheep (karakul) with flat, loose curls. 2. karakul (sheep).

ca·rafe (kə răf/, -räf/), *n.* a glass water bottle.

car·a·mel (kăr/ə məl, -měl/; *Midwest often* kär/məl), *n.* 1. burnt sugar, for coloring and flavoring food, etc. 2. a kind of candy made from sugar, butter, etc.

car·a·pace (kăr/ə pās/), *n.* a shell covering some or all of the dorsal part of an animal.

car·at (kăr/ət), *n.* 1. a unit of weight in gem stones, 200 mg. 2. karat.

car·a·van (kăr/ə văn/), *n.* 1. a group traveling together, as for safety, esp. over deserts in Asia or Africa. 2. a large covered vehicle. 3. a van.

car·a·van·sa·ry (kăr/ə văn/sə rǐ), *n., pl.* **-ries.** 1. (in the Near East) an inn for caravans. 2. any large inn. Also, **car·a·van·se·rai** (kăr/ə văn/sə·rī/, -rä/).

car·a·vel (kăr/ə věl/), *n.* a small ship formerly used esp. by the Spaniards and Portuguese.

car·a·way (kăr/ə wā/), *n.* 1. an herb bearing aromatic seedlike fruit (**caraway seeds**) used in cookery and medicine. 2. the fruit or seeds.

car·bide (kär/bīd, -bǐd), *n.* a compound of carbon with a more positive element.

car·bine (kär/bīn, -bēn), *n.* a type of short rifle.

car·bo·hy·drate (kär/bō hī/drāt), *n.* any of a class of organic compounds which form the supporting tissues of plants and are important food for animals.

car·bo·lat·ed (kär/bə lā/tǐd), *adj.* containing carbolic acid.

car·bol·ic acid (kär bŏl/ǐk), phenol (def. 1).

car·bon (kär/bən), *n.* 1. *Chem.* a widely distributed element which occurs in a pure state as the diamond and in an impure state as charcoal. *Symbol:* C; *at. wt.:* 12.010; *at. no.:* 6; *sp. gr.:* (of diamond) 3.51 at 20°C. 2. a duplicate copy made by using carbon paper. —**car/bo·na/ceous,** *adj.*

car·bon·ate (*n.* kär/bə nāt/, -nǐt; *v.* kär/bə·nāt/), *n., v.*, **-ated, -ating.** —*n.* 1. *Chem.* a salt of carbonic acid. —*v.t.* 2. to form into a carbonate. 3. to charge with carbon dioxide. —**car/bon·a/tion,** *n.*

carbon dioxide, a colorless, odorless, incombustible gas, CO_2, used as dry ice, in carbonated beverages, fire extinguishers, etc.

car·bon·ic (kär bŏn/ǐk), *adj.* *Chem.* containing tetravalent carbon.

carbonic acid, the acid, H_2CO_3, formed when carbon dioxide dissolves in water.

car·bon·if·er·ous (kär/bə nǐf/ər əs), *adj.* producing coal.

car·bon·ize (kär/bə nīz/), *v.t.*, **-ized, -izing.** 1. to char, forming carbon. 2. to coat or enrich with carbon. —**car/bon·i·za/tion,** *n.*

carbon monoxide, a colorless, odorless, poisonous gas, CO, formed when carbon burns with an insufficient supply of air.

carbon paper, paper faced with carbon or other material, used to reproduce a copy upon a second sheet underneath.

carbon tetrachloride, a noninflammable, colorless liquid, CCl_4, used in medicine, and as a fire extinguisher, cleaning fluid, solvent, etc.

car·bo·run·dum (kär/bə rŭn/dəm), *n.* 1. silicon carbide, SiC, an important abrasive. 2. (*cap.*) a trademark for this substance.

car·boy (kär/boi), *n.* a large bottle, esp. one protected by basketwork or a wooden box, as for acids.

car·bun·cle (kär/bŭng kəl), *n.* 1. a painful circumscribed inflammation of the subcutaneous tissue (like a boil, but more serious). 2. a garnet cut in a rounded form.

car·bu·ret (kär/bə rāt/, -byə rět/), *v.t.*, **-reted, -reting** or (*esp. Brit.*) **-retted, -retting.** to combine or mix with carbon or hydrocarbons. —**car·bu·re·tion** (kär/bə rā/shən, kär/byə rěsh/ən), *n.*

car·bu·re·tor (kär/bə rā/tər, -byə rět/ər), *n.* an apparatus for adding hydrocarbons to nonluminous gases or to air to produce an illuminating or explosive gas. Also, *esp. Brit.,* **car·bu·ret·tor** (kär/byə rět/ər).

car·cass (kär/kəs), *n.* 1. the dead body of an animal or (in contempt) of a human being. 2. (in contempt or humor) a living body. 3. anything from which life and power are gone. Also, **car/case.**

car·cin·o·gen (kär sǐn/ə jən), *n.* *Pathol.* any substance which tends to produce a cancer in a body.

car·ci·no·ma (kär/sə nō/mə), *n., pl.* **-mata** (-mə·tə), **-mas.** a malignant tumor that spreads and often recurs after excision.

card¹ (kärd), *n.* 1. a piece of stiff paper or thin pasteboard, usually rectangular, for various uses.

2. one of a set of small cardboards with spots, figures, etc., for certain games. **3.** (*pl.*) a game played with such a set. **4.** a piece of cardboard with ornamentation, bearing complimentary greeting. **5.** *Colloq.* an amusing person. —*v.t.* **6.** to provide with a card. **7.** to fasten on a card. **8.** to write, etc., on cards.

card² (kärd), *n.* **1.** an implement used in disentangling and combing out fibers of wool, flax, etc., preparatory to spinning. —*v.t.* **2.** to dress (wool, etc.) with a card. —**card′er,** *n.*

car·da·mom (kär′də məm), *n.* **1.** the aromatic seed capsule of various tropical Asiatic plants, used as a condiment and in medicine. **2.** any of the plants. Also, **car·da·mon** (kär′də mən), **car′da·mum.**

card·board (kärd′bôrd′), *n.* a thin, stiff pasteboard, used for signs, boxes, etc.

car·di·ac (kär′dĭ ăk′), *adj.* **1.** pertaining to the heart. —*n.* **2.** a cardiac remedy.

Car·diff (kär′dĭf), *n.* a seaport in SE Wales. 232,450.

car·di·gan (kär′də gən), *n.* a knitted woolen jacket. Also, **cardigan jacket.**

car·di·nal (kär′də nəl), *adj.* **1.** of prime importance; chief. **2.** deep rich red. —*n.* **3.** *Rom. Cath. Ch.* one of the seventy members of the Sacred College, ranking next to the Pope. **4.** a crested North American finch, the male of which is brilliant red. **5.** a deep rich red color.

cardinal flower, a North American plant with showy red flowers.

cardinal number, any of the numbers *one, two,* etc. (in distinction from *first, second,* etc.). Also, **cardinal numeral.**

cardinal points, the four chief directions of the compass: north, south, east, and west.

card·ing (kär′dĭng), *n.* the process of preparing fibers as wool, cotton, etc., for spinning.

car·di·o·graph (kär′dĭ ə grăf′, -grăf′), *n.* an instrument for recording by a line graph the movements of the heart. —**car′di·o·graph′ic,** *adj.*

card·sharp (kärd′shärp′), *n.* a person who cheats at card games.

care (kâr), *n., v.,* **cared, caring.** —*n.* **1.** worry; anxiety. **2.** a cause of worry, anxiety, etc. **3.** serious attention; caution. **4.** charge. **5.** an object of concern. —*v.i.* **6.** to be concerned or solicitous. **7.** to make provision or look out. **8.** to have an inclination or affection.

ca·reen (kə rēn′), *v.t.* **1.** to cause (a ship) to lie wholly or partly on its side, as for repair. **2.** to cause (a ship) to heel over. —*v.i.* **3.** to lean, sway, or tip to one side. —*n.* **4.** a careening.

ca·reer (kə rĭr′), *n.* **1.** general course of a person through life, as in some profession. **2.** an occupation, profession, etc., followed as one's lifework. **3.** success in a profession, etc. **4.** a course, esp. a swift one. **5.** speed. —*v.i.* **6.** to run or move rapidly along. —**ca·reer′ist,** *n.*

care·free (kâr′frē′), *adj.* without anxiety or worry.

care·ful (kâr′fəl), *adj.* **1.** cautious in one's actions. **2.** exact; thorough. **3.** done with accuracy or caution. **4.** solicitously mindful. —**care′-ful·ly,** *adv.* —**care′ful·ness,** *n.*

care·less (kâr′lĭs′), *adj.* **1.** not paying enough attention to what one does. **2.** not exact or thorough. **3.** done or said heedlessly. **4.** unconcerned. —**care′less·ly,** *adv.* —**care′less·ness,** *n.*

ca·ress (kə rĕs′), *n.* **1.** an expression of affection, as an embrace, kiss, etc. —*v.t.* **2.** to touch or pat gently to show affection. —**ca·ress′ing·ly,** *adv.*

car·et (kar′ət), *n.* a mark (∧) made in written or printed matter to show the place where something is to be inserted.

care·tak·er (kâr′tā′kər), *n.* a person who takes care of a thing, place, or person.

car·go (kär′gō), *n., pl.* **-goes, -gos.** **1.** the freight of a ship or airplane. **2.** load.

Car·ib (kar′ĭb), *n.* a member of an Indian people of NE South America. —**Car′ib·an,** *adj.*

Car·ib·be·an (kar′ə bē′ən, kə rĭb′ĭ-), *adj.* **1.** pertaining to the Caribbean Sea. —*n.* **2.** a Carib. **3.** Also, **Caribbean Sea.** a sea between Central America, the West Indies, and South America. ab. 750,000 sq. mi.

car·i·bou (kar′ə bōō′), *n., pl.* **-bous,** (*esp. collectively*) **bou.** any of several North American species or varieties of reindeer.

car·i·ca·ture (kar′ĭ kə chər, -chŏŏr′), *n., v.,* **-tured, -turing.** —*n.* **1.** a picture, description,

etc., ludicrously exaggerating the peculiarities or defects of persons or things. **2.** the art or process of making such pictures, etc. —*v.t.* **3.** to make a caricature of. —**car′i·ca·tur·ist,** *n.*

car·ies (kâr′ēz, -ĭ ēz′), *n.* decay, esp. of bone or teeth. —**car·i·ous** (kâr′ĭ əs), *adj.*

car·il·lon (kar′ə lŏn′, -lən, kə rĭl′yən), *n., v.,* **-lonned, -lonning.** —*n.* **1.** a set of stationary bells in a tower, sounded by manual or pedal action, or by machinery. **2.** a melody played on such bells. —*v.i.* **3.** to play a carillon. —**car·il·lon·neur** (kar′ə lə nûr′), *n.*

car·i·ole (kar′ĭ ōl′), *n.* **1.** a small, open, two-wheeled vehicle. **2.** a covered cart.

car·load (kär′lōd′), *n.* *Chiefly U.S.* the amount carried by a car, esp. a freight car.

Car·lyle (kär līl′), *n.* **Thomas,** 1795–1881, Scottish essayist and historian.

Car·mel·ite (kär′mə līt′), *n.* **1.** a mendicant friar of a religious order founded in the 12th century. **2.** a nun belonging to this order.

car·mine (kär′mĭn, -mīn), *n.* **1.** a crimson red color. **2.** a crimson pigment obtained from cochineal. —*adj.* **3.** crimson.

car·nage (kär′nĭj), *n.* the slaughter of a great number, as in battle; massacre.

car·nal (kär′nəl), *adj.* **1.** not spiritual; temporal; worldly. **2.** sensual. **3.** sexual. —**car·nal′i·ty,** *n.* —**car′nal·ly,** *adv.*

car·na·tion (kär nā′shən), *n.* **1.** any of numerous cultivated varieties of clove pink with fragrant flowers of various colors. **2.** pink.

car·nel·ian (kär nēl′yən), *n.* a red or reddish variety of chalcedony, used in jewelry, etc.

car·ni·val (kär′nə vəl), *n.* **1.** an amusement show, usually traveling from place to place, having side shows, merry-go-rounds, etc. **2.** any merrymaking or revelry.

car·ni·vore (kär′nə vôr′), *n.* *Zool.* one of the order of mammals, chiefly flesh-eating, that includes the cats, dogs, bears, etc.

car·niv·o·rous (kär nĭv′ə rəs), *adj.* flesh-eating. —**car·niv′o·rous·ly,** *adv.*

car·ol (kar′əl), *n., v.,* **-oled, -oling** or (*esp. Brit.*) **-olled, -olling. 1.** a song, esp. of joy. **2.** a Christmas song or hymn. —*v.i., v.t.* **3.** to sing, esp. in a lively, joyous manner. —**car′ol·er;** *esp. Brit.,* **car′ol·ler,** *n.*

Car·ol II (kar′əl), born 1893, king of Rumania, 1930–40.

Car·o·line Islands (kar′ə lĭn′, -lĭn), a group of over 500 islands in the Pacific, E of the Philippine Islands: now under U.S. administration. 54,900 pop.; 525 sq. mi.

car·om (kar′əm), *n.* **1.** *Billiards.* a shot in which the ball struck with the cue is made to hit two balls in succession. **2.** any strike and rebound. —*v.i.* **3.** to make a carom.

ca·rot·id (kə rŏt′ĭd), *Anat.* —*n.* **1.** either of the two great arteries, one on each side of the neck, which carry blood to the head. —*adj.* **2.** pertaining to the carotids. —**ca·rot′id·al,** *adj.*

ca·rous·al (kə rou′zəl), *n.* a noisy or drunken feast or other social gathering; jovial revelry.

ca·rouse (kə rouz′), *n., v.,* **-roused, -rousing.** —*n.* **1.** a noisy or drunken feast; jovial revelry. —*v.i.* **2.** to engage in a carouse.

car·ou·sel (kar′ə zĕl′, -sĕl′), *n.* carrousel.

carp¹ (kärp), *v.i.* to find fault; cavil.

carp² (kärp), *n., pl.* **carps,** (*esp. collectively*) **carp.** a large, coarse fresh-water food fish, commonly bred in ponds.

carp., carpentry.

car·pal (kär′pəl), *Anat.* —*adj.* **1.** pertaining to the carpus. —*n.* **2.** a carpale.

car·pa·le (kär pā′lĭ), *n., pl.* **-lia** (-lĭ ə). *Anat.* any of the bones of the wrist.

Car·pa·thi·an Mountains (kär pā′thĭ ən), a mountain system extending 800 mi. from N Czechoslovakia to central Rumania. Highest peak, 8737 ft. Also, **Carpathians.**

car·pel (kär′pəl), *n.* *Bot.* a simple pistil, or a single member of a compound pistil: regarded as a modified leaf. —**car′pel·lar·y,** *adj.*

car·pen·ter (kär′pən tər), *n.* **1.** a workman who builds houses and does other types of woodwork. —*v.i.* **2.** to do carpenter's work. —*v.t.* **3.** to make by carpentry. —**car′pen·ter·ing, car′-pen·try,** *n.*

car·pet (kär′pĭt), *n.* **1.** a heavy fabric, commonly of wool, for covering floors. **2.** a covering of this material. **3.** any covering like a carpet. —*v.t.* **4.** to cover with a carpet.

car·pet·bag (kär′pĭt băg′), *n.* a bag for traveling, esp. one made of carpeting.

car·pet·bag·ger (kär′pĭt băg/ər), n. 1. a person who takes up residence in a place, with no more property than he brings in a carpetbag, to seek special advantages. 2. a Northerner who went to the South after the Civil War to seek advantages made possible by the disorganized condition of affairs.

car·pet·ing (kär′pĭt ĭng), n. 1. material for carpets. 2. carpets in general.

car·pus (kär′pəs), n., pl. -pi (-pī). Anat. 1. the wrist. 2. the wrist bones collectively.

car·riage (kär′ĭj; also for 6 kâr′ĭ ĭj), n. 1. a wheeled vehicle for conveying persons, usually drawn by horses. 2. Brit. a railway car. 3. a wheeled support, as for a cannon. 4. posture; bearing. 5. conveyance. 6. the price or cost of transportation. 7. management.

car·ri·er (kâr′ĭ ər), n. 1. a person or thing that carries. 2. a person, company, etc., that undertakes to convey goods or persons for hire. 3. a mechanism by which something is carried or moved. 4. an individual harboring specific organisms who may transmit the disease to others. 5. Also, **carrier wave**. Radio. the wave whose amplitude, frequency, or phase is to be varied or modulated to transmit a signal.

carrier pigeon, a pigeon trained to fly home from great distances and thus transport written messages.

car·ri·on (kăr′ĭ ən), n. 1. dead and putrefying flesh. —adj. 2. feeding on carrion. 3. of or like carrion.

Car·roll (kăr′əl), n. Lewis, (Charles Lutwidge Dodgson) 1832–98, British writer.

car·rot (kăr′ət), n. 1. a plant of an umbelliferous genus including one species which is valued for its yellowish edible root. 2. the root.

car·rot·y (kăr′ət ĭ), adj. yellowish-red.

car·rou·sel (kăr′ə zĕl′, -sĕl′), n. a merry-go-round (def. 1).

car·ry (kăr′ĭ), v., -ried, -rying, n., pl. -ries. —v.t. 1. to convey from one place to another. 2. to bear the weight, etc., of. 3. U.S. to take a (part) in singing. 4. to hold (the body, head, etc.) in a certain manner. 5. to behave (oneself). 6. to take, esp. by force; win. 7. to secure the election or adoption of. 8. to extend in a given direction. 9. to have as an attribute, etc. 10. Com. a. to keep on hand or in stock. b. to keep on one's account books, etc. —v.i. 11. to act as a bearer. 12. to have or exert propelling force. 13. to be transmitted, propelled, or sustained. 14. **carry off, a.** to win (the prize, etc.). **b.** to face consequences boldly. 15. **carry on, a.** to manage. **b.** U.S. to behave in an excited, foolish, or improper manner. **c.** Chiefly Brit. to continue. 16. **carry out,** to accomplish (a plan, etc.). —n. 17. range, as of a gun. 18. Golf. the distance traversed by a ball before it alights. 19. U.S. a portage.

car·ry·all (kăr′ĭ ôl′), n. a light, covered, one-horse family carriage, with two seats.

car·ry·o·ver (kăr′ĭ ō′vər), n. the part left over to a later period, account, etc.

Car·son (kär′sən), n. Christopher, ("Kit") 1809–68, U.S. frontiersman and scout.

Carson City, the capital of Nevada, in the W part. 2478.

cart (kärt), n. 1. a two-wheeled vehicle usually for the conveyance of heavy goods. 2. any small vehicle moved by hand. —v.t. 3. to convey in a cart. —v.i. 4. to drive a cart. —**cart′er,** n.

cart·age (kär′tĭj), n. the cost of carting.

carte blanche (kärt′ blänsh′), pl. **cartes blanches** (kärts′ blänsh′), unconditional authority; full power.

car·tel (kär tĕl′, kär′təl), n. 1. an international syndicate, combine, or trust generally formed to regulate prices and output in some field. 2. a written agreement between belligerents.

Car·te·sian (kär tē′zhən), adj. pertaining to Descartes, or to his dualistic philosophy.

Car·thage (kär′thĭj), n. an ancient city-state in N Africa, near modern Tunis: destroyed by the Romans, 146 B.C. —**Car·tha·gin·i·an** (kär′thə jĭn′ĭ ən), adj., n.

Car·thu·sian (kär thōō′zhən), n. 1. a member of an austere monastic order founded in 1086. —adj. 2. belonging to this order.

car·ti·lage (kär′tə lĭj, kärt′lĭj), n. Anat., Zool. 1. a firm, elastic, flexible connective tissue. 2. a part composed of cartilage.

car·ti·lag·i·nous (kär′tə lăj′ə nəs), adj. 1. of or resembling cartilage. 2. having the skeleton composed mostly of cartilage.

cartog., cartography.

car·tog·ra·phy (kär tŏg′rə fĭ), n. the production of maps. —**car·tog′ra·pher,** n. —**car·to·graph·ic** (kär′tə grăf′ĭk), adj.

car·ton (kär′tən), n. a cardboard box.

car·toon (kär tōōn′), n. 1. a sketch or drawing as in a newspaper or periodical, usually caricaturing some subject or persons of current interest. 2. Fine Arts. a full-scale model drawing for mosaic, tapestry, etc. 3. a comic strip. 4. an animated cartoon. —v.t. 5. to represent by a cartoon. —**car·toon′ist,** n.

car·tridge (kär′trĭj), n. 1. a cylindrical case of pasteboard, metal, or the like, for holding a complete charge of powder, and often also the bullet or the shot, for a rifle, machine gun, or other small arm. 2. Photog. a case or holder for a roll of camera film.

cart·wheel (kärt′hwēl′), n. 1. a somersault performed sidewise. 2. Slang. any large coin.

carve (kärv), v., carved, carving. —v.t. 1. to fashion or produce by cutting. —v.i. 2. to decorate by cutting designs, etc. 3. to cut meat. —**carv′er,** n.

car·vel (kär′vəl), n. caravel.

carv·ing (kär′vĭng), n. 1. act of fashioning or producing by cutting. 2. carved work.

car·y·at·id (kăr′ĭ ăt′ĭd), n., pl. -ids, -ides (-ə dēz′). Archit. a figure of a woman used like a supporting column.

ca·sa·ba (kə sä′bə), n. a kind of winter muskmelon, having a yellow rind and sweet, juicy flesh.

Ca·sa·blan·ca (kä′sä blăng′kä, kăs′ə blăng′kə), n. a seaport in NW Morocco. 257,430.

Cas·a·no·va (kăz′ə nō′və, kăs′-), n. Giovanni Jacopo, 1725–98, Italian adventurer and writer.

Cas·bah (käz′bä), n. Kashbah.

cas·cade (kăs kād′), n., v., -caded, -cading. —n. 1. a waterfall over steep rocks, or a series of small waterfalls. 2. an arrangement of lace, etc., in folds falling one over another in a zigzag fashion. —v.i. 3. to fall in or like a cascade.

Cascade Range, a mountain range from N California to British Columbia. Highest peak, Mt. Rainier, 14,408 ft.

cas·car·a (kăs kâr′ə), n. a species of buckthorn, of the Pacific coast of the U.S., yielding cascara sagrada.

cascara sa·gra·da (sə grä′də), the bark of the cascara, used as a cathartic or laxative.

case[1] (kās), n. 1. an instance of the occurrence, existence, etc., of something. 2. the actual state of things. 3. situation; condition. 4. a state of things involving a question for discussion or decision. 5. a statement of facts, reasons, etc. 6. an instance of disease, etc., requiring medical attention. 7. a medical patient. 8. Law. a. a suit or action. b. a set of facts giving rise or defense to a legal claim. 9. Gram. a category in the inflection of nouns, pronouns, and adjectives, denoting the syntactic relation of these words to other words in the sentence. 10. Colloq. a peculiar or unusual person. 11. **in any case,** anyhow. 12. **in case,** if. 13. **in case of,** in the event of.

case[2] (kās), n., v., cased, casing. —n. 1. a thing for containing something; receptacle. 2. a sheath. 3. a box with its contents. 4. the amount contained in a box. 5. a framework, as of a door. 6. Print. a tray divided into compartments for holding type, arranged into two parts: the **upper case** for capitals, etc., and the **lower case** for small letters, etc. —v.t. 7. to put in a case.

case·hard·en (kās′här′dən), v.t. 1. Metall. to make the outside surface of hard. 2. to harden in spirit.

ca·se·in (kā′sĭ ĭn, -sēn), n. Biochem. a protein precipitated from milk, as by rennet, and forming the basis of cheese and certain plastics.

case·mate (kās′māt′), n. an armored enclosure for guns in a warship, fortress, etc. —**case′mat·ed,** adj.

case·ment (kās′mənt), n. a window opening on hinges like a door.

ca·se·ous (kā′sĭ əs), adj. of or like cheese.

cash (kăsh), n. 1. money, esp. money on hand. 2. money, or an equivalent (as a check), paid at the time of making a purchase. —v.t. 3. to give or obtain cash for (a check, etc.). —v.i. 4. U.S. Colloq. to die (fol. by in).

cash·book (kăsh′bŏŏk′), n. a book in which to record money received and paid out.

cash·ew (kăsh′ōō, kə shōō′), n. 1. a tropical American tree whose bark yields a medicinal gum. 2. its fruit, a small, edible, kidney-shaped nut (cashew nut).

cash·ier[1] (kǎ shǐr/), *n.* one who has charge of cash or money, as in a bank.

cash·ier[2] (kǎ shǐr/), *v.t.* 1. to dismiss, esp. with disgrace. 2. to discard.

cash·mere (kǎsh/mǐr), *n.* 1. the fine wool at the roots of the hair of Kashmir goats. 2. a shawl of this hair. 3. a wool fabric of twill weave.

cas·ing (kā/sǐng), *n.* 1. a case or covering. 2. the framework around a door or window. 3. *U.S.* the outermost covering of an automobile tire.

ca·si·no (kə sē/nō), *n., pl.* -nos. 1. a building or large room for meetings, amusements, gambling, etc. 2. cassino.

cask (kǎsk, käsk), *n.* 1. a barrellike container made of staves, for holding liquids, etc. 2. the quantity such a container holds.

cas·ket (kǎs/kǐt, käs/-), *n.* 1. *Chiefly U.S.* a coffin. 2. a small chest or box, as for jewels.

Cas·pi·an Sea (kǎs/pǐ ən), a salt lake between SE Europe and Asia: the largest inland body of water in the world. ab. 169,000 sq. mi.

Cas·san·dra (kə sǎn/drə), *n. Class. Legend.* a prophetess of ancient Troy, who was fated never to be believed.

cas·sa·va (kə sä/və), *n.* 1. any of several tropical plants of the spurge family, esp. those cultivated for their tuberous roots, which yield important food products. 2. a nutritious starch from the roots, the source of tapioca.

cas·se·role (kǎs/ə rōl/), *n.* a baking dish of glass, pottery, etc., usually with a cover.

cas·sia (kǎsh/ə, kǎs/ʸ ə), *n.* 1. a variety of cinnamon from a species of tree of southern China (**cassia bark**). 2. the tree itself. 3. any of certain herbs, shrubs, and trees, some of which have long pods (**cassia pods**) whose pulp (**cassia pulp**) is a mild laxative, while others yield senna.

cas·si·mere (kǎs/ə mǐr/), *n.* a plain or twilled woolen cloth.

cas·si·no (kə sē/nō), *n.* a kind of card game.

Cas·si·o·pe·ia (kǎs/ʸ ə pē/ə), *n.* 1. a northern circumpolar constellation east of Cepheus. 2. *Gk. Myth.* the mother of Andromeda.

cas·sock (kǎs/ək), *n.* a long, close-fitting garment worn by ecclesiastics and others engaged in church functions.

cas·so·war·y (kǎs/ə wěr/ʸ), *n., pl.* -waries. any of several large, three-toed, flightless birds of Australasian regions, superficially resembling the ostrich.

cast (kǎst, käst), *v.*, **cast, casting,** *n.* —*v.t.* 1. to throw; fling. 2. to throw off or away. 3. to direct (the eye, a glance, light, etc.). 4. to discard or reject. 5. to deposit (a ballot, vote, etc.). 6. *Theat.* to allot parts of (a play) to actors; select (actors) for a play. 7. *Metall.* a. to form (molten metal, etc.) into a particular shape by pouring into a mold. b. to produce (an article) by such a process. 8. to compute. 9. to ponder or plan. —*v.i.* 10. to throw. 11. to calculate. 12. to search this way and that (often fol. by *about*). 13. **cast about, a.** to look about one mentally, as for an excuse. **b.** to scheme. 14. **cast down,** to discourage. 15. **cast up, a.** to compute. **b.** to eject. —*n.* 16. act of casting. 17. that which is cast. 18. the distance to which a thing may be cast. 19. *Games.* a. a throw of dice. b. the number rolled. 20. form; arrangement. 21. *Theat.* the actors to whom the parts in a play are assigned. 22. *Metall.* a. act of casting. b. the quantity of metal cast at one time. 23. something shaped in a mold. 24. *Med.* rigid surgical dressing usually made of plaster of Paris bandage. 25. appearance. 26. sort; style. 27. tendency. 28. a permanent twist. 29. a slight tinge of some color. 30. computation.

cas·ta·net (kǎs/tə nět/), *n.* a pair, or one of a pair, of shells of ivory or hard wood held in the palm and struck together as an accompaniment to music and dancing.

cast·a·way (kǎst/ə wā/, käst/-), *n.* 1. a shipwrecked person. 2. an outcast. —*adj.* 3. cast adrift. 4. thrown away.

caste (kǎst, käst), *n.* 1. one of the social classes into which the Hindus are rigidly separated and of which the privileges or disabilities are transmitted by inheritance. 2. any rigid system of social distinctions.

cas·tel·lat·ed (kǎs/tə lā/tǐd), *adj.* built like a castle, esp. with turrets. —**cas/tel·la/tion,** *n.*

cast·er (kǎs/tər, käs/-), *n.* 1. one that casts. 2. a small wheel on a swivel, set under a piece of furniture, etc.

cas·ti·gate (kǎs/tə gāt/), *v.t.,* -gated, -gating.

to punish in order to correct; criticize severely. —**cas/ti·ga/tion,** *n.* —**cas/ti·ga/tor,** *n.*

Cas·tile (kǎs tēl/), *n.* a former kingdom comprising most of Spain.

Castile soap (kǎs/tēl), a mild soap made with olive oil and soda.

Cas·til·ian (kǎs tǐl/yən), *n.* 1. the accepted standard form of the Spanish language as spoken in Spain. 2. a native or inhabitant of Castile.

cast·ing (kǎs/tǐng, käs/-), *n.* 1. act or process of one that casts. 2. that which is cast.

cast iron, an alloy of iron, carbon, and other elements.

cast-i·ron (kǎst/ī/ərn, käst/-), *adj.* 1. made of cast iron. 2. rigid. 3. hardy.

cas·tle (kǎs/əl, käs/əl), *n., v.,* -tled, -tling. —*n.* 1. a fortified residence, as of a noble in feudal times. 2. a large and stately residence. 3. *Chess.* the rook. —*v.t.* 4. to place in or as in a castle. 5. *Chess.* to move (the king) in castling. —*v.i.* 6. *Chess.* to move the king two squares and bring the castle to the first square the king has passed over. —**cas/tled,** *adj.*

cast·off (kǎst/ôf/, -ŏf/, käst/-), *adj.* 1. thrown away. —*n.* 2. a castoff person or thing.

cas·tor (kǎs/tər, käs/-), *n.* caster (def. 2).

castor oil, a viscid oil obtained from the castor bean, used as a cathartic, lubricant, etc.

castor-oil plant, a tall plant of the spurge family, native to India but widely naturalized, yielding the **castor bean.**

cas·trate (kǎs/trāt), *v.t.,* -trated, -trating. 1. to deprive of the testicles; emasculate. 2. to expurgate. —**cas·tra/tion,** *n.*

cas·u·al (kǎzh/ŏŏ əl), *adj.* 1. happening by chance. 2. unpremeditated. 3. careless; unconcerned. 4. irregular; occasional 5. accidental. —*n.* 6. a worker employed only irregularly. 7. a soldier temporarily at a station or other place of duty. —**cas/u·al·ly,** *adv.* —**cas/u·al·ness,** *n.*

cas·u·al·ty (kǎzh/ŏŏ əl tǐ), *n., pl.* -ties. 1. an unfortunate accident, esp. one involving death. 2. *Mil.* a. a soldier who is missing in action, killed, wounded, or captured. b. (*pl.*) loss in numerical strength through death, wounds, sickness, capture, or desertion. 3. one who is injured or killed in an accident.

cas·u·is·tic (kǎzh/ŏŏ ʸs/tǐk), *adj.* 1. pertaining to casuistry. 2. sophistical. Also, **cas·u·is/ti·cal.**

cas·u·ist·ry (kǎzh/ŏŏ ʸs trǐ), *n., pl.* -ries. the application (or, from an outside point of view, misapplication) of general ethical principles to particular cases of conscience or conduct. —**cas/u·ist,** *n.*

cat (kǎt), *n., v.,* **catted, catting.** —*n.* 1. a domesticated carnivore, widely distributed in a number of breeds. 2. any of a family of digitate carnivores, as the lion, tiger, etc. 3. a spiteful and gossipy woman. —*v.t.* 4. to flog with a cat-o'-nine-tails. —**cat/like/,** *adj.*

ca·tab·o·lism (kə tăb/ə lǐz/əm), *n. Physiol., Biol.* a breaking down process. —**cat·a·bol·ic** (kăt/ə bŏl/ʸk), *adj.*

cat·a·clysm (kăt/ə klǐz/əm), *n.* 1. any violent change or upheaval. 2. *Phys. Geog.* a sudden and violent change in the earth's surface. 3. an extensive flood. —**cat/a·clys/mic, cat/a·clys/mal,** *adj.*

cat·a·comb (kăt/ə kōm/), *n.* (*usually pl.*) an underground cemetery.

cat·a·falque (kăt/ə fălk/), *n.* a raised structure on which a dead body lies or is carried in state.

cat·a·lep·sy (kăt/ə lĕp/sǐ), *n. Pathol.* a bodily condition marked esp. by suspension of sensation, muscular rigidity, and fixity of posture. —**cat/a·lep/tic,** *adj., n.*

cat·a·log (kăt/ə lôg/, -lŏg/), *n., v.t.* catalogue. —**cat/a·log/er, cat/a·log/ist,** *n.*

cat·a·logue (kăt/ə lôg/, -lŏg/), *n., v.,* -logued, -loguing. —*n.* 1. a list, usually in alphabetical order, with brief notes on the names, articles, etc., listed. 2. a record of the books of a library, indicated on cards. —*v.t.* 3. to make a catalogue of; enter in a catalogue. —**cat/a·logu/er, cat/a·logu/ist,** *n.*

ca·tal·pa (kə tăl/pə), *n.* any of certain trees of America and Asia, one common species of which has large cordate leaves and bell-shaped white flowers.

ca·tal·y·sis (kə tăl/ə sǐs), *n., pl.* -ses (-sēz/). *Chem.* the causing or accelerating of a change by a substance (**catalyst**) which is not permanently affected by the reaction. —**cat·a·lyt·ic** (kăt/ə lǐt/ʸk), *adj., n.*

cat·a·lyst (kăt/ə lĭst), *n.* *Chem.* a substance that causes catalysis.

cat·a·lyze (kăt/ə līz/), *v.t.*, **-lyzed, -lyzing.** *Chem.* to act upon by catalysis.

cat·a·ma·ran (kăt/ə mə răn/), *n.* **1.** *Naut.* **a.** a raft. **b.** any craft with twin parallel hulls. **2.** *Colloq.* a quarrelsome person.

cat·a·mount (kăt/ə-mount/), *n.* a wild animal of the cat family, as (in America) the cougar or lynx.

Catamaran

Ca·ta·nia (kä tä/nyä), *n.* a seaport in E Sicily. 269,-102.

cat·a·pult (kăt/ə pŭlt/), *n.* **1.** an ancient military engine for throwing darts, stones, etc. **2.** a device for launching an airplane from the deck of a ship. —*v.t.* **3.** to hurl as from a catapult.

cat·a·ract (kăt/ə răkt/), *n.* **1.** a waterfall, esp. a large one. **2.** any downpour or deluge. **3.** an abnormality of the eye, characterized by opacity of the lens.

ca·tarrh (kə tär/), *n.* inflammation of a mucous membrane, esp. of the respiratory tract, accompanied by excessive secretions. —**ca·tarrh/al,** *adj.*

ca·tas·tro·phe (kə tăs/trə fī), *n.* **1.** a sudden and widespread disaster. **2.** the dénouement. **3.** a cataclysm. —**cat·a·stroph·ic** (kăt/ə strŏf/-ĭk), *adj.*

Ca·taw·ba (kə tô/bə), *n.* **1.** a reddish grape of the eastern U.S. **2.** a light, dry, white wine made from this grape.

cat·bird (kăt/bûrd/), *n.* a slate-colored North American songbird, having a call resembling the mewing of a cat.

cat·boat (kăt/bōt/), *n.* a boat with one forward mast and a single sail.

cat·call (kăt/kôl/), *n.* a cry like that of a cat, used to express disapproval at a meeting, etc.

catch (kăch), *v.,* **caught, catching,** *n., adj.* —*v.t.* **1.** to capture, esp. after pursuit. **2.** to entrap or deceive. **3.** to be in time to reach (a train, etc.). **4.** to surprise or detect, as in some action. **5.** to hit. **6.** to intercept and seize (a ball, etc.). **7.** to check (one's breath, etc.). **8.** to get or contract. **9.** to snatch. **10.** to be entangled with. **11.** to charm. **12.** to understand. —*v.i.* **13.** to become fastened or entangled. **14.** to take hold. **15.** to overtake something moving. **16.** to become lighted. **17.** to spread or be communicated, as a disease. —*n.* **18.** act of catching. **19.** anything that catches, esp. a device for checking motion. **20.** that which is caught, as a quantity of fish. **21.** a fragment. **22.** *Music.* a round, esp. one in which the words are so arranged as to produce ludicrous effects. —*adj.* **23.** catchy.

catch·all (kăch/ôl/), *n.* a general receptacle.

catch·er (kăch/ər), *n.* **1.** one that catches. **2.** *Baseball.* the player who stands behind the home base to catch the pitched ball.

catch·ing (kăch/ĭng), *adj.* **1.** infectious. **2.** attractive; fascinating; alluring.

catch·pen·ny (kăch/pĕn/ĭ), *adj., n., pl.* **-nies.** —*adj.* **1.** made to sell readily at a low price, regardless of value. —*n.* **2.** anything cheap and of little value.

catch·up (kăch/əp, kĕch/-), *n. Now U.S.* a sauce, usually of tomatoes, for meat, fish, etc.

catch·word (kăch/wûrd/), *n.* **1.** a word or phrase repeated for effect, as by a political party. **2.** a word printed at the top of a page in a dictionary or other book to indicate the first or last article on that page.

catch·y (kăch/ĭ), *adj.,* **catchier, catchiest. 1.** pleasing and easily remembered. **2.** tricky; deceptive.

cate (kāt), *n. Archaic.* a choice food.

cat·e·chism (kăt/ə kĭz/əm), *n.* **1.** an elementary book on the principles of a religion, in the form of questions and answers. **2.** the contents of such a book. —**cat/e·chis/tic, cat/e·chis/ti·cal,** *adj.*

cat·e·chize (kăt/ə kīz/), *v.t.,* **-chized, -chizing.** to instruct or examine orally by means of questions and answers. Also, **cat/e·chise/.** —**cat/e·chi·za/tion,** *n.* —**cat·e·chist** (kăt/ə kĭst), **cat/e·chiz/er,** *n.*

cat·e·gor·i·cal (kăt/ə gŏr/ə kəl, -gôr/-), *adj.* **1.** not conditional; direct. **2.** of, pertaining to, or in a category. —**cat/e·gor/i·cal·ly,** *adv.*

cat·e·go·ry (kăt/ə gōr/ĭ), *n., pl.* **-ries. 1.** a division in any field of knowledge, as a phylum or any of its subdivisions in biology. **2.** any general division.

ca·ter (kā/tər), *v.i.* **1.** to provide food, service, etc. **2.** to provide means of amusement, pleasure, etc. —**ca/ter·er,** *n.*

cat·er-cor·nered (kăt/ə kôr/nərd, kăt/ər-), *adj.* **1.** diagonal. —*adv.* **2.** diagonally.

cat·er·pil·lar (kăt/ə pĭl/ər, kăt/ər-), *n.* **1.** the wormlike larva of a butterfly or a moth. **2.** Also, **caterpillar tractor.** a tractor having the driving wheels inside endless tracks, thus being capable of hauling over rough or soft ground. **3.** (*cap.*) a trademark for this tractor.

cat·er·waul (kăt/ər wôl/), *v.i.* **1.** to cry as cats in rutting time. **2.** to howl or screech. —*n.* Also, **cat/er·waul/ing. 3.** the cry of a cat in rutting time. **4.** any similar sound.

cat·fish (kăt/fĭsh/), *n., pl.* **-fishes,** (*esp. collectively*) **-fish.** any of numerous fishes having some fancied resemblance to a cat, such as one of the North American fresh-water fishes characterized by long barbels.

cat·gut (kăt/gŭt/), *n.* the intestines of sheep or other animals, dried and twisted, used as strings for musical instruments, etc.

Cath., Catholic.

ca·thar·sis (kə thär/sĭs), *n.* **1.** *Aesthetics.* the effect of art in purifying the emotions. **2.** *Med.* a purging.

ca·thar·tic (kə thär/tĭk), *adj.* **1.** Also, **ca·thar/-ti·cal.** evacuating the bowels. —*n.* **2.** a purgative.

Ca·thay (kă thā/), *n. Archaic or Poetic.* China.

ca·the·dral (kə thē/drəl), *n.* **1.** the principal church of a diocese, containing the bishop's throne. **2.** any of various important churches. —*adj.* **3.** pertaining to or containing a bishop's throne.

Cath·er·ine II (kăth/rĭn, -ər ĭn), (*"the Great"*) 1729–96, empress of Russia, 1762–96.

cath·e·ter (kăth/ə tər), *n. Med.* a hollow tube employed to drain fluids from body cavities or to distend body passages.

cath·ode (kăth/ōd), *n.* **1.** (in a voltaic cell, etc.) the electrode which emits electrons or gives off negative ions and toward which positive ions move or collect. **2.** the negative pole of a battery or other source of electric current. —**ca·thod·ic** (kə thŏd/ĭk), *adj.*

cathode ray, a stream of electrons generated at the cathode during an electric discharge in a vacuum tube.

cath·o·lic (kăth/ə lĭk, kăth/lĭk), *adj.* **1.** pertaining to the whole Christian body or church. **2.** universal. **3.** broad-minded; liberal.

Cath·o·lic (kăth/ə lĭk, kăth/lĭk), *adj.* **1.** of or belonging to the Catholic Church (which see). **2.** denoting or pertaining to the orthodox churches which have kept the apostolic succession of bishops. **3.** pertaining to the Western Church. —*n.* **4.** a member of a catholic church, esp. of the Church of Rome.

Catholic Church, *Rom. Cath. Ch.* a visible society of baptized, professing the same faith under the authority of the invisible Head (Christ) and the authority of the visible head (the pope and the bishops in communion with him).

Ca·thol·i·cism (kə thŏl/ə sĭz/əm), *n.* the faith, system, and practice of the Catholic Church.

cath·o·lic·i·ty (kăth/ə lĭs/ə tĭ), *n.* universality; broad-mindedness.

cat·kin (kăt/kĭn), *n. Bot.* an ament.

cat nap, *U.S.* a short, light nap or doze.

cat·nip (kăt/nĭp), *n.* a plant of the mint family, with strongly scented leaves of which cats are fond.

Ca·to (kā/tō), *n.* **1.** Marcus Porcius, (*"the Elder"*) 234–149 B.C., Roman statesman, soldier, and writer. **2.** his great-grandson Marcus Porcius, (*"the Younger"*) 95–46 B.C., Roman statesman, soldier, and Stoic philosopher.

cat-o'-nine-tails (kăt/ə nīn/tālz/), *n., pl.* **-tails.** a whip, usually having nine knotted lines or cords fastened to a handle, used to flog offenders.

Cats·kill Mountains (kăts/kĭl), a range of low mountains in E New York. Highest peak, 4204 ft. Also, **Catskills.**

cat's-paw (kăts/pô/), *n.* a person used by another to serve his purposes. Also, **cats/paw/.**

cat·sup (kăt/səp, kĕch/əp), *n.* catchup.

cat·tail (kăt/tāl/), *n.* a tall reedlike marsh plant with flowers in long, dense cylindrical spikes.

cat·tish (kăt/ĭsh), *adj.* 1. catlike. 2. spiteful. —**cat/tish·ly,** *adv.* —**cat/tish·ness,** *n.*

cat·tle (kăt/əl), *n.* 1. *U.S.* ruminants of the bovine kind. 2. *Brit.* such animals together with horses and other domesticated animals. 3. *Contemptuous.* human beings.

cat·tle·man (kăt/əl mən), *n., pl.* **-men.** 1. a person employed in tending or rearing cattle. 2. *U.S.* the owner of a cattle ranch.

cat·ty (kăt/ĭ), *adj.,* **-tier, -tiest.** 1. catlike. 2. slyly malicious. —**cat/ti·ly,** *adv.* —**cat/ti·ness,** *n.*

Ca·tul·lus (kə tŭl/əs), *n.* **Gaius Valerius,** 84?-54? B.C., Roman lyric poet.

cat·walk (kăt/wôk/), *n.* any narrow walking space on a bridge, or in an aircraft.

Cau·ca·sia (kô kā/zhə, -shə), *n.* a region in the Soviet Union between the Black and Caspian seas. Also, **Caucasus.**

Cau·ca·sian (kô kā/zhən, -shən, -kăzh/ən, -kăsh/ən), *adj.* 1. pertaining to the so-called "white race," embracing the chief peoples of Europe, southwestern Asia, and northern Africa. —*n.* 2. a member of the Caucasian race.

Cau·ca·sus (kô/kə səs), *n.* a mountain range in the S Soviet Union in Europe. Highest peak, Mt. Elbrus, 18,465 ft.

cau·cus (kô/kəs), *n.* 1. *U.S.* a meeting of the local members of a political party to nominate candidates, etc., or of legislators of the same party to determine party policies. —*v.i.* 2. to hold or meet in a caucus.

cau·dal (kô/dəl), *adj. Zool.* 1. of, at, or near the tail. 2. taillike. —**cau/dal·ly,** *adv.*

cau·date (kô/dāt), *adj. Zool.* having a tail or taillike appendage. Also, **cau/dat·ed.**

cau·dle (kô/dəl), *n.* a warm drink for the sick, as wine mixed with eggs, bread, spices, etc.

caul (kôl), *n.* a part of the amnion sometimes covering the head of a child at birth.

caul·dron (kôl/drən), *n.* caldron.

cau·li·flow·er (kô/lə flou/ər; *Colloq. often* kŏl/ĭ-), *n.* 1. a cultivated plant whose inflorescence forms a compact, fleshy head. 2. the head, used as a vegetable.

caus·al (kô/zəl), *adj.* 1. of, constituting, or implying a cause. 2. *Gram.* expressing a cause, as a conjunction. —**caus/al·ly,** *adv.*

cau·sal·i·ty (kô zăl/ə tĭ), *n., pl.* **-ties.** 1. the relation of cause and effect. 2. causal quality or agency.

cau·sa·tion (kô zā/shən), *n.* 1. the action of causing. 2. the relation of cause to effect. 3. a cause.

caus·a·tive (kô/zə tĭv), *n.* 1. *Gram.* a word (usually a verb) denoting causation. —*adj.* 2. *Gram.* a. pertaining to an affix or other form by which causatives are derived from an underlying word. b. pertaining to a word or words so derived. 3. productive. —**caus/a·tive·ly,** *adv.*

cause (kôz), *n., v.,* **caused, causing.** —*n.* 1. the thing, person, etc., from which something results. 2. the reason; motive. 3. good or sufficient reason. 4. *Law.* a. a ground of legal action. b. a case for judicial decision. 5. any subject of discussion or debate. 6. the aim, purpose, etc., of a group. —*v.t.* 7. to bring about. —**cause/less,** *adj.* —**caus/er,** *n.*

cau·se·rie (kō/zə rē/), *n.* 1. a talk or chat. 2. a short, informal essay, etc.

cause·way (kôz/wā/), *n.* 1. a raised road, as across wet ground. 2. a highway or paved way.

caus·tic (kôs/tĭk), *adj.* 1. capable of burning, corroding, or destroying living tissue. 2. severely critical or sarcastic. —*n.* 3. a caustic substance. —**caus/ti·cal·ly,** *adv.* —**caus·tic·i·ty** (kôs tĭs/ə tĭ), *n.*

cau·ter·ize (kô/tə rīz/), *v.t.,* **-ized, -izing.** to burn with a hot iron, or with fire or a caustic, esp. for curative purposes. —**cau/ter·i·za/tion,** *n.*

cau·ter·y (kô/tə rĭ), *n., pl.* **-teries.** 1. a caustic substance or a hot iron used to destroy tissue. 2. the process of destroying tissue with a cautery.

cau·tion (kô/shən), *n.* 1. prudence in regard to danger or evil; carefulness. 2. a warning against danger or evil. 3. *Colloq.* a person or thing that is unusual, odd, etc. —*v.t.* 4. to give warning to. —**cau/tion·ar/y,** *adj.*

cau·tious (kô/shəs), *adj.* having or showing caution. —**cau/tious·ly,** *adv.* —**cau/tious·ness,** *n.*

cav·al·cade (kăv/əl kād/, kăv/əl kād/), *n.* a procession, esp. one of persons on horseback.

cav·a·lier (kăv/ə lĭr/), *n.* 1. a horseman, esp. a mounted soldier; a knight. 2. a courtly gentleman. 3. (*cap.*) an adherent of Charles I of England in his contest with Parliament. —*adj.* 4. haughty. 5. offhand. 6. (*cap.*) of or pertaining to the Cavaliers. —**cav/a·lier/ly,** *adv.*

cav·al·ry (kăv/əl rĭ), *n., pl.* **-ries.** *Mil.* 1. troops that serve on horseback. 2. (in armored forces) an element having reconnaissance in force as its principal mission. —**cav·al·ry·man** (kăv/əl rĭ mən), *n.*

cave (kāv), *n., v.,* **caved, caving.** —*n.* 1. a hollow in the earth, esp. one opening horizontally into a hill, etc. —*v.t.* 2. to cause to fall. —*v.i.* 3. to fall or sink, as ground. 4. *Colloq.* to give or yield.

cave-in (kāv/ĭn/), *n.* a collapse, as of a mine.

cave man, 1. a cave dweller of the Old Stone Age. 2. *Colloq.* a man who behaves in a rough, primitive manner, esp. toward women.

cav·ern (kăv/ərn), *n.* a cave, esp. a large cave. —**cav/ern·ous,** *adj.*

cav·i·ar (kăv/ĭ är/, kä/vĭ-, kăv/ĭ är/), *n.* the roe of sturgeon and other large fish, pressed and salted as a relish. Also, **cav/i·are/.**

cav·il (kăv/əl), *v.,* **-iled, -iling** or (*esp. Brit.*) **-illed, -illing,** *n.* —*v.i.* 1. to find fault unnecessarily. —*n.* 2. a trivial and annoying objection. —**cav/il·er;** *esp. Brit.,* **cav/il·ler,** *n.*

cav·i·ty (kăv/ə tĭ), *n., pl.* **-ties.** 1. any hollow place. 2. *Anat.* a hollow space within the body, a bone, a tooth, etc.

ca·vort (kə vôrt/), *v.i. U.S. Colloq.* to prance or caper about.

ca·vy (kā/vĭ), *n., pl.* **-vies.** any of various short-tailed South American rodents, including the domesticated guinea pig.

caw (kô), *n.* 1. the cry of the crow, raven, etc. —*v.i.* 2. to utter this cry or a similar sound.

Cax·ton (kăk/stən), *n.* **William,** 1422?-91. first British printer.

cay (kā, kē), *n.* a small island; key.

cay·enne (kī ĕn/, kā-), *n.* a hot, biting condiment composed of the ground pods and seeds of capsicums. Also, **cayenne pepper.**

Cay·enne (kī ĕn/, kā-), *n.* a seaport in and the capital of French Guiana. 11,700.

cay·man (kā/mən), *n., pl.* **-mans.** any of several tropical American crocodilians.

Ca·yu·ga (kā ū/gə, kī-), *n., pl.* **-ga, -gas.** a member of a tribe of North American Indians, the smallest tribe of the Iroquois Confederacy.

cay·use (kī ūs/), *n. Western U.S.* an Indian pony.

Cb, *Chem.* columbium.

cc., cubic centimeter or centimeters. Also, **c.c.**

Cd, *Chem.* cadmium.

Ce, *Chem.* cerium.

cease (sēs), *v.,* **ceased, ceasing,** *n.* —*v.i.* 1. to stop (moving, speaking, etc.). 2. to end. —*v.t.* 3. to put a stop or end to. —*n.* 4. cessation.

cease·less (sēs/lĭs), *adj.* without stop or pause; incessant. —**cease/less·ly,** *adv.*

Ce·cro·pi·a moth (sĭ krō/pĭ ə), a large North American silk-producing moth.

ce·dar (sē/dər), *n.* 1. any of certain coniferous trees including the **cedar of Lebanon,** a stately tree native in Asia Minor, etc. 2. any of various junipers, as the **red cedar,** an American tree with a fragrant reddish wood used for making lead pencils, etc.

cedar bird, *Ornith.* a waxwing of North America. Also, **cedar waxwing.**

Cedar Rapids, a city in E Iowa. 62,120.

cede (sēd), *v.t.,* **ceded, ceding.** to yield or formally resign and surrender to another, as by treaty.

ce·dil·la (sĭ dĭl/ə), *n.* a mark placed under *c,* as in *façade,* to show that it has the sound of *s.*

ceil (sēl), *v.t.* 1. to overlay (the interior upper surface) with plaster, etc. 2. to provide with a ceiling.

ceil·ing (sē/lĭng), *n.* 1. the overhead interior lining of a room. 2. top limit. 3. *Aeron.* a. the maximum altitude from which the earth can be seen on a particular day. b. the maximum altitude to which a particular aircraft can rise under specified conditions.

cel·an·dine (sĕl/ən dīn/), *n.* a plant of the poppy family with yellow flowers.

cel·a·nese (sĕl/ə nēz/), *n.* **1.** an acetate rayon fabric. **2.** (*cap.*) a trademark for this.

Cel·e·bes (sĕl/ə bēz/), *n.* an island in the Dutch East Indies, separated from the Philippine Islands by the **Celebes Sea.** With adjacent islands, 4,-231,900 pop.; 72,986 sq. mi.

cel·e·brant (sĕl/ə brənt), *n.* **1.** the officiating priest in the celebration of the Eucharist. **2.** a participant in a public religious ceremony.

cel·e·brate (sĕl/ə brāt/), *v.*, **-brated, -brating.** —*v.t.* **1.** to observe (a day) or commemorate (an event) with ceremonies or festivities. **2.** to proclaim. **3.** to extol. **4.** to solemnize. —*v.i.* **5.** to observe a day or commemorate an event with ceremonies or festivities. **6.** to perform a religious ceremony, esp. Mass. —**cel/e·bra/tion,** *n.* —**cel/e·bra/tor,** *n.*

cel·e·brat·ed (sĕl/ə brā/tĭd), *adj.* famous.

ce·leb·ri·ty (sə lĕb/rə tĭ), *n.*, *pl.* **-ties.** **1.** a famous person. **2.** fame; renown.

ce·ler·i·ty (sə lĕr/ə tĭ), *n.* swiftness; speed.

cel·er·y (sĕl/ə rĭ), *n.* a plant of the parsley family, whose blanched leafstalks are used raw for salad, and cooked as a vegetable.

ce·les·tial (sə lĕs/chəl), *adj.* **1.** pertaining to the spiritual heaven; divine. **2.** pertaining to the sky. **3.** (*cap.*) of or pertaining to the former Chinese Empire (**Celestial Empire**) or the Chinese people. —*n.* **4.** an inhabitant of heaven. **5.** (*cap.*) Humorous. a Chinese. —**ce·les/tial·ly,** *adv.*

cel·i·ba·cy (sĕl/ə bə sĭ), *n.*, *pl.* **-cies.** **1.** the unmarried state. **2.** abstention by vow from marriage.

cel·i·bate (sĕl/ə bĭt, -bāt/), *n.* **1.** one who remains unmarried. —*adj.* **2.** unmarried.

cell (sĕl), *n.* **1.** a small room in a convent, prison, etc. **2.** any small compartment, etc. **3.** a small unit within a larger organization. **4.** *Biol.* a plant or animal structure, usually microscopic, containing nuclear and cytoplasmic material. **5.** *Elect.* a device which generates electricity, consisting in one of its simplest forms of two plates, each of a different metal, placed in a jar containing a dilute acid or other electrolyte (**voltaic cell**). **6.** *Phys. Chem.* a device for producing electrolysis, consisting essentially of the electrolyte, its container, and the electrodes (**electrolytic cell**).

cel·lar (sĕl/ər), *n.* a room or set of rooms for the storage of foodstuffs, etc., usually beneath a building.

cel·lar·age (sĕl/ər ĭj), *n.* **1.** cellar space. **2.** charges for storage in a cellar.

Cel·li·ni (chə lē/nĭ), *n.* **Benvenuto** (bĕn/vĕ nōō/tō), 1500–71, Italian artist.

cel·list (chĕl/ĭst), *n.* a player on the cello. Also, **'cel/list.**

cel·lo (chĕl/ō), *n.*, *pl.* **-los.** the baritone of the violin family, which is rested vertically on the floor between the player's knees. Also, **'cel/lo.**

cel·lo·phane (sĕl/ə fān/), *n.* **1.** a transparent, paperlike product of viscose. **2.** (*cap.*) a trademark for this product.

cel·lu·lar (sĕl/yə lər), *adj.* pertaining to or characterized by cellules or cells.

cel·lule (sĕl/ūl), *n.* a little cell.

cel·lu·loid (sĕl/yə loid/), *n.* **1.** a substance consisting essentially of soluble guncotton and camphor, used as a substitute for ivory, etc. **2.** (*cap.*) a trademark for this substance.

cel·lu·lose (sĕl/yə lōs/), *n.* *Chem.* an inert substance, a carbohydrate, the chief constituent of the cell walls of plants, and forming an essential part of wood, cotton, hemp, paper, etc.

Celt (sĕlt), *n.* a member of an Indo-European people now represented chiefly by the Irish, Gaels, Welsh, and Bretons.

Celt·ic (sĕl/tĭk), *n.* **1.** a group of Indo-European languages including Irish, Scotch, Gaelic, Welsh, Breton, etc. —*adj.* **2.** of the Celts or their language.

ce·ment (sĭ mĕnt/), *n.* **1.** any of various substances which are soft when first prepared but later become stonelike, used for making floors, etc. **2.** anything that binds or unites. —*v.t.* **3.** to unite by cement. **4.** to coat with cement. —*v.i.* **5.** to cohere. —**ce·ment/er,** *n.*

cem·e·ter·y (sĕm/ə tĕr/ĭ), *n.*, *pl.* **-teries.** a burial ground; graveyard.

ce·no·bite (sē/nə bīt/, sĕn/ə-), *n.* one of a religious order living in a convent or community.

cen·o·taph (sĕn/ə tăf/, -täf/), *n.* a sepulchral monument in memory of a person buried elsewhere. —**cen/o·taph/ic,** *adj.*

cen·ser (sĕn/sər), *n.* a container in which incense is burned.

cen·sor (sĕn/sər), *n.* **1.** an official who examines books, plays, news reports, etc., for parts objectionable on moral, political, military, or other grounds. **2.** any person who supervises the manners or morality of others. **3.** an adverse critic. **4.** a member of the board of two officials of republican Rome who kept the register of the citizens, supervised manners and morals, etc. —*v.t.* **5.** to examine and act upon as a censor does.

Acolyte with censer

cen·so·ri·ous (sĕn sōr/ĭ əs), *adj.* severely critical. —**cen·so/ri·ous·ly,** *adv.* —**cen·so/ri·ous·ness,** *n.*

cen·sor·ship (sĕn/sər shĭp/), *n.* **1.** act of censoring. **2.** the office or power of a censor.

cen·sure (sĕn/shər), *n.*, *v.*, **-sured, -suring.** —*n.* **1.** an expression of disapproval. —*v.t., v.i.* **2.** to criticize adversely. —**cen/sur·er,** *n.*

cen·sus (sĕn/səs), *n.* an official enumeration of inhabitants, with details as to age, sex, pursuits, etc.

cent (sĕnt), *n.* **1.** the hundredth part of the U.S. dollar. **2.** a bronze coin of this value. **3.** the hundredth part of monetary units elsewhere.

cent., **1.** centigrade. **2.** central. **3.** century.

cen·taur (sĕn/tôr), *n.* *Gk. Legend.* one of a race of monsters having the head, trunk, and arms of a man, and the body and legs of a horse.

cen·ta·vo (sĕn tä/vō), *n.*, *pl.* **-vos** (-vōz). a small coin or monetary unit equal to the hundredth part of a particular monetary unit, as of a peso in Mexico, the Philippine Islands, Cuba, etc.

cen·te·nar·i·an (sĕn/tə nâr/ĭ ən), *adj.* **1.** pertaining to or having lived 100 years. —*n.* **2.** one who has reached the age of a hundred.

cen·te·nar·y (sĕn/tə nĕr/ĭ), *adj., n.*, *pl.* **-naries.** —*adj.* **1.** pertaining to a period of 100 years. **2.** recurring once in every 100 years. —*n.* **3.** a 100th anniversary. **4.** a period of 100 years.

cen·ten·ni·al (sĕn tĕn/ĭ əl), *adj.* **1.** pertaining to, or marking the completion of, 100 years. **2.** pertaining to a 100th anniversary. **3.** lasting 100 years. **4.** 100 years old. —*n.* **5.** a 100th anniversary. **6.** its celebration. —**cen·ten/ni·al·ly,** *adv.*

cen·ter (sĕn/tər), *n.* **1.** *Geom.* the middle point, as the point within a circle equally distant from all points of the circumference. **2.** a point, pivot, axis, etc., round which anything revolves. **3.** a principal point, place, or object. **4.** a person, thing, group, etc., occupying the middle position, esp. troops. **5.** (*usually cap.*) (in continental Europe) that part of a legislative assembly holding views intermediate between those of the conservatives (or Right) and the liberals (or Left). **6.** *Football, etc.* the middle player in the forward line. **7.** *Basketball.* a player who attempts to tap the ball to a teammate when a jump ball is thrown by a referee at the beginning of play. **8.** *Physiol.* a cluster of nerve cells governing a specific organic process. —*v.t.* **9.** to place in or on a center. **10.** to collect at a center. **11.** to determine or mark the center of. **12.** to adjust (an object, etc.) so that its axis or the like is in a central position. —*v.i.* **13.** to be at or come to a center.

cen·ter·board (sĕn/tər bōrd/), *n.* *Naut.* a movable keel that can be drawn up in shoal water.

center of gravity, *Mech.* that point of a body from which it could be suspended or on which it could be supported and be in equilibrium in any position in a uniform gravitational field.

cen·ter·piece (sĕn/tər pēs/), *n.* an ornamental piece for the center of a table, etc.

cen·tes·i·mal (sĕn tĕs/ə məl), *adj.* hundredth.

cen·ti·grade (sĕn/tə grād/), *adj.* **1.** divided into 100 degrees, as a scale. **2.** pertaining to the centigrade thermometer.

centigrade thermometer, a thermometer based on a scale of equal degrees between zero (fixed at the melting point of ice) and 100° (fixed at the boiling point of water) at a pressure of 760 mm. of mercury.

cen·ti·gram (sĕn/tə grăm/), *n.* one hundredth of a gram. Also, *esp. Brit.*, **cen/ti·gramme/.**

cen·ti·li·ter (sĕn/tə lē/tər), *n.* one one-hundredth of a liter. Also, *esp. Brit.*, **cen/ti·li/tre.**

cen·time (sän/tēm), n. the hundredth part of a franc.

cen·ti·me·ter (sĕn/tə mē/tər), n. one hundredth of a meter. Also, esp. Brit., **cen/ti·me/tre**.

centimeter-gram-second, adj. a system of units employed in science, based on the centimeter, gram, and second as the primary units of length, mass, and time.

cen·ti·pede (sĕn/tə pēd/), n. any member of the class of active, predacious insects having numerous legs.

cen·tral (sĕn/trəl), adj. 1. of or forming the center. 2. in, at, or near the center. 3. principal; chief. 4. pertaining to the brain and spinal cord of the nervous system. —n. 5. the central office of a telephone system. —**cen/tral·ly,** adv.

Central America, continental North America S of Mexico, comprising Guatemala, Honduras, El Salvador, Nicaragua, Costa Rica, Panama, and British Honduras. —**Central American.**

cen·tral·ize (sĕn/trə līz/), v.t., -ized, -izing. 1. to draw to or toward a center. 2. to bring under one control, esp. in government. —v.i. 3. to come together at a center. —**cen/tral·i·za/tion,** n. —**cen/tral·iz/er,** n.

cen·tre (sĕn/tər), n., v., -tred, -tring. Chiefly Brit. center.

cen·tric (sĕn/trĭk), adj. central. Also, **cen/tri·cal.** —**cen/tri·cal·ly,** adv.

cen·trif·u·gal (sĕn trĭf/yə gəl), adj. 1. moving or directed outward from the center. 2. pertaining to or operated by centrifugal force. —n. 3. a cylinder rotated rapidly to separate solids from liquids. —**cen·trif/u·gal·ly,** adv.

centrifugal force or **action,** the force outward exerted by a body moving in a curved path.

cen·tri·fuge (sĕn/trə fūj/), n. a machine consisting of a rotating container in which substances of different densities may be separated by centrifugal force.

cen·trip·e·tal (sĕn trĭp/ə təl), adj. 1. proceeding or directed toward the center. 2. operating by centripetal force. —**cen·trip/e·tal·ly,** adv.

centripetal force or **action,** a force acting on a body, which is directed toward the center of a circle or curve, which causes it to move in the circle or curve.

cen·tu·ple (sĕn/tyə pəl, -tə-), adj., v., -pled, -pling. —adj. 1. a hundred times as great; hundredfold. —v.t. 2. to increase 100 times.

cen·tu·ri·on (sĕn tyŏŏr/Y ən, -tŏŏr/-), n. (in the ancient Roman army) a commander.

cen·tu·ry (sĕn/chə rY), n., pl. -ries. a period of one hundred years.

century plant, a Mexican species of agave, cultivated for ornament.

ce·phal·ic (sə făl/Yk), adj. of or pertaining to the head.

ceph·a·lo·pod (sĕf/ə lə pŏd/), n. a member of the most highly organized class of mollusks, including the squid, octopus, etc., the members of which have tentacles attached to the head. —ceph/a·lop/o·dan, adj., n.

ceph·a·lo·tho·rax (sĕf/ə lō thôr/ăks), n. Zool. (in certain arachnids and crustaceans) the coalesced head and thorax.

ce·ram·ic (sə răm/Yk), adj. pertaining to products made from clay and similar materials, such as pottery, brick, etc., or to their manufacture.

ce·ram·ics (sə răm/Yks), n. 1. (construed as sing.) the art of making clay products and similar ware. 2. (construed as pl.) articles of earthenware, etc.

Cer·ber·us (sûr/bər əs), n. Class. Myth. a dog, usually represented as having three heads, which guarded the entrance to the infernal regions.

ce·re·al (sYr/Y əl), n. 1. any of certain plants yielding an edible grain, as wheat, rye, oats, rice, maize, etc. 2. the grain itself. 3. some edible preparation of it. —adj. 4. of or pertaining to grain or the plants producing it.

cer·e·bel·lum (sĕr/ə bĕl/əm), n., pl. -bellums, -bella (-bĕl/ə). Anat., Zool. a large expansion of the hindbrain, concerned with voluntary movements, posture, and equilibration. —cer/e·bel/lar, adj.

cer·e·bral (sĕr/ə brəl, sə rē/brəl), adj. 1. Anat., Zool. of or pertaining to the cerebrum or the brain. 2. intellectual.

cer·e·brate (sĕr/ə brāt/), v., -brated, -brating. —v.i. 1. to use the brain. —v.t. 2. to perform by brain action. —cer/e·bra/tion, n.

cer·e·bro·spi·nal (sĕr/ə brō spī/nəl), adj.

Anat., Physiol. pertaining to or affecting both the brain and the spinal cord.

cer·e·brum (sĕr/ə brəm), n., pl. -brums, -bra (-brə). Anat., Zool. the anterior and upper part of the brain, consisting of two hemispheres, concerned with voluntary and conscious processes.

cer·e·mo·ni·al (sĕr/ə mō/nY əl), adj. 1. pertaining to, marked by, or of the nature of ceremonies or ceremony. —n. 2. a system of ceremonies, rites, or formalities. 3. a rite or ceremony. —cer/e·mo/ni·al·ism, n. —cer/e·mo/ni·al·ist, n. —cer/e·mo/ni·al·ly, adv.

cer·e·mo·ni·ous (sĕr/ə mō/nY əs), adj. 1. formally or elaborately polite. 2. pertaining to, marked by, or consisting of ceremony. —cer/e·mo/ni·ous·ly, adv. —cer/e·mo/ni·ous·ness, n.

cer·e·mo·ny (sĕr/ə mō/nY), n., pl. -nies. 1. the formalities observed on some solemn or important occasion. 2. any formal act or observance, esp. a meaningless one. 3. strict adherence to conventional forms; formality.

Ce·res (sYr/ēz), n. the Roman goddess of agriculture.

ce·rise (sə rēz/, -rēs/), n., adj. bright red; cherry.

ce·ri·um (sYr/Y əm), n. Chem. a steel-gray, ductile metallic element. Symbol: Ce; at. wt.: 140.13; at. no.: 58.

cer·tain (sûr/tən), adj. 1. having no doubt; confident. 2. inevitable; bound to come. 3. established as true or sure. 4. agreed upon. 5. definite, but not specified. 6. trustworthy; reliable. 7. some though not much. —n. 8. for certain, surely.

cer·tain·ly (sûr/tən lY), adv. 1. with certainty; assuredly. —interj. 2. yes! of course!

cer·tain·ty (sûr/tən tY), n., pl. -ties. 1. state of being certain. 2. something certain.

certif., certificate. Also, **cert.**

cer·tif·i·cate (n. sər tYf/ə kYt; v. sər tYf/ə kāt/), n., v., -cated, -cating. —n. 1. a writing on paper certifying to the truth of something. 2. a document issued to a person completing an educational course. —v.t. 3. to attest by a certificate. 4. to furnish with or authorize by a certificate.

cer·ti·fi·ca·tion (sûr/tə fə kā/shən, sər tYf/ə-), n. 1. act of certifying. 2. state of being certified. 3. a certified statement; certificate.

cer·ti·fy (sûr/tə fī/), v.t., -fied, -fying. 1. to guarantee as certain. 2. to testify to or vouch for in writing. 3. to assure. 4. to guarantee. 5. to acknowledge in writing upon (a check) that the bank on which it is drawn has funds of the drawer sufficient to pay it. —v.i. 6. to testify; vouch. —cer/ti·fi/er, n.

cer·ti·tude (sûr/tə tūd/, -tōōd/), n. certainty.

ce·ru·le·an (sə rōō/lY ən), adj., n. sky blue.

ce·ru·men (sə rōō/mən), n. Anat. a waxlike secretion in the outer ear.

Cer·van·tes Sa·a·ve·dra (sər văn/tēz sä/ä·vē/drä), **Miguel de,** 1547–1616, Spanish novelist.

cer·vi·cal (sûr/və kəl), adj. Anat. pertaining to the cervix or neck.

cer·vine (sûr/vYn, -vYn), adj. 1. deerlike. 2. of deer or the deer family. 3. tawny.

cer·vix (sûr/vYks), n., pl. cervixes, cervices (sər vī/sēz). 1. the neck. 2. any necklike part.

ce·si·um (sē/zY əm), n. Chem. a rare, soft, monovalent metallic element. Symbol: Cs; at. wt.: 132.91; at. no.: 55; sp. gr.: 1.9 at 20°C.

ces·sa·tion (sĕ sā/shən), n. a ceasing; pause.

ces·sion (sĕsh/ən), n. 1. act of ceding, as by treaty. 2. something, as territory, ceded.

cess·pool (sĕs/pōōl/), n. a cistern, well, or pit for receiving the filth of a water closet, etc.

ce·ta·cean (sə tā/shən), adj. 1. belonging to an order of aquatic mammals, including the whales, dolphins, etc. —n. 2. a cetacean mammal.

Cey·lon (sY lŏn/), n. an island in the Indian Ocean, S of India: a British self-governing colony. 6,197,000 pop.; 25,232 sq. mi. Cap.: Colombo.

Cé·zanne (sY zän/), n. **Paul,** 1839–1906, French painter.

cf., (L confer) compare.

cg., centigram; centigrams.

cgs, centimeter-gram-second (system). Also, **c.g.s.**

Ch., 1. chapter. 2. church. Also, **ch.**

Chad (chăd), n. **Lake,** a lake in N Africa at the junction of French Equatorial Africa, French West Africa, and Nigeria. 10,000 to 20,000 sq. mi. (seasonal variation).

chafe (chāf), v., chafed, chafing, n. —v.t. 1. to

warm by rubbing. **2.** to wear or make sore by rubbing. **3.** to annoy. **4.** to heat; make warm. —*v.i.* **5.** to rub. **6.** to become worn or sore by rubbing. **7.** to be annoyed. —*n.* **8.** annoyance. **9.** heat, wear, or soreness caused by rubbing.

chaff¹ (chăf, chäf), *n.* **1.** the husks of grains and grasses separated from the seed. **2.** worthless matter; rubbish. —**chaff′y,** *adj.*

chaff² (chăf, chäf), *v.t., v.i.* **1.** to ridicule or tease good-naturedly. —*n.* **2.** good-natured raillery.

chaf·fer (chăf′ər), *n.* **1.** bargaining; haggling. —*v.i.* **2.** to bargain. **3.** to bandy words. —*v.t.* **4.** to barter. —**chaf′fer·er,** *n.*

chaf·finch (chăf′ĭnch), *n.* a common European finch often kept as a cage bird.

chaf·ing dish (chā′fĭng), an apparatus for cooking food or keeping it hot.

cha·grin (shə grĭn′), *n.* **1.** a feeling of vexation and disappointment or humiliation. —*v.t.* **2.** to vex by disappointment or humiliation.

chain (chān), *n.* **1.** a connected series of metal or other links for connecting, confining, etc. **2.** something that binds or restrains. **3.** (*pl.*) bonds or fetters. **4.** (*pl.*) bondage. **5.** a series of things in succession. **6.** a range of mountains. **7.** *Chem.* a linkage of atoms of the same element. **8.** *Survey.* a measuring instrument consisting of 100 wire rods or links, each 7.92 inches long (**surveyor's** or **Gunter's chain**), or one foot long (**engineer's chain**). —*v.t.* **9.** to fasten or secure with a chain. **10.** to fetter.

chain gang, *Chiefly U.S.* a group of prisoners usually chained together when in camp, in transit, etc.

chain reaction, *Physics.* a molecular or atomic process which, once started, automatically continues and spreads. —**chain′-re·act′ing,** *adj.*

chain stitch, a kind of chainlike ornamental stitching.

chain store, 1. a group of retail stores under the same management. **2.** one such store.

chair (châr), *n.* **1.** a seat with a back and legs, usually for one person. **2.** a seat of office or authority. **3.** the position of a judge, chairman, etc. **4.** the chairman of a meeting. —*v.t.* **5.** to place or seat in a chair.

chair·man (châr′mən), *n., pl.* **-men.** the presiding officer of a meeting, committee, etc. —**chair′man·ship,** *n.* —**chair′wom′an,** *n. fem.*

chaise (shāz), *n.* **1.** a light, open carriage, usually with a hood. **2.** a post chaise.

chaise longue (shāz′ lông′), a couch with seat prolonged to form a full-length leg rest.

chal·ced·o·ny (kăl sĕd′ə nĭ, kăl′sə dō′nĭ), *n., pl.* **-nies.** a translucent variety of quartz, often milky or grayish.

Chal·de·a (kăl dē′ə), *n.* an ancient region in S Babylonia. —**Chal·de′an,** *n., adj.*

cha·let (shă lā′, shăl′ā), *n.* **1.** a herdsman's hut in the Swiss mountains. **2.** a kind of cottage, low and with wide eaves.

chal·ice (chăl′ĭs), *n.* **1.** *Poet.* a drinking cup. **2.** *Eccles.* **a.** a cup for the wine of the Eucharist or Mass. **b.** the wine contained in it. **3.** a cuplike blossom.

chalk (chôk), *n.* **1.** a soft powdery limestone consisting chiefly of fossil shells. **2.** a prepared piece of chalk or chalklike substance for marking. —*v.t.* **3.** to mark or write with chalk. **4.** to rub over or whiten with chalk. **5.** to treat or mix with chalk. —**chalk′like,** *adj.* —**chalk′y,** *adj.* —**chalk′i·ness,** *n.*

chal·lenge (chăl′ĭnj), *n., v.,* **-lenged, -lenging.** —*n.* **1.** a call to engage in a contest of skill, strength, etc., or in a fight. **2.** a demand to explain. **3.** *Mil.* the demand of a sentry for identification. **4.** *Law.* a formal objection to the qualifications of a juror or jury. **5.** *U.S.* the assertion that a vote is invalid or that a voter is not legally qualified. —*v.t.* **6.** to summon to a contest of skill, strength, etc. **7.** to demand defiantly. **8.** to call in question. **9.** *Mil.* to halt and demand identification or countersign from. **10.** *Law.* to take formal exception to (a juror or jury). **11.** *U.S.* to assert that (a vote) is invalid or (a voter) is not qualified to vote. —*v.i.* **13.** to make or issue a challenge. —**chal′lenge·a·ble,** *adj.* —**chal′leng·er,** *n.*

chal·lis (shăl′ĭ), *n.* a printed fabric of plain weave in wool, cotton, or rayon. Also, **chal′lie.**

cham·ber (chām′bər), *n.* **1.** a room or apart-

ment, esp. a bedroom. **2.** (*pl.*) *Brit.* rooms for residence in the house of another. **3.** a room in a palace or official residence. **4.** the meeting hall of a legislative or other assembly. **5.** (*pl.*) a place where a judge hears matters not requiring action in court. **6.** a legislative, judicial, or other like body. **7.** a cavity. **8.** a receptacle for one or more cartridges in a firearm, or for a shell in a gun or other cannon. —*v.t.* **9.** to put in a chamber. **10.** to provide with a chamber. —**cham′bered,** *adj.*

cham·ber·lain (chām′bər lĭn), *n.* **1.** an official manager of a sovereign's or nobleman's living quarters. **2.** a treasurer. **3.** the high steward of a nobleman. **4.** a high official of a royal court.

cham·ber·maid (chām′bər mād′), *n.* a female servant who takes care of bedrooms.

chamber music, music suited for performance in a room or a small concert hall.

cham·bray (shăm′brā), *n.* a fine variety of gingham, commonly plain.

cha·me·le·on (kə mē′lĭ ən, -mēl′yən), *n.* **1.** any of a group of lizards characterized by the power of changing the color of the skin. **2.** an inconstant person.

cham·fer (chăm′fər), *n.* an oblique surface cut on the edge or corner of a solid, usually sloping at 45°.

African chameleon (8 in. long)

cham·ois (shăm′ĭ), *n., pl.* **-ois. 1.** an agile goatlike antelope of high mountains of Europe and southwestern Russia. **2.** a soft, pliable leather made from various skins dressed with oil.

champ¹ (chămp), *v.t.* **1.** to bite upon, esp. impatiently. **2.** to crush with the teeth and chew vigorously or noisily. —*v.i.* **3.** to chew impatiently or noisily. —*n.* **4.** act of champing.

champ² (chămp), *n. Slang.* a champion.

cham·pagne (shăm pān′), *n.* a sparkling white wine produced in the wine region of Champagne, France, or elsewhere.

cham·paign (shăm pān′), *n.* level, open country.

cham·pi·on (chăm′pĭ ən), *n.* **1.** a person or thing that holds first place in any sport, etc., usually won in competition. **2.** one who fights for or defends any person or cause. —*v.t.* **3.** to defend; support. —*adj.* **4.** first among all competitors. **5.** *Colloq.* first-rate.

cham·pi·on·ship (chăm′pĭ ən shĭp′), *n.* **1.** the position or honor of being a champion. **2.** advocacy or defense.

Cham·plain (shăm plān′), *n.* **Lake,** a lake between New York and Vermont. ab. 600 sq. mi.

chance (chăns, chäns), *n., v.,* **chanced, chancing,** *adj.* —*n.* **1.** the absence of any known reason why an event should turn out one way rather than another. **2.** fate; luck. **3.** a possibility or probability. **4.** an opportunity. **5.** *Baseball.* an opportunity for a put-out or assist. **6.** a risk. **7. by chance,** accidentally. —*v.i.* **8.** to occur by chance. **9.** to come by chance. —*v.t.* **10.** *Colloq.* to risk. —*adj.* **11.** due to chance.

chan·cel (chăn′səl, chän′-), *n.* the space about a church altar, usually enclosed, for the clergy.

chan·cel·ler·y (chăn′sə lə rĭ, -slə rĭ, chän′-), *n., pl.* **-leries. 1.** the position or department of a chancellor. **2.** the building or room occupied by a chancellor's department.

chan·cel·lor (chăn′sə lər, chän′-), *n.* **1.** the title of various judges and high officials. **2.** (formerly) the chief minister of state in Germany or Austria. **3.** a secretary, as of a king or embassy. **4.** the chief administrative officer in certain American universities. —**chan′cel·lor·ship′,** *n.*

chan·cer·y (chăn′sə rĭ, chän′-), *n., pl.* **-ceries. 1.** the office or department of a chancellor. **2.** a chancellery. **3.** an office of public records. **4.** *Law.* **a.** court having jurisdiction in equity. **b.** equity. **5. in chancery, a.** *Law.* in litigation in a court of chancery. **b.** *Boxing.* (of a contestant's head) held under his opponent's arm. **c.** in a helpless position.

chan·cre (shăng′kər), *n.* the initial lesion of syphilis.

chan·de·lier (shăn′də lĭr′), *n.* a branched lighting fixture, suspended from a ceiling.

chan·dler (chăn′dlər, chän′-), *n.* **1.** a dealer. **2.** one who makes or sells candles. **3.** a retailer of groceries, etc. —**chan′dler·y,** *n.*

Chang·chun (chäng′chŏŏn′), *n.* a city in NE China: the capital of Manchuria. 395,900.

change (chānj), *v.*, **changed, changing,** *n.* —*v.t.* **1.** to alter in condition, appearance, etc. **2.** to substitute for something else. **3.** to give or get smaller or different money in return for. **4.** to interchange. **5.** to remove and replace the coverings of. —*v.i.* **6.** to become different. **7.** to make a change or exchange. **8.** to change one's clothes. —*n.* **9.** alteration; modification. **10.** the substitution of one thing for another. **11.** variety or novelty. **12.** a fresh set of clothing. **13.** money given in exchange for an equivalent of higher denomination. **14.** a balance of money that is returned when the sum tendered in payment is larger than the sum due. **15.** coins of low denomination. **16.** Also, **'change.** *Com.* an exchange for securities, etc. **17.** any of the various sequences in which a peal of bells may be rung. —**chang′er,** *n.*

change·a·ble (chān′jə bəl), *adj.* **1.** liable to change; variable. **2.** of changing color or appearance. —**change′a·bil′i·ty, change′a·ble·ness,** *n.* —**change′a·bly,** *adv.*

chan·nel (chăn′əl), *n., v.,* **-neled, -neling** or (*esp. Brit.*) **-nelled, -nelling.** —*n.* **1.** the bed of a stream. **2.** the deeper part of a waterway. **3.** a wide strait. **4.** a means of access. **5.** a course into which something may be directed. **6.** a route through which anything passes. **7.** a frequency band wide enough for one-way communication. **8.** a tubular passage for liquids or fluids. **9.** a groove or furrow. —*v.t.* **10.** to convey through a channel. **11.** to direct toward or into some particular course. **12.** to form a channel in; groove.

Channel Islands, a British island group in the English Channel, including Alderney, Guernsey, Jersey, etc. 93,205 pop.; 75 sq. mi.

chant (chănt, chänt), *n.* **1.** a song. **2.** a short, simple melody, specif. one used in singing the psalms, etc., in the church service. **3.** a psalm or the like, chanted or for chanting. —*v.t.* **4.** to sing. **5.** to sing in the manner of a chant, esp. in the church service. —*v.i.* **6.** to sing. **7.** to sing a chant. —**chant′er,** *n.*

chant·ey (shăn′tǐ, chăn′-), *n., pl.* **-eys.** a sailors' song, sung in rhythm to work. Also, **chant′y.**

chan·ti·cleer (chăn′tə klǐr′), *n.* a rooster.

cha·os (kā′ŏs), *n.* **1.** utter confusion or disorder. **2.** the infinity of space or formless matter before the existence of the ordered universe.

cha·ot·ic (kā ŏt′ǐk), *adj.* in utter disorder.

chap[1] (chăp), *v.*, **chapped, chapping,** *n.* —*v.t.* **1.** to crack, roughen, and redden (the skin). **2.** to split. —*v.i.* **3.** to become chapped. —*n.* **4.** a fissure or crack, esp. in the skin.

chap[2] (chăp), *n. Colloq.* a fellow; man or boy.

chap., **1.** Chaplain. **2.** chapter. Also, **Chap.**

chap·ar·ral (chăp′ə răl′), *n. Southwestern U.S.* **1.** a close growth of low evergreen oaks. **2.** any dense thicket.

chap·el (chăp′əl), *n.* **1.** a private or subordinate place of prayer. **2.** a room or building for worship in a college, royal court, etc.

chap·er·on (shăp′ə rōn′), *n.* **1.** an older woman, who, for propriety, attends a young unmarried woman in public or accompanies a party of young unmarried men and women. —*v.t.* **2.** to attend as chaperon. Also, **chap′er·one′.**

chap·lain (chăp′lǐn), *n.* an ecclesiastic attached to a royal court, college, military unit, etc.

chap·let (chăp′lǐt), *n.* **1.** a wreath or garland for the head. **2.** a string of beads.

chaps (chăps, shăps), *n.pl. Western U.S.* strong leather overalls, having no seat, worn esp. by cowboys.

chap·ter (chăp′tər), *n.* **1.** a main division of a book, treatise, or the like. **2.** a branch of a society or fraternity.

char[1] (chär), *v.*, **charred, charring.** —*v.t.* **1.** to burn or reduce to charcoal. **2.** to burn slightly; scorch. —*v.i.* **3.** to become charred. —**char′ry,** *adj.*

char[2] (chär), *n., v.*, **charred, charring.** *Chiefly Brit.* —*n.* **1.** a charwoman. **2.** an odd job; chore. —*v.i.* **3.** to do small jobs. **4.** to do housework by the day. —*v.t.* **5.** to do (odd jobs).

char·ac·ter (kăr′ǐk tər), *n.* **1.** the aggregate of qualities that distinguishes one person or thing from others. **2.** one such quality. **3.** good moral constitution or status. **4.** reputation. **5.** a formal statement concerning the qualities of a former employee. **6.** status or capacity. **7.** a person. **8.** *Colloq.* an odd person. **9.** a person represented in a drama, story, etc. **10.** a significant visual mark or symbol, as a letter of the alphabet. —*v.t.* **11.** to portray; describe. —**char′ac·ter·less,** *adj.*

char·ac·ter·is·tic (kăr′ǐk tə rǐs′tǐk), *adj.* **1.** of or indicating the character or peculiar quality; typical. —*n.* **2.** a distinguishing feature. —**char′ac·ter·is′ti·cal·ly,** *adv.*

char·ac·ter·ize (kăr′ǐk tə rīz′), *v.t.*, **-ized, -izing. 1.** to mark or distinguish as a characteristic. **2.** to describe the character of. **3.** to give character to. —**char′ac·ter·i·za′tion,** *n.* —**char′ac·ter·iz′er,** *n.*

cha·rade (shə rād′), *n.* a parlor game in which a player or players act out in pantomime a word or phrase for the others to guess.

char·coal (chär′kōl′), *n.* **1.** the carbonaceous material obtained by the imperfect combustion of wood or other organic substances. **2.** a pencil of charcoal for drawing. **3.** a drawing made with such a pencil.

charge (chärj), *v.*, **charged, charging,** *n.* —*v.t.* **1.** to put a load on or in. **2.** to furnish (a thing) with the quantity, as of fuel, that it is fitted to receive. **3.** to supply with a quantity of electricity or electrical energy. **4.** to command. **5.** to instruct authoritatively, as a judge does a jury. **6.** to impute as a fault. **7.** to blame; accuse. **8.** to hold liable for payment. **9.** to enter as a debit. **10.** to impose or ask as a price. **11.** to attack by rushing violently against. —*v.i.* **12.** to rush, as to an attack. —*n.* **13.** a load or burden. **14.** the quantity of anything which an apparatus is fitted to hold, or holds, at one time. **15.** a quantity of explosive to be set off at one time. **16.** care, custody, or superintendence. **17.** anything or anybody committed to one's care. **18.** a command. **19.** an accusation. **20.** *Law.* an address by a judge to a jury at the close of a trial, instructing them as to the legal points affecting their verdict. **21.** expense or cost. **22.** a sum or price charged. **23.** an attack, as of soldiers. **24.** *Her.* a device on a coat of arms. **25. in charge,** having supervision. —**charge′a·ble,** *adj.*

charg·er (chär′jər), *n.* **1.** one who charges. **2.** a horse intended to be ridden in battle. **3.** *Elect.* an apparatus which charges storage batteries.

char·i·ly (châr′ə lǐ), *adv.* **1.** warily. **2.** sparingly.

char·i·ness (châr′ǐ nǐs), *n.* chary quality.

char·i·ot (chăr′ǐ ət), *n.* a two-wheeled vehicle used by the ancients in war, racing, etc.

char·i·ot·eer (chăr′ǐ ə tǐr′), *n.* a chariot driver.

char·i·ta·ble (chăr′ə tə bəl), *adj.* **1.** generous in gifts to relieve the needs of others. **2.** kindly in judging others. **3.** pertaining to or concerned with charity. —**char′i·ta·ble·ness,** *n.* —**char′i·ta·bly,** *adv.*

char·i·ty (chăr′ə tǐ), *n., pl.* **-ties. 1.** the relief of unfortunate or needy persons. **2.** something given to a person or persons in need. **3.** a charitable act. **4.** a charitable institution. **5.** benevolent feeling. **6.** Christian love.

char·la·tan (shär′lə tən), *n.* one who pretends to more knowledge or skill than he possesses. —**char′la·tan·ism′, char′la·tan·ry,** *n.*

Char·le·magne (shär′lə mān′), *n.* ("*Charles the Great*") A.D. 742–814, king of the Franks, A.D. 768–814: as Charles I, emperor of the Holy Roman Empire, A.D. 800–814.

Charles I (chärlz), **1.** Charlemagne. **2.** 1600–49, king of Great Britain and Ireland from 1625 until executed in 1649.

Charles II, 1630–85, king of Great Britain and Ireland, 1660–85.

Charles·ton (chärlz′tən), *n.* **1.** the capital of West Virginia, in the W part. 67,914. **2.** a seaport in SE South Carolina. 71,275.

Char·lotte (shär′lət), *n.* a city in S North Carolina. 100,899.

Char·lot·te A·ma·li·e (shär lŏt′ə ä mä′lǐ ə), a seaport and capital of the Virgin Islands, on St. Thomas island. 9801.

char·lotte russe (shär′lət rōōs′), a mold of sponge cake filled with whipped cream or the like.

charm (chärm), *n.* **1.** an irresistible power to please and attract. **2.** some quality exerting a fascinating influence. **3.** something with this power. **4.** a trinket to be worn on a chain, etc. **5.** an amulet. **6.** any action, verse, or formula credited with magical power. —*v.t.* **7.** to attract powerfully by beauty, etc. **8.** to enchant. **9.** to endow with or protect by supernatural powers. —*v.i.* **10.** to be fascinating or pleasing. **11.** to use charms. **12.** to act as a charm. —**charm′er,** *n.*

charm·ing (chär′mĭng), *adj.* delightful.

char·nel house (chär′nəl), a house or place in which the bodies or bones of the dead are deposited.

chart (chärt), *n.* 1. a sheet exhibiting information in tabulated, methodical, or other graphic form. 2. a map, esp. a hydrographic or marine map. —*v.t.* 3. to make a chart of. 4. to plan.

char·ter (chär′tər), *n.* 1. the articles or certificate of incorporation taken in connection with the law under which a corporation is organized. 2. authorization from a parent organization to establish a new branch, etc. 3. a contract by which a ship is leased for a stated time. —*v.t.* 4. to establish by charter. 5. to lease or hire by charter. 6. to hire (a car, etc.).

char·treuse (shär trœz′), *n.* 1. an aromatic liqueur made by the Carthusian monks, at Grenoble, France, and Tarragona, Spain. 2. a light yellowish green.

char·wom·an (chär′wŏŏm′ən), *n., pl.* -women. a woman hired to do odd jobs of household work.

char·y (châr′ĭ), *adj.,* **charier, chariest.** 1. careful; wary. 2. shy. 3. fastidious. 4. sparing.

chase[1] (chās), *v.,* **chased, chasing,** *n.* —*v.t.* 1. to pursue in order to seize, overtake, capture, kill, etc. 2. to drive by pursuing. 3. to put to flight. —*v.i.* 4. to follow in pursuit. 5. *Colloq.* to run or hasten. —*n.* 6. pursuit. 7. an object of pursuit. 8. the sport of hunting.

chase[2] (chās), *n., v.,* **chased, chasing.** —*n.* 1. a rectangular iron frame in which composed type, etc., is locked, as for printing. 2. a groove, furrow, or trench. —*v.t.* 3. to groove or indent. —**chas′er,** *n.*

chase[3] (chās), *v.t.,* **chased, chasing.** to ornament (metal) by engraving or embossing.

chas·er (chā′sər), *n.* 1. one that chases. 2. *U.S. Colloq.* a drink of water or the like, after a drink of liquor.

chasm (kăz′əm), *n.* 1. a yawning fissure or deep cleft in the earth's surface. 2. any breach, fissure or gap. —**chas·mal** (kăz′məl), *adj.*

chas·sis (shăs′ĭ, -ĭs, chăs′ĭ), *n., pl.* **chassis** (shăs′ĭz, chăs′-). 1. *Auto.* the frame, wheels, and machinery of a motor vehicle, on which the body is supported. 2. that portion of the landing gear that supports an aircraft.

chaste (chāst), *adj.* 1. pure; virtuous. 2. decent. 3. pure in style; simple. —**chaste′ly,** *adv.* —**chaste′ness,** *n.*

chas·ten (chā′sən), *v.t.* to punish for the sake of moral improvement. —**chas′ten·er,** *n.*

chas·tise (chăs tīz′), *v.t.,* **-tised, -tising.** to inflict corporal punishment upon. —**chas·tise·ment** (chăs′tĭz mənt, chăs tīz′-), *n.*

chas·ti·ty (chăs′tə tĭ), *n.* quality of being chaste.

chas·u·ble (chăz′yə bəl, chăs′-), *n. Eccles.* a sleeveless outer vestment worn by the celebrant at Mass.

chat (chăt), *v.,* **chatted, chatting,** *n.* —*v.i.* 1. to converse in an informal manner. —*n.* 2. informal conversation. 3. any of several passerine birds, as the **yellow-breasted chat** of the U.S., known for their chattering cries.

cha·teau (shä tō′), *n., pl.* -teaux (-tōz′). 1. a French castle. 2. a stately residence or a country estate.

Chā·teau-Thier·ry (shä tō′ tē′ə rĭ), *n.* a town in N France: heavy fighting, 1918. 7.413.

chat·e·laine (shăt′ə lān′), *n.* 1. the mistress of a castle. 2. a woman's lapel ornament.

Chat·ta·noo·ga (chăt′ə nōō′gə), *n.* a city in SE Tennessee: two battles, 1863. 128,163.

chat·tel (chăt′əl), *n.* 1. a movable or tangible property other than land, buildings, and other things annexed to land. 2. a slave.

chat·ter (chăt′ər), *v.i.* 1. to utter a succession of quick, inarticulate, speechlike sounds. 2. to talk rapidly and to little purpose; jabber. 3. to make a rapid clicking noise by striking together, as the teeth from cold. —*n.* 4. idle or foolish talk. 5. act or sound of chattering.

chat·ter·box (chăt′ər bŏks′), *n.* a very talkative person.

chat·ty (chăt′ĭ), *adj.,* **-tier, -tiest.** given to or full of familiar talk; conversational.

Chau·cer (chô′sər), *n.* Geoffrey (jĕf′rĭ), 1340?-1400, British poet.

chauf·feur (shō′fər, shō fûr′), *n.* the paid and licensed operator of a private motor car.

chau·vin·ism (shō′və nĭz′əm), *n.* blind enthusiasm for military glory; zealous patriotism. —**chau′vin·ist,** *n., adj.* —**chau′vin·is′tic,** *adj.*

cheap (chēp), *adj.* 1. of a relatively low price. 2. costing little labor or trouble. 3. charging low prices. 4. of small value; mean. 5. embarrassed. 6. obtainable at a low rate in interest. 7. of decreased purchasing power. —*adv.* 8. at a low price. —**cheap′ly,** *adv.* —**cheap′ness,** *n.*

cheap·en (chē′pən), *v.t.* 1. to make cheap. 2. to belittle. —*v.i.* 3. to become cheap.

cheat (chēt), *n.* 1. a fraud; swindle. 2. a person who defrauds. —*v.t.* 3. to defraud; swindle. 4. to deceive. 5. to beguile. —*v.i.* 6. to practice fraud. —**cheat′er,** *n.*

check (chĕk), *v.t.* 1. to stop the motion of suddenly. 2. to restrain or control. 3. to investigate or verify as to correctness. 4. to note with a mark, as to indicate correctness. 5. to leave in temporary custody. 6. to accept for temporary custody. 7. to mark in a pattern of checks or squares. 8. *Chess.* to place an opponent's king under direct attack. —*v.i.* 9. to correspond accurately. 10. *U.S.* to make an inquiry for verification, etc. 11. to crack or split, usually in small checks. 12. *U.S.* to leave and pay for one's quarters at a hotel. —*n.* 13. a person or thing that restrains. 14. **in check,** under restraint. 15. a sudden stoppage. 16. control with a view to ascertaining performance, etc. 17. a mark put against an item or the like to indicate that it has been examined or verified. 18. a written order directing a bank to pay money. 19. a ticket showing amount owed for food or beverages consumed, or goods purchased. 20. a token given as a means of identification. 21. a pattern formed of squares, as on a checkerboard. 22. *Chess.* the exposure of the king to direct attack. —*adj.* 23. serving to check, control, verify, etc. 24. checkered. —*interj.* 25. *Chess.* an optional call to warn one's opponent that his king is exposed to direct attack. —**check′er,** *n.*

check·er (chĕk′ər), *n.* 1. one of the pieces used in checkers. 2. a checkered pattern. 3. one of the squares of a checkered pattern. —*v.t.* 4. to mark like a checkerboard. 5. to diversify in appearance or character.

check·er·board (chĕk′ər bōrd′), *n.* a board marked off into sixty-four squares of alternating colors, on which checkers and chess are played.

check·ers (chĕk′ərz), *n.* a game played on a checkerboard by two persons.

check·mate (chĕk′māt′), *n., v.,* **-mated, -mating,** *interj.* —*n.* 1. *Chess.* a. act of putting the opponent's king into an inextricable check. b. the position of the pieces when a king is checkmated. 2. defeat. —*v.t.* 3. *Chess.* to put into inextricable check. 4. to defeat. —*interj.* 5. *Chess.* the announcing by a player that he has put his opponent's king into inextricable check.

check·rein (chĕk′rān′), *n.* a short rein attached to the saddle of a harness to prevent a horse from lowering its head.

cheek (chēk), *n.* 1. either side of the face below eye level. 2. something resembling the human cheek in form or position. 3. *Colloq.* impudence.

cheek·y (chē′kĭ), *adj.,* **cheekier, cheekiest.** *Colloq.* impudent. —**cheek′i·ness,** *n.*

cheep (chēp), *v.i., v.t., n.* chirp.

cheer (chĭr), *n.* 1. a shout of encouragement, approval, etc. 2. that which gives joy; encouragement. 3. state of spirits. 4. gladness, gaiety, or animation. 5. food; provisions. —*v.t.* 6. to salute with shouts of approval, etc. 7. to gladden. 8. to encourage. —*v.i.* 9. to utter cheers of approval, etc. 10. to become cheerful. —**cheer′er,** *n.*

cheer·ful (chĭr′fəl), *adj.* 1. full of cheer. 2. pleasant. 3. arising from good spirits. —**cheer′-ful·ly,** *adv.* —**cheer′ful·ness,** *n.*

cheer·less (chĭr′lĭs), *adj.* joyless; gloomy. —**cheer′less·ly,** *adv.*

cheer·y (chĭr′ĭ), *adj.,* **cheerier, cheeriest.** 1. gay. 2. enlivening. —**cheer′i·ly,** *adv.* —**cheer′-i·ness,** *n.*

cheese[1] (chēz), *n.* 1. the curd of milk separated from the whey and prepared as a food. 2. a mass of this substance.

cheese[2] (chēz), *v.t.,* **cheesed, cheesing.** *Slang.* to stop (esp. in **cheese it!,** look out!).

cheese·cloth (chēz′klŏth′, -klôth′), *n.* a coarse cotton fabric of open texture.

chees·y (chē′zĭ), *adj.,* **cheesier, cheesiest.** 1. like cheese. 2. *U.S. Slang.* of poor quality.

chee·tah (chē′tə), *n.* an animal of the cat family, of southwestern Asia and Africa, resembling the leopard, often trained for hunting deer, etc.

chef (shĕf), *n.* a cook, esp. a head cook.

Che·khov (chĕk/ŏf, -ŏf), *n.* **Anton Pavlovich,** 1860–1904, Russian writer.

che·la (kē/lə), *n., pl.* **-lae** (-lē). the nipperlike organ or claw terminating certain limbs of crustaceans and arachnids.

che·late (kē/lāt), *adj. Zool.* having a chela.

Chel·sea (chĕl/sĭ), *n.* a city in E Massachusetts, near Boston. 41,259.

chem., 1. chemical. 2. chemistry.

chem·i·cal (kĕm/ə kəl), *adj.* 1. of or concerned with the science or the operations or processes of chemistry. —*n.* 2. a substance produced by or used in a chemical process. —**chem/i·cal·ly,** *adv.*

che·mise (shə mēz/), *n.* a woman's loose-fitting shirtlike undergarment.

chem·ist (kĕm/ĭst), *n.* 1. one versed in chemistry. 2. *Brit.* druggist.

chem·is·try (kĕm/ĭs trĭ), *n., pl.* **-tries.** 1. the science that treats of the composition of substances and various elementary forms of matter. 2. chemical properties, reactions, etc.

chem·ur·gy (kĕm/ûr jĭ), *n.* a division of applied chemistry concerned with the industrial use of organic substances, as soybeans, peanuts, etc. —**chem·ur/gic, chem·ur/gi·cal,** *adj.*

che·nille (shə nēl/), *n.* 1. a velvety cord used in embroidery, fringe, etc. 2. fabric made with a fringed thread as the weft with wool or cotton.

cheque (chĕk), *n. Brit.* a bank check.

cheq·uer (chĕk/ər), *n. Brit.* checker.

Cher·bourg (shâr/bŏŏrg), *n.* a seaport in NW France. 39,760.

cher·ish (chĕr/ĭsh), *v.t.* 1. to treat as dear. 2. to nurture. 3. to cling fondly to (ideas, etc.).

Cher·o·kee (chĕr/ə kē/, chĕr/ə kē/), *n., pl.* **-kee, -kees.** a member of an important tribe of North American Indians of Iroquoian family.

che·root (shə rōōt/), *n.* a cigar having open, unpointed ends.

cher·ry (chĕr/ĭ), *n., pl.* **-ries,** *adj.* —*n.* 1. the fruit of any of certain trees, consisting of a pulpy, globular drupe enclosing a one-seeded smooth stone. 2. the tree itself. 3. its wood. 4. bright red. —*adj.* 5. bright-red.

cher·ub (chĕr/əb), *n., pl.* **cherubs** *for 3, 4;* **cherubim** (chĕr/ə bĭm, -yŏŏ bĭm) *for 1, 2.* 1. *Bible.* a kind of celestial being. 2. *Theol.* an angel, often represented as a beautiful winged child. 3. a beautiful or innocent person, esp. a child. 4. a person with a chubby, innocent face. —**che·ru·bic** (chə rōō/bĭk), *adj.* —**che·ru/bi·cal·ly,** *adv.*

Ches·a·peake Bay (chĕs/ə pēk/), a large inlet of the Atlantic, in Maryland and Virginia. ab. 200 mi. long; 4–40 mi. wide.

Chesh·ire cat (chĕsh/ər, -ĭr), a constantly grinning cat, in *Alice in Wonderland.*

chess (chĕs), *n.* a game played by two persons, each with sixteen pieces, on a checkerboard (or **chess/board/**).

chess·man (chĕs/măn/, -mən), *n., pl.* **-men** (-mĕn/, -mən). one of the pieces used in chess.

chest (chĕst), *n.* 1. the trunk of the body from the neck to the belly. 2. a box, usually a large, strong one, for the safekeeping of valuables. 3. the place where the funds of a public institution, etc., are kept. 4. the funds themselves. 5. a box in which certain goods, as tea, are packed for transit. 6. the quantity contained in such a box.

Ches·ter (chĕs/tər), *n.* a city in SE Pennsylvania. 59,285.

Ches·ter·field (chĕs/tər fēld/), *n.* 1. **Philip Dormer Stanhope, 4th Earl of,** 1694–1773, British statesman. 2. (*l.c.*) an overcoat, usually single-breasted, with concealed buttons.

chest·nut (chĕs/nŭt/, -nət), *n.* 1. the edible nut of certain trees of the beech family. 2. any of the trees. 3. the wood. 4. reddish brown. 5. *Colloq.* an old joke, anecdote, etc. —*adj.* 6. reddish-brown.

chev·a·lier (shĕv/ə lĭr/), *n.* 1. a member of certain orders of honor or merit. 2. a knight.

chev·i·ot (shĕv/ĭ ət), *n.* a worsted fabric in a coarse twill weave, used for coats, suits, etc.

chev·ron (shĕv/rən), *n.* a badge consisting of stripes meeting at an angle, worn on the sleeve (by noncommissioned officers, policemen, etc.) as an indication of rank, etc.

chew (chōō), *v.t., v.i.* 1. to crush or grind with the teeth. 2. to meditate. —*n.* 3. act of chewing. 4. that which is chewed. —**chew/er,** *n.*

che·wink (chĭ wĭngk/), *n.* a bird of the finch family, common in eastern North America.

Chey·enne (shī ĕn/), *n.* the capital of Wyoming, in the SE part. 22,474.

Chey·enne (shī ĕn/), *n., pl.* **-enne, -ennes.** an Indian of a tribe of the Algonquian family, formerly in Minnesota, North and South Dakota, etc.

chi (kī), *n.* the twenty-second letter (X,χ) of the Greek alphabet.

Chiang Kai·shek (chyäng/ kī/shĕk/), born 1886, president of China, 1943–1949.

Chi·an·ti (kĭ än/tĭ), *n.* a dry, red, full-bodied Italian table wine.

chic (shēk, shĭk), *adj.* 1. cleverly attractive in style. —*n.* 2. cleverly attractive style.

Chi·ca·go (shĭ kô/gō, -kä/-), *n.* a city in NE Illinois. With suburbs, 4,499,126.

chi·can·er·y (shĭ kā/nə rĭ), *n., pl.* **-eries.** 1. trickery or sophistry. 2. a quibble or subterfuge.

chick (chĭk), *n.* a young chicken or bird.

chick·a·dee (chĭk/ə dē/), *n.* any of several North American birds, esp. the black-capped titmouse.

chick·en (chĭk/ən, -ĭn), *n.* 1. the young of the domestic fowl (or certain other birds). 2. a domestic fowl of any age, or its flesh. 3. *Colloq.* a young girl.

chick·en-heart·ed (chĭk/ən här/tĭd, chĭk/-ĭn-), *adj.* timid; cowardly.

chicken pox, a mild, contagious eruptive disease, commonly of children.

chick·weed (chĭk/wēd/), *n.* any of various plants of the pink family, esp. one whose leaves and seeds are relished by birds.

chic·le (chĭk/əl), *n.* a gumlike substance from certain tropical American trees, as the sapodilla, used in the manufacture of chewing gum, etc.

Chic·o·pee (chĭk/ə pē/), *n.* a city in S Massachusetts, on the Connecticut river. 41,664.

chic·o·ry (chĭk/ə rĭ), *n., pl.* **-ries.** a perennial plant with bright-blue flowers, cultivated as a salad plant and for its root, which is used roasted and ground as a substitute for or adulterant for coffee.

chide (chīd), *v.t., v.i.,* **chided** or **chid; chided, chid** or **chidden; chiding.** to scold. —**chid/er,** *n.*

chief (chēf), *n.* 1. the head or leader of a body of men, a clan, or a tribe. 2. *Her.* the upper third of an escutcheon. —*adj.* 3. highest in rank or authority. 4. most important. 5. standing at the head. —**chief/ly,** *adv.*

chief·tain (chēf/tən, -tĭn), *n.* the chief, as of a tribe. —**chief/tain·cy, chief/tain·ship/,** *n.*

chif·fon (shĭ fŏn/, shĭf/ŏn), *n.* sheer fabric of silk or rayon in plain weave.

chif·fo·nier (shĭf/ə nĭr/), *n.* a high bureau, often having a mirror. Also, **chif/fon·nier/.**

chig·ger (chĭg/ər), *n.* 1. the parasitic larva of certain kinds of mites, which causes severe itching when attached to the skin. 2. chigoe.

chig·oe (chĭg/ō), *n.* a flea of the West Indies, South America, Africa, etc., the female of which buries itself in the skin of men and animals.

Chi·hua·hua (chĭ wä/wä), *n.* the smallest type of dog, originating in Mexico.

chil·blain (chĭl/blān/), *n.* (*usually pl.*) *Pathol.* an inflammation on the hands and feet caused by exposure to cold and moisture.

child (chīld), *n., pl.* **children.** 1. a baby. 2. a boy or girl. 3. a son or daughter. 4. any person or thing regarded as the product of particular influences, etc. —**child/hood,** *n.* —**child/less, adj.** —**child/less·ness,** *n.* —**child/like/,** *adj.*

child·birth (chīld/bûrth/), *n.* parturition. Also, **child/bed/.**

child·ish (chīl/dĭsh), *adj.* 1. of, like, or befitting a child. 2. puerile; weak; silly. —**child/ish·ly,** *adv.* —**child/ish·ness,** *n.*

Chil·e (chĭl/ĭ), *n.* a republic in SW America, on the Pacific coast. 5,237,432 pop.; 286,396 sq. mi. *Cap.:* Santiago. —**Chil/e·an,** *adj., n.*

chil·e con car·ne (chĭl/ĭ kŏn kär/nĭ), a Mexican dish made from meat and chopped red pepper, served with beans.

chil·i (chĭl/ĭ), *n., pl.* **chilies.** the pod of certain species of capsicum. Also, **chil/e, chili pepper.**

chill (chĭl), *n.* 1. coldness, esp. a moderate but penetrating coldness. 2. a sensation of cold, usually with shivering. 3. a depressing influence or sensation. —*adj.* 4. cold. 5. shivering with cold. 6. depressing or discouraging. 7. not hearty.

—*v.i.* **8.** to become cold. **9.** *Metall.* to become hard, esp. on the surface, by sudden cooling. —*v.t.* **10.** to make cold or cool. **11.** to depress; discourage. **12.** *Metall.* to harden (cast iron or steel) on the surface by casting in a metal mold. —**chill′er,** *n.*

chil·ly (chĭl′ĭ), *adj.,* **-lier, -liest,** *adv.* —*adj.* **1.** producing a sensation of cold. **2.** feeling cold. **3.** without warmth of feeling. —*adv.* **4.** in a chill manner. —**chil′li·ness,** *n.*

chime (chīm), *n., v.,* **chimed, chiming.** —*n.* **1.** an arrangement for striking a bell. **2.** a set of vertical metal tubes struck with a hammer, as used in the modern orchestra. **3.** carillon (def. 1). **4.** harmonious music; melody. —*v.i., v.t.* **5.** to sound harmoniously, as a set of bells. **6.** to harmonize; agree. —**chim′er,** *n.*

chi·me·ra (kĭ mĭr′ə, kī-), *n., pl.* **-ras. 1.** (*often cap.*) a mythological fire-breathing monster with a lion's head, a goat's body, and a serpent's tail. **2.** a horrible or unreal creature of the imagination.

chi·mer·i·cal (kĭ měr′ə kəl, -mĭr′-, kī-), *adj.* **1.** imaginary. **2.** wildly fanciful. Also, **chi·mer′ic.**

chim·ney (chĭm′nĭ), *n., pl.* **-neys. 1.** a structure, usually vertical, containing a passage by which the smoke, gases, etc., of a fire are carried off. **2.** that part of such a structure which rises above a roof. **3.** a tube, commonly of glass, surrounding the flame of a lamp.

chimney sweep, one whose business it is to clean out chimneys. Also, **chimney sweeper.**

chim·pan·zee (chĭm′păn zē′, chĭm păn′zĭ), *n.* a highly intelligent anthropoid ape of equatorial Africa.

chin (chĭn), *n., v.,* **chinned, chinning.** —*n.* **1.** the lower extremity of the face, below the mouth. **2.** the point of the under jaw. —*v.i.* **3.** *Colloq.* to talk.

chi·na (chī′nə), *n.* **1.** a vitreous ceramic ware, orig. produced in China. **2.** any porcelain ware.

Chi·na (chī′nə), *n.* a republic in E Asia. ab. 457,835,000 pop.; ab. 4,475,000 sq. mi. *Cap.:* Nanking.

Chi·na·man (chī′nə mən), *n., pl.* **men.** *Offensive.* a native or inhabitant of China.

Chi·na·town (chī′nə toun′), *n.* the Chinese quarter of a city.

chi·na·ware (chī′nə wâr′), *n.* dishes, etc., of china.

chinch bug (chĭnch), a small American hemipterous insect, destructive to wheat, etc.

chin·chil·la (chĭn chĭl′ə), *n.* **1.** a small South American rodent whose valuable skin is dressed as a fur. **2.** a thick, napped, woolen fabric, esp. for children's coats.

Chi·nese (chī nēz′, -nēs′), *n., pl.* **-nese,** *adj.* —*n.* **1.** the standard language of China, based on the speech of Peking. **2.** a native of China. —*adj.* **3.** of or pertaining to China, its inhabitants, or their language.

chink[1] (chĭngk), *n.* a crack, cleft, or fissure.

chink[2] (chĭngk), *v.t., v.i.* **1.** to make, or cause to make, a short, sharp, ringing sound, as of glasses striking together. —*n.* **2.** a chinking sound.

Chi·nook (chĭ nŏŏk′, -nŏŏk′), *n., pl.* **-nook, -nooks. 1.** a member of a North American Indian tribe living on the north side of the Columbia river. **2.** a North American Indian linguistic family of the northwest U.S. **3.** (*l.c.*) a warm, dry wind which blows down the eastern slopes of the Rocky Mountains.

chin·qua·pin (chĭng′kə pĭn), *n.* **1.** the dwarf chestnut, a small tree of the U.S., bearing a small, edible nut. **2.** a tree of the beech family, on the Pacific coast. **3.** the nut of either of these trees.

chintz (chĭnts), *n.* a printed cotton fabric, used esp. for draperies.

chip (chĭp), *n., v.,* **chipped, chipping.** —*n.* **1.** a small piece, as of wood, separated by chopping, cutting, or breaking. **2.** a very thin slice of food, candy, etc. **3.** (*pl.*) *Brit.* French fried potatoes. **4.** a mark made by chipping. **5.** *Games.* a counter, as of ivory or bone. **6.** anything trivial or worthless, or dried up or without flavor. **7.** a piece of dried dung. —*v.t.* **8.** to cut with an ax, chisel, etc. **9.** to cut or break off (bits or fragments). **10.** *Colloq.* to contribute. —*v.i.* **11.** to break off in small pieces. **12. chip in,** to contribute money, etc.

chip·munk (chĭp′mŭngk), *n.* any of various small striped terrestrial squirrels of America and Europe.

chip·per (chĭp′ər), *adj. U.S. Colloq.* lively.

Chip·pe·wa (chĭp′ə wä′, -wā′, -wə), *n.* **1.** an Ojibwa Indian. **2.** the Ojibwa language.

chi·rop·o·dy (kĭ rŏp′ə dĭ, kī-), *n.* the treatment of minor foot ailments, such as corns, bunions, etc. —**chi·rop′o·dist,** *n.*

chi·ro·prac·tic (kī′rə prăk′tĭk), *n.* a therapeutic system based upon adjusting body structures, esp. the spine.

chi·ro·prac·tor (kī′rə prăk′tər), *n.* one who practices chiropractic.

chirp (chûrp), *v.i., v.t.* **1.** to make or utter with a short, sharp sound, as small birds and certain insects. —*n.* **2.** a chirping sound. —**chirp′er,** *n.*

chirr (chûr), *v.i.* **1.** to make a shrill trilling sound, as a grasshopper. —*n.* **2.** such a sound.

chir·rup (chĭr′əp, chûr′-), *v.,* **-ruped, -ruping,** *n.* —*v.i., v.t.* **1.** to chirp. —*n.* **2.** a chirping sound.

chis·el (chĭz′əl), *n., v.,* **-eled, -eling** or (*esp. Brit.*) **-elled, -elling.** —*n.* **1.** a tool with a cutting edge at the extremity, for shaping wood, stone, etc. —*v.t., v.i.* **2.** to cut, shape, etc., with a chisel. **3.** *Now U.S. Slang.* **a.** to cheat. **b.** to get by cheating. —**chis′el·er;** *esp. Brit.,* **chis′el·ler,** *n.*

chit[1] (chĭt), *n.* **1.** a voucher of money owed for food, etc. **2.** *Chiefly Brit.* a note.

chit[2] (chĭt), *n.* a pert girl.

chit·chat (chĭt′chăt′), *n.* light conversation.

chi·tin (kī′tĭn), *n.* a characteristic horny organic component of the shell of arthropods. —**chi′tin·ous,** *adj.*

chit·ter·ling (chĭt′ər lĭng), *n.* (*usually pl.*) the small intestine of swine, etc., cooked for food.

chiv·al·ric (shĭv′əl rĭk, shĭ văl′rĭk), *adj.* **1.** pertaining to chivalry. **2.** chivalrous.

chiv·al·rous (shĭv′əl rəs), *adj.* **1.** having the qualities of chivalry, such as courage, courtesy, etc. **2.** chivalric. —**chiv′al·rous·ly,** *adv.* —**chiv′al·rous·ness,** *n.*

chiv·al·ry (shĭv′əl rĭ), *n.* **1.** the ideal qualifications of a knight, such as courtesy, generosity, valor, etc. **2.** the rules and customs of medieval knighthood.

chive (chīv), *n.* a small bulbous plant, related to the onion, with long, slender leaves which are used as a seasoning in cookery.

chlo·ral (klōr′əl), *n.* *Chem.* **1.** a colorless, mobile liquid, first prepared from chlorine and alcohol and used as a hypnotic. **2.** a white, crystalline substance (**chloral hydrate**) formed by combining liquid chloral with water, used as a hypnotic.

chlo·rate (klōr′āt, -ĭt), *n.* *Chem.* a salt of chloric acid.

chlo·ric (klōr′ĭk), *adj.* *Chem.* of or containing chlorine in the pentavalent state.

chlo·ride (klōr′īd, -ĭd), *n.* a compound containing chlorine.

chlo·rin·ate (klōr′ə nāt′), *v.t.,* **-ated, -ating.** *Chem.* to combine, treat, or disinfect with chlorine. —**chlo′rin·a′tion,** *n.* —**chlo′rin·a′tor,** *n.*

chlo·rine (klōr′ēn, -ĭn), *n.* *Chem.* a greenish-yellow gaseous element, used as a bleaching agent, etc. *Symbol:* Cl; *at. wt.:* 35.46; *at. no.:* 17. Also, **chlo·rin** (klōr′ĭn).

chlo·ro·form (klōr′ə fôrm′), *n.* **1.** *Chem., etc.* a colorless volatile liquid, $CHCl_3$, used esp. as an anesthetic. —*v.t.* **2.** to administer chloroform to.

chlo·ro·phyll (klōr′ə fĭl), *n. Bot., Biochem.* the green coloring substance of leaves and plants. Also, **chlo′ro·phyl.**

chlo·ro·plast (klōr′ə plăst′), *n. Bot.* a plastid containing chlorophyll.

chock (chŏk), *n.* **1.** a block or wedge of wood, etc., for preventing movement, as of a wheel or a cask. **2.** *Naut.* a fitting through which a mooring line or the like passes, usually on or in the rail. —*v.t.* **3.** to furnish with or secure by a chock or chocks. —*adv.* **4.** as close or tight as possible.

chock-full (chŏk′fŏŏl′), *adj.* crammed.

choc·o·late (chŏk′ə lĭt, chŏk′-, chôk′lĭt, chôk′-), *n.* **1.** a preparation of the seeds of cacao, roasted, husked, and ground, often sweetened and flavored. **2.** a beverage or a candy made from this. **3.** dark brown. —*adj.* **4.** made with chocolate.

Choc·taw (chŏk′tô), *n., pl.* **-taw, -taws.** a member of a large tribe of North American Indians, formerly living chiefly in southern Mississippi.

choice (chois), *n., adj.,* **choicer, choicest.** —*n.* **1.** act of choosing; selection. **2.** power of choosing; option. **3.** the person or thing chosen. **4.** an abundance from which to choose. **5.** that which is preferred or preferable. 6. an alternative. 7. a well-chosen supply. —*adj.* 8. excellent. 9. carefully selected. —**choice/ness,** *n.*

choir (kwĭr), *n.* 1. a company of singers, esp. in church service. 2. any company or band. 3. *Archit.* that part of a church used by the singers.

choke (chōk), *v.,* **choked, choking,** *n.* —*v.t.* 1. to stop the breath of, by squeezing or obstructing the windpipe; suffocate. 2. to check the growth, progress, or action of. 3. to obstruct; clog. 4. to suppress, as an emotion. 5. to fill chock-full. 6. (in internal-combustion engines) to enrich the fuel mixture by diminishing the air supply to the carburetor. —*v.i.* 7. to suffer strangling or suffocation. 8. to be obstructed or clogged. —*n.* 9. act or sound of choking. 10. any mechanism which, by blocking a passage, regulates the flow of air, etc., as in an automobile carburetor. 11. a narrowed part.

choke·damp (chōk/dămp/), *n.* mine atmosphere so high in carbon dioxide as to cause choking.

chok·er (chō/kər), *n.* *Colloq.* a necklace worn tightly around the neck.

chol·er (kŏl/ər), *n.* 1. irascibility; anger; wrath; irritability. 2. *Old Physiol.* bile.

chol·er·a (kŏl/ər ə), *n.* *Pathol.* 1. an acute disorder of the digestive tract, marked by diarrhea, vomiting, cramps, etc. 2. an acute, infectious disease, marked by profuse diarrhea, vomiting, cramps, etc., and often fatal (**Asiatic cholera**).

chol·er·ic (kŏl/ər ĭk), *adj.* irascible; angry.

choose (chooz), *v.,* **chose, chosen** or (*Obs.*) **chose, choosing.** —*v.t.* 1. to select from a number. 2. to prefer and decide (to do something). 3. to want. —*v.i.* 4. to make a choice. —**choos/-er,** *n.*

chop¹ (chŏp), *v.,* **chopped, chopping,** *n.* —*v.t.* 1. to cut with a quick, heavy blow or series of blows, using an ax, etc. 2. to make by so cutting. 3. to cut in pieces. 4. *Tennis, etc.* to hit (a ball) with a chop stroke. —*v.i.* 5. to make a quick, heavy stroke or a series of strokes, as with an ax. —*n.* 6. act of chopping. 7. a cutting blow. 8. a slice of lamb, veal, etc., usually one containing a rib. 9. a short, irregular, broken motion of waves. —**chop/per,** *n.*

chop² (chŏp), *v.i.,* **chopped, chopping.** to turn, shift, or change suddenly, as the wind.

chop³ (chŏp), *n.* (*usually pl.*) a jaw.

Cho·pin (shō/păn), *n.* **Frédéric François,** 1810?–49, Polish-French composer.

chop·py (chŏp/ĭ), *adj.,* **-pier, -piest.** (of the sea, etc.) forming short, irregular waves.

chop·stick (chŏp/stĭk/), *n.* one of the pair of small sticks, used by the Chinese, etc., to raise food to the mouth.

chop su·ey (chŏp/ soo/ĭ), *U.S.* a mixed dish served in Chinese restaurants, consisting of meat, onions, bean sprouts, green peppers, etc., cooked together in a sauce, eaten commonly with rice. Also, **chop/ soo/y.**

cho·ral (*adj.* kōr/əl; *n.* kə rǎl/, kō-, kōr/əl), *adj.* 1. of a chorus or a choir. 2. sung by or adapted for a chorus or a choir. —*n.* 3. a choral composition. 4. a simple sacred tune.

cho·rale (kə rǎl/, -rǎl/, kō-, kōr/əl), *n.* choral.

chord¹ (kôrd), *n.* 1. a string of a musical instrument. 2. a feeling or emotion. 3. *Geom.* that part of a straight line between two of its intersections with a curve. 4. *Anat.* a cord. —**chord/al,** *adj.*

'chord² (kôrd), *n.* *Music.* a combination of simultaneous tones in harmonic relation.

chore (chōr), *n.* *U.S.* 1. a small or odd job. 2. (*pl.*) routine work around a house or farm. 3. a hard or unpleasant task.

cho·re·a (kə rē/ə, kō-), *n.* *Pathol.* an acute disease of children characterized by involuntary movements in the face or extremities.

cho·re·og·ra·phy (kōr/ĭ ŏg/rə fĭ), *n.* the art of composing ballets, etc., or of dancing. —**cho/re·og/ra·pher,** *n.*

chor·is·ter (kôr/ĭs tər, kŏr/-), *n.* 1. a singer in a choir, esp. a male one. 2. a choir leader.

chor·tle (chôr/təl), *v.,* **-tled, -tling,** *n.* —*v.t., v.i.* 1. to chuckle with glee. —*n.* 2. a gleeful chuckle.

cho·rus (kōr/əs), *n., pl.* **-ruses,** *v.,* **-rused, -rusing.** —*n.* 1. *Music.* a. a group of persons singing in concert. b. a piece of music for singing in concert. c. a recurring refrain. 2. simultaneous utterance in singing, speaking, etc. 3. the sounds uttered. 4. (in musical shows) a. the company of dancers and singers. b. the singing

or song of such a company. 5. (in ancient Greek use) a dance by a company of persons accompanied with song or narration. —*v.t., v.i.* 6. to sing or utter in chorus.

chow (chou), *n.* 1. one of a Chinese breed of dogs of medium size, with a thick, even coat of hair. 2. *U.S. Slang.* food.

chow·der (chou/dər), *n.* *U.S.* a soup containing clams or fish with potatoes, onions, etc.

chow mein (chou/ mān/), a stew of mushrooms, celery, shredded chicken, etc., served with fried noodles.

chrism (krĭz/əm), *n.* a consecrated oil used in baptism, confirmation, etc. —**chris/mal,** *adj.*

Christ (krĭst), *n.* *Bible.* 1. the Messiah expected by the Jews. 2. Jesus of Nazareth, as fulfilling this expectation.

chris·ten (krĭs/ən), *v.t.* 1. to baptize. 2. to give a name to at baptism. —**chris/ten·ing,** *n.*

Chris·ten·dom (krĭs/ən dəm), *n.* 1. Christians collectively. 2. the Christian world.

Chris·tian (krĭs/chən), *adj.* 1. pertaining to or derived from Jesus Christ or his teachings. 2. believing in or belonging to the religion of Jesus Christ. 3. pertaining to Christianity or Christians. 4. exhibiting a spirit proper to a follower of Jesus Christ. —*n.* 5. an adherent of Christianity.

Chris·ti·an·i·ty (krĭs/chĭ ăn/ə tĭ), *n., pl.* **-ties.** 1. the Christian religion. 2. Christian quality or character. 3. state of being a Christian.

Chris·tian·ize (krĭs/chə nīz/), *v.t., v.i.,* **-ized, -izing.** to make or become Christian.

Christian name, the name given at baptism.

Christian Science, a system of religious teaching, based on the Scriptures, the most notable application of which is the treatment of disease by mental and spiritual means, founded about 1866 by Mrs. Mary Baker Glover Eddy. —**Christian Scientist.**

Christ·like (krīst/līk/), *adj.* showing the spirit of Christ. Also, **Christ/ly.** —**Christ/like/ness,** *n.*

Christ·mas (krĭs/məs), *n.* the annual festival of the Christian church commemorating the birth of Jesus: celebrated on December 25.

chro·mate (krō/māt), *n.* a salt of chromic acid.

chro·mat·ic (krō măt/ĭk), *adj.* 1. pertaining to color or colors. 2. *Music.* a. involving a modification of the normal scale by the use of accidentals. b. progressing by semitones. —**chro·mat/i·cal·ly,** *adv.*

chro·ma·tin (krō/mə tĭn), *n.* *Biol.* that portion of the cell nucleus which readily takes on stains.

chrome (krōm), *n.* chromium, esp. as a source of various pigments, as **chrome yellow** and **chrome green.**

chro·mic (krō/mĭk), *adj.* *Chem.* of or containing chromium, esp. in the trivalent state.

chro·mi·um (krō/mĭ əm), *n.* *Chem.* a lustrous, hard, brittle metallic element used in certain alloys, as a mordant, etc. *Symbol:* Cr; *at. wt.:* 52.01; *at. no.:* 24; *sp. gr.:* 7.1.

chro·mo·lith·o·graph (krō/mō lĭth/ə grăf/, -gräf/), *n.* a picture produced by chromolithography.

chro·mo·li·thog·ra·phy (krō/mō lĭ thŏg/rə fĭ), *n.* the process of lithographing in colors.

chro·mo·some (krō/mə sōm/), *n.* *Biol.* each of several threadlike, rodlike, or beadlike bodies which contain the chromatin during cell division.

Chron., *Bible.* Chronicles.

chron·ic (krŏn/ĭk), *adj.* 1. inveterate; constant. 2. continuing a long time. 3. having long had a disease, habit, or the like. Also, **chron/i·cal.** —**chron/i·cal·ly,** *adv.*

chron·i·cle (krŏn/ə kəl), *n., v.,* **-icled, -icling.** —*n.* 1. a record of events in the order of time. 2. **Chronicles,** two historical books of the Old Testament. —*v.t.* 3. to record in a chronicle. —**chron/i·cler,** *n.*

chron·o·log·i·cal (krŏn/ə lŏj/ə kəl), *adj.* 1. arranged in the order of time. 2. pertaining to or in accordance with chronology. Also, **chron/o·log/-ic.** —**chron/o·log/i·cal·ly,** *adv.*

chro·nol·o·gy (krə nŏl/ə jĭ), *n., pl.* **-gies.** 1. a particular statement of the supposed or accepted order of past events. 2. the science of arranging time in periods and ascertaining the dates and historical order of past events. —**chro·nol/o·gist,** *n.*

chro·nom·e·ter (krə nŏm/ə tər), *n.* a timepiece with special mechanism for ensuring accuracy.

chrys·a·lis (krĭs'ə lĭs), *n.*, *pl.* **chrysalises,** **chrysalides** (krĭ săl'ə dēz'). the hard-shelled pupa of a moth or butterfly. Also, **chrys'a·lid.**

chry·san·the·mum (krĭ săn'thə məm), *n.* any of certain perennial plants of the aster family, usually having large, colorful flowers.

chub (chŭb), *n.*, *pl.* **chubs,** (*esp. collectively*) **chub.** **1.** a common fresh-water fish of Europe with a thick fusiform body. **2.** any of several unrelated American fishes, esp. the deep-water whitefishes of the Great Lakes.

chub·by (chŭb'ĭ), *adj.*, **-bier, -biest.** plump.

chuck[1] (chŭk), *v.t.* **1.** to pat or tap lightly. **2.** *Brit.* to throw with a quick motion. —*n.* **3.** a light pat or tap, as under the chin.

chuck[2] (chŭk), *n.* **1.** the cut of beef between the neck and the shoulder blade. **2.** a chock. **3.** a mechanical device for holding tools or work in a machine.

chuck-full (chŭk'fŏŏl'), *adj.* chock-full.

chuck·le (chŭk'əl), *v.*, **chuckled, chuckling,** *n.* —*v.i.* **1.** to laugh in a soft, amused manner. —*n.* **2.** a soft, amused laugh. —**chuck'ler,** *n.*

chug (chŭg), *n.*, *v.*, **chugged, chugging.** —*n.* **1.** a short, dull explosive sound. —*v.i.* **2.** to make this sound.

chuk·ker (chŭk'ər), *n.* *Polo.* one of the periods of play. Also, **chuk'kar.**

chum (chŭm), *n.*, *v.*, **chummed, chumming.** —*n.* **1.** a very close friend. **2.** a roommate, as at college. —*v.i.* **3.** to associate intimately.

chum·my (chŭm'ĭ), *adj.*, **-mier, -miest.** intimate; sociable. —**chum'mi·ly,** *adv.*

chump (chŭmp), *n.* **1.** *Colloq.* a blockhead. **2.** a short, thick piece of wood. **3.** *Slang.* the head.

Chung·king (chŏŏng'kĭng'), *n.* a city in central China, on the Yangtze. 535,000.

chunk (chŭngk), *n.* **1.** a thick mass or lump of anything. **2.** a substantial amount (of something).

chunk·y (chŭn'gkĭ), *adj.*, **chunkier, chunkiest.** stout; stocky. —**chunk'i·ness,** *n.*

church (chûrch), *n.* **1.** an edifice for public Christian worship. **2.** public worship of God in a church. **3.** the whole body of Christian believers. **4.** a Christian denomination. **5.** the ecclesiastical organization or power as distinguished from the state. **6.** any non-Christian religious society, organization, or congregation.

Church·ill (chûrch'ĭl, -əl), *n.* **1.** **Winston,** 1871–1947, U.S. novelist. **2.** **Winston Leonard Spencer,** born 1874, British statesman and writer: prime minister, 1940–45 and since 1951. **3.** a river in Canada, from E Saskatchewan NE to Hudson Bay. ab. 1000 mi.

church·man (chûrch'mən), *n.*, *pl.* **-men.** an ecclesiastic; clergyman.

Church of England, the established church of England.

church·ward·en (chûrch'wôr'dən), *n.* a lay officer who looks after the secular affairs of a church.

church·yard (chûrch'yärd'), *n.* the yard adjoining a church, often used as a graveyard.

churl (chûrl), *n.* **1.** a peasant; rustic. **2.** a rude, boorish, or surly person. —**churl'ish,** *adj.* —**churl'ish·ly,** *adv.* —**churl'ish·ness,** *n.*

churn (chûrn), *n.* **1.** a vessel or machine in which cream or milk is agitated to make butter. —*v.t.* **2.** to stir or agitate, esp. in order to make into butter. **3.** to make by the agitation of cream. —**churn'er,** *n.*

chute (shōōt), *n.* **1.** a channel, tube, etc., for conveying water, coal, etc., to a lower level. **2.** a waterfall or rapid. **3.** a steep slope. **4.** parachute.

chut·ney (chŭt'nĭ), *n.*, *pl.* **-neys.** a relish of East Indian origin containing fruits, herbs, spices, etc.

chyle (kīl), *n.* a milky fluid containing emulsified fat and other products of digestion, formed in the small intestine and conveyed to the veins. —**chy'lous,** *adj.*

chyme (kīm), *n.* the pulpy matter into which food is converted by gastric digestion. —**chy'mous,** *adj.*

ci·bo·ri·um (sĭ bōr'ĭ əm), *n.*, *pl.* **-boria** (-bōr'ĭ ə). **1.** a permanent canopy over an altar. **2.** any vessel for the sacred wafers for the Eucharist.

ci·ca·da (sĭ kā'də, -kä'-), *n.*, *pl.* **-das, -dae** (-dē). any of a family which comprises large homopterous insects noted for the shrill sound produced by the male by means of vibrating membranes or drums on the under side of the abdomen.

cic·a·trix (sĭk'ə trĭks, sĭ kā'trĭks), *n.*, *pl.* **cica-**

trices (sĭk'ə trī'sēz). the new tissue which forms over a wound or the like, and later contracts into the scar. Also, **cic·a·trice** (sĭk'ə trĭs).

cic·a·trize (sĭk'ə trīz'), *v.t.*, *v.i.*, **-trized, -trizing.** to heal or become healed by the formation of a cicatrix. —**cic'a·tri·za'tion,** *n.*

Cic·e·ro (sĭs'ə rō'), *n.* **1. Marcus Tullius,** 106–43 B.C., Roman statesman and orator. **2.** a city in NE Illinois, near Chicago. 64,712. —**Cic·e·ro·ni·an** (sĭs'ə rō'nĭ ən), *adj.*

ci·der (sī'dər), *n.* the expressed juice of apples, used for drinking, either before fermentation (**sweet cider**) or after fermentation (**hard cider**), or for making applejack, vinegar, etc.

ci·gar (sĭ gär'), *n.* a small, shaped roll of tobacco leaves prepared for smoking.

cig·a·rette (sĭg'ə rĕt', sĭg'ə rĕt'), *n.* a roll of finely cut tobacco for smoking, enclosed in thin paper. Also, **cig'a·ret'.**

cil·i·a (sĭl'ĭ ə), *n.pl.*, *sing.* **cilium** (sĭl'ĭ əm). **1.** the eyelashes. **2.** *Zool.* short hairs, as on the surface of protozoans, for locomotion. **3.** *Bot.* minute, hairlike processes.

cil·i·ar·y (sĭl'ĭ ĕr'ĭ), *adj.* **1.** noting or pertaining to a delicate ring of tissue in the eye from which the lens is suspended by fine ligaments. **2.** pertaining to cilia.

cinch (sĭnch), *U.S.* —*n.* **1.** a strong girth for a saddle or pack. **2.** *Colloq.* a firm hold. **3.** *Slang.* something sure or easy. —*v.t.* **4.** to gird, bind, or seize firmly.

cin·cho·na (sĭn kō'nə), *n.* **1.** any of certain trees of the madder family, native in the Andes and cultivated in Java, the bark yielding quinine. **2.** the bark.

Cin·cin·nat·i (sĭn'sə năt'ĭ, -nät'ə), *n.* a city in SW Ohio, on the Ohio river. 455,610.

cinc·ture (sĭngk'chər), *n.*, *v.*, **-tured, -turing.** —*n.* **1.** a belt or girdle. **2.** something surrounding. —*v.t.* **3.** to encircle; encompass.

cin·der (sĭn'dər), *n.* **1.** a burned-out or partially burned piece of coal, wood, etc. **2.** (*pl.*) ashes. —*v.t.* **3.** to reduce to cinders. —**cin'der·y,** *adj.*

Cin·der·el·la (sĭn'də rĕl'ə), *n.* beautiful heroine of a well-known fairy tale, forced to be a household drudge until seen and wed by the prince.

cin·e·ma (sĭn'ə mə), *n.* **1.** a motion picture. **2. the cinema,** motion pictures collectively. **3.** a motion-picture theater. —**cin·e·mat·ic** (sĭn'ə măt'ĭk), *adj.* —**cin'e·mat'i·cal·ly,** *adv.*

cin·e·mat·o·graph (sĭn'ə măt'ə grăf', -gräf'), *Brit.* —*n.* **1.** a motion-picture projector or camera. —*v.t.*, *v.i.* **2.** to take motion pictures (of).

cin·e·rar·i·um (sĭn'ə râr'ĭ əm), *n.*, *pl.* **-raria** (-râr'ĭ ə). a place for the ashes of the dead after cremation. —**cin·er·ar·y** (sĭn'ə rĕr'ĭ), *adj.*

cin·na·bar (sĭn'ə bär'), *n.* **1.** a mineral, mercuric sulfide, occurring in red crystals or masses: the principal ore of mercury. **2.** red mercuric sulfide, used as a pigment.

cin·na·mon (sĭn'ə mən), *n.* **1.** the aromatic inner bark of any of several trees of the laurel family of the East Indies, etc., much used as a spice. **2.** a tree yielding cinnamon. **3.** reddish brown.

cinque·foil (sĭngk'foil'), *n.* **1.** any of certain plants of the rose family, having a calyx of five sepals and a corolla of five petals. **2.** a decorative design or feature resembling the leaf of cinquefoil.

CIO, Congress of Industrial Organizations. Also, **C.I.O.**

ci·on (sī'ən), *n.* scion (def. 2).

ci·pher (sī'fər), *n.* **1.** an arithmetical symbol (0) which denotes naught; or no quantity or magnitude. **2.** something of no value. **3.** a person of no influence. **4.** a secret method of writing, as by a specially formed code of symbols. **5.** writing done by such a method. **6.** the key to a secret method of writing. **7.** a monogram. —*v.i.* **8.** to use numerals arithmetically. —*v.t.* **9.** to calculate numerically. **10.** to write in, or as in, cipher.

cir·ca (sûr'kə), *prep.*, *adv.* about (used esp. in approximate dates). *Abbr.:* ca., c. or c, cir.

Cir·ce (sûr'sĭ), *n.* *Gk. Legend.* the enchantress who turned the companions of Odysseus into swine by a magic drink.

cir·cle (sûr'kəl), *n.*, *v.*, **-cled, -cling.** —*n.* **1.** a closed plane curve consisting of all points equally distant from a center point. **2.** the portion of a plane bounded by such a curve. **3.** any circular object, formation, or arrangement. **4.** a ring. **5.** a section of seats in a theater. **6.** the area within which something acts, exerts influence, etc.

7. a series perpetually repeated. **8.** a complete series forming a connected whole; cycle. **9.** a number of persons bound by a common tie. **10.** *Geog.* a parallel of latitude. **11.** *Astron.* the orbit of a heavenly body. —*v.t., v.i.* **12.** to enclose or move in a circle. —**cir′cler,** *n.*

cir·clet (sûr′klĭt), *n.* **1.** a small circle. **2.** a ring.

cir·cuit (sûr′kĭt), *n.* **1.** act of going around. **2.** a circular or roundabout journey or course. **3.** a periodical journey from place to place, to perform certain duties, as of judges or ministers. **4.** the route followed, places visited, or district covered by such a journey. **5.** *Elect.* **a.** the complete path of an electric current. **b.** an arrangement of conductors, electronic tubes, and other devices, for the investigation or utilization of electrical phenomena. —*v.t., v.i.* **6.** to make the circuit (of).

cir·cu·i·tous (sər kū′ə təs), *adj.* roundabout. —**cir′cu′i·tous·ly,** *adv.*

cir·cu·lar (sûr′kyə lər), *adj.* **1.** of or pertaining to a circle. **2.** round. **3.** moving in or forming a circle. **4.** circuitous; roundabout. **5.** (of a letter, etc.) addressed to a number of persons. —*n.* **6.** a letter, notice, or statement for circulation among the general public. —**cir′cu·lar·ly,** *adv.*

cir·cu·lar·ize (sûr′kyə lə rīz′), *v.t.,* -ized, -izing. to send circulars to. —**cir′cu·lar·i·za′tion,** *n.*

cir·cu·late (sûr′kyə lāt′), *v.i., v.t.,* -lated, -lating. **1.** to move in a circle or circuit. **2.** to pass from place to place, from person to person, etc. —**cir′cu·la·tive,** *adj.* —**cir′cu·la·tor,** *n.* —**cir·cu·la·to·ry** (sûr′kyə lə tôr′ĭ), *adj.*

cir·cu·la·tion (sûr′kyə lā′shən), *n.* **1.** act of moving in a circle or circuit. **2.** the recurrent movement of the blood through the various vessels of the body. **3.** the passage of anything from place to place, person to person, etc. **4.** the distribution of copies of a publication among readers. **5.** the number of copies distributed.

cir·cum·am·bi·ent (sûr′kəm ăm′bĭ ənt), *adj.* surrounding.

cir·cum·cise (sûr′kəm sīz′), *v.t.,* -cised, -cising. to remove the foreskin of (males), esp. as a religious rite. —**cir′cum·cis′er,** *n.* —**cir·cum·ci·sion** (sûr′kəm sĭzh′ən), *n.*

cir·cum·fer·ence (sər kŭm′fər əns), *n.* **1.** the outer boundary, esp. of a circular area. **2.** the length of such a boundary.

cir·cum·flex (sûr′kəm flĕks′), *adj.* **1.** noting or having a particular accent (^, ^, ~), indicating quality of sound, etc. **2.** bending or winding around. —*n.* **3.** the circumflex accent. —*v.t.* **4.** to bend around.

cir·cum·lo·cu·tion (sûr′kəm lō kū′shən), *n.* a roundabout way of speaking or expression.

cir·cum·nav·i·gate (sûr′kəm năv′ə gāt′), *v.t.,* -gated, -gating. to sail around.

cir·cum·scribe (sûr′kəm skrīb′), *v.t.,* -scribed, -scribing. **1.** to draw a line around; encircle. **2.** to limit or confine, esp. narrowly. **3.** *Geom.* **a.** to draw (a figure) around another figure so as to touch as many points as possible. **b.** (of a figure) to enclose (another figure) in this manner. —**cir′cum·scrib′er,** *n.* —**cir·cum·scrip·tion** (sûr′kəm skrĭp′shən), *n.*

cir·cum·spect (sûr′kəm spĕkt′), *adj.* **1.** cautious; prudent. **2.** well-considered. —**cir′cum·spect′ly,** *adv.* —**cir′cum·spec′tion, cir′cum·spect′ness,** *n.*

cir·cum·stance (sûr′kəm stăns′), *n., v.,* -stanced, -stancing. —*n.* **1.** a condition, with respect to time, place, manner, etc., which accompanies, determines, or modifies a fact or event. **2.** a secondary or minor detail. **3.** (*pl.*) the state of a person with respect to material welfare. **4.** an incident or occurrence. **5.** detailed narration. **6.** *Archaic.* ceremonious display. **7. under no circumstances,** never. —*v.t.* **8.** to place in particular circumstances.

cir·cum·stan·tial (sûr′kəm stăn′shəl), *adj.* **1.** of, pertaining to, or derived from circumstances. **2.** incidental. **3.** detailed. —**cir′cum·stan′tial·ly,** *adv.*

cir·cum·vent (sûr′kəm vĕnt′), *v.t.* **1.** to gain advantage over by artfulness or deception; outwit. **2.** to entrap. **3.** to go around. —**cir′cum·vent′er, cir′cum·ven′tor,** *n.* —**cir′cum·ven′tion,** *n.*

cir·cus (sûr′kəs), *n.* **1.** a company of performers, animals, etc., esp. a traveling company. **2.** (in ancient Rome) a large, roofless enclosure, surrounded by tiers of seats, for chariot races, etc.

cir·rho·sis (sĭ rō′sĭs), *n. Pathol.* a disease of the liver characterized by increase of connective tissue and alteration in make-up. —**cir·rhot·ic** (sĭ rŏt′ĭk), *adj.*

cir·ro·cu·mu·lus (sĭr′ō kū′myə ləs), *n. Meteorol.* a cloud of high altitude, consisting of small fleecy balls or flakes, often in rows or ripples.

cir·ro·stra·tus (sĭr′ō strā′təs), *n. Meteorol.* a high veillike cloud, often giving rise to halos around the sun and moon.

cir·rus (sĭr′əs), *n., pl.* **cirri** (sĭr′ī). **1.** *Bot.* a tendril. **2.** *Zool.* a filament serving as a tentacle, etc. **3.** *Meteorol.* a cloud having a thin, fleecy appearance, normally occurring at great altitudes and consisting of minute ice crystals. —**cir·rose** (sĭr′ōs, sĭ rōs′), **cir·rous** (sĭr′əs), *adj.*

Cis·ter·cian (sĭs tûr′shən), *n.* **1.** a member of an order of monks and nuns founded in 1098 in France. —*adj.* **2.** belonging to this order.

cis·tern (sĭs′tərn), *n.* a reservoir, tank, or vessel for holding water or other liquid.

cit·a·del (sĭt′ə dəl, -dĕl′), *n.* **1.** a fortress in or near a city. **2.** any strongly fortified place; stronghold.

ci·ta·tion (sī tā′shən), *n.* **1.** act of citing. **2.** the quoting of a passage, book, author, etc. **3.** a quotation. **4.** mention or enumeration. **5.** a summons, esp. to appear in court. **6.** *Mil.* mention of a soldier or unit, in orders, usually for gallantry.

cite (sīt), *v.t.,* cited, citing. **1.** to quote (a passage, book, author, etc.), esp. as an authority. **2.** to mention in support, proof, or confirmation. **3.** to summon, esp. to appear in court. **4.** to mention. **5.** *Mil.* to mention (a soldier, unit, etc.) in orders, as for gallantry. —**cit′a·ble, cite′a·ble,** *adj.*

cit·i·zen (sĭt′ə zən, -sən), *n.* **1.** a person, native or naturalized, owing allegiance to a government and entitled to its protection. **2.** an inhabitant of a city. **3.** a civilian (as distinguished from a soldier, police officer, etc.).

cit·i·zen·ry (sĭt′ə zən rĭ, -sən-), *n., pl.* -ries. citizens collectively.

cit·i·zen·ship (sĭt′ə zən shĭp′, -sən-), *n.* the status of a citizen, with its rights and duties.

cit·rate (sĭt′rāt, sī′trāt), *n. Chem.* a salt or ester of citric acid.

cit·ric acid (sĭt′rĭk), *Chem.* an acid contained in many fruits, especially in limes and lemons.

cit·ron (sĭt′rən), *n.* **1.** a pale-yellow fruit resembling the lemon, borne by a small Asiatic tree allied to the lemon and lime. **2.** the tree itself. **3.** the rind of the fruit, candied or preserved.

cit·ron·el·la (sĭt′rə nĕl′ə), *n.* a fragrant grass of southern Asia, cultivated as the source of an oil (**citronella oil**) used in making liniment, perfume, and soap.

cit·rus (sĭt′rəs), *n.* **1.** any tree or shrub of the genus which includes the citron, lemon, lime, orange, grapefruit, etc. —*adj.* **2.** Also, **cit′rous.** of or pertaining to such trees or shrubs.

cit·y (sĭt′ĭ), *n., pl.* cities. **1.** a large or important town. **2.** *U.S.* an incorporated municipality, usually governed by a mayor and a board of aldermen or councilmen. **3.** *Canada.* a municipality of high rank, usually based on population.

cit·y-state (sĭt′ĭ stāt′), *n.* a sovereign state consisting of an autonomous city with its dependencies.

Ciu·dad Tru·jil·lo (sū däd′ trōō hē′yô), the capital of the Dominican Republic, on the S coast. 131,271.

civ·et (sĭv′ĭt), *n.* **1.** a yellowish unctuous substance with a musklike odor, obtained from a pouch in the genital region of civets and used in perfumery. **2.** Also, **civet cat.** a catlike carnivorous mammal of southern Asia and Africa.

civ·ic (sĭv′ĭk), *adj.* **1.** municipal. **2.** of or pertaining to citizenship; civil. **3.** of citizens.

civ·ics (sĭv′ĭks), *n.* the science of civic affairs.

civ·ies (sĭv′ĭz), *n.pl. Colloq.* civilian clothes. Also, **civ′vies.**

civ·il (sĭv′əl), *adj.* **1.** of or consisting of citizens. **2.** of the commonwealth or state. **3.** of citizens in their ordinary capacity (distinguished from *military, ecclesiastical, etc.*). **4.** of the citizen as an individual. **5.** befitting a citizen. **6.** civilized. **7.** polite. **8.** (of divisions of time) legally recognized. —**civ′il·ly,** *adv.*

ci·vil·ian (sĭ vĭl′yən), *n.* **1.** one engaged in civil pursuits (distinguished from a soldier, etc.). —*adj.* **2.** of or pertaining to civilians.

ci·vil·i·ty (sĭ vĭl′ə tĭ), *n., pl.* -ties. **1.** courtesy. **2.** a polite attention or expression.

civ·i·li·za·tion (sĭv′ə lə zā′shən), *n.* **1.** an advanced state of society, in which a high level of art, science, religion, and government has been reached. **2.** those who have reached such a state. **3.** the culture, etc., of a specific group. **4.** act or process of civilizing.

civ·i·lize (sĭv′ə līz′), *v.t.*, **-lized, -lizing.** to bring out of a savage state; enlighten; refine.

civil service, the public service concerned with all affairs not military, naval, legislative, or judicial.

civil war, a war between parties, regions, etc., within their own country as (*cap.*) the American war between the North and South (1861–65).

Cl, *Chem.* chlorine.

cl., **1.** carload. **2.** centiliter. **3.** clause.

clab·ber (klăb′ər), *n.* **1.** milk turned thick in souring. —*v.i.* **2.** (of milk) to become thick in souring.

clack (klăk), *v.i.* **1.** to make a quick, sharp sound, as by striking. **2.** to chatter. —*v.t.* **3.** to utter by clacking. —*n.* **4.** a clacking sound. **5.** something that clacks. —**clack′er,** *n.*

clad (klăd), *v.* a pt. and pp. of **clothe.**

claim (klām), *v.t.* **1.** to demand as a right or as due. **2.** to assert and demand the recognition of (a title, etc.). **3.** to assert as a fact. **4.** to require as due or fitting. —*n.* **5.** a demand for something as due. **6.** an assertion of something as a fact. **7.** a right to claim or demand. **8.** that which is claimed. —**claim′er,** *n.*

claim·ant (klā′mənt), *n.* one who makes a claim.

clair·voy·ant (klâr voi′ənt), *adj.* **1.** having the power of seeing objects or actions beyond the range of vision. —*n.* **2.** a clairvoyant person. —**clair·voy′ance,** *n.*

clam (klăm), *n., v.,* **clammed, clamming.** —*n.* **1.** any of various bivalve mollusks, esp. certain edible species. —*v.i.* **2.** to gather or dig clams.

clam·ber (klăm′bər), *v.i., v.t.* **1.** to climb, using both feet and hands. —*n.* **2.** a clambering.

clam·my (klăm′ĭ), *adj.,* **-mier, -miest.** covered with a cold, sticky moisture. —**clam′mi·ness,** *n.*

clam·or (klăm′ər), *n.* **1.** a loud outcry. **2.** a vehement expression of desire or dissatisfaction. **3.** popular outcry. **4.** any loud and continued noise. —*v.i.* **5.** to raise an outcry. —*v.t.* **6.** to drive, force, put, etc., by clamoring. **7.** to utter noisily. Also, *Brit.,* **clam′our.**

clam·or·ous (klăm′ər əs), *adj.* **1.** vociferous; noisy. **2.** vigorous in demands or complaints.

clamp (klămp), *n.* **1.** a device for supporting, fastening, holding, or compressing objects. —*v.t.* **2.** to fasten with or put in a clamp.

clan (klăn), *n.* **1.** a group of related families or households. **2.** a clique, set, society, or party.

Clamp

clan·des·tine (klăn dĕs′tĭn), *adj.* secret; private. —**clan·des′tine·ly,** *adv.*

clang (klăng), *v.i., v.t.* **1.** to ring loudly or harshly. —*n.* **2.** a clanging sound.

clan·gor (klăng′gər, klăng′ər), *n.* **1.** loud, resonant sound. **2.** clamorous noise. —*v.i.* **3.** to make a clangor. Also, *Brit.,* **clan′gour.** —**clan′gor·ous,** *adj.*

clank (klăngk), *n.* **1.** sharp, hard, metallic sound. —*v.i.* **2.** to make or move with such a sound. —*v.t.* **3.** to cause to resound sharply.

clan·nish (klăn′ĭsh), *adj.* **1.** of or like a clan. **2.** associating only with one's own narrow clique. —**clan′nish·ly,** *adv.* —**clan′nish·ness,** *n.*

clans·man (klănz′mən), *n., pl.* **-men.** a member of a clan.

clap (klăp), *v.,* **clapped, clapping,** *n.* —*v.t.* **1.** to strike with a quick, smart blow. **2.** to strike (the hands) together in applause. **3.** to put, etc., promptly and effectively. —*v.i.* **4.** to make an abrupt, sharp sound. **5.** to clap the hands, as in applause. —*n.* **6.** act or sound of clapping. **7.** a slap. **8.** a loud and abrupt or explosive noise, as of thunder.

clap·board (klăb′ərd, klăp′bôrd′), *n.* **1.** *U.S.* a long, thin board, used in covering the outer walls of buildings being laid horizontally. —*adj.* **2.** of or pertaining to clapboard. —*v.t.* **3.** to cover with clapboards.

clap·per (klăp′ər), *n.* **1.** one that claps. **2.** the tongue of a bell.

claque (klăk), *n.* a set of hired applauders in a theater.

clar·et (klăr′ət), *n.* **1.** a red table wine. **2.** Also,

claret red. deep purplish red. —*adj.* **3.** deep purplish red.

clar·i·fy (klăr′ə fī′), *v.t., v.i.,* **-fied, -fying.** to make or become clear, pure, or intelligible. —**clar′i·fi·ca′tion,** *n.* —**clar′i·fi′er,** *n.*

clar·i·net (klăr′ə nĕt′), *n.* a wind instrument in the form of a cylindrical tube with a single reed attached to its mouthpiece. —**clar′i·net′ist, clar·i·net′tist,** *n.*

clar·i·on (klăr′ĭ ən), *adj.* **1.** clear and shrill. —*n.* **2.** an old kind of trumpet. **3.** *Poetic.* the sound of this instrument.

clar·i·ty (klăr′ə tĭ), *n.* clearness.

Clarks·burg (klärks′bûrg), *n.* a city in N West Virginia. 30,579.

clash (klăsh), *v.i.* **1.** to make a loud, harsh noise. **2.** to collide, esp. noisily. **3.** to conflict. —*v.t.* **4.** to strike with a resounding or violent collision. **5.** to produce (sound, etc.) by collision. —*n.* **6.** the noise of a collision. **7.** a collision. **8.** a conflict, esp. of views or interests.

clasp (klăsp, kläsp), *n.* **1.** a device for fastening things or parts together. **2.** a grasp; an embrace. —*v.t.* **3.** to fasten with a clasp. **4.** to furnish with a clasp. **5.** to take hold of with an enfolding grasp. —**clasp′er,** *n.*

class (klăs, kläs), *n.* **1.** a number of persons or things, regarded as forming one group through the possession of similar qualities. **2.** any division of persons or things according to rank or grade. **3.** the system of dividing society; caste. **4.** social rank, esp. high rank. **5.** *Chiefly U.S. Slang.* excellence. **6.** *U.S.* a number of students ranked together or graduated in the same year. **7.** a type of accommodation on railroads and steamers. **8.** *Zool., Bot.* the usual major subdivision of a phylum or subphylum, commonly comprising a plurality of orders. —*v.t.* **9.** to arrange, place, or rate as to class. —*v.i.* **10.** to take or have a place in a particular class. —**class′a·ble,** *adj.* —**class′er,** *n.*

class., **1.** classic. **2.** classical.

clas·sic (klăs′ĭk), *adj.* **1.** of the highest class or rank. **2.** serving as a standard or model. **3.** of or characteristic of Greek and Roman antiquity. **4.** in the style of the ancient Greek and Roman literature or art. —*n.* **5.** an author, artist, etc., or production of the first rank. **6.** (*pl.*) the literature of ancient Greece and Rome.

clas·si·cal (klăs′ə kəl), *adj.* **1.** classic. **2.** versed in the ancient classics. **3.** marked by classicism. **4.** teaching or relating to the humanities, general sciences, etc., distinguished from technical subjects. **5.** accepted as standard in a given field of knowledge. —**clas′si·cal·ly,** *adv.*

clas·si·cism (klăs′ə sĭz′əm), *n.* the principles of classic literature or art, or adherence to them, characterized esp. by regularity, simplicity, balance, proportion, and controlled emotion.

clas·si·cist (klăs′ə sĭst), *n.* **1.** an adherent of classicism in literature or art. **2.** an authority on Greek and Roman studies.

clas·si·fi·ca·tion (klăs′ə fə kā′shən), *n.* **1.** act or the result of classifying. **2.** *Zool., Bot.* the assignment of plants and animals to groups within a system of categories distinguished by structure, origin, etc.

clas·si·fy (klăs′ə fī′), *v.t.,* **-fied, -fying.** to arrange or distribute in classes. —**clas′si·fi′a·ble,** *adj.*

class·mate (klăs′māt′, kläs′-), *n.* a member of the same class, as at school or college.

class·room (klăs′rōōm′, -rŏŏm′, kläs′-), *n.* a room in a school or college in which classes meet.

clat·ter (klăt′ər), *v.i.* **1.** to make a rattling sound. **2.** to move rapidly with such a sound. —*v.t.* **3.** to cause to clatter. —*n.* **4.** a clattering noise. —**clat′ter·er,** *n.*

clause (klôz), *n.* **1.** *Gram.* a group of words containing a subject and a predicate, forming part of a compound or complex sentence, or coextensive with a simple sentence. **2.** part of a document containing complete sense in itself, as of a will. —**claus′al,** *adj.*

claus·tro·pho·bi·a (klôs′trə fō′bĭ ə), *n.* *Psychiatry.* a morbid dread of closed or narrow places.

cla·vate (klā′vāt), *adj.* club-shaped.

clav·i·chord (klăv′ə kôrd′), *n.* an ancient keyboard instrument.

clav·i·cle (klăv′ə kəl), *n.* *Anat.* either of two slender bones each articulating with the sternum and a scapula and forming the anterior part of a shoulder.

clav·i·er (klăv′ĭ ər, klə vîr′), *n.* the keyboard of a musical instrument.

claw (klô), *n.* **1.** a sharp, usually curved, nail on the foot of an animal. **2.** any part or thing resembling a claw. —*v.t.* **3.** to tear, scratch, seize, make, etc., with claws.

clay (klā), *n.* **1.** a natural earthy material, essentially of hydrated silicates of aluminum, used for making bricks, pottery, etc. **2.** earth; mud. **3.** the human body. —**clay·ey** (klā′Y), *adj.*

Clay (klā), *n.* **Henry,** 1777–1852, U.S. statesman.

clay·more (klā′mōr′), *n.* a heavy two-edged sword formerly used by the Scottish Highlanders.

clean (klēn), *adj.* **1.** free from dirt or filth. **2.** free from foreign matter; pure. **3.** free from blemish. **4.** free from obstructions. **5.** morally pure; innocent. **6.** free from dirty habits, as an animal. **7.** shapely; trim. **8.** dexterous; adroit. **9.** complete; perfect. —*adv.* **10.** in a clean manner. **11.** wholly. —*v.t.* **12.** to make clean. —*v.i.* **13.** to perform or to undergo a process of cleaning. **14.** to get rid of dirt, etc. —**clean′a·ble,** *adj.* —**clean′er,** *n.* —**clean′ness,** *n.*

clean-cut (klēn′kŭt′), *adj.* **1.** sharply outlined. **2.** definite. **3.** neat and wholesome.

clean·ly (*adj.* klĕn′lY; *adv.* klēn′lY), *adj.,* **-lier, -liest,** *adv.* —*adj.* **1.** careful to keep or make clean. **2.** habitually clean. —*adv.* **3.** in a clean manner. —**clean·li·ness** (klĕn′lY nYs), *n.*

cleanse (klĕnz), *v.t.,* **cleansed, cleansing.** to make clean. —**cleans′er,** *n.*

clear (klîr), *adj.* **1.** free from darkness, obscurity, or cloudiness. **2.** bright. **3.** transparent. **4.** of a pure, even color. **5.** easily seen, heard, or understood. **6.** evident; plain. **7.** free from confusion or doubt. **8.** perceiving distinctly. **9.** convinced. **10.** free from guilt or blame. **11.** serene. **12.** free from obstacles; open. **13.** unentangled; free. **14.** emptied of contents, cargo, etc. **15.** without limitation. **16.** without obligation. —*adv.* **17.** in a clear manner. —*v.t.* **18.** to free from darkness, indistinctness, uncertainty, obstruction, contents, guilt, etc. **19.** to pass without entanglement. **20.** to pay (a debt) in full. **21.** to gain as clear profit. **22.** to free (a ship, etc.) from detention at a port. —*v.i.* **23.** to become clear. —*n.* **24.** a clear or unobstructed space. **25. in the clear,** a. between the bounding parts. b. free. —**clear′-a·ble,** *adj.* —**clear′ness,** *n.*

clear·ance (klîr′əns), *n.* **1.** act of clearing. **2.** a clear space; clearing. **3.** the clearing of a ship at a port.

clear-cut (klîr′kŭt′), *adj.* distinctly defined.

clear·ing (klîr′Yng), *n.* a tract of cleared land, as in a forest.

clearing house, *Banking.* a place or institution where mutual claims and accounts are settled.

cleat (klēt), *n.* **1.** a small wedge-shaped block, as one fastened to a spar or the like as a support, check, etc. **2.** *Naut.* a piece of wood or iron consisting of a bar with arms, to which ropes are belayed. **3.** a piece of iron fastened under a shoe to preserve the sole. —*v.t.* **4.** to fasten to or with a cleat.

cleav·age (klē′vYj), *n.* **1.** act of cleaving. **2.** state of being cleft or split. **3.** *Biol.* the total or partial division of the egg into smaller cells.

cleave¹ (klēv), *v.i.,* **cleaved** or (*Archaic*) **clave, cleaved, cleaving.** to adhere; cling (fol. by *to*).

cleave² (klēv), *v.t.,v.i.,* **cleft** or **cleaved** or **clove, cleft** or **cleaved** or **cloven, cleaving. 1.** to part by a cutting blow. **2.** to pass through (air, water, etc.). —**cleav′a·ble,** *adj.*

cleav·er (klē′vər), *n.* **1.** one that cleaves. **2.** a hatchet used by butchers.

clef (klĕf), *n. Music.* a symbol placed upon a staff to indicate the name and pitch of the notes corresponding to its lines and spaces.

cleft (klĕft), *n.* a space or opening made by cleavage; split.

clem·a·tis (klĕm′ə tĭs), *n.* any of certain flowering vines or erect shrubs of the crowfoot family.

Treble Clef   Bass Clef

Cle·men·ceau (klĕm′ən sō′), *n.* **Georges Eu·gène Benjamin,** 1841–1929; premier of France, 1906–09 and 1917–20.

Clem·ens (klĕm′ənz), *n.* **Samuel Langhorne,** ("*Mark Twain*") 1835–1910, U.S. author.

clem·ent (klĕm′ənt), *adj.* **1.** merciful in disposition; lenient. **2.** (of the weather, etc.) mild. —**clem′en·cy,** *n.*

clench (klĕnch), *v.t.* **1.** to close (the hands, teeth, etc.) tightly. **2.** to grasp firmly. **3.** to clinch. —*n.* **4.** act of clenching. **5.** a tight hold. **6.** that which holds fast or clenches.

Cle·o·pa·tra (klē′ə pā′trə, -păt′rə, -pä′trə), *n.* 69?–30 B.C., queen of Egypt, 47–30 B.C.

clere·sto·ry (klîr′stōr′Y), *n., pl.* **-ries.** the upper part of the nave, transepts, and choir of a building, esp. a church, perforated with windows.

cler·gy (klûr′jY) *n., pl.* **-gies.** the body of men ordained for religious work.

cler·gy·man (klûr′jY mən), *n., pl.* **-men.** a member of the clergy; a minister. Also, **cler·ic** (klĕr′Yk).

cler·i·cal (klĕr′ə kəl), *adj.* **1.** pertaining to clerks. **2.** of, pertaining to, or characteristic of the clergy. **3.** upholding the power of the clergy in politics. —*n.* **4.** a clergyman. **5.** a person or a party trying to extend the power of the church in government. —**cler′i·cal·ly,** *adv.*

cler·i·cal·ism (klĕr′ə kə lYz′əm), *n.* clerical power in politics. —**cler′i·cal·ist,** *n.*

clerk (klûrk; *Brit.* klärk), *n.* **1.** one employed in an office, court, shop, etc., to keep records, attend to correspondence, etc. **2.** *U.S.* a retail salesman or saleswoman. **3.** *Chiefly Legal.* a clergyman. **4.** a layman charged with various minor ecclesiastical duties. —*v.i.* **5.** to act or serve as a clerk. —**clerk′ship′,** *n.*

Cleve·land (klēv′lənd), *n.* **1. (Stephen) Gro·ver,** 1837–1908, 22nd and 24th president of the U.S., 1885–89, 1893–97. **2.** a city in NE Ohio. 878,336; with suburbs, 1,210,316.

Cleveland Heights, a city in NE Ohio. 54,992.

clev·er (klĕv′ər), *adj.* **1.** bright mentally. **2.** dexterous or nimble. **3.** showing ingenuity. —**clev′er·ly,** *adv.* —**clev′er·ness,** *n.*

clew (kloo), *n.* **1.** a ball of thread, yarn, etc. **2.** clue.

cli·ché (klē shā′), *n.* a trite, stereotyped expression, idea, practice, etc.

click (klYk), *n.* **1.** a slight, sharp sound. **2.** some clicking mechanism, as a pawl. —*v.i.* **3.** to emit or make a slight, sharp sound. **4.** *Slang.* to succeed. —*v.t.* **5.** to cause to click. —**click′er,** *n.*

cli·ent (klī′ənt), *n.* **1.** one who applies to a lawyer for advice or aid. **2.** a customer.

cli·en·tele (klī′ən tĕl′), *n.* the customers, patients, etc., as a whole.

cliff (klYf), *n.* the high, steep face of a rocky mass; precipice.

Clif·ton (klYf′tən), *n.* a city in NE New Jersey. 48,827.

cli·mac·ter·ic (klī măk′tər Yk, klī′măk tĕr′Yk), *adj.* **1.** crucial. —*n.* **2.** a year in which important changes in health, fortune, etc., occur. **3.** any critical period.

cli·mac·tic (klī măk′tYk), *adj.* pertaining to or forming a climax. Also, **cli·mac′ti·cal.**

cli·mate (klī′mYt), *n.* the composite weather conditions of a region, as temperature, humidity, sunshine, and winds, averaged over a series of years. —**cli·mat·ic** (klī măt′Yk), *adj.*

cli·ma·tol·o·gy (klī′mə tŏl′ə jY), *n.* the science that deals with climatic conditions. —**cli·ma·to·log·ic** (klī′mə tə lŏj′Yk), *adj.*

cli·max (klī′măks), *n.* **1.** the highest point of anything; culmination. **2.** *Rhet.* **a.** a figure consisting in a series of related ideas arranged in increasing intensity. **b.** the last member of this figure. —*v.i., v.t.* **3.** to reach, or bring to, the climax.

climb (klīm), *v.,* **climbed** or (*Archaic*) **clomb, climbed** or (*Archaic*) **clomb, climbing,** *n.* —*v.i., v.t.* **1.** to ascend, esp. by using both hands and feet. **2.** to rise slowly by continued effort. **3.** to slope upward. **4. climb down,** to descend, esp. by using both hands and feet. —*n.* **5.** a climbing; an ascent by climbing. **6.** a place to be climbed. —**climb′er,** *n.*

clime (klīm), *n. Poetic.* **1.** a region. **2.** climate.

clinch (klYnch), *v.t.* **1.** to secure (a driven nail, etc.) by beating down the point. **2.** to fasten (work) together thus. **3.** to settle decisively. —*v.i.* **4.** *Boxing, etc.* to grasp tightly. —*n.* **5.** act of clinching. **6.** *Boxing, etc.* a grasp.

clinch·er (klYnch′ər), *n.* **1.** a nail, etc., for clinching. **2.** something decisive.

cling (klYng), *v.i.,* **clung, clinging. 1.** to adhere closely; stick. **2.** to hold fast, as by grasping. **3.** to be or remain close. **4.** to remain attached (to an idea, hope, etc.). —**cling′ing·ly,** *adv.*

cling·stone (klYng′stōn′), *adj.* **1.** having a

stone to which the pulp adheres closely, as certain peaches. —*n.* 2. a clingstone peach.

clin·ic (klĭn′ĭk), *n.* 1. a place, as in connection with a hospital, for the treatment of nonresident patients. 2. the instruction of medical students by treating patients in their presence.

clin·i·cal (klĭn′ə kəl), *adj.* 1. pertaining to a clinic. 2. pertaining to or used in a sickroom. 3. concerned with observation and treatment of disease in the patient. —**clin′i·cal·ly**, *adv.*

clink[1] (klĭngk), *v.i., v.t.* 1. to make, or cause to make, a light, sharp, ringing sound. —*n.* 2. a clinking sound.

clink[2] (klĭngk), *n. Colloq.* a prison; jail.

clink·er (klĭng′kər), *n.* 1. a hard brick, used for paving,etc. 2. a mass of incombustible matter fused together, as in the burning of coal.

cli·nom·e·ter (klī nŏm′ə tər, klĭ-), *n.* an instrument used to determine inclination.

Cli·o (klī′ō), *n. Class. Myth.* the Muse of history.

clip[1] (klĭp), *v.,* **clipped, clipping,** *n.* —*v.t.* 1. to cut, as with shears. 2. to cut or trim the hair or fleece of. 3. to curtail. 4. to omit sounds of (a word) in pronouncing. 5. *Colloq.* to hit with a quick, sharp blow. —*v.i.* 6. to cut something. 7. to cut items from a newspaper, etc. 8. to move swiftly. —*n.* 9. act of clipping. 10. anything clipped off.

clip[2] (klĭp), *n., v.,* **clipped, clipping.** —*n.* 1. a clasp, esp. a metal one for papers, letters, etc. 2. a metal cartridge-holder for an automatic pistol, etc. —*v.t., v.i.* 3. to grip tightly.

clip·per (klĭp′ər), *n.* 1. one that clips. 2. (*often pl.*) a cutting tool, esp. shears. 3. a sailing vessel built and rigged for speed.

clip·ping (klĭp′ĭng), *n.* 1. act of one that clips. 2. a piece clipped out, as from a newspaper.

clique (klēk, klĭk), *n.* a small, snobbishly exclusive group. —**cli′quish,** *adj.* —**cli′quish·ly,** *adv.* —**cli′quish·ness,** *n.*

cli·to·ris (klī′tə rĭs, klĭt′ə rĭs), *n. Anat.* the erectile organ of the vulva.

clo·a·ca (klō ā′kə), *n., pl.* -**cae** (-sē). 1. a sewer. 2. a privy. 3. a place or receptacle of moral filth. 4. *Zool.* the cavity into which the intestinal, urinary, and generative canals open in certain animals. —**clo·a′cal,** *adj.*

cloak (klōk), *n.* 1. a loose outer garment. 2. that which covers or conceals. —*v.t.* 3. to cover with a cloak. 4. to hide.

cloche (klōsh), *n.* a bell-shaped, close-fitting woman's hat.

clock[1] (klŏk), *n.* 1. an instrument for measuring and indicating time, esp. one not carried on the person. —*v.t.* 2. to time, test, or ascertain by the clock.

clock[2] (klŏk), *n.* an ornament on each side of a stocking, from the ankle upward.

clock·wise (klŏk′wīz′), *adv., adj.* in the direction of rotation of the hands of a clock.

clock·work (klŏk′wûrk′), *n.* 1. the mechanism of a clock. 2. like **clockwork,** with perfect precision.

clod (klŏd), *n.* 1. a lump or mass, esp. of earth. 2. earth; soil. 3. a blockhead; dolt. —**clod′dy,** *adj.*

clog (klŏg, klôg), *v.,* **clogged, clogging,** *n.* —*v.t.* 1. to hamper; hinder. 2. to obstruct, esp. by sticky matter. —*v.i.* 3. to become clogged or choked up. 4. to stick together. 5. to do a clog dance. —*n.* 6. anything that impedes motion or action. 7. a kind of shoe with a thick sole usually of wood. 8. a similar but lighter shoe worn in the **clog dance.**

clois·ter (klois′tər), *n.* 1. a covered walk, esp. one adjoining a church, running round an open court. 2. a monastery or nunnery. 3. any quiet, secluded place. —*v.t.* 4. to confine in a cloister. —**clois·tral** (klois′trəl), *adj.*

close (*v.* klōz; *adj., adv.* klōs; *n.* klōz *for 36–39,* klōs *for 40*), *v., closed, closing, adj., closer, closest, adv., n.* —*v.t.* 1. to stop or obstruct (a gap, etc.). 2. to stop the entrances, apertures, or gaps in. 3. to enclose. 4. to join; unite. 5. to bring to an end. —*v.i.* 6. to shut. 7. to come together; unite. 8. to grapple. 9. to come to terms. 10. to agree. 11. to come to an end. —*adj.* 12. shut; not open. 13. shut in; enclosed. 14. completely enclosing. 15. with all openings closed. 16. confined; narrow. 17. lacking fresh or freely circulating air. 18. oppressive. 19. narrowly confined, as a prisoner. 20. secretive; reticent. 21. stingy. 22. scarce, as money. 23. not open to general admission, competition, etc. 24. under prohibition as to hunting or fish-

ing. 25. having the parts near together. 26. compact; condensed. 27. near, or near together, in space, time, or relation. 28. intimate; confidential. 29. based upon a strong uniting feeling of love, honor, etc. 30. fitting tightly, as a cap. 31. strict; minute. 32. not deviating from a model or original. 33. nearly even or equal. 34. strictly logical. —*adv.* 35. in a close manner. —*n.* 36. act of closing. 37. the end. 38. a junction; union. 39. a grapple. 40. an enclosure. —**close·ly** (klōs′lĭ), *adv.* —**close·ness** (klōs′nĭs), *n.*

closed shop, a shop in which union membership is a condition of employment.

close-fist·ed (klōs′fĭs′tĭd), *adj.* miserly.

close-hauled (klōs′hôld′), *adj. Naut.* sailing as close to the wind as a vessel will sail.

clos·et (klŏz′ĭt), *n.* 1. a small room, recess, or cabinet for clothing, food, etc. 2. a small private room. 3. a toilet. —*v.t.* 4. to shut up in a private room for a conference, etc.

clo·sure (klō′zhər), *n.* 1. act of closing or shutting. 2. state of being closed. 3. conclusion. 4. that which closes or shuts. 5. *Parl. Proc.* a method of closing a debate and causing an immediate vote to be taken on the question under discussion.

clot (klŏt), *n., v.,* **clotted, clotting.** —*n.* 1. a mass or lump, as of coagulated blood. —*v.i.* 2. to form into clots. —*v.t.* 3. to cause to clot.

cloth (klôth, klŏth), *n., pl.* **cloths** (klôthz, klŏthz; klôths, klŏths). 1. a fabric formed by weaving, felting, etc., from wool, silk, cotton, or other fiber, used for garments, upholstery, etc. 2. a piece of such a fabric for a particular purpose. 3. a particular profession, esp. that of a clergyman. 4. **the cloth,** the clergy.

clothe (klōth), *v.t.,* **clothed** or **clad, clothing.** 1. to dress. 2. to provide with clothing.

clothes (klōz, klōthz), *n.pl.* 1. garments for the body; wearing apparel. 2. bedclothes.

clothes·pin (klōz′pĭn′, klōthz′-), *n.* a forked piece of wood or other device for hanging articles on a line.

cloth·ier (klōth′yər, -ĭ ər), *n.* a maker or seller of woolen cloth or of clothes.

cloth·ing (klō′thĭng), *n.* 1. garments collectively; clothes; apparel. 2. a covering.

clo·ture (klō′chər), *n. U.S.* closure.

cloud (kloud), *n.* 1. a visible collection of particles of water or ice suspended in the air, usually at an elevation above the earth's surface. 2. any similar mass, as of dust. 3. a dim or obscure part. 4. a patch or spot. 5. anything that obscures, or causes gloom, disgrace, etc. —*v.t.* 6. to overspread with a cloud or clouds. 7. to obscure; darken. 8. to make gloomy. 9. to place under suspicion, disgrace, etc. —*v.i.* 10. to grow cloudy. —**cloud′less,** *adj.*

cloud·burst (kloud′bûrst′), *n.* a sudden and very heavy rainfall.

cloud·y (klou′dĭ), *adj.,* **cloudier, cloudiest.** 1. overcast with clouds. 2. not clear or transparent. 3. obscure; indistinct. —**cloud′i·ness,** *n.*

clout (klout), *n. Colloq. or Dial.* —*n.* 1. a blow, esp. with the hand. —*v.t.* 2. to strike, esp. with the hand.

clove[1] (klōv), *n.* 1. the dried flower bud of a tropical tree of the myrtle family, used whole or ground as a spice. 2. the tree.

clove[2] (klōv), *n.* one of the bulbs in the axils of the scales of a mother bulb, as in garlic.

clo·ven (klō′vən), *adj.* cleft; split.

clo·ver (klō′vər), *n.* any of various herbs of the bean family, with trifoliolate leaves and dense flower heads, many species of which, as **red clover,** are cultivated as forage plants.

clown (kloun), *n.* 1. a jester or buffoon in a circus, pantomime, etc. 2. a rustic. 3. a boor. —*v.i.* 4. to act like a clown. —**clown′ish,** *adj.*

cloy (kloi), *v.t.* to weary by an excess of food, sweetness, pleasure, etc.; surfeit; satiate. —**cloy′ing·ly,** *adv.* —**cloy′ing·ness,** *n.*

club (klŭb), *n., v.,* **clubbed, clubbing.** —*n.* 1. a heavy stick, usually thicker at one end than at the other; cudgel. 2. a stick or bat used to drive a ball, etc., in various games. 3. a group of persons organized for a social, political, or other purpose. 4. the place occupied by such a group. 5. a black trefoil-shaped figure on a playing card. 6. a card bearing such figures. 7. (*pl.*) the suit so marked. —*v.t., v.i.* 8. to beat with a club. 9. to unite; join together.

club·foot (klŭb′fŏŏt′), *n.* 1. a deformed foot. 2. the condition of such a foot.

cluck (klŭk), *v.i.* **1.** to utter the cry of a hen brooding or calling her chicks. —*n.* **2.** this sound.

clue (kloo), *n.* **1.** anything that guides in the solution of a problem, mystery, etc. **2.** clew.

clump (klŭmp), *n.* **1.** a cluster, esp. of trees or other plants. **2.** a lump or mass. **3.** a clumping tread, sound, etc. —*v.i.* **4.** to walk heavily and clumsily. —**clump′y, clump′ish,** *adj.*

clum·sy (klŭm′zǐ), *adj.,* **-sier, -siest. 1.** awkward in movement or action. **2.** awkwardly done or made. —**clum′si·ly,** *adv.* —**clum′si·ness,** *n.*

clus·ter (klŭs′tər), *n.* **1.** a number of things of the same kind, growing or held together; a bunch. —*v.t.* **2.** to gather into a cluster. —*v.i.* **3.** to form a cluster. —**clus′ter·y,** *adj.*

clutch (klŭch), *v.t.* **1.** to seize with the hands or claws; snatch. **2.** to hold tightly. —*v.i.* **3.** to try to seize. —*n.* **4.** the hand, claw, etc., when grasping. **5.** (*chiefly pl.*) power of control; mastery. **6.** grasp. **7.** a tight hold. **8.** a device for gripping something. **9.** a coupling or appliance by which working parts of machinery may be made to engage or disengage.

clut·ter (klŭt′ər), *v.t.* **1.** to heap, litter, or strew in a disorderly manner. —*n.* **2.** a disorderly heap or assemblage. **3.** confusion; disorder.

Cly·tem·nes·tra (klǐ′təm nĕs′trə), *n. Gk. Legend.* the wife of Agamemnon.

cm., centimeter; centimeters.

co-, a prefix signifying association and accompanying action, occurring before vowels and before *h* and *gn,* as in *coauthor.*

Co, *Chem.* cobalt.

Co., 1. Company. **2.** County. Also, **co.**

c.O., 1. care of. **2.** carried over. Also, **c/o**

C.O., Commanding Officer.

coach (kōch), *n.* **1.** a large, closed, four-wheeled carriage. **2.** an enclosed automobile. **3.** a public bus. **4.** a railroad passenger car. **5.** a person who trains athletes for a contest, etc. **6.** a private tutor. —*v.t.* **7.** to give instruction or advice to. —*v.i.* **8.** to act as a coach.

coach·man (kōch′mən), *n., pl.* **-men.** a man employed to drive a coach or carriage.

co·ad·ju·tor (kō ăj′ə tər, kō′ə joo′tər), *n.* an assistant, esp. to a bishop or other ecclesiastic.

co·ag·u·late (kō ăg′yə lāt′), *v.i., v.t.,* **-lated, -lating.** to change from a fluid into a thickened mass; congeal. —**co·ag′u·la′tion,** *n.* —**co·ag′u·la′tive,** *adj.* —**co·ag′u·la′tor,** *n.*

coal (kōl), *n.* **1.** a black or dark-brown combustible mineral substance consisting of carbonized vegetable matter, used as a fuel: **hard coal** (anthracite), **soft coal** (bituminous coal), **brown coal** (lignite). **2.** a piece of wood or other combustible substance either glowing, charred, or burned out. —*v.t., v.i.* **3.** to provide with or take on coal.

co·a·lesce (kō′ə lĕs′), *v.i.,* **-lesced, -lescing. 1.** to grow together or into one body. **2.** to unite. —**co′a·les′cence,** *n.* —**co′a·les′cent,** *adj.*

co·a·li·tion (kō′ə lǐsh′ən), *n.* **1.** union into one mass; fusion. **2.** a combination or alliance.

coal oil, kerosene.

coal tar, a thick, black, viscid liquid formed during the distillation of coal which is further processed for dyes and synthetic compounds.

coam·ing (kō′mǐng), *n.* a raised border around an opening in a deck, etc., to keep water out.

coarse (kōrs), *adj.,* **coarser, coarsest. 1.** of inferior or faulty quality; base. **2.** composed of relatively large parts. **3.** lacking in delicacy. **4.** harsh. **5.** vulgar; not refined. —**coarse′ly,** *adv.* —**coarse′ness,** *n.*

coars·en (kōr′sən), *v.t., v.i.* to make or become coarse.

coast (kōst), *n.* **1.** the land next to the sea; seashore. **2.** the region nearby. **3.** a slope down which one may slide on a sled. **4.** a slide or ride down a hill, etc. —*v.i.* **5.** *U.S.* to slide on a sled down an incline. **6.** *U.S.* to move effortlessly, as on a bicycle without using pedals. **7.** to sail along a coast. —*v.t.* **8.** to proceed along the coast of. **9.** to go along or near to (a coast). —**coast′al,** *adj.*

coast·er (kōs′tər), *n.* **1.** one that coasts. **2.** a vessel engaged in coastwise trade. **3.** a sled for coasting. **4.** a small dish placed under glasses, etc., to protect a table.

coast guard, a government organization employed in the coastal lifesaving service, antismuggling patrol, etc.

coast·wise (kōst′wīz′), *adv.* **1.** along the coast. —*adj.* **2.** following the coast.

coat (kōt), *n.* **1.** an outer garment with sleeves, covering the upper part of the body. **2.** a natural integument or covering, as hair, fur, bark, etc. **3.** anything that covers or conceals. —*v.t.* **4.** to cover or provide with a coat.

co·a·ti (kō ä′tǐ), *n., pl.* **-tis.** any of certain tropical American plantigrade carnivores closely related to the raccoon, and having a long ringed tail and a flexible snout.

coat·ing (kō′tǐng), *n.* a layer of any substance spread over a surface.

coat of arms, the heraldic bearings of a person.

coat of mail, *pl.* **coats of mail.** a defensive garment made of interlinked metal rings, overlapping metal plates, etc.

coax (kōks), *v.t., v.i.* **1.** to influence by gentle persuasion, flattery, etc. **2.** to get or win by coaxing. —**coax′er,** *n.* —**coax′ing·ly,** *adv.*

co·ax·i·al (kō ăk′sǐ əl), *adj.* having a common axis or coincident axes. Also, **co·ax·al** (kō ăk′səl).

cob (kŏb), *n.* **1.** *U.S.* a corncob. **2.** a male swan. **3.** a short-legged, thick-set horse.

co·balt (kō′bôlt), *n. Chem.* a silver-white metallic element with a faint pinkish tinge. *Symbol:* Co; *at. wt.:* 58.94; *at. no.:* 27; *sp. gr.:* 8.9 at 20°C.

co·bal·tic (kō bôl′tǐk), *adj. Chem.* of or containing cobalt, esp. in the trivalent state (Co^{+3}).

co·bal·tous (kō bôl′təs), *adj. Chem.* containing divalent cobalt (Co^{+2}).

cob·ble (kŏb′əl), *n., v.,* **-bled, -bling.** —*n.* **1.** a cobblestone. —*v.t.* **2.** to mend (shoes, etc.).

cob·bler (kŏb′lər), *n.* **1.** one who mends shoes. **2.** *U.S.* a deep-dish fruit pie.

cob·ble·stone (kŏb′əl stōn′), *n.* a natural rounded stone, large enough for use in paving.

co·bra (kō′brə), *n.* any of certain snakes exceedingly venomous and characterized by the ability to dilate its neck so that it assumes a hoodlike form.

cob·web (kŏb′wĕb′), *n.* **1.** a web spun by a spider to catch its prey. **2.** anything flimsy or entangling.

co·ca (kō′kə), *n.* either of two shrubs, native in the Andes and cultivated in Java and elsewhere, whose dried leaves yield cocaine.

co·caine (kō kān′, kō′kān), *n.* a bitter crystalline alkaloid obtained from coca leaves, used as a local anesthetic. Also, **co·cain′.**

coc·cyx (kŏk′sǐks), *n., pl.* **coccyges** (kŏk sī′jēz). a small triangular bone forming the lower extremity of the spinal column in man.

coch·i·neal (kŏch′ə nēl′, kŏch′ə nēl′), *n.* a red dye prepared from the dried bodies of females of a scale insect of Mexico, Central America, etc.

coch·le·a (kŏk′lǐ ə), *n., pl.* **-leae** (-lǐ ē′). a division, spiral in form, of the internal ear, in man and most other mammals. —**coch′le·ar,** *adj.*

cock[1] (kŏk), *n.* **1.** a rooster. **2.** the male of any bird. **3.** a weathercock. **4.** a leader; chief person. **5.** a faucet, tap, or stop valve. **6.** (in a firearm) **a.** that part of the lock which causes the discharge. **b.** the position into which this part is brought, preparatory to firing. —*v.t.* **7.** to set the cock of (a firearm) preparatory to firing. —*v.i.* **8.** to cock the firing mechanism of a gun.

cock[2] (kŏk), *v.t.* to set or turn up or to one side, often in a jaunty manner.

cock[3] (kŏk), *n.* **1.** a conical pile of hay, etc. —*v.t.* **2.** to pile (hay, etc.) in such piles.

cock·ade (kŏ kād′), *n.* a knot of ribbon, etc., worn on the hat as a badge or a part of a uniform. —**cock·ad′ed,** *adj.*

Cock·aigne (kŏ kān′), *n.* a fabulous land of luxury and idleness.

cock·a·too (kŏk′ə too′), *n.* any of the colorful crested parrots of the East Indies, Australia, etc.

cock·a·trice (kŏk′ə trǐs), *n.* a fabulous serpent with deadly glance, commonly represented with the head, legs, and wings of a cock and the body and tail of a serpent.

cock·boat (kŏk′bōt′), *n.* a small boat.

cock·crow (kŏk′krō′), *n.* dawn.

cocked hat (kŏkt), a hat having the brim turned up on two or three sides.

cock·er·el (kŏk′ər əl, kŏk′rəl), *n.* a young domestic cock.

cock·er spaniel (kŏk′ər), one of a breed of small spaniels trained for use in hunting or kept as pets. Also, **cocker.**

cock·eyed (kŏk′īd′), *adj.* **1.** having a squinting eye; cross-eyed. **2.** *Slang.* twisted or slanted to one side. **3.** *Slang.* foolish; absurd.

cock·horse (kŏk′hôrs′), *n.* a child's rocking horse or hobbyhorse.

cock·le (kŏk′əl), *n.*, *v.*, **-led, -ling.** —*n.* **1.** any of certain bivalve mollusks with somewhat heart-shaped, radially ribbed valves. **2.** cockleshell. **3.** the inmost parts or depths (of the heart). **4.** a small shallow or light boat. —*v.i.*, *v.t.* **5.** to wrinkle or pucker.

cock·le·bur (kŏk′əl bûr′), *n.* any of certain coarse weeds with spiny burs.

cock·le·shell (kŏk′əl shĕl′), *n.* **1.** a shell, esp. of the cockle. **2.** a small, light boat.

cock·ney (kŏk′nĭ), *n.*, *pl.* **-neys,** *adj.* ♦—*n.* (*often cap.*) **1.** a native or resident of London, especially those of the East End who have marked peculiarities of pronunciation and dialect. **2.** their pronunciation or dialect. —*adj.* **3.** of cockneys or their dialect.

cock·pit (kŏk′pĭt′), *n.* **1.** (in some airplanes) an enclosed space for the pilot and copilot. **2.** a low recess aft in the deck of a boat. **3.** a pit for fights between cocks.

cock·roach (kŏk′rōch′), *n.* any of various orthopterous insects, usually nocturnal, that have a flattened body, esp. the pale, yellowish-brown one that is a common household pest.

cocks·comb (kŏks′kōm′), *n.* **1.** the comb of a cock. **2.** a garden plant of the amaranth family with flowers, commonly crimson or purple, in a broad spike. **3.** a coxcomb.

cock·sure (kŏk′shŏŏr′), *adj.* **1.** perfectly certain. **2.** overconfident.

cock·tail (kŏk′tāl′), *n.* **1.** any of various short drinks, consisting typically of gin, whiskey, or brandy mixed with vermouth, fruit juices, etc. **2.** a portion of oysters, clams, etc., served in a small glass with a sauce. **3.** a mixture of fruits served in a glass.

cock·y (kŏk′ĭ), *adj.*, **cockier, cockiest.** *Colloq.* arrogantly smart. —**cock′i·ness,** *n.*

co·co (kō′kō), *n.*, *pl.* **-cos. 1.** a tall, slender tropical palm which produces the coconut. **2.** the coconut fruit or seed.

co·coa (kō′kō), *n.* **1.** the roasted, husked, and ground seeds of the cacao from which much of the fat has been removed. **2.** a beverage made from cocoa powder. **3.** brown. —*adj.* **4.** of or pertaining to cocoa.

co·co·nut (kō′kə nŭt′, -nət), *n.* the seed of the coco palm, hard-shelled, lined with a white edible pulp, and containing a milky liquid.

co·coon (kə kōōn′), *n.* the silky envelope spun by the larva of many insects, as silkworms, as a covering while they are in the pupal state.

cod (kŏd), *n.*, *pl.* **cods,** (*esp. collectively*) **cod.** one of the most important North Atlantic food fishes.

Cod (kŏd), *n.* **Cape,** a sandy peninsula in SE Massachusetts in the Atlantic.

C.O.D., *U.S.* collect on delivery. Also, **c.o.d.**

cod·dle (kŏd′əl), *v.t.*, **-dled, -dling. 1.** to boil gently. **2.** to pamper.

code (kōd), *n.*, *v.*, **coded, coding.** —*n.* **1.** any systematic collection or digest of laws, as of a country. **2.** any system of rules. **3.** a system of signals for communication by telegraph, etc. **4.** a system of arbitrarily chosen words, etc., used for brevity or secrecy. —*v.t.* **5.** to arrange or enter in a code.

co·deine (kō′dēn), *n.* a white, crystalline alkaloid, obtained from opium, used as an analgesic, sedative, and hypnotic. Also, **co·de·in** (kō′dĭ ĭn).

co·dex (kō′dĕks), *n.*, *pl.* **codices** (kō′də sēz′, kŏd′ə-). a manuscript volume of the Scriptures, etc.

cod·fish (kŏd′fĭsh′), *n.*, *pl.* **-fishes,** (*esp. collectively*) **-fish. cod.**

codg·er (kŏj′ər), *n.* *Colloq.* an odd person.

cod·i·cil (kŏd′ə səl), *n.* **1.** a supplement to a will, containing an addition, explanation, etc., of something in the will. **2.** some similar supplement.

cod·i·fy (kŏd′ə fī′, kō′də-), *v.t.*, **-fied, -fying.** to arrange (laws, etc.) into a systematic collection. —**cod′i·fi·ca′tion,** *n.* —**cod′i·fi′er,** *n.*

cod·ling (kŏd′lĭng), *n.* an unripe apple. Also, **cod·lin** (kŏd′lĭn).

codling moth, a small moth whose larva feeds on apples, etc. Also, **codlin moth.**

cod-liv·er oil (kŏd′lĭv′ər), a fixed oil, extracted from the liver of the common cod or of allied species, used as a source of vitamins A and D.

co·ed (kō′ĕd′), *n.* *U.S. Colloq.* a female student in a coeducational institution. Also, **co′-ed′.**

co·ed·u·ca·tion (kō′ĕj ə kā′shən), *n.* joint education, esp. of both sexes in the same institution and classes. —**co′ed·u·ca′tion·al,** *adj.*

co·ef·fi·cient (kō′ə fĭsh′ənt), *n.* **1.** *Math.* a number placed before and multiplying another quantity. **2.** *Physics.* a quantity, constant for a given substance, body, or process under certain specified conditions, that serves as a measure of some one of its properties. —*adj.* **3.** coöperating.

coe·len·ter·ate (sĭ lĕn′tə rāt′, -tər ĭt), *n.* *Zool.* a member of a phylum of invertebrates that includes hydras, jellyfishes, corals, etc., and is characterized by a single internal cavity for digestion, excretion, etc.

co·e·qual (kō ē′kwəl), *adj.* **1.** equal in rank, ability, etc. —*n.* **2.** a coequal person or thing.

co·erce (kō ûrs′), *v.t.*, **-erced, -ercing. 1.** to restrain. **2.** to force or compel. —**co·er′ci·ble,** *adj.* —**co·er′cive,** *adj.*

co·er·cion (kō ûr′shən), *n.* **1.** act or power of coercing. **2.** government by force.

co·e·val (kō ē′vəl), *adj.* **1.** of the same age, date, or duration. **2.** contemporary.

co·ex·ist (kō′ĭg zĭst′), *v.i.* to exist together or at the same time. —**co′ex·ist′ent,** *adj.*

co·ex·tend (kō′ĭk stĕnd′), *v.t.*, *v.i.* to extend equally through the same space or duration. —**co′ex·ten′sion,** *n.* —**co′ex·ten′sive,** *adj.*

cof·fee (kôf′ĭ, kŏf′ĭ), *n.* **1.** a beverage, consisting of a decoction or infusion of the roasted and ground seeds (**coffee beans**) of the two-seeded fruit (**coffee berry**) of certain tropical trees and shrubs of the madder family. **2.** the berry or seed of such plants. **3.** the tree or shrub itself. **4.** dark brown.

cof·fer (kôf′ər, kŏf′ər), *n.* **1.** a chest, esp. one for valuables. **2.** (*pl.*) a treasury; funds. **3.** any of various boxlike enclosures.

cof·fin (kôf′ĭn, kŏf′ĭn), *n.* the box or case in which a corpse is placed for burial.

cog (kŏg), *n.* a tooth or projection on a wheel, etc., for transmitting motion to, or receiving motion from, a corresponding part.

co·gent (kō′jənt), *adj.* compelling belief; convincing. —**co′gen·cy,** *n.* —**co′gent·ly,** *adv.*

cog·i·tate (kŏj′ə tāt′), *v.*, **-tated, -tating.** —*v.i.* **1.** to ponder; meditate. —*v.t.* **2.** to think about. —**cog′i·ta′tion,** *n.* —**cog′i·ta′tive,** *adj.* —**cog′-i·ta′tor,** *n.*

co·gnac (kōn′yăk, kŏn′-), *n.* (*often cap.*) a French brandy.

cog·nate (kŏg′nāt), *adj.* **1.** of the same parentage, descent, origin, nature, etc. —*n.* **2.** a person or thing cognate with another.

cog·ni·tion (kŏg nĭsh′ən), *n.* **1.** act or process of knowing; perception. **2.** the product of such a process. —**cog·ni·tive** (kŏg′nə tĭv), *adj.*

cog·ni·zance (kŏg′nə zəns, kŏn′ə-), *n.* **1.** knowledge; notice; perception. **2.** *Law.* **a.** judicial notice. **b.** the right of taking judicial notice. **c.** admission. **3.** the scope of knowledge, etc.

cog·ni·zant (kŏg′nə zənt, kŏn′ə-), *adj.* having cognizance; aware (fol. by *of*).

cog·no·men (kŏg nō′mən), *n.* **1.** a surname. **2.** any name, esp. a nickname.

cog·wheel (kŏg′hwēl′), *n.* a wheel with cogs, for transmitting or receiving motion.

co·hab·it (kō hăb′ĭt), *v.i.* to live together as husband and wife. —**co·hab′i·ta′tion,** *n.*

co·here (kō hĭr′), *v.i.*, **-hered, -hering. 1.** to stick together; be united. **2.** to be connected.

Cogwheels

co·her·ence (kō hĭr′əns), *n.* **1.** act or state of cohering. **2.** logical connection. Also, **co·her′-en·cy.**

co·her·ent (kō hĭr′ənt), *adj.* **1.** sticking together. **2.** connected. **3.** logical. —**co·her′ent·ly,** *adv.*

co·he·sion (kō hē′zhən), *n.* **1.** act or state of uniting or sticking together. **2.** *Physics.* the state or process by which the particles of a body or substance are bound together.

co·he·sive (kō hē′sĭv), *adj.* cohering.

co·hort (kō′hôrt), *n.* **1.** one of the ten divisions in an ancient Roman legion. **2.** any group, esp. of warriors.

coif (koif), *n.* **1.** a hood-shaped cap worn under a veil, as by nuns. —*v.t.* **2.** to furnish with a coif.

coif·fure (kwä fyŏŏr′), *n.* **1.** a style of arranging or combing the hair. **2.** a headdress.

coign of vantage (koin), an advantageous position.

coil[1] (koil), *v.t., v.i.* **1.** to twist or wind spirally. —*n.* **2.** a connected series of spirals into which a rope or the like is wound. **3.** a single such ring. **4.** *Elect.* a conductor, as a copper wire, wound up in a spiral or other form.

coil[2] (koil), *n.* **1.** tumult. **2.** trouble.

coin (koin), *n.* **1.** a piece of metal stamped and issued by a government for use as money. **2.** such pieces collectively. **3.** *Archit.* **a.** a corner. **b.** a cornerstone. **c.** a wedge-shaped stone of an arch. —*v.t.* **4.** to make (money) by stamping metal. **5.** to convert (metal) into money. **6.** *Colloq.* to make (money) rapidly. **7.** to invent. —**coin′er,** *n.*

coin·age (koi′nĭj), *n.* **1.** act, process, or right of coining. **2.** that which is coined.

co·in·cide (kō′ĭn sīd′), *v.i.,* **-cided, -ciding. 1.** to occupy the same place, time, or position. **2.** to correspond exactly.

co·in·ci·dence (kō ĭn′sə dəns), *n.* **1.** condition or fact of coinciding. **2.** a striking occurrence of events at the same time apparently by chance.

co·in·ci·dent (kō ĭn′sə dənt), *adj.* coinciding in place, time, or position. —**co·in′ci·dent·ly,** *adv.*

co·in·ci·den·tal (kō ĭn′sə dĕn′təl), *adj.* showing coincidence. —**co·in′ci·den′tal·ly,** *adv.*

co·i·tion (kō ĭsh′ən), *n.* sexual intercourse. Also, **co·i·tus** (kō′ĭ təs).

coke (kōk), *n., v.,* **coked, coking.** —*n.* **1.** the solid carbon product resulting from the distillation of coal in an oven or closed chamber. —*v.t., v.i.* **2.** to convert into or become coke.

Col., 1. Colorado. **2.** Colonel. **3.** (*l.c.*) column.

co·la (kō′lə), *n.* kola.

col·an·der (kŭl′ən dər, kŏl′-), *n.* a strainer for draining off liquids, esp. in cookery.

cold (kōld), *adj.* **1.** having a temperature lower than the normal temperature of the body. **2.** having, producing, or feeling little or no warmth. **3.** dead. **4.** *U.S.* unconscious. **5.** deficient in emotion, ardor, etc. **6.** not cordial or friendly. **7.** failing to excite feeling or interest. **8.** imperturbable. **9.** depressing. **10.** faint; weak. **11.** *Art.* blue in effect. —*n.* **12.** the relative absence of heat. **13.** the sensation produced by loss of heat from the body. **14.** an indisposition caused by exposure to cold, characterized by catarrh, coughing, etc. —**cold′ish,** *adj.* —**cold′ly,** *adv.* —**cold′ness,** *n.*

cold-blood·ed (kōld′blŭd′ĭd), *adj.* **1.** without feeling; cruel. **2.** designating or pertaining to animals, as fishes and reptiles, whose blood temperature ranges from the freezing point upward. —**cold′-blood′ed·ly,** *adv.* —**cold′-blood′ed·ness,** *n.*

cold war, intense economic and political rivalry just short of military conflict.

cole (kōl), *n.* any of various plants of the same genus as cabbage, esp. rape. Also, **cole·wort** (kōl′wûrt′).

co·le·op·ter·ous (kō′lĭ ŏp′tər əs, kŏl′ĭ-), *adj.* belonging or pertaining to the order of insects including beetles.

Cole·ridge (kōl′rĭj), *n.* **Samuel Taylor,** 1772–1834, British poet, critic, and philosopher.

cole·slaw (kōl′slô′), *n. U.S.* a salad of finely sliced cabbage.

col·ic (kŏl′ĭk), *n.* **1.** paroxysmal pain in the abdomen or bowels. —*adj.* **2.** pertaining to or affecting the colon or bowels. —**col′ick·y,** *adj.*

col·i·se·um (kŏl′ə sē′əm), *n.* **1.** an amphitheater, stadium, large theater, etc. **2.** (*cap.*) Colosseum.

coll., 1. college. **2.** colloquial.

col·lab·o·rate (kə lăb′ə rāt′), *v.i.,* **-rated, -rating. 1.** to work, one with another. **2.** to coöperate treacherously. —**col·lab′o·ra′tion,** *n.* —**col·lab′o·ra′tor, col·lab′o·ra′tion·ist,** *n.*

col·lapse (kə lăps′), *v.,* **-lapsed, -lapsing,** *n.* —*v.i.* **1.** to fall or cave in. **2.** to be made so that parts can be folded, placed, etc., together. **3.** to fail. **4.** to lose strength, etc., suddenly. —*v.t.* **5.** to cause to collapse. —*n.* **6.** a falling in or together. **7.** a sudden, complete failure. —**col·laps′i·ble,** *adj.*

col·lar (kŏl′ər), *n.* **1.** anything worn around the neck. **2.** the part of a shirt, coat, etc., around the neck, usually folded over. **3.** a band put around an animal's neck to restrain or identify it. **4.** part of a harness around the horse's neck. —*v.t.* **5.** to put a collar on. **6.** to seize by the collar or neck.

col·lar·bone (kŏl′ər bōn′), *n.* clavicle.

col·late (kŏ lāt′, kə-, kŏl′āt), *v.t.,* **-lated, -lating. 1.** to compare (texts, etc.). **2.** *Bookbinding.* to verify the arrangment of (the gathered sheets of a book, etc.). —**col·la′tor,** *n.*

col·lat·er·al (kə lăt′ər əl), *adj.* **1.** situated at the side. **2.** running side by side. **3.** *Bot.* standing side by side. **4.** auxiliary. **5.** additional. **6.** secured by collateral. **7.** aside from the main subject, etc. **8.** descended from the same stock, but in a different line. —*n.* **9.** security pledged for the payment of a loan. **10.** a collateral kinsman. —**col·lat′er·al·ly,** *adv.*

col·la·tion (kŏ lā′shən, kə-), *n.* **1.** act of collating. **2.** description of the technical features of a book. **3.** a light meal.

col·league (kŏl′ēg), *n.* an associate in office, professional employment, etc.

col·lect[1] (kə lĕkt′), *v.t.* **1.** to gather together. **2.** to accumulate. **3.** to receive or compel payment of. **4.** to regain control of (one's faculties, etc., or oneself). —*v.i.* **5.** to gather together. **6.** to accumulate. —*adj., adv.* **7.** to be paid for on delivery. —**col·lect′a·ble, col·lect′i·ble,** *adj.* —**col·lec·tion** (kə lĕk′shən), *n.*

col·lect[2] (kŏl′ĕkt), *n.* any of certain brief prayers used in Western churches, as those before the epistle in the communion service.

col·lect·ed (kə lĕk′tĭd), *adj.* composed; self-possessed. —**col·lect′ed·ly,** *adv.* —**col·lect′ed·ness,** *n.*

col·lec·tive (kə lĕk′tĭv), *adj.* **1.** formed by collection. **2.** forming a collection; combined. **3.** pertaining to a group of individuals. —*n.* **4.** a collective noun. **5.** a collective body. **6.** a unit in a collectivist system. —**col·lec′tive·ly,** *adv.*

collective bargaining, the process by which wages, hours, rules, etc., are negotiated and agreed upon by a union with an employer for all the employees it represents.

collective noun, *Gram.* a noun that under the singular form expresses a grouping of individual objects or persons, as *herd, jury,* and *clergy.*

col·lec·tiv·ism (kə lĕk′tə vĭz′əm), *n.* the socialistic principle of control by the people collectively of all means of production, etc. —**col·lec′tiv·ist,** *n., adj.*

col·lec·tor (kə lĕk′tər), *n.* **1.** one that collects. **2.** a person employed to collect debts, taxes, etc. —**col·lec′tor·ship′,** *n.*

col·lege (kŏl′ĭj), *n.* **1.** an institution of higher learning, esp. one affording a general or liberal education. **2.** an institution for special instruction, as in medicine, agriculture, etc. **3.** the building or buildings occupied by a college. **4.** an organized association having certain powers, rights, duties, or pursuits.

col·le·gian (kə lē′jən, -jĭ ən), *n.* a student in, or a graduate of, a college.

col·le·giate (kə lē′jĭt, -jĭ ĭt), *adj.* **1.** of or pertaining to a college. **2.** of, for, or like college students.

col·lide (kə līd′), *v.i.,* **-lided, -liding. 1.** to come into violent contact; crash. **2.** to conflict.

col·lie (kŏl′ĭ), *n.* a dog of any of certain intelligent varieties much used for tending sheep.

col·lier (kŏl′yər), *n. Chiefly Brit.* **1.** a ship for carrying coal. **2.** a coal miner.

col·lier·y (kŏl′yə rĭ), *n., pl.* **-lieries.** a coal mine, including all buildings and equipment.

col·li·mate (kŏl′ə māt′), *v.t.,* **-mated, -mating. 1.** to make parallel. **2.** to adjust accurately the line of sight of (a telescope). —**col′li·ma′tion,** *n.*

col·li·sion (kə lĭzh′ən), *n.* **1.** act of colliding; crash. **2.** a clash; conflict.

col·lo·cate (kŏl′ō kāt′), *v.t.,* **-cated, -cating. 1.** to set together. **2.** to arrange in proper order. —**col′lo·ca′tion,** *n.*

col·loid (kŏl′oid), *n. Phys. Chem.* a gelatinous or other substance which when dissolved in a liquid will not diffuse readily through vegetable or animal membranes. —**col·loi·dal** (kə loi′dəl), *adj.*

colloq., 1. colloquial. **2.** colloquialism.

col·lo·qui·al (kə lō′kwĭ əl), *adj.* **1.** characteristic of or appropriate to ordinary conversation rather than formal speech or writing. **2.** conversational. —**col·lo′qui·al·ly,** *adv.*

col·lo·qui·al·ism (kə lō′kwĭ ə lĭz′əm), *n.* **1.** a colloquial expression. **2.** colloquial style or usage.

col·lo·quy (kŏl'ə kwĭ), n., pl. -quies. 1. a conversation. 2. a conference. —col'lo·quist, n.

col·lu·sion (kə lōō'zhən), n. secret agreement for a fraudulent purpose; conspiracy. —col·lu'sive, adj. —col·lu'sive·ly, adv.

Colo., Colorado.

co·logne (kə lōn'), n. a perfumed toilet water.

Co·logne (kə lōn'), n. a city in W Germany. 772,221.

Co·lom·bi·a (kə lŭm'bǐ ə), n. a republic in NW South America. 9,807,432 pop.; 439,828 sq. mi. Cap.: Bogotá. —Co·lom'bi·an, adj., n.

Co·lom·bo (kō lŏm'bō), n. a seaport in and the capital of Ceylon, on the W coast. 284,155.

co·lon¹ (kō'lən), n. a point of punctuation (:) marking off a main portion of a sentence, introducing a list, etc.

co·lon² (kō'lən), n., pl. -lons, -la (-lə). Anat. that portion of the large intestine from the caecum to the rectum. —co·lon·ic (kə lŏn'ĭk), adj.

Co·lón (kō lōn'), n. a seaport in Panama at the Atlantic end of the Panama Canal. 44,393.

colo·nel (kûr'nəl), n. an officer ranking in most armies below a brigadier general. —colo'nel·cy, colo'nel·ship', n.

co·lo·ni·al (kə lō'nǐ əl), adj. 1. of or pertaining to a colony or colonies. 2. pertaining to the thirteen British colonies which became the United States of America. 3. Ecol. forming a colony. —n. 4. an inhabitant of a colony.

col·o·nist (kŏl'ə nǐst), n. 1. an inhabitant of a colony. 2. a member of a colonizing expedition.

col·o·nize (kŏl'ə nīz'), v.t., v.i., -nized, -nizing. 1. to plant or establish a colony (in). 2. to form a colony (of). —col'o·ni·za'tion, n. —col'o·niz'er, n.

col·on·nade (kŏl'ə nād'), n. Archit. a series of columns set at regular intervals, usually supporting a roof, series of arches, etc. —col'on·nad'ed, adj.

col·o·ny (kŏl'ə nǐ), n., pl. -nies. 1. a group of people who leave their native country to form a settlement subject to the parent state. 2. the country colonized. 3. any people or territory separated from but subject to a ruling power. 4. any group of individuals of similar occupation, status, etc., usually living in a community of their own. 5. Ecol. a group of animals or plants living or growing together in close association.

col·o·phon (kŏl'ə fŏn', -fən), n. an inscription at the front or close of a book usually identifying the publisher.

col·or (kŭl'ər), n. 1. the evaluation by the visual sense of that quality of light which is basically determined by its spectral composition. 2. complexion. 3. a ruddy complexion. 4. racial complexion other than white. 5. a blush. 6. vivid quality, as of literary work. 7. details in description included for the sake of realism. 8. pigment; paint; dye. 9. any distinctive color, badge, etc., of identification. 10. (pl.) a. a flag, ensign, etc., as of a military body. b. U.S. Navy. the ceremony of hoisting the national flag at 8 A.M. and of lowering it at sunset. 11. outward appearance. —v.t. 12. to give or apply color to. 13. to cause to appear different from the reality. 14. to give a special character or quality to. —v.i. 15. to take on or change color. —col'or·er, n. —col'or·less, adj.

col·or·a·ble (kŭl'ər ə bəl), adj. 1. capable of being colored. 2. specious. 3. deceptive.

Col·o·rad·o (kŏl'ə răd'ō, -rä'dō), n. 1. a State in the W United States. 1,137,581 pop.; 104,247 sq. mi. Cap.: Denver. Abbr.: Colo. 2. a river from N Colorado to the Gulf of California. 1360 mi. —Col'o·rad'an, adj., n.

Colorado Springs, a city in central Colorado. 36,789.

col·or·a·tion (kŭl'ə rā'shən), n. coloring.

col·o·ra·tu·ra (kŭl'ə rə tyŏŏr'ə, -tŏŏr'ə), n. 1. runs, trills, etc., in vocal music. 2. a lyric soprano who specializes in such music.

color blindness, defective color perception. —col'or-blind', adj.

col·ored (kŭl'ərd), adj. 1. having color. 2. belonging to some other race than the white. 3. pertaining to the Negro race. 4. biased.

col·or·ful (kŭl'ər fəl), adj. 1. full of color. 2. richly picturesque. —col'or·ful·ly, adv.

col·or·ing (kŭl'ər ĭng), n. 1. act or method of applying color. 2. appearance as to color. 3. specious appearance.

co·los·sal (kə lŏs'əl), adj. gigantic; vast.

Col·os·se·um (kŏl'ə sē'əm), n. 1. an amphitheater in Rome, the greatest in antiquity, begun by Vespasian. 2. (l.c.) coliseum.

Co·los·sian (kə lŏsh'ən), n. 1. an inhabitant of Colossae, an ancient city of Phrygia. 2. (pl.) the book of the New Testament called The Epistle of Paul the Apostle to the Colossians.

co·los·sus (kə lŏs'əs), n., pl. -lossi (-lŏs'ī), -lossuses. 1. (cap.) the legendary bronze statue of Apollo at Rhodes. 2. anything colossal or gigantic.

col·our (kŭl'ər), n., v.t., v.i. Brit. color.

colt (kōlt), n. a young horse, esp. a male.

col·ter (kōl'tər), n. a sharp blade attached to the beam of a plow, used to cut the ground.

Co·lum·bi·a (kə lŭm'bǐ ə), n. 1. the capital of South Carolina, in the central part, 62,396. 2. a river flowing from SE British Columbia through Washington and Oregon into the Pacific. 1214 mi. 3. the United States. —Co·lum'bi·an, adj., n.

col·um·bine (kŏl'əm bīn'), n. any of certain erect branching herbs of the crowfoot family having handsome, colorful flowers.

co·lum·bi·um (kə lŭm'bǐ əm), n. Chem. a steel-gray metallic element; niobium. Symbol: Cb (or Nb); at. wt.: 92.91; at. no.: 41; sp. gr.: 8.4 at 20°C.

Co·lum·bus (kə lŭm'bəs), n. 1. Christopher, 1446?–1506, Italian navigator in Spanish service: discoverer of America, 1492. 2. the capital of Ohio, in the central part. 306,087. 3. a city in W Georgia. 53,208.

Columbus Day, a holiday, Oct. 12, in honor of the discovery of America.

col·umn (kŏl'əm), n. 1. Archit. an upright shaft, usually serving as a support; pillar. 2. any columnlike object, mass, or formation. 3. one of the vertical rows of printed matter of a page. 4. a regular contribution to a newspaper, usually signed, and consisting of comment, news, or feature material. 5. a line of ships or troops following one after another. —co·lum·nar (kə lŭm'nər), adj. —col·umned (kŏl'əmd), adj.

col·umn·ist (kŏl'əm ĭst, -əm nĭst), n. the editor or conductor of a special column in a newspaper.

Com., 1. Commander. 2. (l.c.) commerce.

co·ma¹ (kō'mə), n., pl. -mas. a state of prolonged unconsciousness, due to disease, etc.

co·ma² (kō'mə), n., pl. -mae (-mē). Astron. the nebulous envelope around the nucleus of a comet.

Co·man·che (kō măn'chĭ), n., pl. -ches. a member of an Indian tribe, formerly ranging from Wyoming to Texas.

comb (kōm), n. 1. a toothed piece of bone, metal, etc., for arranging the hair. 2. a card for dressing wool, etc. 3. the fleshy, serrated growth on the head of the domestic fowl. 4. the crest of a wave. —v.t. 5. to dress (the hair, wool, etc.) with a comb. 6. to search everywhere in.

com·bat (v., n. kŏm'băt, kŭm'-; v. also kəm-băt'), v., -bated, -bating or (esp. Brit.) -batted, -batting, n. —v.t., v.i. 1. to fight; battle. —n. 2. a fight between two men, armies, etc.

com·bat·ant (kŏm'bə tənt, kŭm'-), n. 1. a person or group that fights. —adj. 2. fighting.

com·ba·tive (kŏm'bə tĭv, kŭm'-, kəm băt'ĭv), adj. ready or inclined to fight.

comb·er (kō'mər), n. 1. one who or that which combs. 2. a long, curling wave.

com·bi·na·tion (kŏm'bə nā'shən), n. 1. act of combining. 2. state of being combined. 3. a number of things combined. 4. something formed by combining. 5. an alliance of persons or parties. 6. the set of numbers or letters dialed to operate a certain type of lock (combination lock) used on safes, etc. 7. a suit of underwear in one piece.

com·bine (v. kəm bīn'; n. kŏm'bīn, kəm bīn' for 6, kŏm'bīn for 7), v., -bined, -bining. —v.t. 1. to unite; coalesce. 2. to possess or exhibit in union. —v.i. 3. to unite; coalesce. 4. to join forces. 5. to enter into chemical union. —n. 6. a combination. 7. U.S. a machine for cutting and threshing ripe standing grain and seed. —com·bin'a·ble, adj. —com·bin'er, n.

com·bus·ti·ble (kəm bŭs'tə bəl), adj. 1. inflammable. 2. easily excited. —n. 3. a combustible substance.

com·bus·tion (kəm bŭs'chən), n. 1. act or process of burning. 2. Chem. oxidation.

come (kŭm), v.i., came, come, coming. 1. to approach or arrive, as in time, succession, place, etc. 2. to appear. 3. to extend; reach. 4. to take place; happen. 5. to be available, produced, etc. **6.** to occur to the mind. **7.** to issue; emanate. **8.** to be the result. **9.** to enter into a specified state. **10.** to be born. **11.** to become. **12.** to turn out to be. **13. come across, a.** to meet with. **b.** *Colloq.* to pay or give. **14. come out, a.** to be published. **b.** to be revealed. **c.** to make a debut. **d.** to reach the end. —**com'-er,** *n.*

come·back (kŭm'băk'), *n.* **1.** *Colloq.* a return to a former position, etc. **2.** *Slang.* a retort.

co·me·di·an (kə mē'dĭ ən), *n.* **1.** an actor in comedy. **2.** a writer of comedy. **3.** a comic person.

co·me·di·enne (kə mē'dĭ ĕn'), *n.* an actress in comedy.

come·down (kŭm'doun'), *n.* *Colloq.* a humiliating descent from dignity, etc.

com·e·dy (kŏm'ə dĭ), *n., pl.* **-dies. 1.** a play, movie, etc., of light and humorous character. **2.** any comic or humorous incident or series of incidents.

come·ly (kŭm'lĭ), *adj.,* **-lier, -liest. 1.** pleasing in appearance. **2.** proper. —**come'li·ness,** *n.*

co·mes·ti·ble (kə mĕs'tə bəl), *adj.* edible.

com·et (kŏm'ĭt), *n.* a celestial body moving about the sun in an elongated orbit, usually a central mass surrounded by a misty envelope which extends into a stream away from the sun.

com·fit (kŭm'fĭt, kŭm'-), *n.* a bonbon.

com·fort (kŭm'fərt), *v.t.* **1.** to console; cheer. —*n.* **2.** consolation; solace. **3.** a person or thing that affords consolation. **4.** a state of complete physical and mental ease. —**com'fort·ing·ly,** *adv.* —**com'fort·less,** *adj.*

com·fort·a·ble (kŭmf'tə bəl, kŭm'fər tə bəl), *adj.* **1.** giving comfort. **2.** being in a state of comfort. **3.** adequate. —**com'fort·a·bly,** *adv.*

com·fort·er (kŭm'fər tər), *n.* **1.** one that comforts. **2.** *U.S.* a quilted bedcover.

com·ic (kŏm'ĭk), *adj.* **1.** of or pertaining to comedy. **2.** humorous; funny. —*n.* **3.** a comic actor. **4.** *Colloq.* a comic periodical. **5.** (*pl.*) *Colloq.* the comic strips.

com·i·cal (kŏm'ə kəl), *adj.* provoking laughter; funny. —**com'i·cal·ly,** *adv.*

comic strip, a series of several drawings relating a comic incident, an adventure story, etc.

Com·in·form (kŏm'ĭn fôrm'), *n.* an organization established in 1947 by the Communist parties of nine European countries for mutual advice and coördinated activity.

com·ing (kŭm'ĭng), *n.* **1.** approach. —*adj.* **2.** approaching. **3.** on the way to success.

Com·in·tern (kŏm'ĭn tûrn', kŏm'ĭn tûrn'), *n.* the Third Communist International, dissolved 1943.

com·i·ty (kŏm'ə tĭ), *n., pl.* **-ties.** courtesy; civility.

Comm., 1. commission. **2.** committee.

com·ma (kŏm'ə), *n.* a mark of punctuation (;) used to indicate the smallest interruptions in continuity of thought or grammatical construction.

com·mand (kə mănd', -mänd'), *v.t.* **1.** to order with authority. **2.** to demand. **3.** to be in control over. **4.** to overlook. **5.** to deserve and get (respect, etc.). —*v.i.* **6.** to issue commands. **7.** to occupy a dominating position. —*n.* **8.** act of ordering. **9.** an order given by a commander. **10.** a body of troops, etc., under a commander. **11.** control. —**com·mand'ing·ly,** *adv.*

com·man·dant (kŏm'ən dănt', -dänt'), *n.* the commanding officer of a place, etc.

com·man·deer (kŏm'ən dĭr'), *v.t.* **1.** to order into military service. **2.** to seize (property) for military use. **3.** *Colloq.* to seize arbitrarily.

com·mand·er (kə mǎn'dər, -mǎn'-), *n.* **1.** one who commands. **2.** a chief officer. **3.** *U.S. Navy.* an officer ranking just below a captain.

commander in chief, *pl.* **commanders in chief.** (*sometimes caps.*) the supreme commander of the armed forces of a nation.

com·mand·ment (kə mănd'mənt, -mänd'-), *n.* **1.** a command. **2.** any one of the precepts of God (the Ten Commandments).

com·man·do (kə mǎn'dō, -mǎn'-), *n., pl.* **-dos, -does.** (in World War II) **1.** a military unit for organized raids against Axis forces. **2.** *Chiefly U.S.* a member of this unit.

com·mem·o·rate (kə mĕm'ə rāt'), *v.t.,* **-rated, -rating. 1.** to serve as a memento of. **2.** to honor the memory of. —**com·mem'o·ra'tion,** *n.* —**com·mem·o·ra·tive** (kə mĕm'ə rā'tĭv, -rə tĭv), *adj.*

com·mence (kə mĕns'), *v.i., v.t.,* **-menced, -mencing.** to begin; start. —**com·menc'er,** *n.*

com·mence·ment (kə mĕns'mənt), *n.* **1.** beginning. **2.** (in colleges, etc.) the awarding of degrees or diplomas at the end of the academic year. **3.** the day on which this takes place.

com·mend (kə mĕnd'), *v.t.* **1.** to mention as worthy of confidence, notice, etc. **2.** to entrust. —**com·mend'a·ble,** *adj.* —**com·mend'a·bly,** *adv.*

com·men·da·tion (kŏm'ən dā'shən), *n.* **1.** act of commending. **2.** something that commends.

com·mend·a·to·ry (kə mĕn'də tôr'ĭ), *adj.* serving to commend; approving; praising.

com·men·su·rate (kə mĕn'shə rĭt, -sə-), *adj.* **1.** of equal extent or duration. **2.** corresponding in amount, magnitude, or degree. —**com·men'su·rate·ly,** *adv.*

com·ment (kŏm'ĕnt), *n.* **1.** a note in explanation, expansion, or criticism of a passage in a writing, book, etc. **2.** a remark, observation, or criticism. —*v.i.* **3.** to write notes upon a text. **4.** to make remarks. —*v.t.* **5.** to annotate.

com·men·tar·y (kŏm'ən tĕr'ĭ), *n., pl.* **-taries. 1.** a series of comments. **2.** an explanatory essay or treatise.

com·men·ta·tor (kŏm'ən tā'tər), *n.* a person who discusses news events, etc.

com·merce (kŏm'ərs), *n.* **1.** interchange of commodities, as between different countries or different parts of the same country. **2.** social relations.

com·mer·cial (kə mûr'shəl), *adj.* **1.** of or engaged in commerce. **2.** prepared merely for sale. —*n.* **3.** *Radio.* a commercial announcement or program. —**com·mer'cial·ly,** *adv.*

com·mer·cial·ism (kə mûr'shə lĭz'əm), *n.* the principles, methods, and practices of commerce.

com·mer·cial·ize (kə mûr'shə līz'), *v.t.,* **-ized, -izing.** to make commercial in character. —**com·mer'cial·i·za'tion,** *n.*

com·min·gle (kə mĭng'gəl), *v.t., v.i.,* **-gled, -gling.** to mingle together; blend.

com·mis·er·ate (kə mĭz'ə rāt'), *v.t.,* **-ated, -ating.** to feel or express sympathy for. —**com·mis'er·a'tion,** *n.*

com·mis·sar (kŏm'ə sär'), *n.* head of a government department in the U.S.S.R.

com·mis·sar·i·at (kŏm'ə sär'ĭ ət), *n.* **1.** the supply department of an army. **2.** any of the governmental divisions of the U.S.S.R.

com·mis·sar·y (kŏm'ə sĕr'ĭ), *n., pl.* **-saries. 1.** a store that supplies food and equipment, as in an army. **2.** *Mil.* an officer of the commissariat. **3.** one to whom some charge is delegated.

com·mis·sion (kə mĭsh'ən), *n.* **1.** act of committing. **2.** an authoritative order. **3.** authority granted for a particular action. **4.** a document granting authority. **5.** a body of persons charged with particular functions. **6.** the condition of being placed under special charge. **7.** the condition of anything in active service or use. **8.** a matter committed to one's charge. **9.** authority to act as agent for another or others. **10.** the perpetrating of a crime, etc. **11.** that which is committed. **12.** a sum allowed to an agent for his services. **13.** the position of an officer in the army or navy. —*v.t.* **14.** to give a commission to. **15.** to authorize. **16.** to put (a ship, etc.) into active service. **17.** to give an order for.

com·mis·sion·er (kə mĭsh'ən ər), *n.* **1.** one commissioned to act officially. **2.** a government official in charge of a department.

com·mit (kə mĭt'), *v.t.,* **-mitted, -mitting. 1.** to give in trust or charge; consign. **2.** to consign to custody. **3.** to hand over for treatment, disposal, etc. **4.** *Parl. Proc.* to refer (a bill, etc.) to a committee for consideration. **5.** to do; perpetrate. **6.** to pledge. —**com·mit'ta·ble,** *adj.*

com·mit·ment (kə mĭt'mənt), *n.* **1.** act of committing. **2.** state of being committed. **3.** consignment, as to prison. **4.** perpetration, as of a crime. Also, **com·mit'tal** for defs. 1, 3, 4.

com·mit·tee (kə mĭt'ĭ), *n.* a person or a group of persons elected or appointed to investigate, report, or act in special cases.

com·mode (kə mōd'), *n.* **1.** a piece of furniture containing drawers. **2.** a stand containing a chamber pot or washbasin.

com·mo·di·ous (kə mō'dĭ əs), *adj.* roomy; spacious. —**com·mo'di·ous·ly,** *adv.*

com·mod·i·ty (kə mŏd'ə tĭ), *n., pl.* **-ties. 1.** a thing that is of use. **2.** an article of commerce.

com·mo·dore (kŏm'ə dôr'), *n.* **1.** *U.S.* an officer of a rank next below that of rear admiral. **2.** the head of a yacht club.

com·mon (kŏm'ən), *adj.* **1.** belonging equally to, or shared alike by, two or more or all in question. **2.** joint; united. **3.** public. **4.** generally known; notorious. **5.** general; ordinary. **6.** of frequent occurrence; usual. **7.** trite. **8.** inferior. **9.** coarse; vulgar. **10.** ordinary. —*n.* **11.** a tract of land owned or used by all members of a community. **12. in common**, jointly. —**com'·mon·ly**, *adv.* —**com'mon·ness**, *n.*

com·mon·er (kŏm'ən ər), *n.* one of the common people.

common law, the unwritten law, based on custom or court decision.

common noun, *Gram.* a noun that can be preceded by a limiting modifier, in meaning applicable to any one or all of the members of a class, as *man, city*, in contrast to *Lincoln, New York.*

com·mon·place (kŏm'ən plās'), *adj.* **1.** ordinary; uninteresting. **2.** trite. —*n.* **3.** a trite saying. **4.** anything common. —**com'mon·place·ness**, *n.*

com·mons (kŏm'ənz), *n.pl.* **1.** the common people. **2.** (*cap.*) the elective house of the Parliament of Great Britain and Northern Ireland, Canada, and some of the other Dominions. **3.** food or provisions. **4.** a large dining room, esp. at a university.

com·mon·weal (kŏm'ən wēl'), *n.* the public welfare. Also, **common weal.**

com·mon·wealth (kŏm'ən wĕlth'), *n.* **1.** the whole body of people of a nation or state. **2.** a democratic state.

com·mo·tion (kə mō'shən), *n.* **1.** violent or tumultuous agitation. **2.** sedition; insurrection.

com·mu·nal (kŏm'yə nəl, kə mū'nəl), *adj.* **1.** pertaining to a community. **2.** of or belonging to the people of a community. —**com'mu·nal·ly**, *adv.*

com·mune¹ (*v.* kə mūn'; *n.* kŏm'ūn), *v.,* -**muned**, -**muning**, *n.* —*v.i.* **1.** to talk together. —*n.* **2.** friendly conversation.

com·mune² (kə mūn'), *v.i.,* -**muned**, -**muning**. to partake of the Eucharist.

com·mune³ (kŏm'ūn), *n.* the smallest administrative division in France, Italy, Switzerland, etc.

com·mu·ni·ca·ble (kə mū'nə kə bəl), *adj.* capable of being communicated.

com·mu·ni·cant (kə mū'nə kənt), *n.* **1.** one who partakes, or is entitled to partake, of the Eucharist. **2.** one who communicates.

com·mu·ni·cate (kə mū'nə kāt'), *v.,* -**cated**, -**cating**. —*v.t.* **1.** to impart; transmit. **2.** to make known. —*v.i.* **3.** to interchange thoughts, impart information, etc. **4.** to have or form a connecting passage. **5.** to partake of the Eucharist. —**com·mu'ni·ca'tor**, *n.*

com·mu·ni·ca·tion (kə mū'nə kā'shən), *n.* **1.** act or fact of communicating. **2.** that which is communicated or imparted. **3.** a message imparting views, information, etc. **4.** passage between places. **5.** (*pl.*) the means of sending messages, orders, etc.

com·mu·ni·ca·tive (kə mū'nə kā'tĭv), *adj.* **1.** inclined to communicate. **2.** talkative. **3.** of or pertaining to communication.

com·mun·ion (kə mūn'yən), *n.* **1.** act of sharing; participation. **2.** state of things so held. **3.** fellowship. **4.** communication. **5.** *Eccles.* **a.** a body of persons of one faith. **b.** reception of the Eucharist. **c.** the Eucharist.

com·mu·ni·qué (kə mū'nə kā', kə mū'nə kā'), *n.* an official bulletin or communication.

com·mu·nism (kŏm'yə nĭz'əm), *n.* a system of social organization based on the holding of all property in common, actual ownership being ascribed to the community as a whole or to the state.

com·mu·nist (kŏm'yə nĭst), *n.* **1.** an advocate of communism. **2.** (*often cap.*) a person who belongs to a political party advocating communism. —*adj.* **3.** pertaining to communists or communism. —**com'mu·nis'tic, com'mu·nis'ti·cal**, *adj.*

com·mu·ni·ty (kə mū'nə tĭ), *n., pl.* -**ties**. **1.** a social group whose members reside in a specific locality, share government, and have a cultural and historical heritage. **2.** the public. **3.** *Ecol.* a group of organisms, both plant and animal, living together in an ecologically related fashion. **4.** joint possession, enjoyment, liability, etc. **5.** identity.

com·mu·ta·tion (kŏm'yə tā'shən), *n.* **1.** act of substituting one thing for another. **2.** *U.S.* regu-

lar travel between home (usually distant) and work. **3.** the lessening of a penalty, etc.

commutation ticket, *U.S.* a ticket issued at a reduced rate, as by a railroad company, valid for a specified number of trips.

com·mu·ta·tor (kŏm'yə tā'tər), *n. Elect.* a device for reversing the direction of a current.

com·mute (kə mūt'), *v.,* -**muted**, -**muting**. —*v.t.* **1.** to exchange for something else. **2.** to change (a penalty, etc.) for one less severe. —*v.i.* **3.** *U.S.* to travel regularly between home (usually distant) and work. —**com·mut'er**, *n.*

comp., **1.** compare. **2.** compiled.

com·pact¹ (*adj., v.* kəm păkt'; *n.* kŏm'păkt), *adj.* **1.** joined or packed together; dense. **2.** pithy; terse. **3.** composed. —*v.t.* **4.** to join or pack closely together. **5.** to make by close union or conjunction. —*n.* **6.** a small case containing a mirror, face powder, a puff, and (sometimes) rouge. —**com·pact'ly**, *adv.* —**com·pact'ness**, *n.*

com·pact² (kŏm'păkt), *n.* an agreement between parties; a covenant; a contract.

com·pan·ion (kəm păn'yən), *n.* **1.** one who accompanies or associates with another. **2.** a person employed to assist another. **3.** a mate or match for a thing. **4.** a handbook. —*v.t.* **5.** to be a companion to. —**com·pan'ion·less**, *adj.* —**com·pan'ion·ship'**, *n.*

com·pan·ion·a·ble (kəm păn'yən ə bəl), *adj.* sociable. —**com·pan'ion·a·bly**, *adv.*

com·pan·ion·ate (kəm păn'yən ĭt), *adj.* of, by, or like companions.

com·pan·ion·way (kəm păn'yən wā'), *n. Naut.* the steps from the deck down to a cabin.

com·pa·ny (kŭm'pə nĭ), *n., pl.* -**nies**, *v.,* -**nied**, -**nying**. —*n.* **1.** a number of individuals assembled or associated together, as for social purposes. **2.** companionship. **3.** a guest or guests. **4.** a number of persons united for joint action, esp. for business. **5.** *Mil.* a subdivision of a regiment or battalion. **6.** *Naut.* a ship's crew, including the officers. —*v.i.* **7.** to associate.

compar., comparative.

com·pa·ra·ble (kŏm'pə rə bəl), *adj.* **1.** capable of being compared. **2.** worthy of comparison. —**com'pa·ra·ble·ness**, *n.* —**com'pa·ra·bly**, *adv.*

com·par·a·tive (kəm păr'ə tĭv), *adj.* **1.** of or pertaining to comparison. **2.** proceeding by or founded on comparison. **3.** estimated by comparison; relative. **4.** *Gram.* denoting the intermediate degree of the comparison of adjectives and adverbs. —*n.* **5.** *Gram.* **a.** the comparative degree. **b.** a form in it, as English *lower* in contrast to *low* and *lowest.* —**com·par'a·tive·ly**, *adv.*

com·pare (kəm pâr'), *v.,* -**pared**, -**paring**, *n.* —*v.t.* **1.** to represent as similar. **2.** to note the similarities and differences of. **3.** *Gram.* to form the degrees of comparison of. —*v.i.* **4.** to bear comparison. —*n.* **5.** comparison. —**com·par'er**, *n.*

com·par·i·son (kəm păr'ə sən), *n.* **1.** act of comparing. **2.** state of being compared. **3.** a comparative estimate. **4.** *Gram.* that function of an adverb or adjective used to indicate degrees of superiority or inferiority in quality, quantity, or intensity, as in *mild, milder, mildest.*

com·part·ment (kəm pärt'mənt), *n.* a separate room, section, space, etc.

com·pass (kŭm'pəs), *n.* **1.** an instrument for determining directions, consisting of a needle indicating magnetic north. **2.** extent; range; scope. **3.** (*usually pl.*) an instrument for describing circles, etc., consisting generally of two movable legs hinged at one end. —*v.t.* **4.** to go or move round. **5.** to encircle. **6.** to accomplish. —**com'pass·a·ble**, *adj.*

com·pas·sion (kəm păsh'ən), *n.* **1.** a feeling of sorrow or pity for the sufferings or misfortunes of another. —*v.t.* **2.** to pity.

com·pas·sion·ate (*adj.* kəm păsh'ən ĭt; *v.* kəm·păsh'ə nāt'), *adj., v.,* -**ated**, -**ating**. —*adj.* **1.** having or showing compassion. —*v.t.* **2.** to pity. —**com·pas'sion·ate·ly**, *adv.* —**com·pas'sion·ate·ness**, *n.*

com·pat·i·ble (kəm păt'ə bəl), *adj.* capable of existing together in harmony. —**com·pat'i·bil'i·ty**, *n.* —**com·pat'i·bly**, *adv.*

com·pa·tri·ot (kəm pā'trĭ ət), *n.* a fellow countryman or countrywoman.

com·peer (kəm pîr', kŏm'pîr), *n.* an equal; comrade.

com·pel (kəm pĕl'), *v.t.,* -**pelled**, -**pelling**. **1.** to force, esp. to a course of action. **2.** to secure or bring about by force. —**com·pel'ler**, *n.*

com·pen·di·ous (kəm pĕn′dĬ əs), *adj.* covering the subject briefly; concise. —**com·pen′di·ous·ly,** *adv.*

com·pen·di·um (kəm pĕn′dĬ əm), *n., pl.* **-di·ums, -dia** (-dĬ ə). a full summary of a subject.

com·pen·sate (kŏm′pən sāt′), *v.,* **-sated, -sat·ing.** —*v.t.* 1. to offset; make up for. 2. to recompense or pay. —*v.i.* 3. to make amends (fol. by *for*). —**com′pen·sa′tor,** *n.* —**com·pen·sa·to·ry** (kŏm pĕn′sə tōr′Ĭ), *adj.*

com·pen·sa·tion (kŏm′pən sā′shən), *n.* 1. act of compensating. 2. an equivalent for services, debt, loss, suffering, etc. 3. behavior which offsets some personal trait, such as inferiority.

com·pete (kəm pēt′), *v.i.,* **-peted, -peting.** to contend with another for a prize, profit, etc.

com·pe·tence (kŏm′pə təns), *n.* 1. adequate qualification or capacity. 2. sufficiency. 3. an income sufficient to furnish the necessities of life. Also, **com′pe·ten·cy.**

com·pe·tent (kŏm′pə tənt), *adj.* 1. fitting, suitable, or sufficient. 2. *Law.* having legal capacity or qualification. —**com′pe·tent·ly,** *adv.*

com·pe·ti·tion (kŏm′pə tĬsh′ən), *n.* 1. act of competing; rivalry. 2. a contest. 3. the rivalry between business enterprises.

com·pet·i·tive (kəm pĕt′ə tĬv), *adj.* of, pertaining to, involving, or decided by competition. —**com·pet′i·tive·ly,** *adv.* —**com·pet′i·tive·ness,** *n.*

com·pet·i·tor (kəm pĕt′ə tər), *n.* a rival.

com·pile (kəm pĬl′), *v.t.,* **-piled, -piling.** 1. to put together in one book or work. 2. to make (a book, etc.) from various sources. —**com·pi·la·tion** (kŏm′pə lā′shən), *n.* —**com·pil′er,** *n.*

com·pla·cen·cy (kəm plā′sən sĬ), *n., pl.* **-cies.** a feeling of quiet pleasure; satisfaction. Also, **com·pla′cence.**

com·pla·cent (kəm plā′sənt), *adj.* pleased, esp. with oneself; self-satisfied. —**com·pla′cent·ly,** *adv.*

com·plain (kəm plān′), *v.i.* 1. to express grief, pain, dissatisfaction, etc. 2. to tell of one's ailments, etc. 3. to state a grievance or accusation. —**com·plain′er,** *n.* —**com·plain′ing·ly,** *adv.*

com·plain·ant (kəm plā′nənt), *n.* one who makes a complaint, as in a legal action.

com·plaint (kəm plānt′), *n.* 1. an expression or cause of grief, regret, pain, etc. 2. *U.S. Law.* the first pleading of the plaintiff in a civil action.

com·plai·sant (kəm plā′zənt, kŏm′plə zănt′), *adj.* obliging; gracious. —**com·plai′sance,** *n.* —**com·plai′sant·ly,** *adv.*

com·ple·ment (*n.* kŏm′plə mənt; *v.* kŏm′plə·mĕnt′), *n.* 1. that which completes. 2. the quantity that completes anything. 3. either of two parts or things needed to complete each other. 4. full amount. 5. a word or words used to complete a grammatical construction, esp. in the predicate, as an object, predicate adjective, or predicate noun. 6. *Geom.* the angular amount needed to bring a given angle to a right angle. —*v.t.* 7. to complete. —**com′ple·men′tal, com′ple·men′ta·ry,** *adj.*

com·plete (kəm plēt′), *adj., v.,* **-pleted, -pleting.** —*adj.* 1. having all its parts; entire. 2. finished. 3. thorough; perfect. —*v.t.* 4. to make whole or entire. 5. to make perfect. 6. to end or fulfill. —**com·plete′ly,** *adv.* —**com·plete′ness,** *n.* —**com·plet′er,** *n.*

com·ple·tion (kəm plē′shən), *n.* 1. act of completing. 2. state of being completed. 3. fulfillment.

com·plex (*adj.* kəm plĕks′, kŏm′plĕks; *n.* kŏm′plĕks), *adj.* 1. composed of interconnected parts. 2. intricate. 3. *Gram.* containing one or more dependent clauses. —*n.* 4. a complex whole or system. 5. *Colloq.* an obsessing notion. —**com·plex′ly,** *adv.* —**com·plex′ness,** *n.*

com·plex·ion (kəm plĕk′shən), *n.* 1. the natural color and appearance of the skin, esp. of the face. 2. appearance. —**com·plex′ion·al,** *adj.*

com·plex·i·ty (kəm plĕk′sə tĬ), *n., pl.* **-ties.** 1. complex quality; intricacy. 2. something complex.

com·pli·ance (kəm plī′əns), *n.* 1. act of complying. 2. a disposition to yield to others. 3. base subservience. 4. accordance. Also, **com·pli′an·cy** for 1-3.

com·pli·ant (kəm plī′ənt), *adj.* complying; yielding. Also, **com·pli′a·ble.** —**com·pli′ant·ly,** *adv.*

com·pli·cate (*v.* kŏm′plə kāt′; *adj.* kŏm′plə·kĬt), *v.,* **-cated, -cating,** *adj.* —*v.t.* 1. to make

com·plex, intricate, or involved. 2. to **combine** intricately. —*adj.* 3. complex.

com·pli·cat·ed (kŏm′plə kā′tĬd), *adj.* 1. not simple; complex. 2. difficult to analyze, explain, etc.

com·pli·ca·tion (kŏm′plə kā′shən), *n.* 1. act of complicating. 2. a complicated state. 3. a complex combination of elements or things. 4. a complicating element. 5. *Pathol.* a concurrent disease or condition which aggravates the original disease.

com·plic·i·ty (kəm plĬs′ə tĬ), *n., pl.* **-ties.** state of being an accomplice.

com·pli·ment (*n.* kŏm′plə mənt; *v.* kŏm′plə·mĕnt′), *n.* 1. an expression of praise or commendation. —*v.t.* 2. to pay a compliment to.

com·pli·men·ta·ry (kŏm′plə mĕn′tə rĬ, -trĬ), *adj.* 1. of the nature of, conveying, or addressing a compliment. 2. *U.S.* free.

com·ply (kəm plī′), *v.i.,* **-plied, -plying.** to act in accordance (with wishes, requirements, etc.). —**com·pli′er,** *n.*

com·po·nent (kəm pō′nənt), *adj.* 1. composing; constituent. —*n.* 2. a constituent part.

com·port (kəm pōrt′), *v.t.* 1. to conduct. —*v.i.* 2. to suit. —**com·port′ment,** *n.*

com·pose (kəm pōz′), *v.,* **-posed, -posing.** —*v.t.* 1. to form by uniting parts. 2. to be the parts of. 3. to make up. 4. to put in proper form or order. 5. to devise (a literary or musical production). 6. to settle, as a quarrel. 7. to calm; quiet. 8. *Print.* **a.** to set (type). **b.** to set the types for (an article, etc.). —*v.i.* 9. to practice composition.

com·posed (kəm pōzd′), *adj.* calm. —**com·pos·ed·ly** (kəm pō′zĬd lĬ), *adv.*

com·pos·er (kəm pō′zər), *n.* 1. a writer of music. 2. an author.

com·pos·ite (kəm pŏz′Ĭt), *adj.* 1. made up of various parts. 2. *Bot.* belonging to a family of plants, including the daisy, aster, etc., in which the florets are borne in a close head. —*n.* 3. something composite. —**com·pos′ite·ly,** *adv.*

com·po·si·tion (kŏm′pə zĬsh′ən), *n.* 1. act of combining parts to form a whole. 2. manner in which such parts are combined. 3. resulting state or product. 4. constitution. 5. a compound. 6. organization of the parts of a work of art so as to achieve a unified whole. 7. the art or act of putting words and sentences together in accordance with the rules of grammar and rhetoric. 8. the art or result of composing music. 9. a short essay written as a school exercise. 10. a settlement. 11. the setting up of type for printing.

com·pos·i·tor (kəm pŏz′ə tər), *n.* typesetter.

com·post (kŏm′pōst), *n.* a decaying mixture, as of dung, dead leaves, etc., for fertilizing land.

com·po·sure (kəm pō′zhər), *n.* calmness.

com·pote (kŏm′pōt), *n.* a preparation or dish of fruit stewed in a syrup.

com·pound[1] (*adj.* kŏm′pound, kŏm pound′; *n.* kŏm′pound; *v.* kəm pound′), *adj.* 1. composed of two or more parts, or involving two or more functions, etc. 2. *Gram.* containing two or more coördinate independent clauses. —*n.* 3. something formed by combining parts, etc. 4. *Chem.* a pure substance composed of two or more elements whose composition is constant. 5. *Gram.* a compound word. —*v.t.* 6. to combine. 7. to form by combining parts, etc. 8. to constitute. 9. to settle. 10. *Law.* to agree, for a consideration, not to prosecute or punish a wrongdoer for. —**com·pound′a·ble,** *adj.* —**com·pound′er,** *n.*

com·pound[2] (kŏm′pound), *n.* (in Asia) an enclosure containing a residence of Europeans.

compound interest, interest paid, not only on the principal, but on the interest after it has periodically come due and, remaining unpaid, been added to the principal.

com·pre·hend (kŏm′prĬ hĕnd′), *v.t.* 1. to understand. 2. to include; comprise. —**com′pre·hend′i·ble,** *adj.* —**com′pre·hend′ing·ly,** *adv.*

com·pre·hen·si·ble (kŏm′prĬ hĕn′sə bəl), *adj.* intelligible. —**com′pre·hen′si·bil′i·ty, com′·pre·hen′si·ble·ness,** *n.* —**com′pre·hen′si·bly,** *adv.*

com·pre·hen·sion (kŏm′prĬ hĕn′shən), *n.* 1. act or fact of comprehending. 2. comprehensiveness. 3. understanding.

com·pre·hen·sive (kŏm′prĬ hĕn′sĬv), *adj.* 1. inclusive; of large scope. 2. having a wide mental grasp. —**com′pre·hen′sive·ly,** *adv.* —**com′·pre·hen′sive·ness,** *n.*

com·press (*v.* kəm prĕs′; *n.* kŏm′prĕs), *v.t.* 1. to press together; force into less space. —*n.* 2.

Med. a soft pad used to supply moisture, cold, heat, etc. —com·pressed', *adj.* —com·press'·i·ble, *adj.* —com·press'i·bil'i·ty, *n.*

com·pres·sion (kəm prĕsh'ən), *n.* **1.** act of compressing. **2.** compressed state. **3.** the increase of air pressure. —com·pres'sive, *adj.*

com·pres·sor (kəm prĕs'ər), *n.* **1.** *Anat.* a muscle that compresses some part of the body. **2.** *Surg.* an instrument for compressing a part of the body. **3.** a machine by which a gas is compressed.

com·prise (kəm prīz'), *v.t.*, -prised, -prising. **1.** to include; contain. **2.** to consist of. Also, com·prize'. —com·pris'al, *n.*

com·pro·mise (kŏm'prə mīz'), *n.*, *v.*, -mised, -mising. —*n.* **1.** a settlement of differences by mutual concessions. **2.** anything resulting from compromise. **3.** something intermediate between different things. **4.** an endangering, esp. of reputation. —*v.t.*, *v.i.* **5.** to settle by a compromise. **6.** to endanger the reputation of. —com'pro·mis'er, *n.*

comp·trol·ler (kən trō'lər), *n.* controller.

com·pul·sion (kəm pŭl'shən), *n.* **1.** act of compelling; coercion. **2.** *Psychol.* a strong irrational impulse to carry out a given act. —com·pul'sive, *adj.*

com·pul·so·ry (kəm pŭl'sə rĭ), *adj.* **1.** using compulsion; compelling. **2.** compelled; forced. —com·pul'so·ri·ly, *adv.* —com·pul'so·ri·ness, *n.*

com·punc·tion (kəm pŭngk'shən), *n.* uneasiness of conscience; remorse.

com·pu·ta·tion (kŏm'pyə tā'shən), *n.* act, process, method, or result of computing.

com·pute (kəm pūt'), *v.t.*, *v.i.*, -puted, -puting. to determine by calculation; calculate. —com·put'a·bil'i·ty, *n.* —com·put'er, *n.*

com·rade (kŏm'răd), *n.* **1.** an associate; close companion. **2.** a fellow member of a political party, etc. —com'rade·ship', *n.*

con[1] (kŏn), *adv.* **1.** opposed. —*n.* **2.** the argument, voter, etc., against (something).

con[2] (kŏn), *v.t.*, conned, conning. to study.

con[3] (kŏn), *adj.*, *v.*, conned, conning. *U.S. Slang.* —*adj.* **1.** confidence. —*v.t.* **2.** to swindle.

con·cat·e·na·tion (kŏn kăt'ə nā'shən), *n.* **1.** connection, as in a chain. **2.** a series of interconnected things or events.

con·cave (*adj.*, *v.* kŏn kāv', kŏn'kāv; *n.* kŏn'kāv), *adj.*, *n.*, *v.*, -caved, -caving. —*adj.* **1.** curved like the interior of a circle. —*n.* **2.** a concave surface, part, line, etc. —*v.t.* **3.** to make concave. —con·cave'ly, *adv.* —con·cave'ness, *n.*

con·cav·i·ty (kŏn kăv'ə tĭ), *n.*, *pl.* -ties. **1.** state of being concave. **2.** a concave surface or thing.

con·ceal (kən sēl'), *v.t.* **1.** to hide. **2.** to keep secret. —con·ceal'a·ble, *adj.* —con·ceal'er, *n.* —con·ceal'ment, *n.*

con·cede (kən sēd'), *v.*, -ceded, -ceding. —*v.t.* **1.** to admit as true, just, or proper. **2.** to grant or yield. —*v.i.* **3.** to yield or admit. —con·ced'ed·ly, *adv.*

con·ceit (kən sēt'), *n.* **1.** an exaggerated estimate of one's own ability, importance, etc. **2.** esteem. **3.** personal opinion. **4.** a thought; idea. **5.** imagination; fancy. **6.** a whim. **7.** a fanciful idea or expression. —*v.t.* **8.** to flatter. **9.** to apprehend. **10.** to imagine.

con·ceit·ed (kən sē'tĭd), *adj.* having an exaggerated opinion of one's abilities, importance, etc. —con·ceit'ed·ly, *adv.*

con·ceive (kən sēv'), *v.*, -ceived, -ceiving. —*v.t.* **1.** to form (a notion, purpose, etc.). **2.** to form a notion of. **3.** to understand. **4.** to believe. **5.** to become pregnant with. —*v.i.* **6.** to form an idea. **7.** to become pregnant. —con·ceiv'a·ble, *adj.* —con·ceiv'a·bly, *adv.* —con·ceiv'er, *n.*

con·cen·trate (kŏn'sən trāt'), *v.*, -trated, -trating. —*v.t.* **1.** to bring or draw to a common center or point of union; focus. **2.** to intensify by removing or reducing certain parts. —*v.i.* **3.** to converge to a center. **4.** to become more intense or purer. **5.** to direct one's attention fully on something. —*n.* **6.** a product of concentration. —con'cen·tra'tor, *n.*

con·cen·tra·tion (kŏn'sən trā'shən), *n.* **1.** act of concentrating. **2.** concentrated state. **3.** exclusive attention. **4.** something concentrated.

concentration camp, a guarded enclosure for political prisoners, aliens, refugees, etc.

con·cen·tric (kən sĕn'trĭk), *adj.* having a common center. —con·cen'tri·cal·ly, *adv.*

con·cept (kŏn'sĕpt), *n.* **1.** a general notion. **2.** a complex of characters.

con·cep·tion (kən sĕp'shən), *n.* **1.** act of conceiving. **2.** state of being conceived. **3.** a notion; idea. —con·cep'tion·al, *adj.*

con·cep·tu·al (kən sĕp'chŏŏ əl), *adj.* pertaining to conception or to concepts. —con·cep'tu·al·ly, *adv.*

con·cern (kən sûrn'), *v.t.* **1.** to relate to; be connected with. **2.** to interest, engage, or involve. **3.** to disquiet or trouble. —*n.* **4.** business; affair. **5.** a matter that involves one's attention, interest, welfare, or happiness. **6.** solicitude or anxiety. **7.** important bearing. **8.** a commercial or manufacturing firm.

con·cern·ing (kən sûr'nĭng), *prep.* relating to; regarding; about.

con·cern·ment (kən sûrn'mənt), *n.* **1.** importance. **2.** interest; participation. **3.** bearing. **4.** anxiety; solicitude.

con·cert (*n.* kŏn'sûrt, -sərt; *v.* kən sûrt'), *n.* **1.** a public musical performance in which several singers or players, or both, participate. **2.** accord or harmony. —*v.t.* **3.** to arrange by agreement. **4.** to devise. —*v.i.* **5.** to plan or act together.

con·cert·ed (kən sûr'tĭd), *adj.* contrived by agreement; prearranged.

con·cer·ti·na (kŏn'sər tē'nə), *n.*, *pl.* -ni (-nē) a small hexagonal accordion.

con·cer·to (kən chĕr'tō), *n.*, *pl.* -tos, *It.* -ti (-tē) a composition for one or more principal instruments, with orchestral accompaniment.

con·ces·sion (kən sĕsh'ən), *n.* **1.** act of conceding or yielding. **2.** the thing yielded. **3.** something conceded, as a grant of land, a privilege, or a franchise.

conch (kŏngk, kŏnch), *n.*, *pl.* conchs (kŏngks), conches (kŏn'chĭz). the spiral shell of a gastropod, often used as a trumpet.

Man playing a concertina

con·cil·i·ate (kən sĭl'ĭ āt'), *v.t.*, -ated, -ating. **1.** to overcome the distrust or hostility of. **2.** to reconcile. —con·cil'i·a'tion, *n.* —con·cil'i·a'tor, *n.*

con·cil·i·a·to·ry (kən sĭl'ĭ ə tôr'ĭ), *adj.* tending to conciliate. Also, con·cil·i·a·tive (kən sĭl'ĭ ā'tĭv).

con·cise (kən sīs'), *adj.* expressing much in few words; succinct; terse. —con·cise'ly, *adv.* —con·cise'ness, *n.*

con·clave (kŏn'klāv, kŏng'-), *n.* **1.** any private meeting. **2.** the place in which the cardinals meet privately to elect a Pope. **3.** the assembly of the cardinals for the election of a Pope.

con·clude (kən klŏŏd'), *v.*, -cluded, -cluding. —*v.t.* **1.** to bring to an end; finish. **2.** to say in conclusion. **3.** to settle or arrange finally. **4.** to deduce; infer. **5.** to decide. —*v.i.* **6.** to finish. **7.** to decide. —con·clud'er, *n.*

con·clu·sion (kən klŏŏ'zhən), *n.* **1.** the end; the final part. **2.** a result or outcome. **3.** final settlement or decision. **4.** a deduction or inference.

con·clu·sive (kən klŏŏ'sĭv), *adj.* serving to settle a question; decisive. —con·clu'sive·ly, *adv.* —con·clu'sive·ness, *n.*

con·coct (kŏn kŏkt', kən-), *v.t.* **1.** to make by combining ingredients, as in cookery. **2.** to contrive. —con·coc'tion, *n.*

con·com·i·tant (kŏn kŏm'ə tənt, kən-), *adj.* **1.** accompanying. —*n.* **2.** a concomitant quality, circumstance, or thing. —con·com'i·tant·ly, *adv.*

con·cord (kŏn'kôrd, kŏng'-), *n.* **1.** agreement; accord. **2.** peace. **3.** a treaty. **4.** harmony.

Con·cord (kŏng'kərd), *n.* **1.** a town in E Massachusetts: battle, April 19, 1775. 7972. **2.** the capital of New Hampshire, in the S part. 27,171.

con·cord·ance (kŏn kôr'dəns, kən-), *n.* **1.** agreement; harmony. **2.** an alphabetical index of the principal words of a book.

con·cord·ant (kŏn kôr'dənt, kən-), *adj.* agreeing; harmonious. —con·cord'ant·ly, *adv.*

con·cor·dat (kŏn kôr'dăt), *n.* **1.** an agreement. **2.** an agreement between the Pope and a secular government regarding ecclesiastical matters.

con·course (kŏn'kôrs, kŏng'-), *n.* **1.** assemblage. 2. a driveway or promenade in a park. 3. an open space in a railroad station. 4. confluence.

con·crete (kŏn'krēt, kŏn krēt' *for 1–9, 12;* kŏn-krēt' *for 10, 11*), *adj., n., v.,* **-creted, -creting.** —*adj.* 1. actual; real. 2. pertaining to or concerned with realities rather than abstractions. 3. representing or applied to an actual substance or thing. 4. made of concrete. 5. formed by coalescence of separate particles into a mass. —*n.* 6. a concrete idea or thing. 7. a mass formed by coalescence of particles. 8. an artificial stonelike material, made by mixing cement, sand, broken stones, etc. —*v.t.* 9. to treat with concrete. 10. to render solid. —*v.i.* 11. to become solid; harden. 12. to use or apply concrete. —**con·crete'ly,** *adv.* —**con·crete'ness,** *n.*

con·cre·tion (kŏn krē'shən), *n.* 1. act or process of concreting. 2. state of being concreted. 3. a solid mass formed by coalescence.

con·cu·bine (kŏng'kyə bīn', kŏn'-), *n.* a woman living with a man but not married to him.

con·cu·pis·cent (kŏn kū'pə sənt), *adj.* lustful; sensual. —**con·cu'pis·cence,** *n.*

con·cur (kən kûr'), *v.i.,* **-curred, -curring.** 1. to agree. 2. to coöperate; combine. 3. to coincide. 4. to unite.

con·cur·rence (kən kûr'əns, -kŭr'-), *n.* 1. act of concurring. 2. agreement. 3. coöperation. 4. coincidence.

con·cur·rent (kən kûr'ənt, -kŭr'-), *adj.* 1. occurring together or side by side. 2. coöperating. 3. having equal authority. 4. agreeing. —*n.* 5. a rival. —**con·cur'rent·ly,** *adv.*

con·cus·sion (kən kŭsh'ən), *n.* 1. act of shaking or shocking, as by a blow. 2. shock occasioned by a blow or collision. 3. *Pathol.* jarring of the brain, etc., from a blow, etc. —**con·cus'sive,** *adj.*

con·demn (kən dĕm'), *v.t.* 1. to express strong disapproval of. 2. to pronounce guilty. 3. to judge to be unfit for use or service.. 4. *U.S. Law.* to acquire ownership of for a public purpose. —**con·dem·na·ble** (kən dĕm'nə bəl), *adj.* —**dem·na·to·ry** (kən dĕm'nə tōr'ĭ), *adj.* —**condemn·er** (kən dĕm'ər), *n.* —**con·demn'ing·ly,** *adv.*

con·dem·na·tion (kŏn'dĕm nā'shən, -dəm-), *n.* 1. act of condemning. 2. strong censure. 3. cause for condemning.

con·den·sa·tion (kŏn'dĕn sā'shən), *n.* 1. act of condensing. 2. condensed state or form. 3. a condensed mass. 4. act of reducing a gas or vapor to a liquid or solid form.

con·dense (kən dĕns'), *v.,* **-densed, -densing.** —*v.t.* 1. to make compact. 2. to reduce to another and denser form, as a gas to a liquid state. —*v.i.* 3. to become compact. 4. to become liquid or solid, as a vapor. —**con·den'sa·ble,** *adj.*

con·dens·er (kən dĕn'sər), *n.* 1. one that condenses. 2. an apparatus for reducing gases or vapors to liquid or solid form. 3. a lens used to concentrate the rays of light and direct them upon the object. 4. *Elect.* a device for accumulating and holding a charge of electricity.

con·de·scend (kŏn'dĭ sĕnd'), *v.i.* 1. to waive ceremony voluntarily and assume equality with an inferior. 2. to deign. —**con·de·scen·sion** (kŏn'dĭ sĕn'shən), **con'de·scend'ence,** *n.* —**con'-de·scend'ing·ly,** *adv.*

con·di·ment (kŏn'də mənt), *n.* something used to add flavor to food, as a sauce.

con·di·tion (kən dĭsh'ən), *n.* 1. particular mode of being of a person or thing. 2. state of health. 3. fit state. 4. social position. 5. a restricting circumstance. 6. something demanded as an essential part, as of an agreement. —*v.t.* 7. to put in proper state. 8. to be a condition of. 9. to make conditional. —*v.i.* 10. to make conditions. —**con·di'tion·er,** *n.*

con·di·tion·al (kən dĭsh'ən əl), *adj.* imposing, containing, or depending on a condition or conditions. —**con·di'tion·al·ly,** *adv.*

con·dole (kən dōl'), *v.i.,* **-doled, -doling.** to express sympathy with one in affliction. —**con·do'lence, con·dole'ment,** *n.*

con·done (kən dōn'), *v.t.,* **-doned, -doning.** to pardon or overlook (an offense). —**con·do·na·tion** (kŏn'dō nā'shən), *n.* —**con·don'er,** *n.*

con·dor (kŏn'dər), *n.* a large vulture of the New World, as the **Andean condor** and **California condor.**

con·duce (kən dūs', -dōōs'), *v.i.,* **-duced, -ducing.** to lead or contribute. —**con·du'cive,** *adj.*

con·duct (*n.* kŏn'dŭkt; *v.* kən dŭkt'), *n.* 1. per-

sonal behavior; deportment. 2. management; execution. 3. guidance; escort. —*v.t.* 4. to behave (oneself). 5. to manage; carry on. 6. to direct as leader. 7. to escort. 8. to serve as a channel or medium for (heat, sound, etc.). —*v.i.* 9. to lead. 10. to act as conductor. —**con·duct'i·ble,** *adj.* —**con·duct'i·bil'i·ty,** *n.* —**con·duc'tive,** *adj.*

con·duct·ance (kən dŭk'təns), *n. Elect.* conducting power of a conductor.

con·duc·tion (kən dŭk'shən), *n.* 1. a conducting. 2. *Physics.* a. transmission through a conductor. b. conductivity.

con·duc·tiv·i·ty (kŏn'dŭk tĭv'ə tĭ), *n., pl.* **-ties.** *Physics.* the property or power of conducting heat, electricity, or sound.

con·duc·tor (kən dŭk'tər), *n.* 1. a leader, guide, or director. 2. the official in charge of a railroad train, bus, or streetcar. 3. the director of an orchestra or chorus. 4. a substance, body, or device that readily conducts heat, sound, etc.

con·duit (kŏn'dĭt, -dōō ĭt), *n.* 1. a pipe, tube, etc., for conveying water or other fluid. 2. some similar natural passage.

cone (kōn), *n., v.,* **coned, coning.** —*n.* 1. a form that tapers from its circular base to a single point. 2. *Geom.* a solid whose surface is generated by the straight lines joining a fixed point to the points of a plane curve whose plane does not contain the fixed point. 3. *Mach.* a mechanical part having the shape of a cone. 4. *Bot.* a. the conical multiple fruit of the pine, fir, etc., consisting of scales bearing naked ovules or seeds. b. a similar fruit. 5. anything cone-shaped. —*v.t.* 6. to shape like a cone.

con·fab (kŏn'făb), *n., v.,* **-fabbed, -fabbing.** *Colloq.* —*n.* 1. confabulation. —*v.i.* 2. to confabulate.

con·fab·u·late (kən făb'yə lāt'), *v.i.,* **-lated, -lating.** to converse. —**con·fab'u·la'tion,** *n.*

con·fec·tion (kən fĕk'shən), *n.* 1. a candy. 2. a sweet preparation of fruit or the like, as a preserve. 3. the process of making.

con·fec·tion·er (kən fĕk'shən ər), *n.* one who makes or sells candies, ice cream, etc.

con·fec·tion·er·y (kən fĕk'shə nĕr'ĭ), *n., pl.* **-eries.** 1. confections collectively. 2. the work of a confectioner. 3. a confectioner's shop.

con·fed·er·a·cy (kən fĕd'ər ə sĭ, -fĕd'rə sĭ), *n., pl.* **-cies.** 1. a body of confederated persons, parties, or states. 2. a conspiracy. 3. the **Confederacy,** the Confederate States of America.

con·fed·er·ate (*adj., n.* kən fĕd'ər ĭt, -fĕd'rĭt; *v.* kən fĕd'ə rāt'), *adj., n., v.,* **-ated, -ating.** —*adj.* 1. united in a league or conspiracy. 2. (*cap.*) denoting or pertaining to the Confederacy. —*n.* 3. an ally. 4. an accomplice. 5. (*cap.*) an adherent of the Confederacy. —*v.t., v.i.* 6. to unite in a league or conspiracy.

Confederate States of America, the eleven Southern States which seceded from the American Union in 1860–61.

con·fed·er·a·tion (kən fĕd'ə rā'shən), *n.* 1. act of confederating. 2. state of being confederated. 3. a league or alliance. 4. a body of confederates. 5. the **Confederation,** the union of the American colonies from 1781 to 1789 under the **Articles of Confederation.**

con·fer (kən fûr'), *v.,* **-ferred, -ferring.** —*v.t.* 1. to bestow. —*v.i.* 2. to consult together. —**con·fer'ment,** *n.* —**con·fer'ra·ble,** *adj.* —**con·fer'rer,** *n.*

con·fer·ee (kŏn'fə rē'), *n. U.S.* one who is conferred with or takes part in a conference.

con·fer·ence (kŏn'fər əns), *n.* 1. a meeting for consultation or discussion. 2. consultation. 3. *U.S. Sports.* an organization of teams.

con·fess (kən fĕs'), *v.t., v.i.* 1. to acknowledge or avow. 2. to admit. 3. to declare (one's sins), esp. to a priest, for the obtaining of absolution.

con·fes·sion (kən fĕsh'ən), *n.* 1. acknowledgment or avowal. 2. disclosing of sins to a priest to obtain forgiveness. 3. that which is confessed.

con·fes·sion·al (kən fĕsh'ən əl), *adj.* 1. of confession. —*n.* 2. the place set apart for the hearing of confessions by a priest.

con·fes·sor (kən fĕs'ər), *n.* 1. one who confesses. 2. a priest who hears confessions.

con·fet·ti (kən fĕt'ĭ), *n.pl., sing.* **-fetto** (-fĕt'tô). 1. small bits of colored paper, thrown at carnivals, etc. 2. confections.

con·fi·dant (kŏn'fə dănt'), *n.* one to whom secrets are confided. —**con'fi·dante',** *n. fem.*

con·fide (kən fīd'), *v.,* **-fided, -fiding.** —*v.i.* 1. to show trust by imparting secrets. —*v.t.* 2. to tell in assurance of secrecy. 3. to entrust. —con·fid′er, n.

con·fi·dence (kŏn′fə dəns), n. 1. full trust. 2. self-reliance, assurance, or boldness. 3. certitude. 4. a ground of trust.

confidence game, the obtaining of money by fraud, after winning the victim's confidence. —confidence man.

con·fi·dent (kŏn′fə dənt), adj. 1. having strong belief or assurance; sure. 2. bold. —con′fi·dent·ly, adv.

con·fi·den·tial (kŏn′fə dĕn′shəl), adj. 1. spoken or written in confidence. 2. betokening confidence. 3. entrusted with secrets or private affairs. —con′fi·den′tial·ly, adv.

con·fig·u·ra·tion (kən fĭg′ə rā′shən), n. 1. the relative disposition of parts. 2. external form.

con·fine (v. kən fīn′; n. kŏn′fīn), v., -fined, -fining, n. —v.t. 1. to enclose within bounds. 2. to imprison. 3. to be in childbed. —n. 4. (usually pl.) a boundary. —con·fine′ment, n. —con·fin′er, n.

con·firm (kən fûrm′), v.t. 1. to make sure; verify. 2. to make valid or binding. 3. to strengthen, as in habit, opinion, etc. 4. Eccles. to administer the rite of confirmation to. —con·firm′a·ble, adj.

con·fir·ma·tion (kŏn′fər mā′shən), n. 1. act of confirming. 2. that which confirms. 3. Eccles. a rite for confirming and strengthening the recipient in his faith.

con·firm·a·to·ry (kən fûr′mə tōr′ĭ), adj. serving to confirm. Also, con·firm′a·tive.

con·firmed (kən fûrmd′), adj. 1. settled; ratified. 2. inveterate. 3. (of a disease) chronic.

con·fis·cate (kŏn′fĭs kāt′, kən fĭs′kāt), v., -cated, -cating, adj. —v.t. 1. to seize as forfeited to the public treasury. 2. to seize as if by authority. —adj. 3. confiscated. —con′fis·ca′tion, n. —con′fis·ca′tor, n.

con·fla·gra·tion (kŏn′flə grā′shən), n. a large and destructive fire.

con·flict (v. kən flĭkt′; n. kŏn′flĭkt), v.i. 1. to come into collision or opposition; clash. —n. 2. a battle or struggle. 3. controversy. 4. discord or antagonism.

con·flu·ence (kŏn′flŏŏ əns), n. 1. a flowing together of two or more streams. 2. a throng. —con′flu·ent, adj.

con·form (kən fôrm′), v.i., v.t. to act in, or bring into, accord. 2. to become or make similar in form or character. —con·form′er, n.

con·form·a·ble (kən fôr′mə bəl), adj. 1. similar. 2. exhibiting agreement or harmony. 3. compliant or submissive. —con·form′a·bly, adv.

con·for·ma·tion (kŏn′fôr mā′shən), n. 1. form. 2. symmetrical arrangement of parts. 3. act of conforming. 4. state of being conformed.

con·form·ist (kən fôr′mĭst), n. one who conforms to a usage or practice.

con·form·i·ty (kən fôr′mə tĭ), n., pl. -ties. 1. correspondence in form or character; accordance. 2. compliance. Also, con·form′ance.

con·found (kŏn found′, kən-), v.t. 1. to mingle completely. 2. to mix or associate by mistake. 3. to confuse. 4. to perplex. 5. (in mild oaths) to damn. —con·found′er, n.

con·found·ed (kŏn foun′dĭd, kən-), adj. 1. damned. 2. Colloq. detestable. —con·found′ed·ly, adv.

con·front (kən frŭnt′), v.t. 1. to stand or meet facing. 2. to oppose. 3. to set face to face.

Con·fu·cius (kən fū′shəs), n. 551–478 B.C., Chinese philosopher and teacher of principles of conduct. —Con·fu′cian, adj., n. —Con·fu′cian·ism, n. —Con·fu′cian·ist, n., adj.

con·fuse (kən fūz′), v.t., -fused, -fusing. 1. to combine without order; jumble. 2. to throw into disorder. 3. to associate by mistake. 4. to perplex. 5. to disconcert. —con·fus·ed·ly (kənfū′zĭd lĭ, -fūzd′lĭ), adv. —con·fus′ing·ly, adv.

con·fu·sion (kən fū′zhən), n. 1. act of confusing. 2. state of being confused. 3. disorder. 4. lack of clearness. 5. embarrassment. 6. perplexity.

con·fute (kən fūt′), v.t., -futed, -futing. 1. to disprove. 2. to prove to be wrong. 3. to confound. —con·fu·ta·tion (kŏn′fyŏŏ tā′shən), n. —con·fut′er, n.

Cong., 1. Congress. 2. Congressional.

con·geal (kən jēl′), v.t., v.i. 1. to change to a solid or rigid state, as by freezing. 2. to coag-

---

ulate. 3. to make or become fixed, as principles, etc. —con·geal′a·ble, adj. —con·geal′er, n. —con·geal′ment, n.

con·gen·ial (kən jēn′yəl), adj. 1. suited or adapted in spirit, temper, etc. 2. agreeable or pleasing. —con·ge·ni·al·i·ty (kən jē′nĭ ăl′ə tĭ), n. —con·gen′ial·ly, adv.

con·gen·i·tal (kən jĕn′ə təl), adj. existing at or from one's birth. —con·gen′i·tal·ly, adv.

con·ger (kŏng′gər), n. a large edible marine eel along the coast of Europe. Also, conger eel.

con·gest (kən jĕst′), v.t. 1. to overcrowd. 2. Pathol. to cause an unnatural accumulation of blood in the vessels of. —v.i. 3. to become congested. —con·ges′tion, n.

con·glom·er·ate (n., adj., kən glŏm′ər ĭt; v. -ə rāt′), n., adj., v., -ated, -ating. —m. 1. anything composed of heterogeneous elements. 2. Geol. a rock consisting of pebbles, etc., embedded in a finer cementing material. —adj. 3. gathered into a rounded mass, or consisting of parts so gathered. 4. Geol. of the nature of a conglomerate. —v.t., v.i. 5. to collect into a cohering or rounded mass. —con·glom′er·a′tion, n.

Con·go (kŏng′gō), n. a river from central Africa into the Atlantic. ab. 3000 mi.

congo snake, either of two eel-shaped salamanders of the southern U.S. Also, congo eel.

con·grat·u·late (kən grăch′ə lāt′), v.t., -lated, -lating. to express sympathetic joy to (a person), as on a happy occasion. —con·grat′u·la·tor, n. —con·grat·u·la·to·ry (kən grăch′ə lətōr′ĭ), adj.

con·grat·u·la·tion (kən grăch′ə lā′shən), n. 1. act of congratulating. 2. (usually pl.) a congratulatory expression; felicitation.

con·gre·gate (kŏng′grə gāt′), v., -gated, -gating, adj. —v.i., v.t. 1. to assemble, esp. in large numbers. —adj. 2. assembled. —con′gre·ga·tive, adj.

con·gre·ga·tion (kŏng′grə gā′shən), n. 1. act of congregating. 2. an assemblage, as for religious worship. 3. an organization formed for religious purposes.

con·gre·ga·tion·al (kŏng′grə gā′shən əl), adj. 1. of or pertaining to a congregation. 2. (cap.) pertaining to a form of church government in which each local church acts as an independent body.

con·gre·ga·tion·al·ism (kŏng′grə gā′shən ə-lĭz′əm), n. 1. the type of church government in which each local religious society is self-governing. 2. (cap.) the system and doctrine of the Congregational churches. —con′gre·ga′tion·al·ist, n., adj.

con·gress (kŏng′grĭs), n. 1. the national legislative body, esp. (cap.) of the U.S., consisting of the Senate and House of Representatives. 2. a formal meeting for the discussion of some matter of common interest. —v.i. 3. to meet in congress. —con·gres·sion·al (kən grĕsh′ən əl), adj.

con·gress·man (kŏng′grĭs mən), n., pl. -men. (often cap.) a member of the U.S. Congress, esp. of the House of Representatives. —con′gress·wom′an, n. fem.

Congress of Industrial Organizations, a federation of industrial labor unions, originally (1935) within the American Federation of Labor, but independent from it since 1938.

con·gru·ent (kŏng′grŏŏ ənt), adj. 1. agreeing. 2. Geom. coinciding exactly when superposed. —con′gru·ence, con′gru·en·cy, n. —con′gru·ent·ly, adv.

con·gru·i·ty (kən grŏŏ′ə tĭ), n., pl. -ties. 1. agreement; appropriateness. 2. Geom. capacity of figures of being exactly superposed. 3. a point of agreement.

con·gru·ous (kŏng′grŏŏ əs), adj. 1. agreeing or harmonious. 2. exhibiting harmony of parts. 3. appropriate. —con′gru·ous·ly, adv. —con′gru·ous·ness, n.

con·ic (kŏn′ĭk), adj. Also, con′i·cal. having the form of, resembling, or pertaining to a cone. —con′i·cal·ly, adv.

co·ni·fer (kō′nə fər, kŏn′ə-), n. any of certain (mostly evergreen) trees and shrubs, including the pine, fir, and other cone-bearing trees and shrubs. —co·nif·er·ous (kō nĭf′ər əs), adj.

conj., 1. conjugation. 2. conjunction.

con·jec·tur·al (kən jĕk′chər əl), adj. 1. of the nature of, or involving conjecture. 2. given to making conjectures. —con·jec′tur·al·ly, adv.

con·jec·ture (kən jĕk′chər), n., v., -tured, -turing. —n. 1. the formation or expression of an opinion without sufficient proof. 2. such an opinion. —*v.t.* **3.** to conclude or suppose from insufficient evidence. —*v.i.* **4.** to form conjectures.

con·join (kən join′), *v.t.*, *v.i.* to join together. —**con·join′er**, *n.*

con·joint (kən joint′), *adj.* **1.** joined together; united. **2.** joint. —**con·joint′ly**, *adv.*

con·ju·gal (kŏn′jə gəl), *adj.* of, or of the nature of, marriage. —**con′ju·gal·ly**, *adv.*

con·ju·gate (*v.* kŏn′jə gāt′; *adj.*, *n.* kŏn′jə gĭt, -gāt′), *v.*, **-gated, -gating**, *adj.*, *n.* —*v.t.* **1.** *Gram.* **a.** to inflect (a verb). **b.** to recite or display the inflected forms of (a verb) in a fixed order. —*v.i.* **2.** *Biol.* to unite temporarily. —*adj.* **3.** joined together; coupled. —*n.* **4.** one of a group of conjugate words. —**con′ju·ga′tive**, *adj.*

con·ju·ga·tion (kŏn′jə gā′shən), *n.* **1.** *Gram.* **a.** the inflection of verbs. **b.** the whole set of inflected forms of a verb. **c.** a class of verbs having similar sets of inflected forms. **2.** act of conjugating; union; conjunction.

con·junc·tion (kən jŭngk′shən), *n.* **1.** combination; union; association. **2.** a combination of events or circumstances. **3.** *Gram.* **a.** one of the major form classes, or parts of speech, comprising words used to link together words, phrases, clauses, or sentences. **b.** such a word. **4.** *Astron.* the meeting of heavenly bodies in the same longitude or right ascension.

con·junc·ti·va (kŏn′jŭngk tī′və), *n.*, *pl.* **-vas, -vae** (-vē). *Anat.* the mucous membrane which lines the inner surface of the eyelids.

con·junc·tive (kən jŭngk′tĭv), *adj.* **1.** connective. **2.** joint. **3.** *Gram.* of the nature of a conjunction. —*n.* **4.** *Gram.* a conjunction. —**con·junc′tive·ly**, *adv.*

con·junc·ti·vi·tis (kən jŭngk′tə vī′tĭs), *n.* *Pathol.* inflammation of the conjunctiva.

con·jur·a·tion (kŏn′jŏŏ rā′shən), *n.* **1.** invocation by a sacred name. **2.** a spell or charm.

con·jure (kŭn′jər, kŏn′-), *v.*, **-jured, -juring.** —*v.t.* **1.** to call upon (a devil or spirit) by invocation or spell. **2.** to effect by invocation or spell. **3.** to produce, etc., by magic. **4. conjure up, a.** to call or cause by magic. **b.** to recall. —*v.i.* **5.** to invoke a devil or spirit. **6.** to practice magic. —**con′jur·er, con′jur·or**, *n.*

con·nect (kə nĕkt′), *v.t.* **1.** to join or unite; link. **2.** to associate. —*v.i.* **3.** to join or unite. **4.** (of trains, etc.) to run so as to make connections. —**con·nect′ed·ly**, *adv.* —**con·nect′er, con·nec′tor**, *n.* —**con·nec′tive**, *adj.*, *n.*

Con·nec·ti·cut (kə nĕt′ə kət), *n.* a State in the NE United States. 1,963,519 pop.; 5009 sq. mi. *Cap.:* Hartford. *Abbr.:* **Conn.**

con·nec·tion (kə nĕk′shən), *n.* **1.** act of connecting. **2.** state of being connected. **3.** anything that connects. **4.** association. **5.** a circle of associates, or a member of such a circle. **6.** relation or sequence. **7.** the meeting of means of conveyance for transfer of passengers without delay. **8.** a relative, as by marriage. Also, *Brit.*, **con·nex′ion.**

con·ning tower (kŏn′ĭng), the armored pilothouse of a warship.

con·niv·ance (kə nī′vəns), *n.* **1.** act of conniving. **2.** *Law.* tacit encouragement or assent to wrongdoing by another. Also, **con·niv′ence.**

con·nive (kə nīv′), *v.i.*, **-nived, -niving.** **1.** to aid wrongdoing, etc., by forbearing to act or speak. **2.** to coöperate secretly. —**con·niv′er**, *n.*

con·nois·seur (kŏn′ə sûr′), *n.* a competent judge in an art, esp. one of the fine arts.

con·no·ta·tion (kŏn′ə tā′shən), *n.* **1.** act or fact of connoting. **2.** that which is connoted. —**con·no·ta·tive** (kŏn′ə tā′tĭv, kə nō′tə-), *adj.*

con·note (kə nōt′), *v.t.*, **-noted, -noting.** to signify in addition to the primary meaning.

con·nu·bi·al (kə nū′bĭ əl), *adj.* of marriage; matrimonial. —**con·nu′bi·al·ly**, *adv.*

con·quer (kŏng′kər), *v.t.* **1.** to acquire by force of arms. **2.** to subdue. **3.** to gain by effort. **4.** to surmount. —*v.i.* **5.** to make conquests. —**con′quer·a·ble**, *adj.* —**con′quer·or**, *n.*

con·quest (kŏn′kwĕst, kŏng′-), *n.* **1.** act of conquering. **2.** captivation. **3.** vanquishment. **4.** that which is acquired by conquering.

con·quis·ta·dor (kŏn kwĭs′tə dôr′; *Sp.* kông-kēs′tä dôr′), *n.*, *pl.* **-dors**, *Sp.* **-dores** (-dô′rĕs). one of the Spanish conquerors of Mexico and Peru in the 16th century.

Con·rad (kŏn′răd), *n.* **Joseph**, 1857–1924, Polish-born British novelist.

con·san·guin·e·ous (kŏn′săng gwĭn′ĭ əs), *adj.*

related by birth; akin. —**con′san·guin′e·ous·ly**, *adv.* —**con′san·guin′i·ty**, *n.*

con·science (kŏn′shəns), *n.* the internal recognition of right and wrong as regards one's actions and motives. —**con′science·less**, *adj.*

con·sci·en·tious (kŏn′shĭ ĕn′shəs, kŏn′sĭ-), *adj.* controlled by or done according to conscience. —**con′sci·en′tious·ly**, *adv.* —**con′sci·en′tious·ness**, *n.*

con·scion·a·ble (kŏn′shən ə bəl), *adj.* conformable to conscience; just. —**con′scion·a·bly**, *adv.*

con·scious (kŏn′shəs), *adj.* **1.** awake to one's own existence, sensations, etc. **2.** inwardly aware. **3.** known to oneself; felt. **4.** self-conscious. **5.** deliberate. —**con′scious·ly**, *adv.*

con·scious·ness (kŏn′shəs nĭs), *n.* **1.** state of being conscious. **2.** the thoughts and feelings, collectively, of an individual or aggregate of people.

con·script (*adj.*, *n.* kŏn′skrĭpt; *v.* kən skrĭpt′), *adj.* **1.** enrolled or formed by conscription; drafted. —*n.* **2.** a recruit obtained by conscription. —*v.t.* **3.** to draft for military or naval service. —**con·scrip′tion**, *n.*

con·se·crate (kŏn′sə krāt′), *v.*, **-crated, -crating**, *adj.* —*v.t.* **1.** to make or declare sacred. **2.** to devote or dedicate. —*adj.* **3.** *Archaic.* sacred. —**con′se·cra′tion**, *n.* —**con′se·cra′tor**, *n.*

con·sec·u·tive (kən sĕk′yə tĭv), *adj.* **1.** uninterrupted in succession; successive. **2.** marked by logical sequence. —**con·sec′u·tive·ly**, *adv.* —**con·sec′u·tive·ness**, *n.*

con·sen·sus (kən sĕn′səs), *n.* general agreement.

con·sent (kən sĕnt′), *v.i.* **1.** to agree; comply or yield. —*n.* **2.** assent; permission. **3.** agreement in opinion, etc. —**con·sent′er**, *n.*

con·se·quence (kŏn′sə kwĕns′), *n.* **1.** act or fact of following as an effect or result upon something antecedent. **2.** an effect or result. **3.** the conclusion of an argument or inference. **4.** importance.

con·se·quent (kŏn′sə kwĕnt′), *adj.* **1.** following as an effect or result. **2.** following as a logical conclusion. —*n.* **3.** anything that follows upon something else.

con·se·quen·tial (kŏn′sə kwĕn′shəl), *adj.* **1.** following as an effect or result. **2.** pompous. **3.** of importance. —**con′se·quen′tial·ly**, *adv.*

con·se·quent·ly (kŏn′sə kwĕnt′lĭ), *adv.* by way of consequence; therefore.

con·ser·va·tion (kŏn′sər vā′shən), *n.* **1.** act of conserving. **2.** official supervision of forests, etc.

con·serv·a·tive (kən sûr′və tĭv), *adj.* **1.** disposed to preserve existing conditions, institutions, etc. **2.** cautious or moderate. **3.** preservative. **4.** (*often cap.*) noting a political party whose characteristic principle is opposition to change. —*n.* **5.** a person of conservative principles. **6.** a member of a conservative party in politics. **7.** a preservative. —**con·serv′a·tive·ly**, *adv.* —**con·serv′a·tism, con·serv′a·tive·ness**, *n.*

con·serv·a·to·ry (kən sûr′və tōr′ĭ), [*n.*, *pl.* **-ries**, *adj.* —*n.* **1.** *U.S.* a place for instruction in music and theatrical arts. **2.** *Chiefly Brit.* a greenhouse. —*adj.* **3.** preservative.

con·serve (*v.* kən sûrv′; *n.* kŏn′sûrv, kən-sûrv′), *v.*, **-served, -serving**, *n.* —*v.t.* **1.** to keep in a safe or sound state. **2.** to preserve, as fruit, with sugar, etc. —*n.* **3.** (*often pl.*) a mixture of several fruits, cooked to jamlike consistency with sugar. —**con·serv′er**, *n.*

con·sid·er (kən sĭd′ər), *v.t.* **1.** to contemplate mentally. **2.** to deem to be. **3.** to think; suppose. **4.** to make allowance for. **5.** to pay attention to. **6.** to respect. —*v.i.* **7.** to reflect.

con·sid·er·a·ble (kən sĭd′ər ə bəl), *adj.* **1.** worthy of consideration; important. **2.** fairly large or great. —*n.* **3.** *U.S. Colloq.* much. —**con·sid′er·a·bly**, *adv.*

con·sid·er·ate (kən sĭd′ər ĭt), *adj.* **1.** showing consideration for another's feelings, etc. **2.** deliberate. —**con·sid′er·ate·ly**, *adv.* —**con·sid′-er·ate·ness**, *n.*

con·sid·er·a·tion (kən sĭd′ə rā′shən), *n.* **1.** act of considering. **2.** regard or account. **3.** a thought. **4.** a recompense for service rendered, etc. **5.** thoughtfulness for others. **6.** importance. **7.** esteem.

con·sid·er·ing (kən sĭd′ər ĭng), *prep.* taking into account; in view of.

con·sign (kən sīn′), *v.t.* **1.** to deliver formally (fol. by *to*). **2.** to entrust. **3.** to set apart, as to a purpose. **4.** *Com.* to transmit, as by public car rier, esp. for sale. —con·sign'a·ble, *adj.* —con·sign·ee (kŏn'sī nē', -sĭ nē'), *n.* —con·sign·or, con·sign·er (kən sī'nər), *n.*

con·sign·ment (kən sīn'mənt), *n.* 1. act of consigning. 2. that which is consigned.

con·sist (kən sĭst'), *v.i.* 1. to be composed. 2. to be contained. 3. to be compatible.

con·sist·en·cy (kən sĭs'tən sĭ), *n.*, *pl.* -cies. 1. solidity or firmness. 2. degree of density or viscosity. 3. constant adherence to the same principles, etc. 4. agreement. Also, con·sist'·ence.

con·sist·ent (kən sĭs'tənt), *adj.* 1. agreeing or compatible. 2. constantly adhering to the same principles, etc. 3. cohering. —con·sist'ent·ly, *adv.*

con·sis·to·ry (kən sĭs'tə rĭ), *n.*, *pl.* -ries. 1. any of various ecclesiastical councils. 2. the place where it meets.

con·so·la·tion (kŏn'sə lā'shən), *n.* 1. act of consoling. 2. state of being consoled. 3. one that consoles. —con·sol·a·to·ry (kən sŏl'ə tōr'ĭ), *adj.*

con·sole¹ (kən sōl'), *v.t.*, -soled, -soling. to alleviate the sorrow of; comfort. —con·sol'a·ble, *adj.* —con·sol'er, *n.* —con·sol'ing·ly, *adv.*

con·sole² (kŏn'sōl), *n.* 1. a desklike structure containing the keyboards, pedals, etc., of an organ. 2. a floor-model radio cabinet. 3. a console table. 4. a bracket or bracketlike support.

con·sole table (kŏn'sōl), a table supported by brackets fixed to a wall.

con·sol·i·date (kən sŏl'ə dāt'), *v.t.*, *v.i.*, -dated, -dating. 1. to make or become solid or firm. 2. *Mil.* to strengthen by rearranging troops after a successful attack. 3. to unite; combine. —con·sol'i·da'tion, *n.*

con·som·mé (kŏn'sə mā'), *n.* a strong, clear soup made by boiling meat slowly.

con·so·nant (kŏn'sə nənt), *n.* 1. *Phonet.* a sound made with more or less obstruction of the breath stream in its passage outward, as the *l*, *s*, and *t* of *list*. 2. a letter which usually represents such a sound. —*adj.* 3. in agreement; consistent. 4. corresponding in sound, as words. 5. harmonious. —con'so·nance, *n.* —con'so·nant·ly, *adv.*

con·so·nan·tal (kŏn'sə năn'təl), *adj.* of, of the nature of, or marked by a consonant.

con·sort (*n.* kŏn'sôrt; *v.* kən sôrt'), *n.* 1. a husband or wife. 2. one ship accompanying another. —*v.i.*, *v.t.* 3. to associate. 4. to agree or harmonize.

con·sor·ti·um (kən sôr'shĭ əm), *n.*, *pl.* -tia (-shĭ ə). a combination of banks, etc., for carrying into effect some operation requiring much capital.

con·spic·u·ous (kən spĭk'yŏŏ əs), *adj.* 1. easy to be seen. 2. readily attracting attention. —con·spic'u·ous·ly, *adv.* —con·spic'u·ous·ness, *n.*

con·spir·a·cy (kən spĭr'ə sĭ), *n.*, *pl.* -cies. 1. act of conspiring. 2. a plot. —con·spir'a·tor, *n.*

con·spire (kən spīr'), *v.*, -spired, -spiring. —*v.i.* 1. to combine for an evil or unlawful purpose. 2. to act in combination. —*v.t.* 3. to plot. —con·spir'er, *n.*

con·sta·ble (kŏn'stə bəl, kŭn'-), *n.* 1. any of various officers of the peace. 2. *Eng.* a policeman.

con·stab·u·lar·y (kən stăb'yə lĕr'ĭ), *n.*, *pl.* -laries. the police of a district.

con·stant (kŏn'stənt), *adj.* 1. invariable; uniform. 2. continuing without intermission. 3. regularly recurrent. 4. steadfast; faithful. 5. resolute. —*n.* 6. something constant, invariable, or unchanging. —con·stan·cy (kŏn'stən sĭ), *n.* —con'stant·ly, *adv.*

Con·stan·tine I (kŏn'stən tīn', -tēn'), ("the Great") A.D. 288?–337, Roman emperor, A.D. 324–337; built Constantinople.

Con·stan·ti·no·ple (kŏn'stăn tə nō'pəl), *n.* former name of Istanbul.

con·stel·la·tion (kŏn'stə lā'shən), *n.* *Astron.* 1. any of various groups of stars to which definite names have been given. 2. a division of the heavens occupied by such a group.

con·ster·na·tion (kŏn'stər nā'shən), *n.* utter amazement; paralyzing dismay.

con·sti·pate (kŏn'stə pāt'), *v.t.*, -pated, -pating. to cause constipation in. —con'sti·pat'ed, *adj.*

con·sti·pa·tion (kŏn'stə pā'shən), *n.* a condition of the bowels marked by difficult evacuation.

con·stit·u·en·cy (kən stĭch'ŏŏ ən sĭ), *n.*, *pl.*

-cies. 1. the body of voters in a district represented by an elective officer. 2. the district itself.

con·stit·u·ent (kən stĭch'ŏŏ ənt), *adj.* 1. serving to make up a thing; component. 2. having power to frame or alter a political constitution. —*n.* 3. a constituent element, etc. 4. a voter in a district represented by an elective officer.

con·sti·tute (kŏn'stə tūt', -tōōt'), *v.t.*, -tuted, -tuting. 1. to compose; form. 2. to appoint to a function; make. 3. to establish. 4. to give legal form to. 5. to frame.

con·sti·tu·tion (kŏn'stə tū'shən, -tōō'-), *n.* 1. make-up or composition. 2. the physical character of the body. 3. disposition. 4. establishment. 5. any established arrangement or custom. 6. the system of fundamental principles according to which a nation, corporation, etc., is governed. 7. the document embodying these principles.

con·sti·tu·tion·al (kŏn'stə tū'shən əl, -tōō'-), *adj.* 1. inherent in a person's constitution of body or mind. 2. beneficial to the bodily constitution. 3. essential. 4. having the power of, or existing by virtue of and subject to, a constitution. —*n.* 5. a walk or other exercise for health. —con'sti·tu'tion·al·ly, *adv.*

con·sti·tu·tion·al·i·ty (kŏn'stə tū'shə năl'ə tĭ, -tōō'-), *n.* quality of being constitutional.

con·strain (kən strān'), *v.t.* 1. to force, compel, or oblige. 2. to confine forcibly. 3. to restrain. —con·strain'a·ble, *adj.* —con·strain'er, *n.*

con·strained (kən strānd'), *adj.* forced.

con·straint (kən strānt'), *n.* 1. confinement. 2. repression of natural feelings. 3. unnatural restraint in manner, etc. 4. something that constrains.

con·strict (kən strĭkt'), *v.t.* to draw together; compress; cause to contract or shrink. —con·stric'tion, *n.*

con·stric·tor (kən strĭk'tər), *n.* 1. a snake that crushes its prey in its coils. 2. one who or that which constricts.

con·struct (*v.* kən strŭkt'; *n.* kŏn'strŭkt), *v.t.* 1. to build; devise. 2. *Geom.*, *etc.* to draw, as a figure, so as to fulfill given conditions. —*n.* 3. something constructed. —con·struc'tor, con·struct'er, *n.*

con·struc·tion (kən strŭk'shən), *n.* 1. act or art of constructing. 2. structure. 3. *Gram.* the arrangement of two or more forms in a grammatical unit. 4. explanation. —con·struc'tion·al, *adj.*

con·struc·tive (kən strŭk'tĭv), *adj.* 1. tending to construct. 2. structural. 3. deduced by interpretation. —con·struc'tive·ly, *adv.* —con·struc'tive·ness, *n.*

con·strue (kən strōō' *or*, *esp.* *Brit.* kŏn'strōō), *v.*, -strued, -struing. —*v.t.* 1. to explain or interpret. 2. to deduce by interpretation; infer. 3. to translate. 4. to explain the syntax of. —*v.i.* 5. to admit of grammatical analysis. —con·stru'a·ble, *adj.*

con·sul (kŏn'səl), *n.* 1. an agent appointed by an independent state to reside in a foreign state and discharge certain administrative duties. 2. either of the two chief magistrates of the ancient Roman republic. —con'su·lar, *adj.* —con'sul·ship', *n.*

con·su·late (kŏn'sə lĭt), *n.* 1. the premises occupied by a consul. 2. consulship.

con·sult (kən sŭlt'), *v.t.* 1. to ask advice of. 2. to refer to for information. 3. to have regard for (a person's interest, etc.) in making plans. —*v.i.* 4. to confer. —con·sult'a·tive, *adj.* —con·sult'er, *n.*

con·sult·ant (kən sŭl'tənt), *n.* 1. one who consults. 2. one who gives expert advice.

con·sul·ta·tion (kŏn'səl tā'shən), *n.* conference.

con·sume (kən sōōm'), *v.*, -sumed, -suming. —*v.t.* 1. to use up. 2. to devour. 3. to destroy. 4. to spend (money, etc.) wastefully. 5. to engross. —*v.i.* 6. to be consumed. —con·sum'a·ble, *adj.*, *n.*

con·sum·er (kən sōō'mər), *n.* 1. one who consumes. 2. one who uses up a commodity or service.

con·sum·mate (*v.* kŏn'sə māt'; *adj.* kən sŭm'-ĭt), *v.*, -mated, -mating, *adj.* —*v.t.* 1. to bring to completion. —*adj.* 2. complete or perfect. —con·sum'mate·ly, *adv.* —con·sum·ma'tor, *n.*

con·sum·ma·tion (kŏn'sə mā'shən), *n.* completion or perfection.

con·sump·tion (kən sŭmp'shən), *n.* 1. act of consuming. 2. destruction by use. 3. the amount

consumed. **4.** the using up of goods and services. **5.** *Pathol.* **a.** a wasting disease, esp. tuberculosis of the lungs. **b.** progressive wasting of the body.
con·sump·tive (kən sŭmp′tĭv), *adj.* **1.** destructive; wasteful. **2.** *Pathol.* **a.** pertaining to or of the nature of consumption. **b.** affected with consumption. —*n.* **3.** one who suffers from consumption.
cont., **1.** containing. **2.** continued.
con·tact (kŏn′tăkt), *n.* **1.** state or fact of touching. **2.** immediate proximity or association. **3.** *Elect.* a junction between electric conductors which permits current flow. **4.** *Med.* one who has lately been exposed to an infected person. —*v.t.* **5.** to put into contact. **6.** *Colloq.* to get in touch with. —*v.i.* **7.** to enter into or be in contact.
con·ta·gion (kən tā′jən), *n.* **1.** the communication of disease by contact. **2.** a disease so communicated. **3.** influence.
con·ta·gious (kən tā′jəs), *adj.* **1.** communicable to other individuals, as a disease. **2.** causing or involving contagion. —**con·ta′gious·ly,** *adv.* —**con·ta′gious·ness,** *n.*
con·tain (kən tān′), *v.t.* **1.** to have within itself. **2.** to have capacity for. **3.** to comprise. **4.** to restrain. **5.** *Math.* to be divisible by, without a remainder. —**con·tain′a·ble,** *adj.*
con·tain·er (kən tā′nər), *n.* a receptacle, as a box, bottle, or other containing structure.
con·tam·i·nate (kən tăm′ə nāt′), *v.t.,* **-nated, -nating.** to render impure by contact or mixture. —**con·tam′i·na′tion,** *n.*
con·temn (kən těm′), *v.t.* to treat scornfully. —**con·temn·er** (kən těm′nər), *n.*
con·tem·plate (kŏn′təm plāt′), *v.,* **-plated, -plating.** —*v.t.* **1.** to observe thoughtfully. **2.** to consider attentively. **3.** to intend. **4.** to have in view as a future event. —*v.i.* **5.** to meditate. —**con′tem·pla′tive,** *adj.* —**con′tem·pla′tor,** *n.*
con·tem·pla·tion (kŏn′təm plā′shən), *n.* **1.** act of contemplating; reflection. **2.** religious meditation. **3.** intention. **4.** prospect.
con·tem·po·ra·ne·ous (kən těm′pə rā′nĭ əs), *adj.* contemporary.
con·tem·po·rar·y (kən těm′pə rěr′ĭ), *adj., n., pl.* **-raries.** —*adj.* **1.** existing or occurring at the same time. **2.** of the same age. —*n.* **3.** one belonging to the same time or period with another or others. **4.** a person of the same age as another.
con·tempt (kən těmpt′), *n.* **1.** act of despising. **2.** the feeling toward anything considered mean, vile, or worthless; scorn. **3.** dishonor; disgrace. **4.** *Law.* disobedience to, or open disrespect of, a court or legislature.
con·tempt·i·ble (kən těmp′tə bəl), *adj.* deserving of or held in contempt. —**con·tempt′i·bly,** *adv.*
con·temp·tu·ous (kən těmp′chŏŏ əs), *adj.* expressing contempt; scornful. —**con·temp′tu·ous·ly,** *adv.*
con·tend (kən těnd′), *v.i.* **1.** to struggle in opposition. **2.** to compete; vie. **3.** to dispute earnestly. —*v.t.* **4.** to assert earnestly. —**con·tend′er,** *n.*
con·tent[1] (kŏn′těnt; *rarely* kən těnt′), *n.* **1.** (*usually pl.*) that which is contained. **2.** substance, as of a document. **3.** capacity. **4.** area. **5.** the amount contained.
con·tent[2] (kən těnt′), *adj.* **1.** satisfied. **2.** easy in mind. **3.** willing; assenting. —*v.t.* **4.** to make content. —*n.* **5.** contentment.
con·tent·ed (kən těn′tĭd), *adj.* satisfied. —**con·tent′ed·ly,** *adv.* —**con·tent′ed·ness,** *n.*
con·ten·tion (kən těn′shən), *n.* **1.** strife, competition, or controversy. **2.** a point made or upheld in controversy. —**con·ten′tious,** *adj.*
con·tent·ment (kən těnt′mənt), *n.* state of being contented; satisfaction; ease of mind.
con·test (*n.* kŏn′těst; *v.* kən těst′), *n.* **1.** struggle for victory or superiority. **2.** a competition. **3.** controversy. —*v.t.* **4.** to fight for, as in battle. **5.** to argue against. —*v.i.* **6.** to dispute or compete. —**con·test′a·ble,** *adj.*
con·test·ant (kən těs′tənt), *n.* **1.** one who takes part in a contest or competition. **2.** one who contests the result of an election, etc.
con·text (kŏn′těkst), *n.* the parts of a discourse or writing which precede or follow, and are directly connected with, a given passage or word. —**con·tex·tu·al** (kən těks′chŏŏ əl), *adj.* —**con·tex′tu·al·ly,** *adv.*
con·ti·gu·i·ty (kŏn′tə gū′ə tĭ), *n., pl.* **-ties.** state of being contiguous.

con·tig·u·ous (kən tĭg′yŏŏ əs), *adj.* **1.** touching; in contact. **2.** near. —**con·tig′u·ous·ly,** *adv.*
con·ti·nence (kŏn′tə nəns), *n.* self-restraint, esp. in regard to sexual passion.
con·ti·nent (kŏn′tə nənt), *n.* **1.** one of the main land masses of the globe (Europe, Asia, Africa, North America, South America, and Australia). **2.** the mainland. **3. the Continent,** the mainland of Europe. **4.** a continuous tract of land. —*adj.* **5.** exercising restraint in desire or passion. —**con′ti·nent·ly,** *adv.*
con·ti·nen·tal (kŏn′tə něn′təl), *adj.* **1.** of, or of the nature of, a continent. **2.** (*usually cap.*) or pertaining to the mainland of Europe. **3.** (*cap.*) of the colonies during and immediately after the Revolutionary War. —*n.* **4.** (*cap.*) a soldier of the Continental army. **5.** a piece of paper money issued during the American Revolution.
con·tin·gen·cy (kən tĭn′jən sĭ), *n., pl.* **-cies.** **1.** dependence on chance or on the fulfillment of a condition. **2.** a contingent event.
con·tin·gent (kən tĭn′jənt), *adj.* **1.** dependent for existence, etc., on something not yet certain. **2.** uncertain; possible. **3.** accidental. —*n.* **4.** a share to be contributed. **5.** a quota of troops furnished. **6.** a representative group at an assemblage. **7.** a contingency. —**con·tin′gent·ly,** *adv.*
con·tin·u·al (kən tĭn′yŏŏ əl), *adj.* **1.** proceeding without interruption or cessation. **2.** of regular or frequent recurrence. —**con·tin′u·al·ly,** *adv.*
con·tin·u·ance (kən tĭn′yŏŏ əns), *n.* **1.** continuation. **2.** *Law.* adjournment.
con·tin·u·a·tion (kən tĭn′yŏŏ ā′shən), *n.* **1.** act or fact of continuing. **2.** state of being continued. **3.** extension to a further point. **4.** that by which anything is continued, as a sequel.
con·tin·ue (kən tĭn′ū), *v.,* **-tinued, -tinuing.** —*v.i.* **1.** to go forward or onward in any course or action. **2.** to go on after interruption. **3.** to endure. **4.** to abide; stay. —*v.t.* **5.** to go on with or persist in. **6.** to extend or prolong. **7.** to resume. **8.** to say in continuation. **9.** to cause to endure. **10.** to carry over, postpone, or adjourn.
con·ti·nu·i·ty (kŏn′tə nū′ə tĭ, -nŏŏ′-), *n., pl.* **-ties.** **1.** state or quality of being continuous. **2.** a continuous whole. **3.** a scenario or script.
con·tin·u·ous (kən tĭn′yŏŏ əs), *adj.* **1.** having the parts in immediate connection. **2.** uninterrupted. —**con·tin′u·ous·ly,** *adv.* —**con·tin′u·ous·ness,** *n.*
con·tin·u·um (kən tĭn′yŏŏ əm), *n., pl.* **-tinua** (-tĭn′yŏŏ ə). a continuous extent, series, or whole.
con·tort (kən tôrt′), *v.t.* to twist; distort. —**con·tor′tion,** *n.*
con·tor·tion·ist (kən tôr′shən ĭst), *n.* one whose gymnastic feats involve contorted postures.
con·tour (kŏn′tŏŏr), *n.* **1.** the outline of a figure or body. —*v.t.* **2.** to mark with lines indicating the contour of.
con·tra·band (kŏn′trə bănd′), *n.* **1.** anything prohibited by law from being imported or exported. **2.** goods imported or exported illegally. **3.** smuggling. **4.** goods which neutrals cannot supply to one belligerent except at the risk of seizure by the other. —*adj.* **5.** prohibited from export or import.
con·tra·bass (kŏn′trə bās′), *Music.* —*n.* **1.** (in any family of instruments) the member below the bass. **2.** (in the violin family) the double bass. —*adj.* **3.** denoting such instruments.
con·tra·cep·tion (kŏn′trə sěp′shən), *n.* the prevention, by deliberate measures, of conception. —**con′tra·cep′tive,** *adj., n.*
con·tract (kŏn′trăkt; *v.* kən trăkt′), *n.* **1.** an agreement between two or more parties for the doing or not doing of some definite thing. **2.** the writing containing such an agreement. **3.** the formal agreement of marriage. **4.** Also, **contract bridge.** a modification of auction bridge in which the side which wins the bid can earn towards game only that number of tricks bid. **5.** (in auction or contract bridge) **a.** the highest bid. **b.** the number of tricks so bid. —*v.t.* **6.** to draw together. **7.** to wrinkle. **8.** to shorten (a word, etc.), as by omitting some elements. **9.** to acquire or incur. —*v.i.* **10.** to be drawn together or reduced; shrink. **11.** to enter into an agreement. —**con·tract′ed,** *adj.* —**con·tract′i·ble,** *adj.* —**con·trac′tive,** *adj.*
con·trac·tile (kən trăk′təl, -tĭl), *adj.* capable of contraction.
con·trac·tion (kən trăk′shən), *n.* **1.** act of con-

tracting. 2. state of being contracted. 3. a shortened form of a word, etc.

con·trac·tor (kŏn′trăk tər, kən trăk′tər), *n.* one who contracts to furnish supplies or perform work.

con·trac·tu·al (kən trăk′chŏŏ əl), *adj.* of, or of the nature of, a contract.

con·tra·dict (kŏn′trə dĭkt′), *v.t.* 1. to assert or be the contrary or opposite of. 2. to deny the words of (a person). —*v.i.* 3. to utter a contrary statement. —**con′tra·dict′a·ble**, *adj.* —**con′tra·dic′tive**, *adj.*

con·tra·dic·tion (kŏn′trə dĭk′shən), *n.* 1. act of contradicting. 2. assertion of the contrary. 3. a statement, fact, etc., that contradicts another or itself. 4. inconsistency.

con·tra·dic·to·ry (kŏn′trə dĭk′tə rĭ), *adj.* 1. asserting the contrary or opposite; inconsistent. 2. given to contradiction.

con·tra·dis·tinc·tion (kŏn′trə dĭs tĭngk′shən), *n.* distinction by opposition or contrast.

con·tral·to (kən trăl′tō), *n., pl.* **-tos**, *adj. Music.* —*n.* 1. the lowest female voice or voice part. 2. the highest male voice or voice part. 3. a singer with a contralto voice. —*adj.* 4. pertaining to the contralto.

con·trap·tion (kən trăp′shən), *n. Colloq.* a contrivance; a device.

con·tra·pun·tal (kŏn′trə pŭn′təl), *adj.* 1. of or pertaining to counterpoint. 2. composed of relatively independent melodies sounded together.

con·tra·ri·wise (kŏn′trĕr ĭ wīz′), *adv.* 1. in the opposite way. 2. on the contrary. 3. perversely.

con·tra·ry (kŏn′trĕr ĭ; *for 4 also* kən trâr′ĭ), *adj., n., pl.* **-ries**, *adv.* —*adj.* 1. opposite in nature or character. 2. opposite in direction or position. 3. unfavorable. 4. perverse. —*n.* 5. that which is opposite. 6. either of two contrary things. —*adv.* 7. contrariwise. —**con′tra·ri·ly**, *adv.* —**con′tra·ri·ness**, *n.*

con·trast (*v.* kən trăst′; *n.* kŏn′trăst), *v.t.* 1. to set in opposition in order to show unlikeness. 2. to form a contrast to. —*v.i.* 3. to form a contrast. —*n.* 4. act of contrasting. 5. state of being contrasted. 6. a striking exhibition of unlikeness. 7. something strikingly unlike.

con·tra·vene (kŏn′trə vēn′), *v.t.,* **-vened, -vening.** 1. to go or act counter to; oppose. 2. to violate or infringe. —**con·tra·ven·tion** (kŏn′trə vĕn′shən), *n.*

con·trib·ute (kən trĭb′ūt), *v.,* **-uted, -uting.** —*v.t.* 1. to give in common with others. 2. to furnish to a magazine, etc. —*v.i.* 3. to make contribution. —**con·trib′u·tive, con·trib′u·to′ry,** *adj.* —**con·trib′u·tive·ly,** *adv.* —**con·trib′u·tor,** *n.*

con·tri·bu·tion (kŏn′trə bū′shən), *n.* 1. act of contributing. 2. something contributed. 3. an article contributed to a magazine, etc. 4. a levy.

con·trite (kən trīt′, kŏn′trīt), *adj.* deeply penitent. —**con·trite′ly,** *adv.* —**con·trite′ness,** **con·tri·tion** (kən trĭsh′ən), *n.*

con·triv·ance (kən trī′vəns), *n.* 1. a device, esp. a mechanical one. 2. act, manner, or power of contriving.

con·trive (kən trīv′), *v.,* **-trived, -triving.** —*v.t.* 1. to plan with ingenuity; devise. 2. to plot (evil, etc.). 3. to bring about, as by a plan or scheme. —*v.i.* 4. to plan. 5. to plot. —**con·triv′er,** *n.*

con·trol (kən trōl′), *v.,* **-trolled, -trolling,** *n.* —*v.t.* 1. to exercise direction over; dominate. 2. to curb, restrain, or check. —*n.* 3. act or power of controlling; regulation. 4. check or restraint. 5. something that serves to control. 6. a device for regulating and guiding a machine. 7. (*pl.*) a coördinated arrangement of such devices. —**con·trol′la·ble,** *adj.* —**con·trol′la·bil′i·ty,** *n.*

con·trol·ler (kən trō′lər), *n.* 1. one employed to check expenditures, etc. 2. one who regulates. 3. a regulating mechanism. —**con·trol′ler·ship′,** *n.*

con·tro·ver·sial (kŏn′trə vûr′shəl), *adj.* 1. of, or of the nature of, controversy. 2. debatable. 3. disputatious. —**con′tro·ver′sial·ist,** *n.* —**con′tro·ver′sial·ly,** *adv.*

con·tro·ver·sy (kŏn′trə vûr′sĭ), *n., pl.* **-sies.** dispute, debate, or contention.

con·tro·vert (kŏn′trə vûrt′, kŏn′trə vûrt′), *v.t.* 1. to dispute; deny. 2. to debate; discuss.

con·tu·ma·cious (kŏn′tyŏŏ mā′shəs, -tŏŏ-), *adj.* stubbornly perverse or disobedient. —**con′tu·ma′cious·ly,** *adv.* —**con′tu·ma′cious·ness,** **con·tu·ma·cy** (kŏn′tyŏŏ mə sĭ, -tŏŏ-), *n.*

con·tu·me·ly (kŏn′tyŏŏ mə lĭ, -tŏŏ-, kən tū′mə lĭ, -tōō-; *formerly* kŏn′tyŏŏ mē′lĭ), *n., pl.* **-lies.** 1. contemptuous or humiliating treatment. 2. a humiliating insult. —**con·tu·me·li·ous** (kŏn′tyŏŏ mē′lĭ əs, -tōō-), *adj.*

con·tuse (kən tūz′, -tōōz′), *v.t.,* **-tused, -tusing.** to bruise.

con·tu·sion (kən tū′zhən, -tōō′-), *n.* a bruise.

co·nun·drum (kə nŭn′drəm), *n.* 1. a riddle the answer to which involves a pun. 2. any puzzle.

con·va·lesce (kŏn′və lĕs′), *v.i.,* **-lesced, -lescing.** to progress toward recovery of health.

con·va·les·cence (kŏn′və lĕs′əns), *n.* the gradual recovery of health and strength after illness. —**con′va·les′cent,** *adj., n.*

con·vec·tion (kən vĕk′shən), *n.* the transference of heat by the circulation or movement of the heated parts of a liquid or gas. —**con·vec′tion·al,** *adj.* —**con·vec′tive,** *adj.*

con·vene (kən vēn′), *v.i., v.t.,* **-vened, -vening.** to come together; assemble. —**con·ven′er,** *n.*

con·ven·ience (kən vēn′yəns), *n.* 1. quality of being convenient. 2. a situation or time convenient for one. 3. advantage. 4. anything convenient.

con·ven·ient (kən vēn′yənt), *adj.* 1. agreeable to the needs or purpose; favorable, easy, or comfortable for use. 2. easily accessible. —**con·ven′ient·ly,** *adv.*

con·vent (kŏn′vĕnt), *n.* 1. a community of persons devoted to religious life under a superior. 2. a society of monks, friars, or nuns. 3. a monastery or nunnery.

con·ven·ti·cle (kən vĕn′tə kəl), *n.* 1. a secret or unauthorized meeting, esp. for religious worship. 2. a place of meeting.

con·ven·tion (kən vĕn′shən), *n.* 1. a meeting or assembly, as of delegates. 2. an agreement or contract. 3. an international agreement, as one dealing with postal service, etc. 4. general agreement; accepted usage. 5. a rule, method, or practice established by general usage.

con·ven·tion·al (kən vĕn′shən əl), *adj.* 1. conforming to accepted standards, as of conduct. 2. pertaining to convention; established by general usage. 3. formal, rather than spontaneous or original. —**con·ven′tion·al·ism′,** *n.* —**con·ven′tion·al·ly,** *adv.*

con·ven·tion·al·i·ty (kən vĕn′shə năl′ə tĭ), *n., pl.* **-ties.** 1. conventional quality. 2. adherence to convention. 3. a conventional practice, form, etc.

con·verge (kən vûrj′), *v.,* **-verged, -verging.** —*v.i.* 1. to tend to meet in a point or line. —*v.t.* 2. to cause to converge.

con·ver·gence (kən vûr′jəns), *n.* 1. act or fact of converging. 2. convergent state or quality. 3. degree or point of convergence. —**con·ver′gent,** *adj.*

con·ver·sant (kŏn′vər sənt, kən vûr′-), *adj.* 1. familiar by use or study. 2. acquainted. —**con′ver·sant·ly,** *adv.*

con·ver·sa·tion (kŏn′vər sā′shən), *n.* 1. informal interchange of thoughts by spoken words. 2. association; intimate acquaintance.

con·ver·sa·tion·al (kŏn′vər sā′shən əl), *adj.* 1. of or characteristic of conversation. 2. given to conversation. —**con′ver·sa′tion·al·ly,** *adv.*

con·ver·sa·tion·al·ist (kŏn′vər sā′shən əl ĭst), *n.* one given to or excelling in conversation.

con·verse¹ (*v.* kən vûrs′; *n.* kŏn′vûrs), *v.,* **-versed, -versing,** *n.* —*v.i.* 1. to talk informally with another. —*n.* 2. conversation. —**con·vers′er,** *n.*

con·verse² (*adj.* kən vûrs′, kŏn′vûrs; *n.* kŏn′vûrs), *adj.* 1. opposite or contrary in direction or action. —*n.* 2. a thing which is the opposite or contrary of another. —**con·verse′ly** (kən vûrs′lĭ, kŏn′vûrs-), *adv.*

con·vert (*v.* kən vûrt′; *n.* kŏn′vûrt), *v.t.* 1. to change into something of different form or properties. 2. to cause to adopt a different religion, opinion, etc. 3. to divert from the proper or intended use. 4. *Law.* to assume unlawful rights of ownership of (personal property). 5. to exchange for an equivalent. —*v.i.* 6. to be converted. —*n.* 7. one who has been converted. —**con·ver′sion** (kən vûr′zhən, -shən), *n.*

con·vert·er (kən vûr′tər), *n.* 1. one who or that which converts. 2. an oval vessel in which molten pig iron is converted into steel. Also, **con·ver′tor.**

con·vert·i·ble (kən vûr′tə bəl), *adj.* 1. capable

of being converted. **2.** *Auto.* having a folding top. **—n. 3.** *Colloq.* a convertible automobile. —con·vert'i·bil'i·ty, *n.*

con·vex (*adj.* kŏn věks', kən-; *n.* kŏn'věks), *adj.* **1.** curved outward. **—n. 2.** a convex surface or thing. —con·vex'i·ty, *n.* —con·vex'ly, *adv.*

con·vey (kən vā'), *v.t.* **1.** to carry or transport from one place to another. **2.** to transmit. **3.** to communicate. **4.** *Law.* to transfer.

con·vey·ance (kən vā'əns), *n.* **1.** act of conveying. **2.** a means of conveyance, esp. a vehicle. **3.** *Law.* the transfer of property from one person to another.

con·vey·or (kən vā'ər), *n.* **1.** one that conveys. **2.** a contrivance for transporting material from one place to another. Also, **con·vey'er.**

con·vict (*v.* kən vĭkt'; *n.* kŏn'vĭkt), *v.t.* **1.** to prove or declare guilty of an offense. **—n. 2.** a convicted person serving a prison sentence.

con·vic·tion (kən vĭk'shən), *n.* **1.** act of convicting. **2.** state of being convicted. **3.** act of convincing. **4.** state of being convinced. **5.** a firm belief.

con·vince (kən vĭns'), *v.t.,* -vinced, -vincing. to persuade by argument or proof. —con·vinc'er, *n.* —con·vin'ci·ble, *adj.* —con·vinc'ing·ly, *adv.*

con·viv·i·al (kən vĭv'ĭ əl), *adj.* fond of feasting, drinking, and merry company.

con·vo·ca·tion (kŏn'və kā'shən), *n.* **1.** act of convoking. **2.** fact or state of being convoked. **3.** an assembly. —con'vo·ca'tion·al, *adj.*

con·voke (kən vōk'), *v.t.,* -voked, -voking. to call together; summon to meet. —con·vok'er, *n.*

con·vo·lu·tion (kŏn'və lōō'shən), *n.* **1.** a rolled up or coiled condition. **2.** a whorl. **3.** one of the sinuous ridges of the surface of the brain.

con·voy (*v.* kən voi', kŏn'voi; *n.* kŏn'voi), *v.t.* **1.** to escort, now usually for protection. **—n. 2.** act of convoying. **3.** a warship, etc., that escorts, esp. for protection. **4.** a formation of ships, etc., accompanied by a protecting escort.

con·vulse (kən vŭls'), *v.t.,* -vulsed, -vulsing. **1.** to shake violently. **2.** to cause to laugh violently.

con·vul·sion (kən vŭl'shən), *n.* **1.** contortion of the body caused by violent muscular contractions. **2.** violent disturbance. **3.** a violent fit of laughter. —con·vul'sive, *adj.* —con·vul'sive·ly, *adv.*

co·ny (kō'nĭ, kŭn'ĭ), *n., pl.* -nies. **1.** the fur of a rabbit, esp. when dyed to simulate Hudson seal. **2.** *Archaic.* a rabbit.

coo (kōō), *v.,* cooed, cooing, *n.* —v.i. **1.** to utter the soft, murmuring sound of doves, or a similar sound. **2.** to murmur amorously. —v.t. **3.** to utter by cooing. —n. **4.** a cooing sound. —coo'·er, *n.*

cook (kŏŏk), *v.t.* **1.** to prepare (food) by boiling, baking, roasting, etc. **2.** to subject (anything) to heat. **3.** *Colloq.* to concoct. **4.** *Slang.* to ruin. —v.i. **5.** to prepare food by heat. **6.** to undergo cooking. **—n. 7.** one whose occupation is the preparation of food for the table. —cook'er, *n.*

cook·book (kŏŏk'bŏŏk'), *n.* a book containing recipes and instructions for cooking.

cook·er·y (kŏŏk'ə rĭ), *n., pl.* -eries. **1.** the art of cooking. **2.** a place for cooking.

cook·y (kŏŏk'ĭ), *n., pl.* cookies. *U.S.* a small cake of stiff sweet dough. Also, **cook'ie.**

cool (kōōl), *adj.* **1.** moderately cold. **2.** imparting or permitting a sensation of moderate coldness. **3.** calm; deliberate. **4.** lacking in enthusiasm or cordiality. **5.** calmly audacious. **—n. 6.** the cool part, place, time, etc. **7.** coolness. —v.t., v.i. **8.** to make or become cool. —cool'·ish, *adj.* —cool'ly, *adv.* —cool'ness, *n.*

cool·er (kōōl'ər), *n.* **1.** an apparatus for cooling or keeping cool. **2.** a refrigerant. **3.** *Slang.* a jail.

Cool·idge (kōōl'ĭj), *n.* Calvin, 1872–1933, 30th president of the U.S., 1923–29.

coo·lie (kōōl'ĭ), *n.* (in India, China, etc.) an unskilled native laborer. Also, **coo'ly.**

coon (kōōn), *n.* raccoon.

coop (kōōp, kŏŏp), *n.* **1.** an enclosure, cage, or pen in which fowls, etc., are confined. **2.** any small place. **3.** *Slang.* a prison. —v.t. **4.** to place or keep in a coop.

coop·er (kōō'pər, kŏŏp'ər), *n.* **1.** one who makes or repairs casks, barrels, etc. —v.t. **2.** to make or repair (casks, etc.). —v.i. **3.** to work as a cooper.

Coo·per (kōō'pər, kŏŏp'ər), *n.* **James Fenimore,** 1789–1851, U.S. novelist.

coop·er·age (kōō'pər ĭj, kŏŏp'ər-), *n.* **1.** the work of a cooper. **2.** his place of work.

co·öp·er·ate (kō ŏp'ə rāt'), *v.i.,* -ated, -ating. to work or act together. Also, **co-op'er·ate',** **co·op'er·ate'.** —co·öp'er·a'tor, *n.*

co·öp·er·a·tion (kō ŏp'ə rā'shən), *n.* **1.** joint operation or action. **2.** activity shared for mutual benefit. Also, **co-op'er·a'tion, co·op'er·a'tion.**

co·öp·er·a·tive (kō ŏp'ə rā'tĭv, -ŏp'rə tĭv), *adj.* **1.** coöperating; of coöperation. **2.** pertaining to economic coöperation. **—n. 3.** a coöperative society or store. Also, **co-op'er·a'tive, co·op'er·a'tive.** —co·öp'er·a·tive·ly, *adv.* —co·öp'er·a·tive·ness, *n.*

coöperative store, a retail store owned and managed by consumer-customers.

co·ör·di·nate (*adj., n.* kō ôr'də nĭt, -nāt'; *v.* kō ôr'də nāt'), *adj., n., v.,* -nated, -nating. —adj. **1.** equal in rank or importance. **2.** involving coördination. **3.** *Math.* using or pertaining to systems of coördinates. **—n. 4.** an equal. **5.** *Math.* a magnitude used in defining the position of a point, line, etc. —v.t. **6.** to place in the same order, rank, etc. **7.** to place in due order or proper position. **8.** to combine in harmonious relation or action. —v.i. **9.** to become coördinate. **10.** to assume proper order or relation. **11.** to act in harmonious combination. Also, **co·or'di·nate, co·or'di·nate.** —co·ör'di·nate·ly, *adv.* —co·ör'di·na'tion, *n.* —co·ör'di·na'tive, *adj.* —co·ör'di·na'tor, *n.*

coot (kōōt), *n.* **1.** any of certain aquatic birds characterized by lobate toes and short wings and tail. **2.** *Colloq.* a fool.

coot·ie (kōō'tĭ), *n.* *Orig. Brit. Colloq.* a louse.

cop (kŏp), *n., v.,* copped, copping. **—n. 1.** *Colloq.* a policeman. —v.t. *Slang.* **2.** to catch. **3.** to steal.

cope¹ (kōp), *v.i.,* coped, coping. to struggle or contend, esp. on even terms.

cope² (kōp), *n., v.,* coped, coping. **—n. 1.** a long mantle worn by ecclesiastics in processions and on other occasions. **2.** any canopylike covering. **3.** the sky. —v.t. **4.** to furnish with a cope.

Co·pen·ha·gen (kō'pən hā'gən), *n.* the capital of Denmark. 890,130.

Co·per·ni·cus (kō pûr'nə kəs, kə-), *n.* **Nicolaus,** 1473–1543, Polish astronomer.

cope·stone (kōp'stōn'), *n.* **1.** the top stone, as of a building. **2.** a stone used for or in coping.

cop·i·er (kŏp'ĭ ər), *n.* one who copies; copyist.

cop·ing (kō'pĭng), *n.* the uppermost course of a wall, usually made sloping to carry off water.

co·pi·ous (kō'pĭ əs), *adj.* **1.** abundant. **2.** exhibiting abundance. —co'pi·ous·ly, *adv.* —co'·pi·ous·ness, *n.*

cop·per (kŏp'ər), *n.* **1.** *Chem.* a malleable, ductile metallic element having a characteristic reddish-brown color. *Symbol:* Cu; *at. wt.:* 63.57; *at. no.:* 29; *sp. gr.:* 8.92 at 20°C. **2.** a copper coin, as the U.S. cent. **3.** a metallic reddish brown. —cop'per·y, *adj.*

cop·per·as (kŏp'ər əs), *n.* ferrous sulfate, used in dyeing, medicine, photography, etc.

cop·per·head (kŏp'ər hĕd'), *n.* **1.** a venomous snake of the U.S., having a copper-colored head. **2.** (*cap.*) a Northern sympathizer with the South during the U.S. Civil War.

cop·per·plate (kŏp'ər plāt'), *n.* **1.** a plate of polished copper on which writing, etc., is engraved or etched. **2.** a print or an impression from such a plate. **3.** engraving or printing of this kind.

cop·pice (kŏp'ĭs), *n.* *Chiefly Brit.* a wood or thicket of small trees or bushes. Also, **copse** (kŏps).

cop·ra (kŏp'rə), *n.* the dried kernel or meat of the coconut, from which coconut oil is expressed.

cop·u·la (kŏp'yə lə), *n., pl.* -las, -lae (-lē'). **1.** something that links together. **2.** *Gram.* a word (in English the verb *be*) which acts as a link between subject and predicate. —cop'u·lar, *adj.*

cop·u·late (kŏp'yə lāt'), *v.i.,* -lated, -lating. to unite in sexual intercourse. —cop'u·la'tion, *n.*

cop·u·la·tive (kŏp'yə lā'tĭv), *adj.* **1.** serving to couple. **2.** involving or consisting of connected words or clauses. **3.** of the nature of a copula. **4.** of or pertaining to copulation. **—n. 5.** a copulative word. —cop'u·la'tive·ly, *adv.*

cop·y (kŏp'ĭ), *n., pl.* copies, *v.,* copied, copying. **—n. 1.** a transcript, reproduction, or imitation of an original. 2. that which is to be transcribed, reproduced, or imitated. 3. material intended to be reproduced in print. 4. one of the specimens of the same engraving or the like. 5. an example of penmanship to be copied by a pupil. —*v.t.* 6. to make a copy of. 7. to imitate. —*v.i.* 8. to make a copy or copies.

cop·y·ist (kŏp′Ĭ Ĭst), *n.* a transcriber.

cop·y·right (kŏp′Ĭ rīt′), *n.* 1. the exclusive right, granted by law for a term of years, to make and dispose of copies of, and otherwise control, a literary, musical, or artistic work. —*adj.* 2. protected by copyright. —*v.t.* 3. to secure a copyright on.

co·quet (kō kĕt′), *v.*, **-quetted, -quetting,** *adj.* —*v.i.* 1. to flirt. 2. to trifle; dally. —*adj.* 3. coquettish.

co·quet·ry (kō′kə trĭ, kō kĕt′rĬ), *n.*, *pl.* **-ries.** 1. flirtation. 2. trifling.

co·quette (kō kĕt′), *n.* a flirt. —**co·quet′tish,** *adj.* —**co·quet′tish·ly,** *adv.* —**co·quet′tish·ness,** *n.*

cor·al (kŏr′əl, kŏr′-), *n.* 1. the hard, calcareous (red, white, black, etc.) skeleton of any of various marine coelenterate animals, the individual polyps of which come forth by budding. 2. such skeletons collectively, forming reefs, etc. 3. an animal of this kind. 4. a reddish yellow. —*adj.* 5. made of coral. 6. making coral. 7. resembling coral, esp. in color.

Coral Sea, a part of the S Pacific, partially enclosed by NE Australia, New Guinea, the Solomon Islands, and the New Hebrides.

cor·bel (kôr′bəl), *n.*, *v.*, **-beled, -beling** or (*esp. Brit.*) **-belled, -belling.** *Archit.* —*n.* 1. a supporting projection of stone, wood, etc., on the face of a wall. —*v.t.* 2. to furnish with corbels.

cord (kôrd), *n.* 1. a string or small rope. 2. *Elect.* a small, very flexible insulated cable. 3. *Anat.* a cordlike structure. 4. a cordlike rib on the surface of cloth. 5. a ribbed fabric, esp. corduroy. 6. (*pl.*) corduroy trousers. 7. a unit of volume used chiefly for fuel wood, now generally equal to 128 cubic feet. —*v.t.* 8. to furnish with a cord. 9. to bind or fasten with cords. 10. to pile (wood) in cords. —**cord′ed,** *adj.*

cord·age (kôr′dĬj), *n.* 1. cords or ropes collectively. 2. a quantity of wood measured in cords.

cor·date (kôr′dāt), *adj.* heart-shaped. —**cor′·date·ly,** *adv.*

cor·di·al (kôr′jəl), *adj.* 1. hearty; warmly friendly. 2. stimulating. —*n.* 3. anything that invigorates. 4. a liqueur. —**cor/dial·ly,** *adv.* —**cor·di·al·i·ty** (kär jăl′ə tĬ), **cor/dial·ness,** *n.*

cor·dil·le·ra (kôr′dĬl yâr′ə, kôr dĬl′ə rə), *n.* a chain of mountains.

cord·ite (kôr′dīt), *n.* a smokeless powder composed of nitroglycerin, nitrocellulose, and mineral jelly.

Cór·do·ba (kôr′dō bä), *n.* 1. Also, **Cor·do·va** (kôr′də və). a city in S Spain. 143,206. 2. a city in central Argentina. 339,375.

cor·don (kôr′dən), *n.* 1. a cord or braid worn for ornament. 2. a ribbon worn, usually diagonally across the breast, as a badge of a knightly or honorary order. 3. a line of sentinels, military posts, or the like, guarding a particular area.

cor·do·van (kôr′də vən), *adj.* 1. designating or made of a leather made orig. at Córdoba. —*n.* 2. cordovan leather.

cor·du·roy (kôr′də roi′, kôr′də roi′), *n.* 1. a cotton pile fabric with lengthwise ridges. 2. (*pl.*) trousers made of this. —*adj.* 3. of or like corduroy. 4. constructed of logs laid together transversely, as a road across swampy ground.

core (kôr), *n.*, *v.*, **cored, coring.** —*n.* 1. the central part of a fleshy fruit, containing the seeds. 2. the central or most essential part. 3. *Elect.* the piece of iron, bundle of iron wires, or the like, forming the central or inner portion of an electromagnet, induction coil, or the like. —*v.t.* 4. to remove the core of (fruit). —**cor′er,** *n.*

Cor·inth (kôr′Ĭnth, kŏr′-), *n.* an ancient city in Greece, famed for its luxury.

Co·rin·thi·an (kə rĬn′thĬ ən), *adj.* 1. of Corinth. 2. luxurious. 3. *Archit.* designating or pertaining to one of the three Greek orders, distinguished by a bell-shaped capital with rows of acanthus leaves. —*n.* 4. a native or inhabitant of Corinth. 5. (*pl.*) the two epistles of the New Testament addressed by St. Paul to the Christian community at Corinth.

cork (kôrk), *n.* 1. the outer bark of a species of oak of Mediterranean countries, used for making stoppers of bottles, floats, etc. 2. the tree itself.

3. something made of cork. 4. a piece of cork, or of other material (as rubber), used as a stopper, etc. 5. *Angling.* a small float. 6. *Bot.* an outer tissue of bark. —*v.t.* 7. to provide with a cork. 8. to stop with a cork. 9. to blacken with burnt cork. —**cork′y,** *adj.*

Cork (kôrk), *n.* a seaport in S Republic of Ireland. 75,484.

cork·screw (kôrk′skrōō′), *n.* 1. an instrument consisting of a metal spiral with a sharp point, used to draw corks from bottles. —*adj.* 2. spiral.

cor·mo·rant (kôr′mə rənt), *n.* 1. any bird of a family comprising large, voracious water birds with a long neck and a pouch under the beak in which they hold captured fish. 2. a greedy or rapacious person. —*adj.* 3. greedy.

corn[1] (kôrn), *n.* 1. maize. 2. any edible grain, esp. wheat in England, and oats in Scotland. 3. a single seed of certain plants, esp. of cereal plants. —*v.t.* 4. to preserve and season with salt in grains. 5. to preserve or cure in brine, as meat. —**corned,** *adj.*

corn[2] (kôrn), *n.* a horny callosity of the epidermis, caused by pressure or friction, esp. on the toes or feet.

corn-cob (kôrn′kŏb′), *n. U.S.* 1. the woody core in which the grains of an ear of maize are embedded. 2. a tobacco pipe with a bowl made of this.

cor·ne·a (kôr′nĬ ə), *n. Anat.* the transparent anterior part of the external coat of the eye, covering the iris and the pupil. —**cor′ne·al,** *adj.*

cor·ner (kôr′nər), *n.* 1. the meeting place of two converging lines or surfaces. 2. an angle. 3. a projecting angle. 4. the place where two streets meet. 5. a margin; edge. 6. any narrow, secluded, or secret place. 7. an awkward position, esp. one from which escape is impossible. 8. any part, even the least or the most remote. 9. *Finance.* a monopoly of the available supply of a commodity, to a point permitting control of price. 10. a piece to protect the corner of anything. —*v.t.* 11. to furnish with corners. 12. to place in, or drive into, a corner. 13. to form a corner in (a stock, etc.). —*v.i.* 14. *U.S.* to meet in a corner.

cor·ner·stone (kôr′nər stōn′), *n.* 1. a stone at the corner of two walls, serving to unite them. 2. a stone built into a corner of an edifice as the starting point in building, usually laid with formal ceremonies. 3. something of fundamental importance.

cor·net (kôr nĕt′ *for 1;* kôr′nĬt, kôr nĕt′ *for 2*), *n.* 1. a wind instrument of the trumpet class, with valves or pistons. 2. a little cone of paper twisted at the end, used for enclosing small wares. —**cor·net′ist,** **cor·net/tist,** *n.*

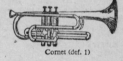
Cornet (def. 1)

corn·flow·er (kôrn′flou′ər), *n.* any of several plants growing in grain fields, as one with blue flowers, growing wild in Europe and often cultivated for ornament.

cor·nice (kôr′nĬs), *n.*, *v.*, **-niced, -nicing.** *Archit.* —*n.* 1. a horizontal molded projection which crowns or finishes a wall, building, etc. 2. the uppermost division of an entablature, resting on the frieze. —*v.t.* 3. to furnish with a cornice.

Cor·nish (kôr′nĬsh), *adj.* 1. of Cornwall (county in SW England), its inhabitants or the language formerly spoken by them. —*n.* 2. the old Celtic language of Cornwall. —**Cor′nish·man,** *n.*

corn-starch (kôrn′stärch′), *n.* a starch made from corn, used for making puddings, etc.

cor·nu·co·pi·a (kôr′nə kō′pĬ ə), *n.* 1. the fabulous goat horn which suckled Zeus, represented as overflowing with flowers, fruit, etc., and symbolizing plenty. 2. a horn-shaped receptacle or ornament.

Corn·wal·lis (kôrn wŏl′Ĭs, -wôl′Ĭs), *n.* **Charles, 1st Marquis,** 1738–1805, British general: surrendered to Washington at Yorktown, 1781.

corn·y (kôr′nĬ), *adj.*, **cornier, corniest.** 1. of or abounding in corn. 2. *Slang.* of poor quality.

co·rol·la (kə rŏl′ə), *n. Bot.* the internal envelope or floral leaves of a flower.

cor·ol·lar·y (kôr′ə lĕr′Ĭ, kŏr′-), *n.*, *pl.* **-laries.** 1. a proposition incidentally proved in proving another. 2. a natural consequence.

co·ro·na (kə rō′nə), *n.*, *pl.* **-nas, -nae** (-nē). 1. a white or colored circle of light seen round a luminous body, esp. the sun or moon. 2. *Anat.* the upper portion, as of the head. 3. *Bot.* a crownlike appendage. **4.** *Elect.* a discharge, frequently luminous, at the surface of a conductor. —cor·o·nal (kə rō'nəl, kôr'ə nəl, kôr'-), *adj.*

Co·ro·na·do (kôr'ə nä'dō), *n.* **Francisco Vásquez de**, 1510–1554?, Spanish explorer.

cor·o·nar·y (kôr'ə nĕr'ĭ, kôr'-), *adj.* **1.** of or like a crown. **2.** *Anat.* pertaining to the arteries which supply the heart tissues.

cor·o·na·tion (kôr'ə nā'shən, kôr'-), *n.* act or ceremony of investing a king, etc., with a crown.

cor·o·ner (kôr'ə nər, kôr'-), *n.* a local official whose chief function is to investigate by inquest (often before a **coroner's jury**) any death not clearly natural. —cor'o·ner·ship', *n.*

cor·o·net (kôr'ə nĭt, -nĕt', kôr'-), *n.* **1.** a small or inferior crown. **2.** a crownlike ornament for the head.

Co·rot (kô rō'), *n.* **Jean Baptiste Camille**, 1796–1875, French painter.

Corp., 1. Corporal. **2.** Corporation. Also, **corp.**

cor·po·ral[1] (kôr'pə rəl), *adj.* of the body; physical. —cor'po·ral'i·ty, *n.* —cor'po·ral·ly, *adv.*

cor·po·ral[2] (kôr'pə rəl), *n.* (in the army) a noncommissioned officer of lowest rank.

cor·po·rate (kôr'pə rĭt, -prĭt) *adj.* **1.** of or forming a corporation. **2.** united in one body. —cor'po·rate·ly, *adv.*

cor·po·ra·tion (kôr'pə rā'shən), *n.* **1.** an association of individuals, created by law or under authority of law, having a continuous existence irrespective of that of its members. **2.** *Slang.* a large abdomen.

cor·po·re·al (kôr pōr'ĭ əl), *adj.* **1.** bodily. **2.** material; tangible. —cor·po're·al'i·ty, cor·po're·al·ness, *n.* —cor·po're·al·ly, *adv.*

corps (kôr), *n., pl.* **corps** (kōrz). **1.** an organized military body. **2.** a military unit of ground combat forces consisting of two or more divisions. **3.** a group of persons acting together.

corpse (kôrps), *n.* a dead body.

cor·pu·lent (kôr'pyə lənt), *adj.* portly; fat. —cor'pu·lence, *n.*

cor·pus (kôr'pəs), *n., pl.* **-pora** (-pə rə). **1.** a body. **2.** a large or complete collection of writings, etc.

Cor·pus Chris·ti (kôr'pəs krĭs'tĭ), a seaport in S Texas. 57,301.

cor·pus·cle (kôr'pəs əl, -pŭs əl), *n.* *Physiol.* one of the minute bodies which form a constituent of the blood, etc. —cor·pus·cu·lar (kôr pŭs'kyə lər), *adj.*

cor·pus de·lic·ti (kôr'pəs dĭ lĭk'tī), *Law.* the fact that a crime has actually been committed.

cor·ral (kə rǎl'), *n., v.,* **-ralled, -ralling.** —*n.* **1.** a pen for horses, cattle, etc. —*v.t.* **2.** to confine in a corral. **3.** *U.S. Colloq.* to capture.

cor·rect (kə rěkt'), *v.t.* **1.** to remove the errors of. **2.** to mark the errors in. **3.** to admonish or rebuke. **4.** to counteract the effect of (something hurtful). **5.** *Math., Physics., etc.* to alter or adjust to accord with some required condition. —*adj.* **6.** free from error; accurate. **7.** proper. —cor·rec'tive, *adj., n.* —cor·rect'ly, *adv.* —cor·rect'ness, *n.* —cor·rec'tor, *n.*

cor·rec·tion (kə rěk'shən), *n.* **1.** act of correcting. **2.** that which is substituted for what is wrong. **3.** punishment; reproof. —cor·rec'tion·al, *adj.*

Cor·reg·i·dor (kə rěg'ə dōr'), *n.* a fortified island in Manila Bay, in the Philippine Islands: heroic U.S. resistance, 1942. 2 sq. mi.

cor·re·late (kôr'ə lāt', kôr'-), *v.,* **-lated, -lating,** *adj., n.* —*v.t., v.i.* **1.** to bring into or have a mutual or reciprocal relation. —*adj.* **2.** correlated. —*n.* **3.** either of two related things. —cor're·la'tion, *n.*

cor·rel·a·tive (kə rěl'ə tĭv), *adj.* **1.** so related that each implies or complements the other. **2.** mutually related. —*n.* **3.** either of two things which are correlative. —cor·rel'a·tive·ly, *adv.*

cor·re·spond (kôr'ə spŏnd'), *v.i.* **1.** to be in agreement or conformity. **2.** to be similar or analogous (fol. by *to*). **3.** to communicate by letters. —cor're·spond'ing·ly, *adv.*

cor·re·spond·ence (kôr'ə spŏn'dəns, kôr'-), *n.* **1.** act or fact of corresponding. **2.** agreement; conformity. **3.** communication by exchange of letters. **4.** letters between correspondents.

cor·re·spond·ent (kôr'ə spŏn'dənt, kôr'-), *n.* **1.** one who communicates by letters. **2.** one employed to contribute news, etc., regularly from a distant place. **3.** a thing that corresponds to something else. —*adj.* **4.** corresponding.

cor·ri·dor (kôr'ə dər, -dôr', kôr'-), *n.* **1.** a pas-

sage connecting parts or rooms of a building. **2.** a narrow tract of land forming a passageway.

cor·rob·o·rate (kə rŏb'ə rāt'), *v.t.,* **-rated, -rating.** to make more certain; confirm. —cor·rob'o·ra'tion, *n.* —cor·rob'o·ra'tive, *adj.* —cor·rob'o·ra'tive·ly, *adv.* —cor·rob'o·ra'tor, *n.*

cor·rode (kə rōd'), *v.,* **-roded, -roding.** —*v.t.* **1.** to eat away gradually as if by gnawing, esp. by chemical action. —*v.i.* **2.** to become corroded. —cor·ro·sive (kə rō'sĭv), *adj., n.*

cor·ro·sion (kə rō'zhən), *n.* **1.** act or process of corroding. **2.** a product of corroding, as rust.

cor·ru·gate (kôr'ə gāt', kôr'-), *v.t., v.i.,* **-gated, -gating. 1.** to draw or bend into folds or alternate furrows and ridges. **2.** to wrinkle, as the skin, etc. —cor'ru·ga'tion, *n.*

cor·rupt (kə rŭpt'), *adj.* **1.** dishonest. **2.** debased in character; evil. **3.** putrid. **4.** tainted. —*v.t.* **5.** to cause to be dishonest, disloyal, etc. **6.** to lower morally. **7.** to taint. **8.** to make putrid. —*v.i.* **9.** to become corrupted or corrupt. —cor·rupt'er, *n.* —cor·rupt'i·ble, *adj.* —cor·rupt'i·bil'i·ty, *n.* —cor·rup'tive, *adj.* —cor·rupt'ly, *adv.* —cor·rupt'ness, *n.*

cor·rup·tion (kə rŭp'shən), *n.* **1.** act of corrupting. **2.** state of being corrupt. **3.** depravity. **4.** dishonest proceedings. **5.** bribery. **6.** debasement. **7.** putrefactive decay. **8.** any corrupting influence.

cor·sage (kôr säzh'), *n.* **1.** a small bouquet worn at the waist or shoulder. **2.** a bodice.

cor·sair (kôr'sâr), *n.* **1.** a privateer. **2.** a pirate. **3.** a fast vessel used for piracy.

cor·se·let (kôr'sə lĕt' *for 1;* kôrs'lĭt *for 2*), *n.* **1.** a supporting undergarment worn by women. **2.** armor for the body. Also, **cors·let** (kôrs'lĭt).

cor·set (kôr'sĭt), *n.* (*often pl.*) a close-fitting inner garment worn, chiefly by women, to give shape and support to the body.

Cor·si·ca (kôr'sə kə), *n.* an island in the Mediterranean, SE of and forming a department in France. 267,971 pop.; 3367 sq. mi. *Cap.:* Ajaccio. —Cor'si·can, *adj., n.*

cor·tege (kôr täzh', -tězh'), *n.* **1.** a retinue. **2.** a procession. Also, *French,* **cor·tège** (kôr tězh').

Cor·tés (kôr těz'), *n.* **Hernando,** 1485–1547, Spanish conqueror of Mexico. Also, **Cor·tez'.**

cor·tex (kôr'těks), *n., pl.* **-tices** (-tə sēz'). **1.** *Bot.* bark. **2.** *Anat., Zool.* **a.** the rind of an organ, as of the kidney. **b.** the layer of gray matter which invests the surface of the cerebrum and the cerebellum. —cor·ti·cal (kôr'tə kəl), *adj.*

co·run·dum (kə rŭn'dəm), *n.* a common mineral, aluminum oxide, Al_2O_3, notable for its hardness: used as an abrasive.

cor·us·cate (kôr'ə skāt', kôr'-), *v.i.,* **-cated, -cating.** to sparkle; gleam. —cor'us·ca'tion, *n.*

cor·vette (kôr vět'), *n.* **1.** a warship of the old sailing class, usually with only one tier of guns. **2.** *Brit.* a small lightly armed, fast vessel, used mostly for convoy escort. Also, **cor·vet** (kôr vět', kôr'vět).

cor·ymb (kôr'ĭmb, -ĭm, kôr'-), *n.* *Bot.* a form of inflorescence in which the flowers form a flat-topped cluster, the outermost flowers being the first to expand.

co·ry·za (kə rī'zə), *n.* a cold in the head.

co·se·cant (kō sē'kənt, -kănt), *n.* *Trig.* the secant of the complement, or the reciprocal of the sine, of a given angle or arc.

co·sine (kō'sīn), *n.* *Trig.* the sine of the complement of a given angle or arc.

cos·met·ic (kŏz mět'ĭk), *n.* **1.** a preparation for beautifying the skin, etc. —*adj.* **2.** serving to beautify.

cos·mic (kŏz'mĭk), *adj.* **1.** of or pertaining to the cosmos. **2.** immeasurably vast. —cos'mi·cal·ly, *adv.*

cosmic rays, rays of extremely high penetrating power that seem to originate beyond the earth's atmosphere, and that consist, at least in part, of particles moving in velocities approaching the speed of light.

cos·mog·o·ny (kŏz mŏg'ə nĭ), *n., pl.* **-nies.** a theory of the origin of the universe.

cos·mog·ra·phy (kŏz mŏg'rə fĭ), *n., pl.* **-phies.** the science which describes the heavens and earth, embracing astronomy, geography, and geology.

cos·mol·o·gy (kŏz mŏl'ə jĭ), *n.* the branch of philosophy that concerns itself with the origin and structure of the universe.

cos·mo·pol·i·tan (kŏz′mə pŏl′ə tən), *adj.* **1.** belonging to all parts of the world. **2.** free from local or national ideas, prejudices, or attachments. —*n.* **3.** one who is free from provincial or national prejudices.

cos·mos (kŏz′məs, -mŏs), *n.* **1.** the universe as an embodiment of order and harmony. **2.** a complete and harmonious system. **3.** any plant of a composite genus of tropical America, some species of which are cultivated for their showy flowers.

Cos·sack (kŏs′ăk, -ək), *n.* one of a people of the southern Soviet Union, noted as horsemen.

cost (kôst, kŏst), *n.*, *v.*, **cost, costing.** —*n.* **1.** the price paid to acquire, produce, accomplish, or maintain anything. **2.** a sacrifice, loss, or penalty. **3.** outlay of money, labor, etc. **4.** expenses incurred in litigation. —*v.i.* **5.** to require the expenditure of money, time, labor, etc., in exchange, purchase, or payment. **6.** to result in a particular sacrifice, loss, or penalty. —*v.t.* **7.** to determine the cost of.

Cos·ta Ri·ca (kŏs′tə rē′kə, kôs′-, kōs′-), a republic in Central America between Panama and Nicaragua. 672,043 pop.; 19,238 sq. mi. *Cap.*: San José. —**Cos′ta Ri′can.**

cos·ter·mon·ger (kŏs′tər mŭng′gər, kôs′-), *n. Chiefly Brit.* a hawker of fruit, fish, etc.

cos·tive (kŏs′tĭv, kôs′-), *adj.* constipated.

cost·ly (kôst′lĭ, kŏst′-), *adj.*, **-lier, -liest.** **1.** costing much. **2.** *Archaic.* lavish. —**cost′li·ness,** *n.*

cos·tume (*n.* kŏs′tūm, -tōōm; *v.* kŏs tūm′, -tōōm′), *n.*, *v.*, **-tumed, -tuming.** —*n.* **1.** the style of dress, including ornaments and the way of wearing the hair. **2.** dress belonging to another period, place, etc., as worn on the stage, etc. **3.** a set of garments, esp. for a woman. —*v.t.* **4.** to furnish with a costume.

cos·tum·er (kŏs tū′mər, -tōō′-), *n.* one who makes or deals in costumes.

co·sy (kō′zĭ), *adj.*, **-sier, -siest,** *n.*, *pl.* **-sies.** cozy. —**co′si·ly,** *adv.* —**co′si·ness,** *n.*

cot[1] (kŏt), *n.* **1.** a light portable bed, esp. one of canvas. **2.** *Brit.* a crib.

cot[2] (kŏt), *n.* **1.** a cottage; hut. **2.** a small place of shelter.

co·tan·gent (kō tăn′jənt), *n. Trig.* the tangent of the complement, or the reciprocal of the tangent, of a given angle or arc.

cote (kōt), *n.* **1.** a shelter for sheep, pigs, pigeons, etc. **2.** *N. Eng.* a cottage.

co·te·rie (kō′tə rĭ), *n.* **1.** a set of persons who associate together, esp. socially. **2.** a clique.

co·til·lion (kō tĭl′yən, kə-), *n.* **1.** a lively French social dance. **2.** *U.S.* a complex dance consisting of elaborate figures, with changing of partners and giving of favors.

cot·tage (kŏt′ĭj), *n.* **1.** a small, humble house. **2.** a small country or suburban house. **3.** *U.S.* a temporary residence at a vacation resort.

cottage cheese, *U.S.* a kind of soft white cheese made of skim milk curds without rennet.

cot·tag·er (kŏt′ĭj ər), *n.* one who lives in a cottage, esp. (*U.S.*) at a vacation resort.

cot·ter[1] (kŏt′ər), *n.* **1.** a pin, or the like, fitted into an opening to hold something together. **2.** cotter pin.

cot·ter[2] (kŏt′ər), *n. Scot.* a person occupying a plot of land under a system of competitive tenure. Also, **cot′tar.**

cotter pin, *Mech.* a cotter having a split end which is spread after being pushed through a hole.

cot·ton (kŏt′ən), *n.* **1.** a soft, white, downy substance, consisting of the hairs attached to the seeds of plants of the mallow family, used in making fabrics, etc. **2.** a plant yielding cotton. **3.** such plants collectively, as a cultivated crop. **4.** cloth, thread, etc., made of cotton. —*v.i.* **5.** *Colloq.* to become attached or friendly. —**cot′ton·y,** *adj.*

cot·ton·mouth (kŏt′ən mouth′), *n.* the water moccasin, a venomous snake of the southern U.S.

cot·ton·seed (kŏt′ən sēd′), *n.*, *pl.* **-seeds,** (*esp. collectively*) **-seed.** the seed of the cotton plant, yielding a brown-yellow oil (**cottonseed oil**) used in pharmacology and cooking.

cot·ton·tail (kŏt′ən tāl′), *n.* the common rabbit of the U.S., having a fluffy white tail.

cot·ton·wood (kŏt′ən wŏŏd′), *n.* any of several American species of poplar with cottonlike tufts on the seeds.

cot·y·le·don (kŏt′ə lē′dən), *n. Bot.* the primary or rudimentary leaf of the embryo of plants.

couch (kouch), *n.* **1.** a bed or other place of rest; a lounge. **2.** the lair of a wild beast. —*v.t.* **3.** to put into words; express. **4.** to lower, as the head. **5.** to lower (a spear, etc.), as for attack. **6.** to lay or put down. —*v.i.* **7.** to lie at rest; recline. **8.** to crouch; stoop. **9.** to lurk.

couch·ant (kou′chənt), *adj.* lying down.

cou·gar (kōō′gər), *n. Zool.* a large tawny feline of North and South America; puma; panther.

cough (kôf, kŏf), *v.i.* **1.** to expel the air from the lungs suddenly and with a characteristic noise. —*v.t.* **2.** to expel by coughing. —*n.* **3.** act or sound of coughing. **4.** an illness characterized by frequent coughing.

Cougar
(Total length 8 ft.)

could (kŏŏd), *v.* pt. of **can**[1].

cou·lee (kōō′lĭ), *n.* **1.** *Western N. Amer.* a deep ravine or gulch, usually dry. **2.** a stream of lava.

cou·lomb (kōō lŏm′), *n.* the usual unit of quantity of electricity: the quantity transferred by a current of one ampere in one second.

coun·cil (koun′səl), *n.* **1.** an assembly convened for consultation, deliberation, or advice. **2.** an ecclesiastical assembly for deciding matters of doctrine or discipline. **3.** a body of persons specially selected to act in an advisory, administrative, or legislative capacity.

Council Bluffs, a city in SW Iowa. 41,439.

coun·cil·man (koun′səl mən), *n.*, *pl.* **-men.** a member of a council, esp. a local legislative body.

coun·ci·lor (koun′sə lər), *n.* a member of a council. Also, *esp. Brit.*, **coun′cil·lor.**

coun·sel (koun′səl), *n.*, *v.*, **-seled, -seling** or (*esp. Brit.*) **-selled, -selling.** —*n.* **1.** advice; opinion or instruction given to another. **2.** interchange of opinions; consultation; deliberation. **3.** plan; design. **4.** a legal adviser; lawyer. —*v.t.* **5.** to give advice to; advise. **6.** to recommend (a plan, etc.). —*v.i.* **7.** to give advice. **8.** to take counsel.

coun·se·lor (koun′sə lər), *n.* **1.** one who advises; adviser. **2.** a lawyer, esp. a trial lawyer. Also, *esp. Brit.*, **coun′sel·lor.**

count[1] (kount), *v.t.* **1.** to check over (the individuals of a collection) to ascertain their total number. **2.** to compute. **3.** to list the numerals up to. **4.** to take into account. **5.** to ascribe. **6.** to esteem; consider. —*v.i.* **7.** to count the items of a collection to ascertain the total. **8.** to list the numerals in order. **9.** to rely. **10.** to be worth. **11.** to enter into consideration. —*n.* **12.** act of counting. **13.** the total number. **14.** accounting. **15.** *Law.* a distinct charge, as in an indictment. —**count′a·ble,** *adj.*

count[2] (kount), *n.* (in Europe) a nobleman corresponding in rank to the English earl.

coun·te·nance (koun′tə nəns), *n.*, *v.*, **-nanced, -nancing.** —*n.* **1.** appearance, esp. the expression of the face. **2.** the face. **3.** composed expression of face. **4. out of countenance,** visibly disconcerted. **5.** encouragement. —*v.t.* **6.** to encourage; support.

count·er[1] (koun′tər), *n.* **1.** a table on which money is counted, business is transacted, etc. **2.** a piece of metal, etc., used in keeping account, as in games. **3.** an imitation coin or token.

count·er[2] (koun′tər), *n.* **1.** one who counts. **2.** an apparatus for counting.

coun·ter[3] (koun′tər), *adv.* **1.** in the wrong way. **2.** contrary (chiefly with *run* or *go*). —*adj.* **3.** opposite; contrary. —*n.* **4.** that which is contrary to something else. **5.** a blow delivered in receiving or parrying another blow, as in boxing. **6.** that portion of the stern of a boat from the water line to the full outward swell. **7.** the piece of stiff leather forming the back of a shoe or boot around the heel. —*v.t.* **8.** to go counter to; oppose. **9.** to meet (a blow, etc.) by another in return. —*v.i.* **10.** to make an opposing move.

coun·ter·act (koun′tər ăkt′), *v.t.* to frustrate by contrary action. —**coun′ter·ac′tion,** *n.*

coun·ter·at·tack (*n.* koun′tər ə tăk′; *v.* koun′tər ə tăk′), *n.* **1.** an attack designed to counteract another. —*v.t.*, *v.i.* **2.** to deliver a counterattack (to).

coun·ter·bal·ance (*n.* koun′tər băl′əns; *v.* koun′tər băl′əns), *n.*, *v.*, **-anced, -ancing.** —*n.* **1.** a weight, power, or influence that balances another. —*v.t.* **2.** to weight or act against with an equal weight or force.

coun·ter·claim (*n.* koun′tər klăm′; *v.* koun′-

tər klām′), *n.* **1.** a claim set up against another claim. —*v.i.* **2.** to set up a counterclaim.

coun·ter·clock·wise (koun′tər klŏk′wīz′), *adj., adv.* in a direction opposite to that of the rotation of the hands of a clock.

coun·ter·es·pi·o·nage (koun′tər ĕs′pĭ ə nĭj, -näzh′), *n.* the detection of enemy espionage.

coun·ter·feit (koun′tər fĭt), *adj.* **1.** made to imitate, and pass for, something else; not genuine. —*n.* **2.** an imitation designed to pass as an original; a forgery. —*v.t.* **3.** to imitate fraudulently; forge. —*v.i.* **4.** to make counterfeits, as of money. **5.** to feign. —**coun′ter·feit′er,** *n.*

coun·ter·mand (*v.* koun′tər mănd′, -mänd′; *n.* koun′tər mănd′, -mänd′), *v.t.* **1.** to revoke (a command, etc.). **2.** to recall by a contrary order. —*n.* **3.** a command, etc., revoking another.

coun·ter·of·fen·sive (koun′tər ə fĕn′sĭv), *n. Mil.* an attack by an army against an enemy force which has been and may still be attacking.

coun·ter·pane (koun′tər pān′), *n.* a quilt.

coun·ter·part (koun′tər pärt′), *n.* **1.** a duplicate. **2.** a thing that complements something else. **3.** a person or thing closely resembling another.

coun·ter·plot (koun′tər plŏt′), *n., v.,* -**plotted,** -**plotting.** —*n.* **1.** a plot directed against another plot. —*v.i.* **2.** the devise a counterplot. —*v.t.* **3.** to plot against (a plot or plotter).

coun·ter·point (koun′tər point′), *n. Music.* **1.** the art of combining melodies. **2.** the texture resulting from the combining of individual melodic lines. **3.** a melody composed to be combined with another melody.

coun·ter·poise (koun′tər poiz′), *n., v.,* -**poised,** -**poising.** —*n.* **1.** a counterbalancing weight. **2.** any equal and opposing force. **3.** equilibrium. —*v.t.* **4.** to balance by an opposing weight.

coun·ter·rev·o·lu·tion (koun′tər rĕv′ə lōō′-shən), *n.* a revolution opposed to a preceding one. —**coun′ter·rev′o·lu′tion·ar·y,** *adj.* —**coun′ter·rev′o·lu′tion·ist,** *n.*

coun·ter·sign (koun′tər sīn′), *n.* **1.** *Mil.* a password given to a guard. **2.** a sign in reply to another. **3.** a signature added to another, esp. for authentication. —*v.t.* **4.** to sign (a document) in addition to another signature, esp. in authentication.

coun·ter·sink (*v., n.* koun′tər sĭngk′; *v. also* koun′tər sĭngk′), *v.,* -**sunk, -sinking,** *n.* —*v.t.* **1.** to enlarge the upper part of (a hole) to receive the cone-shaped head of a screw, etc. **2.** to cause (the head of a screw, etc.) to sink flush with or below the surface. —*n.* **3.** a tool for countersinking a hole. **4.** a countersunk hole.

coun·ter·weight (koun′tər wāt′), *n.* a counterbalancing weight.

count·ess (koun′tĭs), *n.* **1.** the wife or widow of a count in the nobility of continental Europe, or of an earl in the British peerage. **2.** a woman having the rank of a count or earl in her own right.

count·less (kount′lĭs), *adj.* innumerable.

coun·tri·fied (kŭn′trĭ fīd′), *adj.* rustic or rural. Also, **coun′try·fied′.**

coun·try (kŭn′trĭ), *n., pl.* -**tries,** *adj.* —*n.* **1.** a tract of land; region; district. **2.** the territory of a nation. **3.** a state. **4.** the people of a district, state, or nation. **5.** the land of one's birth or citizenship. **6.** rural districts (as opposed to cities). —*adj.* **7.** rural. **8.** rude; unpolished.

coun·try-dance (kŭn′trĭ dăns′, -däns′), *n.* a dance of rural (or native) English origin, esp. one in which the partners stand facing each other in two lines.

coun·try·man (kŭn′trĭ mən), *n., pl.* -**men.** **1.** a man of one's own country. **2.** a man who lives in the country. —**coun′try·wom′an,** *n. fem.*

coun·try·side (kŭn′trĭ sīd′), *n.* **1.** a particular section of a country, esp. rural. **2.** its inhabitants.

coun·ty (koun′tĭ), *n., pl.* -**ties.** **1.** the political unit next below the State in the U.S. **2.** one of the chief administrative divisions of a country or state, as in Great Britain and Ireland.

coup (kōō), *n., pl.* **coups** (kōōz). an unexpected and successful stroke.

coup de grâce (kōō də gräs′), **1.** a death blow, usually a bullet in the head to make sure an executed person is dead. **2.** a finishing stroke.

coup d'é·tat (kōō dĕ tä′), a sudden change of government illegally or by force.

cou·pé (kōō pā′; *for 1, also* kōōp), *n.* **1.** a closed automobile having a trunk compartment or

rumble seat in the rear. **2.** a short four-wheeled closed carriage with an outside seat for the driver.

cou·ple (kŭp′əl), *n., v.,* -**pled, -pling.** —*n.* **1.** a pair. **2.** two of the same sort connected or considered together. **3.** a man and a woman united by marriage or betrothal, associated as partners in a dance, etc. —*v.t.* **4.** to fasten, link, or associate together. —*v.i.* **5.** to unite. —**cou′pler,** *n.*

cou·plet (kŭp′lĭt), *n.* **1.** a pair of successive lines of verse, esp. such as rhyme together and are of the same length. **2.** a pair; couple.

cou·pling (kŭp′lĭng), *n.* **1.** act of one that couples. **2.** any mechanical device for connecting parts or things. **3.** a device used in joining railroad cars, etc. **4.** *Elect.* **a.** the association of two circuits in such a way that power may be transferred from one to the other. **b.** a device to insure coupling.

cou·pon (kōō′pŏn, kū′-), *n.* **1.** a separable part of a certificate, ticket, etc., entitling the holder to something. **2.** one of a number of such parts calling for periodical payments on a bond.

cour·age (kûr′ĭj, kŭr′), *n.* the quality of mind that enables one to face danger, etc., without fear; bravery.

cou·ra·geous (kə rā′jəs), *adj.* brave; valiant. —**cou·ra′geous·ly,** *adv.* —**cou·ra′geous·ness,** *n.*

cour·i·er (kûr′ĭ ər, kŏŏr′-), *n.* **1.** a messenger sent in haste. **2.** a person hired by travelers to take charge of the arrangements of a journey.

course (kōrs), *n., v.,* **coursed, coursing.** —*n.* **1.** advance in a particular direction. **2.** the path, route, or channel along which anything moves. **3.** the ground, water, etc., on which a race is run, sailed, etc. **4.** the continuous passage or progress through time or a succession of stages. **5.** regular or natural order of events. **6.** behavior. **7.** a particular manner of proceeding. **8.** a systematized series, as of studies. **9.** any one of the studies in such a series. **10.** a part of a meal served at one time. **11.** a continuous horizontal range of stones, bricks, or the like, in a wall, etc. **12. of course, a.** certainly. **b.** in the natural order. —*v.t.* **13.** to run through or over. **14.** to pursue. **15.** to cause (dogs) to pursue game. —*v.i.* **16.** to follow a course. **17.** to run; race.

cours·er (kōr′sər), *n. Poetic.* a swift horse.

court (kōrt), *n.* **1.** an open space enclosed by a wall, buildings, etc. **2.** a short street. **3.** a smooth, level area on which to play tennis, handball, etc. **4.** one of the divisions of such an area. **5.** the residence of a sovereign or other high dignitary; palace. **6.** the body of persons forming his retinue. **7.** a sovereign and his councilors. **8.** a formal assembly held by a sovereign. **9.** homage paid. **10.** assiduous attention directed to gain favor, etc. **11.** *Law.* **a.** a place where justice is administered. **b.** a judicial tribunal for the determination of cases. **c.** a session of a judicial assembly. —*v.t.* **12.** to endeavor to win the favor of. **13.** to woo. **14.** to attempt to gain (applause, etc.). —*v.i.* **15.** to woo.

cour·te·ous (kûr′tĭ əs), *adj.* having good manners; polite. —**cour′te·ous·ly,** *adv.* —**cour′te·ous·ness,** *n.*

cour·te·san (kōr′tə zən, kûr′-), *n.* a prostitute. Also, **cour′te·zan.**

cour·te·sy (kûr′tə sĭ), *n., pl.* -**sies. 1.** excellence of manners; politeness. **2.** a courteous act or expression. **3.** indulgence. **4.** a curtsy.

court·house (kōrt′hous′), *n.* **1.** a building in which courts of law are held. **2.** *U.S.* a county seat.

cour·ti·er (kōr′tĭ ər), *n.* **1.** one in attendance at the court of a sovereign. **2.** one who seeks favor.

court·ly (kōrt′lĭ), *adj.,* -**lier, -liest. 1.** polite; elegant. **2.** flattering. **3.** of the court of a sovereign. —**court′li·ness,** *n.*

court-mar·tial (kōrt′mär′shəl), *n., pl.* **courts-martial,** *v.,* -**tialed, -tialing** *or* (*esp. Brit.*) -**tialled, -tialling.** —*n.* **1.** a court consisting of military or naval personnel appointed by a commander to try charges of offense against military or naval law. —*v.t.* **2.** to arraign and try by court-martial.

court·room (kōrt′rōōm′, -rŏŏm′), *n.* a room in which the sessions of a law court are held.

court·ship (kōrt′shĭp), *n.* **1.** the wooing of a woman. **2.** solicitation, esp. of favors.

court·yard (kōrt′yärd′), *n.* a space enclosed by walls, next to or within a castle, large house, etc.

cous·in (kŭz′ən), *n.* **1.** the son or daughter of an

uncle or aunt. **2.** one related by descent in a diverging line from a known common ancestor. **3.** a kinsman or kinswoman. **4.** a person related to another by similar natures, etc. **5.** a term of address from one sovereign to another or to a great noble. —**cous'in·ly,** *adj., adv.*

cous·in-ger·man (kŭz'ən jûr'mən), *n., pl.* **cousins-german.** a first cousin; the child of an uncle or aunt.

cou·tu·rier (kōō tY ryĕ'), *n.* a dressmaker (man).

cove (kōv), *n., v.,* **coved, coving.** —*n.* **1.** a small recess in the shore of a sea, lake, etc. **2.** a sheltered nook. —*v.t., v.i.* **3.** to form into a cove.

cov·e·nant (kŭv'ə nənt), *n.* **1.** an agreement between two or more persons; contract. **2.** *Eccles.* a solemn agreement between the members of a church. **3.** (in Biblical usage) the agreement of God with man as set forth in the Old and the New Testament. **4.** *Law.* a formal agreement of legal validity. —*v.i.* **5.** to enter into a covenant. —*v.t.* **6.** to agree to by covenant. —**cov'e·nant·er,** *n.*

Cov·en·try (kŏv'ən trĭ, kŭv'-), *n.* a city in central England. 233,000.

cov·er (kŭv'ər), *v.t.* **1.** to put something over or upon, as for protection or concealment. **2.** to occupy the surface of. **3.** to clothe. **4.** to put one's hat on. **5.** to bring upon (oneself). **6.** to shelter; protect. **7.** to hide from view. **8.** to aim directly at, as with a pistol. **9.** to have within range. **10.** to include; comprise. **11.** to suffice to meet (a charge, etc.) or offset (a loss, etc.). **12.** to deposit the equivalent of (money deposited), as in wagering; accept (a bet, etc.). **13.** to act as reporter of. **14.** to pass or travel over. **15.** to brood or sit on (eggs or chicks). —*n.* **16.** that which covers. **17.** protection; concealment. **18.** woods, etc., sheltering and concealing game. **19.** a set of articles (plate, knife, fork, etc.) laid at table for one person. **20.** *Philately.* an envelope or outer wrapping for mail. —**cov'er·er,** *n.* —**cov'er·less,** *adj.*

cov·er·age (kŭv'ər Yj), *n.* **1.** the total extent of risk covered in a policy of insurance. **2.** *Finance.* the value of funds held to meet liabilities.

covered wagon, *U.S.* a large wagon with a canvas top, esp. a prairie schooner.

cov·er·ing (kŭv'ər Yng), *n.* something over or around a thing, esp. for concealment, protection, or warmth.

cov·er·let (kŭv'ər lYt), *n.* **1.** the outer covering of a bed. **2.** any cover.

cov·ert (kŭv'ərt), *adj.* **1.** covered; sheltered. **2.** concealed; secret. —*n.* **3.** a cover. **4.** shelter; concealment. **5.** *Hunting.* a thicket giving shelter to wild animals or game. **6.** (*pl.*) *Ornith.* the smaller feathers that cover the bases of the large feathers of the wing and tail. **7.** covert cloth. —**cov'ert·ly,** *adv.* —**cov'ert·ness,** *n.*

covert cloth, a cotton or worsted fabric of twill weave.

cov·et (kŭv'Yt), *v.t., v.i.* to desire inordinately or wrongfully. —**cov'et·a·ble,** *adj.* —**cov'et·er,** *n.*

cov·et·ous (kŭv'ə təs), *adj.* inordinately or wrongly desirous. —**cov'et·ous·ly,** *adv.* —**cov'et·ous·ness,** *n.*

cov·ey (kŭv'Y), *n., pl.* -**eys. 1.** a brood or small flock of partridges or similar birds. **2.** a group.

Cov·ing·ton (kŭv'Yng tən), *n.* a city in N Kentucky, on the Ohio river. 62,018.

cow¹ (kou), *n., pl.* **cows,** (*Archaic*) **kine. 1.** the female of a bovine animal that has produced a calf. **2.** the female of various other large animals, as the elephant, whale, etc.

cow² (kou), *v.t.* to intimidate.

cow·ard (kou'ərd), *n.* **1.** one who lacks courage. —*adj.* **2.** lacking courage; timid. **3.** proceeding from or expressive of fear or timidity.

cow·ard·ice (kou'ər dYs), *n.* lack of courage.

cow·ard·ly (kou'ərd lY), *adj.* **1.** lacking courage. **2.** of or befitting a coward. —*adv.* **3.** like a coward. —**cow'ard·li·ness,** *n.*

cow·boy (kou'boi), *n. U.S.* a man employed in the care of the cattle of a ranch, doing his work largely on horseback.

cow·catch·er (kou'kăch'ər), *n. U.S.* a triangular frame at the front of a locomotive, etc., for clearing the track of obstructions.

cow·er (kou'ər), *v.i.* to crouch in fear or shame.

cow hand, one employed on a cattle ranch.

cow·herd (kou'hûrd'), *n.* one whose occupation is the tending of cows.

cow·hide (kou'hYd'), *n., v.,* -**hided,** -**hiding.** —*n.* **1.** the hide of a cow. **2.** the leather made from it. **3.** *U.S.* a whip made of rawhide or of braided leather. —*v.t.* **4.** to whip with a cowhide.

cowl (koul), *n.* **1.** a hooded garment worn by monks. **2.** the hood of this garment. **3.** a hood-shaped covering for a chimney, to increase the draft. **4.** the part of the automobile body supporting the rear of the hood and the windshield, and housing the instrument panel. —*v.t.* **5.** to put a monk's cowl on. **6.** to cover with a cowl. —**cowled,** *adj.*

cow·lick (kou'lYk'), *n.* a tuft of hair turned up, usually over the forehead.

cowl·ing (kou'lYng), *n. Aeron.* a streamlined housing for an aircraft engine.

cow·man (kou'mən), *n., pl.* -**men.** *Western U.S.* an owner of cattle; a rancher.

cow·pea (kou'pē'), *n.* **1.** an annual plant extensively cultivated in the southern U.S. esp. for forage, etc. **2.** the seed.

cow·pox (kou'pŏks'), *n.* an eruptive disease of cows in which pustules form which contain a virus used in the vaccination of man against smallpox.

cow·punch·er (kou'pŭn'chər), *n. U.S. Colloq.* a cowboy.

cow·rie (kou'rY), *n.* the shell of certain marine gastropods, as one species with a small shell used as money in certain parts of Asia and Africa. Also, **cow'ry.**

cow·slip (kou'slYp), *n.* **1.** an English primrose bearing yellow flowers. **2.** *U.S.* the marsh marigold.

cox (kŏks), *n. Colloq.* coxswain.

cox·comb (kŏks'kōm'), *n.* **1.** a conceited dandy. **2.** *Bot.* cockscomb. **3.** the cap, resembling a cock's comb, formerly worn by professional fools.

cox·swain (kŏk'sən, -swān), *n.* the steersman of a boat.

coy (koi), *adj.* **1.** shy; modest. **2.** affectedly shy. —**coy'ly,** *adv.* —**coy'ness,** *n.*

coy·o·te (kĭ ō'tY, kĪ'ōt), *n.* a wild animal of the wolf kind, of western North America, noted for loud and prolonged howling at night.

coy·pu (koi'pōō), *n., pl.* -**pus,** (*esp. collectively*) -**pu.** a large South American aquatic rodent, yielding the fur nutria.

coz·en (kŭz'ən), *v.t., v.i.* to cheat. —**coz'en·er,** *n.*

co·zy (kō'zY), *adj.,* -**zier,** -**ziest,** *n., pl.* -**zies.** —*adj.* **1.** snug; comfortable. —*n.* **2.** a padded covering for a teapot, etc., to retain the heat. —**co'zi·ly,** *adv.* —**co'zi·ness,** *n.*

C.P.A., Certified Public Accountant.

Cpl., Corporal. Also, **cpl.**

Cr, *Chem.* chromium.

cr., 1. credit. **2.** creditor.

crab¹ (krăb), *n., v.,* **crabbed, crabbing.** —*n.* **1.** any of certain crustaceans, having a short, broad, flattened body, the abdomen or so-called tail being small and folded under the thorax. **2.** (*cap.*) the zodiacal constellation or sign Cancer. **3.** a grouchy person. **4.** any of various mechanical contrivances for hoisting or pulling. —*v.i.* **5.** to catch crabs. —**crab'ber,** *n.*

crab² (krăb), *n.* a crab apple (fruit or tree).

crab³ (krăb), *v.i., v.t.,* **crabbed, crabbing.** *Colloq.* to find fault (with).

crab apple, 1. a small, sour wild apple. **2.** a kind of small, sour apple, used for making jelly. **3.** any tree bearing such fruit.

crab·bed (krăb'Yd), *adj.* **1.** Also, **crab'by.** perverse; grouchy. **2.** intricate. **3.** difficult to decipher. —**crab'bed·ly,** *adv.* —**crab'bed·ness,** *n.*

crab grass, an annual grass that is a common weedy pest in lawns.

crack (krăk), *v.i.* **1.** to make a sudden, sharp sound in, or as in, breaking. **2.** to break with a sudden, sharp sound. **3.** to break without complete separation of parts. **4.** (of the voice) to break abruptly and discordantly. **5.** *Colloq.* to fail. **6. crack down,** *U.S. Colloq.* to take severe measures. **7. crack up, a.** to suffer a breakdown. **b.** to crash. —*v.t.* **8.** *Colloq.* to cause to make a sudden, sharp sound. **9.** to break without complete separation of parts. **10.** *Colloq.* to break into (a safe, etc.). **11.** to open and drink (a bottle of wine, etc.). **12.** to make unsound mentally. **13.** to tell (a joke, etc.). **14. crack up, a.** *Colloq.* to praise. **b.** to crash. —*n.* **15.** a sudden, sharp noise, esp. of something breaking. **16.** *Colloq.* a shot, as with a rifle. **17.** *Colloq.* a resounding blow. **18.** a break without complete separation of parts. **19.** a slight opening. **20.** *Colloq.* a try. **21.** *Slang.* a joke. —*qdj.* **22.** *Colloq.* first-rate.

crack·brained (krăk'brānd'), *adj.* crazy.

cracked (krăkt), *adj.* **1.** broken. **2.** broken without separation of parts. **3.** damaged. **4.** *Colloq.* mentally unsound. **5.** broken in tone.

crack·er (krăk'ər), *n.* **1.** a thin, crisp biscuit. **2.** a firecracker. **3.** a small paper roll containing an explosive and usually a candy, motto, etc., which explodes when pulled sharply at both ends. **4.** one of a class of poor whites in parts of the southeastern U.S. **5.** one that cracks.

crack·er·jack (krăk'ər jăk'), *Slang.* —*n.* **1.** *U.S.* an excellent person or thing. —*adj.* **2.** excellent.

crack·ing (krăk'ĭng), *n.* (in the distillation of petroleum or the like) the process of breaking down certain hydrocarbons into simpler ones by excess heat, etc.

crack·le (krăk'əl), *v.,* -led, -ling, *n.* —*v.i.* **1.** to make slight, sudden, sharp noises, rapidly repeated. —*v.t.* **2.** to cause to crackle. **3.** to break with a crackling noise. —*n.* **4.** act of crackling. **5.** a crackling noise. **6.** a network of fine cracks, as in the glaze of some kinds of porcelain.

crack·ling (krăk'lĭng), *n.* **1.** the making of crackling sounds. **2.** the crisp browned skin or rind of roast pork. **3.** (*usually pl.*) *Dial.* the crisp residue left when fat, especially hogs' fat, is rendered.

crack·up (krăk'ŭp'), *n.* **1.** a crash. **2.** *Colloq.* a breakdown in health. **3.** collapse.

Crac·ow (krăk'ou, krä'kō), *n.* a city in S Poland: capital of Poland, 1320–1609. 300,000.

cra·dle (krā'dəl), *n., v.,* -dled, -dling. —*n.* **1.** a little bed or cot for an infant, usually on rockers. **2.** the place where anything is nurtured. **3.** any contrivance similar to a child's cradle, as the framework on which a ship rests during repair. **4.** a framework with swivel wheels, on which a mechanic can lie beneath an automobile. **5.** *Agric.* a frame of wood with a row of long curved teeth projecting above and parallel to a scythe, for laying grain in bunches as it is cut. **6.** a box on rockers used by miners for washing auriferous gravel or sand to separate the gold. —*v.t.* **7.** to place or rock in a cradle. **8.** to nurture during infancy. **9.** to cut (grain) with a cradle. **10.** to wash in a miner's cradle. —*v.i.* **11.** to lie in a cradle.

craft (krăft, kräft), *n.* **1.** skill; dexterity. **2.** skill applied to bad purposes; cunning. **3.** an art, trade, or occupation requiring special skill. **4.** the members of a trade collectively; guild. **5.** (*construed as pl.*) vessels or aircraft collectively. **6.** a single vessel or aircraft.

crafts·man (krăfts'mən, kräfts'-), *n., pl.* -men. one who practices a craft. —**crafts'man·ship'**, *n.*

craft·y (krăf'tĭ, kräf'-), *adj.,* craftier, craftiest. cunning; deceitful; sly. —**craft'i·ly**, *adv.* —**craft'i·ness**, *n.*

crag (krăg), *n.* a steep, rugged rock; rough, broken, projecting part of a rock. —**crag'gy**, **crag·ged** (krăg'ĭd), *adj.* —**crag'gi·ness**, *n.*

cram (krăm), *v.,* crammed, cramming, *n.* —*v.t.* **1.** to fill (something) tightly. **2.** to force or stuff (fol. by *into*, etc.). **3.** to fill with an excess of food. —*v.i.* **4.** to eat greedily. **5.** *Colloq.* to prepare for an examination by hastily storing the memory with facts. —*n.* **6.** *Colloq.* act or result of cramming. —**cram'mer**, *n.*

cramp¹ (krămp), *n.* **1.** a sudden involuntary contraction of a muscle or group of muscles, sometimes with severe pain. **2.** (*often pl.*) piercing pains in the abdomen. —*v.t.* **3.** to affect with a cramp.

cramp² (krămp), *n.* **1.** a small metal bar with bent ends, for holding together timbers, masonry, etc. **2.** a clamp. **3.** anything that confines or restrains. —*v.t.* **4.** to fasten or hold with a cramp. **5.** to restrict or hamper. —*adj.* **6.** difficult. **7.** contracted; narrow.

cran·ber·ry (krăn'bĕr'ĭ), *n., pl.* -ries. **1.** the red, acid fruit or berry of any of certain plants of the heath family, used in making sauce, jelly, etc. **2.** the plant itself.

crane (krān), *n., v.,* craned, craning. —*n.* **1.** any of a group of large wading birds with very long legs, bill, and neck, and elevated hind toe. **2.** any of various similar birds of other families, as the great blue heron. **3.** a device for moving heavy weights, consisting essentially of a post bearing a projecting arm on which the hoisting tackle is fitted. **4.** any similar device, as a swing-

ing arm by a fireplace for suspending pots over the fire. —*v.t.* **5.** to hoist, lower, or move by a crane. **6.** to stretch (the neck) as a crane does. —*v.i.* **7.** to stretch out one's neck.

Crane (krān), *n.* **Stephen,** 1871–1900, U.S. writer.

cra·ni·ol·o·gy (krā'nĭ ŏl'ə jĭ'), *n.* the science that deals with the characteristics of skulls.

cra·ni·om·e·try (krā'nĭ ŏm'ə trĭ'), *n.* the science of measuring skulls. —**cra'ni·om'e·trist**, *n.*

cra·ni·um (krā'nĭ əm), *n., pl.* -niums, -nia (-nĭ ə). the skull. —**cra'ni·al**, *adj.*

crank (krăngk), *n.* **1.** a device for communicating or changing motion, consisting in its simplest form of an arm at right angles at the end of the shaft which receives or imparts the motion. **2.** *U.S. Colloq.* a grouchy person. **3.** *U.S. Colloq.* an eccentric person. —*v.i.* **4.** to bend into a crank. **5.** to turn or operate with a crank. —*v.i.* **6.** to turn a crank. —*adj.* **7.** unsteady.

crank·case (krăngk'kās'), *n.* the housing which encloses the crankshaft, etc.

crank·shaft (krăngk'shăft', -shäft'), *n. Mach.* a shaft driving or driven by a crank.

crank·y (krăng'kĭ), *adj.,* crankier, crankiest. **1.** ill-tempered; cross. **2.** eccentric. **3.** unsteady. —**crank'i·ly**, *adv.* —**crank'i·ness**, *n.*

cran·ny (krăn'ĭ), *n., pl.* -nies. a small, narrow opening (in a wall, etc.). —**cran'nied**, *adj.*

Cran·ston (krăn'stən), *n.* a city in E Rhode Island, near Providence. 47,085.

crap (krăp), *n. U.S.* **1.** a losing throw in the game of craps. **2.** the game of craps.

crap·pie (krăp'ĭ), *n.* a small sunfish.

craps (krăps), *n. U.S.* a gambling game played with two dice.

crap·shoot·er (krăp'shōō'tər), *n. U.S.* a person who plays the game of craps.

crash¹ (krăsh), *v.t.* **1.** to break in pieces violently and noisily. **2.** to force with violence and noise. **3.** *Colloq.* to come uninvited to (a party, etc.). **4.** *Colloq.* to enter without a ticket. **5.** to land (an aircraft) with some damage. —*v.i.* **6.** to break or fall to pieces with noise. **7.** to move or go with a crash. **8.** to land an aircraft with some damage. —*n.* **9.** a breaking or falling to pieces with loud noise. **10.** the shock of collision and breaking. **11.** a sudden collapse. **12.** a sudden, loud noise. **13.** *Aeron.* act of crashing. —**crash'·er**, *n.*

crash² (krăsh), *n.* a rough fabric used as toweling, dress fabric, etc.

crass (krăs), *adj.* **1.** gross; stupid. **2.** thick; coarse. —**crass'ly**, *adv.*

crate (krāt), *n., v.,* crated, crating. —*n.* **1.** a box or framework for packing fruit, furniture, etc. **2.** a basket of wickerwork. —*v.t.* **3.** to put in a crate.

cra·ter (krā'tər), *n.* **1.** the cup-shaped depression around the orifice of a volcano. **2.** any large hole or pit in the ground.

cra·vat (krə văt'), *n.* **1.** a necktie. **2.** a scarf.

crave (krāv), *v.,* craved, craving. —*v.t.* **1.** to desire eagerly. **2.** to require. **3.** to ask or beg for. —*v.i.* **4.** to beg (fol. by *for*).

cra·ven (krā'vən), *adj.* **1.** cowardly. —*n.* **2.** a coward. —*v.t.* **3.** to make cowardly. —**cra'ven·ly**, *adv.* —**cra'ven·ness**, *n.*

crav·ing (krā'vĭng), *n.* eager desire; longing.

craw (krô), *n.* **1.** the crop of a bird or insect. **2.** the stomach of an animal.

craw·fish (krô'fĭsh'), *n., pl.* -fishes, (*esp. collectively*) -fish. any of numerous fresh-water crustaceans closely related to the lobsters but smaller.

crawl (krôl), *v.i.* **1.** to move slowly by dragging the body along the ground, as a worm. **2.** to progress slowly, laboriously, or timorously. **3.** to be, or feel as if, overrun with crawling things. —*n.* **4.** act of crawling. **5.** *Swimming.* a stroke characterized by alternate overarm movements. —**crawl'er**, *n.*

cray·fish (krā'fĭsh'), *n., pl.* -fishes, (*esp. collectively*) -fish. *Chiefly Brit.* crawfish.

cray·on (krā'ən, -ŏn), *n., v.,* -oned, -oning. —*n.* **1.** a stick of colored clay, chalk, etc., used for drawing. —*v.t.* **2.** to draw with a crayon or crayons.

craze (krāz), *v.,* crazed, crazing, *n.* —*v.t.* **1.** to make insane. **2.** to make small cracks on the surface of (pottery, etc.). —*v.i.* **3.** to become insane. **4.** to become minutely cracked, as the glaze of pottery. —*n.* **5.** a mania; a popular fashion, etc. **6.** insanity. **7.** a minute crack in the glaze of pottery, etc. —**crazed,** *adj.*

cra·zy (krā′zĭ), *adj.,* **-zier, -ziest. 1.** insane. **2.** *Colloq.* too excited. **3.** liable to break. —**cra′zi·ly,** *adv.* —**cra′zi·ness,** *n.*

crazy quilt, *U.S.* a patchwork quilt.

creak (krēk), *v.i.* **1.** to make a sharp, squeaking sound. **2.** to move with creaking. —*v.t.* **3.** to cause to creak. —*n.* **4.** a creaking sound.

creak·y (krē′kĭ), *adj.,* **creakier, creakiest.** creaking. —**creak′i·ly,** *adv.* —**creak′i·ness,** *n.*

cream (krēm), *n.* **1.** the fatty part of milk. **2.** something containing or resembling this substance. **3.** (*usually pl.*) a soft-centered confection coated with chocolate. **4.** a soup containing cream sauce. **5.** the best part of anything. **6.** yellowish white. —*v.i.* **7.** to form cream. **8.** to froth. —*v.t.* **9.** to work to a smooth, creamy mass. **10.** to prepare (chicken, etc.) with cream.

cream·er (krē′mər), *n.* **1.** one who or that which creams. **2.** a small jug for cream.

cream·er·y (krē′mə rĭ), *n., pl.* **-eries. 1.** an establishment producing butter and cheese. **2.** a place for the sale of milk and its products.

cream of tartar, purified and crystallized tartar, used in baking powder, etc.

cream·y (krē′mĭ); *adj.,* **creamier, creamiest. 1.** containing cream. **2.** resembling cream. **3.** cream-colored. —**cream′i·ness,** *n.*

crease[1] (krēs), *n., v.,* **creased, creasing.** —*n.* **1.** a mark produced by folding; a ridge or furrow. **2.** *Cricket.* one of certain lines on the ground to define the positions of the bowler and the batsman. —*v.t.* **3.** to make a crease or creases in or on. —*v.i.* **4.** to become creased.

crease[2] (krēs), *n.* creese.

cre·ate (krē āt′), *v.,* **-ated, -ating,** *adj.* —*v.t.* **1.** to cause to exist; produce. **2.** to evolve from one's own thought. **3.** to be the first to represent (a role). **4.** to invest with new character or functions; appoint. —*adj.* **5.** *Poetic.* created.

cre·a·tion (krē ā′shən), *n.* **1.** act of creating. **2.** fact of being created. **3. the Creation,** the original bringing into existence of the universe by the Deity. **4.** that which is created. —**cre·a′tion·al,** *adj.*

cre·a·tive (krē ā′tĭv), *adj.* **1.** having the quality or power of creating. **2.** productive (fol. by *of*). —**cre·a′tive·ly,** *adv.* —**cre·a′tive·ness,** *n.*

cre·a·tor (krē ā′tər), *n.* **1.** one that creates. **2. the Creator,** God. —**cre·a′tor·ship′,** *n.*

crea·ture (krē′chər), *n.* **1.** anything created. **2.** an animate being. **3.** an animal, as distinct from man. **4.** a person controlled by another.

cre·dence (krē′dəns), *n.* **1.** belief. **2.** something giving a claim to confidence.

cre·den·tial (krĭ dĕn′shəl), *n.* **1.** that which gives a title to belief or confidence. **2.** (*usually pl.*) a testimonial attesting the bearer's right to confidence or authority.

cred·i·ble (krĕd′ə bəl), *adj.* **1.** capable of being believed. **2.** trustworthy. —**cred′i·bil′i·ty, cred′i·ble·ness,** *n.* —**cred′i·bly,** *adv.*

cred·it (krĕd′ĭt), *n.* **1.** belief; trust. **2.** influence or authority resulting from the confidence of others. **3.** trustworthiness. **4.** reputation. **5.** commendation or honor for some quality, etc. **6.** a source of commendation or honor. **7.** the ascription of something as due to a person, etc. **8.** *Educ.* **a.** official recording of the work of a student in a particular course. **b.** a unit of a curriculum. **9.** time allowed for payment for goods, etc., obtained on trust. **10.** confidence in a purchaser's ability and intention to pay, displayed by entrusting him with goods, etc., without immediate payment. **11.** reputation of solvency and probity. **12.** anything on the credit side of an account. **13.** the balance in one's favor in an account. **14.** *Bookkeeping.* **a.** the acknowledgment of payment received, in an account. **b.** the side (right-hand) of an account on which such entries are made. **c.** an entry, or the total shown, on the credit side. —*v.t.* **15.** to believe; trust. **16.** to reflect credit upon. **17.** to ascribe (something) to a (person, etc.). **18.** *Bookkeeping,* to give credit for or to. **19.** to give credit to.

cred·it·a·ble (krĕd′ĭt ə bəl), *adj.* bringing credit, honor, reputation, or esteem. —**cred′it·a·ble·ness,** *n.* —**cred′it·a·bly,** *adv.*

cred·i·tor (krĕd′ĭ tər), *n.* **1.** one who gives credit. **2.** one to whom money is due.

cre·do (krē′dō, krā′dō), *n., pl.* **-dos. 1.** the Apostles' Creed. **2.** any creed.

cre·du·li·ty (krə dū′lə tĭ, -dōō′-), *n.* a disposition to believe too readily.

cred·u·lous (krĕj′ə ləs), *adj.* **1.** disposed to believe too readily. **2.** marked by or arising from credulity. —**cred′u·lous·ly,** *adv.* —**cred′u·lous·ness,** *n.*

creed (krēd), *n.* **1.** an authoritative formulated statement of the chief articles of Christian belief. **2. the Apostles' Creed. 3.** any formula or system of belief, esp. religious belief.

creek (krēk, krĭk), *n.* **1.** *U.S., Canada, and Australia.* a small stream, as a branch of a river. **2.** *Chiefly Brit.* a small inlet or bay.

creel (krēl), *n.* a wickerwork basket, esp. one used by anglers for holding fish.

creep (krēp), *v.,* **crept, creeping,** *n.* —*v.i.* **1.** to move with the body close to the ground. **2.** to move slowly or stealthily. **3.** to move or behave timidly or servilely. **4.** to have a sensation as of something creeping over the skin. **5.** to grow along the ground, a wall, etc., as a plant. —*v.t.* **6.** *Poetic.* to creep along or over. —*n.* **7.** act of creeping. **8.** (*usually pl.*) a sensation as of something creeping over the skin.

creep·er (krē′pər), *n.* **1.** one that creeps. **2.** (*pl.*) a loose garment worn by infants. **3.** *Bot.* a plant which grows along a surface, sending out rootlets from the stem, as ivy.

creep·y (krē′pĭ), *adj.,* **creepier, creepiest. 1.** that creeps. **2.** having or causing a creeping sensation of the skin, as from horror.

creese (krēs), *n.* a heavy dagger with a wavy blade, used by the Malays.

cre·mate (krē′māt), *v.t.,* **-mated, -mating.** to reduce (a corpse) to ashes. —**cre·ma′tion,** *n.*

cre·ma·to·ry (krē′mə tōr′ĭ, krĕm′-), *adj., n., pl.* **-ries.** —*adj.* **1.** of or pertaining to cremation. —*n.* **2.** a furnace or an establishment for cremating.

cre·nate (krē′nāt), *adj.* having the margin notched or scalloped, as a leaf. —**cre′nate·ly,** *adv.*

cren·el·ate (krĕn′ə lāt′), *v.t.,* **-ated, -ating.** to furnish with battlements. Also, *esp. Brit.,* **cren′el·late′.** —**cren′el·at·ed,** *adj.*

Cre·ole (krē′ōl), *n.* **1.** (in the West Indies and Spanish America) one born in the region but of European, usually Spanish, ancestry. **2.** (in Louisiana and elsewhere) a person born in the region but of French ancestry. **3.** the French language of Louisiana. **4.** (*l.c.*) a person of mixed Creole and Negro ancestry speaking a form of French or Spanish. —*adj.* **5.** of or pertaining to Creoles.

cre·o·sote (krē′ə sōt′), *n., v.,* **-soted, -soting.** —*n.* **1.** an oily liquid obtained by the distillation of wood tar: used as a preservative and antiseptic. **2.** coal-tar creosote. —*v.t.* **3.** to treat with creosote.

crêpe (krāp), *n., v.,* **creped, creping.** —*n.* **1.** a thin, light fabric of silk, cotton, or other fiber, with a finely crinkled surface. **2.** Also, **crepe paper.** thin paper wrinkled to resemble crepe. **3.** a black (or white) silk fabric, used for mourning veils, etc. —*v.t.* **4.** to cover, clothe, or drape with crepe. Also, **crêpe.**

crêpe su·zette (krāp′ sōō zĕt′), a thin dessert pancake, often flavored with liqueur.

crep·i·tate (krĕp′ə tāt′), *v.i.,* **-tated, -tating.** to crackle. —**crep′i·ta′tion,** *n.*

cre·pus·cu·lar (krĭ pŭs′kyə lər), *adj.* **1.** of, pertaining to, or resembling twilight; dim; indistinct. **2.** *Zool.* appearing or flying in the twilight.

cre·scen·do (krə shĕn′dō, -sĕn′dō), *n., pl.* **-dos** (-dōz), *adj., adv.* —*n.* **1.** a gradual increase in force or loudness. **2.** *Music.* a crescendo passage. —*adj., adv.* **3.** gradually increasing in force or loudness.

cres·cent (krĕs′ənt), *n.* **1.** the arc-shaped figure of the moon in its first or last quarter. **2.** the emblem of the Turkish Empire. **3.** the Turkish or Mohammedan power. **4.** any crescent-shaped object. —*adj.* **5.** shaped like a crescent. **6.** increasing.

cress (krĕs), *n.* any of various plants of the mustard family with pungent-tasting leaves, often used for salad, esp. the **water cress.**

cres·set (krĕs′ĭt), *n.* a mounted or suspended metal cup containing oil, pitch, etc., which is burned for light or as a beacon.

crest (krĕst), *n.* **1.** a tuft or growth on an animal's head, as the comb of a cock. **2.** anything resembling such a tuft. **3.** a plume or other ornament on the top of a helmet. **4.** a helmet. **5.** *Her.* a figure borne above the escutcheon in a coat of arms, and also used separately as a distinguishing device. **6.** the head or top of anything. **7.** the foamy top of a wave. —*v.t.* **8.** to furnish with a crest. —**crest′ed,** *adj.*

crest·fall·en (krĕst′fô′lən), *adj.* **1.** dejected; dispirited; depressed. **2.** with drooping crest.

cre·ta·ceous (krĭ tā′shəs), *adj.* of the nature of, resembling, or containing chalk.

Crete (krēt), *n.* a Greek island in the Mediterranean, SE of Greece. 441,687 pop.; 3235 sq. mi. *Cap.:* Canea. —**Cre′tan,** *adj.*, *n.*

cre·tin (krē′tĭn), *n.* a person afflicted with cretinism. —**cre′tin·ous,** *adj.*

cre·tin·ism (krē′tə nĭz′əm), *n.* a chronic disease, due to deficiency of thyroid secretion, characterized by deformity, dwarf size, and idiocy.

cre·tonne (krĭ tŏn′, krē′tŏn), *n.* a heavy cotton material in printed designs, used esp. for drapery.

cre·vasse (krə văs′), *n.*, *v.*, -vassed, -vassing. —*n.* **1.** a fissure in a glacier. **2.** *U.S.* a breach in a levee. —*v.t.* **3.** to fissure with crevasses.

crev·ice (krĕv′ĭs), *n.* a crack; cleft; fissure.

crew (krōō), *n.* **1.** a group of persons engaged upon a particular work. **2.** *Naut.* **a.** the men who man a ship. **b.** the sailors of a ship's company. **3.** any group of armed men. **4.** (often in derogatory use) crowd.

crib (krĭb), *n.*, *v.*, cribbed, cribbing. —*n.* **1.** a child's bed with enclosed sides. **2.** a stall or pen for cattle. **3.** a rack for fodder. **4.** a small house or room. **5.** any of various frameworks, as of timbers, used in construction work. **6.** a bin for storing grain, salt, etc. **7.** *Colloq.* a petty theft, plagiarism, etc. —*v.t.* **8.** to confine in or provide with a crib or cribs. **9.** *Colloq.* to steal.

crib·bage (krĭb′ĭj), *n.* a kind of card game.

crick (krĭk), *n.* **1.** a sharp, painful spasm of the muscles, as of the neck, making it difficult to move the part. —*v.t.* **2.** to give a crick to.

crick·et[1] (krĭk′ĭt), *n.* any of certain orthopterous insects characterized by their long antennae, ability to leap, and the ability of the males to produce shrill sounds by friction of their leathery forewings.

crick·et[2] (krĭk′ĭt), *n.* **1.** an open-air game played with ball, bats, and wickets, by two sides of eleven players each. **2.** *Colloq.* fair play. —*v.i.* **3.** to play cricket. —**crick′et·er,** *n.*

cri·er (krī′ər), *n.* **1.** one who cries. **2.** an official who makes public announcements. **3.** a hawker.

crime (krīm), *n.* **1.** an act committed or an omission of duty, injurious to the public welfare, for which punishment is prescribed by law. **2.** serious violation of law. **3.** any offense, wrongdoing, or sin.

Cri·me·a (krī mē′ə, krī-), *n.* a large peninsula in the SW Soviet Union, separating the Black Sea from the Sea of Azov. —**Cri·me′an,** *adj.*

crim·i·nal (krĭm′ə nəl), *adj.* **1.** of crime or its punishment. **2.** of the nature of or involving crime. **3.** guilty of crime. —*n.* **4.** a person guilty of a crime. —**crim′i·nal′i·ty,** *n.* —**crim′i·nal·ly,** *adv.*

crim·i·nol·o·gy (krĭm′ə nŏl′ə jĭ), *n.* the science dealing with the causes and treatment of crimes and criminals. —**crim′i·nol′o·gist,** *n.*

crimp (krĭmp), *v.t.* **1.** to press into small regular folds; make wavy. —*n.* **2.** act of crimping. **3.** crimped condition or form. **4.** (*usually pl.*) something crimped, as a lock of hair. **5.** put a crimp in, *Colloq.* to hinder. —**crimp′er,** *n.* —**crimp′y,** *adj.*

crim·son (krĭm′zən), *adj.* **1.** deep purplish-red. —*n.* **2.** a crimson color, pigment, or dye. —*v.t.* **3.** to make crimson.

cringe (krĭnj), *v.*, cringed, cringing, *n.* —*v.i.* **1.** to shrink or crouch, esp. from fear or servility. **2.** to fawn. —*n.* **3.** servile obeisance.

crin·kle (krĭng′kəl), *v.*, -kled, -kling, *n.* —*v.t.*, *v.i.* **1.** to wind or turn in and out. **2.** to wrinkle; ripple. **3.** to rustle. —*n.* **4.** a wrinkle; ripple. **5.** a crinkling sound. —**crin′kly,** *adj.*

cri·noid (krī′noid, krĭn′oid), *adj.* **1.** lilylike. —*n.* **2.** one of a class of marine animals with radiating arms on an attached stalk, including the sea lilies and numerous fossil forms.

crin·o·line (krĭn′ə lĭn, -lēn), *n.* **1.** a petticoat of stiff material, formerly worn under a full dress skirt. **2.** a hoop skirt. **3.** stiff coarse cotton material for interlining.

crip·ple (krĭp′əl), *n.*, *v.*, -pled, -pling. —*n.* **1.** one who is partially or wholly deprived of the use of one or more of his limbs; a lame person.

—*v.t.* **2.** to make a cripple of. **3.** to disable. —**crip′pler,** *n.*

cri·sis (krī′sĭs), *n.*, *pl.* -ses (-sēz). **1.** a decisive stage in the course of anything. **2.** the point in the course of a disease at which a decisive change occurs, leading either to recovery or to death.

crisp (krĭsp), *adj.* **1.** hard but easily breakable; brittle. **2.** firm and fresh. **3.** brisk; sharp. **4.** lively; pithy; sparkling. **5.** bracing. **6.** crinkled, wrinkled, or rippled. **7.** curly. —*v.t.*, *v.i.* **8.** to make or become crisp. **9.** to curl. —**crisp′ly,** *adv.* —**crisp′ness,** *n.*

crisp·y (krĭs′pĭ), *adj.*, crispier, crispiest. **1.** brittle; crisp. **2.** curly or wavy. **3.** brisk.

criss·cross (krĭs′krôs′, -krŏs′), *adj.* **1.** crossed; marked by crossings. —*n.* **2.** a crisscross mark, pattern, etc. —*adv.* **3.** crosswise. —*v.t.*, *v.i.* **4.** to mark with or form crossing lines.

Cris·to·bal (krĭs tō′bəl), *n.* a seaport in the Canal Zone at the Atlantic end of the Panama Canal, adjacent to Colón. 826.

cri·te·ri·on (krī tĭr′ĭ ən), *n.*, *pl.* -teria (-tĭr′ĭ ə), -terions. a standard of judgment or criticism.

crit·ic (krĭt′ĭk), *n.* **1.** a person skilled in judging the qualities of some class of things. **2.** one who censures or finds fault.

crit·i·cal (krĭt′ə kəl), *adj.* **1.** inclined to find fault or judge with severity. **2.** occupied with or skilled in criticism. **3.** involving skillfull judgment. **4.** of or pertaining to critics or criticism. **5.** pertaining to, or of the nature of, a crisis; crucial. **6.** involving suspense, risk, peril, etc. —**crit′i·cal·ly,** *adv.* —**crit′i·cal·ness,** *n.*

crit·i·cism (krĭt′ə sĭz′əm), *n.* **1.** act or art of criticizing. **2.** a critical comment, article, or essay.

crit·i·cize (krĭt′ə sīz′), *v.*, -cized, -cizing. —*v.i.* **1.** to make judgments as to merits and faults. **2.** to find fault. —*v.t.* **3.** to judge or discuss the merits and faults of. **4.** to find fault with. Also, *Brit.*, **crit′i·cise′.** —**crit′i·ciz′a·ble,** *adj.* —**crit′i·ciz′er,** *n.*

cri·tique (krĭ tēk′), *n.* **1.** an article criticizing a literary or other work. **2.** art of criticism.

croak (krōk), *v.i.* **1.** to utter a low, hoarse, dismal cry, as a frog or raven. **2.** to speak with a low, hollow voice. **3.** to forebode evil; grumble. **4.** *Slang.* to die. —*v.t.* **5.** to utter by croaking. **6.** *Slang.* to kill. —*n.* **7.** act or sound of croaking.

croak·er (krō′kər), *n.* **1.** one that croaks. **2.** any of various fishes that make a croaking noise.

Cro·a·tia (krō ā′shə, -shĭ′ə), *n.* a constituent republic of Yugoslavia, in the NW part: a medieval kingdom. 3,360,500 pop.; 19,817 sq. mi. *Cap.:* Zagreb. —**Cro·at** (krō′ăt), *n.* —**Cro·a·tian** (krō ā′shən), *adj.*, *n.*

cro·chet (krō shā′), *n.*, *v.*, -cheted (-shād′), -cheting (-shā′ĭng). —*n.* **1.** a kind of needle-work done with a hooked needle for drawing the thread into loops. —*v.t.*, *v.i.* **2.** to form by crochet.

crock (krŏk), *n.* an earthen pot or jar.

crock·er·y (krŏk′ə rĭ), *n.* crocks collectively.

Crock·ett (krŏk′ĭt), *n.* David, 1786–1836, U.S. frontiersman: killed in defense of Alamo.

croc·o·dile (krŏk′ə dīl′), *n.* any of the large, thick-skinned reptiles inhabiting the waters of tropical Africa, Asia, Australia, and America.

crocodile tears, false or insincere tears.

croc·o·dil·i·an (krŏk′ə dĭl′ĭ ən), *n.* **1.** any of an order of reptiles including crocodiles, alligators, etc. —*adj.* **2.** of or pertaining to the crocodile.

cro·cus (krō′kəs), *n.*, *pl.* crocuses. any of certain small bulbous plants of the iris family, much cultivated for their showy, solitary flowers.

Croe·sus (krē′səs), *n.* king of Lydia, 560–546 B.C., noted for his great wealth.

croft (krôft, krŏft), *n.* *Brit.* a small piece of enclosed ground for tillage, etc.

Cro-Mag·non (krō măg′nŏn), *adj.* belonging to a prehistoric race of Europe, believed to be of the same species as modern man.

Crom·well (krŏm′wəl, -wĕl, krŭm′-), *n.* **1.** Oliver, 1599–1658, British general, Puritan statesman, and Lord Protector of the Commonwealth, 1653–58. **2.** his son, Richard, 1626–1712, British soldier, politician, Lord Protector of the Commonwealth, 1658–59.

crone (krōn), *n.* an ugly old woman.

cro·ny (krō′nĭ), *n.*, *pl.* -nies. an intimate friend.

crook (krŏōk), *n.* **1.** a bent or curved implement, piece, appendage, etc. **2.** an implement having a bent or curved part, as a shepherd's staff or the crosier of a bishop. 3. any bend, turn, or curve. 4. *Colloq.* a dishonest person, esp. a swindler. —*v.t.*, *v.i.* 5. to bend; curve.

crook·ed (krŏŏk′ĭd), *adj.* 1. bent; curved. 2. deformed. 3. not honest. —**crook′ed·ly**, *adv.* —**crook′ed·ness**, *n.*

croon (krōōn), *v.i.*, *v.t.* 1. to sing softly, esp. with exaggerated feeling. —*n.* 2. act or sound of crooning. —**croon′er**, *n.*

crop (krŏp), *n.*, *v.*, **cropped, cropping.** —*n.* 1. the cultivated produce of the ground, as grain or fruit, while growing or when gathered. 2. the yield of such produce for a particular season. 3. the yield of some other product in a season. 4. the stock or handle of a whip. 5. a short riding whip with a loop instead of a lash. 6. act of cropping. 7. a mark produced by clipping the ears, as of an animal. 8. a style of wearing the hair cut short. 9. a special pouchlike enlargement of the gullet of many birds, in which food is held, and may undergo partial preparation for digestion. 10. the craw. —*v.t.* 11. to remove the head or top of (a plant, etc.). 12. to cut off the ends or a part of. 13. to cut short. 14. to clip the ears, hair, etc., of. —*v.i.* 15. to bear or yield a crop or crops. 16. to appear unexpectedly (fol. by *up* or *out*).

crop·per (krŏp′ər), *n.* 1. one that crops. 2. one who raises a crop. 3. one who cultivates land for its owner in return for part of the crop. 4. *Colloq.* a heavy fall, esp. from a horse. 5. a failure; collapse.

cro·quet (krō kā′), *n.* an outdoor game played by knocking wooden balls through a series of iron arches by means of mallets.

cro·quette (krō kĕt′), *n.* a small mass of minced meat or fish, or of other material, often coated with egg and bread crumbs, and fried.

cro·sier (krō′zhər), *n.* the pastoral staff of a bishop or an abbot, hooked like a shepherd's crook.

cross (krôs, krŏs), *n.* 1. a structure consisting essentially of an upright and a transverse piece, upon which persons were formerly put to death. 2. the Cross, the cross upon which Jesus died. 3. a figure of the cross as a Christian emblem, badge, etc. 4. the cross as the symbol of Christianity. 5. a crucifix. 6. a structure or monument in the form of a cross, set up for prayer, etc. 7. any of various modifications of the Christian emblem as used in heraldry, art, etc. 8. any object, figure, or mark resembling a cross, as two intersecting lines. 9. such a mark made instead of a signature by a person unable to write. 10. misfortune; trouble. 11. a mixing of breeds. 12. a crossbred. 13. something intermediate in character between two things. —*v.t.* 14. to make the sign of the cross upon or over. 15. to cancel by marking with a cross or lines. 16. to place in the form of a cross or crosswise. 17. to put or draw across. 18. to lie or pass across; intersect. 19. to move, pass, or extend from one side to the other side of (a street, etc.). 20. to transport across something. 21. to meet and pass. 22. to oppose; thwart. 23. *Biol.* to cause (members of different breeds, varieties, or the like) to produce offspring. —*v.i.* 24. to lie or be athwart. 25. to move, pass, or extend from one side to another. 26. to meet and pass. 27. to interbreed. —*adj.* 28. athwart; transverse. 29. contrary; opposite. 30. ill-humored; snappish. 31. crossbred; hybrid. —**cross′ly**, *adv.* —**cross′ness**, *n.*

cross·bar (krôs′bär′, krŏs′-), *n.* a transverse bar, line, or stripe.

cross·bones (krôs′bōnz′, krŏs′-), *n.pl.* two bones placed crosswise, symbolizing death.

cross·bow (krôs′bō′, krŏs′-), *n.* an old weapon for shooting missiles, consisting of a bow fixed transversely on a stock. —**cross′bow′man**, *n.*

cross·bred (krôs′brĕd′, krŏs′-), *adj.* 1. produced by crossbreeding. —*n.* 2. an animal or group of animals produced by hybridization.

cross·breed (krôs′brēd′, krŏs′-), *v.*, **-bred, -breeding**, *n.* —*v.t.* 1. to produce (a hybrid) within a species, using two breeds or varieties. —*v.i.* 2. to undertake or engage in hybridizing, esp. within a single species. —*n.* 3. a crossbred.

cross·cut (krôs′kŭt′, krŏs′-), *adj.*, *n.*, *v.*, **-cut, -cutting.** —*adj.* 1. made or used for cutting crosswise. 2. cut across the grain or on the bias. —*n.* 3. a direct course between two points, as one diagonal to a main way. —*v.t.* 4. to cut across.

cross·ex·am·ine (krôs′ĭg zăm′ĭn, krŏs′-), *v.t.*, **-ined, -ining.** 1. to examine closely or minutely. 2. to examine (a witness called by the opposing

side). —**cross′-ex·am′i·na′tion**, *n.* —**cross′-ex·am′in·er**, *n.*

cross-eye (krôs′ī′, krŏs′-), *n.* strabismus, esp. the form in which both eyes turn toward the nose. —**cross′-eyed′**, *adj.*

cross-fer·ti·li·za·tion (krôs′fûr′tə lə zā′shən, krŏs′-), *n.* 1. *Biol.* fertilization of an organism by the fusion of an egg from one individual with a sperm of a different individual. 2. *Bot.* fertilization of one flower or plant by pollen from another.

cross-fer·ti·lize (krôs′fûr′tə līz′, krŏs′-), *v.t.*, **-lized, -lizing.** to cause the cross-fertilization of.

cross·hatch (krôs′hăch′, krŏs′-), *v.t.* to shade with intersecting sets of parallel lines.

cross·ing (krôs′ĭng, krŏs′ĭng), *n.* 1. act of one that crosses. 2. a place where lines, tracks, etc., cross each other. 3. a place at which a road, river, etc., may be crossed.

cross·patch (krôs′păch′, krŏs′-), *n.* *Colloq.* an ill-humored person.

cross·piece (krôs′pēs′, krŏs′-), *n.* a piece of any material placed across something.

cross·pol·li·nate (krôs′pŏl′ə nāt′, krŏs′-), *v.t.*, **-nated, -nating.** to cross-fertilize. —**cross′-pol′li·na′tion**, *n.*

cross-pur·pose (krôs′pûr′pəs, krŏs′-), *n.* an opposing purpose.

cross-ques·tion (krôs′kwĕs′chən, krŏs′-), *v.t.* to cross-examine.

cross-re·fer (krôs′rĭ fûr′, krŏs′-), *v.t.*, *v.i.*, **-ferred, -ferring.** to refer by a cross reference.

cross reference, a reference from one part of a book, etc., to a word, item, etc., in another part.

cross·road (krôs′rōd′, krŏs′-), *n.* 1. a road that crosses another road. 2. a by-road. 3. (*often pl., construed as sing.*) the place where roads intersect.

cross section, 1. a section made by a plane cutting anything transversely, esp. at right angles to the longest axis. 2. a piece so cut off. 3. a typical selection or sample.

cross-stitch (krôs′stĭch′, krŏs′-), *n.* 1. a kind of stitching employing pairs of diagonal stitches crossing each other in the middle at right angles. —*v.t.*, *v.i.* 2. to work in cross-stitch.

cross·tree (krôs′trē′, krŏs′-), *n.* *Naut.* one of the horizontal transverse pieces fastened to the head of a lower mast or topmast to support the top, spread the shrouds, etc.

cross·wise (krôs′wīz′, krŏs′-), *adv.* 1. across. 2. in the form of a cross. 3. contrarily. Also, **cross′ways′.**

cross·word puzzle (krôs′wûrd′, krŏs′-), a puzzle in which words corresponding to given meanings are to be supplied and fitted into a figure divided into spaces, the letters forming horizontal and vertical words at the same time.

C. Crosstree

crotch (krŏch), *n.* 1. a forked piece, part, support, etc. 2. a forking or place of forking, as of the human body between the legs.

crotch·et (krŏch′ĭt), *n.* 1. a small hook. 2. a hooklike device or part. 3. an odd fancy or whimsical notion. 4. *Chiefly Brit. Music.* a quarter note.

crotch·et·y (krŏch′ĭt ĭ), *adj.* given to odd fancies. —**crotch′et·i·ness**, *n.*

cro·ton (krō′tən), *n.* 1. any of certain chiefly tropical plants of the spurge family, many species of which have important medicinal properties. 2. any plant of a related genus cultivated for the ornamental foliage.

Cro·ton bug (krō′tən), the common cockroach.

crouch (krouch), *v.i.* 1. to stoop or bend low. 2. to bend close to the ground, as an animal preparing to spring. 3. to bow or stoop servilely. —*v.t.* 4. to bend low. —*n.* 5. act of crouching.

croup¹ (krōōp), *n.* *Pathol.* any affection of the larynx or trachea characterized by a hoarse cough and difficult breathing. —**croup′y**, *adj.*

croup² (krōōp), *n.* the rump or buttocks of certain animals, esp. of a horse.

crou·pi·er (krōō′pĭ ər), *n.* an attendant who collects and pays the money at a gaming table.

crou·ton (krōō′tŏn), *n.* a small piece of fried or toasted bread, used in soups, etc.

crow¹ (krō), *n.* 1. certain of the oscine birds with lustrous black plumage and a characteristic harsh cry of "caw." **2.** any of various similar birds of other families. **3.** a crowbar. **4. eat crow,** to be compelled to do or say something humiliating.

crow[2] (krō), v., **crowed** (or **crew** for 1), **crowed, crowing,** n. —v.i. **1.** to utter the characteristic cry of a cock. **2.** to utter an inarticulate cry of pleasure. **3.** to boast. —n. **4.** the cry of the cock.

Crow (krō), n. a member of a North American Indian tribe located in eastern Montana.

crow·bar (krō′bär′), n. a bar of iron, often with a wedge-shaped end, for use as a lever, etc.

crowd (kroud), n. **1.** a large number of persons gathered closely together. **2.** the masses. **3.** any group or set of persons. —v.i. **4.** to throng; swarm. **5.** to press forward. —v.t. **6.** to push. **7.** to press closely together. **8.** to fill to excess. **9.** *Colloq.* to urge. —**crowd′ed,** adj.

crow·foot (krō′fŏŏt′), n., pl. -foots for 1 and 2. **1.** any plant of the buttercup family, esp. one with divided leaves suggestive of a crow's foot. **2.** any of various other plants with leaves or other parts suggestive of a bird's foot.

crown (kroun), n. **1.** an ornamental garland for the head, conferred by the ancients as a mark of victory or distinction. **2.** honorary distinction. **3.** a decorative covering for the head, worn as a symbol of sovereignty. **4.** the power or dominion of a sovereign. **5. the Crown,** the sovereign as head of the state. **6.** any crownlike emblem or design. **7.** a coin generally bearing a crown. The English crown is worth five shillings. **8.** something having the form of a crown, as the corona of a flower. **9.** the top of anything, as of the head, a hat, etc. **10.** the head itself. **11.** *Dentistry.* an artificial substitute, as of gold or porcelain, for the enamel part of a tooth. **12.** the highest or most perfect state of anything. **13.** an exalting or chief attribute. **14.** the acme or supreme source of honor, beauty, etc. **15.** *Naut.* the part of an anchor where the arms join the shank. —v.t. **16.** to place a crown upon the head of. **17.** to invest with regal power. **18.** to honor or reward. **19.** to surmount as with a crown. **20.** to complete worthily. **21.** *Checkers.* to change (a checker) into a king by putting another piece on it. —**crown′er,** n.

crown prince, the heir apparent of a monarch.

crown princess, the wife of a crown prince.

crow's-foot (krōz′fŏŏt′), n., pl. -feet. *(usually pl.)* a wrinkle at the outer corner of the eye.

crow's-nest (krōz′nĕst′), n. *Naut.* **1.** a box or shelter for the lookout, secured near the top of a mast. **2.** a similar lookout station ashore.

Croy·don (kroi′dən), n. a city in SE England, near London: airport. 234,640.

cru·cial (krōō′shəl), adj. **1.** involving a final and supreme decision; decisive. **2.** severe; trying. **3.** cross-shaped. —**cru′cial·ly,** adv.

cru·ci·ble (krōō′sə bəl), n. **1.** a vessel of refractory material employed for heating substances to high temperatures. **2.** a severe, searching test.

cru·ci·fix (krōō′sə fĭks), n. **1.** a cross with the figure of Jesus crucified upon it. **2.** any cross.

cru·ci·fix·ion (krōō′sə fĭk′shən), n. **1.** act of crucifying. **2.** *(cap.)* the death of Jesus upon a cross.

cru·ci·form (krōō′sə fôrm′), adj. cross-shaped.

cru·ci·fy (krōō′sə fī′), v.t., -fied, -fying. **1.** to put to death by nailing or binding the body to a cross. **2.** to torment. —**cru′ci·fi′er,** n.

crude (krōōd), adj., **cruder, crudest. 1.** in a raw state; unrefined. **2.** unripe. **3.** lacking finish or completeness. **4.** lacking culture, tact, etc. **5.** blunt; bare. —**crude′ly,** adv. —**crude′ness, cru′di·ty,** n.

cru·el (krōō′əl), adj. **1.** disposed to inflict suffering; pitiless. **2.** causing, or marked by, great pain or distress. —**cru′el·ly,** adj. —**cru′el·ness,** n.

cru·el·ty (krōō′əl tĭ), n., pl. -ties. **1.** cruel quality or conduct. **2.** a cruel act.

cru·et (krōō′ĭt), n. a glass bottle, esp. one for holding vinegar, oil, etc., for the table.

cruise (krōōz), v., **cruised, cruising,** n. —v.i. **1.** to sail around, as for pleasure. **2.** to fly at a practical (rather than high) speed. —v.t. **3.** to cruise over. —n. **4.** a voyage made by cruising.

cruis·er (krōō′zər), n. **1.** one who or that which cruises. **2.** a warship of medium tonnage, designed for speed and long cruising radius. **3.** a boat, usually power-driven, for pleasure trips.

crul·ler (krŭl′ər), n. a light, sweet cake fried in deep fat, often ring-shaped or twisted.

crumb (krŭm), n. **1.** a small particle of bread, cake, etc., such as breaks off. **2.** any small particle. **3.** the soft inner portion of a bread. —v.t. **4.** *Cookery.* to cover or prepare with bread crumbs. **5.** to break into crumbs.

crum·ble (krŭm′bəl), v., -bled, -bling, n. —v.t., v.i. **1.** to break into small fragments. **2.** to decay. —n. **3.** something crumbling or crumbled. —**crum′bly,** adj.

crum·pet (krŭm′pĭt), n. *Chiefly Brit.* a soft bread resembling a muffin.

crum·ple (krŭm′pəl), v., -pled, -pling, n. —v.t., v.i. **1.** to draw or press into irregular folds; rumple. **2.** *Colloq.* to collapse. —n. **3.** a wrinkle produced by crumpling.

crunch (krŭnch), v.t., v.i. **1.** to chew with a crushing noise. **2.** to crush noisily. **3.** to produce, or proceed with, a crushing noise. —n. **4.** act or sound of crunching.

crup·per (krŭp′ər, krŏŏp′-), n. a leather strap on the back of the saddle of a harness, passing in a loop under a horse's tail.

cru·sade (krōō sād′), n., v., -saded, -sading. —n. **1.** *(often cap.)* any of the military expeditions undertaken by the Christians of Europe in the 11th, 12th, and 13th centuries for the recovery of the Holy Land from the Mohammedans. **2.** any vigorous movement for a noble idea, cause, etc. —v.i. **3.** to go on or engage in a crusade. —**cru·sad′er,** n.

cruse (krōōz, krōōs), n. an earthen pot, bottle, etc.

crush (krŭsh), v.t. **1.** to press and bruise between two hard bodies. **2.** to break into small fragments. **3.** to force out by squeezing. **4.** to subdue or overwhelm. —v.i. **5.** to become crushed. **6.** to press or crowd forcibly. —n. **7.** act of crushing. **8.** state of being crushed. **9.** *Colloq.* a great crowd. —**crush′er,** n.

crust (krŭst), n. **1.** the hard outer portion of bread. **2.** a piece of this. **3.** the outside covering of a pie. **4.** any hard external covering, as the hard shell of certain animals, the exterior portion of the earth, etc. —v.t. **5.** to cover with a crust. —v.i. **6.** to form a crust.

crus·ta·cean (krŭs tā′shən), adj. **1.** belonging to a class of (chiefly aquatic) arthropods, including the lobsters, shrimps, crabs, barnacles, etc., commonly having the body covered with a hard shell or crust. —n. **2.** a crustacean animal.

crust·y (krŭs′tĭ), adj., **crustier, crustiest. 1.** of the nature of, like, or having a crust. **2.** harsh. —**crust′i·ly,** adv. —**crust′i·ness,** n.

crutch (krŭch), n. **1.** a staff to assist a lame person in walking, usually with a crosspiece that fits under the armpit. **2.** any of various devices resembling this. —v.t. **3.** to support on crutches.

crux (krŭks), n., pl., **cruxes, cruces** (krōō′sēz). **1.** a vital, basic, or decisive point. **2.** a cross. **3.** something that puzzles or perplexes.

cry (krī), v., **cried, crying,** n., pl. **cries.** —v.i. **1.** to utter inarticulate sounds, as of grief or suffering, usually with tears. **2.** to shed tears. **3.** to shout. **4.** to give forth characteristic calls, as animals. —v.t. **5.** to utter loudly; call out. **6.** to announce or sell by outcry. **7.** to beg for or implore in a loud voice. **8.** to belittle (fol. by down). —n. **9.** act or sound of crying; a shout, scream, or wail. **10.** clamor; outcry. **11.** an appeal. **12.** an oral proclamation. **13.** a call of wares for sale, etc. **14.** a fit of weeping. **15.** the characteristic call of an animal.

cry·ing (krī′ĭng), adj. **1.** that cries; weeping. **2.** demanding attention or remedy.

crypt (krĭpt), n. a subterranean chamber, esp. one beneath a church, used as a burial place, etc.

cryp·tic (krĭp′tĭk), adj. hidden; secret; occult. Also, **cryp′ti·cal.** —**cryp′ti·cal·ly,** adv.

cryp·to·gam (krĭp′tə găm′), n. *Bot.* **1.** any of an old primary division of plants comprising those without true flowers and seeds, as the ferns. **2.** a plant without a true seed. —**cryp′to·gam′-ic, cryp·tog·a·mous** (krĭp tŏg′ə məs), adj.

cryp·to·gram (krĭp′tə grăm′), n. a message or writing in secret characters or otherwise occult.

cryp·to·graph (krĭp′tə grăf′, -gräf′), n. **1.** a cryptogram. **2.** a system of secret writing.

cryp·tog·ra·phy (krĭp tŏg′rə fĭ), n. process or art of writing in secret characters or in cipher. —**cryp·tog′ra·pher,** n.

crys·tal (krĭs′təl), n. **1.** a clear, transparent mineral or glass resembling ice. **2.** the trans-

parent form of crystallized quartz. **3.** *Chem.,*
Mineral. a solid body with symmetrically arranged plane surfaces. **4.** anything of or like
such a substance. **5.** a single grain or mass of a
crystalline substance. **6.** glass of a high degree
of brilliance. **7.** cut glass. **8.** the glass or plastic
cover over the face of a watch. **9.** *Radio.* the
piece of galena, or the like, forming the essential
part of a crystal detector. —*adj.* **10.** composed
of crystal. **11.** resembling crystal; clear.

crys·tal·line (krĭs′tə lĭn, -līn′), *adj.* **1.** of or
like crystal; clear; transparent. **2.** formed by
crystallization. **3.** composed of crystals, as
rocks. **4.** pertaining to crystals or their formation.

crys·tal·lize (krĭs′tə līz′), *v.,* -lized, -lizing.
—*v.t.* **1.** to form into crystals. **2.** to give definite
form to. —*v.i.* **3.** to become crystalline in form.
4. to assume definite form. —**crys′tal·liz′a-
ble,** *adj.* —**crys′tal·li·za′tion,** *n.*

crys·tal·log·ra·phy (krĭs′tə lŏg′rə fĭ), *n.* the
science dealing with crystallization and crystals.

crys·tal·loid (krĭs′tə loid′), *adj.* **1.** resembling
a crystal. —*n.* **2.** a substance which, when dissolved in a liquid, will diffuse readily through
vegetable or animal membranes. —**crys′tal-
loi′dal,** *adj.*

Cs, *Chem.* cesium.

C.S.T., Central Standard Time. Also, **CST**

Cu, *Chem.* cuprum.

cu., cubic.

cub (kŭb), *n.* **1.** the young of certain animals,
as the fox, bear, etc. **2.** *Humorous or Contemptuous.* an awkward or unmannerly youth. **3.**
Colloq. an inexperienced reporter.

Cu·ba (kū′bə), *n.* a republic S of Florida: largest
island in the West Indies. 4,778,583 pop.; 44,218
sq. mi. *Cap.:* Havana. —**Cu′ban,** *adj., n.*

cub·by·hole (kŭb′ĭ hōl′), *n.* small enclosed
space.

cube (kūb), *n., v.,* **cubed, cubing.** —*n.* **1.** a solid
bounded by six equal squares. **2.** *Arith., Alg.* the
third power of a quantity. —*v.t.* **3.** to make into
a cube or cubes. **4.** to raise to the third power.

cu·beb (kū′bĕb), *n.* the fruit of an East Indian
climbing shrub of the pepper family, dried in an
unripe state, and used for urinary and bronchial
disorders.

cube root, the quantity of which a given quantity is the cube.

cu·bic (kū′bĭk), *adj.* **1.** of three dimensions,
solid, or pertaining to solid content. **2.** having
the form of a cube. **3.** *Arith., Alg.* being of the
third power. Also, **cu′bi·cal.** —**cu′bi·cal·ly,**
adv.

cu·bi·cle (kū′bə kəl), *n.* **1.** a bedroom, esp. one
of a number in a dormitory. **2.** any small compartment.

cubic measure, 1. the measurement of volume in cubic units. **2.** a system of such units,
esp. that in which 1728 cubic inches = 1 cubic
foot.

cub·ism (kū′bĭz əm), *n.* *Art.* one of the aspects
of postimpressionism, which aims to express the
artist's emotions through arrangements on his
canvas of geometrical forms in various colors and
textures. —**cub′ist,** *n., adj.* —**cu·bis′tic,** *adj.*

cu·bit (kū′bĭt), *n.* an ancient linear unit based
on the length of the forearm, usually 17 to 21
inches.

cuck·old (kŭk′əld), *n.* **1.** the husband of an unfaithful wife. —*v.t.* **2.** to make a cuckold of.

cuck·oo (kŏŏk′ōō), *n., pl.* -os, *v.,* -ooed, -ooing,
adj. —*n.* **1.** any of certain small birds, esp. a
common European migratory bird noted for its
characteristic call, and for its habit of laying eggs
in the nests of other birds to be hatched by them.
2. the call of the cuckoo. **3.** a fool. —*v.i.* **4.** to
utter the call of the cuckoo. —*adj.* **5.** *U.S.
Slang.* crazy; foolish.

cu·cum·ber (kū′kŭm bər), *n.* **1.** a creeping
plant yielding a long fleshy fruit eaten in salads
and used for pickling. **2.** the fruit of this plant.

cud (kŭd), *n.* the portion of food which a rumi-
nating animal returns from the first stomach to
the mouth to chew a second time.

cud·dle (kŭd′əl), *v.,* -dled, -dling, *n.* —*v.t.* **1.** to
hold or hug tenderly; fondle. —*v.i.* **2.** to lie close
and snug; nestle. —*n.* **3.** a hug; embrace.
—**cud′dly,** *adj.*

cudg·el (kŭj′əl), *n., v.,* -eled, -eling, or (*esp.
Brit.*) -elled, -elling. —*n.* **1.** a short, thick stick
used as a weapon. —*v.t.* **2.** to strike with a
cudgel. **3.** cudgel one's brains, to think hard.

cue[1] (kū), *n.* **1.** anything said or done on stage
that is followed by a specific line or action. **2.** a
hint. **3.** the part one is to play. **4.** disposition.

cue[2] (kū), *n., v.,* **cued, cuing.** —*n.* **1.** a long
tapering rod used to strike the ball in billiards,
pool, etc. **2.** a queue of hair. **3.** a queue of persons. —*v.t.* **4.** to tie into a queue or tail.

cuff[1] (kŭf), *n.* **1.** a fold, band, or other piece
trimming the bottom of a sleeve. **2.** a turned-up
fold at the bottom of trouser legs, etc.

cuff[2] (kŭf), *v.t.* **1.** to strike with the open hand.
—*n.* **2.** such a blow. **3.** a handcuff.

cui·rass (kwĭ răs′), *n.* **1.** a piece of defensive
armor combining a breastplate and a piece for the
back. **2.** the breastplate alone.

cui·sine (kwĭ zēn′), *n.* **1.** the kitchen. **2.** style
of cooking; cookery.

cuisse (kwĭs), *n.* a piece of armor for the thigh.

cul-de-sac (kŭl′də săk′, kŏŏl′-), *n.* **1.** a saclike cavity, tube, or the like, open only at one
end. **2.** a street, lane, etc., closed at one end;
blind alley.

cu·lex (kū′lĕks), *n., pl.* -lices (-lə sēz′). the
common house mosquito.

cu·li·nar·y (kū′lə nĕr′ĭ), *adj.* pertaining to the
kitchen or to cookery; used in cooking.

cull (kŭl), *v.t.* **1.** to choose; select. **2.** to collect;
gather. —*n.* **3.** act of culling. **4.** something
culled, esp. something picked out and put aside
as inferior.

culm[1] (kŭlm), *n.* **1.** coal dust. **2.** anthracite.

culm[2] (kŭlm), *n.* **1.** the jointed and usually hollow stem of grasses. —*v.i.* **2.** to grow into a culm.

cul·mi·nate (kŭl′mə nāt′), *v.i.,* -nated, -nat-
ing. to reach the highest point or development.

cul·mi·na·tion (kŭl′mə nā′shən), *n.* **1.** act or
fact of culminating. **2.** the highest point; acme.

cul·pa·ble (kŭl′pə bəl), *adj.* deserving blame or
censure; blameworthy. —**cul′pa·bil′i·ty, cul′-
pa·ble·ness,** *n.* —**cul′pa·bly,** *adv.*

cul·prit (kŭl′prĭt), *n.* **1.** a person arraigned for
an offense. **2.** one guilty of an offense or fault.

cult (kŭlt), *n.* **1.** a particular system of religious
worship. **2.** an instance of an almost religious
veneration for a person or thing. **3.** the object
of such devotion.

cul·ti·va·ble (kŭl′tə və bəl), *adj.* capable of
being cultivated. Also, **cul·ti·vat·a·ble** (kŭl′tə-
vā′tə bəl). —**cul′ti·va·bil′i·ty,** *n.*

cul·ti·vate (kŭl′tə vāt′), *v.t.,* -vated, -vating.
1. to prepare and care for (land) in raising crops;
till. **2.** to use a cultivator on. **3.** to produce by
culture. **4.** to develop or improve by education
or training. **5.** to promote the development of
(an art, science, etc.). **6.** to devote oneself to (an
art, etc.). **7.** to seek to foster (friendship, etc.).
8. to seek the friendship of. —**cul′ti·vat′ed,**
adj. —**cul′ti·va′tion,** *n.*

cul·ti·va·tor (kŭl′tə vā′tər), *n.* **1.** one that
cultivates. **2.** an implement for loosening the
earth and destroying weeds.

cul·tur·al (kŭl′chər əl), *adj.* of or pertaining to
culture or cultivation. —**cul′tur·al·ly,** *adv.*

cul·ture (kŭl′chər), *n., v.,* -tured, -turing. —*n.*
1. action or practice of cultivating the soil. **2.**
the raising of plants or animals. **3.** development
by education. **4.** the resulting enlightenment or
refinement. **5.** a particular state or stage of
civilization. **6.** *Biol.* a. the cultivation of micro-
organisms, tissues, etc., for scientific study, medicinal use, etc. b. the product resulting from
such cultivation. —*v.t.* **7.** to subject to culture.
8. *Biol.* to develop (microörganisms, tissues, etc.)
in an artificial medium.

cul·tured (kŭl′chərd), *adj.* **1.** cultivated. **2.**
enlightened; refined.

cul·vert (kŭl′vərt), *n.* a drain or channel crossing under a road, etc.: a sewer; a conduit.

cum·ber (kŭm′bər), *v.t.* **1.** to hamper. **2.** to
burden. **3.** to trouble. —*n.* **4.** hindrance.
—**cum′ber·er,** *n.*

Cum·ber·land (kŭm′bər lənd), *n.* **1.** a city in
NW Maryland. 39,483. **2.** a river from SE Ken-
tucky through N Tennessee to the Ohio near
Paducah, Kentucky. 687 mi.

cum·ber·some (kŭm′bər səm), *adj.* **1.** burdensome. **2.** unwieldy. Also, **cum·brous** (kŭm′brəs).
—**cum′ber·some·ly,** *adv.*

cu·mu·late (*v.* kū′myə lāt′; *adj.* kū′myə lĭt,
-lāt′), *v.,* -lated, -lating, *adj.* —*v.t.* **1.** to accumulate. —*adj.* **2.** heaped up. —**cu′mu·la′tion,**
n.

cu·mu·la·tive (kū′myə lā′tĭv), *adj.* **1.** increasing or formed by accumulation. **2.** of a dividend

or interest which accumulates if not paid when due. —**cu·mu·la·tive·ly**, *adv.* —**cu·mu·la·tive·ness**, *n.*

cu·mu·lus (kū′myə ləs), *n.*, *pl.* **-li** (-lī′). **1.** a heap. **2.** *Meteorol.* a cloud made up of rounded heaps and with a flat base. —**cu′mu·lous**, *adj.*

cu·ne·ate (kū′nĭ ĭt, -āt′), *adj.* wedge-shaped.

cu·ne·i·form (kū nē′ə fôrm′, kū′nĭ ə fôrm′), *adj.* **1.** wedge-shaped, as the characters anciently used in writing in Persia, Assyria, etc. —*n.* **2.** cuneiform characters or writing. Also, **cu·ni·form** (kū′nə fôrm′).

cun·ning (kŭn′ĭng), *n.* **1.** ability; skill. **2.** craftiness; guile. —*adj.* **3.** exhibiting or wrought with ingenuity. **4.** crafty; sly. **5.** *U.S. Colloq.* quaintly pleasing or attractive. —**cun′ning·ly**, *adv.* —**cun′ning·ness**, *n.*

cup (kŭp), *n.*, *v.*, **cupped, cupping.** —*n.* **1.** a small, open container, esp. of porcelain, used mainly to drink from. **2.** an ornamental cup or other article offered as a prize in a contest. **3.** the containing part of a goblet or the like. **4.** a cup with its contents. **5.** a cupful. **6.** a unit of capacity, equal to 8 fluid ounces. **7.** any of various beverages, as a mixture containing wine. **8.** the chalice used in the Eucharist. **9.** the wine of the Eucharist. **10.** something to be endured. **11.** any cuplike utensil, part, etc. **12.** *Golf.* the hole. **13. in one's cups,** intoxicated. —*v.t.* **14.** to take or place in a cup.

cup·bear·er (kŭp′bâr′ər), *n.* an attendant who fills and hands the cups in which drink is served.

cup·board (kŭb′ərd), *n.* **1.** a closet with shelves for dishes, etc. **2.** *Brit.* any small closet.

cup·cake (kŭp′kāk′), *n.* a small cup-shaped cake.

Cu·pid (kū′pĭd), *n.* **1.** the Roman god of love, son of Venus, represented as a winged boy with bow and arrows. **2.** (*l.c.*) a representation of a similar winged being, esp. as symbolic of love.

cu·pid·i·ty (kū pĭd′ə tĭ), *n.* eager or inordinate desire, esp. to possess something.

cu·po·la (kū′pə lə), *n.* **1.** a rounded dome constituting, or built upon, a roof. **2.** any of various domelike structures, organs, etc. **3.** *Metall.* a vertical, circular furnace for melting cast iron.

cu·pre·ous (kū′prĭ əs), *adj.* **1.** copper-colored. **2.** consisting of or containing copper; copperlike.

cu·pric (kū′prĭk), *adj. Chem.* of or containing copper, esp. in the divalent state (Cu^{+2}).

cu·prous (kū prəs), *adj. Chem.* containing monovalent copper (Cu^{+1}).

cu·prum (kū′prəm), *n.* copper. *Chem. abbr.:* Cu

cur (kûr), *n.* **1.** a snarling, worthless, or outcast dog. **2.** a low, despicable person.

cur·a·ble (kyŏŏr′ə bəl), *adj.* that may be cured. —**cur′a·bil′i·ty**, *n.* —**cur′a·bly**, *adv.*

Cu·ra·çao (kyŏŏr′ə sō′, kōō′rä sou′), *n.* **1.** a Dutch colony in the West Indies, consisting of a group of islands north of Venezuela. 124,800 pop.; 403 sq. mi. *Cap.* Willemstad. **2.** the main island of this colony. 75,500 pop.; 210 sq. mi. **3.** (*l.c.*) a liqueur flavored with the peel of the (bitter) **Curaçao orange.**

cu·ra·cy (kyŏŏr′ə sĭ), *n.*, *pl.* **-cies.** the office or position of a curate.

cu·ra·re (kyŏŏ rä′rĭ), *n.* a blackish resinlike substance from certain tropical plants, used by South American Indians for poisoning arrows, and employed in physiological experiments, etc. Also, **cu·ra′ri.**

cu·rate (kyŏŏr′ĭt), *n. Chiefly Brit.* a clergyman employed as assistant of a rector or vicar.

cur·a·tive (kyŏŏr′ə tĭv), *adj.* **1.** serving to cure or heal; remedial. —*n.* **2.** a remedy.

cu·ra·tor (kyŏŏ rā′tər *for 1, 2*; kyŏŏr′ə tər *for 3*), *n.* **1.** the person in charge of a museum, etc. **2.** a manager. **3.** a guardian.

curb (kûrb), *n.* **1.** a chain or strap attached to the upper ends of the branches of a bit and passing under the horse's lower jaw, used in restraining the horse. **2.** anything that restrains or controls. **3.** an enclosing framework or border. **4.** a line of stones, concrete, etc., at the edge of a sidewalk, etc. **5.** the sidewalk as a market for the sale of securities not listed on the stock exchange. —*v.t.* **6.** to control or restrain. **7.** to put a curb on.

curb bit, a bit for a horse, which, by slight effort, produces great pressure on the mouth to control the animal.

curb·ing (kûr′bĭng), *n.* the material forming a curb.

curb·stone (kûrb′stōn′), *n.* one of the stones, or a range of stones, forming a curb, as along the outer edge of a sidewalk, etc.

curd (kûrd), *n.* **1.** (*often pl.*) a substance obtained from milk by coagulation, used esp. for making into cheese. —*v.t.*, *v.i.* **2.** to turn into curd. —**curd′y**, *adj.*

cur·dle (kûr′dəl), *v.t.*, *v.i.*, **-dled, -dling. 1.** to change into curd. **2. curdle the blood,** to terrify.

cure (kyŏŏr), *n.*, *v.*, **cured, curing.** —*n.* **1.** a method or course of remedial treatment, as for disease. **2.** restoration to health. **3.** a remedy. **4.** act or a method of curing meat, etc. **5.** spiritual charge of the people in a certain district. **6.** the office or district of one exercising such oversight. —*v.t.* **7.** to restore to health. **8.** to rid of something undesirable. **9.** to prepare (meat, etc.) for preservation, by salting, drying, etc. —*v.i.* **10.** to effect a cure. **11.** to become cured. —**cur′er**, *n.*

cu·ré (kyŏŏ rā′), *n.* a parish priest.

cure-all (kyŏŏr′ôl′), *n.* a cure for all ills.

cur·few (kûr′fū), *n.* **1.** the giving of a signal, esp. by a bell, at a certain hour in the evening, as for children to retire from the streets. **2.** the time of ringing such a bell. **3.** the bell itself. **4.** (in medieval Europe) the ringing of a bell at a fixed hour in the evening as a signal for covering or extinguishing fires. **5.** the ringing of an evening bell.

cu·ri·a (kyŏŏr′ĭ ə), *n.*, *pl.* **curiae** (kyŏŏr′ĭ ē′). the Pope and those about him at Rome engaged in the administration of the papal authority.

cu·rie (kyŏŏr′ē, kyŏŏ rē′), *n. Chem., Physics.* the amount of radioactivity associated with the radon in equilibrium with one gram of radium.

Cu·rie (kyŏŏr′ē, kyŏŏ rē′), *n.* **1. Marie,** 1867–1934, Polish physicist and chemist, in France. **2.** her husband, **Pierre,** 1859–1906, French physicist and chemist.

cu·ri·o (kyŏŏr′ĭ ō′), *n.*, *pl.* **curios.** any article, object of art, etc., valued as a curiosity.

cu·ri·os·i·ty (kyŏŏr′ĭ ŏs′ə tĭ), *n.*, *pl.* **-ties. 1.** the desire to know about anything; inquisitiveness. **2.** interesting quality, as from strangeness. **3.** a curious thing.

cu·ri·ous (kyŏŏr′ĭ əs), *adj.* **1.** desirous of learning or knowing; inquisitive. **2.** prying. **3.** exciting interest because of strangeness. **4.** *Colloq.* odd; eccentric. —**cu′ri·ous·ly**, *adv.* —**cur′i·ous·ness**, *n.*

cu·ri·um (kyŏŏr′ĭ əm), *n. Chem.* an element discovered among the products of the bombardment of uranium and plutonium by very energetic helium ions. *Symbol:* Cm; *at. no.:* 96.

curl (kûrl), *v.t.*, *v.i.* **1.** to form into ringlets, as the hair. **2.** to form into a spiral; coil. —*n.* **3.** a ringlet of hair. **4.** anything of a spiral or curved shape. **5.** a coil. **6.** act of curling. **7.** state of being curled. —**curl′er**, *n.*

cur·lew (kûr′lōō), *n.* any of certain shore birds with long slender downward curved bill.

curl·i·cue (kûr′lĭ kū′), *n.* a fantastic curl.

curl·ing (kûr′lĭng), *n.* a Scottish game played on the ice, in which large, smooth, rounded stones are slid toward a mark.

curl·y (kûr′lĭ), *adj.*, **curlier, curliest. 1.** curling or tending to curl. **2.** having curls.

cur·mudg·eon (kər mŭj′ən), *n.* an irascible, churlish fellow. —**cur·mudg′eon·ly**, *adj.*

cur·rant (kûr′ənt), *n.* **1.** a small seedless raisin, produced chiefly in California and in the Levant, used in cookery, etc. **2.** the small, edible, acid, round berry of certain wild or cultivated shrubs. **3.** the shrub itself.

cur·ren·cy (kûr′ən sĭ), *n.*, *pl.* **-cies. 1.** that which is current as a medium of exchange. **2.** general acceptance; prevalence. **3.** circulation.

cur·rent (kûr′ənt), *adj.* **1.** belonging to the time actually passing. **2.** passing from one to another; circulating, as coin. **3.** publicly reported or known. **4.** prevalent. **5.** generally accepted. —*n.* **6.** a flowing; flow, as of a river. **7.** that which flows, as a stream. **8.** a portion of a large body of water, or of air, etc., moving in a certain direction. **9.** *Elect.* **a.** a movement of electricity. **b.** the rate of flow, in amperes. **10.** course, as of events; the general tendency. —**cur′rent·ly**, *adv.*

cur·ric·u·lum (kə rĭk′yə ləm), *n.*, *pl.* **-lums, -la** (-lə). **1.** the aggregate of courses of study given in a school, etc. **2.** the course of study in a school, etc. —**cur·ric′u·lar**, *adj.*

cur·ry¹ (kûr′ĭ), *n.*, *pl.* **-ries**, *v.*, **-ried, -rying.** —*n.* **1.** an East Indian sauce or relish in many varieties, containing a mixture of spices, fruits, etc. **2.** a dish prepared with curry sauce or powder. —*v.t.* **3.** to prepare with curry sauce or powder.

cur·ry² (kûr´ Y), *v.t.*, **-ried, -rying. 1.** to rub and clean (a horse, etc.) with a comb. **2.** to dress (tanned hides) by soaking, scraping, coloring, etc. **3.** to beat. **4.** curry favor, to seek favor by flattery, etc. —**cur´ri·er,** *n.*

cur·ry·comb (kûr´Y kōm´), *n.* a comb, usually with rows of metal teeth, for currying horses, etc.

curse (kûrs), *n., v.,* **cursed** or **curst, cursing.** —*n.* **1.** the expression of a wish that evil, etc., befall another. **2.** an ecclesiastical censure or anathema. **3.** a profane oath. **4.** evil invoked upon one. **5.** something accursed. **6.** the cause of evil, misfortune, or trouble. —*v.t.* **7.** to wish or invoke evil upon. **8.** to swear at. **9.** to blaspheme. **10.** to afflict with great evil. **11.** to excommunicate. —*v.i.* **12.** to utter curses. —**curs´er,** *n.*

curs·ed (kûr´sYd, kûrst), *adj.* **1.** under a curse. **2.** hateful; abominable. —**curs´ed·ly,** *adv.*

cur·sive (kûr´sYv), *adj.* **1.** (of writing or printing type) in flowing strokes, with the letters joined together. —*n.* **2.** a cursive letter or printing type.

cur·so·ry (kûr´sə rY), *adj.* going rapidly over something, without noticing details; hasty; superficial. —**cur´so·ri·ly,** *adv.* —**cur´so·ri·ness,** *n.*

curt (kûrt), *adj.* **1.** short or brief. **2.** rudely brief. —**curt´ly,** *adv.* —**curt´ness,** *n.*

cur·tail (kər tāl´), *v.t.* to cut short; abridge; reduce. —**cur·tail´er,** *n.* —**cur·tail´ment,** *n.*

cur·tain (kûr´tən, -tYn), *n.* **1.** a hanging piece of fabric used to shut out the light from a window, adorn a room, etc. **2.** anything that shuts off, covers, or conceals. —*v.t.* **3.** to provide, shut off, conceal, or adorn with a curtain.

curt·sey (kûrt´sY), *n., pl.* **-seys,** *v.,* **-seyed, -seying.** curtsy.

curt·sy (kûrt´sY), *n., pl.* **-sies,** *v.,* **-sied, -sying.** —*n.* **1.** a bow by women, consisting of bending the knees and lowering the body. —*v.i.* **2.** to make a curtsy.

cur·va·ture (kûr´və chər), *n.* **1.** act of curving. **2.** curved condition, often abnormal. **3.** degree of curving. **4.** something curved.

curve (kûrv), *n., v.,* **curved, curving,** *adj.* —*n.* **1.** a continuously bending line, without angles. **2.** a curving. **3.** any curved outline, form, thing, or part. **4.** *Baseball.* the curved course given to a ball by the pitcher; a curved ball. —*v.i., v.t.* **5.** to bend in a curve; take, or cause to take, the course of a curve. —*adj.* **6.** curved. —**curv·ed·ly** (kûr´vYd lY), *adv.* —**curv´ed·ness,** *n.*

cur·vet (*n.* kûr´vYt; *v.* kər vĕt´, kûr´vYt), *n., v.,* **-vetted, -vetting** or **-veted, -veting.** —*n.* **1.** a leap of a horse in which all the legs are off the ground at once. —*v.i.* **2.** to leap in a curvet. **3.** to leap and frisk. —*v.t.* **4.** to cause to make a curvet.

cur·vi·lin·e·ar (kûr´və lYn´Y ər), *adj.* consisting of or bounded by curved lines. Also, **cur´vi·lin´e·al.**

cush·ion (kŏŏsh´ən), *n.* **1.** a soft bag filled with feathers, air, etc., to sit, kneel, or lie on. **2.** anything similar in appearance or use. **3.** the elastic raised rim encircling the top of a billiard table. **4.** something to absorb a shock, jar, or jolt, as a body of air. —*v.t.* **5.** to place on or support by a cushion. **6.** to furnish with a cushion or cushions. **7.** to check the motion of (a piston, etc.) by a cushion, as of steam.

cusp (kŭsp), *n.* **1.** a pointed end. **2.** a point, projection, or elevation, as on the crown of a tooth. **3.** *Astron.* a point of a crescent, esp. of the moon. —**cus·pi·dal** (kŭs´pə dəl), *adj.*

cus·pid (kŭs´pYd), *n.* a canine tooth.

cus·pi·date (kŭs´pə dāt´), *adj.* having a sharp and stiff point or cusp. Also, **cus´pi·dat´ed.**

cus·pi·dor (kŭs´pə dôr´), *n.* a spittoon.

cuss (kŭs), *U.S. Colloq.* —*n.* **1.** a curse. **2.** a person or animal. —*v.t., v.i.* **3.** to curse.

cus·tard (kŭs´tərd), *n.* a dish made of eggs and milk, sweetened and baked or boiled.

Cus·ter (kŭs´tər), *n.* George Armstrong, 1839–76, U.S. general and Indian fighter.

cus·to·di·an (kŭs tō´dY ən), *n.* a person who has custody. —**cus·to´di·an·ship´,** *n.*

cus·to·dy (kŭs´tə dY), *n., pl.* **-dies. 1.** keeping; guardianship; care. **2.** imprisonment. —**cus·to·di·al** (kŭs tō´dY əl), *adj.*

cus·tom (kŭs´təm), *n.* **1.** a habitual practice;

usual way of acting. **2.** habits or usages collectively. **3.** a long-continued habit so established that it has the force of law. **4.** such habits collectively. **5.** (*pl.*) duties imposed by law on imported or, less commonly, exported goods. **6.** (*pl.*) the government department that collects these duties. **7.** habitual patronage of a particular shop, etc. **8.** customers or patrons collectively. —*adj.* **9.** made specially for individual customers. **10.** dealing in things so made, or doing work to order.

cus·tom·ar·y (kŭs´tə měr´Y), *adj., n., pl.* **-aries.** —*adj.* **1.** according to custom; habitual. **2.** of or established by custom. —*n.* **3.** a book containing the legal customs of a locality. —**cus´tom·ar´i·ly** or, for emphasis, **cus´tom·ar´i·ly,** *adv.* —**cus´tom·ar´i·ness,** *n.*

cus·tom·er (kŭs´təm ər), *n.* **1.** one who purchases goods from another. **2.** *Colloq.* a fellow.

custom house, a government office at a seaport for collecting customs, clearing vessels, etc.

cut (kŭt), *v.,* **cut, cutting,** *adj., n.* —*v.t.* **1.** to penetrate with a sharp-edged instrument. **2.** to strike sharply. **3.** to wound severely the feelings of. **4.** to sever; carve. **5.** to hew or saw down. **6.** to separate from the main body; lop off. **7.** to reap; mow. **8.** to trim by clipping, shearing, paring, or pruning. **9.** to intersect; cross. **10.** to shorten by omitting a part. **11.** to lower; reduce. **12.** to dissolve; dilute. **13.** to make by cutting. **14.** to excavate; dig. **15.** *Colloq.* to renounce. **16.** *Colloq.* to refuse to recognize socially. **17.** to perform. **18.** *Colloq.* to absent oneself from. **19.** *Cards.* to divide (a pack of cards) at random. **20.** *Sports.* to hit (a ball) so as to change its course and cause it to spin. —*v.i.* **21.** to penetrate or divide something as with a sharp-edged instrument. **22.** to admit of being cut. **23.** to pass, go, or come, esp. in the most direct way. **24.** to strike sharply. **25.** (of the teeth) to grow through the gums. **26.** to interrupt (fol. by *in*). **27. cut back,** *Football.* to reverse direction suddenly. **28. cut off, a.** to intercept. **b.** to interrupt. **c.** to bring to a sudden end. **d.** to shut out. **e.** to disinherit. **29. cut out, a.** to omit; delete. **b.** to supplant. **c.** to be fit for. **d.** to cease. **e.** to prepare. **f.** to make. —*adj.* **30.** that has been subjected to cutting. **31.** *Bot.* incised; cleft. **32.** fashioned by cutting. **33.** reduced by cutting. **34. cut and dried, a.** settled in advance. **b.** lacking spontaneity. —*n.* **35.** act of cutting. **36.** a piece cut off. **37.** *U.S. Colloq.* share. **38.** the result of cutting, as an incision, wound, channel, etc. **39.** manner in which anything is cut. **40.** style. **41.** a passage straight across. **42.** an excision or omission of a part. **43.** a part excised or omitted. **44.** a reduction in price, salary, etc. **45.** an act, speech, etc., which wounds the feelings. **46.** an engraved block or plate for printing, or an impression from it.

cu·ta·ne·ous (kū tā´nY əs), *adj.* of, pertaining to, or affecting the skin.

cut·a·way (kŭt´ə wā´), *adj.* **1.** (of a coat) having the skirt cut away from the waist in front. —*n.* **2.** a cutaway coat.

cute (kūt), *adj.,* **cuter, cutest. 1.** *U.S. Colloq.* pleasingly pretty or dainty. **2.** *Archaic or Dial.* clever. —**cute´ly,** *adv.* —**cute´ness,** *n.*

cut glass, glass ornamented by cutting with abrasive wheels. —**cut´glass´,** *adj.*

cu·ti·cle (kū´tə kəl), *n.* **1.** the epidermis. **2.** a superficial membrane, or the like. **3.** the non-living epidermis which surrounds the edges of the finger nail or toenail.

cut·lass (kŭt´ləs), *n.* a short, heavy, slightly curved sword. Also, **cut´las.**

cut·ler (kŭt´lər), *n.* one who makes, sells, or repairs knives, etc.

cut·ler·y (kŭt´lə rY), *n.* **1.** art or business of a cutler. **2.** cutting instruments collectively.

cut·let (kŭt´lYt), *n.* **1.** a slice of meat for broiling or frying cut from the leg, esp. of veal or mutton. **2.** a flat croquette of minced chicken or the like.

cut·off (kŭt´ôf´, -ŏf´), *n.* **1.** a shorter passage or way. **2.** the arresting of the passage of steam or working fluid to the cylinder of an engine, or the mechanisms effecting it.

cut·out (kŭt´out´), *n.* **1.** something cut out from something else. **2.** a valve in the exhaust pipe of an internal-combustion engine, which permits the engine to exhaust directly into the air.

cut·purse (kŭt´pûrs´), *n.* **1.** one who stole by cutting purses from the girdle. **2.** a pickpocket.

cut·ter (kŭt´ər), *n.* **1.** one that cuts. **2.** a small sailing vessel with a deep hull, square stern, and sloop rig. **3.** a medium-sized boat or launch belonging to a warship. **4.** a light-armed government vessel used to prevent smuggling, etc. **5.** a small, single-seated sleigh, usually for one horse.

cut·throat (kŭt′thrōt′), *n.* **1.** a murderer. —*adj.* **2.** murderous. **3.** relentless.

cut·ting (kŭt′ĭng), *n.* **1.** act of one that cuts. **2.** something cut off. **3.** *Hort.* a piece of plant, commonly a root, shoot, or leaf, cut from a plant to reproduce an entire new plant. —*adj.* **4.** that cuts. **5.** piercing, as a wind. **6.** sarcastic. —**cut′-ting·ly,** *adv.*

cut·tle·fish (kŭt′əl fĭsh′), *n., pl.* **-fishes,** (*esp. collectively*) **-fish.** any of various decapod cephalopods, having sucker-bearing arms and the power of ejecting a black, inklike fluid when pursued. Also, **cut′tle.**

cut·wa·ter (kŭt′wô′tər, -wŏt′ər), *n.* the fore part of a ship's stem or prow, which cuts the water.

cut·worm (kŭt′wûrm′), *n.* any of various caterpillars which feed at night on the young plants of corn, cabbage, etc.

cwt., hundredweight.

-cy, **1.** a suffix of abstract nouns, paired usually with adjectives ending in *-t, -te, -tic,* especially *-nt* (as *democracy, accuracy, expediency*), with other adjectives (as *fallacy*), or with a noun (as *lunacy*), and sometimes forming (in extended suffixes) action nouns, as *vacancy* (*vacate*). **2.** a suffix of nouns denoting a rank or dignity, as in *magistracy.*

Cuttlefish (5 in. long)

cy·an·ic (sī ăn′ĭk), *adj.* blue.

cyanic acid, *Chem.* a poisonous compound, HOCN, isomeric with fulminic acid.

cy·a·nide (sī′ə nīd′, -nĭd), *n., v.,* **-nided, -niding.** —*n.* **1.** Also, **cy·a·nid** (sī′ə nĭd). a salt of hydrocyanic acid. —*v.t.* **2.** to treat with a cyanide.

cy·an·o·gen (sī ăn′ə jən), *n.* **1.** a poisonous, inflammable gas, C₂N₂. **2.** a univalent radical, CN.

cy·a·no·sis (sī′ə nō′sĭs), *n.* *Pathol.* blueness of the skin, as from imperfectly oxygenated blood.

cy·cad (sī′kăd), *n.* any of an order of gymnospermous plants intermediate in appearance between ferns and the palms.

cyc·la·men (sĭk′lə mən, -měn′), *n.* any of certain plants of the primula family, comprising low-growing herbs with tuberous rootstocks and nodding white, purple, pink, or crimson flowers with reflexed petals.

cy·cle (sī′kəl), *n., v.,* **-cled, -cling.** —*n.* **1.** a round of years or a recurring period of time. **2.** any complete course or series. **3.** any long period of years. **4.** a series of poetic or prose narratives about some central event, figure, etc. **5.** a bicycle, tricycle, etc. **6.** a period pertaining to the recurrence of astronomical phenomena. **7.** *Physics.* a complete or double alternation or reversal of an alternating electric current. —*v.i.* **8.** to ride or travel by a bicycle, etc. **9.** to move or revolve in cycles.

cy·clic (sī′klĭk, sĭk′lĭk), *adj.* **1.** of or pertaining to a cycle or cycles; revolving or recurring in cycles. **2.** *Chem.* pertaining to a compound whose structural formula contains a closed chain or ring of atoms. **3.** *Bot.* arranged in whorls. Also, **cy′-cli·cal.**

cy·clist (sī′klĭst), *n.* *Chiefly Brit.* one who rides a bicycle, etc. Also, **cy′cler.**

cy·clom·e·ter (sī klŏm′ə tər), *n.* a device for recording the revolutions of a wheel and hence the distance traversed by a wheeled vehicle.

cy·clone (sī′klōn), *n.* **1.** an atmospheric pressure system characterized by relatively low pressure at its center, and by counterclockwise wind motion in the northern hemisphere, clockwise in the southern. **2.** a tropical hurricane. —**cy·clon·ic** (sī klŏn′ĭk), **cy·clon′i·cal,** *adj.*

cy·clo·pe·di·a (sī′klə pē′dĭ ə), *n.* an encyclopedia. Also, **cy′clo·pae′di·a.** —**cy′clo·pe′dic, cy′clo·pae′dic,** *adj.* —**cy′clo·pe′dist,** *n.*

Cy·clops (sī′klŏps), *n., pl.* **Cyclopes** (sī klō′pēz). *Class. Myth.* one of a race of lawless giants with but one eye, who forged thunderbolts for Zeus and who assisted Vulcan in his workshops.

cy·clo·ram·a (sī′klə răm′ə, -rä′mə), *n.* a pictorial representation, in natural perspective, on the wall of a room, the spectators being in the center.

cy·clo·tron (sī′klə trŏn′, sĭk′lə-), *n.* *Physics.* a device for imparting very high speed to electrified

particles by successive electric impulses at high frequency.

cyg·net (sĭg′nĭt), *n.* a young swan.

cyl·in·der (sĭl′ĭn dər), *n.* **1.** *Geom.* a solid which may be conceived as generated by the revolution of a rectangle about one of its sides. **2.** any cylinderlike object or part. **3.** the rotating part of a revolver, which contains the chambers for the cartridges. **4.** the body of a pump. **5.** the chamber in an engine in which the working medium acts upon the piston. —*v.t.* **6.** to furnish with a cylinder. —**cy·lin·dri·cal** (sĭ lĭn′drə kəl), **cy·lin′dric,** *adj.* —**cy·lin′dri·cal·ly,** *adv.*

cym·bal (sĭm′bəl), *n.* one of a pair of concave plates of brass or bronze struck together to produce a sharp, ringing sound. —**cym′bal·ist,** *n.*

Cym·ry (kĭm′rĭ), *n.pl.* the Welsh, or the branch of the Celtic race to which the Welsh belong. —**Cym·ric** (kĭm′rĭk, sĭm′-), *adj.*

cyn·ic (sĭn′ĭk), *n.* **1.** one who doubts or denies the goodness of human motives and often displays his attitude by sneers, sarcasm, etc. **2.** (*cap.*) one of a sect of Greek philosophers founded by Antisthenes of Athens (born about 444 B.C.), who sought to develop the ethical teachings of Socrates. —*adj.* **3.** cynical. **4.** (*cap.*) of or pertaining to the Cynics or their doctrines.

cyn·i·cal (sĭn′ə kəl), *adj.* of or like a cynic; distrusting the motives of others. —**cyn′i·cal·ly,** *adv.*

cyn·i·cism (sĭn′ə sĭz′əm), *n.* **1.** cynical disposition or character. **2.** a cynical remark. **3.** (*cap.*) the doctrines of the Cynics.

cy·no·sure (sī′nə shōōr′, sĭn′ə-), *n.* **1.** something that strongly attracts attention by its brilliance, etc. **2.** (*cap.*) the constellation of the Little Bear (Ursa Minor). **3.** (*cap.*) the polestar.

Cyn·thi·a (sĭn′thĭ ə), *n.* **1.** Artemis (Diana). **2.** *Poetic.* the moon, the emblem of Artemis.

cy·pher (sī′fər), *n., v.i., v.t.* cipher.

cy·press (sī′prəs), *n.* **1.** any of certain evergreen trees of the pine family, distinguished by dark-green, scalelike, overlapping leaves. **2.** any of various other allied coniferous trees. **3.** the wood of these trees.

cyp·ri·noid (sĭp′rə noid′, sĭ prī′noid), *adj.* **1.** resembling a carp; belonging to the group of fishes including the carps, suckers, loaches, etc. —*n.* **2.** a cryprinoid fish.

Cy·prus (sī′prəs), *n.* an island in the Mediterranean, S of Turkey: a British colony. 395,000 pop.; 3572 sq. mi. *Cap.:* Nicosia.

Cy·re·na·i·ca (sīr′ə nā′ə kə, sī′rə-), *n.* an ancient district in N Africa, W of Egypt.

Cy·rus (sī′rəs), *n.* (*"the Elder"* or *"the Great"*) died 529 B.C., king of Persia, 558?-529 B.C.

cyst (sĭst), *n.* **1.** *Pathol.* a closed bladderlike sac formed in animal tissues, containing fluid or semifluid morbid matter. **2.** a bladder, sac, or vesicle. **3.** *Bot.* a sporelike cell with a resistant protective wall. **4.** *Zool.* a sac surrounding an animal that has passed into a dormant condition. —**cyst′ic,** *adj.*

Cyth·er·e·a (sĭth′ə rē′ə), *n.* *Gk. Myth.* a surname of Aphrodite (Venus). —**Cyth′er·e′an,** *adj.*

cy·tol·o·gy (sī tŏl′ə jĭ), *n.* the scientific study of cells, esp. their formation, structure, and functions. —**cy·tol′o·gist,** *n.*

cy·to·plasm (sī′tə plăz′əm), *n.* *Biol.* the protoplasm of a cell exclusive of the nucleus. Also, **cy·to·plast** (sī′tə plăst′). —**cy′to·plas′mic,** *adj.*

C.Z., Canal Zone (Panama).

czar (zär), *n.* **1.** an emperor or king. **2.** (*usually cap.*) the emperor of Russia.

cza·ri·na (zä rē′nə), *n.* a Russian empress.

czar·ism (zär′ĭz əm), *n.* dictatorship.

Czech (chĕk), *n.* **1.** a member of the most westerly branch of the Slavs, living mainly in Czechoslovakia. **2.** the Slavic language of many of the people of Czechoslovakia. —**Czech, Czech′ic, Czech′ish,** *adj.*

Czech., Czechoslovakia. Also, **Czechosl.**

Czech·o·slo·vak (chĕk′ə slō′văk, -väk), *n.* **1.** a member of the branch of the Slavic race comprising the Czechs proper, the Slovaks, etc. —*adj.* **2.** of or pertaining to the Czechoslovaks. Also, **Czech·o-Slo′vak.**

Czech·o·slo·va·ki·a (chĕk′ə slō vä′kĭ ə, -văk′-ĭ-), *n.* a republic in central Europe. 13,791,000 pop.; 49,379 sq. mi. *Cap.:* Prague. Also, **Czech′o-Slo·va′ki·a.** —**Czech·o·slo·vak′i·an,** *adj., n.*

D

D, d (dē), *n.*, *pl.* **D's** or **Ds, d's** or **ds.** **1.** the 4th letter of the English alphabet. **2.** (as a symbol) the fourth in order. **3.** *Music.* the second tone of the scale of C.

D, 1. Roman numeral for 500. **2.** *Chem.* deuterium.

D., 1. Democrat. **2.** *Physics.* density.

d., 1. delete. **2.** *Brit.* (L *denarius*) penny; (L *denarii*) pence. **3.** *Physics.* density. **4.** died.

D.A., District Attorney.

dab¹ (dăb), *v.*, **dabbed, dabbing,** *n.* —*v.t.* **1.** to strike, pat, or tap gently. **2.** to apply by light strokes. —*v.i.* **3.** to strike lightly. —*n.* **4.** a quick or light blow; pat. **5.** a small moist lump or mass. **6.** a small quantity. —**dab′ber,** *n.*

dab² (dăb), *n.* a European flatfish.

dab·ble (dăb′əl), *v.*, **-bled, -bling.** —*v.t.* **1.** to wet slightly or repeatedly; splash; spatter. —*v.i.* **2.** to play in water. **3.** to do anything in a slight or superficial manner. —**dab′bler,** *n.*

dace (dās), *n.*, *pl.* **daces,** (*esp. collectively*) **dace.** a small fresh-water fish, resembling a carp.

Da·chau (dä′кнou), *n.* a Nazi concentration camp, scene of mass murders, in S Germany.

dachs·hund (dăks′hŏŏnd′, dăsh′-), *n.* one of a German breed of small hounds with a long body and very short legs.

da·coit (də koit′), *n.* one of a class of robbers in India and Burma, who plunder in bands.

dac·tyl (dăk′təl, -tĭl), *n.* *Pros.* a foot of three syllables, one long (or accented) followed by two short (or unaccented). —**dac·tyl·ic** (dăk tĭl′ĭk), *adj.*, *n.*

dad (dăd), *n.* (in familiar use) father.

dad·dy (dăd′ĭ), *n.*, *pl.* **-dies.** (in childish or familiar use) dad.

dad·dy-long·legs (dăd′ĭ lông′lĕgz′, -lŏng′-), *n.* *U.S.* a harvestman.

da·do (dā′dō), *n.*, *pl.* **-does, -dos.** **1.** *Archit.* the part of a pedestal between the base and the cornice. **2.** the lower part of an interior wall, separately decorated.

Daed·a·lus (dĕd′ə ləs), *n.* *Gk. Myth.* an Athenian architect who built the labyrinth for Minos and made wings for himself and his son Icarus.

dae·mon (dē′mən), *n.* **1.** *Gk. Myth.* **a.** a god. **b.** a subordinate deity. **2.** a demon. —**dae·mon·ic** (dē mŏn′ĭk), *adj.*

daf·fo·dil (dăf′ə dĭl), *n.* a plant with single or double yellow nodding flowers, blooming in the spring.

daff·y (dăf′ĭ), *adj.*, **daffier, daffiest.** *U.S. Colloq.* or *Brit. Dial.* silly; crazy.

daft (dăft, däft), *adj.* **1.** insane. **2.** foolish. —**daft′ly,** *adv.* —**daft′ness,** *n.*

dag·ger (dăg′ər), *n.* **1.** a short, knifelike weapon, used for stabbing. **2.** *Print.* a mark (†) used for references, etc.

da·guerre·o·type (də gĕr′ə tīp′), *n.*, *v.*, **-typed, -typing.** —*n.* **1.** an early type of photograph, made on a silver surface. **2.** this process. —*v.t.* **3.** to photograph by this process.

dahl·ia (dăl′yə, däl′- or, *esp. Brit.*, dāl′-), *n.* **1.** any of certain composite plants, native in Mexico and Central America, widely cultivated for their showy, variously colored flowers. **2.** the flower of such a plant.

Dáil Eir·eann (dôl âr′ən), the lower house of parliament of Republic of Ireland. Also, **Dáil.**

dai·ly (dā′lĭ), *adj.*, *n.*, *pl.* **-lies,** *adv.* —*adj.* **1.** of, done, occurring, or issued each day or weekday. —*n.* **2.** a newspaper appearing each day or weekday. —*adv.* **3.** every day; day by day.

dain·ty (dān′tĭ), *adj.*, **-tier, -tiest,** *n.*, *pl.* **-ties.** —*adj.* **1.** of delicate beauty or charm. **2.** pleasing to eat; delicious. **3.** fastidious. **4.** too particular; squeamish. —*n.* **5.** something delicious; a delicacy. —**dain′ti·ly,** *adv.* —**dain′ti·ness,** *n.*

dair·y (dâr′ĭ), *n.*, *pl.* **dairies.** **1.** a room or building where milk and cream are made into butter and cheese. **2.** a shop or company that sells milk, butter, etc. **3.** the business of producing milk, butter, etc.

dair·y·man (dâr′ĭ mən), *n.*, *pl.* **-men.** **1.** owner or manager of a dairy. **2.** employee in a dairy.

da·is (dā′ĭs, dās), *n.* a raised platform for a throne, seats of honor, a lecturer's desk, etc.

dai·sy (dā′zĭ), *n.*, *pl.* **-sies,** *adj.* —*n.* **1.** any of various composite plants whose flower heads have a yellow disk and white rays. **2.** *Slang.* something fine. —*adj.* **3.** *Slang.* fine. —**dai′sied,** *adj.*

Da·kar (dä kär′), *n.* a seaport in and the capital of French West Africa. With dependencies, 141,000 pop.; 68 sq. mi.

Da·lai La·ma (dä lī′ lä′mə), the chief pontiff and governmental ruler of Tibet.

dale (dāl), *n.* a vale; valley.

Da·li (dä′lē), *n.* **Salvador** (săl′və dôr′), born 1904, Spanish painter in U.S.

Dal·las (dăl′əs), *n.* a city in NE Texas. 294,734.

dal·li·ance (dăl′ĭ əns), *n.* **1.** a trifling away of time; dawdling. **2.** flirtation.

dal·ly (dăl′ĭ), *v.*, **-lied, -lying.** —*v.i.* **1.** to sport or play, esp. amorously. **2.** to trifle. **3.** to waste time; delay. —*v.t.* **4.** to waste (time). —**dal′li·er,** *n.*

Dal·ma·tian (dăl mā′shən), *n.* one of a breed of white dogs profusely marked with small black spots; coach dog.

dal·ton·ism (dôl′tə nĭz′əm), *n.* color blindness.

dam¹ (dăm), *n.*, *v.*, **dammed, damming.** —*n.* **1.** a barrier to obstruct the flow of water. **2.** a body of water confined by a dam. —*v.t.* **3.** to furnish, obstruct, or confine with a dam.

dam² (dăm), *n.* a female parent (used esp. of quadrupeds).

dam·age (dăm′ĭj), *n.*, *v.*, **-aged, -aging.** —*n.* **1.** injury or harm that impairs value or usefulness. **2.** (*pl.*) *Law.* the estimated money equivalent for detriment or injury sustained. —*v.t.* **3.** to cause damage to. —*v.i.* **4.** to suffer damage. —**dam′age·a·ble,** *adj.* —**dam′ag·ing·ly,** *adv.*

dam·a·scene (dăm′ə sēn′, dăm′ə sēn′), *v.t.*, **-scened, -scening.** **1.** to produce wavy lines on, as in the welding of iron and steel in the swords of Damascus. **2.** to ornament (objects of iron and steel) by inlaying with precious metals.

Da·mas·cus (də măs′kəs), *n.* the capital of Syria, in the SW part. 261,010.

dam·ask (dăm′əsk), *n.* **1.** a reversible fabric of linen, silk, cotton, or wool, woven with patterns. **2.** damascened steel. **3.** the pink color of the damask rose. —*adj.* **4.** made of or like damask. **5.** pink (like the damask rose). —*v.t.* **6.** to damascene.

damask rose, a fragrant pink rose.

dame (dām), *n.* **1.** *Archaic.* a woman of rank or authority. **2.** (in Great Britain) **a.** the legal title of the wife of a knight or baronet. **b.** (since 1917) the title of a woman upon whom a dignity corresponding to that of a knight has been conferred. **3.** *U.S.* a married woman. **4.** *Slang.* a woman. **5.** *Archaic* or *Dial.* the mistress of a household.

damn (dăm), *v.t.* **1.** to declare (something) to be bad, unfit, invalid, or illegal. **2.** to condemn as a failure. **3.** to bring condemnation upon. **4.** to doom to eternal punishment. **5.** to curse, using the word "damn." —*v.i.* **6.** to swear. —*n.* **7.** the utterance of the word "damn" in swearing or for emphasis.

dam·na·ble (dăm′nə bəl), *adj.* **1.** worthy of damnation. **2.** detestable. —**dam′na·bly,** *adv.*

dam·na·tion (dăm nā′shən), *n.* **1.** act of damning. **2.** state of being damned. **3.** a cause of being damned. **4.** *Theol.* sin as incurring or deserving eternal punishment. —**dam·na·to·ry** (dăm′nə tôr′ĭ), *adj.*

damned (dămd), *adj.* **1.** condemned, esp. to eternal punishment. **2.** detestable. —*adv.* **3.** very.

Dam·o·cles (dăm′ə klēz′), *n. Gk. Legend.* a flatterer, who, having extolled the happiness of the ruler of Syracuse, was placed at a banquet, with a sword suspended over his head by a single hair, to show him the perilous nature of that happiness.

Da·mon (dā′mən), *n. Rom. Legend.* a man who barely escaped suffering the death penalty as voluntary hostage for his friend Pythias.

damp (dămp), *adj.* 1. moderately wet; moist. —*n.* 2. moisture; humidity. 3. a noxious or stifling vapor or gas, esp. in a mine. 4. dejection. —*v.t.* 5. to make damp; moisten. 6. to check the energy, etc., of. 7. to stifle or extinguish. —**damp′ly,** *adv.* —**damp′ness,** *n.*

damp·en (dăm′pən), *v.t.* 1. to moisten. 2. to deaden or depress. —*v.i.* 3. to become damp. —**damp′en·er,** *n.*

damp·er (dăm′pər), *n.* 1. one that damps. 2. a movable plate for regulating the draft in a stove, furnace, etc. 3. *Music.* a device in stringed keyboard instruments to deaden the vibration of the strings.

dam·sel (dăm′zəl), *n.* a young woman; girl.

dam·son (dăm′zən), *n.* 1. the small dark-blue or purple fruit of a plum tree introduced into Europe from Asia Minor. 2. the tree.

Dan (dăn), *n.* 1. one of the twelve sons of Jacob. 2. one of the twelve Hebrew tribes. 3. a city at the northern end of Palestine; hence, **from Dan to Beersheba** (the two limits of Palestine).

Dan·a·üs (dăn′ əs), *n. Gk. Myth.* a king who married his daughters, the **Danaides** (də nā′ə-dēz′), to their fifty cousins, but made them slay their husbands on the wedding night.

dance (dăns, däns), *v.*, **danced, dancing,** *n.* —*v.i.* 1. to move with the feet or body rhythmically, esp. to music. 2. to leap, skip, etc., as from excitement. —*v.t.* 3. to perform in (a dance). 4. to cause to dance. —*n.* 5. a successive group of rhythmical steps, generally to music. 6. an act or round of dancing. 7. a social gathering for dancing. 8. a suitable piece of music for dancing. —**danc′er,** *n.* —**danc′ing·ly,** *adv.*

dan·de·li·on (dăn′də lī′ən), *n.* a common composite plant, abundant as a weed, having deeply toothed leaves and yellow flowers.

dan·der (dăn′dər), *n. Colloq.* anger or temper.

dan·di·fy (dăn′də fī′), *v.t.*, **-fied, -fying.** to make foppish. —**dan′di·fi·ca′tion,** *n.*

dan·dle (dăn′dəl), *v.t.*, **-dled, -dling.** 1. to move lightly up and down, as a child on the knees. 2. to pet; pamper. —**dan′dler,** *n.*

dan·druff (dăn′drəf), *n.* a scurf which forms on the scalp and comes off in small scales.

dan·dy (dăn′dĭ), *n.*, *pl.* **-dies,** *adj.*, **-dier, -diest.** —*n.* 1. a fop. 2. *Colloq.* something very fine. —*adj.* 3. foppish. 4. *U.S. Colloq.* fine.

Dane (dān), *n.* 1. a native or inhabitant of Denmark. 2. a person of Danish descent.

Dane·law (dān′lô′), *n.* 1. the laws in force in that part of England which the Danes controlled in the ninth century. 2. that part of England.

dan·ger (dān′jər), *n.* 1. liability or exposure to harm or injury; peril. 2. instance or cause of peril.

dan·ger·ous (dān′jər əs), *adj.* full of danger. —**dan′ger·ous·ly,** *adv.* —**dan′ger·ous·ness,** *n.*

dan·gle (dăng′gəl), *v.*, **-gled, -gling,** *n.* —*v.i.* 1. to hang loosely with a swaying motion. 2. to hang about a person, as if seeking favor. —*v.t.* 3. to cause to dangle. —*n.* 4. act of dangling. —**dan′gler,** *n.*

Dan·iel (dăn′yəl), *n. Bible.* 1. a Jewish prophet in Babylon. 2. a book in the Old Testament.

Dan·ish (dā′nĭsh), *adj.* 1. of or pertaining to the Danes, their country, or their language. —*n.* 2. the language of Denmark.

dank (dăngk), *adj.* unpleasantly damp. —**dank′ly,** *adv.* —**dank′ness,** *n.*

Dan·te (dăn′tĭ), *n.* (*Dante Alighieri*) 1265–1321, Italian poet: author of *Divine Comedy.*

Dan·ube (dăn′ūb), *n.* a river in Europe, flowing from SW Germany E to the Black Sea. 1725 mi. —**Dan·u·bi·an** (dăn ū′bĭ ən), *adj.*

Dan·ville (dăn′vĭl), *n.* 1. a city in E Illinois. 36,919. 2. a city in S Virginia. 32,749.

Dan·zig (dăn′sĭg), *n.* a seaport in N Poland, on Bay of Danzig (inlet of the Baltic). 118,000.

Daph·ne (dăf′nĭ), *n. Gk. Myth.* a nymph who, pursued by Apollo, was saved by being changed into a laurel tree.

dap·per (dăp′ər), *adj.* 1. neat; trim. 2. small

and active. —**dap′per·ly,** *adv.* —**dap′per·ness,** *n.*

dap·ple (dăp′əl), *n.*, *adj.*, *v.*, **-pled, -pling.** —*n.* 1. mottled marking, as of an animal's skin. 2. an animal with a mottled skin. —*adj.* 3. dappled; spotted. —*v.t.*, *v.i.* 4. to mark or become marked with spots. —**dap′pled,** *adj.*

D.A.R., Daughters of the American Revolution.

Dar·da·nelles (där′də nĕlz′), *n.pl.* the strait between European and Asiatic Turkey, connecting the Aegean with the Sea of Marmara. 40 mi. long; 1–5 mi. wide. Ancient, Hellespont.

dare (dâr), *v.*, **dared** or **durst, dared, daring,** *n.* —*v.i.* 1. to be bold enough. —*v.t.* 2. to have the necessary courage for. 3. to meet defiantly. 4. to challenge, esp. by doubting one's courage. —*n.* 5. challenge. —**dar′er,** *n.*

dare·dev·il (dâr′dĕv′əl), *n.* 1. a recklessly daring person. —*adj.* 2. recklessly daring.

Dar·i·en (dâr′Ĭ ĕn′, där′Ĭ ĕn′), *n.* 1. Gulf of, an arm of the Caribbean between the NE coast of Panama and Colombia. 2. **Isthmus of,** former name of the **Isthmus of Panama.**

dar·ing (dâr′ĭng), *n.* 1. adventurous courage. —*adj.* 2. bold; adventurous. —**dar′ing·ly,** *adv.*

Da·ri·us I (də rī′əs), ("the Great") 558?–486? B.C., king of Persia, 521–486? B.C.

dark (därk), *adj.* 1. with little or no light. 2. radiating or reflecting little light. 3. approaching black in hue. 4. not pale or fair. 5. gloomy; dismal. 6. sullen. 7. destitute of knowledge or culture. 8. hard to understand; obscure. 9. hidden; secret. 10. silent; reticent. —*n.* 11. the absence of light. 12. night; nightfall. 13. a dark place. 14. a dark color. 15. obscurity. 16. secrecy. 17. ignorance. —**dark′ly,** *adv.* —**dark′ness,** *n.*

Dark Ages, the time in history from about A.D. 476 to about A.D. 1000.

dark·en (där′kən), *v.t.*, *v.i.* to make or become dark or darker.

dark horse, a race horse, competitor, etc., that is little known or who unexpectedly wins.

dark lantern, a lantern whose light can be obscured by a dark slide or cover at the opening.

dark·ling (därk′lĭng), *adv.*, *adj.* in the dark.

dark·room (därk′rōōm′, -rŏŏm′), *n. Photog.* a darkened room used when developing film, etc.

dar·ling (där′lĭng), *n.* 1. a person dearly loved. —*adj.* 2. dearly loved.

darn[1] (därn), *v.t.* 1. to mend with rows of stitches. —*n.* 2. a darned place in a garment, etc. 3. act of darning. —**darn′er,** *n.*

darn[2] (därn), *adj.*, *adv.* 1. darned. —*v.t.* 2. *U.S. Colloq.* to confound (as a mild oath). —*n.* 3. not give a darn, to be utterly indifferent.

darned (därnd), *U.S. Colloq.* —*adj.* 1. confounded. —*adv.* 2. extremely; remarkably.

darning needle, 1. a long needle with a long eye, used in darning. 2. a dragonfly.

dart (därt), *n.* 1. a slender, pointed, missile weapon propelled by the hand or otherwise. 2. something resembling such a weapon, as the sting of an insect. 3. act of darting. 4. a seam used where a wedge-shaped piece has been cut out. —*v.i.* 5. to move swiftly. 6. to throw a dart or other missile weapon. —*v.t.* 7. to throw suddenly.

dart·er (där′tər), *n.* 1. one that darts. 2. a snakebird. 3. any of certain small, fresh-water fishes of the perch family which dart quickly when disturbed.

Dar·win (där′wĭn), *n.* **Charles,** 1809–82, British naturalist. —**Dar·win′i·an,** *adj.*, *n.*

Dar·win·ism (där′wə nĭz′əm), *n.* the biological doctrine of Charles Darwin respecting the origin of species as derived by descent from parent forms through the natural selection of those best adapted to survive in the struggle for existence. —**Dar′win·ist,** *n.*, *adj.*

dash (dăsh), *v.t.* 1. to strike violently, esp. so as to break to pieces. 2. to throw violently or suddenly. 3. to bespatter. 4. to apply roughly. 5. to mix. 6. to ruin or frustrate. 7. to depress. 8. to abash. 9. to write, make, sketch, etc., hastily. —*v.i.* 10. to strike with violence. 11. rush. —*n.* 12. a violent and rapid blow. 13. a check or discouragement. 14. the throwing of water, etc., against a thing. **15.** the sound of the splashing. **16.** a small quantity mixed with something else. **17.** a horizontal line (—) used as a mark of punctuation to note an abrupt break in a sentence, to begin and end a parenthetic clause, as an indication of omission of words, etc. **18.** a rush. **19.** *Sports.* a short race. **20.** vigor. **21.** a dashboard. **22.** *Teleg.* a signal of longer duration than a dot, as in Morse code. —**dash/er,** *n.*

dash·board (dăsh/bōrd/), *n.* **1.** the instrument board of an automobile. **2.** a board on the front of a vehicle, to protect the occupants from mud, etc.

dash·ing (dăsh/ĭng), *adj.* **1.** spirited; lively. **2.** stylish. —**dash/ing·ly,** *adv.*

dash·y (dăsh/ĭ), *adj.*, **dashier, dashiest.** showy.

das·tard (dăs/tərd), *n.* **1.** a mean, sneaking coward. —*adj.* **2.** cowardly. —**das/tard·ly,** *adj.* —**das/tard·li·ness,** *n.*

dat., dative.

da·ta (dā/tə, dăt/ə, dä/tə), *n.* **1.** pl. of **datum.** **2.** facts, etc., known or available.

date[1] (dāt), *n., v.,* **dated, dating.** —*n.* **1.** a particular time when something happens or happened. **2.** an inscription on a writing, coin, etc., that shows the time of writing, casting, delivery, etc. **3.** the period of an event or to which anything belongs. **4.** duration. **5.** *U.S. Colloq.* an appointment. —*v.i.* **6.** to have a date. **7.** to belong to a particular period. —*v.t.* **8.** to furnish with a date. **9.** to ascertain the date of. —**dat/er,** *n.*

date[2] (dāt), *n.* the oblong, fleshy fruit of the **date palm:** a staple food in northern Africa, Arabia, etc., and an important export.

dat·ed (dā/tĭd), *adj.* out-of-date.

date·less (dāt/lĭs), *adj.* **1.** without a date. **2.** endless. **3.** of permanent interest.

date line, 1. a line in a letter, newspaper, or the like, giving the date of origin. **2.** a line, theoretically coinciding with the meridian of 180° from Greenwich, the regions on either side of which are counted as differing by one day in their calendar dates.

da·tive (dā/tĭv), *Gram.* —*adj.* **1.** denoting a case having as one function indication of the indirect object of a verb. —*n.* **2.** the dative case. **3.** a word in that case.

da·tum (dā/təm), *n., pl.* **-ta** (-tə). **1.** any proposition assumed or given, from which conclusions may be drawn. **2.** (*often pl.*) a fact.

daub (dôb), *v.t., v.i.* **1.** to cover with soft, adhesive matter, as mud, etc. **2.** to spread (mud, etc.) on or over something. **3.** to paint unskillfully. —*n.* **4.** material for daubing walls, etc. **5.** anything daubed on. **6.** act of daubing. **7.** a crude, inartistic painting. —**daub/er,** *n.*

daugh·ter (dô/tər), *n.* **1.** a female child or person in relation to her parents. **2.** any female descendant. **3.** one related as if by the ties binding daughter to parent. **4.** anything (personified as female) considered with respect to its origin. —**daugh/ter·ly,** *adj.*

daugh·ter-in-law (dô/tər ĭn lô/), *n., pl.* **daughters-in-law.** the wife of one's son.

daunt (dônt, dänt), *v.t.* **1.** to overcome with fear. **2.** to dishearten.

daunt·less (dônt/lĭs, dänt/-), *adj.* fearless; bold. —**daunt/less·ly,** *adv.* —**daunt/less·ness,** *n.*

dau·phin (dô/fĭn), *n.* the title of the eldest son of the king of France, from 1349 to 1830.

dav·en·port (dăv/ən pōrt/), *n.* *U.S.* a large sofa, often one convertible into a bed.

Dav·en·port (dăv/ən pōrt/), *n.* a city in E Iowa, on the Mississippi. 66,039.

Da·vid (dā/vĭd), *n.* **1.** fl. c1000 B.C., the second king of the Hebrews. **2. Saint,** died A.D. 601?, Welsh bishop: patron saint of Wales.

Da·vis (dā/vĭs), *n.* **Jefferson,** 1808–89, president of Confederate States, 1861–65.

dav·it (dăv/ĭt, dā/vĭt), *n.* *Naut.* a projecting piece of wood or iron on the side or stern of a vessel, fitted with a tackle, etc., for raising, lowering, or suspending a small boat, anchor, or other weight.

Da·vy (dā/vĭ), *n.* **Sir Humphry,** 1778–1829, British chemist.

Da·vy Jones (dā/vĭ jōnz/), *Naut.* the spirit of the sea; the sailor's devil.

Davy Jones's locker, the ocean's bottom, esp. as the grave of all who perish at sea.

daw (dô), *n.* a jackdaw.

daw·dle (dô/dəl), *v.i., v.t.,* **-dled, -dling.** to waste (time); loiter. —**daw/dler,** *n.*

dawn (dôn), *n.* **1.** the first appearance of daylight in the morning. **2.** the beginning of anything. —*v.i.* **3.** to begin to grow light in the morning. **4.** to begin to develop. **5.** to begin to be perceived (fol. by *on*).

Daw·son (dô/sən), *n.* a town in NW Canada: capital of Yukon Territory. 1043.

day (dā), *n.* **1.** the interval of light between two successive nights. **2.** daylight. **3.** *Astron.* **a.** the period during which the earth makes one revolution on its axis. **b.** the average length of this interval, twenty-four hours (**mean solar day**). **4.** the portion of a day allotted to labor. **5.** a day as a point or unit of time, or on which something occurs. **6.** a day assigned to a particular purpose. **7.** a contest. **8.** (*often pl.*) a particular period. **9.** (*often pl.*) period of activity. **10.** period of power or influence.

day·book (dā/bŏŏk/), *n.* a book in which daily transactions are entered.

day·break (dā/brāk/), *n.* dawn.

day·dream (dā/drēm/), *n.* **1.** a visionary fancy indulged in while awake; reverie. —*v.i.* **2.** to have daydreams. —**day/dream/er,** *n.*

day laborer, an unskilled worker paid by the day.

day·light (dā/līt/), *n.* **1.** the light of day. **2.** openness; publicity. **3.** daytime. **4.** daybreak.

day·light-sav·ing time (dā/līt/ sā/vĭng), time one or more hours later than the standard time, usually used during summer months to give more hours of daylight to the working day.

day·star (dā/stär/), *n.* the morning star.

day·time (dā/tīm/), *n.* the time between sunrise and sunset.

Day·ton (dā/tən), *n.* a city in SW Ohio. 210,718.

daze (dāz), *v.,* **dazed, dazing,** *n.* —*v.t.* **1.** to stun with a blow, shock, etc. **2.** to confuse. —*n.* **3.** a dazed condition. —**daz·ed·ly** (dā/zĭd lĭ), *adv.*

daz·zle (dăz/əl), *v.,* **-zled, -zling,** *n.* —*v.t., v.i.* **1.** to overpower (the vision) by intense light. **2.** to bewilder by brilliancy. —*n.* **3.** act or fact of dazzling. **4.** bewildering brightness. —**daz/zler,** *n.*

D.C., 1. Also, **d.c.** direct current. **2.** District of Columbia.

D.D., Doctor of Divinity.

D-day (dē/dā/), *n.* *Mil.* the day, usually unspecified, for beginning an attack.

D.D.S., Doctor of Dental Surgery.

DDT, a very powerful insecticide.

dea·con (dē/kən), *n.* **1.** (in hierarchical churches) a member of the clerical order next below that of priest. **2.** (in other churches) an officer having variously defined duties. —**dea/con·ry, dea/-con·ship/,** *n.*

dead (dĕd), *adj.* **1.** no longer living. **2.** not alive. **3.** resembling death. **4.** insensible; numb. **5.** no longer in existence or use. **6.** without spiritual life. **7.** *Colloq.* exhausted. **8.** infertile. **9.** lacking animation, force, or any other characteristic quality. **10.** extinguished. **11.** tasteless or flat, as liquor. **12.** complete. **13.** sure; unerring. **14.** *Sports.* out of play. —*n.* **15.** one who is dead. **16.** dead persons collectively. **17.** the period of greatest darkness, coldness, etc. —*adv.* **18.** completely. **19.** with abrupt and complete stoppage of motion, etc. **20.** exactly. —**dead/ness,** *n.*

dead beat, 1. *U.S. Colloq.* one who has a reputation for not paying his bills. **2.** *Slang.* a sponger.

dead center, (in a gasoline engine, etc.) either of two positions of the crank in which the connecting rod has no power to turn it.

dead·en (dĕd/ən), *v.t.* **1.** to make less sensitive, active, or forcible. **2.** to retard. **3.** to make impervious to sound, as a floor. —*v.i.* **4.** to become dead.

dead end, a street closed at one end.

dead letter, 1. a law, etc., which has lost its force, though not formally abolished. **2.** a letter which, because of faulty address, etc., cannot be delivered.

dead·line (dĕd/līn/), *n.* the latest time for finishing something.

dead·lock (dĕd/lŏk/), *n.* **1.** complete standstill. —*v.t., v.i.* **2.** to bring or come to a deadlock.

dead·ly (dĕd/lĭ), *adj.,* **-lier, -liest,** *adv.* —*adj.* **1.** causing or tending to cause death; fatal. **2.** implacable. **3.** like death. —*adv.* **4.** in a manner resembling death. **5.** *Colloq.* excessively. —**dead/li·ness,** *n.*

dead reckoning, *Naut.* the calculation of a ship's position without astronomical observations, by means of the distances sailed on the various courses.

Dead Sea, a salt lake on E border of Palestine. 46 mi. long; 10 mi. wide; 1293 feet below sea level.

dead·wood (dĕd'wŏŏd'), *n.* 1. dead branches or trees. 2. anything useless.

deaf (dĕf; *now less often* dēf), *adj.* 1. unable to hear. 2. heedless of; inattentive. —deaf'ly, *adv.* —deaf'ness, *n.*

deaf·en (dĕf'ən), *v.t.* 1. to make deaf. 2. to stun with noise. 3. to render (a sound) inaudible. —deaf'en·ing·ly, *adv.*

deaf-mute (dĕf'mūt'), *n.* a person who is deaf and dumb.

deal[1] (dēl), *v.*, **dealt, dealing,** *n.* —*v.i.* 1. to occupy oneself or itself. 2. to act with respect to a thing or person. 3. to conduct oneself toward persons. 4. to do business. 5. to distribute cards, etc. —*v.t.* 6. to give to one as his share. 7. to distribute. 8. to deliver (blows, etc.). —*n.* 9. *Colloq.* a business transaction. 10. a bargain or arrangement, often a secret or underhand one. 11. treatment; arrangement. 12. a quantity or degree. 13. an indefinite but large amount or extent. 14. *Cards.* **a.** the distribution to the players of the cards. **b.** the set of cards in one's hands. **c.** the turn of a player to deal. —deal'·er, *n.*

deal[2] (dēl), *n.* a board or plank, esp. of fir or pine.

deal·ing (dē'lĭng), *n.* (*usually pl.*) relations.

dean (dēn), *n.* 1. *Educ.* **a.** the head of a faculty in a college. **b.** an official in an American college having charge of student personnel services. 2. *Eccles.* the head of the chapter of a cathedral or a collegiate church. 3. the senior member, in length of service, of any body. —dean'ship, *n.*

dean·er·y (dē'nə rĭ), *n., pl.* **-eries.** 1. the office or jurisdiction of a dean. 2. the residence of a dean.

dear (dĭr), *adj.* 1. loved. 2. (in the salutation of a letter) highly esteemed. 3. precious in one's regard. 4. expensive. 5. charging high prices. 6. high. —*n.* 7. one who is dear. 8. beloved one. —*adv.* 9. fondly. 10. at a high price. —*interj.* 11. an exclamation of surprise, etc. —dear'ly, *adv.* —dear'ness, *n.*

Dear·born (dĭr'bärn, -bôrn), *n.* a city in SE Michigan, near Detroit. 63,584.

dearth (dûrth), *n.* 1. scarcity. 2. famine.

death (dĕth), *n.* 1. the end of life. 2. (*often cap.*) the annihilating power personified, usually represented as a skeleton. 3. state of being dead. 4. extinction. 5. the time at which a person dies. 6. manner of dying. 7. loss of spiritual life. 8. bloodshed or murder.

death·bed (dĕth'bĕd'), *n.* 1. the bed on which a person dies. 2. the last hours before death.

death·blow (dĕth'blō'), *n.* a fatal blow.

death cup, 1. a poisonous mushroom, part of which persists around the base of the stipe as a definite membranous cup. 2. the cup.

death·less (dĕth'lĭs), *adj.* 1. immortal. 2. perpetual. —death'less·ly, *adv.*

death·ly (dĕth'lĭ), *adj.* 1. deadly; fatal. 2. like death. 3. *Poetic.* of death. —*adv.* 4. in the manner of death. 5. very.

death's-head (dĕths'hĕd'), *n.* a human skull, esp. as a symbol of mortality.

Death Valley, an arid basin in E California; lowest land in the Western Hemisphere. 276 ft. below sea level.

death·watch (dĕth'wŏch', -wôch'), *n.* 1. a vigil beside a dying or dead person. 2. a guard set over a condemned person before execution.

de·ba·cle (dā bä'kəl, -bäk'əl, dĭ-), *n.* 1. a general breakup or rout. 2. a breaking up of ice in a river. 3. a violent rush of waters.

de·bar (dĭ bär'), *v.t.*, **-barred, -barring.** 1. to exclude from a place or condition. 2. to prevent (an action, etc.). —de·bar'ment, *n.*

de·bark (dĭ bärk'), *v.t., v.i.* to disembark. —de·bar·ka·tion (dē'bär kā'shən), *n.*

de·base (dĭ bās'), *v.t.*, **-based, -basing.** to reduce in quality or value. —de·base'ment, *n.*

de·bate (dĭ bāt'), *n., v.*, **-bated, -bating.** —*n.* 1. a discussion, esp. of a public question in an assembly. 2. consideration. 3. a systematic contest of speakers in which two points of view of a proposition are advanced with proof. —*v.i.* 4. to engage in discussion. 5. to consider, discuss, or

argue. —*v.t.* 6. to discuss or argue (a question). 7. to dispute about. 8. to consider. —de·bat'a·ble, *adj.* —de·bat'er, *n.*

de·bauch (dĭ bôch'), *v.t.* 1. to corrupt or pervert. —*v.i.* 2. to indulge in a debauch. —*n.* 3. a period of debauchery. 4. debauchery. —de·bauch'er, *n.* —de·bauch'ment, *n.*

deb·au·chee (dĕb'ô chē', -shē'), *n.* one given to debauchery.

de·bauch·er·y (dĭ bô'chə rĭ), *n., pl.* **-eries.** 1. seduction from morality. 2. excessive indulgence in sensual pleasures. 3. seduction from duty.

de·ben·ture (dĭ bĕn'chər), *n.* a certificate of indebtedness.

de·bil·i·tate (dĭ bĭl'ə tāt'), *v.t.*, **-tated, -tating.** to weaken. —de·bil'i·ta'tion, *n.* —de·bil'i·ta'tive, *adj.*

de·bil·i·ty (dĭ bĭl'ə tĭ), *n., pl.* **-ties.** weakness.

deb·it (dĕb'ĭt), *n.* 1. the recording of debt in an account. 2. a recorded item of debt. 3. any entry, or the total shown, on the debit side. —*v.t.* 4. to charge with or as a debt. 5. to enter upon the debit side of an account.

deb·o·nair (dĕb'ə nâr'), *adj.* 1. courteous. 2. gay. Also, **deb·o·naire', deb·on·naire'.** —deb'·o·nair'ly, *adv.* —deb'o·nair'ness, *n.*

de·bouch (dĭ bōōsh'), *v.i.* 1. to march out into open country. 2. to issue; emerge. —de·bouch'·ment, *n.*

de·bris (də brē', dā'brē), *n.* 1. the remains of anything broken down or destroyed; ruins. 2. *Geol.* an accumulation of loose fragments of rock, etc.

Debs (dĕbz), *n.* **Eugene Victor,** 1855–1926, U.S. labor leader.

debt (dĕt), *n.* 1. that which is owed. 2. an obligation to pay or render something. 3. the condition of being under such an obligation. 4. *Theol.* a sin.

debt·or (dĕt'ər), *n.* one who is in debt.

de·bunk (dĭ bŭngk'), *v.t.* *U.S. Colloq.* to remove false sentiments, opinions, etc., about.

De·bus·sy (də bü'sĭ'), *n.* **Claude Achille,** 1862–1918, French composer.

de·but (dĭ bū', dā-, dā'bū), *n.* 1. a first public appearance on a stage, etc. 2. a formal introduction and entrance into society.

deb·u·tante (dĕb'yōō tänt', dĕb'yə tänt'), *n.* a woman making a debut.

Dec., December.

dec., 1. deceased. 2. decimeter.

dec·ade (dĕk'ād), *n.* 1. a period of ten years. 2. a group, set, or series of ten.

dec·a·dence (dĭ kā'dəns, dĕk'ə-), *n.* act or process of falling into an inferior state; decay; deterioration. Also, **de·ca·den·cy** (dĭ kā'dən sĭ, dĕk'ə-). —de·ca'dent, *adj., n.* —de·ca'dent·ly, *adv.*

dec·a·gon (dĕk'ə gŏn'), *n.* *Geom.* a polygon having 10 angles and 10 sides.

dec·a·gram (dĕk'ə grăm'), *n.* *Metric System.* a unit of 10 grams, equivalent to 0.3527 ounce avoirdupois.

dec·a·he·dron (dĕk'ə hē'drən), *n., pl.* **-drons, -dra** (-drə). *Geom.* a solid figure having 10 faces.

dec·al·co·ma·ni·a (dĭ kăl'kə mā'nĭ ə), *n.* 1. the art or process of transferring pictures or designs from specially prepared paper to wood, metal, china, glass, etc. 2. the prepared paper bearing such a picture or design. Also, **de·cal'.**

dec·a·li·ter (dĕk'ə lē'tər), *n.* *Metric System.* a unit of 10 liters.

Dec·a·logue (dĕk'ə lôg', -lŏg'), *n.* the Ten Commandments. Also, **dec'a·logue, Dec'a·log', dec'a·log'.**

dec·a·me·ter (dĕk'ə mē'tər), *n.* *Metric System.* a measure of length equal to 10 meters.

de·camp (dĭ kămp'), *v.i.* 1. to break camp. 2. to depart quickly or secretly.

de·cant (dĭ kănt'), *v.t.* to pour off gently.

de·cant·er (dĭ kăn'tər), *n.* 1. a bottle for decanting. 2. an ornamental bottle from which wine, water, etc., are served at table.

de·cap·i·tate (dĭ kăp'ə tāt'), *v.t.*, **-tated, -tating.** to behead. —de·cap'i·ta'tion, *n.*

dec·a·pod (dĕk'ə pŏd'), *n.* 1. any crustacean of an order including crabs, lobsters, crawfish, shrimps, etc., characterized by their five pairs of walking legs. —*adj.* 2. belonging to this order.

dec·a·syl·la·ble (dĕk'ə sĭl'ə bəl), *n.* a verse of ten syllables. —dec'a·syl·lab'ic, *adj.*

de·cath·lon (dĭ kăth′lŏn), *n.* an athletic contest comprising ten different exercises or events, won by the contestant having the highest total score.

De·ca·tur (dĭ kā′tər), *n.* **1.** a city in central Illinois. 59,305. **2. Stephen,** 1779–1820, U.S. naval officer.

de·cay (dĭ kā′), *v.i.* **1.** to fall away from a state of excellence, prosperity, health, etc. **2.** to rot. —*v.t.* **3.** to cause to decay. —*n.* **4.** progressive decline. **5.** loss of health, intellect, etc. **6.** rotting.

de·cease (dĭ sēs′), *n., v.,* **-ceased, -ceasing.** —*n.* **1.** death. —*v.i.* **2.** to die. —**de·ceased′,** *adj., n.*

de·ce·dent (dĭ sē′dənt). *n.* **1.** *Law.* a deceased person. —*adj.* **2.** left by a deceased person.

de·ceit (dĭ sēt′), *n.* **1.** act or practice of deceiving; fraud; cheating. **2.** a trick; stratagem. **3.** falseness.

de·ceit·ful (dĭ sēt′fəl), *adj.* **1.** full of deceit. **2.** fraudulent. —**de·ceit′ful·ly,** *adv.* —**de·ceit′-ful·ness,** *n.*

de·ceive (dĭ sēv′), *v.,* **-ceived, -ceiving.** —*v.t.* **1.** to mislead by a false appearance or statement. —*v.i.* **2.** to act deceitfully. —**de·ceiv′er,** *n.*

de·cel·er·ate (dē sĕl′ə rāt′), *v.t., v.i.,* **-ated, -ating.** to decrease in velocity. —**de·cel′er·a′tion,** *n.*

De·cem·ber (dĭ sĕm′bər), *n.* the twelfth month of the year, containing 31 days.

de·cen·cy (dē′sən sĭ), *n., pl.* **-cies. 1.** state or quality of being decent. **2.** something decent or proper.

de·cen·ni·al (dĭ sĕn′ĭ əl), *adj.* **1.** of or for ten years. **2.** occurring every ten years. —*n.* **3.** a decennial anniversary. —**de·cen′ni·al·ly,** *adv.*

de·cent (dē′sənt), *adj.* **1.** fitting; appropriate. **2.** conforming to the recognized standard of propriety, good taste, etc. **3.** respectable. **4.** of seemly appearance. **5.** fair; passable. —**de′-cent·ly,** *adv.* —**de′cent·ness,** *n.*

de·cen·tral·ize (dē sĕn′trə līz′), *v.t.,* **-ized, -izing.** to undo the centralization of (administrative powers, etc.). —**de·cen′tral·i·za′tion,** *n.*

de·cep·tion (dĭ sĕp′shən), *n.* **1.** act of deceiving. **2.** state of being deceived. **3.** something that deceives; a sham; a cheat.

de·cep·tive (dĭ sĕp′tĭv), *adj.* apt or tending to deceive. —**de·cep′tive·ly,** *adv.* —**de·cep′tive·ness,** *n.*

dec·i·bel (dĕs′ə bĕl′), *n. Physics.* the unit of power ratio equal to one tenth of a bel.

de·cide (dĭ sīd′), *v.t., v.i.,* **-cided, -ciding.** to settle (a question, struggle, etc.) by giving victory to one side. —**de·cid′a·ble,** *adj.*

de·cid·ed (dĭ sī′dĭd), *adj.* **1.** free from ambiguity; unmistakable. **2.** resolute. —**de·cid′ed·ly,** *adv.*

de·cid·u·ous (dĭ sĭj′ŏŏ əs), *adj.* **1.** shedding the leaves annually, as trees, etc. **2.** falling off or shed at a particular season, stage, etc., as horns, etc.

dec·i·gram (dĕs′ə grăm′), *n. Metric System.* a unit of weight of one tenth of a gram.

dec·i·li·ter (dĕs′ə lē′tər), *n. Metric System.* a unit of capacity of one tenth of a liter.

dec·i·mal (dĕs′ə məl), *adj.* **1.** pertaining to tenths, or to the number ten. **2.** proceeding by tens. —*n.* **3.** a decimal fraction. —**dec′i·mal·ly,** *adv.*

decimal fraction, a fraction whose denominator is some power of ten, usually indicated by a dot (the **decimal point**) before the numerator.

dec·i·mate (dĕs′ə māt′), *v.t.,* **-mated, -mating. 1.** to destroy a great number or proportion of. **2.** to select by lot and kill every tenth man of. —**dec′i·ma′tion,** *n.* —**dec′i·ma′tor,** *n.*

dec·i·me·ter (dĕs′ə mē′tər), *n. Metric System.* a unit of length of one tenth of a meter.

de·ci·pher (dĭ sī′fər), *v.t.* **1.** to make out the meaning of (poor writing, etc.). **2.** to discover the meaning of (anything obscure or difficult). **3.** to interpret by the use of a key, as something written in cipher. —**de·ci′pher·a·ble,** *adj.* —**de·ci′pher·ment,** *n.*

de·ci·sion (dĭ sĭzh′ən), *n.* **1.** act of deciding. **2.** a judgment, as by a court. **3.** that which is decided. **4.** firmness, as of character.

de·ci·sive (dĭ sī′sĭv), *adj.* **1.** having the power or quality of determining. **2.** resolute; determined. —**de·ci′sive·ly,** *adv.* —**de·ci′sive·ness,** *n.*

deck (dĕk), *n.* **1.** a platform on a ship, covering the space below and serving as a floor. **2.** a platform or part resembling this. **3.** a pack of playing cards. —*v.t.* **4.** to clothe in something ornamental; array.

deck hand, a sailor working on deck.

deck·le (dĕk′əl), *n.* **1.** (in paper making) a frame which forms the paper pulp, fixing the size of a sheet of paper. **2.** deckle edge. Also, **deck′el.**

deckle edge, the untrimmed edge of handmade paper. —**deck′le-edged′,** *adj.*

de·claim (dĭ klām′), *v.i., v.t.* **1.** to speak aloud rhetorically. **2.** to inveigh. —**de·claim′er,** *n.*

dec·la·ma·tion (dĕk′lə mā′shən), *n.* **1.** act or art of declaiming. **2.** an exercise in oratory. **3.** speech or writing for oratorical effect. —**de·clam·a·to·ry** (dĭ klăm′ə tōr′ĭ), *adj.*

dec·la·ra·tion (dĕk′lə rā′shən), *n.* **1.** a positive or formal statement, announcement, etc. **2.** a proclamation. **3.** that which is proclaimed. **4.** the document embodying the proclamation. **5.** *Bridge.* a bid, esp. the successful bid.

Declaration of Independence, *U.S. Hist.* **1.** the public act by which the Second Continental Congress, on July 4, 1776, declared the Colonies to be free and independent of Great Britain. **2.** the document embodying it.

de·clare (dĭ klâr′), *v.,* **-clared, -claring.** —*v.t.* **1.** to make known, esp. in formal terms. **2.** to affirm. **3.** to reveal. **4.** to make due statement of (dutiable goods, etc.). **5.** to make (a dividend) payable. **6.** *Bridge.* to signify (a certain suit) as trumps or to establish the bid at no-trump. —*v.i.* **7.** to make a declaration. **8.** to proclaim oneself. —**de·clar′a·tive, de·clar′a·to′ry,** *adj.* —**de·clar′er,** *n.*

de·clen·sion (dĭ klĕn′shən), *n.* **1.** act or fact of declining. **2.** a bending, sloping, or moving downward. **3.** deterioration; decline. **4.** *Gram.* **a.** the inflection of nouns, and of words similarly inflected, for categories such as case and number. **b.** the whole set of inflected forms of such a word. **c.** a class of such words having similar sets of inflected forms. —**de·clen′sion·al,** *adj.*

dec·li·na·tion (dĕk′lə nā′shən), *n.* **1.** a bending, sloping, or moving downward. **2.** deterioration; decline. **3.** a deviating. **4.** a polite refusal. **5.** *Astron.* the angular distance of a heavenly body from the celestial equator, measured on a great circle passing through the celestial pole and the body. **6.** the horizontal angle between the direction of true north and magnetic north at any place.

de·cline (dĭ klīn′), *v.,* **-clined, -clining,** *n.* —*v.t.* **1.** to refuse. **2.** to cause to slope downward. **3.** *Gram.* **a.** to inflect (a noun, pronoun, or adjective). **b.** to recite or display the inflected forms of a noun, pronoun, or adjective in a fixed order. —*v.i.* **4.** to refuse. **5.** to bend or slant down. **6.** to draw toward·the close, as the day. **7.** to condescend. **8.** to fail in strength, value, etc. —*n.* **9.** a downward incline or slope. **10.** deterioration; diminution. **11.** progress downward or toward a close. **12.** the last part. —**de·clin′a·ble,** *adj.*

de·cliv·i·ty (dĭ klĭv′ə tĭ), *n., pl.* **-ties.** a downward slope, as of ground.

de·coct (dĭ kŏkt′), *v.t.* to boil (a medicinal substance, etc.) in water, etc., to extract the essence. —**de·coc′tion** (dĭ kŏk′shən), *n.*

de·code (dē kōd′), *v.t.,* **-coded, -coding.** to translate from code into the original language.

dé·col·le·té (dā′kŏl tā′), *adj.* **1.** (of a garment) low-necked. **2.** wearing a low-necked garment.

de·com·pose (dē′kəm pōz′), *v.t., v.i.,* **-posed, -posing. 1.** to separate into constituent parts. **2.** to rot. —**de·com·po·si·tion** (dē′kŏm pə zĭsh′-ən), *n.*

de·con·tam·i·nate (dē′kən tăm′ə nāt′), *v.t.,* **-nated, -nating.** to free (an object or area) of dangerous gases, etc. with which it has been in contact. —**de·con·tam′i·na′tion,** *n.*

dé·cor (dā kôr′), *n.* decoration.

dec·o·rate (dĕk′ə rāt′), *v.t.,* **-rated, -rating. 1.** to deck with something becoming; embellish. **2.** to confer distinction upon by a medal, etc. —**dec′o·ra′tive,** *adj.* —**dec′o·ra′tive·ly,** *adv.* —**dec′o·ra′tor,** *n.*

dec·o·ra·tion (dĕk′ə rā′shən), *n.* **1.** act of decorating. **2.** adornment. **3.** a badge of an order, medal, etc., conferred as a mark of honor.

Decoration Day, *U.S.* Memorial Day.

dec·o·rous (dĕk′ə rəs, dĭ kōr′əs), *adj.* proper

in conduct, appearance, etc. —dec′o·rous·ly, adv. —dec′o·rous·ness, n.

de·co·rum (dĭ kōr′əm), n. **1.** propriety of behavior, dress, etc. **2.** that which is proper.

de·coy (n. dĭ koi′, dē′koi; v. dĭ koi′), n. **1.** one who or that which entices, as into a trap, etc. **2.** an image of a bird used to entice game. **3.** a pond into which wild fowl are lured. —v.t. **4.** to lure by a decoy. —v.i. **5.** to be decoyed. —de·coy′er, n.

de·crease (v. dĭ krēs′; n. dē′krēs, dĭ krēs′), v., -creased, -creasing, n. —v.i., v.t. **1.** to diminish gradually in extent, quantity, etc. —n. **2.** gradual diminution. **3.** the amount by which a thing is lessened.

de·cree (dĭ krē′), n., v., -creed, -creeing. —n. **1.** an ordinance or edict. —v.t., v.i. **2.** to ordain.

de·crep·it (dĭ krĕp′ĭt), adj. weakened by old age; feeble; infirm. —de·crep′it·ly, adv.

de·crep·i·tude (dĭ krĕp′ə tūd′, -tŏod′), n. decrepit condition; feebleness, esp. from old age.

de·cre·scen·do (dē′krə shĕn′dō, dā′-), adj., adv., n., pl. -dos. Music. —adj., adv. **1.** gradually reducing force or loudness. —n. **2.** a gradual reduction in force or loudness.

de·cry (dĭ krī′), v.t., -cried, -crying. to speak disparagingly of. —de·cri′al, n.

de·cum·bent (dĭ kŭm′bənt), adj. **1.** lying down. **2.** Bot. (of stems, etc.) lying on the ground with the extremity tending to ascend.

ded·i·cate (dĕd′ə kāt′), v.t., -cated, -cating. **1.** to set apart for a sacred purpose. **2.** to give up wholly or earnestly. **3.** to inscribe (a book, etc.) to a friend, etc., as in appreciation. —ded′i·ca′tive, ded·i·ca·to·ry (dĕd′ə kə tōr′ĭ), adj. —ded′i·ca′tor, n.

ded·i·ca·tion (dĕd′ə kā′shən), n. **1.** act of dedicating. **2.** fact of being dedicated. **3.** an inscription in a book, etc., dedicating it.

de·duce (dĭ dūs′, -dōos′), v.t., -duced, -ducing. **1.** to derive as a conclusion from something known or assumed. **2.** to trace the course of. —de·duc′i·ble, adj.

de·duct (dĭ dŭkt′), v.t. to take away, as from a sum or amount. —de·duct′i·ble, adj.

de·duc·tion (dĭ dŭk′shən), n. **1.** act of deducting. **2.** that which is deducted. **3.** the process of deducing. **4.** Logic. inference by reasoning from generals to particulars. —de·duc′tive, adj. —de·duc′tive·ly, adv.

deed (dēd), n. **1.** that which is done; an act. **2.** an achievement. **3.** action, as contrasted with words. **4.** Law. a document executed under seal and delivered to effect a conveyance, esp. of real estate. —v.t. **5.** to convey or transfer by deed.

deem (dēm), v.i., v.t. to think or judge.

deep (dēp), adj. **1.** extending far downward, inward, or backward. **2.** situated far down, in, or back. **3.** extending to or coming from a depth. **4.** difficult to understand. **5.** profound. **6.** serious. **7.** heartfelt. **8.** absorbing. **9.** intense; extreme. **10.** low in pitch, as sound. **11.** having penetrating intellectual powers. **12.** much involved. **13.** absorbed. —n. **14.** the deep part of the sea, etc. **15.** any deep space or place. **16.** the part of greatest intensity, as of winter. —adv. **17.** to or at a considerable or specified depth. **18.** far on (in time). **19.** profoundly. —deep′ly, adv. —deep′ness, n.

deep·en (dē′pən), v.t., v.i. to make or become deep or deeper. —deep′en·er, n.

deep-freeze (dēp′frēz′), n., v., -freezed, -freezing. —n. **1.** a locker in which foods are stored at a temperature of 0° F. **2.** (cap.) a trademark for this. —v.t. **3.** to store or freeze in a deep-freeze.

deep-root·ed (dēp′rōo′tĭd, -rŏot′ĭd), adj. firmly implanted. Also, deep′-seat′ed.

deer (dĭr), n., pl. deer, (occasionally) deers. any animal of a family comprising ruminants most of which have solid deciduous horns or antlers (usually in the male only).

deer·hound (dĭr′hound′), n. a shaggy hound allied to the greyhound.

deer·skin (dĭr′skĭn′), n. **1.** the skin of a deer. **2.** leather made from this. **3.** a garment made of such leather.

def., **1.** defendant. **2.** definite. **3.** definition.

de·face (dĭ fās′), v.t., -faced, -facing. to mar the face or appearance of. —de·face′a·ble, adj. —de·face′ment, n. —de·fac′er, n.

de fac·to (dē făk′tō), in fact; in reality.

de·fame (dĭ fām′), v.t., -famed, -faming. to attack the reputation of, as by uttering or pub-

lishing maliciously anything injurious. —def·a·ma·tion (dĕf′ə mā′shən, dē′fə-), n. —de·fam·a·to·ry (dĭ făm′ə tōr′ĭ), adj. —de·fam′er, n.

de·fault (dĭ fôlt′), n. **1.** failure to act; neglect. **2.** failure to perform an act or obligation, as to pay a debt, to appear in court, etc. **3.** Sports. failure to participate in or complete a scheduled match. —v.i. **4.** to fail to fulfill an engagement, claim, or obligation. **5.** Law. to fail to appear in court. **6.** Sports. to fail to participate in or complete a match. —v.t. **7.** to fail to perform or pay. **8.** Sports. to fail to compete in. —de·fault′er, n.

de·feat (dĭ fēt′), v.t. **1.** to overcome in a contest, battle, etc. **2.** to thwart. —n. **3.** act of overcoming in a contest. **4.** an overthrow. **5.** frustration. —de·feat′er, n.

de·feat·ism (dĭ fē′tĭz əm), n. the spirit or policy of those who despair of success. —de·feat′ist, n., adj.

def·e·cate (dĕf′ə kāt′), v., -cated, -cating. —v.t. **1.** to purify. —v.i. **2.** to void excrement. —def′e·ca′tion, n.

de·fect (dĭ fĕkt′, dē′fĕkt), n. **1.** a fault or imperfection. **2.** lack, esp. of an essential.

de·fec·tion (dĭ fĕk′shən), n. **1.** a falling away from duty, virtue, etc. **2.** failure; lack.

de·fec·tive (dĭ fĕk′tĭv), adj. **1.** faulty; imperfect. **2.** Psychol. characterized by subnormal intelligence or behavior. **3.** Gram. lacking one or more of the inflected forms proper to most words of the same class in the language. —n. **4.** one that is defective. —de·fec′tive·ly, adv. —de·fec′tive·ness, n.

de·fence (dĭ fĕns′), n. Brit. defense.

de·fend (dĭ fĕnd′), v.t. **1.** to ward off attack from. **2.** to uphold. **3.** to contest. —v.i. **4.** Law. to enter or make a defense. —de·fend′a·ble, adj. —de·fend′er, n.

de·fend·ant (dĭ fĕn′dənt), n. Law. the party against whom a claim or charge is brought.

de·fense (dĭ fĕns′), n. **1.** resistance against attack; protection. **2.** something that defends. **3.** the defending of a cause or the like by speech, etc. **4.** a speech, etc., in vindication. **5.** Law. a. the denial or pleading of the defendant. b. a defendant and his legal agents collectively. **6.** the practice or art of defending oneself or one's goal. —de·fense′less, adj. —de·fense′less·ly, adv. —de·fense′less·ness, n. —de·fen′si·ble, adj. —de·fen′si·bly, adv.

de·fen·sive (dĭ fĕn′sĭv), adj. **1.** serving to defend; protective. **2.** made or carried on to resist attack. **3.** of or pertaining to defense. —n. **4.** something that serves to defend. **5.** defensive position or attitude. —de·fen′sive·ly, adv. —de·fen′sive·ness, n.

de·fer¹ (dĭ fûr′), v.t., v.i., -ferred, -ferring. to put off to a future time. —de·fer′ment, n. —de·fer′rer, n.

de·fer² (dĭ fûr′), v.i., -ferred, -ferring. to yield in opinion (fol. by to).

def·er·ence (dĕf′ər əns), n. submission to or regard for the opinion, will, etc., of another.

def·er·en·tial (dĕf′ə rĕn′shəl), adj. showing deference. —def′er·en′tial·ly, adv.

de·fi·ance (dĭ fī′əns), n. **1.** a bold resistance to authority or to any opposing force. **2.** open disregard. **3.** a challenge to combat.

de·fi·ant (dĭ fī′ənt), adj. characterized by defiance. —de·fi′ant·ly, adv.

de·fi·cien·cy (dĭ fĭsh′ən sĭ), n., pl. -cies. **1.** state or fact of being deficient. **2.** the deficit.

de·fi·cient (dĭ fĭsh′ənt), adj. **1.** lacking some element or characteristic. **2.** insufficient.

def·i·cit (dĕf′ə sĭt), n. the amount by which a sum of money falls short.

de·fi·er (dĭ fī′ər), n. one who defies.

de·file¹ (dĭ fīl′), v.t., -filed, -filing. **1.** to make foul, dirty, or unclean. **2.** to violate the chastity of. **3.** to desecrate. **4.** to sully (a reputation, etc.). —de·file′ment, n. —de·fil′er, n.

de·file² (dĭ fīl′, dē′fīl′), n., v., -filed, -filing. —n. **1.** any narrow passage, esp. between mountains. —v.i. **2.** to march in a line, or by files; file off.

de·fine (dĭ fīn′), v.t., -fined, -fining. **1.** to state the meaning of (a word, etc.). **2.** to describe. **3.** to determine or fix the extent of. **4.** to make clear the form of. **5.** to specify distinctly. —de·fin′a·ble, adj. —de·fin′a·bly, adv. —de·fin′er, n.

def·i·nite (dĕf′ə nĭt), adj. **1.** clearly determined; exact. **2.** having fixed limits. **3.** limiting. **4.** Bot. (of an inflorescence) determinate. —def′i·nite·ly, adv. —def′i·nite·ness, n.

definite article, the article (Eng. *the*) which classes as "identified" the noun it modifies.

def·i·ni·tion (děf′ə nǐsh′ən), *n.* **1.** act of defining. **2.** the statement of the meaning of a word, etc. **3.** sharpness of the image formed by an optical system.

de·fin·i·tive (dǐ fǐn′ə tǐv), *adj.* **1.** conclusive; final. **2.** serving to specify definitely. —*n.* **3.** a limiting word, as an article, a demonstrative, or the like. —**de·fin′i·tive·ly,** *adv.* —**de·fin′i·tive·ness,** *n.*

de·flate (dǐ flāt′), *v.t.,* **-flated, -flating. 1.** to release the air or gas from (something inflated). **2.** to reduce (prices, etc.) from an inflated condition.

de·fla·tion (dǐ flā′shən), *n.* **1.** act of deflating. **2.** an abnormal decline in the level of prices, esp. one not accompanied by an equal reduction in the costs of production. —**de·fla′tion·ar′y,** *adj.*

de·flect (dǐ flěkt′), *v.t., v.i.* to bend or turn from a true course or right line. —**de·flec′tion,** *n.* —**de·flec′tive,** *adj.* —**de·flec′tor,** *n.*

de·flow·er (dǐ flou′ər), *v.t.* **1.** to deprive of flowers. **2.** to ravish.

De·foe (dǐ fō′), *n.* **Daniel,** 1661?–1731, British novelist and essayist.

de·for·est (dē fôr′ǐst, -fŏr′-), *v.t.* to divest of forests. —**de·for′est·a′tion,** *n.*

de·form (dǐ fôrm′), *v.t.* **1.** to mar the form of; disfigure. **2.** to mar the beauty of; spoil. **3.** to transform. —**de·for·ma·tion** (dē′fôr mā′shən, děf′ər-), *n.* —**de·formed′,** *adj.* —**de·form′-er,** *n.*

de·form·i·ty (dǐ fôr′mə tǐ), *n., pl.* **-ties. 1.** state of being deformed. **2.** a deformed person or thing. **3.** ugliness.

de·fraud (dǐ frôd′), *v.t.* to deprive of a right or property by fraud. —**de·fraud′er,** *n.*

de·fray (dǐ frā′), *v.t.* to bear or pay (the costs, etc.). —**de·fray′a·ble,** *adj.* —**de·fray′al, de·fray′ment,** *n.* —**de·fray′er,** *n.*

de·frost (dē frôst′, -frŏst′), *v.t.* to remove the frost or ice from. —**de·frost′er,** *n.*

deft (děft), *adj.* dexterous; skillful; clever. —**deft′ly,** *adv.* —**deft′ness,** *n.*

de·funct (dǐ fŭngkt′), *adj.* **1.** dead. —*n.* **2.** a dead person. —**de·funct′ness,** *n.*

de·fy (*v.* dǐ fī′; *n.* dǐ fī′, dē′fī), *v.,* **-fied, -fying,** *n., pl.* **-fies.** —*v.t.* **1.** to challenge or resist boldly. **2.** to offer effective resistance to. **3.** to challenge (one) to do something deemed impossible. —*n.* **4.** *U.S. Slang.* a challenge.

De·gas (də gäs′), *n.* **Hilaire Germain Edgar,** 1834–1917, French painter.

de·gauss·ing (dǐ gou′sǐng, -gō′zǐng), *n.* a process used to neutralize a ship's magnetic field as a protection against magnetic mines.

de·gen·er·a·cy (dǐ jěn′ər ə sǐ), *n.* degenerate state of character; degeneration.

de·gen·er·ate (*v.* dǐ jěn′ə rāt′; *adj., n.* dǐ jěn′-ər ǐt), *v.,* **-ated, -ating,** *adj., n.* —*v.i.* **1.** to decline in physical, mental, or moral qualities; deteriorate. **2.** *Biol.* to revert to a less highly organized or simpler type. —*adj.* **3.** having declined in physical or moral qualities. **4.** having lost the qualities proper to the kind. **5.** characterized by degeneracy. —*n.* **6.** a degenerate person. —**de·gen′er·ate·ly,** *adv.* —**de·gen′er·ate·ness,** *n.* —**de·gen′er·a′tion,** *n.* —**de·gen′er·a′tive,** *adj.*

de·grade (dǐ grād′), *v.t.,* **-graded, -grading. 1.** to reduce in rank, degree, etc. **2.** to debase. **3.** to lower in dignity or estimation. **4.** *Phys. Geog.* to wear down by erosion. —**deg·ra·da·tion** (děg′rə dā′shən), *n.* —**de·grad′er,** *n.*

de·gree (dǐ grē′), *n.* **1.** a step or stage in an ascending or descending scale. **2.** *Genetics, etc.* a certain distance in the line of descent, determining the proximity of blood. **3.** relative rank, station, etc. **4.** a stage in a scale of intensity or amount. **5.** *Geom., etc.* the 360th part of a complete angle or turn (often indicated by the sign °, as 45°). **6.** *Alg.* the sum of the exponents of the variables in an algebraic expression. **7.** a unit in the measurement of temperature. **8.** a unit on an arbitrary scale of measurement. **9.** *Law.* a relative measure of criminality. **10.** *Educ.* a title conferred by colleges as an indication of the completion of a course of study, or as an honorary recognition of achievement. **11.** *Gram.* one of the three parallel formations (positive, compara-

Degrees (def. 5)
of a circle

tive, and superlative) of adjectives and adverbs, showing differences in quality, quantity, or intensity in the attribute referred to. **12.** *Music.* a tone, or step, of the scale. **13. by degrees,** gradually.

de·his·cence (dǐ hǐs′əns), *n. Bot.* the natural bursting open of capsules, fruits, anthers, etc., for the discharge of contents. —**de·his′cent,** *adj.*

de·hy·drate (dē hī′drāt), *v.t., v.i.,* **-drated, -drating.** to deprive of or lose water or moisture. —**de′hy·dra′tion,** *n.*

de·ic·er (dē ī′sər), *n.* a device preventing or removing ice formation.

de·i·fy (dē′ə fī′), *v.t.,* **-fied, -fying. 1.** to make a god of. **2.** to adore or regard as a deity. —**de·i·fi·ca·tion** (dē′ə fə kā′shən), *n.* —**de·i·fi′er,** *n.*

deign (dān), *v.i.* **1.** to think fit or in accordance with one's dignity. —*v.t.* **2.** to condescend to give or grant.

de·ism (dē′ǐz əm), *n.* **1.** belief in the existence of a God on the evidence of reason and nature only. **2.** belief in a God who created the world but has since remained indifferent to His creation. —**de′ist,** *n.* —**de·is′tic,** *adj.*

de·i·ty (dē′ə tǐ), *n., pl.* **-ties. 1.** a god or goddess. **2.** divine nature. **3.** the rank of a god. **4. the Deity,** God.

de·ject·ed (dǐ jěk′tǐd), *adj.* disheartened. —**de·ject′ed·ly,** *adv.* —**de·ject′ed·ness,** *n.*

de·jec·tion (dǐ jěk′shən), *n.* lowness of spirits.

de ju·re (dē jŏŏr′ǐ), *Latin.* by right or law.

Del., Delaware.

Del·a·ware (děl′ə wâr′), *n.* **1.** a State in the eastern United States, on the Atlantic coast. 286,527 pop.; 2057 sq. mi. *Cap.:* Dover. **2.** a river flowing from SE New York along the boundary between Pennsylvania and New Jersey into Delaware Bay. 296 mi. —**Del·a·war·e·an** (děl′-ə wâr′Y ən), *adj., n.*

de·lay (dǐ lā′), *v.t.* **1.** to put off to a later time; postpone. **2.** to impede the progress of; hinder. —*v.i.* **3.** to linger; loiter. —*n.* **4.** act of delaying. **5.** fact of being delayed. —**de·lay′er,** *n.*

de·le (dē′lǐ), *v.t.,* **deled, deleing.** *Print.* to omit.

de·lec·ta·ble (dǐ lěk′tə bəl), *adj.* delightful; enjoyable. —**de·lec′ta·ble·ness,** *n.* —**de·lec′-ta·bly,** *adv.*

de·lec·ta·tion (dē′lěk tā′shən), *n.* delight.

del·e·gate (*n.* děl′ə gāt′, -gǐt; *v.* děl′ə gāt′), *n., v.,* **-gated, -gating.** —*n.* **1.** one delegated to act for or represent another or others; deputy. **2.** *U.S. Govt.* **a.** the representative of a Territory in the House of Representatives of the U.S. **b.** a member of the lower house of the State legislatures of Maryland, Virginia, and West Virginia. —*v.t.* **3.** to send or appoint (a person) as representative. **4.** to commit (functions, etc.) to another.

del·e·ga·tion (děl′ə gā′shən), *n.* **1.** act of delegating. **2.** fact of being delegated. **3.** the body of delegates chosen to represent others.

de·lete (dǐ lēt′), *v.t.,* **-leted, -leting.** to take out (anything written or printed); cancel; erase. —**de·le·tion** (dǐ lē′shən), *n.*

del·e·te·ri·ous (děl′ə tǐr′Y əs), *adj.* harmful.

delft (dělft), *n.* glazed earthenware decorated in colors, esp. in blue, made at Delft, Netherlands. Also, **delf** (dělf), **delft′ware′.**

Del·hi (děl′Y), *n.* **1.** a province in N India. 918,000 pop.; 574 sq. mi. **2.** the capital of this province: former capital of the old Mogul Empire. 521,849.

de·lib·er·ate (*adj.* dǐ lǐb′ər Yt; *v.* dǐ lǐb′ə rāt′), *adj., v.,* **-ated, -ating.** —*adj.* **1.** carefully considered; intentional. **2.** characterized by deliberation. **3.** slow; unhurried. —*v.t.* **4.** to consider. —*v.i.* **5.** to think carefully. **6.** to confer formally. —**de·lib′er·ate·ly,** *adv.* —**de·lib′er·ate·ness,** *n.* —**de·lib′er·a′tor,** *n.*

de·lib·er·a·tion (dǐ lǐb′ə rā′shən), *n.* **1.** careful consideration before decision. **2.** formal consultation. **3.** deliberate quality.

de·lib·er·a·tive (dǐ lǐb′ə rā′tǐv), *adj.* **1.** having the function of deliberating. **2.** having to do with policy.

del·i·ca·cy (děl′ə kə sǐ), *n., pl.* **-cies. 1.** fineness of texture, quality, etc. **2.** fineness of perception or feeling. **3.** the quality of requiring or involving great care. **4.** nicety of action or operation. **5.** bodily weakness. **6.** something pleasing, esp. to the palate.

del·i·cate (děl′ə kǐt), *adj.* **1.** fine in texture, quality, etc. **2.** dainty or choice, as food. **3.** soft or faint, as color. **4.** subtle. **5.** fragile. **6.** requiring great care. **7.** fine in action. **8.** regardful of what is becoming, proper, etc. **9.** sensitive. —**del′i·cate·ly,** *adv.* —**del′i·cate·ness,** *n.*

del·i·ca·tes·sen (dĕl′ə kə tĕs′ən), *n.* **1.** a store selling foods that require little or no preparation for serving. **2.** (*construed as pl.*) the foods sold.

de·li·cious (dĭ lĭsh′əs), *adj.* **1.** highly pleasing to the senses, esp. to taste. **2.** delightful. —*n.* **3.** (*cap.*) a variety of red eating apple, widely grown in the U.S. —**de·li′cious·ly,** *adv.* —**de·li′cious·ness,** *n.*

de·light (dĭ līt′), *n.* **1.** a high degree of pleasure; joy. **2.** something that gives great pleasure. —*v.t.* **3.** to please highly. —*v.i.* **4.** to have great pleasure. —**de·light′ed,** *adj.* —**de·light′ed·ly,** *adv.*

de·light·ful (dĭ līt′fəl), *adj.* highly pleasing. —**de·light′ful·ly,** *adv.* —**de·light′ful·ness,** *n.*

De·li·lah (dĭ lī′lə), *n. Bible.* Samson's mistress, who betrayed him to the Philistines.

de·lim·it (dĭ lĭm′ĭt), *v.t.* to mark the limits of. —**de·lim′i·ta′tion,** *n.* —**de·lim′i·ta′tive,** *adj.*

de·lin·e·ate (dĭ lĭn′ĭ āt′), *v.t.,* **-ated, -ating.** **1.** to sketch or trace in outline. **2.** to describe. —**de·lin′e·a′tion,** *n.* —**de·lin′e·a′tive,** *adj.* —**de·lin′e·a′tor,** *n.*

de·lin·quen·cy (dĭ lĭng′kwən sĭ), *n., pl.* **-cies.** **1.** neglect of duty; fault; guilt. **2.** a misdeed.

de·lin·quent (dĭ lĭng′kwənt), *adj.* **1.** neglectful of a duty; guilty of a misdeed. **2.** of or pertaining to delinquents. —*n.* **3.** one who is delinquent. —**de·lin′quent·ly,** *adv.*

del·i·quesce (dĕl′ə kwĕs′), *v.i.,* **-quesced, -quescing.** **1.** to melt away. **2.** to become liquid. —**del′i·ques′cence,** *n.* —**del′i·ques′cent,** *adj.*

de·lir·i·ous (dĭ lĭr′ĭ əs), *adj.* affected with or characteristic of delirium. —**de·lir′i·ous·ly,** *adv.*

de·lir·i·um (dĭ lĭr′ĭ əm), *n., pl.* **-liriums, -liria** (-lĭr′ĭ ə). **1.** a temporary mental disorder, as in fevers, characterized by excitement, hallucinations, etc. **2.** a state of violent emotion.

delirium tre·mens (trē′mənz), a delirium due to excessive indulgence in alcohol.

De·li·us (dē′lĭ əs, dēl′yəs), *n.* **Frederick,** 1862–1934, British composer.

de·liv·er (dĭ lĭv′ər), *v.t.* **1.** to give up or surrender. **2.** to carry and turn over (letters, goods, etc.) to intended recipients. **3.** to utter or pronounce. **4.** to give forth or emit; direct. **5.** to liberate. **6.** to release or save. **7.** to disburden (a woman) of a child in childbirth. —**de·liv′er·a·ble,** *adj.* —**de·liv′er·er,** *n.*

de·liv·er·ance (dĭ lĭv′ər əns), *n.* **1.** act of delivering. **2.** fact of being delivered. **3.** a formal pronouncement.

de·liv·er·y (dĭ lĭv′ə rĭ), *n., pl.* **-eries.** **1.** the delivering of letters, goods, etc. **2.** a surrender. **3.** the utterance of words. **4.** vocal and bodily behavior during a speech. **5.** act or manner of giving or sending forth. **6.** release or rescue. **7.** childbirth; parturition. **8.** something delivered.

dell (dĕl), *n. Literary in U.S.* a small valley.

de·louse (dē lous′, -louz′), *v.t.,* **-loused, -lousing.** to free of lice; remove lice from.

Del·phi (dĕl′fī), *n.* an ancient city in central Greece: the site of an oracle of Apollo (**Delphic oracle**). —**Del·phic** (dĕl′fĭk), **Del·phi·an** (dĕl′-fĭ ən), *adj.*

del·phin·i·um (dĕl fĭn′ĭ əm), *n.* any of numerous garden flowers of the crowfoot family, having handsome, usually blue, irregular flowers; larkspur.

del·ta (dĕl′tə), *n.* **1.** the fourth letter (Δ, δ) of the Greek alphabet. **2.** anything triangular. **3.** a plain of alluvial deposit between diverging branches of the mouth of a river, often triangular.

del·toid (dĕl′toid), *n.* **1.** a large triangular muscle covering the joint of the shoulder and serving to raise the arm away from the side of the body. —*adj.* **2.** triangular.

de·lude (dĭ lōōd′), *v.t.,* **-luded, -luding.** to mislead; deceive. —**de·lud′er,** *n.*

del·uge (dĕl′ūj), *n., v.,* **-uged, -uging.** —*n.* **1.** a great flood; downpour. **2.** anything that overwhelms like a flood. **3. the Deluge,** the great flood in the days of Noah. —*v.t.* **4.** to flood. **5.** to overwhelm.

de·lu·sion (dĭ lōō′zhən), *n.* **1.** act of deluding. **2.** fact of being deluded. **3.** a false opinion. **4.** *Psychiatry.* a fixed, dominating, or persistent false mental conception resistant to reason with regard to actual things or matters of fact.

de·lu·sive (dĭ lōō′sĭv), *adj.* **1.** deceptive. **2.** false; unreal. —**de·lu′sive·ly,** *adv.*

de luxe (də lōōks′, lŭks′), of special elegance, sumptuousness, or fineness.

delve (dĕlv), *v.i., v.t.,* **delved, delving. 1.** to carry on intensive research for information, etc. **2.** *Archaic or Dial.* to dig. —**delv′er,** *n.*

Dem., **1.** Democrat. **2.** Democratic.

de·mag·net·ize (dē măg′nə tīz′), *v.t.,* **-ized, -izing.** to remove magnetic properties from. —**de·mag′net·i·za′tion,** *n.* —**de·mag′net·iz′-er,** *n.*

dem·a·gog·ic (dĕm′ə gŏj′ĭk, -gŏg′ĭk), *adj.* of or characteristic of a demagogue. Also, **dem′a·gog′i·cal.**

dem·a·gogue (dĕm′ə gŏg′, -gŏg′), *n.* a leader who uses the passions or prejudices of the populace for his own interests. Also, **dem′a·gog′.** —**dem′a·gogu′er·y,** *n.*

de·mand (dĭ mănd′, -mänd′), *v.t.* **1.** to ask for with authority; claim as a right. **2.** to ask for urgently. **3.** to require as proper or necessary. —*v.i.* **4.** to inquire or ask. —*n.* **5.** act of demanding. **6.** that which is demanded. **7.** an urgent or pressing requirement. **8.** an inquiry or question. **9.** the state of being in request for purchase or use. **10.** *Econ.* **a.** the desire and ability to purchase. **b.** the quantity which buyers will take at a particular price. —**de·mand′a·ble,** *adj.* —**de·mand′er,** *n.*

de·mar·ca·tion (dē′mär kā′shən), *n.* **1.** the marking off of the boundaries of something. **2.** separation by boundaries. Also, **de′mar·ka′tion.**

de·mean[1] (dĭ mēn′), *v.t.* to debase.

de·mean[2] (dĭ mēn′), *v.t.* to conduct (oneself).

de·mean·or (dĭ mē′nər), *n.* conduct; behavior.

de·ment·ed (dĭ mĕn′tĭd), *adj.* crazed; insane. —**de·ment′ed·ly,** *adv.* —**de·ment′ed·ness,** *n.*

de·men·tia (dĭ mĕn′shə, -shĭ ə), *n.* a state of mental disorder characterized by impairment or loss of the mental powers.

dementia prae·cox (prē′kŏks), a form of insanity characterized especially by introversion and odd, distorted behavior.

de·mer·it (dē mĕr′ĭt), *n.* **1.** fault. **2.** a mark against a person for misconduct or deficiency.

de·mesne (dĭ mān′, -mēn′), *n.* **1.** possession (of land) as one's own. **2.** an estate possessed. **3.** the land attached to a manor house, reserved for the owner's use. **4.** the dominion of a sovereign or state. **5.** a region.

De·me·ter (dĭ mē′tər), *n. Gk. Myth.* goddess of the fruitful earth and protectress of marriage, identified by the Romans with Ceres.

dem·i·god (dĕm′ĭ gŏd′), *n.* one partly divine and partly human. —**dem′i·god′dess,** *n. fem.*

dem·i·john (dĕm′ĭ jŏn′), *n.* a large smallnecked bottle, usually cased in wickerwork.

de·mil·i·ta·rize (dē mĭl′ə tə rīz′), *v.t.,* **-rized, -rizing.** to free from militarism or military control. —**de·mil′i·ta·ri·za′tion,** *n.*

dem·i·monde (dĕm′ĭ mŏnd′), *n.* the class of women who have doubtful reputations.

de·mise (dĭ mīz′), *n., v.,* **-mised, -mising.** —*n.* **1.** death. **2.** *Law.* a transfer of an estate. **3.** *Govt.* transfer of sovereignty, as by the death of the sovereign. —*v.t.* **4.** *Law.* to transfer (an estate, etc.) for a limited time. **5.** *Govt.* to transfer (sovereignty). —*v.i.* **6.** *Law.* to pass by bequest, inheritance, or succession to the Crown.

dem·i·tasse (dĕm′ĭ tăs′, -täs′), *n.* **1.** a small cup for serving black coffee after dinner. **2.** the coffee contained in such a cup.

de·mo·bi·lize (dē mō′bə līz′), *v.t.,* **-lized, -lizing.** to disband (an army). —**de·mo′bi·li·za′tion,** *n.*

de·moc·ra·cy (dĭ mŏk′rə sĭ), *n., pl.* **-cies.** **1.** a form of government in which the supreme power is vested in the people and exercised by them or by their elected agents under a free electoral system. **2.** a state having such a government. **3.** a state of society characterized by formal equality of rights and privileges. **4.** political or social equality. **5.** (*cap.*) *U.S.* **a.** the principles of the Democratic party. **b.** the members of this party collectively.

dem·o·crat (dĕm′ə krăt′), *n.* **1.** an advocate of democracy. **2.** (*cap.*) *U.S.* a member of the Democratic party.

dem·o·crat·ic (dĕm′ə krăt′ĭk), *adj.* **1.** pertaining to or of the nature of democracy or a democracy. **2.** advocating or upholding democracy. **3.** (*cap.*) *U.S.* of, pertaining to, or characteristic of

the Democratic party. Also, **dem'o·crat'i·cal.**
—**dem'o·crat'i·cal·ly,** *adv.*

Democratic party, one of the two major
political parties in the U.S., founded in 1828.

de·moc·ra·tize (dĭ mŏk'rə tīz'), *v.t., v.i.,* -tized,
-tizing. to make or become democratic.

de·mol·ish (dĭ mŏl'ĭsh), *v.t.* **1.** to reduce to
ruins. **2.** to destroy. —**de·mol'ish·er,** *n.* —**de·**
mol'ish·ment, *n.*

dem·o·li·tion (dĕm'ə lĭsh'ən, dē'mə-), *n.* **1.**
act of demolishing. **2.** state of being demolished.

demolition bomb, *Mil.* a bomb containing a
large charge to destroy material objects.

de·mon (dē'mən), *n.* **1.** an evil spirit; a devil.
2. an atrociously wicked or cruel person. **3.** a
person of great energy, etc. **4.** daemon.

de·mon·e·tize (dĭ mŏn'ə tīz', -mŭn'-), *v.t.,*
-tized, -tizing. to divest of value as money.

de·mo·ni·ac (dĭ mō'nĭ ăk'), *adj.* Also, **de·mo·**
ni·a·cal (dē'mə nī'ə kəl). **1.** of, pertaining to, or
like a demon. **2.** raging; frantic. —*n.* **3.** one
seemingly possessed by a demon. —**de·mo·ni·a·**
cal·ly (dē'mə nī'ĭk lĭ), *adv.*

de·mon·ic (dĭ mŏn'ĭk), *adj.* of, pertaining to,
or of the nature of a demon.

de·mon·ol·o·gy (dē'mə nŏl'ə jĭ), *n.* the study
of demons or of beliefs about demons.

de·mon·stra·ble (dĭ mŏn'strə bəl, dĕm'ən-),
adj. capable of being demonstrated. —**de·mon'·**
stra·bil'i·ty, *n.* —**de·mon'stra·bly,** *adv.*

dem·on·strate (dĕm'ən strāt'), *v.,* -strated,
-strating. —*v.t.* **1.** to prove. **2.** to describe and
explain with the help of specimens, etc. **3.** to
manifest. —*v.i.* **4.** to make, give, or take part in
a demonstration. —**dem'on·stra'tor,** *n.*

dem·on·stra·tion (dĕm'ən strā'shən), *n.* **1.**
the proving of anything conclusively. **2.** proof.
3. a description or explanation, given with the
help of specimens, etc. **4.** exhibition of an article
to advertise or sell it. **5.** a display; manifestation.
6. a public exhibition of sympathy, opposition,
etc., as a mass meeting. **7.** a show of military
force, made to deceive the enemy. **8.** *Math.* a
logical presentation of the way in which given
assumptions imply a certain result.

dem·on·stra·tive (dĭ mŏn'strə tĭv), *adj.* **1.**
characterized by open exhibition or expression of
feelings, etc. **2.** explanatory or illustrative.
3. indubitably conclusive. **4.** *Gram.* indicating
or specifying the thing referred to. —*n.* **5.** *Gram.*
a demonstrative word. —**de·mon'stra·tive·ly,**
adv.

de·mor·al·ize (dĭ môr'ə līz', -mŏr'-), *v.t.,* -ized,
-izing. **1.** to corrupt the morals of. **2.** to deprive
of courage, discipline, etc. **3.** to reduce to disorder. —**de·mor'al·i·za'tion,** *n.* —**de·mor'al·**
iz'er, *n.*

De·mos·the·nes (dĭ mŏs'thə nēz'), *n.* 384?–
322 B.C., Athenian statesman and orator.

de·mote (dĭ mōt'), *v.t.,* -moted, -moting. to
reduce to a lower grade or class. —**de·mo'tion,** *n.*

de·mur (dĭ mûr'), *v.,* -murred, -murring, *n.*
—*v.i.* **1.** to object. —*n.* **2.** act of making objection. **3.** an objection raised.

de·mure (dĭ myŏŏr'), *adj.,* -murer, -murest.
1. affectedly modest, decorous, or prim. **2.** serious; decorous. —**de·mure'ly,** *adv.* —**de·mure'·**
ness, *n.*

de·mur·rage (dĭ mûr'ĭj), *n.* *Com.* the detention of a vessel, railroad car, etc., as in loading
or unloading, beyond the agreed time.

de·mur·rer (dĭ mûr'ər), *n.* **1.** an objector. **2.**
Law. a pleading that even if the facts are as alleged, they do not sustain the contention based
on them. **3.** an objection.

den (dĕn), *n., v.,* denned, denning. —*n.* **1.** a retired place, as a cave, serving as the habitation
of a beast. **2.** a cave as a shelter, etc. **3.** a
squalid place. **4.** a cozy private room. —*v.i.* **5.**
to live in a den.

de·nar·i·us (dĭ nâr'ĭ əs), *n., pl.* -narii (-nâr'-
ĭ ī'). (in English monetary reckoning) a penny.

de·nat·u·ral·ize (dē năch'ə rə līz'), *v.t.,* -ized,
-izing. **1.** to deprive of the original nature. **2.**
to deprive of citizenship. —**de·nat'u·ral·i·za'·**
tion, *n.*

de·na·ture (dē nā'chər), *v.t.,* -tured, -turing.
1. to deprive of its peculiar nature. **2.** to render
unfit for drinking or eating.

de·na·zi·fy (dē nät'sə fī', -nät'-), *v.t.,* -fied,
-fying. to rid of Nazism. —**de·na'zi·fi·ca'-**
tion, *n.*

den·drite (dĕn'drīt), *n.* *Anat., Physiol.* the

branching portion of a neuron which picks up the
stimulus.

den·gue (dĕng'gā, -gĭ), *n.* *Pathol.* an infectious,
eruptive, usually epidemic fever of warm climates, characterized esp. by severe pains.

de·ni·al (dĭ nī'əl), *n.* **1.** contradiction of a
statement, etc. **2.** refusal to believe a doctrine,
etc. **3.** the refusal of a claim, request, etc. **4.**
refusal to recognize or acknowledge.

de·ni·er[1] (dĭ nī'ər), *n.* one who denies.

de·nier[2] (də nĭr'), *n.* a unit of weight to indicate fineness of silk, rayon, or nylon yarn.

den·im (dĕn'əm), *n.* a heavy twilled cotton for
overalls, etc.

den·i·zen (dĕn'ə zən), *n.* **1.** an inhabitant. **2.**
anything adapted to a new place, condition, etc.
—*v.t.* **3.** to make a denizen of.

Den·mark (dĕn'märk), *n.* a kingdom in N
Europe, on Jutland peninsula and the adjacent
islands. 4,077,747 pop.; 16,576 sq. mi. *Cap.:*
Copenhagen.

de·nom·i·nate (dĭ nŏm'ə nāt'), *v.t.,* -nated,
-nating. to give a name to, esp. a specific name.

de·nom·i·na·tion (dĭ nŏm'ə nā'shən), *n.* **1.** a
name or designation, esp. one for a class of things.
2. a class or grade of persons or things distinguished by a specific name. **3.** a religious sect.
—**de·nom'i·na'tion·al,** *adj.* —**de·nom'i·na'-**
tion·al·ly, *adv.*

de·nom·i·na·tive (dĭ nŏm'ə nā'tĭv, -nə tĭv),
adj. **1.** conferring or constituting a distinctive
name. **2.** *Gram.* (esp. of verbs) formed from a
noun. —*n.* **3.** *Gram.* a denominative verb or
other word.

de·nom·i·na·tor (dĭ nŏm'ə nā'tər), *n.* **1.** that
term of a fraction (usually under the line) which
shows the number of equal parts into which the
unit is divided. **2.** one that denominates.

de·no·ta·tion (dē'nō tā'shən), *n.* **1.** the meaning of a term when it merely identifies its referent
(cf. *connotation*). **2.** act or fact of denoting.

de·note (dĭ nōt'), *v.t.,* -noted, -noting. **1.** to be
a mark or symbol of; indicate. **2.** to be a name
for.

de·noue·ment (dā'nōō mäN'), *n.* **1.** the final
disentangling of the intricacies of a plot, as of a
drama. **2.** outcome; solution.

de·nounce (dĭ nouns'), *v.t.,* -nounced, -nounc-
ing. **1.** to condemn openly. **2.** to inform against.
3. to give formal notice of the termination of (a
treaty, etc.). —**de·nounce'ment,** *n.* —**de·**
nounc'er, *n.*

dense (dĕns), *adj.,* denser, densest. **1.** having
the component parts closely together; compact.
2. thick-headed; stupid. **3.** intense. **4.** *Photog.*
(of a negative) relatively opaque. —**dense'ly,**
adv. —**dense'ness,** *n.*

den·si·ty (dĕn'sə tĭ), *n., pl.* -ties. **1.** state or
quality of being dense; compactness. **2.** stupid-
ity. **3.** *Physics.* the mass per unit of volume.

dent (dĕnt), *n.* **1.** a hollow or depression in a
surface, as from a blow. —*v.t.* **2.** to make a dent
in or on. —*v.i.* **3.** to become indented.

den·tal (dĕn'təl), *adj.* **1.** of or pertaining to the
teeth. **2.** of or pertaining to dentistry. **3.**
Phonet. with the tongue tip touching or near the
upper front teeth. —*n.* **4.** *Phonet.* a dental sound.

den·tate (dĕn'tāt), *adj.* *Bot., Zool.* having a
toothed margin or toothlike projections.

den·ti·frice (dĕn'tə frĭs), *n.* a powder, paste,
or other preparation for cleaning the teeth.

den·tin (dĕn'tĭn), *n.* *Anat.* the hard calcareous
tissue that forms the greatest part of a tooth.
Also, **den·tine** (dĕn'tēn, -tĭn).

den·tist (dĕn'tĭst), *n.* one whose profession is
dentistry.

den·tist·ry (dĕn'tĭs trĭ), *n.* the science dealing
with the prevention and treatment of oral disease, esp. the filling of teeth, etc.

den·ti·tion (dĕn tĭsh'ən), *n.* the kind, number,
and arrangement of the teeth.

den·ture (dĕn'chər), *n.* an artificial restoration
of several or of all the teeth of either jaw.

de·nude (dĭ nūd', -nōōd'), *v.t.,* -nuded, -nuding.
1. to make bare; strip. **2.** *Geol.* to lay (rock)
bare by erosion. —**den·u·da·tion** (dĕn'yŏŏ dā'-
shən, dē'nyŏŏ-, -nōō-), *n.*

de·nun·ci·a·tion (dĭ nŭn'sĭ ā'shən, -shĭ-), *n.*
1. open and vehement condemnation. **2.** an accusation of crime. **3.** notice of the termination of
an international agreement. **4.** warning. —**de·**
nun'ci·a·to'ry, *adj.*

Den·ver (dĕn'vər), *n.* the capital of Colorado,
in the central part. 322,412.

de·ny (dĭ nī'), *v.t.*, **-nied, -nying. 1.** to declare not to be true. **2.** to refuse to believe (a doctrine, etc.). **3.** to refuse (a claim, request, etc.). **4.** to disown; repudiate.

de·o·dor·ant (dē ō'dər ənt), *n.* **1.** an agent for destroying odors. —*adj.* **2.** destroying odors.

de·o·dor·ize (dē ō'də rīz'), *v.t.*, **-ized, -izing.** to deprive of odor. —**de·o'dor·iz'er,** *n.*

dep., 1. department. **2.** deputy.

de·part (dĭ pärt'), *v.i.* **1.** to go away, as from a place. **2.** to turn aside or away; diverge (fol. by *from*). **3.** to die. —*v.i.* **4.** to leave. —**de·part'ed,** *adj.*, *n.*

de·part·ment (dĭ pärt'mənt), *n.* **1.** a distinct part of anything arranged in divisions. **2.** one of the administrative districts of a country, as France. **3.** one of the principal branches of a governmental organization. —**de·part·men·tal** (dē'pärt měn'təl), *adj.* —**de'part·men'tal·ly,** *adv.*

de·par·ture (dĭ pär'chər), *n.* **1.** a going away. **2.** divergence. **3.** death.

de·pend (dĭ pĕnd'), *v.i.* **1.** to rely; trust. **2.** to rely for support, help, etc. **3.** to be contingent. **4.** *Gram.* (of a word) to be subordinate (to another).

de·pend·a·ble (dĭ pĕn'də bəl), *adj.* that may be depended on; reliable. —**de·pend'a·bil'i·ty,** de·pend'a·ble·ness, *n.* —**de·pend'a·bly,** *adv.*

de·pend·ence (dĭ pĕn'dəns), *n.* **1.** state of depending for aid, support, etc. **2.** trust. **3.** state of being contingent on something. **4.** subordination. **5.** an object of reliance or trust.

de·pend·en·cy (dĭ pĕn'dən sĭ), *n.*, *pl.* **-cies. 1.** dependence. **2.** something dependent. **3.** an annex. **4.** a subject territory which is not an integral part of the ruling country.

de·pend·ent (dĭ pĕn'dənt), *adj.* **1.** depending on something else for aid, support, etc. **2.** contingent. **3.** subordinate. **4.** (of linguistic forms) not used in isolation. **5.** hanging down. —*n.* **6.** one who depends on another for support, etc.

de·pict (dĭ pĭkt'), *v.t.* **1.** to represent by painting; portray. **2.** to describe. —**de·pict'er,** *n.* —**de·pic'tion,** *n.*

de·pil·a·to·ry (dĭ pĭl'ə tōr'ĭ), *adj.*, *n.*, *pl.* **-ries.** —*adj.* **1.** capable of removing hair. —*n.* **2.** a depilatory agent.

de·plete (dĭ plēt'), *v.t.*, **-pleted, -pleting.** to reduce the stock or amount of. —**de·ple'tion,** *n.*

de·plor·a·ble (dĭ plōr'ə bəl), *adj.* **1.** lamentable. **2.** grievous; wretched. —**de·plor'a·bly,** *adv.*

de·plore (dĭ plōr'), *v.t.*, **-plored, -ploring.** to feel or express deep grief for or in regard to.

de·ploy (dĭ ploi'), *v.t.*, *v.i.* *Mil.* to spread out and form an extended front. —**de·ploy'ment,** *n.*

de·po·nent (dĭ pō'nənt), *adj.* **1.** *Gk. and Lat. Gram.* (of a verb) appearing only in the passive voice forms, but with active meaning. —*n.* **2.** *Law.* one who testifies under oath, esp. in writing. **3.** deponent verb.

de·pop·u·late (dē pŏp'yə lāt'), *v.t.*, **-lated, -lating.** to deprive of inhabitants. —**de·pop'-u·la'tion,** *n.* —**de·pop'u·la'tor,** *n.*

de·port (dĭ pōrt'), *v.t.* **1.** to transport forcibly, as to a penal colony. **2.** to conduct (oneself).

de·por·ta·tion (dē'pōr tā'shən), *n.* an expulsion of undesired aliens and others from a state.

de·port·ment (dĭ pōrt'mənt), *n.* conduct.

de·pose (dĭ pōz'), *v.*, **-posed, -posing.** —*v.t.* **1.** to remove from office, esp. high office. **2.** to declare or testify, esp. under oath. —*v.i.* **3.** to bear witness.

de·pos·it (dĭ pŏz'ĭt), *v.t.* **1.** to put or lay down; place. **2.** to place for safekeeping. **3.** to give as security or part payment. —*n.* **4.** anything laid down; sediment. **5.** a coating of metal deposited by an electric current. **6.** an accumulation, or occurrence, of ore, oil, etc. **7.** anything laid away for safekeeping. **8.** money placed in a bank. **9.** anything given as security or part payment.

de·pos·i·tar·y (dĭ pŏz'ə tĕr'ĭ), *n.*, *pl.* **-taries. 1.** one to whom anything is given in trust. **2.** a depository.

dep·o·si·tion (dĕp'ə zĭsh'ən, dē'pə-), *n.* **1.** removal from an office. **2.** act of depositing. **3.** that which is deposited. **4.** *Law.* a. the giving of testimony under oath. b. the testimony so given.

de·pos·i·tor (dĭ pŏz'ĭ tər), *n.* **1.** one that deposits. **2.** one who deposits money in a bank.

de·pos·i·to·ry (dĭ pŏz'ə tōr'ĭ), *n.*, *pl.* **-ries. 1.** a place where anything is deposited. **2.** a depositary.

de·pot (dē'pō; *Mil. or Brit.* dĕp'ō), *n.* **1.** *U.S.* a railroad station. **2.** *Mil.* a. a place where supplies are stored. b. a place where recruits receive their first training.

de·prave (dĭ prāv'), *v.t.*, **-praved, -praving.** to make bad or worse; corrupt. —**de·praved',** *adj.* —**de·prav'er,** *n.*

de·prav·i·ty (dĭ prăv'ə tĭ), *n.*, *pl.* **-ties. 1.** state of being depraved. **2.** a depraved act or practice.

dep·re·cate (dĕp'rə kāt'), *v.t.*, **-cated, -cating.** to express earnest disapproval of. —**dep're·cat'ing·ly,** *adv.* —**dep're·ca'tion,** *n.* —**dep're·ca'tor,** *n.* —**dep·re·ca·to·ry** (dĕp'rə kə tōr'ĭ), *adj.*

de·pre·ci·ate (dĭ prē'shĭ āt'), *v.*, **-ated, -ating.** —*v.t.* **1.** to reduce the value of. **2.** to belittle. —*v.i.* **3.** to decline in value. —**de·pre'ci·a'tor,** *n.*

de·pre·ci·a·tion (dĭ prē'shĭ ā'shən), *n.* **1.** decrease in value due to wear, etc. **2.** decrease in purchasing value of money. **3.** disparagement.

dep·re·da·tion (dĕp'rə dā'shən), *n.* a preying upon or plundering; robbery; ravage.

de·press (dĭ prĕs'), *v.t.* **1.** to lower in spirits; deject. **2.** to lower in force, etc.; weaken. **3.** to lower in amount or value. **4.** to put into a lower position. **5.** to press down. —**de·press'i·ble,** *adj.*

de·pres·sant (dĭ prĕs'ənt), *Med.* —*adj.* **1.** sedative. —*n.* **2.** a sedative.

de·pressed (dĭ prĕst'), *adj.* **1.** dejected. **2.** pressed down. **3.** lowered in force, etc. **4.** *Bot., Zool.* flattened.

de·pres·sion (dĭ prĕsh'ən), *n.* **1.** act of depressing. **2.** state of being depressed. **3.** a depressed place or part. **4.** dejection of spirits. **5.** inactivity, as of trade. **6.** period during which there is a decline in business. —**de·pres'sive,** *adj.*

dep·ri·va·tion (dĕp'rə vā'shən), *n.* **1.** act of depriving. **2.** fact of being deprived. **3.** loss.

de·prive (dĭ prīv'), *v.t.*, **-prived, -priving. 1.** to divest of something. **2.** to keep something from (a person, etc.).

dept., department.

depth (dĕpth), *n.* **1.** distance downward, inward, or backward. **2.** safe or suitable deepness. **3.** abstruseness. **4.** gravity. **5.** emotional profundity. **6.** intensity, as of silence, color, etc. **7.** lowness of pitch. **8.** sagacity or profundity. **9.** a deep or unfathomable part or place. **10.** the part of greatest intensity, as of night.

depth charge, an antisubmarine bomb dropped or thrown from a ship or an airplane. Also, **depth bomb.**

dep·u·ta·tion (dĕp'yə tā'shən), *n.* **1.** appointment to represent or act for another or others. **2.** the person or body of persons so appointed.

de·pute (dĭ pūt'), *v.t.*, **-puted, -puting. 1.** to appoint as one's substitute or agent. **2.** to assign (a charge, etc.) to a deputy.

dep·u·tize (dĕp'yə tīz'), *v.t.*, *v.i.*, **-tized, -tizing.** to appoint or act as a deputy.

dep·u·ty (dĕp'yə tĭ), *n.*, *pl.* **-ties,** *adj.* —*n.* **1.** a person appointed to act for another or others. **2.** a representative in any of certain legislative bodies. —*adj.* **3.** acting as deputy for another.

De Quin·cey (dĭ kwĭn'sĭ), **Thomas,** 1785–1859, British essayist.

der., 1. derivative. **2.** derived.

de·rail (dē rāl'), *v.t.* to cause (a train, etc.) to run off the rails. —**de·rail'ment,** *n.*

de·range (dĭ rānj'), *v.t.*, **-ranged, -ranging. 1.** to disarrange. **2.** to make insane. —**de·ranged',** *adj.* —**de·range'ment,** *n.*

Der·by (dûr'bĭ; *Brit.* där'bĭ), *n.*, *pl.* **-bies. 1.** a horse race in the United States, run annually at Churchill Downs, Kentucky. **2.** a horse race in England, run annually at Epsom Downs, near London. **3.** (*l.c.*) a stiff felt hat with rounded crown, worn chiefly by men.

der·e·lict (dĕr'ə lĭkt), *adj.* **1.** abandoned, as by the owner (said esp. of a ship at sea). **2.** neglectful of duty. —*n.* **3.** personal property abandoned by the owner. **4.** a ship abandoned at sea. **5.** a person abandoned, esp. by society.

der·e·lic·tion (dĕr'ə lĭk'shən), *n.* **1.** culpable neglect, as of duty. **2.** act of abandoning. **3.** state of being abandoned.

de·ride (dĭ rīd'), *v.t.*, **-rided, -riding.** to laugh at in contempt; mock. —**de·rid'er,** *n.*

de·ri·sion (dĭ rĭzh'ən), *n.* **1.** act of deriding; mockery. **2.** an object of ridicule.

de·ri·sive (dĭ rī'sĭv), *adj.* characterized by derision; ridiculing; mocking. Also, **de·ri·so·ry** (dĭ-rĭ/sə rĭ/). **—de·ri/sive·ly,** *adv.* **—de·ri/sive-ness,** *n.*

deriv., 1. derivation. **2.** derivative.

der·i·va·tion (dĕr/ə vā/shən), *n.* **1.** act of deriving. **2.** fact of being derived. **3.** origin. **4.** *Gram.* **a.** the composing of new words by the addition of prefixes or suffixes to existing root words. **b.** the systematic description of such processes in a particular language.

de·riv·a·tive (dĭ rĭv/ə tĭv), *adj.* **1.** derived. **2.** not original; secondary. **—n. 3.** something derived. **4.** *Gram.* a form derived from another. **5.** *Chem.* a substance obtained or derived from another. **—de·riv/a·tive·ly,** *adv.*

de·rive (dĭ rĭv/), *v.,* **-rived, -riving. —v.t. 1.** to receive or obtain from a source or origin. **2.** to trace, as from a source or origin. **3.** to deduce. **4.** *Chem.* to produce (a compound) from another compound by replacement of elements or radicals. **—v.i. 5.** to originate.

der·ma (dûr/mə), *n.* **1.** the true skin, beneath the epidermis. **2.** the skin in general. **—der/-mal,** *adj.*

der·ma·tol·o·gy (dûr/mə tŏl/ə jĭ), *n.* science of the skin and its diseases. **—der/ma·tol/o·gist,** *n.*

der·mis (dûr/mĭs), *n.* derma. **—der/mic,** *adj.*

der·o·gate (dĕr/ə gāt/), *v.i.,* **-gated, -gating. 1.** to detract. **2.** to degenerate. **—der/o·ga/-tion,** *n.*

de·rog·a·to·ry (dĭ rŏg/ə tôr/ĭ), *adj.* tending to derogate or detract; depreciating. Also, **de·rog/-a·tive. —de·rog/a·to/ri·ly,** *adv.*

der·rick (dĕr/ĭk), *n.* **1.** any of various devices for lifting and moving heavy weights. **2.** the towerlike framework over an oil well or the like.

der·ring-do (dĕr/ĭng dōō/), *n.* *Archaic.* daring deeds; heroic daring.

der·rin·ger (dĕr/ĭn jər), *n.* *U.S.* a short-barreled pistol of large caliber.

der·vish (dûr/vĭsh), *n.* a member of certain Mohammedan ascetic orders, some of which carry on ecstatic observances, as violent dancing.

des·cant (*n.* dĕs/kănt; *v.* dĕs kănt/, dĭs-), *n.* **1.** *Music.* **a.** a melody or counterpoint accompanying a simple musical theme. **b.** a song or melody. **—v.i. 2.** *Music.* to sing. **3.** to discourse at length.

Des·cartes (dĕ kärt/), *n.* **René,** 1596–1650, French philosopher and mathematician.

de·scend (dĭ sĕnd/), *v.i.* **1.** to pass, go, or come down. **2.** to come down by transmission, as from ancestors. **3.** to be derived by birth or extraction. **4.** to come down in a hostile manner, as an army. **5.** to come down from a certain intellectual, moral, or social standard. **6.** *Astron.* to move toward the horizon. **—v.t. 7.** to move or go down.

de·scend·ant (dĭ sĕn/dənt), *n.* **1.** one descended from an ancestor. **—adj. 2.** Also, **de·scend/-ent.** descending.

de·scent (dĭ sĕnt/), *n.* **1.** act or fact of descending. **2.** a downward slope. **3.** a passage or stairway leading down. **4.** extraction; lineage. **5.** a sudden attack.

de·scribe (dĭ skrĭb/), *v.t.,* **-scribed, -scribing. 1.** to set forth in written or spoken words. **2.** *Geom.* to draw, as an arc. **—de·scrib/a·ble,** *adj.* **—de·scrib/er,** *n.*

de·scrip·tion (dĭ skrĭp/shən), *n.* **1.** representation by written or spoken words. **2.** sort; kind. **3.** *Geom.* act of describing a figure.

de·scrip·tive (dĭ skrĭp/tĭv), *adj.* having the quality or function of describing. **—des·crip/-tive·ly,** *adv.* **—de·scrip/tive·ness,** *n.*

de·scry (dĭ skrī/), *v.t.,* **-scried, -scrying. 1.** to make out by looking. **2.** to perceive; detect.

des·e·crate (dĕs/ə krāt/), *v.t.,* **-crated, -crating.** to divest of sacred character or office. **—des/e·crat/er, des/e·cra/tor,** *n.* **—des/e·cra/tion,** *n.*

de·sen·si·tize (dē sĕn/sə tīz/), *v.t.,* **-tized, -tizing.** to lessen the sensitiveness of.

des·ert[1] (dĕz/ərt), *n.* **1.** an area so arid as to support little or no vegetation. **2.** any area in which few forms of life can exist. **—adj. 3.** of or like a desert; desolate; barren.

de·sert[2] (dĭ zûrt/), *v.t.* **1.** to abandon or forsake. **2.** (of a soldier or sailor) to leave (the service, etc.) without intention of coming back. **3.** to fail (one). **—v.i. 4.** to forsake one's duty, etc. **—de·sert/er,** *n.*

de·sert[3] (dĭ zûrt/), *n.* **1.** a due reward or punishment. **2.** worthiness of reward or punishment.

de·ser·tion (dĭ zûr/shən), *n.* **1.** act of deserting. **2.** state of being deserted.

de·serve (dĭ zûrv/), *v.t., v.i.,* **-served, -serving.** to merit (reward, punishment, etc.) in return for actions, etc. **—de·serv/er,** *n.*

de·serv·ed·ly (dĭ zûr/vĭd lĭ), *adv.* justly.

de·serv·ing (dĭ zûr/vĭng), *adj.* worthy of reward or praise.

des·ic·cate (dĕs/ə kāt/), *v.t., v.i.,* **-cated, -cating. 1.** to dry thoroughly. **2.** to preserve by depriving of moisture. **—des/ic·ca/tion,** *n.*

de·sid·er·a·tum (dĭ sĭd/ə rā/təm), *n., pl.* **-ta** (-tə). something wanted or needed.

de·sign (dĭ zīn/), *v.t.* **1.** to prepare the plans for (a work to be executed). **2.** to fashion artistically or skillfully. **3.** to contrive; plan. **—v.i. 4.** to make drawings, sketches, or plans. **5.** to fashion a work of art, etc. **—n. 6.** an outline, sketch, or plan. **7.** the pattern or arrangement of an artistic work. **8.** the art of designing. **9.** a plan; project. **10.** a hostile or crafty scheme. **11.** purpose.

des·ig·nate (*v.* dĕz/ĭg nāt/; *adj.* dĕz/ĭg nĭt, -nāt/), *v.,* **-nated, -nating,** *adj.* **—v.t. 1.** to indicate or specify. **2.** to name or style. **3.** to appoint or assign. **—adj. 4.** designated. **—des/ig·na/tor,** *n.*

des·ig·na·tion (dĕz/ĭg nā/shən), *n.* **1.** act of designating. **2.** a name. **3.** nomination; appointment.

de·sign·ed·ly (dĭ zī/nĭd lĭ), *adv.* purposely.

de·sign·er (dĭ zī/nər), *n.* **1.** one who designs (works of art, dresses, machines, etc.). **2.** a schemer.

de·sign·ing (dĭ zī/nĭng), *adj.* **1.** contriving schemes. **2.** showing forethought. **—n. 3.** act or art of making designs. **—de·sign/ing·ly,** *adv.*

de·sir·a·ble (dĭ zīr/ə bəl), *adj.* worthy to be desired; pleasing, excellent, or fine. **—de·sir/a·bil/i·ty, de·sir/a·ble·ness,** *n.* **—de·sir/a·bly,** *adv.*

de·sire (dĭ zīr/), *v.,* **-sired, -siring,** *n.* **—v.t. 1.** to wish or long for; crave. **2.** to ask for; request. **—n. 3.** a longing or craving. **4.** a request. **5.** something desired. **6.** passion or lust.

de·sir·ous (dĭ zīr/əs), *adj.* having desire; desiring.

de·sist (dĭ zĭst/), *v.i.* to cease; stop.

desk (dĕsk), *n.* a table specially adapted for convenience in writing or reading.

Des Moines (də moin/, moinz/), the capital of Iowa, in the central part. 159,819.

des·o·late (*adj.* dĕs/ə lĭt; *v.* dĕs/ə lāt/), *adj., v.,* **-lated, -lating. —adj. 1.** barren or devastated. **2.** without inhabitants; deserted. **3.** left alone; lonely. **4.** dreary; dismal. **—v.t. 5.** to lay waste. **6.** to deprive of inhabitants. **7.** to make disconsolate. **8.** to abandon. **—des/o·lat/er, des/o·la/tor,** *n.* **—des/o·late·ly,** *adv.* **—des/o·late-ness,** *n.*

des·o·la·tion (dĕs/ə lā/shən), *n.* **1.** act of desolating. **2.** state of being desolated. **3.** devastation; ruin. **4.** dreariness. **5.** loneliness. **6.** a desolate place.

De So·to (də sō/tō), **Hernando** or **Fernando,** 1500–42, Spanish explorer in America.

de·spair (dĭ spâr/), *n.* **1.** loss of hope; hopelessness. **2.** that which causes hopelessness. **—v.i. 3.** to lose or be without hope. **—de·spair/ing,** *adj.*

des·patch (dĭs pāch/), *v.t., v.i., n.* dispatch.

des·per·a·do (dĕs/pə rā/dō, -rä/dō), *n., pl.* **-does, -dos.** a desperate or reckless criminal.

des·per·ate (dĕs/pər ĭt), *adj.* **1.** reckless from despair. **2.** characterized by the recklessness of despair. **3.** leaving little or no hope; very serious. **4.** extremely bad. **—des/per·ate·ly,** *adv.* **—des/-per·ate·ness,** *n.*

des·per·a·tion (dĕs/pə rā/shən), *n.* **1.** state of being desperate. **2.** despair.

des·pi·ca·ble (dĕs/pĭ kə bəl; *less often* dĕs pĭk/-ə bəl), *adj.* contemptible. **—des/pi·ca·bly,** *adv.*

de·spise (dĭ spīz/), *v.t.,* **-spised, -spising.** to scorn; hold in contempt. **—de·spis/er,** *n.*

de·spite (dĭ spīt/), *prep., n., v.,* **-spited, -spiting. —prep. 1.** in spite of; notwithstanding. **—n. 2.** contemptuous treatment; insult. **3.** in despite of, notwithstanding. **—v.t. 4.** *Obs.* to spite.

de·spoil (dĭ spoil/), *v.t.* to rob; plunder. **—de·spoil/er, de·spoil/ment, de·spo·li·a·tion** (dĭ spō/lĭ ā/shən), *n.*

de·spond (dĭ spŏnd/), *v.i.* to lose courage or hope.

de·spond·en·cy (dĭ spŏn/dən sĭ), *n.* depression from loss of courage or hope. Also, **de·spond'-ence.** **—de·spond'ent,** *adj.*

des·pot (dĕs'pət, -pŏt), *n.* **1.** an absolute ruler. **2.** a tyrant.

des·pot·ic (dĕs pŏt'ĭk), *adj.* of or of the nature of a despot; tyrannical. **—des·pot'i·cal·ly,** *adv.*

des·pot·ism (dĕs'pə tĭz'əm), *n.* **1.** the exercise of absolute authority. **2.** an absolute or autocratic government. **3.** tyranny.

des·sert (dĭ zûrt'), *n.* a final course including pies, puddings, etc.

des·ti·na·tion (dĕs'tə nā'shən), *n.* **1.** the predetermined end of a journey. **2.** the purpose for which anything is destined; ultimate end.

des·tine (dĕs'tĭn), *v.t.,* **-tined, -tining. 1.** to set apart for a particular use, etc. **2.** to ordain beforehand.

des·ti·ny (dĕs'tə nĭ), *n., pl.* **-nies. 1.** that which is to happen to a particular person or thing. **2.** the predetermined course of events. **3.** the power which determines the course of events.

des·ti·tute (dĕs'tə tūt', -tōōt'), *adj.* **1.** lacking means or resources. **2.** deprived or devoid.

des·ti·tu·tion (dĕs'tə tū'shən, -tōō'-), *n.* **1.** utter poverty. **2.** deprivation; want; absence.

de·stroy (dĭ stroi'), *v.t.* **1.** to ruin; spoil; demolish. **2.** to put an end to. **3.** to kill; slay. **4.** to nullify; invalidate. **—de·stroy'a·ble,** *adj.*

de·stroy·er (dĭ stroi'ər), *n.* **1.** one who or that which destroys. **2.** a torpedo-boat destroyer.

de·struct·i·ble (dĭ strŭk'tə bəl), *adj.* that may be destroyed. **—de·struct'i·bil'i·ty,** *n.*

de·struc·tion (dĭ strŭk'shən), *n.* **1.** act of destroying. **2.** fact or condition of being destroyed. **3.** a cause or means of destroying.

de·struc·tive (dĭ strŭk'tĭv), *adj.* **1.** causing destruction (fol. by *of* or *to*). **2.** tending to overthrow, disprove, or discredit. **—de·struc'tive·ly,** *adv.* **—de·struc'tive·ness,** *n.*

des·ue·tude (dĕs'wə tūd', -tōōd'), *n.* state of being no longer used or practiced.

des·ul·to·ry (dĕs'əl tōr'ĭ), *adj.* **1.** disconnected, unmethodical, or fitful. **2.** random. **—des'ul·to'ri·ly,** *adv.* **—des'ul·to'ri·ness,** *n.*

de·tach (dĭ tăch'), *v.t.* **1.** to unfasten and separate; disunite. **2.** to send away (a regiment, ship, etc.) on a special mission. **—de·tach'a·ble,** *adj.*

de·tached (dĭ tăcht'), *adj.* **1.** standing apart; separate. **2.** not interested.

de·tach·ment (dĭ tăch'mənt), *n.* **1.** act of detaching. **2.** condition of being detached. **3.** aloofness, as from worldly affairs. **4.** freedom from partiality. **5.** sending out of a detached force of troops or naval ships. **6.** something detached, as troops for some special task.

de·tail (*n.* dĭ tāl', dē'tāl; *v.* dĭ tāl'), *n.* **1.** an individual or minute part. **2.** particulars collectively. **3.** a dealing with part by part or item by item. **4.** a narrative or report. **5.** any small section of a larger structure considered as a unit. **6.** *Mil.* **a.** a detailing for a special service. **b.** the party or person so selected. **c.** a particular assignment. **7. in detail,** item by item. **—v.t. 8.** to relate or report in particulars. **9.** *Mil.* to appoint for some particular duty.

de·tain (dĭ tān'), *v.t.* **1.** to keep from proceeding; keep waiting; delay. **2.** to keep under restraint or in custody. **—de·tain'er,** *n.* **—de·tain'ment,** *n.*

de·tect (dĭ tĕkt'), *v.t.* **1.** to catch (a person) in some act. **2.** to find out the action or character of. **3.** to discover the presence, existence, or fact of. **4.** *Radio.* to subject to the action of a detector. **—de·tect'a·ble, de·tect'i·ble,** *adj.*

de·tec·tion (dĭ tĕk'shən), *n.* **1.** act of detecting. **2.** fact of being detected. **3.** discovery. **4.** *Radio.* rectification of alternating currents in a radio receiver.

de·tec·tive (dĭ tĕk'tĭv), *n.* **1.** a member of the police force whose function it is to obtain information and evidence, as of offenses against the law. **—adj. 2.** pertaining to detection or detectives.

de·tec·tor (dĭ tĕk'tər), *n.* **1.** one that detects. **2.** *Radio.* **a.** a device for detecting electric oscillations or waves. **b.** a device, as a vacuum tube, which rectifies the alternating currents in a receiver.

de·ten·tion (dĭ tĕn'shən), *n.* **1.** act of detaining. **2.** state of being detained. **3.** confinement.

de·ter (dĭ tûr'), *v.t.,* **-terred, -terring.** to discourage or restrain (one) from acting or proceeding through fear, doubt, etc. **—de·ter'ment,** *n.*

de·ter·gent (dĭ tûr'jənt), *adj.* **1.** cleansing. **—n. 2.** a detergent substance or agent.

de·te·ri·o·rate (dĭ tĭr'ĭ ə rāt'), *v.t., v.i.,* **-rated, -rating.** to make or become worse. **—de·te'ri·o·ra'tion,** *n.* **—de·te'ri·o·ra'tive,** *adj.*

de·ter·mi·na·ble (dĭ tûr'mə nə bəl), *adj.* capable of being determined.

de·ter·mi·nant (dĭ tûr'mə nənt), *n.* a determining agent or factor.

de·ter·mi·nate (dĭ tûr'mə nĭt), *adj.* **1.** having defined limits; definite. **2.** settled. **3.** conclusive; final. **4.** resolute. **5.** *Bot.* (of an inflorescence) having the primary and each secondary axis ending in a flower or bud. **—de·ter'mi·nate·ly,** *adv.* **—de·ter'mi·nate·ness,** *n.*

de·ter·mi·na·tion (dĭ tûr'mə nā'shən), *n.* **1.** act of coming to a decision. **2.** ascertainment. **3.** a solution. **4.** the settlement of a dispute, etc., by authoritative decision. **5.** the decision arrived at. **6.** firmness of purpose.

de·ter·mi·na·tive (dĭ tûr'mə nā'tĭv), *adj.* **1.** determining. **—n. 2.** something that determines.

de·ter·mine (dĭ tûr'mĭn), *v.,* **-mined, -mining. —v.t. 1.** to settle (a dispute, etc.) by an authoritative decision. **2.** to conclude or ascertain. **3.** *Geom.* to fix the position of. **4.** to decide causally. **5.** to give direction or tendency to; impel. **6.** to decide upon. **—v.i. 7.** to decide. **—de·ter'min·er,** *n.*

de·ter·mined (dĭ tûr'mĭnd), *adj.* resolute; firm. **—de·ter'mined·ly,** *adv.*

de·ter·min·ism (dĭ tûr'mə nĭz'əm), *n.* the doctrine that outer events and human choices are the results of antecedent conditions, physical or psychological. **—de·ter'min·ist,** *n., adj.*

de·ter·rent (dĭ tûr'ənt, -tĕr'-), *adj.* **1.** deterring. **—n. 2.** a thing that deters. **—de·ter'rence,** *n.*

de·test (dĭ tĕst'), *v.t.* to hate or dislike intensely. **—de·test'a·ble,** *adj.* **—de·test'a·bly,** *adv.* **—de·test'er,** *n.*

de·tes·ta·tion (dē'tĕs tā'shən), *n.* **1.** abhorrence; hatred. **2.** a person or thing detested.

de·throne (dē thrōn'), *v.t.,* **-throned, -throning.** to remove from the throne. **—de·throne'-ment,** *n.*

det·o·nate (dĕt'ə nāt', dē'tə-), *v.i., v.t.,* **-nated, -nating.** to explode, esp. with suddenness or violence. **—det'o·na'tion,** *n.* **—det'o·na'tor,** *n.*

de·tour (dē'tŏŏr, dĭ tŏŏr'), *n.* **1.** a roundabout course, esp. one used temporarily instead of the main route. **—v.i. 2.** to make a detour. **—v.t. 3.** to cause to make a detour.

de·tract (dĭ trăkt'), *v.t.* **1.** to take away. **2.** to divert. **—v.i. 3.** to take away a part. **—de·trac'-tion,** *n.* **—de·trac'tive,** *adj.* **—de·trac'tor,** *n.*

det·ri·ment (dĕt'rə mənt), *n.* **1.** loss, damage, or injury. **2.** a cause of loss or damage.

det·ri·men·tal (dĕt'rĭ mĕn'təl), *adj.* injurious; prejudicial. **—det'ri·men'tal·ly,** *adv.*

de·tri·tus (dĭ trī'təs), *n.* *Geol.* particles of rock or other material worn or broken away from a mass, as by the action of water.

De·troit (dĭ troit'), *n.* a city in SE Michigan, on the Detroit river. 1,623,452.

deuce¹ (dūs, dōōs), *n.* **1.** *Cards, Dice.* a card, or the side of a die, having two pips. **2.** *Tennis.* a score in which each side has three points (the score 40) in a game, or five games in a set.

deuce² (dūs, dōōs), *n.* *Colloq.* bad luck; devil.

deu·ced (dū'sĭd, dōō'-; dūst, dōōst), *adj.* *Brit. Colloq.* excessive. **—deu'ced·ly,** *adv.*

Deut., Deuteronomy.

deu·te·ri·um (dū tĭr'ĭ əm, dōō-), *n.* *Chem.* an isotope of hydrogen, having twice the mass of ordinary hydrogen. *Symbol:* D; *at. no.:* 1; *at. wt.:* 2.01.

Deu·ter·on·o·my (dū'tə rŏn'ə mĭ, dōō'-), *n.* *Bible.* the fifth book of the Pentateuch.

De Va·le·ra (dĕv'ə lâr'ə, -lĭr'ə), **Eamon,** born 1882, Irish statesman.

de·val·u·ate (dē văl'yŏŏ āt'), *v.t.,* **-ated, -ating.** to reduce the value of. **—de·val'u·a'tion,** *n.*

dev·as·tate (dĕv'ə stāt'), *v.t.,* **-tated, -tating.** to lay waste; render desolate. **—dev'as·tat'ing·ly,** *adv.* **—dev'as·ta'tion,** *n.* **—dev'as·ta'tor,** *n.*

de·vel·op (dĭ vĕl'əp), *v.t.* **1.** to bring out the capabilities or possibilities of. **2.** to disclose; reveal. **3.** to bring into being or activity. **4.** *Photog.* **a.** to render visible (the latent image) in the exposed sensitized film. **b.** to treat (a photographic plate, etc.) with chemical agents so as to bring out the latent image. **—v.i. 5.** to grow into a more mature or advanced state. **6.** to come gradually into existence or operation. **7.** to come out or be disclosed. —**de·vel'op·a·ble,** adj.

de·vel·op·er (dĭ vĕl'əp ər), n. **1.** one that develops. **2.** Photog. the solution used to develop a photographic film or plate.

de·vel·op·ment (dĭ vĕl'əp mənt), n. **1.** act of developing. **2.** a developed state, form, or product. —**de·vel'op·men'tal,** adj.

de·vi·ate (dē'vĭ āt'), v.i., v.t., **-ated, -ating.** to turn aside (from the way or course); digress. —**de'vi·a'tion,** n.

de·vice (dĭ vīs'), n. **1.** an invention or contrivance. **2.** a plan. **3.** a crafty scheme. **4.** an artistic figure or design used as a heraldic bearing, trademark, or the like. **5.** a motto. **6.** (pl.) will; desire.

dev·il (dĕv'əl), n., v., **-iled, -iling** or (esp. Brit.) **-illed, -illing.** —n. **1.** Theol. **a.** (sometimes cap.) the supreme spirit of evil; Satan. **b.** a subordinate evil spirit at enmity with God. **2.** an atrociously wicked person. **3.** a person of great cleverness or recklessness. **4.** the errand boy or apprentice in a printing office. **5.** a fellow. —v.t. **6.** Colloq. to harass, torment, or plague. **7.** Cookery. to prepare with hot or savory seasoning.

dev·il·fish (dĕv'əl fĭsh'), n., pl. **-fishes** (esp. collectively) **-fish. 1.** any of various marine animals, as the manta rays. **2.** any of various large cephalopods, as the octopus.

Devilfish (def. 1)
(Total length 20 ft.)

dev·il·ish (dĕv'əl ĭsh, dĕv'-lĭsh), adj. **1.** of, like, or befitting a devil. **2.** Colloq. very great. —adv. **3.** Colloq. extremely. —**dev'il·ish·ly,** adv. —**dev'il·ish·ness,** n.

dev·il·ment (dĕv'əl mənt), n. devilish conduct.

dev·il·try (dĕv'əl trĭ), n., pl. **-tries. 1.** wicked or reckless mischief. **2.** extreme wickedness.

de·vi·ous (dē'vĭ əs), adj. **1.** departing from the direct way; circuitous. **2.** straying. —**de'vi·ous·ly,** adv. —**de'vi·ous·ness,** n.

de·vise (dĭ vīz'), v., **-vised, -vising,** n. —v.t. **1.** to plan; contrive; invent. **2.** Law. to assign or transmit (property, property) specif. real property) by will. —v.i. **3.** to plan; contrive. —n. **4.** Law. **a.** act of disposing of property by will. **b.** a will or clause in a will disposing of property. **c.** the property disposed of. —**de·vis'a·ble,** adj. —**de·vis'er,** n.

de·vi·tal·ize (dē vī'tə līz'), v.t., **-ized, -izing.** to deprive of vitality. —**de·vi'tal·i·za'tion,** n.

de·void (dĭ void'), adj. destitute (fol. by of).

de·volve (dĭ vŏlv'), v., **-volved, -volving.** —v.t. **1.** to transfer or delegate (a duty, etc.) to or upon another. —v.i. **2.** to fall as a duty or responsibility on a person. —**dev·o·lu·tion** (dĕv'ə lōō'shən), **de·volve'ment,** n.

de·vote (dĭ vōt'), v.t., **-voted, -voting. 1.** to appropriate to a particular pursuit, cause, person, etc. **2.** to appropriate by or as by a vow.

de·vot·ed (dĭ vō'tĭd), adj. **1.** zealous or ardent in attachment. **2.** dedicated; consecrated. —**de·vot'ed·ly,** adv. —**de·vot'ed·ness,** n.

dev·o·tee (dĕv'ə tē'), n. one ardently devoted to anything, esp. to religion.

de·vo·tion (dĭ vō'shən), n. **1.** consecration. **2.** earnest attachment or dedication to a cause, person, etc. **3.** Theol. the ready will to perform what belongs to the service of God. **4.** (often pl.) Eccles. religious observance or worship. —**de·vo'tion·al,** adj. —**de·vo'tion·al·ly,** adv.

de·vour (dĭ vour'), v.t. **1.** to eat up ravenously. **2.** to consume destructively, recklessly, or wantonly. **3.** to engulf. **4.** to take in greedily with the intellect.

de·vout (dĭ vout'), adj. **1.** pious; religious. **2.** expressing devotion or piety. **3.** earnest or sincere. —**de·vout'ly,** adv. —**de·vout'ness,** n.

dew (dū, dōō), n. **1.** moisture condensed from the atmosphere, esp. at night, and deposited in the form of small drops upon any cool surface. **2.** something likened to dew. **3.** moisture in small drops, as tears, perspiration, etc. —v.t. **4.** to wet with dew. —**dew'less,** adj.

dew·ber·ry (dū'bĕr'ĭ, dōō'-), n., pl. **-ries. 1.** (in North America) the fruit of several species of running, trailing blackberries. **2.** a plant bearing this fruit.

dew·claw (dū'klô', dōō'-), n. a functionless inner claw or digit in the foot of some dogs.

dew·drop (dū'drŏp', dōō'-), n. a drop of dew.

Dew·ey (dū'ĭ, dōō'ĭ), n. **1. George,** 1837–1917, U.S. admiral: defeated Spanish fleet in Manila Bay in the Spanish-American War. **2. John,** 1859–1952, U.S. philosopher and educator. **3. Thomas Edmund,** born 1902, U.S. lawyer and political leader.

dew·lap (dū'lăp', dōō'-), n. the pendulous fold of skin under the throat of cattle.

dew point, the temperature of the air at which dew begins to be deposited.

dew·y (dū'ĭ, dōō'ĭ), adj., **dewier, dewiest. 1.** moist with dew. **2.** having the quality of dew.

dex·ter·i·ty (dĕks tĕr'ə tĭ), n. **1.** skill in using the hands or body. **2.** mental adroitness; cleverness.

dex·ter·ous (dĕks'trəs, -tər əs), adj. **1.** skillful in the use of the hands or body. **2.** having mental adroitness; clever. **3.** done with dexterity. —**dex'ter·ous·ly,** adv. —**dex'ter·ous·ness,** n.

dex·trin (dĕks'trĭn), n. Chem. a soluble gummy substance formed from starch: used as a substitute for gum arabic, as a mucilage, etc. Also, **dex·trine** (dĕks'trĭn, -trēn).

dex·trose (dĕks'trōs), n. Chem. a sugar, commercially obtainable from starch by acid hydrolysis.

dex·trous (dĕks'trəs), adj. dexterous. —**dex'trous·ly,** adv. —**dex'trous·ness,** n.

di·a·be·tes (dī'ə bē'tĭs, -tēz), n. Pathol. **1.** a disease in which sugar appears abnormally in the urine. **2.** a disease in which there is a persistent abnormal amount of urine. —**di·a·bet·ic** (dī'ə bĕt'ĭk, -bē'tĭk), adj., n.

di·a·bol·ic (dī'ə bŏl'ĭk), adj. **1.** fiendish; outrageously wicked. **2.** pertaining to or actuated by the devil. Also, **di'a·bol'i·cal** (esp. for def. 1). —**di'a·bol'i·cal·ly,** adv.

di·a·co·nate (dī ăk'ə nĭt, -nāt'), n. **1.** the office or dignity of a deacon. **2.** a body of deacons.

di·a·crit·ic (dī'ə krĭt'ĭk), n. **1.** a diacritical mark. —adj. **2.** diacritical.

di·a·crit·i·cal (dī'ə krĭt'ə kəl), adj. **1.** distinctive. **2.** capable of distinguishing.

diacritical mark, a mark attached to a letter to distinguish it from another of similar form, to give it a particular phonetic value, etc.

di·a·dem (dī'ə dĕm'), n. **1.** a crown. **2.** a cloth headband, sometimes jeweled, formerly worn by Oriental kings. **3.** royal dignity or authority.

di·aer·e·sis (dī ĕr'ə sĭs), n., pl. **-ses** (-sēz'). dieresis.

di·ag·nose (dī'əg nōs', -nōz'), v.t., v.i., **-nosed, -nosing.** to make a diagnosis of (a disease, etc.).

di·ag·no·sis (dī'əg nō'sĭs), n., pl. **-ses** (-sēz). **1.** Med. **a.** the process of determining by examination the nature of a diseased condition. **b.** the decision reached. **2.** Biol. a description which classifies precisely. **3.** any examination or analysis. —**di·ag·nos·tic** (dī'əg nŏs'tĭk), adj. —**di·ag·nos·ti·cian** (dī'əg nŏs tĭsh'ən), n.

di·ag·o·nal (dī ăg'ə nəl), adj. **1.** Math. connecting, as a straight line, two nonadjacent angles of a quadrilateral, polygon, or polyhedron. **2.** having an oblique direction. **3.** having oblique lines, ridges, etc. —n. **4.** a diagonal line or plane. **5.** a diagonal row, part, etc. **6.** diagonal cloth. —**di·ag'o·nal·ly,** adv.

di·a·gram (dī'ə grăm'), n., v., **-gramed, -graming** or (esp. Brit.) **-grammed, -gramming.** —n. **1.** a figure, or set of lines, marks, etc., to give the outlines of an object, show a process, etc. **2.** a chart, plan, or scheme. —v.t. **3.** to represent by a diagram; make a diagram of. —**di·a·gram·mat·ic** (dī'ə grə măt'ĭk), **di'a·gram·mat'i·cal,** adj. —**di'a·gram·mat'i·cal·ly,** adv.

di·al (dī'əl, dīl), n., v., **dialed, dialing** or (esp. Brit.) **dialled, dialling.** —n. **1.** a face upon which time is indicated by pointers or shadows. **2.** a disk with figures, as for the indication of pressure, etc., as by a pointer. **3.** a plate or disk with letters and numbers, used in tuning a radio or making telephone connections. —v.t. **4.** to measure with a dial. **5.** to indicate on or call by a telephone dial. —v.i. **6.** to use a telephone dial.

dial., 1. dialect. **2.** dialectal.

di·a·lect (dī'ə lĕkt'), n. **1.** the language of a particular district or class. **2.** a special variety or branch of a language. —**di'a·lec'tal,** adj. —**di'a·lec'tal·ly,** adv.

di·a·lec·tic (dī'ə lĕk'tĭk), adj. **1.** of, pertaining to, or of the nature of logical argumentation. **2.** of a dialect. —n. **3.** the art or practice of logical argumentation. **4.** (often pl.) logic.

di·a·lec·ti·cal (dī/ə lĕk/tə kəl), *adj.* **1.** dialectic. **2.** of a dialect. —**di/a·lec/ti·cal·ly,** *adv.*

di·a·logue (dī/ə lôg/, -lŏg/), *n., v.,* **-logued, -loguing.** —*n.* **1.** conversation between two or more persons. **2.** a literary work in the form of a conversation. —*v.i.* **3.** to converse. Also, **di/a·log/.**

diam., diameter.

di·am·e·ter (dī ăm/ə tər), *n.* **1.** *Geom.* a straight line passing through the center of a circle. **2.** the length of such a line; thickness.

di·a·met·ri·cal (dī/ə mĕt/rə kəl), *adj.* **1.** pertaining to or along a diameter. **2.** direct; complete. Also, **di/a·met/ric.** —**di/a·met/ri·cal·ly,** *adv.*

dia·mond (dī/mənd, dī/ə-), *n.* **1.** a pure or nearly pure form of carbon, crystallized in the isometric system, of extreme hardness and, when used as a precious stone, of great brilliancy. **2.** *Geom.* an equilateral quadrilateral; a rhombus. **3.** *Cards.* **a.** a red lozenge-shaped figure on a playing card. **b.** a card of the suit bearing such figures. **c.** (*pl.*) the suit. **4.** *Baseball.* the space enclosed by the home plate and three bases. —*adj.* **5.** made of or with a diamond or diamonds. —*v.t.* **6.** to adorn with diamonds.

dia·mond·back (dī/mənd băk/, dī/ə-), *n.* **1.** any rattlesnake with diamond-shaped marking. **2.** Also, **diamondback terrapin.** an edible turtle living in salt-water marshes of the eastern and southern U.S. and having diamond-shaped markings on the back.

Di·an·a (dī ăn/ə), *n.* an ancient Italian deity, goddess of the moon and of hunting, and protectress of women, identified by the Romans with the Greek Artemis.

di·a·pa·son (dī/ə pā/zən, -sən), *n. Music.* **1.** a melody. **2.** the compass of a voice or instrument. **3.** either of two principal timbres or stops of a pipe organ: **a.** the **open diapason,** giving full, majestic tones. **b.** the **stopped diapason,** giving powerful flutelike tones.

di·a·per (dī/ə pər), *n.* **1.** a piece of cloth which forms part of a baby's underclothing. —*v.t.* **2.** to put a diaper on (a baby).

di·aph·a·nous (dī ăf/ə nəs), *adj.* transparent.

di·a·phragm (dī/ə frăm/), *n.* **1.** *Anat.* a muscular, membranous or ligamentous wall, as the partition separating the thoracic from the abdominal cavity in mammals. **2.** a vibrating membrane or disk, as in a telephone. **3.** an optical device with an adjustable hole to regulate light entering a camera, etc. —*v.t.* **4.** to furnish with a diaphragm. —**di·a·phrag·mat·ic** (dī/ə frăg-măt/ĭk), *adj.*

di·ar·rhe·a (dī/ə rē/ə), *n.* an intestinal disorder characterized by morbid frequency and fluidity of fecal evacuations. Also, **di/ar·rhoe/a.**

di·a·ry (dī/ə rĭ), *n., pl.* **-ries. 1.** a daily record, esp. of the writer's own experiences. **2.** a book for such a record. —**di·a·rist** (dī/ə rĭst), *n.*

di·a·stase (dī/ə stās/), *n. Biochem.* an enzyme present in germinated barley, potatoes, etc., which converts starch into dextrin and maltose.

di·as·to·le (dī ăs/tə lē/), *n. Physiol., etc.* the normal rhythmical dilatation of the heart. —**di·as·tol·ic** (dī/ə stŏl/ĭk), *adj.*

di·as·tro·phism (dī ăs/trə fĭz/əm), *n. Geol.* **1.** the action of the forces which cause the earth's crust to be deformed, producing continents, mountains, etc. **2.** any such deformation. —**di·a·stroph·ic** (dī/ə strŏf/ĭk), *adj.*

di·a·ther·my (dī/ə thûr/mĭ), *n. Med.* the production of heat in body tissues by high currents for therapeutic purposes. —**di/a·ther/mic,** *adj.*

di·a·ton·ic (dī/ə tŏn/ĭk), *adj. Music.* involving only the tones, intervals, or harmonies of a major or minor scale without chromatic alteration.

di·a·tribe (dī/ə trīb/), *n.* a bitter and violent denunciation.

Di·az (dē/äs), *n.* **Porfirio,** 1830–1915, president of Mexico, 1877–80, 1884–1911.

di·ba·sic (dī bā/sĭk), *adj. Chem.* **1.** containing two hydrogen atoms that can be replaced or ionized. **2.** having two univalent, basic atoms.

dib·ble (dĭb/əl), *n., v.,* **-bled, -bling.** —*n.* **1.** an implement for making holes in the ground for planting seeds, bulbs, etc. —*v.t.* **2.** to make a hole in (the ground) with a dibble. —**dib/bler,** *n.*

dice (dīs), *n. pl., sing.* **die,** *v.,* **diced, dicing.** —*n.* **1.** small cubes whose sides are marked with different numbers of spots, used esp. in some gambling games. **2.** the game played. **3.** any small cubes. —*v.t.* **4.** to cut into small cubes. —*v.i.* **5.** to play at dice. —**dic/er,** *n.*

di·chot·o·my (dī kŏt/ə mĭ), *n., pl.* **-mies. 1.** division into two parts or halves. **2.** *Logic.* classification by division into two sections. —**di·chot/o·mous,** *adj.*

di·chro·mat·ic (dī/krō măt/ĭk), *adj.* **1.** having two colors. **2.** *Zool.* exhibiting two color phases within a species not due to age or season.

dick (dĭk), *n. U.S. Slang.* a detective.

Dick·ens (dĭk/ĭnz), *n.* **Charles** (**John Huffam**), 1812–70, British novelist.

dick·ens (dĭk/ĭnz), *n., interj.* devil.

dick·er (dĭk/ər), *Chiefly U.S.* —*v.i., v.t.* **1.** to trade by barter; haggle. —*n.* **2.** a barter.

dick·ey (dĭk/ĭ), *n., pl.* **-eys.** a waist without sides or sleeves, to be worn under a dress or suit. Also, **dick/y, dick/ie.**

Dick·in·son (dĭk/ĭn sən), *n.* **Emily,** 1830–86, U.S. poet.

di·cot·y·le·don (dī kŏt/ə lē/dən, dī/kŏt-), *n.* a plant with two cotyledons. —**di·cot/y·le/don·ous,** *adj.*

dict., **1.** dictation. **2.** dictionary.

dic·ta·phone (dĭk/tə fōn/), *n.* **1.** a phonographic instrument that records and reproduces dictation. **2.** (*cap.*) a trademark for this device.

dic·tate (*v.* dĭk/tāt, dĭk tāt/; *n.* dĭk/tāt), *v.,* **-tated, -tating,** *n.* —*v.t., v.i.* **1.** to say (something) to be taken down in writing or otherwise. **2.** to command with authority. —*n.* **3.** a command.

dic·ta·tion (dĭk tā/shən), *n.* **1.** act of dictating. **2.** words dictated. **3.** something commanded.

dic·ta·tor (dĭk/tā tər, dĭk tā/tər), *n.* **1.** a person exercising absolute power, esp. in government. **2.** one who dictates. —**dic/ta·tor·ship/,** *n.*

dic·ta·to·ri·al (dĭk/tə tōr/ĭ əl), *adj.* **1.** of a dictator. **2.** absolute; unlimited. **3.** imperious; overbearing. —**dic/ta·to/ri·al·ly,** *adv.* —**dic/·ta·to/ri·al·ness,** *n.*

dic·tion (dĭk/shən), *n.* **1.** style of speaking or writing as dependent upon choice of words. **2.** distinctness of speech; enunciation.

dic·tion·ar·y (dĭk/shə nĕr/ĭ), *n., pl.* **-aries. 1.** a book containing a selection of the words of a language, usually arranged alphabetically, with information on their meaning, pronunciation, spelling, etc. **2.** a book giving information on a particular subject, under alphabetically arranged headings.

dic·tum (dĭk/təm), *n., pl.* **-ta** (-tə), **-tums. 1.** an authoritative pronouncement. **2.** a maxim.

di·dac·tic (dī dăk/tĭk), *adj.* **1.** instructive. **2.** inclined to lecture others too much. —**di·dac/·ti·cal·ly,** *adv.* —**di·dac/ti·cism,** *n.*

did·dle (dĭd/əl), *v.i.,* **-dled, -dling.** *Colloq.* to waste time. —**did/dler,** *n.*

did·n't (dĭd/nt), contraction of *did not.*

Di·do (dī/dō), *n.* the legendary queen of Carthage who killed herself when abandoned by Aeneas.

di·do (dī/dō), *n., pl.* **-dos, -does.** (*often pl.*) *U.S. Colloq.* a prank; an antic.

die[1] (dī), *v.i.,* **died, dying. 1.** to cease to live or exist. **2.** to lose force, etc. **3.** to fade (fol. by *away, down, out,* etc.). **4.** to suffer as if dying. **5.** to pine with desire, love, etc.

die[2] (dī), *n., pl.* **dies** for 1, 2; **dice** for 3; *v.,* **died, dieing.** —*n.* **1.** *Mach.* any of various devices for cutting or forming material, as in a press. **2.** an engraved stamp for impressing a design, etc. **3.** a small cube whose sides have different numbers of spots, used in certain games. —*v.t.* **4.** to impress, shape, or cut with a die.

die-hard (dī/härd/), *n.* **1.** one who resists vigorously to the last, esp. a conservative in politics. —*adj.* **2.** resisting vigorously to the last.

di·e·lec·tric (dī/ĭ lĕk/trĭk), *Elect.* —*adj.* **1.** nonconducting. —*n.* **2.** a dielectric substance. —**di/e·lec/tri·cal·ly,** *adv.*

di·er·e·sis (dī ĕr/ə sĭs), *n., pl.* **-ses** (-sēz/). a sign (··) placed over the second of two adjacent vowels to indicate separate pronunciation.

Die·sel engine (dē/zəl), a type of internal-combustion engine in which fuel oil is ignited in a cylinder into which air has been compressed to about 1000°F. Also, **Diesel motor.**

die·sink·er (dī/sĭngk/ər), *n.* an engraver of dies for stamping or embossing. —**die/sink/ing,** *n.*

Di·es I·rae (dī/ēz ī/rē), *Latin.* a famous medieval Latin hymn on the Day of Judgment.

di·et[1] (dī/ət), *n., v.,* **-eted, -eting.** —*n.* **1.** food considered in relation to its effects. **2.** a particular selection of food, esp. one to improve health. **3.** manner of living as regards food. —*v.t.* **4.** to regulate the food of. —*v.i.* **5.** to adhere to a particular diet. —**di′et·er,** *n.* —**di·e·tet·ic** (dī′ə tĕt′ĭk), *adj.*

di·et² (dī′ət), *n.* a formal assembly for discussing or acting upon public or state affairs.

di·e·tar·y (dī′ə tĕr′ĭ), *adj.*, *n.*, *pl.* **-taries.** —*adj.* **1.** pertaining to diet. —*n.* **2.** a diet.

di·e·tet·ics (dī′ə tĕt′ĭks), *n.* the art or science concerned with the regulation of diet.

di·e·ti·tian (dī′ə tĭsh′ən), *n.* one versed in regulating diets or planning meals. Also, **di′e·ti′-cian.**

dif·fer (dĭf′ər), *v.i.* **1.** to be unlike in nature (fol. by *from*). **2.** to disagree (fol. by *with* or *from*).

dif·fer·ence (dĭf′ər əns, dĭf′rəns), *n.*, *v.*, **-enced, -encing.** —*n.* **1.** state or relation of being different. **2.** an instance or a degree of unlikeness. **3.** act of distinguishing. **4.** a disagreement; quarrel. **5.** the amount by which one quantity is greater or less than another. —*v.t.* **6.** to make different.

dif·fer·ent (dĭf′ər ənt, dĭf′rənt), *adj.* **1.** having unlike qualities (fol. by *from*, often *to*, sometimes *than*; use of *to* and *than* is considered improper by many; but the use of *to* is especially common in England). **2.** not identical; various. **3.** unusual. —**dif′fer·ent·ly,** *adv.*

dif·fer·en·tial (dĭf′ə rĕn′shəl), *adj.* **1.** of or pertaining to difference. **2.** distinctive. **3.** exhibiting or depending upon a difference. **4.** *Physics, Mach., etc.* pertaining to or involving the difference of two or more motions, forces, etc. —*n.* **5.** *Mach.* a set of gears designed to permit two or more shafts to revolve at different speeds, as a set in an automobile permitting rear wheels to revolve at different speeds when the car is turning. **6.** *Com.* **a.** the difference involved in a special lower rate. **b.** a special lower rate. —**dif′fer·en′tial·ly,** *adv.*

dif·fer·en·ti·ate (dĭf′ə rĕn′shĭ āt′), *v.*, **-ated, -ating.** —*v.t.* **1.** to distinguish; alter; change. **2.** to perceive the difference in or between. —*v.i.* **3.** to become unlike. **4.** to make a distinction. —**dif′fer·en′ti·a′tion,** *n.* —**dif′fer·en′ti·a′tor,** *n.*

dif·fi·cult (dĭf′ə kŭlt′, -kəlt), *adj.* **1.** hard to do; not easy. **2.** hard to understand or solve. **3.** hard to deal with. **4.** hard to satisfy. **5.** hard to persuade. —**dif′fi·cult′ly,** *adv.*

dif·fi·cul·ty (dĭf′ə kŭl′tĭ, -kəl tĭ), *n.*, *pl.* **-ties.** **1.** fact or condition of being difficult. **2.** trouble or embarrassment, esp. financial. **3.** a cause of trouble or embarrassment. **4.** reluctance. **5.** objection. **6.** that which is hard to do, understand, or surmount.

dif·fi·dent (dĭf′ə dənt), *adj.* lacking confidence in oneself; timid; shy. —**dif′fi·dence,** *n.* —**dif′-fi·dent·ly,** *adv.*

dif·fract (dĭ frăkt′), *v.t.* to break up by diffraction.

dif·frac·tion (dĭ frăk′shən), *n.* *Physics.* **1.** a modification that light undergoes when passing by the edge of an opaque body or through small apertures, resulting in the formation of a series of prismatic colors, etc. **2.** an analogous modification produced upon sound waves. —**dif·frac′-tive,** *adj.*

dif·fuse (*v.* dĭ fūz′; *adj.* dĭ fūs′), *v.*, **-fused, -fusing,** *adj.* —*v.t.*, *v.i.* **1.** to pour out and spread, as a fluid. **2.** to spread or scatter widely. **3.** *Physics.* to spread or intermingle by diffusion. —*adj.* **4.** discursive; wordy. **5.** widely spread or scattered. —**dif·fuse′ly** (dĭ fūs′lĭ), *adv.* —**dif·fuse′ness,** *n.* —**dif·fus′er, dif·fu·sor** (dĭ fū′zər), *n.*

dif·fu·sion (dĭ fū′zhən), *n.* **1.** act of diffusing. **2.** state of being diffused. **3.** wordiness. **4.** *Physics.* **a.** the gradual permeation of any region by a fluid, owing to the thermal agitation of its particles or molecules. **b.** the process of being scattered.

dig (dĭg), *v.*, **dug** or **digged, digging,** *n.* —*v.i.* **1.** to break up, turn over, or remove earth, etc., as with a spade. **2.** to make one's way by digging. **3.** *Colloq.* to work hard. —*v.t.* **4.** to break up or penetrate (the ground) with a spade, etc. **5.** to make (a hole, etc.) by removing material. **6.** to obtain or remove by digging. **7.** to find by effort. **8.** to force (fol. by *into*). —*n.* *Colloq.* **9.** a poke. **10.** a cutting, sarcastic remark.

di·gest (*v.* dĭ jĕst′, dī-; *n.* dī′jĕst), *v.t.* **1.** to prepare (food) in the alimentary canal for assimilation into the system. **2.** to assimilate mentally.

---

3. to arrange methodically in the mind. **4.** to arrange in a system; classify. **5.** *Chem.* to keep (a substance) in contact with a liquid to soften or to disintegrate it. —*v.i.* **6.** to digest food. **7.** to undergo digestion, as food. —*n.* **8.** a collection or summary. **9.** a systematic abstract of some body of law. —**di·gest′er,** *n.* —**di·gest′i·ble,** *adj.* —**di·gest′i·bil′i·ty,** *n.*

di·ges·tion (dĭ jĕs′chən, dī-), *n.* **1.** the act or power of digesting food. **2.** the resulting state.

di·ges·tive (dĭ jĕs′tĭv, dī-), *adj.* **1.** serving for or pertaining to digestion. **2.** promoting digestion.

dig·ger (dĭg′ər), *n.* **1.** a person or an animal that digs. **2.** a tool, part of a machine, etc., for digging.

dig·gings (dĭg′ĭngz *for 1, 2;* dĭg′ənz *for 3*), *n.pl.* **1.** a place where digging is carried on. **2.** that which is dug out. **3.** *Chiefly Brit. Colloq.* lodgings.

dight (dīt), *v.t.*, **dight** or **dighted, dighting.** *Archaic.* **1.** to prepare. **2.** to adorn.

dig·it (dĭj′ĭt), *n.* **1.** a finger or toe. **2.** any of the Arabic figures 0, 1, . . . 9. —**dig′it·al,** *adj.*

dig·i·tal·is (dĭj′ə tăl′ĭs, -tā′lĭs), *n.* **1.** any plant of the figwort family, esp. the common foxglove. **2.** the dried leaves of the foxglove, used as a heart stimulant.

dig·i·tate (dĭj′ə tāt′), *adj.* having digits or digitlike parts.

dig·ni·fied (dĭg′nə fīd′), *adj.* marked by dignity; noble; stately. —**dig′ni·fied′ly,** *adv.*

dig·ni·fy (dĭg′nə fī′), *v.t.*, **-fied, -fying.** to confer honor or dignity upon; honor; ennoble.

dig·ni·tar·y (dĭg′nə tĕr′ĭ), *n.*, *pl.* **-taries.** one who holds a high rank, esp. in the church.

dig·ni·ty (dĭg′nə tĭ), *n.*, *pl.* **-ties.** **1.** nobility of manner or style. **2.** worthiness. **3.** honorable place. **4.** degree of excellence. **5.** rank. **6.** a high office or title. **7.** the person holding it.

di·gress (dĭ grĕs′, dī-), *v.i.* to wander away from the main purpose, argument, etc.

di·gres·sion (dĭ grĕsh′ən, dī-), *n.* **1.** act of digressing. **2.** a portion of a discourse, etc., that digresses.

di·gres·sive (dĭ grĕs′ĭv, dī-), *adj.* tending to digress. —**di·gres′sive·ly,** *adv.* —**di·gres′-sive·ness,** *n.*

di·he·dral (dī hē′drəl), *Math.* —*adj.* **1.** having, or formed by, two planes. —*n.* **2.** Also, **dihedral angle.** the figure made by two planes which intersect.

dike (dīk), *n.*, *v.*, **diked, diking.** —*n.* **1.** an embankment for restraining the waters of the sea or a river. **2.** a ditch. **3.** a ridge of earth as thrown up in excavating. **4.** a causeway. **5.** *Geol.* a long, narrow, mass of igneous or eruptive rock intruded into a fissure in older rock. —*v.t.* **6.** to furnish or drain with a dike. Also, **dyke.**

di·lap·i·dat·ed (dĭ lăp′ə dā′tĭd), *adj.* reduced to or fallen into ruin or decay.

di·lap·i·da·tion (dĭ lăp′ə dā′shən), *n.* dilapidated condition; ruin.

dil·a·ta·tion (dĭl′ə tā′shən, dī′lə-), *n.* **1.** act of dilating. **2.** state of being dilated. **3.** a dilated part.

di·late (dī lāt′, dī-), *v.*, **-lated, -lating.** —*v.t.* **1.** to make wider or larger. **2.** to enlarge upon. —*v.i.* **3.** to expand. **4.** to speak at length. —**di·lat′a·ble,** *adj.* —**di·la′tion,** *n.* —**di·la′tor,** *n.*

dil·a·to·ry (dĭl′ə tōr′ĭ), *adj.* **1.** inclined to delay; slow; tardy. **2.** intended to bring about delay. —**dil′a·to′ri·ly,** *adv.* —**dil′a·to′ri·ness,** *n.*

di·lem·ma (dĭ lĕm′ə), *n.* **1.** a situation requiring a choice between equally undesirable alternatives. **2.** *Logic.* a form of argument in which alternatives (**the horns of the dilemma**) are presented, each of which has undesirable consequences.

dil·et·tan·te (dĭl′ə tăn′tĭ, -ə tänt′), *n.*, *pl.* **-tes, -ti** (-tē), *adj.* —*n.* **1.** one who pursues an art or science in an amateur or superficial way. **2.** a lover of an art. —*adj.* **3.** of or pertaining to dilettantes. —**dil′et·tan′tish,** *adj.* —**dil′et·tant′ism,** *n.*

dil·i·gence¹ (dĭl′ə jəns), *n.* constant and earnest effort to accomplish what is undertaken.

dil·i·gence² (dĭl′ə jəns), *n.* a public stagecoach.

dil·i·gent (dĭl′ə jənt), *adj.* **1.** constant in effort to accomplish something. **2.** pursued with persevering attention. —**dil′i·gent·ly,** *adv.*

dill (dĭl), *n.* **1.** a plant of the parsley family bearing a seedlike fruit used in medicine and for flavoring pickles, etc.   2. its aromatic seeds or leaves.

dil·ly-dal·ly (dĭl'ĭ dăl'ĭ), *v.i.*, **-lied, -lying.** to waste time, esp. by indecision; trifle; loiter.

di·lute (dĭ lōōt', dī-; *adj. also* dī'lōōt), *v.*, **-luted, -luting,** *adj.* —*v.t.* 1. to make thinner or weaker by the addition of water or the like. —*v.i.* 2. to become diluted. —*adj.* 3. reduced in strength; weak.

di·lu·tion (dĭ lōō'shən, dī-), *n.* 1. act of diluting.   2. state of being diluted.   3. something diluted.

di·lu·vi·al (dĭ lōō'vĭ əl), *adj.* pertaining to a deluge or flood. Also, **di·lu'vi·an.**

dim (dĭm), *adj.*, **dimmer, dimmest,** *v.*, **dimmed, dimming.** —*adj.* 1. not bright; obscure.   2. indistinct.   3. vague.   4. dull in luster.   5. not seeing clearly.   6. not clearly understanding. —*v.t.*, *v.i.* 7. to make or become dim. —**dim'ly,** *adv.* —**dim'ness,** *n.*

dim., diminuendo. Also, **dimin.**

dime (dīm), *n.* a silver coin of the U.S., of the value of 10 cents or ¹/₁₀ dollar.

di·men·sion (dĭ mĕn'shən), *n.* magnitude, esp. as measured in a particular direction. —**di·men'·sion·al,** *adj.* —**di·men'sion·less,** *adj.*

di·min·ish (dĭ mĭn'ĭsh), *v.t.* 1. to make smaller; lessen; reduce.   2. *Music.* to make smaller by a half step than the corresponding perfect or minor interval. —*v.i.* 3. to lessen. —**di·min'ish·a·ble,** *adj.*

di·min·u·en·do (dĭ mĭn'yōō ĕn'dō), *adj.*, *n.*, *pl.* **-dos.** *Music.* —*adj.* 1. gradually reducing in force or loudness. —*n.* 2. a gradual reduction of force or loudness.

dim·i·nu·tion (dĭm'ĭ nū'shən, -nōō'-), *n.* act, fact, or process of diminishing; reduction.

di·min·u·tive (dĭ mĭn'yə tĭv), *adj.* 1. small; tiny.   2. *Gram.* denoting smallness, affection, or triviality. —*n.* 3. a small thing or person.   4. *Gram.* a diminutive element or formation. —**di·min'u·tive·ly,** *adj.* —**di·min'u·tive·ness,** *n.*

dim·i·ty (dĭm'ə tĭ), *n.*, *pl.* **-ties.** a thin cotton fabric, woven with a stripe or check of heavier yarn.

dim·mer (dĭm'ər), *n.* 1. one that dims.   2. a device for controlling light intensity.

dim-out (dĭm'out'), *n.* a reduction or concealment of night lighting.

dim·ple (dĭm'pəl), *n.*, *v.*, **-pled, -pling.** —*n.* 1. a small natural hollow in some part of the body, esp. in the cheek. —*v.t.* 2. to mark with dimples. —*v.i.* 3. to form dimples.

dim·wit (dĭm'wĭt'), *n.* *Slang.* a stupid person.

din (dĭn), *n.*, *v.*, **dinned, dinning.** —*n.* 1. a loud, confused noise. —*v.t.* 2. to assail with din.   3. to say with persistent repetition. —*v.i.* 4. to make a din.

dine (dīn), *v.*, **dined, dining.** —*v.i.* 1. to eat dinner. —*v.t.* 2. to entertain at dinner.

din·er (dī'nər), *n.* 1. one who dines.   2. *U.S.* a railroad dining car, or a restaurant like one.

di·nette (dī nĕt'), *n.* a small dining room.

ding (dĭng), *v.i.*, *v.t.* 1. to sound, as a bell; ring.   2. *Colloq.* to impress by reiteration. —*n.* 3. the sound of a bell.

ding-dong (dĭng'dông', -dŏng'), *n.* 1. the repeated sound of a bell. —*adj.* 2. *Colloq.* vigorously fought.

din·ghy (dĭng'gĭ), *n.*, *pl.* **-ghies.** a small boat, esp. one used as a tender. Also, **din'gey, din'gy.**

din·gy (dĭn'jĭ), *adj.*, **-gier, -giest.** dark, dull, or dirty. —**din'gi·ly,** *adv.* —**din'gi·ness,** *n.*

dink·ey (dĭngk'ĭ), *n.*, *pl.* **dinkeys.** anything small, esp. a small locomotive. Also, **dink'y.**

dink·y (dĭngk'ĭ), *adj.*, **dinkier, dinkiest.** *Colloq.* of small size.

din·ner (dĭn'ər), *n.* 1. the main meal, esp. as taken about noon or (now) in the evening.   2. a formal meal in honor of some person or occasion.

di·no·saur (dī'nə sôr'), *n.* *Paleontol.* any member of extinct groups of Mesozoic reptiles, mostly of gigantic size.

dint (dĭnt), *n.* 1. force; power.   2. a dent. —*v.t.* 3. to make a dint in. —**dint'less,** *adj.*

di·oc·e·san (dī ŏs'ə sən, dī'ə sē'sən), *adj.* 1. of or pertaining to a diocese. —*n.* 2. the bishop in charge of a diocese.

di·o·cese (dī'ə sēs', -sĭs), *n.* the district under the pastoral care of a bishop.

di·oe·cious (dī ē'shəs), *adj.* *Biol.* (esp. of plants) having separate sexes.

Di·og·e·nes (dī ŏj'ə nēz'), *n.* c412–c323 B.C., Greek Cynic philosopher.

Di·o·ny·sus (dī'ə nī'səs), *n.* *Gk. Myth.* the youthful and beautiful god of wine, identified with the Roman god Bacchus. Also, **Di'o·ny·sos.**

di·o·ram·a (dī'ə răm'ə, -rä'mə), *n.* 1. a miniature scene reproduced in three dimensions.   2. a partly translucent picture, viewed through an aperture.

di·ox·ide (dī ŏk'sīd, -sĭd), *n.* *Chem.* an oxide containing two atoms of oxygen per molecule. Also, **di·ox·id** (dī ŏk'sĭd).

dip (dĭp), *v.*, **dipped** or **dipt, dipping,** *n.* —*v.t.* 1. to plunge temporarily into a liquid.   2. to lift by bailing or scooping.   3. to lower and raise. —*v.i.* 4. to plunge into a liquid and emerge quickly.   5. to plunge a ladle, etc., into water, etc., esp. to remove something.   6. to sink or drop down.   7. to slope downward.   8. to engage slightly in a subject.   9. to read here and there in a book. —*n.* 10. act of dipping.   11. that which is taken up by dipping.   12. a liquid into which something is dipped.   13. a lowering.   14. downward slope.

diph·the·ri·a (dĭf thĭr'ĭ ə, dĭp-), *n.* *Pathol.* a febrile infectious disease caused by a specific bacillus, characterized by the formation of a false membrane in the air passages, esp. the throat.

diph·the·rit·ic (dĭf'thə rĭt'ĭk, dĭp'-), *adj.* of or affected by diphtheria. Also, **diph·the'ri·al.**

diph·thong (dĭf'thông, -thŏng, dĭp'-), *n.* a vowel speech sound that ends so differently from its beginning that two letters are needed to represent it adequately. —**diph·thon'gal,** *adj.*

di·plo·ma (dĭ plō'mə), *n.*, *pl.* **-mas,** *Lat.* **-mata** (-mə tə). a document conferring some honor, privilege, or power, as one given by a university at graduation.

di·plo·ma·cy (dĭ plō'mə sĭ), *n.*, *pl.* **-cies.** 1. the conduct by government officials of international relations.   2. skill in negotiations.

dip·lo·mat (dĭp'lə măt'), *n.* one employed or skilled in diplomacy. Also, *Brit.*, **di·plo·ma·tist** (dĭ plō'mə tĭst).

dip·lo·mat·ic (dĭp'lə măt'ĭk), *adj.* 1. of, pertaining to, or engaged in diplomacy.   2. skilled in diplomacy; tactful. —**dip'lo·mat'i·cal·ly,** *adv.*

dip·per (dĭp'ər), *n.* 1. one that dips.   2. a container with a handle, used to dip liquids.   3. (*cap.*) *Astron.* a. Also, **Big Dipper.** the group of seven bright stars in Ursa Major resembling such a vessel in outline. b. Also, **Little Dipper.** a similar group in Ursa Minor.

dip·so·ma·ni·a (dĭp'sə mā'nĭ ə), *n.* an irresistible periodic craving for intoxicating drink. —**dip'so·ma'ni·ac,** *n.*

dip·ter·ous (dĭp'tər əs), *adj.* 1. *Zool.* belonging or pertaining to the order that includes houseflies, gnats, mosquitoes, etc., characterized typically by a single pair of membranous wings.   2. *Bot.* having two winglike appendages.

dire (dīr), *adj.*, **direr, direst.** 1. dreadful; awful.   2. utmost. —**dire'ly,** *adv.* —**dire'ness,** *n.*

di·rect (dĭ rĕkt', dī-), *v.t.* 1. to guide with advice; manage; control.   2. to command; order.   3. to tell (a person) the way to a place, etc.   4. to point or aim toward a place or an object.   5. to address (words, a letter, etc.) to a person. —*v.i.* 6. to act as a guide.   7. to give commands or orders. —*adj.* 8. proceeding in the shortest course; straight.   9. proceeding in an unbroken line of descent.   10. immediate; personal.   11. straightforward.   12. exact.   13. *Gram.* (of quotation or discourse) consisting exactly of the words originally used.   14. *Govt.* of or by action of voters, which takes effect without any intervening agency such as representatives. —*adv.* 15. in a direct manner; straight. —**di·rect'ness,** *n.*

direct current, *Elect.* a relatively steady current in one direction in a circuit.

di·rec·tion (dĭ rĕk'shən, dī-), *n.* 1. act of directing, pointing, aiming, etc.   2. the line along which anything lies, faces, moves, etc.   3. guidance.   4. command.   5. management. —**di·rec'tive,** *adj.*, *n.*

di·rec·tion·al (dĭ rĕk'shən əl, dī-), *adj.* 1. of or pertaining to direction in space.   2. *Radio.* adapted for determining the direction of signals received or transmitting signals in a given direction.

di·rect·ly (dĭ rĕkt'lĭ, dī-), *adv.* 1. in a direct line, way, or manner.   2. *Chiefly Brit.* without delay.

direct object, *Gram.* the person or thing upon which the action of the verb is expended or toward which it is directed.

di·rec·tor (dĭ rĕk′tər, dī-), *n.* **1.** one that directs. **2.** one of a body of persons chosen to control the affairs of a company. **—di·rec′tor·ship′,** *n.*

di·rec·to·rate (dĭ rĕk′tə rĭt, dī), *n.* **1.** the office of a director. **2.** a body of directors.

di·rec·to·ry (dĭ rĕk′tə rĭ, dī-), *n., pl.* **-ries,** *adj.* **—n. 1.** a book or billboard containing a list of the names and addresses of people in a city, building, profession, etc. **2.** a book of directions. **—adj. 3.** directing.

dire·ful (dīr′fəl), *adj.* dreadful; awful. **—dire′ful·ly,** *adv.* **—dire′ful·ness,** *n.*

dirge (dûrj), *n.* a funeral song or tune, or one expressing mourning.

dir·i·gi·ble (dĭr′ə jə bəl), *n.* **1.** an airship. **—adj. 2.** that may be steered. **—dir′i·gi·bil′-i·ty,** *n.*

dirk (dûrk), *n.* **1.** a dagger. **—v.t. 2.** to stab.

dirn·dl (dûrn′dəl), *n.* **1.** a dress with full skirt and close-fitting bodice, commonly of colorful material. **2.** a skirt in such a style.

dirt (dûrt), *n.* **1.** any filthy substance, as dust, mud, etc. **2.** *U.S. and Brit. Dial.* earth, esp. when loose. **3.** something vile or mean. **4.** scurrilous language. **5.** gossip.

dirt·y (dûr′tĭ), *adj.,* **dirt·i·er, dirt·i·est,** *v.,* **dir·tied, dirty·ing.** **—adj. 1.** soiled with dirt; unclean. **2.** soiling. **3.** vile; mean. **4.** indecent. **5.** stormy. **6.** dingy. **—v.t., v.i. 7.** to make or become dirty. **—dirt′i·ly,** *adv.* **—dirt′i·ness,** *n.*

dis·a·bil·i·ty (dĭs′ə bĭl′ə tĭ), *n., pl.* **-ties.** **1.** lack of physical or mental ability. **2.** legal incapacity.

dis·a·ble (dĭs ā′bəl), *v.t.,* **-bled, -bling. 1.** to weaken or destroy the capability of. **2.** to disqualify. **—dis·a′ble·ment,** *n.*

dis·a·buse (dĭs′ə būz′), *v.t.,* **-bused, -busing.** to free from deception or error.

dis·ad·van·tage (dĭs′əd văn′tĭj, -vän′-), *n., v.,* **-taged, -taging. —n. 1.** any unfavorable circumstance or condition. **2.** injury to reputation, credit, etc. **—v.t. 3.** to subject to disadvantage. **—dis·ad·van·ta·geous** (dĭs ăd′vən tā′jəs, dĭs′-ăd-), *adj.* **—dis·ad′van·ta′geous·ly,** *adv.* **—dis·ad′van·ta′geous·ness,** *n.*

dis·af·fect (dĭs′ə fĕkt′), *v.t.* to make unfriendly, discontented, or disloyal. **—dis′af·fec′tion,** *n.*

dis·a·gree (dĭs′ə grē′), *v.i.,* **-greed, -greeing.** to fail to agree; differ. **2.** to quarrel. **3.** to conflict in action or effect.

dis·a·gree·a·ble (dĭs′ə grē′ə bəl), *adj.* **1.** unpleasant; offensive. **2.** unamiable. **—dis′a·gree′a·ble·ness,** *n.* **—dis′a·gree′a·bly,** *adv.*

dis·a·gree·ment (dĭs′ə grē′mənt), *n.* **1.** act, state, or fact of disagreeing. **2.** diversity; unlikeness. **3.** difference of opinion. **4.** quarrel.

dis·al·low (dĭs′ə lou′), *v.t.* to refuse to allow. **—dis′al·low′ance,** *n.*

dis·ap·pear (dĭs′ə pĭr′), *v.i.* **1.** to vanish from sight. **2.** to cease to exist or be known. **—dis′-ap·pear′ance,** *n.*

dis·ap·point (dĭs′ə point′), *v.t.* **1.** to fail to fulfill the expectations or wishes of. **2.** to thwart.

dis·ap·point·ment (dĭs′ə point′mənt), *n.* **1.** act or fact of disappointing. **2.** state or feeling of being disappointed. **3.** something that disappoints.

dis·ap·pro·ba·tion (dĭs′ăp rə bā′shən), *n.* disapproval.

dis·ap·prov·al (dĭs′ə prōō′vəl), *n.* act or state of disapproving; censure.

dis·ap·prove (dĭs′ə prōōv′), *v.,* **-proved, -proving. —v.t. 1.** to think wrong; condemn. **2.** to withhold approval from. **—v.i. 3.** to have an unfavorable opinion. **—dis′ap·prov′ing·ly,** *adv.*

dis·arm (dĭs ärm′), *v.t.* **1.** to deprive of arms. **2.** to divest of hostility, suspicion, etc. **—v.i. 3.** to lay down arms. **4.** to reduce or limit the national armed power.

dis·ar·ma·ment (dĭs är′mə mənt), *n.* **1.** act of disarming. **2.** the reduction or limitation of the national armed power.

dis·ar·range (dĭs′ə rānj′), *v.t.,* **-ranged, -ranging.** to disorder; unsettle. **—dis′ar·range′ment,** *n.*

dis·ar·ray (dĭs′ə rā′), *v.t.* **1.** to put out of order. **—n. 2.** disorder; confusion. **3.** disorder of apparel.

dis·as·sem·ble (dĭs′ə sĕm′bəl), *v.t.,* **-bled, -bling.** to take apart. **—dis′as·sem′bly,** *n.*

dis·as·ter (dĭ zăs′tər, -zäs′-), *n.* any unfortunate event, esp. a sudden or great misfortune.

dis·as·trous (dĭ zăs′trəs, -zäs′-), *adj.* ruinous; calamitous. **—dis·as′trous·ly,** *adv.*

dis·a·vow (dĭs′ə vou′), *v.t.* to disclaim knowledge of, connection with, or responsibility for; disown. **—dis′a·vow′al,** *n.* **—dis′a·vow′er,** *n.*

dis·band (dĭs bănd′), *v.t.* **1.** to break up or dissolve (a group). **—v.i. 2.** to break up. **—dis·band′ment,** *n.*

dis·bar (dĭs bär′), *v.t.,* **-barred, -barring.** *Law.* to expel from the legal profession or from the bar of a particular court. **—dis·bar′ment,** *n.*

dis·be·lieve (dĭs′bĭ lēv′), *v.t.,* **-lieved, -lieving.** to reject as untrue. **—dis′be·lief′,** *n.*

dis·bur·den (dĭs bûr′dən), *v.t.* **1.** to remove a burden from. **2.** to relieve of anything oppressive or annoying. **3.** to get rid of (a burden). **—v.i. 4.** to unload a burden. **—dis·bur′den·ment,** *n.*

dis·burse (dĭs bûrs′), *v.t.,* **-bursed, -bursing.** to pay out (money); expend. **—dis·burs′a·ble,** *adj.* **—dis·burse′ment,** *n.*

disc (dĭsk), *n.* disk.

dis·card (*v.* dĭs kärd′; *n.* dĭs′kärd), *v.t.* **1.** to cast aside; reject. **2.** *Cards.* **a.** to throw out (a card or cards) from one's hand. **b.** to play (a card, not a trump, of a different suit from that of the card led). **—v.i. 3.** *Cards.* to discard a card or cards. **—n. 4.** act of discarding. **5.** one that is cast out. **6.** *Cards.* the card or cards discarded.

dis·cern (dĭ zûrn′, -sûrn′), *v.t., v.i.* **1.** to see, recognize, or apprehend clearly. **2.** to distinguish or discriminate. **—dis·cern′er,** *n.* **—dis·cern′i·ble,** *adj.* **—dis·cern′i·bly,** *adv.*

dis·cern·ing (dĭ zûr′nĭng, -sûr′-), *adj.* showing discernment. **—dis·cern′ing·ly,** *adv.*

dis·cern·ment (dĭ zûrn′mənt, -sûrn′-), *n.* faculty of discerning; acuteness of judgment.

dis·charge (dĭs chärj′; *n. also* dĭs′chärj), *v.,* **-charged, -charging. —v.t. 1.** to relieve of a load. **2.** to remove, send forth, or get rid of (a charge, lead, etc.). **3.** to fire; shoot. **4.** to pour forth. **5.** to relieve oneself of (an obligation, etc.). **6.** to relieve of obligation, etc. **7.** to fulfill (a duty, etc.). **8.** to dismiss from service. **9.** to send away or allow to go. **10.** to pay (a debt). **—v.i. 11.** to get rid of or deliver a load. **12.** to come or pour forth. **—n. 13.** act of discharging a ship, load, etc. **14.** act of firing a weapon. **15.** ejection; emission. **16.** rate or amount of issue. **17.** something discharged. **18.** *Law.* acquittal. **b.** annulment. **19.** a relieving or being relieved of obligation. **20.** dismissal from employment, etc. **21.** *Elect.* **a.** the withdrawing or transference of an electric charge. **b.** the equalization of the difference of potential between two terminals or the like. **—dis·charge′a·ble,** *adj.* **—dis·charg′er,** *n.*

dis·ci·ple (dĭ sī′pəl), *n., v.,* **-pled, -pling. —n. 1.** one of the followers of Jesus Christ. **2.** any adherent of the doctrines of another. **—v.t. 3.** to convert into a disciple. **—dis·ci′ple·ship′,** *n.*

dis·ci·pli·nar·i·an (dĭs′ə plə när′ĭ ən), *n.* **1.** one who enforces discipline. **—adj. 2.** disciplinary.

dis·ci·pli·nar·y (dĭs′ə plə nĕr′ĭ), *adj.* of or for discipline; promoting discipline.

dis·ci·pline (dĭs′ə plĭn), *n., v.,* **-plined, -plining. —n. 1.** training to act in accordance with rules. **2.** instruction designed to train to proper conduct or action. **3.** punishment. **4.** subjection to rules of behavior. **5.** a set or system of rules. **6.** *Eccles.* the rules of a church as distinguished from its doctrine. **7.** a branch of learning. **—v.t. 8.** to train by instruction. **9.** to punish or correct. **—dis′ci·plin′a·ble,** *adj.* **—dis′ci·plin·er,** *n.*

dis·claim (dĭs klām′), *v.t.* to deny interest in or connection with; disavow; disown.

dis·claim·er (dĭs klā′mər), *n.* **1.** act of disclaiming. **2.** one who disclaims.

dis·close (dĭs klōz′), *v.t.,* **-closed, -closing. 1.** to make known; reveal. **2.** to uncover; lay open to view. **—dis·clos′er,** *n.*

dis·clo·sure (dĭs klō′zhər), *n.* **1.** act of disclosing. **2.** that which is disclosed.

dis·coid (dĭs′koid), *adj.* disk-shaped.

dis·col·or (dĭs kŭl′ər), *v.t.* **1.** to change or spoil the color of. **—v.i. 2.** to change color; become faded or stained. **—dis·col′or·a′tion,** *n.*

dis·com·fit (dĭs kŭm′fĭt), *v.t.* **1.** to defeat utterly. **2.** to foil. **3.** to disconcert.

dis·com·fi·ture (dĭs kŭm′fĭ chər), *n.* **1.** utter defeat. **2.** frustration. **3.** confusion.

dis·com·fort (dĭs kŭm′fərt), *n.* **1.** absence of comfort; uneasiness. **2.** anything that disturbs the comfort. —*v.t.* **3.** to make uncomfortable.

dis·com·mode (dĭs′kə mōd′), *v.t.*, **-moded, -moding.** to put to inconvenience; trouble.

dis·com·pose (dĭs′kəm pōz′), *v.t.*, **-posed, -posing. 1.** to disarrange; unsettle. **2.** to perturb. —**dis′com·pos′ed·ly**, *adv.* —**dis′com·pos′ing·ly**, *adv.* —**dis·com·po·sure** (dĭs′kəm pō′zhər), *n.*

dis·con·cert (dĭs′kən sûrt′), *v.t.* **1.** to perturb; ruffle. **2.** to disarrange. —**dis′con·cert′ing·ly**, *adv.*

dis·con·nect (dĭs′kə nĕkt′), *v.t.* to sever the connection of; detach. —**dis′con·nec′tion**, *n.*

dis·con·nect·ed (dĭs′kə nĕk′tĭd), *adj.* **1.** disjointed; broken. **2.** incoherent. —**dis′con·nect′ed·ly**, *adv.* —**dis′con·nect′ed·ness**, *n.*

dis·con·so·late (dĭs kŏn′sə lĭt), *adj.* **1.** unhappy; inconsolable. **2.** cheerless; gloomy. —**dis·con′so·late·ly**, *adv.* —**dis·con′so·la′tion**, **dis·con′so·late·ness**, *n.*

dis·con·tent (dĭs′kən tĕnt′), *adj.* **1.** not content; dissatisfied. —*n.* **2.** Also, **dis′con·tent′-ment.** the lack of content; dissatisfaction. —*v.t.* **3.** to dissatisfy.

dis·con·tent·ed (dĭs′kən tĕn′tĭd), *adj.* dissatisfied; unhappy. —**dis′con·tent′ed·ly**, *adv.*

dis·con·tin·ue (dĭs′kən tĭn′yōō), *v.*, **-tinued, -tinuing.** —*v.t.* **1.** to put an end to. **2.** to cease to take, use, etc. **3.** *Law.* to terminate or abandon (a suit, etc.). —*v.i.* **4.** to come to an end; stop. —**dis′con·tin′u·ance, dis′con·tin′u·a′-tion**, *n.* —**dis′con·tin′u·er**, *n.*

dis·con·tin·u·ous (dĭs′kən tĭn′yōō əs), *adj.* not continuous; interrupted. —**dis′con·tin′u·ous·ly**, *adv.* —**dis·con·ti·nu·i·ty** (dĭs′kŏn tə nū′ə tĭ, -nōō′-), *adj.* —**dis′con·tin′u·ous·ness**, *n.*

dis·cord (*n.* dĭs′kôrd; *v.* dĭs kôrd′), *n.* **1.** lack of concord or harmony. **2.** difference of opinions. **3.** strife; war. **4.** *Music.* an inharmonious combination of musical tones sounded together. **5.** any harsh noise. —*v.i.* **6.** to disagree.

dis·cord·ant (dĭs kôr′dənt), *adj.* **1.** disagreeing; incongruous. **2.** dissonant; harsh. —**dis·cord′ance, dis·cord′an·cy**, *n.* —**dis·cord′ant·ly**, *adv.*

dis·count (*v.* dĭs′kount, dĭs kount′; *n.* dĭs′-kount), *v.t.* **1.** to deduct; make a reduction of. **2.** to advance money with deduction of interest on. **3.** to disregard. **4.** to allow for exaggeration in. **5.** to take (an event, etc.) into account in advance. —*v.i.* **6.** to advance money after deduction of interest. —*n.* **7.** act of discounting. **8.** amount deducted for prompt payment or other special reason. **9.** any deduction from the nominal value. **10.** a payment of interest in advance upon a loan of money. —**dis′count·a·ble**, *adj.*

dis·coun·te·nance (dĭs koun′tə nəns), *v.*, **-nanced, -nancing**, *n.* —*v.t.* **1.** to disconcert; abash. **2.** to show disapproval of. —*n.* **3.** disapproval.

dis·cour·age (dĭs kûr′ĭj), *v.t.*, **-aged, -aging. 1.** to deprive of courage; dispirit. **2.** to dissuade (fol. by *from*). **3.** to hinder. **4.** to express disapproval of. —**dis·cour′age·ment**, *n.* —**dis·cour′ag·er**, *n.* —**dis·cour′ag·ing·ly**, *adv.*

dis·course (*n.* dĭs′kōrs, dĭs kōrs′; *v.* dĭs kōrs′), *n.*, *v.*, **-coursed, -coursing.** —*n.* **1.** talk; conversation. **2.** a formal discussion of a subject, as a treatise, sermon, etc. —*v.i.* **3.** to talk; converse. **4.** to treat a subject formally in speech or writing.

dis·cour·te·ous (dĭs kûr′tĭ əs), *adj.* lacking courtesy; rude. —**dis·cour′te·ous·ly**, *adv.*

dis·cour·te·sy (dĭs kûr′tə sĭ), *n.*, *pl.* **-sies. 1.** lack of courtesy. **2.** a discourteous act. Also, **dis·cour′te·ous·ness.**

dis·cov·er (dĭs kŭv′ər), *v.t.* **1.** to gain sight or knowledge of (something previously unseen or unknown). **2.** *Archaic.* to reveal. —**dis·cov′er-a·ble**, *adj.* —**dis·cov′er·er**, *n.*

dis·cov·er·y (dĭs kŭv′ə rĭ), *n.*, *pl.* **-eries. 1.** act of discovering. **2.** something discovered.

dis·cred·it (dĭs krĕd′ĭt), *v.t.* **1.** to injure the reputation of. **2.** to destroy confidence in. **3.** to give no credit to. —*n.* **4.** loss or lack of belief. **5.** disrepute. **6.** something that damages a good reputation.

dis·cred·it·a·ble (dĭs krĕd′ĭt ə bəl), *adj.* such as to bring discredit. —**dis·cred′it·a·bly**, *adv.*

dis·creet (dĭs krēt′), *adj.* wise or judicious; prudent. —**dis·creet′ly**, *adv.* —**dis·creet′-ness**, *n.*

dis·crep·an·cy (dĭs krĕp′ən sĭ), *n.*, *pl.* **-cies. 1.** state or quality of being discrepant; incon-

sistency. **2.** an instance of difference or inconsistency.

dis·crep·ant (dĭs krĕp′ənt), *adj.* disagreeing; discordant; inconsistent. —**dis·crep′ant·ly**, *adv.*

dis·crete (dĭs krēt′), *adj.* **1.** separate; distinct. **2.** consisting of distinct parts. —**dis·crete′ly**, *adv.*

dis·cre·tion (dĭs krĕsh′ən), *n.* **1.** freedom of judgment or choice. **2.** quality of being discreet; prudence.

dis·cre·tion·ar·y (dĭs krĕsh′ə nĕr′ĭ), *adj.* subject or left to one's discretion.

dis·crim·i·nate (*v.* dĭs krĭm′ə nāt′; *adj.* dĭs-krĭm′ə nĭt), *v.*, **-nated, -nating**, *adj.* —*v.i.* **1.** to make a distinction, as in favor of or against a person or thing. **2.** to distinguish accurately. —*v.t.* **3.** to differentiate. **4.** to distinguish as different. —*adj.* **5.** marked by discrimination. —**dis·crim′i·nate·ly**, *adv.* —**dis·crim′i·nat′-ing·ly**, *adv.* —**dis·crim′i·na′tor**, *n.*

dis·crim·i·na·tion (dĭs krĭm′ə nā′shən), *n.* **1.** act of discriminating. **2.** the resulting state. **3.** the making of a difference in particular cases, as in favor of or against a person or thing. **4.** the power of making nice distinctions.

dis·crim·i·na·tive (dĭs krĭm′ə nā′tĭv), *adj.* **1.** characteristic. **2.** making distinctions; discriminating. Also, **dis·crim′i·na·to·ry** (dĭs krĭm′ə nə-tōr′ĭ). —**dis·crim′i·na′tive·ly**, *adv.*

dis·cur·sive (dĭs kûr′sĭv), *adj.* passing from one subject to another; rambling. —**dis·cur′-sive·ly**, *adv.* —**dis·cur′sive·ness**, *n.*

dis·cus (dĭs′kəs), *n.*, *pl.* **discuses, disci** (dĭs′ī). *Gymnastics.* a circular stone or metal plate for throwing to a distance.

dis·cuss (dĭs kŭs′), *v.t.* to examine the considerations for and against; talk over.

dis·cus·sion (dĭs kŭsh′ən), *n.* critical examination by argument; debate.

dis·dain (dĭs dān′), *v.t.* **1.** to despise; scorn. **2.** to think unworthy of notice, etc. —*n.* **3.** haughty contempt; scorn.

dis·dain·ful (dĭs dān′fəl), *adj.* full of or showing disdain; scornful. —**dis·dain′ful·ly**, *adv.*

dis·ease (dĭ zēz′), *n.*, *v.*, **-eased, -easing.** —*n.* **1.** a morbid condition of the body, or of some organ or part; illness; sickness; ailment. —*v.t.* **2.** to affect with disease.

dis·em·bark (dĭs′ĕm bärk′), *v.t.*, *v.i.* to put or go on shore from a ship; land. —**dis·em·bar·ka·tion** (dĭs′ĕm bär kā′shən), *n.*

dis·em·bod·y (dĭs′ĕm bŏd′ĭ), *v.t.*, **-bodied, -bodying.** to divest (a soul, etc.) of the body.

dis·em·bow·el (dĭs′ĕm bou′əl), *v.t.*, **-eled, -eling** or (*esp. Brit.*) **-elled, elling.** to remove the bowels from. —**dis′em·bow′el·ment**, *n.*

dis·en·chant (dĭs′ĕn chănt′, -chänt′), *v.t.* to free from enchantment. —**dis′en·chant′ment**, *n.*

dis·en·cum·ber (dĭs′ĕn kŭm′bər), *v.t.* to free from encumbrance; disburden.

dis·en·fran·chise (dĭs′ĕn frăn′chīz), *v.t.*, **-chised, -chising.** to disfranchise.

dis·en·gage (dĭs′ĕn gāj′), *v.*, **-gaged, -gaging.** —*v.t.* **1.** to release from attachment or connection. **2.** to free from engagement, pledge, etc. —*v.i.* **3.** to free oneself. —**dis′en·gage′ment**, *n.*

dis·en·tan·gle (dĭs′ĕn tăng′gəl), *v.t.*, *v.i.*, **-gled, -gling.** to free or become free from entanglement; untangle. —**dis′en·tan′gle·ment**, *n.*

dis·es·tab·lish (dĭs′ĕs tăb′lĭsh), *v.t.* **1.** to deprive of the character of being established. **2.** to withdraw exclusive state recognition or support from (a church). —**dis′es·tab′lish·ment**, *n.*

dis·es·teem (dĭs′ĕs tēm′), *v.t.* **1.** to hold in low esteem. —*n.* **2.** lack of esteem; disregard.

dis·fa·vor (dĭs fā′vər), *n.* **1.** displeasure; disesteem. **2.** lack of favor. **3.** an act of disregard, dislike, or unkindness. —*v.t.* **4.** to regard or treat with disfavor.

dis·fig·ure (dĭs fĭg′yər), *v.t.*, **-ured, -uring. 1.** to mar the figure, appearance, or beauty of. **2.** to mar the effect or excellence of. —**dis·fig′ure-ment**, *n.* —**dis·fig′ur·er**, *n.*

dis·fran·chise (dĭs frăn′chīz), *v.t.*, **-chised, -chising. 1.** to deprive (persons) of rights of citizenship. **2.** to deprive of a franchise. —**dis-fran·chise·ment** (dĭs frăn′chĭz mənt), *n.*

dis·gorge (dĭs gôrj′), *v.*, **-gorged, -gorging.** —*v.t.* **1.** to vomit forth; discharge. **2.** to give up unwillingly. —*v.i.* **3.** to disgorge something.

dis·grace (dĭs grās′), *n.*, *v.*, **-graced, -gracing.** —*n.* **1.** state of being in dishonor; shame. **2.** a cause of shame or dishonor. **3.** exclusion from favor, confidence, or trust. —*v.t.* **4.** to bring shame or reproach upon. **5.** to dismiss with discredit. —**dis·grac'er**, *n.*

dis·grace·ful (dĭs grās'fəl), *adj.* bringing or deserving disgrace; shameful; dishonorable. —**dis·grace'ful·ly**, *adv.* —**dis·grace'ful·ness**, *n.*

dis·grun·tle (dĭs grŭn'təl), *v.t.*, **-tled, -tling.** to make discontent. —**dis·grun'tle·ment**, *n.*

dis·guise (dĭs gīz'), *v.*, **-guised, -guising**, *n.* —*v.t.* **1.** to conceal the identity of by means of a misleading garb, etc. **2.** to conceal or cover up the real state or character of. —*n.* **3.** that which disguises. **4.** the make-up, mask, or costume of an entertainer. **5.** act of disguising. **6.** state of being disguised.

dis·gust (dĭs gŭst'), *v.t.* **1.** to cause nausea or loathing in. **2.** to offend the good taste, moral sense, etc., of. —*n.* **3.** strong distaste; nausea; loathing. **4.** repugnance; strong aversion. —**dis·gust'ed·ly**, *adv.* —**dis·gust'ing·ly**, *adv.*

dish (dĭsh), *n.* **1.** an open, shallow container of pottery, etc., for holding food, etc. **2.** that which is in a dish. **3.** a particular article of food. **4.** as much as a dish will hold. —*v.t.* **5.** to put into or serve in a dish.

dis·ha·bille (dĭs'ə bēl'), *n.* **1.** negligee. **2.** a loose morning dress.

dish·cloth (dĭsh'klôth', -klŏth'), *n.* a cloth for use in washing dishes. Also, **dish·clout** (dĭsh'klout').

dis·heart·en (dĭs här'tən), *v.t.* to discourage. —**dis·heart'en·ing·ly**, *adv.* —**dis·heart'en·ment**, *n.*

di·shev·el (dĭ shĕv'əl), *v.t.*, **-eled, -eling** or (*esp. Brit.*) **-elled, -elling.** to let hang in loose disorder. —**di·shev'el·ment**, *n.*

dis·hon·est (dĭs ŏn'ĭst), *adj.* **1.** not honest. **2.** fraudulent. —**dis·hon'est·ly**, *adv.*

dis·hon·es·ty (dĭs ŏn'ĭs tĭ), *n.*, *pl.* **-ties. 1.** lack of honesty. **2.** a dishonest act.

dis·hon·or (dĭs ŏn'ər), *n.* **1.** lack of honor. **2.** disgrace; shame. **3.** an insult. **4.** a cause of shame. **5.** *Com.* failure or refusal of the drawee or acceptor of a bill of exchange or note to accept it, or, if it is accepted, to pay and retire it. —*v.t.* **6.** to disgrace; bring shame on. **7.** *Com.* to fail or refuse to honor (a draft, etc.) by payment.

dis·hon·or·a·ble (dĭs ŏn'ər ə bəl), *adj.* **1.** showing lack of honor; shameful. **2.** having no honor. —**dis·hon'or·a·bly**, *adv.*

dis·il·lu·sion (dĭs'ĭ lōō'zhən), *v.t.* **1.** to free from illusion. —*n.* **2.** a freeing or a being freed from illusion. —**dis·il·lu'sion·ment**, *n.* —**dis·il·lu·sive** (dĭs'ĭ lōō'sĭv), *adj.*

dis·in·cline (dĭs'ĭn klīn'), *v.t.*, *v.i.*, **-clined, -clining.** to make or be averse or indisposed. —**dis·in'cli·na'tion**, *n.*

dis·in·fect (dĭs'ĭn fĕkt'), *v.t.* to destroy disease germs in. —**dis·in·fec'tion**, *n.* —**dis·in·fec'tor**, *n.*

dis·in·fect·ant (dĭs'ĭn fĕk'tənt), *n.* **1.** anything that destroys bacteria. —*adj.* **2.** disinfecting.

dis·in·gen·u·ous (dĭs'ĭn jĕn'yŏŏ əs), *adj.* lacking frankness, candor, or sincerity.

dis·in·her·it (dĭs'ĭn hĕr'ĭt), *v.t.* *Law.* to exclude from inheritance. —**dis·in·her'it·ance**, *n.*

dis·in·te·grate (dĭs ĭn'tə grāt'), *v.*, **-grated, -grating.** —*v.t.* **1.** to reduce to particles, fragments, or parts. —*v.i.* **2.** to separate into component parts. —**dis·in·te·gra·ble** (dĭs ĭn'tə grə bəl), *adj.* —**dis·in'te·gra'tion**, *n.* —**dis·in'te·gra'tor**, *n.*

dis·in·ter (dĭs'ĭn tûr'), *v.t.*, **-terred, -terring. 1.** to exhume. **2.** to bring from obscurity into view. —**dis·in·ter'ment**, *n.*

dis·in·ter·est (dĭs ĭn'tər ĭst, -trĭst), *n.* absence of interest; indifference.

dis·in·ter·est·ed (dĭs ĭn'tə rĕs'tĭd, -trĭs tĭd), *adj.* **1.** unbiased by selfish motives. **2.** *U.S. Colloq.* not interested. —**dis·in'ter·est'ed·ly**, *adv.* —**dis·in'ter·est'ed·ness**, *n.*

dis·join (dĭs join'), *v.t.*, *v.i.* to disunite; separate.

dis·joint (dĭs joint'), *v.t.* **1.** to separate the joints of. **2.** to derange. —*v.i.* **3.** to come apart. **4.** to be dislocated.

dis·joint·ed (dĭs join'tĭd), *adj.* **1.** having the joints separated. **2.** disconnected; incoherent. —**dis·joint'ed·ly**, *adv.* —**dis·joint'ed·ness**, *n.*

dis·junc·tive (dĭs jŭngk'tĭv), *adj.* **1.** serving or tending to disjoin. **2.** *Gram.* **a.** syntactically setting two or more expressions in opposition to each other or expressing an alternative. **b.** not

syntactically dependent upon some particular expression. —**dis·junc'tive·ly**, *adv.*

disk (dĭsk), *n.* **1.** any thin, flat, circular plate, object, or surface. **2.** a phonograph record. **3.** *Bot., Zool., etc.* any of various roundish, flat structures. **4.** *Bot.* (in the daisy and other composite plants) the central portion of the flower head, composed of tubular florets.

disk harrow, a harrow having sharp-edged disks set at such an angle that they pulverize and turn the soil.

disk jockey, a radio announcer on an all-record program.

dis·like (dĭs līk'), *v.*, **-liked, -liking**, *n.* —*v.t.* **1.** to regard with displeasure or aversion. —*n.* **2.** the feeling of disliking; distaste. —**dis·lik'a·ble**, *adj.*

dis·lo·cate (dĭs'lō kāt'), *v.t.*, **-cated, -cating. 1.** to displace; put out of proper position. **2.** to derange; upset; disorder. —**dis'lo·ca'tion**, *n.*

dis·lodge (dĭs lŏj'), *v.t.*, *v.i.*, **-lodged, -lodging.** to drive, or be driven, from a place of lodgment. —**dis·lodg'ment**, *n.*

dis·loy·al (dĭs loi'əl), *adj.* not loyal; false to one's obligations or allegiance. —**dis·loy'al·ly**, *adv.*

dis·loy·al·ty (dĭs loi'əl tĭ), *n.*, *pl.* **-ties. 1.** quality of being disloyal. **2.** violation of allegiance or duty. **3.** a disloyal act.

dis·mal (dĭz'məl), *adj.* **1.** gloomy; dreary. **2.** terrible; dreadful. —**dis'mal·ly**, *adv.* —**dis'mal·ness**, *n.*

dis·man·tle (dĭs măn'təl), *v.t.*, **-tled, -tling. 1.** to deprive of equipment, defenses, etc. **2.** to pull down; take apart. —**dis·man'tle·ment**, *n.*

dis·may (dĭs mā'), *v.t.* **1.** to dishearten utterly; daunt. —*n.* **2.** sudden or complete loss of courage; utter disheartenment.

dis·mem·ber (dĭs mĕm'bər), *v.t.* **1.** to deprive of limbs. **2.** to separate into parts. —**dis·mem'ber·ment**, *n.*

dis·miss (dĭs mĭs'), *v.t.* **1.** to direct or allow to go. **2.** to discharge, as from service. **3.** to discard or reject. —**dis·miss'al**, *n.*

dis·mount (dĭs mount'), *v.i.* **1.** to get off (from a horse, bicycle, etc.). —*v.t.* **2.** to throw down, as from a horse. **3.** to remove from its mounting, setting, etc. **4.** to take (a piece of mechanism) to pieces. —**dis·mount'a·ble**, *adj.*

dis·o·be·di·ent (dĭs'ə bē'dĭ ənt), *adj.* neglecting or refusing to obey. —**dis'o·be'di·ence**, *n.* —**dis'o·be'di·ent·ly**, *adv.*

dis·o·bey (dĭs'ə bā'), *v.t.*, *v.i.* to neglect or refuse to obey. —**dis'o·bey'er**, *n.*

dis·o·blige (dĭs'ə blīj'), *v.t.*, **-bliged, -bliging. 1.** to refuse or neglect to oblige. **2.** to affront. —**dis'o·blig'ing**, *adj.* —**dis'o·blig'ing·ly**, *adv.*

dis·or·der (dĭs ôr'dər), *n.* **1.** lack of order or regular arrangement. **2.** an irregularity. **3.** breach of order. **4.** a derangement of physical or mental health. —*v.t.* **5.** to destroy the order of. **6.** to derange the physical or mental health of.

dis·or·der·ly (dĭs ôr'dər lĭ), *adj.* **1.** untidy; confused. **2.** unruly; tumultuous. **3.** *Law.* contrary to public order or morality. —*adv.* **4.** without order; confusedly. —**dis·or'der·li·ness**, *n.*

dis·or·gan·ize (dĭs ôr'gə nīz'), *v.t.*, **-ized, -izing.** to throw into confusion or disorder. —**dis·or'gan·i·za'tion**, *n.* —**dis·or'gan·iz'er**, *n.*

dis·own (dĭs ōn'), *v.t.* to refuse to acknowledge as belonging or pertaining to oneself; repudiate.

dis·par·age (dĭs pär'ĭj), *v.t.*, **-aged, -aging. 1.** to lower the estimation of. **2.** to belittle. —**dis·par'age·ment**, *n.* —**dis·par'ag·er**, *n.* —**dis·par'ag·ing·ly**, *adv.*

dis·pa·rate (dĭs'pə rĭt), *adj.* dissimilar; unlike.

dis·par·i·ty (dĭs pär'ə tĭ), *n.*, *pl.* **-ties.** lack of similarity or equality; inequality; difference.

dis·pas·sion·ate (dĭs păsh'ən ĭt), *adj.* free from personal feeling; impartial; calm. —**dis·pas'sion·ate·ly**, *adv.* —**dis·pas'sion·ate·ness**, *n.*

dis·patch (dĭs păch'), *v.t.* **1.** to send off. **2.** to dismiss (a person), as after an audience. **3.** to kill. **4.** to transact (business, etc.) quickly. —*n.* **5.** the sending off of a messenger, letter, etc. **6.** dismissal. **7.** killing. **8.** speedy transaction. **9.** speed. **10.** a written message, esp. one sent in haste. **11.** a news account transmitted by a reporter. —**dis·patch'er**, *n.*

dis·pel (dĭs pĕl'), *v.t.*, **-pelled, -pelling.** to scatter; disperse. —**dis·pel'ler**, *n.*

dis·pen·sa·ble (dĭs pĕn'sə bəl), *adj.* **1.** unimportant. **2.** capable of being administered.

dis·pen·sa·ry (dĭs pĕn'sə rĭ), *n.*, *pl.* -ries. a place where something is dispensed, esp. medicines.

dis·pen·sa·tion (dĭs'pən sā'shən, -pĕn-), *n.* **1.** act of dispensing. **2.** that which is distributed. **3.** a certain order or system. **4.** *Theol.* **a.** the divine ordering of affairs. **b.** a divinely appointed system. **5.** *Rom. Cath. Ch.* an official relaxation of a law in a particular case. **—dis'pen·sa'tor,** *n.*

dis·pen·sa·to·ry (dĭs pĕn'sə tōr'Ĭ), *n.*, *pl.* -ries. **1.** a book in which medicinal substances are described. **2.** a dispensary.

dis·pense (dĭs pĕns'), *v.*, -pensed, -pensing. **—v.t. 1.** to deal out; distribute. **2.** to administer (laws, etc.). **3.** *Pharm.* to put up (medicine). **4.** *Rom. Cath. Ch.* to grant a dispensation to, for, or from. **—v.i. 5.** to grant dispensation. **6. dispense with, a.** to forgo. **b.** to do away with (a need, etc.). **—dis·pens'er,** *n.*

dis·perse (dĭs pûrs'), *v.*, -persed, -persing. **—v.t. 1.** to scatter abroad. **2.** to spread; diffuse. **3.** to dispel. **—v.i. 4.** to become scattered. **5.** to vanish. **—dis·pers'ed·ly,** *adv.* **—dis·pers'er,** *n.*

dis·per·sion (dĭs pûr'shən, -zhən), *n.* **1.** act of dispersing. **2.** state of being dispersed. **3.** *Optics.* the separation of white or complex light into its constituent colors. Also, *for defs. 1 and 2,* **dis·per'sal.**

dis·pir·it (dĭs pĭr'Ĭt), *v.t.* to discourage; dishearten. **—dis·pir'it·ed,** *adj.* **—dis·pir'it·ed·ly,** *adv.*

dis·place (dĭs plās'), *v.t.*, -placed, -placing. **1.** to put out of the usual or proper place. **2.** to replace. **3.** to remove from a position, office, or dignity.

displaced person, (esp. in Europe) a person removed from his homeland for use as a slave laborer or driven from it by an invasion.

dis·place·ment (dĭs plās'mənt), *n.* **1.** act of displacing. **2.** state of being displaced. **3.** the weight or volume of fluid displaced by a floating or submerged body, equivalent to the weight of the floating body or to the volume of the submerged body.

dis·play (dĭs plā'), *v.t.* **1.** to show; exhibit. **2.** to reveal; betray. **3.** to unfold. **4.** to show ostentatiously. **—n. 5.** exhibition; show. **6.** an ostentatious show. **—dis·play'er,** *n.*

dis·please (dĭs plēz'), *v.*, -pleased, -pleasing. **—v.t. 1.** to offend; annoy. **—v.i. 2.** to be unpleasant.

dis·pleas·ure (dĭs plĕzh'ər), *n.*, *v.*, -ured, -uring. **—n. 1.** dissatisfaction; annoyance. **—v.t. 2.** *Archaic.* to displease.

dis·port (dĭs pōrt'), *v.t.*, *v.i.* **1.** to divert or amuse (oneself). **—n. 2.** diversion; amusement.

dis·pos·a·ble (dĭs pō'zə bəl), *adj.* capable of being disposed of; subject to disposal.

dis·pos·al (dĭs pō'zəl), *n.* **1.** act of disposing, or of disposing of, something. **2.** bestowal or assignment. **3.** control.

dis·pose (dĭs pōz'), *v.*, -posed, -posing. **—v.t. 1.** to put in a particular arrangement or place. **2.** to incline. **—v.i. 3.** to arrange or decide matters. **4. dispose of, a.** to deal with or get rid of. **b.** to give or sell. **—dis·pos'er,** *n.*

dis·po·si·tion (dĭs'pə zĭsh'ən), *n.* **1.** mental or moral constitution. **2.** inclination or tendency. **3.** arrangement, as of troops. **4.** final settlement. **5.** regulation. **6.** bestowal, as by gift or sale. **7.** control.

dis·pos·sess (dĭs'pə zĕs'), *v.t.* to put out of possession. **—dis'pos·ses'sion,** *n.* **—dis'pos·ses'sor,** *n.*

dis·praise (dĭs prāz'), *v.*, -praised, -praising. *n.* **—v.t. 1.** to censure; disparage. **—n. 2.** censure.

dis·proof (dĭs prōōf'), *n.* refutation.

dis·pro·por·tion (dĭs'prə pōr'shən), *n.* **1.** lack of proportion. **2.** something out of proportion. **—v.t. 3.** to make disproportionate.

dis·pro·por·tion·ate (dĭs'prə pōr'shə nĭt), *adj.* not proportionate. Also, **dis'pro·por'tion·al.** **—dis'pro·por'tion·ate·ly,** *adv.* **—dis'pro·por'tion·ate·ness,** *n.*

dis·prove (dĭs prōōv'), *v.t.*, -proved, -proving. to prove to be false. **—dis·prov'a·ble,** *adj.*

dis·put·a·ble (dĭs pū'tə bəl, dĭs'pyōō tə bəl), *adj.* that may be disputed; questionable. **—dis·put'a·bil'i·ty,** *n.* **—dis·put'a·bly,** *adv.*

dis·pu·tant (dĭs'pyōō tənt, dĭs pū'tənt), *adj.* **1.** disputing. **—n. 2.** one who disputes; a debater.

dis·pu·ta·tion (dĭs'pyōō tā'shən), *n.* a controversy or debate.

dis·pu·ta·tious (dĭs'pyōō tā'shəs), *adj.* argumentative; contentious. Also, **dis·put·a·tive** (dĭs·pū'tə tĭv). **—dis'pu·ta'tious·ly,** *adv.*

dis·pute (dĭs pūt'), *v.*, -puted, -puting, *n.* **—v.i.**, *v.t.* **1.** to engage in argument. **2.** to quarrel (about). **—n. 3.** argument; quarrel.

dis·qual·i·fi·ca·tion (dĭs kwŏl'ə fə kā'shən), *n.* **1.** act of disqualifying. **2.** state of being disqualified. **3.** something that disqualifies.

dis·qual·i·fy (dĭs kwŏl'ə fĭ'), *v.*, -fied, -fying. **—v.t. 1.** to deprive of qualification. **2.** to deprive of rights or privileges.

dis·qui·et (dĭs kwī'ət), *v.t.* **1.** to disturb; make uneasy. **—n. 2.** disturbance; uneasiness.

dis·qui·e·tude (dĭs kwī'ə tūd', -tōōd'), *n.* state of disquiet; uneasiness.

dis·qui·si·tion (dĭs'kwə zĭsh'ən), *n.* a formal discourse or treatise on a subject.

Dis·rae·li (dĭz rā'lĭ), *n.* **Benjamin,** (*Earl of Beaconsfield*) 1804–81, British statesman.

dis·re·gard (dĭs'rĭ gärd'), *v.t.* **1.** to pay no attention to. **2.** to treat without due regard. **—n. 3.** lack of regard; neglect. **—dis're·gard'ful,** *adj.*

dis·re·pair (dĭs'rĭ pâr'), *n.* impaired condition.

dis·rep·u·ta·ble (dĭs rĕp'yə tə bəl), *adj.* **1.** not reputable. **2.** discreditable. **—dis·rep'u·ta·bil'i·ty,** *n.* **—dis·rep'u·ta·bly,** *adv.*

dis·re·pute (dĭs'rĭ pūt'), *n.* ill repute; discredit.

dis·re·spect (dĭs'rĭ spĕkt'), *n.* **1.** lack of respect. **—v.t. 2.** to regard or treat without respect. **—dis're·spect'ful,** *adj.* **—dis're·spect'ful·ly,** *adv.*

dis·robe (dĭs rōb'), *v.t.*, *v.i.*, -robed, -robing. to undress. **—dis·robe'ment,** *n.* **—dis·rob'er,** *n.*

dis·rupt (dĭs rŭpt'), *v.t.* to break up. **—dis·rupt'er,** *n.* **—dis·rup'tion,** *n.* **—dis·rup'tive,** *adj.*

dis·sat·is·fac·tion (dĭs'săt Ĭs făk'shən), *n.* lack of satisfaction; state of not being satisfied.

dis·sat·is·fy (dĭs săt'Ĭs fĭ'), *v.t.*, -fied, -fying. to make ill-satisfied, ill-pleased, or discontented.

dis·sect (dĭ sĕkt'), *v.t.* **1.** to cut apart (an animal body, plant, etc.) to examine it. **2.** to analyze. **—dis·sec'tion,** *n.* **—dis·sec'tor,** *n.*

dis·sem·ble (dĭ sĕm'bəl), *v.*, -bled, -bling. **—v.t. 1.** to conceal the real nature of. **2.** to feign. **3.** to ignore. **—v.i. 4.** to conceal one's motives, etc. **—dis·sem'bler,** *n.*

dis·sem·i·nate (dĭ sĕm'ə nāt'), *v.t.*, -nated, -nating. to scatter, as seed in sowing; spread abroad. **—dis·sem'i·na'tion,** *n.* **—dis·sem'i·na'tor,** *n.*

dis·sen·sion (dĭ sĕn'shən), *n.* **1.** violent disagreement; discord. **2.** difference in opinion.

dis·sent (dĭ sĕnt'), *v.i.* **1.** to disagree. **2.** to differ in religious opinion. **—n. 3.** difference in opinion. **4.** separation from an established church. **—dis·sent'er,** *n.*

dis·sen·tient (dĭ sĕn'shənt), *adj.* **1.** dissenting. **—n. 2.** one who dissents. **—dis·sen'tience,** *n.*

dis·ser·ta·tion (dĭs'ər tā'shən), *n.* a written essay, treatise, or thesis, esp. a formal one.

dis·serv·ice (dĭs sûr'vĭs), *n.* harm; injury.

dis·sev·er (dĭ sĕv'ər), *v.t.*, *v.i.* **1.** to separate. **2.** to divide into parts. **—dis·sev'er·ance,** *n.*

dis·si·dent (dĭs'ə dənt), *adj.* **1.** dissenting. **—n. 2.** a dissenter. **—dis'si·dence,** *n.*

dis·sim·i·lar (dĭ sĭm'ə lər), *adj.* not similar. **—dis·sim·i·lar·i·ty** (dĭ sĭm'ə lăr'ə tĭ), *n.* **—dis·sim'i·lar·ly,** *adv.*

dis·si·mil·i·tude (dĭs'sĭ mĭl'ə tūd', -tōōd'), *n.* **1.** unlikeness; difference. **2.** a point of difference.

dis·sim·u·late (dĭ sĭm'yə lāt'), *v.t.*, *v.i.*, -lated, -lating. to disguise or dissemble. **—dis·sim'u·la'tion,** *n.*

dis·si·pate (dĭs'ə pāt'), *v.*, -pated, -pating. **—v.t. 1.** to scatter. **2.** to scatter wastefully; squander. **—v.i. 3.** to be scattered. **4.** to indulge in dissolute pleasure. **—dis'si·pat'er, dis'si·pa'tor,** *n.*

dis·si·pat·ed (dĭs'ə pā'tĭd), *adj.* dissolute. **—dis'si·pat'ed·ly,** *adv.* **—dis'si·pat'ed·ness,** *n.*

dis·si·pa·tion (dĭs'ə pā'shən), *n.* **1.** act of dissipating. **2.** state of being dissipated. **3.** waste. **4.** dissolute living.

dis·so·ci·ate (dĭ sō'shĭ āt'), *v.t.*, *v.i.*, -ated, -ating. **1.** to disunite; separate. **2.** *Chem.* to subject to or undergo dissociation. —**dis·so'ci·a'tive,** *adj.*

dis·so·ci·a·tion (dĭ sō'sĭ ā'shən, -shĭ ā'-), *n.* **1.** separation; disunion. **2.** *Chem.* the decomposition of a complex substance into simpler constituents.

dis·sol·u·ble (dĭ sŏl'yə bəl), *adj.* capable of being dissolved. —**dis·sol'u·bil'i·ty,** *n.*

dis·so·lute (dĭs'ə loot'), *adj.* indifferent to moral restraints; licentious. —**dis'so·lute'ly,** *adv.* —**dis'so·lute'ness,** *n.*

dis·so·lu·tion (dĭs'ə loo'shən), *n.* **1.** act of resolving into parts. **2.** the resulting state. **3.** the breaking up of a tie, bond, assembly, organization, etc. **4.** an order by the head of the state terminating a parliament. **5.** death. **6.** destruction. **7.** the legal termination of business activity. **8.** *Chem.* solution in a liquid substance.

dis·solve (dĭ zŏlv'), *v.,* **-solved, -solving.** —*v.t.* **1.** to make a solution of. **2.** to break up (a connection, union, assembly, organization, etc.). **3.** to order the termination of a parliament. **4.** to end; destroy. **5.** to resolve into parts or elements. **6.** *Law.* to annul. —*v.i.* **7.** to become dissolved. **8.** to disappear gradually. —**dis·solv'a·ble,** *adj.* —**dis·solv'er,** *n.*

dis·so·nance (dĭs'ə nəns), *n.* **1.** an inharmonious sound. **2.** *Music.* a simultaneous combination of tones conventionally accepted as being in a state of unrest and needing completion.

dis·so·nant (dĭs'ə nənt), *adj.* **1.** harsh in sound. **2.** out of harmony. —**dis'so·nant·ly,** *adv.*

dis·suade (dĭ swād'), *v.t.,* **-suaded, -suading.** **1.** to deter by advice. **2.** to urge against. —**dis·sua·sion** (dĭ swā'zhən), *n.* —**dis·sua·sive** (dĭ swā'sĭv), *adj.*

dist., **1.** distance. **2.** district.

dis·taff (dĭs'tăf, -täf), *n.* **1.** a staff with a cleft end, used for holding wool, flax, etc., in spinning. **2.** the female sex. **3.** a woman.

distaff side, the female side of a family.

dis·tance (dĭs'təns), *n., v.,* **-tanced, -tancing.** —*n.* **1.** the extent of space between things or points. **2.** remoteness. **3.** the interval between two points of time. **4.** a distant point or place. **5.** reserve or aloofness. **6.** *Music.* interval. —*v.t.* **7.** to surpass.

dis·tant (dĭs'tənt), *adj.* **1.** far off or apart; remote. **2.** apart. **3.** reserved. **4.** to a distance. —**dis'tant·ly,** *adv.*

dis·taste (dĭs tāst'), *n.* **1.** dislike. **2.** aversion for food or drink.

dis·taste·ful (dĭs tāst'fəl), *adj.* **1.** causing dislike. **2.** unpleasant to the taste. —**dis·taste'·ful·ly,** *adv.* —**dis·taste'ful·ness,** *n.*

dis·tem·per[1] (dĭs tĕm'pər), *n.* **1.** a specific infectious disease of young dogs caused by a filterable virus. **2.** a disorder or disease. **3.** disturbance. —*v.t.* **4.** to derange.

dis·tem·per[2] (dĭs tĕm'pər), *n.* **1.** a method of painting in which the colors are mixed with some binding medium. **2.** a painting by this method. —*v.t.* **3.** to paint in distemper.

dis·tend (dĭs tĕnd'), *v.t., v.i.* **1.** to stretch apart or out. **2.** to expand by stretching. —**dis·ten·si·ble** (dĭs tĕn'sə bəl), *adj.* —**dis·ten'si·bil'i·ty,** *n.* —**dis·ten'tion,** *n.*

dis·tich (dĭs'tĭk), *n. Pros.* a couplet.

dis·till (dĭs tĭl'), *v.t., v.i.,* **-tilled, -tilling.** *Chiefly Brit.* distill.

dis·till (dĭs tĭl'), *v.t.* **1.** to subject to, extract by, or obtain by distillation. **2.** to let fall in drops. —*v.i.* **3.** to undergo distillation. **4.** to fall in drops. —**dis·till'a·ble,** *adj.*

dis·til·late (dĭs'tə lĭt, -lāt'), *n.* the product obtained from condensation of vapors in distillation.

dis·til·la·tion (dĭs'tə lā'shən), *n.* **1.** the volatilizing or evaporation and subsequent condensation of a liquid. **2.** the purification or concentration of a substance. **3.** a distillate. **4.** act or process of distilling. **5.** fact of being distilled.

dis·till·er (dĭs tĭl'ər), *n.* **1.** an apparatus for distilling. **2.** one who extracts spirituous liquors by distillation.

dis·till·er·y (dĭs tĭl'ə rĭ), *n., pl.* **-eries.** a place or establishment where distilling is carried on.

dis·tinct (dĭs tĭngkt'), *adj.* **1.** not identical. **2.** different in nature. **3.** clear; plain. **4.** distinguishing clearly. —**dis·tinct'ness,** *n.*

dis·tinc·tion (dĭs tĭngk'shən), *n.* **1.** a distinguishing as different. **2.** the noting of differences; discrimination. **3.** a difference. **4.** a distinguishing characteristic. **5.** a mark of special favor. **6.**

marked superiority; eminence. **7.** distinguished appearance.

dis·tinc·tive (dĭs tĭngk'tĭv), *adj.* distinguishing. —**dis·tinc'tive·ly,** *adv.* —**dis·tinc'tive·ness,** *n.*

dis·tinct·ly (dĭs tĭngkt'lĭ), *adv.* **1.** in a distinct manner; clearly. **2.** without doubt.

dis·tin·gué (dĭs'tăng gā', dĭs tăng'gā), *adj.* distinguished. —**dis'tin·gué,** *adj. fem.*

dis·tin·guish (dĭs tĭng'gwĭsh), *v.t.* **1.** to mark off as different. **2.** to recognize as different. **3.** to perceive clearly. **4.** to be a distinctive characteristic of. **5.** to make eminent. **6.** to classify. —*v.i.* **7.** to show a difference. **8.** to discriminate. —**dis·tin'guish·a·ble,** *adj.* —**dis·tin'guish·a·bly,** *adv.* —**dis·tin'guish·er,** *n.*

dis·tin·guished (dĭs tĭng'gwĭsht), *adj.* **1.** conspicuous. **2.** eminent. **3.** distingué.

dis·tort (dĭs tôrt'), *v.t.* **1.** to twist awry or out of shape. **2.** to pervert. —**dis·tort'ed,** *adj.* —**dis·tort'er,** *n.* —**dis·tor'tion,** *n.*

dis·tract (dĭs trăkt'), *v.t.* **1.** to divert, as the attention. **2.** to trouble greatly in mind. **3.** to rend by dissension. —**dis·tract'ed,** *adj.* —**dis·tract'ed·ly,** *adv.* —**dis·tract'er,** *n.* —**dis·tract'ing,** *adj.* —**dis·tract'ing·ly,** *adv.* —**dis·trac'tive,** *adj.*

dis·trac·tion (dĭs trăk'shən), *n.* **1.** act of distracting. **2.** state of being distracted. **3.** mental derangement. **4.** tumult.

dis·trait (dĭs trā'), *adj.* absent-minded.

dis·traught (dĭs trôt'), *adj.* **1.** distracted; bewildered; deeply agitated. **2.** crazed.

dis·tress (dĭs trĕs'), *n.* **1.** great pain, anxiety, or sorrow. **2.** a state of extreme necessity. **3.** the state of a ship requiring immediate assistance. —*v.t.* **4.** to afflict with pain, anxiety, or sorrow. —**dis·tress'ful,** *adj.* —**dis·tress'ful·ly,** *adv.* —**dis·tress'ing,** *adj.* —**dis·tress'ing·ly,** *adv.*

dis·trib·ute (dĭs trĭb'ūt), *v.t.,* **-uted, -uting.** **1.** to divide in shares; allot. **2.** to spread; scatter. **3.** to sort or classify. —**dis·trib'ut·a·ble,** *adj.*

dis·tri·bu·tion (dĭs'trə bū'shən), *n.* **1.** act of distributing. **2.** state or manner of being distributed. **3.** arrangement; classification. **4.** that which is distributed. —**dis·tri·bu'tion·al,** *adj.*

dis·trib·u·tive (dĭs trĭb'yə tĭv), *adj.* **1.** that distributes. **2.** *Gram.* treating the members of a group individually. —**dis·trib'u·tive·ly,** *adv.*

dis·trib·u·tor (dĭs trĭb'yə tər), *n.* **1.** one that distributes. **2.** one engaged in general marketing of some goods. **3.** a device in an engine which distributes the igniting voltage to the spark plugs in a definite sequence. Also, **dis·trib'u·ter.**

dis·trict (dĭs'trĭkt), *n.* **1.** a division of a country, county, etc., for administrative, electoral, or other purposes. **2.** a region or locality. —*v.t.* **3.** to divide into districts.

district attorney, an attorney for the government within a specified district.

District of Columbia, a federal area in the E United States, on the Potomac, coextensive with the federal capital, Washington: governed by Congress. 843,451 pop.; 69 sq. mi. *Abbr.:* D. C.

dis·trust (dĭs trŭst'), *v.t.* **1.** to regard with doubt or suspicion. —*n.* **2.** doubt; suspicion. —**dis·trust'ful,** *adj.* —**dis·trust'ful·ly,** *adv.*

dis·turb (dĭs tûrb'), *v.t.* **1.** to interrupt the quiet, rest, or peace of. **2.** to interfere with. **3.** to disarrange; unsettle. **4.** to trouble. —**dis·turb'er,** *n.* —**dis·turb'ing·ly,** *adv.*

dis·turb·ance (dĭs tûr'bəns), *n.* **1.** act of disturbing. **2.** state of being disturbed. **3.** something that disturbs. **4.** an outbreak of disorder.

dis·un·ion (dĭs ūn'yən), *n.* **1.** severance of union; separation. **2.** lack of union; dissension.

dis·u·nite (dĭs'ū nīt'), *v.t., v.i.,* **-nited, -niting.** **1.** to separate; disjoin. **2.** to alienate. —**dis·u·ni·ty** (dĭs ū'nə tĭ), *n.*

dis·use (*n.* dĭs ūs'; *v.* dĭs ūz'), *n., v.,* **-used, -using.** —*n.* **1.** discontinuance of use or practice. —*v.t.* **2.** to cease to use.

ditch (dĭch), *n.* **1.** a long, narrow channel in the earth, as for irrigating land. **2.** any channel or waterway. —*v.t.* **3.** to dig a ditch or ditches in. **4.** *Slang.* to get rid of. —**ditch'er,** *n.*

dith·er (dĭth'ər), *n.* **1.** a trembling. **2.** *Colloq.* a state of trembling excitement or fear.

dith·y·ramb (dĭth'ə răm', -rămb'), *n.* a vehement or wild choral song, orig. one in honor of Dionysus. —**dith·y·ram·bic** (dĭth'ə răm'bĭk), *adj.*

dit·to (dĭt'ō), *n., pl.* **-tos,** *adv., v.,* **-toed, -toing.**

—n. 1. the aforesaid; the same. **—adv. 2.** as already stated. **—v.t. 3.** to duplicate.

ditto marks, two small marks (") indicating repetition, placed beneath the thing repeated.

dit·ty (dĭt′ĭ), *n., pl.* **-ties. 1.** a poem intended to be sung. **2.** a short, simple song.

ditty bag, a bag used by sailors to hold sewing implements and other necessaries. Also, **ditty box.**

di·u·ret·ic (dī′yŏŏ rĕt′ĭk), *Med.* **—adj. 1.** increasing the urine. **—n. 2.** a diuretic medicine.

di·ur·nal (dī ûr′nəl), *adj.* **1.** daily. **2.** of the daytime. **—di·ur′nal·ly,** *adv.*

div., 1. divided. **2.** dividend. **3.** division.

di·va (dē′vä), *n., pl.* **-vas.** a prima donna.

di·va·lent (dī vā′lənt), *adj. Chem.* having a valence of two.

di·van (dī′văn, dī văn′), *n.* a sofa or couch.

dive (dīv), *v.,* **dived** or (*U.S. Colloq. and Brit. Dial.*) **dove; dived; diving;** *n.* **—v.i. 1.** to plunge, esp. headfirst, as into water. **2.** to go below the surface of the water, as a submarine. **3.** to plunge deeply. **4.** (of an airplane) to plunge downward at a sharp angle. **—n. 5.** act of diving. **6.** *Colloq.* a disreputable place. **—div′er,** *n.*

dive bomber, an airplane of the pursuit type which drops its bombs while diving temporarily at the target. **—dive bombing.**

di·verge (dĭ vûrj′, dī-), *v.i.,* **-verged, -verging. 1.** to move or lie in different directions from a common point. **2.** to differ. **—di·ver′gence,** *n.* **—di·ver′gent,** *adj.* **—di·ver′gent·ly,** *adv.*

di·vers (dī′vərz), *adj.* several; sundry.

di·verse (dĭ vûrs′, dī-, dī′vûrs), *adj.* **1.** of a different kind, form, etc. **2.** of various kinds or forms. **—di·verse′ly,** *adv.* **—di·verse′ness,** *n.*

di·ver·si·fy (dĭ vûr′sə fī′, dī-), *v.t.,* **-fied, -fying. 1.** to give variety or diversity to. **2.** to vary. **—di·ver′si·fi·ca′tion,** *n.*

di·ver·sion (dĭ vûr′zhən, -shən, dī-), *n.* **1.** act of diverting, as from a course. **2.** recreation; pastime.

di·ver·si·ty (dĭ vûr′sə tĭ, dī-), *n., pl.* **-ties. 1.** state of being diverse; difference. **2.** variety.

di·vert (dĭ vûrt′, dī-), *v.t.* **1.** to turn aside; deflect. **2.** to draw off to a different object, etc. **3.** to entertain or amuse. **—di·vert′er,** *n.*

di·ver·tisse·ment (dē vĕr tēs män′), *n.* a diversion or entertainment.

di·vest (dĭ vĕst′, dī-), *v.t.* **1.** to strip of clothing, etc. **2.** to deprive of anything; dispossess.

di·vide (dĭ vīd′), *v.,* **-vided, -viding,** *n.* **—v.t. 1.** to separate into parts. **2.** to sunder; cut off. **3.** to apportion; share. **4.** to cause to disagree. **5.** to classify. **6.** *Math.* to separate into equal parts by the process of division. **—v.i. 7.** to become divided. **8.** to share something with others. **—n. 9.** the zone separating two drainage basins.

di·vid·ed (dĭ vī′dĭd), *adj.* **1.** separated; shared. **2.** *Bot.* (of a leaf) cut into distinct portions by incisions extending to the midrib or base.

div·i·dend (dĭv′ə dĕnd′), *n.* **1.** *Math.* a number to be divided by another. **2.** a pro-rata share in an amount to be distributed. **3.** a share of anything divided.

di·vid·er (dĭ vī′dər), *n.* **1.** one that divides. **2.** (*pl.*) compasses for dividing lines, etc.

div·i·na·tion (dĭv′ə nā′shən), *n.* **1.** the discovering of what is obscure or future, as by supernatural means. **2.** prophecy. **—di·vin·a·to·ry** (dĭ vĭn′ə tôr′ĭ), *adj.*

di·vine (dĭ vīn′), *adj., n., v.,* **-vined, -vining. —adj. 1.** of or pertaining to God or a god. **2.** religious; sacred. **3.** from God. **4.** godlike. **5.** heavenly. **—n. 6.** a theologian. **7.** a priest or clergyman. **—v.t., v.i. 8.** to prophesy. **9.** to perceive by insight; conjecture. **—di·vine′ly,** *adv.* **—di·vine′ness,** *n.* **—di·vin′er,** *n.*

diving bell, a vessel filled with air under pressure, in which persons may work under water.

di·vin·i·ty (dĭ vĭn′ə tĭ), *n., pl.* **-ties. 1.** divine nature. **2.** godhood. **3.** a god. **4. the Divinity,** the Deity. **5.** theology.

di·vis·i·ble (dĭ vĭz′ə bəl), *adj.* capable of being divided. **—di·vis′i·bil′i·ty,** *n.* **—di·vis′i·bly,** *adv.*

di·vi·sion (dĭ vĭzh′ən), *n.* **1.** act of dividing. **2.** state of being divided. **3.** *Math.* the operation inverse to multiplication. **4.** something that divides. **5.** a section. **6.** disagreement; dissension. **7.** *Mil.* a major administrative and tactical unit, usually commanded by a major general. **—di·vi′sion·al,** *adj.*

di·vi·sive (dĭ vī′sĭv), *adj.* creating discord.

di·vi·sor (dĭ vī′zər), *n. Math.* a number by which another number (the dividend) is divided.

di·vorce (dĭ vôrs′), *n., v.,* **-vorced, -vorcing. —n. 1.** a legal dissolution of the marriage bond. **2.** a complete separation of any kind. **—v.t. 3.** to separate by or as by divorce.

di·vor·cee (dĭ vôr′sē′), *n.* a divorced person.

div·ot (dĭv′ət), *n. Golf.* a piece of turf cut out with a club in making a stroke.

di·vulge (dĭ vŭlj′), *v.t.,* **-vulged, -vulging.** to disclose or reveal.

Dix·ie (dĭk′sĭ), *n.* the Southern States of the United States. Also, **Dixie Land.**

diz·en (dīz′ən, dĭz′ən), *v.t.* to deck gaudily.

diz·zy (dĭz′ĭ), *adj.,* **-zier, -ziest,** *v.,* **-zied, -zying. —adj. 1.** affected with a sensation of whirling; giddy. **2.** confused. **3.** causing giddiness. **4.** *Colloq.* foolish. **—v.t. 5.** to make dizzy. **—diz′zi·ly,** *adv.* **—diz′zi·ness,** *n.*

Dji·bou·ti (jē bōō′tē), *n.* a seaport in and the capital of French Somaliland. 16,600.

Dne·pro·pe·trovsk (dně′prŏ pě trôfsk′), *n.* a city in SW Soviet Union, on Dnieper. 500,662.

Dnie·per (nē′pər), *n.* a river in the W Soviet Union, flowing S to the Black Sea. ab. 1400 mi.

Dnies·ter (nē′stər), *n.* a river from Carpathians in SW Soviet Union to Black Sea. 800 mi.

do¹ (dōō), *v., pres. sing.* **1 do, 2** (*Archaic*) **doest** or **dost, 3 does** or (*Archaic*) **doeth** or **doth;** *pt.* **did;** *pp.* **done;** *ppr.* **doing;** *n.* **—v.t. 1.** to perform (acts, a problem, a part, etc.). **2.** to execute (work, etc.). **3.** to accomplish; finish. **4.** to exert. **5.** to be the cause of; effect. **6.** to render (homage, etc.). **7.** to deal with (anything) as the case may require. **8.** to traverse. **9.** *Slang.* to cheat. **10.** to serve. **11.** *Colloq.* to provide. **12. do in,** *Slang.* **a.** to ruin. **b.** to kill. **13. do up, a.** to wrap and tie up. **b.** to comb (hair). **—v.i. 14.** to be in action. **15.** to behave (wisely, etc.). **16.** to fare. **17.** to be as to health. **18.** to suffice. **19.** to treat. **20. do away with,** to abolish. **21.** (used without special meaning in interrogative, negative, and inverted constructions; in imperatives with *you* or *thou* expressed; and occasionally as a metrical expedient in verse). **22.** (used to lend emphasis to a principal verb). **23.** (used to avoid repetition of a verb or full verb expression). **—n. 24.** *Colloq.* a festivity.

do² (dō), *n. Music.* the syllable used for the first tone or keynote of a diatonic scale.

do., ditto.

do·a·ble (dōō′ə bəl), *adj.* that may be done.

dob·bin (dŏb′ĭn), *n.* quiet, plodding horse.

Do·ber·man pin·scher (dō′bər mən pĭn′shər), one of a breed of large smooth-coated terriers, usually black-and-tan or brown.

doc·ile (dŏs′əl; *Brit.* dō′sĭl), *adj.* **1.** readily taught. **2.** tractable. **—doc′ile·ly,** *adv.* **—do·cil·i·ty** (dō sĭl′ə tĭ, dŏ-), *n.*

dock¹ (dŏk), *n.* **1.** a wharf. **2.** the space between two piers, as for a ship. **—v.t. 3.** to bring into a dock. **—v.i. 4.** to come or go into a dock.

dock² (dŏk), *n.* **1.** the fleshy part of an animal's tail. **—v.t. 2.** to cut off the end of. **3.** to deduct from. **4.** to deduct from the wages of.

dock³ (dŏk), *n.* the place in a courtroom where a prisoner is placed during trial.

dock·age¹ (dŏk′ĭj), *n.* **1.** a charge for the use of a dock. **2.** docking accommodations.

dock·age² (dŏk′ĭj), *n.* curtailment; deduction.

dock·et (dŏk′ĭt), *n., v.,* **-eted, -eting. —n. 1.** a list of cases in court for trial. **2.** *U.S.* the list of business to be transacted. **3.** a label or ticket. **—v.t. 4.** *Law.* to abstract and enter in a book.

dock·yard (dŏk′yärd′), *n.* an enclosure where ships are repaired, fitted out, and built.

doc·tor (dŏk′tər), *n.* **1.** a person licensed to practice medicine; physician; surgeon. **2.** a person holding the highest degree conferred by a university. **3.** the academic title possessed by such a person. **4.** a man of great learning. **—v.t. 5.** to treat medicinally. **6.** *Colloq.* to mend. **7.** *Colloq.* to tamper with. **—v.i. 8.** to practice medicine. **9.** to take medicine. **—doc′tor·al,** *adj.*

doc·tor·ate (dŏk′tər ĭt), *n.* the degree of doctor.

doc·tri·naire (dŏk′trə nâr′), *n.* an impractical theorist. Also, **doc′tri·nar′i·an.**

doc·trine (dŏk′trĭn), *n.* **1.** a principle advocated. **2.** teachings collectively. **3.** a body of teachings on a particular subject. —**doc′tri·nal**, *adj.*

doc·u·ment (*n.* dŏk′yə mənt; *v.* dŏk′yə mĕnt′), *n.* 1. a paper furnishing information or evidence. —*v.t.* 2. to furnish with documents, etc. 3. to support by evidence. —**doc′u·men′ta·ry**, *adj.*, *n.* —**doc′u·men·ta′tion**, *n.*

dod·der (dŏd′ər), *v.i.* to shake; tremble.

do·dec·a·gon (dō dĕk′ə gŏn′, -gən), *n.* *Geom.* a polygon having twelve angles and twelve sides.

do·dec·a·he·dron (dō′dĕk ə hē′drən), *n.*, *pl.* **-drons, -dra** (-drə). *Geom.* a solid figure having twelve faces.

Do·dec·a·nese Islands (dō dĕk′ə nēs′, -nēz′, dō′dĕk ə-), a group of twelve Greek islands in the Aegean. 140,848 pop.; 1035 sq. mi.

dodge (dŏj), *v.*, **dodged, dodging**, *n.* —*v.i.* 1. to move suddenly, as to avoid a blow. 2. to prevaricate. —*v.t.* 3. to elude by a sudden shift or by strategy. —*n.* 4. an act of dodging. 5. *Colloq.* an ingenious trick.

dodg·er (dŏj′ər), *n.* 1. one who dodges. 2. a shifty person. 3. *U.S.* a small handbill.

Dodg·son (dŏj′sən), *n.* **Charles Lutwidge**, ("*Lewis Carroll*") 1832–98, British mathematician and author.

do·do (dō′dō), *n.*, *pl.* **-does, -dos.** a clumsy flightless bird of the islands of Mauritius, Réunion, and Rodriguez, but now extinct.

doe (dō), *n.* the female of the deer, antelope, goat, rabbit, and certain other animals.

do·er (dōo′ər), *n.* one who does something.

does (dŭz), *v.* 3rd pers. sing. pres. ind. of **do.**

doe·skin (dō′skĭn′), *n.* 1. the skin of a doe. 2. leather from this. 3. a smooth, closely woven woolen cloth.

Dodo (Ab. 3 ft. long)

does·n't (dŭz′nt), contraction of *does not.*

doff (dŏf, dôf), *v.t.* to remove, as a hat.

dog (dŏg, dôg), *n.*, *v.*, **dogged, dogging**. —*n.* 1. a domesticated carnivore, bred in a great many varieties. 2. any animal of the same family, including wolves, foxes, etc. 3. the male of such an animal. 4. a fellow. 5. (*cap.*) *Astron.* either of two constellations, Canis Major (**Great Dog**) and Canis Minor (**Little Dog**), situated near Orion. 6. a mechanical device for gripping or holding something. 7. an andiron. —*v.t.* 8. to follow closely.

dog·cart (dŏg′kärt′, dôg′-), *n.* 1. a light, two-wheeled vehicle with seats back to back. 2. a cart drawn by dogs.

dog days, a sultry part of the summer, now often reckoned from July 3 to Aug. 11.

doge (dōj), *n.* the chief magistrate of the old republics of Venice and Genoa.

dog-ear (dŏg′ĭr′, dôg′-), *n.* 1. the folded corner of a page in a book. —*v.t.* 2. to disfigure with dog-ears. —**dog′-eared′**, *adj.*

dog·fight (dŏg′fīt′, dôg′-), *n.* a violent engagement of warplanes at close quarters.

dog·fish (dŏg′fĭsh′, dôg′-), *n.*, *pl.* **-fishes**, (*esp. collectively*) **-fish.** any of various small sharks, as the **spiny dogfish** of the northern Atlantic.

dog·ged (dŏg′ĭd, dôg′-), *adj.* persistent; obstinate. —**dog′ged·ly**, *adv.* —**dog′ged·ness**, *n.*

dog·ger·el (dŏg′ər əl, dôg′-), *adj.* 1. (of verse) comic and usually loose in measure. —*n.* 2. doggerel verse. Also, **dog·grel** (dŏg′rəl, dôg′-).

dog·gy (dŏg′ĭ, dôg′ĭ), *n.*, *pl.* **-gies**, *adj.*, **-gier**, **-giest**. —*n.* 1. a little dog. —*adj.* 2. of a dog. 3. ostentatious. Also, **dog′gie.**

dog·house (dŏg′hous′, dôg′-), *n.* 1. a small shelter for a dog. 2. **in the doghouse**, in disfavor.

do·gie (dō′gĭ), *n.* *Western U.S.* a motherless calf in a cattle herd.

dog·ma (dŏg′mə, dôg′-), *n.*, *pl.* **-mas, -mata** (-mə tə). 1. a system of principles or tenets, as of a church. 2. a tenet or prescribed doctrine.

dog·mat·ic (dŏg măt′ĭk, dôg-), *adj.* 1. of or pertaining to dogma. 2. opinionated. Also, **dog·mat′i·cal.** —**dog·mat′i·cal·ly**, *adv.*

dog·ma·tism (dŏg′mə tĭz′əm, dôg′-), *n.* authoritative, positive, or arrogant assertion of opinions. —**dog′ma·tist**, *n.*

dog·ma·tize (dŏg′mə tīz′, dôg′-), *v.i.*, *v.t.*, **-tized, -tizing**. to speak or write dogmatically.

dog's-ear (dŏgz′ĭr′, dôgz′-), *n.*, *v.t.* dog-ear.

Dog Star, 1. Sirius. 2. Procyon.

dog·tooth violet (dŏg′tooth′, dôg′-), a bulbous liliaceous plant bearing yellow or pinkish-white flowers. Also, **dog′s-tooth violet.**

dog·trot (dŏg′trŏt′, dôg′-), *n.* a gentle trot.

dog·watch (dŏg′wŏch′, -wôch′, dôg′-), *n.* *Naut.* either of two short watches on shipboard, from 4 to 6 P.M. and from 6 to 8 P.M.

dog·wood (dŏg′wŏŏd′, dôg′-), *n.* any of a genus of trees or shrubs that includes the **flowering dogwood**, an American ornamental tree with large white or pinkish flowers.

doi·ly (doi′lĭ), *n.*, *pl.* **-lies.** a small ornamental napkin or mat.

do·ing (dōo′ĭng), *n.* 1. action. 2. (*pl.*) deeds.

dol·drum (dŏl′drəm), *n.* 1. a calm, windless area, esp. on the ocean. 2. (*pl.*) dullness; low spirits.

dole (dōl), *n.*, *v.*, **doled, doling.** —*n.* 1. a portion of money, food, etc., given, esp. in charity. 2. a distributing, esp. in charity. 3. a payment by a government to an unemployed person. —*v.t.* 4. to distribute in charity. 5. to give out sparingly.

dole·ful (dōl′fəl), *adj.* full of grief; sorrowful; gloomy. —**dole′ful·ly**, *adv.* —**dole′ful·ness**, *n.*

doll (dŏl), *n.* 1. a toy puppet; a child's toy baby. 2. a pretty but unintelligent woman. —*v.t.*, *v.i.* 3. *Slang.* to dress smartly.

dol·lar (dŏl′ər), *n.* 1. the monetary unit of the U.S., equivalent to 100 cents. 2. a gold or silver coin or a paper note having this value. 3. a corresponding unit, coin, or note elsewhere, as in Canada, China, Mexico, etc.

doll·y (dŏl′ĭ), *n.*, *pl.* **dollies.** 1. a child's name for a doll. 2. a low truck for moving loads.

dol·man (dŏl′mən), *n.*, *pl.* **-mans.** a woman's mantle with capelike arm pieces instead of sleeves.

dol·men (dŏl′mĕn), *n.* a structure usually regarded as a tomb, consisting of two or more large upright stones set with a space between and capped by a horizontal stone.

dol·o·mite (dŏl′ə mīt′), *n.* a common mineral, calcium magnesium carbonate, occurring in crystals and in masses (called **dolomite marble** when coarse-grained).

do·lor (dō′lər), *n.* *Now Chiefly Poetic.* sorrow or grief. Also, *Brit.*, **do′lour.**

dol·or·ous (dŏl′ər əs, dō′lər-), *adj.* full of, expressing, or causing pain or sorrow; grievous. —**dol′or·ous·ly**, *adv.* —**dol′or·ous·ness**, *n.*

dol·phin (dŏl′fĭn), *n.* 1. any of various cetaceans, some of which are commonly called porpoises, esp. one which has a long, sharp nose and abounds in the Mediterranean and the temperate Atlantic. 2. *Naut.* a post, pile cluster, or buoy to which to moor a vessel.

dolt (dōlt), *n.* a blockhead. —**dolt′ish**, *adj.*

-dom, a noun suffix meaning: 1. domain. 2. collection of persons. 3. rank or station. 4. general condition.

do·main (dō mān′), *n.* 1. *Law.* ultimate ownership of land. 2. eminent domain. 3. a realm. 4. a field of action, thought, etc.

dome (dōm), *n.*, *v.*, **domed, doming.** —*n.* 1. *Archit.* **a.** a large, hemispherical vault. **b.** a roof of such shape. 2. anything shaped like a dome. —*v.t.* 3. to cover with a dome. 4. to shape like a dome. —*v.i.* 5. to rise or swell as a dome.

do·mes·tic (də mĕs′tĭk), *adj.* 1. of or pertaining to the home. 2. devoted to home life or affairs. 3. tame. 4. of or pertaining to a particular country apart from others. 5. not foreign. —*n.* 6. a hired household servant. —**do·mes′ti·cal·ly**, *adv.*

do·mes·ti·cate (də mĕs′tə kāt′), *v.*, **-cated, -cating.** —*v.t.* 1. to tame. 2. to attach to home life. 3. to naturalize. —*v.i.* 4. to be domestic. —**do·mes′ti·ca′tion**, *n.*

do·mes·tic·i·ty (dō′mĕs tĭs′ə tĭ), *n.*, *pl.* **-ties.** state of being domestic; domestic or home life.

dom·i·cile (dŏm′ə səl, -sīl′), *n.*, *v.*, **-ciled, -ciling.** —*n.* 1. Also, **dom′i·cil.** a place of residence. —*v.t.* 2. to establish in a domicile. —*v.i.* 3. to dwell.

dom·i·cil·i·ate (dŏm′ə sĭl′ĭ āt′), *v.t.*, *v.i.*, **-ated, -ating.** domicile. —**dom′i·cil′i·a′tion**, *n.*

dom·i·nance (dŏm′ə nəns), *n.* rule; control; authority. Also, **dom′i·nan·cy.**

dom·i·nant (dŏm′ə nənt), *adj.* 1. ruling; most influential. 2. occupying a commanding position. 3. *Genetics.* pertaining to or exhibiting a hereditary character resulting from a more active gene than another. 4. *Music.* pertaining to or based on the dominant. —*n.* 5. *Music.* the fifth tone of a scale. —**dom′i·nant·ly**, *adv.*

dom·i·nate (dŏm′ə nāt′), v., -nated, -nating. —v.t. 1. to rule over. 2. to tower above. —v.i. 3. to rule. 4. to occupy a commanding position.
dom·i·na·tion (dŏm′ə nā′shən), n. 1. act of dominating. 2. rule or sway, often arbitrary.
dom·i·neer (dŏm′ə nĭr′), v.i., v.t. 1. to rule despotically. 2. to tower (over).
dom·i·neer·ing (dŏm′ə nĭr′ĭng), adj. inclined to domineer; tyrannical. —**dom′i·neer′ing·ly,** adv. —**dom′i·neer′ing·ness,** n.
Dom·i·nic (dŏm′ə nĭk), n. Saint, 1170–1221, Spanish priest: founder of Dominican order.
Do·min·i·can (də mĭn′ə kən), adj. 1. of or pertaining to St. Dominic or the mendicant religious order founded by him. 2. of the Dominican Republic. —n. 3. a member of the order of St. Dominic. 4. a native or inhabitant of the Dominican Republic.
Dominican Republic, a republic in the West Indies, occupying E Hispaniola. 2,059,113 pop.; 19,129 sq. mi. Cap.: Ciudad Trujillo.
dom·i·nie (dŏm′ə nĭ, dō′mə-), n. 1. Chiefly Scot. a schoolmaster. 2. a clergyman.
do·min·ion (də mĭn′yən), n. 1. the power or right of governing. 2. a territory under a single rulership. 3. a self-governing commonwealth within a community of nations.
Dominion Day, (in Canada) a legal holiday, July 1, celebrating its formation as a Dominion on July 1, 1867.
dom·i·no¹ (dŏm′ə nō′), n., pl. -noes, -nos. a cloak, usually hooded, worn with a small mask by persons in masquerade.
dom·i·no² (dŏm′ə nō′), n., pl. -noes. 1. (pl. construed as sing.) any of various games played with flat, oblong pieces marked with one to six pips. 2. one of these pieces.
don¹ (dŏn), n. 1. (cap.) Mr., Sir (a Spanish title). 2. a Spanish lord or gentleman. 3. a person of great importance. 4. Colloq. (in the English universities) a head, a fellow, or tutor.
don² (dŏn), v.t., donned, donning. to put on.
Don (dŏn), n. a river flowing from the central Soviet Union in Europe S through a wide arc to the Sea of Azov. ab. 1300 mi.
do·ña (dō′nyä), n. (in Spanish use) 1. a lady. 2. (cap.) a title of respect for a lady.
do·nate (dō′nāt), v.t., -nated, -nating. Chiefly U.S. to make a gift cf, as to a fund or cause.
do·na·tion (dō nā′shən), n. act of presenting something as a gift. 2. a gift, as to a fund.
Don·cas·ter (dŏng′kăs tər; Brit. -kəs tər), n. a city in central England, in S Yorkshire. 75,690.
done (dŭn), v. 1. pp. of do¹. —adj. 2. cooked.
Do·nets (dŏ nĕts′), n. a river in the SW Soviet Union, flowing SE to the Don river. ab. 660 mi.
Don·i·zet·ti (dŏn′ə zĕt′ĭ), n. Gaetano, 1797–1848, Italian operatic composer.
don·jon (dŭn′jən, dŏn′-), n. the inner tower, keep, or stronghold of a castle.
Don Ju·an (dŏn jōō′ən; Sp. dôn hwän′), 1. a legendary Spanish nobleman of dissolute life. 2. a libertine or rake.
don·key (dŏng′kĭ, dŭng′-), n., pl. -keys. 1. the ass. 2. a stupid, silly, or obstinate person.
donkey engine, a small steam engine.
don·na (dŏn′ə), n. (in Italian use) 1. a lady. 2. (cap.) a title of respect for a lady.
Donne (dŭn), n. John, 1573–1631, British poet.
do·nor (dō′nər), n. one who gives or donates.
Don Quix·ote (dŏn kwĭk′sət; Sp. dôn kē hō′tĕ), the chivalrous but impractical hero of Cervantes' romance (1605, 1615).
don't (dōnt), contraction of do not.
doo·dad (dōō′dăd), n. Colloq. any trifling ornament or bit of decorative finery.
doo·dle (dōō′dəl), v.t., v.i., -dled, -dling. to draw or scribble idly.
doo·dle·bug¹ (dōō′dəl bŭg′), n. Local U.S. an ant lion larva.
doo·dle·bug² (dōō′dəl bŭg′), n. a device supposedly useful in locating water, oil, minerals, etc., underground.
doom (dōōm), n. 1. fate or destiny, esp. adverse fate. 2. ruin; death. 3. a judgment, as the Last Judgment. —v.t. 4. to destine, esp. to an adverse fate. 5. to pronounce judgment against.
dooms·day (dōōmz′dā′), n. the day of judgment, esp. of the Last Judgment.
door (dōr), n. 1. a movable barrier, commonly turning on hinges or sliding, for closing and opening the entrance to a building, room, cupboard, etc. 2. a doorway.

door·man (dōr′măn′, -mən), n., pl. -men (-mĕn′, -mən). the door attendant of a hotel, etc.
door·nail (dōr′nāl′), n. a large-headed nail.
door·step (dōr′stĕp′), n. a step at a door.
door·way (dōr′wā′), n. the entrance to a building, room, etc., closed and opened by a door.
door·yard (dōr′yärd′), n. a yard near a door.
dope (dōp), n., v., doped, doping. —n. 1. any thick liquid or pasty preparation, as a sauce, lubricant, etc. 2. an absorbent material. 3. Aeron. a varnishlike substance for coating the fabric of airplane wings or the like, to make them waterproof, stronger, etc. 4. Slang. opium or any other stupefying drug. 5. Slang. an opium or drug addict. 6. Slang. information. 7. U.S. Slang. a stupid person. —v.t. 8. Slang. to affect with drugs. 9. dope out, Slang. a. to make by calculation, etc. b. to deduce. —dop′er, n.
dop·ey (dō′pĭ), adj., dopier, dopiest. Slang. affected by or as by a stupefying drug. Also, dop′y.
Do·ré (dō rē′), n. Paul Gustave, 1832?–83, French illustrator and artist.
Dor·ic (dôr′ĭk, dŏr′-), adj. Archit. noting or pertaining to the simplest of the three Greek orders, distinguished esp. by shaft without base and saucer-shaped capital.
dorm (dôrm), n. Colloq. a dormitory.
dor·mant (dôr′mənt), adj. 1. lying asleep or as if asleep. 2. (of a volcano) not erupting. 3. Bot. temporarily inactive. —dor′man·cy, n.
dor·mer (dôr′mər), n. 1. Also, dormer window. a vertical window in a projection from a sloping roof. 2. the whole projecting structure.
dor·mi·to·ry (dôr′mə tōr′ĭ), n., pl. -ries. 1. U.S. a building containing a number of sleeping rooms. 2. Brit. a sleeping room containing a number of beds.

Dormer (def. 1)

dor·mouse (dôr′mous′), n., pl. -mice (-mīs′). any of certain small, furry-tailed old-world rodents which resemble squirrels in appearance and habits.
dor·my (dôr′mĭ), adj. Golf. (of a player or side) being in the lead by as many holes as are still to be played.
dor·sal (dôr′səl), adj. 1. Zool. of, pertaining to, or on the back, as of an organ. 2. Bot. pertaining to the surface away from the axis, as of a leaf. —dor′sal·ly, adv.
Dort·mund (dôrt′mənd), n. a city in W Germany. 542,261.
do·ry (dōr′ĭ), n., pl. -ries. a boat with a narrow, flat bottom, high ends, and flaring sides.
dos·age (dō′sĭj), n. 1. the administration of medicine in doses. 2. the amount given.
dose (dōs), n., v., dosed, dosing. —n. 1. a quantity of medicine to be taken at one time. 2. a quantity of something disagreeable. —v.t. 3. to give doses to.
dos·si·er (dŏs′ĭ ā′, -ĭ ər), n. a bundle of documents all relating to the same matter or subject.
Dos·to·ev·ski (dŏs′tə yĕf′skĭ), n. Feodor Mikhailovich, 1821–81, Russian writer.
dot¹ (dŏt), n., v., dotted, dotting. —n. 1. a small spot, as one made with a pen. 2. anything relatively small. 3. Music. a point after a note or rest to indicate that the duration is to be increased one half. 4. a signal of short duration, used in groups of dots, dashes, and spaces, to represent letters in a Morse or a similar code. —v.t. 5. to mark with a dot or dots. —v.i. 6. to make a dot or dots.
dot² (dŏt), n. Law. dowry. —do·tal (dō′təl), adj.
dot·age (dō′tĭj), n. 1. feebleness of mind, esp. senility. 2. excessive fondness.
do·tard (dō′tərd), n. a senile person.
dote (dōt), v.i., doted, doting. 1. to bestow excessive love (fol. by on or upon). 2. to be weak-minded, esp. from old age. —dot′er, n. —dot′ing, adj. —dot′ing·ly, adv.
doth (dŭth), v. (now only in poetic or solemn use) 3rd per. sing. pres. ind. of do¹.
dot·ty (dŏt′ĭ), adj., -tier, -tiest. 1. Chiefly Brit. Colloq. crazy. 2. marked with dots.
Dou·ay Bible (dōō′ā), an English translation of the Bible, from the Latin Vulgate, prepared by Roman Catholic scholars, the Old Testament being published at Douay (or Douai) in N France, in 1609–10, and the New Testament at Rheims, in 1582. Also, Douay Version.
dou·ble (dŭb′əl), adj., n., v., -bled, -bling, adv.

—*adj.* **1.** twice as great, heavy, etc. **2.** twofold in form, etc. **3.** paired. **4.** *Bot.* having the number of petals largely increased. **5.** ambiguous. **6.** deceitful. **7.** *Music.* duple, as time or rhythm. —*n.* **8.** twice as much. **9.** a duplicate. **10.** a fold or plait. **11.** a sudden backward turn. **12.** an artifice. **13.** a substitute actor or singer. **14.** *Mil.* double time. **15.** *Baseball.* a two-base hit. **16.** a game in which there are two players on each side. **17.** *Bridge.* **a.** a challenge that declarer cannot fulfill his contract. **b.** a bid informing partner of one's strength. —*v.t.* **18.** to make twice as great. **19.** to be or have twice as much as. **20.** to bend or fold (often fol. by *over, up,* etc.). **21.** to clench (the fist). **22.** *Bridge.* to increase (the points) to be won or lost on a declaration. —*v.i.* **23.** to become double. **24.** to bend or fold. **25.** to turn back on a course. **26.** to share quarters, etc. **27.** to serve in two capacities. —*adv.* **28.** twofold; doubly. —**dou′ble·ness,** *n.* —**dou′bler,** *n.*

double bass, the largest instrument of the violin family.

double bassoon, a bassoon an octave lower in pitch than the ordinary bassoon.

dou·ble-breast·ed (dŭb′əl brĕs′tĭd), *adj.* (of a garment) overlapping sufficiently to form two thicknesses of considerable width on the breast.

double cross, *Slang.* a betrayal.

dou·ble-cross (dŭb′əl krôs′, -krŏs′), *v.t. Slang.* to betray. —**dou′ble-cross′er,** *n.*

double dagger, a mark (‡) for references, etc.

dou·ble-deal·ing (dŭb′əl dē′lĭng), *n.* duplicity. —**dou′ble-deal′er,** *n.*

dou·ble-en·ten·dre (dōō blän tän′dr), *n.* a double meaning, one often indelicate.

double entry, *Bookkeeping.* a method in which each transaction is entered to the debit of one account and to the credit of another.

dou·ble-faced (dŭb′əl fāst′), *adj.* hypocritical.

dou·ble-head·er (dŭb′əl hĕd′ər), *n.* the playing of two games, as of baseball, between the same teams on the same day in immediate succession.

dou·ble-quick (dŭb′əl kwĭk′), *adj.* **1.** very rapid. —*adv.* **2.** in a rapid manner. —*n.* **3.** double time.

dou·blet (dŭb′lĭt), *n.* **1.** a close-fitting outer garment, formerly worn by men. **2.** a pair. **3.** one of a pair. **4.** one of two words in the same language, representing the same original, as the English *coy* and *quiet,* one taken from Old French, the other from Latin.

double time, **1.** the fastest rate of marching troops. **2.** *Colloq.* a run at any speed.

dou·bloon (dŭb lōōn′), *n.* a former Spanish gold coin, of varying value.

dou·bly (dŭb′lĭ), *adv.* **1.** in a double manner, measure, or degree. **2.** in two ways.

doubt (dout), *v.t.* **1.** to be uncertain about. —*v.i.* **2.** to feel uncertainty. —*n.* **3.** a state or feeling of uncertainty. —**doubt′er,** *n.* —**doubt′ing·ly,** *adv.*

doubt·ful (dout′fəl), *adj.* **1.** uncertain or ambiguous. **2.** of questionable character. **3.** undecided; hesitating. —**doubt′ful·ly,** *adv.* —**doubt′ful·ness,** *n.*

doubt·less (dout′lĭs), *adv.* **1.** without doubt. **2.** probably. —*adj.* **3.** free from doubt. —**doubt′less·ly,** *adv.* —**doubt′less·ness,** *n.*

douche (dōōsh), *n., v.,* **douched, douching.** —*n.* **1.** a current of water applied to a body part for medicinal purposes. **2.** an instrument for doing this. **3.** a bath taken thus. —*v.t.* **4.** to apply a douche to; douse. —*v.i.* **5.** to receive a douche.

dough (dō), *n.* **1.** flour or meal combined with water, milk, etc., in a mass for baking. **2.** any pasty mass. **3.** *Slang.* money. —**dough′y,** *adj.*

dough·boy (dō′boi′), *n. U.S. Colloq.* an infantryman.

dough·nut (dō′nət, -nŭt′), *n.* a small cake of sweetened dough fried in deep fat.

dough·ty (dou′tĭ), *adj.,* **-tier, -tiest.** *Now Archaic and/or Humorous.* strong; valiant. —**dough′ti·ly,** *adv.* —**dough′ti·ness,** *n.*

Doug·las (dŭg′ləs), *n.* **1.** Stephen Arnold, 1813–61, U.S. political leader. **2.** William Orville, born 1898, associate justice of the U.S. Supreme Court since 1939.

Douglas fir, a coniferous tree of western North America, often over 200 feet high, yielding a strong, durable timber. Also, **Douglas pine.**

dour (dŏŏr, dour), *adj.* **1.** sullen. **2.** *Scot.* stern.

douse (dous), *v.,* **doused, dousing.** —*v.t.* **1.** to plunge into water or the like. **2.** *Slang.* to

extinguish. **3.** *Colloq.* to doff. **4.** *Naut.* to lower in haste. —*v.i.* **5.** to plunge or be plunged into a liquid.

dove[1] (dŭv), *n.* **1.** any bird of the pigeon family, esp. certain small species of terrestrial habits. **2.** (*cap.*) *Theol.* the Holy Ghost. **3.** an innocent, gentle person.

dove[2] (dōv), *v. U.S. Colloq.* pt. of **dive.**

dove·cote (dŭv′kōt′), *n.* a raised structure for domestic pigeons. Also, **dove·cot** (dŭv′kŏt′).

Do·ver (dō′vər), *n.* **1.** a seaport in SE England, nearest to the coast of France. 30,500. **2. Strait of,** a strait between England and France. Least width, 20 mi. **3.** the capital of Delaware, in the central part. 5,517.

dove·tail (dŭv′tāl′), *n.* **1.** *Carp.* a joint formed by tenons and mortises in the shape of a dove's tail. —*v.t., v.i.* **2.** *Carp.* to join by dovetails. **3.** to fit together perfectly.

dow·a·ger (dou′ə jər), *n.* **1.** the widow of a king, duke, or the like. **2.** *Colloq.* a dignified elderly lady.

dow·dy (dou′dĭ), *adj.,* **-dier, -diest,** *n., pl.* **-dies.** —*adj.* **1.** not trim or stylish. —*n.* **2.** an ill-dressed woman. —**dow′di·ly,** *adv.* —**dow′di·ness,** *n.*

dow·el (dou′əl), *n., v.,* **-eled, -eling** or (*esp. Brit.*) **-elled, -elling.** —*n.* **1.** Also, **dowel pin.** *Carp.* a pin fitting into a corresponding hole in an adjacent piece to prevent slipping. —*v.t.* **2.** to furnish with dowels.

dow·er (dou′ər), *n.* **1.** *Law.* the portion of a deceased husband's real property allowed by law to his widow for life. **2.** dowry. **3.** a natural gift. —*v.t.* **4.** to provide with a dower.

down[1] (doun), *adv.* **1.** to or in a lower position or condition. **2.** on or to the ground. **3.** to or at a low point, rate, pitch, bulk, etc. **4.** from an earlier to a later time. **5.** in proper position or state. **6.** on paper or in a book. **7.** in cash. —*prep.* **8.** in a descending direction on, over, or along. —*adj.* **9.** downward. **10.** dejected. **11.** *Football.* (of the ball) not in play. **12.** *Games.* losing or behind. —*n.* **13.** a descent. **14.** a reverse. **15.** *Football.* one of a series of four plays during which a team must advance the ball at least ten yards to keep possession of it. —*v.t.* **16.** to put down; subdue. —*v.i.* **17.** to fall.

down[2] (doun), *n.* **1.** the first feathering of young birds. **2.** the soft under plumage of birds. **3.** a soft hairy growth.

down[3] (doun), *n.* **1.** a dune. **2.** (*usually pl.*) open, rolling, upland country.

down·cast (doun′kăst′, -käst′), *adj.* **1.** directed downward, as the eyes. **2.** dejected. —*n.* **3.** overthrow. **4.** a downward look.

down·fall (doun′fôl′), *n.* **1.** overthrow; ruin. **2.** a fall, as of rain. **3.** a kind of trap or deadfall, in which a weight or missile falls upon the prey. —**down′fall′en,** *adj.*

down·grade (doun′grād′), *n., adj., adv., v.,* **-graded, -grading.** —*n.* **1.** a downward slope. —*adj., adv.* **2.** downhill. —*v.t.* **3.** to assign (a position) to a lower status with a smaller salary.

down·heart·ed (doun′här′tĭd), *adj.* dejected.

down·hill (doun′hĭl′), *adv.* **1.** down a hill. —*adj.* **2.** going or tending downward.

down·pour (doun′pōr′), *n.* a heavy, continuous fall of water, rain, etc.

down·right (doun′rīt′), *adj.* **1.** thorough. **2.** direct. —*adv.* **3.** completely. —**down′right′ly,** *adv.*

down·stairs (doun′stârz′), *adv.* **1.** down the stairs. **2.** to or on a lower floor. —*adj.* **3.** of or on a lower floor. —*n.* **4.** the lower floor of a house.

down·stream (doun′strēm′), *adv.* with or in the direction of the current of a stream.

down town, the business section of a city.

down·town (doun′toun′), *adv.* **1.** to or in the business section of a city. —*adj.* **2.** of, pertaining to, or situated in the business section of a city.

down·trod·den (doun′trŏd′ən), *adj.* trampled upon; tyrannized. Also, **down′trod′.**

down·ward (doun′wərd), *adv.* **1.** Also, **down′wards.** to a lower place or condition. —*adj.* **2.** moving to a lower place or condition. —**down′ward·ly,** *adv.* —**down′ward·ness,** *n.*

down·y (dou′nĭ), *adj.,* **downier, downiest. 1.** of or resembling down; fluffy. **2.** covered with down. **3.** calm. —**down′i·ness,** *n.*

dow·ry (dou′rĭ), *n., pl.* **-ries. 1.** the money, goods, or estate which a woman brings to her husband at marriage. **2.** a natural gift.

dox·ol·o·gy (dŏks ŏl′ə jĭ), *n., pl.* **-gies.** a hymn

or form of words in praise to God, as the Gloria in Excelsis (**great or greater doxology**), the Gloria Patri (**lesser doxology**), or the metrical formula beginning "Praise God from whom all blessings flow."

Doyle (doil), *n.* **Sir Arthur Conan**, 1859–1930, British author of detective stories.

doz., dozen; dozens.

doze (dōz), *v.*, **dozed, dozing,** *n.* —*v.i.* 1. to sleep lightly. —*n.* 2. a light sleep. —**doz′er,** *n.*

doz·en (dŭz′ən), *n., pl.* **dozen, dozens.** a group of twelve units or things. —**doz′enth,** *adj.*

D.P., displaced person. Also, **DP**

Dr., Doctor. Also, **Dr**

dr., 1. debtor. 2. dram; drams.

drab[1] (drăb), *n., adj.,* **drabber, drabbest.** —*n.* 1. dull brownish or yellowish gray. —*adj.* 2. having a drab color. 3. dull. —**drab′ly,** *adv.* —**drab′ness,** *n.*

drab[2] (drăb), *n., v.,* **drabbed, drabbing.** —*n.* 1. an untidy woman. 2. a prostitute. —*v.i.* 3. to associate with drabs.

drachm (drăm), *n. Brit.* dram.

drach·ma (drăk′mə), *n., pl.* **-mas, -mae** (-mē). 1. the monetary unit, or a silver coin, of modern Greece, worth about .02 U.S. cents. 2. the principal silver coin of the ancient Greeks, varying in value.

draft (drăft, dräft), *n.* (*Draft* is the common spelling for the following definitions. See also *draught.*) 1. a drawing, sketch, or design. 2. a preliminary form of any writing. 3. act of drawing. 4. a current of air. 5. a pull; haul. 6. the taking of supplies, forces, etc., from a source. 7. a selection of persons, by lot or otherwise, for military service. 8. a written request by one person (drawer) to another (drawee) that he pay a sum of money to a third person. —*v.t.* 9. to draw the plan of. 10. to draw up in written form. 11. to take by draft, as for military service. —*adj.* 12. used or suited for drawing loads.

draft·ee (drăf tē′, dräf-), *n.* one who is drafted.

drafts·man (drăfts′mən, dräfts′-), *n., pl.* **-men.** one who draws sketches, plans, or designs, as of machines. —**drafts′man·ship′,** *n.*

draft·y (drăf′tĭ, dräf′-), *adj.,* **draftier, draftiest.** characterized by or causing drafts (of air).

drag (drăg), *v.,* **dragged, dragging,** *n.* —*v.t.* 1. to draw heavily or slowly; haul. 2. to search with a grapnel or the like. 3. to break (land) with a harrow. —*v.i.* 4. to be hauled along. 5. to trail on the ground. 6. to move heavily or with effort. 7. to pass with tedious slowness. 8. to dredge. —*n.* 9. *Naut.* something used by or for dragging, as a dragnet. 10. a heavy harrow. 11. a sledge or sled. 12. anything that retards progress. 13. act of dragging. 14. *Aeron.* the force exerted on an airplane, airfoil, etc., tending to reduce its forward motion. 15. *Slang.* influence.

drag·gle (drăg′əl), *v.t., v.i.,* **-gled, -gling.** to soil by dragging over damp ground or in the mud.

drag·net (drăg′nĕt′), *n.* 1. a net to be drawn along the bottom of a river, etc., to catch something. 2. a system for catching a criminal.

drag·o·man (drăg′ə mən), *n., pl.* **-mans, -men.** (in the Orient) a professional interpreter.

drag·on (drăg′ən), *n.* a fabulous monster, generally a huge winged reptile, often spouting fire.

drag·on·fly (drăg′ən flī′), *n., pl.* **-flies.** a large, harmless insect that feeds on mosquitoes and other insects.

dra·goon (drə goon′), *n.* 1. a cavalryman. —*v.t.* 2. to oppress; harass. 3. to force.

drain (drān), *v.t.* 1. to draw off gradually or completely. 2. to make empty or dry by drawing off liquid. 3. to exhaust of possessions, etc. —*v.i.* 4. to flow off, empty, or dry gradually. —*n.* 5. that by which anything is drained, as a pipe. 6. act of draining. —**drain′a·ble,** *adj.* —**drain′er,** *n.*

drain·age (drā′nĭj), *n.* 1. act or process of draining. 2. a system of drains. 3. Also, **drainage basin.** the area drained by a river and its tributaries. 4. that which is drained off.

drake (drāk), *n.* the male of the duck kind.

Drake (drāk), *n.* **Sir Francis**, c1540–1596, British buccaneer and admiral.

dram (drăm), *n., v.,* **drammed, dramming.** —*n.* 1. a unit of apothecaries' weight, equal to 60 grains, 1/8 ounce. 2. *Obs.* 1/16 ounce, avoirdupois weight (27.34 grains). 3. a fluid dram. 4. a small drink of liquor. —*v.i.* 5. to tipple.

dra·ma (drä′mə, drăm′ə), *n.* 1. a composition

presenting in dialogue or pantomime a story to be acted on the stage. 2. dramatic art. 3. any series of events having dramatic interest.

dra·mat·ic (drə măt′ĭk), *adj.* 1. of or pertaining to the drama. 2. employing the form or manner of the drama. 3. characteristic of or appropriate to the drama. —**dra·mat′i·cal·ly,** *adv.*

dra·mat·ics (drə măt′ĭks), *n.* 1. (*construed as sing. or pl.*) the art of producing or acting dramas. 2. (*construed as pl.*) dramatic productions.

dram·a·tis per·so·nae (drăm′ə tĭs pər sō′nē), *Latin.* the persons or characters in a drama.

dram·a·tist (drăm′ə tĭst), *n.* a playwright.

dram·a·tize (drăm′ə tīz′), *v.t.,* **-tized, -tizing.** 1. to put into dramatic form. 2. to express or represent dramatically. —**dram′a·ti·za′tion,** *n.* —**dram′a·tiz′er,** *n.*

dram·a·tur·gy (drăm′ə tûr′jĭ), *n.* the science of dramatic composition or presentation.

drape (drāp), *v.,* **draped, draping,** *n.* —*v.t.* 1. to cover with fabric, esp. in graceful folds. 2. to adjust in graceful folds. —*v.i.* 3. to fall in folds. —*n.* 4. a draped curtain or hanging.

drap·er (drā′pər), *n. Eng.* a dealer in dry goods.

dra·per·y (drā′pə rĭ), *n., pl.* **-peries.** 1. hangings, etc., of fabric, esp. as arranged in loose, graceful folds. 2. the arranging of hangings, etc., in graceful folds. 3. textile fabrics collectively.

dras·tic (drăs′tĭk), *adj.* extreme or violent. —**dras′ti·cal·ly,** *adv.*

draught (drăft, dräft), *n.* (*Draught* is the common spelling for the following definitions. See also *draft.*) 1. a current of air, esp. in a room, chimney, etc. 2. a device for regulating the flow of air or gas, as a damper in a stove. 3. the drawing of a liquid from its receptacle, as of ale from a cask. 4. drinking; a drink. 5. the depth a vessel sinks in water. 6. (*pl. construed as sing.*) the game of checkers. —*adj.* 7. drawn as required.

Dra·vid·i·an (drə vĭd′ĭ ən), *n.* 1. a great linguistic family of India, including Tamil and Kanarese. 2. a member of the Dravidian race. —*adj.* 3. of or pertaining to this people or their language.

draw (drô), *v.,* **drew, drawn, drawing,** *n.* —*v.t.* 1. to pull; drag; lead. 2. to bring or take out, as from a source. 3. to attract. 4. to sketch in lines or words. 5. to mark out; trace. 6. to write or draft. 7. to take in, as by inhaling. 8. to derive; deduce. 9. to produce. 10. to disembowel (a fowl, etc.). 11. to stretch. 12. to wrinkle or shrink by contraction. 13. *Naut.* to displace (a certain depth of water). 14. *Games.* to leave (a contest) undecided. —*v.i.* 15. to exert a pulling, moving, or attracting force. 16. to be drawn. 17. to take out a sword, pistol, etc., for action. 18. to practice pictorial drawing. 19. to shrink. 20. to make a draft or demand. 21. to levy or call (*on*) for money, supplies, etc. 22. to produce or have a draught of air, etc., as in a flue. 23. *Games.* to leave a contest undecided. —*n.* 24. act of drawing. 25. something that draws. 26. that which is drawn. 27. *Games.* an undecided contest.

draw·back (drô′băk′), *n.* a disadvantage.

draw·bridge (drô′brĭj′), *n.* a bridge which may be drawn up or aside, to prevent access, or leave a passage open for boats, etc.

draw·ee (drô ē′), *n. Finance.* one on whom an order, draft, or bill of exchange is drawn.

draw·er (drôr *for 1, 2;* drô′ər *for 3, 4*), *n.* 1. a sliding compartment, as in furniture, that may be drawn out in order to get access to it. 2. (*pl.*) a trouserlike undergarment for the lower part of the body. 3. one that draws. 4. *Finance.* one who draws an order, draft, or bill of exchange.

draw·ing (drô′ĭng), *n.* 1. act of a person or thing that draws. 2. a sketch, plan, or design. 3. the art of making these.

drawing pin, *Brit.* a thumbtack.

drawing room, 1. a room for the reception of company. 2. *U.S.* a private compartment in a railroad car.

draw·knife (drô′nīf′), *n. Carp., etc.* a knife with a handle at each end at right angles to the blade used by drawing over a surface. Also, **drawing knife, draw·shave** (drô′shāv′).

drawl (drôl), *v.t., v.i.* 1. to speak with slow, lingering utterance. —*n.* 2. an utterance of one who drawls. —**drawl′er,** *n.* —**drawl′ing·ly,** *adv.*

drawn work, ornamental work done by drawing threads from a fabric, the remaining portions being formed into patterns by needlework.

dray (drā), *n.* 1. a low, strong cart without fixed

sides, for carrying heavy loads. —*v.t.* 2. to convey on a dray.

dray·age (drā′Yj), *n.* 1. conveyance by dray. 2. a charge made for it.

dray·man (drā′mən), *n.*, *pl.* **-men.** a man who drives a dray.

dread (drĕd), *v.t.*, *v.i.* 1. to fear greatly. —*n.* 2. great fear. 3. deep awe. 4. a person or thing feared. —*adj.* 5. greatly feared. 6. revered.

dread·ful (drĕd′fəl), *adj.* 1. causing great fear. 2. awe-inspiring. 3. *Colloq.* extremely bad, ugly, etc. —**dread′ful·ly,** *adv.* —**dread′ful·ness,** *n.*

dread·nought (drĕd′nôt/), *n.* a type of battleship with the main battery consisting of heavy-caliber guns in turrets. Also, **dread′naught/.**

dream (drēm), *n.*, *v.*, **dreamed** or **dreamt**, **dreaming.** —*n.* 1. a succession of images or ideas present in the mind during sleep. 2. the sleeping state in which this occurs. 3. an object seen in a dream. 4. daydream; reverie. —*v.i.* 5. to have a dream or dreams. 6. to think of something in a very remote way. —*v.t.* 7. to see in sleep or in a vision. 8. to fancy; suppose. —**dream′er,** *n.* —**dream′ing·ly,** *adv.* —**dream′less,** *adj.*

dream·y (drē′mY), *adj.*, **dreamier, dreamiest.** 1. full of or causing dreams. 2. visionary. 3. vague; dim. —**dream′i·ly,** *adv.* —**dream′i·ness,** *n.*

drear·y (drYr′Y), *adj.*, **drearier, dreariest.** 1. causing sadness or gloom. 2. dull. Also, *Poetic,* **drear.** —**drear′i·ly,** *adv.* —**drear′i·ness,** *n.*

dredge[1] (drĕj), *n.*, *v.*, **dredged, dredging.** —*n.* 1. any of various machines for removing earth, etc., as from the bottom of a river, by means of a scoop, suction pipe, or the like. 2. a dragnet. —*v.t.* 3. to clear out with a dredge. 4. to obtain or remove by a dredge. —*v.i.* 5. to use a dredge.

dredge[2] (drĕj), *v.t.*, **dredged, dredging.** *Cookery.* to sprinkle with flour.

dreg (drĕg), *n.* 1. (*usually pl.*) sediment or lees. 2. any worthless residue. —**dreg′gy,** *adj.*

Drei·ser (drī′sər, -zər), *n.* **Theodore,** 1871–1945, U.S. novelist.

drench (drĕnch), *v.t.* 1. to wet thoroughly; soak. 2. to cause to drink. —*n.* 3. act of drenching. 4. something that drenches. 5. a preparation for drenching. 6. a large drink. —**drench′er,** *n.*

Dres·den (drĕz′dən), *n.* 1. a city in E Germany, on the Elbe. 630,216. 2. a fine type of china.

dress (drĕs), *n.*, *adj.*, *v.*, **dressed** or **drest, dressing.** —*n.* .1. the garment worn by women. 2. clothing; garb. 3. outer covering, as the plumage of birds. —*adj.* 4. of or for a dress or dresses. 5. of or for a formal occasion. —*v.t.* 6. to equip with clothing, etc.; attire. 7. to put formal or best clothes on. 8. to ornament. 9. to prepare (food, skins, timber, etc.) by special processes. 10. to comb out and do up (hair). 11. to cultivate (land, etc.). 12. to treat (wounds or sores). 13. to make straight. 14. *Colloq.* to scold. —*v.i.* 15. to clothe oneself, esp. in formal or best clothes. 16. to come into line, as troops.

dress·er[1] (drĕs′ər), *n.* one who dresses.

dress·er[2] (drĕs′ər), *n.* 1. a bedroom table or bureau, often one supporting a mirror. 2. a set of shelves for dishes.

dress·ing (drĕs′Yng), *n.* 1. act of one that dresses. 2. that with which something is dressed. 3. a sauce for food. 4. stuffing for a fowl. 5. an application for a wound. 6. manure, compost, or other fertilizers.

dressing gown, a loose gown or robe worn while making the toilet or when in dishabille.

dress·mak·er (drĕs′mā′kər), *n.* one who makes women's dresses, etc. —**dress′mak′ing,** *n.*

dress parade, the ceremony at which soldiers in dress uniforms take formation under arms.

dress rehearsal, a rehearsal of a play in costume and with scenery, properties, lights, etc.

dress·y (drĕs′Y), *adj.*, **dressier, dressiest.** *Colloq.* showy in dress; stylish. —**dress′i·ness,** *n.*

Drey·fus (drā′fəs, drī′-), *n.* **Alfred,** 1859–1935, French army officer convicted of treason on biased testimony.

drib·ble (drYb′əl), *v.*, **-bled, -bling,** *n.* —*v.i.* 1. to fall or flow in drops; trickle. 2. to drivel. 3. (in men's basketball) to move about a court while bouncing the ball. —*v.t.* 4. to let fall in drops. 5. *Sports.* **a.** (in men's basketball) to bounce (a basketball). **b.** (in some other games) to move (the ball) along by short kicks or pushes. —*n.* 6. a small trickling stream. 7. a small quantity. 8. act of dribbling. —**drib′bler,** *n.*

drib·let (drYb′lYt), *n.* a small part or sum.

dri·er (drī′ər), *adj.* 1. compar. of **dry.** —*n.* Also, **dryer.** 2. one that dries. 3. a substance added to paints, etc., to make them dry quickly. 4. an apparatus for removing moisture.

drift (drYft), *n.* 1. a driving movement or force. 2. *Navig.* course under the impulse of water currents, wind, etc. 3. *Phys. Geog.* a broad and shallow current. 4. *Naut.* the speed in knots of an ocean current. 5. *Aeron.* deviation of an aircraft from a set course due to cross winds. 6. tendency; aim. 7. something driven. 8. a heap of any matter driven together. 9. *Geol.* a deposit of detritus. 10. state or process of being driven. 11. *Mining.* an approximately horizontal passageway in underground mining, etc. —*v.t.*, *v.i.* 12. to carry or be carried along by currents of water or air. 13. to drive or be driven into heaps. —**drift′er,** *n.*

drift·age (drYft′tYj), *n.* 1. action or amount of drifting. 2. drifted matter.

drift·wood (drYft′wŏŏd/), *n.* wood floating on, or cast ashore by, the wate...

drill[1] (drYl), *n.* 1. a tool or machine for boring holes in metal, stone, or other hard substance. 2. *Mil.* training in formal marching or other precise military or naval movements. 3. any strict, methodical training. 4. a gastropod destructive to oysters. —*v.t.* 5. to pierce or bore a hole in. 6. to make (a hole) by boring. 7. *Mil.* to instruct in military conduct and activity. 8. to impart (knowledge) by strict training. —*v.i.* 9. to pierce or bore with a drill. 10. to go through exercise in military or other training. —**drill′er,** *n.*

drill[2] (drYl), *n.* 1. a small furrow to sow seeds in. 2. a machine for sowing seeds in rows. —*v.t.*, *v.i.* 3. to sow (seed) in drills. 4. to plant (ground) in drills. —**drill′er,** *n.*

drill[3] (drYl), *n.* a strong twilled cotton.

drill[4] (drYl), *n.* a baboon of western Africa, smaller than the mandrill.

drill·mas·ter (drYl′mǎs′tər, -mǎs′tər), *n.* one who trains others in anything, esp. soldiers.

dri·ly (drī′lY), *adv.* dryly.

drink (drYngk), *v.*, **drank** (formerly also **drunk**); **drunk** (sometimes **drank,** formerly or as *pred. adj.* **drunken**); **drinking;** *n.* —*v.i.* 1. to swallow water or other liquid. 2. to imbibe alcoholic liquors. 3. to drink in honor of. —*v.t.* 4. to swallow (a liquid). 5. to take in (a liquid) in any manner. 6. to take in through the senses. 7. to drink in honor of. —*n.* 8. any liquid to quench thirst, for nourishment, etc. 9. alcoholic liquor. —**drink′a·ble,** *adj.* —**drink′er,** *n.*

Drink·wa·ter (drYngk′wô′tər, -wŏt′ər), *n.* **John,** 1882–1937, British poet, dramatist, and critic.

drip (drYp), *v.*, **dripped** or **dript, dripping,** *n.* —*v.i.* 1. to let fall drops. 2. to fall in drops. —*v.t.* 3. to let fall in drops. —*n.* 4. act of dripping. 5. the liquid that drips. 6. a projecting part of a cornice to throw off rain water.

drip·ping (drYp′Yng), *n.* 1. act of anything that drips. 2. (*often pl.*) the liquid that drips. 3. fat exuded from meat in cooking: used as shortening.

drive (drīv), *v.*, **drove** or (*Archaic*) **drave; driven; driving;** *n.* —*v.t.* 1. to send away, in, back, etc., by compulsion. 2. to overwork. 3. to cause and guide the movement of. 4. to convey in a vehicle. 5. to keep (machinery) going. 6. to impel; urge. 7. to carry (a bargain, etc.) vigorously through. —*v.i.* 8. to be impelled. 9. to rush violently. 10. to aim (fol. by *at*). 11. to act as driver. 12. to go or travel in a driven vehicle. —*n.* 13. act of driving. 14. an impelling along, as of game, cattle, or floating logs. 15. the animals, etc., thus driven. 16. *Psychol.* a source of motivation. 17. *Sports.* a propelling or forcible stroke. 18. a strong military offensive. 19. a united effort to accomplish some purpose. 20. vigorous pressure or effort. 21. a trip in a driven vehicle. 22. a road for driving. 23. *Mach.* a driving mechanism.

drive-in (drīv′Yn/), *n.* a motion picture theater, refreshment stand, etc., catering to customers who remain in their automobiles.

driv·el (drYv′əl), *v.*, **-eled, -eling** or (*esp. Brit.*) **-elled, -elling,** *n.* —*v.i.* 1. to let saliva flow from the mouth. 2. to issue like spittle. 3. to talk foolishly. —*v.t.* 4. to utter foolishly. —*n.* 5. saliva flowing from the mouth. 6. childish talk. —**driv′el·er;** *esp. Brit.,* **driv′el·ler,** *n.*

driv·er (drī′vər), *n.* 1. one that drives. 2. one who drives an animal, vehicle, etc. 3. *Mach.* a part that transmits motion. 4. *Golf.* a wooden-headed club, used for long shots.

drive·way (drīv′wā/), *n.* 1. a private road from a house to the street. 2. any road.

driz·zle (drĭz′əl), v., -zled, -zling, n. —v.i., v.t. 1. to rain gently and steadily in fine drops. —n. 2. a light rain. —**driz′zly,** adj.

droll (drōl), adj. amusingly queer; comical.

droll·er·y (drō′lə rĭ), n., pl. -eries. 1. something amusingly queer. 2. a jest. 3. droll quality. 4. jesting.

drom·e·dar·y (drŏm′ə dĕr′ĭ, drŭm′-), n., pl. -daries. the one-humped or Arabian camel, light swift types of which are bred for riding and racing.

drone[1] (drōn), n. 1. the male of the honeybee and other bees, stingless and making no honey. 2. an idler. 3. a remotely controlled mechanism, as a radio-controlled airplane.

Dromedary
(6 ft. high at the shoulder)

drone[2] (drōn), v., droned, droning, n. —v.i. 1. to make a dull, monotonous sound. 2. to speak in a monotonous tone. —v.t. 3. to say in a monotonous tone. —n. 4. Music. a. a continuous low tone produced by bass pipes or strings. b. the pipes (esp. of the bagpipe) or strings producing this tone. 5. a monotonous tone.

drool (drōōl), v., n. Colloq. drivel.

droop (drōōp), v.i. 1. to sink, bend, or hang down, as from weakness or exhaustion. 2. Poetic. to sink; descend, as the sun. 3. to fall into a state of physical weakness; flag; fail. 4. to lose spirit or courage. —v.t. 5. to let sink or drop. —n. 6. a drooping. —**droop′ing·ly,** adv. —**droop′y,** adj.

drop (drŏp), n., v., dropped or dropt, dropping. —n. 1. a small quantity of liquid which falls in a spherical mass. 2. the quantity in such a mass. 3. a very small quantity. 4. (usually pl.) liquid medicine given in drops. 5. something like a drop, as a confection, pendant, etc. 6. act of dropping; fall. 7. the distance or depth to which anything drops. 8. a steep slope. 9. that which drops, as a theater curtain. 10. a trap door. 11. a slit into which to drop mail. —v.i. 12. to fall in globules, as water or other liquid. 13. to have an abrupt descent. 14. to fall wounded, dead, etc. 15. to end; cease. 16. to withdraw; disappear. 17. to fall lower in condition, degree, etc. 18. to pass without effort into some condition. 19. to move (back, to the rear, etc.). 20. to visit informally. 21. to give birth. —v.t. 22. to let fall in drops. 23. to let fall; lower. 24. to give birth to (young). 25. to express casually. 26. to send (a note, etc.). 27. to bring to the ground by a blow or shot. 28. to set down, as from a car, etc. 29. to omit (a letter or syllable). 30. to cease to have to do with. 31. U.S. to dismiss. 32. Football. to score (a goal) by a drop kick. 33. Cookery. to poach.

drop-forge (drŏp′fôrj′), v.t., -forged, -forging. Metall. to forge by the impact of a falling weight. —**drop forging.**

drop hammer, an apparatus for forging, in which a heavy weight drops on the metal to be worked, which is placed on an anvil or in dies.

drop kick, Football. a kick given the ball as it bounces after being dropped by the kicker. —**drop′-kick′,** v.t., v.i.

drop·let (drŏp′lĭt), n. a little drop.

drop·per (drŏp′ər), n. 1. one that drops. 2. a glass tube with a small orifice for expelling medicine in drops.

drop·si·cal (drŏp′sə kəl), adj. of, like, or affected with dropsy. —**drop′si·cal·ly,** adv.

drop·sy (drŏp′sĭ), n. Pathol. an excessive accumulation of serous fluid, as in a serous cavity.

drosh·ky (drŏsh′kĭ), n., pl. -kies. a light, low, four-wheeled, open vehicle, used in Russia. Also, **dros·ky** (drŏs′kĭ).

Dro·soph·i·la (drō sŏf′ə lə), n.pl. a genus of flies, one species of which (the fruit fly) is widely used in laboratory studies of inheritance.

dross (drôs, drŏs), n. 1. Metall. a waste product taken off molten metal during smelting. 2. refuse.

drought (drout), n. dry weather. Also, **drouth** (drouth). —**drought′y,** adj.

drove[1] (drōv), v. pt. of drive.

drove[2] (drōv), n., v., droved, droving. —n. 1. a number of oxen, sheep, or swine driven in a group. 2. a large crowd of human beings, esp. in motion. —v.t., v.i. 3. to drive or deal in (cattle) as a drover.

dro·ver (drō′vər), n. 1. one who drives cattle, sheep, etc., to market. 2. a dealer in cattle.

drown (droun), v.i. 1. to be suffocated by immersion in water or other liquid. —v.t. 2. to suffocate by immersion in water or other liquid. 3. to get rid of. 4. to flood. 5. to overpower.

drowse (drouz), v., drowsed, drowsing, n. —v.i. 1. to be sleepy. —v.t. 2. to make sleepy. 3. to spend (time) in drowsing. —n. 4. a sleepy condition.

drow·sy (drou′zĭ), adj., -sier, -siest. 1. inclined to sleep. 2. sluggish. 3. inducing sleepiness. —**drow′si·ly,** adv. —**drow′si·ness,** n.

drub (drŭb), v., drubbed, drubbing, n. —v.t. 1. to beat, esp. with a stick. 2. to defeat decisively. —n. 3. a blow. —**drub′ber,** n.

drub·bing (drŭb′ĭng), n. a beating or defeat.

drudge (drŭj), n., v., drudged, drudging. —n. 1. one who does hard, uninteresting work. —v.i. 2. to perform such work.

drudg·er·y (drŭj′ə rĭ), n., pl. -eries. tedious, hard, or uninteresting work.

drug (drŭg), n., v., drugged, drugging. —n. 1. a chemical substance used to protect or improve the health. 2. a narcotic. 3. (formerly) any ingredient used in chemistry, dyeing, etc. 4. a commodity that is overabundant in the market. —v.t. 5. to mix (food or drink) with a drug. 6. to affect with a drug.

drug·gist (drŭg′ĭst), n. U.S. one who prepares drugs according to medical prescriptions.

drug store, U.S. the store of a druggist, often also selling cosmetics, light meals, etc.

Dru·id (drōō′ĭd), n. (often l.c.) one of an order of priests among the ancient Celts of Gaul, Britain, and Ireland. —**dru·id′ic, dru·id′i·cal,** adj. —**dru′id·ism′,** n.

drum (drŭm), n., v., drummed, drumming. —n. 1. a musical instrument consisting of a hollow cylinder covered at one or both ends with a tight membrane which is struck with the hand, a stick, or pair of sticks. 2. the sound of a drum, or a similar sound. 3. something resembling a drum in shape or structure, or in the noise it produces. 4. Anat., Zool. a. the tympanum. b. the tympanic membrane. —v.i. 5. to beat or play a drum. 6. to beat on anything rhythmically. —v.t. 7. to beat rhythmically. 8. to call by, or as by, beating a drum. 9. to force by persistent repetition. 10. to solicit (trade, etc.).

drum·lin (drŭm′lĭn), n. Geol. a long narrow or oval hill of unstratified glacial drift.

drum major, leader of a drum corps or band.

drum·mer (drŭm′ər), n. 1. one who plays a drum. 2. U.S. a traveling salesman.

drum·stick (drŭm′stĭk′), n. 1. a stick for beating a drum. 2. the leg of a cooked chicken, etc.

drunk (drŭngk), adj. 1. intoxicated. —n. Colloq. 2. a drunken person. 3. a spree. —v. 4. pp. and former pt. of drink.

drunk·ard (drŭngk′ərd), n. a person who is habitually or frequently drunk.

drunk·en (drŭngk′ən), adj. 1. intoxicated; drunk. 2. given to drunkenness. 3. pertaining to, proceeding from, or marked by intoxication. —**drunk′en·ly,** adv. —**drunk′en·ness,** n.

dru·pa·ceous (drōō pā′shəs), adj. Bot. 1. of or resembling a drupe. 2. producing drupes.

drupe (drōōp), n. Bot. a fruit, as the peach, cherry, etc., consisting of an outer skin, a pulpy and succulent layer, and a hard inner stone which encloses a single seed.

drupe·let (drōōp′lĭt), n. Bot. a little drupe, as one of the pericarps composing the blackberry.

dry (drī), adj., drier, driest, v., dried, drying, n., pl. drys. —adj. 1. free from moisture; not wet. 2. having little or no rain. 3. not under, in, or on water. 4. not yielding water or other liquid. 5. not yielding milk. 6. free from tears. 7. wiped or drained away. 8. thirsty. 9. without butter or the like. 10. plain; unadorned. 11. dull; uninteresting. 12. humorous in an unemotional way. 13. (of wines) not sweet. 14. of or pertaining to nonliquid substances. 15. U.S. Colloq. characterized by or favoring prohibition of the manufacture and sale of alcoholic liquors for use as beverages. —v.t. 16. to make dry. —v.i. 17. to become dry; lose moisture. —n. 18. U.S. Colloq. a prohibitionist. —**dry′ly,** adv. —**dry′ness,** n.

dry·ad (drī′əd, -ăd), n., pl. -ads, -ades (-ə dēz′). Gk. Myth. (often cap.) a nymph of the woods. —**dry·ad·ic** (drī ăd′ĭk), adj.

dry battery, Elect. a dry cell or group of cells.

dry cell, Elect. a cell in which the electrolyte exists in the form of a paste or is otherwise restrained from flowing from its original position.

dry-clean (drī′klēn′), *v.t.* to clean (garments, etc.) with benzine, gasoline, etc. —**dry cleaner.**

Dry·den (drī′dən), *n.* **John,** 1631–1700, British poet, dramatist, and critic.

dry dock, a structure from which water can be removed after entrance of a ship: used when making repairs, etc. —**dry′-dock′,** *v.t., v.i.*

dry·er (drī′ər), *n.* drier.

dry farming, a mode of farming in regions having little rainfall, depending largely upon till-age methods which reduce evaporation. —**dry farmer.**

dry goods, textile fabrics and related articles of trade, in distinction from groceries, hardware, etc.

dry ice, 1. solid carbon dioxide, used as a re-frigerant. 2. (*cap.*) a trademark for this sub-stance.

dry measure, the system of units of capacity ordinarily used in measuring dry commodities, such as grain, fruit, etc. In the U.S. 2 pints = 1 quart; 8 quarts = 1 peck; 4 pecks = 1 bushel.

dry nurse, a nurse who takes care of a child but does not suckle it.

dry-nurse (drī′nûrs′), *v.t.,* **-nursed, -nursing.** to act as a dry nurse to.

dry point, 1. a needle used on copper plates to produce furrows with raised edges that print with a fuzzy, velvety black. 2. an engraving so made.

dry rot, a decay of seasoned timber causing it to become brittle and powdery.

Ds, *Chem.* dysprosium.

D.S., Doctor of Science.

D. Sc., Doctor of Science.

D.S.T., Daylight Saving Time.

d.t., delirium tremens. Also, **d.t.'s.**

du·al (dū′əl, dōō′-), *adj.* 1. of or pertaining to two. 2. twofold; double. 3. *Gram.* designating a number category which implies two persons or things. —*n.* 4. *Gram.* **a.** the dual number. **b.** a form therein. —**du·al·i·ty** (dū ăl′ə tĭ, dōō-), *n.* —**du′al·ly,** *adv.*

du·al·ism (dū′ə lĭz′əm, dōō′-), *n.* 1. state of being dual. 2. *Philos.* a theory holding that there are two basic principles, as mind and body. —**du′al·ist,** *n.* —**du′al·is′tic,** *adj.*

dub[1] (dŭb), *v.t.,* **dubbed, dubbing.** 1. to make, or designate as, a knight. 2. to name; call. 3. to strike, cut, rub, etc., to make smooth.

dub[2] (dŭb), *n. Slang.* an unskillful person.

dub[3] (dŭb), *v.,* **dubbed, dubbing,** *n. Motion Pic-tures.* —*v.t.* 1. to change the sound record on a film or to add sounds. —*n.* 2. the new sounds added.

Du Bar·ry (dū băr′ĭ, dōō), **Comtesse** (*Marie Jeanne Bécu*) 1746–93, mistress of Louis XV of France.

du·bi·e·ty (dū bī′ə tĭ, dōō-), *n., pl.* **-ties.** 1. doubtfulness; doubt. 2. a matter of doubt.

du·bi·ous (dū′bĭ əs, dōō′-), *adj.* 1. doubtful. 2. questionable. 3. of uncertain outcome. 4. in-clined to doubt. —**du′bi·ous·ly,** *adv.* —**du′bi-ous·ness,** *n.*

Dub·lin (dŭb′lĭn), *n.* the capital of the Republic of Ireland, in the E part. 495,074.

Du·buque (də būk′), *n.* a city in E Iowa, on the Mississippi. 43,892.

du·cal (dū′kəl, dōō′-), *adj.* of a duke.

duc·at (dŭk′ət), *n.* 1. any of various gold coins formerly in use in European countries, usually worth $2.27 to $2.32. 2. *Slang.* a ticket.

du·ce (dōō′chě), *n.* 1. leader. 2. il Duce, the leader (applied esp. to Benito Mussolini).

duch·ess (dŭch′ĭs), *n.* 1. the wife or widow of a duke. 2. *Hist.* a woman who holds in her own right the sovereignty or titles of a duchy.

duch·y (dŭch′ĭ), *n., pl.* **duchies.** the territory ruled by a duke or duchess.

duck[1] (dŭk), *n.* 1. any of numerous wild or do-mesticated web-footed swimming birds of a fam-ily characterized by a flat bill, short legs, and stout body. 2. the female of this fowl. 3. *Colloq.* a darling; pet.

duck[2] (dŭk), *v.i.* 1. to plunge momentarily un-der water. 2. to bob. 3. to avoid a blow, task, etc. —*v.t.* 4. to plunge in water momentarily. 5. to lower (the head, etc.) suddenly. 6. to avoid (a blow, task, etc.). —*n.* 7. act of ducking.

duck[3] (dŭk), *n.* 1. a heavy plain cotton fabric for tents, clothing, etc. 2. (*pl.*) clothes, esp. trousers, made of it.

duck[4] (dŭk), *n.* (in World War II) a military truck for amphibious use.

duck·bill (dŭk′bĭl′), *n.* a small, aquatic, egg-laying mammal of Australia and Tasmania, hav-ing webbed feet and the muzzle like the beak of a duck. Also, **duck′billed′ platypus.**

duck·ling (dŭk′lĭng), *n.* a young duck.

duck·weed (dŭk′wēd′), *n.* any of certain small aquatic plants which float free on still water.

duct (dŭkt), *n.* a tube, canal, or conduit by which substances are conveyed, as glandular se-cretions.

duc·tile (dŭk′təl, -tĭl), *adj.* 1. capable of being hammered out thin or drawn out into wire or threads. 2. plastic. 3. compliant; tractable. —**duc·til′i·ty,** *n.*

duct·less gland (dŭkt′lĭs), *Anat., Zool.* a gland with no excretory duct, but whose secretion is absorbed directly into the blood or lymph, as the thyroid and pituitary gland.

dud (dŭd), *n. Colloq.* 1. an article of clothing. 2. (*pl.*) clothes. 3. belongings. 4. a failure. 5. *Mil.* a shell that has failed to explode.

dude (dūd, dōōd, *n.* 1. a fop. 2. *Slang.* a person raised in a large city. —**dud′ish,** *adj.*

dude ranch, a ranch operated also as a resort.

dudg·eon (dŭj′ən), *n.* resentment; anger.

due (dū, dōō), *adj.* 1. payable or owing. 2. rightful; proper. 3. adequate. 4. attributable, as to a cause. 5. expected to be ready or present. —*n.* 6. that which is due or owed. —*adv.* 7. di-rectly or straight.

du·el (dū′əl, dōō′-), *n., v.,* **-eled, -eling** or (*esp. Brit.*) **-elled, -elling.** —*n.* 1. a prearranged com-bat between two persons, fought with deadly weapons, esp. to settle a private quarrel. 2. any contest between two sides. —*v.i., v.t.* 3. to fight in a duel. —**du′el·er;** *esp. Brit.,* **du′el·ler,** *n.* —**du′el·ist;** *esp. Brit.,* **du′el·list,** *n.*

du·en·na (dū ĕn′ə, dōō-), *n.* 1. (in Spain and Portugal) an older woman serving as escort or protector of a young lady. 2. a governess; chap-eron.

du·et (dū ĕt′, dōō-), *n. Music.* a composition for two voices or performers.

duff (dŭf), *n.* a flour pudding boiled in a bag.

duf·fel (dŭf′əl), *n.* a camper's outfit.

duffel bag, a canvas bag used esp. by military personnel for personal effects. Also, **duf′fle bag.**

duff·er (dŭf′ər), *n.* 1. *Brit. Colloq.* a plodding or incompetent person. 2. *Slang or Dial.* peddler.

dug[1] (dŭg), *v.* pt. and pp. of **dig.**

dug[2] (dŭg), *n.* the nipple of a female.

dug·out (dŭg′out′), *n.* 1. a rough shelter formed by an excavation in the ground. 2. a boat made by hollowing out a log. 3. *Baseball.* an enclosure from which inactive players watch the game.

Duis·burg-Ham·born (dys′bōōrkH hăm′-bōrn), *n.* a city in W Germany at the junction of the Rhine and Ruhr rivers. 434,646.

duke (dūk, dōōk), *n.* 1. a sovereign ruler of a duchy. 2. a nobleman ranking just below a prince. 3. (*chiefly pl.*) *Slang.* the fist. —**duke′-dom,** *n.*

dul·cet (dŭl′sĭt), *adj.* pleasing; melodious.

dul·ci·mer (dŭl′sə mər), *n. Music.* a zither with metal strings struck by light hammers.

dull (dŭl), *adj.* 1. slow of understanding; stupid. 2. lacking keenness of perception or feeling. 3. not acute. 4. not brisk. 5. spiritless. 6. tedious; uninteresting. 7. not sharp; blunt. 8. lacking richness or intensity of color. 9. dim. —*v.t., v.i.* 10. to make or become dull. —**dull′ish, adj.** —**dull′ness, dul′ness,** *n.* —**dul′ly,** *adv.*

dull·ard (dŭl′ərd), *n.* a dull or stupid person.

dulse (dŭls), *n.* a coarse, edible, red seaweed.

Du·luth (də lōōth′, dŏŏ-), *n.* a city in E Min-nesota: a port on Lake Superior. 101,065.

du·ly (dū′lĭ, dōō′-), *adv.* 1. properly; fitly. 2. in due season; punctually. 3. adequately.

du·ma (dōō′mä), *n.* (in Russia prior to 1917) a council or legislative assembly.

Du·mas (dy mä′), *n.* 1. **Alexandre,** 1802–70, French novelist and dramatist. 2. his son, **Alexandre,** 1824–95, French dramatist and novelist.

dumb (dŭm), *adj.* 1. without the power of speech. 2. that does not speak much or at all. 3. made, done, etc., without speech. 4. lacking some usual characteristic, etc. 5. *U.S. Colloq.* stupid. —**dumb′ly,** *adv.* —**dumb′ness,** *n.*

dumb·bell (dŭm'bĕl'), *n.* **1.** gymnasium apparatus consisting of a bar with weights at each end. **2.** *U.S. Slang.* a stupid person.

dumb show, 1. a pantomime. **2.** gesture without speech.

dumb·wait·er (dŭm'wā'tər), *n. U.S.* an elevator for bringing food, rubbish, etc., from one floor to another.

dum·dum (dŭm'dŭm), *n.* a hollow-nosed bullet that expands on impact.

dum·found (dŭm found'), *v.t.* to strike dumb with amazement. Also, **dumb·found'**.

dum·my (dŭm'Y), *n., pl.* **-mies,** *adj.* **—n. 1.** a model or copy of something, as for display of clothes. **2.** *Colloq.* a stupid person. **3.** an agent ostensibly acting for himself. **4.** a mute. **5.** *Cards.* **a.** (in bridge) the dealer's partner whose hand is exposed and played by the dealer. **b.** an exposed hand which serves as partner to one of the players. **—adj. 6.** acting for others while ostensibly acting for oneself. **7.** counterfeit.

dump[1] (dŭmp), *v.t.* **1.** to throw down or drop heavily. **2.** to empty out. **3.** to sell (goods) in large quantities at a low price. **—v.i. 4.** to fall or drop suddenly. **5.** to unload. **6.** to sell in large quantities at a low price. **—n. 7.** anything, as rubbish, dumped. **8.** a place where it is deposited. **9.** a collection of ammunition, etc., as near a battle front. **10.** *U.S. Slang.* a dilapidated place. **—dump'er,** *n.*

dump[2] (dŭmp), *n.* (*now only pl.*) *Colloq.* a dull, gloomy state of mind.

dump·ling (dŭmp'lYng), *n.* **1.** a rounded mass of steamed dough (often served with stewed meat, etc.). **2.** a pudding consisting of dough enclosing a fruit, and boiled or baked.

dump·y (dŭmp'Y), *adj.,* **dumpier, dumpiest.** short and stout; squat. **—dump'i·ness,** *n.*

dun[1] (dŭn), *v.,* **dunned, dunning,** *n.* **—v.t. 1.** to ask repeatedly, as for the payment of a debt. **—n. 2.** one who duns. **3.** a demand for payment.

dun[2] (dŭn), *adj., n.* dull or grayish brown.

dunce (dŭns), *n.* a dull-witted or stupid person.

dunce cap, a tall paper cone put on the head of a slow or lazy student. Also, **dunce's cap.**

Dun·dee (dŭn dē'), *n.* a seaport in E Scotland. 170,500.

dun·der·head (dŭn'dər hĕd'), *n.* a dunce.

dune (dūn, dōōn), *n.* a sand hill or ridge formed by the wind, in deserts, near lakes, etc.

dung (dŭng), *n.* **1.** manure; excrement. **—v.t. 2.** to manure (ground). **—dung'y,** *adj.*

dun·ga·ree (dŭng'gə rē'), *n.* a coarse cotton fabric used esp. for work clothes, etc. (**dungarees**).

dun·geon (dŭn'jən), *n.* any strong, close cell, esp. underground.

dung·hill (dŭng'hYl'), *n.* a heap of dung.

dunk (dŭngk), *v.t., v.i.* to dip (doughnuts, etc.) into coffee, milk, etc. **—dunk'er,** *n.*

Dun·kirk (dŭn'kûrk), *n.* a seaport in N France: scene of the evacuation under German fire of the British expeditionary force of over 330,-000 men. May 29–June 4, 1940. 10,575.

dun·lin (dŭn'lYn), *n.* a widely distributed sandpiper of the northern hemisphere.

dun·nage (dŭn'Yj), *n.* **1.** baggage or personal effects. **2.** *Naut.* material placed around cargo to prevent injury from water, etc.

Dun·sa·ny (dŭn sā'nY), *n.* **Edward, 18th Baron,** born 1878, Irish dramatist and writer.

du·o (dōō'ō), *n., pl.* **duos, dui** (dōō'ē). a duet.

du·o·dec·i·mal (dū'ə dĕs'ə məl, dōō'-), *adj.* **1.** pertaining to twelfths or twelve. **—n. 2.** one of a system of numerals the base of which is twelve. **3.** one of twelve equal parts.

du·o·dec·i·mo (dū'ə dĕs'ə mō', dōō'-), *n., pl.* **-mos,** *adj.* **—n. 1.** a book size (about 5 x 7½ inches) determined by folding sheets into twelve leaves. **—adj. 2.** in duodecimo.

du·o·de·num (dū'ə dē'nəm, dōō'-), *n. Anat., Zool.* the first portion of the small intestine, from the stomach to the jejunum. **—du'o·de'nal,** *adj.*

dupe (dūp, dōōp), *n., v.,* **duped, duping. —n. 1.** a person who is deceived or tricked. **—v.t. 2.** to deceive; trick.

du·ple (dū'pəl, dōō'-), *adj.* double; twofold.

duple time, *Music.* characterized by two beats to the measure.

du·plex (dū'plĕks, dōō'-), *adj.* **1.** double. **2.** *Mach.* including two identical working parts in a single framework. **—n. 3.** duplex house.

duplex apartment, an apartment, or suite of rooms, on two floors or stories.

duplex house, *U.S.* a house for two families.

du·pli·cate (*adj., n.* dū'plə kYt, dōō'-; *v.* dū'plə kāt', dōō'-), *adj., n., v.,* **-cated, -cating. —adj. 1.** exactly like or corresponding to something else. **2.** double. **3.** *Cards.* denoting a game in which the same cards are replayed by another team. **—n. 4.** an exact copy. **5.** *Cards.* a duplicate game. **—v.t. 6.** to copy exactly. **7.** to double. **—du'pli·ca'tion,** *n.* **—du'pli·ca'tor,** *n.*

du·plic·i·ty (dū plYs'ə tY, dōō-), *n., pl.* **-ties.** deceitfulness in speech or conduct.

du·ra·ble (dyŏŏr'ə bəl, dōōr'-), *adj.* lasting or enduring. **—du'ra·bil'i·ty, du'ra·ble·ness,** *n.* **—du'ra·bly,** *adv.*

du·ral·u·min (dyŏŏ răl'yə mYn, dōō-), *n.* **1.** an aluminum-base alloy. **2.** (*cap.*) a trademark for this alloy.

dur·ance (dyŏŏr'əns, dōōr'-), *n.* imprisonment.

du·ra·tion (dyŏŏ rā'shən, dōō-), *n.* **1.** continuance in time. **2.** length of time anything continues.

Dur·ban (dûr'bən), *n.* a seaport in the E part of the Union of South Africa, in Natal. 259,606.

dur·bar (dûr'bär), *n.* (in India) **1.** the court of a native ruler. **2.** a public audience held by a native prince or a British governor or viceroy.

Dü·rer (dY'rər), *n.* **Albrecht** or **Albert,** 1471–1528, German painter and engraver.

du·ress (dyŏŏr'Ys, dōōr'-, dyŏŏ rĕs', dōō-), *n.* **1.** compulsion. **2.** imprisonment.

Dur·ham (dûr'əm), *n.* a city in N North Carolina. 60,195.

dur·ing (dyŏŏr'Yng, dōōr'-), *prep.* **1.** throughout the continuance of. **2.** in the course of. ,

du·rum wheat (dyŏŏr'əm, dōōr'-), an important species of wheat, the flour from which is used for macaroni, etc. Also, **durum.**

Du·se (dōō'zĕ), *n.* **Eleonora,** (*Signora Checchi*) 1859–1924, Italian actress.

dusk (dŭsk), *n.* **1.** partial darkness; shade. **2.** the darker stage of twilight. **—adj. 3.** dark. **—v.t., v.i. 4.** to darken.

dusk·y (dŭs'kY), *adj.,* **duskier, duskiest. 1.** somewhat dark. **2.** dim. **3.** gloomy. **—dusk'i·ly,** *adv.* **—dusk'i·ness,** *n.*

Düs·sel·dorf (dōōs'əl dôrf'), *n.* a city in W Germany. 541,410.

dust (dŭst), *n.* **1.** earth or other matter in fine, dry particles. **2.** the human body. **3.** a dead body. **4.** a low or humble condition. **5.** anything worthless. **—v.t. 6.** to free from dust. **7.** to sprinkle with dust. **8.** to strew or sprinkle as dust. **9.** to make dusty. **—v.i. 10.** to wipe dust from a table, etc. **11.** to become dusty. **—dust'·er,** *n.* **—dust'less,** *adj.*

dust bowl, an area subject to dust storms.

dust·pan (dŭst'păn'), *n.* a utensil in which dust is collected and removed.

dust storm, a storm of wind which raises dense masses of dust into the air.

dust·y (dŭs'tY), *adj.,* **dustier, dustiest. 1.** filled or covered with dust. **2.** dustlike. **3.** gray. **—dust'i·ly,** *adv.* **—dust'i·ness,** *n.*

Dutch (dŭch), *adj.* **1.** of, pertaining to, or characteristic of the people of the Netherlands or Holland, or their country or language. **2.** *Archaic or Slang.* German; Teutonic. **3. in Dutch,** *Slang.* in trouble. **—n. 4.** the people of the Netherlands or Holland. **5.** a Germanic language, the language of the Netherlands. **—Dutch'man,** *n.*

Dutch East Indies, the former island possessions of the Netherlands in the Malay Archipelago, including Sumatra, Java, Celebes, parts of Borneo and New Guinea, the Moluccas, and other islands. See **Indonesia.** 60,727,000 pop.; 735,195 sq. mi.

Dutch Guiana, Surinam.

Dutch Harbor, a U.S. naval base in the Aleutian Islands.

Dutch·man's-breech·es (dŭch'mənz brYch'-Yz), *n. sing. and pl.* a delicate herb with pale-yellow, two-spurred flowers.

Dutch oven, a heavily constructed kettle with a close-fitting lid, used for pot roasts, etc.

Dutch treat, *U.S. Colloq.* a meal or entertainment in which each person pays for himself.

Dutch uncle, a severe and frank critic.

du·te·ous (dū′tĭ əs, dōō′-), *adj.* dutiful; obedient. —**du′te·ous·ly**, *adv.* —**du′te·ous·ness**, *n.*

du·ti·a·ble (dū′tĭ ə bəl, dōō′-), *adj.* subject to duty, as imported goods.

du·ti·ful (dū′tĭ fəl, dōō′-), *adj.* **1.** performing one's duties. **2.** required by duty. —**du′ti·ful·ly**, *adv.* —**du′ti·ful·ness**, *n.*

du·ty (dū′tĭ, dōō′-), *n.*, *pl.* **-ties.** **1.** that which one is bound to do by moral or legal obligation. **2.** moral obligation. **3.** office or function. **4.** homage; respect. **5.** an act of respect. **6.** a levy, esp. one imposed on the import or export of goods.

du·ve·tyn (dōō′və tēn′), *n.* a napped fabric of cotton, wool, silk, or rayon. Also, **du′ve·tine′**.

D.V., Deo volente (God willing).

Dvo·rák (dvôr′zhäk), *n.* **Anton**, 1841–1904, Czech composer.

dwarf (dwôrf), *n.* **1.** an abnormally small person, animal, or plant. —*adj.* **2.** abnormally small. —*v.t.* **3.** to cause to seem small. **4.** to prevent the growth of. —*v.i.* **5.** to become stunted or smaller. —**dwarf′ish**, *adj.*

dwell (dwĕl), *v.i.*, **dwelt** or **dwelled, dwelling. 1.** to reside permanently. **2.** to continue for a time. **3.** to emphasize. —**dwell′er**, *n.*

dwell·ing (dwĕl′ĭng), *n.* residence or abode.

dwin·dle (dwĭn′dəl), *v.i.*, *v.t.*, **-dled, -dling.** to make or become smaller; shrink; diminish.

dwt., pennyweight.

Dy, *Chem.* dysprosium.

dye (dī), *n.*, *v.*, **dyed, dyeing.** —*n.* **1.** a coloring material. **2.** color or hue produced by dyeing. —*v.t.* **3.** to color with a dye. —*v.i.* **4.** to impart or take color. —**dye′ing**, *n.* —**dy′er**, *n.*

dyed-in-the-wool (dīd′ĭn ᵗhə wŏŏl′), *adj.* **1.** dyed before weaving. **2.** complete.

dye·stuff (dī′stŭf′), *n.* a material used as a dye.

dy·ing (dī′ĭng), *adj.* **1.** ceasing to live. **2.** pertaining to or just preceding death. —*n.* **3.** death.

dyke (dīk), *n.*, *v.*, **dyked, dyking.** dike.

dy·nam·ic (dī năm′ĭk), *adj.* **1.** of or pertaining to force, esp. force not in equilibrium. **2.** pertaining to dynamics. **3.** energetic; forceful. Also, **dy·nam′i·cal.** —**dy·nam′i·cal·ly**, *adv.*

dy·nam·ics (dī năm′ĭks), *n.* **1.** that branch of physics which deals with the action of force on bodies in motion or at rest. **2.** (*construed as pl.*) the forces at work in any field.

dy·na·mite (dī′nə mīt′), *n.*, *v.*, **-mited, -miting.** —*n.* **1.** a high explosive of nitroglycerin with some absorbent. —*v.t.* **2.** to blow up or destroy with dynamite. —**dy′na·mit′er**, *n.*

dy·na·mo (dī′nə mō′), *n.*, *pl.* **-mos.** any rotating machine in which mechanical energy input may be converted into electrical energy output, or electrical input may be converted into mechanical output.

dy·na·mo·e·lec·tric (dī′nə mō ĭ lĕk′trĭk), *adj.* pertaining to the conversion of mechanical energy into electric energy, or vice versa.

dy·na·mom·e·ter (dī′nə nŏm′ə tər), *n.* a device for measuring force or power.

dy·nas·ty (dī′nəs tĭ; *Brit.* also dĭn′əs tĭ), *n.*, *pl.* **-ties.** a sequence of rulers from the same family.

dyne (dīn), *n.* *Physics.* the unit of force in the centimeter-gram-second system: that force which, acting on a body of mass of one gram for one second, gives it a velocity of one centimeter per second.

dys·en·ter·y (dĭs′ən tĕr′ĭ), *n.* an infectious disease of the lower part of the bowels, with diarrhea that becomes mucous and hemorrhagic. —**dys′en·ter′ic**, *adj.*

dys·pep·sia (dĭs pĕp′shə, -sĭ ə), *n.* indigestion.

dys·pep·tic (dĭs pĕp′tĭk), *adj.* **1.** of or suffering from dyspepsia. **2.** morbidly gloomy. —*n.* **3.** a dyspeptic person. Also, **dys·pep′ti·cal.** —**dys·pep′ti·cal·ly**, *adv.*

dys·pro·si·um (dĭs prō′sĭ əm, -shĭ-), *n.* *Chem.* a rare-earth metallic element. *Symbol:* Dy; *at. wt.:* 162.46; *at. no.:* 66.

dz., dozen; dozens.

E

E, e (ē), *n.*, *pl.* **E's** or **Es, e's** or **es. 1.** the 5th letter of the English alphabet. **2.** *Music.* the third tone in the scale of C major.

E, **1.** east. **2.** eastern. **3.** English.

E., 1. Earl. **2.** east. **3.** eastern. **4.** English.

ea., each.

each (ēch), *adj.* **1.** every individual. —*pron.* **2.** every individual one. —*adv.* **3.** apiece.

ea·ger (ē′gər), *adj.* **1.** keen or ardent in feeling. **2.** intensely earnest. —**ea′ger·ly**, *adv.* —**ea′ger·ness**, *n.*

ea·gle (ē′gəl), *n.* **1.** any of certain large diurnal birds of prey of the falcon family, esp. the **golden eagle** of the northern hemisphere, and the **bald eagle** of North America, noted for their size, strength, powerful flight, and keenness of vision. **2.** a standard, seal, etc., bearing the figure of an eagle. **3.** a gold coin of the United States, the value of ten dollars. **4.** *Golf.* a score two below par on any but par-three holes.

ea·glet (ē′glĭt), *n.* a young eagle.

ear[1] (ĭr), *n.* **1.** the organ of hearing. **2.** the external part alone. **3.** the sense of hearing. **4.** sensitive perception of the differences of sound. **5.** attention. **6.** any object resembling the external ear.

ear[2] (ĭr), *n.* **1.** that part of a cereal plant, as corn, wheat, etc., which contains the fruit, grains, or kernels. —*v.i.* **2.** to form ears.

ear·ache (ĭr′āk′), *n.* pain in the ear.

ear·drum (ĭr′drŭm′), *n.* tympanic membrane.

earl (ûrl), *n.* a British nobleman of a rank next below that of marquis. —**earl′dom**, *n.*

ear·ly (ûr′lĭ), *adv.*, **-lier, -liest,** *adj.* —*adv.* **1.** in the first part of some time, course, or series. **2.** before the usual time. —*adj.* **3.** occurring in the first part of some time, course, or series. **4.** occurring before the usual time. **5.** belonging to a period far back in time. **6.** occurring in the near future. —**ear′li·ness**, *n.*

ear·mark (ĭr′märk′), *n.* **1.** a mark of identification made on the ear of an animal. **2.** any identifying mark. —*v.t.* **3.** to mark with an earmark. **4.** to set aside for a specific use.

earn (ûrn), *v.t.* **1.** to gain by labor. **2.** to merit; deserve. **3.** to get as one's due. **4.** to gain as due return. —**earn′er**, *n.*

ear·nest[1] (ûr′nĭst), *adj.* **1.** serious in effort. **2.** showing depth of feeling. **3.** having serious importance. —*n.* **4.** seriousness. —**ear′nest·ly**, *adv.* —**ear′nest·ness**, *n.*

ear·nest[2] (ûr′nĭst), *n.* a portion given or done in advance as a pledge of the remainder.

earn·ing (ûr′nĭng), *n.* **1.** act of one who earns. **2.** (*pl.*) money earned; wages; profits.

ear·phone (ĭr′fōn′), *n.* a receiver in a headset.

ear·ring (ĭr′rĭng′), *n.* a ring or other ornament worn in or on the lobe of the ear.

ear·shot (ĭr′shŏt′), *n.* reach or range of hearing.

earth (ûrth), *n.* **1.** the planet we inhabit, the third in order from the sun. **2.** the inhabitants of this planet. **3.** this planet as the habitation of man, in contrast to heaven and hell. **4.** the dry land; the ground. **5.** soil; dirt. **6.** worldly matters. **7.** *Chem.* any of certain difficultly reducible metallic oxides, as alumina, etc. **8.** *Elect.* a ground.

earth·en (ûr′thən), *adj.* **1.** composed of earth. **2.** made of baked clay.

earth·en·ware (ûr′thən wâr′), *n.* earthen pottery; vessels, etc., of baked or hardened clay.

earth·ly (ûrth′lĭ), *adj.*, **-lier, -liest. 1.** of or pertaining to the earth. **2.** possible. **—earth′- li·ness,** *n.*

earth·quake (ûrth′kwāk′), *n.* a vibration or movement of a part of the earth's surface.

earth·ward (ûrth′wərd), *adv.* toward the earth. Also, **earth′wards. —earth′ward,** *adj.*

earth·work (ûrth′wûrk′), *n.* the excavating and embanking of earth involved in engineering construction, fortification, etc.

earth·worm (ûrth′wûrm′), *n.* any one of numerous annelid worms that burrow in soil.

earth·y (ûr′thĭ), *adj.*, **earthier, earthiest. 1.** of or characteristic of earth. **2.** worldly. **3.** coarse. **—earth′i·ness,** *n.*

ear·wax (ĭr′wăks′), *n.* cerumen.

ear·wig (ĭr′wĭg′), *n.*, *v.*, **-wigged, -wigging. —n. 1.** an insect of an order having the forceps or pincers at the end of the abdomen. **—v.t. 2.** to bias.

ease (ēz), *n.*, *v.*, **eased, easing. —n. 1.** freedom from labor, pain, or annoyance; comfort. **2.** freedom from worry. **3.** facility. **4.** freedom from stiffness or formality. **—v.t. 5.** to make comfortable. **6.** to free from care. **7.** to lessen. **8.** to release from pressure, tension, or the like. **9.** to facilitate. **—v.i. 10.** to be eased. **—eas′er,** *n.*

ea·sel (ē′zəl), *n.* a stand for supporting an artist's canvas, a blackboard, or the like.

ease·ment (ēz′mənt), *n.* **1.** an easing. **2.** something that gives ease. **3.** *Law.* a right held by one person to make use of the land of another.

eas·i·ly (ē′zə lĭ, ēz′lĭ), *adv.* in an easy manner.

eas·i·ness (ē′zĭ nĭs), *n.* easy quality.

east (ēst), *n.* **1.** a cardinal point of the compass, corresponding to the point where the sun is seen to rise. **2.** the direction in which this point lies. **3.** (*l.c. or cap.*) a region in this direction. **4. the East, a.** the Orient. **b.** the eastern part of the United States. **—adj. 5.** toward, in, or from the east. **—adv. 6.** toward, in, or from the east.

East Chicago, a city in NW Indiana. 54,637.

East Cleveland, a city in NE Ohio. 39,495.

East·er (ēs′tər), *n.* an annual Christian festival in commemoration of the resurrection of Jesus Christ, observed on the first Sunday after the full moon that occurs on or next after March 21.

Easter Island, an island in the S Pacific, ab. 2000 mi. W of and belonging to Chile.

east·er·ly (ēs′tər lĭ), *adj.*, *adv.* **1.** toward the east. **2.** from the east.

east·ern (ēs′tərn), *adj.* **1.** lying toward or in the east. **2.** directed toward the east. **3.** coming from the east. **4.** (*l.c. or cap.*) of or pertaining to the East. **5.** (*usually cap.*) Oriental. **—east′- ern·most,** *adj.*

Eastern Church, 1. the church of the countries in the eastern part of Roman Empire. **2.** any body of Christians belonging to the Greek Church.

East·ern·er (ēs′tərn ər), *n.* a person of or from the eastern U.S.

East Indies, 1. a collective name of India, Indo-China, and the Malay Archipelago. **2.** the Malay Archipelago. **—East Indian.**

Eas·ton (ēs′tən), *n.* a city in E Penn. 33,589.

East Orange, city in NE New Jersey. 68,945.

East Providence, a town in NE Rhode Island, near Providence. 32,165.

East Saint Louis, a city in SW Illinois, across the Mississippi from St. Louis. 75,609.

east·ward (ēst′wərd), *adv.* toward the east. Also, **east′wards. —east′ward,** *adj.* **—east′- ward·ly,** *adv.*

eas·y (ē′zĭ), *adj.*, **easier, easiest,** *adv.* **—adj. 1.** not difficult. **2.** free from pain, worry, etc. **3.** conducive to comfort. **4.** fond of ease. **5.** lenient. **6.** not burdensome. **7.** compliant. **8.** free from formality or embarrassment. **9.** not tight. **10.** moderate. **—adv. 11.** *Colloq.* in an easy manner.

eas·y·go·ing (ē′zĭ gō′ĭng), *adj.* taking matters in an easy way; comfortably unconcerned.

eat (ēt), *v.*, **ate** (āt; *esp. Brit.* ĕt) or (*Archaic*) **eat** (ĕt, ēt); **eaten** or (*Archaic*) **eat** (ĕt, ēt); **eating;** *n.* **—v.t. 1.** to take into the mouth and swallow, as food. **2.** to consume by devouring. **3.** to devastate. **4.** to wear away. **5.** to make (a hole, etc.). **—v.i. 6.** to consume food. **7.** to make a way as by gnawing or corrosion. **—n. 8.** (*pl.*) *Slang.* food. **—eat′er,** *n.*

eat·a·ble (ē′tə bəl), *adj.* **1.** edible. **—n. 2.** (*usually pl.*) an article of food.

eau de Co·logne (ō′ də kə lōn′), **1.** cologne. **2.** (*cap.*) a trademark for a certain type of cologne.

eaves (ēvz), *n.pl.* the overhanging lower edge of a roof.

eaves·drop (ēvz′drŏp′), *v.i.*, **-dropped, -dropping.** to listen clandestinely. **—eaves′drop′- per,** *n.*

ebb (ĕb), *n.* **1.** the falling of the tide. **2.** decline or decay. **3.** a point of decline. **—v.i. 4.** to flow back or away. **5.** to decline or decay.

eb·on·ite (ĕb′ə nīt′), *n.* vulcanite.

eb·on·y (ĕb′ən ĭ), *n.*, *pl.* **-onies,** *adj.* **—n. 1.** a hard, heavy, durable wood, most highly prized when black, from various tropical trees of southern India and Ceylon. **2.** any tree yielding such wood. **—adj. 3.** made of ebony. **4.** like ebony; black. Also, *Poetic,* **eb′on.**

e·bul·lient (ĭ bŭl′yənt), *adj.* **1.** seething with fervor, enthusiasm, etc. **2.** boiling up. **—e·bul′- lience,** *n.* **—e·bul′lient·ly,** *adv.*

eb·ul·li·tion (ĕb′ə lĭsh′ən), *n.* **1.** an outburst. **2.** ebullient state. **3.** act of boiling up.

ECA, Economic Coöperation Administration.

ec·cen·tric (ĭk sĕn′trĭk, ĕk-), *adj.* **1.** deviating from the usual character, practice, etc.; odd. **2.** *Math.* not concentric. **3.** not in the center. **4.** *Mach.* having the axis or support away from the center. **5.** *Astron.* deviating from a circular form. **—n. 6.** one that is unusual or odd. **7.** *Mach.* a device for converting circular into reciprocating rectilinear motion. **—ec·cen′tri·cal·ly,** *adv.*

ec·cen·tric·i·ty (ĕk′sən trĭs′ə tĭ, ĕk′sĕn-), *n.*, *pl.* **-ties. 1.** an oddity. **2.** eccentric quality.

Eccl., Ecclesiastes. Also, **Eccles.**

eccl., (*also cap.*) ecclesiastical. Also, **eccles.**

Ec·cle·si·as·tes (ĭ klē′zĭ ăs′tēz), *n.* a book of the Old Testament traditionally ascribed to Solomon.

ec·cle·si·as·tic (ĭ klē′zĭ ăs′tĭk), *n.* **1.** a clergyman. **—adj. 2.** ecclesiastical.

ec·cle·si·as·ti·cal (ĭ klē′zĭ ăs′tə kəl), *adj.* of or pertaining to the church or the clergy.

Ec·cle·si·as·ti·cus (ĭ klē′zĭ ăs′tə kəs), *n.* one of the books of the Apocrypha.

ech·e·lon (ĕsh′ə lŏn′), *n.* **1.** a level of command. **2.** a steplike formation of troops, ships, planes, etc. **—v.t., v.i. 3.** to form in echelon.

e·chid·na (ĭ kĭd′nə), *n.*, *pl.* **-nas, -nae** (-nē). any of certain spine-covered insectivorous mammals of New Guinea and Australia with claws and a slender snout.

ech·o (ĕk′ō), *n.*, *pl.* **echoes,** *v.*, **echoed, echoing. —n. 1.** a repetition of sound, produced by the reflection of sound waves. **2.** a sound heard after reflection. **3.** any repetition or close imitation. **4.** one who imitates another. **5.** (*cap.*) *Class. Myth.* a mountain nymph who pined away for Narcissus until only her voice remained. **—v.i. 6.** to emit an echo. **7.** to be repeated by an echo. **—v.t. 8.** to repeat by an echo. **9.** to repeat or imitate the words, etc., of. **—ech′o·er,** *n.*

é·clair (ā klâr′), *n.* an iced, finger-shaped cake having a cream or custard filling.

é·clat (ā klä′), *n.* brilliance, as of success.

ec·lec·tic (ĕk lĕk′tĭk), *adj.* **1.** choosing from various sources. **2.** made up of what is selected from diverse sources. **—n. 3.** one who follows an eclectic method. **—ec·lec′ti·cism′,** *n.*

e·clipse (ĭ klĭps′), *n.*, *v.*, **eclipsed, eclipsing. —n. 1.** the obscuration of the light of a satellite by the intervention of its primary planet between it and the sun. **2.** any obscuration. **—v.t. 3.** to cause to suffer eclipse. **4.** to obscure; darken. **5.** to surpass.

e·clip·tic (ĭ klĭp′tĭk), *n.* **1.** the apparent annual path of the sun in the heavens. **2.** an analogous great circle. **—adj. 3.** Also, **e·clip′ti·cal.** pertaining to an eclipse or the ecliptic.

ec·logue (ĕk′lôg, -lŏg), *n.* a pastoral poem.

e·col·o·gy (ĭ kŏl′ə jĭ), *n.* the branch of biology which treats of the relations between organisms and their environment. **—e·col′o·gist,** *n.*

econ., 1. economic. **2.** economics.

e·co·nom·ic (ē′kə nŏm′ĭk, ĕk′ə-), *adj.* **1.** pertaining to the production, distribution, and use

Diagram of ecliptic
A, Ecliptic; B, Celestial equator; C, Orbit of earth; D, Sun

of wealth. 2. of or pertaining to the science of economics. 3. utilitarian.

e·co·nom·i·cal (ē/kə nŏm/ə kəl, ĕk/ə-), *adj.* 1. avoiding waste or extravagance; thrifty. 2. economic. —**e/co·nom/i·cal·ly,** *adv.*

Economic Coöperation Administration, the U.S. government agency (estab. 1948) in charge of economic aid to foreign nations.

e·co·nom·ics (ē/kə nŏm/ĭks, ĕk/ə-), *n.* the science of the production, distribution, and consumption of goods and services.

e·con·o·mist (Ĭ kŏn/ə mĭst), *n.* 1. an expert in economics. 2. an economical person.

e·con·o·mize (Ĭ kŏn/ə mīz/), *v.,* -mized, -mizing. —*v.t.* 1. to use sparingly or frugally. —*v.i.* 2. to avoid waste or extravagance. —**e·con/o·miz/er,** *n.*

e·con·o·my (Ĭ kŏn/ə mĭ), *n., pl.* -mies. 1. thrifty management. 2. a saving. 3. the efficient management of the resources of a community, etc. 4. an organized system or method.

ec·ru (ĕk/rōō, ā/krōō), *adj., n.* very light brown. Also, **é/cru.**

ec·sta·sy (ĕk/stə sĭ), *n., pl.* -sies. 1. overpowering emotion. 2. rapturous delight. 3. the frenzy of poetic inspiration. 4. mystic rapture. —**ec·stat·ic** (ĕk stăt/Ĭk), *adj., n.* —**ec·stat/i·cal·ly,** *adv.*

ec·to·plasm (ĕk/tə plăz/əm), *n.* 1. *Biol.* the outer portion of the cytoplasm. 2. *Spiritualism.* the supposed emanation from the body of a medium.

Ec·ua·dor (ĕk/wə dôr/), *n.* a republic in NW South America. 3,171,367 pop.; 104,510 sq. mi. *Cap.:* Quito. —**Ec/ua·do/ri·an,** *adj., n.*

ec·u·men·i·cal (ĕk/yŏō mĕn/ə kəl *or, esp. Brit.,* ē/kyŏō-), *adj.* 1. general. 2. pertaining to the whole Christian church. Also, **ec/u·men/ic.**

ec·ze·ma (ĕk/sə mə, ĕg zē/-), *n.* an inflammatory, itching disease of the skin.

-ed[1], a suffix forming the past tense.

-ed[2], a suffix forming: 1. the past participle. 2. participial adjectives indicating a resultant condition or quality.

-ed[3], a suffix forming adjectives from nouns.

ed., 1. edited. 2. edition. 3. (*pl.* **eds.**) editor.

Edam cheese (ē/dăm, -dəm), a hard, round cheese, usually red outside. Also, **Edam.**

Ed·da (ĕd/ə), *n., pl.* **Eddas.** 1. Elder or Poetic Edda, a collection of old Icelandic poems on mythical and religious subjects. 2. Younger or Prose Edda, an old Icelandic work containing ancient myths, etc.

Ed·ding·ton (ĕd/Ĭng tən), *n.* **Sir Arthur Stanley,** 1882–1944, British astronomer.

ed·dy (ĕd/Ĭ), *n., pl.* -dies, *v.,* -died, -dying. —*n.* 1. a current at variance with the main current of liquid, gas, dust, etc. —*v.i., v.t.* 2. to whirl in eddies.

Ed·dy (ĕd/Ĭ), *n.* **Mrs. Mary Baker,** 1821–1910, U.S. religious leader.

e·del·weiss (ā/dəl vīs/), *n.* a small composite herb with white woolly leaves and flowers, growing in the high altitudes of the Alps.

E·den (ē/dən), *n.* 1. the garden which was the first home of Adam and Eve. 2. any paradise.

e·den·tate (ē dĕn/tāt), *adj.* 1. belonging or pertaining to an order of New World mammals, comprising the armadillos, sloths, and anteaters. —*n.* 2. an edentate mammal.

edge (ĕj), *n., v.,* edged, edging. —*n.* 1. the border or margin. 2. a brink or verge. 3. the narrow surface of a thin, flat object. 4. the thin, sharp side of a blade. 5. sharpness or keenness. —*v.t.* 6. to sharpen. 7. to border. 8. to move edgewise. —*v.i.* 9. to move edgewise. —**edged,** *adj.*

edge·wise (ĕj/wīz/), *adv.* with the edge directed forward. Also, **edge·ways** (ĕj/wāz/).

edg·ing (ĕj/Ĭng), *n.* border; trimming for edges.

edg·y (ĕj/Ĭ), *adj.* 1. sharp-edged. 2. irritable.

ed·i·ble (ĕd/ə bəl), *adj.* 1. fit to be eaten. —*n.* 2. (*usually pl.*) anything edible. —**ed/i·bil/i·ty,** *n.*

e·dict (ē/dĭkt), *n.* a decree issued by a sovereign or other authority. —**e·dic/tal,** *adj.*

ed·i·fice (ĕd/ə fĭs), *n.* a building, esp. a large one.

ed·i·fy (ĕd/ə fī/), *v.t.,* -fied, -fying. to instruct or benefit, esp. morally. —**ed·i·fi·ca·tion** (ĕd/ə fə kā/shən), *n.*

e·dile (ē/dĭl), *n.* aedile.

Ed·in·burgh (ĕd/ən bûr/ō *or, esp. Brit.,* -brə), *n.* the capital of Scotland, in the SE part. 463,100.

Ed·i·son (ĕd/ə sən), *n.* **Thomas Alva,** 1847–1931, U.S. inventor.

ed·it (ĕd/Ĭt), *v.t.* 1. to direct the preparation of (a newspaper, etc.). 2. to prepare for publication.

edit., 1. edited. 2. edition. 3. editor.

e·di·tion (Ĭ dĭsh/ən), *n.* 1. one of a number of printings of a book, etc., issued at different times, and differing from another by alterations. 2. the format in which a work is published.

ed·i·tor (ĕd/Ĭ tər), *n.* 1. the director of a newspaper, etc. 2. one who writes editorials. 3. one who edits material for publication. —**ed/i·tor·ship/,** *n.*

ed·i·to·ri·al (ĕd/ə tōr/Ĭ əl), *n.* 1. an article, as in a newspaper, presenting the opinion of the periodical. —*adj.* 2. of or written by an editor. —**ed/i·to/ri·al·ly,** *adv.*

ed·i·to·ri·al·ize (ĕd/ə tōr/Ĭ ə līz/), *v.i.,* -ized, -izing. to inject one's opinion.

Ed·mon·ton (ĕd/mən tən), *n.* a city in SW Canada: the capital of Alberta. 93,817.

E.D.T., Eastern daylight time. Also, **e.d.t.**

educ., 1. educated. 2. education.

ed·u·ca·ble (ĕj/ŏō kə bəl), *adj.* capable of being educated.

ed·u·cate (ĕj/ŏō kāt/), *v.t.,* -cated, -cating. 1. to develop by instruction. 2. to send to school. —**ed/u·ca/tive,** *adj.* —**ed/u·ca/tor,** *n.*

ed·u·ca·tion (ĕj/ŏō kā/shən), *n.* 1. act or process of instruction or training. 2. the result produced. 3. the science or art of teaching. —**ed/u·ca/tion·al,** *adj.*

e·duce (Ĭ dūs/, Ĭ dōōs/), *v.t.,* educed, educing. to elicit. —**e·duc/i·ble,** *adj.* —**e·duc·tion** (Ĭ dŭk/shən), *n.*

Ed·ward (ĕd/wərd), *n.* 1. (*"the Black Prince"*) Prince of Wales, 1330–76 (son of Edward III). 2. **VIII,** (*Duke of Windsor*) born 1894, King of England in 1936 (son of George V).

Ed·wards (ĕd/wərdz), *n.* **Jonathan,** 1703–58, colonial American clergyman and metaphysician.

Edward the Confessor, c1004–66, king of England, 1042–66.

-ee, a suffix of nouns denoting one who is the object of some action or who receives something.

E.E., Electrical Engineer.

eel (ēl), *n.* a snakelike fish. —**eel/like, eel/y,** *adj.*

e'en (ēn), *adv. Poet.* or *Dial.* even.

e'er (âr), *adv. Poetic.* ever.

ee·rie (Ĭr/Ĭ), *adj.,* -rier, -riest. 1. weird, strange, or uncanny. 2. affected with superstitious fear. —**ee/ri·ly,** *adv.* —**ee/ri·ness,** *n.*

ee·ry (Ĭr/Ĭ), *adj.,* -rier, -riest. eerie.

ef·face (Ĭ fās/), *v.t.,* -faced, -facing. 1. to destroy. 2. to obliterate (traces, etc.). 3. to make inconspicuous. —**ef·face/ment,** *n.* —**ef·fac/er,** *n.*

ef·fect (Ĭ fĕkt/), *n.* 1. a result; consequence. 2. power to produce results. 3. operation or execution. 4. a mental impression produced, as by a speech. 5. intent; significance. 6. (*pl.*) personal property. 7. **in effect,** in fact. —*v.t.* 8. to bring about. 9. to produce.

ef·fec·tive (Ĭ fĕk/tĭv), *adj.* 1. producing the intended or expected result. 2. actually in effect. 3. impressive; striking. —*n.* 4. a soldier or sailor fit for duty. —**ef·fec/tive·ly,** *adv.* —**ef·fec/tive·ness,** *n.*

ef·fec·tu·al (Ĭ fĕk/chŏō əl), *adj.* producing, or capable of producing, an intended effect. —**ef·fec/tu·al/i·ty,** *n.* —**ef·fec/tu·al·ly,** *adv.*

ef·fem·i·nate (Ĭ fĕm/ə nĭt), *adj.* delicate to an unmanly degree in tastes, habits, etc. —**ef·fem·i·na·cy** (Ĭ fĕm/ə nə sĭ), *n.*

ef·fen·di (Ĭ fĕn/dĬ), *n., pl.* -dis. a Turkish title of respect for government officials, etc.

ef·fer·ent (ĕf/ər ənt), *adj. Anat.* carrying away.

ef·fer·vesce (ĕf/ər vĕs/), *v.i.,* -vesced, -vescing. 1. to give off bubbles of gas, as fermenting liquors. 2. to exhibit excitement, liveliness, etc. —**ef/fer·ves/cence, ef/fer·ves/cen·cy,** *n.* —**ef/fer·ves/cent,** *adj.*

ef·fete (Ĭ fēt/), *adj.* 1. exhausted; worn out. 2. unable to produce. —**ef·fete/ness,** *n.*

ef·fi·ca·cious (ĕf/ə kā/shəs), *adj.* effective as a means, measure, remedy, etc. —**ef/fi·ca/cious·ly,** *adv.* —**ef·fi·ca·cy** (ĕf/ə kə sĭ), *n.* —**ef/fi·ca/cious·ness,** *n.*

ef·fi·cien·cy (Ĭ fĬsh/ən sĭ), *n., pl.* -cies. fact or quality of being efficient.

ef·fi·cient (Ĭ fĬsh/ənt), *adj.* 1. competent in

operation or performance. **2.** producing an effect. —ef·fi′cient·ly, *adv.*

ef·fi·gy (ĕf′ə jĭ), *n., pl.* **-gies. 1.** an image, esp. sculptured, as on a monument. **2.** a representation of an obnoxious person.

ef·flo·resce (ĕf′lō rĕs′), *v.i.,* **-resced, -rescing. 1.** to blossom. **2.** *Chem.* **a.** to change to a powdery substance upon exposure to air. **b.** to become covered with crystals of salt or the like through evaporation, etc. —ef′flo·res′cence, *n.* —ef′flo·res′cent, *adj.*

ef·flu·ence (ĕf′lōō əns), *n.* **1.** outward flow. **2.** something that flows out. —ef′flu·ent, *adj., n.*

ef·flu·vi·um (ĭ flōō′vĭ əm), *n., pl.* **-via** (-vĭ ə), **-viums.** a slight or invisible vapor, esp. one that is disagreeable or noxious. —ef·flu′vi·al, *adj.*

ef·fort (ĕf′ərt), *n.* **1.** exertion of physical or mental power. **2.** an attempt. **3.** an achievement.

ef·fort·less (ĕf′ərt lĭs), *adj.* **1.** requiring or involving no effort; easy. **2.** making no effort; passive.

ef·fron·ter·y (ĭ frŭn′tə rĭ), *n., pl.* **-teries.** shameless or impudent boldness; barefaced audacity.

ef·ful·gent (ĭ fŭl′jənt), *adj.* shining forth brilliantly. —ef·ful′gence, *n.* —ef·ful′gent·ly, *adv.*

ef·fuse (*v.* ĭ fūz′; *adj.* ĭ fūs′), *v.,* **-fused, -fusing,** *adj.* —*v.t.* **1.** to pour out or forth. —*v.i.* **2.** to exude. —*adj.* **3.** *Bot.* spread out loosely.

ef·fu·sion (ĭ fū′zhən), *n.* **1.** act of pouring forth. **2.** that which is effused. **3.** unrestrained expression of feelings, etc.

ef·fu·sive (ĭ fū′sĭv), *adj.* unduly demonstrative. —ef·fu′sive·ly, *adv.* —ef·fu′sive·ness, *n.*

eft (ĕft), *n.* *U.S.* the newt in its land stage.

eft·soon (ĕft sōōn′), *adv.* *Archaic.* **1.** soon afterward. **2.** again. **3.** forthwith. Also, **eft·soons′.**

e.g., (L *exempli gratia*) for example.

egg[1] (ĕg), *n.* **1.** the roundish reproductive body produced by the female of animals, esp. by the domestic hen. **2.** anything resembling a hen's egg. **3.** Also, **egg cell.** *Biol.* the female reproductive cell.

egg[2] (ĕg), *v.t.* to incite or urge; encourage.

egg·nog (ĕg′nŏg′), *n.* a drink made of eggs, milk, sugar, and, usually, wine or spirits.

egg·plant (ĕg′plănt′, -plänt′), *n.* **1.** a plant cultivated for its edible, egg-shaped fruit, usually dark-purple in color. **2.** the fruit.

eg·lan·tine (ĕg′lən tīn′, -tēn′), *n.* the sweetbrier.

e·go (ē′gō, ĕg′ō), *n., pl.* **egos. 1.** the "I" or self of any person. **2.** *Colloq.* conceit; egotism.

e·go·ism (ē′gō ĭz′əm, ĕg′ō-), *n.* **1.** the habit of valuing everything only in reference to one's personal interest. **2.** egotism. —e′go·ist, *n.* —e′go·is′tic, e′go·is′ti·cal, *adj.* —e′go·is′ti·cal·ly, *adv.*

e·go·tism (ē′gə tĭz′əm, ĕg′ə-), *n.* **1.** the habit of talking too much about oneself; conceit. **2.** selfishness. —e′go·tist, *n.* —e′go·tis′tic, e′go·tis′ti·cal, *adj.* —e′go·tis′ti·cal·ly, *adv.*

e·gre·gious (ĭ grē′jəs, -jĭ əs), *adj.* remarkably flagrant. —e·gre′gious·ly, *adv.*

e·gress (ē′grĕs), *n.* **1.** act of going out. **2.** an exit. **3.** the right of going out.

e·gret (ē′grĭt, ĕg′rĭt), *n.* any of various herons, as the **snowy egret** of North America, bearing during the breeding season tufts of long plumes.

E·gypt (ē′jĭpt), *n.* a kingdom in NE Africa: divided into **Lower Egypt** (the Nile delta) and **Upper Egypt** (from near Cairo S to the Sudan). 17,423,000 pop.; 386,100 sq. mi. *Cap.:* Cairo. —E·gyp′tian (ĭ jĭp′shən), *adj., n.*

E·gyp·tol·o·gy (ē′jĭp tŏl′ə jĭ), *n.* the science of Egyptian antiquities. —E′gyp·tol′o·gist, *n.*

Ehr·lich (ār′lĭкн), *n.* Paul, 1854–1915, German physician, bacteriologist, and chemist.

E.I., 1. East Indian. **2.** East Indies.

ei·der (ī′dər), *n.* eider duck or eider down.

eider duck, any of several large sea ducks of the northern hemisphere, generally black and white, and yielding **eider down.**

Eif·fel Tower (ī′fəl), a tower of skeletal iron construction in Paris, France. 984 ft. high.

eight (āt), *n.* **1.** a cardinal number, seven plus one. **2.** a symbol for this number. **3.** a set of this many persons or things. —*adj.* **4.** amounting to eight in number. —**eighth** (ātth), *adj., n.*

eight·een (ā′tēn′), *n.* **1.** a cardinal number, ten plus eight. **2.** a symbol for this number. —**eight·eenth** (ā′tēnth′), *adj., n.*

eighth note, *Music.* a note having one eighth of the time value of a whole note.

eight·y (ā′tĭ), *n., pl.* **eighties,** *adj.* —*n.* **1.** a cardinal number, ten times eight. **2.** a symbol for this number. —*adj.* **3.** amounting to eighty in number. —**eight·i·eth** (ā′tĭ ĭth), *adj., n.*

Ein·stein (īn′stīn), *n.* **Albert,** born 1879, U.S. physicist, born in Germany.

Eir·e (âr′ə), *n.* former name of **Republic of Ireland.**

Ei·sen·how·er (ī′zən hou′ər), *n.* **Dwight David,** born 1890, 34th president of the U.S., since 1953; general and educator.

ei·ther (ē′thər or, esp. Brit., ī′thər), *adj.* **1.** one or the other of two. **2.** each of the two. —*pron.* **3.** one or the other. —*conj.* **4.** (used as one of two coördinate alternatives). —*adv.* **5.** (used after negative sentences coördinated by *and, or, nor*).

e·jac·u·late (ĭ jăk′yə lāt′), *v.t.,* **-lated, -lating. 1.** to exclaim. **2.** to eject suddenly and swiftly. —e·jac′u·la′tion, *n.* —e·jac′u·la′tor, *n.* —e·jac·u·la·to·ry (ĭ jăk′yə lə tōr′ĭ), *adj.*

e·ject (ĭ jĕkt′), *v.t.* **1.** to drive or force out. **2.** to dismiss. **3.** to evict. —e·jec′tion, *n.* —e·jec′tive, *adj.* —e·jec′tor, *n.*

eke[1] (ēk), *v.t.,* **eked, eking.** (fol. by *out*) **1.** to supplement. **2.** to contrive to make (a living).

eke[2] (ēk), *adv., conj.* *Archaic.* also.

el (ĕl), *n.* **1.** elevated railroad. **2.** ell[1].

e·lab·o·rate (*adj.* ĭ lăb′ə rĭt; *v.* ĭ lăb′ə rāt′), *adj., v.,* **-rated, -rating.** —*adj.* **1.** worked out with great care and detail. —*v.t.* **2.** to work out minutely. **3.** to produce by labor. —*v.i.* **4.** to give additional treatment. —e·lab′o·rate·ly, *adv.* —e·lab′o·rate·ness, *n.* —e·lab′o·ra′tion, *n.* —e·lab′o·ra′tor, *n.*

El A·la·mein (ĕl ä′lä mān′), a town on the N coast of Egypt: decisive British victory, 1942.

é·lan (ĕ län′), *n.* dash; impetuous ardor.

e·land (ē′lənd), *n.* a large, heavily built antelope of southern and eastern Africa.

e·lapse (ĭ lăps′), *v.i.,* **elapsed, elapsing.** (of time) to slip by or pass away.

e·las·mo·branch (ĭ lăs′mə brăngk′, ĭ lăz′-), *adj.* **1.** of the group of vertebrates including the sharks and rays, with cartilaginous skeletons and five to seven pairs of gill openings. —*n.* **2.** an elasmobranch fish.

e·las·tic (ĭ lăs′tĭk), *adj.* **1.** recovering shape after deformation. **2.** flexible. **3.** springy. **4.** buoyant. —*n.* **5.** material made elastic with strips of India rubber. **6.** a piece of this material. **7.** rubber band. —e·las′ti·cal·ly, *adv.*

e·las·tic·i·ty (ĭ lăs′tĭs′ə tĭ, ē′lăs-), *n.* **1.** elastic state or quality. **2.** flexibility. **3.** buoyancy.

e·late (ĭ lāt′), *v.,* **elated, elating,** *adj.* —*v.t.* **1.** to put in high sprits. —*adj.* **2.** in high spirits. —e·la′tion, *n.*

el·a·ter (ĕl′ə tər), *n.* *Bot.* an elastic filament serving to disperse spores.

El·ba (ĕl′bə), *n.* Italian island in Mediterranean between Corsica and Italy: scene of Napoleon's first exile, 1814–15. 31,641 pop.; 94 sq. mi.

El·be (ĕl′bə), *n.* a river from W Czechoslovakia NW through Germany to the North Sea. 725 mi.

El·bert Peak (ĕl′bərt), a mountain in central Colorado. 14,431 ft.

el·bow (ĕl′bō), *n.* **1.** the joint of the arm between upper arm and forearm. **2.** something bent like or resembling the elbow. —*v.t.* **3.** to jostle. **4.** to make (one's way) by so pushing. —*v.i.* **5.** to jostle one's way.

el·bow·room (ĕl′bō rōōm′, -rōōm′), *n.* ample room; free scope.

El·brus (ĕl′brōōs, ăl′brōōs), *n.* a mountain in the S Soviet Union in Europe, in the Caucasus Mountains. 18,465 ft. Also, **El′brus.**

eld (ĕld), *n.* *Archaic.* **1.** age. **2.** old age. **3.** antiquity.

eld·er[1] (ĕl′dər), *adj.* **1.** older. **2.** senior. **3.** earlier. —*n.* **4.** a person older than oneself. **5.** an aged person. **6.** one of the older and more influential men of a tribe or community, often a ruler. **7.** a presbyter. **8.** (in certain Protestant churches) a governing officer, either with or without teaching or pastoral functions.

el·der[2] (ĕl′dər), *n.* any of certain shrubs and small trees of the honeysuckle family bearing clusters of small white or light-colored flowers and a black or red fruit.

el·der·ber·ry (ĕl′dər bĕr′ĭ), *n., pl.* **-ries. 1.** the fruit of the elder. **2.** elder[2].

eld·er·ly (ĕl/dər lĭ), *adj.* **1.** somewhat old. **2.** of later life. —**eld/er·li·ness,** *n.*

eld·est (ĕl/dĭst), *adj.* oldest.

El Do·ra·do (ĕl də rä/dō, -rä/-), **1.** a legendary treasure city of South America. **2.** any place of reputed fabulous wealth.

e·lect (ĭ lĕkt/), *v.t.* **1.** to select by vote. **2.** to determine in favor of (a course of action, etc.). **3.** to choose. —*adj.* **4.** selected for an office, but not yet inducted. **5.** chosen. **6.** select or choice. **7.** *Theol.* chosen by God, esp. for eternal life. —*n.* **8.** the persons chosen by God, esp. for eternal life.

elect., 1. electric. **2.** electricity.

e·lec·tion (ĭ lĕk/shən), *n.* **1.** the selection of a person or persons for office by vote. **2.** a public vote upon a proposition submitted. **3.** act of electing.

e·lec·tion·eer (ĭ lĕk/shə nĭr/), *v.i.* to work for a candidate, party, ticket, etc., in an election.

e·lec·tive (ĭ lĕk/tĭv), *adj.* **1.** pertaining to the principle of electing to office, etc. **2.** appointed by election. **3.** bestowed by election. **4.** having the power of electing to office, etc., as a body of persons. **5.** optional. —*n.* **6.** an optional study, as at college.

e·lec·tor (ĭ lĕk/tər), *n.* **1.** one who elects. **2.** *U.S.* a member of the electoral college. **3.** (*usually cap.*) (in the Holy Roman Empire) one of the princes entitled to elect the emperor. —**e·lec/tor·al,** *adj.*

electoral college, a body of electors chosen by voters in the several States to elect the president and vice-president of the United States.

e·lec·tor·ate (ĭ lĕk/tər ĭt), *n.* **1.** the body of persons entitled to vote in an election. **2.** the dignity or territory of an elector of the Holy Roman Empire.

E·lec·tra (ĭ lĕk/trə), *n. Gk. Legend.* the daughter of Agamemnon and Clytemnestra. She incited her brother Orestes to avenge the murder of his father.

e·lec·tric (ĭ lĕk/trĭk), *adj.* **1.** pertaining to, derived from, produced by, or involving electricity. **2.** producing, transmitting, or operated by electric currents. **3.** thrilling; exciting. —*n.* **4.** a railroad, truck, etc., operated by electricity.

e·lec·tri·cal (ĭ lĕk/trə kəl), *adj.* **1.** electric. **2.** concerned with electricity. —**e·lec/tri·cal·ly,** *adv.*

electrical transcription, 1. a radio broadcast from a phonograph record made for the purpose. **2.** the phonograph record itself.

electric chair, 1. an electrified chair used to execute criminals. **2.** the electrocution.

electric eel, an eellike South American fish, giving strong electric discharges.

electric eye, a photoelectric cell.

e·lec·tri·cian (ĭ lĕk/trĭsh/ən, ē/lĕk-), *n.* one who installs, operates, or repairs electric devices.

e·lec·tric·i·ty (ĭ lĕk/trĭs/ə tĭ, ē/lĕk-), *n.* **1.** an agency producing various physical phenomena, as attraction and repulsion, luminous and heating effects, shock to the body, chemical decomposition, etc., which are due to the presence and movements of electrons and other particles. **2.** the science dealing with this agency. **3.** electric current.

e·lec·tri·fy (ĭ lĕk/trə fī/), *v.t.,* **-fied, -fying. 1.** to charge with or subject to electricity. **2.** to equip for the use of electric power. **3.** to excite or thrill. —**e·lec/tri·fi·ca/tion,** *n.*

e·lec·tro·chem·is·try (ĭ lĕk/trō kĕm/ĭs trĭ), *n.* the branch of chemistry that deals with the relation between chemical changes and electricity. —**e·lec/tro·chem/i·cal,** *adj.*

e·lec·tro·cute (ĭ lĕk/trə kūt/), *v.t.,* **-cuted, -cuting.** to kill or execute by electricity. —**e·lec/tro·cu/tion,** *n.*

e·lec·trode (ĭ lĕk/trōd), *n. Elect.* a conductor through which a current enters or leaves an electrolytic cell, vacuum tube, etc.

e·lec·tro·dy·nam·ics (ĭ lĕk/trō dī năm/ĭks), *n.* the branch of electricity that deals with the mutual action of electric currents and the interaction of currents and magnets. —**e·lec/tro·dy·nam/ic,** *adj.*

e·lec·tro·lier (ĭ lĕk/trə lĭr/), *n.* a chandelier.

e·lec·trol·y·sis (ĭ lĕk/trŏl/ə sĭs), *n.* **1.** the decomposition of a chemical compound by an electric current. **2.** *Surg.* the destruction of tumors, hair roots, etc., by an electric current.

e·lec·tro·lyte (ĭ lĕk/trə līt/), *n.* **1.** *Elect.* a conducting medium in which the flow of current is

accompanied by the movement of matter. **2.** *Chem.* any substance which dissociates into ions when dissolved in a suitable medium or when melted, thus forming a conductor of electricity. —**e·lec·tro·lyt·ic** (ĭ lĕk/trə lĭt/ĭk), **e·lec/tro·lyt/i·cal,** *adj.* —**e·lec/tro·lyt/i·cal·ly,** *adv.*

e·lec·tro·lyze (ĭ lĕk/trə līz/), *v.t.,* **-lyzed, -lyzing.** to decompose by electrolysis.

e·lec·tro·mag·net (ĭ lĕk/trō măg/nĭt), *n.* a device, consisting of an iron or steel core which is magnetized by electric current in a coil which surrounds it. —**e·lec/tro·mag·net/ic,** *adj.*

e·lec·tro·mag·net·ism (ĭ lĕk/trō măg/nə tĭz/əm), *n.* **1.** the phenomena resting upon the relations between electric currents and magnetism. **2.** the science that deals with these relations.

e·lec·trom·e·ter (ĭ lĕk/trŏm/ə tər, ē/lĕk-), *n.* an instrument for detecting or measuring a potential difference by means of the mechanical forces exerted between electrically charged bodies.

e·lec·tro·mo·tive (ĭ lĕk/trə mō/tĭv), *adj.* pertaining to or producing a flow of electricity.

electromotive force, the amount of energy supplied to an electric circuit in one second by a voltaic cell or other source of electrical energy when one ampere of current flows in the circuit.

e·lec·tro·mo·tor (ĭ lĕk/trə mō/tər), *n.* electric motor.

e·lec·tron (ĭ lĕk/trŏn), *n.* an extremely small, negatively charged particle, having about one thousandth the mass of a hydrogen atom, supposed to be or contain the unit of negative electricity. —**e·lec·tron·ic** (ĭ lĕk/trŏn/ĭk, ē/lĕk-), *adj.*

e·lec·tro·neg·a·tive (ĭ lĕk/trō nĕg/ə tĭv), *adj.* **1.** containing negative electricity. **2.** assuming negative potential when in contact with a dissimilar substance. **3.** nonmetallic.

e·lec·tron·ics (ĭ lĕk/trŏn/ĭks, ē/lĕk-), *n.* the investigation and application of phenomena involving the movement of free electrons, as in radio, television, etc., and applications involving ions.

electron tube, *Electronics.* a vacuum tube.

e·lec·tro·plate (ĭ lĕk/trə plāt/), *v.,* **-plated, -plating,** *n.* —*v.t.* **1.** to coat with a metal by electrolysis. —*n.* **2.** electroplated articles or ware. —**e·lec/tro·plat/er,** *n.* —**e·lec/tro·plat/ing,** *n.*

e·lec·tro·pos·i·tive (ĭ lĕk/trə pŏz/ə tĭv), *adj.* **1.** containing positive electricity. **2.** assuming positive potential when in contact with another substance. **3.** basic, as an element or radical.

e·lec·tro·scope (ĭ lĕk/trə skōp/), *n.* a device for detecting the presence of electricity, and whether it is positive or negative.

e·lec·tro·stat·ics (ĭ lĕk/trə stăt/ĭks), *n.* the science of static electricity. —**e·lec/tro·stat/ic,** *adj.*

e·lec·tro·type (ĭ lĕk/trə tīp/), *n., v.,* **-typed, -typing.** —*n.* **1.** a facsimile, for use in printing, of a block of type, an engraving, or the like. —*v.t.* **2.** to make an electrotype of. —**e·lec/tro·typ/er,** *n.*

e·lec·trum (ĭ lĕk/trəm), *n.* an amber-colored alloy of gold and silver known to the ancients.

el·ee·mos·y·nar·y (ĕl/ə mŏs/ə nĕr/ĭ, ĕl/ĭ ə-), *adj.* **1.** charitable. **2.** derived from or provided by charity. **3.** dependent on charity.

el·e·gance (ĕl/ə gəns), *n.* **1.** elegant quality. **2.** something elegant. Also, **el/e·gan·cy.**

el·e·gant (ĕl/ə gənt), *adj.* **1.** tastefully fine or luxurious. **2.** gracefully refined. **3.** *Colloq.* excellent; superior. —**el/e·gant·ly,** *adv.*

el·e·gi·ac (ĕl/ə jī/ăk, -ək, ĭ lē/jĭ ăk/), *adj.* Also, **el/e·gi/a·cal. 1.** *Ancient Pros.* noting a distich the first line of which is a dactylic hexameter and the second a pentameter. **2.** belonging to an elegy or to elegy. **3.** expressing sorrow. —*n.* **4.** an elegiac verse. **5.** a poem or poems in such verses.

el·e·gize (ĕl/ə jīz/), *v.t., v.i.,* **-gized, -gizing.** to lament in or as in an elegy.

el·e·gy (ĕl/ə jĭ), *n., pl.* **-gies. 1.** a mournful, melancholy, or plaintive poem. **2.** a poem written in elegiac meter.

elem., 1. elementary. **2.** elements.

el·e·ment (ĕl/ə mənt), *n.* **1.** a constituent part of a whole. **2.** a rudimentary principle. **3.** one of the substances (usually earth, water, air, and fire) early regarded as constituting the material universe. **4.** one of these four substances regarded as the natural habitat of something. **5.** the most suitable environment. **6.** (*pl.*) atmospheric forces. **7.** one of a class of substances which have hitherto

resisted analysis by any known chemical means.
8. *Elect.* either of the two dissimilar substances which constitute a voltaic couple. **9.** *(pl.)* the bread and wine used in the Eucharist.

el·e·men·tal (ĕl/ə mĕn/təl), *adj.* 1. of the nature of an ultimate constituent. 2. pertaining to rudiments. 3. of or pertaining to the elements or any one of them. 4. pertaining to the forces or phenomena of physical nature. 5. comparable to the great forces of nature. 6. pertaining to chemical elements. —el/e·men/tal·ly, *adv.*

el·e·men·ta·ry (ĕl/ə mĕn/tə rĭ, -trĭ), *adj.* 1. pertaining to or dealing with rudiments. 2. elemental. —el/e·men/ta·ri·ly, *adv.* —el/e·men/ta·ri·ness, *n.*

el·e·phant (ĕl/ə fənt), *n., pl.* -phants, *(esp. collectively)* -phant. any of the large mammals of Africa and India, with long prehensile trunk and long tusks of ivory.

el·e·phan·ti·a·sis (ĕl/ə fən tī/ə sĭs, -făn-), *n.* a disease, due to lymphatic obstruction, characterized by enormous enlargement of affected parts.

el·e·phan·tine (ĕl/ə făn/tĭn, -tīn, -tēn), *adj.* 1. of or like an elephant. 2. huge; clumsy.

el·e·vate (ĕl/ə vāt/), *v.* -vated, -vating, *adj.* —*v.t.* 1. to move or raise to a higher place. 2. to exalt. 3. to put in high spirits. —*adj.* 4. *Poetic.* raised.

el·e·va·tion (ĕl/ə vā/shən), *n.* 1. an elevated place. 2. the height to which anything is elevated. 3. loftiness; nobleness. 4. act of elevating. 5. state of being elevated. 6. a drawing which represents an object geometrically on a vertical plane.

el·e·va·tor (ĕl/ə vā/tər), *n.* 1. one who or that which raises. 2. a moving platform for conveying goods, persons, etc., from one level to another. 3. *U.S.* a building for storing grain. 4. a hinged horizontal plane on an airplane, etc., used to control inclination.

el·ev·en (ĭ lĕv/ən), *n.* 1. a cardinal number, ten plus one. 2. a symbol for this number. —*adj.* 3. amounting to eleven in number. —e·lev/enth, *adj., n.*

elf (ĕlf), *n., pl.* **elves** (ĕlvz). 1. a tiny imaginary being with magical powers. 2. a dwarf. 3. a small, mischievous person. —elf/ish, *adj.*

elf·in (ĕl/fĭn), *adj.* 1. pertaining to elves. 2. elflike. —*n.* 3. an elf.

El·gar (ĕl/gər, -gär), *n.* Sir Edward, 1857–1934, British composer.

El·gin (ĕl/jĭn), *n.* a city in NE Illinois. 38,333.

El Gre·co (ĕl grä/kō, grĕk/ō), *(Domingo Theotocopouli)* 1548?–1614, painter, architect, and sculptor in Spain and Italy, born in Crete.

e·lic·it (ĭ lĭs/ĭt), *v.t.* to draw forth; evoke. —e·lic/i·ta/tion, *n.* —e·lic/i·tor, *n.*

e·lide (ĭ līd/), *v.t.,* elided, eliding. 1. to omit (a vowel, etc.) in pronunciation. 2. to suppress.

el·i·gi·bil·i·ty (ĕl/ə jə bĭl/ə tĭ), *n.* 1. worthiness or fitness to be chosen. 2. legal qualification for election or appointment.

el·i·gi·ble (ĕl/ə jə bəl), *adj.* 1. fit to be chosen. —*n.* 2. a person or thing that is eligible. —el/i·gi·bly, *adv.*

E·li·jah (ĭ lī/jə), *n.* a great Hebrew prophet of the 9th century B.C.

e·lim·i·nate (ĭ lĭm/ə nāt/), *v.t.,* -nated, -nating. 1. to get rid of. 2. to ignore. 3. *Physiol.* to void. 4. *Math.* to remove (a quantity) from an equation by removing certain variables. —e·lim/i·na/tion, *n.* —e·lim/i·na/tor, *n.*

El·i·ot (ĕl/ĭ ət), *n.* 1. Charles William, 1834–1926, U.S. educator. 2. George, *(Mary Ann Evans)* 1819–80, British novelist. 3. T(homas) S(tearns), born 1888, British writer, born in the U.S.

E·li·sha (ĭ lī/shə), *n.* a Hebrew prophet of the 9th century B.C., the successor of Elijah.

e·li·sion (ĭ lĭzh/ən), *n.* the omission of a vowel in pronunciation.

e·lite (ĭ lēt/, ā-), *n.* the choice or best part.

e·lix·ir (ĭ lĭk/sər), *n.* 1. an alchemic preparation for transmuting base metals into gold or for prolonging life. 2. a panacea. 3. the quintessence. 4. *Pharm.* a tincture with more than one base, or some similar compound medicine.

E·liz·a·beth (ĭ lĭz/ə bəth), *n.* 1. I, 1533–1603, queen of England 1558–1603, daughter of Henry VIII. 2. II, born 1926, queen of England since 1952; daughter of George VI. 3. a city in NE New Jersey. 109,912.

E·liz·a·be·than (ĭ lĭz/ə bē/thən, -bĕth/ən), *adj.* 1. of or pertaining to Queen Elizabeth or to her

times. —*n.* 2. one who lived in England during the Elizabethan period.

elk (ĕlk), *n., pl.* **elks,** *(esp. collectively)* **elk.** 1. the largest existing European and Asiatic deer, the male of which has large palmate antlers. 2. (in America) the wapiti.

Elk·hart (ĕlk/härt/; *commonly* ĕl/kärt), *n.* a city in N Indiana. 33,434.

ell¹ (ĕl), *n.* an extension to a building, usually at right angles to one end.

ell² (ĕl), *n.* a measure of length, now little used, varying in different countries.

el·lipse (ĭ lĭps/), *n.* *Geom.* a plane curve such that the sums of the distances of each point in its periphery from two fixed points, the foci, are equal.

el·lip·sis (ĭ lĭp/sĭs), *n., pl.* -ses (-sēz). 1. *Gram.* the omission from a sentence of a word or words which would complete the construction. 2. *Print.* a mark or marks as ——, . . . , * * *, to indicate such an omission.

el·lip·ti·cal (ĭ lĭp/tə kəl), *adj.* 1. pertaining to or having the form of an ellipse. 2. pertaining to or marked by grammatical ellipsis. Also, **el·lip/tic.** —el·lip/ti·cal·ly, *adv.*

El·lis (ĕl/ĭs), *n.* (Henry) Havelock, 1859–1939, British scientific writer.

El·lis Island (ĕl/ĭs), a small island in upper New York Bay: a former U.S. immigrant station.

elm (ĕlm), *n.* 1. any of the trees of a genus including the **English elm,** the **white** or **American elm,** etc., some of which are widely cultivated for shade and ornament. 2. the wood of such a tree.

El·mi·ra (ĕl mī/rə), *n.* city in S New York. 45,106.

e·lo·cu·tion (ĕl/ə kū/shən), *n.* 1. manner of speaking or reading in public. 2. *Speech.* the study and practice of delivery. —el/o·cu/tion·ar/y, *adj.* —el/o·cu/tion·ist, *n.*

e·lon·gate (ĭ lông/gāt, ĭ lŏng/-), *v.,* -gated, -gating, *adj.* —*v.t., v.i.* 1. to lengthen. —*adj.* 2. lengthened. —e·lon/ga/tion, *n.*

e·lope (ĭ lōp/), *v.i.,* eloped, eloping. to run away with a lover. —e·lope/ment, *n.* —e·lop/er, *n.*

el·o·quence (ĕl/ə kwəns), *n.* 1. the action or art of using language with fluency, power, and aptness. 2. eloquent language.

el·o·quent (ĕl/ə kwənt), *adj.* 1. having the power of fluent, forcible speech. 2. characterized by forcible and appropriate expression. 3. movingly expressive. —el/o·quent·ly, *adv.*

El Pas·o (ĕl păs/ō), a city in W Texas. 96,810.

El Sal·va·dor (ĕl săl/və dôr/), a republic in W Central America. 1,997,000 pop.; 13,176 sq. mi. *Cap.:* San Salvador.

else (ĕls), *adv.* 1. instead. 2. in addition. 3. other. 4. otherwise.

else·where (ĕls/hwâr/), *adv.* somewhere else.

e·lu·ci·date (ĭ lōō/sə dāt/), *v.t.,* -dated, -dating. to make clear; explain. —e·lu/ci·da/tion, *n.* —e·lu/ci·da/tive, *adj.* —e·lu/ci·da/tor, *n.*

e·lude (ĭ lōōd/), *v.t.,* eluded, eluding. 1. to avoid or escape by dexterity. 2. to evade. 3. to baffle. —e·lud/er, *n.* —e·lu·sion (ĭ lōō/zhən), *n.*

e·lu·sive (ĭ lōō/sĭv), *adj.* 1. eluding clear perception. 2. dexterously evasive. Also, **e·lu·so·ry** (ĭ lōō/sə rĭ). —e·lu/sive·ly, *adv.* —e·lu/sive·ness, *n.*

elv·ish (ĕl/vĭsh), *adj.* elfish. —elv/ish·ly, *adv.*

E·ly·si·um (ĭ lĭzh/ĭ əm, ĭ lĭz/-), *n.* 1. Also, **Elysian fields.** *Gk. Myth.* the abode of the blessed after death. 2. any place or state of perfect happiness. —**E·ly·sian** (ĭ lĭzh/ən), *adj.*

em (ĕm), *n., pl.* **ems.** 1. the letter M, m. 2. *Print.* the square of any size of type.

e·ma·ci·ate (ĭ mā/shĭ āt/), *v.t.,* -ated, -ating. to make lean by a gradual wasting away of flesh. —e·ma/ci·a/tion, *n.*

em·a·nate (ĕm/ə nāt/), *v.i.,* -nated, -nating. to come forth; originate. —em/a·na/tion, *n.*

e·man·ci·pate (ĭ măn/sə pāt/), *v.t.,* -pated, -pating. to free from restraint. —e·man/ci·pa/tion, *n.* —e·man/ci·pa/tive, *adj.* —e·man/ci·pa/tor, *n.*

e·mas·cu·late (*v.* ĭ măs/kyə lāt/; *adj.* ĭ măs/kyə lĭt, -lāt/), *v.,* -lated, -lating, *adj.* —*v.t.* 1. to castrate. 2. to deprive of strength or vigor. —*adj.* 3. emasculated. —e·mas/cu·la/tion, *n.* —e·mas/cu·la/tor, *n.*

em·balm (ĕm bäm/), *v.t.* 1. to treat (a dead body) with chemicals, etc., to prevent decay.

2. to keep in memory. —em·balm′er, *n*. —embalm′ment, *n*.

em·bank (ĕm băngk′), *v.t.* to enclose, confine, or protect with a bank, mound, dike, or the like.

em·bank·ment (ĕm băngk′mənt), *n.* 1. a mound, dike, or the like, raised to hold back water, carry a roadway, etc. 2. act of embanking.

em·bar·go (ĕm bär′gō), *n., pl.* -goes, *v.*, -goed, -going. —*n.* 1. an order of a government prohibiting the movement of merchant vessels from or into its ports. 2. an injunction to refuse freight for shipment, in case of congestion, etc. 3. a restraint or prohibition. —*v.t.* 4. to impose an embargo on.

em·bark (ĕm bärk′), *v.t., v.i.* 1. to put or receive on board a ship. 2. to involve or invest in an enterprise. —em′bar·ka′tion, *n.*

em·bar·rass (ĕm băr′əs), *v.t.* 1. to make self-conscious, etc. 2. to complicate. 3. to impede. 4. to beset with financial difficulties. —em·bar′rass·ing, *adj.* —em·bar′rass·ing·ly, *adv.* —em·bar′rass·ment, *n.*

em·bas·sy (ĕm′bə sĭ), *n., pl.* -sies. 1. an ambassador and his staff. 2. the official headquarters of an ambassador. 3. the function or office of an ambassador. 4. the sending of ambassadors.

em·bat·tle[1] (ĕm băt′əl), *v.t.*, -tled, -tling. 1. to prepare for battle. 2. to fortify.

em·bat·tle[2] (ĕm băt′əl), *v.t.*, -tled, -tling. to furnish with battlements.

em·bed (ĕm bĕd′), *v.t.*, -bedded, -bedding. 1. to fix in a surrounding mass. 2. to lay in a bed.

em·bel·lish (ĕm bĕl′ĭsh), *v.t.* 1. to ornament; adorn. 2. to enhance with fictitious additions. —em·bel′lish·er, *n.* —em·bel′lish·ment, *n.*

em·ber (ĕm′bər), *n.* a small live coal, brand of wood, etc., as in a dying fire.

Ember days, a quarterly season of fasting and prayer observed in many churches.

em·bez·zle (ĕm bĕz′əl), *v.t.*, -zled, -zling. to appropriate fraudulently to one's own use. —em·bez′zle·ment, *n.* —em·bez′zler, *n.*

em·bit·ter (ĕm bĭt′ər), *v.t.* to make bitter.

em·bla·zon (ĕm blā′zən), *v.t.* 1. to inscribe on a heraldic shield. 2. to extol. —em·bla′zon·ment, em·bla′zon·ry, *n.*

em·blem (ĕm′bləm), *n.* a symbol of a quality, class of persons, etc.

em·blem·at·ic (ĕm′blə măt′ĭk), *adj.* symbolic. Also, em′blem·at′i·cal. —em′blem·at′i·cal·ly, *adv.*

em·bod·y (ĕm bŏd′ĭ), *v.t.*, -bodied, -bodying. 1. to invest with a body, as a spirit. 2. to give a concrete form to. 3. to organize; incorporate. 4. to comprise. —em·bod′i·ment, *n.*

em·bold·en (ĕm bōl′dən), *v.t.* to make bold.

em·bo·lism (ĕm′bə lĭz′əm), *n. Pathol.* the occlusion of a blood vessel by an embolus.

em·bo·lus (ĕm′bə ləs), *n., pl.* -li (-lī′). *Pathol.* undissolved material in the vascular system.

em·bos·om (ĕm bŏoz′əm, -bŏo′zəm), *v.t.* 1. to enfold. 2. to embrace. 3. to cherish; foster.

em·boss (ĕm bôs′, -bŏs′), *v.t.* to raise surface designs in relief on. —em·boss′er, *n.* —em·boss′ment, *n.*

em·bou·chure (äm′bŏŏ shŏŏr′), *n.* 1. the mouth of a river. 2. the mouthpiece of a wind instrument.

em·bow·er (ĕm bou′ər), *v.t., v.i.* to shelter in or as in a bower; cover or surround with foliage.

em·brace (ĕm brās′), *v.*, -braced, -bracing, *n.* —*v.t.* 1. to take or clasp in the arms; hug. 2. to accept willingly. 3. to avail oneself of. 4. to adopt (a religion, etc.). 5. to include. —*v.i.* 6. to join in an embrace. —*n.* 7. act of embracing; a hug. —em·brace′a·ble, *adj.*

em·bra·sure (ĕm brā′zhər), *n.* a flared opening in a wall or parapet through which a gun may be fired.

em·bro·cate (ĕm′brō kāt′), *v.t.*, -cated, -cating. to moisten and rub with a liniment or lotion. —em′bro·ca′tion, *n.*

em·broi·der (ĕm broi′dər), *v.t.* 1. to decorate with ornamental needlework. 2. to form in needlework. 3. to adorn rhetorically. —*v.i.* 4. to do embroidery. —em·broi′der·er, *n.*

em·broi·der·y (ĕm broi′də rĭ), *n., pl.* -deries. 1. the art of making raised designs in threads of silk, gold, etc. 2. embroidered work.

em·broil (ĕm broil′), *v.t.* 1. to involve in strife. 2. to complicate. —em·broil′er, *n.* —em·broil′ment, *n.*

em·brown (ĕm broun′), *v.t., v.i.* to make or become brown or dark.

em·bry·o (ĕm′brĭ ō′), *n., pl.* -os, *adj.* —*n.* 1. an organism or being in the earlier stages of its development, as before emergence from the egg, etc. 2. *Bot.* the rudimentary plant usually contained in the seed. 3. the beginning of anything. —*adj.* 4. embryonic.

em·bry·ol·o·gy (ĕm′brĭ ŏl′ə jĭ), *n.* the science of the embryo, its genesis, development, etc. —em′bry·o·log·i·cal (ĕm′brĭ ə lŏj′ə kəl), em′·bry·o·log′ic, *adj.* —em′bry·ol′o·gist, *n.*

em·bry·on·ic (ĕm′brĭ ŏn′ĭk), *adj.* 1. of or in the state of an embryo. 2. rudimentary.

e·mend (ĭ mĕnd′), *v.t.* to correct. Also, e·men·date (ē′mən dāt′). —e·mend′a·ble, *adj.* —e·men·da′tion, *n.*

em·er·ald (ĕm′ər əld, ĕm′rəld), *n.* 1. a rare green variety of beryl, highly valued as a gem. 2. clear deep green. —*adj.* 3. having a clear, deep-green color.

e·merge (ĭ mûrj′), *v.i.*, emerged, emerging. 1. to rise or come forth from. 2. to come into view or notice. 3. to arise, as a question. —e·mer′gence, *n.* —e·mer′gent, *adj.*

e·mer·gen·cy (ĭ mûr′jən sĭ), *n., pl.* -cies. a sudden and urgent occasion for action.

e·mer·i·tus (ĭ mĕr′ə təs), *adj.* retired from active duty but retaining rank.

e·mer·sion (ĭ mûr′shən, -zhən), *n.* emergence.

Em·er·son (ĕm′ər sən), *n.* Ralph Waldo, 1803–82, U.S. essayist and poet.

em·er·y (ĕm′ə rĭ, ĕm′rĭ), *n.* a granular mineral substance used for grinding and polishing.

e·met·ic (ĭ mĕt′ĭk), *adj.* 1. inducing vomiting. —*n.* 2. an emetic medicine or agent.

E.M.F., electromotive force. Also, e.m.f., emf

em·i·grate (ĕm′ə grāt′), *v.i.*, -grated, -grating. to leave one place to settle in another. —em′i·grant, *n., adj.* —em′i·gra′tion, *n.*

é·mi·gré (ĕm′ə grā′), *n.* an emigrant.

em·i·nence (ĕm′ə nəns), *n.* 1. high rank or repute. 2. a high place or part. 3. (*cap.*) *Rom. Cath. Ch.* the title of honor of a cardinal.

em·i·nent (ĕm′ə nənt), *adj.* 1. high in rank or repute. 2. noteworthy. 3. lofty. —em′i·nent·ly, *adv.*

eminent domain, the authority of the state by which it can appropriate private property for public use, compensation being given for it.

e·mir (ə mĭr′), *n.* an Arabian chieftain or prince.

em·is·sar·y (ĕm′ə sĕr′ĭ), *n., pl.* -saries, *adj.* —*n.* 1. an agent on a mission. —*adj.* 2. sent forth.

e·mis·sion (ĭ mĭsh′ən), *n.* 1. act of emitting. 2. that which is emitted. —e·mis′sive, *adj.*

e·mit (ĭ mĭt′), *v.t.*, emitted, emitting. 1. to send forth; discharge. 2. to issue, as an order. 3. to utter. —e·mit′ter, *n.*

e·mol·lient (ĭ mŏl′yənt), *adj.* 1. soothing, esp. to the skin. —*n.* 2. an emollient medicine.

e·mol·u·ment (ĭ mŏl′yə mənt), *n.* salary or fees.

e·mo·tion (ĭ mō′shən), *n.* 1. an affective state of consciousness in which joy, sorrow, fear, hate, or the like, is experienced. 2. any of the feelings of joy, sorrow, fear, hate, love, etc. —e·mo′tion·al, *adj.* —e·mo′tion·al·ly, *adv.*

e·mo·tion·al·ism (ĭ mō′shən ə lĭz′əm), *n.* emotional character, appeal, or tendency.

Emp., 1. Emperor. 2. Empress.

em·pan·el (ĕm păn′əl), *v.t.*, -eled, -eling or (*esp. Brit.*) -elled, -elling. impanel.

em·pa·thy (ĕm′pə thĭ), *n. Psychol.* mental entering into the feeling or spirit of a person or thing.

Em·ped·o·cles (ĕm pĕd′ə klēz′), *n.* c490–c430 B.C., Greek philosopher and statesman.

em·per·or (ĕm′pər ər), *n.* the sovereign or supreme ruler of an empire. —em′per·or·ship′, *n.*

em·pha·sis (ĕm′fə sĭs), *n., pl.* -ses (-sēz′). 1. stress. 2. stress on particular words or syllables.

em·pha·size (ĕm′fə sīz′), *v.t.*, -sized, -sizing. to give emphasis to; lay stress upon; stress.

em·phat·ic (ĕm făt′ĭk), *adj.* 1. uttered with emphasis. 2. using emphasis in speech or action. 3. marked; striking. —em·phat′i·cal·ly, *adv.*

em·pire (ĕm′pīr), *n.* 1. an aggregate of nations or peoples ruled by a single sovereign. 2. a government under an emperor. 3. imperial power; sovereignty. 4. supreme control; absolute sway. —*adj.* **5.** (*cap.*) developed or in vogue during the first French empire (1804–15).

em·pir·ic (ĕm pĭr′ĭk), *n.* **1.** a follower of empirical method. **2.** quack. —*adj.* **3.** empirical.

em·pir·i·cal (ĕm pĭr′ə kəl), *adj.* derived from or depending upon experience or observation alone. —**em·pir′i·cal·ly,** *adv.*

em·pir·i·cism (ĕm pĭr′ə sĭz′əm), *n.* **1.** empirical method. **2.** the doctrine that all knowledge is derived from experience. **3.** quackery.

em·place·ment (ĕm plās′mənt), *n.* **1.** *Fort.* the space, platform, or the like, for a gun or battery and its accessories. **2.** a putting in position.

em·ploy (ĕm ploi′), *v.t.* **1.** to use the services of. **2.** to make use of. **3.** to devote (time, etc.). —*n.* **4.** employment. —**em·ploy′a·ble,** *adj.*

em·ploy·ee (ĕm ploi′ē, ĕm′ploi ē′), *n.* a person hired by another. Also, **em·ploy′e, em·ploy′é.**

em·ploy·er (ĕm ploi′ər), *n.* one who employs.

em·ploy·ment (ĕm ploi′mənt), *n.* **1.** act of employing. **2.** state of being employed. **3.** work.

em·po·ri·um (ĕm pōr′ĭ əm), *n., pl.* **-poriums, -poria** (-pōr′ĭ ə). **1.** a principal center of trade. **2.** a large store selling a great variety of articles.

em·pow·er (ĕm pou′ər), *v.t.* **1.** to authorize. **2.** to enable. —**em·pow′er·ment,** *n.*

em·press (ĕm′prĭs), *n.* **1.** a woman ruler of an empire. **2.** the consort of an emperor.

emp·ty (ĕmp′tĭ), *adj.,* **-tier, -tiest,** *v.,* **-tied, -tying,** *n., pl.* **-ties.** —*adj.* **1.** containing nothing. **2.** vacant; unoccupied. **3.** without load. **4.** devoid. **5.** without force, effect, or significance. **6.** *Colloq.* hungry. —*v.t.* **7.** to deprive of contents. **8.** to discharge (contents). —*v.i.* **9.** to become empty. **10.** to discharge contents. —*n.* **11.** *Colloq.* something empty. —**emp′ti·ly,** *adv.* —**emp′ti·ness,** *n.*

em·pur·ple (ĕm pûr′pəl), *v.t.,* **-pled, -pling.** to tinge or color with purple.

em·pyr·e·al (ĕm pĭr′ĭ əl, ĕm′pə rē′əl, -pī-), *adj.* **1.** pertaining to the highest heaven. **2.** celestial.

em·py·re·an (ĕm′pə rē′ən, -pī-), *n.* **1.** the highest heaven. **2.** the visible heavens. —*adj.* **3.** empyreal.

e·mu (ē′mū), *n.* either of two large, flightless, three-toed Australian birds closely related to the ostrich.

em·u·late (ĕm′yə lāt′), *v.t.,* **-lated, -lating. 1.** to try to equal or excel. **2.** to rival. —**em′u·la′tion,** *n.* —**em′u·la·tive,** *adj.* —**em′u·la′tor,** *n.*

em·u·lous (ĕm′yə ləs), *adj.* desirous of emulating. —**em′u·lous·ly,** *adv.* —**em′u·lous·ness,** *n.*

e·mul·si·fy (ĭ mŭl′sə fī′), *v.t.,* **-fied, -fying.** to make into an emulsion. —**e·mul′si·fi·ca′tion,** *n.*

e·mul·sion (ĭ mŭl′shən), *n.* **1.** a liquid preparation of the color and consistency of milk. **2.** *Chem.* any colloidal suspension of a liquid in another liquid. **3.** *Photog.* the light-sensitive layer on a photographic film, plate, or paper.

en (ĕn), *n.* **1.** the letter N, n. **2.** *Print.* half of the width of an em.

en·a·ble (ĕn ā′bəl), *v.t.,* **-bled, -bling. 1.** to give power, means, or ability to. **2.** to make possible or easy.

en·act (ĕn ăkt′), *v.t.* **1.** to make into law. **2.** to decree. **3.** to act the part of.

en·act·ment (ĕn ăkt′mənt), *n.* **1.** act of enacting. **2.** a law; statute.

e·nam·el (ĭ năm′əl), *n., v.,* **-eled, -eling** or (*esp. Brit.*) **-elled, -elling.** —*n.* **1.** a glassy substance, usually opaque, applied by fusion to the surface of metal, pottery, etc. **2.** utensils with an enamel surface. **3.** an enamellike paint, etc. **4.** any enamellike surface with a bright luster. **5.** the hard, glossy, calcareous outer surface of the teeth. —*v.t.* **6.** to inlay or overlay with enamel. —**e·nam′el·er;** *esp. Brit.,* **e·nam′el·ler,** *n.* —**e·nam′el·work′,** *n.*

en·am·or (ĕn ăm′ər), *v.t.* to inflame with love.

enc., 1. enclosed. **2.** enclosure.

en·camp (ĕn kămp′), *v.i., v.t.* to settle or lodge in a camp. —**en·camp′ment,** *n.*

en·case (ĕn kās′), *v.t.,* **-cased, -casing.** incase.

-ence, a noun suffix equivalent to **-ance,** and corresponding to **-ent** in adjectives, as in *abstinence.*

en·ceph·a·li·tis (ĕn sĕf′ə lī′tĭs), *n. Pathol.* inflammation of the substance of the brain.

en·ceph·a·lon (ĕn sĕf′ə lŏn′), *n., pl.* **-la** (-lə). the brain. —**en·ce·phal·ic** (ĕn′sə făl′ĭk), *adj.*

en·chain (ĕn chān′), *v.t.* **1.** to fasten with chains. **2.** to hold fast, as the attention. —**en·chain′ment,** *n.*

en·chant (ĕn chănt′, -chänt′), *v.t.* **1.** to subject to magical influence; bewitch. **2.** to charm. —**en·chant′er,** *n.* —**en·chant′ing,** *adj.* —**en·chant′ing·ly,** *adv.* —**en·chant′ment,** *n.* —**en·chant′ress,** *n.fem.*

en·cir·cle (ĕn sûr′kəl), *v.t.,* **-cled, -cling. 1.** to form a circle round; surround. **2.** to make a circuit of. —**en·cir′cle·ment,** *n.*

encl., 1. enclosed. **2.** enclosure.

en·clave (ĕn′klāv), *n.* a country entirely or mostly surrounded by another.

en·close (ĕn klōz′), *v.t.,* **-closed, -closing. 1.** to close in on all sides. **2.** to surround, as with a fence. **3.** to insert in the same envelope, etc., with the main letter, etc. **4.** to contain. Also, inclose.

en·clo·sure (ĕn klō′zhər), *n.* **1.** act of enclosing. **2.** that which encloses, as a fence. **3.** that which is enclosed.

en·co·mi·ast (ĕn kō′mĭ ăst′), *n.* a eulogist.

en·co·mi·as·tic (ĕn kō′mĭ ăs′tĭk), *adj.* eulogistic.

en·co·mi·um (ĕn kō′mĭ əm), *n., pl.* **-miums, -mia** (-mĭ ə). a formal expression of praise; eulogy.

en·com·pass (ĕn kŭm′pəs), *v.t.* **1.** to encircle. **2.** to contain. —**en·com′pass·ment,** *n.*

en·core (äng′kōr, än′-), *interj., n., v.,* **-cored, -coring.** —*interj.* **1.** again; once more. —*n.* **2.** a demand, as by applause, for a repetition of a song, etc., or for an additional number. **3.** that which is given in response to such a demand. —*v.t.* **4.** to call for an encore from or by.

en·coun·ter (ĕn koun′tər), *v.t.* **1.** to meet, esp. unexpectedly. **2.** to contend against. —*v.i.* **3.** to meet, esp. in conflict. —*n.* **4.** a meeting, esp. casually or unexpectedly. **5.** battle; combat.

en·cour·age (ĕn kûr′ĭj), *v.t.,* **-aged, -aging. 1.** to inspire with courage or confidence. **2.** to stimulate by assistance, etc. —**en·cour′age·ment,** *n.* —**en·cour′ag·er,** *n.* —**en·cour′ag·ing·ly,** *adv.*

en·croach (ĕn krōch′), *v.i.* **1.** to advance beyond proper limits. **2.** to trespass. —**en·croach′·ment,** *n.* —**en·croach′er,** *n.*

en·crust (ĕn krŭst′), *v.t.* incrust.

en·cum·ber (ĕn kŭm′bər), *v.t.* **1.** to impede or hamper. **2.** to block up or fill with what is obstructive or superfluous. **3.** to burden with debt, etc.

en·cum·brance (ĕn kŭm′brəns), *n.* **1.** that which encumbers. **2.** a dependent person, esp. a child. **3.** *Law.* a claim on property.

-ency, a noun suffix, equivalent to **-ence.**

ency., encyclopedia. Also, **encyc.**

en·cyc·li·cal (ĕn sĭk′lə kəl, -sī′klə-), *n.* **1.** a letter addressed by the Pope to all bishops in communion with the Holy See. —*adj.* **2.** intended for general circulation. Also, **en·cyc′lic.**

en·cy·clo·pe·di·a (ĕn sī′klə pē′dĭ ə), *n.* a work treating separately various topics from all branches of knowledge, usually in alphabetical arrangement. Also, **en·cy′clo·pae′di·a.** —**en·cy′clo·pe′dic, en·cy′clo·pae′dic,** *adj.* —**en·cy′·clo·pe′dist, en·cy′clo·pae′dist,** *n.*

en·cyst (ĕn sĭst′), *v.t., v.i. Biol.* to enclose or become enclosed in a cyst. —**en·cyst′ment,** *n.*

end (ĕnd), *n.* **1.** an extremity of anything. **2.** an extreme part of anything extended in space. **3.** a limit. **4.** termination. **5.** the concluding part. **6.** a purpose. **7.** result. **8.** death. **9.** a cause of death, destruction, or ruin. **10.** a remnant. **11.** *Football, etc.* either of the players at the ends of the forward line. —*v.t.* **12.** to bring or put an end to. **13.** to form the end of. —*v.i.* **14.** to come to an end. **15.** to issue or result. —**end′er,** *n.*

en·dan·ger (ĕn dān′jər), *v.t.* to expose to danger; imperil. —**en·dan′ger·ment,** *n.*

en·dear (ĕn dĭr′), *v.t.* to make dear, esteemed, or beloved. —**en·dear′ing·ly,** *adv.*

en·dear·ment (ĕn dĭr′mənt), *n.* **1.** act of endearing. **2.** state of being endeared. **3.** action or utterance manifesting affection.

en·deav·or (ĕn dĕv′ər), *v.i.* **1.** to make an effort; strive. —*v.t.* **2.** to try. —*n.* **3.** an attempt. Also, *Brit.,* **en·deav′our.** —**en·deav′or·er,** *n.*

en·dem·ic (ĕn dĕm′ĭk), *adj.* **1.** Also, **en·dem′i·cal.** peculiar to a particular people or locality. —*n.* **2.** an endemic disease. —**en·dem′i·cal·ly,** *adv.*

end·ing (ĕn′dĭng), *n.* **1.** termination; close.

2. death. 3. *Gram.* an inflectional element at the end of a word form, as -*s* in *cuts.*

en·dive (ĕn′dīv, än′dēv), *n.* U.S. a plant of two main types, one with finely divided, much curled leaves and one with broad, fleshy leaves, both used for salads.

end·less (ĕnd′lĭs), *adj.* **1.** having no end; boundless; incessant. **2.** made continuous. —**end′less·ly,** *adv.* —**end′less·ness,** *n.*

end·most (ĕnd′mōst), *adj.* furthest.

en·do·carp (ĕn′dō kärp′), *n.* *Bot.* the inner layer of a pericarp, as the stone of certain fruits.

en·do·crine (ĕn′dō krĭn′, -krĭn), *n.* **1.** an endocrine gland. **2.** an internal secretion. —*adj.* **3.** of the endocrine glands or their secretions.

endocrine gland, any of various glands or organs (as the thyroid gland, etc.) which produce certain important internal secretions.

en·dog·e·nous (ĕn dŏj′ə nəs), *adj.* *Biol.* originating within. —**en·dog′e·nous·ly,** *adv.*

en·do·plasm (ĕn′dō plăz′əm), *n.* *Biol.* the inner portion of the cytoplasm. —**en′do·plas′mic,** *adj.*

en·dorse (ĕn dôrs′), *v.t.,* -**dorsed,** -**dorsing.** **1.** to approve, support, or sustain. **2.** to write or sign on the back of a document, etc. —**en·dors′a·ble,** *adj.* —**en·dors′er,** *n.*

en·dorse·ment (ĕn dôrs′mənt), *n.* **1.** approval. **2.** the placing of one's signature, etc., on a document. **3.** the signature, etc.

en·do·sperm (ĕn′dō spûrm′) *n.* nutritive matter in seed plant ovules, derived from the embryo sac.

en·dow (ĕn dou′), *v.t.* **1.** to provide with a permanent fund. **2.** to equip. —**en·dow′er,** *n.*

en·dow·ment (ĕn dou′mənt), *n.* **1.** act of endowing. **2.** that with which an institution, person, etc., is endowed. **3.** (*usually pl.*) a talent.

en·due (ĕn dū′, -dōō′), *v.t.,* -**dued,** -**duing.** to invest with some gift, quality, or faculty.

en·dur·ance (ĕn dyŏŏr′əns, -dōōr′-), *n.* **1.** fact or power of enduring anything. **2.** lasting quality. **3.** something endured.

en·dure (ĕn dyŏŏr′, -dōōr′), *v.,* -**dured,** -**during.** —*v.t.* **1.** to sustain or undergo. **2.** to tolerate. —*v.i.* **3.** to continue to exist. **4.** to suffer without yielding; suffer patiently. —**en·dur′a·ble,** *adj.* —**en·dur′a·bly,** *adv.* —**en·dur′ing,** *adj.* —**en·dur′ing·ly,** *adv.*

end·ways (ĕnd′wāz′), *adv.* **1.** on end. **2.** with the end upward or forward. **3.** lengthwise. **4.** end to end. Also, **end·wise** (ĕnd′wīz′).

en·e·ma (ĕn′ə mə), *n., pl.* **enemas, enemata** (ĕnĕm′ə tə). *Med.* a fluid injected into the rectum.

en·e·my (ĕn′ə mĭ), *n., pl.* -**mies,** *adj.* —*n.* **1.** an adversary or opponent. **2.** an armed foe. **3.** a hostile nation. **4.** something harmful. —*adj.* **5.** belonging to a hostile power.

en·er·get·ic (ĕn′ər jĕt′ĭk), *adj.* **1.** forcible; vigorous. **2.** effective. —**en′er·get′i·cal·ly,** *adv.*

en·er·gize (ĕn′ər jīz′), *v.,* -**gized,** -**gizing.** —*v.t.* **1.** to give energy to. —*v.i.* **2.** to exert energy.

en·er·gy (ĕn′ər jĭ), *n., pl.* -**gies.** **1.** capacity or habit of vigorous activity. **2.** operation; activity. **3.** power as exerted. **4.** ability to produce action or effect. **5.** vigor of expression. **6.** *Physics.* the property of a system which diminishes, when the system does work on any other system, by an amount equal to the work so done.

en·er·vate (*v.* ĕn′ər vāt′; *adj.* ĭ nûr′vĭt), *v.,* -**vated,** -**vating,** *adj.* —*v.t.* **1.** to destroy the vigor of; weaken. —*adj.* **2.** enervated. —**en′er·va′tion,** *n.*

en·fant ter·ri·ble (än fän tĕ rē′bl), *French.* **1.** a child that makes embarrassing remarks. **2.** an indiscreet and irresponsible person.

en·fee·ble (ĕn fē′bəl), *v.t.,* -**bled,** -**bling.** to make feeble. —**en·fee′ble·ment,** *n.* —**en·fee′bler,** *n.*

en·fi·lade (ĕn′fə lād′), *n., v.,* -**laded,** -**lading.** *Mil.* —*n.* **1.** sweeping fire from along the length of a line of troops, a trench, a battery, etc. —*v.t.* **2.** to attack with an enfilade.

en·fold (ĕn fōld′), *v.t.* infold. —**en·fold′er,** *n.*

en·force (ĕn fōrs′), *v.t.,* -**forced,** -**forcing.** **1.** to compel obedience to. **2.** to obtain (payment, etc.) by force. **3.** to impose (a course of action) upon a person. **4.** to lay stress upon. —**en·force′a·ble,** *adj.* —**en·for·ced·ly** (ĕn fōr′sĭd lĭ), *adv.* —**en·force′ment,** *n.* —**en·forc′er,** *n.*

en·fran·chise (ĕn frăn′chīz), *v.t.,* -**chised,** -**chising.** **1.** to admit to citizenship. **2.** to set free; liberate. —**en·fran′chis·er,** *n.*

Eng., 1. England. **2.** English.

eng., 1. engineering. **2.** engraving.

en·gage (ĕn gāj′), *v.,* -**gaged,** -**gaging.** —*v.t.* **1.** to occupy the attention or efforts of. **2.** to secure for aid, use, etc.; hire. **3.** to attract and hold fast. **4.** to please. **5.** to bind, as by pledge. **6.** to betroth. **7.** to enter into conflict with. **8.** *Mech.* to interlock with. —*v.i.* **9.** to become involved. **10.** to take employment. **11.** to assume an obligation. **12.** to enter into conflict. **13.** *Mech.* to interlock. —**en·gag′er,** *n.*

en·gaged (ĕn gājd′), *adj.* **1.** busy; involved. **2.** pledged. **3.** betrothed. **4.** entered into conflict with. **5.** *Mech.* interlocked.

en·gage·ment (ĕn gāj′mənt), *n.* **1.** act of engaging. **2.** state of being engaged. **3.** an obligation or agreement. **4.** betrothal. **5.** employment, or a period or post of employment. **6.** an affair of business. **7.** a conflict or battle. **8.** *Mech.* act or state of interlocking.

en·gag·ing (ĕn gā′jĭng), *adj.* attractive; pleasing. —**en·gag′ing·ly,** *adv.* —**en·gag′ing·ness,** *n.*

En·gels (ĕng′əls), *n.* **Friedrich,** 1820–95, German socialist writer in England, associated with Karl Marx.

en·gen·der (ĕn jĕn′dər), *v.t.* **1.** to cause. **2.** to beget. —*v.i.* **3.** to come into existence.

en·gine (ĕn′jən), *n.* **1.** any machine designed to convert energy into mechanical work. **2.** a railroad locomotive. **3.** any mechanical contrivance. **4.** an instrument used in warfare, as a battering ram.

en·gi·neer (ĕn′jə nĭr′), *n.* **1.** one versed in the design, construction, and use of engines or in any branch of engineering. **2.** one who manages a locomotive. **3.** a member of the army or navy especially trained in engineering work. —*v.t.* **4.** to plan, construct, or manage as an engineer. **5.** to manage.

en·gi·neer·ing (ĕn′jə nĭr′ĭng), *n.* the art or science of practical application of the knowledge of pure sciences such as physics, chemistry, biology, etc.

Eng·land (ĭng′glənd), *n.* the largest division of the United Kingdom, occupying all of the island of Great Britain except Scotland and Wales. 38,468,000 pop.; 50,327 sq. mi. *Cap.:* London.

Eng·lish (ĭng′glĭsh), *adj.* **1.** of, pertaining to, or characteristic of England or its inhabitants, etc. **2.** of or pertaining to the English language. —*n.* **3.** the people of England collectively. **4.** the Germanic language of the British Isles, widespread and standard also in the U.S. and most of the British Empire, historically termed **Old English** or **Anglo-Saxon** (to 1150), **Middle English** (to 1450), and **Modern English.** **5.** (*l.c.*) U.S. *Billiards.* a spinning motion imparted to a ball. —*v.t.* **6.** to translate into English.

English Channel, an arm of the Atlantic between England and France. ab. 350 mi. long; 20–100 mi. wide.

English horn, the alto of the oboe family, richer in tone, and a fifth lower in pitch than the oboe.

Eng·lish·man (ĭng′glĭsh mən), *n., pl.* -**men.** **1.** a native or a naturalized citizen of England. **2.** an English ship. —**Eng′lish·wo′man,** *n.fem.*

engr., 1. engineer. **2.** engraved. **3.** engraver.

en·graft (ĕn grăft′, -gräft′), *v.t.* to insert, as a scion of one tree into another, for propagation.

en·grave (ĕn grāv′), *v.t.,* -**graved,** -**graving.** **1.** to chase (letters, designs, etc.) on a hard surface. **2.** to print from such a surface. **3.** to mark with incised letters, designs, etc. **4.** to impress deeply. —**en·grav′er,** *n.*

Man playing an English horn

en·grav·ing (ĕn grā′vĭng), *n.* **1.** act or art of one that engraves. **2.** the design engraved. **3.** an engraved plate or block. **4.** a print from this.

en·gross (ĕn grōs′), *v.t.* **1.** to occupy wholly; absorb. **2.** to write or copy in a fair, large hand or in a formal manner. **3.** to monopolize. —**en·gross′er,** *n.* —**en·gross′ing,** *adj.* —**en·gross′ment,** *n.*

en·gulf (ĕn gŭlf′), *v.t.* to swallow up; submerge.

en·hance (ĕn häns′, -häns′), *v.t.,* -**hanced,** -**hancing.** **1.** to intensify. **2.** to raise the value of. —**en·hance′ment,** *n.* —**en·hanc′er,** *n.*

e·nig·ma (ĭ nĭg′mə), *n.* **1.** something puzzling

or inexplicable. 2. a riddle. —en·ig·mat·ic (ĕn′-ĭg măt′ĭk, ē′nĭg-), en′ig·mat′i·cal, *adj.* —en′-ig·mat′i·cal·ly, *adv.*

en·join (ĕn join′), *v.t.* 1. to order or direct. 2. *Law.* to prohibit by injunction.

en·joy (ĕn joi′), *v.t.* 1. to take pleasure in. 2. to have and use with satisfaction. 3. to find pleasure for (oneself). —en·joy′a·ble, *adj.* —en·joy′-a·bly, *adv.* —en·joy′er, *n.*

en·joy·ment (ĕn joi′mənt), *n.* 1. the possession or use of anything with pleasure. 2. a form or source of pleasure.

en·kin·dle (ĕn kĭn′dəl), *v.t., v.i.*, -dled, -dling. to kindle. —en·kin′dler, *n.*

en·lace (ĕn lās′), *v.t.*, -laced, -lacing. 1. to bind or encircle. 2. to interlace. —en·lace′-ment, *n.*

en·large (ĕn lärj′), *v.*, -larged, -larging. —*v.t.* 1. to make larger. 2. to expand. —*v.i.* 3. to grow larger. 4. to extend in detail. —en·large′-ment, *n.* —en·larg′er, *n.*

en·light·en (ĕn lī′tən), *v.t.* to impart knowledge to. —en·light′en·er, *n.* —en·light′en-ment, *n.*

en·list (ĕn lĭst′), *v.i., v.t.* 1. to enroll for military or naval service. 2. to secure (a person, services, etc.) for some cause, enterprise, etc. —en·list′er, *n.* —en·list′ment, *n.*

enlisted man, any male member of the armed services who is not an officer or cadet.

en·liv·en (ĕn lī′vən), *v.t.* to make vigorous, active, or gay. —en·liv′en·er, *n.* —en·liv′en-ment, *n.*

en masse (ĕn măs′; *Fr.* äN mȧs′), *French.* in a mass or body; all together.

en·mesh (ĕn mĕsh′), *v.t.* to entangle.

en·mi·ty (ĕn′mə tĭ), *n., pl.* -ties. hatred; ill will.

en·no·ble ((ĕn nō′bəl), *v.t.*, -bled, -bling. 1. to exalt. 2. to confer a title of nobility on. —en·no′ble·ment, *n.* —en·no′bler, *n.*

en·nui (än′wē), *n.* boredom.

e·nor·mi·ty (ĭ nôr′mə tĭ), *n., pl.* -ties. 1. atrociousness. 2. something outrageous. 3. hugeness.

e·nor·mous (ĭ nôr′məs), *adj.* 1. huge; immense. 2. atrocious. —e·nor′mous·ly, *adv.* —e·nor′mous·ness, *n.*

e·nough (ĭ nŭf′), *adj.* 1. adequate. —*n.* 2. an adequate quantity. —*adv.* 3. sufficiently. 4. fully or quite. 5. tolerably. —*interj.* 6. it is enough!

en·quire (ĕn kwīr′), *v.t., v.i.*, -quired, -quiring. inquire. —en·quir′y, *n.*

en·rage (ĕn rāj′), *v.t.*, -raged, -raging. to put into a rage; infuriate. —en·rage′ment, *n.*

en·rap·ture (ĕn răp′chər), *v.t.*, -tured, -turing. to move to rapture; delight beyond measure.

en·rich (ĕn rĭch′), *v.t.* 1. to supply with riches, wealth, etc. 2. to make finer in quality. —en·rich′er, *n.* —en·rich′ment, *n.*

en·rol (ĕn rōl′), *v.t., v.i.*, -rolled, -rolling. enroll.

en·roll (ĕn rōl′), *v.t.* 1. to place upon a list. 2. to enlist (oneself). 3. to record. —en·roll′er, *n.* —en·roll′ment, en·rol′ment, *n.*

en route (än rōōt′; *Fr.* äN), on the way.

Ens., Ensign.

en·sconce (ĕn skŏns′), *v.t.*, -sconced, -sconcing. 1. to hide securely. 2. to settle snugly.

en·sem·ble (än säm′bəl), *n.* 1. all the parts of a thing taken together. 2. the entire costume of an individual. 3. the general effect. 4. *Music.* a. the united performance of the full number of singers, musicians, etc. b. the group so performing. —*adv.* 5. together.

en·shrine (ĕn shrīn′), *v.t.*, -shrined, -shrining. 1. to enclose in or as in a shrine. 2. to cherish as sacred. —en·shrine′ment, *n.*

en·shroud (ĕn shroud′), *v.t.* to shroud; conceal.

en·sign (ĕn′sīn; *Mil.* ĕn′sən), *n.* 1. a flag or banner. 2. a badge of office or authority. 3. the lowest commissioned naval officer. 4. a standard-bearer. —en′sign·ship′, en′sign·cy, *n.*

en·si·lage (ĕn′sə lĭj), *n., v.*, -laged, -laging. —*n.* 1. the preservation of green fodder in a silo. 2. fodder thus preserved. —*v.t.* 3. to ensile.

en·sile (ĕn sīl′, ĕn′sīl), *v.t.*, -siled, -siling. to preserve (green fodder) in a silo.

en·slave (ĕn slāv′), *v.t.*, -slaved, -slaving. to make a slave of. —en·slave′ment, *n.* —en·slav′er, *n.*

en·snare (ĕn snâr′), *v.t.*, -snared, -snaring. to

capture in, or involve as in, a snare. —en·snare′-ment, *n.* —en·snar′er, *n.*

en·sue (ĕn sōō′), *v.i.*, -sued, -suing. 1. to follow in order. 2. to follow as a result.

en·sure (ĕn shōōr′), *v.t.*, -sured, -suring. 1. to secure, as to a person. 2. to make sure to come, occur, etc. 3. to make secure or safe.

-ent, a suffix equivalent to -ant, in adjectives and nouns, as in *ardent, dependent.*

en·tab·la·ture (ĕn tăb′lə chər), *n.* that part of a classic architectural order which rests horizontally upon the columns and consists of the architrave, frieze, and cornice.

en·tail (ĕn tāl′), *v.t.* 1. to involve. 2. to limit the inheritance of. —*n.* 3. act of entailing. 4. state of being entailed. 5. any predetermined order of succession. 6. that which is entailed, as an estate. —en·tail′ment, *n.*

en·tan·gle (ĕn tăng′gəl), *v.t.*, -gled, -gling. 1. to make tangled. 2. to ensnare. 3. to embarrass; perplex. —en·tan′gle·ment, *n.*

en·tente (än tänt′), *n.* 1. understanding. 2. the parties to an understanding.

en·ter (ĕn′tər), *v.i.* 1. to come or go in. 2. to make an entrance. 3. to be admitted. 4. to begin. 5. **enter into, a.** to take part in. **b.** to become a party to. —*v.t.* 6. to come or go into. 7. to penetrate or pierce. 8. to insert. 9. to join. 10. to cause to be admitted. 11. to begin upon. 12. to record. —en′ter·a·ble, *adj.*

en·ter·ic (ĕn tĕr′ĭk), *adj.* intestinal.

en·ter·prise (ĕn′tər prīz′), *n.* 1. a project, esp. an important or challenging one. 2. boldness or readiness in undertaking.

en·ter·pris·ing (ĕn′tər prī′zĭng), *adj.* bold and energetic in undertaking. —en′ter·pris·ing·ly, *adv.*

en·ter·tain (ĕn′tər tān′), *v.t.* 1. to divert; amuse. 2. to receive as a guest. 3. to consider. 4. to harbor; cherish. —*v.i.* 5. to exercise hospitality. —en′ter·tain′er, *n.* —en′ter·tain′ing-ly, *adv.*

en·ter·tain·ment (ĕn′tər tān′mənt), *n.* 1. act of entertaining. 2. something affording diversion or amusement.

en·thral (ĕn thrōl′), *v.t.*, -thralled, -thralling. enthrall. —en·thral′ment, *n.*

en·thrall (ĕn thrôl′), *v.t.* 1. to charm. 2. to subjugate. Also, **inthrall, inthral.** —en·thrall′-er, *n.* —en·thrall′ment, *n.*

en·throne (ĕn thrōn′), *v.t.*, -throned, -throning. to place on a throne. —en·throne′ment, *n.*

en·thuse (ĕn thōōz′), *v.*, -thused, -thusing. *U.S. Colloq.* —*v.i.* 1. to show enthusiasm. —*v.t.* 2. to move to enthusiasm.

en·thu·si·asm (ĕn thōō′zĭ ăz′əm), *n.* lively interest.

en·thu·si·ast (ĕn thōō′zĭ ăst′), *n.* 1. a person of ardent zeal. 2. a religious visionary or fanatic.

en·thu·si·as·tic (ĕn thōō′zĭ ăs′tĭk), *adj.* 1. full of enthusiasm; ardent. 2. pertaining to or of the nature of enthusiasm. —en·thu′si·as′ti·cal·ly, *adv.*

en·tice (ĕn tīs′), *v.t.*, -ticed, -ticing. to allure; inveigle. —en·tice′ment, *n.* —en·tic′er, *n.* —en·tic′ing·ly, *adv.*

en·tire (ĕn tīr′), *adj.* 1. whole; complete. 2. intact. 3. unimpaired. 4. undivided; continuous. 5. *Bot.* without notches or indentations. 6. full or thorough. 7. not gelded. —*n.* 8. the whole. —en·tire′ly, *adv.* —en·tire′ness, *n.*

en·tire·ty (ĕn tīr′tĭ), *n., pl.* -ties. 1. state of being entire; completeness. 2. the whole.

en·ti·tle (ĕn tī′təl), *v.t.*, -tled; -tling. 1. to give a title, right, or claim to something. 2. to name or designate.

en·ti·ty (ĕn′tə tĭ), *n., pl.* -ties. 1. something that has a real existence; a thing. 2. existence.

en·tomb (ĕn tōōm′), *v.t.* to place in a tomb; bury; inter. —en·tomb′ment, *n.*

en·to·mol·o·gy (ĕn′tə mŏl′ə jĭ), *n.* the branch of zoölogy that treats of insects. —en·to·mo·log·i·cal (ĕn′tə mə lŏj′ə kəl), en·to·mo·log′ic, *adj.* —en′to·mol′o·gist, *n.*

en·tou·rage (än′tōō räzh′), *n.* 1. attendants, as of a person of rank. 2. environment.

en·tr′acte (än träkt′), *n.* 1. the interval between two consecutive acts of a play or opera. 2. a performance, as of music or dancing, given during such an interval.

en·trails (ĕn′trālz, -trəlz), *n.pl.* 1. the internal parts of the trunk of an animal body. 2. the intestines.

en·train (ĕn trān′), *v.i.* to put or go aboard a train. —**en·train′ment**, *n.*

en·trance[1] (ĕn′trəns), *n.* **1.** act of entering. **2.** a point or place of entering. **3.** admission.

en·trance[2] (ĕn träns′, -träns′), *v.t.*, **-tranced, -trancing. 1.** to enrapture. **2.** to put into a trance. —**en·trance′ment**, *n.* —**en·tranc′ing·ly**, *adv.*

en·trant (ĕn′trənt), *n.* one who enters.

en·trap (ĕn trăp′), *v.t.*, **-trapped, -trapping.** to catch in a trap. —**en·trap′ment**, *n.*

en·treat (ĕn trēt′), *v.t.* **1.** to beseech; implore. **2.** to ask earnestly for. —*v.i.* **3.** to make an earnest request. —**en·treat′ing·ly**, *adv.*

en·treat·y (ĕn trē′tĭ), *n.*, *pl.* **-treaties.** earnest request or petition; supplication.

en·tree (än′trā), *n.* **1.** *U.S.* any food other than a roast, served as the main course. **2.** a dish served at dinner before the main course or between the regular courses. **3.** the right or privilege of entering.

en·trench (ĕn trĕnch′), *v.t.* **1.** to dig defensive trenches around. **2.** to establish in a strong position. —*v.i.* **3.** to trespass. **4.** to verge. —**en·trench′ment**, *n.*

en·tre·pre·neur (än′trə prə nûr′), *n.* **1.** a contractor. **2.** one who undertakes any enterprise.

en·trust (ĕn trŭst′), *v.t.* **1.** to invest with a responsibility. **2.** to commit in trust (*to*).

en·try (ĕn′trĭ), *n.*, *pl.* **-tries. 1.** entrance. **2.** act of recording. **3.** the statement, etc., recorded. **4.** a contestant. **5.** *Law.* act of taking possession of lands or tenements by entering them.

en·twine (ĕn twīn′), *v.t.*, *v.i.*, **-twined, -twining.** to twine about or together. —**en·twine′ment**, *n.*

e·nu·mer·ate (ĭ nū′mə rāt′, ĭ nōō′-), *v.t.*, **-ated, -ating. 1.** to specify as in a list. **2.** to count. —**e·nu′mer·a′tion**, *n.* —**e·nu′mer·a′tive**, *adj.* —**e·nu′mer·a′tor**, *n.*

e·nun·ci·ate (ĭ nŭn′sĭ āt′, -shĭ-), *v.t.*, *v.i.*, **-ated, -ating. 1.** to utter (words, etc.). **2.** to state as a theory. **3.** to announce. —**e·nun′ci·a′tion**, *n.*

en·vel·op (ĕn vĕl′əp), *v.*, **-oped, -oping**, *n.* —*v.t.* **1.** to wrap. **2.** to surround. —*n.* **3.** envelope. —**en·vel′op·ment**, *n.*

en·ve·lope (ĕn′və lōp′, än′-), *n.* **1.** a cover for a letter or the like. **2.** a wrapper or surrounding cover.

en·ven·om (ĕn vĕn′əm), *v.t.* **1.** to make poisonous. **2.** to embitter.

en·vi·a·ble (ĕn′vĭ ə bəl), *adj.* that is to be envied. —**en′vi·a·ble·ness**, *n.* —**en′vi·a·bly**, *adv.*

en·vi·ous (ĕn′vĭ əs), *adj.* full of or expressing envy. —**en′vi·ous·ly**, *adv.* —**en′vi·ous·ness**, *n.*

en·vi·ron (ĕn vī′rən), *v.t.* to surround.

en·vi·ron·ment (ĕn vī′rən mənt), *n.* **1.** the aggregate of surrounding things, conditions, or influences. **2.** an environing. —**en·vi′ron·men′tal**, *adj.*

en·vi·rons (ĕn vī′rənz), *n.pl.* outskirts; suburbs.

en·vis·age (ĕn vĭz′ĭj), *v.t.*, **-aged, -aging. 1.** to contemplate; visualize. **2.** to face.

en·voy (ĕn′voi), *n.* **1.** a diplomatic agent of the rank after an ambassador. **2.** a diplomatic agent. **3.** any messenger.

en·vy (ĕn′vĭ), *n.*, *pl.* **-vies**, *v.*, **-vied, -vying.** —*n.* **1.** discontent, usually with ill will, at another's superiority or success. **2.** an object of envious feeling. —*v.t.* **3.** to regard with envy. —**en′vi·er**, *n.* —**en′vy·ing·ly**, *adv.*

en·wrap (ĕn răp′), *v.t.*, **-wrapped, -wrapping. 1.** to wrap. **2.** to absorb in thought, etc.

en·zy·mat·ic (ĕn′zī măt′ĭk, -zī′-), *adj.* of or pertaining to an enzyme.

en·zyme (ĕn′zīm, -zĭm), *n.* any of various substances, as pepsin, originating from living cells and capable of producing certain chemical changes in organic substances.

e·o·lith·ic (ē′ə lĭth′ĭk), *adj.* noting or pertaining to the earliest stage of human culture, characterized by the use of amorphous stone implements.

e·on (ē′ən, ē′ŏn), *n.* **1.** an aeon. **2.** the largest division of geologic time.

E·os (ē′ŏs), *n.* the Greek goddess of the dawn, identified with the Roman Aurora.

e·o·sin (ē′ə sĭn), *n.* a coal-tar product used for dyeing silk, etc., rose-red. —**e′o·sin·like′**, *adj.*

-eous, var. of **-ous,** occurring in adjectives taken from Latin or derived from Latin nouns.

ep·au·let (ĕp′ə lĕt′, -lĭt), *n.* a shoulder piece worn on military uniforms. Also, **ep′au·lette′.**

é·pée (ā pā′), *n.* *Fencing.* a thin sword.

Eph., Ephesians.

e·phah (ē′fə), *n.* a Hebrew unit of dry measure, equal to about a bushel. Also, **e′pha.**

e·phed·rine (ĭ fĕd′rĭn), *n.* a crystalline alkaloid used esp. for relief of colds, asthma, and hay fever.

e·phem·er·al (ĭ fĕm′ər əl), *adj.* short-lived; transitory. —**e·phem′er·al·ly**, *adv.*

e·phem·er·id (ĭ fĕm′ər ĭd), *n.* a May fly.

E·phe·sians (ĭ fē′zhənz), *n.* the book of the New Testament called in full *The Epistle of Paul the Apostle to the Ephesians.* *Abbr.:* **Ephes.**

eph·od (ĕf′ŏd, ē′fŏd), *n.* a kind of Hebrew priestly vestment, esp. that worn by the high priest.

E·phra·im (ē′frĭ əm), *n.* *Bible.* **1.** the younger son of Joseph. **2.** the tribe of Israel traditionally descended from him. **3.** the Kingdom of Israel.

ep·ic (ĕp′ĭk), *adj.* **1.** Also, **ep′i·cal.** denoting or resembling elevated poetic composition in which heroic events are described. —*n.* **2.** an epic poem. etc. —**ep′i·cal·ly**, *adv.*

ep·i·carp (ĕp′ə kärp′), *n.* *Bot.* the outermost layer of a pericarp, as the peel of certain fruits.

ep·i·cen·ter (ĕp′ə sĕn′tər), *n.* *Geol.* a point from which earthquake waves seem to go out.

ep·i·cure (ĕp′ə kyōōr′), *n.* one with a refined taste in eating and drinking. **2.** a glutton.

ep·i·cu·re·an (ĕp′ə kyōō rē′ən), *adj.* **1.** of luxurious tastes or habits. **2.** fit for an epicure. **3.** (*cap.*) of or pertaining to Epicureanism. —*n.* **4.** an epicure. **5.** (*cap.*) a disciple of Epicur···

Ep·i·cu·re·an·ism (ĕp′ə kyōō rē′ə nĭz′əm), *n.* **1.** the philosophical system of Epicurus, who claimed that the highest good in life is freedom from disturbance or pain. **2.** (*l.c.*) epicurean habits.

Ep·i·cu·rus (ĕp′ə kyōōr′əs), *n.* 342?–270 B.C., Greek philosopher.

ep·i·dem·ic (ĕp′ə dĕm′ĭk), *adj.* **1.** Also, **ep′i·dem′i·cal.** affecting at the same time a large number of persons in a locality. —*n.* **2.** an epidemic disease. —**ep′i·dem′i·cal·ly**, *adv.*

ep·i·der·mis (ĕp′ə dûr′mĭs), *n.* **1.** *Anat., Zool.* the outer, nonsensitive layer of the skin. **2.** *Bot.* a thin outer layer of cells of seed plants and ferns. —**ep′i·der′mal, ep′i·der′mic,** *adj.*

ep·i·glot·tis (ĕp′ə glŏt′ĭs), *n.* *Anat.* a thin, valvelike cartilaginous structure that covers the glottis during swallowing.

ep·i·gram (ĕp′ə grăm′), *n.* **1.** a witty and terse saying. **2.** a short poem usually ending with a witty turn and often satirical. —**ep·i·gram·mat·ic** (ĕp′ə grə măt′ĭk), *adj.* —**ep′i·gram·mat′i·cal·ly**, *adv.*

ep·i·lep·sy (ĕp′ə lĕp′sĭ), *n.* a nervous disease usually characterized by convulsions and loss of consciousness. —**ep·i·lep·tic** (ĕp′ə lĕp′tĭk), *adj.*, *n.*

ep·i·logue (ĕp′ə lôg′, -lŏg′), *n.* **1.** a speech by one of the actors after the conclusion of a play. **2.** the person or persons speaking this. **3.** a concluding part added to a literary work. Also, **ep′i·log′.**

ep·i·neph·rine (ĕp′ə nĕf′rĭn, -rēn), *n.* *Chem.* adrenalin. Also, **ep·i·neph·rin** (ĕp′ə nĕf′rĭn).

E·piph·a·ny (ĭ pĭf′ə nĭ), *n.* a festival, Jan. 6, commemorating the manifestation of Christ to the Magi.

ep·i·phyte (ĕp′ə fīt′), *n.* *Bot.* a plant which grows upon another but does not get food, water, or minerals from it. —**ep·i·phyt·ic** (ĕp′ə fĭt′ĭk), **ep′i·phyt′i·cal,** *adj.* —**ep′i·phyt′i·cal·ly**, *adv.*

Epis., Episcopal. Also, **Episc.**

e·pis·co·pa·cy (ĭ pĭs′kə pə sĭ), *n.*, *pl.* **-cies. 1.** government of the church by bishops. **2.** the office or incumbency of a bishop. **3.** the order of bishops.

e·pis·co·pal (ĭ pĭs′kə pəl), *adj.* **1.** pertaining to a bishop. **2.** (*often cap.*) based on or recognizing a governing order of bishops. **3.** (*cap.*) designating the Anglican Church or a branch of it.

E·pis·co·pa·lian (ĭ pĭs′kə pāl′yən), *adj.* **1.** pertaining or adhering to the Episcopal Church. **2.** (*l.c.*) episcopal. —*n.* **3.** a member of the Episcopal Church. —**E·pis′co·pa′lian·ism**, *n.*

e·pis·co·pate (ĭ pĭs′kə pĭt, -pāt′), *n.* **1.** a bishopric. **2.** the order or body of bishops. **3.** the incumbency of a bishop.

ep·i·sode (ĕp/ə sōd/, -zōd/), *n.* **1.** an incident, as in a person's life. **2.** an incidental digression in a story, etc. —**ep·i·sod·ic** (ĕp/ə sŏd/ĭk, -zŏd/-), **ep/i·sod/i·cal,** *adj.* —**ep/i·sod/i·cal·ly,** *adv.*

e·pis·tle (ĭ pĭs/əl), *n.* **1.** a letter, esp. a formal or didactic one. **2.** (*usually cap.*) one of the apostolic letters in the New Testament.

e·pis·to·lar·y (ĭ pĭs/tə lĕr/ĭ), *adj.* **1.** in, or carried on by, letters. **2.** of or pertaining to letters.

ep·i·taph (ĕp/ə tăf/, -täf/), *n.* a commemorative inscription on a tomb or mortuary monument.

ep·i·the·li·um (ĕp/ə thē/lĭ əm), *n., pl.* **-liums,** **-lia** (-lĭ ə). *Biol.* any tissue which covers a surface, or lines a cavity or the like, and which performs protective, secreting, or other functions, as the epidermis, the lining of blood vessels, etc. —**ep/i·the/li·al,** *adj.*

ep·i·thet (ĕp/ə thĕt/), *n.* a descriptive term applied to a person or thing, as in Alexander *the Great.*

e·pit·o·me (ĭ pĭt/ə mĭ), *n.* **1.** a summary or abstract. **2.** a typical representation.

e·pit·o·mize (ĭ pĭt/ə mīz/), *v.t.,* **-mized, -mizing.** to make an epitome of. —**e·pit/o·miz/er,** *n.*

ep·i·zo·öt·ic (ĕp/ə zō ŏt/ĭk), *adj.* **1.** prevalent temporarily among animals. —*n.* **2.** an epizoötic disease.

e plu·ri·bus u·num (ē plŏŏr/ə bəs ū/nəm), *Latin.* one out of many (motto of the United States).

ep·och (ĕp/ək *or, esp. Brit.,* ē/pŏk), *n.* **1.** a particularly distinctive period. **2.** the beginning of any distinctive period in the history of anything. **3.** *Geol.* the main division of a geological period. —**ep/och·al,** *adj.*

ep·ode (ĕp/ōd), *n. Anc. Pros.* the part of a lyric ode following the strophe and antistrophe.

ep·on·y·mous (ĕ pŏn/ə məs), *adj.* giving one's name to a tribe, place, etc.

ep·si·lon (ĕp/sə lŏn/, -lən), *n.* the fifth letter (E, ε) of the Greek alphabet.

Ep·som (ĕp/səm), *n.* a town in SE England: site of **Epsom Downs,** a famous race track where the annual Derby is held.

Epsom salt, (*often pl.*) hydrated magnesium sulfate, used as a cathartic, etc.

Ep·stein (ĕp/stīn), *n.* **Jacob,** born 1880, English sculptor, born in U.S.

eq., **1.** equal. **2.** equation. **3.** equivalent.

eq·ua·ble (ĕk/wə bəl, ē/kwə-), *adj.* **1.** free from variations. **2.** uniform. **3.** tranquil. —**eq/ua·bil/i·ty, eq/ua·ble·ness,** *n.* —**eq/ua·bly,** *adv.*

e·qual (ē/kwəl), *adj., n., v.,* **equaled, equaling** or (*esp. Brit.*) **equalled, equalling.** —*adj.* **1.** as great as another. **2.** alike in quantity, value, rank, ability, etc. **3.** evenly proportioned. **4.** uniform. **5.** adequate. **6.** having adequate means. **7.** level. —*n.* **8.** one who or that which is equal. —*v.t.* **9.** to be or become equal to. **10.** to make or do something equal to. —**e/-qual·ly,** *adv.*

e·qual·i·ty (ĭ kwŏl/ə tĭ), *n., pl.* **-ties.** **1.** state of being equal. **2.** uniform character.

e·qual·ize (ē/kwə līz/), *v.t.,* **-ized, -izing.** **1.** to make equal. **2.** to make uniform. —**e/qual·i·za/tion,** *n.* —**e/qual·iz/er,** *n.*

e·qua·nim·i·ty (ē/kwə nĭm/ə tĭ, ĕk/wə-), *n.* evenness of mind or temper; calmness; composure.

e·quate (ĭ kwāt/), *v.t.,* **equated, equating. 1.** to state the equality of or between. **2.** to make equal.

e·qua·tion (ĭ kwā/zhən, -shən), *n.* **1.** act of making equal. **2.** equally balanced state. **3.** *Math.* an expression of the equality of two quantities, employing the sign = between them. **4.** *Chem.* a symbolic representation of a reaction.

e·qua·tor (ĭ kwā/tər), *n.* **1.** that great circle of a heavenly body whose plane is equidistant from the poles and perpendicular to the axis. **2.** the great circle of the earth.

e·qua·to·ri·al (ē/kwə tôr/ĭ əl, ĕk/wə-), *adj.* **1.** of or near an equator. **2.** of or like the regions at the equator. —**e/qua·to/ri·al·ly,** *adv.*

eq·uer·ry (ĕk/wə rĭ), *n., pl.* **-ries. 1.** an officer of a royal household, in charge of horses. **2.** an officer who attends on the British sovereign.

e·ques·tri·an (ĭ kwĕs/trĭ ən), *adj.* **1.** of or pertaining to horsemen or horsemanship. **2.** mount-

ed on horseback. —*n.* **3.** a rider on horseback. —**e·ques·tri·enne** (ĭ kwĕs/trĭ ĕn/), *n.fem.*

e·qui·an·gu·lar (ē/kwĭ ăng/gyə lər), *adj.* having all the angles equal.

e·qui·dis·tant (ē/kwə dĭs/tənt), *adj.* equally distant. —**e/qui·dis/tance,** *n.* —**e/qui·dis/-tant·ly,** *adv.*

e·qui·lat·er·al (ē/kwə lăt/ər əl), *adj.* **1.** having all the sides equal. —*n.* **2.** a figure having all its sides equal. —**e/qui·lat/er·al·ly,** *adv.*

e·quil·i·brant (ĭ kwĭl/ə brənt), *n. Physics.* a counterbalancing force or system of forces.

e·qui·li·brate (ē/kwə lī/brāt, ĭ kwĭl/ə brāt/), *v.t., v.i.,* **-brated, -brating. 1.** to balance equally. **2.** to be in equilibrium with. —**e/qui·li·bra/-tion,** *n.*

e·qui·lib·ri·um (ē/kwə lĭb/rĭ əm), *n.* **1.** a state of balance between any powers, forces, influences, etc. **2.** mental balance.

e·quine (ē/kwīn), *adj.* **1.** of, pertaining to, or resembling a horse. —*n.* **2.** a horse.

e·qui·noc·tial (ē/kwə nŏk/shəl), *adj.* **1.** pertaining to an equinox or the equinoxes. **2.** occurring at the time of an equinox. —*n.* **3.** the celestial equator. **4.** an equinoctial gale or storm.

e·qui·nox (ē/kwə nŏks/), *n.* the time when the sun crosses the plane of the earth's equator, making night and day all over the earth of equal length, occurring about March 21 (**vernal equinox**) and Sept. 22 (**autumnal equinox**).

e·quip (ĭ kwĭp/), *v.t.,* **equipped, equipping. 1.** to furnish or provide. **2.** to array.

eq·ui·page (ĕk/wə pĭj), *n.* **1.** a carriage. **2.** a carriage with horses and servants. **3.** equipment.

e·quip·ment (ĭ kwĭp/mənt), *n.* **1.** anything used in or provided for some purpose. **2.** act of equipping. **3.** state of being equipped. **4.** a person's knowledge and skill necessary for a task, etc.

e·qui·poise (ē/kwə poiz/, ĕk/wə-), *n.* **1.** an even balance; equilibrium. **2.** a counterpoise.

eq·ui·se·tum (ĕk/wə sē/təm), *n., pl.* **-tums, -ta** (-tə). a horsetail (plant).

eq·ui·ta·ble (ĕk/wə tə bəl), *adj.* just; fair; reasonable. —**eq/ui·ta·bly,** *adv.*

eq·ui·ty (ĕk/wə tĭ), *n., pl.* **-ties. 1.** fairness; impartiality. **2.** that which is fair and just. **3.** *Law.* a system of jurisprudence serving to supplement and remedy the limitations of the common law. **4.** the interest of a shareholder.

equiv., equivalent.

e·quiv·a·lent (ĭ kwĭv/ə lənt), *adj.* **1.** equal in value, measure, force, effect, significance, etc. **2.** corresponding in position, function, etc. **3.** *Geom.* having the same extent, as a triangle and a square of equal area. **4.** *Chem.* having the same capacity to combine or react chemically. —*n.* **5.** that which is equivalent. —**e·quiv/a·lence, e·quiv/a·len·cy,** *n.* —**e·quiv/a·lent·ly,** *adv.*

e·quiv·o·cal (ĭ kwĭv/ə kəl), *adj.* **1.** uncertain. **2.** questionable; suspicious. **3.** ambiguous. —**e·quiv/o·cal·ly,** *adv.*

e·quiv·o·cate (ĭ kwĭv/ə kāt/), *v.i.,* **-cated, -cating.** to use ambiguous expressions, esp. to mislead. —**e·quiv/o·ca/tion,** *n.* —**e·quiv/o·ca/-tor,** *n.*

-er¹, a suffix: **1.** forming nouns designating persons from the object of their occupation or labor, as in *hatter,* or from their place of origin or abode, as in *Icelander,* or designating either persons or things from some special characteristic, as in *six-footer.* **2.** serving as the regular English formative of agent nouns (being attached to verbs of any origin), as in *bearer, distributer, harvester, theorizer.*

-er², a suffix of nouns denoting persons or things connected with something, as in *grocer.*

-er³, a suffix forming the comparative degree of adjectives, as in *harder, smaller.*

-er⁴, a suffix forming the comparative degree of adverbs, as in *faster.*

Er, *Chem.* erbium.

e·ra (ĭr/ə, ē/rə), *n.* **1.** a period of time marked by distinctive character, events, etc. **2.** a system of chronological notation reckoned from a given date. **3.** a period so reckoned. **4.** *Geol.* a major division of geological time.

e·rad·i·ca·ble (ĭ răd/ə kə bəl), *adj.* that may be eradicated.

e·rad·i·cate (ĭ răd/ə kāt/), *v.t.,* **-cated, -cating. 1.** to remove or destroy utterly. **2.** to uproot. —**e·rad/i·ca/tion,** *n.* —**e·rad/i·ca/tor,** *n.*

e·rase (ĭ rās'), *v.t.*, erased, erasing. to rub out, as letters written, etc. —**e·ras'a·ble**, *adj.*

e·ras·er (ĭ rā'zər), *n.* an instrument, as a piece of rubber or cloth, for erasing marks made with pen, pencil, chalk, etc.

E·ras·mus (ĭ răz'məs), *n.* Desiderius, 1466?–1536, Dutch humanist and satirist.

e·ra·sure (ĭ rā'shər), *n.* 1. act of erasing. 2. something erased.

er·bi·um (ûr'bĭ əm), *n.* a rare-earth metallic element. *Symbol:* Er; *at. wt.:* 167.2; *at. no.:* 68.

ere (âr), *prep., conj.* before.

Er·e·bus (ĕr'ə bəs), *n. Gk. Myth.* a place of darkness through which the dead pass to Hades.

e·rect (ĭ rĕkt'), *adj.* 1. upright in position or posture. —*v.t.* 2. to build. 3. to raise to an upright position. 4. *Geom.* to draw (a line or figure) upon a given line, base, or the like. 5. *Mach.* to assemble. —**e·rect'er, e·rec'tor,** *n.* —**e·rec'tion,** *n.* —**e·rect'ly,** *adv.* —**e·rect'ness,** *n.*

ere·long (âr lông', -lŏng'), *adv.* before long.

erg (ûrg), *n. Physics.* the unit of work or energy in the cgs system: the work done by one dyne moving through a distance of one centimeter.

er·go (ûr'gō), *conj., adv. Latin.* therefore.

er·got (ûr'gət, -gŏt), *n.* 1. a disease of rye and other cereals, due to a fungus. 2. the resulting growths, used medicinally.

Er·ic·son (ĕr'ĭk sən), *n.* Leif, fl. A.D. 1000, Scandinavian navigator (son of Eric the Red).

Er·ic the Red (ĕr'ĭk), born A.D. about 950, Norseman who discovered and colonized Greenland.

E·rie (ĭr'ĭ), *n.* 1. Lake, one of the five Great Lakes, between the U.S. and Canada. 239 mi. long; 9940 sq. mi. 2. a city in NW Pennsylvania. 116,955. 3. a member of a tribe of American Indians formerly living along the southern shore of Lake Erie.

Erie Canal, a canal in New York, extending from Albany to Buffalo and connecting the Hudson with Lake Erie.

Er·in (âr'ĭn, ĭr'ĭn), *n. Poetic.* Ireland.

E·ris (ĭr'ĭs, ĕr'ĭs), *n. Gk. Myth.* goddess of discord.

Er·i·tre·a (ĕr'ĭ trē'ə), *n.* a former Italian colony in NE Africa. 865,000 pop.; 45,900 sq. mi. —**Er'i·tre'an,** *adj., n.*

erl·king (ûrl'kĭng'), *n. Ger. and Scand. Myth.* a spirit which works mischief, esp. to children.

er·mine (ûr'mĭn), *n., pl.* -mines, (*esp. collectively*) -mine. 1. a brown weasel which turns white in winter. 2. its lustrous white winter fur. 3. the office or dignity of a judge.

erne (ûrn), *n.* a sea eagle. Also, **ern.**

e·rode (ĭ rōd'), *v.t.*, eroded, eroding. 1. to eat away. 2. to form (a channel, etc.) by eating or wearing away.

E·ros (ĭr'ŏs, ĕr'ŏs), *n.* the Greek god of love, identified by the Romans with Cupid.

e·rose (ĭ rōs'), *adj.* 1. uneven as if gnawed. 2. *Bot.* having the margin irregularly incised.

e·ro·sion (ĭ rō'zhən), *n.* 1. act of eroding. 2. state of being eroded. —**e·ro·sive** (ĭ rō'sĭv), *adj.*

e·rot·ic (ĭ rŏt'ĭk), *adj.* of or pertaining to sexual love; amatory. —**e·rot'i·cal·ly,** *adv.*

e·rot·i·cism (ĭ rŏt'ə sĭz'əm), *n.* erotic character.

ERP, European Recovery Program. Also, **E.R.P.**

err (ûr), *v.i.* 1. to be mistaken. 2. to sin.

er·rand (ĕr'ənd), *n.* 1. a short trip for a specific purpose. 2. a special business entrusted to a messenger.

er·rant (ĕr'ənt), *adj.* 1. roving adventurously. 2. erring. —**er'rant·ly,** *adv.*

er·rant·ry (ĕr'ənt rĭ), *n., pl.* -ries. conduct or performance like that of a knight-errant.

er·rat·ic (ĭ răt'ĭk), *adj.* 1. eccentric; queer. 2. wandering; not fixed. —**er·rat'i·cal·ly,** *adv.*

er·ra·tum (ĭ rā'təm, ĭ rä'-), *n., pl.* -ta (-tə). an error in writing or printing.

err·ing (ûr'ĭng, ĕr'-), *adj.* 1. wrong. 2. sinning.

erron., 1. erroneous. 2. erroneously.

er·ro·ne·ous (ə rō'nĭ əs, ĕ-), *adj.* containing error; incorrect. —**er·ro'ne·ous·ly,** *adv.*

er·ror (ĕr'ər), *n.* 1. a mistake, as in action, speech, etc. 2. belief of what is not true. 3. a moral offense. 4. *Baseball.* a faulty play which prolongs a batsman's time at bat or allows a runner to be safe or to advance.

er·satz (ĕr zäts'), *adj., n.* substitute.

Erse (ûrs), *n.* Gaelic, esp. Scotch Gaelic.

erst (ûrst), *adv. Archaic.* before the present time; formerly.

erst·while (ûrst'hwīl'), *adj.* former.

e·ruct (ĭ rŭkt'), *v.t., v.i.* to belch forth; emit.

e·ruc·tate (ĭ rŭk'tāt), *v.t., v.i.*, -tated, -tating. eruct. —**e·ruc·ta·tion** (ĭ rŭk'tā'shən, ē'rŭk-), *n.*

e·ru·dite (ĕr'ŏŏ dīt', ĕr'yŏŏ-), *adj.* scholarly.

er·u·di·tion (ĕr'ŏŏ dĭsh'ən, ĕr'yŏŏ-), *n.* acquired knowledge; learning; scholarship.

e·rupt (ĭ rŭpt'), *v.i.* 1. to burst forth, as volcanic matter. —*v.t.* 2. to cause to burst forth. 3. (of a volcano, etc.) to eject. —**e·rup'tive,** *adj.*

e·rup·tion (ĭ rŭp'shən), *n.* 1. an issuing forth suddenly and violently. 2. *Geol.* the ejection of molten rock, water, etc. 3. *Pathol.* **a.** the breaking out of a rash or the like. **b.** a rash.

-ery, a suffix of nouns denoting occupation, business, calling, or condition, place or establishment, goods or products, things collectively, qualities, actions, etc., as in *archery, bakery, prudery, scenery, witchery.*

er·y·sip·e·las (ĕr'ə sĭp'ə ləs, ĭr'ə-), *n. Pathol.* an acute, febrile, infectious disease, characterized by inflammation of the skin or mucous membranes.

E·sau (ē'sô), *n. Bible.* a son of Isaac and Rebecca.

es·ca·drille (ĕs'kə drĭl'), *n.* 1. a squadron of airplanes. 2. a small naval squadron.

es·ca·lade (ĕs'kə lād'), *n., v.*, -laded, -lading. —*n.* 1. a mounting by ladders, esp. in assault. —*v.t.* 2. to mount thus.

es·ca·la·tor (ĕs'kə lā'tər), *n.* 1. a moving continuous stairway. 2. (*cap.*) a trademark for this.

escalator clause, a provision in a contract between a labor union and a company permitting wage increases or decreases under specified conditions.

es·ca·pade (ĕs'kə pād', ĕs'kə pād'), *n.* 1. a reckless proceeding; a wild prank. 2. an escape.

es·cape (ĕs kāp'), *v.*, -caped, -caping, *n.* —*v.i.* 1. to get away, as from restraint. 2. to slip away from pursuit or peril. 3. to issue forth. —*v.t.* 4. to elude (pursuit, notice, etc.). 5. to slip from (a person) inadvertently, as a remark. —*n.* 6. act of escaping. 7. fact of having escaped. 8. a means of escaping. 9. avoidance of reality. 10. leakage, as of water, gas, etc. —**es·cap'a·ble,** *adj.* —**es·cap'er,** *n.*

es·cape·ment (ĕs kāp'mənt), *n.* 1. a way of escape. 2. *Horol.* the portion of a watch or clock which measures beats and controls the speed. 3. a mechanism for regulating the motion of a typewriter carriage.

es·cap·ism (ĕs kā'pĭz əm), *n.* the avoidance of reality. —**es·cap'ist,** *n.*

es·ca·role (ĕs'kə rōl'), *n.* a broad-leaved kind of endive, used for salads.

es·carp·ment (ĕs kärp'mənt), *n.* 1. a long, clifflike ridge. 2. a steep slope about a fortification.

-escence, a suffix of nouns denoting action, change, condition, etc., and corresponding to verbs ending in *-esce* or adjectives in *-escent*, as in *convalescence.*

-escent, a suffix of adjectives meaning "beginning to be or do something," as in *convalescent.*

es·cheat (ĕs chēt'), *Law.* —*n.* 1. the "return" of property to the state when there are no legally qualified heirs. 2. property which reverts thus. —*v.i., v.t.* 3. to "return" by escheat.

es·chew (ĕs chōō'), *v.t.* to shun; avoid.

es·cort (*n.* ĕs'kôrt; *v.* ĕs kôrt'), *n.* 1. an accompanying person or persons for protection, guidance, or courtesy. 2. protection, safeguard, or guidance. —*v.t.* 3. to accompany as an escort.

es·cri·toire (ĕs'krĭ twär'), *n.* a writing desk.

es·crow (ĕs'krō, ĕs krō'), *n. Law.* a contract, deed, bond, or other written agreement deposited with a third person, by whom it is to be delivered to the grantee or promisee on the fulfillment of some condition.

es·cu·do (ĕs kōō'dō), *n., pl.* -dos. 1. the gold monetary unit of Portugal. 2. any of various coins of Portugal, Spain, Chile, etc.

es·cu·lent (ĕs'kyə lənt), *adj.* 1. edible. —*n.* 2. something edible, esp. a vegetable.

es·cutch·eon (ĕs kŭch′ən), *n.* the shield or surface on which armorial bearings are shown.

Es·dras (ĕz′drəs), *n.* either of the first two books of the Apocrypha. *Abbr.*: **Esd.**

-ese, a noun and adjective suffix referring to locality, nationality, language, literary style, etc., as in *Chinese.*

Es·ki·mo (ĕs′kə mō′), *n., pl.* **-mos, -mo,** *adj.* —*n.* 1. one of a people inhabiting the arctic coasts of America. 2. their language. —*adj.* 3. of or pertaining to the Eskimos or their language.

Eskimo dog, one of a breed of strong dogs used by the Eskimos to draw sleds.

e·soph·a·gus (ē sŏf′ə gəs), *n., pl.* **-gi** (-jī′). a tube connecting the mouth with the stomach.

es·o·ter·ic (ĕs′ə tĕr′ĭk), *adj.* 1. profound; recondite. 2. belonging to the select few. 3. private. 4. intended to be communicated only to the initiated.

esp., especially. Also, **espec.**

es·pal·ier (ĕs păl′yər), *n.* a fruit tree trained to grow flat against a trellis, wall, etc.

es·pe·cial (ĕs pĕsh′əl), *adj.* 1. special; exceptional. 2. of a particular kind. —**es·pe′cial·ly,** *adv.*

Es·pe·ran·to (ĕs′pə rän′tō, -răn′tō), *n.* an artificial language for international auxiliary use.

es·pi·al (ĕs pī′əl), *n.* a spying or keeping watch.

es·pi·o·nage (ĕs′pĭ ə nĭj′, ə spī′-, ĕs′pĭ ə näzh′), *n.* the work or use of spies.

es·pla·nade (ĕs′plə näd′, -näd′), *n.* any open, level space, esp. one serving for walks or drives.

es·pous·al (ĕs pou′zəl), *n.* 1. adoption or advocacy, as of a cause. 2. a marriage ceremony.

es·pouse (ĕs pouz′), *v.t.,* **-poused, -pousing.** 1. to adopt or advocate. 2. to marry.

es·prit (ĕs prē′), *n. French.* wit; sprightliness.

es·prit de corps (ĕs prē′ də kôr′), *French.* a sense of group unity and honor.

es·py (ĕs pī′), *v.t.,* **-pied, -pying.** to see at a distance; catch sight of. —**es·pi′er,** *n.*

Esq., Esquire.

es·quire (ĕs kwīr′), *n., v.,* **-quired, -quiring.** —*n.* 1. *Brit.* a polite title after a man's last name. 2. (in the Middle Ages) a squire attendant upon a knight. 3. a man belonging to the order of English gentry ranking next below a knight. —*v.t.* 4. to raise to the rank of esquire.

-ess, a suffix forming distinctively feminine nouns.

es·say (*n.* ĕs′ā *for 1;* ĕs′ā, ĕ sā′ *for 2; v.* ĕ sā′), *n.* 1. a short literary composition. 2. an attempt. —*v.t.* 3. to try.

es·say·ist (ĕs′ā ĭst), *n.* a writer of essays.

Es·sen (ĕs′ən), *n.* a city in W Germany. 666,743.

es·sence (ĕs′əns), *n.* 1. intrinsic nature. 2. a substance obtained from a plant, drug, or the like, in concentrated form. 3. an alcoholic solution of an essential oil. 4. a perfume.

es·sen·tial (ə sĕn′shəl), *adj.* 1. absolutely necessary. 2. pertaining to or constituting the essence of a thing. —*n.* 3. an indispensable element. —**es·sen′tial·ly,** *adv.*

essential oil, any of a class of oils obtained from plants, possessing the odor and other properties of the plant, and volatilizing completely when heated: used in making perfumes, flavors, etc.

-est, a suffix forming the superlative degree of adjectives and adverbs, as in *warmest.*

EST, Eastern Standard Time. Also, **E.S.T., e.s.t.**

est., 1. Also, **estab.** established. 2. estimated.

es·tab·lish (ĕs tăb′lĭsh), *v.t.* 1. to set up on a firm or permanent basis. 2. to settle in a position, business, etc. 3. to prove. 4. to make (a church) a national institution.

es·tab·lish·ment (ĕs tăb′lĭsh mənt), *n.* 1. act of establishing. 2. state or fact of being established. 3. something established. 4. a household. 5. the building and equipment of a business concern. 6. a permanent civil, military, or other organization. 7. institution. 8. the recognition by the state of a church as the state church. 9. the church so recognized.

es·tate (ĕs tāt′), *n.* 1. a piece of landed property. 2. *Law.* property or possessions. 3. period or condition of life. 4. a political or social group or class. 5. social status or rank.

es·teem (ĕs tēm′), *v.t.* 1. to regard, esp. highly or favorably. 2. to value. —*n.* 3. favorable opinion or regard. 4. opinion or estimation.

es·ter (ĕs′tər), *n. Chem.* a compound formed by

the reaction between an acid and an alcohol with the elimination of a molecule of water.

Esth., Esther.

Es·ther (ĕs′tər), *n.* one of the books of the Old Testament, named from its principal character.

es·thete, etc. (ĕs′thēt), *n.* See **aesthete,** etc.

es·ti·ma·ble (ĕs′tə mə bəl), *adj.* 1. worthy of esteem. 2. that can be estimated. —**es′ti·ma·bly,** *adv.*

es·ti·mate (*v.* ĕs′tə māt′; *n.* ĕs′tə mĭt, -māt′), *v.,* **-mated, -mating,** *n.* —*v.t.* 1. to form an approximate opinion regarding the value, amount, size, weight, etc., of. 2. to judge. —*v.i.* 3. to submit approximate figures. —*n.* 4. an approximate calculation. 5. a judgment or opinion. —**es′ti·ma′tor,** *n.*

es·ti·ma·tion (ĕs′tə mā′shən), *n.* 1. judgment or opinion. 2. esteem. 3. estimate.

Es·to·ni·a (ĕs tō′nĭ ə), *n.* a constituent republic of the Soviet Union, on the Baltic: independent republic, 1918–40. —**Es·to′ni·an,** *adj., n.*

es·trange (ĕs trānj′), *v.t.,* **-tranged, -tranging.** 1. to alienate the affections of. 2. to keep at a distance. 3. to divert from the original use or possessor. —**es·trange′ment,** *n.* —**es·trang′-er,** *n.*

es·tu·ar·y (ĕs′chŏŏ ĕr′Y), *n., pl.* **-aries.** 1. that part of a river in which its current meets the sea's tides. 2. an inlet of the sea.

e·ta (ā′tə, ē′tə), *n.* the seventh letter (H, η) of the Greek alphabet.

et al., (L *et alii*) and others.

et cet·er·a (ĕt sĕt′ər ə, -sĕt′rə), *Latin.* and others; and so forth; and so on. *Abbr.*: **etc.**

etch (ĕch), *v.t.* 1. to engrave (metals, etc.) with an acid or the like. 2. to produce or copy by this method. —*v.i.* 3. to practice the art of etching. —**etch′er,** *n.*

etch·ing (ĕch′ĭng), *n.* 1. a process of making designs or pictures on a metal plate, glass, etc., by the corrosion of an acid instead of by a tool. 2. an impression, as on paper, taken from an etched plate.

e·ter·nal (Y tûr′nəl), *adj.* 1. without beginning or end. 2. ceaseless. 3. immutable. —*n.* 4. that which is eternal. 5. **the Eternal,** God. —**e·ter′-nal·ly,** *adv.* —**e·ter′nal·ness,** *n.*

e·ter·ni·ty (Y tûr′nə tY), *n., pl.* **-ties.** 1. time without beginning or end. 2. eternal existence. 3. a seemingly endless time.

-eth, a form of *-th,* the ordinal suffix.

eth·ane (ĕth′ān), *n. Chem.* an odorless, gaseous hydrocarbon, C_2H_6, of the methane series, present in illuminating gas and crude petroleum.

e·ther (ē′thər), *n.* 1. *Chem.* a highly volatile and inflammable colorless liquid, $(C_2H_5)_2O$, used as a solvent and anesthetic. 2. the upper regions of space. 3. an all-pervading medium formerly postulated for the transmission of light, heat, etc.

e·the·re·al (Y thĭr′Y əl), *adj.* 1. light and airy. 2. extremely delicate. 3. heavenly. 4. of or pertaining to the ether. —**e·the·re·al·ly,** *adv.*

e·the·re·al·ize (Y thĭr′Y ə līz′), *v.t.,* **-ized, -izing.** to make ethereal. —**e·the′re·al·i·za′tion,** *n.*

e·ther·ize (ē′thə rīz′), *v.t.,* **-ized, -izing.** to put under the influence of ether. —**e′ther·i·za′tion,** *n.*

eth·i·cal (ĕth′ə kəl), *adj.* 1. pertaining to or dealing with principles of morality. 2. in accordance with the rules or standards of a profession. —**eth′i·cal·ly,** *adv.* —**eth′i·cal·ness,** *n.*

eth·ics (ĕth′ĭks), *n.pl.* 1. the science of morality. 2. the rules of conduct for a particular group. 3. moral principles.

E·thi·o·pi·a (ē′thY ō′pY ə), *n.* a kingdom in E Africa. 6,800,000 pop.; ab. 350,000 sq. mi. *Cap.*: Addis Ababa. —**E′thi·o′pi·an,** *adj., n.*

eth·nic (ĕth′nĭk), *adj.* 1. pertaining to or peculiar to a population, esp. to a speech group, loosely also to a race. 2. heathen or pagan. Also, **eth′-ni·cal.** —**eth′ni·cal·ly,** *adv.*

eth·nol·o·gy (ĕth nŏl′ə jY), *n.* the science that treats of the distinctive subdivisions of mankind, their origin, relations, peculiarities, institutions, etc. —**eth·no·log·i·cal** (ĕth′nə lŏj′ə kəl), **eth′no·log′-ic,** *adj.* —**eth′no·log′i·cal·ly,** *adv.* —**eth·nol′o·gist,** *n.*

eth·yl (ĕth′əl), *n.* 1. *Chem.* a univalent radical, C_2H_5, from ethane. 2. a type of fluid, containing tetraethyl lead, etc., added to gasoline for more even combustion. 3. (*cap.*) a trademark for this fluid. —**e·thyl·ic** (Y thĭl′Yk), *adj.*

eth·yl·ene (ĕth/ə lēn/), *n.* a colorless, inflammable gas, C₂H₄, with an unpleasant odor.

e·ti·ol·o·gy (ē/tĭ ŏl/ə jĭ), *n.* the study of the causes of diseases. —e/ti·ol/o·gist, *n.*

et·i·quette (ĕt/ə kĕt/), *n.* conventional requirements as to social behavior or formal ceremony.

Et·na (ĕt/nə), *n.* Mount, an active volcano in E Sicily. 10,758 ft.

E·ton (ē/tən), *n.* a town in S England: site of Eton College. 4399. —E·to·ni·an (ē tō/nĭ ən), *n.*, *adj.*

E·tru·ri·a (ĭ trŏŏr/ĭ ə), *n.* an ancient country in W Italy, roughly corresponding to modern Tuscany. —E·trus·can (ĭ trŭs/kən), *adj.*, *n.*

et seq., (L *et sequens*) and the following.

é·tude (ā tūd/, ā tōōd/), *n. Music.* a composition intended mainly for the practice of some point of technique.

et·y·mol·o·gy (ĕt/ə mŏl/ə jĭ), *n.*, *pl.* -gies. 1. the study of historical linguistic change, esp. as applied to individual words. 2. an account of the history of a particular word. 3. the derivation of a word. —et·y·mo·log·i·cal (ĕt/ə mə lŏj/ə kəl), et/y·mo·log/ic, *adj.* —et/y·mo·log/i·cal·ly, *adv.* —et/y·mol/o·gist, *n.*

Eu, *Chem.* europium.

eu·ca·lyp·tus (ū/kə lĭp/təs), *n.*, *pl.* -ti (-tī), -tuses. a tree of the myrtle family, native in Australia and cultivated elsewhere, which yields a valuable timber and bears leaves containing an oil used in medicine.

Eu·cha·rist (ū/kə rĭst), *n.* 1. the sacrament of the Lord's Supper; the communion. 2. the consecrated elements of the Lord's Supper. —Eu/cha·ris/tic, *adj.*

eu·chre (ū/kər), *n.*, *v.*, -chred, -chring. —*n.* 1. a variety of card game. —*v.t.* 2. *U.S. Colloq.* to outwit.

Eu·clid (ū/klĭd), *n.* fl. c300 B.C., Greek geometrician at Alexandria. —Eu·clid/e·an, *adj.*

eu·gen·ic (ū jĕn/ĭk), *adj.* 1. of or producing improvement in the offspring. 2. having good inherited characteristics. Also, **eu·gen/i·cal.** —eu·gen/i·cal·ly, *adv.*

eu·gen·ics (ū jĕn/ĭks), *n.* the science of improving the qualities of the human race.

Eu·gé·nie (œ zhĕ nē/), *n.* Empress, 1826–1920, wife of Napoleon III.

eu·lo·gize (ū/lə jīz/), *v.t.*, -gized, -gizing. to praise highly. —eu/lo·giz/er, eu/lo·gist, *n.*

eu·lo·gy (ū/lə jĭ), *n.*, *pl.* -gies. a speech or writing in praise of a person or thing. —eu/lo·gis/tic, eu/lo·gis/ti·cal, *adj.* —eu/lo·gis/ti·cal·ly, *adv.*

eu·nuch (ū/nək), *n.* a castrated man, esp. one formerly employed as a harem attendant.

eu·pep·sia (ū pĕp/shə, -sĭ ə), *n.* good digestion. —eu·pep·tic (ū pĕp/tĭk), *adj.*

eu·phe·mism (ū/fə mĭz/əm), *n. Rhet.* 1. the substitution of a mild, indirect, or vague expression for a harsh or blunt one. 2. the expression so substituted. —eu/phe·mist, *n.* —eu/phe·mis/tic, eu/phe·mis/ti·cal, *adj.* —eu/phe·mis/ti·cal·ly, *adv.*

eu·pho·ni·ous (ū fō/nĭ əs), *adj.* characterized by euphony; agreeable to the ear. —eu·pho/ni·ous·ly, *adv.* —eu·pho/ni·ous·ness, *n.*

eu·pho·ni·um (ū fō/nĭ əm), *n.* baritone tuba.

eu·pho·ny (ū/fə nĭ), *n.*, *pl.* -nies. agreeableness or pleasant effect of sound.

eu·pho·ri·a (ū fōr/ĭ ə), *n. Psychol.* a feeling or state of well-being.

Eu·phra·tes (ū frā/tēz), *n.* a river from E Turkey through Syria and Iraq. 1700 mi.

Eur., 1. Europe. 2. European.

Eur·a·sia (yŏŏ rā/zhə, -shə), *n.* Europe and Asia considered as a whole. —Eur·a/sian, *adj.*, *n.*

eu·re·ka (yŏŏ rē/kə), *interj.* I have found (it): the reputed exclamation of Archimedes when he finally found the answer to a problem.

Eu·rip·i·des (yŏŏ rĭp/ə dēz/), *n.* 480?–406? B.C., Athenian tragic poet.

Eu·rope (yŏŏr/əp), *n.* a continent in the W part of Eurasia, separated from Asia by the Ural Mountains on the E and the Caucasus Mountains and the Black and Caspian Seas on the SE. ab. 550,000,000 pop.; ab. 3,754,000 sq. mi. —Eu·ro·pe·an (yŏŏr/ə pē/ən), *adj.*, *n.*

Eu·ro·pe·an·ize (yŏŏr/ə pē/ə nīz/), *v.t.*, -ized, -izing. to make European.

European Recovery Program, a broad plan for aiding the European nations in their economic recovery, first proposed by Secretary of State George C. Marshall in 1947.

eu·ro·pi·um (yŏŏ rō/pĭ əm), *n. Chem.* a rare-earth metallic element with light pink salts. Symbol: Eu; at. wt.: 152; at. no.: 63.

Eu·ryd·i·ce (yŏŏ rĭd/ə sē/), *n. Gk. Myth.* the wife of Orpheus. See **Orpheus.**

Eu·sta·chi·an tube (ū stā/kĭ ən), *Anat.* a canal from the middle ear to the pharynx.

Eu·ter·pe (ū tûr/pĭ), *n. Class. Myth.* the Muse of music and lyric poetry.

eu·tha·na·sia (ū/thə nā/zhə), *n.* painless death, esp. to one suffering from a painful disease.

Eux·ine Sea (ūk/sĭn, -sīn), Black Sea.

e·vac·u·ate (ĭ văk/yŏŏ āt/), *v.*, -ated, -ating. —*v.t.* 1. to leave empty; vacate. 2. to remove (troops, etc.) from a place. 3. *Physiol.* to discharge, esp. from the bowels. —*v.i.* 4. to leave a town because of air-raid threats, etc. —e·vac/u·a/tion, *n.* —e·vac/u·a/tor, *n.*

e·vac·u·ee (ĭ văk/yŏŏ ē/, ĭ văk/yŏŏ ē/), *n.* a person removed from a place of danger.

e·vade (ĭ vād/), *v.*, evaded, evading. —*v.t.* 1. to escape from by trickery or cleverness. 2. to avoid. 3. to baffle. —*v.i.* 4. to practice evasion. —e·vad/er, *n.* —e·vad/ing·ly, *adv.*

e·val·u·ate (ĭ văl/yŏŏ āt/), *v.t.*, -ated, -ating. to appraise carefully. —e·val/u·a/tion, *n.*

ev·a·nesce (ĕv/ə nĕs/), *v.i.*, -nesced, -nescing. to vanish; fade away. —ev/a·nes/cence, *n.* —ev/a·nes/cent, *adj.*

e·van·gel (ĭ văn/jəl), *n.* 1. tidings of the redemption of the world through Christ. 2. (cap.) any of the Gospels.

e·van·gel·i·cal (ē/văn jĕl/ə kəl, ĕv/ən-), *adj.* pertaining to or in keeping with the Gospel and its teachings. Also, **e/van·gel/ic.** —e/van·gel/i·cal·ism/, *n.* —e/van·gel/i·cal·ly, *adv.*

e·van·ge·lism (ĭ văn/jə lĭz/əm), *n.* the preaching or promulgation of the Gospel.

e·van·ge·list (ĭ văn/jə lĭst), *n.* 1. a preacher of the Gospel. 2. (cap.) any of the writers (Matthew, Mark, Luke, and John) of the four Gospels. 3. a revivalist. —e·van/ge·lis/tic, *adj.*

e·van·ge·lize (ĭ văn/jə līz/), *v.t.*, *v.i.*, -lized, -lizing. 1. to preach the gospel (to). 2. to convert to Christianity. —e·van/ge·li·za/tion, *n.*

Ev·ans·ton (ĕv/ən stən), *n.* a city in NE Illinois, near Chicago. 65,389.

Ev·ans·ville (ĕv/ənz vĭl/), *n.* a city in SW Indiana, on the Ohio river. 97,062.

e·vap·o·rate (ĭ văp/ə rāt/), *v.*, -rated, -rating. —*v.i.* 1. to pass off in vapor. 2. to give off moisture. 3. to disappear. —*v.t.* 4. to convert into a vapor. 5. to extract moisture from. —e·vap/o·ra/tion, *n.* —e·vap/o·ra/tor, *n.*

evaporated milk, thick, unsweetened, canned milk with most of the water removed.

e·va·sion (ĭ vā/zhən), *n.* 1. act of escaping or avoiding something by trickery or cleverness. 2. a means of evading.

e·va·sive (ĭ vā/sĭv), *adj.* tending to evade. —e·va/sive·ly, *adv.* —e·va/sive·ness, *n.*

eve (ēv), *n.* 1. the evening or day before a church festival, etc. 2. the period just preceding any event, etc. 3. *Poetic.* evening.

Eve (ēv), *n. Bible.* the first woman.

e·ven¹ (ē/vən), *adj.* 1. level; smooth. 2. parallel. 3. regular. 4. uniform. 5. equal in measure or quantity. 6. divisible by 2. 7. denoted by such a number. 8. expressible without fractional parts. 9. leaving no debt on either side. 10. calm; placid. 11. impartial. —adv. 12. evenly. 13. yet (to emphasize a comparative). 14. (to suggest an extreme unlikelihood). 15. just. 16. fully. 17. indeed. —v.t. 18. to make even. 19. to balance. —e/ven·ly, *adv.* —e/ven·ness, *n.*

e·ven² (ē/vən), *n. Archaic.* evening; eve.

e·ven-hand·ed (ē/vən hăn/dĭd), *adj.* fair.

eve·ning (ēv/nĭng), *n.* 1. the latter part of the day and early part of the night. 2. any concluding period. —adj. 3. of or occurring in the evening.

evening primrose, a plant with yellow flowers that open at nightfall.

evening star, a bright planet seen in the west after sunset, esp. Venus.

e·ven·song (ē/vən sŏng/, -sŏng/), *n.* 1. *Anglican Ch.* a form of worship to be said or sung at evening. 2. *Rom. Cath. Ch.* vespers.

e·vent (ĭ vĕnt/), *n.* 1. anything that happens. 2. fact of happening. 3. the result. 4. *Sports.* each of the items in a program of races, etc.

e·vent·ful (Y vĕnt′fəl), *adj.* **1.** full of events. **2.** momentous. —**e·vent′ful·ly**, *adv.* —**e·vent′ful·ness**, *n.*

e·ven·tide (ē′vən tīd′), *n. Now Poetic.* evening.

e·ven·tu·al (Y vĕn′chŏŏ əl), *adj.* **1.** ultimate; final. **2.** contingent. —**e·ven′tu·al·ly**, *adv.*

e·ven·tu·al·i·ty (Y vĕn′chŏŏ ăl′ə tY), *n., pl.* **-ties.** a contingent event.

e·ven·tu·ate (Y vĕn′chŏŏ āt′), *v.i.*, **-ated, -ating.** to result. —**e·ven′tu·a′tion**, *n.*

ev·er (ĕv′ər), *adv.* **1.** at all times. **2.** continuously. **3.** at any time. **4.** (with emphatic force) at all.

Ev·er·est (ĕv′ər Yst), *n.* **Mount,** a peak of the Himalayas, in E Nepal: the highest mountain in the world. 29,141 ft.

Ev·er·ett (ĕv′ər Yt), *n.* **1.** a city in E Massachusetts, near Boston. 46,784. **2.** a seaport in NW Washington. 30,224.

ev·er·glade (ĕv′ər glād′), *n. Southern U.S.* a tract of low, swampy land.

Ev·er·glades (ĕv′ər glādz′), *n.* a swampy and partly forested region in S Florida. 5000 sq. mi.

ev·er·green (ĕv′ər grēn′), *adj.* **1.** having green leaves throughout the entire year. —*n.* **2.** an evergreen plant.

ev·er·last·ing (ĕv′ər lăs′tYng, -läs′-), *adj.* **1.** lasting forever; eternal. **2.** continuing indefinitely. **3.** incessant. **4.** wearisome. —*n.* **5.** eternity. **6. the Everlasting,** God. **7.** any of various plants or flowers which retain their shape, color, etc., when dried. —**ev′er·last′ing·ly**, *adv.*

ev·er·more (ĕv′ər môr′), *adv.* forever.

e·vert (Y vûrt′), *v.t.* to turn outward, or inside out. —**e·ver′si·ble**, *adj.* —**e·ver′sion**, *n.*

ev·er·y (ĕv′rY), *adj.* **1.** each. **2.** all possible.

ev·er·y·bod·y (ĕv′rY bŏd′Y), *pron.* every person.

ev·er·y·day (ĕv′rY dā′), *adj.* **1.** of or suitable for every day; daily. **2.** of or for ordinary days. **3.** usual.

ev·er·y·one (ĕv′rY wŭn′), *n.* everybody.

ev·er·y·thing (ĕv′rY thYng′), *pron.* every thing or particular of an aggregate or total; all.

ev·er·y·where (ĕv′rY hwâr′), *adv.* in every place or part; in all places.

e·vict (Y vYkt′), *v.t.* to expel from a building, etc., by legal process. —**e·vic′tion**, *n.* —**e·vic′tor**, *n.*

ev·i·dence (ĕv′ə dəns), *n., v.*, **-denced, -dencing.** —*n.* **1.** ground for belief; proof. **2.** an indication. **3.** *Law.* the data offered to the court or jury in proof of the facts in issue. —*v.t.* **4.** to make evident or clear. —**ev·i·den′tial** (ĕv′ə dĕn′shəl), *adj.*

ev·i·dent (ĕv′ə dənt), *adj.* plain or clear to the sight or understanding. —**ev′i·dent·ly**, *adv.*

e·vil (ē′vəl), *adj.* **1.** violating the moral law; wicked. **2.** harmful. **3.** unfortunate; disastrous. **4.** due to (actual or imputed) bad character or conduct. —*n.* **5.** that which is evil. **6.** harm; misfortune. **7.** anything causing injury or harm. —*adv.* **8.** badly. —**e′vil·ly**, *adv.* —**e′vil·ness**, *n.*

e·vil·do·er (ē′vəl dŏŏ′ər), *n.* one who does evil. —**e·vil·do·ing** (ē′vəl dŏŏ′Yng), *n.*

evil eye, the power, superstitiously attributed to certain persons, of inflicting injury or bad luck by a look. —**e′vil-eyed′**, *adj.*

e·vil-mind·ed (ē′vəl mīn′dYd), *adj.* **1.** having an evil mind. **2.** excessively sex-minded.

e·vince (Y vYns′), *v.t.*, **evinced, evincing. 1.** to show clearly; prove. **2.** to reveal. —**e·vin′ci·ble**, *adj.*

e·vis·cer·ate (Y vYs′ə rāt′), *v.t.*, **-ated, -ating.** to disembowel. —**e·vis′cer·a′tion**, *n.*

e·voke (Y vōk′), *v.t.*, **evoked, evoking. 1.** to produce (memories, feelings, etc.). **2.** to summon. —**ev′o·ca′tion**, *n.* —**e·vok′er**, *n.*

ev·o·lu·tion (ĕv′ə lŏŏ′shən; *Brit. also* ē′və-), *n.* **1.** any process of formation or growth. **2.** something evolved. **3.** *Biol.* the continuous genetic adaptation of organisms or species to the environment by the integrating agencies of selection, hybridization, inbreeding, and mutation. **4.** a movement or maneuver of troops, ships, etc. **5.** a giving off of gas, heat, etc. —**ev′o·lu′tion·al**, *adj.* —**ev′o·lu′tion·al·ly**, *adv.* —**ev′o·lu′tion·ar′y**, *adj.*

ev·o·lu·tion·ist (ĕv′ə lŏŏ′shən Yst; *Brit. also* ē′və-), *n.* a believer in the doctrine of evolution.

e·volve (Y vŏlv′), *v.*, **evolved, evolving.** —*v.t.* **1.** to develop gradually. **2.** *Biol.* to develop to a more highly organized condition. **3.** to emit, as

vapors, etc. —*v.i.* **4.** to develop. —**e·volve′ment**, *n.* —**e·volv′er**, *n.*

ewe (ū; *dial.* yō), *n.* a female sheep.

ew·er (ū′ər), *n.* a pitcher with a wide spout.

ex (ĕks), *prep. Finance.* without.

ex-, a prefix used to indicate a former title, status, etc., as in *ex-president.*

Ex., **1.** Exodus. **2.** (*l.c.*) example. **3.** except.

ex·act (Yg zăkt′), *adj.* **1.** strictly accurate. **2.** precise. **3.** strict or rigorous. —*v.t.* **4.** to demand or require. **5.** to force or compel. —**ex·ac′tion**, *n.* —**ex·act′ness, ex·act′i·tude**′, *n.*

ex·act·ing (Yg zăk′tYng), *adj.* **1.** severe. **2.** requiring close application. **3.** extortionate. —**ex·act′ing·ly**, *adv.* —**ex·act′ing·ness**, *n.*

ex·act·ly (Yg zăkt′lY), *adv.* **1.** in an exact manner. **2.** quite so; that's right.

ex·ag·ger·ate (Yg zăj′ə rāt′), *v.*, **-ated, -ating.** —*v.t.* **1.** to magnify beyond truth. **2.** to increase abnormally. —*v.i.* **3.** to employ exaggeration. —**ex·ag′ger·at′ed**, *adj.* —**ex·ag′ger·a′tion**, *n.* —**ex·ag′ger·a′tor**, *n.*

ex·alt (Yg zôlt′), *v.t.* **1.** to elevate in rank, power, quality, etc. **2.** to extol. **3.** to elate. —**ex′al·ta′tion**, *n.* —**ex·alt′ed·ly**, *adv.* —**ex·alt′er**, *n.*

ex·am (Yg zăm′), *n. Colloq.* an examination.

exam., **1.** examination. **2.** examined.

ex·am·i·na·tion (Yg zăm′ə nā′shən), *n.* **1.** act of examining. **2.** state of being examined. **3.** act of testing pupils, candidates, etc., as by questions. **4.** the test itself. **5.** the statements, etc., made by one examined. **6.** *Law.* formal interrogation.

ex·am·ine (Yg zăm′Yn), *v.t.*, **-ined, -ining. 1.** to inspect carefully; investigate. **2.** to test the knowledge, reactions, or qualifications of. **3.** *Law.* to interrogate. —**ex·am′in·a·ble**, *adj.* —**ex·am′i·nee′**, *n.* —**ex·am′in·er**, *n.*

ex·am·ple (Yg zăm′pəl, -zăm′-), *n., v.*, **-pled, -pling.** —*n.* **1.** one or a part taken to show the character of the whole. **2.** a pattern or model. **3.** a specimen. **4.** an instance illustrating a rule or method. **5.** a warning. **6.** a precedent. —*v.t.* **7.** to give or be an example of.

ex·as·per·ate (Yg zăs′pə rāt′), *v.t.*, **-ated, -ating.** to annoy extremely; infuriate. —**ex·as′per·at′ing·ly**, *adv.* —**ex·as′per·a′tion**, *n.*

exc., **1.** except. **2.** (*cap.*) Excellency.

Ex·cal·i·bur (ĕks kăl′ə bər), *n.* the magic sword of King Arthur.

ex ca·the·dra (ĕks kə thē′drə, kăth′Y drə), *Latin.* with authority. —**ex′-ca·the′dra**, *adj.*

ex·ca·vate (ĕks′kə vāt′), *v.t.*, **-vated, -vating. 1.** to make a hole or cavity in. **2.** to make (a tunnel, etc.) by removing material. **3.** to dig out (earth, etc.). **4.** to unearth. —**ex′ca·va′tion**, *n.* —**ex′ca·va′tor**, *n.*

ex·ceed (Yk sēd′), *v.t.* **1.** to go beyond the limits of. **2.** to surpass. —*v.i.* **3.** to be greater. **4.** to surpass others. —**ex·ceed′er**, *n.*

ex·ceed·ing (Yk sē′dYng), *adj.* extraordinary; excessive. —**ex·ceed′ing·ly**, *adv.*

ex·cel (Yk sĕl′), *v.t., v.i.*, **-celled, -celling.** to surpass; be superior to; outdo.

ex·cel·lence (ĕk′sə ləns), *n.* **1.** fact or state of excelling. **2.** an excellent quality.

ex·cel·len·cy (ĕk′sə lən sY), *n., pl.* **-cies. 1.** (*usually cap.*) a title of honor, as to governors. **2.** excellence.

ex·cel·lent (ĕk′sə lənt), *adj.* remarkably good. —**ex′cel·lent·ly**, *adv.*

ex·cel·si·or (n. Yk sĕl′sY ər; *adj.* -sY ôr′), *n.* **1.** a kind of fine wood shavings, used for stuffing, packing, etc. —*adj.* **2.** *Latin.* higher.

ex·cept[1] (Yk sĕpt′), *prep.* **1.** Also, **ex·cept′ing.** excluding; but. —*conj.* **2.** with the exception (that). **3.** otherwise than.

ex·cept[2] (Yk sĕpt′), *v.t.* **1.** to exclude. —*v.i.* **2.** to object.

ex·cep·tion (Yk sĕp′shən), *n.* **1.** act of excepting. **2.** fact of being excepted. **3.** something excepted. **4.** an objection.

ex·cep·tion·a·ble (Yk sĕp′shən ə bəl), *adj.* objectionable. —**ex·cep′tion·a·bly**, *adv.*

ex·cep·tion·al (Yk sĕp′shən əl), *adj.* unusual; extraordinary. —**ex·cep′tion·al·ly**, *adv.*

ex·cerpt (n. ĕk′sûrpt; v. Yk sûrpt′), *n.* **1.** a passage from a book or the like. —*v.t.* **2.** to take (a passage) from a book or the like.

ex·cess (n. Yk sĕs′; *adj.* ĕk′sĕs, Yk sĕs′), *n.* **1.** fact of exceeding something in amount. **2.** the amount by which one thing exceeds another. **3.** an extreme or excessive amount. **4.** immoderate indulgence. —*adj.* 5. more than is necessary, usual, or specified.

ex·ces·sive (ĭk sĕs′ĭv), *adj.* exceeding the usual or proper limit. —**ex·ces′sive·ly**, *adv.* —**ex·ces′sive·ness**, *n.*

exch., 1. exchange. 2. exchequer.

ex·change (ĭks chānj′), *v.*, **-changed, -changing,** *n.* —*v.t.* 1. to part with for some equivalent. 2. to change for another. 3. to interchange. —*v.i.* 4. to make an exchange. 5. to pass or be taken in exchange. —*n.* 6. act or process of exchanging. 7. that which is given or received in return. 8. a place for buying and selling commodities, securities, etc. 9. a central office. 10. the system by which debits and credits in different places are settled by documents (**bills of exchange**) representing money. 11. the reciprocal transference of equivalent sums of money, as in the currencies of two different countries. 12. the varying rate or sum, in one currency, given for a fixed sum in another currency. —**ex·change′a·ble**, *adj.* —**ex·chang′er**, *n.*

ex·cheq·uer (ĭks chĕk′ər, ĕks′chĕk ər), *n.* 1. a treasury, as of a nation. 2. (in Great Britain) (*often cap.*) the governmental department in charge of the public revenues. 3. *Colloq.* finances.

ex·cise[1] (*n.* ĭk sīz′, ĕk′sīz; *v.* ĭk sīz′), *n., v.,* **-cised, -cising.** —*n.* 1. a tax on the manufacture, sale, or consumption of certain commodities, as tobacco, etc. —*v.t.* 2. to impose an excise on.

ex·cise[2] (ĭk sīz′), *v.t.*, **-cised, -cising.** to remove or cut out. —**ex·cis′a·ble**, *adj.* —**ex·ci·sion** (ĭk sĭzh′ən), *n.*

ex·cit·a·ble (ĭk sī′tə bəl), *adj.* easily excited. —**ex·cit′a·bil′i·ty, ex·cit′a·ble·ness**, *n.* —**ex·cit′a·bly**, *adv.*

ex·ci·ta·tion (ĕk′sī tā′shən), *n.* 1. act of exciting. 2. state of being excited.

ex·cite (ĭk sīt′), *v.t.*, **-cited, -citing.** 1. to stir up. 2. to cause. 3. *Physiol.* to stimulate. —**ex·cit′ed**, *adj.* —**ex·cit′ed·ly**, *adv.* —**ex·cite′ment**, *n.* —**ex·cit′er**, *n.* —**ex·cit′ing·ly**, *adv.*

ex·claim (ĭks klām′), *v.i., v.t.* to cry out suddenly, as in surprise, protest, etc.

exclam., 1. exclamation. 2. exclamatory.

ex·cla·ma·tion (ĕks′klə mā′shən), *n.* 1. act of exclaiming; outcry. 2. interjection. —**ex·clam·a·to·ry** (ĭks klăm′ə tō′rĭ), *adj.*

exclamation point or **mark**, a punctuation mark (!) used after an exclamation.

ex·clude (ĭk sklōōd′), *v.t.*, **-cluded, -cluding.** 1. to shut or keep out. 2. to expel. —**ex·clud′er**, *n.* —**ex·clu′sion**, *n.*

ex·clu·sive (ĭk sklōō′sĭv), *adj.* 1. not admitting of something else. 2. excluding from account. 3. undivided. 4. in which no others have or may have a share. 5. single or sole. 6. disposed to exclude outsiders to association, etc. 7. *Colloq.* fashionable. —**ex·clu′sive·ly**, *adv.* —**ex·clu′sive·ness**, *n.*

ex·com·mu·ni·cate (ĕks′kə mū′nə kāt′), *v.*, **-cated, -cating,** *n., adj.* —*v.t.* 1. to cut off from communion or membership, esp. in a church. —*n.* 2. an excommunicated person. —*adj.* 3. excommunicated. —**ex′com·mu′ni·ca′tion**, *n.* —**ex′com·mu′ni·ca′tor**, *n.*

ex·co·ri·ate (ĭk skōr′ĭ āt′), *v.t.*, **-ated, -ating.** 1. *Physiol.* to remove the skin from. 2. to denounce. —**ex·co′ri·a′tion**, *n.*

ex·cre·ment (ĕks′krə mənt), *n.* waste matter from the body, esp. the feces. —**ex·cre·men·tal** (ĕks′krə mĕn′təl), *adj.*

ex·cres·cence (ĭk skrĕs′əns), *n.* 1. abnormal growth or increase. 2. an outgrowth, usually abnormal. Also, **ex·cres′cen·cy**. —**ex·cres′cent**, *adj.*

ex·cre·ta (ĭk skrē′tə), *n.pl.* excreted matters, as sweat, urine, etc. —**ex·cre′tal**, *adj.*

ex·crete (ĭk skrēt′), *v.t.*, **-creted, -creting.** to separate and eliminate from the body, as waste matters. —**ex·cre′tion**, *n.* —**ex·cre′tive**, *adj.* —**ex·cre·to·ry** (ĕks′krə tōr′ĭ, ĭk skrē′tə rĭ), *adj.*

ex·cru·ci·ate (ĭk skrōō′shĭ āt′), *v.t.*, **-ated, -ating.** to torture. —**ex·cru′ci·at′ing**, *adj.* —**ex·cru′ci·at′ing·ly**, *adv.*

ex·cul·pate (ĕks′kŭl pāt′, ĭk skŭl′pāt), *v.t.*, **-pated, -pating.** to clear from a charge of guilt or fault. —**ex′cul·pa′tion**, *n.*

ex·cur·sion (ĭk skûr′zhən, -shən), *n.* 1. a short trip for a special purpose. 2. a trip on a train, etc., at a reduced rate. 3. the persons (**excursionists**) who make such a journey. 4. deviation or digression.

ex·cur·sive (ĭk skûr′sĭv), *adj.* wandering; digressive. —**ex·cur′sive·ly**, *adv.*

ex·cuse (*v.* ĭks kūz′; *n.* ĭk skūs′), *v.*, **-cused, -cusing,** *n.* —*v.t.* 1. to pardon or forgive (a fault, etc.). 2. to apologize for. 3. to justify. 4. to release from an obligation. 5. to seek or obtain release for (oneself). —*n.* 6. that which is offered as a reason for being excused. 7. act of excusing. —**ex·cus′a·ble**, *adj.* —**ex·cus′a·bly**, *adv.* —**ex·cus′er**, *n.*

exec., 1. executive. 2. executor.

ex·e·cra·ble (ĕk′sə krə bəl), *adj.* 1. abominable. 2. *Colloq.* very bad. —**ex′e·cra·bly**, *adv.*

ex·e·crate (ĕk′sə krāt′), *v.t., v.i.*, **-crated, -crating.** 1. to abominate. 2. to curse. —**ex′e·cra′tion**, *n.* —**ex′e·cra′tor**, *n.*

ex·e·cute (ĕk′sə kūt′), *v.t.*, **-cuted, -cuting.** 1. to carry out; accomplish. 2. to perform or do. 3. to put to death according to law. 4. to produce in accordance with a plan. 5. *Law.* to give effect or force to (a law, sentence, etc.). —**ex′e·cut′er**, *n.*

ex·e·cu·tion (ĕk′sə kū′shən), *n.* 1. act or process of executing. 2. state or fact of being executed. 3. capital punishment. 4. mode or skill of performance. 5. effective action.

ex·e·cu·tion·er (ĕk′sə kū′shən ər), *n.* one who executes (criminals, etc.).

ex·ec·u·tive (ĭg zĕk′yə tĭv), *adj.* 1. suited for practical performance or direction. 2. charged with or pertaining to execution of laws or administration of affairs. —*n.* 3. a person or body charged with or skilled in administrative work. 4. the executive branch of a government. —**ex·ec′u·tive·ly**, *adv.*

executive mansion, the official residence of the President, a governor, etc.

ex·ec·u·tor (ĭg zĕk′yə tər), *n.* 1. one who performs, fulfills, etc. 2. *Law.* a person named by a decedent in his will to carry out the provisions of his will. —**ex·ec′u·trix** (ĭg zĕk′yə trĭks′), *n.fem.*

ex·e·ge·sis (ĕk′sə jē′sĭs), *n., pl.* **-ses** (-sēz). critical explanation or interpretation, esp. of Scripture. —**ex·e·get·ic** (ĕk′sə jĕt′ĭk), *adj.*

ex·em·plar (ĭg zĕm′plər, -plär), *n.* 1. a model or pattern. 2. a typical instance.

ex·em·pla·ry (ĭg zĕm′plə rĭ, ĕg′zəm plĕr′ĭ), *adj.* 1. worthy of imitation. 2. warning. 3. serving for a model. 4. typical.

ex·em·pli·fy (ĭg zĕm′plə fī′), *v.t.*, **-fied, -fying.** 1. to show by example. 2. to serve as an example of. —**ex·em′pli·fi·ca′tion**, *n.*

ex·em·pli gra·ti·a (ĭg zĕm′plī grā′shĭ ə), *Latin.* for example. *Abbr.:* e.g.

ex·empt (ĭg zĕmpt′), *v.t.* 1. to free from an obligation or liability to which others are subject. —*adj.* 2. released from an obligation, liability, etc. —*n.* 3. one who is exempt. —**ex·emp′tion**, *n.*

ex·er·cise (ĕk′sər sīz′), *n., v.*, **-cised, -cising.** —*n.* 1. bodily or mental exertion, esp. for training or improvement. 2. something done for practice or training. 3. a putting into action, use, operation, or effect. 4. (*often pl.*) a ceremony. —*v.t.* 5. to put through exercises. 6. to put (faculties, rights, etc.) into action, practice, or use. 7. to use or display. 8. to perform. 9. to have as an effect. 10. to worry. —*v.i.* 11. to go through exercises. —**ex′er·cis′er**, *n.*

ex·ert (ĭg zûrt′), *v.t.* to put forth, as power; put into vigorous action. —**ex·er′tive**, *adj.*

ex·er·tion (ĭg zûr′shən), *n.* 1. vigorous action or effort. 2. an effort. 3. exercise.

Ex·e·ter (ĕk′sə tər), *n.* a city in SW England. 73,990.

ex·e·unt (ĕk′sĭ ənt), *Latin.* they go out.

ex·hale (ĕks hāl′, ĭg zāl′), *v.i., v.t.*, **-haled, -haling.** 1. to emit (breath or vapor). 2. to pass off as vapor. —**ex·ha·la·tion** (ĕks′hə lā′shən, ĕg′zə-), *n.*

ex·haust (ĭg zôst′), *v.t.* 1. to empty of contents. 2. to create a vacuum in. 3. to draw out or drain off. 4. to use up completely. 5. to fatigue greatly. 6. to treat or study thoroughly. 7. to deprive wholly of useful or essential properties, etc. —*v.i.* 8. to pass out. —*n.* 9. *Mach.* a. the escape of the gases from the cylinder of an engine after expansion. b. the gases ejected. c. the parts of an engine through which the exhaust is ejected. —**ex·haust′i·ble**, *adj.* —**ex·haust′i·bil′i·ty**, *n.*

ex·haus·tion (ĭg zôs′chən), *n.* 1. act or process of exhausting. 2. state of being exhausted. 3. extreme weakness or fatigue.

ex·haus·tive (ĭg zôs′tĭv), *adj.* 1. comprehensive; thorough. 2. tending to exhaust or drain. —ex·haus'tive·ly, adv. —ex·haus'tive·ness, n.

ex·hib·it (ĭg zĭb'ĭt), v.t. 1. to offer or expose to view. 2. to display. —v.i. 3. to present something to view. —n. 4. an exhibiting. 5. that which is exhibited. —ex·hib'i·tor, ex·hib'it·er, n.

ex·hi·bi·tion (ĕk'sə bĭsh'ən), n. 1. an exhibiting. 2. a public display.

ex·hi·bi·tion·ism (ĕk'sə bĭsh'ə nĭz'əm), n. 1. a tendency to display one's abilities or to behave so as to attract attention. 2. Psychiatry. the attaining of sexual gratification by exhibiting and attracting attention to the genitals. —ex'hi·bi'tion·ist, n.

ex·hil·a·rate (ĭg zĭl'ə rāt'), v.t., -rated, -rating. to make cheerful or merry. —ex·hil'a·rat'ing, adj. —ex·hil'a·rat'ing·ly, adv. —ex·hil'a·ra'tion, n.

ex·hort (ĭg zôrt'), v.t., v.i. to urge, advise, or caution earnestly. —ex·hor'ta·tive, ex·hor'ta·to'ry, adj. —ex·hort'er, n.

ex·hor·ta·tion (ĕg'zôr tā'shən, ĕk'sôr-), n. 1. act of exhorting. 2. an utterance conveying urgent advice.

ex·hume (ĭg zūm', ĕks hūm'), v.t., -humed, -huming. to dig (esp. a body) out of the earth. —ex·hu·ma·tion (ĕks'hyŏŏ mā'shən), n.

ex·i·gen·cy (ĕk'sə jən sĭ), n., pl. -cies. 1. urgency. 2. (usually pl.) a need, demand, or requirement. 3. an emergency. Also, ex'i·gence. —ex'i·gent, adj.

ex·ig·u·ous (ĭg zĭg'yŏŏ əs, ĭk sĭg'-), adj. scanty; small. —ex·i·gu·i·ty (ĕk'sə gū'ə tĭ), n.

ex·ile (ĕg'zīl, ĕk'sīl), n., v., -iled, -iling. —n. 1. prolonged separation or expulsion from one's country or home. 2. any one separated or expelled from his country or home. 3. fact or state of such expulsion. —v.t. 4. to separate or expel from country, home, etc.

ex·ist (ĭg zĭst'), v.i. 1. to have actual being; be. 2. to live. 3. to occur. —ex·ist'ent, adj.

ex·ist·ence (ĭg zĭs'təns), n. 1. state or fact of existing; being. 2. life. 3. mode of existing. 4. all that exists. 5. something that exists.

ex·is·ten·tial·ism (ĕg'zĭs tĕn'shə lĭz'əm, ĕk'sĭs-), n. Philos. a recent movement which stresses personal decision in the face of a universe without purpose.

ex·it (ĕg'zĭt, ĕk'sĭt), n. 1. a way out. 2. a departure. —v. 3. he (or she, or the person named) goes out.

ex li·bris (ĕks lī'brĭs, lē'-), Latin. (on bookplates) from the library (of). Abbr.: ex lib.

Exod., Exodus.

ex·o·dus (ĕk'sə dəs), n. 1. a departure or emigration. 2. (often cap.) the departure of the Israelites from Egypt. 3. (cap.) the second book of the Old Testament.

ex of·fi·ci·o (ĕks ə fĭsh'ĭ ō'), by virtue of office or official position. —ex'-of·fi'ci·o', adj.

ex·og·e·nous (ĕks ŏj'ə nəs), adj. 1. derived externally. 2. Bot. having stems which grow by the addition of an annual layer of wood to the outside beneath the bark.

ex·on·er·ate (ĭg zŏn'ə rāt'), v.t., -ated, -ating. to clear, as from blame. —ex·on'er·a'tion, n.

ex·or·bi·tant (ĭg zôr'bə tənt), adj. exceeding the bounds of custom, propriety, or reason. —ex·or'bi·tance, n. —ex·or'bi·tant·ly, adv.

ex·or·cise (ĕk'sôr sīz'), v.t., -cised, -cising. to expel or deliver of (an evil spirit) by solemn ceremonies. Also, ex'or·cize'.

ex·or·cism (ĕk'sôr sĭz'əm), n. 1. act of exorcising. 2. the ceremony used. —ex'or·cist, n.

ex·or·di·um (ĭg zôr'dĭ əm, ĭk sôr'-), n., pl. -diums, -dia (-dĭ ə). 1. the beginning. 2. the introductory part of an oration, etc.

ex·ot·ic (ĭg zŏt'ĭk), adj. 1. of foreign origin or character. 2. Colloq. strikingly unusual. —n. 3. anything exotic. —ex·ot'i·cal·ly, adv.

exp., 1. expired. 2. export. 3. express.

ex·pand (ĭk spănd'), v.t., v.i. 1. to increase in extent, size, etc. 2. to spread out. 3. to express in fuller detail. —ex·pand'er, n.

ex·panse (ĭk spăns'), n. 1. wide extent of anything. 2. expansion.

ex·pan·si·ble (ĭk spăn'sə bəl), adj. capable of being expanded.

ex·pan·sion (ĭk spăn'shən), n. 1. act of expanding. 2. state of being expanded. 3. the amount of expanding. 4. an expanded portion or form.

ex·pan·sive (ĭk span'sĭv), adj. 1. capable of expanding. 2. extensive. 3. effusive; unrestrained. —ex·pan'sive·ly, adv. —ex·pan'sive·ness, n.

ex·pa·ti·ate (ĭk spā'shĭ āt'), v.i., -ated, -ating. to enlarge in discourse or writing. —ex·pa'ti·a'tion, n. —ex·pa'ti·a'tor, n.

ex·pa·tri·ate (v. ĕks pā'trĭ āt'; adj., n. ĕks pā'trĭ ĭt, -āt/-), v., -ated, -ating, adj., n. —v.t. 1. to exile. —adj. 2. exiled. —n. 3. an exile. —ex·pa'tri·a'tion, n.

ex·pect (ĭk spĕkt'), v.t. 1. to look forward to. 2. to look for with justification. 3. Colloq. to suppose.

ex·pect·an·cy (ĭk spĕk'tən sĭ), n., pl. -cies. 1. expectation. 2. something expected. Also, ex·pec'tance.

ex·pect·ant (ĭk spĕk'tənt), adj. 1. expecting. 2. expecting the birth of a child. 3. characterized by expectations. 4. expected. —n. 5. one who expects. —ex·pect'ant·ly, adv.

ex·pec·ta·tion (ĕk'spĕk tā'shən), n. 1. act of expecting. 2. state of expecting. 3. state of being expected. 4. expectant mental attitude. 5. something expected. 6. (often pl.) a good prospect.

ex·pec·to·rant (ĭk spĕk'tə rənt), adj. 1. promoting the secretion of fluid from the respiratory tract. —n. 2. an expectorant medicine.

ex·pec·to·rate (ĭk spĕk'tə rāt'), v.t., v.i., -rated, -rating. to expel (phlegm, etc.); spit. —ex·pec'to·ra'tion, n.

ex·pe·di·en·cy (ĭk spē'dĭ ən sĭ), n., pl. -cies. 1. quality of being expedient. 2. a regard for what is politic or advantageous. 3. something expedient. Also, ex·pe'di·ence.

ex·pe·di·ent (ĭk spē'dĭ ənt), adj. 1. suitable for the purpose. 2. conducive to advantage. 3. acting in accordance with expediency. —n. 4. a means to an end. 5. a means employed in an exigency. —ex·pe'di·ent·ly, adv.

ex·pe·dite (ĕks'pə dīt'), v., -dited, -diting, adj. —v.t. 1. to speed up. 2. to accomplish promptly. 3. to issue officially. —adj. 4. ready. —ex'pe·dit'er, n.

ex·pe·di·tion (ĕks'pə dĭsh'ən), n. 1. a journey for some specific purpose, as of exploration. 2. the body of persons or ships, etc., engaged in it. 3. promptness.

ex·pe·di·tion·ar·y (ĕks'pə dĭsh'ə nĕr'ĭ), adj. pertaining to or composing an expedition.

ex·pe·di·tious (ĕks'pə dĭsh'əs), adj. prompt. —ex'pe·di'tious·ly, adv.

ex·pel (ĭk spĕl'), v.t., -pelled, -pelling. 1. to force out or eject. 2. to cut off from membership or relations. —ex·pel'la·ble, adj. —ex·pel'ler, n.

ex·pend (ĭk spĕnd'), v.t. 1. to use up. 2. to spend. —ex·pend'a·ble, adj. —ex·pend'er, n.

ex·pend·i·ture (ĭk spĕn'dĭ chər), n. 1. act of expending. 2. expense.

ex·pense (ĭk spĕns'), n. 1. cost. 2. a cause of spending. 3. act of expending. 4. loss or injury due to any detracting cause.

ex·pen·sive (ĭk spĕn'sĭv), adj. entailing great expense; costly. —ex·pen'sive·ly, adv. —ex·pen'sive·ness, n.

ex·pe·ri·ence (ĭk spĭr'ĭ əns), n., v., -enced, -encing. —n. 1. a particular encounter or undergoing of something. 2. the process or fact of personally observing, encountering, or undergoing something. 3. knowledge gained thus. 4. Philos. all that is perceived, understood, and remembered. —v.t. 5. to have experience of.

ex·pe·ri·enced (ĭk spĭr'ĭ ənst), adj. 1. having had experience. 2. wise or skillful through experience.

ex·per·i·ment (n. ĭk spĕr'ə mənt; v. -mĕnt'), n. 1. a test for discovering something unknown or checking a principle, supposition, etc. 2. experimentation. —v.i. 3. to try or test in order to find something out. —ex·per'i·ment·er, n.

ex·per·i·men·tal (ĭk spĕr'ə mĕn'təl), adj. 1. pertaining to, derived from, or founded on experiment. 2. empirical. 3. tentative. —ex·per'i·men'tal·ly, adv.

ex·per·i·men·ta·tion (ĭk spĕr'ə mĕn tā'shən), n. act or process of making experiments.

ex·pert (n. ĕks'pûrt; adj. ĭk spûrt', ĕks'pûrt), n. 1. a person with special knowledge in some field. —adj. 2. skillful or skilled. 3. pertaining to, coming from, or characteristic of an expert. —ex·pert'ly, adv. —ex·pert'ness, n.

ex·pi·ate (ĕks'pĭ āt'), v.t., -ated, -ating. to

atone or make amends for. **—ex'pi·a·ble,** *adj.*
—ex'pi·a'tion, *n.* **—ex'pi·a'tor,** *n.*

ex·pi·a·to·ry (ĕks'pĭ ə tōr'ĭ), *adj.* able to make atonement or expiation.

ex·pi·ra·tion (ĕk'spə rā'shən), *n.* **1.** end; close. **2.** act of expiring. **—ex·pir·a·to·ry** (ĭk spīr'ə tōr'ĭ), *adj.*

ex·pire (ĭk spīr'), *v.*, **-pired, -piring. —v.i. 1.** to end; terminate. **2.** to die. **—v.t. 3.** to breathe out. **4.** to emit or eject. **—ex·pir'er,** *n.*

ex·plain (ĭk splān'), *v.t.* **1.** to make plain or clear. **2.** to assign a meaning to. **3.** to account for. **—v.i. 4.** to give an explanation. **—explain'a·ble,** *adj.* **—ex·plain'er,** *n.* **—ex·plan·a·to·ry** (ĭk splăn'ə tōr'ĭ), *adj.*

ex·pla·na·tion (ĕk'splə nā'shən), *n.* **1.** act or process of explaining. **2.** that which explains. **3.** a meaning.

ex·ple·tive (ĕks'plə tĭv), *adj.* **1.** added merely for completion, emphasis, etc. **—n. 2.** an expletive syllable, word, or phrase. **3.** an exclamatory oath. **—ex'ple·tive·ly,** *adv.*

ex·pli·ca·ble (ĕks'plĭ kə bəl), *adj.* capable of being explained.

ex·pli·cate (ĕks'plə kāt'), *v.t.*, **-cated, -cating. 1.** to develop. **2.** to explain. **—ex'pli·ca'tion,** *n.*

ex·plic·it (ĭk splĭs'ĭt), *adj.* **1.** clearly expressed; unequivocal. **2.** unreserved; outspoken. **—ex·plic'it·ly,** *adv.* **—ex·plic'it·ness,** *n.*

ex·plode (ĭk splōd'), *v.*, **-ploded, -ploding. —v.i. 1.** to burst or blow up violently with a loud report. **2.** to burst forth with laughter, violent speech, etc. **—v.t. 3.** to cause to explode. **4.** to discredit or disprove. **—ex·plod'er,** *n.*

ex·ploit[1] (ĕks'ploit, ĭk sploit'), *n.* a striking or notable deed; a feat; a spirited or heroic act.

ex·ploit[2] (ĭk sploit'), *v.t.* **1.** to turn to practical account. **2.** to use selfishly. **—ex·ploit'a·ble,** *adj.* **—ex'ploi·ta'tion,** *n.* **—ex·ploit·a·tive** (ĭk sploi'tə tĭv), *adj.* **—ex·ploit'er,** *n.*

ex·plore (ĭk splōr'), *v.t., v.i.*, **-plored, -ploring. 1.** to range over (a region, etc.) for the purpose of discovery. **2.** to scrutinize; examine. **—ex'plo·ra'tion,** *n.* **—ex·plor'a·to·ry, ex·plor'a·tive,** *adj.* **—ex·plor'er,** *n.*

ex·plo·sion (ĭk splō'zhən), *n.* **1.** act of exploding. **2.** the noise itself. **3.** a violent outburst of laughter, anger, etc.

ex·plo·sive (ĭk splō'sĭv), *adj.* **1.** tending or serving to explode. **2.** pertaining to or of the nature of an explosion. **—n. 3.** an explosive agent or substance, as dynamite. **—ex·plo'sive·ly,** *adv.* **—ex·plo'sive·ness,** *n.*

ex·po·nent (ĭk spō'nənt), *n.* **1.** one that expounds or explains. **2.** one who or that which stands as a representative or symbol of something. **3.** *Alg.* a symbol placed above and at the right of another to denote to what power the latter is to be raised, as in X^3. **—ex·po·nen·tial** (ĕks'pōnĕn'shəl), *adj.*

ex·port (*v.* ĭk spōrt', ĕks'pōrt; *n.* ĕks'pōrt), *v.t.* **1.** to send (commodities) to other countries. **—n. 2.** act of exporting. **3.** an article exported. **—ex·port'a·ble,** *adj.* **—ex'por·ta'tion,** *n.* **—ex·port'er,** *n.*

ex·pose (ĭk spōz'), *v.t.*, **-posed, -posing. 1.** to lay open (to danger, harm, etc.). **2.** to bare to the air, cold, etc. **3.** to display. **4.** to reveal or unmask. **5.** to subject, as to the action of something. **—ex·pos'er,** *n.*

ex·po·sé (ĕks'pō zā'), *n.* an exposure, as of something discreditable.

ex·po·si·tion (ĕks'pə zĭsh'ən), *n.* **1.** a public exhibition or show. **2.** explanation. **3.** display.

ex·pos·i·tor (ĭk spŏz'ə tər), *n.* one who expounds, or gives an exposition.

ex·pos·i·to·ry (ĭk spŏz'ə tōr'ĭ), *adj.* serving to expound or explain. Also, **ex·pos'i·tive.**

ex post fac·to (ĕks' pōst' făk'tō), *Latin.* retroactive.

ex·pos·tu·late (ĭk spŏs'chə lāt'), *v.i.*, **-lated, -lating.** to reason earnestly with a person against something he intends to do or has done. **—ex·pos'tu·la'tion,** *n.* **—ex·pos'tu·la'tor,** *n.* **—ex·pos·tu·la·to·ry** (ĭk spŏs'chə lə tōr'ĭ), *adj.*

ex·po·sure (ĭk spō'zhər), *n.* **1.** act of exposing. **2.** disclosure or unmasking. **3.** a laying open to view, action, influence, etc. **4.** *Photog.* act of subjecting a film, plate, or paper to actinic rays of light. **5.** state of being exposed. **6.** situation with regard to sunlight or wind.

ex·pound (ĭk spound'), *v.t.* **1.** to state in detail. **2.** to explain. **—ex·pound'er,** *n.*

ex·press (ĭk sprĕs'), *v.t.* **1.** to put into words.

2. to show or reveal. **3.** *U.S.* to send express. **4.** to press or squeeze out. **—adj. 5.** clearly indicated; definite. **6.** special. **7.** specially direct or fast, as a train, highway, etc. **—adv. 8.** by express. **9.** specially. **—n. 10.** an express train, elevator, etc. **11.** a messenger or a message specially sent. **12.** a system of sending parcels, money, etc. **13.** a company engaged in this business. **—ex·press'er,** *n.* **—ex·press'i·ble,** *adj.* **—ex·press'i·bly,** *adv.*

ex·press·age (ĭk sprĕs'ĭj), *n.* **1.** the business of transmitting parcels, money, etc., by express. **2.** the charge for such transmission.

ex·pres·sion (ĭk sprĕsh'ən), *n.* **1.** act of setting forth in words. **2.** a particular word or phrase. **3.** wording; phrasing. **4.** power of expressing in words. **5.** indication of feeling, spirit, etc., as on the face. **6.** a look or intonation as expressing feeling, etc. **7.** *Math.* a symbol or a combination of symbols serving to express something. **8.** act of pressing out. **—ex·pres'sion·less,** *adj.*

ex·pres·sive (ĭk sprĕs'ĭv), *adj.* **1.** serving to express. **2.** full of expression. **—ex·pres'sive·ly,** *adv.* **—ex·pres'sive·ness,** *n.*

ex·press·ly (ĭk sprĕs'lĭ), *adv.* **1.** explicitly. **2.** specially.

ex·press·man (ĭk sprĕs'mən), *n., pl.* **-men.** a delivery man for an express company.

ex·pro·pri·ate (ĕks prō'prĭ āt'), *v.t.*, **-ated, -ating.** to take or condemn, esp. for public use by the right of eminent domain. **—ex·pro'pri·a'tion,** *n.*

ex·pul·sion (ĭk spŭl'shən), *n.* **1.** act of driving out or expelling. **2.** state of being expelled. **—ex·pul·sive** (ĭk spŭl'sĭv), *adj.*

ex·punge (ĭk spŭnj'), *v.t.*, **-punged, -punging.** to erase; obliterate. **—ex·pung'er,** *n.*

ex·pur·gate (ĕks'pər gāt', ĭk spûr'gāt), *v.t.*, **-gated, -gating.** to amend by removing objectionable matter. **—ex'pur·ga'tion,** *n.*

ex·qui·site (ĕks'kwĭ zĭt, ĭk skwĭz'ĭt), *adj.* **1.** extremely beautiful, delicate, or charming. **2.** extraordinarily fine. **3.** intense, as pleasure, pain, etc. **—n. 4.** a dandy. **—ex'qui·site·ly,** *adv.* **—ex'qui·site·ness,** *n.*

ext., **1.** extension. **2.** extra.

ex·tant (ĕks'tənt, ĭk stănt'), *adj.* still existing; not destroyed or lost.

ex·tem·po·ra·ne·ous (ĭk stĕm'pə rā'nĭ əs), *adj.* done or spoken extempore; impromptu. Also, **ex·tem·po·rar·y** (ĭk stĕm'pə rĕr'ĭ). **—ex·tem'po·ra'ne·ous·ly,** *adv.* **—ex·tem'po·ra'ne·ous·ness,** *n.*

ex·tem·po·re (ĭk stĕm'pə rĭ), *adv.* **1.** without preparation; offhand. **2.** without notes. **—adj. 3.** extemporaneous.

ex·tem·po·rize (ĭk stĕm'pə rīz'), *v.i., v.t.*, **-rized, -rizing.** to speak, sing, or play extempore. **—ex·tem'po·ri·za'tion,** *n.* **—ex·tem'po·riz'er,** *n.*

ex·tend (ĭk stĕnd'), *v.t.* **1.** to stretch out. **2.** to offer or grant. **3.** to postpone (the payment of a debt). **—v.i. 4.** to be or become extended. **5.** to reach, as to a particular point. **6.** to increase in length, scope, etc. **—ex·tend'ed,** *adj.* **—ex·tend'i·ble,** *adj.*

ex·ten·si·ble (ĭk stĕn'sə bəl), *adj.* capable of being extended. **—ex·ten'si·bil'i·ty,** *n.*

ex·ten·sion (ĭk stĕn'shən), *n.* **1.** act of extending. **2.** state of being extended. **3.** that by which something is extended. **4.** something extended. **5.** extent. **6.** *Physics, etc.* that property of a body by which it occupies a portion of space. **—ex·ten'sion·al,** *adj.*

ex·ten·sive (ĭk stĕn'sĭv), *adj.* **1.** wide; broad. **2.** far-reaching; thorough. **—ex·ten'sive·ly,** *adv.* **—ex·ten'sive·ness,** *n.*

ex·ten·sor (ĭk stĕn'sər, -sôr), *n.* a muscle which extends or straightens a part of the body.

ex·tent (ĭk stĕnt'), *n.* **1.** the space or degree to which a thing extends. **2.** something extended; an extended space.

ex·ten·u·ate (ĭk stĕn'yŏŏ āt'), *v.t.*, **-ated, -ating.** to represent (fault, offense, etc.) as less serious. **—ex·ten'u·a'tion,** *n.*

ex·te·ri·or (ĭk stĭr'ĭ ər), *adj.* **1.** outer. **2.** situated or being outside. **—n. 3.** the outside. **4.** *(pl.)* externals. **—ex·te'ri·or·ly,** *adv.*

ex·ter·mi·nate (ĭk stûr'mə nāt'), *v.t.*, **-nated, -nating.** to destroy totally. **—ex·ter'mi·na'tion,** *n.* **—ex·ter'mi·na'tor,** *n.*

ex·ter·nal (ĭk stûr'nəl), *adj.* **1.** outer. **2.** to be applied to the outside of a body, as a remedy. **3.** situated or being outside of something. **4.** per-

taining to the outward appearance. **5.** foreign.
—*n.* **6.** the outside. **7.** that which is external.
8. (*pl.*) external features, etc. —**ex·ter'nal·ly**,
adv.

ex·tinct (Ĭk stĬngkt'), *adj.* **1.** extinguished or
inactive. **2.** obsolete. **3.** no longer existing.

ex·tinc·tion (Ĭk stĬngk'shən), *n.* **1.** act of extinguishing. **2.** fact of being extinguished. **3.**
suppression; abolition.

ex·tinc·tive (Ĭk stĬngk'tĬv), *adj.* tending or
serving to extinguish.

ex·tin·guish (Ĭk stĬng'gwĬsh), *v.t.* **1.** to put
out (a fire, light, etc.). **2.** to put an end to. **3.** to
obscure or eclipse. —**ex·tin'guish·a·ble**, *adj.*
—**ex·tin'guish·a·bly**, *adv.* —**ex·tin'guish·er**, *n.*
—**ex·tin'guish·ment**, *n.*

ex·tir·pate (ĕk'stər pāt', Ĭk stûr'pāt), *v.t.*,-**pat**-
ed, -**pating.** **1.** to remove or destroy totally.
2. to root up. —**ex'tir·pa'tion**, *n.*

ex·tol (Ĭk stōl', -stŏl'), *v.t.*, -**tolled**, -**tolling.** to
praise highly. Also, *esp. Brit.*, **ex·toll'.**

ex·tort (Ĭk stôrt'), *v.t.* to obtain (money, information, etc.) by force, torture, threat, or the like.
—**ex·tort'er**, *n.*

ex·tor·tion (Ĭk stôr'shən), *n.* **1.** act of extorting. **2.** anything extorted.

ex·tor·tion·a·ry (Ĭk stôr'shə nĕr'Ĭ), *adj.* characterized by or given to extortion.

ex·tor·tion·ate (Ĭk stôr'shən Ĭt), *adj.* characterized by extortion. —**ex·tor'tion·ate·ly**, *adv.*

ex·tor·tion·er (Ĭk stôr'shən ər), *n.* one who
practices extortion. Also, **ex·tor'tion·ist.**

ex·tra (ĕks'trə), *adj.* **1.** beyond what is usual,
expected, or necessary; additional. —*n.* **2.** something additional. **3.** a special edition of a newspaper. **4.** *Motion Pictures.* a person hired by the
day to play a minor part. —*adv.* **5.** in excess of
the usual or specified amount. **6.** unusually.

extra-, a prefix meaning "outside," "beyond,"
"besides," freely used as an English formative,
as in *extrajudicial.*

ex·tra·bold (ĕks'trə bōld'), *n.* *Print.* unusually heavy boldface.

ex·tra·cel·lu·lar (ĕks'trə sĕl'yə lər), *adj.* *Biol.*
outside a cell or cells.

ex·tract (*v.* Ĭk străkt'; *n.* ĕks'trăkt), *v.t.* **1.** to
draw out by force. **2.** to deduce. **3.** to derive or
obtain. **4.** to make excerpts from. —*n.* **5.** something extracted. **6.** an excerpt. **7.** a preparation
containing the active principles of a drug, etc.
—**ex·tract'a·ble**, **ex·tract'i·ble**, *adj.* —**ex-
trac'tive**, *adj.* —**ex·trac'tor**, *n.*

ex·trac·tion (Ĭk străk'shən), *n.* **1.** act of extracting. **2.** state or fact of being extracted.
3. descent. **4.** something extracted.

ex·tra·cur·ric·u·lar (ĕks'trə kə rĬk'yə lər),
adj. outside the regular curriculum.

ex·tra·dite (ĕks'trə dīt'), *v.t.*, -**dited**, -**diting.**
1. to give up (a fugitive or prisoner) to another
nation or authority. **2.** to obtain the extradition
of. —**ex'tra·dit'a·ble**, *adj.* —**ex·tra·di·tion**
(ĕks'trə dĬsh'ən), *n.*

ex·tra·ju·di·cial (ĕks'trə jōō dĬsh'əl), *adj.* outside of judicial proceedings; not valid in the action or
authority of a court. —**ex'tra·ju·di'cial·ly**, *adv.*

ex·tra·ne·ous (Ĭk strā'nĬ əs), *adj.* introduced
or coming from without; external. —**ex·tra'ne-
ous·ly**, *adv.* —**ex·tra'ne·ous·ness**, *n.*

ex·traor·di·nar·y (Ĭk strôr'də nĕr'Ĭ, ĕks'trə-
ôr'də nĕr'Ĭ), *adj.* **1.** beyond what is ordinary.
2. unusual; remarkable. **3.** special. —**ex·traor'-
di·nar·i·ly**, *adv.* —**ex·traor'di·nar·i·ness**, *n.*

ex·tra·sen·so·ry (ĕks'trə sĕn'sə rĬ), *adj.* outside of the normal sense perception.

ex·tra·ter·ri·to·ri·al (ĕks'trə tĕr'ə tōr'Ĭ əl),
adj. beyond local territorial jurisdiction.

ex·tra·ter·ri·to·ri·al·i·ty (ĕks'trə tĕr'ə tōr'-
Ĭ ăl'ə tĬ), *n.* the possession or exercise of political
rights by a foreign power within a state having
its own government.

ex·trav·a·gance (Ĭk străv'ə gəns), *n.* **1.** excessive expenditure or outlay of money. **2.** unrestrained excess.

ex·trav·a·gant (Ĭk străv'ə gənt), *adj.* **1.** going beyond prudence or necessity in expenditure;
wasteful. **2.** exorbitant. **3.** exceeding the bounds
of reason. —**ex·trav'a·gant·ly**, *adv.*

ex·trav·a·gan·za (Ĭk străv'ə găn'zə), *n.* an
elaborate, expensive musical or dramatic composition.

ex·treme (Ĭk strēm'), *adj.*, -**tremer**, -**tremest**,
n. —*adj.* **1.** farthest from the ordinary. **2.** exceedingly great. **3.** outermost. **4.** going to the

utmost lengths. **5.** last or final. —*n.* **6.** the
utmost or highest degree. **7.** the furthest or
utmost length, or an excessive length, beyond the
ordinary or average. —**ex·treme'ly**, *adv.* —**extreme'ness**, *n.*

extreme unction, *Rom. Cath. Ch.* a sacrament in which a dying person is anointed with oil
by a priest for the health of his soul and body.

ex·trem·ism (Ĭk strē'mĬz əm), *n.* tendency to
go to extremes. —**ex·trem'ist**, *n.*

ex·trem·i·ty (Ĭk strĕm'ə tĬ), *n.*, *pl.* -**ties.** **1.** the
extreme or terminal point, limit, or part. **2.** a
limb of the body. **3.** the end part of a limb, as a
hand or foot. **4.** a condition of extreme need,
distress, etc. **5.** the utmost degree. **6.** an extreme measure.

ex·tri·cate (ĕks'trə kāt'), *v.t.*, -**cated**, -**cating.**
to disentangle; free. —**ex·tri·ca·ble** (ĕks'trə kə-
bəl), *adj.* —**ex'tri·ca·bly**, *adv.* —**ex'tri·ca-
bil'i·ty**, *n.* —**ex'tri·ca'tion**, *n.*

ex·trin·sic (ĕks trĬn'sĬk), *adj.* **1.** unessential.
2. being or coming from without. —**ex·trin'si-
cal·ly**, *adv.*

ex·tro·ver·sion (ĕks'trō vûr'zhən, -shən), *n.*
Psychol. interest directed outward or to things
outside the self. —**ex'tro·vert'**, *n.*, *adj.*

ex·trude (Ĭk strōōd'), *v.*, -**truded**, -**truding.**
—*v.t.* **1.** to expel. —*v.i.* **2.** to protrude. —**ex-
tru·sion** (Ĭk strōō'zhən), *n.* —**ex·tru'sive**, *adj.*

ex·u·ber·ant (Ĭg zōō'bər ənt), *adj.* **1.** lavish.
2. luxuriant; superabundant. —**ex·u'ber·ance**,
ex·u'ber·an·cy, *n.* —**ex·u'ber·ant·ly**, *adv.*

ex·ude (Ĭg zōōd', Ĭk sōōd'), *v.i.*, *v.t.*, -**uded**, -**ud**-
ing. to ooze out. —**ex'u·da'tion**, *n.*

ex·ult (Ĭg zült'), *v.i.* to rejoice exceedingly; be
jubilant. —**ex'ul·ta'tion**, *n.* —**ex·ult'ing·ly**,
adv.

ex·ult·ant (Ĭg zül'tənt), *adj.* exulting; highly
elated; triumphant. —**ex·ult'ant·ly**, *adv.*

-ey, var. of **-y**, used esp. after *y*, as in *clayey.*

eye (ī), *n.*, *pl.* **eyes.** (*Archaic*) *v.*, **eyed**,
eying or **eyeing**. —*n.* **1.** the organ of sight.
2. power of seeing; appreciative or keen visual
perception. **3.** a look. **4.** close watch. **5.** regard,
view, or intention. **6.** something resembling the
eye. —*v.t.* **7.** to view. **8.** to watch narrowly.

eye·ball (ī'bôl'), *n.* the ball or globe of the eye.

eye·brow (ī'brou'), *n.* **1.** the ridge forming
the upper part of the orbit of the eye. **2.** the
fringe of hair growing upon it.

eye·glass (ī'glăs', ī'gläs'), *n.* **1.** (*pl.*) a pair of
lenses to correct a refractive error of the eye.
2. the eyepiece of an optical instrument.

eye·hole (ī'hōl'), *n.* **1.** eye socket. **2.** a hole to
look through, as in a mask or a curtain. **3.** a circular opening for the insertion of a pin, hook,
rope, etc.

eye·lash (ī'lăsh'), *n.* one of the short, curved
hairs on the edge of an eyelid.

eye·less (ī'lĬs), *adj.* **1.** lacking eyes. **2.** blind.

eye·let (ī'lĬt), *n.* **1.** a small hole for the passage
of a lace or cord. **2.** a metal ring for lining a small
hole.

eye·lid (ī'lĬd'), *n.* the movable lid of skin which
serves to cover and uncover the eyeball.

eye opener, *U.S.* **1.** something that causes
the eyes to open, as an enlightening or startling
disclosure or experience. **2.** *Colloq.* a drink of
liquor, esp. one taken early in the day.

eye·piece (ī'pēs'), *n.* (in an optical instrument)
the lens to which the eye is applied.

eye·shot (ī'shŏt'), *n.* range of vision.

eye·sight (ī'sīt'), *n.* **1.** the power of seeing.
2. action or fact of seeing.

eye·sore (ī'sōr'), *n.* an unpleasant sight.

eye·strain (ī'strān'), *n.* discomfort produced
in the eyes by excessive or faulty use.

eye·tooth (ī'tōōth'), *n.*, *pl.* -**teeth** (-tēth'). a
canine tooth, esp. of the upper jaw.

eye·wash (ī'wŏsh', ī'wôsh'), *n.* a lotion for
the eyes.

eye·wink·er (ī'wĬngk'ər), *n.* eyelash.

eye·wit·ness (ī'wĬt'nĬs), *n.* one who actually
beholds some act or occurrence.

ey·rie (âr'Ĭ, Ĭr'Ĭ), *n.* aerie. Also, **ey'ry.**

E·ze·ki·el (Ĭ zē'kĬ əl), *n.* **1.** fl. 6th century B.C.,
one of the Hebrew prophets. **2.** a book of the
Old Testament, written by him.

Ez·ra (ĕz'rə), *n.* **1.** fl. 5th century B.C., Hebrew
scribe and priest who with Nehemiah led the
revival of Judaism in Palestine. **2.** a short book
of chronicles of the Old Testament.

F

F, f (ĕf), *n., pl.* **F's or Fs, f's or fs.** **1.** the sixth letter of the English alphabet. **2.** *Music.* the fourth tone in the scale of C major.

F, *Chem.* fluorine.

F., **1.** Fahrenheit. **2.** February. **3.** Friday.

f., **1.** (*pl.* **ff.**) folio. **2.** following.

fa (fä), *n.* *Music.* the syllable used for the fourth tone of a scale.

Fa·bi·an (fā′bĭ ən). *adj.* avoiding battle; purposely delaying; cautiously dilatory.

fa·ble (fā′bəl), *n., v.,* **-bled, -bling.** —*n.* **1.** a short tale to teach a moral, often with animals as characters. **2.** a story not founded on fact. —*v.i.* **3.** to tell or write fables. **4.** to lie. —*v.t.* **5.** to invent (stories). —**fa′bler,** *n.*

fab·ric (făb′rĭk), *n.* **1.** a cloth made by weaving, knitting, or felting fibers. **2.** framework; structure. **3.** a building.

fab·ri·cate (făb′rə kāt′), *v.t.,* **-cated, -cating.** **1.** to construct. **2.** to make by assembling standard parts. **3.** to devise (a lie, etc.). **4.** to fake. —**fab′ri·ca′tion,** *n.* —**fab′ri·ca′tor,** *n.*

fab·u·lous (făb′yə ləs), *adj.* **1.** almost unbelievable. **2.** told about in fables. **3.** known about only through myths or legends. **4.** based on fables. —**fab′u·lous·ly,** *adv.* —**fab′u·lous·ness,** *n.*

fa·çade (fə säd′, fä-), *n.* the front part, esp. of a building.

face (fās), *n., v.,* **faced, facing.** —*n.* **1.** the front part of the head. **2.** presence. **3.** a look or expression. **4.** *Colloq.* impudence. **5.** outward appearance. **6.** prestige. **7.** the amount specified in a bill or note. **8.** surface. **9.** the side or part of a side upon which the use of a thing depends. **10.** the front. **11.** *Print.* the working surface of a type, plate, etc. —*v.t.* **12.** to look or front toward. **13.** to confront. **14.** to oppose confidently or defiantly. **15.** to cover with a different material. —*v.i.* **16.** to be turned or placed. —**face′a·ble,** *adj.* —**face′less,** *adj.*

fac·et (făs′ĭt), *n., v.,* **-eted, -eting** or (*esp. Brit.*) **-etted, -etting.** —*n.* **1.** one of the polished surfaces of a cut gem. **2.** aspect. —*v.t.* **3.** to cut facets on.

fa·ce·tious (fə sē′shəs), *adj.* amusing; humorous. —**fa·ce′tious·ly,** *adv.* —**fa·ce′tious·ness,** *n.*

face value, par or apparent value.

fa·cial (fā′shəl), *adj.* **1.** of the face. **2.** for the face. —*n.* **3.** *Colloq.* a massage or treatment for the face. —**fa′cial·ly,** *adv.*

fac·ile (făs′ĭl), *adj.* **1.** moving, working, etc., with ease. **2.** easily done, used, etc. **3.** affable, agreeable, or complaisant. —**fac′ile·ly,** *adv.* —**fac′ile·ness,** *n.*

fa·cil·i·tate (fə sĭl′ə tāt′), *v.t.,* **-tated, -tating.** **1.** to make easier. **2.** to assist. —**fa·cil′i·ta′tion,** *n.*

fa·cil·i·ty (fə sĭl′ə tĭ), *n., pl.* **-ties.** **1.** something that makes easier the performance of any action. **2.** ease. **3.** dexterity.

fac·ing (fā′sĭng), *n.* **1.** a covering in front, for ornament, protection, etc. **2.** material applied on the edge of a garment for ornament or protection.

fac·sim·i·le (făk sĭm′ə lĭ, -lē′), *n., adj., v.,* **-led, -leing.** —*n.* **1.** an exact copy. —*adj.* **2.** of a facsimile. **3.** producing facsimiles. —*v.t.* **4.** to reproduce in facsimile.

fact (făkt), *n.* **1.** truth; reality. **2.** something known to have happened. **3.** something said to be true.

fac·tion (făk′shən), *n.* **1.** a small group of people within a larger group. **2.** party strife or intrigue. —**fac′tion·al,** *adj.*

fac·tious (făk′shəs), *adj.* **1.** inclined to act for party purposes. **2.** caused by party spirit or strife. —**fac′tious·ly,** *adv.* —**fac′tious·ness,** *n.*

fac·tor (făk′tər), *n.* **1.** one of the elements that contribute to bring about any given result. **2.**

Math. one of two or more numbers, algebraic expressions, or the like, which when multiplied together produce a given product. **3.** an agent. —*v.t.* **4.** *Math.* to express (a quantity) as a product of two or more quantities of like kind. —**fac′tor·ship′,** *n.*

fac·to·ry (făk′tə rĭ), *n., pl.* **-ries.** a building or group of buildings where goods are manufactured.

fac·to·tum (făk tō′təm), *n.* one employed to do all kinds of work for another.

fac·tu·al (făk′chŏŏ əl), *adj.* pertaining to or based on fact; real. —**fac′tu·al·ly,** *adv.*

fac·ul·ty (făk′əl tĭ), *n., pl.* **-ties.** **1.** an ability for a particular kind of action. **2.** one of the powers of the mind or body. **3.** *Educ.* **a.** one of the departments of learning in a university. **b.** the teaching body in any of these departments. **c.** the entire teaching and administrative force of a university.

fad (făd), *n.* a temporary fashion, etc. —**fad′dish,** *adj.* —**fad′dist,** *n.*

fade (fād), *v.,* **faded, fading.** —*v.i.* **1.** to lose freshness, strength, or health. **2.** to lose brightness or vividness. **3.** to disappear gradually. —*v.t.* **4.** to cause to fade. —**fad′a·ble,** *adj.*

fa·ër·ie (fā′ə rĭ, fâr′ĭ), *n.* **1.** fairyland. **2.** *Archaic.* a fairy. —*adj.* **3.** *Archaic.* fairy. Also, **fa′ër·y.**

Faer·oe Islands (fâr′ō), a group of 21 islands in the N Atlantic between Great Britain and Iceland. 29,178 pop.; 540 sq. mi. *Cap.:* Torshaven.

fag (făg), *v.,* **fagged, fagging,** *n.* —*v.t.* **1.** to tire by labor; exhaust. —*n.* **2.** a drudge. **3.** *Chiefly Brit. Slang.* a cigarette.

fag end, the last part of something.

fag·ot (făg′ət), *n.* **1.** a bundle of sticks, twigs, etc., bound together, used for fuel, etc. —*v.t.* **2.** to bind into a fagot. Also, *Brit.,* **fag′got.**

fag·ot·ing (făg′ət ĭng), *n.* a type of decorative joining used to combine cloth or lace.

Fahr·en·heit (fâr′ən hīt′), *adj.* denoting or pertaining to a thermometric scale in which the melting point of ice is 32 degrees above zero, and the boiling point of water 212 degrees above zero.

fail (fāl), *v.i.* **1.** to be unsuccessful or lacking in action, supply, detail, or result. **2.** to dwindle or die away. **3.** to become weaker. **4.** to become insolvent or bankrupt. —*v.t.* **5.** to neglect to perform or observe. **6.** to prove of no use or help to. **7.** to declare (a person) unsuccessful in a test, course of study, etc. —*n.* **8.** failure as to performance, etc.

fail·ing (fā′lĭng), *n.* **1.** failure. **2.** a defect; weakness. —*prep.* **3.** in the absence or default of.

faille (fil, fāl), *n.* a soft, transversely ribbed silk or rayon fabric.

fail·ure (fāl′yər), *n.* **1.** act of failing; lack of success. **2.** nonperformance of something required. **3.** insufficiency. **4.** loss of strength, vigor, etc. **5.** condition of being bankrupt. **6.** one who or that which proves unsuccessful.

fain (fān), *adv.* **1.** *Poetic.* gladly. —*adj.* **2.** *Rare.* willing. **3.** *Archaic. or Dial.* eager.

faint (fānt), *adj.* **1.** lacking brightness, loudness, strength, etc. **2.** feeble. **3.** feeling weak, dizzy, or exhausted. **4.** lacking courage. —*v.i.* **5.** to lose consciousness temporarily. —*n.* **6.** temporary loss of consciousness. —**faint′ly,** *adv.* —**faint′ness,** *n.*

faint-heart·ed (fānt′här′tĭd), *adj.* lacking courage. —**faint′-heart′ed·ly,** *adv.*

fair[1] (fâr), *adj.* **1.** free from dishonesty or injustice. **2.** legitimately sought, done, etc. **3.** moderately good, large, or satisfactory. **4.** likely; promising. **5.** *Meteorol.* **a.** bright; sunny. **b.** not stormy. **6.** free from blemish. **7.** clear; easy to read. **8.** of a light hue. **9.** attractive. **10.** courteous. —*adv.* **11.** in a fair manner. —**fair′ish,** *adj.* —**fair′ness,** *n.*

fair[2] (fâr), *n.* **1.** a competitive exhibition of farm products, livestock, etc. **2.** an exhibition and sale of articles to raise money, often for some charitable purpose.

fair ball, *Baseball.* any batted ball other than a foul.

fair·ly (fâr/lĭ), *adv.* **1.** justly; impartially. **2.** moderately. **3.** actually. **4.** legitimately. **5.** clearly.

fair-spo·ken (fâr/spō/kən), *adj.* courteous, civil, or plausible in speech; smooth-tongued.

fair·way (fâr/wā/), *n.* **1.** an unobstructed way. **2.** *Golf.* that part of the links between tees and putting greens where the grass is kept short.

fair·y (fâr/ĭ), *n.*, *pl.* **fairies**, *adj.* —*n.* **1.** one of a class of diminutive supernatural beings, having magical powers for good or evil in human affairs. **2.** a male homosexual. —*adj.* **3.** having to do with fairies. **4.** fairylike. —**fair/y·like/**, *adj.*

fair·y·land (fâr/ĭ lănd/), *n.* **1.** the realm of fairies. **2.** any enchanting region.

faith (fāth), *n.* **1.** confidence or trust. **2.** belief in the doctrines of religion. **3.** a system of religious belief. **4.** loyalty or fidelity.

faith·ful (fāth/fəl), *adj.* **1.** strict in the performance of duty. **2.** true to one's promises, etc. **3.** full of or showing loyalty or fidelity. **4.** reliable. **5.** accurate. —*n.* **6.** the body of loyal members of any party or religion. —**faith/ful·ly**, *adv.* —**faith/ful·ness**, *n.*

faith·less (fāth/lĭs), *adj.* **1.** not adhering to allegiance, promises, vows, or duty. **2.** that cannot be trusted. **3.** without belief. —**faith/less·ly**, *adv.* —**faith/less·ness**, *n.*

fake (fāk), *v.*, **faked**, **faking**, *n.*, *adj. Colloq.* —*v.t., v.i.* **1.** to make (something specious, deceptive, or fraudulent). **2.** to pretend. —*n.* **3.** something faked. **4.** one who fakes. —*adj.* **5.** designed to deceive or cheat. —**fak/er**, *n.*

fa·kir (fə kĭr/, fā/kər), *n.* a Mohammedan or Hindu ascetic or monk. Also, **fa·keer/.**

Fa·lange (fā/lănj), *n.* the fascist party in power in Spain since the Civil War of 1936–39. —**Fa·lan·gist** (fə lăn/jĭst), *n.*

fal·cate (făl/kāt), *adj.* hooked; curved.

fal·chion (fôl/chən, -shən), *n.* a broad, short sword having a curved edge.

fal·con (fôl/kən, fô/kən), *n.* **1.** any of various diurnal birds of prey of the family including the **peregrine falcon,** which has long, pointed wings and a notched bill. **2.** any of various hawks used in falconry.

fal·con·ry (fôl/kən rĭ, fô/-), *n.* **1.** the art of training falcons to attack wild fowl or game. **2.** the sport of hawking. —**fal/con·er**, *n.*

Falk·land Islands (fôk/lənd), a group of about 200 islands in the S Atlantic, ab. 300 mi. E of the Strait of Magellan: a British crown colony. 2239 pop.; 4618 sq. mi. *Cap.*: Stanley.

fall (fôl), *v.*, **fell**, **fallen**, **falling**. —*v.i.* **1.** to descend; drop. **2.** to come down suddenly from a standing or erect position. **3.** to hang down. **4.** to be cast down. **5.** to succumb. **6.** to lose high position, character, etc. **7.** to drop down wounded or dead. **8.** to pass into some condition or relation. **9.** to become. **10.** to come by chance. **11.** to occur; happen. **12.** to become less or lower. **13. fall back,** to give way; retreat. **14. fall in, a.** to take one's place in line, as a soldier. **b.** to meet. **15. fall out, a.** to drop out of one's place in line, as a soldier. **b.** to quarrel. **16. fall through,** to fail. —*v.t.* **17.** to fell. —*n.* **18.** act of falling; descent. **19.** the quantity that descends. **20.** *Chiefly U.S.* autumn. **21.** (*usually pl.*) a cataract or waterfall. **22.** lapse into sin. **23.** surrender or capture.

fal·la·cious (fə lā/shəs), *adj.* **1.** deceptive; misleading. **2.** logically unsound. —**fal·la/cious·ly**, *adv.* —**fal·la/cious·ness**, *n.*

fal·la·cy (făl/ə sĭ), *n.*, *pl.* **-cies. 1.** a deceptive, misleading, or false notion, belief, etc. **2.** an unsound argument.

fall·en (fô/lən), *v.* **1.** pp. of **fall.** —*adj.* **2.** that has dropped. **3.** prostrate. **4.** degraded. **5.** overthrown. **6.** dead.

fall guy, *U.S. Slang.* a scapegoat.

fal·li·ble (făl/ə bəl), *adj.* **1.** liable to err. **2.** liable to be false. —**fal/li·bil/i·ty**, **fal/li·ble·ness**, *n.* —**fal/li·bly**, *adv.*

falling star, an incandescent meteor.

Fal·lo·pi·an tubes (fə lō/pĭ ən), a pair of slender ducts from the body cavity to the uterus.

fal·low (făl/ō), *adj.* **1.** plowed and left unseeded. —*n.* **2.** land unseeded after plowing. —*v.t.* **3.** to make (land) fallow.

fallow deer, a Eurasian deer with yellowish coat.

Fall River, a seaport in SE Massachusetts. 115,428.

false (fôls), *adj.*, **falser**, **falsest. 1.** not true or correct. **2.** uttering what is untrue. **3.** deceitful; faithless. **4.** deceptive. **5.** not genuine. **6.** substitute or supplementary. **7.** inaccurate in pitch. —**false/ly**, *adv.* —**false/ness**, *n.*

false·hood (fôls/hŏŏd), *n.* **1.** lack of conformity to truth or fact. **2.** an untrue idea, belief, etc. **3.** a lie. **4.** act of lying.

Fallow deer
(3 ft. high at the shoulder)

fal·set·to (fôl sĕt/ō), *n.*, *pl.* **-tos**, *adj.*, *adv.* —*n.* **1.** an unnaturally high-pitched voice, esp. in a man. —*adj.* **2.** singing in a falsetto. —*adv.* **3.** in a falsetto.

fal·si·fy (fôl/sə fī/), *v.*, **-fied**, **-fying.** —*v.t.* **1.** to make false. **2.** to alter fraudulently. **3.** to misrepresent. **4.** to disprove. —*v.i.* **5.** to make false statements. —**fal·si·fi·ca·tion** (fôl/sə fə kā/shən), *n.* —**fal/si·fi/er**, *n.*

fal·si·ty (fôl/sə tĭ), *n.*, *pl.* **-ties. 1.** quality of being false. **2.** a falsehood.

falt·boat (fält/bōt/), *n.* a folding boat.

fal·ter (fôl/tər), *v.i.* **1.** to hesitate or waver. **2.** to speak hesitatingly. **3.** to become unsteady. —*v.t.* **4.** to utter hesitatingly. —*n.* **5.** act of faltering. **6.** a faltering sound. —**fal/ter·ing·ly**, *adv.*

fame (fām), *n.*, *v.*, **famed**, **faming.** —*n.* **1.** widespread favorable reputation. **2.** reputation. —*v.t.* **3.** to make famous. —**fame/less**, *adj.*

famed (fāmd), *adj.* famous.

fa·mil·iar (fə mĭl/yər), *adj.* **1.** commonly known or seen. **2.** well-acquainted. **3.** easy; informal. **4.** closely intimate. —*n.* **5.** a familiar friend or associate. —**fa·mil/iar·ly**, *adv.*

fa·mil·i·ar·i·ty (fə mĭl/ĭ ăr/ə tĭ), *n.*, *pl.* **-ties. 1.** close acquaintance. **2.** undue intimacy. **3.** informality.

fa·mil·iar·ize (fə mĭl/yə rīz/), *v.t.*, **-ized**, **-izing. 1.** to make familiarly acquainted, as with something. **2.** to make well-known. —**fa·mil/iar·i·za/tion**, *n.*

fam·i·ly (făm/ə lĭ, făm/lĭ), *n.*, *pl.* **-lies. 1.** parents and their children. **2.** one's children collectively. **3.** any group of close relatives. **4.** all those persons descended from a common progenitor. **5.** *Chiefly Brit.* descent. **6.** *Biol.* the usual major subdivision of an order or suborder, commonly comprising a plurality of genera.

fam·ine (făm/ĭn), *n.* **1.** extreme scarcity, esp. of food. **2.** starvation.

fam·ish (făm/ĭsh), *v.t., v.i.* **1.** to starve. **2.** to starve to death. —**fam/ished**, *adj.*

fa·mous (fā/məs), *adj.* **1.** renowned; well-known. **2.** *Colloq.* excellent. —**fa/mous·ly**, *adv.* —**fa/mous·ness**, *n.*

fan[1] (făn), *n.*, *v.*, **fanned**, **fanning.** —*n.* **1.** any device for causing a current of air by the movement of a broad surface. —*v.t., v.i.* **2.** to move (the air) with a fan. **3.** to cause air to blow upon, as from a fan. **4.** to stir to activity. **5.** *Agric.* to winnow. **6.** *Baseball.* to strike out.

fan[2] (făn), *n. Colloq.* a devotee.

fa·nat·ic (fə năt/ĭk), *n.* **1.** a person with an extreme and unreasoning enthusiasm or zeal, esp. in religious matters. —*adj.* **2.** fanatical. —**fa·nat/i·cism** (fə năt/ə sĭz/əm), *n.*

fa·nat·i·cal (fə năt/ə kəl), *adj.* **1.** actuated or characterized by an extreme, unreasoning enthusiasm or zeal, esp. in religious matters. **2.** pertaining to or characteristic of a fanatic. —**fa·nat/i·cal·ly**, *adv.*

fan·ci·er (făn/sĭ ər), *n.* a person having an interest in something, as dogs, etc.

fan·ci·ful (făn/sĭ fəl), *adj.* **1.** quaint or odd in appearance. **2.** imaginary; unreal. **3.** whimsical. —**fan/ci·ful·ly**, *adv.* —**fan/ci·ful·ness**, *n.*

fan·cy (făn/sĭ), *n.*, *pl.* **-cies**, *adj.*, **-cier**, **-ciest**, *v.*, **-cied**, **-cying.** —*n.* **1.** imagination. **2.** the faculty of creating illustrative or decorative imagery. **3.** a hallucination. **4.** a caprice; whim. **5.** capricious preference. **6.** taste. —*adj.* **7.** of superior quality. **8.** ornamental. **9.** imaginative.

—*v.t.* **10.** to picture to oneself. **11.** to believe without being sure. **12.** to like.

fan·cy-free (făn′sĭ frē′), *adj.* free from any influence, esp. love.

fan·dan·go (făn dăng′gō), *n., pl.* **-gos.** a lively Spanish dance in triple time.

fane (fān), *n. Archaic or Poetic.* temple.

fan·fare (făn′fâr), *n.* **1.** a flourish played on trumpets or the like. **2.** an ostentatious flourish or parade.

fang (făng), *n.* **1.** one of the long teeth of a snake, by which venom is injected. **2.** a canine tooth. **3.** the root of a tooth. —**fanged** (făngd), *adj.*

fan·light (făn′lĭt′), *n.* a fan-shaped or other window above a door or other opening.

fan·tail (făn′tāl′), *n.* **1.** a tail or part shaped like a fan. **2.** a fancy breed of domestic pigeons with a fan-shaped tail.

fan-tan (făn′tăn′), *n.* **1.** a kind of card game. **2.** a Chinese gambling game using coins or counters.

fan·ta·si·a (făn tā′zhĭ ə, -zhə, făn′tə zē′ə), *n. Music.* **1.** a composition in fanciful or irregular style. **2.** a potpourri of well-known airs.

fan·tas·tic (făn tăs′tĭk), *adj.* **1.** odd, quaint, or grotesque. **2.** fanciful. **3.** imaginary. Also, **fan·tas′ti·cal.** —**fan·tas′ti·cal·ly,** *adv.*

fan·ta·sy (făn′tə sĭ, -zĭ), *n., pl.* **-sies.** **1.** imagination. **2.** a mental image, esp. when grotesque. **3.** *Psychol.* an imaginative sequence fulfilling a psychological need; a daydream. **4.** a hallucination.

far (fär), *adv., adj.,* **farther, farthest.** —*adv.* **1.** at or to a great distance. **2.** remote in time, degree, desire, etc. **3.** very much. **4. by far,** very much. **5. in so far,** to such an extent. —*adj.* **6.** at or to a great distance. **7.** more distant of the two.

far·ad (făr′əd, -ăd), *n. Elect.* a unit of capacitance equal to the change in the number of coulombs of charge per volt of change of potential.

Far·a·day (făr′ə dĭ, -dā′), *n.* **Michael,** 1791–1867, British physicist and chemist.

far·a·way (fär′ə wā′), *adj.* **1.** distant; remote. **2.** abstracted or dreamy, as a look.

farce (färs), *n., v.,* **farced, farcing.** —*n.* **1.** a play, light in tone, full of absurd situations. **2.** a ridiculous sham. —*v.t.* **3.** to season with wit.

far·ci·cal (fär′sə kəl), *adj.* ludicrous; absurd. —**far′ci·cal·i·ty,** *n.* —**far′ci·cal·ly,** *adv.*

fare (fâr), *n., v.,* **fared, faring.** —*n.* **1.** the price of conveyance or passage. **2.** a paying passenger. **3.** food. —*v.i.* **4.** to eat. **5.** to get along; do. **6.** to go. —**far′er,** *n.*

Far East, the countries of E and SE Asia: China, Japan, Korea, Siam, etc.

fare·well (fâr′wĕl′), *interj.* **1.** good-by. —*n.* **2.** an expression of good wishes at parting. **3.** leave-taking. —*adj.* **4.** parting.

far-fetched (fär′fĕcht′), *adj.* remotely connected; forced; strained.

far-flung (fär′flŭng′), *adj.* flung or extending over a great distance.

Far·go (fär′gō), *n.* a city in SE North Dakota. 32,580.

fa·ri·na (fə rē′nə), *n.* flour or meal made from cereal grains, cooked as cereal, etc.

far·i·na·ceous (făr′ə nā′shəs), *adj.* **1.** consisting or made of flour or meal. **2.** mealy.

farm (färm), *n.* **1.** a tract of land devoted to agriculture or the like. —*v.t.* **2.** to cultivate (land). **3.** to let or lease. —*v.i.* **4.** to operate a farm. —**farm′er,** *n.*

farm·house (färm′hous′), *n.* a house on a farm.

farm·ing (fär′mĭng), *n.* **1.** the operation of a farm. —*adj.* **2.** of, for, or pertaining to farms.

farm·stead (färm′stĕd′), *n. Chiefly Brit.* a farm with its buildings.

farm·yard (färm′yärd′), *n.* a yard surrounded by or connected with farm buildings.

far·o (fâr′ō), *n. Cards.* a gambling game.

far-off (fär′ôf′, -ŏf′), *adj.* distant; remote.

Fa·rouk I (fä rook′), born 1920, king of Egypt since 1936.

far·ra·go (fə rā′gō, -rä′-), *n., pl.* **-goes.** a confused mixture; a hodgepodge; a medley.

far-reach·ing (fär′rē′chĭng), *adj.* extending far in influence, effect, etc.

far·ri·er (făr′ĭ ər), *n. Brit.* **1.** a blacksmith. **2.** a doctor for horses. —**far′ri·er·y,** *n.*

far·row (făr′ō), *n.* **1.** a litter of pigs. —*v.t., v.i.* **2.** (of swine) to bring forth (young).

far-see·ing (fär′sē′ĭng), *adj.* **1.** having foresight. **2.** far-sighted.

far-sight·ed (fär′sī′tĭd), *adj.* **1.** seeing to a great distance. **2.** seeing objects at a distance more clearly than those near at hand. **3.** foreseeing future results wisely. —**far′-sight′ed·ly,** *adv.* —**far′-sight′ed·ness,** *n.*

far·ther (fär′thər), *compar. of* **far.** —*adv.* **1.** at or to a greater distance, point, or extent. **2.** additionally. —*adj.* **3.** more distant. **4.** additional.

far·ther·most (fär′thər mōst′, -məst), *adj.* most distant or remote; farthest.

far·thest (fär′thĭst), *superl. of* **far.** —*adj.* **1.** most distant or remote. **2.** longest. —*adv.* **3.** to or at the greatest distance.

far·thing (fär′thĭng), *n.* an English coin of bronze, worth one fourth of a penny, or about half a U.S. cent.

far·thin·gale (fär′thĭng gāl′), *n.* a kind of hoop skirt worn in the 16th and 17th centuries.

fas·ces (făs′ēz), *n.pl., sing.* **fascis** (făs′ĭs). a bundle of rods containing an ax with the blade projecting, borne before Roman magistrates as an emblem of official power.

fas·ci·cle (făs′ə kəl), *n.* **1.** a bundle. **2.** a part of a printed work. —**fas′ci·cled,** *adj.*

fas·ci·nate (făs′ə nāt′), *v.t.* **-nated, -nating.** to attract and hold irresistibly. —**fas′ci·nat′ing·ly,** *adv.* —**fas′ci·na′tor,** *n.*

fas·ci·na·tion (făs′ə nā′shən), *n.* **1.** act of fascinating. **2.** state of being fascinated. **3.** fascinating quality; charm.

fas·cism (făsh′ĭz əm), *n.* a governmental system with strong centralized power, permitting no opposition, controlling all affairs of the nation, emphasizing an aggressive nationalism, and anti-communist. —**fas′cist,** *n., adj.*

fash·ion (făsh′ən), *n.* **1.** a prevailing style of dress, etiquette, etc. **2.** fashionable people collectively. **3.** manner; way. **4.** a kind; sort. —*v.t.* **5.** to form; make. **6.** to adapt. —**fash′ion·er,** *n.*

fash·ion·a·ble (făsh′ən ə bəl), *adj.* **1.** conforming to the fashion. **2.** of or patronized by the world of fashion. —*n.* **3.** a fashionable person. —**fash′ion·a·ble·ness,** *n.* —**fash′ion·a·bly,** *adv.*

fast¹ (făst, fäst), *adj.* **1.** quick; swift; rapid. **2.** indicating a time in advance of the correct time, as a clock. **3.** extremely active or unrestrained. **4.** resistant. **5.** firmly in place; securely attached, closed, or held. **6.** firm in adherence. **7.** permanent; lasting. —*adv.* **8.** tightly. **9.** soundly. **10.** quickly, swiftly, or rapidly. **11.** in quick succession. **12.** in an energetic or dissipated way.

fast² (făst, fäst), *v.i.* **1.** to abstain from all food. **2.** to eat sparingly or of certain foods. —*n.* **3.** a fasting. **4.** a day or period of fasting.

fas·ten (făs′ən, fäs′-), *v.t.* **1.** to fix firmly or securely in place; attach securely. **2.** to make secure. **3.** to enclose securely. **4.** to attach by any connecting agency. **5.** to direct (the eyes, thoughts, etc.) intently. —*v.i.* **6.** to become fast, fixed, or firm. **7.** to seize. —**fas′ten·er,** *n.*

fas·ten·ing (făs′ən ĭng, fäs′-), *n.* something that fastens, as a lock or clasp.

fas·tid·i·ous (făs tĭd′ĭ əs), *adj.* hard to please; excessively critical. —**fas·tid′i·ous·ly,** *adv.* —**fas·tid′i·ous·ness,** *n.*

fast·ness (făst′nĭs, fäst′-), *n.* **1.** a secure or fortified place. **2.** state of being fast.

fat (făt), *adj.,* **fatter, fattest,** *n., v.,* **fatted, fatting.** —*adj.* **1.** fleshy; plump. **2.** of, like, or containing fat. **3.** profitable; advantageous. **4.** thick. **5.** plentiful. **6.** dull; stupid. —*n.* **7.** a white or yellowish, greasy substance forming the chief part of the adipose tissue of animals and also found in plants. **8.** the richest or best part of anything. —*v.t., v.i.* **9.** to make or become fat.

fa·tal (fā′təl), *adj.* **1.** causing death or ruin. **2.** decisively important. —**fa′tal·ly,** *adv.* —**fa′tal·ness,** *n.*

fa·tal·ism (fā′tə lĭz′əm), *n.* the doctrine that all events are subject to inevitable predetermination. —**fa′tal·ist,** *n.* —**fa′tal·is′tic,** *adj.* —**fa′tal·is·ti·cal·ly,** *adv.*

fa·tal·i·ty (fā tăl′ə tĭ, fə-), *n., pl.* **-ties.** **1.** a disaster resulting in death; calamity. **2.** deadliness. **3.** predetermined liability to disaster. **4.** the fate or destiny of a person or thing.

fate (fāt), *n., v.,* **fated, fating.** —*n.* **1.** fortune; destiny. **2.** a divine decree or a fixed sentence by which the order of things is prescribed. **3.** death, destruction, or ruin. —*v.t.* **4.** to destine.

fat·ed (fā′tĭd), *adj.* destined.

fate·ful (fāt′fəl), *adj.* **1.** decisively important. **2.** deadly or disastrous. **3.** controlled by irresistible destiny. **4.** prophetic; ominous. —**fate′ful·ly**, *adv.* —**fate′ful·ness**, *n.*

Fates (fāts), *n.pl. Gk. and Roman Myth.* the three goddesses of destiny.

fat·head (făt′hĕd′), *n.* a stupid person.

fa·ther (fä′thər), *n.* **1.** a male parent. **2.** any male ancestor. **3.** a fatherly protector or provider. **4.** one of the leading men of a city, etc. **5.** a person or thing who originates or establishes something. **6.** (*cap.*) God. **7.** any of the chief early Christian writers. **8.** a priest. —*v.t.* **9.** to beget. **10.** to originate. —**fa′ther·hood′**, *n.* —**fa′ther·less**, *n.*

fa·ther-in-law (fä′thər ĭn lô′), *n.*, *pl.* **fathers-in-law.** the father of one's spouse.

fa·ther·land (fä′thər lănd′), *n.* **1.** one's native country. **2.** the land of one's ancestors.

fa·ther·ly (fä′thər lĭ), *adj.* **1.** of, like, or befitting a father. —*adv.* **2.** in the manner of a father. —**fa′ther·li·ness**, *n.*

fath·om (făth′əm), *n.*, *pl.* **fathoms**, (*esp. collectively*) **fathom**, *v.* —*n.* **1.** *Chiefly Naut.* a unit of length equal to 6 feet. —*v.t.* **2.** to measure the depth of. **3.** to understand thoroughly. —**fath′om·a·ble**, *adj.* —**fath′om·er**, *n.* —**fath′om·less**, *adj.*

fa·tigue (fə tēg′), *n.*, *v.*, **-tigued**, **-tiguing**, *adj.* —*n.* **1.** weariness from exertion. **2.** *Mil.* a. Also, **fatigue duty.** nonmilitary labor by soldiers, such as cleaning up an area. b. (*pl.*) work clothes. —*v.t.* **3.** to weary or exhaust. —*adj.* **4.** of or pertaining to fatigue. —**fa·tigue′less**, *adj.*

Fat·i·ma (făt′ĭ mə, fä′tə mä′), *n.* A.D. c606–632, daughter of Mohammed.

fat·ling (făt′lĭng), *n.* a young animal, as a calf or a lamb, fattened for slaughter.

fat·ness (făt′nĭs), *n.* **1.** condition of being fat. **2.** corpulence. **3.** oiliness. **4.** richness; fertility.

fat·ten (făt′ən), *v.t.*, *v.i.* to make or grow fat. —**fat′ten·er**, *n.*

fat·ty (făt′ĭ), *adj.*, **-tier**, **-tiest**. consisting of, containing, or resembling fat. —**fat′ti·ness**, *n.*

fa·tu·i·ty (fə tū′ə tĭ, -tōō′-), *n.*, *pl.* **-ties**. **1.** foolishness. **2.** something foolish.

fat·u·ous (făch′ōō əs), *adj.* **1.** foolish; silly. **2.** unreal; illusory. —**fat′u·ous·ly**, *adv.* —**fat′u·ous·ness**, *n.*

fau·ces (fô′sēz), *n.pl. Anat.* the cavity at the back of the mouth, leading into the pharynx. —**fau·cal** (fô′kəl), **fau·cial** (fô′shəl), *adj.*

fau·cet (fô′sĭt), *n.* any device for controlling the flow of liquid from a pipe or the like.

fault (fôlt), *n.* **1.** a defect; flaw. **2.** an error. **3.** a misdeed. **4.** *Geol.* a break in a body of rock or of a vein, with dislocation along the plane of fracture. **5.** to a fault, excessively. —*v.i.* **6.** *Geol.* to undergo a fault. —*v.t.* **7.** *Geol.* to cause a fault in. —**fault′less**, *adj.* —**fault′less·ly**, *adv.*

fault·find·ing (fôlt′fīn′dĭng), *n.* **1.** act of pointing out faults; carping. —*adj.* **2.** given to finding fault. —**fault′find′er**, *n.*

fault·y (fôl′tĭ), *adj.*, **faultier**, **faultiest**. having faults or defects. —**fault′i·ly**, *adv.* —**fault′i·ness**, *n.*

faun (fôn), *n. Rom. Myth.* one of a class of rural deities represented as men with the ears, horns, tail, and legs of a goat.

fau·na (fô′nə), *n.* the animals of a given region or period, collectively. —**fau′nal**, *adj.*

Faust (foust), *n.* the character in a famous German story who sold his soul to the devil for power or knowledge.

faux pas (fō pä′), *pl.* **faux pas** (fō päz′). a slip in manners or conduct.

fa·vor (fā′vər), *n.* **1.** a kind act. **2.** kindness; kind approval. **3.** state of being held in regard. **4.** a gift bestowed as a token of good will, love, etc. **5. in favor of**, a. in support of. b. to the advantage of. —*v.t.* **6.** to regard with favor or preference. **7.** to oblige. **8.** to facilitate. **9.** *Colloq.* to resemble. Also, *Brit.*, **fa′vour**. —**fa′vor·er**, *n.* —**fa′vor·ing·ly**, *adv.*

fa·vor·a·ble (fā′vər ə bəl), *adj.* **1.** affording aid or advantage. **2.** inclined to aid or approve. **3.** granting what is desired. **4.** promising well. —**fa′vor·a·ble·ness**, *n.* —**fa′vor·a·bly**, *adv.*

fa·vored (fā′vərd), *adj.* **1.** regarded or treated with favor. **2.** enjoying special advantages. **3.** of specified appearance.

fa·vor·ite (fā′vər ĭt), *n.* **1.** a person or thing

regarded with special favor or preference. —*adj.* **2.** regarded with particular favor or preference.

fa·vor·it·ism (fā′vər ə tĭz′əm), *n.* **1.** the favoring of one person or group over others. **2.** state of being a favorite.

fawn¹ (fôn), *n.* **1.** a young deer. —*adj.* **2.** light yellowish-brown.

fawn² (fôn), *v.i.* to seek notice or favor by servile demeanor. —**fawn′er**, *n.* —**fawn′ing·ly**, *adv.*

fay (fā), *n.* a fairy.

faze (fāz), *v.t.*, **fazed**, **fazing**. *U.S. Colloq.* to disturb; discomfit; daunt.

FBI, Federal Bureau of Investigation.

FCC, Federal Communications Commission.

Fe, *Chem.* (L *ferrum*) iron.

fe·al·ty (fē′əl tĭ), *n.*, *pl.* **-ties**. fidelity, esp. to a lord, usually sworn by a vassal.

fear (fĭr), *n.* **1.** a painful feeling of impending danger, evil, trouble, etc. **2.** anxiety; solicitude. **3.** reverential awe. —*v.t.*, *v.i.* **4.** to be afraid (of). **5.** to have reverential awe (of). —**fear′er**, *n.* —**fear′less**, *adj.* —**fear′less·ly**, *adv.* —**fear′less·ness**, *n.*

fear·ful (fĭr′fəl), *adj.* **1.** causing fear. **2.** feeling fear. **3.** showing or caused by fear. —**fear′ful·ly**, *adv.* —**fear′ful·ness**, *n.*

fear·some (fĭr′səm), *adj.* **1.** causing fear. **2.** afraid; timid. —**fear′some·ly**, *adv.* —**fear′some·ness**, *n.*

fea·si·ble (fē′zə bəl), *adj.* **1.** capable of being done or effected. **2.** suitable. **3.** likely. —**fea′si·bil′i·ty**, **fea′si·ble·ness**, *n.* —**fea′si·bly**, *adv.*

feast (fēst), *n.* **1.** a periodical celebration of some event, etc. **2.** a sumptuous entertainment or meal, esp. one for many guests. —*v.i.* **3.** to have, or partake of, a feast. **4.** to dwell with delight. —*v.t.* **5.** to provide with a feast. **6.** to delight. —**feast′er**, *n.*

feat (fēt), *n.* a noteworthy act or achievement, displaying boldness, skill, etc.

feath·er (fĕth′ər), *n.* **1.** one of the epidermal appendages which together constitute the plumage of birds. **2.** plumage. **3.** condition, as of health, spirits, etc. **4.** kind or character. —*v.t.* **5.** to provide or cover with feathers. **6.** *Rowing.* to turn (an oar) after a stroke so that the blade becomes nearly horizontal. —**feath′ered**, *adj.* —**feath′er·less**, *adj.* —**feath′er·like′**, *adj.*

feath·er·brain (fĕth′ər brān′), *n.* a giddy or weak-minded person.

feath·er·weight (fĕth′ər wāt′), *n.* a boxer or other contestant weighing between 118 and 126 lbs.

feath·er·y (fĕth′ə rĭ), *adj.* **1.** covered with feathers. **2.** light; airy.

fea·ture (fē′chər), *n.*, *v.*, **-tured**, **-turing**. —*n.* **1.** any part of the face, as the nose, chin, etc. **2.** (*pl.*) the face. **3.** a prominent part. **4.** the main picture in a movie program. **5.** a special article, column, cartoon, etc., in a newspaper or magazine. —*v.t.* **6.** to be a feature of. **7.** to give prominence to. —**fea′ture·less**, *adj.*

fea·tured (fē′chərd), *adj.* given prominence.

Feb., February.

feb·ri·fuge (fĕb′rə fūj′), *adj.* **1.** serving to dispel or reduce fever. —*n.* **2.** a febrifuge medicine or agent. —**fe·brif·u·gal** (fĭ brĭf′yə gəl, fĕb′rə fū′gəl), *adj.*

fe·brile (fē′brəl, fĕb′rəl), *adj.* feverish.

Feb·ru·ar·y (fĕb′rōō ĕr′ĭ), *n.* the second month of the year, containing ordinarily 28 days, in leap years 29.

fe·ces (fē′sēz), *n. pl.* **1.** excrement. **2.** dregs; sediment. —**fe·cal** (fē′kəl), *adj.*

fe·cund (fē′kŭnd, fĕk′ŭnd), *adj.* prolific; fruitful; productive. —**fe·cun·di·ty** (fĭ kŭn′də tĭ), *n.*

fed·er·al (fĕd′ər əl), *adj.* **1.** of or pertaining to a league between nations or states. **2.** of or pertaining to a central government distinct from state and city governments. **3.** (*cap.*) (in the Civil War) pertaining to or supporting the Union government. **4.** (*cap.*) relating to, or adhering to, the support of the Constitution. —*n.* **5.** an advocate of federation or federalism. **6.** (*cap.*) an adherent of the Union government during the Civil War. —**fed′er·al·ly**, *adv.*

fed·er·al·ism (fĕd′ər ə lĭz′əm), *n.* **1.** the federal principle of government. **2.** (*cap.*) the principles of the Federalist party.

fed·er·al·ist (fĕd′ər əl ĭst), *n.* **1.** an advocate of federalism. **2.** (*cap.*) a member or supporter of the Federalist party. —*adj.* **3.** of federalism or the Federalists.

Federalist party, *U.S. Hist.* **1.** a political group that favored the adoption of the Constitution. **2.** a political party advocating a strong central government. Also, **Federal party.**

fed·er·al·ize (fĕd'ər ə līz'), *v.t.*, **-ized, -izing.** to unite in a federal union.

fed·er·ate (*v.* fĕd'ə rāt'; *adj.* fĕd'ər ĭt), *v.,* **-ated, -ating,** *adj.* —*v.t., v.i.* **1.** to unite in a league. **2.** to organize on a federal basis. —*adj.* **3.** federated; allied.

fed·er·a·tion (fĕd'ə rā'shən), *n.* **1.** act of federating. **2.** a league or confederacy. —**fed'er·a'tive,** *adj.*

fe·do·ra (fĭ dōr'ə), *n.* a soft felt hat for a man.

fee (fē), *n., v.,* **feed, feeing.** —*n.* **1.** a payment for services. **2.** a sum paid for a privilege. **3.** a tip. **4.** ownership. **5.** *Law.* an estate of inheritance in land. —*v.t.* **6.** to give a fee to.

fee·ble (fē'bəl), *adj.,* **-bler, -blest. 1.** weak. **2.** ineffective. —**fee'ble·ness,** *n.* —**fee'blish,** *adj.* —**fee'bly,** *adv.*

fee·ble-mind·ed (fē'bəl mīn'dĭd), *adj.* lacking the normal mental powers. —**fee'ble-mind'ed·ness,** *n.*

feed (fēd), *v.,* **fed, feeding,** *n.* —*v.t.* **1.** to give food to. **2.** to provide with any requisite materials. **3.** to satisfy; gratify. —*v.i.* **4.** to eat. **5.** to subsist. —*n.* **6.** food, esp. for cattle, horses, etc. **7.** *Colloq.* **a** meal. **8.** a feeding mechanism. —**feed'er,** *n.*

feel (fēl), *v.,* **felt, feeling,** *n.* —*v.t.* **1.** to perceive or examine by touch. **2.** to have any sensation. **3.** to find (one's way) by touch. **4.** to be or become conscious of. **5.** to be emotionally affected by. **6.** to experience. **7.** to have a sensation, impression, or conviction of. —*v.i.* **8.** to have perception by touch. **9.** to grope. **10.** to have emotions. **11.** to be consciously, in emotion, opinion, etc. **12.** to have compassion. **13.** to have a sensation or experience of being. —*n.* **14.** a quality perceived by touching. **15.** a vague mental impression or feeling. **16.** the sense of touch.

feel·er (fē'lər), *n.* **1.** one that feels. **2.** a proposal, hint, etc., designed to bring out the opinions or purposes of others. **3.** *Zool.* an organ of touch.

feel·ing (fē'lĭng), *n.* **1.** the function or the power of perceiving by touch. **2.** a particular sensation of this kind. **3.** a consciousness or impression. **4.** an emotion. **5.** opinion. **6.** (*pl.*) sensibilities. —*adj.* **7.** that feels. **8.** emotional or sympathetic. —**feel'ing·ly,** *adv.*

feet (fēt), *n.* pl. of **foot.**

feign (fān), *v.t., v.i.* **1.** to invent fictitiously. **2.** to pretend. —**feigned,** *adj.* —**feign'er,** *n.* —**feign'ing·ly,** *adv.*

feint (fānt), *n.* **1.** a deliberately deceptive movement. **2.** a feigned appearance. —*v.i.* **3.** to make a feint.

feld·spar (fĕld'spär', fĕl'-), *n.* any of a group of minerals, principally aluminum silicates, characterized by two cleavages at nearly right angles.

fe·lic·i·tate (fĭ lĭs'ə tāt'), *v.t.,* **-tated, -tating.** to congratulate. —**fe·lic'i·ta'tion,** *n.*

fe·lic·i·tous (fĭ lĭs'ə təs), *adj.* apt or appropriate, as action or expression. —**fe·lic'i·tous·ly,** *adv.* —**fe·lic'i·tous·ness,** *n.*

fe·lic·i·ty (fĭ lĭs'ə tĭ), *n., pl.* **-ties. 1.** happiness. **2.** a source of happiness. **3.** a skillful faculty. **4.** an instance or display of this.

fe·line (fē'līn), *adj.* **1.** belonging or pertaining to the cat family, which includes domestic cats, lions, tigers, etc. **2.** catlike. **3.** sly; stealthy. —*n.* **4.** an animal of the cat family. —**fe'line·ly,** *adv.*

fell[1] (fĕl), *v.t.* **1.** to knock, strike, or cut down. **2.** to finish (a seam) by sewing the edge down flat. —**fell'er,** *n.*

fell[2] (fĕl), *adj.* **1.** cruel. **2.** deadly.

fell[3] (fĕl), *n.* the skin or hide of an animal.

fel·lah (fĕl'ə), *n.* a native peasant or laborer in Egypt, Syria, etc.

fel·loe (fĕl'ō), *n.* the rim of a wheel, into which spokes are inserted.

Wheel
F, Felloe; S, Spokes; H, Hub

fel·low (fĕl'ō), *n.* **1.** a man; boy. **2.** *Colloq.* beau. **3.** a companion. **4.** an equal; peer. **5.** one of a pair. **6.** a graduate student of a university to whom an allowance is granted. **7.** a member of any of certain learned societies. —*adj.* **8.** belonging to the same class or group.

fel·low·ship (fĕl'ō shĭp'), *n.* **1.** companionship. **2.** community of interest, feeling, etc. **3.** an association of persons having similar tastes, interests, etc. **4.** the position of a fellow of a university, etc., or the sum of money he receives.

fellow traveler, a sympathetic nonmember of a political party.

fel·on[1] (fĕl'ən), *n.* **1.** one who has committed a felony. —*adj.* **2.** wicked; malicious.

fel·on[2] (fĕl'ən), *n.* an inflammation of the deeper tissues of a finger or toe, usually near the nail.

fel·o·ny (fĕl'ə nĭ), *n., pl.* **-nies.** *Law.* any of various serious offenses, as murder, burglary, etc. —**fe·lo·ni·ous** (fĭ lō'nĭ əs), *adj.* —**fe·lo'ni·ous·ly,** *adv.*

felt (fĕlt), *n.* **1.** a nonwoven fabric of wool, fur, or hair, matted together by pressure. —*adj.* **2.** pertaining to or made of felt. —*v.t.* **3.** to make into felt; mat or press together.

fem., feminine.

fe·male (fē'māl), *n.* **1.** a person or animal of the sex which brings forth young. **2.** *Bot.* a pistillate plant. —*adj.* **3.** belonging to the sex which brings forth young. **4.** pertaining to or characteristic of this sex; feminine. **5.** *Bot.* pistillate. **6.** *Mech.* designating some part, etc., into which a corresponding part fits.

fem·i·nine (fĕm'ə nĭn), *adj.* **1.** pertaining to a woman. **2.** like a woman; gentle. **3.** effeminate. **4.** belonging to the female sex. **5.** *Gram.* denoting or pertaining to one of the genders to which many nouns denoting females belong. —*n.* **6.** *Gram.* **a.** the feminine gender. **b.** a noun of that gender. —**fem'i·nine·ly,** *adv.* —**fem·i·nin·i·ty** (fĕm'ə nĭn'ə tĭ), **fem'i·nine·ness,** *n.*

fe·mur (fē'mər), *n., pl.* **femurs, femora** (fĕm'ə rə). *Anat.* the thigh bone. —**fem·o·ral** (fĕm'ə rəl), *adj.*

fen (fĕn), *n.* *Brit.* boggy land; marsh.

fence (fĕns), *n., v.,* **fenced, fencing.** —*n.* **1.** an enclosure around or along a field, yard, etc. **2.** on the fence, *U.S. Colloq.* undecided or neutral. **3.** a person who receives and disposes of stolen goods. —*v.t.* **4.** to enclose or separate by some barrier. —*v.i.* **5.** to use a sword, foil, etc., in defense and attack. **6.** to parry arguments. —**fenc'er,** *n.*

fenc·ing (fĕn'sĭng), *n.* **1.** act, practice, or art of using a sword, foil, etc., for defense and attack. **2.** fences collectively. **3.** material for fences.

fend (fĕnd), *v.t.* **1.** to ward off. —*v.i.* **2.** to make defense. **3.** to parry. **4.** *Colloq.* to provide.

fend·er (fĕn'dər), *n.* **1.** the sheet metal part over the road wheel of an automobile, etc. **2.** a device, as a metal bar, on an automobile, ship, etc., for cushioning the shock of a collision.

Fe·ni·an (fē'nĭ ən, fēn'yən), *n.* a member of an Irish revolutionary organization, founded in New York in 1858, which had for its aim the establishment of an independent Irish republic.

fen·nel (fĕn'əl), *n.* an umbelliferous plant having yellow flowers and bearing aromatic fruits used in cookery and medicine.

fe·ral (fĭr'əl), *adj.* wild or untamed.

fer-de-lance (fĕr də läns'), *n.* a large, very venomous snake of tropical America.

Fer·di·nand V (fûr'dĭ nănd'), 1452–1516, Spanish king who commissioned Columbus to make his voyages.

fer·ment (*n.* fûr'mĕnt; *v.* fər mĕnt'), *n.* **1.** any of various agents or substances which cause fermentation, as yeasts, molds, pepsin, etc. **2.** fermentation. **3.** agitation; tumult. —*v.t.* **4.** to act upon as a ferment. **5.** to agitate; excite. —*v.i.* **6.** to undergo fermentation. **7.** to seethe with agitation or excitement.

fer·men·ta·tion (fûr'mĕn tā'shən), *n.* **1.** act or process of fermenting. **2.** *Chem.* a change, as effervescence or decomposition, brought about by a ferment. **3.** agitation; excitement.

fern (fûrn), *n.* *Bot.* any of an order of nonflowering plants that have delicate, feathery, spore-bearing leaves.

fern·er·y (fûr'nə rĭ), *n., pl.* **-eries.** a place in which ferns are grown for ornament.

fe·ro·cious (fə rō'shəs), *adj.* savagely fierce; violently cruel. —**fe·ro'cious·ly,** *adv.* —**fe·roc·i·ty** (fə rŏs'ə tĭ), **fe·ro'cious·ness,** *n.*

fer·ret (fĕr'ĭt), *n.* **1.** a domesticated form of the polecat, used in hunting rabbits, rats, etc. —*v.t., v.i.* **2.** to drive out by or hunt with ferrets. **3.** to search. —**fer'ret·er,** *n.*

fer·ric (fĕr′ĭk), *adj. Chem.* of or containing iron, esp. in the trivalent state (Fe+3).

Fer·ris wheel (fĕr′ĭs), an amusement device consisting of a rotating upright wheel with seats suspended around its rim.

fer·ro·con·crete (fĕr′ō kŏn′krēt, -kŏn krēt′), *n.* reinforced concrete.

fer·rous (fĕr′əs), *adj. Chem.* of or containing iron, esp. in the divalent state (Fe+2).

fer·ru·gi·nous (fĕ rōō′jə nəs), *adj.* iron-bearing.

fer·ry (fĕr′ĭ), *n., pl.* **-ries,** *v.,* **-ried, -rying.** —*n.* 1. a place where ferryboats operate. 2. a ferryboat. —*v.t., v.i.* 3. to carry or pass over a river, etc., in a boat.

fer·ry·boat (fĕr′ĭ bōt′), *n.* a boat used to convey passengers, etc., across a river or the like.

fer·ry·man (fĕr′ĭ mən), *n., pl.* **-men.** one who owns or runs a ferry.

fer·tile (fûr′təl or, *esp. Brit.,* -tīl), *adj.* 1. producing abundantly; prolific, as in crops, ideas, etc. 2. *Biol.* a. fertilized, as an egg. b. capable of producing eggs, etc.

fer·til·i·ty (fər tĭl′ə tĭ), *n.* 1. fertile state or quality. 2. ability to produce offspring.

fer·ti·lize (fûr′tə līz′), *v.t.,* **-lized, -lizing.** 1. *Biol.* a. to render (an egg, etc.) capable of development by union with the male element. b. to impregnate. 2. to make fertile or enrich (soil, etc.). —**fer′ti·liz′a·ble,** *adj.* —**fer′ti·li·za′tion,** *n.*

fer·ti·liz·er (fûr′tə lī′zər), *n.* any material used to fertilize the soil, esp. a manure.

fer·ule (fĕr′əl, -ōōl), *n., v.,* **-uled, -uling.** —*n.* 1. a rod for the punishment of children. —*v.t.* 2. to punish with a ferule.

fer·vent (fûr′vənt), *adj.* 1. having or showing great warmth and earnestness of feeling. 2. hot; glowing. —**fer′ven·cy, fer′vent·ness,** *n.* —**fer′vent·ly,** *adv.*

fer·vid (fûr′vĭd), *adj.* 1. heated or vehement in spirit, enthusiasm, etc. 2. glowing; hot. —**fer′vid·ly,** *adv.* —**fer′vid·ness,** *n.*

fer·vor (fûr′vər), *n.* 1. great warmth and earnestness of feeling. 2. intense heat.

fess (fĕs), *n. Her.* a wide horizontal band across the middle of an escutcheon. Also, **fesse.**

fes·tal (fĕs′təl), *adj.* pertaining to or befitting a feast or gala occasion. —**fes′tal·ly,** *adv.*

fes·ter (fĕs′tər), *v.i.* 1. to generate pus. 2. to rankle, as a feeling of resentment. —*v.t.* 3. to cause to fester. —*n.* 4. a small purulent sore.

fes·ti·val (fĕs′tə vəl), *n.* 1. a periodic religious or other feast. 2. any course of festive activities. —*adj.* 3. of, pertaining to, or befitting a feast or holiday.

fes·tive (fĕs′tĭv), *adj.* pertaining to or suitable for a feast or festival. —**fes′tive·ly,** *adv.*

fes·tiv·i·ty (fĕs tĭv′ə tĭ), *n., pl.* **-ties.** 1. a festive celebration. 2. (*pl.*) festive proceedings. 3. festive gaiety or pleasure.

fes·toon (fĕs tōōn′), *n.* 1. a chain of flowers, etc., suspended in a curve between two points. —*v.t.* 2. to adorn with festoons.

fe·tal (fē′təl), *adj.* of, pertaining to, or having the character of a fetus.

fetch (fĕch), *v.t.* 1. to go and bring. 2. to bring (a price, etc.). 3. *Colloq.* to take. 4. to take (a breath). 5. to deal (a blow, etc.). —*v.i.* 6. to go and bring things. —*n.* 7. act of fetching.

fetch·ing (fĕch′ĭng), *adj. Colloq.* charming; captivating. —**fetch′ing·ly,** *adv.*

fete (fāt), *n., v.,* **feted, feting.** —*n.* 1. a feast or festival. 2. a holiday. —*v.t.* 3. to honor with a fete. Also, **fête.**

fet·id (fĕt′ĭd, fē′tĭd), *adj.* having an offensive odor; stinking. —**fet′id·ly,** *adv.*

fet·ish (fĕt′ĭsh, fē′tĭsh), *n.* 1. an inanimate object regarded with awe as the embodiment or habitation of a potent spirit or as having magical potency. 2. any object of blind reverence. Also, **fe′tich.** —**fe′tish-like′,** *adj.*

fe·tish·ism (fĕt′ĭsh ĭz′əm, fē′tĭsh-), *n.* 1. belief in or use of fetishes. 2. *Psychiatry.* the compulsive use of some inanimate object in attaining sexual gratification, such as a lock of hair, etc. Also, **fe′tich·ism′.**

fet·lock (fĕt′lŏk), *n.* 1. a part of a horse's leg behind the joint between the cannon bone and the great pastern bone, and bearing a tuft of hair. 2. this tuft of hair.

fet·ter (fĕt′ər), *n.* 1. a shackle on the feet. 2. (*usually pl.*) anything that restrains. —*v.t.* 3. to put fetters upon. 4. to restrain.

fet·tle (fĕt′əl), *n.* state; condition.

fe·tus (fē′təs), *n.* the young of an animal in the womb or egg, esp. in its later stages.

feud (fūd), *n.* 1. a bitter, continuous hostility. 2. a quarrel.

feu·dal (fū′dəl), *adj.* of or pertaining to the feudal system. —**feu′dal·ly,** *adv.*

feu·dal·ism (fū′də lĭz′əm), *n.* the feudal system or its principles and practices.

feudal system, the system in Europe during the Middle Ages, based on the holding of lands in return for services to a lord by the vassal.

feu·da·to·ry (fū′də tōr′ĭ), *n., pl.* **-ries.** a vassal in the feudal system.

fe·ver (fē′vər), *n.* 1. a morbid condition of the body characterized by undue rise of temperature, quickening of the pulse, and disturbance of various bodily functions. 2. intense nervous excitement. —*v.t.* 3. to affect with fever.

fe·ver·ish (fē′vər ĭsh), *adj.* 1. excited or restless. 2. having fever. 3. pertaining to, of the nature of, or resembling fever. —**fe′ver·ish·ly,** *adv.* —**fe′ver·ish·ness,** *n.*

fever sore, a cold sore.

few (fū), *adj., fewer, fewest, n.* —*adj.* 1. not many. —*n.* 2. **the few,** the minority. 3. **quite a few,** *Colloq.* a fairly large number. —**few′ness,** *n.*

fez (fĕz), *n., pl.* **fezzes.** a felt cap, usually red, with a long black tassel, formerly the national headdress of the Turks.

ff., and the following (pages, verses, etc.).

fi·an·cé (fē′än sā′, fē än′sā), *n.* a man engaged to be married. —**fi′an·cée′,** *n. fem.*

fi·as·co (fĭ ăs′kō), *n., pl.* **-cos, -coes.** an ignominious failure.

fi·at (fī′ət, -ăt), *n.* an authoritative decree, sanction, or order.

Turkish **fez**

fiat money, *U.S.* paper currency made legal tender but not convertible into coin.

fib (fĭb), *n., v.,* **fibbed, fibbing.** —*n.* 1. a trivial falsehood. —*v.i.* 2. to tell a fib. —**fib′ber,** *n.*

fi·ber (fī′bər), *n.* 1. a fine threadlike piece, as of cotton. 2. a slender filament. 3. matter composed of filaments. 4. character. 5. a slender threadlike root of a plant. Also, **fi′bre.**

fi·ber·board (fī′bər bōrd′), *n.* 1. a building material made of wood or other plant fibers compressed and cemented into rigid sheets. 2. a sheet of fiberboard.

fi·ber·glas (fī′bər glăs′, -gläs′), *n.* 1. a material consisting of extremely fine filaments of glass which are combined in yarn and woven into fabrics, or are used in masses as an insulator. 2. (*cap.*) a trademark for this material.

fi·bril (fī′brəl), *n.* a small or fine fiber.

fi·brin (fī′brĭn), *n.* a white, tough, strongly elastic, fibrous protein, formed in the coagulation of blood.

fi·broid (fī′broid), *adj.* 1. resembling fiber or fibrous tissue. 2. composed of fibers.

fi·brous (fī′brəs), *adj.* containing, consisting of, or resembling fibers.

fib·u·la (fĭb′yə lə), *n., pl.* **-lae** (-lē), **-las.** *Anat.* the outer and thinner of the two bones from the knee to the ankle.

-fication, a suffix of nouns of action or state corresponding to verbs ending in -*fy,* as in *deification.*

fich·u (fĭsh′ōō), *n.* a kerchief worn about the neck by women, with the ends drawn together on the breast.

fick·le (fĭk′əl), *adj.* likely to change from caprice, irresolution, etc. —**fick′le·ness,** *n.*

fic·tion (fĭk′shən), *n.* 1. the branch of literature comprising works of imaginative narration, as novels or tales. 2. something feigned, invented, or imagined. —**fic′tion·al,** *adj.*

fic·ti·tious (fĭk tĭsh′əs), *adj.* 1. false; not genuine. 2. imaginatively produced or set forth. —**fic·ti′tious·ly,** *adv.* —**fic·ti′tious·ness,** *n.*

fid·dle (fĭd′əl), *n., v.,* **-dled, -dling.** —*n.* 1. a violin (now chiefly in familiar or contemptuous use). —*v.i., v.t.* 2. *Colloq.* to play on the fiddle. 3. to trifle. —**fid′dler,** *n.*

fid·dle·stick (fĭd′əl stĭk′), *n.* a fiddle bow.

fid·dle·sticks (fĭd′əl stĭks′), *interj.* nonsense!

fi·del·i·ty (fĭ dĕl′ə tĭ, fə-), *n., pl.* **-ties.** 1. strict observance of promises, duties, etc. 2. loyalty. 3. conjugal faithfulness. 4. accuracy.

fidg·et (fĭj'ĭt), v.i. 1. to move about restlessly or impatiently. —v.t. 2. to make uneasy. —n. 3. (often pl.) restlessness or uneasiness. —fidg'-et·y, adj.

fi·du·ci·ar·y (fĭ dū'shĭ ĕr'ĭ, -dōō'-), adj., n., pl. -aries. —adj. 1. Law. of or pertaining to the relation between a trustee of property and his principal. 2. depending on public confidence for value. —n. 3. Law. a person to whom property is entrusted to hold or manage for another.

fie (fī). interj. an exclamation expressing disgust, disapprobation, etc.

fief (fēf), n. a tenure of land subject to feudal obligations.

field (fēld), n. 1. a piece of open ground, esp. one suitable for pasture or tillage. 2. Sports. a. a piece of ground devoted to sports. b. all the contestants. 3. Baseball. that part of the ground on which the fielders play. 4. Mil. the scene of active military operations. 5. an expanse of anything. 6. any region characterized by a particular feature or product. 7. the surface of a canvas, shield, etc., on which something is portrayed. 8. a sphere or range of activity, interest, etc. 9. Physics. a region of space influenced by some agent. —v.t., v.i. 10. Baseball, etc. to stop, or catch, and throw (the ball) as a fielder. —adj. 11. of or occurring on a field.

field·er (fēl'dər), n. Baseball. any of the players stationed around and outside the diamond.

field glass, a compact binocular telescope.

field goal, Football. a goal earned by a kick from the field.

Field·ing (fēl'dĭng), n. Henry, 1707–54, British novelist.

field marshal, an officer of the highest military rank in the British and other armies.

field·piece (fēld'pēs'), n. Mil. a cannon mounted on a carriage for service in the field.

field·work (fēld'wûrk'), n. Fort. a temporary fortification constructed in the field.

field work, work done in the field, as by a surveyor, geologist, etc.

fiend (fēnd), n. 1. Satan; the devil. 2. a cruel or wicked person. 3. an addict or devotee.

fiend·ish (fēn'dĭsh), adj. cruel and wicked. —fiend'ish·ly, adv. —fiend'ish·ness, n.

fierce (fîrs), adj., fiercer, fiercest. 1. wild or vehement in temper, appearance, or action. 2. violent in force, etc. 3. furiously intense. 4. Slang. extremely bad, etc. —fierce'ly, adv. —fierce'ness, n.

fier·y (fîr'ĭ, fī'ə rĭ), adj., fierier, fieriest. 1. of, with, like, or containing fire. 2. intensely hot. 3. intensely ardent, impetuous, or passionate. 4. easily angered. —fier'i·ly, adv. —fier'i·ness, n.

fi·es·ta (fĭ ĕs'tə); n. 1. a religious celebration. 2. a holiday or festival.

fife (fīf), n., v., fifed, fifing. —n. 1. a high-pitched flute much used in military music. —v.i., v.t. 2. to play on a fife. —fif'er, n.

fif·teen (fĭf'tēn'), n. 1. a cardinal number, ten plus five. 2. a symbol for this number. —adj. 3. amounting to fifteen in number. —fif'teenth', adj., n.

fifth (fĭfth), adj. 1. next after the fourth. 2. being one of five equal parts. —n. 3. a fifth part, esp. of one (¹⁄₅). 4. the fifth member of a series.

fifth column, a body of persons in a country who are in sympathy with its enemies, and who are serving enemy interests or are ready to assist an enemy attack. —fifth columnist.

fif·ty (fĭf'tĭ), n., pl. -ties, adj. —n. 1. a cardinal number, ten times five. 2. a symbol for this number. —adj. 3. amounting to fifty in number. —fif'ti·eth, adj., n.

fig (fĭg), n. 1. a pear-shaped fruit, eaten fresh or preserved or dried, growing on a small tree (fig tree) native in SW Asia. 2. the least bit.

fig., 1. figurative. 2. figure; figures.

fight (fīt), n., v., fought, fighting. —n. 1. a battle or combat. 2. ability or inclination to fight. —v.i., v.t. 3. to engage in battle or in single combat (with). 4. to contend in any manner (with). 5. to carry on (a battle, duel, etc.). —fight'er, n.

fig·ment (fĭg'mənt), n. a product of the imagination, as a story, theory, etc.

fig·ur·a·tion (fĭg'yə rā'shən), n. 1. act of shaping into a particular figure. 2. the resulting shape.

fig·ur·a·tive (fĭg'yər ə tĭv), adj. 1. of the nature of or involving a figure of speech; not literal. 2. abounding in or addicted to figures of speech. —fig'ur·a·tive·ly, adv. —fig'ur·a·tive·ness, n.

fig·ure (fĭg'yər; Brit. fĭg'ər), n., v., -ured, -uring. —n. 1. a written symbol other than a letter, esp. a numerical symbol. 2. an amount or value expressed in numbers. 3. (pl.) arithmetic. 4. form or shape. 5. a character or personage, esp. one of distinction. 6. the appearance or impression made. 7. a representation, pictorial or sculptured, of something. 8. an emblem or type. 9. Rhet. a figure of speech. 10. a device or pattern, as in cloth. 11. a movement or pattern in skating or dancing. 12. Music. a short succession of musical notes which produces a single impression. —v.t. 13. to compute or calculate. 14. to mark or adorn with figures. 15. Colloq. to conclude or judge. 16. to solve; understand. —v.i. 17. to compute with numerical figures. 18. to be conspicuous. 19. figure on, Colloq. a. to rely on. b. to take into consideration. —fig'ure·less, adj. —fig'ur·er, n.

fig·ured (fĭg'yərd), adj. 1. formed or shaped. 2. ornamented with a pattern.

fig·ure·head (fĭg'yər hĕd'), n. 1. a person who is only nominally the head of a society, community, etc. 2. Naut. a statue or bust at the prow of a ship.

figure of speech, a literary mode of expression, as a metaphor, simile, etc., in which words are used out of their literal sense or out of ordinary locutions for special effect.

fig·ur·ine (fĭg'yə rēn'), n. a small ornamental figure of pottery, metalwork, etc.

Fi·ji (fē'jē), n. a British colony in the S Pacific, N of New Zealand, comprising the Fiji Islands and a dependent group to the NW. 234,000 pop.; 7435 sq. mi. Cap.: Suva.

fil·a·ment (fĭl'ə mənt), n. 1. a very fine thread or fiber. 2. Elect. (in an incandescent lamp) the threadlike conductor in the bulb which is raised to incandescence by the passage of current. —fil·a·men·ta·ry (fĭl'ə mĕn'tə rĭ), fil·a·men·tous (fĭl'ə mĕn'təs), adj.

fil·bert (fĭl'bərt), n. 1. the thick-shelled, edible nut of certain varieties of hazel. 2. a tree or shrub bearing such nuts.

filch (fĭlch), v.t., v.i. to steal (esp. something of small value); pilfer. —filch'er, n.

file¹ (fīl), n., v., filed, filing. —n. 1. any device, as a cabinet, in which papers, etc., are kept. 2. a collection of papers so kept. 3. a line of persons or things arranged one behind another. —v.t. 4. to arrange and keep (papers, etc.) methodically. —v.i. 5. to march in a file. 6. to make application. —fil'er, n.

file² (fīl), n., v., filed, filing. —n. 1. a metal tool with numerous small ridges on its surface, for smoothing or cutting. —v.t. 2. to reduce, smooth, cut, or remove with a file. —fil'er, n.

fi·let (fĭ lā', fĭl'ā), n., v.t. fillet (defs. 3, 5).

fil·i·al (fĭl'ĭ əl), adj. pertaining to or befitting a son or daughter. —fil'i·al·ly, adv.

fil·i·bus·ter (fĭl'ə bŭs'tər), n. 1. U.S. (in a legislative assembly) a process used by a minority to obstruct legislation by prolonged speeches, etc. 2. a freebooter or buccaneer. —v.i. 3. U.S. to engage in a filibuster (against). 4. to act as a freebooter or buccaneer. —fil'i·bus'ter·er, n.

fil·i·gree (fĭl'ə grē'), n., v., -greed, -greeing. —n. 1. ornamental work of fine wires. 2. anything very delicate or fanciful. —v.t. 3. to adorn with filigree.

fil·ings (fī'lĭngz), n.pl. particles removed by a file.

Fil·i·pi·no (fĭl'ə pē'nō), n., pl. -nos (-nōz), adj. —n. 1. a native of the Philippine Islands. —adj. 2. Philippine.

fill (fĭl), v.t. 1. to make full. 2. to occupy to the full capacity. 3. to supply plentifully. 4. to satisfy, as food does. 5. to put into a receptacle. 6. to be plentiful throughout. 7. to pervade. 8. to furnish with an occupant or incumbent. 9. to execute (a business order). 10. to supply (a blank space) with written matter, etc. 11. to meet (requirements, etc.). 12. to make up (a medical prescription). 13. to stop up. 14. to perform the duties of (a position, etc.). —v.i. 15. to become full. —n. 16. a full supply. 17. a mass of earth, etc., used to fill a hollow, etc.

fill·er (fĭl'ər), n. 1. one that fills. 2. a thing or quantity of a material put in to fill something. 3. a liquid, paste, or the like, used to coat a surface or to give solidity, bulk, etc., to a substance.

fil·let (fĭl′ĭt; *usually* fĭl′ā *for 3, 5*), *n.* **1.** a narrow ribbon round the head or hair. **2.** any narrow strip. **3.** a slice of meat, fish, etc., usually without bones. —*v.t.* **4.** to bind or adorn with a fillet. **5.** to cut (meat, etc.) as a fillet.

fill·ing (fĭl′ĭng), *n.* that which is put in to fill something, as in a tooth cavity.

filling station, a place where gasoline and oil are retailed for automobiles.

fil·lip (fĭl′əp), *v.t.* **1.** to strike with the nail of a finger snapped from the end of the thumb. **2.** to tap smartly. —*n.* **3.** act of filliping. **4.** anything that tends to rouse, excite, or revive.

Fill·more (fĭl′mōr), *n.* **Millard,** 1800–74, 13th president of the U.S., 1850–53.

fil·ly (fĭl′ĭ), *n., pl.* **-lies. 1.** a female colt or young mare. **2.** *Colloq.* a young girl.

film (fĭlm), *n.* **1.** a thin layer or coating. **2.** a cellulose roll or sheet coated with a photographically sensitive emulsion. **3.** a motion picture. **4.** a thin skin or membrane. —*v.t.* **5.** to cover with a film. **6.** to photograph with a camera. —**film′y,** *adj.*

fil·ter (fĭl′tər), *n.* **1.** any device in which cloth, paper, porous porcelain, etc., is held and through which something is passed to remove suspended impurities, recover solids, etc. **2.** *Photog.* a screen of dyed gelatin or glass used to control the rendering of color, etc. —*v.t., v.i.* **3.** to remove by a filter. **4.** to act as a filter for. **5.** to pass through a filter.

fil·ter·a·ble (fĭl′tər ə bəl), *adj.* **1.** capable of being filtered. **2.** *Bacteriol.* capable of passing through bacteria-retaining filters. Also, **fil·tra·ble** (fĭl′trə bəl).

filth (fĭlth), *n.* **1.** foul matter. **2.** obscenity.

filth·y (fĭl′thĭ), *adj.,* **filthier, filthiest. 1.** disgustingly dirty. **2.** obscene. —**filth′i·ly,** *adv.* —**filth′i·ness,** *n.*

fil·trate (fĭl′trāt), *v.,* **-trated, -trating,** *n.* —*v.t., v.i.* **1.** to filter. —*n.* **2.** liquid passed through a filter. —**fil·tra′tion,** *n.*

fin (fĭn), *n., v.,* **finned, finning.** —*n.* **1.** a membranous winglike organ on the body of fishes, used for propulsion, steering, or balancing. **2.** anything resembling a fin. —*v.i.* **3.** to move the fins.

fi·na·gle (fĭ nā′gəl), *v.i., v.t.,* **-gled, -gling.** *Colloq.* **1.** to cheat (a person); get (something) by trickery. **2.** to wangle.

fi·nal (fī′nəl), *adj.* **1.** last in place, order, or time. **2.** ultimate. **3.** decisive. —*n.* **4.** something final.

fi·na·le (fĭ nä′lĭ), *n.* the last part, esp. of a concert, opera, or composition.

fi·nal·ist (fī′nə lĭst), *n.* one who takes part in the final trial, as of a contest.

fi·nal·i·ty (fĭ năl′ə tĭ), *n., pl.* **-ties. 1.** state, quality, or fact of being final; decisiveness. **2.** a final act, utterance, etc.

fi·nal·ly (fī′nə lĭ), *adv.* **1.** in the end. **2.** in a final manner; decisively.

fi·nance (fĭ năns′, fī′năns), *n., v.,* **-nanced, -nancing.** —*n.* **1.** the management of money matters. **2.** (*pl.*) pecuniary resources. —*v.t.* **3.** to supply with means of payment.

fi·nan·cial (fĭ năn′shəl, fī-), *adj.* pertaining to or dealing with money matters; pecuniary. —**fi·nan′cial·ly,** *adv.*

fin·an·cier (fĭn′ən sîr′, fī′nən-), *n.* one engaged in financial operations.

finch (fĭnch), *n.* any of numerous small passerine birds of the family including the buntings, sparrows, etc.

find (fīnd), *v.,* **found, finding,** *n.* —*v.t.* **1.** to come upon; meet with. **2.** to learn, attain, or obtain by search or effort. **3.** to discover. **4.** to recover (something lost). **5.** *Law.* to determine after judicial inquiry. —*v.i.* **6.** to determine an issue after judicial inquiry. —*n.* **7.** act of finding. **8.** a discovery.

find·er (fīn′dər), *n.* **1.** one that finds. **2.** a camera attachment enabling a photographer to determine what will be included in the picture.

find·ing (fīn′dĭng), *n.* **1.** discovery. **2.** *Law.* a decision or verdict.

fine¹ (fīn), *adj.,* **finer, finest,** *adv., v.,* **fined, fining.** —*adj.* **1.** choice, excellent, or admirable. **2.** consisting of minute particles. **3.** very thin or slender. **4.** keen or sharp. **5.** delicate. **6.** affectedly elegant. **7.** showy or smart. **8.** good-looking. **9.** (of gold, etc.) having a high proportion of pure metal. —*adv.* **10.** *Colloq.* in a fine manner. —*v.i., v.t.* **11.** to become or make fine. —**fine′ly,** *adv.* —**fine′ness,** *n.*

fine² (fīn), *n., v.,* **fined, fining.** —*n.* **1.** a sum of money exacted as a penalty. —*v.t.* **2.** to subject to a fine.

fine arts, those arts which seek expression through beautiful or significant modes, as architecture, sculpture, painting, etc.

fin·er·y (fī′nə rĭ), *n., pl.* **-eries.** fine or showy dress, ornaments, etc.

fine-spun (fīn′spŭn′), *adj.* **1.** drawn out to a fine thread. **2.** highly refined or subtle.

fi·nesse (fĭ nĕs′), *n., v.,* **-nessed, -nessing.** —*n.* **1.** delicacy of execution. **2.** artful management. **3.** *Cards.* an attempt to win a trick with a card while holding a higher card not in sequence with it, in the hope that a card between will not be played. —*v.i.* **4.** to use finesse. **5.** to make a finesse at cards.

fin·ger (fĭng′gər), *n.* **1.** any of the five terminal members of the hand. **2.** something like a finger. —*v.t., v.i.* **3.** to touch or use with the fingers. —**fin′ger·er,** *n.* —**fin′ger·less,** *adj.*

finger bowl, a small bowl to hold water for rinsing the fingers at table.

fin·ger·nail (fĭng′gər nāl′), *n.* the nail at the end of a finger.

fin·ger·print (fĭng′gər prĭnt′), *n.* **1.** an impression of the markings of the inner surface of the last joint of the thumb or a finger. —*v.t.* **2.** to take the fingerprints of.

fin·i·al (fĭn′ĭ əl, fī′nĭ-), *n.* *Archit.* the ornamental termination of a pinnacle, gable, etc.

fin·i·cal (fĭn′ə kəl), *adj.* **1.** too particular or fussy. **2.** overelaborate. Also, **fin·ick·y** (fĭn′ə kĭ). —**fin′i·cal·ly,** *adv.*

fi·nis (fī′nĭs), *n.* *Latin.* end; conclusion.

fin·ish (fĭn′ĭsh), *v.t.* **1.** to bring to an end or to completion. **2.** to come to the end of. **3.** to use up completely. **4.** to perfect. —*v.i.* **5.** to come to an end. **6.** to complete a course, etc. —*n.* **7.** the end or conclusion. **8.** educational or social polish. **9.** the manner in which a thing is finished in preparation. —**fin′ished,** *adj.* —**fin′ish·er,** *n.*

fi·nite (fī′nīt), *adj.* **1.** having bounds or limits. —*n.* **2.** that which is finite. —**fi′nite·ly,** *adv.*

finite verb, a verb limited by person, number, tense, mood, and aspect.

Fin·land (fĭn′lənd), *n.* a republic in N Europe. 3,816,000 pop.; ab. 118,000 sq. mi. *Cap.:* Helsinki. —**Fin′land·er, Finn** (fĭn), *n.*

fin·nan had·die (fĭn′ən hăd′ĭ), smoked haddock. Also, **finnan haddock.**

Finn·ish (fĭn′ĭsh), *n.* **1.** the principal language of Finland. —*adj.* **2.** of or pertaining to Finland or its inhabitants.

fiord (fyōrd), *n.* a long, narrow arm of the sea, bordered by steep cliffs.

fir (fûr), *n.* any of certain evergreen coniferous trees, as the **balsam fir.**

fire (fīr), *n., v.,* **fired, firing.** —*n.* **1.** burning or combustion. **2.** a burning mass of material. **3.** the destructive burning of a building, town, forest, etc. **4.** passion; ardor. **5.** the discharge of firearms. **6. on fire, a.** burning. **b.** eager; ardent. —*v.t.* **7.** to set on fire. **8.** to supply with fuel. **9.** to inflame or inspire. **10.** to discharge, as a gun. **11.** *Slang.* to eject or dismiss. —*v.i.* **12.** to take fire. **13.** to go off, as a gun. **14.** to discharge a gun, etc.

fire·arm (fīr′ärm′), *n.* **1.** a gun from which a projectile is fired. **2.** small arms.

fire·box (fīr′bŏks′), *n.* the chamber in which the fire of a steam boiler, etc., is placed.

fire·brand (fīr′brănd′), *n.* **1.** a piece of burning wood. **2.** one who kindles strife, etc.

fire·brick (fīr′brĭk′), *n.* a brick made of clay capable of resisting great heat (**fire clay**).

fire·bug (fīr′bŭg′), *n.* *U.S. Colloq.* an incendiary.

fire·crack·er (fīr′krăk′ər), *n.* a paper cylinder filled with a loud explosive, used in merrymaking, etc.

fire·damp (fīr′dămp′), *n.* a combustible gas formed esp. in coal mines.

fire·dog (fīr′dôg′, -dŏg′), *n.* andiron.

fire engine, a motor truck equipped for fire fighting.

fire escape, an apparatus or structure used to escape from a burning building.

fire extinguisher, a portable apparatus containing chemicals for putting out a fire.

fire·fly (fīr′flī′), *n., pl.* **-flies.** any of certain soft-bodied, nocturnal beetles which possess abdominal light-producing organs.

fire·man (fīr/mən), n., pl. **-men.** 1. a man employed to extinguish or prevent fires. 2. a man employed to tend fires; a stoker.

fire·place (fīr/plās/), n. that part of a chimney which opens into a room and in which fuel is burned.

fire·proof (fīr/prōōf/), adj. 1. proof against fire. —v.t. 2. to make fireproof.

fire·side (fīr/sīd/), n. 1. the space about a fire or hearth. 2. home; home life.

fire·trap (fīr/trăp/), n. a building which is especially dangerous in case of fire.

fire·wa·ter (fīr/wô/tər, -wŏt/ər), n. liquor.

fire·weed (fīr/wēd/), n. any of various plants appearing in recently burned areas.

fire·wood (fīr/wŏŏd/), n. wood for fuel.

fire·work (fīr/wûrk/), n. (usually pl.) a combustible or explosive device for producing a striking display of light or a loud noise, often also used in signaling at night, etc.

firm[1] (fûrm), adj. 1. comparatively solid, hard, stiff, or rigid. 2. securely fixed in place. 3. steady. 4. unalterable. 5. steadfast. —v.t., v.i. 6. to make or become firm. —adv. 7. firmly. —**firm/ly,** adv. —**firm/ness,** n.

firm[2] (fûrm), n. a company of two or more persons for carrying on a business.

fir·ma·ment (fûr/mə mənt), n. the sky.

first (fûrst), adj. 1. being before all others in time, order, importance, etc. 2. Music. highest or chief among several voices or instruments of the same class. —adv. 3. before all others in time, order, etc. 4. in the first place. —n. 5. that which is first in time, order, rank, etc. 6. the beginning. 7. the first part. 8. the first place in a race, etc.

first aid, emergency aid or treatment given to persons suffering from accident, etc.

first-born (fûrst/bôrn/), adj. 1. eldest. —n. 2. a first-born child.

first-class (fûrst/klăs/, -kläs/), adj. 1. of the highest or best cl ss or quality. —adv. 2. by first-class conveyance.

first-hand (fûrst/hănd/), adv., adj. from the original source.

first lieutenant, Mil. an officer ranking next below a captain.

first·ling (fûrst/lĭng), n. 1. the first of its kind. 2. first offspring. 3. the first result.

first·ly (fûrst/lĭ), adv. in the first place; first.

first-rate (fûrst/rāt/), adj. 1. of the first rate or class. 2. excellent. —adv. 3. Colloq. excellently.

firth (fûrth), n. Chiefly Scot. a long, narrow indentation of the sea coast.

fis·cal (fĭs/kəl), adj. of or pertaining to the public treasury or to financial matters in general. —**fis/cal·ly,** adv.

fish (fĭsh), n., pl. **fishes,** (esp. collectively) **fish.** 1. any of various cold-blooded, aquatic vertebrates, typically having an elongated body usually covered with scales. 2. Colloq. (with an adjective) a person. —v.t., v.i. 3. to catch or attempt to catch (fish or the like). 4. to search or draw as if by fishing.

fish·er (fĭsh/ər), n. 1. a fisherman. 2. a dark-brown somewhat foxlike marten of northern North America.

fish·er·man (fĭsh/ər mən), n., pl. **-men.** 1. one engaged in fishing. 2. a fishing boat.

fish·er·y (fĭsh/ə rĭ), n., pl. **-eries.** 1. the occupation or industry of catching fish. 2. a place where such an industry is regularly carried on.

fish hawk, osprey.

fish·hook (fĭsh/hŏŏk/), n. a hook used with fishing tackle.

fish·ing (fĭsh/ĭng), n. art or practice of catching fish.

fish·mon·ger (fĭsh/mŭng/gər), n. Chiefly Brit. a dealer in fish.

fish·wife (fĭsh/wīf/), n., pl. **-wives.** 1. a woman who sells fish. 2. a woman who uses abusive language.

fish·y (fĭsh/ĭ), adj., fishier, fishiest. 1. like a fish in shape, smell, taste, etc. 2. consisting of or abounding in fish. 3. Colloq. improbable or questionable. —**fish/i·ness,** n.

fis·sion (fĭsh/ən), n. 1. act of splitting into parts. 2. Biol. the division of an organism into new organisms as a process of reproduction.

fis·sion·a·ble (fĭsh/ən ə bəl), adj. capable of undergoing nuclear fission.

fis·sure (fĭsh/ər), n., v., **-sured, -suring.** —n. 1. a narrow opening produced by separation; cleft. 2. cleavage. —v.t., v.i. 3. to cleave; split.

fist (fĭst), n. the hand closed tightly, with the fingers doubled into the palm.

fist·ic (fĭs/tĭk), adj. pugilistic.

fist·i·cuff (fĭs/tə kŭf/), n. 1. a blow with the fist. 2. (pl.) combat with the fists.

fis·tu·la (fĭs/chŏŏ lə), n., pl. **-las, -lae** (-lē/). a narrow passage formed by disease or injury, as one leading from an abscess to a free surface. —**fis·tu·lous** (fĭs/chŏŏ ləs), **fis/tu·lar,** adj.

fit[1] (fĭt), adj., fitter, fittest, v., fitted, fitting, n. —adj. 1. well suited. 2. proper. 3. competent. 4. worthy. 5. ready. 6. in good physical condition. —v.t. 7. to be suitable or proper for. 8. to conform or adjust to. 9. to make competent. 10. to prepare. 11. to provide; equip. —v.i. 12. to be suitable or proper. 13. to be of the right size or shape. —n. 14. the manner in which a thing fits. 15. something that fits. —**fit/ly,** adv. —**fit/ness,** n. —**fit/ter,** n.

fit[2] (fĭt), n. 1. a sudden, acute attack of a disease. 2. an access or period of feeling, activity, etc.

fitch (fĭch), n. the European polecat.

Fitch·burg (fĭch/bûrg/), n. a city in N Massachusetts. 41,284.

fit·ful (fĭt/fəl), adj. irregularly intermittent. —**fit/ful·ly,** adv. —**fit/ful·ness,** n.

fit·ting (fĭt/ĭng), adj. 1. suitable or proper. —n. 2. (pl.) furnishings, etc. —**fit/ting·ly,** adv.

Fitz·Ger·ald (fĭts jĕr/əld), n. **Edward,** 1809–83, British poet: translated Omar Khayyam.

Fiu·me (fū/mĕ), n. a seaport in NW Yugoslavia. 53,000.

five (fīv), n. 1. a cardinal number, four plus one. 2. a symbol for this number. 3. a set of this many persons or things. —adj. 4. amounting to five in number. —**five/fold/,** adj., adv.

Five Nations, U.S. Hist. a confederacy of Iroquoian Indians: the Mohawks, Oneidas, Onondagas, Cayugas, and Senecas.

fix (fĭks), v., fixed or fixt, fixing, n. —v.t. 1. to make fast, firm, or stable. 2. to settle. 3. to direct (the eyes, etc.) steadily. 4. to put or place (blame, etc.) on a person. 5. to repair. 6. Colloq. to arrange matters with, esp. privately or dishonestly. 7. U.S. to prepare. 8. Colloq. to get revenge upon. —v.i. 9. to become fixed. —n. 10. Colloq. a predicament. —**fix/a·ble,** adj. —**fix/er,** n.

fix·a·tion (fĭk sā/shən), n. 1. act of fixing. 2. state of being fixed. 3. Psychoanal. a partial arrest of emotional and instinctual development at an early point in life, due to a severe traumatic experience or an overwhelming gratification.

fix·a·tive (fĭk/sə tĭv), adj. 1. serving to fix. —n. 2. a fixative substance.

fixed (fĭkst), adj. 1. made fast, firm, or permanent. 2. steadily directed; set or rigid. 3. definitely and permanently placed. 4. not varying. 5. put in order. 6. Colloq. arranged privately or dishonestly. —**fix·ed·ly** (fĭk/sĭd lĭ), adv. —**fix/ed·ness,** n.

fixed star, Astron. any of the stars which apparently always retain the same position with respect to one another.

fix·ing (fĭk/sĭng), n. 1. act of one that fixes. 2. (pl.) U.S. Colloq. trimmings.

fix·i·ty (fĭk/sə tĭ), n., pl. **-ties.** 1. state or quality of being fixed. 2. something fixed.

fix·ture (fĭks/chər), n. 1. something securely fixed in position. 2. a person or thing long established in the same place or position.

fizz (fĭz), v.i. 1. to make a hissing sound. —n. 2. a hissing sound. Also, **fiz.** —**fizz/y,** adj.

fiz·zle (fĭz/əl), v., **-zled, -zling,** n. —v.i. 1. to make a hissing sound, esp. one that dies out weakly. 2. Colloq. to fail ignominiously. —n. 3. a fizzling. 4. Colloq. a failure.

Fl, Chem. fluorine.

fl., 1. (L floruit) flourished. 2. fluid.

Fla., Florida.

flab·ber·gast (flăb/ər găst/), v.t. Colloq. to overcome with surprise; astound.

flab·by (flăb/ĭ), adj., **-bier, -biest.** 1. soft; weak; limp. 2. lacking firmness, as character, etc. —**flab/bi·ness,** n.

flac·cid (flăk/sĭd), adj. flabby; limp; not firm.

—**flac·cid/i·ty, flac/cid·ness,** *n.* —**flac/cid·ly,** *adv.*

flag[1] (flăg), *n., v.,* **flagged, flagging.** —*n.* **1.** a piece of cloth used as an ensign, signal, etc. —*v.t.* **2.** to decorate with flags. **3.** to signal or warn by a flag.

flag[2] (flăg), *n.* any of various plants with long, sword-shaped leaves.

flag[3] (flăg), *v.i.,* **flagged, flagging. 1.** to hang loosely or limply; droop. **2.** to fall off in vigor, interest, etc.

flag[4] (flăg), *n., v.,* **flagged, flagging.** —*n.* **1.** a flat slab of stone used for paving, etc. —*v.t.* **2.** to lay or pave with flags. —**flag/less,** *adj.*

Flag Day, June 14, the anniversary of the day (June 14, 1777) when Congress adopted the Stars and Stripes as the national emblem.

flag·el·lant (flăj/ə lənt, flə jĕl/ənt), *n.* **1.** one who scourges himself for religious discipline. —*adj.* **2.** flagellating.

flag·el·late (flăj/ə lāt/), *v.,* **-lated, -lating,** *adj.* —*v.t.* **1.** to whip; scourge; flog. —*adj.* **2.** Also, **flag/el·lat/ed.** *Biol.* having flagellums. —**flag/el·la/tion,** *n.*

fla·gel·lum (flə jĕl/əm), *n., pl.* **-gella** (-jĕl/ə), **-gellums. 1.** *Biol.* a lashlike appendage serving as an organ of locomotion in certain bacteria, etc. **2.** *Bot.* a runner.

flag·eo·let (flăj/ə lĕt/), *n.* a small end-blown flute.

flag·ging[1] (flăg/ĭng), *adj.* drooping; failing. —**flag/ging·ly,** *adv.*

flag·ging[2] (flăg/ĭng), *n.* **1.** flagstones collectively. **2.** a pavement of flagstones.

fla·gi·tious (flə jĭsh/əs), *adj.* **1.** shamefully wicked. **2.** infamous. —**fla·gi/tious·ly,** *adv.*

flag·on (flăg/ən), *n.* **1.** a large bottle. **2.** a vessel for liquids, as for use at table.

flag·pole (flăg/pōl/), *n.* a staff or pole on which a flag is displayed. Also, **flag·staff** (flăg/stăf/, -stäf/).

fla·grant (flā/grənt), *adj.* glaring; notorious. —**fla/gran·cy, fla/grance,** *n.* —**fla/grant·ly,** *adv.*

flag·ship (flăg/shĭp/), *n.* a ship which bears the commanding officer of a fleet, squadron, or the like, and displays his flag.

flag·stone (flăg/stōn/), *n.* a flat slab of stone used for paving, etc.

flail (flāl), *n.* **1.** an instrument for threshing grain by hand. —*v.t.* **2.** to strike with, or as if with, a flail.

flair (flâr), *n.* talent; aptitude.

flak (flăk), *n.* anti-aircraft fire.

flake (flāk), *n., v.,* **flaked, flaking.** —*n.* **1.** a small, flat, thin piece of anything. —*v.i., v.t.* **2.** to separate in flakes.

flak·y (flā/kĭ), *adj.,* **flakier, flakiest. 1.** consisting of flakes. **2.** cleaving off in flakes. **3.** flakelike. —**flak/i·ly,** *adv.* —**flak/i·ness,** *n.*

flam·beau (flăm/bō), *n., pl.* **-beaux** (-bōz), **-beaus.** a flaming torch.

flam·boy·ant (flăm boi/ənt), *adj.* **1.** flaming. **2.** florid; ornate. **3.** *Archit.* characterized by wavy, flamelike tracery, as in windows. —**flam·boy/ance, flam·boy/an·cy,** *n.* —**flam·boy/ant·ly,** *adv.*

flame (flām), *n., v.,* **flamed, flaming.** —*n.* **1.** burning gas or vapor, as from wood, etc. **2.** *(often pl.)* state of blazing combustion. **3.** *Slang.* sweetheart. —*v.i.* **4.** to burn with a flame or flames; blaze. **5.** to break into open anger, etc.

flame thrower, *Mil.* an apparatus that throws a spray of oil that ignites in the air.

flam·ing (flā/mĭng), *adj.* **1.** blazing. **2.** brilliant. **3.** passionate. —**flam/ing·ly,** *adv.*

fla·min·go (flə mĭng/gō), *n., pl.* **-gos, -goes.** any of certain aquatic birds with very long neck and legs, webbed feet, and pinkish to scarlet plumage.

Flan·ders (flăn/dərz), *n.* a medieval county in W Europe, extending along the North Sea from the Strait of Dover to the mouth of the Scheldt river: the corresponding modern regions include the provinces of **East Flanders** and **West Flanders** in W Belgium, and the adjacent parts of N France and SW Netherlands.

Florida flamingo
(Ab. 4 ft. long)

flange (flănj), *n., v.,* **flanged, flanging.** —*n.* **1.** a projecting rim, collar, edge, ridge, or the like, on an object, for keeping it in place, etc. —*v.i.* **2.** to project like, or take the form of, a flange.

flank (flăngk), *n.* **1.** the side of an animal or a human being between the ribs and hip. **2.** the side of anything, as of a building. **3.** *Mil., Naval.* the extreme right or left side of an army, fleet, or fortification. —*v.t.* **4.** to be at the side of. **5.** to pass round or turn the flank of. —*v.i.* **6.** to occupy a position at the side. —**flank/er,** *n.*

flan·nel (flăn/əl), *n.* **1.** a warm, soft fabric of wool. **2.** *(pl.)* a garment made of flannel. —**flan/nel·ly,** *adj.*

flan·nel·et (flăn/ə lĕt/), *n.* a cotton fabric, napped on one side. Also, **flan/nel·ette/.**

flap (flăp), *v.,* **flapped, flapping,** *n.* —*v.i., v.t.* **1.** to swing about loosely, esp. with noise. **2.** to move (wings, etc.) up and down. —*n.* **3.** a flapping motion or noise. **4.** something that hangs loosely, attached at one side only.

flap·jack (flăp/jăk/), *n.* griddlecake.

flap·per (flăp/ər), *n.* **1.** a flap. **2.** *Colloq.* a frivolous young woman.

flare (flâr), *v.,* **flared, flaring,** *n.* —*v.i.* **1.** to burn with an unsteady, swaying flame. **2.** to blaze with a sudden burst of flame. **3.** to burst out in sudden fierce activity, passion, etc. **4.** to spread gradually outward. —*v.t.* **5.** to cause (something) to spread gradually outward. —*n.* **6.** a swaying flame or light. **7.** a sudden blaze or burst of flame. **8.** a substance burned to produce a signal fire. **9.** a sudden burst, as of temper. **10.** a gradual spread outward.

flare-up (flâr/ŭp/), *n.* *Colloq.* a sudden outburst of anger.

flash (flăsh), *n.* **1.** a sudden, brief outburst of flame or light. **2.** a sudden, brief display of joy, wit, etc. **3.** an instant. **4.** ostentatious display. **5.** *Journ.* a brief telegraphic dispatch. —*v.i.* **6.** to break forth into sudden flame or light. **7.** to gleam. **8.** to burst suddenly into view or perception. —*v.t.* **9.** to emit (fire or light) in sudden flashes. **10.** to cause to flash. **11.** to communicate instantaneously. **12.** *Colloq.* to make ostentatious display of. —*adj.* **13.** ostentatious. **14.** sham. —**flash/er,** *n.*

flash·light (flăsh/līt/), *n.* a small portable electric lamp powered by dry batteries.

flash·y (flăsh/ĭ), *adj.,* **flashier, flashiest. 1.** sparkling, esp. in a superficial way. **2.** gaudy. —**flash/i·ly,** *adv.* —**flash/i·ness,** *n.*

flask (flăsk, fläsk), *n.* a bottle-shaped container made of glass, metal, etc.

flat[1] (flăt), *adj.,* **flatter, flattest,** *n., v.,* **flatted, flatting,** *adv.* —*adj.* **1.** level or even. **2.** horizontal or prone. **3.** not deep or thick. **4.** spread out, as an unrolled map. **5.** collapsed; deflated. **6.** unqualified, downright, or positive. **7.** uninteresting; dull. **8.** stale; tasteless or insipid. **9.** pointless, as a joke, etc. **10.** lacking relief, contrast, or shading, as a painting. **11.** *Music.* **a.** (of a tone) lowered a half step in pitch. **b.** below an intended pitch, as a note. —*n.* **12.** something flat. **13.** a flat surface, side, or part. **14.** level ground. **15.** *Music.* (in musical notation) the character ♭, which when attached to a note lowers its significance one chromatic half step. **16.** *Colloq.* a deflated tire. —*v.t., v.i.* **17.** to make or become flat. —*adv.* **18.** in a flat position. **19.** in a flat manner. **20.** *Music.* below the true pitch. —**flat/ly,** *adv.* —**flat/ness,** *n.* —**flat/tish,** *adj.*

flat[2] (flăt), *n.* a suite of rooms on one floor forming a complete residence.

flat·boat (flăt/bōt/), *n.* a large flat-bottomed boat for use in shallow water.

flat·car (flăt/kär/), *n.* *U.S.* a railroad car consisting of a platform without sides or top.

flat·fish (flăt/fĭsh/), *n., pl.* **-fishes,** (*esp. collectively*) **-fish.** any of a group of fishes including the halibut, flounder, etc., having a flat body and (in the adult) having both eyes on the upper side.

flat·i·ron (flăt/ī/ərn), *n.* an iron with a flat face, for smoothing cloth.

flat·ten (flăt/ən), *v.t., v.i.* to make or become flat. —**flat/ten·er,** *n.*

flat·ter (flăt/ər), *v.t.* **1.** to compliment or praise insincerely. **2.** to represent too favorably. **3.** to cajole, wheedle, or beguile. **4.** to gratify by compliments or attentions. **5.** to beguile with hopes. —*v.i.* **6.** to use flattery. —**flat/ter·er,** *n.* —**flat/ter·ing·ly,** *adv.*

flat·ter·y (flăt/ə rĭ), *n., pl.* **-teries. 1.** act of flattering. **2.** a flattering compliment or speech.

flat·top (flăt/tŏp/), *n.* *U.S.* an aircraft carrier.

flat·u·lent (flăch′ə lənt), *adj.* **1.** generating gas in the alimentary canal, as food. **2.** suffering from such gas. **3.** pretentious; empty. —**flat′u·lence, flat′u·len·cy,** *n.* —**flat′u·lent·ly,** *adv.*

Flau·bert (flō bĕr′), *n.* **Gustave,** 1821–80, French novelist.

flaunt (flônt), *v.i.*, *v.t.* **1.** to display (oneself, etc.) conspicuously or boldly. —*n.* **2.** act of flaunting. —**flaunt′er,** *n.* —**flaunt′ing·ly,** *adv.*

flau·tist (flō′tĭst), *n.* a flutist.

fla·vor (flā′vər), *n.* **1.** taste of a thing. **2.** a flavoring substance. **3.** the characteristic quality of a thing. —*v.t.* **4.** to give flavor to. Also, *Brit.,* **fla′vour.** —**fla′vor·less,** *adj.*

fla·vor·ing (flā′vər ĭng), *n.* something that gives flavor.

flaw (flô), *n.* **1.** a defect; fault. **2.** a crack, break, breach, or rent. —*v.t.* **3.** to produce a flaw in. —**flaw′less,** *adj.* —**flaw′less·ly,** *adv.* —**flaw′less·ness,** *n.*

flax (flăks), *n.* **1.** a slender annual plant with narrow leaves and blue flowers. **2.** the fiber of this plant, manufactured into linen yarn.

flax·en (flăk′sən), *adj.* **1.** made of flax. **2.** resembling flax. **3.** pertaining to flax. **4.** pale yellow. Also, **flax′y.**

flay (flā), *v.t.* **1.** to strip off the skin of. **2.** to criticise with scathing severity.

flea (flē), *n.* any of numerous small, wingless, blood-sucking insects, parasitic upon mammals and birds.

fleck (flĕk), *n.* **1.** a spot or patch of color, light, etc. **2.** a speck. —*v.t.* **3.** to spot; dapple.

flec·tion (flĕk′shən), *n.* **1.** act of bending. **2.** state of being bent. **3.** a bend. —**flec′tion·al,** *adj.*

fledge (flĕj), *v.,* **fledged, fledging.** —*v.t.* **1.** to bring up (a bird) until it is able to fly. **2.** to furnish with feathers. —*v.i.* **3.** (of a bird) to acquire the feathers necessary for flight.

fledg·ling (flĕj′lĭng), *n.* **1.** a young bird just fledged. **2.** an inexperienced person.

flee (flē), *v.i.*, *v.t.*, **fled, fleeing. 1.** to run away from (danger, pursuers, etc.). **2.** to move swiftly.

fleece (flēs), *n., v.,* **fleeced, fleecing.** —*n.* **1.** the coat of wool that covers a sheep. **2.** the wool shorn at one time. **3.** something resembling a fleece. **4.** a fabric with a soft, silky pile. —*v.t.* **5.** to deprive of the fleece. **6.** to plunder; swindle. —**fleec′er,** *n.*

fleec·y (flē′sĭ), *adj.,* **fleecier, fleeciest.** of, covered with, or resembling a fleece.

fleet[1] (flēt), *n.* **1.** the largest organized unit of naval ships. **2.** a number of airplanes, automobiles, ships, etc., moving or operating in company.

fleet[2] (flēt), *adj.* **1.** swift; rapid. —*v.i.* **2.** to move swiftly. —**fleet′ly,** *adv.* —**fleet′ness,** *n.*

fleet·ing (flē′tĭng), *adj.* transitory.

Flem·ing (flĕm′ĭng), *n.* **1.** a native of Flanders. **2.** a Flemish-speaking Belgian.

Flem·ish (flĕm′ĭsh), *adj.* **1.** of or pertaining to Flanders, its people, or their language. —*n.* **2.** the people of Flanders. **3.** their language.

flesh (flĕsh), *n.* **1.** the soft substance of an animal body, consisting of muscle and fat. **2.** the body, esp. as distinguished from the soul. **3.** mankind. **4.** living creatures generally. **5.** one's kindred or family. **6.** *Bot.* the soft pulpy portion of a fruit, vegetable, etc. **7. in the flesh, a.** alive. **b.** in person.

flesh·ly (flĕsh′lĭ), *adj.,* **-lier, -liest. 1.** of or pertaining to the body. **2.** carnal; sensual. **3.** worldly. —**flesh′li·ness,** *n.*

flesh·pot (flĕsh′pŏt′), *n.* **1.** a pot or vessel containing meat. **2.** (*pl.*) good living; luxuries.

flesh·y (flĕsh′ĭ), *adj.,* **fleshier, fleshiest. 1.** plump; fat. **2.** of or like flesh. **3.** *Bot.* pulpy. —**flesh′i·ness,** *n.*

fleur-de-lis (flœr′də lē′), *n., pl.* **fleurs-de-lis** (flœr′də lēz′). **1.** a heraldic device resembling three petals encircled by a band. **2.** the distinctive bearing of the royal family of France. **3.** the iris (flower or plant).

flex (flĕks), *v.t.*, *v.i.* to bend.

flex·i·ble (flĕk′sə bəl), *adj.* **1.** easily bent. **2.** adaptable. **3.** disposed to yield. —**flex′i·bil′i·ty,** *n.* —**flex′-i·bly,** *adv.*

flex·ion (flĕk′shən), *n.* *Chiefly Brit.* flection.

Fleur-de-lis

flex·or (flĕk′sər), *n.* *Anat.* a muscle which serves to flex or bend a part of the body.

flex·ure (flĕk′shər), *n.* **1.** act of bending. **2.** state of being bent. **3.** a bend.

flib·ber·ti·gib·bet (flĭb′ər tĭ jĭb′ĭt), *n.* a chattering or flighty person.

flick (flĭk), *n.* **1.** a sudden light blow or stroke. —*v.t.* **2.** to strike lightly. **3.** to remove with such a stroke.

flick·er[1] (flĭk′ər), *v.i.*, *v.t.* **1.** to burn or shine unsteadily. **2.** to vibrate; quiver. —*n.* **3.** an unsteady flame or light. **4.** a flickering movement. —**flick′er·ing·ly,** *adv.*

flick·er[2] (flĭk′ər), *n.* any of several North American woodpeckers with bright wing and tail linings.

fli·er (flī′ər), *n.* **1.** something that flies or moves rapidly. **2.** an aviator. **3.** *U.S. Colloq.* a financial venture.

flight[1] (flīt), *n.* **1.** act, manner, or power of flying. **2.** the distance covered by a flying object. **3.** a number of things flying through the air together. **4.** a journey by airplane. **5.** a transcending of ordinary bounds. **6.** the series of steps between two landings or floors.

flight[2] (flīt), *n.* fleeing; hasty departure.

flight·y (flī′tĭ), *adj.,* **flightier, flightiest. 1.** capricious; frivolous. **2.** mildly crazy. —**flight′-i·ly,** *adv.* —**flight′i·ness,** *n.*

flim·sy (flĭm′zĭ), *adj.,* **-sier, -siest,** *n., pl.* **-sies.** —*adj.* **1.** without material strength. **2.** weak; inadequate. —*n.* **3.** a thin kind of paper. —**flim′-si·ly,** *adv.* —**flim′si·ness,** *n.*

flinch (flĭnch), *v.i.* **1.** to shrink from what is dangerous, difficult, or unpleasant. **2.** to wince. —*n.* **3.** act of flinching.

flin·ders (flĭn′dərz), *n.pl.* splinters.

fling (flĭng), *v.,* **flung, flinging,** *n.* —*v.t.* **1.** to throw with force or violence. **2.** to send forth suddenly and rapidly. —*v.i.* **3.** to move with haste or violence. —*n.* **4.** act of flinging. **5.** a spell of unrestrained indulgence of one's impulses. **6.** a lively Scotch dance. —**fling′er,** *n.*

flint (flĭnt), *n.* **1.** a hard kind of silica, used for striking fire. **2.** something very hard.

Flint (flĭnt), *n.* a city in SE Michigan. 151,543.

flint·lock (flĭnt′lŏk′), *n.* **1.** a gunlock in which a piece of flint striking against steel produces sparks which ignite the priming. **2.** a firearm with such a lock.

flint·y (flĭn′tĭ), *adj.,* **flintier, flintiest. 1.** of or like flint; hard. **2.** cruel; unmerciful.

flip[1] (flĭp), *v.,* **flipped, flipping,** *n.* —*v.t.* **1.** to put in motion with a snap of a finger and thumb. —*n.* **2.** a smart tap or strike.

flip[2] (flĭp), *n.* a drink made with liquor or wine, sugar, and egg, powdered with nutmeg.

flip[3] (flĭp), *adj.,* **flipper, flippest.** *Colloq.* smart; pert; flippant.

flip·pant (flĭp′ənt), *adj.* **1.** smart or pert in speech. **2.** disrespectful. —**flip′pan·cy, flip′-pant·ness,** *n.* —**flip′pant·ly,** *adv.*

flip·per (flĭp′ər), *n.* **1.** a broad, flat limb, as of a seal, whale, etc., especially adapted for swimming. **2.** *Slang.* the hand.

flirt (flûrt), *v.i.* **1.** to trifle in love. **2.** to toy (with an idea, etc.). —*v.t.* **3.** to move or throw suddenly. —*n.* **4.** a person given to flirting. **5.** a quick throw or motion.

flir·ta·tion (flûr tā′shən), *n.* **1.** act of flirting. **2.** a love affair which is not serious. —**flir-ta′tious,** *adj.*

flit (flĭt), *v.,* **flitted, flitting,** *n.* —*v.i.* **1.** to move lightly and swiftly. **2.** to flutter. —*n.* **3.** a light, swift movement; flutter.

flitch (flĭch), *n.* **1.** the side of a hog salted and cured. —*v.t.* **2.** to cut into flitches.

fliv·ver (flĭv′ər), *n.* *Slang.* a small, inexpensive automobile.

float (flōt), *v.i.* **1.** to rest or move on or in a liquid, the air, etc. **2.** to move or drift about free from attachment. **3.** to be launched, as a company, scheme, etc. —*v.t.* **4.** to cause to float. **5.** to launch (a company, scheme, etc.). **6.** to sell on the market, as a stock or a bond. —*n.* **7.** something that floats. **8.** a piece of cork for supporting a baited line in the water. **9.** a platform on wheels, bearing a display, and drawn in a procession. —**float′a·ble,** *adj.*

float·er (flō′tər), *n.* **1.** one that floats. **2.** *Colloq.* one who is continually changing his place of abode, employment, etc. **3.** *U.S.* one who fraudulently votes, usually for pay, in different places in the same election.

float·ing (flō′tĭng), *adj.* 1. that floats. 2. free from attachment. 3. *Pathol.* away from its proper position. 4. not fixed or settled.

floating ribs, *Anat.* the two lowest pairs of ribs in man, attached neither to the sternum nor to the cartilages of other ribs.

flock (flŏk), *n.* 1. a number of animals of one kind keeping, feeding, or herded together. 2. a crowd. 3. a congregation in relation to its pastor. —*v.i.* 4. to gather or go in a flock, company, or crowd.

floe (flō), *n.* a field of floating ice formed on the surface of the sea, etc.

flog (flŏg, flôg), *v.t.*, **flogged, flogging.** to beat with a whip, stick, etc. —**flog′ger,** *n.*

flood (flŭd), *n.* 1. a great overflowing of water over land not usually submerged. 2. **the Flood,** the universal deluge in the days of Noah. 3. *Poetic.* the sea; a river. 4. any great outpouring. 5. the flowing in of the tide. —*v.t.* 6. to overflow in or cover with a flood. 7. to cover or overwhelm as with a flood. —*v.i.* 8. to overflow.

flood·gate (flŭd′gāt′), *n.* 1. a gate designed to regulate the flow of water. 2. anything serving to control flow or passage.

flood·light (flŭd′līt′), *n.* 1. an artificial light giving illumination over a large area. —*v.t.* 2. to illuminate with a floodlight.

floor (flōr), *n.* 1. that part of a room or the like upon which one walks. 2. a story of a building. 3. the flat bottom of a place. 4. the part of a legislative chamber, etc., where members sit and speak. 5. the right of one member to speak from such a place. 6. the bottom, base, or minimum charged or paid. —*v.t.* 7. to furnish with a floor. 8. to knock down. 9. *Colloq.* to defeat. 10. *Colloq.* to confound.

floor·ing (flōr′ĭng), *n.* 1. a floor. 2. floors collectively. 3. materials for making floors.

floor leader, *U.S.* the member in either the Senate or the House who directs the activities of his party on the floor.

floor·walk·er (flōr′wô′kər), *n.* a person employed in a store to direct customers, supervise salesmen, etc.

flop (flŏp), *v.*, **flopped, flopping,** *n. Colloq.* —*v.i.* 1. to fall suddenly, esp. with noise. 2. to change suddenly. 3. to fail. 4. to flap, as in the wind. —*v.t.* 5. to drop, throw, etc., with a sudden bump. —*n.* 6. act of flopping. 7. the sound of flopping. 8. a failure. —**flop′per,** *n.* —**flop′py,** *adj.*

flop·house (flŏp′hous′), *n.* a cheap hotel.

flo·ra (flōr′ə), *n.*, *pl.* **floras, florae** (flōr′ē). 1. the plants of a particular region or period. 2. (*cap.*) the Roman goddess of flowers.

flo·ral (flōr′əl), *adj.* pertaining to or consisting of flowers. —**flo′ral·ly,** *adv.*

Flor·ence (flôr′əns, flŏr′-), *n.* a city in central Italy. 307,945. —**Flor·en·tine** (flôr′ən tēn′, flŏr′-), *adj.*, *n.*

flo·res·cence (flō rĕs′əns), *n.* act, state, or period of flowering. —**flo·res′cent,** *adj.*

flo·ret (flōr′ĭt), *n.* 1. a small flower. 2. *Bot.* one of the closely clustered small flowers that make up the flower head of a composite flower.

flo·ri·cul·ture (flōr′ə kŭl′chər), *n.* the cultivation of flowers. —**flo′ri·cul′tur·al,** *adj.*

flor·id (flôr′ĭd, flŏr′-), *adj.* 1. high-colored or ruddy, as cheeks, persons, etc. 2. flowery; ornate. —**flor′id·ly,** *adv.*

Flor·i·da (flôr′ə də, flŏr′-), *n.* a State in the SE United States between the Atlantic and the Gulf of Mexico. 2,310,303 pop.; 58,560 sq. mi. *Cap.:* Tallahassee. *Abbr.:* Fla.

flor·in (flôr′ĭn, flŏr′-), *n.* 1. an English silver coin worth 2 shillings. 2. any of various other European coins.

flo·rist (flōr′ĭst, flôr′-), *n.* one who cultivates flowers, esp. for sale; a dealer in flowers.

floss (flôs, flŏs), *n.* 1. the cottony fiber yielded by the silk-cotton trees. 2. silk filaments with little or no twist, used in embroidery. —**floss′y,** *adj.*

flo·ta·tion (flō tā′shən), *n.* 1. act of floating. 2. state of floating.

flo·til·la (flō tĭl′ə), *n.* 1. a number of small naval vessels. 2. a small fleet.

flot·sam (flŏt′səm), *n.* wreckage of a ship and its cargo as found floating on the water.

flounce[1] (flouns), *v.*, **flounced, flouncing,** *n.* —*v.i.* 1. to go with an angry fling of the body. —*n.* 2. a flouncing movement.

flounce[2] (flouns), *n.*, *v.*, **flounced, flouncing.** —*n.* 1. a wide ruffle used for trimming, esp. on women's skirts. —*v.t.* 2. to trim with a flounce.

floun·der[1] (floun′dər), *v.i.* 1. to struggle with stumbling or plunging movements. 2. to struggle clumsily or helplessly in embarrassment or confusion. —*n.* 3. action of floundering.

floun·der[2] (floun′dər), *n.*, *pl.* **-ders,** (*esp. collectively*) **-der.** any of various edible flatfishes.

flour (flour), *n.* 1. the finely ground meal of grain, esp. of wheat. —*v.t.* 2. to make into flour. 3. to sprinkle or dredge with flour. —**flour′y,** *adj.*

flour·ish (flûr′ĭsh), *v.i.* 1. to thrive; prosper. 2. to be at the height of fame or excellence. 3. to grow luxuriantly. 4. to make strokes with a brandished weapon or the like. 5. to make a display. 6. to add embellishments to writing, letters, etc. —*v.t.* 7. to brandish or wave. 8. to display. —*n.* 9. a brandishing or waving, as of a sword. 10. a display. 11. a decoration in writing. 12. *Music.* an elaborate passage largely for display.

flout (flout), *v.t.*, *v.i.* 1. to mock; scoff (at). —*n.* 2. a mocking insult; gibe.

flow (flō), *v.i.* 1. to move along in a stream. 2. to issue or proceed from a source. 3. to proceed continuously and smoothly. 4. to fall or hang loosely at full length, as hair. 5. to abound with something. 6. to rise and advance, as the tide. —*v.t.* 7. to cause or permit to flow. 8. to flood. —*n.* 9. act of flowing. 10. movement in or as in a stream. 11. the rate of flowing. 12. an outpouring or discharge of something. 13. the rise of the tide.

flow·er (flou′ər), *n.* 1. the blossom of a plant. 2. *Bot.* that part of a seed plant comprising the reproductive organs. 3. a plant considered with reference to its blossom or floral beauty. 4. state of bloom. 5. the finest or most flourishing state or period. 6. the best member or part. —*v.i.* 7. to blossom. 8. to come out into full development or display. —*v.t.* 9. to decorate with a floral design.

flow·er·et (flou′ər ĭt), *n.* a small flower.

flowering dogwood, a North American tree, widely planted, bearing in the spring a profusion of white or pale pink flowers.

flow·er·pot (flou′ər pŏt′), *n.* a pot to hold earth for a plant to grow in.

flow·er·y (flou′ə rĭ), *adj.*, **-erier, -eriest.** 1. abounding in or covered with flowers. 2. highly ornate. 3. decorated with floral designs. —**flow′er·i·ness,** *n.*

flu (flōō), *n. Colloq.* influenza.

fluc·tu·ate (flŭk′chŏŏ āt′), *v.i.*, **-ated, -ating.** to change continually from one course, condition, etc., to another; vary irregularly. —**fluc′tu·a′tion,** *n.*

flue (flōō), *n.* 1. the smoke passage in a chimney. 2. any duct for air, gases, etc.

flu·ent (flōō′ənt), *adj.* 1. flowing smoothly and easily. 2. able to speak or write readily. 3. easy; graceful. 4. flowing, as a stream. —**flu′en·cy,** *n.* —**flu′ent·ly,** *adv.*

fluff (flŭf), *n.* 1. light, downy particles, as of cotton. 2. a downy mass. —*v.t.*, *v.i.* 3. to make into fluff. 4. to make or become fluffy.

fluff·y (flŭf′ĭ), *adj.*, **fluffier, fluffiest.** of, like, or covered with fluff; soft and light as fluff. —**fluff′i·ly,** *adv.* —**fluff′i·ness,** *n.*

flu·id (flōō′ĭd), *n.* 1. a substance, as a liquid or a gas, which is capable of flowing, and which usually does not resist forces tending to change its shape but not its volume. —*adj.* 2. capable of flowing; liquid or gaseous. 3. consisting of or pertaining to fluids. 4. not fixed, stable, or rigid. —**flu·id′i·ty,** *n.*

fluid dram, one eighth of a fluid ounce.

fluid ounce, a measure of capacity equal to $1/16$ pint in the U.S.

fluke[1] (flōōk), *n.* 1. the flat triangular piece at the end of each arm of an anchor, which catches in the ground. 2. a barb of a harpoon, etc.

fluke[2] (flōōk), *n.* any lucky chance, stroke, etc.

fluke[3] (flōōk), *n.* a flounder[2].

fluk·y (flōō′kĭ), *adj.*, **flukier, flukiest.** *Colloq.* obtained by chance rather than skill.

flume (flōōm), *n.* 1. a deep, narrow defile, esp. one containing a mountain torrent. 2. an artificial channel or trough for conducting water, as one in which logs, etc., are transported.

flunk (flŭngk), *U.S. Colloq.* —*v.i.*, *v.t.* 1. to fail in (a recitation, etc.). —*n.* 2. a failure.

flun·key (flŭng/kĭ), n., pl. **-keys.** flunky.

flun·ky (flŭng/kĭ), n., pl. **-kies.** 1. a male servant in livery. 2. a servile follower.

flu·o·res·cence (floo/ə rĕs/əns), n. Physics, Chem. the property possessed by certain substances of emitting light upon exposure to external radiation or bombardment by a stream of particles. —**flu/o·res/cent,** adj.

fluorescent lamp, an electric lamp in which light is produced by the passage of electricity through a vapor or gas in a tube.

flu·o·ride (floo/ə rīd/), n. Chem. a compound containing fluorine. Also, **flu·o·rid** (floo/ə rĭd).

flu·o·rine (floo/ə rēn/ -rĭn), n. Chem. a nonmetallic element, a pale yellow corrosive gas. Symbol: F; at. wt.: 19.0; at. no.: 9. Also, **flu·o·rin** (floo/ə rĭn). —**flu·or·ic** (floo ôr/ĭk, -ŏr/-), adj.

flu·o·rite (floo/ə rīt/), n. a common mineral, calcium fluoride, CaF₂: the principal source of fluorine. Also, **flu·or·spar** (floo/ôr spär/, -ər-).

fluor·o·scope (floor/ə skōp/, floo/ə rə-), n. a device fitted with a fluorescent screen, the shadows of bodies being examined by means of x-rays.

flur·ry (flûr/ĭ), n., pl. **-ries,** v., **-ried, -rying.** —n. 1. a sudden gust of wind. 2. a light shower or snowfall. 3. commotion. —v.t. 4. to fluster.

flush¹ (flŭsh), n. 1. a blush; rosy glow. 2. a rushing flow, as of water. 3. elation. 4. glowing freshness or vigor. —v.t., v.i. 5. to redden. 6. to flood with water. 7. to animate or elate.

flush² (flŭsh), adj. 1. even or level. 2. wellsupplied. 3. abundant. 4. full of vigor. —adv. 5. so as to be flush. —v.t. 6. to make flush.

flush³ (flŭsh), Hunting. —v.t. 1. to cause to start up. —n. 2. a flushed bird.

flush⁴ (flŭsh), n. Cards. a hand or set of cards all of one suit.

flus·ter (flŭs/tər), v.t. 1. to confuse; make nervous. —v.i. 2. to become flustered. —n. 3. confusion; excitement.

flute (floot), n., v., **fluted, fluting.** —n. 1. a musical wind instrument consisting of a tube with a series of finger holes or keys. 2. Archit., etc. a groove or furrow, as in a pillar. 3. a groove in any material, as in a woman's ruffle. —v.i. 4. to produce flutelike sounds. 5. to play on a flute. —v.t. 6. to utter in flutelike tones. 7. to form flutes in. —**flut/ed,** adj.

flut·ing (floo/tĭng), n. 1. act of playing on the flute. 2. the sound of a flute. 3. fluted work.

flut·ist (floo/tĭst), n. a flute player.

flut·ter (flŭt/ər), v.i. 1. to wave in the air, as a flag. 2. to flap the wings, or fly with flapping movements. 3. to move in quick, irregular motions. 4. to beat fast and irregularly. —n. 5. a fluttering movement. 6. nervous excitement or mental agitation. 7. sensation; stir. —**flut/ter·ing·ly,** adv. —**flut/ter·y,** adj.

flux (flŭks), n. 1. a flowing or flow. 2. the flowing in of the tide. 3. continuous change. 4. an abnormal discharge of blood or other matter from the body. 5. the rate of flow of a fluid, heat, or the like. 6. a substance, as borax, used to promote the fusion of metals or minerals. —v.t. 7. to melt; fuse.

flux·ion (flŭk/shən), n. a flow or flux.

fly¹ (flī), v., **flew** or (for def. 5) **flied; flown; flying;** n., pl. **flies.** —v.i. 1. to move through the air on wings or by the wind or any other force or agency. 2. to flutter in the air, as a flag. 3. to travel in an aircraft. 4. to move or pass swiftly. 5. Baseball. to bat a fly ball. —n. 6. a strip along one edge of a garment to conceal the buttons or other fasteners. 7. a flap forming the door of a tent. 8. Baseball. a ball knocked high in the air. —**fly/er,** n.

fly² (flī), n., pl. **flies.** 1. any of certain twowinged insects, esp. the housefly. 2. a fishhook dressed with silk, tinsel, etc., to resemble an insect.

fly-by-night (flī/bī nīt/), adj. irresponsible.

fly·catch·er (flī/kăch/ər), n. any of numerous small, insectivorous birds.

fly·ing (flī/ĭng), adj. 1. that flies. 2. floating, waving, hanging, or moving in the air. 3. moving swiftly. 4. hasty. —n. 5. flight.

flying boat, an aircraft whose main body consists of a single hull or boat.

flying buttress, (in Gothic architecture) an arch which carries the thrust of the nave wall over the aisle to a solid pier buttress.

flying fish, any of certain fishes with winglike pectoral fins which help them to glide through the air after leaping from the water.

flying machine, an airplane or the like.

flying saucer, any of various disk-shaped planes or missiles allegedly seen flying at high speeds and altitudes.

fly·leaf (flī/lēf/), n., pl. **-leaves** (-lēvz/). a blank leaf in the front or the back of a book.

fly·speck (flī/spĕk/), n. a speck or tiny stain, as one from the excrement of a fly.

fly·weight (flī/wāt/), n. a boxer of 112 pounds or less.

fly·wheel (flī/hwēl/), n. a heavy wheel which by its momentum tends to equalize the speed of machinery with which it is connected.

FM, Radio. frequency modulation.

foal (fōl), n. 1. a colt or filly. —v.t., v.i. 2. to bring forth (a foal).

foam (fōm), n. 1. a mass of minute bubbles formed on the surface of a liquid by agitation, fermentation, etc. —v.i., v.t. 2. to foam or cause to foam. —**foam/y,** adj. —**foam/i·ness,** n.

fob (fŏb), n. 1. a small pocket in trousers for a watch, etc. 2. a short chain or ribbon with a seal or the like, attached to a watch and worn hanging from the pocket.

F.O.B., free on board. Also, **f.o.b.**

fo·cal (fō/kəl), adj. of or pertaining to a focus. —**fo/cal·ly,** adv.

focal distance, (of a mirror or lens) the distance from a point near its center to the focal point. Also, **focal length.**

fo·cal·ize (fō/kə līz/), v.t., **-ized, -izing.** to focus. —**fo/cal·i·za/tion,** n.

fo·cus (fō/kəs), n., pl. **-cuses, -ci** (-sī), v., **-cused, -cusing** or (esp. Brit.) **-cussed, -cussing.** —n. 1. a point at which rays of light, heat, or other radiation, meet after being refracted or reflected. 2. the focal distance of a lens. 3. the position of a viewed object necessary to produce a clear image. 4. a central point, as of attention. —v.t. 5. to bring to a focus or into focus. 6. to concentrate. —v.i. 7. to become focused.

fod·der (fŏd/ər), n. coarse roughages used as feed for livestock, as hay.

foe (fō), n. an enemy or opponent.

foe·tus (fē/təs), n. fetus. —**foe/tal,** adj.

fog (fŏg, fôg), n., v., **fogged, fogging.** —n. 1. a thick mist. 2. mental confusion or obscurity. 3. Photog. a darkening of a developed plate or print by accidental light. —v.t. 4. to envelop with fog. 5. Photog. to affect by fog. 6. to confuse. —v.i. 7. to become fogged.

fo·gey (fō/gĭ), n., pl. **-geys.** fogy.

fog·gy (fŏg/ĭ, fôg/ĭ), adj., **-gier, -giest.** 1. abounding in fog; misty. 2. dim; obscure. —**fog/gi·ly,** adv. —**fog/gi·ness,** n.

fog·horn (fŏg/hôrn/, fôg/-), n. a horn for warning ships, as in bad weather.

fo·gy (fō/gĭ), n., pl. **-gies.** an old-fashioned or excessively conservative person.

foi·ble (foi/bəl), n. a weak point or whimsy.

foil¹ (foil), v.t. to frustrate; balk.

foil² (foil), n. 1. a metallic substance formed into very thin sheets. 2. anything that sets off another to advantage by contrast.

foil³ (foil), n. a blunt sword with a button at the point, for use in fencing.

foist (foist), v.t. to impose or bring in fraudulently or unwarrantably.

fol., 1. folio. 2. following. 3. followed.

fold¹ (fōld), v.t. 1. to bend (paper, etc.) over upon itself. 2. to bring together (the arms, etc.). 3. to enclose; wrap. 4. to embrace. —v.i. 5. to be folded or be capable of folding. 6. to collapse or fail. —n. 7. a part that is folded. 8. a hollow made by folding.

fold² (fōld), n. 1. an enclosure for sheep. 2. the church.

-fold, a suffix attached to numerals and other quantitative words or stems to denote multiplication by or division into a certain number, as in twofold, manifold.

fold·er (fōl/dər), n. 1. one that folds. 2. a folded printed sheet. 3. an outer cover, usually of light cardboard, for papers.

fo·li·a·ceous (fō/lĭ ā/shəs), adj. 1. leaflike. 2. bearing leaves or leaflike parts.

fo·li·age (fō/lĭ ĭj), n. 1. the leaves of a plant. 2. leaves in general. —**fo/li·aged,** adj.

fo·li·ate (adj. fō/lĭ ĭt, -āt/; v. fō/lĭ āt/), adj., v., **-ated, -ating.** —adj. 1. having leaves. 2. leaflike. —v.i. 3. to put forth leaves.

fo·li·a·tion (fō/lĭ ā/shən), n. 1. act of putting forth leaves. 2. state of being in leaf. 3. the arrangement of leaves within the bud. **4.** the consecutive numbering of the leaves of a book or manuscript. **5.** ornamentation with foliage.

fo·li·o (fō′lǐ ō′), n., pl. **-lios,** adj., v., **-lioed, -lioing.** —n. **1.** a sheet of paper folded once to make two leaves. **2.** a volume having pages of the largest size. **3.** a leaf of a manuscript or book numbered only on the front side. **4.** Print. the page number of a book. —adj. **5.** pertaining to or having the format of a folio. —v.t. **6.** to number the leaves of (a book).

folk (fōk), n., pl. **folk, folks,** adj. —n. **1.** (often pl.) people in general. **2.** (usually pl.) people of a specified group. **3.** (pl.) Colloq. one's relatives. —adj. **4.** originating among the common people.

folk·lore (fōk′lōr′), n. the traditional beliefs, customs, etc., of a people.

folk·sy (fōk′sǐ), adj. **1.** sociable. **2.** simple; unsophisticated.

foll., following.

fol·li·cle (fŏl′ə kəl), n. **1.** Bot. a dry one-celled seed vessel consisting of a single carpel. **2.** Anat. a small cavity, sac, or gland. —**fol·lic·u·lar** (fə lĭk′yə lər), adj.

fol·low (fŏl′ō), v.t. **1.** to come or go after. **2.** to accept as a guide or leader. **3.** to conform to or comply with. **4.** to move along (a path, etc.). **5.** to result from. **6.** to go in pursuit of. **7.** to be concerned with as an occupation, etc. **8.** to watch the movements or course of. **9.** to understand. —v.i. **10.** to come or occur next after something or someone else. **11.** to result. —n. **12.** act of following. —**fol′low·a·ble,** adj.

fol·low·er (fŏl′ō ər), n. **1.** one that follows. **2.** a disciple or adherent.

fol·low·ing (fŏl′ō ĭng), n. **1.** a body of followers, etc. **2.** the following, things, lines, etc., that follow. —adj. **3.** that follows.

fol·ly (fŏl′ĭ), n., pl. **-lies. 1.** state or quality of being foolish. **2.** a foolish action, idea, etc.

fo·ment (fō mĕnt′), v.t. to instigate or foster (discord, rebellion, etc.). —**fo′men·ta′tion,** n. —**fo·ment′er,** n.

fond (fŏnd), adj. **1.** liking (fol. by of). **2.** loving. **3.** doting. **4.** cherished. —**fond′ly,** adv. —**fond′ness,** n.

fon·dant (fŏn′dənt), n. a thick, creamy sugar paste, the basis of many candies.

fon·dle (fŏn′dəl), v.t., **-dled, -dling.** to handle or touch fondly; caress. —**fon′dler,** n.

fon·due (fŏn′dōō, fŏn dōō′), n. a baked dish of grated cheese, butter, eggs, etc.

font[1] (fŏnt), n. **1.** a receptacle for the water used in baptism. **2.** a receptacle for holy water.

font[2] (fŏnt), n. Print. a complete assortment of type of one style and size.

Foo·chow (fōō′chou′), n. a seaport in SE China. 348,280.

food (fōōd), n. **1.** what is eaten or taken in for nourishment. **2.** solid nourishment (as opposed to drink).

food·stuff (fōōd′stŭf′), n. a substance or material suitable for food.

fool (fōōl), n. **1.** a silly or stupid person. **2.** a professional jester. —v.t. **3.** to trick; deceive. **4.** to spend foolishly. —v.i. **5.** to joke; play. **6.** to waste time.

fool·er·y (fōō′lə rǐ), n., pl. **-eries. 1.** foolish conduct. **2.** a foolish action or thing.

fool·har·dy (fōōl′här′dǐ), adj., **-dier, -diest.** foolishly bold or rash. —**fool′har′di·ly,** adv. —**fool′har′di·ness,** n.

fool·ish (fōō′lǐsh), adj. **1.** silly; without sense. **2.** unwise. —**fool′ish·ly,** adv. —**fool′ish·ness,** n.

fool·proof (fōōl′prōōf′), adj. Colloq. **1.** involving no risk or harm. **2.** never-failing.

fools·cap (fōōlz′kăp′), n. writing paper, usually folded, about 12 x 15 inches.

fool's gold, iron pyrites, sometimes mistaken for gold.

foot (fōōt), n., pl. **feet,** v. —n. **1.** the terminal part of the leg on which the body stands and moves. **2.** a unit of length divided into 12 inches. **3.** infantry. **4.** walking or running motion. **5.** any thing or part resembling a foot. **6.** the lowest part, as of a hill, ladder, page, etc. **7.** the last, as of a series. **8.** Pros. a group of syllables constituting a metrical unit. —v.i. **9.** to walk. **10.** to total, as an account. —v.t. **11.** Colloq. to pay, as a bill.

foot·age (fōōt′ĭj), n. length or extent in feet.

foot-and-mouth disease (fōōt′ən mouth′),

a contagious virus disease of cattle and other cloven-footed animals.

foot·ball (fōōt′bôl′), n. **1.** a game played with a large, inflated leather ball on a field at either end of which there is a goal post. **2.** the ball itself.

foot·board (fōōt′bōrd′), n. **1.** a board on which to support the foot or feet. **2.** an upright piece across the foot of a bedstead.

foot·bridge (fōōt′brĭj′), n. a bridge intended for pedestrians only.

foot·can·dle (fōōt′kăn′dəl), n. a unit of illumination equivalent to that produced by a standard candle at the distance of one foot.

foot·fall (fōōt′fôl′), n. a footstep.

foot·hill (fōōt′hĭl′), n. a minor elevation at the base of a mountain or mountain range.

foot·hold (fōōt′hōld′), n. **1.** a hold or support for the feet. **2.** secure position.

foot·ing (fōōt′ĭng), n. **1.** secure position. **2.** the basis on which anything is established. **3.** place or support for the feet. **4.** reciprocal relation.

foot·lights (fōōt′līts′), n.pl. **1.** a row of lights at the front of a stage. **2.** the acting profession.

foot·man (fōōt′mən), n., pl. **-men.** a male servant who attends the door or the carriage, waits at table, etc.

foot·note (fōōt′nōt′), n. a note at the foot of a page, referring to a part of the text.

foot·pad (fōōt′păd′), n. a highwayman.

foot·path (fōōt′păth′, -päth′), n. **1.** a path for pedestrians only. **2.** Brit. a sidewalk.

foot·pound (fōōt′pound′), n. Mech. a unit of energy or work, the equivalent to that produced by a force of one pound moving through a distance of one foot.

foot·print (fōōt′prĭnt′), n. a mark left by the foot.

foot soldier, an infantryman.

foot·sore (fōōt′sōr′), adj. having sore or tender feet, as from much walking.

foot·step (fōōt′stĕp′), n. a step of the foot, or the sound produced by it.

foot·stool (fōōt′stōōl′), n. a low stool upon which to rest one's feet.

foot·work (fōōt′wûrk′), n. the use of the feet, as in tennis, boxing, etc.

foo·zle (fōō′zəl), v., **-zled, -zling,** n. —v.t., v.i. **1.** to play clumsily. —n. **2.** act of foozling.

fop (fŏp), n. a man who is excessively concerned about his manners and appearance. —**fop′pish,** adj.

for (fôr; unstressed fər), prep. **1.** with the purpose of. **2.** suited to; used by or with. **3.** in order to obtain. **4.** with inclination toward. **5.** in return for. **6.** appropriate or adapted to. **7.** with respect to. **8.** during. **9.** in favor of. **10.** in place of. **11.** in the interest of. **12.** as an offset to. **13.** in honor of. **14.** with the purpose of reaching. **15.** conducive to. **16.** in order to save. **17.** to allow of. **18.** because of. **19.** in spite of. **20.** to the extent of. **21.** that. —conj. **22.** since. **23.** because.

for·age (fôr′ĭj, fŏr′-), n., v., **-aged, -aging.** —n. **1.** food for horses and cattle. **2.** searching for provisions. —v.i. **3.** to wander in search of supplies. **4.** to make a raid. —**for′ag·er,** n.

for·as·much (fôr′əz mŭch′), conj. in view of the fact that; seeing that; since (fol. by as).

for·ay (fôr′ā, fŏr′ā), n. **1.** a plundering raid. —v.i., v.t. **2.** to raid; pillage.

for·bear[1] (fôr bâr′), v.t., v.i., **-bore, -borne, -bearing. 1.** to refrain (from). **2.** to be patient.

for·bear[2] (fôr′bâr′), n. forebear.

for·bear·ance (fôr bâr′əns), n. **1.** act of forbearing. **2.** patient endurance.

for·bid (fər bĭd′), v.t., **-bade or -bad, -bidden or -bid, -bidding. 1.** to command not to do, have, use, etc., something. **2.** to prohibit.

for·bid·ding (fər bĭd′ĭng), adj. **1.** causing fear. **2.** dangerous-looking. —**for·bid′ding·ly,** adv.

force (fōrs), n., v., **forced, forcing.** —n. **1.** strength; impetus. **2.** might. **3.** physical coercion. **4.** Law. violence. **5.** power to influence, affect, or control. **6.** mental or moral strength. **7.** (often pl.) an army. **8.** any body of persons combined for joint action. **9.** operation. **10.** Physics. an influence which produces or tends to produce motion or change of motion. **11.** any influence. **12.** binding power. **13.** meaning. —v.t. **14.** to compel. **15.** to drive or propel against resistance. **16.** to bring about by force.

17. to impose. 18. to obtain by force. 19. to overpower. 20. to break open (a lock, etc.).

forced (fōrst), *adj.* 1. compulsory. 2. strained, unnatural, or affected. 3. emergency. —**forced·ly** (fōr'sĭd lĭ), *adv.*

force·ful (fōrs'fəl), *adj.* powerful; vigorous. —**force'ful·ly**, *adv.* —**force'ful·ness**, *n.*

force·meat (fōrs'mēt'), *n.* meat chopped fine and seasoned, used as stuffing, etc.

for·ceps (fōr'səps), *n.*, *pl.* **-ceps, -cipes** (-sə-pēz'). an instrument, as pincers or tongs, for seizing and holding objects, as in surgical operations.

for·ci·ble (fōr'sə bəl), *adj.* 1. effected by force. 2. having force; effective. 3. convincing. —**for'ci·bly**, *adv.*

ford (fōrd), *n.* 1. a place where a river may be crossed by wading. —*v.t.* 2. to cross by a ford. —**ford'a·ble**, *adj.*

fore[1] (fōr), *adj.* 1. situated at or toward the front. 2. forward; earlier. —*adv.* 3. *Naut.* at or toward the bow. —*n.* 4. the front.

fore[2] (fōr), *interj. Golf.* a cry of warning to persons liable to be struck by the ball.

fore and aft, *Naut.* in, at, or to both ends of a ship.

fore-and-aft (fōr'ənd äft'), *adj. Naut.* in a line with the keel of a ship.

fore·arm[1] (fōr'ärm'), *n.* the part of the arm between the elbow and the wrist.

fore·arm[2] (fōr ärm'), *v.t.* to arm beforehand.

fore·bear (fōr'bâr'), *n.* an ancestor.

fore·bode (fōr bōd'), *v.t.*, *v.i.*, **-boded, -boding.** to predict; portend, esp. evil. —**fore·bod'ing**, *n.*, *adj.*

fore·cast (fōr'kăst', -käst'), *v.*, **-cast** or **-casted, -casting**, *n.* —*v.t.*, *v.i.* 1. to predict. 2. to foreshadow. —*n.* 3. a prediction. —**fore'cast'-er**, *n.*

fore·cas·tle (fōk'səl, fōr'kăs'əl), *n. Naut.* 1. the seamen's quarters in a merchant vessel, usually in the forward part. 2. that part of the upper deck forward of the foremast.

fore·close (fōr klōz'), *v.t.*, *v.i.*, **-closed, -closing.** *Law.* to deprive (a mortgagor or pledgor) of the right to redeem his property. —**fore·clo·sure** (fōr klō'zhər), *n.*

fore·doom (fōr dōōm'), *v.t.* to doom beforehand.

fore·fa·ther (fōr'fä'ᵺər), *n.* an ancestor.

fore·fin·ger (fōr'fĭng'gər), *n.* the first finger, next to the thumb.

fore·foot (fōr'fŏŏt'), *n.*, *pl.* **-feet** (-fēt'). one of the front feet of an animal.

fore·front (fōr'frŭnt'), *n.* the foremost part or place.

fore·go (fōr gō'), *v.t.*, *v.i.*, **-went, -gone, -going.** to go before; precede. —**fore·go'er**, *n.* —**fore·go'ing**, *adj.*, *n.*

fore·gone (fōr gôn', -gŏn', fōr'gôn', -gŏn'), *adj.* previous; past.

fore·ground (fōr'ground'), *n.* the parts in or toward the front.

fore·hand (fōr'hănd'), *adj.* 1. made to the right side of the body (when the player is right-handed). —*n.* 2. *Tennis, etc.* a forehand stroke.

fore·hand·ed (fōr'hăn'dĭd), *adj.* 1. forehand, as a stroke in tennis, etc. 2. prudent. —**fore'hand'ed·ness**, *n.*

fore·head (fōr'ĭd, fōr'-, fōr'hĕd'), *n.* the part of the face above the eyes; the brow.

for·eign (fōr'ĭn, fŏr'-), *adj.* 1. pertaining to, characteristic of, or derived from another country. 2. pertaining to relations with other countries. 3. external to one's own country. 4. carried on with other countries. 5. not belonging. 6. unfamiliar. —**for'eign·ness**, *n.*

for·eign·er (fōr'ĭn ər, fŏr'-), *n.* a citizen of a different country; alien.

fore·know (fōr nō'), *v.t.*, **-knew, -known, -knowing.** to know beforehand. —**fore'knowl'edge**, *n.*

fore·land (fōr'lănd'), *n.* 1. a cape, headland, or promontory. 2. land lying in front.

fore·leg (fōr'lĕg'), *n.* one of the front legs of a quadruped, an insect, etc.

fore·lock (fōr'lŏk'), *n.* the lock of hair that grows from the fore part of the head.

fore·man (fōr'mən), *n.*, *pl.* **-men.** 1. a man in charge of a group of workers. 2. the chairman of a jury.

fore·mast (fōr'măst', -mäst'; *Naut.* -məst), *n.* the mast nearest the bow of a ship.

fore·most (fōr'mōst', -məst), *adj.*, *adv.* first in place, order, rank, etc.

fore·noon (fōr'nōōn'), *n.* the period of daylight before noon.

fo·ren·sic (fə rĕn'sĭk), *adj.* pertaining to, connected with, or used in public discussion.

fore·or·dain (fōr'ôr dān'), *v.t.* to ordain or appoint beforehand; predestinate. —**fore'or·dain'ment, fore·or·di·na·tion** (fōr'ôr də nā'shən), *n.*

fore·run (fōr rŭn'), *v.t.*, **-ran, -run, -running.** to precede. —**fore'run'ner**, *n.*

fore·sail (fōr'sāl'; *Naut.* -səl), *n.* 1. the sail bent to the lower yard on the foremast of a square-rigged vessel. 2. the principal sail on the foremast.

fore·see (fōr sē'), *v.t.*, **-saw, -seen, -seeing.** to see beforehand. —**fore·see'a·ble**, *adj.*

fore·shad·ow (fōr shăd'ō), *v.t.* to shadow or indicate beforehand. —**fore·shad'ow·er**, *n.*

fore·shore (fōr'shōr'), *n.* the part of the shore between the high-water and low-water marks.

fore·short·en (fōr shôr'tən), *v.t. Drawing.* to reduce the length of (certain lines, etc.) to give the proper impression to the eye by means of perspective.

fore·show (fōr shō'), *v.t.*, **-showed, -shown, -showing.** to show beforehand; foretell.

fore·sight (fōr'sīt'), *n.* 1. provision for the future. 2. act or power of foreseeing. —**fore'-sight'ed**, *adj.*

fore·skin (fōr'skĭn'), *n. Anat.* the prepuce.

for·est (fōr'ĭst, fŏr'-), *n.* 1. a large tract of land covered with trees. 2. the trees alone. —*v.t.* 3. to cover with trees. —**for'est·ed**, *adj.*

fore·stall (fōr stôl'), *v.t.* to prevent, hinder, or thwart by action in advance.

for·est·a·tion (fōr'ĭs tā'shən, fŏr'-), *n.* the planting of forests.

for·est·er (fōr'ĭs tər, fŏr'-), *n.* 1. an expert in forestry. 2. an officer in charge of a forest.

for·est·ry (fōr'ĭs trĭ, fŏr'-), *n.* the science of planting and taking care of forests.

fore·taste (*n.* fōr'tāst'; *v.* fōr tāst'), *n.*, *v.*, **-tasted, -tasting.** —*n.* 1. a taste beforehand. —*v.t.* 2. to taste beforehand.

fore·tell (fōr tĕl'), *v.t.*, *v.i.*, **-told, -telling.** to predict or prophesy.

fore·thought (fōr'thôt'), *n.* 1. prudence. 2. previous consideration; anticipation.

fore·to·ken (*n.* fōr'tō'kən; *v.* fōr tō'kən), *n.* 1. an omen. —*v.t.* 2. to foreshadow.

fore·top (fōr'tŏp', *Naut.* -təp), *n.* a platform at the head of a foremast.

for·ev·er (fôr ĕv'ər), *adv.* 1. eternally; without ever ending. 2. incessantly.

for·ev·er·more (fôr ĕv'ər mōr'), *adv.* for ever hereafter.

fore·warn (fōr wôrn'), *v.t.* to warn beforehand.

fore·word (fōr'wûrd'), *n.* a preface or introductory statement in a book, etc.

for·feit (fôr'fĭt), *n.* 1. a fine; a penalty. —*v.t.* 2. to lose as a forfeit. —*adj.* 3. forfeited.

for·fei·ture (fôr'fĭ chər), *n.* 1. act of forfeiting. 2. that which is forfeited; a fine.

for·gath·er (fôr găᵺ'ər), *v.i.* to convene; assemble.

forge[1] (fôrj), *n.*, *v.*, **forged, forging.** —*n.* 1. the special fireplace or furnace in which metal is heated before shaping. 2. a smithy. —*v.t.* 3. to form, esp. by heating and hammering. 4. to imitate (a signature, etc.) fraudulently. —*v.i.* 5. to commit forgery. —**forg'er**, *n.*

forge[2] (fôrj), *v.i.*, **forged, forging.** to move ahead slowly or with difficulty.

forg·er·y (fôr'jə rĭ), *n.*, *pl.* **-geries.** 1. the making of a fraudulent imitation of a thing. 2. something produced by forgery. 3. the fraudulent imitation of another's signature.

for·get (fər gĕt'), *v.t.*, *v.i.*, **-got** or (*Archaic*) **-gat; -gotten** or **-got; -getting.** to cease or fail to remember.

for·get·ful (fər gĕt'fəl), *adj.* 1. apt to forget. 2. heedless. —**for·get'ful·ly**, *adv.* —**for·get'-ful·ness**, *n.*

for·get-me-not (fər gĕt'mĭ nŏt'), *n.* a small plant bearing a light-blue flower.

for·give (fər gĭv'), *v.t.*, *v.i.*, **-gave, -given, -giving.** 1. to grant pardon for or remission of (an offense, debt, etc.). **2.** to grant pardon to (a person). —**for·giv′a·ble,** adj. —**for·giv′er,** n.

for·give·ness (far gĭv′nĭs), n. **1.** act of forgiving. **2.** state of being forgiven. **3.** disposition or willingness to forgive.

for·go (fôr gō′), v.t., **-went, -gone, -going.** to abstain from; do without; give up, renounce, or resign.

fork (fôrk), n. **1.** an instrument having two or more prongs, for holding, lifting, etc. **2.** the point at which a thing, as a road, divides into branches. **3.** each of the branches. —v.t. **4.** Slang. to hand. —v.i. **5.** to divide into branches. —**forked,** adj.

for·lorn (fôr lôrn′), adj. **1.** abandoned. **2.** miserable or wretched. **3.** hopeless. —**for·lorn′ly,** adv. —**for·lorn′ness,** n.

form (fôrm), n. **1.** external shape considered apart from color or material. **2.** something that gives shape; mold. **3.** a particular structural condition. **4.** the style of arranging parts for a pleasing or effective result, as in literary composition. **5.** proper shape or arrangement. **6.** a set or customary method of doing something. **7.** a document with blank spaces to be filled in with particulars. **8.** a formality or ceremony. **9.** conventional observance of social usages. **10.** condition, esp. with reference to fitness. **11.** Gram. any word, part of a word, or group of words arranged in a construction, which recurs in various contexts in a language with relatively constant meaning. **12.** Brit. a grade or class of pupils in a school. **13.** an assemblage of type, etc., secured in a chase to print from. —v.t. **14.** to construct or produce. **15.** to serve for or constitute. **16.** to place in order; arrange. **17.** to frame (ideas, etc.) in the mind. **18.** to contract (habits, friendships, etc.). **19.** to shape; fashion. —v.i. **20.** to take form. **21.** to be formed.

for·mal (fôr′məl), adj. **1.** being in accordance with conventional requirements. **2.** ceremonious. **3.** perfunctory. **4.** made or done in accordance with forms ensuring validity. **5.** rigorously methodical. **6.** denoting language whose grammar and syntax are correct, and speech whose sounds are carefully formed without sounding stilted. **7.** Philos. pertaining to the form of a thing, esp. as distinguished from the matter. —**for′mal·ly,** adv.

form·al·de·hyde (fôr măl′də hīd′), n. a gas, CH_2O, used most often in an aqueous solution, as a disinfectant and preservative.

for·mal·ism (fôr′mə lĭz′əm), n. strict adherence to prescribed or customary forms.

for·mal·i·ty (fôr măl′ə tĭ), n., pl. **-ties. 1.** accordance with prescribed, customary, or due forms. **2.** an established mode of proceeding. **3.** a formal act or observance.

for·mal·ize (fôr′mə līz′), v., **-ized, -izing.** —v.t. **1.** to make formal. **2.** to give a definite form to. —v.i. **3.** to be formal.

for·mat (fôr′măt), n. the physical appearance of a book, based on the type face, binding, margins, etc.

for·ma·tion (fôr mā′shən), n. **1.** act or process of forming. **2.** state of being formed. **3.** the manner in which a thing is formed. **4.** a particular disposition of troops, ships, planes, etc. **5.** something formed. **6.** Geol. a body of rocks classed as a unit for purposes of geologic mapping.

form·a·tive (fôr′mə tĭv), adj. **1.** giving form or shape. **2.** pertaining to formation.

form class, Gram. a class of words or forms in a language with one or more grammatical features in common.

for·mer (fôr′mər), adj. **1.** prior or earlier. **2.** past or long past. **3.** preceding. **4.** being the first-mentioned of two.

for·mer·ly (fôr′mər lĭ), adv. in time past; heretofore; of old.

for·mic acid (fôr′mĭk), Chem. a colorless irritant liquid, once obtained from insects but now manufactured synthetically.

for·mi·da·ble (fôr′mĭ də bəl), adj. **1.** that is to be feared or dreaded. **2.** of alarming strength, difficulty, etc. —**for′mi·da·bly,** adv.

form·less (fôrm′lĭs), adj. lacking form; shapeless. —**form′less·ly,** adv. —**form′less·ness,** n.

For·mo·sa (fôr mō′sə), n. an island off the SE coast of China. 5,895,864 pop.; 13,807 sq. mi.

for·mu·la (fôr′myə lə), n., pl. **-las, -lae** (-lē′). **1.** a set form of words, as for stating something, for indicating procedure, or for ceremonial use. **2.** Math. a rule or principle frequently expressed in algebraic symbols. **3.** Chem. an expression of

the constituents of a compound by symbols and figures. **4.** a recipe or prescription.

for·mu·late (fôr′myə lāt′), v.t., **-lated, -lating. 1.** to state definitely or systematically. **2.** to reduce to a formula. —**for′mu·la′tion,** n. —**for′mu·la′tor,** n.

for·ni·cate (fôr′nə kāt′), v.i., **-cated, -cating.** (of unmarried persons) to have illicit sexual intercourse. —**for′ni·ca′tion,** n. —**for′ni·ca′tor,** n.

for·sake (fôr sāk′), v.t., **-sook, -saken, -saking. 1.** to leave entirely; desert. **2.** to give up (a habit, etc.).

for·sooth (fôr sōōth′), adv. in truth; indeed.

for·swear (fôr swâr′), v.t., **-swore, -sworn, -swearing. 1.** to reject or renounce upon oath or with protestations. **2.** to perjure (oneself).

for·syth·i·a (fôr sĭth′ĭ ə, -sī′thĭ ə), n. any of certain shrubs cultivated for their showy yellow flowers, appearing in early spring before the leaves.

fort (fôrt), n. a strong or fortified place.

fort., 1. fortification. **2.** fortified.

forte¹ (fôrt), n. that in which one excels.

for·te² (fôr′tĕ), Music. —adj. **1.** loud. —adv. **2.** loudly. —n. **3.** a loud passage.

forth (fôrth), adv. **1.** forward; onward. **2.** out; into view. **3.** abroad.

forth·com·ing (fôrth′kŭm′ĭng), adj. **1.** about to appear. **2.** ready or available when required or expected.

forth·right (fôrth′rīt′; adv. also fôrth′rīt′), adj. **1.** outspoken. **2.** direct; straightforward. —adv. **3.** directly forward. **4.** immediately.

forth·with (fôrth′wĭth′, -wĭth′), adv. immediately; at once; without delay.

for·ti·eth (fôr′tĭ ĭth), adj. **1.** next after the thirty-ninth. —n. **2.** one (or the last) of forty parts.

for·ti·fi·ca·tion (fôr′tə fə kā′shən), n. **1.** act of fortifying. **2.** that which fortifies. **3.** the science of constructing defensive military works. **4.** a fortified place.

for·ti·fy (fôr′tə fī′), v.t., **-fied, -fying. 1.** to strengthen or protect against attack. **2.** to furnish with a means of resisting strain, wear, etc. **3.** to impart strength to. **4.** to confirm.

for·tis·si·mo (fôr tĭs′ə mō′), Music. —adj. **1.** very loud. —adv. **2.** very loudly.

for·ti·tude (fôr′tə tūd′, -tōōd′), n. patient courage under affliction, privation, etc.

fort·night (fôrt′nīt′, -nĭt), n. Chiefly Brit. two weeks.

fort·night·ly (fôrt′nīt′lĭ), adj., adv., n., pl. **-lies.** —adj. **1.** occurring or appearing once a fortnight. —adv. **2.** once a fortnight. —n. **3.** a periodical issued every two weeks.

for·tress (fôr′trĭs), n. a large fortified place.

Fort Smith, a city in W Arkansas. 36,584.

for·tu·i·tous (fôr tū′ə təs, -tōō′-), adj. happening by chance; accidental. —**for·tu′i·tous·ly,** adv.

for·tu·nate (fôr′chə nĭt), adj. **1.** having good fortune; lucky. **2.** bringing or presaging good fortune. —**for′tu·nate·ly,** adv.

for·tune (fôr′chən), n., v., **-tuned, -tuning.** —n. **1.** position in life as determined by wealth. **2.** amount of wealth. **3.** great wealth. **4.** chance; luck. **5.** lot; destiny. **6.** good luck. —v.t. **7.** to endow with a fortune.

for·tune·tell·er (fôr′chən tĕl′ər), n. one who professes to tell people what will happen in the future. —**for′tune·tell′ing,** adj.

Fort Wayne (wān), a city in NE Indiana. 118,410.

Fort William, a city in S Canada. 30,585.

Fort Worth (wûrth), a city in N Texas. 177,-662.

for·ty (fôr′tĭ), n., pl. **-ties,** adj. —n. **1.** a cardinal number, ten times four. **2.** a symbol for this number. —adj. **3.** amounting to forty in number.

for·ty-nin·er (fôr′tĭ nī′nər), n. (sometimes cap.) one of those who went to California in 1849, during the gold rush, in search of fortune.

fo·rum (fōr′əm), n., pl. **forums, fora** (fōr′ə). **1.** an assembly for the discussion of questions of public interest. **2.** a court or tribunal. **3.** the public square of an ancient Roman city.

for·ward (fôr′wərd), adv. Also, **for′wards. 1.** onward; ahead. **2.** towards the front. **3.** out; into view. —adj. **4.** moving ahead; onward. **5.** well-advanced. **6.** ready, prompt, or eager. **7.** pert or bold. **8.** situated in the front. —n. **9.**

Sports. a player stationed in advance of others on his team. —*v.t.* **10.** to transmit, esp. to a new address. **11.** to hasten; promote. **—for′ward·ly,** *adv.* **—for′ward·ness,** *n.*

for·ward·er (fôr′wər dər), *n.* one who sees that the goods of another are transported.

fos·sil (fŏs′əl), *n.* **1.** any remains, impression, or trace of an animal or plant of a former geological age. **2.** *Colloq.* an old-fashioned person. **—adj. 3.** of the nature of a fossil.

fos·sil·if·er·ous (fŏs′ə lĭf′ər əs), *adj.* bearing or containing fossils, as rocks or strata.

fos·sil·ize (fŏs′ə līz′), *v.*, **-ized, -izing. —v.t. 1.** to convert into a fossil. **—v.i. 2.** to become a fossil. **—fos′sil·i·za′tion,** *n.*

fos·ter (fôs′tər, fŏs′-), *v.t.* **1.** to promote the growth of. **2.** to rear, as a child. **3.** to cherish. **—adj. 4.** unrelated by birth but accepted in the family.

Fos·ter (fôs′tər, fŏs′-), *n.* **Stephen Collins,** 1826–64, U.S. song writer and composer.

foul (foul), *adj.* **1.** disgustingly offensive. **2.** filthy or dirty. **3.** clogged. **4.** unfavorable or stormy. **5.** abominable, as crime, slander, etc. **6.** scurrilous, profane, or obscene. **7.** contrary to the rules of a game; unfair. **8.** in collision. **9.** entangled. **—adv. 10.** in a foul manner. **—n. 11.** that which is foul. **12.** a violation of the rules of a game. **13.** *Baseball.* a ball knocked outside the base lines. **—v.t. 14.** to make foul. **15.** to clog. **16.** to collide with. **17.** to cause to become entangled. **18.** to defile; disgrace. **—v.i. 19.** to become foul. **20.** *Naut.* to collide. **21.** to become entangled or clogged. **22.** *Sports.* to make a foul play; give a foul blow. **23.** *Baseball.* to knock a foul. **—foul′ly,** *adv.* **—foul′ness,** *n.*

fou·lard (fŏō lärd′, fə-), *n.* a soft silk with printed design, for neckties, etc.

found¹ (found), *v.t.* **1.** to establish on a firm basis. **2.** to base or ground. **—found′er,** *n.*

found² (found), *v.t.* **1.** to pour (molten metal, etc.) into a mold. **2.** to form of molten material in a mold. **—found′er,** *n.*

foun·da·tion (foun dā′shən), *n.* **1.** that on which something is founded. **2.** the basis of anything. **3.** the ground on which some structure rests. **4.** act of founding. **5.** state of being founded. **6.** an endowed institution.

foun·der (foun′dər), *v.i.* **1.** to fill with water and sink. **2.** to fall down. **3.** to stumble, break down, or go lame.

found·ling (found′lĭng), *n.* an infant found abandoned.

found·ry (foun′drĭ), *n.*, *pl.* **-ries. 1.** an establishment in which molten metal is cast. **2.** the founding of metal, etc. **3.** things made by founding.

fount (fount), *n.* **1.** a fountain. **2.** a source.

foun·tain (foun′tən), *n.* **1.** a spring or source of water. **2.** the source of anything. **3.** a jet of water (or other liquid) from a structure, as to afford water for use, etc. **4.** a structure for discharging such a jet.

foun·tain·head (foun′tən hĕd′), *n.* **1.** the source of a stream. **2.** a primary source.

fountain pen, a writing pen with a reservoir for supplying ink continuously.

four (fôr), *n.* **1.** a cardinal number, three plus one. **2.** a symbol of this number. **3.** a set of this many persons or things. **—adj. 4.** amounting to four in number.

four-flush·er (fôr′flŭsh′ər), *n.* *Slang.* one who makes pretensions that he cannot bear out.

four freedoms, freedom of speech, freedom of worship, freedom from want, and freedom from fear: listed by Franklin D. Roosevelt.

four-in-hand (fôr′ĭn hănd′), *n.* a long scarf or necktie to be tied in a slipknot with the ends left hanging.

four-post·er (fôr′pōs′tər), *n.* a bed with four posts, as for supporting curtains.

four·score (fôr′skôr′), *adj.* eighty.

four·some (fôr′səm), *n.* **1.** *Golf, etc.* a match played by four persons, two on each side. **2.** a group of four.

four·square (fôr′skwâr′), *adj.* **1.** square. **2.** firm; steady. **3.** frank; blunt.

four·teen (fôr′tēn′), *n.* **1.** a cardinal number, ten plus four. **2.** a symbol for this number. **—adj. 3.** amounting to fourteen in number. **—four′teenth′,** *adj.*, *n.*

fourth (fôrth), *adj.* **1.** next after the third. **2.** being one of four equal parts. **—n. 3.** one (or the last) of four parts.

fourth estate, the newspapers.

Fourth of July, *U.S.* the date of the adoption of the Declaration of Independence, in 1776, observed as a legal holiday.

fowl (foul), *n.*, *pl.* **fowls,** (*esp. collectively*) **fowl,** *v.* **—n. 1.** the domestic hen or rooster. **2.** any various similar birds, as the duck. **—v.i. 3.** to hunt fowl. **—fowl′er,** *n.*

fowling piece, a shotgun for shooting wild fowl.

fox (fŏks), *n.* **1.** any of certain carnivores of the dog family, smaller than the wolves. **2.** a cunning person. **—v.t. 3.** *Colloq.* to deceive or trick.

fox·glove (fŏks′glŭv′), *n.* any of certain plants having upright stems with many bell-shaped flowers. The leaves are used as digitalis.

fox·hole (fŏks′hōl′), *n.* a small pit, usually for one or two men, used for cover in a battle area.

fox·hound (fŏks′hound′), *n.* one of a breed of fleet, keen-scented hounds trained to hunt foxes.

fox terrier, one of a breed of small, active terriers, sometimes used for driving foxes from their holes, but kept chiefly as pets.

fox trot, a social dance, in $^4/_4$ time, performed by couples.

fox-trot (fŏks′trŏt′), *v.i.*, **-trotted, -trotting.** to dance a fox trot.

fox·y (fŏk′sĭ), *adj.*, **foxier, foxiest.** cunning or crafty. **—fox′i·ly,** *adv.* **—fox′i·ness,** *n.*

Fox terrier
(15 in. high at the shoulder)

foy·er (foi′ər, foi′ā), *n.* **1.** the lobby of a theater or hotel. **2.** an entrance hall.

Fr., 1. Father. **2.** French. **3.** Friday.

fr., 1. (*pl.* **fr., frs.**) franc. **2.** from.

Fra (frä), *n.* brother (a title of a friar).

fra·cas (frā′kəs), *n.* a disorderly noise, disturbance, or fight; uproar.

frac·tion (frăk′shən), *n.* **1.** *Math.* one or more aliquot parts of a unit or whole number. **2.** a part as distinct from the whole of anything. **—frac′tion·al,** *adj.*

frac·tious (frăk′shəs), *adj.* **1.** cross, fretful, or peevish. **2.** unruly. **—frac′tious·ly,** *adv.*

frac·ture (frăk′chər), *n.*, *v.*, **-tured, -turing. —n. 1.** the breaking of a bone, cartilage, etc., or the resulting condition. **2.** act of breaking. **3.** state of being broken. **—v.t.**, *v.i.* **4.** to break or crack.

frag·ile (frăj′əl), *adj.* easily broken, shattered, or damaged; delicate. **—frag′ile·ly,** *adv.* **—fra·gil·i·ty** (frə jĭl′ə tĭ), **frag′ile·ness,** *n.*

frag·ment (frăg′mənt), *n.* **1.** a part broken off or detached. **2.** a bit or scrap.

frag·men·tar·y (frăg′mən tĕr′ĭ), *adj.* composed of fragments; broken; incomplete.

frag·men·ta·tion (frăg′mən tā′shən), *adj.* *Mil.* denoting a bomb, etc., that scatters fragments of its case or contents over a wide area.

fra·grant (frā′grənt), *adj.* **1.** having a pleasant odor. **2.** pleasant. **—fra′grance, fra′gran·cy,** *n.* **—fra′grant·ly,** *adv.*

frail (frāl), *adj.* **1.** weak; not robust. **2.** fragile. **3.** morally weak. **—frail′ly,** *adv.* **—frail′ness,** *n.*

frail·ty (frāl′tĭ), *n.*, *pl.* **-ties. 1.** quality or state of being frail. **2.** moral weakness.

frame (frām), *n.*, *v.*, **framed, framing. —n. 1.** an enclosing border, as for a picture. **2.** the sustaining parts of a structure fitted and joined together. **3.** the body with reference to its build. **4.** a particular state, as of the mind. **5.** form, constitution, or structure in general. **6.** one of the successive small pictures on a strip of motion-picture film. **—v.t. 7.** to form or construct. **8.** to devise or compose, as a plan, law, poem, etc. **9.** to conceive, as ideas, etc. **10.** *Colloq.* to prearrange fraudulently. **11.** *Colloq.* to incriminate unjustly. **12.** to provide with a frame. **—fram′er,** *n.*

frame-up (frām′ŭp′), *n.* *Orig. U.S. Slang.* that which is fraudulently prearranged.

frame·work (frām′wûrk′), *n.* a structure designed to support or enclose something.

franc (frăngk), *n.* **1.** a French monetary unit and coin, equal at present to 0.84 U.S. cent. **2.** the corresponding coin and unit of Switzerland, Belgium, Italy, etc.

France (frăns, fräns), *n.* a republic in W Europe, 40,517,923 pop.; 212,736 sq. mi. *Cap.*: Paris.

France (fräns), *n.* **Anatole**, (*Jacques Anatole Thibault*) 1844–1924, French novelist.

fran·chise (frăn′chīz), *n.* **1.** the right to vote. **2.** a privilege granted by a government, a manufacturer, a corporation, etc. —**fran′chised**, *adj.*

Fran·cis (frăn′sĭs, frän′-), *n.* **Saint**, (*Francis of Assisi*) 1181?–1226, Italian friar.

Fran·cis·can (frăn sĭs′kən), *adj.* **1.** of or pertaining to the mendicant religious order founded by St. Francis of Assisi. —*n.* **2.** a member of this order.

Franck (frängk), *n.* **César Auguste**, 1822–1890, French composer, born in Belgium.

Fran·co (fräng′kō), *n.* **Francisco**, born 1892, Spanish chief of state, 1939–47; regent of the kingdom of Spain since 1947.

fran·gi·ble (frăn′jə bəl), *adj.* capable of being broken; breakable. —**fran′gi·bil′i·ty**, *n.*

frank (frängk), *adj.* **1.** candid or outspoken; sincere. **2.** undisguised; downright. —*n.* **3.** a signature or mark affixed by special privilege to a letter, package, or the like, to ensure its transmission free of charge. —*v.t.* **4.** to mark (a letter, package, etc.) for free transmission. —**frank′ly**, *adv.* —**frank′ness**, *n.*

Frank (frängk), *n.* a member of a group of ancient Germanic peoples who conquered Gaul about A.D. 500.

Frank·en·stein (frängk′ən stīn′), *n.* **1.** one who creates a monster that he cannot control or that brings about his own ruin. **2.** the monster itself.

Frank·fort (frängk′fôrt), *n.* the capital of Kentucky, in the N part. 11,442.

Frankfort on the Main (mān), a city in W Germany. 553,464.

frank·furt·er (frängk′fər tər), *n.* a reddish variety of sausage made of beef and pork. Also, **frank′furt.**

Frank·furt·er (frängk′fər tər), *n.* **Felix**, born 1882, U.S. jurist: associate justice U.S. Supreme Court since 1939, born in Austria.

frank·in·cense (frängk′ĭn sĕns′), *n.* an aromatic gum resin from certain Asiatic and African trees: burned as incense.

Frank·lin (frängk′lĭn), *n.* **Benjamin**, 1706–90, American statesman and inventor.

frank·lin (frängk′lĭn), *n.* (in the Middle Ages) a non-noble freeholder.

fran·tic (frăn′tĭk), *adj.* wild with excitement, passion, fear, pain, etc. —**fran′ti·cal·ly**, *adv.*

frap·pé (frä pā′), *U.S.* —*n.* **1.** a fruit juice mixture frozen to a mush, to be sipped as an appetizer. —*adj.* **2.** chilled; iced; frozen.

fra·ter·nal (frə tûr′nəl), *adj.* **1.** brotherly. **2.** being, or pertaining to, a society of men associated for mutual aid, etc. —**fra·ter′nal·ly**, *adv.*

fra·ter·ni·ty (frə tûr′nə tĭ), *n.*, *pl.* **-ties.** **1.** *U.S.* a student society organized for social and other purposes. **2.** a body of persons associated by ties of common purpose, interest, etc. **3.** brotherhood.

frat·er·nize (frăt′ər nīz′), *v.i.*, **-nized, -nizing.** **1.** to associate in a fraternal or friendly way. **2.** to associate intimately with citizens of an enemy or conquered country. —**frat′er·ni·za′tion**, *n.* —**frat′er·niz′er**, *n.*

frat·ri·cide (frăt′rə sīd′, frā′trə-), *n.* act of killing one's brother. —**frat′ri·cid′al**, *adj.*

Frau (frou), *n.*, *pl.* **Fraus** (frouz), *Ger.* **Frauen** (frou′ən). *German.* a married woman (as title, equivalent to *Mrs.*).

fraud (frôd), *n.* **1.** deceit, trickery, sharp practice, or breach of confidence. **2.** *U.S. Colloq.* an imposter.

fraud·u·lent (frô′jə lənt), *adj.* **1.** cheating; dishonest. **2.** involving fraud. —**fraud′u·lence**, *n.* —**fraud′u·len·cy**, *n.* —**fraud′u·lent·ly**, *adv.*

fraught (frôt), *adj.* involving; full of.

Fräu·lein (froi′līn), *n.*, *pl.* **Fräuleins**, *Ger.* **Fräulein.** *German.* an unmarried woman (as a title, equivalent to *Miss*).

fray¹ (frā), *n.* a noisy quarrel; brawl.

fray² (frā), *v.t.* **1.** to wear (cloth, rope, etc.) to loose, raveled threads at the edge. **2.** to rub. —*v.i.* **3.** to become frayed.

fraz·zle (frăz′əl), *v.*, **-zled, -zling**, *n.* *Chiefly U.S.* —*v.i.*, *v.t.* **1.** to fray. **2.** to tire out. —*n.* **3.** state of being frazzled.

freak (frēk), *n.* **1.** a person or animal on exhibition as an example of some strange deviation

from nature. **2.** any abnormal or unusual object. **3.** a sudden change of the mind. —*adj.* **4.** unusual. —**freak′ish**, *adj.*

freck·le (frĕk′əl), *n.*, *v.*, **-led, -ling.** —*n.* **1.** a small brownish-yellow spot in the skin. —*v.t.* **2.** to cover with freckles. —*v.i.* **3.** to become freckled. —**freck′led**, **freck′ly**, *adj.*

Fred·er·ick the Great (frĕd′ər ĭk, frĕd′rĭk), (*Frederick II*) 1712–86, king of Prussia, 1740–86.

free (frē), *adj.*, **freer, freest**, *adv.*, **freed, freeing.** —*adj.* **1.** enjoying or characterized by personal rights or liberty. **2.** pertaining to or reserved for those who enjoy personal liberty. **3.** having political independence. **4.** exempt from external authority, etc., as the will, thought, etc. **5.** at liberty, permitted, or able at will (to do something). **6.** not subject to restrictions or duties, as trade. **7.** not literal. **8.** not subject to rules, set forms, etc. **9.** clear of obstructions. **10.** exempt or released from. **11.** uncombined chemically. **12.** open. **13.** easy, firm, or swift in movement. **14.** loose. **15.** acting without self-restraint. **16.** frank. **17.** liberal or lavish. **18.** given without consideration of a return, as a gift. **19.** provided without charge. —*adv.* **20.** in a free manner. **21.** without charge. —*v.t.* **22.** to make free. —**free′ly**, *adv.* —**free′ness**, *n.*

free·boot·er (frē′boo̅′tər), *n.* a pirate.

free·born (frē′bôrn′), *adj.* born free, rather than in slavery, bondage, or vassalage.

free·dom (frē′dəm), *n.* **1.** civil or personal liberty. **2.** political independence. **3.** a particular immunity or other privilege. **4.** exemption from the presence of anything specified. **5.** ease or facility of action. **6.** frankness. **7.** the right of enjoying all the privileges of citizenship, etc.

free·hold (frē′hōld′), *n.* *Law.* an estate which may only be owned for life or transferred by inheritance. —**free′hold′er**, *n.*

free lance, a contributor to periodicals, etc., who is not regularly employed by them.

free·man (frē′mən), *n.*, *pl.* **-men.** **1.** a man who is free. **2.** one who is entitled to citizenship, franchise, etc.

Free·ma·son (frē′mā′sən, frē′mā′-), *n.* a member of a widely distributed secret order (**Free and Accepted Masons**), having for its object mutual assistance and fellowship.

free on board, *Com.* delivered aboard the carrier without extra charge to the buyer.

free silver, *Econ.* the free coinage of silver, esp. at a fixed ratio with gold.

free-soil (frē′soil′), *adj.* *U.S. Hist.* opposing the extension of slavery into the Territories or those parts not yet States.

free-spo·ken (frē′spō′kən), *adj.* speaking without reserve. —**free′-spo′ken·ness**, *n.*

free·stone (frē′stōn′), *adj.* having a stone from which the pulp is easily separated, as certain peaches.

free·think·er (frē′thĭng′kər), *n.* one who forms his religious opinions independently of authority or tradition. —**free′think′ing**, *n.*, *adj.* —**free thought.**

free verse, *Pros.* verse unhampered by fixed metrical forms.

free will, free choice; voluntary decision.

free-will (frē′wĭl′), *adj.* voluntary.

freeze (frēz), *v.*, **froze, frozen, freezing**, *n.* —*v.i.* **1.** to become hardened into ice or into a solid body. **2.** to be of the degree of cold at which water freezes. **3.** to suffer the effects of intense cold. **4.** to die of frost or cold. **5.** to be chilled with fear, etc. —*v.t.* **6.** to harden into ice. **7.** to obstruct by the formation of ice. **8.** to cause to suffer intense cold. **9.** to kill by frost or cold. **10.** to chill with fear, etc. **11.** *U.S. Colloq.* to exclude from society, business, etc., as by chilling behavior, severe competition, etc. **12.** to fix (rents, prices, etc.) at a specific amount, usually by government order. —*n.* **13.** act of freezing. **14.** state of being frozen. **15.** a frost. —**freez′a·ble**, *adj.*

freez·er (frē′zər), *n.* **1.** one that freezes or chills. **2.** a machine containing cold brine, etc., for freezing ice-cream mix or the like. **3.** a refrigerator held at temperatures at or below 32°F.

freezing point, the temperature at which a liquid freezes.

freight (frāt), *n.* **1.** the ordinary conveyance of goods afforded by common carriers. **2.** the price paid for such transportation. **3.** the cargo of a vessel. **4.** *U.S. and Canada.* cargo or lading carried for pay either by water, land, or air. —*v.t.* **5.** to load. **6.** to transport or send as freight.

freight·age (frā'tǐj), *n.* **1.** transportation of goods. **2.** the price for this. **3.** freight.

freight·er (frā'tər), *n.* a vessel engaged chiefly in the transportation of goods.

French (french), *adj.* **1.** of, pertaining to, or characteristic of, France, its inhabitants, or their language. —*n.* **2.** the people of France. **3.** a Romance language, the language of France. —**French'man**, *n.*

French chalk, a talc for marking lines on cloth, etc.

French Equatorial Africa, a French territory in central Africa. 3,423,000 pop.; 960,230 sq. mi. *Cap.*: Brazzaville.

French Guiana, a French possession on the NE coast of South America. 31,000 pop.; 7720 sq. mi. *Cap.*: Cayenne.

French Guinea, a colony in French West Africa, on the Atlantic coast. 2,100,000 pop.; ab. 96,900 sq. mi. *Cap.*: Conakry.

French horn, a brass-wind instrument consisting of a coiled tube ending in a flaring bell.

French Indo-China, a French colonial possession in SE Asia. 23,030,000 pop.; ab. 285,900 sq. mi. *Cap.*: Hanoi. See **Viet Nam.**

French leave, departure without ceremony, permission, or notice.

French Revolution, *French Hist.* the movement (1789–99) that overthrew the absolute monarchy of the Bourbons.

French toast, bread covered with an egg and milk mixture and sautéed.

French West Africa, a French territory in W Africa. 15,336,000 pop.; 1,815,278 sq. mi. *Cap.*: Dakar.

French West Indies, the French islands in the West Indies, comprising Guadeloupe and dependencies, and Martinique. 551,000 pop.; 1114 sq. mi.

fre·net·ic (frə nět'ĭk), *adj.* frantic; frenzied.

fren·zy (frĕn'zĭ), *n., pl.* **-zies,** *v.,* **-zied, -zying.** —*n.* **1.** wild excitement or enthusiasm. **2.** mental derangement. —*v.t.* **3.** to make frantic. —**fren'zied,** *adj.*

freq., **1.** frequent. **2.** frequently.

fre·quen·cy (frē'kwən sĭ), *n., pl.* **-cies.** **1.** Also, **fre'quence.** state or fact of being frequent. **2.** rate of recurrence. **3.** *Physics.* the number of periods or regularly recurring events of any given kind in unit time.

frequency modulation, *Electronics.* a broadcasting system, relatively free from static, in which the frequency of the transmitted wave is modulated or varied in accordance with the amplitude and pitch of the signal.

fre·quent (*adj.* frē'kwənt; *v.* frĭ kwĕnt'), *adj.* **1.** occurring at short intervals. **2.** constant or regular. —*v.t.* **3.** to visit often. —**fre·quent'er,** *n.* —**fre'quent·ly,** *adv.*

fres·co (frĕs'kō), *n., pl.* **-coes, -cos,** *v.,* **-coed, -coing.** —*n.* **1.** a method of painting on a wall, ceiling, or the like, usually before the plaster is dry. **2.** a picture so painted. —*v.t.* **3.** to paint in fresco.

fresh (frĕsh), *adj.* **1.** newly made, arrived, obtained, etc. **2.** new; novel. **3.** additional. **4.** not salt, as water. **5.** brisk; vigorous. **6.** not faded, worn, impaired, etc. **7.** pure, cool, or refreshing, as air. **8.** *Meteorol.* (of wind) moderately strong or brisk. **9.** inexperienced. **10.** *Slang.* presumptuous. —*adv.* **11.** freshly. —**fresh'ly,** *adv.* —**fresh'ness,** *n.*

fresh·en (frĕsh'ən), *v.t., v.i.* to make or become fresh. —**fresh'en·er,** *n.*

fresh·et (frĕsh'ĭt), *n.* **1.** a sudden flood, due to heavy rains, melting snow, etc. **2.** a fresh-water stream flowing into the sea.

fresh·man (frĕsh'mən), *n., pl.* **-men.** a student in the first year at a college or school.

fresh-wa·ter (frĕsh'wô'tər, -wŏt'ər), *adj.* of or living in water that is fresh, not salt.

Fres·no (frĕz'nō), *n.* a city in central California. 63,672.

fret[1] (frĕt), *v.,* **fretted, fretting,** *n.* —*v.i.* **1.** to be irritated, discontented, worried, or the like. —*v.t.* **2.** to irritate, annoy, or vex. —*n.* **3.** an irritated state of mind; vexation.

fret[2] (frĕt), *n., v.,* **fretted, fretting.** —*n.* **1.** an interlaced, angular design. —*v.t.* **2.** to ornament with a fret.

fret[3] (frĕt), *n.* any of the ridges across the finger board of a lute or similar instrument.

fret·ful (frĕt'fəl), *adj.* disposed to fret; irritable. —**fret'ful·ly,** *adv.* —**fret'ful·ness,** *n.*

fret·work (frĕt'wûrk'), *n.* ornamental work consisting of interlacing parts.

Freud (froid), *n.* **Sigmund,** 1856–1939, Austrian physician and psychoanalyst.

Freud·i·an (froi'dĭ ən), *adj.* **1.** of or pertaining to Freud or his doctrines, esp. in respect to the causes and treatment of neurotic and psychopathic states, the interpretation of dreams, etc. —*n.* **2.** an adherent of the essential doctrines of Freud. —**Freud'i·an·ism,** *n.*

Fri., Friday.

fri·a·ble (frī'ə bəl), *adj.* easily crumbled; crumbly. —**fri'a·bil'i·ty, fri'a·ble·ness,** *n.*

fri·ar (frī'ər), *n. Rom. Cath. Ch.* a brother or member of one of certain religious orders.

fri·ar·y (frī'ə rĭ), *n., pl.* **-aries.** **1.** a convent of friars. **2.** a brotherhood of friars.

fric·as·see (frĭk'ə sē'), *n., v.,* **-seed, -seeing.** —*n.* **1.** meat cut up, stewed, and served in its own gravy. —*v.t.* **2.** to prepare as a fricassee.

fric·tion (frĭk'shən), *n.* **1.** *Physics.* the resistance to the relative motion of surfaces of bodies in contact. **2.** the rubbing of two surfaces together. **3.** conflict, as of opinions, etc. —**fric'tion·al,** *adj.*

Fri·day (frī'dĭ), *n.* the sixth day of the week, following Thursday.

fried·cake (frīd'kāk'), *n.* a doughnut.

friend (frĕnd), *n.* **1.** one attached to another by feelings of personal regard. **2.** a patron or supporter. **3.** a member of the same nation, party, etc. **4.** (*cap.*) a member of the **Society of Friends,** a Christian sect opposed to taking oaths and to war; Quaker. —**friend'less,** *adj.*

friend·ly (frĕnd'lĭ), *adj.,* **-lier, -liest,** *adv.* —*adj.* **1.** of, like, or befitting a friend. **2.** favorably disposed. **3.** not hostile. —*adv.* **4.** in a friendly manner. —**friend'li·ness,** *n.*

friend·ship (frĕnd'shĭp), *n.* **1.** friendly feeling or relation. **2.** state of being a friend.

frieze (frēz), *n.* **1.** that part of an entablature between the architrave and the cornice, commonly ornamented with sculpture. **2.** any similar decorative band.

frig·ate (frĭg'ĭt), *n.* an old type of sailing war vessel, designed for high speed.

fright (frīt), *n.* **1.** sudden fear or terror. **2.** a person or thing of shocking, grotesque, or ridiculous appearance. —*v.t.* **3.** *Poetic.* to frighten.

fright·en (frī'tən), *v.t.* **1.** to throw into a fright; terrify. **2.** to drive by scaring. —**fright'ened,** *adj.*

fright·ful (frīt'fəl), *adj.* **1.** dreadful; terrible. **2.** horrible; revolting. **3.** *Colloq.* disagreeable. **4.** *Colloq.* very great. —**fright'ful·ly,** *adv.* —**fright'ful·ness,** *n.*

frig·id (frĭj'ĭd), *adj.* **1.** very cold. **2.** without warmth of feeling. **3.** stiff or formal. —**frigid'i·ty, frig'id·ness,** *n.* —**frig'id·ly,** *adv.*

Frigid Zone, the regions between the poles and the polar circles.

frill (frĭl), *n.* **1.** a ruffle. **2.** any useless ornament. —*v.t.* **3.** to trim with a frill or frills. —**frill'y,** *adj.*

fringe (frĭnj), *n., v.,* **fringed, fringing.** —*n.* **1.** an ornamental border of lengths of thread, cord, etc. **2.** anything resembling this. —*v.t.* **3.** to furnish with a fringe. **4.** to serve as a fringe for.

frin·gil·line (frĭn jĭl'ĭn, -ĭn), *adj.* belonging or pertaining to the finch family which includes the sparrows, canaries, finches, etc.

frip·per·y (frĭp'ə rĭ), *n., pl.* **-peries.** **1.** tawdry finery in dress. **2.** ostentation. **3.** trifles.

frisk (frĭsk), *v.i.* **1.** to dance, leap, skip, or gambol. —*v.t.* **2.** *Slang.* to search (a person) for concealed weapons, etc.

frisk·y (frĭs'kĭ), *adj.,* **friskier, friskiest.** lively; frolicsome; playful. —**frisk'i·ly,** *adv.* —**frisk'i·ness,** *n.*

frit·ter[1] (frĭt'ər), *v.t.* to squander or waste little by little. —**frit'ter·er,** *n.*

frit·ter[2] (frĭt'ər), *n.* a small cake of batter fried in deep fat.

friv·o·lous (frĭv'ə ləs), *adj.* **1.** not worthy of serious notice. **2.** lacking seriousness or sense. **3.** given to trifling or levity. —**fri·vol'i·ty** (frĭvŏl'ə tĭ), **friv'o·lous·ness,** *n.* —**friv'o·lous·ly,** *adv.*

friz (frĭz), *v.,* **frizzed, frizzing,** *n., pl.* **frizzes.** —*v.t., v.i.* **1.** to form into small, crisp curls. —*n.* **2.** something frizzed.

friz·zle[1] (frĭz′əl), *v.t., v.i.,* -zled, -zling, *n.* friz.

friz·zle[2] (frĭz′əl), *v.i.,* -zled, -zling. to make a sizzling noise in frying or the like.

friz·zly (frĭz′lĭ), *adj.* curly. Also, **friz′zy.**

fro (frō), *adv.* 1. from; back. 2. **to and fro, a.** back and forth. **b.** hither and thither.

frock (frŏk), *n.* 1. a gown or dress. 2. a smock. 3. a coarse outer garment worn by monks. —*v.t.* 4. to provide with a frock.

frock coat, a man's coat, usually double-breasted, extending to about the knees.

frog[1] (frŏg, frôg), *n., v.,* **frogged, frogging.** —*n.* 1. any of various tailless amphibians, esp. of a web-footed aquatic species. 2. a slight hoarseness. —*v.i.* 3. to hunt frogs.

frog[2] (frŏg, frôg), *n.* 1. an ornamental button and loop. 2. a device at the intersection of two railway tracks to permit the wheels and flanges on one track to cross or branch from the other.

frol·ic (frŏl′ĭk), *n., v.,* -icked, -icking, *adj.* —*n.* 1. gaiety; fun. 2. a merrymaking. —*v.i.* 3. to play merrily. —*adj.* 4. gay; merry. —**frol′ick·er,** *n.* —**frol′ic·some,** *adj.*

from (frŏm; *unstressed* frəm), *prep.* a particle specifying a starting point, and hence used to express removal or separation in space, time, order, etc., discrimination or distinction, source or origin, instrumentality, and cause or reason.

frond (frŏnd), *n. Bot.* 1. a finely divided leaf, esp. of a fern. 2. a leaflike expansion not differentiated into stem and foliage, as in lichens.

front (frŭnt), *n.* 1. the foremost part. 2. the part which seems to be directed forward. 3. the place where active military operations are carried on. 4. land facing a road, river, etc. 5. *Colloq.* a person listed as an official of an organization merely for the sake of prestige. 6. *Colloq.* outward impression of rank, position, or wealth. 7. bearing or demeanor. 8. impudence. 9. a coalition to achieve a particular end, usually political. 10. something attached or worn at the fore part. 11. *Meteorol.* a surface of discontinuity separating two dissimilar air masses. —*adj.* 12. of, pertaining to, in, or at the front. —*v.t.* 13. to face. 14. to confront. —*v.i.* 15. to have or turn the front in some specified direction.

front·age (frŭn′tĭj), *n.* 1. the front of a building or lot. 2. the lineal extent of this front. 3. land abutting on a river, street, etc.

fron·tal (frŭn′təl), *adj.* 1. of, in, or at the front. 2. noting or pertaining to the forehead. —*n.* 3. a bone of the forehead. —**front′al·ly,** *adv.*

fron·tier (frŭn tĭr′, frŏn′tĭr), *n.* 1. the border of a country. 2. *U.S.* that part of a country which forms the border of its settled regions. —*adj.* 3. of or on the frontier.

fron·tiers·man (frŭn tĭrz′mən), *n., pl.* -men. a man who lives on the frontier.

fron·tis·piece (frŭn′tĭs pēs′, frŏn′-), *n.* an illustrated leaf preceding the title page of a book.

frost (frôst, frŏst), *n.* 1. a state of the temperature which occasions the freezing of water. 2. a covering of minute ice needles. 3. act or process of freezing. 4. coldness. —*v.t.* 5. to cover with frost. 6. to give a frostlike surface to. 7. to ice (a cake, etc.).

Frost (frôst, frŏst), *n.* **Robert,** born 1875, U.S. poet.

frost·bite (frôst′bīt′, frŏst′-), *n., v.,* -bit, -bitten, -biting. —*n.* 1. the inflamed, gangrenous effect of excessive exposure to extreme cold. —*v.t.* 2. to injure by frost.

frost·ing (frôs′tĭng, frŏs′-), *n.* 1. a preparation of sugar, water, etc., for covering cakes. 2. a lusterless finish, as of metal or glass.

frost·y (frôs′tĭ, frŏs′-), *adj.,* frostier, frostiest. 1. freezing; very cold. 2. like or covered with a frost. 3. lacking warmth of feeling. —**frost′i·ly,** *adv.* —**frost′i·ness,** *n.*

froth (frôth, frŏth), *n.* 1. a mass of bubbles, as on a fermented liquid; foam. 2. a foam of saliva. 3. something unsubstantial. —*v.t.* 4. to cover with froth. 5. to cause to foam. 6. to emit like froth. —*v.i.* 7. to foam. —**froth′y,** *adj.* —**froth′i·ness,** *n.*

fro·ward (frō′wərd, frō′ərd), *adj.* perverse.

frown (froun), *v.i.* 1. to contract the brow as in displeasure or deep thought; scowl. 2. to look displeased. —*n.* 3. a frowning look; scowl.

frowz·y (frou′zĭ), *adj.,* frowzier, frowziest. 1. slovenly. 2. musty. Also, **frows′y.**

fro·zen (frō′zən), *adj.* 1. congealed by cold; covered with ice, as a stream. 2. very cold. 3. injured or killed by frost. 4. obstructed by ice,

as pipes. 5. chilly or cold in manner. 6. *Finance, Colloq.* rendered impossible of liquidation.

fruc·ti·fy (frŭk′tə fī′), *v.,* -fied, -fying. —*v.i.* 1. to bear fruit. —*v.t.* 2. to make fruitful or productive. —**fruc′ti·fi·ca′tion,** *n.*

fru·gal (frōō′gəl), *adj.* 1. economical in use or expenditure. 2. costing little. —**fru·gal·i·ty** (frōō găl′ə tĭ), **fru′gal·ness,** *n.* —**fru′gal·ly,** *adv.*

fruit (frōōt), *n.* 1. any product of vegetable growth useful to men or animals. 2. *Bot.* **a.** the developed ovary of a seed plant, as the pea pod, nut, tomato, pineapple, etc. **b.** the edible part of a plant developed from a flower, as the peach, banana, etc. 3. product, result, or effect. —*v.i., v.t.* 4. to bear or bring to bear fruit.

fruit·ful (frōōt′fəl), *adj.* 1. abounding in fruit. 2. productive of results; profitable. —**fruit′ful·ly,** *adv.* —**fruit′ful·ness,** *n.*

fru·i·tion (frōō ĭsh′ən), *n.* 1. attainment of anything desired. 2. enjoyment. 3. state of bearing fruit.

fruit·less (frōōt′lĭs), *adj.* 1. useless; vain. 2. barren. —**fruit′less·ly,** *adv.* —**fruit′less·ness,** *n.*

fruit·y (frōō′tĭ), *adj.,* fruitier, fruitiest. resembling fruit; having the taste of fruit.

frump (frŭmp), *n.* a dowdy woman. —**frump′ish, frump′y,** *adj.*

frus·trate (frŭs′trāt), *v.t.,* -trated, -trating. 1. to make (plans, efforts, etc.) of no avail. 2. to thwart (a person). —**frus·tra′tion,** *n.*

frus·tum (frŭs′təm), *n., pl.* -tums, -ta (-tə). *Geom.* 1. the part of a conical solid left after cutting off a top portion by a plane parallel to the base. 2. the part of a conical solid between two cutting planes.

fry[1] (frī), *v.,* fried, frying, *n., pl.* fries. —*v.t., v.i.* 1. to cook in fat, usually over direct heat. —*n.* 2. a dish of something fried.

fry[2] (frī), *n., pl.* fry. the young of fishes.

fry·er (frī′ər), *n.* 1. one that fries. 2. something, as a young chicken, for frying.

ft., 1. feet. 2. foot. 3. fort.

fuch·sia (fū′shə), *n.* any plant of a genus which includes varieties cultivated for their handsome drooping flowers.

fud·dle (fŭd′əl), *v.,* -dled, -dling. —*v.t.* 1. to intoxicate. —*v.i.* 2. to tipple.

fudge[1] (fŭj), *n.* a candy composed of sugar, butter, milk, and chocolate.

fudge[2] (fŭj), *n., v.,* fudged, fudging. —*n.* 1. nonsense. —*v.i.* 2. to talk nonsense.

fu·el (fū′əl), *n., v.,* -eled, -eling or (*esp. Brit.*) -elled, -elling. —*n.* 1. combustible matter used to maintain fire, as coal, wood, oil, etc. 2. means of sustaining or increasing ardor, etc. —*v.t.* 3. to supply with fuel. —*v.i.* 4. to procure or take in fuel.

fu·gi·tive (fū′jə tĭv), *n.* 1. a person who is fleeing. —*adj.* 2. having taken flight. 3. transitory or ephemeral. 4. wandering. —**fu′gi·tive·ly,** *adv.* —**fu′gi·tive·ness,** *n.*

fugue (fūg), *n. Music.* a composition whose themes are enunciated by the several voices or parts in turn, subjected to contrapuntal treatment, and gradually built up into a complex form.

Füh·rer (fy′rər), *n. German.* 1. leader. 2. **der** (dĕr) **Führer,** the leader (applied esp. to Adolph Hitler).

Fu·ji (fōō′jē), *n.* an extinct volcano in central Japan, on Honshu island. 12,395 ft. Also, **Fu·ji·ya·ma** (fōō′jē yä′mä).

Fu·ku·o·ka (fōō′kōō ô′kä), *n.* a city in SW Japan, on Kyushu island. 288,794.

-ful, a suffix meaning: 1. full of or characterized by. 2. tending or able to. 3. as much as will fill.

ful·crum (fŭl′krəm), *n., pl.* -crums, -cra (-krə). the support upon which a lever turns in moving a body.

ful·fill (fŏŏl fĭl′), *v.t.* 1. to carry out, as a promise, etc. 2. to perform or obey. 3. to satisfy. Also, **ful·fil′.** —**ful·fill′ment, ful·fil′ment,** *n.*

F, Fulcrum; L, Lever

full (fŏŏl), *adj.* 1. filled to utmost capacity. 2. complete. 3. of the maximum size, amount, volume, etc. **4.** (of garments, etc.) ample. **5.** abundant; well-supplied. **6.** rounded out, as in form. **7.** *Music.* ample in volume or richness. —*adv.* **8.** completely. **9.** exactly. **10.** very. —*v.t., v.i.* **11.** to make or become full. —*n.* **12. in full,** without reduction or contraction. —**full'ness,** *n.* —**ful'ly,** *adv.*

full·back (fŏol'băk'), *n.* *Football.* the player usually farthest behind the line of scrimmage.

full dress, the formal attire customarily worn in the evening.

ful·ler's earth (fŏol'ərz), an absorbent clay, used for cleaning cloth, in medicine, etc.

full house, *Poker.* a hand consisting of three of a kind and a pair.

ful·mi·nate (fŭl'mə nāt'), *v.,* -**nated, -nating,** *n.* —*v.i., v.t.* **1.** to explode with a loud noise. **2.** to denounce vehemently. —*n.* **3.** *Chem.* one of a group of unstable, explosive salts. —**ful'mi·na'tion,** *n.*

ful·some (fŏol'səm, fŭl'-), *adj.* **1.** excessive; gross. **2.** disgusting. —**ful'some·ly,** *adv.*

Ful·ton (fŏol'tən), *n.* **Robert,** 1765–1815, U.S. inventor: built first profitable steamboat.

fum·ble (fŭm'bəl), *v.,* -**bled, -bling,** *n.* —*v.i.* **1.** to feel or grope about clumsily. **2.** *Sports.* to fail to catch and hold the ball. —*v.t.* **3.** to handle clumsily. **4.** *Sports.* to fail to catch and hold (a ball). —*n.* **5.** act of fumbling. —**fum'bler,** *n.*

fume (fūm), *n., v.,* **fumed, fuming.** —*n.* **1.** (*often pl.*) a smokelike or vaporous exhalation. **2.** an angry mood. —*v.t.* **3.** to treat with fumes. —*v.i.* **4.** to emit fumes. **5.** to show anger.

fu·mi·gate (fū'mə gāt'), *v.t.,* -**gated, -gating.** to expose to smoke or fumes, as in disinfecting. —**fu'mi·ga'tion,** *n.* —**fu'mi·ga'tor,** *n.*

fun (fŭn), *n., v.,* **funned, funning.** —*n.* **1.** merry amusement; joking. **2. for or in fun,** playfully. **3. make fun of,** to ridicule. —*v.i.* **4.** *Colloq.* to joke.

func·tion (fŭngk'shən), *n.* **1.** the action or activity proper to a person, thing, or institution. **2.** any ceremonious gathering or occasion. **3.** *Math.* a quantity whose value depends upon the values of other quantities. **4.** *Gram.* the grammatical role which a linguistic form plays. —*v.i.* **5.** to perform a function; act; operate.

func·tion·al (fŭngk'shən əl), *adj.* **1.** of or pertaining to a function or functions. **2.** designed or adapted primarily to perform some operation or duty. **3.** pertaining to an algebraic operation. —**func'tion·al·ly,** *adv.*

func·tion·ar·y (fŭngk'shə něr'ĭ), *n., pl.* -**aries.** an official.

fund (fŭnd), *n.* **1.** a stock of money or pecuniary resources. **2.** a stock of anything. **3.** (*pl.*) money in hand. —*v.t.* **4.** to convert (general outstanding debts) into a more or less permanent debt represented by bonds.

fun·da·men·tal (fŭn'də měn'təl), *adj.* **1.** basic; underlying. **2.** of or affecting the foundation or basis. **3.** original. —*n.* **4.** a basic principle, rule, law, or the like. **5.** *Physics.* the component of lowest frequency in a composite wave. —**fun'da·men'tal·ly,** *adv.*

fun·da·men·tal·ism (fŭn'də měn'tə lĭz'əm), *n.* **1.** a movement in American Protestantism which stresses the rigid, literal acceptance of the Bible. **2.** the faith in the Bible so stressed. —**fun'da·men'tal·ist,** *n., adj.*

Fun·dy (fŭn'dĭ), *n.* **Bay of,** a deep inlet of the Atlantic in SE Canada.

fu·ner·al (fū'nər əl), *n.* **1.** the ceremonies connected with the disposition of the body of a dead person. —*adj.* **2.** of or pertaining to a funeral.

fu·ne·re·al (fū nĭr'ĭ əl), *adj.* **1.** of a funeral. **2.** mournful. —**fu·ne're·al·ly,** *adv.*

fun·gi·cide (fŭn'jə sīd'), *n.* an agent, such as a spray, for destroying fungi. —**fun'gi·cid'al,** *adj.*

fun·gous (fŭng'gəs), *adj.* of, like, or caused by fungi.

fun·gus (fŭng'gəs), *n., pl.* **fungi** (fŭn'jī), **funguses,** *adj.* —*n.* **1.** any of a group of thallophytes including the mushrooms, molds, mildews, etc., characterized chiefly by absence of chlorophyll. —*adj.* **2.** fungous.

funk (fŭngk), *Colloq.* —*n.* **1.** cowering fear or terror. —*v.t.* **2.** to be afraid of. **3.** to frighten. —*v.i.* **4.** to shrink in fear.

fun·nel (fŭn'əl), *n., v.,* -**neled, -neling** or (*esp. Brit.*) -**nelled, -nelling.** —*n.* **1.** a cone-shaped utensil for conducting liquid, etc., through a

small opening. **2.** a smokestack. **3.** a flue or shaft, as for ventilation. —*v.t.* **4.** to converge.

fun·ny (fŭn'ĭ), *adj.,* -**nier, -niest.** **1.** amusing; comical. **2.** *Colloq.* strange; queer; odd. —**fun'ni·ly,** *adv.* —**fun'ni·ness,** *n.*

funny bone, a part of the elbow which, when struck, causes a tingling sensation in the arm and hand.

fur (fûr), *n., v.,* **furred, furring.** —*n.* **1.** the skin of certain animals, covered with a fine, soft, thick, hairy coating. **2.** (*usually pl.*) an article of apparel made of such material. **3.** any coating resembling fur. —*v.t.* **4.** to line or trim with fur.

fur·be·low (fûr'bə lō'), *n.* **1.** a plaited or gathered trimming on a woman's gown or the like. **2.** any bit of showy trimming.

fur·bish (fûr'bĭsh), *v.t.* **1.** to restore to freshness. **2.** to polish. —**fur'bish·er,** *n.*

fu·ri·ous (fyŏor'ĭ əs), *adj.* **1.** full of fury. **2.** intensely violent, as storms, etc. **3.** of unrestrained energy, speed, etc. —**fu'ri·ous·ly,** *adv.* —**fu'ri·ous·ness,** *n.*

furl (fûrl), *v.t., v.i.* **1.** to draw into a compact roll, as a flag against its staff. —*n.* **2.** a roll resulting from being furled.

fur·long (fûr'lông, -lŏng), *n.* a unit of distance, equal to 220 yards or ⅛ mi.

fur·lough (fûr'lō), *Mil.* —*n.* **1.** vacation granted to an enlisted man. —*v.t.* **2.** to grant a furlough to.

fur·nace (fûr'nĭs), *n.* a structure in which to generate heat, as for heating houses.

fur·nish (fûr'nĭsh), *v.t.* **1.** to provide or supply. **2.** to fit up (a room, etc.) with furniture, etc. —**fur'nish·er,** *n.*

fur·nish·ings (fûr'nĭsh ĭngz), *n.pl.* **1.** furniture, etc., for a house or room. **2.** accessories of dress.

fur·ni·ture (fûr'nə chər), *n.* **1.** the tables, chairs, bedsteads, cabinets, etc., required in a house, office, or the like. **2.** necessary accessories for something.

fu·ror (fyŏor'ôr), *n.* **1.** a general outburst of enthusiasm or excitement. **2.** a prevailing mania or craze. **3.** fury; rage.

furred (fûrd), *adj.* **1.** having fur. **2.** made with or of fur, as garments.

fur·ri·er (fûr'ĭ ər), *n.* a dealer in or dresser of furs.

fur·ring (fûr'ĭng), *n.* **1.** act of lining, trimming, or clothing with fur. **2.** the fur used.

fur·row (fûr'ō), *n.* **1.** a narrow trench made by a plow. **2.** a narrow, trenchlike depression in any surface. —*v.t.* **3.** to plow (land, etc.). **4.** to make wrinkles in (the face, etc.).

fur·ry (fûr'ĭ), *adj.,* -**rier, -riest.** made of or covered with fur. —**fur'ri·ness,** *n.*

fur·ther (fûr'thər), *compar. adv. and adj., superl.* **furthest,** *v.* —*adv.* **1.** farther. **2.** to a greater extent. **3.** moreover. —*adj.* **4.** farther. **5.** more extended. **6.** more. —*v.t.* **7.** to promote; forward.

fur·ther·ance (fûr'thər əns), *n.* act of furthering; promotion; advancement.

fur·ther·more (fûr'thər mōr'), *adv.* moreover; besides; in addition.

fur·ther·most (fûr'thər mōst'), *adj.* most distant.

fur·tive (fûr'tĭv), *adj.* **1.** stealthy; secret. **2.** sly; shifty. —**fur'tive·ly,** *adv.* —**fur'tive·ness,** *n.*

fu·ry (fyŏor'ĭ), *n., pl.* -**ries.** **1.** frenzied or unrestrained violent passion, esp. anger. **2.** violence; vehemence. **3.** (*cap.*) *Class. Myth.* one of the avenging deities (in female form, with serpents twined in her hair).

furze (fûrz), *n.* a low, much-branched, spiny shrub with yellow flowers, common on waste lands in Europe.

fuse¹ (fūz), *n.* **1.** *Elect.* a protective device with a part that melts under excessive current, thus opening the circuit. **2.** a tube, ribbon, or the like, filled or saturated with combustible matter, for igniting an explosive. **3.** fuze.

fuse² (fūz), *v.t., v.i.,* **fused, fusing.** to combine or blend, esp. by melting together.

fu·see (fū zē'), *n.* **1.** a kind of match with a large head, for igniting by friction. **2.** a red flare light, used as a warning signal.

fu·se·lage (fū'zə lĭj, fū'zə läzh', -sə-), *n.* the framework of the body of an airplane.

fu·sel oil (fū'zəl, -səl), a mixture of amyl alcohols obtained as a by-product in the fermentation of grains.

fu·si·ble (fū′zə bəl), *adj.* capable of being fused or melted. —**fu′si·ble·ness, fu/si·bil′i·ty,** *n.*

fu·sil·ier (fū′zə lĭr′), *n.* a soldier armed with a light musket.

fu·sil·lade (fū′zə lād′), *n., v.,* **-laded, -lading.** —*n.* **1.** a simultaneous or continuous discharge of firearms. —*v.t.* **2.** to attack or shoot by a fusillade.

fu·sion (fū′zhən), *n.* **1.** act of fusing. **2.** state of being fused. **3.** that which is fused.

fu·sion·ism (fū′zhə nĭz′əm), *n.* the principle, policy, or practice of political coalition. —**fu′sion·ist,** *n., adj.*

fuss (fŭs), *n.* **1.** needless or useless bustle. —*v.i.* **2.** to make a fuss. —*v.t.* **3.** to put into a fuss.

fuss-budg·et (fŭs′bŭj′ĭt), *n.* *Colloq.* a fussy person.

fuss·y (fŭs′ĭ), *adj.,* **fussier, fussiest. 1.** excessively particular about petty details. **2.** (of clothes, etc.) elaborate. **3.** full of details. —**fuss′i·ly,** *adv.* —**fuss′i·ness,** *n.*

fus·tian (fŭs′chən), *n.* **1.** a stout cotton fabric. **2.** bombast. —*adj.* **3.** made of fustian. **4.** bombastic, as language. **5.** worthless.

fust·y (fŭs′tĭ), *adj.,* **fustier, fustiest. 1.** moldy; musty. **2.** old-fashioned. —**fust′i·ness,** *n.*

fut., future.

fu·tile (fū′təl, -tĭl; *Brit.* fū′tīl), *adj.* **1.** useless; not successful. **2.** trifling. —**fu′tile·ly,** *adv.* —**fu·til′i·ty, fu/tile·ness,** *n.*

fu·ture (fū′chər), *n.* **1.** time that is to be hereafter. **2.** what will exist or happen in future time. **3.** *Gram.* the future tense. **4.** (*usually pl.*) a speculative purchase or sale of commodities for future receipt or delivery. —*adj.* **5.** that is to be or come hereafter. **6.** connected with time to come. **7.** *Gram.* designating a tense, or other verb formation or construction, which refers to events or states in time to come.

fu·tu·ri·ty (fū tyŏŏr′ə tĭ, -tŏŏr′-), *n., pl.* **-ties. 1.** future time. **2.** a future state or event. **3.** quality of being future.

fuze (fūz), *n.* **1.** a device to detonate an explosive charge. **2.** fuse[1].

fuzz (fŭz), *n.* **1.** loose, light, fluffy matter. **2.** a mass or coating of such matter.

fuzz·y (fŭz′ĭ), *adj.,* **fuzzier, fuzziest. 1.** of or like fuzz. **2.** covered with fuzz. **3.** indistinct. —**fuzz′i·ness,** *n.*

G

G, g (jē), *n., pl.* **G's or Gs, g's or gs. 1.** the 7th letter of the English alphabet. **2.** *Music.* the fifth tone in the scale of C major.

g., 1. *Elect.* conductance. **2.** gram.

Ga, *Chem.* gallium.

Ga., Georgia.

gab (găb), *v.,* **gabbed, gabbing,** *n.* *Colloq.* —*v.i.* **1.** to talk idly; chatter. —*n.* **2.** idle talk; chatter. **3.** glib speech.

gab·ar·dine (găb′ər dēn′, găb′ər dēn′), *n.* a firm, woven fabric of worsted, cotton, or spun rayon. Also, **gab′er·dine′.**

gab·ble (găb′əl), *v.,* **-bled, -bling,** *n.* —*v.i., v.t.* **1.** to jabber. —*n.* **2.** rapid, unintelligent talk. —**gab′bler,** *n.*

gab·by (găb′ĭ), *adj.,* **-bier, -biest.** loquacious.

ga·ble (gā′bəl), *n., v.,* **-bled, -bling.** *Archit.* —*n.* **1.** the end of a ridged roof together with the triangular expanse of wall from the level of the eaves to the apex of the roof. —*v.t.* **2.** to build with a gable or gables; form as a gable.

Ga·bri·el (gā′brĭ əl), *n.* one of the archangels, appearing usually as a divine messenger.

Gables

gad[1] (găd), *v.i.,* **gadded, gadding.** to move restlessly or idly about.

gad[2] (găd), *n.* a goad for driving cattle.

Gad (găd), *n., interj.* *Archaic.* a euphemistic form of *God* used as a mild oath. Also, **gad.**

gad·a·bout (găd′ə bout′), *n.* *Colloq.* one who gads, esp. for curiosity or gossip.

gad·fly (găd′flī′), *n., pl.* **-flies.** any fly that goads or stings domestic animals.

gadg·et (găj′ĭt), *n.* *Colloq.* a mechanical contrivance or device; any ingenious article.

gad·o·lin·i·um (găd′ə lĭn′ĭ əm), *n.* *Chem.* a rare-earth metallic element. *Symbol:* Gd; *at. wt.:* 156.9; *at. no.:* 64.

Gael (gāl), *n.* **1.** a Scottish Celt or Highlander. **2.** *Rare.* an Irish Celt.

Gael·ic (gā′lĭk), *n.* **1.** the Celtic language of ancient Ireland and any of the languages that developed from it (Irish, Scotch Gaelic, and Manx). —*adj.* **2.** of the Gaels or their language.

gaff (găf), *n.* **1.** a strong hook with a handle, used for landing large fish. **2.** *U.S. Slang.* hard-

ship or strain. **3.** *Naut.* the spar extending the upper edge of a fore-and-aft sail. —*v.t.* **4.** to hook or land with a gaff.

gag[1] (găg), *v.,* **gagged, gagging,** *n.* —*v.t.* **1.** to stop up the mouth to prevent speech. **2.** to restrain from freedom of speech. **3.** to cause to heave with nausea. —*v.i.* **4.** to heave with nausea. —*n.* **5.** something thrust into the mouth to prevent speech. **6.** any suppression of freedom of speech.

gag[2] (găg), *n.* a joke.

gage[1] (gāj), *n.* **1.** something, as a glove, thrown down in token of challenge to combat. **2.** a pledge or security.

gage[2] (gāj), *n., v.t.,* **gaged, gaging.** gauge.

gai·e·ty (gā′ə tĭ), *n., pl.* **-ties. 1.** state of being gay or cheerful. **2.** (*often pl.*) festivity. **3.** showiness; finery.

gai·ly (gā′lĭ), *adv.* **1.** merrily. **2.** showily.

gain (gān), *v.t.* **1.** to obtain; acquire. **2.** to win. **3.** to obtain as a profit. **4.** to arrive at. —*v.i.* **5.** to improve. **6.** to get nearer, as in pursuit. —*n.* **7.** profit; advantage. **8.** an increase or advance. **9.** acquisition. —**gain′er,** *n.*

gain·ful (gān′fəl), *adj.* profitable; lucrative. —**gain′ful·ly,** *adv.* —**gain′ful·ness,** *n.*

gain·say (gān′sā′), *v.t.,* **-said, -saying. 1.** to deny. **2.** to speak or act against.

Gains·bor·ough (gānz′bŭr′ō; *Brit.* -bə rə), *n.* Thomas, 1727–88, British painter.

'gainst (gĕnst *or, esp. Brit.,* gänst), *prep., conj.* against. Also, **gainst.**

gait (gāt), *n.* the manner of walking or stepping, esp. of a horse. —**gait′ed,** *adj.*

gai·ter (gā′tər), *n.* **1.** a covering of cloth, leather, etc., for the lower leg, worn over the shoe, etc. **2.** a shoe with elastic insertions at the sides.

gal., gallon; gallons.

ga·la (gā′lə, găl′ə; *Brit.* gä′lə), *adj.* **1.** festive; festal. —*n.* **2.** a festive occasion.

ga·lac·tic (gə lăk′tĭk), *adj.* *Astron.* pertaining to the Galaxy or Milky Way.

Gal·a·had (găl′ə hăd′), *n.* Sir, *Arthurian Romance.* the noblest and purest knight of the Round Table, fated to retrieve the Holy Grail.

Ga·lá·pa·gos Islands (gə lä′pə gōs′), an archipelago on the equator in the Pacific, ab. 600 mi. W of and belonging to Ecuador. 661 pop.; 3029 sq. mi.

Ga·la·tia (gə lā′shə, -shĭ ə), *n.* an ancient country in central Asia Minor: later a Roman province. —**Ga·la'tian,** *adj.*, *n.*

Ga·la·tians (gə lā'shənz), *n. pl.* the book of the New Testament addressed by St. Paul to the Galatians.

gal·ax·y (găl'ək sĭ), *n., pl.* **-axies. 1.** *Astron.* (*usually cap.*) the Milky Way. **2.** any brilliant or splendid assemblage.

gale (gāl), *n.* **1.** a strong wind. **2.** *Meteorol.* a wind with a velocity between 30 and 65 miles per hour. **3.** *Colloq.* a noisy outburst.

Ga·len (gā'lən), *n.* Claudius, A.D. c130–c200, Greek physician.

ga·le·na (gə lē'nə), *n.* a very common heavy (sp. gr. 7.6) mineral, lead sulfide, PbS: the principal ore of lead.

Gal·i·le·an (găl'ə lē'ən), *adj.* **1.** of or pertaining to Galilee. —*n.* **2.** a native or inhabitant of Galilee. **3.** a Christian. **4. the Galilean,** Jesus.

Gal·i·le·an (găl'ə lē'ən), *adj.* of or pertaining to Galileo.

Gal·i·lee (găl'ə lē'), *n.* **1.** an ancient Roman province in N Palestine. **2. Sea of,** a lake in NE Palestine. 14 mi. long.

Gal·i·le·o (găl'ə lē'ō), *n.* (*Galileo Galilei*) 1564–1642, Italian physicist and astronomer.

gall[1] (gôl), *n.* **1.** something very bitter or severe. **2.** rancor. **3.** bile. **4.** *U.S. Slang.* impudence.

gall[2] (gôl), *v.t.* **1.** to chafe severely. **2.** to irritate. —*v.i.* **3.** to be or become chafed. —*n.* **4.** a sore due to rubbing. **5.** something irritating.

gall[3] (gôl), *n.* any abnormal vegetable growth or excrescence on plants, caused by insects, fungi, etc.

gal·lant (*adj.* găl'ənt *for 1, 2;* gə länt', găl'ənt *for 3; n.* găl'ənt, gə länt'), *adj.* **1.** brave or chivalrous. **2.** stately. **3.** polite and attentive to women. —*n.* **4.** a gay and dashing man. **5.** a man particularly attentive to women. —**gal'lant·ly,** *adv.*

gal·lant·ry (găl'ən trĭ), *n., pl.* **-ries. 1.** dashing courage. **2.** courtly attention to women.

gall bladder, *Anat.* a vesicle attached to the liver which receives bile, concentrates it, and discharges it after meals.

gal·le·on (găl'ĭ ən, găl'yən), *n.* a large sailing vessel used esp. by the Spaniards.

gal·ler·y (găl'ə rĭ, găl'rĭ), *n., pl.* **-leries. 1.** a covered walk. **2.** *Southern U.S.* a veranda. **3.** a corridor. **4.** a balcony. **5.** any body of spectators. **6.** a place devoted to the exhibition of art. **7.** a room or building in which to take pictures, practice shooting, etc. **8.** *Naut.* a balcony-like structure at the stern of old ships.

gal·ley (găl'ĭ), *n., pl.* **-leys. 1.** an early seagoing vessel propelled by oars or by oars and sails. **2.** the kitchen of a ship. **3.** *Print.* a long, narrow tray for composed type.

galley proof, *Print.* proof from type on a galley.

galley slave, 1. a person condemned to work at the oar on a galley. **2.** a drudge.

Gal·lic (găl'ĭk), *adj.* **1.** pertaining to the Gauls or Gaul. **2.** French.

gallic acid, *Chem.* an acid, a white or yellowish crystalline powder, found in nutgalls, mangoes, and other plants.

Gal·li·cism (găl'ə sĭz'əm), *n.* **1.** a French linguistic peculiarity. **2.** a French expression used in another language. Also, **gal'li·cism.**

gal·li·na·ceous (găl'ə nā'shəs), *adj.* pertaining to or like the domestic fowls.

Gal·lip·o·li (gə lĭp'ə lĭ), *n.* a peninsula in European Turkey between the Dardanelles and the Aegean. ab. 60 mi. long.

gal·li·pot (găl'ə pŏt'), *n.* a small glazed pot used by druggists for medicines, etc.

gal·li·um (găl'ĭ əm), *n. Chem.* a rare, bluish-white metallic element. Sym.: Ga; *at. wt.:* 69.72; *at. no.:* 31; *sp. gr.:* 5.91 at 20°C.

gal·li·vant (găl'ə vănt'), *v.i.* to gad gaily or frivolously.

gall·nut (gôl'nŭt'), *n.* a nutlike gall.

gal·lon (găl'ən), *n.* a common unit of capacity in English-speaking countries, the U.S. gallon being equal to 231 cu. in. (3.7853 liters).

gal·lop (găl'əp), *v.i.* **1.** to ride or run at full speed. —*v.t.* **2.** to cause (a horse, etc.) to gallop. —*n.* **3.** a fast gait of a horse, etc., in which in the course of each stride all four feet are off the ground at once. —**gal'lop·er,** *n.*

gal·lows (găl'ōz, -əz), *n., pl.* **-lowses, -lows.** a wooden frame, consisting of a crossbeam on two

uprights, on which condemned persons are executed by hanging.

gall·stone (gôl'stōn'), *n. Pathol.* a calculus or stone formed in the bile or gall passages.

ga·lore (gə lōr'), *adv.* in abundance.

ga·losh (gə lŏsh'), *n.* (*usually pl.*) an overshoe or rubber. Also, **ga·loshe'.**

gals., gallons.

Gals·wor·thy (gôlz'wûr'thĭ, gălz'-), *n.* **John,** 1867–1933, British writer.

gal·van·ic (găl văn'ĭk), *adj.* pertaining to or produced by galvanism; producing or caused by an electric current.

gal·va·nism (găl'və nĭz'əm), *n.* electricity, esp. as produced by chemical action.

gal·va·nize (găl'və nīz'), *v.t.,* **-nized, -nizing. 1.** to stimulate by a galvanic current. **2.** to startle into sudden activity. **3.** to coat (metal, esp. iron or steel) with zinc. —**gal'va·niz'er,** *n.*

gal·va·nom·e·ter (găl'və nŏm'ə tər), *n.* an instrument for determining the strength and direction of an electric current. —**gal'va·nom'e·try,** *n.*

Gal·ves·ton (găl'vəs tən), *n.* a seaport in SE Texas. 60,862.

Ga·ma (gä'mə, gä'mə), *n.* **Vasco da,** c1469–1524, Portuguese navigator.

gam·bit (găm'bĭt), *n. Chess.* an opening in which the player seeks by sacrificing a pawn or piece to obtain some advantage.

gam·ble (găm'bəl), *v.,* **-bled, -bling,** *n.* —*v.i.* **1.** to play at any game of chance for stakes. —**2.** to risk money or anything of value on the outcome of something involving chance. —*v.t.* **3.** to lose by betting. —*n.* **4.** *Colloq.* any matter or thing involving risk or uncertainty. —**gam'bler,** *n.* —**gam'bling,** *n.*

gam·boge (găm bōj', -bōōzh'), *n.* a gum resin from certain trees of Siam, etc.: used as a yellow pigment and as a cathartic.

gam·bol (găm'bəl), *v.,* **-boled, -boling** or (*esp. Brit.*) **-bolled, -bolling,** *n.* —*v.i.* **1.** to skip about, as in dancing or playing; frolic. —*n.* **2.** a skipping or frisking about; frolic.

gam·brel (găm'brəl), *n.* the hock of an animal, esp. of a horse.

gambrel roof, a roof whose sides have two slopes. —**gam'brel-roofed',** *adj.*

game[1] (gām), *n., adj.,* **gamer, gamest,** *v.,* **gamed, gaming.** —*n.* **1.** an amusement or pastime. **2.** the apparatus employed in playing any of certain games. **3.** a contest of chance, skill, or endurance. **4.** a single portion of play. **5.** wild animals, including birds and fishes, such as are hunted or taken for sport or profit. —*adj.* **6.** pertaining to animals hunted or taken as game. **7.** plucky. **8.** *Colloq.* willing. —*v.i.* **9.** to gamble. —**game'ly,** *adv.* —**game'ness,** *n.*

game[2] (gām), *adj. Colloq.* lame.

game·cock (gām'kŏk'), *n.* a cock bred and trained for fighting.

game·some (gām'səm), *adj.* frolicsome.

game·ster (gām'stər), *n.* a gambler.

gam·ete (găm'ēt, gə mēt'), *n. Biol.* either of the two germ cells which unite to form a new organism; a mature reproductive cell. —**ga·met·ic** (gə mĕt'ĭk), *adj.*

gam·in (găm'ĭn), *n.* a neglected boy left to run about the streets.

gam·ing (gā'mĭng), *n.* gambling.

gam·ma (găm'ə), *n.* the third letter (Γ, γ, = English G, g) of the Greek alphabet.

gamma rays, *Physics.* rays similar to x-rays, but of higher frequency and penetrating power, forming part of the radiation of radioactive substance.

gam·mon[1] (găm'ən), *n.* **1.** the game of backgammon. **2.** *Backgammon.* a victory in which the winner throws off all his men before his opponent throws off any.

gam·mon[2] (găm'ən), *n. Brit. Colloq.* bosh.

gam·ut (găm'ət), *n.* **1.** the whole scale or range. **2.** *Music.* **a.** the whole series of recognized musical notes. **b.** the major scale.

gam·y (gā'mĭ), *adj.,* **gamier, gamiest. 1.** having the flavor of game. **2.** plucky. —**gam'i·ly,** *adv.* —**gam'i·ness,** *n.*

gan (găn), *v. Archaic and Poetic.* began.

gan·der (găn'dər), *n.* the male goose.

Gan·dhi (gän'dē), *n.* **Mohandas Karamchand,** (*Mahatma Gandhi*) 1869–1948, Hindu religious and political leader.

gang (găng), *n.* **1.** a band or group, as of criminals. **2.** a squad or shift. —*v.i.* **3.** *Colloq.* to form or act as a gang.

Gan·ges (găn'jēz), *n.* a river flowing from the Himalayas in N India SE to the Bay of Bengal: sacred to the Hindus. ab. 1500 mi.

gan·gling (găng'glĭng), *adj.* awkwardly tall and spindly. Also, **gan'gly.**

gan·gli·on (găng'glĭ ən), *n.*, *pl.* **-glia** (-glĭ ə), **-glions.** **1.** *Anat.* gray matter outside the brain and spinal cord. **2.** *Pathol.* a cyst in connection with the sheath of a tendon. —**gan·gli·on·ic** (găng'glĭ ŏn'ĭk), *adj.*

gang·plank (găng'plăngk'), *n.* a plank or temporary bridge used in passing into and out of a ship, etc.

gan·grene (găng'grēn, găng grēn'), *n.*, *v.*, **-grened, -grening.** *Pathol.* —*n.* **1.** the dying of tissue. —*v.t.*, *v.i.* **2.** to affect or become affected with gangrene. —**gan·gre·nous** (găng'grə nəs), *adj.*

gang·ster (găng'stər), *n.* *Colloq.* a member of a gang of criminals.

gang·way (găng'wā'), *n.* **1.** a passageway. **2.** *Brit.* an aisle in a theater, restaurant, etc. —*interj.* **3.** clear the way!

gan·net (găn'ĭt), *n.* any of certain coastal birds of the family which includes the boobies.

gan·oid (găn'oid), *adj.* belonging to a certain grouping of fishes, many of which have hard, smooth scales, as the sturgeons, etc.

gant·let (gănt'lĭt, gônt'-), *n.* a former punishment, chiefly military, in which the offender ran between two rows of men who struck at him as he passed.

Gan·y·mede (găn'ə mēd'), *n.* *Class. Myth.* a Trojan youth carried off to become cupbearer to Zeus.

gaol (jāl), *n.*, *v.t.* *Brit.* jail. —**gaol'er,** *n.*

gap (găp), *n.*, *v.*, **gapped, gapping.** —*n.* **1.** a break or opening, as in a wall. **2.** a vacant space or interval. **3.** a ravine or cleft cutting a mountain ridge. —*v.t.* **4.** to make a gap in.

gape (gāp, găp), *v.*, **gaped, gaping,** *n.* —*v.i.* **1.** to open the mouth, as in absorbed attention. **2.** to stare with open mouth, as in wonder. **3.** to open as a gap. —*n.* **4.** a breach. **5.** act of gaping. —**gap'er,** *n.* —**gap'ing·ly,** *adv.*

gapes (gāps, găps), *n.pl.* a disease of poultry attended with frequent gaping.

gar (gär), *n.*, *pl.* **gars,** (*esp. collectively*) **gar.** a predacious fish covered with smooth, shiny scales and having large teeth.

G.A.R., Grand Army of the Republic.

ga·rage (gə räzh', -räj'), *n.*, *v.*, **-raged, -raging.** —*n.* **1.** a building for sheltering, cleaning, or repairing motor vehicles. —*v.t.* **2.** to put or keep in a garage.

Gar·and rifle (găr'ənd), a semiautomatic, clip-fed rifle: adopted as standard equipment in the U.S. Army.

garb (gärb), *n.* **1.** mode of dress. **2.** clothes. —*v.t.* **3.** to clothe.

gar·bage (gär'bĭj), *n.* refuse animal and vegetable matter from a kitchen.

gar·ble (gär'bəl), *v.t.*, **-bled, -bling.** to make unfair or misleading selections from.

gar·den (gär'dən), *n.* **1.** a plot of ground devoted to the cultivation of plants. —*v.i.* **2.** to cultivate a garden. —**gar'den·er,** *n.*

gar·de·nia (gär dē'nyə, -nĭ ə), *n.* any of certain evergreen trees and shrubs cultivated for their fragrant, waxlike, white flowers.

Gar·field (gär'fēld), *n.* James Abram, 1831–81, twentieth president of the United States, in 1881.

gar·fish (gär'fĭsh'), *n.*, *pl.* **-fishes,** (*esp. collectively*) **-fish. gar.**

Gar·gan·tu·a (gär găn'chŏŏ ə), *n.* the amiable, gluttonous giant in Rabelais' *Gargantua and Pantagruel.* —**Gar·gan'tu·an,** *adj.*

gar·gle (gär'gəl), *v.*, **-gled, -gling.** —*v.t.*, *v.i.* **1.** to rinse (the throat or mouth) with a liquid held in the throat and kept in motion by a stream of air from the lungs. —*n.* **2.** any liquid used for gargling.

gar·goyle (gär'goil), *n.* a spout, often terminating in a grotesque head, for carrying off water.

Gar·i·bal·di (găr'ə bôl'dĭ, -bäl'-), *n.* Giuseppe, 1807–82, Italian patriot.

gar·ish (gâr'ĭsh), *adj.* **1.** glaring. **2.** exces-

sively showy or ornate. —**gar'ish·ly,** *adv.* —**gar'ish·ness,** *n.*

gar·land (gär'lənd), *n.* **1.** a wreath of flowers, leaves, etc. —*v.t.* **2.** to crown or deck with a garland.

gar·lic (gär'lĭk), *n.* a hardy plant of the lily family whose strong-scented, pungent bulb is used in cookery and medicine. —**gar'lick·y,** *adj.*

gar·ment (gär'mənt), *n.* **1.** any article of clothing. —*v.t.* **2.** to clothe.

gar·ner (gär'nər), *v.t.* **1.** to collect or store. —*n.* **2.** a granary.

Gar·ner (gär'nər), *n.* John Nance, born 1869, vice-president of the U.S., 1933–41.

gar·net (gär'nĭt), *n.* **1.** any of a group of hard, vitreous minerals. A deep-red transparent variety is used as a gem. **2.** deep red.

gar·nish (gär'nĭsh), *v.t.* **1.** to adorn. **2.** to decorate (a dish) for the table. —*n.* **3.** adornment or decoration. —**gar'nish·er,** *n.*

gar·nish·ee (gär'nĭ shē'), *v.*, **-nisheed, -nish-eeing,** *n.* *Law.* —*v.t.* **1.** to attach by garnishment. —*n.* **2.** a person served with a garnishment.

gar·nish·ment (gär'nĭsh mənt), *n.* **1.** decoration. **2.** *Law.* a warning to a third party to hold, subject to the court's direction, money or property of a defendant.

gar·ni·ture (gär'nĭ chər), *n.* adornment.

gar·ret (găr'ĭt), *n.* attic (def. 1).

gar·ri·son (găr'ə sən), *n.* **1.** a body of troops stationed in a fortified place. **2.** the place where they are stationed. —*v.t.* **3.** to provide with a garrison. **4.** to occupy (a fort, etc.).

Gar·ri·son (găr'ə sən), *n.* William Lloyd, 1805–79, U.S. abolitionist.

gar·rote (gə rŏt', -rōt'), *n.*, *v.*, **-roted, -roting.** —*n.* **1.** a Spanish mode of capital punishment, orig. by strangulation. **2.** strangulation. —*v.t.* **3.** to strangle. —**gar·rot'er,** *n.*

gar·ru·lous (găr'ə ləs, -yə ləs), *adj.* **1.** talkative, esp. about trifles. **2.** wordy. —**gar·ru·li·ty** (gə rōō'lə tĭ), **gar'ru·lous·ness,** *n.* —**gar'ru·lous·ly,** *adv.*

gar·ter (gär'tər), *n.* **1.** a fastening, as an elastic band, to keep up the stocking. —*v.t.* **2.** to fasten with a garter.

garter snake, any of certain harmless snakes, usually with three light stripes.

Gar·y (gâr'ĭ), *n.* city in NW Indiana. 111,719.

gas (găs), *n.*, *pl.* **gases,** *v.*, **gassed, gassing.** —*n.* **1.** *Physics.* a substance possessing perfect molecular mobility and the property of indefinite expansion. **2.** any such fluid except air, as a gas that is burned for illumination and heating. **3.** *U.S. Colloq.* gasoline. **4.** *Slang.* empty talk. —*v.t.* **5.** to supply with gas. **6.** to affect or overcome with gas. —*v.i.* **7.** to give off gas. **8.** *Slang.* to indulge in empty talk idly. —**gas'less,** *adj.*

gas·con·ade (găs'kə nād'), *n.*, *v.*, **-aded, -ading.** —*n.* **1.** boastful talk. —*v.i.* **2.** to boast.

gas·e·ous (găs'ĭ əs), *adj.* having the nature of, in the form of, or pertaining to gas.

gash (găsh), *n.* **1.** a long, deep wound or cut. —*v.t.* **2.** to make a long, deep cut in.

gas·i·fy (găs'ə fī'), *v.t.*, *v.i.*, **-fied, -fying.** to convert into or become a gas.

gas·ket (găs'kĭt), *n.* anything used as a packing, as a rubber or metal ring.

gas mask, a masklike device worn to protect against noxious gases, fumes, etc.

gas·o·line (găs'ə lēn', găs'ə lēn'), *n.* a volatile, inflammable, liquid mixture of hydrocarbons, obtained in the distillation of petroleum, and used as a solvent, as fuel, etc. Also, **gas'o·lene'.**

gas·om·e·ter (găs ŏm'ə tər), *n.* an apparatus for measuring or storing gas.

gasp (găsp, gäsp), *n.* **1.** a sudden, short breath. —*v.i.* **2.** to catch the breath with open mouth. —*v.t.* **3.** to utter with gasps.

Gaspé Peninsula (găs pā'), a peninsula in SE Canada, in Quebec province.

gas·sy (găs'ĭ), *adj.*, **-sier, -siest. 1.** full of or containing gas. **2.** like gas.

gas·tric (găs'trĭk), *adj.* pertaining to the stomach.

gastric juice, *Biochem.* the digestive fluid secreted by the glands of the stomach.

gas·tri·tis (găs trī'tĭs), *n.* inflammation of the stomach, esp. of its mucous membrane.

gas·tron·o·my (găs trŏn'ə mĭ), *n.* the art of

good eating. —**gas·tro·nom·ic** (găs′trə nŏm′Ĭk), **gas′tro·nom′i·cal**, *adj.* —**gas′tro·nom′i·cal·ly**, *adv.*

gas·tro·pod (găs′trə pŏd′), *n.* any of a class of mollusks comprising the snails, having a shell of a single valve and a ventral muscular foot on which they glide about.

gat (găt), *n. Slang.* a gun or pistol.

gate (gāt), *n.* 1. a movable barrier, as in a fence. 2. an opening for passage into an enclosure. 3. a device for regulating the passage of water, steam, or the like. 4. the number of persons who pay for admission to an athletic contest or other exhibition.

gate·way (gāt′wā′), *n.* 1. a passage or entrance having a gate. 2. any means of entering or leaving a place.

gath·er (găth′ər), *v.t.* 1. to bring together into one company or aggregate. 2. to infer. 3. to pick or harvest (any crop or natural yield). 4. to take. 5. to collect (one's energies or oneself) as for an effort. 6. to contract, as into wrinkles or folds. —*v.i.* 7. to come together. 8. to accumulate. 9. to increase. 10. to come to a head, as a sore in suppurating. —*n.* 11. a fold or pucker, as in cloth. —**gath′er·er**, *n.*

gath·er·ing (găth′ər Ĭng), *n.* 1. act of one that gathers. 2. that which is gathered together. 3. an assembly or crowd. 4. a collection of anything.

gauche (gōsh), *adj.* clumsy; tactless.

Gau·cho (gou′chō), *n.* a native of the South American pampas.

gaud (gôd), *n.* a showy ornament.

gaud·y (gô′dĬ), *adj.*, **gaudier, gaudiest.** excessively or vulgarly showy. —**gaud′i·ly**, *adv.* —**gaud′i·ness**, *n.*

gauge (gāj), *v.*, **gauged, gauging**, *n.* —*v.t.* 1. to appraise, estimate, or judge. 2. to measure. —*n.* 3. a standard of measure. 4. extent; capacity. 5. the distance between the rails of a railroad. Also, **gage.** —**gaug′er**, *n.*

Gau·guin (gō găn′), *n.* Paul, 1848–1903, French painter.

Gaul (gôl), *n.* 1. a vast ancient region in W Europe, including what is now N Italy, France, Belgium, and parts of the Netherlands, Germany, and Switzerland. 2. an inhabitant of this country. 3. a Frenchman.

gaunt (gônt), *adj.* 1. emaciated; haggard. 2. bleak; desolate. —**gaunt′ly**, *adv.* —**gaunt′ness**, *n.*

gaunt·let (gônt′lĬt, gänt′-), *n.* 1. a medieval glove, as of mail or plate, to protect the hand. 2. a glove with a large cuff.

Gau·ta·ma (gô′tə mə, gou′-), *n.* 563?–483? **B.C.**, Buddha.

gauze (gôz), *n.* a thin transparent fabric.

gauz·y (gô′zĬ), *adj.*, **gauzier, gauziest.** like gauze; thin as gauze. —**gauz′i·ness**, *n.*

gav·el (găv′əl), *n.* a small mallet used by a presiding officer, etc.

ga·votte (gə vŏt′), *n.* 1. an old French dance in moderately quick ⁴/₄ time. 2. a piece of music for this dance. Also, **ga·vot′.**

Ga·wain (gä′wĬn, gô′-), *n.* Sir, *Arthurian Romance.* one of the knights of the Round Table.

gawk (gôk), *n.* 1. an awkward, foolish person. —*v.i.* 2. *Colloq.* to stare stupidly.

gawk·y (gô′kĬ), *adj.*, **gawkier, gawkiest.** awkward; clumsy. —**gawk′i·ness**, *n.*

gay (gā), *adj.*, **gayer, gayest.** 1. joyous; merry. 2. bright or showy. 3. licentious. —**gay′ly**, *adv.* —**gay′ness**, *n.*

gaze (gāz), *v.*, **gazed, gazing**, *n.* —*v.i.* 1. to look steadily or intently. —*n.* 2. a steady or intent look. —**gaz′er**, *n.*

ga·zelle (gə zĕl′), *n.* any of certain small antelopes, noted for their graceful movements and lustrous eyes.

ga·zette (gə zĕt′), *n.* 1. a newspaper. 2. an official government journal.

gaz·et·teer (găz′ə tĬr′), *n.* 1. a geographical dictionary. 2. a journalist.

Gd, *Chem.* gadolinium.

Gdy·nia (gdĬ′nyä), *n.* a seaport in N Poland, on the Bay of Danzig. 79,000.

Ge, *Chem.* germanium.

gear (gĬr), *n.* 1. *Mach.* a. a mechanism for transmitting or changing motion, as by toothed wheels. b. a toothed wheel which engages with another wheel or part. 2. implements, tools, or apparatus. 3. *Naut.* the ropes, blocks, etc., be-

longing to a particular sail or spar. 4. personal equipment, as clothes. —*v.t.* 5. to provide with or connect by gearing. 6. to supply 7. to accommodate or adjust.

gear·ing (gĬr′Ĭng), *n. Mach.* the parts by which motion is transmitted, esp. a train of toothed wheels.

gear·shift (gĬr′shĬft′), *n.* a device for connecting gears for transmitting power.

gear·wheel (gĬr′hwēl′), *n.* a cogwheel.

geck·o (gĕk′ō), *n.*, *pl.* **geckos, geckoes.** a small, harmless lizard.

gee (jē), *interj.*, *n.*, *v.*, **geed, geeing.** —*interj.*, *n.* 1. a word of command to horses, etc., to turn to the right. —*v.i.*, *v.t.* 2. to turn to the right.

gee·zer (gē′zər), *n. Slang.* a queer person.

Ge·hen·na (gĬ hĕn′ə), *n.* 1. *Old Test.* a place for burning refuse. 2. *New Test.* hell.

Gei·ger counter (gī′gər), *Physics.* an instrument for detecting and counting ionizing particles: used in measuring radioactivity, etc.

gei·sha (gā′shə), *n.*, *pl.* **-sha, -shas.** a Japanese singing and dancing girl.

gel (jĕl), *n.*, *v.*, **gelled, gelling.** *Phys. Chem.* —*n.* 1. a semirigid colloidal dispersion of a solid with a liquid or gas, as jelly. —*v.i.* 2. to form or become a gel.

gel·a·tin (jĕl′ə tĬn), *n.* 1. a nearly transparent substance, obtained by boiling the bones, skin, etc., of animals, and forming the basis of jellies, glues, and the like. 2. any of various similar substances, as vegetable gelatin. 3. a preparation in which gelatin is the essential constituent. Also, **gel′a·tine.**

ge·lat·i·nous (jĬ lăt′ə nəs), *adj.* 1. jellylike. 2. of or pertaining to gelatin.

geld (gĕld), *v.t.*, **gelded or gelt, gelding.** to castrate (esp. animals).

geld·ing (gĕl′dĬng), *n.* a castrated animal.

gel·id (jĕl′Ĭd), *adj.* very cold; icy. —**ge·lid′i·ty, gel′id·ness**, *n.* —**gel′id·ly**, *adv.*

gem (jĕm), *n.*, *v.*, **gemmed, gemming.** —*n.* 1. a stone used in jewelry. 2. something prized for its beauty or worth. —*v.t.* 3. to adorn with gems. —**gem′like′**, *adj.*

gem·i·nate (*v.* jĕm′ə nāt′; *adj.* jĕm′ə nĬt, -nāt′), *v.*, **-nated, -nating**, *adj.* —*v.t.*, *v.i.* 1. to make or become double or paired. —*adj.* 2. twin; coupled. —**gem′i·nate·ly**, *adv.* —**gem′i·na′tion**, *n.*

Gem·i·ni (jĕm′ə nī′), *n.pl.*, *gen.* **Geminorum** (jĕm′ə nōr′əm). 1. *Astron.* the Twins, a zodiacal constellation containing two bright stars. 2. the third sign of the zodiac.

gems·bok (gĕmz′bŏk′), *n.* a large antelope of South Africa, having long, straight horns.

Gen., 1. General. 2. Genesis.

gen·darme (zhän′därm), *n.* one of a corps of military police, esp. in France.

gen·der (jĕn′dər), *n.* 1. *Gram.* a set of classes which together include all nouns, membership in a particular class being shown by the form of the noun itself or by the form or choice of words that modify, replace, or otherwise refer to the noun. 2. *Colloq.* sex.

gene (jēn), *n. Biol.* the unit of inheritance, which is transmitted by the chromosome and which develops into a hereditary character.

ge·ne·al·o·gy (jē′nĬ ăl′ə jĬ, jĕn′Ĭ-, -ŏl′-), *n.*, *pl.* **-gies.** 1. an account of family ancestors or relatives. 2. the investigation of family pedigrees. —**ge·ne·a·log·i·cal** (jē′nĬ ə lŏj′ə kəl, jĕn′Ĭ-), *adj.* —**ge′ne·a·log′ic**, *adj.* —**ge′ne·a·log′i·cal·ly**, *adv.* —**ge·ne·al·o·gist** (jē′nĬ ăl′ə jĬst, jĕn′Ĭ-, -ŏl′-), *n.*

gen·er·a (jĕn′ər ə), *n.* pl. of **genus.**

gen·er·al (jĕn′ər əl), *adj.* 1. pertaining to, affecting, including, or participated in by all. 2. prevalent; usual. 3. miscellaneous. 4. not specific or special. 5. indefinite. —*n.* 6. a highranking army officer, usually (as in the U.S. Army) above a colonel. 7. *Eccles.* the chief of a religious order. 8. in general, commonly.

gen·er·al·is·si·mo (jĕn′ər ə lĬs′ə mō′), *n.*, *pl.* **-mos.** the supreme commander of several or all armies acting together.

gen·er·al·i·ty (jĕn′ə răl′ə tĬ), *n.*, *pl.* **-ties.** 1. a general or vague statement. 2. general principle. 3. the greater part or majority. 4. state or quality of being general.

gen·er·al·ize (jĕn′ər ə līz′), *v.*, **-ized, -izing.** —*v.t.* 1. to give a general character to. 2. to infer (a general principle, etc.) from facts, etc. 3. to make general. —*v.i.* 4. to form general notions. —**gen′er·al·i·za′tion**, *n.*

gen·er·al·ly (jĕn′ər ə lĭ), *adv.* **1.** with respect to the larger part. **2.** usually. **3.** without reference to particular persons or things.

General of the Army, *U.S.* the highest ranking general.

gen·er·al·ship (jĕn′ər əl shĭp′), *n.* **1.** skill as a general. **2.** management. **3.** the rank or functions of a general.

gen·er·ate (jĕn′ə rāt′), *v.t.,* -**ated, -ating. 1.** to bring into existence. **2.** to produce.

gen·er·a·tion (jĕn′ə rā′shən), *n.* **1.** the whole body of individuals born about the same time. **2.** the average period of a generation (commonly 30 years). **3.** a single step in natural descent. **4.** procreation. **5.** production by natural or artificial processes. —**gen′er·a′tive,** *adj.*

gen·er·a·tor (jĕn′ə rā′tər), *n.* **1.** a machine which converts mechanical energy into electrical energy. **2.** *Chem.* an apparatus for producing a gas or vapor. **3.** one that generates.

ge·ner·ic (jĭ nĕr′ĭk), *adj.* **1.** pertaining to a genus. **2.** applicable or referring to all the members of a genus or class. —**ge·ner′i·cal·ly,** *adv.*

gen·er·os·i·ty (jĕn′ə rŏs′ə tĭ), *n., pl.* -**ties. 1.** readiness or liberality in giving. **2.** freedom from meanness of character. **3.** a generous act.

gen·er·ous (jĕn′ər əs), *adj.* **1.** bountiful; unselfish. **2.** free from meanness of character. **3.** abundant. **4.** rich. —**gen′er·ous·ly,** *adv.* —**gen′er·ous·ness,** *n.*

Gen·e·sis (jĕn′ə sĭs), *n.* **1.** the first book of the Old Testament, telling of the beginnings of the world. **2.** (*l.c.*) origin; creation.

ge·net·ic (jə nĕt′ĭk), *adj.* **1.** *Biol.* pertaining or according to genetics. **2.** pertaining to genesis or origin. —**ge·net′i·cal·ly,** *adv.*

ge·net·ics (jə nĕt′ĭks), *n. Biol.* the science of heredity. —**ge·net·i·cist** (jə nĕt′ə sĭ′st), *n.*

Ge·ne·va (jə nē′və), *n.* **1.** a city in SW Switzerland: seat of League of Nations, 1920–46. 132,200. **2.** a lake between SW Switzerland and France. 45 mi. long; 225 sq. mi.

Gen·ghis Khan (jĕng′gĭs kän′), 1162–1227, Mongol conqueror of most of Asia and of E Europe to the Dnieper river.

gen·ial (jēn′yəl), *adj.* **1.** sympathetically cheerful; cordial. **2.** enlivening; supporting life. —**gen′ial·ly,** *adv.* —**ge·ni·al·i·ty** (jē′nĭ ăl′ə tĭ), **gen′ial·ness,** *n.*

ge·nie (jē′nĭ), *n.* a jinni.

gen·i·tal (jĕn′ə təl), *adj.* pertaining to generation or the organs of generation.

gen·i·tals (jĕn′ə təlz), *n.pl.* the reproductive organs, esp. the external organs.

gen·i·tive (jĕn′ə tĭv), *Gram.* —*adj.* **1.** denoting the case of nouns generally used to modify other nouns, usually indicating possession. —*n.* **2.** the genitive case.

gen·ius (jēn′yəs), *n., pl.* **geniuses** for 1–4, 7, **genii** (jē′nĭ ī′) for 5, 6. **1.** exceptional natural creative capacity. **2.** a person having such capacity. **3.** natural ability. **4.** distinctive character, as of a nation, period, etc. **5.** the guardian spirit of a place, etc. **6.** either of two spirits, one good and the other evil, supposed to attend a person throughout his life. **7.** a person who strongly influences another.

Gen·o·a (jĕn′ə wə), *n.* a seaport in NW Italy. 648,480. —**Gen·o·ese** (jĕn′ō ēz′, -ēs′), *adj., n.*

gen·o·cide (jĕn′ə sīd′), *n.* extermination of a national or racial group as a planned move.

gen·re (zhäN′r), *n.* **1.** kind; style. **2.** the category of subject matter, as in painting, that represents scenes from ordinary life.

gent (jĕnt), *n.* (in humorous or vulgar use) gentleman.

gen·teel (jĕn tēl′), *adj.* **1.** belonging or suited to polite society. **2.** well-bred; polite. —**gen·teel′ly,** *adv.* —**gen·teel′ness,** *n.*

gen·tian (jĕn′shən), *n.* any plant of a large genus comprising herbs commonly having blue flowers.

gen·tile (jĕn′tīl), *adj.* **1.** not Jewish. **2.** Christian. **3.** heathen or pagan. —*n.* **4.** a non-Jewish person, esp. a Christian. **5.** (among Mormons) one not a Mormon. **6.** a heathen or pagan. Also, **Gen′tile.**

gen·til·i·ty (jĕn tĭl′ə tĭ), *n., pl.* -**ties. 1.** superior refinement or elegance. **2.** (*usually pl.*) an instance of this. **3.** gentle birth.

gen·tle (jĕn′təl), *adj.,* -**tler, -tlest,** *v.,* -**tled, -tling.** —*adj.* **1.** mild, kindly, or amiable. **2.** moderate. **3.** wellborn. **4.** respectable. **5.** eas-

ily managed. **6.** soft or low. **7.** polite; refined. **8.** *Archaic.* chivalrous. —*v.t.* **9.** *Colloq.* to tame. —**gen′tle·ness,** *n.* —**gen′tly,** *adv.*

gen·tle·folk (jĕn′təl fōk′), *n.pl.* persons of good breeding. Also, **gen′tle·folks′.**

gen·tle·man (jĕn′təl mən), *n., pl.* -**men. 1.** a man of good breeding, education, and manners. **2.** any man. **3.** a valet.

gen·tle·man·ly (jĕn′təl mən lĭ), *adj.* like or befitting a gentleman; well-bred.

gentlemen's agreement, an agreement binding only as a matter of honor.

gen·tle·wom·an (jĕn′təl wŏŏm′ən), *n., pl.* -**women.** a woman of good breeding.

gen·try (jĕn′trĭ), *n.* **1.** wellborn and well-bred people. **2.** (in England) the upper middle class. **3.** (in humorous use) folks.

gen·u·flect (jĕn′yŏŏ flĕkt′), *v.i.* to bend the knee in reverence. —**gen′u·flec′tion,** *n.*

gen·u·ine (jĕn′yŏŏ ĭn), *adj.* **1.** real; authentic. **2.** sincere. —**gen′u·ine·ly,** *adv.* —**gen′u·ine·ness,** *n.*

ge·nus (jē′nəs), *n., pl.* **genera** (jĕn′ər ə), **genuses. 1.** a kind; class. **2.** *Biol.* the usual major subdivision of a family or subfamily, usually consisting of more than one species, essentially very similar to one another and regarded as very closely related. **3.** *Logic.* a class or group of individuals including subordinate groups called *species.*

ge·o·cen·tric (jē′ō sĕn′trĭk), *adj.* **1.** *Astron.* as viewed from the center of the earth. **2.** having the earth as a center. Also, **ge/o·cen/tri·cal.**

ge·od·e·sy (jĭ ŏd′ə sĭ), *n.* that branch of applied mathematics which determines the shape and area of large tracts of country, the exact position of geographical points, and the curvature, shape, and dimensions of the earth. Also, **ge·o·det·ics** (jē′ō dĕt′ĭks). —**ge/o·det/ic,** *adj.*

geog., geography.

ge·og·ra·phy (jĭ ŏg′rə fĭ), *n., pl.* -**phies.** the study of the surface of the earth, its climate, relief soil, vegetation, population, etc. —**ge·og′·ra·pher,** *n.* —**ge·o·graph·i·cal** (jē′ə grăf′ə kəl), **ge/o·graph/ic,** *adj.* —**ge/o·graph/i·cal·ly,** *adv.*

geol., **1.** geologic. **2.** geology.

ge·ol·o·gy (jĭ ŏl′ə jĭ), *n., pl.* -**gies.** the science which treats of the earth, the rocks of which it is composed, and the changes which it has undergone or is undergoing. —**ge·o·log·ic** (jē′ə lŏj′ĭk), **ge/o·log/i·cal,** *adj.* —**ge/o·log/i·cal·ly,** *adv.* —**ge·ol/o·gist,** *n.*

geom., **1.** geometric. **2.** geometry.

ge·om·e·trid (jĭ ŏm′ə trĭd), *n.* any of a certain family of moths, the larvae of which are called measuring worms.

ge·om·e·try (jĭ ŏm′ə trĭ), *n.* that branch of mathematics which deduces the properties of figures in space from their defining conditions by means of assumed properties of space. —**ge·o·met·ric** (jē′ə mĕt′rĭk), **ge/o·met/ri·cal,** *adj.* —**ge/o·met/ri·cal·ly,** *adv.*

ge·o·pol·i·tics (jē′ō pŏl′ə tĭks), *n.* the application of geography to the external political problems of states.

George (jôrj), *n.* **1. Saint,** died A.D. 303?, Christian martyr: patron saint of England. **2. III,** 1738–1820, king of England, 1760–1820. **3. VI,** 1895–1952, king of England, 1936–52.

Geor·gette (jôr jĕt′), *n.* sheer silk or rayon crepe of dull texture.

Geor·gia (jôr′jə), *n.* **1.** a State in the SE United States. 3,128,302 pop.; 58,876 sq. mi. *Cap.:* Atlanta. *Abbr.:* Ga. **2.** a constituent republic of the Soviet Union, bordering on the Black Sea. 3,542,289 pop.; ab. 26,800 sq. mi. *Cap.:* Tiflis. —**Geor·gian** (jôr′jən), *adj., n.*

ge·ot·ro·pism (jĭ ŏt′rə pĭz′əm), *n. Biol.* a tropism oriented with respect to gravitation. —**ge·o·trop·ic** (jē′ə trŏp′ĭk), *adj.*

Ger., **1.** German. **2.** Germany. **3.** (*l.c.*) gerund.

ge·ra·ni·um (jĭ rā′nĭ əm), *n.* **1.** any of the plants of the genus *Geranium,* most of which have pink or purple flowers. **2.** a plant of the allied genus *Pelargonium,* many species of which are cultivated for their showy flowers.

ger·fal·con (jûr′fôl′kən, -fô′-), *n.* any of various large arctic and subarctic falcons.

ger·i·at·rics (jĕr′ĭ ăt′rĭks), *n.* the science of the medical and hygienic care of, or the diseases of, aged persons.

germ (jûrm), *n.* **1.** a microörganism, esp. when disease-producing. **2.** that from which anything springs as if from a seed.

Ger·man (jûr′mən), *adj.* **1.** of or pertaining to Germany, its inhabitants, or their language. —*n.* **2.** a native or inhabitant of Germany. **3.** the language of Germany and Austria and an official language of Switzerland.

ger·man (jûr′mən), *adj.* **1.** sprung from the same father and mother. **2.** sprung from the brother or sister of one's parent.

ger·mane (jər mān′), *adj.* pertinent.

Ger·man·ic (jər măn′ĭk), *adj.* **1.** pertaining to the Teutonic race or any of the peoples belonging to it, or to the group of languages spoken by these peoples. **2.** German. —*n.* **3.** a group of Indo-European languages, including English, German, Dutch, and the Scandinavian languages.

ger·ma·ni·um (jər mā′nĭ om), *n. Chem.* a rare metallic element. *Symbol:* Ge; *at. wt.:* 72.6; *at. no.:* 32; *sp. gr.:* 5.36 at 20°C.

German measles, a contagious disease, usually mild, accompanied by fever, often some sore throat, and a rash.

German shepherd dog, police dog.

German silver, a white alloy of copper, zinc, and nickel.

Ger·ma·ny (jûr′mə nĭ), *n.* a country in central Europe. 65,285,900 pop.; 137,975 sq. mi. Now divided into four zones of occupation: **British Zone,** 23,026,000 pop.; 37,877 sq. mi.; **French Zone,** 5,787,081 pop.; 16,491 sq. mi.; **Russian Zone,** 19,693,600 pop.; 42,235 sq. mi.; **U.S. Zone,** 16,980,763 pop.; 41,371 sq. mi. *Cap.:* Berlin.

ger·mi·cide (jûr′mə sīd′), *n.* an agent that kills germs or microörganisms. —**ger′mi·cid′al,** *adj.*

ger·mi·nal (jûr′mə nəl), *adj.* **1.** pertaining to a germ or germs. **2.** of the nature of a germ or germ cell. **3.** in the earliest stage.

ger·mi·nate (jûr′mə nāt′), *v.,* **-nated, -nating.** —*v.i.* **1.** to begin to grow or develop. **2.** *Bot.* **a.** to develop into a plant or individual. **b.** to sprout. —*v.t.* **3.** to produce. —**ger′mi·na′tion,** *n.*

ger·ry·man·der (gĕr′ĭ măn′dər, jĕr′-), *v.t.* to subject (a State, county, etc.) to an arbitrary arrangement of its political divisions so as to give one party an unfair advantage in elections.

Gersh·win (gûrsh′wĭn), *n.* George, 1898–1937, U.S. composer.

ger·und (jĕr′ənd), *n. Gram.* a derived noun form of verbs.

ge·run·dive (jĭ rŭn′dĭv), *n.* **1.** (in Latin) the future passive participle, similar to the gerund in formation. —*adj.* **2.** resembling a gerund.

gest (jĕst), *n. Archaic.* **1.** a metrical romance. **2.** a story. **3.** a deed. Also, **geste.**

Ge·sta·po (gə stä′pō), *n.* secret state police of Nazi Germany.

ges·tate (jĕs′tāt), *v.t.,* **-tated, -tating.** to carry in the womb during the period from conception to delivery. —**ges·ta′tion,** *n.*

ges·tic·u·late (jĕs tĭk′yə lāt′), *v.,* **-lated, -lating.** —*v.i.* **1.** to make gestures, esp. when speaking excitedly. —*v.t.* **2.** to express by gesturing. —**ges·tic′u·la′tor,** *n.* —**ges·tic·u·la·to·ry** (jĕs tĭk′yə lə tōr′ĭ), **ges·tic′u·la′tive,** *adj.*

ges·tic·u·la·tion (jĕs tĭk′yə lā′shən), *n.* **1.** act of gesticulating. **2.** an animated gesture.

ges·ture (jĕs′chər), *n., v.,* **-tured, -turing.** —*n.* **1.** a movement of the body, head, arms, hands, or face expressive of an idea. **2.** any demonstration. —*v.i.* **3.** to make gestures. —*v.t.* **4.** to express by gestures.

get (gĕt), *v.,* got or (*Archaic*) gat; got or gotten; getting. —*v.t.* **1.** to obtain, gain, or acquire. **2.** to learn. **3.** to cause to be or do. **4.** to capture. **5.** *Colloq.* to be obliged to. **6.** to prevail on. **7.** to prepare. **8.** *Slang.* to hit. **9.** *Colloq.* to kill. **10.** *Colloq.* to puzzle; irritate. **11.** *Chiefly U.S. Colloq.* to understand. —*v.i.* **12.** to arrive. **13.** to become. **14.** to succeed in coming or going.

get·a·way (gĕt′ə wā′), *n. Colloq.* **1.** an escape. **2.** the start of a race.

Geth·sem·a·ne (gĕth sĕm′ə nĭ), *n.* a garden east of Jerusalem: the scene of Christ's agony and betrayal.

Get·tys·burg (gĕt′ĭz bûrg′), *n.* a borough in S Pennsylvania: crucial defeat of Confederate forces near here, July 1, 2, and 3, 1863. 5916.

get·up (gĕt′ŭp′), *n. Colloq.* **1.** appearance. **2.** style of dress; costume.

gew·gaw (gū′gô), *n.* **1.** a bit of gaudy finery. —*adj.* **2.** showy, but without value.

gey·ser (gī′zər, -sər), *n.* a hot spring which intermittently sends up fountainlike jets of water and steam into the air.

ghast·ly (găst′lĭ, gäst′-), *adj.,* **-lier, -liest,** *adv.* —*adj.* **1.** frightful; horrible. **2.** deathly pale. **3.** *Colloq.* bad. —*adv.* **4.** horribly. **5.** with a deathlike aspect. —**ghast′li·ness,** *n.*

ghat (gôt), *n.* (in India) a passage or stairway descending to a river.

Ghent (gĕnt), *n.* a city in NW Belgium. 160,141.

gher·kin (gûr′kĭn), *n.* a small, immature cucumber, used in pickling.

ghet·to (gĕt′ō), *n., pl.* **ghettos, ghetti** (gĕt′ē). **1.** any quarter inhabited chiefly by Jews. **2.** a quarter in a city in which Jews were formerly required to live.

ghost (gōst), *n.* **1.** a disembodied soul imagined as wandering among or haunting living persons. **2.** a mere shadow or semblance. **3.** (*cap.*) a spiritual being. —**ghost′ly,** *adj.* —**ghost′li·ness,** *n.*

ghost writer, one who does literary work for someone else who takes the credit.

ghoul (gōōl), *n.* **1.** an evil demon of Oriental legend, supposed to feed on corpses, etc. **2.** a grave robber. **3.** one who revels in what is revolting. —**ghoul′ish,** *adj.* —**ghoul′ish·ly,** *adv.* —**ghoul′ish·ness,** *n.*

G.H.Q., *Mil.* General Headquarters.

G.I., *Colloq.* **1.** an enlisted man of the U.S. Army. **2.** *U.S. Army.* government issue. Also, **GI**

gi·ant (jī′ənt), *n.* **1.** an imaginary being of human form but superhuman size, strength, etc. **2.** a person or thing of unusually great size, importance, etc. —*adj.* **3.** gigantic. —**gi·ant·ess** (jī′ən tĭs), *n. fem.*

gib·ber (jĭb′ər, gĭb′-), *v.i.* **1.** to speak inarticulately. —*n.* **2.** gibbering utterance.

gib·ber·ish (jĭb′ər ĭsh, gĭb′-), *n.* rapid, unintelligible talk.

gib·bet (jĭb′ĭt), *n., v.,* **-beted, -beting.** —*n.* **1.** a gallows with a projecting arm at the top. —*v.t.* **2.** to hang on a gibbet.

gib·bon (gĭb′ən), *n.* any of the small, slender, long-armed anthropoid apes of arboreal habits, found in the East Indies and southern Asia.

Gib·bon (gĭb′ən), *n.* Edward, 1737–94, British historian.

gib·bous (gĭb′əs), *adj.* **1.** hump-backed. **2.** (of a heavenly body) so viewed as to appear convex on both margins. —**gib′bous·ly,** *adv.* —**gib′bous·ness,** *n.*

gibe (jīb), *v.,* **gibed, gibing,** *n.* —*v.i.* **1.** to scoff; jeer. —*v.t.* **2.** to taunt. —*n.* **3.** a taunting remark. —**gib′er,** *n.*

gib·let (jĭb′lĭt), *n.* (*usually pl.*) the heart, liver, or gizzard of a fowl.

Gi·bral·tar (jĭ brôl′tər), *n.* **1.** a British crown colony comprising a fortress and seaport located on a narrow promontory near the S tip of Spain. 20,000 pop.; 1⁷⁄₈ sq. mi. **2. Rock of,** a long, precipitous mountain nearly coextensive with this colony. 1396 ft. high; 2¹⁄₂ mi. long. **3. Strait of,** a strait between Europe and Africa at the Atlantic entrance to the Mediterranean. 8¹⁄₂–23 mi. wide.

gid·dy (gĭd′ĭ), *adj.,* **-dier, -diest,** *v.,* **-died, -dying.** —*adj.* **1.** frivolously light. **2.** dizzy. **3.** attended with or causing dizziness. —*v.t., v.i.* **4.** to make or become giddy. —**gid′di·ly,** *adv.* —**gid′di·ness,** *n.*

Gide (zhēd), *n.* André, 1869–1951, French novelist, essayist, and critic.

gift (gĭft), *n.* **1.** a present. **2.** act, power, or right of giving. **3.** a special ability; talent. —*v.t.* **4.** to present with.

gift·ed (gĭf′tĭd), *adj.* talented.

gig (gĭg), *n.* **1.** a long, fast-pulling boat used esp. for racing. **2.** a light, two-wheeled, one-horse carriage.

gi·gan·tic (jī găn′tĭk), *adj.* **1.** of, like, or befitting a giant. **2.** very large; huge.

gig·gle (gĭg′əl), *v.,* **-gled, -gling.** —*v.i.* **1.** to laugh in a silly, undignified way. —*n.* **2.** a silly, spasmodic laugh. —**gig′gler,** *n.* —**gig′gly,** *adj.*

gig·o·lo (jĭg′ə lō′), *n., pl.* **-los. 1.** a man supported by a woman. **2.** a male professional escort.

Gi·la monster (hē'lə), a large, venomous lizard of the southwestern U.S., having the skin studded with yellow- or orange-and-black headlike tubercles.

Gil·bert (gĭl'bərt), n. Sir **William Schwenck**, 1836–1911, British dramatist.

Gilbert and El·lice Islands (ĕl'ĭs), a British colony in the central Pacific, comprising many widely scattered islands. 35,000 pop.; 203 sq. mi. Cap.: Ocean Island.

gild (gĭld), v.t., **gilded** or **gilt, gilding.** 1. to coat with gold. 2. to give a bright, pleasing, or specious aspect to. —**gild'er,** n. •

gill¹ (gĭl), n. an aquatic respiratory organ, as on fish. —**gilled,** adj.

gill² (jĭl), n. a unit of liquid measure equal to ¼ pint.

gil·ly·flow·er (jĭl'ĭ flou'ər), n. a name for various flowers, as the wallflower.

gilt (gĭlt), adj. 1. gilded. —n. 2. the gold or other material applied in gilding.

gilt-edged (gĭlt'ĕjd'), adj. 1. having the edges gilded. 2. of the highest order or quality.

gim·bals (jĭm'bəlz, gĭm'-), n. a contrivance for keeping a suspended object, as a ship's compass, horizontal.

gim·crack (jĭm'krăk'), n. 1. a showy, useless trifle. —adj. 2. showy but useless.

gim·let (gĭm'lĭt), n. a small tool for boring holes, consisting of a shaft with a pointed screw at one end and a handle at the other.

gim·mick (gĭm'ĭk), n. U.S. Slang. a device by which a magician or carnival pitchman works a trick.

gimp (gĭmp), n. a flat trimming of silk, wool, or other cord.

gin¹ (jĭn), n. an alcoholic beverage obtained by redistilling spirits with flavoring agents, esp. juniper berries, orange peel, etc.

gin² (jĭn), n., v., **ginned, ginning.** —n. 1. a machine for separating cotton from its seeds, as a **cotton gin.** 2. a trap or snare for game, etc. —v.t. 3. to clear (cotton) of seeds with a gin. 4. to catch (game, etc.) in a gin.

gin³ (jĭn), n. Cards. a variety of rummy. Also, **gin rummy.**

gin·ger (jĭn'jər), n. 1. the pungent, spicy rhizome of any of certain reedlike plants, used in cookery and medicine. 2. Colloq. animation. —gin'ger·y, adj.

ginger ale, a drink similar to ginger beer.

ginger beer, a nonalcoholic effervescing drink flavored with ginger.

gin·ger·bread (jĭn'jər brĕd'), n. 1. a kind of cake or cooky flavored with ginger and molasses. 2. something showy.

gin·ger·ly (jĭn'jər lĭ), adv. warily.

gin·ger·snap (jĭn'jər snăp'), n. a small, thin, brittle cooky spiced with ginger.

ging·ham (gĭng'əm), n. yarn-dyed, plainweave cotton fabric, usually checked.

gink·go (gĭngk'gō, jĭngk'gō), n., pl. **-goes.** a large, ornamental, gymnospermous tree, native to China, with fan-shaped leaves.

gin·seng (jĭn'sĕng), n. either of two plants, one of China, Korea, etc., and one of North America, yielding an aromatic root extensively used in medicine.

gip (jĭp), v.t., **gipped, gipping,** n. gyp.

Gip·sy (jĭp'sĭ), n., pl. **-sies,** adj. Chiefly Brit. Gypsy.

gi·raffe (jə răf'), n. a tall, long-necked, spotted ruminant of Africa, the tallest of existing quadrupeds.

gird (gûrd), v.t., **girt** or **girded, girding.** 1. to encircle with a belt or girdle. 2. to surround. 3. to prepare (oneself) mentally for action.

gird·er (gûr'dər), n. (in structural work) any main horizontal supporting member or beam, as of wood or iron.

gir·dle (gûr'dəl), n., v., **-dled, -dling.** —n. 1. a belt, cord, sash, or the like, worn about the waist. 2. a lightweight undergarment which supports the abdominal region of the body. 3. any encircling band. —v.t. 4. to encircle, as with a belt. —gir'dler, n.

girl (gûrl), n. 1. a female child or young person. 2. a young unmarried woman. 3. a female servant. 4. Colloq. a sweetheart. —girl'hood, n. —girl'ish, adj. —girl'ish·ly, adv. —girl'ish·ness, n.

girl scout, a member of an organization of girls (**Girl Scouts**), founded in the U.S. in 1912, aiming to develop good health, citizenship, character, and home-making ability.

girth (gûrth), n. 1. the measure around anything; circumference. 2. a band passed under the belly of a horse, etc., to secure a saddle or pack on its back. —v.t. 3. to bind or fasten with a girth. 4. to encircle.

gist (jĭst), n. the essential part.

give (gĭv), v., **gave, given, giving,** n. —v.t. 1. to deliver freely; bestow. 2. to deliver to another in exchange for something. 3. to grant permission or opportunity to. 4. to show. 5. to suppose; assume. 6. to provide. 7. to produce. 8. to make, do, or perform. 9. to issue or utter. 10. to impart or communicate. 11. to administer. 12. to surrender. 13. to emit. —v.i. 14. to yield. 15. to fail. 16. **give out, a.** to become worn out or used up. **b.** to emit. **c.** to distribute. 17. **give up, a.** to lose all hope. **b.** to abandon as hopeless. **c.** to forsake. **d.** to surrender. **e.** to devote entirely. —n. 18. elasticity. —giv'er, n.

give-and-take (gĭv'ən tāk'), n. 1. compromise or mutual concession. 2. good-humored exchange of talk, etc.

give·a·way (gĭv'ə wā'), n. Colloq. 1. a betrayal, usually unintentional. 2. a premium given to promote sales, etc.

giv·en (gĭv'ən), adj. 1. specified. 2. addicted. 3. conferred. 4. assigned as a basis of calculation, reasoning, etc. 5. Math. known.

given name, the name given to one, not inherited; first name.

giz·zard (gĭz'ərd), n. the grinding or muscular stomach of birds.

Gk., Greek.

Gl, Chem. glucinum.

gla·brous (glā'brəs), adj. hairless.

gla·cé (glȧ sĕ'), adj. 1. frozen. 2. frosted or iced. 3. candied.

gla·cial (glā'shəl), adj. 1. characterized by the presence of ice in extensive masses or glaciers. 2. caused by ice or glaciers. 3. icy. 4. Chem. of or tending to assume an icelike form, as certain acids. —gla'cial·ly, adv.

gla·ci·ate (glā'shĭ āt'), v.t., **-ated, -ating.** 1. to cover with ice or glaciers. 2. to affect by glacial action. —gla·ci·a·tion (glā'sĭ ā'shən,-shĭ-), n.

gla·cier (glā'shər), n. an extended mass of ice formed from snow and moving very slowly down high mountains.

Glacier National Park, a mountain and forest reserve in NW Montana: numerous glaciers and lakes. 1534 sq. mi.

glad (glăd), adj., **gladder, gladdest.** 1. delighted or pleased. 2. characterized by or showing cheerfulness, joy, or pleasure. 3. attended with or causing joy or pleasure. —glad'ly, adv. —glad'ness, n.

glad·den (glăd'ən), v.t. to make glad.

glade (glād), n. an open space in a forest.

glad·i·a·tor (glăd'ĭ ā'tər), n. Rom. Hist. a person, often a slave or captive, who fought in public with a sword or other weapon to entertain the people.

glad·i·o·la (glăd'ĭ ō'lə), n. gladiolus.

glad·i·o·lus (glăd'ĭ ō'ləs), n., pl. **-li** (-lī), **-luses.** any of certain plants with erect, sword-shaped leaves and spikes of variously colored flowers.

glad·some (glăd'səm), adj. 1. delightful. 2. glad. —glad'some·ly, adv.

Glad·stone (glăd'stōn, -stən), n. **William Ewart,** 1809–98, British statesman.

Gladstone bag, a light traveling bag hinged to open into two compartments.

glair (glâr), n. 1. the white of an egg. 2. a glaze or size made of it. —glair'y, adj.

glam·our (glăm'ər), n. 1. alluring and often illusory charm. 2. witchery. Also, **glam'or.** —glam'or·ous, adj. —glam'or·ous·ly, adv.

glance (glăns, gläns), v., **glanced, glancing,** n. —v.i., v.t. 1. to look quickly or briefly. 2. to flash. 3. to go off in an oblique direction from an object struck. —n. 4. a quick or brief look. 5. a gleam or flash of light. 6. a glancing off, as of a missile after striking. 7. a reference in passing.

gland (glănd), n. Anat. 1. an organ by which certain constituents are separated from the blood for use in the body or for ejection from it, or by which certain changes are produced in the blood or lymph. **2.** any of various organs or structures likened to true glands.

glan·ders (glăn'dərz), *n.* a contagious disease of horses, etc., communicable to man, characterized by swellings beneath the jaw.

glan·du·lar (glăn'jə lər), *adj.* **1.** of, containing, or bearing glands. **2.** of, pertaining to, or resembling a gland.

glans (glănz), *n.* *Anat.* the head of the penis or clitoris.

glare[1] (glâr), *n.*, *v.*, **glared, glaring.** —*n.* **1.** a strong, dazzling light. **2.** showiness. **3.** a fierce or piercing look. —*v.i.* **4.** to shine with a strong, dazzling light. **5.** to look with a fierce or piercing stare.

glare[2] (glâr), *n.* **1.** a bright, smooth surface, as of ice. —*adj.* **2.** glassy.

glar·ing (glâr'ĭng), *adj.* **1.** that glares. **2.** garish. **3.** very conspicuous.

Glas·gow (glăs'gō, -kō, glăs'-), *n.* a seaport in SW Scotland. 1,061,000.

glass (glăs, gläs), *n.* **1.** a hard, brittle, transparent substance produced by fusion, usually consisting of mutually dissolved silica and silicates. **2.** something made of glass. **3.** (*pl.*) eyeglasses. **4.** glassware. **5.** a glass container for drinking water, etc. **6.** glassful. —*adj.* **7.** made of glass. —*v.t.* **8.** to cover with glass.

glass blowing, the art or process of forming glass into ware by blowing by mouth or mechanically. —**glass blower.**

glass·ful (glăs'fŏŏl', gläs'-), *n.*, *pl.* **-fuls.** as much as a glass holds.

glass·ware (glăs'wâr', gläs'-), *n.* articles of glass.

glass·y (glăs'ĭ, gläs'ĭ), *adj.*, **glassier, glassiest. 1.** resembling glass. **2.** having a fixed, unintelligent stare. **3.** vitreous. —**glass'i·ly,** *adv.*

glau·co·ma (glô kō'mə), *n.* a disease of the eye, characterized by pressure within the eyeball with progressive loss of vision.

glau·cous (glô'kəs), *adj.* **1.** bluish-green. **2.** *Bot.* covered with a whitish bloom, as a plum.

glaze (glāz), *v.*, **glazed, glazing.** —*v.t.* **1.** to furnish with glass. **2.** to produce a vitreous or glossy surface on (pottery, etc.). **3.** *Painting.* to cover with a thin layer of transparent color in order to modify the tone. —*v.i.* **4.** to become glazed or glassy. —*n.* **5.** a smooth, glossy surface or coating. —**glaz'ing,** *n.*

gla·zier (glā'zhər), *n.* one who fits windows, etc., with glass.

gleam (glēm), *n.* **1.** a flash or beam of light. **2.** a brief manifestation. —*v.i.* **3.** to send forth a gleam or gleams.

glean (glēn), *v.t.*, *v.i.* **1.** to gather slowly and laboriously in bits. **2.** to gather (grain, etc.) after the reapers or regular gatherers. —**glean'er,** *n.*

glee (glē), *n.* **1.** demonstrative joy. **2.** a song for three or more voices.

glee club, a group for singing.

glee·ful (glē'fəl), *adj.* full of glee; merry. —**glee'ful·ly,** *adv.* —**glee'ful·ness,** *n.*

glen (glĕn), *n.* a narrow, secluded valley.

Glen·dale (glĕn'dāl'), *n.* a city in SW California, near Los Angeles. 96,495.

glib (glĭb), *adj.*, **glibber, glibbest.** ready and fluent, often insincerely so. —**glib'ly,** *adv.* —**glib'ness,** *n.*

glide (glīd), *v.*, **glided, gliding,** *n.* —*v.i.* **1.** to move smoothly along, as a bird, skater, etc. **2.** to pass by gradual change. **3.** *Aeron.* to move in the air, esp. at an easy angle downward, as by the action of gravity. **4.** *Music.* to pass from tone to tone without a break. —*v.t.* **5.** to cause to glide. —*n.* **6.** a gliding movement.

glid·er (glī'dər), *n.* **1.** one that glides. **2.** *Aeron.* a motorless heavier-than-air craft for gliding.

glim·mer (glĭm'ər), *n.* **1.** a faint or unsteady light. **2.** an inkling. —*v.i.* **3.** to shine or appear faintly or unsteadily. —**glim'mer·ing,** *n.*, *adj.*

glimpse (glĭmps), *n.*, *v.*, **glimpsed, glimpsing.** —*n.* **1.** a momentary view or appearance. **2.** an inkling. —*v.t.*, *v.i.* **3.** to catch a glimpse (of). —**glimps'er,** *n.*

glint (glĭnt), *n.* **1.** a gleam. **2.** luster. —*v.i.* **3.** to gleam.

glis·ten (glĭs'ən), *v.i.* **1.** to shine with a sparkling light or a faint intermittent glow. —*n.* **2.** a glistening. —**glis'ten·ing·ly,** *adv.*

glit·ter (glĭt'ər), *v.i.* **1.** to shine with a brilliant, sparkling light or luster. **2.** to make a brilliant

show. —*n.* **3.** glittering light or luster; splendor. —**glit'ter·ing·ly,** *adv.*

gloam·ing (glō'mĭng), *n.* *Poetic.* dusk.

gloat (glōt), *v.i.* to gaze with exultation.

globe (glōb), *n.*, *v.*, **globed, globing.** —*n.* **1.** the earth. **2.** any celestial body. **3.** a sphere on which is depicted a map of the earth or of the heavens. **4.** a sphere. —*v.t.* **5.** to form into a globe. —*v.i.* **6.** to take the form of a globe. —**glob'al,** *adj.* —**glob'al·ly,** *adv.*

globe·fish (glōb'fĭsh'), *n.*, *pl.* **-fishes,** (*esp. collectively*) **-fish.** a puffer (def. 2).

globe·trot·ter (glōb'trŏt'ər), *n.* *Colloq.* one who travels widely, esp. for sightseeing.

glob·u·lar (glŏb'yə lər), *adj.* **1.** globe-shaped. **2.** composed of globules.

glob·ule (glŏb'ūl), *n.* a small spherical body.

glock·en·spiel (glŏk'ən spēl'), *n.* *Music.* a set of steel bars mounted in a frame and struck with hammers, used by military bands.

glom·er·ate (glŏm'ər ĭt), *adj.* compactly clustered. —**glom'er·a'tion,** *n.*

gloom[1] (glōōm), *n.* **1.** darkness; dimness. —*v.i.*, *v.t.* **2.** to become or make dark.

gloom[2] (glōōm), *n.* **1.** melancholy; low spirits. —*v.i.* **2.** to make gloomy or sad.

gloom·y[1] (glōō'mĭ), *adj.*, **gloomier, gloomiest.** dark; deeply shaded.

gloom·y[2] (glōō'mĭ), *adj.*, **gloomier, gloomiest. 1.** causing gloom. **2.** melancholy. —**gloom'i·ly,** *adv.* —**gloom'i·ness,** *n.*

Glo·ri·a (glôr'ĭ ə), *n.* **1.** (in Christian liturgical worship) one of several hymns beginning with "Gloria." **2.** (*l.c.*) a halo.

glo·ri·fy (glôr'ə fī'), *v.t.*, **-fied, -fying. 1.** to magnify with praise; extol. **2.** to transform into something more splendid. **3.** to make glorious. —**glor'i·fi·ca'tion,** *n.* —**glor'i·fi'er,** *n.*

glo·ri·ous (glôr'ĭ əs), *adj.* **1.** delightful. **2.** conferring glory. **3.** full of glory. **4.** brilliantly beautiful. —**glo'ri·ous·ly,** *adv.*

glo·ry (glôr'ĭ), *n.*, *pl.* **glories,** *v.*, **gloried, glorying.** —*n.* **1.** exalted praise, honor, or distinction, accorded by common consent. **2.** something that makes honored or illustrious. **3.** adoring praise. **4.** resplendent beauty. **5.** magnificence. **6.** heaven. —*v.i.* **7.** to rejoice proudly. **8.** to exult arrogantly.

gloss[1] (glôs, glŏs), *n.* **1.** a superficial luster. **2.** an external show. —*v.t.* **3.** to put a gloss upon.

gloss[2] (glôs, glŏs), *n.* **1.** an explanation, by means of a note, of an expression in a text. —*v.t.*, *v.i.* **2.** to annotate. **3.** to explain away.

glos·sa·ry (glôs'ə rĭ, glŏs'ə-), *n.*, *pl.* **-ries.** a list of basic difficult terms in a subject, with definitions.

gloss·y (glôs'ĭ, glŏs'ĭ), *adj.*, **glossier, glossiest. 1.** lustrous. **2.** plausible. —**gloss'i·ly,** *adv.* —**gloss'i·ness,** *n.*

glot·tis (glŏt'ĭs), *n.* the opening at the upper part of the larynx, between the vocal cords. —**glot'tal,** *adj.*

Glouces·ter (glŏs'tər, glôs'-), *n.* a city in SW England. 63,500.

glove (glŭv), *n.*, *v.*, **gloved, gloving.** —*n.* **1.** a covering for the hand, with a separate sheath for each finger. **2.** a boxing glove. —*v.t.* **3.** to cover with a glove.

glov·er (glŭv'ər), *n.* one who makes or sells gloves.

glow (glō), *n.* **1.** light emitted by a substance heated to luminosity. **2.** brightness of color. **3.** a state of bodily heat. **4.** warmth of emotion. —*v.i.* **5.** to emit bright light and heat without flame. **6.** to shine like something intensely heated. **7.** to exhibit a strong, bright color. **8.** to be excessively hot. **9.** to be animated with emotion. —**glow'ing,** *adj.* —**glow'ing·ly,** *adv.*

glow·er (glou'ər), *v.i.* **1.** to look with sullen dislike or discontent. —*n.* **2.** a frown.

glow·worm (glō'wûrm'), *n.* any of certain fireflies, esp. a European beetle, the wingless female of which emits a greenish light.

gloze (glōz), *v.t.*, **glozed, glozing.** to explain away.

glu·ci·num (glōō sī'nəm), *n.* beryllium. *Sym.* Gl. Also, **glu·cin·i·um** (glōō sĭn'ĭ əm).

glu·cose (glōō'kōs), *n.* a sugar, $C_6H_{12}O_6$, the common form occurring in many fruits, animal tissues and fluids, etc., and having a sweetness about one half that of ordinary sugar.

glue (glōō), *n.*, *v.*, **glued, gluing.** —*n.* **1.** an impure gelatin obtained by boiling skins, hoofs, etc.

used esp. as an adhesive. **2.** any similar adhesive material. —*v.t.* **3.** to join or fasten with glue. —**glue′y**, *adj.*

glum (glŭm), *adj.*, **glummer, glummest.** gloomily sullen. —**glum′ly**, *adv.* —**glum′ness**, *n.*

glut (glŭt), *v.*, **glutted, glutting,** *n.* —*v.t.* **1.** to feed or fill to satiety. **2.** to cloy. —*n.* **3.** a full supply. **4.** a surfeit.

glu·ten (glōō′tən), *n.* the tough, viscid nitrogenous substance remaining when the flour of wheat or other grain is washed to remove the starch. —**glu′te·nous**, *adj.*

glu·ti·nous (glōō′tə nəs), *adj.* gluey; viscid; sticky. —**glu′ti·nous·ly**, *adv.*

glut·ton¹ (glŭt′ən), *n.* one who indulges in something excessively, esp. food. —**glut′ton·ous**, *adj.* —**glut′ton·ous·ly**, *adv.* —**glut′ton·y**, **glut′ton·ous·ness**, *n.*

glut·ton² (glŭt′ən), *n.* a thick-set, voracious mammal of the weasel family, inhabiting northern regions.

glyc·er·in (glĭs′ər ĭn), *n.* a colorless, odorless, liquid alcohol, of syrupy consistency and sweet taste, used in medicine, the arts, etc. Also, **glyc·er·ine** (glĭs′ər ĭn, -ə rēn′).

gly·co·gen (glī′kə jən), *n.* a white, tasteless substance, usually stored in the liver.

gm., gram; grams.

G-man (jē′măn′), *n.* *U.S.* an FBI agent.

gnarl (närl), *n.* a knotty protuberance on a tree. —**gnarled, gnarl′y**, *adj.*

gnash (năsh), *v.t., v.i.* to grind (the teeth) together, esp. in rage or pain.

gnat (năt), *n.* any of certain small flies, esp. the biting gnats and the midges.

gnaw (nô), *v.t.*, **gnawed, gnawed** or **gnawn, gnawing. 1.** to wear away or remove by persistent biting. **2.** to torment.

gneiss (nīs), *n.* a metamorphic rock, generally made up of bands which differ in color and composition. —**gneiss′ic**, *adj.*

gnome (nōm), *n.* one of a species of diminutive beings fabled to inhabit the interior of the earth and to act as guardians of its treasures.

gno·mon (nō′mŏn), *n.* a vertical shaft or the like used as an astronomical instrument by noting the length of its shadow cast at noon.

gnos·tic (nŏs′tĭk), *adj.* Also, **gnos′ti·cal. 1.** pertaining to or possessing knowledge. **2.** (*cap.*) pertaining to the Gnostics. —*n.* **3.** (*cap.*) a member of any of certain sects among the early Christians who claimed to have superior knowledge of spiritual things. —**Gnos′ti·cism**, *n.*

gnu (nōō, nū), *n., pl.* **gnus, (***esp. collectively***) gnu.** any of certain African antelopes characterized by an oxlike head and curved horns.

go (gō), *v.*, **went, gone, going,** *n., pl.* **goes.** —*v.i.* **1.** to move or proceed. **2.** to depart. **3.** to act, work, or run. **4.** to become. **5.** to be habitually. **6.** to be known. **7.** to extend. **8.** (of time) to pass. **9.** to be sold. **10.** to result. **11.** to belong. **12.** to harmonize. **13.** to explode. **14.** to begin. —*n.* **15.** act of going. **16.** *Colloq.* energy. **17.** *Colloq.* an attempt. **18.** *Colloq.* a success. **19.** *Colloq.* a bargain. **20. on the go,** *Colloq.* very active. —**go′er,** *n.*

goad (gōd), *n.* **1.** a stick with a pointed end, for driving cattle, etc. **2.** a stimulus. —*v.t.* **3.** to prick or drive with a goad.

goal (gōl), *n.* **1.** aim or end. **2.** the terminal point in a race. **3.** a pole or other object by which this is marked. **4.** a bound or structure toward which the players strive to advance the ball, etc. **5.** act of throwing or kicking the ball through or over the goal. **6.** the score made by accomplishing this. —**goal′less**, *adj.*

goal·keep·er (gōl′kē′pər), *n.* a player whose duty it is to prevent the ball from going through or over the goal. Also, **goal·ie** (gō′lĭ).

goat (gōt), *n.* **1.** any of various agile hollow-horned ruminants closely related to the sheep. **2.** (*cap.*) *Astron.* the zodiacal constellation or sign Capricorn. **3.** *U.S. Slang.* the scapegoat. **4. get one's goat,** *U.S. Slang.* to make one lose his temper.

goat·ee (gō tē′), *n.* a man's tuftlike beard.

goat·herd (gōt′hûrd′), *n.* one who tends goats.

goat·skin (gōt′skĭn′), *n.* **1.** the skin or hide of a goat. **2.** leather made from it.

goat·suck·er (gōt′sŭk′ər), *n.* a nonpasserine nocturnal bird of Europe, with flat head and wide mouth, formerly supposed to suck the milk of goats; whippoorwill.

gob¹ (gŏb), *n.* a mass or lump.

gob² (gŏb), *n. Slang.* a seaman in the navy.

gob·bet (gŏb′ĭt), *n.* a fragment or hunk.

gob·ble¹ (gŏb′əl), *v.*, **-bled, -bling.** —*v.t.* **1.** to swallow hastily in large pieces. **2.** *U.S. Slang.* to seize upon eagerly. —*v.i.* **3.** to eat hastily. —**gob′bler**, *n.*

gob·ble² (gŏb′əl), *v.*, **-bled, -bling,** *n.* —*v.i.* **1.** to make the characteristic throaty cry of a turkey cock. —*n.* **2.** this sound.

gob·ble·de·gook (gŏb′əl dĭ gŏŏk′), *n. Colloq.* language full of circumlocution and jargon.

gob·bler (gŏb′lər), *n.* a male turkey.

Gob·e·lin (gŏb′ə lĭn), *adj.* made at the tapestry factory of the Gobelins in Paris.

go·be·tween (gō′bə twēn′), *n.* one who acts as agent between persons or parties.

Go·bi (gō′bī), *n.* a desert in E Asia, mostly in Mongolia. ab. 500,000 sq. mi.

gob·let (gŏb′lĭt), *n.* a drinking glass with a foot and stem.

gob·lin (gŏb′lĭn), *n.* a grotesque, mischievous sprite or elf.

go·cart (gō′kärt′), *n.* a small, wheeled vehicle for small children to ride in.

God (gŏd), *n.* **1.** the one Supreme Being, the creator and ruler of the universe. **2.** (*l.c.*) a deity, esp. a male deity. **3.** (*l.c.*) any deified person or object.

god·child (gŏd′chīld′), *n., pl.* **-children.** one whom a person sponsors at baptism. —**god′-daugh′ter**, *n.* —**god′son′**, *n.*

god·dess (gŏd′ĭs), *n.* **1.** a female god or deity. **2.** an adored woman.

god·fa·ther (gŏd′fä′thər), *n.* a man who sponsors a child at baptism.

God·head (gŏd′hĕd′), *n.* **1.** the Supreme Being. **2.** (*l.c.*) godhood or godship.

god·hood (gŏd′hŏŏd), *n.* divine character.

god·less (gŏd′lĭs), *adj.* **1.** having or acknowledging no God. **2.** wicked. —**god′less·ly**, *adv.* —**god′less·ness**, *n.*

god·like (gŏd′līk′), *adj.* like or befitting a god, or God. —**god′like′ness**, *n.*

god·ly (gŏd′lĭ), *adj.*, **-lier, -liest.** conforming to God's laws. —**god′li·ness**, *n.*

god·moth·er (gŏd′mŭth′ər), *n.* a woman who sponsors a child at baptism.

god·par·ent (gŏd′pâr′ənt), *n.* a godfather or godmother.

god·send (gŏd′sĕnd′), *n.* something unexpected but particularly welcome.

god·ship (gŏd′shĭp), *n.* the rank or character of a god.

God·speed (gŏd′spēd′), *n.* God speed you (a wish of success).

Goeb·bels (gœb′əls), *n.* **Paul Joseph,** 1897–1945, German Nazi propaganda leader.

Goe·ring (gœ′rĭng), *n.* **Hermann,** 1893–1946, German field marshal and Nazi leader.

Goe·thals (gō′thəlz), *n.* **George Washington,** 1858–1928, U.S. general and engineer, in charge of building the Panama Canal.

Goe·the (gœ′tə), *n.* **Johann Wolfgang von,** 1749–1832, German writer.

go-get·ter (gō′gĕt′ər), *n. U.S. Colloq.* an enterprising, aggressive person.

gog·gle (gŏg′əl), *n., v.*, **-gled, -gling.** —*n.* **1.** (*pl.*) spectacles so devised as to protect the eyes from injury. **2.** a goggling look. —*v.i., v.t.* **3.** to roll (the eyes). **4.** (of the eyes) to roll; bulge and stare. —**gog′gle-eyed′**, *adj.*

Gogh (gō, gôⲕ), *n.* **Vincent van,** 1853–90, Dutch painter.

go·ing (gō′ĭng), *n.* **1.** a departure. **2.** condition of roads. —*adj.* **3.** moving or operating.

goi·ter (goi′tər), *n. Pathol.* an enlargement of the thyroid gland, on the front and sides of the neck. Also, **goi′tre.**

gold (gōld), *n.* **1.** a precious yellow metal, highly malleable and ductile. *Sym.:* Au; *at. wt.:* 197.2; *at. no.:* 79; *sp. gr.:* 19.3 at 20°C. **2.** money; wealth. **3.** bright metallic yellow. —*adj.* **4.** of, like, or pertaining to gold.

gold brick, *Colloq.* **1.** a brick-shaped mass of imitation gold sold by a swindler. **2.** anything of spurious value. **3.** a loafer.

gold-brick (gōld′brĭk′), *Colloq.* —*v.t.* **1.** to swindle. —*v.i.* **2.** to loaf on the job or evade responsibility. —**gold′-brick′er**, *n.*

Gold Coast, a British territory in W Africa. 3,572,000 pop.; 91,843 sq. mi. *Cap.:* Accra.

Gold Coast Colony, a British colony in W Africa, on the Gulf of Guinea. 1,573,000 pop.; 23,937 sq. mi. *Cap.*: Accra.

gold·en (gōl'dən), *adj.* **1.** of the color of gold; metallic yellow. **2.** made or consisting of gold. **3.** most excellent. **4.** joyous. **5.** indicating the 50th event of a series, as a wedding anniversary.

Golden Fleece, the fleece of gold which Jason and the Argonauts recovered from the father of Medea.

Golden Gate, a strait in W California between San Francisco Bay and the Pacific.

golden mean, the happy medium between extremes; moderate course of action.

gold·en·rod (gōl'dən rŏd'), *n.* any of certain composite plants, most species of which bear numerous small yellow flowers.

golden rule, the rule of conduct: "*Whatsoever ye would that men should do to you, do ye even so to them.*"

gold-filled (gōld'fĭld'), *adj.* containing a filling of cheaper metal within a layer of gold.

gold·finch (gōld'fĭnch'), *n.* **1.** a European fringilline songbird having wings marked with yellow. **2.** any of certain small, yellow American finches.

gold·fish (gōld'fĭsh'), *n.*, *pl.* **-fishes**, (*esp. collectively*) **-fish**. a small gold-colored fish of the carp family, prized for aquariums.

gold leaf, gold beaten into a very thin sheet, used for gilding, etc.

gold rush, a large-scale emigration of people to a region where gold has been discovered, as that to California in 1849.

gold·smith (gōld'smĭth'), *n.* one who makes or sells articles of gold.

Gold·smith (gōld'smĭth'), *n.* **Oliver,** 1728-74, British poet, novelist, and dramatist.

gold standard, a monetary system with gold of specified weight and fineness as the unit of value.

golf (gŏlf, gôlf), *n.* **1.** an outdoor game, in which a small ball is driven with special clubs into a series of holes, distributed at various distances over a course having natural or artificial obstacles, the object being to get the ball into each hole in as few strokes as possible. —*v.i.* **2.** to play golf. —**golf'er,** *n.*

Gol·go·tha (gŏl'gə thə), *n.* **1.** Calvary. **2.** a place of suffering or sacrifice.

Go·li·ath (gə lī'əth), *n.* the giant whom David killed with a stone from a sling.

gol·ly (gŏl'ĭ), *interj. Colloq.* a mild expletive expressing surprise, etc.

Go·mor·rah (gə môr'ə, -mŏr'ə), *n.* an ancient city destroyed for its wickedness.

Gom·pers (gŏm'pərz), *n.* **Samuel,** 1850-1924, U.S. labor leader.

gon·ad (gŏn'ăd), *n. Anat.* the sex gland, male or female, in which germ cells develop and appropriate sex hormones are produced.

gon·do·la (gŏn'də lə), *n.* **1.** a long, narrow boat with a high peak at each end, used on the Venetian canals. **2.** the car of a dirigible.

gondola car, *U.S.* a railway freight car with sides but no top.

gon·do·lier (gŏn'də lĭr'), *n.* a man who rows or poles a gondola.

gone (gôn, gŏn), *adj.* **1.** departed. **2.** hopeless. **3.** dead. **4.** weak and faint. **5. far gone, a.** deeply involved. **b.** dying.

gon·er (gôn'ər, gŏn'ər), *n. Colloq.* a person or thing that is dead, lost, or past recovery.

gon·fa·lon (gŏn'fə lən), *n.* a banner suspended from a crossbar, often with streamers.

gong (gông, gŏng), *n. Music.* an Oriental bronze disk struck with a soft-headed stick.

gon·or·rhe·a (gŏn'ə rē'ə), *n. Pathol.* a contagious, purulent inflammation of the urethra or the vagina. Also, *esp. Brit.*, **gon'or·rhoe'a.**

goo (gōō), *n. U.S. Slang.* sticky matter.

goo·ber (gōō'bər), *n. U.S.* the peanut.

good (gŏŏd), *adj.*, **better, best,** *n.*, *interj.*, *adv.* —*adj.* **1.** morally excellent. **2.** excellent. **3.** right; proper. **4.** well-behaved. **5.** kind. **6.** honorable or worthy. **7.** reliable; safe. **8.** genuine. **9.** pleasant. **10.** sufficient. **11.** full. **12.** competent or skillful. **13.** fairly great. **14. as good as,** in effect. —*n.* **15.** profit; benefit. **16.** excellence, righteousness, or kindness. **17.** (*pl.*) possessions. **18.** (*pl.*) wares. **19.** (*pl.*) *U.S.* cloth. **20. for good,** forever. **21. make good, a.** to pay

for. **b.** to fulfill. **c.** to be successful. **d.** to substantiate. —*interj.* **22.** an expression of approval or satisfaction. —*adv.* **23.** *Colloq.* well.

good-by (gŏŏd'bī'), *interj.*, *n.*, *pl.* **-bys.** farewell: a conventional expression used at parting. Also, **good'-bye'.**

Good Friday, the Friday before Easter, observed as the anniversary of the crucifixion of Jesus.

good-heart·ed (gŏŏd'här'tĭd), *adj.* kind.

good humor, a cheerful or amiable mood.

good-hu·mored (gŏŏd'hū'mərd, -ū'mərd), *adj.* having or showing a pleasant, amiable mood. —**good'-hu'mored·ly,** *adv.*

good·ish (gŏŏd'ĭsh), *adj.* fairly good.

good-look·ing (gŏŏd'lŏŏk'ĭng), *adj.* of good appearance; handsome.

good·ly (gŏŏd'lĭ), *adj.*, **-lier, -liest. 1.** of a good quality. **2.** of good appearance. **3.** of good size. —**good'li·ness,** *n.*

good nature, pleasant disposition.

good-na·tured (gŏŏd'nā'chərd), *adj.* having or showing good nature. —**good'-na'tured·ly,** *adv.* —**good'-na'tured·ness,** *n.*

Good Neighbor Policy, a diplomatic policy of the U.S. first presented in 1933 by President Roosevelt for the encouragement of friendly relations and mutual defense by the nations of the Western Hemisphere.

good·ness (gŏŏd'nĭs), *n.* **1.** moral excellence. **2.** kindness; generosity. **3.** excellence.

good Samaritan, a person who is compassionate and helpful to one in distress.

good-tem·pered (gŏŏd'tĕm'pərd), *adj.* having or showing amiability.

good will, 1. friendly disposition; favor. **2.** cheerful acquiescence. **3.** *Com.* an intangible asset arising from the reputation of a business.

good·y (gŏŏd'ĭ), *n.*, *pl.*, **goodies,** *adj.*, *interj. Colloq.* —*n.* **1.** (*pl.*) sweet food; candy. —*adj.* **2.** affecting goodness. —*interj.* **3.** wonderful!

goo·ey (gōō'ĭ), *adj.*, **gooier, gooiest.** *Slang.* like goo; sticky; viscid.

goof (gōōf), *n. Slang.* a foolish or stupid person. —**goof'y,** *adj.* —**goof'i·ness,** *n.*

goon (gōōn), *n. U.S. Slang.* **1.** a stupid person. **2.** a hired thug used in a labor dispute.

goose (gōōs), *n.*, *pl.* **geese** for 1-2; **gooses** for 3. **1.** any of certain wild or domesticated web-footed birds, most of them larger and with a longer neck than the ducks. **2.** a simpleton. **3.** a tailor's smoothing iron with a curved handle. —**goose'-like',** *adj.*

goose·ber·ry (gōōs'bĕr'ĭ, gōōz'-, -bə rĭ), *n.*, *pl.* **-ries. 1.** the small, edible, acid, globular berry of certain prickly shrubs. **2.** the shrub itself.

goose flesh, a rough condition of the skin induced by cold or fear. Also, **goose pimples.**

goose·neck (gōōs'nĕk'), *n.* something curved like the neck of a goose, as a flexible stand for a desk lamp.

goose step, a marching step, esp. of the German infantry, in which the legs are swung high with straight, stiff knees. —**goose'-step',** *v.i.*

G.O.P., the "Grand Old Party," an epithet for the Republican party since 1880.

go·pher (gō'fər), *n.* **1.** any of various ground squirrels of western North America. **2.** any of various other burrowing rodents of western and southern North America and Central America, with large external fur-lined cheek pouches.

Gor·di·an (gôr'dĭ ən), *adj.* pertaining to Gordius, ancient king of Phrygia, who tied a knot (**Gordian knot**) to be undone only by one who should rule Asia; it was cut by Alexander the Great.

gore[1] (gōr), *n.* blood that is shed.

gore[2] (gōr), *v.t.*, **gored, goring.** (of an animal) to pierce with the horns or tusks.

gore[3] (gōr), *n.*, *v.*, **gored, goring.** —*n.* **1.** a triangular piece of cloth, etc., inserted in a garment, a sail, etc., as to give greater width. —*v.t.* **2.** to make or furnish with a gore.

gorge (gôrj), *n.*, *v.*, **gorged, gorging.** —*n.* **1.** a narrow cleft with steep, rocky walls. **2.** *Archaic.* the throat. —*v.t.* **3.** to stuff (oneself) with food.

gor·geous (gôr'jəs), *adj.* splendid in appearance or coloring. —**gor'geous·ly,** *adv.* —**gor'geous·ness,** *n.*

Gor·gon (gôr'gən), *n. Gk. Legend.* any of three sisters whose heads were covered with snakes instead of hair, and whose glance turned the beholder to stone.

Gor·gon·zo·la (gôr'gən zō'lə), *n.* a strongly flavored Italian cheese.

go·ril·la (gə ril'ə), *n.* **1.** the largest of the anthropoid apes, ground-living and vegetarian, esp. of western equatorial Africa. **2.** an ugly, brutal fellow.

Gor·ki (gôr'kǐ), *n.* **1.** Maxim, 1868–1936, Russian writer. **2.** a city in the central Soviet Union in Europe. 644,116.

gor·mand·ize (gôr'məndīz'), *v.i., v.t.* **-ized, -iz·ing.** to eat like a glutton. —**gor'mand·iz'er**, *n.*

gorse (gôrs), *n. Chiefly Brit.* furze. —**gors'y**, *adj.*

gor·y (gôr'ǐ), *adj.*, **gor·i·er, gor·i·est.** bloody.

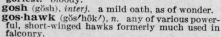
Gorilla (def. 1)
(6 ft. high)

gosh (gŏsh), *interj.* a mild oath, as of wonder.

gos·hawk (gŏs'hôk'), *n.* any of various powerful, short-winged hawks formerly much used in falconry.

Go·shen (gō'shən), *n.* **1.** a pastoral region in Lower Egypt, colonized by the Israelites before the Exodus. **2.** a place of plenty and comfort.

gos·ling (gŏz'lĭng), *n.* **1.** a young goose. **2.** a foolish, inexperienced person.

gos·pel (gŏs'pəl), *n.* **1.** the body of doctrine taught by Christ and the apostles. **2.** the story of Christ's life and teachings, as contained in the first four books (**Gospels**) of the New Testament. **3.** *Colloq.* something implicitly believed. —*adj.* **4.** pertaining to the gospel. **5.** evangelical.

gos·sa·mer (gŏs'ə mər), *n.* **1.** a fine filmy cobweb, seen on grass and bushes, or floating in the air in calm weather, esp. in autumn. —*adj.* **2.** Also, **gos·sa·mer·y** (gŏs'ə mə rǐ). of or like gossamer.

gos·sip (gŏs'əp), *n., v.,* **-siped, -sip·ing.** —*n.* **1.** idle talk, esp. about the affairs of others. **2.** light, familiar talk or writing. **3.** a person given to tattling or idle talk. —*v.i., v.t.* **4.** to talk idly, esp. about the affairs of others. —**gos'sip·er**, *n.* —**gos'sip·y**, *adj.*

Gö·te·borg (yœ'tə bôr'y), *n.* a seaport in SW Sweden, on the Kattegat. 315,474.

Goth (gŏth), *n.* **1.** one of a Teutonic people who, in the 3rd to 5th century, invaded and settled in parts of the Roman Empire. **2.** a barbarian.

Goth·am (gŏth'əm, gō'thəm), *n.* the city of New York.

Goth·ic (gŏth'ĭk), *adj.* **1.** *Archit.* denoting or pertaining to a style common in western Europe from the 12th to the 16th century, characterized by great height, the pointed arch, and the flying buttress. **2.** medieval. **3.** (esp. in literature) stressing irregularity and details, usually of a grotesque or horrible nature. —*n.* **4.** Gothic architecture, sculpture, or decoration. **5.** an extinct Germanic language. **6.** (*l.c.*) U.S. a square-cut printing type, without serifs or hairlines.

gouache (gwäsh), *n.* **1.** a method of painting with opaque water colors. **2.** an opaque color so used. **3.** a work executed in this medium.

gouge (gouj), *n., v.,* **gouged, gouging.** —*n.* **1.** a chisel whose blade has a concavo-convex cross section. **2.** a groove made by gouging. —*v.t.* **3.** to scoop out with a gouge. **4.** to dig or force out. **5.** *U.S. Colloq.* to impose upon or swindle. —**goug'er**, *n.*

gou·lash (gōo'läsh, -lash), *n.* a stew of beef, veal, etc., esp. with paprika.

Gou·nod (gōo'nō), *n.* Charles François, 1818–93, French composer.

gourd (gōrd, gōord), *n.* **1.** the fruit of certain plants of the cucumber family, esp. one whose dried shell is used for bottles, bowls, etc. **2.** a plant bearing such a fruit.

gour·mand (gōor'mənd), *n.* one fond of good eating.

gour·met (gōor'mā), *n.* a connoisseur in the delicacies of the table; an epicure.

gout (gout), *n.* a disease characterized by painful inflammation of the joints, esp. those in the great toe. —**gout'y**, *adj.* —**gout'i·ness**, *n.*

Gov., Governor. Also, **gov.**

gov·ern (gŭv'ərn), *v.t., v.i.* **1.** to rule by right of authority. **2.** to influence; guide. **3.** to hold

in check. **4.** to serve as a law for. **5.** *Gram.* to be accompanied by (a particular form). —**gov'erna·ble**, *adj.*

gov·ern·ess (gŭv'ər nĭs), *n.* a woman who directs the education of children, generally in their own homes.

gov·ern·ment (gŭv'ərn mənt, -ər-), *n.* **1.** political rule and administration. **2.** the system of rule by which a state, etc., is governed. **3.** the governing body of persons in a state, etc. **4.** direction; control. **5.** the district governed. —**gov·ern·men·tal** (gŭv'ərn mĕn'təl, -ər-), *adj.* —**gov'ern·men'tal·ly**, *adv.*

gov·er·nor (gŭv'ər nər), *n.* **1.** the executive head of a State in the U.S. **2.** *Chiefly Brit.* a director of an institution, society, etc. **3.** a person appointed to govern a province, town, fort, or the like. **4.** *Mach.* a device for regulating a supply of fuel for ensuring uniform speed. —**gov'er·nor·ship'**, *n.*

governor general, *pl.* **governors general.** a governor who has under him subordinate governors.

Govt., Government. Also, **govt.**

gown (goun), *n.* **1.** a woman's dress or robe. **2.** a loose outer garment worn as distinctive of office, etc. —*v.t., v.i.* **3.** to dress in, or put on, a gown.

Go·ya (gô'yä), *n.* Francisco de, 1746–1828, Spanish painter and etcher.

Gr., **1.** Greek. **2.** (*l.c.*) grain. **3.** (*l.c.*) gram.

grab (grăb), *v.,* **grabbed, grabbing,** *n.* —*v.t.* **1.** to seize suddenly and eagerly. **2.** to take illegal possession of. —*n.* **3.** a sudden, eager grasp. **4.** seizure by violent or illegal means. **5.** that which is grabbed. —**grab'ber**, *n.*

grace (grās), *n., v.,* **graced, gracing.** —*n.* **1.** elegance or beauty of form, manner, motion, or act. **2.** a pleasing quality. **3.** favor or good will. **4.** mercy; pardon. **5.** *Law.* an allowance of additional time to a debtor. **6.** *Theol.* the free, unmerited favor and love of God. **7.** a short prayer of thanks before or after a meal. **8.** (*usually cap.*) a formal title for a duke, duchess, or archbishop. **9.** (*cap.*) *Class. Myth.* one of three sister goddesses, presiding over all beauty and charm. **10.** Also, **grace note.** *Music.* an embellishment not essential to the harmony or melody. —*v.t.* **11.** to lend grace to. **12.** to favor or honor. —**grace'less**, *adj.*

grace·ful (grās'fəl), *adj.* characterized by grace; elegant. —**grace'ful·ly**, *adv.* —**grace'-ful·ness**, *n.*

gra·cious (grā'shəs), *adj.* **1.** kind; courteous. **2.** indulgent in a condescending way. **3.** merciful. —*interj.* **4.** an exclamation of surprise, etc. —**gra'cious·ly**, *adv.* —**gra'cious·ness**, *n.*

grack·le (grăk'əl), *n.* any of various dark birds of the Old World (starlings) or of America (American starlings, blackbirds, etc.).

grad., **1.** graduate. **2.** graduated.

gra·da·tion (grā dā'shən), *n.* **1.** any process or change taking place gradually. **2.** (*usually pl.*) a stage in such a series. **3.** the gradual passing of one shade of color to another, or one surface to another, as in painting, etc. **4.** act of grading.

grade (grād), *n., v.,* **graded, grading.** —*n.* **1.** a degree in a scale, as of rank, quality, value, etc. **2.** a class of persons or things of the same relative rank, quality, etc. **3.** a stage in a course or process. **4.** a single division of a school classified according to the progress of the pupils. **5.** (*pl.*) Also, **grade school.** *U.S.* elementary school. **6.** *U.S.* a number, letter, etc., indicating the relative quality of a student's work. **7.** inclination with the horizontal of a road, railroad, etc. —*v.t.* **8.** to arrange in grades. **9.** to determine the grade of. **10.** to cause to pass by degrees. **11.** to reduce to a level. —*v.i.* **12.** to be graded. —**grad'er**, *n.*

grade crossing, a crossing of a railroad and a highway, etc., at the same level.

gra·di·ent (grā'dǐ ənt), *n.* **1.** the degree or rate of ascent or descent. **2.** an inclined surface. —*adj.* **3.** rising or descending by regular degrees. **4.** progressing by walking, as an animal.

grad·u·al (grăj'ŏŏ əl), *adj.* **1.** taking place, changing, moving, etc., by degrees. **2.** rising or descending at an even, moderate inclination. —*n.* **3.** *Eccles.* an antiphon sung between the epistle and the gospel in the Eucharistic service. —**grad'u·al·ly**, *adv.* —**grad'u·al·ness**, *n.*

grad·u·ate (*n., adj.* grăj'ŏŏ ǐt, -āt'; *v.* grăj'ŏŏ āt'), *n., adj., v.,* **-ated, -ating.** —*n.* **1.** one who has received a degree or diploma, as from a university. **2.** a glass vessel for measuring. —*adj.* **3.** that has been graduated. **4.** of or pertaining to graduates. —*v.i.* **5.** to receive a degree or diploma. **6.** to change gradually. —*v.t.* **7.** to confer a degree upon or to grant a diploma to. **8.** to arrange in grades. **9.** to divide into degrees. —**grad′u·a′tion,** *n.*

graft[1] (gräft, gräft), *n.* **1.** *Hort.* a shoot or part of a plant inserted in a slit or the like in another plant or tree so as to become nourished by and united with it. **2.** *Surg.* a portion of living tissue surgically transplanted. —*v.t.* **3.** to make (a graft). —*v.i.* **4.** to become grafted. —**graft′er,** *n.*

graft[2] (gräft, gräft), *U.S. Colloq.* —*n.* **1.** the acquisition of gain through the abuse of one's position or influence in politics, business, etc. —*v.i.* **2.** to practice graft. —**graft′er,** *n.*

gra·ham (grā′əm), *adj.* made of **graham flour** (unbolted wheat flour).

grail (grāl), *n.* a cup which according to medieval legend was used by Jesus at the Last Supper, and in which Joseph of Arimathaea received the last drops of Jesus' blood at the Cross.

grain (grān), *n.* **1.** a small hard seed, esp. of one of the cereal plants. **2.** the gathered seeds of cereal plants in the mass. **3.** the plants themselves. **4.** any small particle, as of sand, gold, etc. **5.** the smallest unit of weight in most systems. In an avoirdupois ounce there are 437.5 grains; in the troy and apothecaries' ounces there are 480 grains. **6.** the smallest possible amount of anything. **7.** the direction of fibers in wood. **8.** texture. **9.** temper or natural character. —*v.t.* **10.** to form into grains. **11.** to give a granular appearance to. —**grain′y,** *adj.*

grain alcohol, alcohol made from grain.

gram (gräm), *n.* a metric unit of mass, defined as one thousandth of a kilogram and equal to 15,432 grains. Also, *esp. Brit.,* **gramme.**

gram., 1. grammar. **2.** grammatical.

gram·mar (gräm′ər), *n.* **1.** the features of a language considered systematically as a whole. **2.** an account of the preceding. **3.** speech or writing in accordance with standard usage. **4:** the elements of any subject. —**gram′mar·less,** *adj.*

gram·mar·i·an (grə mâr′ĭ ən), *n.* a specialist in the study of grammar.

grammar school, 1. *U.S.* a graded school intermediate between a primary school and a high school. **2.** *Brit.* a secondary school corresponding to an American high school.

gram·mat·i·cal (grə mät′ə kəl), *adj.* **1.** of or pertaining to grammar. **2.** conforming to standard usage. —**gram·mat′i·cal·ly,** *adv.*

gram molecule, *Chem.* that quantity of a substance whose weight in grams is numerically equal to the number which expresses the molecular weight of the substance. Also, **gram′-mo·lec′u·lar weight.**

gram·o·phone (gräm′ə fōn′), *n.* **1.** a phonograph. **2.** (*cap.*) a trade name for this.

gram·pus (gräm′pəs), *n.* a cetacean of the dolphin family, widely distributed in northern seas.

Gra·na·da (grə nä′də), *n.* a city in S Spain. 155,405.

gran·a·ry (grän′ə rĭ, grā′nə-), *n., pl.* **-ries.** a storehouse or repository for grain.

grand (gränd), *adj.* **1.** imposing in size or general effect. **2.** stately; dignified. **3.** lofty. **4.** magnificent. **5.** noble or fine. **6.** main or chief. **7.** of great importance. **8.** complete. —**grand′ly,** *adv.* —**grand′ness,** *n.*

grand·aunt (gränd′ănt′, -änt′), *n.* a greataunt.

Grand Banks, an extensive shoal SE of Newfoundland: fishing grounds.

Grand Canyon, a gorge of the Colorado river in N Arizona. Over 200 mi. long; 2000 to 6000 ft. deep.

grand·child (gränd′chīld′), *n., pl.* **-children.** a child of one's son or daughter.

Grand Cou·lee (kōō′lĭ), **1.** a dry canyon in central Washington. 52 mi. long. **2.** a dam on the Columbia river at the N end of this canyon: the largest concrete dam in the world. 550 ft. high.

grand·daugh·ter (gränd′dô′tər), *n.* a daughter of one's son or daughter.

grand duke, 1. the sovereign of a territory called a **grand duchy,** ranking next below a king. **2.** a son of a czar or of a czar's son.

gran·dee (gran dē′), *n.* a Spanish nobleman of the highest rank.

gran·deur (grän′jər, -jŏŏr), *n.* imposing greatness; exalted dignity or importance.

grand·fa·ther (gränd′fä′thər), *n.* **1.** the father of one's father or mother. **2.** a forefather.

gran·dil·o·quent (gran dĭl′ə kwənt), *adj.* speaking or expressed in a lofty or pompous style. —**gran·dil′o·quence,** *n.* —**gran·dil·o·quent·ly,** *adv.*

gran·di·ose (grän′dĭ ōs′), *adj.* **1.** grand in an impressive way. **2.** pompous. —**gran′di·ose′·ly,** *adv.*

grand jury, a jury of from 12 to 23 persons designated to ascertain whether the evidence of alleged violations is sufficient to warrant trial by a petty jury.

grand·moth·er (gränd′mŭth′ər), *n.* **1.** the mother of one's father or mother. **2.** an ancestress.

grand·neph·ew (gränd′nĕf′ū, -nĕv′ū), *n.* a son of one's nephew or niece.

grand·niece (gränd′nēs′), *n.* a daughter of one's nephew or niece.

grand opera, a drama interpreted by music, the text being sung throughout.

grand·par·ent (gränd′pâr′ənt), *n.* a parent of a parent.

Grand Rapids, city in SW Michigan. 164,292.

grand·sire (gränd′sīr′), *n.* *Archaic.* **1.** a grandfather. **2.** a forefather. **3.** an old man.

grand·son (gränd′sŭn′), *n.* a son of one's son or daughter.

grand·stand (gränd′ständ′), *n.* the principal stand for spectators at an athletic field, etc.

grand·un·cle (gränd′ŭng′kəl), *n.* an uncle of one's father or mother.

grange (grānj), *n.* **1.** a farm. **2.** (*cap.*) *U.S.* a local branch of an association for promoting the interests of agriculture. **3.** (*cap.*) the association itself.

grang·er (grān′jər), *n.* **1.** a farmer. **2.** (*cap.*) *U.S.* a member of a Grange.

gran·ite (grän′ĭt), *n.* a granular igneous rock much used in building, etc.

gran·ny (grän′ĭ), *n., pl.* **-nies.** *Colloq.* **1.** a grandmother. **2.** an old woman.

granny's knot, a square knot in which the second part is crossed the wrong way.

grant (gränt, gränt), *v.t.* **1.** to bestow or accord. **2.** to agree or accede to. **3.** to admit or concede. **4.** to transfer. —*n.* **5.** that which is granted. **6.** act of granting. **7.** *Law.* an instrument which conveys property. —**gran·tee′,** *n.* —**grant′er, grant′or,** *n.*

Grant (gränt), *n.* Ulysses Simpson, 1822–85, Union general in the Civil War and 18th president of the U.S., 1869–77.

gran·u·lar (grän′yə lər), *adj.* **1.** of the nature of granules. **2.** composed of or bearing granules. **3.** showing a granulated structure.

gran·u·late (grän′yə lāt′), *v.,* **-lated, -lating.** —*v.t.* **1.** to form into granules or grains. **2.** to make rough on the surface. —*v.i.* **3.** to become granular. —**gran′u·la′tion,** *n.*

gran·ule (grän′ūl), *n.* **1.** a little grain. **2.** a small particle.

grape (grāp), *n.* **1.** an edible, pulpy, smooth-skinned berry which grows in clusters on certain vines, and from which wine is made. **2.** any vine bearing this fruit. **3.** dull, dark purplish red.

grape·fruit (grāp′frōōt′), *n.* a large roundish, yellow-skinned edible citrus fruit with a juicy, acid pulp, grown mainly in the U.S.

grape·shot (grāp′shŏt′), *n.* *Archaic.* a cluster of small cast-iron balls used as a charge for a cannon.

grape sugar, dextrose.

grape·vine (grāp′vīn′), *n.* **1.** a vine that bears grapes. **2.** *U.S. Colloq.* **a.** a person-to-person method of relaying secret reports. **b.** rumor.

graph (gräf), *n.* a diagram representing a system of connections or interrelations among two or more things by a number of distinctive dots, lines, bars, etc.

graph·ic (gräf′ĭk), *adj.* **1.** lifelike; vivid. **2.** pertaining to the use of diagrams, graphs, etc. **3.** pertaining to writing. **4.** pertaining to painting, etching, engraving, and closely related arts. Also, **graph′i·cal.** —**graph′i·cal·ly,** *adv.*

graph·ite (gräf′īt), *n.* a very common mineral, soft native carbon: used in lead pencils, as a lubricant, etc.

graph·ol·o·gy (grä fŏl′ə jĭ), *n.* the study of

handwriting, esp. as regarded as an expression of the writer's character. —**graph·ol/o·gist**, *n.*

grap·nel (gräp/nəl), *n.*　**1.** a device consisting essentially of one or more hooks or clamps, for grasping something.　**2.** a small anchor with three or more flukes.

grap·ple (gräp/əl), *n., v.,* -**pled, -pling.**　—*n.* **1.** a hook or an iron instrument by which one thing, as a ship, fastens on another.　**2.** a gripping.　**3.** a grip in wrestling.　—*v.t.* **4.** to seize, hold, or fasten with a grapple.　**5.** to engage in a struggle with.　—*v.i.* **6.** to hold or make fast to something, as with a grapple.　**7.** to seize another, or each other, in a firm grip, as in wrestling.　**8.** to try to deal.　—**grap/pler**, *n.*

grappling iron,　a grapnel.

grasp (gräsp, gräsp), *v.t.*　**1.** to seize and hold, as by clasping with the fingers.　**2.** to understand.　—*v.i.* **3.** to seize something firmly or eagerly.　**4.** to try to seize.　—*n.* **5.** a gripping.　**6.** power of seizing and holding.　**7.** hold, possession, or mastery.　**8.** comprehension.　—**grasp/er**, *n.*

grasp·ing (gräs/pĭng, gräs/-), *adj.*　**1.** that grasps.　**2.** greedy.　—**grasp/ing·ly**, *adv.*

grass (gräs, gräs), *n.*　**1.** any of a family of plants characterized by jointed stems, sheathing leaves, flower spikelets, and fruit consisting of a seedlike grain.　**2.** herbage.　**3.** the grass-covered ground.　**4.** pasture.

grass·hop·per (gräs/hŏp/ər, gräs/-), *n.* any of numerous orthopterous insects which are terrestrial, herbivorous, and have their hind legs fitted for leaping.

grass·y (gräs/ĭ, gräs/ĭ), *adj.,* **grassier, grassiest.**　**1.** covered with grass.　**2.** of or like grass.　—**grass/i·ness**, *n.*

grate[1] (grāt), *n., v.,* **grated, grating.** —*n.* **1.** a frame of metal bars for holding fuel when burning, as in a fireplace.　**2.** a framework of bars used as a partition, guard, etc.　**3.** a fireplace.　—*v.t.* **4.** to furnish with a grate or grates.　—**grate/less,** *adj.*　—**grate/like/,** *adj.*

grate[2] (grāt), *v.,* **grated, grating.** —*v.i.* **1.** to have an irritating or unpleasant effect on the feelings.　**2.** to make a sound as of rough scraping.　**3.** to sound harshly.　—*v.t.* **4.** to rub together with a harsh, jarring sound.　**5.** to reduce to small particles by rubbing against a rough surface. —**grat/er**, *n.*

grate·ful (grāt/fəl), *adj.*　**1.** deeply appreciative; thankful.　**2.** actuated by or betokening gratitude.　**3.** pleasing or refreshing. —**grate/ful·ly**, *adv.*　—**grate/ful·ness**, *n.*

grat·i·fy (grăt/ə fī/), *v.t.,* -**fied, -fying.**　**1.** to give pleasure to (persons) by satisfying desires.　**2.** to satisfy.　—**grat/i·fi·ca/tion**, *n.*

grat·ing (grā/tĭng), *n.* a partition or frame of crossing bars serving as a cover or guard.

gra·tis (grā/tĭs, grăt/ĭs), *adv.*　**1.** gratuitously. —*adj.* **2.** free; gratuitous.

grat·i·tude (grăt/ə tūd/, -tōōd/), *n.* quality or feeling of being grateful or thankful.

gra·tu·i·tous (grə tū/ə təs, -tōō/-), *adj.*　**1.** freely bestowed or obtained; free.　**2.** being without reason, cause, or justification.　—**gra·tu/i·tous·ly**, *adv.*

gra·tu·i·ty (grə tū/ə tĭ, -tōō/-), *n., pl.* -**ties.** a gift of money over and above payment due for service; tip.

grave[1] (grāv), *n.*　**1.** an excavation in the earth to receive a dead body in burial.　**2.** any place of interment.

grave[2] (grāv), *adj.,* **graver, gravest,** *n.*　—*adj.* **1.** dignified; solemn.　**2.** weighty or important.　**3.** critical.　**4.** *Phonet.* noting or having a particular accent (`) indicating a comparatively low pitch, quality of sound, distinct syllabic value, etc.　—*n.* **5.** the grave accent. —**grave/ly**, *adv.* —**grave/ness**, *n.*

grave[3] (grāv), *v.t.,* **graved, graved or graven, graving.**　**1.** to incise or engrave.　**2.** to impress deeply.　—**grav/er**, *n.*

grave·clothes (grāv/klōz/, -klōthz/), *n.pl.* the clothes in which a dead body is interred.

grav·el (grăv/əl), *n., v.,* -**eled, -eling** or (*esp. Brit.*) -**elled, -elling.**　—*n.* **1.** small stones and pebbles, or a mixture of these with sand.　**2.** *Pathol.* multiple small calculi formed in the kidneys.　—*v.t.* **3.** to cover with gravel.　—**grav/el·ly**, *adj.*

grav·en image (grā/vən),　an idol.

grave·stone (grāv/stōn/), *n.* a stone marking a grave.

grave·yard (grāv/yärd/), *n.*　a cemetery.

grav·i·tate (grăv/ə tāt/), *v.i.,* -**tated, -tating.**　**1.** to move under the influence of gravitational force.　**2.** to sink; fall.　**3.** to be strongly attracted.

grav·i·ta·tion (grăv/ə tā/shən), *n.*　**1.** *Physics.* that force of attraction between all particles or bodies, or that acceleration of one toward another, of which the fall of bodies to the earth is an instance.　**2.** natural tendency toward some point.　—**grav/i·ta/tion·al**, *adj.*

grav·i·ty (grăv/ə tĭ), *n., pl.* -**ties.**　**1.** the force of attraction by which terrestrial bodies tend to fall toward the center of the earth.　**2.** heaviness or weight.　**3.** solemnity.　**4.** serious or critical character.

gra·vure (grə vyŏŏr/, grā/vyər), *n.*　**1.** a process of photomechanical printing, such as rotogravure.　**2.** a plate or print produced by this process.

gra·vy (grā/vĭ), *n., pl.* -**vies.** the fat and juices that drip from cooking meat, often made into a dressing for meat, etc.

gray (grā), *adj.*　**1.** of a color between white and black.　**2.** dark, dismal, or gloomy.　—*n.* **3.** any color in the range from white to black.　**4.** gray material or clothing.　—*v.t., v.i.* **5.** to make or become gray. Also, *esp. Brit.*, **grey.**　—**gray/ly**, *adv.*　—**gray/ness**, *n.*

Gray (grā), *n.*　**Thomas,** 1716–71, British poet.

gray·beard (grā/bĭrd/), *n.* an old man; sage. Also, *Brit.*, **grey/beard/.**

gray·ish (grā/ĭsh), *adj.* having a tinge of gray. Also, *esp. Brit.*, **greyish.**

gray·ling (grā/lĭng), *n.* any of certain freshwater fishes allied to the trout, but having a longer and higher dorsal fin of resplendent color.

gray matter,　**1.** *Anat.* nervous tissue, esp. of the brain and spinal cord, containing both fibers and nerve cells, and of a dark reddish-gray color.　**2.** *Colloq.* intellect.

Graz (gräts), *n.* a city in SE Austria. 208,016.

graze[1] (grāz), *v.i., v.t.,* **grazed, grazing.**　**1.** to feed on (growing herbage), as cattle, sheep, etc., do.　**2.** to put cattle, etc., to feed on (grass, etc.).

graze[2] (grāz), *v.,* **grazed, grazing,** *n.* —*v.t., v.i.* **1.** to touch (something) lightly in passing.　**2.** to scrape.　—*n.* **3.** a grazing.

graz·ing (grā/zĭng), *n.* pasture land.

grease (*n.* grēs; *v.* grēs, grēz), *n., v.,* **greased, greasing.**　—*n.* **1.** the melted fat of animals.　**2.** any lubricant.　—*v.t.* **3.** to put grease on; lubricate.　**4.** to smear with grease.　**5.** *Slang.* to bribe.

grease·wood (grēs/wŏŏd/), *n.* a shrub of the alkaline regions of the western U.S., containing a small amount of oil and used for fuel.

greas·y (grē/sĭ, -zĭ), *adj.,* **greasier, greasiest.**　**1.** smeared with grease.　**2.** of or containing grease; oily.　**3.** greaselike.　—**greas/i·ly**, *adv.*　—**greas/i·ness**, *n.*

great (grāt), *adj.*　**1.** unusually large.　**2.** considerable in degree.　**3.** notable.　**4.** famous.　**5.** important.　**6.** chief or principal.　**7.** of high position or standing.　**8.** of noble or lofty character.　**9.** being such in an extreme degree.　**10.** skillful or expert.　**11.** *Colloq.* first-rate.　**12.** more remote in direct ascent or descent than a specified relationship.　—**great/ly**, *adv.*　—**great/ness**, *n.*

Great Bear,　*Astron.* Ursa Major.

Great Britain,　an island off NW Europe, separated from the mainland by the English Channel and the North Sea: since 1707 the name has applied politically to England, Scotland, and Wales. 45,890,200 pop.; 88,139 sq. mi.

great circle,　**1.** a circle on a sphere the plane of which passes through the center of the sphere.　**2.** the line of shortest distance between two points on the surface of the earth.

great·coat (grāt/kōt/), *n.* *Chiefly Brit.* a heavy overcoat.

Great Dane,　one of a breed of large, powerful, short-haired dogs, somewhat resembling the mastiff.

Great Divide,　the continental divide of North America: the Rocky Mountains.

great·en (grā/tən), *v.t., v.i. Archaic.* to make or become greater.

great-heart·ed (grāt/här/tĭd), *adj.*　**1.** generous; magnanimous.　**2.** courageous.

Great Lakes,　a series of five large lakes between the United States and Canada, connected with the Atlantic by the St. Lawrence: Lakes Erie, Huron, Michigan, Ontario, and Superior.

Great Plains,　a semiarid region E of the Rocky Mountains in the United States and Canada.

Great Salt Lake, a shallow salt lake in NW Utah. ab. 2300 sq. mi.

great seal, the principal seal of a government or state.

Great Smoky Mountains, a mountain range in North Carolina and Tennessee. Highest peak, 6642 ft.

greave (grēv), *n.* armor for the leg from knee to ankle.

grebe (grēb), *n.* any of several diving birds related to the loons, but having lobate rather than webbed toes, and a rudimentary tail.

Gre·cian (grē′shən), *adj.*, *n.* Greek.

Greece (grēs), *n.* a kingdom in S Europe at the S end of the Balkan Peninsula. 7,108,814 pop.; 50,147 sq. mi. *Cap.:* Athens.

greed (grēd), *n.* inordinate or rapacious desire, esp. for wealth.

greed·y (grē′dĭ), *adj.*, **greedier, greediest. 1.** very eager for wealth. **2.** greatly desiring, esp. of food or drink. —**greed′i·ly,** *adv.* —**greed′i·ness,** *n.*

Greek (grēk), *adj.* **1.** of or pertaining to Greece, the Greeks, or their language. —*n.* **2.** a native or inhabitant of Greece. **3.** the language of the ancient Greeks and any of the languages which have developed from it.

Greek Orthodox Church, 1. the Christian church of the countries in doctrinal agreement with the patriarch of Constantinople. **2.** Also, **Greek Church.** that part of this church which constitutes the established church in Greece.

Gree·ley (grē′lĭ), *n.* **Horace,** 1811–72, U.S. journalist and politician.

green (grēn), *adj.* **1.** of the color of growing foliage. **2.** covered with herbage or foliage. **3.** unseasoned, unripe, or immature. **4.** inexperienced. —*n.* **5.** green color. **6.** grassy land. **7.** *Golf.* **a.** the whole course on which golf is played. **b.** a putting green alone. **8.** a piece of grassy ground constituting a town common. **9.** (*pl.*) **a.** fresh leaves or branches of trees, shrubs, etc., used for decoration. **b.** the leaves and stems of plants, as spinach, used for food. —*v.i.*, *v.t.* **10.** to become or make green. —**green′ish,** *adj.* —**green′ness,** *n.*

Green (grēn), *n.* **William,** born 1873, U.S. labor leader: president of the A.F.L. since 1924.

green·back (grēn′băk′), *n.* a United States legal-tender note, usually printed in green on the back.

Green Bay, a port in E Wisconsin, on Lake Michigan. 46,235.

green·bri·er (grēn′brī′ər), *n.* a climbing liliaceous plant of the eastern U.S., with prickly stem and thick leaves.

Greene (grēn), *n.* **Nathanael,** 1742–86, American Revolutionary general.

green·er·y (grē′nə rĭ), *n.*, *pl.* **-eries. 1.** green foliage or vegetation; verdure. **2.** a place where green plants are reared or kept.

green-eyed (grēn′īd′), *adj.* jealous.

green·gage (grēn′gāj′), *n.* one of several varieties of light-green plums.

green·gro·cer (grēn′grō′sər), *n.* *Brit.* a retailer of fresh vegetables and fruit.

green·horn (grēn′hôrn′), *n.* *Colloq.* a raw, inexperienced person.

green·house (grēn′hous′), *n.* a house for the cultivation of plants.

green·ing (grē′nĭng), *n.* any of several varieties of apple the skin of which is green even when ripe.

Green·land (grēn′lənd), *n.* a Danish colony NE of North America: the largest island in the world. 18,431 pop.; ab. 840,000 sq. mi. (over 700,000 sq. mi. ice-capped).

Green Mountains, a mountain range in Vermont. Highest peak, 4393 ft.

Greens·bor·o (grēnz′bûr′ō), *n.* a city in N North Carolina. 59,319.

green tea, a tea which has been subjected to a heating process without previous special withering and fermenting.

Green·wich Time (grĭn′ĭj, grĕn′-, -ĭch), the standard of time as designated at the Observatory in Greenwich, England.

Green·wich Village (grĕn′ĭch), a section of New York City: artists' and writers' center.

green·wood (grēn′wŏŏd′), *n.* a wood or forest when green, as in summer.

greet (grēt), *v.t.* **1.** to address with some form of salutation. **2.** to manifest itself to. —*v.i.* **3.** to give salutations on meeting. —**greet′er,** *n.*

greet·ing (grē′tĭng), *n.* **1.** act or words of one who greets. **2.** (*usually pl.*) a friendly message.

gre·gar·i·ous (grĭ gâr′ĭ əs), *adj.* **1.** living in flocks or herds. **2.** *Bot.* growing in open clusters. **3.** fond of company; sociable. —**gre·gar′i·ous·ly,** *adv.* —**gre·gar′i·ous·ness,** *n.*

Gre·go·ri·an calendar (grĭ gōr′ĭ ən), the calendar now in use, according to which the ordinary year consists of 365 days, and a leap year of 366 days occurs in every year whose number is exactly divisible by 4 except centenary years whose numbers are not exactly divisible by 400.

Greg·o·ry I (grĕg′ə rĭ), **Saint,** (*"Gregory the Great"*) A.D. c540–604, Italian cleric; pope, A.D. 590–604.

grem·lin (grĕm′lĭn), *n.* a mischievous invisible being, said by airplane pilots to cause engine trouble and mechanical difficulties.

gre·nade (grĭ nād′), *n.* a small explosive shell thrown by hand or fired from a rifle.

gren·a·dier (grĕn′ə dĭr′), *n.* **1.** (in the British army) a member of the first regiment of household infantry. **2.** (formerly) a soldier who threw grenades.

gren·a·dine[1] (grĕn′ə dēn′, grĕn′ə dēn′), *n.* a thin dress fabric of silk, rayon, or wool.

gren·a·dine[2] (grĕn′ə dēn′, grĕn′ə dēn′), *n.* a syrup made from pomegranate juice.

Gret·na Green (grĕt′nə), a village in S Scotland, near the English border, to which many runaway English couples formerly eloped.

grey (grā), *adj.*, *n.*, *v.* *Chiefly Brit.* gray.

grey·hound (grā′hound′), *n.* one of a breed of tall, slender dogs, notable for keen sight and for fleetness.

grid (grĭd), *n.* **1.** a grating. **2.** *Elect.* a metallic framework in a storage cell or battery for conducting the electric current and supporting the active material. **3.** *Electronics.* the electrode in an electron tube which controls the electron flow between the other electrodes.

grid·dle (grĭd′əl), *n.*, *v.*, **-dled, -dling.** —*n.* **1.** a handled frying pan with only a slight ledge at the edge, for cooking pancakes, etc. —*v.t.* **2.** to cook on a griddle.

grid·dle·cake (grĭd′əl kāk′), *n.* a thin cake of batter cooked on a griddle; flapjack.

grid·i·ron (grĭd′ī′ərn), *n.* **1.** a utensil consisting of parallel metal bars to broil meat, etc., on. **2.** *Football.* the field of play.

grief (grēf), *n.* **1.** keen sorrow; painful regret. **2. come to grief,** to turn out badly.

Grieg (grēg), *n.* **Edvard,** 1843–1907, Norwegian composer.

griev·ance (grē′vəns), *n.* **1.** a wrong, real or fancied, considered as grounds for complaint. **2.** complaint against an unjust act.

grieve (grēv), *v.i.*, *v.t.*, **grieved, grieving.** to feel, or cause to feel, grief or sorrow.

griev·ous (grē′vəs), *adj.* **1.** causing grief or sorrow. **2.** flagrant. **3.** sorrowful. —**griev′ous·ly,** *adv.* —**griev′ous·ness,** *n.*

grif·fin (grĭf′ĭn), *n.* *Gk. Myth.* a fabulous monster, usually having the head and wings of an eagle and the body of a lion. Also, **grif·fon** (grĭf′-ən).

grig (grĭg), *n.* *Dial.* **1.** a cricket or grasshopper. **2.** a small or young eel.

grill (grĭl), *n.* **1.** a grated utensil for broiling meat, etc., over a fire. **2.** a grillroom. —*v.t.*, *v.i.* **3.** to broil on a gridiron. **4.** to torment with heat. **5.** *U.S. Colloq.* to subject to severe and persistent questioning.

grille (grĭl), *n.* a grating or barrier, as for a gate. —**grilled,** *adj.*

grill·room (grĭl′rōōm′, -rŏŏm′), *n.* a room where meats, etc., are grilled and served.

grilse (grĭls), *n.*, *pl.* **grilse.** a salmon which is ready to return, or has returned, from the sea to the river for the first time.

grim (grĭm), *adj.*, **grimmer, grimmest. 1.** stern; unrelenting. **2.** sinister or ghastly. **3.** forbidding. **4.** fierce, savage, or cruel. —**grim′ly,** *adv.* —**grim′ness,** *n.*

gri·mace (grĭ mās′), *n.*, *v.*, **-maced, -macing.** —*n.* **1.** a wry face; facial contortion. —*v.i.* **2.** to make grimaces.

gri·mal·kin (grĭ măl′kĭn, -môl′-), *n.* **1.** a cat. **2.** an old female cat.

grime (grīm), *n.*, *v.*, **grimed, griming.** —*n.*

1. dirt or foul matter, esp. on or ingrained in a surface. —*v.t.* **2.** to cover with dirt; soil.

Grimm (grĭm), *n.* **Jakob Ludwig Karl,** 1785–1863, or his brother, **Wilhelm Karl,** 1786–1859, German philologists and collectors of fairy tales.

grim·y (grī′mĭ), *adj.,* **grimier, grimiest.** covered with grime; dirty. —**grim′i·ly,** *adv.* —**grim′i·ness,** *n.*

grin (grĭn), *v.,* **grinned, grinning,** *n.* —*v.i.* **1.** to smile broadly. —*n.* **2.** a broad smile.

grind (grīnd), *v.,* **ground** or (*Rare*) **grinded, grinding,** *n.* —*v.t.* **1.** to wear, smooth, or sharpen by friction. **2.** to reduce to fine particles. **3.** to oppress. **4.** to grit. **5.** to operate by turning a crank. —*v.i.* **6.** to perform the operation of reducing to fine particles. **7.** to grate. **8.** *Colloq.* to work or study laboriously. —*n.* **9.** act of grinding. **10.** *Colloq.* laborious work.

grind·er (grīn′dər), *n.* **1.** one that grinds. **2.** a molar tooth.

grind·stone (grīnd′stōn′), *n.* a rotating stone wheel used for grinding, sharpening, etc.

grin·go (grĭng′gō), *n., pl.* **-gos.** (among Spanish Americans) a foreigner, esp. an Anglo-Saxon.

grip (grĭp), *n., v.,* **gripped** or **gript, gripping.** —*n.* **1.** firm grasp. **2.** the power of gripping. **3.** control. **4.** *U.S.* a small suitcase. **5.** a special mode of clasping hands. **6.** something which seizes and holds. **7.** a handle or hilt. **8.** a sudden, sharp pain. **9.** *Theat. Slang.* a stagehand. —*v.t.* **10.** to grasp or seize firmly. **11.** to hold the interest of. —*v.i.* **12.** to hold fast. —**grip′per,** *n.*

gripe (grīp), *v.,* **griped, griping,** *n.* —*v.t., v.i.* **1.** to grasp; clutch. **2.** to produce or suffer pain in the bowels. **3.** *U.S. Colloq.* to complain constantly. —*n.* **4.** a firm hold; clutch. **5.** *U.S. Colloq.* a complaint. **6.** (*usually pl.*) an intermittent spasmodic pain in the bowels. —**grip′er,** *n.*

grippe (grĭp), *n.* influenza.

gris·ly (grĭz′lĭ), *adj.,* **-lier, -liest. 1.** such as to cause a shuddering horror; gruesome. **2.** grim. —**gris′li·ness,** *n.*

grist (grĭst), *n.* **1.** grain to be ground. **2.** ground grain; meal produced from grinding.

gris·tle (grĭs′əl), *n.* cartilage. —**gris·tly** (grĭs′lĭ), *adj.*

grist·mill (grĭst′mĭl′), *n.* a mill for grinding grain, esp. the customer's own grain.

grit (grĭt), *n., v.,* **gritted, gritting.** —*n.* **1.** fine, hard particles such as are deposited like dust from the air. **2.** a coarse-grained siliceous rock. **3.** *U.S.* indomitable spirit; pluck. —*v.t., v.i.* **4.** to grate or grind. —**grit′ty,** *adj.* —**grit′ti·ness,** *n.*

grits (grĭts), *n.pl.* **1.** grain, hulled and often coarsely ground. **2.** *U.S.* coarsely ground hominy.

griz·zled (grĭz′əld), *adj.* gray.

griz·zly (grĭz′lĭ), *adj.,* **-zlier, -zliest,** *n., pl.* **-zlies.** —*adj.* **1.** grayish. **2.** gray-haired. —*n.* **3.** a grizzly bear.

grizzly bear, a large, ferocious bear of western North America, varying in color from grayish to brownish.

groan (grōn), *n.* **1.** a low, mournful sound uttered in pain, grief, derision, or disapprobation. —*v.i.* **2.** to utter or make such a sound. —**groan′er,** *n.*

groat (grōt), *n.* an English silver coin, issued 1351–1662, worth fourpence.

gro·cer (grō′sər), *n.* a dealer in food supplies and other articles of household use.

gro·cer·y (grō′sə rĭ), *n., pl.* **-ceries. 1.** *U.S.* a grocer's store. **2.** (*usually pl.*) a commodity sold by grocers. **3.** the business of a grocer.

grog (grŏg), *n.* **1.** a mixture of alcoholic liquor and water. **2.** strong drink.

grog·gy (grŏg′ĭ), *adj.,* **-gier, -giest.** *Colloq.* **1.** staggering, as from exhaustion or blows. **2.** drunk. —**grog′gi·ness,** *n.*

grog·ram (grŏg′rəm), *n.* a coarse fabric of silk, of silk and mohair or wool, or of wool.

groin (groin), *n.* **1.** *Anat.* the fold or hollow on either side of the body where the thigh joins the abdomen. **2.** *Archit.* the curved line or edge formed by the intersection of two vaults.

grom·met (grŏm′ĭt), *n.* a ring or eyelet of metal, etc.

Gro·my·ko (grō mē′kō), *n.* **Andrei Andreievich,** born 1909, Russian diplomat.

groom (grōōm, grŏŏm), *n.* **1.** a man or boy in charge of horses or the stable. **2.** a bridegroom. —*v.t.* **3.** to make neat or tidy. **4.** to tend (horses). **5.** *U.S.* to prepare for a position, election, etc.

grooms·man (grōōmz′mən, grŏŏmz′-), *n., pl.* **-men.** a best man at a wedding.

groove (grōōv), *n., v.,* **grooved, grooving.** —*n.* **1.** a furrow or channel, esp. one cut by a tool. **2.** a fixed routine. **3. in the groove,** *Jazz.* played perfectly. —*v.t.* **4.** to cut a groove in.

grope (grōp), *v.,* **groped, groping.** —*v.i.* **1.** to feel one's way. **2.** to search blindly or uncertainly. —*v.t.* **3.** to seek by feeling. —**grop′er,** *n.* —**grop′ing·ly,** *adv.*

gros·beak (grōs′bēk′), *n.* any of various finches having a large, stout conical bill.

gros·grain (grō′grān′), *n.* heavy, corded, silk or rayon ribbon or cloth.

gross (grōs), *adj., n., pl.* **grosses** for **6, gross** for **7;** *v.* —*adj.* **1.** total, esp. without having been subjected to deduction, as for charges, loss, etc. **2.** flagrant. **3.** coarse or indecent. **4.** large or bulky. **5.** dense. —*n.* **6.** the main body, bulk, or mass. **7.** a unit consisting of twelve dozen, or 144. —*v.t.* **8.** to make a gross profit of. —**gross′-ly,** *adv.* —**gross′ness,** *n.*

gross ton, 2,240 lbs.

gro·tesque (grō tĕsk′), *adj.* **1.** fantastic in the shaping and combination of forms. **2.** bizarre. —*n.* **3.** any grotesque object or thing. —**grotesque′ly,** *adv.* —**gro·tesque′ness,** *n.*

grot·to (grŏt′ō), *n., pl.* **-toes, -tos. 1.** a cave. **2.** an artificial cavernlike recess or structure.

grouch (grouch), *U.S. Colloq.* —*v.i.* **1.** to be sulky or discontent; complain. —*n.* **2.** a sulky or morose person. **3.** a sulky or morose mood. —**grouch′y,** *adj.* —**grouch′i·ly,** *adv.* —**grouch′i·ness,** *n.*

ground (ground), *n.* **1.** the earth's solid surface; land. **2.** soil. **3.** (*often pl.*) a tract of land for a special use. **4.** (*often pl.*) the motive or reason. **5.** the underlying surface, or background, in painting, lace, etc. **6.** (*pl.*) dregs or sediment. **7.** *Elect.* **a.** a conducting connection between an electric circuit and the earth. **b.** the terminal to which the grounding lead is attached. —*adj.* **8.** on, at, or adjacent to the surface of the earth. **9.** pertaining to the ground. —*v.t.* **10.** to set on the ground. **11.** to settle or establish. **12.** to instruct in elements. **13.** to furnish with a ground. **14.** *Naut.* to run aground. —*v.i.* **15.** to come to or strike the ground.

ground·er (groun′dər), *n. Baseball, etc.* a ball knocked or thrown along the ground.

ground hog, woodchuck.

ground·less (ground′lĭs), *adj.* without basis or reason. —**ground′less·ness,** *n.*

ground·ling (ground′lĭng), *n.* **1.** a plant or animal that lives on or close to the ground. **2.** an uncritical or uncultured person.

ground·nut (ground′nŭt′), *n.* **1.** any of various plants with edible underground portions, as the peanut. **2.** its edible tuber, pod, or the like.

ground squirrel, any of various terrestrial rodents of the squirrel family, as the chipmunk.

ground swell, a broad, deep swell or rolling of the sea, due to a distant storm or gale.

ground·work (ground′wûrk′), *n.* the foundation, base, or basis.

group (grōōp), *n.* **1.** any assemblage of persons or things. **2.** a number of persons or things belonging or classed together. **3.** *Chem.* a number of atoms in a molecule connected or arranged together in some special manner. —*v.t.* **4.** to place or arrange in a group. —*v.i.* **5.** to form a group.

grouse[1] (grous), *n., pl.* **grouse.** any of certain gallinaceous birds, including such important game species as the **red grouse** of Great Britain and **ruffed grouse** of North America.

grouse[2] (grous), *v.,* **groused, grousing,** *n. Slang.* —*v.i.* **1.** to complain. —*n.* **2.** a complaint. —**grous′er,** *n.*

grove (grōv), *n.* a small wood or orchard.

grov·el (grŭv′əl, grŏv′-), *v.i.,* **-eled, -eling** or (*esp. Brit.*) **-elled, -elling. 1.** to humble oneself or act in an abject manner, as in fear. **2.** to lie or move with the face downward, esp. in abject humility, fear, etc.

grow (grō), *v.,* **grew, grown, growing.** —*v.i.* **1.** to increase in size or substance. **2.** to arise or issue as from a germ, stock, or originating source. **3.** to increase in influence or effect (fol. by *on* or *upon*). **4.** to become by degrees. —*v.t.* **5.** to cause or allow to grow. —**grow′er,** *n.*

growl (groul), *v.i.* **1.** to utter a deep guttural sound of anger or hostility. —*v.t.* **2.** to express by growling. —*n.* **3.** act or sound of growling. —**growl′er,** *n.*

grown (grōn), *adj.* **1.** advanced in growth. **2.** arrived at full growth or maturity.

grown-up (grōn′ŭp′), *n.* an adult.

grown-up (grōn′ŭp′), *adj.* **1.** having reached maturity. **2.** of or for adults.

growth (grōth), *n.* **1.** act, process, or manner of growing; development. **2.** something that has grown. **3.** *Pathol.* a morbid mass of tissue, as a tumor.

grub (grŭb), *n., v.,* **grubbed, grubbing.** —*n.* **1.** the bulky larva of certain insects, esp. of beetles. **2.** a drudge. **3.** *Slang.* food. —*v.t., v.i.* **4.** to dig. **5.** to uproot. —**grub′ber,** *n.*

grub·by (grŭb′ĭ), *adj.,* **-bier, -biest.** dirty; slovenly. —**grub′bi·ness,** *n.*

grub·stake (grŭb′stāk′), *n., v.,* **-staked, -staking.** *U.S.* —*n.* **1.** provisions, outfit, etc., furnished to a prospector on condition of participating in the profits of his discoveries. —*v.t.* **2.** to furnish with a grubstake.

grudge (grŭj), *n., v.,* **grudged, grudging.** —*n.* **1.** a feeling of ill will excited by a personal insult, etc. —*v.t.* **2.** to give or permit with reluctance. —*v.i.* **3.** to feel ill will. —**grudg′ing·ly,** *adv.*

gru·el (grōō′əl), *n., v.,* **-eled, -eling** or (*esp. Brit.*) **-elled, -elling.** —*n.* **1.** a light, usually thin, cooked cereal made by boiling meal, esp. oatmeal, in water or milk. —*v.t.* **2.** to exhaust; disable. —**gru′el·ing,** *adj., n.*

grue·some (grōō′səm), *adj.* inspiring horror; revolting. —**grue′some·ly,** *adv.* —**grue′some·ness,** *n.*

gruff (grŭf), *adj.* **1.** low and harsh; hoarse. **2.** rough; surly. —**gruff′ly,** *adv.*

grum·ble (grŭm′bəl), *v.,* **-bled, -bling,** *n.* —*v.i.* **1.** to murmur in discontent; complain. **2.** to growl. **3.** to rumble. —*n.* **4.** an ill-humored complaining. **5.** a rumble. —**grum′bler,** *n.* —**grum′bling·ly,** *adv.*

grump·y (grŭm′pĭ), *adj.,* **grumpier, grumpiest.** surly; ill tempered. —**grump′i·ly,** *adv.*

grunt (grŭnt), *v.i.* **1.** to utter the deep guttural sound characteristic of a hog. —*v.t.* **2.** to express with a grunt. —*n.* **3.** the sound of grunting. **4.** any of certain marine fishes which can emit a grunt. —**grunt′er,** *n.*

Gru·yère cheese (grĭ yâr′, grōō-), a firm, pale-yellow variety of Swiss cheese.

Gua·da·la·ja·ra (gwä′dä lä hä′rä), *n.* a city in W Mexico. 227,631.

Gua·dal·ca·nal (gwä′dəl kə năl′, -däl kä näl′), *n.* one of the Solomon Islands, in the S Pacific: U.S. victory over the Japanese, 1942–43. 14,300 pop.; abt. 2500 sq. mi.

Gua·de·loupe (gwä′də lōōp′), *n.* two French islands in the Leeward Islands of the West Indies. 304,000 pop.; 687 sq. mi. *Cap.:* Basse-Terre.

Guam (gwäm), *n.* an island belonging to the U.S. in the N Pacific, E of the Philippine Islands: the largest of the Marianas group; U.S. naval station. 22,290 pop.; 206 sq. mi. *Cap.:* Agaña.

gua·no (gwä′nō), *n., pl.* **-nos.** a manure composed chiefly of the excrement of sea birds, found esp. on islands near the Peruvian coast.

guar·an·tee (găr′ən tē′), *n., v.,* **-teed, -teeing.** —*n.* **1.** a warrant, pledge, or formal assurance given by way of security. **2.** one who gives a formal assurance or guaranty. —*v.t.* **3.** to secure, as by giving security. **4.** to make oneself answerable for. **5.** to undertake to secure to another, as rights. **6.** to engage to protect or indemnify.

guar·an·tor (găr′ən tôr′, -tər), *n.* one who makes or gives a guarantee.

guar·an·ty (găr′ən tĭ), *n., pl.* **-ties,** *v.,* **-tied, -tying.** —*n.* **1.** a warrant, pledge, or promise given by way of security. **2.** act of giving security. **3.** one who acts as a guarantee. —*v.t.* **4.** to guarantee.

guard (gärd), *v.t.* **1.** to protect. **2.** to watch in order to prevent escape, etc. —*v.i.* **3.** to take precautions. **4.** to give protection. **5.** to keep watch. —*n.* **6.** one who guards. **7.** a body of men, esp. soldiers, guarding a place from theft, fire, etc. **8.** close watch. **9.** a part for guarding against injury, loss, etc. **10.** a posture of defense or readiness, as in fencing, boxing, etc. **11.** *Football.* either of two players holding a position of defense at the right and the left of the center. **12.** *Basketball.* one of the defensive players on a team.

guard·ed (gär′dĭd), *adj.* **1.** cautious; wary. **2.** protected or watched. —**guard′ed·ly,** *adv.* —**guard′ed·ness,** *n.*

guard·house (gärd′hous′), *n.* a military jail.

guard·i·an (gär′dĭ ən), *n.* **1.** one who guards, protects, or preserves. **2.** one who is entrusted by law with the care of the person or property, or both, of another, as of a minor. —*adj.* **3.** guarding. —**guard′i·an·ship′,** *n.*

guards·man (gärdz′mən), *n., pl.* **-men.** **1.** a guard. **2.** *U.S.* a member of the National Guard.

Gua·te·ma·la (gwä′tə mä′lə), *n.* **1.** a republic in Central America. 3,283,209 pop.; 42,042 sq. mi. **2.** Also, **Guatemala City.** the capital of this republic. 163,826. —**Gua·te·ma′lan,** *adj., n.*

gua·va (gwä′və), *n.* **1.** any of various trees or shrubs of the myrtle family, natives of tropical or subtropical America, with a fruit used for jelly, etc. **2.** the fruit.

Guay·a·quil (gwä′yä kēl′), *n.* a seaport in W Ecuador. 172,948.

gua·yu·le (gwä yōō′lĕ), *n.* **1.** a rubber-yielding bushlike composite plant of northern Mexico, etc. **2.** the rubber obtained from this plant.

gu·ber·na·to·ri·al (gū′bər nə tôr′ĭ əl), *adj.* *Chiefly U.S.* pertaining to a governor.

gudg·eon (gŭj′ən), *n.* **1.** a small European fresh-water fish of the minnow family, much used for bait. **2.** one who is easily duped. **3.** a bait. —*v.t.* **4.** to dupe.

guer·don (gûr′dən), *Poetic.* —*n.* **1.** a reward. —*v.t.* **2.** to reward.

Guern·sey (gûrn′zĭ), *n., pl.* **-seys.** one of a breed of dairy cattle of average size.

guer·ril·la (gə rĭl′ə), *n.* a member of a small independent band of soldiers which harasses the enemy by surprise raids, etc. Also, **gue·ril′la.**

guess (gĕs), *v.t.* **1.** to form an opinion of without certainty. **2.** to conjecture correctly. **3.** to think. —*v.i.* **4.** to form a conjecture. **5.** to conjecture correctly. —*n.* **6.** a notion, judgment, or conclusion based on uncertain knowledge. —**guess′er,** *n.*

guess·work (gĕs′wûrk′), *n.* conjecture.

guest (gĕst), *n.* **1.** a person entertained at the house or table of another. **2.** one who receives the hospitality of a club, a city, or the like. **3.** a person who pays for lodging, and sometimes food, at a hotel, etc.

guf·faw (gŭ fô′), *n.* **1.** a loud, coarse burst of laughter. —*v.i.* **2.** to laugh loudly and boisterously.

Gui·an·a (gē ăn′ə, -ä′nə), *n.* a vast tropical region in NE South America, including British Guiana, French Guiana, and Surinam.

guid·ance (gī′dəns), *n.* **1.** act of guiding; leadership. **2.** something that guides.

guide (gīd), *v.,* **guided, guiding,** *n.* —*v.t.* **1.** to lead or show the way to. **2.** to direct the movement or course of. —*n.* **3.** one who guides tourists, hunters, etc. **4.** a directional marker. —**guid′er,** *n.*

guide·book (gīd′bŏŏk′), *n.* a book of directions and information for tourists, etc.

guide·post (gīd′pōst′), *n.* a roadside post bearing a sign for the guidance of travelers.

gui·don (gī′dən), *n.* *Mil.* a small flag for marking, signaling, or identification.

guild (gĭld), *n.* an organization of persons with common professional or cultural interests formed for mutual aid and protection.

guil·der (gĭl′dər), *n.* gulden.

guild·hall (gĭld′hôl′), *n.* *Brit.* the hall used by a guild for its assemblies.

guilds·man (gĭldz′mən), *n., pl.* **-men.** a member of a guild.

guile (gīl), *n.* insidious cunning. —**guile′ful,** *adj.* —**guile′less,** *adj.*

guil·le·mot (gĭl′ə mŏt′), *n.* any of certain narrow-billed northern oceanic birds.

guil·lo·tine (*n.* gĭl′ə tēn′; *v.* gĭl′ə tēn′), *n., v.,* **-tined, -tining.** —*n.* **1.** a machine for beheading persons by means of a heavy blade falling in two grooved posts. —*v.t.* **2.** to behead by the guillotine.

guilt (gĭlt), *n.* **1.** fact or state of having committed an offense or crime. **2.** guilty conduct. —**guilt′less,** *adj.*

guilt·y (gĭl′tĭ), *adj.,* **guiltier, guiltiest.** **1.** justly chargeable with guilt. **2.** characterized by, connected with, or involving guilt. **3.** affected with or showing a sense of guilt. —**guilt′i·ly**, *adv.* —**guilt′i·ness**, *n.*

guimpe (gĭmp, gămp), *n.* a piece of lace, etc., worn at the throat of a low-cut dress.

Guin·ea (gĭn′ĭ), *n.* **1.** a coastal region in W Africa, of indefinite boundaries. **2.** (*l.c.*) a British gold coin worth 21 shillings.

guinea fowl, an African gallinaceous bird which has (usually) dark-gray plumage with small white spots, one species of which is now domesticated throughout the world and valued for its flesh and eggs.

guinea hen, 1. the female of the guinea fowl. **2.** any guinea fowl.

guinea pig, a short-eared, short-tailed rodent, much used in scientific experiments, commonly regarded as the domesticated form of one of the South American wild species of cavy.

Guin·e·vere (gwĭn′ə vĭr′), *n. Arthurian Romance.* wife of King Arthur and mistress of Lancelot. Also, **Guin·e·ver** (gwĭn′ə vər).

guise (gīz), *n.* **1.** external appearance. **2.** mere semblance.

gui·tar (gĭ tär′), *n.* a musical stringed instrument with a long neck and a flat, somewhat violinlike body.

gulch (gŭlch), *n. U.S.* a deep, narrow ravine.

gul·den (gŏŏl′dən), *n., pl.* **-dens, -den. 1.** the gold monetary unit of the Netherlands, equal to 37.7 U.S. cents. **2.** a Dutch silver coin of this value.

gules (gūlz), *n. Her.* red.

Man playing a guitar

gulf (gŭlf), *n.* **1.** a portion of an ocean or sea partly enclosed by land. **2.** a chasm or abyss. **3.** any wide separation, as in education, etc. —*v.t.* **4.** to engulf.

Gulf Stream, a warm oceanic current issuing from the Gulf of Mexico, flowing northward along the U.S. coast and thence northeasterly toward the British Isles.

gull[1] (gŭl), *n.* any of certain long-winged, web-footed, aquatic birds, usually white with gray back and wings.

gull[2] (gŭl), *v.t.* **1.** to trick; cheat. —*n.* **2.** a dupe.

Gul·lah (gŭl′ə), *n.* **1.** a member of a Negro people settled as slaves on the sea islands and coastal region of Georgia and South Carolina. **2.** their English dialect.

gul·let (gŭl′ĭt), *n.* **1.** the esophagus. **2.** the throat or pharynx.

gul·li·ble (gŭl′ə bəl), *adj.* easily deceived. —**gul′li·bil′i·ty**, *n.* —**gul′li·bly**, *adv.*

gul·ly (gŭl′ĭ), *n., pl.* **-lies**, *v.,* **-lied, -lying.** —*n.* **1.** a small valley or canyon cut by running water. —*v.t.* **2.** to make gullies in.

gulp (gŭlp), *v.i.* **1.** to gasp or choke as when taking large drafts of liquids. —*v.t.* **2.** to swallow in large drafts or pieces. —*n.* **3.** act of gulping. **4.** the amount swallowed at one time.

gum[1] (gŭm), *n., v.,* **gummed, gumming.** —*n.* **1.** any of various viscid, amorphous exudations from plants, hardening on exposure to air, and soluble in, or forming a viscid mass with, water. **2.** chewing gum. —*v.t.* **3.** to smear, stiffen, or stick together with gum.

gum[2] (gŭm), *n.* (*often pl.*) the firm, fleshy tissue covering the alveolar parts of either jaw and enveloping the necks of the teeth.

gum arabic, a gum obtained from certain species of acacia: used in calico printing, in medicine, etc.

gum·bo (gŭm′bō), *n., pl.* **-bos. 1.** the okra plant. **2.** its mucilaginous pods. **3.** a soup, usually chicken, thickened with okra pods.

gum·boil (gŭm′boil′), *n.* a small abscess on the gum.

gum·drop (gŭm′drŏp′), *n. U.S.* a droplike confection of gum arabic, gelatin, or the like.

gum·my (gŭm′ĭ), *adj.,* **-mier, -miest. 1.** of the nature of gum; viscid. **2.** covered with gum. **3.** exuding gum. —**gum′mi·ness,** *n.*

gump·tion (gŭmp′shən), *n. Colloq.* **1.** resourcefulness. **2.** shrewd, practical sense.

gum·shoe (gŭm′shōō), *n., v.,* **-shoed, -shoeing.** —*n.* **1.** a rubber overshoe. **2.** (*pl.*) sneakers. **3.** *U.S. Slang.* a detective. —*v.i.* **4.** *U.S. Slang.* to move or act stealthily.

gum tree, any tree that exudes or yields gum, as the eucalyptus, sapodilla, etc.

gun (gŭn), *n., v.,* **gunned, gunning.** —*n.* **1.** a

device having a metal tube through which missiles are thrown by the force of gunpowder, etc. **2.** any portable firearm except a pistol or revolver, as a rifle. **3.** a long-barreled cannon, having a flat trajectory. **4.** *U.S. Colloq.* a pistol or revolver. **5.** any similar device for projecting something. —*v.i., v.t.* **6.** to hunt or shoot with a gun. **7.** *Slang.* to accelerate quickly.

gun·boat (gŭn′bōt′), *n.* a small vessel carrying mounted guns.

gun·cot·ton (gŭn′kŏt′ən), *n.* an explosive cellulose nitrate, made by digesting clean cotton in a mixture of nitric and sulfuric acids.

gun·lock (gŭn′lŏk′), *n.* the mechanism of a firearm by which the charge is exploded.

gun·man (gŭn′mən), *n., pl.* **-men.** *U.S.* a man armed with a gun, esp. to rob or kill.

gun metal, 1. any of various dark gray alloys used for chains, belt buckles, etc. **2.** a dark gray with bluish tinge. **3.** a bronze formerly much employed for cannon.

gun·ner (gŭn′ər), *n.* **1.** one who works a gun or cannon. **2.** a hunter with a gun.

gun·ner·y (gŭn′ə rĭ), *n.* **1.** the art and science of constructing and managing guns, esp. large guns. **2.** the firing of guns. **3.** guns collectively.

gun·ning (gŭn′ĭng), *n.* act, practice, or art of shooting with guns.

gun·ny (gŭn′ĭ), *n., pl.* **-nies. 1.** a strong, coarse material made commonly from jute, used for bagging, etc. **2.** Also, **gunny bag** or **sack.** a bag or sack made of this material.

gun·pow·der (gŭn′pou′dər), *n.* an explosive mixture of saltpeter (potassium nitrate), sulfur, and charcoal, used esp. in gunnery.

gun·run·ning (gŭn′rŭn′ĭng), *n.* the smuggling of guns, etc. —**gun′run′ner,** *n.*

gun·shot (gŭn′shŏt′), *n.* **1.** a shot fired from a gun. **2.** the range of a gun. **3.** the shooting of a gun.

gun·smith (gŭn′smĭth′), *n.* one who makes or repairs firearms.

gun·stock (gŭn′stŏk′), *n.* the stock in which the barrel of a shoulder weapon is fixed.

gun·wale (gŭn′əl), *n. Naut.* the upper edge of a vessel's or boat's side.

gup·py (gŭp′ĭ), *n., pl.* **-pies.** a live-bearing top minnow, commonly kept in household aquariums.

gur·gle (gûr′gəl), *v.,* **-gled, -gling,** *n.* —*v.i.* **1.** to flow in a broken, irregular, noisy current. —*n.* **2.** act or noise of gurgling.

gush (gŭsh), *v.i.* **1.** to flow suddenly and copiously. **2.** *Colloq.* to talk effusively. —*v.t.* **3.** to emit suddenly, forcibly, or copiously. —*n.* **4.** a sudden and violent emission of a fluid. **5.** *Colloq.* effusive language. —**gush′ing·ly,** *adv.*

gush·er (gŭsh′ər), *n.* **1.** *Chiefly U.S.* a flowing oil well. **2.** a person who gushes.

gush·y (gŭsh′ĭ), *adj.,* **gushier, gushiest.** effusive. —**gush′i·ness,** *n.*

gus·set (gŭs′ĭt), *n.* **1.** an angular piece of material inserted in a shirt, etc., usually under the armhole. **2.** a metallic plate used for connections.

gust (gŭst), *n.* **1.** a sudden blast of wind. **2.** an outburst of passionate feeling.

gus·ta·to·ry (gŭs′tə tōr′ĭ), *adj.* of taste.

Gus·ta·vus V (gŭs tā′vəs), 1858–1950, king of Sweden, 1907–1950.

gus·to (gŭs′tō), *n., pl.* **-tos.** keen enjoyment.

gust·y (gŭs′tĭ), *adj.,* **gustier, gustiest. 1.** blowing in gusts, as wind, rain, etc. **2.** marked by gusts of wind, etc. —**gust′i·ly,** *adv.*

gut (gŭt), *n., v.,* **gutted, gutting.** —*n.* **1.** the intestine. **2.** (*pl.*) the bowels or entrails. **3.** (*pl.*) *Slang.* courage. **4.** intestinal tissue or fiber. **5.** a preparation of the intestines of an animal used for violin strings, tennis rackets, fishing lines, etc. —*v.t.* **6.** to disembowel. **7.** to plunder. **8.** to destroy the interior of.

gut·buck·et (gŭt′bŭk′ĭt), *adj. Jazz.* in a primitive style.

Gu·ten·berg (gōō′tən bûrg′), *n.* **Johannes,** c1398–1468, German printer.

gut·ta-per·cha (gŭt′ə pûr′chə), *n.* the concrete milky juice of certain Asiatic and Malayan trees, used in the arts, medicine, and manufactures.

gut·ter (gŭt′ər), *n.* **1.** a channel at the side of a street, for leading off surface water. **2.** any channel, trough, or the like. —*v.i., v.t.* **3.** to flow in streams. **4.** to form gutters (in).

gut·ter·snipe (gŭt/ər snīp/), n. Colloq. a street child of the lowest class; gamin.

gut·tur·al (gŭt/ər əl), adj. 1. pertaining to the throat. 2. throaty. 3. Phonet. pertaining to sounds articulated in the back of the mouth. —n. 4. a guttural sound. —**gut/tur·al·ly**, adv.

guy[1] (gī), n., v., **guyed, guying.** —n. 1. Slang. a person. —v.t. 2. Slang. to ridicule.

guy[2] (gī), n., v., **guyed, guying.** —n. 1. a rope or appliance used to guide and steady a thing being hoisted or lowered. —v.t. 2. to guide, steady, or secure with a guy or guys.

guz·zle (gŭz/əl), v.i., v.t., **-zled, -zling.** to drink greedily. —**guz/zler**, n.

gym (jĭm), n. gymnasium.

gym·na·si·um (jĭm nā/zĭ əm), n., pl. **-siums, -sia** (-zĭ ə). 1. a building or room for physical education activities. 2. a place where Greek youths met for exercise and discussion.

gym·nast (jĭm/năst), n. one trained and skilled in, or a teacher of, gymnastics.

gym·nas·tic (jĭm năs/tĭk), adj. pertaining to exercises which develop flexibility, strength, and agility.

gym·nas·tics (jĭm năs/tĭks), n. 1. (construed as pl.) gymnastic exercises. 2. (construed as sing.) the practice or art of gymnastic exercises.

gym·no·sperm (jĭm/nə spûrm/), n. Bot. a plant having its seeds exposed or naked, not enclosed in an ovary. —**gym/no·sper/mous**, adj.

gy·ne·col·o·gy (gī/nə kŏl/ə jĭ, jī/nə-, jĭn/ə-), n. that department of medical science which deals with the functions and diseases peculiar to women. Also, **gy/nae·col/o·gy.** —**gy/ne·col/o·gist**, n.

gyp (jĭp), v., **gypped, gypping,** n. U.S. Slang. —v.t. 1. to swindle; cheat. —n. 2. a swindle. 3. a swindler.

gyp·sum (jĭp/səm), n. a very common mineral, hydrated calcium sulfate: used to make plaster of Paris, as a fertilizer, etc.

Gyp·sy (jĭp/sĭ), n., pl. **-sies,** adj. —n. 1. one of a nomadic Caucasian minority race of Hindu origin. 2. the language of the Gypsies. —adj. 3. pertaining to the Gypsies.

gypsy moth, a moth, introduced from Europe, whose caterpillar is destructive to trees.

gy·rate (jī/rāt, jī rāt/), v.i., **-rated, -rating.** to move in a circle or spiral; whirl. —**gy·ra/tion**, n. —**gy·ra·to·ry** (jī/rə tôr/ĭ), adj.

gy·ro·com·pass (jī/rō kŭm/pəs), n. a compass employing a continuously driven gyroscope instead of a magnetized needle.

gy·ro·scope (jī/rə skōp/), n. an apparatus consisting of a rotating wheel so mounted that its axis can turn freely in certain or all directions, and capable of maintaining the same absolute direction in space in spite of movements of the mountings and surrounding parts. —**gy·ro·scop·ic** (jī/rə skŏp/ĭk), adj.

gy·ro·sta·bi·liz·er (jī/rō stā/bə lī/zər), n. a gyroscopic device for stabilizing a seagoing vessel by counteracting its rolling motion from side to side.

gyve (jīv), n., v., **gyved, gyving.** —n. 1. (usually pl.) a shackle; fetter. —v.t. 2. to shackle.

H

H, h (āch), n., pl. **H's** or **Hs, h's** or **hs.** a consonant, the 8th letter of the English alphabet.

H, 1. Elect. henry. 2. Chem. hydrogen.

h., 1. high. 2. Baseball. hits. 3. hour.

ha (hä), interj. an exclamation of surprise, interrogation, suspicion, triumph, etc.

Haa·kon VII (hō/kōōn), born 1872, king of Norway since 1905; exiled in England, 1940–45.

Hab., Habakkuk.

Ha·bak·kuk (hə băk/ək, hăb/ə kŭk/), n. 1. a Hebrew prophet. 2. his book of prophecies, in the Old Testament.

ha·be·as cor·pus (hā/bĭ əs kôr/pəs), Law. a writ requiring an imprisoned person to be brought before a judge or court.

hab·er·dash·er (hăb/ər dăsh/ər), n. U.S. a dealer in men's furnishings.

hab·er·dash·er·y (hăb/ər dăsh/ə rĭ), n., pl. **-eries.** 1. a haberdasher's shop. 2. the goods sold there.

ha·bil·i·ment (hə bĭl/ə mənt), n. 1. (pl.) clothes or garments. 2. dress; attire.

hab·it (hăb/ĭt), n. 1. a tendency, constantly shown, to act in a certain way. 2. a particular practice, custom, or usage. 3. customary practice or use. 4. garb of a particular rank, profession, etc. 5. a woman's riding dress. —v.t. 6. to clothe; array.

hab·it·a·ble (hăb/ə tə bəl), adj. capable of being inhabited. —**hab/it·a·bly,** adv.

hab·it·ant (hăb/ə tənt), n. an inhabitant.

hab·i·tat (hăb/ə tăt/), n. 1. the kind of place where a given animal or plant naturally lives or grows. 2. place of abode.

hab·i·ta·tion (hăb/ə tā/shən), n. 1. a place of abode. 2. act of inhabiting.

ha·bit·u·al (hə bĭch/ōō əl), adj. 1. fixed by or resulting from habit. 2. being such by habit. 3. usual. —**ha·bit/u·al·ly,** adv.

ha·bit·u·ate (hə bĭch/ōō āt/), v.t., **-ated, -ating.** to accustom (a person, the mind, etc.). —**ha·bit/u·a/tion,** n.

hab·i·tude (hăb/ə tūd/, -tōōd/), n. customary condition, character, or habit.

ha·bit·u·é (hə bĭch/ōō ā/), n. a habitual frequenter of a place.

ha·ci·en·da (hä/sĭ ĕn/də), n. (in Spanish America) a landed estate; country house.

hack[1] (hăk), v.t., v.i. 1. to cut, notch, or chop irregularly, as with heavy blows. 2. to emit short, frequently repeated coughs. —n. 3. a cut, gash, or notch. —**hack/er,** n.

hack[2] (hăk), n. 1. Brit. a horse kept for common hire or general work. 2. an old or worn-out horse. 3. a person who hires himself out for general work, esp. literary work. 4. U.S. a carriage kept for hire. 5. Colloq. a taxi. —v.t. 6. to make a hack of. —v.i. 7. Colloq. to drive a taxi. —adj. 8. hired. 9. hackneyed.

hack·a·more (hăk/ə môr/), n. a coil of rope or a halter used in breaking horses.

hack·le (hăk/əl), n., v., **-led, -ling.** —n. 1. one of the long, slender feathers on the neck of certain birds, as the rooster. 2. the whole neck plumage of the rooster, etc. 3. Angling. an artificial fly made with hackles (def. 1). 4. a comb for dressing flax or hemp. —v.t. 5. Angling. to supply with a hackle. 6. to comb, as flax or hemp.

hack·ney (hăk/nĭ), n., pl. **-neys,** adj., v., **-neyed, -neying.** —n. 1. a horse for ordinary riding or driving. 2. a horse kept for hire. 3. a carriage kept for hire. —adj. 4. let out, employed, or done for hire. —v.t. 5. to make trite by frequent use.

hack·neyed (hăk/nĭd), adj. trite; stale.

hack·saw (hăk/sô/), n. a saw used for cutting metal, consisting typically of a narrow, fine-toothed blade fixed in a frame.

had·dock (hăd/ək), n., pl. **-docks,** (esp. collectively) **-dock.** a food fish of the northern Atlantic, related to but smaller than the cod.

Ha·des (hā/dēz), n. 1. Gk. Myth. the gloomy subterranean abode of departed spirits. 2. (l.c.) Colloq. hell.

haf·ni·um (hăf/nĭ əm, häf/-), n. Chem. a metallic element found in zirconium ores. Symbol: Hf; at. wt.: 178.6; at. no.: 72; sp. gr.: 12.1.

haft (hăft, häft), n. 1. a handle, esp. of a knife, sword, etc. —v.t. 2. to furnish with a haft.

hag (hăg), *n.* **1.** a repulsive, often vicious or malicious, old woman. **2.** a witch.

Ha·gar (hā′gär, -gər), *n. Bible.* Egyptian concubine of Abraham, mother of Ishmael.

Ha·gers·town (hā′gərz toun′), *n.* a city in NW Maryland. 32,491.

Hag·ga·dah (hə gä′də), *n., pl.* **-doth** (-dōth). *Jewish Lit.* **1.** the nonlegal part of Jewish traditional literature. **2.** the free exposition or illustration, chiefly homiletic, of the Scripture. **3.** the ritual used on the first two nights of Passover. **4.** a book containing it also, **Hag·ga′da.**

Hag·ga·i (hăg′ī ī′, hăg′ī), *n.* **1.** fl. 520 B.C., a tenth of the minor prophets of Israel. **2.** his book in the Old Testament.

hag·gard (hăg′ərd), *adj.* wild-looking, as from prolonged suffering, anxiety, etc.; gaunt. —**hag′gard·ness,** *n.*

hag·gis (hăg′ĭs), *n. Chiefly Scot.* a dish made of the heart, liver, etc., of a sheep, etc., minced with suet and oatmeal, seasoned, and boiled in the stomach of the animal.

hag·gle (hăg′əl), *v.,* **-gled, -gling,** *n.* —*v.i.* **1.** to bargain in a petty manner. **2.** to wrangle. —*n.* **3.** act of haggling. —**hag′gler,** *n.*

hag·rid·den (hăg′rĭd′ən), *adj.* worried or tormented, as by a witch.

Hague (hāg), *n.* **The,** a city in W Netherlands, near the North Sea: seat of the government, royal residence, and World Court. 482,840.

Hai·fa (hī′fə), *n.* a seaport in NW Israel. 128,800.

hail¹ (hāl), *v.t.* **1.** to salute or greet. **2.** to call out to. —*v.i.* **3.** to call out in order to greet, attract attention, etc. **4.** to belong to or come from. —*n.* **5.** to shout to attract attention. **6.** a salutation or greeting. —*interj.* **7.** *Poetic and Literary.* an exclamation of salutation or greeting.

hail² (hāl), *n.* **1.** pellets of ice falling from the clouds in a shower. —*v.i.* **2.** to pour down hail. —*v.t.* **3.** to pour down as or like hail.

Hail Mary, Ave Maria.

hail·stone (hāl′stōn′), *n.* a pellet of hail.

hail·storm (hāl′stôrm′), *n.* a storm with hail.

hair (hâr), *n.* **1.** the natural covering of the human head and of the body of most mammals. **2.** the aggregate of hairs which grow on an animal. **3.** any fine, filamentous outgrowth. **4.** a very small measure, degree, etc.

hair·cloth (hâr′klôth′, -klŏth′), *n.* cloth woven of hair from horses' tails and manes.

hair·cut (hâr′kŭt′), *n.* act or style of cutting the hair.

hair·do (hâr′dōō′), *n., pl.* **-dos.** method of arranging a woman's hair.

hair·dress·er (hâr′drĕs′ər), *n.* one who arranges or cuts hair, esp. women's hair.

hair·line (hâr′līn′), *n.* **1.** a very slender line. **2.** *Print.* a very thin line on the face of a type.

hair·pin (hâr′pĭn′), *n.* **1.** a slender U-shaped piece of wire, shell, etc., used by women to fasten the hair. —*adj.* **2.** (of a road, track, etc.) doubling back in a U-shape.

hair·rais·ing (hâr′rā′zĭng), *adj.* terrifying.

hair's-breadth (hârz′bredth′), *n.* **1.** a very small distance. —*adj.* **2.** extremely close. Also, **hairs′breadth′, hair′breadth′.**

hair trigger, a trigger that operates a firearm by very slight pressure.

hair·y (hâr′ĭ), *adj.,* **hairier, hairiest. 1.** covered with hair; having much hair. **2.** of or like hair. —**hair′i·ness,** *n.*

Hai·ti (hā′tĭ), *n.* a republic in the West Indies, occupying the W part of the island of Hispaniola. 3,000,000 pop.; 10,714 sq. mi. *Cap.:* Port-au-Prince. **2.** former name of **Hispaniola.** —**Hai·ti·an** (hā′tĭ ən, -shən), *adj., n.*

hake (hāk), *n., pl.* **hakes** (*esp. collectively*) **hake.** any of certain marine fishes related to the cod.

hal·berd (hăl′bərd), *n.* a shafted weapon with an axlike cutting blade, beak, and apical spike, used esp. in the 15th and 16th centuries. Also, **hal·bert** (hăl′bərt).

hal·berd·ier (hăl′bər dĭr′), *n.* a soldier, guard, or attendant armed with a halberd.

hal·cy·on (hăl′sĭ ən), *adj.* calm; peaceful.

hale¹ (hāl), *adj.,* **haler, halest.** healthy.

hale² (hāl), *v.t.,* **haled, haling.** to haul or bring. —**hal′er,** *n.*

Hale (hāl), *n.* **Nathan,** 1755–76, American soldier hanged as a spy by the British.

half (hăf, häf), *n., pl.* **halves** (hăvz, hävz), *adj., adv.* —*n.* **1.** one of the two equal parts of anything. —*adj.* **2.** being one of the two equal parts. **3.** being equal to only about half of the full measure. **4.** incomplete. —*adv.* **5.** to the extent or measure of half. **6.** partly.

half-and-half (hăf′ənd hăf′, häf′ənd häf′), *adj.* **1.** half one thing and half another. —*adv.* **2.** in two equal portions. —*n.* **3.** a mixture of two things. **4.** *Chiefly Brit.* a mixture of two malt liquors, esp. porter and ale.

half·back (hăf′băk′, häf′-), *n. Football, etc.* one of the players behind the forward line.

half-baked (hăf′bākt′, häf′-), *adj.* **1.** insufficiently cooked. **2.** not completed. **3.** lacking mature judgment or experience.

half-blood (hăf′blŭd′, häf′-), *n.* **1.** a half-breed. **2.** a person related to only one of the parents. —**half′blood′ed,** *adj.*

half-breed (hăf′brēd′, häf′-), *n.* the offspring of parents of different races.

half brother, a brother by one parent only.

half-caste (hăf′kăst′, häf′käst′), *n.* **1.** a person of mixed race. **2.** one of mixed European and Hindu or Mohammedan parentage.

half-cocked (hăf′kŏkt′, häf′-), *adj.* premature.

half dollar, a silver coin of the United States worth 50 cents.

half-heart·ed (hăf′här′tĭd, häf′-), *adj.* showing little enthusiasm. —**half′-heart′ed·ly,** *adv.* —**half′-heart′ed·ness,** *n.*

half hitch, a hitch formed by passing the end of a rope round its standing part and bringing it up through the bight.

half-mast (hăf′măst′, häf′mäst′), *n.* **1.** a position halfway below the top of a mast. —*v.t.* **2.** to place (a flag) at half-mast (as a mark of respect for the dead or as a signal of distress).

half note, *Music.* a note equivalent in time value to one half of a semibreve.

half·pen·ny (hā′pə nĭ, hāp′nĭ), *n., pl.* **halfpennies** (hā′pə nĭz, hāp′nĭz) for 1; **halfpence** (hā′pəns) for 2; *adj.* —*n.* **1.** a British bronze coin of half the value of a penny. **2.** the sum of half a penny. —*adj.* **3.** of the price or value of a halfpenny. **4.** of trifling value.

half sister, a sister by one parent only.

half step, 1. *Music.* a semitone. **2.** *Mil.* a step fifteen inches long in quick time.

half-tone (hăf′tōn′, häf′-), *n.* **1.** *Painting, Photog., etc.* a value intermediate between high light and deep shade. **2.** *Photoengraving.* a process in which gradation of tone is obtained by a system of minute dots of varying size and density. —*adj.* **3.** pertaining to, using, or used in the halftone process.

half tone, *Music.* a semitone.

half-track (hăf′trăk′, häf′-), *n.* a truck with its driving wheels on caterpillar treads.

half·way (hăf′wā′, häf′-), *adv.* **1.** half over the way. —*adj.* **2.** midway. **3.** partial.

half-wit (hăf′wĭt′, häf′-), *n.* one who is feebleminded. —**half′-wit′ted,** *adj.*

hal·i·but (hăl′ə bət, hŏl′-), *n., pl.* **-buts,** (*esp. collectively*) **-but.** either of two species of large flatfishes widely used for food.

Hal·i·fax (hăl′ə făks′), *n.* a seaport in SE Canada: capital of Nova Scotia. 70,488.

hal·i·to·sis (hăl′ə tō′sĭs), *n.* bad or offensive breath.

hall (hôl), *n.* **1.** *U.S.* a corridor or vestibule in a building. **2.** a large room for public assemblies, etc. **3.** a large building of a college.

Hal·le (hăl′ə), *n.* a city in central Germany. 220,092.

hal·le·lu·jah (hăl′ə lōō′yə), *interj.* **1.** Praise ye the Lord! —*n.* **2.** an exclamation of "hallelujah!" Also, **hal′le·lu′iah.**

hall·mark (hôl′märk′), *n.* **1.** an official mark indicating a standard of purity, used in marking gold and silver articles assayed by the Goldsmith's Company of London. **2.** any mark of genuineness, good quality, etc.

hal·loo (hə lōō′), *interj., n., pl.* **-loos,** *v.* —*interj.* **1.** an exclamation used to attract attention, etc. —*n.* **2.** the cry "halloo!" —*v.i.* **3.** to shout.

hal·low (hăl′ō), *v.t.* **1.** to make holy; sanctify; consecrate. **2.** to honor as holy.

Hal·low·een (hăl′ō ēn′, hŏl′-), *n.* the evening of Oct. 31; the eve of All Saints' Day. Also, **Hal′low·e′en′.**

hal·lu·ci·na·tion (hə lōō′sə nā′shən), *n.* an apparent perception, as by sight or hearing, for which there is no real external cause.

hall·way (hôl′wā′), *n.* *U.S.* a corridor.

ha·lo (hā′lō), *n., pl.* **-los, -loes,** *v.,* **-loed, -loing.** —*n.* 1. a radiance surrounding the head in the representation of a sacred personage. 2. *Meteorol.* a circle of light appearing around the sun or moon. —*v.t.* 3. to surround with a halo. —*v.i.* 4. to form a halo.

hal·o·gen (hăl′ə jən, hā′lə-), *n.* *Chem.* any of the negative elements fluorine, chlorine, iodine, and bromine, which form binary salts by direct union with metals.

Hals (häls), *n.* **Frans,** 1580?-1666, Dutch portrait painter.

halt[1] (hôlt), *v.i., v.t.* 1. to stop temporarily, as in marching, etc. —*n.* 2. temporary stop. —**halt′er,** *n.*

halt[2] (hôlt), *v.i.* 1. to proceed in a faulty way, as in speech, etc. 2. to hesitate. 3. *Archaic.* to limp. —*adj.* 4. *Archaic.* lame. —*n.* 5. *Archaic.* lameness. —**halt′er,** *n.*

hal·ter (hôl′tər), *n.* 1. a rope or strap for leading or fastening horses or cattle. 2. a noose for hanging criminals. 3. a woman's sports waist, tied behind the neck and across the back. —*v.t.* 4. to put a halter on.

halve (hăv, häv), *v.t.,* **halved, halving.** 1. to divide in halves. 2. to reduce to half.

hal·yard (hăl′yərd), *n.* a rope or tackle used to hoist or lower a sail, yard, flag, etc.

ham (hăm), *n., v.,* **hammed, hamming.** —*n.* 1. one of the rear quarters of a hog, esp. the heavy-muscled part, between hip and hock. 2. the part of the leg back of the knee. 3. *Theat. Slang.* an actor who overacts. 4. *Slang.* an amateur. —*v.i.* 5. *Theat. Slang.* to overact.

Ham (hăm), *n.* *Bible.* second son of Noah.

Ham·burg (hăm′bûrg), *n.* a seaport in N Germany. 1,711,877.

ham·burg·er (hăm′bûr′gər), *n.* 1. Hamburg steak. 2. a bun containing such meat.

Ham·burg steak (hăm′bûrg), (*sometimes l.c.*) chopped beef, fried or broiled in cakes.

Ham·il·ton (hăm′əl tən), *n.* 1. **Alexander,** 1757-1804, American statesman and writer on government. 2. a city in SE Canada. 166,337; with suburbs, 176,110. 3. a city in SW Ohio. 50,592. 4. the capital of Bermuda. 1863.

Ham·it·ic (hă mĭt′ĭk, hə-), *n.* 1. a family of languages related to the Semitic, spoken in North Africa, including ancient Egyptian and modern Berber. —*adj.* 2. of this family.

ham·let (hăm′lĭt), *n.* a small village.

ham·mer (hăm′ər), *n.* 1. an instrument consisting of a solid head, usually of metal, set crosswise on a handle, used for beating metals, driving nails, etc. 2. anything like a hammer in form, action, or use. 3. *Firearms.* that part of the lock which by its fall or action causes the discharge. —*v.t.* 4. to beat or drive with a hammer. 5. to fasten by using a hammer. 6. to work out laboriously. —*v.i.* 7. to strike blows with a hammer. 8. to make laborious attempts. —**ham′mer·er,** *n.*

ham·mer·head (hăm′ər hĕd′), *n.* any of certain sharks characterized by a head expanded laterally so as to resemble a double-headed hammer.

ham·mock (hăm′ək), *n.* a kind of hanging bed made of canvas or the like.

Ham·mond (hăm′ənd), *n.* a city in NW Indiana, near Chicago. 70,184.

ham·per[1] (hăm′pər), *v.t.* to impede; hinder.

ham·per[2] (hăm′pər), *n.* a large basket or wickerwork receptacle, usually with a cover.

ham·string (hăm′strĭng′), *n., v.,* **-strung, -stringing.** —*n.* 1. (in man) any of the tendons which bound the ham, or hollow of the knee. 2. (in quadrupeds) the great tendon at the back of the hock. —*v.t.* 3. to cut the hamstring or hamstrings of and thus disable. 4. to cripple or disable.

Ham·tramck (hăm trăm′ĭk), *n.* a city in SE Michigan, within limits of Detroit. 49,839.

Han·cock (hăn′kŏk), *n.* **John,** 1737-93, American statesman: first signer of the Declaration of Independence.

hand (hănd), *n.* 1. the terminal part of the arm, consisting of the palm and five fingers. 2. something resembling a hand in shape or function. 3. a worker; laborer. 4. the persons of any company or group. 5. (*often pl.*) possession, control, or care. 6. active coöperation. 7. side. 8. a side of a subject, question, etc. 9. a person considered as a source, as of information. 10. style of handwriting. 11. skill. 12. a person, with reference to action, ability, or skill. 13. a round of applause. 14. a pledge of marriage. 15. a linear measure used in giving the height of horses, etc., equal to four inches. 16. *Cards.* the cards dealt to or held by each player at one time. 17. **at hand,** a. near by. b. near in time. c. ready for use. 18. **on hand,** a. in immediate possession. b. before one for attention. c. *U.S.* present. —*v.t.* 19. to deliver or pass with the hand. 20. to transmit. —*adj.* 21. of the hand. 22. done or made by hand. 23. that may be carried in, or worn on, the hand. 24. operated by hand.

hand·bag (hănd′băg′), *n.* 1. a small valise. 2. a woman's purse.

hand·ball (hănd′bôl′), *n.* 1. a game in which a ball is batted against a wall with the hand. 2. the ball used in this game.

hand·bar·row (hănd′băr′ō), *n.* a frame with handles at each end.

hand·bill (hănd′bĭl′), *n.* a small printed bill or announcement.

hand·book (hănd′bŏŏk′), *n.* 1. a small book for guidance, as in an occupation. 2. a guidebook for travelers.

hand·cuff (hănd′kŭf′), *n.* 1. (*usually pl.*) a ring-shaped shackle for the wrist, usually one of a pair connected by a chain. —*v.t.* 2. to put handcuffs on.

hand·ed (hăn′dĭd), *adj.* 1. having a hand or hands. 2. having a hand characterized in some specified manner.

Han·del (hăn′dəl), *n.* **George Frederick,** (*Georg Friedrich Händel*) 1685-1759, German composer.

hand·ful (hănd′fŏŏl′), *n., pl.* **-fuls.** 1. as much or as many as the hand can contain. 2. a small quantity or number.

hand·i·cap (hăn′dĭ kăp′), *n., v.,* **-capped, -capping.** —*n.* 1. a race or other contest in which certain disadvantages or advantages are placed upon competitors to equalize their chances of winning. 2. the disadvantage or advantage itself. 3. any encumbrance or disadvantage. —*v.t.* 4. to serve as a handicap to. 5. to subject to a disadvantageous handicap.

hand·i·craft (hăn′dĭ krăft′, -kräft′), *n.* 1. manual skill. 2. a manual art or occupation. —**hand′i·crafts′man,** *n.*

hand·i·ly (hăn′də lĭ), *adv.* 1. dexterously; expertly. 2. conveniently.

hand·i·work (hăn′dĭ wûrk′), *n.* 1. work done or made by the hands. 2. the action of a particular doer or maker. 3. the result of one's action.

hand·ker·chief (hăng′kər chĭf, -chēf′), *n.* 1. a small piece of fabric, usually square, for wiping the face, nose, etc. 2. a neckerchief.

han·dle (hăn′dəl), *n., v.,* **-dled, -dling.** —*n.* 1. a part of a thing which is to be grasped by the hand in using or moving it. 2. opportunity. —*v.t.* 3. to touch or feel with the hand. 4. to manipulate or manage. 5. to deal with or treat, as a subject. 6. to deal or trade in (goods, etc.).

handle bar, (*often pl.*) the curved steering bar of a bicycle, etc., in front of the rider.

han·dler (hănd′lər), *n.* 1. a person or thing that handles. 2. *Boxing.* a trainer or second.

hand·made (hănd′mād′), *adj.* made by hand, rather than by machine.

hand·maid (hănd′mād′), *n.* a female servant or attendant. Also, **hand′maid′en.**

hand-me-down (hănd′mĭ doun′, hăn′-), *n.* *Now U.S. Colloq.* an article of clothing handed down to one who is younger, smaller, etc.

hand organ, a portable barrel organ played by means of a crank turned by hand.

hand·out (hănd′out′), *n.* *U.S. Slang.* a portion of food or the like given to a beggar.

hand-pick (hănd′pĭk′), *v.t.* 1. to pick by hand. 2. to select carefully. 3. to select for ulterior purposes. —**hand′-picked′,** *adj.*

hand·saw (hănd′sô′), *n.* a saw used with one hand.

hand·some (hăn′səm), *adj.,* **-somer, -somest.** 1. of fine or admirable appearance. 2. considerable. 3. generous. 4. *U.S. Colloq.* dexterous. —**hand′some·ly,** *adv.* —**hand′some·ness,** *n.*

hand·spike (hănd′spīk′), *n.* a bar used as a lever.

hand-to-hand, *adj.* at close quarters.

hand-to-mouth (hănd'tə mouth'), *adj.* precarious; unsettled.

hand·writ·ing (hănd'rī'tĭng), *n.* 1. writing done by hand. 2. style of writing.

hand·y (hăn'dĭ), *adj.,* **handier, handiest.** 1. conveniently accessible. 2. skillful with the hands; dexterous. 3. convenient to handle. 4. useful. —**hand'i·ness,** *n.*

handy man, a man hired to do various kinds of work.

hang (hăng), *v.,* **hung** or (esp. for capital punishment and suicide) **hanged; hanging;** *n.* —*v.t.* 1. to fasten (a thing) so that it is supported only from above. 2. to suspend by the neck until dead. 3. to let droop. 4. to furnish with something suspended. 5. to fasten into position. 6. to attach (paper, etc.) to walls. —*v.i.* 7. to be suspended. 8. to be suspended from a cross or gallows. 9. to bend forward or downward. 10. to be contingent. 11. to hold fast, cling, or adhere. 12. to be doubtful or undecided. 13. to loiter. 14. to be imminent. —*n.* 15. the way in which a thing hangs. 16. *U.S. Colloq.* the precise manner of doing, using, etc., something. 17. *U.S. Colloq.* meaning. 18. the least bit of care.

hang·ar (hăng'ər), *n.* 1. a shed or shelter. 2. a shed for airplanes or airships.

hang·bird (hăng'bûrd'), *n.* a bird that builds a hanging nest, esp. the Baltimore oriole.

Hang·chow (hăng'chou'), *n.* a seaport in E China. 600,023.

hang·dog (hăng'dôg', -dŏg'), *adj.* 1. mean; sneaking. 2. ashamed; abashed.

hang·er (hăng'ər), *n.* a contrivance that hangs things, as a shaped support for a garment.

hang·er-on (hăng'ər ŏn'), *n., pl.* **hangers-on.** a follower, esp. a parasitic one.

hang·ing (hăng'ĭng), *n.* 1. capital punishment by strangulation on a gallows. 2. (*often pl.*) something hung on walls, as a drapery, etc. —*adj.* 3. deserving of or punishable by death by hanging. 4. that hangs.

hang·man (hăng'mən), *n., pl.* **-men.** one who hangs persons condemned to death.

hang·nail (hăng'nāl'), *n.* a small piece of partly detached skin at the side or base of a fingernail.

hang·out (hăng'out'), *n. Slang.* a place where one lives or frequently visits.

hang·o·ver (hăng'ō'vər), *n. U.S. Colloq.* 1. something remaining from a former time. 2. the effect on a person after excessive indulgence in alcoholic liquor.

hank (hăngk), *n.* 1. a skein, as of yarn. 2. a coil, knot, or loop.

han·ker (hăng'kər), *v.i.* to have a restless or incessant longing. —**han'ker·ing,** *n.*

Han·kow (hăn'kou'), *n.* a city in E China: a port on the Yangtze. 725,185.

Han·ni·bal (hăn'ə bəl), *n.* 247–183? B.C. Carthaginian general who crossed the Alps and invaded Italy.

Han·o·ver (hăn'ō vər), *n.* 1. a city in NW Germany. 470,950. 2. the name of the English royal family from 1714 to 1901. —**Han·o·ve·ri·an** (hăn'ō vĭr'ĭ ən), *adj., n.*

Han·se·at·ic League (hăn'sĭ ăt'ĭk), a medieval league of towns of northern Germany and adjacent countries for the promotion and protection of commerce.

han·som (hăn'səm), *n.* a two-wheeled covered vehicle drawn by one horse, the driver being mounted on an elevated seat behind.

Ha·nuk·kah (hä'nŏŏ kä'), *n.* a Jewish festival in commemoration of the victory of the Maccabees.

hap (hăp), *n., v.,* **happed, happing.** *Archaic.* —*n.* 1. one's lot. 2. an occurrence or accident. —*v.i.* 3. to happen.

hap·haz·ard (*adj., adv.* hăp'hăz'ərd; *n.* hăp'·hăz'ərd), *adj.* 1. determined by mere chance. —*adv.* 2. at random; by chance. —*n.* 3. mere chance. —**hap'haz'ard·ly,** *adv.* —**hap'haz'·ard·ness,** *n.*

hap·less (hăp'lĭs), *adj.* unlucky.

hap·ly (hăp'lĭ), *adv. Archaic.* by chance.

hap·pen (hăp'ən), *v.i.* 1. to take place; occur. 2. to occur by chance. 3. to have the fortune (to). 4. to befall. 5. to come by chance.

hap·pen·ing (hăp'ən ĭng, hăp'nĭng), *n.* an occurrence; event.

hap·py (hăp'ĭ), *adj.,* **-pier, -piest.** 1. charac-

terized by or indicative of pleasure, content, or gladness. 2. delighted, pleased, or glad. 3. fortunate or lucky. 4. apt or felicitous. —**hap'pi·ly,** *adv.* —**hap'pi·ness,** *n.*

hap·py-go-luck·y (hăp'ĭ gō lŭk'ĭ), *adj.* 1. trusting to luck. —*adv.* 2. haphazard.

Haps·burg (hăps'bûrg), *n.* a German princely family which has furnished sovereigns to the Holy Roman Empire, Austria, Spain, etc.

ha·ra-ki·ri (hä'rə kĭr'ĭ), *n.* suicide by ripping open the abdomen with a knife: the form of honorable suicide in Japan when in disgrace or under sentence of death.

ha·rangue (hə răng'), *n., v.,* **-rangued, -ranguing.** —*n.* 1. a passionate, vehement speech. —*v.t.* 2. to address in a harangue. —*v.i.* 3. to deliver a harangue.

har·ass (hăr'əs, hə răs'), *v.t.* 1. to trouble by repeated attacks, etc.; harry. 2. to disturb persistently. —**har'ass·er,** *n.* —**har'ass·ment,** *n.*

Har·bin (här'bēn', -bĭn), *n.* a city in NE China, in central Manchuria. 637,573.

har·bin·ger (här'bĭn jər), *n.* 1. one who goes before and makes known the approach of another. —*v.t.* 2. to herald the coming of.

har·bor (här'bər), *n.* 1. a portion of a body of water along the shore providing shelter for ships. 2. any place of shelter. —*v.t.* 3. to give shelter to. 4. to conceal. 5. to have in mind; cherish. Also, *Brit.,* **har'bour.**

har·bor·age (här'bər ĭj), *n.* 1. shelter for ships, as in a harbor. 2. shelter.

hard (härd), *adj.* 1. solid to the touch; not soft. 2. firmly formed. 3. difficult or troublesome. 4. carried on with great exertion. 5. laborious; energetic. 6. violent; severe. 7. oppressive or harsh. 8. incapable of being denied or explained away. 9. unfriendly. 10. unpleasant to the eye, ear, or aesthetic sense. 11. rigorous in terms. 12. not swayed easily; shrewd. 13. in coin rather than in paper currency. 14. *U.S.* intoxicating. 15. (of water) containing mineral salts which interfere with the action of the soap. 16. *Phonet.* (of *c* and *g*) pronounced as in *come* and *go.* —*adv.* 17. with great exertion. 18. intently. 19. harshly or severely. 20. solid or firm.

hard-bit·ten (härd'bĭt'ən), *adj.* tough.

hard-boiled (härd'boild'), *adj.* 1. boiled until hard, as an egg. 2. *Colloq.* hardened by experience. 3. *Slang.* rough or tough.

hard coal, anthracite.

hard·en (här'dən), *v.t.* 1. to make hard or harder. 2. to make unyielding or unfeeling. 3. to strengthen or toughen. —*v.i.* 4. to become hard or harder. —**hard'en·er,** *n.*

hard-fist·ed (härd'fĭs'tĭd), *adj.* stingy.

hard-head·ed (härd'hĕd'ĭd), *adj.* 1. practical; shrewd. 2. obstinate; willful. —**hard'-head'·ed·ness,** *n.*

hard-heart·ed (härd'här'tĭd), *adj.* unfeeling; pitiless. —**hard'-heart'ed·ness,** *n.*

har·di·hood (här'dĭ hŏŏd'), *n.* hardy spirit or character; boldness or daring.

har·di·ly (här'də lĭ), *adv.* in a hardy manner.

har·di·ness (här'dĭ nĭs), *n.* 1. robustness; strength. 2. hardihood; audacity.

Har·ding (här'dĭng), *n.* **Warren Gamaliel,** 1865–1923, 29th president of the U.S., 1921–23.

hard·ly (härd'lĭ), *adv.* 1. barely; almost not at all. 2. not quite. 3. with little likelihood. 4. with difficulty. 5. harshly.

hard·ness (härd'nĭs), *n.* state or quality of being hard.

hard·pan (härd'păn'), *n. Chiefly U.S.* 1. any layer of firm detrital matter, as of clay, underlying soft soil. 2. hard, unbroken ground.

hard·ship (härd'shĭp), *n.* 1. severe toil, trial, oppression, or need. 2. an instance of this.

hard·tack (härd'tăk'), *n.* a kind of hard biscuit much used by sailors and soldiers.

hard·ware (härd'wâr'), *n.* metalware as tools, locks, hinges, cutlery, etc.

hard·wood (härd'wŏŏd'), *n.* the hard, compact wood of the oak, maple, etc.

har·dy (här'dĭ), *adj.,* **-dier, -diest.** 1. fitted for enduring fatigue, hardship, exposure, etc. 2. requiring great physical endurance. 3. bold or daring.

Har·dy (här'dĭ), *n.* **Thomas,** 1840–1928, British novelist and poet.

hare (hâr), *n., pl.* **hares,** (*esp. collectively*) **hare.** 1. a mammal of the same genus as the rabbit, resembling it very closely but larger in size. **2.** a rabbit.

hare·brained (hâr'brānd'), *adj.* giddy; reckless.

hare·lip (hâr'lĭp'), *n.* a congenitally deformed lip, in which there is a vertical fissure.

har·em (hâr'əm, hăr'-), *n.* **1.** that part of an Oriental palace reserved for women. **2.** the women in an Oriental household.

ha·ri·ka·ri (hä'rĭ kä'rĭ), *n.* hara-kiri.

bark (härk), *v.i.* **1.** to listen. **2.** hark back, to revert.

hark·en (här'kən), *v.i.* *Poetic.* to listen; give heed to what is said. —**hark'en·er,** *n.*

Har·lem (här'ləm), *n.* the chief Negro section of New York City.

Har·le·quin (här'lə kwĭn, -kĭn), *n.* **1.** (*sometimes l. c.*) a droll character in comedy and pantomime, usually masked, dressed in colorful tights, and bearing a wooden sword. **2.** (*l.c.*) a buffoon. —*adj.* **3.** (*l.c.*) fancifully varied in color, decoration, etc.

har·lot (här'lət), *n.* a prostitute.

har·lot·ry (här'lə trĭ), *n.,* *pl.* **-ries.** **1.** prostitution. **2.** a harlot.

harm (härm), *n.* **1.** injury; damage. **2.** moral injury; evil. —*v.t.* **3.** to injure; damage. —**harm'er,** *n.*

harm·ful (härm'fəl), *adj.* doing harm.—**harm'-ful·ly,** *adv.* —**harm'ful·ness,** *n.*

harm·less (härm'lĭs), *adj.* doing no harm. —**harm'less·ly,** *adv.* —**harm'less·ness,** *n.*

har·mon·ic (här mŏn'ĭk), *adj.* **1.** pertaining to or marked by harmony. **2.** *Physics.* denoting an integral multiple of a given frequency. —*n.* **3.** an overtone.

har·mon·i·ca (här mŏn'ə kə), *n.* a musical instrument having a set of small metallic reeds mounted in a case and played by the breath.

har·mo·ni·ous (här mō'nĭ əs), *adj.* **1.** marked by agreement or congruity. **2.** tuneful; melodious. —**har·mo'ni·ous·ly,** *adv.* —**har·mo'ni·ous·ness,** *n.*

har·mo·ni·um (här mō'nĭ əm), *n.* a reed organ.

har·mo·nize (här'mə nīz'), *v.,* **-nized, -nizing.** —*v.t.* **1.** to bring into harmony or agreement. **2.** *Music.* to accompany with appropriate harmony. —*v.i.* **3.** to be in agreement in action, sense, or feeling. —**har'mo·niz'er,** *n.*

har·mo·ny (här'mə nĭ), *n.,* *pl.* **-nies.** **1.** agreement; accord. **2.** congruity. **3.** *Music.* a. simultaneous combination of tones. b. the science of the structure, relations, and practical combination of chords.

har·ness (här'nĭs), *n.* **1.** the combination of straps, bands, and other parts forming the working gear of a horse or other draft animal. —*v.t.* **2.** to put harness on. **3.** to bring under conditions for working.

Har·old II (hăr'əld), c1022–1066, king of England in 1066: defeated by William the Conqueror.

harp (härp), *n.* **1.** a musical instrument consisting of a triangular frame holding strings that are plucked with the fingers. —*v.i.* **2.** to play on a harp. **3.** to dwell persistently. —**harp'ist, harp'er,** *n.*

har·poon (här poon'), *n.* **1.** a barbed, spearlike missile attached to a rope, used in capturing whales, etc. —*v.t.* **2.** to strike, catch, or kill with a harpoon. —**har·poon'er,** *n.*

harp·si·chord (härp'sĭ kôrd'), *n.* a keyboard instrument, precursor of the piano.

Har·py (här'pĭ), *n.,* *pl.* **-pies.** **1.** *Gk. Myth.* a ravenous, filthy monster having a woman's head and a bird's body. **2.** (*l.c.*) a rapacious, grasping person.

har·que·bus (här'kwə bəs), *n.* a light hand gun, common before the musket.

har·ri·dan (har'i dən), *n.* a disreputable violent woman; vicious old hag.

har·ri·er[1] (hăr'ĭ ər), *n.* **1.** one that harries. **2.** any of certain predatory hawks.

har·ri·er[2] (hăr'ĭ ər), *n.* **1.** a breed of hounds used in hunting hares. **2.** a cross-country runner.

Har·ris (hăr'ĭs), *n.* Joel Chandler, 1848–1908, U.S. author.

Har·ris·burg (hăr'ĭs bûrg'), *n.* the capital of Pennsylvania, in the S part. 83,893.

Har·ri·son (har'ə sən), *n.* **1.** Benjamin, 1833–1901, 23rd president of the U.S., 1889–93. **2.** his grandfather, **William Henry,** 1773–1841, 9th president of the U.S., in 1841.

har·row (hăr'ō), *n.* **1.** a wheelless agricultural implement set with teeth, upright disks, etc., drawn over plowed land to level it, break clods etc. —*v.t.* **2.** to draw a harrow over. **3.** to disturb or distress.

har·ry (hăr'ĭ), *v.,* **-ried, -rying.** —*v.t.* **1.** to harass; torment. **2.** to devastate. —*v.i.* **3.** to make harassing incursions.

harsh (härsh), *adj.* **1.** rough to the touch or to any of the senses. **2.** ungentle and unpleasant. **3.** inartistic. —**harsh'ly,** *adv.* —**harsh'ness,** *n.*

hart (härt), *n.,* *pl.* **harts,** (*esp. collectively*) **hart.** a male of the deer, esp. the red deer.

Harte (härt), *n.* (Francis) Bret, 1839–1902, U.S. author.

har·te·beest (här'tə bēst', härt'bēst'), *n.* a large South African antelope.

Hart·ford (härt'fərd), *n.* the capital of Connecticut, in the central part. 166,267.

har·um-scar·um (hâr'əm skâr'əm), *adj.* **1.** reckless; rash. —*adv.* **2.** recklessly. —*n.* **3.** a reckless person. **4.** reckless conduct.

har·vest (här'vĭst), *n.* **1.** the gathering of crops. **2.** the season of gathering ripened crops. **3.** a crop or yield. **4.** the product or result of any labor or process. —*v.t.* **5.** to gather, as a crop. **6.** to gather the crop from. —*v.i.* **7.** to reap. —**har'vest·er,** *n.*

har·vest·man (här'vĭst mən), *n.,* *pl.* **-men.** **1.** one who harvests. **2.** any of certain spiderlike creatures usually with very long legs; daddylonglegs.

Har·vey (här'vĭ), *n.* **William,** 1578–1657, British physician, discoverer of the circulation of the blood.

has-been (hăz'bĭn'), *n.* *Colloq.* a person who is no longer successful, popular, etc.

hash (hăsh), *n.* **1.** a dish of chopped meat and potatoes. **2.** a mess or jumble. —*v.t.* **3.** to chop into small pieces; mince.

hash·ish (hăsh'ēsh, -ĭsh), *n.* the flowering tops, leaves, etc., of East Indian hemp, used as a narcotic and intoxicant.

has·n't (hăz'ənt), contraction of *has not.*

hasp (hăsp, häsp), *n.* a clasp for a door, lid, etc., esp. one passing over a staple and fastened by a pin or a padlock.

has·sock (hăs'ək), *n.* **1.** a thick cushion used as a footstool, etc. **2.** a tuft of coarse grass.

haste (hāst), *n.,* *v.,* **hasted, hasting.** —*n.* **1.** energetic speed; hurry. —*v.t., v.i.* **2.** *Poetic.* to hasten.

has·ten (hā'sən), *v.i.* **1.** to move or act with haste; hurry. —*v.t.* **2.** to cause to hasten.

hast·y (hās'tĭ), *adj.,* **hastier, hastiest. 1.** speedy; quick; hurried. **2.** rash. **3.** quick-tempered; irascible. —**hast'i·ly,** *adv.* —**hast'-i·ness,** *n.*

hasty pudding, 1. a mush made of flour or oatmeal. **2.** *U.S.* corn-meal mush.

hat (hăt), *n.,* *v.,* **hatted, hatting.** —*n.* **1.** a shaped covering for the head. **2.** pass (round) the hat, to ask for contributions. —*v.t.* **3.** to provide with a hat.

hatch[1] (hăch), *v.t.* **1.** to bring forth (young) from the egg. **2.** to cause young to emerge from (the egg). **3.** to contrive; concoct. —*v.i.* **4.** to be hatched. —*n.* **5.** act of hatching. **6.** that which is hatched.

hatch[2] (hăch), *n.* **1.** a cover for an opening in a deck, floor, roof, or the like. **2.** (*often pl.*) a hatchway.

hatch[3] (hăch), *v.t.* to mark with lines, esp. closely set parallel lines, as for shading.

hatch·er·y (hăch'ə rĭ), *n.,* *pl.* **-eries.** a place for hatching eggs of hens, fish, etc.

hatch·et (hăch'ĭt), *n.* a small, short-handled ax for use with one hand.

hatch·way (hăch'wā'), *n.* an opening in a ship's deck, for passage to parts below.

hate (hāt), *v.,* **hated, hating,** *n.* —*v.t.* **1.** to dislike; detest. —*v.i.* **2.** to feel hatred. —*n.* **3.** strong dislike. **4.** the object of hatred. —**hat'er,** *n.*

hate·ful (hāt'fəl), *adj.* detestable; odious. —**hate'ful·ly,** *adv.* —**hate'ful·ness,** *n.*

ha·tred (hā'trĭd), *n.* intense dislike.

hat·ter (hăt'ər), *n.* a maker or seller of hats.

hau·berk (hô'bûrk), *n.* a long coat of mail.

haugh·ty (hô'tĭ), *adj.,* **-tier, -tiest.** disdainfully proud; arrogant. —**haugh'ti·ly,** *adv.* —**haugh'ti·ness,** *n.*

haul (hôl), *v.t., v.i.* **1.** to pull or draw with force.

2. haul up, *Colloq.* to change the course of (a ship). —*n.* **3.** a strong pull or tug. **4.** that which is hauled. **5.** the distance through which anything is hauled. **6.** the quantity taken, caught, won, etc., at one time. —**haul′er,** *n.*

haunch (hônch, hänch), *n.* **1.** the hip. **2.** the fleshy part of the body about the hip. **3.** the leg and loin of an animal.

haunt (hônt; hänt), *v.t.* **1.** to visit habitually, esp. as a spirit or ghost. **2.** to recur persistently to. —*n.* **3.** (*often pl.*) a place of frequent resort.

haut·boy (hō′boi, ō′boi), *n.* oboe.

hau·teur (hō tûr′), *n.* haughtiness.

Ha·van·a (hə văn′ə), *n.* a seaport in and the capital of Cuba, on the NW coast. 676,376.

have (hăv), *v.*, *pres.* 1 **have,** 2 **have** or **hast,** 3 **has** or **hath,** *pl.* **have;** *pt.* and *past part.* **had;** *pres. part.* **having.** —*v.t.* **1.** to possess; own; contain. **2.** to hold in some relation, position, etc. **3.** to get, receive, or take. **4.** to be required or obliged. **5.** to experience. **6.** to hold in mind, sight, etc. **7.** to require or cause. **8.** to show in action. **9.** to engage in or perform. **10.** to permit. **11.** to assert. **12.** to know. **13.** to give birth to. **14.** to wear. **15.** *Colloq.* to hold at a disadvantage. **16.** have **rather,** to consider as preferable. —*aux. v.* **17.** (used with the past participle of a verb to form a compound or perfect tense).

ha·ven (hā′vən), *n.* **1.** a harbor or port. **2.** any place of shelter. —*v.t.* **3.** to shelter.

have·n't (hăv′ənt), contraction of *have not.*

Ha·ver·hill (hā′vər Yl, -vrəl), *n.* a city in NE Massachusetts. 46,752.

hav·er·sack (hăv′ər săk′), *n.* a bag for rations, provisions, etc.

hav·oc (hăv′ək), *n.*, *v.*, **-ocked, -ocking.** —*n.* **1.** devastation; ruinous damage. **2.** play **havoc with,** to ruin. —*v.t.*, *v.i.* **3.** to work havoc (upon).

haw[1] (hô), *n.* the fruit of the hawthorn.

haw[2] (hô), *interj.* **1.** an utterance marking hesitation in speech. —*n.* **2.** the utterance "haw." —*v.i.* **3.** to utter "haw."

haw[3] (hô), *interj.* **1.** a command to horses, etc., directing them to turn left. —*v.t.*, *v.i.* **2.** to turn to the left.

Ha·wai·i (hə wī′ē, -wä′yə), *n.* **1.** Hawaiian Islands. **2.** the largest of the Hawaiian Islands. 73,276 pop.; 4021 sq. mi. —**Ha·wai′ian,** *adj.*, *n.*

Hawaiian Islands, a group of islands belonging to the United States, in the N Pacific, 2090 mi. SW of San Francisco, forming (with the Midway Islands) the **Territory of Hawaii.** 458,177 pop.; 6454 sq. mi. *Cap.:* Honolulu.

hawk[1] (hôk), *n.* **1.** any of certain diurnal birds of prey, as the falcons, buzzards, etc. —*v.i.* **2.** to hunt with hawks trained to pursue game. —**hawk′er,** *n.* —**hawk′ing,** *n.*

hawk[2] (hôk), *v.t.*, *v.i.* to offer (goods) for sale by outcry in a street or from door to door. —**hawk′er,** *n.*

hawk[3] (hôk), *v.i.* **1.** to clear the throat noisily. —*n.* **2.** a noisy effort to clear the throat.

hawk moth, any of certain moths noted for their very swift flight.

hawks·bill (hôks′bĭl′) *n.* a marine turtle yielding tortoise shell and having a mouth shaped like the bill of a hawk.

hawse·hole (hôz′hōl′, hôs′-), *n.* a hole in the bow of a ship, through which a cable is passed.

haw·ser (hô′zər, -sər), *n.* *Naut.* a cable or large rope used in mooring, towing, etc.

haw·thorn (hô′thôrn′), *n.* any of certain small trees of the rose family with stiff thorns, cultivated in hedges for fragrant blossoms and bright-colored fruits.

Haw·thorne (hô′thôrn′), *n.* **Nathaniel,** 1804–64, U.S. author.

hay (hā), *n.* **1.** grass cut and dried for use as fodder. —*v.t.* **2.** to convert (grass) into hay.

hay·cock (hā′kŏk′), *n.* *Chiefly Brit.* a small conical pile of hay in a hayfield.

Hay·dn (hā′dən), *n.* **Franz Joseph,** 1732–1809, Austrian composer.

Hayes (hāz), *n.* **Rutherford Birchard,** 1822–93, 19th president of the U.S., 1877–81.

hay fever, a catarrhal affection of the mucous membranes of the eyes and respiratory tract, attacking susceptible persons (usually) during the summer, and caused by the pollen of certain plants.

hay·field (hā′fēld′), *n.* a field in which grass is grown or cut for hay.

hay·loft (hā′lôft′, -lŏft′), *n.* a loft in a stable or barn, for the storage of hay.

hay·mak·er (hā′mā′kər), *n.* **1.** one who makes hay. **2.** a swinging, knockout blow.

hay·mow (hā′mou′), *n.* **1.** a mass of hay stored in a barn. **2.** the place in a barn where hay is stored. **3.** a stack of hay.

hay·seed (hā′sēd′), *n.* **1.** grass seed, esp. that shaken out of hay. **2.** *U.S. Slang.* a rustic.

hay·stack (hā′stăk′), *n.* a stack of hay with a conical or ridged top. Also, *esp. Brit.,* **hay·rick** (hā′rĭk′).

hay·wire (hā′wīr′), *n.* **1.** wire used to bind bales of hay. —*adj. Slang.* **2.** out of order. **3.** crazy.

haz·ard (hăz′ərd), *n.* **1.** exposure to danger; risk; peril. **2.** chance. **3.** *Golf.* an obstacle on the course. **4.** a game played with two dice. —*v.t.* **5.** to venture to offer (a conjecture, etc.). **6.** to expose to risk. **7.** to run the risk of.

haz·ard·ous (hăz′ər dəs), *adj.* full of risk; perilous. —**haz′ard·ous·ly,** *adv.*

haze[1] (hāz), *n.* **1.** a mistlike aggregation of minute particles of vapor, dust, etc., in the air. **2.** vagueness of the mind.

haze[2] (hāz), *v.t.*, **hazed, hazing.** to subject (freshmen, etc.) to abusive tricks. —**haz′er,** *n.* —**haz′ing,** *n.*

ha·zel (hā′zəl), *n.* **1.** any of certain shrubs or small trees of the birch family which bear edible nuts. **2.** light reddish brown. —*adj.* **3.** of, pertaining to, or made of hazel. **4.** having a hazel color.

ha·zel·nut (hā′zəl nŭt′), *n.* the nut of the hazel.

Ha·zle·ton (hā′zəl tən), *n.* a city in E Pennsylvania. 38,009.

Haz·litt (hăz′lYt), *n.* **William,** 1778–1830, British critic and essayist.

ha·zy (hā′zĭ), *adj.*, **-zier, -ziest. 1.** characterized by the presence of haze. **2.** vague; confused. —**ha′zi·ly,** *adv.* —**ha′zi·ness,** *n.*

he (hē; *unstressed* ē, Y), *pron.* **1.** the male being mentioned. **2.** anyone; that person. —*n.* **3.** a man. **4.** a male, esp. of an animal.

He, *Chem.* helium.

head (hĕd), *n.* **1.** the upper part of the human body, joined to the trunk by the neck. **2.** the corresponding part of an animal's body. **3.** the head considered as the seat of thought, memory, etc. **4.** the position of leadership. **5.** a leader or chief. **6.** that part of anything which forms the top. **7.** the foremost or projecting part. **8.** a person or individual. **9.** culmination or crisis. **10.** the hair covering the head. **11.** something resembling a head in form. **12.** a rounded or compact part of a plant, usually at the top of the stem. **13.** the maturated part of an abscess, boil, etc. **14.** the obverse of a coin, bearing a head (opposed to *tail*). **15.** a major section or topic. **16.** the source of a river. **17.** froth or foam. **18.** a headline. **19.** the stretched membrane covering the end of a drum. **20.** *Mach.* a device holding one or more cutting tools to the work. —*adj.* **21.** situated at the top or front. **22.** leading; principal. **23.** coming from in front. —*v.t.* **24.** to lead; precede. **25.** to be the head or chief of. **26.** to turn or direct. —*v.i.* **27.** to move toward a point specified. —**head′less,** *adj.*

head·ache (hĕd′āk′), *n.* a pain located in the head.

head·band (hĕd′bănd′), *n.* a band worn around the head; fillet.

head·cheese (hĕd′chēz′), *n.* a jellied mass or loaf of parts of the head and feet of hogs cut up and cooked.

head·dress (hĕd′drĕs′), *n.* **1.** a covering or decoration for the head. **2.** a hairdo.

head·er (hĕd′ər), *n.* **1.** a person or apparatus that removes or puts a head on something. **2.** *Colloq.* a plunge or dive headfirst.

head·first (hĕd′fûrst′), *adv.* **1.** with the head in front or bent forward. **2.** rashly. Also, **head·fore·most** (hĕd′fōr′mōst′, -məst).

head·gear (hĕd′gĭr′), *n.* any covering for the head.

head·hunt·ing (hĕd′hŭn′tĭng), *n.* (among certain savage tribes) the practice of taking enemy heads as trophies or for use in religious ceremonies. —**head′-hunt·er,** *n.*

head·ing (hĕd′ĭng), *n.* **1.** something that serves as a head, top, or front. **2.** a title or caption. **3.** a section or topic.

head·land (hĕd′lənd), *n.* a promontory extending into a large body of water.

head·light (hĕd/līt/), *n.* a lamp on the front of an automobile, locomotive, etc.

head·line (hĕd/līn/), *n., v.* **-lined, -lining.** —*n.* **1.** a display line over an article, etc., as in a newspaper. —*v.t.* **2.** to furnish with a headline.

head·long (hĕd/lông/, -lŏng/), *adv.* **1.** head-first. **2.** hastily. **3.** rashly. —*adj.* **4.** done or going with the head foremost. **5.** hasty. **6.** rash. **7.** steep.

head·man (hĕd/mən), *n., pl.* **-men.** a chief or leader.

head·mas·ter (hĕd/mäs/tər, -mäs/tər), *n. Chiefly Brit.* the principal of a school or seminary.

head·on (hĕd/ŏn/, -ŏn/), *adj.* with the head foremost.

head·phone (hĕd/fōn/), *n.* a headset.

head·piece (hĕd/pēs/), *n.* **1.** a helmet. **2.** any covering for the head. **3.** a headset.

head·quar·ters (hĕd/kwôr/tərz), *n.pl. or sing.* **1.** any center from which official orders are issued. **2.** any center of operations.

head·set (hĕd/sĕt/), *n. Radio, Teleph., etc.* a device consisting of one or two receivers, with attachments for holding them over the ears.

head·ship (hĕd/shĭp), *n.* the position of head or chief; chief authority; leadership.

heads·man (hĕdz/mən), *n., pl.* **-men.** one who beheads condemned persons.

head·stall (hĕd/stôl/), *n.* that part of a bridle or halter which encompasses the head.

head·stock (hĕd/stŏk/), *n.* the part of a machine containing the working members.

head·stone (hĕd/stōn/), *n.* a stone set at the head of a grave.

head·strong (hĕd/strông/, -strŏng/), *adj.* willful; stubborn.

head·wa·ters (hĕd/wô/tərz, -wŏt/ərz), *n.pl.* the upper tributaries of a river.

head·way (hĕd/wā/), *n.* **1.** motion forward. **2.** progress. **3.** clear space in height, as under an arch.

head·work (hĕd/wûrk/), *n.* mental labor.

head·y (hĕd/ĭ), *adj.,* **headier, headiest. 1.** rashly impetuous. **2.** intoxicating.

heal (hēl), *v.t.* **1.** to restore to health. **2.** to mend. —*v.i.* **3.** to effect a cure. **4.** to get well. —**heal/er,** *n.*

health (hĕlth), *n.* **1.** soundness of body; freedom from disease or ailment. **2.** the general condition of the body. **3.** a wish for a person's health, happiness, etc., esp. as a toast.

health·ful (hĕlth/fəl), *adj.* **1.** conducive to health; wholesome. **2.** healthy. —**health/ful·ly,** *adv.* —**health/ful·ness,** *n.*

health·y (hĕl/thĭ), *adj.,* **healthier, healthiest. 1.** possessing health. **2.** of or characteristic of health. **3.** conducive to health. —**health/i·ness,** *n.*

heap (hēp), *n.* **1.** an assemblage of things lying one on another; a pile. **2.** *Colloq.* a great quantity. —*v.t.* **3.** to pile. **4.** to amass. **5.** to cast or bestow in great quantity. **6.** to load or supply abundantly.

hear (hĭr), *v.,* **heard** (hûrd) **hearing.** —*v.t.* **1.** to perceive by the ear. **2.** to listen to. **3.** to be informed of. **4.** to give a formal, official, or judicial hearing to. —*v.i.* **5.** to have perception of sound by the ear. **6.** to listen or take heed. **7.** to receive information. **8.** to listen with favor or assent. —**hear/er,** *n.*

hear·ing (hĭr/ĭng), *n.* **1.** the sense by which sound is perceived. **2.** act of perceiving sound. **3.** opportunity to be heard. **4.** *Law.* a presentation of testimony and arguments. **5.** earshot.

hark·en (här/kən), *v.i.* harken. —**hark/en·er,** *n.*

hear·say (hĭr/sā/), *n.* gossip; rumor.

hearse (hûrs), *n.* a funeral vehicle for conveying a dead person to the place of burial.

Hearst (hûrst), *n.* William Randolph, 1863–1951, U.S. editor and publisher.

heart (härt), *n.* **1.** a hollow muscular organ which by rhythmic contractions and relaxations keeps the blood in circulation throughout the body. **2.** this organ considered as the seat of life, thought, or emotion. **3.** capacity for sympathy. **4.** courage

Section of human heart
A, Vena cava; B, Right auricle; C, Right ventricle; D, Aorta; E, Pulmonary artery; F, Left auricle; G, Left ventricle

or enthusiasm. **5.** the innermost or most essential part. **6.** the breast or bosom. **7.** a figure with rounded sides meeting in a point at the bottom and curving inward to a cusp at the top. **8.** a playing card of a suit marked with heart-shaped figures in red. **9. at heart,** inwardly; in reality. **10. by heart,** by memory.

heart·ache (härt/āk/), *n.* mental anguish.

heart·break (härt/brāk/), *n.* crushing sorrow or grief. —**heart/break/ing,** *adj.*

heart·bro·ken (härt/brō/kən), *adj.* crushed with sorrow or grief.

heart·burn (härt/bûrn/), *n.* an uneasy, burning sensation in (chiefly) the stomach.

heart·en (här/tən), *v.t.* to encourage; cheer.

heart·felt (härt/fĕlt/), *adj.* earnest; sincere.

hearth (härth), *n.* **1.** that part of the floor of a room on which the fire is made or above which is a stove, fireplace, furnace, etc. **2.** the fireside; home.

hearth·stone (härth/stōn/), *n.* **1.** a stone forming a hearth. **2.** the fireside; home.

heart·less (härt/lĭs), *adj.* **1.** unfeeling; cruel. **2.** without courage or enthusiasm. —**heart/less·ly,** *adv.* —**heart/less·ness,** *n.*

heart·rend·ing (härt/rĕn/dĭng), *adj.* causing mental anguish. —**heart/-rend/ing·ly,** *adv.*

heart·sick (härt/sĭk/), *adj.* grievously depressed or unhappy. —**heart/sick/ness,** *n.*

heart·sore (härt/sōr/), *adj.* grieved.

heart·strick·en (härt/strĭk/ən), *adj.* deeply or keenly affected.

heart·strings (härt/strĭngz/), *n.pl.* the deepest feelings; the strongest affections.

heart·throb (härt/thrŏb/), *n.* a passionate or sentimental emotion.

heart-to-heart (härt/ə härt/), *adj.* frank.

heart·wood (härt/wŏŏd/), *n.* the hard central wood of the trunk of an exogenous tree.

heart·y (här/tĭ), *adj.,* **heartier, heartiest,** *n., pl.* **hearties.** —*adj.* **1.** cordial; friendly. **2.** genuine; sincere. **3.** enthusiastic or vigorous. **4.** physically vigorous. **5.** substantial. —*n.* **6.** a good fellow. **7.** a sailor. —**heart/i·ly,** *adv.* —**heart/i·ness,** *n.*

heat (hēt), *n.* **1.** warmth or hotness. **2.** a form of energy resident in the random motion of molecules, which will raise the temperature of a body to which it is added. **3.** hot season or weather. **4.** intensity of feeling. **5.** a fit of passion. **6.** the greatest intensity. **7.** a single course or trial in a contest. **8.** *Zool.* **a.** sexual excitement in female animals. **b.** the period of such excitement. —*v.t.* **9.** to make hot or warm. **10.** to excite. —*v.i.* **11.** to become hot or warm. **12.** to become excited.

heat·ed (hē/tĭd), *adj.* vehement; angry.

heat·er (hē/tər), *n.* an apparatus for heating, as a furnace.

heath (hēth), *n.* **1.** *Brit.* a tract of waste land overgrown with shrubs. **2.** any of various low evergreen shrubs common on such waste land. **3.** any of several plants of the same family.

hea·then (hē/thən), *n., pl.* **-thens, -then,** *adj.* —*n.* **1.** an unconverted individual of a people which does not acknowledge the God of the Bible; a gentile or pagan. —*adj.* **2.** pagan; pertaining to the heathen. —**hea/then·ish,** *adj.* —**hea/then·ism/,** *n.*

heath·er (hĕth/ər), *n.* any of various heaths, esp. those of Scotland. —**heath/er·y,** *adj.*

heat lightning, flashes of light near the horizon, reflections of more distant lightning.

heat·stroke (hēt/strōk/), *n.* collapse or fever caused by exposure to excessive heat.

heat wave, a prolonged period of excessively warm weather.

heave (hēv), *v.,* **heaved** or (*esp. Naut.*) **hove; heaving;** *n.* —*v.t.* **1.** to raise with effort or force. **2.** to lift and throw. **3.** to utter laboriously. **4.** to cause to rise and fall. —*v.i.* **5.** to rise and fall with a swelling motion. **6.** to pant. **7.** to vomit; retch. **8.** to swell or bulge. **9.** *Naut.* **a.** to haul or pull. **b.** heave to, to stop. —*n.* **10.** act of heaving. **11.** (*pl. construed as sing.*) a disease of horses, characterized by difficult breathing.

heav·en (hĕv/ən), *n.* **1.** the abode of God, the angels, and the spirits of the righteous after death. **2.** (*cap., often pl.*) God. **3.** (*chiefly pl.*) the sky. **4.** a place or state of supreme bliss.

heav·en·ly (hĕv/ən lĭ), *adj.* **1.** blissful; beautiful. **2.** of or in the heavens. **3.** divine.

heav·en·ward (hĕv/ən wərd), *adv.* **1.** Also, **heav/en·wards.** toward heaven. —*adj.* **2.** directed toward heaven.

Heav·i·side layer (hěv′ĭ sīd′), the lower region, or regions, of the ionosphere chiefly responsible for the reflection of radio waves of certain frequencies, thus making long-distance short wave radio communication possible.

heav·y (hěv′ĭ), adj., **heavier, heaviest**, n., pl. **heavies**, adv. —adj. **1.** of great weight. **2.** of great amount, force, intensity, etc. **3.** burdensome; harsh. **4.** broad, thick, or coarse. **5.** Mil. **a.** heavily armed or equipped. **b.** of the larger sizes. **6.** serious or intense. **7.** trying; difficult. **8.** being such in an unusual degree. **9.** laden. **10.** full of or showing sorrow. **11.** overcast or cloudy. **12.** clumsy. **13.** ponderous; dull. **14.** loud and deep. **15.** not easily digested. **16.** pregnant. **17.** Chem. referring to that isotope of greater atomic weight. —n. **18.** Theat. **a.** a villainous part. **b.** an actor of villainous parts. —adv. **19.** in a heavy manner. —**heav′i·ly**, adv. —**heav′i·ness**, n.

heav·y·weight (hěv′ĭ wāt′), n. **1.** one of more than average weight. **2.** a boxer of more than 175 pounds. **3.** Colloq. a very intelligent or influential person.

Heb., **1.** Hebrew. **2.** Hebrews.

He·bra·ic (hĭ brā′ĭk), adj. Hebrew.

He·bra·ism (hē′brā ĭz′əm, -brĭ-), n. **1.** a Hebrew idiom. **2.** Hebrew thought.

He·brew (hē′brōō), n. **1.** a member of that branch of the Semitic race descended from the line of Abraham; Israelite; Jew. **2.** a Semitic language, the language of the Hebrews. —adj. **3.** of or pertaining to the Hebrews or their language.

He·brews (hē′brōōz), n. a New Testament epistle, preserved among the Epistles of Paul.

Heb·ri·des (hěb′rə dēz′), n.pl. a group of islands off the W coast of and belonging to Scotland. 61.800 pop.; ab. 2900 sq. mi.

Hec·a·te (hěk′ə tĭ), n. Gk. Myth. a goddess of the moon, earth, and infernal regions, associated with witchcraft.

hec·a·tomb (hěk′ə tōm′, -tōōm′), n. **1.** a great public sacrifice, orig. of a hundred oxen, as to the Greek gods. **2.** any great slaughter.

heck·le (hěk′əl), v.t., **-led, -ling.** to harass with questions and jibes. —**heck′ler**, n.

hec·tare (hěk′târ), n. the common unit of land measure in the metric system, equivalent to 2.471 acres.

hec·tic (hěk′tĭk), adj. **1.** characterized by great excitement, passions, etc. **2.** marking a condition of the body when attended by flushed cheeks, hot skin, and emaciation. **3.** consumptive. —n. **4.** a consumptive person. —**hec′ti·cal·ly**, adv.

hec·to·gram (hěk′tə grăm′), n. Metric System. a unit of 100 grams. Also, esp. Brit., **hec′to·gramme′**.

hec·to·graph (hěk′tə grăf′, -gräf′), n. **1.** a process for making copies of a writing, etc., from a prepared gelatin surface. **2.** the apparatus used.

hec·to·li·ter (hěk′tə lē′tər), n. Metric System. a unit of capacity of 100 liters. Also, esp. Brit., **hec′to·li′tre**.

hec·to·me·ter (hěk′tə mē′tər), n. Metric System. a measure of length equal to 100 meters. Also, esp. Brit., **hec′to·me′tre**.

Hec·tor (hěk′tər), n. **1.** Gk. Legend. the eldest son of Priam and the noblest of Homer's heroes; slain by Achilles. **2.** (l.c.) a bully. —v.t. **3.** (l.c.) to bully.

hedge (hěj), n., v., **hedged, hedging.** —n. **1.** a row of bushes or small trees forming a fence. —v.t. **2.** to enclose with a hedge. **3.** to surround. **4.** to obstruct. —v.i. **5.** to avoid an open or decisive course. **6.** to protect a bet, speculation, etc., by taking some offsetting risk.

hedge·hog (hěj′hŏg′, -hôg′), n. **1.** an insectivorous European mammal frequenting hedges and gardens, having spiny hairs on the back and sides. **2.** U.S. the porcupine.

hedge·hop (hěj′hŏp′), v.i., **-hopped, -hopping.** to fly an airplane very low. —**hedge′hop′per**, n.

hedge·row (hěj′rō′), n. a hedge (def. 1).

he·don·ism (hē′də nĭz′əm), n. the doctrine that pleasure or happiness is the highest good. —**he′don·ist**, n., adj. —**he′do·nis′tic**, adj.

heed (hēd), v.t., v.i. **1.** to give attention (to); notice. —n. **2.** careful attention; notice. —**heed′ful**, adj. —**heed′ing·ly**, adv. —**heed′less**, adj.

heel[1] (hēl), n. **1.** the back part of the foot, below and behind the ankle. **2.** the part of a stocking,

shoe, or the like, covering the heel. **3.** a solid part of wood, rubber, etc., attached to the sole of a shoe, under the heel. **4.** something resembling the human heel in position, shape, etc. **5.** the last part of anything. —v.t. **6.** to follow closely. **7.** to furnish with heels.

heel[2] (hēl), v.i. **1.** (of a ship, etc.) to lean to one side. —v.t. **2.** to cause to lean. —n. **3.** a heeling movement.

heel[3] (hēl), n. Colloq. a cad.

heel·tap (hēl′tăp′), n. a layer of leather or the like in a shoe heel; a lift.

heft (hěft), n. **1.** U.S. and Brit. Dial. weight; heaviness. —v.t. **2.** to try the weight of by lifting.

heft·y (hěf′tĭ), adj., **heftier, heftiest.** Colloq. **1.** heavy; weighty. **2.** powerful.

He·gel (hā′gəl), n. **Georg Wilhelm Friedrich**, 1770–1831, German philosopher.

he·gem·o·ny (hĭ jěm′ə nĭ, hěj′ə mō′nĭ), n., pl. **-nies.** leadership or predominance.

He·gi·ra (hĭ jī′rə, hěj′ə rə), n. the flight of Mohammed from Mecca, A.D. 622.

Hei·del·berg (hī′dəl bûrg′), n. a city in SW Germany. 86,467.

heif·er (hěf′ər), n. a female cow under three years of age that has not produced a calf.

height (hīt), n. **1.** state of being high. **2.** extent upward; altitude. **3.** a hill or mountain. **4.** the highest part or point; apex.

height·en (hī′tən), v.t., v.i. **1.** to make or become higher. **2.** to increase the intensity (of).

heil (hīl), interj. German. hail! (a greeting).

Hei·ne (hī′nə), n. **Heinrich**, 1797–1856, German poet, journalist, and critic.

hei·nous (hā′nəs), adj. hateful; odious. —**hei′nous·ly**, adv. —**hei′nous·ness**, n.

heir (âr), n. one who inherits the property of a deceased person. —**heir′ess**, n. fem. —**heir′less**, adj.

heir apparent, pl. **heirs apparent.** an heir whose right is indefeasible.

heir·loom (âr′lōōm′), n. a possession transmitted from generation to generation.

heir presumptive, an heir whose expectation may be defeated by the birth of a nearer heir.

He·jaz (hē jäz′), n. a former independent kingdom in W Arabia. ab. 1,500,000 pop.; ab. 150,000 sq. mi. Cap.: Mecca.

Hel·en (hěl′ən), n. Gk. Legend. the beautiful daughter of Zeus and wife of Menelaus of Sparta. Her abduction by Paris caused the Trojan War.

Hel·e·na (hěl′ə nə), n. the capital of Montana, in the W part. 15,056.

hel·i·cal (hěl′ə kəl), adj. pertaining to or having the form of a helix. —**hel′i·cal·ly**, adv.

Hel·i·con (hěl′ə kŏn′, -kən), n. Gk. Myth. a mountain in S Greece, regarded as the source of poetic inspiration.

hel·i·cop·ter (hěl′ə kŏp′tər; Aeron. often hē′lə-), n. an airplane which is lifted in the air by horizontal propellers.

he·li·o·cen·tric (hē′lĭ ō sěn′trĭk), adj. Astron. **1.** as viewed or measured from the center of the sun. **2.** having the sun as a center.

he·li·o·graph (hē′lĭ ə grăf′, -gräf′), n. **1.** a device for signaling by means of a movable mirror which flashes beams of light to a distance. —v.t., v.i. **2.** to communicate by heliograph.

He·li·os (hē′lĭ ŏs′), n. Gk. Myth. the sun god.

he·li·o·trope (hē′lĭ ə trōp′, hēl′yə- or, esp. Brit., hěl′yə-), n. **1.** any of certain herbs or shrubs with small, fragrant purple flowers. **2.** reddish lavender.

he·li·um (hē′lĭ əm), n. Chem. an inert gaseous element: used as a substitute for inflammable gases in dirigible balloons. Symbol: He; at. wt.: 4.003; at. no.: 2; density: 0.1785 at 0°C. and 760 mm. pressure.

he·lix (hē′lĭks), n., pl. **helices** (hěl′ə sēz′), **helixes.** **1.** any spiral. **2.** a spiral object.

hell (hěl), n. **1.** the abode of evil and condemned spirits. **2.** any place or state of torment or misery. **3.** Hades.

Hel·las (hěl′əs), n. Greece.

hell·bend·er (hěl′běn′dər), n. a large aquatic salamander of certain American rivers.

hell·cat (hěl′kăt′), n. **1.** an evil-tempered, unmanageable woman. **2.** a hag or witch.

Hel·lene (hěl′ēn), n. a Greek. —**Hel·len·ic** (hě lěn′ĭk, -lē′nĭk), adj., n.

Hel·len·ism (hĕl′ə nĭz′əm), *n.* **1.** ancient Greek culture or ideals. **2.** adoption of Greek speech, ideas, or customs. —**Hel′len·ist,** *n.*

Hel·len·is·tic (hĕl′ə nĭs′tĭk), *adj.* pertaining to the Greeks or their culture, etc., after the time of Alexander the Great.

Hel·les·pont (hĕl′ə spŏnt′), *n.* ancient name of the **Dardanelles.**

hel·lion (hĕl′yən), *n. Colloq.* a troublesome, mischief-making person.

hell·ish (hĕl′ĭsh), *adj.* of, like, or befitting hell; infernal; wicked. —**hell′ish·ly,** *adv.*

hel·lo (hĕ lō′, hə-, hĕl′ō), *interj., n., pl.* **-los,** *v.* **-loed, -loing.** —*interj.* **1.** an exclamation to attract attention or express greeting. —*n.* **2.** the call "hello." —*v.i.* **3.** to call "hello."

helm[1] (hĕlm), *n.* **1.** the tiller or wheel by which the rudder of a vessel is controlled. **2.** the entire steering apparatus. **3.** the place or post of control. —*v.t.* **4.** to steer; direct.

helm[2] (hĕlm), *n. Archaic.* a helmet.

hel·met (hĕl′mĭt), *n.* a protective covering for the head, usually of metal.

helms·man (hĕlmz′mən), *n., pl.* **-men.** the man at the helm who steers a ship.

hel·ot (hĕl′ət, hē′lət), *n.* **1.** one of the serfs in ancient Sparta. **2.** a serf or slave.

help (hĕlp), *v.,* helped or (*Archaic*) holp; helped or (*Archaic*) holpen; helping; *n.* —*v.t., v.i.* **1.** to aid; assist. **2.** to succor; save. **3.** to relieve (someone) in need, sickness, pain, or distress. **4.** to avoid. **5.** to remedy, stop, or prevent. —*n.* **6.** aid or assistance. **7.** relief or succor. **8.** a person or thing that helps. **9.** *U.S.* a domestic servant or a farm laborer. —**help′er,** *n.*

help·ful (hĕlp′fəl), *adj.* giving help; useful. —**help′ful·ly,** *adv.* —**help′ful·ness,** *n.*

help·ing (hĕl′pĭng), *n.* **1.** act of one that helps. **2.** a single portion.

help·less (hĕlp′lĭs), *adj.* **1.** unable to help oneself. **2.** without help. —**help′less·ly,** *adv.* —**help′less·ness,** *n.*

help·mate (hĕlp′māt′), *n.* **1.** a companion and helper. **2.** a wife or husband. Also, **help′meet′.**

Hel·sin·ki (hĕl′sĭng kē), *n.* a seaport in and the capital of Finland, on the S coast. 319,939.

hel·ter-skel·ter (hĕl′tər skĕl′tər), *adv.* **1.** in disorderly haste. —*adj.* **2.** disorderly.

helve (hĕlv), *n., v.,* **helved, helving.** *Chiefly Brit.* —*n.* **1.** the handle of an ax or the like. —*v.t.* **2.** to furnish with a helve.

Hel·ve·tia (hĕl vē′shə), *n. Poetic.* Switzerland. —**Hel·ve′tian,** *adj., n.*

hem[1] (hĕm), *v.,* **hemmed, hemming.** *n.* —*v.t.* **1.** to enclose or confine. **2.** to fold back and sew down the edge of (cloth, etc.). —*n.* **3.** the edge made by folding back a margin of cloth and sewing it down.

hem[2] (hĕm), *interj., n., v.,* **hemmed, hemming.** —*interj.* **1.** an utterance resembling a slight clearing of the throat, used to attract attention, express doubt, etc. —*n.* **2.** the utterance of "hem." —*v.i.* **3.** to utter the sound "hem."

hem·a·tite (hĕm′ə tīt′, hē′mə-), *n.* a very common mineral, iron oxide, Fe_2O_3: the principal ore of iron.

Hem·ing·way (hĕm′ĭng wā′), *n.* **Ernest,** born 1898, U.S. author.

he·mip·ter·ous (hĭ mĭp′tər əs), *adj.* belonging or pertaining to insects of the order *Hemiptera,* including the true bugs (whose forewings are in part thickened and leathery) and the cicadas, leaf hoppers, aphids, etc. (whose wings are entirely membranous).

hem·i·sphere (hĕm′ə sfĭr′), *n.* **1.** half of the terrestrial globe or celestial sphere. **2.** half of a sphere. **3.** *Anat.* either of the lateral halves of the cerebrum. —**hem·i·spher·i·cal** (hĕm′ə sfĕr′ə-kəl), *adj.*

hem·lock (hĕm′lŏk), *n.* **1.** *U.S.* Also, **hemlock spruce.** any of certain coniferous trees. **2.** *Chiefly Brit.* a poisonous umbelliferous herb with spotted stems, finely divided leaves, and small white flowers. **3.** a poisonous drink made from this herb.

hem·mer (hĕm′ər), *n.* **1.** one that hems. **2.** a sewing-machine attachment for hemming.

he·mo·glo·bin (hē′mə glō′bĭn, hĕm′ə-), *n.* the protein coloring matter of the red blood corpuscles, which conveys oxygen to the tissues.

he·mo·phil·i·a (hē′mə fĭl′ĭ ə, hĕm′ə-), *n. Pathol.* a morbid condition, usually congenital, characterized by a tendency to bleed immoderately, as from an insignificant wound, caused by

improper coagulation of the blood. —**he′mo·phil′i·ac′,** *n.*

hem·or·rhage (hĕm′ə rĭj, hĕm′rĭj), *n.* a discharge of blood, as from a ruptured blood vessel. —**hem·or·rhag·ic** (hĕm′ə răj′ĭk), *adj.*

hem·or·rhoid (hĕm′ə roid′, hĕm′roid), *n. Pathol.* a dilation of the veins under the skin of the anus; pile. —**hem′or·rhoi′dal,** *adj.*

hemp (hĕmp), *n.* **1.** a tall, annual (orig. Asiatic) herb of the mulberry family. **2.** the tough fiber of this plant, used for making coarse fabrics, ropes, etc. **3.** an East Indian variety of common hemp, yielding hashish. —**hemp′en,** *adj.*

hem·stitch (hĕm′stĭch′), *v.t.* **1.** to hem along a line from which threads have been drawn out, stitching the cross threads into a series of little groups. —*n.* **2.** the stitch used or the needlework done in hemstitching.

hen (hĕn), *n.* **1.** the female of the domestic fowl. **2.** the female of any bird.

hen·bane (hĕn′bān′), *n.* an Old World herb bearing sticky, hairy foliage of a disagreeable odor, and yellowish-brown flowers, and possessing poisonous properties.

hence (hĕns), *adv.* **1.** therefore. **2.** from this time onward. **3.** at the end of a given period. **4.** from this source or origin. **5.** from this place. —*interj.* **6.** depart!

hence·forth (hĕns′fôrth′), *adv.* from now on. Also, **hence·for·ward** (hĕns′fôr′wərd).

hench·man (hĕnch′mən), *n., pl.* **-men.** a trusty attendant or follower.

hen·e·quen (hĕn′ə kĭn), *n.* the fiber of an agave of Yucatan, used for making ropes, coarse fabrics, etc. Also, **hen′e·quin.**

hen·na (hĕn′ə), *n.* **1.** a shrub or small tree of Asia and the Levant from whose leaves is made a reddish-orange dye or cosmetic. **2.** reddish or orange brown. —*v.t.* **3.** to tint or dye with henna.

hen·ner·y (hĕn′ə rĭ), *n., pl.* **-neries.** a place where fowls are kept.

hen·peck (hĕn′pĕk′), *v.t.* (of a wife) to domineer over (her husband). —**hen′pecked′,** *adj.*

hen·ry (hĕn′rĭ), *n., pl.* **-ries, -rys.** *Elect.* the practical unit of inductance: equivalent to the inductance of a circuit in which an electromotive force of one volt is produced by a current in the circuit which varies at the rate of one ampere per second.

Hen·ry (hĕn′rĭ), *n.* **1. O.,** (*William Sidney Porter*) 1862–1910, U.S. writer. **2. Patrick,** 1736–99, American patriot. **3. VIII,** 1491–1547, king of England, 1509–47, and of Ireland, 1541–47.

hep (hĕp), *adj. U.S. Slang.* having inside knowledge, or being informed (fol. by *to*).

he·pat·ic (hĭ păt′ĭk), *adj.* **1.** of or acting on the liver, as a medicine. —*n.* **2.** a medicine acting on the liver.

he·pat·i·ca (hĭ păt′ə kə), *n., pl.* **-cas, -cae** (-sē′). any of certain herbs of the crowfoot family, with delicate purplish, pink, or white flowers.

hep·cat (hĕp′kăt′), *n. Jazz Slang.* an expert performer, or a knowing admirer, of jazz.

Hep·ple·white (hĕp′əl hwīt′), *n.* **1. George,** died 1786, British furniture designer. —*adj.* **2.** in the style of Hepplewhite.

hep·ta·gon (hĕp′tə gŏn′), *n.* a polygon having seven angles and seven sides. —**hep·tag·o·nal** (hĕp tăg′ə nəl), *adj.*

hep·tam·e·ter (hĕp tăm′ə tər), *n. Pros.* a verse of seven metrical feet.

her (hûr), *pron.* **1.** the objective case of *she.* —*adj.* **2.** a possessive form of *she.* **3.** of, belonging to, or having to do with a female person or personified thing.

her., **1.** heraldic. **2.** heraldry.

He·ra (hĭr′ə), *n. Gk. Myth.* a goddess, wife of Zeus and queen of heaven. Also, **He·re** (hĭr′ē).

Her·a·cles (hĕr′ə klēz′), *n.* Greek name of **Hercules.** Also, **Her′a·kles′.**

her·ald (hĕr′əld), *n.* **1.** a messenger, forerunner, or harbinger. **2.** one who proclaims or announces. **3.** an officer who regulates the use of armorial bearings. —*v.t.* **4.** to proclaim. **5.** to usher in.

he·ral·dic (hĕ răl′dĭk), *adj.* of or pertaining to heralds or heraldry.

her·ald·ry (hĕr′əl drĭ), *n., pl.* **-ries.** **1.** the art of blazoning armorial bearings, of settling the right of persons to use certain bearings, of tracing and recording genealogies, etc. **2.** a heraldic device. **3.** a coat of arms.

herb (ûrb, hûrb), *n.* **1.** a flowering plant whose stem above ground does not become woody and persistent. **2.** such a plant when valued for its medicinal properties, flavor, scent, or the like. —**her·ba·ceous** (hûr bā′shəs), *adj.*

herb·age (ûr′bĭj, hûr′-), *n.* **1.** nonwoody vegetation. **2.** the leaves and stems of herbs.

herb·al (hûr′bəl, ûr′-), *adj.* **1.** of herbs. —*n.* **2.** a treatise on herbs or plants.

herb·al·ist (hûr′bəl ĭst, ûr′-), *n.* one who collects or deals in herbs, esp. medicinal herbs.

her·bar·i·um (hûr bâr′ĭ əm), *n., pl.* **-bariums, -baria** (-bâr′ĭ ə). a collection of dried plants systematically arranged.

Her·bert (hûr′bərt), *n.* Victor, 1859–1924, U.S. composer.

her·biv·o·rous (hûr bĭv′ə rəs), *adj.* feeding on plants.

her·cu·le·an (hûr kū′lĭ ən, hûr′kyə lē′ən), *adj.* requiring strength, courage, or size.

Her·cu·les (hûr′kyə lēz′), *n. Class. Myth.* a hero of great strength and courage who performed twelve extraordinary tasks.

herd[1] (hûrd), *n.* **1.** a number of animals kept, feeding, or traveling together. **2.** a large crowd. **3.** the rabble. —*v.i.* **4.** to unite or go in a herd. —*v.t.* **5.** to form into a herd.

herd[2] (hûrd), *n.* **1.** Also, **herds′man.** the keeper of a herd. —*v.t.* **2.** to tend, drive, or lead a herd. —**herd′er,** *n.*

here (hĭr), *adv.* **1.** in or at this place. **2.** to or toward this place. **3.** present. **4.** here's to, a formula in offering a toast. —*n.* **5.** this place. **6.** this world; this life.

here·a·bout (hĭr′ə bout′), *adv.* about this place. Also, **here′a·bouts′.**

here·af·ter (hĭr ăf′tər, -äf′-), *adv.* **1.** at some future time. **2.** in the world to come. —*n.* **3.** a future life. **4.** the future.

here·by (hĭr bī′), *adv.* by means of this.

he·red·i·ta·ble (hĭ rĕd′ə tə bəl), *adj.* heritable. —**he·red′i·ta·bil′i·ty,** *n.*

he·red·i·tar·y (hĭ rĕd′ə tĕr′ĭ), *adj.* **1.** passing naturally from parents to offspring. **2.** pertaining to inheritance or heredity. **3.** being such through feelings, etc., derived from predecessors. **4.** descending by inheritance. —**he·red′i·tar′i·ly,** *adv.*

he·red·i·ty (hĭ rĕd′ə tĭ), *n., pl.* **-ties.** *Biol.* the transmission of genetic characters from parents to progeny.

Her·e·ford (hĕr′ə fərd, hûr′fərd), *n.* one of a breed of beef cattle originating in England, characterized by a red body, white face, and other white markings.

here·in (hĭr ĭn′), *adv.* **1.** in or into this place. **2.** in view of this.

here·in·af·ter (hĭr′ĭn ăf′tər, -äf′-), *adv.* afterward in this document, statement, etc.

here·of (hĭr ŏv′), *adv.* of or about this.

here·on (hĭr ŏn′, -ôn′), *adv.* hereupon.

her·e·sy (hĕr′ə sĭ), *n., pl.* **-sies.** **1.** doctrine at variance with the accepted doctrine, esp. of a church. **2.** the maintaining of such a doctrine.

her·e·tic (hĕr′ə tĭk), *n.* **1.** a professed believer who maintains religious opinions contrary to those accepted by his church. —*adj.* **2.** heretical.

he·ret·i·cal (hə rĕt′ə kəl), *adj.* of, pertaining to, or like heresy. —**he·ret′i·cal·ly,** *adv.*

here·to (hĭr tōō′), *adv.* to this place, thing, document, proposition, etc.

here·to·fore (hĭr′tə fōr′), *adv.* before this time.

here·up·on (hĭr′ə pŏn′, -pôn′), *adv.* upon this; following immediately upon this.

here·with (hĭr wĭth′, -wĭth̸′), *adv.* **1.** along with this. **2.** by means of this.

her·it·a·ble (hĕr′ə tə bəl), *adj.* **1.** capable of being inherited. **2.** capable of inheriting. —**her′it·a·bil′i·ty,** *n.* —**her′it·a·bly,** *adv.*

her·it·age (hĕr′ə tĭj), *n.* an inheritance; inherited lot or portion.

her·maph·ro·dite (hûr măf′rə dīt′), *n.* **1.** an animal or a flower having normally both the male and female organs of generation. **2.** a person or thing in which two opposite qualities are combined. —*adj.* **3.** of or like a hermaphrodite. —**her·maph·ro·dit·ic** (hûr măf′rə dĭt′ĭk), *adj.*

Her·mes (hûr′mēz), *n. Gk. Myth.* a deity, herald, and messenger of the gods, and god of roads, commerce, invention, cunning, and theft: identified by Romans with Mercury.

her·met·ic (hûr mĕt′ĭk), *adj.* made airtight by fusion or sealing. Also, **her·met′i·cal.** —**her·met′i·cal·ly,** *adv.*

her·mit (hûr′mĭt), *n.* one who has retired to a solitary place, esp. for a life of religious seclusion.

her·mit·age (hûr′mə tĭj), *n.* the habitation of a hermit.

hermit crab, any of certain decapod crustaceans which protect their soft uncovered rear by occupying the castoff shell of a univalve mollusk.

her·ni·a (hûr′nĭ ə), *n., pl.* **-nias, -niae** (-nĭ ē′). *Pathol.* the protrusion of an organ or tissue through an opening in its surrounding walls, esp. in the abdominal region.

he·ro (hĭr′ō), *n., pl.* **heroes.** **1.** a man of distinguished valor or performance. **2.** the principal male character in a story, play, etc.

Her·od (hĕr′əd), *n. (the Great)* died 4 B.C., king of the Jews from 37 to 4 B.C.

Herod An·ti·pas (ăn′tĭ păs′), died after A.D. 39, ruler of Galilee, A.D. 4–39; presided at the trial of Jesus.

He·rod·o·tus (hĭ rŏd′ə təs), *n.* 484?–425? B.C., Greek historian.

he·ro·ic (hĭ rō′ĭk), *adj.* Also, **he·ro′i·cal. 1.** of or pertaining to heroes. **2.** noble. **3.** intrepid; determined. **4.** dealing with heroes, as literature. **5.** magniloquent; grand. **6.** *Arts.* of a size larger than life. —*n.* **7.** (*usually pl.*) heroic verse. **8.** (*pl.*) bombast. —**he·ro′i·cal·ly,** *adv.*

heroic verse, a form of verse adapted to the treatment of heroic or exalted themes: in classical poetry, the hexameter; in English, the iambic pentameter.

her·o·in (hĕr′ō ĭn), *n. Pharm.* **1.** a derivative of morphine, used as a sedative, etc. **2.** (*cap.*) a trademark for this drug.

her·o·ine (hĕr′ō ĭn), *n.* **1.** a female hero. **2.** the principal female character in a story, play, etc.

her·o·ism (hĕr′ō ĭz′əm), *n.* **1.** the qualities of a hero or heroine. **2.** heroic conduct.

her·on (hĕr′ən), *n.* any of certain long-legged, long-necked, long-billed wading birds.

her·on·ry (hĕr′ən rĭ), *n., pl.* **-ries.** a place where a colony of herons breeds.

her·pes (hûr′pēz), *n. Pathol.* any of certain inflammatory infections of the skin or mucous membrane, characterized by clusters of vesicles which tend to spread.

her·pe·tol·o·gy (hûr′pə tŏl′ə jĭ), *n.* the branch of zoölogy that treats of reptiles and amphibians. —**her′pe·tol′o·gist,** *n.*

Herr (hĕr), *n., pl.* **Herren** (hĕr′ən). *German.* Mr.

her·ring (hĕr′ĭng), *n., pl.* **-rings,** (*esp. collectively*) **-ring. 1.** an important food fish of the north Atlantic, occurring in enormous shoals in the North Sea and on the northern American coast. **2.** any of various related fish.

her·ring·bone (hĕr′ĭng bōn′), *n.* **1.** a pattern of parallel lines, set obliquely, with each successive line slanting away from the other: used in masonry, textiles, embroidery, etc. —*adj.* **2.** having or resembling a herringbone pattern.

Her·ri·ot (ĕ ryō′), *n.* Édouard, born 1872, French statesman.

Herringbone pattern

hers (hûrz), *pron.* **1.** a form of the possessive her. **2.** the person(s) or thing(s) belonging to her.

her·self (hər sĕlf′), *pron.* **1.** an emphatic form of her or she. **2.** a reflexive form of her.

hertz·i·an wave (hĕrt′sĭ ən), an electromagnetic wave, artificially produced as a means of transmission in radio telegraphy.

hes·i·tan·cy (hĕz′ə tən sĭ), *n., pl.* **-cies.** hesitation; indecision. Also, **hes′i·tance.**

hes·i·tant (hĕz′ə tənt), *adj.* hesitating; undecided. —**hes′i·tant·ly,** *adv.*

hes·i·tate (hĕz′ə tāt′), *v.i.,* **-tated, -tating. 1.** to hold back in doubt or indecision. **2.** to be unwilling. **3.** to pause. **4.** to stammer. —**hes′i·tat′ing·ly,** *adv.*

hes·i·ta·tion (hĕz′ə tā′shən), *n.* **1.** act or state of hesitating. **2.** a halting or faltering in speech.

Hes·per·i·des (hĕs pĕr′ə dēz′), *n.pl. Gk. Myth.* certain nymphs fabled to guard a garden in which grew golden apples.

Hes·per·us (hĕs′pər əs), *n.* the evening star, esp. Venus.

Hes·sian (hĕsh′ən), *n.* U.S. a German mercenary used by England during the American Revolution.

Hessian fly, a small dipterous insect whose

larva is one of the most destructive pests of wheat.

het·er·o·dox (hĕt′ər ə dŏks′), *adj.* holding or reflecting unorthodox doctrines or opinions.

het·er·o·dox·y (hĕt′ər ə dŏk′sĭ), *n., pl.* **-dox·ies.** 1. heterodox state or quality. 2. a heterodox opinion, etc.

het·er·o·dyne (hĕt′ər ə dīn′), *adj.* denoting or pertaining to a method of receiving continuous-wave radiotelegraph signals by impressing upon the continuous radio-frequency oscillations another set of radio-frequency oscillations of a slightly different frequency.

het·er·o·ge·ne·ous (hĕt′ər ə jē′nĭ əs), *adj.* 1. different in kind; unlike. 2. composed of widely unlike elements. —**het·er·o·ge·ne·i·ty** (hĕt′ər ə-jə nē′ə tĭ), **het′er·o·ge′ne·ous·ness**, *n.*

het·er·o·sex·u·al (hĕt′ər ə sĕk′shŏŏ əl), *adj.* pertaining to or exhibiting sexual feeling for a person (or persons) of opposite sex. —**het′er·o·sex′u·al′i·ty**, *n.*

hew (hū), *v.t., v.i.*, **hewed, hewed** or **hewn, hewing.** 1. to chop or cut with an ax, sword, or the like. 2. to cut down; fell. —**hew′er**, *n.*

hex (hĕks), *U.S. Colloq. or Dial.* —*v.t.* 1. to bewitch. —*n.* 2. a witch. 3. a spell.

hex·a·gon (hĕk′sə gŏn′, -gən), *n.* a polygon having six angles and six sides. —**hex·ag·o·nal** (hĕks ăg′ə nəl), *adj.*

hex·am·e·ter (hĕks ăm′ə tər), *Pros.* —*n.* 1. a verse consisting of six metrical feet. —*adj.* 2. consisting of six metrical feet.

hex·a·pod (hĕk′sə pŏd′), *n.* 1. an insect. —*adj.* 2. having six feet.

hey (hā), *interj.* an exclamation to express pleasure, surprise, etc., or to call attention.

hey·day (hā′dā′), *n.* the stage or period of highest vigor or fullest strength.

Hez·e·ki·ah (hĕz′ə kī′ə), *n.* a king of Judah of the 8th–7th centuries B.C.

Hf., *Chem.* hafnium.

Hg, *Chem.* (L *hydrargyrum*) mercury.

hhd., hogshead.

hi (hī), *interj.* an exclamation, esp. of greeting.

H.I., Hawaiian Islands.

hi·a·tus (hī ā′təs), *n., pl.* **-tuses, -tus.** 1. a break, with a part missing; lacuna. 2. a gap.

hi·ber·nal (hī bûr′nəl), *adj.* wintry.

hi·ber·nate (hī′bər nāt′), *v.i.*, **-nated, -nating.** to spend the winter in a dormant condition, as certain animals. —**hi′ber·na′tion**, *n.*

Hi·ber·ni·a (hī bûr′nĭ ə), *n.* Latin or literary name of Ireland. —**Hi·ber′ni·an**, *adj., n.*

hi·bis·cus (hī bĭs′kəs, hĭ′-), *n.* any of certain herbs, shrubs, or trees of the mallow family, many of which have large showy flowers.

hic·cup (hĭk′ŭp, -əp), *n.* 1. a quick, involuntary drawing in of breath. —*v.i.* 2. to make the sound of a hiccup. 3. to have hiccups. Also, **hic·cough** (hĭk′ŭp, -əp).

hick (hĭk), *Slang.* —*n.* 1. an unsophisticated person. 2. a farmer. —*adj.* 3. pertaining to or characteristic of hicks.

hick·o·ry (hĭk′ə rĭ), *n., pl.* **-ries.** 1. any of certain North American trees, some of which bear sweet, edible nuts (**hickory nuts**) and yield valuable hard wood. 2. the wood of such a tree.

hi·dal·go (hĭ dăl′gō), *n., pl.* **-gos.** (in Spain) a man of the lower nobility.

hide¹ (hīd), *v.*, **hid, hidden** or **hid, hiding.** —*v.t.* 1. to conceal from sight. 2. to keep secret. —*v.i.* 3. to conceal oneself. —**hid·den** (hĭd′ən), *adj.* —**hid′er**, *n.*

hide² (hīd), *n., v.*, **hided, hiding.** —*n.* 1. the skin of an animal. —*v.t.* 2. *Colloq.* to flog or thrash.

hide·bound (hīd′bound′), *adj.* narrow and rigid in opinion.

hid·e·ous (hĭd′ĭ əs), *adj.* 1. horrible to the senses; very ugly. 2. shocking or revolting to the moral sense. —**hid′e·ous·ly**, *adv.* —**hid′e·ous·ness**, *n.*

hide·out (hīd′out′), *n.* a safe place for hiding (usually from the law).

hid·ing¹ (hī′dĭng), *n.* 1. concealment. 2. a place or means of concealment.

hid·ing² (hī′dĭng), *n. Colloq.* a flogging.

hie (hī), *v.i.*, **hied, hieing** or **hying.** to go hastily.

hi·er·ar·chy (hī′ə rär′kĭ), *n., pl.* **-chies.** 1. any system of persons or things in a graded order, etc. 2. *Science.* a series of successive terms of different rank. —**hi′er·ar′chi·cal**, **hi′er·ar′chic**, *adj.*

hi·er·at·ic (hī′ə răt′ĭk), *adj.* priestly.

hi·er·o·glyph·ic (hī′ər ə glĭf′ĭk, hī′rə-), *adj.* Also, **hi′er·o·glyph′i·cal.** 1. designating or pertaining to a writing system, esp. of the ancient Egyptians, in which many symbols are conventionalized pictures of the thing named. 2. inscribed with hieroglyphic symbols. 3. hard to decipher. —*n.* 4. a hieroglyphic symbol. 5. (*usually pl.*) hieroglyphic writing. 6. a symbol with a hidden meaning. 7. (*pl.*) writing difficult to decipher.

hig·gle (hĭg′əl), *v.i.*, **-gled, -gling.** to bargain, esp. in a petty way; haggle.

hig·gle·dy-pig·gle·dy (hĭg′əl dĭ pĭg′-əl dĭ), *Colloq.* —*adv.* 1. in a jumbled confusion. —*adj.* 2. jumbled. —*n.* 3. a jumble.

Hieroglyphics

high (hī), *adj.* 1. lofty; tall. 2. having a specified extent upward. 3. exceeding the common degree or measure. 4. expensive. 5. greater in rank, station, estimation, etc. 6. *Music.* a. acute in pitch. b. a little sharp. 7. shrill. 8. extending to or from an elevation. 9. of great amount, degree, force, etc. 10. chief; main. 11. grave; serious. 12. arrogant. 13. merry or hilarious. 14. *Colloq.* excited with drink. 15. remote. 16. (of meat) slightly tainted. 17. on **high**, a. above. b. in heaven. —*adv.* 18. at or to a high point, place, or level, or a high rank or estimate, a high amount or price, or a high degree. —*n.* 19. *Meteorol.* a pressure system characterized by relatively high pressure at its center.

high·ball (hī′bôl′), *n. U.S.* a drink of whiskey or other liquor diluted with water, seltzer, or ginger ale, and served with ice in a tall glass.

high·born (hī′bôrn′), *adj.* of noble birth.

high·boy (hī′boi′), *n.* a tall chest of drawers supported on legs.

high·bred (hī′brĕd′), *adj.* 1. of superior breed. 2. characteristic of superior breeding.

high·brow (hī′brou′), *Colloq.* —*n.* 1. a person of intellectual tastes. —*adj.* 2. of highbrows. 3. being a highbrow.

High Church, a party in the Anglican Church which lays great stress on church authority and jurisdiction, ritual, etc. —**High′-Church′**, *adj.* —**High Churchman.**

high·fa·lu·tin (hī′fə lōō′tən), *adj. Colloq.* pompous; pretentious. Also, **high′fa·lu′ting.**

high-fi·del·i·ty (hī′fĭ dĕl′ə tĭ), *adj. Electronics.* (of an amplifier, radio receiver, etc.) reproducing the full audio range of the original signal of sounds with relatively little distortion.

high·fli·er (hī′flī′ər), *n.* one who goes to extremes in aims, pretensions, opinions, etc. Also, **high′fly′er.**

high-flown (hī′flōn′), *adj.* 1. extravagant in aims, pretensions, etc. 2. bombastic.

high-fre·quen·cy (hī′frē′kwən sĭ), *adj.* noting or pertaining to frequencies above the audible range, as in radio.

high-hand·ed (hī′hăn′dĭd), *adj.* overbearing; arbitrary. —**high′-hand′ed·ly**, *adv.* —**high′-hand′ed·ness**, *n.*

high-hat (*v.* hī′hăt′; *adj.* hī′hăt′), *v.*, **-hatted, -hatting,** *adj. U.S. Slang.* —*v.t.* 1. to snub or treat condescendingly. —*adj.* 2. snobbish. 3. fashionable.

high·land (hī′lənd), *n.* 1. an elevated region. 2. (*pl.*) a mountainous or hilly region.

High·land·er (hī′lən dər), *n.* a member of the Gaelic race of the Highlands.

Highland fling, a vigorous Scotch dance.

Highland Park (hī′lənd), a city in SE Michigan, within limits of Detroit. 50,810.

High·lands (hī′ləndz), *n.pl.* a mountainous region in Scotland, N of the Grampians.

high·light (hī′līt′), *v.*, **-lighted, -lighting,** *n.* —*v.t.* 1. to emphasize. —*n.* 2. Also, **high light,** a conspicuous part. 3. an important event, scene, etc. 4. *Art.* the point of most intense light.

high·ly (hī′lĭ), *adv.* 1. in or to a high degree. 2. with high appreciation or praise. 3. at or to a high price.

High Mass, *Rom. Cath. Ch.* a Mass celebrated according to the complete rite by a priest or prelate attended by a deacon and subdeacon, parts of the Mass being chanted or sung by the ministers and parts by the choir.

high-mind·ed (hī′mīn′dĭd), *adj.* 1. having or showing high principles or feelings. 2. proud. —**high′-mind′ed·ness**, *n.*

high·ness (hī′nĭs), *n.* 1. state of being high.

2. (*cap.*) a title of honor given to royal or princely personages (prec. by *His, Your,* etc.).

High Point, a city in central North Carolina. 38,495.

high-pres·sure (hī/prĕsh/ər), *adj.* **1.** having or involving a pressure above the normal. **2.** vigorous; persistent.

high·road (hī/rōd/), *n.* **1.** a main road; highway. **2.** an easy or certain course.

high school, *U.S.* a school following the ordinary grammar school and corresponding to grades 9 through 12.

high seas, the open, unenclosed waters of any sea or ocean, outside the jurisdiction of any nation.

high-sound·ing (hī/soun/dĭng), *adj.* having an imposing or pretentious sound.

high-spir·it·ed (hī/spĭr/ə tĭd), *adj.* having a high, proud, or bold spirit.

high-strung (hī/strŭng/), *adj.* at great tension; highly nervous.

hight (hīt), *adj. Archaic.* named.

high-test (hī/tĕst/), *adj.* (of gasoline) boiling at a comparatively low temperature.

high tide, 1. the tide at its greatest elevation. **2.** the time of such a tide. Also, **high water.**

high time, 1. the time just before it is too late. **2.** *Slang.* a gay time.

high-toned (hī/tōnd/), *adj.* **1.** high in tone. **2.** dignified. **3.** *U.S. Colloq.* fashionable.

high·way (hī/wā/), *n.* **1.** a main road, as one between towns. **2.** a waterway.

high·way·man (hī/wā/mən), *n., pl.* **-men.** a robber on the highway.

hi·jack (hī/jăk/), *U.S. Slang.* —*v.t.* **1.** to steal (liquor or other goods) from bootleggers or smugglers while it is in transit. —*v.i.* **2.** to engage in such stealing. —**hi/jack/er,** *n.*

hike (hīk), *v.,* **hiked, hiking,** *n.* —*v.i.* **1.** to march or walk a great distance. **2.** *Slang.* to raise. —*n.* **3.** a long march or walk. **4.** *Slang.* an increase. —**hik/er,** *n.*

hi·lar·i·ous (hī lâr/ē əs, hĭ-), *adj.* **1.** boisterously gay. **2.** cheerful. —**hi·lar/i·ous·ly,** *adv.* —**hi·lar/i·ous·ness, hi·lar/i·ty,** *n.*

hill (hĭl), *n.* **1.** a conspicuous natural elevation of the earth's surface. **2.** an artificial heap or pile. **3.** a little heap of earth about a cultivated plant or a cluster of such plants. —*v.t.* **4.** to surround with hills. —**hill/y,** *adj.* —**hill/i·ness,** *n.*

hill·bil·ly (hĭl/bĭl/ī), *n., pl.* **-lies.** *U.S. Colloq.* a person living in the backwoods or mountains.

hill·ock (hĭl/ək), *n.* a little hill or mound.

hilt (hĭlt), *n.* **1.** the handle of a sword or dagger. **2.** to the hilt, fully. —**hilt/ed,** *adj.*

hi·lum (hī/ləm), *n., pl.* **-la** (-lə). *Bot.* the scar on a seed produced by separation from its stalk.

him (hĭm), *pron.* objective case of *he.*

Hi·ma·la·yas (hĭ mäl/yəz, hĭm/ə lā/əz), *n.pl.* **The,** a lofty mountain system along the border between India and Tibet. Highest peak (in the world), Mt. Everest, 29,141 ft. Also, **The Himalaya** or **Himalaya Mountains.** —**Hi·ma·la·yan** (hĭ mäl/yən, hĭm/ə lā/ən), *adj.*

Himm·ler (hĭm/lər), *n.* **Heinrich,** 1900–45, head of the Gestapo in Nazi Germany.

him·self (hĭm sĕlf/), *pron.* **1.** a reflexive form of *him.* **2.** an emphatic form of *him* or *he.* **3.** his normal self.

hind[1] (hīnd), *adj.,* **hinder, hindmost** or **hindermost.** rear or back; posterior.

hind[2] (hīnd), *n. Zool.* the female of the deer, chiefly the red deer.

hind[3] (hīnd), *n. Archaic.* a peasant.

hind·brain (hīnd/brān/), *n. Anat.* the cerebellum, pons, and medulla oblongata.

Hin·de·mith (hĭn/də mĭt), *n.* **Paul,** born 1895, German composer, now in U.S.

Hin·den·burg (hĭn/dən bûrg/), *n.* **Paul von,** 1847–1934, German field marshal: president of Germany, 1925–34.

hin·der[1] (hĭn/dər), *v.t.* **1.** to check; retard. **2.** to stop. —**hin/der·ing·ly,** *adv.*

hind·er[2] (hīn/dər), *adj.* rear; back.

hind·most (hīnd/mōst/), *adj.* furthest behind; last. Also, **hind·er·most** (hīn/dər mōst/).

hind·quar·ter (hīnd/kwôr/tər), *n.* the posterior end of a halved carcass of beef, etc.

hin·drance (hĭn/drəns), *n.* **1.** an impeding, stopping, or preventing. **2.** a means or cause of hindering.

hind·sight (hīnd/sīt/), *n.* perception of the nature of a case after the event.

Hin·du (hĭn/dōō), *n.* **1.** a native of India or Hindustan, esp. one who adheres to a form of the ancient national religion, which recognizes the primacy of the Brahman caste. —*adj.* **2.** of or pertaining to Hindus or Hinduism. Also, **Hin/doo.**

Hin·du·ism (hĭn/dōō ĭz/əm), *n.* the religious and social doctrines and rites of the Hindus.

Hin·du·stan (hĭn/dōō stän/, -stän/), *n.* **1.** Persian name of India. **2.** the predominantly Hindu areas of the peninsula of India.

Hin·du·sta·ni (hĭn/dōō stä/nĭ, -stän/ĭ), *n.* **1.** a standard language or lingua franca of northern India. —*adj.* **2.** of Hindustan, its people, or their languages.

hinge (hĭnj), *n., v.,* **hinged, hinging.** —*n.* **1.** the joint on which a door, shutter, lid, or the like, moves. —*v.i.* **2.** to depend on. —*v.t.* **3.** to furnish with a hinge. **4.** to cause to depend. —**hinged,** *adj.*

hin·ny (hĭn/ĭ), *n., pl.* **-nies.** the offspring of a stallion and she-donkey.

hint (hĭnt), *n.* **1.** an indirect suggestion; intimation. —*v.t.* **2.** to give a hint of. —*v.i.* **3.** to make a hint (usually fol. by *at*). —**hint/er,** *n.*

hin·ter·land (hĭn/tər länd/), *n.* **1.** the area on the landward side of a port that it serves. **2.** the remote or less developed parts of a country.

hip[1] (hĭp), *n.* the projecting part of each side of the body formed by the side of the pelvis and the upper part of the femur, with the flesh covering them.

hip[2] (hĭp), *n.* the ripe fruit of a rose.

hipped (hĭpt), *adj. U.S. Slang.* having an obsession.

Hip·poc·ra·tes (hĭ pŏk/rə tēz/), *n.* 460?–357 B.C., Greek physician.

Hip·po·crat·ic oath (hĭp/ə krăt/ĭk), an oath embodying the duties of physicians, usually taken by those about to enter upon the practice of medicine.

Hip·po·crene (hĭp/ə krēn/, hĭp/ə krē/nĭ), *n. Gk. Myth.* a spring on Mount Helicon, regarded as a source of poetic inspiration.

hip·po·drome (hĭp/ə drōm/), *n.* an arena for equestrian and other spectacles.

hip·po·pot·a·mus (hĭp/ə pŏt/ə məs), *n., pl.* **-muses, -mi** (-mī/). a large herbivorous mammal having a thick hairless body, short legs, and large head and muzzle, found in and near the rivers, lakes, etc., of Africa, and able to remain under water for a considerable time.

hip roof, *Archit.* a roof with sloping ends and sides.

hire (hīr), *v.,* **hired, hiring,** *n.* —*v.t.* **1.** to obtain for pay the services or use of. —*n.* **2.** the price or compensation paid for use or services.

hire·ling (hīr/lĭng), *n.* one serving for hire (now usually in contempt).

Hir·o·hi·to (hĭr/ō hē/tō), *n.* born 1901, emperor of Japan since 1926.

Hir·o·shi·ma (hĭr/ə shē/mə), *n.* a seaport in SW Japan: first military use of atomic bomb, Aug. 6, 1945. 171,902 (1946); 343,968 (1940).

hir·sute (hûr/sōōt), *adj.* hairy; bristly.

his (hĭz), *pron.* **1.** the possessive form of *he.* **2.** the person(s) or thing(s) belonging to him. —*adj.* **3.** belonging or pertaining to him.

His·pa·ni·a (hĭs pā/nĭ ə, -nyə), *n. Poetic.* Spain. —**His·pan·ic** (hĭs păn/ĭk), *adj.*

His·pan·io·la (hĭs/pən yō/lə), *n.* an island in the West Indies, including the republic of Haiti and the Dominican Republic.

hiss (hĭs), *v.i., v.t.* **1.** to make a sound like that of the letter *s* prolonged. **2.** to express disapproval or contempt (of) by making this sound. —*n.* **3.** a hissing sound, esp. in disapproval. —**hiss/er,** *n.*

hist., 1. historical. **2.** history.

his·tol·o·gy (hĭs tŏl/ə jĭ), *n.* the science that treats of organic tissues. —**his·tol/o·gist,** *n.*

his·to·ri·an (hĭs tōr/ĭ ən), *n.* **1.** a writer of history. **2.** an authority on history.

his·tor·ic (hĭs tôr/ĭk, -tŏr/-), *adj.* **1.** famous or important in history. **2.** historical.

his·tor·i·cal (hĭs tôr/ə kəl, -tŏr/-), *adj.* **1.** relating to or concerned with history. **2.** narrated or mentioned in history. —**his·tor/i·cal·ly,** *adv.*

his·to·ri·og·ra·pher (hĭs tōr/ĭ ŏg/rə fər), *n.* a historian, esp. an official one. —**his·to/ri·og/ra·phy,** *n.*

his·to·ry (hĭs/tə rĭ), *n., pl.* **-ries. 1.** the branch of knowledge dealing with past events. **2.** the record of past events. **3.** the aggregate of past events. **4.** a past worthy of record or out of the ordinary.

his·tri·on·ic (hĭs′trĭ ŏn′ĭk), *adj.* **1.** of or pertaining to actors or acting. **2.** artificial.

his·tri·on·ics (hĭs′trĭ ŏn′ĭks), *n.pl.* **1.** dramatic representation. **2.** artificial behavior, speech, etc., for effect.

hit[1] (hĭt), *v.*, **hit, hitting,** *n.* —*v.t.* **1.** to deal a blow to. **2.** to collide or come in forcible contact with. **3.** to succeed in striking. **4.** to drive or propel by a stroke. **5.** to affect severely. **6.** to assail sharply. —*v.i.* **7.** to strike with a missile, etc.; deal a blow. —*n.* **8.** an impact or collision. **9.** a stroke or blow. **10.** *Baseball.* a ball so hit that the batter reaches base safely. —**hit′ter,** *n.*

hit[2] (hĭt), *v.*, **hit, hitting,** *n.* —*v.t.* **1.** to come upon; meet. **2.** to suit exactly. **3.** to guess correctly. **4.** *U.S. Colloq.* to arrive at. **5. hit it off,** *Colloq.* to agree. —*v.i.* **6.** to come into collision. **7.** to find. —*n.* **8.** a successful stroke, performance, or production.

hitch (hĭch), *v.t.* **1.** to fasten with a hook, rope, strap, etc. **2.** to harness to a vehicle. **3.** to raise with jerks. **4.** to fasten oneself or itself to something. **5.** to move jerkily. —*n.* **6.** a making fast, as to something. **7.** *Naut., etc.* any of various forms of knot made with rope. **8.** an obstruction. **9.** a jerk or pull. **10.** a hobble or limp.

hitch·hike (hĭch′hīk′), *v.i.*, **-hiked, -hiking.** *Colloq.* to travel by walking, with occasional rides in passing automobiles. —**hitch′hik′er,** *n.*

hith·er (hĭth′ər), *adv.* **1.** to or toward this place. —*adj.* **2.** nearer. **3.** earlier.

hith·er·to (hĭth′ər tōō′), *adv.* until now.

hith·er·ward (hĭth′ər wərd), *adv.* hither. Also, **hith′er·wards.**

Hit·ler (hĭt′lər), *n.* **Adolf,** 1889–1945?, Nazi leader and dictator of Germany, born in Austria: German chancellor, 1933–45; president, 1934–45.

Hit·tite (hĭt′īt), *n.* **1.** one of a powerful, civilized ancient people who flourished in Asia Minor and adjoining regions (1900–1200 B.C.). —*adj.* **2.** having to do with the Hittites.

hive (hīv), *n.*, *v.*, **hived, hiving.** —*n.* **1.** an artificial shelter for honeybees. **2.** the bees inhabiting a hive. **3.** something resembling a beehive in structure, use, or activity. —*v.t.*, *v.i.* **4.** to gather into a hive.

hives (hīvz), *n.* any of various eruptive diseases of the skin.

H.M., His (or Her) Majesty.

H.M.S., **1.** His, or Her, Majesty's Service. **2.** His, or Her, Majesty's Ship.

ho (hō), *interj.* an exclamation of surprise, etc., or, when repeated, derisive laughter.

Ho, *Chem.* holmium.

hoar (hōr), *adj.* **1.** gray or white, as with age or frost. **2.** old. —*n.* **3.** hoariness.

hoard (hōrd), *n.* **1.** an accumulation for preservation or future use. —*v.t.*, *v.i.* **2.** to accumulate (food, money, etc.) for preservation or future use. —**hoard′er,** *n.*

hoar·frost (hōr′frôst′, -frŏst′), *n.* white frost.

hoar·hound (hōr′hound′), *n.* horehound.

hoarse (hōrs), *adj.*, **hoarser, hoarsest.** having a gruff, husky vocal tone. —**hoarse′ly,** *adv.* —**hoarse′ness,** *n.*

hoar·y (hōr′ĭ), *adj.*, **hoarier, hoariest. 1.** gray or white, esp. with age. **2.** ancient. —**hoar′i·ness,** *n.*

hoax (hōks), *n.* **1.** a humorous or mischievous deception, esp. a practical joke. —*v.t.* **2.** to deceive by a hoax. —**hoax′er,** *n.*

hob[1] (hŏb), *n.* **1.** a shelf at the back or side of a fireplace. **2.** a peg or pin used as a target in certain games.

hob[2] (hŏb), *n.* **1.** a hobgoblin or elf. **2.** *Colloq.* mischief.

Hobbes (hŏbz), *n.* **Thomas,** 1588–1679, British philosopher.

hob·ble (hŏb′əl), *v.*, **-bled, -bling,** *n.* —*v.i.* **1.** to walk lamely. **2.** to proceed irregularly. —*v.t.* **3.** to cause to limp. **4.** to fasten together the legs of (a horse, etc.) so as to prevent free motion. —*n.* **5.** a rope, strap, etc., used to hobble an animal.

hob·ble·de·hoy (hŏb′əl dĭ hoi′), *n.* **1.** an adolescent boy. **2.** an awkward boy.

hob·by (hŏb′ĭ), *n.*, *pl.* **-bies. 1.** a favorite occupation, topic, etc., pursued for amusement. **2.** a hobbyhorse.

hob·by·horse (hŏb′ĭ hôrs′), *n.* a stick with a

horse's head, or a rocking horse, ridden by children.

hob·gob·lin (hŏb′gŏb′lĭn), *n.* **1.** anything causing superstitious fear. **2.** a goblin.

hob·nail (hŏb′nāl′), *n.* a short, large-headed nail for protecting the soles of heavy boots and shoes.

hob·nob (hŏb′nŏb′), *v.i.*, **-nobbed, -nobbing. 1.** to associate on very friendly terms. **2.** to drink together.

ho·bo (hō′bō), *n.*, *pl.* **-bos, -boes.** *U.S.* **1.** a tramp or vagrant. **2.** a wandering worker.

Ho·bo·ken (hō′bō kən), *n.* a seaport in NE New Jersey. 50,115.

Hob·son's choice (hŏb′sənz), the choice of taking either the thing offered or nothing.

hock[1] (hŏk), *n.* the joint in the hind leg of the horse, etc., above the fetlock joint.

hock[2] (hŏk), *n.* *Chiefly Brit.* any white Rhine wine.

hock[3] (hŏk), *v.t.*, *n.* *U.S. Slang.* pawn.

hock·ey (hŏk′ĭ), *n.* a game in which opposing sides seek with clubs (**hockey sticks**) curved at one end to drive a ball or disk into their opponent's goal.

ho·cus-po·cus (hō′kəs pō′kəs), *n.*, *v.*, **-cused, -cusing** or (*esp. Brit.*) **-cussed, -cussing.** —*n.* **1.** a formula used in conjuring. **2.** sleight of hand. **3.** trickery or deception. —*v.i.* **4.** to perform tricks.

hod (hŏd), *n.* **1.** a portable trough for carrying mortar, bricks, etc. **2.** a coal scuttle.

hodge·podge (hŏj′pŏj′), *n.* a jumble.

hoe (hō), *n.*, *v.*, **hoed, hoeing.** —*n.* **1.** a long-handled implement used to break up the surface of the ground, destroy weeds, etc. —*v.t.*, *v.i.* **2.** to dig, scrape, weed, cultivate, etc., with a hoe.

hoe·cake (hō′kāk′), *n.* *Southern U.S.* a cake made with corn meal.

hog (hŏg, hôg), *n.*, *v.*, **hogged, hogging.** —*n.* **1.** any of certain omnivorous, nonruminant mammals whose flesh is used as food; pig, sow, or boar. **2.** *Colloq.* a selfish, gluttonous, or filthy person. —*v.t.* **3.** *Slang.* to take more than one's share of.

Ho·garth (hō′gärth), *n.* **William,** 1697–1764, British painter and engraver.

hog·gish (hŏg′ĭsh, hôg′ĭsh), *adj.* **1.** like or befitting a hog. **2.** selfish; gluttonous; filthy. —**hog′gish·ly,** *adv.* —**hog′gish·ness,** *n.*

hog·nose snake (hŏg′nōz′, hôg′-), any of certain harmless American snakes with hoglike snouts.

hogs·head (hŏgz′hĕd′, hôgz′-), *n.* **1.** a large cask, esp. one containing from 63 to 140 gallons. **2.** a varying unit of liquid measure, esp. one containing 63 gallons.

hog-tie (hŏg′tī′, hôg′-), *v.t.*, **-tied, -tying.** to tie with all four feet together.

hog·wash (hŏg′wŏsh′, -wôsh′, hôg′-), *n.* **1.** refuse given to hogs; swill. **2.** nonsense.

Hoh·en·zol·lern (hō′ən zŏl′ərn), *n.* a German princely family of Prussia: rulers of the German Empire, 1871–1918, and of Rumania, 1866–1948.

hoi pol·loi (hoi′ pə loi′), the masses.

hoist (hoist), *v.t.* **1.** to lift, esp. by some mechanical appliance. —*n.* **2.** an apparatus for hoisting, as an elevator. **3.** act of hoisting; a lift.

hoi·ty-toi·ty (hoi′tĭ toi′tĭ), *interj.* **1.** an exclamation denoting somewhat contemptuous surprise. —*adj.* **2.** assuming; haughty. —*n.* **3.** haughtiness.

ho·kum (hō′kəm), *n.* *Slang.* nonsense.

Hol·bein (hōl′bīn), *n.* **1. Hans,** c1460–1524, German painter. **2.** his son, **Hans,** 1497?–1543, German painter.

hold[1] (hōld), *v.*, **held; held** or (*Archaic*) **holden; holding;** *n.* —*v.t.* **1.** to have or keep in the hand. **2.** to bear, sustain, or support with the hand, arms, etc., or by any means. **3.** to keep in a specified state, etc. **4.** to engage in; observe or celebrate. **5.** to hinder or restrain. **6.** to occupy. **7.** to contain. **8.** to think or believe; entertain. **9.** to consider. **10.** to decide legally. —*v.i.* **11.** to continue in a specified state. **12.** to adhere; cling. **13.** to keep a grasp on something. **14.** to continue in resistance. **15. hold** or **keep back,** to restrain or check. **16. hold forth, a.** to propose. **b.** to harangue. **17. hold off, a.** to keep aloof or at a distance. **b.** to refrain from action. **18. hold out, a.** to offer. **b.** to extend. **c.** to keep out. **d.** to continue to endure or resist. **19. hold over,** to postpone. **20. hold up, a.** to display. **b.** to stop. **c.** to rob. **d.** to support or uphold. **e.** to endure. —*n.* **21.** grasp; grip. **22.** a handle. **23.** a dominating influence. **24.** *Music.* a pause (symbol). **25.** a prison.

hold² (hōld), *n.* the interior of a ship below deck, esp. where the cargo is stowed.

hold·back (hōld/băk′), *n.* a restraint.

hold·er (hōl/dər), *n.* **1.** something to hold a thing with. **2.** one who has the ownership, possession, or use of something. **3.** *Law.* one who has the right to enforce a negotiable instrument.

hold·fast (hōld/făst′, -fäst′), *n.* something used to hold or secure a thing in place.

hold·ing (hōl/dĭng), *n.* **1.** act of one that holds. **2.** (*often pl.*) property owned, esp. stocks, bonds, and real estate.

holding company, *Finance.* a company controlling other companies by virtue of stock ownership.

hold·up (hōld/ŭp′), *n.* *U.S. Colloq.* a forcible stopping and robbing of a person.

hole (hōl), *n.*, *v.*, holed, holing. —*n.* **1.** an opening through anything. **2.** a cavity. **3.** a burrow. **4.** a small, dingy, or mean abode. **5.** a dungeon. **6.** *Colloq.* an embarrassing predicament. **7.** *Colloq.* a flaw. —*v.t.* **8.** to make a hole in. **9.** to put or drive into a hole. —*v.i.* **10.** to retire for the winter, as a hibernating animal. —hole/y, *adj.*

hol·i·day (hŏl/ə dā′), *n.* **1.** a day on which ordinary business is suspended in commemoration of some event, etc. **2.** any day of exemption from labor. **3.** (*often pl.*) *Chiefly Brit.* a vacation. —*adj.* **4.** festive; joyous. **5.** suited only to a holiday.

ho·li·ness (hō/lĭ nĭs), *n.* **1.** state or character of being holy. **2.** (*cap.*) a title of the Pope (prec. by *his* or *your*).

Hol·land (hŏl/ənd), *n.* the Netherlands. —Hol/land·er, *n.*

Hol·lands gin (hŏl/əndz), gin in which the juniper is mixed in the mash.

hol·ler (hŏl/ər), *Dial.* —*v.i.*, *v.t.* **1.** to shout (something). —*n.* **2.** a loud cry of pain, surprise, etc.

hol·low (hŏl/ō), *adj.* **1.** having a hole or cavity within. **2.** having a concavity. **3.** sunken. **4.** not resonant; dull. **5.** unreal; vain. **6.** insincere. **7.** hungry. —*n.* **8.** a depression or cavity. **9.** a valley. —*v.t.*, *v.i.* **10.** to make or become hollow. —*adv.* **11.** in a hollow manner. **12.** *Colloq.* utterly. —hol/low·ness, *n.*

hol·ly (hŏl/ĭ), *n.*, *pl.* -lies. **1.** any of certain trees or shrubs having glossy leaves and bright-red berries. **2.** the foliage and berries, much used for Christmas decoration.

hol·ly·hock (hŏl/ĭ hŏk′, -hōk′), *n.* a tall plant of the mallow family having showy flowers of various colors.

Hol·ly·wood (hŏl/ĭ wŏŏd′), *n.* a part of Los Angeles, California: center of American motion-picture industry.

Holmes (hōmz), *n.* **1.** Oliver Wendell, 1809–94, U.S. author and physician. **2.** his son, Oliver Wendell, 1841–1935, associate justice of the U.S. Supreme Court, 1902–32.

hol·mi·um (hōl/mĭ əm), *n.* *Chem.* a rare-earth element. *Symbol:* Ho; *at. wt.:* 164.94; *at. no.:* 67.

holm oak (hōm), an evergreen oak of southern Europe, with foliage like that of the holly.

hol·o·caust (hŏl/ə kôst′), *n.* **1.** great destruction of life, esp. by fire. **2.** a burnt offering.

hol·o·graph (hŏl/ə grăf′, -gräf′), *adj.* **1.** wholly written by the person in whose name it appears. —*n.* **2.** a holograph writing.

Hol·stein (hōl/stīn, -stēn), *n.* one of a breed of large, black-and-white dairy cattle, originating in North Holland and Friesland. Also, **Hol/stein-Frie/sian.**

hol·ster (hōl/stər), *n.* a leather case for a pistol, attached to a belt or a saddle.

ho·ly (hō/lĭ), *adj.*, -lier, -liest, *n.*, *pl.* -lies. —*adj.* **1.** specially recognized as or declared sacred. **2.** dedicated to the service of God. **3.** saintly or devout. **4.** of religious purity, etc. **5.** religious. —*n.* **6.** a sacred place.

Holy Communion. See communion.

holy day, a consecrated day or religious festival, esp. one other than Sunday.

Holy Ghost, the third person of the Trinity.

Holy Land, Palestine.

holy of holies, **1.** a place of special sacredness. **2.** the inner chamber of the Jewish temple entered only by the high priest only once a year.

Hol·yoke (hōl/yōk), *n.* a city in S Massachusetts, on the Connecticut river. 53,750.

holy orders, **1.** the rite of ordination. **2.** the

rank of a minister. **3.** the major grades of a ministry.

Holy Roman Empire, the empire in western and central Europe which began in A.D. 962 and ended in 1806, regarded theoretically as the temporal form of a universal dominion whose spiritual head was the Pope.

Holy See, **1.** the office or jurisdiction of the Pope. **2.** the papal court.

Holy Spirit, the Holy Ghost.

ho·ly·stone (hō/lĭ stōn′), *n.*, *v.*, -stoned, -stoning. —*n.* **1.** a soft sandstone for scrubbing decks. —*v.t.* **2.** to scrub with a holystone.

Holy Roman Empire, A.D. 1200

Holy Week, the week preceding Easter Sunday.

Holy Writ, the Scriptures.

hom·age (hŏm/ĭj, ŏm/-), *n.* **1.** respect or reverence. **2.** the formal acknowledgment by a feudal tenant or vassal of owing his lord faith and service.

hom·burg (hŏm/bûrg), *n.* a man's felt hat with a soft crown dented lengthwise.

home (hōm), *n.*, *adj.*, *adv.*, *v.*, homed, homing. —*n.* **1.** a house, apartment, or other shelter that is the fixed residence of a person or family. **2.** an institution for the homeless, sick, etc. **3.** the dwelling place or habitat of an animal, etc. **4.** one's native place or own country. **5.** the goal. **6.** *Baseball.* the plate to which the batter must return after running around the bases, in order to score a run. **7.** at home, a. in one's own house or country. b. at ease. c. prepared to receive social visits. —*adj.* **8.** domestic. —*adv.* **9.** to, toward, or at home. **10.** deep; effectively and completely. **11.** to the mark or point aimed at. —*v.i.* **12.** to go home. —*v.t.* **13.** to bring or send home. —home/less, *adj.* —home/like/, *adj.*

home economics, the art and science of home management, covering matters of food, clothing, furniture, child care, etc.

home·land (hōm/lănd′), *n.* one's native land.

home·ly (hōm/lĭ), *adj.*, -lier, -liest. **1.** plain; unpretentious. **2.** *U.S.* not good-looking; ugly. **3.** not having elegance or cultivation. —home/-li·ness, *n.*

home·made (hōm/mād′), *adj.* made at home.

ho·me·op·a·thy (hō/mĭ ŏp/ə thĭ), *n.* the method of treating disease by drugs, given in minute doses, which would produce in a healthy person symptoms similar to those of the disease. —ho·me·o·path·ic (hō/mĭ ə păth/ĭk), *adj.* —home·op·a·thist (hō/mĭ ŏp/ə thĭst), ho·me·o·path (hō/mĭ ə păth/), *n.*

Ho·mer (hō/mər), *n.* **1.** c10th cent. B.C., Greek poet: author of *Iliad* and *Odyssey.* **2.** Winslow, 1836–1910, U.S. painter.

hom·er (hō/mər), *n.* *Colloq.* **1.** *Baseball.* a home run. **2.** a homing pigeon.

Ho·mer·ic (hō mĕr/ĭk), *adj.* of, pertaining to, or suggestive of Homer or his poetry.

home rule, self-government in local matters.

home run, *Baseball.* a run made on a hit which enables the batter to make a nonstop circuit of the bases.

home·sick (hōm/sĭk′), *adj.* depressed by a longing for home. —home/sick/ness, *n.*

home·spun (hōm/spŭn′), *adj.* **1.** spun or made at home. **2.** plain; simple. —*n.* **3.** cloth made at home. **4.** cloth of similar appearance to that hand-spun and hand-woven.

home·stead (hōm/stĕd, -stĭd), *n.* **1.** *U.S.* a dwelling with its land and buildings exempted by law (homestead law) from seizure or sale for debt. **2.** any dwelling. —home/stead/er, *n.*

home stretch, the straight part of a race track leading to the finish line.

home·ward (hōm/wərd), *adv.* **1.** Also, home/wards. toward home. —*adj.* **2.** directed toward home.

home·work (hōm/wûrk′), *n.* **1.** the part of a lesson prepared at home. **2.** any work done at home.

home·y (hō′mĭ), *adj.*, **homier, homiest.** *Colloq.* comfortable; cozy.

hom·i·cide (hŏm′ə sīd′), *n.* the killing of one human being by another. —**hom′i·cid′al,** *adj.*

hom·i·let·ics (hŏm′ə lĕt′ĭks), *n.* the art of preaching. —**hom′i·let′ic,** *adj.*

hom·i·ly (hŏm′ə lĭ), *n., pl.* **-lies. 1.** a sermon. **2.** an admonitory or moralizing discourse.

homing pigeon, a pigeon trained to fly home from a distance, employed to carry messages.

hom·i·ny (hŏm′ə nĭ), *n.* white corn hulled and crushed or coarsely ground: prepared for use as food by boiling.

Ho·mo (hō′mō), *n., pl.* **Homines** (hŏm′ə nēz′). the primate genus that includes modern man, *Homo sapiens,* and some related extinct species.

ho·mo·ge·ne·ous (hō′mə jē′nĭ əs, hŏm′ə-), *adj.* **1.** composed of parts all of the same kind. **2.** essentially alike. —**ho′mo·ge′ne·ous·ly,** *adv.* —**ho·mo·ge·ne·i·ty** (hō′mə jə nē′ə tĭ, hŏm′ə-), *n.*

ho·mog·e·nize (hō mŏj′ə nīz′, hŏ′mə jə-), *v.t.,* **-nized, -nizing.** to form by mixing and emulsifying.

hom·o·graph (hŏm′ə grăf′, -gräf′), *n.* a word of the same written form as another, but of different origin and signification.

ho·mol·o·gous (hō mŏl′ə gəs), *adj.* similar or corresponding, as in position, structure, origin, etc.

hom·o·logue (hŏm′ə lôg′, -lŏg′), *n.* something homologous.

ho·mol·o·gy (hō mŏl′ə jĭ), *n., pl.* **-gies.** state of being homologous.

hom·o·nym (hŏm′ə nĭm), *n.* a word like another in sound and perhaps in spelling, but different in meaning.

hom·o·phone (hŏm′ə fōn′), *n.* a word pronounced the same as another, whether spelled the same or not.

ho·mop·ter·ous (hō mŏp′tər əs), *adj.* pertaining or belonging to a suborder of hemipterous insects having wings of the same texture throughout, comprising the aphids, cicadas, etc.

Ho·mo sa·pi·ens (hō′mō sā′pĭ ĕnz′), modern man, the single surviving species of the genus *Homo.*

ho·mo·sex·u·al (hō′mə sĕk′shŏŏ əl, hŏm′ə-), *adj.* **1.** pertaining to or exhibiting sexual feeling for a person of the same sex. —*n.* **2.** a homosexual person. —**ho′mo·sex′u·al′i·ty,** *n.*

ho·mun·cu·lus (hō mŭng′kyə ləs), *n., pl.* **-li** (-lī′). a little man; a dwarf.

Hon., 1. Honorable. **2.** Honorary.

Hon·du·ras (hŏn dŏŏr′əs, -dyŏŏr′-), *n.* **1.** a republic in Central America. 1,173,032 pop.; 59,161 sq. mi. *Cap.:* Tegucigalpa. **2.** See **British Honduras.** —**Hon·du′ran,** *adj., n.*

hone (hōn), *n., v.,* **honed, honing.** —*n.* **1.** a whetstone of fine texture, for sharpening razors, etc. —*v.t.* **2.** to sharpen on a hone.

hon·est (ŏn′ĭst), *adj.* **1.** honorable in principles, intentions, and actions. **2.** showing uprightness and fairness. **3.** sincere. **4.** genuine or unadulterated. **5.** virtuous. —**hon′est·ly,** *adv.*

hon·es·ty (ŏn′ĭs tĭ), *n.* **1.** quality or fact of being honest. **2.** truthfulness.

hon·ey (hŭn′ĭ), *n., pl.* **honeys,** *adj., v.,* **honeyed** or **honied, honeying.** —*n.* **1.** a sweet, viscid fluid produced by bees from the nectar collected from flowers. **2.** something sweet, delicious, or delightful. **3.** darling. —*adj.* **4.** of or like honey. —*v.t.* **5.** *Archaic or U.S.* to talk sweetly or endearingly.

hon·ey·bee (hŭn′ĭ bē′), *n.* a bee that collects and stores honey.

hon·ey·comb (hŭn′ĭ kōm′), *n.* **1.** a structure of wax containing rows of hexagonal cells, formed by bees for honey and their eggs. **2.** anything resembling this. —*v.t.* **3.** to reduce to a honeycomb. **4.** to penetrate in all parts.

hon·ey·dew (hŭn′ĭ dū′, -dōō′), *n.* the sweet material which exudes from the leaves of certain plants in hot weather.

honeydew melon, a sweet-flavored, white-fleshed muskmelon with a pale-green rind.

hon·eyed (hŭn′ĭd), *adj.* **1.** dulcet or ingratiating. **2.** of or resembling honey.

honey locust, a thorny North American tree bearing pods with a sweet pulp.

hon·ey·moon (hŭn′ĭ mōōn′), *n.* **1.** a holiday spent by a newly married couple in traveling. —*v.i.* **2.** to spend one's honeymoon. —**hon′ey·moon′er,** *n.*

hon·ey·suck·le (hŭn′ĭ sŭk′əl), *n.* any of certain upright or climbing shrubs, some species of which are cultivated for their fragrant white, yellow, or red tubular flowers.

Hong Kong (hŏng′ kŏng′), a British crown colony in SE China, comprising the island of Hong Kong (32 sq. mi.) and the adjacent mainland. 980,000 pop.; 390 sq. mi. *Cap.:* Victoria. Also, **Hong′kong′.**

honk (hŏngk, hôngk), *n.* **1.** the cry of the wild goose. **2.** any similar sound, as of an automobile horn. —*v.i.* **3.** to emit a honk.

honk·y-tonk (hŏng′kĭ tôngk′, hông′kĭ-tôngk′), *n.* *U.S. Slang.* a cheap, sordid saloon, cabaret, etc.

Hon·o·lu·lu (hŏn′ə lōō′lōō), *n.* a seaport in the Hawaiian Islands, on Oahu: capital of the Territory of Hawaii. 179,326.

hon·or (ŏn′ər), *n.* **1.** high public esteem; fame; glory. **2.** reputation for worthy behavior. **3.** a source of credit or distinction. **4.** a special privilege or favor. **5.** (*usually pl.*) high rank, dignity, or distinction. **6.** a deferential title, esp. of judges and mayors (prec. by *his, your,* etc.). **7.** high-minded character or principles. **8.** chastity. **9.** *Bridge, etc.* any one of the five highest trump cards. —*v.t.* **10.** to hold in high respect; revere. **11.** to confer honor upon. **12.** to worship. **13.** to show a courteous regard for. **14.** *Com.* to accept and pay (a draft, etc.) when due. Also, *Brit.* **hon′our.**

hon·or·a·ble (ŏn′ər ə bəl), *adj.* **1.** in accordance with principles of honor. **2.** noble or distinguished. **3.** (as a title of respect prefixed to the names of certain officials and others). **4.** bringing honor. —**hon′or·a·ble·ness,** *n.* —**hon′or·a·bly,** *adv.*

hon·o·rar·i·um (ŏn′ə râr′ĭ əm), *n., pl.* **-rariums, -raria** (-râr′ĭ ə). **1.** an honorary token fee. **2.** a fee for professional services.

hon·or·ar·y (ŏn′ə rĕr′ĭ), *adj.* **1.** given for honor only, without the usual duties, etc. **2.** holding a title or position conferred for honor only.

Hon·shu (hŏn′shōō), *n.* the chief island of Japan. 55,194,449 pop.; 88,851 sq. mi.

hooch (hōōch), *n.* *U.S. Slang.* **1.** alcoholic beverages. **2.** liquor illicitly made and sold.

hood[1] (hŏŏd), *n.* **1.** a soft covering for the head and neck. **2.** something resembling this. **3.** the cover over an automobile engine. —*v.t.* **4.** to cover with a hood. —**hood′ed,** *adj.*

hood[2] (hŏŏd), *n.* *Slang.* a hoodlum.

Hood (hŏŏd), *n.* **Mount,** a volcanic peak in N Oregon, in the Cascade Range. 11,253 ft.

-hood, a suffix denoting state, condition, character, nature, etc. (as in *childhood*) or a body of persons of a particular character or class (as in *sisterhood*).

hood·lum (hōōd′ləm), *n.* *U.S.* a petty gangster; ruffian. —**hood′lum·ism,** *n.*

hoo·doo (hōō′dōō), *n., pl.* **-doos,** *v.,* **-dooed, -dooing.** —*n.* **1.** voodoo. **2.** *Colloq.* a person or thing that brings bad luck. —*v.t.* **3.** *Colloq.* to cause bad luck to.

hood·wink (hŏŏd′wĭngk′), *v.t.* **1.** to deceive; humbug. **2.** to blindfold.

hoo·ey (hōō′ĭ), *U.S. Slang.* —*interj.* **1.** an exclamation of disapproval. —*n.* **2.** nonsense.

hoof (hŏŏf, hōōf), *n., pl.* **hoofs,** (*Rare*) **hooves;** *v.* —*n.* **1.** the horny covering of the foot of certain animals, as the ox, horse, etc. **2.** the entire foot of a horse, etc. —*v.i.* **3.** *Colloq.* to walk. **4.** *Colloq.* to dance. —**hoofed,** *adj.* —**hoof′er,** *n.*

hook (hŏŏk), *n.* **1.** a curved piece of metal or the like for catching, pulling, or sustaining something. **2.** a fishhook. **3.** a snare; trap. **4.** a sharp curve in the course of anything. **5.** a curved spit of land. **6.** *Golf.* a stroke which curves to the left of the player striking the ball. **7.** *Baseball.* a curve. **8.** *Boxing.* a swinging stroke or blow. **9.** *Music.* a stroke or line attached to the stem of eighth notes, etc. **10. by hook or by crook,** by any means. **11. on one's own hook,** *Slang.* on one's own responsibility. —*v.t.* **12.** to seize, fasten, or catch with a hook. **13.** *Slang.* to steal. **14.** to connect. —*v.i.* **15.** to become attached by a hook. **16.** to curve like a hook.

hook·ah (hŏŏk′ə), *n.* a tobacco pipe with a long, flexible tube by which the smoke is drawn through a vase of water and thus cooled. Also, **hook′a.**

hooked (hŏŏkt), *adj.* hook-shaped.

hooked rug, *U.S.* a rug made by drawing

loops of yarn or cloth through a foundation of burlap or the like.

hook·up (hŏŏk′ŭp′), *n.* **1.** *Radio.* a diagram of radio apparatus. **2.** connection.

hook·worm (hŏŏk′wûrm′), *n.* any of certain bloodsucking nematode worms, parasitic in the intestines.

hook·y (hŏŏk′ĭ), *n.* **—play hooky,** to be unjustifiably absent from school.

hoo·li·gan (hōō′lə gən), *Slang.* **—n. 1.** a hoodlum. **—adj. 2.** of or like hooligans. **—hoo′li·gan·ism,** *n.*

hoop (hŏŏp, hōōp), *n.* **1.** a circular band, esp. one to hold together the staves of a cask, etc. **2.** something resembling a hoop. **3.** a circular band of stiff material used to expand a woman's skirt. **—v.t. 4.** to bind with a hoop.

hoop skirt, a woman's skirt, made to stand out by an undergarment of flexible hoops connected by tapes.

hoo·ray (hŏŏ rā′), *interj., v.i., n.* hurrah.

hoose·gow (hōōs′gou), *n.* *U.S. Slang.* jail.

Hoo·sier (hōō′zhər), *n.* *U.S.* an inhabitant of Indiana.

hoot (hōōt), *v.i.* **1.** to shout, esp. in derision. **2.** (of an owl) to utter its cry. **—v.t. 3.** to assail with shouts of derision. **4.** to drive (*out, away, off*, etc.) by hooting. **—n. 5.** the cry of an owl. **6.** any similar sound. **7.** a shout, esp. of derision. **8.** a thing of no value.

Hoo·ver (hōō′vər), *n.* **Herbert Clark,** born 1874, 31st president of the U.S., 1929–33.

Hoover Dam, official name of **Boulder Dam.**

hop[1] (hŏp), *v.,* **hopped, hopping,** *n.* **—v.i. 1.** to leap, esp. on only one foot. **2.** to make a flight. **3.** *Colloq.* (of an airplane, etc.) to leave the ground. **—v.t. 4.** *Colloq.* to hop about, off, or over. **5.** to jump onto. **—n. 6.** a short leap, esp. on one foot. **7.** *Colloq.* a flight of an airplane. **8.** *Colloq.* a dance.

hop[2] (hŏp), *n., v.,* **hopped, hopping. —n. 1.** any of certain twining plants whose dried ripe cones are used in brewing, etc. **2.** (*pl.*) the cones. **—v.t. 3.** to treat with hops.

hope (hōp), *n., v.,* **hoped, hoping. —n. 1.** expectation of something desired. **2.** a particular instance of such expectation or desire. **3.** confidence in a future event. **4.** a person or thing that expectations are centered in. **—v.t. 5.** to look forward to with desire and confidence. **6.** to trust in the truth of a matter. **—v.i. 7.** to have an expectation of something desired.

hope·ful (hōp′fəl), *adj.* **1.** full of hope. **2.** exciting hope. **—n. 3.** a promising young person. **—hope′ful·ly,** *adv.* **—hope′ful·ness,** *n.*

hope·less (hōp′lĭs), *adj.* **1.** affording no hope. **2.** without hope; despairing. **—hope′less·ly,** *adv.* **—hope′less·ness,** *n.*

Ho·pi (hō′pĭ), *n., pl.* **-pis.** a member of a Pueblo tribe inhabiting stone-built towns in northern Arizona.

Hop·kins (hŏp′kĭnz), *n.* **1. Gerard Manley,** 1844–89, British poet. **2. Harry Lloyd,** 1890–1946, U.S. political official.

hopped up, *U.S. Slang.* very excited.

hop·per (hŏp′ər), *n.* **1.** one that hops. **2.** any one of various jumping insects. **3.** a funnel-shaped chamber in which materials are stored temporarily and later discharged through the bottom.

hop·scotch (hŏp′skŏch′), *n.* a children's game in which the player hops from one compartment to another of an oblong figure traced on the ground, without resting on a line.

Hor·ace (hŏr′ĭs, hŏr′-), *n.* 65–8 B.C., Roman lyric poet and satirist.

Ho·ra·tius (hə rā′shəs, hŏ-), *n.* *Rom. Legend.* a hero celebrated for his defense of the bridge over the Tiber against the Etruscans.

horde (hôrd), *n., v.,* **horded, hording. —n. 1.** a great multitude. **2.** a nomadic group. **—v.i. 3.** to gather in a horde.

hore·hound (hôr′hound′), *n.* **1.** a perennial herb with downy leaves and small whitish flowers containing a bitter medicinal juice. **2.** a brittle candy flavored with the extract of the herb.

ho·ri·zon (hə rī′zən), *n.* **1.** the line or circle which forms the apparent boundary between earth and sky. **2.** the limit or range of knowledge.

hor·i·zon·tal (hôr′ə zŏn′təl, hŏr′-), *adj.* **1.** at right angles to the vertical. **2.** flat; level. **—n.**

3. a horizontal line, plane, etc. **—hor′i·zon′tal·ly,** *adv.*

hor·mone (hôr′mōn), *n.* *Physiol.* any of various substances, formed in endocrine organs, which activate specifically receptive organs when transported to them by the body fluids.

horn (hôrn), *n.* **1.** a hard, often curved and pointed growth (usually one of a pair) on the heads of cattle, sheep, goats, antelope, etc. **2.** any hornlike projection or extremity. **3.** something formed from or resembling the horn of an animal. **4.** *Music.* a wind instrument usually made of metal. **5.** an instrument for sounding a warning signal. **6.** one of the extremities of the crescent moon. **—v.t. 7.** to furnish with horns. **—v.i. 8. horn in,** *U.S. Slang.* to intrude. **—adj. 9.** made of horn. **—horned,** *adj.*

Horn (hôrn), *n.* **Cape,** a headland on a small island at the S extremity of South America.

horn·blende (hôrn′blĕnd′), *n.* any of the common black or dark-colored aluminous varieties of certain hydrous silicate minerals.

horn·book (hôrn′bŏŏk′), *n.* **1.** a page containing the alphabet, etc., covered with a transparent sheet and fixed in a frame with a handle, formerly used in teaching children to read. **2.** a primer.

horned pout, a large-headed fresh-water catfish, one of the bullheads.

horned toad, any of various small, harmless lizards of western North America, with hornlike spines on the head and body.

hor·net (hôr′nĭt), *n.* any of certain large, strong, social wasps having an exceptionally severe sting.

horn of plenty, the cornucopia.

horn·pipe (hôrn′pīp′), *n.* **1.** an English folk clarinet. **2.** a lively dance, popular among sailors. **3.** a piece of music for or in the style of such a dance.

horn·swog·gle (hôrn′swŏg′əl), *v.t.,* **-gled, -gling.** *Slang.* to swindle, cheat, or hoax.

horn·y (hôr′nĭ), *adj.,* **hornier, horniest. 1.** hornlike through hardening; callous. **2.** consisting of a horn. **3.** having a horn or horns.

horol., horology.

ho·rol·o·gy (hō rŏl′ə jĭ), *n.* the art or science of making timepieces or of measuring time.

hor·o·scope (hôr′ə skōp′, hŏr′-), *n.* **1.** a diagram of the heavens for use in calculating nativities, etc. **2.** the art of foretelling events by observation of the stars and planets.

hor·ren·dous (hŏ rĕn′dəs, hŏ-), *adj.* dreadful; horrible. **—hor·ren′dous·ly,** *adv.*

hor·ri·ble (hôr′ə bəl, hŏr′-), *adj.* **1.** causing horror; dreadful. **2.** extremely unpleasant. **—hor′ri·ble·ness,** *n.* **—hor′ri·bly,** *adv.*

hor·rid (hôr′ĭd, hŏr′-), *adj.* **1.** dreadful; abominable. **2.** *Colloq.* extremely unpleasant. **—hor′rid·ly,** *adv.* **—hor′rid·ness,** *n.*

hor·ri·fy (hôr′ə fī′, hŏr′-), *v.t.,* **-fied, -fying.** to cause to feel horror; shock intensely.

hor·ror (hôr′ər, hŏr′-), *n.* **1.** a shuddering fear or abhorrence. **2.** anything that excites such a feeling. **3.** a painful or intense aversion or repugnance.

hors d'oeu·vre (ôr dœ′vr), *pl.* **d'oeuvres** (dœ′vr). a relish such as olives or radishes, served before or between the regular courses of a meal.

horse (hôrs), *n., pl.* **horses,** (*esp. collectively*) **horse,** *v.,* **horsed, horsing,** *adj.* **—n. 1.** a large, domesticated quadruped, employed as a beast of draft and burden and for carrying a rider. **2.** cavalry. **3.** something on which a person rides, sits, or exercises, as if on a horse's back. **4.** a frame, block, etc., with legs on which something is mounted. **—v.t. 5.** to provide with a horse or horses. **6.** to set on horseback. **—v.i. 7.** to mount or go on a horse. **8.** *Slang.* to joke boisterously. **—adj. 9.** unusually large for one of its kind.

horse·back (hôrs′băk′), *n.* **1.** the back of a horse. **—adv. 2.** on horseback.

horse·car (hôrs′kär′), *n.* *U.S.* a streetcar drawn by a horse or horses.

horse chestnut, 1. the shiny, brown, nutlike seed of certain ornamental trees bearing large leaves and upright clusters of showy flowers. **2.** the tree itself.

horse·fly (hôrs′flī′), *n., pl.* **-flies.** any of certain flies that bite horses; gadfly.

horse·hair (hôrs′hâr′), *n.* a hair, or the hair, of a horse, esp. from the mane or tail.

horse latitudes, *Naut.* the areas lying between the regions of westerly winds and of trade winds, marked by light variable winds and occasional calms.

horse·laugh (hôrs′lăf′, -läf′), *n.* a loud, coarse laugh.

horse·man (hôrs′mən), *n., pl.* **-men.** a rider on horseback. **—horse′man·ship′,** *n.*

horse·play (hôrs′plā′), *n.* rough or boisterous play.

horse·pow·er (hôrs′pou′ər), *n.* a unit for measuring power, or rate of work, equivalent to 550 foot-pounds per second.

horse·rad·ish (hôrs′răd′ĭsh), *n.* a cultivated plant whose pungent root is ground and used as a condiment and in medicine.

horse sense, *Colloq.* plain, practical sense.

horse·shoe (hôrs′shoo′), *n., v.,* **-shoed, -shoe-ing. —**n. 1. a U-shaped iron plate nailed to a horse's hoof to protect it. 2. something shaped like a horseshoe. 3.(*pl. construed as sing.*) a game using horseshoes or similar pieces, the object being to throw the piece so as to encircle an iron stake 30 or 40 feet away. **—**v.t. 4. to put horseshoes on.

horse·tail (hôrs′tāl′), *n.* any of certain perennial, herbaceous plants, characterized by hollow, jointed stems.

horse·whip (hôrs′hwĭp′), *n., v.,* **-whipped, -whipping. —**n. 1. a whip for controlling horses. **—**r.t. 2. to beat with a horsewhip.

hors·y (hôr′sĭ), *adj.,* **horsier, horsiest.** 1. of or like horses. 2. interested in horses, horse racing, etc. 3. *Slang.* gross in size, appearance, etc.

hort., 1. horticultural. 2. horticulture.

hor·ta·to·ry (hôr′tə tōr′ĭ), *adj.* encouraging; inciting. Also, **hor·ta·tive** (hôr′tə tĭv).

hor·ti·cul·ture (hôr′tə kŭl′chər), *n.* 1. the cultivation of a garden. 2. the science and art of cultivating garden plants. **—hor′ti·cul′tur·al,** *adj.* **—hor′ti·cul′tur·ist,** *n.*

ho·san·na (hō zăn′ə), *interj.* 1. an exclamation in praise of God or Christ. **—**n. 2. a cry of "hosanna." 3. an acclamation.

hose (hōz), *n., pl.* **hose** or (*Archaic*) **hosen,** *v.,* **hosed, hosing. —**n. 1. a stocking. 2. tights or breeches, formerly worn by men. 3. a flexible tube for conveying water, etc., to a desired point. **—**v.t. 4. to water, wash, or drench by means of a hose.

Ho·se·a (hō zē′ə, -zā′ə), *n.* 1. a Hebrew prophet of the 8th century B.C. 2. the first of the books of the minor prophets in the Old Testament.

ho·sier·y (hō′zhə rĭ), *n.* stockings.

hos·pice (hŏs′pĭs), *n.* a house of shelter or rest for pilgrims, strangers, etc.

hos·pi·ta·ble (hŏs′pĭ tə bəl *or, esp. Brit.,* hŏs-pĭt′ə bəl), *adj.* 1. inclined to or characterized by hospitality. 2. favorably receptive. **—hos′pi·ta·bly,** *adv.*

hos·pi·tal (hŏs′pĭ təl), *n.* an institution in which sick or injured persons are given medical or surgical treatment.

hos·pi·tal·i·ty (hŏs′pə tăl′ə tĭ), *n., pl.* **-ties.** the reception and entertainment of guests or strangers with liberality and kindness.

hos·pi·tal·ize (hŏs′pĭ tə līz′), *v.t.,* **-ized, -izing.** to place for care in a hospital. **—hos′pi·tal·i·za′-tion,** *n.*

host[1] (hōst), *n.* 1. one who entertains guests in his own home or elsewhere. 2. the landlord of an inn. 3. an animal or plant from which a parasite obtains nutrition.

host[2] (hōst), *n.* a great number.

Host (hōst), *n. Eccles.* the bread consecrated in the celebration of the Eucharist.

hos·tage (hŏs′tĭj), *n.* a person given or held as a security for the performance of certain actions. **—hos′tage·ship′,** *n.*

hos·tel (hŏs′təl), *n.* a supervised lodging place for young people traveling by bicycle or walking.

hos·tel·ry (hŏs′təl rĭ), *n., pl.* **-ries.** *Archaic.* an inn.

host·ess (hōs′tĭs), *n.* 1. a female host. 2. a woman employed in a restaurant or place of amusement to seat the guests, etc. 3. a paid dancing partner.

hos·tile (hŏs′təl; *Brit.* -tīl), *adj.* 1. opposed in feeling, action, or character; unfriendly. 2. of an enemy. **—hos′tile·ly,** *adv.*

hos·til·i·ty (hŏs tĭl′ə tĭ), *n., pl.* **-ties.** 1. enmity; antagonism. 2. (*pl.*) acts of warfare.

hos·tler (hŏs′lər, ŏs′lər), *n. Archaic,* one who takes care of horses, esp. at an inn.

hot (hŏt), *adj.,* **hotter, hottest,** *adv.* **—**adj. 1. having a high temperature. 2. actively conducting current. 3. having a sensation of great bodily heat. 4. sharp-tasting, as pepper. 5. ardent or vehement. 6. lustful. 7. violent. 8. strong or fresh, as a scent. 9. new. 10. following very closely. 11. *Jazz.* performed in an enthusiastic manner, with improvised or decorative additions to the original melody. 12. *Slang.* recently stolen or otherwise illegally obtained. **—**adv. 13. in a hot manner. **—hot′ly,** *adv.* **—hot′ness,** *n.*

hot air, *Slang.* empty, pretentious talk.

hot·bed (hŏt′bĕd′), *n.* 1. a bed of earth, heated by fermenting manure, etc., and usually covered with glass, for growing plants out of season. 2. a place favoring rapid growth.

hot·blood·ed (hŏt′blŭd′ĭd), *adj.* excitable; impetuous.

hot·box (hŏt′bŏks′), *n.* an overheated journal box, in a railroad car or locomotive.

hot cross bun, a bun with a cross of frosting on it, eaten chiefly during Lent.

hot dog, *Colloq.* a hot frankfurter or wiener (sausage), esp. as served in a split roll.

ho·tel (hō tĕl′), *n.* a house offering lodging, food, etc., for travelers, etc.

hot·foot (hŏt′foot′), *adv.* 1. with great speed. **—**v.i. 2. to go in great haste.

hot·head (hŏt′hĕd′), *n.* a hot-headed person.

hot·head·ed (hŏt′hĕd′ĭd), *adj.* impetuous; rash. **—hot′-head·ed·ly,** *adv.* **—hot′-head′-ed·ness,** *n.*

hot·house (hŏt′hous′), *n.* an artificially heated greenhouse for cultivating tender plants.

hot rod, *U.S. Slang.* a car (usually an old one) whose engine has been altered for increased speed.

Hot·ten·tot (hŏt′ən tŏt′), *n.* a member of a native South African yellowish-brown race.

hound (hound), *n.* 1. a dog of any of various breeds used in hunting. 2. *Slang.* an addict. **—**v.t. 3. to hunt or track, esp. with hounds. 4. to incite (a hound, etc.) to pursuit or attack; urge on.

hour (our), *n.* 1. a space of time equal to one 24th part of a day; 60 minutes. 2. a particular or appointed time. 3. the present time.

hour·glass (our′glăs′, -gläs′), *n.* an instrument for measuring time, consisting of two bulbs of glass joined by a narrow passage through which a quantity of sand runs in just an hour.

hou·ri (hoor′ĭ, hour′ĭ), *n., pl.* **-ris.** one of the beautiful virgins provided in paradise to all faithful Mohammedans.

hour·ly (our′lĭ), *adj.* 1. of, occurring, or done each successive hour. 2. continual. **—**adv. 3. every hour. 4. frequently.

house (*n.* hous; *v.* houz), *n., pl.* **houses** (hou′zĭz), *v.,* **housed, housing. —**n. 1. a building for habitation, rest, etc. 2. a household. 3. a building for any purpose. 4. a theater. 5. the audience of a theater, etc. 6. a family regarded as consisting of ancestors and descendants. 7. the building in which a legislative or deliberative body meets. 8. the body itself. 9. a commercial establishment. **—**v.t. 10. to provide with a house. 11. to shelter.

house·boat (hous′bōt′), *n.* a boat fitted up for use as a floating dwelling.

house·break·er (hous′brā′kər), *n.* one who breaks into and enters a house with a felonious intent. **—house′break′ing,** *n.*

house·bro·ken (hous′brō′kən), *adj.* trained to live indoors, as a dog.

house·fly (hous′flī′), *n., pl.* **-flies.** a common dipterous insect, found nearly all over the world.

house·hold (hous′hōld′, -ōld′), *n.* 1. the people of a house collectively. **—**adj. 2. domestic. **—house′hold′er,** *n.*

house·keep·er (hous′kē′pər), *n.* a woman who does or directs the work of a household. **—house′keep′ing,** *n.*

house·maid (hous′mād′), *n.* a female servant employed in general work in a household.

House of Commons, the elective house of the Parliament of Great Britain and Northern Ireland.

House of Delegates, the lower house of the General Assembly in Virginia, West Virginia, and Maryland.

House of Lords, the nonelective house of the Parliament of Great Britain and Northern Ireland.

House of Representatives, the lower legislative branch in national and state governing bodies, as in the United States, Australia, etc.

house·warm·ing (hous/wôr/mĭng), *n.* a party to celebrate occupancy of a new house.

house·wife (hous/wīf/), *n., pl.* **-wives** (-wīvz/). the woman in charge of a household. **—house/-wife/ly,** *adj.*

house·wif·er·y (hous/wī/fə rĭ, -wīf/rĭ, hŭz/ʔf-rĭ), *n.* the function or work of a housewife.

house·work (hous/wûrk/), *n.* the cleaning, cooking, etc., to be done in housekeeping.

hous·ing (hou/zĭng), *n.* 1. a shelter, covering, or the like. 2. houses collectively. 3. *Mach.* a frame, plate, or the like, that supports a part of a machine, etc.

Hous·man (hous/mən), *n.* **Alfred Edward,** 1859–1936, British poet.

Hous·ton (hū/stən), *n.* 1. **Sam,** 1793–1863, U.S. frontier hero and soldier. 2. a city in SE Texas. 384,415.

hov·el (hŭv/əl, hŏv/-), *n., v.,* **-eled, -eling,** or (*esp. Brit.*) **-elled, -elling.** *—n.* 1. a small, mean dwelling house. *—v.t.* 2. to lodge in a hovel.

hov·er (hŭv/ər, hŏv/-), *v.i.* 1. to hang fluttering or suspended in the air. 2. to keep lingering about. 3. to waver. *—n.* 4. act of hovering. 5. state of hovering.

how (hou), *adv.* 1. in what way or manner. 2. to what extent, degree, etc. 3. at what price. 4. in what condition. 5. why. 6. with what meaning. 7. what? *—n.* 8. a question beginning with "how." 9. way or manner of doing.

how·be·it (hou bē/ĭt), *adv.* nevertheless.

Howe (hou), *n.* **Elias,** 1819–67, U.S. inventor (of the sewing machine).

How·ells (hou/əlz), *n.* **William Dean,** 1837–1920, U.S. novelist and editor.

how·ev·er (hou ĕv/ər), *conj.* 1. nevertheless. *—adv.* 2. to whatever extent or degree. 3. in whatever manner.

how·itz·er (hou/ĭt sər), *n.* a short-barreled cannon, used esp. for curved fire.

howl (houl), *v.i.* 1. to utter a loud, prolonged, mournful cry, as that of a wolf. 2. to wail. *—v.t.* 3. to utter with howls. *—n.* 4. the cry of a dog, wolf, etc. 5. a wail.

howl·er (hou/lər), *n.* 1. one that howls. 2. *Colloq.* an especially ludicrous blunder.

how·so·ev·er (hou/sō ĕv/ər), *adv.* 1. to whatsoever extent. 2. in whatsoever manner.

hoy·den (hoi/dən), *n.* 1. a tomboy. *—adj.* 2. boisterous.

HP, horsepower. Also, **hp, H.P., h.p.**

H.Q., headquarters. Also, **h.q.**

hr., *pl.* **hrs.** hour; hours.

H.R., House of Representatives.

H.R.H., His (or Her) Royal Highness.

ht., height.

hub (hŭb), *n.* 1. the central part of a wheel, as that part into which the spokes are inserted. 2. the part in central position around which all else revolves. 3. **the Hub,** Boston, Mass.

hub·ba hub·ba (hŭb/ə hŭb/ə), *U.S. Slang.* an exclamation of liking or approval.

hub·bub (hŭb/ŭb), *n.* 1. a loud, confused noise, as of many voices. 2. tumult.

huck·a·back (hŭk/ə băk/), *n.* toweling of linen or cotton. Also, **huck.**

huck·le·ber·ry (hŭk/əl bĕr/ĭ), *n., pl.* **-ries.** 1. the dark-blue or black edible berry of any of certain shrubs of the heath family. 2. a shrub yielding such a berry.

huck·ster (hŭk/stər), *n.* Also, **huck/ster·er.** 1. a hawker or peddler. 2. *U.S. Slang.* an advertising man. *—v.i.* 3. to deal in small articles.

hud·dle (hŭd/əl), *v.,* **-dled, -dling,** *n.* *—v.t., v.i.* 1. to crowd together confusedly. 2. to draw (oneself) closely together. *—n.* 3. a confused heap, mass, or crowd. 4. *Colloq.* a secret conference. 5. *Football.* a gathering of the team behind the scrimmage line for instructions, signals, etc.

Hud·son (hŭd/sən), *n.* 1. **Henry,** died 1611?, British navigator and explorer in North America. 2. **William Henry,** 1841–1922, British author. 3. a river in E New York, flowing S to New York Bay. 306 mi.

Hudson Bay, a large inland sea in N Canada. ab. 850 mi. long; ab. 600 mi. wide.

Hudson seal, muskrat fur which has been plucked and dyed to resemble seal.

hue¹ (hū), *n.* 1. that property of color by which the various regions of the spectrum are distinguished, as red, blue, etc. 2. variety of a color. 3. color.

hue² (hū), *n.* outcry, as of pursuers.

hue and cry, the pursuit of an offender with outcries to give an alarm.

hued (hūd), *adj.* having a hue or color.

huff (hŭf), *n.* 1. a sudden fit of anger. *—v.t., v.i.* 2. to make or become angry. **—huff/y,** *adj.*

hug (hŭg), *v.,* **hugged, hugging,** *n.* *—v.t.* 1. to clasp tightly in the arms, esp. with affection. 2. to cling firmly to. 3. to keep close to. *—v.i.* 4. to cling together. *—n.* 5. a tight clasp with the arms.

huge (hūj), *adj.,* **huger, hugest.** extraordinarily large in bulk, quantity, or extent. **—huge/ly,** *adv.* **—huge/ness,** *n.*

hug·ger-mug·ger (hŭg/ər mŭg/ər), *n.* 1. disorder or confusion. *—adj.* 2. secret. 3. disorderly or confused. *—v.t.* 4. to keep secret. *—v.i.* 5. to act secretly.

Hughes (hūz), *n.* **Charles Evans,** 1862–1948, U.S. statesman: chief justice of U.S. Supreme Court, 1930–41.

Hu·go (hū/gō), *n.* **Victor Marie,** 1802–85, French poet, novelist, and dramatist.

Hu·gue·not (hū/gə nŏt/), *n.* a member of the Reformed or Calvinistic communion of France in the 16th and 17th centuries.

hu·la-hu·la (hōō/lə hōō/lə), *n.* a native Hawaiian dance with intricate arm movements which tell a story in pantomime. Also, **hu/la.**

hulk (hŭlk), *n.* 1. the body of an old or dismantled ship. 2. a dismasted wreck. 3. a bulky person or mass. *—v.i.* 4. to loom in bulky form.

hulk·ing (hŭl/kĭng), *adj.* bulky; heavy and clumsy. Also, **hulk/y.**

hull¹ (hŭl), *n.* 1. the husk, shell, or outer covering of a seed or fruit. *—v.t.* 2. to remove the hull of.

hull² (hŭl), *n.* 1. the frame or body of a ship. 2. *Aeron.* the fuselage of a flying boat.

Hull (hŭl), *n.* **Cordell,** born 1871, U.S. statesman.

hul·la·ba·loo (hŭl/ə bə lōō/), *n.* a clamorous noise or disturbance; an uproar.

hum (hŭm), *v.,* **hummed, humming,** *n.* *—v.i., v.t.* 1. to make a low, continuous, droning sound. 2. to sing with closed lips, without articulating words. 3. *Colloq.* to be in a state of busy activity. *—n.* 4. an inarticulate or indistinct murmur.

hu·man (hū/mən), *adj.* 1. of or pertaining to man. 2. having the nature of man. 3. of or pertaining to mankind generally. *—n.* 4. *Colloq.* or *Humorous.* a human being.

hu·mane (hū mān/), *adj.* 1. characterized by tenderness and compassion. 2. tending to refine; polite. **—hu·mane/ly,** *adv.* **—hu·mane/ness,** *n.*

hu·man·ism (hū/mə nĭz/əm), *n.* 1. any system or mode of thought or action in which human interests predominate. 2. devotion to or study of the humanities. **—hu/man·ist,** *n.* **—hu/man·is/tic,** *adj.*

hu·man·i·tar·i·an (hū măn/ə târ/ĭ ən), *adj.* 1. having regard to the interests of all mankind; broadly philanthropic. *—n.* 2. a philanthropist. **—hu·man/i·tar/i·an·ism/,** *n.*

hu·man·i·ty (hū măn/ə tĭ), *n., pl.* **-ties.** 1. the human race; mankind. 2. condition or quality of being human. 3. kindness; benevolence. 4. **the humanities, a.** the study of the Latin and Greek classics. **b.** the study of literature, philosophy, art, etc., as distinguished from the social and physical sciences.

hu·man·ize (hū/mə nīz/), *v.t., v.i.,* **-ized, -izing.** 1. to make or become humane. 2. to make or become human. **—hu/man·i·za/tion,** *n.*

hu·man·kind (hū/mən kīnd/), *n.* the human race.

hu·man·ly (hū/mən lĭ), *adv.* 1. by human means. 2. according to human knowledge.

hum·ble (hŭm/bəl, ŭm/-), *adj.,* **-bler, -blest,** *v.,* **-bled, -bling.** *—adj.* 1. low in station, grade of importance, etc. 2. modest; meek. 3. courteously respectful. 4. low in height, level, etc. *—v.t.* 5. to abase. 6. to make meek. **—hum/ble·ness,** *n.* **—hum/bly,** *adv.*

hum·bug (hŭm/bŭg), *n., v.,* **-bugged, -bugging.** *—n.* 1. a hoax; fraud. 2. quality of falseness or deception. 3. a cheat; impostor. *—v.t., v.i.* 4. to hoax; delude.

hum·bug·er·y (hŭm/bŭg/ə rĭ), *n.* sham.

hum·ding·er (hŭm dĭng/ər), *n.* *Slang.* a person or thing remarkable of its kind.

hum·drum (hŭm/drŭm/), *adj.* 1. lacking variety; dull. *—n.* 2. monotony. 3. tedious talk. 4. a dull boring fellow.

hu·mer·us (hū′mər əs), *n.*, *pl.* **-meri** (-mə rī′). *Anat.* the single long bone in the arm which extends from the shoulder to the elbow. —**hu′mer·al**, *adj.*

hu·mid (hū′mĭd), *adj.* moist or damp. —**hu′mid·ly**, *adv.* —**hu′mid·ness**, *n.*

hu·mid·i·fy (hū mĭd′ə fī′), *v.t.*, **-fied, -fying.** to make humid. —**hu·mid′i·fi·ca′tion**, *n.* —**hu·mid′i·fi′er**, *n.*

hu·mid·i·ty (hū mĭd′ə tY), *n.* **1.** humid condition. **2.** *Meteorol.* the ratio of the water vapor in the atmosphere to the amount required to saturate it at the same temperature.

hu·mi·dor (hū′mə dôr′), *n.* a container for tobacco, esp. cigars, fitted with means for keeping the tobacco suitably moist.

hu·mil·i·ate (hū mĭl′Y āt′), *v.t.*, **-ated, -ating.** to lower the pride or self-respect of. —**hu·mil′i·at′ing·ly**, *adv.* —**hu·mil′i·a′tion**, *n.*

hu·mil·i·ty (hū mĭl′ə tY), *n.*, *pl.* **-ties.** a modest sense of one's own significance.

hum·ming·bird (hŭm′ĭng bûrd′), *n.* any of certain very small American birds characterized by narrow wings whose rapid vibration produces a hum.

hum·mock (hŭm′ək), *n.* **1.** a knoll or hillock. **2.** a ridge in an ice field.

hu·mor (hū′mər, ū′-), *n.* **1.** the quality of being funny. **2.** the faculty of perceiving or expressing the amusing. **3.** speech or writing showing this faculty. **4.** mental disposition. **5.** whim or caprice. **6.** *Biol.* any animal or plant fluid, such as the blood or lymph. —*v.t.* **7.** to indulge. **8.** to accommodate oneself to. Also, *Brit.*, **hu′mour.** —**hu′mor·less**, *adj.*

hu·mor·esque (hū′mə rĕsk′), *n.* a humorous or capricious musical composition.

hu·mor·ist (hū′mər Yst, ū′-), *n.* **1.** one who exercises the faculty of humor. **2.** a humorous writer, actor, etc.

hu·mor·ous (hū′mər əs, ū′-), *adj.* amusing; funny. —**hu′mor·ous·ly**, *adv.* —**hu′mor·ous·ness**, *n.*

hump (hŭmp), *n.* **1.** a rounded protuberance, esp. on the back, as that of the camel. **2.** a low, rounded rise of ground. —*v.t.* **3.** to raise (the back, etc.) in a hump. **4.** *U.S. Slang.* to exert (oneself) in a great effort. —*v.i.* **5.** to rise in a hump. **6.** *U.S. Slang.* to exert oneself.

hump·back (hŭmp′băk′), *n.* **1.** a back with a hump. **2.** one who has such a back. —**hump′-backed′**, *adj.*

humph (hŭmf), *interj.* an expression of disbelief, dissatisfaction, contempt, etc.

hu·mus (hū′məs), *n.* the dark organic material in soils, produced by the decomposition of vegetable or animal matter.

Hun (hŭn), *n.* **1.** a member of a warlike Asiatic people who devastated Eurppe in the 4th and 5th centuries. **2.** a destructive person.

hunch (hŭnch), *v.t.* **1.** to thrust out or up in a hump. —*v.i.* **2.** to lunge forward. —*n.* **3.** a hump. **4.** *U.S. Colloq.* a premonition or suspicion.

hunch·back (hŭnch′băk′), *n.* humpback (def. 2). —**hunch′backed′**, *adj.*

hun·dred (hŭn′drəd), *n.*, *pl.* **-dreds,** (*as after a numeral*) **-dred,** *adj.* —*n.* **1.** a cardinal number, ten times ten. **2.** a symbol for this number, as 100. **3.** a set of a hundred persons or things. —*adj.* **4.** amounting to one hundred in number.

hun·dred·fold (hŭn′drəd fōld′), *adj.*, *adv.* a hundred times as great or as much.

hun·dredth (hŭn′drədth), *adj.* **1.** next after the ninety-ninth. **2.** being one of a hundred equal parts. —*n.* **3.** a hundredth part, esp. of one ($^1/_{100}$). **4.** the hundredth of a series.

hun·dred·weight (hŭn′drəd wāt′), *n.*, *pl.* **-weights, -weight.** a unit of avoirdupois weight commonly equivalent in the U.S. to 100 pounds.

Hun·ga·ry (hŭng′gə rY), *n.* a republic in central Europe. 9,467,000 pop.; 35,926 sq. mi. *Cap.:* Budapest. —**Hun·gar·i·an** (hŭng gâr′Y ən), *adj.*, *n.*

hun·ger (hŭng′gər), *n.* **1.** the painful sensation caused by need of food. **2.** a need for food. **3.** strong or eager desire. —*v.i.* **4.** to be hungry. **5.** to have a strong desire. —*v.t.* **6.** to starve.

hunger strike, a persistent refusal to eat, as a form of protest.

hun·gry (hŭng′grY), *adj.*, **-grier, -griest. 1.** craving food. **2.** indicating hunger. **3.** strongly or eagerly desirous. —**hun′gri·ly**, *adv.* —**hung′-ri·ness**, *n.*

hunk (hŭngk), *n.* *Colloq.* a large piece.

hunk·y (hŭngk′Y), *adj.* *U.S. Slang.* **1.** Also, **hunk·y·do·ry** (hŭngk′Y dōr′Y). satisfactory; well. **2.** even; leaving no balance.

hunt (hŭnt), *v.t.*, *v.i.* **1.** to chase (game or other wild animals) for the purpose of catching or killing. **2.** to pursue with force, hostility, etc. **3.** to search (for); seek. —*n.* **4.** act of hunting game or other wild animals. **5.** a body of hunters. **6.** a search.

hunt·er (hŭn′tər), *n.* **1.** one who hunts game or other wild animals. **2.** a dog or horse used in hunting. —**hunt′ress**, *n. fem.*

Hun·ting·ton (hŭn′tĭng tən), *n.* a city in W West Virginia. 78,836.

hunts·man (hŭnts′mən), *n.*, *pl.* **-men.** *Chiefly Brit.* a hunter.

hur·dle (hûr′dəl), *n.*, *v.*, **-dled, -dling.** —*n.* **1.** a barrier in a race track, to be leaped by the contestants. **2.** a difficult problem. —*v.t.*, *v.i.* **3.** to leap over (a hurdle, etc.) as in a race. **4.** to master (a problem, etc.). —**hur′dler**, *n.*

hur·dy-gur·dy (hûr′dY gûr′dY), *n.*, *pl.* **-dies.** a barrel organ or similar instrument played by turning a crank.

hurl (hûrl), *v.t.*, *v.i.* **1.** to drive or throw (something) with great force. —*n.* **2.** a forcible or violent throw; a fling. —**hurl′er**, *n.*

hurl·y-burl·y (hûr′lY bûr′lY), *n.*, *pl.* **-burlies.** commotion; tumult.

Hu·ron (hyŏŏr′ən), *n.* **1.** Lake, a lake between Lakes Michigan and Erie. ab. 23,000 sq. mi. **2.** a member of an Indian tribe of the Iroquoian family, living east of Lake Huron.

hur·rah (hə rä′, -rô′), *interj.* **1.** an exclamation of joy, applause, or the like. —*v.i.* **2.** to shout "hurrah." —*n.* **3.** the exclamation "hurrah." Also, **hur·ray** (hə rā′).

hur·ri·cane (hûr′Y kān′), *n.* a violent tropical cyclonic storm.

hurricane deck, a light upper deck on passenger steamers, etc.

hur·ried (hûr′Yd), *adj.* **1.** driven to hurry. **2.** hasty. —**hur′ried·ly**, *adv.*

hur·ry (hûr′Y), *v.*, **-ried, -rying,** *n.*, *pl.* **-ries.** —*v.i.* **1.** to move, proceed, or act with haste. —*v.t.* **2.** to drive or move with speed. **3.** to hasten. —*n.* **4.** need or desire for haste. **5.** haste.

hur·ry-scur·ry (hûr′Y skûr′Y), *n.*, *pl.* **-ries.** headlong, disorderly haste. Also, **hur′ry-skur′ry.**

hurt (hûrt), *v.*, **hurt, hurting,** *n.* —*v.t.* **1.** to cause bodily injury or pain to. **2.** to damage or harm. **3.** to offend or grieve. —*v.i.* **4.** to cause pain, injury, damage, or harm. —*n.* **5.** an injury, damage, or harm.

hurt·ful (hûrt′fəl), *adj.* injurious; harmful. —**hurt′ful·ly**, *adv.* —**hurt′ful·ness**, *n.*

hur·tle (hûr′təl), *v.*, **-tled, -tling.** —*v.i.* **1.** to strike or rush violently. —*v.t.* **2.** to fling, dash, or collide with violently.

hus·band (hŭz′bənd), *n.* **1.** the man of a married pair. —*v.t.* **2.** to manage, esp. with prudent economy.

hus·band·man (hŭz′bənd mən), *n.*, *pl.* **-men.** a farmer.

hus·band·ry (hŭz′bən drY), *n.* **1.** agriculture; farming. **2.** frugality; thrift.

hush (hŭsh), *interj.* **1.** a command to be silent. —*v.i.* **2.** to become or be silent. —*v.t.* **3.** to make silent. **4.** to suppress mention of. —*n.* **5.** silence or quiet.

hush money, a bribe to keep silent about something.

husk (hŭsk), *n.* **1.** the dry external covering of certain fruits or seeds, esp. (*U.S.*) of an ear of corn. **2.** the outer part of anything, esp. when worthless. —*v.t.* **3.** to remove the husk from. —**husk′er**, *n.*

husking bee, *U.S.* a gathering of persons to assist in husking corn.

husk·y (hŭs′kY), *adj.*, **huskier, huskiest,** *n.*, *pl.* **huskies.** —*adj.* **1.** *U.S. Colloq.* big and strong. **2.** somewhat hoarse. **3.** abounding in husks. **4.** like husks. —*n.* **5.** *U.S. Colloq.* a big and strong person. —**husk′i·ly**, *adv.* —**husk′i·ness**, *n.*

Husk·y (hŭs′kY), *n.*, *pl.* **Huskies.** an Eskimo dog. Also, **husk′y.**

Huss (hŭs), *n.* **John,** 1369?–1415, Bohemian religious reformer and martyr.

hus·sar (hŏŏ zär′), *n.* (formerly) a member of a body of light cavalry, in European armies.

hus·sy (hŭs′ĭ, hŭz′ĭ), *n.*, *pl.* **-sies.** 1. an ill-behaved girl. 2. a worthless woman.

hus·tings (hŭs′tĭngz), *n. pl. or sing. Brit.* an electioneering platform.

hus·tle (hŭs′əl), *v.*, **-tled, -tling,** *n.* —*v.i.* 1. *Colloq.* to proceed or work rapidly or energetically. 2. to push or force one's way. —*v.t.* 3. to force or shove roughly or hurriedly. —*n.* 4. *Colloq.* energetic activity, as in work. 5. discourteous shoving, pushing, or jostling. —**hus′tler,** *n.*

hut (hŭt), *n.*, *v.*, **hutted, hutting.** —*n.* 1. a small, rough, or humble dwelling. —*v.t.*, *v.i.* 2. to lodge in a hut.

hutch (hŭch), *n.* 1. a pen for small animals. 2. a chest, box, or trough. —*v.t.* 3. to put away in a hutch; hoard.

Hux·ley (hŭks′lĭ), *n.* **Thomas Henry,** 1825–95, British biologist and writer.

huz·za (hə zä′), *interj.*, *n.*, *pl.* **-zas,** *v.*, **-zaed, -zaing.** —*interj.* 1. an exclamation of exultation, applause, or the like. —*n.* 2. the exclamation "huzza." —*v.i.* 3. to shout "huzza."

hy·a·cinth (hī′ə sĭnth), *n.* any of certain bulbous plants of the lily family, widely cultivated for their spikes of fragrant, bell-shaped flowers.

hy·brid (hī′brĭd), *n.* 1. the offspring of two animals or plants of different races, breeds, varieties, species, or genera. 2. anything derived from heterogeneous sources. —*adj.* 3. bred from two distinct races, breeds, varieties, etc. —**hy′brid·ism′,** *n.*

hy·brid·ize (hī′brə dīz′), *v.t.* **-ized, -izing.** 1. to cause to produce hybrids. 2. to form in a hybrid manner. —**hy′brid·i·za′tion,** *n.*

Hyde Park (hīd), 1. a park in London, England. 2. a village in SE New York: site of burial place of Franklin D. Roosevelt.

Hy·der·a·bad (hī′dər ə bäd′, -băd′, hī′drə-), *n.* 1. a province in the S part of India. 16,338,500 pop.; 82,313 sq. mi. 2. the capital of this province, in the central part. 739,159.

hy·dra (hī′drə), *n.*, *pl.* **-dras, -drae** (-drē). 1. (*cap. or l.c.*) *Gk. Myth.* a monstrous serpent, slain by Hercules, having nine heads, each of which was replaced by two after being cut off, unless the wound was cauterized. 2. *Zool.* any of certain fresh-water polyps. 3. any persistent evil. 4. (*cap.*) *Astron.* a southern constellation, representing a sea serpent.

hy·dran·gea (hī drān′jə, -drăn′jĭ ə), *n.* any of certain shrubs cultivated for their large showy flower clusters.

hy·drant (hī′drənt), *n.* a water pipe with a spout, nozzle, or other outlet, usually in the street.

hy·drate (hī′drāt), *n.*, *v.*, **-drated, -drating.** *Chem.* —*n.* 1. any of a class of compounds containing chemically combined water. —*v.t.* 2. to combine chemically with water. —**hy·dra′tion,** *n.*

hydraul., hydraulics.

hy·drau·lic (hī drô′lĭk), *adj.* 1. of, operated by, or employing water or other liquid. 2. pertaining to hydraulics. —**hy·drau′li·cal·ly,** *adv.*

hy·drau·lics (hī drô′lĭks), *n.* the science treating of the laws governing water or other liquids in motion and their applications in engineering.

hy·dride (hī′drīd, -drĭd), *n. Chem.* a compound of hydrogen with another element or a radical. Also, **hy·drid** (hī′drĭd).

hy·dro·car·bon (hī′drə kär′bən), *n. Chem.* any of a class of compounds containing only hydrogen and carbon, such as methane.

hy·dro·chlo·ric acid (hī′drə klôr′ĭk), a colorless gas, HCl, or an aqueous solution of it: much used industrially.

hy·dro·cy·an·ic acid (hī′drō sī ăn′ĭk), a colorless, poisonous liquid, HCN, with an odor like that of bitter almonds.

hy·dro·e·lec·tric (hī′drō ĭ lĕk′trĭk), *adj.* pertaining to the generation and distribution of electric energy derived from the energy of falling water or any other hydraulic source. —**hy·dro·e·lec·tric·i·ty** (hī′drō ĭ lĕk trĭs′ə tĭ), *n.*

hy·dro·flu·or·ic acid (hī′drō floo ôr′ĭk, -ŏr′-), a colorless, corrosive, volatile liquid.

hy·dro·gen (hī′drə jən), *n. Chem.* a colorless, odorless, inflammable gas, which combines chemically with oxygen to form water. *Symbol:* H; *at. wt.:* 1.008; *at. no.:* 1; *weight of one liter at 760 mm. pressure and 0°C.:* .08987 g. —**hy·drog·e·nous** (hī drŏj′ə nəs), *adj.*

hy·dro·gen·ate (hī′drə jə nāt′), *v.t.*, **-ated,**

-ating. to combine or treat with hydrogen. —**hy′dro·gen·a′tion,** *n.*

hydrogen bomb, a bomb whose potency is based on the release of nuclear energy resulting from the fusion of hydrogen isotopes in the formation of helium. It will, reputedly, be many times more powerful than the atom bomb.

hydrogen peroxide, a colorless, unstable, oily liquid, H_2O_2, the aqueous solution of which is used as an antiseptic and a bleaching agent.

hy·drog·ra·phy (hī drŏg′rə fĭ), *n.* the science of the measurement, description, and mapping of the surface waters of the earth. —**hy·drog′ra·pher,** *n.* —**hy·dro·graph·ic** (hī′drə grăf′ĭk), **hy′dro·graph′i·cal,** *adj.*

hy·drol·y·sis (hī drŏl′ə sĭs), *n.*, *pl.* **-ses** (-sēz′). chemical decomposition by which a compound is resolved into other compounds by taking up the elements of water. —**hy·dro·lyt·ic** (hī′drə lĭt′ĭk), *adj.* —**hy·dro·lyze** (hī′drə līz′), *v.t.*, *v.i.*

hy·drom·e·ter (hī drŏm′ə tər), *n.* a sealed cylinder with weighted bulb and graduated stem for determining the specific gravity of liquids by reading the level of the liquid on the emerging stem. —**hy·dro·met·ric** (hī′drə mĕt′rĭk), **hy′dro·met′ri·cal,** *adj.* —**hy·drom′e·try,** *n.*

hy·drop·a·thy (hī drŏp′ə thĭ), *n.* the treatment of disease by the external or internal use of water. —**hy·dro·path·ic** (hī′drə păth′ĭk), *adj.*

hy·dro·pho·bi·a (hī′drə fō′bĭ ə), *n. Pathol.* 1. rabies. 2. a morbid or unnatural dread of water. —**hy·dro·pho·bic** (hī′drə fō′bĭk, -fōb′ĭk), *adj.*

hy·dro·plane (hī′drə plān′), *n.*, *v.*, **-planed, -planing.** —*n.* 1. an airplane equipped to light upon or ascend from water. 2. a light, high-powered boat, designed to plane along the surface of water at very high speeds. —*v.i.* 3. to travel in a hydroplane.

hy·dro·pon·ics (hī′drə pŏn′ĭks), *n.* the cultivation of plants by placing the roots in liquid nutrient solutions rather than in soil.

hy·dro·sphere (hī′drə sfïr′), *n.* the water on the surface of the globe.

hy·dro·stat·ics (hī′drə stăt′ĭks), *n.* the statics of fluids, a branch of science usually confined to the equilibrium and pressure of liquids. —**hy′dro·stat′ic,** *adj.*

hy·dro·ther·a·py (hī′drə thĕr′ə pĭ), *n.* treatment of disease by means of water. —**hy·dro·the·rap·ic** (hī′drō thə răp′ĭk), *adj.*

hy·drous (hī′drəs), *adj.* containing water or its elements.

hy·drox·ide (hī drŏk′sīd, -sĭd), *n. Chem.* a compound containing the hydroxyl (OH) group. Also, **hy·drox·id** (hī drŏk′sĭd).

hy·drox·yl radical or **group** (hī drŏk′sĭl), *Chem.* a univalent radical or group, OH, containing hydrogen and oxygen.

hy·dro·zo·an (hī′drə zō′ən), *adj.* 1. pertaining to a class of coelenterates that comprises polyps and free-swimming medusae. —*n.* 2. a member of this class.

hy·e·na (hī ē′nə), *n.* any of certain nocturnal carnivores, which feed chiefly on carrion, found chiefly in Africa.

Hy·ge·ia (hī jē′ə), *n. Class. Myth.* the goddess of health.

hy·giene (hī′jēn, -jĭ ēn′), *n.* the science which deals with the preservation of health. —**hy′gi·en·ist,** *n.*

hy·gi·en·ic (hī′jĭ ĕn′ĭk, -jē′nĭk), *adj.* 1. sanitary. 2. pertaining to hygiene.

hy·gro·scope (hī′grə skōp′), *n.* an instrument indicating the approximate humidity of the air.

hy·gro·scop·ic (hī′grə skŏp′ĭk), *adj.* absorbing or attracting moisture from the air.

hy·la (hī′lə), *n.* a tree toad.

hy·men (hī′mən), *n. Anat.* a fold of mucous membrane partially closing the external orifice of the vagina in a virgin.

Hy·men (hī′mən), *n. Gk. Myth.* the god of marriage.

hy·me·ne·al (hī′mə nē′əl), *adj.* 1. pertaining to marriage. —*n.* 2. a marriage song.

hy·me·nop·ter·on (hī′mə nŏp′tər ən), *n.* a hymenopterous insect.

hy·me·nop·ter·ous (hī′mə nŏp′tər əs), *adj.* belonging or pertaining to an order of insects having (when winged) four membranous wings, and including the wasps, bees, ants, etc.

hymn (hĭm), *n.* 1. a song or ode in praise or honor of God, a deity, a nation, etc. —*v.t.* 2. to praise or express in a hymn. —*v.i.* **3.** to sing hymns.

hym·nal (hĭm′nəl), *n.* **1.** Also, **hymn′book′.** a book of hymns for use in divine worship. —*adj.* **2.** of or pertaining to hymns.

hym·nol·o·gy (hĭm nŏl′ə jĭ), *n.* the study of hymns, their history, etc,

hy·per·a·cid·i·ty (hī′pər ə sĭd′ə tĭ), *n.* excessive acidity, as of the gastric juice.

hy·per·bo·la (hī pûr′bə lə), *n., pl.* **-las.** *Geom.* a curve consisting of two distinct and similar branches, formed by the intersection of a plane with a right circular cone when the plane makes a greater angle with the base than does the generator of the cone.

hy·per·bo·le (hī pûr′bə lē′, -lĭ), *n.* *Rhet.* obvious exaggeration, for effect.

hy·per·bol·ic (hī′pər bŏl′ĭk), *adj.* **1.** exaggerated. **2.** exaggerating. —**hy′per·bol′i·cal·ly,** *adv.*

Hy·per·bo·re·an (hī′pər bōr′ĭ ən), *n.* **1.** *Gk. Legend.* one of a people supposed to live in a land of perpetual sunshine and plenty beyond the north wind. —*adj.* **2.** of or pertaining to the Hyperboreans. **3.** arctic or frigid.

hy·per·crit·i·cal (hī′pər krĭt′ə kəl), *adj.* excessively critical; overcritical.

hy·per·me·tro·pi·a (hī′pər mə trō′pĭ ə), *n.* *Pathol.* a condition of the eye in which parallel rays are focused behind the retina, distant objects being seen more distinctly than near ones; farsightedness.

hy·per·sen·si·tive (hī′pər sĕn′sə tĭv), *adj.* **1.** excessively sensitive. **2.** *Pathol.* allergic to a substance to which a normal individual does not react. —**hy′per·sen′si·tive·ness, hy′per·sen′si·tiv′i·ty,** *n.*

hy·per·ten·sion (hī′pər tĕn′shən), *n.* *Pathol.* **1.** elevation of the blood pressure, especially the diastolic pressure. **2.** an arterial disease of which this is the outstanding sign.

hy·per·thy·roid·ism (hī′pər thī′roi dĭz′əm), *n.* *Pathol.* overactivity of the thyroid gland. —**hy′per·thy′roid,** *n.*

hy·phen (hī′fən), *n.* **1.** a short line (-) used to connect the parts of a compound word or the parts of a word divided for any purpose, as for syllabication. —*v.t.* **2.** to hyphenate.

hy·phen·ate (hī′fə nāt′), *v.,* **-ated, -ating,** *adj.* —*v.t.* **1.** to join by a hyphen. **2.** to write with a hyphen. —*adj.* **3.** hyphenated. —**hy′phen·a′tion,** *n.*

hyp·no·sis (hĭp nō′sĭs), *n., pl.* **-ses** (-sēz). *Psychol.* a condition or state, allied to normal sleep, which can be artificially produced and is characterized by marked susceptibility to suggestion, loss of will power, etc.

hyp·not·ic (hĭp nŏt′ĭk), *adj.* **1.** pertaining to hypnosis or hypnotism. **2.** inducing sleep. —*n.* **3.** an agent or drug that produces sleep. **4.** one subject to hypnotic influence. —**hyp·not′i·cal·ly,** *adv.*

hyp·no·tism (hĭp′nə tĭz′əm), *n.* the science dealing with the induction of hypnosis.

hyp·no·tize (hĭp′nə tīz′), *v.t.,* **-tized, -tizing.** to put in a hypnotic state. —**hyp′no·tist,** *n.*

hy·po[1] (hī′pō), *n.* *Chem.* sodium thiosulfate, a photographic fixing agent.

hy·po[2] (hī′pō), *n.* *Slang.* a hypodermic needle or injection.

hy·po·chlo·rous acid (hī′pə klōr′əs, hĭp′ə-), *Chem.* an acid, HClO, whose solutions have strong bleaching properties.

hy·po·chon·dri·a (hī′pə kŏn′drĭ ə, hĭp′ə-), *n.* *Psychiatry.* a morbid condition characterized by depressed spirits and fancies of ill health.

hy·po·chon·dri·ac (hī′pə kŏn′drĭ ăk′, hĭp′ə-), *adj.* **1.** Also, **hy·po·chon·dri·a·cal** (hī′pō kŏn drī′ə kəl, hĭp′ō-). pertaining to or suffering from hypochondria. —*n.* **2.** a person suffering from hypochondria.

hy·poc·ri·sy (hĭ pŏk′rə sĭ), *n., pl.* **-sies.** **1.** act of pretending to have a character or beliefs, principles, etc., that one does not possess. **2.** pretense of virtue or piety; false goodness.

hyp·o·crite (hĭp′ə krĭt), *n.* one given to hypocrisy; one who feigns virtue or piety; a pretender. —**hyp′o·crit′i·cal,** *adj.* —**hyp′o·crit′i·cal·ly,** *adv.*

hy·po·der·mic (hī′pə dûr′mĭk), *adj.* **1.** characterized by the introduction of medical remedies under the skin. **2.** introduced under the skin, as a needle or syringe. **3.** pertaining to parts under the skin. —*n.* **4.** a hypodermic remedy or injection. **5.** a hypodermic syringe. —**hy′po·der′mi·cal·ly,** *adv.*

hy·po·gas·tri·um (hī′pə găs′trĭ əm, hĭp′ə-), *n., pl.* **-tria** (-trĭ ə). *Anat.* the lower part of the abdomen. —**hy′po·gas′tric,** *adj.*

hy·po·sul·fite (hī′pə sŭl′fīt), *n.* *Chem.* sodium thiosulfate, a bleach and photographic fixing agent.

hy·pot·e·nuse (hī pŏt′ə nūs′, -nōōs′), *n.* *Geom.* the side of a right triangle opposite the right angle. Also, **hy·poth·e·nuse** (hī pŏth′ə nūs′, -nōōs′, hĭ-).

hy·poth·e·cate (hī pŏth′ə kāt′, hĭ-), *v.t.,* **-cated, -catˀng.** to pledge as security without delivering over; mortgage. —**hy·poth′e·ca′tion,** *n.*

hy·poth·e·sis (hī pŏth′ə sĭs, hĭ-), *n., pl.* **-ses** (-sēz′). **1.** a proposed explanation for some phenomenon. **2.** a proposition assumed as a premise in an argument. **3.** a mere guess.

hy·poth·e·size (hī pŏth′ə sīz′, hĭ-), *v.,* **-sized, -sizing.** —*v.i.* **1.** to form a hypothesis. —*v.t.* **2.** to suppose by hypothesis.

hy·po·thet·i·cal (hī′pə thĕt′ə kəl), *adj.* **1.** assumed by hypothesis; supposed. **2.** involving hypothesis. **3.** conditional or conjectural. Also, **hy′po·thet′ic.** —**hy′po·thet′i·cal·ly,** *adv.*

hy·po·thy·roid·ism (hī′pō thī′roi dĭz′əm, hĭp′ō-), *n.* *Pathol.* abnormally diminished activity of the thyroid gland.

hy·son (hī′sən), *n.* a Chinese green tea.

hys·sop (hĭs′əp), *n.* an aromatic labiate herb with blue flowers.

hys·ter·ec·to·my (hĭs′tə rĕk′tə mĭ), *n., pl.* **-mies.** *Surg.* the excision of the uterus.

hys·te·ri·a (hĭs tĭr′ĭ ə, -tĕr′-), *n.* **1.** morbid or senseless emotionalism. **2.** a psychoneurotic disorder characterized by violent emotional outbreaks, perversion of sensory and motor functions, and various morbid effects due to autosuggestion.

hys·ter·ic (hĭs tĕr′ĭk), *n.* **1.** (*usually pl.*) a fit of hysteria; hysteria. —*adj.* **2.** hysterical.

hys·ter·i·cal (hĭs tĕr′ə kəl), *adj.* **1.** emotionally disordered. **2.** of, pertaining to, or characteristic of hysteria. **3.** suffering from or subject to hysteria. —**hys·ter′i·cal·ly,** *adv.*

hys·ter·ot·o·my (hĭs′tə rŏt′ə mĭ), *n., pl.* **-mies.** *Surg.* the operation of cutting into the uterus, as used in Caesarean section.

I

I[1], **i** (ī), *n., pl.* **I's or Is, i's or is.** **1.** the 9th letter of the English alphabet. **2.** Roman numeral for 1.

I[2] (ī), *pron., n., pl.* **I's.** —*pron.* **1.** the subject form of the singular pronoun of the first person, used by a speaker of himself. —*n.* **2.** the pronoun *I* used as a noun.

I, *Chem.* iodine.

I., **1.** Island; Islands. **2.** Isle; Isles.

Ia., Iowa.

i·amb (ī′ămb), *n.* *Pros.* a metrical foot of two syllables, a short followed by a long, or an unaccented by an accented.

i·am·bic (ī ăm′bĭk), *Pros.* —*adj.* **1.** pertaining to the iamb. **2.** consisting of or employing iambs. —*n.* **3.** an iamb. **4.** (*usually pl.*) a verse or poem consisting of iambs.

-ian, var. of **-an,** as in *Grecian.*

I·be·ri·a (ī bĭr′ĭ ə), *n.* a peninsula in SW Europe, comprising Spain and Portugal. Also, **Iberian Peninsula.** —**I·be′ri·an,** *adj., n.*

i·bex (ī′bĕks), *n., pl.* **ibexes, ibices** (ĭb′ə sēz′, ī′bə-), *(esp. collectively)* **ibex.** any of various Old World wild goats with large recurved horns.

i·bi·dem (ĭ bī′dĕm), *adv. Latin.* in the same book, chapter, page, etc. *Abbr.:* **ibid., ib.**

i·bis (ī′bĭs), *n., pl.* **ibises** (ī′bĭs ĭz), *(esp. collectively)* **ibis.** any of certain large wading birds of warm regions, allied to the herons and storks.

-ible, var. of **-able,** occurring in words taken from the Latin (as in *legible*), or modeled on the Latin type (as in *reducible*).

ibn-Sa·ud (ĭb′ən sä ōōd′), *n.* Abdul-Aziz, born 1880, king of Saudi Arabia since 1932.

Ib·sen (ĭb′sən), *n.* Henrik, 1828–1906, Norwegian dramatist and poet.

-ic, a suffix: **1.** forming adjectives from nouns or stems not used as words themselves, meaning "pertaining or belonging to" (*poetic, metallic, Homeric*), found extensively in adjective nouns of a similar type (*public, magic*), and in nouns the adjectives of which end in *-ical* (*music, critic*). **2.** *Chem.* showing that an element is present in a compound at a high valence, at least higher than when the suffix *-ous* is used.

-ical, a compound suffix forming adjectives from nouns, providing synonyms to words ending in *-ic,* and providing an adjective with additional meanings to those in the *-ic* form.

Ic·a·rus (ĭk′ə rəs, ī′kə-), *n. Gk. Legend.* the son of Daedalus. Together they escaped from Crete using wax wings, but Icarus, flying so high that the sun melted his wings, drowned in the Aegean.

I.C.C., Interstate Commerce Commission.

ice (īs), *n., v.,* **iced, icing,** *adj.* —*n.* **1.** the solid form of water, produced by freezing. **2.** any substance resembling this. **3.** *U.S.* a frozen dessert made of sweetened water and fruit juice. **4.** icing. **5.** formality. **6.** *Slang.* a diamond or diamonds. —*v.t., v.i.* **7.** to cover with ice. **8.** to change into ice. **9.** to cool with ice. —*adj.* **10.** of or pertaining to ice.

-ice, a suffix used in many nouns to indicate state or quality, as in *service, justice.*

ice·berg (īs′bûrg′), *n.* a large mass of ice, detached from a glacier and floating out to sea.

ice·boat (īs′bōt′), *n.* **1.** a triangular frame with runners, sails, etc., for sailing on ice. **2.** ice-breaker (def. 1).

ice·bound (īs′bound′), *adj.* **1.** held fast or hemmed in by ice. **2.** obstructed by ice.

ice·box (īs′bŏks′), *n.* a box or chest to hold ice for keeping food, etc., cool.

ice·break·er (īs′brā′kər), *n.* **1.** a strong ship for breaking channels through ice. **2.** a tool or machine for chopping ice into small pieces.

ice·cap (īs′kăp′), *n.* a cap of ice over an area (sometimes vast), sloping in all directions from the center.

ice cream, a frozen food made of cream (or a substitute), sweetened and variously flavored.

Ice·land (īs′lənd), *n.* a large island in the N Atlantic between Greenland and Denmark: formerly Danish, it has been an independent republic since 1944. 130,356 pop.; 39,698 sq. mi. *Cap.:* Reykjavik. —**Ice·land·er** (īs′lăn′dər, -lən dər), *n.*

Ice·lan·dic (īs lăn′dĭk), *adj.* **1.** pertaining to Iceland, its inhabitants, or their language. —*n.* **2.** the language of Iceland, a Scandinavian language.

ice·man (īs′măn′), *n., pl.* **-men** (-mĕn′). *U.S.* a man dealing in or delivering ice.

ice skate, (*usually pl.*) **1.** a thin metal runner attached to the shoe, for skating on ice. **2.** a shoe fitted with such a runner.

ice-skate (īs′skāt′), *v.i.,* **-skated, -skating.** to skate on ice.

ich·neu·mon (ĭk nū′mən, -nōō′-), *n.* a slender carnivorous mammal of Egypt, resembling the weasel in form and habits.

ichneumon fly, a hymenopterous insect whose larvae are parasitic on other larvae.

ich·thy·ol·o·gy (ĭk′thĭ ŏl′ə jĭ), *n.* the branch of zoölogy that treats of fishes. —**ich′thy·ol′o·gist,** *n.*

ich·thy·o·saur (ĭk′thĭ ə sôr′), *n.* any of an extinct order of fishlike marine reptiles.

ich·thy·o·sau·rus (ĭk′thĭ ə sôr′əs), *n., pl.* **-sauri** (-sôr′ī). ichthyosaur.

i·ci·cle (ī′sĭ kəl), *n.* a pendent tapering mass of

ice formed by the freezing of dripping water. —**i′ci·cled,** *adj.*

i·ci·ly (ī′sə lĭ), *adv.* in an icy manner.

i·ci·ness (ī′sĭ nĭs), *n.* state of being icy.

ic·ing (ī′sĭng), *n.* a preparation of sugar, egg whites, etc., as for covering cakes.

i·con (ī′kŏn), *n., pl.* **icons, icones** (ī′kə nēz′). **1.** a picture, image, or other representation. **2.** *Eastern Ch.* a representation of some sacred personage, itself venerated as sacred.

i·con·o·clast (ī kŏn′ə klăst′), *n.* **1.** an opponent of icon worship. **2.** one who attacks cherished beliefs as based on error or superstition. —**i·con′o·clas′tic,** *adj.*

i·cy (ī′sĭ), *adj.,* **icier, iciest. 1.** made of or covered with ice. **2.** resembling ice. **3.** cold. **4.** slippery. **5.** without warmth of feeling.

id (ĭd), *n. Psychoanal.* the part of the psyche residing in the unconscious which is the source of instinctive energy.

I'd (īd), contraction of *I would, I should,* or *I had.*

id., idem.

I·da·ho (ī′də hō′), *n.* a State in the NW United States. 472,314 pop.; 83,557 sq. mi. *Cap.:* Boise. *Abbr.:* Id., Ida. —**I′da·ho′an,** *n., adj.*

i·de·a (ī dē′ə), *n.* **1.** any conception existing in the mind. **2.** a thought or notion. **3.** an impression. **4.** an opinion, view, or belief.

i·de·al (ī dē′əl, ī dēl′), *n.* **1.** a conception of something in its highest perfection. **2.** a standard or model of perfection. —*adj.* **3.** constituting a standard of perfection. **4.** regarded as perfect in its kind. **5.** not real or practical; visionary.

i·de·al·ism (ī dē′ə lĭz′əm), *n.* **1.** the cherishing or pursuing of ideals. **2.** *Philos.* any theory which maintains that the real is of the nature of thought, or that the object of external perception consists of ideas. —**i·de′al·ist,** *n., adj.* —**i·de′al·is′tic,** *adj.*

i·de·al·ize (ī dē′ə līz′), *v.t.,* **-ized, -izing.** to represent in an ideal form; exalt to an ideal perfection. —**i·de′al·i·za′tion,** *n.*

i·de·al·ly (ī dē′ə lĭ), *adv.* **1.** in accordance with an ideal; perfectly. **2.** in idea.

i·dem (ī′dĕm, ĭd′ĕm), *pron., adj. Latin.* the same.

i·den·ti·cal (ī dĕn′tə kəl), *adj.* **1.** agreeing exactly. **2.** the same or being the same one. —**i·den′ti·cal·ly,** *adv.*

identical twin, one of a pair of twins of the same sex which develop from one fertilized ovum.

i·den·ti·fy (ī dĕn′tə fī′), *v.t.,* **-fied, -fying. 1.** to recognize or establish as being a particular person or thing. **2.** to make, represent to be, or regard or treat as identical. **3.** to associate in feeling, interest, action, etc. —**i·den′ti·fi′a·ble,** *adj.* —**i·den′ti·fi·ca′tion,** *n.*

i·den·ti·ty (ī dĕn′tə tĭ), *n., pl.* **-ties. 1.** state or fact of remaining the same one, as under varying conditions. **2.** condition of being oneself or itself. **3.** who a person or what a thing is. **4.** state or fact of being the same one. **5.** exact likeness.

i·de·ol·o·gy (ī′dĭ ŏl′ə jĭ, ĭd′ĭ-), *n., pl.* **-gies.** the body of doctrine, myth, and symbols of a social movement, institution, class, or large group.

ides (īdz), *n.pl.* (in the ancient Roman calendar) the 15th day of March, May, July, or October, and the 13th day of the other months.

id·i·o·cy (ĭd′ĭ ə sĭ), *n., pl.* **-cies. 1.** condition of being an idiot. **2.** senseless folly.

id·i·om (ĭd′ĭ əm), *n.* **1.** a form of expression peculiar to a language. **2.** a dialect. **3.** the language peculiar to a people. **4.** a distinct style or character, as in music, art, etc. —**id′i·o·mat′ic,** *adj.* —**id′i·o·mat′i·cal·ly,** *adv.*

id·i·o·syn·cra·sy (ĭd′ĭ ə sĭng′krə sĭ, -sĭn′-), *n., pl.* **-sies.** any tendency, characteristic, or the like, peculiar to an individual. —**id·i·o·syn·crat·ic** (ĭd′ĭ ə sĭn krăt′ĭk), *adj.*

id·i·ot (ĭd′ĭ ət), *n.* **1.** an utterly foolish person. **2.** one lacking the capacity to develop beyond the mental level of three or four years.

id·i·ot·ic (ĭd′ĭ ŏt′ĭk), *adj.* of or like an idiot; senselessly foolish. —**id′i·ot′i·cal·ly,** *adv.*

i·dle (ī′dəl), *adj.,* **idler, idlest,** *v.,* **idled, idling.** —*adj.* **1.** unemployed; doing nothing. **2.** unoccupied. **3.** of no real worth or importance. **4.** baseless or groundless. **5.** frivolous or vain. **6.** futile or ineffective. —*v.i.* **7.** to pass time in idleness. **8.** to move idly. **9.** *Mach.* to operate while the transmission is disengaged. —*v.t.* **10.** to pass (time) in idleness. —**i′dle·ness,** *n.* —**i′dler,** *n.* —**i′dly,** *adv.*

idle wheel, *Mach.* a cogwheel placed between two other cogwheels in order to transfer the motion of one to the other without changing the direction of rotation.

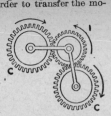

I. Idle wheel; C. Cogwheel

i·dol (ī′dəl), *n.* 1. an image or object to which religious worship is addressed. 2. *Bible.* a false god. 3. any person or thing blindly adored. 4. a fallacy.

i·dol·a·ter (ī dŏl′ə tər), *n.* 1. a worshiper of idols. 2. an adorer or devotee.

i·dol·a·try (ī dŏl′ə trĭ), *n., pl.* **-tries.** 1. the worship of idols. 2. blind adoration, reverence, or devotion. —**i·dol′a·trous,** *adj.* —**i·dol′a·trous·ly,** *adv.*

i·dol·ize (ī′də līz′), *v.t.* **-ized, -izing.** to worship as an idol. —**i′dol·i·za′tion,** *n.*

i·dyl (ī′dəl), *n.* 1. a poem or prose composition describing a charmingly simple pastoral scene or event. 2. material suitable for an idyl. Also, **i′dyll.**

i·dyl·lic (ī dĭl′ĭk), *adj.* 1. suitable for or suggestive of an idyl. 2. of, pertaining to, or of the nature of an idyl.

i.e., (Latin *id est*) that is.

if (ĭf), *conj.* 1. in case that; on condition that. 2. even though. 3. whether. —*n.* 4. a condition or supposition.

if·fy (ĭf′ĭ), *adj. Colloq.* doubtful.

ig·loo (ĭg′lōō), *n., pl.* **-loos.** an Eskimo hut, dome-shaped, built of snow. Also, **ig′lu.**

Ig·na·tius of Loy·o·la (ĭg nā′shəs, loi ō′lə), Saint, 1491–1556, Spanish soldier and priest: founder of the Jesuit order.

ig·ne·ous (ĭg′nĭ əs), *adj.* 1. *Geol.* produced under conditions involving intense heat, as rocks of volcanic origin. 2. of fire.

ig·nite (ĭg nīt′), *v.,* **-nited, -niting.** —*v.t.* 1. to set on fire; kindle. 2. *Chem.* to heat intensely. —*v.i.* 3. to take fire. —**ig·nit′er,** *n.*

ig·ni·tion (ĭg nĭsh′ən), *n.* 1. act of igniting. 2. state of being ignited. 3. (in an internal-combustion engine) the process which ignites the fuel in the cylinder.

ig·no·ble (ĭg nō′bəl), *adj.* 1. of low character, aims, quality, etc.; base. 2. of humble birth or station. —**ig·no′bly,** *adv.*

ig·no·min·i·ous (ĭg′nə mĭn′ĭ əs), *adj.* 1. discreditable; humiliating. 2. contemptible. —**ig′no·min′i·ous·ly,** *adv.*

ig·no·min·y (ĭg′nə mĭn′ĭ), *n., pl.* **-minies.** 1. disgrace; dishonor. 2. base quality or conduct.

ig·no·ra·mus (ĭg′nə rā′məs), *n., pl.* **-muses.** an ignorant person.

ig·no·rance (ĭg′nə rəns), *n.* lack of knowledge, learning, or information.

ig·no·rant (ĭg′nə rənt), *adj.* 1. lacking knowledge, learning, or information. 2. uninformed; unaware. 3. showing lack of knowledge. —**ig′no·rant·ly,** *adv.*

ig·nore (ĭg nōr′), *v.t.,* **-nored, -noring.** to refrain from noticing or recognizing.

Ig·o·rot (ĭg′ə rōt′, ē′gə-), *n., pl.* **-rot, -rots.** a member of a people of the Malay stock in northern Luzon, Philippine Islands. Also, **Ig·or·ro·te** (ē′gôr rō′tĕ).

i·gua·na (ĭ gwä′nə), *n.* any of certain large, arboreal, herbivorous lizards of tropical America, esteemed as food.

IHS, shortening of Greek ΙΗΣΟΤΣ Jesus.

i·kon (ī′kŏn), *n.* icon.

Il, *Chem.* illinium.

il·e·um (ĭl′ĭ əm), *n. Anat.* the third and lowest division of the small intestine.

i·lex (ī′lĕks), *n.* the holm oak.

Il·i·ad (ĭl′ĭ əd), *n.* a Greek epic poem describing the siege of Troy, ascribed to Homer.

-ility, a compound suffix making abstract nouns from adjectives by replacing the adj. suffixes: *-il(e)*, *-le*, as in *civility, sterility, ability.*

il·i·um (ĭl′ĭ əm), *n., pl.* **ilia** (ĭl′ĭ ə). *Anat.* the broad upper portion of either innominate bone.

ilk (ĭlk), *adj.* 1. same. 2. *Scot. and N. Eng.* each; every. —*n.* 3. family, class, or kind.

ill (ĭl), *adj.,* **worse, worst,** *n., adv.* —*adj.* 1. physically unwell; sick. 2. evil; wicked. 3. objection-

able; poor. 4. hostile. 5. unfavorable. —*n.* 6. evil. 7. harm or injury. 8. a disease or ailment. —*adv.* 9. wickedly. 10. unsatisfactorily or poorly. 11. with difficulty.

I'll (īl), contraction of *I will* or *I shall.*

Ill., Illinois.

ill., 1. illustrated. 2. illustration.

ill-ad·vised (ĭl′əd vīzd′), *adj.* acting or done without due consideration; imprudent.

ill-bred (ĭl′brĕd′), *adj.* showing or due to lack of proper breeding; rude.

il·le·gal (ĭ lē′gəl), *adj.* not legal; unauthorized. —**il·le·gal·i·ty** (ĭl′ē găl′ə tĭ), *n.* —**il·le′gal·ly,** *adv.*

il·leg·i·ble (ĭ lĕj′ə bəl), *adj.* impossible or hard to read or decipher. —**il·leg′i·bil′i·ty, il·leg′i·ble·ness,** *n.* —**il·leg′i·bly,** *adv.*

il·le·git·i·mate (ĭl′ĭ jĭt′ə mĭt), *adj.* 1. not legitimate; unlawful. 2. born out of wedlock. 3. irregular. —**il·le·git′i·mate·ly,** *adv.* —**il·le·git′i·ma·cy,** *n.*

ill-fat·ed (ĭl′fā′tĭd), *adj.* 1. destined to an unhappy fate. 2. bringing bad fortune.

ill-fa·vored (ĭl′fā′vərd), *adj.* not pleasant in appearance; ugly.

ill-got·ten (ĭl′gŏt′ən), *adj.* acquired by evil means.

ill humor, a disagreeable mood. —**ill′-hu′mored,** *adj.* —**ill′-hu′mored·ly,** *adv.*

il·lib·er·al (ĭ lĭb′ər əl), *adj.* 1. not generous. 2. narrow-minded. 3. without culture.

il·lic·it (ĭ lĭs′ĭt), *adj.* not licensed; unlawful. —**il·lic′it·ly,** *adv.*

il·lim·it·a·ble (ĭ lĭm′ĭt ə bəl), *adj.* limitless; boundless. —**il·lim′it·a·bly,** *adv.*

il·lin·i·um (ĭ lĭn′ĭ əm), *n. Chem.* a rare-earth element. *Symbol:* Il; *at. no.:* 61.

Il·li·nois (ĭl′ə noi′, -noiz′), *n.* a State in the central United States. 8,028,453 pop.; 56,400 sq. mi. *Cap.:* Springfield. *Abbr.:* Ill. —**Il′li·nois′an,** *n., adj.*

il·lit·er·a·cy (ĭ lĭt′ər ə sĭ), *n.* lack of ability to read and write.

il·lit·er·ate (ĭ lĭt′ər ĭt), *adj.* 1. unable to read and write. 2. lacking education. 3. showing lack of culture. —*n.* 4. an illiterate person. —**il·lit′er·ate·ly,** *adv.* —**il·lit′er·ate·ness,** *n.*

ill-man·nered (ĭl′măn′ərd), *adj.* having bad manners; impolite; rude.

ill-na·tured (ĭl′nā′chərd), *adj.* cross; unkindly; unpleasant. —**ill′-na′tured·ly,** *adv.*

ill·ness (ĭl′nĭs), *n.* 1. a state of bad health; sickness. 2. an attack of sickness.

il·log·i·cal (ĭ lŏj′ə kəl), *adj.* not logical; unreasonable. —**il·log′i·cal·ly,** *adv.*

ill-starred (ĭl′stärd′), *adj.* 1. ill-fated; unlucky. 2. disastrous.

ill temper, bad disposition. —**ill′-tem′pered,** *adj.* —**ill′-tem′pered·ness,** *n.*

ill-treat (ĭl′trēt′), *v.t.* to treat badly. —**ill′-treat′ment,** *n.*

il·lu·mi·nant (ĭ lōō′mə nənt), *n.* an illuminating agent or material.

il·lu·mi·nate (ĭ lōō′mə nāt′), *v.,* **-nated, -nating.** —*v.t.* 1. to supply with light. 2. to make lucid or clear. 3. to enlighten. 4. to decorate (a letter, page, etc.) with color, gold, or the like. —*v.i.* 5. to become illuminated. —**il·lu′mi·na′tive,** *adj.* —**il·lu′mi·na′tor,** *n.*

il·lu·mi·na·tion (ĭ lōō′mə nā′shən), *n.* 1. act of illuminating. 2. fact or condition of being illuminated. 3. a supply of light. 4. decoration with a painted design in color, gold, etc.

il·lu·mine (ĭ lōō′mĭn), *v.t., v.i.,* **-mined, -mining.** to illuminate or be illuminated.

illus., 1. illustrated. 2. illustration.

ill-use (*v.* ĭl′ūz′; *n.* ĭl′ūs′), *v.,* **-used, -using,** —*n.* —*v.t.* 1. to treat badly, unjustly, or cruelly. —*n.* 2. Also, **ill-us·age** (ĭl′ū′sĭj, -zĭj). bad, unjust, or cruel treatment.

il·lu·sion (ĭ lōō′zhən), *n.* 1. something that deceives by producing a false impression. 2. deception. 3. a false impression or belief. 4. *Psychol.* a perception of a thing which misrepresents it, or gives it qualities not present in reality. 5. a very thin, delicate kind of tulle.

il·lu·sive (ĭ lōō′sĭv), *adj.* illusory. —**il·lu′sive·ly,** *adv.* —**il·lu′sive·ness,** *n.*

il·lu·so·ry (ĭ lōō′sə rĭ), *adj.* causing illusion; deceptive; unreal. —**il·lu′so·ri·ly,** *adv.*

il·lus·trate (ĭl′ə strāt′, ĭ lŭs′trāt), *v.t.,* **-trated,**

illustration 225 **impairment**

-trating. 1. to make clear by examples. **2.** to furnish (a book, etc.) with pictures. —**il/lus·tra/tor,** *n.*

il·lus·tra·tion (ĭl/ə strā/shən), *n.* **1.** that which illustrates, as a picture in a book, etc. **2.** a comparison or example. **3.** explanation; elucidation.

il·lus·tra·tive (ĭ lŭs/trə tĭv, ĭl/ə strā/tĭv), *adj.* serving to illustrate. —**il·lus/tra·tive·ly,** *adv.*

il·lus·tri·ous (ĭ lŭs/trĭ əs), *adj.* **1.** renowned; famous. **2.** glorious, as deeds, etc. —**il·lus/tri·ous·ly,** *adv.* —**il·lus/tri·ous·ness,** *n.*

ill will, hostile or unfriendly feeling.

il·ly (ĭl/ĭ, ĭl/lĭ), *adv.* ill.

I'm (īm), contraction of *I am.*

im·age (ĭm/ĭj), *n., v.,* **-aged, -aging.** —*n.* **1.** a likeness of a person, animal, or thing. **2.** an optical counterpart. **3.** an idea or conception. **4.** *Psychol.* the reliving of a sensation in the absence of the original stimulus. **5.** *Rhet.* a figure of speech, esp. a metaphor or a simile. —*v.t.* **6.** to imagine; conceive. **7.** to make an image of. **8.** to describe. **9.** to mirror. **10.** to symbolize.

im·age·ry (ĭm/ĭj rĭ, ĭm/ĭj ə rĭ), *n., pl.* **-ries. 1.** the formation of images, or such images collectively. **2.** the use of rhetorical images. **3.** rhetorical images collectively.

im·ag·i·na·ble (ĭ măj/ə nə bəl), *adj.* capable of being imagined. —**im·ag/i·na·bly,** *adv.*

im·ag·i·nar·y (ĭ măj/ə nĕr/ĭ), *adj.* existing only in the imagination.

im·ag·i·na·tion (ĭ măj/ə nā/shən), *n.* **1.** the action or faculty of imagining. **2.** the product of imagining; a mental creation.

im·ag·i·na·tive (ĭ măj/ə nā/tĭv, -nə tĭv), *adj.* **1.** characterized by or showing imagination. **2.** pertaining to imagination. **3.** given to imagining. **4.** fanciful. —**im·ag/i·na·tive·ly,** *adv.*

im·ag·ine (ĭ măj/ĭn), *v.t., v.i.,* **-ined, -ining. 1.** to form a mental image of (something not actually present to the senses). **2.** to think, suppose, or guess. —**im·ag/in·er,** *n.*

im·ag·ism (ĭm/ə jĭz/əm), *n.* a method or movement in poetic composition, originating about 1912, which aimed particularly at clear pictures of what the poet has in mind without vagueness or symbolism. —**im/ag·ist,** *n., adj.*

im·be·cile (ĭm/bə sĭl), *n.* **1.** a person of defective mentality above the grade of idiocy. —*adj.* **2.** mentally feeble. **3.** absurd. —**im/be·cil/i·ty,** *n.*

im·bed (ĭm bĕd/), *v.t.,* **-bedded, -bedding.** embed.

im·bibe (ĭm bīb/), *v.t., v.i.,* **-bibed, -bibing. 1.** to drink. **2.** to absorb. —**im·bib/er,** *n.*

im·bro·glio (ĭm brōl/yō), *n., pl.* **-glios. 1.** a complicated situation. **2.** a complicated misunderstanding or disagreement.

im·brue (ĭm broō/), *v.t.,* **-brued, -bruing.** to stain, esp. with blood.

im·bue (ĭm bū/), *v.t.,* **-bued, -buing. 1.** to inspire, as with feelings. **2.** to saturate or impregnate.

im·i·ta·ble (ĭm/ə tə bəl), *adj.* that may be imitated. —**im/i·ta·bil/i·ty,** *n.*

im·i·tate (ĭm/ə tāt/), *v.t.,* **-tated, -tating. 1.** to follow or copy in action or manner. **2.** to mimic or counterfeit. —**im/i·ta/tor,** *n.*

im·i·ta·tion (ĭm/ə tā/shən), *n.* **1.** a result or product of imitating. **2.** act of imitating. —*adj.* **3.** made to imitate a genuine or superior article or thing.

im·i·ta·tive (ĭm/ə tā/tĭv), *adj.* **1.** imitating or copying. **2.** made in imitation of something. —**im/i·ta·tive·ly,** *adv.* —**im/i·ta·tive·ness,** *n.*

im·mac·u·late (ĭ măk/yə lĭt), *adj.* **1.** spotlessly clean, as linen. **2.** pure; undefiled. **3.** free from fault or flaw. —**im·mac/u·late·ly,** *adv.*

Immaculate Conception, *Rom. Cath. Ch.* the unique privilege by which the Virgin Mary was conceived in her mother's womb without the stain of original sin, through the anticipated merits of Jesus Christ.

im·ma·nent (ĭm/ə nənt), *adj.* remaining within; inherent. —**im/ma·nence, im/ma·nen·cy,** *n.* —**im/ma·nent·ly,** *adv.*

Im·man·u·el (ĭ măn/yōō əl), *n.* a name to be given to Christ as the son of a virgin.

im·ma·te·ri·al (ĭm/ə tĭr/ĭ əl), *adj.* **1.** unimportant. **2.** incorporeal; spiritual. —**im/ma·te/ri·al·ly,** *adv.*

im·ma·ture (ĭm/ə tyōōr/, -tōōr/), *adj.* not mature, ripe, developed, or perfected. —**im/ma·ture/ly,** *adv.* —**im/ma·tu/ri·ty,** *n.*

im·meas·ur·a·ble (ĭ mĕzh/ər ə bəl), *adj.* incapable of being measured; limitless. —**im·meas/ur·a·bly,** *adv.*

im·me·di·a·cy (ĭ mē/dĭ ə sĭ), *n.* the character of being immediate.

im·me·di·ate (ĭ mē/dĭ ĭt), *adj.* **1.** occurring or done without delay; instant. **2.** present. **3.** nearest or next. **4.** direct. —**im·me/di·ate·ly,** *adv.*

im·me·mo·ri·al (ĭm/ə mōr/ĭ əl), *adj.* extending back beyond memory, record, or knowledge. —**im/me·mo/ri·al·ly,** *adv.*

im·mense (ĭ mĕns/), *adj.* **1.** vast; huge. **2.** boundless. **3.** *Slang.* very good or fine. —**im·mense/ly,** *adv.* —**im·mense/ness, im·men/si·ty,** *n.*

im·merse (ĭ mûrs/), *v.t.,* **-mersed, -mersing. 1.** to plunge into a liquid; dip. **2.** to baptize by immersion. **3.** to involve deeply; absorb. —**im·mer·sion** (ĭ mûr/shən), *n.*

im·mi·grant (ĭm/ə grənt), *n.* **1.** one who immigrates. —*adj.* **2.** immigrating.

im·mi·grate (ĭm/ə grāt/), *v.i.,* **-grated, -grating.** to come into a new habitat or place of residence. —**im/mi·gra/tion,** *n.*

im·mi·nent (ĭm/ə nənt), *adj.* likely to occur at any moment; impending. —**im/mi·nence,** *n.* —**im/mi·nent·ly,** *adv.*

im·mo·bile (ĭ mō/bĭl, -bēl), *adj.* **1.** immovable. **2.** motionless. —**im/mo·bil/i·ty,** *n.*

im·mo·bi·lize (ĭ mō/bə līz/), *v.t.,* **-lized, -lizing.** to make immovable or motionless.

im·mod·er·ate (ĭ mŏd/ər ĭt), *adj.* excessive; extreme. —**im·mod/er·ate·ly,** *adv.*

im·mod·est (ĭ mŏd/ĭst), *adj.* **1.** indecent; shameless. **2.** forward; impudent. —**im·mod/est·ly,** *adv.* —**im·mod/es·ty,** *n.*

im·mo·late (ĭm/ə lāt/), *v.t.,* **-lated, -lating. 1.** to sacrifice. **2.** to kill as a sacrificial victim. —**im/mo·la/tion,** *n.* —**im/mo·la/tor,** *n.*

im·mor·al (ĭ mŏr/əl, ĭ môr/-), *adj.* not conforming to the moral law. —**im·mor/al·ly,** *adv.*

im·mo·ral·i·ty (ĭm/ə răl/ə tĭ), *n., pl.* **-ties. 1.** wickedness; vice. **2.** sexual impurity. **3.** an immoral act.

im·mor·tal (ĭ môr/təl), *adj.* **1.** not subject to death. **2.** imperishable or everlasting. **3.** perpetual. —*n.* **4.** an immortal being. **5.** a person, esp. an author, of enduring fame. **6.** (*usually pl.*) one of the gods of classical mythology. —**im·mor/tal·ly,** *adv.*

im·mor·tal·i·ty (ĭm/ôr tăl/ə tĭ), *n.* **1.** unending life. **2.** enduring fame.

im·mor·tal·ize (ĭ môr/tə līz/), *v.t.,* **-ized, -izing. 1.** to make immortal. **2.** to bestow unending fame upon. —**im·mor/tal·iz/er,** *n.*

im·mov·a·ble (ĭ moō/və bəl), *adj.* **1.** fixed; stationary. **2.** motionless. **3.** not subject to change. **4.** emotionless. **5.** steadfast; unyielding. **6.** not changing from one date to another in different years. —*n.* **7.** something immovable. **8.** (*pl.*) *Law.* lands and the appurtenances thereof, as trees, buildings, etc. —**im·mov/a·bil/i·ty,** *n.* —**im·mov/a·bly,** *adv.*

im·mune (ĭ mūn/), *adj.* **1.** protected from a disease or the like, as by inoculation. **2.** exempt. —*n.* **3.** one who is immune.

im·mu·ni·ty (ĭ mū/nə tĭ), *n., pl.* **-ties. 1.** state of being immune. **2.** exemption from obligation, service, taxation, etc.

im·mu·nize (ĭm/yə nīz/, ĭ mū/nīz), *v.t.,* **-nized, -nizing.** to make immune. —**im/mu·ni·za/tion,** *n.*

im·mu·nol·o·gy (ĭm/yōō nŏl/ə jĭ), *n.* that branch of medical science which deals with immunity from disease.

im·mure (ĭ myōōr/), *v.t.,* **-mured, -muring. 1.** to enclose within walls. **2.** to confine. **3.** to imprison. —**im·mure/ment,** *n.*

im·mu·ta·ble (ĭ mū/tə bəl), *adj.* unchangeable; unalterable. —**im·mu/ta·bil/i·ty,** *n.* —**im·mu/ta·bly,** *adv.*

imp (ĭmp), *n.* **1.** a little devil or demon. **2.** a mischievous child.

imp., 1. imperative. **2.** imperfect.

im·pact (*n.* ĭm/păkt; *v.* ĭm păkt/), *n.* **1.** the striking of one body against another. **2.** an impinging. —*v.t.* **3.** to drive or press closely or firmly into something.

im·pact·ed (ĭm păk/tĭd), *adj.* *Dentistry.* denoting a tooth incapable of growing out or erupting and remaining within the jawbone.

im·pair (ĭm pâr/), *v.t., v.i.* to diminish in value, excellence, etc.; weaken. —**im·pair/ment,** *n.*

im·pale (Ĭm pāl′), *v.t.*, **-paled, -paling. 1.** to fix upon a sharpened stake or the like. **2.** to pierce with a sharpened stake thrust up through the body, as for torture. —**im·pale′ment,** *n.*

im·pal·pa·ble (Ĭm păl′pə bəl), *adj.* **1.** incapable of being perceived by the sense of touch. **2.** incapable of being readily grasped by the mind. —im·pal′pa·bil′i·ty, *n.* —im·pal′pa·bly, *adv.*

im·pan·el (Ĭm păn′əl), *v.t.*, **-eled, -eling** or (*esp. Brit.*) **-elled, -elling. 1.** to enter on a list for jury duty. **2.** to select (a jury).

im·part (Ĭm pärt′), *v.t.* **1.** to tell. **2.** to give; bestow. —**im·part′er,** *n.*

im·par·tial (Ĭm pär′shəl), *adj.* unbiased; just. —im·par·ti·al·i·ty (Ĭm′pär shĭ ăl′ə tĭ), *n.* —im·par′tial·ly, *adv.*

im·pass·a·ble (Ĭm păs′ə bəl, -päs′-), *adj.* that cannot be passed over, through, or along. —im·pass′a·bil′i·ty, *n.* —im·pass′a·bly, *adv.*

im·passe (Ĭm păs′, Ĭm′păs), *n.* a position from which there is no escape.

im·pas·sioned (Ĭm păsh′ənd), *adj.* passionate; ardent. —**im·pas′sioned·ly,** *adv.*

im·pas·sive (Ĭm păs′Ĭv), *adj.* **1.** without emotion; apathetic. **2.** calm. —**im·pas′sive·ly,** *adv.* —im·pas·siv·i·ty (Ĭm′pă sĬv′ə tĬ), *n.*

im·pa·tience (Ĭm pā′shəns), *n.* **1.** lack of patience. **2.** restlessness. **3.** intolerance of anything that thwarts or hinders.

im·pa·tient (Ĭm pā′shənt), *adj.* **1.** not patient; not bearing pain, opposition, etc., with composure. **2.** indicating lack of patience. **3.** intolerant. **4.** restless in desire or expectation. —**im·pa′tient·ly,** *adv.*

im·peach (Ĭm pēch′), *v.t.* **1.** to accuse (a public official) before a tribunal of misconduct in office. **2.** to challenge the credibility of; doubt. —im·peach′a·ble, *adj.* —**im·peach′ment,** *n.*

im·pec·ca·ble (Ĭm pĕk′ə bəl), *adj.* **1.** faultless or irreproachable. **2.** not liable to sin. —im·pec′ca·bil′i·ty, *n.* —im·pec′ca·bly, *adv.*

im·pe·cu·ni·ous (Ĭm′pə kū′nĬ əs), *adj.* penniless; poor. —**im·pe·cu′ni·ous·ly,** *adv.*

im·ped·ance (Ĭm pē′dəns), *n. Elect.* the apparent resistance, or total opposition to current of an alternating-current circuit, consisting of two components, reactance and true or ohmic resistance.

im·pede (Ĭm pēd′), *v.t.*, **-peded, -peding.** to retard in progress; obstruct; hinder.

im·ped·i·ment (Ĭm pĕd′ə mənt), *n.* **1.** some physical defect. **2.** hindrance; obstacle.

im·ped·i·men·ta (Ĭm pĕd′ə mĕn′tə), *n.pl.* supplies carried with an army.

im·pel (Ĭm pĕl′), *v.t.*, **-pelled, -pelling.** to drive or urge forward. —**im·pel′ler,** *n.*

im·pend (Ĭm pĕnd′), *v.i.* **1.** to be imminent. **2.** to hang or be suspended.

im·pend·ing (Ĭm pĕn′dĬng), *adj.* **1.** about to happen; imminent. **2.** overhanging.

im·pen·e·tra·ble (Ĭm pĕn′ə trə bəl), *adj.* **1.** that cannot be penetrated, pierced, or entered. **2.** inaccessible to ideas, influences, etc. **3.** incomprehensible. —im·pen′e·tra·bil′i·ty, *n.* —im·pen′e·tra·bly, *adv.*

im·pen·i·tent (Ĭm pĕn′ə tənt), *adj.* not repentant; obdurate. —im·pen′i·tence, *n.* —im·pen′i·tent·ly, *adv.*

imper., imperative.

im·per·a·tive (Ĭm pĕr′ə tĬv), *adj.* **1.** not to be avoided or evaded. **2.** commanding. **3.** *Gram.* designating or pertaining to the verb mode specialized for use in command, requests, and the like, or a verb inflected for this mode. —*n.* **4.** a command. **5.** *Gram.* **a.** the imperative mode. **b.** a verb therein. —**im·per′a·tive·ly,** *adv.*

im·pe·ra·tor (Ĭm′pə rā′tər), *n.* **1.** an absolute or supreme ruler. **2.** an emperor.

im·per·cep·ti·ble (Ĭm′pər sĕp′tə bəl), *adj.* **1.** very slight, gradual, or subtle. **2.** not perceptible. —im′per·cep′ti·bly, *adv.*

imperf., imperfect.

im·per·fect (Ĭm pûr′fĬkt), *adj.* **1.** having a defect or defects. **2.** incomplete. **3.** *Gram.* denoting action or state still in process at some temporal point of reference. —*n.* **4.** *Gram.* **a.** the imperfect tense. **b.** a form therein. —im·per′fect·ly, *adv.* —**im·per′fect·ness,** *n.*

im·per·fec·tion (Ĭm′pər fĕk′shən), *n.* **1.** an imperfect detail. **2.** imperfect condition.

im·per·fo·rate (Ĭm pûr′fə rĬt, -rāt′), *adj.* having no perforation. Also, **im·per′fo·rat′ed.**

im·pe·ri·al (Ĭm pĬr′Ĭ əl), *adj.* **1.** of or pertaining to an empire, emperor, or empress. **2.** of a commanding quality, manner, or aspect. **3.** domineering; imperious. **4.** very fine or grand; magnificent. **5.** (of weights and measures) conforming to the standards legally established in Great Britain. —im·pe′ri·al·ly, *adv.*

im·pe·ri·al·ism (Ĭm pĬr′Ĭ ə lĬz′əm), *n.* the policy of extending the rule or authority of an empire or nation over foreign countries. —im·pe′ri·al·ist, *n., adj.* —im·pe′ri·al·is′tic, *adj.* —im·pe′ri·al·is′ti·cal·ly, *adv.*

im·per·il (Ĭm pĕr′əl), *v.t.*, **-iled, -iling** or (*esp. Brit.*) **-illed, -illing.** to endanger.

im·pe·ri·ous (Ĭm pĬr′Ĭ əs), *adj.* domineering; dictatorial, or overbearing. —im·pe′ri·ous·ly, *adv.* —im·pe′ri·ous·ness, *n.*

im·per·ish·a·ble (Ĭm pĕr′Ĭsh ə bəl), *adj.* not perishable; enduring. —im·per′ish·a·bly, *adv.*

im·per·ma·nent (Ĭm pûr′mə nənt), *adj.* not permanent. —im·per′ma·nen·cy, *n.*

im·per·me·a·ble (Ĭm pûr′mĬ ə bəl), *adj.* **1.** not passable. **2.** (of substances) not permitting the passage of a fluid through the pores, interstices, etc. —im·per′me·a·bil′i·ty, *n.* —im·per′me·a·bly, *adv.*

impers., impersonal.

im·per·son·al (Ĭm pûr′son əl), *adj.* **1.** without personal reference or connection. **2.** having no personality. **3.** *Gram.* (of a verb) having only third person singular forms. —*n.* **4.** *Gram.* an impersonal verb. —im·per′son·al·ly, *adv.*

im·per·son·ate (Ĭm pûr′sə nāt′), *v.t.*, **-ated, -ating. 1.** to pretend to be; act the part of. **2.** to personify; typify. —im·per′son·a′tion, *n.* —im·per′son·a′tor, *n.*

im·per·ti·nence (Ĭm pûr′tə nəns), *n.* **1.** unmannerly intrusion or presumption; insolence. **2.** irrelevance. Also, **im·per′ti·nen·cy.**

im·per·ti·nent (Ĭm pûr′tə nənt), *adj.* **1.** intrusive or presumptuous. **2.** not relevant. —im·per′ti·nent·ly, *adv.*

im·per·turb·a·ble (Ĭm′pər tûr′bə bəl), *adj.* not easily excited; calm. —im′per·turb′a·bil′i·ty, *n.* —im′per·turb′a·bly, *adv.*

im·per·vi·ous (Ĭm pûr′vĬ əs), *adj.* **1.** not pervious; impermeable. **2.** impenetrable. —im·per′vi·ous·ly, *adv.* —im·per′vi·ous·ness, *n.*

im·pet·u·ous (Ĭm pĕch′ŏŏ əs), *adj.* **1.** acting with sudden or rash energy. **2.** having great impetus; violent. —im·pet′u·ous·ly, *adv.* —im·pet′u·ous·ness, im·pet·u·os·i·ty (Ĭm pĕch′ŏŏ ŏs′ə tĬ), *n.*

im·pe·tus (Ĭm′pə təs), *n.* **1.** impulse; stimulus. **2.** the force with which a moving body tends to maintain its velocity and overcome resistance.

im·pi·e·ty (Ĭm pī′ə tĬ), *n., pl.* **-ties. 1.** lack of piety; ungodliness. **2.** lack of respect.

im·pinge (Ĭm pĬnj′), *v.i.*, **-pinged, -pinging. 1.** to strike; collide. **2.** to encroach. —im·pinge′ment, *n.*

im·pi·ous (Ĭm′pĬ əs), *adj.* lacking reverence for God. —im′pi·ous·ly, *adv.* —im′pi·ous·ness, *n.*

imp·ish (Ĭmp′Ĭsh), *adj.* of or like an imp; mischievous. —imp′ish·ly, *adv.* —imp′ish·ness, *n.*

im·pla·ca·ble (Ĭm plā′kə bəl, -plăk′ə-), *adj.* not to be appeased or pacified; inexorable. —im·pla′ca·bly, *adv.*

im·plant (Ĭm plănt′, -plänt′), *v.t.* **1.** to instill or inculcate. **2.** to insert. **3.** to plant. —im′plan·ta′tion, *n.*

im·ple·ment (*n.* Ĭm′plə mənt; *v.* -mĕnt′), *n.* **1.** an instrument, tool, or utensil. —*v.t.* **2.** to provide with implements. **3.** to execute or fulfill.

im·pli·cate (Ĭm′plə kāt′), *v.t.*, **-cated, -cating. 1.** to involve in some matter. **2.** to imply. **3.** to intertwine; interlace.

im·pli·ca·tion (Ĭm′plə kā′shən), *n.* **1.** act of implying. **2.** state of being implied. **3.** something implied or suggested; hint.

im·plic·it (Ĭm plĬs′Ĭt), *adj.* **1.** unquestioning, unreserved, or absolute. **2.** implied, rather than expressly stated. —im·plic′it·ly, *adv.*

im·plied (Ĭm plīd′), *adj.* involved, indicated, or suggested by implying.

im·plore (Ĭm plōr′), *v.t.*, **-plored, -ploring. 1.** to beseech; entreat. **2.** to make urgent supplication for (aid, mercy, etc.). —im·plor′ing·ly, *adv.*

im·ply (Ĭm plī′), *v.t.*, **-plied, -plying. 1.** to involve necessarily. **2.** to signify or mean. **3.** to indicate or suggest.

im·po·lite (Ĭm′pə līt′), *adj.* not courteous; uncivil; rude. —im′po·lite′ly, *adv.* —im′po·lite′ness, *n.*

im·pol·i·tic (Ĭm pŏl'ə tĭk), *adj.* inexpedient; injudicious. —**im·pol'i·tic·ly,** *adv.*

im·pon·der·a·ble (Ĭm pŏn'dər ə bəl), *adj.* **1.** that cannot be weighed or estimated. —*n.* **2.** an imponderable thing, force, or agency.

im·port (*v.* Ĭm pôrt', Ĭm'pôrt; *n.* Ĭm'pôrt), *v.t.* **1.** to bring in from a foreign country, as merchandise. **2.** to make known or mean. —*v.i.* **3.** to matter. —*n.* **4.** an imported commodity or article. **5.** act of importing. **6.** meaning. **7.** importance. —**im·port'er,** *n.*

im·por·tance (Ĭm pôr'təns), *n.* the quality or fact of being important; consequence.

im·por·tant (Ĭm pôr'tənt), *adj.* **1.** of much significance or consequence. **2.** prominent. **3.** of considerable influence or authority. **4.** pompous. —**im·por'tant·ly,** *adv.*

im·por·ta·tion (Ĭm'pôr tā'shən), *n.* **1.** the bringing in of merchandise from foreign countries. **2.** something imported.

im·por·tu·nate (Ĭm pôr'chə nĭt), *adj.* urgent or persistent in solicitation. —**im·por'tu·nate·ly,** *adv.* —**im·por'tu·nate·ness,** *n.*

im·por·tune (Ĭm'pôr tūn', -tōōn', Ĭm pôr'chən), *v.t., v.i.,* **-tuned, -tuning.** to beg urgently or persistently.

im·por·tu·ni·ty (Ĭm'pôr tū'nə tĭ, -tōō'-), *n., pl.* **-ties. 1.** persistence in solicitation. **2.** (*pl.*) importunate solicitations.

im·pose (Ĭm pōz'), *v.,* **-posed, -posing.** —*v.t.* **1.** to set (a tax, punishment, etc.) to be obeyed, fulfilled, etc. —*v.i.* **2.** to obtrude oneself or one's requirements, as upon others. **3.** to presume, as upon patience, etc. **4.** to deceive.

im·pos·ing (Ĭm pō'zĭng), *adj.* impressive in size, stateliness, etc. —**im·pos'ing·ly,** *adv.*

im·po·si·tion (Ĭm'pə zĭsh'ən), *n.* **1.** the laying on of something as a burden, obligation, etc. **2.** something imposed. **3.** an imposing upon a person, as by taking undue advantage of his good nature. **4.** act of imposing fraudulently or deceptively on others.

im·pos·si·bil·i·ty (Ĭm pŏs'ə bĭl'ə tĭ, Ĭm'pŏs-), *n., pl.* **-ties. 1.** the quality of being impossible. **2.** something impossible.

im·pos·si·ble (Ĭm pŏs'ə bəl), *adj.* **1.** that cannot be, exist, or happen. **2.** that cannot be done or effected. **3.** that cannot be true. **4.** not to be done, endured, etc. **5.** hopelessly difficult. —**im·pos'si·bly,** *adv.*

im·post (Ĭm'pōst), *n.* **1.** a tax, tribute, or duty. —*v.t.* **2.** to determine duties on.

im·pos·tor (Ĭm pŏs'tər), *n.* **1.** one who practices deception under an assumed character or name. **2.** a swindler.

im·pos·ture (Ĭm pŏs'chər), *n.* fraud; deception.

im·po·tence (Ĭm'pə təns), *n.* **1.** the condition or quality of being impotent; weakness. **2.** complete failure of sexual power, esp. in the male. **3.** *Obs.* lack of self-restraint. Also, **im'po·ten·cy.**

im·po·tent (Ĭm'pə tənt), *adj.* **1.** lacking power, ability, or effectiveness. **2.** feeble. **3.** wholly lacking in sexual power. —**im'po·tent·ly,** *adv.*

im·pound (Ĭm pound'), *v.t.* **1.** to shut up in a pound, as a stray animal. **2.** to confine. **3.** to seize and retain in custody of the law.

im·pov·er·ish (Ĭm pŏv'ər Ĭsh, -pŏv'rĬsh), *v.t.* **1.** to reduce to poverty. **2.** to exhaust the strength or richness of. —**im·pov'er·ish·ment,** *n.*

im·prac·ti·ca·ble (Ĭm prăk'tə kə bəl), *adj.* **1.** that cannot be put into practice with the available means. **2.** unsuitable for practical use. —**im·prac'ti·ca·bil'i·ty,** *n.* —**im·prac'ti·ca·bly,** *adv.*

im·prac·ti·cal (Ĭm prăk'tə kəl), *adj.* not practical.

im·pre·cate (Ĭm'prə kāt'), *v.t.,* **-cated, -cating.** to invoke (esp. evil or curses). —**im'pre·ca'tion,** *n.*

im·preg·na·ble (Ĭm prĕg'nə bəl), *adj.* **1.** strong enough to resist attack. **2.** not to be controverted. —**im·preg'na·bil'i·ty,** *n.* —**im·preg'na·bly,** *adv.*

im·preg·nate (*v.* Ĭm prĕg'nāt; *adj.* Ĭm prĕg'nĭt, -nāt), *v.,* **-nated, -nating,** *adj.* —*v.t.* **1.** to make pregnant. **2.** to fertilize. **3.** to fill with; saturate. —*adj.* **4.** impregnated. —**im'preg·na'tion,** *n.*

im·pre·sa·ri·o (Ĭm'prə sär'Ĭ ō'), *n., pl.* **-rios.** the manager of an opera or concert company.

im·press[1] (*v.* Ĭm prĕs'; *n.* Ĭm'prĕs), *v.,* **-pressed** or (*Archaic*) **-prest; -pressing;** *n.* —*v.t.* **1.** to affect or influence deeply. **2.** to fix firmly in the mind. **3.** to stamp; imprint. —*n.* **4.** act of impressing. **5.** a stamp; imprint. **6.** a distinctive character or effect imparted. —**im·press'i·ble,** *adj.*

im·press[2] (Ĭm prĕs'), *v.t.,* **-pressed** or (*Archaic*) **-prest, -pressing.** to force into public service, as seamen. —**im·press'ment,** *n.*

im·pres·sion (Ĭm prĕsh'ən), *n.* **1.** a strong effect produced on the intellect, feelings, or conscience. **2.** a notion, remembrance, or belief. **3.** a mark, indentation, figure, etc., produced by pressure. **4.** *Print., etc.* **a.** a printed copy from type, a plate, etc. **b.** one of a number of printings made at different times from the same set of type, without alteration. **5.** act of impressing. **6.** state of being impressed.

im·pres·sion·a·ble (Ĭm prĕsh'ən ə bəl, -prĕsh'-nə-), *adj.* easily impressed or influenced; susceptible. —**im·pres'sion·a·bil'i·ty,** *n.*

im·pres·sion·ism (Ĭm prĕsh'ə nĭz'əm), *n.* **1.** a way of painting (developed 1865–75) with informal subject matter and effects of light noted directly as they impress the artist. **2.** a late 19th and early 20th century method of musical composition, marked by the use of unorthodox means to express impressions or emotions. —**im·pres'sion·ist,** *n., adj.* —**im·pres'sion·is'tic,** *adj.*

im·pres·sive (Ĭm prĕs'Ĭv), *adj.* such as to impress the mind; remarkable. —**im·pres'sive·ly,** *adv.* —**im·pres'sive·ness,** *n.*

im·pri·ma·tur (Ĭm'prĬ mā'tər, -prī-), *n.* an official license to print a book, etc.

im·print (*n.* Ĭm'prĬnt; *v.* Ĭm prĬnt'), *n.* **1.** a mark made by pressure. **2.** the name and address of the printer or publisher, the date of publication, etc., usually on the title page. —*v.t.* **3.** to impress (a quality or mark). **4.** to fix firmly on the mind, memory, etc.

im·pris·on (Ĭm prĬz'ən), *v.t.* to put into a prison. —**im·pris'on·ment,** *n.*

im·prob·a·ble (Ĭm prŏb'ə bəl), *adj.* not likely to be true or to happen. —**im·prob'a·bil'i·ty,** *n.* —**im·prob'a·bly,** *adv.*

im·promp·tu (Ĭm prŏmp'tū, -tōō), *adj.* **1.** made or done without previous preparation. **2.** suddenly or hastily prepared, made, etc. —*adv.* **3.** without preparation. —*n.* **4.** something impromptu.

im·prop·er (Ĭm prŏp'ər), *adj.* **1.** not strictly belonging, applicable, or right. **2.** not in accordance with propriety of behavior, manners, etc. **3.** unsuitable or inappropriate. —**im·prop'er·ly,** *adv.*

improper fraction, a fraction with a numerator greater than the denominator.

im·pro·pri·e·ty (Ĭm'prə prī'ə tĬ), *n., pl.* **-ties. 1.** quality of being improper. **2.** inappropriateness. **3.** unseemliness.

im·prove (Ĭm prōōv'), *v.,* **-proved, -proving.** —*v.t.* **1.** to bring into a more desirable or excellent condition. **2.** to increase the value of (real property) by betterments. **3.** to make good use of. —*v.i.* **4.** to increase in value, excellence, etc. —**im·prov'a·ble,** *adj.* —**im·prov'er,** *n.*

im·prove·ment (Ĭm prōōv'mənt), *n.* **1.** the act of improving. **2.** the state of being improved. **3.** a change whereby a thing is improved.

im·prov·i·dent (Ĭm prŏv'ə dənt), *adj.* **1.** lacking foresight; incautious. **2.** neglecting to provide for future needs. —**im·prov'i·dence,** *n.* —**im·prov'i·dent·ly,** *adv.*

im·pro·vise (Ĭm'prə vīz'), *v.t., v.i.,* **-vised, -vising. 1.** to prepare offhand or hastily. **2.** to compose, recite, sing, etc., extemporaneously. —**im·pro·vi·sa·tion** (Ĭm'prə vĭ zā'shən, Ĭm'prŏv ə-), *n.* —**im'pro·vis'er,** *n.*

im·pru·dent (Ĭm prōō'dənt), *adj.* lacking prudence or discretion. —**im·pru'dence,** *n.* —**im·pru'dent·ly,** *adv.*

im·pu·dent (Ĭm'pyə dənt), *adj.* characterized by a shameless boldness, assurance, or effrontery. —**im'pu·dence, im'pu·den·cy,** *n.* —**im'pu·dent·ly,** *adv.*

im·pugn (Ĭm pūn'), *v.t.* to assail by words or arguments, as statements, motives, veracity, etc.

im·pulse (Ĭm'pŭls), *n.* **1.** the inciting influence of a particular feeling, mental state, etc. **2.** sudden, involuntary inclination prompting to action. **3.** an impelling action or force. **4.** *Physiol.* a stimulus conveyed by the nervous system, muscle fibers, etc. **5.** *Elect.* a single, usually sudden, flow of current in one direction.

im·pul·sion (Ĭm pŭl'shən), *n.* **1.** the act of impelling. **2.** impulse; impetus.

im·pul·sive (Ĭm pŭl'sĬv), *adj.* **1.** moved by impulses; impetuous. **2.** impelling. —**im·pul'sive·ly,** *adv.* —**im·pul'sive·ness,** *n.*

im·pu·ni·ty (ĭm pū'nə tĭ'), *n.* exemption from punishment.

im·pure (ĭm pyŏŏr'), *adj.* **1.** not pure; mixed with something else. **2.** ceremonially unclean. **3.** immoral or corrupt. —**im·pure'ly**, *adv.* —**im·pure'ness**, *n.*

im·pu·ri·ty (ĭm pyŏŏr'ə tĭ'), *n., pl.* **-ties. 1.** the quality or state of being impure. **2.** (*often pl.*) that which is or makes impure.

im·pute (ĭm pūt'), *v.t.*, **-puted, -puting.** to attribute, esp. something discreditable to (a person). —**im·pu·ta·tion** (ĭm'pyŏŏ tā'shən), *n.*

in (ĭn), *prep.* **1.** a particle expressing inclusion, situation, presence, existence, action, etc., within limits, as of place, time, circumstances, etc. —*adv.* **2.** in or into some place, position, state, relation, etc. **3.** within. **4.** in one's house or office. —*adj.* **5.** internal; inward; inbound. —*n.* **6.** (*pl.*) the political party in power.

in-, a prefix of Latin origin corresponding to English *un-*, having a negative or privative force, meaning "not or lacking" (as in *inexpensive, inconvenient*) or "the lack of" (as in *inaccuracy, indecorum*).

In, *Chem.* indium.

in., inch; inches.

in ab·sen·ti·a (ĭn ăb sĕn'shĭ ə), *Latin.* in or during (one's) absence.

in·ac·ti·vate (ĭn ăk'tə vāt'), *v.t.*, **-vated, -vating.** to make inactive.

in·ad·vert·ent (ĭn'əd vûr'tənt), *adj.* **1.** not attentive; heedless. **2.** characterized by lack of attention, as actions, etc. **3.** unintentional. —**in'ad·vert'ence, in'ad·vert'en·cy**, *n.* —**in'ad·vert'ent·ly**, *adv.*

in·al·ien·a·ble (ĭn āl'yən ə bəl), *adj.* not alienable; that cannot be transferred to another. —**in·al'ien·a·bil'i·ty**, *n.* —**in·al'ien·a·bly**, *adv.*

in·am·o·ra·ta (ĭn ăm'ə rä'tə, ĭn/ăm-), *n., pl.* **-tas.** a woman who loves or is loved.

in·am·o·ra·to (ĭn ăm'ə rä'tō, ĭn/ăm-), *n.* a male lover.

in·ane (ĭn ān'), *adj.* **1.** lacking sense; silly. **2.** empty; void. —*n.* **3.** that which is inane or void. —**in·ane'ly**, *adv.*

in·a·ni·tion (ĭn/ə nĭsh'ən), *n.* **1.** exhaustion from lack of nourishment. **2.** emptiness.

in·an·i·ty (ĭn ăn'ə tĭ'), *n., pl.* **-ties. 1.** lack of sense; silliness. **2.** an inane remark, etc. **3.** emptiness.

in·as·much as (ĭn'əz mŭch'), **1.** in view of the fact that; since. **2.** in so far as.

in·au·gu·ral (ĭn ô' ̣ə yə rəl, -gə rəl), *adj.* **1.** of or pertaining to an inauguration. —*n.* **2.** an address, as of a president, at the beginning of a term of office. **3.** inaugural ceremonies.

in·au·gu·rate (ĭn ô'gyə rāt', -gə-), *v.t.*, **-rated, -rating. 1.** to make a formal beginning of; begin. **2.** to induct into office with formal ceremonies. —**in·au'gu·ra'tion**, *n.* —**in·au'gu·ra'tor**, *n.*

in·board (ĭn'bōrd'), *adv., adj. Naut.* within the hull, or toward the center, of a ship.

in·born (ĭn'bôrn'), *adj.* native; innate.

in·bound (ĭn'bound'), *adj.* inward bound.

in·bred (ĭn'brĕd'), *adj.* **1.** innate; native. **2.** resulting from or involved in inbreeding.

in·breed (ĭn brēd'), *v.t.*, **-bred, -breeding.** to breed together closely related members of a family.

inc., 1. inclosure. **2.** including. **3.** inclusive. **4.** (*also cap.*) incorporated.

In·ca (ĭng'kə), *n.* one of the dominant groups of Peruvian Indians prior to the Spanish conquest. —**In'can**, *n., adj.*

in·can·desce (ĭn'kən dĕs'), *v.i., v.t.*, **-desced, -descing.** to glow or cause to glow.

in·can·des·cence (ĭn/kən dĕs'əns), *n.* the state of a body caused by approximately white heat, when it may be used as a source of artificial light.

in·can·des·cent (ĭn/kən dĕs'ənt), *adj.* **1.** (of light, etc.) produced by incandescence. **2.** glowing or white with heat. **3.** brilliant.

in·can·ta·tion (ĭn/kăn tā'shən), *n.* **1.** the chanting of words purporting to have magical power. **2.** a spell or charm. **3.** magical ceremonies.

in·ca·pac·i·tate (ĭn/kə păs'ə tāt'), *v.t.*, **-tated, -tating.** to make incapable or unfit; disqualify. —**in/ca·pac'i·ta'tion**, *n.*

in·car·cer·ate (ĭn kär'sə rāt'), *v.t.*, **-ated, -ating. 1.** to imprison; confine. **2.** to enclose. —**in·car/cer·a'tion**, *n.*

in·car·na·dine (ĭn kär'nə dīn', -dĭn), *adj., n., v.*, **-dined, -dining.** —*adj.* **1.** flesh-colored; pale red. **2.** crimson. —*n.* **3.** an incarnadine color. —*v.t.* **4.** to make incarnadine.

in·car·nate (*adj.* ĭn kär'nĭt, -nāt; *v.* ĭn kär'nāt), *adj., v.*, **-nated, -nating.** —*adj.* **1.** embodied in flesh. **2.** personified or typified. **3.** flesh-colored. —*v.t.* **4.** to put into concrete form. **5.** to be the embodiment or type of. **6.** to embody in flesh.

in·car·na·tion (ĭn/kär nā'shən), *n.* **1.** an incarnate being or form. **2.** assumption of human form, as by a divine being. **3.** a person or thing representing some quality, idea, etc., in typical form.

in·case (ĭn kās'), *v.t.*, **-cased, -casing.** to enclose in a case. —**in·case'ment**, *n.*

in·cen·di·a·rism (ĭn sĕn'dĭ ə rĭz'əm), *n.* act or practice of an incendiary.

in·cen·di·ar·y (ĭn sĕn'dĭ ĕr'ĭ), *adj., n., pl.* **-aries.** —*adj.* **1.** used for setting property on fire. **2.** of or pertaining to the criminal setting on fire of property. **3.** tending to arouse strife, sedition, etc. —*n.* **4.** one who maliciously sets fire to property. **5.** *Mil.* a shell containing phosphorus or similar material producing great heat. **6.** an agitator.

in·cense¹ (ĭn'sĕns), *n., v.*, **-censed, -censing.** —*n.* **1.** an aromatic gum or other substance producing a sweet odor when burned. **2.** a pleasant perfume or fragrance. —*v.t., v.i.* **3.** to burn incense (for).

in·cense² (ĭn sĕns'), *v.t.*, **-censed, -censing.** to make angry; enrage. —**in·cense'ment**, *n.*

in·cen·tive (ĭn sĕn'tĭv), *n.* **1.** that which incites to action, etc. —*adj.* **2.** inciting; provocative. —**in·cen'tive·ly**, *adv.*

in·cep·tion (ĭn sĕp'shən), *n.* beginning.

in·ces·sant (ĭn sĕs'ənt), *adj.* continuing without interruption. —**in·ces'sant·ly**, *adv.*

in·cest (ĭn'sĕst), *n.* sexual intercourse between persons related by blood or marriage within the degrees in which marriage is prohibited. —**in·ces·tu·ous** (ĭn sĕs'chŏŏ əs), *adj.*

inch (ĭnch), *n.* **1.** a unit of length, $1/12$ foot equivalent to 2.54 centimeters. **2.** a very small amount of anything. —*v.i., v.t.* **3.** to move by small degrees.

in·cho·ate (ĭn kō'ĭt), *adj.* just begun; incipient. —**in·cho'ate·ly**, *adv.*

inch·worm (ĭnch'wûrm'), *n.* measuring worm.

in·ci·dence (ĭn'sə dəns), *n.* **1.** the range or occurrence or influence of a thing, or the extent of its effects. **2.** the falling, or direction or manner of falling, of a ray of light, etc., on a surface

in·ci·dent (ĭn'sə dənt), *n.* **1.** an occurrence or event. **2.** an episode, as in a story. **3.** something that occurs casually in connection with some

in/a·bil'i·ty
in/ac·ces/si·bil'i·ty
in/ac·ces/si·ble
in/ac·ces/si·bly
in·ac'cu·ra·cy
in·ac'cu·rate
in·ac'cu·rate·ly
in·ac'cu·rate·ness
in·ac'tion
in·ac'tive
in·ac'tive·ly
in·ac'tiv·i·ty
in/ad·e'qua·cy
in·ad'e·quate
in·ad'e·quate·ly
in·ad'e·quate·ness
in/ad·mis/si·bil'i·ty
in/ad·mis/si·ble

in/ad·mis/si·bly
in/ad·vis/a·ble
in/ad·vis/a·bly
in·al/ien·a·bil'i·ty
in·al'ien·a·ble
in·al'ien·a·bly
in·an'i·mate
in·an'i·mate·ly
in/ap·pli·ca·bil'i·ty
in·ap'pli·ca·ble
in·ap'pli·ca·bly
in·ap'po·site
in/ap·pre'ci·a·ble
in/ap·pre'ci·a·bly
in/ap·pre'ci·a·tive
in/ap·proach'a·ble

in/ap·pro'pri·ate
in/ap·pro'pri·ate·ly
in/ap·pro'pri·ate·ness
in·apt'
in·apt'i·tude'
in·apt'ly
in·apt'ness
in/ar·tic'u·late
in/ar·tic'u·late·ly
in/ar·tic'u·late·ness
in/ar·tis'tic
in/ar·tis'ti·cal
in/ar·tis'ti·cal·ly
in/at·ten'tion
in/at·ten'tive
in/at·ten'tive·ly

in/at·ten'tive·ness
in·au/di·bil'i·ty
in·au'di·ble
in·au'di·bly
in/aus·pi'cious
in/aus·pi'cious·ly
in·cal/cu·la·ble
in·cal'cu·la·bly
in/ca·pa·bil'i·ty
in·ca'pa·ble
in·ca'pa·ble·ness
in·ca'pa·bly
in/ca·pac'i·ty
in·cau'tion
in·cau'tious
in·cau'tious·ly
in·cau'tious·ness
in·cer'ti·tude'

thing else. **—adj. 4.** likely or apt to happen. **5.** naturally belonging or connected.

in·ci·den·tal (ĭn/sə dĕn/təl), *adj.* **1.** happening or likely to happen in conjunction with something else. **2.** occurring by chance. **3.** subsidiary; secondary. **—n. 4.** something incidental.

in·ci·den·tal·ly (ĭn/sə dĕn/tə lĭ/), *adv.* **1.** in an incidental manner. **2.** by the way.

in·cin·er·ate (ĭn sĭn/ə rāt/), *v.t., v.i.,* **-ated, -ating.** to burn or reduce to ashes; cremate. **—in·cin/er·a/tion,** *n.*

in·cin·er·a·tor (ĭn sĭn/ə rā/tər), *n.* a furnace or apparatus for incinerating.

in·cip·i·ent (ĭn sĭp/ĭ ənt), *adj.* beginning to exist or appear. **—in·cip/i·ence, in·cip/i·en·cy,** *n.* **—in·cip/i·ent·ly,** *adv.*

in·cise (ĭn sīz/), *v.t.,* **-cised, -cising. 1.** to cut into. **2.** to engrave; carve.

in·ci·sion (ĭn sĭzh/ən), *n.* **1.** a cut, gash, or notch. **2.** act of incising. **3.** keenness.

in·ci·sive (ĭn sī/sĭv), *adj.* **1.** penetrating or biting. **2.** sharp; keen; acute. **—in·ci/sive·ly,** *adv.* **—in·ci/sive·ness,** *n.*

in·ci·sor (ĭn sī/zər), *n.* a tooth in the anterior part of the jaw adapted for cutting.

in·cite (ĭn sīt/), *v.t.,* **-cited, -citing.** to urge on; prompt to action. **—in·cite/ment,** *n.* **—in·cit/er,** *n.*

incl., 1. inclosure. **2.** including. **3.** inclusive.

in·cli·na·tion (ĭn/klə nā/shən), *n.* **1.** a bent, liking, or preference. **2.** act of inclining. **3.** state of being inclined. **4.** deviation from a normal direction or position. **5.** an inclined surface.

in·cline (*v.* ĭn klīn/; *n.* ĭn/klīn, ĭn klīn/), *v.,* **-clined, -clining,** *n.* **—v.i. 1.** to have a particular tendency. **2.** to deviate from the vertical or horizontal. **3.** to approximate. **4.** to lean; bend. **—v.t. 5.** to dispose (a person) in mind, etc. **6.** to bow or bend. **—n. 7.** an inclined surface; slope.

inclined plane, a plane surface inclined to the horizon, or forming with a horizontal plane any angle but a right angle.

in·cli·nom·e·ter (ĭn/klə nŏm/ə tər), *n.* **1.** *Aeron.* an instrument for measuring the angle an aircraft makes with the horizontal. **2.** an instrument for determining the inclination or dip of the earth's magnetic force by the dip of a magnetic needle.

in·close (ĭn klōz/), *v.t.,* **-closed, -closing.** enclose. **—in·clo·sure** (ĭn klō/zhər), *n.*

in·clude (ĭn klōōd/), *v.t.,* **-cluded, -cluding. 1.** to contain or comprise. **2.** to place in an aggregate, class, or the like. **3.** to involve as a factor.

in·clu·sion (ĭn klōō/zhən), *n.* **1.** act of including. **2.** state of being included. **3.** that which is included.

in·clu·sive (ĭn klōō/sĭv), *adj.* **1.** including the stated extremes. **2.** comprehensive. **3.** enclosing; embracing. **—in·clu/sive·ly,** *adv.* **—in·clu/sive·ness,** *n.*

in·cog·ni·to (ĭn kŏg/nə tō/), *adj., adv., n., pl.* **-tos. —adj. 1.** having one's identity concealed, as under an assumed name. **—n. 2.** with the real identity concealed. **—n. 3.** one who is incognito. **4.** state of being incognito.

in·come (ĭn/kŭm), *n.* the money that comes in periodically from property, business, labor, etc.; revenue.

in·com·ing (ĭn/kŭm/ĭng), *adj.* **1.** coming in. **2.** succeeding. **3.** entering.

in·com·mode (ĭn/kə mōd/), *v.t.,* **-moded, -mod-**

ing. 1. to inconvenience or discomfort. **2.** to impede; hinder.

in·com·mu·ni·ca·do (ĭn/kə mū/nə kä/dō), *adj.* (esp. of a prisoner) deprived of communication with others.

in·com·pa·ra·ble (ĭn kŏm/pə rə bəl, -prə bəl), *adj.* **1.** matchless or unequaled. **2.** not comparable. **—in·com/pa·ra·bly,** *adv.*

in·com·pe·tent (ĭn kŏm/pə tənt), *adj.* **1.** not competent; without ability. **2.** unqualified. **—n. 3.** an incompetent person. **—in·com/pe·tence,** *n.* **—in·com/pe·tent·ly,** *adv.*

in·con·ven·ience (ĭn/kən vēn/yəns), *n., v.,* **-ienced, -iencing. —n. 1.** quality or state of being inconvenient. **2.** an inconvenient circumstance or thing. **—v.t. 3.** to put to inconvenience.

in·con·ven·ient (ĭn/kən vēn/yənt), *adj.* awkward, inopportune, disadvantageous, or troublesome. **—in·con·ven/ient·ly,** *adv.*

in·cor·po·rate (*v.* ĭn kôr/pə rāt/; *adj.* ĭn kôr/pə rĭt, -prĭt), *v.,* **-rated, -rating,** *adj.* **—v.t., v.i. 1.** to create or form (a corporation). **2.** to put into a body or mass as an integral part or parts. **3.** to include as a part or parts, as the body or mass does. **—adj. 4.** incorporated, as a company. **—in·cor/po·ra/tion,** *n.* **—in·cor/po·ra/tor,** *n.*

in·cor·ri·gi·ble (ĭn kôr/ĭ jə bəl, -kŏr/-), *adj.* **1.** bad beyond correction or reform. **2.** willful; uncontrollable. **3.** firmly fixed. **—n. 4.** one who is incorrigible. **—in·cor/ri·gi·bil/i·ty,** *n.* **—in·cor/ri·gi·bly,** *adv.*

in·crease (*v.* ĭn krēs/; *n.* ĭn/krēs), *v.,* **-creased, -creasing,** *n.* **—v.t., v.i. 1.** to make or become greater in any respect; add to. **2.** to make or become more numerous. **3.** to multiply by propagation. **4.** *Poetic.* to wax, as the moon. **—n. 5.** growth or augmentation in numbers. **6.** production of offspring. **7.** act or process of increasing. **8.** that by which something is increased. **9.** the result of increasing. **—in·creas/er,** *n.* **—in·creas/ing·ly,** *adv.*

in·cred·i·ble (ĭn krĕd/ə bəl), *adj.* **1.** seeming too extraordinary to be possible. **2.** not credible. **—in·cred/i·bil/i·ty,** *n.* **—in·cred/i·bly,** *adv.*

in·cre·du·li·ty (ĭn/krə dū/lə tĭ, -dōō/-), *n.* quality of being incredulous; a refusal of belief.

in·cred·u·lous (ĭn krĕj/ə ləs), *adj.* **1.** indisposed to believe; skeptical. **2.** indicating unbelief. **—in·cred/u·lous·ly,** *adv.*

in·cre·ment (ĭn/krə mənt, ĭng/-), *n.* **1.** something added or gained. **2.** profit.

in·crim·i·nate (ĭn krĭm/ə nāt/), *v.t.,* **-nated, -nating. 1.** to charge with a crime or fault. **2.** to involve in an accusation. **—in·crim/i·na/tion,** *n.* **—in·crim/i·na/tor,** *n.* **—in·crim·i·na·to·ry** (ĭn krĭm/ə na tōr/ĭ), *adj.*

in·crust (ĭn krŭst/), *v.t.* **1.** to cover or line with a crust or hard coating. **2.** to form into a crust. **3.** to deposit as a crust. Also, **encrust. —in/crus·ta/tion,** *n.*

in·cu·bate (ĭn/kyə bāt/, ĭng/-), *v.t., v.i.,* **-bated, -bating. 1.** to sit upon (eggs) for the purpose of hatching. **2.** to hatch (eggs), as by sitting upon them or by artificial heat. **3.** to maintain (bacterial cultures, etc.) at the most favorable temperature for development. **—in/cu·ba/tion,** *n.*

in·cu·ba·tor (ĭn/kyə bā/tər, ĭng/-), *n.* **1.** an apparatus for hatching eggs artificially, consisting essentially of a case heated by a lamp or the like. **2.** a boxlike apparatus in which prematurely born infants are kept. **3.** one who or that which incubates.

---

in/ci·vil/i·ty	in/com·mu/ni·ca/-tive	in/con·gru/i·ty	in/con·stant·ly
in·clem/en·cy	in/com·pat/i·bil/i·ty	in·con/gru·ous	in/con·test/a·ble
in·clem/ent	in/com·pat/i·ble	in·con/gru·ous·ly	in/con·test/a·bly
in·clem/ent·ly	in/com·pat/i·bly	in/con·se/quence/	in·con/ti·nence
in·cog/ni·zant	in/com·plete/	in/con·se/quent	in·con/ti·nent
in/co·her/ence	in/com·plete/ly	in/con·se·quen/tial	in·con/ti·nent·ly
in/co·her/en·cy	in/com·plete/ness	in/con·se/quent·ly	in/con·tro·vert/i·ble
in/co·her/ent	in·com·ple/tion	in/con·sid/er·a·ble	in/con·tro·vert/i·bly
in/com·bus/ti·ble	in/com·pre·hen/si-bil/i·ty	in/con·sid/er·ate	in/con·vert/i·bil/i·ty
in/com·bus/ti·bly		in/con·sid/er·ate·ly	in/con·vert/i·ble
in/com·men/su·ra-ble	in/com·pre·hen/si-ble	in/con·sid/er·ate-ness	in/cor·po/re·al
in/com·men/su·ra-bly	in/com·pre·hen/si-bly	in/con·sist/en·cy	in/cor·po/re·al/i·ty
in/com·men/su·rate	in/com·press/i·ble	in/con·sist/ent	in/cor·po/re·al·ly
in/com·men/su·rate-ly	in/con·ceiv/a·ble	in/con·sist/ent·ly	in/cor·rect/
in/com·mo/di·ous	in/con·ceiv/a·bly	in/con·sol/a·ble	in/cor·rect/ly
in/com·mo/di·ous-ly	in/con·clu/sive	in/con·sol/a·bly	in/cor·rect/ness
in/com·mu/ni·ca·ble	in/con·clu/sive·ly	in/con·so/nant	in/cor·rupt/
in/com·mu/ni·ca·bly	in/con·gru/ence	in/con·spic/u·ous	in/cor·rupt/i·bil/i-ty
	in/con·gru/ent	in/con·spic/u·ous·ly	in/cor·rupt/i·ble
		in/con/stan·cy	in/cor·rupt/i·bly
		in/con/stant	in/cor·rupt/ly

in·cu·bus (ĭn′kyə bəs, ĭng′-), *n.*, *pl.* **-bi** (-bī′), **-buses.** 1. a demon supposed to descend upon sleeping persons. 2. something that oppresses one like a nightmare. 3. a nightmare.

in·cul·cate (ĭn kŭl′kāt, ĭn′kŭl kāt′), *v.t.*, **-cated, -cating.** to impress by repeated statement; teach persistently and earnestly. —**in′cul·ca′tion**, *n.* —**in·cul′ca·tor**, *n.*

in·cul·pate (ĭn kŭl′pāt, ĭn′kŭl pāt′), *v.t.*, **-pated, -pating.** 1. to blame; accuse. 2. to incriminate. —**in′cul·pa′tion**, *n.*

in·cum·ben·cy (ĭn kŭm′bən sĭ), *n.*, *pl.* **-cies.** 1. state of being incumbent. 2. that which is incumbent. 3. the position or term of an incumbent.

in·cum·bent (ĭn kŭm′bənt), *adj.* 1. obligatory. 2. lying, leaning, or pressing on something. —*n.* 3. the holder of an office.

in·cum·ber (ĭn kŭm′bər), *v.t.* encumber.

in·cu·nab·u·la (ĭn′kyŏŏ năb′yə lə), *n.pl.*, *sing.* **-lum** (-ləm). 1. books produced in the infancy of printing (before 1500). 2. the earliest stages of anything. —**in′cu·nab′u·lar**, *adj.*

in·cur (ĭn kûr′), *v.t.*, **-curred, -curring.** 1. to run or fall into (some consequence, usually undesirable). 2. to bring upon oneself.

in·cur·a·ble (ĭn kyŏŏr′ə bəl), *adj.* 1. not curable. —*n.* 2. one suffering from an incurable disease. —**in·cur′a·bil′i·ty**, *n.* —**in·cur′a·bly**, *adv.*

in·cur·sion (ĭn kûr′zhən, -shən), *n.* 1. a sudden, hostile invasion or raid. 2. a harmful inroad.

in·curve (*v.* ĭn kûrv′; *n.* ĭn′kûrv′), *v.*, **-curved, -curving**, *n.* *Baseball.* —*v.t.* 1. to curve inward. —*n.* 2. a ball curving toward the batter.

Ind., 1. India. 2. Indian. 3. Indiana.

ind., 1. independent. 2. indicative.

in·debt·ed (ĭn dĕt′əd), *adj.* under obligation for benefits, favors, assistance, etc., received. —**in·debt′ed·ness**, *n.*

in·deed (ĭn dēd′), *adv.* 1. in fact; in reality; truly. —*interj.* 2. an expression of surprise, irony, etc.

indef., indefinite.

in·de·fat·i·ga·ble (ĭn′dĭ făt′ə gə bəl), *adj.* incapable of being tired out; tireless. —**in′de·fat′-i·ga·bil′i·ty**, *n.* —**in′de·fat′i·ga·bly**, *adv.*

in·de·fea·si·ble (ĭn′dĭ fē′zə bəl), *adj.* not to be annulled or made void; not forfeitable. —**in′-de·fea′si·bil′i·ty**, *n.* —**in′de·fea′si·bly**, *adv.*

in·def·i·nite (ĭn dĕf′ə nĭt), *adj.* 1. not definite; without fixed or specified limit. 2. not clearly defined or determined; not precise. 3. *Gram.* not specifying precisely. —**in·def′i·nite·ly**, *adv.* —**in·def′i·nite·ness**, *n.*

indefinite article, *Gram.* the article (as *a, an*) which classes as "single and unidentified" the noun it modifies.

in·del·i·ble (ĭn dĕl′ə bəl), *adj.* 1. incapable of being deleted or obliterated. 2. making indelible marks. —**in·del′i·bil′i·ty**, *n.* —**in·del′i·bly**, *adv.*

in·dem·ni·fy (ĭn dĕm′nə fī′), *v.t.*, **-fied, -fying.** 1. to compensate for damage, loss, expense, etc. 2. to engage to make good or secure against anticipated loss. —**in·dem′ni·fi·ca′tion**, *n.*

in·dem·ni·ty (ĭn dĕm′nə tĭ), *n.*, *pl.* **-ties.** 1. protection against or compensation for damage or loss. 2. legal exemption from liabilities or penalties incurred by one's actions.

in·dent (*v.* ĭn dĕnt′; *n.* ĭn′dĕnt, ĭn dĕnt′), *v.t.* 1. to form deep recesses in. 2. to set in or back from the margin, as the first line of a paragraph. 3. to notch. —*n.* 4. an indentation. 5. an indention.

in·den·ta·tion (ĭn′dĕn tā′shən), *n.* 1. a cut, notch, or deep recess. 2. an indention.

in·den·tion (ĭn dĕn′shən), *n.* 1. an indentation. 2. an indenting, as of a line.

in·den·ture (ĭn dĕn′chər), *n.*, *v.*, **-tured, -turing.** —*n.* 1. a contract by which a person, as an apprentice, is bound to service. 2. the formal agreement between a group of bondholders and the debtor as to the terms of the debt. 3. indentation. —*v.t.* 4. to bind by indenture, as an apprentice.

in·de·pend·ence (ĭn′dĭ pĕn′dəns), *n.* 1. state or quality of being independent. 2. freedom from subjection to or the influence of others.· 3. exemption from external control or support. Also, **in′de·pend′en·cy.**

In·de·pend·ence (ĭn′dĭ pĕn′dəns), *n.* a city in W Missouri: starting point of the Santa Fe and Oregon trails. 16,066.

Independence Day, *U.S.* July 4, a holiday commemorating the adoption of the Declaration of Independence on July 4, 1776.

in·de·pend·ent (ĭn′dĭ pĕn′dənt), *adj.* 1. not influenced in matters of opinion, conduct, etc. 2. not subject to another's authority; free. 3. not influenced by the thought or action of others. 4. not dependent on something else for existence, operation, etc. 5. not relying on another or others for aid or support. 6. declining others' aid or support. 7. self-confident; unconstrained. 8. free from party commitments in voting. —*n.* 9. an independent person or thing. —**in′de·pend′ent·ly**, *adv.*

in·dex (ĭn′dĕks), *n.*, *pl.* **-dexes, -dices** (-də sēz′), *v.* —*n.* 1. a detailed alphabetical list of names, places, and topics in a book with page references. 2. a sign, token, or indication. 3. a guiding principle. 4. a pointer or indicator, as in a scientific instrument. 5. *Print.*, *etc.* a sign (☞) used to point out a particular note, etc. 6. the forefinger. 7. *Science.* a number or formula expressing some property, ratio, etc., of a thing indicated. 8. (*cap.*) a list of books which Roman Catholics are forbidden by Church authority to read without special permission. —*v.t.* 9. to provide with an index, as a book. 10. to enter in an index, as a word.

In·di·a (ĭn′dĭ ə), *n.* 1. a large peninsula in southern Asia, S of the Himalayas and projecting into the Indian Ocean: politically divided into the two states of India and Pakistan, and the smaller areas of French India and Portuguese India. The state of India became an independent republic on Jan. 26, 1950. Pakistan has dominion status in the British Commonwealth of Nations. 2. an independent republic occupying most of

India, May, 1949

the peninsula of India. ab. 337,000,000 pop.; ab. 1,246,000 sq. mi. *Cap.:* New Delhi.

India ink, 1. a black pigment, consisting chiefly of lampblack. 2. a liquid ink from this.

In·di·a·man (ĭn′dĭ ə mən), *n.*, *pl.* **-men.** a ship in the India trade, esp. a large one of the East India Company.

In·di·an (ĭn′dĭ ən), *n.* 1. a member of the aboriginal race of America or of any of the aboriginal North and South American stocks (**American Indian**). 2. *Colloq.* any of the American Indian languages. 3. a member of any of the native races of India or the East Indies (**East Indian**). —*adj.* 4. of or pertaining to the race embracing the aborigines of America. 5. of or pertaining to India or the East Indies.

In·di·an·a (ĭn′dĭ ăn′ə), *n.* a State in the central United States. 3,767,313 pop.; 36,291 sq. mi. *Cap.:* Indianapolis. *Abbr.:* Ind. —**In·di·an·i·an** (ĭn′dĭ-ăn′ĭ ən), *adj.*, *n.*

In·di·an·ap·o·lis (ĭn′dĭ ə năp′ə lĭs), *n.* the capital of Indiana, in the central part. 386,972.

in·cul′pa·ble	in′de·ci′sive·ness	in′de·fen′si·bly	in′de·scrib′a·ble
in·cul′pa·bly	in′de·clin′a·ble	in′de·fin′a·ble	in′de·scrib′a·bly
in·cu′ri·ous	in·dec′o·rous	in′de·fin′a·ble·ness	in′de·struct′i·bil′i-
in·cu′ri·ous·ly	in·dec′o·rous·ly	in′de·fin′a·bly	ty
in·de′cen·cy	in·dec′o·rous·ness	in′de·his′cence	in′de·struct′i·ble
in·de′cent	in·de·co′rum	in′de·his′cent	in′de·struct′i·bly
in·de′cent·ly	in·de·fec′tive	in·del′i·ca·cy	in′de·ter′mi·na·ble
in′de·ci′pher·a·ble	in′de·fen′si·bil′i-	in·del′i·cate	in′de·ter′mi·nate·
in′de·ci′sion	ty	in·del′i·cate·ly	in′de·ter′mi·nate-
in′de·ci′sive	in′de·fen′si·ble	in′de·mon′stra-	ly
in′de·ci′sive·ly	in′de·fen′si·ble·ness	ble	in′de·ter′mi·na′tion

Indian club, a gymnasium hand apparatus, bottle-shaped, usually used in pairs.

Indian corn, *Chiefly Brit.* maize.

Indian file, single file.

Indian giver, *U.S. Colloq.* one who takes back a gift.

Indian Ocean, an ocean S of Asia, E of Africa, and W of Australia. ab. 28,350,000 sq. mi.

Indian pipe, a leafless plant of North America and Asia, having a solitary flower.

Indian summer, a period of mild, dry weather occurring in the late autumn.

India paper, a thin, tough, opaque paper.

India rubber, a highly elastic substance obtained from the milky juice of numerous tropical plants; rubber. Also, **india rubber.**

indic., indicative. Also, **ind.**

in·di·cate (ĭn′də kāt′), *v.t.,* -cated, -cating. 1. to be a sign of; betoken. 2. to point out or point to. 3. to show. 4. to state or express.

in·di·ca·tion (ĭn′də kā′shən), *n.* 1. anything serving to indicate or point out, as a sign, token, etc. 2. *Med.* a special symptom or the like.

in·dic·a·tive (ĭn dĭk′ə tĭv), *adj.* 1. that indicates; suggestive. 2. *Gram.* designating or pertaining to the verb mode of ordinary statements, questions, etc., in contrast to hypothetical statements or those made without reference to a specific actor or time of action. —*n.* 3. *Gram.* **a.** the indicative mode. **b.** a verb therein. —**in·dic′a·tive·ly,** *adv.*

in·di·ca·tor (ĭn′də kā′tər), *n.* 1. one who or that which indicates. 2. a pointer on an instrument. 3. an instrument which indicates the condition of a machine, etc. 4. a pressure gauge. 5. *Chem.* a substance used to indicate the condition of a solution, etc.

in·di·ces (ĭn′də sēz′), *n.* a pl. of **index.**

in·dict (ĭn dīt′), *v.t.* 1. to charge with an offense; accuse. 2. (of a grand jury) to bring a formal accusation against, as a means of bringing to trial. —**in·dict′a·ble,** *adj.* —**in·dict′er, in·dict′or,** *n.*

in·dict·ment (ĭn dīt′mənt), *n.* 1. act of indicting. 2. *Law.* a formal accusation presented by a grand jury. 3. an accusation.

In·dies (ĭn′dēz), *n.pl.* 1. the West Indies. 2 the East Indies.

in·dif·fer·ence (ĭn dĭf′ər əns), *n.* 1. lack of interest or concern. 2. unimportance. 3. quality or fact of being indifferent.

in·dif·fer·ent (ĭn dĭf′ər ənt), *adj.* 1. without interest or concern; apathetic. 2. impartial. 3. neutral in character or quality. 4. of only moderate amount, excellence, etc. —**in·dif′fer·ent·ly,** *adv.*

in·dig·e·nous (ĭn dĭj′ə nəs), *adj.* 1. originating in and characterizing a particular region or country; native. 2. innate; natural. —**in·dig′e·nous·ly,** *adv.*

in·di·gent (ĭn′də jənt), *adj.* 1. needy; poor. 2. destitute. —**in·di·gence,** *n.* —**in′di·gent·ly,** *adv.*

in·di·ges·tion (ĭn′də jĕs′chən, -dī-), *n.* incapability of, or difficulty in, digesting food; dyspepsia.

in·dig·nant (ĭn dĭg′nənt), *adj.* full of indignation. —**in·dig′nant·ly,** *adv.*

in·dig·na·tion (ĭn′dĭg nā′shən), *n.* displeasure at something deemed unworthy, unjust, or base; righteous anger.

in·dig·ni·ty (ĭn dĭg′nə tĭ), *n., pl.* -ties. a humiliating affront, insult, or injury.

in·di·go (ĭn′də gō′), *n., pl.* -gos, -goes. 1. a blue dye obtained from certain plants, chiefly Asiatic. 2. deep violet blue.

indigo bunting, a North American songbird of the finch family, the male of which is indigo. Also, **indigo bird.**

in·di·rec·tion (ĭn′də rĕk′shən, -dī-), *n.* 1. action or procedure that is not direct. 2. a roundabout course or method. 3. deceitful or crooked dealing.

indirect object, *Gram.* the object with reference to which (for whose benefit, in whose interest, etc.) the action of a verb is performed.

in·dis·cre·tion (ĭn′dĭs krĕsh′ən), *n.* 1. lack of

discretion; imprudence. 2. an indiscreet act or step.

in·dis·crim·i·nate (ĭn′dĭs krĭm′ə nĭt), *adj.* 1. not discriminating. 2. not discriminate; confused. —**in·dis·crim′i·nate·ly,** *adv.* —**in·dis·crim′i·nate·ness,** *n.*

in·dis·pen·sa·ble (ĭn′dĭs pĕn′sə bəl), *adj.* 1. absolutely necessary or requisite. 2. that cannot be disregarded or neglected. —*n.* 3. one who or that which is indispensable. —**in/dis·pen/sa·bil/i·ty, in/dis·pen/sa·ble·ness,** *n.* —**in/dis·pen/sa·bly,** *adv.*

in·dis·pose (ĭn′dĭs pōz′), *v.t.,* -posed, -posing. 1. to make unfit; disqualify. 2. to make ill, esp. slightly. 3. to render averse or unwilling. —**in·dis·po·si·tion** (ĭn′dĭs pə zĭsh′ən), *n.*

in·dis·posed (ĭn′dĭs pōzd′), *adj.* 1. sick or ill, esp. slightly. 2. disinclined or unwilling.

in·dite (ĭn dīt′), *v.t.,* -dited, -diting. to write, as a speech, poem, etc. —**in·dit′er,** *n.*

in·di·um (ĭn′dĭ əm), *n. Chem.* a rare metallic element, soft, white, malleable and easily fusible. *Symbol:* In; *at. wt.:* 114.76; *at. no.:* 49; *sp. gr.:* 7.3 at 20°C.

in·di·vid·u·al (ĭn′də vĭj′ŏŏ əl), *adj.* 1. single; particular; separate. 2. pertaining or peculiar to a single person or thing. 3. intended for the use of one person only. 4. distinguished by peculiar and marked characteristics. 5. of which each is different from the others. —*n.* 6. a single human being, animal, or thing. 7. a person.

in·di·vid·u·al·ism (ĭn′də vĭj′ŏŏ ə lĭz′əm), *n.* 1. a social theory advocating the liberty, rights, or independent action of the individual. 2. the principle or habit of independent thought or action. 3. egoism; selfishness. 4. individual character. —**in/di·vid/u·al·ist,** *n.* —**in/di·vid/u·al·is/tic,** *adj.*

in·di·vid·u·al·i·ty (ĭn′də vĭj′ŏŏ ăl′ə tĭ), *n., pl.* -ties. 1. the particular character, or aggregate of qualities, which distinguishes one person or thing from others. 2. a person or thing of individual or distinctive character. 3. state or quality of being individual.

in·di·vid·u·al·ize (ĭn′də vĭj′ŏŏ ə līz′), *v.,* -ized, -izing. —*v.t.* 1. to give an individual or distinctive character to. 2. to specify; particularize. —*v.i.* 3. to become individual. 4. to particularize.

in·di·vid·u·al·ly (ĭn′də vĭj′ŏŏ ə lĭ), *adv.* 1. in an individual manner. 2. separately. 3. personally.

in·di·vis·i·ble (ĭn′də vĭz′ə bəl), *adj.* 1. not divisible; incapable of being divided. —*n.* 2. something indivisible. —**in/di·vis/i·bil/i·ty,** *n.* —**in/di·vis/i·bly,** *adv.*

In·do-Chi·na (ĭn′dō chī′nə), *n.* 1. a peninsula in SE Asia comprising French Indo-China, Siam, the Malay Peninsula, and Burma. 2. See **French Indo-China.** —**In/do-Chi·nese′,** *adj., n.*

in·doc·tri·nate (ĭn dŏk′trĭ nāt′), *v.t.,* -nated, -nating. 1. to instruct (in a doctrine, etc.). 2. to teach or inculcate. —**in·doc′tri·na′tion,** *n.*

In·do-Eu·ro·pe·an (ĭn′dō yŏŏr′ə pē′ən), *adj.* 1. of or pertaining to a major family of languages that includes most of the languages of Europe (now spread to other parts of the world), of Asia, and a few scattered others. —*n.* 2. this family of languages. Also, **In·do-Ger·man·ic** (ĭn′dō jər mán′ĭk).

in·do·lent (ĭn′də lənt), *adj.* 1. having or showing a disposition to avoid exertion. 2. *Pathol.* causing little or no pain. —**in′do·lence,** *n.* —**in′do·lent·ly,** *adv.*

in·dom·i·ta·ble (ĭn dŏm′ə tə bəl), *adj.* that cannot be subdued or overcome, as persons, pride, courage, etc. —**in·dom′i·ta·bly,** *adv.*

In·do·ne·sia (ĭn′dō nē′shə, -zhə), *n.* 1. the East Indies. 2. **United States of,** a federation, constituted Dec. 1949, of states in the Malay Archipelago, including Sumatra, Java, Celebes, parts of Borneo and Timor, the Moluccas, and other islands: officially a Dutch-Indonesian union under the Crown. *Cap.:* Jakarta. Formerly, **Dutch East Indies.** —**In/do·ne/sian,** *n., adj.*

in·door (ĭn′dōr′), *adj.* occurring, used, etc., inside a house or building.

in·doors (ĭn'dōrz'), *adv.* in or into a house or building.

in·dorse (ĭn dôrs'), *v.t.*, -dorsed, -dorsing. endorse.

in·du·bi·ta·ble (ĭn dū'bə tə bəl, -dōō'-), *adj.* that cannot be doubted; certain. —**in·du'bi·ta·ble·ness,** *n.* —**in·du'bi·ta·bly,** *adv.*

in·duce (ĭn dūs', -dōōs'), *v.t.*, -duced, -ducing. 1. to lead or move by persuasion or influence. 2. to bring about, produce, or cause. —**in·duce'-ment,** *n.* —**in·duc'er,** *n.* —**in·duc'i·ble,** *adj.*

in·duct (ĭn dŭkt'), *v.t.* 1. to lead or bring in; introduce, esp. formally, as into a place, office, etc. 2. *U.S.* to bring into military service. —**in'-duc·tee',** *n.*

in·duct·ance (ĭn dŭk'təns), *n. Elect.* that property of a circuit by virtue of which electromagnetic induction takes place.

in·duc·tion (ĭn dŭk'shən), *n.* 1. *Logic.* **a.** the process of discovering explanations for a set of particular facts, by estimating the weight of observational evidence in favor of a proposition which (usually) asserts something about that entire class of facts. **b.** a conclusion reached by this process. 2. a bringing forward of facts, evidence, etc. 3. the act of causing. 4. introduction or initiation, as into an office or benefice; installation. 5. a prelude. 6. *Elect.* the process by which a body having electrical or magnetic properties calls forth similar properties in a neighboring body without direct contact.

induction coil, *Elect.* a transformer designed as two concentric coils with a common soft iron core, with the inner coil (primary) of few turns and the outer coil (secondary) of a great number of turns.

in·duc·tive (ĭn dŭk'tĭv), *adj.* 1. pertaining to or employing logical induction. 2. pertaining to or involving electrical or magnetic induction. —**in·duc'tive·ly,** *adv.*

in·duc·tor (ĭn dŭk'tər), *n. Elect.* a device, the primary purpose of which is to introduce inductance into an electric circuit.

in·due (ĭn dū', -dōō'), *v.t.*, -dued, -duing. endue.

in·dulge (ĭn dŭlj'), *v.*, -dulged, -dulging. —*v.i.* 1. to yield to an inclination. —*v.t.* 2. to yield to, satisfy, or gratify (desires, etc.). 3. to allow (oneself) to follow one's will. —**in·dulg'ing·ly,** *adv.*

in·dul·gence (ĭn dŭl'jəns), *n., v.,* -genced, -gencing. —*n.* 1. gratification of desire. 2. indulgent allowance or tolerance. 3. *Rom. Cath. Ch.* a remission of the temporal punishment still due to sin after it has been forgiven. —*v.t.* 4. *Rom. Cath. Ch.* to furnish with an indulgence.

in·dul·gent (ĭn dŭl'jənt), *adj.* characterized by or showing indulgence. —**in·dul'gent·ly,** *adv.*

in·du·rate (*v.* ĭn'dyŏŏ rāt', -dōō-; *adj.* ĭn'dyŏŏ-rĭt), *v.*, -rated, -rating, *adj.* —*v.t.*, *v.i.* 1. to make or become hard; inure. —*adj.* 2. hardened; inured.

In·dus (ĭn'dəs), *n.* a river flowing from W Tibet through Kashmir and SW through Pakistan to the Arabian Sea. ab. 2000 mi.

in·dus·tri·al (ĭn dŭs'trĭ əl), *adj.* 1. of or pertaining to industry or productive labor. 2. having highly developed industries. 3. engaged in industry. —*n.* 4. (*pl.*) stocks or bonds of industrial enterprises. —**in·dus'tri·al·ly,** *adv.*

in·dus·tri·al·ism (ĭn dŭs'trĭ ə lĭz'əm), *n.* an economic organization of society built largely on mechanized industry rather than agriculture, craftsmanship, or commerce.

in·dus·tri·al·ist (ĭn dŭs'trĭ əl ĭst), *n.* one who conducts or owns an industrial enterprise.

in·dus·tri·al·ize (ĭn dŭs'trĭ ə līz'), *v.t.*, -ized, -izing. to introduce industry (into an area) on a large scale. —**in·dus'tri·al·i·za'tion,** *n.*

in·dus·tri·ous (ĭn dŭs'trĭ əs), *adj.* hard-working; diligent. —**in·dus'tri·ous·ly,** *adv.* —**in·dus'tri·ous·ness,** *n.*

in·dus·try (ĭn'dəs trĭ), *n., pl.* -tries. 1. a trade or manufacture. 2. the ownership and management of companies, factories, etc. 3. systematic work or labor. 4. assiduous activity at any work or task.

in·e·bri·ate (*v.* ĭn ē'brĭ āt'; *n., adj.* -ĭt), *v.*, -ated, -ating, *n., adj.* —*v.t.* 1. to make drunk; intoxicate. 2. to exhilarate. —*n.* 3. an intoxicated person. 4. a habitual drunkard. —*adj.* 5. Also, **in·e'bri·at'ed.** drunk; intoxicated. —**in·e'bri·a'tion,** *n.*

in·e·bri·e·ty (ĭn'ĭ brī'ə tĭ), *n.* drunkenness.

in·ef·fa·ble (ĭn ĕf'ə bəl), *adj.* 1. that cannot be expressed; inexpressible. 2. that must not be uttered. —**in·ef'fa·bil'i·ty, in·ef'fa·ble·ness,** *n.* —**in·ef'fa·bly,** *adv.*

in·ef·fec·tu·al (ĭn'ĭ fĕk'chŏŏ əl), *adj.* 1. without satisfactory or decisive effect. 2. unavailing; futile. 3. powerless or impotent. —**in'ef·fec'-tu·al·ly,** *adv.*

in·el·i·gi·ble (ĭn ĕl'ĭ jə bəl), *adj.* 1. not eligible; not proper or suitable for choice. 2. legally disqualified. —*n.* 3. one who is ineligible. —**in·el'i·gi·bil'i·ty,** *n.* —**in·el'i·gi·bly,** *adv.*

in·ept (ĭn ĕpt'), *adj.* 1. not apt, fitted, or suitable. 2. inappropriate. 3. absurd or foolish. —**in·ept'ly,** *adv.* —**in·ept'ness,** *n.*

in·ept·i·tude (ĭn ĕp'tə tūd', -tōōd'), *n.* 1. quality of being inept. 2. an inept act or remark.

in·ert (ĭn ûrt'), *adj.* 1. having no inherent power of action, motion, or resistance. 2. without active properties, as a drug. 3. of an inactive or sluggish habit or nature. —**in·ert'ly,** *adv.* —**in·ert'ness,** *n.*

in·er·tia (in ûr'shə), *n.* 1. inert condition; inactivity; sluggishness. 2. *Physics.* **a.** that property of matter by which it retains its state of rest or of uniform rectilinear motion so long as it is not acted upon by an external force. **b.** an analogous property of a force.

in·es·ti·ma·ble (ĭn ĕs'tə mə bəl), *adj.* 1. that cannot be estimated, or too great to be estimated. 2. of incalculable value. —**in·es'ti·ma·bly,** *adv.*

in·ev·i·ta·ble (ĭn ĕv'ə tə bəl), *adj.* 1. that cannot be avoided, evaded, or escaped; necessary. 2. sure to befall, happen, or come. —*n.* 3. that which is unavoidable. —**in·ev'i·ta·bil'i·ty, in·ev'i·ta·ble·ness,** *n.* —**in·ev'i·ta·bly,** *adv.*

in·ex·o·ra·ble (ĭn ĕk'sə rə bəl), *adj.* 1. unyielding or unalterable. 2. not to be persuaded, moved, or affected by prayers or entreaties. —**in·ex'o·ra·bil'i·ty, in·ex'o·ra·ble·ness,** *n.* —**in·ex'o·ra·bly,** *adv.*

in·ex·pli·ca·ble (ĭn ĕks'pli kə bəl), *adj.* —explicable; incapable of being explained. —**in·ex'pli·ca·bly,** *adv.*

in ex·tre·mis (ĭn ĭk strē'mĭs), *Latin.* 1. in extremity. 2. near death.

inf., 1. (*also cap.*) infantry. 2. infinitive. 3. information. 4. (L *infra*) below; after.

in·fal·li·ble (ĭn făl'ə bəl), *adj.* 1. not liable to error, as persons, their judgment, pronouncements, etc. 2. absolutely trustworthy. 3. unfailing; certain. 4. *Rom. Cath. Ch.* immune from fallacy or liability to error in expounding matters of faith or morals in virtue of the promise made by Christ to the Church. —*n.* 5. an infallible person or thing. —**in·fal'li·bil'i·ty, in·fal'li·ble·ness,** *n.* —**in·fal'li·bly,** *adv.*

in·fa·mous (ĭn'fə məs), *adj.* 1. of evil fame or repute. 2. detestable; shamefully bad. —**in'fa·mous·ly,** *adv.* —**in'fa·mous·ness,** *n.*

in·fa·my (ĭn'fə mĭ), *n., pl.* -mies. 1. evil fame, shameful notoriety, or public reproach. 2. infamous character or conduct. 3. an infamous act or circumstance.

in·duc'tile	in·el'e·gan·cy	in·ex·act'ly	in'ex·pert'ly
in·ed'i·bil'i·ty	in·el'e·gant	in·ex·act'ness	in'ex·pert'ness
in·ed'i·ble	in·el'e·gant·ly	in·ex·cus'a·ble	in·ex·pi·a·ble
in·ef·face'a·ble	in·el'o·quent	in·ex·cus·a·bly	in·ex·press'i·ble
in·ef·face'a·bly	in·e'luc'ta·ble	in·ex·haust'i·ble	in·ex·press'i·bly
in·ef·fec'tive	in·e·qual'i·ty	in·ex·ist'ent	in·ex·pres'sive
in·ef·fec'tive·ly	in·eq'ui·ta·ble	in·ex·pe'di·ence	in·ex·pres'sive·ly
in·ef·fec'tive·ness	in·eq'ui·ta·bly	in·ex·pe'di·en·cy	in·ex·ten'si·ble
in·ef·fi·ca'cious	in·eq'ui·ty	in·ex·pe'di·ent	in·ex·tin'guish·a-ble
in·ef·fi·ca'cious·ly	in·e·rad'i·ca·ble	in·ex·pe'di·ent·ly	ble
in·ef'fi·ca·cy	in·e·ras'a·ble	in·ex·pen'sive	in·ex·tin'guish·a-bly
in·ef·fi'cien·cy	in·er'rant	in·ex·pen'sive·ly	bly
in·ef'fi·cient	in·es·cap'a·ble	in·ex·pen'sive·ness	in·ex'tri·ca·bil'i·ty
in·ef·fi'cient·ly	in·es·sen'tial	in·ex·pe'ri·ence	ty
in·e·las'tic	in·ex·act'	in·ex·pe'ri·enced	in·ex'tri·ca·ble
in·el'e·gance	in·ex·act'i·tude'	in·ex·pert'	in·ex'tri·ca·bly

in·fan·cy (ĭn/fən sĭ), n., pl. **-cies. 1.** state or period of being an infant; early childhood. **2.** the corresponding period in the existence of anything. **3.** Law. the period of life to the age of majority (in the common law, through 21).

in·fant (ĭn/fənt), n. **1.** a child during the earliest period of its life; baby. **2.** Law. a person who is not of full age, esp. one who is under 21. **3.** a beginner. —adj. **4.** of or pertaining to infants or infancy. **5.** being in infancy.

in·fan·ta (ĭn fän/tə), n. **1.** a daughter of the king of Spain or of Portugal. **2.** an infante's wife.

in·fan·te (ĭn fän/tā), n. a son of the king of Spain or of Portugal, not heir to the throne.

in·fan·ti·cide[1] (ĭn fän/tə sīd/), n. the killing of an infant. —**in·fan/ti·cid/al,** adj.

in·fan·ti·cide[2] (ĭn fän/tə sīd/), n. ·one who kills an infant.

in·fan·tile (ĭn/fən tīl/, -tĭl/), adj. **1.** babyish; childish. **2.** of or pertaining to infants.

infantile spinal paralysis, Pathol. an acute disease, most common in infants, characterized by inflammation of the nerve cells, mainly of the spinal cord, resulting in a motor paralysis, followed by muscular atrophy, etc., and often by permanent deformities if not treated. Also, **infantile paralysis.**

in·fan·ti·lism (ĭn fän/tə lĭz/əm), n. the persistence in an adult of markedly childish anatomical, physiological, or psychological characteristics.

in·fan·try (ĭn/fən trĭ), n. soldiers or military units that fight on foot, with bayonets, rifles, machine guns, grenades, mortars, etc.

in·fan·try·man (ĭn/fən trĭ mən), n., pl. **-men.** a soldier of the infantry.

in·fat·u·ate (v. ĭn fäch/ōō āt/; adj., n. ĭn fäch/ōō ĭt, -āt/), v., **-ated, -ating,** adj., n. —v.t. **1.** to inspire or possess with a foolish or unreasoning passion, as of love. **2.** to affect with folly. —adj. **3.** infatuated. —n. **4.** a person who is infatuated. —**in·fat/u·a/tion,** n.

in·fat·u·at·ed (ĭn fäch/ōō ā/tĭd), adj. made foolish by love; blindly in love.

in·fect (ĭn fĕkt/), v.t. **1.** to impregnate (a person, organ, wound, etc.) with disease-producing germs. **2.** to taint, contaminate, or affect.

in·fec·tion (ĭn fĕk/shən), n. **1.** action of infecting. **2.** an infecting with germs of disease, as through the medium of infected insects, air, water, clothing, etc. **3.** an infecting agency or influence. **4.** an infectious disease. **5.** an influence.

in·fec·tious (ĭn fĕk/shəs), adj. **1.** communicable by infection, as diseases. **2.** causing or communicating infection. **3.** tending to spread from one to another. —**in·fec/tious·ly,** adv. —**in·fec/tious·ness,** n.

in·fer (ĭn fûr/), v., **-ferred, -ferring.** —v.t. **1.** to derive by reasoning; conclude or judge from premises or evidence. **2.** to imply or hint. —v.i. **3.** to draw a conclusion, as by reasoning. —**in·fer·a·ble** (ĭn fûr/ə bəl, ĭn/fər-), adj. —**in·fer/a·bly,** adv.

in·fer·ence (ĭn/fər əns), n. **1.** act or process of inferring. **2.** that which is inferred.

in·fer·en·tial (ĭn/fə rĕn/shəl), adj. pertaining to or depending on inference. —**in/fer·en/tial·ly,** adv.

in·fe·ri·or (ĭn fĭr/ĭ ər), adj. **1.** lower in station, rank, degree, or grade. **2.** poor in quality. **3.** less important, valuable, or excellent. **4.** lower in place or position. **5.** Print. lower than the main line of type, as the figures in chemical formulas. —n. **6.** one inferior to another or others, as in rank or merit. —**in·fe·ri·or·i·ty** (ĭn fĭr/ĭ ôr/ə tĭ, -ŏr/-), n.

inferiority complex, feelings arising from one's real or imagined inferiorities. Also, **inferiority feelings.**

in·fer·nal (ĭn fûr/nəl), adj. **1.** of or pertaining to the lower world of classical mythology. **2.** of, inhabiting, or befitting hell. **3.** hellish; fiendish; diabolical. **4.** Colloq. outrageous. —**in·fer/nal·ly,** adv.

infernal machine, an explosive apparatus intended to destroy life or property.

in·fer·no (ĭn fûr/nō), n., pl. **-nos. 1.** hell. **2.** a hell-like region.

in·fest (ĭn fĕst/), v.t. **1.** to overrun in a trouble-

some manner, as destructive animals, vermin, etc., do. **2.** to be numerous in, as anything troublesome. —**in/fes·ta/tion,** n. —**in·fest/-er,** n.

in·fi·del (ĭn/fə dəl), n. **1.** an unbeliever. **2.** one who does not accept a particular faith, esp. Christianity or Mohammedanism. —adj. **3.** without religious faith. **4.** not accepting a particular faith, esp. Christianity or Mohammedanism.

in·fi·del·i·ty (ĭn/fə dĕl/ə tĭ), n., pl. **-ties. 1.** unfaithfulness. **2.** adultery. **3.** lack of religious faith. **4.** a breach of trust.

in·field (ĭn/fēld/), n. Baseball. **1.** the diamond. **2.** the three basemen and the shortstop.

in·field·er (ĭn/fēl/dər), n. Baseball. an infield player.

in·fil·trate (ĭn fĭl/trāt), v., **-trated, -trating,** n. —v.t. **1.** to filter into or through; permeate. **2.** to cause to pass in by, or as by, filtering. —v.i. **3.** to pass in or through a substance, etc., by or as by filtering. —n. **4.** that which infiltrates. —**in/fil·tra/tion,** n.

infin., infinitive.

in·fi·nite (ĭn/fə nĭt), adj. **1.** immeasurably or exceedingly great. **2.** perfect. **3.** endless; inexhaustible. —n. **4.** that which is infinite. **5.** the Infinite or the Infinite Being, God. —**in/fi·nite·ly,** adv. —**in/fi·nite·ness,** n.

in·fin·i·tes·i·mal (ĭn/fĭn ə tĕs/ə məl), adj. **1.** indefinitely or exceedingly small; minute. **2.** immeasurably small. —n. **3.** an infinitesimal quantity. —**in/fin·i·tes/i·mal·ly,** adv.

in·fin·i·tive (ĭn fĭn/ə tĭv), Gram. —n. **1.** (in many languages) a noun form derived from verbs, which names the action or state without specifying the subject. **2.** (in English) the simple form of the verb (come, eat) used after certain other verbs (I didn't come), or this simple form preceded by to (the marked infinitive, I wanted to come). —adj. **3.** of or pertaining to the infinitive or its meaning. —**in·fin/i·tive·ly,** adv.

in·fin·i·tude (ĭn fĭn/ə tūd/, -tōōd/), n. **1.** infinity. **2.** an infinite extent or amount.

in·fin·i·ty (ĭn fĭn/ə tĭ), n., pl. **-ties. 1.** state of being infinite. **2.** that which is infinite. **3.** infinite space, time, quantity, extent, amount, or number. **4.** an indefinitely great amount or number.

in·firm (ĭn fûrm/), adj. **1.** feeble in body or health. **2.** not steadfast or resolute, as persons, the mind, etc. **3.** not firm, solid, or strong. —**in·firm/ly,** adv. —**in·firm/ness,** n.

in·fir·ma·ry (ĭn fûr/mə rĭ), n., pl. **-ries. 1.** a hospital. **2.** a dispensary.

in·fir·mi·ty (ĭn fûr/mə tĭ), n., pl. **-ties. 1.** a physical weakness or ailment. **2.** state of being infirm. **3.** a moral weakness.

in·fix (v. ĭn fĭks/; n. ĭn/fĭks/), v.t. **1.** to fix, fasten, or drive in. **2.** to implant. **3.** to impress. **4.** Gram. to add as an infix. —v.i. **5.** Gram. (of a linguistic form) to admit an infix. —n. **6.** Gram. an affix which is inserted within the body of the element to which it is added.

in·flame (ĭn flām/), v., **-flamed, -flaming.** —v.t. **1.** to set aflame or afire. **2.** to light or redden. **3.** to excite (a person, the passions, etc.). **4.** to cause inflammation in. **5.** to raise (the blood, bodily tissue, etc.) to a morbid or feverish heat. —v.i. **6.** to take fire. **7.** to be excited, as passion.

in·flam·ma·ble (ĭn flăm/ə bəl), adj. **1.** capable of being set on fire; combustible. **2.** easily roused to passion; excitable. —n. **3.** something inflammable. —**in·flam/ma·bil/i·ty,** n. —**in·flam/-ma·bly,** adv.

in·flam·ma·tion (ĭn/flə mā/shən), n. **1.** act of inflaming. **2.** state of being inflamed. **3.** Pathol. a reaction of the body to injurious agents, commonly characterized by heat, redness, swelling, pain, etc., and disturbed function.

in·flam·ma·to·ry (ĭn flăm/ə tōr/ĭ), adj. **1.** kindling passion, anger, etc. **2.** Pathol. pertaining to or attended with inflammation.

in·flate (ĭn flāt/), v., **-flated, -flating.** —v.t. **1.** to swell or puff out; dilate. **2.** to expand (currency, prices, etc.) unduly. —v.i. **3.** to cause inflation. **4.** to become inflated. —**in·flat/a·ble,** adj. —**in·flat/er, in·fla/tor,** n.

in·fla·tion (ĭn flā/shən), n. **1.** undue expansion or increase of the currency of a country, esp. by

---

in·fea/si·ble	in/fe·cun/di·ty	in/fe·lic/i·tous·ly	in·fer/tile
in·fe/cund	in/fe·lic/i·tous	in/fe·lic/i·ty	in·fer/til·i·ty

the issuing of paper money not redeemable in specie. **2.** a substantial rise of prices caused by an undue expansion in paper money or bank credit. **3.** act of inflating. **4.** state of being inflated.

in·fla·tion·ar·y (ĭn flā′shə nĕr′Ĭ), *adj.* of or causing inflation.

in·fla·tion·ism (ĭn flā′shə nĭz′əm), *n.* the policy or practice of inflation through expansion of currency or bank deposits. **—in·fla′tion·ist**, *n.*

in·flect (ĭn flĕkt′), *v.t.* **1.** to bend. **2.** to modulate (the voice). **3.** *Gram.* **a.** to apply inflection to (a word). **b.** to recite or display all, or a distinct set of, the inflections of (a word), in a fixed order. *—v.i.* **4.** *Gram.* to be characterized by inflection.

in·flec·tion (ĭn flĕk′shən), *n.* **1.** modulation of the voice. **2.** *Gram.* the existence in a language of sets of forms built normally on a single stem, having different syntactical functions and meanings, but all those of a single stem being members of the same fundamental part of speech and constituting forms of the same "word." **3.** a bend. Also, *Brit.,* **in·flex′ion. —in·flec′tion·al,** *adj.*

in·flict (ĭn flĭkt′), *v.t.* **1.** to lay on. **2.** to impose as something that must be borne or suffered. **3.** to impose (anything unwelcome).

in·flic·tion (ĭn flĭk′shən), *n.* **1.** act of inflicting. **2.** something inflicted, as punishment, suffering, etc.

in·flo·res·cence (ĭn′flō rĕs′əns), *n.* **1.** a flowering. **2.** *Bot.* **a.** the arrangement of flowers on the axis. **b.** the flowering part of a plant. **c.** a flower cluster. **d.** flowers collectively. **e.** a single flower. **—in′flo·res′cent,** *adj.*

in·flu·ence (ĭn′flŏŏ əns), *n., v.,* **-enced, -encing.** *—n.* **1.** action exerted by one thing or person on another. **2.** power of producing effects on another. **3.** a thing or person that affects another. *—v.t.* **4.** to modify, affect, or sway. **5.** to move or impel to, or to do, something. **—in′flu·enc·er,** *n.*

in·flu·en·tial (ĭn′flŏŏ ĕn′shəl), *adj.* having or exerting influence. **—in′flu·en·tial·ly,** *adv.*

in·flu·en·za (ĭn′flŏŏ ĕn′zə), *n. Pathol.* an acute, extremely contagious disease occurring in several forms with varying symptoms, usually with nasal catarrh and bronchial inflammation, and due to a specific microörganism.

in·flux (ĭn′flŭks′), *n.* **1.** act of flowing in. **2.** the place or point at which one stream flows into another or into the sea.

in·fold (ĭn fōld′), *v.t.* **1.** to wrap up; envelop. **2.** to clasp; embrace.

in·form (ĭn fôrm′), *v.t., v.i.* **1.** to impart knowledge (to). **2.** to supply (oneself) with knowledge. **—in·form′er,** *n.* **—in·form′ing·ly,** *adv.*

in·for·mal (ĭn fôr′məl), *adj.* **1.** not according to prescribed or customary forms. **2.** unceremonious. **3.** denoting speech characterized by colloquial usage, having the flexibility of grammar, syntax, and pronunciation allowable in conversation. **—in·for·mal·i·ty** (ĭn′fôr măl′ə tĬ), *n.* **—in·for′mal·ly,** *adv.*

in·form·ant (ĭn fôr′mənt), *n.* one who gives information.

in·for·ma·tion (ĭn′fər mā′shən), *n.* **1.** knowledge concerning some fact or circumstance. **2.** act of informing. **3.** state of being informed. **—in′for·ma′tion·al,** *adj.*

in·form·a·tive (ĭn fôr′mə tĭv), *adj.* affording information; instructive.

in·frac·tion (ĭn frăk′shən), *n.* breach; violation; infringement.

in·fra·red (ĭn′frə rĕd′), *n.* **1.** the part of the invisible spectrum contiguous to the red end of the visible spectrum, comprising radiation of greater wave length than that of red light. *—adj.* **2.** denoting or pertaining to the infrared or its component rays.

in·fringe (ĭn frĭnj′), *v.,* **-fringed, -fringing.** *—v.t.* **1.** to violate or transgress. *—v.i.* **2.** to encroach or trespass. **—in·fringe′ment,** *n.* **—in·fring′er,** *n.*

in·fu·ri·ate (*v.* ĭn fyŏŏr′Ĭ āt′; *adj.* -Ĭt), *v.,* **-ated, -ating,** *adj.* *—v.t.* **1.** to make furious; enrage. *—adj.* **2.** infuriated. **—in·fu′ri·at′ing·ly,** *adv.* **—in·fu′ri·a′tion,** *n.*

in·fuse (ĭn fūz′), *v.t.,* **-fused, -fusing.** **1.** to cause to penetrate; instill. **2.** to imbue or inspire.

3. to pour in. **4.** to steep or soak (a plant, etc.) in a liquid so as to extract its soluble properties or ingredients. **—in·fu·sion** (ĭn fū′zhən), *n.*

in·fu·so·ri·an (ĭn′fyŏŏ sōr′Ĭ ən), *n.* any of certain protozoans, mostly microscopic and aquatic, having vibratile cilia.

-ing[1], a suffix of nouns formed from verbs, expressing the action of the verb or its result, product, material, etc., as in *the art of building.*

-ing[2], a suffix forming the present participle of verbs, such participles being often used as adjectives (participial adjectives), as in *warring factions.*

in·gen·ious (ĭn jēn′yəs), *adj.* **1.** showing cleverness of invention or construction. **2.** skillful in contriving or constructing. **—in·gen′ious·ly,** *adv.* **—in·gen′ious·ness,** *n.*

in·gé·nue (ăn zhĕ nY′), *n., pl.* **-nues** (-nYz′). **1.** (in a play) the part of an ingenuous girl. **2.** the actress who plays such a part.

in·ge·nu·i·ty (ĭn′jə nū′ə tĬ, -nōō′-), *n., pl.* **-ties. 1.** quality of being ingenious. **2.** skillfulness of contrivance or design.

in·gen·u·ous (ĭn jĕn′yŏŏ əs), *adj.* **1.** free from reserve, restraint, or dissimulation. **2.** artless; innocent. **—in·gen′u·ous·ly,** *adv.* **—in·gen′u·ous·ness,** *n.*

in·gest (ĭn jĕst′), *v.t. Physiol.* to put or take (food, etc.) into the body. **—in·ges′tion,** *n.*

in·gle·nook (ĭng′gəl nŏŏk′), *n. Chiefly Brit.* a corner by the fire.

in·glo·ri·ous (ĭn glōr′Ĭ əs), *adj.* shameful; disgraceful. **—in·glo′ri·ous·ly,** *adv.*

in·go·ing (ĭn′gō′Ĭng), *adj.* entering.

in·got (ĭng′gət), *n.* **1.** the casting obtained when melted metal is poured into a mold. **2.** a cast metal mass, formed by rolling, etc.

in·graft (ĭn grăft′, -gräft′), *v.t.* engraft.

in·grained (ĭn grānd′, ĭn′grānd′), *adj.* **1.** fixed firmly; deep-rooted. **2.** inveterate.

in·grate (ĭn′grāt), *n.* an ungrateful person.

in·gra·ti·ate (ĭn grā′shĬ āt′), *v.t.,* **-ated, -ating.** to establish (oneself) in the favor or good graces of others. **—in·gra′ti·at′ing·ly,** *adv.* **—in·gra′ti·a′tion,** *n.*

in·gre·di·ent (ĭn grē′dĬ ənt), *n.* something that enters as an element into a mixture.

in·gress (ĭn′grĕs), *n.* **1.** act or right of entering. **2.** an entrance.

in·grown (ĭn′grōn′), *adj.* **1.** having grown into the flesh. **2.** grown inward.

in·gui·nal (ĭng′gwə nəl), *adj.* of, pertaining to, or situated in the groin.

in·gulf (ĭn gŭlf′), *v.t.* engulf.

in·hab·it (ĭn hăb′Ĭt), *v.t., v.i.* to live or dwell in (a place). **—in·hab′it·a·ble,** *adj.*

in·hab·it·ant (ĭn hăb′ə tənt), *n.* a person or an animal that inhabits a place.

in·hal·ant (ĭn hā′lənt), *adj.* **1.** serving for inhalation. *—n.* **2.** an apparatus or medicine used for inhaling.

in·hale (ĭn hāl′), *v.t., v.i.,* **-haled, -haling.** to breathe in (air, smoke of cigarettes, etc.). **—in·ha·la·tion** (ĭn′hə lā′shən), *n.*

in·hal·er (ĭn hā′lər), *n.* **1.** an apparatus used in inhaling medicinal vapors, anesthetics, etc. **2.** a respirator. **3.** one who inhales.

in·here (ĭn hĬr′), *v.i.,* **-hered, -hering.** to exist permanently and inseparably (in), as a quality, attribute, or element.

in·her·ent (ĭn hĬr′ənt), *adj.* existing in something as a permanent and inseparable element, quality, or attribute. **—in·her′ence,** *n.* **—in·her′ent·ly,** *adv.*

in·her·it (ĭn hĕr′Ĭt), *v.t.* to receive (property, etc.) as the heir of the former owner. **—in·her′it·a·ble,** *adj.* **—in·her′i·tor,** *n.*

in·her·it·ance (ĭn hĕr′ə təns), *n.* **1.** that which is or may be inherited, as property, a quality, a tradition, etc. **2.** act or fact of inheriting. **3.** the right of inheriting.

in·hib·it (ĭn hĭb′Ĭt), *v.t.* **1.** to restrain, hinder, arrest, or check (an action, impulse, etc.). **2.** to forbid. **—in·hib′it·er,** *n.* **—in·hib·i·to·ry** (ĭn·hĬb′ə tōr′Ĭ), **in·hib′i·tive,** *adj.*

in·hi·bi·tion (ĭn′Ĭ bĬsh′ən, ĭn′hĬ-), *n.* **1.** act of inhibiting. **2.** state of being inhibited. **3.** *Psychol.* the blocking of any psychological process by another psychological process.

in·flex′i·bil′i·ty	in·fran′gi·ble	in·fre′quent	in·grat′i·tude′
in·flex′i·ble	in·fre′quence	in·fre′quent·ly	in′har·mon′ic
in·flex′i·bly	in·fre′quen·cy	in·fu′si·ble	in′har·mo′ni·ous

in·hu·man (ĭn hū′mən), *adj.* **1.** lacking natural human feeling or sympathy for others; brutal. **2.** not human. —**in·hu′man·ly,** *adv.*

in·hu·man·i·ty (ĭn′hū măn′ə tĭ), *n.,* *pl.* **-ties. 1.** state or quality of being inhuman or inhumane; cruelty. **2.** an inhuman or inhumane act.

in·im·i·cal (ĭn ĭm′ə kəl), *adj.* **1.** adverse in tendency or effect. **2.** unfriendly or hostile. —**in·im′i·cal·ly,** *adv.*

in·im·i·ta·ble (ĭn ĭm′ə tə bəl), *adj.* incapable of being imitated. —**in·im′i·ta·bil′i·ty,** *n.* —**in·im′i·ta·bly,** *adv.*

in·iq·ui·ty (ĭ nĭk′wə tĭ), *n.,* *pl.* **-ties. 1.** gross injustice; wickedness. **2.** an unjust or wicked action; a sin. —**in·iq′ui·tous,** *adj.* —**in·iq′ui·tous·ly,** *adv.* —**in·iq′ui·tous·ness,** *n.*

in·i·tial (ĭ nĭsh′əl), *adj., n., v.,* **-tialed, -tialing** or (*esp. Brit.*) **-tialled, -tialling.** —*adj.* **1.** of or pertaining to the beginning; incipient. **2.** at the beginning of a word or syllable. —*n.* **3.** an initial letter, as of a word. —*v.t.* **4.** to sign with an initial or initials. —**in·i′tial·ly,** *adv.*

in·i·ti·ate (*v.* ĭ nĭsh′ĭ āt′; *n.* ĭ nĭsh′ĭ ĭt, -āt′), *v.,* **-ated, -ating,** *n.* —*v.t.* **1.** to begin or originate. **2.** to introduce into the knowledge of some subject. **3.** to admit with formal rites into secret knowledge, a society, etc. **4.** to propose (a measure) by initiative procedure. —*n.* **5.** one who has been initiated. —**in·i′ti·a′tor,** *n.*

in·i·ti·a·tion (ĭ nĭsh′ĭ ā′shən), *n.* **1.** formal admission into a society, etc. **2.** the ceremonies of admission. **3.** act of initiating.

in·i·ti·a·tive (ĭ nĭsh′ĭ ə tĭv, -ĭ ā′tĭv), *n.* **1.** an introductory act or step. **2.** readiness and ability in initiating action; enterprise. **3.** *Govt.* procedure by which a specified number of voters may propose a statute, etc., and compel a popular vote on its adoption. —*adj.* **4.** serving to initiate.

in·i·ti·a·to·ry (ĭ nĭsh′ĭ ə tōr′ĭ), *adj.* **1.** introductory; initial. **2.** serving to admit into a society, etc. —**in·i′ti·a·to′ri·ly,** *adv.*

in·ject (ĭn jĕkt′), *v.t.* **1.** to force (a fluid, etc.) into a passage, cavity, or tissue. **2.** to introduce (something), often arbitrarily or inappropriately. —**in·jec′tion,** *n.* —**in·jec′tor,** *n.*

in·junc·tion (ĭn jŭngk′shən), *n.* **1.** *Law.* a judicial process or order requiring the person or persons to whom it is directed to do or (more commonly) not to do a particular thing. **2.** a command, order, or admonition.

in·jure (ĭn′jər), *v.t.,* **-jured, -juring. 1.** to damage; hurt; impair. **2.** to do wrong or injustice to. —**in′jur·er,** *n.*

in·ju·ri·ous (ĭn jŏŏr′ĭ əs), *adj.* **1.** harmful, hurtful, or detrimental. **2.** wrongful. —**in·ju′ri·ous·ly,** *adv.* —**in·ju′ri·ous·ness,** *n.*

in·ju·ry (ĭn′jə rĭ), *n.,* *pl.* **-juries. 1.** harm of any kind done or sustained. **2.** a particular form or instance of harm. **3.** wrong or injustice done or suffered.

in·jus·tice (ĭn jŭs′tĭs), *n.* **1.** quality or fact of being unjust. **2.** unjust action or treatment. **3.** an unjust act or circumstance.

ink (ĭngk), *n.* **1.** a fluid or viscous substance used for writing or printing. —*v.t.* **2.** to mark, stain, cover, or smear with ink. —**ink′er,** *n.* —**ink′less,** *adj.* —**ink′like′,** *adj.*

ink·ling (ĭngk′lĭng), *n.* **1.** a hint or slight suggestion. **2.** a vague idea or notion.

ink·stand (ĭngk′stănd′), *n.* **1.** a stand for ink, pens, etc. **2.** Also, **ink·well** (ĭngk′wəl′). a container for ink.

ink·y (ĭngk′ĭ), *adj.,* **inkier, inkiest. 1.** black as ink. **2.** resembling ink. **3.** stained with ink. —**ink′i·ness,** *n.*

in·laid (ĭn′lād′, ĭn lād′), *adj.* **1.** set in the surface of a thing. **2.** decorated or made with a design set in the surface.

in·land (*adj.* ĭn′lənd; *adv., n.* ĭn′lănd′, -lənd), *adj.* **1.** pertaining to or situated in the interior part of a country or region. **2.** domestic; not foreign. —*adv.* **3.** in or toward the interior of a country. —*n.* **4.** the interior part of a country.

in-law (ĭn′lô′), *n.* *Colloq.* a relative by marriage.

in·lay (*v.* ĭn lā′; *n.* ĭn′lā′), *v.,* **-laid, -laying,** *n.* —*v.t.* **1.** to decorate (an object) with veneers of fine materials set in its surface. **2.** to insert or

apply (layers of fine materials) in a surface of an object. —*n.* **3.** inlaid work. **4.** material inserted in something else, esp. for ornament. **5.** *Dentistry.* a filling of metal, porcelain, or plastic which is fitted and fastened into a tooth as a solid mass.

in·let (*n.* ĭn′lĕt; *v.* ĭn lĕt′), *n., v.,* **-let, -letting.** —*n.* **1.** a narrow indentation of a shore line, or a narrow passage between islands. **2.** an entrance. —*v.t.* **3.** to insert.

in·ly (ĭn′lĭ), *adv.* *Now Poetic.* inwardly.

in·mate (ĭn′māt′), *n.* **1.** one who dwells with another or others in the same house. **2.** one of those confined in a hospital, prison, etc.

in me·mo·ri·am (ĭn mə mōr′ĭ ăm′), in memory (of); as a memorial (to).

in·most (ĭn′mōst′, -məst), *adj.* **1.** situated furthest within. **2.** most intimate.

inn (ĭn), *n.* **1.** a small hotel. **2.** a tavern.

in·nate (ĭ nāt′, ĭn′āt), *adj.* **1.** existing in one from birth; inborn. **2.** arising from the constitution of the mind, rather than acquired from experience. —**in·nate′ly,** *adv.*

in·ner (ĭn′ər), *adj.* **1.** situated farther within; interior. **2.** more intimate, private, or secret. **3.** mental or spiritual. **4.** not obvious; esoteric.

in·ner·most (ĭn′ər mōst′, -məst), *adj.* **1.** farthest inward. —*n.* **2.** innermost part.

in·ning (ĭn′ĭng), *n.* **1.** *Baseball.* a round in which both teams bat, with each side getting three outs. **2.** an opportunity for activity; a turn.

inn·keep·er (ĭn′kē′pər), *n.* the owner or manager of an inn.

in·no·cence (ĭn′ə səns), *n.* **1.** freedom from moral or legal wrong; guiltlessness. **2.** simplicity or guilelessness. Also, **in′no·cen·cy.**

in·no·cent (ĭn′ə sənt), *adj.* **1.** free from any moral or legal wrong; guiltless. **2.** not involving evil intent or motive. **3.** harmless. **4.** having or showing the simplicity or naiveté of an unworldly person. —*n.* **5.** an innocent person. **6.** a guileless person. —**in′no·cent·ly,** *adv.*

in·noc·u·ous (ĭ nŏk′yŏŏ əs), *adj.* not harmful or injurious. —**in·noc′u·ous·ly,** *adv.*

in·nom·i·nate bone (ĭ nŏm′ə nĭt), *Anat.* either of the two bones forming the sides of the pelvis.

in·no·vate (ĭn′ə vāt′), *v.,* **-vated, -vating.** —*v.i.* **1.** to bring in something new. —*v.t.* **2.** to bring in (something new) for the first time. —**in′no·va′tor,** *n.*

in·no·va·tion (ĭn′ə vā′shən), *n.* **1.** something new introduced. **2.** act of innovating.

in·nu·en·do (ĭn′yŏŏ ĕn′dō), *n.,* *pl.* **-does.** an indirect intimation about a person or thing, esp. of a derogatory nature.

in·nu·mer·a·ble (ĭ nū′mər ə bəl, -nŏŏ′-), *adj.* **1.** very numerous. **2.** incapable of being numbered or counted. —**in·nu′mer·a·bly,** *adv.*

in·oc·u·late (ĭ nŏk′yə lāt′), *v.t.,* **-lated, -lating. 1.** to implant (a disease) in a person or animal by the introduction of germs or virus, as through a puncture, in order to produce a mild form of the disease and thus secure immunity. **2.** to impregnate (a person or animal) thus. —**in·oc′u·la′tion,** *n.* —**in·oc′u·la′tor,** *n.*

in·or·di·nate (ĭn ôr′də nĭt), *adj.* **1.** excessive. **2.** disorderly. **3.** unrestrained in conduct, etc. **4.** irregular. —**in·or′di·nate·ly,** *adv.*

in·or·gan·ic (ĭn′ôr găn′ĭk), *adj.* **1.** not having the organization which characterizes living bodies. **2.** not characterized by vital processes. **3.** *Chem.* noting or pertaining to compounds not containing carbon, excepting cyanides and carbonates. **4.** not fundamental. —**in′or·gan′i·cal·ly,** *adv.*

in·pa·tient (ĭn′pā′shənt), *n.* a patient who is lodged and fed as well as treated in a hospital.

in·put (ĭn′pŏŏt′), *n.* **1.** that which is put in. **2.** the power supplied to a machine.

in·quest (ĭn′kwĕst), *n.* **1.** a legal or judicial inquiry, esp. before a jury. **2.** an inquiry made by a coroner (**coroner's inquest**).

in·quire (ĭn kwīr′), *v.,* **-quired, -quiring.** —*v.t.* **1.** to seek to learn by asking. —*v.i.* **2.** to seek information by questioning; ask. **3.** to make investigation. —**in·quir′er,** *n.* —**in·quir′ing·ly,** *adv.*

in·quir·y (ĭn kwīr′ĭ, ĭn′kwə rĭ), *n.,* *pl.* **-quiries.**

in·hos′pi·ta·ble	in′ju·di′cious	in′ob·serv′ance	in′of·fen′sive·ness
in·hos′pi·ta·bly	in′ju·di′cious·ly	in′ob·serv′ant	in·op′er·a·ble
in′hos·pi·tal′i·ty	in′ju·di′cious·ness	in·o′dor·ous	in·op′er·a′tive
in′hu·mane′	in·nox′ious	in′of·fen′sive	in·op′por·tune′
in′hu·mane′ly	in′nu·tri′tion	in′of·fen′sive·ly	in·qui′e·tude′

1. a seeking for truth, information, or knowledge. **2.** interrogation. **3.** a question or query.

in·qui·si·tion (ĭn'kwə zĭsh'ən), *n.* **1.** act of inquiring; inquiry; research. **2.** an investigation. **3.** (*cap.*) *Rom. Cath. Ch.* a special tribunal for the defense of Catholic teaching in faith and morals, the judgment of heresy, the application of canonical punishment, etc. —**in'qui·si'tion·al,** *adj.*

in·quis·i·tive (ĭn kwĭz'ə tĭv), *adj.* **1.** given to inquiry or research; curious. **2.** unduly curious; prying. —*n.* **3.** an inquisitive person. —**in·quis'i·tive·ly,** *adv.* —**in·quis'i·tive·ness,** *n.*

in·quis·i·tor (ĭn kwĭz'ə tər), *n.* **1.** one who makes inquisition. **2.** a questioner.

in·quis·i·to·ri·al (ĭn kwĭz'ə tōr'ē əl), *adj.* pertaining to an inquisitor or inquisitors, or to inquisition.

in re (ĭn rē'), *Latin.* in the matter of.

in·road (ĭn'rōd'), *n.* **1.** forcible or serious encroachment. **2.** a raid; foray.

in·rush (ĭn'rŭsh'), *n.* a rushing in; influx.

ins., **1.** inches. **2.** inspector.

in·sane (ĭn sān'), *adj.* **1.** mentally deranged. **2.** characteristic of one mentally deranged. **3.** set apart for the use of mentally deranged persons. **4.** utterly senseless. —**in·sane'ly,** *adv.* —**in·sane'ness,** *n.*

in·san·i·ty (ĭn săn'ə tĭ), *n., pl.* **-ties. 1.** condition of being insane. **2.** extreme folly.

in·scribe (ĭn skrīb'), *v.t.* **-scribed, -scribing. 1.** to write or engrave (words, characters, etc.). **2.** to mark (a surface) with words, characters, etc. **3.** to address or dedicate (a book, photograph, etc.) informally. **4.** to enroll. **5.** *Geom.* to draw (one figure) within another figure so that the inner lies in the boundary of the outer at as many points as possible. —**in·scrib'a·ble,** *adj.* —**in·scrib'er,** *n.*

in·scrip·tion (ĭn skrĭp'shən), *n.* **1.** something inscribed. **2.** a brief, informal dedication, as of a book.

in·scru·ta·ble (ĭn skrōō'tə bəl), *adj.* **1.** incapable of being scrutinized; impenetrable to investigation. **2.** impenetrable or unfathomable physically. —**in·scru'ta·bil'i·ty,** *n.* —**in·scru'ta·bly,** *adv.*

in·sect (ĭn'sĕkt), *n.* **1.** *Zool.* any animal of the class *Insecta,* a group of small, air-breathing arthropods characterized by a body clearly divided into three parts: head, thorax, and abdomen. **2.** any arthropod having superficial similarity to the *Insecta.* **3.** a contemptible person. —**in'sect·like',** *adj.*

in·sec·ti·cide (ĭn sĕk'tə sīd'), *n.* a substance or preparation used for killing insects. —**in·sec'ti·cid'al,** *adj.*

in·sec·ti·vore (ĭn sĕk'tə vōr'), *n.* **1.** an insectivorous animal or plant. **2.** any of the mammalian order that includes the moles, shrews, and Old World hedgehogs.

in·sec·tiv·o·rous (ĭn'sĕk tĭv'ə rəs), *adj.* adapted to feeding on insects, as shrews, moles, hedgehogs, etc.

in·sem·i·nate (ĭn sĕm'ə nāt'), *v.t.* **-nated, -nating. 1.** to inject seed into. **2.** to impregnate. **3.** to sow as seed in something; implant. —**in·sem'i·na'tion,** *n.*

in·sen·sate (ĭn sĕn'sāt, -sĭt), *adj.* **1.** not endowed with sensation. **2.** unfeeling. **3.** without sense, understanding, or judgment. —**in·sen'sate·ly,** *adv.*

in·sep·a·ra·ble (ĭn sĕp'ə rə bəl), *adj.* **1.** incapable of being separated, parted, or disjoined. —*n.* (*usually pl.*) **2.** something inseparable. **3.** an inseparable companion or friend. —**in·sep'a·ra·bly,** *adv.*

in·sert (*v.* ĭn sûrt'; *n.* ĭn'sûrt), *v.t.* **1.** to put or set in. **2.** to introduce into the body of something. —*n.* **3.** something inserted, or to be inserted.

in·ser·tion (ĭn sûr'shən), *n.* **1.** act of inserting. **2.** something inserted.

in·ses·so·ri·al (ĭn'sĕ sōr'ē əl), *adj.* **1.** adapted for perching. **2.** habitually perching.

in·set (*n.* ĭn'sĕt'; *v.* ĭn sĕt'), *n., v.,* **-set, -setting.** —*n.* **1.** an insert. **2.** influx. —*v.t.* **3.** to insert.

in·shore (ĭn'shōr'), *adj.* **1.** close to the shore.

2. lying or operating close to the shore. —*adv.* **3.** toward the shore.

in·side (*prep.,* *adv.* ĭn'sīd'; *n., adj.* ĭn'sīd'), *prep.* **1.** within. —*adv.* **2.** in or into the inner part. **3.** within the space or period. **4.** on the inside. —*n.* **5.** the inner part; interior. **6.** the inner side or surface. **7.** (*often pl.*) *Colloq.* the inward parts of the body. **8.** the inward nature. —*adj.* **9.** interior; internal. **10.** acting, employed, done, or originating within a building or place. **11.** derived from the inner circle of those concerned in and having private knowledge of a case.

in·sid·er (ĭn'sī'dər), *n.* **1.** one who is inside some place, society, etc. **2.** *Colloq.* one who is within a limited circle of persons who understand the actual facts in a case.

in·sid·i·ous (ĭn sĭd'ē əs), *adj.* **1.** intended to entrap or beguile. **2.** stealthily treacherous. **3.** operating or proceeding inconspicuously but with grave effect. —**in·sid'i·ous·ly,** *adv.* —**in·sid'i·ous·ness,** *n.*

in·sight (ĭn'sīt'), *n.* **1.** a sight had or given into something. **2.** penetrating mental discernment.

in·sig·ni·a (ĭn sĭg'nĭ ə), *n. pl., sing.* **insigne** (-nē). **1.** badges or distinguishing marks of office or honor. **2.** distinguishing marks or signs.

in·sig·nif·i·cant (ĭn'sĭg nĭf'ə kənt), *adj.* **1.** unimportant, trifling, or petty. **2.** too small to be important. **3.** of no consequence, influence, or distinction. **4.** contemptible. **5.** meaningless. —*n.* **6.** a word, thing, or person without significance. —**in'sig·nif'i·cance,** *n.* —**in'sig·nif'i·cant·ly,** *adv.*

in·sin·u·ate (ĭn sĭn'yōō āt'), *v.,* **-ated, -ating.** —*v.t.* **1.** to suggest or hint slyly. **2.** to instill or infuse subtly or artfully into the mind. **3.** to bring into a position by artful methods. —*v.i.* **4.** to make insinuations. —**in·sin'u·at'ing·ly,** *adv.* —**in·sin'u·a'tive,** *adj.* —**in·sin'u·a'tor,** *n.*

in·sin·u·a·tion (ĭn sĭn'yōō ā'shən), *n.* **1.** covert or artful hinting, as of something not plainly stated. **2.** a hint of this kind. **3.** subtle or artful instillment into the mind. **4.** act of insinuating. **5.** ingratiation. **6.** the art or power of stealing into the affections and pleasing. **7.** an ingratiating act or speech.

in·sip·id (ĭn sĭp'ĭd), *adj.* **1.** without distinctive, interesting, or attractive qualities. **2.** without sufficient taste to be pleasing. —**in'si·pid'i·ty,** **in·sip'id·ness,** *n.* —**in·sip'id·ly,** *adv.*

in·sist (ĭn sĭst'), *v.i.* to be emphatic, firm, or pertinacious on some matter of desire, demand, intention, etc.

in·sist·ent (ĭn sĭs'tənt), *adj.* **1.** earnest or emphatic in dwelling upon, maintaining, or demanding something; persistent. **2.** compelling attention or notice. —**in·sist'ence, in·sist'en·cy,** *n.* —**in·sist'ent·ly,** *adv.*

in·snare (ĭn snâr'), *v.t.,* **-snared, -snaring.** ensnare.

in·sole (ĭn'sōl'), *n.* the inner sole of a shoe.

in·so·lent (ĭn'sə lənt), *adj.* boldly rude or disrespectful. —**in'so·lence,** *n.* —**in'so·lent·ly,** *adv.*

in·sol·vent (ĭn sŏl'vənt), *Law.* —*adj.* **1.** unable to satisfy creditors or discharge liabilities. **2.** pertaining to bankrupt persons or bankruptcy. —*n.* **3.** one who is insolvent. —**in·sol'ven·cy,** *n.*

in·som·ni·a (ĭn sŏm'nĭ ə), *n.* inability to sleep, esp. when chronic; sleeplessness.

in·so·much (ĭn'sō mŭch'), *adv.* **1.** to such an extent (*that*); so (*that*). **2.** inasmuch (*as*).

in·sou·ci·ant (ĭn sōō'sĭ ənt), *adj.* free from concern; carefree. —**in·sou'ci·ance,** *n.*

in·spect (ĭn spĕkt'), *v.t.* **1.** to view closely and critically. **2.** to examine formally or officially. —**in·spec·tion** (ĭn spĕk'shən), *n.*

in·spec·tor (ĭn spĕk'tər), *n.* **1.** one who inspects. **2.** an officer of police, usually ranking next below a superintendent.

in·spi·ra·tion (ĭn'spə rā'shən), *n.* **1.** an inspiring or animating action or influence. **2.** something inspired, as a thought. **3.** *Theol.* a divine influence directly and immediately exerted upon the mind or soul of a man. **4.** inhalation. **5.** act of inspiring. —**in'spi·ra'tion·al,** *adj.*

in·spire (ĭn spīr'), *v.,* **-spired, -spiring.** —*v.t.* **1.** to infuse an animating, quickening, or exalting influence into. **2.** to produce or arouse (a feeling,

in·san'i·tar'y	in'se·cure'ly	in·sen'si·tive	in'sin·cer'i·ty
in·sa'tia·ble	in'se·cu'ri·ty	in·sen'ti·ence	in'so·bri'e·ty
in·sa'tia·bly	in·sen'si·bil'i·ty	in·sen'ti·ent	in·sol'u·bil'i·ty
in·sa'ti·ate	in·sen'si·ble	in'sin·cere'	in·sol'u·ble
in'se·cure'	in·sen'si·bly	in'sin·cere'ly	in·solv'a·ble

thought, etc.). **3.** to affect with a specified feeling, thought, etc. **4.** to influence or impel. **5.** to prompt or instigate (utterances, etc.) by influence. **6.** to inhale. —*v.i.* **7.** to give inspiration. **8.** to inhale. —**in·spir′er,** *n.*

in·spir·it (ĭn spĭr′ĭt), *v.t.* to infuse (new) spirit or life into. —**in·spir′it·ing·ly,** *adv.*

in·spis·sate (ĭn spĭs′āt), *v.t.*, *v.i.*, **-sated, -sat·ing.** to thicken, as by evaporation.

inst., **1.** instant. **2.** (*also cap.*) institute. **3.** (*also cap.*) institution.

in·stall (ĭn stôl′), *v.t.* **1.** to place in position for service or use, as a system of electric lighting, etc. **2.** to establish in any office, position, or place. —**in·stal·la·tion** (ĭn stə lā′shən), *n.*

in·stall·ment[1] (ĭn stôl′mənt), *n.* **1.** any of several parts into which a debt or other sum payable is divided for payment at successive fixed times. **2.** a single portion of something furnished or issued by parts at successive times. Also, **in·stal′ment.**

in·stall·ment[2] (ĭn stôl′mənt), *n.* installation. Also, **in·stal′ment.**

in·stance (ĭn′stəns), *n.*, *v.*, **-stanced, -stancing.** —*n.* **1.** a case of anything. **2.** an example put forth in proof or illustration. **3. for instance,** for example. **4.** urging or suggestion. **5.** legal process. —*v.t.* **6.** to cite as an instance or example.

in·stant (ĭn′stənt), *n.* **1.** a very short space of time; a moment. **2.** the present or specified point of time. —*adj.* **3.** immediate. **4.** present; current. —*adv.* **5.** *Poetic.* instantly.

in·stan·ta·ne·ous (ĭn′stən tā′nĭ əs), *adj.* **1.** occurring, done, or completed in an instant. **2.** existing at or pertaining to a particular instant. —**in′stan·ta′ne·ous·ly,** *adv.*

in·stan·ter (ĭn stăn′tər), *adv.* instantly.

in·stant·ly (ĭn′stənt lĭ), *adv.* immediately; at once. **2.** *Archaic.* urgently.

in·state (ĭn stāt′), *v.t.*, **-stated, -stating.** to put into a certain state or position. —**in·state′-ment,** *n.*

in·stead (ĭn stĕd′), *adv.* **1.** in the place; in lieu (fol. by *of*). **2.** in one's (its, their, etc.) stead.

in·step (ĭn′stĕp′), *n.* the arched upper surface of the human foot between the toes and the ankle.

in·sti·gate (ĭn′stə gāt′), *v.t.*, **-gated, -gating.** **1.** to spur on or incite to some action. **2.** to foment. —**in′sti·ga′tion,** *n.* —**in′sti·ga′tive,** *adj.* —**in′sti·ga′tor,** *n.*

in·still (ĭn stĭl′), *v.t.*, **-stilled, -stilling.** **1.** to infuse slowly into the mind or feelings. **2.** to put in drop by drop. Also, **in·stil′.** —**in·still′ment,** *n.*

in·stinct[1] (ĭn′stĭngkt), *n.* **1.** an inborn pattern of activity and response common to a given biological stock; innate impulse. **2.** a natural aptitude. —**in·stinc′tu·al,** *adj.*

in·stinct[2] (ĭn stĭngkt′), *adj.* urged or animated from within (fol. by *with*).

in·stinc·tive (ĭn stĭngk′tĭv), *adj.* **1.** pertaining to or of the nature of instinct. **2.** prompted by instinct. —**in·stinc′tive·ly,** *adv.*

in·sti·tute (ĭn′stə tūt′, -tōōt′), *v.*, **-tuted, -tuting,** *n.* —*v.t.* **1.** to set up or establish. **2.** to inaugurate; initiate. **3.** to set in operation. **4.** to bring into use or practice. —*n.* **5.** a society or organization, as of literary, scientific, or educational character. **6.** an established principle, law, custom, or organization. **7.** (*pl.*) an elementary textbook of law.

in·sti·tu·tion (ĭn′stə tū′shən, -tōō′-), *n.* **1.** an organization for the promotion of a particular object. **2.** any established law, custom, practice, etc. **3.** act of instituting; establishment.

in·sti·tu·tion·al (ĭn′stə tū′shən əl, -tōō′-), *adj.* **1.** of, pertaining to, or established by institution. **2.** *Advertising.* having good will and a wider reputation as the primary object rather than the securing of present purchasers. —**in′sti·tu′-tion·al·ly,** *adv.*

instr., **1.** instructor. **2.** instrument.

in·struct (ĭn strŭkt′), *v.t.* **1.** to direct; furnish with orders. **2.** to teach; train; educate.

in·struc·tion (ĭn strŭk′shən), *n.* **1.** act or practice of instructing. **2.** knowledge imparted. **3.** (*usually pl.*) an order or direction. —**in·struc′-tion·al,** *adj.*

in·struc·tive (ĭn strŭk′tĭv), *adj.* serving to instruct or inform. —**in·struc′tive·ly,** *adv.*

in·struc·tor (ĭn strŭk′tər), *n.* **1.** one who instructs; teacher. **2.** the academic rank given in American colleges to a teacher ranking below the lowest grade of professor.

in·stru·ment (ĭn′strə mənt), *n.* **1.** a tool; implement. **2.** a contrivance for producing musical sounds. **3.** a thing with or by which something is effected; a means. **4.** a formal legal document.

in·stru·men·tal (ĭn′strə mĕn′təl), *adj.* **1.** serving as a means. **2.** of or pertaining to an instrument. **3.** helpful; useful. **4.** performed on or written for musical instruments. **5.** *Gram.* denoting a case which has as chief function the indication of means or agency. —*n.* **6.** *Gram.* the instrumental case.

in·stru·men·tal·ist (ĭn′strə mĕn′təl ĭst), *n.* one who performs on a musical instrument.

in·stru·men·tal·i·ty (ĭn′strə mĕn tăl′ə tĭ), *n.*, *pl.* **-ties.** **1.** quality of being instrumental. **2.** fact or function of serving some purpose. **3.** a means or agency. **4.** helpfulness; usefulness.

in·stru·men·tal·ly (ĭn′strə mĕn′tə lĭ), *adv.* **1.** by the use of an instrument. **2.** with or on an instrument.

in·stru·men·ta·tion (ĭn′strə mĕn tā′shən), *n.* **1.** the arranging of music for instruments, esp. for an orchestra. **2.** instrumentality.

in·suf·fer·a·ble (ĭn sŭf′ər ə bəl), *adj.* not to be endured; unbearable. —**in·suf′fer·a·ble·ness,** *n.* —**in·suf′fer·a·bly,** *adv.*

in·su·lar (ĭn′sə lər), *adj.* **1.** of or pertaining to an island or islands. **2.** dwelling or situated on an island. **3.** narrow or illiberal. —**in·su·lar·i·ty** (ĭn′sə lăr′ə tĭ), *n.* —**in′su·lar·ly,** *adv.*

in·su·late (ĭn′sə lāt′), *v.t.*, **-lated, -lating.** **1.** to cover or surround (an electric wire, etc.) with nonconducting material. **2.** *Physics, etc.* to separate by the interposition of a nonconductor, in order to prevent or reduce the transfer of electricity, heat, or sound. **3.** to isolate or segregate.

in·su·la·tion (ĭn′sə lā′shən), *n.* **1.** material used for insulating. **2.** act of insulating. **3.** resulting state.

in·su·la·tor (ĭn′sə lā′tər), *n.* insulating material, often glass or porcelain, in a form so designed as to support a charged conductor and electrically isolate it.

in·su·lin (ĭn′sə lĭn), *n.* **1.** *Med.* an extract obtained from the pancreas of animals, used in the treatment of diabetes, and causing a reduction of sugar in the blood and urine. **2.** (*cap.*) a trademark for this extract.

in·sult (*v.* ĭn sŭlt′; *n.* ĭn′sŭlt), *v.t.* **1.** to treat insolently or with contemptuous rudeness; affront. —*n.* **2.** an insolent or contemptuously rude action or speech; affront. —**in·sult′ing,** *adj.*

in·su·per·a·ble (ĭn sōō′pər ə bəl), *adj.* incapable of being passed over, overcome, or surmounted. —**in·su′per·a·bil′i·ty, in·su′per·a·ble·ness,** *n.* —**in·su′per·a·bly,** *adv.*

in·sup·port·a·ble (ĭn′sə pōr′tə bəl), *adj.* not endurable; insufferable.

in·sur·a·ble (ĭn shŏŏr′ə bəl), *adj.* capable of being insured, as against risk of loss.

in·sur·ance (ĭn shŏŏr′əns), *n.* **1.** the act, system, or business of insuring property, life, etc., against loss or harm arising in specified contingencies, as fire, accident, death, disablement, or the like, in consideration of a payment proportioned to the risk involved. **2.** the contract thus made. **3.** the amount for which anything is insured. **4.** the premium paid for insuring a thing.

in·sure (ĭn shŏŏr′), *v.*, **-sured, -suring.** —*v.t.* **1.** to make sure, secure, or certain. **2.** to guarantee against risk of loss or harm. **3.** to secure indemnity to or on, in case of loss, damage, or death. **4.** to issue an insurance policy on. —*v.i.* **5.** to issue an insurance policy.

in·sured (ĭn shŏŏrd′), *n.* a person covered by an insurance policy.

in·sur·er (ĭn shŏŏr′ər), *n.* one who or that which insures.

in·sur·gent (ĭn sûr′jənt), *n.* **1.** one who rises in forcible opposition to lawful authority. **2.** *U.S. Pol.* a member of a political party who revolts against the methods or policies of the party. —*adj.* **3.** rising in revolt; rebellious. —**in·sur′-gence,** *in·sur′gen·cy,* *n.*

in·sur·rec·tion (ĭn′sə rĕk′shən), *n.* **1.** act of rising in arms against established authority. **2.**

in′sta·bil′i·ty	in′sub·or′di·nate·ly	in′suf·fi′cien·cy	in′sup·press′i·bly
in·sta′ble	in′sub·or′di·na′tion	in′suf·fi′cient	in′sur·mount′a·ble
in′sub·or′di·nate	in′sub·stan′tial	in′sup·press′i·ble	in′sur·mount′a·bly

a revolt. —**in/sur·rec/tion·ar/y,** *adj., n.* —**in/sur·rec/tion·ist,** *n.*

in·swept (ĭn/swĕpt/), *adj.* tapering at the front or tip, as an airplane wing.

int., 1. interest. 2. interior. 3. internal. 4. international. 5. intransitive.

in·tact (ĭn tăkt/), *adj.* remaining uninjured, unaltered, sound, or whole; unimpaired.

in·tagl·io (ĭn tăl/yō, -tăl/-), *n., pl.* **intaglios.** 1. a gem, seal, piece of jewelry, or the like, cut with an incised or sunken design. 2. incised carving, as opposed to carving in relief.

in·take (ĭn/tāk/), *n.* 1. the point at which a fluid is taken into a channel, pipe, etc. 2. act of taking in. 3. that which is taken in. 4. quantity taken in.

in·tan·gi·ble (ĭn tăn/jə bəl), *adj.* 1. incapable of being perceived by the sense of touch. 2. not definite or clear to the mind. —*n.* 3. something intangible. —**in·tan/gi·bil/i·ty, in·tan/gi·ble·ness,** *n.* —**in·tan/gi·bly,** *adv.*

in·te·ger (ĭn/tə jər), *n.* 1. one of the numbers 0, 1, 2, 3, 4, etc.; a whole number, as distinguished from a fraction or a mixed number. 2. a complete entity.

in·te·gral (ĭn/tə grəl), *adj.* 1. of or pertaining to a whole; constituent or component. 2. necessary to the completeness of the whole. 3. entire or complete. 4. *Arith.* pertaining to or being an integer; not fractional. —*n.* 5. an integral whole. —**in/te·gral·ly,** *adv.*

in·te·grate (ĭn/tə grāt/), *v.t.,* -**grated,** -**grating.** 1. to bring together (parts) into a whole. 2. to make up or complete as a whole. —**in/te·gra/tion,** *n.*

in·teg·ri·ty (ĭn tĕg/rə tĭ), *n.* 1. soundness of moral character; uprightness. 2. state of being whole, entire, or undiminished. 3. sound, unimpaired, or perfect condition.

in·teg·u·ment (ĭn tĕg/yə mənt), *n.* 1. a skin, shell, rind, or the like. 2. a covering.

in·tel·lect (ĭn/tə lĕkt/), *n.* 1. the power or faculty of the mind by which one knows or understands; understanding. 2. mental capacity, esp. of a high order. 3. a person of high mental capacity.

in·tel·lec·tu·al (ĭn/tə lĕk/chŏŏ əl), *adj.* 1. appealing to or engaging the intellect. 2. of or pertaining to the intellect. 3. directed or inclined toward things that involve the intellect. 4. possessing or showing intellect or mental capacity, esp. to a high degree. —*n.* 5. an intellectual being or person. —**in·tel·lec·tu·al·i·ty** (ĭn/tə lĕk/chŏŏ-ăl/ə tĭ), *n.* —**in/tel·lec/tu·al·ly,** *adv.*

in·tel·lec·tu·al·ism (ĭn/tə lĕk/chŏŏ ə lĭz/əm), *n.* 1. devotion to intellectual pursuits. 2. *Philos.* the doctrine that knowledge is wholly or chiefly derived from pure reason.

in·tel·li·gence (ĭn tĕl/ə jəns), *n.* 1. capacity for understanding and for other forms of adaptive behavior. 2. good mental capacity. 3. news; information. 4. the gathering or distribution of information, esp. secret information. 5. a staff of persons engaged in obtaining such information.

intelligence quotient, the mental age divided by the actual age.

intelligence test, any of several psychological tests which attempt to measure the mental development of an individual.

in·tel·li·gent (ĭn tĕl/ə jənt), *adj.* having or showing a good understanding or mental capacity. —**in·tel/li·gent·ly,** *adv.*

in·tel·li·gent·si·a (ĭn tĕl/ə jĕnt/sĭ ə, -gĕnt/sĭ ə), *n.pl.* a group of persons having or claiming special enlightenment; the intellectuals.

in·tel·li·gi·ble (ĭn tĕl/ə jə bəl), *adj.* capable of being understood; comprehensible. —**in·tel·li·gi·bil·i·ty** (ĭn tĕl/ə jə bĭl/ə tĭ), *n.* —**in/tel/li·gi·bly,** *adv.*

in·tend (ĭn tĕnd/), *v.t.* 1. to have in mind as something to be done or brought about. 2. to design or mean for a particular purpose, recipient, etc. —*v.i.* 3. to have a purpose or design.

in·tend·an·cy (ĭn tĕn/dən sĭ), *n., pl.* -**cies.** the office or function of an intendant.

in·tend·ant (ĭn tĕn/dənt), *n.* a director, manager, or superintendent.

in·tend·ed (ĭn tĕn/dĭd), *adj.* 1. purposed or designed. 2. prospective. —*n.* 3. *Colloq.* an intended husband or wife.

in·tense (ĭn tĕns/), *adj.* 1. existing or occurring in a high or extreme degree. 2. acute, strong, or

vehement, as emotions. 3. very great, strong, keen, severe, etc. 4. strenuous or earnest, as activity. 5. having or showing great strength of feeling, as language. 6. emotional. —**in·tense/ly,** *adv.* —**in·tense/ness,** *n.*

in·ten·si·fy (ĭn tĕn/sə fī/), *v.t., v.i.,* -**fied,** -**fying.** to make or become intense or more intense. —**in·ten/si·fi·ca/tion,** *n.* —**in·ten/si·fi/er,** *n.*

in·ten·si·ty (ĭn tĕn/sə tĭ), *n., pl.* -**ties.** 1. quality or condition of being intense. 2. great energy, strength, vehemence, etc. 3. high or extreme degree. 4. the degree to which something is intense. 5. loudness or softness of vocal tone. 6. *Physics.* a. the strength of an electric current in amperes. b. voltage. c. the strength of an electrical or magnetic field. d. the magnitude, as of a force, etc.

in·ten·sive (ĭn tĕn/sĭv), *adj.* 1. of, pertaining to, or characterized by intensity. 2. *Gram.* indicating increased emphasis or force. —*n.* 3. something that intensifies. 4. *Gram.* an intensive element or formation. —**in·ten/sive·ly,** *adv.*

in·tent[1] (ĭn tĕnt/), *n.* 1. an intending or purposing. 2. purpose; aim.

in·tent[2] (ĭn tĕnt/), *adj.* 1. firmly or steadfastly fixed or directed. 2. having the gaze or thoughts earnestly fixed on something. 3. bent, as on some purpose. 4. earnest. —**in·tent/ly,** *adv.* —**in·tent/ness,** *n.*

in·ten·tion (ĭn tĕn/shən), *n.* 1. a purpose or design. 2. the end or object intended. 3. (*pl.*) *Colloq.* purposes with respect to a proposal of marriage. 4. meaning.

in·ten·tion·al (ĭn tĕn/shən əl), *adj.* done with intention or on purpose. —**in·ten/tion·al·ly,** *adv.*

in·ter (ĭn tûr/), *v.t.,* -**terred,** -**terring.** to bury, esp. with ceremonies.

inter-, a prefix meaning "between," "among," "mutually," "reciprocally," "together," as in *interweave.*

in·ter·act (ĭn/tər ăkt/), *v.i.* to act on each other. —**in/ter·ac/tion,** *n.* —**in/ter·ac/tive,** *adj.*

in·ter·breed (ĭn/tər brēd/), *v.t., v.i.,* -**bred,** -**breeding.** to breed by the crossing of different animal or plant species, breeds, varieties, or individuals.

in·ter·cede (ĭn/tər sēd/), *v.i.,* -**ceded,** -**ceding.** to interpose in behalf of one in difficulty or trouble, as by pleading or petition.

in·ter·cel·lu·lar (ĭn/tər sĕl/yə lər), *adj.* situated between or among cells or cellules.

in·ter·cept (ĭn/tər sĕpt/), *v.t.* 1. to cut off from the intended destination. 2. to stop the natural course of (light, water, etc.). 3. to stop or check (passage, etc.). 4. *Chiefly Math.* to mark off or include, as between two points or lines. —**in/ter·cep/tion,** *n.* —**in/ter·cep/tor,** *n.*

in·ter·ces·sion (ĭn/tər sĕsh/ən), *n.* act of interceding. —**in·ter·ces·sor** (ĭn/tər sĕs/ər), *n.* —**in/ter·ces/so·ry,** *adj.*

Arc of circle intercepted by line between points X and Y

in·ter·change (*v.* ĭn/tər chānj/; *n.* ĭn/tər chānj/), *v.t.,* -**changed,** -**changing,** *n.* —*v.t.* 1. to put each of (two things) in the place of the other. 2. to exchange. 3. to cause to alternate. —*v.i.* 4. to alternate. 5. to change places. —*n.* 6. act of interchanging. —**in/ter·change/a·ble,** *adj.* —**in/ter·change/a·bil/i·ty,** *n.*

in·ter·col·le·gi·ate (ĭn/tər kə lē/jĭ ĭt, -jĭt), *adj.* between colleges.

in·ter·com (ĭn/tər kŏm/), *n.* *Slang.* an intercommunication system, as of an airplane.

in·ter·com·mu·ni·cate (ĭn/tər kə mū/nə kāt/), *v.t., v.i.,* -**cated,** -**cating.** to communicate mutually. —**in/ter·com·mu/ni·ca/tion,** *n.*

in·ter·con·nect (ĭn/tər kə nĕkt/), *v.t.* to connect, one with another. —**in/ter·con·nec/tion,** *n.*

in·ter·cos·tal (ĭn/tər kŏs/təl, -kôs/təl), *adj.* 1. pertaining to muscles, parts, or intervals between the ribs. 2. situated between the ribs. —*n.* 3. an intercostal muscle, part, or space.

in·ter·course (ĭn/tər kōrs/), *n.* 1. dealings between individuals. 2. interchange of thoughts, etc. 3. sexual relations.

in·ter·de·nom·i·na·tion·al (ĭn/tər dĭ nŏm/ə nā/shən əl), *adj.* between (religious) denominations.

---

in/sus·cep/ti·ble | in·tem/per·ance | in·tem/per·ate | in·tem/per·ate·ly

in·ter·de·pend·ent (Ĭn'tər dĬ pĕn'dənt), *adj.* mutually dependent. —**in'ter·de·pend'ence,** **in'ter·de·pend'en·cy,** *n.* —**in'ter·de·pend'ent·ly,** *adv.*

in·ter·dict (*n.* Ĭn'tər dĬkt'; *v.* Ĭn'tər dĬkt'), *n.* **1.** a prohibitory act or decree of a court or an administrative officer. **2.** *Rom. Cath. Ch.* a punishment by which the faithful, remaining in communion with the Church, are prohibited from participation in certain sacred acts. —*v.t.* **3.** *Eccles.* to cut off authoritatively from certain ecclesiastical functions and privileges. **4.** to forbid; prohibit. —**in'ter·dic'tion,** *n.* —**in'ter·dic'to·ry,** *adj.*

in·ter·est (Ĭn'tər Ĭst, -trĬst), *n.* **1.** the feeling of one whose attention or curiosity is particularly engaged by something. **2.** a particular feeling of this kind. **3.** the power of exciting such feeling. **4.** importance. **5.** a business, cause, or the like, in which a number of persons are interested. **6.** a share in the ownership of property or the like. **7.** a group of persons having a common interest. **8.** something in which one has an interest. **9.** benefit or advantage. **10. in the interest** (or **interests) of,** on behalf of. **11.** *Com.* payment, or a sum paid, for the use of money borrowed. —*v.t.* **12.** to engage or excite the attention, curiosity, or participation of. **13.** to involve.

in·ter·est·ed (Ĭn'tər Ĭs tĬd, -trĬs tĬd, -tə rĕs'tĬd), *adj.* **1.** involved or concerned. **2.** having an interest or share. **3.** having the attention or curiosity engaged. **4.** characterized by a feeling of interest. **5.** influenced by personal or selfish motives. —**in'ter·est·ed·ly,** *adv.* —**in'ter·est·ed·ness,** *n.*

in·ter·est·ing (Ĭn'tər Ĭs tĬng, -trĬs tĬng, -tə rĕs'tĬng). *adj.* **1.** arousing a feeling of interest. **2.** engaging or exciting and holding the attention or curiosity. —**in'ter·est·ing·ly,** *adv.*

in·ter·fere (Ĭn'tər fĬr'), *v.i.* **1.** to clash; be in opposition. **2.** to come into opposition, esp. with the effect of hampering. **3.** to intervene for a particular purpose. **4.** to meddle. **5.** *Football, etc.* to obstruct the action of an opposing player in a way barred by the rules. **6.** *Physics.* to cause interference. —**in'ter·fer'er,** *n.* —**in'ter·fer'ing·ly,** *adv.*

in·ter·fer·ence (Ĭn'tər fĬr'əns), *n.* **1.** act or fact of interfering. **2.** *Physics.* the reciprocal action of waves (as of light, sound, etc.), when meeting, by which they reinforce or cancel each other. **3.** *Radio.* **a.** the jumbling of radio signals because signals other than the desired ones are being received. **b.** the signals which produce the incoherence.

in·ter·fold (Ĭn'tər fōld'), *v.t.* to fold, one within another; fold together.

in·ter·fuse (Ĭn'tər fūz'), *v.t., v.i.,* **-fused, -fusing.** **1.** to diffuse throughout or permeate. **2.** to blend or fuse, one with another. —**in'ter·fu'sion,** *n.*

in·ter·im (Ĭn'tər Ĭm), *n.* **1.** an intervening time; the meantime. —*adj.* **2.** temporary.

in·te·ri·or (Ĭn tĬr'Ĭ ər), *adj.* **1.** inside; internal. **2.** situated inside of and at a distance from the coast or border. **3.** inland or domestic. **4.** mental or spiritual. **5.** *Geom.* (of an angle) inner, as an angle formed between two parallel lines when cut by a third line. —*n.* **6.** the internal part; the inside. **7.** the inland parts of a region, country, etc. **8.** the domestic affairs of a country as distinguished from its foreign affairs. —**in·te'ri·or·ly,** *adv.*

interj., interjection.

in·ter·ject (Ĭn'tər jĕkt'), *v.t.* **1.** to include abruptly. **2.** to interpolate. —**in'ter·jec'tor,** *n.*

in·ter·jec·tion (Ĭn'tər jĕk'shən), *n.* **1.** act of interjecting. **2.** an exclamation. **3.** something, as a remark, interjected. **4.** *Gram.* **a.** a form class, or part of speech, comprising words which constitute utterances or clauses in themselves, without grammatical connection. **b.** such a word. —**in'ter·jec'tion·al,** *adj.* —**in'ter·jec'tion·al·ly,** *adv.*

in·ter·lace (Ĭn'tər lās'), *v.i., v.t.,* **-laced, -lacing.** to cross (threads, strips, etc.) as if woven together; blend intricately. —**in'ter·lace'ment,** *n.*

in·ter·lard (Ĭn'tər lärd'), *v.t.* **1.** to diversify with something intermixed or interjected. **2.** to be intermixed in.

in·ter·lay (Ĭn'tər lā'), *v.t.,* **-laid, -laying.** **1.** to lay between. **2.** to diversify with something laid between.

in·ter·leave (Ĭn'tər lēv'), *v.t.,* **-leaved, -leav-**

ing. **1.** to provide blank leaves in (a book) for notes. **2.** to insert blank leaves between (the regular printed leaves).

in·ter·line[1] (Ĭn'tər lĬn'), *v.t.,* **-lined, -lining.** to write between the lines of a book, manuscript, etc.

in·ter·line[2] (Ĭn'tər lĬn'), *v.t.,* **-lined, -lining.** to provide (a garment) with a lining between the ordinary lining and the outer fabric.

in·ter·lin·e·ar (Ĭn'tər lĬn'Ĭ ər), *adj.* **1.** situated between the lines. **2.** having interpolated lines.

in·ter·lin·ing (Ĭn'tər lĬ'nĬng), *n.* an inner lining placed between the ordinary lining and the outer fabric of a garment.

in·ter·link (Ĭn'tər lĬngk'), *v.t.* to link, one with another.

in·ter·lock (Ĭn'tər lŏk'), *v.i.* **1.** to lock or connect with each other. —*v.t.* **2.** to lock, one with another.

in·ter·loc·u·tor (Ĭn'tər lŏk'yə tər), *n.* **1.** the man in a minstrel troupe who carries on a conversation with the end men. **2.** one who takes parts in a conversation.

in·ter·loc·u·to·ry (Ĭn'tər lŏk'yə tōr'Ĭ), *adj.* **1.** of or occurring in conversation. **2.** *Law.* not finally decisive of a case.

in·ter·lope (Ĭn'tər lōp'), *v.i.,* **-loped, -loping.** to intrude, as into some field without a proper license. —**in'ter·lop'er,** *n.*

in·ter·lude (Ĭn'tər lōōd'), *n.* **1.** an intervening episode, period, space, etc. **2.** a short dramatic piece, esp. of a light or farcical character. **3.** a performance or entertainment, as between the acts of a play. **4.** an instrumental passage or a piece of music rendered between the parts of a song, church service, drama, etc.

in·ter·mar·ry (Ĭn'tər măr'Ĭ), *v.i.,* **-ried, -rying.** **1.** to become connected by marriage, as two families, tribes, or castes. **2.** to marry within the limits of the family. —**in'ter·mar'riage,** *n.*

in·ter·med·dle (Ĭn'tər mĕd'əl), *v.i.,* **-dled, -dling.** to interfere officiously; meddle.

in·ter·me·di·ar·y (Ĭn'tər mē'dĬ ĕr'Ĭ), *adj., n., pl.* **-aries.** —*adj.* **1.** intermediate. **2.** acting between persons, parties, etc. —*n.* **3.** an intermediate agent or agency. **4.** a means.

in·ter·me·di·ate (Ĭn'tər mē'dĬ Ĭt), *adj.* being, situated, or acting between two points, stages, things, persons, etc.

in·ter·ment (Ĭn tûr'mənt), *n.* burial.

in·ter·mez·zo (Ĭn'tər mĕt'sō, -mĕd'zō), *n., pl.* **-zos, -zi** (-sē, -zē). **1.** a short dramatic, musical, or other entertainment of light character introduced between the acts of a drama or opera. **2.** a short musical composition between main divisions of an extended musical work. **3.** an independent musical composition of similar character.

in·ter·mi·na·ble (Ĭn tûr'mə nə bəl), *adj.* unending; endless. —**in·ter'mi·na·bly,** *adv.*

in·ter·min·gle (Ĭn'tər mĬng'gəl), *v.t., v.i.,* **-gled, -gling.** to mingle, one with another.

in·ter·mis·sion (Ĭn'tər mĬsh'ən), *n.* **1.** an interval between periods of action or activity. **2.** act of intermitting. **3.** state of being intermitted.

in·ter·mit·tent (Ĭn'tər mĬt'ənt), *adj.* **1.** that ceases for a time. **2.** alternately ceasing and beginning again. —**in'ter·mit'tent·ly,** *adv.*

in·ter·mix (Ĭn'tər mĬks'), *v.t., v.i.* to intermingle. —**in'ter·mix'ture,** *n.*

in·tern[1] (*v.* Ĭn tûrn'; *n.* Ĭn'tûrn), *v.t.* **1.** to oblige to reside within prescribed limits, as enemy aliens. **2.** to hold within a country until the termination of a war. —*n.* **3.** someone interned.

in·tern[2] (Ĭn'tûrn), *n.* Also, **interne.** **1.** a resident member of the medical staff of a hospital, commonly a recent medical graduate acting as assistant. **2.** an inmate. —*v.i.* **3.** to be or perform the duties of an intern. —**in'tern·ship',** *n.*

in·ter·nal (Ĭn tûr'nəl), *adj.* **1.** situated or occurring inside something; interior. **2.** of or pertaining to the inside or inner part. **3.** to be taken inwardly. **4.** existing or occurring within a country; domestic. **5.** pertaining to the domestic affairs of a country. **6.** mental or spiritual; subjective. **7.** *Anat., Zool.* inner. —*n.* **8.** *(pl.)* entrails. **9.** inner or intrinsic attribute. —**in·ter'nal·ly,** *adv.*

internal-combustion engine, an engine of one or more working cylinders in which the process of combustion takes place within the cylinder.

internat., international.

in·ter·na·tion·al (Ĭn'tər năsh'ən əl), *adj.* **1.** between or among nations. **2.** of or pertaining to different nations or their citizens. 3. pertaining to the relations between nations. —*n.* 4. (*cap.*) any of a series of socialistic or communistic associations uniting groups or parties of various countries. —in′ter·na′tion·al′i·ty, *n.* —in′ter·na′tion·al·ly, *adv.*

In·ter·na·tio·nale (ăn těr nå syô nål′), *n.* a popular revolutionary song, first sung in France in 1871.

in·ter·na·tion·al·ism (ĭn′tər năsh′ən ə lĭz′əm), *n.* 1. the principle of coöperation among nations. 2. international character, relations, etc. —in′ter·na′tion·al·ist, *n.*

in·ter·na·tion·al·ize (ĭn′tər năsh′ən ə līz′), *v.t.*, -ized, -izing. to make international; bring under international control. —in′ter·na′tion·al·i·za′tion, *n.*

in·terne (ĭn′tûrn), *n.* intern[2].

in·ter·ne·cine (ĭn′tər nē′sīn, -sĭn), *adj.* 1. mutually destructive. 2. characterized by great slaughter.

in·tern·ee (ĭn′tûr nē′), *n.* one who is or has been interned, as a prisoner of war.

in·tern·ment (ĭn·tûrn′mənt), *n.* confinement, as of prisoners of war.

in·ter·o·ce·an·ic (ĭn′tər ō′shĭ ăn′ĭk), *adj.* between oceans.

in·ter·pel·late (ĭn′tər pĕl′āt, ĭn tûr′pə lāt′), *v.t.*, -lated, -lating. to call formally upon (a minister or member of the government) to explain some official act or policy. —in′ter·pel·la′tion, *n.*

in·ter·pen·e·trate (ĭn′tər pĕn′ə trāt′), *v.t.*, *v.i.*, -trated, -trating. 1. to penetrate thoroughly; permeate. 2. to penetrate reciprocally. —in′ter·pen′e·tra′tion, *n.*

in·ter·phone (ĭn′tər fōn′), *n.* a telephone connecting offices, etc., in the same building, ship, etc.

in·ter·plan·e·tar·y (ĭn′tər plăn′ə těr′Y), *adj.* *Astron.* situated within the solar system, but not within the atmosphere of the sun or any planet.

in·ter·play (ĭn′tər plā′), *n.* reciprocal play, action, or influence.

in·ter·po·late (ĭn tûr′pə lāt′), *v.*, -lated, -lating. —*v.t.* 1. to alter (a text, etc.) by the insertion of new matter. 2. to insert (new or spurious matter) thus. 3. to interject; interpose. 4. *Math.* to insert or find intermediate terms in (a sequence). —*v.i.* 5. to make interpolations. —in·ter′po·la′tion, *n.*

in·ter·pose (ĭn′tər pōz′), *v.*, -posed, -posing. —*v.t.* 1. to place between; cause to intervene. 2. to bring (influence, action, etc.) to bear between parties, or in behalf of a person. 3. to interrupt with (a remark, etc.). —*v.i.* 4. to assume an intervening position or relation. 5. to mediate. 6. to interrupt. —in·ter·po·si·tion (ĭn′tər pə zĭsh′ən), *n.*

in·ter·pret (ĭn tûr′prĭt), *v.t.*, *v.i.* 1. to explain or elucidate. 2. to construe or understand in a particular way. 3. to bring out the meaning of (a dramatic work, music, etc.) by performance or execution. 4. to translate. —in·ter′pret·er, *n.* —in·ter′pre·tive, *adj.*

in·ter·pre·ta·tion (ĭn tûr′prə tā′shən), *n.* 1. act of interpreting. 2. an explanation given. 3. a construction placed upon something. 4. the rendering of a dramatic part, music, etc., so as to bring out the meaning or to indicate one's particular conception of it. 5. translation. —in·ter′pre·ta′tive, *adj.*

in·ter·ra·cial (ĭn′tər rā′shəl), *adj.* of, for, between, or pertaining to persons of different races.

in·ter·reg·num (ĭn′tər rĕg′nəm), *n., pl.* -nums, -na (-nə). 1. an interval of time between the reign of one sovereign and that of his successor. 2. any similar interval. 3. any pause or interruption.

in·ter·re·late (ĭn′tər rĭ lāt′), *v.t.*, -lated, -lating. to bring into reciprocal relation. —in′ter·re·lat′ed, *adj.* —in′ter·re·la′tion, *n.* —in′ter·re·la′tion·ship, *n.*

interrog., interrogative.

in·ter·ro·gate (ĭn tĕr′ə gāt′), *v.*, -gated, -gating. —*v.t.* 1. to question (a person). —*v.i.* 2. to ask questions. —in·ter′ro·ga′tor, *n.*

in·ter·ro·ga·tion (ĭn těr′ə gā′shən), *n.* 1. act of questioning. 2. a question.

interrogation point, question mark. Also, **interrogation mark.**

in·ter·rog·a·tive (ĭn′tə rŏg′ə tĭv), *adj.* 1. pertaining to or conveying a question. 2. *Gram.* (of

an element or construction) forming or constituting a question. —*n.* 3. *Gram.* an interrogative word, element, or construction. —in′ter·rog′a·tive·ly, *adv.*

in·ter·rog·a·to·ry (ĭn′tə rŏg′ə tōr′Y), *adj., n., pl.* -tories. —*adj.* 1. questioning. —*n.* 2. a question or inquiry.

in·ter·rupt (ĭn′tə rŭpt′), *v.t.* 1. to make a break in (an otherwise continuous extent, process, etc.). 2. to stop (a person) in the midst of doing or saying something. —*v.i.* 3. to interrupt action or speech. —in′ter·rupt′er, *n.*

in·ter·rup·tion (ĭn′tə rŭp′shən), *n.* 1. act of interrupting. 2. state of being interrupted. 3. something that interrupts.

in·ter·scho·las·tic (ĭn′tər skə lăs′tĭk), *adj.* between elementary or secondary schools.

in·ter·sect (ĭn′tər sĕkt′), *v.t.* 1. to cut or divide by passing through or lying across. —*v.i.* 2. to cross, as lines. 3. *Geom.* to have one or more points in common.

in·ter·sec·tion (ĭn′tər sĕk′shən), *n.* act, fact, or place of intersecting.

in·ter·sperse (ĭn′tər spûrs′), *v.t.*, -spersed, -spersing. 1. to scatter here and there among other things. 2. to diversify with something introduced here and there. —in·ter·sper·sion (ĭn′tər spûr′shən, -zhən), *n.*

in·ter·state (ĭn′tər stāt′), *adj.* between or jointly involving states.

in·ter·stel·lar (ĭn′tər stĕl′ər), *adj.* among the stars.

in·ter·stice (ĭn tûr′stĭs), *n.* 1. an intervening space. 2. a chink, crevice, or opening. —in·ter·sti·tial (ĭn′tər stĭsh′əl), *adj.*

in·ter·trib·al (ĭn′tər trī′bəl), *adj.* between tribes.

in·ter·twine (ĭn′tər twīn′), *v.t.*, *v.i.*, -twined, -twining. to twine together.

in·ter·twist (ĭn′tər twĭst′), *v.t.*, *v.i.* to twist together. —in′ter·twist′ing·ly, *adv.*

in·ter·ur·ban (ĭn′tər ûr′bən), *adj.* 1. between cities. —*n.* 2. an interurban train or car.

in·ter·val (ĭn′tər val), *n.* 1. an intervening period of time. 2. a pause. 3. a space intervening between things, points, etc. 4. *Music.* the difference in pitch between two tones.

in·ter·vene (ĭn′tər vēn′), *v.i.*, -vened, -vening. 1. to come or be between, as in place, time, or a series. 2. to intercede or mediate. —in·ter·ven·tion (ĭn′tər vĕn′shən), *n.* —in′ter·ven′tion·ist, *n.*

in·ter·view (ĭn′tər vū′), *n.* 1. the conversation of a writer or reporter with a person or persons from whom material for a news story or other writing is sought. 2. the report of such conversation. 3. a meeting or conference. —*v.t.* 4. to have an interview with. —in′ter·view′er, *n.*

in·ter·weave (ĭn′tər wēv′), *v.*, -wove or -weaved; -woven or -wove or -weaved; -weaving. —*v.t.* 1. to weave together, one with another. —*v.i.* 2. to become woven together.

in·tes·tate (ĭn tĕs′tāt, -tĭt), *adj.* 1. dying without having made a will. 2. not disposed of by will. —*n.* 3. one who dies intestate. —in·tes·ta·cy (ĭn tĕs′tə sY), *n.*

in·tes·tine (ĭn tĕs′tĭn), *n.* 1. *Anat.* **a.** the lower part of the alimentary canal, from the pylorus to the anus. **b.** a definite portion of this part. The small intestine comprises the duodenum, jejunum, and ileum; the large intestine comprises the caecum, colon, and rectum. —*adj.* 2. internal; civil. —in·tes′ti·nal, *adj.*

in·thrall (ĭn thrôl′), *v.t.* enthrall.

in·throne (ĭn thrōn′), *v.t.*, -throned, -throning. enthrone.

in·ti·ma·cy (ĭn′tə mə sY), *n., pl.* -cies. 1. intimate association or friendship. 2. an instance of this. 3. illicit sexual relations.

in·ti·mate[1] (ĭn′tə mĭt), *adj.* 1. associated in close personal relations. 2. characterized by or involving personally close or familiar association. 3. private; personal. 4. maintaining illicit sexual relations. 5. detailed; deep. 6. thorough. 7. inmost. —*n.* 8. an intimate friend or associate. —in′ti·mate·ly, *adv.* —in′ti·mate·ness, *n.*

in·ti·mate[2] (ĭn′tə māt′), *v.t.*, -mated, -mating to hint; suggest. —in′ti·ma′tion, *n.*

in·tim·i·date (ĭn tĭm′ə dāt′), *v.t.*, -dated, -dating. 1. to make timid; overawe. 2. to force or deter by fear. —in·tim′i·da′tion, *n.* —in·tim′i·da′tor, *n.*

in·ti·tle (ĭn tī′təl), *v.t.*, -tled, -tling. entitle.

in·to (Ĭn'tōō; *unstressed* Ĭn'tŏŏ, -tə), *prep.* **1.** to the inside of. **2.** *Math.* by (with *divide* implied).

in·to·na·tion (Ĭn'tō nā'shən), *n.* **1.** the pattern or melody of pitch changes revealed in connected speech. **2.** act of intoning.

in·tone (Ĭn tōn'), *v.*, -toned, -toning. —*v.t.* **1.** to utter with a particular tone. **2.** to utter in a singing voice. **3.** to recite in monotone. —*v.i.* **4.** to speak or recite in a singing voice, esp. in monotone.

in·tox·i·cant (Ĭn tŏk'sə kənt), *adj.* **1.** intoxicating. —*n.* **2.** an intoxicating agent.

in·tox·i·cate (Ĭn tŏk'sə kāt'), *v.*, -cated, -cating. —*v.t.* **1.** to affect temporarily with loss of control over the physical and mental powers, by means of alcoholic liquor, a drug, or other substance. **2.** to excite mentally beyond self-control or reason. —*v.i.* **3.** to cause or produce intoxication. —**in·tox'i·cat'ed,** *adj.*

in·tox·i·ca·tion (Ĭn tŏk'sə kā'shən), *n.* **1.** inebriation; drunkenness. **2.** *Pathol.* poisoning. **3.** overpowering effect upon the mind.

intra-, a prefix meaning "within," freely used as an English formative, esp. in scientific terms, sometimes in opposition to *extra-*.

in·trac·ta·ble (Ĭn trăk'tə bəl), *adj.* **1.** not docile; stubborn. **2.** unmanageable. —**in·trac'ta·bil'i·ty, in·trac'ta·ble·ness,** *n.* —**in·trac'ta·bly,** *adv.*

in·tra·dos (Ĭn trā'dŏs), *n. Archit.* the interior curve or surface of an arch or vault.

in·tra·mu·ral (Ĭn'trə myŏŏr'əl), *adj.* **1.** engaged in or pertaining to a single college, or its students. **2.** within the walls or enclosing limits.

intrans., intransitive. Also, **intr.**

in·tran·si·gent (Ĭn trăn'sə jənt), *adj.* **1.** uncompromising, esp. in politics. —*n.* **2.** one who is irreconcilable, esp. in politics. —**in·tran'si·gence, in·tran'si·gen·cy,** *n.* —**in·tran'si·gent·ly,** *adv.*

in·tran·si·tive (Ĭn trăn'sə tĭv), *adj.* **1.** (of a verb) never accompanied by a direct object. —*n.* **2.** an intransitive verb. —**in·tran'si·tive·ly,** *adv.*

in·tra·state (Ĭn'trə stāt'), *adj.* within a state, esp. one of the United States.

in·tra·ve·nous (Ĭn'trə vē'nəs), *adj.* **1.** within a vein or the veins. **2.** noting or pertaining to an injection into a vein. —**in'tra·ve'nous·ly,** *adv.*

in·treat (Ĭn trēt'), *v.t., v.i.* entreat.

in·trench (Ĭn trĕnch'), *v.t., v.i.* entrench.

in·trep·id (Ĭn trĕp'Ĭd), *adj.* fearless; dauntless. —**in'tre·pid'i·ty,** *n.* —**in·trep'id·ly,** *adv.*

in·tri·ca·cy (Ĭn'trə kə sĭ), *n., pl.* -cies. **1.** intricate character or state. **2.** an intricate part, action, etc.

in·tri·cate (Ĭn'trə kĭt), *adj.* **1.** perplexingly entangled or involved. **2.** confusingly complex; complicated. —**in'tri·cate·ly,** *adv.* —**in'tri·cate·ness,** *n.*

in·trigue (*v.* Ĭn trēg'; *n.* Ĭn trēg', Ĭn'trēg), *v.*, -trigued, -triguing, *n.* —*v.t.* **1.** to excite the curiosity or interest of by puzzling, novel, or otherwise arresting qualities. **2.** to bring or force by crafty plotting. —*v.i.* **3.** to plot craftily. —*n.* **4.** the use of underhand machinations to accomplish designs. **5.** a plot or crafty dealing. **6.** a clandestine or illicit love affair. —**in·tri'guer,** *n.* —**in·tri'guing·ly,** *adv.*

in·trin·sic (Ĭn trĭn'sĭk), *adj.* belonging to a thing by its very nature. Also, **in·trin'si·cal.** —**in·trin'si·cal·ly,** *adv.*

in·tro, introduction. Also, **introd.**

in·tro·duce (Ĭn'trə dūs', -dōōs'), *v.t.*, -duced, -ducing. **1.** to bring into notice, knowledge, use, vogue, etc. **2.** to bring forward for consideration, as a proposed legislative bill, etc. **3.** to bring forward with preliminary matter. **4.** to bring (a person) to the knowledge of something. **5.** to insert; put in. **6.** to bring (a person) into the acquaintance of another. **7.** to present formally. —**in'tro·duc'er,** *n.*

in·tro·duc·tion (Ĭn'trə dŭk'shən), *n.* **1.** act of introducing. **2.** a formal presentation of one person to another or others. **3.** something introduced. **4.** a preliminary part, as of a book, leading up to the main part. **5.** an elementary treatise.

in·tro·duc·to·ry (Ĭn'trə dŭk'tə rĭ), *adj.* preliminary; prefatory. Also, **in·tro·duc'tive.**

in·tro·spect (Ĭn'trə spĕkt'), *v.i.* **1.** to consider one's own internal state or feelings. —*v.t.* **2.** to examine. —**in'tro·spec'tive,** *adj.* —**in'tro·spec'tive·ly,** *adv.* —**in'tro·spec'tive·ness,** *n.*

in·tro·spec·tion (Ĭn'trə spĕk'shən), *n.* observation or examination of one's own mental states or processes.

in·tro·ver·sion (Ĭn'trə vûr'shən, -zhən), *n.* **1.** act of introverting. **2.** introverted state. **3.** *Psychol.* interest directed inward or upon the self.

in·tro·vert (*n., adj.* Ĭn'trə vûrt'; *v.* Ĭn'trə vûrt'), *n.* **1.** *Psychol.* a person concerned chiefly with his own thoughts. —*adj.* **2.** marked by introversion. —*v.t.* **3.** to turn inward. **4.** to direct (the mind, etc.) inward or upon the self.

in·trude (Ĭn trōōd'), *v.*, -truded, -truding. —*v.t.* **1.** to thrust or bring in without reason, permission, or welcome. **2.** *Geol.* to thrust or force in. —*v.i.* **3.** to thrust oneself in; come uninvited. —**in·trud'er,** *n.* —**in·tru·sion** (Ĭn trōō'zhən), *n.* —**in·tru·sive** (Ĭn trōō'sĭv), *adj.* —**in·tru'sive·ly,** *adv.*

in·trust (Ĭn trŭst'), *v.t.* entrust.

in·tu·i·tion (Ĭn'tyŏŏ ĭsh'ən, -tōō-), *n.* direct perception of truths, facts, etc., independently of any reasoning process. —**in·tu·i'tion·al,** *adj.*

in·tu·i·tive (Ĭn tū'ə tĭv, -tōō'-), *adj.* **1.** perceiving by intuition. **2.** perceived by, resulting from, or involving intuition. **3.** of the nature of intuition. —**in·tu'i·tive·ly,** *adv.* —**in·tu'i·tive·ness,** *n.*

in·un·date (Ĭn'ən dāt', -ŭn-, Ĭn ŭn'dāt), *v.t.*, -dated, -dating. **1.** to flood; deluge. **2.** to overwhelm. —**in'un·da'tion,** *n.*

in·ure (Ĭn yŏŏr'), *v.t.*, -ured, -uring. to toughen or harden by exercise; accustom.

inv., 1. invented. **2.** invoice.

in·vade (Ĭn vād'), *v.*, -vaded, -vading. —*v.t.* **1.** to enter as an enemy. **2.** to enter as if to take possession. **3.** to intrude upon. **4.** to encroach or infringe upon. —*v.i.* **5.** to make an invasion. —**in·vad'er,** *n.*

in·va·lid[1] (Ĭn'və lĭd), *n.* **1.** an infirm or sickly person. —*adj.* **2.** deficient in health; sick. **3.** of or for invalids. —*v.t., v.i.* **4.** to make or become an invalid.

in·val·id[2] (Ĭn văl'Ĭd), *adj.* not valid; of no force, weight, or cogency; weak. —**in·va·lid·i·ty** (Ĭn'və lĭd'ə tĭ), *n.*

in·val·i·date (Ĭn văl'ə dāt'), *v.t.*, -dated, -dating. to render invalid. —**in·val'i·da'tion,** *n.*

in·va·lid·ism (Ĭn'və lĭd Ĭz'əm), *n.* prolonged ill health.

in·val·u·a·ble (Ĭn văl'yŏŏ ə bəl), *adj.* of inestimable value. —**in·val'u·a·bly,** *adv.*

in·var·i·a·ble (Ĭn vâr'Ĭ ə bəl), *adj.* not changing or not capable of being changed; always the same. —**in·var'i·a·bil'i·ty,** *n.* —**in·var'i·a·bly,** *adv.*

in·va·sion (Ĭn vā'zhən), *n.* **1.** act of entering as an enemy. **2.** the entrance or advent of anything troublesome or harmful, as disease. **3.** entrance as if to take possession or overrun. **4.** infringement by intrusion. —**in·va·sive** (Ĭn vā'sĭv), *adj.*

in·vec·tive (Ĭn vĕk'tĭv), *n.* **1.** vehement denunciation, censure, or reproach. **2.** vituperation. —*adj.* **3.** censoriously abusive; vituperative; denunciatory.

in·veigh (Ĭn vā'), *v.i.* to attack vehemently in words; rail. —**in·veigh'er,** *n.*

in·vei·gle (Ĭn vē'gəl, -vā'gəl), *v.t.*, -gled, -gling. to draw, allure, win, or seduce by beguiling.

in·vent (Ĭn vĕnt'), *v.t., v.i.* **1.** to devise or contrive (something new). **2.** to create with the imagination. —**in·ven'tor, in·vent'er,** *n.*

in·ven·tion (Ĭn vĕn'shən), *n.* **1.** act of inventing. **2.** anything invented or devised. **3.** the exercise of imaginative or creative power in literature or art. **4.** the power of inventing, devising, or originating. **5.** something fabricated, as a false statement.

in·ven·tive (Ĭn vĕn'tĭv), *adj.* **1.** apt at inventing, devising, or contriving. **2.** having the function of inventing. **3.** pertaining to, involving, or showing invention. —**in·ven'tive·ly,** *adv.* —**in·ven'tive·ness,** *n.*

in·ven·to·ry (Ĭn'vən tōr'Ĭ), *n., pl.* -tories, *v.*, -toried, -torying. —*n.* **1.** a detailed descriptive list of articles, with number, quantity, and value of each. **2.** a formal list of movables, as of a

in·tol'er·a·bil'i·ty	in·tol'er·a·ble·ness	in·tol'er·ance	in·tol'er·ant·ly
in·tol'er·a·ble	in·tol'er·a·bly	in·tol'er·ant	in·ur·bane'

merchant's stock. **3.** the value of a stock of goods. —*v.t.* **4.** to make an inventory of.

in-ver-ness (ĭn'vər-nĕs'), *n.* an overcoat with a long, removable cape. Also, **Inverness cape.**

in-verse (ĭn vûrs', ĭn'vûrs), *adj.* **1.** reversed in position, direction, or tendency. **2.** opposite to in nature or effect. **3.** inverted. —*n.* **4.** an inverted state or condition. **5.** that which is inverse. —**in-verse'ly,** *adv.*

in-ver-sion (ĭn vûr'zhən, -shən), *n.* **1.** act of inverting. **2.** an inverted state. **3.** *Rhet.* reversal of the usual or natural order of words. **4.** *Music.* the process, or result, of transposing the tones of an interval or chord so that the original bass becomes an upper voice. **5.** *Psychiatry.* assumption of the sexual role of the opposite sex. **6.** something inverted.

in-vert (*v.* ĭn vûrt'; *n.* ĭn'vûrt), *v.t.* **1.** to turn upside down. **2.** to reverse in position, direction, or order. **3.** to turn or change to the opposite or contrary, as in nature, bearing, or effect. —*n.* **4.** one who or that which is inverted.

in-ver-te-brate (ĭn vûr'tə brĭt, -brāt'), *adj.* **1.** *Zool.* not vertebrate; without a backbone. **2.** without strength of character. —*n.* **3.** an invertebrate animal. **4.** one who lacks strength of character.

in-vest (ĭn vĕst'), *v.t.* **1.** to put (money) to use, by purchase or expenditure, in something offering profitable returns. **2.** to spend. **3.** to clothe. **4.** to cover or adorn. **5.** to surround or besiege. **6.** to endow. **7.** to furnish with power, authority, rank, etc. —*v.i.* **8.** to invest money. —**in-ves'tor,** *n.*

in-ves-ti-gate (ĭn vĕs'tə gāt'), *v.,* **-gated, -gating.** —*v.t.* **1.** to search or inquire into; examine in detail. —*v.i.* **2.** to make inquiry, examination, or investigation. —**in-ves'ti-ga'tor,** *n.*

in-ves-ti-ga-tion (ĭn vəs'tə gā'shən), *n.* act or process of investigating; detailed or careful examination.

in-ves-ti-ture (ĭn vĕs'tə chər), *n.* **1.** act of investing. **2.** state of being invested, as with a garment, quality, etc.

in-vest-ment (ĭn vĕst'mənt), *n.* **1.** the investing of money or capital in order to secure profitable returns. **2.** a particular instance or mode of investing. **3.** a thing invested in. **4.** that which is invested. **5.** act of investing.

in-vet-er-ate (ĭn vĕt'ər ĭt), *adj.* **1.** confirmed in a habit, practice, feeling, or the like. **2.** firmly established by long continuance, as a habit; chronic. —**in-vet'er-ate-ly,** *adv.*

in-vid-i-ous (ĭn vĭd'ĭ əs), *adj.* **1.** such as to bring odium, unpopularity, or envious dislike. **2.** offensive or unfairly discriminating. —**in-vid'i-ous-ly,** *adv.* —**in-vid'i-ous-ness,** *n.*

in-vig-or-ate (ĭn vĭg'ə rāt'), *v.t.,* **-ated, -ating.** to give vigor to. —**in-vig'or-a'tion,** *n.* —**in-vig'or-a'tive,** *adj.*

in-vin-ci-ble (ĭn vĭn'sə bəl), *adj.* **1.** that cannot be conquered or vanquished. **2.** insuperable; insurmountable. —**in-vin'ci-bil'i-ty,** *n.* —**in-vin'ci-bly,** *adv.*

in-vi-o-la-ble (ĭn vī'ə lə bəl), *adj.* **1.** that must not be violated; that is to be treated as if sacred. **2.** that cannot be violated or injured. —**in-vi'o-la-bil'i-ty,** *n.* —**in-vi'o-la-bly,** *adv.*

in-vi-o-late (ĭn vī'ə lĭt, -lāt'), *adj.* **1.** free from violation, injury, desecration, or outrage. **2.** undisturbed. **3.** unbroken. **4.** not infringed. —**in-vi'o-late-ly,** *adv.*

in-vis-i-ble (ĭn vĭz'ə bəl), *adj.* **1.** not perceptible by the eye. **2.** withdrawn from or out of sight. **3.** not discernible by the mind. —*n.* **4.** an invisible thing or being. **5.** (prec. by *the*) **a.** the unseen or spiritual world. **b.** (*cap.*) God. —**in-vis'i-bil'i-ty, in-vis'i-ble-ness,** *n.* —**in-vis'i-bly,** *adv.*

in-vi-ta-tion (ĭn'və tā'shən), *n.* **1.** act of inviting. **2.** the written or spoken form with which a person is invited. **3.** attraction or allurement.

in-vite (*v.* ĭn vīt'; *n.* ĭn'vīt), *v.,* **-vited, -viting,** *n.* —*v.t.* **1.** to ask in a courteous way, to come or go to some place, gathering, etc., or to do something. **2.** to request formally. **3.** to act so as to bring on or render probable. **4.** to attract, allure, or tempt. —*v.i.* **5.** to give invitation. —*n.* **6.** *Slang.* an invitation. —**in-vit'er,** *n.*

in-vit-ing (ĭn vī'tĭng), *adj.* that invites; esp., attractive, alluring, or tempting. —**in-vit'ing-ly,** *adv.*

in-vo-ca-tion (ĭn'və kā'shən), *n.* **1.** act of calling upon a deity, etc., for aid, inspiration, etc.

2. a form of words used in invoking. **3.** a calling upon a spirit by incantation.

in-voice (ĭn'vois), *n., v.,* **-voiced, -voicing.** —*n.* **1.** a written list of merchandise, with prices, delivered or sent to a buyer. —*v.t.* **2.** to make an invoice of. **3.** to enter in an invoice.

in-voke (ĭn vōk'), *v.t.,* **-voked, -voking. 1.** to make supplication or prayer for. **2.** to call on (a divine being, etc.), as in prayer. **3.** to appeal to. **4.** to conjure.

in-vol-un-tar-y (ĭn vŏl'ən tĕr'Y), *adj.* **1.** not acting, done, or made by one's own will or choice. **2.** unintentional. **3.** *Physiol.* acting independently of, or done or occurring without, conscious control. —**in-vol'un-tar'i-ly,** *adv.* —**in-vol'un-tar'i-ness,** *n.*

in-volve (ĭn vŏlv'), *v.t.,* **-volved, -volving. 1.** to include as a necessary circumstance, condition, or consequence; entail. **2.** to include or contain. **3.** to bring into an intricate form or condition. **4.** to bring into difficulty, embarrassment, etc. **5.** to implicate, as in crime. **6.** to be highly or excessively interested in. **7.** to roll, wrap, or envelop. —**in-volve'ment,** *n.* —**in-volv'er,** *n.*

in-vul-ner-a-ble (ĭn vŭl'nər ə bəl), *adj.* **1.** incapable of being wounded, hurt, or damaged. **2.** proof against attack. —**in-vul'ner-a-bil'i-ty,** *n.* —**in-vul'ner-a-bly,** *adv.*

in-ward (ĭn'wərd), *adv.* Also, **in'wards. 1.** toward the inside or interior. **2.** in or into the mind or soul. —*adj.* **3.** proceeding or directed toward the inside or interior. **4.** interior; internal. **5.** pertaining to the inside or inner part. **6.** located within the body. **7.** inland. **8.** intrinsic; inherent; essential. **9.** mental or spiritual. —*n.* **10.** the internal part; the inside. **11.** (*pl.*) the inward parts of the body.

in-ward-ly (ĭn'wərd lY), *adv.* **1.** in or on, or with reference to, the inner part. **2.** privately; secretly. **3.** not aloud.

in-ward-ness (ĭn'wərd nYs), *n.* **1.** state of being inward or internal. **2.** earnestness. **3.** spirituality.

in-wrap (ĭn răp'), *v.t.,* **-wrapped, -wrapping.** enwrap.

in-wrought (ĭn rôt'), *adj.* **1.** worked with something by way of decoration. **2.** worked in, as a decorative pattern. **3.** closely combined with something.

Io, *Chem.* ionium.

i-o-dide (ī'ə dīd', -dYd), *n. Chem.* a compound usually of two elements only, one of which is iodine. Also, **i-o-did** (ī'ə dYd).

i-o-dine (ī'ə dīn', -dYn; *Chem.* -dēn'), *n. Chem.* a nonmetallic element occurring as a grayish-black crystalline solid, which sublimes to a dense violet vapor when heated: used in medicine as an antiseptic, and in the arts. *Symbol:* I; *at. wt.:* 126.92; *at. no.:* 53; *sp. gr.:* (solid) 4.93 at 20°C. Also, **i-o-din** (ī'ə dYn).

i-o-do-form (ī ō'də fôrm', ī ŏd'ə-), *n. Chem.* a yellowish crystalline compound, CHI_3: used as an antiseptic.

i-on (ī'ən, ī'ŏn), *n. Physics, Chem.* **1.** an electrically charged atom, radical, or molecule, formed by the loss or gain of one or more electrons. **2.** one of the electrically charged particles formed in a gas by the action of an electric discharge, etc. —**i-on-ic** (ī ŏn'Yk), *adj.*

-ion, a suffix of nouns denoting action or process, state or condition, or sometimes things or persons, as in *fusion, suspicion.*

I-o-ni-a (ī ō'nY ə), *n.* an ancient region on the W coast of Asia Minor and adjacent islands: colonized by the ancient Greeks. —**I-o'ni-an,** *adj., n.*

Ionian Sea, an arm of the Mediterranean between S Italy, E Sicily, and Greece.

I-on-ic (ī ŏn'Yk), *adj.* **1.** *Archit.* noting or pertaining to one of the three Greek orders, distinguished by the spiral scroll-like ornaments on the capitals. **2.** *Pros.* noting or employing one of two feet consisting of two long and two short syllables. **3.** pertaining to the Ionians. —*n.* **4.** *Pros.* an Ionic foot, verse, or meter.

i-o-ni-um (ī ō'nY əm), *n. Chem.* a radioactive element formed in the decay of uranium. *Symbol:* Io; *at. no.:* 90; *at. wt.:* about 230.

i-on-ize (ī'ə nīz'), *v.t., v.i.,* **-ized, -izing. 1.** to separate or change into ions. **2.** to produce ions (in). —**i-on-i-za-tion** (ī'ə nə zā'shən), *n.* —**i'on-iz'er,** *n.*

i-on-o-sphere (ī ŏn'ə sfYr'), *n.* the succession of ionized layers that constitute the outer regions of the earth's atmosphere beyond the stratosphere, considered as beginning with the Heaviside layer at about 60 miles, and extending several hundred miles up.

i·o·ta (ī ō′tə), *n.* **1.** the ninth letter (I, *ι*, = English I, i) of the Greek alphabet (the smallest letter). **2.** a very small quantity; jot.

I O U (ī′ō′ū′), a written acknowledgment of a debt, containing the expression *I O U* (I owe you). Also, **I.O.U.**

-ious, a termination consisting of the suffix **-ous** with a preceding original or euphonious vowel i.

I·o·wa (ī′ə wə; *locally* ī′ə wā′), *n.* a State in the central United States. 2,543,502 pop.; 56,280 sq. mi. *Cap.:* Des Moines. *Abbr.:* **Ia.** **—I·o·wan** (ī′ə wən), *adj., n.*

ip·e·cac (ĭp′ə kăk′), *n.* **1.** the dried root of two small, shrubby South American plants, used as an emetic, purgative, etc. **2.** a drug consisting of the roots of these plants. Also, **ip·e·cac·u·an·ha** (ĭp′ə kăk′yŏŏ ăn′ə).

Iph·i·ge·ni·a (ĭf′ə jĭ nī′ə), *n. Gk. Legend.* the daughter of Agamemnon and Clytemnestra.

ip·se dix·it (ĭp′sĭ dĭk′sĭt), *Latin.* **1.** he himself said it. **2.** an assertion without proof.

ip·so fac·to (ĭp′sō făk′tō), *Latin.* by the fact itself; by that very fact.

Ips·wich (ĭps′wĭch), *n.* a seaport in E England. 98,020.

IQ, intelligence quotient. Also, **I.Q.**

Ir, *Chem.* iridium.

Ir., **1.** Ireland. **2.** Irish.

I·ran (ĭ rän′, ĭ-), *n.* a kingdom in SW Asia. ab. 15,000,000 pop.; ab. 635,000 sq. mi. *Cap.:* Teheran. Formerly, **Persia.** **—I·ra·ni·an** (ĭ rā′nĭ ən), *adj., n.*

I·raq (ĭ räk′), *n.* a kingdom in SW Asia, N of Saudi Arabia and W of Iran, centering in the Tigris-Euphrates basin of Mesopotamia. 4,150,-000 pop.; 116,600 sq. mi. *Cap.:* Bagdad. Also, **I·rak′.**

I·ra·qi (ē rä′kē), *n., pl.* **-qis,** *adj.* **—n. 1.** a native of Iraq. **—adj. 2.** of or pertaining to Iraq or its inhabitants.

i·ras·ci·ble (ĭ răs′ə bəl, ĭ răs′-), *adj.* **1.** easily provoked to anger. **2.** characterized by, excited by, or arising from anger. **—i·ras′ci·bil′i·ty,** **i·ras′ci·ble·ness,** *n.* **—i·ras′ci·bly,** *adv.*

i·rate (ī′rāt, ī rāt′), *adj.* angry; enraged. **—i′rate·ly,** *adv.*

ire (īr), *n.* anger; wrath. **—ire′ful,** *adj.* **—ire′ful·ly,** *adv.* **—ire′less,** *adj.*

Ire., Ireland.

Ire·land (īr′lənd), *n.* **1.** a large western island of the British Isles, comprising the Republic of Ireland and Northern Ireland. ab. 4,277,000 pop; 32,375 sq. mi. **2. Republic of,** an independent republic occupying most of Ireland: still maintaining certain reciprocal relations within the British Commonwealth of Nations. 2,949,713 pop.; 27,137 sq. mi. *Cap.:* Dublin. Formerly, **Eire.**

ir·i·des·cence (ĭr′ə dĕs′əns), *n.* a play of lustrous, changing colors. **—ir′i·des′cent,** *adj.* **—ir′i·des′cent·ly,** *adv.*

i·rid·i·um (ĭ rĭd′ĭ əm, ī rĭd′-), *n. Chem.* a precious metallic element resembling platinum. *Symbol; Ir; at. wt.:* 193.1; *at. no.:* 77; *sp. gr.:* 22.4 at 20°C.

i·ris (ī′rĭs), *n., pl.* **irises, irides** (ĭr′ə dēz′, ī′rə-). **1.** *Anat.* the contractile circular diaphragm forming the colored portion of the eye and containing a circular opening (the pupil) in its center. **2.** *Bot.* **a.** a family of plants comprising certain perennial herbs with handsome flowers and sword-shaped leaves. **b.** a plant of this family. **3.** (*cap.*) *Gk. Myth.* a messenger of the gods, regarded as the goddess of the rainbow. **4.** a rainbow.

I·rish (ī′rĭsh), *adj., n., pl.* **Irish.** **—adj. 1.** of, pertaining to, or characteristic of Ireland or its people. **—n. 2.** the inhabitants of Ireland and their immediate descendants elsewhere. **3.** the Celtic language of Ireland.

Irish Free State, former name of the **Republic of Ireland** (1922–37).

I·rish·man (ī′rĭsh mən), *n., pl.* **-men.** a man born in Ireland or of Irish ancestry. **—I′rish·wom′an,** *n. fem.*

Irish potato, the common white potato.

Irish Sea, a part of the Atlantic between Ireland and England.

Irish setter, a dark mahogany-red variety of setter.

Irish stew, a stew usually made of mutton, lamb, or beef, with potatoes, onions, etc.

Irish terrier, one of a breed of small, active, intelligent dogs with wiry hair, usually of a reddish tinge.

irk (ûrk), *v.t.* to weary, annoy, or trouble.

irk·some (ûrk′səm), *adj.* causing weariness, disgust, or annoyance. **—irk′some·ly,** *adv.* **—irk′some·ness,** *n.*

Ir·kutsk (ĭr kōōtsk′), *n.* a city in the S Soviet Union in Asia. 243,380.

i·ron (ī′ərn), *n.* **1.** *Chem.* a ductile, malleable, silver-white metallic element, scarcely known in a pure condition, but abundantly used in its crude or impure forms containing carbon for making tools, machinery, etc. *Symbol:* Fe (Lat. *ferrum*); *at. wt.:* 55.85; *at. no.:* 26; *sp. gr.:* 7.86 at 20°C. **2.** something hard, strong, rigid, unyielding, or the like. **3.** an instrument, utensil, weapon, etc., made of iron. **4.** an iron implement used heated for pressing cloth, etc. **5.** an iron-headed golf club intermediate between a cleek and a mashie. **6.** (*pl.*) an iron shackle or fetter. **—adj. 7.** made of iron. **8.** resembling iron in color, firmness, etc. **9.** stern, harsh, or cruel. **—v.t., v.i. 10.** to press (clothes, etc.) with a heated iron. **11.** to furnish, mount, or arm with iron. **12.** to shackle or fetter with irons.

i·ron·clad (ī′ərn klăd′), *adj.* **1.** covered with iron plates, as a warship; armor-plated. **2.** very rigid or strict. **—n. 3.** one of the first naval ships fitted with armor.

iron curtain, a state of rigid censorship and secrecy.

i·ron·i·cal (ī rŏn′ə kəl), *adj.* **1.** pertaining to, of the nature of, or characterized by irony. **2.** using or addicted to irony. Also, **i·ron′ic.** **—i·ron′i·cal·ly,** *adv.* **—i·ron′i·cal·ness,** *n.*

iron lung, a chamber in which alternate pulsations of high and low pressure can be used to force normal lung movements, used esp. in some cases of infantile paralysis.

iron pyrites, 1. fool's gold. **2.** marcasite.

i·ron·side (ī′ərn sīd′), *n.* **1.** a person with great power of endurance or resistance. **2.** (*cap., usually pl.*) **a.** Edmund II of England. **b.** Oliver Cromwell. **c.** one of Cromwell's troopers. **3.** (*pl.*) an ironclad.

i·ron·ware (ī′ərn wâr′), *n.* articles of iron, as pots, kettles, tools, etc.; hardware.

i·ron·wood (ī′ərn wŏŏd′), *n.* **1.** any of certain trees with hard, heavy wood found on the islands off the coast of southern California. **2.** the wood.

i·ron·work (ī′ərn wûrk′), *n.* **1.** work in iron. **2.** parts or articles made of iron. **—i′ron·work′er,** *n.*

i·ron·works (ī′ərn wûrks′), *n.pl. or sing.* an establishment where iron is smelted or where it is cast or wrought.

i·ro·ny (ī′rə nĭ), *n., pl.* **-nies. 1.** a figure of speech in which the literal meaning of a locution is the opposite of that intended: used in ridicule or humor. **2.** an outcome of events contrary to what was, or what might have been, expected. **3.** an ironical quality.

Ir·o·quoi·an (ĭr′ə kwoi′ən), *adj.* belonging to or constituting a linguistic family of North American Indians, of Canada and the eastern U.S., including the Iroquois confederacy, the Cherokees, Hurons, Erie, and others.

Ir·o·quois (ĭr′ə kwoi′, -kwoiz′), *n.sing. and pl.* a member of the Indian confederacy (the Five Nations), comprising the Mohawks, Oneidas, Onondagas, Cayugas, and Senecas, with, later, the Tuscaroras.

ir·ra·di·ate (*v.* ĭ rā′dĭ āt′; *adj.* -ĭt, -āt′), *v., -ated, -ating, adj.* **—v.t. 1.** to illuminate. **2.** to radiate (light, etc.). **3.** to heat with radiant energy. **4.** to cure by being exposed to radiation, as of ultraviolet light. **—v.i. 5.** to emit rays; shine. **—adj. 6.** bright. **—ir·ra′di·a′tion,** *n.*

ir·ra·tion·al (ĭ răsh′ən əl), *adj.* **1.** without the faculty of reason. **2.** without, or deprived of, sound judgment. **3.** utterly illogical. **—ir·ra′tion·al·ly,** *adv.* **—ir·ra′tion·al′i·ty, ir·ra′tion·al·ness,** *n.*

Ir·ra·wad·dy (ĭr′ə wŏd′ĭ), *n.* a river flowing S through Burma to the Bay of Bengal. ab. 1250 mi.

ir·re·claim·a·ble (ĭr′ĭ klā′mə bəl), *adj.* incapable of being reclaimed. **—ir′re·claim′a·bly,** *adv.*

ir·rec·on·cil·a·ble (ĭ rĕk′ən sī′lə bəl), *adj.* **1.** that cannot be harmonized or adjusted; incompatible. 2. implacably opposed. —**ir·rec'on·cil'a·bly,** *adv.*

ir·re·cov·er·a·ble (Ir'Y kŭv'ər ə bəl), *adj.* 1. that cannot be regained. 2. that cannot be remedied or rectified. —**ir're·cov'er·a·bly,** *adv.*

ir·re·deem·a·ble (Ir'Y dē'mə bəl), *adj.* 1. incapable of being bought back or paid off. 2. not convertible into specie, as paper money. 3. beyond redemption. 4. hopeless. —**ir're·deem'a·bly,** *adv.*

Ir·re·den·tist (Ir'Y dĕn'tYst), *n.* (*also l.c.*) a member of an Italian association advocating the redemption, or the incorporation into Italy, of certain neighboring regions having a primarily Italian population.

ir·re·duc·i·ble (Ir'Y dū'sə bəl, -dōō'-), *adj.* 1. incapable of being reduced or diminished. 2. incapable of being brought into a different condition or form. —**ir're·duc'i·bly,** *adv.*

ir·re·fra·ga·ble (Y rĕf'rə gə bəl), *adj.* not to be refuted; undeniable. —**ir·ref'ra·ga·bly,** *adv.*

ir·ref·u·ta·ble (Y rĕf'yə tə bəl, Ir'Y fū'tə bəl), *adj.* not refutable; incontrovertible. —**ir·ref'u·ta·bil'i·ty,** *n.* —**ir·ref'u·ta·bly,** *adv.*

irreg., 1. irregular. 2. irregularly.

ir·reg·u·lar (Y rĕg'yə lər), *adj.* 1. without symmetry, formal arrangement, etc. 2. not characterized by any fixed principle, method, or rate. 3. not conformed or conforming to rules of justice or morality, as conduct, etc. 4. *Gram.* not conforming to the most prevalent pattern of formation, inflection, construction, etc. 5. *Mil.* not belonging to the established forces. —*n.* 6. one who or that which is irregular. —**ir·reg'u·lar·ly,** *adv.*

ir·reg·u·lar·i·ty (Y rĕg'yə lăr'ə tY), *n., pl.* **-ties.** 1. state or fact of being irregular. 2. something irregular.

ir·rel·e·vant (Y rĕl'ə vənt), *adj.* not relevant; not applicable or pertinent. —**ir·rel'e·vant·ly,** *adv.* —**ir·rel'e·vance,** **ir·rel'e·van·cy,** *n.*

ir·re·li·gion (Ir'Y lYj'ən), *n.* 1. lack of religion. 2. impiety.

ir·re·li·gious (Ir'Y lYj'əs), *adj.* not religious; impious; ungodly. —**ir're·li'gious·ly,** *adv.*

ir·re·me·di·a·ble (Ir'Y mē'dY ə bəl), *adj.* not remediable; irreparable. —**ir're·me'di·a·ble·ness,** *n.* —**ir're·me'di·a·bly,** *adv.*

ir·re·mis·si·ble (Ir'Y mYs'ə bəl), *adj.* 1. not remissible; unpardonable, as a sin. 2. that cannot be remitted, as a duty.

ir·re·mov·a·ble (Ir'Y mōō'və bəl), *adj.* not removable. —**ir're·mov'a·bly,** *adv.*

ir·rep·a·ra·ble (Y rĕp'ə rə bəl), *adj.* incapable of being rectified, remedied, or made good. —**ir·rep'a·ra·bly,** *adv.*

ir·re·place·a·ble (Ir'Y plā'sə bəl), *adj.* that cannot be replaced.

ir·re·press·i·ble (Ir'Y prĕs'ə bəl), *adj.* not repressible. —**ir're·press'i·bil'i·ty, ir're·press'i·ble·ness,** *n.* —**ir're·press'i·bly,** *adv.*

ir·re·proach·a·ble (Ir'Y prō'chə bəl), *adj.* free from blame. —**ir're·proach'a·bly,** *adv.*

ir·re·sist·i·ble (Ir'Y zYs'tə bəl), *adj.* that cannot be resisted or withstood. —**ir're·sist'i·bil'i·ty, ir're·sist'i·ble·ness,** *n.* —**ir're·sist'i·bly,** *adv.*

ir·res·o·lute (Y rĕz'ə lōōt'), *adj.* doubtful or undecided; vacillating. —**ir·res'o·lute'ly,** *adv.* —**ir·res'o·lute'ness, ir·res'o·lu'tion,** *n.*

ir·re·spec·tive (Ir'Y spĕk'tYv), *adj.* without regard to something else, esp. something specified; independent. —**ir're·spec'tive·ly,** *adv.*

ir·re·spon·si·ble (Ir'Y spŏn'sə bəl), *adj.* 1. not responsible or accountable. —*n.* 2. an irresponsible person. —**ir're·spon'si·bil'i·ty,** *n.* —**ir're·spon'si·bly,** *adv.*

ir·re·triev·a·ble (Ir'Y trē'və bəl), *adj.* 1. irrecoverable. 2. irreparable. —**ir're·triev'a·bly,** *adv.*

ir·rev·er·ent (Y rĕv'ər ənt), *adj.* not reverent; deficient in veneration or respect. —**ir·rev'er·ent·ly,** *adv.* —**ir·rev'er·ence,** *n.*

ir·re·vers·i·ble (Ir'Y vûr'sə bəl), *adj.* that cannot be reversed. —**ir're·vers'i·bly,** *adv.*

ir·rev·o·ca·ble (Y rĕv'ə kə bəl), *adj.* not to be revoked, repealed, or annulled. —**ir·rev'o·ca·bil'i·ty,** *n.* —**ir·rev'o·ca·bly,** *adv.*

ir·ri·ga·ble (Ir'Y gə bəl), *adj.* that may be irrigated.

ir·ri·gate (Ir'ə gāt'), *v.t.,* **-gated, -gating.** 1. to supply (land) with water by means of streams passing through it. 2. *Med.* to supply (a wound, etc.) with a constant flow of some liquid.

ir·ri·ga·tion (Ir'ə gā'shən), *n.* 1. the supplying of land with water from artificial channels to promote vegetation. 2. *Med.* the covering or washing out of anything with water or other liquid for the purpose of making or keeping it moist.

ir·ri·ta·bil·i·ty (Ir'ə tə bYl'ə tY), *n., pl.* **-ties.** 1. quality of being irritable. 2. an irritable state or condition. 3. *Physiol., Biol.* the ability to be excited to a characteristic action or function by the application of some stimulus.

ir·ri·ta·ble (Ir'ə tə bəl), *adj.* 1. easily excited to impatience or anger. 2. *Physiol., Biol.* displaying irritability (def. 3). 3. *Pathol.* susceptible to physical irritation. —**ir'ri·ta·bly,** *adv.*

ir·ri·tant (Ir'ə tənt), *adj.* 1. irritating. —*n.* 2. anything that irritates.

ir·ri·tate (Ir'ə tāt'), *v.t.,* **-tated, -tating.** 1. to excite to impatience or anger. 2. *Physiol., Biol.* to excite (a living system) to some characteristic action or function. 3. *Pathol.* to bring (a bodily part, etc.) to an abnormally excited or sensitive condition. —**ir'ri·ta'tion,** *n.* —**ir'ri·ta'tive,** *adj.*

ir·rup·tion (Y rŭp'shən), *n.* a breaking or bursting in; a violent incursion. —**ir·rup'tive,** *adj.*

Ir·ving (ûr'vYng), *n.* **Washington,** 1783–1859, U.S. writer.

Ir·ving·ton (ûr'vYng tən), *n.* a town in NE New Jersey, near Newark. 55,328.

is (Yz), *v.* 3rd pers. sing. pres. indic. of **be.**

Is., 1. Also, **Isa.** Isaiah. 2. Also, **is.** Island. 3. Isle.

I·saac (I'zək), *n.* a patriarch, son of Abraham and Sarah, and father of Jacob.

Is·a·bel·la I (Yz'ə bĕl'ə), 1451–1504, joint ruler, 1474–1504, of Castile and León in Spain with her husband Ferdinand V, and patron of Columbus.

I·sa·iah (I zā'ə, I zī'ə), *n.* 1. a major Hebrew prophet of the eighth century B.C. 2. a long book of the Old Testament.

Is·car·i·ot (Ys kăr'Y ət), *n.* 1. the surname of Judas, the betrayer of Jesus. 2. a traitor.

I·seult (Y sōōlt'), *n.* *Arthurian Romance.* 1. the wife of Mark, king of Cornwall, loved by Tristram (Tristan). 2. daughter of the king of Brittany, and wife of Tristram.

-ish, 1. a suffix used to form adjectives from nouns, with the sense of: a. "belonging to" (a people, country, etc.), as in *Spanish.* b. "after the manner of," "having the characteristics of," "like," as in *girlish.* c. "addicted to," "inclined or tending to," as in *bookish.* 2. a suffix used to form adjectives from other adjectives, with the sense of "somewhat," "rather," as in *reddish.*

Ish·ma·el (Ysh'mY əl), *n.* 1. the outcast son of Abraham and Hagar. 2. any outcast.

Ish·ma·el·ite (Ysh'mY ə līt'), *n.* 1. a descendant of Ishmael (from whom the Arabs claim descent). 2. an outcast.

i·sin·glass (I'zYng glăs', -gläs'), *n.* 1. a pure, transparent or translucent form of gelatin, esp. that derived from the air bladders of certain fishes. 2. mica.

I·sis (I'sYs), *n.* an Egyptian goddess.

isl., 1. (*pl.* **isls.**) island. 2. isle.

Is·lam (Ys'ləm, Ys läm'), *n.* 1. the religious system of Allah according to Mohammed; Mohammedanism. 2. the whole body of Mohammedan believers, their civilization, and their lands. —**Is·lam·ic** (Ys läm'Yk, -lä'mYk), *adj.*

is·land (I'lənd), *n.* 1. a small tract of land completely surrounded by water. 2. something resembling an island. 3. a platform in the middle of a street, at a crossing, for the safety of pedestrians. 4. *Physiol., Anat.* an isolated portion of tissue or aggregation of cells.

is·land·er (I'lən dər), *n.* a native or inhabitant of an island.

isle (īl), *n.* a small island. Also, **is·let** (I'lYt).

ism (Yz'əm), *n.* a distinctive doctrine, theory, system, or practice.

-ism, a suffix of nouns denoting action or practice, state or condition, principles, doctrines, a usage or characteristic, etc., as in *baptism, Darwinism.*

is·n't (Yz'nt), contraction of *is not.*

i·so·bar (I'sə bär'), *n.* 1. *Meteorol., etc.* a line drawn on a weather map, etc., connecting all points having the same barometric pressure. 2. *Physics, Chem.* one of two atoms of different atomic number, but having the same atomic weight.

i·so·bar·ic (I'sə băr'Yk), *adj.* 1. having or showing equal barometric pressure. **2.** of or pertaining to isobars.

i·so·late (ī′sə lāt′, ĭs′ə-), *v.t.*, **-lated, -lating. 1.** to set apart; separate so as to be alone. **2.** *Med.* to keep (an infected person) from contact with noninfected ones. **3.** *Chem.* to obtain (a substance) in an uncombined or pure state. **—i·so·la·tion** (ī′sə lā′shən, ĭs′ə-), *n.*

i·so·la·tion·ist (ī′sə lā′shən ĭst, ĭs′ə-), *n.* one who favors nonparticipation in international affairs. **—i′so·la′tion·ism,** *n.*

I·solde (ĭ sōld′, ĭ sōl′də), *n.* Iseult.

i·so·mer (ī′sə mər), *n.* *Chem.* a compound which is isomeric with one or more other compounds.

i·so·mer·ic (ī′sə mĕr′ĭk), *adj.* *Chem.* (of compounds) composed of the same kinds and numbers of atoms which differ from each other in the arrangement of the atoms and, therefore, in one or more properties.

i·som·er·ism (ī sŏm′ə rĭz′əm), *n.* state or condition of being isomeric.

i·so·met·ric (ī′sə mĕt′rĭk), *adj.* pertaining to or having equality of measure. Also, **i′so·met′-ri·cal. —i′so·met′ri·cal·ly,** *adv.*

i·sos·ce·les (ī sŏs′ə lēz′), *adj.* (of a triangle) having two sides equal.

i·so·therm (ī′sə thûrm′), *n.* a line connecting points on the earth's surface having the same (mean) temperature. **—i′so·ther′mal,** *adj.*

i·so·tope (ī′sə tōp′), *n.* *Chem.* any of two or more forms of a chemical element, occupying the same place in the periodic table and nearly identical in properties, but differing by one or more units in atomic weight. **—i·so·top·ic** (ī′sə-tŏp′ĭk), *adj.*

i·so·trop·ic (ī′sə trŏp′ĭk, -trō′pĭk), *adj.* *Physics.* having one or more properties that are the same in all directions.

Is·ra·el (ĭz′rĭ əl), *n.* **1.** the Hebrew or Jewish people. **2.** God's chosen people; the elect. **3.** the northern kingdom of the ancient Hebrews. **4.** a republic (formed as a Jewish state May 15, 1948) comprising a part of Palestine. ab. 900,000 pop.; ab. 5500 sq. mi. *Cap.:* Hakirya (suburb of Tel Aviv). **5.** a name given to Jacob after he had wrestled with the angel. **6.** the Christian church.

Is·rae·li (ĭz rā′lĭ), *n., pl.* **-lis,** *adj.* **—n. 1.** a native or inhabitant of Israel. **—adj. 2.** of or pertaining to Israel.

Is·ra·el·ite (ĭz′rĭ ə līt′), *n.* **1.** a Hebrew; Jew. **2.** one of God's chosen people. **—adj. 3.** pertaining to Israel; Jewish.

Is·sei (ēs′sā′), *n., pl.* **-sei.** a person of Japanese ancestry, born in Japan, who has come to the United States to live, but retains his allegiance to Japan.

is·su·ance (ĭsh′ŏŏ əns), *n.* act of issuing.

is·sue (ĭsh′ŏŏ or, *esp. Brit.,* ĭs′ū), *n., v.,* **-sued, -suing. —n. 1.** act of sending; delivery; emission. **2.** that which is issued. **3.** a quantity issued at one time. **4.** a point in question or dispute. **5.** a stage at which a matter is ready for decision. **6.** a product, effect, result, or consequence. **7.** a distribution of food (rations), clothing, equipment, or ammunition. **8.** offspring or progeny. **9.** a going, coming, passing, or flowing out. **10.** an outlet or vent. **11. at issue, a.** in controversy. **b.** in disagreement. **c.** inconsistent. **12. take issue,** to disagree. **—v.t. 13.** to send out; deliver; put into circulation. **14.** to print (a publication) for sale or distribution. **15.** to distribute (food, clothing, etc.). **16.** to discharge; emit. **—v.i. 17.** to go, pass, or flow out; emerge. **18.** to come or proceed from any source. **19.** to result. **—is′su·a·ble,** *adj.* **—is′su·er,** *n.*

-ist, a suffix of nouns, often accompanying verbs ending in *-ize* or nouns ending in *-ism,* denoting one who does, practices, or is concerned with something, or holds certain principles, doctrines, etc., as in *apologist, socialist.*

Is·tan·bul (ĭs′tăn bŏŏl′, -tän-), *n.* a city in European Turkey, on the Bosporus. 793,949.

isth·mus (ĭs′məs), *n., pl.* **-muses, -mi** (-mī). a narrow strip of land, bordered on both sides by water, connecting two larger bodies of land. **—isth·mi·an** (ĭs′mĭ ən), *adj.*

-istic, a suffix of adjectives (and in the plural of nouns from adjectives) formed from nouns in *-ist,* and having reference to such nouns, or to associated nouns in *-ism,* as in *theistic, puristic.* In nouns it has usually a plural form.

-istical. See **-istic, -al**[1].

it (ĭt), *pron.* **1.** a personal pronoun of the third person and neuter gender, corresponding to *he* and *she.* **—n. 2.** (in children's games) the player called upon to perform some task.

Ital., 1. Italian. **2.** Italy. Also, **It.**

ital., italic (type).

I·tal·ian (ĭ tăl′yən), *adj.* **1.** of or pertaining to Italy, its people, or their language. **—n. 2.** a native or inhabitant of Italy. **3.** a Romance language, the language of Italy, official also in Switzerland.

i·tal·ic (ĭ tăl′ĭk), *adj.* **1.** designating or pertaining to a style of printing types in which the letters usually slope to the right (thus, *italic*). **—n. 2.** (*often pl.*) italic type.

i·tal·i·cize (ĭ tăl′ə sīz′), *v.,* **-cized, -cizing. —v.t. 1.** to print in italic type. **2.** to underscore with a single line, as in indicating italics. **—v.i. 3.** to use italics.

It·a·ly (ĭt′ə lĭ), *n.* a republic in S Europe, comprising a peninsula S of the Alps, and the islands of Sicily, Sardinia, Elba, etc. 45,527,000 pop.; 119,772 sq. mi. *Cap.:* Rome.

itch (ĭch), *v.i.* **1.** to have or feel a peculiar irritation of the skin which causes a desire to scratch the part affected. **2.** to have a desire to do or to get something. **—n. 3.** the sensation of itching. **4. the itch,** a contagious disease caused by the **itch mite,** which burrows into the skin; scabies. **5.** a restless desire or longing. **—itch′y,** *adj.*

-ite, a suffix of nouns denoting esp. **(a)** persons associated with a place, tribe, leader, doctrine, system, etc., as in *Israelite.*; **(b)** minerals and fossils; **(c)** explosives; **(d)** chemical compounds, esp. salts of acids whose names end in *-ous;* **(e)** pharmaceutical and commercial products; **(f)** a member or component of a part of the body.

i·tem (ī′təm), *n.* **1.** a separate article or particular. **2.** a separate piece of information or news, as in a newspaper.

i·tem·ize (ī′tə mīz′), *v.t.,* **-ized, -izing.** to state by items; give the particulars of. **—i′tem·i·za′-tion,** *n.* **—i′tem·iz′er,** *n.*

it·er·ate (ĭt′ə rāt′), *v.t.,* **-ated, -ating. 1.** to utter again or repeatedly. **2.** to do (something) over again or repeatedly. **—it′er·a′tion,** *n.*

it·er·a·tive (ĭt′ə rā′tĭv), *adj.* repeating; repetitious.

i·tin·er·ant (ī tĭn′ər ənt, ĭ tĭn′-), *adj.* **1.** traveling from place to place, or on a circuit, as a preacher, judge, or peddler. **—n. 2.** one who travels from place to place, esp. for duty or business. **—i·tin′er·ant·ly,** *adv.* **—i·tin′er·an·cy, i·tin′er·a·cy,** *n.*

i·tin·er·ar·y (ī tĭn′ə rĕr′ĭ, ĭ tĭn′-), *n., pl.* **-aries,** *adj.* **—n. 1.** a route. **2.** an account of a journey. **3.** a book describing a route or routes of travel, with information for travelers. **4.** a plan of travel. **—adj. 5.** pertaining to traveling or travel routes. **6.** itinerant.

-ition, a noun suffix, as in *expedition, extradition,* etc., being *-tion* with a preceding original or formative vowel, or, in other words, *-ite + -ion.*

-itious, an adjective suffix occurring in adjectives associated with nouns in *-tion,* as *expeditious,* etc.

its (ĭts), *adj.* possessive form of **it.**

it's (ĭts), contraction of *it is.*

it·self (ĭt sĕlf′), *pron.* emphatic or reflexive form of *it.*

-ity, a suffix forming abstract nouns of condition, characteristics, etc., as in *jollity, civility.*

I·van III (ī′vən), (*the Great*) 1440–1505, grand duke of Muscovy, 1462–1505.

Ivan IV, (*the Terrible*) 1530–84, grand duke of Muscovy, 1533–47, and first czar of Russia, 1547–84.

-ive, a suffix of adjectives (and nouns of adjectival origin) expressing tendency, disposition, function, connection, etc., as in *active, corrective.*

I've (īv), contraction of *I have.*

Ives (īvz), *n.* **James Merritt,** 1824–95, U.S. lithographer.

i·vied (ī′vĭd), *adj.* covered or overgrown with ivy.

i·vo·ry (ī′və rĭ, ī′vrĭ), *n., pl.* **-ries,** *adj.* **—n.**

1. the hard white substance, a variety of dentine, composing the main part of the tusks of the elephant, walrus, etc. **2.** an article made of ivory, as a billiard ball. **3.** (*pl.*) *Slang.* **a.** the keys of a piano, accordion, etc. **b.** dice. **4.** creamy or yellowish white. —*adj.* **5.** consisting or made of ivory. **6.** of the color ivory.

Ivory Coast, a colony in French West Africa. 4,014,000 pop.; 184,222 sq. mi. *Cap.:* Abidjan.

ivory tower, 1. a place withdrawn from the world and worldly acts and attitudes. **2.** an attitude of aloofness.

i·vy (ī′vĭ), *n.*, *pl.* **ivies. 1.** Also, **English Ivy.** a climbing vine with smooth, shiny, evergreen leaves, inconspicuous yellowish flowers, and black berries, widely grown as an ornamental. **2.** any of various other climbing or trailing plants.

I·wo Ji·ma (ē′wə jē′mə), one of a group of islands in the N Pacific, S of Japan: taken by U.S. forces, Feb.-Mar., 1945.

-ization, a suffix combination of **-ize** with **-ation.**

-ize, a suffix of verbs having the sense **(a)** intransitively, of following some line of action, practice, policy, etc., as in *theorize*, or of becoming (as indicated), as in *crystallize*, and **(b)** transitively, of acting toward or upon, treating, or affecting in a particular way, as in *colonize*, or of making or rendering (as indicated), as in *civilize*.

iz·zard (ĭz′ərd), *n.* *Colloq.* **1.** the letter *Z*. **2.** from A to izzard, completely.

J

J, j (jā), *n.*, *pl.* **J's** or **Js, j's** or **js.** a consonant, the 10th letter of the English alphabet.

J, *Physics.* joule.

Ja., January.

jab (jăb), *v.*, **jabbed, jabbing,** *n.* —*v.t.*, *v.i.* **1.** to poke; thrust smartly or sharply. —*n.* **2.** a poke; smart or sharp thrust.

jab·ber (jăb′ər), *v.i.*, *v.t.* **1.** to talk or utter rapidly, indistinctly, or nonsensically; chatter. —*n.* **2.** jabbering talk or utterance; gibberish. —**jab′ber·er,** *n.* —**jab′ber·ing·ly,** *adv.*

ja·bot (zhă bō′), *n.* a falling ruffle, cascade, or other arrangement of lace, embroidery, or the like, worn at the neck or front of the waist.

ja·cinth (jā′sĭnth, jăs′ĭnth), *n.* a reddish-orange zircon.

jack (jăk), *n.* **1.** any of various mechanical contrivances or devices, as a contrivance for raising great weights small distances. **2.** a man or fellow. **3.** (*cap. or l.c.*) a sailor. **4.** *U.S.* any of the four knaves in playing cards. **5.** jackstone. **6.** a small union or ensign used by a ship or vessel as a signal, etc., and flown from the jack staff as an indication of nationality. **7.** jackass. **8.** jack rabbit. **9.** *Elect.* a connecting device to which the wires of a circuit may be attached and which is arranged for the insertion of a plug. **10.** *Naut.* a horizontal bar or crosstree of iron at the topgallant masthead, to spread the royal shrouds. —*v.t.* **11.** to lift or move with a jack. **12.** *Colloq.* to raise (prices, wages, etc.).

jack·al (jăk′ôl, -əl), *n.* **1.** a kind of wild dog of Asia and Africa, which hunts in packs at night. **2.** one who does drudgery for another.

jack·a·napes (jăk′ə nāps′), *n.* a pert, presuming man; whippersnapper.

jack·ass (jăk′ăs′), *n.* **1.** a male donkey. **2.** a very stupid or foolish person.

jack·boot (jăk′bo͞ot′), *n.* a large leather boot reaching up over the knee, orig. one serving as armor.

jack·daw (jăk′dô′), *n.* **1.** a glossy black European bird of the crow family. **2.** a large glossy blackbird of the southern U.S. and Mexico.

jack·et (jăk′ĭt), *n.* **1.** a short coat, in various forms, worn by both sexes. **2.** an outer covering. —*v.t.* **3.** to cover with a jacket.

jack-in-the-box (jăk′ĭn ᵺə bŏks′), *n.* a toy consisting of a figure, enclosed in a box, which springs out when the lid is unfastened.

jack-in-the-pul·pit (jăk′ĭn ᵺə po͝ol′pĭt), *n.* a North American herb of the arum family, having an upright spadix arched over by a spathe.

jack·knife (jăk′nīf′), *n.*, *pl.* **-knives.** *U.S.* **1.** a large pocketknife. **2.** a type of dive in which the diver assumes a folded position of the body while moving through the air, and straightens out before entering the water.

jack-of-all-trades (jăk′əv ôl′trādz′), *n.* one who can do any kind of work or business.

jack-o'-lan·tern (jăk′ə lăn′tərn), *n.* a lantern made of a rind, as a pumpkin shell, with holes cut to represent human eyes, nose, mouth, etc.

jack pot, *Poker.* a pot that accumulates until a player opens the betting with a pair of jacks or better.

jack rabbit, any of various large hares of western North America, having very long limbs and ears.

Jack·son (jăk′sən), *n.* **1. Andrew,** 1767–1845, U.S. general, 7th president of the U.S., 1829–37. **2. Robert Houghwout,** born 1892, U.S. jurist: associate justice of U.S. Supreme Court since 1941. **3. Thomas Jonathan,** ("*Stonewall Jackson*") 1824–63, Confederate general in the U.S. Civil War. **4.** the capital of Mississippi, in the central part. 62,107. **5.** a city in S Michigan. 49,656.

Jack·son·ville (jăk′sən vĭl′), *n.* a seaport in NE Florida. 173,065.

jack·stone (jăk′stōn′), *n.* **1.** one of a set of shaped pieces of iron used in children's play. **2.** (*pl. construed as sing.*) a game thus played.

jack·straw (jăk′strô′), *n.* one of a number of straws, strips of wood, etc., used in a game (**jackstraws**) in which they are thrown on a table in confusion and are to be picked up singly without disturbing the others.

Ja·cob (jā′kəb), *n.* the second son of Isaac, the twin brother of Esau, and father of the 12 patriarchs.

Jac·o·be·an (jăk′ə bē′ən), *adj.* **1.** of or pertaining to James I of England or his times. —*n.* **2.** a Jacobean writer, personage, etc.

Jac·o·bin (jăk′ə bĭn), *n.* **1.** a member of a club of French revolutionists organized in 1789. **2.** an extreme radical.

Jac·o·bite (jăk′ə bīt′), *n.* an adherent of James II of England after his overthrow (1688), or of his descendants.

Jacob's ladder, *Naut.* a rope ladder with wooden steps.

jade¹ (jād), *n.* **1.** either of two minerals, sometimes green, highly esteemed as an ornamental stone for carvings, jewelry, etc. **2.** Also, **jade green.** bluish green.

jade² (jād), *n.*, *v.*, **jaded, jading.** —*n.* **1.** a horse, esp. an inferior or worn-out one. **2.** (in opprobrious use) a woman. —*v.t.*, *v.i.* **3.** to weary or tire.

jad·ed (jā′dĭd), *adj.* **1.** worn-out. **2.** sated.

Jaf·fa (jăf′ə), *n.* a seaport in W Israel. 94,310.

jag¹ (jăg), *n.*, *v.*, **jagged, jagging.** —*n.* **1.** a sharp projection on an edge or surface. —*v.t.* **2.** to cut or slash; form notches or ragged points in.

jag² (jăg), *n.* *U.S. Slang.* a fit of intoxication.

jag·ged (jăg′ĭd), *adj.* having notches, teeth, or ragged edges. —**jag′ged·ly,** *adv.*

jag·uar (jăg′wär), *n.* a large, ferocious, spotted feline of tropical America.

Jah·veh (yä′vĕ), *n.* Yahweh. Also, **Jah′ve, Jah** (yä).

jai a·lai (hī ä lī′), a game resembling handball, esp. popular in Cuba, played on an indoor court with basketlike rackets.

jail (jāl), *n.* **1.** a prison. —*v.t.* **2.** to take into or hold in custody. —**jail′less**, *adj.* —**jail′like′**, *adj.*

jail·bird (jāl′bûrd′), *n.* one who is or has been confined in jail.

jail·er (jā′lər), *n.* the keeper of a jail. Also, **jail′or.**

ja·lop·y (jə löp′Y), *n., pl.* **-lopies.** *Colloq.* an old, decrepit, or unpretentious automobile.

jam¹ (jăm), *v.,* **jammed, jamming,** *n.* —*v.t.* **1.** to press or squeeze tightly between bodies or surfaces. **2.** to bruise or crush by squeezing. **3.** to press, push, or thrust violently. **4.** to fill or block up by crowding. **5.** to cause to become wedged, caught, or displaced, so that it cannot work, as a machine, etc. **6.** *Radio.* to interfere with (signals, etc.) by sending out others of approximately the same frequency. —*v.i.* **7.** to become wedged or fixed. **8.** to press or push violently. **9.** (of a machine, etc.) to become unworkable as through the wedging or displacement of a part. **10.** *Jazz Slang.* to enliven a composition by impromptu variations and improvisations. —*n.* **11.** act of jamming. **12.** state of being jammed. **13.** mass of persons or objects jammed together. **14.** *Colloq.* a difficult situation.

jam² (jăm), *n.* a preserve of whole fruit, slightly crushed, boiled with sugar. —**jam′like′,** *adj.*

Ja·mai·ca (jə mā′kə), *n.* an island in the West Indies, S of Cuba: with dependencies it forms a British colony. 1,237,000 pop.; 4540 sq. mi. *Cap.*: Kingston. —**Ja·mai′can,** *adj., n.*

jamb¹ (jăm), *n.* vertical piece forming the side of a doorway, window, or the like. Also, **jambe.**

jamb² (jăm), *v.t., v.i., n.* jam¹ (defs. 1–9, 11–13).

jam·bo·ree (jăm′bə rē′), *n.* *U.S. Slang.* a carousal; any noisy merrymaking.

J. Jamb

James (jāmz), *n.* **1.** an apostle, son of Zebedee and brother of the apostle John. **2. Henry,** 1843–1916, U.S. novelist in England. **3. Jesse,** 1847–82, U.S. bandit. **4. William,** 1842–1910, U.S. psychologist and philosopher (brother of Henry James).

James I, 1566–1625, king of England, 1603–25.

James II, 1633–1701, king of England, 1685–88.

James·town (jāmz′toun′), *n.* **1.** a ruined village in E Virginia: the first permanent English settlement in North America, 1607. **2.** a city in SW New York. 42,638.

jam session, a meeting of musicians for a spontaneous and improvised performance of swing music without scores.

Jan., January.

jan·gle (jăng′gəl), *v.,* **-gled, -gling,** *n.* —*v.i.* **1.** to sound harshly or discordantly. **2.** to wrangle. —*v.t.* **3.** to cause to sound harshly or discordantly. —*n.* **4.** a harsh or discordant sound. **5.** a quarrel. —**jan′gler,** *n.*

jan·i·tor (jăn′ə tər), *n.* **1.** a person employed to take care of a building, offices, etc. **2.** a doorkeeper or porter. —**jan·i·tress** (jăn′ə trĭs), *n. fem.*

Jan·u·ar·y (jăn′yŏŏ ĕr′Y, -ə rĭ), *n., pl.* **-aries.** the first month of the year, containing 31 days.

Ja·nus (jā′nəs), *n.* an ancient Italian deity, regarded by the Romans as presiding over doors and gates, commonly represented with two faces in opposite directions.

Jap (jăp), *adj., n. Colloq. and Derogatory.* Japanese.

Jap., Japanese.

Ja·pan (jə păn′), *n.* an empire on a chain of islands off the E coast of Asia. 73,110,995 pop.; 142,267 sq. mi. *Cap.*: Tokyo. —**Jap·a·nese** (jăp′ə nēz′, -nēs′), *adj., n.*

ja·pan (jə păn′), *n., adj., v.,* **-panned, -panning.** —*n.* **1.** any of various hard, durable, black varnishes for coating wood, metal, etc. **2.** work varnished and figured in the Japanese manner. —*adj.* **3.** of or pertaining to japan. —*v.t.* **4.** to varnish with japan.

Japanese beetle, a beetle, orig. native in Japan, injurious to the foliage of fruit and other trees.

jape (jāp), *v.i.,* **japed, japing,** *n.* joke; jest.

ja·pon·i·ca (jə pŏn′ə kə), *n.* **1.** the camellia. **2.** the Japanese quince, an Asiatic shrub with clusters of scarlet flowers and yellowish fruit.

jar¹ (jär), *n.* a broad-mouthed earthen or glass vessel, commonly cylindrical in form.

jar² (jär), *v.,* **jarred, jarring,** *n.* —*v.i.* **1.** to produce a harsh, grating sound. **2.** to have a harshly unpleasant effect upon the nerves, feelings, etc. **3.** to vibrate or shake. **4.** to conflict; clash. —*v.t.* **5.** to cause to sound harshly or discordantly. **6.** to cause to rattle or shake. **7.** to have a harshly unpleasant effect upon (the feelings, nerves, etc., or the person). —*n.* **8.** a harsh, grating sound. **9.** a discordant sound. **10.** a vibrating movement. **11.** a harshly unpleasant effect upon the mind or feelings due to physical or other shock. **12.** a quarrel; conflict.

jar·di·niere (jär′də nĭr′), *n.* an ornamental stand for plants.

jar·gon (jär′gən, -gŏn), *n.* **1.** unintelligible or meaningless talk or writing; gibberish. **2.** the language peculiar to a trade, profession, or other group. —*v.i.* **3.** to utter or talk jargon.

Jas., James.

jas·mine (jăs′mĭn, jăz′-), *n.* **1.** any of certain fragrant-flowered shrubs of the olive family. **2.** any of certain other plants of America, as the **yellow jasmine, Cape jasmine** (gardenia), etc.

Ja·son (jā′sən), *n. Gk. Legend.* the leader of the Argonauts in quest of the Golden Fleece.

jas·per (jăs′pər), *n.* a compact, opaque, often highly colored variety of quartz.

jaun·dice (jôn′dĭs, jän′-), *n., v.,* **-diced, -dicing.** —*n.* **1.** *Pathol.* a condition due to the presence of bile pigments in the blood, characterized by yellowness of the skin, lassitude, and loss of appetite. **2.** state of feeling in which views are colored or judgment is distorted. —*v.t.* **3.** to affect with jaundice. **4.** to affect with envy, jealousy, etc.

jaunt (jônt, jänt), *v.i.* **1.** to make a short journey, esp. for pleasure. —*n.* **2.** such a journey.

jaun·ty (jôn′tĭ, jän′-), *adj.* **-tier, -tiest.** **1.** sprightly in manner or bearing. **2.** smartly trim. —**jaun′ti·ly,** *adv.* —**jaun′ti·ness,** *n.*

Ja·va (jä′və), *n.* **1.** an island in the Dutch East Indies. 39,755,902 pop.; 48,920 sq. mi. *Cap.*: Batavia. **2.** *U.S. Slang.* coffee. —**Jav·a·nese** (jăv′ə nēz′, -nēs′), *adj., n.*

jave·lin (jăv′lYn, jăv′ə lYn), *n.* **1.** a spear to be thrown by hand. —*v.t.* **2.** to strike or pierce with a javelin.

jaw (jô), *n.* **1.** one of the two bones or structures (upper and lower) which form the framework of the mouth. **2.** the mouth. **3.** anything likened to the mouth. **4.** one of two or more parts, as of a machine, which grasp or hold something. **5.** *Slang.* offensive talk. —*v.i., v.t.* **6.** *Slang.* to talk; gossip. **7.** *Slang.* to scold.

jaw·bone (jô′bōn′), *n.* **1.** any bone of the jaws. **2.** the bone of the lower jaw.

jaw·break·er (jô′brā′kər), *n.* *Colloq.* a word hard to pronounce.

jay (jā), *n.* **1.** any of certain crested or uncrested birds of the crow family, all of them robust, noisy, and mischievous, as the **common jay** of Europe and the **blue jay** of America. **2.** *Slang.* simpleton.

Jay (jā), *n.* **John,** 1745–1829, American statesman and jurist.

Jay·hawk·er (jā′hô′kər), *n.* a native of Kansas.

jay·walk (jā′wôk′), *v.i.* *Colloq.* to cross a street otherwise than by a regular crossing or in a heedless manner, as against traffic lights. —**jay′walk′er,** *n.* —**jay′walk′ing,** *n.*

jazz (jăz), *n.* **1.** dance music, usually of a "hot" improvised nature, with syncopated rhythms. **2.** *Slang.* liveliness; spirit. —*adj.* **3.** of the nature of or pertaining to jazz. —*v.t.* **4.** *Slang.* to enliven.

Je., June.

jeal·ous (jĕl′əs), *adj.* **1.** feeling envious resentment of another's success, advantages, etc. **2.** characterized by or proceeding from suspicious fears or envious resentment. **3.** suspicious or fearful of rivalry, as in love. **4.** vigilant in maintaining or guarding something. **5.** (in Biblical use) intolerant of unfaithfulness. —**jeal′ous·ly,** *adv.* —**jeal′ous·ness,** *n.*

jeal·ous·y (jĕl′ə sY), *n., pl.* **-ousies.** **1.** envious resentment of another's success, advantage, etc. **2.** suspicion or fear of rivalry, as in love. **3.** state or feeling of being jealous. **4.** an instance of jealous feeling.

jean (jēn, jān), *n.* **1.** a stout twilled cotton fabric. **2.** (*pl.*) trousers; overalls.

Jeans (jēnz), *n.* **Sir James Hopwood,** 1877–1946, British physicist and astronomer.

jeep (jēp), *n.* a small (chiefly) military motor vehicle.

jeer (jĭr), *v.i.* **1.** to speak or shout derisively. —*v.t.* **2.** to treat with derision. —*n.* **3.** a derisive or rude gibe. —**jeer′ing·ly,** *adv.*

Jef·fer·son (jĕf′ər sən), *n.* **Thomas,** 1743–1826, American statesman and 3rd president of the U.S., 1801–09: important in framing the Declaration of Independence. —**Jef·fer·so·ni·an** (jĕf′ər sō′nĭ ən), *adj., n.*

Je·ho·vah (jĭ hō′və), *n.* a name of God in the Old Testament.

Jehovah's Witnesses, a sect of Christians who are pacifists and do not recognize the authority of the state when in conflict with religious principles.

Je·hu (jē′hū), *n.* **1.** a prophet of Judah in the 9th century B.C. **2.** (*l.c.*) a fast driver. **3.** (*l.c.*) *Slang.* any driver.

je·june (jĭ jōōn′), *adj.* **1.** deficient in nourishing or substantial qualities. **2.** unsatisfying to the mind. —**je·june′ly,** *adv.*

je·ju·num (jĭ jōō′nəm), *n.* *Anat.* the middle portion of the small intestine, between the duodenum and the ileum.

jell (jĕl), *v.i.* *Colloq.* to form a jelly.

jel·lied (jĕl′ĭd), *adj.* **1.** brought to the consistency of jelly. **2.** containing or spread over with jelly.

jel·ly (jĕl′ĭ), *n., pl.* **-lies,** *v.,* **-lied, -lying.** —*n.* **1.** a food preparation of a soft, elastic consistency due to the presence of gelatin, pectin, etc., as fruit juice boiled down with sugar. **2.** anything of the consistency of jelly. —*v.t., v.i.* **3.** to bring or come to the consistency of jelly.

jel·ly·fish (jĕl′ĭ fĭsh′), *n., pl.* **-fishes,** (*esp. collectively*) **-fish.** any of various invertebrate marine animals of a soft, gelatinous structure, esp. one with an umbrellalike body and long, trailing tentacles.

Je·na (yā′nä), *n.* a city in central Germany: Napoleon decisively defeated Prussians near here, 1806. 70,573.

Jen·ghis Khan (jĕn′gĭz kän′, jĕng′-), Genghis Khan. Also, **Jen′ghiz Khan′.**

jen·net (jĕn′ĭt), *n.* a small Spanish horse.

jen·ny (jĕn′ĭ), *n., pl.* **-nies.** **1.** a spinning jenny. **2.** the female of certain animals.

jeop·ard·ize (jĕp′ər dīz′), *v.t.,* **-ized, -izing.** to risk or imperil. Also, **jeop′ard.**

jeop·ard·y (jĕp′ər dĭ), *n.* **1.** hazard or risk of loss or harm. **2.** danger. **3.** *Law.* the state of criminal defendants on trial.

Jer., **1.** Jeremiah. **2.** Jersey.

jer·bo·a (jər bō′ə), *n.* any of various mouselike rodents of North Africa and Asia with long hind legs used for jumping.

jer·e·mi·ad (jĕr′ə mī′ăd), *n.* a prolonged lamentation; lugubrious complaint.

Jer·e·mi·ah (jĕr′ə mī′ə), *n.* **1.** one of the major Hebrew prophets, fl. about 650 to 585 B.C. **2.** a book of the Old Testament.

Jer·i·cho (jĕr′ə kō′), *n.* an ancient city of Palestine, N of the Dead Sea.

jerk¹ (jûrk), *n.* **1.** a quick, sharp thrust, pull, throw, or the like. **2.** *Physiol.* a sudden movement of an organ or a part. **3.** *Slang.* an unsophisticated or unconventional person. —*v.t.* **4.** to give a sudden thrust, pull, or twist to. —*v.i.* **5.** to give a jerk or jerks. **6.** to move with a quick, sharp motion.

jerk² (jûrk), *v.t.* **1.** to preserve meat, esp. beef (jerked beef) by cutting in strips and curing by drying in the sun. —*n.* **2.** jerked meat, esp. beef.

jer·kin (jûr′kĭn), *n.* a close-fitting jacket or short coat.

jerk·wa·ter (jûrk′wô′tər, -wŏt′ər), *U.S. Colloq.* —*n.* **1.** a train not running on the main line. —*adj.* **2.** off the main line. **3.** of minor importance.

jerk·y (jûr′kĭ), *adj.,* **jerkier, jerkiest.** characterized by jerks or sudden starts. —**jerk′i·ly,** *adv.* —**jerk′i·ness,** *n.*

Je·rome (jə rōm′, jĕr′əm), *n.* **Saint,** A.D. c340–420, monk who made the Latin version of the Bible known as the Vulgate.

jer·ry-build (jĕr′ĭ bĭld′), *v.t.,* **-built, -building.** to build cheaply and flimsily.

Jer·sey (jûr′zĭ), *n., pl.* **-seys.** **1.** a British island in the English Channel. 50,462 pop.; 45

sq. mi. *Cap.*: St. Helier. **2.** one of a breed of dairy cattle whose milk is very rich in butterfat.

jer·sey (jûr′zĭ), *n., pl.* **-seys.** a close-fitting knitted jacket or shirt, of wool, silk, etc.

Jersey City, a seaport in NE New Jersey, opposite New York City. 301,173.

Je·ru·sa·lem (jĭ rōō′sə ləm), *n.* a city in central Palestine: an ancient holy city and place of pilgrimage for Jews, Christians, and Moslems. 157,080.

Jerusalem artichoke, **1.** a species of sunflower having edible tuberous underground stems or rootstocks. **2.** the tuber itself.

Jes·se (jĕs′ĭ), *n.* *Bible.* father of David.

jest (jĕst), *n.* **1.** a witticism or joke. **2.** sport or fun. **3.** the object of laughter, sport, or mockery. —*v.i.* **4.** to joke. **5.** to speak or act in mere sport. **6.** to gibe or scoff. —*v.t.* **7.** to deride; banter.

jest·er (jĕs′tər), *n.* **1.** one who jests. **2.** a professional fool or clown, kept by a prince or noble, esp. during the Middle Ages.

Je·su (jē′zōō, -sōō), *n.* *Poetic.* Jesus.

Jes·u·it (jĕzh′ōō ĭt, jĕz′yōō-), *n.* a member of a Roman Catholic religious order (**Society of Jesus**) founded by Ignatius Loyola in 1534. —**Jes′u·it′ic, Jes′u·it′i·cal,** *adj.*

Je·sus (jē′zəs), *n.* born ca. 6 B.C. and crucified ca. A.D. 29, the founder of the Christian religion. Also, **Jesus Christ.**

jet¹ (jĕt), *v.,* **jetted, jetting.** —*n.* **1.** a stream of fluid, gas, etc., from a nozzle, orifice, etc. **2.** that which so issues, as water or gas. **3.** the spout used. **4.** jet plane. —*v.i., v.t.* **5.** to spout.

jet² (jĕt), *n.* **1.** a compact black coal, susceptible of a high polish, used for making jewelry, etc. **2.** a deep, glossy black. —*adj.* **3.** consisting or made of jet. **4.** black as jet.

jet plane, an airplane whose engine is operated by jet propulsion.

jet propulsion, a method of producing a propelling force upon an air or water craft through the reaction of a high-velocity jet, usually of heated gases, discharged toward the rear. —**jet-pro·pelled** (jĕt′prə pĕld′), *adj.*

jet·sam (jĕt′səm), *n.* **1.** goods thrown overboard to lighten a vessel in distress. **2.** such goods when washed ashore.

jet·ti·son (jĕt′ə sən, -zən), *n.* **1.** act of casting overboard. **2.** jetsam. —*v.t.* **3.** to throw (cargo, etc.) overboard, esp. to lighten a vessel in distress.

jet·ty (jĕt′ĭ), *n., pl.* **-ties.** **1.** a structure of stones, piles, or the like, projecting into the sea or other body of water so as to deflect the current, etc. **2.** a wharf or landing pier.

Jew (jōō), *n.* **1.** one of the Hebrew or Jewish people. —*adj.* **2.** Jewish. —**Jew′ess,** *n. fem.*

Jew-bait·ing (jōō′bā′tĭng), *n.* active anti-Semitism. —**Jew′-bait′er,** *n.*

jew·el (jōō′əl), *n., v.,* **-eled, -eling** or (*esp. Brit.*) **-elled, -elling.** —*n.* **1.** a cut and polished stone; gem. **2.** a fashioned ornament for personal adornment, usually set with gems. **3.** a thing or person of great worth or excellence. **4.** a precious stone (or some substitute) used as a bearing in a watch or delicate instrument. —*v.t.* **5.** to set or adorn with jewels.

jew·el·er (jōō′əl ər), *n.* one who makes, or deals in, jewelry. Also, *esp. Brit.,* **jew′el·ler.**

jew·el·ry (jōō′əl rĭ), *n.* articles made of gold, silver, precious stones, etc., for personal adornment. Also, *esp. Brit.,* **jew′el·ler·y.**

jew·fish (jōō′fĭsh′), *n., pl.* **-fishes,** (*esp. collectively*) **-fish.** any of certain large marine fishes frequenting southern waters and reaching a weight of several hundred pounds.

Jew·ish (jōō′ĭsh), *adj.* **1.** of or pertaining to the Jews; Hebrew. —*n.* **2.** Yiddish.

Jew·ry (jōō′rĭ), *n., pl.* **-ries.** **1.** the Jewish people. **2.** a ghetto.

jew's-harp (jōōz′härp′), *n.* a steel tongue within an iron frame, held between the jaws and plucked while the varying position of the mouth changes the tone. Also, **jews′-harp′.**

Jez·e·bel (jĕz′ə bəl), *n.* **1.** the wife of Ahab, king of Israel, notorious for her conduct. **2.** a shameless, abandoned woman.

jg, junior grade. Also, **j.g.**

jib¹ (jĭb), *n.* *Naut.* **1.** a triangular sail set in front of the forward (or single) mast. **2.** any of certain similar sails set beyond the jib proper, as a **flying jib.**

jib² (jĭb), *v.i., v.t.,* **jibbed, jibbing.** jibe¹.

jib³ (jĭb), *v.,* **jibbed, jibbing,** *n.* —*v.i.* **1.** *Chiefly*

Brit. to move restively sidewise or backward; balk. —*n.* **2.** a horse or other animal that jibs.

jib boom, *Naut.* a spar forming a continuation of a bowsprit.

jibe[1] (jīb), *v.*, **jibed, jibing,** *n. Naut.* —*v.i., v.t.* **1.** to shift (a sail, etc.) from one side to the other when running before the wind. —*n.* **2.** act of jibing.

jibe[2] (jīb), *v.t., v.i.,* **jibed, jibing,** *n.* gibe.

jibe[3] (jīb), *v.i.,* **jibed, jibing.** *U.S. Colloq.* to agree; be in harmony or accord.

jif·fy (jĭf′ĭ), *n., pl.* **-fies.** *Colloq.* a very short time. Also, **jiff.**

jig[1] (jĭg), *n.* a device for holding the work in a machine tool, esp. one for accurately guiding a drill.

jig[2] (jĭg), *n., v.,* **jigged, jigging.** —*n.* **1.** a rapid, lively, springy, irregular dance. **2.** a piece of music for such a dance. **3. the jig is up,** there is no further chance. —*v.t., v.i.* **4.** to dance (a jig or any lively dance). **5.** to move with a jerky or bobbing motion.

jig·ger[1] (jĭg′ər), *n.* **1.** *Naut.* a small sail set in the stern of a canoe, yawl, etc. **2.** any of various mechanical devices, many of which have a jerky or jolting motion. **3.** *Colloq.* some contrivance, article, or part that one cannot name more precisely. **4.** *U.S.* a 1½ oz. measure used in cocktail recipes.

jig·ger[2] (jĭg′ər), *n.* a chigoe.

jig·gered (jĭg′ərd), *adj.* (as a euphemism) damned.

jig·gle (jĭg′əl), *v.,* **-gled, -gling,** *n.* —*v.t., v.i.* **1.** to move up and down or to and fro with short, quick jerks. —*n.* **2.** a jiggling movement.

jig saw, a narrow saw mounted vertically in a frame, used for cutting curves, etc.

jig·saw puzzle (jĭg′sô′), a picture sawed or cut up into small irregular pieces to form a puzzle.

jilt (jĭlt), *v.t.* **1.** to cast off (a lover or sweetheart) after encouragement or engagement. —*n.* **2.** a woman who jilts a lover.

Jim Crow (jĭm krō′), *U.S.* a practice or policy of segregating Negroes, as in public places, etc. Also, **Jim Crowism.**

jim·my (jĭm′ĭ), *n., pl.* **-mies,** *v.,* **-mied, -mying.** —*n.* **1.** a short crowbar used esp. by burglars. —*v.t.* **2.** to force open by a jimmy.

jim·son weed (jĭm′sən), a coarse, ill-smelling weed with white flowers and poisonous leaves. Also, **Jimson weed.**

jin·gle (jĭng′gəl), *v.,* **-gled, -gling,** *n.* —*v.i.* **1.** to make clinking sounds, as coins, keys, etc., when struck together. —*v.t.* **2.** to cause to jingle. —*n.* **3.** a clinking or tinkling sound. **4.** a musical succession of like sounds, as in rhyme or alliteration, without particular regard for sense. **5.** a piece of such verse. —**jin′gly,** *adj.*

jin·go (jĭng′gō), *n., pl.* **-goes,** *adj.* —*n.* **1.** one who favors a bellicose or blustering foreign policy; chauvinist. —*adj.* **2.** of or pertaining to jingoes. **3.** characterized by jingoism. —**jin′go·ism′,** *n.* —**jin′go·is′tic,** *adj.*

jinn (jĭn), *n.pl., sing.* **jinni. 1.** *Mohammedan Myth.* a class of spirits lower than the angels, capable of appearing in human and animal forms and influencing mankind for good and evil. **2.** (*construed as sing. with pl.* **jinns**) a spirit of this class.

jin·rik·i·sha (jĭn rĭk′shô, -shä), *n.* a small two-wheeled hooded vehicle drawn by one or more men, used in Japan and elsewhere. Also, **jin·rick′sha.**

jinx (jĭngks), *n. Colloq.* a person, thing, or influence supposed to bring bad luck.

Jinrikisha

jit·ney (jĭt′nĭ), *n., pl.* **-neys,** *v.,* **-neyed, -neying.** —*n.* **1.** *U.S. Colloq.* an automobile which carries passengers for a small fare. **2.** *U.S. Slang.* a five-cent piece. —*v.t., v.i.* **3.** to carry or ride in a jitney.

jit·ter (jĭt′ər), *U.S. Slang.* —*n.* **1.** (*pl.*) nervousness. —*v.i.* **2.** to behave nervously.

jit·ter·bug (jĭt′ər bŭg′), *n., v.,* **-bugged, -bugging.** —*n.* **1.** one whose enthusiastic responses to the rhythms of swing music take the form of violent and unpredictable dance motions. —*v.i.* **2.** to dance in such a manner.

jit·ter·y (jĭt′ə rĭ), *adj. U.S. Slang.* nervous.

jiu·jit·su (jōō jĭt′sōō), *n.* jujitsu. Also, **jiu·jut′su.**

jive (jīv), *n. Slang.* **1.** the talk of swing enthusiasts. **2.** swing music.

Joan of Arc (jōn, ärk), 1412–31, French heroine who aroused the spirit of nationality in France against the English and was burned by them as a witch. In 1920 she was canonized.

job (jŏb), *n., v.,* **jobbed, jobbing.** —*n.* **1.** a piece of work. **2.** *U.S.* a post of employment. **3.** *Colloq.* an affair, matter, occurrence, or state of affairs. **4.** *Slang.* a robbery or other criminal deed. —*v.i.* **5.** to do business as a jobber. —*v.t.* **6.** to buy in large quantities and sell to dealers in smaller lots. **7.** to let out (work) in separate portions. —**job′less,** *adj.* —**job′less·ness,** *n.*

Job (jōb), *n.* **1.** the much-afflicted hero of a book of the Old Testament. **2.** the book itself.

job·ber (jŏb′ər), *n.* **1.** a wholesale merchant, esp. one selling to retailers. **2.** a pieceworker.

job lot, **1.** any large lot of goods handled by a jobber. **2.** a sundry amount, usually of poor quality.

Jo·cas·ta (jō kăs′tə), *n. Gk. Legend.* the mother, and later the wife, of Oedipus.

jock·ey (jŏk′ĭ), *n., pl.* **-eys,** *v.,* **-eyed, -eying.** —*n.* **1.** one who rides horses professionally in races. —*v.t.* **2.** to bring, put, etc., by skillful maneuvering. **3.** to trick or cheat. —*v.i.* **4.** to aim at an advantage by skillful maneuvering. **5.** to act trickily.

jock·strap (jŏk′străp′), *n.* an athletic supporter worn by men.

jo·cose (jō kōs′), *adj.* jesting; humorous; playful. —**jo·cose′ly,** *adv.* —**jo·cose′ness, jo·cos·i·ty** (jō kŏs′ə tĭ′), *n.*

joc·u·lar (jŏk′yə lər), *adj.* joking or jesting; waggish; facetious. —**joc·u·lar·i·ty** (jŏk′yə lăr′ə tĭ), *n.* —**joc′u·lar·ly,** *adv.*

joc·und (jŏk′ənd, jō′kənd), *adj.* cheerful; merry; gay; glad. —**joc′und·ly,** *adv.*

jodh·purs (jŏd′pərz, jōd′-), *n.pl.* riding breeches fitting closely from the knee to the ankle.

Jo·el (jō′əl), *n.* a minor Hebrew prophet of the postexilian period.

joe-pye weed (jō′pī′), a tall composite weed of North America with clusters of pinkish or purple flowers.

Jof·fre (zhôf′r), *n.* **Joseph Jacques Césaire,** 1852–1931, French general.

jog[1] (jŏg), *v.,* **jogged, jogging,** *n.* —*v.t.* **1.** to move or shake with a push or jerk. **2.** to nudge. **3.** to stir up by hint or reminder. —*v.i.* **4.** to move with a jolt or jerk. **5.** to go with a jolting motion. **6.** to go in a steady or humdrum fashion. —*n.* **7.** a shake; nudge. **8.** a slow, steady walk, trot, etc.

jog[2] (jŏg), *n. Chiefly U.S.* an irregularity of line or surface; projection; notch.

jog·gle (jŏg′əl), *v.,* **-gled, -gling,** *n.* —*v.t.* **1.** to shake slightly. **2.** to join or fasten by a joggle or joggles. —*v.i.* **3.** to move irregularly; shake. —*n.* **4.** act of joggling. **5.** a slight shake; jolt. **6.** a moving with jolts or jerks. **7.** a projection on one of two joining surfaces, or a notch on the other, to prevent slipping.

jog trot, a slow, regular pace.

Jo·han·nes·burg (jō hăn′ĭs bûrg′), *n.* a city in the N part of the Union of South Africa: gold mines. With suburbs, 727,943.

John (jŏn), *n.* **1.** one of the apostles, to whom is attributed the authorship of the fourth Gospel, three Epistles, and the Book of Revelation. **2.** the fourth Gospel, in the New Testament. **3.** one of the three Epistles of John, referred to as 1, 2, and 3 John. **4.** John the Baptist. **5.** 1167?–1216, king of England, 1199–1216, who signed the Magna Charta in 1215.

John Bull, **1.** the English people. **2.** the typical Englishman.

john·ny·cake (jŏn′ĭ kāk′), *n. U.S.* a cake made of corn meal, water or milk, etc.

John·ny-jump-up (jŏn′ĭ jŭmp′ŭp′), *n. U.S.* **1.** any of certain violets. **2.** a small form of the pansy.

John·son (jŏn′sən), *n.* **1. Andrew,** 1808–75, 17th president of the U.S., 1865–69. **2. Samuel,** 1709–84, British author and lexicographer.

Johns·town (jōnz′toun′), *n.* a city in SW Pennsylvania: disastrous flood, 1889. 66,668.

John the Baptist, *Bible.* the baptizer and forerunner of Jesus.

Jo·hore (jə hōr′), *n.* a native state in the

Malayan Union. 605,416 pop.; 7330 sq. mi. *Cap.*: Johore.

join (join), *v.t.* **1.** to bring or put together. **2.** to come into contact, connection, or union with. **3.** to become a member of. **4.** to come into the company of. **5.** to unite in marriage. **6.** to adjoin. —*v.i.* **7.** to come into or be in contact or connection. **8.** to associate or ally oneself. **9.** to take part with others. —*n.* **10.** joining. **11.** a place or line of joining.

join·er (joi′nər), *n.* **1.** one who or that which joins. **2.** a carpenter.

joint (joint), *n.* **1.** the place or part in which two things are joined or united. **2.** (in an animal body) the movable place or part where two bones or segments join. **3. out of joint**, **a.** dislocated. **b.** out of order. **4.** *Biol.* a portion between two articulations, nodes, or the like. **5.** *Bot.* the part of a stem from which a branch or a leaf grows. **6.** one of the portions into which a carcass is divided by a butcher. **7.** *U.S. Slang.* **a.** a cheap, sordid place, as for the illicit sale of liquor. **b.** any resort or abode. —*adj.* **8.** shared by two or more. **9.** sharing or acting in common. **10.** associated, as in action. —*v.t.* **11.** to unite by a joint or joints. **12.** to divide at a joint.

joint·ly (joint′lY), *adv.* together; in common.

join·ture (join′chər), *n.* *Law.* an estate or property settled on a widow.

joist (joist), *n.* **1.** one of the pieces of timber to which are fastened the boards of a floor, the laths of a ceiling, or the like. —*v.t.* **2.** to furnish with or fix on joists. —**joist′less,** *adj.*

joke (jōk), *n., v.,* **joked, joking.** —*n.* **1.** something said or done to excite laughter or amusement. **2.** an amusing or ridiculous circumstance. **3.** an object of joking or jesting. **4.** a trifling matter. —*v.i.* **5.** to speak or act in a playful or merry way. —*v.t.* **6.** to banter, rally, or chaff. —**jok′ing·ly,** *adv.*

jok·er (jō′kər), *n.* **1.** one who jokes. **2.** an extra playing card in a pack, used in some games. **3.** a hidden clause in a paper, document, etc., which largely changes its apparent nature.

Jo·li·et (jō′lY ĕt′, jō′lY ĕt′), *n.* a city in NE Illinois. 42,365.

jol·li·fi·ca·tion (jŏl′ə fə kā′shən), *n.* jolly merrymaking; a jolly festivity.

jol·li·ty (jŏl′ə tY), *n., pl.* **-ties.** **1.** jolly state, mood, or proceedings. **2.** (*pl.*) jolly festivities.

jol·ly (jŏl′Y), *adj.,* **-lier, -liest,** *v.,* **-lied, -lying,** *adv.* —*adj.* **1.** in good spirits; gay. **2.** cheerfully festive. **3.** *Chiefly Brit. Colloq.* fine; pleasing. **4.** *Brit. Colloq.* big or great. —*v.t.* **5.** *Colloq.* to banter pleasantly. **6.** *Colloq.* to make fun of. —*v.i.* **7.** *Colloq.* to jolly a person. —*adv.* **8.** *Brit. Colloq.* extremely; very. —**jol′li·ly,** *adv.* —**jol′-li·ness,** *n.*

jolly boat, a ship's work boat, hoisted at the stern of a sailing vessel.

Jolly Rog·er (rŏj′ər), the pirates' flag.

jolt (jōlt), *v.t., v.i.* **1.** to jar or shake roughly. —*n.* **2.** a jolting shock or movement.

Jo·nah (jō′nə), *n.* **1.** a Hebrew prophet who, thrown overboard to allay a tempest, was swallowed by a large fish and lived in its belly for three days before he was vomited up. **2.** a short book of the Old Testament bearing his name.

Jon·a·than (jŏn′ə thən), *n.* **1.** son of Saul, and friend of David. **2.** *Hort.* a variety of red apple that matures in early fall.

Jones (jōnz), *n.* **John Paul,** 1747–92, American naval commander in the Revolutionary War, born in Scotland.

jon·gleur (jŏng′glər), *n.* (in medieval France and Norman England) an itinerant minstrel or entertainer.

jon·quil (jŏng′kwĭl, jŏn′-), *n.* a species of narcissus with long, narrow, rushlike leaves and fragrant yellow or white flowers.

Jon·son (jŏn′sən), *n.* **Ben,** 1573?–1637, British dramatist and poet.

Jop·lin (jŏp′lĭn), *n.* city in SW Missouri. 37,144.

Jor·dan (jôr′dən), *n.* a river flowing from S Lebanon through the Sea of Galilee and S along the boundary between Palestine and Trans-Jordan into the Dead Sea. ab. 200 mi.

Jo·seph (jō′zəf), *n.* **1.** a Hebrew patriarch, the first son of Jacob by Rachel. **2.** the husband of Mary, the mother of Jesus.

Jo·se·phine (jō′zə fēn′), *n.* 1763–1814, first wife of Napoleon Bonaparte.

Joseph of Ar·i·ma·thae·a (ăr′ə mə thē′ə), a

rich Israelite who believed in Christ and who laid the body of Jesus in the tomb.

josh (jŏsh), *U.S. Slang.* —*v.t., v.i.* **1.** to chaff; banter in a teasing way. —*n.* **2.** a chaffing remark; banter. —**josh′er,** *n.*

Josh·u·a (jŏsh′ōō ə), *n.* **1.** the successor of Moses as leader of the Israelites. **2.** a book of the Old Testament.

joss (jŏs), *n.* a Chinese deity or idol.

joss house, a Chinese temple for idol worship.

joss stick, a slender stick of a dried fragrant paste, burned by the Chinese as incense, etc.

jos·tle (jŏs′əl), *v.,* **-tled, -tling,** *n.* —*v.t.* **1.** to strike or push roughly or rudely against. —*v.i.* **2.** to push or elbow one's way rudely. —*n.* **3.** a collision, shock, or push, as in jostling.

jot (jŏt), *n., v.,* **jotted, jotting.** —*n.* **1.** the least bit. —*v.t.* **2.** to write or mark (*down*) briefly.

joule (joul, jōōl), *n.* *Physics.* a unit of work or energy equal to 107 ergs.

jounce (jouns), *v.,* **jounced, jouncing,** *n.* —*v.i., v.t.* **1.** to move violently up and down. —*n.* **2.** a jouncing movement.

journ., journalism.

jour·nal (jûr′nəl), *n.* **1.** a daily record, as of occurrences. **2.** a newspaper, magazine, or the like. **3.** *Bookkeeping.* a daybook. **4.** *Naut.* a logbook. **5.** *Mach.* that part of a shaft or axle in actual contact with a bearing.

jour·nal·ese (jûr′nə lēz′, -lēs′), *n.* the style of writing supposed to characterize newspapers.

jour·nal·ism (jûr′nə lYz′əm), *n.* the occupation of writing for, editing, and conducting newspapers and other periodicals. —**jour′nal·is′tic,** *adj.*

jour·nal·ist (jûr′nəl Yst), *n.* one engaged in journalism.

jour·ney (jûr′nY), *n., pl.* **-neys,** *v.,* **-neyed, -neying.** —*n.* **1.** a course of travel from one place to another. **2.** a distance traveled in a specified time. —*v.i.* **3.** to travel.

jour·ney·man (jûr′nY mən), *n., pl.* **-men.** one who has served his apprenticeship at a trade and who works at it for another.

joust (jŭst, joust), *n.* **1.** a combat in which two armored knights on horseback opposed each other with lances. **2.** (*pl.*) a tournament. —*v.i.* **3.** to contend in a joust or tournament.

Jove (jōv), *n.* Jupiter. —**Jo′vi·an,** *adj.*

jo·vi·al (jō′vY əl), *adj.* endowed with or characterized by a hearty, joyous humor or a spirit of good-fellowship. —**jo′vi·al·ly,** *adv.* —**jo′vi·al·ness, jo·vi·al·i·ty** (jō′vY ăl′ə tY), *n.*

jowl (joul, jōl), *n.* **1.** a jaw, esp. the under jaw. **2.** the cheek.

joy (joi), *n.* **1.** keen or lively pleasure; gladness; delight. **2.** a source of gladness or delight. **3.** a state of happiness. —*v.i.* **4.** to be glad; rejoice.

Joyce (jois), *n.* **James,** 1882–1941, Irish author.

joy·ful (joi′fəl), *adj.* **1.** full of joy; glad; delighted. **2.** showing or expressing joy. **3.** causing or bringing joy; delightful. —**joy′ful·ly,** *adv.* —**joy′ful·ness,** *n.*

joy·less (joi′lYs), *adj.* **1.** destitute of joy or gladness. **2.** causing no joy or pleasure.

joy·ous (joi′əs), *adj.* joyful. —**joy′ous·ly,** *adv.* —**joy′ous·ness,** *n.*

joy ride, *Colloq.* a pleasure ride in an automobile, esp. when the car is driven recklessly.

joy stick, the control stick of an airplane.

J.P., Justice of the Peace.

Jr., Junior. Also, **jr.**

ju·bi·lant (jōō′bə lənt), *adj.* **1.** rejoicing; exultant. **2.** expressing, exciting, or manifesting joy. —**ju′bi·lant·ly,** *adv.*

ju·bi·la·tion (jōō′bə lā′shən), *n.* **1.** rejoicing; exultation. **2.** a joyful celebration.

ju·bi·lee (jōō′bə lē′), *n.* **1.** the celebration of any of certain anniversaries. **2.** the completion of the 50th year of any continuous course or period. **3.** any season or occasion of rejoicing or festivity. **4.** rejoicing or jubilation.

Jud., **1.** Judges. **2.** Judith (Apocrypha).

Ju·dah (jōō′də), *n.* **1.** the fourth son of Jacob and Leah. **2.** the powerful tribe of his descendants. **3.** an ancient kingdom in S Palestine, including the tribes of Judah and Benjamin.

Ju·da·ic (jōō dā′Yk), *adj.* of or pertaining to the Jews; Jewish.

Ju·da·ism (jōō′dY Yz′əm), *n.* the religious system and polity of the Jews.

Ju·das (jōō′dəs), *n.* **1.** Judas Iscariot, the disciple who betrayed Jesus. **2.** one treacherous enough to betray a friend.

Jude (jōōd), *n.* a short book of the New Testament, written by a "brother of James" (and possibly of Jesus).

Ju·de·a (jōō dē′ə), *n.* the S part of Palestine under the Romans. —**Ju·de′an,** *adj., n.*

Judg., Judges.

judge (jŭj), *n., v.,* **judged, judging.** —*n.* **1.** a public officer authorized to hear and determine causes in a court of law. **2.** any authorized arbiter. **3.** one qualified to pass a critical judgment. —*v.t.* **4.** to pass sentence on or in. **5.** to decide upon critically; estimate. **6.** to decide authoritatively. **7.** to infer, think, or hold as an opinion. —*v.i.* **8.** to pass judgment. **9.** to form an opinion. —judg′er, *n.* —judge′ship, *n.*

Judg·es (jŭj′Yz), *n.* a book of the Old Testament, containing the history of Israel under the leaders from Deborah to Samuel.

judg·ment (jŭj′mənt), *n.* **1.** act of judging. **2.** *Law.* **a.** the judicial decision of a cause in court. **b.** the obligation, esp. a debt, arising from a judicial decision. **3.** good sense; discretion. **4.** the forming of an opinion or estimate. **5.** the opinion formed. **6.** the final trial of all mankind, both the living and the dead, at the end of the world. Also, *esp. Brit.,* **judge′ment.**

ju·di·ca·ture (jōō′də kə chər), *n.* **1.** the administration of justice, as by judges. **2.** the office, function, or authority of a judge.

ju·di·cial (jōō dYsh′əl), *adj.* **1.** pertaining to the administration of justice. **2.** pertaining to courts of law or to judges. **3.** judgelike. **4.** critical; discriminating. **5.** decreed, sanctioned, or enforced by a court. —**ju·di′cial·ly,** *adv.*

ju·di·ci·ar·y (jōō dYsh′Y ĕr′Y, -dYsh′ə rY), *adj., n., pl.* **-aries.** —*adj.* **1.** pertaining to judgment in courts of justice, or to courts or judges; judicial. —*n.* **2.** the judicial branch of government. **3.** the judges collectively.

ju·di·cious (jōō dYsh′əs), *adj.* **1.** discreet, prudent, or politic. **2.** wise, sensible, or well-advised. —**ju·di′cious·ly,** *adv.* —**ju·di′cious·ness,** *n.*

Ju·dith (jōō′dYth), *n.* **1.** an apocryphal book of the Old Testament. **2.** its heroine.

ju·do (jōō′dō), *n.* jujitsu.

jug (jŭg), *n., v.,* **jugged, jugging.** —*n.* **1.** a container in various forms for holding liquids. **2.** *Slang.* a prison. —*v.t.* **3.** to put into a jug. **4.** *Slang.* to imprison.

Jug·ger·naut (jŭg′ər nôt′), *n.* **1.** the eighth incarnation of Vishnu. **2.** an idol of this deity, in India, annually drawn on an enormous car under whose wheels devotees are said to have thrown themselves to be crushed.

jug·gle (jŭg′əl), *v.,* **-gled, -gling,** *n.* —*v.t., v.i.* **1.** to perform conjuring tricks with (balls, knives, etc.). **2.** to manipulate. —*n.* **3.** a trick; deception. —jug′gler, *n.* —jug′gler·y, *n.*

Ju·go·slav (ū′gō släv′, -släv′), *n., adj.* Yugoslav. Also, **Ju′go-Slav′.** —**Ju′go·slav′ic,** *adj.*

Ju·go·sla·vi·a (ū′gō slä′vY ə), *n.* Yugoslavia. —**Ju′go·sla′vi·an,** *adj., n.*

jug·u·lar (jŭg′yə lər, jōō′gyə-), *Anat.* —*adj.* **1.** of or pertaining to the throat or neck. **2.** noting or pertaining to any of certain large veins of the neck. —*n.* **3.** a jugular vein.

juice (jōōs), *n.* **1.** the liquid part of plant or animal substance. **2.** any extracted liquid. **3.** *U.S. Slang.* electric power.

juic·y (jōō′sY), *adj.,* **juicier, juiciest. 1.** full of juice. **2.** interesting; vivacious; colorful. —**juic′i·ly,** *adv.* —**juic′i·ness,** *n.*

ju·jit·su (jōō jYt′sōō), *n.* a Japanese method of wrestling which employs the strength and weight of the opponent to his disadvantage. Also, **ju·jut′su.**

juke box (jōōk), *U.S. Slang.* a coin-operated phonograph permitting selection of the record to be played.

Jukes (jōōks), *n.* the fictitious name of an actual New York family whose history over several generations showed a high incidence of disease, delinquency, and poverty.

Jul., July.

ju·lep (jōō′lYp), *n.* See **mint julep.**

Ju·li·an·a Lou·i·se Em·ma Ma·rie Wil·hel·mi·na (jōō′lY än′ə lōō ē′sə ĕm′ä mä rē′ vYl′-hĕl mē′nä), born 1909, queen of the Netherlands since 1948.

Jul·ian calendar (jōōl′yən), the calendar established by Julius Caesar in 46 B.C. which

fixed the length of the year at 365 days, with 366 days in every fourth year (leap year).

ju·li·enne (jōō′lY ĕn′), *adj.* **1.** (of vegetables) cut into thin strips or small pieces. —*n.* **2.** a clear soup containing vegetables cut into thin strips or small pieces.

Ju·ly (jōō lī′), *n., pl.* **-lies.** the seventh month of the year, containing 31 days.

jum·ble (jŭm′bəl), *v.,* **-bled, -bling,** *n.* —*v.t.* **1.** to mix in a confused mass. **2.** to confuse mentally. —*v.i.* **3.** to be mixed up. —*n.* **4.** a confused mixture. **5.** a state of confusion or disorder.

jum·bo (jŭm′bō), *n., pl.* **-bos,** *adj. Colloq.* —*n.* **1.** a big, clumsy person, animal, or thing. —*adj.* **2.** very large.

jump (jŭmp), *v.i.* **1.** to spring clear of the ground or other support by a sudden muscular effort; leap. **2.** *Checkers.* to jump, and thus capture, an opponent's piece. **3.** to rise suddenly in amount, price, etc. —*v.t.* **4.** to pass over by a leap. **5.** to cause to jump or leap. **6.** *Checkers.* to capture (an opponent's man) by leaping over it to an unoccupied square. **7.** *Bridge.* to raise (the bid) by more than necessary. **8.** to abscond from, or evade by absconding. **9.** to leave (the track), as trains do. **10.** *U.S.* to get on or off (a train, etc.) by jumping. —*n.* **11.** act of jumping; a leap. **12.** a space or obstacle or apparatus cleared in a leap. **13.** a sudden rise in amount, price, etc. **14.** *U.S. Colloq.* a head start.

jump·er¹ (jŭmp′ər), *n.* **1.** one who or that which jumps. **2.** a boring tool or device worked with a jumping motion.

jump·er² (jŭmp′ər), *n.* **1.** a one-piece, sleeveless dress worn with blouse by women and children. **2.** a loose outer jacket.

jumping bean, the seed of any of certain Mexican plants of the spurge family, which is inhabited by the larvae of a small moth whose movements cause the seed to move about or jump.

jumping jack, a toy consisting of a jointed figure of a man which is made to jump, as by pulling a string attached to its limbs.

jump·y (jŭmp′Y), *adj.,* **jumpier, jumpiest. 1.** characterized by or inclined to sudden, involuntary starts, esp. from nervousness, fear, etc. **2.** causing to jump or start. —**jump′i·ness,** *n.*

Jun., **1.** June. **2.** Junior.

Junc., Junction.

jun·co (jŭng′kō), *n., pl.* **-cos.** any of certain small finches of North America, all with white on the outer tail feathers.

junc·tion (jŭngk′shən), *n.* **1.** combination; union. **2.** a place or station where railroad lines meet or cross. **3.** a place of joining or meeting.

junc·ture (jŭngk′chər), *n.* **1.** a point of time, esp. one made critical or important by a concurrence of circumstances. **2.** a crisis. **3.** a joint, articulation, or seam. **4.** junction.

June (jōōn), *n.* the sixth month of the year, containing 30 days.

Ju·neau (jōō′nō), *n.* a seaport in and the capital of Alaska, in the SE part. 5729.

June bug, 1. (in the northern U.S.) any of certain large brown beetles which appear about June. **2.** (in the southern U.S.) a large, greenish scarabaeid beetle. Also, **June beetle.**

Jung (yŏŏng), *n.* **Carl Gustav,** born 1875, Swiss psychiatrist and psychologist.

jun·gle (jŭng′gəl), *n.* **1.** wild land overgrown with dense, rank vegetation. **2.** *U.S. Slang.* a camp for hobos or tramps.

jun·ior (jōōn′yər), *adj.* **1.** younger (often used after the name of a son having the same name as his father). **2.** of lower rank or standing. **3.** (in American universities, colleges, and schools) noting or pertaining to the third-year class. —*n.* **4.** a person who is younger than another. **5.** one who is of more recent entrance into, or of lower standing in, an office, class, profession, etc. **6.** a student who is in the next to the final year of a course of study.

junior college, a collegiate institution extending through the first one or two years of college instruction and granting a certificate of title instead of a degree.

ju·ni·per (jōō′nə pər), *n.* any of certain coniferous evergreen shrubs or trees whose cones form purple berries used in making gin and in medicine as a diuretic.

junk¹ (jŭngk), *n.* **1.** any old or discarded material, as metal, paper, rags, etc. —*v.t.* **2.** *Colloq.* to discard as no longer of use.

junk² (jŭngk), *n.* a kind of seagoing ship used in Chinese and other waters, having square sails spread by battens, a high stern, and usually a flat bottom.

Jun·ker (yŏŏng′kər), *n.* a member of a class of aristocratic landholders, esp. in Prussia.

jun·ket (jŭng′kĭt), *n.* **1.** a sweet custardlike food of flavored milk curded with rennet. **2.** (*cap.*) a trademark for this food. **3.** a trip by a legislative committee ostensibly to obtain information. **4.** a picnic; pleasure excursion. —*v.i.* **5.** to go on a junket. —*v.i.* **6.** to entertain; regale.

Ju·no (jōō′nō), *n. Rom. Myth.* an ancient Roman goddess, the wife of Jupiter, presiding over marriage and women.

jun·ta (jŭn′tə), *n.* **1.** a meeting. **2.** a deliberative or administrative council, esp. in Spain. **3.** a junto.

jun·to (jŭn′tō), *n., pl.* **-tos.** a self-appointed committee, esp. with political aims.

Ju·pi·ter (jōō′pə tər), *n.* **1.** the supreme deity of the ancient Romans, the god of the heavens; Jove. **2.** the largest planet, fifth in order from the sun.

Ju·ra Mountains (jōōr′ə), a mountain range between France and Switzerland. Highest peak, 5654 ft.

ju·rid·i·cal (jŏŏ rĭd′ə kəl), *adj.* **1.** of or pertaining to the administration of justice. **2.** legal. Also, **ju·rid′ic.**

ju·ris·dic·tion (jŏŏr′ĭs dĭk′shən), *n.* **1.** the right, power, or authority to administer justice by hearing and determining controversies. **2.** authority; control. **3.** the extent or range of authority. —**ju·ris·dic′tion·al,** *adj.* —**ju·ris·dic′tion·al·ly,** *adv.*

ju·ris·pru·dence (jŏŏr′ĭs prōō′dəns), *n.* **1.** the science or philosophy of law. **2.** a body or system of laws. **3.** a department of law.

ju·rist (jŏŏr′ĭst), *n.* **1.** one who professes the science of law. **2.** one versed in the law. **3.** one who writes on the subject of law.

ju·ris·tic (jŏŏ rĭs′tĭk), *adj.* relating to law; juridical; legal. Also, **ju·ris′ti·cal.**

ju·ror (jŏŏr′ər), *n.* a member of any jury.

ju·ry¹ (jŏŏr′ĭ), *n., pl.* **juries. 1.** a body of persons sworn to render a verdict or true answer on a question or questions officially submitted to them. **2.** a body of persons chosen to adjudge prizes, etc., as in a competition.

ju·ry² (jŏŏr′ĭ), *adj. Naut.* makeshift.

ju·ry·man (jŏŏr′ĭ mən), *n., pl.* **-men.** a juror:

just (jŭst), *adj.* **1.** actuated by truth and justice. **2.** equitable; even-handed. **3.** rightful; lawful. **4.** true; correct. **5.** deserved, as a sentence, reward, etc. **6.** proper or right. **7.** righteous. —*adv.* **8.** within a brief preceding time. **9.** exactly. **10.** barely. **11.** only or merely. **12.** *Colloq.* truly. —**just′ly,** *adv.* —**just′ness,** *n.*

jus·tice (jŭs′tĭs), *n.* **1.** righteousness; equitableness; moral rightness. **2.** justness of ground or reason. **3.** the moral principle determining just conduct. **4.** just conduct, dealing, or treatment. **5.** the requital of desert as by punishment or reward. **6.** the administration of law. **7.** judicial process. **8.** a judge or magistrate. —**jus′tice·ship′,** *n.*

justice of the peace, a local officer having authority to try minor cases, solemnize marriages, etc.

jus·ti·fi·a·ble (jŭs′tə fī′ə bəl), *adj.* capable of being justified; defensible. —**jus′ti·fi·a·bly,** *adv.*

jus·ti·fi·ca·tion (jŭs′tə fə kā′shən), *n.* **1.** something that justifies; an excuse. **2.** act of justifying. **3.** state of being justified.

jus·ti·fy (jŭs′tə fī′), *v.t.,* **-fied, -fying. 1.** to show (an act, claim, statement, etc.) to be just, right, or warranted. **2.** to defend or uphold as blameless, just, or right. **3.** to absolve; acquit. —**jus′ti·fi′er,** *n.*

Jus·tin·i·an I (jŭs tĭn′ĭ ən), A.D. 483–565, Byzantine emperor, A.D. 527–565, whose leading jurists formulated a code of laws called the **Justinian Code.**

jut (jŭt), *v.,* **jutted, jutting,** *n.* —*v.i.* **1.** to project; protrude. —*n.* **2.** a projection.

jute (jōōt), *n.* **1.** a strong fiber used for making fabrics, cordage, etc., obtained from certain East Indian plants. **2.** one of these plants.

Jute (jōōt), *n.* a member of a Germanic tribe which invaded Britain from the continent and settled there in the 5th century A.D.

Jut·land (jŭt′lənd), *n.* a peninsula comprising the continental portion of Denmark.

ju·ve·ni·e (jōō′və nəl, -nĭl, -nīl′), *adj.* **1.** pertaining to, suitable for, or intended for young persons. **2.** young. —*n.* **3.** a young person; youth. **4.** *Theat.* a. a youthful male role. b. an actor who plays such parts. **5.** a book for young people.

jux·ta·pose (jŭks′tə pōz′), *v.t.,* **-posed, -posing.** to place in close proximity or side by side. —**jux′ta·po·si′tion,** *n.*

Jy., July.

K

K, k (kā), *n., pl.* **K's** or **Ks, k's** or **ks.** a consonant, the 11th letter of the English alphabet.

K, *Chem.* potassium.

K., **1.** King. **2.** Knight.

k., **1.** *Elect.* capacity. **2.** karat. **3.** kilogram.

Kaa·ba (kä′bə, kä′ə bə), *n.* a small building in the Great Mosque at Mecca, containing a sacred stone.

ka·bobs (kə bŏbs′), *n.* an oriental dish of small pieces of meat roasted on a skewer.

Ka·bul (kä′bŏŏl), *n.* the capital of Afghanistan, in the NE part. ab. 120,000.

Kaf·fir (kăf′ər, kä′fər), *n.* a member of a South African Negroid race inhabiting parts of the Cape of Good Hope, Natal, etc.

Kai·ser (kī′zər), *n.* **1.** a German emperor. **2.** an Austrian emperor. **3.** *Hist.* a ruler of the Holy Roman Empire.

Kal·a·ma·zoo (kăl′ə mə zōō′), *n.* a city in SW Michigan. 54,097.

kale (kāl), *n.* **1.** a plant of the mustard family, with leaves not forming a head, used as a potherb. **2.** *U.S. Slang.* money.

ka·lei·do·scope (kə lī′də skōp′), *n.* an optical instrument in which bits of colored glass, etc., in a rotating tube are shown by reflection in continually changing symmetrical forms. —**ka·lei·do·scop·ic** (kə lī′də skŏp′ĭk), *adj.* —**ka·lei·do·scop′i·cal·ly,** *adv.*

Ka·li·nin (kä lē′nĭn), *n.* **Mikhail Ivanovich,** 1875–1946, president of the Praesidium of the Supreme Council of the Soviet Union, 1938–1946.

Kal·li·kaks (kăl′ə kăks′), *n.pl.* the fictitious name of an actual New Jersey family whose history over several generations showed a high incidence of disease, delinquency, and poverty.

kal·so·mine (kăl′sə mīn′, -mĭn), *n., v.t.,* **-mined, -mining.** calcimine.

Kam·chat·ka (kăm chăt′kə), *n.* a peninsula in the E Soviet Union in Asia, extending S between the Bering Sea and the Sea of Okhotsk. ab. 750 mi. long; ab. 104,000 sq. mi.

Ka·mi·ka·ze (kä′mǐ kä′zē), *n.pl. Japanese.* (in World War II) suicide pilots.

Ka·nak·a (kə năk′ə, kän′ə kə), *n.* **1.** a native Hawaiian. **2.** a South Sea islander.

Kan·chen·jun·ga (kän′chən jŏŏng′gə), *n.* a peak of the E Himalayas; third loftiest peak in the world. 28,146 ft.

kan·ga·roo (kăng′gə rōō′), *n., pl.* **-roos,** (*esp. collectively*) **-roo.** any of a family of herbivorous marsupials of the Australian region with powerful hind legs developed for leaping, a sturdy tail serving as a support and balance, a small head, and the forelimbs very short and small.

kangaroo court, *Colloq.* an unauthorized court conducted with a disregard for legal procedure.

kangaroo rat, any of certain small jumping rodents of Mexico and the western U.S.

Kan·sas (kăn′zəs), *n.* 1. a State in the central United States. 1,861,195 pop.; 82,276 sq. mi. *Cap.*: Topeka. *Abbr.*: **Kans.** or **Kan.** 2. a river in NE Kansas, flowing E to the Missouri river. 169 mi. —**Kan′san,** *adj.*, *n.*

Kansas City, 1. a city in W Missouri. 399,178. 2. a city in NE Kansas, adjacent to Kansas City, Missouri. 121,458.

Kant (kănt), *n.* **Immanuel,** 1724–1804, German philosopher.

ka·o·lin (kā′ə lĭn), *n.* a fine white clay used in the manufacture of porcelain. Also, **ka′o·line.**

ka·pok (kā′pŏk, kăp′ək), *n.* the silky down which invests the seeds of a silk-cotton tree (**kapok tree**) of the East Indies, Africa, and tropical America: used for stuffing pillows, etc., and for sound insulation.

kap·pa (kăp′ə), *n.* the tenth letter of the Greek alphabet (Κ, κ).

ka·put (kä poot′), *adj.* *Slang.* ruined.

Ka·ra·chi (kə rä′chĭ), *n.* a seaport in and the capital of Pakistan. 359,492.

kar·a·kul (kăr′ə kəl), *n.* 1. an Asiatic breed of sheep used primarily for the production of lambskin fur. 2. caracul (the fur).

kar·at (kăr′ət), *n.* a twenty-fourth part (used in expressing the fineness of gold, pure gold being 24 karats fine).

Kas·bah (käs′bä), *n.* the older, native quarter of Algiers.

Kash·mir (kăsh mĭr′), *n.* an independent state adjacent to India, Pakistan, Sinkiang province, China, and Tibet. Including feudatories, 4,021,-600 pop.; 82,258 sq. mi. *Cap.*: Srinagar.

Kas·sel (käs′əl), *n.* a city in central Germany. 216,141.

Kat·man·du (kät′män dōō′), *n.* the capital of Nepal. ab. 108,800.

Kat·te·gat (kăt′ə găt′), *n.* the strait between Jutland and Sweden. 40–70 mi. wide.

ka·ty·did (kā′tĭ dĭd), *n.* any of certain large, usually green, long-horned American grasshoppers known for the loud note of the males of some species.

kay·ak (kī′ăk), *n.* an Eskimo hunting craft with a skin cover on a light framework, made watertight by flexible closure around the waist of the occupant.

Kayak

Ka·zak Soviet Socialist Republic (kä zäk′), a constituent republic of the Soviet Union, E and N of the Caspian Sea. 6,145,937 pop.; 1,055,900 sq. mi. *Cap.*: Alma-Ata.

Ka·zan (kä zän′y), *n.* a city in the E Soviet Union in Europe, near the Volga. 401,665.

kc., kilocycle; kilocycles.

ke·a (kā′ə, kē′ə), *n.* a large, greenish New Zealand parrot.

Kear·ny (kär′nĭ), *n.* a city in NE New Jersey, near Newark. 39,467.

Keats (kēts), *n.* **John,** 1795–1821, British poet.

kedge (kĕj), *v.*, **kedged, kedging,** *n.* —*v.t.*, *v.i.* 1. to warp or pull (a ship, etc.) along by means of a rope attached to an anchor. —*n.* 2. Also, **kedge anchor.** a small anchor used in kedging and otherwise.

keel (kēl), *n.* 1. a longitudinal part along the middle of the bottom of a vessel. 2. a ship. 3. a part corresponding to a ship's keel in some other structure, as in a dirigible balloon. —*v.t.*, *v.i.* 4. to turn or upset so as to bring the wrong side or part uppermost.

keel·haul (kēl′hôl′), *v.t.* *Naut.* to haul (a person) under the keel of a vessel, as for punishment.

keel·son (kĕl′sən, kēl′-), *n.* *Naut.* a strengthening line of timbers or iron plates in a ship, above and parallel with the keel.

keen¹ (kēn), *adj.* 1. sharp. 2. piercing or biting. 3. characterized by strength and distinctness of perception, as the eye. 4. having or showing great mental penetration or acumen. 5. intense, as desire, competition, etc. 6. ardent; eager. —**keen′ly,** *adv.* —**keen′ness,** *n.*

keen² (kēn), *Irish.* —*n.* 1. a wailing lament for the dead. —*v.i.* 2. to wail in lamentation for the dead. —**keen′er,** *n.*

keep (kēp), *v.*, **kept, keeping,** *n.* —*v.t.* 1. to maintain in one's action or conduct. 2. to cause to continue in some place, position, state, etc. 3. to hold in custody; detain. 4. to have habitually in stock or for sale. 5. to maintain in one's service or for one's use. 6. to withhold from the knowledge of others. 7. to reserve. 8. to maintain or record by writing, etc. 9. to pay obedient regard to (a law, promise, etc.). 10. to follow; fulfill. 11. to manage. 12. to care for or protect. 13. to continue to hold or have. —*v.i.* 14. to continue in an action, course, position, state, etc. 15. to remain or stay in a place. 16. to continue unimpaired or without spoiling. 17. to hold or restrain oneself or itself. —*n.* 18. board and lodging. 19. the innermost and strongest structure of a medieval castle. 20. **for keeps,** *Colloq.* **a.** for keeping as one's own permanently. **b.** permanently; altogether.

keep·er (kē′pər), *n.* one who guards, watches, or takes care of something or someone.

keep·ing (kē′pĭng), *n.* 1. conformity; agreement. 2. observance, custody, or care.

keep·sake (kēp′sāk′), *n.* anything kept, or given to be kept, for the sake of the giver.

keg (kĕg), *n.* a small cask or barrel, usually holding from 5 to 10 gallons.

Kel·ler (kĕl′ər), *n.* **Helen Adams,** born 1880, U.S. author, blind and deaf, who learned to speak.

kelp (kĕlp), *n.* 1. any of certain large brown seaweeds. 2. the ash of such seaweeds.

kel·pie (kĕl′pĭ), *n.* *Scot.* a fabled water spirit, usually in the form of a horse.

kel·py (kĕl′pĭ), *n.*, *pl.* **-pies.** kelpie.

Kelt (kĕlt), *n.* Celt. —**Kelt′ic,** *n.*, *adj.*

Ke·mal A·ta·türk (kĕ mäl′ ä′tä tyrk′), 1880–1938, president of Turkey, 1923–38.

Kem·pis (kĕm′pĭs), *n.* **Thomas à,** 1380?–1471, German churchman and author.

ken (kĕn), *n.*, *v.*, **kenned** or **kent, kenning.** —*n.* 1. range of vision. 2. knowledge or cognizance. —*v.t.* 3. *Scot.* to have acquaintance with.

Ken., Kentucky.

ken·nel (kĕn′əl), *n.*, *v.*, **-neled, -neling** or (*esp. Brit.*) **-nelled, -nelling.** —*n.* 1. a house for a dog or dogs. 2. (*often pl.*) an establishment where dogs are bred. —*v.t.* 3. to put into or keep in a kennel. —*v.i.* 4. to take shelter or lodge in a kennel.

ke·no (kē′nō), *n.* a game of chance, adapted from lotto for gambling purposes.

Ke·no·sha (kĭ nō′shə), *n.* a city in SE Wisconsin: a port on Lake Michigan. 48,765.

Ken·tuck·y (kən tŭk′ĭ), *n.* 1. a State in the E central United States. 2,745,590 pop.; 40,395 sq. mi. *Cap.*: Frankfort. *Abbr.*: Ky. or Ken. 2. a river flowing from E Kentucky NW to the Ohio river. 259 mi. —**Ken·tuck′i·an,** *adj.*, *n.*

Ken·ya (kēn′yə, kĕn′-), *n.* a British crown colony and protectorate in E Africa. 3,724,000 pop.; 219,730 sq. mi. *Cap.*: Nairobi.

kep·i (kĕp′ĭ), *n.*, *pl.* **kepis.** a military cap with a flat circular top and a visor.

Kep·ler (kĕp′lər), *n.* **Johann** (yō′hän), 1571–1630, German astronomer.

kerb (kûrb), *n.*, *v.t.* *Brit.* curb (defs. 4, 7).

ker·chief (kûr′chĭf), *n.* 1. a cloth worn as a head covering, esp. by women. 2. a cloth worn or carried on the person.

Ke·ren·ski (kĕ rĕn′skĭ), *n.* **Aleksandr Feodorovich,** born 1881, Russian revolutionist; premier, 1917. Also, **Ke·ren′sky.**

kerf (kûrf), *n.* 1. the cut made by a saw or other instrument. 2. that which is cut.

kern (kûrn), *n.* *Print.* a part of the face of a type projecting beyond the body or shank.

ker·nel (kûr′nəl), *n.*, *v.*, **-neled, -neling** or (*esp. Brit.*) **-nelled, -nelling.** —*n.* 1. the softer, usually edible, part contained in the shell of a nut or the stone of a fruit. 2. a grain, as of wheat. 3. the central part of anything; core. —*v.t.* 4. to enclose as a kernel. —**ker′nel·less,** *adj.*

ker·o·sene (kĕr′ə sēn′, kĕr′ə sēn′), *n.* an oil for lamps and heating: a mixture of hydrocarbons, distilled from petroleum, coal, etc.

ketch (kĕch), *n.* a fore-and-aft rigged vessel with a large mainmast and a smaller mast aft, but forward of the rudder post.

ketch·up (kĕch′əp), *n.* catchup.

ke·tone (kē′tōn), *n.* *Chem.* any of a class of organic compounds containing the carbonyl group, CO, attached to two organic radicals.

ket·tle (kĕt′əl), *n.* **1.** a container for boiling liquids, etc.; pot. **2.** teakettle.

ket·tle·drum (kĕt′əl drŭm′), *n.* a drum consisting of a hollow hemisphere of brass or copper with a skin stretched over it.

kew·pie (kū′pĭ), *n.* **1.** a small, very plump doll, usually made of plaster or celluloid. **2.** (*cap.*) a trademark for such a doll.

key[1] (kē), *n., pl.* keys, *adj., v.,* keyed, keying. —*n.* **1.** an instrument for fastening or opening a lock by moving its bolt. **2.** a means of attaining, understanding, solving, etc. **3.** a book or the like containing the solutions or translations of material given elsewhere as exercises. **4.** a systematic explanation of abbreviations, symbols, etc., used in a dictionary, map, etc. **5.** something that controls entrance to a place. **6.** a pin, bolt, wedge, or other piece inserted in a hole or space to lock or hold parts of a mechanism or structure together. **7.** a contrivance for turning a bolt, nut, etc. **8.** one of a set of levers pressed in operating a telegraph, typewriter, etc. **9.** *Music.* **a.** that part of the lever mechanism of piano, organ, or wood wind, which a finger operates. **b.** the keynote or tonic of a scale. **c.** the relationship perceived between all tones in a given unit of music to a single tone or a keynote; tonality. **d.** the principal tonality of a composition. **10.** tone or pitch, as of voice. **11.** style, as of expression. **12.** *Elect.* a device for opening and closing electrical contacts. —*adj.* **13.** of chief importance; fundamental. —*v.t.* **14.** to bring to a particular degree of intensity of excitement, energy, etc. **15.** *Music.* to regulate the pitch of.

key[2] (kē), *n., pl.* keys. a reef or low island.

Key (kē), *n.* Francis Scott, 1780–1843, U.S. lawyer: author of *The Star-Spangled Banner.*

key·board (kē′bōrd′), *n.* the row or set of keys in a piano, typewriter, etc.

key·hole (kē′hōl′), *n.* a hole for a key to a lock.

key·note (kē′nōt′), *n., v.,* -noted, -noting. —*n.* **1.** *Music.* the note or tone on which a system of tones is founded; tonic. **2.** the determining principle or policy governing a speech, action, etc. —*v.t.* **3.** to give the keynote of.

key·stone (kē′stōn′), *n.* the wedge-shaped piece at the summit of an arch, regarded as holding the other pieces in place.

Key West, **1.** an island in S Florida, in the Gulf of Mexico. **2.** a seaport on this island. 12,927.

kg., **1.** keg; kegs. **2.** kilogram; kilograms.

khak·i (kăk′ĭ, kä′kĭ), *n., pl.* khakis, *adj.* —*n.* **1.** dull yellowish brown. **2.** stout uniform cloth of this color. —*adj.* **3.** of the color of khaki. **4.** made of khaki.

khan[1] (kän, kăn), *n.* **1.** the title borne by certain hereditary rulers in Asia. **2.** the supreme ruler of the Tatar tribes, as well as emperor of China, during the Middle Ages. **3.** a title of respect in Iran, Afghanistan, India, etc.

khan[2] (kän, kăn), *n.* an inn or caravansary.

Khar·kov (kär′kŏf, -kŏv), *n.* a city in the S Soviet Union in Europe. 833,423.

Khar·toum (кнär tōōm′), *n.* the capital of the Anglo-Egyptian Sudan: besieged, 1895; retaken by the British, 1898. 44,950.

khe·dive (kə dēv′), *n.* title of the Turkish viceroys in Egypt, 1867–1914. —**khe·di′val, khe·di·vi·al** (kə dē′vĭ əl), *adj.*

Khy·ber Pass (kī′bər), the chief mountain pass between India and Afghanistan, W of Peshawar in Pakistan. 33 mi. long; 6825 ft. high.

kibe (kīb), *n.* a chapped chilblain.

Ki·bei (kē′bā′), *n., pl.* -bei. a person of Japanese descent, born in the U.S., who goes to Japan for an education.

kib·itz (kĭb′ĭts), *v.i.* *Colloq.* to act as a kibitzer.

kib·itz·er (kĭb′ĭt sər), *n.* *Colloq.* a giver of unwanted advice, esp. to card players.

ki·bosh (kī′bŏsh, kĭ bŏsh′), *n.* *Slang.* **1.** nonsense. **2.** put the kibosh on, to foil or stop.

kick (kĭk), *v.t.* **1.** to give a blow or thrust to with the foot. **2.** to drive, force, make, etc., by kicks. —*v.i.* **3.** to strike out with the foot. **4.** *Colloq.* to object or complain. **5.** to recoil, as a firearm when fired. —*n.* **6.** a blow or thrust with the foot. **7.** a recoil, as of a gun. **8.** *Slang.* an

objection or complaint. **9.** *Slang.* a thrill or excitement. —**kick′er,** *n.*

kick·back (kĭk′băk′), *n.* *Colloq.* **1.** a response, usually vigorous. **2.** the practice of a supervisor of taking back a portion of the wages due to workers.

kick·off (kĭk′ôf′, -ŏf′), *n.* *Football.* a place kick from the 40-yard line of the side kicking, as at the beginning of each half.

kick·shaw (kĭk′shô′), *n.* **1.** any fancy dish in cookery. **2.** any trifle.

kid[1] (kĭd), *n., v.,* kidded, kidding. —*n.* **1.** a young goat. **2.** leather made from the skin of a goat. **3.** *Slang.* a child or young person. —*v.i., v.t.* **4.** (of a goat) to give birth to (young).

kid[2] (kĭd), *v.,* kidded, kidding, *n.* *Slang.* —*v.t.* **1.** to tease; jest with. **2.** to fool. —*v.i.* **3.** to jest. —*n.* **4.** humbug; chaffing. —**kid′der,** *n.*

Kidd (kĭd), *n.* **William,** (*"Captain Kidd"*) c1645–1701, British navigator and privateer, hanged for piracy.

kid·nap (kĭd′năp), *v.t.,* -naped, -naping or (*esp. Brit.*) -napped, -napping. to steal or abduct (a child or other person), often for ransom. —**kid′nap·er;** *esp. Brit.,* **kid′nap·per,** *n.*

kid·ney (kĭd′nĭ), *n., pl.* -neys. **1.** (in man) either of a pair of bean-shaped glandular organs, in the back part of the abdominal cavity, which excrete urine. **2.** a corresponding organ in animals. **3.** temperament. **4.** kind.

kidney bean, the kidney-shaped seed of the common bean.

Kiel (kēl), *n.* a seaport in N Germany at the Baltic end of the **Kiel Canal,** a ship canal connecting the North and Baltic Seas. 273,735.

Kier·ke·gaard (kĭr′kə gôr′), *n.* **Soren Aabye,** 1813–55, Danish philosopher.

Ki·ev (kē′ĕf), *n.* a city in the SW Soviet Union, on the Dneiper. 846,293.

kil., kilometer; kilometers.

kill[1] (kĭl), *v.t.* **1.** to cause the death of; slay. **2.** to destroy; extinguish. **3.** to get rid of (time). **4.** to overcome completely. **5.** to cancel (a word, item, etc.). **6.** to defeat or veto (a legislative bill, etc.). —*v.i.* **7.** to cause death. **8.** to commit murder. —*n.* **9.** act of killing (game, etc.). **10.** an animal killed.

kill[2] (kĭl), *n.* *U.S. Dial.* a channel; stream.

Kil·lar·ney (kĭ lär′nĭ), *n.* **1.** a town in SW Republic of Ireland. 5790. **2.** Lakes of, three beautiful lakes nearby.

kill·deer (kĭl′dĭr′), *n.* the largest and commonest of certain plovers of America. Also, **kill·dee** (kĭl′dē′).

kill·er (kĭl′ər), *n.* **1.** one who or that which kills. **2.** any of various ravenous cetaceans of the dolphin family.

kill·ing (kĭl′ĭng), *n.* **1.** act of one that kills. **2.** the total game killed on a hunt. **3.** *Colloq.* a stroke of extraordinary execution, as in business. —*adj.* **4.** that kills. **5.** exhausting. **6.** *Colloq.* irresistibly funny.

kill-joy (kĭl′joi′), *n.* a person or thing that spoils the joy or enjoyment of others.

kiln (kĭl, kĭln), *n.* **1.** a furnace or oven for burning, baking, or drying something. —*v.t.* **2.** to burn, bake, or treat in a kiln.

kil·o (kĭl′ō, kē′lō), *n., pl.* -los. **1.** kilogram. **2.** kilometer.

kil·o·cal·o·rie (kĭl′ə kăl′ə rĭ), *n.* *Physics.* a large calorie: See calorie.

kil·o·cy·cle (kĭl′ə sī′kəl), *n.* a unit equal to 1000 cycles: used esp. in radio as 1000 cycles per second for expressing the frequency of electromagnetic waves.

kil·o·gram (kĭl′ə grăm′), *n.* *Metric System.* a unit of mass and weight equal to 1000 grams, and equivalent to 2.2046 pounds avoirdupois. Also, *esp. Brit.,* **kil′o·gramme′.**

kil·o·li·ter (kĭl′ə lē′tər), *n.* *Metric System.* 1000 liters; a cubic meter. Also, *esp. Brit.,* **kil′o·li′tre.**

kilom., kilometer.

kil·o·me·ter (kĭl′ə mē′tər; *occas.* kĭ lŏm′ə tər), *n.* *Metric System.* a unit of length, the common measure of distances, equal to 1000 meters, and equivalent to 3280.8 feet or 0.621 mile. Also, *esp. Brit.,* **kil′o·me′tre.** —**kil·o·met·ric** (kĭl′ə mĕt′rĭk), **kil′o·met′ri·cal,** *adj.*

kil·o·watt (kĭl′ə wŏt′), *n.* *Elect.* a unit of power, equal to 1000 watts.

kil·o·watt-hour (kĭl′ə wŏt′our′), *n.* *Elect.* a unit of energy equivalent to that transferred or expended in one hour by one kilowatt of power, approx. 1.34 horsepower per hour.

kilt (kĭlt), *n.* any short, plaited skirt, esp. one worn by men in the Scottish highlands. —**kilt′-like′**, *adj.*

kil·ter (kĭl′tər), *n. U.S. Dial.* good condition.

Kim·ber·ley (kĭm′bər lĭ), *n.* a city in the central part of the Union of South Africa: diamond mines. With suburbs, 55,545.

ki·mo·no (kə mō′nə, -nō), *n., pl.* **-nos.** 1. a wide-sleeved robe characteristic of Japanese costume. 2. a woman's loose dressing gown.

kin (kĭn), *n.* 1. one's relatives collectively. 2. family relationship. 3. of kin, related. —*adj.* 4. related. 5. of the same kind or nature.

kind[1] (kīnd), *adj.* 1. of a good nature; benevolent. 2. having, showing, or proceeding from benevolence.

kind[2] (kīnd), *n.* 1. a class or group of individuals (as animals or plants) of the same nature or character. 2. nature or character as determining likeness or difference between things. 3. a person or thing as being of a particular character or class. 4. a more or less adequate example.

kin·der·gar·ten (kĭn′dər gär′tən), *n.* a school for the mental, moral, and physical development of very young children by means of games, etc.

kin·der·gart·ner (kĭn′dər gärt′nər), *n.* a child who attends a kindergarten.

kind·heart·ed (kīnd′här′tĭd), *adj.* having or showing a kind heart. —**kind′heart′ed·ly**, *adv.* —**kind′heart′ed·ness**, *n.*

kin·dle (kĭn′dəl), *v.*, **-dled, -dling.** —*v.t.* 1. to set (a fire, flame, etc.) to burning. 2. to set fire to. 3. to excite, rouse, or inflame. —*v.i.* 4. to begin to burn. 5. to become roused, ardent, or inflamed.

kin·dling (kĭn′dlĭng), *n.* 1. material for starting a fire. 2. act of one who kindles.

kind·ly (kīnd′lĭ), *adj.*, **-lier, -liest,** *adv.* —*adj.* 1. kindhearted; good-natured. 2. gentle or mild, as laws. 3. pleasant, genial, or benign. 4. favorable, as soil. 5. in a kindly or kind manner. 6. cordially or heartily. 7. with pleasure; favorably. —**kind′li·ness**, *n.*

kind·ness (kīnd′nĭs), *n.* 1. state or quality of being kind. 2. a kind act. 3. kind behavior. 4. friendly feeling, or liking.

kin·dred (kĭn′drĭd), *n.* 1. a body of persons related to another, or a family, tribe, or race. 2. one's relatives collectively. 3. relationship by birth or marriage. 4. natural affinity. —*adj.* 5. associated by origin, nature, qualities, etc. 6. related by birth or descent. 7. belonging to relatives.

kine (kīn), *n.pl. Archaic.* pl. of **cow.**

kin·e·mat·ics (kĭn′ə măt′ĭks), *n.* that branch of mechanics which treats of pure motion, without reference to mass or cause. —**kin′e·mat′ic, kin′e·mat′i·cal,** *adj.*

kin·e·scope (kĭn′ə skōp′), *n. Television.* 1. a cathode ray tube with a screen on which the image is reproduced. 2. (*cap.*) a trademark for this tube.

ki·net·ic (kĭ nĕt′ĭk, kī-), *adj.* 1. pertaining to motion. 2. caused by motion.

ki·net·ics (kĭ nĕt′ĭks, kī-), *n.* the branch of mechanics which treats of the action of forces in producing or changing the motion of masses.

kin·folks (kĭn′fōks′), *n.pl. Colloq.* kinsfolk. Also, **kin′folk′.**

king (kĭng), *n.* 1. a man who holds by life tenure (and usually by hereditary right) the chief authority over a country and people. 2. (*cap.*) God or Christ. 3. a person or thing preëminent in its class. 4. a playing card bearing a picture of a king. 5. the chief piece in a game of chess. 6. a piece that has moved entirely across the board in the game of checkers.

King (kĭng), *n.* **William Lyon Mackenzie,** born 1874, Canadian statesman: prime minister, 1921–26, 1926–30, and 1935–48.

king·bird (kĭng′bûrd′), *n.* any of certain flycatchers of the New World.

king·bolt (kĭng′bōlt′), *n.* a vertical bolt connecting the body of a vehicle with the fore axle, truck, etc.

king·dom (kĭng′dəm), *n.* 1. a state or government having a king or queen as its head. 2. anything conceived as an independent realm or sphere.

king·fish (kĭng′fĭsh′), *n., pl.* **-fishes,** (*esp. collectively*) **-fish.** any of various fishes conspicuous for size or some other quality, esp. certain marine food fish of the New England and California coasts.

king·fish·er (kĭng′fĭsh′ər), *n.* any of certain fish- or insect-eating birds that are stout-billed and small-footed, many of which are crested or brilliantly colored.

King James Version. See **Authorized Version.**

king·let (kĭng′lĭt), *n.* a king ruling over a small country or territory.

king·ly (kĭng′lĭ), *adj.*, **-lier, -liest,** *adv.* —*adj.* 1. being a king. 2. consisting of kings or of royal rank. 3. like or befitting a king. —*adv.* 4. in a kingly manner. —**king′li·ness**, *n.*

king·pin (kĭng′pĭn′), *n.* 1. (in bowling games) a. the pin in the center when the pins are in place. b. the pin at the front apex. 2. *Colloq.* the principal person, element, etc.

Kings (kĭngz), *n.pl.* certain books of the Bible which contain the history of the reigns of the kings of Israel and Judah (usually called I Kings and II Kings).

king's English, correct English usage.

king·ship (kĭng′shĭp), *n.* 1. kingly state, office, or dignity. 2. kingly rule.

king snake, any of certain large harmless American snakes, esp. one which feeds on other snakes, including rattlesnakes.

Kings·ton (kĭngz′tən, kĭng′stən), *n.* 1. a seaport in and the capital of Jamaica. 109,000. 2. a city in SE Canada. 30,126.

kink (kĭngk), *n.* 1. a twist or curl, as in a thread, rope, or hair. 2. a crick, as in the neck. 3. an odd notion; crotchet. —*v.i., v.t.* 4. to form or cause to form a kink or kinks, as a rope. —**kink′-y**, *adj.* —**kink′i·ness**, *n.*

kin·ka·jou (kĭng′kə jōō′), *n.* a pale-brown, soft-furred, arboreal, prehensile-tailed mammal of Central and South America, related to the raccoon.

Kin·sey (kĭn′zĭ), *n.* **Alfred Charles,** born 1894, U.S. zoölogist: director of a survey of human sex behavior.

kins·folk (kĭnz′fōk′), *n.pl.* relatives.

kin·ship (kĭn′shĭp), *n.* 1. family relationship. 2. relationship by nature, qualities, etc.; affinity.

kins·man (kĭnz′mən), *n., pl.* **-men.** a male relative. —**kins′wom′an,** *n. fem.*

ki·osk (kĭ ŏsk′, kĭ′ŏsk), *n.* a structure with open sides, used as a bandstand, newsstand, etc.

kip (kĭp), *n.* the hide of a young or small beast.

Kip·ling (kĭp′lĭng), *n.* **Rudyard,** 1865–1936, British writer and poet.

kip·per (kĭp′ər), *v.t.* 1. to cure (herring, salmon, etc.) by cleaning, salting, etc., and drying in the air or in smoke. —*n.* 2. a kippered fish, esp. a herring.

Kir·ghiz (kĭr gēz′), *n., pl.* **-ghiz, -ghizes.** 1. a member of a widespread people of Mongolian physical type and Turkic speech, dwelling chiefly in west central Asia. 2. their language.

kirk (kûrk), *n. Scot. and N. Eng.* a church.

kirsch·was·ser (kĭrsh′väs′ər), *n.* a brandy distilled from wild black cherries. Also, **kirsch.**

kir·tle (kûr′təl), *n.* a woman's gown or skirt. —**kir′tled,** *adj.*

kis·met (kĭz′mĕt, kĭs′-), *n.* fate; destiny.

kiss (kĭs), *v.t.* 1. to touch or press with the lips in token of greeting, affection, etc. 2. to touch gently or lightly. —*v.i.* 3. to kiss someone, something, or each other. —*n.* 4. act of kissing. 5. a piece of toffeelike confectionery. 6. a cooky of egg whites and confectioner's sugar. —**kiss′a-ble,** *adj.* —**kiss′er,** *n.*

kit (kĭt), *n.* 1. a set of tools, supplies, etc., for a special purpose. 2. the case containing these.

kitch·en (kĭch′ən), *n.* a room or place equipped for or appropriated to cooking.

Kitch·en·er (kĭch′ən ər), *n.* a city in SE Canada, in S Ontario. 35,657.

kitch·en·ette (kĭch′ə nĕt′), *n.* a small kitchen.

kitchen police, *Mil.* 1. duty as assistant to the cooks. 2. soldiers on kitchen duty.

kitch·en·ware (kĭch′ən wâr′), *n.* cooking equipment or utensils.

kite (kīt), *n., v.*, **kited, kiting.** —*n.* 1. a light frame covered with some thin material, to be flown in the wind at the end of a long string. 2. any of certain birds of the falcon family which prey on small quarry. 3. *Com.* a fictitious negotiable instrument, used for raising money or sustaining credit. —*v.i.* 4. *Colloq.* to fly or move with a rapid or easy motion. 5. *Com.* to obtain money or credit through kites.

kith (kĭth), *n.* one's friends.

kit·ten (kĭt′ən), *n.* **1.** a young cat. —*v.t.*, *v.i.* **2.** to bring forth (kittens).

kit·ten·ish (kĭt′ən ĭsh), *adj.* kittenlike; artlessly playful. —**kit′ten·ish·ly**, *adv.*

kit·ty[1] (kĭt′ĭ), *n.*, *pl.* **-ties.** a kitten.

kit·ty[2] (kĭt′ĭ), *n.*, *pl.* **-ties.** *Cards.* a pool into which each player puts a certain amount of his winnings, for some special purpose.

ki·wi (kē′wĭ), *n.*, *pl.* **-wis** (-wĭz). **1.** an apteryx. **2.** *Colloq.* a man in an aviation service who does not make flights.

K.K.K., Ku Klux Klan. Also, **KKK**

kl., kiloliter.

Klan (klăn), *n.* Ku Klux Klan.

Klans·man (klănz′mən), *n.*, *pl.* **-men.** a member of the Ku Klux Klan.

klep·to·ma·ni·a (klĕp′tə mā′nĭ ə), *n.* an irresistible desire to steal, without regard to personal needs. —**klep′to·ma′ni·ac′,** *n.*

klieg light (klēg), a floodlight with an arc-light source used in motion-picture studios to project a beam of high actinic power.

Klon·dike (klŏn′dīk), *n.* a region of the Yukon territory in NW Canada: gold rush, 1897–98.

km., kilometer; kilometers.

knack (năk), *n.* **1.** a special ability or skill; aptitude. **2.** a habit or practice.

knap·sack (năp′săk′), *n.* a leather or canvas case for clothes and the like, carried on the back.

knave (nāv), *n.* **1.** an unprincipled or dishonest fellow. **2.** *Cards.* a jack.

knav·er·y (nā′və rĭ), *n.*, *pl.* **-eries.** **1.** action characteristic of a knave. **2.** dishonest dealing. **3.** a knavish act.

knav·ish (nā′vĭsh), *adj.* **1.** like or befitting a knave; dishonest. **2.** waggish. —**knav′ish·ly,** *adv.* —**knav′ish·ness,** *n.*

knead (nēd), *v.t.* **1.** to work (dough, etc.) into a uniform mixture by pressing, folding, and stretching. **2.** to massage. —**knead′er,** *n.*

knee (nē), *n.*, *v.*, **kneed, kneeing.** —*n.* **1.** the joint in man between the thigh and the lower part of the leg. **2.** the corresponding joint in other vertebrates. **3.** the part of a garment covering the knee. **4.** something resembling a knee joint. —*v.t.* **5.** to strike or touch with the knee.

knee action, *Auto.* a method of suspending the front wheels to the chassis by individual spindle and coil-spring mountings for each wheel.

knee·cap (nē′kăp′), *n.* the flat, movable bone at the front of the knee; patella. Also, **knee′pan′.**

kneel (nēl), *v.i.*, **knelt or kneeled, kneeling.** to fall or rest on the knees or a knee, as in supplication. —**kneel′er,** *n.*

knee·pad (nē′păd′), *n.* a pad to protect the knee.

knell (nĕl), *n.* **1.** the sound made by a bell rung slowly for a death or funeral. **2.** any mournful sound. —*v.i.* **3.** to sound, as a bell, esp. as a funeral bell. **4.** to give forth a mournful, ominous, or warning sound. —*v.t.* **5.** to proclaim or summon by, or as by, a bell.

Knick·er·bock·er (nĭk′ər bŏk′ər), *n.* a descendant of the Dutch settlers of New York.

knick·ers (nĭk′ərz), *n.pl.* loosely fitting short breeches gathered in at the knee. Also, **knick·er·bock·ers** (nĭk′ər bŏk′ərz).

knick·knack (nĭk′năk′), *n.* **1.** a trinket; gimcrack. **2.** a bit of bric-a-brac.

knife (nīf), *n.*, *pl.* **knives,** *v.*, **knifed, knifing.** —*n.* **1.** a cutting instrument consisting essentially of a thin blade attached to a handle. **2.** any blade for cutting, as in a tool. —*v.t.* **3.** to cut, stab, etc., with a knife. **4.** *U.S. Slang.* to endeavor to defeat in a secret or underhand way.

knight (nīt), *n.* **1.** *Medieval Hist.* a man of military rank, usually of noble birth, bound to chivalrous conduct. **2.** a man upon whom a non-hereditary honorary rank is conferred by a sovereign because of personal merit or for services rendered to the country. **3.** *Chess.* a piece shaped like a horse's head. —*v.t.* **4.** to dub or create (one) a knight.

knight-er·rant (nīt′ĕr′ənt), *n.*, *pl.* **knights-errant.** *Hist.* a knight who traveled in search of adventures, etc. —**knight′-er·rant·ry,** *n.*

knight·hood (nīt′hŏŏd), *n.* **1.** the rank or dignity of a knight. **2.** the profession of a knight. **3.** the body of knights.

knight·ly (nīt′lĭ), *adj.* **1.** of or characteristic of a knight. **2.** being or resembling a knight. **3.** composed of knights. —*adv.* **4.** in a manner befitting a knight. —**knight′li·ness,** *n.*

knit (nĭt), *v.t.*, *v.i.*, **knitted or knit, knitting.** **1.** to form (fabric) by interlacing loops of yarn with hand needles (**knitting needles**) or a power machine. **2.** to join closely and firmly together. **3.** to contract into folds. —**knit′ter,** *n.* —**knit′ting,** *n.*

knob (nŏb), *n.* **1.** a rounded projecting part forming the handle of a door, drawer, or the like. **2.** a rounded lump or protuberance. **3.** a rounded hill or mountain. —**knobbed,** *adj.* —**knob′by,** *adj.*

knock (nŏk), *v.i.* **1.** to strike a sounding blow with the fist, knuckles, or anything hard, as on a door in seeking admittance. **2.** to make a noise as of striking or pounding, as machinery. **3.** *U.S. Slang.* to make harsh criticisms. **4.** to strike in collision. **5.** *Colloq.* to wander in an aimless way. —*v.t.* **6.** to hit; strike; beat. **7.** to drive, force, or render by a blow or blows. **8.** to strike (a thing) against something else. **9.** *U.S. Slang.* to criticize harshly. **10.** **knock off,** *Colloq.* **a.** to dispose of. **b.** to stop doing something, esp. work. **c.** to disable, overcome, or defeat completely. **11.** **knock out,** to defeat (an opponent) in a pugilistic contest by striking him down with a blow after which he does not rise within a prescribed time. —*n.* **12.** act or the sound of knocking. **13.** a blow or rap. **14.** *U.S. Slang.* an ill-natured criticism.

knock·a·bout (nŏk′ə bout′), *n.* **1.** *Naut.* a small yacht with a jib and mainsail. —*adj.* **2.** suitable for rough use, as a garment. **3.** rough; boisterous.

knock·down (nŏk′doun′), *adj.* **1.** overwhelming; irresistible. **2.** constructed in separate parts, so as to be readily taken apart. —*n.* **3.** a reduction in price.

knock·er (nŏk′ər), *n.* **1.** one who or that which knocks. **2.** a hinged knob, bar, etc., on a door, for use in knocking.

knock-knee (nŏk′nē′), *n.* **1.** inward curvature of the legs, causing the knees to knock together in walking. **2.** (*pl.*) such knees. —**knock′-kneed′,** *adj.*

knock·out (nŏk′out′), *n.* **1.** act of knocking out. **2.** state or fact of being knocked out. **3.** a knockout blow. **4.** *U.S. Slang.* a person or thing of overwhelming success or attractiveness. —*adj.* **5.** that knocks out.

knoll (nōl), *n.* a small, rounded hill.

knot (nŏt), *n.*, *v.*, **knotted, knotting.** —*n.* **1.** an interlacement of a cord, rope, or the like, drawn tight into a lump or knob, as for fastening to something. **2.** a cluster of persons or things. **3.** a protuberance, excrescence, or joint. **4.** the hard, cross-grained mass of wood at the place where a branch joins the trunk of a tree. **5.** *Naut.* **a.** a unit of speed of one nautical mile an hour. **b.** nautical mile. **6.** something involved or intricate. **7.** a bond or tie. —*v.t.* **8.** to tie in or by a knot. —*v.i.* **9.** to become tied or tangled in a knot or knots. —**knot′ted,** *adj.*

knot·hole (nŏt′hōl′), *n.* a hole in a board formed by the falling out of a knot.

knot·ty (nŏt′ĭ), *adj.*, **-tier, -tiest.** **1.** full of knots. **2.** involved, intricate, or difficult. —**knot′ti·ness,** *n.*

knout (nout), *n.* a kind of whip for flogging criminals.

know (nō), *v.*, **knew, known, knowing,** *n.* —*v.t.* **1.** to perceive or understand as fact or truth. **2.** to have fixed in the memory. **3.** to be acquainted with (a thing, place, person, etc.). **4.** to understand from experience or attainment (fol. by *how* before an infinitive). **5.** to be able to distinguish, as one from another. —*v.i.* **6.** to have clear and certain perception, as of fact or truth. **7.** to be cognizant or aware, as of some fact, circumstance, or occurrences. —*n.* **8.** the fact of knowing; knowledge: now chiefly in the colloquial phrase **in the know** (in the circle of those who have inside knowledge). —**know′a·ble,** *adj.* —**know′er,** *n.*

know-how (nō′hou′), *n.* knowledge of how to do something.

know·ing (nō′ĭng), *adj.* **1.** shrewd, sharp, or astute. **2.** having knowledge; intelligent. **3.** conscious; deliberate. —**know′ing·ly,** *adv.*

knowl·edge (nŏl′ĭj), *n.* **1.** acquaintance with facts, truths, or principles, as from study. **2.** familiarity, as with a branch of learning, etc. **3.** perception of fact or truth. **4.** that which is known, or may be known. **5.** cognizance of facts, or range of cognizance.

knowl·edge·a·ble (nŏl′ĭj ə bəl), *adj.* *Colloq.* possessing knowledge; intelligent.

know-noth·ing (nō′nŭth′ĭng), *n.* **1.** an ignoramus. **2.** an agnostic. **3.** (*cap.*) *U.S.* a member of a political party prominent from 1853 to 1856, whose aim was to keep the control of the government in the hands of native citizens.

Knox (nŏks), *n.* **John**, 1505?–1572, leader of the Protestant Reformation in Scotland.

Knox·ville (nŏks′vĭl), *n.* a city in E Tennessee, on the Tennessee river. 111,580.

knuck·le (nŭk′əl), *n., v.,* **-led, -ling.** —*n.* **1.** a joint of a finger. —*v.i.* **2.** to hold the knuckles close to the ground in playing marbles. **3.** to apply oneself vigorously or earnestly, as to a task (fol. by *down*). **4.** to yield (often fol. by *down* or *under*).

knurl (nûrl), *n.* **1.** a small ridge or the like, esp. one of a series, as on the edge of a thumbscrew to assist in obtaining a firm grip. —*v.t.* **2.** to make knurls or ridges on. —**knurl′y,** *adj.*

K.O., knockout. Also, **k.o.**

ko·a·la (kō ä′lə), *n.* a sluggish, tailless, gray, furry, arboreal marsupial of Australia.

Ko·be (kō′bĕ′), *n.* a seaport in S Japan. 443,344.

Koch (kōкн), *n.* **Robert,** 1843–1910, German bacteriologist and physician.

ko·dak (kō′dăk), *n., v.,* **-daked, -daking.** —*n.* **1.** a kind of portable photographic camera. **2.** (*cap.*) a trademark for this camera. —*v.t., v.i.* **3.** to photograph with a kodak. —**ko′dak·er,** *n.*

Koh·i·noor (kō′ə nŏŏr′), *n.* one of the world's large diamonds, 109 carats, first discovered in India and now part of the British crown jewels.

kohl·ra·bi (kōl′rä′bĭ), *n., pl.* **-bies.** a cultivated plant of the cabbage family whose stem above ground is an edible bulblike formation.

Ko·ko·mo (kō′kə mō′), *n.* a city in central Indiana. 33,795.

ko·la (kō′lə), *n.* **1.** the kola nut. **2.** an extract prepared from it. **3.** the tree producing it.

kola nut, a brownish seed produced by certain trees of western tropical Africa, the West Indies, and Brazil: it contains caffein, and is used in soft drinks.

ko·lin·sky (kə lĭn′skĭ), *n.* **1.** the Siberian mink, having fur uniformly buff or tawny, somewhat paler below, varied with black and white on the head. **2.** the fur of such an animal.

Kö·nigs·berg (kœ′nĭgz bûrg′), *n.* a seaport in the W Soviet Union; formerly the capital of East Prussia. 372,164.

Koo·te·nay (kōō′tə nā′), *n.* a river flowing from SE British Columbia, through NW Montana and N Idaho, swinging back into Canada where it enters **Kootenay Lake** (75 mi. long) and empties into the Columbia river. ab. 400 mi. Called **Koo′te·nai′** in the U.S.

ko·peck (kō′pĕk), *n.* a Russian monetary unit and copper coin, ¹⁄₁₀₀ of a ruble. Also, **ko′pek.**

Ko·ran (kō rän′, -răn′), *n.* the sacred scripture of Islam, believed by orthodox Mohammedans to contain revelations made in Arabic by Allah directly to Mohammed.

Ko·re·a (kō rē′ə), *n.* a country in E Asia, on a peninsula SE of Manchuria and between the Sea of Japan and the Yellow Sea: under Japanese rule, 1910–1945; currently divided at 38° N into **South Korea** (21,000,000 pop.; 36,600 sq. mi.; *Cap.:* Seoul) and **North Korea** (9,000,000 pop.; 50,-000 sq. mi.; *Cap.:* Pyongyang). —**Ko·re′an,** *adj., n.*

Korea

ko·ru·na (kō rōō′nä), *n., pl.* **koruny** (kō rōō′nĭ), **ko·run** (kō rōōn′). the monetary unit of Czechoslovakia, stabilized in 1929 to equal $0.03 in the U.S.

Kos·ci·us·ko (kŏs′ĭ ŭs′kō), *n.* **Thaddeus,** 1746–1817, Polish patriot and general who served as an officer in the American Revolutionary army.

ko·sher (kō′shər), *adj.* **1.** fit, lawful, or ritually permitted, according to the Jewish dietary law. **2.** *U.S. Slang.* genuine. —*n.* **3.** *Colloq.* kosher food.

Kous·se·vitz·ky (kōō′sə vĭt′skĭ), *n.* **Serge Alexandrovich,** 1874–1951, Russian-born orchestra conductor in U.S.

kow·tow (kou′tou′, kou′-), *v.i.* **1.** to act in an obsequious manner. **2.** to touch the forehead on the ground while kneeling, as an act of reverence, etc. —*n.* **3.** act of kowtowing.

K.P., Kitchen Police.

Kr, *Chem.* krypton.

kraal (kräl), *n.* **1.** a village of South African natives, usually surrounded by a stockade or the like. **2.** *South African.* an enclosure for cattle, etc. —*v.t.* **3.** to shut up in a kraal, as cattle.

Kra·ka·tau (krä′kä tou′), *n.* a small volcanic island in the Dutch East Indies between Java and Sumatra: violent eruption, 1883. Also, **Kra·ka·to·a** (krä′kä tō′ä).

Kras·no·dar (kräs′nŏ där′), *n.* a city in the S Soviet Union in Europe. 203,946.

K-ra·tion (kā′răsh′ən, -rā′shən), *n. U.S. Army.* one of the emergency field rations used when other rations are not available.

Kreis·ler (krīs′lər), *n.* **Fritz,** born 1875, Austrian violinist, in the U.S.

Krem·lin (krĕm′lĭn), *n.* the citadel of Moscow, including within its walls the chief office of the Soviet government.

krim·mer (krĭm′ər), *n.* a lambskin from the Crimean region, with wool in loose soft curls and usually pale gray.

Krish·na (krĭsh′nə), *n.* the most popular Hindu deity, as an incarnation of Vishnu.

Kriss Krin·gle (krĭs′ krĭng′gəl), Santa Claus.

kro·na (krō′nə), *n., pl.* **-nor** (-nôr). the monetary unit and a silver coin of Sweden and Iceland, equivalent to the krone of Denmark and Norway.

kro·ne (krō′nĕ), *n., pl.* **-ner** (-nĕr). the monetary unit and a silver coin of Denmark and of Norway, equal to about 20.8 U.S. cents.

kryp·ton (krĭp′tŏn), *n. Chem.* an inert monatomic gaseous element. *Symbol:* Kr; *at. wt.:* 83.7; *at. no.:* 36; *weight of one liter at 0°C. and 760 mm. pressure:* 3.708 g.

Kt., 1. Knight. **2.** (*l.c.*) karat.

Kua·la Lum·pur (kwä′lə lŏŏm′pŏŏr′), a city in the SW Malay Peninsula: the capital of the Malayan Union. 111,418.

Ku·blai Khan (kōō′blī kän′), 1216?–94, Mongol emperor, 1259–94: founder of the Mongol dynasty in China.

ku·dos (kū′dŏs), *n.* glory; renown.

Kui·by·shev (kwē′bə shĕf′), *n.* a city in the E Soviet Union in Europe. 390,267.

Ku Klux Klan (kū′ klŭks′ klăn′), **1.** a secret organization in the southern U.S., active for several years after the Civil War, which aimed to suppress the newly acquired powers of the Negroes and to oppose carpetbaggers from the North. **2.** a secret organization (**Knights of the Ku Klux Klan**) founded in 1915, admitting to membership none but native-born, white, Gentile, Protestant Americans, and professing Americanism as its object. Also, **Ku Klux.**

ku·lak (kōō lăk′), *n. Russia.* **1.** (before the revolution) a hard-fisted merchant or a village usurer. **2.** (more recently) any peasant who employed hired labor or possessed any machinery.

ku·miss (kōō′mĭs), *n.* fermented mare's or camel's milk, used as a beverage by Asiatic nomads, etc.

küm·mel (kĭm′əl), *n.* a colorless liqueur flavored with caraway seeds, etc.

kum·quat (kŭm′kwŏt), *n.* **1.** a small, round citrus fruit used chiefly for preserves, being the fruit of certain shrubs native in China. **2.** the plant itself.

Kun·ming (kŏŏn′mĭng′), *n.* a city in SW China: an important transshipment point on the Burma Road in World War II. ab. 150,000.

Kuo·min·tang (kwō′mĭn′tăng′), *n.* a Chinese political party, deriving historically from earlier parties organized or led by Sun Yat-sen, which controlled the larger part of China from 1928 to 1949.

Kurd (kûrd), *n.* a member of a pastoral and warlike people dwelling chiefly in Kurdistan. —**Kurd′ish,** *adj.*

Kur·di·stan (kûr′də stän′), *n.* a mountain and plateau region in SE Turkey, NW Iran, and N Iraq. ab. 74,000 sq. mi.

Ku·rile Islands (kŏŏr′ĭl, kōō rēl′), a chain of small islands off the NE coast of Asia, extending from N Japan to the S tip of Kamchatka: ceded to the Soviet Union by Japan, 1945.

Ku·wait (kŏŏ wīt′), *n.* a sheikdom in NE Arabia: a British protectorate. 100,000 pop.; ab. 1950 sq. mi.

kw., kilowatt.

K.W.H., kilowatt-hour. Also, **kw-hr.**

Ky., Kentucky.

Kyo·to (kyô′tô′), *n.* a city in central Japan: capital of Japan, A.D. 784–1868. 914,655.

L

L¹, l (ĕl), *n.*, *pl.* **L's** or **Ls**, **l's** or **ls**. **1.** a consonant, the 12th letter of the English alphabet. **2.** the Roman numeral for 50.

L², *pl.* **L's. 1.** something having a shape like that of the letter L. **2.** Latin. **3.** *Physics.* length. **4.** (L *libra*) pound.

L., 1. Lake. **2.** Latin. **3.** latitude. **4.** left. **5.** (L *liber*) book. **6.** Liberal.

l., 1. latitude. **2.** law. **3.** leaf. **4.** left. **5.** length. **6.** (*pl.* ll.) line. **7.** liter.

la (lä), *n.* *Music.* the syllable used for the sixth tone of a scale.

La, *Chem.* lanthanum.

La., Louisiana.

lab (lăb), *n.* *U.S. Colloq.* laboratory.

Lab., Labrador.

la·bel (lā'bəl), *n.*, *v.*, **-beled, -beling** or (*esp. Brit.*) **-belled, -belling.** —*n.* **1.** a slip of paper or other material, marked or inscribed, for affixing to something to indicate its nature, ownership, destination, etc. **2.** a short word or phrase of description for a person, group, etc. —*v.t.* **3.** to affix a label to.

la·bi·al (lā'bĭ əl), *adj.* **1.** of or pertaining to the lips or to a liplike part. **2.** *Phonet.* involving lip articulation, as *p, v, m, w,* or a rounded vowel. —**la'bi·al·ly,** *adv.*

la·bi·ate (lā'bĭ āt', -ĭt), *adj.* lipped; having parts shaped or arranged like lips.

la·bi·um (lā'bĭ əm), *n.*, *pl.* **-bia** (-bĭ ə). *Anat., Zool., Bot.* a lip or liplike part.

la·bor (lā'bər), *n.* **1.** bodily toil for the sake of gain or economic production. **2.** those engaged in such toil considered as a class. **3.** hard work. **4.** a task. **5.** the pangs and efforts of childbirth. —*v.i.* **6.** to work; toil. **7.** to strive, as toward a goal. **8.** to be burdened, troubled, or distressed. **9.** to be in childbirth. —*v.t.* **11.** to elaborate. Also, *Brit.*, **labour.** —**la'bor·ing·ly,** *adv.*

lab·o·ra·to·ry (lăb'rə tôr'ĭ, lăb'ə rə-; *Brit.* lə-bôr'ə tə rĭ), *n.*, *pl.* **-ries.** a building or part of a building fitted with apparatus for conducting scientific investigations, etc.

Labor Day, (in most States of the U.S.) a legal holiday, commonly the first Monday in September, in honor of the laboring class.

la·bored (lā'bərd), *adj.* **1.** laboriously formed. **2.** not easy or natural.

la·bor·er (lā'bər ər), *n.* one engaged in work which requires bodily strength rather than skill or training.

la·bo·ri·ous (lə bôr'ĭ əs), *adj.* **1.** requiring much labor, exertion, or perseverance. **2.** diligent in labor. —**la·bo'ri·ous·ly,** *adv.*

labor union, an organization of wage earners or salaried employees for mutual aid and protection, and for dealing collectively with employers.

la·bour (lā'bər), *n.*, *v.i.*, *v.t.* *Brit.* labor.

Labour Party, the British political party representing socialist groups, trade unions, and labor in general.

Lab·ra·dor (lăb'rə dôr'), *n.* **1.** a peninsula in NE North America between Hudson Bay, the Atlantic, and the Gulf of St. Lawrence, containing the Canadian provinces of Quebec and Newfoundland. ab. 500,000 sq. mi. **2.** a territory of Newfoundland in the E part of this peninsula. 4716 pop.; ab. 120,000 sq. mi.

la·bur·num (lə bûr'nəm), *n.* any of several small leguminous trees, having pendulous racemes of yellow flowers.

lab·y·rinth (lăb'ə rĭnth), *n.* **1.** an intricate combination of passages in which it is difficult to find one's way or to reach the exit. **2.** a complicated arrangement. **3.** (*cap.*) *Gk. Myth.* the Cretan labyrinth, constructed by Daedalus, the abode of the fabled Minotaur. **4.** *Anat.* the in-

ternal ear, a complex structure including a bony and a membranous portion.

lab·y·rin·thine (lăb'ə rĭn'thĭn, -thēn), *adj.* **1.** of or forming a labyrinth. **2.** mazy; intricate. Also, **lab·y·rin·thi·an** (lăb'ə rĭn'thĭ ən).

lac¹ (lăk), *n.* a resinous substance deposited on the twigs of various trees in southern Asia by a certain insect, and used in the manufacture of varnishes, etc.

lac² (lăk), *n.* *India.* the sum of 100,000, esp. of rupees.

lace (lās), *n.*, *v.*, **laced, lacing.** —*n.* **1.** ornamental network made of threads by hand or machine. **2.** a cord or string for holding or drawing together. —*v.t.* **3.** to fasten, draw together, or compress by means of a lace. **4.** *Colloq.* to lash, beat, or thrash. **5.** to intermix, as coffee with spirits. —**lace'like',** *adj.*

lac·er·ate (*v.* lăs'ə rāt'; *adj.* lăs'ə rāt', -ər ĭt), *v.*, **-ated, -ating,** *adj.* —*v.t.* **1.** to tear roughly; mangle. **2.** to hurt. —*adj.* **3.** lacerated.

lac·er·a·tion (lăs'ə rā'shən), *n.* **1.** act of lacerating. **2.** a rough, jagged tear.

lach·ry·mal (lăk'rə məl), *adj.* **1.** of, pertaining to, or producing tears. **2.** *Anat., etc.* denoting, pertaining to, or situated near the glands, ducts, or the like, concerned in the secretion or conveyance of tears. —*n.* **3.** (*pl.*) *Anat.* tear-secreting glands.

lach·ry·mose (lăk'rə mōs'), *adj.* **1.** given to shedding tears; tearful. **2.** mournful.

lac·ing (lā'sĭng), *n.* **1.** act of one that laces. **2.** a laced fastening. **3.** a trimming of lace. **4.** a thrashing.

lack (lăk), *n.* **1.** deficiency or absence of something requisite, desirable, or customary. **2.** something lacking or wanting. —*v.t.* **3.** to be entirely or partly without. **4.** to fall short in respect of. —*v.i.* **5.** to be absent, as something requisite or desirable.

lack·a·dai·si·cal (lăk'ə dā'zə kəl), *adj.* languid; weakly sentimental; listless. —**lack'a·dai'si·cal·ly,** *adv.*

lack·ey (lăk'ĭ), *n.*, *pl.* **-eys,** *v.*, **-eyed, -eying.** —*n.* **1.** a manservant. **2.** a servile follower. —*v.t.* **3.** to attend as a lackey does.

lack·lus·ter (lăk'lŭs'tər), *adj.* **1.** lacking brightness; dull. —*n.* **2.** a lack of luster.

la·con·ic (lə kŏn'ĭk), *adj.* using few words; concise. Also, **la·con'i·cal.** —**la·con'i·cal·ly,** *adv.*

lac·quer (lăk'ər), *n.* **1.** a protective coating consisting of a resin and/or a cellulose ester dissolved in a volatile solvent. **2.** any of various resinous varnishes. **3.** ware coated with a lacquer varnish. —*v.t.* **4.** to coat with lacquer.

la·crosse (lə krôs', -krŏs'), *n.* a game of ball played by two teams of 12 players each, who strive to send a ball through a goal by means of long-handled rackets.

La Crosse (lə krôs', -krŏs'), a city in W Wisconsin, on the Mississippi. 42,707.

lac·tate (lăk'tāt), *n.*, *v.*, **-tated, -tating.** —*n.* **1.** *Chem.* an ester or salt of lactic acid. —*v.i.* **2.** to produce milk.

lac·ta·tion (lăk tā'shən), *n.* **1.** the secretion or formation of milk. **2.** the period of milk production.

lac·te·al (lăk'tĭ əl), *adj.* **1.** pertaining to, consisting of, or resembling milk; milky. **2.** *Anat.* conveying or containing chyle. —*n.* **3.** *Anat.* any of the minute lymphatic vessels which convey chyle from the small intestine to the thoracic duct.

lac·tic (lăk'tĭk), *adj.* pertaining to or obtained from milk.

lactic acid, *Chem.* an acid found in sour milk.

lac·to·fla·vin (lăk'tō flā'vĭn), *n.* riboflavin.

lac·tose (lăk'tōs), *n.* *Chem.* a sugar present in milk, used as a food and in medicine.

la·cu·na (lə kū'nə), *n.*, *pl.* **-nae** (-nē) **-nas. 1.** a pit or cavity. **2.** *Anat.* one of the numerous minute cavities in the substance of bone. **3.** a gap or hiatus.

ac·y (lā′sĭ), *adj.*, **lacier, laciest.** resembling lace. —**lac′i·ly,** *adv.* —**lac′i·ness,** *n.*

ad (lăd), *n.* **1.** a boy or youth. **2.** *Colloq.* (in familiar use) any male.

ad·der (lăd′ər), *n.* **1.** a structure of wood, metal, or rope, commonly consisting of two side-pieces between which a series of bars are set at suitable distances, forming a means of ascent or descent. **2.** something resembling a ladder. **3.** a means of rising, as to eminence.

ad·die (lăd′ĭ), *n.* *Chiefly Scot.* a young lad.

ade (lād), *v.*, **laded, laden** or **laded, lading.** —*v.t.* **1.** to put (something) on or in, as a burden, load, or cargo. **2.** to load oppressively. **3.** to fill abundantly. **4.** to lift in or out with a ladle. —*v.i.* **5.** to take on a load. **6.** to lade a liquid.

ad·ing (lā′dĭng), *n.* **1.** act of lading. **2.** load; freight; cargo.

a·dle (lā′dəl), *n.*, *v.*, **-dled, -dling.** —*n.* **1.** a long-handled utensil with a cup-shaped bowl for dipping or conveying liquids. —*v.t.* **2.** to dip or convey with a ladle. —**la′dle·ful′,** *n.* —**la′-dler,** *n.*

.a·do·ga (lä′dŏ gä), *n.* a lake in the NW Soviet Union: largest lake in Europe. ab. 7000 sq. mi.

a·dy (lā′dĭ), *n.*, *pl.* **-dies. 1.** a woman of good breeding, refinement, etc. **2.** a polite term for any woman. **3.** (*cap.*) in Great Britain, the title of any woman whose husband is higher in rank than baronet or knight, or who is the daughter of a nobleman not lower than an earl, etc. **4.** (*cap.*) the Virgin Mary (usually, **Our Lady**). **5.** the mistress of a household. **6.** a woman who is the object of chivalrous devotion.

a·dy·bug (lā′dĭ bŭg′), *n.* a small kind of beetle, usually brown with black spots. The larvae feed upon plant lice and small insects. Also, **lady beetle, la′dy·bird′.**

a·dy·fin·ger (lā′dĭ fĭng′gər), *n.* a small, finger-shaped sponge cake.

ady in waiting, a lady who is in attendance upon a queen or princess.

Ladybug

a·dy·kill·er (lā′dĭ kĭl′ər), *n.* *Slang.* a man supposed to be irresistible to ladies.

a·dy·like (lā′dĭ līk′), *adj.* **1.** like a lady. **2.** befitting a lady. —**la′dy·like′ness,** *n.*

a·dy·love (lā′dĭ lŭv′), *n.* a sweetheart.

a·dy·ship (lā′dĭ shĭp′), *n.* **1.** (*often cap.*) the form used in speaking of or to a woman having the title of *Lady* (prec. by *her, your,* etc.). **2.** the rank of a lady.

a·dy′s-slip·per (lā′dĭz slĭp′ər), *n.* any of certain orchids whose flowers somewhat resemble a slipper. Also, **la′dy-slip′per.**

.a·fa·yette (lăf′ĭ ĕt′, lä′fĭ-), *n.* **Marie Joseph Paul Yves Roch Gilbert du Motier, Marquis de,** 1757–1834, French soldier and statesman who served in the American Revolutionary Army and took a leading part in the French Revolutions of 1789 and 1830.

.a Fol·lette (lə fŏl′ĭt), **Robert Marion,** 1855–1925, U.S. political leader.

.a Fon·taine (lä fôn tĕn′), **Jean de,** 1621–1695, French poet and writer of fables.

ag (lăg), *v.*, **lagged, lagging,** *n.* —*v.i.* **1.** to move slowly; fall behind. —*n.* **2.** a lagging or falling behind. **3.** *Mech.* the amount of retardation of some movement.

a·ger (lä′gər, lô′-), *n.* a beer stored from 6 weeks to 6 months before use. Also, **lager beer.**

ag·gard (lăg′ərd), *adj.* **1.** lagging; backward; slow. —*n.* **2.** Also, **lag′ger.** one who lags. —**lag′gard·ly,** *adv.* —**lag′gard·ness,** *n.*

a·gniappe (lăn yăp′, lăn′yăp), *n.* something given with a purchase to a customer, by way of compliment or for good measure. Also, **la·gnappe′.**

a·goon (lə gōōn′), *n.* **1.** an area of shallow water separated from the sea by low banks. **2.** any small, pondlike body of water.

.a·gos (lä′gōs, lä′gŏs), *n.* the capital of Nigeria, in the SW part. 155,900 pop.; 24 sq. mi.

.a·hore (lə hôr′), *n.* a city in Pakistan, in W Punjab. 671,659.

a·ic (lā′ĭk), *adj.* secular. Also, **la′i·cal.**

air (lâr), *n.* the den of a wild beast.

aird (lârd), *n.* *Scot.* a landed proprietor. —**laird′ship,** *n.*

ais·sez faire (lĕs′ā fâr′), the theory or sys-

tem of government that upholds the autonomous character of the economic order, believing that government should intervene as little as possible in the direction of economic affairs.

la·i·ty (lā′ə tĭ), *n.* laymen, as distinguished from clergymen.

lake¹ (lāk), *n.* a body of water (fresh or salt) of considerable size, surrounded by land.

lake² (lāk), *n.* a red pigment prepared from lac or cochineal.

lake trout, a large, fork-tailed trout, common in the Great Lakes and northward.

Lake·wood (lāk′wŏŏd′), *n.* a city in NE Ohio, on Lake Erie. 69,190.

Lam., Lamentations.

lam¹ (lăm), *v.t.*, **lammed, lamming.** *Slang.* to beat; thrash.

lam² (lăm), *n.*, *v.*, **lammed, lamming.** *Slang.* —*n.* **1.** hasty escape. **2. on the lam,** escaping or fleeing. —*v.i.* **3.** to run off or away.

la·ma (lä′mə), *n.* a priest or monk of Lamaism.

La·ma·ism (lä′mə ĭz′əm), *n.* the form of Buddhism in Tibet and Mongolia. —**La′ma·ist,** *n.*

La·marck (lə märk′), *n.* **Jean Baptiste Pierre Antoine de Monet de,** 1744–1829, French biologist.

la·ma·ser·y (lä′mə sĕr′ĭ), *n.*, *pl.* **-series.** (in Tibet, Mongolia, etc.) a monastery of lamas.

lamb (lăm), *n.* **1.** a young sheep. **2.** one who is young, gentle, meek, innocent, etc. **3. the Lamb,** Christ. —*v.i.* **4.** to give birth to a lamb.

Lamb (lăm), *n.* **Charles,** ("*Elia*") 1775–1834, British essayist and critic.

lam·baste (lăm bāst′), *v.t.*, **-basted, -basting.** *Slang.* to beat severely.

lamb·da (lăm′də), *n.* the eleventh letter of the Greek alphabet (Λ, λ).

lam·bent (lăm′bənt), *adj.* **1.** running or moving lightly over a surface. **2.** playing lightly and brilliantly over a subject. **3.** softly bright. —**lam′ben·cy,** *n.* —**lam′bent·ly,** *adv.*

lamb·kin (lăm′kĭn), *n.* a little lamb.

lamb·skin (lăm′skĭn′), *n.* the skin of a lamb, esp. when dressed with the wool on.

lame (lām), *adj.*, **lamer, lamest,** *v.*, **lamed, laming.** —*adj.* **1.** crippled or disabled, esp. in the foot or leg. **2.** poor or insufficient. —*v.t.* **3.** to make lame or defective. —**lame′ly,** *adv.* —**lame′ness,** *n.*

la·mé (lă mā′), *n.* an ornamental fabric in which metallic threads are woven.

lame duck, *Colloq.* **1.** *U.S.* a Congressman who has failed of reëlection and is serving at the last session of his term. **2.** a person or thing that is disabled, helpless, ineffective, or inefficient.

la·mel·la (lə mĕl′ə), *n.*, *pl.* **-mellae** (-mĕl′ē), **-mellas.** a thin plate, scale, membrane, or layer, as of bone, tissue, etc.

la·mel·li·branch (lə mĕl′ə brăngk′), *n.* *Zool.* any of a class of mollusks comprising the oysters, clams, scallops, etc.

la·ment (lə mĕnt′), *v.t.*, *v.i.* **1.** to feel or express sorrow or regret (for). —*n.* **2.** an expression of grief or sorrow. **3.** an elegy or dirge. —**la·ment′-er,** *n.*

lam·en·ta·ble (lăm′ən tə bəl), *adj.* that is to be lamented. —**lam′en·ta·bly,** *adv.*

lam·en·ta·tion (lăm′ən tā′shən), *n.* **1.** act of lamenting. **2.** a lament. **3. Lamentations,** book of the Old Testament, ascribed by tradition to Jeremiah.

lam·i·na (lăm′ə nə), *n.*, *pl.* **-nae** (-nē′), **-nas.** a thin plate, scale, or layer. —**lam′i·nar,** *adj.*

lam·i·nate (*v.* lăm′ə nāt′; *adj.* lăm′ə nāt′, -nĭt), *v.*, **-nated, -nating,** *adj.* —*v.t.* **1.** to separate into thin layers. **2.** to cover or overlay with laminae. —*v.i.* **3.** to split into thin layers. —*adj.* **4.** Also, **lam′i·nat′ed.** composed of, or having, a lamina or laminae. —**lam′i·na′tion,** *n.*

lamp (lămp), *n.* **1.** any of various devices for using an illuminant, as gas or electricity. **2.** a vessel for containing an inflammable liquid, as oil, which is burned at a wick as a means of illumination.

lamp·black (lămp′blăk′), *n.* a fine black pigment, almost pure carbon, collected as soot from the smoke of burning oil, gas, etc.

lam·poon (lăm pōōn′), *n.* **1.** a malicious or virulent satire upon a person, in either prose or verse. —*v.t.* **2.** to assail in a lampoon. —**lam·poon′er, lam·poon′ist,** *n.*

lam·prey (lăm′prĭ), *n., pl.* **-preys.** any of certain eellike fishes. Some species attach themselves to fishes and rasp a hole in the flesh with their horny teeth so that they can suck the blood of the victim.

Lan·cas·ter (lăng′kə stər), *n.* an English royal house which ruled from 1399 to 1461. —**Lan·cas·tri·an** (lăng kăs′trĭ ən), *adj., n.*

lance (lăns, läns), *n., v.,* **lanced, lancing.** —*n.* 1. a long, shafted weapon with a metal head, used by mounted soldiers in charging. 2. a soldier armed with this weapon. —*v.t.* 3. to open with a lancet.

Lan·ce·lot (lăn′sə lət, -lŏt′, län′-), *n.* **Sir,** *Arthurian Romance.* the greatest of Arthur's knights, and the lover of Queen Guinevere.

lan·ce·o·late (lăn′sĭ ə lāt′, -lĭt), *adj.* shaped like the head of a lance.

lanc·er (lăn′sər, län′-), *n.* a mounted soldier armed with a lance.

lan·cet (lăn′sĭt, län′-), *n.* a small surgical instrument, usually sharp-pointed and two-edged, for opening abscesses, etc.

lance·wood (lăns′wŏŏd′, läns′-), *n.* 1. the tough, elastic wood of certain trees of tropical America, used for carriage shafts, cabinet work, etc. 2. a tree which yields it.

land (lănd), *n.* 1. the solid substance of the earth's surface. 2. the exposed part of the earth's surface, as distinguished from water. 3. ground, esp. with reference to quality or use. 4. *Law.* any part of the earth's surface which can be owned as property, and everything annexed to it, whether by nature or by the hand of man. 5. a region or country. 6. the people of a country; a nation. 7. a realm or domain. —*v.t.* 8. to bring to or put on land. 9. to bring into any place, position, or condition. 10. *Colloq.* to catch or capture. —*v.i.* 11. to come to land or shore. 12. to go or come on land from a ship, airplane, train, etc. 13. to come to rest in any place, position, or condition.

lan·dau (lăn′dô, -dou), *n.* 1. a four-wheeled, two-seated vehicle with a top made in two parts, which may be let down or folded back. 2. a sedan-type automobile with a short convertible back.

land·ed (lăn′dĭd), *adj.* 1. owning land. 2. consisting of land.

land·fall (lănd′fôl′), *n.* 1. an approach to or sighting of land. 2. the land sighted or reached.

land·hold·er (lănd′hōl′dər), *n.* an owner or occupant of land. —**land′hold′ing,** *adj.*

land·ing (lăn′dĭng), *n.* 1. act of one who or that which lands. 2. a place where persons or goods are landed. 3. a platform between flights of stairs.

landing gear, the wheels, floats, etc., of an aircraft, upon which it moves on ground or water.

land·la·dy (lănd′lā′dĭ), *n., pl.* **-dies.** 1. a woman who owns or runs an inn, lodging house, or boarding house. 2. a woman who owns and leases land, buildings, etc.

land·less (lănd′lĭs), *adj.* owning no land.

land·locked (lănd′lŏkt′), *adj.* 1. shut in more or less completely by land. 2. living in waters shut off from the sea, as some fish.

land·lord (lănd′lôrd′), *n.* 1. one who owns and leases land, buildings, etc., to another. 2. the master of an inn, lodging house, etc. 3. a landowner.

land·lub·ber (lănd′lŭb′ər), *n.* *Naut.* a landsman or raw seaman.

land·mark (lănd′märk′), *n.* 1. a conspicuous object on land that serves as a guide, as to vessels at sea. 2. a prominent feature, part, event, etc.

land mine, a large ground-concealed explosive bomb.

Land of Promise, Canaan.

land·own·er (lănd′ō′nər), *n.* an owner or proprietor of land. —**land′own′ing,** *n., adj.*

land·scape (lănd′skāp′), *n., v.,* **-scaped, -scaping.** —*n.* 1. an extensive view of rural scenery. 2. a picture representing natural inland or coastal scenery. —*v.t.* 3. to improve the landscape. —*v.i.* 4. to do landscape gardening as a profession.

Land·seer (lănd′sĭr, -syər), *n.* **Sir Edwin Henry,** 1802–73, British painter.

land·slide (lănd′slīd′), *n.* 1. the sliding down of a mass of soil, detritus, or rock on a steep slope. 2. the mass itself. 3. an overwhelming victory, as in an election. Also, *esp. Brit.,* **land·slip** (lănd′slĭp′) for 1, 2.

lands·man (lăndz′mən), *n., pl.* **-men.** 1. one who lives on land (opposed to *seaman*). 2. *Naut.* a. a sailor on his first voyage. b. an inexperienced seaman, rated below an ordinary seaman.

land·ward (lănd′wərd), *adv.* 1. Also, **land′wards.** toward the land or interior. —*adj.* 2. lying, facing, or tending toward the land or away from the coast. 3. being in the direction of the land.

lane (lān), *n.* 1. a narrow passage, esp. one between hedges, fences, walls, or houses. 2. a fixed route pursued by ocean steamers or airplanes. 3. a part of a highway for traffic moving in one line.

lang., language.

Lang·ley (lăng′lĭ), *n.* **Samuel Pierpont,** 1834–1906, U.S. astronomer, physicist, and pioneer in aeronautics.

Lang·muir (lăng′myŏŏr), *n.* **Irving,** born 1881, U.S. chemist.

lang·syne (lăng′sīn′, -zīn′; *Scot.* läng′sīn′) *Scot.* —*adv.* 1. long since; long ago. —*n.* 2. time long past.

lan·guage (lăng′gwĭj), *n.* 1. communication by voice in the distinctively human manner, using arbitrary, auditory symbols in conventional ways with conventional meanings. 2. communication of meaning in any way. 3. linguistics. 4. form or manner of expression.

lan·guid (lăng′gwĭd), *adj.* 1. drooping or flagging from weakness or fatigue. 2. indifferent. 3. slack; dull. —**lan′guid·ly,** *adv.* —**lan′guidness,** *n.*

lan·guish (lăng′gwĭsh), *v.i.* 1. to become or be weak or feeble. 2. to lose activity and vigor. 3. to pine or suffer. 4. to assume an expression of tender, sentimental melancholy. —*n.* 5. act of languishing. 6. a languishing expression. —**lan′guish·er,** *n.* —**lan′guish·ment,** *n.*

lan·guish·ing (lăng′gwĭsh ĭng), *adj.* 1. becoming languid. 2. lingering. 3. expressive of languor. —**lan′guish·ing·ly,** *adv.*

lan·guor (lăng′gər), *n.* 1. physical weakness or faintness. 2. indolence. 3. emotional tenderness. 4. lack of spirit or vigorous activity. 5. soothing or oppressive stillness. —**lan′guor·ous,** *adj.*

La·nier (lə nĭr′), *n.* **Sidney,** 1842–81, U.S. poet and musician.

lank (lăngk), *adj.* 1. lean; gaunt. 2. (of hair) straight and flat. —**lank′ly,** *adv.* —**lank′ness,** *n.*

lank·y (lăngk′ĭ), *adj.,* **lankier, lankiest.** ungracefully tall and thin. —**lank′i·ly,** *adv.* —**lank′i·ness,** *n.*

lan·o·lin (lăn′ə lĭn), *n.* a fatty substance, extracted from wool, used in ointments.

Lan·sing (lăn′sĭng), *n.* the capital of Michigan, in the S part. 78,753.

lan·tern (lăn′tərn), *n.* 1. a transparent or translucent case for enclosing a light and protecting it from the wind, rain, etc. 2. the chamber at the top of a lighthouse, surrounding the light.

lan·tha·num (lăn′thə nəm), *n.* *Chem.* a rareearth, trivalent, metallic element. *Symbol:* La; *at. wt.:* 138.92; *at. no.:* 57; *sp. gr.:* 6.15 at 20°C.

lan·yard (lăn′yərd), *n.* *Naut.* a short rope or cord for securing or holding something.

Lao-tse (lou′dzŭ′), *n.* born c604 B.C., Chinese philosopher: supposed founder of Taoism. Also **Lao′-tsze′, Lao′-tzu′.**

lap¹ (lăp), *n.* 1. the part of the clothing that lies on the front portion of the body from the waist to the knees when one sits. 2. this portion of the body. 3. the front part of a skirt.

lap² (lăp), *v.,* **lapped, lapping,** *n.* —*v.t., v.i.* 1. to fold over or wrap round something. 2. to nurse fondle, or cherish. 3. to lay (something) partly over something underneath. 4. to lie partly over (something underneath). —*n.* 5. act of lapping. 6. a single round or circuit of the course in racing. 7. act of overlapping. 8. state of overlapping. 9. an overlapping part.

lap³ (lăp), *v.,* **lapped, lapping,** *n.* —*v.t., v.i.* 1. (of water) to wash against (something) with a lapping sound. 2. to take up (liquid) with the tongue. —*n.* 3. act of lapping. 4. the sound of this.

La Paz (lä päs′), a city in W Bolivia: seat of the government (Sucre is the nominal capital). 301,000.

la·pel (lə pĕl′), *n.* a part of a garment folded back on the breast, below the collar.

lap·i·dar·y (lăp′ə dĕr′ĭ), *n., pl.* **-daries.**

workman who cuts, polishes, and engraves precious stones.

lap·in (lăp′ĭn), *n.* **1.** a rabbit. **2.** its fur.

lap·is laz·u·li (lăp′ĭs lăz′yoŏ lī′, -lĭ′), a deep-blue stone, used chiefly for ornamental purposes.

La·place (lä pläs′), *n.* Pierre Simon, **Marquis de**, 1749–1827, French astronomer and mathematician.

Lap·land (lăp′lănd′), *n.* a region inhabited by Lapps in N Norway, N Sweden, N Finland, and part of the NW Soviet Union.

La Pla·ta (lä plä′tä), **1.** a seaport in E Argentina. 256,378. **2.** See **Plata, Rio de la**.

Lapp (lăp), *n.* one of a Finnic people of northern Norway, Sweden, and Finland, and adjacent regions. Also, **Lap·land·er** (lăp′lăn′dər).

lapse (lăps), *n., v.,* **lapsed, lapsing.** —*n.* **1.** a slight error. **2.** a failure or miscarriage through some fault, slip, or negligence. **3.** a gliding or passing away, as of time. **4.** act of falling, slipping, sliding, etc., slowly. **5.** *Law.* the termination of a right or privilege through neglect to exercise it or through failure of some contingency. **6.** a moral fall, as from rectitude. —*v.i.* **7.** to pass slowly, silently, or by degrees. **8.** *Law.* **a.** to pass from one to another by lapse. **b.** to become void. **9.** to sink to a lower grade or condition. **10.** to fall, slip, or glide, esp. downward. **11.** to make an error. **12.** to pass away, as time. —**laps′a·ble**, *adj.*

lap·wing (lăp′wĭng′), *n.* a large Old World plover with strikingly upcurved slender crest, erratic courtship flight, and shrill cries.

lar·board (lär′bōrd′; *Naut.* -bård), *Naut.* —*n.* **1.** the side of a ship to the left of a person looking toward the bow; port. —*adj.* **2.** on or pertaining to the larboard.

lar·ce·ny (lär′sə nĭ), *n., pl.* **-nies.** *Law.* the wrongful taking and carrying away of the personal goods of another from his possession with intent to convert them to the taker's own use. —**lar′ce·nous**, *adj.*

larch (lärch), *n.* **1.** any of certain coniferous trees of the pine family, characterized by a tough, durable wood. **2.** the wood of such a tree.

lard (lärd), *n.* **1.** the rendered fat of hogs. —*v.t.* **2.** to apply lard or grease to. **3.** to prepare or enrich (lean meat, etc.) with pork or bacon.

lard·er (lär′dər), *n.* a room or place where food is kept; pantry.

La·re·do (lə rä′dō), *n.* a city in S Texas, on the Rio Grande. 39,274.

lar·es (lär′ēz, lā′rēz), *n. pl., sing.* **lar** (lär). *Rom. Myth.* household or other tutelary gods.

lares and pe·na·tes (pə nā′tēz), **1.** household gods. **2.** the cherished possessions of a family or household.

large (lärj), *adj.,* **larger, largest**, *n.* —*adj.* **1.** being of more than common size, amount, or number. **2.** extensive or broad. **3.** on a great scale. **4.** grand or pompous. —*n.* **5. at large, a.** at liberty. **b.** at length. **c.** in general. **d.** representing the whole of a state, district, or body, not one division or part of it. —**large′ness**, *n.*

large·ly (lärj′lĭ), *adv.* **1.** to a great extent. **2.** in great quantity; much.

large-scale (lärj′skāl′), *adj.* **1.** very extensive; of great scope. **2.** made to a large scale.

lar·gess (lär′jĭs), *n.* **1.** generous bestowal of gifts. **2.** the gifts or a gift so bestowed. Also, **lar′gesse**.

lar·ghet·to (lär gĕt′ō), *adj., n., pl.* **-ghettos.** *Music.* —*adj.* **1.** somewhat slow. —*n.* **2.** a larghetto movement.

lar·go (lär′gō), *adj., n., pl.* **-gos.** *Music.* —*adj.* **1.** slow. —*n.* **2.** a largo movement.

lar·i·at (lär′ĭ ət), *n.* *U.S.* a long, noosed rope for catching horses, cattle, etc.

lark[1] (lärk), *n.* **1.** any of certain oscine singing birds, mostly of the Old World, characterized by an unusually long, straight hind claw. **2.** any of various similar birds of other families, as the meadow lark of America.

lark[2] (lärk), *Colloq.* —*n.* **1.** a merry adventure; prank. —*v.i.* **2.** to have fun.

lark·spur (lärk′spûr′), *n.* any of certain herbs of the buttercup family whose showy flowers grow, in many species, on tall stalks.

lar·rup (lăr′əp), *v.t.,* **-ruped, -ruping.** *Colloq.* to beat; thrash. —**lar′rup·er**, *n.*

lar·va (lär′və), *n., pl.* **-vae** (-vē). **1.** the young of any insect which undergoes metamorphosis. **2.** any animal in an analogous immature form.

3. the young of any invertebrate animal. —**lar′val**, *adj.*

lar·yn·gi·tis (lăr′ən jī′təs), *n.* *Pathol.* inflammation of the larynx. —**lar·yn·git·ic** (lăr′ən jĭt′ĭk), *adj.*

lar·ynx (lăr′ĭngks), *n., pl.* **larynges** (lə rĭn′jēz), **larynxes.** **1.** *Anat.* the cavity at the upper end of the human windpipe, containing the vocal cords and acting as the organ of voice. **2.** *Zool.* a corresponding structure in other animals. —**la·ryn·ge·al** (lə rĭn′jĭ əl), *adj.*

La Salle (lə săl′), René Robert, **Cavelier de**, 1643–87, French explorer of the Mississippi.

las·car (lăs′kər), *n.* an East Indian sailor.

las·civ·i·ous (lə sĭv′ĭ əs), *adj.* **1.** wanton or lewd. **2.** inciting to lust. —**las·civ′i·ous·ly**, *adv.* —**las·civ′i·ous·ness**, *n.*

lash[1] (lăsh), *n.* **1.** the flexible part of a whip. **2.** a swift stroke or blow, with a whip, etc., as a punishment. —*v.t.* **3.** to strike or beat, usually with a whip. **4.** to beat violently against. **5.** to drive by strokes of a whip or the like. —*v.i.* **6.** to strike vigorously at. —**lash′er**, *n.*

lash[2] (lăsh), *v.t.* to bind or fasten with a rope, cord, or the like. —**lash′er**, *n.*

lash·ing[1] (lăsh′ĭng), *n.* **1.** act of one who or that which lashes. **2.** a whipping.

lash·ing[2] (lăsh′ĭng), *n.* **1.** a binding with a rope or the like. **2.** the rope or the like used.

lass (lăs), *n.* a girl or young woman.

Las·salle (lə säl′), *n.* Ferdinand, 1825–64, German socialist and writer.

las·sie (lăs′ĭ), *n.* a little lass.

las·si·tude (lăs′ə tūd′, -tōōd′), *n.* weariness of body or mind from strain, oppressive climate, etc.; languor.

las·so (lăs′ō; *older* lă sōō′), *n., pl.* **-sos, -soes,** *v.,* **-soed, -soing.** —*n.* **1.** a long rope with a running noose at one end, used for catching horses, cattle, etc. —*v t.* **2.** to catch with a lasso. —**las′so·er**, *n.*

last[1] (lăst, läst), *adj.* **1.** occurring or coming latest, as in time, order, or place. **2.** next before the present. **3.** being the only remaining. **4.** final. **5.** conclusive. —*adv.* **6.** after all others. **7.** on the most recent occasion. **8.** in the end; finally. —*n.* **9.** that which is last. **10.** *Colloq.* the final mention or appearance. **11.** the end or conclusion.

last[2] (lăst, läst), *v.i.* **1.** to continue in progress or existence; endure. **2.** to be enough (*for*). **3.** to continue in force, vigor, effectiveness, etc.

last[3] (lăst, läst), *n.* **1.** a model of the human foot on which shoes are shaped, as in the making. —*v.t.* **2.** to shape on or fit to a last.

last·ing (lăs′tĭng, läs′-), *adj.* enduring; permanent; durable. —**last′ing·ly**, *adv.*

last·ly (lăst′lĭ, läst′-), *adv.* finally.

Last Supper, the supper of Jesus and His apostles on the eve of His crucifixion.

Lat., Latin.

lat., latitude.

latch (lăch), *n.* **1.** a device for holding a door, gate, or the like, closed, consisting basically of a bar falling or sliding into a catch, groove, hole, etc. —*v.t.* **2.** to close or fasten with a latch.

latch·key (lăch′kē′), *n.* a key for drawing back or releasing a latch.

latch·string (lăch′strĭng′), *n.* a string passed through a hole in a door, for raising the latch from the outside.

late (lāt), *adj.,* **later** or **latter, latest** or **last,** *adv.,* **later, latest.** —*adj.* **1.** occurring, coming, or being after the usual or proper time. **2.** continued until after the usual time. **3.** far advanced in time. **4.** belonging to time just before the present. **5.** immediately preceding that which now exists. **6.** recently deceased. **7.** of late, recently. —*adv.* **8.** after the usual or proper time. **9.** at or to an advanced time, period, or stage. **10.** recently but no longer. —**late′ness**, *n.*

la·teen sail (lă tēn′, lə-), a triangular sail extended by a long tapering yard, slung at about one quarter the distance from the lower end.

late·ly (lāt′lĭ), *adv.* of late; recently.

la·tent (lā′tənt), *adj.* **1.** hidden; not visible or apparent. **2.** dormant. **3.** *Psychol.* below the surface, but potentially able to achieve expression. —**la′ten·cy**, *n.* —**la′tent·ly**, *adv.*

lat·er·al (lăt′ər əl), *adj.* **1.** of, toward, at, or from a side. —*n.* **2.** *Football.* a lateral pass. —**lat′er·al·ly**, *adv.*

lateral pass, *Football.* a pass in which the ball

is thrown in a direction almost parallel with the goal line.

Lat·er·an (lăt'ər ən), *n.* **1.** a complex of papal buildings in Rome, containing the Church of St. John in the Lateran (ranking highest of all Roman Catholic churches). —*adj.* **2.** pertaining to the general church councils held there.

la·tex (lā'tĕks), *n.*, *pl.* **latices** (lăt'ə sēz'), **la·texes** (lā'tĕk sĭz'). *Bot.* a milky liquid in certain plants, as milkweeds, the plants yielding India rubber, etc., which coagulates on exposure to the air.

lath (lăth, läth), *n.*, *pl.* **laths** (lăthz, läths, läthz, läths), *v.* —*n.* **1.** a thin, narrow strip of wood used with others like it to form a groundwork for supporting the plastering of a wall, to construct latticework, etc. **2.** wire cloth or the like used in place of laths, as in plastering. —*v.t.* **3.** to cover or line with laths. —**lath'er,** *n.*

lathe (lāth), *n.* a machine for use in working metal, wood, etc., which holds the material and rotates it about a horizontal axis against a tool that shapes it.

lath·er (lăth'ər), *n.* **1.** foam or froth made from soap moistened with water, as by a brush for shaving. **2.** foam or froth formed in profuse sweating, as of a horse. —*v.i.* **3.** to form a lather. **4.** to become covered with lather. —*v.t.* **5.** to cover with lather. —**lath'er·er,** *n.* —**lath'er·y,** *adj.*

lath·ing (lăth'ĭng, läth'ĭng), *n.* **1.** act or process of applying laths. **2.** work consisting of laths; laths collectively.

Lat·in (lăt'ən, -ĭn), *n.* **1.** the language spoken in ancient Rome. **2.** an ancient Roman. **3.** a member of any Latin race. —*adj.* **4.** denoting or pertaining to those peoples (the Italians, French, Spanish, etc.) using languages derived from that of ancient Rome.

Latin America, part of the American continents south of the United States, in which Romance languages are officially spoken. —**Lat'in-A·mer'i·can,** *adj.*, *n.*

La·tin·ist (lăt'ə nĭst), *n.* a specialist in Latin.

Latin Quarter, the quarter of Paris on the south side of the Seine, frequented by students and artists.

lat·ish (lā'tĭsh), *adj.* somewhat late.

lat·i·tude (lăt'ə tūd', -tood'), *n.* **1.** *Geog.* the angular distance north or south from the equator of a point on the earth's surface, measured on the meridian of the point. **2.** freedom from narrow restrictions. **3.** *Photog.* the range of exposures over which proportional representation of subject brightness is obtained. —**lat'i·tu'di·nal,** *adj.*

lat·i·tu·di·nar·i·an (lăt'ə tū'də när'ĭ ən, -too'-), *adj.* **1.** allowing, or characterized by, latitude in opinion or conduct, esp. in religious views. —*n.* **2.** one who is latitudinarian in opinion or conduct.

LATITUDE AND PARALLEL

LONGITUDE AND MERIDIAN

la·trine (lə trēn'), *n.* a privy, esp. in a camp, barracks, factory, or the like.

lat·ter (lăt'ər), *adj.* **1.** being the second mentioned of two. **2.** later. **3.** nearer to the end or close.

Lat·ter-day Saint (lăt'ər dā'), a Mormon.

lat·ter·ly (lăt'ər lĭ), *adv.* **1.** of late; lately. **2.** in the latter part of a period.

lat·tice (lăt'ĭs), *n.*, *v.*, **-ticed, -ticing.** —*n.* **1.** a structure of crossed strips with open spaces between, used as a screen, etc. **2.** a window, gate, or the like, so constructed. —*v.t.* **3.** to furnish with a lattice or latticework.

lat·tice·work (lăt'ĭs wûrk'), *n.* **1.** work consisting of crossed strips with openings between. **2.** a lattice.

Lat·vi·a (lăt'vĭ ə), *n.* a constituent republic of the Soviet Union, in the W part, on the Baltic. 1,950,502 pop.; 25,395 sq. mi. *Cap.:* Riga. —**Lat'vi·an,** *adj.*, *n.*

laud (lôd), *v.t.* to praise; extol.

laud·a·ble (lô'də bəl), *adj.* praiseworthy or commendable. —**laud·a·bil'i·ty, laud'a·ble·ness,** *n.* —**laud'a·bly,** *adv.*

lau·da·num (lô'də nəm, lôd'nəm), *n.* the tincture of opium.

lau·da·tion (lô dā'shən), *n.* praise.

laud·a·to·ry (lô'də tôr'ĭ), *adj.* containing or expressing praise. Also, **laud'a·tive.**

laugh (lăf, läf), *v.i.* **1.** to express mirth, amusement, derision, etc., by an explosive, inarticulate sound of the voice, facial expressions, etc. **2.** laugh at, to deride; ridicule. —*v.t.* **3.** to drive, put, bring, etc., by or with laughter. —*n.* **4.** act or sound of laughing; laughter. —**laugh'er,** *n.*

laugh·a·ble (lăf'ə bəl, läf'ə-), *adj.* such as to cause laughter; funny; ludicrous. —**laugh'a·ble·ness,** *n.* —**laugh'a·bly,** *adv.*

laugh·ing (lăf'ĭng, läf'ĭng), *n.* **1.** laughter. —*adj.* **2.** that laughs. **3. no laughing matter,** a serious matter. —**laugh'ing·ly,** *adv.*

laughing gas, nitrous oxide, N_2O, which when inhaled sometimes produces exhilarating effects: used as an anesthetic in dentistry, etc.

laughing jackass, a harsh-voiced Australian bird (a kind of kingfisher).

laugh·ing·stock (lăf'ĭng stŏk', läf'ĭng-), *n.* a butt for laughter; an object of ridicule.

laugh·ter (lăf'tər, läf'-), *n.* the action or sound of laughing.

launch[1] (lônch, länch), *n.* **1.** a heavy open boat. **2.** the largest boat carried by a warship.

launch[2] (lônch, länch), *v.t.* **1.** to set (a boat) afloat. **2.** to start on a course, career, etc. **3.** to set going. **4.** to send forth forcefully. **5.** to throw or hurl. —*v.i.* **6.** to burst out or plunge boldly into action, speech, etc. **7.** to start out or forth. —**launch'er,** *n.*

laun·der (lôn'dər, län'-), *v.t.*, *v.i.* to wash and iron (clothes, etc.). —**laun'dress,** *n. fem.*

laun·dry (lôn'drĭ, län'-), *n.*, *pl.* **-dries. 1.** articles of clothes, etc., to be washed. **2.** a place where clothes, etc., are laundered.

laun·dry·man (lôn'drĭ mən, län'-), *n.*, *pl.* **-men. 1.** a man who works in or conducts a laundry. **2.** a man who collects and delivers laundry.

lau·re·ate (lôr'ĭ ĭt), *adj.* **1.** crowned with laurel as a mark of honor. **2.** specially recognized, esp. for poetic merit. **3.** consisting of laurel. —*n.* **4.** one crowned with laurel. **5.** a poet laureate. —**lau're·ate·ship',** *n.*

lau·rel (lôr'əl, lŏr'əl), *n.*, *v.*, **-reled, -reling** or (*esp. Brit.*) **-relled, -relling.** —*n.* **1.** a small evergreen tree of Europe (**true laurel**). **2.** any of various similar trees or shrubs, as the **American** or **mountain laurel,** which has glossy leaves and showy flowers. **3.** a branch or wreath of the true laurel, as an emblem of victory or distinction. **4.** (*usually pl.*) honor won, as by achievement. —*v.t.* **5.** to adorn or wreathe with laurel.

Lau·ren·tian Mountains (lô rĕn'shən), a range of low mountains in E Canada between the St. Lawrence and Hudson Bay.

Lau·sanne (lō zăn'), *n.* a city in W Switzerland. 97,800.

la·va (lä'və, lăv'ə), *n.* **1.** the molten rock which issues from a volcano. **2.** the substance formed when this solidifies.

La·val (là vàl'), *n.* **Pierre,** 1883–1945, premier of France, 1931–32, 1935–36; premier of Vichy France, 1942–44; convicted of treason and executed.

lav·a·liere (lăv'ə lĭr'), *n.* an ornamental, usually jeweled, pendant on a small chain, worn by women about the neck. Also, **lav'a·lier'.**

lav·a·to·ry (lăv'ə tôr'ĭ), *n.*, *pl.* **-ries.** a washroom or toilet, as in a school.

lave (lāv), *v.t.*, *v.i.*, **laved, laving.** *Poetic.* to wash or bathe.

lav·en·der (lăv'ən dər), *n.* **1.** pale, bluish purple. **2.** a small Old World shrub with spikes of fragrant pale-purple flowers, yielding an oil (**oil of lavender**) used in medicine and perfumery.

lav·ish (lăv'ĭsh), *adj.* **1.** using or bestowing in great abundance or without stint. **2.** expended, bestowed, or occurring in profusion. —*v.t.* **3.** to expend or bestow in great abundance or without stint. —**lav'ish·er,** *n.* —**lav'ish·ly,** *adv.* —**lav'ish·ness,** *n.*

La·voi·sier (là vwà zyā'), *n.* **Antoine Laurent,** 1743–94, French chemist.

law (lô), *n.* **1.** the principles and regulations emanating from a government and applicable to a people, whether in the form of legislation or of custom and policies recognized and enforced by judicial decision. **2.** any rule, or collection of rules, prescribed under the authority of the state or nation. **3.** the condition of society brought about by the observance of such laws. **4.** a system or collection of such rules. **5.** jurisprudence. **6.** an act of the supreme legislative body of a state or nation. **7.** the profession which deals with law. **8.** legal action; litigation. **9.** any rule or injunction that must be obeyed. **10.** (in philosophical and scientific use) **a.** a statement of a relation or sequence of phenomena invariable under the same conditions. **b.** a mathematical rule. **11.** a commandment or revelation from God. **12. the Law,** the Mosaic law. **13.** the five books of Moses (the Pentateuch).

law·a·bid·ing (lô′ə bī′dĭng), *adj.* abiding by or keeping the law; obedient to law.

law·break·er (lô′brā′kər), *n.* one who violates the law. —**law′break′ing,** *n., adj.*

law·ful (lô′fəl), *adj.* **1.** allowed by law. **2.** legally qualified or entitled. **3.** recognized or sanctioned by law. **4.** valid. —**law′ful·ly,** *adv.* —**law′ful·ness,** *n.*

law·giv·er (lô′gĭv′ər), *n.* one who gives or promulgates a law or a code of laws.

law·less (lô′lĭs), *adj.* **1.** contrary to law. **2.** uncontrolled by law; unbridled. **3.** without law. —**law′less·ly,** *adv.* —**law′less·ness,** *n.*

law·mak·er (lô′mā′kər), *n.* one who makes or enacts laws. —**law′mak′ing,** *n., adj.*

lawn[1] (lôn), *n.* a stretch of grass-covered land, esp. one kept closely mowed, as near a house, in a garden, etc.

lawn[2] (lôn), *n.* a thin or sheer linen or cotton fabric, either plain or printed.

lawn tennis, a form of tennis, played on an unenclosed rectangular plot on a lawn or other level surface.

Law·rence (lôr′əns, lŏr′-), *n.* **1. D(avid) H(erbert),** 1885–1930, British novelist and poet. **2.** a city in NE Massachusetts. 84,323.

law·suit (lô′soot′), *n.* a suit at law; a prosecution of a claim in a law court.

law·yer (lô′yər), *n.* one whose profession it is to conduct suits in court or to give legal advice and aid.

lax (lăks), *adj.* **1.** lacking in strictness; careless. **2.** not precise; vague. **3.** slack; not firm. —**lax′·ly,** *adv.* —**lax′ness,** *n.*

lax·a·tive (lăk′sə tĭv), *Med.* —*adj.* **1.** mildly purgative. —*n.* **2.** a laxative medicine or agent.

lax·i·ty (lăk′sə tĭ), *n.* state or quality of being lax or loose.

lay[1] (lā), *v.,* **laid, laying,** *n.* —*v.t.* **1.** to put in a position of rest or recumbency. **2.** to bring, throw, or beat down. **3.** to cause to subside. **4.** to allay, appease, or suppress. **5.** to smooth down. **6.** to bury. **7.** to bring forth and deposit (an egg or eggs). **8.** to wager; bet. **9.** to put away for future use. **10.** to place, set, or cause to be in a particular situation, state, or condition. **11.** to bring to a person's notice. **12.** to put to; apply. **13.** to set (a trap, etc.). **14.** to locate (a scene). **15.** to present or bring forward, as a claim, charge, etc. **16.** to attribute or ascribe. **17.** to impose as a burden, duty, penalty, or the like. **18.** to set or place in proper position or arrangement. **19.** to cover or spread with something else. **20.** to devise. **21. lay hold of** or **on,** to grasp; seize. **22. lay off, a.** to put aside. **b.** to dismiss, esp. temporarily, as a workman. **c.** to mark off. **23. lay out, a.** to extend at length. **b.** to spread out to the sight, air, etc. **c.** *Slang.* to expend (money) for a particular purpose. **24. lay up, a.** to put away, for future use. **b.** to cause to remain in bed or indoors through illness. —*v.i.* **25.** to lay eggs. **26.** to wager or bet. **27.** to deal or aim blows. **28.** *Colloq.* to lie in wait. —*n.* **29.** the way or position which a thing is laid or lies.

lay[2] (lā), *v.* pt. of **lie**[2].

lay[3] (lā), *adj.* **1.** belonging to, pertaining to, or performed by the people or laity, as distinguished from the clergy. **2.** not belonging to, connected with, or proceeding from a profession, esp. the law or medicine.

lay[4] (lā), *n.* **1.** a short narrative or other poem, esp. one to be sung. **2.** a song.

lay·er (lā′ər), *n.* **1.** a thickness of some material laid on or spread over a surface. **2.** one who or that which lays.

layer cake, a cake made in layers with a cream, jelly, or other filling between layers.

lay·ette (lā ĕt′), *n.* an outfit of clothing, toilet articles, etc., for a newborn child.

lay·man (lā′mən), *n., pl.* **-men.** one who is not

a clergyman or not a member of some particular profession.

lay·off (lā′ôf′, -ŏf′), *n.* **1.** act of laying off. **2.** an interval of enforced unemployment.

lay·out (lā′out′), *n.* **1.** a spreading out. **2.** an arrangement or plan. **3.** the plan or sketch of a page or advertisement.

lay·o·ver (lā′ō′vər), *n.* stopover.

laz·ar (lăz′ər, lā′zər), *n.* *Archaic.* **1.** a person, esp. a beggar, infected with a loathsome disease. **2.** a leper.

laz·a·ret·to (lăz′ə rĕt′ō), *n., pl.* **-tos.** **1.** a hospital for those affected with contagious or loathsome diseases. **2.** a building or a ship set apart for quarantine purposes. **3.** *Naut.* a place in some merchant ships in which provisions and stores are kept. Also, **laz·a·ret** (lăz′ə rĕt′), **laz′a·rette′.**

Laz·a·rus (lăz′ə rəs), *n.* **1.** the beggar, "full of sores," of the parable in Luke 16:19–31. **2.** the brother of Mary and Martha, and friend of Jesus, who raised him from the dead. John 11:1–44; 12:1–18.

la·zy (lā′zĭ), *adj.,* **lazier, laziest. 1.** disinclined to exertion or work; idle. **2.** slow-moving; sluggish. —**la′zi·ly,** *adv.* —**la′zi·ness,** *n.*

la·zy·bones (lā′zĭ bōnz′), *n.* *Colloq.* a lazy person.

lb., *pl.* **lbs., lb.** (L *libra,* pl. *librae*) pound (weight).

l.c., 1. left center. **2.** (L *loco citato*) in the place cited. **3.** *Print.* lower case.

L/C, letter of credit. Also, **l/c.**

lea (lē), *n.* *Poetic.* a meadow.

leach (lēch), *v.t.* **1.** to cause (water, etc.) to percolate through something. **2.** to remove soluble constituents from (ashes, etc.) by percolation. —*v.i.* **3.** (of ashes, etc.) to undergo the action of percolating water. —*n.* **4.** a leaching. **5.** the material leached.

lead[1] (lēd), *v.,* **led, leading,** *n.* —*v.t.* **1.** to go before or with to show the way. **2.** to conduct by holding and guiding. **3.** to influence or induce. **4.** to conduct (water, wire, etc.) in a particular course. **5.** (of a road, etc.) to serve to bring (a person, etc.) to a place. **6.** to take or bring. **7.** to command or direct (an army, organization, etc.). **8.** to go at the head of (a procession, list, etc.). **9.** to begin or open, as a dance. **10.** to act as leader of (an orchestra, etc.). **11.** to go through or pass (life, etc.). **12.** *Cards.* to begin a round, etc., with. —*v.i.* **13.** to act as a guide. **14.** to afford passage (to a place, etc.). **15.** to go or act first. **16.** to take the directing or principal part. **17.** to take the initiative or offensive. —*n.* **18.** the first or foremost place. **19.** the extent of advance. **20.** something that leads. **21.** a guiding indication. **22.** precedence. **23.** *Theat.* **a.** the principal part in a play. **b.** the person who plays it. **24.** *Cards.* the act or right of playing first, as in a round. **25.** *Journ.* a short introduction to an article. **26.** *Elect.* a single conductor, often flexible and insulated, used in connections between pieces of electrical apparatus.

lead[2] (lĕd), *n.* **1.** *Chem.* a heavy, comparatively soft, malleable bluish-gray metal. *Symbol:* Pb; *at. wt.:* 207.21; *at. no.:* 82; *sp. gr.:* 11.34 at 20°C. **2.** a plummet. **3.** bullets; shot. **4.** a small stick of graphite as used in pencils. **5.** *Print.* a thin strip of type metal, less than type high, for increasing the space between lines of type. —*v.t.* **6.** to cover, line, weight, or treat with lead or one of its compounds.

lead·en (lĕd′ən), *adj.* **1.** consisting or made of lead. **2.** inertly heavy. **3.** oppressive, as the air. **4.** sluggish, as the pace. **5.** spiritless or gloomy. **6.** of a dull gray.

lead·er (lē′dər), *n.* **1.** one who or that which leads. **2.** a guiding or directing head, as of an army, movement, etc. **3.** *Music.* a conductor or director, as of an orchestra, band, or chorus. **4.** *Journ.* a principal or important editorial article. **5.** a featured article of trade, esp. one offered at a low price to attract customers. **6.** a pipe for conveying rainwater, etc. **7.** (*pl.*) *Print.* a row of dots or short lines to lead the eye across a space. **8.** *Fishing.* a length of silkworm gut or the like, to which the fly or baited hook is attached. —**lead′er·less,** *adj.* —**lead′er·ship′,** *n.*

lead·ing[1] (lē′dĭng), *n.* **1.** guidance; direction; lead. —*adj.* **2.** directing; guiding. **3.** chief; foremost.

lead·ing[2] (lĕd′ĭng), *n.* *Print.* lead[2] (def. 5).

lead-in wire (lēd′ĭn′), *Radio.* that portion of the antenna connected to the receiving set.

lead pencil (lĕd), an implement for writing made of graphite in a wooden or metal holder.

leaf (lēf), n., pl. **leaves** (lēvz), v. —n. 1. one of the expanded, usually green, organs borne by the stem of a plant. 2. *Bibliog.* a unit comprising two printed pages of a book, one on each side. 3. a thin sheet of metal, etc. 4. a sliding, hinged, or detachable flat part, as of a door, table top, etc. —v.i. 5. to put forth leaves. —v.t. 6. *U.S.* to thumb through the pages of.

leaf·age (lēf′ĭj), n. foliage.

leaf·less (lēf′lĭs), adj. without leaves.

leaf·let (lēf′lĭt), n. 1. one of the separate blades or divisions of a compound leaf. 2. a small or young leaf. 4. a small flat or folded sheet of printed matter.

leaf·stalk (lēf′stôk′), n. petiole (def. 1).

leaf·y (lē′fĭ), adj., **leafier, leafiest.** abounding in, covered with, or consisting of leaves or foliage. —leaf′i·ness, n.

league¹ (lēg), n., v., **leagued, leaguing.** —n. 1. a covenant between persons, parties, states, etc., for mutual assistance, etc. 2. the aggregation of persons, parties, states, etc., associated in such a covenant. 3. **in league,** allied. —v.t. 4. to unite in a league; combine.

league² (lēg), n. a unit of distance, usually estimated roughly at 3 miles.

League of Nations, the organization of nations of the world to promote world peace and coöperation which was created by the Treaty of Versailles (1919) and dissolved, April, 1946, by action of its 21st Assembly.

Le·ah (lē′ə), n. the first wife of Jacob.

leak (lēk), n. 1. an unintended hole, crack, or the like, by which water, etc., enters or escapes. 2. *Elect.* a point where current escapes from a conductor. 3. act of leaking. —v.i. 4. to let water, etc., enter or escape, as through an unintended hole, crack, or the like. 5. to pass in or out in this manner, as water, etc. 6. to become known undesignedly.

leak·age (lē′kĭj), n. 1. act of leaking. 2. that which leaks in or out. 3. the amount that leaks in or out.

leak·y (lē′kĭ), adj., **leakier, leakiest.** allowing water, etc., to leak. —leak′i·ness, n.

leal (lēl), adj. *Archaic or Scot.* loyal.

lean¹ (lēn), v., **leaned** or (*esp. Brit.*) **leant, leaning,** n. —v.i., v.t. 1. to incline or bend from a vertical position. 2. to incline in opinion, action, etc. 3. to rest against or on something for support. 4. to depend. —n. 5. act of leaning; inclination.

lean² (lēn), adj. 1. not plump or fat. 2. (of meat) containing little or no fat. 3. lacking in richness, fullness, quantity, etc. —n. 4. that part of flesh which consists of muscle rather than fat. —lean′ly, adv. —lean′ness, n.

lean·ing (lē′nĭng), n. inclination; tendency.

lean-to (lēn′tōō′), n., pl. **-tos.** 1. a shack or shed supported at one side by trees or posts and with an inclined roof. 2. a roof of single pitch, the higher end abutting a wall or larger building.

leap (lēp), v., **leaped** or **leapt, leaping,** n. —v.i. 1. to spring through the air from one point or position to another. 2. to pass, come, rise, etc., as if with a bound. —v.t. 3. to jump over. 4. to pass over as if by a leap. —n. 5. a spring, jump, or bound. 6. the space cleared in a leap. —leap′er, n.

leap·frog (lēp′frŏg′, -frôg′), n. a game in which one player leaps over another who is in a stooping posture.

leap year, a year containing 366 days, or one day (Feb. 29) more than the ordinary year, to offset the difference in length between the ordinary year and the astronomical year (being, in practice, every year whose number is exactly divisible by 4, as 1948, except centenary years not exactly divisible by 400, as 1900).

learn (lûrn), v., **learned** (lûrnd) or **learnt, learning.** —v.t. 1. to acquire knowledge of or skill in by study, instruction, or experience. 2. to memorize. 3. to ascertain. —v.i. 4. to acquire knowledge or skill. 5. to become informed. —learn′er, n.

learn·ed (lûr′nĭd), adj. 1. having much knowledge. 2. pertaining to or showing learning. —learn′ed·ly, adv.

learn·ing (lûr′nĭng), n. knowledge acquired by systematic study in any field or fields of scholarly application.

lease (lēs), n., v., **leased, leasing.** —n. 1. an instrument conveying property to another for a definite period, usually in consideration of compensation. —v.t. 2. to grant or obtain the temporary possession or use of (lands, tenements, etc.), usually for compensation.

leash (lēsh), n. 1. a thong or line for holding a dog or other animal in check. —v.t. 2. to secure or hold in a leash.

least (lēst), adj. 1. smallest or slightest. 2. lowest in consideration or dignity. —n. 3. the least amount, quantity, degree, etc. 4. **at least, a.** at the lowest estimate. **b.** in any case. 5. **in the least,** in the smallest degree. —adv. 6. to the least extent, amount, or degree.

leath·er (lĕth′ər), n. 1. the skin of animals prepared for use by tanning or a similar process. —v.t. 2. to cover or furnish with leather.

leath·ern (lĕth′ərn), adj. 1. made of leather. 2. resembling leather.

leath·er·neck (lĕth′ər nĕk′), n. *Slang.* a U.S. marine.

leath·er·y (lĕth′ə rĭ), adj. like leather; tough and flexible.

leave¹ (lēv), v., **left, leaving.** —v.t. 1. to go away from; depart from. 2. to let stay or be as specified. 3. to stop. 4. to let (a thing) remain for action or decision. 5. to omit. 6. to allow to remain. 7. to have remaining behind, after ceasing, etc. 8. to have remaining after death. 9. to give for use after one's death or departure. 10. to have as a remainder after subtraction. —v.i. 11. to go away, depart, or set out.

leave² (lēv), n. 1. permission to do something. 2. permission to be absent, as from duty. 3. the time this permission lasts. 4. a farewell.

leave³ (lēv), v.i., **leaved, leaving.** to put forth leaves; leaf.

leav·en (lĕv′ən), n. 1. a mass of fermenting dough reserved for producing fermentation in a new batch of dough. 2. an a ency which produces a gradual change. —v.t. 3. to produce bubbles of gas in (dough or batter) by means of any of a variety of leavening agents. 4. to permeate with an altering influence.

leave-tak·ing (lēv′tā′kĭng), n. the saying of farewell.

leav·ing (lē′vĭng), n. 1. that which is left; residue. 2. (*pl.*) remains; refuse.

Leb·a·non (lĕb′ə nən), n. a republic at the E end of the Mediterranean, N of Palestine. 1,022,-000 pop.; 3927 sq. mi. *Cap.:* Beirut. —**Leb·a·nese** (lĕb′ə nēz′, -nēs′), adj., n.

Le·bens·raum (lā′bəns roum′), n. additional territory desired by a nation for expansion of trade, etc.

lech·er (lĕch′ər), n. a man immoderately given to sexual indulgence; a lewd man. —lech′er·ous, adj. —lech′er·ous·ly, adv. —lech′er·ous·ness, n.

lech·er·y (lĕch′ə rĭ), n. free indulgence of lust; lewdness.

lec·tern (lĕk′tərn), n. a reading desk in a church, from which the lessons are read.

lec·ture (lĕk′chər), n., v., **-tured, -turing.** —n. 1. an instructive discourse read or delivered before an audience. 2. a long, tedious reprimand. —v.i. 3. to give a lecture. —v.t. 4, to deliver a lecture to or before. —lec′tur·er, n.

Le·da (lē′də), n. *Gk. Myth.* the mother by Zeus of Helen, Clytemnestra, Castor, and Pollux.

ledge (lĕj), n. 1. any relatively narrow, horizontal projecting or shelflike surface. 2. a reef.

ledg·er (lĕj′ər), n. 1. *Bookkeeping.* an account book of final entry, containing all the accounts. 2. a horizontal timber fastened to the vertical uprights of a scaffold.

lee¹ (lē), n. 1. shelter. 2. the side or part that is sheltered or away from the wind. —adj. 3. *Chiefly Naut.* pertaining to, situated in, or moving toward the region toward which the wind blows.

lee² (lē), n. (*usually pl.*) sediment or dregs, esp. from wine.

Lee (lē), n. **Robert E.,** 1807–1870, Confederate general in the U.S. Civil War.

leech (lēch), n. 1. any of certain blood-sucking or carnivorous, usually aquatic, worms, some species of which were formerly much used for bloodletting. 2. a parasitic person. —v.t. 3. to apply leeches to so as to bleed.

Leeds (lēdz), n. a city in N England. 483,560.

leek (lēk), n. 1. a plant of the lily family, allied to the onion but having a cylindrical bulb, and used in cookery. 2. any of various allied species.

leer (lĭr), *n*. **1.** a side glance, esp. of sly suggestion or malicious significance. —*v.i.* **2.** to look with a leer. —**leer'ing·ly**, *adv*.

leer·y (lĭr'ĭ), *adj*. *Slang*. **1.** wary; suspicious. **2.** knowing.

lee·ward (lē'wərd; *Naut*. lōō'ərd), *adj*. **1.** pertaining to, situated in, or moving toward the quarter toward which the wind blows. —*n*. **2.** the point or quarter toward which the wind blows. —*adv*. **3.** toward the lee.

Lee·ward Islands (lē'wərd), **1.** a group of islands in the N Lesser Antilles of the West Indies, extending from Puerto Rico SE to Martinique. **2.** a British colony in this group. 98,135 pop.; 421½ sq. mi. *Cap*.: St. John.

lee·way (lē'wā'), *n*. **1.** the lateral movement of a ship or plane to leeward or off its course. **2.** *Colloq*. extra space, time, money, etc.

left (lĕft), *adj*. **1.** of or belonging to the side toward the west when facing north (opposed to *right*). —*n*. **2.** the left side. **3.** persons or groups holding socialistic or radical views.

left-hand (lĕft'hănd'), *adj*. **1.** on or to the left. **2.** of, for, or with the left hand.

left-hand·ed (lĕft'hăn'dĭd), *adj*. **1.** preferably using the left hand. **2.** adapted to or performed by the left hand. **3.** situated on the side of the left hand. **4.** ambiguous or doubtful. **5.** clumsy or awkward. —**left'-hand'ed·ly**, *adv*. —**left'-hand'ed·ness**, *n*.

left·ist (lĕf'tĭst), *n*. **1.** a member of a socialistic or radical party, or a person sympathizing with their views. —*adj*. **2.** having socialistic or radical political ideas.

left·o·ver (lĕft'ō'vər), *n*. something remaining, as food from a meal.

left wing, **1.** members of a socialistic or radical political party. **2.** such a party, or group of such parties. —**left'wing'**, *adj*.

leg (lĕg), *n*., *v*., **legged, legging.** —*n*. **1.** one of the limbs which support the human or animal body. **2.** that part of the limb between the knee and the ankle. **3.** that part of a garment, such as a stocking, trousers, or the like, which covers the leg. **4.** one of the supports of a piece of furniture. **5.** one of the sides of a pair of dividers or compasses. **6.** one of the sides of a triangle other than the base or hypotenuse. **7.** one of the distinct portions of any course. **8.** pull (one's) leg, to make fun of (one). **9.** shake a leg, *Slang*. to hurry up. —*v.i.* **10.** *Colloq*. to walk or run. —**leg'less**, *adj*.

leg., **1.** legal. **2.** legislative.

leg·a·cy (lĕg'ə sĭ), *n*., *pl*. **-cies. 1.** *Law*. a gift of property by will. **2.** anything handed down by an ancestor or predecessor.

le·gal (lē'gəl), *adj*. **1.** appointed, established, or authorized by law. **2.** of or pertaining to law. **3.** permitted by law; lawful. —**le'gal·ly**, *adv*.

le·gal·i·ty (lĭ găl'ə tĭ), *n*., *pl*. **-ties. 1.** conformity with the law; lawfulness. **2.** observance of law.

le·gal·ize (lē'gə līz'), *v.t.*, **-ized, -izing.** to make legal; sanction. —**le'gal·i·za'tion**, *n*.

legal tender, *Law*. currency which may be lawfully offered in payment of debts.

leg·ate (lĕg'ĭt), *n*. **1.** an ecclesiastic delegated by the Pope as his representative. **2.** an envoy. —**leg'ate·ship**, *n*.

leg·a·tee (lĕg'ə tē'), *n*. one to whom a legacy is bequeathed.

le·ga·tion (lĭ gā'shən), *n*. **1.** a diplomatic minister and his staff. **2.** the official residence or office of a minister.

le·ga·to (lĭ gä'tō), *adj*. *Music*. smooth and connected.

leg·end (lĕj'ənd), *n*. **1.** a story handed down by tradition from earlier times and popularly accepted as historical. **2.** such stories collectively. **3.** an inscription, as on a coin or under a picture.

leg·end·ar·y (lĕj'ən dĕr'ĭ), *adj*. **1.** pertaining to or of the nature of a legend or legends. **2.** celebrated or described in legend.

leg·er·de·main (lĕj'ər də mān'), *n*. **1.** sleight of hand. **2.** trickery; deception.

leg·er line (lĕj'ər), *Music*. a short line added when necessary above or below the lines of a staff to increase the range of the staff.

leg·ging (lĕg'ĭng), *n*. (*usually pl*.) an extra outer covering for the leg.

Leg·horn (lĕg'hôrn' *for 1, 2*; lĕg'ərn, -hôrn' *for 3*), *n*. **1.** a seaport in W Italy. 133,521. **2.** (*l.c.*) a hat made of a fine, smooth, plaited straw. **3.**

a Mediterranean breed of the domestic fowl, characterized by prolific laying of white-shelled eggs.

leg·i·ble (lĕj'ə bəl), *adj*. that may be read with ease. —**leg'i·bil'i·ty, leg'i·ble·ness**, *n*. —**leg'-i·bly**, *adv*.

le·gion (lē'jən), *n*. **1.** an infantry brigade in the ancient Roman army, numbering from 3000 to 6000 men, and usually combined with from 300 to 700 cavalry. **2.** a military unit or force. **3.** the Legion, a. the American Legion. b. the French Foreign Legion. **4.** any great multitude.

le·gion·ar·y (lē'jə nĕr'ĭ), *adj*., *n*., *pl*. **-aries.** —*adj*. **1.** pertaining or belonging to a legion. —*n*. **2.** a soldier of a legion.

le·gion·naire (lē'jə nâr'), *n*. (*often cap*.) a member of the American Legion.

leg·is·late (lĕj'ĭs lāt'), *v*., **-lated, -lating.** —*v.i.* **1.** to make or enact laws. —*v.t.* **2.** to effect, bring (*into*), put (*out*), etc., by legislation. —**leg'-is·la'tor**, *n*.

leg·is·la·tion (lĕj'ĭs lā'shən), *n*. **1.** act of making or enacting laws. **2.** a law or a body of laws enacted.

leg·is·la·tive (lĕj'ĭs lā'tĭv), *adj*. **1.** having the function of making laws. **2.** of or pertaining to legislation. **3.** ordained by legislation. **4.** pertaining to a legislature. —*n*. **5.** the legislature. —**leg'is·la'tive·ly**, *adv*.

leg·is·la·ture (lĕj'ĭs lā'chər), *n*. the legislative body of a country or state.

le·git (lə jĭt'), *adj*. *Slang*. legitimate.

le·git·i·ma·cy (lĭ jĭt'ə mə sĭ), *n*. state or fact of being legitimate.

le·git·i·mate (*adj*. lĭ jĭt'ə mĭt; *v*. lĭ jĭt'ə māt'), *adj*., *v*., **-mated, -mating.** —*adj*. **1.** lawful. **2.** in accordance with established rules or standards. **3.** logical. **4.** born of parents legally married. **5.** genuine. —*v.t.* **6.** to make or pronounce lawful. **7.** to show or declare to be legitimate. —**le·git'i·mate·ly**, *adv*.

legitimate drama, drama for the stage (as opposed to motion pictures).

leg·ume (lĕg'ūm, lĭ gūm'), *n*. **1.** any plant of a family that bears pods or seed vessels which are usually dehiscent by both sutures, thus dividing into two parts, as the pea or bean. **2.** the pod or seed vessel itself.

le·gu·mi·nous (lĭ gū'mə nəs), *adj*. pertaining to, of the nature of, or bearing legumes.

Le Ha·vre (lə hä'vrə), a seaport in N France at the mouth of the Seine. 106,934.

le·i (lā'ĭ, lā), *n*., *pl*. **leis.** (in the Hawaiian Islands) a wreath of flowers, leaves, etc., for the neck or head.

Leib·nitz (līb'nĭts), *n*. **Gottfried Wilhelm von,** 1646–1716, German philosopher. Also, **Leib'niz.**

Leices·ter (lĕs'tər), *n*. **1. Robert Dudley, Earl of,** 1532?–88, British statesman. **2.** a city in central England. 269,890.

Leip·zig (līp'sĭg, -sĭk), *n*. a city in central Germany. 707,365.

lei·sure (lē'zhər, lĕzh'ər), *n*. **1.** freedom from the demands of work or duty. **2. at leisure, a.** with free time. **b.** without haste. **c.** unoccupied. —*adj*. **3.** free or unoccupied. **4.** having leisure.

lei·sure·ly (lē'zhər lĭ, lĕzh'ər-), *adj*. **1.** acting, proceeding, or done without haste. **2.** unhurried. —*adv*. **3.** without haste. —**lei'sure·li·ness**, *n*.

leit·mo·tif (līt'mō tēf'), *n*. (in a music drama) a motif or theme associated throughout the work with a particular person, situation, or idea. Also, **leit'mo·tiv'.**

lem·ming (lĕm'ĭng), *n*. any of certain small, mouselike rodents of far northern regions, as Norway, Sweden, etc.

lem·on (lĕm'ən), *n*. **1.** the yellowish acid fruit of certain subtropical trees. **2.** the tree itself. **3.** clear, light yellow color. **4.** *Slang*. something distasteful, disappointing, or unpleasant.

lem·on·ade (lĕm'ə nād'), *n*. a beverage consisting of lemon juice and sweetened water.

le·mur (lē'mər), *n*. any of various small, arboreal, chiefly nocturnal mammals, allied to the monkeys, usually having a foxlike face and woolly fur, and found chiefly in Madagascar. —**le'-mur·like'**, *adj*.

lend (lĕnd), *v*., **lent, lending.** —*v.t.* **1.** to give the temporary use of (money, etc.). **2.** to furnish or impart. **3.** to give obligingly or helpfully. **4.** to accommodate or adapt oneself (or itself) to something. —*v.i.* **5.** to make a loan or loans. —**lend'er**, *n*.

Lend-Lease Act (lĕnd'lēs'), an act (Mar. 11

1941) enabling the U.S. government to furnish material aid to nations at war with Germany and Italy.

length (lĕngkth, lĕngth), *n*. **1.** the linear magnitude of anything as measured from end to end. **2.** extent from beginning to end of a series, book, etc. **3.** extent in time; duration. **4.** a piece or portion of a certain or a known length. **5.** *Pros. and Phonet.* **a.** (of a vowel or syllable) quantity (whether long or short). **b.** the quality of vowels. **6. at length, a.** to or in the full extent. **b.** after a time.

length·en (lĕngk′thən, lĕng′-), *v.t.*, *v.i.* to make or become greater in length.

length·ways (lĕngkth′wāz′, lĕngth′-), *adv.* lengthwise.

length·wise (lĕngkth′wīz′, lĕngth′-), *adv.*, *adj.* in the direction of the length.

length·y (lĕngk′thĭ, lĕng′-), *adj.*, **lengthier**, **lengthiest**. being of great length, esp. speeches, writings, etc. **—length′i·ly**, *adv.* **—length′i·ness**, *n*.

le·ni·ent (lē′nĭ ənt, lēn′yənt), *adj.* mild, clement, or merciful; gentle. **—le′ni·en·cy, le′ni·ence**, *n*. **—le′ni·ent·ly**, *adv.*

Len·in (lĕn′ĭn), *n.* Nikolai, 1870–1924, Russian revolutionary leader: head of Soviet government from 1917 to 1924.

Len·in·grad (lĕn′ĭn grăd′), *n.* a seaport in the NW Soviet Union. 3,191,304.

Len·in·ism (lĕn′ĭ nĭz′əm), *n.* Russian communism as taught by Nikolai Lenin, with emphasis on the "dictatorship of the proletariat."

len·i·ty (lĕn′ə tĭ), *n.*, *pl.* **-ties. 1.** mildness or gentleness. **2.** a lenient act.

lens (lĕnz), *n.*, *pl.* **lenses. 1.** a piece of transparent substance, usually glass, used for changing the convergence of light rays, as in magnifying, or in correcting errors of vision. **2.** *Anat.* a lenslike crystalline part of the eye.

Lent (lĕnt), *n.* an annual season of fasting and penitence, beginning on Ash Wednesday and including the forty weekdays up to Easter, observed by the Roman Catholic, Anglican, and other churches.

Lent·en (lĕn′tən), *adj.* (*often l.c.*) of, pertaining to, or suitable for Lent.

len·til (lĕn′tĭl), *n.* **1.** an annual plant whose flattened seeds constitute a food similar to peas and beans. **2.** the seed.

len·to (lĕn′tō), *Music.* **—adj. 1.** slow. **—adv. 2.** slowly.

Le·o (lē′ō), *n.*, *gen.* **Leonis** (lĭ ō′nĭs). **1.** a zodiacal constellation; the Lion. **2.** the fifth sign of the zodiac.

Le·on·ca·val·lo (lĕ ôn′kä väl′lō), *n.* **Ruggiero**, 1858–1919, Italian operatic composer.

le·o·nine (lē′ə nīn′), *adj.* **1.** of or pertaining to the lion. **2.** lionlike.

leop·ard (lĕp′ərd), *n.* **1.** a large, ferocious, spotted Asiatic or African carnivore of the cat family, usually tawny, with black markings. **2.** any of various related animals, as the jaguar (**American leopard**), the cheetah (**hunting leopard**), and the ounce (**snow leopard**).

Le·o·pold III (lē′ə pōld′), born 1901, king of Belgium since 1934.

Le·o·pold·ville (lē′ə pōld vĭl′), *n.* the capital of the Belgian Congo, in the W part. 102,760.

Le·pan·to (lĭ păn′tō), *n.* a seaport in W Greece: Turkish seapower was destroyed near here in a famous naval battle, 1571.

lep·er (lĕp′ər), *n.* a person affected with leprosy.

lep·i·dop·ter·ous (lĕp′ə dŏp′tər əs), *adj.* belonging or pertaining to an order of insects comprising the butterflies and moths, which in the adult state have four membranous wings.

lep·re·chaun (lĕp′rə kôn′), *n.* *Irish Folklore.* a pygmy, sprite, or goblin.

lep·ro·sy (lĕp′rə sĭ), *n.* a mildly infectious disease due to a microörganism, variously characterized by ulcerations, tubercular nodules, loss of fingers and toes, etc. **—lep·rous** (lĕp′rəs), *adj.*

Les·bi·an (lĕz′bĭ ən), *adj.* **1.** (of a woman) homosexual. **—n. 2.** (*l.c.*) one addicted to Lesbianism.

Les·bi·an·ism (lĕz′bĭ ə nĭz′əm), *n.* homosexual relations between women.

lese maj·es·ty (lēz′ măj′ĭs tĭ), *Law.* any crime or offense against the sovereign power in a state.

le·sion (lē′zhən), *n.* **1.** an injury; wound. **2.**

Pathol. any localized, morbid structural change in the body.

less (lĕs), *adv.* **1.** to a smaller extent, amount, or degree. **—adj. 2.** smaller in size, amount, degree, etc. **3.** lower in importance. **—n. 4.** a smaller amount or quantity. **—prep. 5.** lacking; minus.

-less, a suffix of adjectives meaning "without," "destitute of," as in *childless, peerless.* In adjectives derived from verbs, it indicates failure or inability to perform or be performed, as in *countless.*

les·see (lĕ sē′), *n.* one to whom a lease is granted. **—les·see′ship**, *n*.

less·en (lĕs′ən), *v.i.* **1.** to become less. **—v.t. 2.** to make less. **3.** to depreciate; disparage.

less·er (lĕs′ər), *adj.* **1.** smaller, as in size, amount, importance, etc. **2.** being the smaller or less important of two.

les·son (lĕs′ən), *n.* **1.** something to be learned or studied. **2.** a part of a book or the like assigned for study. **3.** a useful or salutary piece of practical wisdom. **4.** a reproof or punishment. **5.** a portion of Scripture or other sacred writing read at divine service.

les·sor (lĕs′ôr, lĕ sôr′), *n.* one who grants a lease.

lest (lĕst), *conj.* **1.** for fear that. **2.** (after words expressing fear, danger, etc.) that.

let[1] (lĕt), *v.*, **let, letting. —v.t. 1.** to allow or permit. **2.** to grant the occupancy or use of (land, buildings, etc.) for rent or hire. **3.** to contract for performance. **4.** to cause or make. **5. let on, a.** to allow to be known. **b.** *Colloq.* to pretend. **—v.i. 6.** to be rented or leased. **7.** *Colloq.* to be dismissed or ended, as school. **8.** *Colloq.* to cease; stop (fol. by *up*).

let[2] (lĕt), *n.*, *v.*, **letted** or **let, letting. —n. 1.** hindrance or obstacle. **2.** *Tennis, etc.* an interference with the course of the ball on account of which the stroke or point must be played over again. **—v.t. 3.** to hinder.

let·down (lĕt′doun′), *n.* **1.** a decrease in some exertion of force or energy. **2.** disillusion or disappointment.

le·thal (lē′thəl), *adj.* of, pertaining to, or such as to cause death; deadly.

le·thar·gic (lĭ thär′jĭk), *adj.* **1.** drowsy; sluggish. **2.** producing lethargy. Also, **le·thar′gi·cal.** **—le·thar′gi·cal·ly**, *adv.*

leth·ar·gy (lĕth′ər jĭ), *n.*, *pl.* **-gies.** a state of drowsy dullness.

Le·the (lē′thĭ), *n.* **1.** *Gk. Myth.* a river in Hades, whose water caused forgetfulness of the past in those who drank of it. **2.** forgetfulness; oblivion.

Lett (lĕt), *n.* one of a people living on and near the eastern coast of the Baltic Sea, closely related to the Lithuanians.

let·ter (lĕt′ər), *n.* **1.** a communication in writing. **2.** one of the marks used in writing and printing to represent speech sounds. **3.** actual terms or wording, as distinct from general meaning or intent. **4.** (*pl.*) literature in general. **5.** (*pl.*) the profession of literature. **6. to the letter, a.** with close adherence to the actual wording or the literal meaning. **b.** to the fullest extent. **—v.t. 7.** to mark or write with letters. **—let′ter·er**, *n*.

let·tered (lĕt′ərd), *adj.* **1.** educated or learned. **2.** literary. **3.** marked with letters.

let·ter·head (lĕt′ər hĕd′), *n.* **1.** a printed heading on letter paper, esp. one giving the name and address of a business concern, etc. **2.** a sheet of paper with such a heading.

let·ter·ing (lĕt′ər ĭng), *n.* **1.** act or process of inscribing with or making letters. **2.** the letters themselves.

let·ter·per·fect (lĕt′ər pûr′fĭkt), *adj.* without the least error; perfectly.

let·ter·press (lĕt′ər prĕs′), *n.* matter printed from letters or type, rather than from engraved plates.

let·tuce (lĕt′ĭs), *n.* an important salad plant in many varieties, having large, succulent leaves which are much used for salad.

let·up (lĕt′ŭp′), *n.* *Colloq.* cessation; pause.

leu·co·cyte (lōō′kə sīt′), *n.* *Physiol.* one of the white or colorless corpuscles of the blood, concerned in the destruction of disease-producing microörganisms, etc.

leu·ke·mi·a (lōō kē′mĭ ə), *n.* *Pathol.* a serious disease, characterized by excessive production of white blood cells, which are usually found in greatly increased numbers in the blood.

Lev., Leviticus.

Le·vant (lĭ vănt′), *n.* **1.** lands bordering the E shore of the Mediterranean and the Aegean, esp. Syria, Lebanon, and Palestine. **2.** (*l.c.*) a superior grade of morocco. —**Le·van·tine** (lĭ văn′tĭn, lĕv′ən tĭn′, -tēn′), *adj., n.*

lev·ee[1] (lĕv′ĭ), *n. U.S.* an embankment for preventing the overflowing of a river.

lev·ee[2] (lĕv′ĭ, lĕ vē′), *n.* **1.** (in Great Britain) a public court assembly, held in the early afternoon, at which men only are received. **2.** a reception. **3.** a reception of visitors held on rising from bed, as formerly by a royal personage.

lev·el (lĕv′əl), *adj., n., v.,* **-eled, -eling** or (*esp. Brit.*) **-elled, -elling,** *adv.* —*adj.* **1.** having an even surface. **2.** horizontal. **3.** on an equality, as one thing with another. **4.** even, equable, or uniform. **5.** mentally well-balanced. **6. one's level best,** *Colloq.* one's utmost. —*n.* **7.** a device used for determining, or adjusting something to, a horizontal surface. **8.** level position or condition. **9.** a height (*of*). **10.** a position or plane, high or low. —*v.t.* **11.** to make (a surface) even. **12.** to raise or lower to a particular position. **13.** to knock down. **14.** to bring to an equality of status, etc. **15.** to aim at a mark, as a weapon, etc. —*v.i.* **16.** to bring things or persons to a common level. **17.** to aim a weapon, etc. **18.** to direct the mind, purpose, etc., at something. **19.** *Aeron.* to fly parallel to the ground, usually just before landing (fol. by *off*). —*adv.* **20.** in a level, direct, or even way or line. —**lev′el·er;** *esp. Brit.,* **lev′el·ler,** *n.* —**lev′el·ly,** *adv.* —**lev′el·ness,** *n.*

lev·el-head·ed (lĕv′əl hĕd′ĭd), *adj.* having common sense and sound judgment.

lev·er (lĕv′ər, lē′vər), *n.* **1.** a bar or rigid piece acted upon at different points by two forces which generally tend to rotate it in opposite directions about a fixed axis or support. —*v.t., v.i.* **2.** to move with or apply a lever.

lev·er·age (lĕv′ər ĭj, lē′vər ĭj), *n.* **1.** the action of a lever. **2.** the mechanical advantage or power gained by using a lever.

Le·vi (lē′vī), *n.* a son of Jacob and Leah, and ancestor of the Levites.

le·vi·a·than (lĭ vī′ə thən), *n.* **1.** a sea monster mentioned in the Old Testament. **2.** any huge thing, esp. a ship.

Levit., Leviticus.

lev·i·ta·tion (lĕv′ə tā′shən), *n.* (among spiritualists) the alleged phenomenon of bodies heavier than air being by spiritual means rendered buoyant in the atmosphere.

Le·vite (lē′vīt), *n.* **1.** one of the tribe of Levi. **2.** one of those who assisted the priests in the tabernacle and temple.

Le·vit·i·cal (lĭ vĭt′ə kəl), *adj.* of or pertaining to the Levites or the book of Leviticus.

Le·vit·i·cus (lĭ vĭt′ə kəs), *n.* the third book of the Old Testament, containing laws relating to the priests and Levites and to the forms of Jewish ceremonial observance.

lev·i·ty (lĕv′ə tĭ), *n., pl.* **-ties.** **1.** lack of proper seriousness or earnestness. **2.** an instance or exhibition of this. **3.** fickleness.

lev·u·lose (lĕv′yŏŏ lōs′), *n. Chem.* fruit sugar.

lev·y (lĕv′ĭ), *n., pl.* **levies,** *v.,* **levied, levying.** —*n.* **1.** a raising or collecting, as of money or troops, by authority or force. **2.** that which is raised. —*v.t.* **3.** to collect (taxes, contributions, troops, etc.). **4.** to impose as an assessment (*on*). **5.** to start or make (war, etc.).

lewd (lŏŏd), *adj.* **1.** inclined to, characterized by, or inciting to lust. **2.** obscene or indecent. —**lewd′ly,** *adv.* —**lewd′ness,** *n.*

Lew·is (lŏŏ′ĭs), *n.* **1.** John Llewellyn, born 1880, U.S. labor leader. **2.** Meriwether, 1774–1809, U.S. explorer. **3.** Sinclair, 1885–1951, U.S. novelist.

lew·is·ite (lŏŏ′ə sīt′), *n.* a chemical warfare agent characterized by its vesicant action.

Lew·is·ton (lŏŏ′ĭs tən), *n.* a city in SW Maine. 38,598.

lex (lĕks), *n., pl.* **leges** (lē′jēz). law.

lex·i·cog·ra·pher (lĕk′sə kŏg′rə fər), *n.* a writer or compiler of a dictionary.

lex·i·cog·ra·phy (lĕk′sə kŏg′rə fĭ), *n.* the writing or compiling of dictionaries. —**lex·i·co·graph·ic** (lĕk′sə kō grăf′ĭk), **lex′i·co·graph′i·cal,** *adj.* —**lex′i·co·graph′i·cal·ly,** *adv.*

lex·i·con (lĕk′sə kən), *n.* a wordbook or dictionary, esp. of Greek, Latin, or Hebrew.

Lex·ing·ton (lĕk′sĭng tən), *n.* **1.** a town in E Massachusetts, NW of Boston: the first battle of

the American Revolution was fought here, April 19, 1775. 13,187. **2.** a city in N Kentucky. 49,-304.

Ley·den jar (lī′dən), *Elect.* a device for storing electric charge, consisting essentially of a glass jar lined inside and outside, for about two thirds of its height, with tinfoil.

Ley·te (lā′tā), *n.* one of the Philippine Islands, in central part of group. 835,532 pop.; 3085 sq. mi.

Lha·sa (lä′sə, -sä), *n.* the capital of Tibet, in the SE part: sacred city of Lamaism. ab. 50,000 pop.

Li, *Chem.* lithium.

li·a·bil·i·ty (lī′ə bĭl′ə tĭ), *n., pl.* **-ties.** **1.** a debt (opposed to *asset*). **2.** something disadvantageous. **3.** state or fact of being liable.

li·a·ble (lī′ə bəl), *adj.* **1.** subject to something possible or likely, esp. something undesirable. **2.** under legal obligation; responsible or answerable.

li·ai·son (lē′ā zŏn′, lē′ə zŏn′, -zən; lĭ ā′zən), *n.* **1.** the contact maintained between units, groups, etc., in order to ensure concerted action. **2.** an illicit intimacy between a man and woman.

li·ar (lī′ər), *n.* one who lies, or tells lies.

Lib., Liberal.

lib., **1.** (L *liber*) book. **2.** library.

li·ba·tion (lī bā′shən), *n.* **1.** a pouring out of wine or other liquid in honor of a deity. **2.** the liquid poured out.

li·bel (lī′bəl), *n., v.,* **-beled, -beling,** (*esp. Brit.*) **-belled, -belling.** —*n.* **1.** *Law.* **a.** defamation by written or printed words, pictures, or in any form other than by spoken words or gestures. **b.** the crime of publishing it. **2.** anything defamatory. —*v.t.* **3.** to publish a malicious libel against. —**li′bel·er;** *esp. Brit.,* **li′bel·ler,** *n.*

li·bel·ous (lī′bəl əs), *adj.* containing, constituting, or involving a libel. Also, *esp. Brit.,* **li′bel·lous.** —**li′bel·ous·ly,** *adv.*

lib·er·al (lĭb′ər əl, lĭb′rəl), *adj.* **1.** favorable to progress or reform, as in political affairs. **2.** (*often cap.*) noting or pertaining to a political party advocating measures of progressive political reform. **3.** free from prejudice or bigotry; tolerant. **4.** giving freely or in ample measure. **5.** given freely or abundantly. **6.** not strict or rigorous. —*n.* **7.** a person of liberal principles or views. **8.** (*often cap.*) a member of a liberal party in politics, esp. of the Liberal Party in Great Britain. —**lib′er·al·ly,** *adv.* —**lib′er·al·ness,** *n.*

liberal arts, the course of instruction at a modern college granting an academic (as distinguished from a technical) degree.

lib·er·al·ism (lĭb′ər əl ĭz′əm, lĭb′rə-), *n.* **1.** liberal principles, as in politics. **2.** (*sometimes cap.*) the principles and practices of a liberal party in politics. —**lib′er·al·ist,** *n., adj.*

lib·er·al·i·ty (lĭb′ə răl′ə tĭ), *n., pl.* **-ties.** **1.** generosity; bounty. **2.** a liberal gift. **3.** breadth of mind. **4.** liberalism.

lib·er·al·ize (lĭb′ər ə līz′, lĭb′rə-), *v.t., v.i.,* **-ized, -izing.** to make or become liberal. —**lib′er·al·i·za′tion,** *n.*

lib·er·ate (lĭb′ə rāt′), *v.t.,* **-ated, -ating.** to set free; release. —**lib′er·a′tion,** *n.* —**lib′er·a′tor,** *n.*

Li·be·ri·a (lī bĭr′ĭ ə), *n.* a republic in W Africa: founded by freed American slaves, 1847. 2,500,-000 pop.; ab. 46,000 sq. mi. *Cap.:* Monrovia. —**Li·be′ri·an,** *adj., n.*

lib·er·tine (lĭb′ər tēn′), *n.* **1.** one free from restraint or control. **2.** a dissolute man. —*adj.* **3.** free from moral restraints; dissolute; licentious.

lib·er·tin·ism (lĭb′ər tēn ĭz′əm, -tĭn-), *n.* libertine practices or habits of life.

lib·er·ty (lĭb′ər tĭ), *n., pl.* **-ties.** **1.** freedom from arbitrary or despotic government. **2.** freedom from external rule; independence. **3.** freedom from control, interference, obligation, restriction, etc. **4.** freedom from captivity, confinement, or physical restraint. **5.** leave granted to a sailor to go ashore. **6.** the freedom of, or right of frequenting or using, a place, etc. **7.** unwarranted or impertinent freedom in action or speech, or a form or instance of it. **8. at liberty, a.** free from restraint. **b.** unoccupied. **c.** permitted.

Liberty Ship, a U.S. merchant ship built in large numbers during World War II, carrying about 10,000 gross tons.

li·bid·i·nous (lĭ bĭd′ə nəs), *adj.* full of lust; lustful; lewd. —**li·bid·i·nous·ly,** *adv.*

li·bi·do (lĭ bī′dō, -bē′dō), *n.* **1.** *Psychoanal.* all of the instinctual energies and desires which are derived from the *Id*. **2.** the innate impelling force in living beings.

Li·bra (lī/brə), *n.*, *gen.* **-brae** (-brē). **1.** *Astron.* the Balance, a zodiacal constellation. **2.** the seventh sign of the zodiac.

li·brar·i·an (lī brâr/ī ən), *n.* **1.** a person engaged in library service. **2.** an officer in charge of a library.

li·brar·y (lī/brĕr/ĭ, -brə rĭ, -brĭ), *n., pl.* **-braries.** **1.** a place set apart to contain books and other material for reading, study, or reference. **2.** a commercial establishment lending books for a fixed charge. **3.** a collection of manuscripts, publications, and other materials for reading, study, or reference.

li·bret·tist (lĭ brĕt/ĭst), *n.* the writer of a libretto.

li·bret·to (lĭ brĕt/ō), *n., pl.* **-tos, -ti** (-tē). **1.** the text of an opera or other extended musical composition. **2.** a book containing such a text.

Lib·y·a (lĭb/ĭ ə), *n.* a territory in N Africa between Tunisia and Egypt: annexed by Italy, 1912. 817,376 pop.; 679,400 sq. mi. *Cap.:* Tripoli. —**Lib/y·an,** *adj., n.*

li·cense (lī/səns), *n., v.*, **-censed, -censing.** —*n.* **1.** formal permission to do or not to do something. **2.** an official permit. **3.** freedom of action, speech, thought, etc., permitted or conceded. **4.** intentional deviation from rule, convention, or fact, as for the sake of literary or artistic effect. **5.** excessive or undue freedom or liberty. —*v.t.* **6.** to grant authoritative permission to. Also, **li/cence.**

li·cen·ti·ate (lī sĕn/shĭ ĭt, -āt/), *n.* **1.** one who has received a license, as from a university, to practice an art or profession. **2.** the holder of a certain university degree intermediate between that of bachelor and that of doctor.

li·cen·tious (lī sĕn/shəs), *adj.* **1.** libertine; lewd. **2.** lawless; immoral. —**li·cen/tious·ly,** *adv.* —**li·cen/tious·ness,** *n.*

li·chee (lē/chē/), *n.* litchi.

li·chen (lī/kən), *n.* any one of certain compound plants having a vegetative body growing in greenish, gray, yellow, brown, or blackish crustlike patches or bushlike forms on rocks, trees, etc. —**li/chen·ous,** *adj.*

lic·it (lĭs/ĭt), *adj.* permitted; lawful.

lick (lĭk), *v.t.* **1.** to pass the tongue over the surface of. **2.** to make by strokes of the tongue. **3.** *Colloq.* to beat, thrash, or whip. **4.** *Colloq.* to defeat. —*n.* **5.** a stroke of the tongue over something. **6.** a small quantity. **7.** a place to which wild animals resort to lick salt occurring naturally there. **8.** *Colloq.* a blow. **9.** *Colloq.* a brief stroke of activity or endeavor. —**lick/er,** *n.*

lick·spit·tle (lĭk/spĭt/əl), *n.* an abject toady.

lic·o·rice (lĭk/ə rĭs, lĭk/rĭsh), *n.* **1.** a leguminous plant of Europe and Asia, whose sweet-tasting dried root is used in medicine, confectionery, etc. **2.** a black candy made from this root.

lid (lĭd), *n.* **1.** a movable cover for the opening of a vessel, box, etc. **2.** an eyelid. **3.** *Slang.* a hat. —**lid/ded,** *adj.*

Li·do (lē/dō), *n.* a chain of sandy islands in NE Italy, on the Adriatic: fashionable beach resort.

lie¹ (lī), *n., v.*, **lied, lying.** —*n.* **1.** a false statement made with intent to deceive. **2. give the lie (to), a.** to charge with lying. **b.** to imply or show to be false. —*v.i.* **3.** to speak falsely with intent to deceive. —*v.t.* **4.** to bring, put, etc., by lying.

lie² (lī), *v.*, **lay, lain, lying,** *n.* —*v.i.* **1.** to be in a recumbent or prostrate position, as on a bed. **2.** to assume such a position. **3.** to be buried. **4.** to rest (on something). **5.** to be or remain in a specified position or state. **6.** to be or occur (where specified). **7. lie in,** to be confined in childbed. **8. lie to,** *Naut.* (of a ship) to lie comparatively stationary. —*n.* **9.** manner of lying.

Lie (lē), *n.* **Trygve Halvdan,** born 1896, Norwegian statesman: secretary general of United Nations since 1946.

Liech·ten·stein (lĭk/tən stīn/), *n.* a small principality in central Europe between Austria and Switzerland. 11,138 pop.; 65 sq. mi. *Cap.:* Vaduz.

lie·der·kranz (lē/dər kränts/), *n.* **1.** a smooth, strong-smelling cheese. **2.** (*cap.*) a trademark for this cheese. **3.** a German choral society.

lief (lēf), *adv.* **1.** gladly; willingly. —*adj. Archaic.* **2.** willing. **3.** dear.

liege (lēj), *n.* **1.** a lord entitled to allegiance and

service. **2.** a vassal or subject. —*adj.* **3.** entitled to, or owing, allegiance and service.

Li·ège (lĭ äzh/), *n.* a city in E Belgium, on the Meuse river. 157,880.

lien (lēn, lē/ən), *n.* a legal right to hold property or to have it sold or applied for payment of a claim.

li·er (lī/ər), *n.* one who lies (down, etc.).

lieu (lōō), *n.* place; stead.

Lieut., lieutenant.

lieu·ten·ant (lōō tĕn/ənt; *in Brit. use, except in the navy,* lĕf tĕn/ənt), *n.* **1.** *Mil.* a commissioned officer ranking next below a captain. **a. first lieutenant,** an officer ranking between a second lieutenant and a captain. **b. second lieutenant,** the commissioned officer of the lowest rank, ranking below a first lieutenant. **2.** *Nav.* a commissioned officer ranking next below a lieutenant commander. **a. lieutenant junior grade,** a commissioned officer ranking between an ensign and a lieutenant senior grade. **b. lieutenant senior grade,** an officer ranking between lieutenant junior grade and lieutenant commander. **3.** one who acts in place of his superior. —**lieu·ten/an·cy,** *n.*

lieutenant colonel, *Mil.* a commissioned officer ranking next below a colonel.

lieutenant commander, *Nav.* an officer next in rank below a commander.

lieutenant general, *Mil.* an officer ranking next above a major general.

lieutenant governor, *U.S.* a State officer next in rank to the governor.

life (līf), *n., pl.* **lives. 1.** the condition which distinguishes animals and plants from inorganic objects and dead organisms. The manifestations of life are: growth through metabolism, reproduction, and the power of adaptation to environment through changes originating internally. **2.** the existence, or the term of existence, of a person, machine, lease, etc. **3.** a living being. **4.** living things collectively. **5.** course or mode of existence. **6.** a biography. **7.** animation; liveliness. **8.** one who or that which enlivens. **9.** the living form or model as the subject in art. —**life/like,** *adj.*

life belt, a beltlike life preserver.

life·blood (līf/blŭd/), *n.* **1.** the blood necessary to life. **2.** the element that vivifies or animates anything.

life·boat (līf/bōt/), *n.* a small boat carried on a ship for use in the event of disaster.

life buoy, a buoyant device (in various forms) for throwing to persons in the water, to enable them to keep afloat until rescued.

life·guard (līf/gärd/), *n. U.S.* a man employed on a bathing beach to aid in case of accident to bathers.

life insurance, a contract insuring payment of a specific sum of money to a named beneficiary upon the death of the assured or which provides for payment to the policyholder should he survive a specified period of time. Also, **life assurance.**

life·less (līf/lĭs), *adj.* **1.** without life. **2.** destitute of living things. **3.** dead. **4.** without animation, liveliness, or spirit. —**life/less·ly,** *adv.* —**life/less·ness,** *n.*

life line, 1. a line fired across a vessel by which a hawser for a breeches buoy may be hauled aboard. **2.** a line or rope for saving life, as one attached to a lifeboat. **3.** a route over which supplies can be sent to an area otherwise isolated.

life·long (līf/lŏng/, -lông/), *adj.* lasting or continuing through life.

life preserver, a buoyant jacket, belt, or other like device for saving persons in the water from sinking and drowning.

lif·er (lī/fər), *n. Slang.* one sentenced to jail for life.

life·sav·er (līf/sā/vər), *n.* a person who rescues another from danger of death, esp. from drowning. —**life/sav/ing,** *adj., n.*

life-size (līf/sīz/), *adj.* of the size of life or the living original.

life·time (līf/tīm/), *n.* the time that one's life continues; one's term of life.

life·work (līf/wûrk/), *n.* the work, labor, or task of a lifetime.

lift (lĭft), *v.t.* **1.** to move or bring (something) upward; hoist. **2.** to raise or direct upward. **3.** to hold up or display on high. **4.** to raise in rank, estimation, etc. **5.** to send up audibly. **6.** *Colloq.* to steal; plagiarize. —*v.i.* **7.** to give to upward pressure. **8.** to pull or strain in the effort to raise something. **9.** to rise; rise and disperse, as clouds, fog, etc. —*n.* **10.** act of lifting, raising, or rising. **11.** extent of rise. **12.** lifting or raising force. **13.** the weight or load lifted. **14.** help. **15.** a ride in a vehicle, given to help along a traveler on foot. **16.** exaltation, as in feeling. **17.** a device or apparatus for lifting. **18.** *Chiefly Brit.* an elevator. **19.** one of the layers of leather forming the heel of a shoe. —**lift'a·ble,** *adj.* —**lift'er,** *n.*

lig·a·ment (lĭg'ə mənt), *n., pl.* **ligaments, ligamenta** (lĭg'ə mĕn'tə). *Anat.* a band of tissue, usually white and fibrous, serving to connect bones, hold organs in place, etc. —**lig·a·mentous** (lĭg'ə mĕn'təs), *adj.*

lig·a·ture (lĭg'ə chŏŏr', -chər), *n., v.,* -**tured, -turing.** —*n.* **1.** act of binding or tying up. **2.** a band, bandage, or cord. **3.** a tie or bond. **4.** *Print.* a character or type combining two or more letters, as *fi, ffl.* **5.** *Music.* a. a slur. b. a group of notes connected by a slur. **6.** *Surg.* a thread or wire for constriction of blood vessels, etc. —*v.t.* **7.** to bind with a ligature.

light[1] (lĭt), *n., adj., v.,* **lighted** or **lit, lighting.** —*n.* **1.** that which makes things visible or affords illumination. **2.** *Physics.* **a.** electromagnetic radiation to which the organs of sight react. **b.** a similar form of radiant energy which does not affect the retina, as ultraviolet rays. **3.** an illuminating agent or source, as the sun or a lamp. **4.** the radiance or illumination from a particular source. **5.** daylight or daytime. **6.** the aspect in which a thing appears or is regarded. **7.** a gleam or sparkle, as in the eyes. **8.** a means of igniting, as a match. **9.** state of being visible, exposed to view, or revealed to public notice. **10.** mental or spiritual enlightenment. **11.** a person who is a shining example. **12. see the light, a.** to come into existence. **b.** to be made public. **c.** to accept or understand an idea. —*adj.* **13.** having light or illumination, rather than dark. **14.** pale, whitish, or not deep or dark in color. —*v.t.* **15.** to set burning (a candle, lamp, pipe, etc.); kindle; ignite. **16.** to illuminate. **17.** to make bright as with light or color. **18.** to brighten (the face, etc.). —*v.i.* **19.** to take fire or become kindled. **20.** to become bright, as with light or color. **21.** to brighten with animation or joy.

light[2] (lĭt), *adj.* **1.** of little weight; not heavy. **2.** of low specific gravity. **3.** of less than the usual or standard weight. **4.** of small amount, force, intensity, etc. **5.** easy to endure, deal with, or perform. **6.** not profound, serious, or heavy. **7.** trivial. **8.** easily digested, as food. **9.** not heavy or strong, as wine, etc. **10.** spongy or well leavened, as bread. **11.** slender or delicate. **12.** buoyant. **13.** nimble or agile. **14.** free from sorrow or care. **15.** frivolous. **16.** dizzy; slightly delirious. **17.** *Mil.* lightly armed or equipped. **18.** adapted for small loads or swift movement. **19.** (of wind) having a velocity up to 7 mi. per hour. —*adv.* **20.** lightly.

light[3] (lĭt), *v.i.,* **lighted** or **lit, lighting. 1.** to get down or descend as from a horse. **2.** to come to rest; land. **3.** to happen (fol. by *on* or *upon*). **4.** to fall, as a stroke, choice, etc., on a place or person. **5.** *Slang.* to attack (fol. by *into*).

light·en[1] (lī'tən), *v.i.* **1.** to become less dark. **2.** to be bright. **3.** to illuminate. —**light'en·er,** *n.*

light·en[2] (lī'tən), *v.t.* **1.** to lessen the weight of (a load, etc.); reduce the load of (a ship, etc.). **2.** to mitigate. **3.** to cheer.

light·er[1] (lī'tər), *n.* one that lights.

light·er[2] (lī'tər), *n.* **1.** a vessel, commonly a flat-bottomed unpowered barge, used in lightening or unloading and loading ships, etc. —*v.t.* **2.** to convey in or as in a lighter.

light-foot·ed (lī'tfŏŏt'ĭd), *adj.* stepping lightly or nimbly. Also, *Poetic,* **light'-foot'.**

light-head·ed (lī'thĕd'ĭd), *adj.* **1.** having or showing a frivolous or volatile disposition. **2.** giddy, dizzy, or delirious.

light-heart·ed (lī'thär'tĭd), *adj.* carefree; cheerful; gay. —**light'-heart'ed·ly,** *adv.* —**light'-heart'ed·ness,** *n.*

light heavyweight, *Boxing.* a fighter whose weight is between 160 and 175 pounds.

light·house (lī'thous'), *n.* a tower or other structure displaying a light or lights for the guidance of mariners.

light·ing (lī'tĭng), *n.* **1.** act of igniting or illuminating. **2.** arrangement or method of lights. **3.** the way light falls upon a face, object, etc., esp. in a picture.

light·ly (lī'tlĭ), *adv.* **1.** with little weight, intensity, etc. **2.** to but a small degree. **3.** easily.

4. cheerfully. **5.** frivolously. **6.** without due consideration or reason. **7.** nimbly. **8.** indifferently.

light-mind·ed (lī'tmīn'dĭd), *adj.* characterized by levity; frivolous. —**light'-mind'ed·ly,** *adv.* —**light'-mind'ed·ness,** *n.*

light·ness[1] (lī'tnĭs), *n.* **1.** state of being light, illuminated, or whitish. **2.** thin or pale coloration.

light·ness[2] (lī'tnĭs), *n.* **1.** state or quality of being light in weight. **2.** light as to specific gravity. **3.** quality of being agile, nimble, or graceful. **4.** gayness; cheerfulness. **5.** levity in actions, thought, or speech.

light·ning (lī'tnĭng), *n.* a flashing of light, or a sudden illumination of the heavens, caused by the discharge of atmospheric electricity.

lightning bug, *U.S.* a firefly.

lightning rod, a rodlike conductor installed to divert atmospheric electricity away from a structure and protect the structure from lightning by providing a path to earth.

light-ship (lī'tshĭp'), *n.* a ship anchored in a specific location and displaying a light or lights for the guidance of mariners.

light·some (lī'tsəm), *adj.* **1.** airy; buoyant; nimble. **2.** cheerful; gay. **3.** frivolous.

light-weight (lī'twāt'), *adj.* **1.** light in weight. —*n.* **2.** one of less than average weight. **3.** *Colloq.* a person of little mental force or of slight importance. **4.** a boxer who weighs between 127 and 135 pounds.

light-year (lī'tyĭr'), *n.* *Astron.* the distance traversed by light in one year (about 5,880,000,-000,000 miles): used as a unit in measuring stellar distances.

lig·ne·ous (lĭg'nĭ əs), *adj.* of the nature of or resembling wood; woody.

lig·nite (lĭg'nīt), *n.* an imperfectly formed coal, usually dark-brown, and often having a distinct woody texture.

lig·num vi·tae (lĭg'nəm vī'tē), any of certain trees with a very heavy, hard wood.

lik·a·ble (lī'kə bəl), *adj.* such as to be liked; pleasing. Also, **like'a·ble.** —**lik'a·ble·ness,** *n.*

like[1] (līk), *adj.* (*Poetic.* **liker, likest**), *prep., adv., conj., n.* —*adj.* **1.** resembling. **2.** characteristic of. **3.** similar or analogous. **4.** disposed or inclined to. —*prep.* **5.** in like manner with. —*adv.* **6.** *Colloq.* probably. **7.** *Dial.* or *Slang.* as it were. —*conj.* **8.** *Colloq.* like as, just as, or as. **9.** *Colloq.* as if. —*n.* **10.** something of a similar nature (prec. by *the*). **11.** a like person or thing; counterpart, match, or equal.

like[2] (līk), *v.,* **liked, liking,** *n.* —*v.t.* **1.** to find agreeable to one's taste. **2.** to regard with favor or friendly feeling. —*v.i.* **3.** to feel inclined; wish. —*n.* **4.** (*usually pl.*) a favorable feeling; preference.

-like, suffixal use of **like**[1], *adj.,* as in *childlike.*

like·li·hood (līk'lĭ hŏŏd'), *n.* probability. Also, **like'li·ness.**

like·ly (līk'lĭ), *adj.,* -**lier, -liest,** *adv.* —*adj.* **1.** probably or apparently going (to do, be, etc.). **2.** seeming like truth, fact, or certainty; probable. **3.** apparently suitable. **4.** promising. —*adv.* **5.** probably.

like-mind·ed (līk'mīn'dĭd), *adj.* having a like opinion or purpose.

lik·en (lī'kən), *v.t.* to compare.

like·ness (līk'nĭs), *n.* **1.** a representation, picture, or image, esp. a portrait. **2.** the semblance or appearance of something. **3.** state or fact of being like.

like·wise (līk'wīz'), *adv.* **1.** moreover; also; too. **2.** in like manner.

lik·ing (lī'kĭng), *n.* **1.** preference, inclination, or favor. **2.** pleasure or taste.

li·lac (lī'lək), *n.* **1.** any of certain shrubs of the olive family, having large clusters of fragrant purple or white flowers. **2.** pale reddish purple.

lil·i·a·ceous (lĭl'ĭ ā'shəs), *adj.* **1.** of or like the lily. **2.** belonging to the lily family of plants.

Lille (lēl), *n.* a city in N France. 188,871.

Lil·li·put (lĭl'ĭ pŭt', -pət), *n.* an imaginary country inhabited by tiny people, described in Swift's *Gulliver's Travels.*

Lil·li·pu·tian (lĭl'ĭ pū'shən), *adj.* **1.** tiny. —*n.* **2.** an inhabitant of Lilliput. **3.** a tiny being.

lilt (lĭlt), *n.* **1.** rhythmic swing or cadence. **2.** a lilting song or tune. —*v.i., v.t.* **3.** to sing or play in a light, tripping, or rhythmic manner.

lil·y (lĭl'ĭ), *n., pl.* **lilies,** *adj.* —*n.* **1.** any plant of a genus comprising scaly-bulbed herbs with showy funnel-shaped or bell-shaped flowers of various colors. 2. any of various related or similar plants. —*adj.* 3. white as a lily. 4. delicately fair. 5. pure; unsullied. 6. pale. —**lil′y·like′**, *adj.*

lil·y-liv·ered (lĭl′ĭ lĭv′ərd), *adj.* cowardly.

lily of the valley, *pl.* lilies of the valley. a low-growing herb with a raceme of drooping, bell-shaped, fragrant white flowers.

Li·ma (lē′mə *for* 1; lī′mə *for* 2), *n.* 1. the capital of Peru, in the W part. 533,645. 2. a city in NW Ohio. 44,711.

Li·ma bean (lī′mə), 1. a kind of bean with a broad, flat edible seed. 2. the seed, much used for food.

limb (lĭm), *n.* 1. a part of an animal body distinct from the head and trunk, as a leg, arm, or wing. 2. a large or main branch of a tree. 3. a projecting part or member. —**limb′less**, *adj.*

lim·ber[1] (lĭm′bər), *adj.* 1. flexible; pliant. 2. supple; lithe. —*v.i.*, *v.t.* 3. to make limber. —**lim′ber·ly**, *adv.* —**lim′ber·ness**, *n.*

lim·ber[2] (lĭm′bər), *Mil.* —*n.* 1. the detachable forepart of the carriage of a field gun, consisting of two wheels, an axle, a pole, etc. —*v.t.*, *v.i.* 2. to attach the limber to (a gun), in preparation for moving away (usually fol. by *up*).

lim·bo (lĭm′bō), *n.* 1. (*often cap.*) a supposed region on the border of hell or heaven, the abode after death of unbaptized infants or of the righteous who died before the coming of Christ. 2. a place to which persons or things are relegated when cast aside, forgotten, past, or out-of-date.

Lim·burg·er (lĭm′bûrg′ər), *n.* a soft variety of cheese of strong odor and flavor.

lime[1] (līm), *n.*, *v.*, **limed, liming.** —*n.* 1. the oxide of calcium, CaO, a white caustic solid (**unslaked lime**) prepared by calcining limestone, etc.: used in making mortar and cement. When treated with water it produces calcium hydroxide, $Ca(OH)_2$, or **slaked lime.** —*v.t.* 2. to treat (soil, etc.) with lime or compounds of calcium.

lime[2] (līm), *n.* 1. the small, greenish-yellow, acid fruit of a tropical tree allied to the lemon. 2. the tree.

lime[3] (līm), *n.* linden.

lime·kiln (līm′kĭl′, -kĭln′), *n.* a kiln for making lime by calcining limestone.

lime·light (līm′līt′), *n.* 1. a strong light thrown upon the stage to illuminate particular persons or objects. 2. the glare of public observation or notoriety.

li·men (lī′mĕn), *n.*, *pl.* **limens, limina** (lĭm′ə nə). *Psychol.* threshold. —**lim·i·nal** (lĭm′ə nəl, lī′mə-), *adj.*

lim·er·ick (lĭm′ər ĭk), *n.* a humorous verse of five lines.

Lim·er·ick (lĭm′ər ĭk), *n.* a seaport in SW Republic of Ireland. 42,070.

lime·stone (līm′stōn′), *n.* a rock consisting wholly or chiefly of calcium carbonate.

lime·wa·ter (līm′wô′tər, -wŏt′ər), *n.* an aqueous solution of slaked lime, used medicinally and otherwise.

lim·ey (lī′mĭ), *n.*, *pl.* **-eys.** *Colloq.* a British sailor or ship.

lim·it (lĭm′ĭt), *n.* 1. the final or furthest bound as to extent, amount, etc. 2. a boundary, as of a country. —*v.t.* 3. to restrict by fixing limits. 4. to confine or keep within limits. —**lim′it·a·ble,** *adj.*

lim·i·ta·tion (lĭm′ə tā′shən), *n.* 1. a limit or bound; restriction. 2. act of limiting. 3. state of being limited. 4. *Law.* the assignment, as by statute, of a period of time within which an action must be brought.

lim·it·ed (lĭm′ĭt ĭd), *adj.* 1. confined within limits; restricted. 2. *Chiefly Brit.* restricted as to amount of liability. 3. (of trains, buses, etc.) restricted as to passengers, time occupied in transit, etc. —*n.* 4. *U.S.* a limited train, bus, etc.

lim·it·less (lĭm′ĭt lĭs), *adj.* boundless.

limn (lĭm), *v.t.* 1. to represent in drawing or painting. 2. *Archaic.* to portray in words.

Li·moges (lĭ mōzh′), *n.* 1. a city in central France. 107,874. 2. Also, **Limoges ware.** a type of porcelain manufactured at Limoges.

lim·ou·sine (lĭm′ə zēn′, lĭm′ə zēn′), *n.* an automobile having a permanently enclosed compartment for from three to five persons, the roof of which projects forward over the driver's seat in front.

limp[1] (lĭmp), *v.i.* 1. to walk with a labored,

jerky movement, as when lame. —*n.* 2. a lame movement or gait. —**limp′er**, *n.*

limp[2] (lĭmp), *adj.* lacking stiffness or firmness. —**limp′ly**, *adv.* —**limp′ness**, *n.*

lim·pet (lĭm′pĭt), *n.* *Zool.* any of various marine gastropods with a low conical shell open beneath, found adhering to rocks.

lim·pid (lĭm′pĭd), *adj.* 1. clear, transparent, or pellucid, as water, crystal, air, etc. 2. free from obscurity; lucid. —**lim·pid′i·ty, lim′pid·ness,** *n.* —**lim′pid·ly**, *adv.*

lim·y (lī′mĭ), *adj.*, **limier, limiest.** 1. of, containing, or like lime. 2. smeared with birdlime.

lin., 1. lineal. 2. linear.

lin·age (lī′nĭj), *n.* 1. alignment. 2. number of lines of written or printed matter covered.

linch·pin (lĭnch′pĭn′), *n.* a pin inserted through the end of an axletree to keep the wheel on.

Lin·coln (lĭng′kən), *n.* 1. **Abraham,** 1809–65, 16th president of the U.S., 1861–65. 2. the capital of Nebraska, in the SE part. 81,984.

Lind (lĭnd), *n.* **Jenny** (jĕn′ĭ), (*Mrs. Otto Goldschmidt*) 1820–87, Swedish soprano singer.

Lind·bergh (lĭnd′bûrg, lĭn′-), *n.* **Charles Augustus,** born 1902, U.S. aviator who made the first nonstop solo flight from New York to Paris in 1927.

lin·den (lĭn′dən), *n.* any of certain trees which have yellowish or cream-colored flowers and more or less heart-shaped leaves.

line[1] (līn), *n.*, *v.*, **lined, lining.** —*n.* 1. a long mark made with a pen, pencil, tool, etc. 2. something resembling a traced line. 3. a wrinkle on the face, etc. 4. a row or series. 5. a row of written or printed letters, words, etc. 6. a verse of poetry. 7. (*pl.*) the spoken words of a drama, etc., or of an actor's part. 8. a short written message. 9. a boundary; limit. 10. a course of action, procedure, thought, etc. 11. a route. 12. a continuous series of persons, esp. in family descent. 13. (*pl.*) outline or contour. 14. (*pl.*) plan. 15. a kind of occupation or business. 16. any transportation company or system. 17. *Elect.* a wire circuit connecting two or more pieces of electrical apparatus. 18. *Math.* a continuous extent of length, straight or curved, without breadth or thickness. 19. a supply of commercial goods of the same general class. 20. *Music.* one of the straight, horizontal, parallel strokes of the staff, or placed above or below it. 21. *Mil.* a. a trench or rampart. b. a series of military fieldworks. 22. (*pl.*) a distribution of troops, sentries, etc. 23. the line of arrangement of an army or of warships as drawn up ready for battle. 24. a thread, string, cord, rope, or the like. 25. *Football.* the players lined up even with the ball. —*v.i.* 26. to take a position in a line; range. —*v.t.* 27. to bring into a line, or into line with others. 28. to delineate. 29. to mark with a line or lines. 30. to arrange a line along. 31. to form a line along.

line[2] (līn), *v.t.*, **lined, lining.** 1. to cover or fit on the inner side with something. 2. to provide with a layer of material applied to the inner side.

lin·e·age[1] (lĭn′ĭ ĭj), *n.* 1. ancestry or extraction. 2. family or race.

lin·e·age[2] (lī′nĭj), *n.* linage.

lin·e·al (lĭn′ĭ əl), *adj.* 1. being in the direct line, as a descendant. 2. of or transmitted by lineal descent. 3. linear. —**lin′e·al·ly**, *adv.*

lin·e·a·ment (lĭn′ĭ ə mənt), *n.* a feature of a face, body, or figure with respect to its outline or contour.

lin·e·ar (lĭn′ĭ ər), *adj.* 1. extended in a line. 2. involving measurement in one dimension only. 3. of or pertaining to a line or lines.

line·man (līn′mən), *n.*, *pl.* **-men.** 1. one who sets up or keeps in repair telegraph, telephone, or other wires. 2. one who gives sights on line in surveying, etc. 3. *Football.* a player who plays on the forward line.

lin·en (lĭn′ən), *n.* 1. fabric woven from flax yarns. 2. clothes or other articles made of linen cloth or some substitute, as cotton.

lin·er[1] (lī′nər), *n.* 1. one of a commercial line of steamships or airplanes. 2. one who or that which traces by or marks with lines. 3. *Baseball.* a ball batted with much force nearly parallel to the ground.

lin·er[2] (lī′nər), *n.* 1. one who fits or provides linings. 2. something serving as a lining.

lines·man (līnz′mən), *n.*, *pl.* **-men.** 1. a lineman, as on a telegraph line. 2. (in certain games) an official employed to watch the lines which mark out the field, mark the distances gained and lost in play, etc.

line-up (līn′ŭp′), *n.* **1.** a particular order or arrangement. **2.** persons or things in a line. **3.** *Games.* the arrangement of the players. **4.** an organization of people, companies, etc., for some purpose. Also, **line′up′.**

ling (lĭng), *n., pl.* **ling, lings.** an elongated marine food fish of Greenland and northern Europe.

lin·ger (lĭng′gər), *v.i.* **1.** to remain or stay on in a place longer than is usual or expected. **2.** to continue or persist. **3.** to delay; dawdle. —**lin′-ger·er,** *n.*

lin·ge·rie (län′zhə rā′, lăn′zhə rē′, -jə-), *n.* underwear or other garments of silk, rayon, etc., worn by women.

lin·go (lĭng′gō), *n., pl.* **-goes.** (in contemptuous or humorous use) **1.** language. **2.** peculiar or unintelligible language. **3.** jargon.

lin·gua fran·ca (lĭng′gwə frăng′kə), a jargon which is widely used as an international auxiliary language.

lin·gual (lĭng′gwəl), *adj.* of or pertaining to the tongue or some tonguelike part.

lin·guist (lĭng′gwĭst), *n.* **1.** a person who is skilled in foreign languages. **2.** a person who investigates linguistic phenomena.

lin·guis·tic (lĭng gwĭs′tĭk), *adj.* **1.** of or belonging to language. **2.** of or pertaining to linguistics. —**lin·guis′ti·cal·ly,** *adv.*

lin·guis·tics (lĭng gwĭs′tĭks), *n.* the science of language, including among its fields phonetics, phonemics, morphology, and syntax.

lin·i·ment (lĭn′ə mənt), *n.* a liquid preparation, usually oily, for rubbing on or applying to the skin, as for sprains, bruises, etc.

lin·ing (lī′nĭng), *n.* that with which something is lined; a layer of material on the inner side of something.

link (lĭngk), *n.* **1.** one of the rings of which a chain is composed. **2.** a bond or tie. **3.** a ring, loop, or the like. **4.** *Surveying.* a measuring unit, equal to 7.92 in. —*v.t., v.i.* **5.** to join by a link or links; unite.

link·age (lĭngk′ĭj), *n.* **1.** act of linking. **2.** state or manner of being linked. **3.** a system of links.

links (lĭngks), *n.pl.* a golf course.

Link trainer (lĭngk), *Aeron.* a ground training device used in instrument-flight training.

Lin·nae·us (lĭ nē′əs), *n.* **Carolus,** 1707–78, Swedish botanist.

lin·net (lĭn′ĭt), *n.* a small Old World fringilline songbird.

li·no·le·um (lĭ nō′lĭ əm), *n.* a floor covering formed by coating burlap or canvas with linseed oil, powdered cork, and resin.

lin·o·type (lī′nə tīp′), *n.* **1.** a kind of typesetting machine, with keyboard, which casts solid lines of type. **2.** (*cap.*) a trademark for this machine.

lin·seed (lĭn′sēd′), *n.* the seed of flax.

linseed oil, a drying oil obtained by pressing linseed, used in making paints, etc.

lin·sey-wool·sey (lĭn′zĭ wŏŏl′zĭ), *n., pl.* **-seys.** a coarse fabric woven from linen warp and coarse wool filling.

lint (lĭnt), *n.* **1.** a soft material for dressing wounds, etc., procured by scraping or otherwise treating linen cloth. **2.** bits of thread. —**lint′y,** *adj.*

lin·tel (lĭn′təl), *n.* a horizontal supporting member above a door, window, etc.

lint·er (lĭn′tər), *n.* **1.** (*pl.*) short cotton fibers which stick to seeds after a first ginning. **2.** a machine which removes lint from seed.

li·on (lī′ən), *n.* **1.** a large, grayish-tan animal of the cat family, native in Africa and southern Asia. **2.** this animal as the national emblem of Great Britain. **3.** a man of great strength, courage, etc. **4.** a person of note or celebrity who is much sought after. **5.** (*cap.*) *Astron.* Leo. —**li′on·ess,** *n. fem.*

li·on-heart·ed (lī′ən här′tĭd), *adj.* courageous; brave.

li·on·ize (lī′ə nīz′), *v.t.,* **-ized, -izing.** to treat (a person) as a celebrity.

lip (lĭp), *n., adj., v.,* **lipped, lipping.** —*n.* **1.** either of the two fleshy parts or folds forming the margins of the mouth. **2.** a liplike part or structure. **3.** a projecting edge, as of a pitcher. **4.** *Slang.* impudent talk. —*adj.* **5.** of or pertaining to the lips or a lip. **6.** superficial or insincere. —*v.t.* **7.** to touch with the lips. **8.** to utter. —*v.i.*

9. to use the lips in playing a musical wind instrument.

lip reading, the reading, as by a deaf person, of the movements of another's lips when forming words. —**lip reader.**

lip service, insincere profession of devotion or good will.

lip·stick (lĭp′stĭk′), *n.* a stick or elongated piece of a cosmetic preparation for heightening the color of the lips.

liq., **1.** liquid. **2.** liquor.

liq·ue·fac·tion (lĭk′wə făk′shən), *n.* the process of liquefying or making liquid.

liq·ue·fy (lĭk′wə fī′), *v.t., v.i.,* **-fied, -fying.** to make or become liquid. —**liq′ue·fi′a·ble,** *adj.* —**liq′ue·fi′er,** *n.*

li·queur (lĭ kûr′), *n.* any of a class of alcoholic liquors, usually strong, sweet, and highly flavored, as chartreuse, curaçao, etc.

liq·uid (lĭk′wĭd), *adj.* **1.** composed of molecules which move freely among themselves but do not tend to separate like those of gases; neither gaseous nor solid. **2.** of or pertaining to liquids. **3.** flowing or melted. **4.** clear, transparent, or bright. **5.** in cash or easily convertible into cash. —*n.* **6.** a liquid substance. **7.** *Phonet.* either *r* or *l*. —**liq′uid·ly,** *adv.* —**liq′uid·ness, li·quid′i·ty,** *n.*

liq·ui·date (lĭk′wə dāt′), *v.,* **-dated, -dating.** —*v.t.* **1.** to settle or pay (a debt, etc.). **2.** to reduce (accounts) to order. **3.** to convert into cash. **4.** *Slang.* to murder (a person). **5.** to abolish. —*v.i.* **6.** to liquidate debts or accounts. —**liq′ui·da′tion,** *n.*

liquid measure, the system of units of capacity ordinarily used in measuring liquid commodities, such as milk, oil, etc.

liq·uor (lĭk′ər), *n.* **1.** a distilled or spirituous beverage, as brandy or whiskey. **2.** any liquid substance. —*v.t., v.i.* **3.** *Slang.* to furnish with or imbibe liquor.

li·ra (lē′rä), *n., pl.* **lire** (lē′rĕ), **liras.** the monetary unit and a coin of Italy, equal to about .44 U.S. cents.

Lis·bon (lĭz′bən), *n.* a seaport in and the capital of Portugal. 694,389.

lisle (līl), *n.* **1.** knit goods, as hose, made of lisle thread. —*adj.* **2.** made of lisle thread.

lisle thread (līl), a smooth, hard-twisted linen or cotton thread.

lisp (lĭsp), *n.* **1.** a speech defect consisting in pronouncing *s* and *z* like or nearly like the *th* sounds of *thin* and *this,* respectively. **2.** act, habit, or sound of lisping. —*v.t., v.i.* **3.** to pronounce or speak with a lisp. —**lisp′er,** *n.* —**lisp′ing·ly,** *adv.*

lis·some (lĭs′əm), *adj.* **1.** lithe, esp. of body; supple. **2.** agile or active. Also, **lis′som.** —**lis′-some·ness,** *n.*

list¹ (lĭst), *n.* **1.** a record consisting of a series of names, words, or the like. —*v.t., v.i.* **2.** to make a list (of). **3.** to enter in a list with others. **4.** to enlist.

list² (lĭst), *n.* **1.** a border or bordering strip of anything, esp. of cloth. **2.** selvage.

list³ (lĭst), *n.* **1.** a leaning to one side, as of a ship. —*v.i., v.t.* **2.** to incline to one side.

list⁴ (lĭst), *Archaic.* —*v.t.* **1.** to please. **2.** to like or desire. —*v.i.* **3.** to like; wish.

list⁵ (lĭst), *v.i., v.t. Archaic or Poetic.* to listen (to).

lis·ten (lĭs′ən), *v.t., v.i.* **1.** to give attention with the ear. **2.** to give heed; yield to advice. —**lis′-ten·er,** *n.*

Lis·ter (lĭs′tər), *n.* **Joseph, 1st Baron,** 1827–1912, British surgeon: the first to use antiseptics in surgery.

list·less (lĭst′lĭs), *adj.* **1.** feeling no inclination toward or interest in anything. **2.** characterized by or indicating such feeling. —**list′less·ly,** *adv.* —**list′less·ness,** *n.*

lists (lĭsts), *n.pl.* the barriers enclosing the field of combat at a tournament.

Liszt (lĭst), *n.* **Franz,** 1811–86, Hungarian composer and pianist.

lit., **1.** liter. **2.** literal. **3.** literature.

lit·a·ny (lĭt′ə nĭ), *n., pl.* **-nies.** a form of prayer consisting of a series of invocations or supplications with responses which are the same for a number in succession.

li·tchi (lē′chē′), *n., pl.* **-tchis.** **1.** the fruit of a certain kind of Chinese tree, consisting of a thin, brittle shell, enclosing a sweet, jellylike pulp and a single seed. **2.** the tree.

litchi nut, the brownish, dried litchi fruit.

li·ter (lē′tər), *n. Metric System.* a unit of capacity equal to the volume of one kilogram of water at its maximum density, equivalent to 1.0567 U.S. liquid quarts. Also, *esp. Brit.,* **litre.**

lit·er·a·cy (lĭt′ər ə sĭ), *n.* state of being literate; possession of education.

lit·er·al (lĭt′ər əl), *adj.* **1.** following the exact words of the original, as a translation. **2.** (of persons) matter-of-fact; prosaic. **3.** not figurative or metaphorical. **4.** true to fact; not exaggerated. **5.** of or pertaining to the letters of the alphabet. —**lit′er·al·ly,** *adv.* —**lit′er·al·ness,** *n.*

lit·er·ar·y (lĭt′ə rĕr′ĭ), *adj.* **1.** pertaining to or of the nature of books and writings. **2.** versed in or acquainted with literature. **3.** engaged in literature as a profession.

lit·er·ate (lĭt′ər ĭt), *adj.* **1.** able to read and write. **2.** educated. —*n.* **3.** one who can read and write. **4.** a learned person.

lit·e·ra·ti (lĭt′ə rä′tī, -rä′tĭ), *n.pl.* men of learning; scholarly or literary people.

lit·er·a·ture (lĭt′ər ə chər, -chŏŏr′, lĭt′rə-), *n.* **1.** writings in which expression and form, in connection with ideas of permanent and universal interest, are characteristic features, as poetry, essays, etc. **2.** the entire body of writings of a specific language, period, people, subject, etc. **3.** *Colloq.* printed matter of any kind, as circulars.

lithe (līth), *adj.* bending readily; pliant; limber; supple. Also, **lithe·some** (līth′səm). —**lithe′ly,** *adv.* —**lithe′ness,** *n.*

lith·i·um (lĭth′ĭ əm), *n. Chem.* a soft, silver-white metallic element (the lightest of all metals). *Symbol:* Li; *at. wt.:* 6.94; *at. no.:* 3; *sp. gr.:* 0.53 at 20°C.

lith·o·graph (lĭth′ə grăf′, -gräf′), *n.* **1.** a print produced by lithography. —*v.t.* **2.** to produce or copy by lithography.

li·thog·ra·phy (lĭ thŏg′rə fĭ), *n.* **1.** the art or process of producing a picture, writing, or the like, on a flat, specially prepared stone, with some greasy or oily substance, and of taking ink impressions from this as in ordinary printing. **2.** a similar process in which a substance other than stone, as aluminum or zinc, is used. —**li·thog′ra·pher,** *n.* —**lith·o·graph·ic** (lĭth′ə grăf′ĭk), *adj.*

lith·o·sphere (lĭth′ə sfĭr′), *n.* the crust of the earth.

Lith·u·a·ni·a (lĭth′ŏŏ ā′nĭ ə), *n.* a constituent republic of the Soviet Union, in the W part, on the Baltic. 2,550,000 pop.; 24,100 sq. mi. *Cap.:* Vilna. —**Lith·u·a′ni·an,** *adj., n.*

lit·i·ga·ble (lĭt′ə gə bəl), *adj.* subject to litigation.

lit·i·gant (lĭt′ə gənt), *n.* **1.** one engaged in a lawsuit. —*adj.* **2.** involved in a lawsuit.

lit·i·gate (lĭt′ə gāt′), *v.,* -**gated,** -**gating.** —*v.t.* **1.** to contest at law. —*v.i.* **2.** to carry on a lawsuit. —**lit′i·ga′tor,** *n.*

lit·i·ga·tion (lĭt′ə gā′shən), *n.* **1.** the process of litigating. **2.** a lawsuit.

li·ti·gious (lĭ tĭj′əs), *adj.* **1.** of or pertaining to litigation. **2.** overly inclined to litigate.

lit·mus (lĭt′məs), *n.* a blue coloring matter obtained from certain lichens. In alkaline solution litmus turns blue, in acid solution red; hence it is widely used as an indicator, esp. in the form of strips of paper impregnated with a solution of the coloring matter (**litmus paper**).

li·tre (lē′tər), *n. Chiefly Brit.* liter.

lit·ter (lĭt′ər), *n.* **1.** things scattered about. **2.** disorder or untidiness. **3.** a number of young brought forth at one birth. **4.** a kind of stretcher, as for carrying a sick person. **5.** a vehicle carried by men or animals, consisting of a couch suspended between shafts. **6.** straw, hay, etc., used as bedding for animals. —*v.t., v.i.* **7.** to strew (a place) with scattered objects. **8.** to scatter (objects) in disorder. **9.** to give birth to (young).

lit·tle (lĭt′əl), *adj.,* **less** or **lesser, least;** or **littler, littlest;** *adv.,* **less, least;** *n.* —*adj.* **1.** small in size or amount. **2.** short; brief. **3.** being such on a small scale. **4.** small in force; weak. **5.** small in consideration, consequence, etc. **6.** mean, narrow, or illiberal. —*adv.* **7.** not at all (before a verb). **8.** not much. —*n.* **9.** a small amount, quantity, or degree. **10.** a short distance. **11.** a short time. —**lit′tle·ness,** *n.*

Little Rock, the capital of Arkansas, in the central part. 88,039.

lit·to·ral (lĭt′ə rəl), *adj.* **1.** pertaining to the shore of a lake, sea, or ocean. —*n.* **2.** a littoral region.

li·tur·gi·cal (lĭ tûr′jə kəl), *adj.* of or pertaining

---

to public worship. Also, **li·tur′gic.** —**li·tur′gi·cal·ly,** *adv.*

lit·ur·gy (lĭt′ər jĭ), *n., pl.* -**gies.** **1.** a form of public worship; ritual. **2.** a collection of prescribed forms for public worship.

Lit·vi·nov (lĭt vē′nŏf), *n.* **Maksim Maksimovich,** 1876–1951, Soviet statesman.

liv·a·ble (lĭv′ə bəl), *adj.* **1.** suitable for living in; habitable. **2.** companionable. **3.** endurable. Also, **live′a·ble.**

live[1] (lĭv), *v.,* **lived** (lĭvd), **living.** —*v.i.* **1.** to have life; be alive. **2.** to continue in existence, operation, memory, etc. **3.** to rely for maintenance. **4.** to feed or subsist. **5.** to dwell or reside. **6.** to pass life (as specified). —*v.t.* **7.** to pass (life).

live[2] (līv), *adj.* **1.** living; alive. **2.** of or pertaining to life or living beings. **3.** full of life, energy, or activity. **4.** *Colloq.* alert; up-to-date. **5.** *Chiefly U.S. Colloq.* of present interest, as a question or issue. **6.** burning or glowing, as a coal. **7.** vivid or bright, as color. **8.** loaded or unexploded. **9.** carrying an electric current.

live·li·hood (līv′lĭ hŏŏd′), *n.* means of maintaining life; maintenance.

live·long (lĭv′lông′, -lŏng′), *adj.* entire.

live·ly (līv′lĭ), *adj.,* -**lier,** -**liest,** *adv.* —*adj.* **1.** active, vigorous, or brisk. **2.** sprited; sprightly. **3.** eventful; exciting. **4.** strong, keen, or distinct. **5.** vivid or bright. —*adv.* **6.** with activity, vigor, or animation. —**live′li·ly,** *adv.* —**live′li·ness,** *n.*

liv·en (lī′vən), *v.t.* **1.** to rouse; cheer. —*v.i.* **2.** to become livelier; brighten. —**liv′en·er,** *n.*

liv·er[1] (lĭv′ər), *n.* **1.** (in man) a large, reddish-brown glandular organ in the abdominal cavity, secreting bile and performing various metabolic functions. **2.** a similar organ in other animals.

liv·er[2] (lĭv′ər), *n.* **1.** one who lives. **2.** one who leads a life (as specified).

liv·er·ied (lĭv′ər ĭd, lĭv′rĭd), *adj.* clad in livery, as servants.

Liv·er·pool (lĭv′ər pōōl′), *n.* a seaport in W England. 739,000.

liv·er·wort (lĭv′ər wûrt′), *n.* any of a class of mosslike plants which grow mostly on damp ground, in water, or on tree trunks.

liv·er·wurst (lĭv′ər wûrst′, -wōōrst′), *n.* a sausage made mainly of liver.

liv·er·y (lĭv′ə rĭ, lĭv′rĭ), *n., pl.* -**eries.** **1.** a kind of uniform worn by servants, now only menservants, of a person or household. **2.** a distinctive dress worn by an official, a member of a guild, etc. **3.** outward appearance. **4.** the keep, or feeding, stabling, etc., of horses for pay. **5.** *U.S.* a livery stable.

liv·er·y·man (lĭv′ə rĭ mən, lĭv′rĭ-), *n., pl.* -**men.** a keeper of or an employee in a livery stable.

livery stable, a stable where horses and vehicles are cared for or let out for pay.

live·stock (līv′stŏk′), *n.* the horses, cattle, sheep, and other useful animals kept or raised on a farm or ranch.

live wire (līv), *Slang.* an energetic, alert person.

liv·id (lĭv′ĭd), *adj.* **1.** having the discolored bluish appearance due to a bruise, etc. **2.** dark grayish-blue. —**liv′id·ness,** *n.*

liv·ing (lĭv′ĭng), *adj.* **1.** that lives; alive. **2.** in actual existence or use. **3.** active; strong. **4.** burning or glowing. **5.** of or pertaining to living beings. **6.** pertaining to or sufficient for living. —*n.* **7.** act or condition of one that lives. **8.** manner or course of life. **9.** livelihood.

Liv·ing·stone (lĭv′ĭng stən), *n.* **David,** 1813–73, Scottish missionary and explorer in Africa.

living wage, a wage on which it is possible for a wage earner to live according to minimum customary standards.

Liv·y (lĭv′ĭ), *n.* (*Titus Livius*) 59 B.C.–A.D. 17, Roman historian.

liz·ard (lĭz′ərd), *n.* any of certain reptiles usually having long scaly bodies, four legs, and a long tail.

Common lizard
(Total length 5 or 6 in.)

ll., lines.

lla·ma (lä′mə), *n.* any of certain woolly-haired South American ruminants used as beasts of burden.

lla·no (lä/nō), *n.*, *pl.* **-nos.** (in Spanish America) an extensive grassy plain with few trees.

LL.D., (L *Legum Doctor*) Doctor of Laws.

Lloyd George (loid jôrj/), **David,** 1863–1945, British statesman: prime minister, 1916–22.

lo (lō), *interj.* look! see! behold!

load (lōd), *n.* **1.** that which is laid on or placed in anything for conveyance. **2.** the quantity that can be or usually is carried. **3.** anything sustained or supported. **4.** something that oppresses. **5.** the charge of a firearm. **6.** (*pl.*) *Colloq.* a great number. **7.** *Elect.* the power delivered by a generator, motor, power station, or transformer. —*v.t.* **8.** to put a load on or in. **9.** to supply abundantly or excessively with something. **10.** to burden; oppress. **11.** to take on as a load. **12.** to charge (a firearm). —*v.i.* **13.** to put on or take on a load. **14.** to load a firearm. **15.** to become loaded. —**load/er,** *n.*

load·star (lōd/stär/), *n.* lodestar.

load·stone (lōd/stōn/), *n.* **1.** a variety of magnetite which possesses magnetic polarity and attracts iron. **2.** something that attracts.

loaf[1] (lōf), *n.*, *pl.* **loaves** (lōvz). **1.** a portion of bread or cake baked in a mass of definite form. **2.** a shaped mass of sugar, chopped meat, etc.

loaf[2] (lōf), *v.i.* **1.** to lounge or saunter lazily and idly. **2.** to idle away time. —*v.t.* **3.** to idle (*away*). —**loaf/er,** *n.*

loaf·er (lōf/ər), *n.* a moccasinlike shoe.

loam (lōm), *n.* a loose soil composed of clay and sand, esp. a kind containing organic matter and of great fertility. —**loam/y,** *adj.*

loan (lōn), *n.* **1.** act of lending; a grant of the use of something temporarily. **2.** something lent. —*v.t.*, *v.i.* **3.** to lend. —**loan/er,** *n.*

loath (lōth), *adj.* reluctant, averse, or unwilling. —**loath/ly,** *adv.*

loathe (lōth), *v.t.* to feel hatred, disgust, or intense aversion for. —**loath/er,** *n.*

loath·ing (lō/thĭng), *n.* strong dislike mingled with disgust. —**loath/ing·ly,** *adv.*

loath·some (lōth/səm), *adj.* such as to excite loathing; hateful; disgusting. —**loath/some·ly,** *adv.* —**loath/some·ness,** *n.*

lob (lŏb), *n.*, *v.*, **lobbed, lobbing.** *Tennis.* —*n.* **1.** a ball struck high to the back of the opponent's court. —*v.t.*, *v.i.* **2.** to strike (a ball) high into the air to the back of the opponent's court.

lo·bar (lō/bər), *adj.* of or pertaining to a lobe, as of the lungs.

lo·bate (lō/bāt), *adj.* **1.** having a lobe or lobes; lobed. **2.** having the form of a lobe.

lob·by (lŏb/ĭ), *n.*, *pl.* **-bies,** *v.,* **-bied, -bying.** —*n.* **1.** a corridor, vestibule, or entrance hall, as in a public building. **2.** *Chiefly U.S.* the persons who frequent a legislative lobby or chamber, esp. to influence the members. —*v.i.*, *v.t.* **3.** to solicit the votes of (members) of a legislative body in the lobby or elsewhere. —**lob/by·ist,** *n.*

lobe (lōb), *n.* **1.** a roundish projection or division, as of an organ, a leaf, etc. **2.** *Anat.* the soft pendulous lower part of the external ear. —**lobed,** *adj.*

lo·bel·ia (lō bēl/yə), *n.* any of certain herbaceous plants with blue, red, yellow, or white flowers.

lob·lol·ly (lŏb/lŏl/ĭ), *n.*, *pl.* **-lies.** a certain variety of pine of the southern U.S.

lo·bo (lō/bō), *n.*, *pl.* **-bos.** a large gray wolf of the western U.S.

lob·ster (lŏb/stər), *n.* **1.** any of certain large, edible, marine, decapod crustaceans. **2.** any of various similar crustaceans, as certain crawfishes.

lo·cal (lō/kəl), *adj.* **1.** pertaining to, characteristic of, or restricted to a particular place or area. **2.** pertaining to a town or a small district rather than the entire state or country. **3.** stopping at all stations. —*n.* **4.** a local train. **5.** a newspaper item of local interest. **6.** a local branch of a trade union, fraternity, etc. —**lo/cal·ly,** *adv.*

local color, distinctive characteristics or peculiarities of a place or period, esp. as represented in literature, drama, etc.

lo·cale (lō kǎl/, -käl/), *n.* a place or locality, esp. with reference to events or circumstances connected with it.

lo·cal·ism (lō/kə lǐz/əm), *n.* a manner of speaking, a custom, etc., peculiar to one locality.

lo·cal·i·ty (lō kǎl/ə tǐ), *n.*, *pl.* **-ties. 1.** a place, spot, or district. **2.** the place in which a thing is or occurs.

lo·cal·ize (lō/kə līz/), *v.t.*, **-ized, -izing.** to fix in, or assign or restrict to, a particular place. —**lo/cal·i·za/tion,** *n.*

lo·cate (lō/kāt, lō kāt/), *v.,* **-cated, -cating.** —*v.t.* **1.** to discover the place of. **2.** *Chiefly U.S.* to place; settle. **3.** to refer (something), as by opinion, to a particular place. —*v.i.* **4.** *U.S.* to establish oneself in a place; settle.

lo·ca·tion (lō kā/shən), *n.* **1.** a place of settlement or residence. **2.** a place or situation occupied. **3.** *Motion Pictures.* a place, outside of the studio, affording suitable environment for photographing. **4.** act of locating. **5.** state of being located.

loc·a·tive (lŏk/ə tǐv), *Gram.* —*adj.* **1.** denoting a case having as chief function indication of place in or at which. —*n.* **2.** the locative case.

loc. cit., loco citato.

loch (lŏk, lŏкн), *n.* *Scot.* **1.** a lake. **2.** an arm of the sea, esp. when narrow.

lock[1] (lŏk), *n.* **1.** a device for securing a door, gate, lid, drawer, or the like, in position when closed, operated by a key, dial, etc. **2.** the mechanism in a firearm by means of which it can be kept from operating. **3.** an enclosed portion of a canal, river, etc., with gates at each end, for raising or lowering vessels from one level to another. **4.** any of various holds in wrestling. —*v.t.* **5.** to fasten or secure (a door, etc.) by the operation of a lock. **6.** to shut in or out of a place fastened by a lock or locks. **7.** to make fast or immovable by a lock. **8.** to fasten or fix firmly, as by engaging parts. **9.** to join by interlinking or intertwining. —*v.i.* **10.** to become locked.

lock[2] (lŏk), *n.* **1.** a tress of hair. **2.** (*pl.*) the hair of the head. **3.** a portion of wool, flax, etc.

Locke (lŏk), *n.* **John,** 1632–1704, British philosopher.

lock·er (lŏk/ər), *n.* a chest, drawer, closet, or the like, that may be locked.

lock·et (lŏk/ĭt), *n.* a small case for a miniature portrait, a lock of hair, or other keepsake, usually worn on a necklace.

lock·jaw (lŏk/jô/), *n.* *Pathol.* tetanus in which the jaws become firmly locked together.

lock·out (lŏk/out/), *n.* the closing of a business by an employer because the employees refuse to accept his terms.

lock·smith (lŏk/smĭth/), *n.* one who makes or mends locks.

lock·up (lŏk/ŭp/), *n.* a jail.

lo·co (lō/kō), *n.*, *pl.* **-cos,** *v.,* **-coed, -coing,** *adj.* *U.S.* —*n.* **1.** locoweed. **2.** loco disease. —*v.t.* **3.** to poison with locoweed. **4.** to make crazy. —*adj.* **5.** *Slang.* insane; crazy.

lo·co ci·ta·to (lō/kō sǐ tā/tō), *Latin.* in the place, or passage, already mentioned.

loco disease, a disease affecting the brain of animals, caused by eating locoweed.

lo·co·mo·tion (lō/kə mō/shən), *n.* act or power of moving from place to place.

lo·co·mo·tive (lō/kə mō/tǐv), *n.* **1.** a self-propelled vehicle running on a railroad track, designed to pull railroad cars. —*adj.* **2.** moving by means of its own powers. **3.** serving to produce such movement. **4.** of, pertaining to, or having the power of locomotion.

lo·co·mo·tor (lō/kə mō/tər), *adj.* of or pertaining to locomotion.

locomotor a·tax·i·a (ə tǎk/sǐ ə), *Pathol.* a degenerative disease of the spinal cord, marked by loss of control over the muscular movements, mainly in walking.

lo·co·weed (lō/kō wēd/), *n.* any of certain plants of the bean family, of the southwestern U.S., producing loco disease in sheep, horses, etc.

lo·cus (lō/kəs), *n.*, *pl.* **loci** (lō/sī). **1.** a place; locality. **2.** *Math.* a curve or other figure considered as generated by a point, line, or surface, which moves or is placed according to a definite law.

lo·cust (lō/kəst), *n.* **1.** any of certain grasshoppers with short antennae which swarm in immense numbers and strip the vegetation from large areas. **2.** any of various cicadas. **3.** a thorny-branched, white-flowered American tree of the bean family.

lo·cu·tion (lō kū/shən), *n.* **1.** a particular phrase or expression. **2.** style of speech or verbal expression.

lode (lōd), *n.* a veinlike deposit, usually bearing metals.

lode·star (lōd′stär′), *n.* **1.** a star that shows the way. **2.** Polaris. **3.** a guide or center of attention.

lode·stone (lōd′stōn′), *n.* loadstone.

lodge (lŏj), *n.*, *v.*, **lodged, lodging.** —*n.* **1.** a small, slight, or rude habitation; hut. **2.** a house used temporarily, as in the hunting season. **3.** a house or cottage, as on an estate, occupied by a gatekeeper, caretaker, or the like. **4.** the meeting place of a branch of a secret society. **5.** the members composing the branch. **6.** the den of an animal or animals, esp. beavers. —*v.i.* **7.** to have a habitation, esp. temporarily, as in a place or house. **8.** to live in hired quarters in another's house. **9.** to be fixed or implanted. —*v.t.* **10.** to furnish with a habitation or quarters, esp. temporarily. **11.** to furnish with a room or rooms in one's house for payment. **12.** to shelter; harbor. **13.** to put or deposit for storage or keeping. **14.** to bring or send into a particular place or position. **15.** to vest (power, etc.). **16.** to make (a complaint, etc.). —**lodg′er,** *n.*

Lodge (lŏj), *n.* **Henry Cabot,** 1850–1924, U.S. political leader.

lodg·ing (lŏj′ĭng), *n.* **1.** accommodation in a house, esp. in rooms for hire. **2.** a place of abode. **3.** (*pl.*) a room or rooms hired for residence in another's house.

lodging house, a house in which lodgings are let; rooming house.

lodg·ment (lŏj′mənt), *n.* **1.** act of lodging. **2.** state of being lodged. **3.** something lodged or deposited. **4.** a lodging place. Also, *esp. Brit.,* **lodge′ment.**

Lódz (lŏoj), *n.* a city in central Poland. 496,861.

lo·ess (lō′ĭs), *n.* a loamy deposit formed by wind, usually yellowish and calcareous.

loft (lôft, lŏft), *n.* **1.** the story just beneath the roof. **2.** a gallery in a church, hall, etc. **3.** *U.S.* any upper story of a warehouse, mercantile building, or factory. **4.** *Golf.* **a.** the slope of the face of a club backward from the vertical. **b.** act of lofting. —*v.t., v.i.* **5.** *Golf.* to hit (a ball) into the air or over an obstacle.

loft·y (lôf′tĭ, lŏf′-), *adj.,* **loftier, loftiest. 1.** extending high in the air; of imposing height. **2.** exalted in rank, dignity, or character. **3.** elevated in style or sentiment, as writings. **4.** haughty; proud. —**loft′i·ly,** *adv.* —**loft′i·ness,** *n.*

log (lôg, lŏg), *n.*, *v.*, **logged, logging.** —*n.* **1.** an unhewn portion of the trunk or a large limb of a felled tree. **2.** *Naut.* a device for determining the speed of and distance covered by a ship. **3.** a logbook. —*v.t., v.i.* **4.** to cut (trees) into logs. **5.** to record in a logbook.

Lo·gan (lō′gən), *n.* **Mount,** a mountain in W Canada, in SW Yukon Territory: the second highest peak in North America. 19,850 ft.

lo·gan·ber·ry (lō′gən bĕr′ĭ), *n., pl.* **-ries.** a large, dark-red acid fruit, resembling and related to the blackberry.

log·a·rithm (lôg′ə rĭth′əm, -rĭth′əm, lŏg′ə-), *n. Math.* the exponent of that power to which a fixed number must be raised in order to produce a given number. —**log′a·rith′mic,** *adj.*

log·book (lôg′bŏok′, lŏg′-), *n.* **1.** a book in which are officially recorded the speed, distance, weather, and other important particulars of a ship's or plane's voyage. **2.** the record itself.

loge (lōzh), *n.* a box in a theater.

log·ger (lôg′ər, lŏg′ər), *n.* one whose occupation is logging.

log·ger·head (lôg′ər hĕd′, lŏg′ər-), *n.* **1.** a stupid person; blockhead. **2.** Also, **loggerhead** turtle. a large-headed marine turtle of all oceans. **3. at loggerheads,** engaged in dispute.

log·gia (lŏj′ə, lŏj′ĭ ə), *n., pl.* **-gias.** a gallery open to the air on at least one side.

log·ging (lôg′ĭng, lŏg′ĭng), *n.* the process, work, or business of cutting down trees and getting out logs from the forest for timber.

log·ic (lŏj′ĭk), *n.* **1.** the science which investigates the principles governing correct or reliable inference. **2.** reasoning or argumentation. **3.** the system or principles of reasoning applicable to any branch of knowledge. **4.** reasons or sound sense. **5.** convincing force.

log·i·cal (lŏj′ə kəl), *adj.* **1.** according to the principles of logic. **2.** reasoning in accordance with the principles of logic, as a person, etc. **3.** reasonable. **4.** of or pertaining to logic. —**log′i·cal′i·ty, log′i·cal·ness,** *n.* —**log′i·cal·ly,** *adv.*

lo·gi·cian (lō jĭsh′ən), *n.* one skilled in logic.

lo·gis·tic (lō jĭs′tĭk), *adj.* pertaining to military logistics. Also, **lo·gis′ti·cal.**

lo·gis·tics (lō jĭs′tĭks), *n.* the branch of military science concerned with transportation and supply.

log·roll (lôg′rōl′, lŏg′-), *Chiefly U.S.* —*v.t.* **1.** to procure the passage of (a bill) by logrolling. —*v.i.* **2.** to engage in political logrolling.

log·roll·ing (lôg′rō′lĭng, lŏg′-), *n.* **1.** *Chiefly U.S.* the combining of two or more legislators for reciprocal assistance on legislation. **2.** the action of rolling logs to a particular place.

lo·gy (lō′gĭ), *adj.,* **-gier, -giest.** *U.S.* heavy; sluggish; dull.

Lo·hen·grin (lō′ən grĭn, -grēn′), *n. German Legend.* a knight of the grail.

loin (loin), *n.* **1.** (*usually pl.*) the part or parts of the body of man or of a quadruped animal between the false ribs and hipbone. **2.** a cut of meat from this region of an animal.

loin·cloth (loin′klôth′, -klŏth′), *n.* a piece of cloth worn about the loins or hips.

Loire (lwär), *n.* a river flowing from S France into the Bay of Biscay. ab. 625 mi.

loi·ter (loi′tər), *v.i.* **1.** to linger idly or aimlessly in or about a place. **2.** to move in a slow manner. —*v.t.* **3.** to pass (time, etc.) idly. —**loi′ter·er,** *n.*

loll (lŏl), *v.i., v.t.* **1.** to recline or lean in a relaxed or indolent manner. **2.** to hang loosely; droop. —*n.* **3.** act of lolling. —**loll′er,** *n.*

Lol·lard (lŏl′ərd), *n.* an English or Scottish follower of the religious teaching of John Wycliffe from the 14th century to the 16th.

lol·li·pop (lŏl′ĭ pŏp′), *n.* a hard candy on the end of a stick.

Lo·mond (lō′mənd), *n.* **Loch,** a lake in W Scotland. 23 mi. long; 27 sq. mi.

Lon·don (lŭn′dən), *n.* **1.** a metropolis in SE England, on the Thames: capital of the United Kingdom and the British Empire. 7,877,500 pop.; 693 sq. mi. **2.** a city in SE Canada, in S Ontario. 78,264. —**Lon′don·er,** *n.*

lone (lōn), *adj.* **1.** being alone; unaccompanied; solitary. **2.** isolated, as a house.

lone·ly (lōn′lĭ), *adj.,* **-lier, -liest. 1.** lone; solitary. **2.** destitute of friendly companionship or relationships. **3.** remote from men or from places of human habitation or resort. **4.** isolated. **5.** lonesome. —**lone′li·ness,** *n.*

lone·some (lōn′səm), *adj.* **1.** depressed by solitude or by a sense of being alone. **2.** attended with or causing such a state of feeling. **3.** depressingly lonely in situation. —**lone′some·ly,** *adv.* —**lone′some·ness,** *n.*

long¹ (lông, lŏng), *adj.,* **longer** (lông′gər, lŏng′-), **longest** (lông′gĭst, lŏng′-), *n., adv.* —*adj.* **1.** having great extent in space, duration, continuance, etc.; not short. **2.** having a specified extension in space, duration, etc. **3.** beyond the normal extension in space, duration, quantity, etc. **4.** having a long time to run, as a promissory note. **5.** (of the head or skull) of more than ordinary length from front to back. **6.** *Phonet.* **a.** lasting a relatively long time. **b.** belonging to a class of sounds considered as usually longer in duration than another class. **7.** *Com.* **a.** owning some commodity or stock. **b.** depending for profit on a rise in prices. —*n.* **8.** a long time. **9.** something that is long. —*adv.* **10.** for or through a great extent of space or, esp., time. **11.** for or throughout a specified extent, esp. of time. **12.** (in elliptical expressions) gone, occupying, delaying, etc., a long time. **13.** throughout the whole length. **14.** at a point of time far distant from the time indicated. **15. so** (or **as**) **long as,** provided that. —**long′ish,** *adj.*

long² (lông, lŏng), *v.i.* to have a prolonged or unceasing desire, as for something not immediately (if ever) attainable.

long., longitude.

Long Beach, a city in SW California. 241,109.

long·boat (lông′bōt′, lŏng′-), *n.* the largest and strongest boat belonging to a sailing ship.

long·bow (lông′bō′, lŏng′-), *n.* **1.** a bow drawn by hand and discharging a long feathered arrow. **2. draw the longbow,** to tell exaggerated stories.

lon·gev·i·ty (lŏn jĕv′ə tĭ), *n.* **1.** length or duration of life. **2.** long life.

Long·fel·low (lông′fĕl′ō, lŏng′-), *n.* **Henry Wadsworth,** 1807–82, U.S. poet.

long green, *U.S. Slang.* paper currency.

long·hand (lông′hănd′, lŏng′-), *n.* writing of

the ordinary kind, in which the words are written out in full (distinguished from *shorthand*).

long·horn (lông'hôrn', lŏng'-), *n.* one of a kind of cattle predominating on the ranges of northern Mexico and the Great Plains of the U.S. in the early 19th century, characterized by long horns.

long·ing (lông'ĭng, lŏng'-), *n.* 1. prolonged, unceasing, or earnest desire. 2. an instance of it. —*adj.* 3. having a prolonged or earnest desire. 4. characterized by or showing such desire. —**long'ing·ly,** *adv.*

Long Island, an island in SE New York: the boroughs of Brooklyn and Queens of New York City are located at its W end. 118 mi. long; 12–20 mi. wide.

Long Island Sound, an arm of the Atlantic between Connecticut and Long Island. ab. 110 mi. long.

lon·gi·tude (lŏn'jə tūd', -tōōd'), *n. Geog.* angular distance east or west on the earth's surface, measured by the angle contained between the meridian of a particular place and some prime meridian, as that of Greenwich, England.

lon·gi·tu·di·nal (lŏn'jə tū'də nəl, -tōō'-), *adj.* 1. of or pertaining to longitude or length. 2. running lengthwise. —**lon'gi·tu'di·nal·ly,** *adv.*

long·shore·man (lông'shōr'mən, lŏng'-), *n.,* *pl.* **-men.** a man employed on the wharves of a port, as in loading and unloading vessels.

long-sight·ed (lông'sī'tĭd, lŏng'-), *adj.* 1. far-sighted. 2. having great foresight. —**long'-sight'ed·ness,** *n.*

long·stand·ing (lông'stăn'dĭng, lŏng'-), *adj.* existing or occurring for a long time.

long-suf·fer·ing (lông'sŭf'ər ĭng, lŏng'-), *adj.* enduring injury or provocation long and patiently.

long ton, a ton of 2240 pounds.

long-wind·ed (lông'wĭn'dĭd, lŏng'-), *adj.* 1. talking or writing at tedious length. 2. continued to a tedious length. —**long'-wind'ed·ness,** *n.*

look (lŏŏk), *v.i.* 1. to fix the eyes upon something or in some direction in order to see. 2. to glance or gaze, in a manner specified. 3. to use the sight in seeking, examining, etc. 4. to tend, as in significance. 5. to seem (as specified) to the eye or mind. 6. to direct the attention, expectations, or hopes. 7. to face or front. **8. look after,** **a.** to follow with the eye. **b.** to seek. **c.** to take care of. **9. look out, a.** to look forth, as from a window. **b.** to be on guard. **c.** to take watchful care. **10. look up, a.** to direct the eyes upward. **b.** *Colloq.* to improve. **c.** *U.S.* to search for. —*v.t.* 11. to try to find; seek. 12. to express or suggest by looks. —*n.* 13. act of looking. 14. a visual search or examination. 15. (*pl.*) general aspect; appearance. —**look'er,** *n.*

look·er-on (lŏŏk'ər ŏn'), *n.,* *pl.* **lookers-on.** a spectator.

looking glass, a mirror made of glass with a metallic or amalgam backing.

look·out (lŏŏk'out'), *n.* 1. act of looking out. 2. a watch kept, as for something that may happen. 3. a person or group stationed to keep such a watch. 4. a place from which a watch is kept.

loom[1] (lōōm), *n.* 1. a machine or apparatus for weaving yarn or thread into a fabric. —*v.t.* 2. to weave on a loom.

loom[2] (lōōm), *v.i.* 1. to appear indistinctly or in indistinct and enlarged form. —*n.* 2. a looming appearance.

loon[1] (lōōn), *n.* any of certain large, short-tailed, web-footed, fish-eating diving birds of the northern hemisphere.

loon[2] (lōōn), *n.* a worthless, stupid fellow.

loon·y (lōō'nĭ), *adj.,* **loonier, looniest,** *n.,* *pl.* **loonies.** *Slang.* —*adj.* 1. lunatic; crazy. —*n.* 2. a lunatic.

loop (lōōp), *n.* 1. a folding of a portion of a cord, ribbon, etc., upon itself, so as to leave an opening between the parts. 2. anything resembling a loop, as the course of an airplane maneuver. —*v.t.* 3. to form into a loop or loops. 4. to make a loop or loops in. 5. to fasten by forming into a loop. 6. to fly (an airplane) in a loop. —*v.i.* 7. to make or form a loop or loops. —**loop'er,** *n.*

loop·hole (lōōp'hōl'), *n.* 1. a small opening, as in a wall, for looking through, for admitting light and air, or for the discharge of missiles against an enemy outside. 2. a means of escape or evasion.

loose (lōōs), *adj.,* **looser, loosest,** *adv., v.,* **loosed, loosing.** —*adj.* 1. free from bonds, fetters, or restraint. 2. not fastened. 3. uncom-

bined, as a chemical element. 4. not bound together. 5. not put up in a package or other container. 6. open, as the bowels. 7. free from moral restraint. 8. wanton or unchaste. 9. not firm or rigid. 10. not fitting closely, as garments. 11. not close or compact in structure or arrangement. 12. not strict, exact, or precise. —*adv.* 13. in a loose manner. —*v.t.* 14. to free from bonds, restraint, obligation, etc. 15. to shoot or let fly. —**loose'ly,** *adv.* —**loose'ness,** *n.*

loos·en (lōō'sən), *v.t.* 1. to unfasten or undo, as a bond. 2. to slacken or relax. 3. to make less firmly fixed in place. 4. to set free from bonds, restraint, or constraint. 5. to make less close or compact. —*v.i.* 6. to become loose or looser.

loot (lōōt), *n.* 1. plunder taken by pillaging. 2. anything dishonestly and ruthlessly appropriated. 3. act of plundering. —*v.t., v.i.* 4. to take, or carry off, as loot. 5. to plunder. —**loot'-er,** *n.*

lop[1] (lŏp), *v.t., v.i.,* **lopped, lopping.** 1. to cut off the branches, twigs, etc., of (a tree or other plant). 2. to cut off (anything).

lop[2] (lŏp), *v.i., v.t.,* **lopped, lopping.** to hang loosely; droop.

lope (lōp), *v.,* **loped, loping,** *n.* —*v.i.* 1. to move or run with a long, easy stride. —*n.* 2. a long, easy stride. —**lop'er,** *n.*

lop-eared (lŏp'ĭrd'), *adj.* having ears that lop or hang down.

lop-sid·ed (lŏp'sī'dĭd), *adj.* 1. inclining to one side. 2. unsymmetrical. —**lop'sid'ed·ly,** *adv.* —**lop'sid'ed·ness,** *n.*

lo·qua·cious (lō kwā'shəs), *adj.* 1. talking much or freely; talkative. 2. characterized by or showing a disposition to talk much. —**lo·qua'-cious·ly,** *adv.* —**lo·quac·i·ty** (lō kwăs'ə tĭ), *n.*

Lo·rain (lō rān'), *n.* a city in N Ohio: a port on Lake Erie. 44,125.

lo·ran (lôr'ən), *n.* a device by which a navigator can locate his position by determining the time displacement between radio signals from two known stations.

lord (lôrd), *n.* 1. a master, chief, or ruler. 2. a feudal superior. 3. a titled nobleman. 4. (*cap.*) *Brit.* **a.** the title of certain high officials. **b.** the title of a bishop. 5. (*cap.*) God. 6. (*cap.*) Jesus Christ. —*v.i.* 7. to domineer.

lord·ly (lôrd'lĭ), *adj.,* **-lier, -liest,** *adv.* —*adj.* 1. grand or magnificent. 2. insolently imperious. 3. of or befitting a lord. —*adv.* 4. in the manner of a lord. —**lord'li·ness,** *n.*

lord·ship (lôrd'shĭp), *n.* 1. (*often cap.*) *Brit.* the form used in speaking of or to a man having the title of Lord, or of or to a judge. 2. the state or dignity of a lord. 3. *Hist.* **a.** the authority or power of a lord. **b.** the domain of a lord.

Lord's Prayer, the, the prayer given by Jesus to His disciples.

Lord's Supper, 1. the last supper of Jesus and His disciples. 2. the sacrament in commemoration of this; Eucharist.

lore (lôr), *n.* 1. the body of knowledge, esp. of a traditional nature, on a particular subject. 2. learning, knowledge, or erudition.

Lor·e·lei (lôr'ə lī'), *n. German Legend.* an enchantress who, by her singing, caused sailors to wreck their boats on her rock in the Rhine.

lor·gnette (lôr nyĕt'), *n.* 1. a pair of eyeglasses on a long handle. 2. an opera glass.

lorn (lôrn), *adj. Archaic.* forsaken.

lor·ry (lôr'ĭ, lŏr'ĭ), *n., pl.* **-ries.** 1. *Brit.* a motor truck, esp. for heavy work. 2. a long, low, horse-drawn wagon without sides.

Los An·ge·les (lŏs ăng'gə ləs, ăn'jə ləs, -lēz'), a seaport in SW California. With suburbs, 2,904,596 pop.

lose (lōōz), *v.,* **lost, losing.** —*v.t.* 1. to come to be without, by some chance, and not know the whereabouts of. 2. to suffer the deprivation of. 3. to be bereaved of by death. 4. to fail to keep. 5. to cease to have. 6. to bring to destruction or ruin. 7. to have slip from sight, hearing, attention, etc. 8. to become separated from (the way, etc.). 9. to waste. 10. to fail to win. 11. to absorb or engross in something. —*v.i.* 12. to suffer loss. 13. to be defeated. —**los'er,** *n.*

los·ing (lōō'zĭng), *adj.* 1. that loses. —*n.* 2. (*pl.*) losses. —**los'ing·ly,** *adv.*

loss (lôs, lŏs), *n.* 1. detriment or disadvantage from failure to keep, have, or get. 2. that which is lost. 3. amount or number lost. 4. a failure to win. 5. waste. 6. failure to maintain. **7. at a loss, a.** in a state of bewilderment or uncertainty.

b. in a state of embarrassment for lack of something.

loss leader, a popular article sold at a loss to attract trade to a retail store.

lost (lôst, lŏst), *adj.* **1.** no longer possessed or retained. **2.** no longer to be found. **3.** bewildered as to place, direction, etc. **4.** wasted. **5.** that one has failed to win. **6.** destroyed or ruined.

lot (lŏt), *n., v.,* **lotted, lotting.** —*n.* **1.** one of a set of objects drawn from a receptacle, etc., to decide a question or choice by chance. **2.** the drawing of such objects as a method of deciding something. **3.** the decision so made. **4.** allotted share. **5.** a distinct portion or piece of land. **6.** *Motion Pictures.* the site of a motion picture being filmed. **7.** a distinct portion or parcel of anything, as of merchandise. **8.** a number of things or persons collectively. **9.** (*often pl.*) *Colloq.* a great many. —*v.t.* **10.** to draw lots for. **11.** to divide by lot.

Lot (lŏt), *n.* the nephew of Abraham. His wife was changed into a pillar of salt for looking back during their flight from Sodom.

Lo·thar·i·o (lō thâr′Ĭ ō′), *n., pl.* **-tharios.** a jaunty libertine; rake.

Lo·ti (lô tē′), *n.* Pierre, 1850–1923, French novelist.

lo·tion (lō′shən), *n.* a watery liquid containing insoluble medicinal matter applied externally to the skin.

lot·ter·y (lŏt′ə rĬ), *n., pl.* **-teries.** a scheme for raising money, as for some charitable purpose, by the sale of a large number of tickets, certain among which, as determined by chance after the sale, entitle the holders to prizes.

lot·to (lŏt′ō), *n.* a game played by drawing numbered disks from a bag or the like and covering corresponding numbers on cards.

lo·tus (lō′təs), *n.* **1.** *Gk. Legend.* **a.** a plant yielding a fruit which induced dreamy and contented forgetfulness in those who ate it (**lotus-eaters**). **b.** the fruit itself. **2.** any of certain water lilies of Egypt and Asia. **3.** any of certain shrubby herbs with red, pink, or white flowers. Also, **lo′tos.**

loud (loud), *adj.* **1.** striking strongly upon the organs of hearing, as noise, the voice, etc. **2.** making strongly audible sounds. **3.** full of sound or noise. **4.** clamorous, vociferous, or blatant. **5.** emphatic or insistent. **6.** *Colloq.* strong in smell. **7.** excessively showy. **8.** obtrusively vulgar. —*adv.* **9.** loudly. —**loud′ly,** *adv.* —**loud′ness,** *n.*

loud-speak·er (loud′spē′kər), *n.* any of various devices by which speech, music, etc., can be made audible throughout a room, hall, or the like.

Lou·is (lōō′Ĭs), *n.* Joe, born 1914, U.S. heavyweight boxing champion, 1937–49.

Lou·is (lōō′Ĭ, lōō′Ĭs), *n.* **1.** XIV, 1638–1715, king of France, 1643–1715. **2.** XVI, 1754–93, king of France from 1774, deposed in 1792, guillotined in 1793.

Lou·ise (lōō ēz′), *n.* Lake, a glacial lake in the Canadian Rockies, in SW Canada: resort. 5670 ft. high.

Lou·i·si·an·a (lōō ē′zĬ ăn′ə, lōō′Ĭ zĬ-), *n.* a State in the S United States. 2,519,520 pop.; 48,522 sq. mi. *Cap.:* Baton Rouge. *Abbr.:* La. —**Lou·i′si·an′an, Lou·i·si·an·i·an** (lōō ē′zĬ ăn′Ĭ-ən, lōō′Ĭ zĬ-), *adj., n.*

Lou·is·ville (lōō′Ĭ vĬl′), *n.* a city in N Kentucky: a port on the Ohio river. 319,077.

lounge (lounj), *v.,* **lounged, lounging,** *n.* —*v.i.* **1.** to pass time idly and indolently. **2.** to recline indolently; loll. —*n.* **3.** a kind of sofa with a headrest at one end. **4.** a large, public sitting room, as in a hotel. —**loung′er,** *n.*

Lourdes (lōōrd), *n.* a city in SW France: famous shrine. 9399.

Lou·ren·ço Mar·ques (lō rĕn′sō mär′kĕs), the capital of Mozambique. 68,223.

louse (lous), *n., pl.* **lice** (līs), *v.,* **loused, lousing.** —*n.* **1.** any of certain small, wingless, blood-sucking insects, including several species associated with man. **2.** any of various similar insects parasitic on animals or plants. —*v.t.* **3.** *U.S. Slang.* to spoil or defeat.

lous·y (lou′zĬ), *adj.,* **lousier, lousiest. 1.** infested with lice. **2.** *Slang.* mean; contemptible. **3.** *Slang.* well supplied. —**lous′i·ness,** *n.*

Head louse.

lout (lout), *n.* an awkward, stupid person; boor. —**lout′ish,** *adj.* —**lout′ish·ly,** *adv.* —**lout′ish·ness,** *n.*

lou·ver (lōō′vər), *n.* **1.** a certain arrangement of louver boards or the like closing a window or other opening. **2.** a single louver board. **3.** one of a number of slitlike openings in the hood or body of an automobile for the escape of heated air from within.

louver board, one of a series of overlapping, sloping boards, slats, or the like, in an opening, so arranged as to admit air but exclude rain.

Lou·vre (lōō′vr), *n.* a royal palace in Paris, largely occupied since 1793 by a famous museum.

lov·a·ble (lŭv′ə bəl), *adj.* of such a nature as to attract love; amiable. Also, **love′a·ble.** —**lov′a·bil′i·ty, lov′a·ble·ness,** *n.* —**lov′a·bly,** *adv.*

love (lŭv), *n., v.,* **loved, loving.** —*n.* **1.** a strong or passionate affection for a person of the opposite sex. **2.** sexual desire, or its gratification. **3.** a sweetheart. **4.** (*cap.*) a personification of sexual affection, as Eros or Cupid. **5.** a feeling of warm personal affection, as for a parent, child, etc. **6.** strong liking for anything. **7.** *Tennis, etc.* nothing; no score. **8.** in love, feeling deep affection or passion. —*v.t., v.i.* **9.** to have love (for).

love apple, the tomato.

love·bird (lŭv′bûrd′), *n.* any of certain small parrots, remarkable for the fact that the members of each pair keep close together when perching.

love·less (lŭv′lĬs), *adj.* **1.** devoid of love. **2.** feeling no love. **3.** receiving no love.

love-lies-bleed·ing (lŭv′lĭz blē′dĬng), *n.* any of several species of amaranth.

love·lorn (lŭv′lôrn′), *adj.* forsaken by one's love; forlorn or pining from love.

love·ly (lŭv′lĬ), *adj.,* **-lier, -liest. 1.** charmingly or exquisitely beautiful. **2.** having a beauty that appeals to the heart as well as to the eye, as a face, etc. **3.** *Colloq.* delightful. —**love′li·ness,** *n.*

lov·er (lŭv′ər), *n.* **1.** one who is in love with a person of the opposite sex. **2.** one who has a strong liking for something.

love seat, a seat for two persons.

love·sick (lŭv′sĬk′), *adj.* sick or languishing with love. —**love′sick′ness,** *n.*

lov·ing (lŭv′Ĭng), *adj.* affectionate; fond. —**lov′ing·ly,** *adv.*

loving cup, a large cup, as of silver, commonly with handles, awarded as a prize.

low [1] (lō), *adj.* **1.** situated or occurring not far above the ground, floor, or base. **2.** not far above the horizon, as a heavenly body. **3.** lying below the general level. **4.** (of a garment) low-necked. **5.** designating or pertaining to regions near the sea level. **6.** prostrate or dead. **7.** deep, as a bow. **8.** not high or tall. **9.** rising but slightly from a surface. **10.** of less than average height or depth. **11.** feeble; weak. **12.** affording little nourishment, as diet. **13.** small in amount, degree, force, etc. **14.** denoted by a low number. **15.** attributing no great amount, value, or excellence. **16.** depressed or dejected. **17.** humble. **18.** of inferior quality. **19.** mean or base. **20.** coarse or vulgar. **21.** *Biol.* having a relatively simple structure. **22.** *Music.* produced by relatively slow vibrations, as sounds. **23.** not loud. —*adv.* **24.** in or to a low position, point, degree, etc. **25.** cheaply. **26.** at or to a low pitch. **27.** in a low tone. —*n.* **28.** that which is low. **29.** *Meteorol.* a pressure system characterized by relatively low pressure at the center. —**low′ness,** *n.*

low [2] (lō), *v.i.* **1.** to utter the sound characteristic of cattle; moo. —*v.t.* **2.** to utter by lowing. —*n.* **3.** act or sound of lowing.

low·boy (lō′boi′), *n.* a low chest of drawers supported on short legs.

low-bred (lō′brĕd′), *adj.* characterized by or characteristic of low or vulgar breeding.

low-brow (lō′brou′), *Slang.* —*n.* **1.** a person of low intellectual caliber or culture. —*adj.* **2.** being a lowbrow. **3.** pertaining or proper to lowbrows.

Low-Church (lō′chûrch′), *adj.* laying little stress on sacraments and church authority, etc. (used of a party in the Anglican Church). —**Low′-Church′man,** *n.*

low comedy, comedy which depends on physical action and situation rather than on wit and dialogue.

Low Countries, the lowland region near the North Sea, forming the lower basin of the Rhine, Meuse, and Scheldt rivers, corresponding to modern Netherlands, Belgium, and Luxemburg.

low-down (lō′doun′), *n.* **1.** *Slang.* the actual,

unadorned facts or truth on some subject. —*adj.*
2. *Chiefly U.S. Colloq.* low, esp. in the social or moral scale; degraded.

Low·ell (lō′əl), *n.* **1.** Amy Lawrence, 1874–1925, U.S. poet and critic. **2.** James Russell, 1819–91, U.S. poet, essayist, and diplomat. **3.** a city in NE Massachusetts. 101,389.

low·er[1] (lō′ər), *v.t.* **1.** to reduce in amount, price, degree, force, etc. **2.** to make less loud. **3.** to degrade; humble. **4.** to cause to descend. **5.** to make lower in height or level. **6.** *Music.* to make lower in pitch. —*v.i.* **7.** to become lower or less. **8.** to descend.

low·er[2] (lou′ər), *v.i.* **1.** to be dark and threatening, as the sky. **2.** to frown, scowl, or look sullen. —*n.* **3.** a dark, threatening appearance. **4.** a frown or scowl.

Lower California, a narrow peninsula in NW Mexico between the Gulf of California and the Pacific, forming two territories of Mexico. 55,634 sq. mi.

lower case, *Print.* the lower half of a pair of cases, which contains the small letters of the alphabet.

low·er-case (lō′ər kās′), *adj.*, *v.*, **-cased, -casing.** —*adj.* **1.** (of a letter) small (as opposed to *capital*). **2.** *Print.* pertaining to or belonging in the lower case. —*v.t.* **3.** to print or write with a lower-case letter or letters.

Lower House, (*often l.c.*) one of two branches of a legislature, generally more representative than the upper branch.

low·er·ing (lou′ər ĭng), *adj.* **1.** dark and threatening, as the sky, clouds, etc. **2.** frowning or sullen. —**low′er·ing·ly,** *adv.*

low·er·most (lō′ər mōst′), *adj.* lowest.

lower world, the regions of the dead, conceived by the ancients as lying beneath the earth's surface; Hades.

low·land (lō′lənd), *n.* **1.** land low with respect to neighboring country. —*adj.* **2.** of, pertaining to, or characteristic of lowland.

Low Latin, any form of nonclassical Latin.

low·ly (lō′lĭ), *adj.,* **-lier, -liest,** *adv.* —*adj.* **1.** humble in station, condition, or nature. **2.** low in growth or position. **3.** meek. —*adv.* **4.** in a low position, manner, or degree. **5.** humbly. —**low′li·ness,** *n.*

Low Mass, a Mass said, and not sung, by a priest, assisted by a server only.

low-spir·it·ed (lō′spĭr′ĭt ĭd), *adj.* depressed; dejected. —**low′-spir′it·ed·ly,** *adv.*

low tide, 1. the tide at its lowest point. **2.** the time of such a state of the tide.

loy·al (loi′əl), *adj.* **1.** faithful to one's allegiance, as to the government. **2.** faithful to one's oath or obligations. **3.** faithful to any leader, party, cause, or person. —**loy′al·ly,** *adv.*

loy·al·ist (loi′əl ĭst), *n.* **1.** one who is loyal. **2.** (*sometimes cap.*) one who remained loyal to the British government during the American Revolutionary period. **3.** (*cap.*) an adherent of the Republic during the Spanish Civil War (1936–39).

loy·al·ty (loi′əl tĭ), *n., pl.* **-ties.** state or quality of being loyal; faithfulness.

Loy·o·la (loi ō′lə), *n.* Ignatius, 1491–1556, Spanish soldier, priest, and saint; founder of the Jesuit order.

loz·enge (lŏz′ĭnj), *n.* **1.** a small flavored confection of sugar, often medicated, orig. diamond shaped. **2.** *Math.* diamond.

Lt., Lieutenant.

Ltd., *Chiefly Brit.* limited. Also, **ltd.**

Lu, *Chem.* lutecium.

lub·ber (lŭb′ər), *n.* **1.** a big, clumsy, stupid person. **2.** an unskilled seaman.

lub·ber·ly (lŭb′ər lĭ), *adj.* **1.** like or characteristic of a lubber. —*adv.* **2.** in a lubberly manner. —**lub′ber·li·ness,** *n.*

Lü·beck (lȳ′bĕk), *n.* a seaport in N Germany. 154,811.

lu·bri·cant (lōō′brə kənt), *n.* **1.** a lubricating material. —*adj.* **2.** lubricating.

lu·bri·cate (lōō′brə kāt′), *v.t.,* **-cated, -cating. 1.** to apply some oily, greasy, or other substance to, in order to diminish friction. **2.** to make slippery or smooth. —**lu′bri·ca′tion,** *n.* —**lu′bri·ca′tive,** *adj.* —**lu′bri·ca′tor,** *n.*

lu·bric·i·ty (lōō brĭs′ə tĭ), *n., pl.* **-ties. 1.** slipperiness or oily smoothness of surface. **2.** capacity for lubrication. **3.** shiftiness.

lu·cent (lōō′sənt), *adj. Archaic.* shining.

lu·cerne (lōō sûrn′), *n. Chiefly Brit.* alfalfa.

lu·cid (lōō′sĭd), *adj.* **1.** shining or bright. **2.** clear or transparent. **3.** easily understood. **4.** rational or sane. —**lu·cid′i·ty, lu′cid·ness,** *n.* —**lu′cid·ly,** *adv.*

Lu·ci·fer (lōō′sə fər), *n.* **1.** a proud rebellious archangel, identified with Satan, who fell from heaven. **2.** the planet Venus when appearing as the morning star. **3.** (*l.c.*) a friction match.

Lu·cite (lōō′sīt), *n. Trademark.* a plastic compound with unusual optical properties, used for reflectors, airplane windows, etc.

luck (lŭk), *n.* **1.** that which happens to a person, as if by chance. **2.** good fortune.

Luck·now (lŭk′nou), *n.* a city in N India. 387,177.

luck·y (lŭk′ĭ), *adj.,* **luckier, luckiest. 1.** having or attended with good luck; fortunate. **2.** happening fortunately. **3.** bringing or presaging good luck. —**luck′i·ly,** *adv.* —**luck′i·ness,** *n.* —**luck′less,** *adj.*

lu·cra·tive (lōō′krə tĭv), *adj.* profitable; remunerative. —**lu′cra·tive·ly,** *adv.*

lu·cre (lōō′kər), *n.* gain or money as the object of sordid desire.

Lu·cre·tius (lōō krē′shəs), *n.* c96–c55 B.C., Roman poet. —**Lu·cre′tian,** *adj.*

lu·cu·bra·tion (lōō′kyōō brā′shən), *n.* **1.** laborious work, study, etc., esp. at night. **2.** a learned production.

lu·di·crous (lōō′də krəs), *adj.* ridiculous; amusingly absurd. —**lu′di·crous·ly,** *adv.* —**lu′di·crous·ness,** *n.*

luff (lŭf), *Naut.* —*n.* **1.** the forward edge of a fore-and-aft sail. —*v.i.* **2.** to bring the head of a sailing vessel closer to or directly into the wind, with sails shaking.

Luft·waf·fe (lōōft′väf′ə), *n. German.* (under the Nazis) the German Air Force.

lug[1] (lŭg), *v.,* **lugged, lugging,** *n.* —*v.t., v.i.* **1.** to pull or carry with effort. —*n.* **2.** a forcible pull; haul.

lug[2] (lŭg), *n.* a projecting piece by which anything is held or supported.

lug[3] (lŭg), *n.* lugsail.

lug·gage (lŭg′ĭj), *n. Chiefly Brit.* baggage.

lug·ger (lŭg′ər), *n.* a vessel with lugsails.

lug·sail (lŭg′sāl′; *Naut.* -səl), *n. Naut.* a quadrilateral sail bent upon a yard that crosses the mast obliquely.

lu·gu·bri·ous (lōō gū′brĭ əs, -gōō′-), *adj.* mournful; doleful. —**lu·gu′bri·ous·ly,** *adv.* —**lu·gu′bri·ous·ness,** *n.*

Luke (lōōk), *n.* **1.** an early Christian disciple; traditionally, the author of the third Gospel. **2.** the third Gospel, in the New Testament.

luke·warm (lōōk′wôrm′), *adj.* **1.** moderately warm; tepid. **2.** indifferent. —**luke′warm′ly,** *adv.* —**luke′warm′ness,** *n.*

lull (lŭl), *v.t.* **1.** to put to sleep or rest by soothing means. **2.** to soothe or quiet. —*v.i.* **3.** to become lulled, quieted, or stilled. —*n.* **4.** a temporary quiet or stillness. **5.** a soothing sound.

lull·a·by (lŭl′ə bī′), *n., pl.* **-bies,** *v.,* **-bied, -bying.** —*n.* **1.** a song for lulling an infant to sleep. **2.** any lulling song. —*v.t.* **3.** to lull with a lullaby.

lum·ba·go (lŭm bā′gō), *n. Pathol.* rheumatic pain in the muscles of the small of the back.

lum·bar (lŭm′bər), *adj.* **1.** of or pertaining to the loin or loins. —*n.* **2.** a lumbar vertebra, artery, or the like.

lum·ber[1] (lŭm′bər), *n.* **1.** *U.S. and Canada.* timber sawed or split into planks, boards, etc. **2.** miscellaneous useless articles that are stored away. —*v.i.* **3.** *U.S. and Canada.* to cut timber and prepare it for market. —*v.t.* **4.** to heap together in disorder. **5.** to fill up or obstruct with miscellaneous useless articles; encumber. —**lum′ber·er,** *n.* —**lum′ber·ing,** *n.*

lum·ber[2] (lŭm′bər), *v.i.* **1.** to move clumsily or heavily. **2.** to rumble. —**lum′ber·ing,** *adj.*

lum·ber·jack (lŭm′bər jăk′), *n. U.S. and Canada.* one who works at lumbering.

lum·ber·man (lŭm′bər mən), *n., pl.* **-men.** *U.S. and Canada.* **1.** one who cuts and prepares timber. **2.** one who deals in lumber.

lu·men (lōō′mən), *n., pl.* **-mina** (-mə nə). the light emitted by a source of one standard candle in a unit solid angle.

lu·mi·nar·y (lōō′mə nĕr′ĭ), *n., pl.* **-naries. 1.** a celestial body, as the sun. **2.** a body or thing that gives light. **3.** a famous person.

lu·mi·nes·cence (lōō′mə nĕs′əns), *n.* an emission of light not due directly to incandescence and occurring at a temperature below that of incandescent bodies. —lu'mi·nes'cent, *adj.*

lu·mi·nous (loo'mə nəs), *adj.* **1.** radiating or reflecting light; shining. **2.** well lighted. **3.** brilliant intellectually; enlightening. **4.** clear. —lu'mi·nous·ly, *adv.* —lu'mi·nous·ness, lu·mi·nos'i·ty (loo'mə nŏs'ə tĭ), *n.*

lum·mox (lŭm'əks), *n.* *U.S. Colloq.* a clumsy, stupid person.

lump[1] (lŭmp), *n.* **1.** a mass of solid matter without regular shape. **2.** a swelling. **3.** an aggregation. —*adj.* **4.** in the form of a lump or lumps. **5.** including a number of items taken together. —*v.t.* **6.** to unite into one aggregation. **7.** to deal with in the lump or mass. —*v.i.* **8.** to move heavily.

lump[2] (lŭmp), *v.t.* *Colloq.* to endure or put up with (a disagreeable necessity).

lump·ish (lŭmp'ĭsh), *adj.* **1.** like a lump. **2.** clumsy or stupid. —lump'ish·ly, *adv.*

lump·y (lŭmp'ĭ), *adj.*, lumpier, lumpiest. **1.** full of lumps. **2.** covered with lumps. **3.** heavy or clumsy. —lump'i·ness, *n.*

Lu·na (loo'nə), *n.* the moon, personified by the Romans as a goddess.

lu·na·cy (loo'nə sĭ), *n.*, *pl.* -cies. **1.** intermittent insanity. **2.** any form of insanity.

lu·nar (loo'nər), *adj.* **1.** of or pertaining to the moon. **2.** measured by the moon's revolutions. **3.** round or crescent-shaped.

lu·nate (loo'nāt), *adj.* crescent-shaped.

lu·na·tic (loo'nə tĭk), *n.* **1.** an insane person. —*adj.* **2.** insane; crazy. **3.** for or used by the insane.

lunch (lŭnch), *n.* **1.** a light meal between breakfast and dinner. —*v.i.* **2.** to eat lunch. —lunch'er, *n.*

lunch·eon (lŭn'chən), *n.* lunch.

lunch·eon·ette (lŭn'chə nĕt'), *n.* a restaurant where lunches are served.

lung (lŭng), *n.* **1.** either of the two saclike respiratory organs in the thorax of man and the higher vertebrates. **2.** an analogous organ in certain invertebrates.

lunge (lŭnj), *n.*, *v.*, lunged, lunging. —*n.* **1.** a thrust, as in fencing. **2.** any sudden forward movement. —*v.i.* **3.** to make a lunge. —*v.t.* **4.** to thrust; cause to move with a lunge.

lu·pine[1] (loo'pĭn), *n.* any of certain leguminous plants, as a wild species with blue, pink, or white flowers, common in sandy soil.

lu·pine[2] (loo'pĭn), *adj.* **1.** of or like the wolf. **2.** savage; ravenous.

lurch[1] (lûrch), *n.* **1.** sudden leaning or roll to one side. —*v.i.* **2.** to make a lurch; stagger.

lurch[2] (lûrch), *n.* the position of one in a helpless plight.

lure (loor), *n.*, *v.*, lured, luring. —*n.* **1.** anything that attracts, entices, or allures. **2.** a bait, esp. one used in angling. **3.** a feathered decoy, used in falconry to recall the hawk. —*v.t.* **4.** to decoy; entice; allure. **5.** to draw as by a lure. —lur'er, *n.*

lu·rid (loor'ĭd), *adj.* **1.** lighted up with an unnatural (esp. red or fiery) glare. **2.** glaringly sensational. **3.** terrible in fiery intensity, passion, or unrestraint. **4.** wan; pallid. —lu'rid·ly, *adv.* —lu'rid·ness, *n.*

lurk (lûrk), *v.i.* **1.** to remain in or about a place secretly or furtively. **2.** to slink. **3.** to exist unperceived. —lurk'er, *n.* —lurk'ing·ly, *adv.*

lus·cious (lŭsh'əs), *adj.* **1.** highly pleasing to the taste or smell. **2.** sweet to excess; cloying. —lus'cious·ly, *adv.* —lus'cious·ness, *n.*

lush[1] (lŭsh), *adj.* **1.** tender and juicy, as plants; succulent; luxuriant. **2.** characterized by luxuriant vegetation. —lush'ly, *adv.* —lush'ness, *n.*

lush[2] (lŭsh), *Slang.* —*n.* **1.** intoxicating liquor. **2.** a drunken person. —*v.i.*, *v.t.* **3.** to drink (liquor).

lust (lŭst), *n.* **1.** overmastering desire. **2.** sexual desire. —*v.i.* **3.** to have strong desire, esp. sexual desire.

lus·ter (lŭs'tər), *n.* **1.** state or quality of shining by reflecting light; gloss. **2.** some substance used to impart gloss. **3.** radiance. **4.** radiance of beauty, merit, or glory. **5.** a chandelier ornamented with cut-glass pendants. **6.** a fabric of wool and cotton with a lustrous surface. —*v.t.* **7.** to finish with a gloss. Also, *esp. Brit.*, lus'tre.

lust·ful (lŭst'fəl), *adj.* full of lust; libidinous. —lust'ful·ly, *adv.* —lust'ful·ness, *n.*

lus·trous (lŭs'trəs), *adj.* **1.** shining; glossy; bright. **2.** brilliant or splendid. —lus'trous·ly, *adv.* —lus'trous·ness, *n.*

lus·trum (lŭs'trəm), *n.*, *pl.* -trums, -tra (-trə). **1.** a period of five years. **2.** a ceremonial purification of the ancient Roman people performed every five years.

lust·y (lŭs'tĭ), *adj.*, lustier, lustiest. **1.** full of healthy vigor. **2.** hearty, as a meal. —lust'i·ly, *adv.* —lust'i·ness, *n.*

lute (loot), *n.* a stringed musical instrument formerly much used, having a long neck and a hollow, typically pear-shaped body.

lu·te·ci·um (loo tē'shĭ əm), *n.* *Chem.* a rare-earth, trivalent, metallic element. *Symbol:* Lu; *at. wt.:* 174.99; *at. no.:* 71.

Lu·ther (loo'thər), *n.* **Martin**, 1483–1546, German leader of the Protestant Reformation.

Lu·ther·an (loo'thər ən), *adj.* **1.** of or pertaining to Luther, adhering to his doctrines, or belonging to one of the Protestant churches which bears his name. —*n.* **2.** a follower of Luther, or an adherent of his doctrines. —Lu'ther·an·ism', *n.*

Man playing a lute

lut·ist (loo'tĭst), *n.* a lute player.

Lux·em·burg (lŭk'səm bûrg'), *n.* **1.** a grand duchy between Germany, France, and Belgium. 301,367 pop.; 999 sq. mi. **2.** the capital of this duchy. 60,980.

lux·u·ri·ant (lŭg zhŏŏr'ĭ ənt, lŭk shŏŏr'-), *adj.* **1.** abundant in growth, as vegetation. **2.** producing abundantly, as soil. **3.** profuse. **4.** florid, as ornamentation. —lux·u'ri·ance, *n.* —lux·u'ri·ant·ly, *adv.*

lux·u·ri·ate (lŭg zhŏŏr'ĭ āt', lŭk shŏŏr'-), *v.i.*, -ated, -ating. **1.** to indulge in luxury; revel. **2.** to take great delight.

lux·u·ri·ous (lŭg zhŏŏr'ĭ əs, lŭk shŏŏr'-), *adj.* **1.** characterized by luxury. **2.** given to luxury. —lux·u'ri·ous·ly, *adv.* —lux·u'ri·ous·ness, *n.*

lux·u·ry (lŭk'shə rĭ), *n.*, *pl.* -ries. **1.** anything conducive to sumptuous living, usually a refinement of living rather than a necessity. **2.** any form or means of enjoyment. **3.** free indulgence in costly food, clothing, etc.

Lu·zon (loo zŏn'), *n.* the chief island of the Philippine Islands, in the N part of the group. 7,374,798 pop.; 40,420 sq. mi. *Cap.:* Manila.

Lwów (lvoof), *n.* a city in the SW Soviet Union; formerly in Poland. 317,000.

-ly, **1.** the normal adverbial suffix, added to almost any descriptive adjective, e.g., *gladly*, *gradually*. **2.** the adverbial suffix applied to units of time meaning "per," e.g., *hourly*, *daily*. **3.** an adjective suffix meaning "like," e.g., *manly*.

ly·cée (lē sā'), *n.* (in France) a secondary school maintained by the state.

ly·ce·um (lī sē'əm), *n.* **1.** *U.S.* an association for discussion and popular instruction by lectures and other means. **2.** a building, hall, or the like, devoted to instruction by lectures.

lydd·ite (lĭd'īt), *n.* a high explosive consisting chiefly of picric acid.

Lyd·i·a (lĭd'ĭ ə), *n.* an ancient kingdom in W Asia Minor: under Croesus, a wealthy empire including most of Asia Minor. —Lyd'i·an, *adj.*, *n.*

lye (lī), *n.* any solution resulting from leaching, percolation, or the like.

ly·ing[1] (lī'ĭng), *n.* **1.** untruthfulness. —*adj.* **2.** untruthful; false.

ly·ing[2] (lī'ĭng), *v.* pres. part. of lie.

ly·ing-in (lī'ĭng ĭn'), *n.* `1.` confinement in childbed. —*adj.* **2.** of or for childbirth.

lymph (lĭmf), *n.* *Anat.*, *Physiol.* a clear, yellowish, slightly alkaline fluid derived from the tissues of the body and conveyed to the blood stream by the lymphatic vessels.

lym·phat·ic (lĭm făt'ĭk), *adj.* **1.** pertaining to, containing, or conveying lymph. **2.** sluggish in thought and action. —*n.* **3.** a lymphatic vessel.

lynch (lĭnch), *v.t.* to put (a person) to death by some group action without authority or process of law, for some offense known or imputed. —lynch'er, *n.* —lynch'ing, *n.*

Lynch·burg (lĭnch'bûrg), *n.* a city in central Virginia. 45,541.

lynch law, the administration of summary punishment, esp. death, upon an offender (actual or reputed) by private persons acting without authority of law.

Lynn (lĭn), *n.* a seaport in E Massachusetts. 98,123.

lynx (lĭngks), *n.*, *pl.* **lynxes,** (*esp. collectively*) **lynx.** any of certain wildcats having long limbs and short tail, and, usually, tufted ears.

lynx-eyed (lĭngks′īd⸝), *adj.* sharp-sighted.

ly·on·naise (lī′ə nāz′), *adj.* (of food) cooked with pieces of onion.

Ly·ons (lī′ənz), *n.* a city in E France. 460,748.

Ly·ra (lī′rə), *n. Astron.* a northern constellation, containing Vega, one of the brightest stars.

lyre (līr), *n.* 1. a musical instrument of ancient Greece, consisting of a sound box with two curving arms carrying a cross bar from which strings are stretched to the body. 2. (*cap.*) *Astron.* Lyra.

lyre-bird (līr′bûrd⸝), *n.* an Australian passerine bird, the male of which has a long tail which is lyre-shaped when spread.

lyr·ic (lĭr′ĭk), *adj.* Also, **lyr·i·cal.** 1. (of poetry) having the form and musical quality of a song. 2. pertaining to or writing such poetry. 3. characterized by or indulging in a spontaneous, ardent expression of feeling. —*n.* 4. a lyric poem. 5. *Colloq.* the words of a song. —**lyr′i·cal·ly,** *adv.*

lyr·i·cism (lĭr′ə sĭz′əm), *n.* 1. lyric character or style. 2. lyric outpouring of feeling.

Ly·san·der (lī săn′dər), *n.* died 395 B.C., Spartan naval commander and statesman.

-lysis, a word element, especially scientific, meaning "breaking down," "decomposition," as in *analysis, electrolysis.*

-lytic, a termination of adjectives corresponding to nouns in *-lysis,* as in *analytic.*

Lyt·ton (lĭt′ən), *n.* Edward George Earle Lytton Bulwer-Lytton, 1st Baron, 1803–73, British author and politician.

M

M,m(ĕm), *n.*, *pl.* **M's** or **Ms, m's** or **ms.** 1. a consonant, the 13th letter of the English alphabet. 2. the Roman numeral for 1000.

M., 1. (L *meridies*) noon. 2. Monday. 3. (*pl.* **MM.**) Monsieur.

m., 1. male. 2. married. 3. masculine. 4. *Mech.* mass. 5. meter. 6. mile. 7. minim. 8. minute. 9. month.

ma (mä), *n. Colloq.* mamma; mother.

Ma, *Chem.* masurium.

M.A., Master of Arts.

ma'am (măm, mäm; *unstressed* məm), *n. Colloq.* madam.

ma·ca·bre (mə kä′bər, -brə), *adj.* 1. gruesome; ghastly. 2. pertaining to or suggestive of the allegorical dance of death (**danse macabre**) in which a skeleton Death leads people to the grave. Also, **ma·ca′ber.**

mac·ad·am (mə kăd′əm), *n.* 1. a macadamized road or pavement. 2. the broken stone used in making such a road.

mac·ad·am·ize (mə kăd′ə mīz′), *v.t.*, **-ized, -izing.** to construct (a road) by laying and rolling successive layers of broken stone.

Ma·cao (mə kou′), *n.* a Portuguese colony in S China, on a peninsula of **Macao island** and two small adjacent islands. 374,737 pop.; 6 sq. mi.

ma·caque (mə käk′), *n.* any of certain monkeys, found chiefly in Asia, characterized by cheek pouches and, generally, a short tail.

mac·a·ro·ni (măk′ə rō′nĭ), *n.*, *pl.* **-nis, -nies.** 1. a kind of paste of Italian origin, prepared from wheat flour, in the form of dried, hollow tubes, to be cooked for food. 2. an English dandy of the 18th century who affected foreign ways.

mac·a·roon (măk′ə rōōn′), *n.* a sweet drop cooky made of egg whites, sugar, and frequently almond paste, coconut, etc.

Mac·Ar·thur (mək är′thər), *n.* Douglas, born 1880, U.S. general.

Ma·cas·sar (mə kăs′ər), *n.* a seaport in the Dutch East Indies, on SW Celebes island. 84,855.

Ma·cau·lay (mə kô′lĭ), *n.* Thomas Babington Macaulay, Baron, 1800–59, British writer and statesman.

ma·caw (mə kô′), *n.* any of certain large, long-tailed parrots of tropical and subtropical America, noted for their brilliant plumage and harsh voices.

Mac·ca·bees (măk′ə bēz′), *n.pl.* 1. a family of heroes, deliverers of Judea during the Syrian persecutions of 175–164 B.C. 2. the last two books of the Apocrypha, recording the struggle of the Maccabees. —**Mac′ca·be′an,** *adj.*

Mac·Dow·ell (mək dou′əl), *n.* Edward Alexander, 1861–1908, U.S. composer.

mace[1] (mās), *n.* 1. a clublike weapon of war, often with a spiked head. 2. a staff borne before or by certain officials as a symbol of office. 3. the bearer of such a staff.

mace[2] (mās), *n.* a spice ground from the layer between a nutmeg shell and its outer husk.

Mac·e·do·ni·a (măs′ə dō′nĭ ə), *n.* an ancient country in the Balkan Peninsula, N of ancient Greece. —**Mac′e·do′ni·an,** *adj., n.*

mac·er·ate (măs′ə rāt′), *v.t., v.i.,* **-ated, -ating.** to soften or disintegrate by steeping in a liquid, with or without heat. —**mac′er·a′tion,** *n.*

mach., 1. machine. 2. machinery.

ma·che·te (mä chā′tā, mə shĕt′), *n.* a large, heavy knife used esp. in Spanish-American countries as a tool and weapon.

Mach·i·a·vel·li (măk′ĭ ə vĕl′ĭ), *n.* Niccolò di Bernardo, 1469–1527, Italian statesman and writer.

Mach·i·a·vel·li·an (măk′ĭ ə vĕl′ĭ ən), *adj.* 1. of, like, or befitting Machiavelli. 2. being or acting in accordance with Machiavelli's political doctrines, which placed expediency above political morality. 3. wily; astute. —*n.* 4. a follower of Machiavelli or his doctrines. Also, **Mach′i·a·vel′-i·an.** —**Mach′i·a·vel′li·an·ism,** *n.*

ma·chic·o·la·tion (mə chĭk′ə lā′shən), *n. Archit.* an opening in the floor between the corbels of a projecting gallery or parapet, through which missiles, molten lead, etc., might be cast upon an enemy beneath.

mach·i·nate (măk′ə nāt′), *v.i.,* **-nated, -nating.** to contrive or devise, esp. artfully or with evil purpose. —**mach′i·na′tor,** *n.*

mach·i·na·tion (măk′ə nā′shən), *n.* 1. act or process of machinating. 2. (*usually pl.*) a crafty scheme; plot.

ma·chine (mə shēn′), *n., v.,* **-chined, -chining.** —*n.* 1. an apparatus, consisting of interrelated parts, which is used in the performance of some kind of work. 2. a mechanical contrivance. 3. something operated by a mechanical apparatus, as an automobile. 4. *Mech.* a device which transmits and modifies force or motion. 5. any complex agency or operating system. 6. the body of persons conducting and controlling the activities of a political party or other organization. —*v.t.* 7. to make or finish with a machine.

machine gun, a small arm operated by a mechanism, able to deliver a rapid and continuous fire of bullets.

ma·chine-gun (mə shēn′gŭn′), *v.t.,* **-gunned, -gunning.** to shoot at, using a machine gun.

ma·chin·er·y (mə shē′nə rĭ), *n.*, *pl.* **-eries.** 1. machines or mechanical apparatus. 2. the parts of a machine collectively. 3. any system of agencies by which action is maintained.

machine tool, a power-operated machine, as a lathe, milling machine, etc.

ma·chin·ist (mə shē′nĭst), *n.* 1. a person who operates machinery. 2. one who makes and repairs machines. 3. *U.S. Navy.* a warrant officer whose duty is to assist the engineer officer in the engine room.

Mach number (mŏk), a number indicating the ratio between the air speed of an object and the speed of sound at a given altitude, etc.

Mac·ken·zie (mə kĕn′zĭ), *n.* a river in NW Canada, flowing to the Arctic Ocean. ab. 900 mi.; with tributaries, ab. 2525 mi.

mack·er·el (măk′ər əl), *n., pl.* -el, (*occasionally, esp. with reference to different species*) -els. 1. an abundant food fish of the North Atlantic, with wavy cross markings on the back. 2. any of various other similar fishes.

mackerel sky, a sky spotted with small white fleecy clouds.

Mack·i·nac (măk′ə nô′), *n.* **Strait of,** a strait joining Lakes Michigan and Huron. Least width, 4 mi.

mack·i·naw (măk′ə nô′), *n.* a short coat of a thick, blanketlike, commonly plaid, woolen material.

mack·in·tosh (măk′ĭn tŏsh′), *n.* 1. a raincoat made of cloth rendered waterproof by India rubber. 2. such cloth.

Ma·con (mā′kən), *n.* a city in central Georgia. 57,865.

mac·ro·cosm (măk′rə kŏz′əm), *n.* the universe. —**mac′ro·cos′mic,** *adj.*

ma·cron (mā′krŏn, măk′rŏn), *n.* a short horizontal line used as a diacritic over a vowel to indicate that it is a "long" sound, as in *fāte*.

mad (măd), *adj.*, **madder, maddest.** 1. insane. 2. *Colloq.* moved by anger. 3. (of wind, etc.) furious in violence. 4. (of animals) a. abnormally furious. b. affected with rabies. 5. frantic. 6. wildly gay or merry.

Mad·a·gas·car (măd′ə găs′kər), *n.* an island in the Indian Ocean, off the SE coast of Africa: a French colony. 4,227,000 pop.; ab. 228,600 sq. mi. *Cap.:* Tananarive.

mad·am (măd′əm), *n., pl.* **madams, mesdames** (mĕ dăm′). 1. a polite term of address used to a woman. 2. the woman in charge of a brothel.

mad·ame (măd′əm; *Fr.* må dåm′), *n., pl.* **mesdames** (mĕ dăm′). a conventional French title of respect used distinctively to or of a married woman.

mad·cap (măd′kăp′), *adj.* 1. wildly impulsive; lively. —*n.* 2. a madcap person.

mad·den (măd′ən), *v.t.* 1. to make insane. 2. to infuriate. —*v.i.* 3. to become mad.

mad·den·ing (măd′ən ĭng), *adj.* 1. driving to madness. 2. infuriating. 3. raging; furious. —**mad′den·ing·ly,** *adv.*

mad·der (măd′ər), *n.* 1. a European herbaceous climbing plant with panicles of small yellowish flowers. 2. the root of this plant, used for making dyes. 3. the dye itself, usually red. 4. a color produced by such a dye.

mad·ding (măd′ĭng), *adj.* 1. mad; acting as if mad. 2. making mad.

made (mād), *adj.* 1. produced by making, preparing, etc. 2. artificially produced. 3. invented. 4. assured of success or fortune.

Ma·dei·ra (mə dĭr′ə), *n.* 1. a group of five islands off the NW coast of Africa, belonging to Portugal. 249,450 pop.; 308 sq. mi. *Cap.:* Funchal. 2. the chief island of this group. 247,423 pop.; 286 sq. mi. 3. (*often l.c.*) a rich, strong white wine made there.

mad·e·moi·selle (măd′mwə zĕl′), *n., pl.* **mesdemoiselles.** the conventional French title of respect for a girl or unmarried woman.

made-up (mād′ŭp′), *adj.* 1. concocted; invented. 2. artificial. 3. put together; finished.

mad·house (măd′hous′), *n.* 1. an asylum for the insane. 2. a place of commotion.

Mad·i·son (măd′ə sən), *n.* 1. **James,** 1751–1836, 4th president of the U.S., 1809–17. 2. **Dolly,** 1768–1849, wife of James. 3. the capital of Wisconsin, in the S part. 67,447.

mad·ly (măd′lĭ), *adv.* 1. insanely. 2. wildly; furiously. 3. foolishly.

mad·man (măd′măn′, -mən), *n., pl.* -**men.** an insane person.

mad·ness (măd′nĭs), *n.* 1. insanity. 2. rabies. 3. folly. 4. frenzy; rage.

Ma·don·na (mə dŏn′ə), *n.* 1. Virgin Mary. 2. a picture or statue representing the Virgin Mary.

mad·ras (măd′rəs, mə drăs′, -dräs′), *n.* a light cotton fabric used for shirts, etc.

Ma·dras (mə dräs′, -dräs′), *n.* 1. a large province in S India. 49,342,000 pop.; 126,166 sq. mi. 2. a seaport in and the capital of this province, on the Bay of Bengal. 777,481.

mad·re·pore (măd′rə pōr′), *n.* any of certain corals noted for reef-building in tropical seas.

Ma·drid (mə drĭd′), *n.* the capital of Spain, in the central part. 1,141,000.

mad·ri·gal (măd′rĭ gəl), *n.* 1. a lyric poem suitable for musical setting, usually short and often of amatory character. 2. a part song without instrumental accompaniment, usually for five or six voices.

Mae·ce·nas (mē sē′nəs), *n.* 1. **Gaius Cilnius,** c70 B.C.–8 B.C., Roman statesman: patron of Vergil and Horace. 2. a generous patron, esp. of the arts.

Mael·strom (māl′strəm), *n.* 1. a famous whirlpool off the NW coast of Norway. 2. (*l.c.*) any great or violent whirlpool. 3. (*l.c.*) a resistless confusion of affairs, influence, etc.

ma·es·to·so (mä′ĕs tō′sō), *adj., adv. Music.* with majesty; stately.

maes·tro (mīs′trō; *It.* mä ĕs′trō), *n., pl.* -**tri** (-trē). 1. an eminent musical composer, teacher, or conductor. 2. a master of any art.

Mae·ter·linck (mā′tər lĭngk′), *n.* **Maurice,** 1862–1949, Belgian dramatist, essayist, and poet.

Mae West (mā), an inflatable life-preserver vest for aviators who fall in the sea.

Ma·fi·a (mä′fĭ ä′), *n.* a criminal secret society of Sicilians or other Italians, at home or in foreign countries.

mag., 1. magazine. 2. magnitude.

mag·a·zine (măg′ə zēn′, măg′ə zēn′), *n.* 1. a periodical publication containing miscellaneous articles or pieces. 2. a room or place for keeping military stores, as arms, ammunition, etc. 3. a metal receptacle for cartridges in certain types of automatic weapons. 4. a supply chamber in a stove, a camera, etc.

Mag·da·lene (măg′də lēn′, măg′də lē′nē), *n.* 1. **the,** the repentant woman in Luke 7:37–50. 2. (*l.c.*) a reformed prostitute. Also, **Mag·da·len** (măg′də lən).

Mag·de·burg (măg′də bûrg′), *n.* a city in central Germany. 336,838.

mage (māj), *n. Archaic.* a magician.

Ma·gel·lan (mə jĕl′ən), *n.* 1. **Ferdinand,** c1480–1521, Portuguese navigator: discoverer of the Strait of Magellan and the Philippine Islands. 2. **Strait of,** a strait near the S tip of South America connecting the Atlantic and Pacific Oceans. ab. 360 mi. long; 2½–17 mi. wide.

ma·gen·ta (mə jĕn′tə), *n.* 1. a deep red coal-tar dye. 2. reddish purple.

mag·got (măg′ət), *n.* 1. the legless larva of a fly. 2. a whim. —**mag′got·y,** *adj.*

Ma·gi (mā′jī), *n.pl., sing.* -**gus** (-gəs). the three "wise men" who "came from the east" to Jerusalem to do homage to the infant Jesus.

mag·ic (măj′ĭk), *n.* 1. the pretended art of producing effects by means of supernatural or occult forces. 2. the exercise of this art. 3. the effects produced. 4. power exerted through this art. 5. any extraordinary influence. —*adj.* Also, **mag′i·cal.** 6. employed in magic. 7. mysteriously enchanting. 8. of, pertaining to, or due to magic. —**mag′i·cal·ly,** *adv.*

ma·gi·cian (mə jĭsh′ən), *n.* 1. one skilled in magic arts. 2. a juggler; conjurer.

magic lantern, a lantern-slide projector.

Ma·gi·not line (măzh′ə nō′), a zone of French fortifications erected along the German border prior to World War II.

mag·is·te·ri·al (măj′ĭs tĭr′ĭ əl), *adj.* 1. of, pertaining to, or befitting a master; authoritative. 2. imperious; domineering. 3. of, pertaining to, or befitting a magistrate.

mag·is·tra·cy (măj′ĭs trə sĭ), *n., pl.* -**cies.** 1. the office or function of a magistrate. 2. a body of magistrates. 3. the district under a magistrate.

mag·is·trate (măj′ĭs trāt′, -trĭt), *n.* 1. a civil officer charged with the administration of the law. 2. a minor judicial officer, as a justice of the peace.

mag·ma (măg′mə), *n., pl.* -**mata** (-mə tə). 1. any crude mixture of finely divided mineral or organic matters. 2. *Geol.* molten material beneath the solid crust of the earth, from which igneous rock is formed.

Mag·na Char·ta (măg′nə kär′tə), 1. the "great charter" of English liberties, forced from King John by the English barons at Runnymede, June 15, 1215. 2. any fundamental constitution or law guaranteeing rights. Also, **Mag′na Car′ta.**

mag·na·nim·i·ty (măg′nə nĭm′ə tĭ), *n., pl.* -**ties.** 1. quality of being magnanimous. 2. a magnanimous act.

mag·nan·i·mous (măg năn′ə məs), *adj.* 1. generous in forgiving an insult or injury. **2.** high-minded; noble. —**mag·nan′i·mous·ly,** *adv.*

mag·nate (măg′nāt), *n.* a great or dominant person in some field of business.

mag·ne·sia (măg nē′shə, -zhə), *n.* magnesium oxide, a white tasteless substance used in medicine as an antacid and laxative.

mag·ne·si·um (măg nē′shУ əm, -zhəm), *n.* *Chem.* a light, ductile, silver-white metallic element which burns with a dazzling white light. *Symbol:* Mg; *at. wt.:* 24.32; *at. no.:* 12; *sp. gr.:* 1.74 at 20°C.

mag·net (măg′nУt), *n.* **1.** a body (as a piece of steel) which attracts certain substances, esp. iron. **2.** loadstone. **3.** a thing or person that attracts.

mag·net·ic (măg nĕt′Уk), *adj.* **1.** of or pertaining to a magnet or magnetism. **2.** having the properties of a magnet. **3.** capable of being magnetized. **4.** exerting a strong attractive power or charm. —**mag·net′i·cal·ly,** *adv.*

magnetic field, a condition of space in the vicinity of a magnet or electric current which manifests itself as a force on magnetic objects within that space.

magnetic needle, a slender magnetized steel rod which, in a compass, indicates approximate north and south.

magnetic north, the direction in which the needle of a compass points, differing in most places from true north.

magnetic pole, 1. a pole of a magnet. **2.** either of the two points on the earth's surface where the dipping needle stands vertical, one in the arctic regions, and the other in the antarctic.

mag·net·ism (măg′nə tУz′əm), *n.* **1.** the characteristic properties possessed by magnets. **2.** the agency producing magnetic phenomena. **3.** the science dealing with magnetic phenomena. **4.** magnetic or attractive power or charm.

mag·net·ite (măg′nə tīt′), *n.* a very common black iron oxide that is strongly attracted by a magnet: important iron ore.

mag·net·ize (măg′nə tīz′), *v.t.,* -**ized,** -**izing.** **1.** to communicate magnetic properties to. **2.** to attract or influence compellingly. —**mag′net·i·za′tion,** *n.*

mag·ne·to (măg nē′tō), *n., pl.* -**tos.** a small electric generator, the poles of which are permanent magnets, as the generator producing sparks in an internal-combustion engine.

mag·ne·to·e·lec·tric (măg nē′tō У lĕk′trУk), *adj.* pertaining to the induction of electric currents by means of magnets.

mag·ni·fi·ca·tion (măg′nə fə kā′shən), *n.* **1.** act of magnifying. **2.** state of being magnified. **3.** a magnified copy.

mag·nif·i·cence (măg nУf′ə səns), *n.* **1.** splendor; grandeur. **2.** impressiveness of surroundings.

mag·nif·i·cent (măg nУf′ə sənt), *adj.* **1.** making a splendid appearance. **2.** extraordinarily fine; superb. **3.** noble; sublime. —**mag·nif′i·cent·ly,** *adv.*

mag·ni·fy (măg′nə fī′), *v.t., v.i.,* -**fied,** -**fying.** **1.** to increase the apparent size of (an object), as a lens does. **2.** to enlarge. **3.** to cause to seem greater or more important. —**mag′ni·fi′er,** *n.*

mag·nil·o·quent (măg nУl′ə kwənt), *adj.* speaking or expressed in a lofty or grandiose style. —**mag·nil′o·quence,** *n.*

mag·ni·tude (măg′nə tūd′, -tōōd′), *n.* **1.** size; extent. **2.** great amount, size, importance, etc. **3.** *Astron.* the brightness of a star expressed according to an arbitrary numerical system.

mag·no·li·a (măg nō′lУ ə), *n.* **1.** any of certain shrubs and trees with large, usually fragrant flowers and an aromatic bark, much cultivated for ornament. **2.** the magnolia blossom.

mag·num (măg′nəm), *n., pl.* -**nums.** a large bottle for wine or spirits, containing about two quarts.

magnum o·pus (ō′pəs), **1.** a great work. **2.** one's chief work, as a literary work.

mag·pie (măg′pī′), *n.* **1.** any of various noisy, mischievous birds of the crow family, having a long tail and black-and-white plumage. **2.** a chattering person.

mag·uey (măg′wā), *n.* **1.** any of certain species of agave, as the century plant. **2.** the fiber from such a plant.

Mag·yar (măg′yär), *n.* **1.** a member of the ethnic group which forms the predominant element of the population of Hungary. **2.** the Hungarian language. —*adj.* **3.** Hungarian.

ma·ha·ra·jah (mä′hə rä′jə), *n.* the title of certain great Mohammedan ruling princes in India. Also, **ma′ha·ra′ja.**

ma·ha·ra·nee (mä′hə rä′nē), *n. India.* **1.** the wife of a maharajah. **2.** a female sovereign in her own right. Also, **ma′ha·ra′ni.**

ma·hat·ma (mə hät′mə, -hăt′-), *n.* **1.** an adept in Brahmanism. **2.** *Theosophy.* one of a class of reputed beings with preternatural powers.

Ma·hi·can (mə hē′kən), *n.* **1.** a tribe or confederacy of North American Indians of Algonquian speech, centralized formerly in the upper Hudson valley. **2.** an Indian of this confederacy.

mah-jongg (mä′jŏng′, -jŏng′), *n.* a game of Chinese origin, usually for four persons, with dominolike pieces. Also, **mah′-jong′.**

ma·hog·a·ny (mə hŏg′ə nУ), *n., pl.* -**nies,** *adj.* —*n.* **1.** any of certain tropical American trees yielding a hard, reddish-brown wood highly esteemed for making fine furniture, etc. **2.** the wood itself. **3.** any of various related or similar trees, or their wood. **4.** a reddish-brown color. —*adj.* **5.** pertaining to or consisting of mahogany. **6.** of the color mahogany.

Ma·hom·et (mə hŏm′Уt), *n.* Mohammed. —**Ma·hom′et·an,** *adj., n.*

ma·hout (mə hout′), *n.* (in the East Indies) the keeper and driver of an elephant.

Mah·rat·ta (mə răt′ə), *n.* a member of a Hindu people of central and western India.

maid (mād), *n.* **1.** a young unmarried woman. **2.** a spinster. **3.** a female servant.

maid·en (mā′dən), *n.* **1.** a young unmarried woman. —*adj.* **2.** of, pertaining to, or befitting a maiden. **3.** unmarried. **4.** made, tried, appearing, etc., for the first time. **5.** (of a horse, etc.) that never has won a race or a prize.

maid·en·hair (mā′dən hâr′), *n.* any of certain ferns having delicate, finely divided fronds.

maid·en·head (mā′dən hĕd′), *n.* **1.** Also, **maid′en·hood′.** virginity. **2.** the hymen.

maid·en·ly (mā′dən lУ), *adj.* **1.** pertaining to a maiden. **2.** characteristic of or befitting a maiden. —**maid′en·li·ness,** *n.*

maiden name, a woman's surname before marriage.

maid of honor, 1. the chief unmarried attendant of a bride. **2.** an unmarried woman attendant on a queen or princess.

maid-serv·ant (mād′sûr′vənt), *n.* a female servant.

mail[1] (māl), *n.* **1.** letters, packages, etc., arriving or sent by the postal system. **2.** the postal system. —*adj.* **3.** of or pertaining to mail. —*v.t.* **4.** to send by mail. —**mail′a·ble,** *adj.*

mail[2] (māl), *n.* **1.** flexible armor of interlinked rings. **2.** defensive armor. —*v.t.* **3.** to clothe with mail. —**mailed,** *adj.*

mail-box (māl′bŏks′), *n.* **1.** a public box for the mailing of letters. **2.** a private box for the delivery of mail.

mail·man (māl′măn′), *n., pl.* -**men.** one who delivers mail; postman.

mail-or·der house (māl′ôr′dər), a business house conducting a business by receiving orders (**mail orders**) and cash by mail and shipping goods to the buyers.

maim (mām), *v.t.* **1.** to deprive of the use of some bodily member; cripple. **2.** to impair. —**maim′er,** *n.*

main (mān), *adj.* **1.** chief; principal; leading. **2.** sheer; utmost. —*n.* **3.** a principal pipe or duct in a system used to distribute water, gas, etc. **4.** strength; force. **5.** the chief part or point. **6.** *Poetic.* the open ocean. **7.** the mainland. **8.** in the main, for the most part.

Main (mān), *n.* a river flowing from E Germany W to the Rhine. 305 mi.

Maine (mān), *n.* a State in the NE United States, on the Atlantic coast. 876,213 pop.; 33,215 sq. mi. *Cap.:* Augusta. *Abbr.:* Me.

main·land (mān′lănd′, -lənd), *n.* the principal part of a continent.

main·ly (mān′lУ), *adv.* chiefly; mostly.

main·mast (mān′măst′, -mäst′; *Naut.* -məst), *n. Naut.* the principal mast of a ship.

main·sail (mān′sāl′; *Naut.* -səl), *n. Naut.* the principal sail of a ship.

main·sheet (mān′shēt′), *n. Naut.* a sheet of a mainsail.

main·spring (mān′sprУng′), *n.* **1.** the principal spring in a mechanism, as in a watch. **2.** the chief motive power.

main·stay (mān′stā′), *n.* **1.** *Naut.* the stay which secures the mainmast forward. **2.** a chief support.

main·tain (mān tān′), *v.t.* **1.** to keep in existence; preserve; retain. **2.** to keep in a specified state, position, etc. **3.** to affirm or assert. **4.** to support in speech or argument. **5.** to provide with the means of existence. —**main·tain′er,** *n.*

main·te·nance (mān′tə nəns), *n.* **1.** act of maintaining. **2.** state of being maintained. **3.** means of subsistence.

maintenance of membership, an agreement between an employer and a labor union by which employees who are members of the union at the time the agreement is made, or who subsequently join, must either remain members until the agreement expires or be discharged.

main-top·mast (mān′tŏp′məst), *n. Naut.* the mast next above the lower mainmast.

main-top·sail (mān′tŏp′səl), *n. Naut.* the sail set on the main-topmast.

Mainz (mīnts), *n.* a city in W Germany. 158,-533.

maî·tre d'hô·tel (mĕ′tr dō tĕl′), **1.** a head-waiter. **2.** the owner or manager of a hotel. **3.** a steward or butler.

maize (māz), *n. Technical and Brit.* **1.** a widely cultivated cereal plant bearing grain in large ears or spikes; Indian corn. **2.** its grain. **3.** a pale yellow.

Maj., Major.

ma·jes·tic (mə jĕs′tĭk), *adj.* of lofty dignity or imposing aspect; stately; grand. Also, **ma·jes′ti·cal.** —**ma·jes′ti·cal·ly,** *adv.*

maj·es·ty (măj′ĭs tĭ), *n., pl.* **-ties. 1.** regal, lofty, or stately dignity; grandeur. **2.** sovereignty. **3.** a royal personage. **4.** (*usually cap.*) a title used when speaking of or to a sovereign (prec. by *his, your,* etc.)

ma·jol·i·ca (mə jŏl′ə kə, mə yŏl′-), *n.* a kind of pottery coated with enamel and decorated, often in rich colors.

ma·jor (mā′jər), *n.* **1.** *Mil.* a commissioned officer ranking next above a captain. **2.** *U.S.* a subject or field of study chosen by a student to represent his principal interest. **3.** a person of full legal age. —*adj.* **4.** greater, as in size, extent, importance, rank, etc. **5.** of full legal age. **6.** *Music.* **a.** (of an interval) being between the tonic and the second, third, sixth, and seventh degrees of a major scale. **b.** (of a chord) having a major third between the root and the note next above it. **7.** senior (used after a name). **8.** *U.S.* noting or pertaining to educational majors. —*v.i.* **9.** *U.S.* to pursue a principal subject of study (fol. by *in*).

Ma·jor·ca (mə jôr′kə), *n.* a Spanish island in the W Mediterranean. 327,120 pop.; 1405 sq. mi. *Cap.:* Palma.

ma·jor-do·mo (mā′jər dō′mō), *n., pl.* **-mos. 1.** a man in charge of a great household. **2.** a steward or butler.

major general, *Mil.* an officer ranking next below a lieutenant general and next above a brigadier general.

ma·jor·i·ty (mə jôr′ə tĭ, -jŏr′-), *n., pl.* **-ties. 1.** the greater part or number. **2.** the excess whereby the greater number, as of votes, surpasses the remainder. **3.** the state or time of being of full legal age.

major league, either of the two main professional baseball leagues in the U.S.: the American or National Leagues.

major scale, mode, or **key,** *Music.* a scale, mode, or key whose third tone forms a major third with the fundamental tone.

make (māk), *v.,* **made, making,** *n.* —*v.t.* **1.** to bring into existence by shaping material, combining parts, etc. **2.** to cause. **3.** to cause to be or become. **4.** to put into condition. **5.** to induce or compel. **6.** to give rise to; occasion. **7.** to produce, earn, or acquire. **8.** to do; effect. **9.** to establish; enact. **10.** to become by development. **11.** to form in the mind, as a plan. **12.** to judge or infer as to the nature, meaning, etc. **13.** (of material or parts) to compose; form. **14.** to serve for or as. **15.** to assure the success or fortune of. **16.** to deliver. **17.** to accomplish by traveling, etc. **18.** to reach. **19.** *Colloq.* to secure a place on, as a team. —*v.i.* **20.** to act or start (to do, or as if to do, something). **21.** to cause oneself, or something understood, to be as specified. **22.** to show oneself in action or behavior. **23.** to go. **24.** to approach, esp. hostilely. **25. make believe, a.** to pretend. **b.** to cause to believe.

26. make out, a. to write out (a bill, a check, etc.). **b.** to prove. **c.** to discern. **d.** to complete. **e.** *U.S. Colloq.* to manage; succeed. **27. make over, a.** to make anew or alter. **b.** to hand over into the possession or charge of another. **c.** to transfer the title of (property). **28. make time,** *Colloq.* to go fast. **29. make up, a.** to form. **b.** to construct; compile. **c.** to concoct. **d.** to compensate for. **e.** to complete. **f.** to prepare. **g.** to bring to a definite conclusion, as one's mind. **h.** to settle amicably. **i.** to become reconciled. **j.** to beautify artificially, as the face. **30. make up to,** *Colloq.* to fawn on. —*n.* **31.** style or manner of being made. **32.** production with reference to the maker. **33.** disposition; nature. **34.** act or process of making.

make-be·lieve (māk′bə lēv′), *n.* **1.** pretense; feigning; sham. **2.** a pretender. —*adj.* **3.** pretended; feigned; sham.

mak·er (mā′kər), *n.* **1.** one who makes. **2.** (*cap.*) God.

make·shift (māk′shĭft′), *n.* **1.** a temporary expedient or substitute. —*adj.* **2.** serving as or of the nature of a makeshift.

make-up (māk′ŭp′), *n.* **1.** the way in which an actor or other person dresses himself, paints his face, etc., for a part. **2.** the articles used for this purpose, esp. cosmetics, etc. **3.** composition. **4.** physical or mental constitution.

mak·ing (mā′kĭng), *n.* **1.** act of one who or that which makes. **2. in the making,** being made. **3.** structure; constitution. **4.** means or cause of success. **5.** (*often pl.*) material of which something may be made.

Mal·a·bar Coast (măl′ə bär′), a coastal district in SW India. 3,929,000 pop.; 5790 sq. mi.

Ma·lac·ca (mə lăk′ə), *n.* **1.** a settlement in the SW Malay Peninsula: now in the Malayan Union. 212,282 pop.; 640 sq. mi. **2. Strait of,** a strait between Sumatra and the Malay Peninsula. 35-185 mi. wide.

Mal·a·chi (măl′ə kī′), *n.* a Hebrew prophet of the 5th century B.C. and author of the last book of the minor prophets.

mal·a·chite (măl′ə kīt′), *n.* a green mineral, basic copper carbonate: an ore of copper.

mal·ad·just·ed (măl′ə jŭs′tĭd), *adj.* badly adjusted.

mal·ad·just·ment (măl′ə jŭst′mənt), *n.* a faulty adjustment.

mal·ad·min·is·ter (măl′əd mĭn′əs tər), *v.t.* to manage (esp. public affairs) badly. —**mal′ad·min′is·tra′tion,** *n.*

mal·a·droit (măl′ə droit′), *adj.* unskillful; awkward. —**mal′a·droit′ly,** *adv.* —**mal′a·droit′ness,** *n.*

mal·a·dy (măl′ə dĭ), *n., pl.* **-dies. 1.** any bodily disorder or disease, esp. one that is chronic or deep-seated. **2.** any disorder.

Mál·a·ga (măl′ə gə), *n.* a seaport in S Spain, on the Mediterranean. 259,000.

Mal·a·ga (măl′ə gə), *n.* **1.** a sweet strong white wine produced in the province of Málaga, Spain. **2.** any of the grapes grown in or exported from Málaga.

ma·laise (mă lāz′), *n.* a condition of indefinite bodily weakness or discomfort, often marking the onset of a disease.

Mal·a·prop (măl′ə prŏp′), *n.* **Mrs.,** the "old weather-beaten she-dragon" of Sheridan's *Rivals* (1775), noted for her misapplication of words.

mal·a·prop·ism (măl′ə prŏp ĭz′əm), *n.* **1.** ridiculous misuse of words. **2.** a word so misused.

mal·ap·ro·pos (măl′ăp rə pō′), *adj.* **1.** inappropriate. —*adv.* **2.** inappropriately.

ma·lar·i·a (mə lâr′ĭ ə), *n.* a group of diseases characterized by attacks of chills, fever, and sweating, caused by parasitic protozoans which are transferred to the human blood by mosquitoes (genus *Anopheles*). —**ma·lar′i·al, ma·lar′i·an, ma·lar′i·ous,** *adj.*

Ma·lay (mā′lā, mə lā′), *adj.* **1.** of or pertaining to the Malays or their country or language. —*n.* **2.** a member of the dominant people of the Malay Peninsula and adjacent islands. **3.** their language.

Ma·lay·a (mə lā′ə), *n.* **1.** the Malay Peninsula. **2. Federation of,** a federation of political subdivisions of the Malay Peninsula, superseding the **Malayan Union** (formed 1946) in 1948: a British protectorate. ab. 4,652,000 pop.; 53,097 sq. mi. *Cap.:* Kuala Lumpur.

Ma·lay·an (mə lā′ən), *adj.* **1.** Malay. —*n.* **2.** a Malay. **3.** Indonesian.

Malay Archipelago, an extensive archipelago in the Indian and Pacific Oceans, SE of Asia: the islands of the East Indies, including the Moluccas, Borneo, and the Philippine Islands. Also. **Ma·lay·sia** (mə lā′zhə, -shə).

Malay Peninsula, a peninsula in SE Asia, consisting of British Malaya and the S part of Siam.

Malay States, a group of states in the Malay Peninsula, under British protection. ab. 4,079,000 pop.; 51,887 sq. mi. See **Malaya** (def. 2).

mal·con·tent (măl′kən tĕnt′), adj. 1. discontented; dissatisfied. 2. inclined, to rebellion. —n. 3. a malcontent person.

mal de mer (măl də mĕr′), seasickness.

Mal·den (môl′dən), n. a city in E Massachusetts, near Boston, 58,010.

Mal·dive Islands (măl′dīv), a group of coral atolls in the Indian Ocean, SW of India: a dependency of Ceylon. 88,000 pop.; 115 sq. mi.

male (māl), adj. 1. belonging to the sex which begets young. 2. masculine. 3. composed of males. 4. Bot. a. designating or pertaining to any structure which produces fertilization of the female element. b. (of seed plants) staminate. 5. Mach. designating some part, etc., which fits into a corresponding part. —n. 6. a man or boy. 7. any animal of male sex. 8. Bot. a staminate plant.

mal·e·dic·tion (măl′ə dīk′shən), n. 1. a curse. 2. slander. —**mal·e·dic·to·ry** (măl′ə dīk′tə rī′), adj.

mal·e·fac·tor (măl′ə făk′tər), n. 1. an offender against the law. 2. one who does evil.

ma·lef·i·cent (mə lĕf′ə sənt), adj. doing evil; harmful. —**ma·lef′i·cence,** n.

ma·lev·o·lent (mə lĕv′ə lənt), adj. 1. wishing evil to another or others. 2. Astrol. malign influence. —**ma·lev′o·lent·ly,** adv. —**ma·lev′o·lence,** n.

mal·fea·sance (măl fē′zəns), n. Law. the wrongful performance of an act which the person has no right to perform. —**mal·fea′sant,** adj., n.

mal·for·ma·tion (măl′fôr mā′shən), n. faulty or anomalous structure.

mal·formed (măl fôrmd′), adj. faultily or badly formed.

mal·ice (măl′ĭs), n. 1. desire to inflict injury or suffering on another. 2. evil intent.

malice aforethought, Law. (in homicide) a deliberate, premeditated intent to kill, or to do serious bodily harm.

ma·li·cious (mə lĭsh′əs), adj. 1. full of, characterized by, or showing malice. 2. Law. motivated by vicious, wanton, or mischievous purposes. —**ma·li′cious·ly,** adv. —**ma·li′cious·ness,** n.

ma·lign (mə līn′), v.t. 1. to speak ill of; slander. —adj. 2. evil in effect; pernicious. 3. malevolent. —**ma·lign′er,** n. —**ma·lign′ly,** adv. —**ma·lig·ni·ty** (mə lĭg′nə tĭ′), n.

ma·lig·nant (mə lĭg′nənt), adj. 1. disposed to inflict suffering or cause distress. 2. harmful in influence or effect. 3. Pathol. deadly, as a disease, a tumor, etc. —**ma·lig′nance, ma·lig′nan·cy,** n. —**ma·lig′nant·ly,** adv.

ma·lines (mə lēn′), n. a delicate net fabric resembling tulle. Also, **ma·line′.**

ma·lin·ger (mə lĭng′gər), v.i. to feign sickness or injury, esp. in order to avoid duty, work, etc. —**ma·lin′ger·er,** n.

mall (môl, măl), n. a shaded walk, usually public.

mal·lard (măl′ərd), n., pl. -lards, (esp. collectively) -lard. a common, almost cosmopolitan wild duck from which the domestic ducks descended.

mal·le·a·ble (măl′ī ə bəl), adj. 1. capable of being extended or shaped by hammering or by pressure with rollers. 2. adaptable. —**mal′le·a·bil′i·ty, mal′le·a·ble·ness,** n.

mal·let (măl′ĭt), n. 1. a hammerlike tool with a head commonly of wood, used for driving any tool with a wooden handle, as a chisel. 2. the wooden implement used to strike the ball in croquet or polo.

mal·low (măl′ō), n. 1. any of certain herbs with leaves usually angularly lobed or dissected, and purple, pink, or white flowers. 2. any plant of the same family.

Malm·ö (măl′mō), n. a seaport in S Sweden. 171,158.

malm·sey (măm′zĭ), n. a strong sweet wine of a high flavor.

mal·nu·tri·tion (măl′nū trĭsh′ən, -noo-), n. lack of proper nutrition.

mal·o·dor·ous (măl ō′dər əs), adj. having a bad odor. —**mal·o′dor·ous·ly,** adv.

Mal·o·ry (măl′ə rĭ), n. Sir Thomas, fl. 1470, British translator.

mal·prac·tice (măl prăk′tĭs), n. improper professional action or conduct, as from reprehensible ignorance.

malt (môlt), n. 1. germinated grain (usually barley), used in brewing and distilling. 2. liquor produced from malt by fermentation, as beer. —v.t. 3. to convert (grain) into malt. —**malt′y,** adj.

Mal·ta (môl′tə), n. 1. a British island in the Mediterranean between Sicily and Africa: naval station. 222,000 pop.; 95 sq. mi. 2. a British colony consisting of this island and two small adjacent islands. 268,688 pop.; 122 sq. mi. Cap.: Valletta. —**Mal·tese′,** adj., n.

Maltese cat, a bluish-gray domestic cat.

Maltese cross, a cross having four equal arms that expand in width outward.

Mal·thus (măl′thəs), n. Thomas Robert, 1766–1834, British political economist.

malt·ose (môl′tōs), n. Chem. a white crystalline sugar formed by the action of diastase (as in malt) on starch.

mal·treat (măl trēt′), v.t. to treat ill; abuse. —**mal·treat′ment,** n.

ma·ma (mä′mə, mə mä′), n. mother.

mam·ma¹ (mä′mə, mə mä′), n. (esp. in childish use) mother.

mam·ma² (măm′ə), n., pl. **mammae** (măm′ē). the organ, characteristic of mammals, which in the female secretes milk.

mam·mal (măm′əl), n. a member of a class of vertebrates whose young feed upon milk from the mother's breast. —**mam·ma′li·an,** n., adj.

mam·ma·ry (măm′ə rĭ′), adj. Anat., etc. of or pertaining to the mamma or breast.

mam·mon (măm′ən), n. New Testament. riches or material wealth.

mam·moth (măm′əth), n. 1. a large, extinct species of elephant which had a hairy coat and long, curved tusks. —adj. 2. huge; gigantic.

mam·my (măm′ĭ), n., pl. -mies. 1. (in childish use) mother. 2. Southern U.S. a colored female nurse or old family servant.

man (măn), n., pl. **men,** v., **manned, manning.** —n. 1. Anthropol. an individual (genus Homo, family Hominidae, class Mammalia) at the highest level of animal development, mainly characterized by his exceptional mentality. 2. the human race; mankind. 3. a person. 4. the male human being. 5. a husband. 6. one; anyone (prec. by a). 7. a male follower, subordinate, or employee. 8. one having manly qualities. 9. one of the pieces used in playing certain games, as chess or checkers. —v.t. 10. to furnish with men, as for service. 11. to take one's place for service, as at a gun.

Man, n. **Isle of,** an island in the Irish Sea: one of the British Isles. 48,485 pop.; 227 sq. mi. Cap.: Douglas.

Man., 1. Manila. 2. Manitoba.

man·a·cle (măn′ə kəl), n., v., -cled, -cling. —n. (usually pl.) 1. a handcuff. —v.t. 2. to handcuff. 3. to hamper; restrain.

man·age (măn′ĭj), v., -aged, -aging. —v.t. 1. to bring about. 2. to take charge or care of. 3. to influence (a person), as by tact. 4. to handle, direct, or control in action or use. 5. to wield (a weapon, tool, etc.). 6. to succeed in accomplishing (a task, purpose, etc.). —v.i. 7. to conduct affairs. —**man′age·a·ble,** adj. —**man′age·a·bly,** adv.

man·age·ment (măn′ĭj mənt), n. 1. handling, direction, or control. 2. executive ability. 3. the person or persons managing an institution, business, etc.

man·ag·er (măn′ĭj ər), n. one who manages a business, household, etc.

man·a·ge·ri·al (măn′ə jĭr′ĭ əl), adj. pertaining to management or a manager.

Ma·na·gua (mä nä′gwä), n. the capital of Nicaragua, in the W part. 93,032.

ma·ña·na (mä nyä′nä), n., adv. Spanish. tomorrow; the indefinite future.

Ma·nas·sas (mə năs′əs), *n.* a town in NE Virginia: battles of Bull Run (1861, 1862). 1302.

Ma·nas·seh (mə năs′ə), *n.* **1.** son of the patriarch Joseph. **2.** one of the ten tribes of Israel.

man-at-arms (măn′ət ärmz′), *n.*, *pl.* **men-at-arms. 1.** a soldier. **2.** a heavy-armed soldier on horseback.

man·a·tee (măn′ə tē′), *n.* any of various herbivorous, gregarious aquatic mammals having a spoon-shaped tail, of West Indian and Gulf coast waters.

Man·ches·ter (măn′chĕs′tər, -chĭs tər), *n.* **1.** a city in W England. 671,500. **2.** a city in S New Hampshire. 77,685.

Man·chu (măn chōō′), *n.* **1.** one of a Mongolian people inhabiting Manchuria, who conquered China in the 17th century. **2.** the language spoken by the Manchus. —*adj.* **3.** of or pertaining to the Manchus, their country, or their language.

Man·chu·ri·a (măn chŏŏr′ĭ ə), *n.* a territory in E Asia, comprising nine NE provinces of China. 33,942,000 pop.; ab. 413,000 sq. mi. *Cap.:* Changchun. —**Man·chu′ri·an,** *adj.*, *n.*

Man·da·lay (măn′də lā′, măn′də lā′), *n.* a city in central Burma. 134,950.

man·da·mus (măn dā′məs), *n.* *Law.* a writ from a superior court to an inferior court, or to an officer, a corporation, etc., commanding a specified thing to be done.

man·da·rin (măn′də rĭn), *n.* **1.** a member of any of the nine ranks of public officials in the Chinese Empire. **2.** (*cap.*) standard Chinese. **3.** (*cap.*) the north China language, esp. that of Peking. **4.** a small, flattish citrus fruit of which the tangerine is one variety, native in southwestern Asia.

man·da·tar·y (măn′də tĕr′Ĭ), *n.*, *pl.* **-taries.** a person or nation holding a mandate.

man·date (*n.* măn′dāt, -dĬt; *v.* măn′dāt), *n.*, *v.*, **-dated, -dating.** —*n.* **1.** a commission given to one nation by an associated group of nations (such as the League of Nations) to administer the government and affairs of a people in a backward territory. **2.** a mandated territory. **3.** *Pol.* the instruction as to policy given by the electors to a legislative body or to one or more of its members. **4.** a command from a superior court or official to an inferior one. **5.** a command; order. —*v.t.* **6.** to consign (a territory, etc.) under a mandate.

man·da·to·ry (măn′də tōr′Ĭ), *adj.*, *n.*, *pl.* **-ries.** —*adj.* **1.** pertaining to, of the nature of, or containing a mandate. **2.** obligatory. **3.** *Law.* permitting no option. **4.** having received a mandate. —*n.* **5.** mandatary.

man·di·ble (măn′də bəl), *n.* **1.** the bone of the lower jaw. **2.** (in birds) **a.** the lower part of the beak. **b.** (*pl.*) the upper and lower parts of the beak. **3.** (in arthropods) one of the first pair of mouth-part appendages.

man·do·lin (măn′də lĭn′, măn′də lĭn′), *n.* a musical instrument with a pear-shaped wooden body.

man·drag·o·ra (măn drăg′ə rə), *n.* **1.** mandrake. **2.** a mandrake root.

man·drake (măn′drāk, -drĭk), *n.* **1.** a narcotic, short-stemmed European herb of the nightshade family, with a fleshy, often forked root fancied to resemble a human form. **2.** *U.S.* the May apple.

man·drel (măn′drəl), *n.* a spindle, axle, bar, or arbor pressed into a hole in a piece of work to support the work during the machining process. Also, **man·dril.**

man·drill (măn′drĭl), *n.* a large, ferocious-looking baboon of western Africa.

mane (mān), *n.* the long hair growing on the back of or about the neck of some animals, as the horse, lion, etc. —**maned** (mānd), *adj.*

ma·nège (mă nĕzh′, -nāzh′), *n.* **1.** the art of riding horses. **2.** the movements of a trained horse. **3.** a school for teaching horsemanship. Also, **ma·nege′.**

ma·nes (mā′nēz), *n.pl.* (among the ancient Romans) the deified souls of the dead.

Ma·net (mà nĕ′), *n.* Édouard, 1832–83, French impressionist painter.

ma·neu·ver (mə nōō′vər), *n.*, *v.*, **-vered, -vering.** —*n.* **1.** a planned and regulated movement of troops, war vessels, etc. **2.** (*pl.*) a series of tactical exercises by large bodies of troops. **3.** an adroit move. —*v.t.*, *v.i.* **4.** to change the position of (troops, vessels, etc.) by a maneuver. **5.** to bring, put, drive, or make by maneuvers. **6.** to manipulate with skill. —**ma·neu′ver·a·ble,** *adj.*

man·ful (măn′fəl), *adj.* manly; resolute. —**man′ful·ly,** *adv.* —**man′ful·ness,** *n.*

man·ga·nese (măng′gə nēs′, -nēz′), *n.* *Chem.* a hard, brittle, grayish-white metallic element, whose oxide (**manganese oxide**) is a valuable oxidizing agent, used as alloying agent in steel to give it toughness. *Symbol:* Mn; *at. wt.:* 54.93; *at. no.:* 25; *sp. gr.:* 7.2 at 20°C.

mange (mānj), *n.* any of various skin diseases due to parasitic mites affecting animals and sometimes man.

man·gel-wur·zel (măng′gəl wûr′zəl), *n.* *Chiefly Brit.* a coarse variety of the common beet, extensively cultivated as food for cattle, etc. Also, **man′gel.**

man·ger (măn′jər), *n.* a box or trough, as in a stable, from which horses or cattle eat.

man·gle[1] (măng′gəl), *v.t.*, **-gled, -gling. 1.** to cut, slash, or crush so as to disfigure. **2.** to mar; spoil. —**man′gler,** *n.*

man·gle[2] (măng′gəl), *n.*, *v.*, **-gled, -gling.** —*n.* **1.** a machine for smoothing or pressing cloth, household linen, etc., by means of rollers. —*v.t.* **2.** to smooth with a mangle.

man·go (măng′gō), *n.*, *pl.* **-goes, -gos. 1.** the oblong, slightly acid fruit of a tropical tree which is eaten ripe, or preserved or pickled. **2.** the tree itself.

man·grove (măng′grōv, măn′-), *n.* any of certain tropical trees remarkable for a copious development of interlacing adventitious roots above the ground.

man·gy (măn′jĬ), *adj.*, **-gier, -giest. 1.** having, caused by, or like the mange. **2.** contemptible. **3.** squalid. —**man′gi·ness,** *n.*

man·han·dle (măn′hăn′dəl), *v.t.*, **-dled, -dling.** to handle roughly.

Man·hat·tan (măn hăt′ən), *n.* **1.** an island in New York City. 22¼ sq. mi. **2.** a borough of New York City coextensive with Manhattan Island. 1,889,924 pop. **3.** a cocktail of whiskey and sweet vermouth.

man·hole (măn′hōl′), *n.* a hole, usually with a cover, through which a man may enter a sewer, drain, etc., as to make repairs.

man·hood (măn′hŏŏd), *n.* **1.** state of being a man. **2.** manly qualities. **3.** men collectively.

man-hour (măn′our′), *n.* an hour of work by one man, used as an industrial time unit.

ma·ni·a (mā′nĬ ə), *n.* **1.** great excitement or enthusiasm; craze. **2.** *Psychiatry.* a form of insanity characterized by great excitement and, in its acute stage, by great violence.

ma·ni·ac (mā′nĬ ăk′), *n.* **1.** a raving lunatic. —*adj.* **2.** raving with madness.

ma·ni·a·cal (mə nī′ə kəl), *adj.* of or pertaining to mania or a maniac.

ma·nic (mā′nĭk, măn′Ĭk), *adj.* *Med.* pertaining to mania.

man·ic-de·pres·sive (măn′Ĭk dĬ prĕs′Ĭv), *Psychiatry.* —*adj.* **1.** having a mental disorder marked by alternate manifestations of excitation and depression. —*n.* **2.** one who is suffering from this disorder.

man·i·cure (măn′ə kyŏŏr′), *n.*, *v.*, **-cured, -curing.** —*n.* **1.** professional care of the hands and fingernails. —*v.t.*, *v.i.* **2.** to care for (the hands and fingernails). —**man′i·cur′ist,** *n.*

man·i·fest (măn′ə fĕst′), *adj.* **1.** readily perceived; evident; obvious. —*v.t.* **2.** to show plainly. **3.** to prove. —*n.* **4.** a list of a ship's cargo for the use of custom-house officers. —**man′i·fest′ly,** *adv.* —**man′i·fest′ness,** *n.*

man·i·fes·ta·tion (măn′ə fĕs tā′shən), *n.* **1.** act of manifesting. **2.** state of being manifested. **3.** a means of manifesting; indication.

man·i·fes·to (măn′ə fĕs′tō), *n.*, *pl.* **-toes.** a public declaration, as of a government or of any body of persons taking important action, making known objects, motives, etc.

man·i·fold (măn′ə fōld′), *adj.* **1.** of many kinds; numerous and varied. **2.** having many different parts, features, etc. **3.** doing or operating several things at once. —*n.* **4.** something having many different parts. **5.** a copy or facsimile, as of writing. **6.** a pipe with a number of inlets or outlets. —*v.t.* **7.** to make copies of. —**man′i·fold′ly,** *adv.*

man·i·kin (măn′ə kĭn), *n.* **1.** a dwarf; pygmy. **2.** mannequin.

Ma·nil·a (mə nĬl′ə), *n.* **1.** a seaport in and the capital of the Philippine Islands, on W Luzon island. 623,492. **2.** Manila hemp. **3.** Manila paper.

Manila hemp, a fibrous material obtained from the leaves of the abacá, used for making ropes, fabrics, etc.

Manila paper, a strong light-brown paper derived orig. from Manila hemp, but now also from wood-pulp substitutes.

ma·nip·u·late (mə nĭp′yə lāt′), *v.t.*, **-lated, -lating.** 1. to handle, manage, or use, esp. with skill. 2. to adapt (accounts, etc.) to suit one's purpose or advantage. —**ma·nip′u·la′tion,** *n.* —**ma·nip′u·la′tive, ma·nip′u·la·to/ry,** *adj.* —**ma·nip′u·la′tor,** *n.*

man·i·to (măn′ə tō′), *n., pl.* **-tos.** (among the Algonquian Indians) a spirit of supernatural power. Also, **man·i·tou** (măn′ə tōō′).

Man·i·to·ba (măn′ə tō′bə), *n.* a province in central Canada. 729,744 pop.; 246,512 sq. mi. *Cap.:* Winnipeg.

man·kind (măn′kīnd′ *for* 1; măn′kīnd′ *for* 2), *n.* 1. the human race. 2. men, as distinguished from women.

man·like (măn′līk′), *adj.* 1. resembling a man. 2. manly.

man·ly (măn′lĭ), *adj.,* **-lier, -liest.** 1. possessing qualities proper to a man; strong; brave; honorable. 2. pertaining to or befitting a man. —**man′li·ness,** *n.*

Mann (măn *for* 1; män *for* 2), *n.* 1. **Horace,** 1796–1859, U.S. educational reformer. 2. **Thomas,** born 1875, German novelist, in U.S. since 1938.

man·na (măn′ə), *n.* 1. the food miraculously supplied the children of Israel in the wilderness. 2. divine or spirtual food.

man·ne·quin (măn′ə kĭn), *n.* 1. a person employed to wear clothing to exhibit to customers. 2. a figure used by artists, tailors, etc.

man·ner (măn′ər), *n.* 1. way of doing, being done, or happening. 2. customary way of doing. 3. (*pl.*) the prevailing customs, etc., of a people, period, etc. 4. a person's outward bearing. 5. (*pl.*) ways of behaving. 6. (*pl.*) polite ways of behaving. 7. kind; sort. 8. characteristic style. 9. **by all manner of means,** certainly.

man·ner·ism (măn′ə rĭz′əm), *n.* 1. marked or excessive adherence to an unusual manner. 2. a habitual peculiarity of manner. —**man′ner·ist,** *n.*

man·ner·less (măn′ər lĭs), *adj.* without (good) manners.

man·ner·ly (măn′ər lĭ), *adj.* 1. courteous; polite. —*adv.* 2. courteously; politely. —**man′ner·li·ness,** *n.*

Mann·heim (măn′hīm), *n.* a city in SW Germany. 284,957.

man·ni·kin (măn′ə kĭn), *n.* manikin.

man·nish (măn′ĭsh), *adj.* 1. characteristic of or natural to a man. 2. resembling a man. 3. imitating a man. —**man′nish·ly,** *adv.* —**man′nish·ness,** *n.*

ma·noeu·vre (mə nōō′vər), *n., v.t., v.i.,* **-vred, -vring.** maneuver.

man-of-war (măn′əv wôr′), *n., pl.* **men-of-war.** a warship.

man·or (măn′ər), *n.* a landed estate, orig. a feudal holding. —**ma·no·ri·al** (mə nōr′ĭ əl), *adj.*

man power, 1. the power supplied by the physical exertions of a man or men. 2. power in terms of men available or required.

man·sard (măn′särd), *n.* a form of roof with two slopes, the upper slope being nearly flat. Also, **mansard roof.**

manse (măns), *n.* the house and land occupied by a minister or parson.

man·serv·ant (măn′sûr′vənt), *n., pl.* **menservants.** a male servant.

Mans·field (mănz′fēld), *n.* a city in N Ohio. 37,154.

man·sion (măn′shən), *n.* 1. an imposing or stately residence. 2. the house of a manor.

man·slaugh·ter (măn′slô′tər), *n.* 1. homicide. 2. *Law.* the killing of a human being unlawfully but without malice aforethought.

manta ray, a huge tropical ray, reaching a width of twenty feet, with earlike flaps on either side of the head.

man·tel (măn′tel), *n.* 1. the ornamental structure above and about a fireplace, usually having a shelf. 2. Also, **man′tel·piece′.** the shelf.

man·til·la (măn tĭl′ə), *n.* a silk or lace head scarf arranged over a high comb and falling over the back and shoulders, worn in Spain, Mexico, etc.

man·tis (măn′tĭs), *n., pl.* **-tises, -tes** (-tēz). any of certain carnivorous orthopterous insects which hold their forelegs doubled up as if in prayer.

man·tle (măn′təl), *n., v.,* **-tled, -tling.** —*n.* 1. a loose, sleeveless cloak. 2. something that covers, envelops, or conceals. 3. a chemically prepared network hood for a gas jet, which, when the jet is lighted, becomes incandescent and gives a brilliant light. —*v.t.* 4. to cover with a mantle; envelop. —*v.i.* 5. to flush; blush.

man·tu·a (măn′chōō ə), *n.* 1. a loose gown formerly worn by women. 2. a mantle.

Praying mantis
(Ab. 2½ in. long)

man·u·al (măn′yōō əl), *adj.* 1. of, pertaining to, or done by the hand or hands. —*n.* 2. a small book, esp. one giving information. 3. *Mil.* prescribed exercises in the handling of the rifle. 4. *Music.* a keyboard played with the hands. —**man′u·al·ly,** *adv.*

manual training, the training of pupils in woodworking and other crafts and arts.

man·u·fac·ture (măn′yə făk′chər), *n., v.,* **-tured, -turing.** —*n.* 1. the making of goods by manual labor or machinery, esp. on a large scale. 2. the making of anything. 3. the thing manufactured. —*v.t.* 4. to make by hand or machinery, esp. on a large scale. 5. to work up (material) into form for use. 6. to invent fictitiously. —**man′u·fac′tur·a·ble,** *adj.* —**man′u·fac′tur·ing,** *n.*

man·u·fac·tur·er (măn′yə făk′chər ər), *n.* 1. one who owns or runs a manufacturing plant. 2. one who manufactures.

man·u·mit (măn′yə mĭt′), *v.t.,* **-mitted, -mitting.** to release from slavery or servitude. —**man·u·mis·sion** (măn′yə mĭsh′ən), *n.*

ma·nure (mə nyōōr′, -nōōr′), *n., v.,* **-nured, -nuring.** —*n.* 1. any substance for fertilizing the soil. 2. dung or refuse of the stable, etc. —*v.t.* 3. to apply manure to.

man·u·script (măn′yə skrĭpt′), *n.* 1. a book, document, letter, etc., written by hand. 2. writing, as distinguished from print. —*adj.* 3. written or typed by hand (not printed).

Manx (măngks), *adj.* 1. of or pertaining to the Isle of Man, its inhabitants, or their language. —*n.* 2. (construed as *pl.*) the inhabitants of the Isle of Man. 3. the Gaelic of the Isle of Man, virtually extinct.

Manx cat, a tailless variety of the domestic cat.

Manx·man (măngks′mən), *n., pl.* **-men.** a native or inhabitant of the Isle of Man.

man·y (mĕn′ĭ), *adj.,* **more, most,** *n.* —*adj.* 1. constituting a large number. 2. relatively numerous (after *as, so, too,* or *how*). 3. being one of a large number (fol. by *a* or *an*). —*n.* 4. a great number. 5. many persons or things.

Ma·o·ri (mä′ō rĭ, mou′rĭ, mä′rĭ), *n., pl.* **-ris.** 1. a member of the native brown race of Polynesians of New Zealand. 2. their language.

Mao Tse-tung (mou′ dzŭ′dŏŏng′), born 1893, Chinese communist leader.

map (măp), *n., v.,* **mapped, mapping.** —*n.* 1. a representation, on a flat surface, of a part or the whole of the earth's surface, the heavens, or a heavenly body. —*v.t.* 2. to represent in a map. 3. to plan.

ma·ple (mā′pəl), *n.* 1. any of certain trees of the north temperate zone, species of which are valued for shade and ornament, for their wood, or for their sap, from which a syrup (**maple syrup**) and a sugar (**maple sugar**) are obtained. 2. the wood of any such tree.

Ma·quis (mä kē′), *n. sing. and pl.* a member of one of the French underground groups resisting the Germans in World War II.

mar (mär), *v.t.,* **marred, marring.** 1. to damage; ruin. 2. to deface.

Mar., March.

mar., 1. maritime. 2. married.

mar·a·bou (măr′ə bōō′), *n.* 1. any of three large storks of Africa and the East Indies, having under the wings and tail soft, downy feathers that are used in millinery and for making a furlike trimming. 2. one of the feathers. 3. the trimming or material made of them.

Mar·a·cai·bo (măr′ə kī′bō), *n.* a seaport in NW Venezuela. 112,519.

mar·a·schi·no (măr′ə skē′nō), *n.* a cordial or liqueur distilled from certain wild cherries.

maraschino cherries, cherries cooked in colored syrup and flavored with imitation maraschino.

mar·a·thon (măr/ə thŏn/, -thən), *n.* **1.** any long-distance race. **2.** a foot race of about 26 miles. **3.** any long contest with endurance as the primary factor. **4.** (*cap.*) a plain in Attica, NE of Athens, Greece: the Athenians defeated the Persians there, 490 B.C.

ma·raud (mə rôd/), *v.i.*, *v.t.* **1.** to plunder; raid for booty. —*n.* **2.** act of marauding. —**maraud/er,** *n.*

mar·ble (măr/bəl), *n.*, *adj.*, *v.*, **-bled, -bling.** —*n.* **1.** limestone in a crystalline state and capable of taking a polish, much used in sculpture and architecture. **2.** a piece of this stone. **3.** a work of art carved in marble. **4.** *Games.* **a.** a little ball of glass, etc., used in a children's game. **b.** (*pl. construed as sing.*) the game itself. —*adj.* **5.** of or like marble. —*v.t.* **6.** to color or stain like variegated marble.

mar·ca·site (măr/kə sīt/), *n.* a common mineral, iron disulfide, of the same composition as pyrite.

mar·cel (mär sĕl/), *v.*, **-celled, -celling,** *n.* —*v.t.* **1.** to produce regular, continuous waves in (the hair). —*n.* **2.** a marcelling. **3.** a marcelled condition.

march¹ (märch), *v.i.* **1.** to walk with regular and measured tread, as soldiers. **2.** to walk in a stately or deliberate manner. **3.** to advance. —*v.t.* **4.** to cause to march. —*n.* **5.** act or course of marching. **6.** the distance traversed in a single course of marching. **7.** advance. **8.** a piece of music with a rhythm suited to accompany marching. —**march/er,** *n.*

march² (märch), *n.* **1.** a tract of land along a border; frontier. —*v.i.* **2.** to border.

March (märch), *n.* the third month of the year, containing thirty-one days.

mar·chion·ess (mär/shən ĭs, mär/shə nĕs/), *n.* the wife or widow of a marquis.

march·pane (märch/pān/), *n.* marzipan.

Mar·co·ni (mär kō/nĭ), *n.* **Guglielmo,** 1874–1937, Italian inventor of the first successful wireless telegraph.

Mar·cus Au·re·li·us (mär/kəs ô rē/lĭ əs, ô-rēl/yəs), A.D. 121–180, emperor of Rome, A.D. 161–180: Stoic philosopher.

Mar·cy (mär/sĭ), *n.* **Mount,** a mountain in NE New York: the highest peak of the Adirondack Mountains. 5344 ft.

Mar·di gras (mär/dĭ grä/), Shrove Tuesday: the last day of carnival, celebrated in Paris, New Orleans, etc. with festivities.

mare (mâr), *n.* the female of the horse kind.

Ma·ren·go (mə rĕng/gō), *n.* a village in NW Italy: Napoleon defeated the Austrians here, 1800.

mare's-nest (mârz/nĕst/), *n.* something imagined to be an extraordinary discovery but proving to be a delusion or a hoax.

mar·ga·rine (mär/jə rēn/, -rĭn, -gə-), *n.* a butterlike product made by emulsifying vegetable fats or animal fats in ripened milk.

mar·gin (mär/jĭn), *n.* **1.** a border or edge. **2.** (*pl.*) the space bordering the printed or written matter on a page. **3.** a limit beyond which something ceases to exist or be possible. **4.** an amount allowed or available beyond what is actually necessary. **5.** *Finance.* security, as a percentage in money, deposited with a broker as a provision against loss on transactions on behalf of his principal. **6.** *Com.* the difference between the cost and the selling price. —*v.t.* **7.** to provide with a margin or border.

mar·gin·al (mär/jə nəl), *adj.* **1.** pertaining to a margin. **2.** situated on the border or edge. **3.** written or printed in the margin of a page. **4.** *Econ.* **a.** supplying goods at a rate merely covering the cost of production. **b.** of or pertaining to goods produced and marketed at margin. —**mar/gin·al·ly,** *adv.*

mar·gue·rite (mär/gə rēt/), *n.* **1.** the common European daisy. **2.** any of several flowers of the daisy kind.

Ma·ri·a·nas Islands (mä/rē ä/näs), *n.* group of 15 small islands in the Pacific, E of the Philippine Islands: formerly mandated to Japan (except Guam); now under U.S. trusteeship. ab. 66,000 pop.; 453 sq. mi.

Ma·rie An·toi·nette (mə rē/ ăn/twə nĕt/), 1755–93, queen of France, 1774–93, and wife of Louis XVI: executed in the French Revolution.

mar·i·gold (măr/ə gōld/), *n.* any of certain chiefly golden-flowered plants, most of which belong to the composite or aster family.

ma·ri·jua·na (mä/rə hwä/nə), *n.* an Indian hemp, whose dried leaves and flowers are used in cigarettes as a narcotic. Also, **ma/ri·hua/na.**

ma·rim·ba (mə rĭm/bə), *n.* a musical instrument resembling the xylophone.

mar·i·nate (măr/ə nāt/), *v.t.*, **-nated, -nating. 1.** to let stand in a seasoned vinegar-oil mixture. **2.** to apply French dressing to (a food) which will be used later in a salad with mayonnaise. —**mar/i·na/tion,** *n.*

ma·rine (mə rēn/), *adj.* **1.** of, pertaining to, or living in the sea. —*n.* **2.** shipping in general; fleet. **3.** a member of the U.S. Marine Corps.

Marine Corps, a branch of the U.S. Navy usually employed as a landing force.

mar·i·ner (măr/ə nər), *n.* a seaman; sailor.

Mar·i·on (măr/Y ən, mâr/-), *n.* a city in central Ohio. 30,817.

mar·i·o·nette (măr/Y ə nĕt/), *n.* a puppet moved by strings or the hands.

mar·i·tal (măr/ə təl), *adj.* of or pertaining to marriage. —**mar/i·tal·ly,** *adv.*

mar·i·time (măr/ə tīm/), *adj.* **1.** connected with the sea in relation to navigation, shipping, etc. **2.** of or pertaining to the sea. **3.** bordering on the sea.

Maritime Provinces, the Canadian provinces of Nova Scotia, New Brunswick, and Prince Edward Island.

mar·jo·ram (mär/jə rəm), *n.* any of certain plants of the mint family, esp. **sweet marjoram** which is used in cookery.

mark¹ (märk), *n.* **1.** a visible trace, as a line, cut, dent, stain, bruise, etc. **2.** a badge, brand, or other visible sign assumed or imposed. **3.** a symbol used in writing or printing. **4.** a sign, usually a cross, made by an illiterate person by way of signature. **5.** a sign, token, or indication. **6.** a symbol used in rating conduct, proficiency, etc., as of pupils. **7.** a recognized standard. **8.** note, importance, or distinction. **9.** an object aimed at. —*v.t.* **10.** to be a distinguishing feature of. **11.** to put a mark or marks on. **12.** to attach a price, identification, etc., on. **13.** to single out; destine. **14.** to give heed or attention to. **15. mark time, a.** to suspend progress temporarily. **b.** *Mil.* to move the feet alternately as in marching, but without advancing. —*v.i.* **16.** to take notice; consider. —**mark/er,** *n.*

mark² (märk), *n.* the monetary unit and a silver coin of Germany, normally equivalent to about 23.8 U.S. cents.

Mark (märk), *n.* **1.** the evangelist John Mark, traditionally considered the author of the second Gospel. **2.** the second Gospel in the New Testament. **3. King,** *Arthurian Romance.* ruler of Cornwall and husband of Iseult.

mark·down (märk/doun/), *n.* a reduction in price.

marked (märkt), *adj.* **1.** strikingly noticeable; conspicuous. **2.** watched as an object for suspicion or vengeance. **3.** having a mark or marks. —**mark·ed·ly** (mär/kĭd lĭ), *adv.* —**mark/ed·ness,** *n.*

mar·ket (mär/kĭt), *n.* **1.** a meeting of people for selling and buying. **2.** the assemblage of people at such a meeting. **3.** an open space, a covered building, or a store for the sale of food, etc. **4.** trade as regards a particular commodity. **5.** a body of persons carrying on extensive transactions in a specified commodity. **6.** demand for a commodity. **7.** a region where anything is or may be sold. —*v.i.* **8.** to buy or sell in a market. —*v.t.* **9.** to carry or send to market for disposal. **10.** to sell. —**mar/ket·a·ble,** *adj.* —**mar/ket·a·bil/i·ty,** *n.*

market place, a place, esp. an open space in a town, where a market is held.

marks·man (märks/mən), *n.*, *pl.* **-men.** one who shoots well. —**marks/man·ship/,** *n.*

mark·up (märk/ŭp/), *n.* the amount or percentage added to the cost of the article in fixing the selling price.

marl (märl), *n.* **1.** a soil consisting of clay and calcium carbonate, used esp. as a fertilizer. —*v.t.* **2.** to fertilize with marl. —**marl/y,** *adj.*

mar·lin (mär/lĭn), *n.* any of a genus of large, powerful fishes of the warm waters of the Atlantic with a spearlike snout: a favorite big-game fish.

mar·line (mär/lĭn), *n.* *Naut.* small cord of two loosely twisted strands, used for seizing.

mar·line·spike (mär′lĭn spīk′), *n. Naut.* a pointed iron implement used in separating the strands of rope in splicing, etc. Also, **mar′lin·spike′**.

Mar·lowe (mär′lō), *n.* **Christopher,** 1564–93, British dramatist and poet.

mar·ma·lade (mär′mə lād′, mär′mə lād′), *n.* a clear, jellylike preserve with fruit (usually citrus) suspended in small pieces.

Mar·ma·ra (mär′mə rə), *n.* **Sea of,** a sea between European and Asiatic Turkey, connected with the Bosporus and the Dardanelles. ab. 4500 sq. mi. Also, **Mar·mo·ra** (mär′mə rə, mär mōr′ə).

mar·mo·set (mär′mə zĕt′), *n.* any of certain small, squirrellike South and Central American monkeys with soft fur and a long, nonprehensile tail.

mar·mot (mär′mət), *n.* **1.** any of a genus of bushy-tailed, thick-set rodents, as the common woodchuck. **2.** any of certain related animals, as the prairie dogs.

Marne (märn), *n.* a river in NE France, flowing W to the Seine near Paris: battles, 1914; 1918, 1944, 325 mi.

ma·roon¹ (mə rōon′), *n., adj.* dark brownish-red.

ma·roon² (mə rōon′), *v.t.* **1.** to put ashore and leave on a desolate island or coast by way of punishment, as was done by buccaneers, etc. **2.** to isolate completely and helplessly.

marque (märk), *n.* seizure in reprisal.

mar·quee (mär kē′), a rooflike shelter, as of glass, projecting above an outer door and over a sidewalk or a terrace.

mar·quis (mär′kwĭs; *Fr.* mår kē′), *n.* a nobleman ranking next below a duke and above an earl or count. Also, *Brit.,* **mar·quess** (mär′kwĭs).

mar·quise (mär kēz′; *Fr.* mår kēz′), *n.* the wife or widow of a marquis.

mar·qui·sette (mär′kĭ zĕt′, -kwĭ-), *n.* a lightweight open fabric in cotton, rayon, silk, or nylon.

Mar·ra·kech (mär rä′kĕsh), *n.* a city in W Morocco, in the French zone: one of the capitals of the sultanate. 190,314.

mar·riage (mär′ĭj), *n.* **1.** the legal union of a man with a woman for life; wedlock. **2.** the formal declaration or contract by which act a man and a woman join in wedlock. **3.** any intimate union.

mar·riage·a·ble (mär′ĭj ə bəl), *adj.* fit, esp. old enough, for marriage.

mar·ried (mär′ĭd), *adj.* **1.** united in wedlock; wedded. **2.** pertaining to marriage.

mar·row (mär′ō), *n.* **1.** a soft, fatty, vascular tissue in the interior cavities of bones. **2.** the inmost or essential part.

mar·ry¹ (mär′ĭ), *v.,* **-ried, -rying.** —*v.t.* **1.** to take in marriage. **2.** to unite in wedlock. **3.** to give in marriage. —*v.i.* **4.** to take a husband or wife; wed.

mar·ry² (mär′ĭ), *interj. Archaic.* an exclamation of surprise, etc.

Mar·ry·at (mär′ĭ ət), *n.* **Frederick,** 1792–1848, British novelist and naval officer.

Mars (märz), *n.* **1.** the ancient Roman god of war. **2.** *Astron.* the planet next outside the earth, fourth in order from the sun.

Mar·seil·laise (mär′sə lāz′; *Fr.* mår sĕ yĕz′), *n.* the French national song, written in 1792.

Mar·seilles (mär sā′; *older* -sālz′; *Fr.* -sĕ′y), *n.* a seaport in SE France. 635,939.

marsh (märsh), *n.* a tract of low, wet land; swamp.

mar·shal (mär′shəl), *n., v.,* **-shaled, -shaling** or *(esp. Brit.)* **-shalled, -shalling.** —*n.* **1.** a military officer of high rank. **2.** an administrative officer of a U.S. judicial district who performs duties similar to those of a sheriff. **3.** a court officer serving process, attending court, etc. **4.** a person charged with the arrangement or regulation of ceremonies, etc. —*v.t.* **5.** to arrange in due or proper order. **6.** to array for battle, etc. **7.** to usher or lead.

Mar·shall (mär′shəl), *n.* **1. George Catlett,** born 1880, U.S. general and statesman: secretary of state, 1947–49; secretary of defense, 1950–51. **2. John,** 1755–1835, chief justice of the U.S. Supreme Court, 1801–35.

Marshall Islands, a group of 24 islands in the N Pacific: formerly mandated to Japan; now under U.S. trusteeship. 10,684 pop.; 74 sq. mi.

Marshall Plan, former name of **European Recovery Program.**

marsh·mal·low (märsh′măl′ō; -mĕl′), *n.* a sweetened paste or confection containing gum arabic or gelatin, sugar, corn syrup, and flavoring.

marsh marigold, a yellow-flowered plant of the crowfoot family growing in marshes and meadows; cowslip.

marsh·y (mär′shĭ), *adj.,* **marshier, marshiest. 1.** like a marsh; soft and wet. **2.** pertaining to a marsh. —**marsh′i·ness,** *n.*

mar·su·pi·al (mär sōō′pĭ əl), *n.* **1.** any of the order which includes all of the viviparous, but nonplacental, mammals, such as the opossums, kangaroos, etc. Most members have a marsupium containing the mammary glands and serving as a receptacle for the young. —*adj.* **2.** pertaining to, resembling, or having a marsupium. **3.** of or pertaining to the marsupials.

mar·su·pi·um (mär sōō′pĭ əm), *n., pl.* **-pia** (-pĭ ə). the pouch or fold of skin on the abdomen of a female marsupial.

mart (märt), *n.* market; trading center.

mar·ten (mär′tən, -tĭn), *n., pl.* **-tens,** (*esp. collectively*) **-ten. 1.** any of certain slender, furbearing carnivores, as the American **pine marten** of the northern U.S. and Canada. **2.** the fur of such an animal.

Mar·tha (mär′thə), *n.* the sister of Lazarus, whose house Jesus often visited.

mar·tial (mär′shəl), *adj.* **1.** disposed to war; warlike. **2.** pertaining to the army and navy; military. **3.** pertaining to or appropriate for war. —**mar′tial·ly,** *adv.*

Mar·tial (mär′shəl), *n.* A.D. c40–c102, Roman writer of epigrams, born in Spain.

martial law, the law imposed upon an area by state or national military forces when civil authority has broken down.

Mar·tian (mär′shən, -shĭ ən), *adj.* **1.** pertaining to the planet Mars. —*n.* **2.** a supposed inhabitant of the planet Mars.

mar·tin (mär′tən, -tĭn), *n.* any of certain swallows, as the common European **house martin,** which builds its nest about houses.

mar·ti·net (mär′tə nĕt′, mär′tə nĕt′), *n.* a rigid disciplinarian, esp. military or naval.

mar·tin·gale (mär′tən gāl′), *n.* **1.** a strap of a horse's harness passing from the bit or headgear, between the forelegs, to the girth, for holding the head down. **2.** *Naut.* a short, perpendicular spar under the bowsprit end, used for guying down the jib boom.

mar·ti·ni (mär tē′nē), *n., pl.* **-nis.** a cocktail of gin and dry vermouth.

Mar·ti·nique (mär′tə nēk′), *n.* an island in the West Indies, in the Lesser Antilles, forming a department of France. 261,595 pop.; 425 sq. mi. *Cap.:* Fort-de-France.

mar·tyr (mär′tər), *n.* **1.** one who willingly suffers death rather than renounce his religion. **2.** one who is put to death or endures great suffering on behalf of any belief, principle, or cause. —*v.t.* **3.** to put to death as a martyr. **4.** to make a martyr of. —**mar′tyr·dom,** *n.*

mar·tyr·ize (mär′tə rīz′), *v.t.,* **-ized, -izing.** to make a martyr of.

mar·vel (mär′vəl), *n., v.,* **-veled, -veling** or (*esp. Brit.*) **-velled, -velling.** —*n.* **1.** a wonderful thing; a wonder. —*v.t.* **2.** to wonder at. —*v.i.* **3.** to be affected with wonder.

mar·vel·ous (mär′vəl əs), *adj.* such as to excite wonder; surprising; extraordinary. Also, *esp. Brit.,* **mar′vel·lous.** —**mar′vel·ous·ly,** *adv.* —**mar′vel·ous·ness,** *n.*

Marx (märks), *n.* **Karl,** 1818–83, German founder of modern socialism and communism. —**Marx′i·an,** *adj., n.*

Marx·ism (märk′sĭz əm), *n.* the system of thought developed by Karl Marx, esp. the doctrine that the capitalist state will inevitably, after a transitional "dictatorship of the proletariat," be superseded by a socialist order and a classless society. —**Marx′ist,** *n., adj.*

Mar·y (mâr′ĭ), *n. New Testament.* the mother of Jesus. Often called the **Virgin Mary** or **Saint Mary.**

Mar·y·land (mĕr′ə lənd), *n.* a State in the E United States, on the Atlantic coast. 2,186,872 pop.; 10,577 sq. mi. *Cap.:* Annapolis. *Abbr.:* Md.

Mary Stu·art (stū′ərt, stōō′-), 1542–87, queen of Scotland, 1542–67: beheaded for plotting to assassinate her cousin, Queen Elizabeth of England. Also, **Mary, Queen of Scots.**

mar·zi·pan (mär′zə păn′), *n.* a confection made of almond paste with sugar, etc.

Ma·sa·ryk (mä′sä rĭk), *n.* **Tomáš Garrigue**, 1850–1937, Czech statesman: first president of Czechoslovakia, 1918–35.

masc., masculine.

Mas·ca·gni (mäs kä′nyē), *n.* **Pietro**, 1863–1945, Italian operatic composer.

mas·car·a (mäs kăr′ə), *n.* a substance used to color the eyelashes.

mas·cot (mäs′kŏt, -kŏt), *n.* a person, animal, or thing supposed to bring good luck.

mas·cu·line (măs′kyə lĭn), *adj.* **1.** having manlike qualities; manly. **2.** pertaining to or characteristic of a man or men. **3.** *Gram.* denoting or pertaining to the gender to which most or all nouns denoting males belong. —*n.* **4.** *Gram.* the masculine gender. **5.** a noun of that gender. —**mas′cu·lin′i·ty,** *n.*

Mase·field (māz′fēld, māz′-), *n.* **John**, born 1878, British writer: poet laureate since 1930.

mash (mäsh), *n.* **1.** a soft, pulpy mass. **2.** pulpy condition. **3.** a mess of boiled grain, bran, etc., fed warm to horses and cattle. **4.** crushed malt or meal of grain mixed with hot water to form wort. —*v.t.* **5.** to crush. **6.** to reduce to a soft, pulpy mass. **7.** to mix (crushed malt, etc.) with hot water to form wort. **8.** *Obsolesc. Slang.* to flirt with. —**mash′er,** *n.*

mash·ie (mäsh′ĭ), *n.* *Golf.* a club having a short iron head with a sloping face. Also, **mash′y.**

mask (mäsk, mäsk), *n.* **1.** a covering for the face, esp. one worn for disguise. **2.** a covering for the face of an actor, to symbolize the character he represents: used chiefly in Greek and Roman drama. **3.** anything that disguises or conceals. **4.** a masquerade. **5.** a masque. **6.** a likeness of a face, as one molded in plaster after death. **7.** the face or head, as of a fox. **8.** a covering of wire, gauze, etc., to protect the face. **9.** a gas mask. —*v.t.* **10.** to disguise or conceal. **11.** to cover with a mask.

mask·er (mäs′kər, mäs′-), *n.* one who takes part in a masque. Also, **mas′quer.**

mas·och·ism (măz′ə kĭz′əm), *n.* *Psychiatry.* the condition in which sexual gratification depends on suffering, physical pain, and humiliation. —**mas′och·ist,** *n.* —**mas′och·is′tic,** *adj.*

ma·son (mā′sən), *n.* **1.** one who builds with brick, stone, or the like. **2.** (*often cap.*) a Freemason. —*v.t.* **3.** to construct of masonry.

Ma·son-Dix·on line (mā′sən dĭk′sən), the boundary between Pennsylvania and Maryland, popularly considered before the extinction of slavery as a line of demarcation between free and slave States.

ma·son·ic (mə sŏn′ĭk), *adj.* (*often cap.*) pertaining to Freemasons or Freemasonry.

ma·son·ry (mā′sən rĭ), *n.*, *pl.* -ries. **1.** the art or occupation of a mason. **2.** work constructed by a mason. **3.** (*often cap.*) freemasonry.

masque (mäsk, mäsk), *n.* **1.** a form of dramatic entertainment in 16th and 17th century England. **2.** a masquerade.

mas·quer·ade (mäs′kə rād′), *n.*, *v.*, -aded, -ading. —*n.* **1.** an assembly of persons wearing masks and other disguises for dancing, etc. **2.** disguise, esp. one worn at such an assembly. —*v.i.* **3.** to disguise oneself. **4.** to take part in a masquerade. —**mas′quer·ad′er,** *n.*

mass (mäs), *n.* **1.** a body of coherent matter, usually of indefinite shape. **2.** an assemblage, number, or quantity, esp. when large. **3.** an expanse, as of color. **4.** bulk, size, or massiveness. **5.** *Physics.* that property of a body, roughly defined as the measure of the quantity of matter in it, to which its inertia is ascribed. **6. the masses**, the common people. —*v.i.* **7.** to come together in or form a mass or masses. —*v.t.* **8.** to gather into or dispose in a mass or masses.

Mass (mäs), *n.* the celebration of the Eucharist. See **High Mass, Low Mass.**

Mas·sa·chu·setts (mäs′ə chōō′sĭts), *n.* a State in the NE United States, on the Atlantic coast. 4,590,254 pop.; 8257 sq. mi. *Cap.:* Boston. *Abbr.:* Mass.

mas·sa·cre (mäs′ə kər), *n.*, *v.*, -cred, -cring. —*n.* **1.** the unnecessary, indiscriminate killing of a number of human beings, as in barbarous warfare. **2.** a general slaughter. —*v.t.* **3.** to kill in a massacre.

mas·sage (mə säzh′), *n.*, *v.*, -saged, -saging. —*n.* **1.** act or art of treating the body by rubbing, kneading, or the like, to stimulate circulation, etc. —*v.t.* **2.** to treat by massage.

Mas·se·net (mäs nĕ′), *n.* **Jules Émile Frédéric**, 1842–1912, French composer.

mas·seur (mä sœr′), *n.* a man who practises massage. —**mas·seuse** (mä sœz′), *n. fem.*

mas·sive (mäs′ĭv), *adj.* **1.** bulky and heavy. **2.** large, as the forehead. **3.** substantial; imposing. —**mas′sive·ly,** *adv.* —**mas′sive·ness,** *n.*

mass meeting, a large or general assembly of the people to discuss or hear discussed some matter of common interest.

mast¹ (mäst, mäst), *n.* **1.** a tall vertical spar on a vessel, which supports the sails, rigging, etc. **2.** any upright pole. —*v.t.* **3.** to provide with a mast or masts.

mast² (mäst, mäst), *n.* acorns, chestnuts, etc., esp. as food for swine.

mas·ter (mäs′tər, mäs′-), *n.* **1.** one who has the power of controlling, using, or disposing of something at pleasure. **2.** an employer of workmen or servants. **3.** the commander of a merchant vessel. **4.** the male head of a household. **5.** an owner of a slave, horse, dog, etc. **6.** *Chiefly Brit.* a male teacher, tutor, or schoolmaster. **7.** a person whose teachings one follows. **8.** (*cap.*) Christ (prec. by *the, our,* etc.). **9.** a victor. **10.** a workman qualified to teach apprentices and to carry on his trade independently. **11.** a man eminently skilled in something. **12.** *Educ.* a. a person who has taken a certain advanced degree at a college. b. such a degree. **13.** a title of respect for a boy. —*adj.* **14.** being master. **15.** chief or principal. **16.** directing or controlling. **17.** dominating. **18.** being a master of some occupation, art, etc. —*v.t.* **19.** to conquer or subdue. **20.** to become an adept in. —**mas′ter·dom,** *n.*

mas·ter·ful (mäs′tər fəl, mäs′-), *adj.* **1.** authoritative; domineering. **2.** showing mastery or skill. —**mas′ter·ful·ly,** *adv.* —**mas′ter·ful·ness,** *n.*

mas·ter·ly (mäs′tər lĭ, mäs′-), *adj.* **1.** like or befitting a master, as in skill. —*adv.* **2.** in a masterly manner. —**mas′ter·li·ness,** *n.*

Master of Arts, 1. a master's degree, esp. in the liberal arts, granted by a college, usually based on at least one year of study beyond the bachelor's degree. **2.** one holding this degree.

master of ceremonies, a person who directs the entertainment at a party, etc.

mas·ter·piece (mäs′tər pēs′, mäs′-), *n.* **1.** one's most excellent production, as in an art. **2.** any production of masterly skill.

Mas·ters (mäs′tərz, mäs′-), *n.* **Edgar Lee**, born 1869, U.S. poet and novelist.

master sergeant, *U.S. Army.* a noncommissioned officer of the highest rank.

mas·ter·y (mäs′tə rĭ, mäs′-), *n.*, *pl.* -teries. **1.** command or control. **2.** grasp, as of a subject. **3.** victory. **4.** the action of mastering, as a subject. **5.** expert skill or knowledge.

mast·head (mäst′hĕd′, mäst′-), *n.* **1.** the top or head of the mast of a ship. **2.** a statement printed in all issues of a newspaper, etc., giving the name, owner, staff, etc.

mas·tic (mäs′tĭk), *n.* an aromatic, astringent resin obtained from a small evergreen Mediterranean tree.

mas·ti·cate (mäs′tə kāt′), *v.t.*, *v.i.*, -cated, -cating. to chew. —**mas′ti·ca′tion,** *n.* —**mas′ti·ca′tor,** *n.*

mas·tiff (mäs′tĭf, mäs′-), *n.* one of a breed of powerful, stoutly built dogs with large head, drooping ears, and pendulous lips.

mas·to·don (mäs′tə dŏn′), *n.* any of various species of large, extinct mammals of the elephant kind.

mas·toid (mäs′toid), *adj.* **1.** resembling a breast or nipple. **2.** of or denoting the nipplelike process of the temporal bone behind the ear. —*n.* **3.** the mastoid process.

mas·tur·bate (mäs′tər bāt′), *v.i.*, -bated, -bating. to practice sexual self-gratification. —**mas′tur·ba′tion,** *n.* —**mas′tur·ba′tor,** *n.*

ma·su·ri·um (mə sŏŏr′ĭ əm), *n.* *Chem.* a manganese-family element discovered spectroscopically in 1925 but not isolated. *Symbol:* Ma; *at. wt.:* about 98; *at. no.:* 43.

mat¹ (mät), *n.*, *v.*, matted, matting. —*n.* **1.** a piece of fabric made of plaited or woven straw or other material, used to cover a floor, to wipe the shoes on, etc. **2.** a smaller piece of material, often ornamental, set under a dish of food, a lamp, etc. **3.** a thick covering, as of padded canvas, laid on a floor on which wrestlers contend, in order to protect them. **4.** a thickly growing or thick and tangled mass, as of hair. —*v.t.* **5.** to cover with mats or matting. **6.** to form into a mat. —*v.i.* **7.** to become entangled.

mat² (măt), *n.* a framelike piece of material placed in front of a picture.

mat³ (măt), *adj., n., v.,* **matted, matting.** —*adj.* **1.** lusterless and dull in surface. —*n.* **2.** a dull or dead surface, without luster. —*v.t.* **3.** to finish with a mat surface.

mat·a·dor (măt'ə dôr'), *n.* the man who kills the bull in bullfights.

match¹ (măch), *n.* a short, slender piece of wood or other material tipped with a chemical substance which produces fire when rubbed on a rough or chemically prepared surface.

match² (măch), *n.* **1.** a person or thing that equals or resembles another in some respect. **2.** a person or thing that is an exact counterpart of another. **3.** a suitably associated pair. **4.** *Chiefly Brit.* a contest or game. **5.** a matrimonial alliance. —*v.t.* **6.** to equal. **7.** to be the match or counterpart of. **8.** to adapt. **9.** to fit together, as two things. **10.** to procure or produce an equal to. **11.** to place in opposition or conflict. **12.** to provide with a competitor of equal power. **13.** to unite in marriage. —*v.i.* **14.** to be equal or suitable. **15.** to correspond.

match·less (măch'lĭs), *adj.* having no equal; peerless. —**match'less·ly,** *adv.*

match·lock (măch'lŏk'), *n.* an old form of gunlock in which the priming was ignited by a slow match.

match·mak·er¹ (măch'mā'kər), *n.* **1.** one who makes matrimonial matches. **2.** one who makes or arranges matches for contests, etc. —**match'-mak'ing,** *n., adj.*

match·mak·er² (măch'mā'kər), *n.* one who makes matches for burning. —**match'mak'ing,** *n., adj.*

mate¹ (māt), *n., v.,* **mated, mating.** —*n.* **1.** one joined with another in any pair. **2.** a counterpart. **3.** husband or wife. **4.** one of a pair of mated animals. **5.** a habitual associate. **6.** an officer of a merchant vessel who ranks below the captain or master. **7.** an assistant to a warrant officer on a ship. —*v.t.* **8.** to join as a mate or as mates. **9.** to marry. **10.** to pair, as animals. **11.** to join suitably, as two things. —*v.i.* **12.** to marry.

mate² (māt), *n., v.t., v.i.,* **mated, mating.** *Chess.* checkmate.

ma·té (mä'tā, măt'ā), *n.* **1.** a tealike South American beverage made from the léaves of a species of holly native in Paraguay and Brazil. **2.** the plant itself.

ma·ter (mā'tər), *n. Brit. Colloq.* mother.

ma·te·ri·al (mə tîr'ĭ əl), *n.* **1.** the substance or substances of which a thing is made or composed. **2.** any constituent element of a thing. **3.** a textile fabric. **4.** (*pl.*) articles of any kind requisite for making or doing something. —*adj.* **5.** physical; corporeal. **6.** relating to, concerned with, or involving matter. **7.** concerned unduly with corporeal things. **8.** pertaining to the physical rather than the spiritual or intellectual aspect of things. **9.** important. **10.** pertinent or essential. —**ma·te'ri·al·ly,** *adv.*

ma·te·ri·al·ism (mə tîr'ĭ ə lĭz'əm), *n.* **1.** the philosophical theory which regards matter and its motions as constituting the universe, and all phenomena, including those of mind, as due to material agencies. **2.** devotion to material rather than spiritual objects. —**ma·te'ri·al·ist,** *n.* —**ma·te'ri·al·is'tic,** *adj.*

ma·te·ri·al·ize (mə tîr'ĭ ə līz'), *v.,* **-ized, -iz-ing.** —*v.t.* **1.** to give material form to. **2.** to invest with material attributes. —*v.i.* **3.** to assume material form. **4.** to appear. —**ma·te'ri·al·i·za'tion,** *n.*

ma·te·ri·a med·i·ca (mə tîr'ĭ ə měd'ĭ kə), **1.** the remedial substances employed in medicine. **2.** the branch of medicine treating of these.

ma·té·ri·el (mə tîr'ĭ ĕl'), *n.* the aggregate of things used or needed in any business, undertaking, or operation.

ma·ter·nal (mə tûr'nəl), *adj.* **1.** of, befitting, or being a mother. **2.** derived from a mother. **3.** related through a mother. —**ma·ter'nal·ly,** *adv.*

ma·ter·ni·ty (mə tûr'nə tĭ), *n.* state of being a mother; motherhood.

math., mathematics.

math·e·mat·i·cal (măth'ə măt'ĭ kəl), *adj.* **1.** of, pertaining to, or of the nature of mathematics. **2.** employed in the operations of mathematics.

3. having the precision of mathematics. Also, **math'e·mat'ic.** —**math'e·mat'i·cal·ly,** *adv.*

math·e·ma·ti·cian (măth'ə mə tĭsh'ən), *n.* an expert in mathematics.

math·e·mat·ics (măth'ə măt'ĭks), *n.* the science that treats of the measurement, properties, and relations of quantities, including arithmetic, geometry, algebra, etc.

mat·in (măt'ĭn), *n.* **1.** (*pl.*) *Eccles.* **a.** the first of the seven canonical hours, or the service for it. **b.** the order for public morning prayer in the Anglican Church. **2.** *Poetic.* a morning song, esp. of a bird. —*adj.* **3.** Also, **mat'in·al.** pertaining to the morning or to matins.

mat·i·née (măt'ə nā'), *n.* a dramatic or musical performance, usually in the afternoon. Also, **mat'i·nee'.**

Ma·tisse (mȧ tēs'), *n.* **Henri,** born 1869, French painter.

ma·tri·arch (mā'trĭ ärk'), *n.* a woman holding a position analogous to that of a patriarch, as in a family. —**ma'tri·ar'chal,** *adj.*

ma·tri·ar·chy (mā'trĭ är'kĭ), *n., pl.* **-chies.** a form of social organization, as in certain primitive tribes, in which the mother is head of the family, and in which descent is reckoned in the female line.

ma·tri·cide¹ (mā'trə sīd', măt'rə-), *n.* one who kills his mother. —**ma'tri·cid'al,** *adj.*

ma·tri·cide² (mā'trə sīd', măt'rə-), *n.* act of killing one's mother.

ma·tric·u·late (*v.* mə trĭk'yə lāt'; *n.* mə trĭk'-yə lĭt), *v.,* **-lated, -lating,** *n.* —*v.t., v.i.* **1.** to enroll, esp. in a college. —*n.* **2.** one who has been matriculated. —**ma·tric'u·la'tion,** *n.*

mat·ri·mo·ny (măt'rə mō'nĭ), *n., pl.* **-nies.** the rite, ceremony, or sacrament of marriage. —**mat'ri·mo'ni·al,** *adj.* —**mat'ri·mo'ni·al·ly,** *adv.*

ma·trix (mā'trĭks, măt'rĭks), *n., pl.* **matrices** (mā'trĭ sēz', măt'rĭ-), **matrixes.** **1.** that which gives origin or form to a thing enclosed in it. **2.** the womb. **3.** *Print.* a mold for casting type faces.

ma·tron (mā'trən), *n.* **1.** a married woman, esp. an older one. **2.** a woman in charge of the feminine or domestic affairs of an institution or the like. —**ma'tron·ly,** *adj.*

matron of honor, a married woman acting as the principal attendant of the bride at a wedding.

Matt., Matthew.

mat·ter (măt'ər), *n.* **1.** the substance of which physical objects are composed. **2.** physical or corporeal substance in general. **3.** whatever occupies space. **4.** a particular kind of substance. **5.** some substance excreted by a living body, esp. pus. **6.** the substance of a book, etc., as distinguished from the form. **7.** things written or printed. **8.** a thing, affair, or business. **9.** something of consequence. **10.** the trouble or difficulty. **11.** importance. —*v.i.* **12.** to be of importance; signify.

Mat·ter·horn (măt'ər hôrn'), *n.* a peak in the Alps on the Swiss-Italian border. 14,780 ft.

mat·ter-of-fact (măt'ər əv făkt'), *adj.* adhering to actual facts; commonplace.

Mat·thew (măth'ū), *n.* **1.** one of the twelve apostles. **2.** the first Gospel in the New Testament.

Mat·thi·as (mə thī'əs), *n.* a disciple chosen to take the place of Judas Iscariot as one of the apostles.

mat·ting (măt'ĭng), *n.* a coarse fabric of rushes, grass, or the like, for covering floors, etc.

mat·tock (măt'ək), *n.* an instrument shaped like a pickax but having one end broad instead of pointed.

mat·tress (măt'rĭs), *n.* a case filled with hair, straw, cotton, etc., used as or on a bed.

mat·u·rate (măch'ŏŏ rāt', măt'yŏŏ-), *v.i.,* **-rated, -rating.** **1.** to suppurate. **2.** to mature. —**mat'u·ra'tion,** *n.*

ma·ture (mə tyŏŏr', -tŏŏr'), *adj., v.,* **-tured, -turing.** —*adj.* **1.** complete in natural growth or development, as plant and animal forms, cheese, wine, etc. **2.** pertaining to or characteristic of full development. **3.** completed or perfected in full by the mind. **4.** *Com.* having become payable or due, as a note. —*v.t.* **5.** to make mature, esp. to ripen. **6.** to bring to full development. **7.** to complete or perfect. —*v.i.* **8.** to become mature, esp. to ripen. **9.** to come to full development. **10.** *Com.* to become due. —**ma·ture′ly,** *adv.* —**ma·ture′ness,** *n.*

ma·tu·ri·ty (mə tyŏŏr′ə tĭ, -tŏŏr′-), *n.* **1.** state of being mature; ripeness. **2.** full development. **3.** *Com.* **a.** state of being due. **b.** the time when a note or bill of exchange becomes due.

maud·lin (môd′lĭn), *adj.* weakly emotional or sentimental.

Maugham (môm), *n.* **William Somerset,** born 1874, British writer.

Ma·u·i (mä′ōō ē′, mou′ē), *n.* one of the Hawaiian Islands, in the central part of the group. 46,919 pop.; 728 sq. mi.

maul (môl), *n.* **1.** a heavy hammer, as for driving piles. —*v.t.* **2.** to handle or use roughly. —**maul′er,** *n.*

Mau·na Lo·a (mou′nə lō′ə, mô′nə lō′ə), an active volcano on the island of Hawaii. 13,675 ft.

maun·der (môn′dər), *v.i.* to talk in a rambling, foolish, or imbecile way.

Maun·dy Thursday (môn′dĭ) the Thursday of Holy Week.

Mau·pas·sant (mō pä sän′), *n.* **Guy de,** 1850–93, French short-story writer and novelist.

Mau·ri·tius (mô rĭsh′əs, -rĭsh′ĭ əs), *n.* **1.** an island in the Indian Ocean, E of Madagascar. 403,718 pop.; 720 sq. mi. **2.** a British colony consisting of this island and dependencies. 426,-000 pop.; 809 sq. mi. *Cap.:* Port Louis.

mau·so·le·um (mô′sə lē′əm), *n., pl.* -**leums,** -**lea** (-lē′ə). a stately and magnificent tomb.

mauve (mōv), *n., adj.* pale bluish-purple.

mav·er·ick (măv′ər ĭk), *n.* *U.S.* **1.** (in cattle-raising regions) **a.** an animal found without an owner's brand. **b.** a calf separated from its dam. **2.** a dissenter.

ma·vour·neen (mə vŏŏr′nēn, -vōr′-), *n.* *Irish.* my darling. Also, **ma·vour′nin.**

maw (mô), *n.* **1.** the mouth, throat, or gullet as concerned in devouring (now chiefly of animals). **2.** the crop of a fowl. **3.** the stomach.

mawk·ish (mô′kĭsh), *adj.* **1.** slightly nauseating. **2.** sickly sentimental. —**mawk′ish·ly,** *adv.* —**mawk′ish·ness,** *n.*

max., maximum.

max·il·la (măk sĭl′ə), *n., pl.* -**sillae** (-sĭl′ē). a jaw or jawbone, esp. the upper. —**max·il·lar·y** (măk′sə lĕr′ĭ), *adj.*

max·im (măk′sĭm), *n.* **1.** an expression of a general truth, esp. as to conduct. **2.** a principle of conduct.

max·i·mal (măk′sə məl), *adj.* pertaining to or being a maximum; greatest possible.

Max·i·mil·ian (măk′sə mĭl′yən), *n.* 1832–67, archduke of Austria and emperor of Mexico, 1864–67.

max·i·mum (măk′sə məm), *n., pl.* -**ma** (-mə) -**mums,** *adj.* —*n.* **1.** the greatest quantity, value, or degree possible, assignable, allowable, etc. —*adj.* **2.** greatest possible.

may (mā), *v., pt.* **might. 1.** used as an auxiliary to express: **a.** possibility or permission. **b.** wish or prayer. **c.** contingency. **2.** *Law.* (in a statute) must.

May (mā), *n.* the fifth month of the year, containing 31 days.

Ma·ya (mä′yə), *n.* a member of an aboriginal people of Yucatán which had attained a relatively high civilization before the discovery of America. —**Ma′yan,** *adj., n.*

May apple, 1. an American perennial herb bearing an edible, yellowish, egg-shaped fruit. **2.** the fruit.

may·be (mā′bĭ, -bē), *adv.* perhaps.

May Day, the first day of May, long celebrated with various festivities, as dancing round the Maypole, etc., and, in recent years, often marked by labor parades, etc.

May·flow·er (mā′flou′ər), *n.* **1.** the ship in which the Pilgrim Fathers sailed to the New World in 1620. **2.** any of various plants that blossom in May: **a.** (in the U.S.) chiefly the trailing arbutus, hepatica, and anemone. **b.** (in England) the hawthorn, cowslip, etc.

may·hem (mā′hĕm, mā′əm), *n.* *Law.* the crime of violently inflicting a bodily injury rendering a man less able to defend himself.

may·on·naise (mā′ə nāz′), *n.* a thick dressing of egg yolks, vinegar or lemon juice, seasonings, and oil, used esp. for salads.

may·or (mā′ər, mâr), *n.* the principal officer of a municipality. —**may′or·al·ty, may′or·ship′,** *n.*

May·pole (mā′pōl′), *n.* a high pole, decorated with flowers or ribbons, for the merrymakers to dance round at May Day festivities.

Maz·a·rin (măz′ə rĭn), *n.* **Jules,** 1602–61, French cardinal and statesman, born in Italy: chief minister of Louis XIV, 1642–61.

maze (māz), *n.* a confusing network of intercommunicating paths or passages; labyrinth. —**ma′zy,** *adj.*

ma·zur·ka (mə zûr′kə, -zŏŏr′-), *n.* **1.** a lively Polish dance in moderately quick triple rhythm. **2.** music for, or in the rhythm of, this dance. Also, **ma·zour′ka.**

M.C., 1. Master of Ceremonies. **2.** Member of Congress.

Mc·Clel·lan (mə klĕl′ən), *n.* **George Brinton,** 1826–85, Union general in the U.S. Civil War.

Mc·In·tosh (măk′ĭn tŏsh′), *n.* *Hort.* a red eating apple that ripens in early autumn.

Mc·Kees·port (mə kēz′pōrt), *n.* a city in SW Pennsylvania, near Pittsburgh. 55,355.

Mc·Kin·ley (mə kĭn′lĭ), *n.* **1. William,** 1843–1901, 25th president of the U.S., 1897–1901. **2. Mount,** a mountain in central Alaska: the highest peak of North America. 20,300 ft.

Md., Maryland.

M.D., (L *Medicinae Doctor*) Doctor of Medicine.

M-day (ĕm′dā′), *n.* mobilization day.

mdse., merchandise.

me (mē; *unstressed* mĭ), *pers. pron.* objective case of the pronoun I.

Me., Maine.

mead[1] (mēd), *n.* *Poetic.* a meadow.

mead[2] (mēd), *n.* an alcoholic liquor made by fermenting honey and water.

Mead (mēd), *n.* **Lake,** a lake made by Boulder Dam in the Colorado river, in NW Arizona and SE Nevada: largest artificial lake in world. 115 mi. long; 227 sq. mi.

Meade (mēd), *n.* **George Gordon,** 1815–72, Union general in the U.S. Civil War.

mead·ow (mĕd′ō), *n.* **1.** a piece of grassland used for the raising of hay or for pasture. **2.** a low, level tract of uncultivated ground, as along a river. —**mead′ow·y,** *adj.*

meadow lark, a common robust, yellow-breasted songbird of America.

mea·ger (mē′gər), *adj.* **1.** deficient in quantity or quality. **2.** lean or thin. Also, **mea′gre.** —**mea′ger·ly,** *adv.* —**mea′ger·ness,** *n.*

meal[1] (mēl), *n.* **1.** one of the regular repasts of the day, as breakfast, dinner, or supper. **2.** the food eaten or served for a repast.

meal[2] (mēl), *n.* coarse, unbolted grain, cornmeal, or Indian meal.

meal·time (mēl′tīm′), *n.* the usual time for a meal.

meal·y (mē′lĭ), *adj.,* **mealier, mealiest. 1.** soft, dry, and crumbly. **2.** of the nature of, or containing, meal. **3.** pale, as the complexion. —**meal′i·ness,** *n.*

meal·y-mouthed (mē′lĭ mouthd′, -moutht′), *adj.* avoiding plain terms, as from timidity, delicacy, or hypocrisy.

mean[1] (mēn), *v.,* **meant, meaning.** —*v.t.* **1.** to have in the mind as in intention or purpose. **2.** to intend for a particular purpose, destination, etc. **3.** to intend to express. **4.** (of words, etc.) to signify. —*v.i.* **5.** to have intentions.

mean[2] (mēn), *adj.* **1.** inferior in grade, quality, or character. **2.** low in station, rank, or dignity. **3.** of little importance. **4.** shabby. **5.** small-minded or ignoble. **6.** stingy. **7.** *U.S. Colloq.* nasty. **8.** *U.S. Colloq.* ashamed. **9.** *U.S. Colloq.* vicious, as a horse. —**mean′ly,** *adv.* —**mean′-ness,** *n.*

mean[3] (mēn), *n.* **1.** (*usually pl.*) an agency, instrumentality, method, etc., used to attain an end. **2.** (*pl.*) disposable resources, esp. pecuniary resources. **3.** (*pl.*) considerable pecuniary resources. **4.** that which is midway between two extremes. **5.** *Math.* a quantity having a value intermediate between the values of other quantities. **6. by all means, a.** without fail. **b.** certainly. **7. by any means,** in any way. **8. by no means, a.** in no way. **b.** certainly not. —*adj.* **9.** occupying a middle position. **10.** intermediate in kind, quality, degree, time, etc.

me·an·der (mĭ ăn′dər), *v.i.* **1.** to proceed by a winding course. **2.** to wander aimlessly. —*n.* **3.** (*usually pl.*) a winding course. **4.** a circuitous movement.

mean·ing (mē′nĭng), *n.* **1.** that which is intended to be, or actually is, expressed or indicated. —*adj.* **2.** intending. **3.** significant. —**mean'-ing·ful,** *adj.* —**mean'ing·less,** *adj.* —**mean'-ing·less·ly,** *adv.* —**mean'ing·less·ness,** *n.* —**mean'ing·ly,** *adv.*

mean·time (mēn'tīm'), *n.* **1.** the intervening time. —*adv.* **2.** in the intervening time. Also, **mean·while** (mēn'hwīl').

mea·sles (mē'zəlz), *n.* an acute infectious disease occurring mostly in children, characterized by an eruption with small red spots.

mea·sly (mē'zlĭ), *adj.,* **-slier, -sliest. 1.** infected with measles. **2.** *Slang.* wretchedly poor or unsatisfactory.

meas·ure (mĕzh'ər), *n., v.,* **-ured, -uring.** —*n.* **1.** act or process of ascertaining the extent, dimensions, quantity, etc., of something. **2.** size, dimensions, quantity, etc., as thus ascertained. **3.** an instrument for measuring. **4.** a unit or standard of measurement. **5.** a system of measurement. **6.** a legislative bill or enactment. **7.** an action intended as a means to an end. **8.** a short rhythmical movement or arrangement, as in poetry or music. **9.** *Archaic.* a slow, stately dance. **10.** *Music, etc.* the music contained between two bar lines. **11.** (*pl.*) *Geol.* beds; strata. —*v.t.* **12.** to ascertain the extent, dimensions, quantity, etc., of. **13.** to mark off, or deal out, with reference to measure. **14.** to estimate the relative amount, value, etc., of. —*v.i.* **15.** to take measurements. **16.** to be of a specified measure. —**meas'ur·a·ble,** *adj.* —**meas'ur·a·bly,** *adv.* —**meas'ur·er,** *n.*

M. Measure (def. 10)

meas·ured (mĕzh'ərd), *adj.* **1.** ascertained or apportioned by measure. **2.** regular or rhythmical. **3.** deliberate and restrained.

meas·ure·less (mĕzh'ər lĭs), *adj.* without bounds; unlimited; immeasurable.

meas·ure·ment (mĕzh'ər mənt), *n.* **1.** act of measuring. **2.** an ascertained dimension. **3.** extent, size, etc., ascertained by measuring. **4.** a system of measuring.

measuring worm, the larva of any geometrid moth, which progresses by bringing the rear end of the body forward and then advancing the front end.

meat (mēt), *n.* **1.** the flesh of animals as used for food. **2.** food in general. **3.** the edible part of anything, as a fruit, nut, etc. —**meat'less,** *adj.*

meat·y (mē'tĭ), *adj.,* **meatier, meatiest. 1.** of, like, or full of meat. **2.** pithy.

Mec·ca (mĕk'ə), *n.* a city in W Saudi Arabia; the birthplace of Mohammed, and spiritual center of Islam.

mech., **1.** mechanical. **2.** mechanics.

me·chan·ic (mə kăn'ĭk), *n.* **1.** a skilled worker with tools or machines. **2.** one who repairs machinery.

me·chan·i·cal (mə kăn'ə kəl), *adj.* **1.** having to do with machinery. **2.** controlled or operated by a mechanism or machine. **3.** acting or performed without spontaneity, spirit, individuality, etc. **4.** pertaining to or concerned with the use of tools and the like. —**me·chan'i·cal·ly,** *adv.*

mech·a·ni·cian (mĕk'ə nĭsh'ən), *n.* one skilled in contructing, working, or repairing machines.

me·chan·ics (mə kăn'ĭks), *n.* **1.** the branch of knowledge concerned with mechanical appliances. **2.** the science dealing with the action of forces on bodies and with motion. **3.** (construed as *pl.*) the technical aspect.

mech·an·ism (mĕk'ə nĭz'əm), *n.* **1.** a piece of machinery. **2.** the agency or means. **3.** the structure of a machine or similar device or of anything analogous. **4.** the theory that everything in the universe is produced by matter in motion. —**mech'a·nist,** *n.* —**mech'a·nis'tic,** *adj.*

mech·a·nize (mĕk'ə nīz'), *v.t.,* **-nized, -nizing. 1.** to make mechanical. **2.** to introduce machinery into (an industry, etc.). —**mech'a·ni·za'-tion,** *n.*

med., **1.** medical. **2.** medicine. **3.** medieval.

med·al (mĕd'əl), *n., v.,* **-aled, -aling** or (*esp. Brit.*) **-alled, -alling.** —*n.* **1.** a flat piece of metal bearing an inscription, etc., issued to commemorate a person, action, or event, or given as a reward for bravery, merit, or the like. —*v.t.* **2.** to honor with a medal.

med·al·ist (mĕd'əl ĭst), *n.* **1.** a maker of medals. **2.** one to whom a medal has been awarded. Also, *esp. Brit.,* **med'al·list.**

me·dal·lion (mə dăl'yən), *n.* **1.** a large medal. **2.** *Archit.* a tablet, often bearing objects represented in relief.

med·dle (mĕd'əl), *v.i.,* **-dled, -dling.** to concern oneself with something without warrant or necessity; interfere. —**med'dler,** *n.*

med·dle·some (mĕd'əl səm), *adj.* given to meddling. —**med'dle·some·ness,** *n.*

Mede (mēd), *n.* an inhabitant of Media.

Me·de·a (mĭ dē'ə), *n.* *Gk. Legend.* a sorceress, the wife of Jason, whom she assisted in obtaining the Golden Fleece.

Me·del·lín (mĕ'dĕ yĕn'), *n.* a city in W Colombia. 207,450.

Med·ford (mĕd'fərd), *n.* a city in E Massachusetts. 63,083.

me·di·a (mē'dĭ ə), *n.pl., sing.* **medium.** newspapers, etc., used as a means of advertising or publicity.

Me·di·a (mē'dĭ ə), *n.* an ancient country in W Asia, S of the Caspian Sea. —**Me'di·an,** *adj., n.*

me·di·ae·val (mē'dĭ ē'vəl, mĕd'ĭ-), *adj.* medieval.

me·di·al (mē'dĭ əl), *adj.* **1.** situated in or pertaining to the middle. **2.** average. **3.** ordinary. **4.** neither initial nor final. —*n.* **5.** a medial linguistic element. —**me'di·al·ly,** *adv.*

me·di·an (mē'dĭ ən), *adj.* **1.** situated in or pertaining to the middle. —*n.* **2.** the middle number in a given sequence of numbers.

me·di·ate (*v.* mē'dĭ āt'; *adj.* mē'dĭ ĭt), *v.,* **-ated, -ating,** *adj.* —*v.t., v.i.* **1.** to bring about (an agreement, etc.) between parties by acting as mediator. **2.** to settle (disputes, etc.) by mediation. —*adj.* **3.** not direct or immediate. —**me'-di·ate·ly,** *adv.* —**me'di·a'tion,** *n.* —**me'di·a'-tor,** *n.*

med·ic (mĕd'ĭk), *n.* *Slang.* a doctor or medical aid.

med·i·ca·ble (mĕd'ə kə bəl), *adj.* susceptible of medical treatment; curable.

med·i·cal (mĕd'ə kəl), *adj.* **1.** of or pertaining to the science of medicine. **2.** curative; therapeutic. —**med'i·cal·ly,** *adv.*

me·dic·a·ment (mə dĭk'ə mənt, mĕd'ə kə-), *n.* curative or healing substance.

med·i·cate (mĕd'ə kāt'), *v.t.,* **-cated, -cating. 1.** to treat with medicine. **2.** to impregnate with a medicine. —**med'i·ca'tion,** *n.*

Med·i·ci (mĕd'ə chĭ), *n.* **1.** an Italian family of the city of Florence, rich and powerful in the 15th and 16th centuries. **2. Catherine de'** (dĭ), 1519–89, queen of Henry II of France. **3. Lorenzo de'** (dĕ), 1449–1492, ruler of Florence; patron of art and literature.

me·dic·i·nal (mə dĭs'ə nəl), *adj.* used as a medicine; curative; remedial. —**me·dic'i·nal·ly,** *adv.*

med·i·cine (mĕd'ə sən), *n.* **1.** any substance used in treating disease. **2.** the art or science of restoring or preserving health or due physical condition, as by means of drugs, surgical operations, etc. **3.** the medical profession.

medicine ball, a large, solid, leather-covered ball, of considerable weight, thrown from one person to another for exercise.

medicine man, (among American Indians and other primitive peoples) a man supposed to possess supernatural powers.

med·i·co (mĕd'ə kō'), *n., pl.* **-cos.** *Slang.* a doctor.

me·di·e·val (mē'dĭ ē'vəl, mĕd'ĭ-), *adj.* of or pertaining to, characteristic of, or in the style of the Middle Ages.

me·di·e·val·ism (mē'dĭ ē'və lĭz'əm, mĕd'ĭ-), *n.* **1.** the spirit, practices, or methods of the Middle Ages. **2.** devotion to medieval ideals or practices. **3.** a medieval belief, practice, or the like.

me·di·e·val·ist (mē'dĭ ē'vəl ĭst, mĕd'ĭ-), *n.* **1.** an expert in medieval history and affairs. **2.** one in sympathy with the spirit and methods of the Middle Ages.

Me·di·na (mə dē'nä), *n.* a city in W Saudi Arabia, where Mohammed was first accepted as the supreme Prophet from Allah, and where his tomb is located. ab. 30,000.

me·di·o·cre (mē'dĭ ō'kər, mē'dĭ ō'kər), *adj.* of middling quality; ordinary.

me·di·oc·ri·ty (mē'dĭ ŏk'rə tĭ), *n., pl.* **-ties. 1.** state of being mediocre. **2.** mediocre ability. **3.** a person of but moderate ability.

Medit., Mediterranean.

med·i·tate (měd'ə tāt'), v., -tated, -tating. —v.t. 1. to intend or purpose. —v.i. 2. to engage in thought; reflect. —med'i·ta'tion, n. —med'-i·ta'tive, adj. —med'i·ta'tive·ly, adv.

Med·i·ter·ra·ne·an (měd'ə tə rā'nĭ ən), n. 1. the Mediterranean Sea. —adj. 2. pertaining to, situated on or near, or dwelling about the Mediterranean Sea.

Mediterranean Sea, the sea between Africa, Europe, and Asia. ab. 1,145,000 sq. mi.

me·di·um (mē'dĭ əm), n., pl. -diums, -dia (-dĭ ə), adj. —n. 1. a middle state or condition. 2. something intermediate in nature or degree. 3. an intervening substance, as air, etc., through which a force acts or an effect is produced. 4. the element in which an organism has its natural habitat. 5. environment. 6. an agency or means. 7. Painting. a liquid with which pigments are mixed for application. 8. a person conceived of as serving as a means of communicating with the dead. —adj. 9. intermediate in degree, quality, etc.

med·lar (měd'lər), n. 1. a small tree of the apple family. 2. its fruit.

med·ley (měd'lĭ), n., pl. -leys, adj. —n. 1. a mixture or jumble. 2. a piece of music combining passages from various sources. —adj. 3. mixed; motley.

me·dul·la (mĭ dŭl'ə), n., pl. -dullae (-dŭl'ē). 1. Anat. a. the marrow of bones. b. the medulla oblongata. 2. Bot. the pith of plants.

medulla ob·lon·ga·ta (ŏb'lŏng gā'tə), Anat. the lowest or hindmost part of the brain, continuous with the spinal cord.

Me·du·sa (mĭ dū'sə,-zə,-dōō'-), n. Gk. Legend. one of the three Gorgons with snakes for hair.

me·du·sa (mĭ dū'sə, -zə, -dōō'-), n., pl. -sas, -sae (-sē, -zē). Zool. a jellyfish.

meed (mēd), n. Archaic. a reward for service or desert (good or bad).

meek (mēk), adj. 1. humbly patient or submissive. 2. unduly patient or submissive. —meek'-ly, adv. —meek'ness, n.

Meer (mĭr), n. Jan van der, 1632–1675, Dutch painter.

meer·schaum (mĭr'shəm, -shôm), n. 1. a mineral, hydrous magnesium silicate, occurring in white, claylike masses, used for ornamental carvings, for pipe bowls, etc. 2. a tobacco pipe the bowl of which is made of this substance.

meet¹ (mēt), v., met, meeting, n. —v.t. 1. to come into contact with. 2. to come before or to (eye, ear, etc.). 3. to encounter. 4. to go to the place of arrival of, as to welcome. 5. to come into the company or acquaintance of (a person, etc.). 6. to deal effectively with (an objection, etc.). 7. to satisfy (needs, demands, etc.). —v.i. 8. to come together. 9. to assemble, as a committee, society, etc. 10. to become personally acquainted. 11. to experience. —n. 12. a meeting.

meet² (mēt), adj. suitable; proper. —meet'ly, adv.

meet·ing (mē'tĭng), n. 1. a coming together. 2. an assembly, as of persons for some purpose. 3. the persons present.

meeting house, 1. a place for religious worship. 2. a house of worship of Quakers.

meg·a·ce·phal·ic (měg'ə sə făl'ĭk), adj. having a skull with a large cranial capacity or one exceeding the mean.

meg·a·cy·cle (měg'ə sī'kəl), n. Physics. a million cycles, esp. per second.

meg·a·lo·ce·phal·ic (měg'ə lō sə făl'ĭk), adj. megacephalic. —meg'a·lo·ceph'a·ly, n.

meg·a·lo·ma·ni·a (měg'ə lə mā'nĭ ə), n. Psychiatry. a form of mental alienation marked by delusions of greatness, wealth, etc. —meg'a·lo·ma'ni·ac, n.

meg·a·phone (měg'ə fōn'), n. a device for magnifying or directing sound, as a large funnel-shaped instrument.

me·grim (mē'grĭm), n. 1. (pl.) morbid low spirits. 2. migraine.

Me·kong (mā'kŏng'), n. a river flowing from W China SE along most of the boundary between Siam and French Indo-China to the South China Sea. ab. 2600 mi.

mel·an·cho·li·a (měl'ən kō'lĭ ə), n. Psychiatry. mental disease characterized by great depression and gloomy forebodings.

mel·an·chol·y (měl'ən kŏl'ĭ), n., pl. -cholies, adj. —n. 1. a gloomy state of mind; depression.

2. pensiveness. —adj. 3. affected with, characterized by, or showing melancholy. 4. attended with or inducing melancholy. 5. pensive. —mel'-an·chol'ic, adj.

Mel·a·ne·sia (měl'ə nē'shə, -zhə), n. one of the three principal divisions of Oceania, comprising the island groups in the S Pacific, NE of Australia. —Mel'a·ne'sian, adj., n.

mé·lange (mā länzh'), n. a mixture; medley.

mel·a·nism (měl'ə nĭz'əm), n. Ethnol. the condition of having a high amount of dark or black pigment granules in the skin, hair, and eyes.

Mel·ba toast (měl'bə), narrow slices of thin toast.

Mel·bourne (měl'bərn), n. a seaport in SE Australia. With suburbs, 1,107,000 pop.

me·lee (mā'lā, měl'ā), n. a confused, general hand-to-hand fight. Also, mê·lée.

mel·io·rate (mēl'yə rāt'), v.t., v.i., -rated, -rating. to make or become better; improve. —mel'io·ra'tion, n. —mel'io·ra'tive, adj.

mel·lif·lu·ent (mə lĭf'lŏŏ ənt), adj. mellifluous. —mel·lif'lu·ence, n. —mel·lif'lu·ent·ly, adv.

mel·lif·lu·ous (mə lĭf'lŏŏ əs), adj. sweetly or smoothly flowing. —mel·lif'lu·ous·ly, adv.

mel·low (měl'ō), adj. 1. soft and full-flavored from ripeness, as fruit. 2. well-matured, as wines. 3. softened or improved as if by ripening. 4. soft and rich, as sound, color, etc. 5. genial. —v.t., v.i. 6. to make or become mellow. —mel'low·ly, adv. —mel'low·ness, n.

me·lo·de·on (mə lō'dĭ ən), n. 1. a small reed organ. 2. a kind of accordion.

me·lod·ic (mə lŏd'ĭk), adj. 1. melodious. 2. pertaining to melody. —me·lod'i·cal·ly, adv.

me·lo·di·ous (mə lō'dĭ əs), adj. 1. characterized by melody; tuneful. 2. producing melody. —me·lo'di·ous·ly, adv. —me·lo'di·ous·ness, n.

mel·o·dra·ma (měl'ə drä'mə, -drăm'ə), n. a play which intensifies sentiment and exaggerates passion. —mel·o·dra·mat·ic (měl'ə drə măt'ĭk), adj. —mel'o·dra·mat'i·cal·ly, adv. —mel·o·dram·a·tist (měl'ə drăm'ə tĭst), n.

mel·o·dy (měl'ə dĭ), n., pl. -dies. 1. musical sounds in agreeable succession or arrangement. 2. Music. a. the succession of single tones in musical compositions. b. the principal part in a harmonic composition.

mel·on (měl'ən), n. 1. the fruit of any of various plants of the cucumber family, as the muskmelon or watermelon. 2. cut a melon, U.S. Slang. to declare a large extra dividend to shareholders.

Mel·pom·e·ne (měl pŏm'ə nĭ), n. the Muse of tragedy.

melt (mělt), v., melted, melted or molten, melting, n. —v.i. 1. to become liquefied by heat, as ice, butter, metal, etc. 2. to dissolve. 3. to fade gradually. 4. to become softened in feeling by pity, sympathy, love, or the like. —v.t. 5. to reduce to a liquid state by heat. 6. to cause to fade (away). 7. to soften in feeling, as a person. —n. 8. act or process of melting. —melt'er, n.

mel·ton (měl'tən), n. a smooth, heavy woolen cloth, used for overcoats, etc.

Mel·ville (měl'vĭl), n. Herman, 1819–91, U.S. author.

mem., 1. member. 2. memorial.

mem·ber (měm'bər), n. 1. each of the persons composing a society, community, or other body. 2. a part or organ of an animal body; limb. 3. a constituent part. 4. either side of an algebraic equation.

mem·ber·ship (měm'bər shĭp'), n. 1. state of being a member, as of a society. 2. the total number of members.

mem·brane (měm'brān), n. a thin, pliable sheet or layer of animal or vegetable tissue, serving to line an organ, connect parts, etc. —mem·bra·nous (měm'brə nəs), adj.

Me·mel (mā'məl), n. 1. a seaport in the W Soviet Union, in the Lithuanian Republic. 41,297. 2. a territory including this seaport: ceded to Germany by Lithuania, 1939; incorporated into the Soviet Union, 1945. 154,694 pop.; 933 sq. mi.

me·men·to (mĭ měn'tō), n., pl. -tos, -toes. something that serves as a reminder, souvenir, or warning.

mem·o (měm'ō), n., pl. memos. Colloq. memorandum.

mem·oir (měm'wär, -wôr), n. 1. (pl.) records of

facts or events as known to the writer or gathered from special sources. 2. (*pl.*) records of one's own life. 3. a biography.

mem·o·ra·bil·i·a (mĕm'ə rə bĭl'Ĭ ə), *n.pl.*, *sing.* -rabile (-răb'ə lĬ). memorable things.

mem·o·ra·ble (mĕm'ə rə bəl), *adj.* worthy to be remembered; notable. **—mem'o·ra·bil'i·ty,** *n.* **—mem'o·ra·bly,** *adv.*

mem·o·ran·dum (mĕm'ə răn'dəm), *n.*, *pl.* -dums, -da (-də). 1. a note made of something to be remembered, as in future action. 2. a record or written statement of something.

me·mo·ri·al (mə mōr'Ĭ əl), *n.* 1. something designed to preserve the memory of a person, event, etc., as a monument. 2. a written statement of facts presented to a sovereign, a legislative body, etc., as the ground of a petition. **—adj.** 3. commemorative.

Memorial Day, *U.S.* a day, May 30 in most States, set apart for observances in memory of dead soldiers and sailors; Decoration Day.

me·mo·ri·al·ize (mə mōr'Ĭ ə līz'), *v.t.,* -ized, -izing. 1. to commemorate. 2. to present a memorial to. **—me·mo'ri·al·i·za'tion,** *n.* **—memo'ri·al·iz'er,** *n.*

mem·o·rize (mĕm'ə rīz'), *v.t.,* -rized, -rizing. to commit to memory; learn by heart. **—mem'o·ri·za'tion,** *n.*

mem·o·ry (mĕm'ə rĬ), *n.*, *pl.* -ries. 1. the mental faculty of retaining impressions or recalling experiences. 2. remembrance; recollection. 3. the length of time over which recollection extends. 4. the reputation of a person or thing, esp. after death.

Mem·phis (mĕm'fĬs), *n.* a city in SW Tennessee: a port on the Mississippi. 292,942.

mem·sa·hib (mĕm'sä'Ĭb, -sä'hĬb), *n.* (in India) a native's term of respect for a European lady.

men·ace (mĕn'Ĭs), *n.*, *v.,* -aced, -acing. **—n.** 1. something that threatens to cause evil, harm, etc. **—v.t.** 2. to threaten. **—men'ac·ing·ly,** *adv.*

mé·nage (mā näzh'), *n.* a household.

me·nag·er·ie (mə năj'ə rĬ, -näzh'-), *n.* 1. a collection of animals, esp. for exhibition. 2. a place where they are exhibited.

mend (mĕnd), *v.t.* 1. to make whole or sound by repairing. 2. to correct defects or errors in. 3. to remove or correct (a defect, etc.). 4. to progress toward recovery. **—v.i.** 5. (of conditions) to improve. **—n.** 6. repair or improvement. **—mend'a·ble,** *adj.* **—mend'er,** *n.*

men·da·cious (mĕn dā'shəs), *adj.* 1. false. 2. untruthful. **—men·da'cious·ly,** *adv.* **—menda'cious·ness, men·dac·i·ty** (mĕn dăs'ə tĬ), *n.*

Men·del (mĕn'dəl), *n.* Gregor Johann, 1822–84, Austrian biologist. **—Men·de·li·an** (mĕn dē'-lĬ ən), *adj.*

Men·del·ism (mĕn'də lĬz'əm), *n.* the theories of heredity advanced by Mendel. Also, **Men·deli·an·ism** (mĕn dē'lĬ ə nĬz'əm).

Mendel's laws, *Genetics.* the basic principles of heredity discoved by Mendel, showing that alternative hereditary factors of hybrids exhibit a clean-cut separation or segregation from one another.

Men·dels·sohn (mĕn'dəl sən), *n.* Felix, 1809–47, German composer.

men·di·cant (mĕn'də kənt), *adj.* 1. begging; living on alms. 2. pertaining to or characteristic of a beggar. **—n.** 3. a beggar. 4. a mendicant friar. **—men'di·can·cy,** *n.*

Men·e·la·us (mĕn'ə lā'əs), *n. Gk. Legend.* a king of Sparta and husband of Helen: one of the leaders of the Greeks before Troy.

me·ni·al (mē'nĬ əl), *adj.* 1. pertaining to domestic servants. 2. servile. **—n.** 3. a domestic servant. 4. a servile person. **—me'ni·al·ly,** *adv.*

me·nin·ges (mĬ nĬn'jēz), *n.pl.*, *sing.* **meninx** (mē'nĬngks). *Anat.* the three membranes investing the brain and spinal cord.

men·in·gi·tis (mĕn'Ĭn jī'tĬs), *n. Pathol.* inflammation of the meninges.

me·nis·cus (mĬ nĬs'kəs), *n.*, *pl.* -nisci (-nĬs'ī), -niscuses. 1. a crescent or crescent-shaped body. 2. a lens with a crescent-shaped section. 3. the convex or concave upper surface of a column of liquid, the curvature of which is caused by capillarity.

Men·non·ite (mĕn'ə nīt'), *n.* a member of a Christian denomination opposed to infant baptism, the taking of oaths, the holding of public office, and military service.

men·o·pause (mĕn'ə pôz'), *n. Physiol.* the period of irregular menstrual cycles prior to the

final cessation of the menses, occurring normally between the ages of 45 and 50.

men·ses (mĕn'sēz), *n.pl.* monthly discharge of blood from the uterus.

Men·she·vik (mĕn'shĕ vĬk), *n.*, *pl.* -viki (-vĬ-kē'), -viks. (in Russia) a member of a socialistic party opposing the Bolshevik government.

men·stru·al (mĕn'strŏŏ əl), *adj.* 1. of or pertaining to the menses. 2. monthly.

men·stru·ate (mĕn'strŏŏ āt'), *v.i.,* -ated, -ating. to discharge the menses. **—men'stru·a'-tion,** *n.*

men·sur·a·ble (mĕn'shər ə bəl), *adj.* measurable. **—men'sur·a·bil'i·ty,** *n.*

men·su·ra·tion (mĕn'shə rā'shən), *n.* 1. that branch of mathematics which deals with the determination of length, area, and volume. 2. act, art, or process of measuring.

-ment, a suffix of nouns, often concrete, denoting an action or state resulting (*abridgment, refreshment*), a product (*fragment*), or means (*ornament*).

men·tal (mĕn'təl), *adj.* 1. of or pertaining to the mind. 2. performed by or existing in the mind. 3. intellectual.

mental age, *Psychol.* the degree of mental development or intelligence of an individual in comparison with the average intelligence of normal children at different ages.

men·tal·i·ty (mĕn tăl'ə tĬ), *n.*, *pl.* -ties. mental capacity; intellectuality; mind.

men·tal·ly (mĕn'tə lĬ), *adv.* 1. in or with the mind. 2. with regard to the mind.

men·thol (mĕn'thōl, -thôl), *n.* a colorless, crystalline alcohol, present in peppermint oil, used in perfume and confectionery, and for colds and nasal disorders.

men·tho·lat·ed (mĕn'thə lā'tĬd), *adj.* 1. covered or treated with menthol. 2. saturated with or containing menthol.

men·tion (mĕn'shən), *v.t.* 1. to name, specify, or speak of. **—n.** 2. a reference, direct or incidental. **—men'tion·a·ble,** *adj.*

men·tor (mĕn'tər), *n.* a wise and trusted counselor.

men·u (mĕn'ū, mā'nū), *n.* 1. a list of the dishes served at a meal. 2. the dishes served.

me·ow (mĬ ou', myou), *n.* 1. the sound a cat makes. **—v.i.** 2. to make such a sound.

Meph·i·stoph·e·les (mĕf'ə stŏf'ə lēz'), *n. Medieval Demonology.* one of the seven chief devils. He is represented in Goethe's *Faust* as a crafty, sardonic, and scoffing fiend.

me·phit·ic (mĬ fĬt'Ĭk), *adj.* 1. offensive to the smell. 2. noxious; poisonous.

mer·can·tile (mûr'kən tĬl, -tīl'), *adj.* 1. of or pertaining to trade; commercial. 2. engaged in trade or commerce.

mer·can·til·ism (mûr'kən tĬl Ĭz'əm, -tĭl Ĭz'əm), *n.* 1. the mercantile spirit. 2. Also, **mercantile system.** a system of economic and political policy aimed at establishing a favorable balance of trade as a means of securing political supremacy over other nations. **—mer'can·til·ist,** *n.*

Mer·ca·tor's projection (mər kā'tərz), a map projection with rectangular grid which is conformable and on which any curved line is represented as a straight line: particularly useful for navigation, though the scale varies notably with latitude and the shapes of large areas are greatly distorted.

Mercator's projection

mer·ce·nar·y (mûr'sə-nĕr'Ĭ), *adj.*, *n.*, *pl.* -naries. **—adj.** 1. working or acting merely for gain. 2. hired. **—n.** 3. a professional soldier serving in a foreign army. 4. any hireling.

mer·cer (mûr'sər), *n. Brit.* a dealer in textile fabrics, esp. silks, etc.

mer·cer·ize (mûr'sə rīz'), *v.t.,* -ized, -izing. to treat (cotton yarns or fabric) with caustic alkali under tension, increasing strength, luster, and affinity for dye.

mer·chan·dise (*n.* mûr'chən dīz', -dīs'; *v.* mûr'chən dīz'), *n.*, *v.,* -dised, -dising. **—n.** 1. goods; commodities. **—v.i., v.t.** 2. to buy and sell. **—mer'chan·dis'er,** *n.*

mer·chant (mûr'chənt), *n.* 1. one who buys

and sells commodities for profit. **2.** a storekeeper. —*adj.* **3.** pertaining to trade or commerce.

mer·chant·a·ble (mûr/chən tə bəl), *adj.* marketable.

mer·chant·man (mûr/chənt mən), *n.*, *pl.* **-men.** a trading vessel.

merchant marine, 1. the vessels of a nation engaged in commerce. **2.** the officers and crews of merchant vessels.

Mer·ci·a (mûr/shĭ ə, -shə), *n.* an early English kingdom in central Britain. **—Mer/ci·an,** *adj.*, *n.*

mer·ci·ful (mûr/sĭ fəl), *adj.* full of mercy; compassionate. **—mer/ci·ful·ly,** *adv.* **—mer/ci·ful·ness,** *n.*

mer·ci·less (mûr/sĭ lĭs), *adj.* without any mercy; pitiless. **—mer/ci·less·ly,** *adv.* **—mer/ci·less·ness,** *n.*

mer·cu·ri·al (mər kyŏŏr/ĭ əl), *adj.* **1.** pertaining to, containing, or caused by the metal mercury. **2.** sprightly; volatile. **3.** flighty; fickle.

mer·cu·ric (mər kyŏŏr/ĭk), *adj.* *Chem.* of or containing mercury, esp. in the divalent state.

Mer·cu·ro·chrome (mər kyŏŏr/ə krōm/), *n.* *Trademark.* **1.** an iridescent green powder which dissolves in water to furnish a red solution, used as an antiseptic and germicide. **2.** a solution of this compound.

mer·cu·rous (mər kyŏŏr/əs, mûr/kyə rəs), *adj.* *Chem.* containing monovalent mercury.

mer·cu·ry (mûr/kyə rĭ), *n.*, *pl.* **-ries. 1.** *Chem.* a heavy, silver-white metallic element; quicksilver. *Symbol: Hg; at. wt.: 200.6; at. no.: 80; sp. gr.:* 13.546 at 20°C. **2.** (*cap.*) *Astron.* the planet nearest the sun, having a mean distance from the sun of about 36,000,000 miles. **3.** (*cap.*) a Roman deity, messenger of the gods, and god of commerce, dexterity, and eloquence.

mer·cy (mûr/sĭ), *n.*, *pl.* **-cies. 1.** compassion, pity, or benevolence. **2.** discretionary power as to clemency or severity, pardon or punishment, or the like. **3.** an act of forbearance, compassion, or favor.

mere (mĭr), *adj.*, *superl.* **merest.** being nothing more nor better than.

Mer·e·dith (mĕr/ə dĭth), *n.* **George,** 1828–1909, British novelist and poet.

mere·ly (mĭr/lĭ), *adv.* only as specified; simply.

mer·e·tri·cious (mĕr/ə trĭsh/əs), *adj.* showily attractive; tawdry. **—mer/e·tri/cious·ly,** *adv.*

mer·gan·ser (mər găn/sər), *n.*, *pl.* **-sers,** (*esp. collectively*) **-ser.** any of certain saw-billed, fish-eating, diving ducks.

merge (mûrj), *v.*, **merged, merging.** —*v.t.* **1.** to cause to be absorbed; combine. —*v.i.* **2.** to become absorbed or combined.

merg·er (mûr/jər), *n.* **1.** a combination of two or more business enterprises into a single enterprise. **2.** act of merging.

Mer·i·den (mĕr/ə dən), *n.* a city in central Connecticut. 39,494.

me·rid·i·an (mə rĭd/ĭ ən), *n.* **1.** *Geog.* a great circle of the earth passing through the poles and any given point on the earth's surface. **2.** *Astron.* the great circle of the celestial sphere which passes through its poles and the observer's zenith. **3.** the highest point. —*adj.* **4.** of or pertaining to a meridian.

Me·rid·i·an (mə rĭd/ĭ ən), *n.* a city in E [Mississippi. 35,481.

me·ringue (mə răng/), *n.* a mixture of sugar and beaten egg whites formed into small cakes and baked, or spread over pastry, etc.

me·ri·no (mə rē/nō), *n.*, *pl.* **-nos. 1.** a variety of sheep which originated in Spain, valued for its fine wool. **2.** wool from merino sheep.

mer·it (mĕr/ĭt), *n.* **1.** excellence; worth. **2.** a commendable quality, act, etc. **3.** (*pl.*) the substantial right and wrong of a matter. **4.** state or fact of deserving well. **5.** that which is deserved. **6.** (*sometimes pl.*) desert.—*v.t.* **7.** to deserve.

mer·i·to·ri·ous (mĕr/ə tōr/ĭ əs), *adj.* possessing merit. **—mer/i·to/ri·ous·ly,** *adv.* **—mer/i·to/ri·ous·ness,** *n.*

Mer·lin (mûr/lĭn), *n.* *Arthurian Romance.* a venerable magician and seer.

mer·maid (mûr/mād/), *n.* an imaginary female marine creature, typically having the head and trunk of a woman and the tail of a fish. **—mer/man/,** *n. masc.*

Mer·ri·mac (mĕr/ə măk/), *n.* the first ironclad warship: used by the Confederates against the *Monitor* (1862).

mer·ri·ment (mĕr/ĭ mənt), *n.* merry gaiety; mirth; hilarity; laughter.

mer·ry (mĕr/ĭ), *adj.*, **merrier, merriest. 1.** full of cheer or gaiety; joyous. **2.** mirthful; hilarious. **3. make merry,** to be gay or festive. **—mer/ri·ly,** *adv.* **—mer/ri·ness,** *n.*

mer·ry-go-round (mĕr/ĭ gō round/), *n.* a revolving circular platform with hobby-horses, etc., on which children ride for amusement.

mer·ry·mak·ing (mĕr/ĭ mā/kĭng), *n.* **1.** act of making merry. **2.** a merry festivity. —*adj.* **3.** gay; festive. **—mer/ry·ma/ker,** *n.*

me·sa (mā/sə), *n.* a land form having a relatively flat top and bounded wholly or in part with steep, rock walls.

mé·sal·li·ance (mā zăl/ĭ əns), *n.* a marriage with a social inferior.

mes·cal (mĕs kăl/), *n.* **1.** either of two species of cactus of Texas and northern Mexico, whose buttonlike tops (**mescal buttons**) are dried and used as a stimulant, esp. by the Indians. **2.** an intoxicating spirit distilled from the fermented juice of certain species of agave.

mes·en·ceph·a·lon (mĕs/ĕn sĕf/ə lŏn/), *n.* *Anat.* the middle segment of the brain.

mesh (mĕsh), *n.* **1.** one of the open spaces of network of a net. **2.** (*pl.*) means of catching or holding fast. **3.** a net. **4.** *Mach.* the engagement of gear teeth. —*v.t.* **5.** to catch in the meshes of a net; enmesh. **6.** *Mach.* to engage, as gear teeth. —*v.i.* **7.** *Mach.* to become or be engaged, as gear teeth.

mes·mer·ism (mĕs/mə rĭz/əm, mĕz/-), *n.* hypnotism. **—mes·mer·ic** (mĕs mĕr/ĭk, mĕz-), *adj.* **—mes/mer·ist,** *n.*

mes·mer·ize (mĕs/mə rīz/, mĕz/-), *v.t.*, *v.i.*, **-ized, -izing.** to hypnotize. **—mes/mer·i·za/tion,** *n.* **—mes/mer·iz/er,** *n.*

Mes·o·po·ta·mia (mĕs/ə pə tā/mĭ ə), *n.* **1.** an ancient country in Asia between the Tigris and Euphrates rivers. **2.** (loosely) Iraq. **—Mes/o·po·ta/mi·an,** *adj.*, *n.*

mes·o·tron (mĕs/ə trŏn/, mē/sə-), *n.* *Physics.* a constituent particle of cosmic rays, having a mass of the order of 200 times that of an electron and a unit negative or positive charge.

Mes·o·zo·ic (mĕs/ə zō/ĭk, mē/sə-), *Stratig.* —*adj.* **1.** pertaining to the geological era of reptiles. —*n.* **2.** this era.

mes·quite (mĕs kēt/, mĕs/kēt), *n.* a tree or shrub of the mimosa family, of the southwestern U.S., Mexico, etc., whose beanlike pods are rich in sugar and form a valuable fodder.

mess (mĕs), *n.* **1.** a dirty or untidy condition. **2.** embarrassing confusion. **3.** an unpleasant or difficult situation. **4.** a dirty or untidy jumble. **5.** a group regularly taking meals together, as in the army. **6.** the meal so taken. **7.** a quantity of food sufficient for a dish or a single occasion. **8.** a sloppy or unappetizing preparation of food. —*v.t.* **9.** to make dirty or untidy. **10.** to muddle (affairs, etc.). —*v.i.* **11.** to eat in company. **12.** to busy oneself.

mes·sage (mĕs/ĭj), *n.* **1.** a communication transmitted through a messenger or other agency. **2.** an official communication, as from a chief executive to a legislative body. **3.** an inspired communication of a prophet.

mes·sen·ger (mĕs/ən jər), *n.* **1.** one who bears a message or goes on an errand. **2.** a herald or harbinger.

Mes·si·ah (mə sī/ə), *n.* **1.** the title applied to an expected deliverer of the Jewish people, and hence to Jesus. **2.** any expected deliverer. **—Mes·si·an·ic** (mĕs/ĭ ăn/ĭk), *adj.*

Mes·si·na (mĕ sē/nə), *n.* a seaport in NE Sicily. 211,587.

mess·mate (mĕs/māt/), *n.* an associate in a mess, esp. in a ship's mess.

Messrs. messieurs (pl. of *monsieur*).

mess·y (mĕs/ĭ), *adj.*, **messier, messiest. 1.** of the nature of a mess. **2.** being in a mess. **3.** dirty; untidy. **—mess/i·ness,** *n.*

mes·ti·zo (mĕs tē/zō), *n.*, *pl.* **-zos, -zoes. 1.** a person of mixed blood. **2.** (in Spanish America) one who has Spanish and American Indian blood. **—mes·ti·za** (mĕs tē/zə), *n. fem.*

met., 1. metaphor. **2.** metaphysics.

me·tab·o·lism (mə tăb/ə līz/əm), *n.* *Biol.* the sum of the processes in an organism by which food is built up into living protoplasm and by which protoplasm is broken down into simpler compounds with the exchange of energy. **—met·a·bol·ic** (mĕt/ə bŏl/ĭk), *adj.*

met·al (mĕt′əl), *n.*, *v.*, **-aled, -aling** or (*esp. Brit.*) **-alled, -alling.** —*n.* **1.** any of a class of elementary substances, as gold, silver, copper, etc., all of which are crystalline when solid and many of which are characterized by opacity, ductility, conductivity, and a peculiar luster when freshly fractured. **2.** an alloy or mixture composed wholly or partly of such substances. **3.** formative material; mettle. —*v.t.* **4.** to furnish or cover with metal.

metal., **1.** metallurgical. **2.** metallurgy.

metall., metallurgy.

me·tal·lic (mə tăl′ĭk), *adj.* **1.** of, pertaining to, or consisting of metal. **2.** of the nature of metal. —**me·tal′li·cal·ly,** *adv.*

met·al·lur·gy (mĕt′ə lûr′jĭ, mĕ tăl′ər jĭ), *n.* the art or science of separating metals from their ores, of making and compounding alloys, or of treating metals to give them certain desired properties. —**met′al·lur′gic, met′al·lur′gi·cal,** *adj.* —**met′al·lur′gi·cal·ly,** *adv.* —**met·al·lur·gist** (mĕt′ə lûr′jĭst, mĕ tăl′ər jĭst), *n.*

met·al·work·ing (mĕt′əl wûr′kĭng), *n.* act of making metal objects. —**met′al·work′,** *n.* —**met′al·work′er,** *n.*

met·a·mor·phism (mĕt′ə môr′fĭz əm), *n.* **1.** metamorphosis. **2.** *Geol.* a change in the structure or constitution of a rock due to natural agencies, as pressure and heat.

met·a·mor·phose (mĕt′ə môr′fōz, -fōs), *v.t.*, **-phosed, -phosing. 1.** to transform. **2.** to subject to metamorphism.

met·a·mor·pho·sis (mĕt′ə môr′fə sĭs), *n.*, *pl.* **-ses** (-sēz). **1.** change of form, structure, or substance. **2.** any complete change. **3.** a change of form during the postembryonic or embryonic growth of an animal by which it is adapted temporarily to a special environment or way of living usually different from that of the preceding stage. —*met′a·mor′phic, adj.*

met·a·phor (mĕt′ə fər, -fôr′), *n.* a figure of speech in which a resemblance is implied. —**met·a·phor·i·cal** (mĕt′ə fôr′ə kəl, -fŏr′-), **met′a·phor′ic,** *adj.* —**met′a·phor′i·cal·ly,** *adv.*

met·a·phys·i·cal (mĕt′ə fĭz′ə kəl), *adj.* **1.** pertaining to or of the nature of metaphysics. **2.** highly abstract or abstruse. —**met′a·phys′i·cal·ly,** *adv.*

met·a·phys·ics (mĕt′ə fĭz′ĭks), *n.* **1.** that branch of philosophy which treats of first principles, including the sciences of being and of the origin and structure of the universe. **2.** philosophy. —**met·a·phy·si·cian** (mĕt′ə fĭ zĭsh′ən), *n.*

me·tath·e·sis (mə tăth′ə sĭs), *n.*, *pl.* **-ses** (-sēz′). the transposition of letters, syllables, or sounds in a word.

Met·a·zo·a (mĕt′ə zō′ə), *n.pl.* a large zoölogical division comprising all the animals above the protozoans, i.e., those organisms which, although originating from a single cell, are composed of many cells. —**met′a·zo′an,** *adj.*, *n.*

mete[1] (mēt), *v.t.*, **meted, meting.** to distribute or apportion by measure; allot.

mete[2] (mēt), *n.* a limit.

me·temp·sy·cho·sis (mə tĕmp′sə kō′sĭs, mĕt′əm sĭ-), *n.*, *pl.* **-ses** (-sēz). **1.** the passage of the soul from one body to another. **2.** the rebirth of the soul at death in another body either of human or animal form.

me·te·or (mē′tĭ′ ər), *n.* a transient fiery streak in the sky produced by a celestial body passing through the earth's atmosphere; a shooting star.

me·te·or·ic (mē′tĭ ôr′ĭk, -ŏr′ĭk), *adj.* **1.** pertaining to or like a meteor. **2.** consisting of meteors. **3.** transiently brilliant. **4.** swift or rapid. —**me′te·or′i·cal·ly,** *adv.*

me·te·or·ite (mē′tĭ ə rīt′), *n.* **1.** a mass of stone or metal that has reached the earth from outer space. **2.** a meteor.

meteorol., meteorology.

me·te·or·ol·o·gy (mē′tĭ ə rŏl′ə jĭ), *n.* the science dealing with the atmosphere and its phenomena, esp. as relating to weather. —**me′te·or·ol′o·gist,** *n.* —**me·te·or·o·log·i·cal** (mē′tĭ ər ə lŏj′ə kəl), **me′te·or·o·log′ic,** *adj.* —**me′te·or·o·log′i·cal·ly,** *adv.*

me·ter[1] (mē′tər), *n.* the fundamental unit of length in the metric system, equivalent to 39.37 U.S. inches. Also, *esp. Brit.*, **metre.**

me·ter[2] (mē′tər), *n.* **1.** *Pros.* **a.** arrangement of words in regularly measured or rhythmic lines or verses. **b.** a particular form of such arrangement. **2.** *Music.* **a.** the rhythmic element as measured by

division into parts of equal time-value. **b.** the unit of measurement, in terms of number of beats, adopted for a given piece of music. Also, *esp. Brit.*, **metre.**

me·ter[3] (mē′tər), *n.* **1.** an instrument that measures. **2.** one that automatically measures and records the quantity of gas, water, electricity, or the like, passing through it or actuating it. —*v.t.* **3.** to measure by means of a meter.

Meth., Methodist.

meth·ane (mĕth′ān), *n.* *Chem.* a colorless, odorless, inflammable gas, CH_4, the main constituent of marsh gas and the firedamp of coal mines and obtained commercially from natural gas.

meth·a·nol (mĕth′ə nōl′, -nŏl′), *n.* *Chem.* methyl alcohol, or wood alcohol.

me·thinks (mĭ thĭngks′), *v. impers.*; *pt.* **methought.** *Archaic and Poetic.* it seems to me.

meth·od (mĕth′əd), *n.* **1.** a mode of procedure. **2.** order or system in doing anything. **3.** orderly or systematic arrangement.

me·thod·i·cal (mə thŏd′ə kəl), *adj.* systematic; orderly. Also, **me·thod′ic.** —**me·thod′i·cal·ly,** *adv.* —**me·thod′i·cal·ness,** *n.*

Meth·od·ism (mĕth′ə dĭz′əm), *n.* the doctrines, polity, and worship of the Methodist Church.

Meth·od·ist (mĕth′əd ĭst), *n.* **1.** a member of one of the Christian denominations which grew out of the revival of religion led by John Wesley. —*adj.* **2.** of or pertaining to the Methodists or Methodism.

meth·od·ize (mĕth′ə dīz′), *v.t.*, **-ized, -izing. 1.** to reduce to method. **2.** to arrange with method. —**meth′od·iz′er,** *n.*

meth·od·ol·o·gy (mĕth′ə dŏl′ə jĭ), *n.*, *pl.* **-gies.** the science or method, esp. with reference to the conduct of scientific research.

Me·thu·se·lah (mĭ thōō′zə lə), *n.* a Biblical patriarch before the Flood who according to tradition lived 969 years.

meth·yl (mĕth′ĭl), *n.* *Chem.* a univalent hydrocarbon radical, CH_3, derived from methane.

methyl alcohol, *Chem.* a colorless, inflammable, poisonous liquid of the alcohol class, used as a fuel, solvent, etc.; wood alcohol.

me·tic·u·lous (mə tĭk′yə ləs), *adj.* minutely or finically careful. —**me·tic′u·lous·ly,** *adv.*

mé·tier (mĕ tyĕ′), *n.* trade; profession.

me·ton·y·my (mĭ tŏn′ə mĭ), *n.* *Rhet.* the use of the name of one thing for that of another to which it has some logical relation, as "scepter" for "sovereignty."

Met·ra·zol (mĕt′rə zōl′, -zŏl′), *n.* *Trademark.* a drug which increases the activity of the heart and lungs.

me·tre (mē′tər), *n.* *Chiefly Brit.* meter.

met·ric[1] (mĕt′rĭk), *adj.* pertaining to the meter, or to the system of measures and weights originally based upon it.

met·ric[2] (mĕt′rĭk), *adj.* metrical.

met·ri·cal (mĕt′rə kəl), *adj.* **1.** pertaining to poetic measure. **2.** composed in meter or verse. **3.** pertaining to measurement. —**met′ri·cal·ly,** *adv.*

metric system, a decimal system of weights and measures, now widespread over the world. The basic units are the meter (39.37 inches) for length, and the gram (15.432 grains) for mass or weight. Derived units are the liter for capacity, the are for area, and the stere for volume. Names for units larger and smaller than these are formed from the above names by the use of the following prefixes:

| kilo | 1000 | deka | 10 | centi | 0.01 |
| hecto | 100 | deci | 0.1 | milli | 0.001 |

metric ton, a unit of 1000 kilograms, equivalent to 2204.62 avoirdupois pounds.

met·ro·nome (mĕt′rə nōm′), *n.* a mechanical contrivance for marking time, as for music.

me·trop·o·lis (mə trŏp′ə lĭs), *n.*, *pl.* **-lises** (-lĭs′ĭz), **-leis** (-līs′). **1.** the chief city (not necessarily the capital) of a country, state, or region. **2.** a central point, as of some activity.

met·ro·pol·i·tan (mĕt′rə pŏl′ə tən), *adj.* **1.** characteristic of a metropolis or chief city. —*n.* **2.** an inhabitant of a metropolis or chief city. **3.** the next highest rank to Patriarch in the Russian Orthodox Church.

Met·ter·nich (mĕt′ər nĭkH), *n.* **Klemens Wenzel Nepomuk Lothar, Prince von,** 1773–1859, Austrian statesman.

met·tle (mĕt/əl), *n.* **1.** the characteristic disposition or temper. **2.** spirit; courage.

met·tle·some (mĕt/əl səm), *adj.* spirited; courageous. Also, **met·tled** (mĕt/əld).

Metz (mĕts), *n.* a fortress city in NE France. 70,105.

Meuse (mūz), *n.* a river flowing from NE France through E Belgium and S Netherlands into the North Sea. 575 mi.

mew¹ (mū), *n.* **1.** the sound a cat makes. —*v.i.* **2.** to make this sound.

mew² (mū), *n.* a seagull, esp. the common gull of Europe.

mewl (mūl), *v.i.* to cry as a young child.

Mex., **1.** Mexican. **2.** Mexico.

Mexican hairless, a very small dog which grows very little hair.

Mexican War, the war between the United States and Mexico, 1846–48.

Mex·i·co (mĕk/sə kō/), *n.* **1.** a republic in S North America. 22,753,000 pop.; 760,373 sq. mi. *Cap.:* Mexico City. **2.** Gulf of, an arm of the Atlantic between the U.S., Cuba, and Mexico. ab. 716,000 sq. mi. —**Mex/i·can,** *adj., n.*

Mexico City, the capital of Mexico, in the central part. 1,448,422 pop.

Mey·er·beer (mī/ər bār/), *n.* **Giacomo,** 1791–1864, German composer.

mez·za·nine (mĕz/ə nēn/, -nĭn), *n.* a low story between two other stories of greater height, esp. when extending only part way.

mez·zo (mĕt/sō, mĕz/ō), *adj.* middle; medium; half.

mez·zo·so·pran·o (mĕt/sō sə prăn/ō, -prä/nō, mĕz/ō-), *n., pl.* **-pranos, -prani** (-prä/nē). *Music.* **1.** a voice or voice part intermediate in compass between soprano and contralto. **2.** a person having such a voice.

mez·zo·tint (mĕt/sō tĭnt/, mĕz/ō-), *n.* **1.** a method of engraving on copper or steel by burnishing or scraping away a uniformly roughened surface. **2.** a print produced by this method. —*v.t.* **3.** to engrave in mezzotint.

mf., **1.** *Music.* (It. *mezzo forte*), moderately loud. **2.** microfarad.

mfg., manufacturing.

mfr., *pl.* **mfrs.** manufacturer.

Mg, *Chem.* magnesium.

mg., milligram; milligrams.

mgr., **1.** manager. **2.** Monsignor.

mho (mō), *n.* *Elect.* a unit of electrical conductivity, equal to the conductivity of a body whose resistance is one ohm.

mi (mē), *n.* *Music.* the syllable used for the third tone of a scale.

mi., **1.** mile; miles. **2.** mill; mills.

Mi·am·i (mī ăm/Y, -ə), *n.* a city in SE Florida. 172,172.

Miami Beach, a city in SE Florida. 28,012.

mi·as·ma (mī ăz/mə, mY-), *n., pl.* **-mata** (-mə tə), **-mas.** noxious exhalations from putrescent organic matter. —**mi·as/mal,** *adj.*

mi·ca (mī/kə), *n.* any member of a group of minerals, hydrous disilicates of aluminum with other bases, that separate readily into thin, tough layers.

Mi·cah (mī/kə), *n.* **1.** a Hebrew prophet of the 8th century B.C. **2.** the sixth book of the minor prophets, in the Old Testament, which bears his name. *Abbr.:* **Mic.**

Mich., Michigan.

Mi·chael (mī/kəl), *n.* *Bible.* a militant archangel.

Michael I, born 1921, king of Rumania, 1927–30 and 1940–48.

Mich·ael·mas (mYk/əl məs), *n.* *Chiefly Brit.* a festival celebrated on Sept. 29, in honor of the archangel Michael.

Mi·chel·an·ge·lo (mī/kəl ăn/jə lō/, mYk/əl-), *n.* 1475–1564, Italian sculptor, painter, architect, and poet.

Mi·chel·son (mī/kəl sən), *n.* **Albert Abraham,** 1852–1931, U.S. physicist.

Mich·i·gan (mYsh/ə gən), *n.* **1.** a State in the N central United States. 6,064,899 pop.; 58,216 sq. mi. *Cap.:* Lansing. *Abbr.:* **Mich. 2. Lake,** a lake between Wisconsin and Michigan. ab. 22,400 sq. mi.

Mick·ey (mYk/Y), *n., pl.* **-eys.** a drink to which a sleeping drug has been added. Also, **Mickey Finn** (fĭn).

mi·crobe (mī/krōb), *n.* **1.** a microorganism, usually one of vegetable nature; a germ. **2.** a bacterium, esp. one causing disease. —**mi·cro·bi·al** (mī krō/bY əl), **mi·cro/bic,** *adj.*

mi·cro·ce·phal·ic (mī/krō sə făl/Yk), *adj.* having a skull with a small cranial capacity or an abnormally small skull.

mi·cro·cop·y (mī/krə kŏp/Y), *n., pl.* **-copies.** *Library Science.* a greatly reduced photographic copy of a book page, etc.

mi·cro·cosm (mī/krə kŏz/əm), *n.* **1.** a little world. **2.** anything regarded as a world in miniature. **3.** man viewed as an epitome of the universe.

mi·cro·far·ad (mī/krō făr/əd, -ăd), *n.* *Elect.* a unit of capacitance equal to one millionth of a farad.

mi·cro·film (mī/krə fYlm/), *n.* **1.** a narrow film, esp. of motion-picture stock, on which microcopies are made. **2.** microcopy.

mi·crom·e·ter (mī krŏm/ə tər), *n.* **1.** any of various devices for measuring minute distances, angles, etc. **2.** a micrometer caliper.

micrometer caliper, an instrument for measuring thickness (as of wire) with precision.

mi·cron (mī/krŏn), *n., pl.* **-cra** (-krə), **-crons.** one millionth part of a meter. *Symbol:* µ.

Mi·cro·ne·sia (mī/krə nē/zhə, -shə), *n.* groups of small Pacific islands, including the Marianas, the Caroline, and the Marshall Islands. —**Mi/cro·ne/sian,** *adj., n.*

mi·cro·or·gan·ism (mī/krō ôr/gə nYz/əm), *n.* a microscopic organism.

mi·cro·phone (mī/krə fōn/), *n.* an instrument which is capable of transforming the air pressure waves of sound into changes in electric currents or voltages.

mi·cro·scope (mī/krə skōp/), *n.* an optical instrument having a magnifying lens or a combination of lenses for inspecting objects too small to be seen in detail, or at all, by the naked eye.

mi·cro·scop·ic (mī/krə skŏp/Yk), *adj.* **1.** visible or distinct only through a microscope. **2.** tiny. **3.** of the microscope. **4.** suggestive of the use of the microscope. Also, **mi/cro·scop/i·cal.** —**mi/cro·scop/i·cal·ly,** *adv.*

mi·cros·co·py (mī krŏs/kə pY, mī/krə skō/pY), *n.* the use of the microscope.

mi·cro·waves (mī/krō wāvz/), *n.pl.* electromagnetic waves of extremely high frequency.

mic·tu·rate (mYk/chə rāt/), *v.i.* **-rated, -rating.** to urinate.

mid¹ (mYd), *adj.* **1.** at or near its middle point. **2.** occupying a middle place or position.

mid² (mYd), *prep.* amid. Also, **'mid.**

mid., middle.

Mi·das (mī/dəs), *n.* *Gk. Legend.* a Phrygian king who was given the power of turning into gold whatever he touched.

mid·brain (mYd/brān/), *n.* the mesencephalon.

mid·day (mYd/dā/), *n.* **1.** the middle of the day; noon. —*adj.* **2.** of or pertaining to the middle part of the day.

mid·dle (mYd/əl), *adj.* **1.** equally distant from extremes or limits. **2.** intervening or intermediate. **3.** medium. —*n.* **4.** the point, part, etc., equidistant from extremes or limits. **5.** the waist, or middle part of the human body. **6.** something intermediate.

mid·dle-aged (mYd/əl ājd/), *adj.* **1.** intermediate in age between youth and old age. **2.** of or for middle-aged people.

Middle Ages, the time in European history between classical antiquity and the Italian renaissance (from the late 5th century to about A.D. 1350).

middle C, *Music.* the note indicated by the first leger line above the bass staff and the first below the treble staff.

middle class, the people intermediate between the aristocracy or wealthy class and the laboring class.

middle ear, *Anat.* the tympanum.

Middle East, the lands from the E shores of the Mediterranean and Aegean to India.

mid·dle·man (mYd/əl măn/), *n., pl.* **-men.** **1.** an intermediary who distributes goods or securities from producer to consumer on his own account and risk. **2.** any intermediary.

mid·dle·most (mYd/əl mōst/), *adj.* midmost.

Mid·dle·town (mYd/əl toun/), *n.* a city in SW Ohio. 31,220.

mid·dle·weight (mYd/əl wāt/), *n.* a boxer whose weight is between 147 and 160 pounds.

Middle West, that region of the United States bounded on the E by the Allegheny Mountains, on the W by the Rocky Mountains, and on the S by the Ohio river and the S extremities of Missouri and Kansas. —**Middle Western.** —**Middle Westerner.**

mid·dling (mĭd'lĭng), *adj.* **1.** medium in size, quality, rank, etc. **2.** *Colloq.* or *Dial.* in fairly good health. —*adv.* **3.** *Colloq.* or *Dial.* moderately. —*n.* **4.** (*pl.*) the coarser particles of ground wheat mingled with bran.

mid·dy (mĭd'ĭ), *n.*, *pl.* **-dies. 1.** *Colloq.* a midshipman. **2.** a middy blouse.

middy blouse, a loose blouse with a large square back collar, worn by children, girls, etc.

midge (mĭj), *n.* **1.** any of certain minute flies. **2.** a small person.

midg·et (mĭj'ĭt), *n.* **1.** a very small person. **2.** something very small of its kind.

Mi·di (mē dē'), *n.* the south of France.

mid·i·ron (mĭd'ī'ərn), *n. Golf.* an iron club whose face has a medium degree of slope.

mid·land (mĭd'lənd), *n.* **1.** the interior part of a country. —*adj.* **2.** inland.

Mid·lands (mĭd'ləndz), *n.pl.* the central part of England; the midland counties.

mid·most (mĭd'mōst'), *adj.* **1.** being in the very middle. —*adv.* **2.** in the middle part.

mid·night (mĭd'nīt'), *n.* **1.** the middle of the night; 12 o'clock at night. —*adj.* **2.** of, pertaining to, or resembling midnight.

mid·noon (mĭd'nōōn'), *n.* midday; noon.

mid·rib (mĭd'rĭb'), *n. Bot.* the central or middle rib of a leaf.

mid·riff (mĭd'rĭf), *n.* **1.** the diaphragm (in the body). **2.** a dress which exposes the middle part of the body. —*adj.* **3.** denoting or pertaining to such a dress.

mid·ship (mĭd'shĭp'), *adj.* in or belonging to the middle part of a ship.

mid·ship·man (mĭd'shĭp'mən), *n.*, *pl.* **-men. 1.** *U.S.* one of the rank held by men attending the Naval or Coast Guard academies. **2.** *Brit.* an officer of the rank held by young men on leaving the government naval schools.

mid·ships (mĭd'shĭps'), *adv.* amidships.

midst (mĭdst), *n.* **1.** the position of anything being or occurring in the middle. **2.** the middle point, part, or stage.

mid·stream (mĭd'strēm'), *n.* the middle of the stream.

mid·sum·mer (mĭd'sŭm'ər), *n.* the middle of summer.

mid·way (mĭd'wā'), *adv.*, *adj.* **1.** in or to the middle. —*n.* **2.** a place for side shows and other amusements at a fair or the like.

Midway Islands, several islets in the N Pacific, ab. 1200 mi. NW of and forming a part of the Territory of Hawaii: Japanese naval defeat, 1942. 437 pop.; 2 sq. mi.

Mid·west (mĭd'wĕst'), *U.S.* —*n.* **1.** Middle West. —*adj.* **2.** Middle Western. Also, **Mid·west·ern** (mĭd'wĕs'tərn). —**Mid'west'ern·er,** *n.*

mid·wife (mĭd'wīf'), *n.*, *pl.* **-wives** (-wīvz'). a woman who assists women in childbirth.

mid·wife·ry (mĭd'wīf'ə rĭ, -wīf'rĭ), *n.* the assistance of women in childbirth.

mid·win·ter (mĭd'wĭn'tər), *n.* the middle of winter.

mid·year (mĭd'yĭr'), *n.* **1.** the middle of the year. **2.** (*pl.*) *Colloq.* midyear examinations. —*adj.* **3.** of or occurring in midyear.

mien (mēn), *n.* air, bearing, or aspect.

miff (mĭf), *Colloq.* —*n.* **1.** a petty quarrel. —*v.t.* **2.** to offend. —*v.i.* **3.** to take offense.

might[1] (mīt), *v.* pt. of **may.**

might[2] (mīt), *n.* **1.** power to do or accomplish; ability. **2.** superior power.

might·y (mī'tĭ), *adj.*, **mightier, mightiest. 1.** having, characterized by, or showing might or power. **2.** huge. **3.** *Colloq.* great in amount, extent, or importance. —*adv.* **4.** *Colloq.* very. —**might'i·ly,** *adv.* —**might'i·ness,** *n.*

mi·gnon·ette (mĭn'yə nĕt'), *n.* a garden plant having racemes of small, fragrant, greenish-white flowers with prominent reddish-yellow or brownish anthers.

mi·graine (mī'grān, mĭ grān'), *n.* a paroxysmal headache on one side of the head, usually associated with nausea.

mi·grant (mī'grənt), *adj.* **1.** migrating. —*n.* **2.** one that migrates.

mi·grate (mī'grāt), *v.i.*, **-grated, -grating. 1.** to go from one country, region, or abode to settle in another. **2.** to pass periodically from one region to another, as certain birds.

mi·gra·tion (mī grā'shən), *n.* **1.** action of migrating. **2.** a migratory movement. **3.** a number or body of persons or animals migrating together.

mi·gra·to·ry (mī'grə tōr'ĭ), *adj.* **1.** migrating. **2.** pertaining to a migration. **3.** roving.

mi·ka·do (mĭ kä'dō), *n.*, *pl.* **-dos.** (*often cap.*) a title of the emperor of Japan.

mike (mīk), *n. Slang.* microphone.

mil (mĭl), *n.* a unit of length equal to .001 of an inch, used in measuring the diameter of wires.

mil., 1. military. **2.** militia.

mi·la·dy (mĭ lā'dĭ), *n.*, *pl.* **-dies.** a Continental rendering of English *my lady*, used in speaking to or of an English lady.

Mi·lan (mĭ lăn', mĭl'ən), *n.* a city in N Italy. 1,255,026.

milch (mĭlch), *adj.* denoting a cow, goat, or other milk-giving animal.

mild (mīld), *adj.* **1.** amiably gentle or temperate in feeling or behavior toward others. **2.** characterized by or showing such gentleness, as speech. **3.** not cold, severe, or extreme, as weather. **4.** moderate in force, effect, intensity, etc. —**mild'·ly,** *adv.* —**mild'ness,** *n.*

mil·dew (mĭl'dū', -dōō'), *n.* **1.** a coating or discoloration on plants, fabrics, paper, etc., caused by any of various parasitic fungi. **2.** any of these fungi. —*v.t., v.i.* **3.** to affect or become affected with mildew. —**mil'dew'y,** *adj.*

mile (mīl), *n.* a unit of distance: **1. statute mile,** 5280 ft. **2. nautical mile,** 6080.20 feet. **3. international nautical** or **air mile,** 6076.097 feet.

mile·age (mī'lĭj), *n.* **1.** the aggregate number of miles made or traveled over in a given time. **2.** distance in miles. **3.** an allowance for traveling expenses at a fixed rate per mile. Also, **mil'age.**

mile·post (mīl'pōst'), *n.* a post set up to mark distance by miles, as along a highway.

mile·stone (mīl'stōn'), *n.* **1.** a stone set up to mark distance by miles, as along a highway. **2.** an event marking a stage in life, history, etc.

Mil·haud (mē yō'), *n.* **Darius,** born 1892, French composer, now in the U.S.

mi·lieu (mē lyœ'), *n.* medium or environment.

mil·i·tant (mĭl'ə tənt), *adj.* **1.** combative; aggressive. **2.** warring. —*n.* **3.** a militant person. —**mil'i·tan·cy,** *n.* —**mil'i·tant·ly,** *adv.*

mil·i·ta·rism (mĭl'ə tə rĭz'əm), *n.* **1.** military spirit or policy. **2.** the principle of maintaining a large military establishment. **3.** the tendency to regard military efficiency as the supreme ideal of the state. —**mil'i·ta·rist,** *n.* —**mil'i·ta·ris'tic,** *adj.*

mil·i·ta·rize (mĭl'ə tə rīz'), *v.t.*, **-rized, -rizing.** to make military or militaristic. —**mil'i·ta·ri·za'tion,** *n.*

mil·i·tar·y (mĭl'ə tĕr'ĭ), *adj.* **1.** of or pertaining to the armed forces or a state of war. **2.** of or befitting a soldier. —*n.* **3.** the army. —**mil'i·tar'i·ly,** *adv.*

military attaché, an army officer on the staff of an ambassador or minister.

military police, soldiers who perform police duties within the army.

mil·i·tate (mĭl'ə tāt'), *v.i.*, **-tated, -tating.** to operate (*against* or *in favor of*).

mi·li·tia (mĭ lĭsh'ə), *n.* a body of men enrolled for military service, called out periodically for drill and exercise but for actual service only in emergencies. —**mi·li'tia·man,** *n.*

milk (mĭlk), *n.* **1.** an opaque white liquid secreted by the mammary glands of female mammals, serving for the nourishment of their young, and, in the case of the cow and some other animals, used by human beings as food. **2.** any liquid resembling this. —*v.t.* **3.** to draw milk from the udder of (a cow or other animal). **4.** to extract information, wealth, etc., from.

milk·er (mĭl'kər), *n.* **1.** one who milks. **2.** a milking machine. **3.** a cow or other animal that gives milk.

milk·maid (mĭlk'mād'), *n.* a woman who milks cows or is employed in a dairy.

milk·man (mĭlk'măn'), *n.*, *pl.*, **-men.** a man who sells or delivers milk.

milk of magnesia, *Pharm.* an antacid or laxative composed of a magnesium-hydroxide suspension in water.

milk·sop (mĭlk'sŏp'), *n.* a soft, effeminate man or youth. —**milk'sop'ism,** *n.*

milk tooth, a temporary tooth of a mammal later replaced by a permanent tooth.

milk·weed (mĭlk'wēd'), *n.* any of certain plants with a milky juice.

milk·y (mĭl'kĭ), *adj.,* **milkier, milkiest.** of or like milk. —**milk'i·ness,** *n.*

Milky Way, *Astron.* the faintly luminous band stretching across the heavens, composed of innumerable stars too faint for unassisted vision.

mill[1] (mĭl), *n.* **1.** a place in which any of various mechanical operations or forms of manufacture is carried on. **2.** a mechanical appliance for grinding, crushing, or pulverizing any solid substance, esp. grain. **3.** any of various apparatuses for working materials into due form or performing other mechanical operations. —*v.t.* **4.** to grind, work, treat, or shape in or with a mill. **5.** to finish the edge of (a coin, etc.) with a series of transverse grooves. —*v.i.* **6.** to move confusedly in a circle, as a herd of cattle.

mill[2] (mĭl), *n.* a U.S. money of account, equal to one tenth of a cent.

Mill (mĭl), *n.* **John Stuart,** 1806–73, British philosopher and economist.

Mil·lay (mĭ lā'), *n.* **Edna St. Vincent,** 1892–1950, U.S. poet.

mill·dam (mĭl'dăm'), *n.* a dam built in a stream to furnish water for turning a mill wheel.

mil·len·ni·um (mĭ lĕn'ĭ əm), *n., pl.* **-niums, -nia** (-nĭ ə). **1.** a period of a thousand years. **2.** a thousandth anniversary. **3.** the period during which Christ is to reign on earth. **4.** a period of general righteousness and happiness, esp. in the indefinite future. —**mil·len'ni·al,** *adj.*

mill·er (mĭl'ər), *n.* **1.** one who keeps or operates a mill, esp. a grain mill. **2.** any of various moths that look as if they were powdered with flour.

Mill·er (mĭl'ər), *n.* **Joaquin,** 1841–1913, U.S. poet.

mil·let (mĭl'ĭt), *n.* **1.** a cereal grass cultivated in Europe and Asia for its small grain (used as a food for man and fowls), but in the U.S. grown chiefly for fodder. **2.** any of various related or similar grasses.

Mil·let (mĭ lā'), *n.* **Jean François,** 1814–75, French painter.

mil·li·gram (mĭl'ə grăm'), *n.* a unit of one one-thousandth of a gram, equivalent to 0.0154 grain. Also, *esp. Brit.,* **mil'li·gramme'.**

Mil·li·kan (mĭl'ə kən), *n.* **Robert Andrews,** born 1868, U.S. physicist.

mil·li·li·ter (mĭl'ə lē'tər), *n.* a unit of capacity in the metric system, equal to one thousandth of a liter. Also, *esp. Brit.,* **mil'li·li'tre.**

mil·li·me·ter (mĭl'ə mē'tər), *n.* a unit of length in the metric system equal to one thousandth of a meter. Also, *esp. Brit.,* **mil'li·me'tre.**

mil·li·mi·cron (mĭl'ə mī'krŏn), *n., pl.* **-cra** (-krə). a thousandth part of a micron.

mil·li·ner (mĭl'ə nər), *n.* one who makes or sells hats for women.

mil·li·ner·y (mĭl'ə nĕr'ĭ, -nə rĭ), *n.* **1.** articles made or sold by milliners. **2.** the business or trade of a milliner.

mil·lion (mĭl'yən), *n.* **1.** one thousand times one thousand. **2.** the amount of a thousand thousand units of money. —*adj.* **3.** amounting to one million in numbers. —**mil'lionth,** *adj., n.*

mil·lion·aire (mĭl'yən âr'), *n.* **1.** a person worth a million or millions, as of dollars. **2.** a very rich person. Also, **mil'lion·naire'.**

mil·li·pede (mĭl'ə pēd'), *n.* any of certain arthropods having a cylindrical body of numerous segments, most of which bear two pairs of legs.

mill·pond (mĭl'pŏnd'), *n.* a pond for supplying water to drive a mill wheel.

mill·race (mĭl'rās'), *n.* **1.** the channel in which the current of water (**millstream**) driving a mill wheel flows to the mill. **2.** the current itself.

mill·stone (mĭl'stōn'), *n.* **1.** either of a pair of circular stones between which grain or other substance is ground. **2.** a heavy burden.

mill·work (mĭl'wûrk'), *n.* **1.** ready-made carpentry work from a mill. **2.** work in a mill.

mill·wright (mĭl'rīt'), *n.* one who designs, builds, or sets up mills or mill machinery.

Milne (mĭln), *n.* **Alan Alexander,** born 1882, British writer.

milque·toast (mĭlk'tōst'), *n.* a timid, faint-hearted person.

mil·reis (mĭl'rās'), *n., pl.* **-reis.** a Brazilian

silver coin and monetary unit, equal to 1000 reis or about 5.3 U.S. cents.

milt (mĭlt), *n.* **1.** the secretion of the male generative organs of fishes. **2.** the organs themselves.

milt·er (mĭl'tər), *n.* a male fish in breeding time.

Mil·ton (mĭl'tən), *n.* **John,** 1608–74, British poet. —**Mil·ton·ic** (mĭl tŏn'ĭk), *adj.*

Mil·wau·kee (mĭl wô'kĭ), *n.* a city in SE Wisconsin. 587,472.

mime (mīm), *n., v.,* **mimed, miming.** —*n.* **1.** a jester; clown. **2.** a player in an ancient Greek or Roman kind of farce which depended for effect largely upon ludicrous actions and gestures. **3.** such a farce. —*v.t., v.i.* **4.** to mimic.

Mim·e·o·graph (mĭm'ĭ ə grăf', -gräf'), *n.* **1.** *Trademark.* a stencil device for duplicating letters, circulars, drawings, etc. —*v.t.* **2.** (*l.c.*) to make copies using a Mimeograph.

mim·ic (mĭm'ĭk), *v.,* **-icked, -icking,** *n., adj.* —*v.t.* **1.** to imitate or copy in action, speech, etc. —*n.* **2.** one apt at imitating. —*adj.* **3.** being merely an imitation, often on a smaller scale.

mim·ic·ry (mĭm'ĭk rĭ), *n., pl.* **-ries.** **1.** act, practice, or art of mimicking. **2.** *Zool.* the close external resemblance of an animal to some different animal or to surrounding objects, esp. as serving for protective concealment.

mi·mo·sa (mĭ mō'sə, -zə), *n.* any of certain plants, trees, and shrubs, native in tropical or warm regions, usually having bipinnate leaves, and small flowers in globular heads or cylindrical spikes.

min., **1.** mineralogy. **2.** minim. **3.** minimum. **4.** minor. **5.** minute; minutes.

min·a·ret (mĭn'ə rĕt', mĭn'ə rĕt'), *n.* a lofty, often slender, tower attached to a Mohammedan mosque, from which the muezzin calls the people to prayer.

min·a·to·ry (mĭn'ə tōr'ĭ), *adj.* menacing.

Minaret

mince (mĭns), *v.,* **minced, mincing.** —*v.t.* **1.** to cut or chop into very small pieces. **2.** to moderate (one's words, etc.) to a milder form. **3.** to speak of (matters) in polite or euphemistic terms. **4.** to perform or utter with affected elegance. —*v.i.* **5.** to walk or move with short, affectedly dainty steps. **6.** to act, behave, or speak with affected elegance.

mince·meat (mĭns'mēt'), *n.* a mixture of minced apples, suet (and sometimes meat), candied citron, raisins, etc., for filling a pie (**mince pie**).

minc·ing (mĭn'sĭng), *adj.* affectedly nice or elegant. —**minc'ing·ly,** *adv.*

mind (mīnd), *n.* **1.** that which thinks, feels, wills, etc., as in a human or other conscious being. **2.** the intellect or understanding. **3.** a person considered with reference to intellectual power. **4.** sanity. **5.** disposition, attitude, or temper. **6.** inclination or desire. **7.** intention; will. **8.** psychical or spiritual being, as opposed to matter. **9.** remembrance or recollection. —*v.t.* **10.** to heed or obey (a person, advice, etc.). **11.** to attend to. **12.** to be careful or wary concerning. **13.** to feel disturbed or inconvenienced by. —*v.i.* **14.** to take notice, observe, or understand. **15.** to obey. **16.** to care, feel concern, or object.

Min·da·na·o (mĭn'dä nä'ō, -nou'), *n.* the second largest of the Philippine Islands, in the S part of the group. 1,828,071 pop.; 36,537 sq. mi.

mind·ful (mīnd'fəl), *adj.* attentive; careful (usually fol. by *of*). —**mind'ful·ly,** *adv.* —**mind'ful·ness,** *n.*

mind·less (mīnd'lĭs), *adj.* **1.** without intelligence. **2.** heedless. —**mind'less·ly,** *adv.*

Min·do·ro (mĭn dōr'ō), *n.* one of the Philippine Islands, in the central part of the group. 116,988 pop.; 3922 sq. mi.

mine[1] (mīn), *pron.* **1.** possessive form of *I,* used predicatively or without a noun following. **2.** the person(s) or thing(s) belonging to me. —*adj.* **2.** *Archaic.* my.

mine[2] (mīn), *n., v.,* **mined, mining.** —*n.* **1.** an excavation made in the earth for getting out ores, precious stones, coal, etc. **2.** a deposit of such minerals. **3.** an abounding source or supply. **4.** a device containing a large charge of explosive moored beneath the surface of the water for the purpose of blowing up an enemy vessel which passes near it. **5.** a similar device used on land.

—*v.i.* **6.** to dig in the earth for the purpose of extracting ores, coal, etc. **7.** to lay mines, as in military operations. —*v.t.* **8.** to dig in (earth, etc.) in order to obtain ores, coal, etc. **9.** to extract (ores, coal, etc.) from a mine. **10.** to lay military mines under.

mine field, *Mil., Naval.* an area throughout which mines have been laid.

mine layer, a naval vessel with special equipment for laying underwater mines.

min·er (mī′nər), *n.* **1.** one who works in a mine. **2.** one who lays military mines.

min·er·al (mĭn′ər əl, mĭn′rəl), *n.* **1.** a substance obtained by mining; ore. **2.** any of a class of substances occurring in nature, usually comprising inorganic substances. **3.** any substance neither animal nor vegetable. —*adj.* **4.** of the nature of or pertaining to minerals. **5.** impregnated with a mineral or minerals. **6.** inorganic.

mineral., mineralogy.

min·er·al·ize (mĭn′ər ə līz′, mĭn′rə-), *v.t.,* **-ized, -izing. 1.** to convert into a mineral substance. **2.** to impregnate or supply with mineral substances.

min·er·al·o·gy (mĭn′ə răl′ə jĭ, -rŏl′ə-), *n.* the science of minerals. —**min·er·al·og·i·cal** (mĭn′ər ə lŏj′ə kəl), *adj.* —**min′er·al′o·gist,** *n.*

mineral oil, any of a class of oils of mineral origin, as petroleum, consisting of mixtures of hydrocarbons, and used as illuminants, fuels, etc., and in medicine.

mineral water, water containing dissolved mineral salts or gases, esp. such water for medicinal use.

Mi·ner·va (mĭ nûr′və), *n. Rom. Myth.* the goddess of wisdom, the arts, and war, identified with the Greek Athena.

min·e·stro·ne (mĭn′ə strō′nĭ), *n. Italian.* a soup containing vegetables, herbs, etc., in a broth of chicken or meat.

mine sweeper, a vessel for dragging a body of water in order to remove enemy mines.

Ming (mĭng), *n.* the dynasty which ruled China from 1368 to 1644.

min·gle (mĭng′gəl), *v.,* **-gled, -gling.** —*v.i.* **1.** to become mixed, blended, or united. **2.** to associate in company. **3.** to participate. —*v.t.* **4.** to mix, combine, or blend. **5.** to associate in company. —**min′gler,** *n.*

min·i·a·ture (mĭn′ĭ ə chər, mĭn′ə chər), *n.* **1.** a representation of anything on a very small scale. **2.** greatly reduced from. **3.** a very small painting, esp. a portrait, on ivory, vellum, or the like. —*adj.* **4.** on a very small scale.

miniature camera, a small camera using film of 35 mm. width or less.

min·im (mĭn′əm), *n.* **1.** the smallest unit of liquid measure, the sixtieth part of a fluid dram. **2.** *Music.* a note equivalent in time value to one half of a semibreve. **3.** the least quantity of anything. —*adj.* **4.** very small.

min·i·mize (mĭn′ə mīz′), *v.t.,* **-mized, -mizing. 1.** to reduce to the smallest possible amount or degree. **2.** to belittle.

min·i·mum (mĭn′ə məm), *n., pl.* **-ma (-mə), -mums,** *adj.* —*n.* **1.** the least quantity or amount possible, assignable, allowable, etc. **2.** the lowest amount, value, or degree attained or recorded. —*adj.* **3.** that is a minimum. **4.** least possible. **5.** lowest. **6.** pertaining to a minimum or minimums. —**min′i·mal,** *adj.*

minimum wage, the lowest wage, fixed by agreement with a union or by legal authority, payable to employees of a particular group.

min·ing (mī′nĭng), *n.* **1.** action, process, or industry of extracting ores, etc., from mines. **2.** action of laying mines.

min·ion (mĭn′yən), *n.* **1.** a servile or base favorite of a prince or any patron. **2.** any favorite. —*adj.* **3.** dainty; elegant.

min·is·ter (mĭn′ĭs tər), *n.* **1.** one authorized to conduct religious worship; clergyman. **2.** *Brit. and Continental.* the head of an administrative department of the government. **3.** a diplomatic representative accredited by one government to another. —*v.t.* **4.** to administer or apply. —*v.i.* **5.** to give service, care, or aid. **6.** to contribute, as to comfort, etc.

min·is·te·ri·al (mĭn′ĭs tîr′ĭ əl), *adj.* **1.** pertaining to the ministry of religion or to a minister. **2.** *Brit. and Continental.* pertaining to a ministry or minister of state. **3.** pertaining to or invested with delegated executive authority.

minister plenipotentiary, *pl.* **ministers plenipotentiary.** plenipotentiary.

min·is·trant (mĭn′ə strənt), *adj.* **1.** ministering. —*n.* **2.** one who ministers.

min·is·tra·tion (mĭn′ə strā′shən), *n.* **1.** act of ministering care, aid, religious service, etc. **2.** an instance of it.

min·is·try (mĭn′ĭs trĭ), *n., pl.* **-tries. 1.** the service, functions, or profession of a minister of religion. **2.** the clergy. **3.** the service, function, or office of a minister of state. **4.** the policy-forming executive officials in a country, collectively. **5.** *Brit.* any of the administrative departments of a country. **6.** *Brit.* the building which houses such a department. **7.** *Brit.* the term of office of a minister. **8.** act of ministering.

min·i·ver (mĭn′ə vər), *n.* a fur of white or spotted white and gray used for linings or trimmings.

mink (mĭngk), *n., pl.* **minks,** (*esp. collectively*) **mink.** a semiaquatic weasellike animal yielding a valuable lustrous brown fur.

Min·ne·ap·o·lis (mĭn′ĭ ăp′ə lĭs), *n.* a city in SE Minnesota. 492,370.

min·ne·sing·er (mĭn′ĭ sĭng′ər), *n.* one of a class of German lyric poets and singers of the 12th, 13th, and 14th centuries.

Mink
(Total length 2 ft.)

Min·ne·so·ta (mĭn′ə sō′tə), *n.* a State in the N central United States. 2,821,442 pop.; 84,068 sq. mi. *Cap.:* St. Paul. *Abbr.:* Minn. —**Min′ne·so′tan,** *adj., n.*

min·now (mĭn′ō), *n., pl.* **-nows,** (*esp. collectively*) **-now.** any of various small fresh-water fishes, including the carp.

Mi·no·an (mĭ nō′ən), *adj.* of the ancient advanced civilization of Crete, dating from 3000 to 1100 B.C.

mi·nor (mī′nər), *adj.* **1.** lesser, as in size, extent, or importance. **2.** under legal age. **3.** *Music.* **a.** (of an interval) smaller by a half step than the corresponding major interval. **b.** (of a chord) having a minor third between the root and the note next above it. **4.** *U.S. Educ.* noting or pertaining to educational minors. —*n.* **5.** a person under legal age. **6.** one of inferior rank or importance. **7.** *U.S. Educ.* a subject pursued by a student subordinately to a major subject. **8.** *Music.* a minor interval, chord, scale, etc.

Mi·nor·ca (mĭ nôr′kə), *n.* one of the Balearic Islands, in the W Mediterranean. 43,025 pop.; 271 sq. mi.

mi·nor·i·ty (mĭ nôr′ə tĭ, -nŏr′-, mī-), *n., pl.* **-ties. 1.** the smaller part or number. **2.** a smaller party or group opposed to a majority, as in voting. **3.** the state or period of being under legal age.

minor suit, *Bridge.* diamonds or clubs.

Mi·nos (mī′nəs, -nŏs), *n. Gk. Myth.* a judge in the lower world.

Min·o·taur (mĭn′ə tôr′), *n. Gk. Myth.* a fabulous monster, half bull and half man, confined in the Cretan labyrinth and fed with human flesh.

Minsk (mĕnsk), *n.* a city in the W Soviet Union. 238,772.

min·ster (mĭn′stər), *n. Chiefly Brit.* **1.** a church connected with a monastic establishment. **2.** any large or important church.

min·strel (mĭn′strəl), *n.* **1.** one of a class of medieval musicians who sang or recited to the accompaniment of instruments. **2.** *Poetic.* any musician, singer, or poet. **3.** one of a troupe of comedians, usually white men made up as Negroes, presenting songs, jokes, etc.

min·strel·sy (mĭn′strəl sĭ), *n., pl.* **-sies. 1.** the art or practice of a minstrel. **2.** minstrels' songs, ballads, etc.

mint[1] (mĭnt), *n.* **1.** any of certain aromatic herbs with opposite leaves and small flowers, as the spearmint. **2.** a confection flavored with peppermint or other mint flavoring.

mint[2] (mĭnt), *n.* **1.** a place where money is coined by public authority. **2.** a vast amount, esp. of money. —*adj.* **3.** *Philately.* (of a stamp) as issued by the Post Office. —*v.t.* **4.** to make (coins) by stamping metal. **5.** to fabricate. —**mint′er,** *n.*

mint·age (mĭn′tĭj), *n.* **1.** act or process of minting. **2.** the result of minting. **3.** the charge for or cost of minting or coining.

mint julep, a frosted drink made of bourbon whiskey, sugar, crushed ice, and sprigs of fresh mint.

min·u·end (mĭn′yŏŏ ĕnd′), n. *Math.* the number from which another is to be subtracted.

min·u·et (mĭn′yŏŏ ĕt′), n. **1.** a slow stately dance of French origin. **2.** a piece of music for such a dance or in its rhythm.

mi·nus (mī′nəs), prep. **1.** less by the subtraction of. **2.** lacking. —*adj.* **3.** involving or denoting subtraction. **4.** negative. **5.** *Colloq.* lacking. —*n.* **6.** the minus sign (−). **7.** a minus quantity. **8.** a deficiency or loss.

minus sign, *Math.* the symbol (−) denoting subtraction or a minus quantity.

min·ute[1] (mĭn′ĭt), n., v., -uted, -uting, adj. —*n.* **1.** the sixtieth part of an hour; sixty seconds. **2.** any short space of time. **3.** an instant; moment. **4.** a rough draft, as of a document. **5.** (pl.) the official record of the proceedings at a meeting of a society, committee, or other body. **6.** *Geom.*, etc. the sixtieth part of a degree (often represented by the sign ′). —*v.t.* **7.** to time exactly. —*adj.* **8.** prepared in a very short time.

mi·nute[2] (mī nūt′, -nŏŏt′, mĭ-), adj. **1.** extremely small, as in size, amount, or degree. **2.** of very small scope or importance. **3.** attentive to very small details. —**mi·nute′ly,** adv. —**minute′ness,** n.

min·ute·man (mĭn′ĭt măn′), n., pl. -men (-mĕn′). one of a group of American Revolutionary militiamen who held themselves in readiness for instant military service.

mi·nu·ti·a (mĭ nū′shĭ ə, -shə, -nŏŏ′-), n., pl. -tiae (-shĭ ē′). (usually pl.) a small or trivial detail; a trifling matter.

minx (mĭngks), n. a pert, impudent, or flirtatious girl.

Mir·a·beau (mĭr′ə bō′), n. Honoré Gabriel Victor Riqueti, Count de, 1749–91, French Revolutionary statesman.

mir·a·cle (mĭr′ə kəl), n. **1.** an effect in the physical world which surpasses all known human or natural powers. **2.** a wonderful thing or example.

miracle play, a medieval dramatic form dealing with religious subjects such as Biblical stories or saints' lives, usually presented in a series or cycle by the craft guilds.

mi·rac·u·lous (mĭ răk′yə ləs), adj. **1.** of the nature of a miracle; marvelous. **2.** performed by or involving a supernatural power. **3.** having power to work miracles. —**mi·rac′u·lous·ly,** adv. —**mi·rac′u·lous·ness,** n.

Mi·ra·flo·res (mē′rä flô′rĕs), n.pl. locks on the Panama Canal, near the Pacific entrance.

mi·rage (mĭ räzh′), n. an optical illusion, due to atmospheric conditions, by which reflected images of distant objects are seen.

mire (mīr), n., v., mired, miring. —n. **1.** wet, swampy ground; mud. —*v.t.* **2.** to cause to stick fast in mire. **3.** to involve in difficulties. **4.** to soil with mire or filth. —*v.i.* **5.** to sink in mire.

mirk (mûrk), n., adj. murk.

mir·ror (mĭr′ər), n. **1.** a reflecting surface, usually glass with a metallic backing; a looking glass. **2.** something that gives a faithful reflection or true picture of something else. —*v.t.* **3.** to reflect in a mirror, or as a mirror does.

mirth (mûrth), n. **1.** rejoicing; joyous gaiety; jollity. **2.** humorous amusement. —**mirth′less,** adj. —**mirth′less·ly,** adv.

mirth·ful (mûrth′fəl), adj. **1.** joyous; jolly; laughingly gay or amused. **2.** amusing. —**mirth′ful·ly,** adv. —**mirth′ful·ness,** n.

mir·y (mīr′ĭ), adj., mirier, miriest. **1.** swampy or muddy. **2.** covered with mire. **3.** dirty; filthy. —**mir′i·ness,** n.

mis-, a prefix applied to various parts of speech, meaning "ill," "wrong," or simply negating, as in *mistrial, mistrust.*

mis·ad·ven·ture (mĭs′əd vĕn′chər), n. **1.** a piece of ill fortune; mishap. **2.** ill fortune.

mis·al·li·ance (mĭs′ə lī′əns), n. an improper alliance or association, esp. in marriage.

mis·an·thrope (mĭs′ən thrōp′, mĭz′-), n. a hater of mankind. Also, **mis·an·thro·pist** (mĭs-ăn′thrə pĭst). —**mis·an·throp·ic** (mĭs′ən thrŏp′ĭk), adj.

mis·an·thro·py (mĭs ăn′thrə pĭ), n. hatred, dislike, or distrust of mankind.

mis·ap·ply (mĭs′ə plī′), v.t., -plied, -plying. to make a wrong use of. —**mis·ap·pli·ca·tion** (mĭs′ăp lə kā′shən), n.

mis·ap·pre·hend (mĭs′ăp rĭ hĕnd′), v.t. to misunderstand. —**mis·ap·pre·hen·sion** (mĭs′ăp·rĭ hĕn′shən), n.

mis·ap·pro·pri·ate (mĭs′ə prō′prĭ āt′), v.t., -ated, -ating. **1.** to put to a wrong use. **2.** to apply wrongfully or dishonestly to one's own use, as funds entrusted to one. —**mis′ap·pro′pri·a′tion,** n.

mis·be·got·ten (mĭs′bĭ gŏt′ən), adj. illegitimate. Also, **mis′be·got′.**

mis·be·have (mĭs′bĭ hāv′), v.t., v.i., -haved, -having. to behave badly. —**mis′be·hav′ior,** n.

mis·be·lief (mĭs′bĭ lēf′), n. **1.** erroneous belief. **2.** unorthodox religious belief.

mis·be·lieve (mĭs′bĭ lēv′), v., -lieved, -lieving. —*v.i.* **1.** to hold an erroneous belief. —*v.t.* **2.** to doubt. —**mis′be·liev′er,** n.

misc., **1.** miscellaneous. **2.** miscellany.

mis·cal·cu·late (mĭs kăl′kyə lāt′), v.t., v.i., -lated, -lating. to calculate wrongly. —**mis′cal·cu·la′tion,** n.

mis·call (mĭs kôl′), v.t. to call by a wrong name.

mis·car·riage (mĭs kăr′ĭj), n. **1.** failure to attain the right or desired result. **2.** premature expulsion of a fetus from the uterus, esp. before it is viable.

mis·car·ry (mĭs kăr′ĭ), v.i., -ried, -rying. **1.** to fail to attain the right end. **2.** to be lost in transit, as a letter. **3.** to have a miscarriage.

mis·ce·ge·na·tion (mĭs′ĭ jə nā′shən), n. **1.** mixture of races by sexual union. **2.** interbreeding between different races.

mis·cel·la·ne·ous (mĭs′ə lā′nĭ əs), adj. **1.** consisting of members or elements of different kinds. **2.** of mixed character. **3.** dealing with various subjects. —**mis′cel·la′ne·ous·ly,** adv.

mis·cel·la·ny (mĭs′ə lā′nĭ), n., pl. -nies. **1.** a miscellaneous collection by several authors, assembled in a book. **2.** miscellaneous collection of articles or entries.

mis·chance (mĭs chăns′, -chäns′), n. ill luck; a mishap or misfortune.

mis·chief (mĭs′chĭf), n. **1.** harm or trouble, esp. as due to an agent or cause. **2.** an injury caused by a person or other agent. **3.** a cause or source of harm, evil, or annoyance. **4.** annoying action. **5.** a tendency to tease or annoy.

mis·chie·vous (mĭs′chə vəs), adj. **1.** harmful or injurious. **2.** maliciously or playfully annoying. **3.** fond of mischief. **4.** roguishly teasing. —**mis′chie·vous·ly,** adv. —**mis′chie·vous·ness,** n.

mis·ci·ble (mĭs′ə bəl), adj. capable of being mixed. —**mis·ci·bil′i·ty,** n.

mis·con·ceive (mĭs′kən sēv′), v.t., v.i., -ceived, -ceiving. to misunderstand. —**mis·con·cep·tion** (mĭs′kən sĕp′shən), n.

mis·con·duct (n. mĭs kŏn′dŭkt; v. mĭs′kən-dŭkt′), n. **1.** improper conduct. **2.** unlawful conduct, as by an official in regard to his office. —*v.t.* **3.** to mismanage.

mis·con·strue (mĭs′kən strŏŏ′, mĭs kŏn′strŏŏ), v.t., -strued, -struing. to take in a wrong sense; misinterpret. —**mis·con·struc·tion** (mĭs′kən-strŭk′shən), n.

mis·count (mĭs kount′), v.t., v.i. **1.** to count erroneously. —*n.* **2.** an erroneous counting.

mis·cre·ant (mĭs′krĭ ənt), adj. **1.** depraved; villainous, or base. —*n.* **2.** a vile wretch; villain.

mis·cue (mĭs kū′), n., v., -cued, -cuing. —*n.* **1.** *Billiards,* etc. a slip of the cue, causing it to strike the ball improperly or not at all. —*v.i.* **2.** to make a miscue. **3.** *Theat.* to fail to answer one's cue.

mis·deal (mĭs dēl′), v., -dealt, -dealing. —*n.* —*v.t., v.i.* **1.** to deal wrongly, esp. at cards. —*n.* **2.** a wrong deal. —**mis·deal′er,** n.

mis·deed (mĭs dēd′), n. an evil deed.

mis·de·mean (mĭs′dĭ mēn′), v.t., v.i. to misbehave.

mis·de·mean·or (mĭs′dĭ mē′nər), n. **1.** misbehavior. **2.** *Law.* an offense less serious than a felony.

mis·di·rect (mĭs′dĭ rĕkt′), v.t. to direct wrongly. —**mis′di·rec′tion,** n.

mis·do (mĭs dŏŏ′), v.t., v.i., -did, -done, -doing. to do wrongly. —**mis·do′er,** n.

mis·em·ploy (mĭs′ĕm ploi′), v.t., v.i. to use wrongly or improperly.

mi·ser (mī′zər), n. **1.** one who lives in wretched circumstances in order to save and hoard money. **2.** a niggardly, avaricious person.

mis·er·a·ble (mĭz'ər ə bəl, mĭz'rə-), *adj.* **1.** wretchedly unhappy or uncomfortable. **2.** needy **3.** *Colloq.* ailing. **4.** contemptible. **5.** deplorable. —**mis'er·a·ble·ness**, *n.* —**mis'er·a·bly**, *adv.*

mi·ser·ly (mī'zər lĭ'), *adj.* penurious; niggardly. —**mi'ser·li·ness**, *n.*

mis·er·y (mĭz'ə rĭ'), *n., pl.* **-er·ies. 1.** wretched condition. **2.** distress caused by privation or poverty. **3.** extreme unhappiness. **4.** *Dial.* bodily pain.

mis·fea·sance (mĭs fē'zəns), *n. Law.* **1.** wrong arising from or consisting of affirmative action. **2.** the wrongful and injurious exercise of lawful authority.

mis·fire (mĭs fīr'), *v.,* **-fired, -firing,** *n.* —*v.i.* **1.** to fail to be fired or exploded. —*n.* **2.** a failure in firing.

mis·fit (mĭs fĭt'; *for 3 also* mĭs'fĭt), *v.,* **-fitted, -fitting,** *n.* —*v.t., v.i.* **1.** to fit badly. —*n.* **2.** a bad fit. **3.** a badly adjusted person.

mis·for·tune (mĭs fôr'chən), *n.* **1.** adverse fortune; ill luck. **2.** an instance of this.

mis·give (mĭs gĭv'), *v.,* **-gave, -given, -giving.** —*v.t.* **1.** (of one's mind, etc.) to give doubt to. —*v.i.* **2.** to be apprehensive.

mis·giv·ing (mĭs gĭv'ĭng), *n.* a feeling of doubt, distrust, or apprehension.

mis·gov·ern (mĭs gŭv'ərn), *v.t.* to govern badly. —**mis·gov'ern·ment,** *n.*

mis·guide (mĭs gīd'), *v.t.,* **-guided, -guiding.** to guide wrongly. —**mis·guid'ance,** *n.*

mis·han·dle (mĭs hăn'dəl), *v.t.,* **-dled, -dling.** to handle badly; maltreat.

mis·hap (mĭs'hăp, mĭs hăp'), *n.* an unfortunate accident.

mis·in·form (mĭs'ĭn fôrm'), *v.t.* to give false or misleading information to. —**mis'in·for·ma'·tion,** *n.*

mis·in·ter·pret (mĭs'ĭn tûr'prĭt), *v.t.* to interpret, explain, or understand incorrectly. —**mis'in·ter'pre·ta'tion,** *n.*

mis·judge (mĭs jŭj'), *v.t., v.i.,* **-judged, -judging.** to judge wrongly. —**mis·judg'ment,** *n.*

mis·lay (mĭs lā'), *v.t.,* **-laid, -laying. 1.** to put in a place afterward forgotten. **2.** to misplace. —**mis·lay'er,** *n.*

mis·lead (mĭs lēd'), *v.t.,* **-led, -leading. 1.** to lead or guide wrongly. **2.** to lead into error of conduct, thought, or judgment. —**mis·lead'ing,** *adj.*

mis·man·age (mĭs măn'ĭj), *v.t., v.i.,* **-aged, -aging.** to manage badly. —**mis·man'age·ment,** *n.*

mis·match (mĭs măch'), *v.t.* **1.** to match badly. —*n.* **2.** a bad match.

mis·name (mĭs nām'), *v.t.,* **-named, -naming.** to call by a wrong name.

mis·no·mer (mĭs nō'mər), *n.* a misapplied name or designation.

mi·sog·y·ny (mĭ sŏj'ə nĭ', mī-), *n.* hatred of women. —**mi·sog'y·nist,** *n.* —**mi·sog'y·nous,** *adj.*

mis·place (mĭs plās'), *v.t.,* **-placed, -placing. 1.** to put in a wrong place. **2.** to place or bestow improperly, unsuitably, or unwisely. —**mis·place'ment,** *n.*

mis·play (mĭs plā'), *n.* a wrong play.

mis·print (*n.* mĭs'prĭnt', mĭs'prĭnt'; *v.* mĭs prĭnt'), *n.* **1.** a mistake in printing. —*v.t.* **2.** to print incorrectly.

mis·pri·sion (mĭs prĭzh'ən), *n.* **1.** a wrongful action or commission, esp. of a public official. **2.** neglect to give notice of an act of treason or felony.

mis·pro·nounce (mĭs'prə nouns'), *v.t., v.i.,* **-nounced, -nouncing.** to pronounce incorrectly. —**mis·pro·nun·ci·a·tion** (mĭs'prə nŭn'sĭ ā'shən), *n.*

mis·quote (mĭs kwōt'), *v.t., v.i.,* **-quoted, -quoting.** to quote incorrectly. —**mis'quo·ta'tion,** *n.*

mis·read (mĭs rēd'), *v.t.,* **-read, -reading.** to read wrongly; misinterpret.

mis·rep·re·sent (mĭs'rĕp rĭ zĕnt'), *v.t.* to represent incorrectly, improperly, or falsely. —**mis'rep·re·sen·ta'tion,** *n.*

mis·rule (mĭs rōōl'), *n., v.,* **-ruled, -ruling.** —*n.* **1.** bad or unwise rule. **2.** disorder. —*v.t.* **3.** to misgovern. —**mis·rul'er,** *n.*

miss¹ (mĭs), *v.t., v.i.* **1.** to fail to hit, meet, catch, receive, attain, see, etc. **2.** to fail to perform, attend to, be present at, etc. **3.** to perceive the absence or loss of, often with regret.

4. to escape or avoid. **5.** to fail to understand. —*n.* **6.** a failure to hit, meet, obtain, or accomplish something.

miss² (mĭs), *n., pl.* **misses. 1.** (*cap.*) the conventional title of respect for an unmarried woman. **2.** a young unmarried woman; girl.

Miss., Mississippi.

mis·sal (mĭs'əl), *n.* the book containing the prayers and rites for celebrating Mass.

mis·shape (mĭs shāp'), *v.t.,* **-shaped, -shaped** or **-shapen, -shaping.** to shape ill; deform. —**mis·shap'en,** *adj.*

mis·sile (mĭs'əl), *n.* **1.** an object or weapon that can be thrown, hurled, or shot, as a stone, bullet, lance, or arrow. —*adj.* **2.** capable of being thrown, hurled, or shot.

miss·ing (mĭs'ĭng), *adj.* lacking; absent.

missing link, a hypothetical form of animal assumed to have constituted a connecting link between the anthropoid apes and man.

mis·sion (mĭsh'ən), *n.* **1.** a body of persons sent to a foreign country to conduct negotiations, establish relations, or the like. **2.** the business with which an agent, envoy, etc., is charged. **3.** *U.S.* a permanent diplomatic establishment abroad. **4.** *Mil.* an operation, by one or more war aircraft, against the enemy. **5.** a body of persons sent into a foreign land for religious work among a heathen people. **6.** a missionary post or station. **7.** missionary work. **8.** a self-imposed duty.

mis·sion·ar·y (mĭsh'ə nĕr'ĭ'), *n., pl.* **-aries,** *adj.* —*n.* **1.** a person sent to work for the propagation of his religious faith. **2.** any propagandist. —*adj.* **3.** pertaining to or connected with religious missions.

Mis·sis·sip·pi (mĭs'ə sĭp'ĭ'), *n.* **1.** a State in the S United States. 2,099,533 pop.; 47,716 sq. mi. *Cap.:* Jackson. *Abbr.:* Miss. **2.** a river flowing from N Minnesota S to the Gulf of Mexico. 2470 mi. —**Mis'sis·sip'pi·an,** *adj., n.*

mis·sive (mĭs'ĭv), *n.* **1.** a written message; letter. —*adj.* **2.** sent, esp. from an official source.

Mis·sour·i (mĭ zŏŏr'ĭ', -zŏŏr'ə), *n.* **1.** a State in the central United States. 3,776,250 pop.; 69,674 sq. mi. *Cap.:* Jefferson City. *Abbr.:* Mo. **2.** a river flowing from SW Montana into the Mississippi N of St. Louis, Missouri. 2723 mi. —**Mis·sour'i·an,** *adj., n.*

mis·speak (mĭs spēk'), *v.t., v.i.,* **-spoke, -spoken, -speaking.** to speak, utter, or pronounce incorrectly.

mis·spell (mĭs spĕl'), *v.t., v.i.,* **-spelled** or **-spelt, -spelling.** to spell incorrectly.

mis·spend (mĭs spĕnd'), *v.t.,* **-spent, -spending.** to squander; waste.

mis·state (mĭs stāt'), *v.t.,* **-stated, -stating.** to state wrongly or misleadingly; make a wrong statement about. —**mis·state'ment,** *n.*

mis·step (mĭs stĕp'), *n.* **1.** a wrong step. **2.** an error or slip in conduct.

mist (mĭst), *n.* **1.** a cloudlike aggregation of minute globules of water suspended in the atmosphere at or near the earth's surface. **2.** *Meteorol.* a very thin fog. **3.** something which dims, obscures, or blurs. —*v.i., v.t.* **4.** to become or make misty. **5.** to rain in very fine drops; drizzle.

mis·tak·a·ble (mĭs tā'kə bəl, mə stā'-), *adj.* that may be mistaken, misapprehended, or misunderstood.

mis·take (mĭs tāk', mə stāk'), *n., v.,* **-took, -taken, -taking.** —*n.* **1.** an error in action, opinion, or judgment. **2.** a misconception. —*v.t.* **3.** to take or regard as something or somebody else. **4.** to misunderstand. —*v.i.* **5.** to be in error.

mis·tak·en (mĭs tā'kən, mə stā'-), *adj.* **1.** wrongly conceived, entertained, or done. **2.** erroneous; wrong. **3.** having made a mistake. —**mis·tak'en·ly,** *adv.*

mis·teach (mĭs tēch'), *v.t.,* **-taught, -teaching.** to teach wrongly or badly.

mis·ter (mĭs'tər), *n.* **1.** (*cap.*) the conventional title of respect for a man, prefixed to the name (usually written *Mr.*). **2.** *Colloq.* (in address, without the name) sir. —*v.t.* **3.** *Colloq.* to address or speak of as "mister" or "Mr."

mis·tle·toe (mĭs'əl tō'), *n.* **1.** a European plant with yellowish flowers and white berries, growing parasitically on various trees, much used in Christmas decorations. **2.** any of various other plants of the same family.

mis·tral (mĭs'trəl, mĭs trăl'), *n.* a cold, dry

northerly wind common in southern France and neighboring regions.

mis·treat (mĭs trēt′), *v.t.* to treat badly or wrongly. —**mis·treat′ment,** *n.*

mis·tress (mĭs′trĭs), *n.* **1.** the female head of a household or some other establishment. **2.** a woman employing servants or attendants. **3.** a female owner, as of a slave, dog, etc. **4.** *Brit.* a female teacher. **5.** a woman who illicitly occupies the place of a wife. **6.** *Archaic or Poetic.* sweetheart.

mis·tri·al (mĭs trī′əl), *n.* *Law.* a trial terminated without conclusion on the merits because of some error.

mis·trust (mĭs trŭst′), *n.* **1.** lack of trust or confidence. —*v.t.* **2.** to distrust. —*v.i.* **3.** to be distrustful. —**mis·trust′ful,** *adj.*

mist·y (mĭs′tĭ), *adj.,* **mistier, mistiest. 1.** abounding in or clouded by mist. **2.** indistinct in form or outline. **3.** obscure; vague. —**mist′i·ly,** *adv.* —**mist′i·ness,** *n.*

mis·un·der·stand (mĭs′ŭn dər stănd′), *v.t., v.i.,* **-stood, -standing. 1.** to misinterpret the words or actions of (a person). **2.** to understand wrongly. —**mis′un·der·stand′ing,** *n.*

mis·un·der·stood (mĭs′ŭn dər stoŏd′), *adj.* **1.** improperly interpreted. **2.** unappreciated.

mis·us·age (mĭs ū′sĭj, -zĭj), *n.* **1.** wrong usage, as of words. **2.** bad treatment.

mis·use (*n.* mĭs ūs′; *v.* mĭs ūz′), *n., v.,* **-used, -using.** —*n.* **1.** wrong or improper use. —*v.t.* **2.** to use wrongly or improperly. **3.** to maltreat. —**mis·us′er,** *n.*

Mitch·ell (mĭch′əl), *n.* **Mount,** a mountain in W North Carolina: highest peak in the E United States. 6711 ft.

mite[1] (mīt), *n.* any of various small arachnids with a saclike body, many being parasitic on plants and animals.

mite[2] (mīt), *n.* **1.** a small contribution, but all that one can afford. **2.** a very small creature.

mi·ter (mī′tər), *n.* **1.** the official headdress of a bishop in the Western Church, in its modern form a tall, pointed cap with a top deeply cleft crosswise. **2.** the abutting surface on either of the pieces joined in a miter joint. —*v.t.* **3.** to raise to the rank of bishop. **4.** to join with a miter joint. Also, *esp. Brit.,* **mi′tre.**

miter joint, a joint formed when two pieces of identical cross section are joined at the ends, and where the joined ends are beveled at equal angles.

mit·i·gate (mĭt′ə gāt′), *v.,* **-gated, -gating.** —*v.t.* **1.** to lessen (wrath, pain, etc.) in force or intensity. —*v.i.* **2.** to become milder. —**mit′i·ga′tion,** *n.* —**mit′i·ga′tive,** *adj.* —**mit′i·ga′tor,** *n.*

mitt (mĭt), *n.* **1.** a kind of long glove extending only to, or slightly over, the fingers, worn by women. **2.** *Baseball.* a kind of glove having the side next to the palm of the hand protected by a large, thick mittenlike pad.

mit·ten (mĭt′ən), *n.* a kind of hand covering enclosing the four fingers together and the thumb separately. **2.** a mitt (def. 1). **3.** (*pl.*) *Slang.* boxing gloves.

mix (mĭks), *v.,* **mixed** or **mixt, mixing,** *n.* —*v.t.* **1.** to put together in one mass or assemblage. **2.** to put together indiscriminately or confusedly. **3.** to combine, unite, or join. **4.** to put in as an added element. **5.** to form by combining ingredients. **6.** to confuse completely (fol. by *up*). —*v.i.* **7.** to become mixed. **8.** to associate, as in company. —*n.* **9.** a mixture. **10.** *Colloq.* a muddle or mess. —**mix′er,** *n.*

mixed (mĭkst), *adj.* **1.** put together or formed by mixing. **2.** composed of different constituents, kinds, opinions, etc. **3.** of both sexes. **4.** *Colloq.* mentally confused.

mixed number, a number consisting of a whole number and a fraction, as 4¹/₂.

mix·ture (mĭks′chər), *n.* **1.** a product of mixing. **2.** any combination of differing elements, kinds, qualities, etc.

mix-up (mĭks′ŭp′), *n.* **1.** a confused state of things; muddle. **2.** *Colloq.* a fight.

miz·zen (mĭz′ən), *Naut.* —*n.* **1.** the lower sail set on the mizzenmast. **2.** a mizzenmast. —*adj.* **3.** of, relating to, or set on the mizzenmast. Also, **miz′en.**

miz·zen·mast (mĭz′ən măst′, -mäst′; *Naut.* -most), *n. Naut.* **1.** the third mast on a vessel with three or more masts. **2.** the after of the two masts of a yawl or ketch. Also, **miz′en·mast′.**

ml., **1.** mail. **2.** milliliter.

Mlle., *pl.* **Mlles.** Mademoiselle.

MM., Messieurs.

mm., millimeter; millimeters.

Mme., *pl.* **Mmes.** madame.

Mn, *Chem.* manganese.

mne·mon·ic (nē mŏn′ĭk), *adj.* assisting, or intended to assist, the memory.

mne·mon·ics (nē mŏn′ĭks), *n.* the art of improving or developing the memory.

Mo, *Chem.* molybdenum.

Mo., **1.** Missouri. **2.** Monday.

mo., **1.** *pl.* **mos.** month. **2.** months.

M.O., money order. Also, **m.o.**

mo·a (mō′ə), *n.* any of various extinct, flightless birds of New Zealand, allied to the apteryx but resembling an ostrich.

Mo·ab (mō′ăb), *n.* an ancient kingdom E of the Dead Sea. —**Mo·ab·ite** (mō′ə bīt′), *n., adj.*

moan (mōn), *n.* **1.** a prolonged, low, inarticulate sound uttered from or as if from physical or mental suffering. **2.** any similar sound. —*v.i.* **3.** to utter moans. —*v.t.* **4.** to lament or bemoan. —**moan′ing·ly,** *adv.*

moat (mōt), *Fort.* —*n.* **1.** a deep, wide trench surrounding a fortified place, usually filled with water. —*v.t.* **2.** to surround with a moat.

mob (mŏb), *n., v.,* **mobbed, mobbing.** —*n.* **1.** a disorderly or riotous assemblage of persons. **2.** a crowd bent on or engaged in lawless violence. **3.** a crowd. —*v.t.* **4.** to beset or crowd round tumultuously. **5.** to attack with riotous violence.

mob·cap (mŏb′kăp′), *n.* a large, full cap fitting down over the ears, formerly much worn indoors by women.

mo·bile (mō′bəl, mō′bēl), *adj.* **1.** movable; moving readily. **2.** flowing freely. **3.** changing easily in expression. —**mo·bil·i·ty** (mō bĭl′ə tĭ), *n.*

Mo·bile (mō bēl′), *n.* a seaport in SW Alabama. 78,720.

Mo·bile Bay (mō′bēl), a bay of the Gulf of Mexico in SW Alabama. 36 mi. long.

mo·bi·lize (mō′bə līz′), *v.,* **-lized, -lizing.** —*v.t.* **1.** to put (armed forces) into readiness for active service. **2.** to organize or adapt (industries, etc.) for service to the government in time of war. **3.** to put into motion, circulation, or active use —*v.i.* **4.** to be assembled, organized, etc., for war. —**mo′bi·li·za′tion,** *n.*

moc·ca·sin (mŏk′ə sən, -zən), *n.* **1.** a shoe made entirely of soft leather, as deerskin, worn originally by the American Indians. **2.** Also, **water moccasin.** a venomous snake of the southern U.S., found in or near water.

moccasin flower, the lady's-slipper.

mo·cha (mō′kə), *n.* a choice variety of coffee, originally coming from Arabia.

mock (mŏk), *v.t.* **1.** to assail or treat with ridicule or derision. **2.** to mimic derisively. **3.** *Poetic.* to mimic. **4.** to defy. —*v.i.* **5.** to scoff; jeer. —*n.* **6.** mockery or derision. **7.** an object of derision. **8.** imitation. —*adj.* **9.** being an imitation of something. —**mock′er,** *n.* —**mock′ing·ly,** *adv.*

mock·er·y (mŏk′ə rĭ), *n., pl.* **-eries. 1.** ridicule or derision. **2.** a derisive action or speech. **3.** a subject or occasion of derision. **4.** an imitation, esp. of a ridiculous or unsatisfactory kind. **5.** a mere travesty. **6.** something absurdly or offensively inadequate or unfitting.

mock-he·ro·ic (mŏk′hĭ rō′ĭk), *adj.* **1.** imitating or burlesquing what is heroic. —*n.* **2.** an imitation or burlesque of what is heroic.

mock·ing·bird (mŏk′ĭng bûrd′), *n.* any of certain gray, black, and white song birds remarkable for their imitative powers.

mock-up (mŏk′ŭp′), *n.* a model, built to scale, of a machine, apparatus, or weapon: used in studying the construction or in teaching men how to operate the actual machine, apparatus, or weapon.

mod., **1.** moderate. **2.** *Music.* moderato.

mod·al (mō′dəl), *adj.* of or pertaining to mode, manner, or form. —**mo·dal·i·ty** (mō dăl′ə tĭ), *n.*

mode[1] (mōd), *n.* **1.** manner of acting or doing. **2.** the natural disposition or the manner of existence or action of anything. **3.** *Music.* any of various arrangements of the diatonic tones of an octave, differing from one another in the order of the whole steps and half steps. **4.** *Gram.* a set of categories of verb inflection, whose selection depends either on the syntactic relation of the verb to other verbs in the sentence, or on difference in the speaker's attitude toward the action expressed by the verb.

mode[2] (mōd), *n.* **1.** customary usage in manners, dress, etc. **2.** a prevailing style or fashion.

mod·el (mŏd'əl), *n., adj., v.* **-eled, -eling** or (*esp. Brit.*) **-elled, -elling.** —*n.* **1.** a standard for imitation or comparison. **2.** a representation, generally in miniature. **3.** an image in clay, wax, or the like, to be reproduced in more durable material. **4.** a person or thing that serves as a subject for an artist, etc. **5.** one employed to put on articles of apparel to display them to customers. —*adj.* **6.** serving as a model. **7.** exemplary. —*v.t.* **8.** to plan according to a model. **9.** to give form to. —*v.i.* **10.** to make models. **11.** to produce designs in some plastic material. —**mod'el·er,** *esp. Brit.* **mod'el·ler,** *n.*

mod·er·ate (*adj., n.* mŏd'ər ĭt, mŏd'rĭt; *v.* mŏd'ə rāt'), *adj., n., v.* **-ated, -ating.** —*adj.* **1.** not extreme, excessive, or intense. **2.** of medium quantity, extent, etc. **3.** mediocre; fair. **4.** of or pertaining to moderates, as in politics or religion. —*n.* **5.** one who is moderate in opinion or action. **6.** (*usually cap.*) a member of a political party advocating moderate reform. —*v.t., v.i.* **7.** to make or become less violent, severe, intense, or rigorous. **8.** to preside (over). —**mod'er·ate·ly,** *adv.* —**mod'er·ate·ness,** *n.*

mod·er·a·tion (mŏd'ə rā'shən), *n.* quality of being moderate; restraint; temperance.

mod·e·ra·to (mŏd'ə rä'tō), *adj. Music.* moderate; in moderate time.

mod·er·a·tor (mŏd'ə rā'tər), *n.* a presiding officer, as over a public forum.

mod·ern (mŏd'ərn), *adj.* **1.** of or pertaining to present and recent time. **2.** characteristic of present and recent time. —*n.* **3.** a person of modern times. **4.** one whose views and tastes are modern. **5.** *Print.* a type style differentiated from *old style* by its heavy downstrokes and its straight serifs. —**mod'ern·ness, mo·der·ni·ty** (mŏ dûr'nə tĭ, mō-), *n.*

mod·ern·ism (mŏd'ər nĭz'əm), *n.* **1.** modern character or tendencies. **2.** a modern usage or characteristic. **3.** *Theol.* **a.** (*cap.*) the movement in Roman Catholic thought which sought to interpret church teachings in the light of philosophic and scientific conceptions of the late 19th and early 20th centuries; condemned by Pope Pius in 1907. **b.** the liberal theological tendency in Protestantism. —**mod'ern·ist,** *n., adj.*

mod·ern·is·tic (mŏd'ər nĭs'tĭk), *adj.* **1.** modern. **2.** of or pertaining to modernism or modernists.

mod·ern·ize (mŏd'ər nīz'), *v.t., v.i.* **-ized, -izing.** to make or become modern. —**mod'ern·i·za'tion,** *n.* —**mod'ern·iz'er,** *n.*

mod·est (mŏd'ĭst), *adj.* **1.** having or showing a humble estimate of one's merits, importance, etc. **2.** free from ostentation. **3.** moderate. **4.** decent. —**mod'est·ly,** *adv.*

mod·es·ty (mŏd'əs tĭ), *n., pl.* **-ties. 1.** freedom from vanity, boastfulness, etc. **2.** regard for decency of behavior, speech, dress, etc. **3.** moderation.

mod·i·cum (mŏd'ə kəm), *n.* a moderate or small quantity; a limited amount.

mod·i·fi·ca·tion (mŏd'ə fə kā'shən), *n.* **1.** act of modifying. **2.** state of being modified. **3.** a modified form. **4.** limitation or qualification.

mod·i·fi·er (mŏd'ə fī'ər), *n.* **1.** one who or that which modifies. **2.** *Gram.* a word, phrase, or sentence element which limits or qualifies the sense of another word, phrase, or element in the same construction.

mod·i·fy (mŏd'ə fī'), *v.,* **-fied, -fying.** —*v.t.* **1.** to alter somewhat. **2.** *Gram.* (of a word or larger linguistic form) to stand in a subordinate relation to (another form) usually with descriptive, limiting, or particularizing meaning. **3.** to be the attribute of. **4.** to change (a vowel) by umlaut. **5.** to moderate or qualify. —*v.i.* **6.** to change. —**mod'i·fi'a·ble,** *adj.*

mod·ish (mō'dĭsh), *adj.* fashionable; stylish. —**mod'ish·ly,** *adv.* —**mod'ish·ness,** *n.*

mo·diste (mō dēst'), *n.* a maker of or dealer in articles of fashionable attire, esp. women's dresses, millinery, etc.

mod·u·late (mŏj'ə lāt'), *v.,* **-lated, -lating.** —*v.t.* **1.** to soften; tone down. **2.** to adapt (the voice) fittingly in utterance. **3.** *Music.* to attune to a certain pitch or key. **4.** *Radio.* to cause the amplitude, frequency, phase, or intensity of (the carrier wave) to vary in accordance with the sound waves or other signals. —*v.i.* **5.** *Radio.* to modulate a carrier wave. **6.** *Music.* to pass from one key to another.

mod·u·la·tion (mŏj'ə lā'shən), *n.* **1.** act of modulating. **2.** state of being modulated. **3.** *Music.* transition from one key to another. **4.** *Gram.* the use of a particular distribution of stress or pitch in a construction.

mod·ule (mŏj'ool), *n.* a selected unit of measure, ranging in size from a few inches to several feet, used as a basis for planning and standardization of building materials.

Mo·gul (mō'gŭl, mō gŭl'), *n.* **1.** a Mongolian. **2.** one of the Mongol conquerors of India in the 16th century. **3.** (*l.c.*) an important person.

mo·hair (mō'hâr'), *n.* **1.** the coat or fleece of an Angora goat. **2.** a fabric made of mohair yarn, much used for upholstery.

Moham., Mohammedan.

Mo·ham·med (mō hăm'ĭd), *n.* A.D. 570?–632, Arabian prophet and founder of the Mohammedan religion.

Mo·ham·med·an (mō hăm'ə dən), *adj.* **1.** of or pertaining to Mohammed or his religious system. —*n.* **2.** a follower of Mohammed.

Mo·ham·med·an·ism (mō hăm'ə də nĭz'əm), *n.* the Mohammedan religion; Islam.

Mo·hawk (mō'hôk), *n., pl.* **Mohawk, Mohawks.** a member of a tribe of North American Indians, the most easterly of the Iroquois Five Nations, formerly resident along the Mohawk river, New York.

Mo·hawk (mō'hôk), *n.* a river from central New York E to the Hudson. 148 mi.

Mo·he·gan (mō hē'gən), *n.* a member of a tribe of Algonquian North American Indians, dwelling chiefly in Connecticut in the 17th century.

Mo·hi·can (mō hē'kən), *n.* Mahican.

moi·e·ty (moi'ə tĭ), *n., pl.* **-ties. 1.** a half. **2.** an indefinite portion.

moil (moil), *v.i., n.* toil; labor.

moire (mwär, mōr), *n.* a watered fabric, as of silk or wool.

moi·ré (mwä rā', mōr'ā), *adj.* **1.** watered, as silk; having a wavelike pattern. —*n.* **2.** a design pressed on silk, rayon, etc., by engraved rollers. **3.** moire.

moist (moist), *adj.* **1.** slightly wet; damp. **2.** tearful. —**moist'ly,** *adv.* —**moist'ness,** *n.*

mois·ten (mois'ən), *v.t., v.i.* to make or become moist. —**moist'en·er,** *n.*

mois·ture (mois'chər), *n.* water or other liquid rendering anything moist.

Mo·ja·ve Desert (mō hä'vĭ), a desert in S California. ab. 15,000 sq. mi.

mo·lar (mō'lər), *n.* **1.** one of the three rear teeth on each side of the upper and lower jaws, adapted for grinding. —*adj.* **2.** adapted for grinding.

mo·las·ses (mə lăs'ĭz), *n.* any of various thick, dark-colored syrups, as that produced during the refining of sugar.

mold[1] (mōld), *n.* **1.** a matrix for shaping something in a molten or plastic state. **2.** something formed in or on a mold. **3.** shape or form. —*v.t.* **4.** to shape or form. **5.** to model the style or character of. —**mold'a·ble,** *adj.*

mold[2] (mōld), *n.* **1.** a growth of minute fungi forming on vegetable or animal matter, commonly as a downy or furry coating. **2.** any of the fungi that produce such a growth. —*v.t., v.i.* **3.** to make or become moldy.

mold[3] (mōld), *n.* loose, friable earth, esp. such as is rich in organic matter.

mold·board (mōld'bōrd'), *n.* the curved board or metal plate in a plow, which turns over the earth from the furrow.

mold·er[1] (mōl'dər), *v.i.* to decay; crumble; waste away.

mold·er[2] (mōl'dər), *n.* one who molds.

mold·ing (mōl'dĭng), *n.* **1.** act of one who molds. **2.** something molded. **3.** *Archit., etc.* a decorative contour given to strips of woodwork, etc. **4.** a shaped strip, used for supporting pictures, etc.

mold·y (mōl'dĭ), *adj.,* **moldier, moldiest. 1.** covered with mold. **2.** musty, as from decay. —**mold'i·ness,** *n.*

mole[1] (mōl), *n.* a small congenital spot or blemish on the human skin.

mole[2] (mōl), *n.* any of certain small insectivorous mammals living chiefly underground, and having velvety fur and very small eyes.

mole[3] (mōl), *n.* a massive structure, esp. of stone, as for a breakwater or a pier.

mo·lec·u·lar (mə lĕk′yə lər), *adj.* pertaining to, caused by, or consisting of molecules. —**mo·lec′u·lar·ly,** *adv.*

molecular film, a film or layer one molecule thick.

mol·e·cule (mŏl′ə kūl′), *n.* *Chem., Physics.* the smallest physical unit of an element or compound, consisting of one or more like atoms in the first case, and two or more different atoms in the second case.

mole·hill (mōl′hĭl′), *n.* **1.** a small mound of earth raised up by moles burrowing under the ground. **2.** something insignificant.

mole·skin (mōl′skĭn′), *n.* **1.** the fur of the mole. **2.** a stout napped, twilled cotton fabric.

mo·lest (mə lĕst′), *v.t.* to interfere with annoyingly, injuriously, or with hostile intent. —**mo·les·ta·tion** (mō′lĕs tā′shən, mŏl′ĕs-), *n.* —**mo·lest′er,** *n.*

Mo·lière (mō lyĕr′), *n.* 1622–1673, French writer of comedies.

Mo·line (mō lēn′), *n.* a city in NW Illinois, on the Mississippi. 34,608.

moll (mŏl), *n.* *Slang.* the female companion of a thief, vagrant, or gangster.

mol·li·fy (mŏl′ə fī′), *v.t.,* **-fied, -fying. 1.** to soften in feeling or temper. **2.** to mitigate or appease, as rage. —**mol′li·fi·ca′tion,** *n.* —**mol′li·fi′er,** *n.*

mol·lusk (mŏl′əsk), *n.* any of a large phylum of invertebrates including the snails, bivalves, squids, etc., characterized by the calcareous shell that encloses the body. Also, **mol′lusc.**

mol·ly·cod·dle (mŏl′ĭ kŏd′əl), *n., v.,* **-dled, -dling.** —*n.* **1.** a man or boy who is used to being pampered. —*v.t.* **2.** to pamper.

Mol·nár (mōl′när), *n.* **Ferenc,** 1878–1952, Hungarian dramatist and novelist.

Mo·loch (mō′lŏk), *n.* **1.** a Semitic deity, mentioned in the Bible, whose worship was marked by the sacrifice by burning of children offered by their own parents. **2.** anything requiring frightful sacrifice.

Mo·lo·tov (mô′lŏ tôf), *n.* **Viacheslav Mikhailovich,** born 1890, Soviet statesman.

molt (mōlt), *v.i.* **1.** (of birds, reptiles, etc.) to shed the feathers, skin, or the like, to be succeeded by a new growth. —*v.t.* **2.** to cast or shed (feathers, etc.) in the process of renewal. —*n.* **3.** act or process of molting.

mol·ten (mōl′tən), *adj.* **1.** liquefied by heat. **2.** produced by melting and casting.

mol·to (mōl′tō), *adv.* *Music.* much; very.

Mo·luc·cas (mō lŭk′əz, mə-), *n.pl.* a group of islands in the Dutch East Indies. ab. 428,000 pop.; ab. 30,000 sq. mi.

mo·lyb·de·num (mə lĭb′də nəm, mŏl′ĭb dē′nəm), *n.* *Chem.* a silver-white high-melting metallic element. *Symbol.:* Mo; *at. wt.:* 95.95; *at. no.:* 42; *sp. gr.:* 10.2.

mo·ment (mō′mənt), *n.* **1.** an indefinitely short space of time; an instant. **2.** the present or other particular instant. **3.** importance.

mo·men·tar·y (mō′mən tĕr′ĭ), *adj.* **1.** lasting but a moment; transitory. **2.** occurring at any moment. —**mo′men·tar′i·ly,** *adv.* —**mo′men·tar′i·ness,** *n.*

mo·ment·ly (mō′mənt lĭ), *adv.* **1.** every moment. **2.** for a moment.

mo·men·tous (mō mĕn′təs), *adj.* of great importance or consequence. —**mo·men′tous·ly,** *adv.* —**mo·men′tous·ness,** *n.*

mo·men·tum (mō mĕn′təm), *n., pl.* **-ta** (-tə) **-tums. 1.** *Mech.* the quantity of motion of a moving body, equal to the product of its mass and velocity. **2.** impetus.

Mon., **1.** Monday. **2.** Monsignor.

Mon·a·co (mŏn′ə kō′), *n.* **1.** a principality on the Mediterranean coast, bordering SE France. 23,956 pop.; ½ sq. mi. **2.** the capital of this principality. 1936 pop.

mon·ad (mŏn′ad, mō′năd), *n.* **1.** *Biol.* any simple, single-celled organism. **2.** *Chem.* an element, atom, or radical having a valence of one.

mo·nad·nock (mə năd′nŏk), *n.* a residual hill standing well above the surface of a surrounding peneplain.

mon·arch (mŏn′ərk), *n.* **1.** a hereditary sovereign, as a king or queen. **2.** one who or that which holds a dominating or preëminent position.

mo·nar·chal (mə när′kəl), *adj.* pertaining to,

characteristic of, or befitting a monarch. Also, **mo·nar·chi·al** (mə när′kĭ əl). —**mo·nar′chal·ly,** *adv.*

mo·nar·chi·cal (mə när′kə kəl), *adj.* **1.** of or pertaining to a monarch or monarchy. **2.** favoring monarchy. Also, **mo·nar′chic.** —**mo·nar′chi·cal·ly,** *adv.*

mon·ar·chism (mŏn′ər kĭz′əm), *n.* **1.** the principles of monarchy. **2.** advocacy of monarchical principles. —**mon′ar·chist,** *n., adj.*

mon·ar·chy (mŏn′ər kĭ), *n., pl.* **-chies. 1.** a government or state in which the supreme power is actually or nominally lodged in a monarch. **2.** supreme power wielded by a single person.

mon·as·ter·y (mŏn′ə stĕr′ĭ), *n., pl.* **-teries. 1.** a residence occupied by a community of persons, esp. monks, living in seclusion. **2.** the community of persons living in such a place.

mo·nas·tic (mə năs′tĭk), *adj.* Also, **mo·nas′ti·cal. 1.** of or pertaining to monasteries. **2.** of, pertaining to, or characteristic of monks. —*n.* **3.** a monk.

mo·nas·ti·cism (mə năs′tə sĭz′əm), *n.* the monastic system, condition, or mode of life.

mon·a·tom·ic (mŏn′ə tŏm′ĭk), *adj.* *Chem.* **1.** having one atom in the molecule. **2.** containing one replaceable atom or group. **3.** having a valence of one.

Mon·day (mŭn′dĭ), *n.* the second day of the week, following Sunday.

mo·ne·cious (mə nē′shəs, mō-), *adj.* monoecious.

Mo·nel metal (mō nĕl′), *n.* *Trademark.* a nonrusting, silvery-white alloy containing chiefly nickel and copper.

Mo·net (mō nĕ′), *n.* **Claude,** 1840–1926, French painter.

mon·e·tar·y (mŭn′ə tĕr′ĭ, mŏn′ə-), *adj.* **1.** of or pertaining to the coinage or currency of a country. **2.** pecuniary.

mon·e·tize (mŭn′ə tīz′, mŏn′ə-), *v.t.,* **-tized, -tizing. 1.** to legalize as money. **2.** to coin into money. —**mon′e·ti·za′tion,** *n.*

mon·ey (mŭn′ĭ), *n., pl.* **moneys, monies. 1.** gold, silver, or other metal in pieces of convenient form stamped by public authority and issued as a medium of exchange and measure of value. **2.** coin or certificate (as banknotes, etc.) generally accepted in payment of debts and current transactions. **3.** any article or substance similarly used, as wampum, etc. **4.** wealth.

mon·ey·bag (mŭn′ĭ băg′), *n.* **1.** a bag for money. **2.** (*pl. construed as sing.*) a wealthy person.

mon·eyed (mŭn′ĭd), *adj.* **1.** wealthy. **2.** consisting of or representing money.

money of account, a monetary denomination used in reckoning, esp. one not issued as a coin, as the U.S. mill.

money order, an order for the payment of money, as one issued by one post office and payable at another.

mon·ger (mŭng′gər), *n.* *Brit.* a dealer in some commodity.

Mon·gol (mŏng′gəl, -gŏl, -gōl), *n.* **1.** one of an Asiatic race now living chiefly in Mongolia. **2.** a member of the Mongolian race. **3.** any Mongolian language. —*adj.* **4.** Mongolian.

Mon·go·li·a (mŏng gō′lĭ ə), *n.* **1.** a vast region in Asia, north of China. **2. Inner,** the S part of Mongolia, under Chinese control. **3. Outer,** the N part of Mongolia.

Mon·go·li·an (mŏng gō′lĭ ən), *adj.* **1.** pertaining to Mongolia. **2.** denoting or pertaining to the so-called "yellow" race of Asia, embracing the Chinese, Koreans, Japanese, Siamese, etc. —*n.* **3.** a member of the Mongolian race.

Mon·gol·ism (mŏng′gə lĭz′əm), *n.* an abnormal condition of a child born with a wide, flattened skull, narrow, slanting eyes, and generally a mental deficiency.

Mon·gol·oid (mŏng′gə loid′), *adj.* **1.** resembling the Mongols. **2.** *Anthropol.* **a.** similar or related to the Mongols in physique. **b.** pertaining to the "yellow" race. —*n.* **3.** a person of a Mongoloid race.

mon·goose (mŏng′gōōs), *n., pl.* **-gooses.** a slender ferretlike carnivore, esp. of India, used for destroying rats, etc., and noted for its ability to kill certain venomous snakes without being harmed.

mon·grel (mŭng′grəl, mŏng′-), *n.* **1.** any animal or plant resulting from the crossing of different breeds or varieties. **2.** any cross between different things. —*adj.* **3.** being of mixed breed, origin, nature, etc.

mon·i·ker (mŏn′ə kər), *n. Slang.* a person's name or nickname. Also, **mon/ick·er.**

mon·ism (mŏn′ĭz əm, mō′nĭz əm), *n. Philos.* the doctrine of one ultimate substance or principle, as mind (*idealism*) or matter (*materialism*), or something that is neither mind nor matter but the ground of both. —**mon/ist,** *n.* —**mo·nis·tic** (mō nĭs′tĭk), *adj.*

mo·ni·tion (mō nĭsh′ən), *n.* **1.** warning; caution. **2.** an official or legal notice.

mon·i·tor (mŏn′ə tər), *n.* **1.** a pupil appointed to assist in the conduct of a class or school. **2.** one who admonishes. **3.** something that serves to remind or warn. **4.** (*cap.*) an ironclad warship used by Union forces during the Civil War against the *Merrimac* (1862). —*v.t., v.i.* **5.** *Radio.* **a.** to hear (transmitted signals) using a receiving set in order to check the quality of the transmission. **b.** to listen to (broadcasts) for operating compliance, censorship, propaganda analysis, and similar purposes.

mon·i·to·ry (mŏn′ə tōr′ĭ), *adj.* serving to admonish or warn.

monk (mŭngk), *n.* a man who has withdrawn from the world from religious motives, esp. as a member of an order living under vows of poverty, chastity, and obedience.

mon·key (mŭng′kĭ), *n., pl.* **-keys,** *v.* **-keyed, -keying.** —*n.* **1.** any member of the mammalian order *Primates,* except man, the anthropoid apes and, usually, the lemurs, as the macaque. **2.** a person likened to such an animal, as a mischievous child, a mimic, etc. —*v.i.* **3.** *Colloq.* to play or trifle idly. —*v.t.* **4.** to imitate.

mon·key·shine (mŭng′kĭ shīn′), *n. U.S. Slang.* a mischievous trick or prank.

monkey wrench, a wrench with an adjustable jaw, for turning nuts of different sizes, etc.

monk·ish (mŭngk′ĭsh), *adj.* (often in deprecatory use) of or pertaining to, or characteristic of a monk. —**monk/ish·ly,** *adv.*

Monkey wrench

monks·hood (mŭngks′hŏŏd), *n.* any of certain plants of the aconite family, with hooded flowers.

mon·o·bas·ic (mŏn′ə bā′sĭk), *adj. Chem.* (of an acid) containing one replaceable hydrogen atom.

mon·o·chrome (mŏn′ə krōm′), *n.* a painting or drawing in different shades of a single color. —**mon/o·chrom/ist,** *n.*

mon·o·cle (mŏn′ə kəl), *n.* an eyeglass for one eye. —**mon/o·cled,** *adj.*

mon·o·cot·y·le·don (mŏn′ə kŏt′ə lē′dən), *n. Bot.* a plant with only one cotyledon. —**mon·o·cot·y·le·don·ous** (mŏn′ə kŏt′ə lē′dən əs, -lĕd′-ən-), *adj.*

mon·o·dy (mŏn′ə dĭ), *n., pl.* **-dies. 1.** a Greek ode sung by a single voice. **2.** a poem in which one person laments another's death. **3.** *Music.* a style of composition in which one part or melody predominates. —**mo·nod·ic** (mə nŏd′ĭk), *adj.* —**mon/o·dist,** *n.*

mo·noe·cious (mō nē′shəs), *adj. Biol.* having both male and female organs in the same individual; hermaphroditic.

mo·nog·a·my (mə nŏg′ə mĭ), *n.* **1.** marriage of one woman with one man. **2.** *Zool.* the habit of having only one mate. —**mo·nog/a·mist,** *n.* —**mo·nog/a·mous,** *adj.*

mon·o·gram (mŏn′ə grăm′), *n.* a character consisting of two or more letters combined or interlaced, commonly one's initials, often printed on stationery, etc.

mon·o·graph (mŏn′ə grăf′, -gräf′), *n.* a treatise on a particular subject.

mon·o·lith (mŏn′ə lĭth), *n.* **1.** a large piece of stone, esp. when used in architecture or sculpture. **2.** an obelisk, column, statue, etc., formed of a single block of stone. —**mon/o·lith/ic,** *adj.*

mon·o·logue (mŏn′ə lôg′, -lŏg′), *n.* **1.** a prolonged talk by a single speaker. **2.** any composition, as a poem, in which a single person speaks alone. **3.** a part of a drama in which a single actor speaks alone. **4.** a form of dramatic entertainment by a single speaker. Also, **mon/o·log/.** —**mon/o·logist** (mŏn′ə lôg′ĭst, -lŏg′-), *n.*

mon·o·ma·ni·a (mŏn′ə mā′nĭ ə), *n.* insanity in which the patient is irrational on one subject only. —**mon·o·ma·ni·ac** (mŏn′ə mā′nĭ ăk′), *n.*

mon·o·me·tal·lic (mŏn′ə mə tăl′ĭk), *adj.* **1.**

pertaining to or using one metal. **2.** pertaining to monometallism.

mon·o·met·al·lism (mŏn′ə mĕt′ə lĭz′əm), *n.* **1.** the use of one metal only (as gold or silver) as the monetary standard. **2.** the support of such a standard. —**mon/o·met/al·list,** *n.*

mo·no·mi·al (mō nō′mĭ əl), *adj.* **1.** *Alg.* consisting of one term only. **2.** *Biol.* denoting or pertaining to a name which consists of a single word or term. —*n.* **3.** *Alg.* a monomial expression or quantity.

Mo·non·ga·he·la (mə nŏng′gə hē′lə), *n.* a river flowing from N West Virginia through SW Pennsylvania into the Ohio river at Pittsburgh. 128 mi.

mon·o·plane (mŏn′ə plān′), *n.* an airplane with a single sustaining plane.

mo·nop·o·list (mə nŏp′ə lĭst), *n.* **1.** one who has a monopoly. **2.** an advocate of monopoly. —**mo·nop/o·lis/tic,** *adj.*

mo·nop·o·lize (mə nŏp′ə līz′), *v.t.,* **-lized, -lizing. 1.** to acquire, have, or exercise a monopoly of. **2.** to obtain exclusive possession of. —**mo·nop/o·li·za/tion,** *n.* —**mo·nop/o·liz/er,** *n.*

mo·nop·o·ly (mə nŏp′ə lĭ), *n., pl.* **-lies. 1.** exclusive control of a commodity or service in a particular market, or a control that makes possible the manipulation of prices. **2.** an exclusive grant to carry on a traffic or service. **3.** the exclusive possession or control of something. **4.** a commodity, service, etc., which is exclusively controlled. **5.** a company or the like having a monopoly.

mon·o·syl·la·ble (mŏn′ə sĭl′ə bəl), *n.* a word of one syllable, as *yes* and *no.* —**mon·o·syl·lab·ic** (mŏn′ə sĭ lăb′ĭk), *adj.*

mon·o·the·ism (mŏn′ə thē′ĭz′əm), *n.* the doctrine or belief that there is but one God. —**mon/o·the/ist,** *n., adj.* —**mon/o·the·is/tic,** *adj.*

mon·o·tone (mŏn′ə tōn′), *n.* **1.** a single tone without harmony or variation in pitch. **2.** recitation or singing of words in such a tone. **3.** sameness of style, as in composition. —*adj.* **4.** monotonous.

mo·not·o·nous (mə nŏt′ə nəs), *adj.* **1.** lacking in variety; tiresomely uniform. **2.** characterizing a sound continuing on one note. **3.** limited to a narrow pitch range. —**mo·not/o·nous·ly,** *adv.* —**mo·not/o·nous·ness,** *n.*

mo·not·o·ny (mə nŏt′ə nĭ), *n.* **1.** lack of variety; wearisome uniformity. **2.** the continuance of an unvarying sound. **3.** sameness of tone or pitch, as in utterance.

mon·o·treme (mŏn′ə trēm′), *n.* any member of the lowest order of mammals, comprising only the duckbill and the echidnas, oviparous mammals in which the genital, urinary, and digestive organs have a common opening.

Mon·o·type (mŏn′ə tīp′), *n. Trademark.* **1.** type composed and cast on separate keyboard and casting machines which produce each character on an individual body. **2.** the machine on which such type is set or cast.

mon·o·va·lent (mŏn′ə vā′lənt), *adj. Chem.* having a valence of one.

mon·ox·ide (mŏn ŏk′sīd, mə nŏk′-), *n. Chem.* an oxide containing one oxygen atom to the molecule.

Mon·roe (mən rō′), *n.* **James,** 1758–1831, the 5th president of the United States, 1817–25.

Monroe Doctrine, the doctrine, announced by President Monroe in 1823, that the interference or expansion of any European power in Spanish America should be looked upon as a manifestation of unfriendly disposition toward the U.S.

Mon·ro·vi·a (mən rō′vĭ ə), *n.* a seaport in and the capital of Liberia. ab. 10,000.

Mon·sei·gneur (mōn sĕ nyœr′), *n., pl.* **Messeigneurs** (mĕ sĕ nyœr′). **1.** a French title of honor given to princes, bishops, and other persons of eminence. **2.** a person bearing this title.

mon·sieur (mə syœr′), *n., pl.* **messieurs** (mĕ syœr′). the conventional French title of respect and term of address for a man, corresponding to *Mr.* and *Sir.*

Mon·si·gnor (mŏn sē′nyər), *n., pl.* **Monsignors, Monsignori** (mŏn′sē nyō′rē). *Rom. Cath. Ch.* **1.** a title conferred upon certain dignitaries. **2.** a person bearing this title. Also, **mon·si/gnor.**

mon·soon (mŏn sōōn′), *n.* the seasonal wind of the Indian Ocean and southern Asia, blowing from the southwest in summer and from the northeast in winter.

mon·ster (mŏn′stər), *n.* **1.** a fabulous animal

compounded of brute and human shape, as a centaur. **2.** an animal or a plant of abnormal form or structure. **3.** something unnatural. **4.** a person that excites horror, as by cruelty, etc. **5.** any animal or thing of huge size. —*adj.* **6.** huge; monstrous.

mon·stros·i·ty (mŏn strŏs'ə tĭ), *n., pl.* **-ties.** **1.** state or character of being monstrous. **2.** something monstrous. **3.** a monster.

mon·strous (mŏn'strəs), *adj.* **1.** huge; enormous. **2.** frightful; revolting; shocking. **3.** deviating greatly from the normal type. **4.** having the nature or appearance of a fabulous monster. —**mon'strous·ly,** *adv.* —**mon'strous·ness,** *n.*

Mont., Montana.

mon·tage (mŏn täzh'), *n.* **1.** the art or method of arranging in one composition pictorial elements borrowed from several sources so that the elements are both distinct and blended into a whole. **2.** a picture made in this way.

Mon·taigne (mŏn tān'), *n.* **Michel Eyquem,** 1533–92, French essayist.

Mon·tan·a (mŏn tăn'ə), *n.* a State in the NW United States. 478,477 pop.; 147,138 sq. mi. *Cap.:* Helena. *Abbr.:* Mont. —**Mon·tan'an,** *adj., n.*

Mont·calm (mŏnt käm'), *n.* **Louis Joseph, Marquis de,** 1712–59, French general: defeated by British at Quebec in 1759.

Mont·clair (mŏnt klâr'), *n.* a city in NE New Jersey. 39,807.

Mon·te Car·lo (mŏn'tĭ kär'lō), a town in Monaco principality, SE France: gambling resort. 10,681.

Mon·te·ne·gro (mŏn'tə nē'grō), *n.* a constituent republic of Yugoslavia, in the S part: formerly a kingdom. 360,000 pop.; 5345 sq. mi. *Cap.:* Cetinje. —**Mon·te·ne·grin** (mŏn'tə nē'grĭn), *adj., n.*

Mon·ter·rey (mŏn'tə rā'), *n.* a city in NE Mexico. 185,833.

Mon·te·vi·de·o (mŏn'tə vĭ dā'ō, mŏn'tə vĭd'-ĭ ō'), *n.* a seaport in and the capital of Uruguay. 708,233.

Mon·te·zu·ma II (mŏn'tə zōō'mə), c1477–1520, Aztec emperor of Mexico, 1503–20, conquered by Cortez.

Mont·gom·er·y (mŏnt gŭm'ə rĭ), *n.* **1. Sir Bernard Law,** born 1887, British general. **2.** the capital of Alabama, in the central part. 78,084.

month (mŭnth), *n.* **1.** any of the twelve parts (January, February, etc.) into which the calendar year is divided. **2.** a period of four weeks or 30 days.

month·ly (mŭnth'lĭ), *adj., n., pl.* **-lies,** *adv.* —*adj.* **1.** pertaining to each month. **2.** done, happening, appearing, etc., once a month. **3.** continuing for a month. —*n.* **4.** a periodical published once a month. **5.** (*pl.*) menses. —*adv.* **6.** once a month. **7.** by the month.

Mon·ti·cel·lo (mŏn'tə sĕl'ō), *n.* the home of Thomas Jefferson, in central Virginia.

Mont·mar·tre (môn mär'tr), *n.* a section in N Paris, France: artists' center.

Mont·pel·ier (mŏnt pēl'yər), *n.* the capital of Vermont, in the central part. 8006.

Mont·re·al (mŏnt'rĭ ôl', mŭnt'-), *n.* a seaport in SE Canada, on an island in the St. Lawrence. With suburbs, 1,139,921.

Mont-Saint-Mi·chel (môn săn mē shĕl'), *n.* a rocky islet near the coast in NW France: famous abbey and fortress.

mon·u·ment (mŏn'yə mənt), *n.* **1.** something erected in memory of a person, event, etc., as a statue. **2.** a tomb. **3.** any building, etc., surviving from a past age. **4.** any work, writing, or the like, by a person, regarded as a memorial of him after his death.

mon·u·men·tal (mŏn'yə mĕn'təl), *adj.* **1.** massive or imposing. **2.** *Fine Arts.* of any size larger than that of life. **3.** historically prominent. **4.** *Colloq.* conspicuously great. **5.** of or serving as a monument.

moo (mōō), *v.,* **mooed, mooing,** *n., pl.* **moos.** —*v.i.* **1.** to utter the characteristic cry of a cow. —*n.* **2.** a mooing sound.

mooch (mōōch), *v.t., v.i. Slang.* to get (something) without paying or at another's expense. —**mooch'er,** *n.*

mood[1] (mōōd), *n.* **1.** frame of mind, as at a particular time. **2.** (*pl.*) fits of uncertainty, gloominess, or sullenness.

mood[2] (mōōd), *n. Gram.* mode.

mood·y (mōō'dĭ), *adj.,* **moodier, moodiest. 1.**

given to gloomy or sullen moods. **2.** gloomy; sullen; ill-humored. —**mood'i·ly,** *adv.* —**mood'i·ness,** *n.*

moon (mōōn), *n.* **1.** the body which revolves around the earth monthly at a mean distance of 238,857 miles, accompanying the earth in its annual revolution about the sun. **2.** a month. **3.** any planetary satellite. —*v.i.* **4.** *Colloq.* to wander about or gaze idly or listlessly. —*v.t.* **5.** to spend (time) idly.

moon·beam (mōōn'bēm'), *n.* a ray of moonlight.

moon·calf (mōōn'kăf', -käf'), *n.* a congenital imbecile.

moon·fish (mōōn'fĭsh'), *n., pl.* **-fishes,** (*esp. collectively*) **-fish.** any of certain fishes having a deep, sharply compressed, silvery body.

moon·light (mōōn'līt'), *n.* **1.** the light of the moon. —*adj.* **2.** pertaining to moonlight. **3.** Also, **moon'lit'.** illuminated by moonlight. **4.** occurring by moonlight, or by night.

moon·shine (mōōn'shīn'), *n.* **1.** the light of the moon. **2.** nonsense. **3.** *U.S. Colloq.* smuggled or illicitly distilled liquor.

moon·shin·er (mōōn'shī'nər), *n. U.S. Colloq.* an illicit distiller.

moon·stone (mōōn'stōn'), *n.* a white translucent variety of feldspar with a bluish pearly luster, used as a gem.

moon·struck (mōōn'strŭk'), *adj.* dazed or crazed. Also, **moon·strick·en** (mōōn'strĭk'ən).

moon·y (mōō'nĭ), *adj.,* **moonier, mooniest.** *Colloq.* mooning, listless, or silly.

moor[1] (mōōr), *n. Brit.* **1.** a tract of open, peaty waste land, often overgrown with heath. **2.** a tract of land preserved for shooting game.

moor[2] (mōōr), *v.t., v.i.* **1.** to secure (a ship, etc.) in a particular place, as by cables. **2.** to fix firmly.

Moor (mōōr), *n.* a Mohammedan of the mixed Berber and Arab race inhabiting NW Africa. —**Moor'ish,** *adj.*

Moore (mōōr, mōr), *n.* **1. George,** 1852–1933, Irish novelist, critic, and dramatist. **2. Thomas,** 1779–1852, Irish poet.

moor·ing (mōōr'ĭng), *n.* **1.** act of one that moors. **2.** (*usually pl.*) something by which a ship or the like is moored, as a cable. **3.** (*pl.*) the place where a vessel is moored.

moor·land (mōōr'lănd'), *n. Brit.* moor[1] (def. 1).

moose (mōōs), *n., pl.* **moose.** a large animal of the deer family, inhabiting Canada and the northern U.S., the male of which has enormous antlers.

moot (mōōt), *adj.* **1.** debatable; doubtful. —*v.t.* **2.** to argue (a case, etc.), esp. in a mock court. **3.** to bring forward (any subject, etc.) for discussion.

moot court, a mock court, as for practice for students of law.

mop (mŏp), *n., v.,* **mopped, mopping.** —*n.* **1.** a bundle of coarse yarn, a piece of cloth, or the like, fastened at the end of a handle, used for washing floors, etc. **2.** a thick mass, as of hair. —*v.t.* **3.** to rub, wipe, clean, or remove with a mop. **4.** to wipe. **5.** *Mil.* to clear (ground, etc.) of scattered or remaining enemy combatants, after attacking forces have gone beyond the place.

mope (mōp), *v.,* **moped, moping,** *n.* —*v.i.* **1.** to be sunk in listless apathy or dull dejection. —*n.* **2.** a person who mopes. **3.** (*pl.*) low spirits. —**mop'er,** *n.* —**mop'ish,** *adj.*

mop·pet (mŏp'ĭt), *n.* **1.** *Archaic.* a child. **2.** *Colloq.* a doll.

mo·raine (mə rān'), *n.* a mass of boulders, gravel, sand, and clay deposited by a glacier.

mor·al (mŏr'əl, môr'əl), *adj.* **1.** pertaining to or concerned with right conduct; ethical. **2.** expressing truths or counsel as to right conduct. **3.** founded on the fundamental principles of right conduct rather than on enactment or custom. **4.** conforming to the rules of right conduct. **5.** sexually virtuous. **6.** being practically such through the effect on the mind or on results generally. **7.** resting upon conceiving grounds of probability. —*n.* **8.** the moral teaching in a fable, tale, etc. **9.** (*pl.*) principles or habits with respect to right or wrong conduct; ethics.

mo·rale (mə răl', -räl'), *n.* condition with respect to cheerfulness, confidence, zeal, etc.

mor·al·ist (mŏr'əl ĭst, môr'-), *n.* one who teaches or inculcates morality. —**mor'al·is'tic,** *adj.*

mo·ral·i·ty (mə răl'ə tĭ, mô răl'-), *n., pl.* **-ties.** **1.** conformity to the rules of right conduct.

2. sexual virtue. 3. moral quality. 4. ethics. 5. moral instruction. 6. morality play.

morality play, a form of allegorical drama in vogue from the 14th to the 16th centuries, employing personifications of virtues and vices.

mor·al·ize (môr/ə līz′, mŏr′-), v., -ized, -izing. —v.i. 1. to make moral reflections. —v.t. 2. to draw a moral from. 3. to improve the morals of. —mor′al·i·za′tion, n. —mor′al·iz′er, n.

mor·al·ly (môr/ə lĭ, mŏr′-), adv. 1. in a moral manner. 2. from a moral point of view. 3. virtuously. 4. practically.

mo·rass (mə răs′, mō-), n. 1. a tract of low, soft, wet ground. 2. a marsh or bog.

mor·a·to·ri·um (môr/ə tōr/ĭ əm, mŏr′-), n., pl. -toria (-tōr/ĭ ə), -toriums. 1. a legal authorization to delay payment of money due, as in an emergency. 2. the period during which such authorization is in effect.

mor·bid (môr/bĭd), adj. 1. unwholesomely gloomy, sensitive, etc. 2. affected by, proceeding from, or characteristic of disease. —mor/bid·ly, adv. —mor/bid·ness, mor·bid/i·ty, n.

mor·dant (môr/dənt), adj. 1. caustic or sarcastic, as wit. 2. having the property of fixing colors, as in dyeing. —n. 3. a substance used in dyeing to fix the coloring matter. 4. an acid or other corrosive substance used in etching to eat out the lines, etc. —v.t. 5. to treat with a mordant. —mor/dan·cy, n. —mor/dant·ly, adv.

Mor·de·cai (môr/dĭ kī′), n. (in the book of Esther) a cousin of Esther, who delivered the Jews from Haman.

more (môr), adj., superl. most, n., adv. —adj. 1. in greater quantity, degree, or number (as the comparative of much and many, with the superlative most). 2. additional. —n. 3. an additional quantity or number. 4. a greater quantity or degree. 5. (construed as pl.) a greater number of persons. —adv. 6. in or to a greater degree. 7. in addition; further.

More (môr), n. Sir Thomas, 1478–1535, British statesman and author: canonized in 1935.

more·o·ver (môr ō/vər), adv. beyond what has been said; further; besides.

mo·res (môr/ēz), n.pl. Sociol. folkways of central importance accepted without question and embodying the fundamental moral views of a group.

Mor·gan (môr/gən), n. John Pierpont, 1837–1913, U.S. financier and philanthropist.

mor·ga·nat·ic (môr/gə năt/ĭk), adj. designating or pertaining to a marriage in which a man of high rank marries a woman of lower station with the stipulation that neither she nor the issue shall have any claim to his rank or property. —mor/ga·nat/i·cal·ly, adv.

morgue (môrg), n. 1. a place in which the bodies of persons found dead are exposed for identification. 2. Journ. the reference library of a newspaper, etc.

mor·i·bund (môr/ə bŭnd′, mŏr′-), adj. 1. in a dying state. 2. almost at an end.

mo·ri·on (môr/ĭ ŏn′), n. a helmet with a tall comb and a curved brim.

Mor·mon (môr/mən), n. 1. a member of a religious body in the U.S., founded in 1830 by Joseph Smith and calling itself "The Church of Jesus Christ of Latter-day Saints." —adj. 2. of or pertaining to the Mormons or their religious system. —Mor/mon·ism, n.

morn (môrn), n. Poetic. morning.

morn·ing (môr/nĭng), n. 1. the beginning of day; dawn. 2. the first part of the day, extending from dawn, or from midnight, to noon. —adj. 3. of or pertaining to morning. 4. occurring, used, etc., in the morning.

morn·ing-glo·ry (môr/nĭng glōr/ĭ), n., pl. -ries. any of certain twining plants with funnel-shaped flowers of various colors, common in cultivation.

morning star, a bright planet, seen in the east before sunrise.

Mo·ro (môr/ō), n., pl. -ros. a member of any of various tribes of Mohammedan Malays in the southern Philippine Islands.

Mo·roc·co (mə rŏk/ō), n. a sultanate in NW Africa (traditional capitals: Fez and Marrakech), divided into three administrative zones: French Zone, 6,296,136 pop.; 153,910 sq. mi. (cap.: Rabat); Spanish Zone, 991,954 pop.; 7589 sq. mi. (cap.: Tetuán); Tangier Zone (internationalized). 102,306 pop.; 230 sq. mi. (cap.: Tangier). —Mo·roc·can (mə rŏk/ən), adj., n.

mo·roc·co (mə rŏk/ō), n. a fine leather made from goatskins tanned with sumac.

mo·ron (môr/ŏn), n. a person of arrested intelligence whose mentality is judged incapable of developing beyond that of a normal child of 8 to 12 years of age. —mo·ron·ic (mə rŏn/ĭk), adj.

mo·rose (mə rōs′), adj. gloomily or sullenly ill-humored, as a person, mood, etc. —mo·rose/ly, adv. —mo·rose/ness, n.

Mor·pheus (môr/fĭ əs, môr/fūs), n. Gk. Myth. the god of dreams. —Mor/phe·an, adj.

mor·phine (môr/fēn), n. a bitter crystalline alkaloid, the most important narcotic principle of opium, used in medicine to dull pain, induce sleep, etc.

mor·phol·o·gy (môr fŏl/ə jĭ), n. 1. that branch of biology which deals with the form and structure of animals and plants, without regard to functions. 2. Gram. a. the patterns of word formation in a particular language, including inflection, derivation, and composition. b. the study and description thereof. —mor·pho·log·ic (môr/fə lŏj/ĭk), mor/pho·log/i·cal, adj. —mor/-pho·log/i·cal·ly, adv.

Mor·ris (môr/ĭs, mŏr′-), n. William, 1834–96, British poet, artist, and socialist writer.

Morris chair, a large armchair with an adjustable back and loose cushions.

mor·row (môr/ō, mŏr′-), n. Archaic. 1. morning. 2. the day next after this or after some other particular day or night.

Morse (môrs), n. 1. Samuel Finley Breese, 1791–1872, U.S. inventor (of the telegraph). 2. the Morse code. —adj. 3. noting or pertaining to the Morse code or one resembling it.

Morse code, a system of dots, dashes, and spaces, or the corresponding sounds or the like, used in telegraphy and signaling to represent the letters of the alphabet, numerals, etc.

mor·sel (môr/səl), n. 1. a bite, mouthful, or small portion of food or the like. 2. a scrap; bit.

mor·tal (môr/təl), adj. 1. liable or subject to death. 2. human. 3. belonging to this world. 4. pertaining to death. 5. involving spiritual death. 6. causing death; fatal. 7. to the death. 8. implacable. 9. dire, grievous, or bitter. —n. 10. a human being. —mor/tal·ly, adv.

mor·tal·i·ty (môr tăl/ə tĭ), n., pl. -ties. 1. mortal character, nature, or existence. 2. humanity. 3. relative frequency of death, as in a community.

mor·tar[1] (môr/tər), n. 1. a bowl in which drugs, etc., are reduced to powder with a pestle. 2. a short cannon for shooting shells at high angles.

mor·tar[2] (môr/tər), n. a material which binds stones, bricks, or the like, into a compact mass.

mor·tar·board (môr/tər bôrd′), n. 1. a board, commonly square, used by masons to hold mortar. 2. a kind of academic cap surmounted by a stiff, flat, cloth-covered square piece.

mort·gage (môr/gĭj), n., v., -gaged, -gaging. —n. Law. 1. a conditional conveyance of property to a creditor as security, as for the repayment of money. 2. the deed by which such a transaction is effected. —v.t. 3. to convey or place under a mortgage. 4. to pledge.

mort·ga·gee (môr/gĭ jē′), n. one to whom property is mortgaged.

mort·ga·gor (môr/gĭ jər), n. one who mortgages property. Also, mort/gag·er.

mor·ti·cian (môr tĭsh/ən), n. an undertaker.

mor·ti·fi·ca·tion (môr/tə fə kā/shən), n. 1. humiliation in feeling, as by some wound to pride. 2. a cause or source of such humiliation. 3. the practice of asceticism by penitential discipline to overcome desire for sin and to strengthen the will. 4. Pathol. gangrene.

mor·ti·fy (môr/tə fī′), v., -fied, -fying. —v.t. 1. to humiliate in feeling, as by a wound to the pride. 2. to bring (the body, passions, etc.) into subjection by abstinence, ascetic discipline, and rigorous austerities. 3. Pathol. to affect with gangrene. —v.i. 4. to practice disciplinary austerities. 5. Pathol. to become gangrened. —mor/ti·fi·er, n.

mor·tise (môr/tĭs), n., v., -tised, -tising. —n. 1. a rectangular cavity of considerable depth in one piece of wood, etc., for receiving a corresponding projection (tenon) on another piece, so as to form a joint (mortise and tenon joint). —v.t. 2. to fasten by a mortise. Also, mor/tice.

A. Mortise; B. Tenon

mor·tu·ar·y (môr′chŏŏ ĕr′ĭ), *n.*, *pl.* **-aries,** *adj.*
—*n.* **1.** a place for the temporary reception of
the dead. —*adj.* **2.** of or pertaining to the burial
of the dead. **3.** of or connected with death.

mos., months.

mo·sa·ic (mō zā′ĭk), *n.* **1.** a picture or decoration made of small pieces of stone, glass, etc., of
different colors, inlaid to form a design. **2.** something resembling a mosaic. —*adj.* **3.** pertaining
to or resembling a mosaic or mosaic work.
4. composed of diverse elements combined.

Mo·sa·ic (mō zā′ĭk), *adj.* of or pertaining to
Moses or the writings and institutions attributed
to him. Also, **Mo·sa′i·cal.**

Mosaic Law, **1.** the ancient law of the
Hebrews, attributed to Moses. **2.** the part of
the Scripture containing this law.

Mos·cow (mŏs′kou, -kō), *n.* the capital of the
Soviet Union, in the central part of European
Soviet Russia. 4,137,018.

Mo·selle (mō zĕl′), *n.* **1.** a river flowing from
N E France to the Rhine in W Germany. 320 mi.
2. a light white wine made along the Moselle.

Mo·ses (mō′zĭz, -zĭs), *n.* the liberator of the
Hebrews from Egypt and, according to tradition,
the first lawgiver of Israel.

mo·sey (mō′zĭ), *v.i.*, **-seyed, -seying.** *U.S.
Slang.* **1.** to move along. **2.** to stroll.

Mos·lem (mŏz′ləm, mŏs′-), *adj.*, *n.*, *pl.* **-lems,
-lem.** —*adj.* **1.** pertaining to the Mohammedan
religion, law, or civilization. —*n.* **2.** a Mohammedan.

mosque (mŏsk, môsk), *n.* a Mohammedan
temple or place of worship.

mos·qui·to (mə skē′tō), *n.*, *pl.* **-toes, -tos.** any
of certain dipterous insects, the females of some
species transmitting certain diseases, as malaria
and yellow fever.

mosquito boat, a fast unarmored motorboat
armed with torpedoes and small guns.

moss (môs, mŏs), *n.* **1.** any of certain small
leafy-stemmed plants growing in tufts, sods, or
mats on moist ground, tree trunks, rocks, etc.
2. a growth of such plants. **3.** any of various
similar plants, as certain lichens. —*v.t.* **4.** to
cover with a growth of moss.

moss·back (môs′băk′, mŏs′-), *n.* *U.S. Slang.*
an extreme conservative.

moss rose, a variety of rose with a mosslike
growth on the calyx and stem.

moss·y (môs′ĭ, mŏs′ĭ), *adj.*, **mossier, mossiest.
1.** overgrown with,. or abounding in, moss.
2. resembling moss. —**moss′i·ness,** *n.*

most (mōst), *adj.*, *superl.* of **more,** *n.*, *adv.* —*adj.*
1. in the greatest quantity, degree, or number
(used as the superlative of *much* and *many*, with
the comparative *more*). **2.** in the majority of
instances. **3.** greatest, as in extent. —*n.* **4.** the
greatest quantity, amount, or degree. **5.** the
greatest number or the majority of a class specified. —*adv.* **6.** in or to the greatest extent or
degree. **7.** *Colloq.* almost.

-most, a suffix use of *most* found in a series of
superlatives, e.g., *utmost, foremost.*

most·ly (mōst′lĭ), *adv.* **1.** for the most part; in
the main. **2.** chiefly.

Mo·sul (mō sōōl′), *n.* a city in N Iraq. 108,593.

mot (mō), *n.* a pithy or witty remark.

mote (mōt), *n.* a particle, esp. of dust.

mo·tel (mō tĕl′), *n.* *U.S.* a roadside hotel or cabin
camp for motorists.

moth (môth, mŏth), *n.*, *pl.* **moths** (môthz, mŏthz,
môths, mŏths). any of a very large group of
lepidopterous insects, generally distinguished
from the butterflies by not having their antennae
clubbed and by their (mainly) nocturnal habits.

moth ball, a small ball of naphthalene or
(sometimes) camphor which repels moths and
protects clothing.

moth-eat·en (môth′ē′tən, mŏth′-), *adj.* **1.**
eaten or damaged by moths. **2.** decayed; out of
fashion.

moth·er[1] (mŭth′ər), *n.* **1.** a female parent.
2. (*often cap.*) one's own mother. **3.** the head or
superior of a female religious community. **4.** the
cause, source, or protective influence of something. —*adj.* **5.** that is a mother. **6.** pertaining
to or characteristic of a mother. **7.** native.
8. giving origin or rise, or exercising protective
care. —*v.t.* **9.** to give origin or rise to. **10.** to
care for or protect as a mother does. —**moth′er-
less,** *adj.*

moth·er[2] (mŭth′ər), *n.* a stringy, mucilaginous,
bacterial substance formed on the surface of a

liquid undergoing fermentation (as wine changing to vinegar).

Mother Car·ey's chicken (kâr′ĭz), any of
various small petrels, esp. the stormy petrel.

moth·er·hood (mŭth′ər hŏŏd′), *n.* **1.** state of
being a mother. **2.** mothers collectively. **3.** the
qualities of a mother.

Mother Hub·bard (hŭb′ərd), a full, loose
gown worn by women.

moth·er-in-law (mŭth′ər ĭn lô′), *n.*, *pl.* **moth-
ers-in-law.** the mother of one's husband or wife.

moth·er·land (mŭth′ər lănd′), *n.* one's native
or ancestral country.

moth·er·ly (mŭth′ər lĭ), *adj.* **1.** pertaining to,
characteristic of, or befitting a mother. **2.** having
the character, etc., of a mother. —*adv.* **3.** in the
manner of a mother. —**moth′er·li·ness,** *n.* ·

moth·er-of-pearl (mŭth′ər əv pûrl′), *n.* a
hard, iridescent substance which forms the inner
layer of certain shells, as that of the pearl oyster.

Mother's Day, *U.S.* a day for acts of grateful
affection or remembrance by each person toward
his mother, observed annually on the second
Sunday in May.

mother superior, the head of a female
religious community.

mo·tif (mō tēf′), *n.* a subject or theme for
treatment, as in art or music.

mo·tile (mō′təl, -tĭl), *adj.* *Biol.* moving, or
capable of moving, spontaneously. —**mo·til′i·ty,**
n.

mo·tion (mō′shən), *n.* **1.** the process of changing place or position. **2.** a movement. **3.** power
of movement, as of a living body. **4.** the action
of moving the body in walking, etc. **5.** a gesture.
6. a proposal formally made to a deliberative
assembly. **7.** *Law.* an application made to a
court or judge for an order, ruling, or the like.
—*v.t.*, *v.i.* **8.** to direct by a significant gesture, as
with the hand.

mo·tion·less (mō′shən lĭs), *adj.* without, or
incapable of, motion. —**mo′tion·less·ly,** *adv.*

motion picture, **1.** (*pl.*) consecutive photographs of objects in motion thrown on a screen
by a projector so rapidly as to give the illusion
that the objects are moving as they did in the
original scenes. **2.** a number of such photographs representing an event, play, or the like;
a photoplay.

mo·ti·vate (mō′tə vāt′), *v.t.*, **-vated, -vating.**
to provide with a motive or motives. —**mo′ti-
va′tion,** *n.*

mo·tive (mō′tĭv), *n.*, *adj.*, *v.*, **-tived, -tiving.**
—*n.* **1.** something that prompts a person to act
in a certain way; an incentive. **2.** the goal or
object of one's actions. **3.** (in art, literature, and
music) a motif. —*adj.* **4.** causing motion. **5.** pertaining to motion. **6.** prompting to action.
—*v.t.* **7.** to motivate.

mot·ley (mŏt′lĭ), *adj.*, *n.*, *pl.* **-leys.** —*adj.* **1.**
exhibiting great diversity of elements. **2.** being
of different colors combined. **3.** wearing a parti-
colored garment. —*n.* **4.** the motley or parti-
colored garment of the old-time professional fool
or jester.

mo·tor (mō′tər), *n.* **1.** a comparatively small
and powerful engine, esp. an internal-combustion
engine. **2.** any self-powered vehicle. —*adj.* **3.**
causing or imparting motion. **4.** pertaining to or
operated by a motor. **5.** used in or for motor
vehicles. **6.** *Physiol.* conveying an impulse that
results or tends to result in motion, as a nerve.
—*v.i.* **7.** to ride or travel in an automobile.

mo·tor·boat (mō′tər bōt′), *n.* a boat propelled
by its own mechanical power.

mo·tor·bus (mō′tər bŭs′), *n.* a passenger bus
powered by a motor. Also, **motor coach.**

mo·tor·car (mō′tər kär′), *n.* an automobile.

mo·tor·cy·cle (mō′tər sī′kəl), *n.* a self-propelled bicycle, tricycle, or the like. —**mo·tor-
cy·clist** (mō′tər sī′klĭst), *n.*

mo·tor·ist (mō′tər ĭst), *n.* one who drives an
automobile.

mo·tor·ize (mō′tə rīz′), *v.t.*, **-ized, -izing. 1.** to
furnish with a motor or motors. **2.** to supply
with motor-driven vehicles.

mo·tor·man (mō′tər mən), *n.*, *pl.* **-men.** one
who operates the motor of an electric car or locomotive.

motor ship, a ship driven by internal-combustion engines, usually Diesel engines.

motor truck, an automobile truck.

mot·tle (mŏt′əl), *v.*, **-tled, -tling.** *n.* —*v.t.* **1.** to
diversify with spots or blotches. —*n.* **2.** a diver-

sifying spot or blotch. 3. mottled coloring or pattern.

mot·to (mŏt'ō), *n.*, *pl.* **-toes, -tos.** a maxim adopted as expressing one's guiding principle.

mou·jik (moo zhĭk', moo'zhĭk), *n.* muzhik.

mould (mōld), *n.*, *v.t.*, *v.i. Chiefly Brit.* mold. —**mould'er**, *n.* —**mould'ing**, *n.* —**mould'y**, *adj.* —**mould'i·ness**, *n.*

mould·er (mōl'dər), *n.*, *v.i.*, *v.t.* molder.

moult (mōlt), *v.i.*, *v.t.*, *n. Chiefly Brit.* molt.

mound (mound), *n.* 1. an elevation formed of earth or sand, debris, etc., overlying ruins, a grave, etc. 2. a natural elevation of earth; hillock. —*v.t.* 3. to furnish with a mound of earth. 4. to heap up.

mount[1] (mount), *v.t.* 1. to go up or ascend. 2. to get up on (a platform, a horse, etc.). 3. to set or place at an elevation. 4. to set on horseback. 5. to put into position for use, as a gun. 6. to have (guns) in position for use. 7. to go or put on (guard). 8. to fix on or in a support, setting, etc. 9. to prepare (an animal body or skeleton) as a specimen. —*v.i.* 10. to rise or go to a higher position, degree, etc. 11. to rise in amount. 12. to get up on the back of a horse, etc., for riding. 13. to get up on something, as a platform. —*n.* 14. act or manner of mounting. 15. a horse or other animal used, provided, or available for riding. 16. a support, backing, setting or the like. —**mount'er**, *n.*

mount[2] (mount), *n.* a mountain or hill.

moun·tain (moun'tən, -tĭn), *n.* 1. a natural elevation of the earth's surface rising to a lofty summit. —*adj.* 2. of or pertaining to mountains. 3. living, growing, or found on mountains. 4. resembling a mountain, as in size.

mountain ash, any of certain small trees of the rose family, having small white flowers succeeded by red berries.

moun·tain·eer (moun'tə nĭr'), *n.* 1. an inhabitant of a mountainous district. 2. a climber of mountains. —*v.i.* 3. to climb mountains.

mountain goat, the Rocky Mountain goat.

mountain lion, the cougar.

moun·tain·ous (moun'tə nəs), *adj.* 1. abounding in mountains. 2. of the nature of a mountain. 3. large and high; huge.

mountain sheep, the bighorn of the Rocky Mountains, with massive recurving horns.

moun·te·bank (moun'tə băngk'), *n.* 1. one who sells quack medicines from a platform in public places, appealing to his audience by tricks, storytelling, etc. 2. any charlatan or quack. —*v.i.* 3. to play the mountebank.

mount·ing (moun'tĭng), *n.* 1. act of one that mounts. 2. a support, setting, or the like.

Mount Ver·non (vûr'nən), 1. the home and tomb of George Washington in NE Virginia. 2. a city in SE New York, near New York City. 67,362.

mourn (mōrn), *v.i.*, *v.t.* 1. to feel or express sorrow or grief (for). 2. to grieve or lament for (the dead). —**mourn'er**, *n.*

mourn·ful (mōrn'fəl), *adj.* 1. full of, expressing, or showing sorrow or grief. 2. causing, or attended with, sorrow or mourning. 3. gloomy, somber, or dreary. —**mourn'ful·ly**, *adv.* —**mourn'ful·ness**, *n.*

mourn·ing (mōr'nĭng), *n.* 1. sorrowing or lamentation. 2. the conventional manifestation of sorrow for a person's death, esp. by the wearing of black, etc. 3. the outward tokens of such sorrow, as black garments, etc. —*adj.* 4. of, pertaining to, or used in mourning. —**mourn'ing·ly**, *adv.*

mouse (*n.* mous; *v.* mouz), *n.*, *pl.* **mice** (mīs), *v.*, moused, mousing. —*n.* 1. any of certain small rodents which infest houses. 2. *Slang.* a black eye. —*v.t.* 3. to hunt out, as a cat hunts out mice. —*v.i.* 4. to hunt for or catch mice.

mous·er (mou'zər), *n.* an animal that catches mice.

mousse (moos), *n.* any of various preparations of whipped cream, beaten eggs, gelatin, etc., sweetened and flavored and frozen without stirring.

Mous·sorg·sky (moo sôrg'skĭ), *n.* Modest Petrovich, 1839–81, Russian composer.

mous·tache (məs tăsh', mŭs'tăsh), *n. Chiefly Brit.* mustache.

mous·y (mou'sĭ, mou'zĭ), *adj.*, **mousier, mousiest.** 1. resembling or suggesting a mouse, as in color, odor, behavior, etc. 2. drab.

mouth (*n.* mouth; *v.* mouⁿⁿ), *n.*, *pl.* **mouths** (mouⁿⁿz), *v.* —*n.* 1. the opening through which an animal takes in food. 2. an opening leading out of or into any cavity. 3. a part of a river or the like where its waters are discharged into some other body of water. —*v.t.*, *v.i.* 4. to utter or speak in a sonorous, oratorical, or pompous manner. 5. to press, rub, or mumble with the mouth or lips. 6. to grimace.

mouth·ful (mouth'fool'), *n.*, *pl.* **-fuls.** 1. as much as a mouth can hold. 2. as much as is taken into the mouth at one time. 3. a small quantity. 4. *Slang.* a large amount.

mouth organ, a harmonica.

mouth·piece (mouth'pēs'), *n.* 1. a piece placed at or forming the mouth, as of a receptacle, tube, or the like. 2. a part, as of an instrument, to which the mouth is applied. 3. a person, a newspaper, or the like, that voices the sentiments, decisions, etc., of another or others.

mov·a·ble (moo'və bəl), *adj.* 1. capable of being moved. 2. *Law.* (of property) **a.** not permanent in place. **b.** personal. 3. changing from one date to another in different years. —*n.* 4. an article of furniture which is not fixed in place. 5. (*usually pl.*) *Law.* an article of personal property not attached to land. Also, **move'a·ble.** —**mov'a·ble·ness, mov'a·bil'i·ty**, *n.* —**mov'a·bly**, *adv.*

move (moov), *v.*, **moved, moving**, *n.* —*v.i.* 1. to change place or position. 2. to change one's abode. 3. to advance; progress. 4. to turn; revolve. 5. *Com.* to be disposed of by sale. 6. *Colloq.* to start off. 7. (of the bowels) to operate. 8. to be active in a particular sphere. 9. to take action, as in an affair. 10. to make a formal request, application, or proposal. —*v.t.* 11. to change the place or position of. 12. to set or keep in motion. 13. to prompt, actuate, or impel. 14. to cause (the bowels) to operate. 15. to affect with emotion. 16. to propose formally, as to a court or judge. —*n.* 17. act of moving; movement. 18. a change of abode or residence. 19. an action toward an end. —**mov'er**, *n.*

move·ment (moov'mənt), *n.* 1. act or process of moving. 2. a particular manner of moving. 3. (*chiefly pl.*) an action or activity, as of a person. 4. *Mil., Naval.* a change of position or location of troops or ships. 5. rapid progress of events. 6. the progress of events, as in a drama. 7. the suggestion of action, as in a painting. 8. a series of actions or activities directed toward a particular end. 9. the tendency or trend of affairs in a particular field. 10. an evacuation of the bowels. 11. the material evacuated. 12. the works of a mechanism, as a watch. 13. *Music.* **a.** a principal division or section of a sonata, symphony, or the like. **b.** rhythm; time. 14. *Pros.* rhythmical structure or character.

mov·ie (moo'vĭ), *n. U.S. Colloq.* a motion picture.

mov·ing (moo'vĭng), *adj.* 1. that moves. 2. causing motion. 3. actuating, instigating, or impelling. 4. that affects with emotion. —**mov'ing·ly**, *adv.*

moving picture, motion picture.

mow[1] (mō), *v.*, **mowed, mowed or mown, mowing.** —*v.t.* 1. to cut down (grass, grain, etc.) with a scythe or a machine. 2. to cut grass, grain, etc., from. 3. to kill indiscriminately or in great numbers. —*v.i.* 4. to cut down grass, grain, etc. —**mow'er**, *n.*

mow[2] (mou), *n.* 1. the place in a barn where hay, etc., are stored. 2. a heap of hay or of sheaves of grain in a barn.

Mo·zam·bique (mō'zəm bēk'), *n.* a Portuguese colony in SE Africa. 5,085,630 pop.; 297,731 sq. mi. *Cap.:* Lourenço Marques.

Mo·zart (mō'zärt, mō'tsärt), *n.* Wolfgang Amadeus, 1756–91, Austrian composer.

M.P., 1. melting point. 2. Member of Parliament. 3. Also, **MP,** Military Police.

m.p.h., miles per hour.

Mr. (mĭs'tər), *pl.* **Messrs.** mister: a title prefixed to a man's name or position.

Mrs. (mĭs'ĭz, -ĭs, mĭz'-), *pl.* **Mmes.** mistress: a title prefixed to the name of a married woman.

MS., *pl.* **MSS.** manuscript. Also, **ms.**

Msgr., Monsignor.

m.s.t., mountain standard time.

Mt., *pl.* **Mts.** 1. mount. 2. Also, **mtn.** mountain. Also, **mt.**

M.T., metric ton.

m.t., mountain time.

mu (mū, mōō), *n.* the twelfth letter of the Greek alphabet (M, μ).

much (mŭch), *adj.,* **more, most,** *n., adv.* —*adj.* 1. in great quantity, amount, measure, or degree. —*n.* 2. a great quantity. 3. a great, important, or notable thing. —*adv.* 4. to a great extent; greatly. 5. nearly or about. —**much'ness,** *n.*

mu·ci·lage (mū'sə lĭj), *n.* 1. any of various preparations of gum, glue, or the like, for causing adhesion. 2. any of various gummy secretions or gelatinous substances present in plants.

mu·ci·lag·i·nous (mū'sə lăj'ə nəs), *adj.* 1. of, pertaining to, or secreting mucilage. 2. moist, soft, and viscid.

muck (mŭk), *n.* 1. farmyard dung, decaying vegetable matter, etc., in a moist state; manure. 2. filth; dirt. —*v.t.* 3. to manure. 4. to make dirty; soil. —**muck'y,** *adj.*

muck·er (mŭk'ər), *n. Brit. Slang.* a vulgar, ill-bred person.

muck·rake (mŭk'rāk'), *v.i.,* **-raked, -raking.** *Colloq.* to expose, esp. in print, political or other corruption. —**muck'rak'er,** *n.*

mu·cous (mū'kəs), *adj.* 1. pertaining to, consisting of, or resembling mucus. 2. containing or secreting mucus.

mucous membrane, *Anat., Zool.* a lubricating membrane lining an internal surface or an organ.

mu·cus (mū'kəs), *n.* a viscid secretion of the mucous membranes.

mud (mŭd), *n.* wet, soft earth; mire.

mud·dle (mŭd'əl), *v.,* **-dled, -dling,** *n.* —*v.* 1. to mix up in a confused or bungling way. 2. to render confused mentally, as with drink. 3. to mix or stir. 4. to make muddy or turbid, as water. —*n.* 5. a muddled condition; confusion; mess. —**mud'dler,** *n.*

mud·dy (mŭd'ĭ), *adj.,* **-dier, -diest,** *v.,* **-died, -dying.** —*adj.* 1. abounding in or covered with mud. 2. not clear or pure, as color. 3. dull, as the complexion. 4. not clear mentally. 5. obscure or vague. —*v.t.* 6. to soil with mud. 7. to make turbid. 8. to confuse. —*v.i.* 9. to become muddy. —**mud'di·ly,** *adv.* —**mud'di·ness,** *n.*

mud·guard (mŭd'gärd'), *n.* a shield so placed as to protect riders from mud thrown by the wheels of a vehicle.

mud hen, any of various marsh-inhabiting birds, esp. the American coot.

mud puppy, any of certain North American aquatic salamanders which have bushy red gills and well developed limbs.

mu·ez·zin (mū ĕz'ĭn, mōō-), *n.* (in Mohammedan communities) the crier who intones aloud the call summoning the faithful to prayer.

muff (mŭf), *n.* 1. a thick tubular case covered with fur or other material, in which the hands are placed for warmth. 2. *Baseball.* a failure to hold a ball that comes into one's hands. —*v.t., v.i.* 3. *Colloq.* to bungle. 4. *Baseball.* to fail to hold (a ball that comes into one's hands).

muf·fin (mŭf'ĭn), *n.* 1. a small, round bread made with wheat flour, corn meal, or the like, eaten with butter and usually served hot. 2. such a bread made from yeast dough.

muf·fle (mŭf'əl), *v.,* **-fled, -fling,** *n.* —*v.t.* 1. to wrap in a cloak, scarf, or the like. 2. to wrap with something to deaden or prevent sound. 3. to deaden (sound) by wrappings or other means. —*v.i.* 4. to wrap oneself (up), as in garments. —*n.* 5. something that muffles. 6. muffled sound.

muf·fler (mŭf'lər), *n.* 1. a heavy neck scarf. 2. any of various devices for deadening sound, as the sound of escaping gases of an internal-combustion engine.

muf·ti (mŭf'tĭ), *n., pl.* **-tis.** 1. civilian dress, as opposed to military or other uniform. 2. a Mohammedan legal adviser consulted in applying the religious law.

mug (mŭg), *n., v.,* **mugged, mugging.** —*n.* 1. a drinking cup, commonly with a handle. 2. the quantity it holds. 3. *Slang.* the face. 4. *Slang.* the mouth. —*v.t.* 5. *Slang.* to take a photograph of (a person). 6. *Slang.* (of a thug, etc.) to assault (a victim, etc.) from the rear by locking the forearm around the neck and throttling. —*v.i.* 7. *Slang.* to grimace. —**mug'ger,** *n.*

mug·ger (mŭg'ər), *n.* a broad-snouted crocodile of India, etc., growing to about 12 feet in length. Also, **mug'gar, mug'gur.**

mug·gy (mŭg'ĭ), *adj.,* **-gier, -giest.** (of the weather, etc.) humid and oppressive. —**mug'gi·ness,** *n.*

mug·wump (mŭg'wŭmp'), *n. U.S.* one who acts as an independent, esp. in politics.

mu·jik (mōō zhĭk', mōō'zhĭk), *n.* muzhik.

Muk·den (mōōk'dĕn', mōōk'-), *n.* a city in NE China, in S Manchuria: the former capital of Manchuria. 1,077,500.

mu·lat·to (mə lăt'ō, mū-), *n., pl.* **-toes,** *adj.* —*n.* 1. the offspring of parents of whom one is white and the other a Negro. —*adj.* 2. having a light-brown color (similar to the skin of a mulatto).

mul·ber·ry (mŭl'bĕr'ĭ, -bər ĭ), *n., pl.* **-ries.** 1. any of certain trees, as the **American** and **black mulberries** (which yield edible, berrylike collective fruit) or the **white mulberry** (whose leaves are valued as food for silkworms). 2. the fruit of any such trees.

mulch (mŭlch), *Hort.* —*n.* 1. straw, leaves, loose earth, etc., spread on the ground to protect the roots of newly planted trees, crops, etc. —*v.t.* 2. to cover with mulch.

mulct (mŭlkt), *n.* 1. a fine; penalty. —*v.t.* 2. to punish by fine or forfeiture. 3. to deprive of something by trickery.

mule[1] (mūl), *n.* 1. the offspring of a male donkey and a mare, used esp. as a beast of burden. 2. any hybrid between the donkey and the horse. 3. *Colloq.* a stupid or stubborn person.

mule[2] (mūl), *n.* a kind of slipper which leaves the heel exposed.

mule skinner, *U.S. Colloq.* a driver of mules.

mu·le·teer (mū'lə tĭr'), *n.* a driver of mules.

mul·ish (mū'lĭsh), *adj.* like a mule; stubborn; obstinate. —**mul'ish·ly,** *adv.* —**mul'ish·ness,** *n.*

mull[1] (mŭl), *v.i. U.S. Colloq.* to study or ruminate (*over*).

mull[2] (mŭl), *v.t.* to heat, sweeten, and spice for drinking, as ale, wine, etc.

mul·lein (mŭl'ĭn), *n.* a stout weed with coarse woolly leaves and dense spikes of yellow flowers.

mul·let (mŭl'ĭt), *n., pl.* **-lets,** (*esp. collectively*) **-let.** any of certain marine and fresh-water fishes with a nearly cylindrical body and generally gray coloration.

mul·li·gan (mŭl'ĭ gən), *n. U.S. Slang.* a stew containing meat, vegetables, etc.

mul·li·ga·taw·ny (mŭl'ĭ gə tô'nĭ), *n.* an East Indian soup, flavored with curry.

mul·lion (mŭl'yən), *Archit.* —*n.* 1. a vertical member, as of stone or wood, between the lights of a window or the like. —*v.t.* 2. to furnish with mullions.

multi-, a word element meaning "many."

mul·ti·cel·lu·lar (mŭl'tĭ sĕl'yə lər), *adj.* composed of several to many cells.

mul·ti·col·ored (mŭl'tĭ kŭl'ərd), *adj.* of many colors.

mul·ti·far·i·ous (mŭl'tĭ fâr'ĭ əs), *adj.* 1. having many different parts, forms, etc. 2. numerous and varied; manifold.

mul·ti·form (mŭl'tə fôrm'), *adj.* of many different forms or kinds.

Mul·ti·graph (mŭl'tə grăf', -gräf'), *n. Trademark.* a combined rotary typesetting and printing machine. —*v.t., v.i.* 2. (*l.c.*) to reproduce (matter) with such a machine.

mul·ti·lat·er·al (mŭl'tĭ lăt'ər əl), *adj.* 1. having many sides. 2. multipartite.

mul·ti·mil·lion·aire (mŭl'tə mĭl'yən âr'), *n.* a person worth several millions of dollars.

mul·tip·a·rous (mŭl tĭp'ə rəs), *adj.* producing many, or more than one, at a birth.

mul·ti·par·tite (mŭl'tĭ pär'tĭt), *adj.* 1. having many divisions. 2. denoting an agreement or other instrument in which three or more states participate.

mul·ti·ple (mŭl'tə pəl), *adj.* 1. consisting of, having, or involving many individuals, parts, relations, etc. 2. *Elect.* denoting two or more circuits connected in parallel. 3. *Bot.* (of a fruit) collective. —*n.* 4. *Math.* a number which contains another number some number of times without a remainder.

mul·ti·pli·cand (mŭl'tə plĭ kănd'), *n. Math.* the number to be multiplied by another.

mul·ti·pli·ca·tion (mŭl'tə plə kā'shən), *n.* 1. act or process of multiplying. 2. state of being multiplied. 3. *Arith.* the process of finding the number resulting from the addition of a given number taken as many times as there are units in another given number.

mul·ti·plic·i·ty (mŭl'tə plĭs'ə tĭ), *n., pl.* **-ties.** 1. a great number. 2. manifold variety.

mul·ti·pli·er (mŭl'tə plī'ər), *n.* **1.** one that multiplies. **2.** *Math.* the number by which another is to be multiplied. **3.** *Physics.* a device for intensifying some phenomenon.

mul·ti·ply (mŭl'tə plī'), *v.,* **-plied, -plying.** —*v.t.* **1.** to increase the number, quantity, etc., of. **2.** *Math.* to find the product of by multiplication. **3.** to produce (animals or plants) by propagation. **4.** to increase by procreation. —*v.i.* **5.** to grow in number, quantity, etc. **6.** *Math.* to perform the process of multiplication.

mul·ti·tude (mŭl'tə tūd', -tōōd'), *n.* **1.** a great number. **2.** a crowd or throng.

mul·ti·tu·di·nous (mŭl'tə tū'də nəs, -tōō'-), *adj.* **1.** very numerous. **2.** comprising many items or parts. **3.** *Poetic.* crowded. —**mul'ti·tu'di·nous·ly,** *adv.*

mul·ti·va·lent (mŭl'tə vā'lənt, mŭl tĭv'ə lənt), *adj.* *Chem.* having a valence of three or higher. —**mul'ti·va'lence,** *n.*

mum (mŭm), *adj.* **1.** silent. —*interj.* **2.** Be silent!

mum·ble (mŭm'bəl), *v.,* **-bled, -bling,** *n.* —*v.i., v.t.* **1.** to speak indistinctly or unintelligibly. —*n.* **2.** a low, indistinct utterance or sound. —**mum'bler,** *n.* —**mum'bling·ly,** *adv.*

mum·bo jum·bo (mŭm'bō jŭm'bō), elaborate ritual and incantation.

mum·mer (mŭm'ər), *n.* **1.** one who wears a disguise, esp. at New Year's. **2.** an actor.

mum·mer·y (mŭm'ə rĭ), *n., pl.* **-meries. 1.** performance of mummers. **2.** any mere theatrical performance or ceremony.

mum·mi·fy (mŭm'ə fī'), *v.,* **-fied, -fying.** —*v.t.* **1.** to make (a dead body) into a mummy. —*v.i.* **2.** to shrivel up. —**mum'mi·fi·ca'tion,** *n.*

mum·my (mŭm'ĭ), *n., pl.* **-mies,** *v.,* **-mied, -mying.** —*n.* **1.** the dead body of a human being or animal preserved by the ancient Egyptian (or some similar) method of embalming. —*v.t.* **2.** to make into or like a mummy.

mumps (mŭmps), *n.pl., construed as sing.* a specific infectious disease characterized by inflammatory swelling of the salivary glands.

mun., municipal.

munch (mŭnch), *v.t., v.i.* to chew with steady or vigorous working of the jaws, often audibly. —**munch'er,** *n.*

Mun·cie (mŭn'sĭ), *n.* a city in E Indiana. 49,-720.

mun·dane (mŭn'dān), *adj.* **1.** of or pertaining to the world, universe, or earth. **2.** secular; worldly.

Mu·nich (mū'nĭk), *n.* **1.** a city in S Germany. 829,318. **2.** any dishonorable appeasement. See Munich Pact.

Munich Pact, the pact signed by Germany, Great Britain, France, and Italy on September 29, 1938, by which the Sudetenland was ceded to Germany.

mu·nic·i·pal (mū nĭs'ə pəl), *adj.* of or pertaining to the local government of a town or city. —**mu·nic'i·pal·ly,** *adv.*

mu·nic·i·pal·i·ty (mū nĭs'ə păl'ə tĭ), *n., pl.* **-ties.** a city, town, or other district possessing corporate existence.

mu·nif·i·cent (mū nĭf'ə sənt), *adj.* extremely generous. —**mu·nif'i·cence,** *n.* —**mu·nif'i·cent·ly,** *adv.*

mu·ni·tion (mū nĭsh'ən), *n.* **1.** (*usually pl.*) materials used in war, esp. weapons and ammunition. —*v.t.* **2.** to provide with munitions.

mu·ral (myŏŏr'əl), *adj.* **1.** of, pertaining to, or resembling a wall. **2.** executed on or affixed to a wall. —*n.* **3.** a mural painting.

mur·der (mûr'dər), *n.* **1.** *Law.* the unlawful killing of another human being with malice aforethought. —*v.t., v.i.* **2.** *Law.* to kill unlawfully with malice aforethought. **3.** to spoil by bad performance, etc. —**mur'der·er,** *n.* —**mur'der·ess,** *n. fem.*

mur·der·ous (mûr'dər əs), *adj.* **1.** of the nature of or involving murder. **2.** guilty of, bent on, or capable of murder. **3.** intentionally deadly. —**mur'der·ous·ly,** *adv.* —**mur'der·ous·ness,** *n.*

mu·ri·at·ic acid (myŏŏr'ĭ ăt'ĭk), the commercial name for hydrochloric acid.

Mu·ril·lo (myŏŏ rĭl'ō), *n.* Bartolomé Esteban, 1617–82, Spanish painter.

murk (mûrk), *n.* **1.** darkness. —*adj.* **2.** dark.

murk·y (mûr'kĭ), *adj.,* **murkier, murkiest.** intensely dark, gloomy, and cheerless. —**murk'i·ness,** *n.*

Mur·mansk (mŏŏr mänsk'), *n.* a seaport (ice-free) and railroad terminus in the NW Soviet Union. 117,054.

mur·mur (mûr'mər), *n.* **1.** any low, continuous sound, as of a brook, of low indistinct voices, etc. **2.** a mumbled or private expression of discontent. **3.** *Med.* an abnormal sound heard on listening over the heart, usually through a stethoscope. —*v.i., v.t.* **4.** to make a low, indistinct continuous sound. **5.** to speak in a low tone or indistinctly. **6.** to complain. —**mur'mur·er,** *n.*

Mur·phy (mûr'fĭ), *n.* Frank, born 1890, associate justice of U.S. Supreme Court since 1940.

mur·rain (mûr'ĭn), *n.* any of various diseases of cattle, as anthrax.

Mur·ray (mûr'ĭ), *n.* **1.** Philip, 1886–1952, U.S. labor leader. **2.** a river flowing through SE South Australia into the ocean. ab. 1500 mi.

Mur·rum·bidg·ee (mûr'əm bĭj'ĭ), *n.* a river in SE Australia. ab. 1350 mi.

mur·ther (mûr'thər), *n., v.t., v.i.* *Obs.* murder.

Mus., **1.** museum. **2.** music. **3.** musical.

mus·ca·dine (mŭs'kə dĭn, -dīn'), *n.* a variety of grape indigenous to America.

mus·cat (mŭs'kət, -kăt), *n.* a grape variety with pronounced pleasant sweet aroma and flavor, used for making wine.

Mus·cat (mŭs kät'), *n.* a seaport in SE Arabia. ab. 4200.

mus·ca·tel (mŭs'kə těl', mŭs'kə těl'), *n.* **1.** a sweet wine made from muscat grapes. **2.** the muscat grape.

mus·cle (mŭs'əl), *n., v.,* **-cled, -cling.** —*n.* **1.** a discrete bundle or sheet of contractile fibers having the function of producing movement in the animal body. **2.** the tissue of such a bundle. **3.** brawn. —*v.i.* **4.** *Colloq.* to make one's way by sheer brawn.

mus·cle-bound (mŭs'əl bound'), *adj.* having muscles enlarged and inelastic, as from excessive athletics.

Muscle Shoals, formerly rapids in the Tennessee river, in NW Alabama: now changed into a lake by Wilson Dam, part of the Tennessee Valley Authority.

Mus·co·vy (mŭs'kə vĭ), *n.* *Archaic.* Russia. —**Mus'co·vite',** *n., adj.*

mus·cu·lar (mŭs'kyə lər), *adj.* **1.** of or pertaining to muscle or the muscles. **2.** dependent on or affected by the muscles. **3.** brawny. —**mus·cu·lar·i·ty** (mŭs'kyə lăr'ə tĭ), *n.* —**mus'cu·lar·ly,** *adv.*

mus·cu·la·ture (mŭs'kyə lə chər), *n.* the muscular system of the body or of its parts.

muse (mūz), *v.i., v.t.,* **mused, musing.** to reflect or meditate (on) in silence. —**mus'er,** *n.*

Muse (mūz), *n.* **1.** *Class. Myth.* any of the nine sister goddesses presiding over poetry and song, the drama, dancing, astronomy, etc. **2.** (*sometimes l.c.*) the goddess or the power regarded as inspiring a poet. **3.** (*l.c.*) a poet's characteristic genius or powers.

mu·sette bag (mū zět'), a small bag for personal belongings of army officers, carried by a shoulder strap.

mu·se·um (mū zē'əm), *n.* a place for the exhibition of works of art, etc.

mush¹ (mŭsh), *n.* **1.** *U.S.* meal, esp. corn meal, boiled in water or milk until it forms a thick, soft mass. **2.** any thick, soft matter. **3.** anything unpleasantly lacking in firmness, force, etc. **4.** *Colloq.* maudlin sentiment.

mush² (mŭsh), *v.t.* **1.** to go or travel on foot, esp. over the snow with a dog team. —*interj.* **2.** an order to start or speed up a dog team. —*n.* **3.** a march on foot, esp. over the snow with a dog team. —**mush'er,** *n.*

mush·room (mŭsh'rōōm, -rŏŏm), *n.* **1.** any of various fleshy fungi including the toadstools, etc., esp. certain edible species, usually of umbrella shape. **2.** anything of correspondingly rapid growth. —*adj.* **3.** of, pertaining to, or made of mushrooms. **4.** of rapid growth. —*v.i.* **5.** to gather mushrooms. **6.** to have or assume the shape of a mushroom. **7.** to grow quickly.

mush·y (mŭsh'ĭ), *adj.,* **mushier, mushiest. 1.** mushlike. **2.** *Colloq.* weakly sentimental. —**mush'i·ness,** *n.*

mu·sic (mū'zĭk), *n.* **1.** an art of sound in time

which expresses ideas and emotions in significant forms through the elements of rhythm, melody, harmony, and color. 2. the tones or sounds employed. 3. musical compositions. 4. the written or printed score of a musical composition. 5. such scores collectively.

mu·si·cal (mū′zə kəl), *adj.* 1. of, pertaining to, or producing music. 2. melodious; harmonious. 3. fond of or skilled in music. 4. set to or accompanied by music. —*n.* 5. musical comedy. —**mu′si·cal·ly,** *adv.* —**mu′si·cal·ness,** *n.*

musical comedy, a play with music, often of a whimsical or satirical nature.

mu·si·cale (mū′zĭ kăl′), *n.* a program of music forming part of a social occasion.

music box, a box containing an apparatus for producing music mechanically, as by means of a comblike steel plate with tuned teeth sounded by small pegs in the surface of a revolving cylinder or disk.

music hall, 1. a hall for musical entertainments. 2. *Chiefly Brit.* a theater for vaudeville.

mu·si·cian (mū zĭsh′ən), *n.* 1. one who makes music a profession, esp. as a performer. 2. one skilled in music. —**mu·si′cian·ly,** *adj.*

mus·ing (mū′zĭng), *adj.* 1. absorbed in thought; dreamy. —*n.* 2. contemplation. —**mus′ing·ly,** *adv.*

musk (mŭsk), *n.* 1. a substance secreted in a glandular sac under the skin of the abdomen of the male musk deer, used in perfumery. 2. a similar secretion of other animals, as the civet, etc. 3. the odor of musk.

musk deer, a small, hornless animal of the deer kind, of central Asia, the male of which secretes musk.

Mus·ke·gon (mŭs kē′gən), *n.* a city in W Michigan. 47,697.

mus·kel·lunge (mŭs′kə lŭnj′), *n., pl.* **-lunge.** a large game fish of the pike family, of the lakes and rivers of eastern and middle western North America.

mus·ket (mŭs′kĭt), *n.* a hand gun for infantry soldiers, introduced in the 16th century: the predecessor of the modern rifle.

mus·ket·eer (mŭs′kə tĭr′), *n.* a soldier armed with a musket.

mus·ket·ry (mŭs′kĭt rĭ), *n.* 1. practice in group combat firing with rifles. 2. muskets collectively. 3. troops armed with muskets.

Mus·kho·ge·an (mŭs kō′gĭ ən), *n.* a family of American Indian languages of southeastern U.S., including those of the Choctaw, Chickasaw, and Creek.

musk·mel·on (mŭsk′mĕl′ən), *n.* a kind of melon of many varieties, a round or oblong fruit with a juicy, often aromatically sweet, edible flesh (yellow, white, or green). 2. the plant bearing it.

Mus·ko·gee (mŭs kō′gĭ), *n.* a city in E Oklahoma. 32,332.

musk ox, a bovine ruminant, native to arctic America.

musk·rat (mŭsk′răt′), *n., pl.* **-rats,** (*esp. collectively*) **-rat.** 1. a large aquatic North American rodent with a musky odor. 2. its thick light-brown fur.

musk·y (mŭs′kĭ), *adj.,* **muskier, muskiest.** of or like musk, as odors.

Mus·lem (mŭz′ləm, mŭs′-), *n., adj.* Moslem. Also, **Mus′lim.**

mus·lin (mŭz′lĭn), *n.* a cotton fabric, usually of plain weave, used for sheets, etc.

muss (mŭs), *n. Colloq.* 1. a state of disorder. 2. an untidy or dirty mess. —*v.t.* 3. *U.S. Dial.* to put into disorder; rumple. —**muss′y,** *adj.*

mus·sel (mŭs′əl), *n.* any bivalve mollusk, esp. certain edible marine bivalves and freshwater clams.

Mus·set (my sĕ′), *n.* **Alfred de,** 1810–57, French writer.

Mus·so·li·ni (mōōs′ə lē′nĭ), *n.* **Benito,** 1883–1945, Italian Fascist leader and prime minister of Italy, 1922–43.

Mus·sorg·sky (mōō sôrg′skĭ), *n.* **Modest Petrovich,** 1835–81, Russian composer.

Mus·sul·man (mŭs′əl mən), *n., pl.* **-mans.** a Mohammedan.

must[1] (mŭst), *aux. v.* 1. to be bound by some imperative requirement to. 2. may reasonably be supposed to. —*adj.* 3. necessary; vital. —*n.* 4. anything necessary or vital.

must[2] (mŭst), *n.* new wine; the unfermented juice as pressed from the grape.

mus·tache (mŭs′tăsh, məs tăsh′), *n.* the hair growing on the upper lip of men.

mus·ta·chio (məs tä′shō), *n., pl.* **-chios.** a mustache.

mus·tang (mŭs′tăng), *n.* the small, wild or half-wild horse of the American plains.

mus·tard (mŭs′tərd), *n.* a pungent powder or paste prepared from the seed of the mustard plant, much used as a food seasoning. 2. any of certain plants cultivated for such seeds.

mustard gas, a liquid chemical-warfare agent, producing burns, blindness, and death.

mustard plaster, a powdered black mustard and rubber solution mixture placed on a cloth and used as a counterirritant.

mus·ter (mŭs′tər), *v.t., v.i.* 1. to assemble (troops, a ship's crew, etc.), as for battle, display, etc. 2. to gather. —*n.* 3. an assembling of troops for inspection or other purposes. 4. an assemblage or collection.

mus·ty (mŭs′tĭ), *adj.,* **-tier, -tiest.** 1. having an odor or flavor suggestive of mold, as old buildings, food, etc. 2. antiquated. 3. dull; apathetic. —**mus′ti·ness,** *n.*

mu·ta·ble (mū′tə bəl), *adj.* 1. subject to change. 2. fickle or inconstant. —**mu′ta·bil′i·ty, mu′ta·ble·ness,** *n.* —**mu′ta·bly,** *adv.*

mu·tant (mū′tənt), *adj.* 1. undergoing or resulting from mutation. —*n.* 2. a new type of organism produced as the result of mutation.

mu·ta·tion (mū tā′shən), *n.* 1. act or process of changing. 2. a change or alternation. 3. *Biol.* **a.** a sudden departure from the parent type. **b.** an individual, species, or the like, resulting from such a departure.

mute (mūt), *adj., n., v.,* **muted, muting.** —*adj.* 1. silent; not making sound of any kind. 2. incapable of speech; dumb. 3. *Gram.* (of letters) not pronounced. 4. *Law.* making no response when arraigned. —*n.* 5. one unable to utter words. 6. a device for muffling the tone of a musical instrument. 7. *Phonetics.* a stop. —*v.t.* 8. to deaden the sound of (a musical instrument, etc.). —**mute′ly,** *adv.* —**mute′ness,** *n.*

mu·ti·late (mū′tĭ lāt′), *v.t.,* **-lated, -lating.** 1. to deprive (a person or animal, the body, etc.) of a limb or other important part or parts. 2. to injure, disfigure, or make imperfect by removing or damaging parts. —**mu′ti·la′tion,** *n.* —**mu′ti·la′tor,** *n.*

mu·ti·neer (mū′tə nĭr′), *n.* one guilty of mutiny.

mu·ti·nous (mū′tə nəs), *adj.* 1. disposed to, engaged in, or involving revolt against constituted authority. 2. rebellious. —**mu′ti·nous·ly,** *adv.* —**mu′ti·nous·ness,** *n.*

mu·ti·ny (mū′tə nĭ), *n., pl.* **-nies,** *v.,* **-nied, -nying.** —*n.* 1. revolt against constituted authority, esp. by soldiers or seamen. —*v.i.* 2. to revolt against constituted authority.

mutt (mŭt), *n. Slang.* 1. a dog, esp. a mongrel. 2. a simpleton; a stupid person.

mut·ter (mŭt′ər), *v.i.* 1. to utter words indistinctly or in a low tone, often in making obscure complaints, threats, etc.; murmur. 2. to make a low, rumbling sound. —*v.t.* 3. to utter indistinctly or in a low tone. —*n.* 4. act or utterance of one that mutters.

mut·ton (mŭt′ən), *n.* the flesh of sheep, used as food, esp. that of more mature sheep.

mutton chop, a rib piece of mutton having the bone chopped off at the small end, or some similar piece.

mu·tu·al (mū′chōō əl), *adj.* 1. possessed, experienced, performed, etc., by each of two or more with respect to the other or others; reciprocal. 2. having the same relation each toward the other or others. 3. of or pertaining to each of two or more; common. —**mu′tu·al·ly,** *adv.*

mu·zhik (mōō zhĭk′, mōō′zhĭk), *n.* a Russian peasant. Also, **mu·zjik′.**

muz·zle (mŭz′əl), *n., v.,* **-zled, -zling.** —*n.* 1. the mouth of the barrel of a gun, pistol, etc. 2. the projecting part of the head of an animal, including jaws, mouth, and nose. 3. a cage of straps or wires placed over an animal's mouth to prevent it from biting, eating, etc. —*v.t.* 4. to put a muzzle on (an animal's mouth). 5. to restrain from speech or the expression of opinion; gag.

muz·zle-load·er (mŭz′əl lō′dər), *n.* a firearm which is loaded through the muzzle.

my (mī), *pron.* 1. the possessive form corresponding to *I* and *me,* used before a noun. —*interj.* 2. *Colloq.* an exclamation of surprise.

My·ce·nae (mī sē′nē), *n.* an ancient city in S Greece: advanced civilization, c1400 B.C. to c1100 B.C. —**My′ce·nae′an,** *adj.*

my·col·o·gy (mī kŏl′ə jĭ), *n.* the branch of botany that treats of fungi. —**my·col′o·gist,** *n.*

my·na (mī′nə), *n.* any of certain Asiatic birds of the starling family, some of which are well-known cage birds and learn to talk.

Myn·heer (mīn hâr′, -hĭr′), *n.* **1.** the Dutch term of address and title of respect corresponding to *sir* and *Mr.* **2.** (*l.c.*) *Colloq.* a Dutchman.

my·o·pi·a (mī ō′pĭ ə), *n. Pathol.* a condition of the eye in which parallel rays are focused in front of the retina, objects being seen distinctly only when near to the eye; near-sightedness. —**my·op·ic** (mī ŏp′ĭk), *adj.*

myr·i·ad (mĭr′ĭ əd), *n.* **1.** an indefinitely great number. **2.** ten thousand. —*adj.* **3.** of an indefinitely great number. **4·** having innumerable aspects, etc. **5.** ten thousand.

myr·i·a·pod (mĭr′ĭ ə pŏd′), *n.* any of certain arthropods with long bodies composed usually of many segments, most of which bear three-jointed legs.

Myr·mi·don (mûr′mə dŏn′, -dən), *n., pl.* **Myr·midons, Myrmidones** (mûr mĭd′ə nēz′). **1.** one of the warlike people of ancient Thessaly who accompanied Achilles, their king, to the Trojan War. **2.** (*l.c.*) one who executes without scruple his master's commands.

myrrh (mûr), *n.* an aromatic resinous exudation from certain plants: used for incense, perfume, etc.

myr·tle (mûr′təl), *n.* **1.** a shrub of southern Europe with evergreen leaves, fragrant white flowers, and aromatic berries. **2.** *U.S.* the periwinkle[2].

my·self (mī sĕlf′), *pron., pl.* **ourselves. 1.** an intensifier of *me* or *I.* **2.** a reflexive substitute for *me.*

My·sore (mī sōr′), *n.* **1.** a state in S India. 7,329,140 pop.; 29,458 sq. mi. **2.** the capital of this state. 150,540.

mys·te·ri·ous (mĭs tĭr′ĭ əs), *adj.* **1.** full of, characterized by, or involving mystery. **2.** puzzling; inexplicable. **3.** implying or suggesting a mystery. —**mys·te′ri·ous·ly,** *adv.* —**mys·te′ri·ous·ness,** *n.*

mys·ter·y (mĭs′tə rĭ, -trĭ), *n., pl.* **-teries. 1.** anything that is kept secret or remains unexplained or unknown. **2.** any affair, thing, or person that arouses curiosity or speculation. **3.** puzzling obscurity. **4.** any truth unknowable except by divine revelation. **5.** (in the Christian religion) **a.** a sacramental rite. **b.** (*pl.*) the Eucharistic elements. **c.** the Eucharist. **6.** (*pl.*) rites or secrets known only to those specially initiated. **7.** a miracle play.

mys·tic (mĭs′tĭk), *adj.* **1.** spiritually significant or symbolic. **2.** of or pertaining to mysteries known only to the initiated. **3.** of occult character, power, or significance. **4.** of obscure or mysterious character. **5.** of mystics or mysticism. —*n.* **6.** one initiated into mysteries. **7.** one who believes in mysticism (def. 2).

mys·ti·cal (mĭs′tə kəl), *adj.* **1.** mystic; occult. **2.** of or pertaining to mystics or mysticism. **3.** spiritually symbolic.

mys·ti·cism (mĭs′tə sĭz′əm), *n.* **1.** the beliefs, ideas, or mode of thought of mystics. **2.** the doctrine of an immediate spiritual intuition of truths believed to transcend ordinary understanding through contemplation and love. **3.** obscure thought.

mys·ti·fy (mĭs′tə fī′), *v.t.* **-fied, -fying.** to bewilder purposely; perplex. —**mys′ti·fi·ca′tion,** *n.*

myth (mĭth), *n.* **1.** a traditional or legendary story, usually concerning some superhuman being or beings. **2.** stories or matter of this kind. **3.** any invented story. **4.** an imaginary or fictitious thing or person.

myth., 1. mythological. **2.** mythology.

myth·i·cal (mĭth′ə kəl), *adj.* **1.** pertaining to, of the nature of, or involving a myth or myths. **2.** dealt with in myth. **3.** existing only in myth. **4.** imaginary; fictitious. Also, **myth′ic.** —**myth′i·cal·ly,** *adv.*

my·thol·o·gy (mĭ thŏl′ə jĭ), *n., pl.* **-gies. 1.** a body of myths, as that of a particular people, or that relating to a particular person. **2.** myths collectively. **3.** the science of myths. —**myth′o·log′i·cal,** *adj.* —**myth′o·log′i·cal·ly,** *adv.*

Myt·i·le·ne (mĭt′ə lē′nĭ), *n.* a Greek island in the NE Aegean. 161,832 pop.; 629 sq. mi.

N

N, n (ĕn), *n., pl.* **N's** or **Ns, n's** or **ns. 1.** a consonant, the 14th letter of the English alphabet. **2.** *Math.* an indefinite constant whole number.

N, 1. *Chem.* nitrogen. **2.** north. **3.** northern.

N., 1. Navy. **2.** (*l.c.*) neuter. **3.** (*also l.c.*) New. **4.** (*also l.c.*) Noon. **5.** (*also l.c.*) North; Northern. **6.** (*l.c.*) noun.

Na, *Chem.* (L *natrium*) sodium.

N.A., North America.

nab (năb), *v.t.* **nabbed, nabbing.** *Colloq.* **1.** to catch or seize, esp. suddenly. **2.** to arrest.

na·bob (nā′bŏb), *n.* **1.** an Englishman who has grown rich in India. **2.** any wealthy and luxurious person. **3.** nawab.

na·celle (nə sĕl′), *n.* the enclosed part of an aircraft, in which the engine is housed or passengers, etc., are carried.

na·cre (nā′kər), *n.* mother-of-pearl. —**na·cre·ous** (nā′krĭ əs), *adj.*

na·dir (nā′dər, nā′dĭr), *n.* **1.** the point of the celestial sphere vertically beneath any place or observer, and diametrically opposite to the zenith. **2.** the lowest point.

nae·vus (nē′vəs), *n., pl.* **-vi** (vī). *Dermatology.* any congenital anomaly, including various types of birthmarks.

nag[1] (năg), *v.t., v.i.,* **nagged, nagging.** to torment (someone) by persistent faultfinding, complaints, or importunities. —**nag′ger,** *n.*

nag[2] (năg), *n.* **1.** an old or inferior horse. **2.** *Colloq.* a horse.

Na·ga·sa·ki (nä′gä sä′kē), *n.* a seaport in SW Japan: the second military use of the atomic bomb, Aug. 9, 1945. 174,141.

Na·go·ya (nä′gō yä′), *n.* a city in central Japan. 719,382.

Nag·pur (näg pŏŏr′), *n.* a city in central India. 301,957.

Nah., Nahum.

Na·hum (nā′həm), *n.* **1.** a Hebrew prophet of the late seventh century B.C. **2.** a book of the Old Testament.

nai·ad (nā′ăd, nī′-), *n., pl.* **-ads, -ades** (-ə dēz′). **1.** (*also cap.*) *Class. Myth.* one of a class of water nymphs fabled to dwell in and preside over streams and springs. **2.** a girl swimmer.

na·if (nä ēf′), *adj.* naïve.

nail (nāl), *n.* **1.** a slender piece of metal, usually with one end pointed and the other enlarged, for driving into or through wood, etc., as to hold separate pieces together. **2.** a thin, horny plate, consisting of modified epidermis, growing on the upper side of the end of a finger or toe. —*v.t.* **3.** to fasten with a nail or nails. **4.** to make fast or keep firmly in one place. **5.** *Colloq.* to secure by prompt action. **6.** *Colloq.* to catch or seize. **7.** *Colloq.* to detect and expose (a lie, etc.)

nain·sook (nān′sŏŏk, nān′-), *n.* a fine, soft-finished cotton fabric, usually white.

Nai·ro·bi (nī rō′bĭ), *n.* the capital of Kenya, in British East Africa. ab. 65,000.

na·ïve (nä ēv′), *adj.* naturally simple; unsophisticated; ingenuous. Also, **na·ive′**. —**na·ive′-ly**, *adv.*

na·ive·té (nä ēv′tā′), *n.* **1.** quality of being naïve; artless simplicity. **2.** a naïve action, remark, etc. Also, **na·ive′te′**.

na·ked (nā′kĭd), *adj.* **1.** without clothing or covering; nude. **2.** bare, stripped, or destitute. **3.** without a sheath or customary covering. **4.** without carpets, hangings, or furnishings. **5.** (of the eye, etc.) unassisted by a microscope, telescope, or other instrument. **6.** defenseless or unprotected. **7.** simple; unadorned. **8.** exposed to view or plainly revealed. —**na′ked·ly**, *adv.* —**na′ked·ness**, *n.*

NAM, National Association of Manufacturers. Also, **N. A. M.**

nam·by-pam·by (năm′bĭ′ păm′bĭ′), *adj.*, *n.*, *pl.* **-bies.** —*adj.* **1.** weakly simple or sentimental; insipid. —*n.* **2.** namby-pamby verse or prose. **3.** a namby-pamby person.

name (nām), *n.*, *v.*, **named, naming.** —*n.* **1.** a word or words by which a person, place, or thing, a body or class, or any object of thought, is designated. **2.** mere designation as distinguished from fact. **3.** an appellation, title, or epithet. **4.** a reputation, esp. a distinguished or great reputation. **5.** a famous person. **6. in the name of,** **a.** with appeal to. **b.** by the authority of. **c.** on behalf of. **d.** under the name of. **e.** under the designation of. **7. to one's name,** belonging to one. —*v.t.* **8.** to give a name to. **9.** to call by a specified name. **10.** to mention by name. **11.** to nominate or appoint. **12.** to specify. **13.** to tell the name of. —**nam′a·ble, name′a·ble**, *adj.* —**nam′er**, *n.*

name·less (nām′lĭs), *adj.* **1.** unknown; obscure. **2.** having no name. **3.** left unnamed. **4.** anonymous. **5.** born out of wedlock.

name·ly (nām′lĭ), *adv.* that is to say.

name·sake (nām′sāk′), *n.* **1.** one having the same name as another. **2.** one named after another.

Nan·chang (nän′chäng′), *n.* a city in SE China. 206,400.

nan·keen (năn kēn′), *n.* a firm, durable, yellow or buff fabric. Also, **nan·kin′.**

Nan·king (nän′kĭng′), *n.* the capital of China, in the E part. 1,019,000.

nan·ny (năn′ĭ), *n.*, *pl.* **-nies.** *Brit.* a nurse for children.

nanny goat, a female goat.

Nan·sen (năn′sən, nän′-), *n.* **Fridtjof,** 1861–1930, Norwegian explorer and diplomat.

Nantes (nänts), *n.* **1.** a seaport in W France. 200,265. **2. Edict of,** a law promulgated in 1598, granting considerable religious and civil liberty to the Huguenots: revoked by Louis XIV, 1685.

Nan·tuck·et (năn tŭk′ĭt), *n.* an island off SE Massachusetts. 3401 pop.; 15 mi. long.

Na·o·mi (nā ō′mĭ, nā′ō mī′, -mĭ), *n.* *Bible.* the mother-in-law of Ruth.

nap[1] (năp), *v.*, **napped, napping,** *n.* —*v.i.* **1.** to have a short sleep; doze. **2.** to be off one's guard. —*n.* **3.** a short sleep; doze.

nap[2] (năp), *n.*, *v.*, **napped, napping.** —*n.* **1.** the short fuzzy ends of fibers on the surface of cloth. **2.** any downy coating. —*v.t.* **3.** to raise a nap on.

nape (nāp, năp), *n.* the back (of the neck).

naph·tha (năp′thə, năf′-), *n.* a colorless, volatile liquid, a petroleum distillate, used as a solvent, fuel, etc.

naph·tha·lene (năf′thə lēn′, năp′-), *n.* *Chem.* a white crystalline hydrocarbon, usually prepared from coal tar: used as a moth repellent, etc.

nap·kin (năp′kĭn), *n.* **1.** a rectangular piece of cloth used at table to wipe the lips and hands, and to protect the clothes. **2.** *Chiefly Brit.* a diaper.

Na·ples (nā′pəlz), *n.* a seaport in SW Italy. 959,693.

Na·po·le·on (nə pō′lĭ ən), *n.* **1. Louis,** 1808–73, president of France, 1848–52; as Napoleon III, emperor of France, 1852–70. **2. I.** See **Bonaparte.** —**Na·po·le·on·ic** (nə pō′lĭ ŏn′ĭk), *adj.*

na·po·le·on (nə pō′lĭ ən), *n.* **1.** a piece of pastry consisting of baked puff paste in layers with a cream filling. **2.** a former French gold coin of the value of 20 francs.

nar·cis·sism (när sĭs′ĭz əm), *n.* *Psychoanal.* sexual excitement or erotic gratification through admiration of oneself. —**nar·cis′sist**, *n.*

nar·cis·sus (när sĭs′əs), *n.*, *pl.* **-cissuses, -cissi** (-sĭs′ī). any of certain bulbous plants bearing showy flowers with a cup-shaped corona, including the jonquil and daffodil.

Nar·cis·sus (när sĭs′əs), *n.* *Gk. Legend.* a beautiful youth who fell in love with his own image in water, pined away, and was metamorphosed into the narcissus.

nar·co·sis (när kō′sĭs), *n.* a state of sleep or drowsiness.

nar·co·syn·the·sis (när′kō sĭn′thə sĭs), *n.* a treatment for psychiatric disturbances which uses narcotics.

nar·cot·ic (när kŏt′ĭk), *adj.* **1.** having the power to produce narcosis, as a drug. **2.** pertaining to narcosis or narcotics. —*n.* **3.** any of a class of substances that blunt the senses, relieving pain, etc., and inducing sleep, often used habitually to satisfy morbid appetite. **4.** an individual who uses narcotics habitually.

nard (närd), *n.* **1.** an aromatic Himalayan plant: the source of an ointment used by the ancients. **2.** the ointment.

nar·es (nâr′ēz), *n.pl.*, *sing.* **naris** (nâr′ĭs). *Anat.* the nostrils or the nasal passages.

nar·ghi·le (när′gə lĭ), *n.* an Oriental tobacco pipe in which the smoke is first drawn through water. Also, **nar′gi·le.**

Nar·ra·gan·sett Bay (năr′ə găn′sĭt), an inlet of the Atlantic in E Rhode Island. 28 mi. long.

nar·rate (nă rāt′, năr′āt), *v.t.*, *v.i.*, **-rated, -rating.** to give an account of (events, etc.). —**nar·ra′tor, nar·rat′er**, *n.*

nar·ra·tion (nă rā′shən), *n.* **1.** an account or story. **2.** act or process of narrating. **3.** words or matter narrating something.

nar·ra·tive (năr′ə tĭv), *n.* **1.** a story of events, experiences, or the like. —*adj.* **2.** that narrates. **3.** of or pertaining to narration. —**nar′ra·tive·ly**, *adv.*

nar·row (năr′ō), *adj.* **1.** not broad or wide. **2.** limited in extent or space. **3.** limited in scope. **4.** lacking breadth of view. **5.** limited in amount; meager. **6.** straitened. **7.** barely sufficient or adequate. **8.** careful; minute. —*v.t.*, *v.i.* **9.** to make or become narrower. **10.** to limit or restrict. —*n.* **11.** a narrow part, place, or thing. **12.** (*pl.*) a narrow part of a strait, river, etc. —**nar′row·ly**, *adv.* —**nar′row·ness**, *n.*

nar·row-gauge (năr′ō gāj′), *adj.* (of a railroad track) having less than 56½ inches between rails.

nar·row-mind·ed (năr′ō mīn′dĭd), *adj.* having or showing a prejudiced mind, as persons, opinions, etc. —**nar′row-mind′ed·ly**, *adv.* —**nar′row-mind′ed·ness**, *n.*

nar·whal (när′wəl), *n.* an arctic cetacean, the male of which has a long, straight, spirally twisted tusk extending forward from the upper jaw.

na·sal (nā′zəl), *adj.* **1.** of or pertaining to the nose. **2.** *Phonet.* with the voice issuing through the nose, either partly or entirely. —*n.* **3.** *Phonet.* a nasal speech sound. —**na·sal·i·ty** (nā zăl′ə tĭ), *n.* —**na′sal·ly**, *adv.*

nas·cent (năs′ənt, nā′sənt), *adj.* beginning to exist or develop. —**nas′cen·cy**, *n.*

nascent state, *Chem.* the condition of an element at the instant it is set free from a combination in which it has previously existed.

Nash·u·a (năsh′ŏŏ ə), *n.* a city in S New Hampshire. 32,927.

Nash·ville (năsh′vĭl), *n.* the capital of Tennessee, in the central part. 167,402.

Nas·sau (năs′ô), *n.* a seaport in and the capital of the Bahama Islands. 29,391.

na·stur·tium (nă stûr′shəm, nə-), *n.* any of certain garden plants much cultivated for their showy flowers of yellow, red, and other colors, and for their fruit, which is pickled and used like capers.

nas·ty (năs′tĭ), *adj.*, **-tier, -tiest.** **1.** physically filthy; disgustingly unclean. **2.** offensive; nauseous. **3.** offensive; objectionable. **4.** obscene. **5.** vicious; spiteful. **6.** bad to deal with, encounter, undergo, etc. **7.** very unpleasant. —**nas′ti·ly**, *adv.* —**nas′ti·ness**, *n.*

nat., **1.** national. **2.** native. **3.** natural.

na·tal (nā′təl), *adj.* **1.** of one's birth. **2.** presiding over or affecting one at birth.

Na·tal (nə täl′, -tăl′ for 1; nä täl′, -tôl′ for 2), *n.* **1.** a province of the Union of South Africa, in the E part. 2,182,733 pop.; 35,284 sq. mi. *Cap.:* Pietermaritzburg. **2.** a seaport in E Brazil. 51,896.

na·tant (nā′tənt), *adj.* swimming; floating.

na·ta·to·ri·al (nā′tə tōr′ĭ əl), *adj.* pertaining to, adapted for, or characterized by swimming. Also, **na′ta·to′ry.**

na·ta·to·ri·um (nā/tə tōr/Y əm), *n., pl.* **-to-riums, -toria** (-tōr/Y ə). a swimming pool.

Natch·ez (năch/Yz), *n.* a city in SW Mississippi: a port on the Mississippi. 15,296.

nathe·less (nāth/lĭs, năth/-), *Archaic.* —*adv.* 1. nevertheless. —*prep.* 2. notwithstanding.

na·tion (nā/shən), *n.* 1. an aggregation of persons of the same ethnic family, speaking the same language or cognate languages. 2. a body of people associated with a particular territory who are sufficiently conscious of their unity to seek or to possess a government peculiarly their own.

na·tion·al (năsh/ən əl), *adj.* 1. of, pertaining to, or maintained by a nation as an organized whole. 2. common to the whole people of a country. 3. patriotic. —*n.* 4. a citizen or subject of a particular nation, entitled to its protection. —**na/tion·al·ly,** *adv.*

national bank, 1. a governmentally owned and administered bank. 2. *U.S.* a bank chartered by the national government and formerly authorized to issue notes that served as money.

na·tion·al·ism (năsh/ən ə lYz/əm), *n.* 1. national spirit or aspirations. 2. devotion to the interests of one's own nation. 3. desire for national advancement or independence. —**na/tion·al·ist,** *n., adj.* —**na/tion·al·is/tic,** *adj.*

na·tion·al·i·ty (năsh/ə năl/ə tĭ), *n., pl.* **-ties.** 1. the quality of membership in a particular nation. 2. relationship of property, etc., to a particular nation. 3. national independence. 4. a nation or people.

na·tion·al·ize (năsh/ən ə līz/), *v.t.,* **-ized, -izing.** 1. to bring under the control or ownership of a nation. 2. to make nation-wide. —**na/tion·al·i·za/tion,** *n.*

na·tion-wide (nā/shən wīd/), *adj.* extending throughout the nation.

na·tive (nā/tĭv), *adj.* 1. being the place in which one was born or a thing came into being. 2. belonging to a person or thing by birth or nature; inborn. 3. belonging by birth to a people regarded as natives. 4. indigenous in origin, growth, etc. 5. of, pertaining to, or characteristic of natives. 6. under the rule of natives. 7. occupied by natives. 8. belonging or pertaining to one by reason of one's birthplace or nationality. 9. born in a particular place or country. 10. remaining in a natural state. —*n.* 11. one of the original inhabitants of a place or country, esp. as distinguished from strangers, foreigners, colonizers, etc. 12. one born in a particular place or country. 13. an animal or plant indigenous to a particular region. —**na/tive·ly,** *adv.*

na·tiv·i·ty (nā tĭv/ə tĭ, nə-), *n., pl.* **-ties.** 1. birth. 2. (*cap.*) the birth of Christ. 3. (*cap.*) Christmas.

natl., national.

nat·ty (năt/Y), *adj.,* **-tier, -tiest.** neatly smart in dress or appearance; spruce; trim. —**nat/ti·ly,** *adv.* —**nat/ti·ness,** *n.*

nat·u·ral (năch/ə rəl), *adj.* 1. existing in or formed by nature; not artificial. 2. of or pertaining to nature or the created universe. 3. in a state of nature; uncultivated. 4. growing spontaneously. 5. having a real or physical existence. 6. of, pertaining to, or proper to the nature or essential constitution. 7. proper to the circumstances of the case. 8. free from affectation or constraint. 9. consonant with the nature or character of. 10. in accordance with the nature of things. 11. happening in the ordinary course of things, without the intervention of accident, violence, etc. 12. illegitimate. 13. based on what is learned from nature, rather than on revelation. 14. being such by nature. 15. *Music.* a. neither sharp nor flat. b. changed in pitch by the sign ♮. —*n.* 16. one naturally deficient in intellect. 17. *Colloq.* a thing or a person that is naturally or by nature notably satisfactory or a success. 18. *Music.* a. a white key on the piano, etc. b. the sign ♮, placed before a note canceling the effect of a previous sharp or flat. c. a note affected by a ♮, or a tone thus represented. —**nat/u·ral·ly,** *adv.* —**nat/u·ral·ness,** *n.*

natural gas, combustible gas formed naturally in the earth, as in regions yielding petroleum: used as a fuel, etc.

natural history, the science or study dealing with all objects in nature.

nat·u·ral·ism (năch/ə rə lYz/əm), *n.* 1. (in art or literature) an intention on the part of the artist to represent objects as nearly as possible under their natural and everyday forms. 2. action arising from or based on natural instincts and desires alone. 3. *Philos.* a. the view of the world

which takes account only of natural elements and forces, excluding the supernatural or spiritual. b. the belief that all phenomena are covered by laws of science. 4. adherence to what is natural. —**nat/u·ral·is/tic,** *adj.*

nat·u·ral·ist (năch/ə rəl Yst), *n.* 1. one who is versed in or devoted to natural history. 2. an adherent of naturalism.

nat·u·ral·ize (năch/ə rə līz/), *v.,* **-ized, -izing.** —*v.t.* 1. to confer the rights and privileges of citizenship upon. 2. to introduce (animals or plants) into a region and cause to flourish as if native. 3. to introduce or adopt (foreign words, etc.) into a country. —*v.i.* 4. to become naturalized. —**nat/u·ral·i·za/tion,** *n.*

natural science, science dealing with objects in nature, as distinguished from moral science, abstract mathematics, etc.

natural selection, the elimination of the unfit and the survival of the fit in the struggle for existence, depending upon the adjustment of an organism to a specific environment.

na·ture (nā/chər), *n.* 1. the particular combination of qualities belonging to a person or thing by birth or constitution. 2. the instincts or tendencies directing conduct. 3. character, kind, or sort. 4. a person of a particular character. 5. the material world, esp. as surrounding man and existing independently of his activities. 6. the universe. 7. the sum total of the forces at work throughout the universe. 8. reality.

naught (nôt), *n.* 1. a cipher (0); zero. 2. *Now Archaic or Literary.* nothing. 3. destruction, ruin, or complete failure.

naugh·ty (nô/tĭ), *adj.,* **-tier, -tiest.** 1. disobedient; mischievous. 2. improper; obscene. —**naugh/ti·ly,** *adv.* —**naugh/ti·ness,** *n.*

nau·sea (nô/shə, -shY ə, -sY ə), *n.* 1. a sensation of impending vomiting. 2. sea sickness. 3. extreme disgust.

nau·se·ate (nô/shĭ āt/, -sĭ-), *v.t., v.i.,* **-ated, -ating.** to affect or become affected with nausea. —**nau/se·a/tion,** *n.*

nau·seous (nô/shəs, -shĭ əs), *adj.* 1. causing nausea. 2. disgusting; loathsome. —**nau/seous·ly,** *adv.* —**nau/seous·ness,** *n.*

naut., nautical.

nautch (nôch), *n.* an East Indian exhibition by professional dancing girls (**nautch girls**).

nau·ti·cal (nô/tə kəl), *adj.* of or pertaining to seamen, ships, or navigation. —**nau/ti·cal·ly,** *adv.*

nau·ti·lus (nô/tə ləs), *n., pl.* **-luses, -li** (-lī/). any of certain cephalopods having a spiral, chambered shell with pearly septa.

nav., 1. naval. 2. navigation.

Nav·a·ho (năv/ə hō/), *n., pl.* **-hos, -hoes.** a member of an important tribe of North American Indians located in New Mexico and Arizona, and now constituting the largest tribal group in the U.S. Also, **Nav·a·jo** (năv/ə hō/).

na·val (nā/vəl), *adj.* 1. of or pertaining to ships, esp. ships of war. 2. belonging to, pertaining to, or connected with a navy. 3. possessing a navy.

Na·varre (nə vär/), *n.* a former kingdom in SW France and N Spain.

nave (nāv), *n.* the main body, or middle part, lengthwise, of a church, flanked by the aisles and extending typically from the entrance to the apse or chancel.

na·vel (nā/vəl), *n.* 1. a pit in the middle of the surface of the belly. 2. the central point or middle of any thing or place.

navel orange, a kind of orange having at the apex a navellike formation containing a small secondary fruit.

nav·i·cert (năv/ə sûrt/), *n.* a British consulate certificate, specifying the character of a ship's cargo, etc.

navig., navigation.

nav·i·ga·ble (năv/ə gə bəl), *adj.* that may be navigated, as waters, or vessels or aircraft. —**nav/i·ga·bil/i·ty,** *n.* —**nav/i·ga·bly,** *adv.*

nav·i·gate (năv/ə gāt/), *v.t., v.i.,* **-gated, -gating.** 1. to traverse (the sea, a river, etc.) in a vessel, or (the air) in an aircraft. 2. to direct or manage (a ship or an aircraft) on its course. 3. to pass over (the sea, etc.), as a ship does.

nav·i·ga·tion (năv/ə gā/shən), *n.* 1. act or process of navigating. 2. the art or science of directing the course of a ship or aircraft. —**nav/-i·ga/tion·al,** *adj.*

nav·i·ga·tor (năv/ə gā/tər), *n.* 1. one who navigates. 2. one who conducts explorations by sea.

na·vy (nā′vĭ), *n., pl.* **-vies.** **1.** the whole body of warships and auxiliaries belonging to a country or ruler. **2.** the department of government charged with their management. **3.** Also, **navy blue.** a dark blue.

navy bean, the common small white bean, used for food as dry beans.

navy yard, a government dockyard where naval vessels are built, repaired, and fitted out, and naval stores and munitions of war are laid up.

na·wab (nə wôb′), *n.* a viceroy under the former Mogul empire in India.

nay (nā), *adv.* **1.** no. **2.** also, and not only so, but. —*n.* **3.** a denial or refusal. **4.** a negative vote or voter.

Naz·a·rene (năz′ə rēn′), *n.* **1.** a native or inhabitant of Nazareth, as Jesus Christ (**the Nazarene**). **2.** a Christian. —*adj.* **3.** of or pertaining to Nazareth or the Nazarenes.

Naz·a·reth (năz′ə rəth, -rĭth), *n.* a town in N Israel: childhood home of Jesus. 14,200.

Na·zi (nä′tsĭ, nät′sĭ), *n., pl.* **-zis,** *adj.* —*n.* **1.** a member of the National Socialist German Workers party of Germany, which in 1933, under Adolf Hitler, obtained political control of the country, suppressing all opposition and establishing a dictatorship on the principles of one-party governmental control, belief in the supremacy of Hitler as Führer, anti-Semitism, and the establishment of Germany by superior force as a dominant world power. **2.** one who holds similar views elsewhere. —*adj.* **3.** of or pertaining to the Nazis.

Na·zism (nä′tsĭz əm, nät′sĭz-), *n.* the principles or methods of the Nazis. Also, **Na·zi·ism** (nä′tsĭ ĭz′əm, nät′sĭ-).

Nb, *Chem.* niobium.

N. B., **1.** New Brunswick. **2.** nota bene.

N. C., North Carolina.

N. C. O., Noncommissioned Officer.

Nd, *Chem.* neodymium.

n. d., no date.

N. Dak., North Dakota. Also, **N. D.**

Ne, *Chem.* neon.

NE, **1.** northeast. **2.** northeastern. Also, **n.e., N.E.**

Ne·an·der·thal (nĭ ăn′dər täl′), *adj. Anthropol.* of or pertaining to the **Neanderthal man,** the species of primeval man widespread in Europe in the paleolithic period.

neap (nēp), *adj.* **1.** designating those tides, midway between spring tides, which attain the least height. —*n.* **2.** a neap tide.

Ne·a·pol·i·tan (nē′ə pŏl′ə tən), *adj.* **1.** of or pertaining to Naples. —*n.* **2.** a native or inhabitant of Naples.

near (nĭr), *adv.* **1.** close. **2.** at, within, or to a short distance. **3.** close at hand in time. **4.** close in relation, similarity, etc. —*adj.* **5.** being close by. **6.** less distant. **7.** short or direct. **8.** close in time. **9.** closely related or connected. **10.** intimate or familiar. **11.** narrow. —*prep.* **12.** at, within, or to a short distance, or no great distance, from. **13.** close upon in time. **14.** close upon (a condition, etc.). **15.** close to in similarity, resemblance, etc. **16.** close to (doing something). —*v.t., v.i.* **17.** to come or draw near (to); approach. —**near′ness,** *n.*

near·by (nĭr′bī′), *adj.* close at hand; not far off; adjacent; neighboring.

Near East, **1.** *U.S.* the Balkan States, the Levant, and the countries of SW Asia. **2.** *Brit.* the Balkan States.

near·ly (nĭr′lĭ), *adv.* **1.** all but; almost. **2.** with close approximation. **3.** with close agreement or resemblance. **4.** intimately.

near-sight·ed (nĭr′sī′tĭd), *adj.* seeing distinctly at a short distance only; myopic. —**near′-sight′ed·ly,** *adv.* —**near′-sight′ed·ness,** *n.*

neat (nēt), *adj.* **1.** in a pleasingly orderly condition. **2.** habitually orderly in appearance, etc. **3.** of a simple, pleasing appearance. **4.** cleverly effective. **5.** clever, dexterous, or apt. **6.** unadulterated or undiluted, as liquors. **7.** net. —**neat′ly,** *adv.* —**neat′ness,** *n.*

neath (nēth, nēth), *prep. Poetic or Scot.* beneath. Also, **'neath.**

neat·herd (nēt′hûrd′), *n.* a cowherd.

neb (nĕb), *n.* a bill or beak, as of a bird.

Ne·bras·ka (nə brăs′kə), *n.* a State in the central United States. 1,275,713 pop.; 77,237 sq. mi. *Cap.*: Lincoln. *Abbr.*: Nebr. or Neb. —**Ne·bras′kan,** *adj., n.*

Neb·u·chad·nez·zar (nĕb′yŏŏ kəd nĕz′ər, nĕb′ə-), *n.* a king of Babylonia, 604?–561? B.C.,

and conqueror of Jerusalem. Also, **Neb·u·chad·rez·zar** (nĕb′yŏŏ kəd rĕz′ər, nĕb′ə-).

neb·u·la (nĕb′yə lə), *n., pl.* **-lae** (-lē′), **-las.** *Astron.* a cloudlike, luminous mass composed of gaseous matter or stars far beyond the solar system. —**neb′u·lar,** *adj.*

nebular hypothesis, *Astron.* the theory that the solar system has been evolved from a mass of nebulous matter.

neb·u·lous (nĕb′yə ləs), *adj.* **1.** hazy, vague, indistinct, or confused. **2.** cloudy or cloudlike. **3.** nebular. —**neb′u·lous·ly,** *adv.* —**neb′u·lous·ness,** *n.*

nec·es·sar·i·ly (nĕs′ə sĕr′ə lĭ), *adv.* **1.** by or of necessity. **2.** as a necessary result.

nec·es·sar·y (nĕs′ə sĕr′ĭ), *adj., n., pl.* **-saries.** —*adj.* **1.** that cannot be dispensed with. **2.** happening or existing by necessity. **3.** acting or proceeding from compulsion. —*n.* **4.** something necessary, indispensable, or requisite. **5.** a privy or water closet.

ne·ces·si·tate (nə sĕs′ə tāt′), *v.t.* **-tated, -tating.** **1.** to make necessary. **2.** to compel, oblige, or force. —**ne·ces′si·ta′tion,** *n.*

ne·ces·si·tous (nə sĕs′ə təs), *adj.* needy; indigent. —**ne·ces′si·tous·ly,** *adv.*

ne·ces·si·ty (nə sĕs′ə tĭ), *n., pl.* **-ties.** **1.** something necessary or indispensable. **2.** fact of being necessary. **3.** an imperative requirement or need for something. **4.** state or fact of being necessary or inevitable. **5.** an unavoidable compulsion of doing something. **6.** need; poverty.

neck (nĕk), *n.* **1.** that part of an animal's body which is between the head and the trunk and connects these parts. **2.** the part of a garment covering or encircling the neck. **3.** the slender part of a bottle, retort, or any similar object. **4.** the longer slender part of a violin or the like, extending from the body to the head. **5.** a narrow strip of land, as an isthmus or a cape. —*v.i.* **6.** *U.S. Slang.* to play amorously.

neck·band (nĕk′bănd′), *n.* a band of cloth at the neck of a garment.

neck·cloth (nĕk′klôth′, -klŏth′), *n.* cravat.

neck·er·chief (nĕk′ər chĭf), *n.* a cloth worn round the neck by women or men.

neck·lace (nĕk′lĭs), *n.* an ornament of precious stones, beads, or the like, worn around the neck.

neck·piece (nĕk′pēs′), *n.* a scarf made of fur.

neck·tie (nĕk′tī′), *n.* a narrow band of cloth worn around the neck, commonly under a collar, and tied in front.

neck·wear (nĕk′wâr′), *n.* articles of dress worn round or at the neck.

ne·crol·o·gy (nĕ krŏl′ə jĭ), *n., pl.* **-gies.** **1.** an obituary notice. **2.** a list of persons who have died within a certain time.

nec·ro·man·cy (nĕk′rə măn′sĭ), *n.* **1.** magic; conjuration. **2.** the pretended art of divination through communication with the dead. —**nec′ro·man′cer,** *n.*

ne·crop·o·lis (nĕ krŏp′ə lĭs), *n., pl.* **-lises.** a cemetery, often of large size.

ne·cro·sis (nĕ krō′sĭs), *n.* death of a circumscribed piece of tissue or of an organ. —**ne·crot·ic** (nĕ krŏt′ĭk), *adj.*

nec·tar (nĕk′tər), *n.* **1.** *Bot.* the saccharine secretion of a plant, which attracts the insects or birds that pollinate the flower, collected by bees, in whose body it is elaborated into honey. **2.** the drink of the gods of classical mythology. **3.** any delicious drink.

nec·tar·ine (nĕk′tə rēn′, nĕk′tə rēn′), *n.* a kind of peach, having a skin without down.

nee (nā), *adj.* born. Also, **née.**

need (nēd), *n.* **1.** a case in which some necessity exists; requirement. **2.** urgent want. **3.** necessity arising from the circumstances of a case. **4.** a situation or time of difficulty. **5.** a condition marked by the lack of something requisite. **6.** extreme poverty. —*v.t.* **7.** to require. —*v.i.* **8.** to be necessary. **9.** to be under a necessity. —**need′er,** *n.*

need·ful (nēd′fəl), *adj.* necessary. —**need′ful·ly,** *adv.* —**need′ful·ness,** *n.*

nee·dle (nēd′l), *n., v.,* **-dled, -dling.** —*n.* **1.** a small, slender, pointed instrument with a hole for thread, used in sewing. **2.** a similar implement for use in knitting, crocheting, etc. **3.** *Med.* a slender, pointed, steel instrument used in sewing or piercing tissues. **4.** a small, slender, pointed instrument used to transmit vibratory motions, as from a phonograph record. **5.** anel-

needle. **6.** *Bot.* a needle-shaped leaf, as of a conifer. **7.** an obelisk. —*v.t.* **8.** to sew or pierce with a needle. **9.** to prod or goad. **10.** to tease or heckle.

needle point, canvas which has been embroidered in a certain manner.

need·less (nēd'lĭs), *adj.* not needed; unnecessary. —**need'less·ly,** *adv.* —**need'less·ness,** *n.*

nee·dle·work (nē'dəl wûrk'), *n.* the process or the product of working with a needle as in sewing or embroidery.

needs (nēdz), *adv.* of necessity; necessarily (usually fol. by *must*).

need·y (nē'dĭ), *adj.,* **needier, neediest.** in, or characterized by, need or want; very poor. —**need'i·ness,** *n.*

ne'er (nâr), *adv. Chiefly Poetic.* contraction of *never.*

ne'er-do-well (nâr'dōō wĕl'), *n.* **1.** a worthless person. —*adj.* **2.** worthless.

ne·far·i·ous (nĭ fâr'ĭ əs), *adj.* extremely wicked; iniquitous. —**ne·far'i·ous·ly,** *adv.*

neg., 1. negative. **2.** negatively.

ne·gate (nĭ gāt', nē'gāt), *v.t.,* **-gated, -gating.** to deny; nullify.

ne·ga·tion (nĭ gā'shən), *n.* **1.** act of denying. **2.** a denial. **3.** a negative thing.

neg·a·tive (nĕg'ə tĭv), *adj., n., v.,* **-tived, -tiving.** —*adj.* **1.** expressing or containing negation or denial. **2.** expressing refusal to do something. **3.** refusing consent. **4.** prohibitory. **5.** characterized by the absence of distinguishing qualities. **6.** *Math., Physics.* **a.** minus. **b.** measured or proceeding in the opposite direction to that which is considered as positive. **7.** *Bacteriol.* failing to show a positive result in a test for a specific disease caused by either bacteria or viruses. **8.** *Photog.* denoting an image in which the gradations of light and shade are represented in reverse. **9.** *Elect.* noting or pertaining to the kind of electricity developed on resin, amber, etc., when rubbed with flannel, or that present at the pole from which electrons leave an electric generator or battery, having an excess of electrons. **10.** *Chem.* (of an element or radical) tending to gain electrons and become negatively charged. —*n.* **11.** a negative statement, answer, word, etc. **12.** a refusal of assent. **13.** a veto. **14.** that side of a question which denies what the opposite side affirms. **15.** the negative form of statement. **16.** a negative quality or characteristic. **17.** *Math.* a negative quantity or symbol. **18.** *Photog.* a negative image, as on a film or plate, used chiefly for printing positive pictures. **19.** *Elect.* the negative plate or element in a voltaic cell. —*v.t.* **20.** to deny; contradict. **21.** to disprove. —**neg'a·tive·ly,** *adv.*

neg·a·tiv·ism (nĕg'ə tĭ vĭz'əm), *n.* negativistic behavior.

neg·a·tiv·is·tic (nĕg'ə tĭ vĭs'tĭk), *adj. Psychol.* marked by resistance to a stimulus.

neg·lect (nĭ glĕkt'), *v.t.* **1.** to pay no attention to; disregard. **2.** to be remiss in care for or treatment of. **3.** to omit (doing something), through indifference or carelessness. **4.** to fail to perform (duties, etc.). **5.** to fail to take or use. —*n.* **6.** disregard or negligence. —**neg·lect'er,** *n.*

neg·lect·ful (nĭ glĕkt'fəl), *adj.* disregardful; careless; negligent. —**neg·lect'ful·ly,** *adv.* —**neg·lect'ful·ness,** *n.*

neg·li·gee (nĕg'lə zhā', nĕg'lə zhā'), *n.* **1.** a woman's dressing gown or robe. **2.** easy, informal attire. Also, *French,* **né·gli·gé** (nĕ glē zhě').

neg·li·gent (nĕg'lə jənt), *adj.* guilty of or characterized by neglect, as of duty. —**neg'li·gent·ly,** *adv.* —**neg'li·gence,** *n.*

neg·li·gi·ble (nĕg'lə jə bəl), *adj.* that may be neglected or disregarded. —**neg'li·gi·bil'i·ty,** *n.* —**neg'li·gi·bly,** *adv.*

ne·go·ti·a·ble (nĭ gō'shĭ ə bəl, -shə bəl), *adj.* **1.** capable of being negotiated. **2.** (of bills, etc.) transferable by delivery. —**ne·go'ti·a·bil'i·ty,** *n.*

ne·go·ti·ate (nĭ gō'shĭ āt'), *v.,* **-ated, -ating.** —*v.i.* **1.** to treat with another or others, as in the preparation of a treaty. —*v.t.* **2.** to arrange for by discussion and settlement of terms. **3.** to conduct (an affair, etc.). **4.** *Colloq.* to clear or pass (an obstacle, etc.). **5.** to dispose of by sale or transfer. —**ne·go'ti·a'tion,** *n.* —**ne·go'ti·a'tor,** *n.*

Ne·gri·to (nĭ grē'tō), *n., pl.* **-tos, -toes.** a member of any of certain dwarfish Negroid peoples of SE Asia and of Africa.

Ne·gro (nē'grō), *n., pl.* **-groes,** *adj.* —*n.* **1.** a

member of the Negro race. **2.** a person having more or less Negro blood. —*adj.* **3.** of, denoting, or pertaining to the so-called "black" race of Africa and its descendants elsewhere, characterized by a brown-black complexion. —**Ne·gress** (nē'grĭs), *n. fem.* (often used derogatorily).

Ne·groid (nē'groid), *adj.* **1.** resembling, or akin to, the Negro race and presumably allied to it in origin. Included are African Negroes, Oceanic Negroes, and Negritos. —*n.* **2.** a person of a Negroid race.

Ne·he·mi·ah (nē'ə mī'ə), *n.* **1.** a Hebrew leader of the 5th century **B.C.** **2.** a book of the Old Testament. *Abbr.:* Neh.

Neh·ru (nâr'ōō), *n.* **Jawaharlal,** born 1889, prime minister of the Union of India since 1947.

neigh (nā), *v.i.* **1.** to utter the cry of a horse; whinny. —*n.* **2.** the cry of a horse; whinny.

neigh·bor (nā'bər), *n.* **1.** one who lives near another. **2.** a person or thing that is near another. —*adj.* **3.** living or situated near to another. —*v.t.* **4.** to be near to; adjoin; border on. Also, *Brit.,* **neigh'bour.** —**neigh'bor·ing,** *adj.*

neigh·bor·hood (nā'bər hŏŏd'), *n.* **1.** the region near or about some place or thing; vicinity. **2.** a district or locality. **3.** a number of persons living in a particular locality.

neigh·bor·ly (nā'bər lĭ), *adj.* of or befitting a neighbor; friendly. —**neigh'bor·li·ness,** *n.*

nei·ther (nē'thər or, *esp. Brit.,* nī'thər), *conj.* **1.** not either. **2.** nor yet. —*adj.* **3.** not either; not the one or the other.

Nel·son (nĕl'sən), *n.* **Viscount Horatio,** 1758–1805, British admiral.

nem·a·tode (nĕm'ə tōd'), *n.* any of certain elongated smooth worms of cylindrical shape, parasitic or free-living, as trichinae, etc.

Nem·e·sis (nĕm'ə sĭs), *n., pl.* **-ses** (-sēz'). **1.** the goddess of retribution or vengeance. **2.** (*l.c.*) an agent of retribution or punishment.

ne·o·clas·sic (nē'ō klăs'ĭk), *adj.* belonging to or pertaining to a revival of classic style, as in art or literature. Also, **ne·o·clas'si·cal.**

ne·o·dym·i·um (nē'ō dĭm'ĭ əm), *n. Chem.* a rare-earth, metallic, trivalent element. *Symbol:* Nd; *at. wt.:* 144.27; *at. no.:* 60; *sp. gr.:* 6.9 at 20°C.

ne·o·lith·ic (nē'ə lĭth'ĭk), *adj. Anthropol.* noting or pertaining to the later part of the Old World stone age, characterized by the use of highly finished or polished stone implements and by food raising.

ne·ol·o·gism (nĭ ŏl'ə jĭz'əm), *n.* **1.** a new word or phrase. **2.** the introduction or use of new words, or new senses of words. Also, **ne·ol·o·gy.**

ne·on (nē'ŏn), *n. Chem.* a chemically inert gaseous element: chiefly used in orange-red tubular electrical discharge lamps. *Symbol:* Ne; *at. wt.:* 20.183; *at. no.:* 10; *weight of one liter of the gas at* 0°C *and at* 760 *mm. pressure:* 0.9002 g.

ne·o·phyte (nē'ə fīt'), *n.* **1.** a converted heathen, etc. **2.** a beginner.

Ne·pal (nə pôl'), *n.* a kingdom in the Himalayas between N India and Tibet. ab. 5,600,000 pop.; ab. 54,000 sq. mi. *Cap.:* Katmandu.

neph·ew (nĕf'ū or, *esp. Brit.,* nĕv'ū), *n.* **1.** a son of one's brother or sister. **2.** a son of one's husband's or wife's brother or sister. **3.** (in euphemistic use) an illegitimate son of an ecclesiastic.

ne·phri·tis (nĭ frī'tĭs), *n. Pathol.* inflammation of the kidneys, esp. Bright's disease.

nep·o·tism (nĕp'ə tĭz'əm), *n.* patronage bestowed in consideration of family relationship and not of merit. —**nep'o·tist,** *n.*

Nep·tune (nĕp'tūn, -tōōn), *n.* **1.** *Rom. Myth.* the god of the sea. **2.** the sea or ocean. **3.** *Astron.* the eighth planet in order from the sun. Its mean distance from the sun is 2,793,500,000 miles.

nep·tu·ni·um (nĕp tū'nĭ əm, -tōō'-), *n. Chem.* a radioactive transuranic element, produced artificially by the neutron bombardment of U-238. It decays rapidly to plutonium and then to U-235. *Symbol:* Np; *at. no.:* 93; *at. wt.:* 239.

Ne·re·id (nĭr'ĭ ĭd), *n. Gk. Myth.* a sea nymph. Also, **ne're·id.**

Ne·ro (nĭr'ō), *n.* **A.D.** 37–68, Roman emperor, **A.D.** 54–68.

nerve (nûrv), *n., v.,* **nerved, nerving.** —*n.* **1.** one or more bundles of fibers, forming part of a system which conveys impulses of sensation, motion, etc., between the brain or spinal cord and other parts of the body. **2.** strength, vigor, or energy. **3.** firmness or courage under trying circumstances. **4.** (*pl.*) nervousness. **5. get on**

one's **nerves,** to irritate.   6. *Slang.* impertinent assurance.   7. *Bot.* a vein, as in a leaf.   —*v.t.* 8. to give strength, vigor, or courage to.

nerve·less (nûrv′lĭs), *adj.*   1. *Anat., Bot., etc.* without nerves.   2. lacking strength or vigor.   3. lacking firmness or courage; pusillanimous. —**nerve′less·ly,** *adv.*

nerv·ous (nûr′vəs), *adj.*   1. of or pertaining to the nerves.   2. having or containing nerves of sensation, etc.   3. affecting the nerves.   4. suffering from, characterized by, or proceeding from disordered nerves.   5. highly excitable.   6. unnaturally or acutely uneasy or apprehensive. —**nerv′ous·ly,** *adv.*   —**nerv′ous·ness,** *n.*

nervous system, *Anat., Zool.* the system of nerves and nerve centers in an animal.

nerv·y (nûr′vĭ), *adj.,* **nervier, nerviest.**   1. *U.S. Slang.* audacious; bold.   2. requiring nerve.   3. having or showing courage.   4. *Brit. Colloq.* nervous.

-ness, a suffix used to form, from adjectives and participles, nouns denoting quality or state (also often, by extension, something exemplifying a quality or state) as in *darkness, goodness.*

nest (nĕst), *n.*   1. a structure formed or a place used by a bird for incubation and the rearing of its young.   2. a place used by insects, fishes, turtles, rabbits, or the like, for depositing their eggs or young.   3. a number of birds or other animals inhabiting one nest.   4. a snug retreat.   5. an assemblage of things lying or set close together.   —*v.t.* 6. to settle or place in a nest.   7. to fit or place one within another.   —*v.i.* 8. to build or have a nest.   9. to settle in a nest.   10. to search for nests.

nest egg,   1. an egg left in a nest to induce a hen to continue laying eggs there.   2. money saved, as for emergencies.

nes·tle (nĕs′əl), *v.,* **-tled, -tling.**   —*v.i.* 1. to lie close and snug; cuddle.   2. to lie in a sheltered or pleasant situation.   —*v.t.* 3. to put or press confidingly or affectionately.   —**nes′tler,** *n.*

nest·ling (nĕst′lĭng, nĕs′lĭng), *n.*   1. a young bird in the nest.   2. a young child.

Nes·tor (nĕs′tər), *n.   Gk. Legend.* the wisest and oldest of the Greeks in the Trojan War.

net[1] (nĕt), *n., v.,* **netted, netting.**   —*n.* 1. a lacelike fabric with a uniform mesh of cotton, silk, rayon, or nylon.   2. a bag or other contrivance of strong thread or cord wrought into an open, meshed fabric, for catching fish, birds, or other animals.   3. *Tennis, etc.* a ball that hits the net.   —*v.t.* 4. to cover, screen, or enclose with a net or netting.   5. to take with a net.   6. to catch or ensnare.   7. *Tennis, etc.* to hit (the ball) into the net.

net[2] (nĕt), *adj., n., v.,* **netted, netting.**   —*adj.* 1. exclusive of deductions, as for charges, expenses, loss, discount, etc.   2. sold at net prices.   —*n.* 3. net income, profits, or the like.   —*v.t.* 4. to gain or produce as clear profit.

neth·er (nĕth′ər), *adj.*   1. lying, or conceived as lying, beneath the earth's surface; infernal.   2. lower or under.

Neth·er·lands (nĕth′ər ləndz), *n.pl.*   **The,** a kingdom in W Europe, bordering on the North Sea, Germany, and Belgium. 9,630,000 pop.; 13,-433 sq. mi. *Capitals:* Amsterdam *and* The Hague.

Netherlands Indies, Dutch East Indies.

neth·er·most (nĕth′ər mōst′, -məst), *adj.* lowest.

nether world,   1. hell.   2. the afterworld.

net·ting (nĕt′ĭng), *n.* any of various kinds of net fabric.

net·tle (nĕt′əl), *n., v.,* **-tled, -tling.**   —*n.* 1. any of certain plants armed with stinging hairs.   —*v.t.* 2. to irritate, provoke, or vex.   3. to sting as a nettle does.

net·work (nĕt′wûrk′), *n.*   1. any netlike combination of filaments, lines, veins, passages, or the like.   2. a net.   3. *Radio.* a group of transmitting stations linked by wire so that the same program can be broadcast by all.

neu·ral (nyŏŏr′əl, nŏŏr′-), *adj.* of or pertaining to a nerve or the nervous system.

neu·ral·gia (nyŏŏ răl′jə, nŏŏ-), *n.   Pathol.* sharp and paroxysmal pain along the course of a nerve.   —**neu·ral′gic,** *adj.*

neu·ras·the·ni·a (nyŏŏr′əs thē′nĭ ə, nŏŏr′-), *n. Pathol.* nervous debility or exhaustion, as from overwork or prolonged mental strain.   —**neu·ras·then·ic** (nyŏŏr′əs thĕn′ĭk, nŏŏr′-), *adj., n.*

neu·ri·tis (nyŏŏ rī′tĭs, nŏŏ-), *n.   Pathol.* 1. inflammation of a nerve.   2. continuous pain in a nerve associated with its paralysis and sensory disturbances.   —**neu·rit·ic** (nyŏŏ rĭt′ĭk, nŏŏ-), *adj.*

neu·rol·o·gy (nyŏŏ rŏl′ə jĭ, nŏŏ-), *n.* the science of the nerves or the nervous system, esp. the diseases thereof.   —**neu·ro·log·i·cal** (nyŏŏr′ ə lŏj′ə kəl, nŏŏr′-), *adj.*   —**neu·rol′o·gist,** *n.*

neu·ron (nyŏŏr′ŏn, nŏŏr′-), *n.* a nerve cell. Also, **neu·rone** (nyŏŏr′ōn, nŏŏr′-).

neu·ro·psy·chi·a·try (nyŏŏr′ō sī kī′ə trĭ, nŏŏr′-), *n.* the branch of medicine dealing with diseases involving the mind and nervous system. —**neu·ro·psy·chi·at·ric** (nyŏŏr′ō sī′kĭ ăt′rĭk, nŏŏr′-), *adj.*

neu·rop·ter·ous (nyŏŏ rŏp′tər əs, nŏŏ-), *adj.* belonging to an order of insects characterized by two pairs of membranous wings with netlike venation.

neu·ro·sis (nyŏŏ rō′sĭs, nŏŏ-), *n., pl.* **-ses** (-sēz). psychoneurosis.

neu·rot·ic (nyŏŏ rŏt′ĭk, nŏŏ-), *adj.*   1. having a psychoneurosis.   2. pertaining to the nerves or to nervous disease.   —*n.* 3. a person affected with psychoneurosis.

neut., neuter.

neu·ter (nū′tər, nōō′-), *adj.*   1. *Gram.* denoting or pertaining to one of the genders in various languages, so termed because few if any nouns denoting males or females belong to it.   2. *Zool.* having imperfectly developed sexual organs, as the workers among bees and ants.   3. *Bot.* having neither stamens nor pistils; asexual.   —*n.* 4. *Gram.* a. the neuter gender.   b. a noun of that gender.   5. an animal made sterile by castration.   6. a neuter insect.   7. *Bot.* a plant with neither stamens nor pistils.

neu·tral (nū′trəl, nōō′-), *adj.*   1. refraining from taking part in a controversy or war between others.   2. of no particular kind, color, characteristics, etc.   3. gray; achromatic.   4. *Biol.* neuter.   5. *Chem.* exhibiting neither acid nor alkaline qualities.   6. *Elect., Magnetism.* neither positive nor negative.   —*n.* 7. a person or a state that remains neutral, as in a war.   8. a citizen of a neutral nation.   9. *Mach.* the position or state of disengaged gears or other interconnecting parts.   —**neu′tral·ly,** *adv.*

neu·tral·i·ty (nū trăl′ə tĭ, nōō-), *n.*   1. the state or status of being neutral.   2. the attitude or status of a nation which does not participate in a war between other nations.

neu·tral·ize (nū′trə līz′, nōō′-), *v.t.,* **-ized, -izing.**   1. to make neutral.   2. to render ineffective; counteract.   3. *Mil.* to put out of action or make incapable of action.   4. to declare neutral.   5. *Chem.* to render inert the peculiar properties of.   6. *Elect.* to render electrically neutral.   —**neu′-tral·i·za′tion,** *n.*   —**neu′tral·iz′er,** *n.*

neu·tron (nū′trŏn, nōō′-), *n.   Physics.* a neutral particle with approximately the same mass as a proton.

Ne·vad·a (nə văd′ə, -vä′də), *n.* a State in the W United States. 135,414 pop.; 110,540 sq. mi. *Cap.:* Carson City. *Abbr.:* **Nev.**   —**Ne·vad′an,** *adj., n.*

nev·er (nĕv′ər), *adv.*   1. not ever; at no time.   2. not at all.   3. to no extent.

nev·er·more (nĕv′ər mōr′), *adv.* never again.

nev·er·the·less (nĕv′ər thə lĕs′), *adv.* none the less; notwithstanding; however.

new (nū, nōō), *adj.*   1. of recent origin or production.   2. of a kind now existing or appearing for the first time; novel.   3. having but lately or but now come into knowledge.   4. unfamiliar or strange.   5. having but lately come to a place, position, etc.   6. unaccustomed.   7. further; additional.   8. fresh or unused.   9. being the later or latest of two or more things of the same kind. —*adv.* 10. recently or lately.   11. freshly; anew or afresh.   —*n.* 12. something new.   —**new′-ness,** *n.*

New·ark (nū′ərk, nōō′-), *n.*   1. a city in NE New Jersey. 429,760.   2. a city in central Ohio. 31,487.

New Bed·ford (bĕd′fərd), a seaport in SE Massachusetts. 110,341.

new·born (nū′bôrn′, nōō′-), *adj.*   1. recently or only just born.   2. born anew; reborn.

New Britain,   1. a city in central Connecticut. 68,685.   2. an island in the S Pacific, NE of New Guinea. 90,349 pop.; ab. 14,600 sq. mi. *Cap.:* Rabaul.

New Bruns·wick (brŭnz′wĭk),   1. a province in SE Canada, E of Maine. 457,401 pop.; 27,985 sq. mi. *Cap.:* Fredericton.   2. a city in central New Jersey. 33,180.

New·burgh (nū′bûrg, nŏŏ′-), *n.* a city in SE New York, on the Hudson. 31,883.

New Cal·e·do·ni·a (kăl′ə dō′nĭ ə, -dōn′yə), **1.** an island in the S Pacific, ab. 800 mi. E of Australia. 42,389 pop.; 6224 sq. mi. **2.** a French colony comprising this island and other small islands: formerly a penal colony. 53,000 pop.; 7200 sq. mi. *Cap.:* Nouméa.

New·cas·tle (nū′kăs′əl, -käs′əl, nŏŏ′-), *n.* **1.** Also, **Newcastle-upon-Tyne** (-tīn). a seaport in NE England. 284,750. **2.** a seaport in SE Australia. 104,485.

New Castle, a city in W Pennsylvania. 47,638.

new·com·er (nū′kŭm′ər, nŏŏ′-), *n.* one who has newly come; a new arrival.

New Deal, 1. the principles of the progressive wing of the Democratic party, esp. those advocated under the leadership of President Franklin D. Roosevelt. **2.** the Roosevelt administration. —**New Dealer.**

New Delhi, a city in N India: the capital of the Union of India. 93,733.

new·el (nū′əl, nŏŏ′-), *n.* a post at the head or foot of a stair, supporting the handrail.

New England, six States in the NE United States: Connecticut, Massachusetts, Rhode Island, Vermont, New Hampshire, and Maine. —**New Englander.**

new·fan·gled (nū′făng′gəld, nŏŏ′-), *adj.* **1.** of a new kind. **2.** fond of novelty.

New·found·land (nū′fənd lănd′, nŏŏ′- for 1; nū found′lənd, nŏŏ- for 2), *n.* **1.** a large island in E Canada: became a Canadian province on March 31, 1949. 312,889 pop.; 42,734 sq. mi. **2.** one of a breed of large, shaggy dogs, orig. from Newfoundland, noted for their sagacity, docility, swimming powers, etc.

New Guin·ea (gĭn′Y), **1.** a large island N of Australia: divided into Dutch New Guinea and the recently merged Australian territories of Papua and New Guinea. ab. 900,000 pop.; ab. 316,000 sq. mi. **2. Territory of,** a territory under the trusteeship of Australia, including NE New Guinea, the Bismarck Archipelago, Bougainville, and other islands. 675,000 pop.; ab. 93,000 sq. mi.

New Hamp·shire (hămp′shər, -shĭr), a State in the NE United States. 516,735 pop.; 9304 sq. mi. *Cap.:* Concord. *Abbr.:* N.H.

New Ha·ven (hā′vən), a seaport in S Connecticut. 160,605.

New Heb·ri·des (hĕb′rə dēz′), an island group in the S Pacific, NE of Australia: under joint British and French administration. ab. 43,000 pop.; ab. 5700 sq. mi. *Cap.:* Vila.

New Jer·sey (jûr′zĭ), a State in the E United States, on the Atlantic coast. 4,304,216 pop.; 7836 sq. mi. *Cap.:* Trenton. *Abbr.:* N.J. —**New Jer·sey·ite** (jûr′zĭ ĭt′).

New London, a seaport in SE Connecticut. 30,456.

new·ly (nū′lY, nŏŏ′-), *adv.* **1.** recently; lately. **2.** anew or afresh. **3.** in a new manner or form.

New·man (nū′mən, nŏŏ′-), *n.* **John Henry,** 1801–90, British theologian and author.

New Mexico, a State in the SW United States. 528,997 pop.; 121,666 sq. mi. *Cap.:* Santa Fe. *Abbr.:* N. Mex. *or* N.M. —**New Mexican.**

New Or·le·ans (ôr′lY ənz; *older* ôr lēnz′), a seaport in SE Louisiana, on the Mississippi. 494,537.

New·port (nū′pôrt, nŏŏ′-), *n.* **1.** a city in N Kentucky, on the Ohio river. 30,631. **2.** a seaport and summer resort in SE Rhode Island. 30,532.

Newport News, a seaport in SE Virginia. 37,067.

New Ro·chelle (rō shĕl′, rə-), a city in SE New York, near New York City. 58,408.

news (nūz, nŏŏz), *n.pl.* (*now construed as sing.*) **1.** a report of any recent event, situation, etc. **2.** the report of events published in a newspaper.

news·boy (nūz′boi′, nŏŏz′-), *n.* a boy who sells or delivers newspapers.

news·cast (nūz′kăst′, -käst′, nŏŏz′-), *n.* a radio broadcast of news reports. —**news′cast′-er,** *n.*

news·let·ter (nūz′lĕt′ər, nŏŏz′-), *n.* an informal or confidential report and analysis of the news.

New South Wales, a state in SE Australia. 2,924,654 pop.; 309,433 sq. mi. *Cap.:* Sydney.

news·pa·per (nūz′pā′pər, nŏŏz′-, nŭs′-, nŏŏs′-), *n.* a printed publication issued at regular intervals and commonly containing news, comment, features, and advertisements.

news·print (nūz′prĭnt′, nŏŏz′-), *n.* paper used or made to print newspapers on.

news·reel (nūz′rēl′, nŏŏz′-), *n.* a short motion picture presenting current news events.

news·y (nū′zĭ, nŏŏ′-), *adj.*, **newsier, newsiest,** *n., pl.* **newsies.** *Colloq.* —*adj.* **1.** full of news. —*n.* **2.** *U.S.* a newsboy.

newt (nūt, nŏŏt), *n.* any of certain salamanders of North America, Europe, and northern Asia.

New Testament, those books in the Bible which were produced by the early Christian church, and were added to the Jewish scriptures (Old Testament).

New·ton (nū′tən, nŏŏ′tən), *n.* **1. Sir Isaac,** 1642–1727, British scientist. **2.** a city in E Massachusetts, near Boston. 69,873.

New World, the Western Hemisphere.

new year, 1. the year approaching or newly begun. **2.** (*caps.*) the first day or days of a year. **3.** (*caps.*) New Year's Day.

New Year's Day, January 1. Also, *esp. U.S.,* **New Year's.**

New Year's Eve, the night of December 31, usually observed with merrymaking.

New York, 1. a State in the NE United States. 13,741,836 pop.; 49,576 sq. mi. *Cap.:* Albany. *Abbr.:* N.Y. **2.** Also, **New York City.** a seaport in SE New York at the mouth of the Hudson: the largest city in the Western Hemisphere. 7,454,995; **Greater New York,** 12,684,000. —**New York′er.**

New Zea·land (zē′lənd), a dominion of the British Commonwealth of Nations, consisting of islands (principally North and South Islands) in the S Pacific. 1,761,259 pop.; 103,416 sq. mi. *Cap.:* Wellington. —**New Zea′land·er.**

next (někst), *adj., superl.* of **nigh,** *adv.* —*adj.* **1.** immediately following in time, order, importance, etc. **2.** nearest in place or position. **3.** nearest in relationship or kinship. —*adv.* **4.** in the nearest place, time, importance, etc. **5.** on the first subsequent occasion.

next of kin, a person's nearest relative or relatives.

nex·us (něk′səs), *n., pl.* **nexus. 1.** a tie or link. **2.** a connected series.

N.G., 1. National Guard. **2.** no good. Also, **n.g.**

N.H., New Hampshire.

Ni, *Chem.* nickel.

N.I., Northern Ireland.

Ni·a·cin (nī′ə sən), *n. Trademark.* nicotinic acid.

Ni·ag·a·ra (nī ăg′rə, -ăg′ə rə), *n.* **1.** a river flowing between W New York and Ontario, Canada. 34 mi. **2.** Niagara Falls.

Niagara Falls, 1. the falls of the Niagara river: Horseshoe Falls, in Canada, 158 ft. high; 2600 ft. wide; American Falls, 167 ft. high; 1400 ft. wide. **2.** a city on the New York side of the falls. 78,029. **3.** a city on the Canadian side. 20,589.

nib (nĭb), *n., v.,* **nibbed, nibbing.** —*n.* **1.** a bill or beak, as of a bird. **2.** a penpoint. **3.** a point of anything. —*v.t.* **4.** to mend or trim the nib of.

nib·ble (nĭb′əl), *v.,* **-bled, -bling,** *n.* —*v.i., v.t.* **1.** to bite off small bits of (a thing). **2.** to eat by biting off small pieces. **3.** to bite slightly or gently. **4.** to bite (off, etc.) in small pieces. —*n.* **5.** a small morsel or bit. **6.** act or an instance of nibbling. —**nib′bler,** *n.*

Ni·be·lung·en·lied (nē′bə lŏŏng′ən lēt′), *n.* a medieval German epic about Siegfried's capture of the treasure of the Nibelungs.

nib·lick (nĭb′lĭk), *n. Golf.* a club with a short, rounded, flat iron head whose face slopes greatly from the vertical.

Nic·a·ra·gua (nĭk′ə rä′gwə), *n.* a republic in Central America. 1,082,000 pop.; 57,143 sq. mi. *Cap.:* Managua. —**Nic′a·ra′guan,** *adj., n.*

nice (nīs), *adj.,* **nicer, nicest. 1.** pleasing; agreeable; delightful. **2.** amiably pleasant; kind. **3.** characterized by or requiring great accuracy, precision, skill, or delicacy. **4.** requiring or showing tact or care. **5.** minutely accurate, as instruments. **6.** minute, fine, or subtle. **7.** having or showing delicate and accurate perception. **8.** refined as to manners, language, etc. **9.** suitable or proper. **10.** carefully neat as to dress, habits, etc. **11.** dainty or delicious, as food. **12.** dainty as to food. **13.** *Obs.* foolish. —**nice′ly,** *adv.* —**nice′ness,** *n.*

Nice (nēs), *n.* a city in SE France. 211,165.

ni·ce·ty (nī′sə tY), *n., pl.* **-ties. 1.** a delicate or fine point. **2.** a subtlety. **3.** (*often pl.*) a refinement, as of manners or living. **4.** quality of being nice. **5.** delicacy of character.

niche (nĭch), *n., v.,* **niched, niching.** —*n.* **1.** an ornamental recess in a wall, etc., as for a statue. **2.** a place or position suitable for a person or thing. —*v.t.* **3.** to place in a niche.

Nich·o·las (nĭk′ə ləs), *n.* **1. Saint, a.** Santa Claus. **b.** fl. 4th cent., bishop in Asia Minor: patron saint of Russia, protector of children. **2. II,** 1868–1918, czar of Russia, 1894–1917, executed in the Russian Bolshevik Revolution.

nick (nĭk), *n.* **1.** a notch, groove, or the like, cut into or existing in a thing. **2.** a hollow place produced in an edge or surface, as of a dish, by breaking. **3.** the precise moment or time of some occurrence. —*v.t.* **4.** to make a nick or nicks in. **5.** to hit, guess, catch, etc., exactly. **6.** *Brit. Slang.* to capture or arrest. **7.** to trick, cheat, or defraud.

Nick (nĭk), *n.* the devil (usually **Old Nick**).

nick·el (nĭk′əl), *n., v.,* **-eled, -eling** or (*esp. Brit.*) **-elled, -elling.** —*n.* **1.** *Chem.* a hard, silvery-white, ductile and malleable metallic element: much used in alloys, etc. *Symbol:* Ni; *at. wt.:* 58.6; *at. no.:* 28; *sp. gr.:* 8.9 at 20°C. **2.** *U.S.* a coin composed of or containing nickel, now a five-cent piece. —*v.t.* **3.** to cover or coat with nickel.

nick·el·o·de·on (nĭk′ə lō′dĭ ən), *n.* *U.S.* a place of amusement with motion pictures, etc., to which the price of admission is five cents.

nick·el-plate (nĭk′əl plāt′), *v.t.,* **-plated, -plating.** to coat with nickel by electroplating or otherwise.

nickel silver, German silver.

nick·nack (nĭk′năk′), *n.* knickknack.

nick·name (nĭk′nām′), *n., v.,* **-named, -naming.** —*n.* **1.** a name added to or substituted for the proper name of a person, place, etc., as in ridicule or familiarity. **2.** a familiar form of a proper name. —*v.t.* **3.** to give a nickname to.

nic·o·tine (nĭk′ə tēn′, -tĭn), *n.* a poisonous alkaloid, the active principle of tobacco, obtained as a colorless or nearly colorless, oily, acrid liquid. Also, **nic·o·tin** (nĭk′ə tĭn).

nic·o·tin·ic acid (nĭk′ə tĭn′ĭk), *Chem.* an acid derived from the oxidation of nicotine: found in fresh meat, yeast, etc. It is the component of the vitamin B complex which counteracts pellagra.

nic·ti·tate (nĭk′tə tāt′), *v.i.,* **-tated, -tating.** to wink. —**nic′ti·ta′tion,** *n.*

niece (nēs), *n.* **1.** a daughter of one's brother or sister. **2.** a daughter of one's husband's or wife's brother or sister. **3.** (in euphemistic use) an illegitimate daughter of an ecclesiastic.

Nie·tzsche (nē′chə), *n.* **Friedrich Wilhelm,** 1844–1900, German philosopher.

nif·ty (nĭf′tĭ), *adj.,* **-tier, -tiest,** *n., pl.* **-ties.** *U.S. Slang.* —*adj.* **1.** smart; stylish; fine. —*n.* **2.** a smart or clever remark.

Ni·ger (nī′jər), *n.* **1.** a river in W Africa, flowing through French West Africa and Nigeria into the Gulf of Guinea. ab. 2600 mi. **2.** a colony in NE French West Africa. 1,902,000 pop.; 499,540 sq. mi. *Cap.:* Niamey.

Ni·ge·ri·a (nī jĭr′ĭ ə), *n.* a British colony and protectorate in W Africa, including the Cameroons, under British trusteeship. 21,041,000 pop.; 372,599 sq. mi. *Cap.:* Lagos. —**Ni·ge′ri·an,** *adj., n.*

nig·gard (nĭg′ərd), *n.* **1.** an excessively stingy person. —*adj.* **2.** niggardly.

nig·gard·ly (nĭg′ərd lĭ), *adj.* **1.** parsimonious; stingy. **2.** meanly small or scanty. —*adv.* **3.** in the manner of a niggard. —**nig′gard·li·ness,** *n.*

nig·ger (nĭg′ər), *n.* *Offensive.* a Negro.

nigh (nī), *adv., adj.,* **nigher, nighest** or **next,** *v.* —*adv.* **1.** near in space, time, or relation. **2.** *Chiefly Archaic or Dial.* almost. —*adj.* **3.** being near. **4.** short or direct. —*v.i., v.t.* **5.** *Archaic.* to approach.

night (nīt), *n.* **1.** the interval of darkness between sunset and sunrise. **2.** nightfall. **3.** a state or time of obscurity, ignorance, etc.

night·cap (nīt′kăp′), *n.* **1.** a cap for the head, intended primarily to be worn in bed. **2.** *Colloq.* an alcoholic drink taken before going to bed.

night club, a restaurant, open until very late, furnishing food, drink, entertainment, etc.

night·dress (nīt′drĕs′), *n.* **1.** dress or clothing for wearing in bed. **2.** a nightgown.

night·fall (nīt′fôl′), *n.* the coming of night.

night·gown (nīt′goun′), *n.* **1.** a loose gown,

worn in bed by women or children. **2.** a man's nightshirt.

night·hawk (nīt′hôk′), *n.* **1.** any of certain long-winged American birds of the whippoorwill family, all more or less nocturnal. **2.** *Colloq.* one who is habitually up or prowling about at night.

night·in·gale (nī′tən gāl′, nī′tĭng-), *n.* a small Old World migratory bird of the thrush family, noted for the melodious song of the male given chiefly at night during the breeding season.

Nightingale, *n.* **Florence,** 1820–1910, British reformer of hospital nursing.

night letter, a telegram sent at a reduced charge because subject to the priority in transmission and delivery of regular telegrams.

night·ly (nīt′lĭ), *adj.* **1.** coming, occurring, appearing, or active at night. **2.** coming or occurring each night. —*adv.* **3.** at or by night. **4.** every night.

night·mare (nīt′mâr′), *n.* **1.** a condition or dream during sleep, marked by a feeling of acute fear, anxiety, or other painful emotion. **2.** a condition, thought, or experience suggestive of a nightmare in sleep.

night owl, *Colloq.* a person given to staying up late at night.

night·shade (nīt′shād′), *n.* any of a genus of plants including the **black nightshade,** the **deadly nightshade** (belladonna), and the **stinking nightshade** (henbane).

night·shirt (nīt′shûrt′), *n.* a loose knee-length garment worn in bed by men or boys.

night·time (nīt′tīm′), *n.* the time between evening and morning.

ni·hil·ism (nī′ə lĭz′əm), *n.* **1.** total disbelief in religion or moral principles and obligations, or in established laws and institutions. **2.** *Philos.* **a.** a belief that there is no objective basis of truth. **b.** an extreme form of skepticism, denying all real existence. **c.** nothingness. **3.** (*sometimes cap.*) the principles of a 19th century Russian revolutionary group, holding that existing social and political institutions must be destroyed in order to clear the way for a new state of society. —**ni′hil·ist,** *n.* —**ni′hil·is′tic,** *adj.*

nil (nĭl), *n.* nothing.

Nile (nīl), *n.* **1.** a river in E Africa, flowing N from Lake Victoria to the Mediterranean. 3473 mi. **2. Blue,** a tributary of the Nile, flowing from Ethiopia into the Nile at Khartoum. **3. White,** a part of the Nile above Khartoum.

nim·ble (nĭm′bəl), *adj.,* **-bler, -blest. 1.** quick and light in movement; agile. **2.** quick in apprehending, devising, etc. **3.** cleverly contrived. —**nim′ble·ness,** *n.* —**nim′bly,** *adv.*

nim·bus (nĭm′bəs), *n., pl.* **-bi** (-bī), **-buses. 1.** a bright cloud anciently conceived of as surrounding a deity of the classical mythology when appearing on earth. **2.** *Art.* a disk or other figure representing a radiance about the head of a divine or sacred personage, etc. **3.** *Obs.* a rain cloud.

Nim·rod (nĭm′rŏd), *n.* **1.** *Bible.* a "mighty hunter," the great-grandson of Noah. **2.** one expert in or devoted to hunting.

nin·com·poop (nĭn′kəm pōōp′), *n.* a fool or simpleton.

nine (nīn), *n.* **1.** a cardinal number, eight plus one. **2.** a symbol for this number, as 9 or IX or VIII. **3.** a set of nine persons or things. —*adj.* **4.** amounting to nine in number. —**nine′fold′,** *adj., adv.*

nine·pins (nīn′pĭnz′), *n.pl.* **1.** (*construed as sing.*) a game played with nine wooden pins at which a ball is bowled to knock them down. **2.** (*construed as pl.*) the pins used in this game. **3.** (*construed as sing.*) tenpins played without using a head pin.

nine·teen (nīn′tēn′), *n.* **1.** a cardinal number, ten plus nine. **2.** a symbol for this number, as 19 or XIX or XVIIII. —*adj.* **3.** amounting to nineteen in number. —**nine′teenth′,** *adj., n.*

nine·ty (nīn′tĭ), *n., pl.* **-ties,** *adj.* —*n.* **1.** a cardinal number, ten times nine. **2.** a symbol for this number, as 90 or XC or LXXXX. —*adj.* **3.** amounting to ninety in number. —**nine·ti·eth** (nīn′tĭ ĭth), *adj., n.*

Nin·e·veh (nĭn′ə və), *n.* the ancient capital of Assyria.

nin·ny (nĭn′ĭ), *n., pl.* **-nies.** a fool or simpleton.

ninth (nīnth), *adj.* **1.** next after the eighth. **2.** being one of nine equal parts. —*n.* **3.** a ninth part, esp. of one (¹⁄₉). **4.** the ninth member of a series. —**ninth′ly,** *adv.*

ni·o·bi·um (nī ō′bĭ əm), *n.* *Chem.* columbium.

Symbol: Nb —**ni·o·bic** (nī ō′bĭk, -ŏb′ĭk), **ni·o·bous** (nī ō′bəs), *adj.*

nip[1] (nĭp), *v.*, **nipped, nipping,** *n.* —*v.t.* **1.** to pinch or bite. **2.** to take off by pinching, biting, or snipping. **3.** to check in growth or development. **4.** to affect sharply and painfully or injuriously, as cold does. —*n.* **5.** act of nipping; a pinch. **6.** a sharp or biting remark. **7.** a biting quality, as in frosty air. **8.** sharp cold.

nip[2] (nĭp), *n., v.,* **nipped, nipping.** —*n.* **1.** a small drink of liquor; a sip. —*v.t., v.i.* **2.** to drink (liquor) in small sips, esp. repeatedly.

nip and tuck, *U.S.* (in a race or other contest) with one competitor equaling the speed or efforts of another.

nip·per (nĭp′ər), *n.* **1.** one that nips. **2.** (*usually pl.*) a device for nipping, as forceps. **3.** one of the large claws of a crustacean.

nip·ple (nĭp′əl), *n.* **1.** a protuberance of the mamma or breast where, in the female, the milk ducts discharge; teat. **2.** something resembling it, as the mouthpiece of a nursing bottle. **3.** a short piece of pipe with threads on each end, used for joining valves, etc.

Nip·pon (nĭ′pŏn′, nĭp′ŏn), *n.* Japanese name of Japan. —**Nip′pon·ese′,** *n., adj.*

nip·py (nĭp′ĭ), *adj.,* **-pier, -piest. 1.** sharp; biting. **2.** *Chiefly Brit. Colloq.* nimble.

nir·va·na (nĭr vä′nə, -văn′ə, nər-), *n.* **1.** (*often cap.*) *Buddhism.* **a.** the extinguishment of the restlessness and heat of one's emotions. **b.** the passionless peace of imperturbability, attained through the annihilation of disturbing desires. **2.** freedom from pain, worry, and the external world.

Ni·sei (nē′sā′), *n., pl.* **-sei.** a person of Japanese descent, born in the U.S. and loyal to it.

Nis·sen hut (nĭs′ən), a prefabricated shelter with the shape of a long, slightly flattened cylinder; Quonset hut.

nit (nĭt), *n.* **1.** the egg of a parasitic insect attached to a hair or fiber of clothing, particularly the egg of a louse. **2.** the insect while young.

ni·ter (nī′tər), *n.* **1.** nitrate of potassium, a white salt used in making gunpowder, etc.; saltpeter. **2.** nitrate of sodium, NaNO₃. Also, *esp. Brit.,* **ni′tre.**

ni·trate (nī′trāt), *n., v.,* **-trated, -trating.** —*n.* **1.** *Chem.* a salt or ester of nitric acid. **2.** fertilizer consisting of potassium nitrate or sodium nitrate. —*v.t.* **3.** to treat with nitric acid or a nitrate. **4.** to convert into a nitrate. —**ni·tra′tion,** *n.*

ni·tric (nī′trĭk), *adj.* **1.** *Chem.* containing nitrogen, usually in the pentavalent state. **2.** of or pertaining to niter.

nitric acid, a corrosive liquid, HNO₃, with powerful oxidizing properties.

ni·tri·fy (nī′trə fī′), *v.t.,* **-fied, -fying. 1.** to oxidize (ammonia compounds, etc.) to nitrites or nitrates, esp. by bacterial action. **2.** to impregnate (soil, etc.) with nitrates. **3.** to treat or combine with nitrogen or its compounds.

ni·tro·gen (nī′trə jən), *n. Chem.* a colorless, odorless, gaseous element: used in compounds, as fertilizer, in explosives, and in dyes. *Symbol:* N; *at. wt.:* 14.008; *at. no.:* 7. —**ni·trog·e·nous** (nī·trŏj′ə nəs), *adj.*

ni·tro·glyc·er·in (nī′trə glĭs′ər ĭn), *n.* a colorless, highly explosive oil, a principal constituent of dynamites and certain propelling and rocket powders. Also, **ni·tro·glyc·er·ine** (-ər ĭn, -ə rēn′).

ni·trous (nī′trəs), *adj. Chem.* **1.** pertaining to compounds obtained from niter. **2.** containing nitrogen, usually trivalent.

nitrous oxide, laughing gas.

nit·ty (nĭt′ĭ), *adj.* full of nits.

nit·wit (nĭt′wĭt′), *n.* a slow-witted or foolish person.

nix[1] (nĭks), *Slang.* —*n.* **1.** nothing. —*adv.* **2.** no. —*interj.* **3.** (used as a signal warning of someone's approach).

nix[2] (nĭks), *n., pl.* **nixes.** *Folklore.* a water spirit, usually small, and either good or bad. —**nix·ie** (nĭk′sĭ), *n. fem.*

Nix·on (nĭk′sən), *n.* **Richard,** born 1913, vice-president of the U.S. since 1953.

N.J., New Jersey.

N.M., New Mexico. Also, **N. Mex.**

NNE, north-northeast. Also, **N.N.E.**

NNW, north-northwest. Also, **N.N.W.**

no (nō), *adv., n., pl.* **noes,** *adj.* —*adv.* **1.** a word used: **a.** to express dissent, denial, or refusal, as in response. **b.** to emphasize a previous negative or qualify a previous statement. **2.** not at all

(used with a comparative). **3.** not. —*n.* **4.** an utterance of the word "no." **5.** a denial or refusal. **6.** a negative vote or voter. —*adj.* **7.** not any. **8.** not at all a.

No., **1.** north. **2.** northern. **3.** number. Also, **no.**

No·ah (nō′ə), *n.* a Hebrew patriarch, the builder of **Noah's Ark,** in which, with his family and animals of every species, he survived the deluge.

nob (nŏb), *n. Slang.* the head.

nob·by (nŏb′ĭ), *adj.,* **-bier, -biest.** *Chiefly Brit. Slang.* **1.** fashionable. **2.** first-rate.

No·bel (nō bĕl′), *n.* **Alfred Bernhard,** 1833–96, Swedish inventor of dynamite: established annual prizes for achievement in physics, chemistry, medicine, literature, and the promotion of peace.

no·bil·i·ty (nō bĭl′ə tĭ), *n., pl.* **-ties. 1.** the noble class in a country or state. **2.** (in Great Britain and Ireland) the peerage. **3.** state or quality of being noble. **4.** noble birth or rank.

no·ble (nō′bəl), *adj.,* **nobler, noblest,** *n.* —*adj.* **1.** distinguished by birth, rank, or title. **2.** pertaining to persons so distinguished. **3.** belonging to or constituting a class possessing a hereditary social or political preëminence in a country or state. **4.** of an exalted moral character or excellence. **5.** admirable in dignity of conception, or in the manner of expression or composition. **6.** stately; magnificent. **7.** notably superior. **8.** *Chem.* inert; chemically inactive. —*n.* **9.** a person of noble birth or rank; nobleman. —**no′ble·ness,** *n.*

no·ble·man (nō′bəl mən), *n., pl.* **-men.** a man of noble birth or rank; noble. —**no′ble·wom′an,** *n. fem.*

no·blesse o·blige (nō blĕs′ ô blēzh′), *French.* noble rank requires honorable conduct.

no·bly (nō′blĭ), *adv.* **1.** in a noble manner. **2.** courageously. **3.** splendidly; superbly. **4.** of noble ancestry.

no·bod·y (nō′bŏd′ĭ, -bəd ĭ), *n., pl.* **-bodies. 1.** no person. **2.** a person of no importance.

nock (nŏk), *n.* **1.** a metal or plastic piece at the end of an arrow. **2.** a notch or groove at the end of an arrow into which the bowstring fits.

noc·tu·id (nŏk′chōō ĭd), *n.* **1.** any of a large family of dull-colored moths, the larvae of which are highly injurious. —*adj.* **2.** belonging or pertaining to this family.

noc·tur·nal (nŏk tûr′nəl), *adj.* **1.** of or pertaining to the night. **2.** done, occurring, or coming by night. **3.** active by night. —**noc·tur′nal·ly,** *adv.*

noc·turne (nŏk′tûrn), *n. Music.* **1.** a piece appropriate to the night or evening. **2.** a composition of a dreamy or pensive character.

nod (nŏd), *v.,* **nodded, nodding,** *n.* —*v.i.* **1.** to make a slight, quick inclination of the head, as in assent, greeting, etc. **2.** to let the head fall forward with a sudden, involuntary movement when sleepy. **3.** to grow careless, inattentive, or dull. **4.** (of trees, flowers, plumes, etc.) to droop, bend, or incline with a swaying motion. —*v.t.* **5.** to incline (the head), as in assent, greeting, etc. **6.** to express by such a movement of the head. —*n.* **7.** a short, quick inclination of the head, as in assent, greeting, command, or drowsiness. —**nod′der,** *n.*

nod·al (nō′dəl), *adj.* pertaining to or of the nature of a node.

nod·dle (nŏd′əl), *n. Colloq. and Humorous.* the head.

node (nōd), *n.* **1.** a knot, protuberance, or knob. **2.** a complication; difficulty. **3.** a centering point of component parts. **4.** *Bot.* **a.** a joint in a stem. **b.** a part of a stem which normally bears a leaf. **5.** *Geom.* a point on a curve or surface, at which there can be more than one tangent line or plane. **6.** *Physics.* a point, line, or region in a vibrating medium at which there is comparatively no variation of the disturbance which is being transmitted through the medium. **7.** *Pathol.* a circumscribed swelling.

nod·ule (nŏj′ōōl), *n.* **1.** a small node, knot, or knob. **2.** a small rounded mass or lump. **3.** *Bot.* a tubercle. —**nod·u·lar** (nŏj′ə lər), *adj.*

No·el (nō ĕl′), *n.* **1.** Christmas. **2.** (*l.c.*) a Christmas song or carol.

nog (nŏg), *n. U.S.* any beverage made with beaten eggs and (usually) alcoholic liquor.

nog·gin (nŏg′ĭn), *n.* **1.** a small mug. **2.** a small amount of liquor. **3.** the head.

no·how (nō′hou′), *adv.* (in substandard use) in no manner; not at all.

noise (noiz), *n.*, *v.*, **noised, noising.** —*n.* **1.** sound, esp. of a loud, harsh, or confused kind. **2.** loud shouting; outcry; clamor. **3.** *Archaic.* rumor. —*v.t.* **4.** to spread the report or rumor of. **5.** to spread (a report, rumor, etc.). —*v.i.* **6.** to talk much or publicly. **7.** to make a noise, outcry, or clamor.

noise·less (noiz′lĭs), *adj.* silent; quiet. —**noise′less·ly,** *adv.* —**noise′less·ness,** *n.*

noi·some (noi′səm), *adj.* **1.** offensive or disgusting, often as to odor. **2.** harmful, injurious, or noxious. —**noi′some·ly,** *adv.* —**noi′some·ness,** *n.*

nois·y (noi′zĭ), *adj.*, **noisier, noisiest. 1.** making much noise. **2.** abounding in noise. —**nois′i·ly,** *adv.* —**nois′i·ness,** *n.*

nom., nominative.

no·mad (nō′măd, nŏm′ăd), *n.* **1.** one of a race or tribe moving about from place to place according to the state of the pasturage or food supply. **2.** any wanderer. —*adj.* **3.** nomadic.

no·mad·ic (nō măd′ĭk), *adj.* of, pertaining to, or characteristic of nomads. —**no·mad′i·cal·ly,** *adv.*

no man's land, a disputed tract of land, as one between opposing lines in war.

nom de plume (nŏm′ də ploōm′), pen name.

Nome (nōm), *n.* a seaport in W Alaska. 1559.

no·men·cla·ture (nō′mən klā′chər, nō mĕn′klə-), *n.* **1.** a set or system of names or terms, as those used in a particular science. **2.** the names or terms forming a set or system.

nom·i·nal (nŏm′ə nəl), *adj.* **1.** being such in name only; so-called. **2.** (of a price, consideration, etc.) named as a mere matter of form, being trifling in comparison with the actual value. —**nom′i·nal·ly,** *adv.*

nom·i·nate (nŏm′ə nāt′), *v.t.*, **-nated, -nating. 1.** to propose as a proper person for appointment or election to an office. **2.** to appoint for a duty or office. —**nom′i·na′tion,** *n.* —**nom′i·na′tor,** *n.*

nom·i·na·tive (nŏm′ə nə tĭv, -nā′tĭv, nŏm′nə-), *Gram.* —*adj.* **1.** denoting a case which by its form, position, or function indicates that it serves as the subject of a finite verb. **2.** similar to such a case form in function or meaning. —*n.* **3.** the nominative case, or a word in that case.

nom·i·nee (nŏm′ə nē′), *n.* one nominated, as to fill an office or stand for election.

non-, a prefix meaning "not," freely used as an English formative, usually with a simple negative force as implying mere negation or absence of something (rather than the opposite or reverse of it, as often expressed by **un-**¹), as in *nonadherence, noninterference.*

non·age (nŏn′ĭj, nō′nĭj), *n.* **1.** the period of legal minority. **2.** any period of immaturity.

non·a·ge·nar·i·an (nŏn′ə jə nâr′ĭ ən, nō′nə-jə-), *adj.* **1.** of the age of 90 years, or between 90 and 100 years old. —*n.* **2.** a nonagenarian person.

nonce (nŏns), *n.* the one or particular occasion or purpose (chiefly in *for the nonce*).

non·cha·lant (nŏn′shə lənt, nŏn′shə länt′), *adj.* coolly unconcerned, indifferent, or unexcited; casual. —**non′cha·lant·ly,** *adv.* —**non′cha·lance,** *n.*

non·com (nŏn′kŏm′), *n. Colloq.* a noncommissioned officer.

non·com·bat·ant (nŏn kŏm′bə tənt), *n.* one who is not a combatant; a civilian in time of war.

non·com·mis·sioned (nŏn′kə mĭsh′ənd), *adj.* not commissioned (applied esp. to military officers ranking below warrant officer).

non·com·mit·tal (nŏn′kə mĭt′əl), *adj.* not committing oneself, or not involving committal, to a particular view, course, or the like.

non com·pos men·tis (nŏn kŏm′pəs mĕn′tĭs), *Latin.* not of sound mind.

non·con·duc·tor (nŏn′kən dŭk′tər), *n.* a substance which does not readily conduct or transmit heat, sound, electricity, etc.

non·con·form·ist (nŏn′kən fôr′mĭst), *n.* **1.** one who refuses to conform, as to an established church. **2.** (*often cap.*) one who refuses to conform to the Church of England. —**non′con·form′i·ty,** *n.*

non·de·script (nŏn′dĭ skrĭpt′), *adj.* **1.** of no recognized, definite, or particular type or kind. —*n.* **2.** a person or a thing of no particular type or kind.

none (nŭn), *pron.* **1.** no one; not one. **2.** not any. **3.** no part; nothing. **4.** (*construed as pl.*) no, or not any, persons or things. —*adv.* **5.** in no way; not at all. —*adj.* **6.** not any; no.

non·en·ti·ty (nŏn ĕn′tə tĭ), *n.*, *pl.* **-ties. 1.** a person or thing of no importance. **2.** something which does not really exist.

none·such (nŭn′sŭch′), *n.* a person or thing without equal; paragon.

non·met·al (nŏn′mĕt′əl), *n. Chem.* **1.** an element not having the character of a metal, as carbon, nitrogen, etc. **2.** an element incapable of forming simple positive ions in solution. —**non′-me·tal′lic,** *adj.*

non·ob·jec·tive (nŏn′əb jĕk′tĭv), *adj. Art.* not representing objects known in physical nature; abstract.

non·pa·reil (nŏn′pə rĕl′), *adj.* **1.** having no equal; peerless. —*n.* **2.** a person or thing having no equal. **3.** *Print.* a size of type (6 point).

non·par·ti·san (nŏn pär′tə zən), *adj.* **1.** not

non′ab·sorb′ent	non′con·tin′u·ance	non′ex·port′a·ble	non′in·ter·fer′ence
non′ac·cept′ance	non′con·tin′u·ous	non′ex·tend′ed	non′in·ter·sect′ing
non′ad·ja′cent	non′con·tra·band′	non′ex′tra·dit′a·ble	non′in·ter·ven′tion
non′ag·gres′sion	non′con·tra·dic′to·ry	non′fac′tu·al	non′in·tox′i·cant
non′ag·gres′sive	non′co·öp′er·a′tion	non′fad′ing	non′in·tox′i·cat′ing
non′al·co·hol′ic	non′cor·ro′sive	non′fed′er·al	non′ir·ri·ga·ble
non′ap·pear′ance	non′crit′i·cal	non′fed′er·at′ed	non′ir′ri·tant
non′a·quat′ic	non′crys′tal·line	non′fer′rous	non′ir·ri·tat′ing
non′as·sess′a·ble	non′cu′mu·la·tive	non′fes′tive	non–Jew′
non′as·sim′i·la′tion	non′de·cep′tive	non′fic′tion	non–Jew′ish
non′at·tend′ance	non′de·cid′u·ous	non′fic′tion·al	non·le′gal
non′be·liev′er	non′de·liv′er·y	non′fis′cal	non′lit·er·ar′y
non′bel·lig′er·ent	non′dem·o·crat′ic	non′fis′sion·a·ble	non·liv′ing
non′break′a·ble	non′de·struc′tive	non′freez′ing	non′lu′mi·nous
non·Cath′o·lic	non·dir′i·gi·ble	non′ful·fill′ment	non′mag·net′ic
non·cel′lu·lar	non′dis·crim′i·na′-tion	non′func′tion·al	non·mar′ry·ing
non·cen′tral		non·gas′e·ous	non·mar′tial
non·Chris′tian	non′dis·pos′al	non′green′	non′me·chan′i·cal
non·civ′i·lized′	non′dis·tinc′tive	non′hab·it·a·ble	non·med′i·cal
non·cler′i·cal	non′di·ver′gent	non′he·red′i·tar′y	non·me·dic′i·nal
non′col·laps′i·ble	non′di·vis′i·ble	non′her′it·a·ble	non·me·lo′di·ous
non·com′bat	non·dog·mat′ic	non′his·tor′ic	non·mem′ber
non′com·bust′i·ble	non′dra·mat′ic	non′hu′man	non·met′ri·cal
non·com′mer′cial	non·ed′i·ble	non′hu·mor′ous	non·mi′gra·to·ry
non′com·mu′ni·ca-ble	non′ed·u·ca·ble	non′i·den′ti·cal	non·mil′i·tant
	non′ed·u·ca′tion·al	non′i·den′ti·ty	non·mil′i·tar′y
non′com·pet′i·tive	non·ef·fi′cient	non′id·i·o·mat′ic	non·mor′al
non′com·pli′ance	non′e·las′tic	non′im·mu′ni·ty	non·mor′tal
non′com·pul′sion	non′e·mo′tion·al	non′im·preg′nat-ed	non·mo′tile
non′con·du′cive	non′en·force′ment		non·nat′u·ral
non′con·form′ance	non′e·quiv′a·lent	non′in·clu′sive	non·nav′i·ga·ble
non′con·sec′u·tive	non′es·sen′tial	non′in·dict′a·ble	non′ne·ces′si·ty
non·con′sent′	non·eth′i·cal	non′in·dict′ment	non′ne·go′ti·a·ble
non′con′se·quence′	non′–Eu·clid′e·an	non′in·dus′tri·al	non·neu′tral
non′con·serv′a·tive	non′ex·change′a·ble	non′in·fec′tion	non·nu′tri·tious
non′con·sti·tu′tion-al	non′ex·clu′sive	non′in·fec′tious	non′o·be′di·ence
	non′ex·ist′ence	non′in·flam′ma·ble	non′ob·lig′a·to·ry
non′con·ta′gious	non′ex·ist′ent	non′in·for′a·tive	non·o′dor·ous
non′con·tem·po-rar′y	non′ex·ist′ing	non′in·her′it·a·ble	non·of·fi′cial
	non′ex·plo′sive	non′in·ter·course′	non·or′tho·dox′

partisan; objective. **2.** not supporting any of the regular parties.

non·plus (nŏn plŭs', nŏn'plŭs), *v.*, **-plused, -plusing** or (*esp. Brit.*) **-plussed, -plussing,** *n.* —*v.t.* **1.** to puzzle completely. —*n.* **2.** a state of utter perplexity.

non·pro·duc·tive (nŏn'prə dŭk'tĭv), *adj.* **1.** not producing goods directly, as inspectors, etc. **2.** unproductive.

non·rep·re·sen·ta·tion·al (nŏn'rĕp rĭ zĕn-tā'shən əl), *adj.* not resembling any object in physical nature.

non·res·i·dent (nŏn rĕz'ə dənt), *adj.* **1.** not resident in a particular place. **2.** not residing where official duties require one to reside. —*n.* **3.** one who is nonresident. —**non·res'i·dence, non·res'i·den·cy,** *n.*

non·re·stric·tive (nŏn'rĭ strĭk'tĭv), *adj. Gram.* (of a word or clause) purely descriptive rather than limiting in its application to the sentence element it modifies.

non·sense (nŏn'sĕns), *n.* **1.** that which makes no sense. **2.** senseless or absurd words or action. **3.** absurdity. **4.** anything useless. —**non·sen·si·cal** (nŏn sĕn'sə kəl), *adj.* —**non·sen'si·cal·ly,** *adv.* —**non·sen'si·cal·ness,** *n.*

non se·qui·tur (nŏn sĕk'wə tər), *Latin.* a conclusion which does not logically follow.

non·skid (nŏn'skĭd'), *adj.* having a skid-resistant surface.

non·stop (nŏn'stŏp'), *adj., adv.* without a single stop.

non·such (nŭn'sŭch'), *n.* nonesuch.

non·suit (nŏn'sōōt'), *Law.* —*n.* **1.** a judgment given against a plaintiff who neglects to prosecute or fails to bring sufficient evidence. —*v.t.* **2.** to subject to a nonsuit.

non·sup·port (nŏn'sə pōrt'), *n.* · *Law.* omission to support another, as a wife, child, or other dependent, as required by law.

non·un·ion (nŏn ūn'yən), *adj.* **1.** not belonging to, or not in accordance with the rules of, a trade union. **2.** antiunion. —**non·un'ion·ism,** *n.*

noo·dle[1] (nōō'dəl), *n.* a strip or lump of dough or paste, served in soups, etc.

noo·dle[2] (nōō'dəl), *n.* **1.** *Slang.* the head. **2.** a simpleton.

nook (nŏŏk), *n.* **1.** a corner, as in a room. **2.** any retired or remote spot.

noon (nōōn), *n.* **1.** midday. **2.** twelve o'clock in the daytime. **3.** *Poetic.* midnight.

noon·day (nōōn'dā'), *n.* **1.** midday; noon. —*adj.* **2.** of or at noonday.

no one, no person; nobody.

noon·time (nōōn'tīm'), *n.* the time of noon; midday. Also, **noon'tide'.**

noose (nōōs), *n., v.,* **noosed, noosing.** —*n.* **1.** a loop with a running knot, as in a lasso, which tightens as the rope is pulled. —*v.t.* **2.** to secure by a noose.

nor (nŏr; *unstressed* nər), *conj.* a negative conjunction used: **a.** as the correlative to a preceding *neither.* **b.** *Now Chiefly Poetic.* instead of *neither,* as correlative to a following *nor.* **c.** to continue the force of a negative in a preceding clause.

Nor., **1.** North. **2.** Norway.

Nor·dic (nŏr'dĭk), *adj.* **1.** *Ethnol.* designating, or belonging or pertaining to, a race of men characterized by tall stature, blond hair, and blue eyes, exemplified most markedly by Scandinavians and Britons and their descendants. —*n.* **2.** a member of the Nordic race.

Nor·folk (nŏr'fək), *n.* a seaport in SE Virginia: naval base. 144,332.

norm (nŏrm), *n.* a standard or model.

nor·mal (nŏr'məl), *adj.* **1.** conforming to the standard or the common type; regular; usual. **2.** *Psychol.* approximately average in respect to any psychological trait. **3.** *Math.* being at right angles, as a line; perpendicular. **4.** *Chem.* (of a solution) containing one equivalent weight of the constituent in question in one liter of solution. —*n.* **5.** the standard or type. **6.** the average or mean. **7.** *Math.* a perpendicular line or plane. —**nor·mal·i·ty** (nŏr măl'ə tĭ), **nor'mal·ness,** *n.*

nor·mal·cy (nŏr'məl sĭ), *n.* the character or state of being normal.

nor·mal·ize (nŏr'mə līz'), *v.t.*, **-ized, -izing.** to make normal. —**nor'mal·i·za'tion,** *n.*

nor·mal·ly (nŏr'mə lĭ), *adv.* regularly; according to rule, general custom, etc.

normal school, a school for the preliminary professional education of teachers.

Nor·man (nŏr'mən), *n.* **1.** a member of that branch of the Scandinavians who in the 10th century conquered Normandy. **2.** one of the mixed Scandinavian and French (**Norman French**) race of this region, which conquered England in 1066 (**Norman Conquest**). —*adj.* **3.** of or pertaining to the Normans. **4.** *Archit.* noting or pertaining to a variety of the Romanesque style of architecture introduced into Great Britain by the Normans.

Nor·man·dy (nŏr'mən dĭ), *n.* a region in N France along the English Channel.

Nor·ris·town (nŏr'ĭs toun', nŏr'-), *n.* a borough in SE Pennsylvania. 38,181.

Norse (nŏrs), *adj.* **1.** belonging or pertaining to Norway, esp. ancient Norway with its colonies. —*n.* **2.** (*construed as pl.*) **a.** the Norwegians. **b.** the Northmen. **3.** Norwegian (language).

Norse·man (nŏrs'mən), *n., pl.* **-men.** a Northman.

north (nŏrth), *n.* **1.** a cardinal point of the compass lying to the right of a person facing the setting sun. **2.** the direction in which this point lies. **3.** (*l.c. or cap.*) a territory situated in this direction. **4.** *Chiefly Poetic.* the north wind. **5.** (*cap.*) the northern area of the United States, esp. the States which fought with the Union in the Civil War, lying to the north of the Ohio river, Missouri, and Maryland. —*adj.* **6.** toward or in the north. **7.** from the north, as a wind. **8.** (*cap.*) designating the northern part of a region, nation, country, etc. —*adv.* **9.** toward or in the north.

North America, the northernmost continent of the Western Hemisphere, extending from Central America to the Arctic Ocean. —**North American.**

North Car·o·li·na (kăr'ə lī'nə), a State in the SE United States, on the Atlantic coast. 3,640,645

non'pa·rish'ion·er	non'pro·gres'sive	non'sal'a·ried	non'sus·tain'ing
non'par·lia·men'ta·ry	non'pro·tec'tive	non'sci·en·tif'ic	non'sym·met'ri·cal
non'pa·ro'chi·al	non'Prot'es·tant	non·sea'son·al	
non'par·tic'i·pa·tion	non'pun'ish·a·ble	non'sec·tar'i·an	non'sys·tem·at'ic
non'pas'ser·ine	non·ra'cial	non·sec'tion·al	non·tax'a·ble
non·pay'ing	non're·al'i·ty	non'se·lec'tive	non·teach'a·ble
non·pay'ment	non're·cip'ro·cal	non·sen'si·tive	non·tech'ni·cal
non'per·form'ance	non'rec·og·ni'tion	non·shar'ing	non'ter·ri·to'ri·al
non·per'ma·nent	non're·cur'rent	non·shat'ter	non·tex'tu·al
non·per'me·a·ble	non're·fill'a·ble	non·shrink'a·ble	non·tox'ic
non'per·pen·dic'u·lar	non're·fu'el·ing	non'sig·nif'i·cant	non'trans·fer'a·ble
non'per·sist'ence	non·re'gent	non·sink'a·ble	non·trib'u·tar'y
non'phil·o·soph'i·cal	non're·li'gious	non·slip'ping	non·typ'i·cal
non·po·et'ic	non·re'new·a·ble	non·smok'ing	non'u·nit'ed
non·poi'son·ous	non're·mu'ner·a'tive	non·so'cial	non·us'er
non·po·lit'i·cal	non'res·i·den'tial	non·spark'ling	non·ven'om·ous
non·po'rous	non're·sist'ance	non·spe'cial·ized'	non·ver'ti·cal
non'pred'a·to'ry	non're·sist'ant	non·spir'it·u·al	non·vi·o·la'tion
non'pre·dict'a·ble	non're·strict'ed	non·stain'a·ble	non·vis'u·al
non'pre·scrip'tive	non're·turn'a·ble	non'stan'dard·ized'	non·vo·cal'ic
non'pro·duc'ing	non're·vers'i·ble	non·stim'u·lat'ing	non'vo·ca'tion·al
non'pro·fes'sion·al	non·rhym'ing	non·strik'er	non·vol'a·tile
non·prof'it	non·rhyth'mic	non·strik'ing	non·vol'un·tar'y
non'prof·it·eer'ing	non·rig'id	non'sub·mis'sive	non·vot'er
	non·ru'ral	non'sub·scrib'er	non·vot'ing
	non·sal'a·ble	non·sub·stan'tial	non·work'er
		non'suc·ces'sive	non·yield'ing
		non'sup·port'er	

pop.; 52,712 sq. mi. *Cap.*: Raleigh. *Abbr.*: N.C.
—**North Car·o·lin·i·an** (kär'ə lĭn'ĭ ən).

North Da·ko·ta (də kō'tə). a State in the N central United States. 537,084 pop.; 70,665 sq. mi. *Cap.*: Bismarck. *Abbr.*: N. Dak. —**North Da·ko'tan.**

north·east (nôrth'ēst'; *Naut.* nôr'-), *n.* **1.** the point or direction midway between north and east. **2.** a region in this direction. —*adv.* **3.** in the direction of the northeast. **4.** from this direction. —*adj.* **5.** toward or in the northeast. **6.** from the northeast, as a wind. —**north'east'·ern,** *adj.*

north·east·er (nôrth'ēs'tər; *Naut.* nôr'-), *n.* a wind or gale from the northeast.

north·east·er·ly (nôrth'ēs'tər lǐ; *Naut.* nôr'-), *adj.* **1.** of, in, toward, or from the northeast. —*adv.* **2.** toward or from the northeast.

north·er (nôr'thər), *n.* **1.** (in the U.S. Gulf Coast region) a cold gale from the north, during the winter. **2.** a wind or storm from the north.

north·er·ly (nôr'thər lǐ), *adj.* **1.** moving, directed, or situated toward the north. **2.** coming from the north, as a wind. —*adv.* **3.** toward the north. **4.** from the north.

north·ern (nôr'thərn), *adj.* **1.** toward or in the north. **2.** from the north, as a wind. **3.** of or pertaining to the north, esp. (*cap.*) the North of the U.S. —**north'ern·most',** *adj.*

north·ern·er (nôr'thər nər), *n.* a native or inhabitant of the north, esp. (*cap.*) of the Northern U.S.

Northern Ireland, a political division of the United Kingdom, in the NE part of Ireland. 1,327,000 pop.; 5238 sq. mi. *Cap.*: Belfast.

northern lights, the aurora borealis.

north·land (nôrth'land), *n.* **1.** the land or region in the north. **2.** the northern part of a country. —**north'land·er,** *n.*

North·man (nôrth'mən), *n., pl.* **-men.** a member of the Scandinavian group which from about the 8th to the 11th century made many raids and settlements on Great Britain, Ireland, and other parts of Europe.

North Pole, that end of the earth's axis of rotation marking the northernmost point on the earth.

North Sea, an arm of the Atlantic between Great Britain and the European mainland. ab. 201,000 sq. mi.

North Star, *Astron.* Polaris, the star toward which the north axis of the earth points.

north·ward (nôrth'wərd; *Naut.* nôr'thərd), *adv.* **1.** Also, **north'wards.** toward the north. —*adj.* **2.** moving, bearing, facing, or situated toward the north. —*n.* **3.** the northward part, direction, or point. —**north'ward·ly,** *adj., adv.*

north·west (nôrth'wĕst'; *Naut.* nôr'-), *n.* **1.** the point or direction midway between north and west. **2.** a region in this direction. —*adj.* Also, **north'west·ern. 3.** toward or in the northwest. **4.** from the northwest, as a wind. —*adv.* **5.** in the direction of a point midway between north and west. **6.** from this direction.

north·west·er (nôrth'wĕs'tər; *Naut.* nôr'-), *n.* a wind or gale from the northwest.

north·west·er·ly (nôrth'wĕs'tər lǐ; *Naut.* nôr'-), *adj., adv.* toward or from the northwest.

Northwest Territories, a territory of Canada lying N of the provinces and extending from Yukon territory E to Davis Strait. 12,028 pop.; 1,304,903 sq. mi. *Cap.*: Ottawa.

Norw., **1.** Norway. **2.** Norwegian.

Nor·walk (nôr'wôk), *n.* a city in SW Connecticut. 39,849.

Nor·way (nôr'wā), *n.* a kingdom in N Europe, in the W part of the Scandinavian Peninsula. 3,105,000 pop.; 124,555 sq. mi. *Cap.*: Oslo. —**Nor·we·gian** (nôr wē'jən), *adj., n.*

nor'·west·er (nôr wĕs'tər), *n.* a seaman's oilskin raincoat.

Nor·wich (nôr'ĭch, -ĭj, nôr'-), *n.* a city in E England. 113,270.

Nor·wood (nôr'wŏŏd), *n.* a city in SW Ohio, near Cincinnati. 34,010.

Nos., numbers. Also, **nos.**

nose (nōz), *n., v.,* **nosed, nosing.** —*n.* **1.** the part of the face or head which contains the nostrils, affording passage for air in respiration, etc. **2.** the sense of smell. **3.** a faculty of perceiving or detecting. **4.** something regarded as resembling the nose of a person or animal, as a spout or nozzle. **5.** a projecting part. —*v.t., v.i.* **6.** to smell or sniff.

7. to pry (fol. by *about, into,* etc.). **8.** to move or push forward. **9.** to meddle.

nose·band (nōz'bănd'), *n.* that part of a bridle or halter which passes over the animal's nose.

nose·bleed (nōz'blēd'), *n.* bleeding from the nose.

nose dive, 1. a plunge of an airplane with the fore part of the craft vertically downward. **2.** any sudden drop.

nose-dive (nōz'dīv'), *v.i.,* **-dived** or **-dove, -dived, -diving.** to execute a nose dive.

nose·gay (nōz'gā'), *n.* a bouquet.

nose·piece (nōz'pēs'), *n.* **1.** a protective cover for the nose. **2.** noseband.

nos·tal·gia (nŏs tăl'jə, -jĭ ə), *n.* homesickness or strong desire for family and friends. —**nos·tal'gic,** *adj.*

Nos·tra·da·mus (nŏs'trə dā'məs), *n.* 1503–66, French astrologer.

nos·tril (nŏs'trəl), *n.* an external opening of the nose.

nos·trum (nŏs'trəm), *n.* **1.** a patent medicine. **2.** a quack medicine. **3.** any pet scheme or device.

nos·y (nō'zǐ), *adj.,* **nosier, nosiest.** *Colloq.* prying; inquisitive. Also, **nos'ey.**

not (nŏt), *adv.* a word expressing negation, denial, refusal, or prohibition.

no·ta be·ne (nō'tə bē'nĭ), *Latin.* note well.

no·ta·ble (nō'tə bəl), *adj.* **1.** worthy of note or notice. **2.** prominent; important. —*n.* **3.** a prominent or important person. —**no'ta·ble·ness, no'ta·bil'i·ty,** *n.* —**no'ta·bly,** *adv.*

no·ta·rize (nō'tə rīz'), *v.t.,* **-rized, -rizing.** to authenticate (a contract, etc.).

no·ta·ry public (nō'tə rǐ), *pl.* **notaries public.** a public officer authorized to authenticate contracts, take affidavits, etc. Also, **notary.**

no·ta·tion (nō tā'shən), *n.* **1.** a system of graphic symbols for a specialized use, other than ordinary writing. **2.** a note or record. —**no·ta'tion·al,** *adj.*

notch (nŏch), *n.* **1.** an angular cut in a surface or edge. **2.** *U.S.* a deep, narrow opening or pass between mountains. **3.** *Colloq.* a step, degree, or grade. —*v.t.* **4.** to make a notch or notches in, esp. by way of record. **5.** to record by a notch or notches.

note (nōt), *n., v.,* **noted, noting.** —*n.* **1.** a brief record of something written down, as to assist the memory. **2.** a comment or citation appended to a passage in a book or the like. **3.** a brief written or printed statement giving particulars or information. **4.** a short informal letter. **5.** a formal diplomatic or official communication in writing. **6.** a paper acknowledging a debt and promising payment. **7.** a piece of paper money. **8.** importance or consequence. **9.** notice, observation, or heed. **10.** a musical sound or tone. **11.** *Music.* **a.** a sign used to represent a tone, its position and form indicating the pitch and duration of the tone. **b.** a key, as of a piano. **12.** a signal, announcement, or intimation. —*v.t.* **13.** to mark down, as in writing. **14.** to make particular mention of in a writing. **15.** to annotate. **16.** to give attention or heed to. **17.** to take notice of; perceive. **18.** to set down in or furnish with musical notes. —**not'er,** *n.*

Notes (def. 11a)
A, Breve; B, Whole note;
C, Half note; D, Quarter
note; E, Eighth note;
F, Sixteenth note;
G, Thirty-second note;
H, Sixty-fourth note

note·book (nōt'bŏŏk'), *n.* a book of or for notes.

not·ed (nō'tĭd), *adj.* **1.** celebrated; famous. **2.** specially observed or noticed. —**not'ed·ly,** *adv.*

note·wor·thy (nōt'wûr'thǐ), *adj.* worthy of notice; notable. —**note'wor'thi·ly,** *adv.*

noth·ing (nŭth'ĭng), *n.* **1.** not anything; naught. **2.** no part, share, or trace. **3.** that which is nonexistent. **4.** a trivial action, matter, circumstance, thing, or remark. **5.** an unimportant person. **6.** a cipher or naught. —*adv.* **7.** in no respect or degree; not at all.

noth·ing·ness (nŭth'ĭng nĭs), *n.* **1.** state of being nothing. **2.** nonexistence. **3.** utter insignificance or emptiness.

no·tice (nō'tǐs), *n., v.,* **-ticed, -ticing.** —*n.* **1.** information or intelligence. **2.** an intimation or warning. **3.** a note, placard, or the like, conveying information or warning. **4.** a notification of the termination of an agreement, as for employment. **5.** observation, attention, or heed. —*v.t.* **6.** to pay attention to. **7.** to perceive. **8.** to treat with attention, politeness, or favor. **9.** to acknowledge acquaintance with. **10.** to mention or refer to. **11.** to give notice to.

no·tice·a·ble (nō'tĭs ə bəl), *adj.* that may be noticed; apparent. —**no'tice·a·bly,** *adv.*

no·ti·fi·ca·tion (nō'tə fə kā'shən), *n.* **1.** act of notifying. **2.** a formal notifying. **3.** a notice.

no·ti·fy (nō'tə fī'), *v.t.,* -**fied, -fying. 1.** to give notice to, or inform, of something. **2.** *Chiefly Brit.* to make known. —**no'ti·fi'er,** *n.*

no·tion (nō'shən), *n.* **1.** a general, vague, or imperfect conception of something. **2.** an opinion, view, or belief. **3.** conception or idea. **4.** a whim. **5.** (*pl.*) *U.S.* small wares, esp. pins, needles, thread, tapes, etc.

no·tion·al (nō'shən əl), *adj.* **1.** pertaining to or expressing a notion or idea. **2.** abstract or speculative. **3.** imaginary. **4.** *U.S.* fanciful. —**no'·tion·al·ly,** *adv.*

no·to·ri·e·ty (nō'tə rī'ə tĭ), *n., pl.* -**ties.** state of being notorious or widely known.

no·to·ri·ous (nō tōr'ĭ əs), *adj.* **1.** widely but unfavorably known. **2.** publicly or generally known. —**no·to'ri·ous·ly,** *adv.* —**no·to'ri·ous·ness,** *n.*

Not·ting·ham (nŏt'ĭng əm), *n.* a city in central England. 284,750.

not·with·stand·ing (nŏt'wĭth stăn'dĭng, -wĭth-), *prep.* **1.** in spite of. —*adv.* **2.** nevertheless; yet. —*conj.* **3.** although.

nou·gat (noo'gət, noo'gä), *n.* a pastelike confection containing almonds or other nuts.

nought (nôt), *n., adj., adv.* naught.

noun (noun), *n. Gram.* **1.** one of the major form classes, or parts of speech, comprising words denoting persons, places, things, and such other words as show similar grammatical behavior. **2.** any such word.

nour·ish (nûr'ĭsh), *v.t.* **1.** to sustain with food or nutriment. **2.** to foster or promote. —**nour'·ish·ing·ly,** *adv.*

nour·ish·ment (nûr'ĭsh mənt), *n.* **1.** food; nutriment. **2.** act of nourishing.

nou·veau riche (noo vō rēsh'), *pl.* **nouveaux riches** (noo vō rēsh'). *French.* one who has newly become rich.

Nov., November.

No·va Sco·tia (nō'və skō'shə), a peninsula and province in SE Canada. 577,962 pop.; 21,068 sq. mi. *Cap.:* Halifax. —**No'va Sco'tian.**

nov·el¹ (nŏv'əl), *n.* a fictitious prose narrative of considerable length, portraying characters, actions, and scenes representative of real life in a plot of more or less intricacy.

nov·el² (nŏv'əl), *adj.* of a new kind; new.

nov·el·ist (nŏv'əl ĭst), *n.* a writer of novels.

no·vel·la (nō vĕl'lä), *n., pl.* -**le** (-lĕ). a short story of the type of those contained in the *Decameron* of Boccaccio, etc.

nov·el·ty (nŏv'əl tĭ), *n., pl.* -**ties. 1.** novel character; newness. **2.** a novel thing, experience, or proceeding. **3.** a new or novel article of trade.

No·vem·ber (nō vĕm'bər), *n.* the eleventh month of the year, containing 30 days.

nov·ice (nŏv'ĭs), *n.* **1.** one who is new to the work, etc., in which he is placed. **2.** one who has been received into a religious order or congregation for a period of probation before taking vows.

no·vi·ti·ate (nō vĭsh'ĭ ĭt, -āt), *n.* **1.** state or period of being a novice. **2.** the quarters occupied by religious novices during probation. Also, **no·vi'ci·ate.**

No·vo·caine (nō'və kān'), *n. Trademark.* a synthetic nonirritant local anesthetic. Also, **no'·vo·cain'.**

now (nou), *adv.* **1.** at the present time. **2.** immediately. **3.** at this point or juncture. **4.** at the time only just past. **5.** in these present times; nowadays. **6. now that,** inasmuch as. —*conj.* **7.** since; seeing that. —*n.* **8.** the present time.

now·a·days (nou'ə dāz'), *adv.* **1.** in these times. —*n.* **2.** the present.

no·way (nō'wā'), *adv.* in no way, respect, or degree; not at all. Also, **no'ways'.**

no·where (nō'hwâr'), *adv.* in, at, or to no place; not anywhere.

no·wise (nō'wīz), *adv.* not at all.

nox·ious (nŏk'shəs), *adj.* **1.** harmful or injurious to health. **2.** morally harmful. —**nox'·ious·ly,** *adv.* —**nox'ious·ness,** *n.*

noz·zle (nŏz'əl), *n.* a projecting spout or the like, as of a hose.

nr., near.

N.T., New Testament.

nth (ĕnth), *adj.* **1.** last in a series of infinitely decreasing or increasing values, amounts, etc. **2. the nth degree** or **power,** the utmost extent.

nu (nū, noo), *n.* the thirteenth letter (N, *ν* = English N, n) of the Greek alphabet.

nu·ance (nū äns', noo-, nū'äns, noo'-), *n.* a shade of color, expression, meaning, feeling, etc.

nub (nŭb), *n.* **1.** a knob or protuberance. **2.** *U.S. Colloq.* the gist of anything.

nub·bin (nŭb'ĭn), *n. U.S.* **1.** a small lump or piece. **2.** a small or imperfect ear of maize.

nu·bile (nū'bĭl, noo'-), *adj.* marriageable.

nu·cle·ar (nū'klĭ ər, noo'-), *adj.* of, pertaining to, or forming a nucleus.

nuclear fission, the breakdown of an atomic nucleus of an element of relatively high atomic number into two or more nuclei of lower atomic number, with conversion of part of its mass into energy.

nuclear physics, the branch of physics dealing with the nature of atoms.

nu·cle·ate (nū'klĭ ĭt, -āt', noo'-), *adj.* having a nucleus.

nu·cle·us (nū'klĭ əs, noo'-), *n., pl.* -**clei** (-klĭ ī'), -**cleuses. 1.** a central part or thing about which other parts or things are grouped. **2.** *Biol.* a differentiated mass of protoplasm, encased in a delicate membrane, present in the interior of nearly all living cells. **3.** *Chem.* a fundamental arrangement of atoms which may occur in many compounds by substitution of atoms without a change in structure. **4.** *Physics.* the central core of an atom, composed of protons and neutrons. **5.** *Astron.* the more condensed portion of the head of a comet.

nude (nūd, nood), *adj.* **1.** naked or unclothed. **2.** without the usual coverings, furnishings, etc. **3.** *Law.* made without a consideration. —*n.* **4.** the nude, a. the condition of being undraped. **b.** the undraped human figure. —**nude'ly,** *adv.* —**nude'ness,** *n.*

nudge (nŭj), *v.,* **nudged, nudging,** *n.* —*v.t., v.i.* **1.** to push slightly or jog, esp. with the elbow. —*n.* **2.** a slight push or jog.

nud·ism (nū'dĭz əm, noo'-), *n.* the practice of going naked as a measure of healthful living. —**nud'ist,** *n., adj.*

nu·di·ty (nū'də tĭ, noo'-), *n.* state or fact of being nude; nakedness.

nu·ga·to·ry (nū'gə tōr'ĭ, noo'-), *adj.* **1.** trifling; worthless. **2.** futile; vain.

nug·get (nŭg'ĭt), *n.* **1.** a lump of something. **2.** a lump of native gold.

nui·sance (nū'səns, noo'-), *n.* a highly obnoxious or annoying thing or person.

null (nŭl), *adj.* **1.** of no effect, consequence, or significance. **2. null and void,** having no legal force or effect. **3.** zero.

null·i·fy (nŭl'ə fī'), *v.t.,* -**fied, -fying. 1.** to make null; make ineffective, futile, or of no consequence. **2.** to render or declare legally void or inoperative. —**nul'li·fi·ca'tion,** *n.* —**nul'li·fi'er,** *n.*

nul·li·ty (nŭl'ə tĭ), *n., pl.* -**ties. 1.** nothingness; invalidity. **2.** something null.

Num., Numbers.

numb (nŭm), *adj.* **1.** deprived of or deficient in the power of sensation and movement. **2.** of the nature of numbness. —*v.t.* **3.** to make numb. —**numb'ly,** *adv.* —**numb'ness,** *n.*

num·ber (nŭm'bər), *n.* **1.** the sum, total, count, or aggregate of a collection of units. **2.** a numeral. **3.** (*pl.*) *Obs.* arithmetic. **4.** a single issue of a periodical. **5.** a single part of a program made up of a number of parts. **6.** (*pl.*) considerable collections or quantities. **7.** a large quantity. **8.** *Gram.* (in many languages) a category of the inflection of nouns, verbs, and related word classes, usually expressing the number of persons or objects referred to. **9.** (*pl.*) metrical feet; verse. —*v.t.* **10.** to ascertain the number of. **11.** to mark with a number or numbers. **12.** to enumerate. **13.** to amount to in number. —*v.i.* **14.** *Poetic.* to count. —**num'ber·er,** *n.*

num·ber·less (nŭm'bər lĭs), *adj.* **1.** countless; myriad. **2.** without a number.

Num·bers (nŭm'bərz), *n.* the fourth book of the Old Testament.

nu·mer·a·ble (nū'mər ə bəl, noo'-), *adj.* that may be numbered or counted.

nu·mer·al (nū′mər əl, nōō′-), *n.* **1.** a word or words expressing a number. **2.** a letter or figure denoting a number. **—adj. 3.** of or consisting of numbers. **4.** expressing or denoting number.

nu·mer·ate (nū′mə rāt′, nōō′-), *v.t.,* **-ated, -ating.** to number; count. **—nu′mer·a′tion,** *n.*

nu·mer·a·tor (nū′mə rā′tər, nōō′-), *n.* *Math.* that term (usually written above the line) of a fraction which shows how many parts of a unit are taken.

nu·mer·i·cal (nū měr′ə kəl, nōō′-), *adj.* **1.** of or pertaining to number. **2.** denoting number or a number. **3.** bearing a number. **4.** expressed by a number or figure. **—nu·mer′i·cal·ly,** *adv.*

nu·mer·ous (nū′mər əs, nōō′-), *adj.* **1.** very many. **2.** consisting of or comprising a great number. **—nu′mer·ous·ly,** *adv.* **—nu′mer·ous·ness,** *n.*

nu·mis·mat·ics (nū′mĭz măt′ĭks, -mĭs-, nōō′-), *n.* the science of coins and medals. **—nu′mis·mat′ic,** *adj.* **—nu·mis·ma·tist** (nū mĭz′mə tĭst, -mĭs′-, nōō-), *n.*

num·skull (nŭm′skŭl′), *n.* *Colloq.* a dull-witted person; dunce; dolt.

nun (nŭn), *n.* a woman devoted to a religious life, usually living in a convent under vows.

nun·ci·o (nŭn′shĭ ō′), *n., pl.* **-cios.** a permanent diplomatic representative of the Pope.

nun·ner·y (nŭn′ə rĭ), *n., pl.* **-neries.** a religious house for nuns; convent.

nup·tial (nŭp′shəl), *adj.* **1.** of or pertaining to marriage or the marriage ceremony. **—n. 2.** (*usually pl.*) marriage; wedding.

Nu·rem·berg (nyŏŏr′əm bûrg′, nōŏr′-), *n.* a city in S Germany. 423,383.

nurse (nûrs), *n., v.,* **nursed, nursing. —n. 1.** a person who has the care of the sick or infirm. **2.** a woman who has the general care of a child or children. **3.** a woman employed to suckle an infant. **—v.t. 4.** to tend in sickness or infirmity. **5.** to seek to cure (a cold, etc.) by taking care of oneself. **6.** to look after carefully so as to promote growth, development, etc. **7.** to bring up, train, or nurture. **8.** to suckle (an infant). **—v.i. 9.** to tend the sick or infirm. **10.** to suckle a child. **11.** (of a child) to take the breast. **—nurs′er,** *n.*

nurse·maid (nûrs′mād′), *n.* a woman employed to take care of children.

nurs·er·y (nûr′sə rĭ), *n., pl.* **-eries. 1.** a room or place set apart for young children. **2.** a nursery school. **3.** a place where young trees or other plants are raised for transplanting or for sale.

nurs·er·y·man (nûr′sə rĭ mən), *n., pl.* **-men.** one who owns or conducts a nursery for plants.

nursery school, a prekindergarten school.

nurs·ling (nûrs′lĭng), *n.* an infant or child under a nurse's care. Also, **nurse′ling.**

nur·ture (nûr′chər), *v.,* **-tured, -turing,** *n.* **—v.t. 1.** to feed, nourish, or support during the stages of growth, as children or young; rear. **—n. 2.** upbringing or training. **3.** nourishment or food. **—nur′tur·er,** *n.*

nut (nŭt), *n., v.,* **nutted, nutting. —n. 1.** a dry fruit consisting of an edible kernel or meat enclosed in a shell. **2.** the kernel itself. **3.** *Bot.* a hard, indehiscent, one-seeded fruit, as the chestnut. **4.** *Slang.* the head. **5.** *Slang.* a foolish or crazy person. **6.** a perforated block (usually of metal) with an internal thread, used to screw on the end of a bolt, etc. **—v.i. 7.** to seek for or

gather nuts. **—nut′like′,** *adj.* **—nut′ter,** *n.* **—nut′ting,** *n.*

nut·crack·er (nŭt′krăk′ər), *n.* **1.** (*often pl.*) an instrument for cracking nuts. **2.** any of certain birds of the crow family which feed on nuts.

nut·gall (nŭt′gôl′), *n.* a nutlike gall or excrescence, esp. one formed on an oak.

nut·hatch (nŭt′hăch′), *n.* any of certain small, short-tailed, sharp-beaked birds which feed on small nuts and insects.

nut·meg (nŭt′měg), *n.* **1.** the hard, aromatic seed of the fruit of an East Indian tree, used as a spice. **2.** the tree itself.

nu·tri·a (nū′trĭ ə, nōō′-), *n.* **1.** the coypu. **2.** the fur of this animal, resembling beaver.

nu·tri·ent (nū′trĭ ənt, nōō′-), *adj.* **1.** containing or conveying nutriment. **2.** nourishing. **—n. 3.** a nutrient substance.

nu·tri·ment (nū′trə mənt, nōō′-), *n.* **1.** any matter that, taken into a living organism, serves to sustain it in its existence, promoting growth, replacing loss, and providing energy. **2.** nourishment, food, or aliment.

nu·tri·tion (nū trĭsh′ən, nōō-), *n.* **1.** act or process of nourishing or of being nourished. **2.** food; nutriment. **3.** the process by which the food material taken into an organism is converted into living tissue, etc. **—nu·tri′tion·al,** *adj.* **—nu·tri′tion·al·ly,** *adv.* **—nu·tri′tion·ist,** *n.*

nu·tri·tious (nū trĭsh′əs, nōō-), *adj.* nourishing. **—nu·tri′tious·ly,** *adv.* **—nu·tri′tious·ness,** *n.*

nu·tri·tive (nū′trə tĭv, nōō′-), *adj.* **1.** serving to nourish. **2.** of, pertaining to, or concerned in nutrition. **—nu′tri·tive·ness,** *n.*

nuts (nŭts), *Slang.* **—interj. 1.** an expression of defiance, disgust, etc. **—adj. 2.** crazy.

nut·shell (nŭt′shěl′), *n.* **1.** the shell of a nut. **2. in a nutshell,** in a few words.

nut·ty (nŭt′ĭ), *adj.,* **-tier, -tiest. 1.** abounding in nuts. **2.** nutlike, esp. in taste. **3.** *Slang.* crazy. **—nut′ti·ness,** *n.*

nux vom·i·ca (nŭks vŏm′ə kə), **1.** the strychnine-containing seed (used in medicine) of the orangelike fruit borne by an East Indian tree. **2.** the tree itself.

nuz·zle¹ (nŭz′əl), *v.,* **-zled, -zling. —v.i. 1.** to burrow or root with the nose, as an animal does. **2.** to thrust the nose. **—v.t. 3.** to root up with the nose. **4.** to touch with the nose.

nuz·zle² (nŭz′əl), *v.t., v.i.,* **-zled, -zling.** to snuggle or cuddle.

NW, 1. northwest. **2.** northwestern. Also, **N.W., n.w.**

N.Y., New York.

N.Y.C., New York City.

ny·lon (nī′lŏn), *n.* **1.** a synthetic product capable of extrusion when molten into fibers, sheets, etc., of extreme toughness, strength, and elasticity: used for yarn, bristles, etc. **2.** (*pl.*) stockings made of nylon.

nymph (nĭmf), *n.* **1.** one of a numerous class of inferior divinities of mythology, conceived of as beautiful maidens inhabiting the sea, rivers, woods, trees, mountains, meadows, etc., and frequently mentioned as attending a superior deity. **2.** a beautiful or graceful young woman.

nym·pho·ma·ni·a (nĭm′fə mā′nĭ ə), *n.* *Pathol.* morbid and uncontrollable sexual desire in women. **—nym′pho·ma′ni·ac′,** *adj., n.*

N.Z., New Zealand. Also, **N. Zeal.**

O

O¹, o (ō), *n., pl.* **O's** or **Os, o's, os** or **oes.** a vowel, the 15th letter of the English alphabet.

O² (ō), *interj., n., pl.* **O's. —interj. 1.** a word used before the name in address to lend earnestness to an appeal. **2.** an expression of surprise, pain, gladness, etc. **—n. 3.** the exclamation "O."

o′ (ə, ō), *prep.* an abbreviated form of: **1.** of. **2.** on.

O, 1. *Chem.* oxygen. **2.** Old.

O., **1.** Ocean. **2.** Ohio. **3.** Old.

oaf (ōf), *n.* **1.** a simpleton. **2.** a lout. **—oaf′ish,** *adj.* **—oaf′ish·ly,** *adv.*

O·a·hu (ō ä′hōō), *n.* the third largest and most important of the Hawaiian Islands. 257,664 pop.; 589 sq. mi.

oak (ōk), *n.* **1.** any tree or shrub of a genus including many forest trees with hard, durable wood, bearing the acorn as fruit. **2.** the wood of an oak tree. **—oak′en,** *adj.*

Oak·land (ōk′lənd), *n.* a seaport in W California, on San Francisco Bay. 400,935.

Oak·ley (ōk′lĭ), *n.* **Annie, 1.** 1860–1926, U.S. sharpshooter. **2.** *U.S. Slang.* a free ticket of admittance.

Oak Park, a village in NE Illinois, near Chicago. 66,015.

Oak Ridge, a town in E Tennessee: a center of atomic research. 36,000.

oa·kum (ō′kəm), *n.* loose fiber obtained by untwisting and picking apart old ropes, used for calking the seams of ships, etc.

oar (ōr), *n.* **1.** an instrument for propelling a boat, consisting of a long shaft of wood with a blade at one end. **—v.t., v.i. 2.** to row.

oar·lock (ōr′lŏk′), *n.* a contrivance on a boat's gunwale in or on which the oar rests and swings.

oars·man (ōrz′mən), *n., pl.* **-men.** an expert rower. **—oars′man·ship′,** *n.*

o·a·sis (ō ā′sĭs, ō′ə sĭs), *n., pl.* **-ses** (-sēz, -sēz′). a place in a desert region where ground water brought to the surface, or surface water from other areas, provides for humid vegetation.

oat (ōt), *n.* **1.** (*usually pl.*) a cereal grass cultivated for its edible seed, which is used in making oatmeal and as a food for horses, etc. **2.** (*pl.*) the seeds. **3. feel one's oats,** *U.S. Slang.* **a.** to feel gay or lively. **b.** to be aware of and use one's importance and power. **4. sow one's wild oats,** to indulge in the excesses or follies of youth. **—oat′en,** *adj.*

oat·cake (ōt′kāk′), *n.* a cake, usually thin and brittle, made of oatmeal.

oath (ōth), *n., pl.* **oaths** (ōᵺz). **1.** a solemn attestation of the truth of a statement or the binding character of a promise. **2.** a formally affirmed statement or promise. **3.** a light or blasphemous use of the name of God or anything sacred. **4.** a profane expression; curse.

oat·meal (ōt′mēl′, ōt′mēl′), *n.* **1.** meal made from oats. **2.** porridge of this.

O·ba·di·ah (ō′bə dī′ə), *n.* **1.** a Hebrew prophet. **2.** the Old Testament book which bears his name. *Abbr.:* **Obad.**

ob·bli·ga·to (ŏb′lə gä′tō), *adj., n., pl.* **-tos, -ti** (-tē). *Music.* **—adj. 1.** obligatory or indispensable. **—n. 2.** an obbligato part or accompaniment.

ob·du·rate (ŏb′dyə rĭt, -də-), *adj.* **1.** hardened against persuasions or tender feelings; hardhearted. **2.** persistently impenitent. **—ob·du·ra·cy** (ŏb′dyə rə sĭ), **ob·du·rate·ness,** *n.* **—ob′du·rate·ly,** *adv.*

o·be·di·ent (ō bē′dĭ ənt), *adj.* obeying, or willing to obey; submissive to authority or constraint. **—o·be·di·ence,** *n.* **—o·be·di·ent·ly,** *adv.*

o·bei·sance (ō bā′səns, ō bē′-), *n.* **1.** a movement of the body expressing deep respect; bow or curtsy. **2.** deference or homage. **—o·bei′sant,** *adv.*

ob·e·lisk (ŏb′ə lĭsk), *n.* **1.** a tapering, four-sided shaft of stone, as in ancient Egypt. **2.** *Print.* the dagger (†), used esp. as a reference mark. **—ob′e·lis′cal,** *adj.*

o·bese (ō bēs′), *adj.* excessively fat; corpulent. **—o·bese′ly,** *adv.* **—o·bese′ness, o·bes·i·ty** (ō bē′sə tĭ, ō bēs′ə-), *n.*

o·bey (ō bā′), *v.t.* **1.** to comply with the commands or instructions of. **2.** to comply with (a command, etc.). **3.** (of things) to respond to. **—v.i. 4.** to be obedient. **—o·bey′er,** *n.*

ob·fus·cate (ŏb fŭs′kāt, ŏb′fəs-kāt′), *v.t.,* **-cated, -cating.** to confuse or stupefy. **—ob′fus·ca′tion,** *n.*

ob·i·ter dic·tum (ŏb′ə tər dĭk′təm), *pl.* **obiter dicta** (dĭk′tə). an incidental opinion.

Obelisk

o·bit·u·ar·y (ō bĭch′oo ĕr′ĭ), *n., pl.* **-aries,** *adj.* **—n. 1.** a notice of the death of a person, often with a brief biographical sketch, as in a newspaper. **—adj. 2.** pertaining to or recording a death.

obj., 1. object. **2.** objection. **3.** objective.

ob·ject (*n.* ŏb′jĭkt; *v.* əb jĕkt′), *n.* **1.** something

that may be perceived by the senses, esp. by sight or touch. **2.** a thing or person to which attention or action is directed. **3.** the end toward which effort is directed. **4.** a person or thing which arouses feelings of pity, disgust, etc. **5.** *Gram.* the noun or its substitute which represents the goal of an action (in English either *direct* or *indirect*). **—v.i. 6.** to offer a reason or argument in opposition. **7.** to express or feel disapproval. **—v.t. 8.** to bring as a charge. **—ob·jec′tor,** *n.*

ob·jec·tion (əb jĕk′shən), *n.* **1.** something adduced or said in disagreement or disapproval. **2.** act of objecting. **3.** a feeling of disapproval or dislike.

ob·jec·tion·a·ble (əb jĕk′shən ə bəl), *adj.* that may be objected to; offensive. **—ob·jec′tion·a·bly,** *adv.*

ob·jec·tive (əb jĕk′tĭv), *n.* **1.** something aimed at. **2.** *Gram.* **a.** the objective case. **b.** a word in that case. **3.** (in a telescope, microscope, etc.) the lens which first receives the rays from the object and forms the image viewed through the eyepiece or photographed. **—adj. 4.** being the object of perception or thought. **5.** free from personal feelings or prejudice; unbiased. **6.** of or pertaining to that which can be known. **7.** *Art.* of or pertaining to an object or objects. **8.** *Gram.* **a.** pertaining to the use of a form as object of a verb or preposition. **b.** (in English and some other languages) denoting a case specialized for that use. **—ob·jec′tive·ly,** *adv.* **—ob·jec′tive·ness, ob·jec·tiv·i·ty** (ŏb′jĕk tĭv′ə tĭ), *n.*

ob·ject·less (ŏb′jĭkt lĭs), *adj.* **1.** having no object. **2.** purposeless.

object lesson, a practical illustration of a principle.

ob·jet d'art (ŏb zhĕ där′), *pl.* **objets d'art** (ŏb zhĕ där′). *French.* an object of art.

ob·jur·gate (ŏb′jər gāt′, əb jûr′gāt), *v.t.,* **-gated, -gating.** to reproach vehemently; berate. **—ob′jur·ga′tion,** *n.* **—ob·jur·ga·to·ry** (əb jûr′gə tōr′ĭ), *adj.*

ob·late (ŏb′lāt, ŏb lāt′), *adj.* flattened at the poles. **—ob′late·ly,** *adv.*

ob·la·tion (ŏb lā′shən), *n.* **1.** the offering to God of the elements of bread and wine in the Eucharist. **2.** the whole office of the Eucharist. **3.** the act of making an offering, now esp. to God. **4.** any offering for religious or charitable uses.

ob·li·gate (*v.* ŏb′lə gāt′; *adj.* ŏb′lə gĭt, -gāt′), *v.,* **-gated, -gating,** *adj.* **—v.t. 1.** to oblige or bind morally or legally. **—adj. 2.** obligated, bound, or constrained.

ob·li·ga·tion (ŏb′lə gā′shən), *n.* **1.** a binding requirement as to action; duty. **2.** the binding power of a promise, law, duty, etc. **3.** a binding promise or the like made. **4.** act of binding oneself by a promise, contract, etc. **5.** a benefit, favor, or service, for which gratitude is due. **6.** a debt of gratitude.

ob·lig·a·to·ry (ə blĭg′ə tōr′ĭ, ŏb′lə gə-), *adj.* **1.** imposing obligation. **2.** required as a matter of obligation. **3.** incumbent or compulsory.

o·blige (ə blīj′), *v.t.,* **obliged, obliging. 1.** to require or constrain, as the law, a duty, or necessity does. **2.** to bind (a person, etc.) by a promise, engagement, or contract. **3.** to place under a debt of gratitude for some benefit, favor, or service. **4.** to favor. **—o·blig′er,** *n.* **—o·blig′ing,** *adj.* **—o·blig′ing·ly,** *adv.*

ob·lique (ə blēk′), *adj., v.,* **-liqued, -liquing.** **—adj. 1.** neither perpendicular nor parallel to a given line or surface; slanting. **2.** not straight or direct, as a course, etc. **3.** indirectly stated or expressed. **4.** *Gram.* denoting or pertaining to any case of noun inflection except nominative and vocative, or except these two and accusative. **—v.i. 5.** to slant. **—ob·lique′ly,** *adv.* **—ob·lique′ness, ob·liq·ui·ty** (ə blĭk′wə tĭ), *n.*

oblique angle, an angle that is not a right angle.

ob·lit·er·ate (ə blĭt′ə rāt′), *v.t.,* **-ated, -ating. 1.** to remove all traces of; destroy. **2.** to blot out; cancel; efface. **—ob·lit′er·a′tion,** *n.*

ob·liv·i·on (ə blĭv′ĭ ən), *n.* **1.** state of being forgotten, as by the world. **2.** forgetfulness.

ob·liv·i·ous (ə blĭv′ĭ əs), *adj.* **1.** forgetful. **2.** unmindful; unconscious. **—ob·liv′i·ous·ly,** *adv.* **—ob·liv′i·ous·ness,** *n.*

ob·long (ŏb′lông, -lŏng), *adj.* **1.** elongated. **2.** in the form of an elongated rectangle. **—n. 3.** an oblong figure.

ob·lo·quy (ŏb′lə kwĭ), *n., pl.* **-quies. 1.** the discredit or disgrace resulting from public blame.

2. censure, blame, or abusive language aimed at a person, etc.

ob·nox·ious (ŏb nŏk′shəs), *adj.* **1.** objectionable; offensive. **2.** exposed or liable (to harm, evil, etc.). **3.** *Law.* responsible. **4.** *Obs.* reprehensible. —**ob·nox′ious·ly,** *adv.* —**ob·nox′ious·ness,** *n.*

o·boe (ō′bō, ō′boi), *n.* a wooden wind instrument in the form of a slender conical tube, in which the tone is produced by a double reed. —**o′bo·ist,** *n.*

Obs., obsolete.

ob·scene (əb sēn′, ŏb-), *adj.* offensive to modesty or decency; indecent; lewd. —**ob·scene′ly,** *adv.* —**ob·scene′ness, ob·scen·i·ty** (əb sĕn′ə tĭ, -sē′nə-), *n.*

ob·scur·ant·ism (əb skyŏŏr′ən tĭz′əm), *n.* opposition to inquiry and enlightenment. —**ob·scur′ant·ist,** *n.*, *adj.*

ob·scu·ra·tion (ŏb′skyŏō rā′shən), *n.* **1.** act of obscuring. **2.** state of being obscured.

ob·scure (əb skyŏŏr′), *adj.*, **-scurer, -scurest,** *v.*, **-scured, -scuring,** *n.* **1.** not clear or plain. **2.** inconspicuous or unnoticeable. **3.** of no prominence, note, or distinction. **4.** remote; retired, as a place. **5.** indistinct to the sight, or to some other sense. **6.** dark; murky; dim. —*v.t.* **7.** to make obscure, dark, dim, indistinct, etc. —*n.* **8.** darkness. —**ob·scure′ly,** *adv.* —**ob·scure′ness, ob·scu′ri·ty,** *n.*

ob·se·qui·ous (əb sē′kwĭ əs), *adj.* **1.** servilely compliant or deferential. **2.** showing servile compliance or deference. —**ob·se′qui·ous·ly,** *adv.* —**ob·se′qui·ous·ness,** *n.*

ob·se·quy (ŏb′sə kwĭ), *n.*, *pl.* **-quies.** (*usually pl.*) a funeral rite or ceremony.

ob·serv·a·ble (əb zûr′və bəl), *adj.* **1.** noticeable; noteworthy. **2.** that may be or is to be followed or kept. —**ob·serv′a·bly,** *adv.*

ob·serv·ance (əb zûr′vəns), *n.* **1.** the action of conforming to or following. **2.** a keeping or celebration by appropriate procedure, ceremonies, etc. **3.** a procedure, ceremony, or rite, as for a particular occasion. **4.** a rule or custom to be observed.

ob·serv·ant (əb zûr′vənt), *adj.* **1.** observing or regarding attentively; watchful. **2.** alert. **3.** careful in the observing of a law, custom, or the like. —*n.* **4.** an observer of law or rule. —**ob·serv′ant·ly,** *adv.*

ob·ser·va·tion (ŏb′zər vā′shən), *n.* **1.** act of noticing or perceiving. **2.** act of regarding attentively or watching. **3.** faculty or habit of observing or noticing. **4.** notice. **5.** act of viewing or noting something, for some scientific or other special purpose. **6.** the information or record secured thereby. **7.** an utterance by way of remark or comment. —**ob·ser·va′tion·al,** *adj.*

ob·serv·a·to·ry (əb zûr′və tōr′ĭ), *n.*, *pl.* **-ries.** **1.** a place equipped for making observations of astronomical, meteorological, or other natural phenomena. **2.** a place affording an extensive view.

ob·serve (əb zûrv′), *v.*, **-served, -serving.** —*v.t.* **1.** to see, perceive, or notice. **2.** to regard with attention. **3.** to watch for some scientific, official, or other special purpose. **4.** to remark; comment. **5.** to maintain in one's action, conduct, etc. **6.** to obey. **7.** to show regard for by some appropriate ceremonies, etc. **8.** to perform duly. —*v.i.* **9.** to notice. **10.** to act as an observer. **11.** to remark or comment. —**ob·serv′er,** *n.*

ob·sess (əb sĕs′), *v.t.* to beset, trouble, or dominate; haunt. —**ob·ses′sive,** *adj.*

ob·ses·sion (əb sĕsh′ən), *n.* **1.** the besetting or dominating action or influence of a persistent feeling, idea, or the like, which the person cannot escape. **2.** the feeling or idea itself.

ob·sid·i·an (ŏb sĭd′ĭ ən), *n.* a volcanic glass, usually of a very dark color.

ob·so·les·cent (ŏb′sə lĕs′ənt), *adj.* becoming obsolete. —**ob′so·les′cence,** *n.*

ob·so·lete (ŏb′sə lēt′), *adj.* **1.** no longer in use. **2.** of a discarded type. **3.** *Biol.* imperfectly developed or rudimentary. —**ob′so·lete′ly,** *adv.* —**ob′so·lete′ness,** *n.*

ob·sta·cle (ŏb′stə kəl), *n.* something that stands in the way or obstructs progress.

ob·ste·tri·cian (ŏb′stə trĭsh′ən), *n.* one skilled in obstetrics.

ob·stet·rics (əb stĕt′rĭks), *n.* the branch of medical art or science concerned with caring for and treating women in, before, and after childbirth. —**ob·stet′ric, ob·stet′ri·cal,** *adj.*

ob·sti·nate (ŏb′stə nĭt), *adj.* **1.** firmly and often perversely adhering to one's purpose, opinion, etc. **2.** inflexibly carried out. **3.** not easily controlled. **4.** not yielding readily to treatment. —**ob′sti·nate·ly,** *adv.* —**ob′sti·nate·ness, ob·sti·na·cy** (ŏb′stə nə sĭ), *n.*

ob·strep·er·ous (əb strĕp′ər əs), *adj.* **1.** unruly. **2.** noisy; boisterous. —**ob·strep′er·ous·ly,** *adv.* —**ob·strep′er·ous·ness,** *n.*

ob·struct (əb strŭkt′), *v.t.* **1.** to block or close up, or make difficult of passage, with obstacles. **2.** to interrupt, make difficult, or oppose the passage, course, etc., of. **3.** to come in the way of (a view, etc.). —**ob·struct′er, ob·struc′tor,** *n.* —**ob·struc′tive,** *adj.*

ob·struc·tion (əb strŭk′shən), *n.* **1.** an obstacle or hindrance. **2.** act of obstructing.

ob·struc·tion·ist (əb strŭk′shən ĭst), *n.* a person who obstructs something, esp. legislative business. —**ob·struc′tion·ism′,** *n.*

ob·tain (əb tān′), *v.t.* **1.** to get or acquire; procure. —*v.i.* **2.** to be prevalent, customary, or in vogue. —**ob·tain′a·ble,** *adj.* —**ob·tain′ment,** *n.*

ob·trude (əb trōōd′), *v.*, **-truded, -truding.** —*v.t.* **1.** to thrust forward or upon a person. **2.** to thrust forth; push out. —*v.i.* **3.** to thrust oneself or itself forward; intrude. —**ob·trud′er,** *n.* —**ob·tru′sion,** *n.*

ob·tru·sive (əb trōō′sĭv), *adj.* **1.** having or showing a disposition to obtrude. **2.** (of a thing) obtruding itself. —**ob·tru′sive·ly,** *adv.* —**ob·tru′sive·ness,** *n.*

ob·tuse (əb tūs′, -tōōs′), *adj.* **1.** blunt; not sharp or acute. **2.** (of a leaf, etc.) rounded at the extremity. **3.** dull in perception, feeling, or intellect. **4.** indistinctly felt or perceived. —**ob·tuse′ly,** *adv.* —**ob·tuse′ness,** *n.*

obtuse angle, an angle exceeding 90 degrees but less than 180 degrees.

ob·verse (*n.* ŏb′vûrs; *adj.* ŏb vûrs′, ŏb′vûrs), *n.* **1.** that side of a coin, medal, etc., which bears the principal design. **2.** the front or principal face of anything. **3.** a counterpart. —*adj.* **4.** turned toward or facing one. **5.** corresponding to something else as a counterpart. —**ob·verse′ly,** *adv.*

ob·vi·ate (ŏb′vĭ āt′), *v.t.*, **-ated, -ating.** to meet and dispose of or prevent (difficulties, objections, etc.). —**ob′vi·a′tion,** *n.*

ob·vi·ous (ŏb′vĭ əs), *adj.* open to view or knowledge. —**ob′vi·ous·ly,** *adv.* —**ob′vi·ous·ness,** *n.*

oc·a·ri·na (ŏk′ə rē′nə), *n.* a simple musical wind instrument shaped somewhat like an elongated egg, with finger holes.

oc·ca·sion (ə kā′zhən), *n.* **1.** a particular time, esp. as marked by certain occurrences. **2.** a special or important time, event, or function. **3.** opportunity. **4. on occasion,** occasionally. **5.** the ground, reason, or incidental cause of some action or result. —*v.t.* **6.** to give cause for; bring about.

oc·ca·sion·al (ə kā′zhən əl), *adj.* **1.** occurring or appearing from time to time. **2.** intended for use whenever needed. **3.** arising out of the occasion. —**oc·ca′sion·al·ly,** *adv.*

Oc·ci·dent (ŏk′sə dənt), *n.* **1.** countries in Europe and America. **2.** the Western Hemisphere. **3.** (*l.c.*) the west. —**Oc′ci·den′tal,** *adj.*, *n.*

oc·cip·i·tal (ŏk sĭp′ə təl), *adj.* of or pertaining to the back of the head.

oc·ci·put (ŏk′sə pŭt′, -pət), *n.* *Anat.* the back part of the head or skull.

oc·clude (ə klōōd′), *v.*, **-cluded, -cluding.** —*v.t.* **1.** to close (a passage, etc.). **2.** to shut in, out, or off. **3.** *Chem.* to absorb and retain gases or liquids, in minute pores. —*v.i.* **4.** *Dentistry.* to shut against each other, as opposing teeth of the upper and lower jaws. —**oc·clu·sion** (ə klōō′zhən), *n.* —**oc·clu·sive** (ə klōō′sĭv), *adj.*

oc·cult (ə kŭlt′, ŏk′ŭlt), *adj.* **1.** beyond the bounds of ordinary knowledge. **2.** secret. **3.** involving the alleged knowledge or employment of secret or mysterious agencies. —*n.* **4.** occult studies or sciences. **5.** anything occult. —*v.t.*, *v.i.* **6.** to hide.

oc·cul·ta·tion (ŏk′ŭl tā′shən), *n.* **1.** *Astron.* the passage of one celestial body in front of a second. **2.** disappearance from view.

oc·cult·ism (ə kŭl′tĭz əm), *n.* the doctrine or study of the occult. —**oc·cult′ist,** *n.*, *adj.*

oc·cu·pan·cy (ŏk′yə pən sĭ), *n.* **1.** act of taking possession. **2.** actual possession. **3.** the term during which one is an occupant. **4.** exercise of dominion over a thing which has no owner so as to become legal owner.

oc·cu·pant (ŏk/yə pənt), *n.* **1.** one who occupies. **2.** a tenant of a house, office, etc. **3.** *Law.* an owner through occupancy.

oc·cu·pa·tion (ŏk/yə pā/shən), *n.* **1.** one's business, trade, or calling. **2.** possession, as of a place. **3.** act of occupying. **4.** state of being occupied. **5.** seizure, as by invasion. —oc/cu·pa/tion·al, *adj.*

oc·cu·py (ŏk/yə pī/), *v.t.*, **-pied, -py·ing. 1.** to take up (space, time, etc.). **2.** to engage or employ (the attention, etc.). **3.** to take possession of (a place), as by invasion. **4.** to hold (a position, etc.). —oc/cu·pi/er, *n.*

oc·cur (ə kûr/), *v.i.*, **-curred, -cur·ring. 1.** to take place; happen. **2.** to be met with or found; appear. **3.** to suggest itself in thought.

oc·cur·rence (ə kûr/əns), *n.* **1.** the action or fact of occurring. **2.** an event or incident. —oc·cur/rent, *adj.*

o·cean (ō/shən), *n.* **1.** the vast body of salt water which covers almost three fourths of the earth's surface. **2.** any of the geographical divisions of this body (commonly: the Atlantic, Pacific, Indian, Arctic, and Antarctic oceans). **3.** a vast expanse or quantity. —o·ce·an·ic (ō/shY-ăn/Yk), *adj.*

O·ce·an·i·a (ō/shY ăn/Y ə, -ä/nY ə), *n.* the islands of the central and S Pacific, including Micronesia, Melanesia, and Polynesia.

o·ce·a·nog·ra·phy (ō/shY ə nŏg/rə fY, ō/shən-ŏg/-), *n.* the branch of physical geography dealing with the ocean. —o/ce·a·nog/ra·pher, *n.* —o·ce·a·no·graph·ic (ō/shY ə nə grăf/Yk, ō/shə-nə-), o/ce·a·no·graph/i·cal, *adj.*

o·ce·lot (ō/sə lŏt/, ŏs/ə-), *n.* a spotted, leopard-like cat, some 3 feet in length, ranging from Texas through South America.

o·cher (ō/kər), *n.* **1.** any of a class of natural earths, mixtures of hydrated oxide of iron with various earthy materials, ranging in color from pale yellow to red: used as pigments. —*adj.* **2.** ranging from a pale-yellow to reddish hue. —*v.t.* **3.** to color or mark with ocher. Also, **o/chre.** —o/cher·ous, *adj.*

o'clock (ə klŏk/), of or by the clock (used in referring to the hour of the day).

Oct., October.

oc·ta·gon (ŏk/tə gŏn/, -gən), *n.* a polygon having eight angles and eight sides. —oc·tag·o·nal (ŏk tăg/ə nəl), *adj.*

oc·ta·he·dron (ŏk/tə hē/drən), *n.*, *pl.* **-drons, -dra** (-drə). a solid figure having eight faces. —oc·ta·he·dral (ŏk/tə hē/drəl), *adj.*

oc·tane (ŏk/tān), *n. Chem.* any of eighteen isomeric saturated hydrocarbons, some of which are obtained in the distillation and cracking of petroleum.

oc·tave (ŏk/tYv, -tāv), *Music.* —*n.* **1.** a tone on the eighth degree from a given tone. **2.** the interval between such tones. **3.** a series of tones, or of keys of an instrument, extending through this interval. —*adj.* **4.** pitched an octave higher.

oc·ta·vo (ŏk tā/vō, -tä/-), *n.*, *pl.* **-vos,** *adj.* —*n.* **1.** a book size (about 6 x 9 inches) determined by printing on sheets folded to form eight leaves or sixteen pages. —*adj.* **2.** in octavo.

oc·tet (ŏk tĕt/), *n.* **1.** a company of eight singers or players. **2.** a musical composition for eight voices or instruments. **3.** *Pros.* **a.** a group of eight lines of verse. **b.** the first eight lines of a sonnet. Also, **oc·tette/.**

Oc·to·ber (ŏk tō/bər), *n.* the tenth month of the year, containing 31 days.

oc·to·ge·nar·i·an (ŏk/tə jə nâr/Y ən), *adj.* Also, **oc·tog·e·nar·y** (ŏk tŏj/ə nĕr/Y). **1.** of the age of 80 years. **2.** between 80 and 90 years old. —*n.* **3.** an octogenarian person.

oc·to·pus (ŏk/tə pəs), *n.*, *pl.* **-puses, -pi** (-pī/). any of certain cephalopods with soft, oval bodies, eight sucker-bearing arms, and living mostly on the sea bottom.

oc·to·roon (ŏk/tə-rōōn/), *n.* a person having one-eighth Negro blood.

oc·u·lar (ŏk/yə lər), *adj.* **1.** of or pertaining to the eye. **2.** of the nature of an eye. **3.** performed or perceived

Octopus

by the eye or eyesight. —*n.* **4.** the eyepiece of an optical instrument. —oc/u·lar·ly, *adv.*

oc·u·list (ŏk/yə lYst), *n.* a doctor of medicine skilled in the examination and treatment of the eye; ophthalmologist.

O.D., Officer of the Day.

odd (ŏd), *adj.* **1.** differing in character from what is ordinary or usual. **2.** peculiar in a freakish or eccentric way. **3.** fantastic or bizarre, as things. **4.** being a surplus over a definite quantity. **5.** additional to what is taken into account. **6.** being part of a pair, set, or series of which the rest is lacking. **7.** leaving a remainder of 1 when divided by 2. **8.** occasional. —*n.* **9.** that which is odd. **10.** (*pl.*) odd things, bits, or scraps. See also **odds.** —odd/ly, *adv.* —odd/ness, *n.*

odd·i·ty (ŏd/ə tY), *n.*, *pl.* **-ties. 1.** quality of being odd. **2.** an odd characteristic. **3.** an odd person or thing.

odds (ŏdz), *n.pl. and sing.* **1.** an equalizing allowance, as that given to a weaker side in a contest. **2.** the amount by which the bet of one party to a wager exceeds that of the other. **3.** favorable balance of probability. **4.** advantage or superiority. **5.** disagreement or strife (chiefly in **at odds**).

ode (ōd), *n.* **1.** a lyric poem expressive of exalted or enthusiastic emotion. **2.** (*orig.*) a poem intended to be sung.

O·der (ō/dər), *n.* a river flowing from the Carpathians in N Czechoslovakia through SW Poland and along the German-Polish border into the Baltic. ab. 550 mi.

O·des·sa (ō dĕs/ə), *n.* a seaport in the SW Soviet Union, on the Black Sea. 604,223.

O·din (ō/dYn), *n. Scand. Myth.* the chief deity, being the god of wisdom, culture, war, and the dead.

o·di·ous (ō/dY əs), *adj.* **1.** hateful or detestable. **2.** offensive; disgusting. —o/di·ous·ly, *adv.* —o/-di·ous·ness, *n.*

o·di·um (ō/dY əm), *n.* **1.** hatred; dislike. **2.** the reproach, discredit, or opprobrium attaching to something hated or odious.

o·dor (ō/dər), *n.* **1.** that property of a substance which affects the sense of smell. **2.** agreeable scent; fragrance. **3.** savor characteristic or suggestive of something. **4.** repute. Also, *Brit.,* o/dour. —o/dor·less, *adj.*

o·dor·if·er·ous (ō/də rYf/ər əs), *adj.* yielding or diffusing an odor, esp. a fragrant one.

o·dor·ous (ō/dər əs), *adj.* having or diffusing an odor, esp. a fragrant one. —o/dor·ous·ly, *adv.* —o/dor·ous·ness, *n.*

O·dys·seus (ō dYs/ūs, ō dYs/Y əs), *n. Gk. Legend.* the wisest and wiliest of the Greek leaders in the Trojan War.

Od·ys·sey (ŏd/ə sY), *n.* **1.** Homer's epic poem describing the ten years' wandering of Odysseus after the Trojan War. **2.** (*also l.c.*) any long series of wanderings.

Oed·i·pus (ĕd/ə pəs, ē/də-), *n. Gk. Legend.* a king of Thebes who killed his father involuntarily and unwittingly married his own mother. When the nature of his deeds became apparent, the mother hanged herself, and Oedipus tore out his eyes.

Oedipus complex, *Psychoanal.* **1.** the unresolved desire of a child for sexual gratification through the parent of the opposite sex. **2.** sexual desire of the son for the mother.

o'er (ōr), *prep., adv. Poetic or Dial.* over.

of (ŭv, ŏv; *unstressed* əv), *prep.* a particle indicating: **1.** distance or direction from, separation, deprivation, riddance, etc. **2.** derivation, origin, or source. **3.** cause, occasion, or reason. **4.** material or substance. **5.** a relation of identity. **6.** possession, connection, or association. **7.** inclusion in a number, class, or whole. **8.** objective relation. **9.** reference or respect. **10.** qualities. **11.** time. **12.** to or before (a designated hour of the clock).

off (ôf, ŏf), *adv.* **1.** away from a position occupied. **2.** to or at a distance from a place. **3.** out of association or relation. **4.** deviating from. **5.** as a deduction. **6.** distant (in future time). **7.** out of operation or effective existence. **8.** so as to interrupt or discontinue. **9.** away from employment or service. **10.** completely. **11.** immediately. **12.** with prompt performance. **13.** to fulfillment; into execution. **14.** so as to cause or undergo reduction or diminution. **15.** on one's way or journey. **16. off and on,** intermittently. —*prep.* **17.** so as no longer to be or rest on. **18.** deviating from. **19.** from by subtraction or deduction. **20.** away or disengaged from (duty, work, etc.). **21.** *Slang.* refraining from (some food, activity, etc.). **22.** distant from. **23.** leading out of. **24.** *U.S. Colloq.* from. *—adj.* **25.** *Now Colloq.* in error. **26.** no longer in contemplation. **27.** as to condition, circumstances, supplies, etc. **28.** (of time) on which work is suspended. **29.** not so satisfactory as usual. **30.** (of a chance) remote. *—n.* **31.** state or fact of being off. *—interj.* **32.** be off!

off., **1.** office. **2.** officer. **3.** official.

of·fal (ôf′əl, ŏf′əl), *n.* **1.** the waste or inedible portions of food animals, fowl, and fish. **2.** refuse in general.

off-col·or (ôf′kŭl′ər, ŏf′-), *adj.* **1.** defective in color. **2.** of doubtful propriety.

Of·fen·bach (ôf′ən bäk′, ŏf′-), *n.* **Jacques,** 1819–80, French composer.

of·fend (ə fĕnd′), *v.t.* **1.** to displease greatly in mind or feelings. **2.** to affect (the sense, taste, etc.) disagreeably. *—v.i.* **2.** to give offense. *—of·fend′er,* *n.*

of·fense (ə fĕns′), *n.* **1.** a wrong; sin. **2.** a transgression of law which is not indictable, but is punishable summarily or by the forfeiture of a penalty (**petty offense**). **3.** a cause of transgression or wrong. **4.** something that offends. **5.** act of offending. **6.** the feeling of resentful displeasure caused. **7.** attack or assault. **8.** the persons, side, etc., attacking. Also, *esp. Brit.,* **of·fence′.** *—of·fense′less,* *adj.*

of·fen·sive (ə fĕn′sĭv), *adj.* **1.** causing offense or displeasure; highly annoying. **2.** disagreeable to the sense. **3.** repugnant to the moral sense, good taste, or the like; insulting. **4.** pertaining to or characterized by attack. *—n.* **5.** the position or attitude of attack. **6.** an offensive movement. *—of·fen′sive·ly,* *adv.* *—of·fen′sive·ness,* *n.*

of·fer (ôf′ər, ŏf′ər), *v.t.* **1.** to present for acceptance or rejection. **2.** to propose or volunteer (to do something). **3.** to sacrifice. **4.** to present; put forward. **5.** to attempt to inflict, do, or make. **6.** to present for sale. **7.** to tender or bid as a price. *—v.i.* **8.** to make an offer. **9.** to make an offer of marriage. **10.** to occur. **11.** to sacrifice. *—n.* **12.** act of offering. **13.** a proposal of marriage. **14.** a bid. **15.** an attempt. *—of′fer·er,* *n.*

of·fer·ing (ôf′ər ĭng, ŏf′-), *n.* **1.** something offered in worship or devotion, as to God; sacrifice. **2.** a contribution given to or through the church for a particular purpose. **3.** a gift.

of·fer·to·ry (ôf′ər tōr′ĭ, ŏf′ər-), *n., pl.* **-ries.** **1.** *Rom. Cath. Ch.* the oblation of the unconsecrated elements made by the celebrant at this part of the Mass. **2.** *Eccles.* **a.** the verses, anthem, or music said, sung, or played while the offerings of the people are received at a religious service. **b.** that part of a service at which offerings are made. **c.** the offerings themselves.

off·hand (ôf′hănd′, ŏf′-), *adv.* **1.** without previous thought or preparation; extempore. **2.** cavalier, curt, or brusque. *—adj.* Also, **off′hand′ed.** **3.** done or made offhand. **4.** informal or casual.

of·fice (ôf′ĭs, ŏf′ĭs). *n.* **1.** a place for the transaction of business, the discharge of professional duties, or the like. **2.** a branch of a governmental organization. **3.** the body of persons occupying governmental offices. **4.** a position of duty, trust, or authority, esp. in the public services. **5.** the duty, function, or part of a particular person or agency. **6.** official employment or position. **7.** a service or task to be performed. **8.** *Eccles.* the prescribed form for a service of the church, or the services so prescribed.

of·fi·cer (ôf′ə sər, ŏf′ə-), *n.* **1.** one who holds a position of rank or authority in the army, navy, or any similar organization, esp. one who holds a commission. **2.** a policeman. **3.** a person appointed or elected to some position of responsibility and authority in some corporation, society, or the like. *—v.t.* **4.** to furnish with officers. **5.** to direct, conduct, or manage.

officer of the day, *Mil.* an officer who has charge, for the day, of the guard and prisoners of a military force or camp.

of·fi·cial (ə fĭsh′əl), *n.* **1.** one who holds an office. *—adj.* **2.** of or pertaining to a position of duty, trust, or authority. **3.** authorized; authoritative. **4.** formal. *—of·fi′cial·dom,* *n.* *—of·fi′cial·ly,* *adv.*

of·fi·ci·ate (ə fĭsh′ĭ āt′), *v.i.,* **-ated, -ating.** **1.** to perform the duties of any office or position. **2.** to perform the office of a priest or minister. *—of·fi′ci·a′tion,* *n.* *—of·fi′ci·a′tor,* *n.*

of·fic·i·nal (ə fĭs′ə nəl), *adj.* **1.** kept in stock by apothecaries. **2.** recognized by the pharmacopoeia. *—n.* **3.** an officinal medicine.

of·fi·cious (ə fĭsh′əs), *adj.* **1.** forward in obtruding one's services upon others. **2.** marked by such forwardness. *—of·fi′cious·ly,* *adv.* *—of·fi′cious·ness,* *n.*

off·ing (ôf′ĭng, ŏf′ĭng), *n.* **1.** the more distant part of the sea as seen from the shore. **2.** in the **offing,** not very distant.

off·ish (ôf′ĭsh, ŏf′-), *adj.* *Colloq.* aloof.

off·set (*v.* ôf′sĕt′, ŏf′-; *n., adj.* ôf′sĕt′, ŏf′-), *v.,* **-set, -setting,** *n., adj.* *—v.t.* **1.** to balance by something else as an equivalent. **2.** to compensate for. *—n.* **3.** something that offsets or counterbalances. **4.** the start. **5.** an impression from a lithographic stone or metal plate made on a rubber blanket or roller and then transferred to paper. **6.** *Print.* a faulty transfer of ink on a printed sheet to any adjacent surface. *—adj.* **7.** *Lithog.* pertaining to, or by, offset.

off·shoot (ôf′shōōt′, ŏf′-), *n.* **1.** a shoot from a main stem, as of a plant. **2.** a branch or a descendant of a family or race. **3.** anything coming out from a main stock.

off·shore (ôf′shōr′, ŏf′-), *adv.* **1.** off or away from the shore. **2.** at a distance from the shore. *—adj.* **3.** moving away from the shore. **4.** being at a distance from the shore.

off·side (ôf′sīd′, ŏf′-), *Football, Hockey, etc.* *—adv.* **1.** away from the proper side, as of the ball or of a player who last played or touched it. *—adj.* **2.** being or done offside.

off·spring (ôf′sprĭng′, ŏf′-), *n.* **1.** children or young. **2.** a descendant. **3.** descendants collectively.

off·stage (ôf′stāj′, ŏf′-), *adj.* not in view of the audience; backstage, in the wings, etc.

off-white (ôf′hwīt′, ŏf′-), *adj.* white with a slight touch of gray in it.

oft (ôft, ŏft), *adv.* *Chiefly Poetic.* often.

of·ten (ôf′ən, ŏf′ən), *adv.* **1.** frequently. **2.** in many cases.

of·ten·times (ôf′ən tīmz′, ŏf′ən-), *adv.* *Archaic.* often. Also, **oft′times′.**

Og·den (ŏg′dən), *n.* a city in N Utah. 43,688.

o·gee (ō jē′, ō′jē), *n.* a double curve (like the letter S).

o·gle (ō′gəl), *v.,* **ogled, ogling,** *n.* *—v.t., v.i.* **1.** to look at (someone), esp. with amorous, ingratiating, or impertinently familiar glances. *—n.* **2.** an ogling glance. *—o′gler,* *n.*

o·gre (ō′gər), *n.* a monster or hideous giant, supposed to live on human flesh. *—o·gre·ish* (ō′gər ĭsh), *adj.* *—o·grish* (ō′grĭsh), *adj.* *—o·gress* (ō′grĭs), *n. fem.*

oh (ō), *interj., n., pl.* **oh's, ohs,** *v.* *—interj.* **1.** an expression of surprise, pain, etc. *—n.* **2.** the exclamation "oh." *—v.i.* **3.** to exclaim "oh."

O. Hen·ry (ō hĕn′rĭ), pen name of **William Sydney Porter.**

O·hi·o (ō hī′ō), *n.* **1.** a State in the NE central United States. 7,516,855 pop.; 41,222 sq. mi. *Cap.:* Columbus. **2.** a river flowing SW from Pittsburgh to the Mississippi in S Illinois. 981 mi. *—O·hi′o·an,* *n., adj.*

ohm (ōm), *n.* *Elect.* the unit of resistance: the resistance of a conductor in which one volt produces a current of one ampere. *—ohm·ic* (ō′mĭk), *adj.*

oil (oil), *n.* **1.** any of a large class of substances typically unctuous, viscous, and combustible: used for anointing, lubricating, illuminating, heating, etc. **2.** petroleum. **3.** *Painting.* **a.** an oil color. **b.** a painting done with oil colors. *—v.t.* **4.** to smear, lubricate, or supply with oil. **5.** to bribe. *—adj.* **6.** pertaining to or resembling oil. *—oil′er,* *n.*

oil·cloth (oil′klôth′, -klŏth′), *n.* a cotton fabric made waterproof with oil and pigment: used for tablecloths, etc.

oil color, a color or paint made by grinding a pigment in oil, usually linseed oil.

oil·skin (oil′skĭn′), *n.* **1.** a cotton fabric made waterproof by treatment with oil: used for rain wear, etc. **2.** (*often pl.*) a garment made of it.

oil·y (oi′lĭ), *adj.,* **oilier, oiliest,** *adv. —adj.* **1.** pertaining to or resembling oil. **2.** full of or containing oil. **3.** covered with oil; greasy. **4.** smooth, as in manner or speech. *—adv.* **5.** in an oily manner. *—oil′i·ly,* *adv.* *—oil′i·ness,* *n.*

oint·ment (oint′mənt), *n.* a soft, unctuous preparation, often medicated, for application to the skin.

O·jib·wa (ō jĭb′wä, -wə), *n., pl.* **-wa, -was.** a member of a large tribe of North American Indians in the Lake Superior region. Also, **O·jib′way.**

O.K. (*adj., adv.* ō′kā′; *v., n.* ō′kā′), *adj., adv., v.,* **O.K.'d, O.K.'ing,** *n., pl.* **O.K.'s.** *Orig. U.S. Colloq.* —*adj., adv.* **1.** all right; correct. —*v.t.* **2.** to put "O.K." on (a bill, etc.); approve. —*n.* **3.** an approval or agreement. Also, **OK, o′kay′.**

O·kie (ō′kĭ), *n. Colloq.* **1.** a native or inhabitant of Oklahoma. **2.** a migrant farm worker.

O·ki·na·wa (ō′kə nä′wə), *n.* the largest of the Ryukyu Islands, in the N Pacific: taken by U.S. forces April–June, 1945. 435,681 pop.; 485 sq. mi.

O·kla·ho·ma (ō′klə hō′mə), *n.* a State of the S central United States. 2,224,939 pop.; 69,919 sq. mi. *Cap.:* Oklahoma City. *Abbr.:* **Okla.** —**O′-kla·ho′man,** *adj., n.*

Oklahoma City, the capital of Oklahoma, in the central part. 204,424.

o·kra (ō′krə), *n.* **1.** a tall plant of the mallow family, cultivated for its edible pods, used in soups, etc. **2.** the pod. **3.** the pods collectively.

old (ōld), *adj.,* **older, oldest** or **elder, eldest,** *n.* —*adj.* **1.** far advanced in years or life. **2.** having the characteristics of advanced age. **3.** having reached a specified age. **4.** advanced in years. **5.** having existed long. **6.** long known or in use. **7.** former, past, or ancient. **8.** being the earlier or earliest of two or more things or stages. **9.** worn, decayed, or dilapidated. **10.** of long experience. **11.** *Colloq.* or *Slang.* (implying friendly feeling). —*n.* **12.** old or former time. —**old′ish,** *adj.* —**old′ness,** *n.*

old·en (ōl′dən), *adj. Archaic.* **1.** old. **2.** of old; ancient. **3.** of former days.

Old English, the English language of the period before 1100; Anglo-Saxon.

old-fash·ioned (ōld′făsh′ənd), *adj.* **1.** of a style, kind, or type formerly in vogue. **2.** (of persons) having the ways, ideas, or tastes of a former period.

Old Glory, the flag of the United States.

old maid, 1. an elderly or confirmed spinster. **2.** *Colloq.* a person who is extremely prim, prudish, fastidious, etc. **3.** a game of cards in which the players draw from one another to match pairs. —**old′-maid′ish,** *adj.*

old·ster (ōld′stər), *n. Colloq.* an old person.

old style, *Print.* a type style having uniform thickness of all strokes and slanted serifs.

Old Testament, the collection of Biblical books comprising the Scriptures of "the old covenant." In the Hebrew Bible the three main divisions are the Law, the Prophets, and the Writings. The order in other than Jewish translations follows the Septuagint. In the Vulgate (Latin) translation all but two books of the Apocrypha are included in the Old Testament.

old-tim·er (ōld′tī′mər), *n. Colloq.* one whose residence, membership, etc., dates far back.

Old World, 1. Europe, Asia, and Africa. **2.** the Eastern Hemisphere.

old-world (ōld′wûrld′), *adj.* **1.** of or pertaining to the ancient world. **2.** of or pertaining to the Old World.

o·le·ag·i·nous (ō′lĭ ăj′ə nəs), *adj.* **1.** having the nature or qualities of oil. **2.** containing oil. **3.** producing oil. **4.** oily.

o·le·an·der (ō′lĭ ăn′dər), *n.* a poisonous evergreen shrub with fragrant rose-colored or white flowers.

o·le·o·mar·ga·rine (ō′lĭ ō mär′jə rēn′, -rĭn, -gə-), *n.* a cooking and table fat made from refined vegetable oils, skim milk, and (often) animal fats. Also, **o′le·o′, o·le·o·mar·ga·rin** (ō′lĭ ō mär′-jə rĭn, -gə-).

o·le·o·res·in (ō′lĭ ō rĕz′ən), *n.* a natural mixture of an essential oil and a resin.

ol·fac·tion (ŏl făk′shən), *n.* **1.** act of smelling. **2.** the sense of smell.

ol·fac·to·ry (ŏl făk′tə rĭ, -trĭ), *adj., n., pl.* **-ries.** —*adj.* **1.** of or pertaining to the sense of smell. —*n.* **2.** (*usually pl.*) an olfactory organ.

ol·i·garch (ŏl′ə gärk′), *n.* one of the rulers in an oligarchy.

ol·i·gar·chy (ŏl′ə gär′kĭ), *n., pl.* **-chies. 1.** a form of government in which the power is vested in a small class or clique. **2.** a state so governed. **3.** the ruling group. —**ol′i·gar′chic, ol′i·gar′-chi·cal,** *adj.*

ol·ive (ŏl′ĭv), *n.* **1.** an evergreen tree of Mediterranean and other warm regions, cultivated chiefly for its fruit. **2.** the fruit, a small oval drupe, esteemed as a relish and valuable as a source of oil (**olive oil**). **3.** any of various related or similar trees. **4.** green or yellowish green. —*adj.* **5.** of, pertaining to, or made of olives, their foliage, or their fruit. **6.** green or yellowish green.

olive branch, a branch of the olive tree (an emblem of peace).

O·lym·pi·a (ō lĭm′pĭ ə), *n.* **1.** a plain in ancient Greece where the Olympic games were held. **2.** the capital of Washington, in the W part. 13,254.

O·lym·pi·ad (ō lĭm′pĭ ăd′), *n.* (*often l.c.*) a celebration of the modern Olympic games.

O·lym·pi·an (ō lĭm′pĭ ən), *adj.* **1.** pertaining to or dwelling on Mount Olympus. **2.** pertaining to Olympia (def. 1). **3.** grand; imposing. —*n.* **4.** an Olympian deity.

O·lym·pic (ō lĭm′pĭk), *adj.* **1.** pertaining to Olympia or the games held there. —*n.* **2. the Olympics,** the Olympic games.

Olympic games, 1. the greatest of the games or festivals of ancient Greece, held every four years in Olympia in honor of Zeus. **2.** a modern revival of these games consisting of international competitions in running, swimming, etc.

O·lym·pus (ō lĭm′pəs), *n.* **Mount,** a mountain in NE Greece: fabled abode of the greater Grecian gods. 9730 ft.

O·ma·ha (ō′mə hô′, -hä′), *n.* a city in E Nebraska, on the Missouri river. 223,844.

O·mar Khay·yám (ō′mär kī äm′), died 1123?, Persian poet: wrote *The Rubaiyat.*

o·ma·sum (ō mā′səm), *n., pl.* **-sa** (-sə). the third stomach of a ruminant.

o·me·ga (ō mē′gə, ō mĕg′ə, ō′mĕg ə), *n.* **1.** the last letter (Ω, ω) of the Greek alphabet. **2.** the last or the end.

om·e·let (ŏm′ə lĭt, ŏm′lĭt), *n.* eggs beaten with milk and fried or baked, often with additional ingredients. Also, **om′e·lette.**

o·men (ō′mən), *n.* **1.** anything regarded as giving some indication as to the future. **2.** prophetic significance. —*v.t.* **3.** to portend.

om·i·cron (ŏm′ə krŏn′, ō′mə-), *n.* the fifteenth letter (O, o) of the Greek alphabet.

om·i·nous (ŏm′ə nəs), *adj.* portending evil; inauspicious. —**om′i·nous·ly,** *adv.* —**om′i·nous-ness,** *n.*

o·mit (ō mĭt′), *v.t.,* **omitted, omitting. 1.** to leave out. **2.** to forbear or fail to do, make, use, send, etc. —**o·mis′sion** (ō mĭsh′ən), *n.*

om·ni·bus (ŏm′nə bŭs′, -bəs), *n., pl.* **-buses. 1.** a bus. **2.** an anthology.

om·nip·o·tent (ŏm nĭp′ə tənt), *adj.* **1.** almighty, or infinite in power, as God. **2.** having unlimited or very great authority. —*n.* **3.** an omnipotent being. **4. the Omnipotent,** God. —**om·nip′o·tent·ly,** *adv.* —**om·nip′o·tence,** *n.*

om·ni·pres·ent (ŏm′nə prĕz′ənt), *adj.* present everywhere at the same time. —**om′ni·pres′-ence,** *n.*

om·nis·cient (ŏm nĭsh′ənt), *adj.* **1.** knowing all things. —*n.* **2.** an omniscient being. **3. the Omniscient,** God. —**om·nis′cient·ly,** *adv.* —**om·nis′cience,** *n.*

om·niv·o·rous (ŏm nĭv′ə rəs), *adj.* **1.** eating all kinds of foods. **2.** eating both animal and plant foods. **3.** taking in everything, as with the mind. —**om·niv′o·rous·ly,** *adv.* —**om·niv′o·rous·ness,** *n.*

on (ŏn, ôn), *prep.* **1.** a particle expressing primarily: **a.** position above and in contact with a supporting surface. **b.** immediate proximity. **c.** situation, place, etc. **d.** support, suspension, or reliance. **e.** state, course, etc. **f.** basis. **g.** risk. **h.** occasion. **i.** direction. **j.** encounter. **k.** object of action, thought, etc. **l.** subject, reference, or respect. —*adv.* **2.** on a thing, place, or person. **3.** on oneself or itself. **4.** fast to a thing. **5.** toward a place, point, or object. **6.** forward, onward, or along. **7.** with continuous procedure. **8.** into active operation. —*adj.* **9.** (of a brake) applied. **10.** situated nearer; near. —*n.* **11.** state or fact of being on.

o·nan·ism (ō′nə nĭz′əm), *n.* **1.** withdrawal before occurrence of orgasm. **2.** masturbation. —**o′nan·ist,** *n.*

once (wŭns), *adv.* **1.** formerly. **2.** a single time. **3.** at any time; ever. **4. once for all,** finally and decisively. **5. once in a while,** occasionally. **6. once upon a time,** long ago. —*conj.* **7.** if ever. **8.** whenever. —*n.* **9.** a single occasion. **10.** all

at once, suddenly. **11. at once, a.** immediately. **b.** at the same time.

on·com·ing (ŏn′kŭm′ĭng, ôn′-), *adj.* **1.** approaching. —*n.* **2.** approach.

one (wŭn), *adj.* **1.** being a single unit or individual. **2.** some. **3.** single through union, agreement, or harmony. **4.** the same. **5.** a certain. —*n.* **6.** the first and lowest whole number, or a symbol (as 1, I, or i) representing it. **7.** a unit; a single person or thing. **8. at one,** in a state of unity or agreement. **9. one by one,** singly and in succession. —*pron.* **10.** a person or thing of number or kind indicated or understood. **11.** (in certain pronominal combinations) person. **12.** a person or personified being. **13.** a person indefinitely. **14.** (to avoid repetition) a person or thing of the kind just mentioned.

one-horse (wŭn′hôrs′), *adj.* **1.** using only a single horse. **2.** *U.S. Colloq.* minor.

O·nei·da (ō nī′də), *n.* a member of a tribe of the Iroquois confederacy, former inhabitants of central New York.

O'Neill (ō nēl′), *n.* **Eugene,** born 1888, U.S. dramatist.

one·ness (wŭn′nĭs), *n.* **1.** singleness; unity; sameness. **2.** agreement; concord.

on·er·ous (ŏn′ər əs), *adj.* burdensome, oppressive, or troublesome. —**on′er·ous·ly,** *adv.* —**on′er·ous·ness,** *n.*

one·self (wŭn sĕlf′, wŭnz-), *pron.* a person's self (often used for emphasis or reflexively). Also, **one's self.**

one-sid·ed (wŭn′sī′dĭd), *adj.* **1.** partial, unjust, or unfair. **2.** *Law.* unilateral, as a contract. **3.** unequal. **4.** having but one side.

one-step (wŭn′stĕp′), *n.* a kind of round dance, danced by couples to ragtime.

one-time (wŭn′tīm′), *adj.* former.

one-way (wŭn′wā′), *adj.* moving, or allowing motion, in one direction only.

on·ion (ŭn′yən), *n.* **1.** a widely cultivated plant of the lily family, having an edible succulent bulb of pungent taste and smell. **2.** the bulb.

on·ion·skin (ŭn′yən skĭn′), *n.* a translucent, glazed paper.

on·look·er (ŏn′lŏŏk′ər, ôn′-), *n.* a spectator.

on·ly (ōn′lĭ), *adv.* **1.** alone; solely. **2.** merely; just. **3.** singly. —*adj.* **4.** single; sole. —*conj.* **5.** but.

on·o·mat·o·poe·ia (ŏn′ə măt′ə pē′ə, ō nŏm′ə tə-), *n.* **1.** the formation of a name or word by imitating sound associated with the thing designated. **2.** the use of imitative words for rhetorical effect. —**on′o·mat·o·poe′ic, on·o·mat·o·po·et·ic** (ŏn′ə măt′ə pō ĕt′ĭk), *adj.* —**on′o·mat·o·po·et′i·cal·ly,** *adv.*

on·rush (ŏn′rŭsh′, ôn′-), *n.* a strong forward rush, flow, etc.

on·set (ŏn′sĕt′, ôn′-), *n.* **1.** an attack, esp. a violent one. **2.** a beginning or start.

on·shore (ŏn′shōr′, ôn′-), *adv., adj.* ashore.

on·slaught (ŏn′slôt′, ôn′-), *n.* an onset, assault, or attack, esp. a vigorous one.

Ont., Ontario.

On·tar·i·o (ŏn târ′ĭ ō′), *n.* **1.** a province in S Canada, bordering on the Great Lakes. 3,787,655 pop.; 412,582 sq. mi. *Cap.:* Toronto. **2. Lake,** the smallest of the Great Lakes, between New York and Ontario. ab. 7540 sq. mi.

on·to (ŏn′tōō, ôn′-; *unstressed* -tə), *prep.* to a place or position on; upon; on.

o·nus (ō′nəs), *n.* a burden; responsibility.

on·ward (ŏn′wərd, ôn′-), *adv.* Also, **on′wards. 1.** toward a point ahead or in front. **2.** at a position or point in advance. —*adj.* **3.** directed or moving forward.

on·yx (ŏn′ĭks, ō′nĭks), *n.* a quartz consisting of straight layers or bands which differ in color: used for ornament.

oo·long (ōō′lông, -lŏng), *n.* a variety of semifermented brown or amber tea from Formosa.

ooze[1] (ōōz), *v.,* **oozed, oozing,** *n.* —*v.i.* **1.** (of moisture, etc.) to leak out or exude. **2.** (of a substance) to exude moisture, etc. —*v.t.* **3.** to exude (moisture, etc.). —*n.* **4.** act of oozing. **5.** that which oozes.

ooze[2] (ōōz), *n.* **1.** a calcareous mud covering parts of the ocean bottom. **2.** soft mud; slime.

OP., **1.** opera. **2.** opposite. **3.** opus.

o·pac·i·ty (ō păs′ə tĭ), *n., pl.* **-ties. 1.** state of being opaque. **2.** something opaque.

o·pal (ō′pəl), *n.* a mineral, an amorphous form of silica, found in many varieties and colors, cer-

tain of which are iridescent and valued as gems. —**o·pal·ine** (ō′pəl ĭn, -pə lĭn′), *adj.*

o·pal·esce (ō′pə lĕs′), *v.i.,* **-esced, -escing.** to exhibit a play of colors like that of the opal. —**o′pal·es′cent,** *adj.* —**o′pal·es′cence,** *n.*

o·paque (ō pāk′), *adj.* **1.** not able to transmit, or not transmitting, light. **2.** not shining or bright; dark; dull. **3.** not clear; obscure. —*n.* **4.** something opaque. —**o·paque′ly,** *adv.* —**o·paque′ness,** *n.*

op. cit., opere citato.

ope (ōp), *adj., v.t., v.i.,* **oped, oping.** *Archaic.* open.

o·pen (ō′pən), *adj.* **1.** not shut, as a door, box, drawer, etc. **2.** not enclosed as by barriers. **3.** that may be entered, used, competed for, etc., by all. **4.** available. **5.** unfilled, as a position. **6.** not engaged, as time. **7.** without prohibition as to hunting or fishing. **8.** *U.S. Colloq.* without legal restrictions as to saloons, gambling places, etc. **9.** undecided, as a question. **10.** liable or subject to. **11.** accessible to appeals, offers, etc. **12.** having no cover, roof, etc. **13.** exposed or bare. **14.** unobstructed, as a passage, view, etc. **15.** existing, acting, carried on, etc., without concealment. **16.** candid; frank. **17.** having openings or perforations. **18.** spread out. **19.** generous; liberal. **20.** not yet balanced or adjusted, as an account. **21.** *Phonet.* a. pronounced with a relatively large opening above the tongue. b. (of a syllable) ending with its vowel. —*v.t.* **22.** to make (a house, door, box, drawer, etc.) open. **23.** to render (any space) open to passage or access. **24.** to give access to. **25.** to uncover; lay bare. **26.** to disclose; reveal. **27.** to spread out. **28.** to make less compact. **29.** to establish for the entrance or use of customers, etc. **30.** to begin; start. **31.** to cut or break into. —*v.i.* **32.** to become open, as a door, box, etc. **33.** to afford access (into, to, etc.). **34.** (of a building, etc.) to open its doors. **35.** to begin a session or term. **36.** to begin a season or tour. **37.** to have an opening (into, upon, etc.). **38.** to come apart or asunder. **39.** to spread out or expand. **40.** to become less compact. **41.** to begin; start. —*n.* **42.** an open or clear space. **43.** the open air. **44.** the open water, as of the sea. **45.** the situation of one who does not use or seek concealment. —**o′pen·er,** *n.* —**o′pen·ly,** *adv.* —**o′pen·ness,** *n.*

open air, the unconfined atmosphere; outdoor air. —**o′pen-air′,** *adj.*

o·pen-and-shut (ō′pən ən shŭt′), *adj.* obvious; easily decided.

open city, *Mil.* a city officially declared to be of no military importance and therefore not subject to military attack.

open door, 1. the policy of admitting all nations upon equal terms, esp. for trade. **2.** free admission or access.

o·pen-hand·ed (ō′pən hăn′dĭd), *adj.* generous. —**o′pen-hand′ed·ly,** *adv.*

o·pen-heart·ed (ō pən här′tĭd), *adj.* **1.** candid; frank. **2.** kindly.

o·pen·ing (ō pən ĭng), *n.* **1.** a making or becoming open. **2.** an unobstructed or unoccupied space or place. **3.** a gap, hole, or aperture. **4.** *U.S.* a tract of land thinly wooded as compared with adjoining forest tracts. **5.** act of beginning or starting. **6.** the first part or initial stage. **7.** a vacancy. **8.** an opportunity. **9.** the first performance of a theatrical production.

open shop, a nonunion shop which may or may not employ union members together with nonmembers, but which does not recognize or deal with a union as the representative of the employees.

o·pen·work (ō pən wûrk′), *n.* any kind of work, esp. ornamental, as of metal, lace, etc., showing openings.

op·er·a (ŏp′ər ə, ŏp′rə), *n.* **1.** an extended dramatic composition in which music is an essential and predominant factor. **2.** the branch of musical and dramatic art represented by such compositions. **3.** the score or the words of a musical drama.

op·er·a·ble (ŏp′ər ə bəl), *adj.* **1.** practicable. **2.** admitting of a surgical operation.

opera glasses, a small binocular for use in theaters, etc. Also, **opera glass.**

op·er·ate (ŏp′ə rāt′), *v.,* **-ated, -ating.** —*v.i.* **1.** to work or run, as a machine does. **2.** to exert force or influence. **3.** *Surg.* to treat the body of a patient, usually with instruments, to remedy deformity, injury, or disease. **4.** *Mil., Naval.* to carry on operations in war. —*v.t.* **5.** to manage or use (a machine, etc.) at work. **6.** to keep (a machine, factory, system, etc.) working.

op·er·at·ic (ŏp′ə răt′ĭk), *adj.* of or pertaining to opera. **—op′er·at′i·cal·ly,** *adv.*

op·er·a·tion (ŏp′ə rā′shən), *n.* **1.** act, process, or manner of operating. **2.** state of being operative. **3.** efficacy; influence. **4.** exertion of force or influence. **5.** a process or procedure. **6.** a business transaction. **7.** *Surg.* a process or method of operating on the body of a patient, as with instruments, to remedy injury, etc. **8.** *Math.* a process such as addition. **9.** *Mil., Naval.* **a.** the conduct of a campaign. **b.** a campaign. **—op′er·a′tion·al,** *adj.*

op·er·a·tive (ŏp′ə rā′tĭv, -ər ə tĭv), *n.* **1.** a workman, artisan, or factory hand. **2.** a detective. **—adj. 3.** exerting force or influence. **4.** being in effect or operation. **5.** effective. **6.** *Med.* of or pertaining to remedial operations.

op·er·a·tor (ŏp′ə rā′tər), *n.* **1.** one employed or skilled in operating a machine or apparatus. **2.** one who conducts some industrial establishment, enterprise, or system.

o·per·cu·lum (ō pûr′kyə ləm), *n., pl.* **-la** (-lə), **-lums.** *Bot., Zool., etc.* a part or organ serving as a lid or cover.

o·pe·re ci·ta·to (ŏp′ə rē′ sī tā′tō), *Latin.* in the work cited or quoted. *Abbr.:* op. cit.

op·er·et·ta (ŏp′ə rĕt′ə), *n., pl.* **-erettas, -erretti** (-ə rĕt′ē). a short, light opera.

oph·thal·mi·a (ŏf thăl′mĭ ə), *n.* *Pathol.* inflammation of the eye.

oph·thal·mic (ŏf thăl′mĭk), *adj.* of or pertaining to the eye; ocular.

oph·thal·mol·o·gy (ŏf′thăl mŏl′ə jĭ), *n.* the science dealing with the anatomy, functions, and diseases of the eye. **—oph′thal·mol′o·gist,** *n.*

o·pi·ate (*n., adj.* ō′pĭ ĭt, -āt′; *v.* ō′pĭ āt′), *n., adj., v.,* **-ated, -ating.** *—n.* **1.** a medicine that contains opium; narcotic. **2.** anything that causes dullness or inaction, or that quiets the feelings. *—adj.* **3.** prepared with opium. **4.** inducing sleep; narcotic. *—v.t.* **5.** to subject to an opiate.

o·pine (ō pīn′), *v.t., v.i.,* **opined, opining.** *Obs. except humorously.* to think; deem.

o·pin·ion (ə pĭn′yən), *n.* **1.** what is thought on any subject. **2.** a particular judgment or belief. **3.** a formal or professional judgment. **4.** a judgment or estimate, as to character, merit, etc.

o·pin·ion·at·ed (ə pĭn′yə nā′tĭd), *adj.* conceitedly dogmatic. **—o·pin·ion·at′ed·ness,** *n.*

o·pin·ion·a·tive (ə pĭn′yə nā′tĭv), *adj.* **1.** of or pertaining to opinion. **2.** opinionated.

o·pi·um (ō′pĭ əm), *n.* the inspissated juice of a poppy, containing morphine: a stimulant narcotic used in medicine to relieve pain, induce sleep, etc.

O·por·to (ō pōr′tō), *n.* a city in NW Portugal. 258,548.

o·pos·sum (ə pŏs′əm, pŏs′əm), *n.* a prehensile-tailed, pouched marsupial mammal, about the size of a large cat, common in the southern U.S.

opp., **1.** opposed. **2.** opposite.

Op·pen·heim·er (ŏp′ən hī′mər), *n.* **J. Robert,** born 1904, U.S. nuclear physicist.

op·po·nent (ə pō′nənt), *n.* **1.** one who is on the opposite side in a contest, controversy, or the like. *—adj.* **2.** being opposite, as in position. **3.** adverse; contrary.

op·por·tune (ŏp′ər tūn′, -tōōn′), *adj.* **1.** appropriate or favorable. **2.** timely. **—op′por·tune′ly,** *adv.* **—op′por·tune′ness,** *n.*

op·por·tun·ism (ŏp′ər tū′nĭz əm, -tōō′-), *n.* the policy or practice, as in politics, of adapting actions, etc., to expediency (often at the sacrifice of principle). **—op′por·tun′ist,** *n., adj.* **—op′·por·tun·is′tic,** *adj.*

op·por·tu·ni·ty (ŏp′ər tū′nə tĭ, -tōō′-), *n., pl.* **-ties.** an appropriate or favorable time.

op·pos·a·ble (ə pō′zə bəl), *adj.* **1.** capable of being placed opposite to something else. **2.** that may be opposed.

op·pose (ə pōz′), *v.,* **-posed, -posing.** *—v.t.* **1.** to act against; resist; combat. **2.** to hinder. **3.** to set as an opponent. **4.** to be hostile or adverse to. **5.** to set as an obstacle. **6.** to set in contrast. **7.** to use or take as being opposite or contrary. *—v.i.* **8.** to be or act in opposition. **—op·pos′er,** *n.*

op·po·site (ŏp′ə zĭt), *adj.* **1.** contrary or diametrically different, as in nature, qualities, direction, result, or significance. **—n. 2.** one that is

opposite or contrary. **—op′po·site·ly,** *adv.* **—op′po·site·ness,** *n.*

op·po·si·tion (ŏp′ə zĭsh′ən), *n.* **1.** the action of opposing, resisting, or combating. **2.** antagonism; hostility. **3.** an opposing party or body. **4.** a political party opposed to the party in power.

op·press (ə prĕs′), *v.t.* **1.** to lie heavily upon (the mind, a person, etc.), as care or sorrow. **2.** to burden with cruel or unjust impositions or restraints. **3.** to weigh down, as weariness does. **—op·pres′sor,** *n.*

op·pres·sion (ə prĕsh′ən), *n.* **1.** the exercise of authority or power in a burdensome, cruel, or unjust manner. **2.** act of oppressing. **3.** state of being oppressed. **4.** a weary, depressed feeling.

op·pres·sive (ə prĕs′ĭv), *adj.* **1.** burdensome, unjustly harsh, or tyrannical. **2.** uncomfortably great, intense, etc. **—op·pres′sive·ly,** *adv.* **—op·pres′sive·ness,** *n.*

op·pro·bri·ous (ə prō′brĭ əs), *adj.* **1.** conveying or expressing opprobrium. **2.** disgraceful; shameful. **—op·pro′bri·ous·ly,** *adv.*

op·pro·bri·um (ə prō′brĭ əm), *n.* the disgrace or the reproach incurred by shameful conduct.

opt., **1.** optical. **2.** optional.

op·ta·tive (ŏp′tə tĭv), *Gram.* *—adj.* **1.** designating or pertaining to a verb mood (as in Greek) having among its functions the expression of a wish. *—n.* **2.** the optative mood. **3.** a verb in it.

op·tic (ŏp′tĭk), *adj.* **1.** pertaining to or connected with the eye as the organ of sight, or sight as a function of the brain. **2.** optical. **—n. 3.** (*usually pl.*) the eye.

op·ti·cal (ŏp′tə kəl), *adj.* **1.** acting by means of sight or light, as instruments. **2.** constructed to assist the sight. **3.** visual. **4.** pertaining to optics. **—op′ti·cal·ly,** *adv.*

op·ti·cian (ŏp tĭsh′ən), *n.* **1.** one who makes eyeglasses in accordance with the prescriptions of oculists. **2.** a maker or seller of any optical glasses and instruments.

op·tics (ŏp′tĭks), *n.* the branch of physical science that deals with the properties and phenomena of light and with vision.

op·ti·mism (ŏp′tə mĭz′əm), *n.* **1.** disposition to hope or look for the best. **2.** the belief th t good ultimately predominates over evil in the world. **—op′ti·mist,** *n.* **—op′ti·mis′tic,** *adj.* **—op′ti·mis′ti·cal·ly,** *adv.*

op·ti·mum (ŏp′tə məm), *n., pl.* **-ma** (-mə), **-mums,** *adj.* *—n.* **1.** the best point, degree, amount, etc., for the purpose. *—adj.* **2.** best; most favorable.

op·tion (ŏp′shən), *n.* **1.** power or liberty of choosing. **2.** something chosen; choice. **3.** a privilege of demanding, within a specified time, the carrying out of a transaction upon stipulated terms.

op·tion·al (ŏp′shən əl), *adj.* **1.** left to one's choice. **2.** leaving something to choice. **—op′·tion·al·ly,** *adv.*

op·tom·e·try (ŏp tŏm′ə trĭ), *n.* the practice or art of testing the eyes for eyeglasses by means of suitable instruments. **—op·tom′e·trist,** *n.*

op·u·lent (ŏp′yə lənt), *adj.* **1.** wealthy, rich, or affluent, as persons or places. **2.** richly supplied; abundant or plentiful. **—op′u·lent·ly,** *adv.* **—op′u·lence, op′u·len·cy,** *n.*

o·pus (ō′pəs), *n., pl.* **opera** (ŏp′ə rə). **1.** a work. **2.** a musical composition.

or (ôr; *unstressed* ər), *conj.* a particle used: **1.** to connect words, phrases, or clauses representing alternatives. **2.** to connect alternative terms. **3.** as the correlative to a preceding *either.*

-or, a suffix of nouns denoting one who or that which does something, or has some particular function or office, as in *actor, confessor, creditor.* In some cases -or is used as an alternative or a substitute for -er[1], esp. in legal terms, as in *lessor, assignor.*

or·a·cle (ôr′ə kəl, ŏr′-), *n.* **1.** (in ancient Greece and elsewhere) an utterance, often ambiguous or obscure, given by a priest or priestess at a shrine as the response of the god to an inquiry. **2.** the agency or medium giving such responses. **3.** a shrine or place at which they were given.

o·rac·u·lar (ō răk′yə lər), *adj.* **1.** of the nature of or resembling an oracle. **2.** uttered as if divinely inspired or infallible. **3.** ambiguous or obscure. **—o·rac′u·lar·ly,** *adv.*

o·ral (ōr′əl), *adj.* **1.** uttered; spoken. **2.** employing speech. **3.** of or pertaining to the mouth. **4.** done, taken, or administered by the mouth. **—n. 5.** an oral examination in a college, school, etc. **—o′ral·ly,** *adv.*

O·ran (ō rän′), *n.* a seaport in NW Algeria. 200,671.

or·ange (ôr′ĭnj, ŏr′-), *n.* **1.** a round reddish-yellow edible citrus fruit of which there are two principal kinds, the bitter and sweet, the latter comprising the most important of the citrus fruits. **2.** any of the white-flowered evergreen trees of warm countries yielding it. **3.** reddish yellow. —*adj.* **4.** of or pertaining to the orange. **5.** of a reddish-yellow color.

Or·ange (ôr′ĭnj, ŏr′-), *n.* **1.** a city in NE New Jersey. 35,717. **2.** a princely family of Europe, including the present royal family of The Netherlands.

or·ange·ade (ôr′ĭnj ād′, ŏr′-), *n.* a drink made of orange juice and sweetened water.

Or·ange·man (ôr′ĭnj mən, ŏr′-), *n., pl.* **-men.** a member of a secret society formed in the north of Ireland in 1795, having for its object the maintenance of the Protestant religion and political ascendancy.

orange pekoe, a black tea composed of only the smallest top leaves: grown in India and Ceylon.

o·rang-u·tan (ō răng′ŏŏ tăn′), *n.* a large, long-armed anthropoid ape of arboreal habits, found in Borneo and Sumatra. Also, **o·rang-ou·tang** (ō-răng′ŏŏ tăng′), **o·rang′.**

Orang-utan (4½ ft. high)

o·rate (ō rāt′, ōr′āt), *v.i.*, **orated, orating.** *Chiefly Humorous.* to make an oration.

o·ra·tion (ō rā′shən), *n.* a formal speech, as at academic exercises.

or·a·tor (ôr′ə tər, ŏr′-), *n.* a public speaker, esp. one of great eloquence.

or·a·to·ri·o (ôr′ə tōr′ĭ-ō, ŏr′-), *n., pl.* **-rios.** an extended musical composition, usually based upon a religious theme, for solo voices, chorus, and orchestra.

or·a·to·ry[1] (ôr′ə tōr′ĭ, ŏr′-), *n.* **1.** eloquent speaking. **2.** the art of public speaking. —**or/a·tor′i·cal,** *adj.* —**or/a·tor′i·cal·ly,** *adv.*

or·a·to·ry[2] (ôr′ə tōr′ĭ, ŏr′-), *n., pl.* **-ries.** a place of prayer, as a small chapel.

orb (ôrb), *n.* **1.** *Chiefly Poetic.* any of the heavenly bodies. **2.** a sphere or globe. **3.** *Chiefly Poetic.* the eyeball or eye. —*v.t.* **4.** to form into a circle or a sphere.

or·bic·u·lar (ôr bĭk′yə lər), *adj.* circular; ringlike or spherical. Also, **or·bic·u·late** (ôr bĭk′yə-lĭt, -lāt/).

or·bit (ôr′bĭt), *n.* **1.** the elliptical or curved path described by a planet, etc., about another body. **2.** a course regularly pursued, as in life. **3.** *Anat.* the bony cavity of the skull which contains the eye. —**or/bit·al,** *adj.*

orch., orchestra.

or·chard (ôr′chərd), *n.* **1.** a piece of ground devoted to the cultivation of fruit trees. **2.** a collection of such trees.

or·ches·tra (ôr′kĭs trə), *n.* **1.** a company of performers on various musical instruments for playing concert music. **2.** (in a modern theater, etc.) **a.** the space reserved for the musicians. **b.** the entire main-floor space for spectators. —**or·ches·tral** (ôr kĕs′trəl), *adj.* —**or·ches′tral·ly,** *adv.*

or·ches·trate (ôr′kĭs trāt′), *v.t., v.i.,* **-trated, -trating.** to arrange (music) for performance by an orchestra. —**or·ches·tra′tion,** *n.*

or·chid (ôr′kĭd), *n.* **1.** any of certain perennial herbs of temperate and tropical regions with beautiful flowers of unusual form. **2.** purple, varying from bluish to reddish.

or·chi·da·ceous (ôr′kĭ dā′shəs), *adj.* belonging to the orchid family of plants.

ord., **1.** order. **2.** ordinance. **3.** ordinary.

or·dain (ôr dān′), *v.t.* **1.** *Eccles.* to invest with ministerial or sacerdotal functions. **2.** to appoint authoritatively. **3.** to decree. —**or·dain′er,** *n.* —**or·dain′ment,** *n.*

or·deal (ôr dēl′, -dē′əl, ôr′dēl), *n.* **1.** any severe test or trial. **2.** a primitive form of trial, as by the effect of fire upon the accused, the result being regarded as a divine judgment.

or·der (ôr′dər), *n.* **1.** an authoritative direction, injunction, or mandate. **2.** *Law.* a command of a court or judge. **3.** the disposition of things following one after another, as in space, time, etc. **4.** methodical or harmonious arrangement. **5.**

formal disposition or array. **6.** proper or satisfactory condition. **7.** state or condition generally. **8.** *Gram.* the arrangement of the elements of a construction in a particular sequence. **9.** any distinctive class, kind, or sort. **10.** *Biol.* the usual major subdivision of a class or subclass. **11.** a body of persons of the same profession, occupation, or pursuits. **12.** a body of persons living by common consent under the same religious, moral, or social regulations. **13.** a monastic society or fraternity. **14.** (*usually pl.*) the rank or status of an ordained Christian minister. **15.** (*usually pl.*) the rite or sacrament of ordination. **16.** a prescribed form of divine service. **17.** *Hist.* a society of knights, of combined military and monastic character, as in the Middle Ages. **18.** a modern society resembling the knightly orders. **19.** conformity to law or established authority. **20.** absence of revolt, disturbance, etc. **21.** customary mode of procedure. **22.** an established system or regime. **23.** an order to make or furnish something. **24.** a quantity of goods purchased. **25.** *Archit.* **a.** a series of columns with their entablature arranged in given proportions. **b.** any one of the typical variations of such an arrangement distinguished by proportion, capital types, and other characteristics. **26. in order that,** to the end that. **27. in order to,** as a means to. **28. in short order,** immediately. **29. on order,** ordered but not yet received. **30. on the order of,** resembling to some extent. —*v.t.* **31.** to give a direction or command to. **32.** to command to go or come. **33.** to give an order for. **34.** to prescribe. **35.** to regulate, conduct, or manage. **36.** to arrange methodically or suitably. —*v.i.* **37.** to issue orders. —**or·der′er,** *n.*

or·der·ly (ôr′dər lĭ), *adj., adv., n., pl.* **-lies.** —*adj.* **1.** arranged or disposed in order. **2.** systematic; methodical. **3.** well-behaved; proper. —*adv.* **4.** according to established order or rule. —*n.* **5.** *Mil.* a soldier attending on a superior officer to carry orders, etc. **6.** an attendant in a hospital. —**or′der·li·ness,** *n.*

or·di·nal[1] (ôr′də nəl), *adj.* **1.** pertaining to an order, as of animals or plants. —*n.* **2.** an ordinal number or numeral.

or·di·nal[2] (ôr′də nəl), *n.* **1.** a directory of ecclesiastical services. **2.** a book containing the forms for the ordination of priests, etc.

ordinal number, any of the numbers *first, second, third,* etc. (in distinction from *one, two, three,* etc.). Also, **ordinal numeral.**

or·di·nance (ôr′də nəns), *n.* an authoritative rule or law; a decree.

or·di·nar·i·ly (ôr′də nĕr′ə lĭ; *emphatic* ôr′də-när′ə lĭ), *adv.* **1.** in ordinary cases; usually. **2.** in the ordinary way.

or·di·nar·y (ôr′də nĕr′ĭ), *adj., n., pl.* **-naries.** —*adj.* **1.** of the usual kind. **2.** somewhat inferior. **3.** customary; normal. —*n.* **4.** the ordinary condition, degree, run, or the like. **5.** a high bicycle of an early type, with one large wheel in front and one small wheel behind. **6. in ordinary,** (of officials, etc.) in regular service. —**or·di·nar′i·ness,** *n.*

or·di·nate (ôr′də nāt′, -nĭt), *n.* *Math.* the y Cartesian coördinate. See **abscissa.**

or·di·na·tion (ôr′də nā′shən), *n.* **1.** *Eccles.* act or ceremony of ordaining. **2.** fact of being ordained.

ordn., ordnance.

ord·nance (ôrd′nəns), *n.* **1.** cannon or artillery. **2.** military weapons of all kinds.

or·dure (ôr′jər, -dyŏŏr), *n.* filth; dung.

ore (ōr), *n.* **1.** a metal-bearing mineral or rock. **2.** a mineral or natural product serving as a source of some nonmetallic substance, as sulfur.

Or·e·gon (ôr′ə gŏn′, -gən, ŏr′-), *n.* a State in the NW United States, on the Pacific coast. 1,452,618 pop.; 96,981 sq. mi. *Cap.*: Salem. *Abbr.*: Oreg. *or* Ore. —**Or·e·go·ni·an** (ôr′ə gō′nĭ ən, ŏr′-), *adj., n.*

org., **1.** organic. **2.** organized.

or·gan (ôr′gən), *n.* **1.** Also, **pipe organ.** a musical instrument consisting of one or more sets of pipes sounded by means of compressed air, played by means of keys arranged in one or more keyboards. **2.** a reed organ. **3.** (in an animal or a plant) a part, as the heart, having some specific function. **4.** an instrument or means, as of performance. **5.** a means of communicating thoughts, etc., as a newspaper serving as the voice of a political party.

or·gan·dy (ôr′gən dĭ), *n., pl.* **-dies.** a fine, thin, stiff cotton fabric usually having a durable crisp finish: used for neckwear, dresses, curtains, etc. Also, **or′gan·die.**

or·gan·ic (ôr găn′ĭk), *adj.* **1.** noting or pertaining to a class of chemical compounds which consists of those existing in or derived from living organisms and includes all other compounds of carbon. **2.** characteristic of, pertaining to, or derived from living organisms. **3.** of or pertaining to an organ or the organs of an animal or a plant. **4.** organized; systematic. **5.** constitutional; structural. **—or·gan/i·cal·ly,** *adv.*

or·gan·ism (ôr′gə nĭz′əm), *n.* **1.** a living individual composed of mutually dependent parts. **2.** any form of animal or plant life. **3.** any organized body or system.

or·gan·ist (ôr′gən ĭst), *n.* a player on an organ.

or·gan·i·za·tion (ôr′gən ə zā′shən), *n.* **1.** act or process of organizing. **2.** state or manner of being organized. **3.** that which is organized. **4.** a body of persons organized for some end or work. **—or′gan·i·za′tion·al,** *adj.*

or·gan·ize (ôr′gə nīz′), *v.,* **-ized, -izing. —***v.t.* **1.** to form into a whole consisting of coördinated parts. **2.** to systematize. **3.** to give organic character to. **4.** to build a trade union among. **5.** to enlist the employees of into a trade union. **—***v.i.* **6.** to combine in an organized company, party, or the like. **7.** to assume organic structure. **—or′gan·iz′er,** *n.*

or·gasm (ôr′găz əm), *n.* *Physiol.* a complex series of responses of the genitals and skin at the culmination of a sexual act.

or·gy (ôr′jĭ), *n., pl.* **-gies. 1.** wild, drunken, or licentious revelry. **2.** any proceedings marked by unbridled indulgence of passions. **3.** (*pl.*) *Class. Myth.* secret rites connected with the worship of certain deities (esp. Dionysus) celebrated with wild dancing and singing, drinking, etc. **—or·gi·as·tic** (ôr′jĭ ăs′tĭk), *adj.*

o·ri·el (ôr′Ĭ əl), *n.* a bay window.

o·ri·ent (*n., adj.* ôr′Ĭ ənt, ōr′Ĭ ĕnt′; *v.* ôr′Ĭ ĕnt′), *n.* **1.** the east. **2. the Orient, a.** the countries to the E (and SE) of the Mediterranean. **b.** the countries of Asia generally, especially E Asia. **—***adj.* **3.** rising. **4.** *Now Poetic.* eastern. **—***v.t.* **5.** to place so as to face the east. **6.** to place in any definite position. **7.** to adjust with relation to surroundings, circumstances, facts, etc. **8.** *Survey.* to turn a map so that north on the map is parallel to north on the ground. **—***v.i.* **9.** to turn toward the east, or in any specified direction.

O·ri·en·tal (ōr′Ĭ ĕn′təl), *adj.* **1.** (*also l.c.*) of, pertaining to, or characteristic of the Orient. **2.** (*l.c.*) eastern. **—***n.* **3.** (*sometimes l.c.*) a native or inhabitant of the Orient, esp. one belonging to a native race.

O·ri·en·tal·ism (ōr′Ĭ ĕn′tə lĬz′əm), *n.* **1.** an Oriental peculiarity. **2.** oriental character. **3.** the knowledge and study of Oriental languages, literature, etc. Also, **orientalism. —O′ri·en′tal·ist,** *n.*

o·ri·en·ta·tion (ōr′Ĭ ən tā′shən), *n.* **1.** act or process of orienting. **2.** state of being oriented. **3.** *Psychol.* the ability to locate oneself in one's environment with reference to time, place, and people.

or·i·fice (ôr′ə fĬs, ŏr′-), *n.* a mouth or aperture, as of a tube or pipe; vent.

orig., **1.** origin. **2.** original. **3.** originally.

or·i·gin (ôr′ə jĬn, ŏr′-), *n.* **1.** that from which anything arises or is derived; source. **2.** rise or derivation from a particular source. **3.** the beginning. **4.** birth; parentage; extraction.

o·rig·i·nal (ə rĬj′ə nəl), *adj.* **1.** belonging or pertaining to the origin or beginning; first. **2.** new; fresh; novel. **3.** arising or proceeding independently. **4.** capable of or given to thinking or acting independently. **5.** proceeding from a person as the inventor, maker, composer, or author. **6.** being that from which a copy, a translation, or the like, is made. **—***n.* **7.** a primary form or type from which varieties are derived. **8.** an original work, writing, or the like (as opposed to any copy or imitation). **9.** the person or thing represented by a picture, description, etc. **—o·rig′i·nal·ly,** *adv.*

o·rig·i·nal·i·ty (ə rĬj′ə năl′ə tĭ), *n., pl.* **-ties. 1.** state or quality of being original. **2.** ability to think or act independently. **3.** freshness or novelty.

original sin, *Theol.* **1.** a tendency to evil held to be innate in mankind and transmitted from Adam to the race in consequence of his sin. **2.** *Rom. Cath. Theol.* the privation of sanctifying grace in consequence of Adam's sin.

o·rig·i·nate (ə rĬj′ə nāt′), *v.,* **-nated, -nating. —***v.i.* **1.** to take its origin; arise; spring. **—***v.t.* **2.** to give origin to; initiate; invent. **—o·rig′i·na′tion,** *n.* **—o·rig′i·na′tor,** *n.*

O·ri·no·co (ō′rē nō′kō), *n.* a large river in N South America, flowing from S Venezuela into the Atlantic. ab. 1600 mi.

o·ri·ole (ôr′Ĭ ōl′), *n.* **1.** any of certain Old World passerine birds, mostly bright-yellow with black on the head, wings and tail, as the **golden oriole** of Europe and Africa. **2.** any of various brightly colored American passerine birds, as the **Baltimore oriole.**

O·ri·on (ō rī′ən), *n., gen.* **Orionis** (ôr′Ĭ ō′nĬs, ōr′-). *Astron.* a constellation containing two bright supergiant stars.

o·ri·son (ôr′Ĭ zən, ŏr′-), *n.* a prayer.

Ork·ney Islands (ôrk′nĬ), an island group off the NE tip of Scotland. 21,600 pop.; 376 sq. mi. *Co. seat:* Kirkwall.

Or·lan·do (ôr lăn′dō), *n.* a city in central Florida. 36,736.

Or·lé·ans (ôr′lĬ ənz), *n.* a city in N France: seige raised by Joan of Arc (1428). 70,240.

or·mo·lu (ôr′mə lōō′), *n.* an alloy of copper and zinc, used to imitate gold.

or·na·ment (*n.* ôr′nə mənt; *v.* ôr′nə mĕnt′), *n.* **1.** an accessory, article, or detail used to beautify the appearance or general effect. **2.** a person who adds luster, as to surroundings, society, etc. **—***v.t.* **3.** to furnish with ornaments. **4.** to be an ornament to.

or·na·men·tal (ôr′nə mĕn′təl), *adj.* **1.** of or used for ornament. **2.** decorative. **—***n.* **3.** something ornamental. **4.** a plant cultivated for decorative purposes. **—or′na·men′tal·ly,** *adv.*

or·na·men·ta·tion (ôr′nə mĕn tā′shən), *n.* **1.** act of ornamenting. **2.** state of being ornamented. **3.** that with which a thing is ornamented.

or·nate (ôr nāt′), *adj.* **1.** elaborately or showily adorned. **2.** embellished with rhetoric. **—or·nate′ly,** *adv.* **—or·nate′ness,** *n.*

or·ner·y (ôr′nə rĭ), *adj. Chiefly U.S. Dial.* **1.** disagreeable in disposition. **2.** stubborn.

ornith., **1.** ornithological. **2.** ornithology.

or·ni·thol·o·gy (ôr′nə thŏl′ə jĬ), *n.* the branch of zoölogy that deals with birds. **—or·ni·tho·log·i·cal** (ôr′nə thə lŏj′ə kəl), *adj.* **—or′ni·thol′o·gist,** *n.*

o·ro·tund (ōr′ə tŭnd′), *adj.* **1.** (of the voice or utterance) characterized by strength, fullness, richness, and clearness. **2.** (of a style of utterance) pompous or bombastic.

O·roz·co (ō rôs′kō), *n.* **José Clemente,** born 1883, Mexican painter.

or·phan (ôr′fən), *n.* **1.** a child bereaved by death of both parents. **—***adj.* **2.** of or for orphans. **3.** bereaved of parents. **—***v.t.* **4.** to bereave of parents. **—or′phan·hood′,** *n.*

or·phan·age (ôr′fən Ĭj), *n.* an institution for orphans.

Or·phe·us (ôr′fĬ əs, -fūs), *n.* *Gk. Myth.* a son of Apollo and Calliope: a singer and an entrancing player of the lyre. **—Or·phic** (ôr′fĬk), *adj.*

or·ris (ôr′Ĭs, ŏr′-), *n.* any of certain species of iris with a fragrant rootstock.

or·ris·root (ôr′Ĭs rōōt′, -rŏŏt′, ŏr′-), *n.* the rootstock of the orris, used as a perfume, etc.

or·tho·clase (ôr′thə klās′, -klāz′), *n.* a very common mineral of the feldspar group, potassium aluminum silicate: used in the manufacture of porcelain.

or·tho·don·tia (ôr′thə dŏn′shə, -shĬ ə), *n.* the branch of dentistry concerned with straightening irregular teeth. **—or′tho·don′tic,** *adj.* **—or′tho·don′tist,** *n.*

or·tho·dox (ôr′thə dŏks′), *adj.* **1.** sound or correct in opinion or doctrine, esp. theological or religious doctrine. **2.** conforming to the Christian faith as represented in the primitive ecumenical creeds. **3.** (*cap.*) **a.** designating the Eastern or Greek Church. **b.** of or pertaining to the Greek Church. **4.** approved; conventional. **—or′tho·dox′ly,** *adv.*

Orthodox Church, the Christian church of the countries formerly comprised in the Eastern Roman Empire, and of countries evangelized from it, as Russia.

or·tho·dox·y (ôr′thə dŏk′sĬ), *n., pl.* **-doxies. 1.** orthodox practice. **2.** orthodox character.

or·tho·ë·py (ôr thō′ə pĬ, ôr′thō-), *n.* the study of correct pronunciation.

or·thog·ra·phy (ôr thŏg′rə fĬ), *n., pl.* **-phies.**

the art of spelling words according to accepted usage. —**or·tho·graph·ic** (ôr/thə gräf/ĭk), **or/-tho·graph/i·cal,** adj.

or·tho·pe·dics (ôr/thə pē/dĭks), n. the correction or cure of deformities and diseases of the spine, bones, joints, muscles, or other parts of the skeletal system. Also, **or/tho·pe/dy.** —**or/tho-pe/dic,** adj. —**or/tho·pe/dist,** n.

or·thop·ter·ous (ôr thŏp/tər əs), adj. belonging or relating to an order of insects that includes the crickets, grasshoppers, cockroaches, etc., characterized usually by leathery fore wings and longitudinally folded, membranous hind wings. —**or·thop/ter·an,** adj., n.

or·to·lan (ôr/tə lən), n. an Old World bunting, esteemed as a table delicacy.

-ory, a suffix of adjectives meaning "having the function or effect of," as in compulsory.

Os, Chem. osmium.

O·sa·ka (ō sä/kə), n. a seaport in S Japan. 1,293,501.

os·cil·late (ŏs/ə lāt/), v.i., -lated, -lating. **1.** to swing or move to and fro, as a pendulum does; vibrate. **2.** to fluctuate between states, opinions, purposes, etc. **3.** Physics. to have, produce, or generate oscillations. —**os/cil·la/tor,** n.

os·cil·la·tion (ŏs/ə lā/shən), n. **1.** act or fact of oscillating. **2.** a single movement in one direction of an oscillating body, etc. **3.** fluctuation between states, opinions, etc. **4.** Physics. **a.** a single forward and backward surge of electric charge. **b.** a rapid change in electromotive force. **c.** one complete cycle of an electric wave.

os·cine (ŏs/ĭn, -īn), adj. of or pertaining to a large group of passerine birds, containing those with the most highly developed vocal organs, and commonly termed the singing birds.

os·cu·late (ŏs/kyə lāt/), v.t., v.i., -lated, -lating. **1.** to kiss. **2.** to bring or come into close contact. —**os/cu·la/tion.** —**os·cu·la·to·ry** (ŏs/kyə lə-tōr/ĭ), adj.

-ose, an adjective suffix meaning "full of," "abounding in," "given to," "like," as in verbose.

Osh·kosh (ŏsh/kŏsh), n. a city in E Wisconsin. 39,089.

o·sier (ō/zhər), Chiefly Brit. —n. **1.** any of various willows with tough flexible twigs or branches which are used for wickerwork. **2.** a twig from such a willow. —adj. **3.** pertaining to or made of osiers.

O·si·ris (ō sī/rĭs), n. one of the principal Egyptian gods, brother and husband of Isis.

-osity, a noun suffix equivalent to -ose (or -ous) plus -ity.

Os·lo (ŏz/lō, ŏs/-), n. a seaport in and the capital of Norway, in the SE part. 275,160.

os·mi·um (ŏz/mĭ əm), n. Chem. a hard, heavy metallic element used for electric-light filaments, etc. Symbol: Os; at. wt.: 190.2; at. no.: 76; sp. gr.: 22.48 at 20°C.

os·mo·sis (ŏz mō/sĭs, ŏs-), n. Phys. Chem., etc. **1.** the tendency of a fluid to pass through a semipermeable membrane into a solution where its concentration is lower, thus equalizing the conditions on either side of the membrane. **2.** the diffusion of fluids through membranes or porous partitions. —**os·mot·ic** (ŏz mŏt/ĭk, ŏs-), adj. —**os·mot/i·cal·ly,** adv.

os·prey (ŏs/prĭ), n., pl. -preys. a large hawk which feeds on fish.

Os·sa (ŏs/ə), n. Gk. Myth. a mountain in E Greece. When attacking the Olympian gods, the giants tried to reach heaven by piling Mount Pelion on Olympus and Ossa on Pelion. 6405 ft.

os·se·ous (ŏs/ĭ əs), adj. composed of, containing, or resembling bone; bony.

os·si·fy (ŏs/ə fī/), v., -fied, -fying. —v.t. **1.** to convert into, or harden like, bone. —v.i. **2.** to become bone or hard like bone. —**os/si·fi·ca/tion,** n.

Ost·end (ŏst ĕnd/), n. a seaport in NW Belgium. 44,303.

os·ten·si·ble (ŏs tĕn/sə bəl), adj. apparent; professed; pretended. —**os·ten/si·bly,** adv.

os·ten·ta·tion (ŏs/tĕn tā/shən), n. pretentious show; display intended to impress others. Also, **os/ten·ta/tious·ness.**

os·ten·ta·tious (ŏs/tĕn tā/shəs), adj. **1.** pretentious; showing off. **2.** intended to attract notice. —**os/ten·ta/tious·ly,** adv.

os·te·ol·o·gy (ŏs/tĭ ŏl/ə jĭ), n. the branch of anatomy that treats of the skeleton and its parts. —**os·te·o·log·i·cal** (ŏs/tĭ ə lŏj/ə kəl), adj. —**os/te·ol/o·gist,** n.

os·te·o·my·e·li·tis (ŏs/tĭ ō mī/ə lī/tĭs), n. Pathol. a purulent inflammation of the bone.

os·te·op·a·thy (ŏs/tĭ ŏp/ə thĭ), n. a theory of disease and a method of treatment resting upon the supposition that most diseases are due to deformation of some part of the body and can be cured by some kind of manipulation. —**os·te·o-path** (ŏs/tĭ ə päth/), **os/te·op/a·thist,** n. —**os-te·o·path·ic** (ŏs/tĭ ə päth/ĭk), adj.

os·tra·cism (ŏs/trə sĭz/əm), n. **1.** act of ostracizing. **2.** fact or state of being ostracized.

os·tra·cize (ŏs/trə sīz/), v.t., -cized, -cizing. **1.** to banish or exile. **2.** to exclude by general consent from society, privileges, etc.

os·trich (ŏs/trĭch, ŏs/-), n. any of certain large two-toed, swift-footed, flightless birds of Africa and Arabia, now extensively reared for the plumage.

Os·tro·goth (ŏs/trə gŏth/), n. a member of the easterly division of the Goths, which maintained a monarchy in Italy from A.D. 493 to 555. —**Os/-tro·goth/ic,** adj.

OT, Old Testament. Also, **OT., O.T.**

oth·er (ŭth/ər), adj. **1.** additional or further. **2.** different or distinct from the one or ones mentioned or implied. **3.** different in nature or kind. **4.** being the remaining one of two or more. **5.** (with plural nouns) being the remaining ones of a number. **6.** former. **7. the other day** (night, etc.), a day (night, etc.) or two ago. **8. every other,** every alternate. —pron. **9.** the other one. **10.** another person or thing. **11.** some person or thing else.

oth·er·wise (ŭth/ər wīz/), adv. **1.** under other circumstances. **2.** differently. **3.** in other respects. —adj. **4.** other or different. **5.** that would otherwise be or exist.

other world, the world of the future life.

oth·er·world·ly (ŭth/ər wûrld/lĭ), adj. of, pertaining to, or devoted to another world.

o·ti·ose (ō/shĭ ōs/, -tĭ-), adj. **1.** at leisure; idle. **2.** futile. **3.** useless.

Ot·ta·wa (ŏt/ə wə), n. **1.** the capital of Canada, in SE Ontario. With suburbs, 215,022. **2.** a river in SE Canada, flowing into the St. Lawrence at Montreal. 685 mi. **3.** a member of a tribe of Algonquian Indians of Canada.

ot·ter (ŏt/ər), n., pl. -ters, (esp. collectively) -ter. any of certain aquatic, fur-bearing, carnivorous mammals of the weasel family, having webbed feet adapted for swimming, and a long tail slightly flattened horizontally, acting as a rudder.

Ot·to·man (ŏt/ə mən), adj., n., pl. -mans. —adj. **1.** of or pertaining to the Turkish dynasty or empire founded about 1300 (**Ottoman Empire**) and replaced in 1922 by the republic of Turkey. **2.** of or pertaining to the lands, peoples; and possessions of the Ottoman Empire. —n. **3.** a Turk. **4.** (l.c.) a low cushioned seat or footstool.

ouch (ouch), interj. an exclamation expressing sudden pain.

ought[1] (ôt), aux. v. was (were) or am (is, are) bound by obligation, justice, propriety, fitness, or the like.

ought[2] (ôt), n. a cipher (0).

ought[3] (ôt), n., adv. aught[1].

ounce[1] (ouns), n. **1.** a unit of weight equal to 1/16 lb. avoirdupois. **2.** a unit of 1/12 lb. troy or apothecaries' weight. **3.** a fluid ounce. **4.** a small quantity.

ounce[2] (ouns), n. a long-haired leopardlike feline inhabiting the mountain ranges of central Asia.

our (our), pron. or adj. the possessive form corresponding to we and us, used before a noun.

ours (ourz), pron. the form of our used predicatively or without a noun following.

our·self (our sĕlf/), pron. a form corresponding to ourselves, used of a single person, esp. (like we for I) in the regal or formal style.

our·selves (our sĕlvz/), pron.pl. **1.** a substitute for reflexive of us. **2.** an intensifier of we or us.

-ous, 1. an adjective suffix meaning "full of," "given to," "characterized by," "having," "of the nature of," "like," etc., as in glorious, wondrous. **2.** a suffix used in chemical terms to imply a lower valence than in the case of a corresponding term in -ic.

oust (oust), v.t. **1.** to expel from a place or position occupied. **2.** Law. to eject.

oust·er (ous/tər), n. **1.** Law. ejection; dispossession. **2.** one who ousts.

out (out), adv. **1.** not in a place, position, state, etc. **2.** away from one's home, country, etc. **3.** to exhaustion, extinction, or conclusion. **4.** to or at an end or conclusion. **5.** extinguished. **6.** not in fashion. **7.** into public notice. **8.** seeking openly and energetically to do or have. **9.** into or in society. **10.** for hire. **11.** on strike. **12.** so as to project or extend. **13.** into or in existence or activity. **14.** from a source, cause, material, etc. **15.** from a state of composure, satisfaction, or harmony. **16.** in or into a state of confusion, vexation, dispute, or unfriendliness. **17.** so as to deprive or be deprived. **18.** having used the last. **19.** from a number, stock, or store. **20.** aloud. **21.** with completeness or effectiveness. **22.** completely. **23.** Baseball, etc. from a turn at bat. **24. out and away,** by far. —adj. **25.** external; exterior. **26.** Baseball, etc. not having its inning. **27.** away from one's work. **28.** exposed; made bare. **29.** at a pecuniary loss. **30.** removed from or not in effective operation, play, a turn at bat, or the like, as in a game. —prep. **31.** out or forth from. **32.** outside of. —interj. **33.** Begone! away! —n. **34.** projection; projecting corner. **35.** a means of escaping from a place, punishment, responsibility, etc. **36.** Baseball. a put-out. **37.** Polit. a person not in office. **38.** (pl.) Colloq. odds; bad terms. —v.i. **39.** to go or come out. —v.t. **40.** to expel; oust.

out-, prefixal use of **out,** adv., prep., or adj., occurring in various senses in compounds, as in outcast, outcome, outside, and serving also to form many transitive verbs denoting a going beyond, surpassing, or outdoing in the particular action indicated, as in outbid, outdo, outlast, and many other words in which the meaning is readily perceived, the more important of these being entered below.

out-and-out (out'/and out'), adj. thoroughgoing; thorough; complete; unqualified.

out·bid (out bǐd'), v.t., **-bid, -bidden** or **-bid, -bidding.** to outdo in bidding.

out·board (out'bōrd'), adv., adj. Naut. on the outside, or away from the center, of a ship or boat.

outboard motor, a small portable gasoline engine with propeller and tiller, clamped on the stern of a boat.

out·bound (out'bound'), adj. outward bound.

out·break (out'brāk'), n. **1.** an outburst. **2.** a sudden and active manifestation. **3.** a public disturbance; riot.

out·build·ing (out'bǐl'dǐng), n. a detached building subordinate to a main building.

out·burst (out'bûrst'), n. **1.** a bursting forth. **2.** a sudden and violent appearance.

out·cast (out'kǎst', -käst'), n. **1.** a person who is cast out, as from society. **2.** a vagabond. —adj. **3.** cast out, as from one's home. **4.** pertaining to or characteristic of an outcast. **5.** rejected or discarded.

out·class (out klǎs', -kläs'), v.t. to surpass (a competitor, etc.).

out·come (out'kŭm'), n. that which results from something; consequence.

out·crop (n. out'krǒp'; v. out krǒp'), n., v., **-cropped, -cropping.** —n. **1.** a cropping out, as of a stratum at the surface of the earth. **2.** the emerging part. —v.i. **3.** to crop out, as strata.

out·cry (n. out'krī'; v. out krī'), n., pl. **-cries,** v., **-cried, -crying.** —n. **1.** a crying out. **2.** a cry of distress, indignation, or the like. **3.** loud clamor. —v.t. **4.** to cry louder than.

out·date (out dāt'), v.t., **-dated, -dating.** to make antiquated or obsolete.

out·dis·tance (out dǐs'tans), v.t., **-tanced, -tancing.** to leave far behind; outstrip.

out·do (out dōō'), v.t., **-did, -done, -doing.** to surpass in performance; surpass.

out·door (out'dōr'), adj. occurring or used in the open air.

out·doors (out dōrz'), adv. **1.** in the open air. —n. **2.** the open air.

out·er (ou'tǝr), adj. **1.** farther out; external. **2.** of or pertaining to the outside. —**out'er·most',** adj.

out·face (out fās'), v.t., **-faced, -facing. 1.** to face or stare down. **2.** to defy.

out·field (out'fēld'), n. Baseball. **1.** the part of the field beyond the diamond. **2.** the players stationed in it.

out·field·er (out'fēl'dǝr), n. Baseball. one of the players stationed in the outfield.

out·fit (out'fǐt'), n., v., **-fitted, -fitting.** —n. **1.** an assemblage of articles for equipping. **2.** a set of articles for any purpose. **3.** U.S. Colloq. a group associated in any undertaking, as a mili-

tary body, etc. —v.t. **4.** to equip. —v.i. **5.** to furnish oneself with an outfit. —**out'fit'ter,** n.

out·flank (out flăngk'), v.t. **1.** to go or extend beyond the flank of (an opposing army, etc.). **2.** to turn the flank of.

out·gen·er·al (out jěn'ǝr ǝl), v.t., **-aled, -aling** or (esp. Brit.) **-alled, -alling.** to outdo in generalship.

out·go (n. out'gō'; v. out gō'), n., pl. **-goes,** v., **-went, -gone, -going.** —n. **1.** a going out. **2.** expenditure. **3.** that which goes out. —v.t. **4.** to go faster than. **5.** to exceed. **6.** to surpass.

out·go·ing (out'gō'ǐng), adj. departing.

out·grow (out grō'), v.t., **-grew, -grown, -growing. 1.** to grow too large for. **2.** to leave behind or lose in the course of development or time. **3.** to surpass in growing. —v.i. **4.** to protrude.

out·growth (out'grōth'), n. **1.** a natural development, product, or result. **2.** an additional, supplementary result. **3.** a growing out or forth. **4.** an offshoot or excrescence.

out·guess (out gěs'), v.t. to outwit.

out·house (out'hous'), n. **1.** an outbuilding. **2.** an outside privy.

out·ing (ou'tǐng), n. an excursion or pleasure trip.

out·land·er (out'lăn'dǝr), n. a foreigner.

out·land·ish (out lăn'dǐsh), adj. **1.** freakishly or grotesquely odd; bizarre. **2.** foreign-looking. —**out·land'ish·ly,** adv.

out·last (out lăst', -läst'), v.t. to last longer than.

out·law (out'lô'), n. **1.** one excluded from the benefits and protection of the law. **2.** one under sentence of outlawry. **3.** a habitual criminal. —v.t. **4.** to deprive of the benefits and protection of the law, as a person. **5.** to remove from legal jurisdiction. **6.** to prohibit. —**out'law'ry,** n.

out·lay (n. out'lā'; v. out lā'), n., v., **-laid, -laying.** —n. **1.** an expenditure. **2.** an amount expended. —v.t. **3.** to expend.

out·let (out'lět), n. **1.** an opening or passage by which anything is let out; exit. **2.** Elect. **a.** a point on a wiring system at which current is taken to supply electrical devices. **b. outlet box,** a metal box designed to facilitate connections to a wiring system. **3.** Com. **a.** a market for goods. **b.** (of a wholesaler or manufacturer) a store, merchant, or agency selling one's goods.

out·line (out'līn'), n., v., **-lined, -lining.** —n. **1.** the line by which a figure or object is defined or bounded. **2.** a drawing or a style of drawing with merely lines of contour, without shading. **3.** a general sketch, account, or report, indicating only the main features. —v.t. **4.** to draw the outline of. **5.** to sketch the main features of.

out·live (out lǐv'), v.t., **-lived, -living. 1.** to live longer than. **2.** to outlast.

out·look (out'lŏŏk'), n. **1.** the view from a place. **2.** a mental view. **3.** prospect of the future.

out·ly·ing (out'lī'ǐng), adj. **1.** remote; out-of-the-way. **2.** lying outside the boundary.

out·mode (out mōd'), v.t., **-moded, -moding.** to cause to be out of style.

out·num·ber (out nŭm'bǝr), v.t. to exceed in number.

out-of-date (out'ǝv dāt'), adj. of a previous style or fashion; obsolete.

out-of-doors (out'ǝv dōrz'), adj. **1.** Also, **out'-of-door'.** outdoor. —adv., n. **2.** outdoors.

out-of-the-way (out'ǝv thǝ wā'), adj. **1.** remote from much-traveled ways or populous regions; secluded. **2.** unusual. **3.** improper.

out·pa·tient (out'pā'shǝnt), n. a patient receiving treatment at a hospital but not being an inmate.

out·play (out plā'), v.t. to defeat.

out·post (out'pōst'), n. **1.** a station at a distance from the main body of an army to protect it from surprise attack. **2.** the body of troops stationed there.

out·put (out'pŏŏt'), n. **1.** production. **2.** the quantity produced. **3.** the product or yield.

out·rage (out'rāj), n., v., **-raged, -raging.** —n. **1.** any gross violation of law or decency. **2.** anything that outrages the feelings. —v.t. **3.** to subject to grievous violence or indignity. **4.** to affect with a sense of offended right or decency. **5.** to offend against (right, decency, feelings, etc.) grossly or shamelessly.

out·ra·geous (out rā'jǝs), adj. **1.** of the nature of or involving gross injury or wrong. **2.** grossly offensive to the sense of right or decency. **3.** intolerable or shocking. —**out·ra'geous·ly**, *adv.* —**out·ra'geous·ness**, *n.*

out·rank (out răngk'), *v.t.* to rank above.

out·rig·ger (out'rĭg'ər), *n.* a framework extended outboard from the side of a boat, esp., as in South Pacific canoes, supporting a float which gives stability.

out·right (*adj.* out'rīt'; *adv.* out'rīt'), *adj.* **1.** complete or total. **2.** downright. **3.** directed straight out or on. —*adv.* **4.** completely. **5.** without restraint or concealment. **6.** at once.

out·run (out rŭn'), *v.t.*, **-ran, -run, -running. 1.** to outstrip in running. **2.** to exceed.

out·set (out'sĕt'), *n.* the beginning or start.

out·shine (out shīn'), *v.t.*, **-shone, -shining. 1.** to surpass in shining. **2.** to surpass in splendor, excellence, etc.

out·side (*n., adj., adv.* out'sīd'; *prep.* out'sīd'), *n.* **1.** the outer side, surface, or part. **2.** the external aspect or appearance. **3.** something merely external. **4.** the space beyond an enclosure, boundary, etc. —*adj.* **5.** being, acting, done, or originating beyond an enclosure, boundary, etc. **6.** not belonging to or connected with an institution, society, etc. **7.** extreme. —*adv.* **8.** on or to the outside. **9.** *U.S. Colloq.* with the exception. —*prep.* **10.** outside of. **11.** *Colloq.* except.

out·sid·er (out'sī'dər), *n.* **1.** one not within an enclosure, boundary, etc. **2.** one not belonging to a particular group, set, party, etc.

out·size (out'sīz'), *n.* an uncommon or irregular size.

out·skirt (out'skûrt'), *n.* (often *pl.*) an outer or bordering part or district.

out·smart (out smärt'), *v.t. U.S. Colloq.* to prove too clever for.

out·spo·ken (out'spō'kən), *adj.* candid; frank. —**out'spo'ken·ly**, *adv.* —**out'spo'ken·ness**, *n.*

out·spread (*v.* out sprĕd'; *n., adj.* out'sprĕd'), *v.*, **-spread, -spreading,** *n., adj.* —*v.t., v.i.* **1.** to extend. —*adj.* **2.** spread out. **3.** diffused abroad. —*n.* **4.** a spreading out. **5.** an expanse.

out·stand·ing (out stăn'dĭng), *adj.* **1.** prominent; conspicuous; striking. **2.** that remains unsettled, unpaid, etc.

out·stretch (out strĕch'), *v.t.* **1.** to extend. **2.** to stretch beyond (a limit, etc.).

out·strip (out strĭp'), *v.t.*, **-stripped, -stripping. 1.** to surpass; excel. **2.** to outdo in running or swift travel.

out·ward (out'wərd), *adj.* **1.** being, or pertaining to, only what is seen or apparent. **2.** toward or on the outside or exterior. —*adv.* Also, **out'-wards. 3.** toward the outside; out. **4.** away from port. **5.** visibly; openly.

out·ward·ly (out'wərd lĭ), *adv.* **1.** as regards appearance. **2.** toward the outside. **3.** on the outside.

out·wear (out wâr'), *v.t.*, **-wore, -worn, -wearing.** to wear or last longer than.

out·weigh (out wā'), *v.t.* to exceed in value, importance, influence, etc.

out·wit (out wĭt'), *v.t.*, **-witted, -witting.** to get the better of by superior cleverness.

ou·zel (ōō'zəl), *n. Brit.* any member of the thrush family, esp. the blackbird.

o·val (ō'vəl), *adj.* **1.** having the general form of an egg; egg-shaped. **2.** ellipsoid or elliptical. —*n.* **3.** any of various oval things, as a geometric figure, a race track, etc.

o·va·ry (ō'və rĭ), *n., pl.* **-ries. 1.** *Anat., Zool.* the female reproductive gland. **2.** *Bot.* the enlarged lower part of the pistil in certain plants, enclosing the ovules or young seeds. —**o·var·i·an** (ō vâr'-ĭ ən), *adj.*

o·vate (ō'vāt), *adj.* egg-shaped.

o·va·tion (ō vā'shən), *n.* an enthusiastic public reception of a person.

ov·en (ŭv'ən), *n.* a chamber or receptacle for baking or heating, or for drying with the aid of heat.

o·ver (ō'vər), *prep.* **1.** above in place or position. **2.** above and to the other side of. **3.** above

in authority, power, etc. **4.** on or upon. **5.** here and there on or in. **6.** through all parts of. **7.** to and fro on or in. **8.** from side to side of. **9.** on the other side of. **10.** reaching higher than, so as to submerge. **11.** in excess of. **12.** above in degree, etc. **13.** in preference to. **14.** from end to end of. **15.** until after the end of. **16.** during. **17.** concerning; about. **18.** while engaged in or concerned with. **19. over and above,** in addition to. —*adv.* **20.** over the top or edge of something. **21.** so as to affect the whole surface. **22.** through a region, area, etc. **23.** at some distance, as in a direction indicated. **24.** from side to side. **25.** across any intervening space. **26.** all through. **27.** from one person, party, etc., to another. **28.** on the other side, as of a sea. **29.** down or upside down. **30.** once more; again. **31.** in excess or addition. **32.** remaining. **33.** throughout a period of time. **34. all over, a.** *U.S. Colloq.* everywhere. **b.** entirely. **c.** finished. **35. over against, a.** opposite to. **b.** as contrasted with. —*adj.* **36.** upper. **37.** higher in authority, etc. **38.** outer. **39.** surplus; extra. **40.** excessive. **41.** at an end; done. —*n.* **42.** an amount in excess or addition.

over-, prefixal use of **over,** *prep., adv.,* or *adj.* occurring in various senses in compounds, as in *overboard, overcoat, overthrow,* and especially employed, with the sense of "over the limit," to excess," "too," to form verbs, adjectives, adverbs, and nouns, as *overact, oversupply,* and many others, mostly self-explanatory.

o·ver·all (ō'vər ôl'), *adj.* **1.** from one extreme limit of a thing to the other. **2.** including everything. —*n.* **3.** (*pl.*) loose, stout trousers, often with a part extending up over the breast, worn by workmen and others.

o·ver·arm (ō'vər ärm'), *adj. Baseball, etc.* delivered or executed with the arm raised above the shoulder.

o·ver·awe (ō'vər ô'), *v.t.*, **-awed, -awing.** to restrain or subdue by inspiring awe; cow.

o·ver·bal·ance (ō'vər băl'əns), *v.*, **-anced, -ancing,** *n.* **1.** to outweigh. **2.** to cause to lose balance. —*n.* **3.** an overbalancing weight or amount.

o·ver·bear (ō'vər bâr'), *v.t.*, **-bore, -borne, -bearing. 1.** to bear down by weight or force. **2.** to treat in a domineering way.

o·ver·bear·ing (ō'vər bâr'ĭng), *adj.* domineering; arrogant. —**o'ver·bear'ing·ly**, *adv.*

o·ver·bid (*v.* ō'vər bĭd'; *n.* ō'vər bĭd'), *v.*, **-bid, -bidden or -bid, -bidding,** *n.* —*v.t., v.i.* **1.** to bid more than the value of (a thing). **2.** to outbid (a person, etc.). —*n.* **3.** a higher bid.

o·ver·board (ō'vər bōrd'), *adv.* over the side of a ship, esp. into the water.

o·ver·cast (ō'vər kăst', -käst', ō'vər kăst', -käst'), *adj., v.*, **-cast, -casting.** —*adj.* **1.** cloudy. **2.** dark; gloomy. —*v.t., v.i.* **3.** to overcloud. **4.** to sew with stitches passing successively over an edge.

o·ver·cloud (ō'vər kloud'), *v.t.* **1.** to overspread with clouds. **2.** to darken; obscure; make gloomy. —*v.i.* **3.** to become clouded over.

o·ver·coat (ō'vər kōt'), *n.* a coat worn over ordinary clothing, as in cold weather.

o·ver·come (ō'vər kŭm'), *v.t.*, *v.i.*, **-came, -come, -coming. 1.** to conquer; defeat. **2.** to prevail over (objections, temptations, etc.). **3.** to surmount (difficulties, etc.). **4.** to overpower (a person, etc.) in body or mind. **5.** to overwhelm in feeling.

o·ver·do (ō'vər dōō'), *v.*, **-did, -done, -doing.** —*v.t.* **1.** to do or carry to excess. **2.** to exaggerate. **3.** to fatigue; exhaust. **4.** to cook too long. —*v.i.* **5.** to do too much.

o·ver·draft (ō'vər drăft', -dräft'), *n.* a draft in excess of one's credit balance, or the amount of the excess.

o·ver·draw (ō'vər drô'), *v.t.*, *v.i.*, **-drew, -drawn, -drawing.** to draw upon (an account, allowance, etc.) in excess of the balance standing to one's credit or at one's disposal.

o·ver·drive (*v.* ō'vər drīv'; *n.* ō'vər drīv'), *v.*, **-drove, -driven, -driving,** *n.* —*v.t.* **1.** to overwork. —*n.* **2.** *Mach.* a device containing a gear set at such ratio and arrangement as to provide (when engaged) a propeller speed greater than the engine crankshaft speed.

o·ver·due (ō′vər dū′, -dōō′), *adj.* past due, as a belated train or an unpaid bill.

o·ver·flow (*v.* ō′vər flō′; *n.* ō′vər flō′), *v.*, **-flowed, -flown, -flowing,** *n.* —*v.i.* **1.** to flow or run over, as rivers, water, etc. **2.** to have the contents flowing over. **3.** to pass from one place or part to another as if flowing from an overfull space. **4.** to be filled or supplied abundantly. —*v.t.* **5.** to flood; inundate. **6.** to flow or run over. —*n.* **7.** an overflowing. **8.** that which flows or runs over. **9.** an excess.

o·ver·grow (ō′vər grō′), *v.*, **-grew, -grown, -growing.** —*v.t.* **1.** to cover with a growth. **2.** to supplant by a more exuberant growth. **3.** to outgrow. —*v.i.* **4.** to grow to excess. —*o′ver-grown′, adj.* —*o′ver·growth′, n.*

o·ver·hand (ō′vər hănd′), *adv.* **1.** with the hand over the object. **2.** with the hand raised above the shoulder, as in pitching a ball. **3.** *Sewing.* with close, shallow stitches over two edges. —*adj.* **4.** done or delivered overhand.

o·ver·hang (*v.* ō′vər hăng′; *n.* ō′vər hăng′), *v.*, **-hung, -hanging,** *n.* —*v.t., v.i.* **1.** to hang over. **2.** to impend (over); threaten. —*n.* **3.** a projection. **4.** the extent of projection.

o·ver·haul (ō′vər hôl′), *v.t.* **1.** to investigate or examine thoroughly, as for repair. **2.** to gain upon or overtake. —*n.* **3.** a thorough examination.

o·ver·head (*adv.* ō′vər hĕd′; *adj., n.* ō′vər-hĕd′), *adv.* **1.** aloft; up in the air or sky. **2.** completely submerged or involved. —*adj.* **3.** situated, operating, or passing overhead. —*n.* **4.** the general cost of running a business.

o·ver·hear (ō′vər hĭr′), *v.t.*, **-heard, -hearing.** to hear (speech, etc., or a speaker) without the speaker's intention or knowledge.

o·ver·joyed (ō′vər joid′), *adj.* overcome with joy; made exceedingly joyful.

o·ver·land (ō′vər lănd′), *adv.* **1.** across the land. **2.** by land. —*adj.* **3.** proceeding or performed overland.

o·ver·lap (*v.* ō′vər lăp′; *n.* ō′vər lăp′), *v.*, **-lapped, -lapping,** *n.* —*v.t.* **1.** to extend over a part of. **2.** to cover and extend beyond (something else). —*v.i.* **3.** to lap over. —*n.* **4.** an overlapping. **5.** the amount of overlapping. **6.** an overlapping part.

o·ver·lay (*v.* ō′vər lā′; *n.* ō′vər lā′), *v.*, **-laid, -laying,** *n.* —*v.t.* **1.** to place (one thing) over another. **2.** to cover or surmount with something, esp. something decorative. —*n.* **3.** a covering. **4.** a layer or decoration of something applied.

o·ver·look (ō′vər lŏŏk′), *v.t.* **1.** to fail to notice, perceive, or consider. **2.** to ignore indulgently, as faults. **3.** to look over, as from a higher position. **4.** to afford a view down over. **5.** to rise above. **6.** to ignore.

o·ver·lord (ō′vər lôrd′), *n.* one who is lord over another or over other lords.

o·ver·ly (ō′vər lĭ′), *adv.* *Colloq.* excessively.

o·ver·night (*adv.* ō′vər nīt′; *n., adj.* ō′vər nīt′), *adv.* **1.** during the night. **2.** on the previous evening. —*adj.* **3.** done, occurring, or continuing during the night. **4.** designed to be used one night or very few nights. **5.** of or pertaining to the previous evening. —*n.* **6.** the previous evening.

o·ver·pass (*n.* ō′vər păs′, -päs′; *v.* ō′vər păs′, -päs′), *n., v.*, **-passed** or **-past, -passing.** —*n.* **1.**

a highway or railway bridge crossing some barrier, as another highway. —*v.t.* **2.** to pass over or traverse.

o·ver·pow·er (ō′vər pou′ər), *v.t.* **1.** to overwhelm in feeling. **2.** to overcome or subdue by superior force. **3.** to overmaster the bodily powers or mental faculties of.

o·ver·pow·er·ing (ō′vər pou′ər ĭng), *adj.* overwhelming. —*o′ver·pow′er·ing·ly, adv.*

o·ver·reach (ō′vər rēch′), *v.t.* **1.** to extend over or beyond. **2.** to reach for or aim at but go beyond. **3.** to defeat (oneself) by overdoing matters, often by excessive eagerness or cunning. **4.** to cheat. —*v.i.* **5.** to extend over something. **6.** to reach too far. **7.** to cheat others.

o·ver·ride (ō′vər rĭd′), *v.t.*, **-rode, -ridden, -riding.** **1.** to ride across (a region, etc.). **2.** to ride roughshod over. **3.** to pursue one's course in disregard of. **4.** to prevail over. **5.** to ride too much.

o·ver·rule (ō′vər rōōl′), *v.t.*, **-ruled, -ruling.** **1.** to rule against the arguments of (a person). **2.** to rule against (a plea, etc.).

o·ver·run (*v.* ō′vər rŭn′; *n.* ō′vər rŭn′), *v.*, **-ran, -run, -running,** *n.* —*v.t.* **1.** to rove over (a country, etc.) as ravaging invaders. **2.** to swarm over in great numbers, as vermin. **3.** to grow rapidly over, as weeds. **4.** to run over so as to injure. **5.** to run beyond. **6.** to exceed. **7.** to overflow. —*v.i.* **8.** to overthrow. **9.** to extend beyond the proper or desired limit. —*n.* **10.** an overrunning. **11.** an amount overrunning.

o·ver·seas (*adv.* ō′vər sēz′; *adj.* ō′vər sēz′), *adv.* **1.** over, across, or beyond the sea. —*adj.* **2.** of or pertaining to passage over the seas. **3.** situated beyond the sea. **4.** foreign. Also, **o·ver·sea** (*adv.* ō′vər sē′; *adj.* ō′vər sē′).

o·ver·see (ō′vər sē′), *v.t.*, **-saw, -seen, -seeing.** to direct or supervise. —*o′ver·see′er, n.*

o·ver·shad·ow (ō′vər shăd′ō), *v.t.* **1.** to diminish the importance of. **2.** to tower over so as to cast a shadow over. **3.** to cast a shadow over.

o·ver·shoe (ō′vər shōō′), *n.* a shoe worn over another shoe for protection against wet, cold, etc.

o·ver·shoot (ō′vər shōōt′), *v.t., v.i.*, **-shot, -shooting.** **1.** to shoot or go over or above (something). **2.** to shoot or go beyond (a limit, etc.). **3.** to shoot a missile over or beyond (what is aimed at). **4.** to go further in any course or matter than is intended or proper.

o·ver·shot (ō′vər shŏt′), *adj.* **1.** driven by water passing over from above, as a vertical water wheel. **2.** having the upper jaw projecting beyond the lower, as a dog.

o·ver·sight (ō′vər sīt′), *n.* **1.** failure to notice or consider. **2.** an error due to inadvertence. **3.** supervision; watchful care.

o·ver·spread (ō′vər sprĕd′), *v.t.*, **-spread, -spreading.** **1.** to spread (one thing) over another. **2.** to cover (a thing) with something else. **3.** to be spread over (something else).

o·ver·state (ō′vər stāt′), *v.t.*, **-stated, -stating.** to exaggerate. —*o′ver·state′ment, n.*

o·ver·stay (ō′vər stā′), *v.t.* to stay beyond the time or duration of.

o·ver·step (ō′vər stĕp′), *v.t.*, **-stepped, -stepping.** to step or pass over or beyond.

o·ver·strung (ō′vər strŭng′), *adj.* too highly strung.

o·ver·stuffed (ō′vər stŭft′), *adj.* *Furnit.* having the entire frame covered by upholstery.

o·vert (ō′vûrt, ō vûrt′), *adj.* open to view or knowledge; not secret. —*o′vert·ly, adv.*

o′ver·ea′ger	o′ver·gen′er·ous	o′ver·play′	o′ver·size′
o′ver·eat′	o′ver·greed′y	o′ver·plump′	o′ver·sized′
o′ver·e·mo′tion·al	o′ver·hast′y	o′ver·pop′u·late′	o′ver·skep′ti·cal
o′ver·em′pha·size′	o′ver·heat′	o′ver·pop′u·lous	o′ver·sleep′
o′ver·en·thu′si·as′-tic	o′ver·high′	o′ver·pow′er·ful	o′ver·spend′
	o′ver·in·dulge′	o′ver·praise′	o′ver·stim′u·late′
o′ver·es′ti·mate′	o′ver·in·dul′gence	o′ver·pro·duce′	o′ver·stock′
o′ver·ex′er·cise′	o′ver·in·dul′gent	o′ver·pro·duc′tion	o′ver·strain′
o′ver·ex·ert′	o′ver·jeal′ous	o′ver·proud′	o′ver·strict′
o′ver·ex·er′tion	o′ver·lad′en	o′ver·rash′	o′ver·stu′di·ous
o′ver·ex·pand′	o′ver·load′	o′ver·rate′	o′ver·stud′y
o′ver·ex·pan′sion	o′ver·long′	o′ver·re·li′gious	o′ver·stuff′
o′ver·ex·pose′	o′ver·meas′ure	o′ver·ripe′	o′ver·sub·scribe′
o′ver·ex·po′sure	o′ver·mer′ry	o′ver·roast′	o′ver·sub·scrip′tion
o′ver·fa·mil′iar	o′ver·mod′est	o′ver·salt′	o′ver·sub′tle
o′ver·fa·tigue′	o′ver·mourn′ful	o′ver·scru′pu·lous	o′ver·suf·fi′cient
o′ver·feed′	o′ver·much′	o′ver·sell′	o′ver·su′per·sti′-tious
o′ver·fit′	o′ver·nice′	o′ver·sen′si·tive	
o′ver·fond′	o′ver·o·be′di·ent	o′ver·se′ri·ous	o′ver·sup·ply′
o′ver·fre′quent	o′ver·pay′	o′ver·sim·plic′i·ty	o′ver·sus·pi′cious
o′ver·full′	o′ver·pay′ment	o′ver·sim′pli·fy′	o′ver·sweet′

o·ver·take (ō′vər tāk′), *v.t.*, **-took**, **-taken**, **-taking**. **1.** to catch up with, as in traveling or in pursuit. **2.** to come upon suddenly (said esp. of night, death, etc.).

o·ver·throw (*v.* ō′vər thrō′; *n.* ō′vər thrō′), *v.*, **-threw**, **-thrown**, **-throwing**, *n.* —*v.t.* **1.** to overcome, defeat, or vanquish. **2.** to put an end to by force, as governments. **3.** to upset; overturn. **4.** to knock down and demolish. **5.** to ruin or destroy. —*n.* **6.** the act of overthrowing. **7.** resulting state.

o·ver·time (*n., adv., adj.* ō′vər tīm′; *v.* ō′vər-tīm′), *n., adv., adj., v.*, **-timed**, **-timing**. —*n.* **1.** time during which one works before or after regularly scheduled working hours. **2.** pay for such time. —*adv.* **3.** during extra time. —*adj.* **4.** of or pertaining to overtime. —*v.t.* **5.** to give too much time to.

o·ver·tone (ō′vər tōn′), *n.* **1.** any frequency emitted by an acoustical instrument that is higher in frequency than the fundamental. **2.** (*usually pl.*) additional meaning.

o·ver·trick (ō′vər trĭk′), *n.* *Cards.* one trick over the number necessary to win the game.

o·ver·ture (ō′vər chər), *n.* **1.** an opening of negotiations: a formal offer. **2.** *Music.* **a.** an orchestral composition forming the prelude or introduction to an opera, oratorio, etc. **b.** an independent piece of similar character.

o·ver·turn (*v.* ō′vər tûrn′; *n.* ō′vər tûrn′), *v.t., v.i.* **1.** to defeat or vanquish. **2.** to turn on its side, face, or back; upset. —*n.* **3.** act of overturning. **4.** state of being overturned.

o·ver·ween·ing (ō′vər wē′nĭng), *adj.* conceited; presumptuous. —**o′ver·ween′ing·ly**, *adv.*

o·ver·weigh (ō′vər wā′), *v.t.* **1.** to exceed in weight. **2.** to weigh down; oppress.

o·ver·weight (*n.* ō′vər wāt′; *adj.* ō′vər wāt′), *n.* **1.** excess of weight. **2.** too great weight. **3.** preponderance. —*adj.* **4.** weighing more than normally or necessarily required.

o·ver·whelm (ō′vər hwĕlm′), *v.t.* **1.** to come, rest, or weigh upon overpoweringly; crush. **2.** to overcome completely in mind or feeling. **3.** to load, heap, treat, or address with an excessive amount of anything. —**o′ver·whelm′ing**, *adj.* —**o′ver·whelm′ing·ly**, *adv.*

o·ver·work (*v.* ō′vər wûrk′; *n.* ō′vər wûrk′), *v.*, **-worked** or **-wrought**, **-working**, *n.* —*v.t.* **1.** to cause to work too hard. —*v.i.* **2.** to work too hard. —*n.* **3.** work beyond one's strength or capacity.

o·ver·wrought (ō′vər rôt′), *adj.* **1.** exhausted by overwork. **2.** excited excessively.

Ov·id (ŏv′ĭd), *n.* 43 B.C.–A.D. 17?, Roman poet. —**O·vid·i·an** (ō vĭd′ī ən), *adj.*

o·vi·duct (ō′vĭ dŭkt′), *n.* *Anat., Zool.* one of a pair of ducts which lead from the body cavity to the exterior in the female and serve to transport and nourish the ovum.

o·vi·form (ō′vĭ fôrm′), *adj.* egg-shaped.

o·vine (ō′vīn, -vĭn), *adj.* pertaining to, of the nature of, or like sheep.

o·vip·a·rous (ō vĭp′ə rəs), *adj.* *Zool.* producing ova or eggs which are matured or hatched after being expelled from the body, as birds, most reptiles and fishes, etc.

o·vi·pos·i·tor (ō′vĭ pŏz′ə tər), *n.* (in certain insects) an organ at the end of the abdomen, by which eggs are deposited.

o·void (ō′void), *adj.* egg-shaped.

o·vule (ō′vūl), *n.* **1.** *Biol.* a small egg. **2.** *Bot.* **a.** a rudimentary seed. **b.** the body containing the female germ cell. —**o·vu·lar** (ō′vyə lər), *adj.*

o·vum (ō′vəm), *n., pl.* **ova** (ō′və). *Biol.* **1.** an egg, in a broad biological sense. **2.** the female reproductive cell or gamete of plants. **3.** the female reproductive cell of animals.

owe (ō), *v.*, **owed**, **owing**. —*v.t.* **1.** to be indebted or obliged for. **2.** to be under obligation to pay or repay. **3.** to have (a certain feeling) toward a person. —*v.i.* **4.** to be in debt.

Ow·en Stan·ley (ō′ĭn stăn′lĭ), a mountain range in SE New Guinea. Highest peak, Mt. Victoria, 13,030 ft.

ow·ing (ō′ĭng), *adj.* **1.** that owes. **2.** owed or due. **3. owing to, a.** because of. **b.** attributable to.

owl (oul), *n.* any of certain birds of prey, chiefly

nocturnal, with a broad head and with large eyes which are usually surrounded by disks of modified feathers and directed forward. They feed on mice, small birds and reptiles, etc. —**owl′ish, owl′-like′**, *adj.*

owl·et (ou′lĭt), *n.* **1.** a young owl. **2.** a small owl.

own (ōn), *adj.* **1.** belonging, pertaining, or relating to oneself or itself. **2.** own property, relatives, etc. **3.** of one's own, belonging to oneself. **4. on one's own**, *Collog.* on one's own account, responsibility, resources, etc. —*v.t.* **5.** to have or possess. **6.** to acknowledge or admit. **7.** to acknowledge as one's own. —*v.i.* **8.** to confess.

own·er (ō′nər), *n.* one who owns; proprietor. —**own′er·ship′**, *n.*

ox (ŏks), *n., pl.* **oxen**. the adult castrated male of the bovine kind, used as a draft animal and for food. —**ox′like′**, *adj.*

Ox., (L *Oxonia*) Oxford.

ox·blood (ŏks′blŭd′), *n.* a deep red color.

ox·bow (ŏks′bō′), *n.* *U.S.* **1.** a bow-shaped piece of wood placed under and around the neck of an ox, with its upper ends inserted in the bar of the yoke. **2.** a bow-shaped bend in a river, or the land embraced by it.

ox·cart (ŏks′kärt′), *n.* an ox-drawn cart.

ox·ford (ŏks′fərd), *n.* a low shoe laced or buttoned over the instep.

Ox·ford (ŏks′fərd), *n.* a city in S England: famous university. 101,040.

Oxford gray, medium to dark gray.

ox·i·date (ŏk′sə dāt′), *v.t., v.i.*, **-dated**, **-dating**. *Chem.* to oxidize. —**ox′i·da′tion**, *n.*

ox·ide (ŏk′sīd, -sĭd), *n.* *Chem.* a compound, usually containing two elements only, one of which is oxygen. Also, **ox·id** (ŏk′sĭd).

ox·i·dize (ŏk′sə dīz′), *v.*, **-dized**, **-dizing**. *Chem.* —*v.t.* **1.** to convert (an element) into its oxide. **2.** to cover with a coating of rust. **3.** to add oxygen or any nonmetal to. **4.** to increase the valence of (an element) in the positive direction. **5.** to remove electrons. —*v.i.* **6.** to become oxidized. —**ox′i·diz′a·ble**, *adj.* —**ox′i·di·za′-tion**, *n.* —**ox′i·diz′er**, *n.*

ox·lip (ŏks′lĭp′), *n.* a species of primrose with pale-yellow flowers.

Ox·o·ni·an (ŏk sō′nĭ ən), *adj.* **1.** of or pertaining to Oxford, England, or Oxford University. —*n.* **2.** a member or graduate of Oxford University.

ox·tail (ŏks′tāl′), *n.* the skinned tail of an ox, used to make a soup.

ox·y·ac·et·y·lene (ŏk′sĭ ə sĕt′ə lēn′), *adj.* of or pertaining to a mixture of oxygen and acetylene, used in a blowtorch (**oxyacetylene blowpipe**) at 3300°C., for cutting steel plates.

ox·y·gen (ŏk′sə jən), *n.* *Chem.* a colorless, odorless gaseous element. It is the supporter of combustion in air, and is the standard of atomic, combining, and molecular weights. *Weight of 1 liter at 0°C. and 760 mm. pressure:* 1.4290 grams. *Symbol:* O; *at. wt.:* 16.0; *at. no.:* 8.

ox·y·gen·ate (ŏk′sə jə nāt′), *v.t.*, **-ated**, **-ating**. to treat or combine, esp. to enrich, with oxygen. Also, **ox′y·gen·ize′**. —**ox′y·gen·a′tion**, *n.*

oxygen mask, a masklike device worn by aviators at great altitudes when inhaling supplementary oxygen from an attached tank.

oxygen tent, a small tent for delivering oxygen to a sick person at critical periods.

ox·y·mo·ron (ŏk′sĭ mōr′ŏn), *n., pl.* **-mora** (-mōr′ə). *Rhet.* a figure by which a locution produces an effect by a seeming self-contradiction, as in *cruel kindness*.

oys·ter (ois′tər), *n.* **1.** any of various edible marine bivalve mollusks with irregularly shaped shells. **2.** *Slang.* a close-mouthed person. —*v.i.* **3.** to dredge for or otherwise take oysters.

oz., *pl.* **ozs.** **1.** ounce. **2.** ounces.

O·zark Mountains (ō′zärk), a group of low mountains in S Missouri, N Arkansas, and NE Oklahoma. Also, **O′zarks**.

o·zone (ō′zōn, ō zōn′), *n.* **1.** a form of oxygen, O₃, with an odor suggesting that of weak chlorine, produced esp. when an electric spark is passed through air. Found in the atmosphere in minute quantities, esp. after a thunderstorm, it is a powerful oxidizing agent. **2.** *Collog.* clear, fresh air. —**o·zon·ic** (ō zŏn′ĭk, ō zō′nĭk), *adj.*

P

P, p (pē), *n.*, *pl.* **P's** or **Ps, p's** or **ps.** a consonant, the 16th letter of the Engish alphabet.

P, 1. *Chem.* phosphorus. 2. *Physics.* pressure.

P., 1. page. 2. participle. 3. past. 4. *Chess.* pawn. 5. *Baseball.* pitcher.

pa (pä), *n.* *Colloq.* papa.

Pa, *Chem.* protoactinium.

Pa., Pennsylvania.

p.a., participial adjective.

pab·u·lum (păb′yə ləm), *n.* that which nourishes an organism; food.

pace (pās), *n.*, *v.*, **paced, pacing.** —*n.* 1. rate of movement. 2. a lineal measure of variable extent, representing the average length of a step. 3. a single step. 4. manner of stepping. 5. a gait of a horse, etc., in which the feet on the same side are lifted and put down together. 6. any of the gaits of a horse, etc. —*v.t.* 7. to set the pace for, as in racing. 8. to traverse with steps. 9. to measure by paces. —*v.i.* 10. to take slow, regular steps. 11. (of a horse) to go at a pace. —**pac′er,** *n.*

pace·mak·er (pās′mā′kər), *n.* one who sets the pace, as in racing. —**pace′mak′ing,** *n.*

pach·y·derm (păk′ə dûrm′), *n.* any of the thick-skinned nonruminant ungulates, as the elephant, hippopotamus, and rhinoceros.

pa·cif·ic (pə sĭf′ĭk), *adj.* 1. tending to make peace. 2. loving peace. 3. peaceful. 4. (*cap.*) designating, or pertaining to, the Pacific Ocean. 5. (*cap.*) of or pertaining to the region bordering on the Pacific Ocean. —*n.* 6. (*cap.*) the Pacific Ocean. —**pa·cif′i·cal·ly,** *adv.*

pa·cif·i·cate (pə sĭf′ə kāt′), *v.t.*, **-cated, -cating.** to pacify. —**pac·i·fi·ca·tion** (păs′ə fə kā′shən), *n.* —**pa·cif′i·ca′tor,** *n.*

Pacific Ocean, the largest ocean, between the American continents and Asia and Australia. ab. 70,000,000 sq. mi.

pac·i·fi·er (păs′ə fī′ər), *n.* 1. one that pacifies. 2. a rubber nipple, etc., given to a baby to suck. 3. a teething ring.

pac·i·fism (păs′ə fĭz′əm), *n.* the principle or policy of maintaining universal peace by negotiated adjustment of differences. —**pac′i·fist,** *n.*, *adj.* —**pac′i·fis′tic,** *adj.*

pac·i·fy (păs′ə fī′), *v.t.*, **-fied, -fying.** 1. to quiet; calm. 2. to appease.

pack[1] (păk), *n.* 1. a bundle or parcel. 2. the quantity of anything packed at one time. 3. a group, esp. of animals. 4. a complete set, as of playing cards (usually 52 in number). 5. a considerable area of pieces of floating ice driven or packed together. 6. *Med.* **a.** a wrapping of the body in wet or dry cloths for therapeutic purposes. **b.** the cloths used. 7. a cosmetic treatment similar to this. —*v.t.* 8. to make into a bundle. 9. to make into a group or compact mass. 10. to fill with anything compactly arranged. 11. to press together; cram. 12. to put or arrange in suitable form for the market. 13. to make airtight, vaportight, or watertight by stuffing. 14. to cover or envelop with something pressed closely around. 15. to carry. 16. to send off summarily. 17. to treat with a therapeutic pack. —*v.i.* 18. to pack goods, etc., in compact form. 19. to admit of being compactly stowed. 20. to become compacted. 21. to leave hastily. —*adj.* 22. used in transporting a pack. 23. made up of pack animals. —**pack′er,** *n.*

pack[2] (păk), *v.t.* to collect, arrange, or manipulate (cards, persons, facts, etc.) so as to serve one's own purposes.

pack·age (păk′ĭj), *n.*, *v.*, **-aged, -aging.** —*n.* 1. a bundle or parcel. 2. that in which anything is packed, as a case, crate, etc. —*v.t.* 3. to put into wrappings or a container.

pack·et (păk′ĭt), *n.* 1. a small package of anything. 2. a boat that carries mail, passengers, and

goods regularly on a fixed route. —*v.t.* 3. to bind up in a package.

pack·ing (păk′ĭng), *n.* 1. act or work of one that packs. 2. any material used for packing or making watertight, steamtight, etc.

pack·sad·dle (păk′săd′əl), *n.* a saddle for supporting the load on a pack animal.

pact (păkt), *n.* an agreement; compact.

pad[1] (păd), *n.*, *v.*, **padded, padding.** —*n.* 1. a cushionlike mass of soft material for comfort, protection, or stuffing. 2. a number of sheets of paper held together at the edge. 3. a soft ink-soaked block of absorbent material for inking a rubber stamp. 4. one of the cushionlike protuberances on the under side of the feet of dogs, foxes, and some other animals. 5. the foot of a fox or other beast of the chase. 6. the large floating leaf of the water lily. —*v.t.* 7. to furnish or stuff with padding. 8. to expand (writing or speech) with unnecessary words or matter.

pad[2] (păd), *n.*, *v.*, **padded, padding.** —*n.* 1. a dull sound, as of footsteps on the ground. —*v.t.* 2. to travel along on foot. —*v.i.* 3. to travel on foot. 4. to go with a dull sound of footsteps.

pad·ding (păd′ĭng), *n.* 1. material, as cotton or straw, with which to pad. 2. unnecessary matter used to expand a speech, etc.

pad·dle[1] (păd′əl), *n.*, *v.*, **-dled, -dling.** —*n.* 1. a short oar held in the hands (not resting in the oarlock). 2. one of the boards on a paddle wheel. 3. a paddle-shaped implement for beating, stirring, etc. —*v.i.*, *v.t.* 4. to propel (a canoe, etc.) by a paddle. 5. to row lightly or gently with oars. 6. *U.S. Colloq.* to beat with a paddle; spank. —**pad′dler,** *n.*

pad·dle[2] (păd′əl), *v.i.*, **-dled, -dling.** to dabble or play in or as in shallow water.

pad·dle·fish (păd′əl fĭsh′), *n.*, *pl.* **-fishes,** (*esp. collectively*) **-fish.** a large fish with a long, flat, paddlelike projection of the snout, abundant in the Mississippi river and its larger tributaries.

paddle wheel, a power-driven wheel with boards (paddles) on its circumference, for propelling a vessel over the water.

pad·dock (păd′ək), *n.* 1. a small field or enclosure, esp. for pasture. 2. a turfed enclosure for horses, esp. at a race track.

pad·dy (păd′ĭ), *n.* 1. rice. 2. rice in the husk, uncut or gathered.

Pa·de·rew·ski (pä′dĕ rĕf′skĭ, păd′ə-), *n.* **Ignace Jan,** 1860–1941, Polish pianist, composer, and statesman.

pad·lock (păd′lŏk′), *n.* 1. a portable lock having a pivoted or sliding hasp which passes through a staple, ring, or the like, and is then made fast. —*v.t.* 2. to fasten with a padlock.

pa·dre (pä′drĭ), *n.* 1. father (used esp. with reference to a priest). 2. (among soldiers and sailors) a chaplain.

Pad·u·a (păj′ŏŏ ə, păd′yŏŏ ə), *n.* a city in NE Italy. 160,921.

Pa·du·cah (pə dū′kə, -dōō′-), *n.* a city in W Kentucky. 33,765.

pae·an (pē′ən), *n.* any song of praise, joy, or triumph.

pa·gan (pā′gən), *n.* 1. one of a people professing some other than the Christian religion. 2. one who is not a Christian, Jew, or Mohammedan. 3. an irreligious or heathenish person. —*adj.* 4. of, pertaining to, or characteristic of pagans. —**pa′gan·ism′,** *n.*

Pa·ga·ni·ni (păg′ə nē′nē), *n.* **Nicolò,** 1784–1840, Italian violinist.

page[1] (pāj), *n.*, *v.*, **paged, paging.** —*n.* 1. one side of a leaf of a book, manuscript, letter, or the like. —*v.t.* 2. to number the pages of.

page[2] (pāj), *n.*, *v.*, **paged, paging.** —*n.* 1. a boy servant or attendant. 2. a youth in attendance on a person of rank, sometimes formerly in the course of training for knighthood. 3. a young male attendant, usually in uniform, in a legislative hall, a hotel, etc. —*v.t.* 4. *U.S.* to seek (a person) by calling out his name, as a hotel page does.

pag·eant (păj'ənt), *n.* an elaborate public spectacle, whether processional or at some fitting spot, illustrative of the history of a place, institution, or other subject.

pag·eant·ry (păj'ən trǐ), *n.*, *pl.* **-ries.** 1. spectacular display; pomp. 2. mere display.

pag·i·na·tion (păj'ə nā'shən), *n.* 1. the sequence or number of pages of a book. 2. the figures by which pages are numbered. 3. act of paging.

pa·go·da (pə gō'də), *n.* (in India, Burma, China, etc.) a temple or sacred building, usually a tower of many stories.

Pa·go Pa·go (päng'ō päng'-ō), the chief harbor and town of American Samoa, on Tutuila island. 934. Also, **Pagopago.**

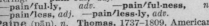

Chinese pagoda

pail (pāl), *n.* a container of wood, metal, etc., nearly or quite cylindrical, with a handle, for holding liquids, etc. —**pail·ful** (pāl'fŏŏl'), *n.*

pain (pān), *n.* 1. bodily or mental suffering or distress. 2. (*pl.*) laborious or careful efforts. 3. penalty or threat. —*v.t.* 4. to hurt; distress. —*v.i.* 5. to cause pain or suffering. —**pain'ful**, *adj.* —**pain'ful·ly**, *adv.* —**pain'ful·ness**, *n.* —**pain'less**, *adj.* —**pain'less·ly**, *adv.*

Paine (pān), *n.* Thomas, 1737–1809, American writer on government, born in England.

pains·tak·ing (pānz'tā'kǐng), *adj.* assiduously careful. —**pains'tak'ing·ly**, *adv.*

paint (pānt), *n.* 1. a substance composed of liquid coloring matter, applied as a coating. —*v.t.* 2. to represent (an object, etc.) or execute (a picture, etc.) in colors. 3. to describe vividly. 4. to cover with color. 5. to apply like paint. —*v.t.* 6. to cover anything with paint. 7. to practice painting.

paint·brush (pānt'brŭsh'), *n.* a brush for applying paint.

paint·er[1] (pān'tər), *n.* 1. an artist who paints pictures. 2. a workman who coats surfaces with paint.

paint·er[2] (pān'tər), *n.* a rope, usually at the bow, for fastening a boat to a ship, stake, etc.

paint·er[3] (pān'tər), *n.* the American panther, or cougar.

paint·ing (pān'tǐng), *n.* 1. a picture executed in paints. 2. act, art, or work of one who paints.

pair (pâr), *n.*, *pl.* **pairs, pair,** *v.* —*n.* 1. two things of a kind, matched together. 2. a combination of two parts joined together. 3. a married or engaged couple. 4. *Govt.* a. two members on opposite sides in a deliberative body who for convenience (as to permit absence) arrange together to forgo voting on a given occasion. b. the arrangement thus made. —*v.t.* 5. to arrange in pairs. 6. to match; mate. —*v.i.* 7. to separate into pairs. 8. to form a pair or pairs. 9. (in a deliberative body) to form a pair to forgo voting.

pais·ley (pāz'lǐ), *n.*, *pl.* **-leys.** 1. a soft fabric made from wool and woven with a colorful and minutely detailed pattern. —*adj.* 2. made of paisley.

pa·jam·as (pə jăm'əz, pə jä'məz), *n.pl.* 1. nightclothes consisting of loose trousers and jacket. 2. loose trousers, worn by both sexes in India, etc. Also, *esp. Brit.*, **pyjamas.**

Pa·ki·stan (pä'kǐ stän'), *n.* a dominion of the British Commonwealth of Nations containing the predominantly Moslem areas of the peninsula of India, concentrated in the northeastern and northwestern parts. ab. 80,500,000 pop.; ab. 350,000 sq. mi. *Cap.*: Karachi.

pal (păl), *n.*, *v.*, **palled, palling.** *Colloq.* —*n.* 1. a comrade; chum. 2. an accomplice. —*v.i.* 3. to associate as a pal or as pals.

pal·ace (păl'ĭs), *n.* 1. the official residence of a sovereign, a bishop, or other exalted personage. 2. a stately mansion or building.

pal·a·din (păl'ə dǐn), *n.* 1. one of the twelve legendary knightly champions in attendance on Charlemagne. 2. any knightly or heroic champion.

pal·an·quin (păl'ən kēn'), *n.* (in India and

other Eastern countries) a covered or boxlike litter borne by means of poles resting on men's shoulders. Also, **pal'an·keen'.**

pal·at·a·ble (păl'ət ə bəl), *adj.* 1. agreeable to the taste; savory. 2. agreeable to the mind. —**pal'at·a·bil'i·ty**, *n.* —**pal'at·a·bly**, *adv.*

pal·a·tal (păl'ə təl), *adj.* 1. *Anat.* of or pertaining to the palate. 2. *Phonet.* with the tongue held close to the hard palate. —*n.* 3. *Phonet.* a palatal sound. —**pal'a·tal·ize'**, *v.t.*

pal·ate (păl'ĭt), *n.* 1. the roof of the mouth, consisting of bone (**hard palate**) in front and of a fleshy structure (**soft palate**) at the back. 2. the sense of taste.

pa·la·tial (pə lā'shəl), *adj.* pertaining to, of the nature of, or befitting a palace. —**pa·la'tial·ly**, *adv.*

pal·a·tine (păl'ə tīn', -tǐn), *adj.* possessing or characterized by royal privileges.

Pa·lau Islands (pä lou'), a group of Pacific islands in the W part of the Caroline group: taken by U.S. forces, 1944; formerly a Japanese mandate, now under U.S. trusteeship. 12,764 pop.; 171 sq. mi.

pa·lav·er (pə lăv'ər, -lä'vər), *n.* 1. a conference, as between travelers and primitive natives. 2. profuse talk; flattery. —*v.i.* 3. to talk profusely and idly. —*v.t.* 4. to cajole.

pale[1] (pāl), *adj.*, **paler, palest,** *v.*, **paled, paling.** —*adj.* 1. without intensity of color. 2. approaching white or gray. 3. dim. 4. faint; feeble. —*v.t.*, *v.i.* 5. to make or become pale. —**pale'ly**, *adv.* —**pale'ness**, *n.*

pale[2] (pāl), *n.*, *v.*, **paled, paling.** —*n.* 1. a stake or picket, as of a fence. 2. any enclosing barrier. 3. limits or bounds. 4. any enclosed area. 5. a district within fixed bounds. —*v.t.* 6. to enclose with pales. 7. to encircle.

pale·face (pāl'fās'), *n.* a white person (an expression attributed to the American Indians).

pa·le·og·ra·phy (pā'lǐ ŏg'rə fǐ, păl'Y-), *n.* 1. ancient forms of writing. 2. the study of ancient writing.

pa·le·o·lith·ic (pā'lǐ ə lǐth'ǐk, păl'Y-), *adj.* noting or pertaining to the earlier part of the Old World Stone Age, marked by exclusive use of chipped stone implements.

paleontol., paleontology.

pa·le·on·tol·o·gy (pā'lǐ ən tŏl'ə jǐ, păl'Y-), *n.* the science of the forms of life existing in former geological periods, as represented by fossil animals and plants. —**pa'le·on·tol'o·gist**, *n.*

Pa·le·o·zo·ic (pā'lǐ ə zō'ǐk, păl'Y-), *adj. Stratig.* pertaining to the oldest geological era or rocks having abundant fossils.

Pa·ler·mo (pä lěr'mō), *n.* a seaport in and the capital of Sicily, in the NW part. 446,384.

Pal·es·tine (păl'ə stīn'), *n.* a former country in SW Asia, on the Mediterranean: now divided into Israel and Arab Palestine; parts of ancient Palestine are now in Syria and Trans-Jordan. 1,912,000 pop.; 10,429 sq. mi. —**Pal·es·tin·i·an** (păl'ə stǐn'Y ən), *adj.*, *n.*

Pa·les·tri·na (păl'ə strē'nə), *n.* Giovanni Pierluigi da, 1526?–1594, Italian composer.

pal·ette (păl'ĭt), *n.* 1. a thin board or tablet with a thumb hole at one end, used by painters to lay and mix colors on. 2. the range of colors used by a particular artist.

pal·frey (pôl'frǐ), *n.*, *pl.* **-freys.** a riding horse, esp. a woman's saddle horse.

pal·imp·sest (păl'ǐmp sěst'), *n.* a parchment or the like from which writing has been erased to make room for another text.

pal·ing (pā'lǐng), *n.* 1. a fence of pales. 2. a pale, as in a fence. 3. pales collectively.

pal·i·sade (păl'ə sād'), *n.*, *v.*, **-saded, -sading.** —*n.* 1. a fence of pales or stakes set firmly in the ground. 2. one of the stakes. 3. (*pl.*) a line of lofty cliffs. —*v.t.* 4. to furnish or fortify with a palisade.

pall[1] (pôl), *n.* 1. a cloth for spreading over a coffin, bier, or tomb. 2. something that covers, shrouds, or overspreads, esp. with darkness or gloom. —*v.t.* 3. to cover with a pall.

pall[2] (pôl), *v.i.* 1. to have a wearying effect. 2. to become insipid, distasteful, or wearisome. —*v.t.* 3. to satiate or cloy.

pal·la·di·um (pə lā'dǐ əm), *n.* *Chem.* a rare metallic element of the platinum group, silverwhite, ductile, and malleable. *Symbol:* Pd; *at. wt.:* 106.7; *at. no.:* 46; *sp. gr.:* 12 at 20°C.

Pal·las (păl'əs), *n.* 1. a name of Athena (often **Pallas Athene**). 2. *Astron.* one of the asteroids.

pall·bear·er (pôl'bâr'ər), *n.* one of those who attend the coffin at a funeral.

pal·let¹ (păl'ĭt), *n.* **1.** a bed or mattress of straw. **2.** a small or poor bed.

pal·let² (păl'ĭt), *n.* **1.** an implement consisting of a flat blade or plate with a handle, used for shaping by potters, etc. **2.** *Horol.* a lever with three projections, two of which intermittently lock and receive impulses from the escape wheel, and one which transmits these impulses to the balance.

pal·li·ate (păl'ĭ āt'), *v.t.*, **-ated, -ating. 1.** to cause (an offense, etc.) to appear less grave; extenuate. **2.** to mitigate or alleviate. —**pal/li·a'tion,** *n.* —**pal'li·a'tive,** *adj.* —**pal'li·a'tive·ly,** *adv.*

pal·lid (păl'ĭd), *adj.* pale; wan. —**pal'lid·ly,** *adv.* —**pal'lid·ness,** *n.*

Pall Mall (pĕl' mĕl', păl' măl'), a street in London, England, famed for its clubs.

pal·lor (păl'ər), *n.* unnatural paleness, as from fear, ill health, or death; wanness.

palm¹ (päm), *n.* **1.** that part of the inner surface of the hand which extends from the wrist to the bases of the fingers. **2.** the corresponding part of the forefoot of an animal. **3.** a linear measure based on either the breadth of the hand (3 to 4 inches) or its length from wrist to fingertips (7 to 10 inches). **4.** a flat, widened part at the end of an armlike projection. —*v.t.* **5.** to conceal in the palm, as in juggling. **6.** to pass fraudulently or deceptively. **7.** to impose (something) fraudulently.

palm² (päm), *n.* **1.** any of certain plants, mostly tall, unbranched trees surmounted by a crown of large pinnate or fan-shaped leaves. **2.** a leaf or branch of a palm tree, esp. as formerly borne as an emblem of victory. —**palm/like',** *adj.*

Pal·ma (päl'mä), *n.* a seaport in and the capital of the Balearic Islands, on W Majorca. 114,405.

pal·mate (păl'māt, -mĭt), *adj.* shaped like an open palm, as a leaf. —**pal'mate·ly,** *adv.*

Palm Beach (päm), a town in SE Florida; seaside winter resort. 3747.

palm·er (pä'mər), *n.* a pilgrim who had returned from the Holy Land, in token of which he bore a palm branch.

pal·met·to (păl mĕt'ō), *n., pl.* **-tos, -toes.** any of certain species of palm with fan-shaped leaves.

palm·is·try (pä'mĭs trĭ), *n.* the art or practice of telling fortunes and interpreting character by the lines and configurations of the palm of the hand. —**palm·ist** (pä'mĭst), *n.*

Palm Sunday, the Sunday next before Easter, celebrated in commemoration of Christ's triumphal entry into Jerusalem.

palm·y (pä'mĭ), *adj.*, **palmier, palmiest. 1.** glorious, prosperous, or flourishing. **2.** abounding in or shaded with palms.

pal·o·mi·no (păl'ə mē'nō), *n., pl.* **-nos.** a tan or cream-colored horse, bred chiefly in the SW United States.

pal·pa·ble (păl'pə bəl), *adj.* **1.** readily or plainly seen, heard, etc.; obvious. **2.** that can be touched or felt; tangible. —**pal'pa·bly,** *adv.*

pal·pi·tate (păl'pə tāt'), *v.i.*, **-tated, -tating. 1.** to pulsate with unnatural rapidity, as the heart, from exertion, emotion, disease, etc. **2.** to quiver. —**pal'pi·ta'tion,** *n.*

pal·sy (pôl'zĭ), *n., pl.* **-sies,** *v.,* **-sied, -sying.** —*n.* **1.** paralysis. —*v.t.* **2.** to paralyze. —**pal'sied,** *adj.*

pal·ter (pôl'tər), *v.i.* **1.** to talk or act insincerely; deal crookedly. **2.** to haggle. **3.** to trifle.

pal·try (pôl'trĭ), *adj.,* **-trier, -triest. 1.** trifling; petty. **2.** worthless. **3.** contemptible. —**pal'tri·ness,** *n.*

pam·pas (păm'pəz; *attributively* păm'pəs), *n. pl.* the vast grassy plains lying in the rain shadow of the Andes and south of the forested lowlands of the Amazon basin, esp. in Argentina. —**pam·pe·an** (păm pē'ən, păm'pĭ ən), *adj.*

pampas grass, a tall ornamental grass, native in South America, having large, thick, feathery, silvery-white panicles.

pam·per (păm'pər), *v.t.* to indulge (a person, one's appetite, etc.) fully or to excess. —**pam'per·er,** *n.*

pam·phlet (păm'flĭt), *n.* **1.** a short essay on some subject of temporary interest. **2.** a small booklet, usually in paper covers.

pam·phlet·eer (păm'flə tĭr'), *n.* **1.** a writer of pamphlets. —*v.i.* **2.** to write pamphlets.

pan (păn), *n., v.,* **panned, panning.** —*n.* **1.** a dish, commonly of metal, usually broad and shallow and often open, used for domestic purposes. **2.** any dishlike part, as the scales of a balance. **3.** (in old guns) the depressed part of the lock, which holds the priming. —*v.t.* **4.** to wash (auriferous gravel, sand, etc.) in a pan to separate the gold or other heavy valuable metal. **5.** *Colloq.* to criticize or reprimand severely. —*v.i.* **6.** *Colloq.* to succeed.

Pan (păn), *n. Gk. Myth.* the god of forests, pastures, flocks, and shepherds, represented with the head, chest, and arms of a man, and the legs and sometimes the horns and ears of a goat.

pan-, a word element or prefix meaning "all," used esp. in terms implying the union, association, or consideration together of all the branches of a race, people, church, or other body, as in *Pan-Christian, Pan-Slavic.*

Pan., Panama.

pan·a·ce·a (păn'ə sē'ə), *n.* a remedy for all diseases; cure-all. —**pan'a·ce'an,** *adj.*

Pan·a·ma (păn'ə mä'), *n.* **1.** a republic in S Central America, enclosing, but not including, the Panama Canal. 622,576 pop.; 28,575 sq. mi. **2.** Also, **Panama City.** the capital of Panama. 111,893. **3. Isthmus of,** an isthmus between North and South America. —**Pan·a·ma·ni·an** (păn'ə mā'nĭ ən, -mä'-), *adj., n.*

Panama Canal, a canal extending SE from the Atlantic to the Pacific across the Isthmus of Panama. 40 mi. long.

Panama hat, a fine plaited hat made of the young leaves of a palmlike plant of Central and South America.

Pan-A·mer·i·can (păn'ə mĕr'ə kən), *adj.* of, pertaining to, or embracing all the countries of North, Central, and South America.

Pan American Union, an organization of the 21 American republics to further understanding and peace.

Pa·nay (pä nī'), *n.* one of the Philippine Islands, in the central part of the group. 1,291,548 pop.; 4446 sq. mi. *Cap.:* Iloilo.

pan·cake (păn'kāk'), *n., v.,* **-caked, -caking.** —*n.* **1.** a flat cake of batter cooked in a pan or on a griddle. **2.** an airplane landing made by pancaking. —*v.i.* **3.** (of an airplane, etc.) to drop flat to the ground after leveling off a few feet above the ground. —*v.t.* **4.** to cause (an airplane) to pancake.

pan·chro·mat·ic (păn'krō măt'ĭk), *adj. Photog.* sensitive to light of all colors.

pan·cre·as (păn'krĭ əs, păng'-), *n. Anat., Zool.* a gland situated near the stomach, secreting an important digestive fluid (**pancreatic juice**). —**pan·cre·at·ic** (păn'krĭ ăt'ĭk, păng'-), *adj.*

pan·da (păn'də), *n.* **1.** Also, **lesser panda.** a carnivore of the Himalayas, somewhat larger than a cat, having reddish-brown fur, the face marked with white, and a long, bushy tail marked with pale rings. **2.** Also, **giant panda.** a large bearlike carnivore of Tibet and southern China, white with black limbs, shoulders, and ears, and a black ring around each eye.

pan·de·mo·ni·um (păn'də mō'nĭ əm), *n.* **1.** wild lawlessness or uproar. **2.** a place of riotous uproar or lawless confusion. **3.** (*often cap.*) the abode of all the demons. **4.** hell.

pan·der (păn'dər), *n.* **1.** a pimp. **2.** one who ministers to the baser passions of others. —*v.t., v.i.* **3.** to act as a pander (for). —**pan'der·er,** *n.*

Pan·do·ra (păn dōr'ə), *n. Class. Myth.* the first mortal woman, on whom all the gods and goddesses bestowed gifts.

pan·dow·dy (păn dou'dĭ), *n., pl.* **-dies.** *U.S.* a pudding or deep pie made with apples, usually sweetened with molasses.

pane (pān), *n.* **1.** one of the divisions of a window, etc., consisting of a single plate of glass in a frame. **2.** a plate of glass for such a division.

pan·e·gyr·ic (păn'ə jĭr'ĭk), *n.* an oration, discourse, or writing in praise of a person or thing; eulogy. —**pan'e·gyr'i·cal,** *adj.* —**pan'e·gyr'i·cal·ly,** *adv.*

pan·el (păn'əl), *n., v.,* **-eled, -eling** or (*esp. Brit.*) **-elled, -elling.** —*n.* **1.** a distinct portion of a wainscot, ceiling, door, etc., or of any surface sunk below or raised above the general level, or enclosed by a border. **2.** a pane. **3.** a comparatively thin, flat piece of wood or the like. **4.** *Painting.* a flat piece of wood of varying kinds on which a picture is painted. **5.** a broad strip of material set vertically in or on a woman's skirt. **6.** *Elect.* a division of a switchboard containing a set of related cords, relays, etc. **7.** a group of speakers in an organized discussion. **8.** *Law.* **a.** the list of persons summoned for service as jurors. **b.** the body of persons composing a jury. —*v.t.* **9.** to arrange in or ornament with panels.

pang (păng), *n.* **1.** a sudden feeling of mental distress. **2.** a sudden, brief, sharp pain.

pan·go·lin (păng gō'lĭn), *n.* any of the scaly anteaters of Africa and tropical Asia, having a covering of broad, overlapping, horny scales.

pan·han·dle[1] (păn'hăn'dəl), *n.* **1.** the handle of a pan. **2.** *U.S.* a narrow projecting strip of land, esp. part of a State.

pan·han·dle[2] (păn'hăn'dəl), *v.i.,* **-dled, -dling.** *Colloq.* to beg. —**pan'han'dler,** *n.*

Pan·hel·len·ic (păn'hə lĕn'ĭk), *adj.* **1.** pertaining to all Greeks. **2.** of or pertaining to collegiate fraternities and sororities.

pan·ic (păn'ĭk), *n., adj., v.,* **-icked, -icking.** —*n.* **1.** demoralizing terror, often as affecting a group of persons or animals. **2.** an instance, outbreak, or period of such fear. **3.** a sudden widespread fear concerning financial affairs leading to credit contraction and widespread sale of securities at depressed prices. —*adj.* **4.** (of fear, terror, etc.) impelling to some frantic action. **5.** of the nature of, due to, or showing panic. —*v.t.* **6.** *Slang.* to keep highly amused. —**pan'ick·y,** *adj.* —**pan·ic·strick·en** (păn'ĭk strĭk'ən), **panic-struck** (păn'ĭk strŭk'), *adj.*

pan·i·cle (păn'ə kəl), *n.* *Bot.* **1.** a compound raceme. **2.** any loose, diversely branching flower cluster.

pan·nier (păn'yər, -ĭ ər), *n.* **1.** a basket, esp. one for carrying on a person's back, or one of a pair across the back of a beast of burden. **2.** a puffed arrangement of drapery about the hips.

pa·no·cha (pə nō'chə), *n.* a candy made of brown sugar, butter, milk, and nuts.

pan·o·ply (păn'ə plĭ), *n., pl.* **-plies.** a complete suit of armor. —**pan·o·plied** (păn'ə plĭd), *adj.*

pan·o·ram·a (păn'ə răm'ə, -rä'mə), *n.* **1.** an unobstructed view over a wide area. **2.** an extended pictorial representation of a landscape or other scene. **3.** a continuously passing or changing scene. —**pan'o·ram'ic,** *adj.*

Pan·pipe (păn'pīp'), *n.* a primitive wind instrument consisting of a series of pipes of graduated length. Also, **Pan's pipes.**

pan·sy (păn'zĭ), *n., pl.* **-sies.** **1.** a species of violet having many cultivated varieties with large, richly and variously colored flowers. **2.** the pansy blossom. **3.** *Slang.* an effeminate or homosexual man.

pant (pănt), *v.i., v.t.* **1.** to breathe hard and quickly, as after exertion. **2.** to gasp, as for air. **3.** to long with intense eagerness. **4.** to throb or heave violently or rapidly; palpitate. —*n.* **5.** act of panting. **6.** a gasp. —**pant'ing·ly,** *adv.*

pan·ta·lets (păn'tə lĕts'), *n.pl.* long drawers with a frill or other finish at the bottom of each leg, and extending below the dress, commonly worn by women and girls in the 19th century. Also, **pan'ta·lettes'.**

pan·ta·loon (păn'tə lōōn'), *n.* **1.** (*pl.*) In *U.S.,* *Archaic except Hist.; in England, formal.* trousers. **2.** (in the modern pantomime) a foolish, vicious old man, the butt and accomplice of the clown.

pan·the·ism (păn'thē ĭz'əm), *n.* **1.** the doctrine that God is the transcendent reality of which the material universe and man are only manifestations. **2.** any religious belief or philosophical doctrine which identifies the universe with God. —**pan'the·ist,** *n.* —**pan'the·is'tic,** **pan'the·is'ti·cal,** *adj.* —**pan'the·is'ti·cal·ly,** *adv.*

Pan·the·on (păn'thĭ ŏn', -ən, păn thē'ən), *n.* **1.** a temple at Rome, erected A.D. 120–124 by Hadrian. **2.** (*l.c.*) a public building containing tombs or memorials of the illustrious dead of a nation. **3.** (*l.c.*) a temple dedicated to all the gods. **4.** (*l.c.*) the gods of a particular mythology.

pan·ther (păn'thər), *n., pl.* **-thers,** (*esp. collectively*) **-ther.** **1.** the cougar or puma. **2.** the leopard.

pan·to·graph (păn'tə grăf', -gräf'), *n.* an instrument for the mechanical copying of plans, diagrams, etc., upon any desired scale.

pan·to·mime (păn'tə mīm'), *n., v.,* **-mimed, -miming.** —*n.* **1.** a play in which the performers express themselves by mute gestures. —*v.t.* **2.** to represent or express by pantomime. —*v.i.* **3.** to express oneself by pantomime. —**pan'to·mim'-ist,** *n.* —**pan·to·mim·ic** (păn'tə mĭm'ĭk), *adj.*

pan·try (păn'trĭ), *n., pl.* **-tries.** a room or closet in which provisions, silverware, dishes, etc., are kept.

pants (pănts), *n.pl.* **1.** *U.S. Colloq.* trousers. **2.** *Brit.* drawers.

pan·zer (păn'zər), *adj.* armored.

pap[1] (păp), *n.* soft food for infants or invalids, as bread soaked in water or milk.

pap[2] (păp), *n.* *Archaic or Dial.* a nipple.

pa·pa (pä'pə, pə pä'), *n.* father.

pa·pa·cy (pā'pə sĭ), *n., pl.* **-cies.** **1.** the office, dignity, or jurisdiction of the Pope (of Rome). **2.** the system of ecclesiastical government in which the Pope is recognized as the supreme head. **3.** the time during which a pope is in office. **4.** the succession or line of the popes.

pa·pal (pā'pəl), *adj.* of or pertaining to the Pope or the Roman Catholic Church.

pa·paw (pô'pô, pə pô'), *n.* **1.** the small fleshy fruit of a certain small temperate North American tree. **2.** the tree itself. Also, **pawpaw.**

pa·pa·ya (pə pä'yə), *n.* **1.** the large yellow melonlike fruit of a tropical American shrub or small tree. **2.** the tree itself.

pa·per (pā'pər), *n.* **1.** a substance made from rags, wood, or other fibrous material, usually in thin sheets, for writing on, wrapping things in, etc. **2.** a written or printed document or instrument. **3.** negotiable notes, bills, etc., collectively. **4.** a document establishing identity, status, or the like. **5.** an essay, article, or dissertation on a particular topic. **6.** a newspaper or journal. —*v.t.* **7.** to write on paper. **8.** to put up in paper. **9.** to decorate with wallpaper. —*adj.* **10.** made or consisting of paper. **11.** Also, **pa'per·y.** thin; flimsy; frail. **12.** existing on paper only and not in reality. —**pa'per·er,** *n.* —**pa'per·like',** *adj.*

paper hanger, one whose business it is to cover or decorate walls with wallpaper.

pa·per·weight (pā'pər wāt'), *n.* a small heavy object laid on papers to keep them from being scattered.

pa·pier-mâ·ché (pā'pər mə shā'), *n.* a substance made of paper pulp mixed with glue and other materials, molded when moist to form various articles.

pa·pil·la (pə pĭl'ə), *n., pl.* **-pillae** (-pĭl'ē). **1.** any small nipplelike process or projection. **2.** one of certain small protuberances concerned with the senses of touch, taste, and smell. **3.** a small vascular process at the root of a hair. **4.** a pimple. —**pap·il·lar·y** (păp'ə lĕr'ĭ), *adj.*

pap·il·lo·ma (păp'ə lō'mə), *n., pl.* **-mata** (-mətə), **-mas.** *Pathol.* a tumor of skin or mucous membrane, as a wart or a corn.

pap·il·lose (păp'ə lōs'), *adj.* full of papillae.

pa·pist (pā'pĭst), *n.* **1.** an adherent of the Pope. **2.** a member of the Roman Catholic Church (usually in disparagement). —*adj.* **3.** papistical.

pa·pis·ti·cal (pā pĭs'tə kəl, pə-), *adj.* of, pertaining to, or characteristic of papists (usually in disparagement). Also, **pa·pis'tic.**

pa·poose (pă pōōs'), *n.* a North American Indian baby or child. Also, **pap·poose'.**

pap·ri·ka (pă prē'kə, păp'rə kə), *n.* the dried fruit of a pepper plant, ground as a condiment.

Pap·u·a (păp'yōō ə, pä'pōō ä'), *n.* **1.** New Guinea. **2. Territory of,** an Australian territory in SE New Guinea, including the adjacent islands: merged with the Territory of New Guinea, 1945. 303,000 pop.; 90,540 sq. mi. *Cap.:* Port Moresby. —**Pap'u·an,** *adj., n.*

pa·py·rus (pə pī'rəs), *n., pl.* **-pyri** (-pī'rī). **1.** a tall aquatic plant of the sedge family, formerly abundant in Egypt. **2.** a material for writing on, prepared from thin strips of the pith of this plant, used by the ancient Egyptians, Greeks, and Romans.

par (pär), *n.* **1.** an equality in value or standing. **2.** an average or normal amount, degree, quality, or the like. **3.** the legally established value of the monetary unit of one country in terms of that of another using the same metal as a standard of value. **4.** *Com.* the state of bonds, stocks, etc., when they may be purchased at their original price or at their face value. **5.** *Golf.* the number of strokes allowed to a hole or course as an expert score. —*adj.* **6.** average or normal. **7.** *Com.* at or pertaining to par.

par., **1.** paragraph. **2.** parallel.

Pa·rá (pä rä´), *n.* Belém.

par·a·ble (păr´ə bəl), *n.* a short allegorical story, conveying some moral lesson.

pa·rab·o·la (pə răb´ə lə), *n.* *Geom.* a plane curve formed by the intersection of a right circular cone with a plane parallel to a generator of the cone.

par·a·bol·ic (păr´ə bŏl´ĭk), *adj.* **1.** having the form of a parabola. **2.** pertaining to or resembling a parabola.

Par·a·cel·sus (păr´ə sĕl´səs), *n.* 1493?–1541, Swiss-German physician and alchemist.

par·a·chute (păr´ə shōōt´), *n.,* *v.,* **-chuted, -chuting.** —*n.* **1.** an umbrellalike apparatus used in descending safely through the air from a great height, esp. from an aircraft. —*v.t.* **2.** to land (troops, equipment, etc.) by parachute. —*v.i.* **3.** to descend by parachute. —**par´a·chut´- ist,** *n.*

pa·rade (pə rād´), *n.,* *v.,* **-raded, -rading.** —*n.* **1.** a public procession for display. **2.** a ceremony involving the marching of troop units and a mass salute at the lowering of the flag at the end of the day. **3.** the orderly assembly of troops for inspection or display. **4.** a place where troops regularly assemble for parade. **5.** display or ostentation. —*v.t.* **6.** to walk up and down on or in. **7.** to display ostentatiously. —*v.i.* **8.** to march or proceed with display. **9.** to promenade in a public place to show oneself. —**pa·rad´er,** *n.*

par·a·digm (păr´ə dĭm, -dīm´), *n.* **1.** *Gram.* **a.** the set of all forms containing a particular element. **b.** a display in fixed arrangement of such a set. **2.** a pattern or example.

par·a·dise (păr´ə dīs´), *n.* **1.** heaven, as the final abode of the righteous. **2.** the garden of Eden. **3.** a place of extreme beauty. **4.** supreme felicity.

par·a·dox (păr´ə dŏks´), *n.* **1.** a statement seemingly self-contradictory but actually expressing a truth. **2.** a self-contradictory and false proposition. —**par´a·dox´i·cal,** *adj.* —**par´a·dox´i·cal·ly,** *adv.* —**par´a·dox´i·cal·ness,** *n.*

par·af·fin (păr´ə fĭn), *n.* **1.** *U.S.* a white or colorless waxy substance obtained chiefly from crude petroleum: used for making candles, waterproofing paper, etc. **2.** *Chem.* any hydrocarbon of the methane series (or **paraffin series**). —*v.t.* **3.** to cover with paraffin. Also, **par·af·fine** (păr´ə fĭn, -fēn´).

par·a·gon (păr´ə gŏn´, -gən), *n.* a model or pattern of excellence.

par·a·graph (păr´ə grăf´, -gräf´), *n.* **1.** a distinct portion of written or printed matter dealing with a particular point, and usually beginning (commonly with indention) on a new line. **2.** a character (now usually ¶) used to indicate the beginning of such a portion. **3.** a note, item, or brief article, as in a newspaper. —*v.t.* **4.** to divide into paragraphs. —**par´a·graph´ic,** *adj.*

Par·a·guay (păr´ə gwā´, -gwī´), *n.* a republic in central South America between Bolivia, Brazil, and Argentina. 1,145,000 pop.; 150,515 sq. mi. *Cap.:* Asunción. —**Par´a·guay´an,** *adj., n.*

par·a·keet (păr´ə kēt´), *n.* any of numerous small slender parrots, usually with long, pointed, graduated tail.

par·al·lax (păr´ə lăks´), *n.* the apparent displacement of an object observed, esp. a heavenly body, due to a change or difference in the position of the observer. —**par·al·lac·tic** (păr´ə lăk´tĭk), *adj.*

par·al·lel (păr´ə lĕl´), *adj., n., v.,* **-leled, -leling** or (*esp. Brit.*) **-lelled, -lelling.** —*adj.* **1.** having the same direction, course, or tendency. **2.** similar. **3.** equally distant at all points. —*n.* **4.** anything parallel in direction, course, or tendency. **5.** a parallel line or plane. **6.** *Geog.* **a.** a circle on the earth surface formed by a plane parallel to the plane of the equator. **b.** the line representing this circle on a map. **7.** a counterpart. **8.** similarity or analogy. **9.** *Print.* a pair of vertical parallel lines (‖) used as a mark of reference. —*v.t.* **10.** to make parallel. **11.** to furnish a parallel for. **12.** to be equivalent to; equal. **13.** to compare.

par·al·lel·ism (păr´ə lĕl´ĭz əm), *n.* **1.** the position or relation of parallels. **2.** agreement in direction, tendency, or character. **3.** a comparison.

par·al·lel·o·gram (păr´ə lĕl´ə grăm´), *n.* a quadrilateral the opposite sides of which are parallel.

pa·ral·y·sis (pə răl´ə sĭs), *n.,* *pl.* **-ses** (-sēz´). **1.** *Pathol.* **a.** loss of power of a voluntary muscular contraction. **b.** a disease characterized by this; palsy. **2.** a standstill or inactivity. —**par·a·lyt·ic** (păr´ə lĭt´ĭk), *n., adj.*

par·a·lyze (păr´ə līz´), *v.t.,* **-lyzed, -lyzing.** to affect with paralysis. —**par´a·ly·za´tion,** *n.*

Par·a·mar·i·bo (păr´ə măr´ĭ bō´), *n.* a seaport in and capital of Surinam. 60,720.

par·a·me·ci·um (păr´ə mē´shĭ əm, -sĭ əm), *n., pl.* **-cia** (-shĭ ə, -sĭ ə). *Zool.* a ciliate infusorian having an oval body and deep long oral groove, inhabiting fresh water and extensively used in experiments on protozoa.

par·a·mount (păr´ə mount´), *adj.* **1.** superior in rank or authority. **2.** supreme; preëminent. —*n.* **3.** a supreme ruler.

par·a·mour (păr´ə mŏor´), *n.* **1.** an illicit lover, esp. of a married person. **2.** any lover.

Pa·ra·ná (pä´rə nä´), *n.* a river from S Brazil along the SE boundary of Uruguay and through E Argentina. ab. 2450 mi.

par·a·noi·a (păr´ə noi´ə), *n.* *Psychiatry.* mental disorder characterized by systematized delusions and the projection of personal conflicts, which are ascribed to the supposed hostility of others. —**par·a·noi·ac** (păr´ə noi´ăk), *adj., n.*

par·a·pet (păr´ə pĭt, -pĕt´), *n.* **1.** *Fort.* **a.** a defensive wall, as of earth or stone. **b.** an elevation raised above the main wall or rampart. **2.** any protective wall at the edge of a balcony, roof, bridge, etc. —**par´a·pet·ed,** *adj.*

par·a·pher·nal·ia (păr´ə fər nāl´yə, -fə nāl´- yə), *n.pl.* **1.** personal belongings. **2.** (*sometimes construed as sing.*) equipment; apparatus.

par·a·phrase (păr´ə frāz´), *n., v.,* **-phrased, -phrasing.** —*n.* **1.** a statement of the sense of a text or passage in other words, as for clearness. **2.** the act of paraphrasing. —*v.t., v.i.* **3.** to restate. —**par´a·phras´er,** *n.*

par·a·ple·gi·a (păr´ə plē´jĭ ə), *n.* *Pathol.* paralysis of both lower or upper limbs. —**par·a·pleg·ic** (păr´ə plĕj´ĭk, -plē´jĭk), *adj., n.*

Pa·rá rubber (pä rä´), India rubber obtained from a tropical South American tree.

par·a·site (păr´ə sīt´), *n.* **1.** an animal or plant which lives on or in an organism of another species (the host), from the body of which it obtains nutriment. **2.** one who lives on the hospitality or patronage of others. —**par·a·sit·ic** (păr´ə sĭt´- ĭk). **par´a·sit´i·cal,** *adj.* —**par´a·sit´i·cal·ly,** *adv.*

par·a·sol (păr´ə sŏl´, -sōl´), *n.* a woman's small or light sun umbrella.

par·a·troop (păr´ə trōōp´), *n.* a force or unit of paratroopers.

par·a·troop·er (păr´ə trōō´pər), *n.* a soldier who reaches battle by landing from a plane by parachute.

par·boil (pär´boil´), *v.t.* to boil partially, or for a short time; precook.

Par·cae (pär´sē), *n.pl.* *Rom. Myth.* the Fates.

par·cel (pär´səl); *n., v.,* **-celed, -celing** or (*esp. Brit.*) **-celled, -celling,** *adv.* —*n.* **1.** a quantity of something wrapped together; bundle. **2.** a quantity of something. **3.** any group or assemblage. **4.** a part or section, as of land. —*v.t.* **5.** to divide into or distribute in portions. —*adv.* **6.** partly.

parcel post, a branch of a postal service charged with conveying parcels.

parch (pärch), *v.t.* **1.** to make dry, esp. to excess. **2.** to make dry and hot, or thirsty. **3.** to dry (peas, beans, etc.) by exposure to heat without burning. —*v.i.* **4.** to become parched.

par·chee·si (pär chē´zĭ), *n.* a game somewhat resembling backgammon. Also, **par·che´si, par·chi´si.**

parch·ment (pärch´mənt), *n.* **1.** the skin of sheep, goats, etc., prepared for use as a writing material, etc. **2.** a manuscript on such material. **3.** a paper resembling this material.

pard[1] (pärd), *n.* *Archaic.* a leopard.

pard[2] (pärd), *n.* *U.S. Slang.* partner.

par·don (pär´dən), *n.* **1.** courteous indulgence, as in excusing fault or seeming rudeness. **2.** *Law.* a remission of penalty. **3.** forgiveness of an offense or offender. —*v.t.* **4.** to remit the penalty of (an offense). **5.** to release (a person) from liability for an offense. **6.** to excuse. —**par´don·a·ble,** *adj.* —**par´don·a·bly,** *adv.* —**par´- don·er,** *n.*

pare (pâr), *v.t.,* **pared, paring. 1.** to cut off the outer part of. **2.** to remove (an outer part) by cutting. **3.** to reduce or diminish.

par·e·gor·ic (păr'ə gôr'ĭk, -gŏr'ĭk), *Pharm.* —*n.* **1.** a soothing medicine. **2.** a camphorated tincture of opium, intended primarily to check diarrhea in children. —*adj.* **3.** assuaging pain; soothing.

paren., *pl.* parens. parenthesis.

pa·ren·chy·ma (pə rĕng'kĭ mə), *n.* **1.** *Bot.* the fundamental cellular tissue of plants, as in the softer parts of leaves, etc. **2.** *Anat., Zool.* the tissue proper of an animal organ as distinguished from its connective or supporting tissue.

par·ent (pâr'ənt), *n.* **1.** a father or a mother. **2.** a progenitor. **3.** a source. —**pa·ren·tal** (pə-rĕn'təl), *adj.* —**pa·ren'tal·ly,** *adv.* —**par'ent·hood',** *n.*

par·ent·age (pâr'ən tĭj), *n.* **1.** birth, lineage, or family. **2.** parenthood.

pa·ren·the·sis (pə rĕn'thə sĭs), *n., pl.* **-ses** (-sēz'). **1.** the upright curves () collectively, or either of them separately, used to mark off an interjected remark. **2.** *Gram.* a qualifying or explanatory word, phrase, clause, sentence, or other sequence of forms which interrupts the syntactic construction without otherwise affecting it, shown in writing by commas, parentheses, or dashes. —**par·en·thet·ic** (păr'ən thĕt'ĭk), **par'en·thet'i·cal,** *adj.* —**par'en·thet'i·cal·ly,** *adv.*

pa·ren·the·size (pə rĕn'thə sīz'), *v.t.,* **-sized, -sizing.** to insert as or in a parenthesis.

pa·re·sis (pə rē'sĭs, păr'ə sĭs), *n. Pathol.* incomplete motor paralysis. —**pa·ret·ic** (pə rĕt'ĭk, pə rē'tĭk), *n., adj.*

par·fait (pär fā'), *n.* a frozen preparation of whipped cream and egg, variously flavored.

par·he·li·on (pär hē'lĭ ən), *n., pl.* **-lia** (-lĭ ə). *Meteorol.* a bright circular spot on a solar halo.

pa·ri·ah (pə rī'ə, pä'rĭ ə, pär'ĭ ə), *n.* **1.** an outcast. **2.** (*cap.*) a member of a low caste in southern India.

pa·ri·e·tal (pə rī'ə təl), *adj.* **1.** *Anat.* referring to any wall or wall-like structure, as the side of the skull. **2.** *Biol.* of or pertaining to structural walls.

par·i·mu·tu·el (păr'ĭ mū'chŏŏ əl), *n.* **1.** a form of betting, as on horseraces, in which those who bet on the winners divide the stakes. **2.** the apparatus that records the bets.

par·ing (pâr'ĭng), *n.* **1.** act of one that pares. **2.** a piece or part pared off.

Par·is (păr'ĭs), *n.* the capital of France, in the N part. 2,725,374. —**Pa·ri·sian** (pə rĭzh'ən, -rĭz'ĭ ən), *adj., n.*

Par·is (păr'ĭs), *n. Gk. Legend.* a Trojan youth, son of King Priam. His abduction of Helen led to the Trojan War.

Paris green, an emerald-green pigment prepared from arsenic trioxide and acetate of copper, now used chiefly as an insecticide.

par·ish (păr'ĭsh), *n.* **1.** an ecclesiastical district having its own church and clergyman. **2.** a local church with its field of activity. **3.** (in Louisiana) a county.

pa·rish·ion·er (pə rĭsh'ən ər), *n.* one of the inhabitants of a parish.

par·i·ty (păr'ə tĭ), *n.* **1.** equality, as in amount, status, or character. **2.** similarity or analogy. **3.** equivalence in value in the currency of another country or at a fixed ratio between moneys of different metals.

park (pärk), *n.* **1.** a tract of land set apart, as by a city, for the benefit of the public. **2.** a tract of land set apart for recreation, sports, etc. **3.** a considerable extent of land forming the grounds of a country house. **4.** a space where vehicles may be assembled or stationed. **5.** *Mil.* **a.** the space occupied by the assembled guns, tanks, etc., of a body of soldiers. **b.** the assemblage formed. —*v.t., v.i.* **6.** to put (an automobile, etc.) for a time in a particular place. **7.** *U.S. Colloq.* to put or leave.

par·ka (pär'kə), *n.* **1.** a fur coat, cut like a shirt, worn in northeastern Asia and in Alaska. **2.** a long woolen shirtlike garment with an attached hood.

Par·kers·burg (pär'kərz bûrg'), *n.* a city in NW West Virginia. 30,103.

Park·man (pärk'mən), *n.* **Francis,** 1823–93, U.S. historian.

park·way (pärk'wā'), *n.* a highway with spaces planted with grass, trees, etc.

Parl., **1.** Parliament. **2.** Parliamentary.

par·lance (pär'ləns), *n.* way of speaking; language.

par·lay (pär'lĭ, pär lā'), *U.S.* —*v.t., v.i.* **1.** to bet (an original amount and its winnings) on another race, etc. —*n.* **2.** such a bet.

par·ley (pär'lĭ), *n., pl.* **-leys,** *v.,* **-leyed, -leying.** —*n.* **1.** a discussion; conference. **2.** an informal conference between enemies under truce, to discuss terms of surrender, etc. —*v.i.* **3.** to hold a parley.

par·lia·ment (pär'lə mənt), *n.* **1.** (*usually cap.*) the legislature of Great Britain, composed of the **House of Lords** and the **House of Commons.** **2.** any one of similar legislative bodies in other countries.

par·lia·men·tar·i·an (pär'lə mĕn târ'ĭ ən), *n.* one skilled in parliamentary law.

par·lia·men·ta·ry (pär'lə mĕn'tə rĭ), *adj.* **1.** of or pertaining to a parliament. **2.** established by a parliament. **3.** characterized by the existence of a parliament. **4.** in accordance with the rules and usages of parliaments or deliberative bodies.

par·lor (pär'lər), *n.* **1.** a room for the reception of visitors; a living room. **2.** a semiprivate room in a hotel, club, or the like, for relaxation, conversation, etc. **3.** *U.S.* an elegant business place or shop. Also, *Brit.,* **par'lour.**

parlor car, a railroad passenger car with comfortable individual reserved seats.

par·lous (pär'ləs), *adj. Archaic.* **1.** perilous. **2.** very great. **3.** clever.

Par·ma (pär'mä), *n.* a city in N Italy. 120,795. —**Par·me·san** (pär'mə zăn'), *adj.*

Parmesan cheese, a hard, dry variety of Italian cheese, made from skim milk.

Par·nas·sus (pär năs'əs), *n.* **Mount,** a mountain in central Greece sacred to Apollo and the Muses, and symbolic of poetic inspiration and achievement. 8068 ft. —**Par·nas'si·an,** *adj., n.*

Par·nell (pär'nəl, pär nĕl'), *n.* **Charles Stewart,** 1846–91, Irish political leader.

pa·ro·chi·al (pə rō'kĭ əl), *adj.* **1.** of or pertaining to a parish or parishes. **2.** narrow, as in viewpoint. —**pa·ro'chi·al·ism',** *n.* —**pa·ro'chi·al·ly,** *adv.*

par·o·dy (păr'ə dĭ), *n., pl.* **-dies,** *v.,* **-died, -dying.** —*n.* **1.** humorous imitation of a serious piece of writing. —*v.t.* **2.** to imitate (a composition, author, etc.) in such a way as to ridicule. —**par'o·dist,** *n.*

pa·role (pə rōl'), *n., v.,* **-roled, -roling.** —*n.* **1.** the liberation of a person from prison, conditional upon good behavior, prior to the end of the maximum sentence imposed upon that person. **2.** such release or its duration. —*v.t.* **3.** to put on parole.

pa·rot·id (pə rŏt'ĭd), *Anat.* —*n.* **1.** either of two saliva-producing glands situated one at the base of each ear. —*adj.* **2.** noting, pertaining to, or situated near either parotid.

par·o·ti·tis (păr'ə tī'tĭs), *n.* mumps.

par·ox·ysm (păr'ək sĭz'əm), *n.* **1.** any sudden, violent outburst. **2.** *Pathol.* a severe attack of a disease, usually recurring. —**par'ox·ys'mal,** *adj.*

par·quet (pär kā', pär kĕt'), *n., v.,* **-queted, -queting** or (*esp. Brit.*) **-quetted, -quetting.** —*n.* **1.** a floor of inlaid design. **2.** the part of the main floor of a theater, etc., between the musicians' space and the parterre. —*v.t.* **3.** to construct (a flooring, etc.) of parquetry.

par·quet·ry (pär'kĭt rĭ), *n.* mosaic work of wood used for floors, etc.

parr (pär), *n., pl.* **parrs,** (*esp. collectively*) **parr.** a young salmon, having dark crossbars on its sides.

par·ra·keet (păr'ə kēt'), *n.* parakeet. Also, **par·ro·ket** (păr'ə kĕt'), **par'ro·quet'.**

par·ri·cide[1] (păr'ə sīd'), *n.* one who kills either of his parents. —**par'ri·cid'al,** *adj.*

par·ri·cide[2] (păr'ə sīd'), *n.* act or crime of killing one's father.

par·rot (păr'ət), *n.* **1.** any of numerous hookbilled, fleshy-tongued, often gaily colored birds, as the cockatoo, parakeet, etc., valued because they can be taught to talk. —*v.t.* **2.** to repeat or imitate like a parrot.

par·ry (păr'ĭ), *v.,* **-ried, -rying,** *n., pl.* **-ries.** —*v.t., v.i.* **1.** to ward off (a stroke, weapon, etc.), as in fencing. **2.** to evade or avoid. —*n.* **3.** an act or mode of parrying. **4.** a defensive movement in fencing.

parse (pärs, pärz), *v.t.,* **parsed, parsing.** to describe (a word or series of words) grammatically, telling the part of speech, etc.

Par·see (pär'sē, pär sē'), *n.* one of a Zoroastrian sect in India, descendants of the Persians who settled in India in the 8th century to escape Mohammedan persecution. Also, **Par'si.**

par·si·mo·ni·ous (pär'sə mō'nĭ əs), *adj.* sparing or frugal, esp. to excess. —**par'si·mo'ni·ous·ly,** *adv.*

par·si·mo·ny (pär'sə mō'nĭ), *n.* excessive economy or frugality; niggardliness.

pars·ley (pärs'lĭ), *n.* a garden herb with aromatic leaves which are much used to garnish or season food.

pars·nip (pärs'nĭp), *n.* **1.** a plant cultivated varieties of which have a large whitish edible root. **2.** the root.

par·son (pär'sən), *n.* **1.** a clergyman or minister. **2.** the holder of a parish benefice.

par·son·age (pär'sən ĭj), *n.* the residence of a parson, provided by the church.

part (pärt), *n.* **1.** a portion of a whole; a piece, fragment, fraction, or section. **2.** an essential portion. **3.** a portion, member, or organ of an animal body. **4.** each of a number of equal portions composing a whole. **5.** a share. **6.** (*usually pl.*) a region or district. **7.** one of the sides to a contest, agreement, etc. **8.** the dividing line formed in parting the hair. **9.** *Music.* a voice, either vocal or instrumental. **10.** a duty, function, or office. **11.** a character sustained in a play; role. **12.** (*usually pl.*) a personal or mental quality. **13. for my** (**his,** etc.) **part,** so far as concerns me (him, etc.). **14. for the most part,** mostly. **15. part and parcel,** an essential part. **16. take part,** to participate. —*v.t.* **17.** to divide (a thing) into parts. **18.** to comb (the hair) away from a dividing line. **19.** to dissolve (a connection, etc.) by separation. **20.** to put or keep asunder; separate. —*v.i.* **21.** to be or become divided into parts. **22.** to separate. **23.** to depart. **24. part with,** to relinquish.

part., **1.** participle. **2.** particular.

par·take (pär tāk'), *v.,* **-took, -taken, -taking.** —*v.i.* **1.** to participate (fol. by *in*). **2.** to receive, take, or have a share (fol. by *of*). **3.** to have something of the nature of (fol. by *of*). —*v.t.* **4.** to share. —**par·tak'er,** *n.*

par·terre (pär târ'), *n.* the part of the main floor of a theater, etc., behind the orchestra, often under the galleries.

par·the·no·gen·e·sis (pär'thə nō jən'ə sĭs), *n. Biol.* development of an egg without fertilization.

Par·the·non (pär'thə nŏn', -nən), *n.* the temple of Athene on the Acropolis of Athens.

Par·thi·a (pär'thĭ ə), *n.* an ancient country in W Asia, SE of the Caspian Sea. —**Par'thi·an,** *adj., n.*

Parthian shot, **1.** a rearward shot by a fleeing mounted archer. **2.** any sharp parting remark.

par·tial (pär'shəl), *adj.* **1.** pertaining to or affecting a part. **2.** not total; incomplete. **3.** *Bot.* secondary or subordinate. **4.** component. **5.** biased or prejudiced. **6.** particularly inclined in liking. —**par·tial·i·ty** (pär shăl'ə tĭ, pär'shY-ăl'-), *n.* —**par'tial·ly,** *adv.*

par·tic·i·pant (pär tĭs'ə pənt), *n.* **1.** one who participates. —*adj.* **2.** participating.

par·tic·i·pate (pär tĭs'ə pāt'), *v.i., v.t.,* **-pated, -pating.** to take or have a part or share (in). —**par·tic'i·pa'tion,** *n.* —**par·tic'i·pa'tor,** *n.*

par·ti·ci·ple (pär'tə sə pəl, -sĭp'əl), *n. Gram.* an adjective form derived from verbs, which ascribes to a noun participation in the action or state of the verb, without specifying person or number of the subject. —**par·ti·cip·i·al** (pär'tə-sĭp'Y əl), *adj.* —**par'ti·cip'i·al·ly,** *adv.*

par·ti·cle (pär'tə kəl), *n.* **1.** a minute portion, piece, or amount. **2.** a clause or article, as of a document. **3.** *Gram.* a word of functional or relational use, such as an article, preposition, or conjunction.

par·ti·col·ored (pär'tĭ kŭl'ərd), *adj.* colored differently in different parts; variegated.

par·tic·u·lar (pər tĭk'yə lər), *adj.* **1.** pertaining to some one person, thing, group, occasion, etc. **2.** individual; single. **3.** noteworthy; unusual. **4.** exceptional or especial. **5.** detailed; minute. **6.** attentive to or exacting about details. —*n.* **7.** an individual part or item. **8.** a detail. **9. in particular,** especially. —**par·tic'u·lar·ly,** *adv.*

par·tic·u·lar·i·ty (pər tĭk'yə lăr'ə tĭ), *n., pl.* **-ties.** **1.** quality or fact of being particular. **2.** special, peculiar, or individual character. **3.** de-

tailed character, as of description. **4.** special carefulness. **5.** fastidiousness. **6.** a particular or characteristic feature.

par·tic·u·lar·ize (pər tĭk'yə lə rīz'), *v.t., v.i.,* **-ized, -izing.** **1.** to make particular (rather than general). **2.** to mention particularly. **3.** to state or treat in detail. —**par·tic'u·lar·i·za'tion,** *n.*

part·ing (pär'tĭng), *n.* **1.** act of one that parts. **2.** division; separation. **3.** departure. —*adj.* **4.** given, taken, done, etc., at parting. **5.** departing.

par·ti·san (pär'tə zən), *n.* **1.** an adherent or supporter of a person, party, or cause. **2.** a guerrilla. —*adj.* **3.** of, pertaining to, or characteristic of partisans. Also, **par'ti·zan.** —**par'ti·san·ship',** *n.*

par·ti·tion (pär tĭsh'ən), *n.* **1.** division into or distribution in portions. **2.** separation. **3.** an interior wall or barrier. —*v.t.* **4.** to divide into parts or portions. **5.** to divide or separate by a partition. —**par·ti'tion·ment,** *n.*

par·ti·tive (pär'tə tĭv), *adj.* **1.** serving to divide into parts. **2.** *Gram.* denoting part of a whole. —*n.* **3.** *Gram.* a partitive word or formation. —**par'ti·tive·ly,** *adv.*

part·ly (pärt'lĭ), *adv.* in part; not wholly.

part·ner (pärt'nər), *n.* **1.** a sharer or associate. **2.** one associated with another or others as an owner of a business. **3.** a husband or a wife. **4.** one's companion in a dance. **5.** a player on the same side with another in a game. —**part'ner·ship',** *n.*

part of speech, *Gram.* any of the mutually exclusive major form classes of a language, which taken together include the entire vocabulary.

par·tridge (pär'trĭj), *n., pl.* **-tridges,** (*esp. collectively*) **-tridge.** **1.** any of various North American gallinaceous birds, as the ruffed grouse and the bob-white quail. **2.** any of various Old World gallinaceous gamebirds.

part song, a song with parts for several voices, esp. one sung without accompaniment.

par·tu·ri·ent (pär tyŏr'Y ənt, -tŏŏr'-), *adj.* **1.** bringing forth young. **2.** pertaining to parturition.

par·tu·ri·tion (pär'tyŏŏ rĭsh'ən, -chŏŏ-), *n.* the act of bringing forth young; childbirth.

par·ty (pär'tĭ), *n., pl.* **-ties,** *adj.* —*n.* **1.** a group gathered together, as for entertainment. **2.** a social gathering. **3.** a detachment of troops assigned to perform some particular service. **4.** a number of persons united in purpose or opinion, in opposition to others, as in politics, etc. **5.** *Law.* **a.** one of the litigants in a legal proceeding. **b.** a signatory to a legal instrument. **6.** *U.S. Colloq.* a person. —*adj.* **7.** of or pertaining to a party or faction.

party line, **1.** a telephone line by which a number of subscribers are connected by one circuit to a central office. **2.** the authoritatively announced policies and practices of a group, usually followed without exception.

par·ve·nu (pär'və nū', -nŏŏ'), *n.* one who has risen to a position above his qualifications.

Pas·a·de·na (păs'ə dē'nə), *n.* a city in SW California, near Los Angeles. 98,279.

pas·chal (păs'kəl), *adj.* pertaining to the Passover, or to Easter.

pa·sha (pə shä', păsh'ə, pä'shə), *n.* a title formerly borne by officials of high rank in Turkish dominions.

pa·sha·lik (pə shä'lYk), *n.* the territory governed by a pasha. Also, **pa·sha'lic.**

pasque·flow·er (păsk'flou'ər), *n.* any of certain plants of the crowfoot family with purple flowers blooming about Easter.

pass (păs, päs), *v.,* **passed** or (*Rare*) **past; passed** or **past; passing;** *n.* —*v.t.* **1.** to go past (something). **2.** to go by without acting upon or noticing. **3.** to omit payment of (a dividend, etc.). **4.** to get through or over (a barrier, etc.). **5.** to undergo successfully (an examination, etc.). **6.** to transcend; exceed; surpass. **7.** to cause to go or move onward. **8.** to cause to go past. **9.** to spend, as time. **10.** to cause to circulate. **11.** to convey or deliver. **12.** to discharge or void, as excrement. **13.** to sanction or approve. **14.** to obtain the approval or sanction of (a legislative body, etc.), as a bill. **15.** to express or pronounce, as an opinion. **16.** *Baseball.* to allow (a batter) to reach first base after four balls. —*v.i.* **17.** to go or move onward; proceed. **18.** to depart. **19.** to elapse or be spent, as time. **20.** to die. **21.** *Colloq.* to faint (fol. by *out*). **22.** to go past, as a procession. **23.** to circulate; be current. **24.** to be accepted or received. **25.** to be interchanged. **26.** to undergo transition or conversion. **27.** to go or get through a barrier, test, examination, etc. **28.** to go unheeded, uncensured, or unchallenged. **29.** to express or pronounce an opinion, verdict, etc. **30.** to be voided, as excrement. **31.** to be ratified or enacted, as a bill or law. **32.** *Law.* to adjudicate. **33.** *U.S.* to throw a ball from one to another. **34.** *Fencing.* to thrust or lunge. **35.** *Cards.* to forgo one's opportunity to bid, play, etc. —*n.* **36.** a narrow route across a relatively low notch or depression in a mountain barrier. **37.** a permission or license to pass, go, come, or enter. **38.** a free ticket. **39.** the transference of a ball, etc., from one player to another, as in football. **40.** *Baseball.* the right to go to first base after four balls. **41.** a thrust or lunge, as in fencing. **42.** *Cards.* an act of not bidding or raising another bid. **43.** a particular stage or state of affairs. **44.** **make a pass,** *Slang.* to make an amorous overture or gesture. —**pass'er,** *n.*

pass., **1.** passenger. **2.** passive.

pass·a·ble (păs'ə bəl, päs'-), *adj.* **1.** that may be passed. **2.** that may be traversed, penetrated, crossed, etc. **3.** fair; moderate. —**pass'a·bly,** *adv.* —**pass'a·ble·ness,** *n.*

pas·sage (păs'ĭj), *n.* **1.** a portion of a writing, speech, or the like. **2.** *Music.* a scalelike series of tones introduced as an embellishment. **3.** act of passing. **4.** liberty, leave, or right to pass. **5.** a way, route, avenue, channel, etc. **6.** movement, transit, or transition. **7.** a voyage across the sea from one port to another. **8.** the privilege of conveyance as a passenger. **9.** lapse, as of time. **10.** progress, as of events. **11.** the passing into law of a legislative measure.

pas·sage·way (păs'ĭj wā'), *n.* a way for passage, as in a building.

Pas·sa·ic (pə sā'ĭk), *n.* a city in NE New Jersey. 61,394.

pass·book (păs'bŏŏk', päs'-), *n.* *Chiefly Brit.* a bankbook.

pas·sé (pă sā', päs'ā), *adj.* **1.** out-of-date. **2.** past. **3.** faded.

pas·sen·ger (păs'ən jər), *n.* one who travels by some form of conveyance.

pass·er-by (păs'ər bī', päs'-), *n., pl.* **passers-by.** one who passes by.

pas·ser·ine (păs'ər ĭn, -ə rīn'), *adj.* **1.** belonging or pertaining to an order of birds, typically perching, including the finches, thrushes, warblers, swallows, crows, larks, etc. —*n.* **2.** any such bird.

pas·si·ble (păs'ə bəl), *adj.* capable of suffering or feeling. —**pas'si·bil'i·ty,** *n.*

pas·sim (păs'ĭm), *adv.* *Latin.* here and there, as in books or writings.

pass·ing (păs'ĭng, päs'-), *adj.* **1.** going by; elapsing. **2.** transitory. **3.** current. **4.** done, given, etc., in passing; cursory. **5.** preëminent; extreme. **6.** indicating that one has passed. —*adv.* **7.** *Archaic.* very. —*n.* **8.** act of one that passes or causes something to pass. **9.** a passage.

pas·sion (păsh'ən), *n.* **1.** any strong feeling or emotion, as hope, fear, joy, grief, anger, love, desire, etc. **2.** passionate sexual love. **3.** an instance or experience of it. **4.** a strong enthusiasm or desire, as for music. **5.** the object of such an enthusiasm or desire. **6.** a passionate outburst. **7.** violent anger. **8.** (*often cap.*) the sufferings of Christ on the Cross, or His sufferings subsequent to the Last Supper. —**pas'sion·less,** *adj.*

pas·sion·ate (păsh'ən ĭt), *adj.* **1.** affected with passion or vehement emotion. **2.** characterized by, expressing, or showing vehement emotion. **3.** vehement, as feelings. **4.** quick-tempered; irascible. —**pas'sion·ate·ly,** *adv.* —**pas'sion·ate·ness,** *n.*

pas·sion-flow·er (păsh'ən flou'ər), *n.* any of certain climbing vines or shrubs, mainly American, bearing showy flowers and a pulpy berry or fruit which in some species is edible.

passion play, a dramatic representation of the passion of Christ.

pas·sive (păs'ĭv), *adj.* **1.** not in open or positive action. **2.** inactive; quiescent; inert. **3.** acted upon; being the object of action. **4.** suffering, receiving, or submitting without resistance. **5.** characterized by or involving doing this. **6.** *Gram.* denoting a voice, or verb inflection, in which the subject is represented as being acted on. —*n.* **7.** *Gram.* **a.** the passive voice. **b.** a form or construction therein. —**pas'sive·ly,** *adv.* —**pas'sive·ness, pas·siv'i·ty,** *n.*

pass·key (păs'kē', päs'-), *n., pl.* **-keys. 1.** a master key. **2.** a private key.

Pass·o·ver (păs'ō'vər, päs'-), *n.* an annual feast of the Jews in commemoration of the deliverance from Egypt, lasting eight days.

pass·port (păs'pōrt, päs'-), *n.* an official document granting permission to the person specified in it to travel, and authenticating his right to protection.

pass·word (păs'wûrd, päs'-) *n.* a secret word, made known only to authorized persons for their use in passing through guards.

past (păst, päst), *adj.* **1.** gone by in time. **2.** belonging to, or having existed or occurred in, time previous to this. **3.** just gone by. **4.** ago. **5.** having served a term in an office. **6.** *Gram.* designating a tense, or other verb formation or construction, which refers to events or states in time gone by. —*n.* **7.** the time gone by. **8.** the events of that time. **9.** a past history, life, career, etc. **10.** a past career which is kept concealed. **11.** *Gram.* **a.** the past tense. **b.** another verb formation or construction with past meaning. **c.** a form therein. —*adv.* **12.** so as to pass by. —*prep.* **13.** after. **14.** beyond in position. **15.** beyond in amount, number, etc. **16.** beyond the reach, scope, influence, or power of.

paste (pāst), *n., v.,* **pasted, pasting.** —*n.* **1.** a mixture of flour and water, used for causing paper, etc., to adhere. **2.** any material in a soft mass. **3.** dough, esp. when prepared with shortening. **4.** any of various food preparations consisting of a smooth, soft mass. **5.** a brilliant, heavy glass, used for making artificial gems. —*v.t.* **6.** to fasten with paste. **7.** *Slang.* to strike; beat soundly.

paste·board (pāst'bōrd'), *n.* a stiff, firm board made of sheets of paper pasted or layers of paper pulp pressed together. **2.** *Slang.* a ticket.

pas·tel (păs tĕl', päs'tĕl), *n.* **1.** a soft subdued shade. **2.** a kind of dried paste used for crayons, made of pigments ground with chalk and compounded with gum water. **3.** a crayon made with such paste.

past·er (pās'tər), *n.* **1.** a slip of paper gummed on the back, to be pasted on or over something. **2.** one that pastes.

pas·tern (păs'tərn), *n.* **1.** that part of the foot of a horse, etc., between the fetlock and the hoof. **2.** either of two bones of this part.

Pas·teur (păs tœr'), *n.* **Louis,** 1822–95, French chemist and bacteriologist.

pas·teur·ize (păs'tə rīz', päs'chə rīz'), *v.t.,* **-ized, -izing.** to expose (milk, etc.) to a high temperature, usually about 140°F., in order to destroy certain microörganisms and prevent or arrest fermentation. —**pas'teur·i·za'tion,** *n.*

pas·tille (păs tĕl', -tŸl'), *n.* **1.** a flavored or medicated lozenge. **2.** a roll or cone of paste containing aromatic substances, burned as a perfume, disinfectant, etc. Also, **pas·til** (păs'tŸl).

pas·time (păs'tīm', päs'-), *n.* a diversion, amusement, or sport.

past master, 1. one who has filled the office of master in a lodge, etc. **2.** one who has ripe experience in any profession, art, etc.

pas·tor (păs'tər, päs'-), *n.* a minister or clergyman with reference to his flock.

pas·to·ral (păs'tə rəl, päs'-), *adj.* **1.** of or pertaining to shepherds. **2.** used for pasture. **3.** having rural simplicity or charm. **4.** pertaining to a minister or clergyman, to his duties, etc. —*n.* **5.** a poem, play, or the like, dealing with the life of shepherds. **6.** a picture or work of art presenting shepherd life. —**pas'to·ral·ly,** *adv.*

pas·tor·ate (păs'tər ĭt, päs'-), *n.* **1.** the office of a pastor. **2.** a body of pastors.

past participle, *Gram.* a participle with past or perfect meaning.

past perfect, *Gram.* pluperfect.

pas·tra·mi (pə strä'mĭ), *n.* a highly seasoned shoulder cut of smoked beef.

pas·try (pās'trĭ), *n., pl.* **-tries.** food made of shortened paste, as pies, tarts, etc.

pas·tur·age (păs'chər ĭj, päs'-), *n.* **1.** growing grass or herbage for cattle, etc. **2.** grazing ground.

pas·ture (păs'chər, päs'-), *n., v.,* **-tured, -turing.** —*n.* **1.** ground covered with grass or herbage, used or suitable for the grazing of cattle, etc. **2.** grass or herbage for feeding cattle, etc. —*v.t.* **3.** to feed (cattle, etc.) by putting them to graze on pasture. **4.** (of cattle, etc.) to graze upon.

past·y (pās'tĭ), *adj.,* **pastier, pastiest.** of or like paste in consistency, appearance, etc.

pat¹ (păt), *v.,* **patted, patting,** *n.* —*v.t.* **1.** to strike lightly with something flat. **2.** to stroke gently as an expression of affection, etc. —*v.i.*

3. to strike lightly or gently. —*n.* **4.** a light stroke or blow with something flat. **5.** the sound of a light stroke, or of light footsteps. **6.** a small mass of something, as butter.

pat² (păt), *adj.* **1.** exactly to the point. **2.** apt; ready. —*adv.* **3.** exactly or perfectly. **4.** aptly. **5. stand pat,** *Colloq.* to stick to one's decision, etc. —**pat′ness,** *n.*

pat., **1.** patent. **2.** patented.

Pat·a·go·ni·a (păt′ə gō′nĭ ə), *n.* **1.** the table-land region constituting the S tip of Argentina. **2.** a region in the extreme S part of South America, extending from the Andes to the Atlantic: mostly in S Argentina, partly in S Chile. —**Pat′a·go′ni·an,** *adj., n.*

patch (păch), *n.* **1.** a piece of material used to mend a hole or to strengthen a weak place. **2.** a piece of material used to cover or protect a wound, an injured part, etc. **3.** any of the pieces of cloth sewed together to form patchwork. **4.** a small piece or scrap of anything. **5.** a piece of land. —*v.t.* **6.** to mend or strengthen with a patch or patches. **7.** to repair in a hasty or makeshift way. **8.** to make by joining patches or pieces together. **9.** to settle; smooth over. —**patch′er,** *n.* —**patch′-y,** *adj.*

patch·work (păch′wûrk′), *n.* **1.** work made of patches sewed together, as a quilt, cushion, etc. **2.** work made up of various parts put together.

patd., patented.

pate (pāt), *n. Humorous.* **1.** the head. **2.** the crown or top of the head. **3.** brains.

pâ·té de foie gras (pä tā′ də fwä grä′), *French.* a paste made with goose livers.

pa·tel·la (pə těl′ə), *n., pl.* **-tellae** (-těl′ē). *Anat.* the kneecap. —**pa·tel′lar,** *adj.*

pat·en (păt′ən), *n.* the plate for the bread in the celebration of the Eucharist.

pat·ent (păt′ənt *or, esp. Brit.,* pā′tənt *for* 1–4, 7; *usually* pā′tənt *for* 5, 6), *n.* **1.** a government grant to an inventor, his heirs or assigns, for a stated period of time, conferring upon him a monopoly of the exclusive right to make, use, and vend the invention. **2.** an invention, process, etc., which has been patented. —*adj.* **3.** of a kind specially protected by a patent. **4.** conferred by a patent. **5.** manifest; evident; plain. **6.** open. —*v.t.* **7.** to obtain the exclusive rights to (an invention) by a patent. —**pat′ent·a·ble,** *adj.* —**pat′ent·a·bil′i·ty,** *n.* —**pat′en·tee′,** *n.* —**pat′ent·ly,** *adv.* —**pat′en·tor′,** *n.*

patent leather, a hard, glossy, smooth leather, usually finished in black.

pa·ter (pā′tər), *n. Brit. Colloq.* father.

pa·ter·nal (pə tûr′nəl), *adj.* **1.** of or befitting a father; fatherly. **2.** related on the father's side. —**pa·ter′nal·ly,** *adj.*

pa·ter·nal·ism (pə tûr′nə lĭz′əm), *n.* the principle or practice of managing the affairs of a country, community, or individuals in the manner of a father dealing with his children. —**pa·ter′nal·is′tic,** *adj.*

pa·ter·ni·ty (pə tûr′nə tĭ), *n.* **1.** derivation from a father. **2.** fatherhood. **3.** origin.

pa·ter·nos·ter (pā′tər nŏs′tər, păt′ər-), *n.* The Lord's Prayer, esp. in the Latin form. Also, **Pater Noster.**

Pat·er·son (păt′ər sən), *n.* a city in NE New Jersey. 139,656.

path (păth, päth), *n.* **1.** a way trodden by the feet of men or beasts. **2.** a walk in a garden or through grounds. **3.** a route, course, or track in which something moves. **4.** a course of action or conduct. —**path′less,** *adj.*

pa·thet·ic (pə thĕt′ĭk), *adj.* **1.** exciting pity or sympathetic sadness. **2.** of or affecting the feelings. Also, **pa·thet′i·cal.** —**pa·thet′i·cal·ly,** *adv.*

path·o·gen·ic (păth′ə jĕn′ĭk), *adj.* disease-producing.

pathol., pathology.

pa·thol·o·gy (pə thŏl′ə jĭ), *n., pl.* **-gies. 1.** the science of the origin, nature, and course of diseases. **2.** the conditions and processes of a disease. —**path·o·log·i·cal** (păth′ə lŏj′ə kəl), **path′o·log′ic,** *adj.* —**path′o·log′i·cal·ly,** *adv.* —**pa·thol′o·gist,** *n.*

pa·thos (pā′thŏs), *n.* the quality or power, as in speech, music, etc., of evoking a feeling of pity or sympathetic sadness.

path·way (păth′wā′, päth′-), *n.* a path.

pa·tience (pā′shəns), *n.* **1.** calm and uncomplaining endurance, as under pain, provocation, etc. **2.** calmness in waiting. **3.** quiet perseverance.

pa·tient (pā′shənt), *n.* **1.** one who is under medical or surgical treatment. **2.** a person or thing that undergoes action. —*adj.* **3.** quietly persevering. **4.** enduring pain, trouble, annoyance, etc., with fortitude, calmness, or quiet submission. **5.** enduring delay with calmness or equanimity. **6.** undergoing the action of another. —**pa′tient·ly,** *adv.*

pat·i·na (păt′ə nə), *n.* **1.** a film or incrustation, usually green, produced by oxidation on the surface of old bronze, and esteemed as ornamental. **2.** a similar film on some other substance.

pa·ti·o (pä′tĭ ō′, păt′ĭ ō′), *n., pl.* **-tios.** an inner court of a house, open to the sky.

Pat. Off., Patent Office.

pat·ois (păt′wä), *n., pl.* **patois** (păt′wäz; *Fr.* pả twä′). any provincial form of speech.

pa·tri·arch (pā′trĭ ärk′), *n.* **1.** any of the earlier Biblical personages regarded as the fathers of the human race. **2.** one of the three great progenitors of the Israelites: Abraham, Isaac, or Jacob. **3.** *Gk. Orthodox Ch.* the bishop of Alexandria, Antioch, Constantinople, Jerusalem, Russia, Rumania, or Serbia. The bishop of Constantinople (**ecumenical patriarch**) is the highest dignitary in the church. **4.** *Rom. Cath. Ch.* **a.** the Pope (**Patriarch of Rome**). **b.** a bishop of the highest rank next after the Pope. **5.** *Mormon Ch.* one of the highest dignitaries who pronounces the blessing of the church. **6.** a venerable old man. **7.** the male head of a family or tribal line. —**pa′tri·ar′chal,** *adj.* —**pa′tri·ar′chal·ly,** *adv.*

pa·tri·ar·chate (pā′trĭ är′kĭt), *n.* the office, dignity, jurisdiction, or residence of an ecclesiastical patriarch.

pa·tri·ar·chy (pā′trĭ är′kĭ), *n., pl.* **-archies.** a form of social organization in which the father is head of the family.

pa·tri·cian (pə trĭsh′ən), *n.* **1.** a member of the original senatorial aristocracy in ancient Rome. **2.** a noble or aristocrat. —*adj.* **3.** of high social rank or noble family. **4.** befitting an aristocrat.

pat·ri·cide¹ (păt′rə sīd′, pā′trə-), *n.* one who kills his father. —**pat′ri·cid′al,** *adj.*

pat·ri·cide² (păt′rə sīd′, pā′trə-), *n.* the killing of one's father.

Pat·rick (păt′rĭk), *n.* **Saint,** A.D. c389–c461, British missionary and bishop in Ireland: patron saint of Ireland.

pat·ri·mo·ny (păt′rə mō′nĭ), *n., pl.* **-nies. 1.** an estate inherited from one's father or ancestors. **2.** the estate or endowment of a church, religious house, etc. —**pat′ri·mo′ni·al,** *adj.*

pa·tri·ot (pā′trĭ ət, -ŏt′ *or, esp. Brit.,* păt′rĭ ət), *n.* a person who loves his country, zealously supporting and defending it and its interests. —**pa′tri·ot′ic,** *adj.* —**pa′tri·ot′i·cal·ly,** *adv.*

pa·tri·ot·ism (pā′trĭ ə tĭz′əm *or, esp. Brit.,* păt′rĭ-), *n.* the spirit or action of a patriot.

pa·tris·tic (pə trĭs′tĭk), *adj.* of or pertaining to the fathers of the Christian church or their writings. Also, **pa·tris′ti·cal.**

pa·trol (pə trōl′), *v.,* **-trolled, -trolling,** *n.* —*v.i.* **1.** to go the rounds in a camp or garrison, as a guard. **2.** to traverse a particular district, as a policeman. —*v.t.* **3.** to go about in for the purpose of guarding or protecting. —*n.* **4.** a person or a body of persons charged with patrolling. **5.** act of patrolling. **6.** (in the Boy Scouts) a unit of eight members.

pa·trol·man (pə trōl′mən), *n., pl.* **-men.** a policeman patrolling a certain district.

pa·tron (pā′trən), *n.* **1.** one who supports with his patronage a shop, hotel, or the like. **2.** a protector or supporter, as of a person, cause, or institution. **3.** a patron saint. —**pa′tron·al,** *adj.* —**pa′tron·ess,** *n. fem.*

pa·tron·age (pā′trən ĭj, păt′rən-), *n.* **1.** the financial support afforded a shop, hotel, etc., by customers. **2.** the position, encouragement, or support of a patron. **3.** the control of appointments to the public service or of other political favors. **4.** offices or other favors so controlled. **5.** condescending favor.

pa·tron·ize (pā′trə nīz′, păt′rə-), *v.t.,* **-ized, -izing. 1.** to favor (a shop, restaurant, etc.) with one's trade. **2.** to treat in a condescending way. **3.** to support. —**pa′tron·iz′ing·ly,** *adv.*

patron saint, a saint regarded as the special guardian of a person, trade, place, etc.

pat·ro·nym·ic (păt′rə nĭm′ĭk), *adj.* **1.** (of names) derived from the name of a father or ancestor. —*n.* **2.** a patronymic name.

pa·troon (pə trōōn′), *n.* one who held an estate in land with certain manorial privileges granted under the old Dutch governments of New York and New Jersey.

pat·ter[1] (păt′ər), *v.i.* **1.** to strike or move with a succession of slight tapping sounds. —*v.t.* **2.** to cause to patter. —*n.* **3.** a pattering sound. **4.** act of pattering.

pat·ter[2] (păt′ər), *n.* **1.** glib or rapid speech. —*v.i.* **2.** to talk or recite glibly or rapidly.

pat·tern (păt′ərn), *n.* **1.** a decorative design, as for china, fabrics, etc. **2.** an original or model proposed for or deserving of imitation. —*v.i.* **3.** to model one's conduct, etc. —*v.t.* **4.** to make after a pattern; model.

Pat·ton (păt′ən), *n.* **George Smith**, 1885–1945, U.S. general.

pat·ty (păt′ĭ), *n., pl.* **-ties. 1.** a little pie. **2.** a thin, round piece.

pau·ci·ty (pô′sə tĭ), *n.* fewness; scantiness.

Paul (pôl), *n.* **Saint**, died A.D. c67, the great Christian missionary: author of several epistles in the New Testament. —**Paul·ine** (pô′lĭn), *adj.*

paunch (pônch, pänch), *n.* **1.** the belly or abdomen. **2.** a large, prominent belly. —**paunch′i·ness**, *n.* —**paunch′y**, *adj.*

pau·per (pô′pər), *n.* a very poor person, esp. one supported by the community.

pau·per·ism (pô′pə rĭz′əm), *n.* poverty.

pau·per·ize (pô′pə rīz′), *v.t.*, **-ized, -izing.** to make a pauper of.

pause (pôz), *n., v.*, **paused, pausing.** —*n.* **1.** a temporary stop, esp. in speech or action. **2.** a cessation proceeding from doubt. **3.** delay; hesitation. **4.** *Music.* the symbol ⌢ or ⌒ placed under or over a note or rest to indicate that it is to be prolonged. —*v.i.* **5.** to make a pause. —**paus′er**, *n.*

pave (pāv), *v.t.*, **paved, paving. 1.** to cover or lay (a road, walk, etc.) with stones, concrete, etc., so as to make a firm, level surface. **2.** to prepare (the way) for. —**pav′er**, *n.*

pave·ment (pāv′mənt), *n.* **1.** a paved road or other surface. **2.** a material used for paving.

pa·vil·ion (pə vĭl′yən), *n.* **1.** a light, open structure for shelter, etc., as in a park. **2.** a projecting element in the front or side of a building. **3.** one of a group of buildings forming a hospital. **4.** a tent.

pav·ing (pā′vĭng), *n.* pavement.

paw (pô), *n.* **1.** the foot of an animal with nails or claws. —*v.t.* **2.** to strike or scrape with the paws. **3.** *Colloq.* to handle clumsily or over-familiarly. —*v.i.* **4.** to beat or scrape the ground, etc., with the paws. **5.** *Colloq.* to use the hands clumsily or rudely on something.

pawl (pôl), *n.* a pivoted bar adapted to engage with the teeth of a rachet wheel or the like so as to prevent movement or to impart motion.

pawn[1] (pôn), *v.t.* **1.** to deposit as security, as for money borrowed. **2.** to pledge. —*n.* **3.** state of being deposited or held as security. **4.** any thing or person serving as security. —**pawn·er** (pô′nər), **pawn·or** (pô′nər, pôn ôr′), *n.*

pawn[2] (pôn), *n.* **1.** *Chess.* one of the 16 pieces of lowest value. **2.** a person used as a tool by another.

pawn·brok·er (pôn′brō′kər), *n.* one who lends money at interest on pledged personal property. —**pawn′bro′king**, *n.*

Paw·nee (pô nē′), *n.* a member of a confederacy of North American Indians now living in N Oklahoma.

pawn·shop (pôn′shŏp′), *n.* the shop of a pawnbroker.

paw·paw (pô′pô), *n.* papaw.

Paw·tuck·et (pô tŭk′ĭt), *n.* a city in NE Rhode Island. 75,797.

pay (pā), *v.*, **paid** or (*Obs.* except for def. 11) **payed, paying,** *n., adj.* —*v.t.* **1.** to discharge (a debt, etc.), as by giving or doing something. **2.** to give (money, etc.), as in discharge of debt. **3.** to satisfy the claims of (a person, etc.), as by giving money due. **4.** to defray (cost). **5.** to give compensation for. **6.** to be profitable to. **7.** to yield as a return. **8.** to requite, as for good, harm, etc. **9.** to give or render (attention, compliments, etc.). **10.** to make (a call, visit, etc.). **11.** *Naut., etc.* to let out (a rope, etc.), as by slackening. —*v.i.* **12.** to give money, etc., due. **13.** to discharge debt. **14.** to yield a profit; be worthwhile. **15.** to give compensation. —*n.* **16.** payment. **17.** wages, salary, or stipend. **18.** paid employ. —*adj.* **19.** (of earth, etc.) containing a sufficient quantity of metal or other value to be profitably worked by the miner. **20.** having a mechanism for

payment when used. —**pay·ee′**, *n.* —**pay′er**, *n.*

pay·a·ble (pā′ə bəl), *adj.* **1.** that is to be paid; due. **2.** that may be paid.

pay·load (pā′lōd′), *n.* the income-producing part of a cargo.

pay·mas·ter (pā′măs′tər, -mäs′-), *n.* an official responsible for the payment of wages.

pay·ment (pā′mənt), *n.* **1.** act of paying. **2.** that which is paid. **3.** requital.

pay·off (pā′ôf′, -ŏf′), *n.* **1.** the payment of a salary. **2.** the time when it is paid. **3.** *Colloq.* a final consequence; settlement.

pay roll, 1. a list of persons to be paid. **2.** the amounts due these persons.

payt., payment.

Pb, *Chem.* (L *plumbum*) lead.

pc., 1. (*pl.* **pcs.**) piece. **2.** prices.

pct., percent. Also, **p.c.**

Pd, *Chem.* palladium.

pd., paid.

pea (pē), *n., pl.* **peas** or (*Archaic or Brit. Dial.*) **pease. 1.** the round, highly nutritious seed of a certain leguminous hardy plant in wide circulation. **2.** the plant bearing such seeds. **3.** any of various related or similar plants, or their seed. **4.** something small as a pea.

peace (pēs), *n.* **1.** freedom from war, hostilities, strife, or commotion. **2.** an agreement between contending parties to abstain from further hostilities.

peace·a·ble (pē′sə bəl), *adj.* **1.** disposed to peace. **2.** peaceful. —**peace′a·ble·ness**, *n.* —**peace′a·bly**, *adv.*

peace·ful (pēs′fəl), *adj.* **1.** characterized by peace; tranquil. **2.** pertaining to or characteristic of a state of peace. **3.** peaceable. —**peace′ful·ly**, *adv.* —**peace′ful·ness**, *n.*

peace·mak·er (pēs′mā′kər), *n.* one who makes peace, as by reconciling parties.

peace pipe, the pipe smoked by the North American Indians in ratification of peace.

peace·time (pēs′tīm′), *n.* **1.** a period of peace. —*adj.* **2.** of or for such a period.

peach[1] (pēch), *n.* **1.** the subacid, juicy drupaceous fruit of a tree widely cultivated in temperate climates. **2.** the tree itself. **3.** a light pinkish yellow, as of a peach. **4.** *Slang.* a person or thing especially admired or liked. —*adj.* **5.** of the color peach. —**peach′like**, *adj.*

peach[2] (pēch), *v.i., v.t. Now Slang.* to inform against (an accomplice or associate).

peach·y (pē′chĭ), *adj.*, **peachier, peachiest. 1.** peachlike. **2.** *Slang.* excellent.

pea·cock (pē′kŏk′), *n., pl.* **-cocks,** (*esp. collectively*) **-cock.** the male of the peafowl, distinguished for its long tail coverts with rich iridescent coloring of green, blue, and gold.

pea·fowl (pē′foul′), *n.* any of certain birds of the pheasant family; a peacock or peahen.

pea·hen (pē′hĕn′), *n.* the female peafowl.

pea jacket, a short coat of thick woolen cloth worn esp. by seamen.

peak (pēk), *n.* **1.** the pointed top of a mountain. **2.** a mountain with a pointed summit. **3.** the pointed top of anything. **4.** the highest point. **5.** the maximum point or degree of anything. **6.** a projecting point. **7.** a projecting front piece, or visor, of a cap.

peaked[1] (pēkt, pē′kĭd), *adj.* having a peak.

peak·ed[2] (pē′kĭd), *adj.* thin; emaciated.

peal (pēl), *n.* **1.** a loud, prolonged sound of bells, or of cannon, thunder, laughter, etc. **2.** a set of bells tuned to one another. —*v.t., v.i.* **3.** to sound loudly and sonorously.

pea·nut (pē′nŭt′), *n.* **1.** the fruit (pod) or the edible seed of a leguminous plant, the pod of which is forced underground in growing, where it ripens. **2.** the plant.

peanut butter, a smooth spread made from finely ground roasted peanuts.

pear (pâr), *n.* **1.** the edible fruit, typically rounded but elongated and growing smaller toward the stem, of a tree of the rose family. **2.** the tree itself.

pearl (pûrl), *n.* **1.** a hard, smooth, often highly lustrous concretion, white or variously colored, secreted within the shell of various bivalve mollusks, and often valuable as a gem. **2.** something similar in form, luster, etc. **3.** something precious or choice. **4.** a very pale bluish gray. **5.** *Print.* a size of type (5 point). —*v.t.* **6.** to adorn with pearls. **7.** to make like pearls. —*v.i.* **8.** to make for pearls. —*adj.* **9.** of the color or form of pearl. —**pearl′y,** *adj.*

Pearl Harbor, a harbor near Honolulu, on the island of Oahu in the Hawaiian Islands: surprise attack by Japan on the U.S. naval base there, Dec. 7, 1941.

Pea·ry (pǐr′ĭ), *n.* **Robert Edwin,** 1856–1920, U.S. explorer: discovered North Pole (1909).

peas·ant (pĕz′ənt), *n.* **1.** one of a class of persons, as in European countries, of inferior social rank, usually engaged in farming. **2.** a rustic.

peas·ant·ry (pĕz′ən trĭ), *n.* **1.** peasants collectively. **2.** the character of a peasant.

pease (pēz), *n., pl.* **pease.** *Archaic or Brit. Dial.* **1.** a pea. **2.** (*pl.*) peas collectively.

peat (pēt), *n.* a highly organic soil (more than fifty percent combustible) dried for use as fuel. —**peat′y,** *adj.*

pea·vey (pē′vĭ), *n., pl.* **-veys.** a lumberman's cant hook with a spike at the end. Also, **pea′vy.**

peb·ble (pĕb′əl), *n., v.,* **-bled, -bling.** —*n.* **1.** a small, rounded stone. **2.** a transparent colorless rock crystal used for the lenses of eyeglasses. —*v.t.* **3.** to prepare (leather, etc.) so as to give it a granulated surface. —**peb′bly,** *adj.*

pe·can (pǐ kän′, pǐ kän′, pē′kän), *n.* **1.** a hickory tree, grown in the southern U.S. for its oval, smooth-shelled nut with a sweet, oily, edible kernel. **2.** the nut.

pec·ca·dil·lo (pĕk′ə dĭl′ō), *n., pl.* **-loes, -los.** a petty sin or offense; trifling fault.

pec·ca·ry (pĕk′ə rĭ), *n., pl.* **-ries,** (*esp. collectively*) **-ry.** any of a number of gregarious, piglike American ungulates.

peck[1] (pĕk), *n.* **1.** a dry measure of 8 quarts. **2.** a container for this quantity. **3.** a considerable quantity.

peck[2] (pĕk), *v.t., v.i.* **1.** to strike with the beak, esp. with quick, repeated movements. **2.** to make (a hole, etc.) by such strokes. **3.** to take (food, etc.) bit by bit, with the beak. —*n.* **4.** a pecking stroke. **5.** *Colloq.* a short, light kiss. —**peck′er,** *n.*

pec·tin (pĕk′tĭn), *n.* *Chem.* an amorphous, colloidal material in ripe fruits which dissolves in boiling water, forming a jelly upon subsequent evaporation.

pec·to·ral (pĕk′tə rəl), *adj.* **1.** of or pertaining to the chest. **2.** worn on the chest.

pec·u·late (pĕk′yə lāt′), *v.i., v.t.,* **-lated, -lating.** to embezzle (entrusted money). —**pec′u·la′tion,** *n.* —**pec′u·la′tor,** *n.*

pe·cu·liar (pǐ kūl′yər), *adj.* **1.** strange, odd, or queer. **2.** uncommon; unusual. **3.** belonging characteristically or exclusively. —**pe·cul′iar·ly,** *adv.*

pe·cu·li·ar·i·ty (pǐ kū′lǐ ăr′ə tǐ), *n., pl.* **-ties. 1.** an odd trait. **2.** singularity. **3.** characteristic quality. **4.** a distinguishing characteristic.

pe·cu·ni·ar·y (pǐ kū′nǐ ĕr′ǐ), *adj.* **1.** consisting of or given or exacted in money. **2.** of or pertaining to money.

ped·a·gog·ic (pĕd′ə gŏj′ĭk, -gō′jǐk), *adj.* of or pertaining to a pedagogue or pedagogy. Also, **ped′a·gog′i·cal.** —**ped′a·gog′i·cal·ly,** *adv.*

ped·a·gogue (pĕd′ə gŏg′, -gôg′), *n.* **1.** a teacher. **2.** a pedantic person. Also, **ped′a·gog′.**

ped·a·go·gy (pĕd′ə gō′jĭ, -gŏg′ĭ), *n.* the function, work, or art of a teacher; teaching.

ped·al (pĕd′əl for 1–4, 6; pē′dəl for 5), *n., v.,* **-aled, -aling or** (*esp. Brit.*) **-alled, -alling,** *adj.* —*n.* **1.** a lever worked by the foot, as in the organ, piano, and harp. **2.** a keyboard attached to the organ, etc., operated by the feet. **3.** a leverlike part worked by the foot, as on a sewing machine, bicycle, etc. —*v.i.* **4.** to work or use the pedals (of). —*adj.* **5.** of or pertaining to a foot or the feet. **6.** of or pertaining to a pedal or pedals.

ped·ant (pĕd′ənt), *n.* one who makes an excessive or tedious show of learning. —**pe·dan·tic** (pǐ dăn′tǐk), *adj.* —**pe·dan′ti·cal·ly,** *adv.*

ped·ant·ry (pĕd′ən trǐ), *n., pl.* **-ries. 1.** an undue display of learning. **2.** slavish attention to rules, details, etc.

ped·dle (pĕd′əl), *v.,* **-dled, -dling.** —*v.t.* **1.** to carry about for sale at retail. —*v.i.* **2.** to travel about retailing small wares. —**ped′dler** (pəd′lər), *n.*

ped·er·as·ty (pĕd′ə răs′tǐ, pē′də-), *n.* unnatural sex relations between males.

ped·es·tal (pĕd′ĭs təl), *n., v.,* **-taled, -taling or** (*esp. Brit.*) **-talled, -talling.** —*n.* **1.** an architectural support for a column, statue, vase, or the like. **2.** any supporting structure. —*v.t.* **3.** to set on a pedestal.

pe·des·tri·an (pə dĕs′trĭ ən), *n.* **1.** one who goes on foot; walker. —*adj.* **2.** walking. **3.** prosaic; dull.

pe·di·a·tri·cian (pē′dǐ ə trǐsh′ən, pĕd′ǐ-), *n.* a physician who specializes in pediatrics. Also, **pe·di·at·rist** (pē′dǐ ăt′rǐst, pĕd′ǐ-).

pe·di·at·rics (pē′dǐ ăt′rǐks, pĕd′ǐ-), *n.* the science of the medical and hygienic care of, or the diseases of, children. —**pe′di·at′ric,** *adj.*

pe·dic·u·lous (pǐ dǐk′yə ləs), *adj.* infested with lice.

ped·i·gree (pĕd′ə grē′), *n.* **1.** an ancestral line, or line of descent, esp. as recorded. **2.** a genealogical table. —**ped′i·greed′,** *adj.*

ped·i·ment (pĕd′ə mənt), *n.* *Archit.* a low triangular gable crowned with a projecting cornice, esp. over a portico or porch.

ped·lar (pĕd′lər), *n.* peddler. Also, **ped′ler.**

pe·dom·e·ter (pǐ dŏm′ə tər), *n.* an instrument for showing approximately the distance walked.

pe·dun·cle (pǐ dŭng′kəl), *n.* *Bot.* a flower stalk, supporting either a cluster or a solitary flower.

peek (pēk), *v.i.* **1.** to peep; peer. —*n.* **2.** a peeking look; peep.

peel (pēl), *v.t.* **1.** to strip off the skin, rind, bark, etc. **2.** to strip off (skin, etc.). —*v.i.* **3.** (of skin, etc.) to come off. **4.** to lose the skin, rind, bark, etc. —*n.* **5.** Also, **peel′ing.** the skin or rind of a fruit, etc. —**peel′er,** *n.*

Peel (pēl), *n.* **Sir Robert,** 1788–1850, British prime minister, 1834–35 and 1841–46.

peen (pēn), *n.* **1.** the sharp or spherical end of the head of a hammer, opposite to the face. —*v.t.* **2.** to strike with the peen.

peep[1] (pēp), *v.i.* **1.** to look through a small aperture. **2.** to look slyly, pryingly, or furtively. **3.** to peer, as from a hiding place. **4.** to begin to appear. —*v.t.* **5.** to show slightly. —*n.* **6.** a peeping look. **7.** the first appearance. —**peep′er,** *n.*

peep[2] (pēp), *v.i.* **1.** to utter the shrill little cry of a young bird, a mouse, etc. **2.** to speak in a thin, weak voice. —*n.* **3.** a peeping cry or sound. —**peep′er,** *n.*

peep·hole (pēp′hōl′), *n.* a hole through which to peep.

Peeping Tom, a prying, furtive observer, often for sexual gratification.

peer[1] (pǐr), *n.* **1.** a person of equal civil rank or standing. **2.** an equal in any respect. **3.** a nobleman.

peer[2] (pǐr), *v.i.* **1.** to look narrowly, as to discern clearly. **2.** to appear slightly.

peer·age (pǐr′ĭj), *n.* **1.** the rank or dignity of a peer. **2.** the body of peers of a country. **3.** a book giving a list of peers, etc.

peer·ess (pǐr′ĭs), *n.* **1.** the wife of a peer. **2.** a woman with the rank of a peer.

peer·less (pǐr′lǐs), *adj.* having no equal; matchless. —**peer′less·ly,** *adv.*

peeve (pēv), *v.,* **peeved, peeving,** *n.* —*v.t.* **1.** *Colloq.* to render peevish. —*n.* **2.** an annoyance.

pee·vish (pē′vǐsh), *adj.* cross, querulous, or fretful, as from vexation or discontent. —**pee′vish·ly,** *adv.* —**pee′vish·ness,** *n.*

peg (pĕg), *n., v.,* **pegged, pegging.** —*n.* **1.** a pin of wood or other material driven or fitted into something, as to fasten parts together, to hang things on, to stop a hole, etc. **2.** *Colloq.* a leg. **3.** *Colloq.* a degree. —*v.t.* **4.** to insert a peg into. **5.** to fasten with pegs. **6.** *Colloq.* to aim or throw. —*v.i.* **7.** to work persistently.

Peg·a·sus (pĕg′ə səs), *n.* **1.** *Class. Myth.* a winged horse, sprung from the blood of Medusa. **2.** *Astron.* a northern constellation represented as the forward half of a flying horse.

peign·oir (pān wär′, pān′wär), *n.* a dressing gown.

Pei·ping (bā′pǐng′), *n.* a city in NE China: former capital of China. 1,500,000 pop. Formerly, **Peking.**

pe·jo·ra·tive (pē′jə rā′tǐv, pǐ jôr′ə tǐv, pǐ jōr′-), *adj.* **1.** depreciative; disparaging. —*n.* **2.** a pejorative form or word. —**pe′jo·ra′tive·ly,** *adv.*

Pe·king (pē′kǐng′), *n.* former name of **Peiping.**

Pe·king·ese (pē′kǐng ēz′), *n.* **1.** a small, long-haired, Chinese dog prized as a pet. —*adj.* **2.** pertaining to Peiping. Also, **Pe·kin·ese** (pē′kə nēz′).

pe·koe (pē′kō *or, esp. Brit.*, pĕk′ō), *n.* a kind of black tea from Ceylon, India, and Java.

pe·lag·ic (pə lăj′ĭk), *adj.* 1. of or pertaining to the oceans. 2. living at or near the surface of the ocean, far from land.

pelf (pĕlf), *n. Usually Contemptuous.* money or riches.

pel·i·can (pĕl′ə kən), *n.* any of certain large birds having a large fish-catching bill.

Pe·li·on (pē′lĭ ən), *n.* **Mount,** *Gk. Myth.* See **Ossa.**

pe·lisse (pə lēs′), *n.* an outer garment lined or trimmed with fur.

pel·la·gra (pə lā′grə, pə lăg′rə), *n. Pathol.* a chronic, noncontagious disease caused by deficient diet. —**pel·la′grous,** *adj.*

pel·let (pĕl′ĭt), *n.* 1. a little ball, as of food or medicine. 2. a bullet or one of a charge of small shot. 3. an imitation bullet, as of wax or paper. —*v.t.* 4. to hit with pellets.

pell-mell (pĕl′mĕl′), *adv.* 1. in a confused mass or crowd. 2. in disorderly, headlong haste. —*adj.* 3. disorderly; tumultuous. —*n.* 4. violent disorder. Also, **pell′mell′.**

pel·lu·cid (pə lōō′sĭd), *adj.* 1. translucent. 2. clear or limpid, as water. 3. clear in meaning. —**pel·lu′cid·ly,** *adv.*

Peloponnesian War, a war between Athens and Sparta from 431 to 404 B.C. which resulted in the transfer of hegemony in Greece from Athens to Sparta.

Pel·o·pon·ne·sus (pĕl′ə pə nē′səs), *n.* the S peninsula of Greece. 8350 sq. mi. Also, **Pel·o·pon·ne′sos.** —**Pel·o·pon·ne·sian** (pĕl′ə pə nē′shən, -zhən), *adj., n.*

pelt[1] (pĕlt), *v.t., v.i.* 1. to assail (a person, thing, etc.) with repeated blows or missiles. 2. to throw (missiles). —*n.* 3. act of pelting. 4. a blow with something thrown. 5. speed. —**pelt′er,** *n.*

pelt[2] (pĕlt), *n.* the skin of a beast.

pel·vis (pĕl′vĭs), *n., pl.* **-ves** (-vēz). *Anat., Zool.* 1. the basinlike cavity in the lower part of the trunk of many vertebrates, formed in man by the innominate bones, sacrum, etc. 2. the bones forming this cavity. —**pel′vic,** *adj.*

pem·mi·can (pĕm′ə kən), *n.* a paste of dried meat pressed into cakes, orig. prepared by North American Indians.

pen[1] (pĕn), *n., v.,* **penned, penning.** —*n.* 1. any instrument for writing with ink. 2. *Ornith.* a large feather of the wing or tail. —*v.t.* 3. to write with a pen.

pen[2] (pĕn), *n., v.,* **penned** or **pent, penning.** —*n.* 1. a small enclosure for domestic animals. 2. any place of confinement. —*v.t.* 3. to confine in a pen.

pe·nal (pē′nəl), *adj.* 1. of or pertaining to punishment. 2. prescribing punishment. 3. constituting punishment. 4. subject to punishment.

pe·nal·ize (pē′nə līz′, pĕn′ə-), *v.t.,* **-ized, -izing.** 1. to subject to a penalty, as a person. 2. to lay under a disadvantage. —**pe′nal·i·za′tion,** *n.*

pen·al·ty (pĕn′əl tĭ), *n., pl.* **-ties.** 1. a punishment for a violation of law or rule. 2. a forfeiture for nonfulfillment of an obligation. 3. that which is forfeited. 4. *Sports.* a disadvantage imposed upon a competitor or side for infraction of the rules.

pen·ance (pĕn′əns), *n.* 1. punishment undergone in token of penitence for sin. 2. a penitential discipline imposed by Church authority.

pe·na·tes (pə nā′tēz), *n.pl. Rom. Myth.* deities of the household and state, worshiped with the lares. Also, **Pe·na′tes.**

pence (pĕns), *n. Brit.* pl. of **penny.**

pen·chant (pĕn′chənt), *n.* a strong inclination; a liking for something.

pen·cil (pĕn′səl), *n., v.,* **-ciled, -ciling** or (*esp. Brit.*) **-cilled, -cilling.** —*n.* 1. a strip of graphite, chalk, or the like, incased in wood, metal, etc., used for drawing or writing. 2. a stick of cosmetic coloring material for use on the eyebrows, etc. 3. a set of lines, light rays, or the like, diverging from or converging to a point. —*v.t.* 4. to use a pencil on. 5. to execute, draw, or write with a pencil. 6. to mark or color with a pencil.

pend (pĕnd), *v.i.* to remain undecided.

pend·ant (pĕn′dənt), *n.* 1. a hanging ornament, as of a necklace or of a vaulted roof. 2. a chandelier. —*adj.* 3. pendent.

pend·ent (pĕn′dənt), *adj.* 1. hanging or suspended. 2. overhanging; jutting or leaning over. 3. impending. 4. undecided. —*n.* 5. pendant.

pend·ing (pĕn′dĭng), *prep.* 1. until. 2. in the

period before the decision or conclusion of. —*adj.* 3. undecided. 4. hanging.

pen·drag·on (pĕn drăg′ən), *n.* chief leader (a title of ancient British chiefs).

pen·du·lous (pĕn′jə ləs), *adj.* 1. hanging. 2. swinging freely. 3. vacillating.

pen·du·lum (pĕn′jə ləm, pĕn′də-), *n.* 1. a body so suspended from a fixed point as to move to and fro by the action of gravity and acquired momentum. 2. a swinging device used for controlling the movement of clockwork.

Pe·nel·o·pe (pə nĕl′ə pĭ), *n.* the faithful wife of Odysseus in the *Odyssey.*

pe·ne·plain (pē′nə plān′), *n. Geol.* an area reduced almost to a plain by erosion.

pen·e·tra·ble (pĕn′ə trə bəl), *adj.* capable of being penetrated. —**pen′e·tra·bil′i·ty,** *n.* —**pen′e·tra·bly,** *adv.*

pen·e·trate (pĕn′ə trāt′), *v.,* **-trated, -trating.** —*v.t.* 1. to pierce into or through. 2. to enter. 3. to permeate. 4. to understand. —*v.i.* 5. to enter, reach, or pass through.

pen·e·trat·ing (pĕn′ə trā′tĭng), *adj.* 1. piercing; sharp. 2. acute; discerning. —**pen′e·trat′ing·ly,** *adv.*

pen·e·tra·tion (pĕn′ə trā′shən), *n.* 1. act or power of penetrating. 2. mental acuteness, discernment, or insight.

pen·guin (pĕn′gwĭn, pĕng′-), *n.* any of certain flightless aquatic birds of the southern hemisphere, with webbed feet, and wings reduced to flippers.

pen·i·cil·lin (pĕn′ə sĭl′ĭn), *n.* a powerful antibacterial substance produced by certain green molds.

Emperor penguin (Total length 4 ft.)

pen·in·su·la (pə nĭn′sə lə, -syə lə), *n.* a piece of land almost surrounded by water. —**pen·in′su·lar,** *adj.*

pe·nis (pē′nĭs), *n., pl.* **-nes** (-nēz), **-nises** (-nĭs ĭz). the male organ of copulation.

pen·i·tent (pĕn′ə tənt), *adj.* 1. repentant; contrite; sorry for sin or fault. —*n.* 2. a penitent person. —**pen′i·tence,** *n.* —**pen′i·tent·ly,** *adv.* —**pen′i·ten′tial,** *adj.*

pen·i·ten·tia·ry (pĕn′ə tĕn′shə rĭ), *n., pl.* **-ries.** 1. a place for imprisonment and reformatory discipline. 2. *U.S.* a State prison.

pen·knife (pĕn′nīf′), *n., pl.* **-knives** (-nīvz′). a small pocketknife.

pen·man (pĕn′mən), *n., pl.* **-men.** 1. one skilled in penmanship. 2. an author.

pen·man·ship (pĕn′mən shĭp′), *n.* the art or style of handwriting.

Penn (pĕn), *n.* **William,** 1644–1718, British Quaker who founded the colony of Pennsylvania.

Penn., Pennsylvania. Also, **Penna.**

pen name, an author's pseudonym.

pen·nant (pĕn′ənt), *n.* a distinctive flag borne on naval or other vessels or used in signaling, etc.

pen·nate (pĕn′āt), *adj.* winged; feathered.

pen·ni·less (pĕn′ĭ lĭs), *adj.* without a penny; destitute of money.

pen·non (pĕn′ən), *n.* 1. a distinctive flag in various forms, orig. one borne on the lance of a knight. 2. *Poetic.* a wing or pinion.

Penn·syl·va·ni·a (pĕn′səl vā′nĭ ə, -vān′yə), *n.* a State in the E United States. 10,023,750; 45,333 sq. mi. *Cap.:* Harrisburg. *Abbr.:* Pa., Penn., or Penna. —**Penn′syl·va′ni·an,** *adj., n.*

pen·ny (pĕn′ĭ), *n., pl.* **pennies** or (*esp. collectively for* 1b) **pence.** 1. any of various coins: a. the U.S. and Canadian cent. b. an English coin, 1/12 of the shilling. 2. a sum of money.

pen·ny·weight (pĕn′ĭ wāt′), *n.* (in troy weight) a unit of 24 grains or 1/20 of an ounce.

pen·ny-wise (pĕn′ĭ wīz′), *adj.* wise or saving in regard to small sums.

Pe·nob·scot (pə nŏb′skŏt), *n.* 1. a river flowing from N Maine S to **Penobscot Bay,** an inlet of the Atlantic. ab. 350 mi. 2. a member of an Algonquian Indian tribe along Penobscot Bay and river.

pe·nol·o·gy (pē nŏl′ə jĭ), *n.* 1. the science of the punishment of crime. 2. the science of the management of prisons. —**pe·nol′o·gist,** *n.*

Pen·sa·co·la (pĕn′sə kō′lə), *n.* a seaport in NW Florida. 37,449.

pen·sile (pĕn′sĭl), *adj.* 1. hanging, as the nests of certain birds. 2. building a hanging nest.

pen·sion (pĕn′shən; *for* 2 *Fr.* päɴ syôɴ′), *n.* 1. a fixed periodical payment made in consideration of past services, injury sustained, etc. **2.** (esp. in France) a boarding house or school. —*v.t.* **3.** to grant a pension to. —**pen'sion·a·ble,** *adj.*

pen·sion·er (pĕn'shən ər), *n.* **1.** one who receives a pension. **2.** a hireling.

pen·sive (pĕn'sĭv), *adj.* deeply, seriously, or sadly thoughtful. —**pen'sive·ly,** *adv.* —**pen'sive·ness,** *n.*

pent (pĕnt), *adj.* **1.** shut in. **2.** confined.

pen·ta·gon (pĕn'tə gŏn'), *n.* **1.** a polygon having five angles and five sides. **2. the Pentagon,** the building in Arlington, Va., containing most U.S. Army headquarters offices. —**pen·tag·o·nal** (pĕn tăg'ə nəl), *adj.*

pen·tam·e·ter (pĕn tăm'ə tər), *n. Pros.* a verse, or line, of five feet.

Pen·ta·teuch (pĕn'tə tūk', -tōŏk'), *n.* the first five books of the Old Testament. —**Pen'ta·teuch'al,** *adj.*

pen·ta·va·lent (pĕn'tə vā'lənt, pĕn tăv'ə-), *adj. Chem.* possessing a valence of 5.

Pen·te·cost (pĕn'tə kôst', -kŏst'), *n.* **1.** a Christian festival commemorating the descent of the Holy Ghost upon the apostles on the day of the Jewish festival; Whitsunday. **2.** a Jewish harvest festival observed on the fiftieth day from the second day of Passover. —**Pen'te·cos'tal,** *adj.*

pent·house (pĕnt'hous'), *n.* a separate apartment or dwelling on a roof.

pent-up (pĕnt'ŭp'), *adj.* confined; restrained.

pe·nult (pē'nŭlt, pĭ nŭlt'), *n.* the last syllable but one in a word. —**pe·nul'ti·mate,** *adj.*

pe·num·bra (pĭ nŭm'brə), *n., pl.* **-brae** (-brē), **-bras.** *Astron.* the partial shadow outside the complete shadow (umbra) of an opaque body. —**pe·num'bral,** *adj.*

pe·nu·ri·ous (pə nyŏŏr'ĭ əs, -nŏŏr'-), *adj.* meanly stingy. —**pe·nu'ri·ous·ly,** *adv.* —**pe·nu'ri·ous·ness,** *n.*

pen·u·ry (pĕn'yə rĭ), *n.* **1.** extreme poverty; destitution. **2.** dearth or insufficiency.

pe·on (pē'ən), *n.* **1.** *Spanish America.* **a.** a day laborer. **b.** one who tends a horse or mule. **2.** *Chiefly Mexico.* one held in servitude to work off debts, etc.

pe·on·age (pē'ən ĭj), *n.* the practice of holding persons in servitude, as to work off debt.

pe·o·ny (pē'ə nĭ), *n., pl.* **-nies. 1.** any of certain perennial herbs and shrubs of the crowfoot family with large showy flowers, familiar in gardens. **2.** the flower.

peo·ple (pē'pəl), *n., pl.* **-ple** or (for 1) **-ples;** *v.,* **-pled, -pling.** —*n.* **1.** the whole body of persons constituting a community, tribe, race, or nation. **2.** the persons of any particular group. **3.** persons in relation to a ruler, leader, etc. **4.** one's relatives. **5.** the common 'people; populace. **6.** persons indefinitely. —*v.t.* **7.** to populate.

Pe·o·ri·a (pĭ ōr'ĭ ə), *n.* a city in central Illinois. 105,087.

pep (pĕp), *n., v.,* **pepped, pepping.** *U.S. Slang.* —*n.* **1.** animation; vigor; energy. —*v.t.* **2.** to give spirit or vigor to.

pep·lum (pĕp'ləm), *n., pl.* **-lums, -la** (-lə). **1.** a short full flounce covering the hips. **2.** a short skirt attached to a bodice or coat.

pep·per (pĕp'ər), *n.* **1.** a pungent condiment obtained from the dried berries of certain plants (affording the **black pepper** and **white pepper** of commerce). **2.** any plant of the genus yielding such berries. **3.** cayenne (**red pepper**). **4.** a common garden plant whose green-to-red fruit is used as a vegetable or seasoning. **5.** its fruit. —*v.t.* **6.** to season with pepper. **7.** to dot; stud. **8.** to pelt with missiles.

pep·per·corn (pĕp'ər kôrn'), *n.* the berry of the pepper plant, often dried and used in pickling.

pep·per·mint (pĕp'ər mĭnt'), *n.* **1.** a labiate herb cultivated for its aromatic pungent oil. **2.** this oil, or some preparation of it. **3.** a lozenge or confection flavored with it.

pepper pot, a spicy West Indian stew.

pep·per·y (pĕp'ə rĭ), *adj.* **1.** like or full of pepper. **2.** sharp or stinging, as speech. **3.** irritable, as persons.

pep·py (pĕp'ĭ), *adj.,* **-pier, -piest.** *Slang.* energetic. —**pep'pi·ness,** *n.*

pep·sin (pĕp'sĭn), *n. Biochem.* an enzyme produced in the stomach which, in the presence of hydrochloric acid, digests proteins. Also, **pep'sine.**

pep·tic (pĕp'tĭk), *adj.* **1.** digestive. **2.** promot-

ing digestion. **3.** of or pertaining to pepsin. —*n.* **4.** a substance promoting digestion.

pep·tone (pĕp'tōn), *n. Biochem.* any of a class of diffusible, soluble substances into which proteins are converted by hydrolysis. —**pep·ton·ic** (pĕp tŏn'ĭk), *adj.*

Pep·ys (pēps, pĕps, pĕp'ĭs), *n.* **Samuel,** 1633–1703, British diarist.

Pe·quot (pē'kwŏt), *n.* a member of a former tribe of Algonquian Indians in S New England.

per (pûr, pər), *prep.* through; by; for each.

per., 1. period. **2.** person.

per·ad·ven·ture (pûr'əd vĕn'chər), *adv.* **1.** maybe; possibly. —*n.* **2.** chance.

per·am·bu·late (pər ăm'byə lāt'), *v.t., v.i.,* **-lated, -lating. 1.** to walk through, about, or over. —**per·am'bu·la'tion,** *n.* —**per·am·bu·la·to·ry** (pər ăm'byə lə tōr'ĭ), *adj.*

per·am·bu·la·tor (pər ăm'byə lā'tər), *n. Brit.* a baby carriage, usually pushed by hand.

per an·num (pər ăn'əm), *Latin.* yearly.

per·cale (pər kāl'), *n.* a closely woven, smooth-finished cambric, plain or printed.

per cap·i·ta (pər kăp'ə tə), *Latin.* by individuals.

per·ceive (pər sēv'), *v.t.,* **-ceived, -ceiving. 1.** to gain knowledge of by seeing, hearing, etc. **2.** to understand. —**per·ceiv'a·ble,** *adj.*

per·cent (pər sĕnt'), *n.* for or in every hundred (used in expressing proportions, rates of interest, etc). Also, **per cent.**

per·cent·age (pər sĕn'tĭj), *n.* **1.** a rate or proportion per hundred. **2.** an allowance, duty, commission, or rate on a hundred. **3.** *Slang.* gain.

per·cen·tile (pər sĕn'tĭl), *Statistics.* —*n.* **1.** one of the values of a variable which divides the distribution of the variable into 100 groups having equal frequencies. —*adj.* **2.** of or pertaining to a percentile.

per·cept (pûr'sĕpt), *n.* **1.** the mental result or product of perceiving. **2.** that which is perceived.

per·cep·ti·ble (pər sĕp'tə bəl), *adj.* capable of being perceived. —**per·cep'ti·bly,** *adv*

per·cep·tion (pər sĕp'shən), *n.* **1.** the action or faculty of perceiving; cognition. **2.** an immediate or intuitive recognition. **3.** a percept.

per·cep·tive (pər sĕp'tĭv), *adj.* **1.** having the power of perceiving. **2.** of or pertaining to perception. **3.** of ready or quick perception.

perch¹ (pûrch), *n.* **1.** a horizontal rod serving as a roost for birds. **2.** anything for a bird to alight upon. **3.** an elevated position. **4.** a linear measure of 5½ yards. **5.** a square rod (30¼ square yards). —*v.i.* **6.** to alight or rest upon a perch. —*v.t.* **7.** to set on a perch.

perch² (pûrch), *n., pl.* **perches,** (*esp. collectively*) **perch. 1.** a common spiny-finned, fresh-water food fish. **2.** any of various other spiny-rayed fishes.

per·chance (pər chăns', -chäns'), *adv. Poetic or Archaic.* **1.** maybe. **2.** by chance.

Per·che·ron (pûr'chə rŏn', -shə-), *n.* one of a breed of draft horses.

per·cip·i·ent (pər sĭp'ĭ ənt), *adj.* **1.** perceiving. **2.** having perception. —*n.* **3.** one that perceives. —**per·cip'i·ence,** *n.*

Per·ci·val (pûr'sə vəl), *n.* **Sir,** *Arthurian Romance.* a knight of King Arthur's court who sought the Holy Grail. Also, **Per'ci·vale.**

per·co·late (*v.* pûr'kə lāt'; *n.* pûr'kə lĭt, -lāt'), *v.,* **-lated, -lating,** *n.* —*v.t., v.i.* **1.** to pass (a liquid) through a porous body; filter. **2.** a percolated liquid. —**per'co·la'tion,** *n.*

per·co·la·tor (pûr'kə lā'tər), *n.* a kind of coffee pot in which boiling water is forced up a hollow stem, filters through ground coffee, and returns to the pot below.

per·cus·sion (pər kŭsh'ən), *n.* **1.** the violent striking of one body against another; impact. **2.** *Med.* the tapping of a part of the body for diagnostic or therapeutic purposes. **3.** the striking of musical instruments to produce tones.

percussion instrument, a musical instrument, as a drum, cymbal, piano, etc., which is struck to produce a sound.

per di·em (pər dī'əm, dĭ'əm), **1.** *Latin.* by the day. **2.** a daily allowance, usually for living expenses while traveling in connection with one's work.

per·di·tion (pər dĭsh'ən), *n.* **1.** final spiritual

ruin or damnation. **2.** hell. **3.** utter destruction or ruin.

per·e·gri·nate (pĕr′ə grə nāt′), *v.,* **-nated, -nating. —***v.i.* **1.** to travel or journey. —*v.t.* **2.** to travel over. —**per′e·gri·na′tion,** *n.*

per·e·grine (pĕr′ə grĭn, -grīn′), *n.* a falcon, formerly much used in Europe for hawking.

per·emp·to·ry (pə rĕmp′tə rĭ, pĕr′əmp tôr′ĭ), *adj.* **1.** leaving no opportunity for denial or refusal; imperative. **2.** imperious or positive. **3.** decisive or final. —**per·emp′to·ri·ly,** *adv.* —**per·emp′to·ri·ness,** *n.*

per·en·ni·al (pə rĕn′ĭ əl), *adj.* **1.** lasting for an indefinitely long time; enduring. **2.** *Bot.* having a life cycle lasting more than two years. —*n.* **3.** a perennial plant. —**per·en′ni·al·ly,** *adv.*

perf., 1. perfect. **2.** perforated.

per·fect (*adj., n.* pûr′fĭkt; *v.* pər fĕkt′, pûr′fĭkt), *adj.* **1.** having all essential elements, characteristics, etc.; complete. **2.** without blemish or defect; faultless. **3.** completely skilled. **4.** exact or correct. **5.** thorough; unqualified. **6.** *Chiefly Colloq.* utter. **7.** *Gram.* denoting action or state brought to a close prior to some temporal point of reference. —*n.* **8.** *Gram.* **a.** the perfect tense. **b.** a verb or other formation or construction with perfect meaning. —*v.t.* **9.** to complete; finish. **10.** to make faultless. **11.** to improve. —**per′fect·er,** *n.* —**per·fect′i·ble,** *adj.* —**per·fect′i·bil′i·ty,** *n.* —**per·fect′ive,** *adj.* —**per′fect·ly,** *adv.*

per·fec·tion (pər fĕk′shən), *n.* **1.** state or quality of being perfect. **2.** the highest degree of proficiency. **3.** a perfect embodiment of something. **4.** a quality, trait, or feature of high excellence. **5.** the highest degree of a quality or trait. **6.** act or fact of perfecting.

per·fi·dy (pûr′fə dĭ), *n., pl.* **-dies.** base breach of faith or trust; faithlessness; treachery. —**per·fid·i·ous** (pər fĭd′ĭ əs), *adj.* —**per·fid′i·ous·ly,** *adv.* —**per·fid′i·ous·ness,** *n.*

per·fo·rate (*v.* pûr′fə rāt′; *adj.* pûr′fə rĭt, -fə rāt′), *v.,* **-rated, -rating,** *adj.* —*v.t.* **1.** to make a hole or holes through. —*adj.* **2.** perforated. —**per′fo·ra′tor,** *n.*

per·fo·ra·tion (pûr′fə rā′shən), *n.* **1.** a hole bored or punched through something, as those between individual postage stamps. **2.** act of perforating. **3.** state of being perforated.

per·force (pər fôrs′), *adv.* of necessity.

per·form (pər fôrm′), *v.t.* **1.** to carry out; execute; do. **2.** to carry into effect; fulfill. **3.** to act (a play, a part, etc.), as on the stage. **4.** to render (music), as by playing. —*v.i.* **5.** to fulfill a command, promise, or undertaking. **6.** to execute or do something. **7.** to act in a play, etc. **8.** to perform music. —**per·form′er,** *n.*

per·form·ance (pər fôr′məns), *n.* **1.** a musical, dramatic, or other entertainment. **2.** the performing of ceremonies, music, a play, or the like. **3.** execution or doing, as of work. **4.** a particular action or deed.

per·fume (*n.* pûr′fūm, pər fūm′; *v.* pər fūm′), *n., v.,* **-fumed, -fuming. —***n.* **1.** a substance, extract, or preparation for diffusing or imparting a sweet smell. **2.** the scent, odor, or volatile particles emitted by sweet-smelling substances. —*v.t.* **3.** to impart fragrance to. **4.** to scent.

per·fum·er (pər fū′mər), *n.* **1.** one that perfumes. **2.** a maker or seller of perfumes.

per·fum·er·y (pər fū′mə rĭ), *n., pl.* **-eries. 1.** perfumes collectively. **2.** a perfume. **3.** the art or business of a perfumer.

per·func·to·ry (pər fŭngk′tə rĭ), *adj.* performed merely as a routine duty; mechanical. —**per·func′to·ri·ly,** *adv.* —**per·func′to·ri·ness,** *n.*

per·go·la (pûr′gə lə), *n.* an arbor formed of horizontal trelliswork supported on posts.

per·haps (pər hăps′), *adv.* maybe; possibly.

per·i·anth (pĕr′ĭ ănth′), *n. Bot.* the envelope of a flower, whether calyx or corolla or both.

per·i·car·di·tis (pĕr′ĭ kär dī′tĭs), *n. Pathol.* inflammation of the pericardium.

per·i·car·di·um (pĕr′ĭ kär′dĭ əm), *n., pl.* **-dia** (-dĭ ə). *Anat.* the membranous sac enclosing the heart. —**per·i·car′di·al, per·i·car′di·ac′,** *adj.*

per·i·carp (pĕr′ĭ kärp′), *n. Bot.* **1.** the walls of a ripened ovary or fruit. **2.** a seed vessel.

Per·i·cles (pĕr′ə klēz′), *n.* c400–429 B.C., Athenian statesman. —**Per·i·cle·an** (pĕr′ə klē′ən), *adj.*

per·i·gee (pĕr′ə jē′), *n. Astron.* the point in the orbit of a heavenly body that is nearest to the earth. —**per′i·ge′al,** *adj.*

per·i·he·li·on (pĕr′ə hē′lĭ ən), *n., pl.* **-lia** (-lĭ ə). *Astron.* the point of a planet's or comet's orbit nearest to the sun.

per·il (pĕr′əl), *n., v.,* **-iled, -iling** or (*esp. Brit.*) **-illed, -illing. —***n.* **1.** exposure to loss or harm. —*v.t.* **2.** to imperil. —**per′il·ous,** *adj.* —**per′il·ous·ly,** *adv.*

per·im·e·ter (pə rĭm′ə tər), *n.* **1.** the outer boundary of a two-dimensional figure. **2.** the length of such a boundary.

pe·ri·od (pĭr′ĭ əd), *n.* **1.** a portion of time, history, life, etc., characterized by certain features or conditions. **2.** *Educ.* a session of classroom study devoted to a single subject. **3.** *Sports, etc.* a definite, timed part of a game. **4.** the time during which anything runs its course. **5.** the mark (.) used to end a complete declarative sentence, indicate an abbreviation, etc. **6.** a full pause such as is made at the end of a complete sentence. **7.** a complete sentence. **8.** (*pl.*) rhetorical language.

pe·ri·od·ic (pĭr′ĭ ŏd′ĭk), *adj.* **1.** characterized by periods or rounds of recurrence. **2.** occurring at regular intervals. **3.** intermittent. **4.** pertaining to or characterized by rhetorical periods or periodic sentences. **5.** (of a sentence) having the sense incomplete until the end is reached. —**pe′ri·od′i·cal·ly,** *adv.*

pe·ri·od·i·cal (pĭr′ĭ ŏd′ə kəl), *adj.* **1.** (of magazines, etc.) issued at regularly recurring intervals. **2.** periodic. —*n.* **3.** a periodical publication.

pe·ri·o·dic·i·ty (pĭr′ĭ ə dĭs′ə tĭ), *n., pl.* **-ties.** tendency to recur at regular intervals.

periodic law, *Chem.* the law that the properties of the elements are periodic functions of their atomic numbers.

periodic table, *Chem.* a table in which the chemical elements, arranged in the order of their atomic numbers, are shown in related groups.

per·i·os·te·um (pĕr′ĭ ŏs′tĭ əm), *n., pl.* **-tea** (-tĭ ə). *Anat.* the normal investment of bone, made up of a dense outer fibrous tissue layer and a more delicate inner layer. —**per′i·os′te·al,** *adj.*

Per·i·pa·tet·ic (pĕr′ə pə tĕt′ĭk), *adj.* **1.** of or pertaining to the philosophy or the followers of Aristotle. **2.** (*l.c.*) *Chiefly Humorous.* itinerant. —*n.* **3.** a member of the Aristotelian school. **4.** (*l.c.*) *Chiefly Humorous.* one who walks or travels about.

pe·riph·er·y (pə rĭf′ə rĭ), *n., pl.* **-eries. 1.** the external boundary of any surface or area. **2.** the external surface of a body. —**pe·riph′er·al,** *adj.*

pe·riph·ra·sis (pə rĭf′rə sĭs), *n., pl.* **-ses** (-sēz′). a roundabout way of speaking; circumlocution.

per·i·phras·tic (pĕr′ə frăs′tĭk), *adj.* **1.** circumlocutory; roundabout. **2.** *Gram.* denoting a construction of two or more words with a class meaning which in other forms of the same language is expressed by inflectional modification of a single word.

per·i·scope (pĕr′ə skōp′), *n.* an optical instrument consisting essentially of a tube with an arrangement of prisms or mirrors by which a view at the surface of water, etc., may be seen from below or behind. —**per·i·scop·ic** (pĕr′ə skŏp′ĭk), *adj.*

per·ish (pĕr′ĭsh), *v.i.* **1.** to suffer death through violence, privation, etc. **2.** to decay and disappear. **3.** to suffer destruction.

per·ish·a·ble (pĕr′ĭsh ə bəl), *adj.* **1.** subject to decay or destruction. —*n.* **2.** (*usually pl.*) a perishable thing, as food. —**per′ish·a·ble·ness, per′ish·a·bil′i·ty,** *n.*

per·i·stal·sis (pĕr′ə stăl′sĭs), *n., pl.* **-ses** (-sēz). *Physiol.* peristaltic movement.

per·i·stal·tic (pĕr′ə stăl′tĭk), *adj. Physiol.* noting or pertaining to the alternate waves of constriction and dilation of a tubular structure, as the alimentary canal.

per·i·style (pĕr′ə stīl′), *n. Archit.* **1.** a range of columns surrounding a building, court, or the like. **2.** a space or court so enclosed.

per·i·to·ne·um (pĕr′ə tə nē′əm), *n., pl.* **-nea** (-nē′ə). *Anat.* the membrane lining the abdominal cavity and investing its viscera. Also, **per′i·to·nae′um.** —**per′i·to·ne′al,** *adj.*

per·i·to·ni·tis (pĕr′ə tə nī′tĭs), *n. Pathol.* inflammation of the peritoneum.

per·i·wig (pĕr′ə wĭg′), *n.* a peruke or wig.

per·i·win·kle[1] (pĕr′ə wĭng′kəl), *n.* any of various edible marine gastropods or sea snails.

per·i·win·kle² (pĕr/ə wĭng/kəl), *n.* a trailing evergreen plant with blue flowers.

per·jure (pûr/jər), *v.t.*, **-jured, -juring.** to render (oneself) guilty of perjury. **—per/jur·er,** *n.*

per·ju·ry (pûr/jə rĭ), *n.*, *pl.* **-ries.** *Law.* the willful utterance of a false statement under oath or affirmation.

perk (pûrk), *v.i.* **1.** to carry oneself, lift the head, or act in a jaunty manner. **2.** to become lively or vigorous. **—v.t. 3.** to raise smartly or briskly. **4.** to dress smartly. **—adj. 5.** perky.

perk·y (pûr/kĭ), *adj.*, **perkier, perkiest.** jaunty; brisk; pert.

per·ma·nent (pûr/mə nənt), *adj.* **1.** lasting or intended to last indefinitely; enduring. **—n. 2.** a permanent wave. **—per/ma·nence, per/ma·nen·cy,** *n.* **—per/ma·nent·ly,** *adv.*

permanent wave, a wave set into the hair by a special technique and remaining for a number of months.

per·man·ga·nate (pər măng/gə nāt/), *n.* *Chem.* a salt of an acid containing manganese, for disinfecting, oxidizing, etc.

per·me·a·ble (pûr/mĭ ə bəl), *adj.* capable of being permeated. **—per/me·a·bil/i·ty,** *n.*

per·me·ate (pûr/mĭ āt/), *v.*, **-ated, -ating. —v.t. 1.** to pass through the substance or mass of. **2.** to penetrate through the pores, etc., of. **3.** to pervade or saturate. **—v.i. 4.** to penetrate; diffuse itself. **—per/me·a/tion,** *n.*

per·mis·si·ble (pər mĭs/ə bəl), *adj.* allowable. **—per·mis/si·bil/i·ty,** *n.* **—per·mis/si·bly,** *adv.*

per·mis·sion (pər mĭsh/ən), *n.* formal or express allowance or consent.

per·mis·sive (pər mĭs/ĭv), *adj.* **1.** permitting or allowing. **2.** allowed; optional.

per·mit (*v.* pər mĭt/; *n.* pûr/mĭt, pər mĭt/), *v.*, **-mitted, -mitting,** *n.* **—v.t. 1.** to allow (a person, etc.) to do something. **2.** to let (something) be done or occur. **3.** to agree to. **4.** to afford opportunity for. **—v.i. 5.** to grant permission. **6.** to afford opportunity. **7.** to allow. **—n. 8.** a written order granting leave to do something. **9.** an authoritative certificate of permission. **10.** permission. **—per·mit/ter,** *n.*

per·mu·ta·tion (pûr/myo tā/shən), *n.* **1.** *Math.* **a.** the act of changing the order of individuals arranged in a particular order (as, *abc* into *acb, bac,* etc.). **b.** any of the resulting arrangements. **2.** alteration.

Per·nam·bu·co (pûr/nəm bū/kō), *n.* Recife.

per·ni·cious (pər nĭsh/əs), *adj.* **1.** highly hurtful. **2.** deadly; fatal. **3.** evil. **—per·ni/cious·ly,** *adv.* **—per·ni/cious·ness,** *n.*

pernicious anemia, *Pathol.* a type of anemia produced by deficient maturation of the red blood cells.

per·nick·et·y (pər nĭk/ə tĭ), *adj.* *Colloq.* fastidious; fussy.

Pe·rón (pĕ rôn/), *n.* Juan Domingo, born 1902, president of Argentina since 1946.

per·o·ra·tion (pĕr/ə rā/shən), *n.* the concluding part of a speech or discourse.

per·ox·ide (pər ŏk/sĭd), *n.*, *v.*, **-ided, -iding. —n.** Also, **per·ox·id** (pər ŏk/sĭd). **1.** *Chem.* **a.** that oxide of an element or radical which contains an unusually large amount of oxygen. **b.** hydrogen peroxide, H_2O_2. **—v.t. 2.** to use peroxide (def. 1b) on (the hair) as a bleach.

per·pen·dic·u·lar (pûr/pən dĭk/yə lər), *adj.* **1.** vertical; upright. **2.** *Geom.* meeting a given line or surface at right angles. **—n. 3.** a perpendicular line or plane. **4.** upright position. **—per/pen·dic/u·lar·ly,** *adv.* **—per/pen·dic·u·lar/i·ty,** *n.*

per·pe·trate (pûr/pə trāt/), *v.t.*, **-trated, -trating.** to perform, execute, or commit (something bad). **—per/pe·tra/tion,** *n.* **—per/pe·tra/tor,** *n.*

per·pet·u·al (pər pĕch/ŏŏ əl), *adj.* **1.** continuing or enduring forever. **2.** continuing without intermission. **—per·pet/u·al·ly,** *adv.*

per·pet·u·ate (pər pĕch/ŏŏ āt/), *v.t.*, **-ated, -ating.** to make perpetual. **—per·pet/u·a/tion,** *n.* **—per·pet/u·a/tor,** *n.*

per·pe·tu·i·ty (pûr/pə tū/ĭ tĭ, -tōō/-), *n.*, *pl.* **-ties.** endless duration or existence.

per·plex (pər plĕks/), *v.t.* to confuse mentally; bewilder; puzzle. **—per/plex/ing·ly,** *adv.*

per·plex·i·ty (pər plĕk/sə tĭ), *n.*, *pl.* **-ties. 1.** perplexed or puzzled condition. **2.** something that perplexes.

per·qui·site (pûr/kwə zĭt), *n.* an incidental

emolument, fee, or profit over and above fixed income, salary, or wages.

Per·ry (pĕr/ĭ), *n.* **1. Oliver Hazard,** 1785–1819, U.S. naval officer. **2. Matthew Calbraith,** 1794–1858, U.S. naval officer; persuaded Japan to open trade with U.S.

pers., 1. person. **2.** personal.

per se (pûr sē/), *Latin.* intrinsically.

per·se·cute (pûr/sə kūt/), *v.t.*, **-cuted, -cuting. 1.** to harass or oppress persistently. **2.** to oppress with injury or punishment for adherence to principles or religious faith. **—per/se·cu/tion,** *n.* **—per/se·cu/tor,** *n.*

Per·seph·o·ne (pər sĕf/ə nĭ), *n.* *Gk. Myth.* daughter of Zeus, kidnapped by Pluto to be his queen of the lower world.

Per·seus (pûr/sūs, pûr/sĭ əs), *n.* **1.** *Gk. Myth.* a hero, the son of Zeus, who slew Medusa. **2.** *Astron.* one of the northern constellations.

per·se·ver·ance (pûr/sə vĭr/əns), *n.* steady persistence in a course of action, a purpose, a state, etc.

per·se·vere (pûr/sə vĭr/), *v.i.*, **-vered, -vering.** to persist in anything undertaken; continue steadfastly. **—per/se·ver/ing·ly,** *adv.*

Per·shing (pûr/shĭng), *n.* **John Joseph,** 1860–1948, U.S. general.

Per·sia (pûr/zhə, -shə), *n.* **1.** an ancient empire centering in W and SW Asia. **2.** former official name of **Iran. —Per/sian,** *adj.*, *n.*

Persian Gulf, an arm of the Arabian Sea, between Arabia and Iran. ab. 600 mi. long.

Persian lamb, 1. the lamb which furnishes caracul. **2.** its skin, bearing closely curled lustrous hairs, usually dyed black.

per·si·flage (pûr/sə fläzh/), *n.* light, bantering talk.

per·sim·mon (pər sĭm/ən), *n.* **1.** any of certain trees, esp. one of North America, with an astringent plumlike fruit becoming sweet and edible when thoroughly ripe. **2.** the fruit.

per·sist (pər sĭst/, -zĭst/), *v.i.* **1.** to continue steadily or firmly in some state, purpose, course of action, or the like, esp. in spite of opposition, remonstrance, etc. **2.** to last or endure.

per·sist·ent (pər sĭst/ənt, -zĭst/-), *adj.* **1.** persisting, esp. in spite of opposition, etc. **2.** lasting or enduring. **3.** continued; constantly repeated. **—per·sist/ent·ly,** *adv.* **—per·sist/ence, per·sist/en·cy,** *n.*

per·son (pûr/sən), *n.* **1.** a human being. **2.** the actual self or individual personality of a human being. **3.** the living body of a human being. **4.** the body in its external aspect. **5. in person,** in one's own bodily presence. **6.** *Gram.* a category of verb inflection and of pronoun classification, distinguishing between the speaker (**first person**), the one addressed (**second person**), and anyone or anything else (**third person**).

per·son·a·ble (pûr/sən ə bəl), *adj.* of pleasing personal appearance; comely.

per·son·age (pûr/sən ĭj), *n.* **1.** a person of distinction or importance. **2.** any person. **3.** a character in a play, story, etc.

per·son·al (pûr/sən əl), *adj.* **1.** of or pertaining to a particular person; private. **2.** relating to, or directed to or aimed at, a particular person. **3.** making personal remarks or attacks. **4.** done, affected, held, etc., in person. **5.** pertaining to or characteristic of a self-conscious being. **6.** of the nature of an individual rational being. **7.** pertaining to the person, body, or bodily aspect. **8.** *Gram.* denoting a class of pronouns classified as referring to the speaker, the one addressed, and anyone or anything else. **9.** *Law.* noting or pertaining to property consisting of movable chattels, money, securities, etc. **—n. 10.** *U.S.* a short news paragraph in a newspaper, referring to a particular person or persons.

per·son·al·i·ty (pûr/sə năl/ə tĭ), *n.*, *pl.* **-ties. 1.** distinctive or notable personal character. **2.** a person as an embodiment of an assemblage of qualities. **3.** existence as a self-conscious being. **4.** a disparaging or offensive statement referring to a particular person.

per·son·al·ize (pûr/sən ə līz/), *v.t.*, **-ized, -izing.** to make personal.

per·son·al·ly (pûr/sən ə lĭ), *adv.* **1.** as regards oneself. **2.** as an individual person. **3.** in person. **4.** as (if) intended personally.

per·son·ate (pûr/sə nāt/), *v.t.*, *v.i.*, **-ated, -ating. 1.** to act or present (a character in a play, etc.). **2.** to assume the character or appearance (of). **—per/son·a/tion,** *n.* **—per/son·a/tor,** *n.*

per·son·i·fy (pər sŏn′ə fī′), v.t., -fied, -fying. 1. to attribute personal nature or character to (an inanimate object or an abstraction), as in speech or writing. 2. to represent (a thing or abstraction) in the form of a person, as in art. 3. to embody (a quality, idea, etc.) in a real person or a concrete thing. 4. to typify. 5. to personate. —per·son′i·fi·ca′tion, n. —per·son′i·fi′er, n.

per·son·nel (pûr′sə nĕl′), n. the persons employed in any work or service.

per·spec·tive (pər spĕk′tĭv), n. 1. the art of depicting landscape, etc., on a flat surface in such a way as to express dimensions and spatial relations. 2. a mental view of events, facts, etc., in proper relationships.

per·spi·ca·cious (pûr′spə kā′shəs), adj. having keen mental perception; discerning. —per′spi·ca′cious·ly, adv. —per·spi·cac·i·ty (pûr′spə kăs′ə tĭ), n.

per·spi·cu·i·ty (pûr′spə kū′ə tĭ), n. 1. clearness or lucidity, as of a statement. 2. quality of being perspicuous.

per·spic·u·ous (pər spĭk′yŏŏ əs), adj. 1. clear to the understanding. 2. lucid. —per·spic′u·ous·ly, adv.

per·spi·ra·tion (pûr′spə rā′shən), n. 1. act of perspiring. 2. sweat.

per·spire (pər spīr′), v., -spired, -spiring. —v.i. 1. to excrete watery fluid through the pores; sweat. —v.t. 2. to exude.

per·suade (pər swād′), v.t., -suaded, -suading. 1. to prevail on (a person, etc.), by advice, reasons, etc., to do something. 2. to convince. —per·suad′a·ble, adj. —per·suad′er, n.

per·sua·sion (pər swā′zhən), n. 1. act of persuading or seeking to persuade. 2. power of persuading. 3. state or fact of being persuaded. 4. a conviction or belief. 5. a form or system of belief, esp. religious belief, or the body of persons adhering to it.

per·sua·sive (pər swā′sĭv), adj. able, fitted, or intended to persuade. —per·sua′sive·ly, adv. —per·sua′sive·ness, n.

pert (pûrt), adj. bold; impertinent; saucy. —pert′ly, adv. —pert′ness, n.

pert., pertaining.

per·tain (pər tān′), v.i. 1. to have reference or relation; relate. 2. to belong or be connected as a part, adjunct, possession, attribute, etc. 3. to belong properly or fittingly.

Perth (pûrth), n. a city in SW Australia. With suburbs, 230,000.

Perth Am·boy (pûrth′ ăm′boi), a seaport in E New Jersey. 41,242.

per·ti·na·cious (pûr′tə nā′shəs), adj. 1. holding tenaciously to a purpose, course of action, or opinion. 2. extremely persistent. —per′ti·na′cious·ly, adv. —per′ti·na′cious·ness, per·ti·nac·i·ty (pûr′tə năs′ə tĭ), n.

per·ti·nent (pûr′tə nənt), adj. pertaining or relating to the matter in hand; relevant. —per′ti·nence, per′ti·nen·cy, n. —per′ti·nent·ly, adv.

per·turb (pər tûrb′), v.t. to disturb greatly; agitate. —per·turb′a·ble, adj. —per·tur·ba·tion (pûr′tər bā′shən), n.

per·tus·sis (pər tŭs′ĭs), n. Pathol. whooping cough. —per·tus′sal, adj.

Pe·ru (pə rōō′), n. a republic in W South America. 6,838,000 pop.; 284,258 sq. mi. Cap.: Lima. —Pe·ru′vi·an, adj., n.

pe·ruke (pə rōōk′), n. a wig, esp. of the kind worn by men in the 17th and 18th centuries.

pe·rus·al (pə rōō′zəl), n. 1. a reading. 2. act of perusing; survey or scrutiny.

pe·ruse (pə rōōz′), v.t., -rused, -rusing. to read, esp. with thoroughness or care. —pe·rus′er, n.

Peruvian bark, cinchona (def. 2).

per·vade (pər vād′), v.t., -vaded, -vading. 1. to extend its presence, activities, influence, etc., throughout. 2. to go everywhere thoroughly (a place), as a person. 3. to go, pass, or spread through. —per·vad′er, n. —per·va·sion (pər vā′zhən), n. —per·va·sive (pər vā′sĭv), adj. —per·va′sive·ly, adv. —per·va′sive·ness, n.

Man wearing a peruke

per·verse (pər vûrs′), adj. 1. determined or disposed to go counter to what is expected or desired; contrary. 2. characterized by or proceeding from such a determination. —per·verse′ly, adv. —per·verse′ness, per·ver′si·ty, n.

per·ver·sion (pər vûr′zhən, -shən), n. 1. act of perverting. 2. state of being perverted. 3. a perverted form of something. 4. Psychiatry. perverted or abnormal condition of the sexual instincts.

per·vert (v. pər vûrt′; n. pûr′vûrt), v.t. 1. to turn away from the right course. 2. to lead astray morally. 3. to turn to an improper use; misapply. 4. to distort. 5. to affect with perversion. —n. 6. one affected with perversion. —per·vert′er, n.

per·vi·ous (pûr′vĭ əs), adj. 1. admitting of passage or entrance; permeable. 2. accessible to reason, feeling, etc. —per′vi·ous·ness, n.

pe·se·ta (pə sā′tə), n. Spanish. 1. the monetary unit of Spain, equivalent to 19.3 U.S. cents. 2. a silver coin nominally of this value.

Pe·sha·war (pĕ shä′wər), n. a city in Pakistan, near the Khyber Pass. 130,967.

pes·ky (pĕs′kĭ), adj., -kier, -kiest. U.S. Colloq. troublesome; annoying.

pe·so (pā′sō), n., pl. -sos (-sōz; Sp. -sôs). 1. the monetary unit and a silver coin of Mexico, equivalent now to about 13 U.S. cents. 2. the monetary unit and a gold or silver coin of Cuba, equal to 100 centavos, or one U.S. dollar. 3. any of various monetary units and coins of Central and South America. 4. the monetary unit and a silver coin of the Philippine Islands, worth 50 U.S. cents.

pes·sa·ry (pĕs′ə rĭ), n., pl. -ries. Med. 1. an instrument worn in the vagina to remedy uterine displacement. 2. a contraceptive device worn in the vagina or uterine cervix.

pes·si·mism (pĕs′ə mĭz′əm), n. 1. disposition to take the gloomiest possible view. 2. the doctrine that the existing world is the worst of all possible worlds, or that all things naturally tend to evil. —pes′si·mist, n. —pes′si·mis′tic, adj. —pes′si·mis′ti·cal·ly, adv.

pest (pĕst), n. 1. a noxious, destructive, or troublesome thing or person; nuisance. 2. a deadly epidemic disease; pestilence.

pes·ter (pĕs′tər), v.t. to harass with petty annoyances; vex; torment.

pest·house (pĕst′hous′), n. a place for persons infected with pestilential disease.

pes·ti·cide (pĕs′tə sīd′), n. a chemical substance for destroying pests, such as mosquitos, flies, etc.

pes·tif·er·ous (pĕs tĭf′ər əs), adj. 1. pestilential. 2. Colloq. troublesome or annoying. —pes·tif′er·ous·ly, adv.

pes·ti·lence (pĕs′tə ləns), n. 1. a deadly epidemic disease. 2. that which produces or tends to produce epidemic disease. 3. the bubonic plague. —pes′ti·len′tial, adj.

pes·ti·lent (pĕs′tə lənt), adj. 1. infectious, as a disease. 2. producing or tending to produce infectious disease. 3. deadly; poisonous. 4. injurious to peace, morals, etc. 5. troublesome or annoying. —pes′ti·lent·ly, adv.

pes·tle (pĕs′əl, pĕs′təl), n., v., -tled, -tling. —n. 1. an instrument for pounding or crushing substances in a mortar. 2. any of various appliances for pounding, stamping, etc. —v.t., v.i. 3. to pound or triturate with a pestle.

pet¹ (pĕt), n., adj., v., petted, petting. —n. 1. any domesticated or tamed animal that is kept as a favorite and cared for affectionately. 2. a favorite. —adj. 3. treated as a pet, as an animal. 4. favorite. 5. showing affection. —v.t. 6. to indulge or pat affectionately. 7. U.S. Slang. to fondle or caress.

pet² (pĕt), n. 1. a fit of peevishness. —v.i. 2. to be peevish; sulk.

Pé·tain (pĕ tăN′), n. Henri Philippe, 1856–1951, French general.

pet·al (pĕt′əl), n. Bot. one of the members of a corolla. —pet′aled, pet′alled, adj.

pe·tard (pĭ tärd′), n. 1. an explosive device formerly used to blow in a gate, breach a wall, etc. 2. hoist on one's own petard, caught in one's own trap.

pet·cock (pĕt′kŏk′), n. a small valve or faucet. Also, **pet cock**.

Pe·ter (pē′tər), n. died A.D. 67?, one of the twelve apostles: reputed author of two New Testament epistles bearing his name.

pe·ter (pē′tər), v.i. U.S. Colloq. to diminish gradually and then disappear or cease (fol. by out).

Peter I, ("the Great") 1672–1725, czar of Russia, 1682–1725.

Peter II, born 1923, king of Yugoslavia, 1934–1945.

Pe·ters·burg (pē'tərz bûrg'), *n.* a city in SE Virginia. 30,631.

Peter the Hermit, c1050–1115, French monk: preacher of the first Crusade.

pet·i·ole (pĕt'ī ōl'), *n. Bot.* the slender stalk by which a leaf is attached to the stem; leafstalk. —**pet·i·o·lar** (pĕt'ī ə lər), *adj.* —**pet·i·o·late** (pĕt'ī ə lāt'), *adj.*

pet·it (pĕt'ī), *adj. Law.* petty.

pe·tite (pə tēt'), *adj. French.* little; tiny.

pet·it four (pĕt'ī fōr'), *pl.* **petits fours** (pĕt'ī fōrz'). a small tea cake, variously frosted and decorated.

pe·ti·tion (pə tĭsh'ən), *n.* 1. a formal request to a person or group in authority or power, soliciting some favor, right, mercy, or benefit. 2. any request, esp. a respectful or humble request. 3. that which is sought by request. —*v.t.* 4. to entreat, supplicate, or beg, as for something desired. —*v.i.* 5. to present a petition. —**pe·ti'tion·er,** *n.*

pet·it jury (pĕt'ī), petty jury.

Pe·trarch (pē'trärk), *n.* 1304–74, Italian poet and scholar.

pet·rel (pĕt'rəl), *n.* any of certain small, long-winged, usually black-and-white, oceanic birds (known as Mother Carey's chickens), esp. the stormy or **storm petrel.**

pet·ri·fy (pĕt'rə fī'), *v.,* **-fied, -fying.** —*v.t.* 1. to convert into stone or a stony substance. 2. to make rigid; stiffen or benumb. 3. to stupefy or paralyze with fear, etc. —*v.i.* 4. to become petrified. —**pet·ri·fac·tion** (pĕt'rə făk'shən), **pet'·ri·fi·ca'tion,** *n.*

Pet·ro·grad (pĕt'rə grăd'), *n.* former name of Leningrad (1914–24).

pe·trog·ra·phy (pĭ trŏg'rə fĭ), *n.* the scientific description and classification of rocks. —**pe·trog'ra·pher,** *n.*

pet·rol (pĕt'rəl), *n. Brit.* gasoline.

pet·ro·la·tum (pĕt'rə lā'təm), *n.* an unctuous substance obtained from petroleum, used as a basis for ointments, etc.

pe·tro·le·um (pə trō'lĭ əm), *n.* an oily, usually dark-colored liquid (a form of bitumen or mixture of various hydrocarbons), occurring naturally in various parts of the world: source of gasoline, naphtha, benzine, kerosene, paraffin, etc.

pe·trol·o·gy (pĭ trŏl'ə jĭ), *n., pl.* **-gies.** the scientific study of rocks, their origin, structure, etc. —**pet·ro·log·ic** (pĕt'rə lŏj'ĭk), **pet'ro·log'i·cal,** *adj.* —**pe·trol'o·gist,** *n.*

pet·ti·coat (pĕt'ī kōt'), *n.* 1. a skirt, esp. an underskirt, worn by women and children. 2. *Chiefly Humorous.* a woman or girl.

pet·ti·fog (pĕt'ī fŏg', -fôg'), *v.i.,* **-fogged, -fogging.** to carry on a petty or shifty law business. —**pet'ti·fog'ger,** *n.*

pet·tish (pĕt'ĭsh), *adj.* peevish; petulant. —**pet'tish·ly,** *adv.*

pet·ty (pĕt'ĭ), *adj.,* **-tier, -tiest.** 1. trifling; trivial. 2. of secondary importance, merit, etc. 3. having or showing narrow ideas, interests, etc. 4. mean or small-minded. —**pet'ti·ly,** *adv.* —**pet'ti·ness,** *n.*

petty jury, a jury, usually of 12 persons, impaneled to determine the facts of a case and render a verdict.

petty officer, a noncommissioned navy officer.

pet·u·lant (pĕch'ə lənt), *adj.* moved to or showing sudden, impatient irritation, esp. over some trifling annoyance. —**pet'u·lant·ly,** *adv.* —**pet'u·lance, pet'u·lan·cy,** *n.*

pe·tu·ni·a (pə tū'nĭ ə, -tōō'-), *n.* any of certain herbs of the nightshade family, bearing funnel-shaped flowers of various colors.

pew (pū), *n.* 1. a fixed benchlike seat with a back, in a church. 2. an enclosure with seats reserved for a particular family or other worshipers.

pe·wee (pē'wē), *n.* 1. wood pewee. 2. the phoebe.

pe·wit (pē'wĭt, pū'ĭt), *n.* 1. the lapwing. 2. the phoebe. 3. the European black-headed gull.

pew·ter (pū'tər), *n.* 1. any of various alloys in which tin is the chief constituent. 2. a utensil made of such an alloy. 3. such utensils collectively. —*adj.* 4. of pewter.

pf., 1. Also, **pfg.** pfennig. 2. preferred.

Pfc., *Mil.* private first class.

pfd., preferred.

pfen·nig (pfĕn'ĭg), *n., pl.* **-nigs, -nige** (-ĭ gə). a small bronze coin and money of account of Germany: 1/100 of a mark.

pha·e·ton (fā'ə tən), *n.* 1. a light four-wheeled carriage, having seats facing forward. 2. an automobile of the touring-car type.

pha·lan·ger (fə lăn'jər), *n.* any of numerous arboreal marsupials of the Australian region.

pha·lanx (fā'lăngks, făl'ăngks), *n., pl.* **pha·lanxes** (fā'lăngk sĭz), **phalanges** (fə lăn'jēz). 1. (in ancient Greece) a body of infantry in close formation with shields joined and long spears overlapping. 2. a compact body of persons, animals, or things. 3. a number of persons, etc., united for a common purpose. 4. *Anat., Zool.* any of the bones of the fingers or toes.

phal·lus (făl'əs), *n., pl.* **phalli** (făl'ī). 1. an image of the male reproductive organ, symbolizing in certain religious systems the generative power in nature. 2. *Anat.* the penis or clitoris. —**phal'lic, phal'li·cal,** *adj.*

phan·tasm (făn'tăz əm), *n.* 1. an apparition or specter. 2. a creation of the imagination. 3. an illusive likeness. —**phan·tas'mal,** *adj.*

phan·tas·ma·go·ri·a (făn tăz'mə gōr'ĭ ə), *n.* a shifting series of phantasms or illusions, as in a dream. —**phan·tas'ma·go'ri·al, phan·tas'·ma·gor'ic,** *adj.*

phan·ta·sy (făn'tə sĭ, -zĭ), *n., pl.* **-sies.** fantasy.

phan·tom (făn'təm), *n.* 1. an image appearing in a dream or imagined. 2. an apparition or specter. —*adj.* 3. unreal; illusive; spectral.

Phar·aoh (fâr'ō, fâr'ĭ ō'), *n.* a title of the ancient Egyptian kings.

Phar·i·sa·ic (făr'ə sā'ĭk), *adj.* 1. of or pertaining to the Pharisees. 2. *(l.c.)* Also, **phar'i·sa'·i·cal.** self-righteous; hypocritical. —**phar'i·sa'·i·cal·ly,** *adv.*

Phar·i·sa·ism (făr'ə sā ĭz'əm), *n.* 1. the doctrine and practice of the Pharisees. 2. *(l.c.)* hypocrisy. Also, **Phar·i·see·ism** (făr'ə sē ĭz'əm).

Phar·i·see (făr'ə sē'), *n.* 1. one of an ancient Jewish sect which believed in the validity of the oral law and in the free interpretation of the written law by seeking to discover its inner meaning. 2. *(l.c.)* a self-righteous or hypocritical person.

Pharm., pharmacy.

phar·ma·ceu·tic (fär'mə sōō'tĭk), *adj.* pertaining to pharmacy. Also, **phar'ma·ceu'ti·cal.** —**phar'ma·ceu'ti·cal·ly,** *adv.*

phar·ma·ceu·tics (fär'mə sōō'tĭks), *n.* pharmacy (def. 1).

phar·ma·cist (fär'mə sĭst), *n.* one skilled in pharmacy; druggist.

phar·ma·col·o·gy (fär'mə kŏl'ə jĭ), *n.* the science of drugs, their preparation, uses, and effects. —**phar·ma·co·log·i·cal** (fär'mə kə lŏj'ə kəl), *adj.* —**phar'ma·col'o·gist,** *n.*

phar·ma·co·poe·ia (fär'mə kə pē'ə), *n.* an authoritative book on drugs and medicines. —**phar'ma·co·poe'ial,** *adj.*

phar·ma·cy (fär'mə sĭ), *n., pl.* **-cies.** 1. the art or practice of preparing and dispensing drugs and medicines. 2. a drug store.

phar·yn·gi·tis (făr'ĭn jī'tĭs), *n.* inflammation of the mucous membrane of the pharynx.

phar·ynx (făr'ĭngks), *n., pl.* **pharynges** (fə rĭn'jēz), **pharynxes.** *Anat.* the tube or cavity which connects the mouth and nasal passages with the esophagus. —**pha·ryn·ge·al** (fə rĭn'jĭ əl), **pha·ryn·gal** (fə rĭng'gəl), *adj.*

phase (fāz), *n.* 1. one aspect or view of a thing. 2. a stage of change or development. 3. *Astron.* the particular appearance presented by a planet, etc., at a given time. 4. *Chem.* a mechanically separate, homogeneous part of a heterogeneous system. 5. *Physics.* a particular stage or point of advancement in a cycle.

Ph. B., Bachelor of Philosophy.

Ph. D., Doctor of Philosophy.

pheas·ant (fĕz'ənt), *n.* any of various large, long-tailed gallinaceous birds, orig. natives of Asia, with brilliant feathers.

phe·nac·e·tin (fə năs'ə tĭn), *n. Pharm.* a crystalline organic compound used as an antipyretic, etc. Also, **phe·nac'e·tine.**

phe·nix (fē'nĭks), *n.* phoenix.

phe·no·bar·bi·tal (fē'nō bär'bə tăl', -tôl'), *n.* a white, odorless powder, used as a sedative or hypnotic.

phe·nol (fē'nŏl, -nōl), *n.* *Chem.* carbolic acid: a hydroxyl derivative of benzene used as a disinfectant, antiseptic, and in organic synthesis. —**phe·no·lic** (fĭ nō'lĭk, -nŏl'ĭk), *adj.*

phe·nol·phthal·ein (fē'nōl thăl'ēn, -fthăl'ĭ-ĭn, fē'nōl-), *n.* a white crystalline compound, used as a laxative.

phe·nom·e·nal (fĭ nŏm'ə nəl), *adj.* **1.** extraordinary or prodigious. **2.** of or pertaining to a phenomenon or phenomena. **3.** cognizable by the senses. —**phe·nom'e·nal·ly,** *adv.*

phe·nom·e·non (fĭ nŏm'ə nŏn'), *n.,* *pl.* **-na** (-nə). **1.** an observed or observable fact, occurrence, or circumstance. **2.** an extraordinary thing or person. **3.** *Philos.* an object of awareness in experience.

phew (fū, pfū), *interj.* an exclamation of disgust, impatience, exhaustion, etc.

phi (fī, fē), *n.* the twenty-first letter (Φ, φ) of the Greek alphabet.

phi·al (fī'əl), *n.* vial (def. 1).

Phil., Philippine.

Phil·a·del·phi·a (fĭl'ə dĕl'fĭ ə), *n.* a city in SE Pennsylvania. With suburbs, 2,898,644.

phi·lan·der (fĭ lăn'dər), *v.i.* (of a man) to make love, esp. without serious intentions. —**phi·lan'der·er,** *n.*

phi·lan·thro·py (fĭ lăn'thrə pĭ), *n.,* *pl.* **-pies.** **1.** love of mankind, esp. as manifested in deeds of practical beneficence. **2.** a benevolent action, work, institution, or the like. —**phil·an·throp·ic** (fĭl'ən thrŏp'ĭk), **phil'an·throp'i·cal,** *adj.* —**phi·lan'thro·pist,** *n.*

phi·lat·e·ly (fĭ lăt'ə lĭ), *n.* the collecting and study of postage stamps, revenue stamps, stamped envelopes, postmarks, post cards, etc. —**phil·a·tel·ic** (fĭl'ə tĕl'ĭk), **phil·a·tel'i·cal,** *adj.* —**phi·lat·e·list** (fĭ lăt'ə lĭst), *n.*

Phi·le·mon (fĭ lē'mən), *n.* **the Epistle of Paul to,** a New Testament epistle, written by Paul.

phil·har·mon·ic (fĭl'här mŏn'ĭk, fĭl'ər-), *adj.* fond of music; music-loving.

Phil·ip (fĭl'ĭp), *n.* **1.** one of the twelve apostles chosen by Jesus. **2.** II, 382–336 B.C., king of Macedonia, 359–336 B.C. (father of Alexander the Great). **3.** Prince, (*Duke of Edinburgh*) born 1921, husband of Queen Elizabeth II of England.

Phi·lip·pi·ans (fĭ lĭp'ĭ ənz), *n.pl.* the epistle of Paul to the Christian community in Philippi (a city in NE Greece), in the New Testament.

Phi·lip·pic (fĭ lĭp'ĭk), *n.* **1.** any of the orations delivered by Demosthenes against Philip of Macedonia. **2.** (*l.c.*) any bitter denunciation.

Phil·ip·pine (fĭl'ə pēn'), *adj.* of or pertaining to the Philippine Islands or their inhabitants.

Philippine Islands, an archipelago of 7083 islands in the Pacific, SE of China: formerly under the guardianship of the U.S., but now an independent republic. 16,000,303 pop.; ab. 115,600 sq. mi. *Cap.:* Manila. Also, **Philippines.** Official name, **Republic of the Philippines.**

Phi·lis·tine (fĭ lĭs'tĭn, fĭl'ə stēn', -stĭn'), –*n.* **1.** a member of a non-Semitic people who settled on the coast of Palestine about 1200 B.C. **2.** one lacking in and indifferent to culture, aesthetic refinement, etc. —*adj.* **3.** lacking in culture. **4.** of the ancient Philistines. —**Phi·lis·tin·ism** (fĭ lĭs'tĭ nĭz'əm, fĭl'ĭ stĭ-), *n.*

phil·o·den·dron (fĭl'ə dĕn' drən), *n.* a common climbing plant, usually with smooth, shiny evergreen leaves.

phi·lol·o·gy (fĭ lŏl'ə jĭ), *n.* **1.** the study of written records. **2.** linguistics. —**phil·o·log·i·cal** (fĭl'ə lŏj'ə kəl), **phil·o·log'ic,** *adj.* —**phi·lol'o·gist,** *n.*

phil·o·mel (fĭl'ə mĕl'), *n.* *Poetic.* the nightingale. Also, **phil'o·me'la.**

phil·o·pro·gen·i·tive (fĭl'ō prō jĕn'ə tĭv), *adj.* fond of young children, esp. one's own.

philos., philosophy.

phi·los·o·pher (fĭ lŏs'ə fər), *n.* **1.** one versed in philosophy. **2.** a person who regulates his actions, judgments, etc., by the light of philosophy or reason. **3.** one who is philosophical (def. 4).

phil·o·soph·i·cal (fĭl'ə sŏf'ə kəl), *adj.* **1.** of or pertaining to philosophy. **2.** versed in or occupied with philosophy. **3.** befitting a philosopher. **4.** rationally calm under trying circumstances. Also, **phil'o·soph'ic.** —**phil'o·soph'i·cal·ly,** *adv.*

phi·los·o·phize (fĭ lŏs'ə fīz'), *v.i.,* **-phized, -phizing.** to speculate or theorize. —**phi·los'o·phiz'er,** *n.*

phi·los·o·phy (fĭ lŏs'ə fĭ), *n., pl.* **-phies.** **1.** the

study or science of the truths or principles underlying all knowledge and being. **2.** a system of philosophical doctrine. **3.** the science of the principles of a particular subject of knowledge.

phil·ter (fĭl'tər), *n., v.,* **-tered, -tering.** —*n.* **1.** a potion, drug, or the like, supposed to induce love. **2.** any magic potion. —*v.t.* **3.** to charm with a philter. Also, *esp. Brit.,* **phil'tre.**

phle·bot·o·my (flĭ bŏt'ə mĭ), *n., pl.* **-mies.** *Med.* act or practice of opening a vein for letting blood; bleeding. —**phle·bot'o·mist,** *n.* —**phle·bot'o·mize,** *v.t.*

phlegm (flĕm), *n.* **1.** *Physiol.* the thick mucus secreted in the respiratory passages and discharged by coughing, etc. **2.** sluggishness or apathy. **3.** coolness or self-possession. —**phlegm'y,** *adj.* —**phleg·mat·ic** (flĕg măt'ĭk), **phleg·mat'i·cal,** *adj.* —**phleg·mat'i·cal·ly,** *adv.*

phlox (flŏks), *n.* any of certain herbs, native to North America, many of which are cultivated for their showy flowers of various colors.

pho·bi·a (fō'bĭ ə), *n.* any obsessing or morbid fear or dread. —**pho'bic,** *adj.*

Phoe·be (fē'bĭ), *n.* **1.** *Gk. Myth.* Artemis as goddess of the moon. **2.** *Poetic.* the moon.

phoe·be (fē'bĭ), *n.* any of certain small American birds; pewit; pewee.

Phoe·bus (fē'bəs), *n.* **1.** *Gk. Myth.* Apollo as the sun god. **2.** *Poetic.* the sun.

Phoe·ni·cia (fĭ nĭsh'ə), *n.* an ancient maritime country on the E coast of the Mediterranean. —**Phoe·ni'cian,** *n., adj.*

phoe·nix (fē'nĭks), *n.* (*also cap.*) a mythical bird of great beauty, the only one of its kind, fabled to live 500 or 600 years, to burn itself on a funeral pile, and to rise from its ashes in the freshness of youth for another cycle of years.

Phoe·nix (fē'nĭks), *n.* the capital of Arizona, in the central part. 65,414.

phone[1] (fōn), *n., v.t., v.i.,* **phoned, phoning.** *Colloq.* telephone.

phone[2] (fōn), *n.* *Phonet.* an individual speech sound.

pho·neme (fō'nēm), *n.* *Phonet.* the smallest distinctive group or class of phones in a language. —**pho·ne'mic,** *adj.*

pho·ne·mics (fō nē'mĭks), *n.* the science of phonemic systems and contrasts. —**pho·ne·mi·cist** (fō nē'mə sĭst), *n.*

phonet., phonetics.

pho·net·ic (fō nĕt'ĭk), *adj.* of or pertaining to speech sounds and their production. Also, **pho·net'i·cal.** —**pho·net'i·cal·ly,** *adv.*

pho·net·ics (fō nĕt'ĭks), *n.* the science of speech sounds and their production. —**pho·ne·ti·cian** (fō'nə tĭsh'ən), *n.*

phon·ic (fŏn'ĭk, fō'nĭk), *adj.* of or pertaining to speech sounds.

phon·ics (fŏn'ĭks, fō'nĭks), *n.* a method of teaching reading, pronunciation, and spelling based upon the phonetic interpretation of ordinary spelling.

pho·no·graph (fō'nə grăf', -grāf'), *n.* any sound-reproducing machine using records. —**pho'no·graph'ic,** *adj.* —**pho'no·graph'i·cal·ly,** *adv.*

pho·nol·o·gy (fō nŏl'ə jĭ), *n.* phonetics or phonemics, or both together. —**pho·no·log·ic** (fō'nə lŏj'ĭk), **pho'no·log'i·cal,** *adj.* —**pho·no·log'i·cal·ly,** *adv.* —**pho·nol'o·gist,** *n.*

pho·ny (fō'nĭ), *adj.,* **-nier, -niest,** *n., pl.* **-nies.** *U.S. Slang.* —*adj.* **1.** not genuine; counterfeit; fraudulent. —*n.* **2.** a counterfeit or fake. **3.** a faker. Also, **pho'ney.**

phos·gene (fŏs'jēn), *n.* *Chem.* carbonyl chloride: a poisonous gas used in chemical warfare and in organic synthesis.

phos·phate (fŏs'fāt), *n.* **1.** *Chem.* a salt or ester of phosphoric acid. **2.** *Agric.* a fertilizer containing phosphorus. **3.** a drink of carbonated water, fruit syrup, and phosphoric acid.

phos·pho·resce (fŏs'fə rĕs'), *v.i.,* **-resced, -rescing.** to be luminous without sensible heat, as phosphorus. —**phos'pho·res'cence,** *n.* —**phos'pho·res'cent,** *adj.*

phos·phor·ic (fŏs fôr'ĭk, -fŏr'-), *adj.* *Chem.* pertaining to or containing the element phosphorus, esp. in its pentavalent state.

phos·pho·rous (fŏs'fə rəs, fŏs fôr'əs), *adj.* *Chem.* containing trivalent phosphorus.

phos·pho·rus (fŏs'fə rəs), *n., pl.* **-ri** (-rī'). *Chem.* a solid nonmetallic element, existing in at least two allotropic forms: a necessary constituent in plant and animal life. *Symbol:* P; *at. wt.:*

photo 359 **picador**

30.98; *at. no.*: 15; *sp. gr.*: (yellow) 1.82 at 20°C., (red) 2.20 at 20°C.

pho·to (fō′tō), *n.*, *pl.* **-tos.** *Colloq.* photograph.

pho·to·e·lec·tric (fō′tō ĭ lĕk′trĭk), *adj.* pertaining to the electronic or other electrical effects produced by light.

photoelectric cell, *Electronics.* a device incorporated in an electric circuit to make the resistance or electromotive force of part of the circuit variable in accordance with variations in the intensity of light falling upon it.

pho·to·en·grav·ing (fō′tō ĕn grā′vĭng), *n.* **1.** a process of preparing printing plates for letterpress printing. **2.** a process of photographic reproduction by which a relief-printing surface is obtained for letterpress printing. **3.** a plate so produced. —**pho′to·en·grav′er,** *n.*

pho·to·flash lamp (fō′tə flăsh′), *Photog.* a bulb that gives an intense light for a fraction of a second.

pho·to·flood lamp (fō′tə flŭd′), *Photog.* an incandescent tungsten lamp, in which high intensity is obtained by overloading.

Photog., photography.

pho·to·gen·ic (fō′tə jĕn′ĭk), *adj.* **1.** *Photog.* suitable for being photographed for artistic purposes, etc. **2.** *Biol.* emitting light; phosphorescent.

pho·to·graph (fō′tə grăf′, -gräf′), *n.* **1.** a picture produced by photography. —*v.t., v.i.* **2.** to take a photograph (of). —**pho·tog·ra·pher** (fə tŏg′rə fər), *n.*

pho·tog·ra·phy (fə tŏg′rə fĭ), *n.* the process or art of producing images of objects on sensitized surfaces by the chemical action of light or of other forms of radiant energy, as x-rays, gamma rays, cosmic rays, etc. —**pho·to·graph·ic** (fō′tə grăf′ĭk), **pho′to·graph′i·cal,** *adj.* —**pho′to·graph′i·cal·ly,** *adv.*

pho·to·gra·vure (fō′tə grə vyŏŏr′, -grāv′yər), *n.* **1.** any of various processes, based on photography, by which an intaglio engraving is formed on a metal printing plate. **2.** the plate.

pho·tom·e·ter (fō tŏm′ə tər), *n.* an instrument for measuring the intensity of light.

pho·tom·e·try (fō tŏm′ə trĭ), *n.* the measurement of the intensity of light. —**pho·to·met·ric** (fō′tə mĕt′rĭk), **pho′to·met′ri·cal,** *adj.* —**pho·tom′e·trist,** *n.*

pho·to·mon·tage (fō′tə mŏn täzh′, -mŏn-), *n.* *Photog.* a combination of several photographs joined together for artistic effect.

pho·to·mu·ral (fō′tə myŏŏr′əl), *n.* a photograph decorating most of a wall.

pho·ton (fō′tŏn), *n.* *Physics.* a quantum of light energy, the energy being proportional to the frequency of the radiation.

pho·to·play (fō′tə plā′), *n.* a play presented in moving pictures.

pho·to·sen·si·tive (fō′tə sĕn′sə tĭv), *adj.* sensitive to light or similar radiation.

Pho·to·stat (fō′tə stăt′), *n.* **1.** *Trademark.* a special camera for making facsimile copies of maps, documents, etc. **2.** (*l.c.*) a copy made with it. —*v.t., v.i.* **3.** (*l.c.*) to make such a copy or copies (of). —**pho′to·stat′ic,** *adj.*

pho·to·syn·the·sis (fō′tə sĭn′thə sĭs), *n.* *Bot.* a process of green plants by which carbohydrates are formed from the carbon dioxide and water of the air under the influence of light.

phrase (frāz), *n., v.,* **phrased, phrasing.** —*n.* **1.** *Gram.* a sequence of two or more words arranged in a grammatical construction and acting as a unit in the sentence. **2.** a characteristic, current, or proverbial expression. **3.** *Music.* a division of a composition, commonly a passage of four or eight measures, forming part of a period. —*v.t.* **4.** to express or word in a particular way. —**phras′al,** *adj.*

phra·se·ol·o·gy (frā′zĭ ŏl′ə jĭ), *n.* **1.** manner or style of verbal expression. **2.** expressions.

phre·net·ic (frĭ nĕt′ĭk), *adj.* **1.** delirious; insane. —*n.* **2.** a phrenetic individual.

phre·nol·o·gy (frĕ nŏl′ə jĭ), *n.* the theory that one's mental powers are indicated by the shape of the skull. —**phren·o·log·ic** (frĕn′ə lŏj′ĭk), **phren′o·log′i·cal,** *adj.* —**phre·nol′o·gist,** *n.*

Phryg·i·a (frĭj′ĭ ə), *n.* an ancient country in central and NW Asia Minor. —**Phryg′i·an,** *adj., n.*

phthis·ic (tĭz′ĭk), *n.* *Pathol.* a wasting disease of the lungs. Also, **phthi·sis** (thī′sĭs, thī′-). —**phthis′i·cal,** *adj.*

Phyfe (fīf), *n.* Duncan, 1768–1854, U.S. furniture maker.

phy·lac·ter·y (fə lăk′tə rĭ), *n., pl.* **-teries.** either of two small leather cases containing slips with Biblical inscriptions, worn by Jews, one on the head and one on the left arm, during certain prayers.

phy·lum (fī′ləm), *n., pl.* **-la** (-lə). **1.** *Biol.* a primary division of the animal or vegetable kingdom. **2.** a group of linguistic stocks or families having no known relations outside the group.

phys., **1.** physical. **2.** physics.

phys·ic (fĭz′ĭk), *n., v.,* **-icked, -icking.** —*n.* **1.** a medicine that purges; cathartic. **2.** any medicine. —*v.t.* **3.** to treat with medicine. **4.** to treat with or to act upon as a cathartic; purge.

phys·i·cal (fĭz′ə kəl), *adj.* **1.** pertaining to the body; bodily. **2.** of matter; material. **3.** pertaining to physics. —**phys′i·cal·ly,** *adv.*

physical chemistry, that branch of chemistry which deals with the relations between the physical (i.e. electrical, optical, etc.) properties of substances and their chemical composition and transformations.

physical education, gymnastic and hygienic instruction.

physical geography, that part of geography concerned with natural features and phenomena of the earth's surface.

physical science, the study of natural laws and processes other than those peculiar to living matter, as in physics, chemistry, astronomy, etc.

phy·si·cian (fə zĭsh′ən), *n.* one legally qualified to practice medicine.

phys·ics (fĭz′ĭks), *n.* the science dealing with natural laws and processes, and the states and properties of matter and energy, other than those restricted to living matter and to chemical changes. —**phys·i·cist** (fĭz′ə sĭst), *n.*

phys·i·og·no·my (fĭz′ĭ ŏg′nə mĭ, -ŏn′ə mĭ), *n., pl.* **-mies.** **1.** the face, esp. as considered as an index to the character. **2.** the art of determining character from the features of the face. —**phys′-i·og′no·mist,** *n.*

phys·i·og·ra·phy (fĭz′ĭ ŏg′rə fĭ), *n.* physical geography. —**phys·i·o·graph·ic** (fĭz′ĭ ə grăf′ĭk), **phys′i·o·graph′i·cal,** *adj.*

physiol., **1.** physiological. **2.** physiology.

phys·i·ol·o·gy (fĭz′ĭ ŏl′ə jĭ), *n.* the science dealing with the functions of living organisms or their parts. —**phys·i·o·log·i·cal** (fĭz′ĭ ə lŏj′ə kəl), **phys′i·o·log′ic,** *adj.* —**phys′i·o·log′i·cal·ly,** *adv.* —**phys′i·ol′o·gist,** *n.*

phys·i·o·ther·a·py (fĭz′ĭ ō thĕr′ə pĭ), *n.* the treatment of disease or bodily weaknesses or defects by physical remedies, such as massage, gymnastics, etc. (rather than by drugs).

phy·sique (fĭ zēk′), *n.* physical or bodily structure, organization, or development.

pi¹ (pī), *n., pl.* **pis.** **1.** the sixteenth letter (Π, π) of the Greek alphabet. **2.** *Math.* the letter π, used as the symbol for the ratio (3.141592+) of the circumference of a circle to its diameter.

pi² (pī), *n., v.,* **pied, piing.** *Print. U.S.* —*n.* **1.** confused type. —*v.t.* **2.** to reduce to confusion.

P.I., Philippine Islands.

pi·a·nis·si·mo (pē′ə nĭs′ə mō′), *adj., adv., n., pl.* **-mos, -mi** (-mē′). *Music.* —*adj.* **1.** very soft. —*adv.* **2.** very softly. —*n.* **3.** a passage or movement played in this way.

pi·an·ist (pĭ ăn′ĭst, pē′ə nĭst), *n.* a performer on the piano.

pi·an·o¹ (pĭ ăn′ō), *n., pl.* **-anos.** a musical instrument in which hammers, operated from a keyboard, strike upon metal strings.

pi·a·no² (pĭ ä′nō), *Music.* —*adj.* **1.** soft; subdued. —*adv.* **2.** softly.

pi·an·o·for·te (pĭ ăn′ə fōr′tĭ, pĭ ăn′ə fôrt′), *n.* the piano.

pi·as·ter (pĭ ăs′tər), *n.* the monetary coin unit of Turkey, worth about 4.4 U.S. cents. Also, **pi·as′tre.**

pi·az·za (pĭ ăz′ə), *n.* **1.** an open square in a city. **2.** *Chiefly U.S.* a veranda of a house.

pi·broch (pē′brŏкн), *n.* (in the Scottish Highlands) a dirge or warlike tune performed on the bagpipe.

pi·ca (pī′kə), *n.* *Print.* **1.** a size of type (12 point). **2.** the depth of this type size (about 1/6 of an inch) as a unit of linear measurement for type, etc.

pic·a·dor (pĭk′ə dôr′), *n.* one of the horsemen

who open a bullfight by enraging the bull with pricks of lances.

Pic·ar·dy (pĭk'ər dĭ), n. a region in N France.

pic·a·resque (pĭk'ə rĕsk'), adj. of or pertaining to rogues: applied to a type of fiction with a rogue or adventurer for hero.

Pi·cas·so (pē käs'sō), n. **Pablo**, born 1881, Spanish-French painter and sculptor.

pic·a·yune (pĭk'ĭ ūn'), n. **1.** U.S. any small coin. **2.** Colloq. an insignificant person or thing. —adj. **3.** Colloq. Also, **pic'a·yun'ish.** small; petty.

Pic·ca·dil·ly (pĭk'ə dĭl'ĭ), n. a street in London, noted for its shops, clubs, etc.

pic·ca·lil·li (pĭk'ə lĭl'ĭ), n., pl. **-lis.** a highly seasoned relish, made of chopped vegetables.

Pic·card (pē kàr'), n. **Auguste**, born 1884, Belgian physicist, born in Switzerland.

pic·co·lo (pĭk'ə lō'), n., pl. **-los.** a small flute, an octave higher than the ordinary flute.

pick[1] (pĭk), v.t. **1.** to choose or select. **2.** to seek and find occasion for. **3.** to seek or find (flaws) in a spirit of faultfinding. **4.** to steal the contents of (a pocket, purse, etc.). **5.** to open (a lock) with a pin, wire, etc., as for robbery. **6.** to pierce, indent, dig into, or break up (something) with a pointed instrument. **7.** to use a pointed instrument, the fingers, teeth, etc., on (a thing), in order to remove something. **8.** to clear (a thing) of something by such action. **9.** to prepare for use by removing feathers, hulls, or other parts. **10.** to pluck or gather. **11.** to take up (bits of food) with the bill or teeth. **12.** to eat in small morsels. **13.** Music. to pluck (the strings) of (an instrument). —v.i. **14.** to strike with or use a pointed instrument on something. **15.** to eat with dainty bites. **16.** to choose. **17. pick on,** Colloq. to annoy; criticize or blame. —n. **18.** choice or selection. **19.** the most desirable part, example, or examples. **20.** the right of selection. **21.** a plectrum.

pick[2] (pĭk), n. **1.** a hand tool consisting of a sharp-pointed iron bar mounted on a wooden handle: used for loosening soil, rock, etc. **2.** any tool or instrument for picking.

pick·a·back (pĭk'ə băk'), adv. piggyback.

pick·a·nin·ny (pĭk'ə nĭn'ĭ), n., pl. **-nies. 1.** a Negro or colored child. **2.** a small child.

pick·ax (pĭk'ăks'), n. a pick, esp. a mattock. Also, **pick'axe'.**

pick·er (pĭk'ər), n. **1.** one who picks. **2.** one who plucks or gathers fruit, flowers, etc.

pick·er·el (pĭk'ər əl), n., pl. **-els,** (esp. collectively) **-el.** U.S., Canada. any of various species of pike, esp. one of the smaller species.

pick·et (pĭk'ĭt), n. **1.** a pointed post, stake, pale, or peg, as for a fence (**picket fence**). **2.** a person or a body of persons stationed by a trade union or the like before a place of work and attempting to dissuade or prevent workers or shoppers from entering the building during a strike. **3.** Mil. a small detached body of troops posted to warn against an enemy's approach. —v.t. **4.** to enclose, fence, or make secure with pickets. **5.** to fasten to a picket. **6.** to place pickets at, as during a strike. —v.i. **7.** to stand or march by a place of employment as a picket. —**pick'et·er,** n.

pick·ing (pĭk'ĭng), n. **1.** act of one that picks. **2.** that which is or may be picked or picked up. **3.** the amount picked. **4.** (pl.) things remaining and worth picking up. **5.** (pl.) pilferings.

pick·le (pĭk'əl), n., v., **-led, -ling.** —n. **1.** a cucumber or other vegetable preserved in vinegar and eaten as a relish. **2.** Metall. an acid or other chemical solution in which metal objects are dipped to remove oxide scale or other adhering substances. **3.** Colloq. a difficult condition or situation. —v.t. **4.** to preserve or steep in brine, vinegar, etc. **5.** to treat with a chemical pickle.

pick·pock·et (pĭk'pŏk'ĭt), n. one who steals from pockets.

pick·up (pĭk'ŭp'), n. **1.** U.S. Slang. an informal or casual acquaintance. **2.** Auto. **a.** capacity for rapid acceleration. **b.** a small open-body delivery truck. **3.** U.S. Slang. improvement. **4.** U.S. Slang. a stimulant. **5.** Radio. act of receiving sound waves in the transmitting set in order to change them into electrical waves. **6.** a device on a phonograph which generates electric or acoustic impulses in accordance with the mechanical variations impressed upon a record.

pic·nic (pĭk'nĭk), n., v., **-nicked, -nicking.** —n. **1.** an outing in which those taking part share a meal in the open air. **2.** Slang. an enjoyable time.

—v.i. **3.** to hold, or take part in, a picnic. —**pic'-nick·er,** n.

pi·cot (pē'kō), n. one of a number of ornamental loops along the edge of lace, ribbon, etc.

pic·ric acid (pĭk'rĭk), Chem. an intensely bitter yellow acid, used as a dye and an explosive.

Pict (pĭkt), n. one of a people who formerly inhabited parts of northern Britain, and in the 9th century became united with the Scots. —**Pict'-ish,** adj., n.

pic·to·ri·al (pĭk tōr'ĭ əl), adj. **1.** of, pertaining to, or expressed in a picture or pictures. **2.** illustrated by or containing pictures. **3.** suggestive of a picture; graphic. —n. **4.** a periodical in which pictures are the leading feature. —**pic-to'ri·al·ly,** adv.

pic·ture (pĭk'chər), n., v., **-tured, -turing.** —n. **1.** a painting, drawing, photograph, or other representation on a flat surface. **2.** any visible image. **3.** a vivid account. **4.** a motion picture. —v.t. **5.** to represent pictorially. **6.** to imagine. **7.** to describe graphically.

pic·tur·esque (pĭk'chə rĕsk'), adj. strikingly interesting; graphic; colorful. —**pic'tur·esque'-ly,** adv. —**pic'tur·esque'ness,** n.

pid·dle (pĭd'əl), v.i., **-dled, -dling.** to do anything in a trifling or ineffective way.

pid·dling (pĭd'lĭng), adj. trifling; petty.

pidg·in English (pĭj'ĭn), an English jargon used in commerce in Chinese ports.

pie[1] (pī), n. a baked dish consisting of fruit, meat, or the like, with an under or an upper crust of pastry, or both.

pie[2] (pī), n. magpie.

pie[3] (pī), n., v., **pied, pieing.** U.S. pi[2].

pie·bald (pī'bôld'), adj. **1.** having patches of black and white or of other colors. —n. **2.** a piebald animal, esp. a horse.

piece (pēs), n., v., **pieced, piecing.** —n. **1.** a limited or individual portion of something. **2.** an amount of work forming a single job. **3.** specimen of artistic production, esp. a short literary composition. **4.** a musical composition, usually a short one. **5.** one of the parts which, assembled together, form a combined whole. **6.** an individual article of a set or collection. **7.** a portion, part, fragment, or shred. **8.** Mil. a. a rifle. **b.** cannon. **9.** a coin. **10.** Dial. a. a while. **b.** a short distance. —v.t. **11.** to mend (a garment, etc.) by applying a piece or pieces; patch. **12.** to complete, enlarge, or extend by something additional. **13.** to make by joining pieces together.

pièce de ré·sis·tance (pyĕs də rĕ zēs täns'), French. **1.** the principal dish of a meal. **2.** the principal event, incident, article, etc.

piece goods, fabrics woven in lengths suitable for sale by linear measure.

piece·meal (pēs'mēl'), adv. **1.** gradually. **2.** done gradually. **3.** into fragments.

piece of eight, the old Spanish dollar.

piece·work (pēs'wûrk'), n. work done and paid for by the piece. —**piece'work'er,** n.

pied (pīd), adj. having patches of two or more colors, as various birds.

Pied·mont (pēd'mŏnt), n. a plateau between the coastal plain and the Appalachian Mountains in Virginia, North Carolina, South Carolina, Georgia, and Alabama.

pie·plant (pī'plănt'), n. U.S. the common rhubarb: so called from its use in pies.

pier (pĭr), n. **1.** a structure built out into the water to serve as a landing place for ships. **2.** a support at the point where the ends of two adjacent bridge spans meet. **3.** a portion of wall between doors, windows, etc.

pierce (pĭrs), v., **pierced, piercing.** —v.t. **1.** to penetrate; run into or through. **2.** to make a hole in. **3.** to make a way into or through. **4.** to affect sharply with some sensation or emotion, as of cold, pain, grief, etc. **5.** to sound sharply through (the air, stillness, etc.), as a cry. —v.i. **6.** to penetrate. —**pierc'er,** n. —**pierc'ing·ly,** adv.

Pierce (pĭrs), n. **Franklin,** 1804–69, 14th president of the U.S., 1853–57.

Pierre (pĭr), n. the capital of South Dakota, in the central part. 4322.

Pi·e·tism (pī'ə tĭz'əm), n. **1.** a movement in the 17th century for the revival of piety in the Lutheran churches in Germany. **2.** (l.c.) depth of religious feeling. **3.** (l.c.) exaggeration or affectation of piety. —**Pi'e·tist,** n.

pi·e·ty (pī'ə tĭ), n., pl. **-ties. 1.** quality or fact of being pious. **2.** dutiful respect for parents or others. **3.** a pious act.

pif·fle (pĭf′əl), *n., v.,* **-fled, -fling.** *Colloq.* —*n.* **1.** nonsense. —*v.i.* **2.** to talk nonsense.

pig (pĭg), *n., v.,* **pigged, pigging.** —*n.* **1.** a young swine of either sex. **2.** any swine or hog. **3.** pork. **4.** *Colloq.* a person or animal of piggish character or habits. **5.** *Metall.* an oblong mass of metal that has been run while still molten into a mold of sand or the like. —*v.i.* **6.** to bring forth pigs.

pi·geon¹ (pĭj′ən), *n.* **1.** any of certain birds characterized by a compact body and short legs, widely distributed throughout the world; dove. **2.** *Slang.* a simpleton or dupe.

pi·geon² (pĭj′ən), *n.* pidgin English.

pi·geon·hole (pĭj′ən hōl′), *n., v.,* **-holed, -holing.** —*n.* **1.** one of a series of small compartments in a desk, cabinet, or the like, used for papers, etc. —*v.t.* **2.** to put away in the proper place for later reference. **3.** to assign a definite place in some system. **4.** to put aside, esp. with the intention of ignoring or forgetting.

pi·geon-toed (pĭj′ən tōd′), *adj.* having the toes or feet turned inward.

pig·ger·y (pĭg′ə rĭ), *n., pl.* **-geries.** *Chiefly Brit.* a place where pigs are kept.

pig·gish (pĭg′ĭsh), *adj.* greedy or filthy. —**pig′gish·ly,** *adv.* —**pig′gish·ness,** *n.*

pig·gy (pĭg′ĭ), *n., pl.* **-gies.** a small pig. Also, **pig′gie.**

pig·gy·back (pĭg′ĭ băk′), *adv.* on the back or shoulders.

piggy bank, a receptacle for saving small coins, often resembling a pig.

pig·head·ed (pĭg′hĕd′ĭd), *adj.* stupidly obstinate.

pig iron, iron produced in a blast furnace, poured into special molds, and used to make wrought iron, cast iron, or steel.

pig·ment (pĭg′mənt), *n.* **1.** a coloring matter or substance. **2.** *Biol.* any substance whose presence in the tissues or cells of animals or plants colors them. —**pig′men·tar′y,** *adj.*

pig·men·ta·tion (pĭg′mən tā′shən), *n.* *Biol.* coloration with or deposition of pigment.

Pig·my (pĭg′mĭ), *n., pl.* **-mies,** *adj. (also l.c.)* Pygmy.

pig·skin (pĭg′skĭn′), *n.* **1.** the skin of a pig. **2.** leather made from it. **3.** *Colloq.* a football.

pig·stick (pĭg′stĭk′), *v.i.* to go wild-boar hunting using a spear. —**pig′stick′er,** *n.*

pig·sty (pĭg′stī′), *n., pl.* **-sties.** a sty or pen for pigs. Also, **pig′pen′.**

pig·tail (pĭg′tāl′), *n.* a braid of hair hanging down the back of the head.

pike¹ (pīk), *n., pl.* **pikes,** *(esp. collectively)* **pike.** **1.** any of various large, slender, voracious freshwater fishes having a long snout, esp. the **northern pike.** **2.** any of various superficially similar fishes.

pike² (pīk), *n., v.,* **piked, piking.** —*n.* **1.** *Hist.* an infantry weapon with a long shaft and small metal head. —*v.t.* **2.** to pierce, wound, or kill with or as with a pike. —**pike′man,** *n.*

pike³ (pīk), *n.* **1.** a country highway. **2.** a tollgate. **3.** the toll paid at a tollgate.

Pike (pīk), *n.* **Zebulon Montgomery,** 1779-1813, U.S. general and explorer.

pik·er (pī′kər), *n.* *U.S. Slang.* **1.** one who gambles, speculates, etc., in a small cautious way. **2.** one who does anything in a contemptibly small or cheap way.

Pike's Peak (pīks), a peak of the Rocky Mountains in central Colorado. 14,108 ft.

pike·staff (pīk′stăf′, -stäf′), *n., pl.* **-staves** (-stāvz′). the shaft of a pike (weapon).

pi·las·ter (pĭ lăs′tər), *n.* *Archit.* a rectangular pillar set in a wall from which it projects.

Pi·late (pī′lət), *n.* **Pontius,** Roman governor of Judea, A.D. 26-36?, when Christ was crucified.

pi·lau (pĭ lô′, -lō′), *n.* an Oriental dish consisting of rice boiled with mutton, fowl, or the like, and flavored with spices, raisins, etc. Also, **pi·laf** (pĭ lăf′), **pi·laff′, pi·law** (pĭ lô′).

pile¹ (pīl), *n., v.,* **piled, piling.** —*n.* **1.** an assemblage of things lying one upon another in a more or less orderly fashion. **2.** *Colloq.* a large amount. **3.** *Nuclear Physics.* a latticework of uranium and various moderating substances used to produce plutonium in the original harnessing of atomic energy. It is essentially a means of controlling the nuclear chain reaction. —*v.t.* **4.** to

lay or dispose in a pile. **5.** to accumulate. **6.** to cover or load with a pile or piles. —*v.i.* **7.** to accumulate, as money, debts, evidence, etc. **8.** to rise in a pile, as snow.

pile² (pīl), *n., v.,* **piled, piling.** —*n.* **1.** a heavy timber or pole driven vertically into the ground or the bed of a river, etc., to support a superstructure or form part of a wall. **2.** any steel or concrete member similarly used. —*v.t.* **3.** to furnish with piles.

pile³ (pīl), *n.* **1.** hair, down, wool, or fur. **2.** a nap. —**piled,** *adj.*

pile⁴ (pīl), *n.* (*usually pl.*) a hemorrhoid.

pi·le·ous (pī′lĭ əs), *adj.* **1.** of or pertaining to hair. **2.** hairy.

pil·fer (pĭl′fər), *v.i., v.t.* to steal, esp. in small quantities. —**pil′fer·er,** *n.*

pil·fer·age (pĭl′fər ĭj), *n.* petty theft.

pil·grim (pĭl′grĭm), *n.* **1.** one who journeys to some sacred place as an act of devotion. **2.** a traveler. **3.** (*cap.*) one of the Pilgrim Fathers.

pil·grim·age (pĭl′grə mĭj), *n.* a journey, esp. one made to some sacred place, as an act of devotion.

Pilgrim Fathers, *U.S. Hist.* the English separatists who founded the colony of Plymouth, Massachusetts, in 1620.

pil·ing (pī′lĭng), *n.* **1.** piles collectively. **2.** a structure composed of piles.

pill (pĭl), *n.* **1.** a small rounded mass of medicinal substance, to be swallowed whole. **2.** *Slang.* a disagreeable person. **3.** *Sports Slang.* a ball. —*v.t.* **4.** to dose with pills.

pil·lage (pĭl′ĭj), *v., v.i.,* **-laged, -laging,** *n.* —*v.t., v.i.* **1.** to rob of money or goods by open violence; plunder. —*n.* **2.** act of plundering. **3.** booty or spoil. —**pil′lag·er,** *n.*

pil·lar (pĭl′ər), *n.* **1.** an upright shaft of stone, brick, or other material, used chiefly as a support. **2.** a person who is a chief supporter of an institution, etc. **3. from pillar to post,** from one difficulty to another. —*v.t.* **4.** to provide with pillars.

pill·box (pĭl′bŏks′), *n.* **1.** a small concrete structure employed as a minor fortress. **2.** a box for pills.

pil·lion (pĭl′yən), *n.* a cushion attached behind a saddle, esp. as a seat for a woman.

pil·lo·ry (pĭl′ə rĭ), *n., pl.* **-ries,** *v.,* **-ried, -rying.** —*n.* **1.** a wooden framework erected on a post, with holes for the head and hands, used to expose an offender to public derision. —*v.t.* **2.** to set in the pillory. **3.** to expose to public ridicule.

pil·low (pĭl′ō), *n.* **1.** a bag filled with feathers, down, or other soft material, commonly used as a support for the head during sleep or rest. **2.** a cushion or pad. —*v.t., v.i.* **3.** to rest on a pillow. —**pil′low·like′,** *adj.*

Pillory

pil·low·case (pĭl′ō kās′), *n.* a removable cotton or linen covering for a pillow.

pi·lose (pī′lōs), *adj.* covered with hair.

pi·lot (pī′lət), *n.* **1.** one duly qualified to steer ships into or out of a harbor or through certain difficult waters. **2.** the steersman of a ship. **3.** one duly qualified to operate an aircraft. **4.** a guide or leader. **5.** *Mach.* a smaller element acting in advance of another and causing the latter to operate when desired. —*v.t.* **6.** to steer. **7.** to guide or conduct.

pi·lot·age (pī′lət ĭj), *n.* **1.** act of piloting. **2.** the fee paid to a pilot (def. 1).

pilot light, a small light kept burning continuously, as beside a large gas burner, to relight a main light whenever desired.

pilot plant, a small factory in which processes planned for full-scale operation are tested in advance to eliminate problems, etc.

Pil·sen (pĭl′zən), *n.* a city in W Czechoslovakia. 114,704.

pi·men·to (pĭ měn′tō), *n., pl.* **-tos. 1.** the dried fruit of a tropical American tree of the myrtle family. **2.** the tree itself. **3.** the pimiento.

pi·mien·to (pĭ myěn′tō), *n., pl.* **-tos.** a garden pepper, used as a vegetable, relish, etc.

pimp (pĭmp), *n.* a pander.

pim·per·nel (pĭm′pər něl′, -nəl), *n.* a small plant of the primrose family with scarlet, purplish, or white flowers that close at the approach of bad weather.

pim·ple (pĭm′pəl), *n.* a small, usually inflammatory swelling of the skin. —**pim′ply, pim′-pled,** *adj.*

pin (pĭn), *n., v.,* **pinned, pinning.** —*n.* **1.** a small, slender, often pointed piece of wood, metal, etc., used to fasten, support, or attach things. **2.** any of various fastenings, ornaments, or badges having a pointed penetrating bar. **3.** a clothespin. **4.** a rolling pin. **5.** one of the bottle-shaped pieces of wood knocked down in ninepins, tenpins, etc. **6.** *Golf.* the flag staff which identifies a hole. **7.** *Colloq.* a leg. —*v.t.* **8.** to fasten or attach with a pin or pins. **9.** to hold fast in a spot or position. **10.** to bind to a course of action, a promise, etc.

pi·na·ceous (pī nā′shəs), *adj.* belonging to the pine family of trees and shrubs, which includes the pine, spruce, fir, etc.

pin·a·fore (pĭn′ə fōr′), *n.* **1.** a child's apron, covering most of the dress. **2.** a sleeveless summer dress.

pin·ball machine (pĭn′bôl′), a machine with a sloping board, used in a game the object of which is usually to shoot a ball, driven by a spring, up a side passage and cause it to roll back down against pins or bumpers and through channels which electrically record the score.

pince-nez (păns′nā′, pĭns′-), *n.* a pair of eyeglasses kept in place by a spring which pinches the nose.

pin·cers (pĭn′sərz), *n.pl. or sing.* **1.** a gripping tool consisting of two pivoted limbs forming a pair of jaws and a pair of handles. **2.** *Zool.* a grasping organ or pair of organs.

pinch (pĭnch), *v.t.* **1.** to compress or squeeze, as between the finger and thumb. **2.** to cramp within narrow bounds. **3.** to render (the face, etc.) unnaturally thin and drawn, as pain or distress does. **4.** to nip (plants) injuriously, as frost does. **5.** to affect with sharp discomfort or distress, as cold, hunger, or need does. **6.** to stint in allowance of money, food, or the like. **7.** *Slang.* to steal. **8.** *Slang.* to arrest. —*v.i.* **9.** to exert a sharp or painful compressing force. **10.** to cause sharp discomfort or distress. **11.** to economize unduly. —*n.* **12.** act of pinching; nip; squeeze. **13.** as much of anything as can be taken up between the finger and thumb. **14.** sharp or painful stress, as of hunger or need. **15.** an emergency. **16.** *Slang.* a raid or an arrest.

pinch·beck (pĭnch′běk), *n.* an alloy of copper and zinc, used in imitation of gold.

pinch·er (pĭn′chər), *n.* **1.** one that pinches. **2.** *(pl.)* pincers.

pinch-hit (pĭnch′hĭt′), *v.i.,* **-hit, -hitting.** *Chiefly Baseball.* to serve as a substitute, esp. in an emergency.

pin·cush·ion (pĭn′kŏŏsh′ən), *n.* a small cushion in which pins are stuck, in readiness for use.

Pin·dar (pĭn′dər), *n.* c522–c443 B.C., Greek lyric poet.

pine[1] (pīn), *n.* **1.** any of certain evergreen coniferous trees varying greatly in size, with long needle-shaped leaves, including many species of economic importance for their timber and as a source of turpentine, tar, pitch, etc. **2.** any of various coniferous pinelike trees. **3.** the wood of the pine tree.

pine[2] (pīn), *v.i.,* **pined, pining. 1.** to long painfully. **2.** to fail gradually in health or vitality from grief, regret, or longing.

pin·e·al body (pĭn′ĭ əl), a body of unknown function present in the brain of all vertebrates having a cranium, believed to be a vestigial sense organ. Also, **pineal gland.**

pine·ap·ple (pīn′ăp′əl), *n.* **1.** the edible juicy fruit of a tropical plant. **2.** the plant itself, having a short stem and rigid, spiny-margined, recurved leaves.

pin·feath·er (pĭn′fĕth′ər), *n.* **1.** an undeveloped feather. **2.** a feather just coming through the skin.

Ping-Pong (pĭng′pŏng′), *n.* *Trademark.* a variety of tennis played on a table with small racquets and a hollow celluloid ball.

pin·head (pĭn′hĕd′), *n.* **1.** the head of a pin. **2.** *Slang.* a stupid person.

pin·ion[1] (pĭn′yən), *n.* *Mach.* a cogwheel engaging with a larger cogwheel or with a rack.

pin·ion[2] (pĭn′yən), *n.* **1.** the distal or terminal segment of a bird's wing. **2.** the wing of a bird. **3.** a feather. —*v.t.* **4.** to bind (a person's arms or hands).

pink[1] (pĭngk), *n.* **1.** a pale reddish purple. **2.** any of certain common garden plants, including the **clove pink,** or carnation. **3.** the flower of

such a plant. **4.** the highest form or degree. **5.** *(often cap.)* a person with radical, but not extreme, political opinions. —*adj.* **6.** of the color pink. —**pink′ish,** *adj.*

pink[2] (pĭngk), *v.t.* **1.** to pierce with a rapier or the like. **2.** to finish with a scalloped, notched, or other ornamental edge.

pink·eye (pĭngk′ī′), *n.* *Pathol.* a contagious form of conjunctivitis.

pink·ie (pĭngk′ĭ), *n.* *Chiefly Eastern U.S.* the little (fifth) finger.

pin money, 1. any small sum set aside for nonessential minor expenditures. **2.** an allowance of money to a wife for personal expenditures.

pin·na (pĭn′ə), *n., pl.* **pinnae** (pĭn′ē), **pinnas.** *Zool.* a feather, wing, or winglike part.

pin·na·cle (pĭn′ə kəl), *n., v.,* **-cled, -cling.** —*n.* **1.** a lofty peak. **2.** a lofty position. **3.** the highest point. **4.** any pointed, towering part or formation, as of rock. —*v.t.* **5.** to place on a pinnacle. **6.** to crown.

pin·nate (pĭn′āt, -ĭt), *adj.* **1.** resembling a feather. **2.** *Bot.* (of a leaf) having leaflets on each side of a common petiole. —**pin′nate·ly,** *adv.*

pi·noch·le (pē′nŭk′əl), *n.* a card game played by two, three, or four persons, with a 48-card deck. Also, **pi′noc′le.**

pi·ñon (pĭn′yən, pēn′yōn), *n.* **1.** any of various pines, esp. of the southern Rocky Mountains, producing large edible seeds. **2.** the seed.

pint (pīnt), *n.* a liquid and a dry measure of capacity, equal to one half a quart.

pin·tle (pĭn′tal), *n.* a pin or bolt, esp. one upon which something turns, as in a hinge.

pin·to (pĭn′tō, pēn′-), *adj., n., pl.* **-tos.** —*adj.* **1.** piebald; mottled; spotted. —*n.* **2.** *Western U.S.* a pinto horse.

pin-up (pĭn′ŭp′), *U.S. Slang.* —*n.* **1.** a picture of a very attractive girl, hung on a wall, usually by personally unknown admirers. **2.** the girl in such a picture. —*adj.* **3.** of or in such a picture.

pin·wheel (pĭn′hwēl′), *n.* a child's toy consisting of a paper wheel fixed by a pin to a stick so as to revolve in the wind.

pin·worm (pĭn′wûrm′), *n.* a small nematode infesting the intestine.

pin·y (pī′nĭ), *adj.,* **pinier, piniest. 1.** abounding in or consisting of pine trees. **2.** of or suggestive of pine trees.

pi·o·neer (pī′ə nĭr′), *n.* **1.** one of those who first enter or settle a region. **2.** one of those who are first in any field of inquiry, enterprise, or progress. **3.** one of a body of advance foot soldiers detailed to make roads, etc. —*v.i., v.t.* **4.** to open or prepare (a way, etc.), as a pioneer does. **5.** to be a pioneer in.

pi·ous (pī′əs), *adj.* **1.** having or showing reverence for God or regard for religious obligations. **2.** practiced or used from religious motives (real or pretended). **3.** sacred. —**pi′ous·ly,** *adv.* —**pi′ous·ness,** *n.*

pip[1] (pĭp), *n.* **1.** *Chiefly Brit.* one of the spots on dice, playing cards, or dominoes. **2.** *Brit. Slang.* a metal insigne of rank on the shoulders of commissioned officers.

pip[2] (pĭp), *n.* a contagious disease of birds, esp. poultry.

pip[3] (pĭp), *n.* a small seed, esp. of a fleshy fruit, as an apple or orange.

pipe (pīp), *n., v.,* **piped, piping.** —*n.* **1.** a hollow cylinder for the conveyance of water, gas, steam, etc. **2.** any of various tubular or cylindrical objects, parts, or formations. **3.** a tube of wood, clay, or other material, with a small bowl at one end, used for smoking tobacco, etc. **4.** *Music.* **a.** a tube used as or in a musical wind instrument. **b.** a musical wind instrument consisting of a single tube, as a flute. **c.** one of the wooden or metal tubes from which the tones of an organ are produced. **5.** *Naut.* a boatswain's whistle. **6.** the note or call of a bird, etc. —*v.i.* **7.** to play on a pipe. **8.** *Naut.* to announce orders, etc., by a boatswain's pipe. **9.** to speak shrilly. —*v.t.* **10.** to convey by means of pipes. **11.** to play (music) on a pipe or pipes. **12.** to summon, order, etc., by sounding the boatswain's whistle. **13.** to utter in a shrill tone. **14.** to finish (a garment, etc.) with piping. —**pipe′ful′,** *n.* —**pip′er,** *n.*

pipe dream, *Slang.* any fantastic notion, story, etc.

pipe line, 1. a conduit of pipe for the transportation of petroleum, natural gas, etc. **2.** a channel of information, usually confidential. Also, **pipe′line′.**

pi·pette (pĭ pĕt′), *n.* a slender graduated tube

for measuring and transferring liquids from one vessel to another.

pip·ing (pī′pĭng), n. 1. pipes collectively. 2. act of one that pipes. 3. the sound of pipes. 4. a tubular band of material for trimming garments, etc., as along edges. —adj. 5. emitting a shrill sound. 6. **piping hot,** very hot.

pip·kin (pĭp′kĭn), n. a small earthen pot.

pip·pin (pĭp′ĭn), n. any of numerous varieties of apple.

pi·quant (pē′kənt), adj. 1. agreeably pungent or sharp; tart. 2. agreeably stimulating, interesting, or attractive. 3. smart or racy. —**pi′quan·cy,** n. —**pi′quant·ly,** adv.

pique (pēk), v., **piqued, piquing,** n. —v.t. 1. to affect with sharp irritation and resentment, esp. by a wound to pride. 2. to excite (interest, curiosity, etc.). 3. to pride (oneself). —n. 4. irritated feeling, as between persons.

pi·qué (pĭ kā′), n. a fabric, usually cotton, woven with raised cords.

pi·ra·cy (pī′rə sĭ), n., pl. **-cies.** 1. robbery or illegal violence at sea. 2. the unauthorized use of a copyrighted or patented work, idea, etc.

Pi·rae·us (pī rē′əs), n. a seaport in SE Greece: the port of Athens. 205,404.

Pi·ran·del·lo (pē′rän dĕl′lō), n. **Luigi,** 1867–1936, Italian dramatist, novelist, and poet.

pi·rate (pī′rət), n., v., **-rated, -rating.** —n. 1. one who robs or commits illegal violence at sea. 2. a vessel employed by such persons. 3. any plunderer. 4. one who uses without authorization for his own profit the work or invention of another. —v.t., v.i. 5. to commit piracy upon. 6. to take by piracy. —**pi·rat·i·cal** (pī răt′ə-kəl), adj. —**pi·rat′i·cal·ly,** adv.

pir·ou·ette (pĭr′ŏŏ ĕt′), n., v., **-etted, -etting.** —n. 1. a whirling about on the toes, as in dancing. —v.i. 2. to perform a pirouette.

Pi·sa (pē′zə), n. a city in NW Italy: leaning tower. 80,784.

pis·ca·to·ri·al (pĭs′kə tōr′ĭ əl), adj. 1. of or pertaining to fishermen or fishing. 2. given or devoted to fishing. Also, **pis′ca·to′ry.**

Pis·ces (pĭs′ēz), n.pl., gen. **Piscium** (pĭsh′ĭ əm). 1. Astron. the Fishes, a zodiacal constellation. 2. the twelfth sign of the zodiac.

pis·mire (pĭs′mīr′), n. an ant.

pis·ta·chi·o (pĭs tä′shĭ ō′, pĭs täsh′ĭ ō′), n., pl. **-chios.** 1. the stone (nut) of the fruit of a small tree of the sumac family, of southern Europe and Asia Minor. 2. its edible greenish kernel. 3. the tree itself. 4. pistachio nut flavor. 5. light yellowish green. Also, **pis·tache** (pĭs täsh′).

pis·til (pĭs′tĭl), n. Bot. the ovule-bearing or seed-bearing organ of a flower, consisting when complete of ovary, style, and stigma. —**pis·til·late** (pĭs′tə lĭt, -lāt′), adj.

pis·tol (pĭs′təl), n., v., **-toled, -toling** or (esp. Brit.) **-tolled, -tolling.** —n. 1. a short firearm intended to be held and fired with one hand. —v.t. 2. to shoot with a pistol.

pis·ton (pĭs′tən), n. a movable disk or cylinder fitting closely within a tube, and capable of being driven alternately forward and backward in the tube by pressure, thus imparting reciprocatory motion to a rod (**piston rod**) attached to it on one side, or of being driven thus by the rod.

pit[1] (pĭt), n., v., **pitted, pitting.** —n. 1. a hole or cavity in the ground. 2. hell, or a part of it. 3. a natural hollow or depression in the body. 4. an enclosure for combats, as of cocks. 5. U.S. that part of the floor of an exchange devoted to a special kind of business. 6. Archit. all that part of the main floor of a theater behind the musicians. —v.t., v.i. 7. to mark, or become marked, with pits. 8. to set in active opposition.

pit[2] (pĭt), n., v., **pitted, pitting.** U.S. —n. 1. the stone of a fruit, as of a cherry. —v.t. 2. to take out the pit from.

Pit·cairn Island (pĭt′kârn), a small British island in the S Pacific: settled by mutineers of the Bounty in 1790. 2 sq. mi.

pitch[1] (pĭch), v.t. 1. to set up or erect (a tent, camp, or the like). 2. to throw, fling, hurl, or toss. 3. Baseball. to deliver or serve (the ball) to the batter. 4. to set at a certain point, degree, level, etc. 5. Music. to determine the key of (a tune, etc.). —v.i. 6. to plunge or fall forward or headlong. 7. to lurch. 8. to throw or toss. 9. Baseball. to deliver or serve the ball to the batter. 10. to slope downward. 11. to plunge with alternate fall and rise of bow and stern, as a ship. —n. 12. point, position, or degree, as in a scale. 13. height in general. 14. Music, Speech, etc. de-

gree of height or depth of a tone or of sound. 15. a particular tonal standard with which given tones may be compared in respect to their relative level. 16. act or manner of pitching. 17. downward inclination or slope.

pitch[2] (pĭch), n. 1. any of various dark-colored tenacious or viscous substances used for making pavements, etc., as the residuum left after the distillation of coal tar. 2. any of various resins. 3. the sap or crude turpentine which exudes from the bark of pines.

pitch·blende (pĭch′blĕnd′), n. an impure mineral occurring in black pitchlike masses: principal ore of uranium and radium.

pitched (pĭcht), adj. fought with all available forces.

pitch·er[1] (pĭch′ər), n. a container, usually with a handle and spout or lip, for holding and pouring liquids.

pitch·er[2] (pĭch′ər), n. 1. one who pitches. 2. Baseball. the player who delivers or throws the ball to the batter.

pitcher plant, any of various plants with leaves modified into a pitcherlike receptacle.

pitch·fork (pĭch′fôrk′), n. 1. a fork for lifting and pitching hay, etc. —v.t. 2. to pitch or throw with a pitchfork.

pitch·y (pĭch′ĭ), adj., **pitchier, pitchiest.** 1. full of pitch. 2. smeared with pitch. 3. of or like pitch. 4. black. —**pitch′i·ness,** n.

pit·e·ous (pĭt′ĭ əs), adj. such as to excite or deserve pity; pathetic. —**pit′e·ous·ly,** adv. —**pit′e·ous·ness,** n.

pit·fall (pĭt′fôl′), n. 1. a concealed pit prepared as a trap for animals or men to fall into. 2. any trap.

pith (pĭth), n. 1. any soft, spongy tissue or substance, as in stems of some plants. 2. the important part; essence. 3. strength, force, or vigor.

Pith·e·can·thro·pus (pĭth′ə kăn thrō′pəs, -kăn′thrə pəs), n., pl. **-pi** (-pī, -pī′). an extinct genus of "apelike" men.

pith·y (pĭth′ĭ), adj., **pithier, pithiest.** 1. full of vigor, substance, or meaning; terse. 2. of, like, or abounding in pith. —**pith′i·ly,** adv. —**pith′i·ness,** n.

pit·i·a·ble (pĭt′ĭ ə bəl), adj. 1. deserving to be pitied; lamentable; deplorable. 2. miserable; contemptible. —**pit′i·a·ble·ness,** n. —**pit′i·a·bly,** adv.

pit·i·ful (pĭt′ĭ fəl), adj. 1. such as to excite or deserve pity. 2. such as to excite contempt by smallness, poor quality, etc. 3. full of pity; compassionate. —**pit′i·ful·ly,** adv. —**pit′i·ful·ness,** n.

pit·i·less (pĭt′ĭ lĭs), adj. feeling or showing no pity; merciless. —**pit′i·less·ly,** adv. —**pit′i·less·ness,** n.

Pitt (pĭt), n. 1. **William,** (1st Earl of Chatham) 1708–1778, British statesman. 2. his son, **William,** 1759–1806, British statesman.

pit·tance (pĭt′əns), n. 1. a small sum for living expenses. 2. a scanty income or wage.

Pitts·burgh (pĭts′bûrg), n. a city in SW Pennsylvania. 671,659.

Pitts·field (pĭts′fēld′), n. a city in W Massachusetts. 49,684.

pi·tu·i·tar·y (pĭ tū′ə tĕr′ĭ, -tŏŏ′-), n., pl. **-taries.** 1. Anat. the pituitary gland. 2. Med. the extract obtained from the pituitary.

pituitary gland, Anat. a small endocrine gland attached to the base of the brain which secretes several hormones.

pit·y (pĭt′ĭ), n., pl. **pities,** v., **pitied, pitying.** —n. 1. sympathetic sorrow for the suffering or misfortune of another. 2. a cause for pity, sorrow, or regret. —v.t., v.i. 3. to feel compassion (for). —**pit′y·ing·ly,** adv.

Pi·us XII (pī′əs), (Eugenio Pacelli) born 1876, pope since 1939.

piv·ot (pĭv′ət), n. 1. a short shaft on which something turns. 2. that on which something turns or depends. 3. the person upon whom a line, as of troops, wheels about. —v.i. 4. to turn on a pivot. —v.t. 5. to mount on, attach by, or provide with a pivot. —**piv′ot·al,** adj.

pix·i·lat·ed (pĭk′sə lā′tĭd), adj. amusingly eccentric.

pix·y (pĭk′sĭ), n., pl. **pixies.** a fairy or sprite. Also, **pix′ie.**

piz·za (pēt′sə), n. Italian. a pielike dish, prepared with tomatoes and cheese.

piz·zi·ca·to (pĭt′sə kä′tō), adj., n., pl. **-ti** (-tĭ)

Music. —*adj.* **1.** played by plucking the strings with the finger. —*n.* **2.** a note or passage so played.

pk., *pl.* **pks. 1.** pack. **2.** park. **3.** peck.

pkg., *pl.* **pkgs.** package.

pl., 1. place. **2.** plate. **3.** plural.

pla·ca·ble (plā′kə bəl, plăk′ə-), *adj.* capable of being appeased; forgiving. —**pla′ca·bil′i·ty,** *n.* —**pla′ca·bly,** *adv.*

plac·ard (*n.* plăk′ärd; *v.* plə kärd′, plăk′ärd), *n.* **1.** a notice to be posted in a public place; poster. —*v.t.* **2.** to post placards on or in.

pla·cate (plā′kāt, plăk′āt), *v.t.,* -**cated,** -**cating.** to appease; pacify. —**pla·ca′tion,** *n.*

place (plās), *n., v.,* **placed, placing.** —*n.* **1.** a particular portion of space. **2.** the portion of space occupied by anything. **3.** a space used for a particular purpose. **4.** any part, as in a body or surface. **5.** a particular passage in a book or writing. **6.** the space or position occupied by a person or thing. **7.** a function or duty. **8.** standing in the social scale. **9.** a short street. **10.** stead; lieu. **11.** a step or point in order of proceeding. **12.** *Sports.* **a.** a position among the leading competitors, usually the first three, at the finish of a race. **b.** the position of the second. **13. take place,** to happen; occur. —*v.t.* **14.** to arrange; dispose. **15.** to put in a particular place, position, situation, or relation. **16.** to find a place, situation, etc., for (a person). **17.** to determine the place of. **18.** to identify by connecting with the proper place, circumstances, etc. —*v.i.* **19.** *Racing.* to finish among the three winners, usually second. —**place′ment,** *n.* —**plac′er,** *n.*

place kick, *Football.* a kick given the ball after it has been held in place on the ground.

pla·cen·ta (plə sĕn′tə), *n., pl.* -**tae** (-tē), -**tas.** *Zool., Anat.* the organ formed in the lining of the mammalian uterus by the union of the uterine mucous membrane with the membranes of the fetus to provide for the nourishment of the fetus and the elimination of its waste products. —**pla·cen′tal,** *adj.*

plac·er (plăs′ər), *n. Mining.* **1.** a superficial gravel or similar deposit containing particles of gold or the like. **2.** a place where such a deposit is washed for gold, etc. (**placer mining**).

plac·id (plăs′ĭd), *adj.* pleasantly calm; tranquil; serene. —**pla·cid·i·ty** (plə sĭd′ə tĭ), **plac′id·ness,** *n.* —**plac′id·ly,** *adv.*

plack·et (plăk′ĭt), *n.* the slit at the top of a skirt, or in a dress or blouse, to facilitate putting it on and off.

pla·gia·rism (plā′jĭ ə rĭz′əm, plā′jə-), *n.* copying or imitating the language, ideas, and thoughts of another author and passing off the same as one's original work. —**pla′gia·rist,** *n.*

pla·gia·rize (plā′jĭ ə rīz′, plā′jə-), *v.,* -**rized,** -**rizing.** —*v.t.* **1.** to appropriate by plagiarism. **2.** to appropriate ideas, passages, etc., from by plagiarism. —*v.i.* **3.** to commit plagiarism. —**pla′gia·riz′er,** *n.*

plague (plāg, plĕg), *n., v.,* **plagued, plaguing.** —*n.* **1.** an epidemic disease of high mortality. **2.** an affliction, calamity, or evil. **3.** any cause of trouble or vexation. —*v.t.* **4.** to trouble or afflict in any manner. **5.** to annoy, bother, or pester. —**pla′guer,** *n.*

pla·guy (plā′gĭ, plĕg′ĭ), *Colloq.* —*adj.* **1.** annoying; vexatious. —*adv.* **2.** vexatiously or excessively. Also, **pla′guey.**

plaid (plăd), *n.* **1.** any fabric woven of different colored yarns in a crossbarred pattern. —*adj.* **2.** having the pattern of a plaid.

plain (plān), *adj.* **1.** clear or distinct. **2.** evident; obvious. **3.** easily understood. **4.** downright. **5.** candid; outspoken. **6.** without special pretensions, elegance, etc. **7.** homely. **8.** without intracacies or difficulties. **9.** ordinary; simple. **10.** without pattern, design, or coloring. **11.** flat or level. —*adv.* **12.** clearly or intelligibly. **13.** candidly. —*n.* **14.** an area with relatively minor differences in elevation. —**plain′ly,** *adv.* —**plain′ness,** *n.*

plain-clothes man (plān′klōz′, -klōᵭhz′), a detective.

Plain·field (plān′fēld′), *n.* a city in N New Jersey. 37,469.

plains·man (plānz′mən), *n., pl.* -**men.** a man or inhabitant of the plains.

plaint (plānt), *n.* **1.** a complaint. **2.** *Archaic and Poetic.* lament.

plain·tiff (plān′tĭf), *n. Law.* one who brings suit in a court (opposed to *defendant*).

plain·tive (plān′tĭv), *adj.* melancholy; mournful. —**plain′tive·ly,** *adv.* —**plain′tive·ness,** *n.*

plait (plāt), *n.* **1.** a braid, as of hair. **2.** a pleat, as of cloth. —*v.t.* **3.** to braid. **4.** to pleat.

plan (plăn), *n., v.,* **planned, planning.** —*n.* **1.** a scheme of action. **2.** a design of arrangement. **3.** a project or definite purpose. **4.** a drawing made to represent a view of a structure or machine. —*v.t.* **5.** to arrange a plan for. **6.** to make a plan of. —*v.i.* **7.** to make plans. —**plan′ner,** *n.*

plane[1] (plān), *n., adj., v.,* **planed, planing.** —*n.* **1.** a flat or level surface. **2.** a level of character, development, or the like. **3.** an airplane. **4.** *Aeron.* a thin extended member of an aircraft affording a supporting surface. —*adj.* **5.** flat or level. **6.** of or pertaining to plane figures. —*v.i.* **7.** to glide. **8.** to lift partly out of water when running at high speed.

plane[2] (plān), *n., v.,* **planed, planing.** —*n.* **1.** a tool with an adjustable blade for smoothing the surface of wood, etc. —*v.t.* **2.** to smooth with a plane or planer. **3.** to remove by a plane. —*v.i.* **4.** to work with a plane. **5.** to function as a plane.

plane[3] (plān), *n. Brit.* a plane tree.

plan·er (plā′nər), *n. Carp.* a power machine for removing rough or excess surface stock from a board.

plan·et (plăn′ĭt), *n. Astron.* any one of the solid heavenly bodies revolving about the sun and shining by reflected light. There are nine **major planets** (Mercury, Venus, the Earth, Mars, Jupiter, Saturn, Uranus, Neptune, and Pluto). —**plan′e·tar′y,** *adj.*

plan·e·tar·i·um (plăn′ə târ′ĭ əm), *n., pl.* -**tari·ums,** -**taria** (-târ′ĭ ə). **1.** a model of the planetary system. **2.** an optical device which projects a representation of the heavens upon a dome through the use of many stereopticons in motion. **3.** the structure in which such a device is housed.

plane tree, any of a certain genus of trees including one which is found wild from Italy to Persia and is much used in Europe for ornament, and the buttonwood or sycamore of North America.

plank (plăngk), *n.* **1.** a long, flat piece of timber. **2.** an article of a platform of political or other principles. —*v.t.* **3.** to lay, cover, or furnish with planks. **4.** *Colloq.* to lay, put, or pay. **5.** to bake or broil and serve (fish, chicken, etc.) on a board.

plant (plănt, plänt), *n.* **1.** any member of the vegetable group of living organisms. **2.** a vegetable. **3.** an herb or other small vegetable growth, in contrast with a tree or shrub. **4.** a seedling or a growing slip. **5.** the equipment, and often the buildings, necessary to carry on any industrial business. **6.** the apparatus for a particular mechanical process. **7.** the buildings, equipment, etc., of an institution. **8.** *Slang.* something intended to trap, decoy, or lure, as criminals. —*v.t.* **9.** to set in the ground for growth, as seeds, etc. **10.** to furnish (land) with plants. **11.** to implant (ideas, etc.) **12.** to set firmly in or on the ground or some other surface. **13.** to put. **14.** *Slang.* to deliver (a blow, etc.). **15.** *Slang.* to conceal, as stolen goods.

Plan·tag·e·net (plăn tăj′ə nĭt), *n.* one of the line of English sovereigns from 1154 to 1399.

plan·tain[1] (plăn′tĭn), *n.* **1.** a tropical herbaceous plant, very similar to the banana. **2.** its fruit.

plan·tain[2] (plăn′tĭn), *n.* a common weed with large, spreading leaves close to the ground and long, slender spikes of small flowers.

plan·ta·tion (plăn tā′shən), *n.* **1.** a farm or estate, esp. in a tropical or semitropical country, on which cotton, tobacco, coffee, or the like, is cultivated, usually by resident laborers. **2.** *Chiefly Brit.* a group of planted trees or plants.

plant·er (plăn′tər, plän′-), *n.* **1.** one who plants. **2.** an implement for planting seeds. **3.** the owner of a plantation.

plaque (plăk), *n.* **1.** a tablet of metal, porcelain, etc., intended for ornament. **2.** a platelike badge of an honorary order.

plas·ma (plăz′mə), *n.* **1.** *Anat., Physiol.* the liquid part of blood or lymph, as distinguished from the corpuscles. **2.** *Biol.* protoplasm.

plas·ter (plăs′tər, pläs′-), *n.* **1.** a pasty composition, as of lime, sand, and water, used for covering walls, ceilings, etc., where it hardens in drying. **2.** calcined gypsum (**plaster of Paris**): a white powdery material which, mixed with water, is used for making casts, molds, etc. **3.** a preparation for spreading upon cloth or the like and applying to the body for some remedial or other purpose. —*v.t.* 4. to cover (walls, etc.) with plaster. 5. to treat with plaster. 6. to overspread thickly or to excess. —**plas′ter·er,** *n.*

plas·tic (plăs′tĭk), *adj.* 1. concerned with or pertaining to molding. 2. capable of being molded. 3. produced by molding. 4. *Surg.* concerned with or pertaining to the remedying or restoring of malformed, injured, or lost parts. 5. pliable; impressionable. —*n.* 6. any of a group of synthetic or natural organic materials which may be shaped when soft and then hardened, including many types of resins, polymers, and cellulose derivatives. —**plas·tic·i·ty** (plăs tĭs′ə-tĭ), *n.*

Pla·ta (plä′tä), *n.* **Río de la** (rē′ō dĕ lä), an estuary on the SE coast of South America between Argentina and Uruguay, formed by the Uruguay and Paraná rivers. ab. 185 mi. long. Also, **Plata River.**

plate (plāt), *n., v.,* **plated, plating.** —*n.* 1. a shallow, usually circular dish from which food is eaten. 2. the contents of such a dish. 3. a service of food for one person at table. 4. *Chiefly Brit.* domestic dishes, utensils, etc., of gold or silver. 5. a dish used for collecting offerings in a church, etc. 6. a thin, flat sheet of metal, etc. 7. a sheet of metal for printing from, formed by stereotyping or electrotyping a page of type. 8. *Dentistry.* a piece of metal, vulcanite, or plastic substance, with artificial teeth attached, to replace natural teeth. 9. *Baseball.* the home base, at which the batter stands. 10. *Photog.* a sensitized sheet of glass, metal, etc. 11. *Anat., Zool., etc.* a platelike part, structure, or organ. —*v.t.* 12. to coat (metal) with a thin film of gold, silver, nickel, etc. 13. to cover or overlay with metal plates for protection, etc. —**plat′er,** *n.*

pla·teau (plă tō′), *n., pl.* **-teaus, -teaux** (-tōz′). 1. a broad, level surface of high elevation, deeply cut by narrow stream valleys or canyons. 2. *Psychol.* a period of little or no progress in an individual's learning.

plate glass, a soda-lime-silica glass formed by rolling the hot glass into a sheet: used in large windows, mirrors, etc.

plat·en (plăt′ən), *n.* 1. a flat plate or rotating cylinder in a printing press, which presses the paper against the inked type. 2. the roller of a typewriter.

plat·form (plăt′fôrm), *n.* 1. a raised flooring or structure for use by public speakers, performers, etc. 2. the raised area alongside the tracks of a railroad station. 3. a body of principles on which a political party or the like takes its stand in appealing to the public.

plat·ing (plā′tĭng), *n.* a thin coating of gold, silver, etc.

plat·i·num (plăt′ə nəm), *n. Chem.* a heavy, grayish-white, highly malleable and ductile metallic element. *Symbol:* Pt; *at. wt.:* 195.23; *at. no.:* 78; *sp. gr.:* 21.5 at 20°C.

plat·i·tude (plăt′ə tūd′, -tŏod′), *n.* a flat, dull, or trite remark. —**plat′i·tu′di·nous,** *adj.*

Pla·to (plā′tō), *n.* 427?-347 B.C., Greek philosopher.

Pla·ton·ic (plə tŏn′ĭk, plā-), *adj.* 1. of or pertaining to Plato or his doctrines. 2. (*l.c. or cap.*) purely spiritual; free from sensual desire.

Pla·to·nism (plā′tə nĭz′əm), *n.* the philosophy or doctrines of Plato or his followers. —**Pla′to·nist,** *n., adj.*

pla·toon (plə tōōn′), *n.* 1. a military unit consisting of two or more squads or sections. 2. a company or set of persons.

Platte (plăt), *n.* a river flowing from central Nebraska E to the Missouri river S of Omaha. 310 mi.

plat·ter (plăt′ər), *n.* a large, shallow dish, commonly oval, for serving meat, etc.

plat·y·pus (plăt′ə pəs), *n., pl.* **-puses, -pi** (-pī′). the duckbill.

plau·dit (plô′dĭt), *n.* (*usually pl.*) 1. a demonstration of applause. 2. any enthusiastic expression of approval.

plau·si·ble (plô′zə bəl), *adj.* 1. having an appearance of truth or reason; specious. 2. apparently worthy of confidence. —**plau′si·bil′i·ty,** *n.* —**plau′si·bly,** *adv.*

Plau·tus (plô′təs), *n.* **Titus Maccius,** c254-c184 B.C., Roman dramatist.

play (plā), *n.* 1. a dramatic composition for performance on the stage. 2. exercise or action by way of amusement or recreation. 3. fun, jest, or

trifling. 4. the carrying on of a game. 5. manner or style of playing. 6. an act or performance in playing. 7. turn to play. 8. the state, as of a ball, of being in use. 9. action or conduct. 10. elusive change, as of colors. 11. a space in which a thing, as a piece of mechanism, can move. 12. freedom of movement or action. —*v.t.* 13. to act the part of. 14. to perform (a drama, etc.) on the stage. 15. to give performances in. 16. to engage in (a game, etc.). 17. to contend against in a game. 18. to represent or imitate in fancy. 19. to perform on (a musical instrument). 20. to perform (music) on an instrument. 21. to do, perform, bring about, or execute. 22. to operate. —*v.i.* 23. to employ oneself in diversion, amusement, or recreation. 24. to amuse oneself or toy; trifle. 25. to engage in a game. 26. to conduct oneself in a specified way. 27. to act on the stage. 28. to perform on a musical instrument. 29. (of the instrument) to sound in performance. 30. to move about lightly or quickly. —**play′a·ble,** *adj.*

play·bill (plā′bĭl′), *n.* a program of a play.

play·boy (plā′boi′), *n. U.S. Colloq.* a wealthy, carefree person who spends most of his time at parties, nightclubs, etc.

play·er (plā′ər), *n.* 1. one who or that which plays. 2. one who takes part or is skilled in some game. 3. an actor. 4. a performer on a musical instrument. 5. a mechanical device by which a musical instrument is played, esp. a piano (**player piano**), is played automatically.

play·fel·low (plā′fĕl′ō), *n.* a playmate.

play·ful (plā′fəl), *adj.* 1. sportive; frolicsome. 2. pleasantly humorous. —**play′ful·ly,** *adv.* —**play′ful·ness,** *n.*

play·go·er (plā′gō′ər), *n.* one who often or habitually attends the theater.

play·ground (plā′ground′), *n.* ground used specifically for open-air recreation.

play·house (plā′hous′), *n.* 1. a theater. 2. a small house for children to play in.

playing card, one of the conventional set of 52 cards used in playing various games of chance and skill.

play·mate (plā′māt′), *n.* a companion in play.

play·off (plā′ôf′, -ŏf′), *n.* the playing of an extra game to break a tie.

play on words, a pun.

play·thing (plā′thĭng′), *n.* a toy.

play·wright (plā′rīt′), *n.* a writer of plays.

pla·za (plă′zə, plăz′ə), *n.* a public square or open space in a city or town.

plea (plē), *n.* 1. that which is alleged, urged, or pleaded in defense or justification. 2. *Law.* **a.** an allegation or defense made by a party to a legal suit. **b.** a suit or action at law. 3. an appeal or entreaty.

plead (plēd), *v.,* **pleaded** or (*Colloq. and Dial.*) **plead** (plĕd) or **pled; pleading.** —*v.i.* 1. to make earnest appeal or entreaty. 2. to use arguments or persuasions, as with a person. 3. *Law.* **a.** to make any allegation or plea. **b.** to address a court as an advocate. —*v.t.* 4. to allege or urge in defense or justification. 5. *Law.* **a.** to maintain (a cause, etc.) before a court. **b.** to allege (something) formally in an action at law. **c.** to cite in defense. —**plead′er,** *n.* —**plead′ing,** *n.*

pleas·ant (plĕz′ənt), *adj.* 1. pleasing; agreeable. 2. (of weather, etc.) fair. 3. gay; merry. 4. jocular. —**pleas′ant·ly,** *adv.* —**pleas′ant·ness,** *n.*

pleas·ant·ry (plĕz′ən trĭ), *n., pl.* **-ries.** 1. pleasant humor in conversation. 2. a humorous remark or action.

please (plēz), *v.,* **pleased, pleasing.** —*v.t.* 1. to act to the pleasure or satisfaction of. 2. to seem good to. 3. (as a polite addition to requests, etc.) if you are willing. 4. to like or wish. —*v.i.* 5. to give pleasure or satisfaction. —**pleas′ing,** *adj.* —**pleas′ing·ly,** *adv.*

pleas·ur·a·ble (plĕzh′ər ə bəl), *adj.* giving pleasure; agreeable. —**pleas′ur·a·bly,** *adv.*

pleas·ure (plĕzh′ər), *n., v.,* **-ured, -uring.** —*n.* 1. state or feeling of being pleased. 2. enjoyment or delight. 3. a cause of enjoyment or delight. 4. one's will, desire, or choice. —*v.t.* 5. to give pleasure to; gratify. —*v.i.* 6. to take pleasure; delight.

pleat (plēt), *n.* 1. a fold made by doubling cloth upon itself. —*v.t.* 2. to fold or arrange in pleats.

ple·be·ian (plĭ bē′ən), *adj.* 1. belonging or pertaining to the common people, orig. those of ancient Rome. **2.** common or vulgar. —*n.* **3.** a plebeian person. —**ple·be/ian·ism**, *n.*

pleb·i·scite (plĕb/ə sīt′, -sĭt), *n.* a direct vote of the qualified voters of a state in regard to some important public question.

plec·trum (plĕk/trəm), *n.*, *pl.* **-tra** (-trə), **-trums.** a small piece of wood, ivory, etc., used for plucking the strings of a lyre, mandolin, etc.

pledge (plĕj), *n.*, *v.*, **pledged, pledging.** —*n.* **1.** a solemn promise of something. **2.** a piece of personal property delivered as security, as for the payment of a debt. **3.** state of being given or held as security. **4.** a person accepted for membership in a club but not yet formally approved. **5.** an assurance of good will conveyed by drinking a person's health; toast. **6.** the solemn vow to abstain from intoxicating drink. —*v.t.* **7.** to bind by a pledge. **8.** to promise solemnly. **9.** to give as a pledge; pawn. —**pledg/er;** *esp. Law*, **pledg/or**, *n.*

Ple·ia·des (plē/ə dēz′, plī/-), *n.*, *pl.* of **pleiad.** *Astron.* a conspicuous cluster of seven stars in the constellation Taurus.

ple·na·ry (plē/nə rĭ, plĕn/ə rĭ), *adj.* **1.** full; complete; absolute. **2.** attended by all qualified members. —**ple/na·ri·ly**, *adv.*

plen·i·po·ten·ti·ar·y (plĕn/ĭ pō tĕn/shĭ ĕr/ĭ, -shə rĭ), *n.*, *pl.* **-aries**, *adj.* **1.** a person, esp. a diplomatic agent, with full authority to transact business. —*adj.* **2.** invested with full authority.

plen·i·tude (plĕn/ĭ tūd′, -tōōd′), *n.* fullness in quantity or degree; abundance.

plen·te·ous (plĕn/tĭ əs), *adj.* plentiful; abundant. —**plen/te·ous·ly**, *adv.* —**plen/te·ous·ness**, *n.*

plen·ti·ful (plĕn/tĭ fəl), *adj.* ample; abundant. —**plen/ti·ful·ly**, *adv.* —**plen/ti·ful·ness**, *n.*

plen·ty (plĕn/tĭ), *n.*, *pl.* **-ties**, *adj.*, *adv.* —*n.* **1.** a full or abundant supply. **2.** abundance. —*adj.* **3.** *Now Chiefly Colloq.* ample; enough. —*adv.* **4.** *Colloq.* fully.

ple·o·nasm (plē/ə năz′əm), *n.* the use of more words than necessary.

pleth·o·ra (plĕth/ə rə), *n.* superabundance.

pleu·ra (plŏor/ə), *n.*, *pl.* **pleurae** (plŏor/ē). a delicate membrane investing each lung in mammals and folded back as a lining of the thorax. —**pleu/ral**, *adj.*

pleu·ri·sy (plŏor/ə sĭ), *n.* *Pathol.* inflammation of the pleura. —**pleu·rit·ic** (plŏo rĭt/ĭk), *adj.*

Plex·i·glas (plĕk/sə glăs′, -gläs′), *n.* *Trademark.* a thermoplastic notable for its permanent transparency, light weight, and resistance to weathering.

plex·us (plĕk/səs), *n.*, *pl.* **plexuses, plexus.** a network, as of nerves or blood vessels.

pli·a·ble (plī/ə bəl), *adj.* **1.** easily bent; flexible. **2.** easily influenced; adaptable. —**pli·a·bil/i·ty**, *n.* —**pli/a·bly**, *adv.*

pli·ant (plī/ənt), *adj.* **1.** bending readily; flexible. **2.** easily influenced. —**pli/an·cy**, *n.* —**pli/ant·ly**, *adv.*

pli·er (plī/ər), *n.* **1.** *pl.* (*sometimes construed as sing.*) small pincers with long jaws, for holding small objects, etc. (often called a **pair of pliers**). **2.** one that plies.

plight[1] (plīt), *n.* condition, state, or situation (now usually bad).

plight[2] (plīt), *v.t.* to pledge or promise.

plinth (plĭnth), *n.* *Archit.* the lower square part of the base of a column.

plod (plŏd), *v.*, **plodded, plodding.** —*v.i.* **1.** to walk heavily; trudge. **2.** to work with dull perseverance. —*v.t.* **3.** to walk heavily over or along. —**plod/der**, *n.*

Plo·eș·ti (plô yĕsht′), *n.* a city in S Rumania: rich oil center. 101,376.

plot[1] (plŏt), *n.*, *v.*, **plotted, plotting.** —*n.* **1.** a secret scheme, esp. one for a hostile, unlawful, or evil purpose. **2.** the main story of a play, novel, poem, or the like. —*v.t.* *v.i.* **3.** to plan secretly (something hostile or evil). **4.** to mark on a plan, map, or chart, as a ship's course. **5.** to make a plot, plan, or map (of). —**plot/ter**, *n.*

plot[2] (plŏt), *n.*, *v.*, **plotted, plotting.** —*n.* **1.** a small area of ground. —*v.t.* **2.** to divide (land) into plots.

plov·er (plŭv/ər, plō/vər), *n.* any of certain shore-inhabiting birds, esp. those with a short tail and a bill like that of a pigeon, as the American **killdeer plover** and the **upland plover**.

plow (plou), *n.* **1.** an agricultural implement for cutting furrows in and turning up the soil. **2.** any of various similar implements, as one for clearing away snow from a road. —*v.t.*, *v.i.* **3.** to make fur-

rows in or turn up (the soil) with a plow. **4.** *Naut.* **a.** to cleave the surface of (the water). **b.** to make (a way) or follow (a course) thus. Also, *esp. Brit.*, **plough.** —**plow/er**, *n.* —**plow/man**, *n.*

plow·share (plou/shâr′), *n.* the blade of a plow.

pluck (plŭk), *v.t.*, *v.i.* **1.** to pull out from the place of growth, as fruit, flowers, feathers, etc. **2.** to pull, esp. with sudden force. **3.** to pull off the feathers, hair, etc., (from). **4.** *Slang.* to rob. **5.** to sound (the strings of a musical instrument) by pulling at them. **6. pluck up, a.** to pull up. **b.** to rouse (courage, etc.). —*n.* **7.** a pull, tug, or jerk. **8.** courage, spirit, or resolution. —**pluck/er**, *n.*

pluck·y (plŭk/ĭ), *adj.*, **pluckier, pluckiest.** having or showing pluck; brave. —**pluck/i·ly**, *adv.* —**pluck/i·ness**, *n.*

plug (plŭg), *n.*, *v.*, **plugged, plugging.** —*n.* **1.** a piece of wood or other material used to stop up a hole. **2.** *Elect.* a device to which may be attached the conductors of a cord and which, by insertion in a socket, establishes contact. **3.** a cake of pressed tobacco. **4.** *Chiefly U.S. Slang.* a worn-out or inferior horse. **5.** *U.S. Slang.* the favorable mention of a product, as in a lecture, radio show, etc. **6.** *Slang.* a man's tall sĭlk hat (**plug hat**). —*v.t.* **7.** to stop with a plug. **8.** to insert a plug into. **9.** *U.S. Slang.* to mention (a product) favorably, as in a lecture, radio show, etc. **10.** *Slang.* to shoot. —*v.i.* **11.** *Colloq.* to work steadily or doggedly. **12.** *Slang.* to shoot. —**plug/ger**, *n.*

plum (plŭm), *n.* **1.** the drupaceous fruit of any of various trees of the rose family, closely related to the cherry. **2.** a tree bearing such fruit. **3.** a raisin. **4.** a deep purple. **5.** a choice thing, appointment, etc. **6.** *Finance.* an extra dividend, generally large.

plum·age (plōō/mĭj), *n.* **1.** the feathery covering of a bird. **2.** feathers collectively.

plumb (plŭm), *n.* **1.** a small mass of lead or heavy material, esp. a plummet. **2.** the vertical. —*adj.* **3.** perpendicular. **4.** *Colloq.* downright. —*adv.* **5.** vertically. **6.** exactly or directly. **7.** *Colloq.* completely. —*v.t.* **8.** to test or adjust by a plumb line. **9.** to make vertical. **10.** to measure the depths of.

plumb·er (plŭm/ər), *n.* one who installs and repairs water pipes, fixtures, etc.

plumb·ing (plŭm/ĭng), *n.* **1.** the system of pipes and apparatus for conveying water, etc., as in a building. **2.** the work of a plumber.

plumb line, a cord to one end of which is attached a metal plumb, used to determine perpendicularity, find the depth of water, etc.

plume (plōōm), *n.*, *v.*, **plumed, pluming.** —*n.* **1.** a feather, esp. a large, long, or conspicuous one. **2.** a feather, a tuft of feathers, or some substitute, worn as an ornament on the hat, helmet, etc. —*v.t.* **3.** to furnish with plumes. **4.** (of a bird) to preen (itself). **5.** to pride (oneself) complacently.

plum·met (plŭm/ĭt), *n.* **1.** Also, **plumb bob.** a piece of lead or other weight attached to a line, used for determining perpendicularity, for sounding, etc. —*v.i.* **2.** to plunge.

plump[1] (plŭmp), *adj.* **1.** somewhat fleshy or fat; chubby. —*v.i.*, *v.t.* **2.** to make or become plump. —**plump/ly**, *adv.* —**plump/ness**, *n.*

plump[2] (plŭmp), *v.i.* **1.** to fall heavily or suddenly and directly. **2.** to vote exclusively for one candidate instead of distributing or splitting one's votes among a number. —*v.t.* **3.** to drop or throw heavily or suddenly. —*n.* **4.** a heavy or sudden fall. —*adv.* **5.** with a heavy or sudden fall. **6.** directly or bluntly. —*adj.* **7.** direct or blunt. —**plump/er**, *n.*

plum·y (plōō/mĭ), *adj.* having or resembling plumes.

plun·der (plŭn/dər), *v.t.*, *v.i.* **1.** to rob by open force, as in war. **2.** to despoil or fleece. —*n.* **3.** pillage or spoliation. **4.** loot. —**plun/der·er**, *n.*

plunge (plŭnj), *v.*, **plunged, plunging**, *n.* —*v.t.* **1.** to cast or thrust suddenly into a liquid, a place, etc. **2.** to bring into some condition. —*v.i.* **3.** to cast oneself, or fall as if cast, into water, a deep place, etc. **4.** to rush or dash. **5.** *Slang.* to bet or speculate recklessly. **6.** to descend abruptly. **7.** to pitch violently forward, esp. with the head downward, as a horse, a ship, etc. —*n.* **8.** act of plunging. **9.** a leap or dive into water or the like. **10.** a rush or dash.

plung·er (plŭn/jər), *n.* **1.** *Mach.* a part of a machine which acts with a plunging motion. **2.** one that plunges. **3.** *Slang.* a reckless bettor or speculator.

plunk (plŭngk), *Colloq. except def. 1.* —*v.t.* **1.** to pluck (a stringed instrument). **2.** to throw, put, etc., heavily or suddenly. —*v.i.* **3.** to plump. —*n.* **4.** act or sound of plunking. —*adv.* **5.** with a plunking sound.

plu·per·fect (plo͞o pûr'fĭkt), *Gram.* —*adj.* **1.** perfect with respect to a temporal point of reference in the past. **2.** designating a tense with such meaning. —*n.* **3.** the pluperfect tense. **4.** a form therein.

plupf., pluperfect.

plur., **1.** plural. **2.** plurality.

plu·ral (plo͝or'əl), *adj.* **1.** consisting of, containing, or pertaining to more than one. **2.** *Gram.* designating the number category that normally implies more than one person, thing, or collection. —*n.* **3.** *Gram.* **a.** the plural number. **b.** a form therein.

plu·ral·i·ty (plo͝o răl'ə tĭ), *n., pl.* **-ties.** **1.** the excess of votes received by the leading candidate over those received by the next candidate. **2.** more than half of the whole; majority. **3.** fact of being numerous. **4.** a large number; multitude. **5.** state or fact of being plural.

plu·ral·ly (plo͝or'ə lĭ), *adv.* as a plural.

plus (plŭs), *prep.* **1.** increased by. **2.** with. —*adj.* **3.** involving or denoting addition. **4.** positive. **5.** *Colloq.* with something in addition. **6.** more (by a certain amount). —*n.* **7.** a plus quantity. **8.** the plus sign (+). **9.** something additional. **10.** a surplus or gain.

plush (plŭsh), *n.* a fabric of silk, cotton, wool, etc., having a long pile.

plus sign, the symbol (+) indicating summation or a positive quantity.

Plu·tarch (plo͞o'tärk), *n.* A.D. c46–c120, Greek biographer.

Plu·to (plo͞o'tō), *n.* **1.** *Gk. Myth.* the lord of the dead and the lower world. **2.** *Astron.* the ninth and outermost planet from the sun.

plu·toc·ra·cy (plo͞o tŏk'rə sĭ), *n., pl.* **-cies.** a government or state in which the wealthy class rules.

plu·to·crat (plo͞o'tə krăt'), *n.* **1.** a member of a plutocracy. **2.** a wealthy person. —**plu'to·crat'ic,** *adj.*

plu·to·ni·um (plo͞o tō'nĭ əm), *n.* a radioactive element, capable of self-maintained explosive fission, formed by bombardment of neptunium. *Symbol:* Pu; *at. no.:* 94.

plu·vi·al (plo͞o'vĭ əl), *adj.* **1.** of or pertaining to rain; rainy. **2.** *Geol.* caused by rain.

ply[1] (plī), *v.t., v.i.,* **plied, plying. 1.** to use or work with. **2.** to carry on. **3.** to treat or assail with something repeatedly applied. **4.** to supply with something pressingly offered. **5.** to importune. **6.** to traverse (a river, etc.), esp. on regular trips.

ply[2] (plī), *n., pl.* **plies.** a fold; thickness.

Plym·outh (plĭm'əth), *n.* **1.** a seaport in SW England: the departing point of the *Mayflower.* 177,200. **2.** a city in SE Massachusetts: founded by the Pilgrims (1620). 13,100.

Plymouth Rock, 1. a rock at Plymouth, Massachusetts, on which the Pilgrim Fathers are said to have landed in 1620. **2.** an American breed of domestic fowls.

ply·wood (plī'wo͝od'), *n.* a material consisting of thin sheets of wood glued together.

P.M., **1.** Postmaster. **2.** (*also l.c.*) post meridiem. **3.** Prime Minister.

pneu·mat·ic (no͞o măt'ĭk, no͞o-), *adj.* **1.** of or pertaining to air, or to gases in general. **2.** pertaining to pneumatics. **3.** operated by air. **4.** containing or filled with air, as a tire. —*n.* **5.** a pneumatic tire. —**pneu·mat'i·cal·ly,** *adv.*

pneu·mat·ics (no͞o măt'ĭks, no͞o-), *n.* the branch of physics that deals with the mechanical properties of air and other gases.

pneu·mo·nia (no͞o mō'nyə, -nĭ ə, no͞o-), *n. Pathol.* inflammation or infection of the lungs.

Po (pō), *n.* a river flowing from the Alps in NW Italy E to the Adriatic. 418 mi.

Po, *Chem.* polonium.

P.O., **1.** postal order. **2.** post office.

poach[1] (pōch), *v.i.* **1.** to take game or fish illegally. **2.** *Chiefly Brit.* to trespass on another's land, etc., esp. to steal game. —**poach'er,** *n.*

poach[2] (pōch), *v.t.* to cook (an egg) in hot water but without the shell.

Po·ca·hon·tas (pō'kə hŏn'təs), *n.* 1595?–1617, American Indian girl said to have prevented the execution of Captain John Smith.

pock (pŏk), *n.* **1.** a pustule on the body in an

eruptive disease, as smallpox. **2.** a mark left by such a pustule.

pock·et (pŏk'ĭt), *n.* **1.** a small bag inserted in a garment, for carrying small articles. **2.** a bag or pouch. **3.** any pouchlike receptacle, hollow, or cavity. **4.** a cavity in the earth, esp. one containing gold or other ore. **5.** a small bag at the corner or side of a billiard table. —*adj.* **6.** suitable for carrying in the pocket. **7.** small; diminutive. —*v.t.* **8.** to put into one's pocket. **9.** to take possession of. **10.** to endure without protest or open resentment. **11.** to suppress.

pocket battleship, a small, heavily armed and armored warship.

pock·et·book (pŏk'ĭt bo͝ok'), *n.* a small bag or case for papers, money, etc.

pock·et·knife (pŏk'ĭt nīf'), *n., pl.* **-knives** (-nīvz'). a small knife with one or more blades which fold into the handle.

pocket veto, the retaining without action, past the time of the adjournment of Congress, by the President of the U.S., of a bill presented to him for signature within ten days of the end of a session, which is equivalent to a veto.

pock·mark (pŏk'märk'), *n.* a mark or pit left by a pustule in smallpox or the like.

po·co (pō'kō), *adj. Music.* somewhat.

pod (pŏd), *n., v.,* **podded, podding.** —*n.* **1.** an elongated, two-valved seed vessel, as that of the pea. **2.** a dehiscent fruit with several seeds. —*v.i.* **3.** to produce pods. **4.** to swell out like a pod.

P.O.D., pay on delivery.

po·di·a·try (pō dī'ə trĭ), *n. Med.* the investigation and treatment of foot disorders. —**po·di'a·trist,** *n.*

po·di·um (pō'dĭ əm), *n., pl.* **-dia** (-dĭ ə). a small dais, esp. one used by an orchestra conductor.

Po·dunk (pō'dŭngk), *n. U.S.* a humorous name for any small or insignificant place.

Poe (pō), *n.* Edgar Allan, 1809–49, U.S. poet, writer of tales, and critic.

po·em (pō'ĭm), *n.* a composition in verse, esp. one characterized by artistic construction and imaginative or elevated thought.

po·e·sy (pō'ə sĭ, -zĭ), *n., pl.* **-sies.** **1.** *Poetic.* poetry. **2.** *Archaic.* the art of poetry.

po·et (pō'ĭt), *n.* one who composes poetry. —**po'et·ess,** *n. fem.*

poet., **1.** poetic. **2.** poetical. **3.** poetry.

po·et·as·ter (pō'ĭt ăs'tər), *n.* an inferior poet.

po·et·ic (pō ĕt'ĭk), *adj.* Also, **po·et'i·cal. 1.** possessing the qualities or the charm of poetry. **2.** of or pertaining to a poet or poets, or to poetry. **3.** characteristic of or befitting a poet. **4.** endowed with the faculty or feeling of a poet. —*n.* **5.** poetics. —**po·et'i·cal·ly,** *adv.*

po·et·ics (pō ĕt'ĭks), *n.* literary criticism treating of the nature and laws of poetry.

poet laureate, *pl.,* **poets laureate.** (in Great Britain) an officer of the royal household, of whom no special duty is required, but who formerly was expected to write odes, etc., in celebration of court and national events.

po·et·ry (pō'ĭt rĭ), *n.* **1.** the art of rhythmical composition, written or spoken, for exciting pleasure by beautiful, imaginative, or elevated thoughts. **2.** literary work in metrical form. **3.** poetic spirit.

po·grom (pō'grəm, pō grŏm'), *n.* an organized massacre, esp. of Jews.

poi (poi, pō'ĭ), *n.* a Hawaiian dish made of the root of the taro.

poign·ant (poin'yənt, poin'ənt), *adj.* **1.** keenly distressing. **2.** strong in mental appeal. **3.** pungent to the taste or smell. —**poign'an·cy,** *n.* —**poign'ant·ly,** *adv.*

poi·lu (pwä'lo͞o), *n.* a French common soldier.

poin·ci·a·na (poin'sĭ ă'nə), *n.* any of certain trees or shrubs of warm areas with showy orange or scarlet flowers.

poin·set·ti·a (poin sĕt'ĭ ə), *n.* a perennial plant of the spurge family, native to Mexico and Central America, with lobed leaves and brilliant scarlet bracts: associated in the U.S. with Christmas festivities.

point (point), *n.* **1.** a sharp or tapering end, as of a dagger. **2.** a projecting part. **3.** a tapering extremity, as a cape. **4.** a pointed tool or instrument. **5.** a mark made with the sharp end of something; dot. **6.** a mark of punctuation. **7.** the period. **8.** a decimal point, etc. **9.** *Phonet., etc.* a diacritical mark indicating a vowel or other modification of sound. **10.** something that has position but not extension, as the intersection of two lines. **11.** a place of which the position alone is considered. **12.** any definite position, as in a scale, course, etc. **13.** each of the 32 positions indicating direction marked at the circumference of the card of a compass. **14.** a degree or stage. **15.** a particular instant of time. **16.** a decisive state of circumstances. **17.** the essential thing or feature. **18.** a particular aim, end, or purpose. **19.** a hint. **20.** a detail or particular. **21.** a distinguishing quality, esp. one of an animal, used as a standard, in stockbreeding, etc. **22.** a single unit, as in counting, scoring, measuring rations allowed, etc. **23.** *Educ.* a single credit, usually corresponding to an hour's class work per week for one semester. **24.** *Elect.* either of a pair of contacts that make or break current flow in a distributor. **25.** *Print.* a unit of measurement: about 1/72 (.0138+) of an inch in the U.S. system. **26. at the point,** close to. **27. in point,** pertinent. **28. in point of,** as regards. **29. make a point of,** to insist upon. **30. on the point of,** on the verge of. **31. to the point,** pertinent. —*v.t.* **32.** to direct (the finger, a weapon, the attention, etc.) at, to, or upon something. **33.** to indicate. **34.** to furnish with a point; sharpen. —*v.i.* **35.** to indicate position or direction, or direct attention, with or as with the finger. **36.** to direct thought in some direction. **37.** to have a specified direction.

point-blank (point′blǎngk′), *adj.* **1.** aimed or fired straight at the mark; direct. **2.** straightforward; plain. —*adv.* **3.** directly; straight. **4.** without circumlocution or deliberation.

point·ed (poin′tǐd), *adj.* **1.** having a point or points. **2.** sharp or piercing. **3.** having force. **4.** directed; aimed. **5.** marked. —**point′ed·ly,** *adv.* —**point′ed·ness,** *n.*

point·er (poin′tər), *n.* **1.** one that points. **2.** a long, tapering stick used by teachers, lecturers, etc., in pointing things out on a map, blackboard, or the like. **3.** the hand on a watch, machine, or instrument. **4.** one of a breed of short-haired hunting dogs trained to indicate game. **5.** *U.S. Colloq.* a hint or suggestion.

point·less (point′lǐs), *adj.* **1.** without a point. **2.** blunt. **3.** without force, meaning, or relevance. **4.** without a point scored. —**point′less·ly,** *adv.* —**point′less·ness,** *n.*

point of view, a viewpoint.

poise (poiz), *n., v.,* **poised, poising.** —*n.* **1.** a state of balance or equilibrium. **2.** composure; self-possession. **3.** stability. —*v.t.* **4.** to balance evenly. **5.** to hold in position for casting, using, etc. —*v.i.* **6.** to be balanced. **7.** to hang supported or suspended. **8.** to hover.

poi·son (poi′zən), *n.* **1.** any substance (liquid, solid, or gaseous) which destroys life or impairs health. —*v.t.* **2.** to administer poison to. **3.** to kill or injure with poison. **4.** to put poison into or upon. **5.** to ruin; corrupt. —*adj.* **6.** containing or being a poison. —**poi′son·er,** *n.* —**poi′son·ous,** *adj.* —**poi′son·ous·ly,** *adv.*

poison ivy, any of several North American shrubs, poisonous to the touch, with shiny trifoliate leaves, green flowers, and whitish berries.

poison oak, any of certain shrubs poisonous to the touch.

poke[1] (pōk), *v.,* **poked, poking,** *n.* —*v.t., v.i.* **1.** to thrust against or into (something) with the finger, a stick, etc. **2.** to make (a hole, one's way, etc.) by thrusting. **3.** to thrust or push. **4.** to force or drive by pushing. **5.** to direct (fun) at a person or thing. **6.** to thrust obtrusively. —*n.* **7.** a thrust or push.

poke[2] (pōk), *n.* **1.** *Now Chiefly Dial.* a bag or sack. **2.** *Archaic.* a pocket.

poke[3] (pōk), *n.* a projecting brim at the front of a woman's bonnet (**poke bonnet**).

pok·er[1] (pō′kər), *n.* **1.** one that pokes. **2.** a metal rod for poking or stirring a fire.

pok·er[2] (pō′kər), *n.* a card game played by two or more persons, in which the players bet on the value of their hand.

poke·weed (pōk′wēd′), *n.* a tall herb of North America, having juicy purple berries (**pokeberries**) and a purple root used in medicine.

Poke bonnet

pok·y (pō′kǐ), *adj.,* **pokier, pokiest.** *Colloq.* **1.** slow; dull. **2.** small and cramped. **3.** dowdy. Also, **poke′y.**

pol., **1.** political. **2.** politics.

Po·land (pō′lənd), *n.* a republic in C Europe.

23,622,334 pop.; ab. 121,000 sq. mi. *Cap.:* Warsaw.

po·lar (pō′lər), *adj.* **1.** of or pertaining to a pole, as of the earth, a magnet, etc. **2.** opposite in character or action. **3.** existing as ions.

polar bear, a large white bear of the arctic regions.

Po·lar·is (pō lâr′ĭs), *n.* *Astron.* a star of the second magnitude situated close to the north pole of the heavens; the polestar or North Star.

po·lar·i·ty (pō lǎr′ə tǐ), *n.* *Physics.* **1.** the possession of an axis with reference to which certain physical properties are determined. **2.** the power or tendency of a magnetized bar, etc., to orient itself along the lines of force. **3.** positive or negative polar condition.

po·lar·i·za·tion (pō′lər ə zā′shən), *n.* **1.** *Optics.* a state, or the production of a state, in which rays of light exhibit different properties in different directions. **2.** *Elect.* the process by which gases produced during electrolysis are deposited on the electrodes of a cell. **3.** the production or acquisition of polarity.

po·lar·ize (pō′lə rīz′), *v.t.,* **-ized, -izing.** to cause polarization in.

Po·lar·oid (pō′lə roid′), *n.* *Trademark.* a sheet of prepared plastic material which polarizes light.

pole[1] (pōl), *n., v.,* **poled, poling.** —*n.* **1.** a long, slender piece of wood or other material. **2.** a unit of length. equal to 16½ ft. **3.** a square rod, 30¼ sq. yards. —*v.t.* **4.** to furnish with poles. **5.** to push, propel, etc., with a pole.

pole[2] (pōl), *n.* **1.** each of the extremities of the axis of the earth or of any spherical body. **2.** each of the two points in which the axis of the earth produced cuts the celestial sphere, about which the stars seem to revolve (**celestial pole**). **3.** *Physics.* each of the two regions or parts of a magnet, electric battery, etc., at which certain opposite forces appear to be concentrated.

Pole (pōl), *n.* a native or inhabitant of Poland.

pole·cat (pōl′kǎt′), *n.* **1.** an ill-smelling, long-haired member of the weasel family, resembling a marten. **2.** any of various North American skunks.

po·lem·ic (pō lěm′ĭk), *n.* **1.** a controversial argument. **2.** Also, **po·lem′i·cal.** controversial. —**po·lem′i·cal·ly,** *adv.*

po·lem·ics (pō lěm′ĭks), *n.* the art or practice of disputation, esp. in theology.

pole·star (pōl′stär′), *n.* **1.** Polaris. **2.** a guide; lodestar.

pole vault, *Sports.* a leap over a horizontal bar with the help of a long pole.

po·lice (pə lēs′), *n., v.,* **-liced, -licing.** —*n.* **1.** an organized civil force for maintaining order, preventing and detecting crime, and enforcing the laws. **2.** (*construed as pl.*) the members of such a force. —*v.t.* **3.** to regulate, control, or keep in order.

police dog, a sheep dog of wolflike appearance, used in police work, as a guide for the blind, etc.

po·lice·man (pə lēs′mən), *n., pl.* **-men.** a member of a body or force of police. —**po·lice′wom′an,** *n. fem.*

pol·i·cy[1] (pŏl′ə sǐ), *n., pl.* **-cies. 1.** a definite course of action adopted and pursued. **2.** action conforming to prudence or expediency. **3.** prudence; practical wisdom. **4.** sagacity; shrewdness.

pol·i·cy[2] (pŏl′ə sǐ), *n., pl.* **-cies. 1.** a document embodying a contract of insurance. **2.** *U.S.* a method of gambling in which bets are made on numbers to be drawn by lottery.

pol·i·o·my·e·li·tis (pŏl′ĭ ō mī′ə lī′tĭs), *n.* *Pathol.* infantile spinal paralysis. Also, *Colloq.,* **po·li·o** (pō′lĭ ō′).

pol·ish (pŏl′ĭsh), *v.t., v.i.* **1.** to make or become smooth and glossy, esp. by friction. **2.** to render or become finished or elegant. **3.** to take or bring by smoothing or refining. **4.** *Slang.* to finish quickly. **5.** *Slang.* to improve. —*n.* **6.** a substance used to give smoothness or gloss. **7.** smoothness and gloss of surface. **8.** refinement; elegance. —**pol′ished,** *adj.* —**pol′ish·er,** *n.*

Pol·ish (pō′lǐsh), *adj.* **1.** of or pertaining to the Poles or Poland. —*n.* **2.** a Slavic language, the principal language of Poland.

polit., **1.** political. **2.** politics.

Po·lit·bu·ro (pŏ lǐt′byŏŏr′ŏ), *n.* a committee in the Communist Party of the Soviet Union, which examines every question before it is referred to the government, and sometimes issues orders independently.

po·lite (pə līt´), *adj.* **1.** showing good manners; courteous. **2.** refined or cultured. **—po·lite´ly**, *adv.* **—po·lite´ness**, *n.*

pol·i·tic (pŏl´ə tĭk), *adj.* **1.** sagacious or prudent. **2.** shrewd; artful. **3.** expedient; judicious. **4.** political. **—pol´i·tic·ly**, *adv.*

po·lit·i·cal (pə lĭt´ə kəl), *adj.* **1.** pertaining to or dealing with politics. **2.** exercising or seeking power in the government. **3.** involving the government. **4.** engaged in or connected with civil administration. **5.** of or pertaining to citizens. **—po·lit´i·cal·ly**, *adv.*

political economy, economics.

political science, the science of the principles and conduct of government.

pol·i·ti·cian (pŏl´ə tĭsh´ən), *n.* **1.** one who is active in party politics. **2.** one who holds a political office. **3.** a statesman.

po·lit·i·co (pə lĭt´ə kō´), *n., pl.* **-cos.** a politician.

pol·i·tics (pŏl´ə tĭks), *n.* **1.** the science of political government. **2.** the practice of conducting political affairs. **3.** political affairs. **4.** political methods. **5.** (*construed as pl.*) political principles.

pol·i·ty (pŏl´ə tĭ), *n., pl.* **-ties. 1.** a particular system of government. **2.** government. **3.** a state or other organized community or body.

Polk (pōk), *n.* **James Knox,** 1795–1849, the 11th president of the U.S., 1845–49.

pol·ka (pōl´kə, pō´kə), *n., v.,* **-kaed, -kaing. —n.** **1.** a lively round dance of Bohemian origin with music in duple time. **2.** a piece of music for such a dance or in its rhythm. **—v.i. 3.** to dance the polka.

polka dot, 1. a dot repeated to form a pattern on a fabric. **2.** a pattern of such dots.

poll (pōl), *n.* **1.** the registering of votes, as at an election. **2.** the voting at an election. **3.** the number of votes cast. **4.** the numerical result of the voting. **5.** a list of individuals, as for taxing or voting. **6.** (*usually pl.*) the place where votes are taken. **7.** an analysis of public opinion on a subject, usually by selective sampling. **8.** the head. **—v.t. 9.** to receive at the polls, as votes. **10.** to take or register the votes of. **11.** to cast at the polls, as a vote. **—v.i. 12.** to give one's vote.

pol·lack (pŏl´ək), *n., pl.* **-lacks,** (*esp. collectively*) **-lack. 1.** a darkly colored North Atlantic food fish of the cod family. **2.** a similar North Pacific cod.

pol·len (pŏl´ən), *n.* the fertilizing element of flowering plants, consisting of fine, powdery, yellowish grains or spores, sometimes in masses.

pol·li·nate (pŏl´ə nāt´), *v.t.,* **-nated, -nating.** *Bot.* to convey pollen for fertilization to. **—pol´li·na´tion**, *n.*

pol·li·wog (pŏl´ĭ wŏg´), *n.* a tadpole.

poll tax, a tax on the individual, the payment of which is a prerequisite to exercise of the right of suffrage.

pol·lute (pə loot´), *v.t.,* **-luted, -luting. 1.** to make foul or dirty. **2.** to defile. **3.** to desecrate. **—pol·lu´tion** (pə loo´shən), *n.*

Pol·ly·an·na (pŏl´ĭ ăn´ə), *n.* a blindly optimistic person.

po·lo (pō´lō), *n.* a game resembling hockey, played on horseback with long-handled mallets and a wooden ball. **—po´lo·ist**, *n.*

Po·lo (pō´lō), *n.* **Marco,** c1254–c1324, Venetian traveler in Asia.

pol·o·naise (pŏl´ə nāz´, pō´lə-), *n.* **1.** a slow dance of Polish origin, in triple rhythm. **2.** a piece of music for such a dance.

po·lo·ni·um (pə lō´nĭ əm), *n. Chem.* a radioactive element. *Symbol:* Po; *at. no.:* 84; *at. wt.:* about 210.

pol·troon (pŏl troon´), *n.* a wretched coward. **—pol·troon´er·y**, *n.*

pol·y·an·dry (pŏl´ĭ ăn´drĭ, pŏl´ĭ ăn´-), *n.* **1.** the practice or the condition of having more than one husband at one time. **2.** *Bot.* the fact of having 20 or more free stamens. **—pol´y·an´drous**, *adj.*

pol·y·an·thus (pŏl´ĭ ăn´thəs), *n.* **1.** a hybrid primrose. **2.** a narcissus, in many varieties, bearing small white or yellow flowers.

pol·y·clin·ic (pŏl´ĭ klĭn´ĭk), *n.* a clinic or a hospital dealing with various diseases.

po·lyg·a·my (pə lĭg´ə mĭ), *n.* the practice or condition of having many or several spouses, esp.

wives, at one time. **—po·lyg´a·mist**, *n.* **—po·lyg´a·mous**, *adj.*

pol·y·glot (pŏl´ĭ glŏt´), *adj.* **1.** knowing several languages. **2.** containing or in several languages. **—n. 3.** a person with a command of a number of languages.

pol·y·gon (pŏl´ĭ gŏn´), *n.* a figure, esp. a closed plane figure, having more than four angles and sides. **—po·lyg·o·nal** (pə lĭg´ə nəl), *adj.*

pol·y·he·dron (pŏl´ĭ hē´drən), *n., pl.* **-drons, -dra** (-drə). a solid figure having many faces. **—pol´y·he´dral**, *adj.*

pol·y·mer (pŏl´ĭ mər), *n. Chem.* a compound of high molecular weight derived either by the combination of many smaller molecules or by the condensation of many smaller molecules eliminating water, alcohol, etc.

pol·y·mer·ic (pŏl´ĭ mĕr´ĭk), *adj. Chem.* (of compounds) having the same elements combined in the same proportions by weight, but differing in molecular weight.

po·lym·er·i·za·tion (pə lĭm´ər ə zā´shən, pŏl´ĭ mər-), *n. Chem.* **1.** act or process of forming a polymer or polymeric compound. **2.** the union of two or more molecules of a compound to form a more complex compound with a higher molecular weight.

pol·y·mer·ize (pŏl´ĭ mə rīz´, pə lĭm´ə rīz´), *v.t., v.i.,* **-ized, -izing. 1.** to combine so as to form a polymer. **2.** to subject to or undergo polymerization.

pol·y·mor·phous (pŏl´ĭ môr´fəs), *adj.* having, assuming, or passing through many or various forms, stages, or the like. Also, **pol´y·mor´phic**. **—pol´y·mor´phism**, *n.*

Pol·y·ne·sia (pŏl´ə nē´shə, -zhə), *n.* one of the three principal divisions of Oceania, comprising those island groups in the Pacific lying E of Melanesia and Micronesia and extending from the Hawaiian Islands S to New Zealand. **—Pol´y·ne´sian**, *adj., n.*

pol·y·no·mi·al (pŏl´ĭ nō´mĭ əl), *adj.* **1.** of or characterized by several terms. **—n. 2.** a polynomial name. **3.** *Alg.* an expression consisting of two or more terms.

pol·yp (pŏl´ĭp), *n.* **1.** *Zool.* a sedentary type of animal form characterized by a more or less fixed base, columnar body, and free end with mouth and tentacles. **2.** *Pathol.* a projecting growth from a mucous surface, as of the nose.

pol·y·phon·ic (pŏl´ĭ fŏn´ĭk), *adj.* **1.** consisting of many voices or sounds. **2.** *Music.* having two or more voices or parts, each with an independent melody, but all harmonizing; contrapuntal. **—po·lyph·o·ny** (pə lĭf´ə nĭ), *n.*

pol·y·syl·lab·ic (pŏl´ĭ sĭ lăb´ĭk), *adj.* **1.** consisting of many syllables. **2.** characterized by such words. **—pol´y·syl´la·ble**, *n.*

pol·y·tech·nic (pŏl´ĭ tĕk´nĭk), *adj.* **1.** pertaining to or dealing with various arts. **—n. 2.** a school for technical subjects.

pol·y·the·ism (pŏl´ĭ thē ĭz´əm), *n.* the doctrine of, or belief in, many gods or more gods than one. **—pol´y·the´ist**, *n.* **—pol´y·the·is´tic**, *adj.*

pom·ace (pŭm´ĭs), *n.* **1.** the pulpy residue from apples or similar fruit after crushing and pressing, as in cider making. **2.** any crushed or ground pulpy substance.

po·made (pō mād´, -mäd´), *n., v.,* **-maded, -mading. —n. 1.** a scented ointment for the scalp and hair. **—v.t. 2.** to apply pomade to.

pome (pōm), *n. Bot.* the fruit of any member of the apple family, as an apple, pear, quince, etc.

pome·gran·ate (pŏm´grăn´ĭt, pŭm´-, pəm-grăn´ĭt), *n.* **1.** a many-seeded fruit with a tough rind (usually red), the edible portion consisting of pleasantly acid flesh developed from the outer seed coat. **2.** the shrub or small tree which yields it, native in southwestern Asia.

Pom·er·a·ni·an (pŏm´ə rā´nĭ ən), *n.* one of a breed of medium-sized or small dogs with sharp nose, pointed ears, and long, thick, silky hair.

pom·mel (pŭm´əl, pŏm´əl), *n., v.,* **-meled, -meling** or (*esp. Brit.*) **-melled, -melling. —n. 1.** a knob, as the protuberant part at the front and top of a saddle. **—v.t. 2.** to strike or beat.

pomp (pŏmp), *n.* **1.** stately display; splendor. **2.** ostentatious display.

pom·pa·dour (pŏm´pə dōr´, -dŏŏr´), *n.* **1.** an arrangement of a man's hair, brushed up from the forehead. **2.** an arrangement of a woman's hair in which it is raised above the forehead.

Pom·pa·dour (pōn pà doŏr´), *n.* **Marquise de,** 1721–64, mistress of Louis XV of France.

pom·pa·no (pŏm′pə nō′), *n.*, *pl.* **-nos.** a deep-bodied food fish of the U.S.

Pom·pe·ii (pŏm pā′ē), *n.* an ancient city in SW Italy at the foot of Mount Vesuvius: buried by an eruption, A.D. 79. **—Pom·pe·ian** (pŏm pā′-ən, -pē′ən), *adj.*, *n.*

Pom·pey (pŏm′pǐ), *n.* 106–48 B.C., Roman general and statesman.

pom·pom (pŏm′pŏm), *n.* an automatic anti-aircraft cannon.

pom·pon (pŏm′pŏn), *n.* **1.** an ornamental tuft or ball of feathers, wool, or the like. **2.** *Hort.* a small globe-shaped flower head that characterizes chrysanthemums and dahlias.

pomp·ous (pŏm′pəs), *adj.* **1.** characterized by an ostentatious parade of importance. **2.** (of language, etc.) ostentatiously lofty. **3.** characterized by pomp. **—pomp′ous·ly,** *adv.* **—pomp′-ous·ness, pom·pos·i·ty** (pŏm pŏs′ə tǐ), *n.*

Pon·ce (pŏn′sě), *n.* a seaport in S Puerto Rico. 65,182.

Ponce de Le·ón (pŏns′də lē′ən), **Juan,** c1460–1521, Spanish explorer of Florida.

pon·cho (pŏn′chō), *n.*, *pl.* **-chos.** a blanketlike cloak with hole in center to put on over the head, worn originally in South America, now widely used as a raincoat.

pond (pŏnd), *n.* a body of water smaller than a lake, esp. one artificially formed.

pon·der (pŏn′dər), *v.i.*, *v.t.* to consider deeply; meditate.

pon·der·ous (pŏn′dər əs), *adj.* **1.** of great weight; heavy. **2.** without graceful lightness or ease. **—pon′der·ous·ly,** *adv.* **—pon·der·ous-ness, pon·der·os·i·ty** (pŏn′də rŏs′ə tǐ), *n.*

pone (pōn), *n.* *Southern U.S.* bread, esp. of a plain kind, made of corn meal.

pon·gee (pŏn jē′), *n.* a fabric woven of wild silk in natural tan color.

pon·iard (pŏn′yərd), *n.* **1.** a dagger. **—***v.t.* **2.** to stab with a poniard.

pons (pŏnz), *n.*, *pl.* **pontes** (pŏn′tēz). *Anat.* a connecting part.

Pon·ti·ac (pŏn′tǐ ăk′), *n.* a city in SE Michigan. 66,626.

pon·tiff (pŏn′tǐf), *n.* **1.** a high or chief priest. **2.** *Eccles.* **a.** a bishop. **b.** the Bishop of Rome (the Pope). **—pon·tif′i·cal** (pŏn tǐf′ə kəl), *adj.*

pon·tif·i·cate (pŏn tǐf′ə kǐt, -kāt′), *n.* **1.** the office, or term of office, of a pontiff. **—***v.i.* **2.** to speak in a pompous manner.

pon·toon (pŏn tōōn′), *n.* **1.** *Mil.* a floating structure used as one of the supports for a temporary bridge (**pontoon bridge**) over a river. **2.** a watertight box used in raising a submerged vessel, etc. **3.** a seaplane float. Also, **pon·ton** (pŏn′tən).

po·ny (pō′nǐ), *n.*, *pl.* **-nies,** *v.*, **-nied, -nying.** **—***n.* **1.** a horse of a small type or breed. **2.** *U.S. Slang.* a translation or other illicit aid. **—***v.t., v.i. U.S. Slang.* **3.** to pay (money), as in settling an account.

pooch (pōōch), *n.* *Slang.* a dog, esp. a mongrel.

poo·dle (pōō′dəl), *n.* one of a breed of pet dogs with thick curly hair often trimmed in an elaborate manner.

pooh-pooh (pōō′pōō′), *v.t.* to express disdain or contempt for; make light of.

pool¹ (pōōl), *n.* **1.** a small body of standing water. **2.** a puddle. **3.** a swimming tank.

pool² (pōōl), *n.* **1.** an association of competitors who agree to control the production, market, and price of a commodity for mutual benefit, although they appear to be rivals. **2.** the combined interests or funds of several persons, firms, etc. **3.** a game played by two or more persons on a billiard table with six pockets. **—***v.t.* **4.** to put (interests, money, etc.) into a common fund.

Poo·na (pōō′nə), *n.* a city in W India, 75 mi. SE of Bombay. 258,197.

poop (pōōp), *n.* **1.** the aftermost part of a ship. **2.** Also, **poop deck.** a deck above the ordinary deck in that part.

poor (pōōr), *adj.* **1.** having little or no wealth, goods, or means of subsistence. **2.** characterized by or showing poverty. **3.** deficient or lacking. **4.** faulty or inferior. **5.** inferior, inadequate, or unsatisfactory; not good. **6.** scanty or paltry. **7.** humble. **8.** unfortunate or hapless. **—***n.* **9.** poor persons collectively. **—poor′ly,** *adv.* **—poor′ness,** *n.*

poor·house (pōōr′hous′), *n.* a house in which paupers are maintained at the public expense.

pop¹ (pŏp), *v.*, **popped, popping,** *n.*, *adv.* **—***v.i.*

1. to make a short, quick, explosive sound. **2.** to burst open with such a sound. **3.** to come or go quickly or suddenly. **4.** to shoot. **—***v.t.* **5.** to cause to make a sudden, explosive sound. **6.** to cause to burst open with such a sound. **7.** to put or thrust quickly or suddenly. **8.** to shoot. **—***n.* **9.** a short, quick, explosive sound. **10.** an effervescent beverage, esp. an unintoxicating one. **—***adv.* **11.** with an explosive sound. **12.** quickly or suddenly.

pop² (pŏp), *adj.* *Colloq.* popular.

pop., **1.** popular. **2.** population.

pop·corn (pŏp′kôrn′), *n.* **1.** any of several varieties of corn whose kernels burst open and puff out when subjected to dry heat. **2.** popped corn.

pope (pōp), *n.* (*often cap.*) the bishop of Rome as head of the Roman Catholic Church.

Pope (pōp), *n.* **Alexander,** 1688–1744, British poet.

pop·gun (pŏp′gŭn′), *n.* a child's toy gun from which a pellet is shot with a loud pop by compressed air.

pop·in·jay (pŏp′ĭn jā′), *n.* a vain, chattering person; fop.

pop·ish (pōp′ĭsh), *adj.* of the Roman Catholic Church (used in a hostile sense).

pop·lar (pŏp′lər), *n.* **1.** any of certain rapidly growing trees yielding a useful, light, soft wood, as the **Lombardy poplar,** a tall, strikingly columnar tree. **2.** the wood itself.

pop·lin (pŏp′lĭn), *n.* a corded fabric of cotton, wool, rayon, or silk.

Po·po·ca·te·pet·l (pō′pə kăt′ə pĕt′əl), *n.* a volcano in S central Mexico, ab. 40 mi. SE of Mexico City. 17,876 ft.

pop·o·ver (pŏp′ō′vər), *n.* a kind of muffin so light as to overflow its pan in cooking.

pop·per (pŏp′ər), *n.* **1.** one that pops. **2.** a utensil for popping corn.

pop·py (pŏp′ĭ), *n.*, *pl.* **-pies.** **1.** any of certain herbs with showy flowers of various colors, including one species which is the source of opium. **2.** an extract, as opium, from such a plant. **3.** orangish-red; scarlet.

pop·py·cock (pŏp′ĭ kŏk′), *n.* *Colloq.* nonsense; bosh.

pop·u·lace (pŏp′yə lĭs), *n.* the common people of a community.

pop·u·lar (pŏp′yə lər), *adj.* **1.** regarded with favor or approval by associates, acquaintances, etc. **2.** of, pertaining to, or representing the people. **3.** generally prevalent. **4.** suited to or intended for ordinary people. **—pop′u·lar·ly,** *adv.*

popular front, an alliance of leftwing, labor, and liberal parties against reactionary government.

pop·u·lar·i·ty (pŏp′yə lăr′ə tǐ), *n.* the quality or fact of being popular.

pop·u·lar·ize (pŏp′yə lə rīz′), *v.t.,* **-ized, -izing.** to make popular. **—pop′u·lar·i·za′tion,** *n.* **—pop′u·lar·iz′er,** *n.*

pop·u·late (pŏp′yə lāt′), *v.t.,* **-lated, -lating.** **1.** to inhabit. **2.** to furnish with inhabitants.

pop·u·la·tion (pŏp′yə lā′shən), *n.* **1.** the total number of persons inhabiting a country, city, or any district or area. **2.** the body of inhabitants of a place. **3.** *Statistics.* an aggregate of statistical items. **4.** act or process of populating.

pop·u·lous (pŏp′yə ləs), *adj.* full of inhabitants. **—pop′u·lous·ness,** *n.*

por·ce·lain (pōr′sə lǐn, pōrs′lǐn), *n.* **1.** a vitreous, more or less translucent, ceramic body or ware; china. **2.** an object made of this material.

porch (pōrch), *n.* **1.** an exterior appendage to a building, forming a covered approach or vestibule to a doorway. **2.** *U.S.* a veranda.

por·cine (pōr′sīn, -sǐn), *adj.* pertaining to or resembling swine.

por·cu·pine (pōr′kyə pīn′), *n.* any of various rodents covered with stout, erectile quills.

pore¹ (pōr), *v.t.,* **pored, poring.** **1.** to meditate or ponder intently. **2.** to read or study with steady attention.

pore² (pōr), *n.* a minute opening or orifice, as in the skin or a leaf, for perspiration, etc.

por·gy (pôr′gǐ), *n.*, *pl.* **-gies,** (*esp. collectively*) **-gy.** any of numerous deep-bodied fishes, esp. a sea bream of Mediterranean and Atlantic waters of Europe (**red porgy**).

pork (pōrk), *n.* the flesh of hogs used as food. **—pork′like′,** *adj.*

pork barrel, *U.S. Slang.* a government appropriation, bill, or policy which supplies funds for local improvements designed to ingratiate legislators with their constituents.

pork·er (pôr′kər), n. a swine.

pork·y (pôr′kĭ), adj. 1. porklike. 2. fat.

por·nog·ra·phy (pôr nŏg′rə fĭ), n. obscene literature or art. **—por·no·graph·ic** (pôr′nə-grăf′ĭk), adj.

po·rous (pôr′əs), adj. 1. full of pores. 2. permeable by water, air, or the like. **—po′rous·ness, po·ros·i·ty** (pō rŏs′ə tĭ), n.

por·phy·ry (pôr′fə rĭ), n., pl. -ries. a very hard rock having a dark purplish-red groundmass containing small crystals of feldspar. **—por′-phy·rit′ic**, adj.

por·poise (pôr′pəs), n., pl. -poises, (esp. collectively) -poise. 1. any of certain gregarious cetaceans, five to eight feet long, usually blackish above and paler beneath. 2. any of several other small cetaceans, as the common dolphin.

por·ridge (pôr′ĭj, pŏr′-), n. Chiefly Brit. a food made of boiled oatmeal or other cereal.

por·rin·ger (pôr′ĭn jər, pŏr′-), n. a dish, deeper than a saucer, for soup, porridge, etc.

port[1] (pôrt), n. 1. a town or place where ships load or unload. 2. a place along the coast where ships may take refuge from storms.

port[2] (pôrt), Naut. —n. 1. the left side of a ship, facing toward the bow. —adj. 2. on or pertaining to the port. —v.t., v.i. 3. to turn or shift to the port.

port[3] (pôrt), n. a very sweet wine, usually dark red, orig. from Portugal.

port[4] (pôrt), n. Naut. a porthole.

port[5] (pôrt), v.t. 1. Mil. to carry (a rifle, etc.), with both hands, in a slanting direction across the front of the body, with the barrel or like part near the left shoulder. —n. 2. Mil. the position of a weapon when ported. 3. carriage or bearing.

Port., 1. Portugal. 2. Portuguese.

port·a·ble (pôr′tə bəl), adj. capable of being easily carried. **—port′a·bil′i·ty**, n.

por·tage (pôr′tĭj), n. 1. act of carrying. 2. the carrying of boats, goods, etc., overland from one navigable water to another. 3. a place over which this is done.

por·tal (pôr′təl), n. a door, gate, or entrance, esp. one of imposing appearance.

Port Ar·thur (är′thər), 1. a seaport on the Yellow Sea in NE China. 162,765. 2. a seaport in SE Texas. 56,065.

Port-au-Prince (pôrt′ō prĭns′), n. a seaport in and the capital of Haiti. 115,000.

port·cul·lis (pôrt kŭl′ĭs), n. a strong grating, as of iron, made to slide in vertical grooves at the sides of a gateway of a fortified place.

por·tend (pôr tĕnd′), v.t. to indicate beforehand, or presage, as an omen does.

por·tent (pôr′tĕnt), n. 1. an indication or omen of something about to happen, esp. something momentous. 2. ominous significance. **—por·ten′tous**, adj. **—por·ten′tous·ly**, adv.

por·ter[1] (pôr′tər), n. 1. one employed to carry baggage, as at a railroad station. 2. U.S. an attendant in a parlor car or sleeping car.

por·ter[2] (pôr′tər), n. a doorkeeper.

por·ter[3] (pôr′tər), n. a heavy, dark-brown beer.

Por·ter (pôr′tər), n. **William Sidney**, (O. Henry) 1862–1910, U.S. short-story writer.

por·ter·house (pôr′tər hous′), n. a choice cut of beef from between the prime ribs and the sirloin. Also, **porterhouse steak.**

port·fo·li·o (pôrt fō′lĭ ō′), n., pl. -lios. 1. a portable case for papers, prints, etc. 2. the post of a minister of state or member of a cabinet.

port·hole (pôrt′hōl′), n. an aperture in the side of a ship, as for admitting light and air.

Port Hu·ron (hyŏŏr′ən), a city in SE Michigan. 32,759.

por·ti·co (pôr′tə kō′), n., pl. -coes, -cos. a structure consisting of a roof supported by columns, usually attached as a porch.

por·tiere (pôr tyâr′, -tǐ âr′), n. a curtain hung at a doorway. Also, **por·tière′.**

por·tion (pôr′shən), n. 1. a part of any whole, whether separate from it or not. 2. the part of a whole allotted to or belonging to a person or group; share. 3. a quantity of food served for one person. —v.t. 4. to divide into or distribute in shares. **—por′tion·less**, adj.

Port·land (pôrt′lənd), n. 1. a seaport in NW Oregon. 305,394. 2. a seaport in SW Maine. 73,643.

Portland cement, a kind of hydraulic cement usually made by burning a mixture of limestone and clay in a kiln.

port·ly (pôrt′lĭ), adj., -lier, -liest. 1. stout; corpulent. 2. stately; imposing. **—port′li·ness,** n.

port·man·teau (pôrt măn′tō), n., pl. -teaus, -teaux (-tōz). Chiefly Brit. a suitcase.

Por·to A·le·gre (pôr′tŏŏ ä lĕ′grə), a seaport in S Brazil. 300,450.

Port-of-Spain (pôrt′əv spān′), n. the capital and seaport of Trinidad. 70,334.

Por·to Ri·co (pôr′tō rē′kō), Puerto Rico.

por·trait (pôr′trāt, -trĭt), n. a likeness of a person, especially of the face, usually made from life.

por·trai·ture (pôr′trĭ chər), n. 1. the art of portraying. 2. a portrait.

por·tray (pôr trā′), v.t. 1. to represent by a drawing, painting, carving, or the like. 2. to represent dramatically, as on the stage. 3. to describe graphically. **—por·tray′al,** n. **—por·tray′er,** n.

Port Sa·id (sä ēd′), a seaport in NE Egypt at the end of the Suez Canal. 126,200.

Ports·mouth (pôrts′məth), n. 1. a seaport in S England. 205,300. 2. a seaport in SE Virginia. 50,745. 4. a city in S Ohio. 40,466.

Por·tu·gal (pôr′chə gəl), n. a republic in SW Europe, W of Spain. (Including the Azores and the Madeira Islands) 8,223,000 pop.; 35,414 sq. mi. Cap.: Lisbon. **—Por·tu·guese** (pôr′chə gēz′, -gēs′), adj., n.

Portuguese Guinea, a Portuguese colony on the W coast of Africa. 351,089 pop.; 13,948 sq. mi. Cap.: Bolama.

Portuguese India, the Portuguese possessions on the W coast of India. 624,177 pop.; 1538 sq. mi. Cap.: Panjim.

por·tu·lac·a (pôr′chə lăk′ə), n. any of certain herbs with thick, succulent leaves and variously colored flowers.

pos., 1. positive. 2. possessive.

pose (pōz), v., posed, posing, n. —v.i. 1. to assume a particular character to impress others. 2. to present oneself before others. 3. to assume or hold a position or attitude for some artistic purpose. —v.t. 4. to place in a suitable position or attitude for a picture, tableau, or the like. 5. to assert, state, or propound. —n. 6. attitude. 7. a position assumed in posing, or exhibited by a figure in a picture, sculptural work, or the like. 8. a studied attitude or mere affectation, as of some character.

Po·sei·don (pō sī′dən), n. Gk. Myth. the god of the sea, identified by the Romans with Neptune.

Po·sen (pō′zən), n. a city in W Poland. 268,000.

pos·er[1] (pō′zər), n. one who poses.

pos·er[2] (pō′zər), n. an embarrassingly difficult question or problem.

po·seur (pō zûr′), n. one who affects a particular character, etc.

pos·it (pŏz′ĭt), v.t. 1. to place. 2. to lay down or assume as a fact or principle.

po·si·tion (pə zĭsh′ən), n. 1. condition with reference to place; location. 2. a place occupied; site. 3. proper place. 4. situation; condition. 5. status or standing. 6. high standing. 7. a post of employment. 8. manner of being placed or arranged. 9. posture. 10. mental attitude. —v.t. 11. to place or locate. **—po·si′tion·al,** adj.

pos·i·tive (pŏz′ə tĭv), adj. 1. explicitly laid down or expressed. 2. admitting of no question. 3. emphatic. 4. confident; fully assured. 5. overconfident or dogmatic. 6. without relation to or comparison with other things; absolute. 7. Colloq. downright. 8. possessing an actual force, being, existence, etc. 9. consisting in or characterized by the presence or possession of distinguishing or marked qualities or features. 10. Elect. having a deficiency of electrons. 11. Chem. (of an element or radical) basic. 12. Photog. showing the lights and shades as seen in the original, as a print from a negative. 13. Gram. denoting the initial degree of the comparison of adjectives and adverbs. 14. Math. denoting a quantity greater than zero. 15. Bacteriol. (of blood, affected tissue, etc.) showing the presence of an organism which causes a disease. —n. 16. something positive. 17. a positive quality or characteristic. 18. a positive quantity or symbol. 19. Photog. a positive picture. **20.** *Gram.* **a.** the positive degree. **b.** a form in it. —**pos′i·tive·ly,** *adv.* —**pos′i·tive-ness,** *n.*

pos·i·tron (pŏz′ə·trŏn′), *n.* *Physics.* a particle of positive electricity with a mass equal to that of the electron.

poss., **1.** possession. **2.** possessive.

pos·se (pŏs′ĭ), *n.* **1.** posse comitatus. **2.** a body or force armed with legal authority.

pos·se co·mi·ta·tus (pŏs′ĭ kŏm′ə tā′təs), the body of men that a peace officer may or does call to assist him in preserving the peace, making arrests, and serving writs.

pos·sess (pə zĕs′), *v.t.* **1.** to have as property; own. **2.** to hold or occupy. **3.** to have as a faculty, quality, or the like. **4.** *Archaic.* to seize or take. **5.** (of a spirit, esp. an evil one) to dominate from within. **6.** to cause to be dominated or influenced, as by a feeling, idea, etc. —**pos-ses′sor,** *n.*

pos·ses·sion (pə zĕsh′ən), *n.* **1.** act or fact of possessing. **2.** state of being possessed. **3.** ownership. **4.** *Law.* actual holding or occupancy. **5.** a thing possessed. **6.** (*pl.*) property or wealth. **7.** a territorial dominion of a state. **8.** control over oneself. **9.** domination or actuation by a feeling, idea, etc. **10.** the feeling or idea itself.

pos·ses·sive (pə zĕs′ĭv), *adj.* **1.** of or pertaining to possession or ownership. **2.** *Gram.* **a.** denoting a possessor. **b.** denoting a case that indicates possession and similar relations. —*n.* **3.** *Gram.* **a.** possessive form. **b.** the possessive case. —**pos·ses′sive·ly,** *adv.*

pos·set (pŏs′ĭt), *n.* a drink made of hot milk curdled with ale, wine, or the like, often sweetened and spiced.

pos·si·bil·i·ty (pŏs′ə bĭl′ə tĭ), *n.*, *pl.* **-ties.** **1.** state or fact of being possible. **2.** a possible thing or person.

pos·si·ble (pŏs′ə bəl), *adj.* that may or can be, exist, happen, be done, be used, etc.

pos·si·bly (pŏs′ə blĭ), *adv.* **1.** perhaps. **2.** in a possible manner. **3.** by any possibility.

pos·sum (pŏs′əm), *n.* *U.S. Colloq.* **1.** opossum. **2. play possum,** to feign.

post¹ (pōst), *n.* **1.** a strong piece of timber, metal, or the like, set upright as a support, a place for displaying notices, etc. —*v.t.* **2.** to affix (a notice, etc.) to a post, wall, or the like. **3.** to bring to public notice. **4.** to enter the name of in a published list. **5.** to placard (a wall, etc.) with notices.

post² (pōst), *n.* **1.** a position of duty, employment, or trust. **2.** the station, or the beat, of a soldier, sentry, or other person on duty. **3.** a military station with permanent buildings. **4.** the body of troops occupying a military station. **5.** *U.S.* a local unit of a veterans' organization. **6.** a trading post. —*v.t.* **7.** to station at a post.

post³ (pōst), *n.* **1.** *Chiefly Brit.* a single dispatch or delivery of mail. **2.** *Chiefly Brit.* the mail itself. **3.** one of a series of stations along a route, for furnishing relays of men and horses for carrying letters, etc. —*v.t.* **4.** *Chiefly Brit.* to mail. **5.** *Bookkeeping.* **a.** to transfer (an entry or item), as from the journal to the ledger. **b.** to enter (an item) in due place and form. **c.** to make all the requisite entries in (the ledger, etc.). —*v.i.* **6.** to travel with speed; hasten. **7.** to inform. —*adv.* **8.** by courier. **9.** with speed.

post-, a prefix meaning "behind," "after," occurring orig. in words from the Latin, but now freely used as an English formative, as in *postgraduate.*

post·age (pōs′tĭj), *n.* the charge for the conveyance of a letter or other matter sent by mail (ordinarily prepaid by a stamp or stamps).

postage stamp, an official stamp in the form of a design on an envelope, etc., or a printed adhesive label to be affixed to a letter, etc., as evidence of prepayment of a designated postage.

post·al (pōs′təl), *adj.* **1.** of or pertaining to the mail service. —*n.* **2.** *U.S. Colloq.* a postal card.

postal card, 1. a card with a printed governmental stamp, for correspondence. **2.** an unofficial post card.

post card, 1. a postal card with a printed governmental stamp. **2.** an unofficial card, often pictorial, mailable when bearing an adhesive postage stamp.

post·date (pōst′dāt′), *v.t.,* **-dated, -dating.** to give a later date to than the true date.

post·er (pōs′tər), *n.* a placard posted in some public place.

pos·te·ri·or (pŏs tĭr′ĭ ər), *adj.* **1.** situated be-

hind; hinder. **2.** coming after in order. **3.** later; subsequent. —*n.* **4.** (*sometimes pl.*) the hinder parts of the body.

pos·ter·i·ty (pŏs tĕr′ə tĭ), *n.* **1.** succeeding generations. **2.** descendants.

pos·tern (pōs′tərn, pŏs′-), *n.* **1.** a back door or gate. **2.** any lesser or private entrance. —*adj.* **3.** like or pertaining to a postern.

Post Exchange, *U.S.* a retail store on an army post selling extra provisions, etc.

post·fix (*v.* pōst fĭks′; *n.* pōst′fĭks), *v.t.* **1.** to append; suffix. —*n.* **2.** something postfixed.

post·grad·u·ate (pōst grăj′ŏŏ ĭt, -āt′), *adj.* **1.** pertaining to or pursuing a course of study after graduation. —*n.* **2.** a postgraduate student.

post·haste (pōst′hāst′), *adv.* with all possible speed.

post·hu·mous (pŏs′chŏŏ məs), *adj.* **1.** published after the death of the author. **2.** born after the death of the father. **3.** arising, existing, or continuing after one's death. —**post′hu·mous·ly,** *adv.*

pos·til·ion (pōs tĭl′yən, pŏs-), *n.* one who rides the left horse of a group used to draw a carriage. Also, *esp. Brit.,* **pos·til′lion.**

post·im·pres·sion·ism (pōst′ĭm prĕsh′ə nĭz′-əm), *n.* the doctrines and methods of certain painters developed between 1875 and 1890, which rejected the casual and momentary effects of the impressionists, but accepted their use of pure color as a means of intensifying permanence and solidity (Cézanne), movement (Van Gogh), etc. —**post′im·pres′sion·ist,** *n., adj.* —**post′im-pres′sion·is′tic,** *adj.*

post·lude (pōst′lōōd′), *n.* *Music.* a concluding piece or movement.

post·man (pōst′mən), *n., pl.* **-men.** a postal employee who delivers mail.

post·mark (pōst′märk′), *n.* **1.** an official mark stamped on a letter or other mail, to cancel the postage stamp, indicate the place and date of sending, etc. —*v.t.* **2.** to stamp with a postmark.

post·mas·ter (pōst′măs′tər, -mäs′tər), *n.* the official in charge of a post office. —**post′mis′-tress,** *n. fem.*

postmaster general, *pl.* **postmasters general.** the executive head of the postal system of a country.

post·me·rid·i·an (pōst′mə rĭd′ĭ ən), *adj.* **1.** occurring after noon. **2.** of the afternoon.

post me·rid·i·em (pōst mə rĭd′ĭ ĕm′), after noon. *Abbr.:* P.M. *or* p.m.

post-mor·tem (pōst môr′təm), *adj.* **1.** subsequent to death, as an examination of the body. —*n.* **2.** a post-mortem examination.

post·na·tal (pōst nā′təl), *adj.* subsequent to birth.

post office, 1. an office of a governmental postal system, for receiving, distributing, and transmitting mail, selling postage stamps, and other service. **2.** (*often cap.*) the governmental department charged with the conveyance of letters, etc.

post·paid (pōst′pād′), *adj.* with the postage prepaid.

post·pone (pōst pōn′), *v.t.,* **-poned, -poning.** to put off to a later time; defer. —**post·pone′-ment,** *n.*

post·pran·di·al (pōst prăn′dĭ əl), *adj.* after-dinner.

post·script (pōst′skrĭpt′), *n.* a paragraph added to a letter which has already been concluded and signed by the writer.

pos·tu·late (*v.* pŏs′chə lāt′; *n.* pŏs′chə lĭt, -lāt′), *v.,* **-lated, -lating,** —*v.t.* **1.** to ask, demand, or claim. **2.** to assume without proof or as self-evident. —*n.* **3.** something postulated. **4.** a fundamental principle. **5.** a prerequisite. —**pos′tu·la′tion,** *n.*

pos·ture (pŏs′chər), *n., v.,* **-tured, -turing.** —*n.* **1.** the position of the body and limbs as a whole. **2.** an affected or unnatural attitude. —*v.t.* **3.** to place in a particular posture. —*v.i.* **4.** to assume a particular posture. **5.** to pose for effect. —**pos′tur·al,** *adj.* —**pos′tur·er,** *n.*

post·war (pōst′wôr′), *adj.* after the war.

po·sy (pō′zĭ), *n., pl.* **-sies.** a flower; nosegay or bouquet.

pot (pŏt), *n., v.,* **potted, potting.** —*n.* **1.** an earthen, metallic, or other container, usually round and deep, used for cooking, growing plants, etc. **2.** a wicker vessel for trapping fish or crustaceans. **3.** the aggregate of bets at stake at one time, as in card playing, esp. poker. **4.** go to

pot, *Slang.* to deteriorate. —*v.t., v.i.* **5.** to put into a pot. **6.** *Hunting.* to shoot (game birds) on the ground or water, or (game animals) at rest, instead of in flight or running.

po·ta·ble (pō′tə bəl), *adj.* **1.** fit for drinking. —*n.* **2.** (*usually pl.*) anything drinkable.

pot·ash (pŏt′ăsh′), *n.* potassium carbonate, K_2CO_3, esp. the crude impure form obtained from wood ashes.

po·tas·si·um (pə tăs′Y əm), *n.* *Chem.* a silvery-white metallic element, which oxidizes rapidly in the air. *Symbol:* K; *at. wt.:* 39,096; *at. no.:* 19; *sp. gr.:* 0.86 at 20°C.

po·ta·tion (pō tā′shən), *n.* **1.** act of drinking. **2.** a drink, esp. of alcoholic liquor.

po·ta·to (pə tā′tō), *n., pl.* **-toes.** **1.** the edible tuber (**white potato** or **Irish potato**) of a widely cultivated plant. **2.** the plant itself.

potato beetle, a widely distributed leaf beetle, one of the most serious agricultural pests in the world. Also, **potato bug.**

pot·bel·ly (pŏt′bĕl′Y), *n., pl.* **-lies.** a protuberant belly. —**pot′bel′lied,** *adj.*

pot·boil·er (pŏt′boi′lər), *n.* *Colloq.* a work of literature or art produced merely for the necessaries of life.

po·tent (pō′tənt), *adj.* **1.** powerful; mighty. **2.** cogent, as reasons, etc. **3.** producing powerful physical or chemical effects, as a drug. **4.** possessed of great power or authority. **5.** exercising great moral influence. **6.** having sexual power. —**po′tent·ly,** *adv.* —**po′tence, po′ten·cy, po′tent·ness,** *n.*

po·ten·tate (pō′tən tāt′), *n.* a sovereign, monarch, or ruler.

po·ten·tial (pə tĕn′shəl), *adj.* **1.** possible as opposed to actual. **2.** latent. **3.** *Gram.* expressing possibility. **4.** *Physics.* denoting energy which is due to position or the like and not to motion. —*n.* **5.** a possibility. **6.** *Elect.* the electrification of a point or body with respect to some arbitrary or hypothetical standard. —**po·ten·ti·al·i·ty** (pə-tən′shY ăl′ə tY), *n.* —**po·ten′tial·ly,** *adv.*

poth·er (pŏth′ər), *n.* **1.** commotion; uproar. **2.** a fuss. —*v.t., v.i.* **3.** to bother.

pot·herb (pŏt′ûrb′, -hûrb′), *n.* any herb prepared as food by cooking in a pot, as spinach, or added as seasoning, as thyme.

pot·hook (pŏt′hŏŏk′), *n.* **1.** a hook for suspending a pot or kettle over an open fire. **2.** an iron rod with a hook at the end, used to lift hot pots, etc. **3.** an S-shaped stroke in writing.

po·tion (pō′shən), *n.* a drink, esp. one of a medicinal, poisonous, or magical kind.

pot·luck (pŏt′lŭk′), *n.* whatever food happens to be at hand without special preparation or buying.

Po·to·mac (pə tō′mək), *n.* a river flowing from West Virginia, between Maryland and Virginia, and past Washington, D.C., into Chesapeake Bay. 287 mi.

pot·pie (pŏt′pī′), *n.* **1.** a baked meat pie. **2.** a stew, as of chicken, with dumplings.

pot·pour·ri (pō pŏŏ rē′, pŏt pŏŏr′Y), *n., pl.* **-ris.** **1.** a mixture of dried petals, spices, etc., kept in a jar for the fragrance. **2.** a musical medley. **3.** a collection of miscellaneous literary extracts.

Pots·dam (pŏts′dăm), *n.* a city in NE Germany, near Berlin: wartime conference of Truman, Churchill (later, Attlee), and Stalin, July-Aug., 1945. 135,892.

pot·sherd (pŏt′shûrd′), *n.* a fragment or broken piece of earthenware.

pot shot, **1.** a shot fired at game merely for food. **2.** a shot at an animal or person within easy range, as from ambush.

pot·tage (pŏt′Yj), *n.* a thick soup made of vegetables, without or with meat.

pot·ted (pŏt′Yd), *adj.* **1.** placed in a pot. **2.** preserved or cooked in a pot. **3.** *Slang.* drunk.

pot·ter¹ (pŏt′ər), *n.* one who makes earthen pots or other vessels.

pot·ter² (pŏt′ər), *v.i.* *Chiefly Brit.* putter¹. —**pot′ter·er,** *n.*

potter's field, a burial place for strangers and the friendless poor.

potter's wheel, a device with a rotating horizontal disk upon which clay is molded.

pot·ter·y (pŏt′ə rY), *n., pl.* **-teries.** **1.** ware fashioned from clay or other earthy material and hardened by heat. **2.** a place where earthen pots are made. **3.** the art or business of a potter.

pouch (pouch), *n.* **1.** a bag, sack, or similar receptacle. **2.** something resembling a bag or pocket. **3.** a baggy fold of flesh under the eye. **4.** *Anat., Zool.* a sac or cyst, as the receptacle for the young of marsupials. —*v.t.* **5.** to put into a pouch. —*v.i.* **6.** to form a pouch. —**pouched,** *adj.*

Pough·keep·sie (pə kYp′sY), *n.* a city in SE New York. 40,478.

poul·ter·er (pōl′tər ər), *n.* *Chiefly Brit.* a dealer in poultry.

poul·tice (pōl′tYs), *n., v.,* **-ticed, -ticing.** —*n.* **1.** a soft, moist mass of bread, meal, herbs, etc., applied as a medicament to the body. —*v.t.* **2.** to apply a poultice to.

poul·try (pōl′trY), *n.* domestic fowls collectively, as chickens, turkeys, guinea fowls, ducks, and geese.

pounce (pouns), *v.,* **pounced, pouncing,** *n.* —*v.i., v.t.* **1.** to swoop down suddenly and lay hold (of), as a bird does on its prey. —*n.* **2.** a sudden swoop.

pound¹ (pound), *v.t.* **1.** to strike repeatedly and with great force. **2.** to crush by beating, as with an instrument. —*v.i.* **3.** to strike heavy blows repeatedly. **4.** to beat or throb violently. —*n.* **5.** act of pounding. **6.** a heavy or forcible blow. —**pound′er,** *n.*

pound² (pound), *n., pl.* **pounds,** (*collectively*) **pound.** **1.** a unit of weight, varying greatly in different periods and countries. **2.** (in the British Empire and the U.S.) either of two legally fixed units, the **pound avoirdupois** (divided into 16 ounces) or the **pound troy** (divided into 12 ounces). **3.** a British money of account (**pound sterling**) of the value of 20 shillings and equivalent to about $4.03.

pound³ (pound), *n.* **1.** an enclosure maintained by authority for confining trespassing or stray cattle, dogs, etc., or for keeping goods seized by distress. —*v.t.* **2.** to impound.

Pound (pound), *n.* Ezra Loomis, born 1885, U.S. poet.

pound·al (poun′dəl), *n.* *Physics.* a unit of force: the force which, acting for one second on a mass of one pound, gives it a velocity of one foot per second.

pound·cake (pound′kāk′), *n.* a kind of rich, sweet cake.

pound·er¹ (poun′dər), *n.* one who or that which pounds, pulverizes, or beats.

pound·er² (poun′dər), *n.* **1.** a person or thing having a weight or value of a pound or a specified number of pounds. **2.** a gun that discharges a missile of a specified weight in pounds.

pound-fool·ish (pound′fŏŏl′Ysh), *adj.* foolish or careless in regard to large sums.

pour (pōr), *v.t.* **1.** to send (a liquid, etc.) flowing or falling, as from a container or into, over, or on something. **2.** to emit (a liquid, etc.) in a stream. **3.** to send forth (words, etc.) profusely. —*v.i.* **4.** to issue, move, or proceed in great quantity. **5.** to flow forth or along. —*n.* **6.** a pouring. **7.** an abundant or continuous flow. **8.** a heavy fall of rain. —**pour′er,** *n.*

pout (pout), *v.i., v.t.* **1.** to protrude (the lips), esp. in sullenness. **2.** to look sullen. —*n.* **3.** a protrusion of the lips, as in pouting. **4.** a fit of sullenness. —**pout′er,** *n.*

pov·er·ty (pŏv′ər tY), *n.* **1.** the condition of being poor. **2.** deficiency or lack.

pov·er·ty-strick·en (pŏv′ər tY strYk′ən), *adj.* suffering from poverty; very poor.

POW, prisoner of war.

pow·der (pou′dər), *n.* **1.** any solid substance in the state of fine, loose particles, as produced by crushing, etc. **2.** a preparation in this form for some special purpose, as gunpowder, a cosmetic powder, etc. —*v.t.* **3.** to reduce to powder. **4.** to cover with powder. —*v.i.* **5.** to use powder as a cosmetic. —**pow′der·er,** *n.* —**pow′der·y,** *adj.*

powder blue, pale gray blue.

pow·er (pou′ər), *n.* **1.** ability to do or act. **2.** (*usually pl.*) a particular faculty of body or mind. **3.** strength; might; force. **4.** the possession of control or command over others; authority. **5.** political control in the government of a country, etc. **6.** legal ability, capacity, or authority. **7.** a person, group, or nation that possesses authority or influence. **8.** (*often pl.*) a deity or divinity. **9.** *Physics.* work done, or energy transferred, per unit of time. **10.** *Mech.* energy or force available for application to work. **11.** mechanical energy as distinguished from hand labor. **12.** *Math.* the product obtained by multiplying a quantity by itself one or more times.

13. *Optics.* the magnifying capacity of a microscope, telescope, or effect.

pow·er·ful (pou'ər fəl), *adj.* **1.** having or exerting great power, force, or effect. **2.** *Colloq.* great in amount. —**pow'er·ful·ly,** *adv.* —**pow'er·ful·ness,** *n.*

pow·er·house (pou'ər hous'), *n. Elect.* a generating station. Also, **power station.**

pow·er·less (pou'ər lĭs), *adj.* lacking power or ability; helpless. —**pow'er·less·ly,** *adv.* —**pow'er·less·ness,** *n.*

power of attorney, *Law.* a written document given by one person or party to another authorizing the latter to act for the former.

Pow·ha·tan (pou'hə tăn'), *n.* c1550–1618, Indian chief in Virginia: father of Pocahontas.

pow·wow (pou'wou'), *n.* **1.** (among North American Indians) a ceremony performed for the cure of disease, success in a hunt, etc. **2.** *Chiefly Colloq.* a council or conference. —*v.i.* **3.** to hold a powwow.

pox (pŏks), *n.* **1.** a disease characterized by skin pustules, as smallpox. **2.** syphilis.

pp., **1.** pages. **2.** past participle.

p.p., **1.** Also, **P.P.** parcel post. **2.** past participle.

ppr., present participle. Also, **p.pr.**

P.P.S., (L *post postscriptum*) a second postscript.

Pr, *Chem.* praseodymium.

pr., *pl.* **prs.** **1.** pair. **2.** present. **3.** price.

P.R., Puerto Rico.

prac·ti·ca·ble (prăk'tə kə bəl), *adj.* capable of being put into practice, done, or effected; feasible. —**prac'ti·ca·bil'i·ty,** *n.* —**prac'ti·ca·bly,** *adv.*

prac·ti·cal (prăk'tə kəl), *adj.* **1.** pertaining or relating to practice or action. **2.** consisting of, involving, or resulting from practice or action. **3.** pertaining to or connected with the ordinary activities, business, or work of the world. **4.** adapted for actual use. **5.** engaged or experienced in actual practice or work. **6.** inclined toward or fitted for actual or useful work. **7.** mindful of the results, usefulness, etc., of action or procedure. **8.** matter-of-fact; prosaic. **9.** virtual. —**prac'ti·cal'i·ty, prac'ti·cal·ness,** *n.*

practical joke, a joke or jest carried out in action; a trick played upon a person.

prac·ti·cal·ly (prăk'tĭk lĭ), *adv.* **1.** in effect; virtually. **2.** in a practical manner.

prac·tice (prăk'tĭs), *n., v.,* **-ticed, -ticing.** —*n.* **1.** habitual or customary performance. **2.** a habit or custom. **3.** repeated performance for the purpose of acquiring skill. **4.** actual performance or operation. **5.** the exercise of a profession or occupation, esp. law or medicine. **6.** the business of a professional man. —*v.t.* **7.** to do or observe habitually or usually. **8.** to exercise or pursue as a profession, art, or occupation. **9.** to do repeatedly in order to acquire skill. **10.** to train or drill. —*v.i.* **11.** to act habitually. **12.** to pursue a profession, esp. law or medicine. **13.** to exercise oneself by performance tending to give proficiency. Also, **practise** for 7–13. —**prac'tic·er,** *n.*

prac·ticed (prăk'tĭst), *adj.* experienced; expert. Also, **prac'tised.**

prac·tise (prăk'tĭs), *v.t., v.i.,* **-tised, -tising.** practice.

prac·ti·tion·er (prăk tĭsh'ən ər), *n.* one engaged in the practice of a profession or the like.

prae·tor (prē'tər), *n. Rom. Hist.* **1.** the title of a consul as leader of the army. **2.** one of a number of elected magistrates. —**prae·to·ri·an** (prē tōr'ĭ an), *adj.*

prag·mat·ic (prăg măt'ĭk), *adj.* **1.** treating historical phenomena with special reference to their causes and results. **2.** *Philos.* of or pertaining to pragmatism. **3.** concerned with practical consequences or values. **4.** meddlesome. Also, **prag·mat'i·cal.** —**prag·mat'i·cal·ly,** *adv.*

prag·ma·tism (prăg'mə tĭz'əm), *n.* **1.** pragmatic character or conduct. **2.** *Philos.* a system of thought in which stress is placed upon practical consequences and values as standards. —**prag'ma·tist,** *n., adj.*

Prague (präg), *n.* the capital of Czechoslovakia, in the W part. 941,398.

prai·rie (prâr'ĭ), *n.* **1.** an extensive, level, treeless tract of highly fertile land in the Mississippi valley. **2.** a meadow.

prairie chicken, a North American bird inhabiting prairies and valued as game.

prairie dog, any of certain gregarious bur-

rowing rodents of American prairies, which utter a barklike cry.

prairie schooner, a small covered wagon, used by pioneers in crossing the prairies and plains of North America.

prairie wolf, the coyote.

praise (prāz), *n., v.,* **praised, praising.** —*n.* **1.** commendation; laudation. **2.** the offering of grateful homage, as an act of worship. —*v.t.* **3.** to express approval or admiration of; extol. **4.** to offer grateful homage to (God or a deity). —**prais'er,** *n.*

praise·wor·thy (prāz'wûr'thĭ), *adj.* deserving of praise; laudable. —**praise'wor'thi·ly,** *adv.* —**praise'wor'thi·ness,** *n.*

pra·line (prä'lēn), *n.* any of various confections of almonds or other nut kernels cooked in a syrup.

pram (prăm), *n. Brit. Colloq.* perambulator.

prance (prăns, präns), *v.,* **pranced, prancing,** *n.* —*v.i.* **1.** to spring from the hind legs, as a horse. **2.** to ride or go about gaily or proudly. —*n.* **3.** act of prancing. —**pranc'er,** *n.*

prank[1] (prăngk), *n.* a playful or mischievous trick. —**prank'ish,** *adj.*

prank[2] (prăngk), *v.t.* to adorn.

pra·se·o·dym·i·um (prä'zĭ ō dĭm'ĭ əm, prä'sĭ-), *n. Chem.* a rare-earth metallic element. *Symbol:* Pr; *at. wt.:* 140.92; *at. no.:* 59; *sp. gr.:* 6.5 at 20°C.

prate (prāt), *v.,* **prated, prating,** *n.* —*v.i.* **1.** to talk much and to little purpose. —*v.t.* **2.** to utter in empty or foolish talk. —*n.* **3.** empty or foolish talk. —**prat'er,** *n.*

prat·tle (prăt'əl), *v.,* **-tled, -tling,** *n.* —*v.i.* **1.** to chatter in a foolish way; babble. —*v.t.* **2.** to utter by chattering or babbling. —*n.* **3.** chatter. **4.** a babbling sound. —**prat'tler,** *n.*

prawn (prôn), *n.* **1.** any of certain shrimplike decapod crustaceans, some of which are used as food. —*v.i.* **2.** to catch prawns.

pray· (prā), *v.t.* **1.** to make earnest or devout petition to. **2.** to make entreaty for; crave. **3.** to offer (a prayer). —*v.i.* **4.** to make entreaty, supplication, or devout petition. **5.** to enter into spiritual communion with God through prayer.

Prawn (3 to 4 in. long)

prayer[1] (prâr), *n.* **1.** a devout petition to, or a spiritual communion with, God, as in supplication, thanksgiving, or adoration. **2.** act, action, or practice of praying. **3.** a form of words used in or appointed for praying. **4.** a religious observance consisting wholly or mainly of prayer. **5.** a petition or entreaty. —**prayer'ful,** *adj.*

pray·er[2] (prā'ər), *n.* one who prays.

pre-, a prefix applied freely to mean "prior to", "in advance of" (*preschool, prewar*), also "early", "beforehand", (*prepay*), "before", "in front of" (*preoral, prepeduncle*), and in many figurative meanings.

preach (prēch), *v.t., v.i.* **1.** to advocate or inculcate (right conduct, etc.) in speech or writing. **2.** to deliver (a sermon or the like). **3.** to give earnest advice, sometimes in a tedious way. —**preach'er,** *n.* —**preach'ing,** *n.*

preach·ment (prēch'mənt), *n.* **1.** act of preaching. **2.** a sermon, esp. a tedious one.

pre·am·ble (prē'ăm'bəl), *n.* **1.** an introductory statement; preface. **2.** the introductory part of a statute, deed, or the like.

pre·ar·range (prē'ə rānj'), *v.t.,* **-ranged, -ranging.** to arrange beforehand. —**pre'ar·range'ment,** *n.*

pre·car·i·ous (prĭ kâr'ĭ əs), *adj.* **1.** uncertain; unstable; insecure. **2.** dependent on the will or pleasure of another. **3.** dangerous; risky. —**pre·car'i·ous·ly,** *adv.* —**pre·car'i·ous·ness,** *n.*

pre·cau·tion (prĭ kô'shən), *n.* **1.** a measure taken beforehand to ward off possible evil. **2.** prudent foresight. —**pre·cau'tion·ar'y,** *adj.*

pre·cede (prē sēd'), *v.t., v.i.,* **-ceded, -ceding.** **1.** to go before, as in place, order, rank, importance, or time. **2.** to preface.

prec·ed·ence (prĭ sē'dəns, prĕs'ə dəns), *n.* **1.** act or fact of preceding. **2.** priority in order, rank, importance, etc. **3.** the right to precede others in ceremonies or social formalities. Also, **prec·ed·en·cy** (prĭ sē'dən sĭ, prĕs'ə dən sĭ).

prec·e·dent[1] (prĕs'ə dənt), *n.* a preceding instance or case which may serve as an example for or a justification in subsequent cases.

pre·ced·ent² (prĭ sē'dənt, prĕs'ə dənt), *adj.* preceding.

pre·ced·ing (prē sē'dĭng), *adj.* that precedes; previous.

pre·cept (prē'sĕpt), *n.* **1.** a commandment or direction given as a rule of action or conduct. **2.** a maxim.

pre·cep·tor (prĭ sĕp'tər), *n.* an instructor; teacher. —**pre·cep·to·ri·al** (prē'sĕp tōr'ĭ əl), **pre·cep'to·ral,** *adj.*

pre·ces·sion (prē sĕsh'ən), *n.* act or fact of preceding; precedence.

pre·cinct (prē'sĭngkt), *n.* **1.** a district for governmental, administrative, or other purposes. **2.** a small electoral area containing one polling place. **3.** a space of definite limits. **4.** (*often pl.*) a boundary or limit.

pre·ci·os·i·ty (prĕsh'ĭ ŏs'ə tĭ), *n., pl.* **-ties.** fastidious or carefully affected refinement, as in language, style, or taste.

pre·cious (prĕsh'əs), *adj.* **1.** of great price or value; valuable. **2.** dear or beloved. **3.** *Colloq.* very great. **4.** affectedly or excessively delicate, refined, or nice. —*n.* **5.** darling. —*adv.* **6.** *Colloq.* very. —**pre'cious·ly,** *adv.* —**pre'cious·ness,** *n.*

prec·i·pice (prĕs'ə pĭs), *n.* a cliff with a vertical or overhanging face.

pre·cip·i·tant (prĭ sĭp'ə tənt), *adj.* **1.** falling or rushing headlong. **2.** hasty; rash. —*n.* **3.** *Chem.* anything that causes precipitation. —**pre·cip'i·tant·ly,** *adv.* —**pre·cip'i·tan·cy, pre·cip'i·tance,** *n.*

pre·cip·i·tate (*v.* prĭ sĭp'ə tāt'; *adj., n.* prĭ sĭp'ə tāt', -tĭt), *v.,* **-tated, -tating,** *adj., n.* —*v.t.* **1.** to hasten the occurrence (of). **2.** *Chem.* to separate (a substance) out in solid form from a solution. **3.** *Physics, Meteorol.* to condense (moisture) from a state of vapor in the form of rain, dew, etc., or be condensed thus. **4.** to fling or fall down. —*adj.* **5.** headlong. **6.** rapid; hasty. **7.** overhasty; rash. —*n.* **8.** *Chem.* a substance precipitated from a solution. **9.** *Physics, Meteorol.* moisture condensed in the form of rain, dew, etc. —**pre·cip'i·tate·ly,** *adv.* —**pre·cip'i·ta·tor,** *n.*

pre·cip·i·ta·tion (prĭ sĭp'ə tā'shən), *n.* **1.** act of precipitating. **2.** state of being precipitated. **3.** a casting down or falling headlong. **4.** haste. **5.** rash rapidity. **6.** *Chem., Physics.* the precipitating of a substance from a solution. **7.** *Meteorol.* **a.** falling products of condensation in the atmosphere, as rain, snow, hail. **b.** the amount precipitated at a given place within a given period.

pre·cip·i·tous (prĭ sĭp'ə təs), *adj.* **1.** like a precipice; full of precipices. **2.** extremely steep. **3.** precipitate. —**pre·cip'i·tous·ly,** *adv.* —**pre·cip'i·tous·ness,** *n.*

pré·cis (prā sē', prā'sē), *n.* a summary.

pre·cise (prĭ sīs'), *adj.* **1.** definite, exact, or accurate. **2.** carefully distinct, as the voice. **3.** strict; puritanical. —**pre·cise'ly,** *adv.* —**pre·cise'ness,** *n.*

pre·ci·sion (prĭ sĭzh'ən), *n.* **1.** quality or state of being precise. **2.** mechanical exactness. —**pre·ci'sion·ist,** *n.*

pre·clude (prĭ klood'), *v.t.,* **-cluded, -cluding.** to prevent the presence, existence, or occurrence of. —**pre·clu·sion** (prĭ kloo'zhən), *n.* —**pre·clu·sive** (prĭ kloo'sĭv), *adj.* —**pre·clu'sive·ly,** *adv.*

pre·co·cious (prĭ kō'shəs), *adj.* **1.** forward in development, esp. mental development, as a child. **2.** prematurely developed. —**pre·co'cious·ly,** *adv.* —**pre·co'cious·ness, pre·coc·i·ty** (prĭ kŏs'ə tĭ), *n.*

pre·con·ceive (prē'kən sēv'), *v.t.,* **-ceived, -ceiving.** to form an idea of in advance. —**pre'con·cep'tion,** *n.*

pre·con·cert (prē'kən sûrt'), *v.t.* to arrange beforehand.

pre·cur·sor (prĭ kûr'sər), *n.* **1.** a predecessor. **2.** a harbinger.

pre·cur·so·ry (prĭ kûr'sə rĭ), *adj.* **1.** introductory. **2.** premonitory.

pred., predicate.

pre·da·cious (prĭ dā'shəs), *adj.* predatory. Also, **pre·da'ceous.**

pred·a·to·ry (prĕd'ə tōr'ĭ), *adj.* **1.** of, pertaining to, or characterized by plundering, pillaging, or robbery. **2.** *Zool.* habitually preying upon other animals.

pred·e·ces·sor (prĕd'ə sĕs'ər, prĕd'ə sĕs'ər), *n.* one who precedes another in an office, position, etc.

pre·des·ti·nate (*v.* prĭ dĕs'tə nāt'; *adj.* prĭ dĕs'tə nĭt, -tə nāt'), *v.,* **-nated, -nating,** *adj.* —*v.t.* **1.** to predetermine, esp. by divine decree or purpose. —*adj.* **2.** predestinated.

pre·des·ti·na·tion (prĭ dĕs'tə nā'shən, prē'dĕs-), *n.* **1.** act of predestining. **2.** the resulting state. **3.** fate or destiny. **4.** *Theol.* **a.** the action of God in foreordaining from eternity whatever comes to pass. **b.** the decree of God by which men are foreordained to everlasting happiness or misery.

pre·des·tine (prĭ dĕs'tĭn), *v.t.,* **-tined, -tining.** to destine beforehand; predetermine.

pre·de·ter·mine (prē'dĭ tûr'mĭn), *v.t.,* **-mined, -mining.** **1.** to determine or decide beforehand. **2.** to ordain beforehand. **3.** to direct or impel beforehand. —**pre'de·ter'mi·na'tion,** *n.*

pred·i·ca·ble (prĕd'ə kə bəl), *adj.* **1.** that may be affirmed; assertable. —*n.* **2.** an attribute.

pre·dic·a·ment (prĭ dĭk'ə mənt), *n.* **1.** an unpleasant, trying, or dangerous situation. **2.** a particular condition or situation.

pred·i·cate (*v.* prĕd'ə kāt'; *adj., n.* prĕd'ə kĭt), *v.,* **-cated, -cating,** *adj., n.* —*v.t.* **1.** to declare or affirm. **2.** *U.S.* to found or base (a statement, action, etc.) on something. —*v.i.* **3.** to make an affirmation or assertion. —*adj.* **4.** predicated. **5.** *Gram.* belonging to the predicate. —*n.* **6.** *Gram.* the active verb in a sentence or clause along with all the words it governs and those which modify it. —**pred'i·ca'tion,** *n.* —**pred'i·ca'tive,** *adj.* —**pred'i·ca'tive·ly,** *adv.*

predicate adjective, an adjective of the predicate bearing a sort of attributive relation to the subject (e.g., *he is dead*) or to the direct object (e.g., *it made him sick*).

predicate noun, a noun following one of a certain group of verbs and designating the same entity as the subject or the direct object.

pre·dict (prĭ dĭkt'), *v.t., v.i.* to foretell; prophesy. —**pre·dict'a·ble,** *adj.* —**pre·dic'tion,** *n.* —**pre·dic'tor,** *n.*

pre·di·gest (prē'dĭ jĕst', -dī-), *v.t.* to treat (food), before introduction into the body, by an artificial process that makes it more easily digestible. —**pre'di·ges'tion,** *n.*

pre·di·lec·tion (prē'də lĕk'shən, prĕd'ə-), *n.* a preference, liking, or partiality.

pre·dis·pose (prē'dĭs pōz'), *v.t.,* **-posed, -posing.** **1.** to dispose beforehand. **2.** to dispose of beforehand. **3.** to give a previous tendency to. **4.** to render subject or liable. —**pre'dis·po·si'tion,** *n.*

pre·dom·i·nant (prĭ dŏm'ə nənt), *adj.* **1.** prevailing. **2.** having power, authority, or influence over others. —**pre·dom'i·nance,** *n.* —**pre·dom'i·nant·ly,** *adv.*

pre·dom·i·nate (prĭ dŏm'ə nāt'), *v.,* **-nated, -nating.** —*v.i.* **1.** to be the stronger or leading element. **2.** to control. **3.** to surpass others in authority or influence. —*v.t.* **4.** to dominate or prevail over. —**pre·dom'i·na'tion,** *n.*

pre·ëm·i·nent (prĭ ĕm'ə nənt), *adj.* superior to others; distinguished beyond others. Also, **pre·em'i·nent.** —**pre·ëm'i·nence, pre·em'i·nence,** *n.* —**pre·ëm'i·nent·ly,** *adv.*

pre·ëmpt (prĭ ĕmpt'), *v.t.* **1.** to acquire beforehand. **2.** to occupy (land) in order to establish a prior right to buy. Also, **pre·empt'.** —**pre·ëmp'tion,** *n.* —**pre·ëmp'tive,** *adj.* —**pre·ëmp'tor** (prĭ ĕmp'tər), *n.*

preen (prēn), *v.t.* **1.** to trim or dress with the beak, as a bird does its feathers. **2.** to dress (oneself) carefully. —**preen'er,** *n.*

pre·ëx·ist (prē'ĭg zĭst'), *v.i.* **1.** to exist beforehand. **2.** to exist in a previous state. Also, **pre'ex·ist'.** —**pre'ëx·ist'ence,** *n.* —**pre'ëx·ist'ent,** *adj.*

pref., **1.** preface. **2.** preferred. **3.** prefix.

pre·fab·ri·cate (prē făb'rə kāt'), *v.t.,* **-cated, -cating.** **1.** to construct beforehand. **2.** to manufacture (houses, etc.) in standardized sections ready for rapid assembling. —**pre·fab'ri·cat'ed,** *adj.* —**pre·fab'ri·ca'tion,** *n.*

pref·ace (prĕf'ĭs), *n., v.,* **-aced, -acing.** —*n.* **1.** a preliminary statement by the author or editor of a book. **2.** any introductory part. —*v.t.* **3.** to provide with a preface. **4.** to serve as a preface to.

pref·a·to·ry (prĕf'ə tōr'ĭ), *adj.* of the nature of a preface; preliminary.

pre·fect (prē'fĕkt), *n.* **1.** a chief magistrate in

ancient Rome. 2. the chief administrative official of a department of France and Italy.

pre·fec·ture (prē′fĕk chər), *n.* the office, jurisdiction, or residence of a prefect.

pre·fer (prĭ fûr′), *v.t.* -ferred, -ferring. 1. to like better; choose rather. 2. *Law.* to give priority to. 3. to present (a statement, suit, charge, etc.).

pref·er·a·ble (prĕf′ər ə bəl), *adj.* 1. worthy to be preferred. 2. more desirable. —**pref′er·a·bil′i·ty,** *n.* —**pref′er·a·bly,** *adv.*

pref·er·ence (prĕf′ər əns), *n.* 1. prior favor or choice. 2. state of being preferred. 3. the object of prior favor or choice. 4. a practical advantage given to one over others.

pref·er·en·tial (prĕf′ə rĕn′shəl), *adj.* 1. pertaining to or of the nature of preference. 2. showing or giving preference. 3. receiving or enjoying preference. —**pref′er·en′tial·ly,** *adv.*

preferential shop, a shop in which union members are preferred.

pre·fer·ment (prĭ fûr′mənt), *n.* 1. act of preferring. 2. state of being preferred. 3. advancement or promotion.

preferred stock, stock which has a priority on dividends and (often) assets.

pre·fig·ure (prē fĭg′yər), *v.t.,* -ured, -uring. 1. to represent beforehand by a figure or type. 2. to represent to oneself beforehand. —**pre·fig′ur·a·tive** (prē fĭg′yər ə tĭv), *adj.* —**pre′fig·u·ra′tion, pre·fig′ure·ment,** *n.*

pre·fix (*n.* prē′fĭks; *v.* prē fĭks′), *n.* 1. *Gram.* an affix which is put before a word, stem, or word element to add to or qualify its meaning (as *un-* in *unkind*). 2. something prefixed. —*v.t.* 3. to put before. 4. *Gram.* to add as a prefix. —**pre·fix·al** (prē′fĭk səl, prē fĭk′səl), *adj.*

preg·na·ble (prĕg′nə bəl), *adj.* 1. capable of being taken by force, as a fortress. 2. open to attack. —**preg′na·bil′i·ty,** *n.*

preg·nan·cy (prĕg′nən sĭ), *n., pl.* -cies. the condition or quality of being pregnant.

preg·nant (prĕg′nənt), *adj.* 1. being with child or young, as a woman. 2. fraught, filled, or abounding. 3. fertile or rich. 4. full of meaning. 5. momentous. —**preg′nant·ly,** *adv.*

pre·hen·sile (prĭ hĕn′sĭl), *adj.* 1. adapted for seizing or grasping. 2. fitted for grasping by folding or wrapping round an object.

pre·his·tor·ic (prē′hĭs tôr′ĭk, -tôr′-), *adj.* of or belonging to a period prior to that of recorded history. Also, **pre′his·tor′i·cal.**

pre·judge (prē jŭj′), *v.t.,* -judged, -judging. to judge beforehand or prematurely. —**pre·judg′ment;** *esp. Brit.,* **pre·judge′ment,** *n.*

prej·u·dice (prĕj′ə dĭs), *n., v.,* -diced, -dicing. —*n.* 1. an opinion formed without knowledge, thought, or reason, esp. an unfavorable opinion. 2. disadvantage or injury. —*v.t.* 3. to affect with a prejudice.

prej·u·di·cial (prĕj′ə dĭsh′əl), *adj.* causing prejudice or disadvantage. —**prej′u·di′cial·ly,** *adv.*

prel·a·cy (prĕl′ə sĭ), *n., pl.* -cies. 1. the office or dignity of a prelate. 2. prelates collectively. 3. the system of church government by prelates.

prel·ate (prĕl′ĭt), *n.* an ecclesiastic of a high order, as an archbishop, bishop, etc.

pre·lim·i·nar·y (prĭ lĭm′ə nĕr′ĭ), *adj., n., pl.* -naries. —*adj.* 1. introductory; preparatory. —*n.* 2. an introductory or preparatory step, measure, or the like. —**pre·lim′i·nar′i·ly,** *adv.*

prel·ude (prĕl′ūd, prē′lōōd), *n., v.,* -uded, -uding. —*n.* 1. a preliminary to an action, event, condition, or work of greater scope and importance. 2. *Music.* **a.** a short composition, free in form and of an improvised character. **b.** a piece which precedes a more important movement. —*v.t., v.i.* 3. to serve as a prelude to or introduction (to).

pre·ma·ture (prē′mə tyŏŏr′, -tŏŏr′, prē′mə-chŏŏr′), *adj.* 1. coming into existence or occurring too soon. 2. mature or ripe before the proper time. 3. overhasty. —**pre′ma·ture′ly,** *adv.* —**pre′ma·ture′ness, pre′ma·tu′ri·ty,** *n.*

pre·med·i·tate (prĭ mĕd′ə tāt′), *v.t., v.i.,* -tated, -tating. to consider or plan beforehand. —**pre′med·i·ta′tion,** *n.*

pre·mier (*n.* prĭ mĭr′, prē′mĭ ər; *adj.* prē′mĭ-ər), *n.* 1. the prime minister, or first minister of state, in France, Great Britain, etc. —*adj.* 2. chief; leading.

pre·mière (prĭ mĭr′), *n.* a first public performance of a play, etc.

prem·ise (prĕm′ĭs), *n., v.,* -ised, -ising. —*n.*

1. (*pl.*) **a.** the property forming the subject of a conveyance. **b.** a building with its grounds, etc. 2. *Logic.* a proposition (or one of several) from which a conclusion is drawn. —*v.t.* 3. to set forth beforehand, as by way of introduction. 4. to assume a proposition as a premise for some conclusion.

pre·mi·um (prē′mĭ əm), *n.* 1. a prize to be won in a competition. 2. a bonus, gift, or sum additional to price, wages, interest, or the like. 3. the amount paid in one sum or periodically as the consideration for a contract of insurance. 4. **at a premium,** in demand.

pre·mo·ni·tion (prē′mə nĭsh′ən), *n.* 1. a forewarning. 2. a presentiment. —**pre·mon·i·to·ry** (prĭ mŏn′ə tôr′ĭ), *adj.*

pre·na·tal (prē nā′təl), *adj.* previous to birth. —**pre·na′tal·ly,** *adv.*

pre·oc·cu·py (prĭ ŏk′yə pī′), *v.t.,* -pied, -pying. 1. to absorb or engross to the exclusion of other things. 2. to occupy or take possession of beforehand or before others. —**pre·oc′cu·pan·cy,** *n.* —**pre·oc′cu·pa′tion,** *n.* —**pre·oc′cu·pied′,** *adj.*

pre·or·dain (prē′ôr dān′), *v.t.* to ordain beforehand; foreordain. —**pre·or·di·na·tion** (prē′ôr də nā′shən), *n.*

prep (prĕp), *adj. Colloq.* preparatory.

prep., 1. preparatory. 2. preposition.

prep·a·ra·tion (prĕp′ə rā′shən), *n.* 1. a proceeding, measure, or provision by which one prepares for something. 2. act of preparing. 3. state of being prepared. 4. something prepared, manufactured, or compounded.

pre·par·a·to·ry (prĭ păr′ə tôr′ĭ), *adj.* 1. serving or designed to prepare. 2. introductory. 3. undergoing preparation for entering college (or, in England, a public school).

pre·pare (prĭ pâr′), *v.,* -pared, -paring. —*v.t.* 1. to make ready for something. 2. to make ready for eating. 3. to manufacture, compound, or compose. —*v.i.* 4. to get ready.

pre·par·ed·ness (prĭ pâr′ĭd nĭs, -pârd′nĭs), *n.* 1. readiness. 2. possession of an adequate army and navy.

pre·pay (prē pā′), *v.t.,* -paid, -paying. 1. to pay beforehand. 2. to pay the charge upon in advance. —**pre·pay′ment,** *n.*

pre·pon·der·ant (prĭ pŏn′dər ənt), *adj.* superior in weight, force influence, number, etc.; predominant. —**pre·pon′der·ant·ly,** *adv.* —**pre·pon′der·ance,** *n.*

pre·pon·der·ate (prĭ pŏn′də rāt′), *v.i.,* -ated, -ating. to be superior in power, force, influence, number, amount, weight, etc.; predominate. —**pre·pon′der·at′ing·ly,** *adv.* —**pre·pon′der·a′tion,** *n.*

prep·o·si·tion (prĕp′ə zĭsh′ən), *n. Gram.* 1. one of the major form classes, or parts of speech, comprising words placed before nouns to indicate their relation to other words or their function in the sentence. 2. any such word, as *by, to, in, from.* —**prep′o·si′tion·al,** *adj.* —**prep′o·si′tion·al·ly,** *adv.*

pre·pos·sess (prē′pə zĕs′), *v.t.* 1. to prejudice or bias, esp. favorably. 2. to impress favorably beforehand or at the outset. —**pre′pos·sess′ing,** *adj.* —**pre′pos·ses′sion,** *n.*

pre·pos·ter·ous (prĭ pŏs′tər əs), *adj.* absurd, senseless, or utterly foolish. —**pre·pos′ter·ous·ly,** *adv.* —**pre·pos′ter·ous·ness,** *n.*

pre·puce (prē′pūs), *n. Anat.* the fold of skin which covers the head of the penis or clitoris; foreskin.

pre·req·ui·site (prē rĕk′wə zĭt), *adj.* 1. required as an antecedent condition. —*n.* 2. something prerequisite.

pre·rog·a·tive (prĭ rŏg′ə tĭv), *n.* an exclusive or special right or privilege attaching to an office or position.

Pres., 1. President. 2. (*l.c.*) present.

pres·age (*n.* prĕs′ĭj; *v.* prĭ sāj′), *n., v.,* -aged, -aging. —*n.* 1. a foreboding. 2. an omen, augury, or prediction. —*v.t., v.i.* 3. to portend. 4. to predict.

pres·by·ter (prĕz′bə tər, prĕs′-), *n.* 1. (in the early Christian church) an office bearer exercising teaching, priestly, and administrative functions. 2. (in hierarchical churches) a priest.

pres·by·te·ri·an (prĕz′bə tĭr′ĭ ən, prĕs′-), *adj.* 1. pertaining to or based on the principle of ecclesiastical government by presbyters or presbyteries. 2. (*cap.*) designating or pertaining to various Protestant churches having this form of government. —*n.* 3. (*cap.*) a member of a Presbyterian church.

Pres·by·te·ri·an·ism (prĕz/bə tǐr/ Y ə nǐz/əm, prĕs/-), n. 1. church government by presbyters or elders, equal in rank and organized into graded administrative courts. 2. the doctrines of Presbyterian churches.

pres·by·ter·y (prĕz/bə tĕr/Y, prĕs/-), n., pl. -teries. 1. a body of presbyters or elders. 2. (in Presbyterian churches) a council consisting of all the ministers and representative lay elders within a district. 3. the churches under the jurisdiction of a presbytery. 4. the part of a church appropriated to the clergy.

pre·sci·ence (prē/shY əns, prĕsh/Y-), n. knowledge of things before they exist or happen. —pre/sci·ent, adj. —pre/sci·ent·ly, adv.

pre·scribe (prǐ skrīb/), v., -scribed, -scribing. —v.t. 1. to order as a rule or a course to be followed. 2. Med. to order for use, as a remedy. —v.i. 3. to lay down rules; direct. 4. Med. to designate remedies or treatment to be used.

pre·scrip·tion (prǐ skrǐp/shən), n. 1. Med. a. a direction (usually written) by the physician for the preparation and use of a medicine. b. medicine prescribed. 2. the act of prescribing. 3. that which is prescribed. —pre·scrip/tive, adj.

pres·ence (prĕz/əns), n. 1. state or fact of being present, as in a place. 2. attendance or company. 3. immediate vicinity. 4. personal appearance or bearing.

pres·ent[1] (prĕz/ənt), adj. 1. being, existing, or occurring at this time or now. 2. for the time being. 3. Gram. a. denoting action or state in process at the moment of speaking. b. designating a tense with such meaning. 4. being with one or others, or in a particular place (opposed to absent). 5. being here or there, rather than elsewhere. 6. existing in a place, thing, combination, or the like. —n. 7. the present time. 8. Gram. the present tense.

pre·sent[2] (v. prǐ zĕnt/; n. prĕz/ənt), v.t. 1. to furnish with a gift or the like. 2. to bring, offer, or give. 3. to afford (an opportunity, etc.). 4. to hand or send in, as a bill for payment. 5. to bring (a person, etc.) before another, esp. a superior, or to the public. 6. to come to show (oneself) before a person, in a place, etc. 7. to show or exhibit. 8. to offer for consideration. 9. to act, as on the stage. —n. 10. a thing bestowed as a gift; gift. —pre·sent/er, n.

pre·sent·a·ble (prǐ zĕn/tə bəl), adj. 1. that may be presented. 2. suitable in appearance, dress, manners, etc. —pre·sent/a·bil/i·ty, n. —pre·sent/a·bly, adv.

pres·en·ta·tion (prĕz/ən tā/shən, prē/zĕn-), n. 1. act of presenting. 2. the state of being presented. 3. introduction, as of a person at court. 4. exhibition or representation. 5. offering, delivering, or bestowal. 6. a gift.

pre·sen·ti·ment (prǐ zĕn/tə mənt), n. a feeling or impression of something about to happen, esp. something evil; foreboding.

pres·ent·ly (prĕz/ənt lY), adv. soon.

pre·sent·ment (prǐ zĕnt/mənt), n. 1. presentation. 2. a representation, picture, or likeness. 3. the presenting of a bill, note, or the like, as for payment.

present participle, a participle with present meaning, as growing.

present perfect, 1. the tense form constructed by using the present tense of have with a past participle, e.g., I have done. 2. a verb in this tense.

pre·serv·a·tive (prǐ zûr/və tǐv), n. 1. something that preserves or tends to preserve. —adj. 2. tending to preserve.

pre·serve (prǐ zûrv/), v., -served, -serving, n. —v.t. 1. to keep alive or in existence. 2. to keep safe from harm or injury. 3. to maintain. 4. to retain. 5. to prepare (food, etc.) so as to resist decomposition or fermentation. 6. to prepare (fruit, etc.) by cooking with sugar. —v.i. 7. to preserve fruit, etc. —n. 8. (usually pl.) fruit, etc., prepared by cooking with sugar. 9. Chiefly Brit. a place set apart for the protection and propagation of game or fish for sport, etc. —pre·serv/a·ble, adj. —pres·er·va·tion (prĕz/ər vā/shən), n. —pre·serv/er, n.

pre·side (prǐ zīd/), v.i., -sided, -siding. 1. to act as chairman or president. 2. to exercise superintendence or control. —pre·sid/er, n.

pres·i·den·cy (prĕz/ə dən sǐ), n., pl. -cies. 1. the office, function, or term of office of a president. 2. (often cap.) the office of President of the United States.

pres·i·dent (prĕz/ə dənt), n. 1. (often cap.) the highest executive officer of a modern republic. 2. an officer chosen to preside over an organized body of persons. 3. the chief officer of a college, society, corporation, etc. —pres·i·den·tial (prĕz/ə dĕn/shəl), adj.

pre·sid·i·um (prǐ sǐd/Y əm), n. (in the Soviet Union) an administrative governmental committee.

press[1] (prĕs), v.t. 1. to act upon with weight or force. 2. to compress or squeeze. 3. to weigh heavily upon. 4. to hold closely, as in an embrace. 5. to iron (clothes, etc.). 6. to extract juice, etc., from by pressure. 7. to beset or harass. 8. to oppress or trouble. 9. to urge or impel. 10. to hurry; hasten. 11. to beseech or entreat. 12. to insist on. —v.i. 13. to exert weight, force, or pressure. 14. to iron clothes, etc. 15. to bear heavily, as upon the mind. 16. to compel haste. 17. to demand immediate attention. 18. to use urgent entreaty. 19. to crowd or throng. —n. 20. printed publications collectively, esp. newspapers and periodicals. 21. the persons writing for or editing newspapers or periodicals. 22. a printing press. 23. an establishment for printing books, etc. 24. any of various instruments or machines for exerting pressure. 25. act of pressing. 26. a crowd, throng, or multitude. 27. a crease caused by pressing. 28. pressure or urgency, as of business. 29. an upright case, or piece of furniture, for holding clothes, books, etc. —press/er, n.

press[2] (prĕs), v.t. to force into service, esp. naval or military service.

press agent, a person employed to attend to the advertising of a theater, performer, etc., through notices in the press.

press·ing (prĕs/Yng), adj. urgent; vital. —press/ing·ly, adv.

press·man (prĕs/mən), n., pl. -men. a man who operates a printing press.

pres·sure (prĕsh/ər), n. 1. the exertion of force upon a body by another body in contact with it. 2. Physics. the force per unit area exerted at a given point. 3. Elect. electromotive force. 4. act of pressing. 5. state of being pressed. 6. harassment. 7. a constraining or compelling force. 8. urgency, as of business.

pressure cooker, a strong, closed vessel in which liquids, meats, vegetables, etc., may be heated above the boiling point under pressure.

pressure group, a group, such as business or labor, which attempts to protect or advance its interests in legislative bodies.

pres·ti·dig·i·ta·tion (prĕs/tə dǐj/ə tā/shən), n. sleight of hand; legerdemain. —pres/ti·dig/i·ta/tor, n.

pres·tige (prĕs tēzh/, prĕs/tǐj), n. reputation or influence arising from success, achievement, rank, or other circumstances.

pres·to (prĕs/tō), adv., adj., n., pl. -tos. —adv. 1. quickly. 2. Music. in quick tempo. —adj. 3. quick. 4. Music. in quick tempo. —n. 5. Music. a movement or piece in quick tempo.

pre·sume (prǐ zoōm/), v., -sumed, -suming. —v.t. 1. to take for granted; assume. 2. Law. to assume as true. 3. to undertake, with unwarrantable boldness. —v.i. 4. to take something for granted. 5. to act with unwarrantable or impertinent boldness. —pre·sum/a·ble, adj. —pre·sum/a·bly, adv. —pre·sum·ed·ly (prǐ zoō/mǐd·lY), adv.

pre·sump·tion (prǐ zŭmp/shən), n. 1. act of presuming. 2. that which is presumed; assumption. 3. a ground or reason for presuming. 4. unwarrantable or impertinent boldness.

pre·sump·tive (prǐ zŭmp/tǐv), adj. 1. affording ground for presumption. 2. based on presumption. 3. presumed. —pre·sump/tive·ly, adv.

pre·sump·tu·ous (prǐ zŭmp/choō əs), adj. 1. full of, characterized by, or showing presumption. 2. unwarrantably or impertinently bold. —pre·sump/tu·ous·ly, adv. —pre·sump/tu·ous·ness, n.

pre·sup·pose (prē/sə pōz/), v.t., -posed, -posing. 1. to take for granted in advance. 2. (of a thing) to require or imply as an antecedent condition. —pre/sup·po·si/tion, n.

pret., preterit.

pre·tend (prǐ tĕnd/), v.t. 1. to make a false appearance of; feign. —v.i. 2. to make believe. 3. to claim. 4. to make pretentious. —pre·tend/ed, adj.

pre·tend·er (prǐ tĕn/dər), n. 1. one who pretends. 2. a claimant to a throne.

pre·tense (prǐ tĕns/, prē/tĕns), n. 1. feigning;

make-believe. 2. a false show of something. 3. act of alleging, now esp. falsely. 4. an alleged or pretended reason; pretext. 5. insincere or false profession. 6. a claim. 7. pretension. Also, esp. Brit., **pre·tence′**.

pre·ten·sion (prĭ tĕn′shən), n. 1. a laying claim to something. 2. a claim. 3. pretentiousness. 4. act of pretending. 5. a pretext.

pre·ten·tious (prĭ tĕn′shəs), adj. 1. full of pretension. 2. characterized by assumption of dignity or importance. 3. ostentatious. —**pre·ten′tious·ly,** adv. —**pre·ten′tious·ness,** n.

pret·er·it (prĕt′ər ĭt), Gram. —adj. 1. denoting past action or state. —n. 2. past. 3. preterit tense. 4. a verb form in the preterit. Also, **pret′er·ite.**

pre·ter·nat·u·ral (prē′tər năch′ə rəl), adj. 1. out of the ordinary course of nature; abnormal. 2. supernatural. —**pre′ter·nat′u·ral·ly,** adv.

pre·text (prē′tĕkst), n. 1. that which is put forward to conceal a true purpose or object. 2. an excuse.

Pre·to·ri·a (prĭ tōr′ĭ ə), n. a city in the NE Union of South Africa: seat of executive government of Union of South Africa. 128,621.

pret·ti·fy (prĭt′ə fī′), v.t., -fied, -fying. to make pretty (often in a disparaging sense).

pret·ty (prĭt′ĭ), adj., -tier, -tiest, n., pl. -ties, adv. —adj. 1. attractive in a feminine or childish way. 2. (of things, places, etc.) pleasing or beautiful. 3. excellent (much used ironically). 4. Colloq. or Dial. considerable. —n. 5. (usually pl.) a pretty trinket or ornament. —adv. 6. moderately. 7. quite; very. —**pret′ti·ly,** adv. —**pret′ti·ness,** n.

pret·zel (prĕt′səl), n. a crisp, dry biscuit, usually in the form of a knot or stick, salted on the outside.

pre·vail (prĭ vāl′), v.i. 1. to be widespread or current. 2. to predominate. 3. to be or prove superior in strength, power, or influence. 4. to operate effectually. 5. to use persuasion successfully.

pre·vail·ing (prĭ vā′lĭng), adj. 1. predominant. 2. generally current. 3. having superior power or influence. 4. effectual. —**pre·vail′ing·ly,** adv. —**pre·vail′ing·ness,** n.

prev·a·lent (prĕv′ə lənt), adj. widespread; in general use or acceptance. —**prev′a·lence,** n. —**prev′a·lent·ly,** adv.

pre·var·i·cate (prĭ văr′ə kāt′), v.i., -cated, -cating. to act or speak evasively. —**pre·var′i·ca′tion,** n. —**pre·var′i·ca′tor,** n.

pre·vent (prĭ vĕnt′), v.t. 1. to keep from occurring; hinder. 2. to stop or thwart. —v.i. 3. to interpose a hindrance. —**pre·vent′a·ble, pre·vent′i·ble,** adj. —**pre·vent′er,** n. —**pre·ven′tion,** n.

pre·ven·tive (prĭ vĕn′tĭv), adj. 1. Med. warding off disease. 2. serving to prevent or hinder. —n. 3. a preventive drug, agent, or measure. Also, **pre·vent·a·tive** (prĭ vĕn′tə tĭv). —**pre·ven′tive·ly,** adv.

pre·view (prē′vū′), n. 1. a view in advance, as of a moving picture. —v.t. 2. to view in advance. Also, U.S., **pre′vue′.**

pre·vi·ous (prē′vĭ əs), adj. 1. coming or occurring before something else; prior. 2. Colloq. premature. —**pre′vi·ous·ly,** adv. —**pre′vi·ous·ness,** n.

pre·vi·sion (prĭ vĭzh′ən), n. foresight.

pre·war (prē′wôr′), adj. before the war.

prey (prā), n. 1. an animal hunted or seized for food, esp. by a carnivorous animal. 2. any victim. 3. action or habit of preying. —v.i. 4. to seek for and seize prey. 5. to plunder. 6. to make profit by activities on a victim. 7. to exert a harmful or oppressive influence. —**prey′er,** n.

Pri·am (prī′əm), n. Gk. Legend. the last king of Troy, at the capture of which he was slain: father of Hector and Paris.

price (prīs), n., v., priced, pricing. —n. 1. the sum or amount of money or its equivalent for which anything is bought, sold, or offered for sale. 2. a reward, as for capturing a criminal. 3. value; worth. —v.t. 4. to set the price of. 5. Colloq. to ask the price of.

price·less (prīs′lĭs), adj. 1. having a value beyond all price; invaluable. 2. Chiefly Brit. Colloq. delightfully amusing; absurd.

prick (prĭk), n. 1. a puncture made by a needle, thorn, or the like. 2. act of pricking. 3. sting or sensation of being pricked. —v.t. 4. to pierce; puncture. 5. to affect with sharp pain, physically or mentally. 6. to urge on. 7. to mark (a sur-

face) with pricks or dots in tracing something. 8. to point upward. —v.i. 9. to point upward. —**prick′er,** n.

prick·le (prĭk′əl), n., v., -led, -ling. —n. 1. a sharp point, as one growing from the bark of a plant. 2. Colloq. a pricking sensation. —v.t. 3. to prick. 4. to cause a pricking sensation in. —v.i. 5. to tingle as if pricked.

prick·ly (prĭk′lĭ), adj., -lier, -liest. 1. full of prickles. 2. troublesome. 3. prickling; smarting. —**prick′li·ness,** n.

prickly heat, Pathol. a cutaneous eruption caused by an inflammation of the sweat glands.

prickly pear, 1. the pear-shaped, prickly, edible fruit of certain species of cactus. 2. the plant itself.

pride (prīd), n., v., prided, priding. —n. 1. high opinion of one's own importance, merit, or superiority. 2. state or feeling of being proud. 3. self-respect; self-esteem. 4. satisfaction taken in something done by or belonging to oneself. 5. that of which a person or group is proud. —v.t. 6. to indulge (oneself) in a feeling of pride.

priest (prēst), n. 1. one whose office it is to perform religious rites. 2. a clergyman; minister. —**priest′ess,** n. fem. —**priest′hood,** n.

priest·craft (prēst′krăft′, -kräft′), n. priestly arts.

Priest·ley (prēst′lĭ), n. Joseph, 1733–1804, British chemist, author, and clergyman.

priest·ly (prēst′lĭ), adj., -lier, -liest. 1. of or pertaining to a priest; sacerdotal. 2. befitting a priest. —**priest′li·ness,** n.

prig (prĭg), n. a self-righteously virtuous person. —**prig′gish,** adj. —**prig′gish·ly,** adv. —**prig′ish·ness,** n.

prim (prĭm), adj., primmer, primmest, v., primmed, primming. —adj. 1. extremely precise or proper, as persons, behavior, etc.; stiffly neat. —v.t., v.i. 2. to make prim, as in appearance. 3. to purse (the mouth, etc.) into a prim expression. —**prim′ly,** adv. —**prim′ness,** n.

prim., primitive.

pri·ma·cy (prī′mə sĭ), n., pl. -cies. 1. state of being first in rank, importance, etc. 2. Brit. Eccles. the office, rank, or dignity of a primate. 3. Rom. Cath. Ch. the jurisdiction of the Pope as supreme bishop.

pri·ma don·na (prē′mə dŏn′ə), pl. prima donnas, a principal female singer of an operatic company.

pri·ma fa·ci·e (prī′mə fā′shĭ ē′, fā′shĭ), Latin. at first view. —**pri′ma-fa′ci·e′,** adj.

pri·mal (prī′məl), adj. 1. first; original. 2. of first importance; fundamental.

pri·ma·ri·ly (prī′mĕr′ə lĭ, prī′mə rə lĭ; emphatically prī mâr′ə lĭ), adv. 1. chiefly; principally. 2. at first; originally.

pri·ma·ry (prī′mĕr′ĭ, -mə rĭ), adj., n., pl. -ries. —adj. 1. first in rank or importance; chief; principal. 2. first in order in any series, sequence, etc. 3. earliest; primitive. 4. constituting or belonging to, the first stage in any process. 5. fundamental; basic. 6. offering elementary instruction. —n. 7. that which is first in order, rank, or importance. 8. Pol. a. U.S. a meeting of the voters of a political party in an election district for nominating candidates for office, etc. b. a preliminary election in which voters of each party nominate candidates for office, etc. 9. one of any set of primary colors. See **primary colors.** 10. Astron. a body in relation to a smaller body or smaller bodies revolving around it, as a planet in relation to its satellites.

primary colors, red, green, and blue lights, which, when properly selected and mixed, can produce any hue, even white, grays, and purples.

pri·mate (prī′mĭt, -māt), n. 1. Brit. Eccles. an archbishop or a bishop ranking first among the bishops of a province, country, etc. 2. any mammal of the order Primates, that includes man, the apes, the monkeys, the lemurs, etc. —**pri′mate·ship′,** n.

prime (prīm), adj., n., v., primed, priming. —adj. 1. first in importance, excellence, or value. 2. first or highest in rank or authority; chief; main. 3. earliest; primitive. 4. original; fundamental. 5. Math. a. not divisible without remainder by any number except itself and unity. b. having no common divisor except unity. —n. 6. the most flourishing stage. 7. the time of early manhood or womanhood. 8. the choicest or best part of anything. 9. the earliest stage of any period. 10. the first hour or period of the day, after sunrise. 11. Math. a prime number. —v.t. 12. to prepare for a particular purpose or operation. **13.** to supply (a firearm) with powder for communicating fire to a charge. **14.** to pour water into (a pump) to make it work effectively. **15.** to cover (a surface) with a preparatory coat, as in painting. **16.** to supply with information, words, etc., for use.

prime·ly (prīm′lĭ), *adv.* *Colloq.* excellently.

prime minister, the principal minister of certain governments.

prim·er[1] (prĭm′ər), *n.* **1.** an elementary book for teaching children to read. **2.** any small elementary book. **3. great primer,** a printing type (18 point). **4. long primer,** a printing type (10 point).

prim·er[2] (prī′mər), *n.* **1.** one that primes. **2.** a cap, cylinder, etc., containing a compound which may be exploded by percussion: used for firing a charge of powder.

pri·me·val (prī mē′vəl), *adj.* of or pertaining to the first age or ages, esp. of the world. —**pri·me′val·ly,** *adv.*

prim·ing (prī′mĭng), *n.* **1.** the material used to ignite a charge. **2.** act of one that primes. **3.** a first coat of paint, size, etc.

prim·i·tive (prĭm′ə tĭv), *adj.* **1.** being the earliest of the kind or in existence. **2.** early in the history of the world or of mankind. **3.** characteristic of early ages; simple; unrefined. **4.** *Anthropol.* of or pertaining to a race, group, etc., having cultural or physical similarities with their early ancestors. —*n.* **5.** something primitive. **6.** *Art.* **a.** an artist belonging to an early period in the development of a style. **b.** a provincial or naïve painter. —**prim′i·tive·ly,** *adv.* —**prim′i·tive·ness,** *n.*

pri·mo·gen·i·tor (prī′mə jĕn′ə tər), *n.* a first ancestor; forefather or ancestor.

pri·mo·gen·i·ture (prī′mə jĕn′ə chər), *n.* **1.** state or fact of being the first-born among the children of the same parents. **2.** *Law.* the principle of inheritance or succession by the firstborn, specif. the eldest son.

pri·mor·di·al (prī môr′dĭ əl), *adj.* **1.** giving origin to something; original; elementary. **2.** *Biol.* initial; first. —**pri·mor′di·al·ly,** *adv.*

primp (prĭmp), *v.t.* **1.** to dress with nicety. —*v.i.* **2.** *Colloq.* to primp oneself.

prim·rose (prĭm′rōz′), *n.* **1.** Also, **prim·u·la** (prĭm′yə lə). any of certain perennial herbs with variously colored flowers, as a common yellow-flowered European species cultivated in many varieties. —*adj.* **2.** pleasant. **3.** of a pale yellow.

prince (prĭns), *n.* **1.** a nonreigning male member of a royal family. **2.** *Hist.* a sovereign or monarch. **3.** one that is chief or preëminent in any class, group, etc. —**prince′dom,** *n.*

Prince Albert, a double-breasted, long frock coat.

prince consort, a prince who is the husband of a reigning female sovereign.

Prince Edward Island, an island in the Gulf of St. Lawrence, forming a province of Canada. 95,047 pop.; 2184 sq. mi. *Cap.:* Charlottetown.

prince·ly (prĭns′lĭ), *adj.,* **-lier, -liest. 1.** greatly liberal; lavish. **2.** royal; noble; magnificent. —**prince′li·ness,** *n.*

Prince of Wales, a title conferred on the eldest son, or heir apparent, of the British sovereign.

prin·cess (prĭn′sĭs), *n.* **1.** a nonreigning female member of a royal family. **2.** a female sovereign. **3.** the consort of a prince.

prin·cesse dress (prĭn sĕs′, prĭn′sĭs), a woman's close-fitting dress cut in one piece from shoulder to hem. Also, **princess dress.**

prin·ci·pal (prĭn′sə pəl), *adj.* **1.** first or highest in rank, importance, value, etc.; chief. —*n.* **2.** a chief or head. **3.** a governing or presiding officer, as of a school. **4.** one who takes a leading part. **5.** *Law.* **a.** a person authorizing another (an agent) to represent him. **b.** a person directly responsible for a crime. **6.** a person primarily liable for an obligation. **7.** *Com.* a capital sum, as distinguished from interest or profit. **8.** the central structure of a roof which determines its shape and supports it. —**prin′ci·pal·ship′,** *n.*

prin·ci·pal·i·ty (prĭn′sə păl′ə tĭ), *n., pl.* **-ties.** a state ruled by a prince, usually a relatively small state.

prin·ci·pal·ly (prĭn′sə pə lĭ, -sĭp′lĭ), *adv.* chiefly; mainly.

principal parts, *Gram.* a set of inflected forms of a verb from which all the other inflected forms can be inferred.

prin·ci·ple (prĭn′sə pəl), *n.* **1.** an accepted or

professed rule of action or conduct. **2.** a fundamental truth on which other truths depend. **3.** a fundamental doctrine. **4.** (*usually pl.*) right rules of conduct. **5.** a rule or law exemplified in natural phenomena, the working of a system, or the like. **6.** *Chem.* a distinctive constituent of a substance.

prink (prĭngk), *v.t.* **1.** to deck or dress for show. —*v.i.* **2.** to deck oneself out.

print (prĭnt), *v.t.* **1.** to produce (a book, etc.) by applying inked types, plates, or the like, to paper or other material. **2.** to cause (a manuscript, etc.) to be reproduced in print. **3.** to write in letters like those commonly used in print. **4.** *Photog.* to produce a positive picture from (a negative) by the transmission of light. —*v.i.* **5.** to take impressions from type, etc. **6.** to produce books, etc., by means of a press. **7.** to give an impression on paper, etc., as type, etc. **8.** to write in characters such as are used in print. —*n.* **9.** state of being printed. **10. in print, a.** in printed form. **b.** still available for purchase from the publisher. **11. out of print,** no longer available for purchase from the publisher. **12.** printed lettering, esp. with reference to character, style, or size. **13.** a picture, design, or the like, printed from a prepared block, plate, etc. **14.** cloth with a design printed on it. **15.** *Photog.* a picture made from a negative. —**print′a·ble,** *adj.* —**print′er,** *n.*

print., printing.

print·ing (prĭn′tĭng), *n.* **1.** the art, process, or business of producing books, newspapers, etc., by impression from movable types, plates, etc. **2.** words, etc., in printed form. **3.** the whole number of copies of a book, etc., printed at one time.

printing press, a machine for printing on paper or the like from type, plates, etc.

pri·or[1] (prī′ər), *adj.* **1.** preceding in time or order; earlier. **2. prior to,** preceding. —*adv.* **3.** previous.

pri·or[2] (prī′ər), *n.* an officer in a monastic order or religious house. —**pri′or·ess,** *n. fem.*

pri·or·i·ty (prī ôr′ə tĭ, -ŏr′-), *n., pl.* **-ties. 1.** state of being earlier in time. **2.** precedence in order, rank, etc.

pri·o·ry (prī′ə rĭ), *n., pl.* **-ries.** a religious house governed by a prior or prioress.

prism (prĭz′əm), *n.* **1.** *Optics.* a transparent body (esp. one with triangular bases) used for decomposing light into its spectrum or for reflecting light beams. **2.** *Geom.* a solid whose bases or ends are congruent and parallel polygons, and whose sides are parallelograms.

pris·mat·ic (prĭz măt′ĭk), *adj.* **1.** of, pertaining to, or like a prism. **2.** formed by a transparent prism. **3.** varied in color; brilliant. Also, **pris·mat′i·cal.**

pris·on (prĭz′ən), *n.* a public building for the confinement or safe custody of criminals and others committed by law.

pris·on·er (prĭz′ə nər, prĭz′nər), *n.* **1.** one who is confined in prison. **2.** one taken by an enemy in war (**prisoner of war**).

pris·sy (prĭs′ĭ), *adj.,* **-sier, -siest.** *U.S. Colloq.* or *Dial.* prim; affectedly nice.

pris·tine (prĭs′tēn, -tĭn), *adj.* **1.** original; primitive. **2.** having its original purity.

prith·ee (prĭ*th*′ĭ), *interj.* *Archaic.* (I) pray thee.

pri·va·cy (prī′və sĭ), *n., pl.* **-cies. 1.** state of being private; retirement or seclusion. **2.** secrecy.

pri·vate (prī′vĭt), *adj.* **1.** belonging to some particular person or persons. **2.** individual; personal. **3.** confidential. **4.** not holding or involving public office or employment. **5.** out of public view or knowledge; secret. **6.** not open to people in general. **7.** alone; secluded. —*n.* **8.** a soldier of lowest rank. —**pri′vate·ly,** *adv.* —**pri′vate·ness,** *n.*

pri·va·teer (prī′və tĭr′), *n.* **1.** a privately owned vessel, commissioned by a government to fight the enemy, esp. his commercial shipping. **2.** the commander, or one of the crew, of such a vessel. —*v.i.* **3.** to cruise as a privateer.

pri·va·tion (prī vā′shən), *n.* **1.** lack of the usual comforts or necessaries of life. **2.** a depriving. **3.** state of being deprived.

priv·a·tive (prĭv′ə tĭv), *adj.* **1.** that deprives. **2.** consisting in or characterized by the depriving, loss, or lack of something. **3.** *Gram.* indicating negation or absence. —**priv′a·tive·ly,** *adv.*

priv·et (prĭv′ĭt), *n.* any of certain shrubs of the olive family, with evergreen leaves and small white flowers, much used for hedges.

priv·i·lege (prĭv′ə lĭj), *n., v.,* **-leged, -leging.** —*n.* **1.** a right enjoyed by a person or persons beyond the common advantages of others. **2.** a prerogative, advantage, or opportunity enjoyed by anyone in a favored position. —*v.t.* **3.** to grant a privilege to. **4.** to exempt. **5.** to authorize (something otherwise forbidden).

priv·i·ly (prĭv′ə lĭ), *adv.* secretly.

priv·y (prĭv′ĭ), *adj., n., pl.* **privies.** —*adj.* **1.** participating in the knowledge of something private or secret. **2.** private. —*n.* **3.** an outhouse serving as a toilet. **4.** *Law.* one participating directly in a legal transaction.

privy council, a board or select body of personal advisers, as of a sovereign.

prize[1] (prīz), *n.* **1.** a reward of victory or superiority, as in a contest. **2.** that which is won in a lottery or the like. **3.** anything striven for, worth striving for, or much valued. **4.** something captured, esp. an enemy's ship with the property in it taken at sea under the law of war. —*adj.* **5.** that has gained a prize. **6.** worthy of a prize. **7.** given as a prize.

prize[2] (prīz), *v.t.,* **prized, prizing. 1.** to esteem highly. **2.** to estimate the value of.

prize[3] (prīz), *v.,* **prized, prizing,** *n.* —*v.t.* **1.** *Chiefly Brit.* to raise, move, or force with a lever. —*n.* **2.** leverage.

prize fight, a contest between boxers for a prize. —**prize fighter.** —**prize fighting.**

prize ring, 1. an enclosed square area for prize fighting. **2.** prize fighting.

pro[1] (prō), *adv., n., pl.* **pros.** —*adv.* **1.** in favor of a proposition, opinion, etc. —*n.* **2.** one who upholds the affirmative. **3.** an argument, vote, etc., for something.

pro[2] (prō), *n., pl.* **pros,** *adj. Colloq.* professional.

pro-, a prefix indicating favor for some party, system, idea, etc., without identity with the group, as in *pro-British.*

prob·a·bil·i·ty (prŏb′ə bĭl′ə tĭ), *n., pl.* **-ties. 1.** quality or fact of being probable. **2.** likelihood. **3.** a probable event, circumstance, etc.

prob·a·ble (prŏb′ə bəl), *adj.* **1.** likely to occur or prove true. **2.** having more evidence for than against. **3.** affording ground for belief. —**prob′a·bly,** *adv.*

pro·bate (prō′bāt), *n., adj., v.,* **-bated, -bating.** *Law.* —*n.* **1.** the official proving of a will as authentic or valid. —*adj.* **2.** of or pertaining to probate or a court of probate. —*v.t.* **3.** to establish the authenticity or validity of (a will).

pro·ba·tion (prō bā′shən), *n.* **1.** act of testing, esp. a person's conduct, character, or the like. **2.** the state or period of such testing. **3.** *Law.* **a.** a method of dealing with offenders, esp. young persons guilty of minor crimes or first offenses, by releasing them conditionally under supervision. **b.** the state of having been conditionally released. **4.** *Educ.* a trial period or condition of students who are being permitted to redeem failures, misconduct, etc. —**pro·ba′tion·al, pro·ba·tion·ar·y** (prō bā′shə nĕr′ĭ), *adj.*

pro·ba·tion·er (prō bā′shən ər), *n.* one undergoing probation or trial.

probe (prōb), *v.,* **probed, probing,** *n.* —*v.t.* **1.** to examine or question thoroughly. **2.** to examine with a probe. —*v.i.* **3.** to penetrate with a probe. —*n.* **4.** a slender surgical instrument for exploring the depth or direction of a wound, sinus, or the like. **5.** *U.S.* an investigation of suspected illegal activity. —**prob′er,** *n.*

pro·bi·ty (prō′bə tĭ, prŏb′ə-), *n.* integrity; uprightness; honesty.

prob·lem (prŏb′ləm), *n.* **1.** any matter involving doubt, uncertainty, or difficulty. **2.** a question proposed for solution or discussion. —*adj.* **3.** difficult to train or guide; unruly.

prob·lem·at·ic (prŏb′lə măt′ĭk), *adj.* doubtful; uncertain. Also, **prob′lem·at′i·cal.** —**prob′lem·at′i·cal·ly,** *adv.*

pro·bos·cis (prō bŏs′ĭs), *n., pl.* **-bos·cis·es** (-bŏs′ĭs ĭz), **-boscides** (-bŏs′ə dēz′). **1.** an elephant's trunk. **2.** any long flexible snout. **3.** *Humorous.* the human nose.

proc., 1. proceedings. **2.** procedure.

pro·caine (prō kān′, prō′kān), *n.* novocaine.

pro·ce·dure (prō sē′jər), *n.* **1.** act or manner of proceeding in any action or process; conduct. **2.** a particular course of action. —**pro·ce′dur·al,** *adj.*

pro·ceed (*v.* prə sēd′; *n.* prō′sēd), *v.i.* **1.** to go forward, esp. after stopping. **2.** to carry on any action or process. **3.** to go on (to do something). **4.** to go or come forth; issue. **5.** to arise,

originate, or result. —*n.* **6.** that which results. **7.** (*usually pl.*) the sum derived from a sale or other transaction.

pro·ceed·ing (prə sē′dĭng), *n.* **1.** an action, course of action, or conduct. **2.** (*pl.*) records of the doings of a society. **3.** *Law.* **a.** the instituting or carrying on of an action at law. **b.** a legal step or measure.

proc·ess (prŏs′ĕs *or, esp. Brit.,* prō′sĕs), *n.* **1.** a systematic series of actions directed to some end. **2.** a continuous action, operation, or series of changes. **3.** *Law.* the summons, mandate, or writ by which a defendant or thing is brought before court for litigation. **4.** *Biol.* a natural outgrowth, projection, or appendage. —*v.t.* **5.** to treat or prepare by some particular process. —*adj.* **6.** prepared or modified by an artificial process.

pro·ces·sion (prə sĕsh′ən), *n.* **1.** a formal or ceremonious parade of persons, animals, vehicles, or other things. **2.** the line or body of persons or things moving along.

pro·ces·sion·al (prə sĕsh′ən əl), *adj.* **1.** of or pertaining to a procession. **2.** sung or recited in procession, as a hymn. —*n.* **3.** a processional hymn. **4.** a book containing hymns, litanies, etc., for use in religious processions.

pro·claim (prō klām′), *v.t.* **1.** to announce publicly or officially. **2.** (of things) to indicate. —*v.i.* **3.** to make a proclamation. —**pro·claim′er,** *n.*

proc·la·ma·tion (prŏk′lə mā′shən), *n.* **1.** a public and official announcement. **2.** act of proclaiming.

pro·cliv·i·ty (prō klĭv′ə tĭ), *n., pl.* **-ties.** natural or habitual inclination or tendency.

pro·con·sul (prō kŏn′səl), *n.* **1.** (among the ancient Romans) a governor of a province with duties and powers similar to those of a consul. **2.** any appointed administrator over a dependency or an occupied area.

pro·cras·ti·nate (prō krăs′tə nāt′), *v.i., v.t.,* **-nated, -nating.** to defer (action); delay. —**pro·cras′ti·na′tion,** *n.* —**pro·cras′ti·na′tor,** *n.*

pro·cre·ate (prō′krĭ āt′), *v.t.,* **-ated, -ating. 1.** to beget (offspring). **2.** to produce. —**pro′cre·a′tion,** *n.* —**pro′cre·a′tive,** *adj.* —**pro′cre·a′tor,** *n.*

proc·tor (prŏk′tər), *n.* **1.** one appointed to keep watch over students at examinations. **2.** *Chiefly Brit.* a college official charged esp. with the maintenance of good order. —*v.t.* **3.** to act as a proctor (def. 1). —**proc·to·ri·al** (prŏk tōr′ĭ əl), *adj.* —**proc′tor·ship′,** *n.*

pro·cum·bent (prō kŭm′bənt), *adj.* **1.** prone; prostrate. **2.** *Bot.* (of a plant or stem) lying along the ground, but without putting forth roots.

proc·u·ra·tor (prŏk′yə rā′tər), *n.* (among the ancient Romans) any of various imperial officers with fiscal or administrative powers.

pro·cure (prō kyōōr′), *v.t., v.i.,* **-cured, -curing. 1.** to obtain by care, effort, or special means. **2.** to bring about; cause. **3.** to obtain (women) for the gratification of lust. —**pro·cur′a·ble,** *adj.* —**pro·cure′ment,** *n.* —**pro·cur′er,** *n.* —**pro·cur′ess,** *n.fem.*

Pro·cy·on (prō′sĭ ŏn′), *n. Astron.* a star of the first magnitude in the constellation Canis Minor.

prod (prŏd), *v.,* **prodded, prodding,** *n.* —*v.t.* **1.** to poke with something pointed. **2.** to rouse or incite. —*n.* **3.** a poke or jab. **4.** any of various pointed instruments, as a goad. —**prod′der,** *n.*

prod·i·gal (prŏd′ə gəl), *adj.* **1.** wastefully or recklessly extravagant. **2.** lavish. —*n.* **3.** a spendthrift. —**prod′i·gal·ly,** *adv.*

prod·i·gal·i·ty (prŏd′ə găl′ə tĭ), *n., pl.* **-ties. 1.** wasteful extravagance in spending. **2.** lavish abundance.

pro·di·gious (prə dĭj′əs), *adj.* **1.** extraordinary in size, amount, extent, degree, force, etc. **2.** wonderful or marvelous. **3.** abnormal; monstrous. —**pro·di′gious·ly,** *adv.* —**pro·di′gious·ness,** *n.*

prod·i·gy (prŏd′ə jĭ), *n., pl.* **-gies. 1.** a person endowed with extraordinary gifts or powers. **2.** a marvelous example. **3.** something wonderful. **4.** something abnormal or monstrous.

pro·duce (*v.* prə dūs′, -dōōs′; *n.* prŏd′ūs, -ōōs *or* prō′dūs, -dōōs), *v.,* **-duced, -ducing,** *n.* —*v.t.* **1.** to bring into existence; create or cause. **2.** *Econ.* to create (something having an exchangeable value). **3.** to bring forth, bear, or yield, as young or natural products. **4.** to present to view; exhibit. **5.** to bring (a play, etc.) before the public. —*v.i.* **6.** to bring forth or yield appropriate offspring, products, etc. **7.** *Econ.* to create value. **—***n.* **8.** yield; product. **9.** agricultural or natural products collectively. **—pro·duc′er,** *n.*

prod·uct (prŏd′ŏkt, -ŭkt), *n.* **1.** a thing produced by any action or operation; result. **2.** *Chem.* a substance obtained from another substance through chemical change. **3.** *Math.* the result obtained by multiplying two or more quantities together.

pro·duc·tion (prə dŭk′shən), *n.* **1.** act of producing; creation; manufacture. **2.** a product. **3.** a work of literature or art. **4.** *Econ.* the producing of articles having an exchangeable value.

pro·duc·tive (prə dŭk′tĭv), *adj.* **1.** having the power of producing; creative. **2.** fertile; prolific. **3.** *Econ.* producing goods and services having exchangeable value. **—pro·duc′tive·ly,** *adv.* **—pro·duc·tiv·i·ty** (prō′dŭk tĭv′ə tĭ), **pro·duc′-tive·ness,** *n.*

pro·em (prō′ĕm), *n.* an introduction.

Prof., Professor. Also, **prof.**

prof·a·na·tion (prŏf′ə nā′shən), *n.* act of profaning; desecration; defilement.

pro·fane (prə fān′), *adj., v.,* **-faned, -faning.** **—***adj.* **1.** characterized by irreverence or contempt for God or sacred things. **2.** secular. **3.** heathen; pagan. **—***v.t.* **4.** to defile; debase. **5.** to treat (anything sacred) with irreverence or contempt. **—pro·fane′ly,** *adv.* **—pro·fane′-ness,** *n.* **—pro·fan′er,** *n.*

pro·fan·i·ty (prə făn′ə tĭ), *n., pl.* **-ties. 1.** quality of being profane; irreverence. **2.** profane conduct, language, etc.

pro·fess (prə fĕs′), *v.t.* **1.** to claim (a feeling, etc.), often insincerely. **2.** to declare openly. **3.** to affirm faith in (a religion, God, etc.). **4.** to make (a thing) one's profession or business. **—***v.i.* **5.** to make profession. **—pro·fess′ed·ly,** *adv.*

pro·fes·sion (prə fĕsh′ən), *n.* **1.** a vocation requiring special knowledge, esp. theology, law, and medicine. **2.** the persons engaged in an occupation. **3.** act of professing; avowal.

pro·fes·sion·al (prə fĕsh′ən əl), *adj.* **1.** following an occupation as a means of livelihood or f gain. **2.** pertaining or appropriate to a profession. **3.** engaged in one of the learned professions. **4.** following as a business an occupation ordinarily engaged in as a pastime. **—***n.* **5.** one belonging to one of the learned professions. **6.** one who makes a business of an occupation ordinarily engaged in as a pastime. **—pro·fes′sion·al·ism′,** *n.* **—pro·fes′sion·al·ly,** *adv.*

pro·fes·sor (prə fĕs′ər), *n.* **1.** a teacher of the highest rank in a university or college. **2.** a teacher. **3.** one who professes his beliefs, etc. **—pro·fes·so·ri·al** (prō′fĕ sōr′ĭ əl, prŏf′ə-), *adj.* **—pro′fes·so′ri·al·ly,** *adv.* **—pro·fes′sor·ship′,** *n.*

prof·fer (prŏf′ər), *v.t.* **1.** to present for acceptance; offer. **—***n.* **2.** an offer.

pro·fi·cient (prə fĭsh′ənt), *adj.* **1.** expert in any art, science, or subject; skilled. **—***n.* **2.** an expert. **—pro·fi′cient·ly,** *adv.* **—pro·fi′cien·cy,** *n.*

pro·file (prō′fīl), *n., v.,* **-filed, -filing. —***n.* **1.** the outline or contour of anything, as the human face, from the side. **2.** *Archit., Engin.* a drawing of a vertical section. **3.** a vivid and concise biography. **—***v.t.* **4.** to draw a profile of. **5.** to shape as to profile.

prof·it (prŏf′ĭt), *n.* **1.** (*often pl.*) pecuniary gain resulting from the employment of capital in any transaction. **2.** the surplus left to the producer or employer after deducting wages, rent, cost of raw materials, etc. **3.** advantage; benefit; gain. **—***v.i., v.t.* **4.** to gain advantage or benefit. **5.** to make profit. **6.** to be of advantage or benefit (to). **—prof′it·less,** *adj.*

prof·it·a·ble (prŏf′ĭt ə bəl), *adj.* **1.** yielding profit. **2.** beneficial or useful. **—prof′it·a·ble-ness,** *n.* **—prof′it·a·bly,** *adv.*

prof·it·eer (prŏf′ə tĭr′), *n.* **1.** one who seeks or exacts exorbitant profits, as by taking advantage of public necessity. **—***v.i.* **2.** to act as a profiteer.

prof·li·gate (prŏf′lə gĭt, -gāt′), *adj.* **1.** utterly and shamelessly immoral. **2.** recklessly extravagant. **—***n.* **3.** a profligate person. **—prof′li-gate·ly,** *adv.* **—prof′li·gate·ness, prof·li·ga·cy** (prŏf′lə gə sĭ), *n.*

pro·found (prə found′), *adj.* **1.** penetrating deeply into subjects of thought or knowledge. **2.** intense; extreme. **3.** being or going far beneath what is superficial, external, or obvious. **4.** low. **5.** deep. **—***n.* **6.** *Poetic.* the ocean. **—pro·found′ly,**

adv. **—pro·found′ness, pro·fun·di·ty** (prə fŭn′-də tĭ), *n.*

pro·fuse (prə fūs′), *adj.* **1.** spending or giving freely; extravagant. **2.** abundant. **—pro·fuse′-ly,** *adv.* **—pro·fuse′ness,** *n.*

pro·fu·sion (prə fū′zhən), *n.* **1.** abundance. **2.** extravagance.

pro·gen·i·tor (prō jĕn′ə tər), *n.* an ancestor in the direct line; forefather.

prog·e·ny (prŏj′ə nĭ), *n., pl.* **-nies.** offspring; issue; descendants.

prog·na·thous (prŏg′nə thəs, prŏg nā′-), *adj.* **1.** (of a jaw) protruding. **2.** (of a skull or a person) having protrusive jaws.

prog·no·sis (prŏg nō′sĭs), *n., pl.* **-noses** (-nō′-sēz). *Med.* a forecast of the probable course and termination of a disease. **—prog·nos·tic** (prŏg-nŏs′tĭk), *adj.*

prog·nos·ti·cate (prŏg nŏs′tə kāt′), *v.t., v.i.,* **-cated, -cating.** to forecast or predict. **—prog-nos′ti·ca′tion,** *n.* **—prog·nos′ti·ca′tor,** *n.*

pro·gram (prō′grăm, -grəm), *n.* **1.** a plan to be followed. **2.** a list of items, performers, etc., in a musical, theatrical, or other entertainment. Also, *esp. Brit.,* **pro′gramme.**

prog·ress (*n.* prŏg′rĕs *or, esp. Brit.,* prō′grĕs; *v.* prə grĕs′), *n.* **1.** a proceeding to a further or higher stage; advancement. **2.** growth or development. **3.** forward movement. **4. in progress,** happening. **—***v.i.* **5.** to advance or to go forward.

pro·gres·sion (prə grĕsh′ən), *n.* **1.** act of progressing. **2.** *Math.* a succession of quantities in which there is a constant relation between each member and the one succeeding it.

pro·gres·sive (prə grĕs′ĭv), *adj.* **1.** advocating improvement or reform, esp. in political matters. **2.** improving or advancing; making progress toward better conditions, etc. **3.** going forward, esp. step by step. **—***n.* **4.** a progressive person. **5.** (*cap.*) a member of the Progressive Party. **—pro·gres′sive·ly,** *adv.* **—pro·gres′-sive·ness,** *n.*

Progressive Party, any of three political parties: one formed in 1912 (led by Theodore Roosevelt), one formed in 1924 (led by Robert M. La Follette), or one formed in 1948 (led by Henry A. Wallace).

pro·hib·it (prō hĭb′ĭt), *v.t.* **1.** to forbid. **2.** to prevent or hinder.

pro·hi·bi·tion (prō′ə bĭsh′ən), *n.* **1.** the interdiction by law of the manufacture and sale of alcoholic drinks for common consumption. **2.** act of prohibiting. **3.** a law or decree that forbids or debars. **—pro′hi·bi′tion·ist,** *n.*

pro·hib·i·tive (prō hĭb′ə tĭv), *adj.* that prohibits or forbids something. Also, **pro·hib′i·to′ry.**

pro·ject (*n.* prŏj′ĕkt; *v.* prə jĕkt′), *n.* **1.** something contemplated, devised, or planned. **—***v.t., v.i.* **2.** to contemplate or plan. **3.** to throw, cast, or impel forward. **4.** to throw upon a surface or into space, as a shadow, an image, etc. **5.** to protrude. **6.** to delineate by any system of correspondence between points.

pro·jec·tile (prə jĕk′tĭl), *n.* **1.** an object fired with an explosive propelling charge, such as a bullet, shell, rocket, or grenade. **2.** any missile. **—***adj.* **3.** impelling forward, as a force. **4.** capable of being impelled forward, as a missile.

pro·jec·tion (prə jĕk′shən), *n.* **1.** a protruding part. **2.** state or fact of protruding. **3.** a causing to protrude. **4.** *Geom., etc.* act, process, or result of projecting. **5.** *Cartog.* a systematic drawing of lines representing meridians and parallels on a plane surface on which the earth surface or some portion of it may be drawn. **6.** *Photog.* the throwing of an image by optical means, as motion pictures. **7.** *Psychol.* the tendency to attribute to another person, or to the environment, what is actually within oneself. **8.** the act of planning or scheming.

pro·jec·tor (prə jĕk′tər), *n.* an apparatus for throwing an image on a screen.

Pro·kof·iev (prō kôf′yĕf), *n.* **Sergei Sergee-vich,** born 1891, Soviet composer.

pro·late (prō′lāt), *adj.* elongated along the polar diameter, as a spheroid.

pro·le·tar·i·an (prō′lə târ′ĭ ən), *adj.* **1.** pertaining or belonging to the proletariat. **—***n.* **2.** a member of the proletariat.

pro·le·tar·i·at (prō′lə târ′ĭ ət), *n.* that class which is dependent for support on daily or casual employment; the working class.

pro·lif·ic (prō lĭf′ĭk), *adj.* abundantly productive or fruitful. **—pro·lif′i·cal·ly,** *adv.*

pro·lix (prō lĭks′, prō′lĭks), *adj.* tediously long and wordy. —**pro·lix·i·ty** (prō lĭk′sə tĭ), *n.*

pro·logue (prō′lôg, -lŏg), *n., v.,* -logued, -loguing. —*n.* 1. an introductory speech, calling attention to the theme of a play. 2. an introductory part of a discourse, poem, or novel. —*v.t.* 3. to introduce with a prologue. Also, **pro′log.**

pro·long (prə lông′, -lŏng′), *v.t.* to extend the duration or length of. —**pro′lon·ga′tion,** *n.*

prom (prŏm), *n. Colloq.* (in American colleges) a ball or dance.

prom·e·nade (prŏm′ə nād′, -näd′), *n., v.,* -naded, -nading. —*n.* 1. a leisurely walk, esp. in a public place. 2. a space or path for such a walk. 3. a march of guests into a ballroom constituting the opening of a formal ball. —*v.i., v.t.* 4. to take a promenade (through or about).

Pro·me·theus (prə mē′thōŏs, -thĭ əs), *n. Gk. Myth.* a Titan who stole fire for mankind from Olympus, in punishment for which he was chained to a rock where his liver was daily gnawed by a vulture. —**Pro·me′the·an,** *adj.*

prom·i·nence (prŏm′ə nəns), *n.* 1. state of being prominent. 2. a projection or protuberance.

prom·i·nent (prŏm′ə nənt), *adj.* 1. conspicuous; especially noticeable. 2. projecting. 3. important; well-known. —**prom′i·nent·ly,** *adv.*

pro·mis·cu·ous (prə mĭs′kyŏŏ əs), *adj.* 1. consisting of all kinds of parts or elements indiscriminately mingled. 2. without discrimination. 3. *Colloq.* casual. —**pro·mis′cu·ous·ly,** *adv.* —**pro·mis′cu·ous·ness, prom·is·cu·i·ty** (prŏm′ĭs kū′ə tĭ), *n.*

prom·ise (prŏm′ĭs), *n., v.,* -ised, -ising. —*n.* 1. a declaration or assurance that one will do, not do, give, not give, etc., something. 2. indication of future excellence or achievement. —*v.t.* 3. to undertake or assure by promise. 4. to afford ground for expecting. —*v.i.* 5. to afford ground for expectation. 6. to make a promise.

Promised Land, 1. Canaan, the land promised by God to Abraham and his descendants. 2. Heaven.

prom·is·ing (prŏm′ə sĭng), *adj.* likely to turn out well. —**prom′is·ing·ly,** *adv.*

prom·is·so·ry (prŏm′ə sōr′ĭ), *adj.* containing or implying a promise.

promissory note, a written promise to pay a specified sum of money to a person designated or to his order, or to the bearer, at a time fixed or on demand.

prom·on·to·ry (prŏm′ən tōr′ĭ), *n., pl.* -ries. a high point of land projecting into the sea.

pro·mote (prə mōt′), *v.t.,* -moted, -moting. 1. to further the growth, development, progress, etc., of. 2. to advance in rank, position, grade, etc. 3. to aid in organizing (financial undertakings). —**pro·mot′er,** *n.* —**pro·mo′tion,** *n.*

prompt (prŏmpt), *adj.* 1. done, delivered, etc., at once or without delay. 2. ready to act as occasion demands. 3. ready and willing. —*v.t., v.i.* 4. to incite to action. 5. to suggest or induce (action, etc.). 6. to assist (an actor, etc.) by suggesting something to be said. —*n.* 7. something that prompts. —**prompt′er,** *n.* —**prompt′ly,** *adv.* —**prompt′ness, promp·ti·tude** (prŏmp′tə tŭd′, -tōōd′), *n.*

pro·mul·gate (prō mŭl′gāt), *v.t.,* -gated, -gating. 1. to proclaim formally or put into operation (a law or decree). 2. to teach publicly (a doctrine, etc.). —**pro·mul·ga·tion** (prō′mŭl gā′shən), *n.* —**pro·mul·ga·tor** (prō mŭl′gā tər), *n.*

pron., 1. pronoun. 2. pronounced. 3. pronunciation.

prone (prōn), *adj.* 1. inclined; disposed; liable. 2. lying face downward. 3. lying flat; prostrate. —**prone′ly,** *adv.* —**prone′ness,** *n.*

prong (prông, prŏng), *n.* 1. one of the pointed divisions or tines of a fork. 2. any pointed projecting part.

prong·horn (prông′hôrn, prŏng′-), *n.* a fleet antelopelike ruminant of the plains of western North America.

pro·noun (prō′noun′), *n. Gram.* 1. one of the major form classes, or parts of speech, comprising words used as substitutes for nouns. 2. any such word. —**pro·nom·i·nal** (prō nŏm′ə nəl), *adj.* —**pro·nom′i·nal·ly,** *adv.*

pro·nounce (prə nouns′), *v.t., v.i.,* -nounced, -nouncing. 1. to enunciate or utter (words, etc.). 2. to declare (a person or thing) to be as specified. 3. to utter or deliver formally or solemnly. 4. to announce authoritatively or officially. —**pro·nounce′a·ble,** *adj.* —**pro·nounc′er,** *n.*

pro·nounced (prə nounst′), *adj.* 1. strongly marked. 2. clearly indicated. 3. decided.

pro·nounce·ment (prə nouns′mənt), *n.* a formal or authoritative statement.

pron·to (prŏn′tō), *adv. U.S. Slang.* promptly.

pro·nun·ci·a·men·to (prə nŭn′sĭ ə mĕn′tō, -shĭ ə-), *n., pl.* -tos. a proclamation.

pro·nun·ci·a·tion (prə nŭn′sĭ ā′shən, -shĭ ā′-), *n.* the act or the result of producing the sounds of speech.

proof (prōōf), *n.* 1. evidence sufficient to establish a thing as true. 2. a test; trial. 3. the establishment of the truth of anything. 4. the arbitrary standard strength, as of alcoholic liquors. 5. *Photog.* a trial print from a negative. 6. *Print.* a trial impression as of composed type, taken to correct errors and make alterations. —*adj.* 7. impenetrable, impervious, or invulnerable.

proof·read (prōōf′rēd′), *v.t., v.i.,* -read (-rĕd), -reading. to read (printers' proofs, etc.) in order to detect and mark errors to be corrected. —**proof′read′er,** *n.* —**proof′read′ing,** *n.*

prop (prŏp), *n., v.,* propped, propping. —*n.* 1. a stick, rod, beam, or other rigid support. 2. any support. —*v.t.* 3. to support with a prop. 4. to rest (a thing) against support. 5. to support.

prop·a·gan·da (prŏp′ə găn′də), *n.* 1. the doctrines propagated by an organization or concerted movement. 2. such an organization or concerted movement. —**prop′a·gan′dism,** *n.* —**prop′a·gan′dist,** *n., adj.*

prop·a·gan·dize (prŏp′ə găn′dīz), *v.t., v.i.,* -dized, -dizing. to spread (principles, etc.) by propaganda.

prop·a·gate (prŏp′ə gāt′), *v.t., v.i.,* -gated, -gating. 1. to cause (plants, animals, etc.) to reproduce. 2. to reproduce (itself, its kind, etc.). 3. to spread (a report, doctrine, etc.). 4. to extend or transmit through space or a medium. —**prop′a·ga′tion,** *n.* —**prop′a·ga′tor,** *n.*

pro·pel (prə pĕl′), *v.t.,* -pelled, -pelling. to drive or move forward.

pro·pel·ler (prə pĕl′ər), *n.* a device having a revolving hub with radiating blades, for propelling a steamship, aircraft, etc.

pro·pen·si·ty (prə pĕn′sə tĭ), *n., pl.* -ties. natural or habitual inclination or tendency.

prop·er (prŏp′ər), *adj.* 1. appropriate; fit; suitable. 2. correct or decorous. 3. fitting; right. 4. belonging or pertaining exclusively or distinctly to a person or thing. 5. strict; accurate. 6. strictly so-called. 7. *Gram.* a. (of a name, noun, or adjective) designating a particular person or thing, written in English with an initial capital letter. b. having the force or function of a proper name. 8. *Chiefly Brit. Colloq.* thorough. —**prop′er·ly,** *adv.*

proper fraction, *Math.* a fraction having the numerator less than the denominator.

prop·er·tied (prŏp′ər tĭd), *adj.* owning property.

prop·er·ty (prŏp′ər tĭ), *n., pl.* -ties. 1. that which one owns; possession. 2. goods, lands, etc., owned. 3. a piece of land or real estate. 4. ownership. 5. an attribute or characteristic, esp. an essential one. 6. *Theat.* an item of furniture or decoration in a stage setting.

proph·e·cy (prŏf′ə sĭ), *n., pl.* -cies. 1. foretelling of what is to come. 2. a prediction. 3. divinely inspired utterance or revelation.

proph·e·sy (prŏf′ə sī), *v.t., v.i.,* -sied, -sying. 1. to foretell or predict. 2. to foretell or declare by divine inspiration. —**proph′e·si′er,** *n.*

proph·et (prŏf′ĭt), *n.* 1. one who speaks for God or a deity, or by divine inspiration. 2. **the Prophets,** the books which form the second of the three Jewish divisions of the Old Testament, comprising all the books from *Joshua* through *Malachi.* 3. one regarded as, or claiming to be, an inspired teacher or leader. 4. one who foretells what is to come. 5. a spokesman of some doctrine, cause, or the like. —**proph′et·ess,** *n. fem.*

pro·phet·ic (prə fĕt′ĭk), *adj.* 1. of or pertaining to a prophet. 2. of or containing prophecy. 3. predicting or ominous. —**pro·phet′i·cal·ly,** *adv.*

pro·phy·lac·tic (prō′fə lăk′tĭk, prŏf′ə-), *adj.* 1. protecting from disease, as a drug. —*n.* 2. a prophylactic medicine or measure.

pro·phy·lax·is (prō′fə lăk′sĭs, prŏf′ə-), *n.* 1. the preventing of disease. 2. prophylactic treatment.

pro·pin·qui·ty (prō pĭng′kwə tĭ), *n.* 1. nearness in place; proximity. **2.** kinship. **3.** similarity.

pro·pi·ti·ate (prə pĭsh'ĭ āt'), *v.t.*, **-ated, -ating.** to appease; conciliate. **—pro·pi'ti·a'tion,** *n.* **—pro·pi'ti·a·to'ry,** *adj.*

pro·pi·tious (prə pĭsh'əs), *adj.* **1.** favorable. **2.** favorably inclined. **—pro·pi'tious·ly,** *adv.* **—pro·pi'tious·ness,** *n.*

pro·po·nent (prə pō'nənt), *n.* **1.** one who puts forward a proposition or proposal. **2.** one who supports a cause or doctrine.

pro·por·tion (prə pōr'shən), *n.* **1.** comparative relation between things or magnitudes as to size, quantity, etc. **2.** proper relation between things or parts. **3.** (*pl.*) dimensions. **4.** a portion. **5.** symmetry; harmony; agreement. **6.** *Math.* a relation of four quantities such that the first divided by the second is equal to the third divided by the fourth. **—v.t. 7.** to adjust in proper relation. **8.** to adjust the proportions of.

pro·por·tion·al (prə pōr'shən əl), *adj.* **1.** having due proportion. **2.** relative. **—pro·por'tion·al·ly,** *adv.*

pro·por·tion·ate (*adj.* prə pōr'shən ĭt; *v.* prəpōr'shə nāt/), *adj., v.*, **-ated, -ating.** **—adj. 1.** being in due proportion. **—v.t. 2.** to make proportionate. **—pro·por'tion·ate·ly,** *adv.*

pro·pos·al (prə pō'zəl), *n.* **1.** act of proposing. **2.** a plan or scheme proposed. **3.** an offer, specif. of marriage.

pro·pose (prə pōz'), *v.*, **-posed, -posing.** **—v.t. 1.** to put forward (a matter) for consideration, acceptance, or action. **2.** to present (a person) for some position, membership, etc. **3.** to intend. **—v.i. 4.** to make a proposal, esp. of marriage. **—pro·pos'er,** *n.*

prop·o·si·tion (prŏp'ə zĭsh'ən), *n.* **1.** act of proposing something to be considered, accepted, adopted, or done. **2.** a plan or scheme proposed. **3.** an offer of terms for a transaction, as in business. **4.** *U.S. Slang.* a thing, matter, or person considered as something dealt with or encountered. **5.** *Math.* a formal statement of either a truth to be demonstrated or an operation to be performed.

pro·pound (prə pound'), *v.t.* to put forward for consideration, acceptance, or adoption. **—pro·pound'er,** *n.*

pro·pri·e·tar·y (prə prī'ə tĕr'ĭ), *adj., n., pl.* **-taries. —adj. 1.** belonging to a proprietor or proprietors. **2.** holding property. **3.** pertaining to property or ownership. **—n. 4.** an owner. **5.** a body of proprietors. **6.** a patent medicine.

pro·pri·e·tor (prə prī'ə tər), *n.* **1.** the owner (or manager) of a business. **2.** an owner, as of property. **—pro·pri'e·tor·ship',** *n.* **—pro·pri·e·tress** (prə prī'ə trĭs), *n. fem.*

pro·pri·e·ty (prə prī'ə tĭ), *n., pl.* **-ties. 1.** conformity to established standards of behavior or manners. **2.** appropriateness or suitability. **3.** rightness or justness.

pro·pul·sion (prə pŭl'shən), *n.* **1.** act of propelling. **2.** state of being propelled. **3.** propelling force. **—pro·pul·sive** (prə pŭl'sĭv), *adj.*

pro ra·ta (prō rā'tə, rä'tə), in proportion.

pro·rate (prō rāt', prō'rāt'), *v.*, **-rated, -rating. —v.i. 1.** to make an arrangement on a basis of proportional distribution. **—v.t. 2.** to divide proportionately.

pros., prosody.

pro·sa·ic (prō zā'ĭk), *adj.* **1.** commonplace; dull. **2.** having the spirit of prose as opposed to poetry. **—pro·sa'i·cal·ly,** *adv.*

pro·sce·ni·um (prō sē'nĭ əm), *n., pl.* **-nia** (-nĭ ə). that part of the stage in front of the curtain, often including the curtain and the framework which holds it.

pro·scribe (prō skrīb'), *v.t.*, **-scribed, -scribing. 1.** to denounce or condemn (a thing) as dangerous. **2.** to outlaw. **3.** to banish or exile. **—pro·scrib'er,** *n.* **—pro·scrip·tion** (prōskrĭp'shən), *n.* **—pro·scrip·tive** (prō skrĭp'tĭv), *adj.*

prose (prōz), *n., adj., v.*, **prosed, prosing. —n. 1.** the ordinary form of spoken or written language, without metrical structure. **2.** matter-of-fact, commonplace, or dull expression, quality, discourse, etc. **—adj. 3.** consisting of or pertaining to prose. **4.** prosaic. **—v.t. 5.** to turn into prose.

pros·e·cute (prŏs'ə kūt'), *v.*, **-cuted, -cuting. —v.t. 1.** *Law.* **a.** to institute or conduct proceedings against. **b.** to seek to enforce or obtain by legal process. **2.** to go on with something begun. **—v.i. 3.** *Law.* **a.** to institute a legal prosecution. **b.** to act as prosecutor. **—pros'e·cu'tion,** *n.* **—pros'e·cu'tor,** *n.*

pros·e·lyte (prŏs'ə līt'), *n., v.*, **-lyted, -lyting. —n. 1.** one who has changed from one opinion, sect, or the like, to another; convert. **—v.t., v.i. 2.** to convert. **—pros'e·lyt·ism,** *n.* **—pros'e·lyt·ize',** *v.t., v.i.*

Pro·ser·pi·na (prō sûr'pə nə), *n. Rom. Myth.* the counterpart of Persephone. Also, **Pro·ser·pi·ne** (prō sûr'pə nē', prŏs'ər pīn'/).

pros·o·dy (prŏs'ə dĭ), *n.* **1.** the study of poetic meters and versification. **2.** a particular system of metrics and versification. **—pros'o·dist,** *n.*

pros·pect (prŏs'pĕkt), *n.* **1.** (*usually pl.*) an apparent probability of advancement, success, etc. **2.** the outlook for the future. **3.** a prospective customer, as in business. **4.** a view or scene. **5.** *Mining.* **a.** an apparent indication of metal, etc. **b.** a spot giving such indications. **—v.t., v.i. 6.** to search (a region), as for gold. **—pros·pec·tor** (prŏs'pĕk tər, prə spĕk'tər), *n.*

pro·spec·tive (prə spĕk'tĭv), *adj.* in prospect or expectation; expected; future. **—pro·spec'tive·ly,** *adv.*

pro·spec·tus (prə spĕk'təs), *n.* a printed circular on a forthcoming literary work, a new security, or the like.

pros·per (prŏs'pər), *v.i.* to be successful; thrive.

pros·per·i·ty (prŏs pĕr'ə tĭ), *n., pl.* **-ties. 1.** prosperous or thriving condition. **2.** (*pl.*) prosperous circumstances.

pros·per·ous (prŏs'pər əs), *adj.* **1.** flourishing; successful. **2.** well-to-do. **3.** favorable. **—pros'per·ous·ly,** *adv.* **—pros'per·ous·ness,** *n.*

pros·tate gland (prŏs'tāt), *Anat.* the composite gland which surrounds the urethra of males at the base of the bladder.

pros·ti·tute (prŏs'tə tūt', -tōōt'), *n., v.*, **-tuted, -tuting. —n. 1.** a woman who engages in sexual intercourse for money as a livelihood. **—v.t. 2.** to submit to sexual intercourse for money as a livelihood. **3.** to put to any base use. **—pros'ti·tu'tion,** *n.* **—pros'ti·tu'tor,** *n.*

pros·trate (prŏs'trāt), *v.*, **-trated, -trating,** *adj.* **—v.t. 1.** to cast (oneself) down in humility. **2.** to lay flat. **3.** to reduce to physical exhaustion. **—adj. 4.** lying flat. **5.** lying with the face to the ground, as in humility. **6.** overthrown; helpless. **7.** in a state of physical exhaustion.

pros·tra·tion (prŏs trā'shən), *n.* **1.** act of prostrating. **2.** state of being prostrated. **3.** extreme mental depression. **4.** extreme physical exhaustion.

pros·y (prō'zĭ), *adj.*, **prosier, prosiest. 1.** of or resembling prose. **2.** commonplace; dull. **—pros'i·ness,** *n.*

Prot., Protestant.

pro·tag·o·nist (prō tăg'ə nĭst), *n.* the leading character, as in a play.

pro·te·an (prō'tĭ ən, prō tē'ən), *adj.* readily assuming different forms; variable.

pro·tect (prə tĕkt'), *v.t.* to defend or guard from attack, invasion, annoyance, insult, etc.

pro·tec·tion (prə tĕk'shən), *n.* **1.** act of protecting. **2.** state of being protected. **3.** something that protects. **4.** *Econ.* the system of fostering home industries by imposing heavy duties on importations from foreign countries. **—pro·tec'tion·ism,** *n.* **—pro·tec'tion·ist,** *n.*

pro·tec·tive (prə tĕk'tĭv), *adj.* **1.** protecting. **2.** designed to protect economically. **—pro·tec'tive·ly,** *adv.*

pro·tec·tor (prə tĕk'tər), *n.* **1.** a defender or guardian. **2.** *Eng. Hist.* one in charge of the kingdom during the sovereign's minority, incapacity, or absence.

pro·tec·tor·ate (prə tĕk'tər ĭt), *n.* **1.** the relation of a strong state toward a weaker one which it protects and partly controls. **2.** a state or territory so protected. **3.** the government of a protector. **4.** (*cap.*) *Eng. Hist.* the period during which Oliver and Richard Cromwell were in power.

pro·té·gé (prō'tə zhā'), *n., pl.* **-gés.** one who is under the friendly patronage of another. **—pro'té·gée',** *n. fem.*

pro·te·in (prō'tē ĭn, prō'tēn), *n. Biochem.* any of a group of nitrogenous organic compounds yielding amino acids, which in animal metabolism are required for all life processes.

pro·test (*n.* prō'tĕst; *v.* prə tĕst'), *n., v.* **1.** the formal expression of objection or disapproval. **—v.i. 2.** to express formal objection or disapproval. **—v.t. 3.** to make a protest against. **4.** to

declare solemnly or formally. —pro·test′er, n.
—pro·test′ing·ly, adv.

Prot·es·tant (prŏt′ĭs tənt), n. **1.** any Western Christian not an adherent of the Roman Catholic Church. **2.** (l.c.) one who protests. —adj. **3.** belonging or pertaining to Protestants or their religion. **4.** (l.c.) protesting.

Prot·es·tant·ism (prŏt′ĭs tən tĭz′əm), n. the religion of Protestants.

prot·es·ta·tion (prŏt′əs tā′shən), n. **1.** act of protesting. **2.** a solemn declaration.

Pro·teus (prō′tūs, prō′tĭ əs), n. Class. Myth. a sea god who had the power of assuming different forms.

pro·to·ac·tin·i·um (prō′tō ăk tĭn′Y əm), n. Chem. an element, a radioactive decay product intermediate between uranium and actinium. Symbol: Pa; at. no.: 91; at. wt.: 231.

pro·to·col (prō′tə kŏl′), n. **1.** an original draft from which a document, esp. a treaty, is prepared. **2.** the etiquette of diplomatic relations. **3.** an agreement between states.

pro·ton (prō′tŏn), n. Physics, Chem. a subatomic particle bearing a positive charge of electricity. The number of protons in the nucleus is different for each element and is called the atomic number of that element.

pro·to·plasm (prō′tə plăz′əm), n. Biol. a complex substance regarded as the physical basis of life, having the power of spontaneous motion, reproduction, etc. —pro′to·plas′mic, adj.

pro·to·type (prō′tə tĭp′), n. **1.** an original or model. **2.** Biol. a primitive form.

pro·to·zo·an (prō′tə zō′ən), adj. **1.** belonging or pertaining to a phylum comprising all those animals that consist of one cell or of a colony of like cells. —n. **2.** any of these animals.

pro·tract (prō trăkt′), v.t. **1.** to extend the duration of. **2.** Anat., etc. to extend or protrude. —pro·trac′tion, n.

pro·trac·tor (prō trăk′tər), n. Math., etc. an instrument, a graduated arc, for plotting or measuring angles on paper.

pro·trude (prō trōōd′), v., -truded, -truding. —v.i. **1.** to project. —v.t. **2.** to cause to project. —pro·tru·sion (prō trōō′zhən), n. —pro·trusive (prō trōō′sĭv), adj.

pro·tu·ber·ance (prō tū′bər əns, -tōō′-), n. protuberant state, form, or part.

pro·tu·ber·ant (prō tū′bər ənt, -tōō′-), adj. bulging out beyond the surrounding surface. —pro·tu′ber·ant·ly, adv.

proud (proud), adj. **1.** pleased or satisfied with something regarded as highly honorable or creditable to oneself. **2.** arrogant; haughty. **3.** self-respecting. **4.** highly honorable or creditable. **5.** majestic; magnificent. —proud′ly, adv.

proud flesh, Pathol. ti:sue formed in the early healing of a wound.

Proust (prōōst), n. **Marcel,** 1871–1922, French novelist.

Prov., **1.** Proverbs. **2.** (l.c.) provincial.

prove (prōōv), v., proved, proved or proven, proving. —v.t. **1.** to establish the truth or genuineness of, as by evidence or argument. **2.** to try or test. —v.i. **3.** to turn out. **4.** to be found to be. —prov′a·ble, adj.

Pro·vence (prō väns′), n. a region in SE France, bordering on the Mediterranean. —Pro·ven·çal (prō′vən säl′), adj., n.

prov·en·der (prŏv′ən dər), n. dry food for beasts, as hay; fodder.

prov·erb (prŏv′ərb), n. **1.** a wise saying or precept, usually a popular, long-current one. **2.** a person or thing that has become a byword. **3.** Proverbs, one of the books of the Old Testament, made up of sayings of wise men of Israel.

pro·ver·bi·al (prə vûr′bY əl), adj. **1.** of or like a proverb. **2.** expressed in a proverb or proverbs. **3.** commonly accepted; well known. —pro·ver′bi·al·ly, adv.

pro·vide (prə vīd′), v., -vided, -viding. —v.t. **1.** to furnish or supply. **2.** to afford or yield. **3.** to prepare, ensure, or procure beforehand. —v.i. **4.** to take measures with due foresight. **5.** to supply means of support, etc. —pro·vid′er, n.

pro·vid·ed (prə vī′dĭd), conj. on the condition or supposition (that).

prov·i·dence (prŏv′ə dəns), n. **1.** the foreseeing care of God. **2.** (cap.) God. **3.** economy.

Prov·i·dence (prŏv′ə dəns), n. a seaport in and the capital of Rhode Island, in the NE part. 253,504.

prov·i·dent (prŏv′ə dənt), adj. **1.** having or showing foresight. **2.** characterized by or proceeding from foresight. **3.** mindful in making provision. **4.** economical or frugal. —prov′i·dent·ly, adv.

prov·i·den·tial (prŏv′ə děn′shəl), adj. **1.** of, pertaining to, or proceeding from divine providence. **2.** fortunate; lucky. —prov′i·den′tial·ly, adv.

pro·vid·ing (prə vī′dĭng), conj. provided.

prov·ince (prŏv′ĭns), n. **1.** an administrative division or unit of a country. **2.** the Provinces, the parts of a country outside of the capital or the largest cities. **3.** a country, territory, district, or region. **4.** a branch of learning or activity. **5.** the sphere or field of action of a person, etc.

Prov·ince·town (prŏv′ĭns toun′), n. a resort town at the tip of Cape Cod, in SE Massachusetts. 3668.

pro·vin·cial (prə vĭn′shəl), adj. **1.** belonging or peculiar to some province or provinces; local. **2.** countrified or rustic. **3.** narrow or illiberal. —n. **4.** one who lives in or comes from the provinces. —pro·vin′cial·ly, adv.

pro·vin·cial·ism (prə vĭn′shə lĭz′əm), n. **1.** provincial character, manner, habit of thought, etc. **2.** a word, expression, or pronunciation peculiar to a province.

pro·vi·sion (prə vĭzh′ən), n. **1.** a clause in a legal instrument, a law, etc., providing for a particular matter. **2.** the providing of something, as of food. **3.** arrangement or preparation beforehand. **4.** something provided. **5.** (pl.) supplies of food. —v.t. **6.** to supply with provisions. —pro·vi′sion·er, n.

pro·vi·sion·al (prə vĭzh′ən əl), adj. for the time being; temporary. —pro·vi′sion·al·ly, adv.

pro·vi·so (prə vī′zō), n., pl. -sos, -soes. **1.** a clause in a statute, contract, or the like, by which a condition is introduced. **2.** a stipulation. —pro·vi′so·ry, adj.

prov·o·ca·tion (prŏv′ə kā′shən), n. **1.** the action of provoking. **2.** something that incites or angers.

pro·voc·a·tive (prə vŏk′ə tĭv), adj. **1.** inciting, stimulating, irritating, or vexing. —n. **2.** something provocative. —pro·voc′a·tive·ly, adv. —pro·voc′a·tive·ness, n.

pro·voke (prə vōk′), v.t., -voked, -voking. **1.** to anger, exasperate, or vex. **2.** to stir up; arouse. **3.** to stimulate. **4.** to give rise to; bring about. —pro·vok′ing·ly, adv.

pro·vost (prō′vŏst), n. one appointed to superintend or preside, as the head of a Scottish town, of certain colleges or churches, etc.

pro·vost marshal (prō′vō), (in the army) an officer acting as head of police.

prow (prou), n. the fore part of a ship or airship.

prow·ess (prou′ĭs), n. **1.** valor; bravery. **2.** superior skill or ability.

prowl (proul), v.i., v.t. **1.** to rove stealthily (over or through) in search of prey, plunder, etc. —n. **2.** act of prowling. —prowl′er, n.

prowl car, a police automobile which patrols a district, receiving instructions from headquarters by shortwave radio.

prox·i·mal (prŏk′sə məl), adj. situated toward the point of origin or attachment, as of a limb. —prox′i·mal·ly, adv.

prox·im·i·ty (prŏk sĭm′ə tĭ), n. nearness in place, time, or relation.

prox·i·mo (prŏk′sə mō′), adv. in or of the coming month. Abbr.: prox.

prox·y (prŏk′sĭ), n., pl. proxies. **1.** the action of a person deputed to act for another. **2.** the person so deputed. **3.** a written authorization empowering another to vote or act for the signer.

prude (prōōd), n. a person who affects extreme modesty or propriety. —prud′ish, adj. —prud′ish·ly, adv. —prud′ish·ness, n.

pru·dence (prōō′dəns), n. **1.** cautious, practical wisdom; discretion. **2.** economy.

pru·dent (prōō′dənt), adj. wisely cautious in practical affairs. —pru′dent·ly, adv.

pru·den·tial (prōō děn′shəl), adj. **1.** of, pertaining to, or characterized by prudence. **2.** exercising prudence. —pru·den′tial·ly, adv.

prud·er·y (prōō′də rĭ), n., pl. -eries. extreme modesty or propriety.

prune¹ (prōōn), n. **1.** a variety of plum which dries without spoiling. **2.** a dried plum used for eating, cooked or uncooked.

prune² (prōōn), v.t., pruned, pruning. **1.** to cut off (twigs, branches, or roots). **2.** to cut undesired twigs, branches, or roots from. **3.** to rid of anything undesirable.

pru·ri·ent (prŏŏr′Ĭ ənt), *adj.* inclined to or characterized by lascivious thought. —**pru′ri·ence, pru′ri·en·cy,** *n.* —**pru′ri·ent·ly,** *adv.*

Prus·sia (prŭsh′ə), *n.* a former state in N Germany. —**Prus·sian,** *adj., n.*

Prussian blue, a dark-blue crystalline, insoluble pigment formed in testing for the ferric ion.

Prussia, 1871–1914.

pry[1] (prī), *v.,* **pried, prying,** *n., pl.* **pries.** —*v.i.* **1.** to look or inquire closely or curiously. —*v.t.* **2.** to find (out) by searching or inquiry. —*n.* **3.** act of prying. **4.** an inquisitive person.

pry[2] (prī), *v.,* **pried, prying,** *n., pl.* **pries.** —*v.t.* **1.** to raise, open, or move by force of leverage. **2.** to get with difficulty. —*n.* **3.** any instrument for raising or moving a thing by leverage, as a crowbar.

Ps., 1. Psalm. **2.** Psalms. Also, **Psa.**

P.S., 1. Also, **p.s.** postscript. **2.** Public School.

psalm (säm), *n.* **1.** a sacred song; hymn. **2.** (*cap.*) any of the 150 songs, hymns, and prayers which form a book of the Old Testament (**Book of Psalms**). —*v.t.* **3.** to celebrate in psalms. —**psalm′ist,** *n.*

psal·mo·dy (sä′mə dĭ, säl′mə dĭ), *n., pl.* **-dies. 1.** the arrangement of psalms for singing. **2.** psalms collectively. **3.** act, practice, or art of singing psalms.

Psal·ter (sôl′tər), *n.* **1.** the Book of Psalms. **2.** (*sometimes l.c.*) a book containing the Psalms for liturgical or devotional use.

pseu·do (sōō′dō), *adj.* false; spurious.

pseudo-, a word element meaning "false," "pretended"; in scientific use, denoting close or deceptive resemblance to the following element.

pseu·do·nym (sōō′də nĭm), *n.* a name adopted by an author to conceal his identity.

pshaw (shô), *interj.* an exclamation expressing impatience, contempt, etc.

psi (sī, psē), *n.* the twenty-third letter (Ψ, ψ) of the Greek alphabet.

psit·ta·co·sis (sĭt′ə kō′sĭs), *n.* a severe infectious disease easily transmissible from parrots to man.

pso·ri·a·sis (sō rī′ə sĭs), *n.* a chronic skin disease characterized by scaly patches. —**pso·ri·at·ic** (sōr′Ĭ ăt′Ĭk), *adj.*

psych., 1. psychological. **2.** psychology.

Psy·che (sī′kĬ), *n.* **1.** *Gk. Myth.* the soul, sometimes represented as a beautiful girl loved by Eros. **2.** (*l.c.*) the human soul, spirit, or mind.

psy·chi·a·try (sī kī′ə trĬ), *n.* the practice or the science of treating mental diseases. —**psy·chi′a·trist,** *n.* —**psy·chi·at·ric** (sī′kĬ ăt′rĬk), *adj.*

psy·chic (sī′kĬk), *adj.* Also, **psy′chi·cal. 1.** of or pertaining to the human soul or mind. **2.** exerted by or proceeding from some nonphysical agency, as in telepathy, etc. —*n.* **3.** a person specially susceptible to psychic influences. —**psy′chi·cal·ly,** *adv.*

psychoanal., psychoanalysis.

psy·cho·a·nal·y·sis (sī′kō ə năl′ə sĭs), *n.* **1.** a systematic structure of theories concerning the relation of conscious and unconscious psychological processes. **2.** a technical procedure for investigating unconscious mental processes and for treating psychoneuroses. —**psy′cho·an′a·lyst,** *n.* —**psy·cho·an·a·lyt·ic** (sī′kō ăn′ə lĬt′Ĭk), **psy′cho·an′a·lyt′i·cal,** *adj.* —**psy′cho·an′a·lyt′i·cal·ly,** *adv.*

psy·cho·an·a·lyze (sī′kō ăn′ə līz′), *v.t.,* **-lyzed, -lyzing.** to investigate or treat by psychoanalysis.

psychol., 1. psychological. **2.** psychology.

psy·chol·o·gy (sī kŏl′ə jĬ), *n., pl.* **-gies. 1.** the science of mental states and processes. **2.** the science of human and animal behavior. **3.** the mental states and processes of a person or of persons, esp. as determining action. —**psy·cho·log·i·cal** (sī′kə lŏj′ə kəl), **psy′cho·log′ic,** *adj.* —**psy′cho·log′i·cal·ly,** *adv.* —**psy·chol′o·gist,** *n.*

psy·cho·neu·ro·sis (sī′kō nyŏŏ rō′sĭs, -nŏŏ-), *n., pl.* **-ses** (-sēz). an emotional disorder in which

feelings of anxiety, obsessional thoughts, compulsive acts, and physical complaints without objective evidence of disease, in various patterns, dominate the personality. —**psy·cho·neu·rot·ic** (sī′kō nyŏŏ rŏt′Ĭk, -nŏŏ-), *adj., n.*

psy·cho·pa·thol·o·gy (sī′kō pə thŏl′ə jĬ), *n.* the science of diseases of the mind.

psy·chop·a·thy (sī kŏp′ə thĬ), *n.* **1.** mental disease or disorder. **2.** the treatment of disease by mental or psychic influence. —**psy·cho·path·ic** (sī′kə păth′Ĭk), *adj.*

psy·cho·sis (sī kō′sĬs), *n., pl.* **-ses** (-sēz). *Pathol.* any major, severe form of mental affection or disease. —**psy·chot·ic** (sī kŏt′Ĭk), *adj., n.*

psy·cho·so·mat·ic (sī′kō sō măt′Ĭk), *adj.* denoting a physical disorder caused or influenced by the emotional state of the patient.

psychosomatic medicine, the application of the principles of psychology in the study and treatment of physical diseases.

psy·cho·ther·a·py (sī′kō thĕr′ə pĬ), *n.* the science of curing psychological disorders. —**psy′cho·ther′a·pist,** *n.*

Pt, *Chem.* platinum.

pt., *pl. (for 1, 3, 4, 5)* **pts. 1.** part. **2.** past. **3.** pint. **4.** point. **5.** port. **6.** preterit.

ptar·mi·gan (tär′mə gən), *n.* any of certain species of grouse characterized by feathered feet, and found in mountainous and cold regions.

PT boat, *U.S.* a small speedy boat used chiefly to torpedo enemy shipping.

pter·i·do·phyte (tĕr′ə dō fīt′), *n.* any of a division of plants which are without seeds, have vascular tissue, and are differentiated into root, stem, and leaf. It includes ferns, horsetails, and club mosses.

pter·o·dac·tyl (tĕr′ə dăk′tĬl), *n.* any of certain extinct flying reptiles.

Ptol·e·ma·ic system (tŏl′ə mā′Ĭk), *Astron.* a system elaborated by Ptolemy according to which the earth was the fixed center of the universe.

Ptol·e·my (tŏl′ə mĬ), *n.* fl. A.D. 127–151, Greek mathematician, astronomer, and geographer, at Alexandria.

pto·maine (tō′mān, tō mān′), *n.* any of a class of basic nitrogenous substances, some of them very poisonous, produced during putrefaction of animal or plant proteins (**ptomaine poisoning**). Also, **pto′main.**

pub (pŭb), *n. Brit. Slang.* a tavern.

pub., 1. public. **2.** published.

pu·ber·ty (pū′bər tĬ), *n.* sexual maturity (in common law, presumed to be 14 years in the male and 12 years in the female).

pu·bes (pū′bēz), *n. Anat.* the lower part of the abdomen. —**pu′bic,** *adj.*

pu·bes·cent (pū bĕs′ənt), *adj.* **1.** arriving at puberty. **2.** *Bot., Zool.* covered with down or fine short hair. —**pu·bes′cence,** *n.*

pub·lic (pŭb′lĬk), *adj.* **1.** of or for the people as a whole, or the community, state, or nation. **2.** pertaining to or engaged in the service of the community or nation. **3.** open to the view or knowledge of all. **4.** known to the public generally. —*n.* **5.** the people constituting a community, state, or nation. **6.** a particular section of the people. **7.** public view or access. —**pub′lic·ly,** *adv.*

pub·li·can (pŭb′lə kən), *n.* **1.** *Brit.* the keeper of a public house. **2.** *Ancient Rome.* a tax collector.

pub·li·ca·tion (pŭb′lə kā′shən), *n.* **1.** the publishing of a book, periodical, etc. **2.** that which is published.

public house, 1. *Brit.* a tavern. **2.** an inn.

pub·li·cist (pŭb′lə sĬst), *n.* **1.** an expert or writer on political affairs or international law. **2.** a press agent or public relations man.

pub·lic·i·ty (pŭb lĬs′ə tĬ), *n.* **1.** state of being public. **2.** public notice as the result of advertising or other special measures. **3.** state of being brought to public notice by mention in the press, on the radio, etc. **4.** the measures, process, or business of securing public notice.

pub·li·cize (pŭb′lĬ sīz′), *v.t.,* **-cized, -cizing.** to bring to public notice; advertise.

public school, 1. *U.S.* a school maintained at public expense for the education of the children and youth of a community or district. **2.** *Eng.* any of certain large, endowed boarding schools.

public utility, a business enterprise performing an essential public service, as supplying electricity or transportation, and either operated or regulated by the government.

pub·lish (pŭb/lĭsh),` v.t.` **1.** to issue (a book, periodical, map, etc.) for sale or distribution to the public. **2.** to announce formally or officially. **3.** to make publicly known. —**pub/lish·a·ble,** *adj.* —**pub/lish·er,** *n.*

Puc·ci·ni (pōōt chē/nē), *n.* **Giacomo,** 1858–1924, Italian operatic composer.

Puck, *n.* **1.** a mischievous fairy in Shakespeare's *Midsummer Night's Dream.* **2.** (*l.c.*) any mischievous spirit. **3.** (*l.c.*) a rubber disk used in place of a ball in ice hockey.

puck·er (pŭk/ər), *v.t., v.i.* **1.** to draw into wrinkles or irregular folds. —*n.* **2.** a wrinkle; irregular fold. **3.** a puckered part.

pud·ding (pŏŏd/ĭng), *n.* a dish made in many forms and of various materials, as flour, milk, and eggs.

pud·dle (pŭd/əl), *n., v.,* **-dled, -dling.** —*n.* **1.** a small pool of water, esp. dirty water. **2.** clay mixed with water and tempered, used as a watertight canal lining, etc. —*v.t.* **3.** to fill with puddles. **4.** to make (clay, etc.) into puddle. **5.** to cover with pasty clay or puddle. **6.** to subject (molten iron) to the process of puddling. —**pud/dler,** *n.*

pud·dling (pŭd/lĭng), *n.* the conversion of pig iron into wrought iron by heating and stirring the molten metal in a furnace, with an oxidizing agent.

pudg·y (pŭj/ĭ), *adj.,* **pudgier, pudgiest.** short and fat or thick. —**pudg/i·ness,** *n.*

pueb·lo (pwĕb/lō), *n., pl.* **-los.** *U.S.* **1.** a village of certain Southwestern Indians whose communal house or group of houses is built of adobe or stone. **2.** (*cap.*) any of certain sedentary, farming, peace-loving Indians living in pueblos in New Mexico and Arizona.

Pueb·lo (pwĕb/lō), *n.* a city in central Colorado. 52,162.

pu·er·ile (pū/ər ĭl), *adj.* **1.** of or pertaining to a child or boy. **2.** childishly foolish. —**pu/er·il/i·ty,** *n.*

pu·er·per·al (pū ûr/pər əl), *adj.* of or consequent on childbirth.

Puer·to Ri·co (pwĕr/tə rē/kō), an island in the West Indies: a territory of the U.S. 2,083,000 pop.; 3435 sq. mi. *Cap.*: San Juan. —**Puer/to Ri/can.**

puff (pŭf), *n.* **1.** a short, quick blast, as of wind or breath. **2.** a small quantity of vapor, smoke, etc., emitted at one blast. **3.** an inflated or distended part. **4.** a commendation, esp. an exaggerated one, of a book, an actor's performance, etc. **5.** a small, soft pad for applying face powder. **6.** a form of light pastry with a filling of cream, jam, or the like. **7.** a portion of material gathered and held down at the edges but left full in the middle, as in a dress, etc. **8.** a cylindrical roll of hair. **9.** a comforter, usually down-filled. —*v.i.* **10.** to blow with short, quick blasts. **11.** to breathe quick and hard, as after violent exertion. **12.** to go with puffing. **13.** to take puffs at a cigar, etc. **14.** to become inflated or distended. —*v.t.* **15.** to send forth (air, vapor, etc.) in short quick blasts. **16.** to smoke (a cigar, etc.). **17.** to inflate or distend. **18.** to inflate with pride, etc. **19.** to praise in exaggerated language. —**puff/y,** *adj.* —**puff/i·ness,** *n.*

puff·ball (pŭf/bôl/), *n.* any of certain fungi characterized by a ball-like fruit body which emits a cloud of spores when broken.

puff·er (pŭf/ər), *n.* **1.** one that puffs. **2.** any of certain fishes capable of inflating the body with water or air until it resembles a globe, with the spines in the skin erected.

puf·fin (pŭf/ĭn), *n.* any of certain sea birds of the auk family, esp. one which abounds on both coasts of the northern Atlantic, nesting in holes in the ground.

puff paste, a very light, flaky, rich paste for pies, tarts, etc.

pug¹ (pŭg), *n.* **1.** one of a breed of dogs, slightly resembling the bulldog but much smaller. **2.** a pug nose. **3.** the fox.

pug² (pŭg), *v.t.,* **pugged, pugging. 1.** to knead (clay, etc.) with water, as in brickmaking. **2.** to stop or fill in with clay or the like.

pug³ (pŭg), *n. Slang.* pugilist.

Pu·get Sound (pū/jĭt), a long, irregularly-shaped arm of the Pacific in NW Washington.

pu·gil·ism (pū/jə lĭz/əm), *n.* the art or practice of fighting with the fists; boxing. —**pu/gil·ist,** *n.* —**pu/gil·is/tic,** *adj.*

pug·na·cious (pŭg nā/shəs), *adj.* given to fighting; quarrelsome. —**pug·na/cious·ly,** *adv.*

—**pug·nac·i·ty** (pŭg năs/ə tĭ), **pug·na/cious·ness,** *n.*

pug nose, a short nose turning up at the tip. —**pug-nosed** (pŭg/nōzd/), *adj.*

pu·is·sant (pū/ə sənt, pū ĭs/ənt, pwĭs/ənt), *adj. Archaic.* powerful; mighty; potent. —**pu/is·sant·ly,** *adv.* —**pu/is·sance,** *n.*

puke (pūk), *v.i., v.t.,* **puked, puking,** *n.* vomit.

Pu·las·ki (pŏŏ läs/kĭ, -kī, pə-), *n.* **Count Casimir,** 1748–79, Polish patriot: general in the American Revolutionary army.

pul·chri·tude (pŭl/krə tūd/, -tŏŏd/), *n.* beauty; comeliness. —**pul/chri·tu/di·nous,** *adj.*

pule (pūl), *v.i.,* **puled, puling.** to cry in a thin voice, as a child; whimper; whine.

Pu·litz·er (pū/lĭt sər, pŏŏl/ĭt sər), *n.* **Joseph,** 1847–1911, U.S. journalist and publisher.

pull (pŏŏl), *v.t.* **1.** to draw or haul. **2.** to tug at with force. **3.** to draw or tear (apart, to pieces, etc.). **4.** to pluck out. **5.** *Slang.* to draw out for use, as a knife. **6.** *Slang.* to carry through (something attempted). **7.** *Print.* to take (a proof) from type, etc. **8.** to propel by rowing, as a boat. **9.** to strain, as a ligament. —*v.i.* **10.** to exert a drawing, tugging, or hauling force. **11.** to get (*in, through,* etc.) as by a pull or effort. **12.** to become, as specified, by pulling. **13.** to row. —*n.* **14.** act of pulling or drawing. **15.** pulling power. **16.** a part or thing to be pulled, as a handle. **17.** a spell at rowing. **18.** *Slang.* influence, as with persons able to grant favors. —**pull/er,** *n.*

pul·let (pŏŏl/ĭt), *n.* a young hen.

pul·ley (pŏŏl/ĭ), *n., pl.* **-leys.** a wheel with a grooved rim in which a rope runs, serving to change the direction of or transmit power, as in pulling at one end of the line to raise a weight at the other end.

Pull·man (pŏŏl/mən), *n., pl.* **-mans.** *Railroads.* a sleeping car or parlor car. Also, **pull/man, Pullman car.**

pul·mo·nar·y (pŭl/mə nĕr/ĭ), *adj.* of, pertaining to, or affecting the lungs.

Pul·mo·tor (pŭl/mō/tər, pŏŏl/-), *n. Trademark.* a mechanical device for artificial respiration where respiration has ceased through asphyxiation, drowning, etc., which forces oxygen into the lungs.

pulp (pŭlp), *n.* **1.** the succulent part of a fruit. **2.** a soft or fleshy part of an animal body. **3.** the inner substance of a tooth containing arteries, veins, etc. **4.** any soft, moist mass, as that into which linen, wood, etc., are converted in the making of paper. **5.** a magazine printed on rough paper, usually devoted to sensational and lurid stories, etc. —*v.t.* **6.** to reduce to pulp. **7.** to remove the pulp from. —*v.i.* **8.** to become reduced to pulp. —**pulp/y,** *adj.* —**pulp/i·ness,** *n.*

pul·pit (pŏŏl/pĭt), *n.* **1.** a platform in a church, from which the clergyman delivers the sermon or conducts the service. **2. the pulpit,** a. preachers collectively. **b.** preaching.

pulp·wood (pŭlp/wŏŏd/), *n.* spruce or other soft wood suitable for making paper.

pul·que (pŏŏl/kĭ), *n.* a fermented milkish drink made from the juice of certain species of Mexican agave.

pul·sate (pŭl/sāt), *v.i.,* **-sated, -sating. 1.** to expand and contract rhythmically, as the heart; throb. **2.** to vibrate; quiver. —**pul·sa/tion,** *n.*

pulse¹ (pŭls), *n., v.,* **pulsed, pulsing.** —*n.* **1.** the regular throbbing of the arteries caused by the successive contractions of the heart, esp. as felt in an artery at the wrist. **2.** the rhythmic recurrence of strokes, vibrations, or undulations. —*v.i.* **3.** to pulsate.

pulse² (pŭls), *n.* the edible seeds of certain leguminous plants, as peas, beans, etc.

pul·ver·ize (pŭl/və rīz/), *v.,* **-ized, -izing.** —*v.t.* **1.** to reduce to dust or powder, as by pounding, etc. **2.** to demolish. —*v.i.* **3.** to become reduced to dust. —**pul/ver·i·za/tion,** *n.* —**pul/ver·iz/er,** *n.*

pu·ma (pū/mə), *n.* **1.** the cougar. **2.** its fur.

pum·ice (pŭm/ĭs), *n., v.,* **-iced, -icing.** —*n.* **1.** a porous form of volcanic glass, used, esp. when powdered, as an abrasive, etc. —*v.t.* **2.** to rub, clean, etc., with pumice.

pum·mel (pŭm/əl), *n., v.t.,* **-meled, -meling** or (*esp. Brit.*) **-melled, -melling.** pommel.

pump¹ (pŭmp), *n.* **1.** an apparatus or machine for raising, driving, exhausting, or compressing fluids. —*v.t., v.i.* **2.** to raise, drive, inflate, etc., with, or as with, a pump. **3.** to operate by action like that on a pump handle. **4.** to seek to elicit information from.· **5.** to elicit (information) by questioning. —**pump′er,** *n.*

pump[2] (pŭmp), *n.* a light, low, slipperlike shoe worn by men and women, orig. for dancing.

pum·per·nick·el (pŭm′pər nĭk′əl), *n.* a coarse, slightly sour bread made of unbolted rye.

pump·kin (pŭmp′kĭn, pŭng′kĭn), *n.* **1.** a large orange-yellow fruit borne by a coarse, decumbent vine: much used for making pies and as food for cattle. **2.** the vine.

pun (pŭn), *n., v.,* **punned, punning.** —*n.* **1.** the humorous use of a word in such a manner as to bring out different meanings, or of words alike or nearly alike in sound but different in meaning. —*v.i.* **2.** to make a pun.

punch[1] (pŭnch), *n.* **1.** a thrusting blow, esp. with the fist. **2.** *Slang.* a vigorous, telling effect. —*v.t.* **3.** to give a sharp thrust to, esp. with the fist. **4.** *Western U.S.* to drive (cattle). —**punch′er,** *n.*

punch[2] (pŭnch), *n.* **1.** a tool or apparatus for piercing or stamping materials, impressing a design, etc. —*v.t.* **2.** to cut, stamp, pierce, form, or drive with such a tool.

punch[3] (pŭnch), *n.* a beverage consisting (usually) of wine or spirits mixed with water, milk, etc., and flavored with sugar, lemon, spices, etc.

Punch (pŭnch), *n.* **1.** the grotesque chief character in the puppet show called "Punch and Judy." **2. pleased as Punch,** delighted.

pun·cheon[1] (pŭn′chən), *n.* a large cask of varying capacity, but usually 111.6 gals.

pun·cheon[2] (pŭn′chən), *n.* a slab of timber, or a piece of a split log, with the face roughly dressed, used for flooring, etc.

pun·chi·nel·lo (pŭn′chə nĕl′ō), *n., pl.* **-los, -loes.** the grotesque chief character in a puppet show of Italian origin: prototype of Punch.

punc·til·i·o (pŭngk tĭl′ĭ ō′), *n., pl.* **-tilios. 1.** a fine detail, as of conduct or procedure. **2.** exactness in the observance of forms.

punc·til·i·ous (pŭngk tĭl′ĭ əs), *adj.* exact in the observance of forms in conduct or actions. —**punc·til′i·ous·ly,** *adv.* —**punc·til′i·ous·ness,** *n.*

punc·tu·al (pŭngk′chŏŏ əl), *adj.* prompt; on time; not late. —**punc′tu·al·ly,** *adv.* —**punc′tu·al·ness, punc·tu·al·i·ty** (pŭngk′chŏŏ ăl′ə tĭ), *n.*

punc·tu·ate (pŭngk′chŏŏ āt′), *v.,* **-ated, -ating.** —*v.t.* **1.** to mark with punctuation marks. **2.** to interrupt at intervals. **3.** to give emphasis to. —*v.i.* **4.** to insert or use marks of punctuation. —**punc′tu·a′tor,** *n.*

punc·tu·a·tion (pŭngk′chŏŏ ā′shən), *n.* the practice, art, or system of inserting commas, semicolons, colons, periods, etc. **(punctuation marks).**

punc·ture (pŭngk′chər), *n., v.,* **-tured, -turing.** —*n.* **1.** act of pricking or perforating with a pointed instrument. **2.** a mark or hole so made. —*v.t.* **3.** to prick, pierce, or perforate. **4.** *Colloq.* to make a puncture in. —*v.i.* **5.** to admit of being punctured.

pun·dit (pŭn′dĭt), *n.* **1.** a Hindu scholar or learned man. **2.** a learned man.

pun·gent (pŭn′jənt), *adj.* **1.** sharp in taste; biting; acrid. **2.** distressing; poignant. **3.** caustic, biting, or sharply expressive. —**pun′gent·ly,** *adv.* —**pun′gen·cy,** *n.*

pun·ish (pŭn′ĭsh), *v.t.* **1.** to subject to pain, loss, confinement, death, etc., for some offense. **2.** to inflict a penalty for (an offense, etc.). **3.** *Colloq.* to handle severely or roughly. —*v.i.* **4.** to inflict punishment. —**pun′ish·a·ble,** *adj.* —**pun′ish·er,** *n.*

pun·ish·ment (pŭn′ĭsh mənt), *n.* **1.** act of punishing. **2.** the penalty in punishing. **3.** *Colloq.* severe treatment.

pu·ni·tive (pū′nə tĭv), *adj.* concerned with or inflicting punishment. Also, **pu·ni·to·ry** (pū′nə tōr′ĭ).

Pun·jab (pŭn jäb′, pŭn′jäb), *n.* a province in NW India: now divided between Pakistan and the Union of India.

punk (pŭngk), *n.* **1.** a preparation that will smolder, used in sticks, as for lighting fireworks. —*adj.* **2.** *U.S. Slang.* poor in quality.

pun·ster (pŭn′stər), *n.* one given to making puns.

punt (pŭnt), *n.* **1.** *Football.* a kick given to a dropped ball before it touches the ground. **2.** *Brit.* a shallow, flat-bottomed, square-ended boat, usually propelled by a pole. —*v.t., v.i.* **3.**

Football. to kick (a dropped ball) before it touches the ground. **4.** to propel (a boat) by a pole or convey (a person, etc.) in a punt. —**punt′er,** *n.*

pu·ny (pū′nĭ), *adj.,* **-nier, -niest. 1.** very small or weakly. **2.** petty; insignificant.

pup (pŭp), *n., v.,* **pupped, pupping.** —*n.* **1.** a puppy. —*v.i.* **2.** to bring forth pups.

pu·pa (pū′pə), *n., pl.* **-pae** (-pē), **-pas.** an insect in the stage between the larva and the winged insect. —**pu′pal,** *adj.*

pu·pil[1] (pū′pəl), *n.* one who is under an instructor or teacher; student.

pu·pil[2] (pū′pəl), *n. Anat.* the opening in the iris of the eye, through which light passes to the retina.

pup·pet (pŭp′ĭt), *n.* **1.** a doll. **2.** an artificial figure moved by wires, etc., as on a miniature stage. **3.** a person controlled by another.

pup·py (pŭp′ĭ), *n., pl.* **-pies. 1.** a young dog. **2.** a presuming, conceited, or empty-headed young man.

pur·blind (pûr′blīnd′), *adj.* nearly blind. —**pur′blind′ly,** *adv.* —**pur′blind′ness,** *n.*

pur·chase (pûr′chəs), *v.,* **-chased, -chasing,** *n.* —*v.t.* **1.** to acquire by payment; buy. **2.** to acquire by effort, sacrifice, flattery, etc. **3.** to haul, draw, or raise, esp. by mechanical power. —*n.* **4..** acquisition by payment; buying. **5.** something bought. **6.** a (good, bad, etc.) bargain. **7.** a tackle or lever to multiply power. **8.** leverage. —**pur′chas·a·ble,** *adj.* —**pur′chas·er,** *n.*

pure (pyŏŏr), *adj.,* **purer, purest. 1.** free from anything of a different, inferior, or contaminating kind. **2.** unmodified; simple. **3.** of unmixed descent. **4.** abstract or theoretical. **5.** without discordant quality. **6.** absolute, utter, or sheer. **7.** being that and nothing else; mere. **8.** clean, spotless, or unsullied. **9.** innocent; chaste. **10.** guiltless. —**pure′ly,** *adv.* —**pure′ness,** *n.*

pu·rée (pyŏŏ rā′, pyŏŏr′ā), *n.* a cooked and sieved food. Also, **pu·ree′.**

pur·ga·tive (pûr′gə tĭv), *adj.* **1.** purging; cleansing. —*n.* **2.** a purgative medicine or agent. —**pur′ga·tive·ly,** *adv.*

pur·ga·to·ry (pûr′gə tōr′ĭ), *n., pl.* **-ries,** *adj.* —*n.* **1.** *Rom. Cath. Theol.* a condition or place in which the souls of those dying penitent are purified from venial sins. **2.** any condition or place of temporary suffering. —*adj.* **3.** serving to purge or purify. —**pur′ga·to′ri·al,** *adj.*

purge (pûrj), *v.,* **purged, purging,** *n.* —*v.t.* **1.** to cleanse; purify. **2.** to rid or free. **3.** to remove by cleansing. **4.** to clear by causing evacuation. —*v.i.* **5.** to become cleansed or purified. —*n.* **6.** act or a process of purging. **7.** something that purges. —**pur·ga·tion** (pûr gā′shən), *n.* —**purg′er,** *n.*

pu·ri·fy (pyŏŏr′ə fī′), *v.t., v.i.,* **-fied, -fying.** to make or become pure or clean. —**pu′ri·fi·ca′tion,** *n.* —**pu′ri·fi′er,** *n.*

pur·ism (pyŏŏr′ĭz əm), *n.* scrupulous observance of purity in language, style, etc. —**pur′ist,** *n.* —**pu·ris′tic,** *adj.*

Pu·ri·tan (pyŏŏr′ə tən), *n.* **1.** one of a class of Protestants who arose in the 16th century within the Church of England, demanding greater strictness in religious discipline. **2.** (*l.c.*) one who affects great strictness of religious principles. —*adj.* **3.** of or pertaining to the Puritans or (*l.c.*) puritans. —**Pu′ri·tan·ism′,** *n.*

pu·ri·tan·i·cal (pyŏŏr′ə tăn′ə kəl), *adj.* **1.** excessively strict, rigid, or austere. **2.** of or pertaining to puritans or (*cap.*) the Puritans. —**pu′ri·tan′i·cal·ly,** *adv.* —**pu′ri·tan′i·cal·ness,** *n.*

pu·ri·ty (pyŏŏr′ə tĭ), *n.* **1.** the condition or quality of being pure. **2.** freedom from any admixture. **3.** careful correctness. **4.** cleanness. **5.** innocence; chastity.

purl[1] (pûrl), *v.i.* **1.** to flow with curling or rippling motions or with a murmuring sound. —*n.* **2.** the action or sound of purling.

purl[2] (pûrl), *v.t., v.i.* **1.** to knit with inversion of the stitch. —*n.* **2.** a stitch used in hand knitting to make a rib effect.

pur·lieu (pûr′lōō), *n.* **1.** a piece of land on the border of a forest. **2.** any bordering, neighboring, or outlying region or district.

pur·loin (pər loin′), *v.t., v.i.* to steal. —**pur·loin′er,** *n.*

pur·ple (pûr′pəl), *n.* **1.** any color having components of both red and blue. **2.** imperial, royal, or other high rank. —*adj.* **3.** of the color of purple. **4.** imperial or regal. **5.** full of literary devices and effects. —**pur′plish,** *adj.*

pur·port (v. par pōrt′, pûr′pōrt; n. pûr′pōrt),
v.t. **1.** to profess or claim. **2.** to express; imply.
—n. **3.** tenor; import; meaning.

pur·pose (pûr′pas), n., v., -posed, -posing. —n.
1. the object for which anything exists or is done,
made, used, etc. **2.** an intended result. **3.** intention. **4.** on purpose, intentionally. —v.t. **5.** to
propose, design, or intend. —**pur′pose·ful,** adj.
—**pur′pose·ful·ly,** adv. —**pur′pose·less,** adj.
—**pur′pose·less·ly,** adv.

pur·pose·ly (pûr′pas lĭ), adv. **1.** intentionally.
2. expressly.

purr (pûr), v.i. **1.** to utter a low, continuous
murmuring sound expressive of satisfaction, as a
cat does. —n. **2.** act or sound of purring.

purse (pûrs), n., v., pursed, pursing. —n. **1.** a
small bag, pouch, or case for carrying money on
the person. **2.** a sum of money collected as a
present or offered as a prize. —v.t. **3.** to pucker.

purs·er (pûr′sar), n. an officer, esp. on a ship,
charged with keeping accounts, etc.

purs·lane (pûrs′lān, -lĭn), n. a widely distributed, yellow-flowered salad plant and potherb.

pur·su·ance (par sōō′ans), n. the following of
some plan, course, etc.

pur·su·ant (par sōō′ant), adj. **1.** proceeding
conformably. —adv. **2.** according.

pur·sue (par sōō′), v., -sued, -suing. —v.t. **1.** to
follow in order to catch, kill, etc.; chase. **2.** to
attend. **3.** to strive to gain. **4.** to proceed in
accordance with (a plan, etc.). **5.** to carry on (a
course of action, studies, etc.). —v.i. **6.** to follow
in pursuit. **7.** to continue. —**pur·su′er,** n.

pur·suit (par sōōt′), n. **1.** act of pursuing. **2.** a
quest. **3.** any form of occupation, pastime, or
the like, regularly pursued.

pu·ru·lent (pyŏŏr′a lant, pyŏŏr′ya-), adj. full
of or discharging pus. —**pu′ru·lence, pu′ru-
len·cy,** n.

pur·vey (par vā′), v.t. Chiefly Brit. to provide,
furnish, or supply (esp. food or provisions).
—**pur·vey′or,** n.

pur·vey·ance (par vā′ans), n. **1.** act of pur-
veying. **2.** that which is purveyed.

pur·view (pûr′vū), n. **1.** range of operation,
activity, concern, view, etc. **2.** the full scope of a
law, document, etc.

pus (pŭs), n. a yellow-white substance found in
abscesses, sores, etc., consisting of a liquid plasma
in which leucocytes, etc., are suspended.

push (pŏŏsh), v.t. **1.** to exert force against (a
thing) in order to move it away. **2.** to shove;
thrust. **3.** to press or urge (a person, etc.). **4.** to
press the adoption, use, sale, etc., of. —v.i. **5.** to
exert a thrusting force upon something; shove.
—n. **6.** act of pushing; a shove or thrust. **7.** a
vigorous onset or effort. **8.** a determined advance.
9. Colloq. persevering energy; enterprise. —**push′-
er,** n. —**push′ing,** n.

Push·kin (pŏŏsh′kĭn), n. **Aleksander Sergee-
vich,** 1799–1837, Russian poet and writer.

push-o·ver (pŏŏsh′ō′var), n. Slang. **1.** anything done easily. **2.** an easily defeated person
or a team.

pu·sil·lan·i·mous (pū′sa lăn′a mas), adj. faint-
hearted; cowardly. —**pu′sil·lan′i·mous·ly,** adv.
—**pu·sil·la·nim·i·ty** (pū′sa la nĭm′a tĭ), n.

puss[1] (pŏŏs), n. a cat.

puss[2] (pŏŏs), n. Slang. **1.** face. **2.** mouth.

puss·y[1] (pŏŏs′ĭ), n., pl. **pussies.** puss[1].

pus·sy[2] (pŭs′ĭ), adj. Med. puslike.

puss·y·foot (pŏŏs′ĭ fŏŏt′), v.i. **1.** to go with a
soft, stealthy tread like that of a cat. **2.** U.S.
Slang. to act cautiously or timidly. —n. **3.** a
person with a soft and stealthy tread. **4.** U.S.
Slang. one who pussyfoots.

puss·y willow (pŏŏs′ĭ), a small American
willow with silky catkins.

pus·tule (pŭs′chŏŏl), n. Pathol. a small elevation of the skin containing pus.

put (pŏŏt), v., put, putting, n. —v.t. **1.** to move
or place. **2.** to bring into some relation, state,
etc. **3.** to subject to. **4.** to set to a duty, task,
action, etc. **5.** to force or drive. **6.** to render or
translate. **7.** to assign or attribute. **8.** to estimate. **9.** to express or state. **10.** to apply, as to
a use. **11.** to submit for answer, consideration,
etc. **12.** to impose, as a burden. **13.** to throw or
cast, esp. with a pushing motion. —v.i. **14.** to
go, move, or proceed. **15. put about,** Naut. to
change direction. **16. put down, a.** to write.
b. to repress or suppress. **17. put off,** to postpone
18. put on, a. to assume. **b.** to pretend. **19. put**

out, a. to extinguish (fire, etc.). **b.** to embarrass.
c. to inconvenience. **d.** to annoy. —n. **20.** a
throw or cast.

pu·ta·tive (pū′ta tĭv), adj. reputed; supposed.
—**pu′ta·tive·ly,** adv.

pu·tre·fy (pū′tra fī′), v., -fied, -fying. —v.t.
1. to cause to rot or decay with an offensive odor.
—v.i. **2.** to rot. —**pu·tre·fac·tion** (pū′tra făk′-
shan), n. —**pu′tre·fac′tive,** adj.

pu·trid (pū′trĭd), adj. in a state of foul decay;
rotten. —**pu·trid′i·ty, pu′trid·ness,** n.

Putsch (pŏŏch), n. German. a minor revolt.

putt (pŭt), Golf. —v.t., v.i. **1.** to strike (the ball)
gently and carefully so as to make it roll along
the putting green into the hole. —n. **2.** an act of
putting. **3.** a stroke made in putting.

put·tee (pŭt′ĭ), n. a strip of cloth wound spirally round the leg from ankle to knee, worn by
sportsmen, soldiers, etc.

put·ter[1] (pŭt′ar), v.i. to busy or occupy oneself in an ineffective manner. —**put′ter·er,** n.

putt·er[2] (pŭt′ar), n. Golf. **1.** one who putts. **2.** a
club used in putting.

put·ty (pŭt′ĭ), n., pl. -ties, v., -tied, -tying. —n.
1. a kind of cement made of whiting and linseed
oil: used for securing panes of glass, etc. **2.** any
of various similar preparations. —v.t. **3.** to
secure, stop up, cover, etc., with putty.

put-up (pŏŏt′ŭp′), adj. Colloq. planned beforehand in a secret or crafty manner.

puz·zle (pŭz′al), n., v., -zled, -zling. —n. **1.** a
contrivance designed to amuse by presenting difficulties to be solved. **2.** a puzzling question,
matter, or person. —v.t. **3.** to render at a loss
what to do, say, or think. —v.i. **4.** to ponder or
study over some perplexing matter. —**puz′zle-
ment,** n. —**puz′zler,** n.

Pvt., Private.

pwt., pennyweight.

PX, Post Exchange.

Pyg·my (pĭg′mĭ), n., pl. -mies. **1.** a member of
any of various Negroid races of small stature of
Africa and Asia. **2.** (l.c.) a dwarf. —adj. **3.** (l.c.)
of very small size, power, etc. Also, **Pigmy.**

py·ja·mas (pa jä′maz, -jäm′az), n.pl. Chiefly
Brit. pajamas.

py·lon (pī′lŏn), n. **1.** a marking post for guiding
aviators, frequently used in races. **2.** a tall structure at either side of a gate, bridge, or avenue
marking an entrance. **3.** a steel tower carrying
high-tension, telephonic, or other cables and lines.
4. Egypt. Archit. a moununental gateway to an
Egyptian edifice, in the shape of a truncated
pyramid through which the passage for the gate
was pierced.

py·lo·rus (pī lōr′as, pī-), n., pl. -lori (-lōr′ī).
Anat. the opening between the stomach and the
intestine. —**py·lor·ic** (pī lôr′ĭk, -lōr′-, pī-), adj.

py·or·rhe·a (pī′a rē′a), n. Pathol. a disease
characterized in its severe forms by the formation
of pus in the pockets between the root of a tooth
and its surrounding tissues. Also, **py′or·rhoe′a.**

pyr·a·mid (pĭr′a mĭd), n. **1.** Archit. a massive
structure built of stone, with square (or polygonal) base, and sloping sides meeting at an apex,
such as those built by the ancient Egyptians as
royal tombs. **2.** Geom. a solid having a triangular, square, or polygonal base, and triangular
sides which meet in a point. —v.i. **3.** to be disposed in the form of a pyramid. —v.t. **4.** to
arrange in the form of a pyramid. **5.** to increase
(costs, wages, etc.) by successively larger additions. —**py·ram·i·dal** (pī răm′a dal), adj.

pyre (pīr), n. **1.** a heap of wood or other combustible material. **2.** such a pile for burning a
dead body.

Pyr·e·nees (pĭr′a nēz′), n.pl. a mountain
range between Spain and France. Highest peak,
11,165 ft. —**Pyr·e·ne′an,** adj.

Py·rex (pī′rĕks), n. Trademark. a heat-resistant
glassware for baking, frying, etc.

py·rite (pī′rīt), n. a very common brass-yellow
mineral, iron disulfide, with a metallic luster;
fool's gold.

py·ri·tes (pī rī′tēz, pa-, pī′rīts), n. **1.** pyrite
(sometimes called iron pyrites). **2.** marcasite
(white iron pyrites). **3.** any of various other
sulfides.

py·ro·e·lec·tric·i·ty (pī′rō ĭ lĕk′trĭs′ a tĭ, -ē′-
lĕk-, pī′rō-), n. the electrified state, or electric
polarity, in some crystals produced by and
changing with temperature. —**py′ro·e·lec′tric,**
adj.

py·rog·ra·phy (pī rŏg′ra fĭ, pī-), n. the burning of designs on wood, leather, etc., with a heated tool. —**py·rog′ra·pher**, *n.*

py·ro·ma·ni·a (pī/rə mā/nĭ ə, pĭr/ə-), *n.* a mania for setting things on fire. —**py/ro·ma/-ni·ac/**, *n.*

py·ro·tech·nics (pī/rə tĕk/nĭks, pĭr/ə-), *n.* **1.** the art of making fireworks. **2.** the use of fireworks for display, military purposes, etc. Also, **py/ro·tech/ny.** —**py/ro·tech/nic**, *adj.*

py·rox·y·lin (pī rŏk/sə lĭn), *n.* a nitrocellulose compound used in the artificial-silk, leather, oilcloth industries, etc.

Pyr·rhic victory (pĭr/ĭk), a victory gained at too great a cost.

Pyth·i·as (pĭth/ĭ əs), *n.* See **Damon.**

py·thon (pī/thŏn, -thən), *n.* any of various large, nonvenomous, Old World tropical snakes which kill by constriction.

Q

Q, q (kū), *n., pl.* **Q's** or **Qs, q's** or **qs.** a consonant, the 17th letter of the English alphabet.

q., 1. quart; quarts. **2.** (*also cap.*) question.

Q.E.D., quod erat demonstrandum (which was to be proved or shown).

Q.M., Quartermaster.

qt., 1. quantity. **2.** (*pl.* **qt., qts.**) quart.

q.t., *Slang.* quiet.

quack[1] (kwăk), *v.i.* **1.** to utter the cry of a duck. —*n.* **2.** the cry of a duck.

quack[2] (kwăk), *n.* **1.** an ignorant or fraudulent pretender to medical skill. **2.** any charlatan. —*adj.* **3.** being or befitting a quack. —**quack/-er·y,** *n.*

quad·ran·gle (kwŏd/răng/gəl), *n.* **1.** a plane figure having four angles and four sides. **2.** a four-sided space surrounded by a building. or buildings. **3.** the building or buildings about such a space. —**quad·ran·gu·lar** (kwŏd răng/gyə lər), *adj.*

quad·rant (kwŏd/rənt), *n.* **1.** one quarter of a circle; an arc of 90°. **2.** the area included between such an arc and two radii drawn one to each extremity. **3.** an instrument used in astronomy, navigation, etc., for measuring altitudes.

quad·rate (*adj., n.* kwŏd/rĭt, -rāt; *v.* kwŏd/rāt), *adj., n., v.,* **-rated, -rating.** —*adj.* **1.** square; rectangular. —*n.* **2.** a square or rectangle. —*v.t., v.i.* **3.** to conform.

quad·rat·ic (kwŏd răt/ĭk), *adj.* **1.** square. **2.** *Alg.* involving the square and no higher power of the unknown quantity. —*n.* **3.** *Alg.* a quadratic equation.

quad·rat·ics (kwŏd răt/ĭks), *n.* the branch of algebra that treats of quadratic equations.

quad·ra·ture (kwŏd/rə chər), *n.* **1.** act of squaring. **2.** act or process of finding a square equal in area to a given surface.

quad·ren·ni·al (kwŏd rĕn/ĭ əl), *adj.* **1.** occurring every four years. **2.** of or for four years. —**quad·ren/ni·al·ly,** *adv.*

quad·ri·lat·er·al (kwŏd/rə lăt/ər əl), *adj.* **1.** having four sides. —*n.* **2.** a plane figure having four sides and four angles.

qua·drille (kwə drĭl/, kə-), *n.* **1.** a square dance for four couples. **2.** the music for such a dance.

quad·roon (kwŏd rōōn/), *n.* a person who is one fourth Negro.

quad·ru·ped (kwŏd/rŏŏ pĕd/), *adj.* **1.** fourfooted. —*n.* **2.** an animal, esp. a mammal, having four feet. —**quad·ru·pe·dal** (kwŏd rōō/pə-dəl, kwŏd/rŏŏ pĕd/əl), *adj.*

quad·ru·ple (kwŏd/rŏŏ pəl, kwŏd rōō/pəl), *adj., n., v.,* **-pled, -pling.** —*adj.* **1.** fourfold. **2.** four times as great. **3.** a number, amount, etc., four times as great as another. —*v.t., v.i.* **4.** to make or become four times as great.

quad·ru·plet (kwŏd/rŏŏ plĭt, kwŏd rōō/-), *n.* one of four children (**quadruplets**) born at a birth.

quad·ru·pli·cate (*v.* kwŏd rōō/plə kāt/; *adj., n.,* kwŏd rōō/plə kĭt, -kāt/), *v.,* **-cated, -cating,** *adj., n.* —*v.t.* **1.** to quadruple. —*adj.* **2.** quadruple. —*n.* **3.** one of four things. —**quad·ru/-pli·ca/tion,** *n.*

quaff (kwăf, kwäf, kwôf), *v.i., v.t.* to drink (wine, etc.) copiously and heartily. —**quaff/er,** *n.*

quag·mire (kwăg/mīr/, kwŏg/-), *n.* a piece of soft, boggy ground.

qua·hog (kwô/hŏg, -hôg, kwə hŏg/, -hôg/), *n.* an edible American clam of the Atlantic coast.

quail[1] (kwāl), *n., pl.* **quails,** (*esp. collectively*) **quail. 1.** a small migratory Old World gallinaceous game bird. **2.** any of certain New World gallinaceous game birds, many of which are locally known as partridges, esp. the bobwhite.

quail[2] (kwāl), *v.i.* to lose courage in difficulty or danger; shrink with fear.

quaint (kwānt), *adj.* **1.** strange or odd in an interesting, pleasing, or amusing way. **2.** having an old-fashioned charm. —**quaint/ly,** *adv.* —**quaint/ness,** *n.*

quake (kwāk), *v.,* **quaked, quaking,** *n. —v.i.* **1.** to shake or tremble, as from cold, fear, convulsion, etc. —*n.* **2.** an earthquake. **3.** a trembling.

Quak·er (kwā/kər), *n.* a member of the Society of Friends. —**Quak/er·ess,** *n. fem.*

qual·i·fi·ca·tion (kwŏl/ə fə kā/shən), *n.* **1.** a quality, accomplishment, etc., which fits for some function or office. **2.** act of qualifying. **3.** modification, limitation, or restriction.

qual·i·fied (kwŏl/ə fīd/), *adj.* **1.** having necessary qualifications. **2.** modified, limited, or restricted in some way.

qual·i·fy (kwŏl/ə fī/), *v.,* **-fied, -fying.** —*v.t.* **1.** to invest with proper or necessary qualities. **2.** to modify; limit. **3.** *Gram.* to modify. **4.** to moderate; mitigate. —*v.i.* **5.** to make or show oneself competent. —**qual/i·fi/er,** *n.*

qual·i·ta·tive (kwŏl/ə tā/tĭv), *adj.* pertaining to or concerned with quality or qualities. —**qual/i·ta/tive·ly,** *adv.*

qual·i·ty (kwŏl/ə tĭ), *n., pl.* **-ties. 1.** a characteristic, property, or attribute. **2.** character with respect to excellence, fineness, etc. **3.** superior excellence. **4.** high social position. **5.** *Acoustics.* the texture of a tone, dependent on its overtone content, which distinguishes it from others of the same pitch and loudness.

qualm (kwäm, kwôm), *n.* **1.** an uneasy scruple as to conduct. **2.** a sudden misgiving. **3.** a sudden sensation of faintness or illness, esp. of nausea. —**qualm/ish,** *adj.*

quan·da·ry (kwŏn/də rĭ, -drĭ), *n., pl.* **-ries.** a state of embarrassing uncertainty; dilemma.

quan·ti·ta·tive (kwŏn/tə tā/tĭv), *adj.* **1.** that is or may be estimated by quantity. **2.** of or pertaining to the measuring of quantity. —**quan/-ti·ta/tive·ly,** *adv.*

quan·ti·ty (kwŏn/tə tĭ), *n., pl.* **-ties. 1.** a particular, indefinite, or considerable amount of anything. **2.** amount or measure. **3.** *Math.* something having magnitude, or size, extent, amount, or the like. **4.** *Music.* the length of a note. **5.** (of sounds or syllables) character as to being long or short, with reference to the time required in uttering them.

quan·tum (kwŏn/təm), *n., pl.* **-ta** (-tə). **1.** quantity or amount. **2.** *Physics.* **a.** one of the discrete quantities of energy or momentum of an atomic system which are characteristic of the **quantum theory. b.** this amount of energy regarded as a unit.

quar·an·tine (kwôr/ən tēn/, kwŏr/-), *n., v.,* **-tined, -tining.** —*n.* **1.** a strict isolation designed to prevent the spread of disease. **2.** a period of detention or isolation imposed upon ships, persons, etc., on arrival when liable or suspected to be bringing some infectious or contagious disease. **3.** the place of detention. —*v.t.* **4.** to put in quarantine. **5.** to isolate politically and commercially.

quar·rel (kwôr/əl, kwŏr/-), n., v., -reled, -rel-ing or (esp. Brit.) -relled, -relling. —n. 1. an angry dispute or altercation. 2. a cause of complaint or hostile feeling. —v.i. 3. to disagree or dispute angrily. —quar/rel·er; esp. Brit., quar/rel·ler, n.

quar·rel·some (kwôr/əl səm, kwŏr/-), adj. inclined to quarrel. —quar/rel·some·ly, adv. —quar/rel·some·ness, n.

quar·ry[1] (kwôr/ī, kwŏr/ī), n., pl. -ries, v., -ried, -rying. —n. 1. an excavation or pit from which building stone, slate, or the like, is obtained. —v.t. 2. to obtain (stone, etc.) from a quarry.

quar·ry[2] (kwôr/ī, kwŏr/ī), n., pl. -ries. 1. a beast or bird hunted or pursued. 2. any object of pursuit or attack.

quart (kwôrt), n. a liquid and a dry measure of capacity, equal to one fourth of a gallon or one eighth of a peck respectively.

quart., 1. quarter. 2. quarterly.

quar·ter (kwôr/tər), n. 1. one of the four equal parts into which anything is or may be divided. 2. U.S. and Canada. a silver coin worth 25 cents. 3. one fourth of an hour (15 minutes). 4. one fourth of a year. 5. Astron. a fourth of the moon's monthly revolution. 6. Sports. any one of the four periods that make up some games. 7. the region of any of the four principal points of the compass or divisions of the horizon. 8. a region, district, or place. 9. (usually pl.) a place of residence. 10. mercy to a vanquished enemy. 11. one of the four parts, each including a leg, of the body of a quadruped. 12. Her. one of the four (or more) parts into which a shield may be divided by horizontal and vertical lines. —v.t., v.i., 13. to divide into four equal parts. 14. to station or lodge. —adj. 15. being one of the four equal parts into which anything is or may be divided.

quar·ter·back (kwôr/tər băk/), n. Football. one of the players behind the forward line.

quar·ter·deck (kwôr/tər dĕk/), n. Naut. the upper deck between the mainmast and the poop or stern.

quar·ter·ly (kwôr/tər lī), adj., n., pl. -lies, adv. —adj. 1. occurring, done, etc., at the end of every quarter of a year. —n. 2. a periodical issued every three months. —adv. 3. once in a quarter of a year.

quar·ter·mas·ter (kwôr/tər măs/tər, -mäs/-tər), n. 1. Mil. an officer charged with providing quarters, clothing, fuel, transportation, etc., for troops. 2. Naval. a petty officer having charge of signals, navigating apparatus, etc.

quarter note, Music. a note equivalent to one fourth of a whole note; crotchet.

quarter section, a square tract of land containing 160 acres.

quar·ter·staff (kwôr/tər stăf/, -stäf/), n., pl. -staves (-stāvz/, -stävz/, -stävz/). 1. a former English weapon consisting of a long pole tipped with iron. 2. exercise or fighting with this weapon.

quar·tet (kwôr tĕt/), n. 1. any group of four persons or things. 2. a composition for four voices or instruments. Also, esp. Brit., quar·tette/.

quar·to (kwôr/tō), n., pl. -tos. a volume printed from sheets folded twice to form four leaves or eight pages.

quartz (kwôrts), n. one of the commonest minerals, silicon dioxide, having many varieties which differ in color, luster, etc.

quash[1] (kwŏsh), v.t. to put down or suppress completely; subdue.

quash[2] (kwŏsh), v.t. to make void, annul, or set aside (a law, indictment, etc.).

qua·si (kwā/sī, -zī, kwä/sī), adj. 1. resembling. —adv. 2. seemingly, but not actually.

quasi-, a prefix form of "quasi."

qua·ter·na·ry (kwə tûr/nə rī), adj., n., pl. -ries. —adj. 1. consisting of four. 2. arranged in fours. —n. 3. a group of four.

quat·rain (kwŏt/rān), n. a stanza or poem of four lines, usually with alternate rhymes.

quat·re·foil (kăt/ər foil/, kăt/rə-), n. 1. a leaf composed of four leaflets, as sometimes a leaf of clover. 2. Archit. an ornament or decorative feature having four foils or lobes.

qua·ver (kwā/vər), v.i., v.t. 1. to shake tremulously; quiver. 2. to

Architectural quatrefoils

sound, speak, or sing tremulously. 3. to perform trills in singing or on a musical instrument. —n. 4. a tremulous shake, esp. in the voice. 5. a quavering tone or utterance. —qua/ver·y, adj.

quay (kē), n. an artificial landing place, as of masonry, built along navigable water.

Que., Quebec.

quean (kwēn), n. 1. a shrew or hussy. 2. a prostitute.

quea·sy (kwē/zī), adj., -sier, -siest. 1. inclined to nausea. 2. uneasy or uncomfortable, as the conscience. 3. squeamish. —quea/si·ly, adv. —quea/si·ness, n.

Que·bec (kwĭ bĕk/), n. 1. a province in E Canada. 3,331,822 pop.; 594,860 sq. mi. 2. the capital of this province. With suburbs, 200,814.

queen (kwēn), n. 1. the wife or consort of a king. 2. a female sovereign or monarch. 3. a woman, or something personified as a woman, that is chief or preëminent in any respect. 4. a playing card bearing a picture of a queen. 5. Chess. the most powerful piece, moving any distance in any straight or diagonal line. 6. a fertile female of ants, bees, or termites. —v.i. 7. to reign as queen. —queen/ly, adj. —queen/li·ness, n.

Queen Anne's lace, a plant with large lacy umbels of minute white flowers.

queen mother, a widowed queen who is mother of a reigning sovereign.

Queens (kwēnz), n. an E borough of New York City, on Long Island. 1,297,634 pop.

Queens·land (kwēnz/lănd/, -lənd), n. a state in NE Australia. 1,091,226 pop.; ab. 670,500 sq. mi. Cap.: Brisbane.

queer (kwĭr), adj. 1. strange or odd. 2. Colloq. suspicious; shady. 3. giddy, faint, or qualmish. 4. Colloq. mentally deranged. —v.t. Slang. 5. to spoil; ruin. —queer/ly, adv. —queer/ness, n.

quell (kwĕl), v.t. 1. to suppress (disorder, etc.); extinguish. 2. to vanquish; subdue. 3. to quiet (feelings, etc.). —quell/er, n.

quench (kwĕnch), v.t. 1. to put an end to; slake, as thirst. 2. to extinguish (fire, etc.). —quench/a·ble, adj. —quench/er, n.

quer·u·lous (kwĕr/ə ləs, kwĕr/yə-), adj. 1. complaining. 2. peevish; fretful. —quer/u·lous·ly, adv. —quer/u·lous·ness, n.

que·ry (kwĭr/ī), n., pl. -ries, v., -ried, -rying. —n. 1. a question; inquiry. —v.t. 2. to ask or inquire. 3. to question (a statement, etc.) as doubtful.

ques., question.

quest (kwĕst), n. 1. a search or hunt. 2. a knightly expedition. —v.i., v.t., 3. to search (for). 4. to go on a quest. —quest/er, n.

ques·tion (kwĕs/chən), n. 1. a sentence in an interrogative form, addressed to someone in order to elicit information. 2. a problem for discussion or investigation. 3. a matter of uncertainty or difficulty. 4. a subject of dispute. 5. beyond (all) question, indisputably. 6. in question, a. under consideration. b. in dispute. 7. out of the question, not to be considered. 8. call in question, a. to dispute, question, or challenge. b. to cast doubt upon. —v.t., v.i. 9. to ask a question or questions (of). 10. to doubt. 11. to dispute. —ques/tion·er, n. —ques/tion·ing·ly, adv.

ques·tion·a·ble (kwĕs/chən ə bəl), adj. 1. of doubtful propriety, honesty, etc. 2. doubtful or uncertain. 3. open to question as to being such. —ques/tion·a·bly, adv.

question mark, a mark (?) indicating a question.

ques·tion·naire (kwĕs/chə nâr/), n. a list of questions, as for statistical purposes.

quet·zal (kĕt säl/), n. a Central American bird having golden-green and scarlet plumage.

queue (kū), n., v., queued, queuing. —n. 1. a braid of hair worn hanging down behind. 2. Chiefly Brit. a file of persons, etc. —v.i. 3. Brit. to form in a line.

quib·ble (kwĭb/əl), n., v., -bled, -bling. —n. 1. a use of ambiguous or irrelevant language or arguments to evade a point at issue. —v.i. 2. to use a quibble or quibbles. —quib/bler, n.

quick (kwĭk), adj. 1. prompt; immediate. 2. completed within a short time. 3. swift or rapid. 4. hasty; impatient. 5. vigorous, lively, or alert. 6. prompt to understand, learn, etc. 7. Archaic or Dial. living. —n. 8. living persons. 9. the tender sensitive flesh of the living body, esp. that under the nails. **10.** the vital or most important part. —*adv.* **11.** quickly. —**quick′ly**, *adv.* —**quick′ness**, *n.*

quick·en (kwĭk′ən), *v.t.* **1.** to accelerate; hasten. **2.** to restore life to. **3.** to stir up, rouse, or stimulate. —*v.i.* **4.** to become more active, sensitive, etc. **5.** to become alive. —**quick′en·er**, *n.*

quick freezing, a process in which food is subjected to sudden and powerful refrigeration, permitting it to be stored almost indefinitely at freezing temperatures.

quick·lime (kwĭk′līm′), *n.* unslaked lime.

quick·sand (kwĭk′sănd′), *n.* an area of soft or loose, wet sand of considerable depth, yielding readily under weight.

quick·set (kwĭk′sĕt′), *n.* *Chiefly Brit.* a plant (esp. of hawthorn) set to grow, as in a hedge.

quick·sil·ver (kwĭk′sĭl′vər), *n.* the metallic element mercury.

quick-tem·pered (kwĭk′tĕm′pərd), *adj.* easily moved to anger.

quick time, 1. a quick rate of marching. **2.** *U.S. Army.* a normal rate of marching in which 120 paces, each of 30 inches, are taken in a minute.

quick-wit·ted (kwĭk′wĭt′ĭd), *adj.* having a nimble, alert intelligence. —**quick′-wit′ted·ly**, *adv.* —**quick′-wit′ted·ness**, *n.*

quid[1] (kwĭd), *n.* a portion of something esp. tobacco, for chewing.

quid[2] (kwĭd), *n.*, *pl.* **quid.** *Brit. Slang.* a sovereign.

quid·nunc (kwĭd′nŭngk′), *n.* one who is curious to know everything that passes; a newsmonger.

quid pro quo (kwĭd′ prō kwō′), *Latin.* one thing in return for another.

qui·es·cent (kwī ĕs′ənt), *adj.* being at rest, quiet, or still; inactive or motionless. —**qui·es′cent·ly**, *adv.* —**qui·es′cence**, *n.*

qui·et[1] (kwī′ət), *n.* freedom from disturbance or tumult; tranquillity.

qui·et[2] (kwī′ət), *adj.* **1.** making no disturbance or trouble. **2.** tranquil; peaceful. **3.** being at rest. **4.** refraining or free from activity. **5.** motionless or moving gently. **6.** making no noise or sound. **7.** free, or comparatively free, from noise. **8.** silent. **9.** restrained in speech, manner, etc. **10.** said, done, etc., in a restrained or unobtrusive way. **11.** not showy. **12.** commercially inactive. —*v.t., v.i.* **13.** to make or become quiet. —**qui′et·ly**, *adv.* —**qui′et·ness**, *n.*

qui·e·tude (kwī′ə tūd′, -tōod′), *n.* state of being quiet; calmness; stillness.

qui·e·tus (kwī ē′təs), *n.* **1.** anything that effectually ends or settles. **2.** discharge or release from life.

quill (kwĭl), *n.* **1.** one of the large feathers of the wing or tail of a bird. **2.** a pen made from a quill. **3.** one of the hollow spines on a porcupine.

quilt (kwĭlt), *n.* **1.** a bed covering made by stitching together two thicknesses of fabric with some soft substance, as wool, between them. —*v.t.* **2.** to stitch together with a soft interlining. —*v.i.* **3.** to make quilts or quilted work.

quilting bee, *U.S.* a social gathering of women to make a quilt or quilts.

quince (kwĭns), *n.* **1.** the hard, yellowish acid fruit of a small, hardy tree of the rose family. **2.** the tree itself.

Quin·cy (kwĭn′zĭ *for 1*; kwĭn′sĭ *for 2*), *n.* **1.** a city in E Massachusetts. 75,810. **2.** a city in W Illinois. 40,469.

qui·nine (kwī′nīn *or, esp. Brit.,* kwĭ nēn′), *n.* *Chem.* a bitter colorless alkaloid used in medicine as a stimulant and to treat malaria. Also, **quin·in** (kwĭn′ĭn).

quin·quen·ni·al (kwĭn kwĕn′ĭ əl), *adj.* of or for five years. **2.** occurring every five years.

quin·sy (kwĭn′zĭ), *n.*, *pl.* **-sies.** *Pathol.* a suppurative inflammation of the tonsils.

quint (kwĭnt), *n.* *Colloq.* a quintuplet.

quin·tes·sence (kwĭn tĕs′əns), *n.* **1.** the pure and concentrated essence of a substance. **2.** the most perfect embodiment of something. —**quin·tes·sen·tial** (kwĭn′tə sĕn′shəl), *adj.*

quin·tet (kwĭn tĕt′), *n.* **1.** any group of five persons or things. **2.** a composition for five voices or instruments. Also, *esp. Brit.,* **quin·tette′.**

Quin·til·ian (kwĭn tĭl′yən, -ĭ ən), *n.* A.D. c35–c95, Roman rhetorician.

quin·tu·ple (kwĭn′tyōō pəl, -tōō-, kwĭn tū′pəl, -tōō′-), *adj., n., v.,* **-pled, -pling.** —*adj.* **1.** fivefold. **2.** five times as great. —*n.* **3.** a number, amount, etc., five times as great as another. —*v.t., v.i.* **4.** to make or become five times as great.

quin·tu·plet (kwĭn′tyōō plĭt, -tōō-, kwĭn tū′plĭt, -tōō′-, -tŭp′lĭt), *n.* **1.** any group of five. **2.** one of five children (**quintuplets**) born at a birth.

quip (kwĭp), *n., v.,* **quipped, quipping.** —*n.* **1.** a sharp, sarcastic remark. **2.** a witty saying. —*v.i.* **3.** to use quips.

quire (kwīr), *n.* a set of 24 uniform sheets of paper.

quirk (kwûrk), *n.* **1.** a peculiarity. **2.** a shift or evasion. **3.** a flourish, as in writing.

quirt (kwûrt), *n.* a short riding whip with a lash of braided leather.

quis·ling (kwĭz′lĭng), *n.* a person who undermines his own country from within.

quit (kwĭt), *v.,* **quit** or **quitted, quitting,** *adj.* —*v.t., v.i.* **1.** to stop; cease. **2.** to depart (from); leave. **3.** to relinquish. —*adj.* **4.** released from obligation, penalty, etc.

quit·claim (kwĭt′klām′), *Law.* —*n.* **1.** a transfer of all one's interest, as in a parcel of real estate. —*v.t.* **2.** to give up claim to.

quite (kwīt), *adv.* **1.** completely; entirely. **2.** actually; really. **3.** *Colloq.* to a considerable degree.

Qui·to (kē′tô), *n.* the capital of Ecuador, in the N part. 165,924 pop.

quits (kwĭts), *adj.* on equal terms by repayment or retaliation.

quit·tance (kwĭt′əns), *n.* **1.** recompense or requital. **2.** discharge from debt.

quit·ter (kwĭt′ər), *n.* *Colloq.* one who quits or gives up easily.

quiv·er[1] (kwĭv′ər), *v.i., v.t.* **1.** to shake or tremble. —*n.* **2.** a tremble; tremor.

quiv·er[2] (kwĭv′ər), *n.* **1.** a case for holding arrows. **2.** the contents of such a case.

Quix·o·te (kĭ hō′tĭ, kwĭk′sət), *n.* See **Don Quixote.**

quix·ot·ic (kwĭks ŏt′ĭk), *adj.* **1.** (*sometimes cap.*) resembling or befitting Don Quixote. **2.** extravagantly chivalrous; impracticable. —**quix·ot′i·cal·ly**, *adv.* —**quix·ot′ism** (kwĭk′sə tĭz′əm), *n.*

quiz (kwĭz), *v., v.,* **quizzed, quizzing,** *n., pl.* **quizzes.** —*v.t.* **1.** to examine by questions. **2.** to question. —*n.* **3.** an informal test of a student or class. **4.** a questioning. —**quiz′zer**, *n.*

quiz·zi·cal (kwĭz′ə kəl), *adj.* **1.** odd or comical. **2.** ridiculing or chaffing. —**quiz′zi·cal·ly**, *adv.*

quoin (koin, kwoin), *n.* **1.** an external solid angle of a wall or the like. **2.** one of the stones forming it. **3.** *Print.* a wedge of wood or metal for securing type in a chase, etc.

quoit (kwoit), *n.* **1.** a flat ring thrown in play to encircle a peg stuck in the ground or to come as close to it as possible. **2.** (*pl. construed as sing.*) the game so played.

quon·dam (kwŏn′dăm), *adj.* former.

Quon·set hut (kwŏn′sĭt), a metal shelter resembling a semicircular arch in cross section.

quo·rum (kwōr′əm), *n.* the number of members of a body required to be present to transact business legally.

quo·ta (kwō′tə), *n.* the proportional part or share of a total due from or to a particular district, state, person, etc.

quo·ta·tion (kwō tā′shən), *n.* **1.** a passage quoted from a book, speech, etc. **2.** act or practice of quoting. **3.** *Com.* a. the statement of the current price of a commodity or security. b. the price so stated.

quotation mark, one of the marks (" or ' at the beginning and " or ' at the end) used to indicate the beginning and end of a quotation.

quote (kwōt), *v.,* **quoted, quoting,** *n.* —*v.t., v.i.* **1.** to repeat (a passage, etc.) from a book, speech, etc., esp. as authority, illustration, etc. **2.** to cite. **3.** *Com.* a. to state (a price). b. to state the current price of. —*n.* **4.** a quotation. **5.** a quotation mark. —**quot′a·ble**, *adj.*

quoth (kwōth), *v.t.* *Archaic.* said.

quo·tid·i·an (kwō tĭd′ĭ ən), *adj.* **1.** daily. **2.** (of a fever, etc.) characterized by daily paroxysms. —*n.* **3.** a quotidian fever.

quo·tient (kwō′shənt), *n.* *Math.* the number of times one quantity is contained in another.

q.v., (L *quod vide*) which see.

R

R, r (är), *n.*, *pl.* **R's** or **Rs, r's** or **rs.** a consonant, the 18th letter of the English alphabet.

R, 1. *Elect.* resistance. 2. *Chess.* rook.

R., 1. Republican. 2. River.

Ra (rä), *n.* the great sun god of the ancient Egyptians.

Ra, *Chem.* radium.

rab·bet (răb′ĭt), *n.*, *v.*, **-beted, -beting.** —*n.* 1. a cut made on the edge of a board to receive the edge of another board similarly shaped. 2. a joint so made. —*v.t.* 3. to cut or form a rabbet in. —*v.i.* 4. to join by a rabbet.

rab·bi (răb′ī), *n.*, *pl.* **-bis.** *Jewish Relig.* a preacher or religious functionary.

rab·bin·i·cal (rə bĭn′ə kəl), *adj.* of or pertaining to the rabbis or their learning, writings, etc. Also, **rab·bin′ic.**

rab·bit (răb′ĭt), *n.* 1. any of certain rodentlike, mammals, esp. the cottontail. 2. a small, long-eared burrowing animal of the hare family.

rab·ble (răb′əl), *n.* 1. a disorderly crowd; mob. 2. (in contemptuous use) the lowest class of people.

Rab·e·lais (răb′ə lā′), *n.* **François,** c1490–1553, French satirist and humorist.

Rab·e·lai·si·an (răb′ə lā′zĭ ən, -zhən), *adj.* of or suggesting Rabelais, whose work is characterized by broad, coarse humor and keen satire.

rab·id (răb′ĭd), *adj.* 1. irrationally extreme in opinion or practice. 2. violently intense. 3. affected with rabies. —**rab′id·ness,** *n.* —**rab′id·ly,** *adv.*

ra·bies (rā′bēz, -bĭ ēz′), *n.* a fatal, infectious disease of the brain which occurs in all warm-blooded animals, esp. dogs, and is transmitted by the bite of an afflicted animal.

rac·coon (ră kōōn′), *n.* a small nocturnal carnivore of North America, arboreal in habit, and having a sharp snout and a bushy ringed tail.

race¹ (rās), *n.*, *v.*, **raced, racing.** —*n.* 1. a contest of speed. 2. an onward or regular course. 3. a strong or rapid current of water. —*v.i.* 4. to engage in a contest of speed. 5. to run, move, or go swiftly. —*v.t.* 6. to try to beat in a contest of speed. 7. to cause to run in a race. —**rac′er,** *n.*

race² (rās), *n.* 1. a group of persons connected by common descent. 2. *Zool.* a variety. 3. a natural kind of living creature. 4. any group, class, or kind. 5. the characteristic taste or flavor of wine. —**ra·cial** (rā′shəl), *adj.*

ra·ceme (rā sēm′, rə-), *n.* *Bot.* a simple inflorescence in which the flowers are borne on short pedicels lying along a common axis, as in the lily of the valley.

race track, 1. a plot of ground laid out for horse-racing. 2. the course for any race.

Ra·chel (rā′chəl), *n.* *Bible.* Jacob's favorite wife, and mother of Joseph and Benjamin.

Rach·ma·ni·noff (räkH mä′nĭ nôf′), *n.* **Sergei Wassilievitch,** 1873–1943, Russian pianist and composer.

Ra·cine (rà sēn′ *for 1;* rə sēn′ *for 2), n.* 1. **Jean Baptiste,** 1639–99, French dramatist. 2. a city in SE Wisconsin. 67,195.

rac·ism (rā′sĭz əm), *n.* a belief that human races have distinctive make-ups that determine their respective cultures, usually involving the idea that one's own race is superior and has the right to rule others. Also, **ra·cial·ism** (rā′shə-lĭz′əm). —**rac′ist,** *n.*

rack¹ (răk), *n.* 1. a framework on which articles are arranged or deposited. 2. a spreading framework set on a wagon for carrying hay, straw, or the like, in large loads. 3. *Mach.* a bar with teeth on one of its sides, adapted to engage with the teeth of a pinion or the like, as for converting circular into rectilinear motion or vice versa. 4. an apparatus formerly in use for torturing persons by stretching the body. 5. torment; anguish. —*v.t.* 6. to torture; torment. 7. to strain.

rack² (răk), *n.* wreck; destruction.

rack·et¹ (răk′ĭt), *n.* 1. a loud noise; din; clamor. 2. *U.S. Slang.* an organized illegal activity, such as bootlegging. 3. *U.S. Slang.* a dishonest scheme, trick, etc.

rack·et² (răk′ĭt), *n.* a light bat having a net of cord or catgut stretched in a frame, used in tennis, etc. Also, **rac′quet.**

rack·et·eer (răk′ə tĭr′), *U.S.* —*n.* 1. one engaged in a racket. —*v.i.* 2. to engage in a racket. —**rack′et·eer′ing,** *n.*

rac·on·teur (răk′ŏn tûr′), *n.* a person skilled in relating stories and anecdotes.

ra·coon (ră kōōn′), *n.* raccoon.

rac·y (rā′sĭ), *adj.*, **racier, raciest.** 1. lively; spirited. 2. sprightly; piquant. 3. agreeably flavored, as wine. 4. risqué. —**rac′i·ly,** *adv.* —**rac′i·ness,** *n.*

ra·dar (rā′där), *n.* *Electronics.* a device to determine the presence and location of an object by measuring the time for the echo of a radio wave to return from it, and the direction from which it returns.

ra·di·al (rā′dĭ əl), *adj.* 1. arranged like radii or rays. 2. of, like, or pertaining to a radius or a ray. —**ra′di·al·ly,** *adv.*

ra·di·ance (rā′dĭ əns), *n.* 1. radiant brightness or light. 2. radiation. Also, **ra′di·an·cy.**

ra·di·ant (rā′dĭ ənt), *adj.* 1. emitting rays of light; shining; bright. 2. bright with joy, hope, etc. 3. *Physics.* emitted in rays or by radiation. —**ra′di·ant·ly,** *adv.*

ra·di·ate (rā′dĭ āt′), *v.*, **-ated, -ating,** *adj.* —*v.i.* 1. to spread like rays from a center. 2. to emit rays, as of light. 3. to issue in rays. —*v.t.* 4. to emit in rays. —*adj.* 5. radiating from a center.

ra·di·a·tion (rā′dĭ ā′shən), *n.* 1. the emission and diffusion of rays of heat, light, electricity, or sounds. 2. radiant energy. 3. a ray or rays.

ra·di·a·tor (rā′dĭ ā′tər), *n.* 1. any of various heating devices, as a series of pipes through which steam passes. 2. a device constructed from thin-walled tubes and metal fins, used for cooling circulating water.

rad·i·cal (răd′ə kəl), *adj.* 1. fundamental. 2. thorough-going or extreme. 3. favoring drastic reforms, esp. in government. 4. *Math.* **a.** pertaining to or forming a root. **b.** denoting or pertaining to the radical sign. —*n.* 5. one who holds extreme principles. 6. one who favors drastic reforms, esp. in government. 7. *Math.* **a.** a quantity expressed as a root of another quantity. **b.** a radical sign. 8. *Chem.* an atom or group of atoms regarded as an important constituent of a molecule, which remains unchanged and behaves as a unit in many reactions. 9. *Gram.* a root. —**rad′i·cal·ism′, rad′i·cal·ness,** *n.* —**rad′i·cal·ly,** *adv.*

radical sign, *Math.* the symbol √ or √‾ indicating extraction of a root of the following quantity.

ra·di·o (rā′dĭ ō′), *n.*, *pl.* **-dios,** *adj.*, *v.*, **-dioed, -dioing.** —*n.* 1. wireless telegraphy or telephony. 2. an apparatus for receiving radio broadcasts. —*adj.* 3. pertaining to, used in, or sent by radio. 4. pertaining to or employing radiations. —*v.t.*, *v.i.* 5. to transmit (a message, etc.) by radio.

ra·di·o·ac·tive (rā′dĭ ō ăk′tĭv), *adj.* *Physics, Chem.* having the property of emitting particles or radiation from an atomic nucleus, as is the case with radium. uranium. etc. —**ra′di·o·ac·tiv′i·ty,** *n.*

radio beacon, a radio station for sending a characteristic signal so as to enable ships or airplanes to determine their position by a receiving instrument.

ra·di·o·fre·quen·cy (rā′dĭ ō frē′kwən sĭ), *n.*, *pl.* **-cies.** 1. the frequency of the transmitting waves of a given radio broadcast. **2.** a frequency within the range of radio transmission.

ra·di·o·gram (rā′dĭ ō grăm′), *n.* a message transmitted by radiotelegraphy.

ra·di·o·graph (rā′dĭ ō grăf′, -gräf′), *n.* **1.** an image produced by the action of x-rays or other rays on a photographic plate. —*v.t.* **2.** to make a radiograph of. —**ra·di·og·ra·phy** (rā′dĭ ŏg′rə-fĭ), *n.*

ra·di·o·phone (rā′dĭ ō fōn′), *n.* **1.** any of various devices for producing sound by the action of radiant energy. **2.** a radiotelephone.

ra·di·o·tel·e·graph (rā′dĭ ō tĕl′ə grăf′, -gräf′), *n.* **1.** a wireless telegraph. —*v.t., v.i.* **2.** to telegraph by radiotelegraphy.

ra·di·o·te·leg·ra·phy (rā′dĭ ō tə lĕg′rə fĭ), *n.* wireless telegraphy, in which messages are transmitted through space by means of the radiated energy of electromagnetic waves.

ra·di·o·tel·e·phone (rā′dĭ ō tĕl′ə fōn′), *n., v.,* **-phoned, -phoning.** —*n.* **1.** a wireless telephone. —*v.t., v.i.* **2.** to telephone by radiotelephony.

ra·di·o·te·leph·o·ny (rā′dĭ ō tə lĕf′ə nĭ), *n.* wireless telephony.

ra·di·o·ther·a·py (rā′dĭ ō thĕr′ə pĭ), *n.* treatment of disease by means of x-rays or of radioactive agencies.

rad·ish (răd′ĭsh), *n.* the crisp, pungent root (red or white) of certain garden plants, eaten raw in salads or as an appetizer.

ra·di·um (rā′dĭ əm), *n. Chem.* a radioactive metallic element which undergoes spontaneous atomic disintegration: used esp. in cancer treatment. *Symbol:* Ra; *at. wt.:* 226.65; *at. no.:* 88.

ra·di·us (rā′dĭ əs), *n., pl.* **-dii** (-dĭ ĭ′), **-diuses. 1.** a straight line extending from the center of a circle or sphere to the circumference or surface. **2.** a circular area of an extent indicated by the length of the radius of its circumscribing circle. **3.** *Anat.* that one of the two bones of the forearm which is on the thumb side.

ra·don (rā′dŏn), *n. Chem.* a rare, chemically inert, radioactive gaseous element produced in the disintegration of radium. *Symbol:* Rn; *at. no.:* 86; *at. wt.:* 222.

R.A.F., Royal Air Force.

raf·fi·a (răf′ĭ ə), *n.* **1.** a species of palm of Madagascar, whose leafstalks yield a fiber much used for tying small packages, for matting, etc. **2.** the fiber.

raf·fle (răf′əl), *n., v.,* **-fled, -fling.** —*n.* **1.** a lottery in which the prize goes to one of the persons buying chances to win it. —*v.t.* **2.** to dispose of by a raffle.

raft¹ (răft, räft), *n.* a floating platform made of logs, planks, casks, etc.

raft² (răft, räft), *n. Colloq.* a great quantity.

raft·er (răf′tər, räf′-), *n.* one of the sloping timbers or members sustaining a roof sheeting or covering.

rag¹ (răg), *n.* **1.** a worthless fragment of cloth, esp. one resulting from tearing or wear. **2.** (*pl.*) tattered clothing. **3.** (in contemptuous or humorous use) an article of cloth, paper, etc., as a newspaper.

rag² (răg), *v.t.,* **ragged, ragging.** *Slang.* **1.** to scold. **2.** to tease.

rag·a·muf·fin (răg′ə mŭf′ĭn), *n.* **1.** a ragged, disreputable person. **2.** a ragged child.

rage (rāj), *n., v.,* **raged, raging.** —*n.* **1.** angry fury; violent anger. **2.** the object of widespread enthusiasm. —*v.i.* **3.** to show or feel violent anger. **4.** to move, continue, or prevail with great violence.

rag·ged (răg′ĭd), *adj.* **1.** clothed in tattered garments. **2.** torn or worn to rags; tattered. **3.** shaggy. **4.** having loose shreds or bits. **5.** rough or sharp. —**rag′ged·ly,** *adv.* —**rag′ged·ness,** *n.*

rag·lan (răg′lən), *n.* a loose overcoat the sleeves of which are cut so as to continue up to the collar.

ra·gout (ră gōō′), *n.* a highly seasoned stew of meat and vegetables.

rag·time (răg′tīm′), *n. Colloq.* (in music) **1.** rhythm marked by frequent syncopation. **2.** music in this rhythm.

rag·weed (răg′wēd′), *n.* any of certain composite herbs whose air-borne pollen is the most prevalent cause of autumnal hay fever.

raid (rād), *n.* **1.** a sudden attack, as upon something to be seized or suppressed. **2.** a sudden attack on an enemy, esp. by airplanes or by a small

force. —*v.t., v.i.* **3.** to make a raid (on). —**raid′-er,** *n.*

rail¹ (rāl), *n.* **1.** a bar of wood or metal fixed horizontally as a support, barrier, fence, etc. **2.** a fence; railing. **3.** one of a pair of steel railroad tracks. **4.** the railroad, as a means of transportation. —*v.t.* **5.** to furnish or enclose with a rail or rails.

rail² (rāl), *v.i.* to utter bitter complaint or vehement denunciation. —**rail′er,** *n.*

rail³ (rāl), *n.* any of certain wading birds characterized by a harsh cry, abounding in marshes in most parts of the world.

rail·ing (rā′lĭng), *n.* a barrier made of rails, rails and supports, etc.

rail·ler·y (rā′lə rĭ), *n., pl.* **-leries.** good-humored ridicule; banter.

rail·road (rāl′rōd′), *n. Chiefly U.S.* **1.** a permanent road, provided with rails on which locomotives and cars transport passengers, freight, and mails. **2.** the company of persons owning or operating such a road and the related buildings, equipment, etc. —*v.t.* **3.** *U.S.* to transport by means of a railroad. **4.** *U.S. Colloq.* to push forward with undue speed. **5.** *Slang.* to imprison on a false charge in order to be rid of.

rail·way (rāl′wā′), *n. Chiefly Brit.* a railroad.

rai·ment (rā′mənt), *n. Archaic or Poetic.* clothing; apparel; attire.

rain (rān), *n.* **1.** water in drops falling from the sky, being condensed from the aqueous vapor in the atmosphere. **2.** a rainfall or shower. —*v.i.* **3.** (of rain) to fall. —*v.t.* **4.** to send down (rain, etc.). **5.** to offer or give abundantly.

rain·bow (rān′bō′), *n.* an arc of prismatic colors appearing in the heavens opposite the sun, due to the refraction and reflection of the sun's rays in drops of rain.

rain·coat (rān′kōt′), *n.* a waterproof coat, worn as a protection from rain.

rain·fall (rān′fôl′), *n.* **1.** a fall of rain. **2.** the amount of water falling in rain, snow, etc., within a given time and area.

Rai·nier (rā nĭr′, rə nĭr′), *n.* **Mount,** a mountain in W Washington. 14,408 ft. Also, **Mount Tacoma.**

rain·y (rā′nĭ), *adj.,* **rainier, rainiest. 1.** characterized by rain. **2.** wet with rain. **3.** bringing rain. —**rain′i·ness,** *n.*

raise (rāz), *v.,* **raised, raising,** *n.* —*v.t.* **1.** to lift up; elevate. **2.** to set upright. **3.** to rouse. **4.** to build; erect. **5.** to cause to be or appear. **6.** to cause or promote the growth of, as crops. **7.** to bring up or about. **8.** to restore to life. **9.** to advance in rank, dignity, etc. **10.** to collect. **11.** to increase in height, degree, intensity, pitch, or force. **12.** to utter (a cry, etc.) in a loud voice. **13.** to cause (the voice) to be heard. **14.** to cause (dough) to rise by expansion and become light, as by the use of yeast. **15.** to increase in amount, as rent, prices, wages, etc. **16.** to bring up; rear. **17.** *Mil.* **a.** to end (a siege) by withdrawing the investing forces. **b.** to end (a siege) by compelling the investing forces to withdraw. —*n.* **18.** an increase in amount, as of wages. **19.** the amount of such an increase.

rai·sin (rā′zən), *n.* a dried, sweet grape used in cookery, etc.

ra·jah (rä′jə), *n.* **1.** *India.* **a.** a king or prince. **b.** a chief or dignitary. **c.** an honorary title conferred on Hindus in India. **2.** a title of rulers, princes, or chiefs in Java, Borneo, etc. Also, **ra′ja.**

rake¹ (rāk), *n., v.,* **raked, raking.** —*n.* **1.** an implement with tines for gathering together hay, breaking and smoothing ground, etc. —*v.t.* **2.** to gather together, draw, or remove with a rake. **3.** to clear, smooth, or prepare with a rake. **4.** to collect, often with difficulty. **5.** to revive. **6.** to fire guns lengthwise on (a place, troops, a ship, etc.). —*v.i.* **7.** to use a rake.

rake² (rāk), *n.* a profligate person; roué.

rake³ (rāk), *n.* inclination or slope away from the perpendicular or the horizontal.

rake-off (rāk′ôf′, -ŏf′), *n. U.S. Slang.* a share, as of profits or illicit gain.

rak·ish (rā′kĭsh), *adj.* **1.** jaunty; dashing. **2.** dissolute. —**rak′ish·ly,** *adv.* —**rak′ish·ness,** *n.*

Ra·leigh (rô′lĭ), *n.* **1. Sir Walter,** 1552?-1618. British explorer, author. **2.** the capital of North Carolina, in the central part. 46,897.

ral·ly¹ (răl′ĭ), *v.,* **-lied, -lying,** *n., pl.* **-lies.** —*v.t.* **1.** to bring into order again. **2.** to call (persons) together for common action. **3.** to concentrate or revive, as one's strength, etc. —*v.i.*

4. to come together for common action. **5.** to come into order again. **6.** to come to the assistance of a person, party, or cause. **7.** to recover partially from illness. **8.** to acquire fresh strength or vigor. —*n.* **9.** a recovery from dispersion or disorder, as of troops. **10.** a renewal of strength, activity, etc. **11.** a coming together of persons, as in a mass meeting. **12.** *Tennis, etc.* the return of the ball by both sides a number of times consecutively.

ral·ly[2] (răl′ĭ), *v.t.*, **-lied, -lying.** to tease.

ram (răm), *n., v.,* **rammed, ramming.** —*n.* **1.** a male sheep. **2.** (*cap.*) the zodiacal constellation or sign Aries. **3.** any of various devices for battering, crushing, driving, or forcing something. —*v.t.* **4.** to drive by heavy blows. **5.** to strike with great force. **6.** to cram. —**ram′mer,** *n.*

ram·ble (răm′bəl), *v.,* **-bled, -bling,** *n.* —*v.i.* **1.** to wander about in a leisurely manner. **2.** to take a course with many turns or windings, as a plant, stream, or path. **3.** to talk or write without sequence of ideas. —*n.* **4.** a leisurely walk without a definite route. —**ram′bler,** *n.*

ram·bunc·tious (răm bŭngk′shəs), *adj.* *U.S. Colloq.* **1.** boisterous. **2.** perverse; unruly.

ram·e·kin (răm′ə kĭn), *n.* **1.** a portion of food baked separately in a small dish. **2.** the dish. Also, **ram′e·quin.**

ram·i·fy (răm′ə fī′), *v.t., v.i.,* **-fied, -fying.** to divide or spread out into branches or branchlike parts. —**ram′i·fi·ca′tion,** *n.*

ram·jet (răm′jĕt′), *n.* a jet-propulsion engine operated by the injection of fuel into a stream of air compressed by the forward speed of the aircraft.

ramp (rămp), *n.* **1.** a sloping surface connecting two different levels. —*v.i.* **2.** to leap or dash with fury.

ram·page (*n.* răm′pāj; *v.* răm pāj′), *n., v.,* **-paged, -paging.** —*n.* **1.** violent or excited behavior. **2.** an instance of this. —*v.i.* **3.** to rush, move, or act furiously or violently.

ramp·ant (răm′pənt), *adj.* **1.** violent in action, spirit, opinion, etc.; raging. **2.** in full sway; prevailing unbridled. **3.** standing on the hind legs. —**ramp′ant·ly,** *adv.*

ram·part (răm′pärt, -pərt), *n.* **1.** *Fort.* a broad mound of earth raised as a fortification about a place, usually having a parapet built upon it. **2.** anything serving as a bulwark or defense. —*v.t.* **3.** to furnish with a rampart.

ram·rod (răm′rŏd′), *n.* **1.** a rod for ramming down the charge of a muzzleloading firearm. **2.** a cleaning rod for the barrel of a rifle, etc.

ram·shack·le (răm′shăk′əl), *adj.* loosely made or held together; rickety; shaky.

ranch (rănch), *n.* **1.** an establishment maintained for production of livestock under range conditions where grass is the main source of feed. —*v.i.* **2.** to own, conduct, or work on a ranch. —**ranch′er, ranch′man,** *n.*

ran·cid (răn′sĭd), *adj.* rank, unpleasant, or stale in smell or taste. —**ran′cid·ness, ran·cid′i·ty,** *n.*

ran·cor (răng′kər), *n.* bitter, rankling resentment or ill-will; hatred; malice. Also, *Brit.,* **ran′cour.** —**ran′cor·ous,** *adj.*

ran·dom (răn′dəm), *adj.* **1.** going, made, occurring, etc., without definite aim, purpose, or reason. —*n.* **2.** at random, in a haphazard way.

range (rānj), *n., adj., v.,* **ranged, ranging.** —*n.* **1.** the limits between which variation is possible. **2.** the extent or scope of the operation or action of something. **3.** the distance of the target from the gun, etc. **4.** a place with targets for practice in shooting. **5.** the compass of a musical instrument or a voice. **6.** a row, line, or series. **7.** the region over which something is found or occurs. **8.** a chain of mountains. **9.** an extensive stretch of grazing ground. **10.** a type of stove for cooking, usually having one or more ovens, and openings on the top for heating various articles at once. —*adj.* **11.** of, or grazing on, a range. —*v.t.* **12.** to put in a row or rows. **13.** to arrange. **14.** to classify. **15.** to pass over (an area) in all directions, as in searching. **16.** to pasture (cattle) on a range. **17.** to vary within certain limits. —*v.i.* **18.** to extend in a line or in a certain direction. **19.** to take up a particular place or position. **20.** to move about or through a region in all directions, as persons, animals, etc. **21.** to rove, roam, or wander. **22.** to extend, be found, or occur.

rang·er (rān′jər), *n.* **1.** a warden employed to patrol a tract of forest. **2.** one of a body of armed men employed in ranging over a region. **3.** (*cap.*)

a U.S. soldier in World War II specially trained for making surprise raids and attacks in small groups.

Ran·goon (răng gōon′), *n.* a seaport in and the capital of Burma, in the S part. 400,415.

rang·y (rān′jĭ), *adj.,* **rangier, rangiest.** slender and long-limbed, as persons.

rank[1] (răngk), *n.* **1.** a number of persons forming a separate class in the social scale or in any graded body. **2.** position or standing. **3.** high position or station. **4.** a row, line, or series. **5.** (*pl.*) the lines or body of an army, etc. **6.** a line of persons standing abreast in close-order formation (distinguished from *file*). **7.** (*pl.*) enlisted men as distinguished from commissioned officers. —*v.t.* **8.** to arrange in a row. **9.** to arrange; classify. **10.** to assign to a particular position, station, class, etc. **11.** *U.S.* to outrank. —*v.i.* **12.** to occupy a place in a particular rank, class, etc. **13.** to have rank or standing. **14.** to be the senior in rank.

rank[2] (răngk), *adj.* **1.** growing with excessive luxuriance. **2.** producing an excessive and coarse growth, as land. **3.** having an offensively strong smell or taste. **4.** offensively strong, as smell. **5.** utter; absolute. —**rank′ly,** *adv.* —**rank′ness,** *n.*

rank and file, the body of an army or other organization, apart from officers.

ran·kle (răng′kəl), *v.i.,* **-kled, -kling.** (of unpleasant feelings, etc.) to keep up keen irritation or bitter resentment.

ran·sack (răn′săk), *v.t.* to search thoroughly or vigorously through (a house, receptacle, etc.), often for plunder.

ran·som (răn′səm), *n.* **1.** the redemption of a prisoner, kidnapped person, etc., for a price. **2.** the sum paid or demanded. —*v.t.* **3.** to redeem from captivity, bondage, detention, etc., by paying a price demanded.

rant (rănt), *v.i., v.t.* **1.** to speak in a wild or vehement way. —*n.* **2.** wild, violent declamation. **3.** a ranting utterance. —**rant′er,** *n.*

rap[1] (răp), *v.,* **rapped, rapping,** *n.* —*v.t., v.i.* **1.** to strike, esp. with a quick, smart blow. —*n.* **2.** a quick, smart, or light blow.

rap[2] (răp), *n.* the least bit.

ra·pa·cious (rə pā′shəs), *adj.* **1.** given to seizing for plunder or the satisfaction of greed. **2.** inordinately greedy; predatory. **3.** (of animals) subsisting by the capture of living prey. —**ra·pa′cious·ly,** *adv.* —**ra·pac·i·ty** (rə păs′ə tĭ), *n.*

rape[1] (rāp), *n., v.,* **raped, raping.** —*n.* **1.** act of seizing and carrying off by force. **2.** the forcible violation of a woman. —*v.t., v.i.* **3.** to seize, take, or carry off by force. **4.** to plunder. **5.** to commit rape (on). —**rap′ist,** *n.*

rape[2] (rāp), *n.* a small plant whose leaves are used as a food for sheep, etc., and whose seeds yield **rape oil.**

Raph·a·el (răf′ĭ əl, rā′fĭ-), *n.* **1.** 1483–1520, Italian painter. **2.** one of the archangels.

rap·id (răp′ĭd), *adj.* **1.** occurring, moving, or acting with great speed; swift. **2.** characterized by speed. —*n.* **3.** (*usually pl.*) a part of a river where the current runs very swiftly, as over a steep slope in the bed. —**rap′id·ly,** *adv.* —**rap′id·ness, ra·pid·i·ty** (rə pĭd′ə tĭ), *n.*

ra·pi·er (rā′pĭ ər), *n.* a sword with a slender blade, used only for thrusting.

rap·ine (răp′ĭn), *n.* the violent seizure of property of others; plunder.

rap·port (ră pôrt′), *n.* harmonious or sympathetic relation.

rap·scal·lion (răp skăl′yən), *n.* a rascal.

rapt (răpt), *adj.* **1.** deeply engrossed or absorbed. **2.** enraptured.

rap·to·ri·al (răp tōr′ĭ əl), *adj.* **1.** predatory. **2.** adapted for seizing prey.

rap·ture (răp′chər), *n.* **1.** ecstatic joy or delight. **2.** (*often pl.*) an utterance or expression of ecstatic delight. —**rap′tur·ous,** *adj.* —**rap′tur·ous·ly,** *adv.*

rare[1] (râr), *adj.,* **rarer, rarest.** **1.** unusual; uncommon. **2.** having the component parts not closely compacted together, as gases. —**rare′ly,** *adv.* —**rare′ness,** *n.*

rare[2] (râr), *adj.,* **rarer, rarest.** (of meat) not thoroughly cooked; underdone.

rare·bit (râr′bĭt), *n.* Welsh rabbit.

rare earth, *Chem.* the oxide of any of the rare-earth elements (a group of closely related metallic elements of atomic number 57 to 71 inclusive).

rar·e·fy (râr′ə fī′), v., -fied, -fying. —v.t. 1. to make rare, more rare, or less dense. 2. to refine. —v.i. 3. to become rare or less dense. —rar·e·fac·tion (râr′ə făk′shən), n.

rar·i·ty (râr′ə tĭ), n., pl. -ties. 1. something unusual or uncommon. 2. rare state or quality. 3. infrequency. 4. thinness, as of a gas.

ras·cal (răs′kəl), n. a base, dishonest person. —ras′cal·ly, adj., adv. —ras·cal·i·ty (răs kăl′ə tĭ), n.

rash[1] (răsh), adj. 1. acting too hastily or without due consideration. 2. characterized by such action. —rash′ly, adv. —rash′ness, n.

rash[2] (răsh), n. an eruption on the skin.

rash·er (răsh′ər), n. a thin slice of bacon or ham for frying or broiling.

rasp (răsp, räsp), v.t. 1. to scrape or abrade with a rough instrument. 2. to irritate (the nerves, feelings, etc.). 3. to utter with a grating sound. —n. 4. act of rasping. 5. a rasping sound. 6. a coarse form of file, having separate pointlike teeth.

rasp·ber·ry (răz′bĕr′ĭ, räz′-), n., pl. -ries. 1. the fruit of certain shrubs of the rose family, consisting of small juicy red, black, or pale-yellow drupelets. 2. Slang. a sound expressing derision or contempt made with the tongue between the lips.

Ras·pu·tin (răs pū′tĭn), n. Grigori Efimovich, 1871–1916, Siberian peasant who exerted great influence over Czar Nicholas II.

rat (răt), n., v., ratted, ratting. —n. 1. any of certain long-tailed rodents, distinguished from the mouse by being larger. 2. any of various similar or related animals. 3. Slang. one who abandons his associates, esp. in time of trouble. 4. U.S. Colloq. a roll of hair or other material used as a pad by women to puff out the hair. —v.i. 5. Slang. to desert one's associates, esp. in time of trouble. 6. Slang. to behave like a mean, cowardly person. 7. to hunt or catch rats.

rat·a·ble (rā′tə bəl), adj. capable of being rated or appraised. —rat′a·bil′i·ty, n.

ratch·et (răch′ĭt), n. a wheel or bar with teeth on the edge, into which a pawl drops or catches, as to prevent reversal of motion or convert reciprocating into rotatory motion.

rate (rāt), n., v., rated, rating. —n. 1. the amount of a charge or payment with reference to some basis of calculation. 2. a fixed charge per unit of quantity. 3. price. 4. degree of speed, progress, etc. 5. degree or comparative extent of action or procedure. 6. grade, class, or sort. 7. at any rate, a. under any circumstances. b. at least. —v.t. 8. to estimate the value of. 9. to consider. 10. to fix at a certain rate. —v.i. 11. to have value, standing, etc. 12. to have position in a certain class.

rath·er (răth′ər, räth′ər), adv. 1. somewhat. 2. (with verbs) in some degree. 3. more properly or justly. 4. sooner or more readily or willingly. 5. in preference. 6. more truly. 7. on the contrary.

raths·kel·ler (räts′kĕl′ər), n. a restaurant of the German type, usually in a cellar or basement.

rat·i·fy (răt′ə fī′), v.t., -fied, -fying. to confirm by expressing consent, approval, or formal sanction. —rat′i·fi·ca′tion, n. —rat′i·fi′er, n.

rat·ing (rā′tĭng), n. 1. classification according to grade or rank. 2. Naut. assigned position in a particular class or grade. 3. a credit standing. 4. an amount fixed as a rate.

ra·tio (rā′shō, -shĭ ō′), n., pl. -tios. the relation between two similar magnitudes in respect to the number of times the first contains the second.

ra·ti·oc·i·na·tion (răsh′ĭ ŏs′ə nā′shən), n. reasoning. —ra′ti·oc′i·na′tive, adj.

ra·tion (răsh′ən, rā′shən), n. 1. a fixed allowance, as of provisions or food. —v.t. 2. to apportion by some method of allowance. 3. to restrict to rations. 4. to supply with rations. —ra′tion·ing, n.

ra·tion·al (răsh′ən əl), adj. 1. agreeable to reason; sensible. 2. having reason or good sense. 3. sane; lucid. 4. endowed with reason. 5. based on reasoning. 6. Arith. expressible as the quotient of two integers. —ra′tion·al·ly, adv. —ra·tion·al·i·ty (răsh′ə năl′ə tĭ), n.

ra·tion·al·ism (răsh′ən ə lĭz′əm, răsh′nə-), n. 1. the principle of accepting reason as the supreme authority in matters of opinion, belief, or conduct. 2. Philos. the theory that reason is in itself a source of knowledge, independent of the senses. —ra′tion·al·ist, n., adj. —ra′tion·al·is′tic, adj.

ra·tion·al·ize (răsh′ən ə līz′, răsh′nə), v., -ized, -izing. —v.t. 1. Psychol. to invent a rational, acceptable explanation for (unconscious behavior). 2. to make rational. —v.i. 3. to employ reason. —ra′tion·al·i·za′tion, n. —ra′tion·al·iz′er, n.

rat·line (răt′lĭn), n. Naut. any of the small ropes which traverse the shrouds horizontally, serving as steps for going aloft.

rats·bane (răts′bān′), n. rat poison.

rat·tan (ră tăn′), n. any of certain climbing palms whose tough stems are used for wickerwork, canes, etc.

rat·tle (răt′əl), v., -tled, -tling, n. —v.i. 1. to make a rapid succession of short, sharp sounds. 2. to move or go, esp. rapidly, with such sounds. 3. to talk rapidly; chatter. —v.t. 4. to cause to rattle. 5. to drive, send, etc., esp. rapidly, with rattling. 6. to utter or perform in a rapid or lively manner. 7. Colloq. to disconcert or confuse (a person). —n. 8. a rapid succession of short, sharp sounds from the collision of hard bodies. 9. a child's toy that makes a rattling sound.

rat·tler (răt′lər), n. 1. a rattlesnake. 2. one that rattles.

rat·tle·snake (răt′əl snāk′), n. any of certain venomous American snakes having several loosely articulated horny rings at the end of the tail, which produce a rattling sound when shaken.

rat·tle·trap (răt′əl trăp′), n. a shaky, rattling object, as a rickety vehicle.

rau·cous (rô′kəs), adj. hoarse; harsh of voice or sound. —rau′cous·ly, adv.

rav·age (răv′ĭj), n., v., -aged, -aging. —n. 1. devastation, havoc, or ruinous damage. —v.t., v.i. 2. to work havoc (upon); ruin. —rav′ag·er, n.

rave (rāv), v., raved, raving, n. —v.i. 1. to talk wildly, as in delirium. 2. (of wind, storms, etc.) to rage. 3. Colloq. to talk with extravagant enthusiasm. —n. 4. act of raving.

rav·el (răv′əl), v., -eled, -eling or (esp. Brit.) -elled, -elling, n. —v.t., v.i. 1. to disengage the threads of (a fabric, a rope, etc.). 2. to tangle or entangle. 3. to perplex. —n. 4. a tangle. 5. an unraveled thread.

Ra·vel (rä vĕl′), n. Maurice, 1875–1937, French composer.

rav·el·ing (răv′əl ĭng), n. something raveled out, as a thread from a knitted fabric. Also, esp. Brit., rav′el·ling.

ra·ven (rā′vən), n. 1. any of several large birds of the crow family with lustrous black plumage and raucous voices. —adj. 2. lustrous black.

rav·en·ing (răv′ən ĭng), adj. 1. rapacious; voracious. —n. 2. rapacity.

rav·en·ous (răv′ən əs), adj. 1. extremely hungry. 2. extremely rapacious. 3. voracious or gluttonous. 4. predatory. —rav′en·ous·ly, adv. —rav′en·ous·ness, n.

ra·vine (rə vēn′), n. a long, deep, narrow valley, esp. one worn by water.

rav·ing (rā′vĭng), adj. 1. delirious. 2. Colloq. extraordinary. —n. 3. irrational, incoherent talk.

ra·vi·o·li (rä′vĭ ō′lĭ, răv′ĭ-), n. pl. small pieces of paste enclosing ground meat (and often spinach), cooked, and served in soup or otherwise.

rav·ish (răv′ĭsh), v.t. 1. to fill with strong emotion, esp. joy. 2. to seize and carry off by force. 3. to rape. —rav′ish·er, n. —rav′ish·ment, n.

rav·ish·ing (răv′ĭsh ĭng), adj. entrancing.

raw (rô), adj. 1. not yet prepared, refined, etc.; in the natural state. 2. uncooked. 3. painfully exposed or open, as a sore, wound, etc. 4. crude in quality or character. 5. ignorant, inexperienced, or untrained. 6. brutally or grossly frank. 7. Slang. brutally unfair. 8. damp and chilly, as the weather. —n. 9. the raw, sore, or naked flesh. —raw′ly, adv. —raw′ness, n.

raw·boned (rô′bōnd′), adj. having little flesh on the bones; gaunt.

raw·hide (rô′hīd′), n., v., -hided, -hiding. —n. 1. the untanned skin of cattle or other animals. 2. a rope or whip made of this. —v.t. 3. to whip with a rawhide.

ray[1] (rā), n. 1. a narrow beam of light. 2. a slight manifestation of intelligence, comfort, etc. 3. Physics. a. any of the lines or streams in which light or radiant energy appears to issue from a luminous object. b. a stream of material particles moving in the same line. 4. any of a system of parts radially arranged. —v.i. 5. to emit rays. —ray′less, adj.

ray[2] (rā), *n.* an elasmobranch fish, with a flat body fitted for life on the sea bottom.

ray·on (rā'ŏn), *n.* a silklike fabric woven of fibers synthetically made from cellulose.

raze (rāz), *v.t.*, **razed, razing.** to tear down, demolish, or level to the ground.

ra·zor (rā'zǝr), *n.* a sharp-edged instrument used esp. for shaving the face.

ra·zor·back (rā'zǝr băk'), *n.* a wild or semi-wild hog with a ridgelike back, common in the southern U.S.

razz (răz), *v.t. U.S. Slang.* to deride.

Rb, *Chem.* rubidium.

R.C. 1. Red Cross. 2. Roman Catholic.

Rd, *Chem.* radium.

rd., 1. (*also cap.*) road. 2. rod; rods.

re[1] (rā, rē), *n. Music.* the syllable used for the second tone of a scale.

re[2] (rē), *prep.* with reference to.

Re, *Chem.* rhenium.

re–, 1. a prefix indicating repetition, as in *reprint*, *rebirth.* 2. a prefix related to the preceding indicating withdrawal or backward motion, often figurative like "back," applied often to stems not used as words, as in *revert, retract.*

reach (rēch), *v.t.* 1. to get or come to; arrive at. 2. to touch or seize with an outstretched hand, a pole, etc. 3. to hold out; extend. 4. to extend so as to touch or meet. 5. to establish communication with. 6. to amount to. 7. to influence. —*v.i.* 8. to stretch, as with the arm. 9. to become outstretched, as the arm. 10. to make a movement or effort as if to touch or seize something. 11. to extend in distance, time, or effect. —*n.* 12. act of reaching. 13. the extent of reaching. 14. range of effective action, power, or capacity. 15. a continuous stretch or extent of something.

re·act (rĭ ăkt'), *v.i.* 1. to act reciprocally upon each other. 2. to act in a reverse direction or manner. 3. to act in opposition. 4. to respond to a stimulus.

re·act·ance (rĭ ăk'tǝns), *n. Elect.* that part of the impedance of an alternating-current circuit which is due to inductance and capacity.

re·ac·tion (rĭ ăk'shǝn), *n.* 1. a reverse movement or tendency, esp. toward political conservatism. 2. action in response to some influence, event, etc. 3. *Physiol.* action in response to a stimulus. 4. *Chem.* the reciprocal action of chemical agents upon each other.

re·ac·tion·ar·y (rĭ ăk'shǝ něr'ĭ), *adj., n., pl.* **-aries.** —*adj.* 1. of, pertaining to, marked by, or favoring reaction, as in politics. —*n.* 2. one who favors reaction.

read[1] (rēd), *v.,* **read** (rĕd), **reading.** —*v.t.* 1. to observe and understand the meaning of (something written or printed, gestures, etc.). 2. to render in speech (something written, printed, etc.). 3. to foresee, foretell, or predict. 4. to understand (something read or observed) in a particular way. 5. to register or indicate, as a thermometer. 6. *Brit.* to study. —*v.i.* 7. to read or peruse writing, printing, etc. 8. to render in speech written or printed words that one is perusing. 9. to admit of being read, esp. properly or well. —**read/a·ble,** *adj.* —**read/a·bil/-i·ty,** *n.* —**read/a·bly,** *adv.*

read[2] (rĕd), *adj.* having knowledge gained by reading.

read·er (rē'dǝr), *n.* 1. one who reads. 2. a schoolbook for instruction in reading. 3. one employed to read critically manuscripts, etc., offered for publication. 4. one who reads or recites before an audience. 5. *Chiefly Brit.* a lecturer or instructor. 6. an assistant to a professor, who grades examinations, etc.

read·ing (rē'dĭng), *n.* 1. the action or practice of one who reads. 2. the oral interpretation of written language. 3. the rendering given to a dramatic part, musical composition, etc. 4. literary knowledge. 5. matter read or for reading. 6. the version of a given passage. 7. the indication of a graduated instrument. —*adj.* 8. pertaining to, or used for, reading. 9. given to reading.

Read·ing (rĕd'ĭng), *n.* a city in SE Pennsylvania. 110,568.

read·y (rĕd'ĭ), *adj.,* **readier, readiest,** *v.,* **readied, readying,** *n.* —*adj.* 1. completely prepared for immediate action or use. 2. duly equipped, completed, adjusted, or arranged. 3. willing. 4. prompt or quick in perceiving, acting, speaking, writing, etc. 5. showing such quickness. 6. inclined, disposed, or apt. 7. likely or liable at any moment (to do something). 8. immediately available. —*v.t.* 9. to make ready; prepare. —*n.* 10. condition or position of being ready. —**read/i·ly,** *adv.* —**read/i·ness,** *n.*

re·a·gent (rē ā'jǝnt), *n.* a substance which, on account of the reactions it causes, is used in chemical analysis.

re·al[1] (rē'ǝl, rēl), *adj.* 1. true; actual. 2. genuine. 3. sincere. 4. *Philos.* a. existent, as opposed to nonexistent. b. actual, as opposed to possible or potential. 5. *Law.* denoting or pertaining to immovable property of a freehold type. —**re/al·ness,** *n.*

re·al[2] (rē'ǝl, rēl; *Sp.* rĕ äl'), *n., pl.* **reals** (rē'ǝlz, rēlz), *Sp.* **reales** (rĕ ä'lĕs). a former Spanish silver coin and money of account, still current in certain Spanish-American countries, equal to one eighth of a peso.

real estate, 1. ownership of lands, etc. 2. land and whatever by annexation is a part of it or is the means of its enjoyment, as minerals, trees, buildings, fences, etc.

re·al·ism (rē'ǝ lĭz'ǝm), *n.* 1. interest in or concern for the actual or real. 2. the tendency to view or represent things as they really are. 3. the treatment of subjects in literature or art with fidelity to nature or real life. 4. *Philos.* a. the doctrine that universals have a real objective existence. b. the doctrine that objects of sense perception have an existence independent of the act of perception. —**re/al·ist,** *n.* —**re/al·is/-tic,** *adj.* —**re/al·is/ti·cal·ly,** *adv.*

re·al·i·ty (rĭ ăl'ǝ tĭ), *n., pl.* **-ties.** 1. state or fact of being real. 2. a real thing or fact. 3. **in reality,** really.

re·al·ize (rē'ǝ līz'), *v.,* **-ized, -izing.** —*v.t.* 1. to grasp or understand clearly. 2. to make real. 3. to convert into cash. 4. to obtain as a profit or income. —*v.i.* 5. to convert property or goods into cash or money. Also, *esp. Brit.,* **re/al·ise/.** —**re/al·iz/a·ble,** *adj.* —**re·al·iz/er,** *n.* —**re·al·i·za·tion** (rē'ǝ lǝ zā'shǝn), *n.*

re·al·ly (rē'ǝ lĭ, rē'lĭ), *adv.* 1. actually. 2. genuinely or truly. 3. indeed.

realm (rĕlm), *n.* 1. a kingdom. 2. the region, sphere, or domain within which anything prevails. 3. the special field of something.

re·al·tor (rē'ǝl tǝr, -tôr'), *n.* a real estate broker.

re·al·ty (rē'ǝl tĭ), *n.* real estate.

ream[1] (rēm), *n.* a standard quantity among paper dealers meaning 20 quires.

ream[2] (rēm), *v.t.* to enlarge (a hole) to size by means of a reamer.

ream·er (rē'mǝr), *n.* a rotating tool with spiral or straight fluted cutting edges for finishing a hole to size and shape.

reap (rēp), *v.t.* 1. to cut (grain, etc.), as in harvest. 2. to gather (a crop, harvest, etc.). 3. to get as a return. —*v.i.* 4. to reap grain, etc. —**reap/er,** *n.*

rear[1] (rĭr), *n.* 1. the back of anything. 2. the space or position behind anything. 3. the hindmost portion. —*adj.* 4. situated at or pertaining to the rear. —**rear/most/,** *adj.*

rear[2] (rĭr), *v.t.* 1. to care for and support up to maturity. 2. to erect. 3. to raise, esp. to an upright position. —*v.i.* 4. to rise on the hind legs, as a horse or other animal.

rear admiral, a naval officer next in rank below a vice-admiral.

rear·ward (rĭr'wǝrd), *adj., adv.* toward or in the rear.

rea·son (rē'zǝn), *n.* 1. a cause for a belief, action, fact, event, etc. 2. a statement in justification or explanation of a belief or action. 3. the mental powers concerned with drawing conclu-

---

re'ab·sorb'	re'ad·dress'	re'ad·vance'	re'ap·point'
re'ab·sorp'tion	re'ad·journ'	re'af·firm'	re'ap·point'ment
re'ac·cept'	re'ad·just'	re'af·fir·ma'tion	re'ap·por'tion
re'ac·com'mo-date'	re'ad·just'ment	re'a·noint'	re·arm'
re'ac·com'pa·ny	re·ad·mis'sion	re'ap·pear'	re·ar'ma·ment
re'ac·cuse'	re·ad·mit'	re'ap·pear'ance	re·ar·range'
re'a·dapt'	re·ad·mit'tance	re'ap·pli·ca'tion	re·ar·range'ment
	re'a·dopt'	re'ap·ply'	re'as·cend'

sions or inferences. **4.** sound judgment. **5.** sanity. —*v.i.* **6.** to think or argue in a logical manner. —*v.t.* **7.** to think out (a problem, etc.) logically. **8.** to conclude or infer. —**rea′son·er,** *n.*

rea·son·a·ble (rē′zən ə bəl, rēz′nə-), *adj.* **1.** agreeable to reason. **2.** not excessive. **3.** moderate, esp. in price. **4.** endowed with reason. —**rea′son·a·ble·ness,** *n.* —**rea′son·a·bly,** *adv.*

rea·son·ing (rē′zən ĭng), *n.* **1.** act or process of one who reasons. **2.** the reasons, proofs, etc., resulting from this process. Also, **rea′beck.**

re·as·sure (rē′ə shŏŏr′), *v.t.,* **-sured, -suring.** to restore (a person, etc.) to assurance or confidence. —**re′as·sur′ance,** *n.* —**re′as·sur′ing·ly,** *adv.*

re·bate (rē′bāt, rĭ bāt′), *n., v.,* **-bated, -bating.** —*n.* **1.** a return of part of an original amount paid for some service or merchandise. **2.** repayment. —*v.t.* **3.** to allow as a discount.

re·bec (rē′bĕk), *n.* a small medieval fiddle having commonly a pear-shaped body and three strings. Also, **re′beck.**

Re·bec·ca (rĭ bĕk′ə), *n. Bible.* the wife of Isaac and. mother of Esau and Jacob.

reb·el (*n., adj.* rĕb′əl; *v.* rĭ bĕl′), *n., adj., v.,* **-belled, -belling.** —*n.* **1.** one who refuses allegiance to. resists, or rises in arms against the rightful government or ruler. **2.** one who resists any authority or control. —*adj.* **3.** rebellious. **4.** of or pertaining to rebels. —*v.i.* **5.** to rise in arms or active resistance against one's government or ruler. **6.** to resist any authority.

re·bel·lion (rĭ bĕl′yən), *n.* **1.** open, organized, and armed resistance to one's government or ruler. **2.** resistance against or defiance of any authority or control.

re·bel·lious (rĭ bĕl′yəs), *adj.* **1.** defying lawful authority. **2.** pertaining to or characteristic of rebels or rebellion. —**re·bel′lious·ly,** *adv.* —**re·bel′lious·ness,** *n.*

re·birth (rē bûrth′, rē′bûrth′), *n.* **1.** being born again. **2.** a new activity or growth.

re·bound (*v.* rĭ bound′; *n.* rē′bound′, rĭ-bound′), *v.i.* **1.** to bound back from force of impact. —*v.t.* **2.** to cause to bound back. —*n.* **3.** act of rebounding; recoil.

re·buff (rĭ bŭf′), *n.* **1.** a blunt or abrupt check, as to one making advances. **2.** a peremptory refusal. —*v.t.* **3.** to check; repel; refuse.

re·buke (rĭ būk′), *v.,* **-buked, -buking,** *n.* —*v.t.* **1.** to reprimand. —*n.* **2.** a reprimand.

re·bus (rē′bəs), *n.* an enigmatical representation of a word or phrase by pictures; symbols, etc., suggesting the word elements or words.

re·but (rĭ bŭt′), *v.t.,* **-butted,-butting.** to refute or oppose.

re·but·tal (rĭ bŭt′əl), *n.* act of rebutting.

rec., **1.** receipt. **2.** recipe. **3.** record.

re·cal·ci·trant (rĭ kăl′sə trənt), *adj.* **1.** resisting authority or control; not obedient or compliant. —*n.* **2.** a recalcitrant person. —**re·cal′ci·trance, re·cal′ci·tran·cy,** *n.*

re·call (*v.* rĭ kôl′; *n.* rĭ kôl′, rē′kôl′), *v.t.* **1.** to recollect or remember. **2.** to call back. **3.** to revoke or withdraw. —*n.* **4.** act of recalling. **5.** the removal of a public official from office by a vote of the people.

re·cant (rĭ kănt′), *v.t., v.i.* to withdraw or disavow (a statement, etc.); retract. —**re·can·ta·tion** (rē′kăn tā′shən), *n.*

re·ca·pit·u·late (rē′kə pĭch′ə lāt′), *v.t., v.i.,* **-lated, -lating.** to review (statements, reasons, etc.) in an orderly summary. —**re′ca·pit′u·la′tion,** *n.*

re·cap·ture (rē kăp′chər), *v.,* **-tured, -turing,** *n.* —*v.t.* **1.** to capture again; retake. —*n.* **2.** recovery or retaking by capture.

re·cast (*v.* rē kăst′, -käst′; *n.* rē′kăst′, -käst′), *v.,* **-cast, -casting,** *n.* —*v.t.* **1.** to cast or form again or anew. —*n.* **2.** a recasting.

recd., received. Also, **rec′d.**

re·cede (rĭ sēd′), *v.i.,* **-ceded, -ceding. 1.** to go or move back. **2.** to become more distant. **3.** to slope backward.

re·ceipt (rĭ sēt′), *n.* **1.** a written acknowledgment of having received money, goods, etc.,

specified. **2.** (*pl.*) the amount received. **3.** act of receiving. **4.** that which is received. **5.** a recipe. —*v.t., v.i.* **6.** to give a receipt (for).

re·ceiv·a·ble (rĭ sē′və bəl), *adj.* **1.** fit for acceptance. **2.** awaiting receipt of payment.

re·ceive (rĭ sēv′), *v.,* **-ceived, -ceiving.** —*v.t.* **1.** to take (something offered or delivered). **2.** to have delivered or brought to oneself. **3.** to get or learn. **4.** to become the support of; sustain. **5.** to contain. **6.** to meet with; experience. **7.** to have inflicted upon one. **8.** to be at home to (visitors). **9.** to welcome (guests, etc.) upon arriving. **10.** to admit to a condition, privilege, membership, etc. **11.** to accept. —*v.i.* **12.** to receive something. **13.** to receive guests. **14.** *Radio.* to convert incoming electromagnetic waves into the original signal, as sound waves.

re·ceiv·er (rĭ sē′vər), *n.* **1.** one that receives. **2.** a device which receives electrical signals, waves, or the like, and renders them perceptible to the senses, as a radio or television set. **3.** *Law.* a person appointed by a court to take charge of a business or property of others, pending litigation. **4.** a receptacle. —**re·ceiv′er·ship′,** *n.*

re·cent (rē′sənt), *adj.* of late occurrence, appearance, or origin. —**re′cen·cy, re′cent·ness,** *n.* —**re′cent·ly,** *adv.*

re·cep·ta·cle (rĭ sĕp′tə kəl), *n.* that which serves to receive or hold something; container.

re·cep·tion (rĭ sĕp′shən), *n.* **1.** act of receiving. **2.** fact of being received. **3.** manner of being received. **4.** a function or occasion when persons are formally received.

re·cep·tion·ist (rĭ sĕp′shən ĭst), *n.* a person employed to receive callers, as in an office.

re·cep·tive (rĭ sĕp′tĭv), *adj.* **1.** having the quality of receiving, taking in, or admitting. **2.** quick to receive ideas, etc.; favorably inclined. —**re·cep′tive·ly,** *adv.* —**re·cep·tiv·i·ty** (rē′sĕp-tĭv′ə tĭ), **re·cep′tive·ness,** *n.*

re·cep·tor (rĭ sĕp′tər), *n. Physiol.* the end organs of sensory or afferent neurons, specialized to be sensitive to stimulating agents.

re·cess (*n.* rĭ sĕs′, rē′sĕs; *v.* rĭ sĕs′), *n.* **1.** temporary withdrawal from the usual work or activity. **2.** a period of such withdrawal. **3.** a receding part, as an alcove or bay. **4.** (*pl.*) a secluded or inner part. —*v.t.* **5.** to place in a recess. **6.** to make a recess or recesses in. —*v.i.* **7.** to take a recess.

re·ces·sion (rĭ sĕsh′ən), *n.* **1.** act of withdrawing. **2.** a receding part of a wall, etc. **3.** a procession at the end of a service. **4.** a temporary decline in business during a period of generally increasing prosperity.

re·ces·sion·al (rĭ sĕsh′ən əl), *adj.* **1.** of or pertaining to a recession of the clergy and choir after the service. —*n.* **2.** a recessional hymn, or music for it.

re·ces·sive (rĭ sĕs′ĭv), *adj.* **1.** tending to recede. **2.** *Biol.* tending to be suppressed by a more active gene.

Re·ci·fe (rĕ sē′fə), *n.* a seaport in E Brazil. 384,422.

rec·i·pe (rĕs′ə pē′), *n.* **1.** any formula, esp. one for preparing a dish in cookery. **2.** a medical prescription.

re·cip·i·ent (rĭ sĭp′ĭ ənt), *n.* **1.** a receiver. —*adj.* **2.** receiving or capable of receiving.

re·cip·ro·cal (rĭ sĭp′rə kəl), *adj.* **1.** given, felt, etc., by each to or toward each; mutual. —*n.* **2.** a thing that is reciprocal to something else. —**re·cip′ro·cal·ly,** *adv.*

re·cip·ro·cate (rĭ sĭp′rə kāt′), *v.t., v.i.,* **-cated, -cating. 1.** to give, feel, etc., in return. **2.** to move, or cause to move, alternately backward and forward. —**re·cip′ro·ca′tion,** *n.*

rec·i·proc·i·ty (rĕs′ə prŏs′ə tĭ), *n.* **1.** reciprocal state or relation. **2.** that relation between countries by which corresponding commercial advantages are mutually granted.

re·cit·al (rĭ sī′təl), *n.* **1.** a musical entertainment given usually by a single performer. **2.** an account, narrative, or description.

rec·i·ta·tive (rĕs′ə tə tēv′), *n. Music.* **1.** a style of vocal music intermediate between speaking and singing. **2.** a passage, part, or piece in this style.

re′as·sem′ble	re′as·so′ci·ate	re·bap′tism	re·cap′i·tal·ize′
re′as·sem′bly	re′as·sume′	re′bap·tize′	re·charge′
re′as·sert′	re′as·sump′-	re·bill′	re·char′ter
re′as·ser′tion	tion	re·bind′	re·check′
re′as·sess′	re′at·tach′	re·born′	re·choose′
re′as·sign′	re′at·tain′	re·broad′cast′	re·chris′ten
re′as·sign′-	re′at·tempt′	re·build′	re·cir′cle
ment	re′a·wak′en	re·built′	re·cir′cu·late′

re·cite (rǐ sīt'), v., -cited, -citing. —v.t. **1.** to repeat the words of, as from memory, esp. in a formal manner. **2.** to repeat (a piece of poetry or prose) before an audience, as for entertainment. **3.** to give an account of. —v.i. **4.** to recite a lesson, or part of a lesson, before a teacher. **5.** to repeat something from memory. —**rec·i·ta·tion** (rĕs'ə tā'shən), n. —**re·cit'er,** n.

reck (rĕk), v.i. to care or heed.

reck·less (rĕk'lĭs), adj. utterly careless or imprudent. —**reck'less·ly,** adv. —**reck'less·ness,** n.

reck·on (rĕk'ən), v.t., v.i. **1.** to count; compute. **2.** to esteem or consider. **3.** Colloq. or Dial. to think or suppose. **4.** to depend or rely (on), as in expectation. **5.** to deal (with), as with something to be taken into account. —**reck'on·er,** n.

reck·on·ing (rĕk'ən ĭng), n. **1.** count; computation. **2.** the settlement of accounts, as between parties. **3.** a bill. **4.** an accounting, as for things received or done.

re·claim (rǐ klām'), v.t. **1.** to bring (land) into a condition for cultivation or other use. **2.** to recover (substances) in a pure or usable form from refuse matter, articles, etc. **3.** to bring back to right living, ideas, etc. —n. **4.** act of reclaiming. —**rec·la·ma·tion** (rĕk'lə mā'shən), n.

re·cline (rǐ klīn'), v.i., -clined, -clining. to lean or lie back.

rec·luse (n. rĕk'lōōs, rǐ klōōs'; adj. rǐ klōōs'), **1.** a person who lives in seclusion, often for religious meditation. —adj. **2.** living in seclusion, often for religious reasons.

rec·og·ni·tion (rĕk'əg nǐsh'ən), n. act of recognizing, or state of being recognized; realization, acknowledgment, or attention.

re·cog·ni·zance (rǐ kŏg'nə zəns, -kŏn'ə-), n. **1.** act of recognizing. **2.** Law. a bond pledging a person to do a particular act. **b.** the sum pledged as surety on such a bond.

rec·og·nize (rĕk'əg nīz'), v., -nized, -nizing. —v.t. **1.** to perceive to be identical with something previously known. **2.** to identify from knowledge of appearance or character. **3.** to perceive as existing or true; realize. **4.** to acknowledge as the person entitled to speak at the particular time. **5.** to acknowledge formally as existing or as entitled to consideration. **6.** to acknowledge or accept formally as being something stated. **7.** to acknowledge or treat as valid. **8.** to acknowledge acquaintance with (a person, etc.), as by a salute. **9.** to show appreciation of (kindness, merit, etc.), as by some reward or tribute. —v.i. **10.** Law. to enter into a recognizance. —**rec'og·niz'a·ble,** adj.

re·coil (rǐ koil' for 1–3; rē- for 4; rē'koil' for 5), v.i. **1.** to draw or shrink back, as in disgust. **2.** to spring back, as a discharged firearm does. **3.** to react. —n. **4.** act of recoiling. **5.** the distance a weapon recoils.

re·col·lect (rĕk'ə lĕkt'), v.t., v.i. to recall to mind; remember. —**rec'ol·lec'tion,** n.

re·col·lect (rē'kə lĕkt'), v.t. **1.** to collect together again. **2.** to compose (oneself).

rec·om·mend (rĕk'ə mĕnd'), v.t. **1.** to commend as worthy of confidence, use, etc. **2.** to urge as advisable or expedient. **3.** to advise. —**rec'om·men·da'tion,** n. —**rec'om·mend·a·to'ry,** adj.

re·com·mit (rē'kə mǐt'), v.t., -mitted, -mitting. **1.** to commit again. **2.** to refer again to a committee. —**re'com·mit'ment,** n.

rec·om·pense (rĕk'əm pĕns'), v., -pensed, -pensing, n. —v.t. **1.** to repay, remunerate, reward, or requite for service, aid, etc. —n. **2.** compensation made, as for service, loss, injury, or wrong.

rec·on·cile (rĕk'ən sīl'), v.t., -ciled, -ciling. **1.** to render no longer opposed. **2.** to win over to friendliness. **3.** to settle (a quarrel, etc.). **4.** to bring into agreement or harmony. —**rec'on·cil'a·ble,** adj. —**rec'on·cil'a·bly,** adv.

rec·on·cil·i·a·tion (rĕk'ən sǐl'ĭ ā'shən), n. **1.** act of reconciling. **2.** state of being reconciled. —**rec'on·cil'i·a·to'ry,** adj.

rec·on·dite (rĕk'ən dīt', rǐ kŏn'dīt), adj. **1.** abstruse; profound. **2.** little known; obscure.

re·con·nais·sance (rǐ kŏn'ə səns), n. **1.** act of reconnoitering. **2.** Mil. a search for useful mili-

tary information in the field, as by a scouting party.

re·con·noi·ter (rē'kə noi'tər, rĕk'ə-), v.t., v.i. to inspect or survey (a region, etc.), esp. to gain information for military purposes. Also, esp. Brit., re**'con·noi'tre.**

re·con·sid·er (rē'kən sǐd'ər), v.t., v.i. to consider again, esp. with a view to a change of decision. —**re'con·sid'er·a'tion,** n.

re·con·struct (rē'kən strŭkt'), v.t. to construct again; rebuild. —**re'con·struc'tive,** adj.

re·con·struc·tion (rē'kən strŭk'shən), n. **1.** act of reconstructing. **2.** (cap.) U.S. Hist. the process by which the States which had seceded were reorganized as a part of the Union after the Civil War.

re·cord (v. rǐ kôrd'; n., adj. rĕk'ərd), v.t. **1.** to set down in writing or the like, as for future use. **2.** to cause to be registered. **3.** to serve to tell of. **4.** to set down, register, or fix by marks, incisions, magnetism, etc., for the purpose of reproduction by a phonograph or magnetic reproducer. —v.i. **5.** to record something. —n. **6.** act of recording. **7.** state or fact of being recorded. **8.** an account in writing or the like preserving knowledge of facts. **9.** information preserved in writing or the like. **10.** a report, list, or aggregate of actions or achievements. **11.** the tracing, marking, or the like, made by a recording instrument. **12.** a cylinder, disk, or other device having characteristic markings or the like for reproducing sound, as in a phonograph. **13.** the best rate, amount, etc., attained, as in some form of sport. **14.** an official writing intended to be preserved. —adj. **15.** making or affording a record. **16.** notable in the degree of attainment.

re·cord·er (rǐ kôr'dər), n. **1.** one who records, esp. as an official duty. **2.** a device to record sound by varying the magnetism in a moving steel wire or tape. **3.** a soft-toned flute played in vertical position.

re·count (rǐ kount'), v.t. **1.** to relate or narrate. **2.** to enumerate.

re·count (v. rē kount'; n. rē'kount', rē kount'), v.t. **1.** to count again. —n. **2.** a second or additional count.

re·coup (rǐ kōōp'), v.t. **1.** to provide or be an equivalent for. **2.** to yield in return. **3.** to reimburse. —n. **4.** act of recouping. —**re·coup'ment,** n.

re·course (rē'kōrs, rǐ kōrs'), n. resort to a person or thing for help or protection.

re·cov·er (rǐ kŭv'ər), v.t. **1.** to regain (something lost or taken away). **2.** to reclaim. —v.i. **3.** to regain health after sickness, etc. **4.** to regain a former (and better) condition. **5.** to regain one's composure, balance, etc. —**re·cov'er·a·ble,** adj.

re·cov·er (rē kŭv'ər), v.t. to cover again.

re·cov·er·y (rǐ kŭv'ə rǐ), n., pl. -eries. **1.** act of recovering. **2.** the regaining of something lost or taken away. **3.** return to health from sickness. **4.** return to a former (and better) condition.

rec·re·ant (rĕk'rǐ ənt), adj. **1.** cowardly. **2.** unfaithful; false. —n. **3.** a coward. **4.** a traitor. —**rec're·ance, rec're·an·cy,** n.

rec·re·ate (rĕk'rǐ āt'), v.t., v.i., -ated, -ating. to refresh (oneself) by means of relaxation and enjoyment, as after work. —**rec're·a'tion,** n. —**rec're·a'tion·al,** adj.

re·cre·ate (rē'krǐ āt'), v.t., -ated, -ating. to create anew. —**re'·cre·a'tion,** n.

re·crim·i·nate (rǐ krǐm'ə nāt'), v.i., v.t., -nated, -nating. to bring a countercharge against (an accuser). —**re·crim'i·na'tion,** n.

re·cruit (rǐ krōōt'), n. **1.** a newly enlisted or drafted soldier or sailor. **2.** a new member of any group, as (U.S. Army) a soldier of the lowest rank. —v.t., v.i. **3.** to enlist (men) for military or naval service. **4.** to raise (a force) by enlistment. **5.** to furnish with a fresh supply. —**re·cruit'er,** n. —**re·cruit'ment,** n.

rec·tan·gle (rĕk'tăng'gəl), n. a parallelogram with all its angles right angles. —**rec·tan'gu·lar,** adj.

rec·ti·fy (rĕk'tə fī'), v.t., -fied, -fying. **1.** to remedy; correct. **2.** to put right by adjustment or calculation. **3.** Chem. to purify (esp. a spirit or liquor) by repeated distillation. **4.** Elect. to

Rectangle

change (an alternating current) into a direct current. —rec′ti·fi′a·ble, *adj.* —rec′ti·fi·ca′-tion, *n.* —rec′ti·fi′er, *n.*

rec·ti·lin·e·ar (rĕk′tə lĭn′ĭ ər), *adj.* 1. forming a straight line. 2. formed by straight lines.

rec·ti·tude (rĕk′tə tūd′, -tŏŏd′), *n.* 1. right-ness of principle or practice. 2. correctness.

rec·tor (rĕk′tər), *n.* 1. *U.S.* a clergyman in charge of a parish in the Protestant Episcopal Church. 2. *Rom. Cath. Ch.* an ecclesiastic in charge of a college, religious house, or congrega-tion. 3. the permanent head in certain univer-sities, colleges, and schools.

rec·to·ry (rĕk′tə rĭ), *n., pl.* -ries. a rector′s house; parsonage.

rec·tum (rĕk′təm), *n., pl.* -ta (-tə), *Anat.* the terminal section of the intestine, ending in the anus. —rec′tal, *adj.*

re·cum·bent (rĭ kŭm′bənt), *adj.* 1. lying down; leaning. 2. inactive; idle. —re·cum′ben·cy, *n.* —re·cum′bent·ly, *adv.*

re·cu·per·ate (rĭ kū′pə rāt′), *v.i.*, -ated, -ating. to regain health or strength. —re·cu′per·a′-tion, *n.* —re·cu′per·a′tive, *adj.*

re·cur (rĭ kûr′), *v.i.*, -curred, -curring. 1. to occur again, as an event, etc. 2. to return to the mind. 3. to return in action, thought, etc. —re·cur′rence, *n.* —re·cur′rent, *adj.* —re-cur′rent·ly, *adv.*

re·curve (rĭ kûrv′), *v.t., v.i.*, -curved, -curving. to curve or bend back or backward.

red (rĕd), *adj.*, redder, reddest, *n.* —*adj.* 1. of a hue beyond orange in the spectrum. 2. ultra-radical politically. —*n.* 3. any of the hues adjacent to orange in the spectrum. 4. an ultra-radical in politics, esp. a communist. 5. see red, *Colloq.* to become infuriated. 6. in the red, hav-ing a loss or deficit. —red′dish, *adj.* —red′-ness, *n.*

red·breast (rĕd′brĕst′), *n.* the robin.

red·cap (rĕd′kăp′), *n.* *U.S.* a porter, esp. in a railroad station.

Red Cross, an international philanthropic or-ganization (Red Cross Society) formed to care for the sick and wounded in war, and active also in relieving suffering occasioned by pestilence, floods, fire, and other calamities.

red deer, 1. a species of deer native in the forests of Europe and Asia, formerly very abun-dant in England. 2. the common American deer in its summer coat.

red·den (rĕd′ən), *v.t.* 1. to make red. —*v.i.* 2. to become red. 3. to blush; flush.

re·deem (rĭ dēm′), *v.t.* 1. to buy or pay off. 2. to buy back, as after a mortgage foreclosure. 3. to recover (something pledged or mortgaged). 4. to convert (paper money) into specie. 5. to fulfill (a pledge, promise, etc.). 6. to make amends for. 7. to obtain the release of, as from captivity, by paying a ransom. 8. to deliver from sin and its consequences by means of a sacrifice offered for the sinner. —re·deem′a·ble, *adj.* —re·deem′er, *n.*

re·demp·tion (rĭ dĕmp′shən), *n.* 1. act of re-deeming. 2. state of being redeemed. 3. deliver-ance; rescue. —re·demp′tive, re·demp′to·ry, *adj.*

red-hand·ed (rĕd′hăn′dĭd), *adj.* in the very act of a crime.

red·head (rĕd′hĕd′), *n.* 1. a person having red hair. 2. an American diving duck, the male of which has a bright chestnut-red head. —red′-head′ed, *adj.*

red herring, 1. something to divert attention. 2. a smoked herring.

red-hot (rĕd′hŏt′), *adj.* 1. very hot. 2. very excited or enthusiastic. 3. violent; furious. 4. fresh; new; most recent.

red lead (lĕd), a heavy, earthy substance, orange to red in color, used as a paint pigment and in the manufacture of glass and glazes.

red-let·ter (rĕd′lĕt′ər), *adj.* 1. marked by red letters, as holidays in the calendar. 2. memora-ble; especially happy.

red-light district, a neighborhood with many houses of prostitution.

red·o·lent (rĕd′ə lənt), *adj.* 1. fragrant. 2. odorous. 3. suggestive; reminiscent. —red′o-lence, *n.*

re·dou·ble (rē dŭb′əl), *v.t., v.i.*, -bled, -bling. to make or become twice as great.

re·doubt (rĭ dout′), *n.* *Fort.* an isolated work forming a complete enclosure of any form used to defend a prominent point.

re·doubt·a·ble (rĭ dou′tə bəl), *adj.* that is to be feared or dreaded; formidable.

re·dound (rĭ dound′), *v.i.* 1. to have a result, as to the advantage, disadvantage, etc., of a per-son or thing. 2. to accrue.

re·dress (*n.* rē′drĕs, rĭ drĕs′; *v.* rĭ drĕs′), *n.* 1. the setting right of what is wrong. —*v.t.* 2. to set right; remedy or reform. —re·dress′er, *n.*

Red River, a river flowing from NW Texas along the S boundary of Oklahoma into the Mississippi in E Louisiana. ab. 1200 mi.

Red Sea, a long narrow arm of the Indian Ocean, extending NW between Africa and Arabia: connected with the Mediterranean by the Suez Canal. ab. 1450 mi. long.

red·skin (rĕd′skĭn′), *n., adj.* North American Indian.

red·start (rĕd′stärt′), *n.* a red, black, and white fly-catching warbler of America.

red tape, excessive attention to formality and routine. —red′-tape′, *adj.*

red·top (rĕd′tŏp′), *n.* a grass, certain forms of which have a reddish panicle.

re·duce (rĭ dūs′, -dōōs′), *v.*, -duced, -ducing. —*v.t.* 1. to bring down to a smaller extent, size, amount, etc. 2. to lower in degree, intensity, rank, etc. 3. to lower in price. 4. to bring to a certain condition, arrangement, etc. 5. to bring under control. 6. *Math.* to change the denomina-tion or form of. 7. *Chem.* a. to deoxidize. b. to add hydrogen to. c. to change (a compound) so that the valence of the positive element is lower. —*v.i.* 8. to become reduced. —re·duc′er, *n.* —re·duc′i·ble, *adj.* —re·duc′tion (rĭ dŭk′shən), *n.*

re·dun·dant (rĭ dŭn′dənt), *adj.* 1. excess; ex-tra. 2. wordy; verbose. —re·dun′dant·ly, *adv.* —re·dun′dan·cy, re·dun′dance; *n.*

re·du·pli·cate (rĭ dū′plə kāt′, -dōō′-), *v.t., v.i.*, -cated, -cating. to double; repeat. —re·du′-pli·ca′tion, *n.* —re·du′pli·ca′tive, *adj.*

red·wood (rĕd′wŏŏd′), *n.* 1. a coniferous tree of California, remarkable for its height (com-monly 200 to 300 feet). 2. its valuable brownish-red timber.

reed (rēd), *n.* 1. the straight stalk of any of various tall grasses growing in marshy places. 2. any of the plants themselves. 3. *Music.* a. a rustic musical pipe made from a hollow stalk. b. a small piece of cane or metal which, attached to the mouths of some wind instruments (reed instruments), helps produce the tone. —*v.t.* 4. to decorate or thatch with reed.

reed organ, a musical keyboard instrument whose tones are produced by small metal reeds.

reed·y (rē′dĭ), *adj.*, reedier, reediest. 1. full of reeds. 2. made of a reed or reeds. 3. like a reed or reeds. 4. having a tone like that of a reed in-strument. —reed′i·ness, *n.*

reef[1] (rēf), *n.* a narrow ridge of rocks or sand at or near the surface of the water.

reef[2] (rēf), *Naut.* —*n.* 1. a part of a sail which is rolled and tied down to reduce the area exposed to the wind. —*v.t.* 2. to shorten (sail) by tying in one or more reefs.

reef·er[1] (rē′fər), *n.* 1. *Naut.* one who reefs. 2. a short coat or jacket of thick cloth.

reef·er[2] (rē′fər), *n.* *U.S. Slang.* a marijuana cigarette.

reek (rēk), *n.* 1. a strong, unpleasant smell. —*v.i.* 2. to smell strongly and unpleasantly. 3. to be wet with sweat, blood, etc.

reel[1] (rēl), *n.* **1.** a cylinder, frame, or other device, turning on an axis, on which to wind something. **2.** *Chiefly Brit.* a bobbin or spool. **3.** *Photog.* **a.** the spool on which film is wound. **b.** a roll of film bearing a series of motion pictures. —*v.t.* **4.** to wind on a reel. **5.** to draw with a reel, or by winding. **6.** to say, write, or produce in an easy, continuous way.

reel[2] (rēl), *v.i.* **1.** to sway or rock under a blow, shock, etc. **2.** to fall back; waver. **3.** to stagger, as from dizziness, intoxication, etc. **4.** to whirl. —*v.t.* **5.** to cause to reel. —*n.* **6.** act of reeling.

reel[3] (rēl), *n.* **1.** a lively Scottish dance. **2.** Virginia reel. **3.** music for either of these.

reeve[1] (rēv), *n.* an administrative officer of a town or district.

reeve[2] (rēv), *v.t.,* **reeved** or **rove, reeving.** *Naut.* to pass (a rope, etc.) through a hole, ring, or the like.

ref., **1.** referee. **2.** reference. **3.** referred.

re·fec·tion (rĭ fĕk/shən), *n.* **1.** refreshment. **2.** a meal or repast.

re·fec·to·ry (rĭ fĕk/tə rĭ), *n., pl.* **-ries.** a dining hall, as in a religious house or college.

re·fer (rĭ fûr/), *v.,* **-ferred, -ferring.** —*v.t.* **1.** to direct the attention or thoughts of. **2.** to direct for information or for anything required. **3.** to submit for information, decision, etc. **4.** to assign to a class, period, etc. —*v.i.* **5.** to direct attention. **6.** to direct anyone for information. **7.** to relate; apply. **8.** to have recourse. **9.** to direct a remark or mention. —**ref·er·a·ble** (rĕf/-ər ə bəl), *adj.*

ref·er·ee (rĕf/ə rē/), *n., v.,* **-eed, -eeing.** —*n.* **1.** one to whom something is referred, esp. for decision or settlement. **2.** a judge in certain games having functions fixed by the rules. —*v.t., v.i.* **3.** to act as referee (in).

ref·er·ence (rĕf/ər əns), *n.* **1.** act or fact of referring. **2.** direction of the attention. **3.** a mention; allusion. **4.** a direction in a book or writing to some book, passage, etc. **5.** use for purposes of information. **6.** a person to whom one refers for testimony as to one's character, abilities, etc. **7.** a written testimonial as to character, abilities, etc. **8.** relation, regard, or respect.

ref·er·en·dum (rĕf/ə rĕn/dəm), *n., pl.* **-dums, -da** (-də). the principle or procedure of submitting measures already passed on by the legislative body to a vote of the electorate.

ref·er·ent (rĕf/ər ənt), *n.* *Rhet., Semantics.* the object to which a term of discourse refers.

re·fill (*v.* rē fĭl/; *n.* rē/fĭl/), *v.t.* **1.** to fill again. —*n.* **2.** something for putting in to refill a thing. —**re·fill/a·ble,** *adj.*

re·fine (rĭ fīn/), *v.t., v.i.,* **-fined, -fining. 1.** to free, or be freed, from impurities. **2.** to purify, or be purified, from what is coarse, vulgar, or debasing. —**re·fin/er,** *n.*

re·fined (rĭ fīnd/), *adj.* **1.** having or showing nice feeling, taste, etc. **2.** freed from coarseness, vulgarity, etc. **3.** freed from impurities. **4.** subtle. **5.** minutely precise; exact.

re·fine·ment (rĭ fīn/mənt), *n.* **1.** fineness of feeling, taste, etc. **2.** elegance of manners or language. **3.** act of refining. **4.** state of being refined. **5.** improvement. **6.** a subtle point or distinction.

re·fin·er·y (rĭ fī/nə rĭ), *n., pl.* **-eries.** an establishment for refining something, as petroleum.

re·fit (rē fĭt/), *v.,* **-fitted, -fitting,** *n.* —*v.t.* **1.** to fit, prepare, or equip again. **2.** to renew supplies. —*n.* **3.** act of refitting.

re·flect (rĭ flĕkt/), *v.t.* **1.** to cast back (light, heat, sound, etc.). **2.** to mirror. **3.** to reproduce; show. **4.** to serve to bring credit, discredit, etc., on. **5.** to think carefully; meditate on. —*v.i.* **6.** to be cast back, as light. **7.** to cast back light, heat, etc. **8.** to be mirrored. **9.** to serve or tend to bring reproach or discredit. **10.** to serve to give a particular aspect.

re·flec·tion (rĭ flĕk/shən), *n.* **1.** act of reflecting. **2.** state of being reflected. **3.** an image. **4.** careful consideration. **5.** a thought. **6.** an

unfavorable remark or observation. —**re·flec/tive,** *adj.* —**re·flec/tive·ly,** *adv.*

re·flec·tor (rĭ flĕk/tər), *n.* a body, surface, or device that reflects light, heat, sound, or the like.

re·flex (*adj., n.* rē/flĕks; *v.* rĭ flĕks/), *adj.* **1.** *Physiol.* noting or pertaining to an involuntary nervous response involving muscular or other activity. **2.** reflected, as light, etc. **3.** bent or turned back. —*n.* **4.** *Physiol.* a reflex action or movement. **5.** the image of an object, as one exhibited by a mirror. —*v.t.* **6.** to bend, turn, or fold back.

re·flex·ive (rĭ flĕk/sĭv), *Gram.* —*adj.* **1.** (of a verb) having identical subject and object, as *shave* in *he shaved himself.* **2.** (of a pronoun) indicating identity of object with subject, as *himself* in the example above. —*n.* **3.** a reflexive verb or pronoun. —**re·flex/ive·ly,** *adv.*

re·flux (rē/flŭks/), *n.* a flowing back; ebb.

re·for·est (rē fôr/ĭst, -fŏr/-), *v.t.* to replant with forest trees. —**re/for·est·a/tion,** *n.*

re·form[1] (rĭ fôrm/), *n.* **1.** the correction of what is wrong, corrupt, etc. **2.** an instance of this. —*v.t.* **3.** to improve by alteration, abolition, etc. —*v.i.* **4.** to abandon evil conduct or error. —**re·form/a·ble,** *adj.* —**re·form/a·tive,** *adj.* —**re·form/er,** *n.*

re·form[2] (rē fôrm/), *v.t., v.i.* to form again.

ref·or·ma·tion (rĕf/ər mā/shən), *n.* **1.** act of reforming. **2.** state of being reformed. **3.** (*cap.*) the religious movement in the 16th century which led to the establishment of the Protestant churches.

re·form·a·to·ry (rĭ fôr/mə tōr/ĭ), *adj., n., pl.* **-ries.** —*adj.* **1.** serving or designed to reform. —*n.* **2.** Also, **reform school.** a penal institution for the reformation of young offenders.

re·formed (rĭ fôrmd/), *adj.* **1.** amended or improved by removal of faults, abuses, etc. **2.** (*cap.*) noting or pertaining to Protestant churches, esp. Calvinist as distinguished from Lutheran.

re·fract (rĭ frăkt/), *v.t.* to subject to refraction. —**re·frac/tor,** *n.*

re·frac·tion (rĭ frăk/shən), *n.* *Physics.* the change of direction of a ray of light, heat, or the like, in passing obliquely from one medium into another in which its speed is different. —**re·frac/tive,** *adj.*

re·frac·to·ry (rĭ frăk/tə rĭ), *adj.* **1.** stubborn; unmanageable. **2.** resisting ordinary methods of treatment. —**re·frac/to·ri·ly,** *adv.* —**re·frac/to·ri·ness,** *n.*

re·frain[1] (rĭ frān/), *v.i.* to keep oneself from.

re·frain[2] (rĭ frān/), *n.* a phrase or verse recurring at intervals in a song or poem.

re·fran·gi·ble (rĭ frăn/jə bəl), *adj.* capable of being refracted, as rays of light.

re·fresh (rĭ frĕsh/), *v.t.* **1.** to reinvigorate by rest, food, etc. **2.** to stimulate (the memory). **3.** to reinvigorate or cheer. —*v.i.* **4.** to take refreshment. **5.** to become fresh or vigorous again. —**re·fresh/ing·ly,** *adv.*

re·fresh·er (rĭ frĕsh/ər), *adj.* **1.** serving as a review of material previously studied. —*n.* **2.** one that refreshes.

re·fresh·ment (rĭ frĕsh/mənt), *n.* **1.** that which refreshes, esp. food or drink. **2.** (*pl.*) articles or portions of food or drink, esp. for a light meal. **3.** act of refreshing.

re·frig·er·ant (rĭ frĭj/ər ənt), *adj.* **1.** refrigerating. **2.** reducing fever. —*n.* **3.** a refrigerant agent, as in a drug. **4.** a liquid capable of vaporizing at a low temperature, as ammonia, used in mechanical refrigeration. **5.** a cooling substance, as ice, etc., used in a refrigerator.

re·frig·er·ate (rĭ frĭj/ə rāt/), *v.t.,* **-ated, -ating.** to make or keep cold or cool. —**re·frig/er·a/tion,** *n.*

re·frig·er·a·tor (rĭ frĭj/ə rā/tər), *n.* a cabinet in which food, drink, etc., are kept cool, as by means of ice or mechanical means.

ref·uge (rĕf/ūj), *n.* shelter or protection from danger, trouble, etc.

re/ë·lect/
re/ë·lec/tion
re/ëm·bark/
re/ë·merge/
re/ë·mer/gence
re·ëm/pha·size/
re/ën·act/
re/ën·act/ment

re/ën·force/
re/ën·gage/
re/ën·gage/ment
re/ën·grave/
re/ën·list/
re/ën·list/ment
re·ën/ter
re·ën/try

re/ës·tab/lish
re/ës·tab/lish·ment
re/ëx·am/i·na/-
  tion
re/ëx·am/ine
re/ëx·hib/it
re/ëx·port/
re·fash/ion

re·fas/ten
re·flow/
re·fold/
re·forge/
re·for/ti·fy/
re·frac/ture
re·frame/
re·fu/el

ref·u·gee (rĕf′yŏŏ jē′), *n.* one who flees for refuge or safety, esp. to a foreign country.

re·ful·gent (rĭ fŭl′jənt), *adj.* shining; radiant; glowing. —**re·ful′gence,** *n.* —**re·ful′gent·ly,** *adv.*

re·fund (*v.* rĭ fŭnd′; *n.* rē′fŭnd), *v.t., v.i.* 1. to give back (money); repay. 2. to reimburse. —*n.* 3. a repayment.

re·fur·bish (rē fûr′bĭsh), *v.t.* to renovate; polish up again; brighten.

re·fus·al (rĭ fū′zəl), *n.* 1. act of refusing. 2. priority in refusing or taking something.

re·fuse¹ (rĭ fūz′), *v., -*fused, -fusing. —*v.t.* 1. to decline to accept (something offered). 2. to deny (a request, etc.). —*v.i.* 3. to decline acceptance, consent, or compliance.

ref·use² (rĕf′ūs), *n.* that which is discarded as worthless or useless; rubbish.

re·fute (rĭ fūt′), *v.t., -*futed, -futing. to prove to be false or erroneous, as an opinion, charge, etc. —**re·fu·ta·ble** (rĕf′yə tə bəl, rĭ fū′tə-), *adj.* —**ref·u·ta·tion** (rĕf′yŏŏ tā′shən), *n.*

reg., 1. regiment. 2. registered. 3. regular. 4. regularly. 5. regulation.

re·gain (rĭ gān′), *v.t.* 1. to get again; recover. 2. to get back to. —**re·gain′er,** *n.*

re·gal (rē′gəl), *adj.* 1. of or befitting a king; royal. 2. stately; splendid. —**re′gal·ly,** *adv.*

re·gale (rĭ gāl′), *v., -*galed, -galing. —*v.t.* 1. to entertain agreeably; delight. 2. to entertain with choice food or drink. —*v.i.* 3. to feast.

re·ga·li·a (rĭ gā′lĭ ə, -gāl′yə), *n.pl.* 1. the emblems of royalty, as the crown, scepter, etc. 2. the decorations or insignia of any office or order.

re·gard (rĭ gärd′), *v.t.* 1. to look upon or think of with a particular feeling. 2. to respect. 3. to think highly of. 4. to consider. 5. to look at. 6. to relate to; concern. —*n.* 7. reference; relation. 8. a point or particular. 9. thought; attention; concern. 10. look. 11. respect. 12. kindly feeling; liking. 13. (*pl.*) sentiments of esteem or affection.

re·gard·ful (rĭ gärd′fəl), *adj.* 1. attentive; heedful. 2. considerate or respectful. —**re·gard′ful·ly,** *adv.*

re·gard·ing (rĭ gär′dĭng), *prep.* with regard to; respecting; concerning.

re·gard·less (rĭ gärd′lĭs), *adj.* 1. heedless; careless. 2. *Colloq.* without regard of expense, danger, etc. —*adv.* 3. anyway. —**re·gard′less·ly,** *adv.*

re·gat·ta (rĭ găt′ə), *n.* 1. a boat race, as of rowboats, yachts, or other vessels. 2. an organized series of such races.

re·gen·cy (rē′jən sĭ), *n., pl. -*cies. 1. the office, jurisdiction, or control of a regent or body of regents. 2. a government consisting of regents.

re·gen·er·ate (*v.* rĭ jĕn′ə rāt′; *adj.* rĭ jĕn′ər ĭt), *v., -*ated, -ating, *adj.* —*v.t.* 1. to effect a complete moral reform in. 2. to make over, esp. in a better form. 3. to generate or produce anew. —*v.i.* 4. to come into existence or be formed again. 5. to reform. —*adj.* 6. made over in a better form. 7. reformed. —**re·gen′er·a′tion,** *n.* —**re·gen′er·a′tive,** *adj.* —**re·gen′er·a′tor,** *n.*

re·gent (rē′jənt), *n.* 1. one who exercises the ruling power in a kingdom during the minority or other disability of the sovereign. 2. *U.S.* a member of the governing board of certain universities and other institutions. —*adj.* 3. acting as regent of a country. —**re′gent·ship′,** *n.*

reg·i·cide¹ (rĕj′ə sīd′), *n.* one who kills a king.

reg·i·cide² (rĕj′ə sīd′), *n.* the killing of a king.

re·gime (rā zhēm′, rĭ-), *n.* 1. a system of rule or government. 2. a prevailing system.

reg·i·men (rĕj′ə mĕn′, -mən), *n.* 1. *Med.* a regulated course of diet, exercise, or manner of living, intended to preserve or restore health. 2. rule or government.

reg·i·ment (*n.* rĕj′ə mənt; *v.* rĕj′ə mĕnt′), *n.* 1. *Mil.* a unit of ground forces, consisting of two or more battalions, a headquarters unit, and certain supporting units. —*v.t.* 2. to form into a regiment or regiments. 3. to subject to strict discipline. —**reg′i·men′tal,** *adj.* —**reg′i·men·ta′tion,** *n.*

Re·gi·na (rĭ jī′nə), *n.* a city in SW Canada: the capital of Saskatchewan. 58,245.

re·gion (rē′jən), *n.* 1. any extensive, continu-

ous part of a surface or space. 2. *Anat.* a place in, or a division of, the body. —**re′gion·al,** *adj.* —**re′gion·al·ly,** *adv.*

reg·is·ter (rĕj′ĭs tər), *n.* 1. a book in which entries of acts, names, or the like, are made for record. 2. any list of such entries. 3. a mechanical device by which certain data are automatically recorded. 4. *Music.* the compass or range of a voice or an instrument. 5. a contrivance for regulating the passage of warm air or the like, esp. a perforated plate in a duct. 6. *Print., etc.* **a.** a precise correspondence, as of lines, columns, etc., esp. on the two sides of a leaf. **b.** correct relation, as of colors in color printing. —*v.t.* 7. to enter or have entered formally in a register. 8. to cause to be recorded, as letters at a post office, for security in transmission, by payment of a special fee. 9. to indicate or show. 10. *Print., etc.* to cause to be in register. —*v.i.* 11. to enroll. 12. to apply for and obtain inclusion of one's name on the list of voters. 13. *Print., etc.* to be in register. —**reg′is·tered,** *adj.*

reg·is·trar (rĕj′ĭs trär′, rĕj′ĭs trär′), *n.* one who keeps a record; an official recorder.

reg·is·tra·tion (rĕj′ĭs trā′shən), *n.* 1. act of registering. 2. an instance of this. 3. an entry in a register. 4. the number registered.

reg·is·try (rĕj′ĭs trĭ), *n., pl. -*tries. 1. act of registering; registration. 2. a place where a register is kept. 3. a register.

reg·nant (rĕg′nənt), *adj.* 1. reigning; ruling. 2. predominant. 3. prevalent.

re·gress (rĭ grĕs′), *v.i.* to move backward. —**re·gres′sion,** *n.*

re·gret (rĭ grĕt′), *v., -*gretted, -gretting, *n.* —*v.t.* 1. to feel sorry about. —*n.* 2. a sense of loss, disappointment, etc. 3. the feeling of being sorry for some fault, act, etc., of one's own. 4. (*pl. or sing.*) a formal expression of regretful feelings. —**re·gret′ta·ble,** *adj.* —**re·gret′ta·bly,** *adv.* —**re·gret′ful,** *adj.* —**re·gret′ful·ly,** *adv.* —**re·gret′ful·ness,** *n.*

reg·u·lar (rĕg′yə lər), *adj.* 1. usual; normal; customary. 2. symmetrical. 3. characterized by fixed principle, uniform procedure, etc. 4. recurring at fixed times. 5. observing fixed times or habits. 6. orderly; well-ordered. 7. conforming to some accepted rule, discipline, etc. 8. formally correct. 9. properly qualified for. 10. *Colloq.* complete. 11. *Gram.* conforming to the most prevalent pattern of formation, inflection, construction, etc. 12. *Mil.* denoting or belonging to the permanently organized or standing army of a state. 13. *Eccles.* belonging to a religious or monastic order. —*n.* 14. *Mil.* a regular soldier. 15. *U.S. Pol.* a party member who faithfully stands by his party. —**reg′u·lar′i·ty,** *n.* —**reg′u·lar·ly,** *adv.*

reg·u·late (rĕg′yə lāt′), *v.t., -*lated, -lating. 1. to control or direct by rule, principle, method, etc. 2. to adjust to some standard or requirement, as amount, degree, etc. 3. to put in good order. —**reg′u·la′tive, reg·u·la·to·ry** (rŏg′yə lə tōr′ĭ), *adj.*

reg·u·la·tion (rĕg′yə lā′shən), *n.* 1. a rule, order, or law. 2. act of regulating. 3. state of being regulated.

reg·u·la·tor (rĕg′yə lā′tər), *n.* 1. one who or that which regulates. 2. *Horol.* **a.** a device in a clock or a watch for causing it to go faster or slower. **b.** a master clock, esp. one of great accuracy, against which other clocks are checked. 3. *Mach.* a governor.

re·gur·gi·tate (rē gûr′jə tāt′), *v., -*tated, -tating. —*v.i.* 1. to surge or rush back, as liquids, gases, undigested food, etc. —*v.t.* 2. to cause to surge or rush back. —**re·gur′gi·ta′tion,** *n.*

re·ha·bil·i·tate (rē′hə bĭl′ə tāt′), *v.t., -*tated, -tating. 1. to restore to a good condition. 2. to reëstablish in good repute. 3. to restore formally to former standing, right, etc. —**re′ha·bil′i·ta′tion,** *n.*

re·hash (*v.* rē hăsh′; *n.* rē′hăsh), *v.t.* 1. to work up (old material) in a new form. —*n.* 2. act of rehashing. 3. something rehashed.

re·hearse (rĭ hûrs′), *v., -*hearsed, -hearsing. —*v.t.* 1. to recite or act (a play, part, etc.) in practice for a public performance. 2. to train (a person, etc.) for some performance. 3. to relate or enumerate. —*v.i.* 4. to rehearse a play, part, etc. —**re·hears′al,** *n.*

Reich (rīk), *n.* Germany.

---

re·fur′nish	re·gird′	re·glue′	re·han′dle
re·gath′er	re·glaze′	re·grade′	re·heat′
re·gild′	re·glo′ri·fy′	re·group′	re·heel′

reichs·mark (rīks′märk′), *n.*, *pl.* **-marks, -mark.** the reconstituted German mark introduced in 1924, worth 23.8 U.S. cents.

Reichs·tag (rīks′täg′), *n.* the elective legislative assembly of Germany.

reign (rān), *n.* **1.** the period of ruling, as of a sovereign. **2.** royal rule. **3.** dominating power. **—v.i.** **4.** to possess sovereign power. **5.** to predominate.

re·im·burse (rē′ĭm bûrs′), *v.t.*, **-bursed, -bursing.** **1.** to repay for expense or loss incurred. **2.** to refund. **—re′im·burse′ment,** *n.*

re·im·port (rē′ĭm pōrt′), *v.t.* to import back into the country of exportation. **—re′im·por·ta′tion,** *n.*

Reims (rēmz), *n.* a city in NE France: surrender of Germany (May 7, 1945). 110,794.

rein (rān), *n.* **1.** a long, narrow strap, fastened to the bridle or bit, by which a rider or driver restrains and guides a horse or other animal. **2.** any of certain other straps of a harness. **3.** a check or restraint. **4.** (*often pl.*) free scope. **—v.t.** **5.** to furnish with a rein or reins. **6.** to check or guide (a horse, etc.) by pulling at the reins. **7.** to curb; control. **—v.i.** **8.** to obey the reins. **9.** to rein a horse.

re·in·car·nate (rē′ĭn kär′nāt), *v.t.*, **-nated, -nating.** to give another body to.

re·in·car·na·tion (rē′ĭn kär nā′shən), *n.* the belief that the soul, upon death of the body, moves to another body or form.

rein·deer (rān′dĭr′), *n.*, *pl.* **-deer,** (*occasionally*) **-deers.** any of certain large deer with branched antlers in both males and females, found in northern or arctic regions, and often domesticated.

re·in·force (rē′ĭn fōrs′), *v.t.*, **-forced, -forcing.** **1.** to strengthen with additional support, material, troops, ships, etc. **2.** to strengthen in effect, supply, etc. Also, **reënforce, re-enforce. —re′in·force′ment,** *n.*

reinforced concrete, concrete poured to embody steel bars for greater strength.

re·in·state (rē′ĭn stāt′), *v.t.*, **-stated, -stating.** to establish again, as in a former position. **—re′in·state′ment,** *n.*

re·it·er·ate (rē ĭt′ə rāt′), *v.t.*, **-ated, -ating.** to repeat; say or do repeatedly. **—re·it′er·a′tion,** *n.*

re·ject (*v.* rĭ jĕkt′; *n.* rē′jĕkt), *v.t.* **1.** to refuse to have, take, recognize, grant, accept, etc. **2.** to throw away; discard. **—n.** **3.** something rejected. **—re·jec·tion** (rĭ jĕk′shən), *n.*

re·joice (rĭ jois′), *v.*, **-joiced, -joicing.** **—v.i.** **1.** to be glad. **—v.t.** **2.** to gladden. **—re·joic′ing,** *n.*

re·join[1] (rē join′), *v.t.*, *v.i.* to join again.

re·join[2] (rĭ join′), *v.t.*, *v.i.* to answer.

re·join·der (rĭ join′dər), *n.* an answer to a reply; response.

re·ju·ve·nate (rĭ jōō′və nāt′), *v.t.*, **-nated, -nating.** to make young again; restore to youthful vigor, etc. **—re·ju′ve·na′tion,** *n.*

rel., religion.

re·lapse (rĭ lăps′), *v.*, **-lapsed, -lapsing,** *n.* **—v.i.** **1.** to fall back into a former state, practice, etc. **2.** to fall back into illness after convalescence or apparent recovery. **3.** to backslide. **—n.** **4.** act of relapsing.

re·late (rĭ lāt′), *v.*, **-lated, -lating.** **—v.t.** **1.** to tell. **2.** to establish association, connection, or relation. **—v.i.** **3.** to have reference to. **—re·lat′er,** *n.*

re·lat·ed (rĭ lā′tĭd), *adj.* **1.** associated; connected. **2.** allied by nature, origin, kinship, marriage, etc. **3.** narrated.

re·la·tion (rĭ lā′shən), *n.* **1.** a connection or association, as between persons, nations, etc. **2.** a relative. **3.** reference; regard; respect. **4.** the action of relating, narrating, or telling. **5.** a narrative; account. **—re·la′tion·al,** *adj.*

re·la·tion·ship (rĭ lā′shən shĭp′), *n.* **1.** connection; a particular connection. **2.** connection or alliance by blood or marriage.

rel·a·tive (rĕl′ə tĭv), *n.* **1.** one who is connected with another or others by blood or marriage. **2.** *Gram.* a relative pronoun, adjective, or adverb. **—adj.** **3.** considered in relation to something else; comparative. **4.** not absolute or independent. **5.** having relation or connection. **6.** relevant; pertinent. **7.** proportionate. **8.** *Gram.* **a.** designating words which introduce subordinate clauses and refer to some element of the principal clause (the antecedent). **b.** (of a clause) introduced by such a word. **—rel′a·tive·ly,** *adv.* **—rel′a·tive·ness,** *n.*

rel·a·tiv·i·ty (rĕl′ə tĭv′ə tĭ), *n.* **1.** state or fact of being relative. **2.** *Physics.* the principle (developed substantially by Einstein) that all observable motion is relative, not absolute. Among the conclusions resulting from this principle are: that time, like motion, is relative and not absolute; that time and space are dependent on each other, time forming with the three dimensions of space a single four-dimensional manifold; that the presence of matter in space is associated with a "warping" of the manifold in its neighborhood, so that a freely moving body describes, not a straight line, but a curve (this effect being what is known as gravitation).

re·lax (rĭ lăks′), *v.t.* **1.** to make less tense, rigid, or firm. **2.** to diminish the force of. **3.** to slacken; abate. **4.** to make less strict, as rules. **—v.i.** **5.** to become less tense, rigid, or firm. **6.** to become less strict. **7.** to slacken in effort, etc.

re·lax·a·tion (rē′lăk sā′shən), *n.* **1.** abatement of bodily or mental effort or application. **2.** something affording such relief. **3.** a loosening or slackening. **4.** diminution of strictness.

re·lay (rē′lā, rĭ lā′), *n.* **1.** a set of persons relieving others or taking turns; shift. **2.** Also, **relay race.** a race of two or more teams of contestants, each contestant running but part of the distance and being relieved by a teammate. **3.** a device that extends or reinforces the action or effect of an apparatus. **—v.t.** **4.** to carry forward by relays. **5.** to provide with or replace by fresh relays.

re·lease (rĭ lēs′), *v.*, **-leased, -leasing,** *n.* **—v.t.** **1.** to free from confinement, bondage, obligation, pain, etc.; let go. **2.** to allow to become known or be issued. **3.** *Law.* to relinquish; surrender. **—n.** **4.** a freeing or releasing from confinement, obligation, pain, etc. **5.** the releasing of something for publication, public exhibition, or sale. **6.** the article so released. **7.** *Law.* the surrender of a right or the like to another.

rel·e·gate (rĕl′ə gāt′), *v.t.*, **-gated, -gating.** **1.** to send or consign to some obscure position, place, or condition. **2.** to turn over (a matter, task, etc.). **3.** to exile; banish. **—rel′e·ga′tion,** *n.*

re·lent (rĭ lĕnt′), *v.i.* to become more mild, compassionate, or forgiving. **—re·lent′less,** *adj.* **—re·lent′less·ly,** *adv.* **—re·lent′less·ness,** *n.*

rel·e·vant (rĕl′ə vənt), *adj.* connected with the matter in hand; pertinent. **—rel′e·vance, rel′e·van·cy,** *n.* **—rel′e·vant·ly,** *adv.*

re·li·a·ble (rĭ lī′ə bəl), *adj.* that may be relied on; trustworthy. **—re·li′a·bil′i·ty, re·li′a·ble·ness,** *n.* **—re·li′a·bly,** *adv.*

re·li·ance (rĭ lī′əns), *n.* **1.** trustful dependence. **2.** confidence.

re·li·ant (rĭ lī′ənt), *adj.* **1.** having or showing reliance. **2.** confident. **3.** trustful.

rel·ic (rĕl′ĭk), *n.* **1.** a surviving memorial, object, trace, etc., of the past. **2.** *Eccles.* the body, a part of the body, or some personal memorial of a saint, martyr, or other sacred person, preserved as worthy of veneration.

rel·ict (rĕl′ĭkt), *n.* *Archaic.* a widow.

re·lief (rĭ lēf′), *n.* **1.** deliverance or alleviation through the removal of pain, distress, oppression, etc. **2.** help given, as to those in poverty. **3.** something affording a pleasing change. **4.** release from a post of duty, as by the coming of a substitute. **5.** prominence, distinctness, or vividness due to contrast. **6.** the projection of a figure or part from the ground or plane on which it is formed, in sculpture or similar work. **7.** a piece or work in such projection. **8.** *Phys. Geog.* the departure of the land surface in any area from that of a level surface.

re·lieve (rĭ lēv′), *v.t.*, **-lieved, -lieving. 1.** to ease or alleviate (pain, distress, need, etc.). **2.** to free from anxiety, fear, pain, etc. **3.** to deliver from poverty, etc. **4.** to bring aid to (a besieged town, etc.). **5.** to make less tedious. **6.** to release (one on duty) by coming as or providing a substitute.

re·li·gion (rĭ lĭj′ən), *n.* **1.** the quest for the values of the ideal life. **2.** a particular system in which the quest for the ideal life has been embodied. **3.** recognition on the part of man of a controlling superhuman power entitled to obedience, reverence, and worship.

re·li·gious (rĭ lĭj′əs), *adj.* **1.** of, pertaining to, or concerned with religion. **2.** pious; devout; godly. **3.** conscientious. —*n.* **4.** a member of a religious order, etc. —**re·li′gious·ly,** *adv.* —**re·li′gious·ness,** *n.*

re·lin·quish (rĭ lĭng′kwĭsh), *v.t.* **1.** to renounce or surrender (a possession, right, etc.). **2.** to let go. —**re·lin′quish·ment,** *n.*

rel·i·quar·y (rĕl′ə kwĕr′ĭ), *n., pl.* **-quaries.** a repository for a relic or relics.

rel·ish (rĕl′ĭsh), *n.* **1.** pleasurable liking, esp. for the taste of something. **2.** something appetizing or savory added to a meal, as pickles or olives. **3.** a pleasing flavor or quality. —*v.t.* **4.** to like; enjoy.

re·luc·tance (rĭ lŭk′təns), *n.* **1.** unwillingness; disinclination. **2.** *Elect.* the resistance offered to the passage of magnetic lines of force.

re·luc·tant (rĭ lŭk′tənt), *adj.* unwilling; disinclined. —**re·luc′tant·ly,** *adv.*

re·ly (rĭ lī′), *v.i.,* **-lied, -lying.** to depend confidently; put trust in.

re·main (rĭ mān′), *v.i.* **1.** to continue to be (as specified). **2.** to stay in a place. **3.** to be left after the removal, loss, etc., of another or others. **4.** to be left to be done, told, etc. —*n. pl.* **5.** that which remains. **6.** a dead body.

re·main·der (rĭ mān′dər), *n.* **1.** that which remains or is left. **2.** a remaining part. **3.** *Arith.* the quantity that remains after subtraction or division. **4.** a copy of a book remaining in the publisher's stock when the sale has practically ceased, frequently sold at a reduced price. —*adj.* **5.** remaining; left. —*v.t.* **6.** to dispose of as a publisher's remainder.

re·mand (rĭ mănd′, -mänd′), *v.t.* **1.** to send back. **2.** *Law.* **a.** to send back (a case) to a lower court from which it was appealed, with instructions as to what further proceedings should be had. **b.** to send back (a prisoner or accused person) into custody. —*n.* **3.** act of remanding.

re·mark (rĭ märk′), *v.t.* **1.** to say casually. **2.** to note; perceive. —*v.i.* **3.** to make an observation. —*n.* **4.** act of remarking; notice. **5.** comment or statement.

re·mark·a·ble (rĭ mär′kə bəl), *adj.* **1.** notably unusual; extraordinary. **2.** worthy of remark or notice. —**re·mark′a·ble·ness,** *n.* —**re·mark′a·bly,** *adv.*

Rem·brandt (rĕm′brănt), *n.* (*Rembrandt Harmenszoon van Rijn* or *van Ryn*) 1606–69, Dutch painter and etcher.

re·me·di·a·ble (rĭ mē′dĭ ə bəl), *adj.* capable of being remedied. —**re·me′di·a·bly,** *adv.*

re·me·di·al (rĭ mē′dĭ əl), *adj.* tending to remedy. —**re·me′di·al·ly,** *adv.*

rem·e·dy (rĕm′ə dĭ), *n., pl.* **-dies,** *v.,* **-died, -dying.** —*n.* **1.** something that cures or relieves a disease or bodily disorder. **2.** something that corrects an evil of any kind. **3.** *Law.* legal redress. —*v.t.* **4.** to cure or heal. **5.** to put right, correct, or eliminate. —**rem′e·di·less,** *adj.*

re·mem·ber (rĭ mĕm′bər), *v.t.* **1.** to recall to the mind by an act or effort of memory. **2.** to retain in the memory. **3.** to have (something) come into the mind again. **4.** to bear (a person) in mind as deserving a gift, reward, or fee. **5.** to mention to another as sending kindly greetings. —*v.i.* **6.** to possess or exercise the faculty of memory.

re·mem·brance (rĭ mĕm′brəns), *n.* **1.** a men-

tal impression retained. **2.** act or fact of remembering. **3.** the faculty of remembering. **4.** commemoration. **5.** something that serves to bring to or keep in mind. **6.** (*pl.*) greetings.

re·mind (rĭ mīnd′), *v.t.* to cause (one) to remember. —**re·mind′er,** *n.*

rem·i·nisce (rĕm′ə nĭs′), *v.i.,* **-nisced, -niscing.** to recall past experiences.

rem·i·nis·cence (rĕm′ə nĭs′əns), *n.* **1.** act or process of remembering one's past. **2.** (*often pl.*) a recollection narrated or told. —**rem′i·nis′cent,** *adj.*

re·miss (rĭ mĭs′), *adj.* **1.** careless, negligent, or slack. **2.** languid; sluggish.

re·mis·si·ble (rĭ mĭs′ə bəl), *adj.* that may be remitted. —**re·mis′si·bil′i·ty,** *n.*

re·mis·sion (rĭ mĭsh′ən), *n.* **1.** act of remitting. **2.** pardon; forgiveness. **3.** abatement, as of diligence, labor, intensity, etc. **4.** the relinquishment of a payment, obligation, etc.

re·mit (rĭ mĭt′), *v.t., v.i.,* **-mitted, -mitting. 1.** to send (money, etc.) to a person or place. **2.** to refrain from inflicting or enforcing, as a punishment. **3.** to refrain from exacting, as a payment. **4.** to pardon or forgive. **5.** to slacken; abate. **6.** to give back. **7.** *Law.* to send back (a case) to an inferior court for further action. **8.** to postpone.

re·mit·tance (rĭ mĭt′əns), *n.* **1.** the remitting of money, etc. **2.** money or its equivalent sent.

re·mit·tent (rĭ mĭt′ənt), *Med.* —*adj.* **1.** abating for a time or at intervals. —*n.* **2.** a remittent fever.

rem·nant (rĕm′nənt), *n.* **1.** a part, quantity, or number (usually small) remaining. **2.** a trace; vestige. —*adj.* **3.** remaining.

re·mon·e·tize (rē mŭn′ə tīz′, -mŏn′-), *v.t.,* **-tized, -tizing.** to restore to use as legal tender. —**re·mon′e·ti·za′tion,** *n.*

re·mon·strance (rĭ mŏn′strəns), *n.* **1.** act of remonstrating; expostulation. **2.** a protest. —**re·mon′strant,** *adj.*

re·mon·strate (rĭ mŏn′strāt), *v.,* **-strated, -strating.** —*v.t.* **1.** to say in remonstrance; protest. —*v.i.* **2.** to present reasons in complaint; plead in protest. —**re·mon·stra·tion** (rē′mŏn·strā′shən, rĕm′ən-), *n.* —**re·mon·stra·tive** (rĭ mŏn′strə tĭv), *adj.* —**re·mon·stra·tor** (rĭ mŏn′strā tər), *n.*

re·morse (rĭ môrs′), *n.* deep and painful regret for wrongdoing; compunction. —**re·morse′ful,** *adj.*

re·mote (rĭ mōt′), *adj.,* **-moter, -motest. 1.** far apart; far distant. **2.** out-of-the-way; secluded. **3.** distant in time. **4.** distant in relationship or connection. **5.** slight or faint. —**re·mote′ly,** *adv.* —**re·mote′ness,** *n.*

re·mount (rē mount′), *v.i., v.t.* **1.** to mount again; reascend. —*n.* **2.** a fresh horse, or a supply of fresh horses.

re·mov·a·ble (rĭ mōō′və bəl), *adj.* that may be removed. —**re·mov′a·bly,** *adv.*

re·mov·al (rĭ mōō′vəl), *n.* **1.** act of removing. **2.** change of residence, position, etc. **3.** dismissal, as from office.

re·move (rĭ mōōv′), *v.,* **-moved, -moving,** *n.* —*v.t.* **1.** to take away or off. **2.** to move to another place or position. **3.** to put out. **4.** to displace from a position or office. **5.** to take, withdraw, or separate (from). **6.** to do away with. **7.** to kill. —*v.i.* **8.** to move from one place to another, esp. to another residence. **9.** *Poetic.* to depart. —*n.* **10.** act of removing. **11.** a removal from one place, as of residence, to another. **12.** the distance by which one place or thing is separated from another. —**re·mov′er,** *n.*

re·mu·ner·ate (rĭ mū′nə rāt′), *v.t.,* **-ated, -ating. 1.** to pay or reward for work, etc. **2.** to yield a recompense for (work, etc.). —**re·mu′ner·a′tion,** *n.* —**re·mu′ner·a′tive,** *adj.*

ren·ais·sance (rĕn′ə säns′, -zäns′, rĭ nā′səns), *n.* **1.** a new birth; revival. **2.** (*cap.*) the activity, spirit, or time of the great revival of art, letters, and learning in Europe during the 14th, 15th, and 16th centuries.

re·nal (rē′nəl), *adj.* of or pertaining to the kidneys or the surrounding regions.

re·nas·cence (rĭ năs′əns), *n.* **1.** rebirth; revival. **2.** (*cap.*) the Renaissance.

---

re·nas·cent (rĭ nǎs′ənt), adj. being reborn; springing again into being or vigor.

rend (rĕnd), v., **rent, rending.** —v.t. **1.** to separate into parts with force or violence. **2.** to tear apart, split, or divide. **3.** to pull or tear violently. **4.** to tear (one's garments or hair) in grief, rage, etc. **5.** to disturb (the air) sharply with loud noise. **6.** to harrow or distress (the heart, etc.) with painful feelings. —v.i. **7.** to tear something. **8.** to become torn.

ren·der (rĕn′dər), v.t. **1.** to make or cause to be or become. **2.** to do; perform. **3.** to furnish. **4.** to exhibit (obedience, attention, etc.). **5.** to present for consideration, payment, etc. **6.** to pay as due (a tax, etc.). **7.** to deliver officially, as judgment. **8.** to translate. **9.** to represent; depict. **10.** to bring out the meaning of by performance, as a piece of music, etc. **11.** to give back; restore. **12.** to melt (fat, etc.).

ren·dez·vous (rän′də vōō′), n., pl. **-vous** (-vōōz′), v., **-voused** (-vōōd′), **-vousing** (-vōō′ǐng). —n. **1.** an appointment to meet. **2.** a place for meeting. —v.i., v.t. **3.** to meet at a place previously appointed.

ren·di·tion (rĕn dǐsh′ən), n. **1.** act of rendering. **2.** interpretation.

ren·e·gade (rĕn′ə gād′), n. **1.** one who deserts a party or cause for another. —adj. **2.** of or like a renegade; traitorous.

re·nege (rǐ nǐg′, -nēg′), v., **-neged, -neging.** —v.i. **1.** Cards. to play a card that is not of the suit led, or to break a rule of play. **2.** Colloq. to go back on one's word. —n. **3.** Cards. an act or instance of reneging.

re·new (rǐ nū′, -nōō′), v.t. **1.** to begin again, as acquaintance. **2.** to make effective for an additional period. **3.** to restore or replenish. **4.** to make, say, or do again. **5.** to reëstablish. **6.** to make new again; restore to a former state. —v.i. **7.** to begin again. **8.** to renew a lease, note, etc. **9.** to become new again. —re·new′a·ble, adj. —re·new′al, n.

Re·no (rē′nō), n. a city in W Nevada: divorce courts. 21,317.

Re·noir (rə nwär′), n. **Pierre Auguste,** 1841–1919, French painter.

re·nounce (rǐ nouns′), v.t., **-nounced, -nouncing. 1.** to give up or put aside voluntarily; often by formal declaration. **2.** to repudiate; disown. —re·nounce′ment, n.

ren·o·vate (rĕn′ə vāt′), v.t., **-vated, -vating. 1.** to make new again; restore to good condition; repair. **2.** to refresh; revive. —ren′o·va′tion, n. —ren′o·va′tor, n.

re·nown (rǐ noun′), n. widespread and high repute; fame. —re·nowned′, adj.

rent[1] (rĕnt), n. **1.** a payment made periodically by a tenant to an owner for the use of land or building. —v.t. **2.** to grant or have the use of (property) in return for payments to be made at agreed times. —v.i. **3.** to be leased or let for rent. —rent′a·ble, adj. —rent′er, n.

rent[2] (rĕnt), n. **1.** an opening made by rending or tearing. **2.** a breach of relations.

rent·al (rĕn′təl), n. **1.** an amount received or paid as rent. —adj. **2.** pertaining to rent.

re·nun·ci·a·tion (rǐ nŭn′sǐ ā′shən, -shǐ-), n. **1.** the formal abandoning of a right, title, etc. **2.** a voluntary giving up, esp. at a sacrifice.

rep (rĕp), n. a transversely corded fabric of wool, silk, rayon, or cotton.

Rep., 1. Representative. **2.** Republican.

re·pair[1] (rǐ pâr′), v.t. **1.** to restore to a good condition, as after decay or damage; mend. **2.** to remedy. —n. **3.** act, process, or work of repairing. **4.** (esp. pl.) an instance, operation, or piece of repairing. **5.** the good condition resulting from repairing. —re·pair′a·ble, adj. —re·pair′man′, n.

re·pair[2] (rǐ pâr′), v.i. to go.

rep·a·ra·ble (rĕp′ə rə bəl), adj. capable of being repaired or remedied.

rep·a·ra·tion (rĕp′ə rā′shən), n. **1.** the making of amends for wrong or injury done. **2.** (usually pl.) compensation in money, material, labor, etc., by a defeated nation for damages. **3.** restoration to good condition. **4.** repairs.

rep·ar·tee (rĕp′ər tē′), n. **1.** a ready and witty reply. **2.** talk full of quick, witty replies. **3.** skill in making witty replies.

re·past (rǐ pǎst′, -päst′), n. food; meal.

re·pa·tri·ate (rē pā′trǐ āt′), v.t., **-ated, -ating.** to bring or send back (a person) to his own country. —re·pa′tri·a′tion, n.

re·pay (rǐ pā′), v.t., **-paid, -paying. 1.** to pay back (money, etc.). **2.** to make return for. **3.** to make return to. —re·pay′a·ble, adj. —re·pay′ment, n.

re·peal (rǐ pēl′), v.t. **1.** to revoke officially. —n. **2.** act of repealing; revocation. —re·peal′a·ble, adj.

re·peat (rǐ pēt′), v.t. **1.** to say again (something one has already said). **2.** to say in reproducing the words, etc., of another. **3.** to reproduce (utterances, sounds, etc.) as a phonograph does. **4.** to tell (something heard) to another or others. **5.** to do, make, etc., again. —v.i. **6.** to do or say something again. —n. **7.** act of repeating. **8.** something repeated. **9.** Music. **a.** a passage to be repeated. **b.** a sign calling for the repetition of a passage. —re·peat′ed, adj. —re·peat′ed·ly, adv.

re·peat·er (rǐ pē′tər), n. **1.** one that repeats. **2.** a firearm that discharges a number of shots without reloading.

re·pel (rǐ pĕl′), v., **-pelled, -pelling.** —v.t. **1.** to drive back (an assailant, invader, etc.). **2.** to thrust away. **3.** to resist effectually (an attack). **4.** to fail to mix with. **5.** to refuse to have to do with. **6.** to reject. **7.** to excite feelings of distaste or aversion. **8.** Mech. to push back or away by a force. —v.i. **9.** to act with a force that drives or keeps away something. **10.** to cause distaste or aversion.

re·pel·lent (rǐ pĕl′ənt), adj. **1.** causing distaste or aversion. **2.** driving back; resistant. —n. **3.** something that repels.

re·pent (rǐ pĕnt′), v.i. **1.** to feel self-reproach, compunction, or contrition for past conduct. **2.** to be penitent. —v.t. **3.** to remember or regard with self-reproach or contrition. **4.** to regret.

re·pent·ance (rǐ pĕn′təns), n. **1.** compunction or contrition for wrongdoing or sin. **2.** regret for any past action. —re·pent′ant, adj. —re·pent′ant·ly, adv.

re·per·cus·sion (rē′pər kŭsh′ən), n. **1.** an effect or result, often indirect, of some event or action. **2.** a rebounding or recoil. **3.** reverberation; echo.

rep·er·toire (rĕp′ər twär′, -twôr′), n. the list of dramas, operas, parts, etc., which a company, actor, singer, or the like, is prepared to perform.

rep·er·to·ry (rĕp′ər tōr′ĭ), n., pl. **-ries. 1.** repertoire. **2.** a stock of things available. **3.** storehouse.

rep·e·ti·tion (rĕp′ə tǐsh′ən), n. repeated action, performance, production, presentation, or utterance.

rep·e·ti·tious (rĕp′ə tǐsh′əs), adj. abounding in tedious repetition. —rep′e·ti′tious·ly, adv.

re·pine (rǐ pīn′), v.i., **-pined, -pining.** to be fretfully discontented; fret; complain.

re·place (rǐ plās′), v.t., **-placed, -placing. 1.** to take the place of; substitute for. **2.** to provide a substitute or equivalent for. **3.** to restore; return. —re·place′a·ble, adj.

re·place·ment (rǐ plās′mənt), n. **1.** act of replacing. **2.** that which replaces.

re·plen·ish (rǐ plĕn′ĭsh), v.t. to restore to fullness or completeness. —re·plen′ish·er, n. —re·plen′ish·ment, n.

re·plete (rǐ plēt′), adj. abundantly supplied or provided. —re·plete′ness, n. —re·ple′tion, n.

rep·li·ca (rĕp′lə kə), n. a copy or reproduction, as of a work of art.

re·ply (rǐ plī′), v., **-plied, -plying,** n., pl. **-plies.** —v.i., v.t. **1.** to answer; respond. —n. **2.** an answer or response.

re·port (rǐ pōrt′), n. **1.** a statement giving the results of investigation, research, etc. **2.** a rumor. **3.** repute; reputation. **4.** a loud noise, as from an explosion. —v.t. **5.** to relate what one has heard, learned, observed, etc. **6.** to make a formal report or statement on. **7.** to lay a charge against

re·nom′i·nate′	re·oc′cu·py′	re·pack′	re·peo′ple
re·nom′i·na′-	re·o′pen	re·pack′er	re·phrase′
tion	re·op·pose′	re·paint′	re·plant′
re·no′ti·fy′	re·or′der	re·pass′	re·play′
re·num′ber	re·or′gan·i·za′-	re·pave′	re·pledge′
re·ob·tain′	tion	re·ped′dle	re·pol′ish
re·oc·cu·pa′tion	re·or′gan·ize′	re·pe′nal·ize′	re·pop′u·late′

(a person), as to a superior. **8.** to present (oneself) to a person in authority. **9.** to take down (a speech, etc.) in writing. **10.** to write an account of (an event, etc.), as for a newspaper. —*v.i.* **11.** to make a report. **12.** to act as a reporter. **13.** to report oneself, as to one in authority. **14.** to present oneself duly, as at a place. —**re·port'·a·ble,** *adj.*

re·port·er (rĭ pōr'tər), *n.* **1.** a person who gathers news for a newspaper. **2.** one who prepares official reports, as of legal proceedings.

re·pose¹ (rĭ pōz'), *n., v.,* **-posed, -posing.** —*n.* **1.** state of rest or sleep. **2.** tranquillity. **3.** dignified calmness. —*v.i.* **4.** to rest or sleep. **5.** to depend or rely. —*v.t.* **6.** to lay to rest. —**re·pose'·ful,** *adj.*

re·pose² (rĭ pōz'), *v.t.,* **-posed, -posing.** to put (trust, etc.) in another.

re·pos·i·to·ry (rĭ pŏz'ə tōr'ĭ), *n., pl.* **-tories.** a receptacle or place where things are deposited, stored, or offered for sale.

re·pos·sess (rē'pə zĕs'), *v.t.* to regain possession of. —**re'·pos·ses'sion,** *n.*

repp (rĕp), *n.* rep.

rep·re·hend (rĕp'rĭ hĕnd'), *v.t.* to find fault with; rebuke; censure; blame. —**rep·re·hen·sion** (rĕp'rĭ hĕn'shən), *n.*

rep·re·hen·si·ble (rĕp'rĭ hĕn'sə bəl), *adj.* deserving to be reprehended; blameworthy. —**rep'·re·hen'si·bly,** *adv.*

rep·re·sent (rĕp'rĭ zĕnt'), *v.t.* **1.** to serve to express, designate, stand for, or denote. **2.** to express or designate by some term, symbol, or the like. **3.** to act in the place of, as a substitute. **4.** to speak and act for by delegated authority. **5.** to act for (a constituency, etc.) by deputed right in exercising a voice in government. **6.** to portray, depict, or state. **7.** to present, produce, or perform (a play, etc.). **8.** to impersonate (a character, etc.). **9.** to serve as an example or specimen of. **10.** to be the equivalent of.

rep·re·sen·ta·tion (rĕp'rĭ zĕn tā'shən), *n.* **1.** act of representing. **2.** state of being represented. **3.** a picture, figure, statue, etc. **4.** a statement of facts, reasons, etc., made in appealing or protesting. —**rep're·sen·ta'tion·al,** *adj.*

rep·re·sent·a·tive (rĕp'rĭ zĕn'tə tĭv), *n.* **1.** one who or that which represents another or others. **2.** one who represents a community in a legislative body, esp. a member of the lower house in the U.S. Congress (**House of Representatives**) or in a State legislature. —*adj.* **3.** serving to represent; representing. **4.** characterized by, founded on, or pertaining to representation of the people in government. **5.** exemplifying a class; typical.

re·press (rĭ prĕs'), *v.t.* **1.** to control, check, or suppress (feelings, tears, etc.). **2.** to quell (sedition, etc.). —**re·press'i·ble,** *adj.* —**re·pres'sive,** *adj.*

re·pres·sion (rĭ prĕsh'ən), *n.* **1.** act of repressing. **2.** state of being repressed. **3.** *Psychoanal.* the rejection from consciousness of painful or disagreeable ideas, memories, feelings, and impulses.

re·prieve (rĭ prēv'), *v., *-prieved, -prieving, *n.* —*v.t.* **1.** to respite (a person) from impending punishment or execution. **2.** to relieve temporarily from any evil. —*n.* **3.** respite from impending punishment or execution. **4.** a warrant authorizing this. **5.** any temporary relief.

rep·ri·mand (rĕp'rə mănd', -mänd'), *n.* **1.** a severe reproof, esp. a formal one. —*v.t.* **2.** to reprove severely.

re·print (*v.* rē prĭnt'; *n.* rē'prĭnt'), *v.t.* **1.** to print again. —*n.* **2.** a reproduction in print of matter already printed.

re·pris·al (rĭ prī'zəl), *n.* the infliction of similar or more severe injury in retaliation, esp. on another nation.

re·proach (rĭ prōch'), *v.t.* **1.** to find fault with; blame. **2.** to upbraid. —*n.* **3.** blame or censure. **4.** disgrace, discredit, or blame incurred. **5.** an object of scorn or contempt.

re·proach·ful (rĭ prōch'fəl), *adj.* full of or expressing reproach; upbraiding. —**re·proach'·ful·ly,** *adv.*

rep·ro·bate (rĕp'rə bāt'), *n., adj., v.,* **-bated, -bating.** —*n.* **1.** a hopelessly wicked, unprincipled, or reprehensible person. —*adj.* **2.** morally depraved; bad. —*v.t.* **3.** to disapprove, condemn, or censure. —**rep'·ro·ba'tion,** *n.*

re·pro·duce (rē'prə dūs', -dōōs'), *v.,* **-duced, -ducing.** —*v.t.* **1.** to make a copy, representation, duplicate, or close imitation of. **2.** to produce another or more individuals of (some animal or plant kind) by generation or propagation, sexual or asexual. —*v.i.* **3.** to propagate. **4.** to turn out (well, etc.) when copied. —**re'pro·duc'er,** *n.* —**re'pro·duc'i·ble,** *adj.*

re·pro·duc·tion (rē'prə dŭk'shən), *n.* **1.** act or process of reproducing. **2.** state of being reproduced. **3.** a copy or duplicate. **4.** the natural process among animals and plants by which new individuals are generated. —**re'pro·duc'tive·ly,** *adv.* —**re'pro·duc'tive·ness,** *n.*

re·proof (rĭ prōōf'), *n.* censure or rebuke.

re·prove (rĭ prōōv'), *v.,* **-proved, -proving.** —*v.t.* **1.** to rebuke; blame. **2.** to disapprove. —*v.i.* **3.** to speak in censure or rebuke. —**re·prov'a·ble,** *adj.* —**re·prov'ing·ly,** *adv.*

rep·tile (rĕp'tĭl *or, esp. Brit.,* -tīl), *n.* **1.** any of various creeping or crawling animals, as the lizards, snakes, etc. **2.** a groveling, mean, or despicable person. —*adj.* **3.** creeping or crawling. **4.** groveling, mean, or despicable.

rep·til·i·an (rĕp tĭl'ĭ ən), *adj.* **1.** belonging or pertaining to a class of cold-blooded vertebrates, including lizards, snakes, turtles, and alligators. **2.** reptilelike. **3.** mean; base; malignant. —*n.* **4.** a reptile.

re·pub·lic (rĭ pŭb'lĭk), *n.* a state in which the supreme power rests in the body of citizens entitled to vote and is exercised by representatives chosen directly or indirectly by them.

re·pub·li·can (rĭ pŭb'lə kən), *adj.* **1.** of. pertaining to, or favoring a republic. **2.** (*cap.*) of or pertaining to the Republican party. —*n.* **3.** one who favors a republican form of government. **4.** (*cap.*) a member of the Republican party. —**re·pub'li·can·ism',** *n.*

Republican party, one of the two major political parties of the United States, originated (1854–56) to combat slavery.

re·pu·di·ate (rĭ pū'dĭ āt'), *v.t.,* **-ated, -ating.** **1.** to reject as having no authority or binding force, as a claim. **2.** to cast off or disown. **3.** to reject with disapproval or condemnation. as a doctrine. **4.** to reject with denial, as a charge. —**re·pu'di·a'tion,** *n.* —**re·pu'di·a'tive,** *adj.* —**re·pu'di·a'tor,** *n.*

re·pug·nant (rĭ pŭg'nənt), *adj.* **1.** distasteful or objectionable. **2.** objecting; averse. **3.** opposed or contrary. —**re·pug'nance,** *n.*

re·pulse (rĭ pŭls'), *v.,* **-pulsed, -pulsing,** *n.* —*v.t.* **1.** to drive back or repel, as an assailant. **2.** to refuse or reject. —*n.* **3.** act of repelling. **4.** fact of being repelled. **5.** refusal or rejection.

re·pul·sion (rĭ pŭl'shən), *n.* **1.** act of repelling. **2.** state of being repelled. **3.** distaste, repugnance, or aversion. **4.** *Physics.* a situation in which bodies are forced apart.

re·pul·sive (rĭ pŭl'sĭv), *adj.* **1.** causing repugnance or aversion. **2.** tending to repel by denial, discourtesy, or the like. **3.** *Physics.* **a.** characterized by physical repulsion. **b.** tending to repel. —**re·pul'sive·ly,** *adv.* —**re·pul'sive·ness,** *n.*

rep·u·ta·ble (rĕp'yə tə bəl), *adj.* held in good repute; honorable; respectable. —**rep'u·ta·bil'i·ty,** *n.* —**rep'u·ta·bly,** *adv.*

rep·u·ta·tion (rĕp'yə tā'shən), *n.* **1.** the estimation in which a person or thing is held, esp. by the community; repute. **2.** favorable repute; good name. **3.** a favorable and publicly recognized standing.

re·pute (rĭ pūt'), *n., v.,* **-puted, -puting.** —*n.* **1.** estimation in the view of others; reputation. **2.** favorable reputation; good name. —*v.t.* **3.** to consider or esteem.

re·put·ed (rĭ pū'tĭd), *adj.* accounted or supposed to be such. —**re·put'ed·ly,** *adv.*

re·quest (rĭ kwĕst'), *n.* **1.** act of asking for something to be given or done. **2.** that which is asked for. **3.** demand. —*v.t.* **4.** to ask for; solicit. **5.** to ask or beg.

Re·qui·em (rē'kwĭ əm, rĕk'wĭ-), *n. Rom. Cath. Ch.* **1.** the Mass celebrated for the repose of the souls of the dead. **2.** a musical setting of this Mass. Also, **re'qui·em.**

re·quire (rĭ kwīr'), *v.,* **-quired, -quiring.** —*v.t.* **1.** to have need of; need. **2.** to call on authoritatively, order, or enjoin. **3.** to demand.

re·pour'	re'·pro·claim'	re·pub'lish	re·pur'pose
re·prime'	re'·pro·mul'gate	re·pur'chase	re·pur'sue'
re·proc'ess	re·prove'	re·pur'i·fy'	re·quick'en

4. to make necessary. 5. to call for as obligatory. 6. to place under an obligation or necessity. —*v.i.* 7. to impose obligation or need.

re·quire·ment (rĭ kwīr′mənt), *n.* 1. that which is demanded or obligatory. 2. act or an instance of requiring. 3. a need.

req·ui·site (rĕk′wə zĭt), *adj.* 1. needed; necessary; indispensable. —*n.* 2. a necessary or indispensable thing.

req·ui·si·tion (rĕk′wə zĭsh′ən), *n.* 1. act of requiring or demanding. 2. a demand made, esp. a formal or authoritative one. —*v.t.* 3. to require or take for use, esp. by official authority.

re·quite (rĭ kwīt′), *v.t.*, -quited, -quiting. 1. to make repayment, return, or retaliation for. 2. to make return to or retaliation on. —**re·quit′-al,** *n.*

re·scind (rĭ sĭnd′), *v.t.* to abrogate; annul; revoke; repeal. —**re·scis·sion** (rĭ sĭzh′ən), *n.*

res·cue (rĕs′kū), *v.*, -cued, -cuing, *n.* —*v.t.* 1. to free or deliver from confinement, violence, danger, or evil. —*n.* 2. act of rescuing. —**res′-cu·er,** *n.*

re·search (rĭ sûrch′, rē′sûrch), *n.* 1. (*often pl.*) diligent inquiry or investigation into a subject. —*v.i.* 2. to investigate carefully. —**re·search′-er,** *n.*

re·seat (rē sēt′), *v.t.* 1. to provide with a new seat or new seats. 2. to seat again.

re·sem·blance (rĭ zĕm′bləns), *n.* similarity; likeness.

re·sem·ble (rĭ zĕm′bəl), *v.t.*, -bled, -bling. to be like or similar to.

re·sent (rĭ zĕnt′), *v.t.* to feel or show displeasure or indignation at. —**re·sent′ful,** *adj.* —**re·sent′ful·ly,** *adv.* —**re·sent′ful·ness,** *n.*

re·sent·ment (rĭ zĕnt′mənt), *n.* displeasure or indignation, as at something regarded as an injury or insult.

res·er·va·tion (rĕz′ər vā′shən), *n.* 1. a keeping back, withholding, or setting apart. 2. an exception or qualification made. 3. *U.S.* a tract of public land set apart for a special purpose, as for the use of an Indian tribe. 4. (*often pl.*) the allotting or the securing of accommodations at a hotel, on a train, etc. 5. the record or assurance of such an arrangement.

re·serve (rĭ zûrv′), *v.*, -served, -serving, *n.*, *adj.* —*v.t.* 1. to keep back or save for future use, disposal, etc. 2. to retain or secure by express stipulation. 3. to set apart for a particular use. —*n.* 4. an amount of capital retained, as by a banker, to meet probable demands. 5. something reserved; stock. 6. a tract of public land set apart for a special purpose. 7. the state of being reserved. 8. *Mil.* a. a fraction of a military force held in readiness to sustain the attack or defense made by the rest of the force. b. (*pl.*) the enrolled but not regular components of the Army of the U.S. 9. avoidance of familiarity in social relationships. 10. reticence or silence. —*adj.* 11. kept in reserve; forming a reserve.

re·served (rĭ zûrvd′), *adj.* 1. set apart for a particular purpose. 2. kept by special arrangement for some person or persons. 3. self-restrained in action or speech. —**re·serv·ed·ly** (rĭ zûr′vĭd lĭ), *adv.*

re·serv·ist (rĭ zûr′vĭst), *n.* a member of a reserve military force of a country.

res·er·voir (rĕz′ər vôr′, -vwâr′), *n.* 1. a natural or artificial place where water is collected and stored for use, esp. water for supplying a community, irrigating land, etc. 2. a place where anything is accumulated. 3. a supply.

re·set (*v.* rē sĕt′; *n.* rē′sĕt′), *v.*, -set, -setting, *n.* —*v.t.* 1. to set again. —*n.* 2. act of resetting. 3. that which is reset. 4. a plant which is replanted.

re·side (rĭ zīd′), *v.i.*, -sided, -siding. 1. to dwell permanently or for a considerable time. 2. to exist. 3. to be vested, as powers.

res·i·dence (rĕz′ə dəns), *n.* 1. dwelling place; dwelling. 2. a large house. 3. act or fact of residing. Also, **res′i·den·cy.**

res·i·dent (rĕz′ə dənt), *n.* 1. one who resides in a place. 2. a diplomatic representative at a foreign court. —*adj.* 3. residing.

res·i·den·tial (rĕz′ə dĕn′shəl), *adj.* 1. of or pertaining to a residence or residences. 2. adapted or used for residence.

re·sid·u·al (rĭ zĭj′ŏŏ əl), *adj.* 1. Also, **re·sid·u·ar·y** (rĭ zĭj′ŏŏ ĕr′ĭ). remaining; left over. 2. *Math.* formed by the subtraction of one quantity from another. —*n.* 3. a remainder.

res·i·due (rĕz′ə dū′, -dōō′), *n.* that which remains; remainder; rest.

re·sid·u·um (rĭ zĭj′ŏŏ əm), *n., pl.* -sidua (-zĭj′-ŏŏ ə). the residue, remainder, or rest.

re·sign (rĭ zīn′), *v.i.*, *v.t.* 1. to give up (an office, position, claim, etc.). 2. to submit; yield.

res·ig·na·tion (rĕz′ĭg nā′shən), *n.* 1. act of resigning. 2. the formal statement, document, etc., stating that one resigns an office, position, etc. 3. submission; unresisting acquiescence.

re·signed (rĭ zīnd′), *adj.* submissive or acquiescent. —**re·sign·ed·ly** (rĭ zī′nĭd lĭ), *adv.*

re·sil·i·ent (rĭ zĭl′ĭ ənt), *adj.* 1. springing back; rebounding. 2. returning to the original form or position after being bent, compressed, or stretched. 3. buoyant; cheerful. —**re·sil′i·ence, re·sil′i·en·cy,** *n.*

res·in (rĕz′ĭn), *n.* 1. any of a class of organic substances obtained directly from certain plants as exudations: used in medicine, varnish-making, etc. 2. rosin. —*v.t.* 3. to treat or rub with resin. —**res′in·ous,** *adj.*

re·sist (rĭ zĭst′), *v.t.* 1. to withstand or oppose. —*v.i.* 2. to offer resistance. —**re·sist′er,** *n.* —**re·sist′i·ble,** *adj.*

re·sist·ance (rĭ zĭs′təns), *n.* 1. act or power of resisting. 2. opposition. 3. *Elect.* that property of a conductor in virtue of which the passage of a current is opposed, causing electric energy to be transformed into heat. —**re·sist′ant,** *adj.*, *n.*

re·sist·less (rĭ zĭst′lĭs), *adj.* 1. irresistible. 2. unresisting. —**re·sist′less·ly,** *adv.*

re·sis·tor (rĭ zĭs′tər), *n. Elect.* a device, the primary purpose of which is to introduce resistance into an electric circuit.

res·o·lute (rĕz′ə lōōt′), *adj.* firmly determined; resolved. —**res′o·lute·ly,** *adv.* —**res′o·lute·ness,** *n.*

res·o·lu·tion (rĕz′ə lōō′shən), *n.* 1. a formal determination or expression of opinion, esp. of a deliberative assembly. 2. a resolve or determination. 3. act of resolving. 4. firmness of purpose. 5. solution or explanation, as of a problem.

re·solve (rĭ zŏlv′), *v.*, -solved, -solving, *n.* —*v.t., v.i.* 1. to determine or decide firmly. 2. to disintegrate, separate, or break up. 3. to determine or state formally in a vote or resolution, as a deliberative assembly. 4. to explain; solve. 5. to clear away or dispel (doubts, etc.). —*n.* 6. a determination made. 7. firmness of purpose. —**re·solv′a·ble,** *adj.* —**re·solv′er,** *n.*

re·solved (rĭ zŏlvd′), *adj.* determined; resolute. —**re·solv·ed·ly** (rĭ zŏl′vĭd lĭ), *adv.*

res·o·nant (rĕz′ə nant), *adj.* 1. resounding or echoing, as sounds, places, etc. 2. deep and full, as a voice. 3. having the property of increasing the intensity of sound by sympathetic vibration. —**res′o·nant·ly,** *adv.* —**res′o·nance,** *n.*

res·o·na·tor (rĕz′ə nā′tər), *n.* an appliance for increasing the intensity of sound by sympathetic vibration.

re·sort (rĭ zôrt′), *v.i.* 1. to have recourse for use, service, or help. 2. to go, esp. frequently. —*n.* 3. a place frequented, esp. by the general public. 4. recourse.

re·sound (rĭ zound′), *v.i.* 1. to echo or ring with sound, as a place. 2. to make an echoing sound or sound loudly. —**re·sound′ing·ly,** *adv.*

re·source (rĭ sōrs′, rē′sōrs), *n.* 1. a source of supply, support, or aid. 2. (*pl.*) the collective wealth of a country. 3. (*often pl.*) money or property; assets. 4. available means afforded by the mind or the personal capabilities. 5. an expedient. 6. capability in dealing with a situation or in meeting difficulties.

re·source·ful (rĭ sōrs′fəl), *adj.* full of resource; fertile in expedients. —**re·source′ful·ly,** *adv.* —**re·source′ful·ness,** *n.*

re·spect (rĭ spĕkt′), *n.* 1. a particular, detail, or point. 2. relation or reference. 3. esteem or

re·rate′	re·sal′a·ble	re·serve′	re·shuf′fle
re·read′	re·sale′	re·set′tle	re·sift′
re·reel′	re·seal′	re·shake′	re·sight′
re·roll′	re·seed′	re·shape′	re·soak′
re·route′	re·seek′	re·sharp′en	re·sol′der
re·run′	re·seize′	re·ship′	re·sole′
re·sad′dle	re·sell′	re·ship′ment	re·so·lid′i·fy′

regard. —*v.t.* **4.** to hold in esteem or honor. **5.** to show esteem, regard, or consideration for. **6.** to relate or have reference to. —**re·spect′er,** *n.*

re·spect·a·ble (rĭ spĕk′tə bəl), *adj.* **1.** worthy of respect; worthy. **2.** of good social standing, reputation, etc. **3.** proper or decent. **4.** fairly good; fair. **5.** considerable in size, number, or amount. —**re·spect′a·bil′i·ty, re·spect′a·ble·ness,** *n.* —**re·spect′a·bly,** *adv.*

re·spect·ful (rĭ spĕkt′fəl), *adj.* showing respect. —**re·spect′ful·ly,** *adv.* —**re·spect′ful·ness,** *n.*

re·spect·ing (rĭ spĕk′tĭng), *prep.* regarding; concerning.

re·spec·tive (rĭ spĕk′tĭv), *adj.* pertaining individually; particular.

re·spec·tive·ly (rĭ spĕk′tĭv lĭ), *adv.* with respect to each of a number.

Re·spi·ghi (rĕ spē′gē), *n.* Ottorino, 1879–1936, Italian composer.

res·pi·ra·tion (rĕs′pə rā′shən), *n.* inhalation and exhalation of air; breathing.

res·pi·ra·tor (rĕs′pə rā′tər), *n.* **1.** a device, usually of gauze, worn over the mouth, or nose and mouth, to prevent the inhalation of noxious substances, etc. **2.** an apparatus to produce artificial respiration.

res·pi·ra·to·ry (rĭ spīr′ə tōr′ĭ, rĕs′pə rə tor′ĭ), *adj.* of or for respiration.

re·spire (rĭ spīr′), *v.i.*, *v.t.*, **-spired, -spiring.** to inhale and exhale (air); breathe.

res·pite (rĕs′pĭt), *n.*, *v.*, **-pited, -piting.** —*n.* **1.** a delay or cessation for a time. **2.** a reprieve. —*v.t.* **3.** to relieve temporarily. **4.** to grant delay in the carrying out of (a punishment, obligation, etc.).

re·splend·ent (rĭ splĕn′dənt), *adj.* shining brilliantly; gleaming. —**re·splend′ent·ly,** *adv.* —**re·splend′ence, re·splend′en·cy,** *n.*

re·spond (rĭ spŏnd′), *v.i.*, *v.t.* **1.** to answer; reply. **2.** to make a return by some action as if in answer. **3.** *Physiol.* to react. **4.** to correspond.

re·spond·ent (rĭ spŏn′dənt), *adj.* **1.** answering; responsive. —*n.* **2.** one who responds. **3.** *Law.* a defendant.

re·sponse (rĭ spŏns′), *n.* **1.** answer or reply, whether in words, action, etc. **2.** *Biol.* any behavior of a living organism which results from stimulation.

re·spon·si·bil·i·ty (rĭ spŏn′sə bĭl′ə tĭ), *n.*, *pl.* **-ties. 1.** state or fact of being responsible. **2.** a particular burden of obligation. **3.** ability to meet debts or payments. **4.** initiative or authority.

re·spon·si·ble (rĭ spŏn′sə bəl), *adj.* **1.** answerable or accountable. **2.** involving accountability. **3.** chargeable with being the author, cause, or occasion of something. **4.** capable of rational thought or action. **5.** able to discharge obligations. **6.** reliable. —**re·spon′si·bly,** *adv.*

re·spon·sive (rĭ spŏn′sĭv), *adj.* **1.** making answer or reply. **2.** *Physiol.* acting in response. —**re·spon′sive·ly,** *adv.* —**re·spon′sive·ness,** *n.*

rest[1] (rĕst), *n.* **1.** refreshing quiet or inactivity, as after work. **2.** tranquillity. **3.** the repose of death. **4.** cessation or absence of motion. **5.** *Music.* **a.** an interval of silence between tones. **b.** a mark or sign indicating it. **6.** a thing to rest (something) on. **7.** a support. —*v.i.* **8.** to refresh oneself, as by sleeping, lying down, cessation of labor, etc. **9.** to be at ease. **10.** to repose in death. **11.** to be quiet or still. **12.** to cease from motion; stop. **13.** to become or remain inactive. **14.** to lie, sit, lean, or be set. **15.** to be imposed as a burden or responsibility. **16.** to rely. **17.** to be based. **18.** to be or exist. **19.** to be fixed or directed on something, as the eyes, etc. **20.** *Law.* to terminate voluntarily the introduction of evidence in a case. —*v.t.* **21.** to give rest to. **22.** to lay or place for rest, ease, or support. **23.** to direct (the eyes, etc.). **24.** to base. **25.** *Law.* to terminate voluntarily the introduction of evidence on.

rest[2] (rĕst), *n.* **1.** that which is left; remainder. **2.** the others. —*v.i.* **3.** to continue to be; remain.

res·tau·rant (rĕs′tə rənt, -ränt′), *n.* an establishment serving meals to customers.

res·tau·ra·teur (rĕs′tə rə tûr′), *n.* the keeper of a restaurant.

rest·ful (rĕst′fəl), *adj.* **1.** full of, or giving, rest. **2.** being at rest; quiet; peaceful. —**rest′ful·ly,** *adv.* —**rest′ful·ness,** *n.*

res·ti·tu·tion (rĕs′tə tū′shən, -tōō′-), *n.* **1.** reparation for loss, damage, or injury. **2.** the restoration of property or rights previously taken away, conveyed, or surrendered.

res·tive (rĕs′tĭv), *adj.* **1.** restless; uneasy. **2.** refractory. **3.** balky, as a horse. —**res′tive·ly,** *adv.* —**res′tive·ness,** *n.*

rest·less (rĕst′lĭs), *adj.* **1.** unable to remain at rest. **2.** unquiet or uneasy. **3.** never motionless or still. **4.** without rest. —**rest′less·ly,** *adv.* —**rest′less·ness,** *n.*

res·to·ra·tion (rĕs′tə rā′shən), *n.* **1.** renewal, revival, or reëstablishment. **2.** restitution. **3. The Restoration, a.** the reëstablishment of the monarchy in England with the return of Charles II in 1660. **b.** the period of the reign of Charles II (1660–85), sometimes extended to include the reign of James II (1685–88).

re·stor·a·tive (rĭ stōr′ə tĭv), *adj.* **1.** serving to restore. **2.** capable of renewing health or strength. —*n.* **3.** a restorative agent. **4.** a means of restoring a person to consciousness.

re·store (rĭ stōr′), *v.t.*, **-stored, -storing. 1.** to bring back into existence, use, or the like; reëstablish. **2.** to bring back to a former, original, or normal condition. **3.** to bring back to a state of health, soundness, or vigor. **4.** to put back in a former position, rank, etc. **5.** to give back. —**re·stor′er,** *n.*

re·strain (rĭ strān′), *v.t.* **1.** to hold back; keep under control; repress. **2.** to deprive of liberty. —**re·strain′a·ble,** *adj.* —**re·strain·ed·ly** (rĭ strā′nĭd lĭ), *adv.* —**re·strain′er,** *n.*

re·straint (rĭ strānt′), *n.* **1.** restraining action or influence. **2.** a means of restraining. **3.** act of restraining. **4.** confinement. **5.** constraint or reserve in feelings.

re·strict (rĭ strĭkt′), *v.t.* to confine or limit. —**re·strict′ed,** *adj.* —**re·strict′ed·ly,** *adv.* —**re·stric′tive,** *adj.*

re·stric·tion (rĭ strĭk′shən), *n.* **1.** something that restricts; restrictive condition or regulation. **2.** act of restricting.

restrictive clause, *Gram.* a relative clause, usually not set off by commas, which identifies the person or object named by the antecedent.

re·sult (rĭ zŭlt′), *n.* **1.** the outcome, consequence, or effect. **2.** *Math.* a quantity, value, etc., obtained by calculation. —*v.i.* **3.** to spring, arise, or proceed as a consequence. **4.** to end.

re·sult·ant (rĭ zŭl′tənt), *adj.* **1.** following as a result or consequence. —*n.* **2.** *Physics.* a force, velocity, etc., equal in result or effect to two or more such forces, velocities, etc. **3.** that which results.

re·sume (rĭ zōōm′), *v.t.*, *v.i.*, **-sumed, -suming. 1.** to go on (with) again after interruption. **2.** to occupy again. **3.** to take again. —**re·sum′a·ble,** *adj.* —**re·sump·tion** (rĭ zŭmp′shən), *n.*

ré·su·mé (rĕz′ŏŏ mā′), *n.* a summary.

re·sur·gent (rĭ sûr′jənt), *adj.* rising or tending to rise again. —**re·sur′gence,** *n.*

res·ur·rect (rĕz′ə rĕkt′), *v.t.* **1.** to bring to life again. **2.** to bring back into use, practice, etc.

res·ur·rec·tion (rĕz′ə rĕk′shən), *n.* **1.** act of rising again from the dead, esp. (*cap.*) of Christ. **2.** state of those risen from the dead. **3.** a revival.

re·sus·ci·tate (rĭ sŭs′ə tāt′), *v.t.*, **-tated, -tating.** to revive, esp. from unconsciousness. —**re·sus′ci·ta′tion,** *n.*

ret (rĕt), *v.t.*, **retted, retting.** to moisten or soak, as flax, in order to soften.

ret., **1.** retired. **2.** Also, **retd.** returned.

re·tail (rē′tāl *for 1–3, 5;* rĭ tāl′ *for 4*), *n.* **1.** the sale of commodities to ultimate consumers. —*adj.* **2.** pertaining to, connected with, or engaged in sale at retail. —*v.t.* **3.** to sell directly to the consumer. **4.** to relate in detail to others. —*v.i.* **5.** to be sold at retail. —**re′tail·er,** *n.*

re·tain (rĭ tān′), *v.t.* **1.** to keep. **2.** to continue to use, etc. **3.** to remember. **4.** to hold in place. **5.** to engage, as a lawyer. —**re·tain′a·ble,** *adj.*

re·tain·er[1] (rĭ tā′nər), *n.* *Hist.* one attached to a noble household and owing it occasional service.

re·tain·er[2] (rĭ tā'nər), *n.* a fee paid to secure services, as of a lawyer.

re·tal·i·ate (rĭ tăl'ĭ āt'), *v.,* -ated, -ating. —*v.i.* 1. to return like for like, esp. evil for evil. —*v.t.* 2. to requite (wrong, injury, etc.) with the like. —**re·tal'i·a'tion,** *n.* —**re·tal'i·a'tive, re·tal·i·a·to·ry** (rĭ tăl'ĭ ə tōr'ĭ), *adj.*

re·tard (rĭ tärd'), *v.t.* 1. to make slow; delay, hinder, or impede. —*v.i.* 2. to be delayed. —*n.* 3. delay. —**re'tar·da'tion,** *n.* —**re·tard'er,** *n.*

retch (rĕch), *v.i.* to make efforts to vomit.

re·ten·tion (rĭ tĕn'shən), *n.* 1. act of retaining. 2. state of being retained. 3. power to retain. 4. memory.

re·ten·tive (rĭ tĕn'tĭv), *adj.* 1. serving to retain. 2. having power to retain. 3. having a good memory. —**re·ten'tive·ness,** *n.*

ret·i·cent (rĕt'ə sənt), *adj.* disposed to say little; reserved. —**ret'i·cence,** *n.* —**ret'i·cent·ly,** *adv.*

re·tic·u·la·tion (rĭ tĭk'yə lā'shən), *n.* a netlike formation, arrangement, or appearance.

ret·i·na (rĕt'ə nə, rĕt'nə), *n., pl.* -nas, -nae (-nē'). *Anat.* the innermost coat of the posterior part of the eyeball, connected with the optic nerve and serving to receive the image. —**ret'i·nal,** *adj.*

ret·i·nue (rĕt'ə nū', -nōō'), *n.* a body of attendants of an important personage.

re·tire (rĭ tīr'), *v.,* -tired, -tiring. —*v.i.* 1. to withdraw; go away or apart. 2. to go to bed. 3. to withdraw from office. business, or active life. 4. to retreat. —*v.t.* 5. to take up and pay, as bonds, bills, etc. 6. to remove from active service, work, etc.

re·tired (rĭ tīrd'), *adj.* 1. no longer active in one's business or profession. 2. due or given a retired person. 3. withdrawn; secluded.

re·tire·ment (rĭ tīr'mənt), *n.* 1. act of retiring. 2. state of being retired. 3. removal or retiring from service, office, or business. 4. privacy or seclusion.

re·tir·ing (rĭ tīr'ĭng), *adj.* 1. that retires. 2. reserved; shy.

re·tort[1] (rĭ tôrt'), *v.t.* 1. to reply in retaliation. —*n.* 2. a severe, incisive, or witty reply.

re·tort[2] (rĭ tôrt'), *n.* *Chem.* a vessel, commonly a glass bulb with a long neck bent downward, used for distilling or decomposing substances by heat.

re·touch (rē tŭch'), *v.t. Photog.* to correct or improve (a negative or print) by the use of a pencil, scraping knife, etc.

A. Retort; B. Receiver

re·trace (rĭ trās'), *v.t.,* -traced, -tracing. to go back over.

re·tract (rĭ trăkt'), *v.t., v.i.* 1. to withdraw (a statement, promise, etc.). 2. to draw back or in. —**re·tract'a·ble,** *adj.* —**re·trac'tion,** *n.* —**re·trac'tor,** *n.*

re·tread (*v.* rē trĕd'; *n.* rē'trĕd'), *v.,* -treaded, -treading, *n.* —*v.t.* 1. to put a new tread on (a worn tire casing). —*n.* 2. a retreaded tire.

re·treat (rĭ trēt'), *n.* 1. the forced or strategic withdrawal of an armed force or fleet. 2. retirement; seclusion. 3. a place of refuge, seclusion, or privacy. 4. a retirement for religious exercises and meditation. 5. a signal given in the army or navy by drum, bugle, or trumpet, at sunset. —*v.i., v.t.* 6. to withdraw; retire. 7. to make a retreat, as an army. 8. to recede.

re·trench (rĭ trĕnch'), *v.t., v.i.* to reduce or curtail (expenses). —**re·trench'ment,** *n.*

ret·ri·bu·tion (rĕt'rə bū'shən), *n.* 1. requital according to merits or deserts. 2. something given or inflicted in requital. —**re·trib·u·tive** (rĭ trĭb'yə tĭv), *adj.*

re·trieve (rĭ trēv'), *v.,* -trieved, -trieving, *n.* —*v.t., v.i.* 1. to recover or regain. 2. to restore. 3. to make amends for (an error, etc.). 4. to make good (a loss, etc.). 5. *Hunting.* (of dogs) to find and fetch (killed or wounded game). —*n.* 6. recovery. —**re·triev'a·ble,** *adj.* —**re·triev'al,** *n.*

re·triev·er (rĭ trē'vər), *n.* 1. one that retrieves. 2. any of several breeds of dog developed or trained for retrieving game.

ret·ro·ac·tive (rĕt'rō ăk'tĭv), *adj.* applying also to what is past. —**ret'ro·ac'tive·ly,** *adv.*

ret·ro·grade (rĕt'rə grād'), *adj., v.,* -graded, -grading. —*adj.* 1. moving backward; retiring. 2. *Chiefly Biol.* exhibiting degeneration or deterioration. —*v.i.* 3. to move backward; retire. 4. *Chiefly Biol.* to decline to a worse condition; degenerate. —**ret'ro·gres'sion,** *n.* —**ret'ro·gres'sive,** *adj.*

ret·ro·spect (rĕt'rə spĕkt'), *n.* contemplation or survey of past events, etc. —**ret'ro·spec'tion,** *n.* —**ret'ro·spec'tive,** *adj.*

ret·rous·sé (rĕt'rōō sā'), *adj.* (esp. of the nose) turned up.

re·turn (rĭ tûrn'), *v.i.* 1. to go or come back, as to a former place, state, etc. 2. to revert or recur. 3. to reply; retort. —*v.t.* 4. to put, bring, take, give, or send back. 5. *Law.* to render (a verdict, etc.). —*n.* 6. act or fact of returning. 7. a recurrence. 8. reciprocation, repayment, or requital. 9. response or reply. 10. (*often pl.*) a yield or profit, as from labor, land, business, investment, etc. 11. a report, esp. a formal or official report. —*adj.* 12. of or pertaining to return or returning. 13. sent, given, or done in return. 14. done or occurring again. 15. denoting a person or thing which is returned or returning to a place. —**re·turn'a·ble,** *adj.*

re·un·ion (rē ūn'yən), *n.* 1. act of uniting again. 2. a gathering of relatives, friends, or associates after separation.

Ré·un·ion (rē ūn'yən), *n.* an island in the Indian Ocean, E of Madagascar, forming a department of France. 212,792 pop.; 970 sq. mi. *Cap.*: St. Denis.

re·u·nite (rē'ū nīt'), *v.t., v.i.,* -nited, -niting. to unite again, as after separation.

rev (rĕv), *n., v.,* **revved, revving.** *Colloq.* —*n.* 1. a revolution (in machinery). —*v.t.* 2. *Chiefly Brit.* to change the speed of. —*v.i.* 3. to undergo revving.

Rev., 1. Revelations. 2. Reverend.

rev., 1. revised. 2. revision.

re·vamp (rē vămp'), *v.t.* to renovate.

re·veal (rĭ vēl'), *v.t.* 1. to make known; disclose. 2. to display; exhibit. —*n.* 3. a revelation; disclosure. —**re·veal'a·ble,** *adj.*

rev·eil·le (rĕv'ə lĭ), *n.* a signal, as on a drum or bugle, at a prescribed hour, to waken soldiers or sailors for the day's duties.

rev·el (rĕv'əl), *v.,* -eled, -eling or (*esp. Brit.*) -elled, -elling, *n.* —*v.i.* 1. to take great pleasure. 2. to make merry. —*n.* 3. merrymaking; revelry. —**rev'e·ler;** *esp. Brit.,* **rev'el·ler,** *n.*

rev·e·la·tion (rĕv'ə lā'shən), *n.* 1. act of disclosing; disclosure. 2. something disclosed. 3. *Theol.* God's disclosure of Himself and of His will to His creatures. 4. **Revelation,** (*often pl.*) "the Revelation of St. John the Divine."

Revelation of St. John the Divine, The, the last book in the New Testament; Apocalypse.

rev·el·ry (rĕv'əl rĭ), *n., pl.* -ries. reveling; boisterous festivity.

re·venge (rĭ vĕnj'), *n., v.,* -venged, -venging. —*n.* 1. retaliation; vengeance. 2. vindictiveness. —*v.t.* 3. to take vengeance on behalf of (a person, etc.) or for (a wrong, etc.). —**re·veng'er,** *n.*

re·venge·ful (rĭ vĕnj'fəl), *adj.* full of revenge; vindictive. —**re·venge'ful·ly,** *adv.*

rev·e·nue (rĕv'ə nū', -nōō'), *n.* 1. the income of a government from taxation, customs, or other sources. 2. any yield or income.

re·ver·ber·ant (rĭ vûr'bər ənt), *adj.* reverberating; reëchoing.

re·ver·ber·ate (rĭ vûr'bə rāt'), *v.i., v.t.,* -ated, -ating. 1. to echo back; resound. 2. to cast back or reflect (light, etc.). —**re·ver'ber·a'tion,** *n.*

re·vere[1] (rĭ vĭr'), *v.t.,* -vered, -vering. to regard with respect and awe; venerate.

re·vere[2] (rĭ vĭr'), *n.* revers.

Re·vere (rĭ vĭr'), *n.* 1. **Paul,** 1735–1818, American patriot. 2. a city in E Massachusetts, near Boston. 34,405.

rev·er·ence (rĕv'ər əns), *n., v.,* -enced, -encing. —*n.* 1. the feeling of deep respect and awe; veneration. 2. an obeisance, bow, or curtsy. 3. (*cap.*) a title used in addressing or mentioning a clergyman (prec. by *your* or *his*). —*v.i.* 4. to regard or treat with reverence.

rev·er·end (rĕv'ər ənd), *adj.* 1. an epithet of respect applied to, or prefixed to the name of, a

re·take'	re·tes'ti·fy'	re·trans'fer	re·type'
re·teach'	re·think'	re'trans·late'	re·use'
re·tell'	re·tie'	re·tri'al	re·u'ti·lize'
re·test'	re·told'	re·try'	re·val'ue

clergyman. 2. entitled to reverence. —*n.* 3. *Colloq.* a clergyman.

rev·er·ent (rĕv′ər ənt), *adj.* feeling, exhibiting, or characterized by reverence; deeply respectful. —**rev′er·ent·ly**, *adv.*

rev·er·en·tial (rĕv′ə rĕn′shəl), *adj.* reverent. —**rev′er·en′tial·ly**, *adv.*

rev·er·ie (rĕv′ə rĭ), *n.* 1. a state of dreamy meditation or fanciful musing. 2. a daydream. 3. a fantastic, visionary, or unpractical idea. Also, rev′er·y.

re·vers (rə vĭr′, -vâr′), *n., pl.* **-vers** (-vĭrz′, -vârz′). a part of a garment turned back to show the lining or facing, as a lapel.

re·ver·sal (rĭ vûr′səl), *n.* 1. act of reversing. 2. an instance of this. 3. state of being reversed.

re·verse (rĭ vûrs′), *adj., n., v.* **-versed, -versing.** —*adj.* 1. opposite or contrary in position, direction, order, action, or character. 2. with the rear part toward one. 3. producing a rearward motion. —*n.* 4. the opposite or contrary of something. 5. the back or rear of anything. 6. a misfortune, check, or defeat. 7. *Auto.* a transmission gear ratio driving a car backwards. —*v.t., v.i.* 8. to turn in an opposite position or in the opposite direction. 9. to turn inside out or upside down. 10. to turn in the opposite order. 11. to change completely. 12. to revoke or annul. 13. *Mach.* to cause to act in an opposite direction or manner. —**re·verse′ly**, *adv.* —**re·vers′er**, *n.* —**re·vers′i·ble**, *adj.*

re·vert (rĭ vûrt′), *v.i.* 1. to return to a former habit, practice, belief, condition, etc. 2. to go back in thought or discourse, as to a subject. 3. *Biol.* to return to an earlier type. —**re·ver·sion** (rĭ vûr′zhən, -shən), *n.*

re·view (rĭ vū′), *n.* 1. a critical article, as in a periodical, on some literary work or the like. 2. a periodical publication; magazine. 3. a second or repeated view of something. 4. an inspection, esp. a formal inspection of any military or naval force. 5. a judicial reëxamination of the decision or proceedings in a case. —*v.t.* 6. to view, look at, or look over again. 7. to inspect, esp. formally or officially. 8. to survey. 9. to discuss (a book, etc.) in a critical review. 10. *Law.* to reëxamine judicially. —*v.i.* 11. to review books, etc. —**re·view′a·ble**, *adj.* —**re·view′er**, *n.*

re·vile (rĭ vīl′), *v.,* **-viled, -viling.** —*v.t.* 1. to assail with contemptuous or opprobrious language. —*v.i.* 2. to speak abusively. —**re·vile′ment**, *n.* —**re·vil′er**, *n.*

re·vise (rĭ vīz′), *v.,* **-vised, -vising.** *n.* —*v.t.* 1. to amend or alter. —*n.* 2. a revised form of something. —**re·vis′er**, *n.* —**re·vi′so·ry**, *adj.*

Revised Version of the Bible, a revision of the King James Version of the Bible, prepared by a committee of British and American scholars, published 1881–85.

re·vi·sion (rĭ vĭzh′ən), *n.* 1. act or work of revising. 2. a revised form or version.

re·viv·al (rĭ vī′vəl), *n.* 1. act of reviving. 2. state of being revived. 3. restoration to life, consciousness, vigor, strength, etc. 4. restoration to use, acceptance, or currency. 5. the reproduction of an old play. 6. a service effecting a religious awakening.

re·viv·al·ist (rĭ vī′vəl ĭst), *n.* 1. one who revives former customs, methods, etc. 2. one who promotes or holds religious revivals.

re·vive (rĭ vīv′), *v.,* **-vived, -viving.** —*v.t.* 1. to set going or in activity again. 2. to make operative or valid again. 3. to bring back into notice, use, or currency. 4. to produce (an old play) again. 5. to restore to life or consciousness. 6. to reanimate or cheer. 7. to quicken or renew in the mind. —*v.i.* 8. to return to life, consciousness, vigor, strength, etc. 9. to be quickened, restored, or renewed, as hope, memories, etc. 10. to return to notice, use, or currency. 11. to become operative or valid again. —**re·viv′er**, *n.*

re·viv·i·fy (rē vĭv′ə fī′), *v.t.,* **-fied, -fying.** to restore to life or give new life to. —**re·viv·i·fi·ca·tion** (rē vĭv′ə fə kā′shən), *n.*

re·voke (rĭ vōk′), *v.,* **-voked, -voking,** *n.* —*v.t.* 1. to withdraw, annul, or repeal. —*v.i.* 2. *Cards.* to fail to follow suit when one can and should do so. —*n.* 3. *Cards.* an act or instance of revoking. —**rev·o·ca·ble** (rĕv′ə kə bəl), **re·vok·a·ble** (rĭ vō′kə bəl), —**rev·o·ca·tion** (rĕv′ə kā′shən), *n.*

re·volt (rĭ vōlt′), *v.i., v.t.* 1. to cast off allegiance or subjection to those in authority; rebel. 2. to feel or affect with disgust or horror. —*n.* 3. insurrection or rebellion. 4. aversion, disgust, or loathing. —**re·volt′er**, *n.*

re·volt·ing (rĭ vōl′tĭng), *adj.* 1. rebellious. 2. disgusting; repulsive. —**re·volt′ing·ly**, *adv.*

rev·o·lu·tion (rĕv′ə lōō′shən), *n.* 1. a complete overthrow of an established government or political system, as the English Revolution (1688), the American Revolution (1775), the French Revolution (1789), the Chinese Revolution (1911), or the Russian Revolution (1917). 2. a complete or marked change. 3. procedure or course as if in a circuit. 4. a turning round or rotating, as on an axis. 5. a moving in a circular or curving course, as about a central point.

rev·o·lu·tion·ar·y (rĕv′ə lōō′shə nĕr′ĭ), *adj., n., pl.* **-aries.** —*adj.* 1. pertaining to, characterized by, or of the nature of a revolution. —*n.* 2. a revolutionist.

rev·o·lu·tion·ist (rĕv′ə lōō′shən ĭst), *n.* one who advocates or takes part in a revolution.

rev·o·lu·tion·ize (rĕv′ə lōō′shə nīz′), *v.t.,* **-ized, -izing.** 1. to bring about a revolution in. 2. to subject to a political revolution.

re·volve (rĭ vŏlv′), *v.i., v.t.,* **-volved, -volving.** 1. to turn round or rotate, as on an axis. 2. to move in a circular or curving course or orbit. 3. to proceed in a cycle. 4. to think about; consider. —**re·volv′a·ble**, *adj.*

re·volv·er (rĭ vŏl′vər), *n.* a pistol having a revolving chambered cylinder for holding a number of cartridges which may be discharged without reloading.

re·vue (rĭ vū′), *n.* 1. a theatrical entertainment in which recent events, popular fads, etc., are parodied. 2. any group of skits, dances, and songs.

re·vul·sion (rĭ vŭl′shən), *n.* a sudden and violent change of feeling or reaction in sentiment, esp. to disgust.

re·ward (rĭ wôrd′), *n.* 1. something given or received in recompense for service, merit, etc. 2. a sum of money offered for the detection or capture of a criminal, the recovery of lost property, etc. —*v.t.* 3. to recompense (a person, etc.) for service, merit, etc. 4. to make return for (service, merit, etc.).

rex (rĕks), *n.* Latin. king.

Rey·kja·vik (rā′kyə vēk′), *n.* a seaport in and the capital of Iceland, in the SW part. 46,578.

Reyn·ard (rĕn′ərd, rā′närd), *n.* a proper name for the fox, orig. in the medieval beast epic, *Reynard the Fox.*

Reyn·olds (rĕn′əldz), *n.* **Sir Joshua,** 1723–92, British portrait painter.

r.f., 1. radio frequency. 2. rapid-fire.

R.F.D., Rural Free Delivery.

Rh, *Chem.* rhodium.

rhap·sod·i·cal (răp sŏd′ə kəl), *adj.* 1. pertaining to, characteristic of, or of the nature of rhapsody. 2. extravagantly enthusiastic; ecstatic. Also, **rhap·sod′ic.** —**rhap·sod′i·cal·ly**, *adv.*

rhap·so·dize (răp′sə dīz′), *v.,* **-dized, -dizing.** —*v.i.* 1. to speak or write rhapsodies. 2. to talk rhapsodically. —*v.t.* 3. to recite as a rhapsody. —**rhap′so·dist**, *n.*

rhap·so·dy (răp′sə dĭ), *n., pl.* **-dies.** 1. an exalted or exaggerated expression of feeling or enthusiasm. 2. *Music.* an instrumental composition irregular in form.

Rhe·a (rē′ə), *n.* 1. *Gk. Myth.* the mother of Zeus and other major deities. 2. (*l.c.*) a South American bird resembling the African ostrich but smaller and having three toes instead of two.

Rheims (rēmz), *n.* Reims.

Rhen·ish (rĕn′ĭsh), *adj.* 1. of or along the river Rhine. —*n.* 2. Rhine wine.

rhe·ni·um (rē′nĭ əm), *n.* *Chem.* a rare metallic element of the manganese subgroup. *Symbol:* Re; *at. no.:* 75; *at. wt.:* 186.31.

rhe·o·stat (rē′ə stăt′), *n.* *Elect.* an adjustable resistor so constructed that its resistance may be changed without opening the circuit in which it may be connected.

rhe·sus (rē′səs), *n.* a macaque, common in India, much used in experimental medicine.

rhet·o·ric (rĕt′ə rĭk), *n.* 1. the art of all spe-

re·vi′brate
re·vict′ual
re·vin′di·cate′
re·vis′it

re·vi′tal·ize′
re·vote′
re·voy′age
re·warm′

re·wash′
re·wa′ter
re·weigh′
re·wind′

re·wire′
re·word′
re·work′
re·write′

cially literary uses of language, including figures of speech. 2. the art of prose as opposed to verse. 3. the use of exaggeration or display (in an unfavorable sense). 4. (orig.) the art of oratory. 5. (in classical oratory) the art of influencing the thought and conduct of one's hearers.

rhe·tor·i·cal (rĭ tôr′ə kəl, -tŏr′-), *adj.* 1. belonging to or concerned with mere style or effect. 2. having the nature of rhetoric. —**rhe·tor′i·cal·ly,** *adv.*

rhetorical question, a question designed to produce an effect and not to draw an answer.

rhet·o·ri·cian (rĕt′ə rĭsh′ən), *n.* 1. one versed in the art of rhetoric. 2. a person who teaches rhetoric.

rheum (rōōm), *n.* 1. *Med.* a thin serous or catarrhal discharge. 2. a cold.

rheu·mat·ic (rōō măt′ĭk), *adj.* 1. pertaining to or of the nature of rheumatism. 2. affected with rheumatism. —*n.* 3. one affected with rheumatism.

rheumatic fever, a disease, usually afflicting children, marked by fever, inflammation of the joints, generalized muscle pains, and frequently associated with pathological changes in the heart.

rheu·ma·tism (rōō′mə tĭz′əm), *n.* a disease commonly affecting the joints and accompanied by constitutional disturbances.

Rh factor, *Biochem.* a substance often present in human blood. Blood containing this factor (**Rh positive**) may cause unfavorable reactions, esp. during pregnancy or after repeated transfusions with blood lacking it (**Rh negative**). In full, **Rhesus factor.**

Rhine (rīn), *n.* a river flowing from SE Switzerland through Germany and the Netherlands into the North Sea. ab. 810 mi.

rhine·stone (rīn′stōn′), *n.* an artificial gem, often cut to imitate the diamond.

Rhine wine, 1. wine (of many varieties) produced in the valley of the Rhine. 2. any of a class of white wines, mostly light and dry.

rhi·ni·tis (rī nī′tĭs), *n. Pathol.* inflammation of the nose or its mucous membrane.

rhi·noc·er·os (rī nŏs′ər əs), *n., pl.* **-oses,** (*esp. collectively*) **-os.** any of various large, ungainly, thick-skinned mammals with one or two upright horns on the snout: found in Africa and Asia.

rhi·zome (rī′zōm), *n. Bot.* a rootlike subterranean stem, commonly horizontal in position, which usually produces roots below and sends up shoots progressively from the upper surface.

rho (rō), *n.* the seventeenth letter (P, ρ) of the Greek alphabet.

Rhode Island (rōd), a state of the NE United States, on the Atlantic coast. 744,986 pop; 1214 sq. mi. *Cap.:* Providence. *Abbr.:* R.I. —**Rhode Islander.**

Rhodes (rōdz), *n.* an island in the Aegean, off the SW coast of Turkey: the largest of the Dodecanese Islands. 61,886 pop.; 542 sq. mi.

Rho·de·sia (rō dē′zhə), *n.* a region in S Africa, comprising the British colonies of **Northern Rhodesia** and **Southern Rhodesia.** —**Rho·de′sian,** *adj., n.*

Rho·di·an (rō′dĭ ən), *adj.* 1. of or pertaining to the island, Rhodes. —*n.* 2. a native or inhabitant of Rhodes.

rho·di·um (rō′dĭ əm), *n. Chem.* a silvery-white metallic element of the platinum family. *Symbol:* Rh; *at. wt.:* 102.91; *at. no.:* 45; *sp. gr.:* 12.5 at 20°C.

rho·do·den·dron (rō′də dĕn′drən), *n.* any of certain evergreen and deciduous shrubs and trees with handsome pink, purple, or white flowers and oval or oblong leaves.

rhom·boid (rŏm′boid), *n.* 1. an oblique-angled parallelogram with only the opposite sides equal. —*adj.* 2. Also, **rhom·boi′dal.** shaped like a rhomboid.

rhom·bus (rŏm′bəs), *n., pl.* **-buses, -bi** (-bī). an oblique-angled equilateral parallelogram.

Rhône (rōn), *n.* a river flowing from S Switzerland through SE France into the Mediterranean. 504 mi.

rhu·barb (rōō′bärb), *n.* 1. any of certain herbs of the buckwheat family, including one variety having a medicinal rhizome and a garden variety having edible leafstalks. 2. the edible fleshy leafstalks of the garden species, used in making pies, etc.

rhyme (rīm), *n., v.,* **rhymed, rhyming.** —*n.* 1. agreement in the terminal sounds of lines of verse, or of words. 2. a word agreeing with another in terminal sound. 3. verse having corre-

spondence in the terminal sounds of the line. 4. a poem having such correspondence. —*v.t.* 5. to treat in rhyme. 6. to use (a word) as a rhyme to another word. —*v.i.* 7. to make rhyme. 8. to form a rhyme, as one word with another. Also, **rime.** —**rhym′er,** *n.*

rhyme·ster (rīm′stər), *n.* a poetaster.

rhythm (rĭth′əm), *n.* 1. movement with uniform recurrence of a beat, accent, or the like. 2. measured movement, as in dancing. 3. *Music.* **a.** the pattern of regular or irregular pulses caused in music by the occurrence of strong and weak melodic and harmonic beats. **b.** a particular form of this. 4. *Pros.* **a.** metrical form. **b.** metrical movement.

rhyth·mi·cal (rĭth′mə kəl), *adj.* 1. periodic, as motion, etc. 2. having a flowing rhythm. 3. of or pertaining to rhythm. Also, **rhyth′mic.** —**rhyth′mi·cal·ly,** *adv.*

R.I., Rhode Island.

ri·al (rĭ′əl), *n.* the monetary unit of Persia.

Ri·al·to (rĭ ăl′tō), *n.* 1. a commercial center in Venice, Italy, consisting of an island and the surrounding district. 2. a bridge spanning the Grand Canal in Venice. 3. the theater district of New York City, along Broadway.

rib[1] (rĭb), *n., v.,* **ribbed, ribbing.** —*n.* 1. one of a series of long, slender, curved bones enclosing the thoracic cavity and articulated with the vertebrae. 2. some thing or part resembling a rib in form, position, or use. 3. an arch forming a support of a vault. 4. a structural member which supports the shape of sofnething. 5. one of the curved timbers in a ship's frame which spring upward and outward from the keel. 6. a primary vein of a leaf. 7. a ridge, as in poplin, caused by heavy yarn. —*v.t.* 8. to furnish with ribs. 9. to enclose as with ribs. 10. to mark with riblike ridges or markings. —**ribbed,** *adj.*

rib[2] (rĭb), *v.t.* **ribbed, ribbing.** *Slang.* to tease; ridicule; make fun of.

rib·ald (rĭb′əld), *adj.* 1. offensive or scurrilous in speech, language, etc. —*n.* 2. a ribald person.

rib·ald·ry (rĭb′əl drĭ), *n.* 1. ribald character, as of language. 2. ribald speech.

rib·and (rĭb′ənd), *n. Archaic and Brit.* ribbon.

rib·bon (rĭb′ən), *n.* 1. a band of silk, rayon, etc., used for ornament, tying, etc. 2. anything resembling a ribbon. 3. a band of material impregnated with ink, used in a typewriter. —*v.t.* 4. to adorn with ribbon.

ri·bo·fla·vin (rī′bō flā′vĭn), *n. Biochem.* a factor of the vitamin B complex, found in milk, fresh meat, eggs, fresh vegetables, etc.; vitamin B_2; vitamin G.

rice (rīs), *n., v.,* **riced, ricing.** —*n.* 1. the edible starchy seeds or grain of a certain species of grass cultivated in warm climates. 2. the plant itself. —*v.t.* 3. to reduce to a form resembling rice. —**ric′er,** *n.*

rice paper, a thin paper made chiefly in China from the straw of rice.

rich (rĭch), *adj.* 1. having wealth or great possessions. 2. abounding in natural resources. 3. abounding. 4. of great worth; valuable. 5. costly; expensively elegant. 6. sumptuous, as a feast. 7. (of food) containing good, nutritious, or choice ingredients, as butter, cream, sugar, etc. 8. (of color) deep, strong, or vivid. 9. full and mellow in tone. 10. producing or yielding abundantly. 11. abundant, plentiful, or ample. 12. *Colloq.* highly amusing. —*n.* 13. rich people collectively. —**rich′ly,** *adv.* —**rich′ness,** *n.*

Rich·ard (rĭch′ərd), *n.* 1. **I,** ("the *Lion-Hearted*") 1157–99, king of England, 1189–99. 2. **II,** 1367–1400, king of England, 1377–99. 3. **III,** 1452–85, king of England, 1483–85.

Rich·e·lieu (rĭsh′ə lōō′), *n.* **Armand Jean du Plessis,** Duke of, 1585–1642, French cardinal and statesman.

rich·es (rĭch′ĭz), *n.pl.* abundant and valuable possessions; wealth.

Rich·mond (rĭch′mənd), *n.* 1. the capital of Virginia, in the E part. 193,042. 2. a SW borough of New York City, comprising Staten Island. 174,441; 64¹/₂ sq. mi. 3. a city in E Indiana. 35,147.

rick (rĭk), *n. Chiefly Brit.* —*n.* 1. a stack of hay, straw, or the like. —*v.t.* 2. to pile up in ricks.

rick·ets (rĭk′ĭts), *n. Pathol.* a disease of childhood, characterized by softening of the bones as a result of a lack of Vitamin D or calcium, often resulting in deformities.

rick·et·y (rĭk′ĭt ĭ), *adj.* 1. liable to fall or col-

lapse; shaky. **2.** tottering; infirm. **3.** suffering from rickets.

rick·ey (rĭk′ĭ), *n.*, *pl.* **-eys.** a drink made principally of spirituous liquor (esp. gin), lime juice, and carbonated water.

rick·shaw (rĭk′shô), *n.* jinrikisha. Also, **rick′-sha.**

ric·o·chet (rĭk′ə shā′, -shĕt′), *n.*, *v.*, **-cheted** (-shād′), **-cheting** (-shā′ĭng) or (*esp. Brit.*) **-chetted** (-shĕt′ĭd), **-chetting** (-shĕt′ĭng). —*n.* **1.** the motion of an object which rebounds from a flat surface over which it is passing. —*v.t.*, *v.i.* **2.** to move in this way.

rid (rĭd), *v.t.*, **rid** or **ridded, ridding. 1.** to clear or free of something objectionable. **2.** to relieve. **3. get rid of, a.** to get relieved of. **b.** to get off one's hands. **c.** to do away with.

rid·dance (rĭd′əns), *n.* **1.** a removal of anything undesirable. **2.** relief or deliverance from something.

rid·dle[1] (rĭd′əl), *n.*, *v.*, **-dled, -dling.** —*n.* **1.** a puzzling question, problem, or matter. —*v.i.* **2.** to propound, or speak in, riddles.

rid·dle[2] (rĭd′əl), *v.*, **-dled, -dling,** *n.* —*v.t.* **1.** to pierce with many holes. **2.** to sift through a riddle, as gravel. —*n.* **3.** a coarse sieve, as one for sifting sand.

ride (rīd), *v.*, **rode** or (*Archaic*) **rid; ridden** or (*Archaic*) **rid; riding;** *n.* —*v.i.* **1.** to be carried on the back of an animal, on or in a vehicle, etc. **2.** to move or float on the water. **3.** to lie at anchor, as a ship. **4.** to turn or rest on something. —*v.t.* **5.** to sit on and manage (a horse, vehicle, or the like) so as to be carried along. **6.** *Slang.* to harass or torment. **7. ride out, a.** to sustain (a gale, etc.) without damage. **b.** to sustain or endure successfully. —*n.* **8.** a journey on a horse, on or in a vehicle, etc.

rid·er (rī′dər), *n.* **1.** one who or that which rides. **2.** an additional clause, usually unrelated to the main body, attached to a legislative bill in passing it.

ridge (rĭj), *n.*, *v.*, **ridged, ridging.** —*n.* **1.** a long, narrow elevation of land. **2.** the long, narrow upper part of an animal's back, a hill, a wave, etc. **3.** the horizontal line in which the tops of the rafters of a roof meet. —*v.t.* **4.** to provide with or form into a ridge or ridges. **5.** to mark with ridges. —*v.i.* **6.** to form ridges.

ridge·pole (rĭj′pōl′), *n.* the horizontal timber at the top of a roof, to which the upper ends of the rafters are fastened.

rid·i·cule (rĭd′ə kūl′), *n.*, *v.*, **-culed, -culing.** —*n.* **1.** words or actions intended to excite contemptuous laughter at a person or thing; derision. —*v.t.* **2.** to deride.

ri·dic·u·lous (rĭ dĭk′yə ləs), *adj.* deserving ridicule; absurd; preposterous. —**ri·dic′u·lous·ly,** *adv.*

rife (rīf), *adj.* **1.** common or frequent; prevalent; widespread. **2.** abounding.

Riff (rĭf), *n.* a member of a northern African people of Barbary and the Sahara.

rif·fle (rĭf′əl), *n.*, *v.*, **-fled, -fling.** —*n.* **1.** *U.S.* a ripple, as upon the surface of water. **2.** the method of riffling cards. —*v.t.*, *v.i.* **3.** to cause a riffle. **4.** to flutter and shift, as pages. **5.** to shuffle (cards) by dividing the deck in two, raising the corners slightly, and allowing them to fall alternately together.

riff·raff (rĭf′răf′), *n.* worthless or disreputable people; rabble.

ri·fle[1] (rī′fəl), *n.*, *v.*, **-fled, -fling.** —*n.* **1.** a shoulder firearm with spiral grooves cut in the inner surface of the gun barrel to give the bullet a rotatory motion and thus render its flight more accurate. —*v.t.* **2.** to cut spiral grooves within (a gun barrel, etc.). —**ri′fle·man,** *n.* —**ri′fling,** *n.*

ri·fle[2] (rī′fəl), *v.t.*, **-fled, -fling. 1.** to ransack and rob. **2.** to search and rob. **3.** to plunder or strip bare of. **4.** to steal.

rift (rĭft), *n.* **1.** a split or cleft. —*v.i.*, *v.t.* **2.** to split.

rig (rĭg), *v.*, **rigged, rigging,** *n.* —*v.t.* **1.** *Chiefly Naut.* **a.** to put in proper order. **b.** to fit (a vessel, a mast, etc.) with the necessary shrouds, stays, etc. **2.** to furnish with equipment, etc. **3.** to put together, esp. as a makeshift. **4.** *Colloq.* to deck with clothes, etc. **5.** *Colloq.* to manipulate fraudulently. —*n.* **6.** the arrangement of the masts, spars, sails, etc., on a boat or ship. **7.** equipment; outfit. **8.** *U.S. Colloq.* a vehicle with a horse or horses. **9.** the equipment used in drilling an oil well. **10.** *Colloq.* costume or dress. —**rig′ger,** *n.*

Ri·ga (rē′gä), *n.* a seaport in the W Soviet Union. 385,063.

rig·ging (rĭg′ĭng), *n.* **1.** the ropes, chains, etc., that support and work the masts, yards, sails, etc., on a ship. **2.** equipment. **3.** *Colloq.* clothing.

right (rīt), *adj.* **1.** in accordance with what is just or good. **2.** correct; true. **3.** correct in judgment, opinion, or action. **4.** sound or normal, as the mind, etc. **5.** in good health or spirits. **6.** in good order. **7.** principal, front, or upper. **8.** most convenient, desirable, or favorable. **9.** appropriate. **10.** genuine; legitimate. **11.** belonging or pertaining to the side of a person or thing which is turned toward the east when the face is toward the north (opposed to *left*). **12.** (of political opinion, etc.) reactionary. **13.** straight. —*n.* **14.** a just claim or title. **15.** that which is due to any one by just claim. **16.** that which is ethically good and proper. **17.** the correct or proper way of thinking. **18.** the right side. **19. the Right,** (*often l.c.*) the political conservatives. —*adv.* **20.** straight; directly. **21.** quite or completely. **22.** immediately. **23.** exactly; just. **24.** uprightly. **25.** correctly. **26.** fittingly. **27.** favorably; well. **28.** toward the right. **29.** *Colloq.* or *Dial.* extremely. **30.** very (used in certain titles). —*v.t.* **31.** to bring or restore to an upright or the proper position. **32.** to set in order. **33.** to correct. **34.** to do justice to. **35.** to redress (wrong, etc.). —*v.i.* **36.** to resume an upright or the proper position. —**right′ly,** *adv.* —**right′ness,** *n.*

right angle, the angle formed by two perpendicular lines intercepting a quarter of a circle drawn about its vertex. —**right′-an′gled,** *adj.*

right·eous (rī′chəs), *adj.* **1.** upright or virtuous; moral. **2.** morally right. —**right′eous·ly,** *adv.* —**right′eous·ness,** *n.*

right·ful (rīt′fəl), *adj.* **1.** having a just claim. **2.** belonging by just claim. **3.** equitable or just. —**right′ful·ly,** *adv.* —**right′ful·ness,** *n.*

right-hand (rīt′hănd′), *adj.* **1.** on or to the right. **2.** of, for, or with the right hand. **3.** most useful as a helper.

right-hand·ed (rīt′hăn′dĭd), *adj.* **1.** using the right hand preferably. **2.** adapted to or performed by the right hand. **3.** *Mach.* moving or rotating from left to right.

right·ist (rī′tĭst), *adj.* **1.** having conservative or reactionary political views. —*n.* **2.** a conservative or reactionary.

right·o (rīt′ō′), *interj. Brit.* yes; all right.

right of way, 1. a legal right to proceed ahead of another. **2.** a path or route which may lawfully be used. **3.** a right of passage, as over another's land. **4.** the strip of land acquired for use by a railroad's tracks.

right triangle, a triangle with a right angle.

right whale, any of certain large toothless whales, including those hunted commercially.

rig·id (rĭj′ĭd), *adj.* **1.** stiff or unyielding; not flexible. **2.** inflexible, strict, or severe. **3.** severely exact; rigorous. **4.** *Aeron.* (of an airship) having its form maintained by a firm internal structure. —**ri·gid′i·ty, rig′id·ness,** *n.* —**rig′id·ly,** *adv.*

rig·ma·role (rĭg′mə rōl′), *n.* a succession of confused or foolish statements.

rig·or (rĭg′ər), *n.* **1.** strictness, severity, or harshness. **2.** severity of life; hardship. **3.** stiffness or rigidity. Also, *Brit.,* **rig′our.**

ri·gor mor·tis (rĭ′gôr môr′tĭs, rĭg′ər), the stiffening of the body after death.

rig·or·ous (rĭg′ər əs), *adj.* **1.** rigidly severe or harsh, as persons, rules, etc. **2.** severely exact or rigidly accurate. **3.** severe or sharp, as weather. —**rig′or·ous·ly,** *adv.* —**rig′or·ous·ness,** *n.*

rile (rīl), *v.t.*, **riled, riling.** *Colloq.* or *Dial.* to irritate or vex.

Ri·ley (rī′lĭ), *n.* **James Whitcomb,** 1849–1916, U.S. poet.

rill (rĭl), *n.* a small rivulet or brook.

rim (rĭm), *n.*, *v.*, **rimmed, rimming.** —*n.* **1.** an outer edge, border, or margin, esp. of a circular object. —*v.t.* **2.** to furnish with a rim.

rime[1] (rīm), *n.*, *v.t.*, *v.i.*, **rimed, riming.** rhyme.

rime[2] (rīm), *n.*, *v.*, **rimed, riming.** *Meteorol.* —*n.* **1.** a rough, white, icy covering deposited on trees, etc., from fog, etc. —*v.t.* **2.** to cover with rime. —**rim′y,** *adj.*

Rim·ski-Kor·sa·kov (rĭm′skĭ kôr′sə kôf′), *n.* **Nikolai Andreevich,** 1844–1908, Russian composer.

rind (rīnd), *n.* a firm outer covering, as of plants, fruits, cheeses, etc.

ring[1] (rĭng), *n., v.,* **ringed, ringing.** —*n.* **1.** a circular band of metal or other material, worn on the finger as an ornament, etc. **2.** anything having the form of a circular band. **3.** a circular line or course. **4.** one of the concentric layers of wood produced yearly in the trunks of certain trees. **5.** a number of persons or things placed in a circle. **6.** an enclosed circular or other area, as one in which a prize fight takes place. **7.** competition; contest. **8.** a group of persons coöperating for selfish, sometimes illicit, purposes. **9.** *Chem.* a number of atoms so united that they may be graphically represented in cyclic form. —*v.t., v.i.* **10.** to encircle. **11.** to form into a ring. **12.** to form a ring or rings. —**ring′er,** *n.*

ring[2] (rĭng), *v.,* **rang, rung, ringing,** *n.* —*v.i.* **1.** to give forth a clear, resonant sound, as a bell does. **2.** to seem (true, false, etc.). **3.** to cause a bell to sound, esp. as a summons. **4.** to sound loudly; resound. **5.** to be filled with sound. **6.** (of the ears) to have the sensation of a continued humming sound. —*v.t.* **7.** to cause to ring, as a bell, etc. **8.** to produce (sound) by ringing. **9.** to announce, summon, signal, etc., by the sound of a bell. **10.** *Slang.* to bring or put (in) artfully or fraudulently. —*n.* **11.** a ringing sound. **12.** any loud sound. **13.** a telephone call. **14.** a characteristic quality, indicating genuineness or the reverse. —**ring′er,** *n.*

ring·lead·er (rĭng′lē′dər), *n.* one who leads others in opposition to law or in anything deemed objectionable.

ring·let (rĭng′lĭt), *n.* **1.** a small ring or circle. **2.** a curled lock of hair.

ring·mas·ter (rĭng′măs′tər, -mäs′-), *n.* one in charge of the performances in a circus.

ring·worm (rĭng′wûrm′), *n.* *Pathol.* any of certain contagious skin diseases due to parasites and characterized by ring-shaped eruptive patches.

rink (rĭngk), *n.* **1.** a sheet of ice for skating, often an indoor one artificially prepared. **2.** a smooth floor for roller skating. **3.** a place containing such a surface.

rinse (rĭns), *v.,* **rinsed, rinsing,** *n.* —*v.t.* **1.** to wash lightly. **2.** to put through clean water, as a final stage in cleansing. —*n.* **3.** a rinsing. —**rins′er,** *n.*

Ri·o de Ja·nei·ro (rē′ō də zhə nâr′ō), a seaport in and the capital of Brazil, in the SE part. 1,941,653.

Ri·o Grande (rē′ō grănd′, grän′dĭ), a river flowing from SW Colorado through central New Mexico and along the Texas-Mexico boundary into the Gulf of Mexico. ab. 1800 mi.

ri·ot (rī′ət), *n.* **1.** a disturbance of the peace by an assembly of persons. **2.** violent or wild disorder or confusion. **3.** a brilliant display. **4. run riot, a.** to act without control or restraint. **b.** to grow luxuriantly. —*v.i.* **5.** to take part in a riot. **6.** to indulge in unrestrained revelry. —**ri′ot·er,** *n.*

ri·ot·ous (rī′ət əs), *adj.* **1.** characterized by or of the nature of rioting. **2.** inciting to or taking part in a riot. **3.** wanton. **4.** boisterous. —**ri′ot·ous·ly,** *adv.* —**ri′ot·ous·ness,** *n.*

rip (rĭp), *v.,* **ripped, ripping,** *n.* —*v.t.* **1.** to cut or tear roughly; slash; slit. —*v.i.* **2.** to become torn apart or split open. —*n.* **3.** a tear made by ripping. —**rip′per,** *n.*

R.I.P., (L *requiescat* or *requiescant in pace*) may he or she (or they) rest in peace.

ri·par·i·an (rĭ pâr′ĭ ən, rī-), *adj.* of, pertaining to, or on the bank of a river or other body of water.

rip cord, *Aeron.* a cord or ring which opens a parachute during a descent.

ripe (rīp), *adj.,* **riper, ripest. 1.** ready for reaping or gathering, as grain, fruits, etc. **2.** fully grown, developed, or mature. **3.** advanced in years. **4.** ready, as for action, execution, etc. —**ripe′ly,** *adv.* —**ripe′ness,** *n.*

rip·en (rī′pən), *v.i., v.t.* **1.** to become or make ripe. **2.** to come or bring to maturity, the proper condition, etc.; mature. —**rip′en·er,** *n.*

rip·ping (rĭp′ĭng), *adj.* *Chiefly Brit. Slang.* excellent; fine.

rip·ple (rĭp′əl), *v.,* **-pled, -pling,** *n.* —*v.i., v.t.* **1.** to form small waves on the surface (of). —*n.* **2.** a small wave or undulation. **3.** any similar movement or appearance. **4.** a sound as of water flowing in ripples.

rip-roar·ing (rĭp′rōr′ĭng), *adj.* *Slang.* riotous; wild and noisy.

rip·saw (rĭp′sô′), *n.* a saw used for sawing timber with the grain.

rip·tide (rĭp′tīd′), *n.* *U.S.* a tide which opposes another or other tides, causing a violent disturbance in the sea.

rise (rīz), *v.,* **rose, risen, rising,** *n.* —*v.i.* **1.** to get up; stand up. **2.** to get up from bed. **3.** to revolt or rebel. **4.** to be built up, erected, or constructed. **5.** to grow, as plants. **6.** to become prominent on a surface, as a blister. **7.** to come into existence; appear. **8.** to come into action, as a wind. **9.** to occur. **10.** to originate; issue. **11.** to move upward; ascend. **12.** to come above the horizon, as a heavenly body. **13.** to extend or slant upward. **14.** to attain higher rank, importance, etc. **15.** to prove oneself equal to (an emergency, etc.). **16.** to increase in height. **17.** to swell or puff up. **18.** to increase in amount, price, or value. **19.** to increase in degree, intensity, or force. **20.** to become louder or of higher pitch. **21.** to return from the dead. —*v.t.* **22.** to cause to rise. —*n.* **23.** upward movement or ascent. **24.** elevation or advance in rank, position, fortune, etc. **25.** origin, source, or beginning. **26.** occasion. **27.** upward slope.

ris·er (rī′zər), *n.* **1.** one who rises, esp. from bed. **2.** the vertical face of a stair step.

ris·i·bil·i·ty (rĭz′ə bĭl′ə tĭ), *n., pl.* **-ties. 1.** ability or disposition to laugh. **2.** (*often pl.*) faculty of laughing.

ris·i·ble (rĭz′ə bəl), *adj.* **1.** inclined to laughter. **2.** laughable or ludicrous.

risk (rĭsk), *n.* **1.** a hazard or dangerous chance. —*v.t.* **2.** to expose to the chance of injury or loss; hazard. **3.** to take the risk of.

risk·y (rĭs′kĭ), *adj.,* **riskier, riskiest. 1.** full of risk; hazardous. **2.** risqué.

ris·qué (rĭs kā′), *adj.* daringly close to indelicacy or impropriety.

rite (rīt), *n.* **1.** a ceremonial act in religious or other solemn use. **2.** a particular system of religious or other ceremonial practice.

rit·u·al (rĭch′ŏŏ əl), *n.* **1.** a form or system of religious or other rites. **2.** observance of set forms in public worship. **3.** a book of rites. —*adj.* **4.** of the nature of, or practiced as, a rite or rites. **5.** of or pertaining to rites. —**rit′u·al·ly,** *adv.*

rit·u·al·ism (rĭch′ŏŏ ə lĭz′əm), *n.* **1.** adherence to or insistence on ritual. **2.** the study of ritual practices or religious rites. **3.** fondness for ritual. —**rit′u·al·is′tic,** *adj.* —**rit′u·al·is′ti·cal·ly,** *adv.*

ri·val (rī′vəl), *n., adj., v.,* **-valed, -valing** or (*esp. Brit.*) **-valled, -valling.** —*n.* **1.** one who is in pursuit of the same object as another; competitor. **2.** equal; match; peer. —*adj.* **3.** being a rival. —*v.t.* **4.** to compete with. **5.** to equal; match.

ri·val·ry (rī′vəl rĭ), *n., pl.* **-ries.** competition.

rive (rīv), *v.,* **rived, rived** or **riven, riving. 1.** to tear apart. **2.** to split; cleave.

riv·er (rĭv′ər), *n.* **1.** a large natural stream of water flowing in a definite course. **2.** any abundant stream or copious flow.

Ri·ve·ra (rē vě′rä), *n.* Diego, born 1886, Mexican painter, esp. of murals.

Riv·er·side (rĭv′ər sīd′), *n.* a city in SW California. 34,696.

riv·et (rĭv′ĭt), *n.* **1.** a metal pin for passing through holes in two or more pieces to hold them together, usually made with a head at one end, the other end being hammered into a head after insertion. —*v.t.* **2.** to fasten with a rivet or rivets. **3.** to fasten firmly. **4.** to hold (the eye, attention, etc.) firmly. —**riv′et·er,** *n.*

Riv·i·er·a (rĭv′ĭ âr′ə), *n.* a famous resort region along the Mediterranean coast of SE France and NW Italy.

riv·u·let (rĭv′yə lĭt), *n.* a small stream.

rm., *pl.* **rms. 1.** ream. **2.** room.

Rn, *Chem.* radon.

R.N., 1. Registered Nurse. **2.** Royal Navy.

roach[1] (rōch), *n.* a cockroach.

roach[2] (rōch), *n., pl.* **roaches,** (*esp. collectively*) **roach.** any of certain fresh-water fishes of the carp family.

road (rōd), *n.* **1.** an open way for passage or travel; highway. **2.** *U.S.* a railroad. **3.** a way or course. **4.** (*often pl.*) Also, **road/stead′.** a protected place near the shore where ships may ride at anchor. **5. on the road, a.** traveling, esp.

as a salesman. **b.** on tour, as a theatrical company.

road·bed (rōd/bĕd/), *n.* the foundation structure of a railroad, on which ties, rails, etc., rest.

road·house (rōd/hous/), *n.* an inn, dance hall, etc., at the roadside.

road·side (rōd/sīd/), *n.* **1.** the side of the road. —*adj.* **2.** on the side of a road.

road·ster (rōd/stər), *n.* an automobile with a top that can be folded back, usually having a single seat for two or more persons.

road·way (rōd/wā/), *n.* **1.** a road. **2.** the part of a road used by vehicles, etc.

roam (rōm), *v.i.* **1.** to ramble; wander; rove. —*v.t.* **2.** to wander over or through. —*n.* **3.** a ramble.

roan (rōn), *adj.* **1.** (chiefly of horses) of a sorrel, chestnut, or bay color sprinkled with gray or white. —*n.* **2.** a roan horse or other animal.

Ro·a·noke (rō/ə nōk/), *n.* a city in W Virginia. 69,287.

roar (rōr), *v.i.* **1.** to utter a loud, deep sound. **2.** to laugh loudly. **3.** to make a loud noise or din. **4.** to function or move with a roar. —*v.t.* **5.** to utter or express in a roar. —*n.* **6.** a loud, deep sound. **7.** a loud outburst of laughter. **8.** a loud noise. —**roar/er,** *n.*

roast (rōst), *v.t.* **1.** to bake or cook (meat or other food) by dry heat, as in an oven. **2.** to brown by exposure to heat, as coffee. **3.** to heat (any material) more or less violently. **4.** *Slang.* to ridicule or criticize severely. —*v.i.* **5.** to roast meat, etc. **6.** to undergo the process of becoming roasted. —*n.* **7.** roasted meat. **8.** a piece of meat for roasting. —*adj.* **9.** roasted.

roast·er (rōs/tər), *n.* **1.** a contrivance for roasting. **2.** a pig, chicken, or other animal fit for roasting. **3.** one that roasts.

rob (rŏb), *v.,* **robbed, robbing.** —*v.t.* **1.** to deprive of something by unlawful force or threat. **2.** to deprive of something unjustly. —*v.i.* **3.** to commit robbery. —**rob/ber,** *n.*

rob·ber·y (rŏb/ə rĭ), *n., pl.* **-beries.** the action or practice, or an instance, of robbing.

robe (rōb), *n., v.,* **robed, robing.** —*n.* **1.** a long, loose gown or outer garment worn for formal or official occasions. **2.** any long, loose garment. **3.** a woman's gown or dress. **4.** (*pl.*) apparel; dress. **5.** a piece of fur, cloth, knitted work, etc., used as a covering or wrap. —*v.t.* **6.** to clothe or apparel. —*v.i.* **7.** to put on a robe.

Robes·pierre (rōbz/pyĭr, -pyĕr/), *n.* **Maximilien François Marie Isidore de,** 1758–94, French Revolutionary leader.

rob·in (rŏb/ĭn), *n.* **1.** a large American thrush with chestnut-red breast and belly. **2.** a small European bird with a yellowish-red breast.

Robin Hood, a traditional English outlaw of the 12th century who robbed the rich to give to the poor.

Rob·in·son (rŏb/ĭn sən), *n.* **Edwin Arlington,** 1869–1935, U.S. poet.

ro·bot (rō/bət, rŏb/ət), *n.* **1.** a manufactured man. **2.** a dull, mechanical person.

ro·bust (rō bŭst/, rō/bŭst), *adj.* **1.** strong and healthy; vigorous. **2.** strongly or stoutly built. —**ro·bust/ly,** *adv.* —**ro·bust/ness,** *n.*

roc (rŏk), *n. Arabian Myth.* a fabulous bird of enormous size and strength.

Roch·es·ter (rŏch/ĕs/tər, -əs tər), *n.* a city in W New York. 324,975.

rock¹ (rŏk), *n.* **1.** a large mass of stone forming an eminence, cliff, or the like. **2.** stone in the mass. **3.** *Dial.* or *Colloq.* a stone of any size. **4.** a firm foundation or support.

rock² (rŏk), *v.i., v.t.* **1.** to move to and fro or from side to side. —*n.* **2.** a rocking movement.

rock-bot·tom (rŏk/bŏt/əm), *adj.* at the lowest limit.

rock-bound (rŏk/bound/), *adj.* hemmed in by rocks; rocky.

rock candy, sugar in hard cohering crystals of considerable size.

rock crystal, transparent quartz.

Rock·e·fel·ler (rŏk/ə fĕl/ər), *n.* **John Davison,** 1839–1937, U.S. philanthropist.

rock·er (rŏk/ər), *n.* **1.** one of the curved pieces on which a cradle or rocking chair rocks. **2.** a rocking chair. **3.** any of various devices that operate with a rocking motion.

rock·et (rŏk/ĭt), *n.* **1.** a cylindrical tube containing combustibles which on being ignited liberate gases whose action propels the tube through

the air: used for pyrotechnic effect, signaling, hurling explosives on the enemy, etc. —*v.i.* **2.** to move like a rocket.

Rock·ford (rŏk/fərd), *n.* a city in N Illinois. 84,637.

rocking chair, a chair mounted on rockers or springs so as to permit a rocking back and forth.

rocking horse, a toy horse mounted on rockers, on which children play.

Rock Island, a city in NW Illinois. 42,775.

rock-rib·bed (rŏk/rĭbd/), *adj.* **1.** having ridges of rock. **2.** unyielding.

rock salt, common salt (sodium chloride), occurring in rocklike masses.

rock·y¹ (rŏk/ĭ), *adj.,* **rockier, rockiest. 1.** full of rocks. **2.** consisting of rock. **3.** like rock. **4.** firm or hard as a rock.

rock·y² (rŏk/ĭ), *adj.,* **rockier, rockiest. 1.** tottering or shaky. **2.** uncertain. **3.** *Colloq. or Slang.* dizzy.

Rocky Mountains, the chief mountain system in North America, extending from N Mexico to Alaska. Highest peak, Mt. McKinley (in Alaska), 20,300 ft. Also, **Rock/ies.**

ro·co·co (rə kō/kō), *n.* **1.** a style of architecture and decoration, originating in France about 1720, distinguished by its elegant and delicate overall ornamentation of shellwork, foliage, etc. —*adj.* **2.** in the rococo style.

rod (rŏd), *n.* **1.** a stick, wand, staff, shaft, or the like. **2.** a pole used in angling or fishing. **3.** a linear measure of 5¹/₂ yards. **4.** *U.S. Slang.* a pistol or revolver.

ro·dent (rō/dənt), *adj.* **1.** belonging or pertaining to the order of gnawing or nibbling mammals that includes the mice, squirrels, beavers, etc. **2.** gnawing. —*n.* **3.** a rodent mammal.

ro·de·o (rō/dĭ ō/, rō dā/ō), *n., pl.* **-deos.** *U.S.* an exhibition of the skills of cowboys for public entertainment.

Ro·din (rō dăn/), *n.* **Auguste,** 1840–1917, French sculptor.

roe¹ (rō), *n.* **1.** the mass of eggs, or spawn, within the ovarian membrane of the female fish (**hard roe**). **2.** the milt or sperm of the male fish (**soft roe**).

roe² (rō), *n., pl.* **roes,** (*esp. collectively*) **roe.** a small, agile Old World deer, the male (**roe/buck/**) of which has three-pointed antlers. Also, **roe deer.**

Roent·gen ray (rĕnt/gən), (*sometimes l.c.*) x-ray.

rog·er (rŏj/ər), *interj. U.S. Slang.* **1.** all right; O.K. **2.** received.

rogue (rōg), *n., v.,* **rogued, roguing.** —*n.* **1.** a dishonest person. **2.** a rascal or scamp. —*v.i.* **3.** to live or act like a rogue. —**ro/guish,** *adj.* —**ro/guish·ly,** *adv.* —**ro/guish·ness,** *n.*

ro·guer·y (rō/gə rĭ), *n., pl.* **-gueries. 1.** roguish conduct. **2.** a rascally act.

roil (roil), *v.t.* **1.** to render (water, etc.) turbid by stirring up sediment. **2.** to irritate; vex. —**roil/y,** *adj.*

roist·er (rois/tər), *v.i.* **1.** to act in a swaggering, boisterous, or uproarious manner. **2.** to revel. —**roist/er·er,** *n.*

role (rōl), *n.* the part or character which an actor presents in a play. Also, **rôle.**

roll (rōl), *v.i.* **1.** to move along a surface by turning over and over, as a wheel. **2.** to move or be moved on wheels. **3.** to move with an undulating motion, as waves. **4.** to extend in undulations, as land **5.** to move or pass, as time. **6.** to have a deep, prolonged sound, as thunder. **7.** *Colloq.* to abound (in wealth, etc.). **8.** to turn round in different directions. **9.** to sway or rock from side to side, as a ship. **10.** to spread out from being rolled up. **11.** to spread out as under a roller. —*v.t.* **12.** to cause to move along a surface by turning over and over. **13.** to move along in a wheeled vehicle. **14.** to drive, impel, or cause to flow onward with a sweeping motion. **15.** to utter or give forth with a full, flowing, continuous sound. **16.** to trill. **17.** to turn round in different directions, as the eyes. **18.** to cause to sway or rock from side to side, as a ship. **19.** to wrap into a roll, ball, or the like. **20.** to make by forming a roll. **21.** to spread out from being rolled up. **22.** to spread out, level, or the like, with a rolling pin, cylinder, etc. **23.** to beat (a drum) with rapid, continuous strokes. —*n.* **24.** a list, register, or catalogue. **25.** anything rolled up in cylindrical form. **26.** a rounded mass of something. **27.** *Cookery.* **a.** thin cake spread with jelly or the like and rolled up. **b.** a small cake of bread. **c.** food which is rolled up. **28.** undulation of surface. **29.** sonorous or rhythmical flow of words. **30.** a deep, prolonged sound, as of thunder or of a drum rapidly beaten. **31.** a rolling motion, as of a ship. **32.** a rolling or swaying gait. **33.** *U.S. Slang.* a wad of paper currency.

roll call, the calling of a list of names, as of students, to find out who is absent.

roll·er (rō′lər), *n.* **1.** a cylinder, wheel, or the like, upon which something is rolled along. **2.** a cylindrical body upon which cloth or other material is rolled up. **3.** a cylindrical body for rolling over something to be spread out, crushed, compacted, inked, etc. **4.** a long, swelling wave advancing steadily.

roller skate, a form of skate with small wheels, for use on a smooth floor, etc. —**roll′er-skate′,** *v.i.*

rol·lick·ing (rŏl′ĭk ĭng), *adj.* swaggering and jolly.

roll·ing (rō′lĭng), *n.* **1.** the action, motion, or sound of anything that rolls. —*adj.* **2.** that rolls. **3.** rising and falling in gentle slopes. **4.** moving in undulating billows, as waves.

rolling pin, a cylinder of wood or other material for rolling out dough, etc.

rolling stock, the vehicles of a railroad, including locomotives, cars, etc.

ro·ly-po·ly (rō′lĭ pō′lĭ), *adj.*, *n.*, *pl.* **-lies.** —*adj.* **1.** short and plumply round. —*n.* **2.** a roly-poly person or thing.

Rom., **1.** Roman. **2.** Romans (N.T.).

ro·maine (rō mān′), *n.* a variety of lettuce with long, comparatively narrow, crisp leaves.

Ro·man (rō′mən), *adj.* **1.** of or pertaining to Rome. **2.** (*usually l.c.*) designating or pertaining to the style of printing types most commonly used in modern books, etc. **3.** of or pertaining to the Roman Catholic Church. —*n.* **4.** a native, inhabitant, or citizen of Rome. **5.** (*usually l.c.*) roman type or letters.

Roman Catholic, **1.** of or pertaining to the Roman Catholic Church. **2.** a member of the Roman Catholic Church.

Roman Catholic Church, the Christian church of which the Pope, or Bishop of Rome, is the supreme head.

ro·mance (*n.* rō măns′, rō′măns; *v.*, *adj.* rōmăns′), *n.*, *v.*, **-manced, -mancing,** *adj.* —*n.* **1.** a tale depicting heroic achievements, colorful events, chivalrous devotion, or other matters appealing to the imagination. **2.** romantic spirit, sentiment, character, or quality. **3.** a romantic affair or experience; love affair. —*v.i.* **4.** to think or talk romantically. —*adj.* **5.** (*cap.*) pertaining to the Romance languages. —**ro·manc′er,** *n.*

Romance language, any of the group of languages which have developed out of Latin, including Rumanian, Italian, French, Spanish, and Portuguese.

Roman Empire, **1.** the lands and peoples subject to ancient Rome. **2.** the imperial form of government established in ancient Rome in 27 B.C.

Ro·man·esque (rō′mə nĕsk′), *adj.* **1.** noting or pertaining to the style of architecture which prevailed in Europe from the late 10th until the 13th century, characterized by the rich outline of the exterior (towers), the clear organization of the interior (bays), heavy walls, small windows, and the use of open timber roofs and groin, barrel, or rib vaults. —*n.* **2.** the Romanesque style.

Ro·man·ize (rō′mə nīz′), *v.t.*, **-ized, -izing.** to render Roman Catholic.

Ro·ma·nov (rō′mə nôf′, -nŏf′), *n.* the imperial dynasty which ruled Russia from 1613 to the abdication of Nicholas II in 1917.

Roman numerals, the numerals in the ancient Roman system of notation, still used for certain limited purposes. The common basic symbols are I(=1), V(=5), X(=10), L(=50), C(=100), D(=500), and M(=1000). If a letter is immediately followed by one of equal or lesser value, the two values are added; thus, XX equals 20, XV equals 15. If a letter is immediately followed by one of greater value, however, the first is subtracted from the second; thus IV equals 4, XL equals 40.

Ro·mans (rō′mənz), *n.* (in the New Testament) one of the doctrinal epistles of Paul, written to the Christian community at Rome.

ro·man·tic (rō măn′tĭk), *adj.* **1.** of, pertaining to, or suggestive of romance. **2.** fanciful; unpractical; quixotic. **3.** imbued with the ideas, spirit,

or sentiment prevailing in romance. **4.** of or pertaining to a style of literature and art characterized by freedom of treatment, subordination of form to matter, imagination, picturesqueness, etc. **5.** imaginary, fictitious, or fabulous. —*n.* **6.** a romantic person. —**ro·man′ti·cal·ly,** *adv.*

ro·man·ti·cism (rō măn′tə sĭz′əm), *n.* **1.** romantic spirit or tendency. **2.** the romantic style or movement in literature and art.

Rom·a·ny (rŏm′ə nĭ), *n.*, *pl.* **-nies,** *adj.* —*n.* **1.** a Gypsy. **2.** Gypsies collectively. **3.** the language of the Gypsies. —*adj.* **4.** pertaining to Gypsies, their language or customs.

Rome (rōm), *n.* **1.** the capital of Italy, in the central part: the ancient capital of the Roman Empire; the site of Vatican City. 1,581,509. **2.** a city in central New York. 34,214.

romp (rŏmp), *v.i.* **1.** to play or frolic in a lively or boisterous manner. —*n.* **2.** a romping frolic. **3.** a romping person, esp. a girl.

romp·ers (rŏm′pərz), *n.pl.* a loose outer garment combining a waist and knickerbockers, worn by young children.

Rom·u·lus (rŏm′yə ləs), *n.* *Rom. Legend.* the founder of Rome (753 B.C.) and its first king.

Rönt·gen ray (rĕnt′gən), Roentgen ray.

rood (rōōd), *n.* **1.** a crucifix, esp. a large one at the entrance to the choir or chancel of a medieval church. **2.** *Archaic.* the cross on which Christ died. **3.** a unit of length varying locally from 5½ to 8 yards. **4.** a unit of land measure, equal to ¼ acre.

roof (rōōf, rŏŏf), *n.* **1.** the external upper covering of a house or other building. **2.** something which in form or position resembles the roof of a house. —*v.t.* **3.** to provide with a roof.

roof·er (rōōf′ər, rŏŏf′-), *n.* one who makes or repairs roofs.

roof·ing (rōōf′ĭng, rŏŏf′-), *n.* **1.** act of covering with a roof. **2.** material for roofs.

rook[1] (rŏŏk), *n.* **1.** a black European crow of a gregarious disposition and given to nesting in colonies in trees about buildings. **2.** a sharper or swindler. —*v.t.* **3.** to cheat; fleece; swindle.

rook[2] (rŏŏk), *n.* *Chess.* a piece having the power to move any unobstructed distance in a straight line forward, backward, or sidewise; castle.

rook·er·y (rŏŏk′ə rĭ), *n.*, *pl.* **-eries.** *Brit.* **1.** a colony of rooks. **2.** a place where rooks congregate to breed. **3.** any breeding place or colony. **4.** a crowded tenement house.

rook·ie (rŏŏk′ĭ), *n.* *Slang.* a raw recruit, as in the army.

room (rōōm, rŏŏm), *n.* **1.** a portion of space within a building or other structure, separated by walls from other parts. **2.** (*pl.*) lodgings or quarters. **3.** space occupied by or available for something. **4.** opportunity or scope. —*v.i.* **5.** to occupy a room or rooms; lodge. —**room′er,** *n.* —**room′ful′,** *n.*

rooming house, a lodging house.

room·mate (rōōm′māt′, rŏŏm′-), *n.* one who shares a room with another or others.

room·y (rōōm′ĭ, rŏŏm′ĭ), *adj.*, **roomier, roomiest.** spacious; large. —**room′i·ness,** *n.*

Roo·se·velt (rō′zə vĕlt′, -vəlt), *n.* **1.** (**Anna**) **Eleanor,** born 1884, U.S. diplomat (wife of Franklin Roosevelt). **2. Franklin Delano,** 1882–1945, 32nd president of the U.S., 1933–45. **3. Theodore,** 1858–1919, 26th president of the U.S., 1901–09.

roost (rōōst), *n.* **1.** a perch upon which domestic fowls rest at night. —*v.i.* **2.** to sit or rest on a roost, perch, etc.

roost·er (rōōs′tər), *n.* a male chicken.

root[1] (rōōt, rŏŏt), *n.* **1.** a part of the body of a plant which, typically, grows downward into the soil, fixing the plant and absorbing nutriment and moisture. **2.** something resembling or suggesting the root of a plant. **3.** the embedded or basal portion of a hair, tooth, nail, etc. **4.** the fundamental or essential part. **5.** the source or origin of a thing. **6.** *Math.* **a.** a quantity which, when multiplied by itself a certain number of times, produces a given quantity. **b.** a quantity which, when substituted for the unknown quantity in an algebraic equation, satisfies the equation. **7.** *Gram.* an element which underlies an inflectional paradigm or is used itself as a word or element of a compound. **8.** *Music.* **a.** the fundamental tone of a compound tone or of a series of harmonics. **b.** the lowest tone of a chord when arranged as a series of thirds; the fundamental. —*v.i.* **9.** to send out roots and begin to grow. **10.** to become established. —*v.t.* **11.** to fix by roots. **12.** to implant deeply. **13.** to pull, tear, or dig by the roots. **14.** to exterminate.

root[2] (rōōt, rŏŏt), *v.i.* **1.** to turn up the soil with the snout, as swine. —*v.t.* **2.** to turn over with the snout.

root[3] (rōōt, rŏŏt), *v.i.* *U.S. Slang.* to encourage or applaud a contestant, etc. —**root′er,** *n.*

root beer, a drink containing the extracted juices of various roots, as of sarsaparilla, sassafras, etc.

root·let (rōōt′lĭt, rŏŏt′-), *n.* a little root.

rope (rōp), *n., v.,* **roped, roping.** —*n.* **1.** a strong, thick line or cord. **2.** a quantity of material or a number of things twisted or strung together in the form of a thick cord. —*v.t.* **3.** to tie, bind, or fasten with a rope. **4.** to catch with a lasso. **5.** *U.S. Slang.* to draw, entice, or inveigle into something.

rop·y (rō′pĭ), *adj.,* **ropier, ropiest. 1.** resembling a rope. **2.** forming viscid or glutinous threads, as a liquid.

Roque·fort cheese (rōk′fərt), a strongly flavored cheese, veined with mold, made of sheep's milk and ripened in caves, orig. at Roquefort, a town in S France.

ro·sa·ry (rō′zə rĭ), *n., pl.* **-ries. 1.** *Rom. Cath. Ch.* **a.** a certain series of prayers. **b.** a string of beads used for counting the prayers in the recitation of the rosary. **2.** a rose garden.

rose (rōz), *n., v.,* **rosed, rosing.** —*n.* **1.** any of certain (usually) prickly-stemmed, showy-flowered shrubs having in the wild state a corolla of five roundish petals. **2.** the red, pink, white, or yellow fragrant flower of such shrubs. **3.** an ornament shaped like or suggesting a rose. **4.** purplish or pinkish red. —*v.t.* **5.** to make rosecolored. **6.** to flush (the cheeks, etc.).

ro·se·ate (rō′zĭ ĭt, -āt′), *adj.* **1.** tinged with rose. **2.** bright or promising. **3.** optimistic.

rose·mar·y (rōz′mâr′ĭ), *n., pl.* **-maries.** an evergreen shrub of the mint family, native in the Mediterranean region, and yielding a fragrant essential oil.

ro·sette (rō zĕt′), *n.* any arrangement, part, object, or formation resembling a rose, as a roseshaped arrangement of ribbon.

rose water, water tinctured with the essential oil of roses.

rose·wood (rōz′wŏŏd′), *n.* **1.** any of various reddish cabinet woods yielded by certain tropical trees. **2.** a tree yielding such wood.

ros·in (rŏz′ĭn), *n.* **1.** the hard, brittle resin left after distilling off the oil of turpentine from the crude oleoresin of the pine: used in making varnish, etc. **2.** resin. —*v.t.* **3.** to rub with rosin.

Ross (rôs, rŏs), *n.* **Betsy,** 1752–1836, American woman who designed and made the first U.S. flag.

Ros·si·ni (rō sē′nĭ), *n.* **Gioachino Antonio,** 1792–1868, Italian composer.

ros·ter (rŏs′tər), *n.* **1.** a list of persons or groups with their turns or periods of duty. **2.** any list, roll, or register.

Ros·tov (rŏ stôf′), *n.* a seaport in the S Soviet Union in Europe, near the Sea of Azov. 510,253.

ros·trum (rŏs′trəm), *n., pl.* **-tra** (-trə), **-trums. 1.** any platform for public speaking. **2.** a pulpit. —**ros′tral,** *adj.*

ros·y (rō′zĭ), *adj.,* **rosier, rosiest. 1.** pink or pinkish-red. **2.** (of the cheeks, etc.) having a fresh, healthy redness. **3.** bright or promising. **4.** cheerful or optimistic. —**ros′i·ly,** *adv.* —**ros′i·ness,** *n.*

rot (rŏt), *v.,* **rotted, rotting,** *n.* —*v.i.* **1.** to undergo decomposition; decay. **2.** to pass or fall by decay. —*v.t.* **3.** to cause to rot. —*n.* **4.** decay; putrefaction. **5.** rotting or rotten matter. **6.** *Pathol.* any disease characterized by malodorous decay. **7.** *Plant Pathol.* any of various diseases or forms of decay produced by fungi or bacteria. **8.** *Chiefly Brit. Slang.* nonsense.

ro·ta·ry (rō′tə rĭ), *adj.* **1.** turning round as on an axis. **2.** taking place round an axis. **3.** having a part or parts that rotate. **4.** noting or pertaining to an internal-combustion engine for an airplane, having radially arranged cylinders which move about a stationary crankshaft.

ro·tate (rō′tāt, rō tāt′), *v.,* **-tated, -tating.** —*v.t.* **1.** to cause to turn round like a wheel on its axis. **2.** to cause to go through a round of changes. —*v.i.* **3.** to turn round, as on an axis. **4.** to proceed in a fixed routine of succession.

ro·ta·tion (rō tā′shən), *n.* **1.** act of turning round, as on an axis. **2.** the turning of the earth daily on its own axis. **3.** regularly recurring succession. **4.** *Agric.* the process or method of varying, in a definite order, the crops grown on the same ground. —**ro·ta′tion·al, ro·ta·to·ry** (rō′tə tōr′ĭ), *adj.*

R.O.T.C., Reserve Officers' Training Corps.

rote (rōt), *n.* **1.** routine; mechanical procedure. **2.** by rote, in a mechanical way without thought of the meaning.

ro·to·gra·vure (rō′tə grə vyŏŏr′, -grā′vyər), *n.* **1.** a photomechanical process in which pictures, letters, etc., are printed from an engraved copper cylinder, the ink-bearing lines, etc., which print, being depressed (etched in) instead of raised as in ordinary metal type, etc. **2.** a print, or newspaper section, made by this process.

ro·tor (rō′tər), *n.* **1.** *Elect.* the rotating member of a machine. **2.** *Aeron.* a system of rotating airfoils, usually horizontal, as those of a helicopter.

rot·ten (rŏt′ən), *adj.* **1.** decaying; putrid; tainted. **2.** corrupt. **3.** *Slang.* wretchedly bad, unsatisfactory, or unpleasant. **4.** contemptible. —**rot′ten·ly,** *adv.* —**rot′ten·ness,** *n.*

rot·ter (rŏt′ər), *n.* *Brit. Slang.* a thoroughly bad or worthless person.

Rot·ter·dam (rŏt′ər dăm′), *n.* a seaport in SW Netherlands. 618,793.

ro·tund (rō tŭnd′), *adj.* **1.** plump. **2.** fulltoned or sonorous. —**ro·tun′di·ty,** *n.*

ro·tun·da (rō tŭn′də), *n.* a round building or room, esp. one with a dome.

rou·ble (rōō′bəl), *n.* ruble.

rou·é (rōō ā′), *n.* a debauchee or rake.

Rou·en (rōō än′), *n.* a city in N France: famous cathedral. 107,739.

rouge (rōōzh), *n., v.,* **rouged, rouging.** —*n.* **1.** any of various red cosmetics for coloring the cheeks or lips. **2.** a reddish powder, chiefly ferric oxide, used for polishing metal, etc. —*v.t.* **3.** to color with rouge.

rough (rŭf), *adj.* **1.** uneven; not smooth. **2.** shaggy. **3.** acting with or characterized by violence. **4.** violently agitated, as the sea. **5.** violently irregular, as motion. **6.** stormy, as weather. **7.** sharp or harsh. **8.** rude. **9.** disorderly. **10.** *Colloq.* severe, hard, or unpleasant. **11.** harsh to the ear; grating; jarring. **12.** harsh to the taste; sharp; astringent. **13.** coarse, as food. **14.** lacking culture. **15.** without luxuries or ordinary comforts. **16.** not perfected or corrected. **17.** made or done without any attempt at exactness or completeness. **18.** crude, unfinished, or unprepared. —*n.* **19.** that which is rough. **20.** *Golf.* any part of the course on which the grass, weeds, etc., are not trimmed. **21.** the rough, hard, or unpleasant part of anything. —*adv.* **22.** in a rough manner. —*v.t.* **23.** to make rough. **24.** to cut, shape, or sketch roughly. —*v.i.* **25.** rough it, to live without the ordinary comforts. —**rough′ly,** *adv.* —**rough′ness,** *n.*

rough·age (rŭf′ĭj), *n.* **1.** rough material. **2.** the coarser kinds or parts of food.

rough-and-read·y (rŭf′ən rĕd′ĭ), *adj.* **1.** rough or crude, but good enough for the purpose. **2.** exhibiting or showing rough vigor.

rough-dry (rŭf′drī′), *v.t.,* **-dried, -drying.** to dry (clothes, etc.) after washing, without smoothing, ironing, etc.

rough·en (rŭf′ən), *v.t., v.i.* to make or become rough.

rough-hew (rŭf′hū′), *v.t.,* **-hewed, hewed** or **-hewn, -hewing. 1.** to hew (timber, stone, etc.) without smoothing or finishing. **2.** to give crude form to.

rough·house (rŭf′hous′), *n., v.,* **-housed, -housing.** *Slang.* —*n.* **1.** rough, disorderly behavior. —*v.i.* **2.** to engage in roughhouse.

rough·neck (rŭf′nĕk′), *n.* *Slang.* a rough, coarse person.

Rough Riders, a volunteer regiment of cavalry organized by Theodore Roosevelt during the Spanish-American War.

rough·shod (rŭf′shŏd′), *adj.* **1.** having horseshoes with projecting nails or points. **2.** ride roughshod over, to override harshly.

rou·lette (rōō lĕt′), *n., v.,* **-letted, -letting.** —*n.* **1.** a gambling game in which bets are placed on the outcome of spinning a disk on which various numbers are printed. **2.** a small wheel, esp. one with sharp teeth, for making lines of marks, dots, or perforations. —*v.t.* **3.** to mark, impress, or perforate with a roulette.

Rou·ma·ni·a (rōō mā′nĭ ə, -mān′yə), *n.* Rumania. —**Rou·ma′ni·an,** *adj., n.*

round (round), *adj.* **1.** circular, ring-shaped, curved, spherical, globular, or plump. **2.** completed by returning to the starting place. **3.** full, complete, or entire. **4.** forming, or expressed by, an integer or whole number (with no fraction). **5.** expressed in tens, hundreds, thousands, or the like. **6.** roughly correct. **7.** considerable in amount. **8.** full and sonorous, as sound. —*n.* **9.** something round. **10.** a complete course, circuit, series, or succession. **11.** a period of activity, commonly one of a series, as in some games. **12.** one of a series of three-minute periods making up a prize fight. **13.** a single discharge of shot by each of a number of guns, rifles, etc., or by a single piece. **14.** a charge of ammunition for a single shot. **15.** a dance with the dancers arranged or moving in a circle or ring. **16.** a form of sculpture in which figures are executed apart from any background. **17.** the portion of the thigh of beef below the rump and above the leg. **18.** *Music.* a short rhythmical canon in which the several voices enter at equal intervals of time. —*adv.* **19.** in a circle, ring, or the like. **20.** on all sides; about. **21.** in circumference. **22.** through a round, circuit, or series. **23.** throughout. **24.** *Chiefly U.S.* in circulation, action, etc. **25.** with change to another or opposite direction, course, opinion, etc. —*prep.* **26.** so as to encircle, surround, or envelop. **27.** on the circuit, border, or outer part of. **28.** around; about. **29.** in all or various directions from. **30.** throughout. **31.** so as to make a partial circuit about or to the other side of. **32.** reached by making a turn about. —*v.t.* **33.** to make round. **34.** to make plump. **35.** to bring to completeness or perfection. **36.** to drive or bring (cattle, etc.) together. **37.** to pass completely round. —*v.i.* **38.** to become round. **39.** to become plump. **40.** to develop to completeness or perfection. —**round′ish,** *adj.* —**round′ness,** *n.*

round·a·bout (round′ə bout′), *adj.* **1.** circuitous or indirect. —*n.* **2.** a short, closely fitting coat or jacket for men or boys. **3.** *Chiefly Brit.* a merry-go-round.

roun·de·lay (roun′də lā′), *n.* **1.** a song in which a phrase, line, or the like, is continually repeated. **2.** the music for such a song.

round·er (roun′dər), *n.* **1.** one that rounds something. **2.** *U.S. Slang.* a habitual drunkard or criminal.

Round·head (round′hĕd′), *n.* *Eng. Hist.* a member or adherent of the Puritan party during the civil wars of the 17th century.

round·house (round′hous′), *n.* a building for locomotives, usually round or semicircular, and built about a turntable.

round·ly (round′lĭ), *adv.* vigorously, severely, or unsparingly.

round robin, a petition or the like, having the signatures arranged in a circle to disguise the order of signing.

round table, **1.** a number of persons, usually seated about a round (or other) table, esp. for discussion of some subject. **2.** (*cap.*) *Arthurian Romance.* **a.** the celebrated table, made round to avoid quarrels as to precedence, about which King Arthur and his knights sat. **b.** King Arthur and his knights.

round·up (round′ŭp′), *n.* **1.** the driving together of cattle, etc., for inspection, branding, or the like. **2.** summary.

rouse (rouz), *v.,* **roused, rousing.** —*v.t.* **1.** to bring or come out of a state of sleep, unconsciousness, inactivity, apathy, depression, etc. **2.** to stir to strong indignation or anger. —*n.* **3.** a rousing. —**rous′er,** *n.*

rous·ing (rou′zĭng), *adj.* **1.** stirring. **2.** active or vigorous. **3.** brisk; lively. **4.** *Colloq.* great or outrageous.

Rous·seau (rōō sō′), *n.* **Jean Jacques,** 1712–78, French philosopher, author, and social reformer.

roust·a·bout (rous′tə bout′), *n.* *U.S.* a wharf laborer or deck hand.

rout (rout), *n.* **1.** a defeat attended with disorderly flight. **2.** a rabble or mob. —*v.t.* **3.** to disperse in defeat and disorderly flight. **4.** to defeat.

route (rōōt, rout), *n., v.,* **routed, routing.** —*n.* **1.** a way or road for passage or travel. —*v.t.* **2.** to fix the route of. **3.** to send by a particular route.

rou·tine (rōō tēn′), *n.* **1.** a customary or regular course of procedure. **2.** regular, unvarying, or mechanical procedure. —*adj.* **3.** of the nature of, proceeding by, or adhering to routine.

rove (rōv), *v.i., v.t.,* **roved, roving.** to wander about without definite destination. —**rov′er,** *n.*

row¹ (rō), *n.* **1.** a number of persons or things

arranged in a line. **2.** a line of adjacent seats, as in a theater. —*v.t.* **3.** to put in a row.

row² (rō), *v.i., v.t.* **1.** to propel (a boat, etc.) by the use of oars. **2.** to convey in a boat, etc., so propelled. —*n.* **3.** act of rowing. **4.** an excursion in a rowboat. —**row′er,** *n.*

row³ (rou), *n.* **1.** a noisy dispute or quarrel. **2.** *Colloq.* clamor. —*v.i.* **3.** *Colloq.* to make or engage in a noisy quarrel.

row·boat (rō′bōt′), *n.* a boat propelled by rowing.

row·dy (rou′dĭ), *n., pl.* **-dies,** *adj.,* **-dier, -diest.** —*n.* **1.** a rough, disorderly person. —*adj.* **2.** rough and disorderly. —**row′di·ly,** *adv.* —**row′di·ness,** *n.* —**row′dy·ish,** *adj.*

row·el (rou′əl), *n.* a small wheel with radiating points, forming the extremity of a horseman's spur.

row·lock (rō′lŏk′, rŭl′ək), *n.* *Chiefly Brit.* oarlock.

roy·al (roi′əl), *adj.* **1.** of or pertaining to a king, queen, or sovereign. **2.** belonging to the royal family. **3.** established, or under the patronage of, a sovereign. **4.** from or by a sovereign. **5.** kinglike; magnificent; splendid. **6.** *Colloq.* fine; excellent. **7.** beyond the ordinary in size, quality, etc. —*n.* **8.** *Naut.* a sail set on the royal mast (next above topgallant mast). —**roy′al·ly,** *adv.*

roy·al·ist (roi′əl ĭst), *n.* **1.** a supporter of a king, esp. in civil war. —*adj.* **2.** of or pertaining to royalists.

roy·al·ty (roi′əl tĭ), *n., pl.* **-ties.** **1.** royal persons collectively. **2.** royal status, dignity, or power. **3.** a portion of proceeds paid to the owner of a patent, or to an author, composer, etc.

r.p.m., revolutions per minute.

R.R., **1.** Railroad. **2.** Right Reverend.

R.S.V.P., (French, *répondez s'il vous plaît*) please reply.

rt., right.

Ru, *Chem.* ruthenium.

rub (rŭb), *v.,* **rubbed, rubbing,** *n.* —*v.t., v.i.* **1.** to subject (an object) to pressure and friction, esp. in order to clean, smooth, polish, etc. **2.** to move, spread, or apply (something) with pressure and friction. **3.** to move (things) with pressure and friction over each other. —*n.* **4.** act of rubbing. **5.** something irritating to the feelings. **6.** an obstacle, impediment, or difficulty.

rub·ber (rŭb′ər), *n.* **1.** an elastic material derived from the latex of certain tropical trees; caoutchouc. **2.** a piece of India rubber, for erasing pencil marks, etc. **3.** (*usually pl.*) an overshoe. **4.** one who rubs. **5.** *Baseball.* the restraining line from which the pitcher delivers the ball. **6.** (in certain games as bridge or whist) **a.** a series of games, usually three, decided when either opposing side wins two games. **b.** the decisive game in a series of this kind. —**rub′ber·y,** *adj.*

rub·ber·ize (rŭb′ə rīz′), *v.t.,* **-ized. -izing.** to coat or impregnate with India rubber or some preparation of it.

rub·ber·neck (rŭb′ər nĕk′), *U.S. Slang.* —*n.* **1.** one who strains to look at things, esp. in curiosity. —*adj.* **2.** pertaining to or for such people. —*v.i.* **3.** to look at things in this manner.

rubber plant, an Asiatic plant of the fig family with oblong, shining leaves, much cultivated in Europe and America as an ornamental house plant.

rub·bish (rŭb′ĭsh), *n.* **1.** waste; debris; litter. **2.** nonsense.

rub·ble (rŭb′əl), *n.* rough fragments of broken stone. —**rub′bly,** *adj.*

rub·down (rŭb′doun′), *n.* massage.

Ru·bens (rōō′bənz), *n.* **Peter Paul,** 1577–1640, Flemish painter.

Ru·bi·con (rōō′bə kŏn′), *n.* **cross the,** to take a decisive, irrevocable step.

ru·bi·cund (rōō′bə kŭnd′), *adj.* red.

ru·bid·i·um (rōō bĭd′ĭ əm), *n.* *Chem.* a silver-white metallic element. *Symbol:* Rb; *at. wt.:* 85.48; *at. no.:* 37; *sp. gr.:* 1.53 at 20°C.

ru·ble (rōō′bəl), *n.* the monetary unit and a silver coin of Russia, equivalent to about 18 U.S. cents.

ru·bric (rōō′brĭk), *n.* **1.** a title, direction, or the like, in a manuscript, book, etc., written or printed in red or otherwise distinguished from the rest of the text. **2.** a direction in liturgical books for the conduct of divine service.

ru·by (rōō′bĭ), *n., pl.* **-bies,** *adj.* —*n.* **1.** a red variety of corundum, highly prized as a gem. **2.** deep red; carmine. —*adj.* **3.** deep-red; carmine.

rud·der (rŭd′ər), *n.* **1.** a movable flat piece hinged vertically at the stern of a ship as a means of steering. **2.** a device like a ship's rudder, for steering an airplane, etc.

R. Rudder (def. 1)

rud·dy (rŭd′ĭ), *adj.*, **-dier,** **-diest.** **1.** of or having a fresh, healthy red color. **2.** reddish. —**rud′di·ness,** *n.*

rude (rood), *adj.,* **ruder, rudest.** **1.** discourteous; impolite. **2.** without culture or refinement. **3.** unmannerly. **4.** rough; harsh. **5.** of a crude make or kind. —**rude′ly,** *adv.* —**rude′ness,** *n.*

ru·di·ment (roo′də mənt), *n.* **1.** the elements of a subject. **2.** (*usually pl.*) a mere beginning or an undeveloped form of something. —**ru′di·men′ta·ry,** *adj.*

rue (roo), *v.,* **rued, ruing,** *n.* —*v.t., v.i.* **1.** to repent; regret bitterly. —*n.* **2.** *Archaic.* sorrow; repentance; regret.

rue·ful (roo′fəl), *adj.* **1.** causing sorrow; deplorable; pitiable. **2.** mournful; doleful. —**rue′-ful′ly,** *adv.* —**rue′ful·ness,** *n.*

ruff[1] (rŭf), *n.* **1.** a collar of lace, etc., gathered into deep, full, regular folds, much worn in the 16th century by both men and women. **2.** a collar, or set of lengthened or specially marked hairs or feathers, on the neck of an animal.

ruff[2] (rŭf), *Cards.* —*n.* **1.** act of trumping when one cannot follow suit. —*v.t., v.i.* **2.** to trump when unable to follow suit.

ruf·fi·an (rŭf′ĭ ən, -yən), *n.* **1.** a tough, lawless person. —*adj.* **2.** Also, **ruf′fi·an·ly.** tough; lawless. —**ruf′fi·an·ism′,** *n.*

ruf·fle[1] (rŭf′əl), *v.,* **-fled, -fling.** —*v.t.* **1.** to destroy the evenness of. **2.** to erect (the feathers), as in anger. **3.** to disturb or irritate. **4.** to gather (cloth, lace, etc.) along one edge. —*v.i.* **5.** to be or become ruffled. —*n.* **6.** a break in the evenness of some surface. **7.** a strip of cloth, lace, etc., gathered along one edge, and used as a trimming on a dress, etc.

ruf·fle[2] (rŭf′əl), *n., v.,* **-fled, -fling.** —*n.* **1.** a low, continuous beating of a drum. —*v.t.* **2.** to beat (a drum) in this manner.

rug (rŭg), *n.* **1.** a piece of carpeting, used as a floor covering or a hanging.

Rug·by (rŭg′bĭ), *n.* **1.** a city in central England. 43,750. **2.** a famous boys' school there.

Rugby football, an English form of football, somewhat like soccer.

rug·ged (rŭg′ĭd), *adj.* **1.** roughly broken, rocky, or hilly. **2.** wrinkled or furrowed. **3.** roughly irregular, heavy, or hard in form. **4.** rough, harsh, or stern. **5.** severe; hard. **6.** tempestuous. —**rug′ged·ly,** *adv.* —**rug′ged·ness,** *n.*

Ruhr (roor), *n.* **1.** a river in W Germany, flowing into the Rhine. 144 mi. **2.** an important mining and industrial region centering in the Ruhr river valley.

ru·in (roo′ĭn), *n.* **1.** (*pl.*) the remains of a fallen building, town, etc. **2.** fallen and wrecked or decayed state. **3.** downfall, decay, or destruction. **4.** the complete loss of means, position, or the like. **5.** something that causes downfall or destruction. —*v.t.* **6.** to reduce to ruin. **7.** to bring (a person, etc.) to financial ruin. **8.** to injure (a thing) irretrievably. —*v.i.* **9.** to fall into ruins. **10.** to come to ruin.

ru·in·a·tion (roo′ə nā′shən), *n.* **1.** act of ruining. **2.** state of being ruined. **3.** something that ruins.

ru·in·ous (roo′ə nəs), *adj.* **1.** bringing ruin; destructive; disastrous. **2.** dilapidated. **3.** consisting of ruins. —**ru′in·ous·ly,** *adv.*

rule (rool), *n., v.,* **ruled, ruling.** —*n.* **1.** a principle or. regulation governing conduct, action, etc. **2.** the code of regulations observed by a religious order or congregation. **3.** control, government, or dominion. **4.** ruler (def. 2). **5.** *Print.* a thin, type-high strip of metal for printing a line. —*v.t., v.i.* **6.** to control, direct, or govern. **7.** to decide judicially or authoritatively. **8.** to mark with lines with the aid of a ruler.

rul·er (roo′lər), *n.* **1.** one that governs. **2.** a strip of wood, metal, or other material with a straight edge, used in drawing lines, measuring, etc.

rul·ing (roo′lĭng), *n.* **1.** an authoritative decision. **2.** act of drawing straight lines with a ruler.

—*adj.* **3.** governing or predominating. **4.** prevalent.

rum (rŭm), *n.* **1.** an alcoholic liquor or spirit distilled from molasses or some other sugar-cane product. **2.** alcoholic drink in general.

Ru·ma·ni·a (roo mā′nĭ ə, -mān′yə), *n.* a republic in SE Europe, bordering on the Black Sea. 16,472,000 pop.; 91,654 sq. mi. *Cap.:* Bucharest. —**Ru·ma′ni·an,** *adj., n.*

rum·ba (rŭm′bə), *n.* **1.** a dance, Cuban Negro in origin and complex in rhythm. **2.** music for this dance.

rum·ble (rŭm′bəl), *v.,* **-bled, -bling,** *n.* —*v.i.* **1.** to make a deep, heavy, continuous sound, as thunder. **2.** to move with such a sound. —*v.t.* **3.** to utter with a rumbling sound. —*n.* **4.** a rumbling sound. **5.** a smaller open-air seat (**rumble seat**) behind the principal roofed seat in an automobile.

ru·mi·nant (roo′mə nənt), *n.* **1.** any of certain animals which comprise the various cloven-hoofed and cud-chewing quadrupeds: cattle, buffalo, sheep, goats, deer, giraffes, camels, etc. —*adj.* **2.** chewing the cud. **3.** meditative.

ru·mi·nate (roo′mə nāt′), *v.,* **-nated, -nating.** —*v.i.* **1.** to chew the cud, as a ruminant does. **2.** to meditate or ponder. —*v.t.* **3.** to chew again. **4.** to meditate on; ponder. —**ru′mi·na′tion,** *n.* —**ru′mi·na′tive,** *adj.*

rum·mage (rŭm′ĭj), *v.,* **-maged, -maging,** *n.* —*v.t., v.i.* **1.** to search thoroughly, esp. by moving about, turning over, etc. —*n.* **2.** miscellaneous articles. **3.** a rummaging search.

rum·my (rŭm′ĭ), *n.* a card game in which the object is to match cards into sets and sequences.

ru·mor (roo′mər), *n.* **1.** a story or statement in general circulation without confirmation or certainty as to facts. **2.** unconfirmed gossip. —*v.t.* **3.** to circulate, report, or assert by a rumor.

rump (rŭmp), *n.* **1.** the hinder part of the body of an animal. **2.** the buttocks. **3.** the last and unimportant or inferior part.

rum·ple (rŭm′pəl), *v.,* **-pled, -pling.** —*v.t.* **1.** to draw or crush into wrinkles. **2.** to ruffle; tousle. —*v.i.* **3.** to become wrinkled. —*n.* **4.** a wrinkle or irregular fold.

rum·pus (rŭm′pəs), *n.* *Colloq.* **1.** disturbing noise; uproar. **2.** a commotion.

rum·run·ner (rŭm′rŭn′ər), *n.* *U.S. Colloq.* a person or ship engaged in smuggling liquor.

run (rŭn), *v.,* **ran, run, running,** *n., adj.* —*v.i.* **1.** to move the legs quickly. **2.** to move swiftly. **3.** to take to flight. **4.** to make a rapid journey for a short stay at a place. **5.** *Racing.* **a.** to take part in a race. **b.** to finish a race in a certain position. **6.** to stand as a candidate for election. **7.** to migrate, as fish, esp. upstream or inshore to spawn. **8.** to sail or be driven (ashore, aground, etc.). **9.** to ply between places. **10.** to move easily, freely, or smoothly. **11.** to flow, as a liquid, a stream, the sea, etc. **12.** to melt and flow, as varnish. **13.** to spread. **14.** to discharge a liquid or fluid. **15.** to overflow or leak. **16.** to creep, trail, or climb, as vines. **17.** to pass quickly. **18.** to continue persistently. **19.** to unravel, as stitches. **20.** to be in operation. **21.** *Law.* to have legal force or effect. **22.** to be played continuously, as a play. **23.** to go or proceed. **24.** to extend or stretch. **25.** to have a specified character, quality, size, etc. **26.** to get or become. —*v.t.* **27.** to perform by running. **28.** to enter (a horse, etc.) in a race. **29.** to run or get past or through. **30.** to pursue; hunt. **31.** to cause to ply between places. **32.** to convey or transport. **33.** to cause to pass quickly. **34.** to keep operating. **35.** to expose oneself to, or be exposed to (a chance, risk, etc.). **36.** to put up (a person) as a candidate for election. **37.** to bring, lead, or force into some state, action, etc. **38.** to cause (a liquid) to flow. **39.** to cause to move easily, freely, or smoothly. **40.** to pierce or stab. **41.** to drive, force, or thrust. **42.** to conduct, as a business. **43.** to extend (a thing). **44.** to draw or trace, as a line. **45.** to smuggle. —*n.* **46.** act or spell of running. **47.** a running pace. **48.** a rapid journey for a short stay at a place. **49.** a period of action, operation, etc. **50.** a line in knitted work where a series of stitches have come undone. **51.** a continuous course of performances, as of a play. **52.** the particular course or tendency of something. **53.** freedom to range over, go through, or use. **54.** a continuous course of some condition of affairs, etc. **55.** any continued or extensive demand, call, or the like. **56.** a small stream. **57.** a kind or class, as of goods. **58.** *Music.* a rapid succession of tones. **59.** a series of sudden and urgent demands, as on a bank, for payment. **60.** a series of successful shots, strokes, or the like, in a game. **61.** *Baseball.* the score unit, made by successfully running around all the bases and reaching the home plate. —*adj.* **62.** melted or liquefied.

run·a·bout (rŭn′ə bout′), *n.* **1.** a roadster. **2.** one who runs about from place to place.

run·a·round (rŭn′ə round′), *n. Slang.* equivocation; evasion.

run·a·way (rŭn′ə wā′), *n.* **1.** a fugitive; deserter. **2.** a horse or team which has broken away from control. —*adj.* **3.** escaped; fugitive. **4.** uncontrolled.

run-down (rŭn′doun′), *adj.* **1.** fatigued; weary. **2.** fallen into disrepair. **3.** (of a spring-operated timepiece) not running because not wound.

rune (rōōn), *n.* any of the characters of an alphabet used by the ancient Germanic-speaking peoples, esp. the Scandinavians. —**ru′nic,** *adj.*

rung (rŭng), *n.* **1.** one of the crosspieces forming the steps of a ladder. **2.** a piece fixed horizontally between the legs of a chair.

run·let (rŭn′lĭt), *n.* a little stream. Also, **run·nel** (rŭn′əl).

run·ner (rŭn′ər), *n.* **1.** one that runs; racer. **2.** a messenger. **3.** something in or on which something else runs or moves. **4.** the blade of a skate. **5.** a long, narrow rug, suitable for a hall. **6.** a smuggler. **7.** a smuggling vessel.

run·ner-up (rŭn′ər ŭp′), *n.* the competitor, player, or team finishing in second place.

run·ning (rŭn′ĭng), *n.* **1.** act of one that runs. **2.** competition. **3.** management. —*adj.* **4.** that runs. **5.** slipping or sliding easily, as a knot. **6.** (of measurement) linear. **7.** current. **8.** going or carried on continuously. **9.** following in succession (placed after the noun). **10.** performed with or during a run. **11.** discharging matter, as a sore.

running board, a small ledge beneath the doors of an automobile, to assist passengers entering or leaving the car.

running head, *Print.* a descriptive heading repeated at the top of (usually) each page.

running knot, a knot made round and so as to slide along a part of the same rope thus forming a noose (**running noose**) which tightens as the rope is pulled.

running mate, **1.** a horse used to establish the pace for another horse in a race. **2.** a candidate for an office linked with another and more important office.

runt (rŭnt), *n.* an undersized animal, person, or thing. —**runt′y,** *adj.*

run·way (rŭn′wā′), *n.* **1.** a way along which something runs. **2.** a paved or cleared strip on which planes land or take off; airstrip.

ru·pee (rōō pē′), *n.* a silver coin and the monetary unit of India, equivalent to about 30 U.S. cents.

rup·ture (rŭp′chər), *n., v.,* **-tured, -turing.** —*n.* **1.** act of breaking. **2.** state of being broken. **3.** hernia. —*v.t.* **4.** to break (a blood vessel, etc.). **5.** to cause a breach of (relations, etc.). **6.** to affect with hernia. —*v.i.* **7.** to suffer a break.

ru·ral (rōōr′əl), *adj.* **1.** of, pertaining to, or characteristic of the country, country life, or country people; rustic. **2.** living in the country. **3.** of or pertaining to agriculture.

rural free delivery, free mail delivery in outlying country areas. *Abbr.:* R.F.D.

ruse (rōōz), *n.* a trick; stratagem.

rush[1] (rŭsh), *v.i.* **1.** to move or go with speed, impetuosity, or violence. **2.** to dash forward for an attack. **3.** to go or plunge with headlong haste. **4.** to go, come, pass, etc., rapidly. —*v.t.* **5.** to send, push, force, carry, etc., with great or undue haste. **6.** to attack with a rush. **7.** *U.S. Slang.* to heap attentions on. —*n.* **8.** act of rushing. **9.** a hostile attack. **10.** an eager rushing of persons to some region to be occupied or exploited, esp. to a new mine field. **11.** a sudden coming. **12.** hurried activity; busy haste. **13.** a hurried state, as from pressure of affairs. **14.** (*pl.*) *Motion Pictures.* the first prints made after shooting a scene or scenes. —*adj.* **15.** requiring haste. **16.** characterized by rush or press of work, traffic, etc. —**rush′er,** *n.*

rush[2] (rŭsh), *n.* **1.** any of certain grasslike herbs with pithy or hollow stems, found in wet or marshy places. **2.** a stem of such a plant, used for making chair bottoms, mats, baskets, etc. —**rush′y,** *adj.*

rusk (rŭsk), *n.* a slice of sweet raised bread dried and browned in the oven.

Rus·kin (rŭs′kĭn), *n.* **John,** 1819–1900, British author, art critic, and social reformer.

Rus·sell (rŭs′əl), *n.* **1. Bertrand, third Earl,** born 1872, British philosopher and mathematician. **2. George William,** (*AE*) 1867–1935, Irish poet and painter.

rus·set (rŭs′ĭt), *n.* **1.** yellowish or reddish brown. **2.** a coarse reddish-brown homespun cloth formerly in use. **3.** a winter apple with a rough brownish skin. —*adj.* **4.** yellowish-brown; reddish-brown.

Rus·sia (rŭsh′ə), *n.* **1.** the Soviet Union. **2.** Also, **Russian Empire.** a former empire in E Europe and N and W Asia: overthrown by the Russian Revolution, 1917. *Cap.:* St. Petersburg (Petrograd). —**Rus′sian,** *adj., n.*

Russian Socialist Federated Soviet Republic, the largest of the constituent republics of the Soviet Union. 108,809,469 pop.; ab. 6,442,700 sq. mi. *Cap.:* Moscow.

rust (rŭst), *n.* **1.** the red or orange coating which forms on the surface of iron when exposed to air and moisture, consisting chiefly of ferric hydroxide and ferric oxide. **2.** *Plant Pathol.* any of the various plant diseases caused by fungi, in which the leaves and stems become spotted and acquire a red-to-brown color. **3.** reddish yellow or brown. —*v.i.* **4.** to grow rusty. —*v.t.* **5.** to affect with rust. —**rust′a·ble,** *adj.* —**rust′less,** *adj.* —**rust′proof′,** *adj.*

rus·tic (rŭs′tĭk), *adj.* **1.** of, pertaining to, or living in the country; rural. **2.** simple; unsophisticated. **3.** uncouth; rude; boorish. **4.** made of roughly dressed limbs or roots of trees, as garden seats. —*n.* **5.** a country person.

rus·ti·cate (rŭs′tə kāt′), *v.,* **-cated, -cating.** —*v.i.* **1.** to go to the country. **2.** to live in the country. —*v.t.* **3.** to send to the country. **4.** to make rustic, as persons, manners, etc. —**rus′ti·ca′tion,** *n.*

rus·tic·i·ty (rŭs tĭs′ə tĭ), *n., pl.* **-ties.** **1.** state or quality of being rustic. **2.** rural character or life.

rus·tle (rŭs′əl), *v.,* **-tled, -tling,** *n.* —*v.i.* **1.** to make a succession of slight, soft sounds, as of parts rubbing gently one on another, as leaves. —*v.t.* **2.** to move so as to cause a rustling sound. **3.** *Western U.S.* to steal (cattle, etc.). —*n.* **4.** the sound made by anything that rustles. —**rus′tler,** *n.*

rust·proof (rŭst′prōōf′), *adj.* not subject to rusting.

rust·y (rŭs′tĭ), *adj.,* **rustier, rustiest.** **1.** covered or affected with rust. **2.** rust-colored. **3.** impaired through disuse or neglect. **4.** having lost agility or alertness. —**rust′i·ly,** *adv.* —**rust′i·ness,** *n.*

rut[1] (rŭt), *n., v.,* **rutted, rutting.** —*n.* **1.** a furrow in the ground, esp. one made by the passage of a vehicle or vehicles. **2.** a fixed or established mode of procedure or course of life. —*v.t.* **3.** to make a rut or ruts in.

rut[2] (rŭt), *n., v.,* **rutted, rutting.** —*n.* **1.** the periodically recurring sexual excitement of the male deer, goat, sheep, etc. —*v.i.* **2.** to be in the condition of rut.

ru·ta·ba·ga (rōō′tə bā′gə, -bĕg′ə), *n.* the yellow turnip.

Ruth (rōōth), *n.* a book of the Old Testament.

Ruth (rōōth), *n.* **George Herman,** ("*Babe*") 1895–1948, U.S. baseball player.

ru·the·ni·um (rōō thē′nĭ əm), *n. Chem.* a steel-gray, rare metallic element. *Symbol:* Ru; *at. wt.:* 101.7; *at. no.:* 44; *sp. gr.:* 12.2 at 20°C.

ruth·less (rōōth′lĭs), *adj.* pitiless; merciless. —**ruth′less·ly,** *adv.* —**ruth′less·ness,** *n.*

rut·ty (rŭt′ĭ), *adj.,* **-tier, -tiest.** full of or abounding in ruts, as a road. —**rut′ti·ness,** *n.*

Ry., Railway.

-ry, a suffix of abstract nouns of condition, practice (*dentistry*) and of collectives (*jewelry*).

rye (rī), *n.* **1.** a widely cultivated cereal grass with two- or three-flowered spikelets. **2.** the seeds or grain of this plant, used for making flour, for livestock feed, and for whiskey. **3.** a straight whiskey distilled from a mash containing 51% or more rye grain.

Ryu·kyu (rū′kū′), *n.* a chain of 55 islands in the W Pacific between Japan and Formosa, formerly belonging to Japan. 839,449 pop.; ab. 1850 sq. mi.

S

S, s (ĕs), *n.*, *pl.* **S's** or **Ss, s's** or **ss.** a consonant, the 19th letter of the English alphabet.

S, 1. South. 2. Southern. 3. *Chem.* sulfur.

S., 1. Sea. 2. South. 3. Southern.

s., 1. second. 2. section. 3. (L *solidus*) shilling. 4. substantive.

Sa, *Chem.* samarium.

S.A., 1. South Africa. 2. South America.

Saar (zär), *n.* a river flowing N from NE France to W Germany. ab. 150 mi.

Saar Basin, a rich coal mining and industrial region in the Saar river valley.

Sab·bath (săb/əth), *n.* 1. the seventh day of the week (Saturday) as the day of rest and religious observance among the Jews and certain Christian sects. 2. the first day of the week (Sunday), similarly observed by most Christians.

Sab·bat·i·cal (sə băt/ə kəl), *adj.* 1. of, pertaining to, or appropriate to the Sabbath. 2. (*l.c.*) bringing a period of rest. —*n.* 3. (*l.c.*) a sabbatical year. —**Sab·bat/i·cal·ly,** *adv.*

sabbatical year, (in certain universities, etc.) a year, usually every seventh, of freedom from teaching, granted to a professor, as for study or travel.

sa·ber (sā/bər), *n.* 1. a heavy one-edged sword, usually slightly curved. —*v.t.* 2. to strike, wound, or kill with a saber. Also, *Brit.,* **sa/bre.**

sa·ble (sā/bəl), *n.* 1. an Old World weasellike mammal of cold regions, valued for its dark-brown fur. 2. a marten. 3. the fur of the sable. —*adj.* 4. made of the fur or hair of the sable. 5. *Poetic.* black; very dark.

sab·ot (săb/ō), *n.* 1. a shoe made of a single piece of wood hollowed out, worn by peasants in France, Belgium, etc. 2. a leather shoe with a thick wooden sole.

sab·o·tage (săb/ə täzh/), *n.*, *v.*, **-taged, -taging.** —*n.* 1. malicious injury to work, tools, etc., or any underhand interference with production or business, as by enemy agents during wartime. —*v.t.* 2. to injure or attack by sabotage.

sab·o·teur (săb/ə tûr/), *n.* one who commits or practices sabotage.

sac (săk), *n.* a baglike structure in an animal or plant, as one containing fluid.

sac·cha·rin (săk/ə rĭn), *n.* a crystalline compound obtained from toluene: used as a sweetening agent in cases of diabetes and obesity.

sac·cha·rine (săk/ə rĭn, -rīn/), *adj.* 1. of a sugary sweetness. 2. pertaining to, of the nature of, or containing sugar. —*n.* 3. saccharin.

sac·er·do·tal (săs/ər dō/təl), *adj.* of or pertaining to priests or the priesthood; priestly.

sac·er·do·tal·ism (săs/ər dō/tə lĭz/əm), *n.* the system or spirit of the priesthood.

sa·chem (sā/chəm), *n.* (among some tribes of American Indians) a chief.

sa·chet (să shā/), *n.* 1. a small bag, case, pad, etc., containing perfuming powder or the like. 2. the powder.

sack[1] (săk), *n.* 1. a large bag of stout woven material, as for grain, potatoes, coal, etc. 2. the amount which a sack will hold, a varying unit of measure. 3. *U.S.* any bag. 4. a loose-fitting coat or jacket. 5. *Brit. Slang.* dismissal from employment. —*v.t.* 6. to put into a sack or sacks. 7. *Brit. Slang.* to dismiss from employment.

sack[2] (săk), *v.t.* 1. to pillage or loot; plunder. —*n.* 2. plundering; pillage.

sack[3] (săk), *n.* any of various strong light-colored wines.

sack·but (săk/bŭt/), *n.* a medieval form of the trombone.

sack·cloth (săk/klôth/, -klŏth/), *n.* 1. sacking. 2. coarse cloth worn as a sign of mourning or penitence.

sack·ing (săk/ĭng), *n.* stout or coarse woven material of hemp, jute, or the like, used for making sacks, etc.

sac·ra·ment (săk/rə mənt), *n.* 1. *Eccles.* a visible sign instituted by Jesus Christ to confer grace or Divine Life on those who worthily receive it. The sacraments of the Protestant Churches are baptism and the Lord's Supper; the sacraments of the Roman and Greek Catholic Churches are baptism, confirmation, the Eucharist, matrimony, penance, holy orders, and extreme unction. 2. (*often cap.*) the Eucharist. 3. something regarded as sacred. 4. an oath; solemn pledge. —**sac/ra·men/tal,** *adj.*

Sac·ra·men·to (săk/rə mĕn/tō), *n.* the capital of California, in the central part. 119,984.

sa·cred (sā/krĭd), *adj.* 1. appropriated or dedicated to a deity or to some religious purpose; consecrated. 2. entitled to veneration or religious respect; holy. 3. pertaining to or connected with religion. 4. reverently dedicated to some person or object. 5. regarded with reverence. 6. secured against violation, infringement, etc., by reverence, sense of right, etc. —**sa/cred·ly,** *adv.* —**sa/cred·ness,** *n.*

sac·ri·fice (săk/rə fīs/), *n.*, *v.*, **-ficed, -ficing.** —*n.* 1. the offering of life or some material possession, etc., to a deity, as in homage. 2. that which is so offered. 3. the surrender or destruction of something for the sake of something considered as having a higher or more pressing claim. 4. a loss incurred in selling something below its value. —*v.t.* 5. to make a sacrifice of. —*v.i.* 6. *Baseball.* to gain a base by a sacrifice hit. —**sac·ri·fi·cial** (săk/rə fĭsh/əl), *adj.* —**sac/ri·fi/cial·ly,** *adv.*

sacrifice hit, *Baseball.* a hit which allows a runner to gain a base while the batter is (or could be) put out before reaching first base.

sac·ri·lege (săk/rə lĭj), *n.* the violation or profanation of anything sacred. —**sac·ri·le·gious** (săk/rə lĭj/əs, -lē/jəs), *adj.* —**sac/ri·le/gious·ly,** *adv.*

sac·ris·tan (săk/rĭs tən), *n.* an official in charge of the sacred vessels, vestments, etc., of a church or a religious house.

sac·ris·ty (săk/rĭs tĭ), *n.*, *pl.* **-ties.** the room in a church or a religious house in which the sacred vessels, vestments, etc., are kept.

sac·ro·sanct (săk/rō săngkt/), *adj.* especially or superlatively sacred or inviolable.

sad (săd), *adj.*, **sadder, saddest.** 1. sorrowful or mournful. 2. causing sorrow. 3. (of color) somber, dark, or dull. 4. *Often Humorous.* deplorably bad; shocking. —**sad/ly,** *adv.* —**sad/ness,** *n.*

sad·den (săd/ən), *v.t.*, *v.i.* to make or become sad.

sad·dle (săd/əl), *n.*, *v.*, **-dled, -dling.** —*n.* 1. a seat for a rider on the back of a horse or other animal, a bicycle, etc. 2. (of mutton, venison, etc.) a cut including part of the backbone and both loins. 3. (of poultry) the posterior part of the back. 4. a ridge connecting two higher elevations. —*v.t.* 5. to put a saddle upon (a horse, etc.). 6. to load, as with a burden. 7. to impose as a responsibility.

sad·dle·bag (săd/əl băg/), *n.* a large bag, usually one of a pair, hung from a saddle.

sad·dle·bow (săd/əl bō/), *n.* the arched front part of a saddle.

sad·dler (săd/lər), *n.* one who makes or deals in saddles, etc.

Sad·du·cee (săj/ə sē/), *n.* one of an ancient Jewish sect which denied the authority of oral tradition, the resurrection of the dead, etc. —**Sad/du·ce/an,** *adj.*, *n.*

sad·ism (săd/ĭz əm, sā/dĭz əm), *n.* *Psychiatry.* 1. sexual gratification gained through causing physical pain and humiliation. 2. any morbid enjoyment in being cruel. —**sad/ist,** *n.*, *adj.* —**sa·dis·tic** (sə dĭs/tĭk, sā-), *adj.*

sad sack, *U.S. Slang.* 1. an ineffective soldier who always blunders despite good intentions. 2. any such ineffective person.

sa·fa·ri (sə fär′Y), *n.*, *pl.* **-ris.** (in eastern Africa) an expedition, esp. for hunting.

safe (sāf), *adj.*, **safer, safest,** *n.* —*adj.* **1.** secure from liability to harm, injury, danger, or risk. **2.** free from hurt, injury, danger, or risk. **3.** involving no risk of mishap, error, etc. **4.** dependable. **5.** cautious in avoiding danger. —*n.* **6.** a steel or iron box for money, jewels, papers, etc. —**safe′ly,** *adv.* —**safe′ness,** *n.*

safe-con·duct (sāf′kŏn′dŭkt), *n.* a document securing a safe passage through a region, esp. in time of war.

safe·guard (sāf′gärd′), *n.* **1.** something serving as a protection or defense, or ensuring safety. —*v.t.* **2.** to guard; protect; secure.

safe·keep·ing (sāf′kē′pĭng), *n.* protection; care.

safe·ty (sāf′tĭ), *n.*, *pl.* **-ties. 1.** freedom from injury or danger. **2.** quality of insuring against hurt, injury, danger, or risk. **3.** a contrivance or device to prevent injury or avert danger. **4.** a locking or cutoff device that prevents a gun from being fired accidentally.

safety belt, *Aeron.* a belt attached to the seat, used for securing the passenger or crew member against sudden bumps, etc.

safety match, a match igniting only when rubbed on a specially prepared surface.

safety pin, a pin bent back on itself to form a spring, with a guard to cover the point.

safety razor, a razor provided with a guard to prevent cutting the skin.

safety valve, 1. a valve in a steam boiler or the like, which, when the pressure becomes abnormal or dangerous, opens and allows the steam or fluid to escape. **2.** a harmless outlet for emotion, nervousness, etc.

saf·fron (sāf′rən), *n.* **1.** a crocus with handsome purple flowers. **2.** an orange-colored product consisting of its dried stigmas, used to color confectionery, for flavoring, etc. **3.** yellow orange.

sag (săg), *v.*, **sagged, sagging,** *n.* —*v.i.* **1.** to sink or bend downward by weight or pressure, esp. in the middle. **2.** to hang loosely or unevenly. **3.** to decline. —*v.t.* **4.** to cause to sag. —*n.* **5.** act or degree of sagging. **6.** a place where anything sags.

sa·ga (sä′gə), *n.* **1.** a medieval Icelandic or Norse prose narrative. **2.** any narrative of heroic exploits.

sa·ga·cious (sə gā′shəs), *adj.* having acute mental discernment and keen practical sense; shrewd. —**sa·ga′cious·ly,** *adv.* —**sa·gac·i·ty** (sə găs′ə tĭ), *n.*

sag·a·more (săg′ə môr′), *n.* (among the American Indians of New England) a chief.

sage¹ (sāj), *n.*, *adj.*, **sager, sagest.** —*n.* **1.** a profoundly wise man. —*adj.* **2.** wise, judicious, or prudent. —**sage′ly,** *adv.* —**sage′ness,** *n.*

sage² (sāj), *n.* **1.** any species of salvia, esp. a perennial herb whose grayish-green leaves are used in medicine and for seasoning in cookery. **2.** sagebrush.

sage·brush (sāj′brŭsh′), *n.* any of certain bushy plants common on the dry plains of the western U.S.

Sag·i·naw (săg′ə nô′), *n.* a city in E Michigan. 82,794.

Sag·it·ta·ri·us (săj′ə târ′Y əs), *n.* **1.** the Archer (a centaur drawing a bow), a zodiacal constellation. **2.** the ninth sign of the zodiac.

sa·go (sā′gō), *n.* a starchy foodstuff derived from the soft interior of the trunk of various palms, used in making puddings, etc.

Sa·har·a (sə hâr′ə, sə hă′rə), *n.* a great desert in N Africa, extending from the Atlantic to the Nile valley. ab. 3,500,000 sq. mi.

sa·hib (sä′ĭb), *n.* (in India) a term of respect applied by natives to a European.

said (sĕd), *adj. Chiefly Law.* named or mentioned before.

Sai·gon (sī gŏn′), *n.* a seaport in S French Indo-China. 111,000.

sail (sāl), *n.* **1.** an expanse of canvas or similar material spread to the wind to make a vessel move through the water. **2.** some similar piece, as an arm of a windmill. **3.** a voyage or excursion. **4. set sail,** to start a voyage. —*v.i.* **5.** to travel in a vessel conveyed by the action of wind, steam, etc. **6.** to move along or be conveyed by wind, steam, etc. **7.** to manage a sailboat. **8.** to begin a journey by water. **9.** to travel or move through the air. **10.** to move

along with dignity. **11.** *Colloq.* to go boldly into action. —*v.t.* **12.** to sail upon, over, or through. **13.** to navigate (a ship, etc.).

sail·boat (sāl′bōt′),· *n.* a boat propelled by sails.

sail·cloth (sāl′klŏth′, -klôth′), *n.* canvas or other material such as is used for making sails.

sail·fish (sāl′fĭsh′), *n.*, *pl.* **-fishes,** (*esp. collectively*) **-fish.** any of certain large marine fishes characterized by a very large dorsal fin likened to a sail, and related to the swordfishes.

sail·or (sā′lər), *n.* **1.** one whose occupation is sailing; seaman. **2.** a seaman below the rank of officer. **3.** a flat-brimmed straw hat with a low, flat crown. —**sail′or·ly,** *adj.*

saint (sānt), *n.* **1.** one of certain exceptionally holy persons formally recognized by the Christian Church as having attained an exalted position in heaven. **2.** (in certain religious bodies) a designation applied by the members to themselves. **3.** a person of great holiness. —**saint′hood,** *n.*

Saint Bernard, one of a breed of large dogs with a massive head, noted for their intelligence: named from the hospice of St. Bernard, in the Alps, where they are kept by the monks for rescuing travelers from the snow.

saint·ed (sān′tĭd), *adj.* **1.** enrolled among the saints. **2.** sacred. **3.** saintly.

Saint-Gau·dens (sānt gō′dənz), *n.* **Augustus,** 1848–1907, U.S. sculptor.

saint·ly (sānt′lĭ), *adj.*, **-lier, -liest.** like or befitting a saint. —**saint′li·ness,** *n.*

Saint-Saëns (săN säns′), *n.* **Charles Camille,** 1835–1921, French composer.

Saint Val·en·tine's Day, Feb. 14, when valentines are given.

Sai·pan (sī pän′), *n.* one of the Marianas Islands, in the N Pacific: taken by U.S. forces, 1944. 23,685 pop.; 71 sq. mi.

saith (sĕth), *v. Archaic or Poetic.* third pers. sing. pres. of **say.**

sake¹ (sāk), *n.* **1.** cause, account, or interest. **2.** purpose or end.

sa·ke² (sä′kĭ), *n.* a Japanese fermented alcoholic beverage made from rice.

Sa·kha·lin (sä′hä lēn′), *n.* an island off the SE coast of the Soviet Union in Asia, N of Japan: formerly (1905–45) divided between Russia and Japan but now entirely Russian. ab. 350,000 pop.; 28,957 sq. mi.

sal (săl), *n. Chiefly Pharm.* salt.

sa·laam (sə läm′), *n.* **1.** (in the Orient) a salutation meaning "peace." **2.** a very low bow or obeisance. —*v.i.*, *v.t.* **3.** to perform a salaam. **4.** to salute (someone) with a salaam.

sal·a·ble (sā′lə bəl), *adj.* subject to or suitable for sale. —**sal′a·bil′i·ty,** *n.*

sa·la·cious (sə lā′shəs), *adj.* **1.** lustful or lecherous. **2.** (of writings, etc.) obscene. —**sa·la′cious·ly,** *adv.* —**sa·la′cious·ness,** *n.*

sal·ad (săl′əd), *n.* **1.** a dish of lettuce or other vegetables, herbs, or meat or fowl, fruit, etc., prepared with various seasonings or dressings and usually served cold. **2.** any plant used for such a dish or eaten raw.

sal·a·man·der (săl′ə măn′dər), *n.* **1.** any of various tailed amphibians, most of which have an aquatic larval stage but are terrestrial as adults. **2.** a mythical reptile or being supposed to be able to live in fire.

sa·la·mi (sə lä′mĭ), *n.* a kind of sausage, originally Italian, often flavored with garlic.

sal·a·ry (săl′ə rĭ), *n.*, *pl.* **-ries.** a fixed compensation periodically paid to a person for regular work or services. —**sal′a·ried,** *adj.*

sale (sāl), *n.* **1.** act of selling. **2.** quantity sold. **3.** opportunity to sell; demand. **4.** a special disposal of goods, as at reduced prices. **5.** transfer of property for money or credit.

sale·a·ble (sā′lə bəl), *adj.* salable.

Sa·lem (sā′ləm), *n.* **1.** a seaport in NE Massachusetts. 41,213. **2.** the capital of Oregon, in the NW part. 30,908.

Sa·ler·no (sə lŭr′nō), *n.* a seaport in SW Italy. 85,368.

sales·man (sālz′mən), *n.*, *pl.* **-men.** a man engaged in selling. —**sales′man·ship′,** *n.* —**sales′la·dy, sales′wom·an,** *n. fem.*

sales·per·son (sālz′pûr′sən), *n.* one engaged in selling goods, esp. in a store. Also, **sales′clerk′.** —**sales′peo′ple,** *n. pl.*

sales·room (sālz′room′, -room′), *n.* a room in which goods are sold.

sales tax, a tax on sales or on receipts from sales.

Sal·ic law (săl′ĭk, sā′lĭk), the alleged fundamental law of the French monarchy by which females were excluded from succession to the crown.

sal·i·cyl·ic acid (săl′ə sĭl′ĭk), *Chem.* an acid used esp. as a remedy for rheumatic and gouty affections.

sa·li·ent (sā′lĭ ənt), *adj.* **1.** prominent or conspicuous. **2.** projecting or pointing outward. —*n.* **3.** a salient angle or part, as the central outward projecting angle of a bastion or an outward projection in a battle line. —**sa′li·ent·ly,** *adv.* —**sa′li·ence,** *n.*

sa·li·en·ti·an (sā′lĭ ĕn′shĭ ən), *n.* **1.** any animal of an amphibian order of which the toads and frogs are typical. —*adj.* **2.** of, pertaining to, or included in the salientians.

sa·line (sā′līn), *adj.* **1.** salty or saltlike. **2.** of or pertaining to a chemical salt, esp. as used as a cathartic. —*n.* **3.** a saline medicine. —**sa·lin·i·ty** (sə lĭn′ə tĭ), *n.*

sa·li·va (sə lī′və), *n.* a fluid consisting of the secretions produced by glands which discharge into the mouth; spittle. —**sal·i·var·y** (săl′ə vĕr′ĭ), *adj.*

sal·i·vate (săl′ə vāt′), *v.i.* **-vated, -vating.** to produce saliva. —**sal′i·va′tion,** *n.*

sal·low (săl′ō), *adj.* **1.** of a yellowish, sickly hue or complexion. —*v.t.* **2.** to make sallow. —**sal′low·ness,** *n.*

sal·ly (săl′ĭ), *n., pl.* **-lies,** *v.,* **-lied, -lying.** —*n.* **1.** a sortie of troops from a besieged place upon an enemy. **2.** a sudden activity or outburst. **3.** a brilliant or clever remark. —*v.i.* **4.** to make a sally.

sal·ma·gun·di (săl′mə gŭn′dĭ), *n.* **1.** a mixed dish of chopped meat, anchovies, eggs, onions, oil, etc. **2.** a miscellany.

salm·on (săm′ən), *n., pl.* **-mons,** (*esp. collectively*) **-mon,** *adj.* —*n.* **1.** a marine and freshwater food fish with pink flesh, common in the northern Atlantic Ocean near the mouths of large rivers, which it ascends to spawn. **2.** a variety of this species confined to lakes, etc. **3.** any of several related food fishes of the North Pacific, as the **chinook salmon;** the **red, sockeye,** or **blueback salmon;** or the **pink salmon. 4.** light yellowish pink. —*adj.* **5.** of the color salmon.

salmon trout, a large trout resembling the salmon.

Sa·lo·me (sə lō′mĭ), *n.* a girl whose dancing so pleased Herod that he gave her the head of John the Baptist at her request, as dictated by her mother.

Sal·o·mon (săl′ə mən), *n.* **Haym,** 1740?–85, American Revolutionary patriot.

sa·lon (sə lŏn′), *n.* **1.** a drawing room in a large house. **2.** an assembly of guests in such a room. **3.** a place for the exhibition of works of art.

Sa·lo·ni·ka (sā·lō nē′kä), *n.* a seaport in NE Greece. 268,140.

sa·loon (sə lōōn′), *n.* **1.** *U.S.* a place for the sale of intoxicating liquors to be drunk on the premises. **2.** a room or place for general use, as by the passengers on a ship.

sal·si·fy (săl′sə fĭ), *n.* a purple-flowered plant whose edible root has an oysterlike flavor.

sal soda, sodium carbonate.

salt (sôlt), *n.* **1.** a crystalline compound, sodium chloride, occurring as a mineral, a constituent of sea water, etc.: used for seasoning food, etc. **2.** *Chem.* a compound which upon ionization yields cations of a metal and anions of an acid radical. **3.** (*pl.*) any of various salts used as purgatives. **4.** that which gives liveliness, piquancy, or pungency to anything. **5.** wit. **6.** *Colloq.* a sailor. **7. salt of the earth,** the best element of people. **8. with a grain of salt,** with reserve or allowance. —*v.t.* **9.** to season, cure, preserve, or treat with salt. **10.** *Colloq.* to store in reserve. —*adj.* **11.** containing or tasting like salt. **12.** cured or preserved with salt. —**salt′er,** *n.* —**salt′ish,** *adj.* —**salt′y,** *adj.* —**salt′i·ness,** *n.*

salt·cel·lar (sôlt′sĕl′ər), *n.* a shaker or dish for salt.

Salt Lake City, the capital of Utah, in the N part, near Great Salt Lake. 149,934.

salt lick, a place to which wild animals resort to lick salt occurring naturally there.

salt·pe·ter (sôlt′pē′tər), *n.* niter (nitrate of potassium). Also, **salt′pe′tre.**

sa·lu·bri·ous (sə lōō′brĭ əs), *adj.* healthful. —**sa·lu′bri·ous·ly,** *adv.*

sal·u·tar·y (săl′yə tĕr′ĭ), *adj.* **1.** conducive to health; healthful. **2.** beneficial; wholesome.

sal·u·ta·tion (săl′yə tā′shən), *n.* **1.** act of saluting. **2.** something uttered, written, or done by way of saluting. **3.** the formal opening of a letter, as "Dear Sir."

sa·lu·ta·to·ri·an (sə lōō′tə tôr′ĭ ən), *n.* (in American schools) the student who delivers the salutatory oration.

sa·lu·ta·to·ry (sə lōō′tə tôr′ĭ), *adj., n., pl.* **-ries.** —*adj.* **1.** pertaining to or of the nature of a salutation. —*n.* **2.** an address of welcome, esp. one given by a member of the graduating class to begin the commencement exercises.

sa·lute (sə lōōt′), *v.,* **-luted, -luting,** *n.* —*v.t.* **1.** to greet with expressions or gestures of good will, respect, etc. **2.** *Mil., Naval.* to pay respect to or honor by some formal act, as by raising the right hand to the side of the headgear, presenting arms, etc. —*v.i.* **3.** to perform or give a salute. —*n.* **4.** an act of saluting; greeting. **5.** *Mil., Naval.* **a.** the special act of respect paid in saluting. **b.** the position of the hand or rifle in saluting.

Sal·va·dor (săl′və dôr′), *n.* **1.** El Salvador. **2.** Official name of São Salvador. —**Sal′va·do′ran,** *adj., n.*

sal·vage (săl′vĭj), *n., v.,* **-vaged, -vaging.** —*n.* **1.** act of saving a ship or its cargo from perils of the seas. **2.** the property so saved. **3.** compensation given to those who voluntarily save a ship or its cargo. **4.** the saving of anything from fire, danger, etc., or the property so saved. —*v.t.* **5.** to save from shipwreck, fire, etc.

Sal·var·san (săl′vər săn′), *n.* **Trademark.** arsphenamine.

sal·va·tion (săl vā′shən), *n.* **1.** act of saving or delivering. **2.** state of being saved or delivered. **3.** a source, cause, or means of deliverance. **4.** *Theol.* deliverance from the power and penalty of sin; redemption.

Salvation Army, a quasi-military religious organization, founded in 1865 to revive religion among the masses.

salve[1] (săv, säv), *n., v.,* **salved, salving.** —*n.* **1.** an ointment for wounds and sores for relief or healing. **2.** anything that soothes or mollifies. —*v.t.* **3.** to soothe as if with salve.

salve[2] (sălv), *v.i., v.t.,* **salved, salving.** to save from loss or destruction; salvage.

sal·ver (săl′vər), *n.* a tray.

sal·vi·a (săl′vĭ ə), *n.* any of certain herbs or shrubs of the mint family, including the common sage.

sal·vo (săl′vō), *n., pl.,* **-vos, -voes. 1.** a discharge of artillery or other firearms, in regular succession. **2.** a round of cheers, applause, etc.

Salz·burg (sôlz′bûrg), *n.* a city in W Austria. 77,170.

Sam., *Bible.* Samuel.

Sa·mar·i·a (sə mâr′ĭ ə), *n.* **1.** an ancient kingdom in N Palestine between the Jordan river and the Mediterranean. **2.** its capital.

Sa·mar·i·tan (sə mâr′ə tən), *n.* **1.** an inhabitant of Samaria. **2.** See **good Samaritan. 3.** one who is compassionate and helpful to a fellow being in distress.

sa·mar·i·um (sə mâr′ĭ əm), *n.* *Chem.* a rare-earth metallic element. *Symbol:* Sm; *at. wt.:* 150.43; *at. no.:* 62.

Sam·ar·kand (săm′ər kănd′), *n.* a city in the SW Soviet Union in Asia: taken by Alexander the Great, 329 B.C. 134,346.

same (sām), *adj.* **1.** identical; not different, or has just been mentioned. **2.** just mentioned or about to be mentioned. **3.** agreeing in kind, amount, etc.; corresponding. **4.** unchanged in character, condition, etc. —*pron.* **5.** the same person or thing. **6. all the same, a.** notwithstanding. **b.** without any material difference. **7. just the same, a.** in the same manner. **b.** nevertheless. —**same′ness,** *n.*

sam·ite (săm′īt, sā′mīt), *n.* a heavy silk fabric, sometimes interwoven with gold, worn in the Middle Ages.

Sa·mo·a (sə mō′ə), *n.* a group of islands in the S Pacific: the islands W of 171° W are a trusteeship of New Zealand (**Territory of Western Samoa**), the rest (**American Samoa**) belong to the U.S. 74,000 pop.; 1209 sq. mi. —**Sa·mo′an,** *adj., n.*

Sam·o·thrace (săm′ə thrās′), *n.* a Greek island in the NE Aegean. 3500 pop.; 68 sq. mi.

sam·o·var (săm/ə vär/, săm/ə vär/), n. a metal urn used esp. in the Soviet Union for heating water for tea.

samp (sămp), n. U.S. **1.** a coarsely ground corn. **2.** a porridge made of it.

sam·pan (săm/păn), n. any of various small boats of China, etc., as one propelled by a single scull over the stern.

Sampan

sam·ple (săm/pəl, säm/-), n., adj., v., **-pled, -pling.** —n. **1.** a small part or one of a number, intended to show the quality, style, etc., of the whole; specimen. —adj. **2.** serving as a specimen. —v.t. **3.** to test or judge by a sample.

sam·pler (săm/plər, säm/-), n. **1.** one who samples. **2.** a cloth embroidered with various devices to show skill in needlework.

Sam·son (săm/sən), n. Bible. a hero of almost supernatural strength.

Sam·u·el (săm/yŏŏ əl), n. **1.** a Hebrew judge and prophet. **2.** either of two Old Testament books bearing his name.

sam·u·rai (săm/ŏŏ rī/), n., pl. **-rai.** (in feudal Japan) a member of the military class.

San An·to·ni·o (săn/ ăn tō/nĭ ō/), a city in S Texas: site of the Alamo. 253,854.

san·a·tive (săn/ə tĭv), adj. curative. Also, **san·a·to·ry** (săn/ə tōr/ĭ).

san·a·to·ri·um (săn/ə tōr/ĭ əm), n., pl. **-toriums, -toria** (-tōr/ĭ ə). sanitarium.

San Ber·nar·di·no (săn/ bûr/nər dē/nō), a city in S California. 56,193.

sanc·ti·fy (săngk/tə fī/), v.t., **-fied, -fying. 1.** to make holy or sacred; consecrate. **2.** to purify or free from sin. **3.** to impart sanction to. —**sanc/ti·fi·ca/tion,** n. —**sanc/ti·fi/er,** n.

sanc·ti·mo·ny (săngk/tə mō/nĭ), n. pretended, affected, or hypocritical holiness or devoutness. —**sanc/ti·mo/ni·ous,** adj. —**sanc/ti·mo/ni·ous·ly,** adv.

sanc·tion (săngk/shən), n. **1.** authoritative permission; approval, support, or ratification. **2.** Law. a provision of a law enacting a penalty for disobedience or a reward for obedience. **3.** Internat. Law. action by one or more states toward another state calculated to force it to comply with legal obligations. —v.t. **4.** to authorize, countenance, or approve. **5.** to ratify or confirm.

sanc·ti·ty (săngk/tə tĭ), n., pl. **-ties. 1.** holiness, saintliness, or godliness. **2.** sacred or hallowed character.

sanc·tu·ar·y (săngk/chŏŏ ĕr/ĭ), n., pl. **-aries. 1.** a holy place. **2.** the part of a church about the altar; chancel. **3.** a place where fugitives are immune from arrest; asylum. **4.** such immunity.

sanc·tum (săngk/təm), n. **1.** a holy place. **2.** an especially private place.

sand (sănd), n. **1.** small, loose, fine grains of rock, as on a beach. **2.** (usually pl.) a region composed principally of sand. **3.** (pl.) moments of time or of one's life. **4.** U.S. Colloq. pluck. **5.** a dull reddish-yellow color. —v.t. **6.** to smooth or polish with sand. **7.** to sprinkle with sand. —**sand/er,** n.

Sand (sănd), n. George, (Madame Amandine Lucile Aurore Dudevant) 1804–76, French novelist.

san·dal (săn/dəl), n., v., **-daled, -daling.** —n. **1.** a kind of shoe, consisting of a sole fastened to the foot by thongs or straps. **2.** a kind of light, low rubber overshoe. —v.t. **3.** to furnish with sandals.

san·dal·wood (săn/dəl wŏŏd/), n. the fragrant heartwood of any of certain Asiatic trees, used for ornamental carving and burned as incense.

sand·bag (sănd/băg/), n., v., **-bagged, -bagging.** —n. **1.** a bag filled with sand, used in fortification, as ballast, etc. —v.t. **2.** to furnish with sandbags. **3.** to hit with a sandbag.

Sand·burg (sănd/bûrg, sänd/-), n. Carl, born 1878, U.S. poet, biographer, and writer.

San Di·e·go (săn/ dĭ ā/gō), a seaport in SW California. 362,658.

sand·man (sănd/măn/), n. the man who, in the fairy tale, makes children sleepy by putting sand in their eyes.

sand·pa·per (sănd/pā/pər), n. **1.** strong paper coated with a layer of sand, used for smoothing or polishing. —v.t., v.i. **2.** to smooth or polish with sandpaper.

sand·pip·er (sănd/pī/pər), n. any of certain shore-inhabiting birds, typically having a piping note and a bill shorter than that of a true snipe.

sand·stone (sănd/stōn/), n. a rock formed by the consolidation of sand.

sand·wich (sănd/wĭch, săn/-), n. **1.** two slices of bread (or toast) with a layer of meat, cheese, or the like, between them. —v.t. **2.** to insert between two other things.

sandwich man, Colloq. a man with advertising boards hung from his shoulders, one before and one behind.

sand·y (săn/dĭ), adj., **sandier, sandiest. 1.** of, containing, or covered with sand. **2.** yellowish red. **3.** having such hair. **4.** shifting or unstable. —**sand/i·ness,** n.

sane (sān), adj., **saner, sanest. 1.** free from mental derangement. **2.** having or showing reason, sound judgment, or good sense. —**sane/ly,** adv. —**sane/ness,** n.

San·for·ize (săn/fə rīz/), v.t., **-ized, -izing.** to shrink (cotton or linen fabrics) mechanically by a patented process before tailoring.

San Fran·cis·co (săn/ frən sĭs/kō), a seaport in W California. With suburbs, 1,428,525.

San Francisco Bay, a large estuary in W California, connected with the Pacific by the Golden Gate. ab. 50 mi. long; 3–12 mi. wide.

sang-froid (sän frwä/), n. French. coolness of mind; calmness; composure.

san·gui·nar·y (săng/gwĭ nĕr/ĭ), adj. **1.** bloody. **2.** bloodthirsty.

san·guine (săng/gwĭn), adj. **1.** naturally cheerful and hopeful. **2.** hopeful or confident. **3.** ruddy. **4.** blood-red; red. —**san/guine·ly,** adv.

san·i·tar·i·an (săn/ə târ/ĭ ən), adj. **1.** sanitary. —n. **2.** an expert in sanitary work.

san·i·tar·i·um (săn/ə târ/ĭ əm), n., pl. **-tariums, -taria** (-târ/ĭ ə). **1.** an establishment for the treatment of invalids, convalescents, etc., esp. in a favorable climate. **2.** a health resort.

san·i·tar·y (săn/ə tĕr/ĭ), adj., n., pl. **-taries.** —adj. **1.** of or pertaining to health or the conditions affecting health, esp. cleanliness, etc. **2.** favorable to health. —n. **3.** a public toilet.

san·i·ta·tion (săn/ə tā/shən), n. the practical application of sanitary measures.

san·i·ty (săn/ə tĭ), n. **1.** soundness of mind. **2.** soundness of judgment.

San Jo·se (săn/ hō zā/), a city in W California. 68,457.

San Jo·sé (săn hô sĕ/), the capital of Costa Rica, in the central part. 70,125.

San Juan (săn hwän/), a seaport in and the capital of Puerto Rico, in the N part. 169,247.

San Ma·ri·no (săn/ mä rē/nō), a small republic in E Italy: the oldest independent country in Europe. 14,545 pop.; 38 sq. mi. Cap.: San Marino.

San Mar·tín (săn/ mär tēn/), José de, 1778–1850, South American patriot, born in Argentina: won independence from Spain for Chile and Peru.

sans (sănz), prep. Archaic. without.

San Sal·va·dor (săn săl/və dôr/), **1.** an island in the E Bahama Islands. 675 pop.; 60 sq. mi. **2.** the capital of El Salvador. 117,776.

sans-cu·lotte (sănz/kyŏŏ lŏt/), n. **1.** (in the French Revolution) a contemptuous designation for a republican of the poorer class, adopted by the revolutionists as a designation of honor. **2.** any radical or revolutionary.

san·se·vi·e·ri·a (săn/sĭ vĭ ēr/ĭ ə), n. any of certain house plants grown for their stiff, sword-shaped leaves.

San·skrit (săn/skrĭt), n. an extinct language, the ancient classical literary language of India.

sans sou·ci (sän sŏŏ sē/), French. carefree.

San·ta An·a (săn/tə ăn/ə), a city in SW California. 38,015.

San·ta Bar·ba·ra (săn/tə bär/bə rə), a city on the SW coast of California. 38,338.

San·ta Claus (săn/tə klôz/), the patron saint of children, dispenser of gifts on Christmas Eve.

San·ta Fe (săn/tə fā/), the capital of New Mexico, in the N part. 20,325.

San·ta Mon·i·ca (săn/tə mŏn/ə kə), a city in SW California. 53,500.

San·tan·der (săn/tän dĕr/), n. a seaport in N Spain. 101,793.

San·ta·ya·na (săn/tĭ än/ə), n. George, 1863–1952, U.S. poet, essayist, and philosopher, born in Spain, lived in Italy.

San·ti·a·go (săn/tē ä/gō), *n.* the capital of Chile, in the central part. 952,075.

San·to Do·min·go (săn/tō də mǐng/gō), **1.** Dominican Republic. **2.** former name of Ciudad Trujillo.

San·tos (săn/tŏós), *n.* a seaport in S Brazil. 158,774.

São Pau·lo (souN pou/lŏó), a city in S Brazil. 1,437,019.

São Sal·va·dor (souN săl/və dôr/), a seaport in E Brazil. 320,694.

sap[1] (săp), *n.* **1.** the juice of a woody plant. **2.** sapwood. **3.** *Slang.* a fool.

sap[2] (săp), *n., v.,* **sapped, sapping. —n. 1.** *Fort.* a deep narrow trench constructed to approach a besieged place or an enemy's position. **—v.t. 2.** *Fort.* to approach (a besieged place, etc.) with deep narrow trenches. **3.** to undermine; weaken or destroy. **—v.i. 4.** *Fort.* to dig a sap. **—sap/per,** *n.*

sap·head (săp/hĕd/), *n. Slang.* a fool.

sa·pi·ent (sā/pǐ ənt), *adj.* wise. **—sa/pi·ence, sa/pi·en·cy,** *n.* **—sa/pi·ent·ly,** *adv.*

sap·ling (săp/lǐng), *n.* a young tree.

sa·pon·i·fy (sə pŏn/ə fī/), *v.,* **-fied, -fying.** *Chem.* **—v.t. 1.** to convert (a fat) into soap by treating with an alkali. **—v.i. 2.** to become converted into soap. **—sa·pon/i·fi·ca/tion,** *n.*

sap·phire (săf/īr), *n.* **1.** a variety of corundum, esp. a transparent blue kind valued as a gem. **2.** a gem of this kind. **3.** deep blue. **—adj. 4.** deep-blue.

Sap·pho (săf/ō), *n.* fl. c600 B.C., a Greek lyric poetess of Lesbos.

sap·py (săp/ī), *adj.* **1.** abounding in sap, as a plant. **2.** *Slang.* silly or foolish.

sap·suck·er (săp/sŭk/ər), *n.* any of certain small American woodpeckers which drill holes in maples, apple trees, etc., drinking the sap and eating the insects which gather there.

sap·wood (săp/wŏŏd/), *n.* the soft wood inside the inner bark.

Sar·a·cen (săr/ə sən), *n.* a Mohammedan or Moslem, esp. with reference to the Crusades. **—Sar·a·cen·ic** (săr/ə sĕn/ǐk), *adj.*

Sar·ah (sâr/ə), *n.* the wife of Abraham and mother of Isaac.

Sa·ra·je·vo (să/rä/yě vô), *n.* a city in central Yugoslavia: assassination of Austrian archduke here precipitated World War I. 78,173.

Sar·a·to·ga (săr/ə tō/gə), *n.* a village in E New York: scene of Burgoyne's defeat in 1777. Now called Schuylerville.

Sa·ra·wak (sə rä/wäk), *n.* a British crown colony in NW Borneo. 442,900 pop.; ab. 50,000 sq. mi. *Cap.:* Kuching.

sar·casm (sär/kăz əm), *n.* **1.** harsh or bitter derision or irony. **2.** an ironical taunt or gibe. **—sar·cas/tic,** *adj.* **—sar·cas/ti·cal·ly,** *adv.*

sar·coph·a·gus (sär kŏf/ə gəs), *n., pl.* **-gi** (-jī/), **-guses.** a stone coffin, often displayed as a monument.

sar·dine (sär dēn/), *n., pl.* **-dines,** (*esp. collectively*) **-dine. 1.** the common pilchard, often preserved in oil as a table delicacy. **2.** any of various allied or similar fishes used in this way.

Sar·din·i·a (sär dǐn/ī ə), *n.* a large island in the Mediterranean, W of Italy: with small nearby islands it comprises a department of Italy. 1,147,500 pop.; 9301 sq. mi. **—Sar·din/i·an,** *adj., n.*

sar·don·ic (sär dŏn/ǐk), *adj.* bitterly ironical; sarcastic; sneering. **—sar·don/i·cal·ly,** *adv.*

sar·do·nyx (sär/də nǐks), *n.* a kind of onyx containing layers or bands of chalcedony.

Sar·gent (sär/jənt), *n.* **John Singer,** 1856–1925, U.S. painter.

sa·ri (să/rē), *n., pl.* **-ris.** a cotton or silk outer garment of Hindu women, worn with one end over the head.

sa·rong (sə rông/), *n.* a skirtlike garment worn by both sexes in the Malay Archipelago, etc.

Sa·roy·an (sə roi/ən), *n.* **William,** born 1908, U.S. author.

sar·sa·pa·ril·la (săr/sə pə rǐl/ə, săs/pə rǐl/ə), *n.* **1.** any of certain tropical American plants having a root which has been much used in medicine as an alterative. **2.** the root. **3.** an extract or other preparation made of it. **4.** a sarsaparilla-flavored soft drink.

Sar·to (sär/tō), *n.* **Andrea del,** 1486–1531, Italian painter.

sar·to·ri·al (sär tōr/ī əl), *adj.* of or pertaining to a tailor or his work.

Sar·tre (sär/tr), *n.* **Jean Paul,** born 1905, French writer and philosopher.

sash[1] (săsh), *n.* a long band of silk, etc., usually worn round the waist for ornament by women and girls.

sash[2] (săsh), *n.* **1.** a movable framework in which panes of glass are set, as in a window or the like. **2.** the part of a window which moves.

sa·shay (să shā/), *v.i. U.S. Colloq.* to glide, move, or go.

Sas·katch·e·wan (săs kăch/ə wän/), *n.* a province in W Canada. 895,922 pop.; 251,700 sq. mi. *Cap.:* Regina.

Sas·ka·toon (săs/kə tōōn/), *n.* a city in SW Canada. 43,027.

sas·sa·fras (săs/ə frăs/), *n.* **1.** an American tree of the laurel family, the aromatic bark of whose root is used medicinally and esp. for flavoring beverages, confectionery, etc. **2.** the bark itself.

sas·sy (săs/ī), *adj.,* **-sier, -siest.** *U.S. Dial.* saucy.

Sat., **1.** Saturday. **2.** Saturn.

Sa·tan (sā/tən), *n.* the chief evil spirit; the great adversary of man; the devil. **—sa·tan·ic** (să tăn/ǐk, sə-), *adj.* **—sa·tan/i·cal·ly,** *adv.*

satch·el (săch/əl), *n.* a small bag, sometimes with a shoulder strap.

sate (sāt), *v.t.,* **sated, sating. 1.** to satisfy (any appetite or desire) to the full. **2.** to surfeit; glut.

sa·teen (să tēn/), *n.* a cotton fabric resembling satin in weave and gloss.

sat·el·lite (săt/ə līt/), *n.* **1.** *Astron.* a small body which revolves round a planet. **2.** an attendant upon a person of importance. **3.** a subservient or obsequious follower.

sa·ti·a·ble (să/shī ə bəl), *adj.* that can be satiated. **—sa/ti·a·bil/i·ty,** *n.*

sa·ti·ate (*v.* să/shī āt/; *adj.* să/shī ǐt, -āt/), *v., -ated, -ating, adj. —v.t.* **1.** to surfeit; cloy. **—adj. 2.** *Archaic or Poetic.* satiated. **—sa/ti·a/tion,** *n.*

sa·ti·e·ty (sə tī/ə tǐ), *n.* surfeit.

sat·in (săt/ən), *n.* **1.** a rayon or silk fabric with a finely woven, glossy surface. **—adj. 2.** of or like satin; smooth; glossy. **—sat/in·y,** *adj.*

sat·in·wood (săt/ən wŏŏd/), *n.* **1.** the satiny wood of an East Indian tree, used for cabinetwork, etc. **2.** the tree itself.

sat·ire (săt/īr), *n.* **1.** the use of irony, sarcasm, ridicule, etc., in exposing vice, folly, etc. **2.** a literary composition in which vices, follies, etc., are held up to scorn, derision, or ridicule. **—sa·tir·i·cal** (sə tǐr/ə kəl), **sa·tir/ic,** *adj.* **—sa·tir/i·cal·ly,** *adv.*

sat·i·rist (săt/ə rǐst), *n.* **1.** a writer of satires. **2.** one who indulges in satire.

sat·i·rize (săt/ə rīz/), *v.t.,* **-rized, -rizing.** to assail with satire. **—sat/i·riz/er,** *n.*

sat·is·fac·tion (săt/ǐs făk/shən), *n.* **1.** act of satisfying. **2.** state of being satisfied. **3.** the cause of being satisfied. **4.** reparation, as of a wrong. **5.** payment, as for debt.

sat·is·fac·to·ry (săt/ǐs făk/tə rǐ), *adj.* fulfilling all demands or requirements. **—sat/is·fac/to·ri·ly,** *adv.*

sat·is·fy (săt/ǐs fī/), *v.,* **-fied, -fying. —v.t. 1.** to fulfill the desires, expectations, needs, or demands of; content. **2.** to fulfill (a desire, need, etc.). **3.** to convince. **4.** to answer sufficiently (an objection, etc.) or solve (a doubt, etc.). **5.** to discharge fully (a debt, etc.). **6.** to make reparation to (a person, etc.) or for (a wrong, etc.). **7.** to pay (a creditor). **—v.i. 8.** to give satisfaction. **—sat/is·fi/er,** *n.* **—sat/is·fy/ing·ly,** *adv.*

sa·trap (să/trăp, săt/răp), *n.* **1.** a governor of a province under the ancient Persian monarchy. **2.** a subordinate, usually despotic, ruler.

sat·u·ra·ble (săch/ə rə bəl), *adj.* that may be saturated. **—sat/u·ra·bil/i·ty,** *n.*

sat·u·rate (*v.* săch/ə rāt/; *adj.* săch/ə rǐt, -rāt/), *v., -rated, -rating, adj. —v.t.* **1.** to soak, impregnate, or imbue thoroughly or completely. **—adj. 2.** *Chiefly Poetic.* saturated.

sat·u·ra·tion (săch/ə rā/shən), *n.* **1.** act or process of saturating. **2.** the resulting state.

saturation point, the point at which a substance will receive no more of another substance in solution, combination, etc.

Sat·ur·day (săt/ər dǐ), *n.* the seventh day of the week, following Friday.

Sat·urn (săt/ərn), n. 1. *Astron.* a major planet, remarkable for the thin rings surrounding it. 2. *Rom. Myth.* the god of agriculture.

Sat·ur·na·li·a (săt/ər nā/lĭ ə), n.pl. 1. (in ancient Rome) the festival of Saturn, observed with unrestrained merrymaking. 2. (*l.c.*) any period of unrestrained revelry. —**Sat'ur·na/li·an**, adj.

sat·ur·nine (săt/ər nīn/), adj. gloomy; taciturn. —**sat/ur·nine/ly**, adv.

sat·yr (săt/ər, sā/tər), n. 1. *Class. Myth.* one of a class of woodland deities, attendant on Bacchus, represented as part human and part goat, and noted for riot and lasciviousness. 2. a lascivious man.

sauce (sôs), n., v., **sauced, saucing.** —n. 1. any preparation, usually liquid or soft, eaten as a relish or appetizing accompaniment to food. 2. *U.S.* stewed fruit. 3. *Colloq.* sauciness. —v.t. 4. to season with sauce. 5. *Colloq.* to speak impertinently to.

sauce·pan (sôs/păn/), n. a metal container, usually having a long handle and a cover, for stewing, etc.

sau·cer (sô/sər), n. a small, round, shallow dish to hold a cup.

sau·cy (sô/sĭ), adj., **-cier, -ciest.** 1. impertinent; insolent. 2. piquantly pert; smart. —**sau/ci·ly**, adv. —**sau/ci·ness**, n.

Sa·u·di Arabia (sä ōō/dĭ), a kingdom in N and central Arabia. 4,750,000 pop.; ab. 600,000 sq. mi. *Capitals:* Mecca *and* Riyadh.

sauer·kraut (sour/krout/), n. cabbage cut fine, salted, and allowed to ferment until sour.

Saul (sôl), n. 1. the first king of Israel. 2. the original name of the apostle Paul.

saun·ter (sôn/tər, sän/-), v.i. 1. to walk with a leisurely gait; stroll. —n. 2. a leisurely walk; stroll. —**saun/ter·er**, n.

sau·ri·an (sôr/ĭ ən), adj. 1. belonging or pertaining to the group of reptiles orig. including the crocodiles, etc., but now technically restricted to the lizards. 2. lizardlike. —n. 3. a saurian animal.

sau·sage (sô/sĭj), n. minced pork, beef, or other meats (often combined), with various added ingredients and seasonings, usually stuffed into linked parts of a prepared intestine or casing.

sau·té (sō tā/), adj., v., **-téed, -téeing**, n. —adj. 1. cooked or browned in a pan containing a little fat. —v.t. 2. to cook in a small amount of fat. —n. 3. a dish of sauté food.

sau·terne (sō tûrn/), n. a sweet white table wine.

sav·age (săv/ĭj), adj. 1. wild or rugged, as country. 2. uncivilized; barbarous. 3. unpolished; rude. 4. fierce, ferocious, or cruel; untamed. —n. 5. an uncivilized human being. 6. a fierce, brutal, or cruel person. —**sav/age·ly**, adv. —**sav/age·ness**, n.

sav·age·ry (săv/ĭj rĭ), n., pl. **-ries.** 1. uncivilized condition. 2. savage nature, conduct, or act.

sa·van·na (sə văn/ə), n. a plain, characterized by coarse grasses and scattered tree growth, esp. on the margins of the tropics. Also, **sa·van/nah.**

Sa·van·nah (sə văn/ə), n. a seaport in E Georgia. 95,966.

sa·vant (să vänt/, săv/ənt), n. a man of learning.

save¹ (sāv), v., **saved, saving.** —v.t. 1. to rescue from danger. 2. to keep safe, intact, or unhurt. 3. to keep from being lost. 4. to avoid the use or waste of. 5. to set apart; reserve. 6. to obviate. 7. *Theol.* to deliver from sin. —v.i. 8. to lay up money, etc. —**sav/a·ble**, adj. —**sav/er**, n.

save² (sāv), prep. 1. except; but. —conj. 2. except; but. 3. *Archaic.* unless.

sav·ing (sā/vĭng), adj. 1. rescuing; preserving. 2. redeeming. 3. economical. 4. making a reservation. —n. 5. economy in expenditure, use, etc. 6. a reduction of expenditure or outlay. 7. that which is saved. 8. (*pl.*) sums of money saved and laid away. —prep. 9. except. 10. with all due respect to or for. —conj. 11. save.

sav·ior (sāv/yər), n. 1. one who saves, rescues, or delivers. 2. (*cap.*) a title of God, esp. of Christ. Also, *esp. Brit.,* **sav/iour.**

sa·voir-faire (săv/wär fâr/), n. knowledge of what to do in any situation; tact.

Sav·o·na·ro·la (săv/ə nə rō/lə), n. **Girolamo,** 1452–98. Italian monk, reformer, and martyr.

sa·vor (sā/vər), n. 1. the quality in a substance which affects the sense of taste or of smell. 2. distinctive quality or property. —v.i. 3. to have taste or odor. 4. to exhibit the peculiar characteristics. —v.t. 5. to season; flavor. 6. to perceive by taste or smell. 7. to show traces of the presence or influence of. Also, *esp. Brit.,* **sa/vour.** —**sa/vor·less**, adj.

sa·vor·y¹ (sā/və rĭ), adj., **-vorier, -voriest.** 1. agreeable in taste or smell. 2. pleasing or agreeable. —**sa/vor·i·ness**, n.

sa·vor·y² (sā/və rĭ), n., pl. **-vories.** any of certain aromatic plants of the mint family, used in cookery.

Sa·voy (sə voi/), n. **House of,** the royal house of Italy from 1861 to 1946.

sav·vy (săv/ĭ), v., **-vied, -vying**, n. *Slang.* —v.t., v.i. 1. to know; understand. —n. 2. understanding; intelligence; sense.

saw¹ (sô), n., v., **sawed, sawed** or **sawn, sawing.** —n. 1. a tool or device for cutting, typically a thin blade of metal with a series of sharp teeth. —v.t., v.i. 2. to cut, or form by cutting, with a saw.

saw² (sô), n. a maxim; proverb.

saw·buck (sô/bŭk/), n. *U.S.* 1. a sawhorse. 2. *Slang.* a ten-dollar bill.

saw·dust (sô/dŭst/), n. small particles of wood produced in sawing.

saw·horse (sô/hôrs/), n. a movable frame for holding wood that is being sawed.

saw·mill (sô/mĭl/), n. an establishment in which timber is sawed into planks, boards, etc., by machinery.

saw·yer (sô/yər), n. one who saws, esp. as an occupation.

Sax·on (săk/sən), n. 1. a member of a Teutonic people anciently dwelling near the mouth of the Elbe, a portion of which invaded and occupied parts of Britain in the 5th and 6th centuries. 2. Continental Saxon (language). 3. a native or inhabitant of Saxony in modern Germany. —adj. 4. of or pertaining to the Saxons.

Sax·o·ny (săk/sə nĭ), n. a state in E Germany. 5,231,739 pop.; 5788 sq. mi. *Cap.:* Dresden.

sax·o·phone (săk/sə fōn/), n. a musical wind instrument consisting of a conical metal tube (usually brass) with keys or valves, and a clarinet mouthpiece. —**sax/o·phon/ist**, n.

say (sā), v., **said, saying**, n. —v.t., v.i. 1. to utter; speak. 2. to express; state; declare. 3. to state as an opinion. 4. to recite. 5. to assume as a hypothesis or an estimate. 6. to report or maintain. —n. 7. what a person says or has to say. 8. *Colloq.* the right or opportunity to speak or decide. —**say/er**, n.

say·ing (sā/ĭng), n. a proverb or apothegm.

say-so (sā/sō/), n. *Colloq.* 1. one's personal statement. 2. final authority. 3. a command.

Sb, *Chem.* (L *stibium*) antimony.

Sc, *Chem.* scandium.

Sc., 1. Scotch. 2. Scottish.

sc., 1. scene. 2. scruple.

S.C., 1. Signal Corps. 2. South Carolina.

s.c., small capitals.

scab (skăb), n., v., **scabbed, scabbing.** —n. 1. the incrustation which forms over a sore during healing. 2. a workman who refuses to join or act with a labor union, who takes a striker's place, or the like. —v.i. 3. to become covered with a scab. 4. to act or work as a scab. —**scab/like/**, adj.

scab·bard (skăb/ərd), n. 1. a sheath or cover for the blade of a sword, dagger, or the like. —v.t. 2. to put into a scabbard.

scab·by (skăb/ĭ), adj., **-bier, -biest.** 1. covered with scabs. 2. consisting of scabs. 3. *Colloq.* mean or contemptible.

sca·bi·es (skā/bĭ ēz/, -bēz), n. any of several infectious skin diseases occurring esp. in sheep and cattle (and in man), caused by parasitic mites; itch.

sca·brous (skā/brəs), adj. 1. rough. 2. harsh; full of difficulties. 3. risqué.

scad (skăd), n. (*usually pl.*) *Slang.* a large quantity.

scaf·fold (skăf/əld, -ōld), n. 1. a temporary structure for holding workmen and materials during the erection, repair, or decoration of a building. **2.** an elevated platform on which a criminal is executed, usually by hanging.

scaf·fold·ing (skăf′əld ĭng), *n.* **1.** a scaffold. **2.** materials for scaffolds.

scal·a·wag (skăl′ə wăg′), *n.* *Colloq.* a scamp or rascal.

scald (skôld), *v.t.* **1.** to burn painfully with hot liquid or steam. **2.** to subject to the action of boiling or hot liquid. **3.** to heat to a temperature just short of the boiling point. —*v.i.* **4.** to be or become scalded. —*n.* **5.** a burn caused by hot liquid or steam.

scale[1] (skāl), *n., v.,* **scaled, scaling.** —*n.* **1.** one of the thin, flat, horny or hard plates that form the covering of certain animals, as fishes. **2.** any thin platelike piece, lamina, or flake. **3.** a scale-like insect injurious to plants. —*v.t.* **4.** to remove the scales from. **5.** to remove in scales or thin layers. —*v.i.* **6.** to come off in scales. **7.** to shed scales. —**scale**′**like**′, *adj.*

scale[2] (skāl), *n., v.,* **scaled, scaling.** —*n.* **1.** the pan, or either of the pans or dishes, of a balance. **2.** (*usually pl.*) a balance for weighing. **3. Scales,** *Astron.* the zodiacal constellation or sign Libra; the Balance. —*v.t.* **4.** to weigh in scales. **5.** to have a weight of.

scale[3] (skāl), *n., v.,* **scaled, scaling.** —*n.* **1.** a succession of steps or degrees. **2.** a point on such a scale. **3.** a series of marks laid down at determinate distances, as along a line, for purposes of measurement. **4.** a graduated line, as on a map, representing proportionate size. **5.** a graduated table of prices, wages, etc. **6.** an instrument with graduated spaces, for measuring, etc. **7.** the proportion which the representation of an object bears to the object. **8.** a certain relative or proportionate size or extent. **9.** *Music.* a succession of tones ascending or descending according to fixed intervals, esp. such a series beginning on a particular note. **10.** anything by which one may ascend. —*v.t., v.i.* **11.** to climb, esp. by a ladder. **12.** to make according to scale: **13.** to reduce in amount according to a fixed proportion. **14.** to measure by a scale.

scal·lion (skăl′yən), *n.* **1.** any onion which does not form a large bulb. **2.** the shallot.

scal·lop (skŏl′əp, skăl′-), *n.* **1.** any of certain bivalve mollusks having fluted shell valves that they clap together to accomplish swimming. **2.** one of the muscles of certain species of such mollusks, esteemed as an article of food. **3.** one of a series of rounded projections along the edge of a garment, cloth, etc. —*v.t.* **4.** to finish (an edge) with scallops.

scalp (skălp), *n.* **1.** the skin and hair of the upper part of the head. —*v.t., v.i.* **2.** to cut or tear the scalp (from). **3.** *Colloq.* to buy and sell so as to make small, quick profits. **4.** *Colloq.* to buy (tickets) cheap and sell at other than official rates. —**scalp**′**er,** *n.*

scal·pel (skăl′pəl), *n.* a small, light, usually straight knife used in surgical and anatomical operations and dissections.

scal·y (skā′lĭ), *adj.,* **scalier, scaliest.** covered with, abounding in, or like scales. —**scal**′**i·ness,** *n.*

scamp (skămp), *n.* **1.** a worthless person; rascal. —*v.t.* **2.** to perform (work, etc.) in a hasty or careless manner.

scam·per (skăm′pər), *v.i.* **1.** to run or go hastily. —*n.* **2.** a quick run.

scan (skăn), *v.,* **scanned, scanning,** *n.* —*v.t.* **1.** to examine minutely. **2.** to glance at hastily. **3.** to analyze (verse) as to its prosodic or metrical structure. **4.** *Television.* to traverse (a surface) with a beam of light or electrons in order to reproduce or transmit a picture. —*v.i.* **5.** to examine the meter of verse. **6.** (of verse) to conform to the rules of meter. **7.** *Television.* to scan a surface. —*n.* **8.** close examination. —**scan**′**ner,** *n.*

scan·dal (skăn′dəl), *n.* **1.** a disgraceful or discreditable action, circumstance, etc. **2.** damage to reputation; disgrace. **3.** defamatory talk; gossip.

scan·dal·ize (skăn′də līz′), *v.t.,* **-ized, -izing.** to shock or offend by something immoral or improper.

scan·dal·mon·ger (skăn′dəl mŭng′gər), *n.* one who spreads scandal.

scan·dal·ous (skăn′dəl əs), *adj.* **1.** disgraceful, shameful, or shocking. **2.** defamatory or libelous. —**scan**′**dal·ous·ly,** *adv.*

Scan·di·na·vi·a (skăn′də nā′vĭ ə), *n.* **1.** the collective name of Norway, Sweden, Denmark, and sometimes also Iceland and the Faeroe Is-

lands. **2.** the peninsula consisting of Norway and Sweden. —**Scan**′**di·na**′**vi·an,** *adj., n.*

scan·di·um (skăn′dĭ əm), *n.* *Chem.* a rare trivalent metallic element. *Symbol:* Sc; *at. wt.:* 45.10; *at. no.:* 21.

scan·sion (skăn′shən), *n.* *Pros.* the metrical analysis of verse.

scant (skănt), *adj.* **1.** barely sufficient; not abundant. **2.** limited; not large. **3.** barely amounting to as much as indicated. **4.** having an inadequate or limited supply. —*v.t.* **5.** to diminish. **6.** to stint; withhold. —**scant**′**ness,** *n.*

scant·ling (skănt′lĭng), *n.* a timber of comparatively small cross section.

scant·y (skăn′tĭ), *adj.,* **scantier, scantiest. 1.** barely sufficient. **2.** meager. **3.** lacking amplitude. —**scant**′**i·ly,** *adv.* —**scant**′**i·ness,** *n.*

Sca·pa Flow (skä′pə, skăp′ə), a sound in the Orkney Islands, N of Scotland. German warships scuttled, 1919.

scape·goat (skāp′gōt′), *n.* one who is made to bear the blame for others or to suffer in their place.

scape·grace (skāp′grās′), *n.* a good-for-nothing person; ne′er-do-well; scamp.

scap·u·la (skăp′yə lə), *n., pl.* **-lae** (-lē′), **-las.** (in man) either of two flat, triangular bones, each forming the back part of a shoulder; shoulder blade.

scap·u·lar (skăp′yə lər), *adj.* **1.** of or pertaining to the shoulders. —*n.* **2.** *Eccles.* a loose, sleeveless monastic garment, hanging from the shoulders. **3.** two small pieces of woolen cloth, joined by strings passing over the shoulders, worn under the ordinary clothing as a badge of affiliation with a religious order, etc.

scar (skär), *n., v.,* **scarred, scarring.** —*n.* **1.** the mark left by a healed wound, sore, or burn. **2.** any blemish remaining as a trace or result. **3.** *Bot.* a mark indicating a former point of attachment, as where a leaf has fallen from a stem. —*v.t.* **4.** to mark with a scar.

scar·ab (skăr′əb), *n.* **1.** any of certain beetles, esp. one species regarded as sacred by the ancient Egyptians. **2.** a representation or image of a beetle, much used among the ancient Egyptians as a symbol, seal, amulet, or the like. **3.** a gem cut in the form of a beetle.

scarce (skârs), *adj.,* **scarcer, scarcest,** *adv.* —*adj.* **1.** insufficient; not abundant. **2.** rare. —*adv.* **3.** *Literary.* scarcely. —**scarce**′**ness,** **scar**′**ci·ty,** *n.*

scarce·ly (skârs′lĭ), *adv.* **1.** barely; hardly. **2.** definitely not. **3.** probably not.

scare (skâr), *v.,* **scared, scaring,** *n.* —*v.t.* **1.** to strike with sudden fear or terror. **2.** to get. —*v.i.* **3.** to become frightened. —*n.* **4.** a sudden fright or alarm.

scare·crow (skâr′krō′), *n.* **1.** an object, usually a figure of a man, set up to frighten crows, etc., away from crops. **2.** a person in ragged clothes.

scare·head (skâr′hĕd′), *n.* *U.S. Colloq.* a newspaper heading in large type.

scarf (skärf), *n., pl.* **scarfs,** (*esp. Brit.*) **scarves** (skärvz). **1.** a long, broad strip of silk, lace, or other material, worn about the neck, shoulders, or head for ornament or protection. **2.** a long cover of cloth for a bureau, table, etc.

scar·i·fy (skăr′ə fī′), *v.t.,* **-fied, -fying. 1.** to make scratches or superficial incisions in (the skin, a wound, etc.). **2.** to lacerate by severe criticism. **3.** to loosen (the soil) with a type of cultivator. **4.** to hasten the sprouting of (seeds) by making incisions in the seed coats. —**scar**′**i·fi·er,** *n.* —**scar**′**i·fi·ca**′**tion,** *n.*

scar·la·ti·na (skär′lə tē′nə), *n.* *Pathol.* scarlet fever, esp. in a mild form.

Scar·lat·ti (skär lät′tē), *n.* **Alessandro,** 1659-1725, Italian composer.

scar·let (skär′lĭt), *n., adj.* bright red inclining toward orange.

scarlet fever, a contagious febrile disease, now chiefly of children, caused by streptococci and characterized by a scarlet eruption.

scarlet tanager, a brightly colored American bird, the male of which is bright red with black wings and tail when in breeding plumage.

scarp (skärp), *n.* a steep slope.

scar·y (skâr′ĭ), *adj.,* **scarier, scariest.** *Colloq.* **1.** causing fright or alarm. **2.** easily frightened; timid.

scat (skăt), *v.i.*, **scatted, scatting.** *U.S. Colloq.* to go off hastily (usually imperative).

scathe (skāŧh), *v.t.*, **scathed, scathing. 1.** to attack with severe criticism. **2.** *Archaic or Dial.* to hurt, harm, or injure.

scath·ing (skā'ŧhĭng), *adj.* **1.** bitterly severe. **2.** that scathes. **—scath'ing·ly,** *adv.*

scat·ter (skăt'ər), *v.t., v.i.* **1.** to throw loosely about. **2.** to separate and drive off in various directions; disperse. **3.** *Physics.* **a.** to reflect or refract (light, etc.) so as to diffuse it in many directions. **b.** to deflect irregularly. **—n. 4.** act of scattering. **—scat'ter·er,** *n.*

scat·ter·brain (skăt'ər brān'), *n.* one incapable of serious, connected thought. **—scat'ter·brained',** *adj.*

scatter rug, a small rug, not meant to carpet a whole room.

scav·enge (skăv'ĭnj), *v.*, **-enged, -enging.** **—v.t. 1.** to cleanse from filth. **—v.i. 2.** to act as a scavenger. **3.** to search for food.

scav·en·ger (skăv'ĭn jər), *n.* **1.** an organism, object, or person that scavenges, esp. any of various animals feeding on dead organic matter. **2.** a street cleaner.

sce·nar·i·o (sĭ när'ĭ ō', -när'-), *n., pl.* **-narios.** an outline of the plot of a dramatic work, giving particulars as to the scenes, characters, situations, etc.

sce·nar·ist (sĭ när'ĭst, -när'-), *n.* a writer of scenarios for motion pictures.

scene (sēn), *n.* **1.** the place where any action occurs. **2.** any view or picture. **3.** an incident or situation in real life. **4.** an exhibition or outbreak of excited feeling before others. **5.** a division of a play or of an act of a play. **6.** scenery (def. 2). **7.** an episode, situation, or the like, as described in writing. **8.** the setting of a story or the like.

scen·er·y (sē'nə rĭ), *n., pl.* **-er·ies. 1.** the general appearance of a place. **2.** hangings, draperies, structures, etc., on the stage representing some place.

sce·nic (sē'nĭk, sĕn'ĭk), *adj.* **1.** of natural scenery; having fine scenery. **2.** dramatic; theatrical. **3.** representing a scene, action, incident, or the like.

scent (sĕnt), *n.* **1.** distinctive odor. **2.** a track or trail as indicated by such an odor. **3.** *Chiefly Brit.* a perfume. **4.** the sense of smell. **—v.t. 5.** to perceive or recognize by the sense of smell. **6.** to perceive in any way. **7.** to perfume.

scep·ter (sĕp'tər), *n.* a rod or wand borne in the hand as an emblem of regal or imperial power. Also, *esp. Brit.*, **scep'tre. —scep'tered,** *adj.*

scep·tic (skĕp'tĭk), *n., adj.* skeptic.

sched·ule (skĕj'ool; *Brit.* shĕd'ūl), *n., v.,* **-uled, -uling. —n. 1.** a timetable. **2.** a statement of details, often in tabular form. **—v.t. 3.** to make a schedule of; enter in a schedule. **4.** *Colloq.* to plan for a certain date.

Scheldt (skĕlt), *n.* a river flowing from N France through W Belgium and SW Netherlands into the North Sea. ab. 250 mi.

sche·mat·ic (skē măt'ĭk), *adj.* pertaining to or of the nature of a diagram or scheme; diagrammatic. **—sche·mat'i·cal·ly,** *adv.*

scheme (skēm), *n., v.,* **schemed, scheming. —n. 1.** a plan or design to be followed. **2.** an underhand plot; intrigue. **3.** a body or system of related doctrines, theories, etc. **4.** any system of correlated things, parts, etc. **—v.t., v.i. 5.** to devise; plan; plot; contrive. **—schem'er,** *n.*

Sche·nec·ta·dy (skə nĕk'tə dĭ), *n.* a city in E New York. 87,549.

scher·zo (skĕr'tsō), *n., pl.* **-zos, -zi** (-tsē). *Music.* a movement or passage of light or playful character.

Schick test (shĭk), *Med.* a diphtheria-immunity test in which diphtheria toxoid is injected cutaneously, nonimmunity being characterized by an inflammation at the injection site.

Schil·ler (shĭl'ər), *n.* **Johann Christoph Friedrich von,** 1759–1805, German poet, dramatist, and writer.

schil·ling (shĭl'ĭng), *n.* the monetary unit and copper-and-nickel coin used in Austria, equal to $0.1407 in the U.S.

schism (sĭz'əm), *n.* division or disunion, esp. into mutually opposed parties. **—schis·mat'ic** (sĭz măt'ĭk), *adj., n.*

schist (shĭst), *n.* any of a class of crystalline rocks whose constituent minerals have a more or less parallel arrangement. **—schis·tose** (shĭs'tōs), *adj.*

schiz·oid (skĭz'oid), *adj.* related to, predisposed to, or afflicted with schizophrenia.

schiz·o·phre·ni·a (skĭz'ə frē'nĭ ə), *n. Psychiatry.* a mental disorder characterized by splitting of the personality, dissociation, and emotional deterioration. **—schiz·o·phren·ic** (skĭz'ə frĕn'ĭk), *adj., n.*

Schles·wig-Hol·stein (shlăs'vĭкн hōl'shtīn), *n.* two duchies of Denmark that were a center of international tension in the 19th century: annexed by Prussia, 1864 (Schleswig) and 1866 (Holstein).

schnapps (shnăps, shnäps), *n.* any spirituous liquor.

schnau·zer (shnou'zər), *n.* one of a German breed of terrier with a wiry gray coat.

schnor·kle (shnôr'kəl), *n.* snorkel.

schol·ar (skŏl'ər), *n.* **1.** a learned or erudite person. **2.** a student; pupil. **—schol'ar·ly,** *adj.* **—schol'ar·li·ness,** *n.*

schol·ar·ship (skŏl'ər shĭp'), *n.* **1.** learning; knowledge acquired by study. **2.** the position of a student who, because of merit, etc., is granted money or other aid to pursue his studies. **3.** the aid granted to such a student.

scho·las·tic (skō lăs'tĭk, skə-), *adj.* **1.** of or pertaining to schools, scholars, or education. **2.** of or pertaining to the medieval schoolmen. **—n. 3.** (*sometimes cap.*) a schoolman, a disciple of the schoolmen, or an adherent of scholasticism. **—scho·las'ti·cal·ly,** *adv.*

scho·las·ti·cism (skō lăs'tə sĭz'əm, skə-), *n.* the system of theological and philosophical teaching predominant in the Middle Ages, based chiefly upon the authority of the church fathers and of Aristotle and his commentators, and characterized by marked formality in methods.

Schön·berg (shœn'bĕrкн), *n.* **Arnold,** 1874–1951, Austrian composer in the U.S.

school[1] (skool), *n.* **1.** a place where instruction is given. **2.** the body of students attending a school. **3.** a regular course of meetings of a teacher and students for instruction. **4.** a session of such a course. **5.** a building, room, etc., in a university, set apart for the use of one of the faculties or for some particular purpose. **6.** the body of followers of a master, system, method, etc. **—adj. 7.** pertaining to or connected with a school or schools. **—v.t. 8.** to educate; teach; train.

school[2] (skool), *n.* a large number of fish, porpoises, whales, or the like, feeding or migrating together.

school·book (skool'book'), *n.* a book for study in schools.

school·boy (skool'boi'), *n.* a boy attending a school.

school·house (skool'hous'), *n.* a building in which a school is conducted.

school·ing (skoo'lĭng), *n.* education.

school·man (skool'mən), *n., pl.* **-men. 1.** one versed in scholastic learning or engaged in scholastic pursuits. **2.** (*sometimes cap.*) one of the medieval writers who dealt with theology and philosophy after the methods of scholasticism.

school·mas·ter (skool'măs'tər, -mäs'-), *n.* a man who teaches in a school. **—school'mis·tress,** *n.fem.*

school·room (skool'room', -room'), *n.* a room in which pupils are taught.

school·teach·er (skool'tē'chər), *n.* a teacher in a school.

schoon·er (skoo'nər), *n.* **1.** a sailing vessel with two or more masts and fore-and-aft rig. **2.** *U.S. Colloq.* a very tall glass, as for beer.

Scho·pen·hau·er (shō'pən hou'ər), *n.* **Arthur,** 1788–1860, German philosopher.

schot·tische (shŏt'ĭsh), *n.* **1.** a round dance resembling the polka. **2.** its music.

Schu·bert (shoo'bərt), *n.* **Franz,** 1797–1828, Austrian composer.

Schu·mann (shoo'män), *n.* **Robert,** 1810–1856, German composer.

Schuyl·kill (skool'kĭl), *n.* a river flowing from E Pennsylvania SE to the Delaware river at Philadelphia. 131 mi.

schwa (shwä), *n. Phonet.* the indeterminate vowel sound of certain unstressed syllables, as of the *a* in *sofa* or the *u* in *circus. Symbol:* ə.

sci., **1.** science. **2.** scientific.

sci·at·ic (sī ăt'ĭk), *adj.* of or affecting the hip.

sci·at·i·ca (sī ăt'ə kə), *n.* pain and tenderness at some points of the sciatic nerve.

sci·ence (sī'əns), *n.* **1.** a branch of knowledge dealing with a body of facts systematically arranged and showing the operation of general laws. **2.** systematic knowledge of the physical world. **3.** knowledge, as of facts. —**sci·en·tif·ic** (sī'ən tĭf'ĭk), *adj.* —**sci'en·tif'i·cal·ly,** *adv.*

sci·en·tist (sī'ən tĭst), *n.* one versed in science, esp. physical or natural science.

scil·i·cet (sĭl'ə sĕt'), *adv.* to wit; namely.

scim·i·tar (sĭm'ə tər), *n.* a curved sword of Oriental origin. Also, **scim'i·ter.**

scin·til·la (sĭn tĭl'ə), *n.* a particle; trace.

scin·til·late (sĭn'tə lāt'), *v.i., v.t.,* **-lat·ed, -lat·ing.** **1.** to emit (sparks). **2.** to sparkle; flash. **3.** to twinkle. —**scin'til·la'tion,** *n.*

sci·on (sī'ən), *n.* **1.** a descendant. **2.** a shoot or twig cut for grafting or planting.

scis·sors (sĭz'ərz), *n.pl. or sing.* a cutting instrument consisting of two blades (with handles) so pivoted together that their edges work against each other (often called *a pair of scissors*).

scle·ro·sis (sklĭ rō'sĭs), *n., pl.* **-ses** (-sēz) *Pathol.* a hardening of a tissue or part. —**scle·rot·ic** (sklĭ rŏt'ĭk), *adj.*

scoff (skôf, skŏf), *n.* **1.** an expression of mockery or derision; jeer. —*v.i.* **2.** to speak derisively; mock; jeer. —**scoff'er,** *n.* —**scoff'ing·ly,** *adv.*

scold (skōld), *v.t., v.i.* **1.** to find fault (with); chide. —*n.* **2.** a person, esp. a woman, addicted to abusive speech. —**scold'er,** *n.* —**scold'ing,** *adj., n.* —**scold'ing·ly,** *adv.*

sconce (skŏns), *n.* a wall bracket for holding one or more candles or other lights.

scone (skōn, skŏn), *n.* a flat, round cake of wheat flour, barley meal, or the like.

scoop (skoop), *n.* **1.** a small, deep shovel with a short handle, for taking up flour, sugar, etc. **2.** the bucket of a steam shovel, etc. **3.** a place scooped out. **4.** act of scooping. **5.** the quantity taken up. **6.** *Colloq.* a big haul, as of money. **7.** *Journ. Slang.* a prior or exclusive news report. —*v.t.* **8.** to take up or out with a scoop. **9.** *Colloq.* to gather. **10.** *Journ. Slang.* to get the better of by a scoop.

scoot (skoot), *Colloq.* —*v.i.* **1.** to go swiftly or hastily. —*v.t.* **2.** to send at high speed. —*n.* **3.** a swift movement or course.

scoot·er (skoo'tər), *n.* **1.** a low vehicle with a tread or footboard between its two wheels, propelled by pushing with one foot. **2.** *U.S.* a sailboat with runners, for use on either water or ice.

scope (skōp), *n.* **1.** extent of view, operation, effectiveness, etc. **2.** space or opportunity for operation. **3.** a tract or area.

scorch (skôrch), *v.t.* **1.** to burn slightly. **2.** to parch or shrivel with heat. **3.** to criticize severely. —*n.* **4.** a superficial burn.

scorch·er (skôr'chər), *n.* **1.** one that scorches. **2.** *Colloq.* a very hot day. **3.** anything caustic or severe.

score (skōr), *n., v., scored, scoring.* —*n.* **1.** the record of points made by the competitors in a game or match. **2.** the scoring of a point or points. **3.** a notch or scratch. **4.** a group or set of twenty. **5.** (*pl.*) a great many. **6.** account, reason, or ground. **7.** pay off or settle a score, **a.** to avenge a wrong. **b.** to fulfill an obligation. **8.** *Music.* a written or printed piece of music with all the vocal and instrumental parts arranged on staves, one under the other. —*v.t.* **9.** to gain for addition to one's score in a game. **10.** to make a score of. **11.** *Music.* **a.** to orchestrate. **b.** to write out in score. **12.** to make notches, cuts, or lines in or on. **13.** to reckon. **14.** to gain or win. **15.** *U.S.* to censure severely. —*v.i.* **16.** to make a point or points in a game. **17.** to keep score. —**scor'er,** *n.*

scorn (skôrn), *n.* **1.** open contempt; disdain. **2.** mockery or derision. —*v.t.* **3.** to treat or regard with scorn. **4.** to reject or refuse with scorn. —**scorn'er,** *n.*

scorn·ful (skôrn'fəl), *adj.* derisive; contemptuous. —**scorn'ful·ly,** *adv.* —**scorn'ful·ness,** *n.*

Scor·pi·o (skôr'pĭ ō'), *n.* **1.** *Astron.* the Scorpion, a zodiacal constellation. **2.** the eighth sign of the zodiac.

scor·pi·on (skôr'pĭ ən), *n.* **1.** any of certain arachnids of the warmer parts of the world, having a long narrow tail terminating in a venomous sting. **2.** (*cap.*) *Astron.* Scorpio.

Scot (skŏt), *n.* a native or inhabitant of Scotland.

Scot., **1.** Scotch. **2.** Scotland. **3.** Scottish.

Scotch (skŏch), *adj.* **1.** of or pertaining to the Scots, Scotland, or the Scottish dialect of Eng-

lish. —*n.* **2.** the people of Scotland collectively. **3.** *Colloq.* barley-malt whiskey distilled in Scotland. **4.** Scots.

scotch (skŏch), *v.t.* **1.** to injure so as to make harmless. **2.** to crush or stamp out.

Scotch·man (skŏch'mən), *n., pl.* **-men.** a native of Scotland. Also, **Scots·man** (skŏts'mən).

Scotch terrier, a breed of terrier with short legs and shaggy hair.

scot-free (skŏt'frē'), *adj.* unhurt; clear.

Scot·land (skŏt'lənd), *n.* a division of the United Kingdom in the N part of Great Britain. 4,933,200 pop.; 29,796 sq. mi. *Cap.:* Edinburgh.

Scotland Yard, **1.** the London (England) police headquarters. **2.** the London police, esp. the branch engaged in crime detection.

Scots (skŏts), *n.* **1.** the Scottish dialect of English. —*adj.* **2.** Scottish or Scotch.

Scott (skŏt), *n.* **Sir Walter,** 1771–1832, Scottish novelist and poet.

Scot·tish (skŏt'ĭsh), *adj.* **1.** Scotch. —*n.* **2.** Scotch. **3.** Scots.

scoun·drel (skoun'drəl), *n.* an unprincipled, dishonorable man; villain. —**scoun'drel·ly,** *adj.*

scour¹ (skour), *v.t.* **1.** to cleanse or polish, esp. by hard rubbing. **2.** to clear out (a channel, etc.).

scour² (skour), *v.i., v.t.* **1.** to move rapidly. **2.** to range about, as in search of something.

scourge (skûrj), *n., v.,* **scourged, scourging.** —*n.* **1.** a whip or lash. **2.** punishment. **3.** a cause of affliction or calamity. —*v.t.* **4.** to lash. **5.** to punish or torment.

scout¹ (skout), *n.* **1.** a soldier, warship, airplane, or the like, sent out to obtain information. **2.** a Boy Scout or Girl Scout. **3.** *Slang.* a fellow. —*v.i.* **4.** to act as a scout. —*v.t.* **5.** to observe for the purpose of obtaining information.

scout² (skout), *v.t., v.i.* to reject with scorn.

scout·mas·ter (skout'măs'tər, -mäs'-), *n.* the adult leader of a troop of Boy Scouts.

scow (skou), *n.* a large flat-bottomed unpowered vessel used chiefly for freight.

scowl (skoul), *v.i.* **1.** to draw the brows in a sullen or angry manner. —*n.* **2.** a scowling expression, look, or aspect. —**scowl'ing·ly,** *adv.*

scrab·ble (skrăb'əl), *v.,* **-bled, -bling,** *n.* —*v.t., v.i.* **1.** to scratch or scrape. **2.** to scrawl; scribble. —*n.* **3.** a scramble. **4.** a scrawled character, writing, etc.

scrag (skrăg), *n., v.,* **scragged, scragging.** —*n.* **1.** a lean or scrawny person or animal. **2.** *Slang.* the neck of a human being. —*v.t.* **3.** *Slang.* to hang or garrote.

scrag·gly (skrăg'lĭ), *adj.,* **-glier, -gliest.** irregular; ragged; shaggy.

scrag·gy (skrăg'ĭ), *adj.,* **-gier, -giest.** **1.** lean or thin. **2.** meager. —**scrag'gi·ness,** *n.*

scram (skrăm), *v.i.,* **scrammed, scramming.** *U.S. Slang.* to get out or away.

scram·ble (skrăm'bəl), *v.,* **-bled, -bling,** *n.* —*v.i.* **1.** to make one's way by a struggling use of the hands and feet, as over rough ground. **2.** to struggle with others for possession. —*v.t.* **3.** to mix together confusedly. **4.** to cook (eggs) in a pan, mixing whites and yolks together. —*n.* **5.** a climb or progression over rough, irregular ground or the like. **6.** a struggle for possession. —**scram'bler,** *n.*

Scran·ton (skrăn'tən), *n.* a city in NE Pennsylvania. 140,404.

scrap¹ (skrăp), *n., adj., v.,* **scrapped, scrapping.** —*n.* **1.** a small piece; fragment. **2.** (*pl.*) pieces of old metal that can be reworked. —*adj.* **3.** consisting of scraps. —*v.t.* **4.** to make into scraps; break up. **5.** to discard as useless or worthless.

scrap² (skrăp), *n., v.i.,* **scrapped, scrapping.** *Slang.* fight or quarrel.

scrap·book (skrăp'book'), *n.* a blank book in which pictures, clippings, etc., are pasted.

scrape (skrāp), *v.,* **scraped, scraping,** *n.* —*v.t.* **1.** to remove an outer layer, adhering matter, etc., from with a sharp or rough instrument. **2.** to remove (an outer layer, etc.) in this way. **3.** to collect laboriously or with difficulty. **4.** to rub harshly on or across. —*v.i.* **5.** to scrape something. **6.** to draw back the foot in making a bow. **7.** to practice laborious economy. —*n.* **8.** act of scraping. **9.** a scraping sound. **10.** a scraped place. **11.** an embarrassing predicament. —**scrap'er,** *n.*

scrap·ple (skrăp'əl), *n.* a sausagelike preparation of minced pork, herbs, corn, or other meal, etc., fried in slices.

scrap·py (skrăp'ĭ), *adj.* **-pier, -piest. 1.** fragmentary; disconnected. **2.** *Slang.* given to fighting. **—scrap'pi·ness,** *n.*

scratch (skrăch), *v.t.*, *v.i.* **1.** to mark slightly by rubbing, scraping, or tearing with something sharp. **2.** to dig, scrape, or tear with the claws, the nails, etc. **3.** to rub or scrape lightly with the fingernails, etc., as to relieve itching. **4.** to erase or strike out (writing, etc.). **5.** to withdraw (a horse, etc.) from a race. **—***n.* **6.** a mark produced by scratching. **7.** an act of scratching. **8.** the sound produced. **9.** the starting place of a race. **10. from scratch,** from the beginning or from nothing. **11.** the standard in ability, courage, etc. **12.** *Billiards and Pool.* **a.** a shot resulting in a penalty. **b.** a fluke. **—***adj.* **13.** used for hasty writing, notes, etc. **14.** *Colloq.* gathered hastily and indiscriminately. **—scratch'er,** *n.* **—scratch'y,** *adj.*

scrawl (skrôl), *v.t.* **1.** to write or draw in a sprawling, awkward manner. **—***n.* **2.** something scrawled. **3.** awkward or careless handwriting.

scraw·ny (skrô'nĭ), *adj.*, **-nier, -niest.** *U.S.* lean; thin; scraggy.

scream (skrēm), *v.i.* **1.** to utter a loud, sharp, piercing cry. **2.** to laugh immoderately. **—***n.* **3.** a loud, sharp, piercing cry. **4.** something hilariously funny. **—scream'er,** *n.*

screech (skrēch), *v.i.*, *v.t.* **1.** to utter (with) a harsh, shrill cry. **—***n.* **2.** a harsh, shrill cry. **—screech'er,** *n.* **—screech'y,** *adj.*

screed (skrēd), *n.* a harangue.

screen (skrēn), *n.* **1.** a covered frame or the like, serving as a shelter, partition, etc. **2.** a surface for displaying motion pictures, etc. **3.** motion pictures collectively. **4.** anything that shelters, protects, or conceals. **5.** wire mesh serving as protection. **6.** a sieve or riddle, as for grain, sand, etc. **7.** *Mil.* a body of men sent out to cover the movement of an army. **8.** *Naval.* a protective formation of small vessels. **9.** *Photoengraving.* a transparent plate containing two sets of fine, parallel lines, one crossing the other, used in the half-tone process. **—***v.t.* **10.** to shelter, protect, or conceal with a screen. **11.** to sift through a screen. **12.** to project (pictures, etc.) on a screen. **—screen'ing,** *n.*

screw (skrōō), *n.* **1.** a metal naillike device having a tapering spiral thread, and driven into wood, etc., with the aid of a screwdriver. **2.** a propeller. **3.** pressure or coercion. **—***v.t.* **4.** to force, press, hold fast, etc., by means of a screw. **5.** to work (a screw, etc.) by turning. **6.** to force. **—***v.i.* **7.** to turn as or like a screw. **8.** to be adapted for being connected or taken apart by means of a screw.

screw·ball (skrōō'bôl'), *n.* *U.S. Slang.* an erratic or eccentric person.

screw·driv·er (skrōō'drī'vər), *n.* a tool for driving in or withdrawing screws by turning them. Also, **screw driver.**

scrib·ble (skrĭb'əl), *v.*, **-bled, -bling,** *n.* **—***v.t.*, *v.i.* **1.** to write hastily or carelessly. **2.** to cover with meaningless marks. **—***n.* **3.** a hasty or careless piece of writing. **—scrib'bler,** *n.*

scribe (skrīb), *n.* **1.** a penman; copyist. **2.** an official of former times who performed clerical duties. **3.** a writer or author.

scrim (skrĭm), *n.* a cotton or linen fabric of open weave, used for curtains, etc.

scrim·mage (skrĭm'ĭj), *n.*, *v.*, **-maged, -maging. —***n.* **1.** a rough struggle. **2.** *Football.* the action between contesting lines of players when the ball is put in play. **—***v.i.* **3.** to engage in a scrimmage. **—scrim'mag·er,** *n.*

scrimp (skrĭmp), *v.t.* **1.** to stint. **2.** to keep on short allowance. **—***v.i.* **3.** to use severe economy.

scrip (skrĭp), *n.* **1.** a writing, esp. a receipt or certificate. **2.** a scrap of paper. **3.** *Finance.* **a.** a certificate representing a fraction of a share of stock. **b.** a certificate to represent a dividend not paid in cash but promised for payment at a later date.

script (skrĭpt), *n.* **1.** handwriting. **2.** *Print.* a type imitating handwriting. **3.** the manuscript of a play, role, or motion picture.

Scrip·ture (skrĭp'chər), *n.* **1.** the sacred writings of the Old and the New Testament or of either of them; the Bible. **2.** (*l.c.*) any sacred writing. **—scrip'tur·al,** *adj.* **—scrip'tur·al·ly,** *adv.*

scriv·en·er (skrĭv'n·ər), *n.* *Archaic.* **1.** a professional or public writer. **2.** a notary.

scrod (skrŏd), *n.* *U.S.* a young codfish, esp. one that is split for cooking.

scrof·u·la (skrŏf'yə·lə), *n.* *Pathol.* a disorder of a tuberculous nature, characterized chiefly by swelling and degeneration of the lymphatic glands, esp. of the neck, and by inflammation of the joints, etc. **—scrof'u·lous,** *adj.*

scroll (skrōl), *n.* **1.** a roll of parchment or paper, esp. one with writing on it. **2.** an ornament resembling a partly unrolled sheet of paper.

scroll saw, a narrow saw mounted vertically in a frame and operated with an up-and-down motion, used for cutting curved ornamental designs.

scro·tum (skrō'təm), *n.*, *pl.* **-ta** (-tə). *Anat.* the pouch of skin that contains the testicles and their coverings. **—scro'tal,** *adj.*

Scroll (def. 1)

scrounge (skrounj), *v.t.*, *v.i.* *Slang.* **1.** to pilfer. **2.** to search. **—scroung'er,** *n.*

scrub[1] (skrŭb), *v.*, **scrubbed, scrubbing,** *n.* **—***v.t.* **1.** to rub hard with a brush, cloth, etc., in washing. **—***v.i.* **2.** to cleanse things by hard rubbing. **—***n.* **3.** act of scrubbing.

scrub[2] (skrŭb), *n.* **1.** low trees or shrubs collectively. **2.** anything undersized or inferior. **—***adj.* **3.** undersized or inferior. **4.** *Sports.* composed of substitute players, as a team. **—scrub'by,** *adj.*

scruff (skrŭf), *n.* the nape of the neck.

scru·ple (skrōō'pəl), *n.*, *v.*, **-pled, -pling. —***n.* **1.** conscientious hesitation or reluctance. **2.** a very small amount. **3.** a unit of weight equal to 20 grains, apothecaries' weight. **—***v.i.*, *v.t.* **4.** to have scruples (about).

scru·pu·lous (skrōō'pyə·ləs), *adj.* **1.** having scruples; conscientious. **2.** minutely careful or exact. **—scru·pu·los·i·ty** (skrōō'pyə·lŏs'ə·tĭ), **scru'pu·lous·ness,** *n.* **—scru'pu·lous·ly,** *adv.*

scru·ti·nize (skrōō'tə·nīz'), *v.t.*, **-nized, -nizing.** to examine closely or critically.

scru·ti·ny (skrōō'tə·nĭ), *n.*, *pl.* **-nies.** searching examination or investigation.

scud (skŭd), *v.*, **scudded, scudding,** *n.* **—***v.i.* **1.** to run or move quickly. **2.** *Naut.* to run before a gale with little or no sail set. **—***n.* **3.** act of scudding. **4.** clouds, spray, or the like, driven by the wind.

scuff (skŭf), *v.i.* **1.** to walk without raising the feet; shuffle. **—***v.t.* **2.** to mar by scraping or hard use. **—***n.* **3.** act or sound of scuffing. **4.** an open type of slipper.

scuf·fle (skŭf'əl), *v.*, **-fled, -fling,** *n.* **—***v.i.* **1.** to struggle in a rough, confused manner. **2.** to shuffle. **—***n.* **3.** a rough, confused struggle. **4.** a shuffling. **—scuf'fler,** *n.*

scull (skŭl), *n.* **1.** an oar worked from side to side over the stern of a boat. **2.** a boat propelled by a scull or sculls. **3.** a light racing boat propelled by one rower with a pair of oars. **—***v.t.*, *v.i.* **4.** to propel (a boat) with a scull or sculls.

scul·ler·y (skŭl'ə·rĭ), *n.*, *pl.* **-leries.** *Chiefly Brit.* a small room where the rough, dirty work of a kitchen is done.

sculp·tor (skŭlp'tər), *n.* one who practices the art of sculpture. **—sculp'tress,** *n. fem.*

sculp·ture (skŭlp'chər), *n.*, *v.*, **-tured, -turing. —***n.* **1.** the fine art of forming figures or designs in relief, in intaglio, or in the round by cutting marble, wood, granite, etc. **2.** a piece of such work. **—***v.t.* **3.** to carve, make, or execute by sculpture. **—sculp'tur·al,** *adj.*

scum (skŭm), *n.*, *v.*, **scummed, scumming. —***n.* **1.** a film of foul or extraneous matter on a liquid. **2.** refuse or offscourings. **3.** low, worthless persons. **—***v.t.* **4.** to remove the scum from. **—***v.i.* **5.** to form scum.

scum·my (skŭm'ĭ), *adj.*, **-mier, -miest. 1.** of or having scum. **2.** despicable.

scup·per (skŭp'ər), *n.* *Naut.* an opening in the side of a ship at or just below the level of the deck, to allow water to run off.

scup·per·nong (skŭp'ər·nông', -nŏng'), *n.* a cultivated grape of the southern U.S.

scurf (skûrf), *n.* scales of dead skin; dandruff. **—scurf'y,** *adj.*

scur·ril·ous (skûr'ə·ləs), *adj.* **1.** grossly or indecently abusive. **2.** coarsely jocular or derisive. **—scur'ril·ous·ly,** *adv.* **—scur'ril·ous·ness,** **scur·ril'i·ty,** *n.*

scur·ry (skûr'ĭ), *v.*, **-ried, -rying,** *n.*, *pl.* **-ries. —***v.i.* **1.** to go in haste. **2.** to send hurrying along. **—***n.* **3.** a scurrying rush.

scur·vy (skûr'vĭ), *n.*, *adj.*, **-vier, -viest. —***n.* **1.** *Pathol.* a disease marked by swollen and bleeding gums, livid spots on the skin, prostration, etc., due to a diet lacking in vitamin C. —*adj.* 2. mean; contemptible. —**scur′vi·ly,** *adv.* —**scur′vi·ness,** *n.*

scut·tle[1] (skŭt′əl), *n.* 1. a deep container for coal. 2. *Brit. Dial.* a broad, shallow basket.

scut·tle[2] (skŭt′əl), *v.i.,* -tled, -tling. to run with quick steps; hurry.

scut·tle[3] (skŭt′əl), *n., v.,* -tled, -tling. —*n.* 1. a small rectangular opening, as in a ship's deck, with a movable cover. —*v.t.* 2. to cut a hole or holes in (a ship or boat), esp. to sink it.

scut·tle·butt (skŭt′əl bŭt′), *n.* 1. *Naut.* a cask for drinking water. 2. *Slang.* rumor; gossip.

scythe (sīth), *n., v.,* **scythed, scything.** —*n.* 1. a long, curving blade fastened at an angle to a handle, for mowing grass, grain, etc., by hand. —*v.t.* 2. to cut with a scythe.

S. Dak., South Dakota. Also, **S.D.**

Se, *Chem.* selenium.

SE, 1. Southeast. 2. Southeastern. Also, **S.E.**

sea (sē), *n.* 1. the salt waters that cover the greater part of the earth's surface. 2. a division of these waters, of considerable extent, marked off by land boundaries. 3. the turbulence of the ocean or other body of water. 4. a copious or overwhelming quantity. 5. **at sea,** a. out on the ocean. b. uncertain or perplexed.

sea anemone, any of certain common marine animals having a columnar body topped by a disk bearing one or more circles of tentacles.

Sea·bees (sē′bēz′), *n.pl.* the construction battalions of the U.S. Navy.

sea·board (sē′bōrd′), *n.* the line where land and sea meet; the seashore.

sea·coast (sē′kōst′), *n.* the land immediately adjacent to the sea.

sea dog, a sailor, esp. one of long experience.

sea·far·er (sē′fâr′ər), *n.* a sailor.

sea·far·ing (sē′fâr′ĭng), *adj.* 1. that travels by sea. 2. following the sea as a calling.

sea·go·ing (sē′gō′ĭng), *adj.* 1. designed or fit for sailing. 2. seafaring.

sea horse, 1. a fish with a prehensile tail and a beaked head that is turned at right angles to the body. 2. a fabulous marine animal with the fore parts of a horse and the hinder parts of a fish.

seal[1] (sēl), *n.* 1. a device impressed on a piece of wax or the like, affixed to a document as evidence of authenticity or attestation. 2. anything that effectively closes a thing. 3. a decorative stamp. —*v.t.* 4. to affix a seal to in authorization, confirmation, etc. 5. to fasten or close by, or as if by, a seal. 6. to decide irrevocably. —**seal′a·ble,** *adj.* —**seal′er,** *n.*

seal[2] (sēl), *n., pl.* **seals,** (*esp. collectively*) **seal** for 1. 1. any of certain marine carnivores having large flippers used in swimming and walking. 2. the skin of the seal. —*v.i.* 3. to hunt seals. —**seal′er,** *n.*

sea legs, *Colloq.* ability to walk with steadiness or ease on a rolling ship.

sea level, the horizontal level corresponding to the surface of the sea when halfway between mean high and low water.

sealing wax, a resinous preparation, soft when heated, used for sealing letters, etc.

sea lion, any of certain large seals of the Pacific coast.

seal·skin (sēl′skĭn′), *n.* the skin or fur of the seal.

seam (sēm), *n.* 1. the line formed by sewing together pieces of cloth, leather, or the like. 2. any line between abutting edges. 3. a wrinkle or a scar. 4. *Geol.* a comparatively thin stratum. —*v.t.* 5. to join with a seam. 6. to mark with wrinkles, scars, etc.

sea·man (sē′mən), *n., pl.* -men. a sailor, specif. one below the rank of officer.

sea·man·ship (sē′mən shĭp′), *n.* the skill necessary for operation, management, and maintenance of ships.

seam·stress (sēm′strĭs), *n.* a woman whose occupation is sewing.

seam·y (sē′mĭ), *adj.,* **seamier, seamiest.** 1. least favorable; worst. 2. having or showing seams. —**seam′i·ness,** *n.*

sé·ance (sā′äns), *n.* 1. a meeting of spiritualists seeking to receive communications from spirits. 2. a session.

sea·plane (sē′plān′), *n.* a hydroplane for use over the sea, esp. one with floats.

sea·port (sē′pōrt′), *n.* 1. a port or harbor pro-

viding accommodation for seagoing vessels. 2. a town or city at such a place.

sear (sîr), *v.t., v.i.* 1. to burn or char the surface (of). 2. to dry up. 3. to brown the surface (of meat) by a brief application of high heat. —*n.* 4. a mark made by searing. —*adj.* 5. *Chiefly Poetic.* dry or withered.

search (sûrch), *v.t.* 1. to go through or examine carefully in seeking to find something. 2. to probe (a wound, etc.). 3. (of wind, gunfire, etc.) to pierce or penetrate. 4. to bring or find (out) by a search. —*v.i.* 5. to make examination or investigation. —*n.* 6. examination or investigation. —**search′a·ble,** *adj.* —**search′er,** *n.* —**search′ing·ly,** *adv.*

search·light (sûrch′līt′), *n.* a light and reflector for throwing a beam of light in any direction.

search warrant, *Law.* a court order authorizing the searching of a house, etc., as for stolen goods.

sea·shore (sē′shōr′), *n.* land along the sea or ocean.

sea·sick (sē′sĭk′), *adj.* affected with seasickness.

sea·sick·ness (sē′sĭk′nĭs), *n.* nausea, etc., caused by the motion of a ship.

sea·side (sē′sīd′), *n.* 1. the seashore; seacoast. —*adj.* 2. at the seaside.

sea·son (sē′zən), *n.* 1. one of the four periods of the year (spring, summer, autumn, and winter). 2. the period of the year when something is best or available. 3. a period of the year marked by certain conditions, activities, etc. 4. a suitable or proper time. —*v.t.* 5. to improve the flavor of (food) by adding spices, herbs, or the like. 6. to mature, ripen, or condition by exposure to suitable conditions or treatment. 7. to dry and harden (timber) by due process. 8. to accustom or harden. —**sea′son·er,** *n.*

sea·son·a·ble (sē′zən ə bəl), *adj.* 1. suitable to the season. 2. timely; opportune. —**sea′son·a·ble·ness,** *n.* —**sea′son·a·bly,** *adv.*

sea·son·al (sē′zən əl), *adj.* pertaining to or dependent on some particular season. —**sea′son·al·ly,** *adv.*

sea·son·ing (sē′zən ĭng), *n.* something that seasons, as salt, spices, herbs, etc.

seat[1] (sēt), *n.* 1. something for sitting on, as a chair. 2. the part of the body on which one sits. 3. manner of sitting, as on horseback. 4. a right to sit as a member in a legislative or similar body. —*v.t.* 5. to place on a seat or seats. 6. to find seats for. 7. to put in a position of authority or in a legislative body.

seat[2] (sēt), *n.* 1. a place in which something prevails or is established. 2. established place or center, as of government. 3. site, location, or locality. 4. abode. —*v.t.* 5. to fix in a particular place.

Se·at·tle (sē ăt′əl), *n.* a seaport in W Washington, on Puget Sound. 368,302.

sea urchin, any of certain marine animals having a globular form and a spine-bearing shell.

sea·ward (sē′wərd), *adv.* 1. Also, **sea′wards.** toward the sea. —*adj.* 2. facing or tending toward the sea. 3. coming from the sea. —*n.* 4. the direction or quarter toward the sea.

sea·way (sē′wā′), *n.* 1. a way over the sea. 2. the open sea. 3. the progress of a ship through the waves. 4. a rough sea.

sea·weed (sē′wēd′), *n.* any plant or plants growing in the ocean.

sea·wor·thy (sē′wûr′thĭ), *adj.* (of a ship) adequately constructed and equipped to sail at sea. —**sea′wor′thi·ness,** *n.*

se·ba·ceous (sĭ bā′shəs), *adj. Physiol.* 1. fatty; greasy. 2. secreting a fatty substance.

SEC, Securities and Exchange Commission.

sec., 1. secant. 2. second. 3. secondary. 4. secretary. 5. section. 6. sector.

se·cant (sē′kant, -kănt), *n.* 1. *Geom.* an intersecting line. 2. *Trig.* a. (orig.) a line from the center of a circle through one extremity of an arc to the tangent from the other extremity. b. the ratio of the length of this line to that of the radius of the circle.

se·cede (sĭ sēd′), *v.i.,* -ceded, -ceding. to withdraw formally from an alliance or organization. —**se·ced′er,** *n.*

se·ces·sion (sĭ sĕsh′ən), *n.* 1. act of seceding. 2. (*often cap.*) the attempted withdrawal from the Union of eleven Southern States in 1860–61, which brought on the Civil War.

se·ces·sion·ist (sĭ sĕsh/ən ĭst), *n.* one who favors secession. —**se·ces/sion·ism/**, *n.*

se·clude (sĭ klōōd/), *v.t.*, **-cluded, -cluding.** to place in solitude; isolate.

se·clu·sion (sĭ klōō/zhən), *n.* **1.** act of secluding. **2.** state of being secluded; solitude. **3.** a secluded place. —**se·clu·sive** (sĭ klōō/sĭv), *adj.* —**se·clu/sive·ness,** *n.*

sec·ond¹ (sĕk/ənd), *adj.* **1.** next after the first in order, time, rank, value, quality, etc. **2.** other or another. —*n.* **3.** one that is second. **4.** one who aids or supports another. **5.** (*pl.*) *Com.* goods below first or perfect quality. —*v.t.* **6.** to support, back up, or assist. **7.** to further or advance. **8.** to express support of (a motion, etc.) as a necessary preliminary to further discussion of the motion or to a vote on it. **9.** to act as second to (a pugilist, etc.). —*adv.* **10.** in the second place, group, etc. —**sec/ond·er,** *n.* —**sec/ond·ly,** *adv.*

sec·ond² (sĕk/ənd), *n.* **1.** the sixtieth part of a minute. **2.** *Geom., etc.* the sixtieth part of a minute of a degree. **3.** a moment or instant.

sec·ond·ar·y (sĕk/ən dĕr/ĭ), *adj., n., pl.* **-aries.** —*adj.* **1.** next after the first in order, place, time, importance, etc. **2.** derived; not original. **3.** of minor importance; subordinate. —*n.* **4.** a subordinate or deputy. —**sec/ond·ar/i·ly,** *adv.*

secondary school, a high school.

sec·ond-class (sĕk/ənd klăs/, -kläs/), *adj.* **1.** of or belonging to the second class. **2.** second-rate; inferior.

sec·ond-hand (sĕk/ənd hănd/), *adj.* **1.** obtained from another; not original. **2.** previously used or owned. **3.** dealing in previously used goods.

second nature, habit, tendency, etc., that is deeply fixed in one's character.

sec·ond-rate (sĕk/ənd rāt/), *adj.* **1.** of the second class, as to size, quality, etc. **2.** inferior; mediocre. —**sec/ond-rat/er,** *n.*

se·cre·cy (sē/krə sĭ), *n., pl.* **-cies.** **1.** state of being secret or concealed. **2.** privacy. **3.** ability to keep a secret. **4.** secretive habits.

se·cret (sē/krĭt), *adj.* **1.** done, made, or conducted without the knowledge of others. **2.** kept from the knowledge of others. **3.** close-mouthed; reticent. **4.** secluded. **5.** beyond ordinary human understanding. —*n.* **6.** something secret, hidden, or concealed. **7.** a hidden reason or explanation. —**se/cret·ly,** *adv.*

sec·re·tar·i·at (sĕk/rə târ/ĭ ət), *n.* the officials or office entrusted with maintaining records and performing secretarial duties.

sec·re·tar·y (sĕk/rə tĕr/ĭ), *n., pl.* **-taries.** **1.** a person who conducts correspondence, keeps records, etc., for an individual or an organization. **2.** an official in charge of a department of government. **3.** a piece of furniture for use as a writing desk. —**sec·re·tar·i·al** (sĕk/rə târ/ĭ əl), *adj.* —**sec/re·tar/y·ship/,** *n.*

se·crete (sĭ krēt/), *v.t.*, **-creted, -creting.** **1.** *Biol.* to separate off, prepare, or elaborate from the blood. **2.** to hide or keep secret.

se·cre·tion (sĭ krē/shən), *n.* **1.** the process or function of an animal body, executed in the glands, by which various substances, as bile, milk, etc., are separated and elaborated from the blood. **2.** the product secreted. —**se·cre·to·ry** (sĭ krē/tə rĭ), *adj.*

se·cre·tive (sĭ krē/tĭv), *adj.* **1.** having a disposition to secrecy; reticent. **2.** secretory. —**se·cre/tive·ly,** *adv.* —**se·cre/tive·ness,** *n.*

secret service, the branch of governmental service charged with secret investigation, espionage, etc., esp. (*caps.*) the branch of the U.S. Treasury Department with the main functions of discovering counterfeiting and of protecting the President.

sect (sĕkt), *n.* a body of persons adhering to a particular religious faith; denomination.

sec·tar·i·an (sĕk târ/ĭ ən), *adj.* **1.** of or pertaining to sectaries or sects. **2.** confined or devoted to a particular sect. —*n.* **3.** a member of a sect. **4.** a bigoted adherent of a sect. —**sec·tar/i·an·ism/,** *n.*

sec·ta·ry (sĕk/tə rĭ), *n., pl.* **-ries.** **1.** a member of a particular sect, esp. one regarded as heretical or schismatic. **2.** one zealously devoted to a particular sect.

sec·tion (sĕk/shən), *n.* **1.** a part cut off or separated. **2.** a distinct portion of a book, writing, or the like. **3.** one of a number of parts that can be fitted together to make a whole. **4.** a distinct part of a country, community, class, or the like.

5. *Railroads.* **a.** a division of a sleeping car containing both an upper and lower berth. **b.** a train scheduled jointly with another or others. —*v.t.* **6.** to cut or divide into sections.

sec·tion·al (sĕk/shən əl), *adj.* **1.** pertaining to a particular section; local. **2.** composed of several independent sections. —**sec/tion·al·ly,** *adv.*

sec·tion·al·ism (sĕk/shən ə lĭz/əm), *n.* excessive regard for local interests, etc.

sec·tor (sĕk/tər), *n.* **1.** *Geom.* a plane figure bounded by two radii and the included arc of a circle, ellipse, or the like. **2.** a mathematical instrument consisting of two flat rulers hinged together at one end. **3.** *Mil.* one of the sections of a forward combat area.

sec·u·lar (sĕk/yə lər), *adj.* of or pertaining to things not religious, sacred, or spiritual; temporal; worldly. —**sec/u·lar·ism/,** *n.* —**sec/u·lar·ist,** *n.* —**sec/u·lar·is/tic,** *adj.* —**sec/u·lar·ly,** *adv.*

sec·u·lar·ize (sĕk/yə lə rīz/), *v.t.*, **-ized, -izing.** **1.** to separate from religious connection or control. **2.** to transfer (property) from ecclesiastical to civil possession or use. —**sec/u·lar·i·za/tion,** *n.*

se·cure (sĭ kyŏŏr/), *adj., v.*, **-cured, -curing.** —*adj.* **1.** free from danger; safe. **2.** not liable to fail, yield, etc., as a support. **3.** free from anxiety. **4.** sure; certain. —*v.t.* **5.** to get or obtain. **6.** to make safe. **7.** to make certain; ensure. **8.** to make firm or fast. **9.** to assure a creditor of payment by the pledge of property. —*v.i.* **10.** to be safe. —**se·cure/ly,** *adv.* —**se·cure/ness,** *n.*

se·cu·ri·ty (sĭ kyŏŏr/ĭ tĭ), *n., pl.* **-ties.** **1.** freedom from danger, risk, etc.; safety. **2.** freedom from care or doubt. **3.** a protection or defense. **4.** an assurance; guarantee. **5.** *Law.* **a.** something given as surety for the fulfillment of a promise, obligation, etc. **b.** an evidence of debt or property, as a certificate of stock.

sec/y., secretary.

se·dan (sĭ dăn/), *n.* **1.** a closed automobile body seating four or more persons. **2.** sedan chair.

sedan chair, a portable wheelless vehicle for one person, borne on poles by two men, one before and one behind.

se·date (sĭ dāt/), *adj.* calm, quiet, or composed; sober. —**se·date/ly,** *adv.* —**se·date/ness,** *n.*

sed·a·tive (sĕd/ə tĭv), *adj.* **1.** tending to calm or soothe. **2.** *Med.* allaying irritability or assuaging pain. —*n.* **3.** a sedative agent or remedy.

Sedan chair

sed·en·tar·y (sĕd/ən tĕr/ĭ), *adj.* **1.** characterized by or requiring a sitting posture. **2.** accustomed to sit much or take little exercise. **3.** *Chiefly Zool.* abiding in one place. —**sed/en·tar/i·ness,** *n.*

sedge (sĕj), *n.* any of certain rushlike or grasslike plants growing in wet places. —**sedg/y,** *adj.*

sed·i·ment (sĕd/ə mənt), *n.* **1.** matter which settles to the bottom of a liquid; lees; dregs. **2.** *Geol.* mineral or organic matter deposited by water, air, or ice. —**sed·i·men·ta·ry** (sĕd/ə mĕn/tə rĭ), *adj.*

se·di·tion (sĭ dĭsh/ən), *n.* incitement of discontent or rebellion against the government. —**se·di/tious,** *adj.* —**se·di/tious·ly,** *adv.*

se·duce (sĭ dūs/, -dōōs/), *v.t.*, **-duced, -ducing.** **1.** to lead astray from duty, rectitude, or principle; corrupt. **2.** to induce to surrender one's chastity. **3.** to entice. —**se·duc/er,** *n.* —**se·duc/i·ble,** *adj.* —**se·duc·tion** (sĭ dŭk/shən), *n.* —**se·duc/tive,** *adj.* —**se·duc/tive·ly,** *adv.* —**se·duc/tive·ness,** *n.*

sed·u·lous (sĕj/ə ləs), *adj.* **1.** diligent; persevering. **2.** persistent. —**sed/u·lous·ly,** *adv.* —**sed/u·lous·ness,** *n.*

see¹ (sē), *v.t., v.i.*, **saw, seen, seeing.** **1.** to perceive with the eyes. **2.** to view. **3.** to discern; understand. **4.** to ascertain; find out. **5.** to have knowledge or experience of. **6.** to make sure. **7.** to meet and converse with. **8.** to receive as a visitor. **9.** to escort. **10.** *Poker, etc.* to meet (a bet), or meet the bet of (a bettor).

see² (sē), *n.* *Eccles.* the seat, center of authority, office, or jurisdiction of a bishop.

seed (sēd), *n., pl.* **seeds, seed,** *v.* —*n.* **1.** the propagating part of a plant. **2.** any small, seedlike part or fruit, as a grain of wheat. **3.** the germ or beginning of anything. **4.** offspring; progeny. **5.** semen or sperm. —*v.t., v.i.* **6.** to sow (land) with seed. **7.** to sow or scatter (seed). **8.** to remove the seeds from (fruit). **9.** to modify (the ordinary drawing of lots for position in a tournament) by distributing ranking players so that they will not meet in the early rounds of play. —**seed'-er**, *n.* —**seed'less**, *adj.*

seed·ling (sēd'lĭng), *n.* a plant or tree grown from a seed.

seed·y (sē'dĭ), *adj.*, **seedier**, **seediest**. **1.** abounding in seed. **2.** shabby. —**seed'i·ly**, *adv.* —**seed'i·ness**, *n.*

see·ing (sē'ĭng), *conj.* in view of the fact (that); considering; inasmuch as.

seek (sēk), *v.*, **sought** (sôt), **seeking**. —*v.t.* **1.** to search for. **2.** to try to obtain. **3.** to try. **4.** to ask for. —*v.i.* **5.** to search. —**seek'er**, *n.*

seem (sēm), *v.i.* **1.** to appear (to be, feel, do, etc.). **2.** to appear to oneself (to be, do, etc.). **3.** to appear to exist. **4.** to appear to be true.

seem·ing (sē'mĭng), *adj.* **1.** apparent; seeming to be such. —*n.* **2.** appearance. —**seem'ing·ly**, *adv.*

seem·ly (sēm'lĭ), *adj.*, **-lier**, **-liest**, *adv.* —*adj.* **1.** in good taste; decent; decorous. **2.** suitable. **3.** *Archaic.* handsome. —*adv.* **4.** fittingly. —**seem'li·ness**, *n.*

seep (sēp), *v.i.* **1.** to pass gradually, as liquid, through a porous substance; ooze. —*n.* **2.** moisture that seeps out.

seep·age (sē'pĭj), *n.* **1.** act or process of seeping. **2.** that which seeps out.

se·er (sē'ər for 1; sĭr for 2, 3), *n.* **1.** one who sees. **2.** a prophet. **3.** a fortune teller. —**seer·ess** (sĭr'ĭs), *n. fem.*

seer·suck·er (sĭr'sŭk'ər), *n.* a cotton fabric with stripes crinkled in the weaving.

see·saw (sē'sô'), *n.* **1.** a children's sport in which they move alternately up and down when seated at opposite ends of a plank balanced at the middle. **2.** such a plank. **3.** an up-and-down or a back-and-forth movement. —*v.i.*, *v.t.* **4.** to move in a seesaw manner.

seethe (sēᵺ), *v.*, **seethed**, **seething**, *n.* —*v.i.*, *v.t.* **1.** to boil. **2.** to surge or foam. **3.** to be in a state of agitation or excitement. —*n.* **4.** act of seething. **5.** state of agitation.

seg·ment (sĕg'mənt), *n.* **1.** one of the parts into which anything is naturally divided. **2.** *Geom.* a part cut off from a figure by a line or a plane. —*v.t.*, *v.i.* **3.** to divide into segments. —**seg·men'tal**, **seg·men·tar·y** (sĕg'mən tĕr'ĭ), *adj.*

seg·men·ta·tion (sĕg'mən tā'shən), *n.* division into segments.

seg·re·gate (*v.* sĕg'rə gāt'; *adj.* sĕg'rə gĭt, -gāt'), *v.*, **-gated**, **-gating**, *adj.* —*v.t.*, *v.i.* **1.** to separate from the others; isolate. —*adj.* **2.** set apart. —**seg're·ga'tion**, *n.*

Seid·litz powder (sĕd'lĭts), an effervescent aperient consisting of tartaric acid, sodium bicarbonate, and Rochelle salt.

Seine (sān), *n.* a river from E France to the English Channel. ab. 480 mi.

seine (sān), *n.*, *v.*, **seined**, **seining**. —*n.* **1.** a fishing net which hangs vertically in the water, having floats at the upper edge and sinkers at the lower. —*v.t.*, *v.i.* **2.** to fish or catch with a seine.

seis·mic (sīz'mĭk, sīs'-), *adj.* of, like, or caused by an earthquake.

seis·mo·graph (sīz'mə grăf', -grăf', sīs'-), *n.* an instrument for recording the phenomena of earthquakes. —**seis'mo·graph'ic**, *adj.* —**seis·mog·ra·phy** (sīz mŏg'rə fĭ, sīs-), *n.*

seize (sēz), *v.*, **seized**, **seizing**. —*v.t.* **1.** to lay hold of suddenly or forcibly; grasp. **2.** to understand. **3.** to take possession of, esp. by force or by legal authority. **4.** to capture; take into custody. **5.** to take advantage of. **6.** *Naut.* to bind, lash, or fasten. —*v.i.* **7.** to lay hold suddenly or forcibly.

sei·zure (sē'zhər), *n.* **1.** act of seizing. **2.** a taking possession, legally or by force. **3.** a sudden attack, as of disease.

sel·dom (sĕl'dəm), *adv.* rarely; not often.

se·lect (sĭ lĕkt'), *v.t.* **1.** to choose; pick out. —*adj.* **2.** selected; chosen in preference to others. **3.** choice; excellent. **4.** exclusive. —**se·lect'-ness**, *n.* —**se·lec'tor**, *n.*

se·lect·ee (sĭ lĕk tē'), *n.* one selected by draft for military or naval service.

se·lec·tion (sĭ lĕk'shən), *n.* **1.** act of selecting or the fact of being selected; choice. **2.** a thing or a number of things selected.

se·lec·tive (sĭ lĕk'tĭv), *adj.* **1.** having the

function or power of selecting. **2.** characterized by selection. **3.** *Radio.* having good selectivity.

selective service, compulsory military service.

se·lec·tiv·i·ty (sĭ lĕk'tĭv'ə tĭ), *n.* **1.** state or quality of being selective. **2.** *Radio.* the ability to receive any one of a band of frequencies to the exclusion of others.

se·lect·man (sĭ lĕkt'mən), *n.*, *pl.* **-men.** *New England.* one of a board of town officers chosen to manage certain public affairs.

Se·le·ne (sĭ lē'nē), *n.* *Gk. Myth.* the goddess of the moon.

sel·e·nite (sĕl'ə nīt', sĭ lē'nīt), *n.* a crystalline variety of gypsum.

se·le·ni·um (sĭ lē'nĭ əm), *n.* *Chem.* a nonmetallic element having an electrical resistance which varies under the influence of light. *Symbol:* Se; *at. wt.:* 78.96; *at. no.:* 34; *sp. gr.:* (gray) 4.80 at 25°C., (red) 4.50 at 25°C.

self (sĕlf), *n.*, *pl.* **selves**, *adj.*, *pron.*, *pl.* **selves.** —*n.* **1.** a person or thing referred to with respect to individuality. **2.** one's nature, character, etc. **3.** personal interest. —*adj.* **4.** uniform; same; identical. —*pron.* **5.** myself, himself, etc.

self-, a prefixal use of *self*, expressing principally reflexive action.

self-ad·dressed (sĕlf'ə drĕst'), *adj.* addressed to oneself.

self-as·ser·tion (sĕlf'ə sûr'shən), *n.* insistence on one's own claims, wishes, opinions, etc. —**self'-as·ser'tive**, *adj.*

self-as·sur·ance (sĕlf'ə shŏŏr'əns), *n.* self-confidence.

self-cen·tered (sĕlf'sĕn'tərd), *adj.* **1.** selfish. **2.** centered in oneself or itself.

self-com·mand (sĕlf'kə mănd', -mänd'), *n.* self-control.

self-com·pla·cent (sĕlf'kəm plā'sənt), *adj.* pleased with oneself; self-satisfied.

self-con·ceit (sĕlf'kən sēt'), *n.* overweening opinion of oneself, one's abilities, etc.

self-con·fi·dence (sĕlf'kŏn'fə dəns), *n.* confidence in one's own judgment, ability, power, etc. —**self'-con'fi·dent**, *adj.* —**self'-con'fi·dent·ly**, *adj.*

self-con·scious (sĕlf'kŏn'shəs), *adj.* excessively or morbidly conscious of oneself as an object of observation to others. —**self'-con'-scious·ly**, *adv.* —**self'-con'scious·ness**, *n.*

self-con·tained (sĕlf'kən tānd'), *adj.* **1.** containing in oneself or itself all that is necessary; independent. **2.** reserved or uncommunicative.

self-con·trol (sĕlf'kən trōl'), *n.* control of oneself or one's actions, feelings, etc.

self-de·fense (sĕlf'dĭ fĕns'), *n.* act of defending one's own person, property, etc.

self-de·ni·al (sĕlf'dĭ nī'əl), *n.* the sacrifice or one's own desires; unselfishness.

self-de·ter·mi·na·tion (sĕlf'dĭ tûr'mə nā'-shən), *n.* **1.** determination by oneself or itself, without outside influence. **2.** the determining by a people of the form of government it shall have.

self-dis·ci·pline (sĕlf'dĭs'ə plĭn), *n.* discipline and training of oneself.

self-ed·u·cat·ed (sĕlf'ĕj'ə kā'tĭd), *adj.* educated by one's own efforts, without formal instruction or financial aid.

self-es·teem (sĕlf'ĕs tēm'), *n.* favorable opinion of oneself; conceit.

self-ev·i·dent (sĕlf'ĕv'ə dənt), *adj.* evident in itself without proof; axiomatic.

self-ex·plan·a·to·ry (sĕlf'ĭk splăn'ə tōr'ĭ), *adj.* needing no explanation; obvious.

self-ex·pres·sion (sĕlf'ĭk sprĕsh'ən), *n.* the expression of one's personality by poetry, music, etc.

self-gov·ern·ment (sĕlf'gŭv'ərn mənt), *n.* government of a state, community, or other body of persons by its members jointly.

self-help (sĕlf'hĕlp'), *n.* act of getting along or the ability to get along without aid.

self-im·por·tant (sĕlf'ĭm pôr'tənt), *adj.* having or showing an exaggerated opinion of one's own importance. —**self'-im·por'tance**, *n.* —**self'-im·por'tant·ly**, *adv.*

self-in·ter·est (sĕlf'ĭn'tər ĭst), *n.* regard for one's own interest or advantage.

self·ish (sĕl'fĭsh), *adj.* **1.** devoted to or caring only for oneself. **2.** characterized by caring only for oneself. —**self'ish·ly**, *adv.* —**self'ish·ness**, *n.*

self·less (sĕlf'lĭs), *adj.* unselfish;

self-love (sĕlf'lŭv'), *n.* the instinct by which man's actions are directed to the promotion of his own welfare.

self-made (sĕlf'mād'), *adj.* having attained success in life unaided.

self-pit·y (sĕlf'pĭt'ĭ), *n.* pity for oneself.

self-pos·sessed (sĕlf'pə zĕst'), *adj.* having or showing control of one's feelings, behavior, etc. —**self'-pos·ses'sion,** *n.*

self-pres·er·va·tion (sĕlf'prĕz'ər vā'shən), *n.* preservation of oneself from harm or destruction.

self-pro·tec·tion (sĕlf'prə tĕk'shən), *n.* protection of oneself or itself.

self-re·li·ance (sĕlf'rĭ li'əns), *n.* reliance on one's own powers. —**self'-re·li'ant,** *adj.*

self-re·spect (sĕlf'rĭ spĕkt'), *n.* proper esteem for the dignity of one's own character. —**self'-re·spect'ing,** *adj.*

self-re·straint (sĕlf'rĭ strānt'), *n.* restraint imposed on one by oneself; self-control.

self-right·eous (sĕlf'rĭ'chəs), *adj.* righteous in one's own esteem.

self-sac·ri·fice (sĕlf'săk'rə fīs'), *n.* sacrifice of one's interests, desires, etc., as for duty or the good of another. —**self'-sac'ri·fic'ing,** *adj.*

self-same (sĕlf'sām'), *adj.* identical.

self-sat·is·fac·tion (sĕlf'săt'ĭs făk'shən), *n.* satisfaction with oneself, one's achievements, etc. —**self'-sat'is·fied',** *adj.*

self-seek·ing (sĕlf'sē'kĭng), *n.* 1. selfishness. —*adj.* 2. selfish.

self-serv·ice (sĕlf'sûr'vĭs), *n.* the serving of oneself in a restaurant, shop, or the like.

self-suf·fi·cient (sĕlf'sə fĭsh'ənt), *adj.* 1. able to supply one's own needs. 2. having undue confidence in one's own powers, etc. —**self'-suf·fi'cien·cy,** *n.*

self-willed (sĕlf'wĭld'), *adj.* obstinately or perversely insistent on one's own will.

sell (sĕl), *v.,* **sold, selling.** —*v.t.* 1. to give to a purchaser for a price. 2. to deal in. 3. to cause acceptance (of). 4. to betray, esp. for a price. —*v.i.* 5. to engage in selling. 6. to find purchasers. —**sell'er,** *n.*

sell·out (sĕl'out'), *n.* 1. *U.S.* betrayal. 2. *Colloq.* a play, show, etc., for which all seats are sold.

Selt·zer (sĕlt'sər), *n.* an effervescent mineral water containing common salt and small quantities of sodium, calcium, and magnesium carbonates.

sel·vage (sĕl'vĭj), *n.* the edge of woven fabric finished to prevent raveling.

se·man·tic (sĭ măn'tĭk), *adj.* pertaining to signification or meaning.

se·man·tics (sĭ măn'tĭks), *n.* 1. the study of meaning and changes of meaning. 2. that branch of modern logic which studies the relations between signs and what they denote.

sem·a·phore (sĕm'ə fôr'), *n.,* *v.,* **-phored, -phoring.** —*n.* 1. an apparatus for conveying information by means of signals. —*v.t.* 2. to signal by semaphore or flags.

sem·blance (sĕm'bləns), *n.* 1. outward appearance. 2. an assumed or unreal appearance. 3. a likeness or copy.

se·men (sē'mən), *n.* the impregnating fluid produced by the male reproductive organs.

se·mes·ter (sĭ mĕs'tər), *n.* one half of a school year.

semi-, a prefix modifying the latter element of the word, meaning "half," as in *semicircle, semiannual.*

Railroad semaphore
A, Proceed;
B, Caution; C, Stop

sem·i·an·nu·al (sĕm'ĭ ăn'yōō əl), *adj.* 1. occurring every half year. 2. lasting for half a year. —**sem'i·an'nu·al·ly,** *adv.*

sem·i·cir·cle (sĕm'ĭ sûr'kəl), *n.* the half of a circle. —**sem'i·cir'cu·lar,** *adj.*

semicircular canal, *Anat.* any of three curved tubular canals in the labyrinth of the ear, concerned with equilibrium.

sem·i·co·lon (sĕm'ĭ kō'lən), *n.* a mark of punctuation (;) used to indicate a more distinct separation between parts of a sentence than that indicated by a comma.

sem·i·con·scious (sĕm'ĭ kŏn'shəs), *adj.* half-conscious; not fully conscious.

sem·i·fi·nal (sĕm'ĭ fī'nəl), *adj.* 1. designating or pertaining to a round, contest, match, etc., which immediately precedes the final and decisive one. —*n.* 2. a semifinal round, contest, etc.

semi·month·ly (sĕm'ĭ mŭnth'lĭ), *adj., n., pl.* **-lies,** *adv.* —*adj.* 1. occurring every half month. —*n.* 2. a semimonthly publication. —*adv.* 3. every half month.

sem·i·nal (sĕm'ə nəl), *adj.* of, pertaining to, or of the nature of semen or seed. —**sem'i·nal·ly,** *adv.*

sem·i·nar (sĕm'ə när'), *n.* a small group of students, as in a university, engaged in advanced study and original research.

sem·i·nar·y (sĕm'ə něr'ĭ), *n., pl.* **-naries.** 1. a school, esp. one of higher grade. 2. a school for the education of men for the ministry. 3. a school for young women.

Sem·i·nole (sĕm'ə nōl'), *n., pl.* **-nole, -noles** (-nōlz), *adj.* —*n.* 1. a member of a tribe of American Indians, resident in Florida and Oklahoma. —*adj.* 2. of or pertaining to this tribe.

sem·i·pre·cious (sĕm'ĭ prĕsh'əs), *adj.* having moderate value, as the amethyst, etc.

Sem·ite (sĕm'īt, sē'mīt), *n.* a member of a speech family comprising the Hebrews, Arabs, Assyrians, etc.

Se·mit·ic (sə mĭt'ĭk), *n.* 1. an important family of languages, including Hebrew, Arabic, and Amharic. —*adj.* 2. of or pertaining to the Semites or their languages.

sem·i·week·ly (sĕm'ĭ wēk'lĭ), *adj., n., pl.* **-lies,** *adv.* —*adj.* 1. occurring or appearing every half week. —*n.* 2. a semiweekly publication. —*adv.* 3. every half week.

sem·o·li·na (sĕm'ə lē'nə), *n.* the large, hard parts of wheat grains retained in the bolting machine after the fine flour has passed through it.

sen (sĕn), *n.* a Japanese monetary unit and copper or bronze coin, worth about half a U.S. cent.

Sen., 1. Senate. 2. Senator. 3. Senior.

sen·ate (sĕn'ĭt), *n.* 1. a legislative assembly of a state or nation. 2. (*cap.*) the upper house of the legislature of certain countries, as the United States, Canada, Australia, etc. 3. the supreme council of state in ancient Rome. 4. a governing, advisory, or disciplinary body, as in certain universities.

sen·a·tor (sĕn'ə tər), *n.* a member of a senate. —**sen'a·tor·ship',** *n.* —**sen·a·to·ri·al** (sĕn'ə tôr'ĭ əl), *adj.*

send (sĕnd), *v.,* **sent, sending.** —*v.t.* 1. to cause to go; order or direct to go. 2. to cause to be conveyed or transmitted to a destination. 3. to compel or force to go. 4. to impel; throw. 5. to give (*forth, out,* etc.), as light, odor, or sound. 6. *Elect.* to transmit. —*v.i.* 7. to dispatch a messenger, agent, message, etc. 8. *Swing Music.* to excite or inspire a jazz performer or listener. —**send'er,** *n.*

Sen·e·ca (sĕn'ə kə), *n.* a member of a large tribe of North American Indians, in western New York.

Sen·e·gal (sĕn'ĭ gôl'), *n.* a colony in W French West Africa. 1,692,000 pop.; 77,683 sq. mi. *Cap.:* St. Louis. —**Sen·e·ga·lese** (sĕn'ə gô lēz', -lēs', -gə-), *adj., n.*

se·nes·cent (sə nĕs'ənt), *adj.* growing old; aging. —**se·nes'cence,** *n.*

sen·es·chal (sĕn'ə shəl), *n.* an officer in the household of a medieval prince or dignitary.

se·nile (sē'nīl, -nĭl), *adj.* of, pertaining to, or characteristic of old age. —**se·nil·i·ty** (sə nĭl'ə tĭ), *n.*

sen·ior (sēn'yər), *adj.* 1. older (used after the name of the older of two persons bearing the same name). 2. of higher rank or standing. 3. (in American colleges and schools) noting or pertaining to the highest class or the last year of the course. —*n.* 4. a person who is older than another. 5. one of higher rank or standing. 6. *U.S.* a member of the senior class in a college or school.

sen·ior·i·ty (sēn yôr'ə tĭ, -yŏr'-), *n., pl.* **-ties.** 1. state or fact of being older. 2. priority or precedence in age or service.

sen·na (sĕn'ə), *n.* 1. a cathartic drug consisting of the dried leaflets of certain cassia plants. 2. any of these plants.

se·ñor (sĕ nyôr'), *n., pl.* **-ñores** (-nyô'rĕs). *Spanish.* 1. a gentleman. 2. (as a term of address) sir. 3. (as a title) Mr.

se·ño·ra (sĕ nyô'rä), *n.* *Spanish.* 1. Mrs.; madame. 2. lady; gentlewoman.

se·ño·ri·ta (sĕ'nyō rē'tä), *n. Spanish.* 1. Miss. 2. young lady.

sen·sa·tion (sĕn sā'shən), *n.* 1. the operation of the senses. 2. a mental condition produced through an organ of sense. 3. *Physiol.* the faculty of perception of stimuli. 4. a state of excited feeling or interest. 5. a cause of such feeling or interest.

sen·sa·tion·al (sĕn sā'shən əl), *adj.* 1. startling or thrilling. 2. aiming at startling or thrilling impressions. —**sen·sa'tion·al·ly,** *adv.*

sen·sa·tion·al·ism (sĕn sā'shən ə lĭz'əm), *n.* 1. matter, language, or style producing startling or thrilling impressions. 2. *Philos.* the doctrine that all ideas are derived from, and are essentially reducible to, sensations. —**sen·sa'tion·al·ist,** *n.*

sense (sĕns), *n., v.,* **sensed, sensing.** —*n.* 1. each of the special faculties by which man and other animals perceive external objects and their own bodily changes (sight, hearing, smell, taste, and touch). 2. a feeling produced through the organs of touch, taste, etc. 3. a faculty or function of the mind or soul. 4. any special capacity for perception, estimation, appreciation, etc. 5. (*usually pl.*) sound mental faculties. 6. any more or less vague perception or impression. 7. the recognition of something as incumbent or fitting. 8. sound practical intelligence. 9. what is sensible. 10. the meaning, or one of the meanings, of a word, group of words, or a passage. —*v.t.* 11. to perceive by the senses.

sense·less (sĕns'lĭs), *adj.* 1. unconscious. 2. stupid or foolish. 3. nonsensical or meaningless. —**sense'less·ly,** *adv.* —**sense'less·ness,** *n.*

sen·si·bil·i·ty (sĕn'sə bĭl'ə tĭ), *n., pl.* **-ties.** 1. capacity for sensation or feeling. 2. mental susceptibility or responsiveness. 3. keen consciousness or appreciation. 4. (*pl.*) emotional capacities. 5. (*sing. or pl.*) sensitive feelings. 6. capacity for refined feelings.

sen·si·ble (sĕn'sə bəl), *adj.* 1. having, using, or showing good judgment. 2. cognizant; aware. 3. considerable. 4. capable of perceiving or being perceived by the senses. 5. conscious. —**sen'si·ble·ness,** *n.* —**sen'si·bly,** *adv.*

sen·si·tive (sĕn'sə tĭv), *adj.* 1. endowed with sensation. 2. readily affected by external agencies or influences. 3. easily affected, pained, annoyed, etc. —**sen'si·tive·ly,** *adv.* —**sen'si·tive·ness,** *n.*

sen·si·tiv·i·ty (sĕn'sə tĭv'ə tĭ), *n., pl.* **-ties.** 1. state or quality of being sensitive. 2. *Radio.* the ability to react to incoming radio waves.

sen·si·tize (sĕn'sə tīz'), *v.t.,* **-tized, -tizing.** 1. to render sensitive. 2. to render sensitive to a serum by a series of injections. —**sen'si·ti·za'·tion,** *n.* —**sen'si·tiz'er,** *n.*

sen·so·ri·um (sĕn sōr'ĭ əm), *n., pl.* **-soriums, -soria** (-sōr'ĭ ə). *Anat.* the supposed seat of sensation in the brain.

sen·so·ry (sĕn'sə rĭ), *adj.* pertaining to sensation or to the senses.

sen·su·al (sĕn'shŏŏ əl), *adj.* 1. excessively inclined to the gratification of the senses. 2. lewd or unchaste. 3. of or pertaining to the senses or physical sensation. —**sen'su·al·ism',** *n.* —**sen'·su·al·ist,** *n.* —**sen·su·al·i·ty** (sĕn'shŏŏ ăl'ə tĭ), *n.* —**sen'su·al·ly,** *adv.*

sen·su·ous (sĕn'shŏŏ əs), *adj.* 1. of or pertaining to the senses. 2. perceived by or affecting the senses. 3. readily affected through the senses. —**sen'su·ous·ly,** *adv.* —**sen'su·ous·ness,** *n.*

sen·tence (sĕn'təns), *n., v.,* **-tenced, -tencing.** —*n.* 1. a word or sequence of grammatically linked words which is not part of any larger construction, typically expressing an independent statement, inquiry, command, or the like. 2. an opinion pronounced on some particular question. 3. *Law.* a. a judicial judgment or decree. b. punishment. —*v.t.* 4. to pronounce sentence upon.

sen·ten·tious (sĕn tĕn'shəs), *adj.* 1. full of pithy sayings or maxims. 2. affectedly judicial or magisterial. 3. using pithy sayings or maxims. 4. of the nature of a maxim; pithy. —**sen·ten'·tious·ly,** *adv.* —**sen·ten'tious·ness,** *n.*

sen·tient (sĕn'shənt), *adj.* 1. that feels. 2. characterized by sensation. —*n.* 3. one that is sentient. —**sen'tience,** *n.*

sen·ti·ment (sĕn'tə mənt), *n.* 1. mental attitude with regard to something; opinion. 2. a mental feeling; emotion. 3. refined or tender emotion. 4. a thought influenced by or proceeding from feeling or emotion.

sen·ti·men·tal (sĕn'tə mĕn'təl), *adj.* 1. expressive of or appealing to the tender emotions.

2. pertaining to or dependent on sentiment. 3. weakly emotional; tender. 4. characterized by or showing sentiment or refined feeling. —**sen'·ti·men'tal·ism',** *n.* —**sen'ti·men'tal·ist,** *n.* —**sen·ti·men·tal·i·ty** (sĕn'tə mĕn tăl'ə tĭ), *n.* —**sen'ti·men·tal·ize,** *v.t., v.i.* —**sen'ti·men'·tal·ly,** *adv.*

sen·ti·nel (sĕn'tə nəl), *n., v.,* **-neled, -neling** or (*esp. Brit.*) **-nelled, -nelling.** —*n.* 1. one that watches. 2. a soldier stationed as a guard to challenge all comers and prevent a surprise attack. —*v.t.* 3. to watch over or guard as a sentinel.

sen·try (sĕn'trĭ), *n., pl.* **-tries.** a soldier stationed at a place to keep guard and prevent the passage of unauthorized persons, watch for fires, etc.

Se·oul (sä'ōōl'), *n.* the capital of Korea, in the W part. 774,000.

Sep., September.

se·pal (sē'pəl), *n. Bot.* each of the individual leaves or parts of the calyx of a flower.

sep·a·ra·ble (sĕp'ə rə bəl), *adj.* capable of being separated. —**sep'a·ra·bil'i·ty,** *n.* —**sep'a·ra·bly,** *adv.*

sep·a·rate (*v.* sĕp'ə rāt'; *adj.* sĕp'ə rĭt), *v.,* **-rated, -rating,** *adj.* —*v.t.* 1. to keep or put apart; divide. 2. to disconnect; disunite. 3. to remove from personal association. —*v.i.* 4. to part company. 5. to come apart; become disconnected or disengaged. —*adj.* 6. separated, disconnected, or disjoined. 7. unconnected or distinct. 8. being or standing apart. —**sep'a·rate·ly,** *adv.* —**sep·a·ra·tive** (sĕp'ə rā'tĭv), *adj.*

sep·a·ra·tion (sĕp'ə rā'shən), *n.* 1. act of separating. 2. state of being separated. 3. *Law.* a. a limited divorce. b. cessation of conjugal cohabitation, as by mutual consent.

sep·a·ra·tist (sĕp'ə rā'tĭst), *n.* one who separates, withdraws, or secedes, as from an established church.

sep·a·ra·tor (sĕp'ə rā'tər), *n.* 1. one that separates. 2. an apparatus for separating one thing from another, as cream from milk, etc.

se·pi·a (sē'pĭ ə), *n.* 1. a brown pigment obtained from the inklike secretion of various cuttlefish: used with brush or pen in drawing. 2. a dark brown. —*adj.* 3. of a brown similar to that from sepia ink.

sep·sis (sĕp'sĭs), *n. Pathol.* local or generalized bacterial invasion of the body.

Sept., September.

Sep·tem·ber (sĕp tĕm'bər), *n.* the ninth month of the year, containing 30 days.

sep·tet (sĕp tĕt'), *n.* 1. any group of seven persons or things. 2. a musical composition for seven voices or instruments.

sep·tic (sĕp'tĭk), *adj.* 1. infective, usually with a pus-forming microbe. 2. infected. —*n.* 3. an agent which causes sepsis. —**sep·tic·i·ty** (sĕp-tĭs'ə tĭ), *n.*

sep·ti·ce·mi·a (sĕp'tə sē'mĭ ə), *n. Pathol.* the invasion and persistence of pathogenic bacteria in the blood stream.

septic tank, a tank in which solid organic sewage is decomposed and purified by anaerobic bacteria.

sep·tu·a·ge·nar·i·an (sĕp'chŏŏ ə jə när'ĭ ən), *adj.* 1. of the age of 70 years, or between 70 and 80 years old. —*n.* 2. a septuagenarian person. Also, **sep·tu·ag·e·nar·y** (sĕp'chŏŏ ăj'ə nĕr'ĭ).

sep·tu·ple (sĕp'tyŏŏ pəl, -tŏŏ-, sĕp tū'pəl, -tŏŏ'-), *adj., v.,* **-pled, -pling.** —*adj.* 1. seven times as great. —*v.t.* 2. to make seven times as great.

sep·ul·cher (sĕp'əl kər), *n.* 1. a tomb, grave, or burial place. —*v.t.* 2. to bury. Also, *esp. Brit.,* **sep'ul·chre.**

se·pul·chral (sə pŭl'krəl), *adj.* 1. of, pertaining to, or serving as a tomb. 2. of or pertaining to burial. 3. funereal or dismal. 4. hollow and deep.

seq., (L *sequens*) the following (one).

se·quel (sē'kwəl), *n.* 1. a literary work, complete in itself, but continuing a preceding work. 2. a subsequent event or circumstance. 3. a result, consequence, or inference.

se·quence (sē'kwəns), *n.* 1. the following of one thing after another; succession. 2. a series. 3. a result; consequence. 4. *Motion Pictures.* a portion of a film story set in the same place and time.

se·ques·ter (sĭ kwĕs'tər), *v.t.* 1. to remove or withdraw into solitude; seclude. 2. *Law.* to seize and hold, as the property and income of a debtor, until legal claims are satisfied. **—se-ques·tra·tion** (sē/kwĕs trā/shən, sĭ kwĕs/-), *n.*

se·quin (sē/kwĭn), *n.* a small spangle used to ornament a dress, etc.

se·quoi·a (sĭ kwoi/ə), *n.* either of two related, extremely large coniferous trees in California (the big tree and redwood).

ser., 1. series. 2. sermon.

se·rag·li·o (sĭ răl/yō, -räl/-), *n., pl.* **-raglios.** a harem.

se·ra·pe (sĕ rä/pĕ), *n.* a kind of shawl worn by Spanish-Americans.

ser·aph (sĕr/əf), *n., pl.* **-aphs, -aphim** (-ə fĭm). a member of the highest order of angels. **—se·raph·ic** (sĭ răf/ĭk), **se·raph/i·cal,** *adj.*

Ser·bi·a (sûr/bĭ ə), *n.* a constituent republic of Yugoslavia, in the SE part. ab. 2,300,000 pop.; ab. 33,500 sq. mi. *Cap.:* Niš. **—Ser/bi·an, Serb,** *adj., n.*

sere (sĭr), *adj.* dry; withered.

ser·e·nade (sĕr/ə nād/), *n., v.,* **-naded, -nad·ing.** *—n.* 1. a complimentary performance of music in the open air at night, as by a lover under the window of his lady. 2. a piece of music suitable for such performance. *—v.t., v.i.* 3. to entertain with or perform a serenade. **—ser/e·nad/-er,** *n.*

se·rene (sə rēn/), *adj.* 1. calm; tranquil. 2. clear; fair. **—se·rene/ly,** *adv.* **—se·rene/ness, se·ren·i·ty** (sə rĕn/ə tĭ), *n.*

serf (sûrf), *n.* a person in a condition of servitude, commonly attached to his lord's land and transferred with it from one owner to another. **—serf/dom,** *n.*

serge (sûrj), *n.* a twilled (usually woolen) fabric used esp. for clothing.

ser·geant (sär/jənt), *n.* 1. a noncommissioned army officer of rank above that of corporal. 2. a police officer of higher rank than a common policeman. **—ser·gean·cy** (sär/jən sĭ), *n.*

sergeant at arms, an executive officer of a legislative or other body, whose duty it is to enforce order, etc.

se·ri·al (sĭr/ĭ əl), *n.* 1. anything published, broadcast, etc., in short installments at regular intervals. *—adj.* 2. published in installments. 3. of, pertaining to, or arranged in a series. **—se/ri·al·ly,** *adv.*

se·ries (sĭr/ĭz), *n., pl.* **-ries.** 1. a number of things, events, etc., in succession; sequence. 2. *Math.* the sum of the terms of a sequence of entities. 3. *Rhet.* a succession of coördinate sentence elements. 4. **in series,** *Elect.* with the positive pole, terminal, or the like, of one, joined to the negative of the next (of batteries, etc.).

ser·if (sĕr/ĭf), *n. Print.* a smaller line used to finish off a main stroke of a letter.

se·ri·o·com·ic (sĭr/ĭ ō kŏm/ĭk), *adj.* partly serious and partly comic.

se·ri·ous (sĭr/ĭ əs), *adj.* 1. of grave or solemn character. 2. weighty or important. 3. critical. **—se/ri·ous·ly,** *adv.* **—se/ri·ous·ness,** *n.*

ser·mon (sûr/mən), *n.* a discourse for the purpose of religious instruction or exhortation.

se·rous (sĭr/əs), *adj.* 1. watery. 2. resembling, containing, or secreting serum.

ser·pent (sûr/pənt), *n.* 1. a snake. 2. a wily, treacherous, or malicious person.

ser·pen·tine (sûr/pən tēn/, -tīn/), *adj.* 1. of or pertaining to a serpent. 2. winding; tortuous. 3. subtle, wily, or cunning.

ser·rate (sĕr/ĭt, -āt), *adj. Chiefly Biol.* having sharp teeth. Also, **ser·rat·ed** (sĕr/ā tĭd).

ser·ra·tion (sĕ rā/shən), *n.* 1. serrated form. 2. a serrated edge. 3. one of the notches of such an edge.

se·rum (sĭr/əm), *n., pl.* **serums, sera** (sĭr/ə). 1. the pale-yellow liquid which separates from the clot in the coagulation of blood. 2. a fluid of this kind obtained from the blood of an animal which has been rendered immune to some disease by inoculation, used as an antitoxic or therapeutic agent.

serv·ant (sûr/vənt), *n.* 1. a person employed in domestic duties. 2. a person in the service of government.

serve (sûrv), *v.,* **served, serving,** *n.* *—v.i.* 1. to act as a servant. 2. to bring food to guests. 3. to help. 4. to do duty as a soldier, congressman, juror, etc. 5. to have definite use. 6. to answer the purpose. 7. *Tennis, etc.* to put the ball in play. *—v.t.* 8. to work for. 9. to help. 10. to go through (a term of service, imprisonment, etc.). 11. to render service to (a king, etc.). 12. to

render obedience or homage to (God, etc.). 13. to perform the duties of (an office, etc.). 14. to be useful to. 15. to suffice. 16. to promote. 17. to set food before. 18. to set (food) on a table. 19. to treat in a specified manner. 20. to gratify (desire, etc.). 21. *Tennis, etc.* to put (the ball) in play. 22. *Law.* to make legal delivery of (a process or writ). *—n.* 23. act, manner, or right of serving. **—serv/er,** *n.*

serv·ice (sûr/vĭs), *n., adj., v.,* **-viced, -vicing.** *—n.* 1. an act of helpful activity. 2. the supplying of articles, activities, etc., required. 3. occupation or employment as a servant. 4. employment in any duties or work for another, a government, etc. 5. a department of public employment, or the body of public servants in it. 6. *Mil.* **a.** the armed forces. **b.** period or duration of active service. 7. public religious worship. 8. a ritual prescribed for public worship or for some particular occasion. 9. a musical setting of the sung portions of a liturgy. 10. a set of dishes, utensils, etc., for a particular use. 11. *Law.* the serving of a process or writ upon a person. 12. *Tennis, etc.* **a.** act or manner of putting the ball in play. **b.** the ball as put in play. *—adj.* 13. useful. *—v.t.* 14. to restore to condition for service.

serv·ice·a·ble (sûr/vĭs ə bəl), *adj.* 1. useful. 2. durable. **—serv/ice·a·bil/i·ty, serv/ice·a·ble·ness,** *n.* **—serv/ice·a·bly,** *adv.*

serv·ice·man (sûr/vĭs măn/), *n., pl.* **-men.** a member of the army, navy, or air force.

serv·i·ette (sûr/vĭ ĕt/), *n.* a napkin.

ser·vile (sûr/vĭl), *adj.* 1. slavishly submissive or obsequious. 2. abject. **—ser/vile·ly,** *adv.* **—ser·vil/i·ty,** **ser/vile·ness,** *n.*

ser·vi·tor (sûr/və tər), *n.* one who is in the service of another; attendant.

ser·vi·tude (sûr/və tĭd/, -tōōd/), *n.* 1. slavery; bondage. 2. compulsory labor as a punishment for criminals.

ses·a·me (sĕs/ə mĭ), *n.* 1. a tropical herbaceous plant whose small oval seeds are edible and yield an oil. 2. the seeds themselves.

ses·qui·cen·ten·ni·al (sĕs/kwĭ sĕn tĕn/ĭ əl), *adj.* 1. pertaining to or marking the completion of 150 years. *—n.* 2. a 150th anniversary, or its celebration.

ses·sion (sĕsh/ən), *n.* 1. the sitting together of a court, council, legislature, or the like, for conference or the transaction of business. 2. a single continuous sitting, or period of sitting, of persons so assembled. 3. a single period of lessons, study, etc., at school. **—ses/sion·al,** *adj.*

set (sĕt), *v.,* **set, setting,** *n., adj.* *—v.t.* 1. to put or place. 2. to put into some condition or relation. 3. to put (a price or value) upon something. 4. to station or appoint. 5. to fix or ordain. 6. to present for others to follow. 7. to prescribe or assign. 8. to adjust or arrange. 9. to fix or mount (a gem, etc.) in gold or the like. 10. to adorn with precious stones. 11. to give an account of. 12. *Surg.* to put (a broken or dislocated bone) back in position. 13. *Music.* to fit, as words to music. 14. to spread (sails) so as to catch the wind. 15. *Print.* **a.** to arrange (type) in the order required for printing. **b.** to put together types corresponding to (copy). 16. to cause to become firm or hard. 17. to cause to be hostile. *—v.i.* 18. to pass below the horizon; sink. 19. to decline. 20. to assume a fixed or rigid state. 21. to become firm or solid. 22. to sit on eggs, as a hen. 23. to fit, as clothes. 24. to begin to move; start. 25. **set about,** to start. 26. **set aside, a.** to put to one side. **b.** to discard. **c.** to annul or quash. 27. **set back,** to hinder; stop. 28. **set down, a.** to put down in writing or printing. **b.** to consider. **c.** to attribute. 29. **set in,** to begin. 30. **set off, a.** to explode. **b.** to start. **c.** to intensify by contrast. 31. **set up,** to start in business, etc. *—n.* 32. a complete assortment, outfit, or collection. 33. a group of persons associating or classed together. 34. the fit. 35. fixed direction, as of the mind, etc. 36. bearing or carriage. 37. a radio receiving apparatus. 38. *Tennis, etc.* a group of games counting as one of the units of a match. 39. *Theat.* a construction representing a place in which action takes place. 40. *Hort.* a young plant, or a slip, tuber, or the like, suitable for planting. 41. *Naut.* **a.** the direction of a wind, current, etc. **b.** the fit and shape of sails. *—adj.* 42. fixed or prescribed beforehand. 43. customary. 44. fixed; rigid. 45. resolved or determined.

set·back (sĕt/băk/), *n.* 1. a check to progress; reverse. 2. *Archit.* a recession at a particular height in a tall building.

Seth (sĕth), *n.* the third son of Adam.

set·tee (sĕ tē′), *n.* a seat for two or more persons, with a back and (usually) arms.

set·ter (sĕt′ər), *n.* **1.** one who sets. **2.** one of a breed of long-haired hunting dogs trained to stand stiffly and point the muzzle toward the scented game.

set·ting (sĕt′ĭng), *n.* **1.** act of one that sets. **2.** surroundings or environment. **3.** that in which something, as a jewel, is set or mounted. **4.** the scenery, etc., of a play. **5.** *Music.* a piece of music composed for certain words.

set·tle[1] (sĕt′əl), *v.,* -tled, -tling. —*v.t.* **1.** to fix definitely; agree upon. **2.** to place in a desired position or order. **3.** to pay (a bill, etc.). **4.** to close (an account) by payment. **5.** to take up residence in. **6.** to cause to take up residence. **7.** to furnish (a place) with inhabitants. **8.** to establish in a way of life, a business, etc. **9.** to quiet (the nerves, stomach, etc.). **10.** to place on a permanent basis. **11.** to cause (a liquid) to deposit dregs. **12.** to cause (dregs, etc.) to sink. **13.** to cause to sink gradually. **14.** to dispose of finally. —*v.i.* **15.** to decide; arrange. **16.** to come to an agreement. **17.** to pay. **18.** to take up residence in a new country or place. **19.** to come to rest. **20.** to become calm or composed. **21.** to set oneself to a regular way of life. **22.** to sink gradually. **23.** to become clear by the sinking of particles, as a liquid. **24.** to sink to the bottom, as sediment. **25.** to become firm or compact. —**set′tler,** *n.*

set·tle[2] (sĕt′əl), *n.* *Chiefly Brit.* a long bench with arms and high back.

set·tle·ment (sĕt′əl mənt), *n.* **1.** act of settling. **2.** state of being settled. **3.** a colony, esp. in its early stages. **4.** a welfare establishment in an underprivileged area providing various facilities for the people in the area.

set-to (sĕt′tōō′), *n., pl.* -tos. *Colloq.* a fight.

set·up (sĕt′ŭp′), *n.* **1.** organization; arrangement. **2.** ice, soda water, etc., for mixing drinks. **3.** *U.S. Slang.* a match or game arranged with an easily defeated opponent.

Se·vas·to·pol (sĭ văs′tə pōl′), *n.* a fortified seaport in the SW Soviet Union. 111,946.

sev·en (sĕv′ən), *n.* **1.** a cardinal number, six plus one. **2.** a symbol for this number, as 7 or VII. **3.** a set of seven persons or things. —*adj.* **4.** amounting to seven in number.

sev·en·fold (sĕv′ən fōld′), *adj.* **1.** seven times as much. —*adv.* **2.** in sevenfold measure.

sev·en·teen (sĕv′ən tēn′), *n.* **1.** a cardinal number, ten plus seven. **2.** a symbol for this number, as 17 or XVII. **3.** amounting to seventeen in number. —**sev′en·teenth′,** *adj., n.*

sev·enth (sĕv′ənth), *adj.* **1.** next after the sixth. **2.** being one of seven equal parts. —*n.* **3.** a seventh part, esp. of one (¹/₇). **4.** the seventh member of a series.

sev·en·ty (sĕv′ən tĭ), *n., pl.* -ties, *adj.* —*n.* **1.** a cardinal number, ten times seven. **2.** a symbol for this number, as 70 or LXX. —*adj.* **3.** amounting to seventy in number. —**sev·en·ti·eth** (sĕv′ən tĭ ĭth), *adj., n.*

sev·er (sĕv′ər), *v.t., v.i.* **1.** to separate. **2.** to divide into parts, esp. forcibly; cut. **3.** to break off (relations, etc.). —**sev′er·a·ble,** *adj.*

sev·er·al (sĕv′ər əl), *adj.* **1.** being more than two or three, but not many. **2.** respective; individual. **3.** separate; different. **4.** single; particular. **5.** various. —*n.* **6.** a few; some. —**sev′er·al·ly,** *adv.*

sev·er·ance (sĕv′ər əns), *n.* **1.** act of severing. **2.** state of being severed.

se·vere (sĭ vĭr′), *adj.,* -verer, -verest. **1.** harsh. **2.** serious; stern. **3.** grave. **4.** rigidly simple; plain. **5.** unpleasantly violent, as wind, a blow, etc. **6.** hard to endure, perform, fulfill, etc. **7.** rigidly exact, accurate, or methodical. —**se·vere′ly,** *adv.* —**se·vere′ness,** **se·ver·i·ty** (sĭ vĕr′ə tĭ), *n.*

Sev·ern (sĕv′ərn), *n.* a river flowing from central Wales through W England into the Bristol Channel. ab. 210 mi.

Se·ville (sə vĭl′, sĕv′ĭl), *n.* a city in SW Spain. 348,000.

sew (sō), *v.t., v.i.,* sewed, sewed or sewn, sewing. **1.** to join or attach by a thread or the like, as with a needle. **2.** to make, repair, etc., (a garment) by this means. —**sew′er,** *n.*

sew·age (sōō′ĭj), *n.* the waste matter which passes through sewers.

sew·er (sōō′ər), *n.* an artificial conduit, usually

underground, for carrying off waste water and refuse, as from a city.

sew·er·age (sōō′ər ĭj), *n.* **1.** the removal of waste water and refuse by means of sewers. **2.** sewage.

sew·ing (sō′ĭng), *n.* **1.** act or work of one who sews. **2.** something sewed or to be sewed.

sex (sĕks), *n.* **1.** the character of being either male or female. **2.** the sum of the anatomical and physiological differences with reference to which the male and the female are distinguished. —**sex′less,** *adj.*

sex·a·ge·nar·i·an (sĕk′sə jə när′ĭ ən), *adj.* **1.** of the age of 60 years, or between 60 and 70 years old. —*n.* **2.** a sexagenarian person. Also, **sex·ag·e·nar·y** (sĕks ăj′ə nĕr′ĭ).

sex appeal, the quality which attracts the opposite sex.

sex·tant (sĕks′tənt), *n.* an astronomical instrument used in measuring angular distances, esp. the altitudes of sun, moon, and stars at sea in determining latitude and longitude.

sex·tet (sĕks tĕt′), *n.* **1.** any group or set of six. **2.** a musical composition for six voices or instruments.

sex·ton (sĕks′tən), *n.* an official of a church charged with taking care of the edifice, ringing its bell, etc.

sex·tu·ple (sĕks′tyŏŏ pəl, -tŏŏ-, sĕks tū′pəl, -tōō′-), *adj., v.,* -pled, -pling. —*adj.* **1.** six times as great. **2.** *Music.* characterized by six beats to the measure. —*v.t., v.i.* **3.** to make or become six times as great.

sex·tu·plet (sĕks′tyŏŏ plĭt, -tŏŏ-, sĕks tū′plĭt, -tōō′-), *n.* one of six children born at one birth.

sex·u·al (sĕk′shŏŏ əl), *adj.* **1.** of or pertaining to sex. **2.** occurring between or involving the two sexes. **3.** having sex or sexual organs. —**sex′u·al·ly,** *adv.*

sex·y (sĕk′sĭ), *adj.,* sexier, sexiest. *Slang.* **1.** sexually attractive. **2.** excessively concerned with sex.

Sfor·za (sfôr′tsä), *n.* **Count Carlo,** 1873–1952, Italian statesman.

Sgt., Sergeant.

shab·by (shăb′ĭ), *adj.,* -bier, -biest. **1.** having the appearance impaired by wear, use, etc. **2.** wearing worn clothes; seedy. **3.** mean; contemptible. —**shab′bi·ly,** *adv.* —**shab′bi·ness,** *n.*

shack (shăk), *n.* *U.S. and Canadian Colloq.* a rough cabin; shanty.

shack·le (shăk′əl), *n., v.,* -led, -ling. —*n.* **1.** a fastening of iron or the like for the wrist, ankle, etc.; fetter. **2.** anything that prevents freedom of procedure, thought, etc. —*v.t.* **3.** to put a shackle on; confine or restrain. —**shack′ler,** *n.*

shad (shăd), *n., pl.* shad, *(for different species)* **shads.** a deep-bodied herring that runs up streams to spawn; valued as a food fish.

shad·bush (shăd′bŏŏsh′), *n.* a shrub or small tree with white flowers and a berrylike fruit **(shadberry),** which blossoms about the time shad appear in the rivers.

shade (shād), *n., v.,* shaded, shading. —*n.* **1.** the comparative darkness caused by the interception of rays of light. **2.** an area of comparative darkness. **3.** (*pl.*) darkness at the close of day. **4.** (*chiefly pl.*) a retired place. **5.** comparative obscurity. **6.** a specter or ghost. **7.** *Class. Myth.* **a.** an inhabitant of Hades. **b.** (*pl.*) the spirits of the dead collectively. **c.** Hades. **8.** degree of darkening of a color by adding black or by decreasing the illumination. **9.** a slight variation, amount, or degree. **10.** something used for protection against excessive light, heat, etc. —*v.t.* **11.** to produce shade in or on. **12.** to obscure, dim, or darken. **13.** to hide from view. **14.** to protect (something) from light, heat, etc., as by a screen. —*v.i.* **15.** to change by slight graduations. —**shade′less,** *adj.*

shad·ing (shā′dĭng), *n.* **1.** a slight variation or difference of color, character, etc. **2.** the representation of the different values in a painting or drawing.

shad·ow (shăd′ō), *n.* **1.** a dark image cast on the ground or some surface by a body intercepting light. **2.** comparative darkness. **3.** (*pl.*) darkness coming after sunset. **4.** shelter. **5.** a trace. **6.** a specter or ghost. **7.** a shadowy image. **8.** a mere semblance. **9.** the dark part of a picture. **10.** a cloud, as on reputation. **11.** an inseparable companion. **12.** one who watches another, as a detective. —*v.t.* **13.** to shade. **14.**

to cast a gloom over. **15.** to screen or protect from light, heat, etc. **16.** to follow (a person) in order to keep watch over his movements. —shad′ow·er, *n.* —shad′ow·less, *adj.*

shad·ow·y (shăd′ō ĭ), *adj.* **1.** dim, unsubstantial, or unreal. **2.** shady.

shad·y (shā′dĭ), *adj.*, **shadier, shadiest. 1.** abounding in shade. **2.** giving shade. **3.** indistinct; spectral. **4.** *Colloq.* uncertain; questionable. —shad′i·ly, *adv.* —shad′i·ness, *n.*

SHAEF, Supreme Headquarters Allied Expeditionary Forces. Also, **Shaef** (shāf).

shaft (shăft, shäft), *n.* **1.** the long, slender rod forming the body of a spear or of an arrow. **2.** something directed as in sharp attack. **3.** a ray or beam. **4.** the handle of a hammer, ax, golf club, or other long implement. **5.** a revolving bar serving to transmit motion, as from an engine. **6.** the body of a column between the base and the capital. **7.** either of the parallel bars of wood between which the animal drawing a vehicle is placed. **8.** any vertical space, as in a building or mine.

shag (shăg), *n., v.,* **shagged, shagging. —n. 1.** rough, matted hair, wool, or the like. **2.** a mass of this. **3.** a cloth with a nap. **4.** a coarse tobacco cut into fine shreds. —*v.t.* **5.** to make rough or shaggy.

shag·gy (shăg′ĭ), *adj.,* **-gier, -giest. 1.** covered with or having long, rough hair. **2.** unkempt. **3.** rough and matted. **4.** having a rough nap. —shag′gi·ness, *n.*

shah (shä), *n.* king: esp. used (*usually cap.*) as a title of the ruler of Persia.

shake (shāk), *v.,* **shook, shaken, shaking,** *n.* —*v.i., v.t.* **1.** to move or sway with short, quick, irregular vibratory movements. **2.** to tremble with emotion, cold, etc. **3.** to fall (*down, off,* etc.) by such motion. **4.** to totter. **5.** *Music.* to trill. **6.** to brandish. **7.** to cause to quiver or tremble. **8.** to cause to totter or wave. **9.** to agitate or disturb profoundly in feeling. **10.** to unsettle. **11.** *Slang.* to get rid of. —*n.* **12.** act of shaking. **13.** tremulous motion. **14.** a tremor. **15.** *Music.* a trill. **16.** a drink made by shaking ingredients together. **17.** *Slang.* an instant. —shak′er, *n.*

Shake·speare (shāk′spĭr), *n.* William, 1564–1616, British poet and dramatist. Also, **Shak′spere, Shak′speare.** —Shake·spear′i·an, **Shake·spear′e·an,** *adj.*

shake-up (shāk′ŭp′), *n.* a thorough change in a business, department, or the like.

shak·o (shăk′ō), *n., pl.* **-os.** a military cap in the form of a cylinder with a visor and a plume.

shak·y (shā′kĭ), *adj.,* **shakier, shakiest. 1.** shaking. **2.** trembling. **3.** insecure. **4.** wavering. —shak′i·ly, *adv.* —shak′i·ness, *n.*

shale (shāl), *n.* a rock of laminated structure formed by the consolidation of clay, etc.

shall (shăl; *unstressed* shəl), *v.t.* **1.** (used, generally, in the first person to indicate simple future time). **2.** (used, generally, in the second and third persons to indicate promise or determination). **3.** (used interrogatively, in questions that admit of *shall* in the answer). **4.** (used conditionally, in all persons to indicate future time).

shal·lot (shə lŏt′), *n.* **1.** a plant of the lily family whose bulb forms bulblets which are used for flavoring in cookery and as a vegetable. **2.** the bulb.

shal·low (shăl′ō), *adj.* **1.** not deep. **2.** superficial. —*n.* **3.** a shallow part of a body of water. —*v.t., v.i.* **4.** to make or become shallow. —shal′low·ly, *adv.* —shal′low·ness, *n.*

shalt (shălt), *v. Poetic.* 2nd pers. sing of **shall.**

sham (shăm), *n., adj., v.,* **shammed, shamming.** —*n.* **1.** a spurious imitation. —*adj.* **2.** pretended; counterfeit. —*v.t., v.i.* **3.** to produce an imitation or pretense (of).

sham·ble[1] (shăm′bəl), *n.* (*pl. often construed as sing.*) **1.** a scene of disorder and confusion. **2.** a slaughter house. **3.** any place of carnage.

sham·ble[2] (shăm′bəl), *v.,* **-bled, -bling,** *n.* —*v.i.* **1.** to walk awkwardly. —*n.* **2.** a shambling gait.

shame (shām), *n., v.,* **shamed, shaming.** —*n.* **1.** the painful feeling arising from the consciousness of something dishonorable, improper, ridiculous, etc. **2.** disgrace; ignominy. —*v.t.* **3.** to cause to feel shame. **4.** to drive, force, etc., through shame.

shame·faced (shām′fāst′), *adj.* **1.** modest or bashful. **2.** showing shame.

shame·ful (shām′fəl), *adj.* **1.** that causes shame. **2.** disgraceful or scandalous. —shame′ful·ly, *adv.* —shame′ful·ness, *n.*

shame·less (shām′lĭs), *adj.* **1.** immodest; audacious. **2.** insensible to disgrace. **3.** showing no shame. —shame′less·ly, *adv.* —shame′less·ness, *n.*

sham·poo (shăm poo′), *v.,* **-pooed, -pooing,** *n.* —*v.t.* **1.** to wash (the head or hair). —*n.* **2.** act of shampooing. **3.** a preparation used for shampooing.

sham·rock (shăm′rŏk), *n.* a plant with trifoliate leaves, taken as the national emblem of Ireland.

Shang·hai (shăng′hī′), *n.* a seaport in E China, near the mouth of the Yangtze. 3,700,000.

shang·hai (shăng′hī, shăng hī′), *v.t.,* **-haied, -haiing.** *Naut.* to render insensible, as by drugs, in order to ship forcibly on a vessel needing sailors.

Shan·gri·la (shăng′grə lä′), *n.* a paradise on earth.

shank (shăngk), *n.* **1.** that part of the leg in man between the knee and the ankle. **2.** a corresponding part in certain animals. **3.** the whole leg. **4.** that portion of an instrument, tool, etc., connecting the acting part with the handle.

Shan·non (shăn′ən), *n.* a river flowing from N Ireland SW to the Atlantic. ab. 240 mi.

shan·tung (shăn′tŭng′), *n.* a silk fabric, a heavy variety of pongee made of rough, spun wild silk.

shan·ty[1] (shăn′tĭ), *n., pl.* **-ties.** a roughly built hut, cabin, or house.

shan·ty[2] (shăn′tĭ), *n., pl.* **-ties.** chantey.

shape (shāp), *n., v.,* **shaped, shaping.** —*n.* **1.** the quality of a thing depending on its external surface. **2.** the form of a particular thing, person, or being. **3.** a phantom. **4.** guise. **5.** a definite form or nature. **6.** condition. **7.** something used to give form. —*v.t.* **8.** to give definite form or character to. **9.** to adjust; adapt. —*v.i.* **10.** to take shape or form. **11.** to come out. —shap′er, *n.*

shape·less (shāp′lĭs), *adj.* having no definite or regular shape. —shape′less·ly, *adv.* —shape′less·ness, *n.*

shape·ly (shāp′lĭ), *adj.,* **-lier, -liest.** having a pleasing shape. —shape′li·ness, *n.*

shard (shärd), *n.* a fragment, esp. of broken earthenware.

share (shâr), *n., v.,* **shared, sharing.** —*n.* **1.** the portion or part allotted or belonging to, or contributed or owed by, an individual or group. **2.** one of the equal parts into which the capital stock of a joint-stock company or a corporation is divided. —*v.t.* **3.** to divide and distribute in shares. **4.** to use, enjoy, etc., jointly. —*v.i.* **5.** to have a share or part. —shar′er, *n.*

share·crop·per (shâr′krŏp′ər), *n.* a tenant farmer who pays as rent a share of the crop.

share·hold·er (shâr′hōl′dər), *n.* one who owns shares in a corporation.

shark[1] (shärk), *n.* any of a group of elongate elasmobranch (mostly marine) fishes, certain species of which are large and ferocious, destructive to other fishes and sometimes dangerous to man.

shark[2] (shärk), *n.* **1.** a person who preys greedily on others. **2.** *Slang.* one who has unusual ability in a particular field.

shark·skin (shärk′skĭn′), *n.* heavy rayon or wool suiting with a dull appearance.

sharp (shärp), *adj.* **1.** having a thin cutting edge or a fine point. **2.** not blunt or rounded. **3.** having sudden change of directions, as a turn. **4.** abrupt, as an ascent. **5.** distinct; marked. **6.** pungent or biting in taste. **7.** shrill. **8.** keenly cold. **9.** intensely painful. **10.** harsh. **11.** fierce or violent. **12.** vigilant. **13.** mentally acute. **14.** shrewd or astute. **15.** shrewd to the point of dishonesty. **16.** *Music.* **a.** above an intended pitch, as a note; too high. **b.** (of a tone) raised a half step in pitch. —*adv.* **17.** keenly or acutely. **18.** suddenly. **19.** punctually. **20.** vigilantly. —*n.* **21.** something sharp. **22.** a sharper. **23.** *Music.* **a.** a tone one half step above a given tone. **b.** the symbol (♯) indicating this. —sharp′ly, *adv.* —sharp′ness, *n.*

sharp·en (shär′pən), *v.t., v.i.* to make or become sharp. —sharp′en·er, *n.*

sharp·er (shär′pər), *n.* a swindler.

sharp·shoot·er (shärp′shoo′tər), *n.* one skilled in shooting, esp. with the rifle.

sharp-wit·ted (shärp/wĭt/ĭd), *adj.* clever or brilliant. —**sharp/-wit/ted·ness,** *n.*

Shas·ta (shăs/tə), *n.* **Mount,** a volcanic peak in N California. 14,161 ft.

shat·ter (shăt/ər), *v.t., v.i.* **1.** to break in pieces. **2.** to damage. **3.** to impair (health, nerves, etc.).

shave (shāv), *v.,* **shaved, shaved** or **shaven, shaving,** *n.* —*v.i.* **1.** to remove hair from (the face, legs, etc.) by cutting it close to the skin. **2.** to cut off (hair) close to the skin. **3.** to cut shavings or thin slices (from). —*n.* **4.** act or process of shaving. **5.** *Colloq.* a narrow escape. **6.** any of various tools for shaving, scraping, removing thin slices, etc.

shav·er (shā/vər), *n.* **1.** one that shaves. **2.** *Colloq.* a small child.

shave·tail (shāv/tāl/), *n.* *U.S. Army Slang.* a second lieutenant.

Sha·vi·an (shā/vĭ ən), *adj.* of or pertaining to George Bernard Shaw.

shav·ing (shā/vĭng), *n.* (*often pl.*) a very thin piece or slice, esp. of wood.

Shaw (shô), *n.* **George Bernard,** 1856–1950, Irish dramatist, critic, and novelist.

shawl (shôl), *n.* a piece of material worn about the shoulders, head, etc., chiefly by women.

Shaw·nee (shô nē/), *n.* a member of an Algonquian-speaking tribe formerly in the east central U.S., now in Oklahoma.

shay (shā), *n.* *Colloq.* a chaise.

she (shē), *pron., n., pl.* **shes.** —*pron.* **1.** the female in question or last mentioned. **2.** the woman. —*n.* **3.** a woman or female.

sheaf (shēf), *n., pl.* **sheaves,** *v.* —*n.* **1.** one of the bundles in which cereal plants, as wheat, rye, etc., are bound after reaping. **2.** any bundle. —*v.t.* **3.** to bind into a sheaf or sheaves.

shear (shĭr), *v.,* **sheared** or (*Archaic*) **shore; sheared** or **shorn; shearing;** *n.* —*v.t.* **1.** to cut with a sharp instrument. **2.** to remove by cutting with a sharp instrument. **3.** to cut the hair, fleece, wool, etc., from. **4.** to deprive. —*n.* **5.** act or process of shearing. —**shear/er,** *n.*

shears (shĭrz), *n.pl.* **1.** scissors of large size (often called a *pair of shears*). **2.** any of various other cutting implements or machines.

sheath (shēth), *n., pl.* **sheaths** (shēthz), *v.* —*n.* **1.** a case or covering for the blade of a sword, dagger, or the like. **2.** any similar covering. —*v.t.* **3.** to sheathe.

sheathe (shēth), *v.t.,* **sheathed, sheathing. 1.** to put (a sword, etc.) into a sheath. **2.** to enclose in a casing or covering.

She·ba (shē/bə) *n.* the Biblical name of an ancient country in S Arabia.

she·bang (shə băng/), *n.* *Slang.* affair.

She·boy·gan (shĭ boi/gən), *n.* a city in E Wisconsin. 40,638.

shed[1] (shĕd), *n.* **1.** a slight or rude structure built for shelter, storage, etc. **2.** a large, strongly built structure, often open at the sides or end.

shed[2] (shĕd), *v.t., v.i.,* **shed, shedding. 1.** to pour forth. **2.** to emit and let fall (tears). **3.** to let flow or cause to flow (blood). **4.** to cast (light, sound, etc.). **5.** to throw off readily. **6.** to cast off by natural process (leaves, hair, feathers, skin, shell, etc.).

sheen (shēn), *n.* luster; brightness.

sheep (shēp), *n., pl.* **sheep. 1.** any of certain ruminant mammals allied to the goats including many domesticated varieties or breeds, valuable for their flesh, fleece, etc. **2.** a meek, timid, or stupid person.

sheep·ish (shē/pĭsh), *adj.* **1.** awkwardly bashful or embarrassed. **2.** meek; timid. —**sheep/-ish·ly,** *adv.* —**sheep/ish·ness,** *n.*

sheep·shank (shēp/shăngk/), *n.* a kind of knot made to shorten a rope temporarily.

sheep·skin (shēp/skĭn/), *n.* **1.** the skin of a sheep. **2.** leather, parchment, or the like, made from the skin of sheep. **3.** *U.S. Colloq.* a diploma.

sheer[1] (shĭr), *adj.* **1.** transparently thin. **2.** unmixed with anything else. **3.** utter. **4.** steep. —*adv.* **5.** completely; quite. **6.** steeply. —**sheer/ly,** *adv.* —**sheer/ness,** *n.*

sheer[2] (shĭr), *v.i., v.t.* **1.** to deviate, or cause to deviate, from a course, as a ship; swerve. —*n.* **2.** a deviation, as of a ship from her course. **3.** the upward longitudinal curve of a ship's deck or bulwarks.

sheet[1] (shēt), *n.* a large rectangular piece of linen, cotton, or other material, used as an article of bedding. **2.** a broad, thin mass, layer, or covering. **3.** an oblong or square piece of paper or parchment.

sheet[2] (shēt), *n.* *Naut.* a rope or chain fastened to a sail to control its trim.

Shef·field (shĕf/ēld), *n.* a city in central England. 501,450.

sheik (shēk), *n.* **1.** (in Arab and other Mohammedan use) **a.** chief or head. **b.** the head of a religious body. **2.** *Slang.* a man of irresistible romantic charm. Also, **sheikh.**

shek·el (shĕk/əl), *n.* the chief silver coin of the ancient Hebrews.

shel·drake (shĕl/drāk/), *n., pl.* **-drakes,** (*esp. collectively*) **-drake. 1.** any of a genus of Old World ducks certain of which are highly variegated in color. **2.** the merganser.

shelf (shĕlf), *n., pl.* **shelves. 1.** a thin slab of wood or other material fixed horizontally to a wall, or in a frame, for supporting objects. **2.** a ledge.

shell (shĕl), *n., pl.* **shells. 1.** a hard outer covering of an animal, as the hard case of a mollusk. **2.** the hard exterior of an egg. **3.** a hard outer covering of a seed, fruit, or the like. **4.** a hollow projectile for a cannon, etc. **5.** a cartridge used in small arms and small artillery pieces. **6.** *Cookery.* the lower pastry crust, baked before the filling is added. **7.** a light, long, narrow racing boat rowed by means of outriggers. —*v.t.* **8.** to take out of the shell, pod, etc. **9.** to remove the shell of. **10.** to bombard. **11. shell out,** *Slang.* to pay up.

shel·lac (shə lăk/), *n., v.,* **-lacked, -lacking.** —*n.* **1.** lac which has been purified and formed into thin plates, used for making varnish. **2.** a varnish (**shellac varnish**) made by dissolving this material in alcohol or a similar solvent. —*v.t.* **3.** to coat with shellac. **4.** *U.S. Colloq.* to whip, defeat, or trounce.

Shel·ley (shĕl/ĭ), *n.* **1. Mary Wollstonecraft Godwin,** 1797–1851, British author: wife of Percy Bysshe Shelley. **2. Percy Bysshe,** 1792–1822, British poet.

shell·fire (shĕl/fīr/), *n.* *Mil.* the firing of explosive shells or projectiles.

shell·fish (shĕl/fĭsh/), *n., pl.* **-fishes,** (*esp. collectively*) **-fish.** an aquatic animal (not a fish in the ordinary sense) having a shell, as the oyster and lobster.

shell shock, *Psychiatry.* nervous or mental disorder characterized by loss of self-command, memory, speech, sight, or other powers.

shel·ter (shĕl/tər), *n.* **1.** a place of refuge or safety. —*v.t.* **2.** to afford shelter to. **3.** to provide with a shelter. **4.** to protect. —*v.i.* **5.** to take shelter. —**shel/ter·er,** *n.* —**shel/ter·less,** *adj.*

shelve[1] (shĕlv), *v.t.,* **shelved, shelving. 1.** to place on a shelf or shelves. **2.** to lay or put aside from consideration. **3.** to remove from active service. **4.** to furnish with shelves.

shelve[2] (shĕlv), *v.i.,* **shelved, shelving.** to slope gradually.

Shen·an·do·ah (shĕn/ən dō/ə), *n.* a river flowing through N Virginia NE to the Potomac at Harpers Ferry, West Virginia. ab. 200 mi.

she·nan·i·gan (shə năn/ə gən), *n.* *Colloq.* (*often pl.*) nonsense or mischief.

shep·herd (shĕp/ərd), *n.* **1.** a man who herds, tends, and guards sheep. **2.** a clergyman. **3. the Shepherd,** Jesus Christ. —*v.t.* **4.** to tend or guard as a shepherd. —**shep·herd·ess** (shĕp/ər-dĭs), *n. fem.*

Sher·a·ton (shĕr/ə tən), *n.* **Thomas,** 1751–1806, British furniture designer.

sher·bet (shûr/bət), *n.* a frozen fruit-flavored mixture containing milk, egg white, etc.

Sher·i·dan (shĕr/ə dən), *n.* **1. Philip Henry,** 1831–88, U.S. general. **2. Richard Brinsley,** 1751–1816, Irish dramatist.

sher·iff (shĕr/ĭf), *n.* the law enforcement officer of a county.

Sher·man (shûr/mən), *n.* **William Tecumseh,** 1820–91, U.S. general.

sher·ry (shĕr/ĭ), *n., pl.* **-ries.** a strong white wine, originally from southern Spain.

Sher·wood Forest (shûr/wŏŏd/), an ancient royal forest in central England: traditional haunt of Robin Hood.

Shet·land Islands (shĕt/lənd), an island group NE of the Orkney Islands, comprising a county of Scotland. 19,100 pop.; 550 sq. mi.

Shetland pony, a pony of a small, sturdy, rough-coated breed, orig. from the Shetland Islands.

shew (shō), *v.t.*, *v.i.*, **shewed, shewn, shewing,** *n.* Chiefly Brit. or Archaic. show.

shib·bo·leth (shĭb′ə-lĕth′), *n.* a test word or pet phrase of a party, sect, etc.

shield (shēld), *n.* 1. a piece of defensive body armor carried on the arm. 2. something shaped like a shield. 3. anything used or serving to protect. —*v.t.*, *v.i.* 4. to protect, esp. with a shield. 5. to serve as a protection for.

Shetland pony
(3 ft. or less high at the shoulder)

shift (shĭft), *v.i.*, *v.t.* 1. to move from one place, position, etc., to another. 2. to manage to get along, esp. by tricks or evasions. 3. to change (gears) in driving an automobile. 4. to change. —*n.* 5. a shifting from one place, person, etc., to another. 6. a work period in a shop, factory, etc. 7. a group of workmen on such a turn. 8. Football. a lateral movement just prior to beginning a play. 9. an expedient; ingenious device. 10. an evasion, artifice, or trick. 11. a change or substitution. —**shift′er,** *n.*

shift·less (shĭft′lĭs), *adj.* 1. lacking in resource. 2. inefficient; lazy. —**shift′less·ly,** *adv.* —**shift′less·ness,** *n.*

shift·y (shĭf′tĭ), *adj.*, **shiftier, shiftiest.** 1. fertile in expedients. 2. evasive or tricky. —**shift′i·ly,** *adv.* —**shift′i·ness,** *n.*

shil·le·lagh (shə-lā′lə, -lĭ), *n.* (in Ireland) a cudgel. Also, **shil·la′lah, shil·le′lah.**

shil·ling (shĭl′ĭng), *n.* a British money of account and silver coin of the value of 12 pence; equivalent to about 24¹/₃ U.S. cents.

shil·ly-shal·ly (shĭl′ĭ shăl′ĭ), *v.*, **-lied, -lying,** *n.*, *adj.*, *adv.* —*v.i.* 1. to be irresolute; vacillate. —*n.* 2. indecision; vacillation. —*adj.* 3. undecided; vacillating. —*adv.* 4. in an irresolute manner.

Shi·loh (shī′lō), *n.* a national military park in SW Tennessee, including a cemetery and battlefield (1862).

shim·mer (shĭm′ər), *v.i.* 1. to shine with a subdued, tremulous light. —*n.* 2. a subdued, tremulous light. —**shim′mer·y,** *adj.*

shim·my (shĭm′ĭ), *n.*, *pl.* **-mies,** *v.*, **-mied, -my·ing.** —*n.* 1. an American ragtime dance, marked by shaking of the hips or shoulders. 2. excessive wobbling in the front wheels of a motor vehicle. —*v.i.* 3. to dance the shimmy. 4. to vibrate.

shin (shĭn), *n.*, *v.*, **shinned, shinning.** —*n.* 1. the front part of the leg from the knee to the ankle. —*v.t.*, *v.i.* 2. to climb by using the hands or arms and legs.

shin·dig (shĭn′dĭg), *n.* U.S. Slang. a dance, party, or other festivity.

shine (shīn), *v.*, **shone** or (*esp. for def. 5*) **shined,** **shining,** *n.* —*v.i.* 1. to give forth, or glow with, light. 2. to glisten; sparkle. 3. to excel. —*v.t.* 4. to cause to shine. 5. to put a polish on. —*n.* 6. radiance; light. 7. luster; polish. 8. sunshine. 9. a polish given to shoes. 10. a giving of such a polish. 11. U.S. Colloq. a liking.

shin·er (shī′nər), *n.* 1. one that shines. 2. Slang. a black eye. 3. any of various small American fresh-water fishes, mostly minnows, with glistening scales.

shin·gle (shĭng′gəl), *n.*, *v.*, **-gled, -gling.** —*n.* 1. a thin piece of wood, asbestos, etc., used in overlapping rows to cover the roofs and sides of houses. 2. a close-cropped haircut. 3. U.S. Colloq. a small signboard. —*v.t.* 4. to cover (a roof, etc.) with shingles. 5. to cut (hair) close to the head. —**shin′gler,** *n.*

shin·gles (shĭng′gəlz), *n. sing. or pl.* Pathol. a cutaneous disease characterized by vesicles about the body.

shin·ing (shī′nĭng), *adj.* 1. radiant; bright. 2. resplendent. 3. conspicuously fine. —**shin′ing·ly,** *adv.*

shin·ny¹ (shĭn′ĭ), *n.*, *pl.* **-nies,** *v.*, **-nied, -nying.** —*n.* 1. a simple variety of hockey, usually played with a ball. 2. the club used. —*v.i.* 3. to play shinny.

shin·ny² (shĭn′ĭ), *v.i.*, **-nied, -nying.** U.S. Colloq. to climb using the shins.

Shin·to (shĭn′tō), *n.* the native religion of Japan, primarily a system of nature and ancestor worship. Also, **Shin′to·ism.** —**Shin′to·ist,** *n.*, *adj.*

shin·y (shī′nĭ), *adj.*, **shinier, shiniest.** bright; glossy. —**shin′i·ness,** *n.*

ship (shĭp), *n.*, *v.*, **shipped, shipping.** —*n.* 1. any vessel intended or used for navigating the water. 2. the personnel of a vessel. 3. an aircraft. —*v.t.* 4. to send or transport by ship, rail, etc. 5. Naut. to take in (water) over the side. 6. to bring (an object) into a ship. 7. to engage for service on a ship. —*v.i.* 8. to embark. 9. to engage to serve on a ship.

-ship, a suffix of nouns denoting condition, character, office, skill, etc., as in clerkship, friendship.

ship·board (shĭp′bōrd′), *n.* 1. a ship. 2. on shipboard, on or in a ship.

ship·build·er (shĭp′bĭl′dər), *n.* one whose occupation is the design and construction of ships. —**ship′build′ing,** *n.*, *adj.*

ship·load (shĭp′lōd′), *n.* a full load for a ship.

ship·mate (shĭp′māt′), *n.* one who serves with another on the same vessel.

ship·ment (shĭp′mənt), *n.* 1. act of shipping goods, etc. 2. that which is shipped.

ship·per (shĭp′ər), *n.* one who ships goods.

ship·ping (shĭp′ĭng), *n.* 1. act of one who ships goods, etc. 2. the action or business of sending or transporting goods, etc., by ship, rail, etc. 3. ships collectively, or their aggregate tonnage.

ship·shape (shĭp′shāp′), *adj.* 1. in good order; trim. —*adv.* 2. in a shipshape manner.

ship·wreck (shĭp′rĕk′), *n.* 1. the destruction or loss of a ship, as by sinking. 2. the remains of a ship. —*v.t.* 3. to destroy; ruin. —*v.i.* 4. to suffer shipwreck.

ship·wright (shĭp′rīt′), *n.* a carpenter employed in the construction or repair of ships.

ship·yard (shĭp′yärd′), *n.* a place near the water in which ships are built or repaired.

shire (shīr), *n.* (in Great Britain) a county.

shirk (shûrk), *v.t.*, *v.i.* 1. to evade (work, duty, etc.). —*n.* 2. Also, **shirk′er.** one who seeks to avoid work, duty, etc.

shirr (shûr), *v.t.* 1. to gather (cloth) on parallel threads. 2. to bake (eggs) in a shallow dish. —*n.* 3. a shirred arrangement of cloth, etc.

shirt (shûrt), *n.* 1. a garment for the upper part of a man's body. 2. an undergarment for the upper part of the body.

shirt·ing (shûr′tĭng), *n.* any of a variety of fabrics suitable for men's shirts.

shirt·waist (shûrt′wāst′), *n.* a waist, worn with a separate skirt.

shiv·er¹ (shĭv′ər), *v.i.* 1. to tremble with cold, fear, etc. —*n.* 2. a tremble or quiver. —**shiv′er·y,** *adj.*

shiv·er² (shĭv′ər), *v.t.*, *v.i.* 1. to break into fragments. —*n.* 2. a fragment; splinter.

shoal¹ (shōl), *n.* 1. a place where the water is shallow. 2. a sandbank or sand bar in the bed of a body of water. —*v.i.*, *v.t.* 3. to become, or cause to become, shallow. —*adj.* 4. shallow.

shoal² (shōl), *n.* 1. a large number or crowd, esp. of fish. —*v.i.* 2. to crowd or throng.

shoat (shōt), *n.* a young weaned pig.

shock¹ (shŏk), *n.* 1. a sudden and violent blow, impact, or encounter. 2. something that upsets mentally, emotionally, etc. 3. Pathol. a sudden collapse of the nervous mechanism caused by violent physical or psychic factors. 4. the physiological effect of an electric current upon the human body. —*v.t.* 5. to strike with great force or with intense surprise, horror, etc. 6. to give an electric shock to. —*v.i.* 7. to collide. —**shock′er,** *n.*

shock² (shŏk), *n.* 1. a group of sheaves of grain placed on end. —*v.t.* 2. to make into shocks.

shock³ (shŏk), *n.* a thick, bushy mass, as of hair.

shock absorber, Mach. a device for deadening shock or concussion.

shock·ing (shŏk′ĭng), *adj.* 1. causing intense surprise, horror, etc. 2. Colloq. very bad. —**shock′ing·ly,** *adv.*

shock therapy, Psychiatry. a recently developed form or method of treating certain psychotic disorders, as schizophrenia, by the use of chemical or electrical means.

shock troops, Mil. troops especially trained and equipped for assault.

shod·dy (shŏd′ĭ), *n.*, *pl.* **-dies,** *adj.*, **-dier, -diest.** —*n.* 1. a fibrous material obtained by shredding woolen rags. 2. anything inferior but pretentious.

—*adj.* **3.** pretending to a superiority not possessed. **4.** of or containing shoddy. —**shod′di·ly**, *adv.* —**shod′di·ness**, *n.*

shoe (shōō), *n., pl.* **shoes,** (*Archaic*) **shoon**; *v.,* **shod, shoeing.** —*n.* **1.** an external covering, usually of leather, for the human foot. **2.** a horseshoe. **3.** the part of a brake mechanism fitting into the drum and expanded for stopping or slowing a car. **4.** the outer casing of a pneumatic automobile tire. —*v.t.* **5.** to provide with a shoe or shoes.

shoe·horn (shōō′hôrn′), *n.* a shaped piece of horn, metal, or the like, inserted in a shoe at the heel to make it slip on more easily.

shoe·lace (shōō′lās′), *n.* a string or lace for fastening a shoe.

shoe·mak·er (shōō′mā′kər), *n.* one who makes or mends shoes.

shoe·string (shōō′strĭng′), *n.* **1.** a shoelace. **2.** *Colloq.* a very small amount of money used to start or carry on a business.

shoe·tree (shōō′trē′), *n.* a device placed in shoes when they are not being worn to maintain the shape.

sho·gun (shō′gŭn′, -gōōn′), *n.* (in Japan) a commander in chief.

shoot (shōōt), *v.,* **shot, shooting,** *n.* —*v.t.* **1.** to hit, wound, or kill with a missile discharged from a weapon. **2.** to send forth (arrows, bullets, etc.). **3.** to discharge (a bow, firearm, etc.). **4.** to send swiftly along. **5.** to pass rapidly through, over, down, etc. **6.** to emit (rays, etc.) swiftly. **7.** to variegate by threads, streaks, etc., of another color. **8.** to project. **9.** to accomplish by kicking or driving the ball, a marble, etc. **10.** *Dice.* to toss (the dice). **11.** to take a picture of with a camera. **12.** to take the altitude of a heavenly body. —*v.i.* **13.** to send forth missiles. **14.** to move or pass suddenly or swiftly. **15.** to come forth from the ground, a stem, etc. **16.** to grow. **17.** to extend. —*n.* **18.** *Chiefly Brit.* an expedition for shooting game. **19.** a contest at shooting. **20.** a growing or sprouting, as of a plant. **21.** a young growth, branch, stem, twig, or the like. —**shoot′er**, *n.*

shooting star, a falling star; meteor.

shop (shŏp), *n., v.,* **shopped, shopping.** —*n.* **1.** a place for selling goods; store. **2.** a workshop. —*v.i.* **3.** to visit shops for purchasing or examining goods. —**shop′per**, *n.*

shop·keep·er (shŏp′kē′pər), *n.* *Chiefly Brit.* one who carries on business in a shop.

shop·lift·er (shŏp′lĭf′tər), *n.* one who steals goods from a shop, as while ostensibly making purchases. —**shop′lift′ing**, *n.*

shop·worn (shŏp′wōrn′), *adj.* worn or marred, as goods handled in a store.

shore[1] (shōr), *n.* **1.** land on or near an ocean, lake, etc. **2.** land. —**shore′less**, *adj.*

shore[2] (shōr), *n., v.,* **shored, shoring.** —*n.* **1.** a supporting post; prop. —*v.t.* **2.** to support by a shore or shores; prop.

shor·ing (shōr′ĭng), *n.* props for a building, a ship, etc.

short (shôrt), *adj.* **1.** not long. **2.** not tall; low. **3.** extending only a little way. **4.** brief or concise. **5.** rudely brief. **6.** scanty. **7.** not reaching a mark or the like, as a throw. **8.** below the standard in extent, quantity, etc. **9.** inferior to. **10.** having an insufficient amount (of money, food, etc.). **11.** breaking or crumbling readily. **12.** *Com.* **a.** not possessing at the time of sale commodities or stocks that one sells. **b.** noting or pertaining to sales of commodities or stocks which the seller does not possess. **13.** *Phonet.* lasting a relatively short time. **14.** (of an alcoholic drink) small. —*adv.* **15.** abruptly or suddenly. **16.** briefly. **17.** on the near side of an intended point. **18.** without going to the length. **19.** *Com.* without possessing at the time the stocks, etc., sold. —*n.* **20.** something that is short, deficient, or lacking. **21.** (*pl.*) breeches, knickerbockers, or short, loose trousers or underwear. **22.** *Elect.* a short circuit. —**short′ness**, *n.*

short·age (shôr′tĭj), *n.* **1.** deficiency in quantity. **2.** an amount deficient.

short·cake (shôrt′kāk′), *n.* **1.** a cake made with butter or other shortening. **2.** a food made of biscuit dough baked or split in layers, with a filling of strawberries or other fruit.

short-change (shôrt′chānj′), *v.t.,* **-changed, -changing.** *Colloq.* **1.** to give less than proper change to. **2.** to cheat.

short circuit, *Elect.* an abnormal connection of relatively low resistance between two points of different potential in a circuit.

short·com·ing (shôrt′kŭm′ĭng), *n.* a defect in conduct, condition, etc.

short cut, a shorter or quicker way.

short·en (shôr′tən), *v.t.* **1.** to make shorter; curtail. **2.** to reduce. **3.** to make (pastry, etc.) short, as with butter. —*v.i.* **4.** to become shorter. —**short′en·er**, *n.*

short·en·ing (shôr′tən ĭng, shôrt′nĭng), *n.* butter, lard, or other fat, used to make pastry, etc., short.

short·hand (shôrt′hănd′), *n.* **1.** a method of rapid handwriting using simple strokes in place of letters, etc. —*adj.* **2.** using shorthand. **3.** written in shorthand.

short-hand·ed (shôrt′hăn′dĭd), *adj.* not having the necessary number of workmen, helpers, etc.

short·horn (shôrt′hôrn′), *n.* one of a breed of beef cattle originating in England.

short-lived (shôrt′lĭvd′, -lĭvd′), *adj.* living or lasting only a little while.

short·ly (shôrt′lĭ), *adv.* **1.** in a short time; soon. **2.** briefly. **3.** rudely.

short shrift, little mercy or delay in dealing with a person, a matter, etc.

short-sight·ed (shôrt′sī′tĭd), *adj.* **1.** lacking in foresight. **2.** near-sighted. —**short′-sight′-ed·ly**, *adv.* —**short′-sight′ed·ness**, *n.*

short·stop (shôrt′stŏp′), *n.* *Baseball.* a fielder between second and third base.

short-tem·pered (shôrt′tĕm′pərd), *adj.* easily irritated or angered.

short-term (shôrt′tûrm′), *adj.* maturing within a short time.

short ton, 2000 pounds.

short wave, *Radio.* electromagnetic waves 60 meters or less in length.

short-wind·ed (shôrt′wĭn′dĭd), *adj.* out of breath quickly.

Sho·sta·ko·vich (shŏ stä kô′vĭch), *n.* **Dimitri Dimitrievich,** born 1906, Russian composer.

shot[1] (shŏt), *n., pl.* **shots** or (for 5, 7) **shot,** *v.,* **shotted, shotting.** —*n.* **1.** the discharge or a discharge of a firearm, bow, etc. **2.** the range of the discharge. **3.** range in general. **4.** act of shooting. **5.** a small pellet of lead, of which a number are used for one charge of a sportsman's gun. **6.** such pellets collectively. **7.** a projectile for discharge from a firearm or cannon. **8.** such projectiles collectively. **9.** a person who shoots. **10.** a heavy metal ball which competitors cast as far as possible in certain athletic contests. **11.** an aimed stroke, throw, or the like, as in games, etc. **12.** an attempt or try. **13.** a guess at something. **14.** *Slang.* an injection or dose. **15.** *Slang.* a drink of liquor. **16.** a photograph. —*v.t.* **17.** to load or supply with shot. **18.** to weight with shot.

shot[2] (shŏt), *adj.* woven so as to present a play of colors, as silk.

shote (shōt), *n.* shoat.

shot·gun (shŏt′gŭn′), *n.* a smooth-bore gun for firing small shot or buckshot.

should (shŏŏd), *v.* **1.** pt. of **shall. 2.** (specially used): **a.** to denote duty, propriety, or expediency. **b.** to make a statement less direct or blunt. **c.** to emphasize the uncertainty in conditional and hypothetical clauses.

shoul·der (shōl′dər), *n.* **1.** either of two parts of the human body extending from the side of the neck to the upper joint of the arm. **2.** (*pl.*) these two parts together with the portion of the back joining them. **3.** a corresponding part in animals. **4.** a shoulderlike part or projection. **5.** the unpaved portion at the edge of a road. —*v.t., v.i.* **6.** to push, as with the shoulder, esp. roughly. **7.** to take upon or support with the shoulder. **8.** to assume as a burden.

shoulder blade, the scapula.

shout (shout), *v.i., v.t.* **1.** to call or cry out loudly and vigorously. **2.** to speak or laugh noisily. —*n.* **3.** a loud call or cry. **4.** a loud burst, as of laughter. —**shout′er**, *n.*

shove (shŭv), *v.,* **shoved, shoving,** *n.* —*v.t., v.i.* **1.** to push, esp. roughly. **2.** **shove off, a.** to push a boat off. **b.** *Slang.* to leave. —*n.* **3.** an act of shoving. —**shov′er**, *n.*

shov·el (shŭv′əl), *n., v.,* **-eled, -eling** or (*esp. Brit.*) **-elled, -elling.** —*n.* **1.** an implement consisting of a broad scoop attached to a handle, used for digging and removing earth, snow, coal, etc. —*v.t.* **2.** to take up and remove with a shovel. **3.** to dig or clear with a shovel. —*v.i.* **4.** to work with a shovel. —**shov′el·er**, *n.*

shov·el·board (shŭv/əl bōrd/), n. shuffleboard.

show (shō), v., **showed, shown** or **showed, showing**, n. —v.t. 1. to exhibit; display. 2. to point out. 3. to guide. 4. to make known; explain. 5. to prove. 6. to indicate. 7. to allege or plead. 8. to accord or grant (favor, etc.). —v.i. 9. to be or become visible. 10. *Racing Slang.* to finish in first, second, or third place in a race. 11. **show off**, a. to display ostentatiously. b. to display one's abilities, cleverness, etc. 12. **show up**, a. to expose (faults, etc.). b. to stand out. c. to appear. —n. 13. a display. 14. ostentatious display. 15. any kind of public exhibition. 16. appearance. 17. an unreal or deceptive appearance. 18. an indication. 19. *Colloq.* a theatrical performance or company. —**show/er,** n.

show·boat (shō/bōt/), n. a boat used as a traveling theater.

show·case (shō/kās/), n. a glass case for the display of articles in shops, etc.

show·down (shō/doun/), n. a forced disclosure of actual resources, power, etc.

show·er (shou/ər), n. 1. a brief fall of rain. 2. a similar fall, as of tears, sparks, or bullets. 3. a large quantity. 4. a bestowal of presents on a prospective bride. 5. a shower bath. —v.t. 6. to pour down in a shower. 7. to bestow liberally. —v.i. 8. to rain in a shower. —**show/er·y,**adj.

shower bath, a bath in which water is showered upon the body from above.

show·ing (shō/ĭng), n. 1. exhibition; show. 2. a presentation, as of facts.

show·man (shō/mən), n., pl. **-men.** 1. one who exhibits a show. 2. one who presents things well. —**show/man·ship/,** n.

show-off (shō/ôf/, -ŏf/), n. 1. pretentious display. 2. one given to pretentious display.

show·room (shō/rōōm/, -rŏŏm/), n. a room for the display of goods.

show·y (shō/ĭ), adj., **showier, showiest.** 1. making an imposing display. 2. ostentatious. —**show/i·ly,** adv. —**show/i·ness,** n.

shrap·nel (shrăp/nəl), n. *Mil.* 1. a hollow projectile containing bullets or the like and a bursting charge, arranged to explode before reaching the object, and to set free a shower of missiles. 2. shell fragments.

shred (shrĕd), n., v., **shredded** or **shred, shredding.** —n. 1. a piece cut or torn off, esp. in a narrow strip. 2. a bit; scrap. —v.t. 3. to reduce to shreds.

Shreve·port (shrēv/pōrt/), n. a city in NW Louisiana. 98,167.

shrew[1] (shrōō), n. a woman of violent temper and speech. —**shrew/ish,** adj.

shrew[2] (shrōō), n. any of certain small insectivorous mammals having a long, sharp snout and a mouselike form.

shrewd (shrōōd), adj. astute in practical matters. —**shrewd/ly,** adv. —**shrewd/ness,** n.

shriek (shrēk), n. 1. a loud, sharp, shrill cry, laugh, or sound. —v.i. 2. to utter or give forth a shriek. —v.t. 3. to cry in a shriek.

shrift (shrĭft), n. *Archaic.* confession to a priest.

shrike (shrīk), n. any of certain predacious oscine birds with a strong hooked and toothed bill, which feed on insects and sometimes on small birds and other animals.

shrill (shrĭl), adj. 1. high-pitched and piercing. —v.t., v.i. 2. to cry shrilly. —n. 3. a shrill sound. —adv. 4. shrilly. —**shrill/ness,** n. —**shril/ly,** adv.

shrimp (shrĭmp), n., pl. **shrimps** or for 1 (*esp. collectively*) **shrimp.** 1. any of certain small, long-tailed, chiefly marine, decapod crustaceans, esteemed as a table delicacy. 2. a small person.

shrine (shrīn), n., v., **shrined, shrining.** —n. 1. a receptacle for sacred relics. 2. any place consecrated or devoted to some saint or deity, as a church. 3. any place hallowed by its history. —v.t. 4. to enshrine.

shrink (shrĭngk), v., **shrank** or **shrunk, shrunk** or **shrunken, shrinking,** n. —v.i., v.t. 1. to draw back, as in retreat. 2. to contract with heat, moisture, etc. 3. to become smaller. —n. 4. a shrinking movement. —**shrink/a·ble,** adj. —**shrink/er,** n. —**shrink/ing·ly,** adv.

shrink·age (shrĭngk/ĭj), n. 1. act or fact of shrinking. 2. the amount of shrinking.

shriv·el (shrĭv/əl), v.t., v.i., **-eled, -eling** or (*esp. Brit.*) **-elled, -elling.** 1. to contract and wrinkle. 2. to wither.

shroud (shroud), n. 1. a white cloth in which a corpse is wrapped for burial. 2. something which covers or conceals. 3. (*usually pl.*) *Naut.* one of a set of strong ropes extended from the mastheads to the sides of a ship to help support the masts. —v.t. 4. to wrap for burial. 5. to cover or hide.

shrub (shrŭb), n. a woody perennial plant smaller than a tree, usually having permanent stems branching from or near the ground. —**shrub/by,** adj.

shrub·ber·y (shrŭb/ə rĭ), n., pl. **-beries.** shrubs collectively.

shrug (shrŭg), v., **shrugged, shrugging,** n. —v.t., v.i. 1. to raise and contract (the shoulders), expressing indifference, disdain, etc. —n. 2. this movement.

shuck (shŭk), n. 1. a husk or pod, as of corn. 2. the shell of an oyster or clam. —v.t. 3. to remove the shucks from. —**shuck/er,** n.

shud·der (shŭd/ər), v.i. 1. to tremble with a sudden convulsive movement, as from horror. —n. 2. such a movement. —**shud/der·ing·ly,** adv.

shuf·fle (shŭf/əl), v., **-fled, -fling,** n. —v.i., v.t. 1. to scrape or drag (the feet) in walking or dancing. 2. to act in a shifting or evasive manner. 3. to mix (cards in a pack). 4. to shift or change. —n. 5. a scraping movement or dragging gait. 6. an evasive trick; evasion. 7. act of shuffling. 8. a shuffling of cards in a pack.

shuf·fle·board (shŭf/əl bōrd/), n. a game in which disks are driven along a smooth surface toward certain lines, etc., on it.

shun (shŭn), v.t., **shunned, shunning.** to avoid (a place, person, etc.), from dislike, caution, etc. —**shun/ner,** n.

shunt (shŭnt), v.t., v.i. 1. to shove or turn aside. 2. to get rid of. 3. *Elect.* to divert (a part of a current) by connecting a circuit element in parallel with another. 4. to shift (a train, or part of it) from one line of rails to another. —n. 5. act of shunting; shift. 6. *Elect.* a conducting element bridged across a circuit, establishing a current path auxiliary to the main circuit. 7. a railroad switch. —**shunt/er,** n.

shut (shŭt), v., **shut, shutting,** adj. —v.t., v.i. 1. to close. 2. to confine; enclose. 3. to exclude. 4. **shut up,** *Colloq.* to stop talking. —adj. 5. closed; fastened up.

shut·down (shŭt/doun/), n. a closing of a factory or the like for a time.

shut-in (shŭt/ĭn/), adj. 1. confined to the house, hospital, etc. —n. 2. a shut-in person.

shut·out (shŭt/out/), n. 1. act of shutting out. 2. a game in which one team does not score.

shut·ter (shŭt/ər), n. 1. a hinged cover for a window. 2. *Photog.* a mechanical device for opening and closing the aperture of a lens. —v.t. 3. to close or provide with shutters.

shut·tle (shŭt/əl), n., v., **-tled, -tling.** —n. 1. a device in a loom, for passing the weft thread from one side of the web to the other. 2. *U.S.* a shuttle train. —v.t., v.i. 3. to move quickly to and fro like a shuttle.

shut·tle·cock (shŭt/əl kŏk/), n. a piece of cork or similar light material with feathers stuck in one end, struck into the air with a battledore in the game of **battledore and shuttlecock.**

shuttle train, a train running for a short distance to and fro, as on a branch line.

Shver·nik (shvĕr/nĭk), n. **Nikolai,** born 1888, president of the Soviet Union since 1946.

shy[1] (shĭ), adj., **shyer, shyest** or **shier, shiest,** v., **shied, shying,** n., pl. **shies.** —adj. 1. bashful; retiring. 2. timid. 3. suspicious. 4. wary. 5. short. —v.i. 6. to start back or aside, as in fear. 7. to recoil. —n. 8. a sudden start aside, as in fear. —**shy/ly,** adv. —**shy/ness,** n.

shy[2] (shĭ), v., **shied, shying,** n., pl. **shies.** —v.i., v.t. 1. to throw with a swift, sudden movement. —n. 2. a quick, sudden throw. 3. *Colloq.* a gibe or sneer. 4. *Colloq.* a try.

Shy·lock (shī/lŏk), n. 1. a relentless moneylender in Shakespeare's *Merchant of Venice.* 2. an extortionate usurer.

shy·ster (shī/stər), n. *U.S. Slang.* a lawyer who uses questionable methods.

Si, *Chem.* silicon.

Si·am (sī ăm/, sī/ăm), n. a kingdom in SE Asia; 15,718,000 pop.; 198,242 sq. mi. *Cap.:* Bangkok. Official name, **Thailand.** —**Si·a·mese** (sī/ə mēz/, -mēs/), adj., n.

Siamese twins, twins who are born joined together in any manner.

Si·be·li·us (sǐ bā'lǐ əs), *n.* **Jean Julius Christian**, born 1865, Finnish composer.

Si·be·ri·a (sī bǐr'ǐ ə), *n.* a part of the Soviet Union, in N Asia, extending from the Ural Mountains to the Pacific. —**Si·be/ri·an**, *adj.*, *n.*

sib·i·lant (sǐb'ə lənt), *adj.* **1.** hissing. —*n.* **2.** a sibilant sound. —**sib/i·lance, sib/i·lan·cy,** *n.* —**sib/i·lant·ly,** *adv.*

sib·yl (sǐb'ǐl), *n.* a prophetess or witch. —**si·byl/ic, sib·yl·line** (sǐb/ə lēn/, -lǐn/, -lǐn), *adj.*

sic¹ (sǐk), *adv.* *Latin.* so; thus.

sic² (sǐk), *v.t.*, **sicked, sicking. 1.** to attack (esp. of a dog). **2.** to incite to attack.

Sic·i·ly (sǐs'ə lǐ), the largest island in the Mediterranean, comprising a department of Italy. 4,242,400 pop.; 9924 sq. mi. *Cap.:* Palermo. —**Si·cil·i·an** (sǐ sǐl/ǐ ən), *adj.*, *n.*

sick (sǐk), *adj.* **1.** ill, unwell, or ailing. **2.** of or attended with sickness. **3.** *Chiefly Brit.* affected with nausea. **4.** deeply affected with sorrow, longing, etc. **5.** *Slang.* disgusted. —*n.* **6.** sick people. —**sick/ish,** *adj.*

sick bay, (in a ship) a compartment used as a hospital.

sick·bed (sǐk/bĕd/), *n.* a bed on which a sick person lies.

sick·en (sǐk/ən), *v.i.*, *v.t.* to become or make sick. —**sick/en·ing,** *adj.* —**sick/en·ing·ly,** *adv.*

sick·le (sǐk/əl), *n.* **1.** an implement for cutting grain, grass, etc., consisting of a curved, hooklike blade mounted in a short handle. **2.** (*cap.*) *Astron.* a group of stars in the constellation Leo, likened to this implement.

sick·ly (sǐk/lǐ), *adj.*, **-lier, -liest,** *adv.*, *v.*, **-lied, -lying.** —*adj.* **1.** unhealthy; ailing. **2.** of or connected with ill health. **3.** mawkish. **4.** faint or feeble. —*adv.* **5.** in a sickly manner. —*v.t.* **6.** to cover with a sickly hue. —**sick/li·ness,** *n.*

sick·ness (sǐk/nǐs), *n.* **1.** a disease or malady. **2.** state of being sick. **3.** nausea.

side (sīd), *n.*, *adj.*, *v.*, **sided, siding.** —*n.* **1.** one of the surfaces or lines bounding a thing. **2.** either of the two surfaces of paper, cloth, etc. **3.** one of the two surfaces or parts other than the front, back, top, and bottom. **4.** an aspect; phase. **5.** region, direction, or position. **6.** a slope. **7.** one of two or more parties in a case, contest, etc. **8.** line of descent. —*adj.* **9.** being at or on one side. **10.** coming from one side. **11.** directed toward one side. **12.** subordinate. —*v.i.* **13.** to place oneself with a side or party.

side arms, *Mil.* weapons (as pistol, sword, etc.) carried at the side or in the belt.

side·board (sīd/bôrd/), *n.* a piece of furniture, as in a dining room, for holding articles of table service.

side·burns (sīd/bûrnz/), *n.pl.* *U.S.* short whiskers extending from the hairline to below the ears and worn with an unbearded chin.

side light, incidental information.

side line, 1. a line at the side of something. **2.** an additional line of goods or business.

side·long (sīd/lông/, -lŏng/), *adj.* **1.** directed to one side. **2.** toward the side.

si·de·re·al (sī dǐr/ǐ əl), *adj.* **1.** determined by stars. **2.** of or pertaining to the stars.

side·sad·dle (sīd/sǎd/əl), *n.* a saddle on which the rider sits with both feet on the same side of the horse: used chiefly by women.

side·slip (sīd/slǐp/), *v.*, **-slipped, -slipping,** *n.* —*v.i.* **1.** to slip to one side. —*n.* **2.** act of sideslipping.

side·step (sīd/stĕp/), *v.i.*, *v.t.*, **-stepped, -stepping. 1.** to step, or avoid by stepping, to one side. **2.** to evade, as decisions, etc.

side·swipe (sīd/swīp/), *v.*, **-swiped, -swiping,** *n.* *U.S.* —*v.t.* **1.** to strike with a sweeping blow along the side. —*n.* **2.** such a blow.

side·track (sīd/trǎk/), *v.t.*, *v.i.* **1.** to move to a siding; as a train. **2.** to distract or divert. —*n.* **3.** a railroad siding.

side·walk (sīd/wôk/), *n.* a walk, esp. a paved one, at the side of a street or road.

side·ways (sīd/wāz/), *adv.*, *adj.* **1.** with the side foremost. **2.** facing to the side. **3.** toward or from one side. Also, **side/way/, side·wise** (sīd/wīz/).

sid·ing (sī/dǐng), *n.* a short track, usually connected by a switch at one or both ends with the main line track.

si·dle (sī/dəl), *v.*, **-dled, -dling.** —*v.i.* **1.** to move sideways. **2.** to edge along furtively. —*n.* **3.** a sidling movement.

siege (sēj), *n.*, *v.*, **sieged, sieging.** —*n.* **1.** the operation of surrounding a place and cutting off supplies, etc., to force surrender. **2.** any prolonged or persistent endeavor to overcome resistance. —*v.t.* **3.** to lay siege to; besiege.

Sieg·fried (sēg/frēd), *n.* *German Legend.* a heroic prince who captures the treasure of the Nibelungs, slays a dragon, and rescues a maiden from an enchanted sleep.

si·en·na (sǐ ĕn/ə), *n.* **1.** an earth used as a yellowish-brown pigment (**raw sienna**) or, after roasting in a furnace, as a reddish-brown pigment (**burnt sienna**). **2.** the color of such a pigment.

si·er·ra (sǐ ĕr/ə), *n.* a chain of hills or mountains with sharp peaks.

si·es·ta (sǐ ĕs/tə), *n.* a midday rest or nap.

sieve (sǐv), *n.*, *v.*, **sieved, sieving.** —*n.* **1.** an instrument with a meshed or perforated bottom, used for separating coarse from fine parts of loose matter, etc. —*v.t.* **2.** to sift.

sift (sǐft), *v.t.* **1.** to separate the coarse parts of (flour, ashes, etc.) with a sieve. **2.** to examine or question closely. —**sift/er,** *n.*

sigh (sī), *v.i.* **1.** to let out one's breath audibly, as from sorrow, weariness, etc. **2.** to yearn. —*v.t.* **3.** to express with a sigh. —*n.* **4.** act or sound of sighing. —**sigh/er,** *n.*

sight (sīt), *n.* **1.** the power or faculty of seeing; vision. **2.** act or fact of seeing. **3.** range of vision. **4.** a view; glimpse. **5.** a spectacle. **6.** an observation taken with a surveying or other instrument. **7.** a device on a firearm, etc., to guide the eye. —*v.t.*, *v.i.* **8.** to get sight of. **9.** to direct by a sight or sights, as a firearm. —**sight/less,** *adj.*

sight draft, a draft payable upon presentation.

sight·ly (sīt/lǐ), *adj.*, **-lier, -liest. 1.** pleasing to the sight. **2.** *U.S.* affording a fine sight or view. —**sight/li·ness,** *n.*

sight·see·ing (sīt/sē/ǐng), *n.* **1.** act of seeing objects or places of interest. —*adj.* **2.** seeing or showing sights. —**sight/se/er,** *n.*

sig·ma (sǐg/mə), *n.* the eighteenth letter (Σ, σ, s) of the Greek alphabet.

sign (sīn), *n.* **1.** a token; indication. **2.** a conventional mark, figure, or symbol, as in musical notation. **3.** a gesture intended to express an idea. **4.** an inscribed board, space, etc., serving for information, advertisement, etc. **5.** *Med.* the objective indications of a disease. **6.** a trace; vestige. **7.** an omen. **8.** *Astron.* any of the twelve divisions of the zodiac. —*v.t.* **9.** to affix a signature to. **10.** to write as a signature. **11.** to engage by written agreement. —*v.i.* **12.** to write one's signature. **13.** to end radio broadcasting (fol. by *off*). **14.** to bind oneself to work by signature (fol. by *on*). —**sign/er,** *n.*

sig·nal (sǐg/nəl), *n.*, *adj.*, *v.*, **-naled, -naling** or (*esp. Brit.*) **-nalled, -nalling.** —*n.* **1.** a gesture, light, etc., to warn, direct, or the like. **2.** *Radio, etc.* **a.** the impulses, waves, sounds, etc., transmitted or received. **b.** the wave which modulates the carrier wave. —*adj.* **3.** serving as a sign. **4.** conspicuous or notable. —*v.t.* **5.** to make a signal to. **6.** to make known by a signal. —*v.i.* **7.** to make communication by a signal or signals. —**sig/nal·er;** *esp. Brit.*, **sig/nal·ler,** *n.*

sig·nal·ize (sǐg/nə līz/), *v.t.*, **-ized, -izing.** to make notable.

sig·nal·ly (sǐg/nə lǐ), *adv.* notably.

sig·na·to·ry (sǐg/nə tōr/ǐ), *adj.*, *n.*, *pl.* **-ries.** —*adj.* **1.** that has signed a document. —*n.* **2.** a signer of a document, as a treaty.

sig·na·ture (sǐg/nə chər), *n.* **1.** a person's name as written by himself or by deputy. **2.** act of signing a document. **3.** *Music.* a sign or set of signs at the beginning of a staff to indicate the key or the time of a piece. **4.** *Radio.* an identifying theme. **5.** *Bookbinding.* a printed sheet folded to form a section of a book. **6.** *Print.* **a.** a symbol at the foot of the first page of every section to guide the binder. **b.** a sheet as thus marked.

sign·board (sīn/bôrd/), *n.* a board bearing an advertisement or the like.

sig·net (sǐg/nǐt), *n.* a small seal.

sig·nif·i·cance (sǐg nǐf/ə kəns), *n.* **1.** importance; consequence. **2.** meaning. **3.** the quality of having a meaning. Also, **sig·nif/i·can·cy.**

sig·nif·i·cant (sǐg nǐf/ə kənt), *adj.* **1.** important. **2.** expressing a meaning. **3.** suggestive. —**sig·nif/i·cant·ly,** *adv.*

sig·ni·fi·ca·tion (sǐg/nə fə kā/shən), *n.* **1.** meaning; sense. **2.** act or fact of signifying. —**sig·nif/i·ca/tive,** *adj.*

sig·ni·fy (sǐg/nə fī/), *v.*, **-fied, -fying.** —*v.t*

1. to make known by signs, speech, or action. **2. to** mean. —*v.i.* **3. to** be of importance or consequence.

Sikh (sēk), *n.* a member of a religious sect mainly in NW India.

si·lage (sī'lĭj), *n.* fodder preserved in a silo.

si·lence (sī'ləns), *n., v.,* **-lenced, -lencing,** *interj.* —*n.* **1.** absence of any sound; stillness. **2.** state or fact of being silent; muteness. **3.** omission of mention. **4.** oblivion. **5.** secrecy. —*v.t.* **6.** to put or bring to silence; still. **7.** to quiet. —*interj.* **8.** be silent! —*si'lenc·er,* *n.*

si·lent (sī'lənt), *adj.* **1.** quiet; still. **2.** refraining from speech. **3.** mute. **4.** taciturn; reticent. **5.** tacit. **6.** not sounded. **7.** taking no active or known part. —**si'lent·ly,** *adv.* —**si'lent·ness,** *n.*

Si·le·sia (sĭ lē'shə, sī-), *n.* a region in central Europe: formerly divided between Germany, Poland, and Czechoslovakia.

si·lex (sī'lĕks), *n.* **1.** silica. **2.** (*cap.*) *Trademark.* a coffee maker of heat-resistant glass.

sil·hou·ette (sĭl'ŏŏ ĕt'), *n., v.,* **-etted, -etting.** —*n.* **1.** an outline drawing, uniformly filled in with black. —*v.t.* **2.** to show in a silhouette.

sil·i·ca (sĭl'ə kə), *n.* silicon dioxide, appearing as quartz, sand flint, and agate.

sil·i·cate (sĭl'ə kĭt, -kāt'), *n.* *Chem.* any salt derived from silica or silica compounds.

sil·i·con (sĭl'ə kən), *n.* *Chem.* a nonmetallic element, constituting more than one fourth of the earth's crust. *Symbol:* Si; *at. wt.:* 28.06; *at. no.:* 14; *sp. gr.:* 2.4 at 20°C.

sil·i·co·sis (sĭl'ə kō'sĭs), *n.* *Pathol.* a disease of the lungs due to inhaling silica particles.

silk (sĭlk), *n.* **1.** the fine, soft, lustrous fiber obtained from the cocoon of the silkworm. **2.** thread made of this fiber. **3.** cloth made of this fiber. **4.** a garment of this cloth. **5.** the hairlike styles on an ear of maize. —*adj.* **6.** Also, **silk'en.** of or like silk.

silk·worm (sĭlk'wûrm'), *n.* the caterpillar of certain moths, which spins a fine, soft filament (silk) to form a cocoon, in which it is enclosed while in the pupal stage.

silk·y (sĭl'kĭ), *adj.,* **silkier, silkiest.** of or like silk; lustrous; smooth. —**silk/i·ness,** *n.*

sill (sĭl), *n.* **1.** a horizontal timber, block, or the like, serving as a foundation of a wall, house, etc. **2.** the horizontal piece beneath a window, door, or other opening.

sil·ly (sĭl'ĭ), *adj.,* **-lier, -liest,** *n., pl.* **-lies.** —*adj.* **1.** foolish; stupid. **2.** absurd or ridiculous. **3.** *Colloq.* stunned. —*n.* **4.** *Colloq.* a silly person. —**sil'li·ness,** *n.*

si·lo (sī'lō), *n., pl.* **-los,** *v.,* **-loed, -loing.** —*n.* **1.** an airproof towerlike structure, in which fermenting green fodder is preserved for future use as silage. —*v.t.* **2.** to put into a silo.

Silo (def. 1)

silt (sĭlt), *n.* **1.** earthy matter, fine sand, or the like, carried by moving water and deposited as a sediment. —*v.i., v.t.* **2.** to fill or become filled with silt. —**silt'y,** *adj.*

sil·van (sĭl'vən), *adj., n.* sylvan.

sil·ver (sĭl'vər), *n.* **1.** *Chem.* a white ductile metallic element, used for coins, ornaments, table utensils, etc. *Symbol:* Ag; *at. wt.:* 107.88; *at. no.:* 47; *sp. gr.:* 10.5 at 20°C. **2.** coin made of this metal; money. **3.** silverware. **4.** a lustrous whitish gray. —*adj.* **5.** of or plated with silver. **6.** clear and soft. **7.** eloquent. **8.** indicating the 25th anniversary. —*v.t.* **9.** to coat with silver or some silverlike substance.

sil·ver·fish (sĭl'vər fĭsh'), *n., pl.* **-fishes,** (*esp. collectively*) **-fish.** any of certain small wingless insects which damage books, wallpaper, etc.

silver fox, the common red fox in a variation in which the fur is black with silver-gray ends.

sil·ver·smith (sĭl'vər smĭth'), *n.* one who makes articles of silver.

sil·ver·ware (sĭl'vər wâr'), *n.* articles, esp. for table use, made of silver.

sil·ver·y (sĭl'və rĭ), *adj.* **1.** resembling silver. **2.** having a clear, ringing sound. **3.** containing or covered with silver. —**sil'ver·i·ness,** *n.*

sim·i·an (sĭm'ĭ ən), *adj.* **1.** of or pertaining to an ape or monkey. —*n.* **2.** an ape or monkey.

sim·i·lar (sĭm'ə lər), *adj.* **1.** having general like-

ness or resemblance. **2.** *Geom.* (of figures) having the same shape. —**sim'i·lar·ly,** *adv.*

sim·i·lar·i·ty (sĭm'ə lăr'ə tĭ), *n., pl.* **-ties. 1.** state of being similar; likeness. **2.** a point of resemblance.

sim·i·le (sĭm'ə lē), *n.* *Rhet.* a figure of speech directly expressing a resemblance.

si·mil·i·tude (sĭ mĭl'ə tūd', -tōōd'), *n.* **1.** likeness; resemblance. **2.** image. **3.** a comparison.

sim·mer (sĭm'ər), *v.i.* **1.** to continue in a state approaching boiling. **2.** to make a gentle murmuring sound. **3.** to continue in a state of subdued activity, excitement, etc. —*v.t.* **4.** to keep in a state approaching boiling. —*n.* **5.** state or process of simmering.

Si·mon (sī'mən), *n.* *Bible.* Also, **Simon Peter.** the original name of Peter.

si·mon-pure (sī'mən pyŏŏr'), *adj.* real; genuine.

si·mo·ny (sī'mə nĭ, sĭm'ə-), *n.* **1.** making profit out of sacred things. **2.** the sin of buying or selling ecclesiastical benefices, etc. —**si'mon·ist,** *n.*

si·moom (sĭ mōōm'), *n.* a hot, suffocating, sandladen wind of the deserts of Arabia, Syria, Africa, etc. Also, **si·moon** (sĭ mōōn').

sim·per (sĭm'pər), *v.i.* **1.** to smile in a silly way. —*v.t.* **2.** to say with a simper. —*n.* **3.** a silly smile.

sim·ple (sĭm'pəl), *adj.,* **-pler, -plest,** *n.* **1.** easy to understand, use, etc. **2.** not elaborate or complex. **3.** not luxurious. **4.** unaffected. **5.** mere; bare. **6.** sincere; innocent. **7.** ordinary. **8.** plain. **9.** humble or lowly. **10.** lacking mental acuteness. **11.** *Chem.* a. composed of but one substance or element. b. not mixed. **12.** *Bot.* not divided into parts. **13.** *Zool.* not compound. **14.** *Music.* single. —*n.* **15.** an ignorant or foolish person. **16.** something unmixed or uncompounded. —**sim'ple·ness,** *n.*

sim·ple-mind·ed (sĭm'pəl mīn'dĭd), *adj.* **1.** lacking in mental acuteness. **2.** mentally deficient. **3.** unsophisticated.

sim·ple·ton (sĭm'pəl tən), *n.* a fool.

sim·plic·i·ty (sĭm plĭs'ə tĭ), *n., pl.* **-ties.** state or quality of being simple.

sim·pli·fy (sĭm'plə fī'), *v.t.,* **-fied, -fying.** to make plainer or easier. —**sim'pli·fi·ca'tion,** *n.*

sim·ply (sĭm'plĭ), *adv.* **1.** in a simple manner. **2.** plainly. **3.** artlessly. **4.** only. **5.** foolishly. **6.** absolutely.

sim·u·late (*v.* sĭm'yə lāt'; *adj.* sĭm'yə lĭt, -lāt'), *v.,* **-lated, -lating,** *adj.* —*v.t.* **1.** to make a pretense of. **2.** to assume or have the appearance of. —*adj.* **3.** simulated. —**sim'u·la'tion,** *n.* —**sim'u·la'tive,** *adj.*

si·mul·ta·ne·ous (sī'məl tā'nĭ əs, sĭm'əl-), *adj.* existing, occurring, or operating at the same time. —**si'mul·ta'ne·ous·ly,** *adv.* —**si'mul·ta'ne·ous·ness,** *n.*

sin (sĭn), *n., v.,* **sinned, sinning.** —*n.* **1.** transgression of divine law. **2.** any serious transgression or offense. —*v.i.* **3.** to do a sinful act. —*v.t.* **4.** to do or perform sinfully.

Si·nai (sī'nī, sī'nī ī'), *n.* **Mount,** the mountain, of uncertain identity, from which the law was given to Moses.

since (sĭns), *adv.* **1.** from then till now. **2.** subsequently. **3.** ago; before now. —*prep.* **4.** from. **5.** between (a past time or event) and the present. —*conj.* **6.** in the period following the time when. **7.** from the time when. **8.** because.

sin·cere (sĭn sēr'), *adj.,* **-cerer, -cerest.** free from deceit or duplicity. —**sin·cere'ly,** *adv.* —**sin·cere'ness,** *n.*

sin·cer·i·ty (sĭn sĕr'ə tĭ), *n., pl.* **-ties.** freedom from deceit or duplicity; honesty.

sine (sīn), *n.* *Math.* (of an angle) a trigonometric function equal to the ratio of the ordinate of the end point of the arc to the radius vector of this end point, the origin being at the center of the circle on which the arc lies and the critical point of the arc being on the x-axis.

si·ne·cure (sī'nĭ kyŏŏr', sĭn'ĭ-), *n.* an office or position requiring little or no work.

sin·ew (sĭn'ū), *n.* **1.** a tendon. **2.** that which supplies strength. **3.** strength; vigor.

sin·ew·y (sĭn'ū ĭ), *adj.* **1.** strong or vigorous. **2.** tough; stringy.

sin·ful (sĭn'fəl), *adj.* wicked. —**sin'ful·ly,** *adv.* —**sin'ful·ness,** *n.*

sing (sĭng), *v.,* **sang** or **sung, sung, singing,** *n.* —*v.i.* **1.** to utter words or sounds in succession with musical modulations of the voice. **2.** to perform a song. **3.** to tell of something in verse.

—v.t. 4. to utter with musical modulations of the voice, as a song. **5.** to proclaim enthusiastically. **6.** to bring, send, put, etc., with or by singing. **—n. 7.** act or performance of singing. **8.** *Colloq.* a meeting of persons for singing. **—sing′er,** *n.*

sing., singular.

Sin·ga·pore (sĭng′gə pōr′, sĭng′ə-), *n.* **1.** a British crown colony in SE Asia, comprising the island of Singapore and its dependencies, Christmas Island and the Cocos Islands. 772,000 pop.; 282 sq. mi. **2.** a seaport in and the capital of this colony. 445,719.

singe (sĭnj), *v.*, **singed, singeing,** *n.* **—v.t. 1.** to burn superficially. **2.** to burn the ends of (hair, etc.). **—n. 3.** a superficial burn. **4.** act of singeing.

sin·gle (sĭng′gəl), *adj., v.,* **-gled, -gling,** *n.* **—adj. 1.** one only; separate; individual. **2.** alone; solitary. **3.** unmarried. **4.** sincere. **5.** having but one set of petals. **—v.t. 6.** to pick out from others. **—v.i. 7.** *Baseball.* to hit the ball so as to reach first base safely. **—n. 8.** something single or separate. **9.** *Baseball.* a hit which allows the batter to reach first base only. **10.** (*pl.*) *Tennis, etc.* a game or match played with one person on each side. **—sing′le·ness,** *n.*

sin·gle-breast·ed (sĭng′gəl brĕs′tĭd), *adj.* (of a garment) overlapping across the breast only enough to allow fastening.

single file, a line of persons or things arranged one behind the other.

sin·gle-foot (sĭng′gəl foŏt′), *n.* **1.** a gait of a horse. **—v.i. 2.** to go at such a gait.

sin·gle-hand·ed (sĭng′gəl hăn′dĭd), *adj.* acting or working alone or unaided. **—sin′gle-hand′ed·ly,** *adv.*

sin·gle·tree (sĭng′gəl trē′, -trĭ′), *n.* whiffletree.

sin·gly (sĭng′glĭ), *adv.* **1.** separately. **2.** one at a time. **3.** single-handed.

Sing Sing (sĭng′ sĭng′), the state prison at Ossining, New York.

sing·song (sĭng′sông′, -sŏng′), *n.* **1.** verse of a jingling or monotonous character. **2.** monotonous rhythmical cadence, tone, or sound. **—adj. 3.** monotonous in rhythm.

sin·gu·lar (sĭng′gyə lər), *adj.* **1.** extraordinary; remarkable. **2.** strange; odd. **3.** unique. **4.** separate. **5.** *Gram.* designating the number category that normally implies one person, thing, or collection. **—n. 6.** *Gram.* the singular number, or a form therein. **—sin′gu·lar·ly,** *adv.* **—sin·gu·lar·i·ty** (sĭng′gyə lăr′ə tĭ), *n.*

sin·is·ter (sĭn′ĭs tər), *adj.* **1.** threatening evil; ominous. **2.** bad; evil; base. **3.** disastrous; unfavorable. **4.** left. **—sin′is·ter·ly,** *adv.* **—sin′is·ter·ness,** *n.*

sink (sĭngk), *v.,* **sank or sunk, sunk or sunken, sinking,** *n.* **—v.i. 1.** to descend gradually to a lower level. **2.** to become submerged. **3.** to fall slowly from weakness, fatigue, etc. **4.** to pass gradually into (slumber, silence, etc.). **5.** to degenerate; decline. **6.** to become lower in tone or pitch. **7.** to enter; permeate. **—v.t. 8.** to cause to fall or descend. **9.** to cause to sink or become submerged. **10.** to depress (a part, area, etc.). **11.** to put down (a pipe, post, etc.). **12.** to bring to a worse state. **13.** to invest (money), now esp. unprofitably. **14.** to make (a hole, shaft, well, etc.) by excavating. **—n. 15.** a basin, esp. in a kitchen, as for receiving dirty water. **16.** a lowlying area where waters collect or where they disappear by sinking down into the ground or by evaporation. **—sink′a·ble,** *adj.*

sink·er (sĭngk′ər), *n.* **1.** one that sinks. **2.** a weight of lead, etc., as for sinking a fishing line. **3.** *U.S. Slang.* a doughnut.

sin·less (sĭn′lĭs), *adj.* free from or without sin. **—sin′less·ly,** *adv.* **—sin′less·ness,** *n.*

sin·ner (sĭn′ər), *n.* one who sins; transgressor.

sin·u·ous (sĭn′yoŏ əs), *adj.* **1.** having many curves, bends, or turns; winding. **2.** indirect; devious. **—sin′u·ous·ness, sin·u·os·i·ty** (sĭn′yoŏ ŏs′ə tĭ), *n.* **—sin′u·ous·ly,** *adv.*

si·nus (sī′nəs), *n.* **1.** *Anat.* any of various cavities, recesses, or passages, as one of the hollow cavities in the skull connecting with the nasal cavities. **2.** *Pathol.* a narrow, elongated abscess with a small orifice. **3.** a curve; bend. **4.** a curving part or recess.

si·nus·i·tis (sī′nə sī′tĭs), *n.* *Pathol.* inflammation of a sinus or sinuses.

-sion, a suffix having the same function as **-tion,** as in *compulsion.*

Sioux (soō), *n., pl.* **Sioux** (soō, soōz). a member of an American Indian tribe, mainly of the U.S. Midwest. **—Siou·an** (soō′ən), *adj.*

Sioux City, a city in W Iowa. 82,364.

Sioux Falls, a city in SE South Dakota. 40,832.

sip (sĭp), *v.,* **sipped, sipping,** *n.* **—v.t., v.i. 1.** to drink a little at a time. **2.** to drink from by sips. **3.** to absorb. **—n. 4.** an act of sipping. **5.** a small quantity taken by sipping. **—sip′per,** *n.*

si·phon (sī′fən), *n.* **1.** a tube or conduit in the form of an inverted U through which liquid flows over the wall of a tank or reservoir to a lower elevation by atmospheric pressure. **2.** a siphon bottle. **—v.t., v.i. 3.** to convey or pass through a siphon.

siphon bottle, a bottle for aerated water, fitted with a siphon through the neck, the water being forced out when a valve is opened.

sir (sûr), *n.* **1.** a respectful or formal term of address used to a man. **2.** (*cap.*) the distinctive title of a knight or baronet.

sire (sīr), *n., v.,* **sired, siring.** **—n. 1.** the male parent of a quadruped. **2.** *Poetic.* a father or forefather. **3.** a respectful term of address. **—v.t. 4.** to beget.

si·ren (sī′rən), *n.* **1.** *Class. Myth.* one of several sea nymphs, part woman and part bird, supposed to lure mariners to destruction by their seductive singing. **2.** any alluring or dangerous woman. **3.** a device that produces a loud, shrill sound by passing compressed air through a rotating perforated disk: used as a police-car signal, etc. **—adj. 4.** dangerously alluring.

Sir·i·us (sĭr′ĭ əs), *n.* the Dog Star, in Canis Major: the brightest star in the heavens.

sir·loin (sûr′loin), *n.* the portion of the loin of beef in front of the rump.

si·roc·co (sə rŏk′ō), *n., pl.* **-cos. 1.** a hot, dry, dust-laden wind blowing from northern Africa and affecting parts of southern Europe. **2.** any hot, oppressive wind.

sir·up (sĭr′əp, sûr′-), *n., v.t.* syrup.

si·sal (sī′səl, sĭs′əl), *n.* **1.** a fiber yielded by an agave of Yucatán, used for making ropes, etc. **2.** a plant yielding such fiber.

sis·sy (sĭs′ĭ), *n., pl.* **-sies. 1.** *Colloq.* an effeminate boy or man. **2.** a little girl.

sis·ter (sĭs′tər), *n.* **1.** a daughter of the same parents or parent. **2.** a nun. **3.** *Brit.* the nurse in charge of a hospital ward. **—adj. 4.** being a sister. **—sis′ter·ly,** *adj.*

sis·ter·hood (sĭs′tər hoŏd′), *n.* **1.** state of being a sister. **2.** a group of sisters.

sis·ter-in-law (sĭs′tər ĭn lô′), *n., pl.* **sisters-in-law. 1.** one's husband's or wife's sister. **2.** one's brother's wife.

sit (sĭt), *v.,* **sat** or (*Archaic*) **sate, sitting.** **—v.i. 1.** to rest on the lower part of the body; be seated. **2.** to be situated; dwell. **3.** to rest or lie. **4.** to pose for an artist, photographer, etc. **5.** to remain inactive. **6.** to cover eggs to hatch them. **7.** to fit. **8.** to occupy a seat in an official capacity, as a judge. **9.** to be in session, as an assembly. **—v.t. 10.** to cause to sit; seat.

sit-down strike (sĭt′doun′), a strike with workers occupying their place of employment and refusing to work or to allow others to work until the strike is settled. Also, **sit′-down′.**

site (sīt), *n.* **1.** the position of a town, building, etc. **2.** the area on which anything is, has been, or is to be located.

sit·ter (sĭt′ər), *n.* **1.** one who sits. **2.** one who stays with young children while the parents go out, usually for the evening.

sit·ting (sĭt′ĭng), *n.* **1.** act of one that sits. **2.** a period of remaining seated, as for a portrait. **3.** a session, as of a legislature.

sit·u·ate (sĭch′oŏ āt′), *v.t.,* **-ated, -ating.** to give a site to; locate.

sit·u·at·ed (sĭch′oŏ ā′tĭd), *adj.* **1.** located; placed. **2.** fixed; supplied.

sit·u·a·tion (sĭch′oŏ ā′shən), *n.* **1.** a location or position. **2.** condition; plight. **3.** the state of affairs. **4.** a position or post of employment.

Si·va (sē′və, shē′və), *n.* *Hinduism.* one of the three chief divinities, the third member of the Hindu trinity.

six (sĭks), *n.* **1.** a cardinal number, five plus one. **2.** a symbol for this number, as 6 or VI. **3.** a set of this many persons or things. **—adj. 4.** amounting to six in number.

six·pence (sĭks′pəns), *n.* **1.** a sum of money of the value of six British pennies. **2.** a British silver coin of this value.

six·pen·ny (sĭks′pĕn′ĭ, -pə nĭ), *adj.* **1.** costing sixpence. **2.** cheap; paltry.

six·teen (sĭks′tēn′), *n.* **1.** a cardinal number, ten plus six. **2.** a symbol for this number. —*adj.* **3.** amounting to sixteen in number. —**six′teenth′**, *adj., n.*

sixteenth note, *Music.* a note having one sixteenth of the time value of a whole note.

sixth (sĭksth), *adj.* **1.** next after the fifth. **2.** being one of six equal parts. —*n.* **3.** a sixth part, esp. of one (¹/₆). **4.** the sixth member of a series.

six·ty (sĭks′tĭ), *n., pl.* **-ties,** *adj.* —*n.* **1.** a cardinal number, ten times six. **2.** a symbol for this number. —*adj.* **3.** amounting to sixty in number. —**six′ti·eth,** *adj., n.*

six·ty-fourth note (sĭks′tĭ fôrth′), *Music.* a note having one sixty-fourth of the time value of a whole note.

siz·a·ble (sī′zə bəl), *adj.* of fair size; fairly large. Also, **size′a·ble.** —**siz′a·ble·ness,** *n.* —**siz′a·bly,** *adv.*

size[1] (sīz), *n., v.,* **sized, sizing.** —*n.* **1.** the dimensions, proportions, or magnitude of anything. **2.** great magnitude. **3.** one of a series of graduated measures for articles. **4.** extent; range. —*v.t.* **5.** to separate or sort according to size. **6. size up,** to form an estimate of.

size[2] (sīz), *n., v.,* **sized, sizing.** —*n.* **1.** any of various preparations made from glue, starch, etc., used for glazing or coating paper, cloth, etc. —*v.t.* **2.** to coat or treat with size.

siz·ing (sī′zĭng), *n.* **1.** act or process of applying size. **2.** size, as for glazing paper.

siz·zle (sĭz′əl), *v.,* **-zled, -zling,** *n.* —*v.i.* **1.** to make a hissing sound, as in frying. **2.** *Colloq.* to be very hot. —*n.* **3.** a sizzling sound.

skate[1] (skāt), *n., v.,* **skated, skating.** —*n.* **1.** a steel runner attached to the bottom of a shoe, enabling a person to glide on ice. **2.** a roller skate. —*v.i.* **3.** to glide over ice, the ground, etc., on skates. —**skat′er,** *n.*

skate[2] (skāt), *n., pl.* **skates,** (*esp. collectively*) **skate.** any of certain rays, usually having a pointed snout and spines down the back.

skein (skān), *n.* a coil of thread or yarn.

skel·e·ton (skĕl′ə tən), *n.* **1.** the bones of a human or other animal body considered together as a framework. **2.** a very lean person or animal. —*adj.* **3.** of or pertaining to a skeleton. —**skel′e·tal,** *adj.*

skep·tic (skĕp′tĭk), *n.* **1.** one who questions the validity or authenticity of something purporting to be knowledge. **2.** one who doubts the truth of the Christian religion or of important elements of it. —*adj.* **3.** pertaining to skeptics or skepticism.

skep·ti·cal (skĕp′tə kəl), *adj.* **1.** having or showing doubt. **2.** denying or questioning the tenets of religion. **3.** of or pertaining to skeptics or skepticism. —**skep′ti·cal·ly,** *adv.*

skep·ti·cism (skĕp′tə sĭz′əm), *n.* doubt or unbelief, esp. with regard to religion.

sketch (skĕch), *n.* **1.** a simply or hastily executed drawing or painting, esp. a preliminary one. **2.** a rough design, plan, or draft. **3.** a short play. —*v.t., v.i.* **4.** to make a sketch (of). —**sketch′er,** *n.*

sketch·book (skĕch′bŏŏk′), *n.* a book for making sketches in.

sketch·y (skĕch′ĭ), *adj.,* **sketchier, sketchiest. 1.** giving only outlines. **2.** slight; imperfect. —**sketch′i·ly,** *adv.* —**sketch′i·ness,** *n.*

skew (skū), *v.i.* **1.** to turn aside or swerve. **2.** to squint. —*v.t.* **3.** to shape obliquely. **4.** to distort. —*adj.* **5.** oblique; slanting. —*n.* **6.** an oblique movement, direction, or position.

skew·er (skū′ər), *n.* **1.** a long pin of wood or metal for putting through meat to hold it together or in place while being cooked. —*v.t.* **2.** to fasten with skewers.

ski (skē; *Nor.* shē), *n., pl.* **skis, ski,** *v.,* **skied, skiing.** —*n.* **1.** one of a pair of long, slender pieces of hard wood, one fastened to each shoe, used for traveling or gliding over snow. —*v.i.* **2.** to travel on or use skis. —**ski′er,** *n.*

skid (skĭd), *n., v.,* **skidded, skidding.** —*n.* **1.** a plank, bar, log, or the like, on which something heavy may be slid along. **2.** a plank on which something is supported. **3.** a device for preventing the wheel of a vehicle from rotating, as when descending a hill. **4.** a runner on the under part of some airplanes, enabling the machine to slide along the ground when alighting. **5.** an act of skidding. —*v.t.* **6.** to place on or slide along a skid or skids. **7.** to check with a skid, as a wheel.

—*v.i.* **8.** to slide along without rotating, as a wheel to which a brake has been applied. **9.** to slip or slide sideways.

skiff (skĭf), *n.* a boat small enough for sailing or rowing by one person.

skill (skĭl), *n.* **1.** the ability that comes from knowledge, practice, aptitude, etc. **2.** expertness; dexterity. —**skilled,** *adj.*

skil·let (skĭl′ĭt), *n.* a frying pan.

skill·ful (skĭl′fəl), *adj.* **1.** having or exercising skill. **2.** showing or involving skill. Also, **skil′ful.** —**skill′ful·ly,** *adv.* —**skill′ful·ness,** *n.*

skim (skĭm), *v.,* **skimmed, skimming,** *n.* —*v.t., v.i.* **1.** to remove (floating matter) from a liquid with a spoon, ladle, etc. **2.** to move or glide lightly along the surface (of). **3.** to go over in reading, treatment, etc., in a superficial manner. —*n.* **4.** act of skimming. **5.** that which is skimmed off. —**skim′mer,** *n.*

skim milk, milk from which the cream has been skimmed.

skimp (skĭmp), *v.t., v.i.* to scrimp.

skimp·y (skĭm′pĭ), *adj.,* **skimpier, skimpiest. 1.** lacking in size, fullness, etc.; scanty. **2.** stingy. —**skimp′i·ly,** *adv.* —**skimp′i·ness,** *n.*

skin (skĭn), *n., v.,* **skinned, skinning.** —*n.* **1.** the external covering of an animal body. **2.** pelt. **3.** any outer coating or surface layer, as the rind or peel of fruit. —*v.t.* **4.** to strip of skin; peel. **5.** to cover with skin. **6.** *Slang.* to fleece, as in gambling. —**skin′ner,** *n.*

skin-deep (skĭn′dēp′), *adj.* **1.** superficial; slight. —*adv.* **2.** slightly; superficially.

skin·flint (skĭn′flĭnt′), *n.* a mean, niggardly person.

skin·ny (skĭn′ĭ), *adj.,* **-nier, -niest. 1.** lean; emaciated. **2.** of or like skin. —**skin′ni·ness,** *n.*

skip (skĭp), *v.,* **skipped, skipping,** *n.* —*v.i.* **1.** to spring, jump, or leap lightly. **2.** to pass from one thing, subject, etc., to another, disregarding or omitting what intervenes. **3.** *Educ.* to be advanced two or more grades. —*v.t.* **4.** to jump lightly over. **5.** to pass over without reading, notice, mention, etc. **6.** *Colloq.* to leave hastily. —*n.* **7.** a light jump. **8.** a passing from one point or thing to another, with disregard of what intervenes. —**skip′per,** *n.*

skip·per (skĭp′ər), *n.* **1.** the master or captain of a ship. —*v.t.* **2.** to act as skipper of.

skirl (skûrl), *Scot. and Brit. Dial.* —*v.i., v.t.* **1.** to sound loudly and shrilly (used esp. of the bagpipe). —*n.* **2.** the sound of the bagpipe.

skir·mish (skûr′mĭsh), *Mil.* —*n.* **1.** a fight between small bodies of troops. —*v.i.* **2.** to engage in a skirmish. —**skir′mish·er,** *n.*

skirt (skûrt), *n.* **1.** the lower part of a gown, coat, or the like, hanging from the waist. **2.** a separate garment worn by women and girls, extending from the waist downward. **3.** (*usually pl.*) the bordering, marginal, or outlying part of a place, group, etc. **4.** *Slang.* a woman or girl. —*v.t.* **5.** to lie on or along the border of. **6.** to pass around the border of.

skit (skĭt), *n.* a short comic play.

skit·tish (skĭt′ĭsh), *adj.* **1.** apt to start or shy. **2.** restlessly or excessively lively. **3.** coy. —**skit′tish·ly,** *adv.* —**skit′tish·ness,** *n.*

skit·tle (skĭt′əl), *n. Chiefly Brit.* **1.** (*pl.*) ninepins. **2.** one of the pins.

skoal (skōl), *n.* a word used in drinking someone's health.

skul·dug·ger·y (skŭl dŭg′ə rĭ), *n. U.S.* dishonorable proceedings; mean trickery.

skulk (skŭlk), *v.i.* **1.** to lie in hiding, as for some evil reason. **2.** to malinger. **3.** to sneak; slink. —*n.* **4.** one who skulks. —**skulk′er,** *n.*

skull (skŭl), *n.* the bony framework of the head, enclosing the brain.

skull·cap (skŭl′kăp′), *n.* a brimless cap fitting closely to the head.

skunk (skŭngk), *n.* **1.** a small, striped, fur-bearing, bushy-tailed North American mammal of the weasel family which ejects a fetid fluid when attacked. **2.** *Colloq.* a thoroughly contemptible person. —*v.t.* **3.** *U.S. Slang.* to defeat completely.

skunk cabbage, a low, fetid, broad-leaved plant growing in moist ground.

sky (skī), *n., pl.* **skies. 1.** (*often pl.*) the region of the clouds or the upper air. **2.** (*often pl.*) the heavens or firmament. **3.** the celestial heaven.

sky·lark (skī′lärk′), *n.* **1.** a European lark famous for its singing in flight. —*v.i.* **2.** *Colloq.* to frolic.

sky·light (skī/līt/), *n.* an opening in a roof or ceiling, fitted with glass, for admitting daylight.

sky·line (skī/līn/), *n.* 1. the outline of something seen against the sky. 2. the apparent horizon.

sky·rock·et (skī/rŏk/ĭt), *n.* 1. a rocket (firework) that ascends into the air and explodes at a height. —*v.i.* 2. *Colloq.* to rise suddenly.

sky·sail (skī/sāl/; *Naut.* -səl), *n.* *Naut.* (in a square-rigged vessel) a light square sail next above the royal.

sky·scrap·er (skī/skrā/pər), *n.* a relatively tall building of many stories.

sky·ward (skī/wərd), *adv., adj.* toward the sky.

sky·writ·ing (skī/rī/tĭng), *n.* 1. the act of writing in the sky with chemically produced smoke released from an airplane. 2. the words, etc., traced.

slab (slăb), *n., v.,* **slabbed, slabbing.** —*n.* 1. a broad, flat, somewhat thick piece of stone, wood, etc. 2. a thick slice of anything. 3. a rough outside piece cut from a log. —*v.t.* 4. to make into a slab or slabs.

slack¹ (slăk), *adj.* 1. not tense or taut; loose. 2. indolent. 3. slow; sluggish. 4. inactive; not brisk. —*adv.* 5. in a slack manner. —*n.* 6. a slack condition, interval, or part. 7. part of a rope, sail, or the like, that hangs loose. 8. a decrease in activity, as in business. —*v.t., v.i.* 9. to slacken. 10. to slake (lime). —**slack/ly,** *adv.* —**slack/ness,** *n.*

slack² (slăk), *n.* small or refuse coal.

slack·en (slăk/ən), *v.t., v.i.* 1. to make or become less active, vigorous, intense, etc. 2. to make or become looser or less taut.

slack·er (slăk/ər), *n.* one who evades his duty, esp. military duty.

slacks (slăks), *n.pl.* loose-fitting trousers worn by men and women as sports costume.

slag (slăg), *n.* the completely fused and vitrified matter separated during the reduction of a metal from its ore. —**slag/gy,** *adj.*

slake (slāk), *v.,* **slaked, slaking.** —*v.t.* 1. to allay (thirst, desire, etc.) by satisfying. 2. to cool or refresh. 3. to disintegrate or treat (lime) with water or moist air.

sla·lom (slä/lōm), *n.* a downhill skiing race in a winding course.

slam¹ (slăm), *v.,* **slammed, slamming,** *n.* —*v.t., v.i.* 1. to shut with force and noise. 2. *U.S. Slang.* to criticize severely. —*n.* 3. a violent and noisy closing, dashing, or impact. 4. the noise made. 5. *U.S. Slang.* a severe criticism.

slam² (slăm), *n.* *Cards.* the winning of all the tricks in one deal (in bridge, called **grand slam**) or of all but one (in bridge, called **little slam**).

slan·der (slăn/dər), *n.* 1. defamation; calumny. 2. a malicious, false, and defamatory statement or report. 3. *Law.* defamation by oral utterance. —*v.t., v.i.* 4. to utter slander (concerning). —**slan/der·er,** *n.* —**slan/der·ous,** *adj.*

slang (slăng), *n.* 1. language of a markedly colloquial character, regarded as below the standard of cultivated speech. 2. the jargon of a particular class, profession, etc. —*v.i.* 3. to use slang. —**slang/y,** *adj.*

slant (slănt, slänt), *v.i., v.t.* 1. to slope. —*n.* 2. slanting direction; slope. 3. a slanting line, surface, etc. 4. a mental view or tendency. —*adj.* 5. slanting; oblique. —**slant/ing·ly,** *adv.*

slant·wise (slănt/wīz/, slänt/-), *adv.* 1. aslant; obliquely. —*adj.* 2. slanting.

slap (slăp), *n., v.,* **slapped, slapping,** *adv.* —*n.* 1. a sharp blow, esp. with the open hand. 2. a rebuke. —*v.t.* 3. to strike sharply, esp. with the open hand. 4. to dash or cast forcibly. —*adv.* 5. smartly; suddenly.

slap·dash (slăp/dăsh/), *adv., adj.* 1. in a hasty, haphazard manner. 2. carelessly hasty.

slap·stick (slăp/stĭk/), *n.* broad comedy in which rough antics prevail.

slash (slăsh), *v.t., v.i.* 1. to cut by striking violently and at random. 2. to lash. 3. to cut, reduce, or alter. 4. to make slits in (a garment) to show an underlying fabric. —*n.* 5. a sweeping stroke. 6. a cut or wound made with such a stroke; gash. 7. an ornamental slit in a garment. —**slash/er,** *n.*

slat¹ (slăt), *n., v.,* **slatted, slatting.** —*n.* 1. a long, thin, narrow strip of wood, metal, etc. —*v.t.* 2. to furnish with slats.

slat² (slăt), *v.,* **slatted, slatting,** *n.* *Dial.* —*v.t.* 1. to dash with force. —*v.i.* 2. to flap violently. —*n.* 3. a sharp blow.

slate (slāt), *n., v.,* **slated, slating.** —*n.* 1. a fine-grained rock formed by the compression of clay, shale, etc., that tends to split along parallel cleavage planes. 2. a thin piece of this rock or a similar material, used esp. for roofing or (when framed) for writing on. 3. a dull, dark bluish gray. 4. *U.S.* a tentative list of candidates, officers, etc., for nomination. —*v.t.* 5. to cover with slate. 6. to set down or list for nomination or appointment. —**slat/y,** *adj.*

slat·tern (slăt/ərn), *n.* a slovenly, untidy woman or girl. —**slat/tern·ly,** *adj., adv.*

slaugh·ter (slô/tər), *n.* 1. the killing or butchering of cattle, sheep, etc., esp. for food. 2. the brutal killing of a person. 3. carnage; massacre. —*v.t.* 4. to kill or butcher (animals), esp. for food. 5. to kill in a brutal or violent manner. 6. to massacre. —**slaugh/ter·er,** *n.*

slaugh·ter·house (slô/tər hous/), *n.* a place where animals are butchered.

Slav (släv, slăv), *n.* 1. one of a race of peoples widely spread over eastern, southeastern, and central Europe, including the Russians, Bulgars, Serbs, Poles, Czechs, etc. —*adj.* 2. of, pertaining to, or characteristic of the Slavs.

slave (slāv), *n., v.,* **slaved, slaving.** —*n.* 1. one who is the property of another. 2. one entirely under the domination of some influence. 3. a drudge. —*v.i.* 4. to work like a slave; drudge.

slav·er¹ (slā/vər), *n.* 1. a dealer in slaves. 2. a vessel used in slave trade.

slav·er² (slăv/ər), *v.i.* 1. to let saliva run from the mouth. —*v.t.* 2. to wet with saliva. —*n.* 3. saliva coming from the mouth.

slav·er·y (slā/və rĭ), *n.* 1. the condition of a slave; bondage. 2. the keeping of slaves as a practice or institution. 3. severe toil; drudgery.

Slav·ic (släv/ĭk, slăv/ĭk), *n.* 1. one of the principal groups of Indo-European languages, spoken by the Slavs. —*adj.* 2. of or pertaining to the Slavs or their languages.

slav·ish (slā/vĭsh), *adj.* 1. of or befitting a slave. 2. abjectly submissive. 3. base; mean. 4. imitative. —**slav/ish·ly,** *adv.* —**slav/ish·ness,** *n.*

slaw (slô), *n.* sliced or chopped cabbage served with seasoning or dressing.

slay (slā), *v.t.,* **slew, slain, slaying.** to kill by violence. —**slay/er,** *n.*

slea·zy (slā/zĭ, slē/zĭ), *adj.,* **-zier, -ziest.** thin or poor in texture; flimsy.

sled (slĕd), *n., v.,* **sledded, sledding.** —*n.* 1. a vehicle mounted on runners for conveying loads over snow, ice, rough ground, etc. 2. a small vehicle of this kind used in coasting, etc. —*v.i., v.t.* 3. to ride or carry on a sled.

sledge¹ (slĕj), *n., v.,* **sledged, sledging.** —*n.* 1. a sled for conveying loads over snow, ice, rough ground, etc. —*v.t., v.i.* 2. to convey or travel by sledge.

sledge² (slĕj), *n., v.,* **sledged, sledging.** —*n.* 1. Also, **sledge hammer.** a large, heavy hammer. —*v.i., v.t.* 2. to strike or beat with a sledge.

sleek¹ (slēk), *adj.* 1. smooth; glossy. 2. smooth of manner; suave. —**sleek/er,** *n.* —**sleek/ly,** *adv.* —**sleek/ness,** *n.*

sleek² (slēk), *v.t.* to smooth.

sleep (slēp), *v.,* **slept, sleeping,** *n.* —*v.i.* 1. to take the rest afforded by a suspension of the voluntary exercise of the bodily functions and the natural suspension of consciousness. 2. to be dormant, quiescent, or inactive, as faculties. —*n.* 3. the state of a person, animal, or plant that sleeps. 4. a period of sleeping. 5. dormancy or inactivity. 6. the repose of death. —**sleep/less,** *adj.* —**sleep/less·ly,** *adv.* —**sleep/less·ness,** *n.*

sleep·er (slē/pər), *n.* 1. one that sleeps. 2. a sleeping car.

sleeping car, a railroad car fitted with berths, compartments, or bedrooms for sleeping.

sleeping sickness, *Pathol.* a form of inflammation of the brain marked by extreme weakness, drowsiness, or sleepiness.

sleep·walk·ing (slēp/wô/kĭng), *n.* state or act of walking while asleep. —**sleep/walk/er,** *n.*

sleep·y (slē/pĭ), *adj.,* **sleepier, sleepiest.** 1. ready to sleep; drowsy. 2. languid. 3. lethargic; sluggish. 4. quiet. —**sleep/i·ly,** *adv.* —**sleep/i·ness,** *n.*

sleet (slēt), *n.* 1. the frozen coating on trees, wires, and other bodies that sometimes forms when rain or sleet falls at a low temperature. 2. *U.S.* frozen or partly frozen rain. —*v.i.* 3. to send down sleet. 4. to fall as or like sleet. —**sleet/y,** *adj.*

sleeve (slēv), *n., v.,* **sleeved, sleeving.** —*n.*

1. the part of a garment that covers the arm.
2. *Mach.* a tubular piece, as of metal, fitting over a rod or the like. **3.** **up one's sleeve,** ready. —*v.t.* **4.** to furnish with sleeves. —**sleeve'less,** *adj.*

sleigh (slā), *n.* **1.** a light, usually open vehicle on runners, generally horse-drawn, used for pleasure driving, etc., in snowy weather. —*v.i.* **2.** to travel or ride in a sleigh.

sleight (slīt), *n.* skill; dexterity.

sleight of hand, 1. skill in feats of jugglery or legerdemain. **2.** such a feat.

slen·der (slĕn'dər), *adj.* **1.** small in circumference. **2.** small in size, amount, extent, etc. **3.** having little value or force. **4.** thin or weak. —**slen'der·ly,** *adv.* —**slen'der·ness,** *n.*

slen·der·ize (slĕn'də rīz'), *v.t.,* **-ized, -izing.** to make slender.

sleuth (slŏŏth), *n. U.S. Colloq.* a detective.

sleuth·hound (slŏŏth'hound'), *n.* a bloodhound.

slew (slŏŏ), *n. Colloq.* a great number.

slice (slīs), *n., v.,* **sliced, slicing.** —*n.* **1.** a thin, broad, flat piece cut from something. **2.** a part; portion. **3.** *Golf.* a slicing stroke. —*v.t., v.i.* **4.** to cut into slices. **5.** *Golf.* to hit (the ball) with a glancing stroke that causes it to curve off to one side. —**slic'er,** *n.*

slick[1] (slĭk), *adj.* **1.** sleek; glossy. **2.** smooth of manners, speech, etc. **3.** sly; shrewdly adroit. **4.** ingenious. **5.** slippery. —*n.* **6.** a smooth place or spot, as an oil-covered area on the ocean. **7.** *U.S. Slang.* a magazine printed on glossy paper. —*adv.* **8.** smoothly; cleverly. —**slick'ly,** *adv.* —**slick'ness,** *n.*

slick[2] (slĭk), *v.t.* **1.** to make sleek or smooth. **2.** *Colloq.* to make smart or fine.

slick·er (slĭk'ər), *n. U.S.* **1.** a long, loose raincoat. **2.** *Colloq.* a swindler.

slide (slīd), *v.,* **slid, slid** or **slidden, sliding,** *n.* —*v.i., v.t.* **1.** to move along a smooth or slippery surface. **2.** to glide or slip easily, quietly, or unobtrusively. **3.** to go unregarded. —*n.* **4.** act of sliding. **5.** a smooth surface for sliding on. **6.** *Geol.* **a.** a landslide or the like. **b.** the mass of matter sliding down. **7.** a single image for projection in a projector. **8.** a plate of glass or other material on which objects are placed for microscopic examination.

slide rule, a device for rapid calculation, consisting essentially of a rule having a sliding piece moving along it, both marked with graduated logarithmic scales.

sliding scale, a variable scale, esp. of industrial costs, as wages, etc.

slight (slīt), *adj.* **1.** small in amount, degree, etc. **2.** trifling. **3.** slender; slim. **4.** frail; flimsy. —*v.t.* **5.** to treat as of slight importance. **6.** to ignore. —*n.* **7.** slighting indifference or treatment. **8.** a snub or an affront. —**slight'ing·ly,** *adv.* —**slight'ly,** *adv.* —**slight'ness,** *n.*

sli·ly (slī'lĭ), *adv.* slyly.

slim (slĭm), *adj.,* **slimmer, slimmest,** *v.,* **slimmed, slimming.** —*adj.* **1.** slender, as in form; slight. **2.** poor. **3.** small; scanty. —*v.t., v.i.* **4.** to make or become slim. —**slim'ly,** *adv.* —**slim'ness,** *n.*

slime (slīm), *n., v.,* **slimed, sliming.** —*n.* **1.** thin, glutinous mud. **2.** any viscous liquid matter, esp. of an offensive kind. **3.** a viscous secretion of animal or vegetable origin. —*v.t.* **4.** to cover with slime.

slim·y (slī'mĭ), *adj.,* **slimier, slimiest. 1.** of or like slime. **2.** covered with slime. **3.** foul. —**slim'i·ly,** *adv.* —**slim'i·ness,** *n.*

sling[1] (slĭng), *n., v.,* **slung, slinging.** —*n.* **1.** an instrument for hurling stones, etc., by hand. **2.** a rope or chain used in hoisting cargo in and out of a ship. **3.** a bandage used to suspend a part, commonly an arm or hand. **4.** a strap by which something is suspended or carried, as on a rifle. **5.** act of slinging. —*v.t.* **6.** to throw, cast, or hurl. **7.** to hang in a sling or so as to swing loosely. —**sling'er,** *n.*

sling[2] (slĭng), *n. U.S.* an iced alcoholic drink, containing gin or the like, water, sugar, and lemon or lime juice.

sling·shot (slĭng'shŏt'), *n.* a Y-shaped stick with an elastic strip between the prongs for shooting stones, etc.

slink (slĭngk), *v.i.,* **slunk, slinking.** to go in a furtive, abject manner, as from fear or shame. —**slink'ing·ly,** *adv.*

slip[1] (slĭp), *v.,* **slipped** or (*Archaic*) **slipt; slipped;**

slipping; *n.* —*v.i.* **1.** to pass or go smoothly or easily; slide. **2.** to slide suddenly and involuntarily. **3.** to move, slide, or start from place, position, etc. **4.** to get away, escape, or be lost. **5.** to go, come, get, etc., easily or quickly. **6.** to pass quickly or imperceptibly. **7.** to make a mistake or error. —*v.t.* **8.** to cause to slip, pass, put, draw, etc., with a smooth, easy, or sliding motion. **9.** to put or draw quickly or stealthily. **10.** to let go. —*n.* **11.** act of slipping. **12.** a slipping of the feet. **13.** a mishap. **14.** a mistake. **15.** an indiscretion. **16.** a woman's underdress. **17.** a pillowcase. **18.** *U.S.* a space between two wharves or in a dock, for vessels to lie in.

slip[2] (slĭp), *n.* **1.** a piece suitable for propagation cut from a plant. **2.** any long, narrow piece or strip, as of wood, paper, land, etc.

slip·knot (slĭp'nŏt'), *n.* a knot which slips easily along the cord round which it is made.

slip·per (slĭp'ər), *n.* a light shoe worn chiefly indoors. —**slip'pered,** *adj.*

slip·per·y (slĭp'ə rĭ), *adj.,* **-perier, -periest. 1.** tending to cause slipping or sliding, as ground. **2.** tending to slip from the hold or from position. **3.** likely to escape. **4.** fickle; shifty, tricky, or deceitful. —**slip'per·i·ness,** *n.*

slip·shod (slĭp'shŏd'), *adj.* untidy.

slip·up (slĭp'ŭp'), *n. Colloq.* a mistake.

slit (slĭt), *v.,* **slit, slitting,** *n.* —*v.t.* **1.** to cut apart or open along a line. **2.** to cut into strips. —*n.* **3.** a straight, narrow cut or opening. —**slit'ter,** *n.*

slith·er (slĭth'ər), *v.i.* **1.** to slide down or along a surface, esp. unsteadily. **2.** to go with a sliding motion. —*n.* **3.** a slide.

sliv·er (slĭv'ər), *n.* **1.** a slender piece, as of wood, split, broken, or cut off; splinter. **2.** a loose, untwisted fiber of wool, cotton, etc. —*v.t., v.i.* **3.** to split or cut into slivers.

slob (slŏb), *n. Slang.* a stupid, clumsy, or slovenly person.

slob·ber (slŏb'ər), *v.i.* **1.** to let saliva, etc., run from the mouth; drivel. **2.** to indulge in mawkish sentimentality. —*n.* **3.** saliva dribbling from the mouth. **4.** mawkishly sentimental speech or actions. —**slob'ber·y,** *adj.*

sloe (slō), *n.* **1.** the small, sour, blackish fruit of the blackthorn. **2.** the shrub itself.

sloe gin, a liqueur flavored with sloe.

slog (slŏg), *v.,* **slogged, slogging.** —*v.t.* **1.** to hit hard, as in boxing. —*v.i.* **2.** to deal heavy blows. **3.** to plod heavily. —**slog'ger,** *n.*

slo·gan (slō'gən), *n.* a distinctive cry or phrase of any party, class, body, or person.

sloop (slŏŏp), *n.* a sailing vessel with a single mast, fitted with a jib and mainsail.

slop[1] (slŏp), *v.,* **slopped, slopping,** *n.* —*v.t., v.i.* **1.** to spill or splash (liquid). **2.** to spill liquid (upon). —*n.* **3.** a quantity of liquid carelessly spilled or splashed about. **4.** (*often pl.*) *Chiefly Brit.* liquid or semiliquid food. **5.** (*often pl.*) the dirty water, liquid refuse, etc., of a household. **6.** swill.

slop[2] (slŏp), *n.* clothing, bedding, etc., supplied to seamen from the ship's stores.

slope (slōp), *v.,* **sloped, sloping,** *n.* —*v.i.* **1.** to take or have an inclined or slanting direction. —*v.t.* **2.** to direct at an inclination. —*n.* **3.** inclination or slant. **4.** an inclined surface. —**slop'ing,** *adj.* —**slop'ing·ly,** *adv.*

slop·py (slŏp'ĭ), *adj.,* **-pier, -piest. 1.** muddy, slushy, or very wet. **2.** *Colloq.* maudling. **3.** *Colloq.* careless. **4.** *Colloq.* untidy. —**slop'pi·ly,** *adv.* —**slop'pi·ness,** *n.*

slosh (slŏsh), *n.* **1.** slush. —*v.i.* **2.** to splash in slush, mud, or water. —**slosh'y,** *adj.*

slot (slŏt), *n., v.,* **slotted, slotting.** —*n.* **1.** a narrow, elongated depression or opening, esp. one to receive something. —*v.t.* **2.** to provide with a slot.

sloth (slŏth, slōth), *n.* **1.** indolence; laziness. **2.** any of certain sluggish arboreal edentates of tropical America.

sloth·ful (slŏth'fəl, slōth'-), *adj.* indolent; lazy. —**sloth'ful·ly,** *adv.* —**sloth'ful·ness,** *n.*

slot machine, a machine for vending small articles, weighing, gambling, etc., operated by dropping a coin in a slot.

slouch (slouch), *v.i.* **1.** to sit or stand in an awkward, drooping posture. **2.** to move or walk with loosely drooping body and careless gait. **3.** to have a droop or downward bend, as a hat. —*n.* **4.** an awkward, drooping carriage of a person. **5.** an awkward, ungainly, or slovenly person. **6.** *U.S. Slang.* an inefficient or inferior person or thing. —**slouch′y,** adj. —**slouch′i·ly,** adv. —**slouch′i·ness,** n.

slough[1] (slou for 1, 3; sloo for 2), n. **1.** a piece of soft, muddy ground. **2.** U.S. and Canada. a marshy or reedy pool, pond, inlet, or the like. **3.** a condition of degradation, embarrassment, or helplessness.

slough[2] (slŭf), n. **1.** the skin of a snake, esp. the outer skin which is shed periodically. **2.** Pathol. a mass of dead tissue which separates from the underlying tissue. —v.i. **3.** to be shed or cast off. **4.** to cast off a slough. —v.t. **5.** to cast or throw. **6.** Bridge. to dispose of (a losing card). —**slough′y,** adj.

Slo·va·ki·a (slō vä′kǐ ə, -väk′ǐ ə), n. a province in E Czechoslovakia. 3,329,793 pop.; 18,921 sq. mi. Cap.: Bratislava. **Slo·vak** (slō′văk, slō-väk′), adj., n.

slov·en (slŭv′ən), n. **1.** an untidy, slovenly person. **2.** a careless worker.

Slo·ve·ni·a (slō vē′nǐ ə), n. a constituent republic of Yugoslavia, in the NW part. 1,144,000 pop.; 6265 sq. mi. Cap.: Ljubljana. **Slo·vene** (slō vēn′, slō′vēn), adj., n.

slov·en·ly (slŭv′ən lǐ), adj., -lier, -liest, adv. —adj. **1.** untidy, careless, or slipshod. —adv. **2.** in a slovenly manner. —**slov′en·li·ness,** n.

slow (slō), adj. **1.** not fast, rapid, or swift. **2.** gradual. **3.** sluggish in nature, disposition, or function. **4.** dull of perception or understanding. **5.** not prompt or readily disposed. **6.** burning or heating with little intensity. **7.** slack, as trade. **8.** running at less than the proper rate of speed. —adv. **9.** in a slow manner. —v.t. **10.** to make slow. **11.** to retard. —v.i. **12.** to become slow. —**slow′ly,** adv. —**slow′ness,** n.

sludge (slŭj), n. **1.** mud; slush. **2.** broken ice, as on the sea.

slue[1] (sloo), v., slued, sluing, n. —v.t., v.i. **1.** to turn or swing round. —n. **2.** act of sluing.

slue[2] (sloo), n. Colloq. slew.

slug[1] (slŭg), n. **1.** any of various slimy, elongated terrestrial gastropods related to the snails, but having no shell. **2.** any heavy piece of crude metal. **3.** a piece of lead or other metal for firing from a gun. **4.** a metal disk used as a coin, generally counterfeit. **5.** Print. **a.** a thick strip of type metal less than type-high. **b.** a line of type in one piece.

slug[2] (slŭg), v., slugged, slugging, n. Colloq. —v.t. **1.** to hit hard, esp. with the fist. —n. **2.** a heavy blow. —**slug′ger,** n.

slug·gard (slŭg′ərd), n. **1.** a lazy person. —adj. **2.** lazy.

slug·gish (slŭg′ĭsh), adj. **1.** inactive, slow, or of little energy. **2.** moving slowly. —**slug′-gish·ly,** adv. —**slug′gish·ness,** n.

sluice (sloos), n., v., sluiced, sluicing. —n. **1.** an artificial channel for water, fitted with a gate (**sluice gate**) for regulating the flow. **2.** the water held back or controlled by a sluice gate. **3.** any contrivance for regulating a flow. **4.** a channel, esp. one carrying off surplus water. —v.t. **5.** to let out (water, etc.) by opening a sluice. **6.** to open a sluice upon. **7.** to flush or cleanse with a rush of water. —v.i. **8.** to flow through a sluice.

slum (slŭm), n., v., slummed, slumming. —n. **1.** (often pl.) a thickly populated, squalid part of a city. —v.i. **2.** to visit slums, esp. from curiosity. —**slum′mer,** n.

slum·ber (slŭm′bər), v.i. **1.** to sleep. **2.** to be in a state of inactivity or calm. —n. **3.** sleep. **4.** a state of inactivity, etc. —**slum′ber·er,** n. —**slum′ber·ous,** adj.

slump (slŭmp), v.i. **1.** to drop heavily. **2.** to fall suddenly and markedly, as prices. —n. **3.** act of slumping. **4.** a decline in prices or sales.

slur (slûr), v., slurred, slurring, n. —v.t. **1.** to pass over lightly. **2.** to pronounce indistinctly. **3.** Music. to sing to a single syllable or play without a break (two or more tones of different pitch). **4.** to calumniate, disparage, or depreciate. —n. **5.** a slurred utterance or sound. **6.** Music. **a.** the combination of two or more tones of different pitch, sung to a single syllable or played without a break. **b.** a curved mark indicating this. **7.** a disparaging remark.

slush (slŭsh), n. **1.** snow in a partly melted state. **2.** liquid mud. **3.** a mixture of grease and other materials for lubricating. **4.** weakly emotional talk, writing, etc. —v.t. **5.** to cover with slush. —**slush′y,** adj.

slut (slŭt), n. **1.** a slovenly woman. **2.** Chiefly U.S. a prostitute. —**slut′tish,** adj.

sly (slī), adj., slyer, slyest or slier, sliest. **1.** cunning or wily. **2.** stealthy. **3.** mischievous; roguish. —**sly′ly,** adv. —**sly′ness,** n.

Sm, Chem. samarium.

smack[1] (smăk), n. **1.** a taste or flavor. **2.** a trace or suggestion. —v.i. **3.** to have a taste, flavor, or trace.

smack[2] (smăk), v.t., v.i. **1.** to separate (the lips) with a sharp sound. **2.** to strike smartly, esp. with the open hand. —n. **3.** a smacking of the lips. **4.** a loud kiss. **5.** a smart, resounding blow. —adv. **6.** Colloq. suddenly and sharply. **7.** Colloq. directly.

smack[3] (smăk), n. a sailing vessel, usually sloop-rigged, used esp. in fishing.

small (smôl), adj. **1.** not big; little. **2.** slender, thin, or narrow. **3.** not great in amount, degree, duration, value, etc. **4.** of minor importance. **5.** ungenerous. **6.** ashamed. **7.** soft. —adv. **8.** in a small manner. **9.** into small pieces. **10.** softly. —n. **11.** that which is small. **12.** the small or narrow part. —**small′ish,** adj. —**small′ness,** n.

small fry, **1.** small or young fish. **2.** young or unimportant persons or objects.

small·pox (smôl′pŏks′), n. an acute, highly contagious febrile disease characterized by a pustular eruption.

smart (smärt), v.i. **1.** to cause or feel a sharp local, and usually superficial, pain. —adj. **2.** sharp or keen, as pain. **3.** sharply severe, as blows, etc. **4.** having or showing quick intelligence; clever. **5.** dashingly or effectively trim in appearance. **6.** socially fashionable. —adv. **7.** in a smart manner. —n. **8.** sharp local pain, as from a wound or sting. —**smart′ly,** adv. —**smart′ness,** n.

smart·en (smär′tən), v.t. to make more trim or spruce; improve in appearance.

smash (smăsh), v.t., v.i. **1.** to break to pieces with violence; shatter. **2.** to overthrow or destroy. **3.** Tennis. to strike (the ball) hard and fast with an overhand stroke. **4.** to crash. **5.** to become financially ruined. —n. **6.** a smashing or shattering, or the sound of it. **7.** a destructive collision. **8.** a process or state of collapse, ruin, or destruction. —**smash′er,** n.

smash-up (smăsh′ŭp′), n. a complete smash.

smat·ter·ing (smăt′ər ĭng), n. a slight or superficial knowledge of something.

smear (smĭr), v.t. **1.** to rub or spread with oil, grease, paint, dirt, etc. **2.** to daub (oil, grease, etc.). **3.** to sully, as one's reputation. **4.** U.S. Slang. to defeat decisively. —n. **5.** a mark or stain made by smearing. **6.** an unfairly derogatory attack.

smell (smĕl), v., smelled or smelt, smelling, n. —v.t. **1.** to perceive (the odor of something) through the nose. **2.** to detect by shrewdness or sagacity. —v.i. **3.** to inhale the odor of a thing. **4.** to give out an odor, esp. an offensive one. —n. **5.** the faculty or sense of smelling. **6.** an odor. —**smell′er,** n. —**smell′y,** adj.

smelling salts, a preparation of ammonium carbonate inhaled in cases of faintness, headache, etc.

smelt[1] (smĕlt), v.t. **1.** to melt (ore) in order to separate the metal contained. **2.** to refine (metal) in this way.

smelt[2] (smĕlt), n., pl. smelts, (esp. collectively) smelt. a small silvery food fish.

smelt·er (smĕl′tər), n. a place where ores are smelted.

smi·lax (smī′lăks), n. **1.** any of certain tropical and temperate vines with woody stems, esp. the sarsaparilla plant. **2.** a delicate, twining plant with glossy, bright-green leaves.

smile (smīl), v., smiled, smiling, n. —v.i. **1.** to assume a facial expression indicative of pleasure, favor, etc. **2.** to look with such an expression. **3.** to have a pleasant or agreeable aspect. —v.t. **4.** to assume or give (a smile). **5.** to express by a smile. —n. **6.** act of smiling. **7.** favoring look or regard. —**smil′er,** n. —**smil′ing·ly,** adv.

smirch (smûrch), v.t. **1.** to discolor or soil. **2.** to sully, as with disgrace. —n. **3.** a dirty smear. **4.** a stain, as on reputation.

smirk (smûrk), v.i. **1.** to smile in an affected or smug way. —n. **2.** such a smile.

smite (smīt), v.t., smote, smitten or smit, smiting. **1.** to strike or hit hard. **2.** to render by, or as by, a blow. **3.** to slay. **4.** to afflict. **5.** to charm; enamor. —**smit′er,** n. —**smit′ten** (smĭt′ən), adj.

smith (smĭth), *n.* a worker in metal.

Smith (smĭth), *n.* **1. Adam,** 1723–90, Scottish political economist. **2. Alfred Emanuel,** 1873–1944, U.S. political leader. **3. Captain John,** 1580–1631, British adventurer: colonist in Virginia. **4. Joseph,** 1805–44, U.S. religious leader who founded the Mormon Church.

smith·er·eens (smĭth′ə rēnz′), *n. pl. Colloq.* small fragments.

smith·y (smĭth′ĭ, smĭth′ĭ), *n., pl.* **smithies.** the workshop of a blacksmith.

smock (smŏk), *n.* **1.** a loose overgarment worn to protect the clothing while at work. —*v.t.* **2.** to draw (a fabric) by needlework into a honeycomb pattern. —**smock′ing,** *n.*

smog (smŏg), *n.* a mixture of smoke and fog.

smoke (smōk), *n., v.,* **smoked, smoking.** —*n.* **1.** the visible gaseous exhalation given off by a burning or smoldering substance. **2.** a cigar or cigarette. —*v.i.* **3.** to emit smoke. **4.** to draw into the mouth and puff out the smoke of tobacco or the like, as from a cigarette. —*v.t.* **5.** to draw into the mouth and puff out the smoke of (tobacco, etc.). **6.** to use (a pipe, etc.) in this process. **7.** to cure (meat, fish, etc.) by exposure to smoke. **8.** to darken by smoke. **9.** to drive (*out*) by smoke. —**smoke′less,** *adj.*

smok·er (smō′kər), *n.* **1.** one that smokes. **2.** Also, **smoking car,** a railroad car for travelers who wish to smoke. **3.** an informal gathering of men.

smoke·stack (smōk′stăk′), *n.* a pipe for the escape of smoke, as on a boat.

smok·y (smō′kĭ), *adj.,* **smokier, smokiest.** **1.** emitting smoke. **2.** hazy or cloudy. **3.** of or like smoke. —**smok′i·ly,** *adv.* —**smok′i·ness,** *n.*

smol·der (smōl′dər), *v.i.* **1.** to burn or smoke without flame. **2.** to exist or continue in a suppressed state. **3.** to display repressed feelings. —*n.* **4.** a smoldering fire.

smooth (smōōth), *adj.* **1.** free from irregularities of surface; not rough. **2.** free from hairs. **3.** free from lumps, as a sauce. **4.** easy and uniform, as motion. **5.** free from hindrances or difficulties. **6.** tranquil, as the feelings. **7.** elegant or polished, as speech. **8.** pleasant or polite, as manner. **9.** bland. —*adv.* **10.** in a smooth manner. —*v.t.* **11.** to make smooth. **12.** to remove (projections, etc.). —*n.* **13.** act of smoothing. **14.** a smooth part or place. —**smooth′er,** *n.* —**smooth′ly,** *adv.* —**smooth′ness,** *n.*

smor·gas·bord (smôr′gŏs bôrd′), *n.* the hors d'œuvres at a Scandinavian dinner.

smoth·er (smŭth′ər), *v.t., v.i.* **1.** to stifle or suffocate. **2.** to extinguish (fire, etc.) by covering so as to exclude air. **3.** to suppress. —*n.* **4.** dust, fog, spray, etc., in a dense or enveloping cloud.

smoul·der (smōl′dər), *v.i., n.* smolder.

smudge (smŭj), *n., v.,* **smudged, smudging.** —*n.* **1.** a dirty smear. **2.** a smoky fire, esp. one for driving away mosquitoes, etc. —*v.t.* **3.** to mark with dirty streaks or smears. —**smudg′y,** *adj.* —**smudg′i·ness,** *n.*

smug (smŭg), *adj.,* **smugger, smuggest. 1.** complacently righteous, clever, etc.; self-satisfied. **2.** trim; sleek. —**smug′ly,** *adv.* —**smug′ness,** *n.*

smug·gle (smŭg′əl), *v.t., v.i.,* **-gled, -gling. 1.** to import or export (goods) secretly in violation of law. **2.** to bring, take, etc., surreptitiously. —**smug′gler,** *n.*

smut (smŭt), *n., v.,* **smutted, smutting.** —*n.* **1.** soot. **2.** a smudge. **3.** obscenity. **4.** a fungous disease of plants, esp. cereals. —*v.t.* **5.** to soil or smudge.

smutch (smŭch), *v.t., n.* smudge.

Smuts (smŭts), *n.* **Jan Christiaan,** 1870–1950, South African statesman.

smut·ty (smŭt′ĭ), *adj.,* **-tier, -tiest. 1.** grimy; dirty. **2.** obscene, as talk. —**smut′ti·ly,** *adv.* —**smut′ti·ness,** *n.*

Smyr·na (smûr′nə), *n.* a seaport in W Turkey. 183,762.

Sn, (L *stannum*) *Chem.* tin.

snack (snăk), *n.* a quick, light meal.

snaf·fle (snăf′əl), *n., v.,* **-fled, -fling.** —*n.* **1.** a slender, jointed bit used on a bridle. —*v.t.* **2.** to put a snaffle on (a horse, etc.).

sna·fu (snă′fōō′), *adj., v.,* **-fued, -fuing.** *Slang.* —*adj.* **1.** in disorder; chaotic. —*v.t.* **2.** to muddle.

snag (snăg), *n., v.,* **snagged, snagging.** —*n.* **1.** a short, projecting stump, as of a branch broken off. **2.** any sharp or rough projection.

3. any obstacle or impediment. —*v.t.* **4.** to catch upon a snag.

snail (snāl), *n.* **1.** a mollusk having a single, usually spirally coiled shell. **2.** a slow or lazy person.

snake (snāk), *n., v.,* **snaked, snaking.** —*n.* **1.** a scaly, limbless, usually slender reptile, occurring in venomous and nonvenomous forms. **2.** a treacherous person. —*v.i.* **3.** to move, twist, or wind in the manner of a snake. —*v.t. U.S.* **4.** to drag or haul. **5.** to jerk.

snak·y (snā′kĭ), *adj.,* **snakier, snakiest. 1.** of or pertaining to snakes. **2.** abounding in snakes. **3.** winding; sinuous. **4.** venomous; insidious.

snap (snăp), *v.,* **snapped, snapping,** *n., adj., adv.* —*v.i.* **1.** to make a sudden, sharp sound. **2.** to move, shut, etc., with a sharp sound. **3.** to break suddenly, esp. something brittle. **4.** to act or move with quick, neat motions of the body. **5.** to photograph. **6.** to make a sudden bite or snatch. **7.** to utter a quick, sharp reproof, retort, etc. —*v.t.* **8.** to seize quickly. **9.** to cause to make a sudden, sharp sound. **10.** to bring, shut, operate, etc., with a sharp sound. **11.** to utter in a quick, sharp manner. **12.** to break suddenly. **13.** to take a photograph of. —*n.* **14.** a sharp, crackling or clicking sound. **15.** a catch operating with such a sound. **16.** a sudden breaking. **17.** a small, thin, brittle or crisp cake. **18.** liveliness; vigor. **19.** a quick or sudden bite or snatch. **20.** a short spell, as of cold weather. **21.** *Photog.* a snapshot. **22.** *Slang.* an easy position, piece of work, or the like. —*adj.* **23.** denoting devices closing by pressure on a spring catch. **24.** made, done, taken, etc., suddenly or offhand. **25.** easy. —*adv.* **26.** in a brisk, sudden manner.

snap·drag·on (snăp′drăg′ən), *n.* an herb long cultivated for its spikes of showy flowers, with a corolla that has been supposed to look like the mouth of a dragon.

snap·per (snăp′ər), *n.* **1.** any of various large marine fishes of warm seas. **2.** a snapping turtle.

snapping turtle, a large and savage turtle of American rivers, having powerful snapping jaws.

snap·pish (snăp′ĭsh), *adj.* **1.** apt to snap or bite. **2.** irritably sharp; curt. —**snap′pish·ly,** *adv.*

snap·py (snăp′ĭ), *adj.,* **-pier, -piest. 1.** snappish. **2.** quick or sudden. **3.** *Colloq.* crisp, smart, lively, brisk, etc. —**snap′pi·ly,** *adv.* —**snap′pi·ness,** *n.*

snap·shot (snăp′shŏt′), *n.* an instantaneous photograph.

snare[1] (snâr), *n., v.,* **snared, snaring.** —*n.* **1.** a device, usually consisting of a noose, for capturing birds or small animals. **2.** any trap. —*v.t.* **3.** to catch with a snare; entrap; entangle. —**snar′er,** *n.*

snare[2] (snâr), *n.* one of the strings of gut stretched across the skin of a snare drum.

snare drum, a small double-headed drum having snares across the lower head to produce a rattling effect.

Snare drum

snarl[1] (snärl), *v.i., v.t.* **1.** to growl viciously, as a dog. **2.** to speak in a savagely angry manner. —*n.* **3.** act of snarling. **4.** a snarling sound or utterance. —**snarl′er,** *n.*

snarl[2] (snärl), *n.* **1.** a tangle, as of hair. **2.** a complicated or confused condition. —*v.t.* **3.** to tangle. **4.** to render complicated or confused. —*v.i.* **5.** to become tangled.

snatch (snăch), *v.i.* **1.** to make a sudden effort to seize something. —*v.t.* **2.** to take, get, secure, rescue, etc., suddenly or hastily. —*n.* **3.** act of snatching. **4.** a sudden motion to seize something. **5.** a scrap; fragment. **6.** a brief period or action. —**snatch′er,** *n.*

sneak (snēk), *v.i., v.t.* **1.** to go or act in a stealthy or furtive manner. —*n.* **2.** one who sneaks. —**sneak′ing,** *adj.* —**sneak′y,** *adj.*

sneak·er (snē′kər), *n.* **1.** *U.S. Colloq.* a shoe with a rubber sole used esp. in gymnasiums. **2.** one who sneaks.

sneer (snĭr), *v.i.* **1.** to smile or act in a manner that shows scorn, contempt, etc. —*n.* **2.** a derisive or scornful look or remark. —**sneer′er,** *n.* —**sneer′ing·ly,** *adv.*

sneeze (snēz), *v.,* **sneezed, sneezing,** *n.* —*v.i.* **1.** to emit breath suddenly, forcibly, and audibly through the nose and mouth by involuntary, spasmodic action. **2.** *Colloq.* to treat with contempt. —*n.* **3.** an act or sound of sneezing. —**sneez'er,** *n.*

snick·er (snĭk'ər), *v.i.* **1.** to laugh in a half-suppressed, often disrespectful, manner. —*n.* **2.** a snickering laugh. Also, *esp. Brit.,* **snig·ger** (snĭg'ər).

snide (snīd), *adj.* derogatory in a nasty, insinuating manner.

sniff (snĭf), *v.i., v.t.* **1.** to draw (air) through the nose in short, audible inhalation. **2.** to clear the nose by so doing. **3.** to smell by short inhalations. **4.** to show disdain, contempt, etc., by a sniff. —*n.* **5.** a single short, audible inhalation.

snif·fle (snĭf'əl), *v.,* **-fled, -fling,** *n.* —*v.i.* **1.** to sniff repeatedly. —*n.* **2.** an act or sound of sniffling. **3. the sniffles,** a mild cold in the head.

snip (snĭp), *v.,* **snipped, snipping,** *n.* —*v.t., v.i.* **1.** to cut with a small, quick stroke, or a succession of such strokes. —*n.* **2.** a small cut. **3.** a small piece snipped off. **4.** (*pl.*) shears for the use of sheet-metal workers.

snipe (snīp), *n., v.,* **sniped, sniping.** —*n.* **1.** any of certain long-billed shore birds frequenting marshes. —*v.i.* **2.** to shoot individual soldiers, etc., from a concealed position. —**snip'er,** *n.*

snip·py (snĭp'ĭ), *adj.,* **-pier, -piest.** *Colloq.* sharp or curt. **2.** fragmentary. —**snip'pi·ness,** *n.*

snitch[1] (snĭch), *v.t. Slang.* to steal.

snitch[2] (snĭch), *Slang.* —*v.i.* **1.** to turn informer. —*n.* **2.** an informer. —**snitch'er,** *n.*

sniv·el (snĭv'əl), *v.i.,* **-eled, -eling** or (*esp. Brit.*) **-elled, -elling. 1.** to weep with sniffling. **2.** to run at the nose. —**sniv'el·er,** *n.*

snob (snŏb), *n.* one who cultivates those with social rank, wealth, etc., and is condescending to others. —**snob'ber·y,** *n.* —**snob'bish,** *adj.* —**snob'bish·ly,** *adv.* —**snob'bish·ness,** *n.*

snood (snōōd), *n.* **1.** a band or fillet for the hair. **2.** a netlike hat or part of a hat.

snoop (snōōp), *Colloq.* —*v.i.* **1.** to prowl or pry. —*n.* **2.** an act or instance of snooping. **3.** one who snoops. —**snoop'er,** *n.*

snoot·y (snōō'tĭ), *adj.,* **snootier, snootiest.** *U.S. Colloq.* snobbish.

snooze (snōōz), *v.i.,* **snoozed, snoozing.** *Colloq.* to sleep; slumber; doze; nap.

snore (snōr), *v.,* **snored, snoring,** *n.* —*v.i.* **1.** to breathe during sleep with harsh sounds. —*n.* **2.** an act of snoring, or the sound made. —**snor'er,** *n.*

snor·kel (snôr'kəl), *n.* a device on a submarine consisting of two vertical tubes for the intake and exhaust of air for Diesel engines and general ventilation, thus permitting cruising at periscope depth for very long periods.

snort (snôrt), *v.i.* **1.** to exhale with a loud, harsh sound, as a horse. **2.** to express contempt, indignation, etc., by such a sound. —*n.* **3.** act or sound of snorting. —**snort'er,** *n.*

snot (snŏt), *n.* mucus from the nose. —**snot'ty,** *adj.*

snout (snout), *n.* the part of an animal's head projecting forward and containing the nose and jaws.

snow (snō), *n.* **1.** the aqueous vapor of the atmosphere falling to the earth in white crystalline flakes. **2.** the fall of these flakes. **3.** *Slang.* cocaine or heroin. —*v.i.* **4.** to fall as snow. —*v.t.* **5.** to cover, obstruct, etc., with snow.

snow·ball (snō'bôl'), *n.* **1.** a ball of snow. **2.** any of certain shrubs with white flowers in large snowball-like clusters. —*v.t.* **3.** to pelt with snowballs. —*v.i.* **4.** to grow larger at an accelerating rate.

snow·drift (snō'drĭft'), *n.* a mass of snow driven together by wind.

snow·fall (snō'fôl'), *n.* a fall of snow.

snow·flake (snō'flāk'), *n.* one of the small feathery flakes in which snow falls.

snow·plow (snō'plou'), *n.* an implement for clearing snow from highways, etc.

snow·shoe (snō'shōō'), *n., v.,* **-shoed, -shoeing.** —*n.* **1.** a racketlike contrivance attached to the foot to enable the wearer to walk on deep snow without sinking in. —*v.i.* **2.** to walk or travel on snowshoes. —**snow'sho·er,** *n.*

snow·storm (snō'stôrm'), *n.* a storm accompanied by a heavy fall of snow.

snow·y (snō'ĭ), *adj.,* **snowier, snowiest.** **1.** abounding in or covered with snow. **2.** snow-white. **3.** immaculate. —**snow'i·ly,** *adv.* —**snow'i·ness,** *n.*

snub (snŭb), *v.,* **snubbed, snubbing,** *n., adj.*

—*v.t.* **1.** to treat with disdain or contempt. **2.** to check or stop suddenly. —*n.* **3.** a sharp rebuke. **4.** a disdainful slight. **5.** a sudden check. —*adj.* **6.** (of the nose) short, and turned up at the tip. —**snub'ber,** *n.* —**snub'by,** *adj.*

snuff[1] (snŭf), *v.t., v.i.* **1.** to inhale. **2.** to smell. —*n.* **3.** an inhalation. **4.** a preparation of powdered tobacco, usually taken into the nostrils by inhalation. —**snuff'er,** *n.*

snuff[2] (snŭf), *n.* **1.** the charred portion of a candlewick. —*v.t.* **2.** to extinguish. —**snuff'er,** *n.*

snuf·fle (snŭf'əl), *v.,* **-fled, -fling,** *n.* —*v.i., v.t.* **1.** to sniff. —*n.* **2.** an act of snuffling. **3. the snuffles,** a cold in the nose. —**snuf'fler,** *n.*

snug (snŭg), *adj.,* **snugger, snuggest,** *v.,* **snugged, snugging,** *adv.* —*adj.* **1.** comfortable or cozy. **2.** trim, neat, or compactly arranged. —*v.i., v.t.* **3.** to nestle. —*adv.* **4.** in a snug manner. —**snug'ly,** *adv.* —**snug'ness,** *n.*

snug·gle (snŭg'əl), *v.i., v.t.,* **-gled, -gling.** to nestle; cuddle.

so[1] (sō), *adv.* **1.** in the way or manner indicated. **2.** in that or this manner. **3.** as stated or reported. **4.** in the aforesaid state. **5.** to that extent. **6.** very. **7.** very greatly. **8.** to such a degree or extent. **9.** having the purpose of. **10.** hence; therefore. **11.** because of. **12.** in such manner as to result from. **13.** in this way. **14.** in such way as to end in. —*conj.* **15.** *Colloq.* consequently. **16.** under the condition that. —*pron.* **17.** such as has been stated. **18.** more or less. —*interj.* **19.** how can that be!

so[2] (sō), *n. Music.* sol.

So., **1.** South. **2.** Southern.

soak (sōk), *v.i.* **1.** to become saturated. **2.** to be thoroughly wet. **3.** to become known slowly (to). —*v.t.* **4.** to saturate thoroughly. **5.** to drench. **6.** to absorb. **7.** *U.S. Slang.* **a.** to beat hard. **b.** to charge exorbitantly, etc. —*n.* **8.** act of soaking. **9.** the state of being soaked. **10.** *Slang.* a heavy drinker. —**soak'er,** *n.*

soap (sōp), *n.* **1.** a substance used for washing and cleansing purposes, usually made by treating a fat with an alkali. —*v.t.* **2.** to rub, cover, or treat with soap. —**soap'y,** *adj.* —**soap'i·ness,** *n.*

soar (sōr), *v.i.* **1.** to fly upward or at a great height. **2.** to rise or aspire to a more exalted level. —*n.* **3.** act of soaring. **4.** the height attained in soaring. —**soar'er,** *n.*

sob (sŏb), *v.,* **sobbed, sobbing,** *n.* —*v.i.* **1.** to weep with a sound caused by a convulsive catching of the breath. —*v.t.* **2.** to utter with sobs. —*n.* **3.** a convulsive catching of the breath in weeping. —**sob'bing·ly,** *adv.*

so·ber (sō'bər), *adj.* **1.** not drunk. **2.** habitually temperate. **3.** quiet or sedate. **4.** marked by seriousness, gravity, solemnity, etc. **5.** not gay or showy. **6.** free from exaggeration. **7.** showing self-control. **8.** sane. —*v.t., v.i.* **9.** to make or become sober. —**so'ber·ly,** *adv.* —**so'ber·ness, so·bri·e·ty** (sō brī'ə tĭ), *n.*

so·bri·quet (sō'brĭ kā'), *n.* a nickname.

Soc., society.

so-called (sō'kôld'), *adj.* **1.** called or designated thus. **2.** incorrectly called thus.

soc·cer (sŏk'ər), *n.* a form of football in which the use of the hands and arms either for playing the ball or for interfering with an opponent is prohibited.

so·cia·ble (sō'shə bəl), *adj.* **1.** inclined to associate with others. **2.** friendly or companionable. —*n.* **3.** *U.S.* an informal social gathering. —**so'cia·ble·ness, so·cia·bil'i·ty,** *n.* —**so'cia·bly,** *adv.*

so·cial (sō'shəl), *adj.* **1.** pertaining or devoted to friendly companionship. **2.** sociable. **3.** living in companionship or in a community. **4.** of or pertaining to human society. **5.** venereal. —*n.* **6.** a social gathering or party. —**so'cial·ly,** *adv.* —**so'cial·ness,** *n.*

so·cial·ism (sō'shə lĭz'əm), *n.* a theory or system of social organization which advocates the vesting of the ownership and control of the means of production, capital, land, etc., in the community as a whole. —**so'cial·ist,** *n., adj.* —**so'cial·is'tic,** *adj.*

so·cial·ize (sō'shə līz'), *v.t.,* **-ized, -izing. 1.** to make social or sociable. **2.** to make socialistic. —**so'cial·i·za'tion,** *n.*

socialized medicine, any of various systems to provide the entire population, especially the lower-income groups, with medical care through federal subsidization of medical and health services, etc.

social security, a plan providing life insurance and old-age pensions, offered by the government to specified groups of the population.

so·ci·e·ty (sə sī'ə tǐ), n., pl. -ties. 1. an organization of persons for religious, literary, patriotic, or other purposes. 2. a community. 3. the body of human beings generally. 4. companionship or company. 5. the people of the polite or fashionable world.

Society of Friends, a sect founded by George Fox about 1650, opposed to oath taking and all war; Quakers.

so·ci·ol·o·gy (sō'sǐ ŏl'ə jǐ, sō'shǐ-), n. the science of the fundamental laws of social relations, institutions, etc. —so'ci·o·log'i·cal, adj. —so'ci·ol'o·gist, n.

sock[1] (sŏk), n. 1. a short stocking. 2. a light shoe worn by ancient comic actors.

sock[2] (sŏk), Slang. —v.t. 1. to strike or hit hard. —n. 2. a hard blow.

sock·et (sŏk'ǐt), n. 1. a hollow part for holding some corresponding part. 2. a device providing a connection with electric wires. —v.t. 3. to place in a socket.

Soc·ra·tes (sŏk'rə tēz'), n. 469?-399 B.C., Athenian philosopher. —So·crat·ic (sō krăt'ǐk), adj., n.

sod (sŏd), n., v., sodded, sodding. —n. 1. a piece of grassland, containing the roots, etc. 2. turf; sward. —v.t. 3. to cover with sods.

so·da (sō'də), n. 1. sodium hydroxide; caustic soda. 2. the oxide of sodium. 3. sodium. 4. soda water. 5. a drink made with soda water, served with fruit or other syrups, ice cream, etc.

so·dal·i·ty (sō dăl'ə tǐ), n., pl. -ties. 1. fellowship. 2. an association or society.

soda water, an effervescent beverage consisting of water charged with carbon dioxide.

sod·den (sŏd'ən), adj. 1. soaked. 2. heavy, doughy, or soggy. 3. dull; stupid. —v.t., v.i. 4. to make or become sodden.

so·di·um (sō'dǐ əm), n. Chem. a soft, silver-white metallic element. Symbol: Na; at. wt.: 22.997; at. no.: 11; sp. gr.: 0.97 at 20°C.

Sod·om (sŏd'əm), n. Bible. an ancient city near the Dead Sea, which was destroyed because of its wickedness.

sod·om·y (sŏd'əm ǐ), n. unnatural sexual intercourse, esp. of one man with another.

so·ev·er (sō ĕv'ər), adv. at all; in any case; of any kind; in any way.

so·fa (sō'fə), n. a long upholstered couch with a back and two arms.

So·fi·a (sō'fǐ ə, sō fē'ə), n. the capital of Bulgaria, in the W part. 434,888.

soft (sôft, sŏft), adj. 1. yielding readily; not hard or stiff. 2. pleasant or comfortable. 3. low or gentle. 4. not glaring, as light. 5. not sharp, as outlines. 6. balmy, as climate. 7. lenient; compassionate. 8. smooth, soothing, or ingratiating. 9. impressionable. 10. sentimental. 11. not strong or robust. 12. Colloq. easy. 13. (of water) relatively free from mineral salts that interfere with the action of soap. 14. Phonet. (of c and g) pronounced as in cent and gem. —n. 15. the soft part; softness. —adv. 16. in a soft manner. —interj. Archaic. 17. hush! —soft'ly, adv. —soft'ness, n.

soft coal, bituminous coal.

soft drink, a drink which is not alcoholic or intoxicating, as root beer, ginger ale, etc.

sof·ten (sôf'ən, sŏf'ən), v.t., v.i. to make or become soft or softer. —soft'en·er, n.

soft soap, Colloq. flattery.

soft-soap (sôft'sōp', sŏft'-), v.t. to flatter.

soft·y (sôf'tǐ, sŏft'-), n., pl. -ties. Colloq. one who is easily imposed upon.

sog·gy (sŏg'ǐ), adj., -gier, -giest. 1. thoroughly wet. 2. damp and heavy. 3. dull; stupid. —sog'gi·ly, adv. —sog'gi·ness, n.

soil[1] (soil), n. 1. that portion of the earth's surface in which plants grow. 2. a particular kind of earth. 3. the ground as producing vegetation. 4. the ground or earth.

soil[2] (soil), v.t. 1. to make dirty. 2. to smudge or stain. 3. to sully or defile morally. —n. 4. a spot, mark, or stain. 5. filth; sewage. 6. manure or compost.

soi·ree (swä rā'), n. an evening party or social gathering. Also, soi·rée'.

so·journ (v. sō jûrn', sō'jûrn; n. sō'jûrn), v.i.

1. to dwell for a time in a place. —n. 2. a temporary stay. —so·journ'er, n.

Sol (sŏl), n. 1. the sun, personified by the Romans as a god. 2. Alchemy. gold.

sol (sōl, sŏl), n. Music. the syllable used for the fifth tone of a scale.

sol·ace (sŏl'ǐs), n., v., -aced, -acing. —n. 1. comfort in sorrow or trouble. —v.t. 2. to comfort, console, alleviate, or relieve.

so·lar (sō'lər), adj. 1. of or pertaining to the sun. 2. determined or operated by the sun. 3. proceeding from the sun, as heat.

so·lar·i·um (sō lâr'ǐ əm), n., pl. -laria (-lâr'ǐə). a room exposed to the sun's rays, as at a seaside hotel.

solar plexus, Anat. a network of nerves situated at the upper part of the abdomen.

solar system, the sun together with all the planets, etc., revolving round it.

sol·der (sŏd'ər), n. 1. any of various fusible alloys applied in a melted state to metal surfaces, joints, etc., to unite them. 2. anything that unites. —v.t., v.i. 3. to unite (metals) with solder. 4. to join closely. —sol'der·er, n.

sol·dier (sōl'jər), n. 1. one who serves in an army. 2. one of the enlisted men in an army. 3. a man of military skill or experience. 4. one who serves in any cause. —v.i. 5. to serve as a soldier. 6. Colloq. to make a mere show of working. —sol'dier·ly, adj.

soldier of fortune, a military adventurer, ready to serve anywhere for pay, etc.

sol·dier·y (sōl'jər ǐ), n., pl. -dieries. 1. soldiers collectively. 2. military training.

sole[1] (sōl), adj. 1. only. 2. unique. 3. exclusive.

sole[2] (sōl), n., v., soled, soling. —n. 1. the bottom of the foot. 2. the corresponding under part of a shoe, boot, or the like. —v.t. 3. to furnish with a sole.

sole[3] (sōl), n., pl. soles, (esp. collectively) sole. any of several flatfishes used as food.

sol·e·cism (sŏl'ə sǐz'əm), n. 1. a substandard intrusion into standard speech. 2. a breach of etiquette. 3. any error. —sol'e·cis'tic, adj.

sole·ly (sōl'lǐ), adv. 1. as the only one or ones. 2. exclusively or only. 3. wholly; merely.

sol·emn (sŏl'əm), adj. 1. grave, sober, or mirthless. 2. serious or earnest. 3. formal or ceremonious. 4. sacred. —sol'emn·ly, adv. —sol'emn·ness, n.

so·lem·ni·ty (sə lĕm'nə tǐ), n., pl. -ties. 1. earnestness; gravity. 2. (often pl.) a solemn observance or ceremonial proceeding.

sol·em·nize (sŏl'əm nīz'), v.t., -nized, -nizing. 1. to observe with rites or ceremonies. 2. to perform (ceremonies, etc.) in due manner. 3. to perform the ceremony of (marriage). —sol'em·ni·za'tion, n.

so·lic·it (sə lǐs'ǐt), v.t., v.i. 1. to seek (for) by entreaty, request, etc. 2. to entreat or importune. 3. to accost (a man) with immoral intention. —so·lic'i·ta'tion, n.

so·lic·i·tor (sə lǐs'ə tər), n. 1. one who solicits. 2. U.S. an officer having charge of the legal business of a city, town, etc. 3. Eng. a lawyer.

so·lic·it·ous (sə lǐs'ə təs), adj. 1. anxious or concerned. 2. eager. —so·lic'it·ous·ly, adv. —so·lic'it·ous·ness, so·lic·i·tude (sə lǐs'ə tūd', -tōōd'), n.

sol·id (sŏl'ǐd), adj. 1. having length, breadth, and thickness. 2. of or pertaining to bodies or figures of three dimensions. 3. filled up; not hollow. 4. without openings or breaks. 5. firm, hard, or compact. 6. dense, thick, or heavy. 7. substantial; not flimsy. 8. not superficial or trifling. 9. entire. 10. uniform in tone or shade. 11. real. 12. sound, as reasons. 13. financially sound. 14. cubic. 15. written without a hyphen. 16. firmly united. 17. U.S. Colloq. on a friendly or favorable footing. 18. U.S. Slang. (of dance music, etc.) perfect. —n. 19. a body or magnitude having length, breadth, and thickness. 20. a solid substance or body. —sol'id·ly, adv. —sol'id·ness, n.

sol·i·dar·i·ty (sŏl'ə dăr'ə tǐ), n., pl. -ties. community of interests, feelings, purposes, action, etc.

so·lid·i·fy (sə lǐd'ə fī'), v.t., v.i., -fied, -fying. to make or become solid. —so·lid'i·fi·ca'tion, n.

so·lid·i·ty (sə lǐd'ə tǐ), n., pl. -ties. state, property, or quality of being solid.

so·lil·o·quize (sə lǐl'ə kwīz'), v.i., -quized, -quizing. to utter a soliloquy.

so·lil·o·quy (sə lĭl′ə kwĭ), *n.*, *pl.* **-quies.** act of talking when alone or as if alone.

sol·i·taire (sŏl′ə târ′), *n.* **1.** a game played by one person alone. **2.** a precious stone, esp. a diamond, set by itself.

sol·i·tar·y (sŏl′ə tĕr′ĭ), *adj.*, *n.*, *pl.* **-taries.** —*adj.* **1.** alone; without companions. **2.** living alone. **3.** single; only. **4.** unfrequented, secluded, or lonely. —*n.* **5.** one who lives alone. —**sol′i·tar′i·ly,** *adv.* —**sol′i·tar′i·ness,** *n.*

sol·i·tude (sŏl′ə tūd′, -tōōd′), *n.* **1.** seclusion. **2.** remoteness from habitations, as of a place. **3.** a lonely, unfrequented place.

so·lo (sō′lō), *n.*, *pl.*, **-los,** *adj.* —*n.* **1.** a musical composition performed by one singer or player. **2.** any performance, as a dance, by one person. **3.** a flight in an airplane during which the student aviator is unaccompanied —*adj.* **4.** *Music.* performing alone. **5.** performed alone. **6.** alone.

so·lo·ist (sō′lō ĭst), *n.* one who performs a solo.

Sol·o·mon (sŏl′ə mən), *n.* a 10th-century B.C. king of Israel, famous for his wisdom.

Solomon Islands, an archipelago in the S Pacific, E of New Guinea: the larger, SE part forms a British protectorate; the NW islands are part of the Australian trusteeship Territory of New Guinea.

So·lon (sō′lən), *n.* **1.** c638–c558 B.C., Athenian statesman. **2.** a wise lawgiver.

so long, *Colloq.* good-by.

sol·stice (sŏl′stĭs), *n. Astron.* either of the two times in the year when the sun is at its greatest distance from the celestial equator: about June 21 and about Dec. 22.

sol·u·ble (sŏl′yə bəl), *adj.* **1.** capable of being dissolved or liquefied. **2.** capable of being solved or explained. —**sol′u·bil′i·ty,** *n.* —**sol′u·bly,** *adv.*

so·lu·tion (sə lōō′shən), *n.* **1.** act of solving a problem, etc. **2.** an explanation or answer. **3.** the act by which a gas, liquid, or solid is dispersed homogeneously in a gas, liquid, or solid without chemical change. **4.** dissolved state. **5.** *U.S.* a watery solution of a potent drug.

solve (sŏlv), *v.t.*, **solved, solving.** to explain; find the answer to. —**solv′a·ble,** *adj.* —**solv′er,** *n.*

sol·vent (sŏl′vənt), *adj.* **1.** able to pay all just debts. **2.** causing solution. —*n.* **3.** the component of a solution which dissolves the other component. —**sol′ven·cy,** *n.*

So·ma·li·land (sō mä′lĭ länd′), *n.* a coastal region in E Africa, including **French Somaliland, British Somaliland, Italian Somaliland,** and part of Ethiopia.

so·mat·ic (sō măt′ĭk), *adj.* bodily; physical.

som·ber (sŏm′bər), *adj.* **1.** gloomily dark. **2.** dark and dull, as color. **3.** depressing; dismal. Also, *esp. Brit.,* **som′bre.** —**som′ber·ly,** *adv.* —**som′ber·ness,** *n.*

som·bre·ro (sŏm brâr′ō), *n.*, *pl.* **-ros.** a broad-brimmed hat worn in Spain, Mexico, the southwestern U.S., etc.

Man wearing a sombrero

some (sŭm; *unstressed* səm), *adj.* **1.** being an undetermined or unspecified one. **2.** certain. **3.** of a certain unspecified number, degree, etc. **4.** unspecified but considerable in number, etc. **5.** about. **6.** *U.S. Slang.* notable. —*pron.* **7.** certain persons, instances, etc., not specified. **8.** an unspecified number, amount, etc. —*adv.* **9.** *Slang.* somewhat. **10.** *U.S. Colloq.* considerably.

some·bod·y (sŭm′bŏd′ĭ, -bŭd′ĭ, -bə dĭ), *pron., n., pl.* **-bodies.** —*pron.* **1.** some person. —*n.* **2.** a person of some note or importance.

some·how (sŭm′hou′), *adv.* in some way not specified, apparent, or known.

some·one (sŭm′wŭn′, -wən), *pron.* some person; somebody.

som·er·sault (sŭm′ər sôlt′), *n.* **1.** an acrobatic movement of the body in which it describes a complete revolution, heels over head. —*v.i.* **2.** to perform a somersault.

Som·er·ville (sŭm′ər vĭl), *n.* a city in E Massachusetts, near Boston. 102,177.

some·thing (sŭm′thĭng), *n.* **1.** a certain undetermined or unspecified thing. **2.** a thing or person of some value or consequence. —*adv.* **3.** to some extent; somewhat.

some·time (sŭm′tīm′), *adv.* **1.** at some indefi-

nite or indeterminate point of time. **2.** at an indefinite future time. —*adj.* **3.** former.

some·times (sŭm′tīmz′), *adv.* on some occasions; at times; now and then.

some·what (sŭm′hwŏt′, -hwət), *adv.* **1.** to some extent. —*n.* **2.** some part, etc.

some·where (sŭm′hwâr′), *adv.* **1.** in, at, or to some place not specified, determined, or known. **2.** at some point of time. —*n.* **3.** an unspecified or uncertain place.

Somme (sôm), *n.* a river in N France, flowing NW to the English Channel. ab. 140 mi.

som·nam·bu·late (sŏm năm′byə lāt′), *v.i., v.t.,* **-lated, -lating.** to walk during sleep.

som·nam·bu·lism (sŏm năm′byə lĭz′əm), *n.* the fact or habit of walking about while asleep; sleepwalking. —**som·nam′bu·list,** *n.*

som·no·lent (sŏm′nə lənt), *adj.* sleepy. —**som′no·lence,** *n.* —**som′no·lent·ly,** *adv.*

son (sŭn), *n.* **1.** a male child in relation to his parents. **2.** any male descendant. **3.** a son-in-law. **4.** a familiar term of address to a man or boy from an older person, an ecclesiastic, etc. **5.** the Son, Jesus Christ.

so·nant (sō′nənt), *adj.* **1.** sounding; having sound. **2.** *Phonet.* voiced. —**so′nance,** *n.*

so·na·ta (sə nä′tə), *n. Music.* an extended instrumental composition usually in several movements.

song (sông, sŏng), *n.* **1.** a short metrical composition for singing; lyric. **2.** poetry. **3.** vocal music. **4. for a song,** at a very low price.

song·bird (sông′bûrd′, sŏng′-), *n.* **1.** a bird that sings. **2.** a woman who sings.

Song of Solomon, The, a book of the Old Testament.

song·ster (sông′stər, sŏng′-), *n.* **1.** one who sings. **2.** a poet. **3.** a songbird. —**song·stress** (sông′strĭs, sŏng′-), *n. fem.*

son-in-law (sŭn′ĭn lô′), *n., pl.* **sons-in-law.** the husband of one's daughter.

son·net (sŏn′ĭt), *n. Pros.* a poem, properly expressive of a single, complete thought, of 14 lines with rhymes arranged according to one of certain definite schemes.

son·net·eer (sŏn′ə tĭr′), *n.* **1.** a composer of sonnets. —*v.i.* **2.** to compose sonnets.

so·no·rous (sə nōr′əs), *adj.* **1.** loud, deep, or resonant. **2.** high-flown; grandiloquent. —**so·no′rous·ly,** *adv.* —**so·no′rous·ness, so·nor·i·ty** (sə nôr′ə tĭ, -nŏr′-), *n.*

Soo·chow (sōō′chou′), *n.* a city in E China. 260,000.

soon (sōōn), *adv.* **1.** within a short period. **2.** in the near future. **3.** promptly. **4.** readily or willingly.

soot (sŏŏt, sōōt), *n.* **1.** a black carbonaceous substance produced during the imperfect combustion of coal, wood, oil, etc. —*v.t.* **2.** to mark or cover with soot. —**soot′y,** *adj.* —**soot′i·ness,** *n.*

soothe (sōōth), *v.t., v.i.,* **soothed, soothing. 1.** to calm, relieve, comfort, or refresh. **2.** to mitigate or allay. —**sooth′ing,** *adj.* —**sooth′ing·ly,** *adv.*

sooth·say·er (sōōth′sā′ər), *n.* one who professes to foretell events. —**sooth′say·ing,** *n.*

sop (sŏp), *n., v.,* **sopped, sopping.** —*n.* **1.** a piece of bread or the like dipped in liquid food. **2.** something given to pacify or quiet. —*v.t.* **2.** to soak (bread, etc.) in some liquid. **4.** to absorb.

soph·ism (sŏf′ĭz əm), *n.* **1.** a specious but fallacious argument. **2.** a fallacy.

soph·ist (sŏf′ĭst), *n.* **1.** (*often cap*) **a.** any of a class of professional teachers in ancient Greece. **b.** any member of this class who concerned himself with specious effectiveness rather than soundness of argument. **2.** one who reasons adroitly and speciously rather than soundly. —**so·phis·tic** (sə fĭs′tĭk), **so·phis′ti·cal,** *adj.* —**so·phis′ti·cal·ly,** *adv.*

so·phis·ti·cate (sə fĭs′tə kāt′, -kĭt), *n.* a sophisticated person.

so·phis·ti·cat·ed (sə fĭs′tə kā′tĭd), *adj.* **1.** (of a person, the ideas, tastes, etc.) altered by education, worldly experience, etc.; artificial. **2.** adapted to the tastes of sophisticates.

so·phis·ti·ca·tion (sə fĭs′tə kā′shən), *n.* **1.** sophisticated character, ideas, tastes, or ways. **2.** change from the natural simplicity.

soph·ist·ry (sŏf′ĭs trĭ), *n., pl.* **-ries.** a subtle, tricky, beguiling but generally fallacious reasoning.

Soph·o·cles (sŏf'ə klēz'), *n.* 495?–406? B.C., Greek poet: writer of tragedies.

soph·o·more (sŏf'ə mōr'), *n.* *Chiefly U.S.* a student in the second year of the course at a university, college, or high school.

soph·o·mor·ic (sŏf'ə môr'ĭk, -mŏr'-), *adj.* *Chiefly U.S.* **1.** of or pertaining to a sophomore or sophomores. **2.** full of immature intellectual pretensions, self-assurance, etc.

so·po·rif·ic (sō'pə rĭf'ĭk, sŏp'ə-), *adj.* **1.** causing sleep. **2.** sleepy; drowsy. —*n.* **3.** something causing sleep.

sop·ping (sŏp'ĭng), *adj.* soaked; drenched.

so·pran·o (sə prăn'ō, -prä'nō), *n.*, *pl.* **-pranos, -prani** (-prä'nē), *adj. Music.* —*n.* **1.** the uppermost part or voice. **2.** the highest singing voice in women and boys. **3.** a part for such a voice. **4.** a singer with such a voice. —*adj.* **5.** of or pertaining to soprano.

sor·cer·er (sôr'sər ər), *n.* one supposed to exercise supernatural powers through evil spirits. —**sor·cer·ess** (sôr'sər ĭs), *n.fem.*

sor·cer·y (sôr'sə rĭ), *n.*, *pl.* **-ceries.** the art, practices, or spells of a sorcerer; witchery.

sor·did (sôr'dĭd), *adj.* **1.** dirty or filthy. **2.** morally mean or ignoble. **3.** meanly selfish or mercenary. —**sor'did·ly,** *adv.* —**sor'did·ness,** *n.*

sore (sōr), *adj.*, **sorer, sorest,** *n.* —*adj.* **1.** physically painful or sensitive, as a wound, etc. **2.** suffering bodily pain from wounds, etc. **3.** grieved, distressed, or sorrowful. **4.** causing very great misery, hardship, etc. **5.** *Colloq.* irritated; offended. —*n.* **6.** a sore spot on the body. **7.** a source or cause of grief, irritation, etc. —**sore'-ly,** *adv.* —**sore'ness,** *n.*

sore·head (sōr'hĕd'), *n.* *U.S. Slang.* an unsportsmanlike loser.

sor·ghum (sôr'gəm), *n.* **1.** a cereal grass of many varieties, used for making molasses and syrup, and for forage, food for man, hay, etc. **2.** the syrup made from sorghum.

so·ror·i·ty (sə rôr'ə tĭ, -rŏr'-), *n.*, *pl.* **-ties.** *U.S.* a club of women or girls, as in a college.

sor·rel[1] (sôr'əl, sŏr'-), *n.* **1.** light reddish brown. **2.** a horse of this color.

sor·rel[2] (sôr'əl, sŏr'-), *n.* any of certain plants having succulent acid leaves used in salads, sauces, etc.

sor·row (sŏr'ō, sôr'ō), *n.* **1.** grief, sadness, or regret. **2.** a cause of grief or regret. **3.** an affliction, misfortune, or trouble. —*v.i.* **4.** to feel sorrow; grieve. —**sor'row·er,** *n.*

sor·row·ful (sŏr'ə fəl, sôr'-), *adj.* **1.** grieved; sad. **2.** mournful; plaintive. **3.** distressing. —**sor'row·ful·ly,** *adv.* —**sor'row·ful·ness,** *n.*

sor·ry (sŏr'ĭ, sôr'ĭ), *adj.*, **-rier, -riest.** **1.** feeling regret, sympathy, pity, etc. **2.** deplorable, pitiable, or miserable. **3.** sorrowful, grieved, or sad. **4.** melancholy; dismal. **5.** wretched; pitiful. —**sor'ri·ly,** *adv.*

sort (sôrt), *n.* **1.** a particular kind, class, or group. **2.** character, quality, or nature. **3.** manner, fashion, or way. —*v.t.* **4.** to arrange according to kind; classify. **5.** to separate or take (out) from other sorts. —**sort'er,** *n.*

sor·tie (sôr'tē), *n.* **1.** a sally of troops from a besieged place to attack the besiegers. **2.** the flying of an airplane on a combat mission.

S O S (ĕs'ō'ĕs'), the letters represented by the radio telegraphic signal used, as by ships in distress, to call for help.

so·so (sō'sō'), *adj.* **1.** neither very good nor very bad. —*adv.* **2.** indifferently; tolerably.

sot (sŏt), *n.* a confirmed drunkard. —**sot'tish,** *adj.* —**sot'tish·ly,** *adv.* —**sot'tish·ness,** *n.*

sou (soo), *n.* a former French bronze coin worth less than 1 U.S. cent.

sou·bri·quet (soo'brə kā'), *n.* sobriquet.

souf·flé (soo flā', soo'flā), *adj.* **1.** puffed up; made light, as by beating. —*n.* **2.** a light, baked dish made fluffy with beaten egg whites.

sough (sŭf, sou), *v.i.* **1.** to make a rushing or murmuring sound. —*n.* **2.** such a sound.

soul (sōl), *n.* **1.** the principle of life, feeling, thought, and action in man, regarded as a distinct entity separate from the body. **2.** the emotional part of man's nature. **3.** noble warmth of feeling, spirit or courage, etc. **4.** the animating principle or essential element of something. **5.** the embodiment of some quality. **6.** a disembodied spirit of a deceased person. **7.** a person.

soul·ful (sōl'fəl), *adj.* of, or expressive of, deep feeling or emotion. —**soul'ful·ly,** *adv.*

soul·less (sōl'lĭs), *adj.* **1.** without a soul. **2.** lacking in nobility, spirit, or courage.

sound[1] (sound), *n.* **1.** the sensation produced in the organs of hearing when certain vibrations are caused in the surrounding air. **2.** the vibrations (**sound waves**) in the air producing this sensation. **3.** the particular auditory effect produced by a given cause. **4.** the distance within which the noise of something may be heard. **5.** mere noise, without meaning. —*v.i.* **6.** to make a sound. **7.** to be heard. **8.** to convey a certain impression. **9.** to give a specific sound. —*v.t.* **10.** to cause to make a sound. **11.** to give forth (a sound). **12.** to announce, order, or direct. **13.** to utter audibly. —**sound'er,** *n.* —**sound'less,** *adj.* —**sound'proof',** *adj.*

sound[2] (sound), *adj.* **1.** free from injury, damage, decay, defect, disease, etc.; healthy. **2.** financially strong. **3.** good or reliable. **4.** substantial or enduring. **5.** without logical or legal defect. **6.** theologically correct or orthodox. **7.** honest; honorable; loyal. **8.** unbroken and deep, as sleep. **9.** vigorous, or thorough. —**sound'ly,** *adv.* —**sound'ness,** *n.*

sound[3] (sound), *v.t.*, *v.i.* **1.** to measure the depth of (water, etc.) by letting down a plummet at the end of a line. **2.** to seek to fathom or ascertain.

sound[4] (sound), *n.* **1.** a relatively narrow passage of water between larger bodies or between the mainland and an island. **2.** an inlet or arm of the sea.

sound·ing[1] (soun'dĭng), *adj.* **1.** emitting a sound or sounds. **2.** sonorous. **3.** high-sounding; pompous.

sound·ing[2] (soun'dĭng), *n.* **1.** (*often pl.*) act or process of measuring depth, etc., with a lead and line. **2.** (*pl.*) parts of the water in which the ordinary sounding lead will reach bottom.

soup (soop), *n.* **1.** a liquid food made by boiling meat, fish, or vegetables, with various added ingredients. —*v.t.* **2.** **soup up,** *U.S. Slang.* to speed up (a motor) by increasing the richness of the fuel mixture.

sour (sour), *adj.* **1.** having an acid taste, such as that of vinegar, lemon juice, etc.; tart. **2.** fermented or spoiled. **3.** disagreeable; unpleasant. **4.** austere; morose; peevish. —*n.* **5.** something sour. **6.** *U.S.* an acid drink, as whiskey with lemon juice, sugar, etc. —*v.i.*, *v.t.* **7.** to become or make sour. —**sour'ish,** *adj.* —**sour'ly,** *adv.* —**sour'ness,** *n.*

source (sōrs), *n.* **1.** any thing or place from which something comes, arises, or is obtained; origin. **2.** the place of origin of a stream or river. **3.** a book, person, etc., supplying information.

sour·dough (sour'dō'), *n.* *Western U.S. and Canada, Alaska.* a prospector or pioneer.

sour grapes, something a person pretends to despise only because he cannot have it.

Sou·sa (soo'zə), *n.* **John Philip,** 1854–1932, U.S. band conductor and composer.

souse (sous), *v.*, **soused, sousing,** *n.* —*v.t.*, *v.i.* **1.** to plunge into water or other liquid. **2.** to drench. **3.** to steep in pickle. **4.** *Slang.* to intoxicate. —*n.* **5.** act of sousing. **6.** something steeped in pickle. **7.** *Slang.* a drunkard.

south (south), *n.* **1.** a cardinal point of the compass directly opposite to the north. **2.** the direction in which this point lies. **3.** (*l.c. or cap.*) a quarter or territory situated in this direction. —*adj.* **4.** lying toward, situated in, or directed toward the south. **5.** coming from the south, as a wind. —*adv.* **6.** toward, in, or from the south.

South Africa. See **Union of South Africa.** —**South African.**

South America, a continent in the S part of the Western Hemisphere. 88,500,000 pop.; ab. 6,900,000 sq. mi. —**South American.**

South·amp·ton (south ămp'tən, -hămp'-), *n.* a seaport in S England. 160,340.

South Australia, a state in S Australia. 636,460 pop.; 380,070 sq. mi. *Cap.:* Adelaide.

South Bend, a city in N Indiana. 101,268.

South Car·o·li·na (kăr'ə lī'nə), a State in the SE United States. 1,909,173 pop.; 31,055 sq. mi. *Cap.:* Columbia. *Abbr.:* S.C. —**South Car·o·lin·i·an** (kăr'ə lĭn'ĭ ən).

South Da·ko·ta (də kō'tə), a State in the N central United States. 547,664 pop.; 77,047 sq. mi. *Cap.:* Pierre. *Abbr.:* S. Dak. —**South Da·ko'tan.**

South·down (south'doun'), *n.* a breed of high-quality mutton sheep.

south·east (south'ēst'; *Naut.* sou'-), *n.* **1.** the point or direction midway between south and east. **2.** a region in this direction. —*adj.* **3.** lying toward, situated in, or directed toward the southeast. **4.** coming from the southeast, as a wind. —*adv.* **5.** in the direction midway between south and east. **6.** from this direction. —**south′east′-ern,** *adj.* —**south′east′ward,** *adj., adv.* —**south′east′ward·ly,** *adv.* —**south′east′-wards,** *adv.*

south·east·er (south′ēs′tər; *Naut.* sou′-), *n.* a wind, gale, or storm from the southeast.

south·east·er·ly (south′ēs′tər lǐ; *Naut.* sou′-), *adj., adv.* toward or from the southeast.

south·er·ly (sǔth′ər lǐ), *adj., adv.* **1.** toward the south. **2.** from the south, as a wind.

south·ern (sǔth′ərn), *adj.* **1.** lying toward, situated in, or directed toward the south. **2.** coming from the south, as a wind. **3.** of or pertaining to the south. **4.** (*cap.*) of or pertaining to the South of the United States.

Southern Cross, *Astron.* the southern constellation Crux, which has its four chief stars arranged in the form of a cross.

south·ern·er (sǔth′ər nər), *n.* a native or inhabitant of the south, esp. (*cap.*) of the United States.

Sou·they (sou′thǐ, sǔth′ǐ), *n.* **Robert,** 1774–1843, British poet and writer.

South Island, the largest island of New Zealand. 552,545 pop.; 58,093 sq. mi.

south·paw (south′pô′), *Sports Slang.* —*n.* **1.** a left-handed pitcher, player, etc. —*adj.* **2.** left-handed.

South Pole, the southern end of the earth's axis of rotation.

south·ward (south′wərd; *Naut.* sǔth′ərd), *adj.* **1.** moving, facing, or situated toward the south. —*adv.* Also, **south′wards. 2.** toward the south. —*n.* **3.** the southward part, direction, or point. —**south′ward·ly,** *adj., adv.*

south·west (south′wěst′; *Naut.* sou′-), *n.* **1.** the point or direction midway between south and west. **2.** a region in this direction. —*adj.* **3.** lying toward, situated in, or directed toward the southwest. **4.** coming from the southwest, as a wind. —*adv.* **5.** toward or from the southwest. —**south′west′ern,** *adj.* —**south′west′er·ly,** *adj., adv.* —**south′west′ward,** *adj., adv.* —**south′west′wards,** *adv.*

south·west·er (south′wěs′tər; *Naut.* sou′-), *n.* **1.** a wind, gale, or storm from the southwest. **2.** a waterproof hat having the brim very broad behind so as to protect the neck, worn esp. by seamen. Also, **sou′·west·er** (sou′wěs′tər).

sou·ve·nir (sōō′və nǐr′, sōō′və nǐr′), *n.* **1.** a remembrance; memento. **2.** a memory.

sov·er·eign (sǒv′rǐn, sǔv′-), *n.* **1.** a monarch; a king or queen. **2.** a British gold coin, worth 1 pound. —*adj.* **3.** belonging to or characteristic of a sovereign. **4.** having supreme rank, power, or authority. **5.** supreme, greatest, or extreme. **6.** efficacious or potent, as a remedy. —**sov′er-eign·ly,** *adv.*

sov·er·eign·ty (sǒv′rǐn tǐ, sǔv′-), *n., pl.* **-ties.** the status, dominion, power, or authority of a sovereign.

so·vi·et (sō′vǐ ět′, -ǐt, sō′vǐ ět′), *n.* **1.** (in the Soviet Union): **a.** a local council. **b.** a council elected by a local council. part of a pyramid of soviets, culminating in the **Supreme Soviet,** which is the "parliament" of the Soviet Union. —*adj.* **2.** of or pertaining to a soviet. **3.** (*cap.*) of or pertaining to the Soviet Union.

so·vi·et·ize (sō′vǐ ə tīz′), *v.t.,* **-ized, -izing.** to bring under the influence of soviets or of the Soviet Union.

Soviet Russia, 1. the Soviet Union. **2.** Russian Socialist Federated Soviet Republic.

Soviet Union, a federal union of sixteen constituent republics, in E Europe and W and N Asia, comprising the larger part of the former Russian Empire. 193,000,000 pop.; ab. 8,350,600 sq. mi. *Cap.:* Moscow. Official name, **Union of Soviet Socialist Republics.**

sow¹ (sō), *v.t., v.i.,* **sowed, sown** or **sowed, sowing. 1.** to scatter (seed) over land, earth etc., for growth. **2.** to scatter seed over (land, etc.). **3.** to propagate or disseminate. —**sow′er,** *n.*

sow² (sou), *n.* an adult female hog.

soy (soi), *n.* **1.** a salty, fermented sauce much used on fish and other dishes in the Orient, prepared from soybeans. **2.** a leguminous plant, orig. Oriental, cultivated for its highly nutritious seed (**soybean**). Also, *esp. Brit.,* **soy·a** (soi′ə).

Sp., 1. Spanish. **2.** (*l.c.*) spelling.

spa (spä), *n.* a mineral spring, or a locality in which such springs exist.

space (spās), *n., v.,* **spaced, spacing.** —*n.* **1.** the unlimited or indefinitely great expanse in which all material objects are located. **2.** the portion of this in a given instance. **3.** a particular extent of surface. **4.** a seat, berth, or room on a train, airplane, etc. **5.** linear distance. **6.** extent or interval of time. —*v.t.* **7.** to divide into spaces. **8.** to set some distance apart. —**spac′er,** *n.*

spa·cious (spā′shəs), *adj.* **1.** containing much space; amply large. **2.** vast. **3.** broad; large; great. —**spa′cious·ly,** *adv.* —**spa′cious·ness,** *n.*

spade¹ (spād), *n., v.,* **spaded, spading.** —*n.* **1.** a tool for digging, having an iron blade adapted for pressing into the ground with the foot. —*v.t.* **2.** to dig, cut, or remove with a spade.

spade² (spād), *n.* **1.** a black figure shaped like an inverted heart with a short stem at the cusp opposite the point, used on playing cards. **2.** a card of the suit bearing such figures. **3.** (*pl.*) the suit of cards bearing this figure.

spa·dix (spā′dǐks), *n., pl.* **spadices** (spā dī′sēz). *Bot.* an inflorescence consisting of a spike with a fleshy or thickened axis, usually enclosed in a spathe.

spa·ghet·ti (spə gět′ǐ), *n.* a kind of food paste of Italian origin in long, slender, solid, cordlike pieces.

Spain (spān), *n.* a country in SW Europe: proclaimed a kingdom by Franco, July, 1947. (Including the Balearic and Canary Islands) 26,246,000 pop.; 194,720 sq. mi. *Cap.:* Madrid.

span¹ (spăn), *n., v.,* **spanned, spanning.** —*n.* **1.** the distance between the tip of the thumb and the tip of the little finger when the hand is fully extended. **2.** a unit of length, commonly 9 inches. **3.** the space between two supports of a bridge. **4.** the full extent of anything. **5.** *Aeron.* the distance between the wing tips of an airplane. **6.** a short space of time. —*v.t.* **7.** to measure by the hand with the thumb and little finger extended. **8.** to extend over, across, or around.

span² (spăn), *n.* a pair of horses or other animals harnessed and driven together.

span·gle (spăng′gəl), *n., v.,* **-gled, -gling.** —*n.* **1.** a small, thin, often circular piece of glittering material for decorating garments, etc. **2.** any small, bright object, spot, or the like. —*v.t.* **3.** to decorate or sprinkle with spangles. —*v.i.* **4.** to glitter.

Span·iard (spăn′yərd), *n.* a native or inhabitant of Spain.

span·iel (spăn′yəl), *n.* a dog of any of various breeds of medium size, usually with a long, silky coat and drooping ears.

Span·ish (spăn′ǐsh), *adj.* **1.** of or pertaining to Spain, its people, or their language. —*n.* **2.** the Spanish people collectively. **3.** a Romance language, the language of Spain, Latin America (except Brazil), and the Philippine Islands.

Spanish America, the Spanish-speaking countries south of the United States. —**Span′ish-A·mer′i·can,** *adj., n.*

Spanish Main, 1. the mainland of America adjacent to the Caribbean Sea. **2.** the Caribbean Sea.

spank (spăngk), *v.t.* **1.** to strike (a child) with the open hand, a slipper, etc., esp. on the buttocks, as in punishment. —*n.* **2.** a blow given in spanking.

spank·ing (spăngk′ǐng), *adj.* **1.** moving rapidly and smartly. **2.** quick and vigorous. **3.** blowing briskly. **4.** *Colloq.* unusually fine, great, large, etc.

span·ner (spăn′ər), *n.* **1.** one that spans. **2.** *Chiefly Brit.* a wrench, esp. one with fixed jaws.

spar¹ (spär), *n., v.,* **sparred, sparring.** —*n.* **1.** *Naut.* a mast, yard, boom, gaff, or the like. —*v.t.* **2.** to provide or make with spars.

spar² (spär), *v., sparred, sparring, n. —v.i.* **1.** to box. **2.** to bandy words. —*n.* **3.** a boxing match. **4.** a dispute.

spar³ (spär), *n.* any of various more or less lustrous crystalline minerals.

Spar (spär), *n.* a woman enlisted in the women's reserve of the U.S. Coast Guard.

spare (spâr), *v., spared, sparing, adj., sparer, sparest, n. —v.t.* **1.** to refrain from harming or destroying. **2.** to deal gently or leniently with. **3.** to save from strain, discomfort, annoyance, or the like. **4.** to refrain from using. **5.** to part with, esp. without inconvenience. **6.** to do without. —*v.i.* **7.** to be frugal. **8.** to forbear. **9.** to exercise lenience or mercy. —*adj.* **10.** kept in reserve, as for possible use. **11.** free for other use. **12.** frugally restricted; meager. **13.** lean or thin. **14.** scanty or scant. —*n.* **15.** a spare thing, part. etc. **16.** *U.S. Bowling.* **a.** the knocking down of all the pins with two bowls. **b.** score so made. —**spare′ly,** *adv.* —**spare′ness,** *n.*

spare·rib (spâr′rĭb′), *n.* a cut of pork containing ribs from the fore end of the row, where there is little meat adhering.

spar·ing (spâr′ĭng), *adj.* **1.** economical. **2.** lenient or merciful. **3.** frugally restricted. **4.** limited. —**spar′ing·ly,** *adv.*

spark[1] (spärk), *n.* **1.** an ignited particle such as is thrown off by burning wood, etc. **2.** *Elect.* the light produced by a sudden discontinuous discharge of electricity, as through air. **3.** a small trace of something. **4.** a trace of life. —*v.i.* **5.** to emit sparks. **6.** to issue as sparks.

spark[2] (spärk), *n.* **1.** a beau, lover, or suitor. —*v.t., v.i.* **2.** *Colloq.* to woo or court.

spar·kle (spär′kəl), *v.,* -**kled,** -**kling,** *n.* —*v.i.* **1.** to issue in little sparks, as fire. **2.** to emit little sparks. **3.** to glisten brightly; glitter. **4.** to effervesce. **5.** to be brilliant, lively, or vivacious. —*n.* **6.** a little spark. **7.** a sparkling appearance. **8.** brilliance, liveliness, or vivacity. —**spar′kler,** *n.*

spark plug, 1. a device inserted in the cylinder of an internal-combustion engine, containing the two terminals between which passes the electric spark for igniting the explosive gases. **2.** *U.S. Colloq.* a person who leads the activities or maintains the morale of a group.

spar·row (spär′ō), *n.* a small, hardy, pugnacious bird of Europe, America, Australia, etc.: a destroyer of insects but now commonly regarded as a pest.

sparse (spärs), *adj.,* **sparser, sparsest. 1.** thinly scattered. **2.** scanty; meager. —**sparse′ly,** *adv.* —**sparse′ness, spar·si·ty** (spär′sə tĭ), *n.*

Spar·ta (spär′tə), *n.* an ancient city in S Greece.

Spar·tan (spär′tən), *adj.* **1.** of or pertaining to Sparta or its people. **2.** rigorously simple, frugal, or austere. —*n.* **3.** a native or inhabitant of Sparta. **4.** a person of Spartan characteristics. —**Spar′tan·ism,** *n.*

Spar·tan·burg (spär′tən bûrg′), *n.* a city in NW South Carolina. 32,249.

spasm (spăz′əm), *n.* **1.** a sudden, abnormal, involuntary muscular contraction. **2.** any sudden, brief spell of unusual energy, activity, etc.

spas·mod·ic (spăz mŏd′ĭk), *adj.* **1.** characterized by spasms. **2.** sudden and violent, but brief; intermittent. Also, **spas·mod′i·cal.** —**spas·mod′i·cal·ly,** *adv.*

spas·tic (spăs′tĭk), *adj. Pathol.* pertaining to, of the nature of, or characterized by spasm.

spat[1] (spăt), *n., v.,* **spatted, spatting.** —*n.* **1.** a petty quarrel. —*v.i. Colloq.* **2.** to engage in a petty quarrel or dispute.

spat[2] (spăt), *n.* (*usually pl.*) a short gaiter worn over the instep.

spathe (spāth), *n. Bot.* a bract or pair of bracts under or enclosing a spadix or flower cluster.

spa·tial (spā′shəl), *adj.* **1.** of or pertaining to space. **2.** existing or occurring in space.

spat·ter (spăt′ər), *v.t., v.i.* **1.** to scatter or dash in small drops. **2.** to splash or sprinkle, esp. with something dirty. —*n.* **3.** act or sound of spattering. **4.** a spot of something spattered. —**spat′ter·ing·ly,** *adv.*

spat·ter·dash (spăt′ər dăsh′), *n.* (*usually pl.*) a kind of long gaiter worn to protect the trousers or stockings from mud, etc.

spat·u·la (spăch′ə lə), *n.* an implement with a broad, flat, flexible blade, used for mixing drugs, spreading, etc. —**spat·u·late** (spăch′ə lĭt, -lāt′), *adj.*

spav·in (spăv′ĭn), *n.* any disease of the hock joint of horses in which enlargements occur. —**spav′ined,** *adj.*

spawn (spôn), *n.* **1.** *Zool.* the mass of sex cells of fishes, amphibians, mollusks, etc., after being emitted. **2.** any offspring. —*v.t., v.i.* **3.** to produce (spawn). —**spawn′er,** *n.*

spay (spā), *v.t.* to remove the ovaries of (a female animal).

speak (spēk), *v.,* **spoke** or (*Archaic*) **spake; spoken** or (*Archaic*) **spoke; speaking.** —*v.i.* **1.** to utter words; talk. **2.** to converse. **3.** to deliver an address, etc. **4.** to make a plea or recommendation. **5.** to mention. —*v.t.* **6.** to utter orally. **7.** to express. **8.** to use in oral utterance, as a language. —**speak′a·ble,** *adj.*

speak·eas·y (spēk′ē′zĭ), *n., pl.* -**easies.** *U.S. Slang.* a place where intoxicating liquors are sold without a license or otherwise contrary to law.

speak·er (spē′kər), *n.* **1.** one who speaks. **2.** (*usually cap.*) the presiding officer of the House of Representatives of the U.S., or of some other similar assembly. **3.** *Radio.* a loud-speaker. —**speak′er·ship′,** *n.*

speak·ing (spē′kĭng), *n.* **1.** the act or utterance of one who speaks. —*adj.* **2.** highly expressive. **3.** lifelike. **4.** used in speaking. **5.** permitting of speaking, as in conversation. **6.** of or pertaining to declamation.

spear[1] (spĭr), *n.* **1.** a weapon for thrusting or throwing, consisting of a long wooden staff to which a sharp head, as of iron, is fixed. **2.** some similar weapon, as one for spearing fish. —*v.t.* **3.** to pierce with a spear. —**spear′man,** *n.*

spear[2] (spĭr), *n.* a blade of grass, etc.

spear·head (spĭr′hĕd′), *n.* **1.** the sharp-pointed head of a spear. **2.** any person or thing that leads an attack, etc. —*v.t.* **3.** to act as a spearhead for.

spear·mint (spĭr′mĭnt′), *n.* an aromatic herb of the mint family: much used for flavoring.

spec., 1. special. **2.** specially.

spe·cial (spĕsh′əl), *adj.* **1.** particular, individual, or certain. **2.** having a particular function, purpose, etc. **3.** specific, as a statement. **4.** distinguished or unusual. **5.** extraordinary; exceptional. **6.** great. —*n.* **7.** a special person or thing. **8.** a special train. **9.** a special edition of a newspaper. —**spe′cial·ly,** *adv.*

spe·cial·ist (spĕsh′əl ĭst), *n.* one who devotes himself to one subject, business, etc.

spe·cial·ize (spĕsh′ə līz′), *v.,* -**ized,** -**izing.** —*v.i.* **1.** to pursue some special line of study, work, etc. —*v.t.* **2.** to render special or specific. **3.** to restrict to specific limits. —**spe′cial·i·za′tion,** *n.*

spe·cial·ty (spĕsh′əl tĭ), *n., pl.* -**ties. 1.** a special subject of study, line of work, or the like. **2.** an article particularly dealt in, manufactured, featured, etc. **3.** a special point, matter, or characteristic.

spe·cie (spē′shĭ), *n.* coin; coined money.

spe·cies (spē′shĭz), *n., pl.* -**cies. 1.** a class of individuals having some common characteristics. **2.** the basic category of biological classification, intended to designate a single kind of animal or plant.

specif., 1. specific. **2.** specifically.

spe·cif·ic (spĭ sĭf′ĭk), *adj.* **1.** explicit; definite. **2.** specified, precise, or particular. **3.** *Biol.* of or pertaining to a species. —*n.* **4.** something specific. **5.** *Med.* a remedy for a specific disease. —**spe·cif′i·cal·ly,** *adv.*

spec·i·fi·ca·tion (spĕs′ə fə kā′shən), *n.* **1.** act of specifying. **2.** a detailed description of dimensions, materials, etc., for a proposed building or the like. **3.** a specified particular.

specific gravity, *Physics.* the ratio of the mass of a given volume of any substance to that of the same volume of some other substance taken as a standard, water being the standard for solids and liquids, and hydrogen or air for gases.

spec·i·fy (spĕs′ə fī′), *v.t., v.i.,* -**fied, -fying.** to mention (something, etc.) specifically.

spec·i·men (spĕs′ə mən), *n.* **1.** a typical animal, plant, mineral, part, etc. **2.** *Colloq.* a person as a specified kind.

spe·cious (spē′shəs), *adj.* superficially pleasing; deceptive; plausible. —**spe′cious·ly,** *adv.* —**spe′cious·ness,** *n.*

speck (spĕk), *n.* **1.** a small spot. **2.** a particle. —*v.t.* **3.** to mark with a speck or specks.

speck·le (spĕk′əl), *n., v.,* -**led, -ling.** —*n.* **1.** a small speck, spot, or mark, as on skin. **2.** speckled coloring or marking. —*v.t.* **3.** to mark with speckles.

spec·ta·cle (spĕk′tə kəl), *n.* **1.** a sight. **2.** a public show or display, esp. on a large scale. **3.** (*pl.*) a set of two glass lenses in a frame, worn in front of the eyes to aid defective vision, protect the eyes, etc. —**spec′ta·cled,** *adj.*

spec·tac·u·lar (spĕk tăk′yə lər), *adj.* pertaining to or of the nature of a spectacle; dramatic; thrilling. —**spec·tac′u·lar·ly,** *adv.*

spec·ta·tor (spĕk′tā tər, spĕk tā′-), *n.* one who looks on; onlooker; observer.

spec·ter (spĕk′tər), *n.* a visible incorporeal spirit; ghost. Also, *esp. Brit.,* **spec′tre.**

spec·tral (spĕk′trəl), *adj.* 1. of or like a specter. 2. of, pertaining to, or produced by a spectrum. —**spec′tral·ly,** *adv.*

spec·tro·scope (spĕk′trə skōp′), *n.* an optical instrument for producing and examining the spectrum of the light or radiation from any source. —**spec·tro·scop·ic** (spĕk′trə skŏp′ĭk), **spec′tro·scop′i·cal,** *adj.* —**spec·tro·scop′i·cal·ly,** *adv.*

spec·tros·co·py (spĕk trŏs′kə pĭ, spĕk′trə-skō′pĭ), *n.* the science dealing with the use of the spectroscope and with spectrum analysis. —**spec·tros·co·pist** (spĕk trŏs′kə pĭst, spĕk′trə-skō′pĭst), *n.*

spec·trum (spĕk′trəm), *n., pl.* **-tra** (-trə), **-trums.** *Physics.* the band of colors formed when a beam of light undergoes dispersion, as by being passed through a prism.

spec·u·late (spĕk′yə lāt′), *v.i.,* **-lated, -lating.** 1. to meditate. 2. to indulge in conjectural thought. 3. to buy and sell commodities, stocks, etc., hazardously in the expectation of great profit. —**spec′u·la′tor,** *n.*

spec·u·la·tion (spĕk′yə lā′shən), *n.* 1. contemplation or consideration. 2. a conclusion or opinion. 3. a conjecture or surmise. 4. act of speculating. 5. a venture or undertaking in which one speculates. —**spec′u·la′tive,** *adj.* —**spec′u·la′tive·ly,** *adv.* —**spec′u·la′tive·ness,** *n.*

spec·u·lum (spĕk′yə ləm), *n., pl.* **-la** (-lə), **-lums.** a mirror or reflector.

speech (spēch), *n.* 1. the faculty or power of speaking. 2. an utterance, remark, or declaration. 3. a form of communication in spoken language made by a speaker before an audience. 4. a language or dialect. 5. manner of speaking.

speech·less (spēch′lĭs), *adj.* 1. temporarily deprived of speech by strong emotion, etc. 2. lacking the faculty of speech. 3. silent. —**speech′less·ly,** *adv.* —**speech′less·ness,** *n.*

speed (spēd), *n., v.,* **sped** or **speeded, speeding.** —*n.* 1. rapidity in moving, acting, etc.; swiftness. 2. rate of motion or progress. —*v.t.* 3. to promote the success of. 4. to increase the rate of speed of. 5. to cause to move, go, or proceed with speed. 6. to expedite the going of. —*v.i.* 7. to go with speed. 8. to increase the rate of speed. —**speed′-er,** *n.*

speed·boat (spēd′bōt′), *n.* a motorboat constructed esp. for speed.

speed·om·e·ter (spē dŏm′ə tər), *n.* a device on an automobile or the like to record the rate of travel in miles per hour.

speed·way (spēd′wā′), *n.* a road or course for fast driving, motoring, or the like.

speed·well (spēd′wĕl), *n.* any of certain herbs having blue flowers.

speed·y (spē′dĭ), *adj.,* **speedier, speediest.** 1. rapid; swift; fast. 2. prompt. —**speed′i·ly,** *adv.* —**speed′i·ness,** *n.*

spell¹ (spĕl), *v.,* **spelled** or **spelt, spelling.** —*v.t.* 1. to name, write, or otherwise give, in order, the letters of (a word, etc.). 2. (of letters) to form (a word, etc.). 3. to read slowly or with difficulty. 4. to signify. —*v.i.* 5. to name, write, or give the letters of words, etc.

spell² (spĕl), *n.* 1. a charm, incantation, or enchantment. 2. fascination.

spell³ (spĕl), *n.* 1. a period of work or other activity. 2. a turn of work so taken. 3. *Colloq.* an attack of some ailment or the like. 4. *Colloq.* an interval, usually indefinite or short. 5. a period of weather of a specified kind. —*v.t.* 6. *Chiefly U.S.* to take the place of (a person, etc.) for a time.

spell·bind (spĕl′bīnd′), *v.t.,* **-bound, -binding.** to render spellbound. —**spell′bind′er,** *n.*

spell·bound (spĕl′bound′), *adj.* enchanted, entranced, or fascinated.

spell·er (spĕl′ər), *n.* 1. one who spells words, etc. 2. a textbook on spelling.

spell·ing (spĕl′ĭng), *n.* the manner in which words are spelled; orthography.

Spell·man (spĕl′mən), *n.* **Francis Joseph,** born 1889, U.S. Roman Catholic clergyman: cardinal since 1946.

Spen·cer (spĕn′sər), *n.* **Herbert,** 1820–1903, British philosopher.

spend (spĕnd), *v.t., v.i.,* **spent, spending.** 1. to pay out (money, etc.); disburse. 2. to employ (labor, time, etc.) on some object, etc. 3. to pass (time) in a particular manner, place, etc. 4. to use up; exhaust. —**spend′er,** *n.*

spend·thrift (spĕnd′thrĭft′), *n.* 1. one who spends extravagantly. —*adj.* 2. wastefully extravagant.

Spen·ser (spĕn′sər), *n.* **Edmund,** c1552–99, British poet. —**Spen·se·ri·an** (spĕn sĭr′ĭ ən), *adj.*

spent (spĕnt), *adj.* used up, consumed, or exhausted.

sperm (spûrm), *n.* 1. spermatic fluid. 2. a male reproductive cell; spermatozoön.

sper·ma·cet·i (spûr′mə sĕt′ĭ, -sē′tĭ), *n.* a whitish, waxy substance obtained from the oil in the head of the sperm whale, used in making ointments, cosmetics, etc.

sper·mat·ic (spûr măt′ĭk), *adj.* of or pertaining to sperm or the sperm gland; seminal.

sper·ma·to·zo·ön (spûr′mə tə zō′ŏn, -ən), *n., pl.* **-zoa** (-zō′ə). *Biol.* one of the minute, motile gametes in semen, which serve to fertilize the ovum.

sperm whale, a large, square-headed whale, valuable for oil and spermaceti.

spew (spū), *v.i., v.t., n.* vomit.

sp. gr., specific gravity.

sphag·num (sfăg′nəm), *n.* any of certain mosses, used in potting and packing plants, etc.

sphere (sfĭr), *n., v.,* **sphered, sphering.** —*n.* 1. a round body whose surface is at all points equidistant from the center. 2. any globular mass, shell, etc. 3. a planet or star. 4. a field of activity or operation. 5. a particular social world. 6. a field of something specified. —*v.t.* 7. to enclose in a sphere. 8. to form into a sphere. —**spher·i·cal** (sfĕr′ə kəl), *adj.*

sphe·roid (sfĭr′oid), *n. Geom.* a solid of revolution obtained by rotating an ellipse about one of its two axes. —**sphe·roi′dal,** *adj.*

sphinc·ter (sfĭngk′tər), *n. Anat.* a circular band of muscle which encircles an orifice or hollow organ.

sphinx (sfĭngks), *n., pl.* **sphinxes, sphinges** (sfĭn′jēz). 1. *Egypt. Antiq.* a. a figure of an imaginary creature having the head of a man and the body of a lion. b. (*usually cap.*) the colossal recumbent stone figure of this kind in N Egypt. 2. (*cap.*) *Gk. Myth.* a fabulous monster which proposed a riddle to passers-by near Thebes, killing those unable to guess it.

spice (spīs), *n., v.,* **spiced, spicing.** —*n.* 1. a pungent or aromatic substance of vegetable origin, as pepper, cinnamon, and the like, used as seasoning, etc. 2. something that gives zest or interest. —*v.t.* 3. to season with spices. 4. to give zest to.

spick-and-span (spĭk′ən spăn′), *adj.* 1. neat and clean. 2. perfectly new; fresh.

spic·ule (spĭk′ūl), *n.* 1. a small, slender, sharp-pointed body or part. 2. *Zool.* one of the small, hard bodies which serve as skeletal elements of various animals. —**spic·u·late** (spĭk′yə lāt′, -lĭt), *adj.*

spic·y (spī′sĭ), *adj.,* **spicier, spiciest.** 1. seasoned with spice. 2. of or resembling spice. 3. aromatic or fragrant. 4. piquant or pungent. 5. somewhat improper. —**spic′i·ly,** *adv.* —**spic′i·ness,** *n.*

spi·der (spī′dər), *n.* 1. any of certain eight-legged, wingless, predacious, insectlike arachnids, most of which spin webs that serve as nests and as traps for prey. 2. a frying pan. —**spi′der·y,** *adj.*

spig·ot (spĭg′ət), *n.* 1. a small plug for stopping the vent of a cask, etc. 2. *U.S.* a faucet.

spike¹ (spīk), *n., v.,* **spiked, spiking.** —*n.* 1. a large, strong nail, esp. of iron. 2. a stiff, sharp-pointed piece or part. —*v.t.* 3. to fasten or provide with a spike or spikes. 4. to pierce with or impale on a spike. 5. to make ineffective; frustrate or stop. 6. *Slang.* to add alcoholic liquor to.

spike² (spīk), *n.* 1. an ear, as of wheat. 2. *Bot.* an inflorescence in which the flowers grow along an elongated, unbranched axis.

spill¹ (spĭl), *v.,* **spilled** or **spilt, spilling.** *n.* —*v.t.* 1. to cause or allow (liquid or any loose matter) to run or fall from a container. 2. to shed (blood). 3. *Naut.* to let the wind out of (a sail).

4. *Colloq.* to cause to fall, as from a horse. **5.** *Slang.* to divulge. —*v.i.* **6.** (of a liquid, etc.) to run from a container. —*n.* **7.** a spilling. **8.** *Colloq.* a fall, as from a horse.

spill² (spĭl), *n.* a splinter.

spill·way (spĭl/wā/), *n.* a passageway through which surplus water escapes from a reservoir.

spin (spĭn), *v.*, **spun** or (*Archaic*) **span; spun; spinning;** *n.* —*v.t.* **1.** to make (yarn) by drawing out, twisting, and winding fibers. **2.** to form (any material) into thread. **3.** (of spiders, silkworms, etc.) to produce (a cobweb, silk, etc.) by secreting a filament. **4.** to twirl; whirl. **5.** to produce; fabricate. **6.** to tell (a story). —*v.i.* **7.** to turn round rapidly, as on an axis. **8.** to produce a thread from the body, as spiders. **9.** to move, go, run, ride, or travel rapidly. —*n.* **10.** the act of causing a spinning. **11.** a spinning motion. **12.** a rapid run, ride, drive, or the like. **13.** *Aeron.* a maneuver in which an airplane descends along a helical path.

spin·ach (spĭn/ĭch, -ĭj), *n.* **1.** a herbaceous annual cultivated for its succulent leaves, which are eaten boiled. **2.** the leaves.

spi·nal (spī/nəl), *adj.* of or pertaining to the spine.

spinal column, (in a vertebrate animal) the bones or vertebrae forming the axis of the skeleton; spine; backbone.

spinal cord, the cord of nervous tissue extending through the spinal column.

spin·dle (spĭn/dəl), *n.*, *v.*, **-dled, -dling.** —*n.* **1.** a rod, tapering toward each end, used in spinning and for holding the thread. **2.** any axle, axis, or shaft. —*v.i.* **3.** to grow tall and slender.

spin·dling (spĭnd/lĭng), *adj.* long or tall and slender. Also, **spin/dly.**

spin·drift (spĭn/drĭft/), *n.* spray blown along the surface of the sea.

spine (spīn), *n.* **1.** the spinal column. **2.** any backbonelike part. **3.** a stiff, pointed process or appendage, as on an animal. **4.** a ridge, as of ground. **5.** a thorn. **6.** the back edge of a book binding.

spine·less (spīn/lĭs), *adj.* **1.** without spines. **2.** having no spine. **3.** without moral force, resolution, or courage. —**spine/less·ly,** *adv.*

spin·et (spĭn/ĭt), *n.* **1.** a small harpsichord. **2.** a small upright piano.

spin·na·ker (spĭn/ə kər), *n.* *Naut.* a large triangular sail carried on the side opposite the mainsail when running before the wind.

spin·ner (spĭn/ər), *n.* **1.** one that spins. **2.** a revolving bait used in trolling or casting for fish.

spin·ner·et (spĭn/ə rĕt/), *n.* an organ by which spiders, etc., spin a silky thread.

spin·ning (spĭn/ĭng), *n.* the technique or act of changing fibrous substances into yarn or thread.

spinning jenny, an early spinning machine having more than one spindle, whereby one person could spin a number of yarns simultaneously.

spinning wheel, an old-fashioned device for spinning wool, flax, etc., consisting essentially of a single spindle driven by a large wheel.

Spi·no·za (spĭ nō/zə), *n.* **Baruch** or **Benedict de,** 1632–77, Dutch philosopher.

spin·ster (spĭn/stər), *n.* a woman still unmarried beyond the usual age of marrying; old maid. —**spin/ster·hood/,** *n.*

spin·y (spī/nĭ), *adj.*, **spinier, spiniest. 1.** abounding in or having spines; thorny. **2.** resembling a spine.

spin·y-finned (spī/nĭ fĭnd/), *adj.* having fins with sharp, bony rays.

spi·ra·cle (spī/rə kəl, spĭr/ə-), *n.* an aperture through which air or water passes in the act of respiration.

spi·rae·a (spī rē/ə), *n.* any of certain herbs or shrubs with small white or pink flowers, certain species of which are much cultivated for ornament.

spi·ral (spī/rəl), *n.*, *adj.*, *v.*, **-raled, -raling** or (*esp. Brit.*) **-ralled, -ralling.** —*n.* **1.** a coil-shaped object, formation, or form. —*adj.* **2.** of or like a spire. **3.** helical. —*v.i.*, *v.t.* **4.** to take a spiral form or move in a spiral course. —**spi/ral·ly,** *adv.*

spire (spīr), *n.*, *v.*, **spired, spiring.** —*n.* **1.** a tall, tapering structure erected on a tower, roof, etc. **2.** such a structure forming the upper part of a steeple. **3.** a tall, sharp-pointed summit, peak, or the like. —*v.i.* **4.** to rise into spirelike form.

spir·it (spĭr/ĭt), *n.* **1.** the vital principle in man,

animating the body or mediating between body and soul. **2.** the incorporeal part of man. **3.** the soul. **4.** a supernatural, incorporeal being, as a fairy, elf, angel, or demon. **5.** an inspiring or animating principle. **6.** (*cap.*) the divine being or influence; God. **7.** the third person of the Trinity; Holy Spirit. **8.** (*pl.*) feelings, esp. with respect to exaltation or depression. **9.** vigor or liveliness. **10.** disposition. **11.** vigorous sense of membership in a group. **12.** the general meaning or intent of a statement, etc. **13.** *Chem.* the essence or active principle of a substance as extracted in liquid form. **14.** (*often pl.*) a strong, distilled, alcoholic liquor. **15.** *Pharm.* a solution in alcohol. —*v.t.* **16.** to animate or inspirit. **17.** to encourage; urge. **18.** to carry (*away, off,* etc.) mysteriously or secretly. —**spir/it·less,** *adj.*

spir·it·ed (spĭr/ĭt ĭd), *adj.* having or showing courage, vigor, liveliness, etc. —**spir/it·ed·ly,** *adv.* —**spir/it·ed·ness,** *n.*

spir·it·u·al (spĭr/ĭ chŏŏ əl), *adj.* **1.** of, pertaining to, or consisting of spirit or incorporeal being. **2.** ethereal or delicately refined. **3.** ecclesiastical; religious; devotional; sacred. —*n.* **4.** a religious song. —**spir/it·u·al·ly,** *adv.* —**spir/it·u·al·ness,** *adv.* (spĭr/ĭ chŏŏ ăl/ə tĭ), *n.*

spir·it·u·al·ism (spĭr/ĭ chŏŏ ə lĭz/əm), *n.* **1.** the belief that the spirits of the dead communicate with the living, esp. through a person (a medium) particularly susceptible to their influence. **2.** the belief that all reality is spiritual. **3.** spiritual quality or tendency. —**spir/it·u·al·ist,** *n.*

spir·it·u·al·ize (spĭr/ĭ chŏŏ ə līz/), *v.t.*, **-ized, -izing.** to make spiritual.

spir·it·u·ous (spĭr/ĭ chŏŏ əs), *adj.* **1.** alcoholic. **2.** (of liquors) distilled. —**spir/it·u·ous·ness,** *n.*

spi·ro·chete (spī/rə kēt/), *n.* a slender, corkscrewlike, bacterial microörganism.

spit¹ (spĭt), *v.*, **spat** or **spit, spitting,** *n.* —*v.i.*, *v.t.* **1.** to eject (saliva, etc.) from the mouth; expectorate. **2.** to throw out or remit. —*n.* **3.** saliva, esp. when ejected. **4.** *Colloq.* the image or likeness of a person, etc. —**spit/ter,** *n.*

spit² (spĭt), *n.*, *v.*, **spitted, spitting.** —*n.* **1.** a sharply pointed, slender rod on which meat is roasted. **2.** a narrow point of land projecting into the water. —*v.t.* **3.** to pierce.

spite (spīt), *n.*, *v.*, **spited, spiting.** —*n.* **1.** keen, ill-natured desire to humiliate, annoy, or injure another. **2.** a grudge. **3. in spite of,** notwithstanding. —*v.t.* **4.** to annoy or thwart, out of spite. —**spite/ful,** *adj.* —**spite/ful·ly,** *adv.* —**spite/ful·ness,** *n.*

spit·fire (spĭt/fīr), *n.* a person of fiery, irritable temper.

Spits·ber·gen (spĭts/bûr/gən), *n.* a group of islands in the Arctic Ocean, N of and belonging to Norway. 550 pop.; 24,293 sq. mi.

spit·tle (spĭt/əl), *n.* saliva; spit.

spit·toon (spĭ tōōn/), *n.* a bowl used as a receptacle for spit.

spitz dog (spĭts), a kind of small dog with long hair and pointed muzzle and ears.

splash (splăsh), *v.t.*, *v.i.* **1.** to wet or soil by dashing water, mud, or the like; spatter. **2.** to dash (water, etc.) about. —*n.* **3.** act of splashing. **4.** the sound of splashing. **5.** a liquid or semiliquid substance splashed upon or in a thing. **6.** a patch, as of color or light. —**splash/er,** *n.* —**splash/y,** *adj.*

splat (splăt), *n.* a broad, flat piece of wood, as the central upright part of the back of a chair.

splat·ter (splăt/ər), *v.t.*, *v.i.* to splash.

splay (splā), *v.t.*, *v.i.* **1.** to spread out; expand; extend. —*n.* **2.** *Archit.* a surface which makes an oblique angle with another. —*adj.* **3.** spread out; wide and flat; turned outward.

spleen (splēn), *n.* **1.** a highly vascular, gland-like but ductless organ, situated in man near the cardiac end of the stomach, in which the blood undergoes certain corpuscular changes. **2.** ill humor. —**spleen/ish, spleen/y,** *adj.*

splen·did (splĕn/dĭd), *adj.* **1.** gorgeous; magnificent. **2.** grand; superb. **3.** glorious. **4.** strikingly admirable or fine. **5.** *Colloq.* excellent. —**splen/did·ly,** *adv.* —**splen/did·ness,** *n.*

splen·dor (splĕn/dər), *n.* **1.** brilliance, magnificence, grandeur, or pomp. **2.** glory. **3.** great brightness. Also, *Brit.,* **splen/dour.**

sple·net·ic (splĭ nĕt/ĭk), *adj.* **1.** of or pertaining to the spleen. **2.** irritable; spiteful.

splice (splīs), *v.*, **spliced, splicing,** *n.* —*v.t.* **1.** to join together or unite, as two ropes by interweaving strands. —*n.* 2. a joining, as of two ropes or parts of a rope by splicing. —**splic′er,** *n.*

splint (splĭnt), *n.* 1. a thin piece of wood or other rigid material used to maintain any part of the body in a fixed position. 2. one of a number of thin strips of wood woven together to make a chair seat, basket, etc. —*v.t.* 3. to hold in position or support by means of a splint or splints.

splin·ter (splĭn′tər), *n.* 1. a thin, sharp piece of wood, bone, etc., split off from a main body. —*v.t., v.i.* 2. to split or break into splinters. —**splin′ter·y,** *adj.*

split (splĭt), *v.,* **split, splitting,** *n., adj.* —*v.t., v.i.* 1. to separate or divide. 2. to burst. 3. to divide into distinct parts. 4. to break up or separate through disagreement, etc. 5. *Chem.* to divide (molecules or atoms) by cleavage into smaller parts. —*n.* 6. act of splitting. 7. a crack; fissure. 8. a breach. 9. *Colloq.* an ice-cream dish made from sliced fruit (usually banana) and ice cream, and covered with syrup and nuts. 10. (*often pl.*) the feat of separating the legs while sinking to the floor, until they extend at right angles to the body. —*adj.* 11. parted; cleft. 12. divided. —**split′ter,** *n.*

split infinitive, a simple infinitive with a word between the *to* and the verb.

split·ting (splĭt′ĭng), *adj.* 1. overpoweringly noisy. 2. violent or severe.

splotch (splŏch), *n.* 1. a large, irregular spot; blot; stain. —*v.t.* 2. to mark with splotches. —**splotch′y,** *adj.*

splurge (splûrj), *n., v.,* **splurged, splurging.** *Colloq.* —*n.* 1. an ostentatious display. —*v.i.* 2. to make a splurge.

splut·ter (splŭt′ər), *v.i., v.t.* 1. to talk or utter hastily and confusedly or incoherently. —*n.* 2. spluttering utterance, talk, noise, or fuss. —**splut′ter·er,** *n.*

spoil (spoil), *v.,* **spoiled or spoilt, spoiling,** *n.* —*v.t.* 1. to damage (a thing) irreparably. 2. to impair in character or disposition by unwise treatment, benefits, etc. —*v.i.* 3. to become spoiled, tainted, or putrid. 4. to plunder, pillage, or rob. —*n.* 5. (*often pl.*) booty, loot, or plunder taken in war or robbery. 6. (*usually pl.*) *Chiefly U.S.* public offices with their emoluments and advantages viewed as won by a victorious political party. 7. treasures won or accumulated. —**spoil′er,** *n.*

spoil·age (spoi′lĭj), *n.* 1. act of spoiling. 2. that which is spoiled.

Spo·kane (spō kăn′), *n.* a city in E Washington. 122,001.

spoke (spōk), *n., v.,* **spoked, spoking.** —*n.* 1. one of the bars, rods, or rungs radiating from the hub of a wheel and supporting the rim. 2. a rung of a ladder. —*v.t.* 3. to fit or furnish with spokes.

spo·ken (spō′kən), *adj.* uttered or expressed by speaking; oral.

spokes·man (spōks′mən), *n., pl.* -men. one who speaks for another or others.

spo·li·a·tion (spō′lĭ ā′shən), *n.* act of spoiling, plundering, or despoiling.

spon·dee (spŏn′dē), *n. Pros.* a foot consisting of two long syllables or two heavy beats.

sponge (spŭnj), *n., v.,* **sponged, sponging.** —*n.* 1. any of a group of aquatic (mostly marine) animals which are characterized by a light, porous, absorbent structure that is used in bathing, in cleansing surfaces, etc. 2. this structure itself, from which the living matter has been removed, used in bathing, etc. 3. *Colloq.* one who persistently lives at the expense of others; parasite. —*v.t., v.i.* 4. to wipe or rub with a wet sponge. 5. to absorb with a sponge. 6. *Colloq.* to get (something) by imposing on another's generosity. —**spong′er,** *n.* —**spon′gy,** *adj.*

spon·sor (spŏn′sər), *n.* 1. one who is responsible for a person or thing. 2. a surety. 3. a godfather or godmother. 4. a person, firm, or other organization that finances a radio program. —*v.t.* 5. to act as sponsor for. —**spon′sor·ship′,** *n.*

spon·ta·ne·ous (spŏn tā′nĭ əs), *adj.* 1. proceeding from a natural impulse; unconstrained. 2. (of impulses, motion, activity, natural processes, etc.) arising from internal forces or causes, or independent of external agencies. —**spon·ta′ne·ous·ly,** *adv.* —**spon·ta′ne·ous·ness, spon·ta·ne·i·ty** (spŏn′tə nē′ə tĭ), *n.*

spoof (spoof), *n., v.t. Slang.* hoax or tease.

spook (spook), *n. Colloq.* a ghost. —**spook′y,** *adj.*

spool (spool), *n.* 1. a cylindrical piece or appliance on which something is wound. —*v.t.* 2. to wind on a spool.

spoon (spoon), *n.* 1. a utensil for taking up or stirring liquid or other food. —*v.t., v.i.* 2. to take up or transfer in a spoon. 3. *Colloq.* to make love (to). —**spoon′ful,** *n.*

spoon·bill (spoon′bĭl′), *n.* any of certain wading birds closely related to the ibises, and having a long, flat bill with spoonlike tip.

spoor (spoor, spōr), *n.* a track or trail, esp. that of a wild animal pursued as game.

spo·rad·ic (spō răd′ĭk), *adj.* 1. periodic or occasional. 2. appearing in scattered instances. 3. isolated. Also, **spo·rad′i·cal.** —**spo·rad′i·cal·ly,** *adv.*

spo·ran·gi·um (spō răn′jĭ əm), *n., pl.* -gia (-jĭ ə). *Bot.* the case or sac within which spores are produced. Also, **spore case.**

spore (spōr), *n., v.,* **spored, sporing.** —*n.* 1. *Biol.* an asexual reproductive cell. 2. a germ, germ cell, seed, or the like. —*v.i.* 3. to bear or produce spores.

spor·ran (spŏr′ən), *n.* (in Scottish Highland costume) a large purse, commonly of fur, worn hanging from the belt in front.

sport (spōrt), *n.* 1. an athletic pastime, as hunting, baseball, tennis, golf, bowling, boxing, etc. 2. diversion; recreation. 3. playful jesting. 4. ridicule. 5. an object of derision. 6. *Slang.* a person of sportsmanlike qualities. 7. *Colloq.* a gambler. 8. *Colloq.* a person who affects fine clothes, etc. 9. *Biol.* an animal or a plant that shows an unusual or singular deviation from the normal or parent type. —*adj.* 10. of or pertaining to sport or sports. 11. suited for athletic wear. —*v.i.* 12. to play, frolic, or gambol. 13. to trifle. 14. to ridicule. —*v.t.* 15. *Colloq.* to display freely or with ostentation.

sport·ing (spōr′tĭng), *adj.* 1. engaging in or interested in athletic sports. 2. sportsmanlike. 3. *Colloq.* involving risk.

spor·tive (spōr′tĭv), *adj.* playful or frolicsome; jesting, jocose, or merry. —**spor′tive·ly,** *adv.* —**spor′tive·ness,** *n.*

sports·man (spōrts′mən), *n., pl.* -men. 1. a man who engages in sports. 2. one who exhibits fairness, self-control, etc., esp. in sports. —**sports′man·like′, sports′man·ly,** *adj.* —**sports′man·ship′,** *n.* —**sports′wom′an,** *n. fem.*

sport·y (spōr′tĭ), *adj.,* **sportier, sportiest.** *Colloq.* vulgarly showy. —**sport′i·ness,** *n.*

spot (spŏt), *n., v.,* **spotted, spotting,** *adj.* —*n.* 1. a stain, blot, or speck, as on a surface. 2. a moral blemish or flaw. 3. a place or locality. 4. *Chiefly Brit.* a small quantity. 5. **on the spot,** a. at once. b. on that very place. c. *U.S. Slang.* in difficulty, danger, or embarrassment. —*v.t., v.i.* 6. to stain with spots. 7. to sully; blemish. 8. *Colloq.* to detect or recognize. 9. *Mil.* to determine (a location) precisely. —*adj.* 10. *Radio.* pertaining to the point of origin of a local broadcast. 11. made, paid, delivered, etc., at once. —**spot′less,** *adj.* —**spot′less·ly,** *adv.* —**spot′less·ness,** *n.*

spot·light (spŏt′līt′), *n.* 1. *Theat.* a strong light thrown upon a particular spot on the stage. 2. an automobile light having a bright, directional beam. 3. conspicuous public attention.

spot·ted (spŏt′ĭd), *adj.* 1. marked with a spot or spots. 2. sullied; blemished.

spotted fever, *Pathol.* any of several fevers characterized by spots on the skin, esp. as in cerebrospinal meningitis or typhus fever.

spot·ter (spŏt′ər), *n.* 1. *Colloq.* one employed to keep watch on others. 2. *Mil.* the person who determines for the gunner the fall of shots in relation to the target.

spot·ty (spŏt′ĭ), *adj.,* **-tier, -tiest.** 1. full of spots; occurring in spots. 2. irregular or uneven. —**spot′ti·ly,** *adv.* —**spot′ti·ness,** *n.*

spous·al (spou′zəl), *n.* 1. (*often pl.*) nuptials. —*adj.* 2. nuptial; matrimonial.

spouse (spouz, spous), *n.* one's husband or wife.

spout (spout), *v.t., v.i.* 1. to discharge or emit (a liquid, etc.) in a stream with some force. 2. *Colloq.* to utter or declaim in an oratorical manner. —*n.* 3. a pipe or tube by which a liquid is discharged or poured. 4. a continuous stream of liquid, etc.

sprain (sprān), *v.t.* 1. to wrench (the ankle, wrist, or other joint) so as to injure without fracture or dislocation. —*n.* 2. a wrench of the parts around a joint, without dislocation. 3. condition of being sprained.

sprat (sprăt), *n.* a small, herringlike marine fish of European waters.

sprawl (sprôl), *v.i.* 1. to be stretched out in an ungraceful posture. 2. to lie or sit with the limbs stretched out in a careless or ungraceful posture. 3. to spread out in a straggling or irregular manner. —*v.t.* 4. to stretch out (the limbs) as in sprawling. 5. to spread out in a straggling manner. —*n.* 6. act of sprawling. 7. sprawling posture.

spray[1] (sprā), *n.* 1. water or other liquid blown or falling through the air in small particles. 2. an appliance for discharging liquid in a jet. 3. a quantity of small objects, flying or discharged through the air. —*v.t.* 4. to scatter in the form of fine particles. 5. to apply as a spray. 6. to sprinkle with a spray. 7. to direct a spray of missiles, etc., upon. —*v.i.* 8. to scatter spray. 9. to issue as spray. —**spray′er,** *n.*

spray[2] (sprā), *n.* a single slender branch with its leaves, flowers, or berries.

spread (sprĕd), *v.,* **spread, spreading,** *n.* —*v.t., v.i.* 1. to stretch out to the full width. 2. to extend over a greater area or period. 3. to arrange or apply in a sheet or layer. 4. to extend or distribute over a region, place, etc. 5. to overlay, cover, or coat. 6. to set (a table, etc.), as for a meal. 7. to send out in various directions, as light. 8. to disseminate, or be disseminated, as news, disease, etc. —*n.* 9. expansion; extension; diffusion. 10. the extent of spreading. 11. capacity for spreading. 12. a stretch, expanse, or extent of something. 13. a cloth covering for a bed, table, or the like, esp. a bedspread. 14. *Colloq.* a meal set out, esp. a feast. 15. any food preparation for spreading on bread, etc., as jam. —**spread′er,** *n.*

spree (sprē), *n.* 1. a lively frolic. 2. a bout or spell of drinking to intoxication.

sprig (sprĭg), *n., v.,* **sprigged, sprigging.** —*n.* 1. a shoot, twig, or small branch. —*v.t.* 2. to decorate (fabrics, etc.) with a design of sprigs. —**sprig′gy,** *adj.*

spright·ly (sprīt′lĭ), *adj.,* **-lier, -liest,** *adv.* —*adj.* 1. animated; vivacious; lively. —*adv.* 2. in a sprightly manner. —**spright′li·ness,** *n.*

spring (sprĭng), *v.,* **sprang** or **sprung, sprung, springing,** *n., adj.* —*v.i.* 1. to rise or move suddenly. 2. to appear suddenly. 3. to come into being. 4. to grow, as plants. 5. to proceed or originate. —*v.t.* 6. to cause to spring. 7. to come to have by cracking, etc. 8. to disclose, produce, etc., suddenly. 9. to leap over. 10. *Slang.* to remove (someone) from prison, by bail or jailbreak. —*n.* 11. a leap, jump, or bound. 12. elasticity. 13. an issue of water from the earth. 14. the first season of the year (in North America taken as comprising March, April, and May). 15. an elastic contrivance, as a strip of steel coiled spirally, which recovers its shape after being compressed, bent, etc. —*adj.* 16. of, pertaining to, characteristic of, or suitable for the season of spring. 17. resting on or containing springs. —**spring′er,** *n.*

Springs (def. 15)
A. Spiral; B. Coil;
C. Volute; D. Leaf

spring·board (sprĭng′bôrd′), *n.* a flexible board used as a take-off in diving, vaulting, etc.

Spring·field (sprĭng′fēld′), *n.* 1. a city in S Massachusetts. 149,554. 2. the capital of Illinois, in the central part. 75,503. 3. a city in W Ohio. 70,662. 4. a city in SW Missouri. 61,238.

spring tide, the large rise and fall of the tide at the new or full moon.

spring·time (sprĭng′tīm′), *n.* the season of spring. Also, **spring′tide′.**

spring·y (sprĭng′ĭ), *adj.,* **springier, springiest.** elastic; resilient. —**spring′i·ness,** *n.*

sprin·kle (sprĭng′kəl), *v.,* **-kled, -kling,** *n.* —*v.t.* 1. to scatter, as a liquid, in drops. 2. to distribute here and there. 3. to overspread with drops of water or the like. 4. to diversify or intersperse. —*v.i.* 5. to be sprinkled. 6. to rain slightly. —*n.* 7. act of sprinkling. 8. that which is sprinkled. —**sprin′kler,** *n.* —**sprin′kling,** *n.*

sprint (sprĭnt), *v.i.* 1. to race at full speed, esp. for a short distance. —*n.* 2. a short race at full

speed. 3. a brief spell of great activity. —**sprint′er,** *n.*

sprit (sprĭt), *n. Naut.* a small spar crossing a fore-and-aft sail diagonally to extend the sail.

sprite (sprīt), *n.* an elf, fairy, or goblin.

sprock·et (sprŏk′ĭt), *n. Mach.* 1. one of a set of projections on the rim of a wheel which engage the links of a chain. 2. such a wheel.

sprout (sprout), *v.i.* 1. to begin to grow. 2. to put forth buds or shoots. 3. to grow quickly. —*v.t.* 4. to cause to sprout. —*n.* 5. a shoot of a plant. 6. (*pl.*) Brussels sprouts.

spruce[1] (sproos), *n.* 1. any of certain coniferous evergreen trees with short, angular, needle-shaped leaves attached singly around twigs. 2. the wood of any such tree.

spruce[2] (sproos), *adj.,* **sprucer, sprucest,** *v.,* **spruced, sprucing.** —*adj.* 1. trim; neat; dapper. —*v.t., v.i.* 2. to make (oneself, etc.) spruce. —**spruce′ly,** *adv.*

spry (sprī), *adj.,* **spryer, spryest** or **sprier, spriest.** active; nimble; brisk. —**spry′ly,** *adv.* —**spry′ness,** *n.*

spud (spŭd), *n., v.,* **spudded, spudding.** —*n.* 1. a narrow spadelike instrument for digging up the roots of weeds. 2. *Colloq.* a potato. —*v.t.* 3. to remove with a spud.

spume (spūm), *n., v.i., v.t.,* **spumed, spuming.** foam; froth.

spu·mo·ne (spə mō′nĭ), *n.* Italian ice cream, usually containing chopped fruit.

spun (spŭn), *adj.* formed by spinning.

spunk (spŭngk), *n.* 1. *Colloq.* pluck; spirit; mettle. 2. touchwood, tinder, or punk.

spunk·y (spŭngk′ĭ), *adj.,* **spunkier, spunkiest.** *Colloq.* plucky; spirited. —**spunk′i·ly,** *adv.* —**spunk′i·ness,** *n.*

spur (spûr), *n., v.,* **spurred, spurring.** —*n.* 1. a pointed device on a boot heel, for goading a horse onward, etc. 2. anything that goads or impels. 3. anything resembling a spur. 4. a ridge projecting from a mountain or mountain range. 5. **on the spur of the moment,** offhand; suddenly. —*v.t., v.i.* 6. to prick (a horse, etc.) with a spur. 7. to furnish with spurs. 8. to urge or impel. —**spurred,** *adj.*

spurge (spûrj), *n.* any of certain plants, some species of which have purgative properties.

spu·ri·ous (spyŏŏr′ĭ əs), *adj.* 1. not genuine, true, or authentic. 2. illegitimate. —**spu′ri·ous·ly,** *adv.* —**spu′ri·ous·ness,** *n.*

spurn (spûrn), *v.t.* 1. to reject with disdain; scorn. —*v.i.* 2. to show disdain. —*n.* 3. disdainful rejection. 4. a kick. —**spurn′er,** *n.*

spurt (spûrt), *v.i., v.t.* 1. to gush or eject suddenly in a stream or jet, as a liquid. 2. to show marked activity or energy for a short period. —*n.* 3. a forcible gush of water, etc. 4. a marked increase of effort for a short period.

spur track, *Railroads.* a short branch track leading from the main track.

spur wheel, *Mach.* a wheel with projecting teeth on the periphery, which are placed radially about and parallel to the axis.

sput·ter (spŭt′ər), *v.i., v.t.* 1. to emit (particles of anything) in an explosive manner. 2. to utter (words or sounds) in an explosive, incoherent manner. —*n.* 3. act or sound of sputtering. 4. explosive, incoherent utterance. —**sput′ter·er,** *n.*

spu·tum (spū′təm), *n., pl.* **-ta** (-tə). 1. spittle mixed with mucus, purulent matter, or the like. 2. that which is expectorated; spittle.

spy (spī), *n., pl.* **spies,** *v.,* **spied, spying.** —*n.* 1. one who keeps secret watch on the actions of others. 2. one employed to obtain secret information, esp. of military affairs of other countries. —*v.i.* 3. to make secret observations. 4. to keep watch. —*v.t.* 5. to catch sight of; see.

spy·glass (spī′glăs′, -gläs′), *n.* a small telescope.

sq., square.

squab (skwŏb), *n.* a nestling pigeon, marketed when fully grown but still unfledged.

squab·ble (skwŏb′əl), *v.,* **-bled, -bling,** *n.* —*v.i.* 1. to engage in a petty quarrel. —*n.* 2. a petty quarrel. —**squab′bler,** *n.*

squad (skwŏd), *n., v.,* **squadded, squadding.** —*n.* 1. a small number of soldiers (about ten men). 2. any small group engaged in a common enterprise, etc. —*v.t.* 3. to form into squads. 4. to assign to a squad.

squad car, an automobile used by the police for patrolling.

squad·ron (skwŏd'rən), *n.* **1.** a portion of a naval fleet. **2.** an armored cavalry unit consisting of two or more troops (companies). **3.** the basic administrative and tactical unit of the Air Force. **4.** any special group.

squal·id (skwŏl'ĭd), *adj.* **1.** dirty; filthy. **2.** wretched; miserable; degraded. —**squal'id·ly**, *adv.* —**squal'id·ness**, *n.*

squall[1] (skwôl), *n.* **1.** a sudden, violent gust of wind, often accompanied by rain, snow, or sleet. **2.** *Colloq.* a commotion. —*v.i.* **3.** to blow in a squall. —**squall'y**, *adj.*

squall[2] (skwôl), *v.i.*, *v.t.* **1.** to cry out loudly; scream violently. —*n.* **2.** act or sound of squalling. —**squall'er**, *n.*

squal·or (skwŏl'ər), *n.* squalid state.

squan·der (skwŏn'dər), *v.t.* **1.** to spend (money, time, etc.) extravagantly. —*n.* **2.** extravagant expenditure. —**squan'der·er**, *n.*

square (skwâr), *n.*, *v.*, **squared, squaring,** *adj.*, **squarer, squarest,** *adv.* —*n.* **1.** a plane figure having four equal sides and four right angles. **2.** anything having this form. **3.** an area in a city marked off by streets along each side. **4.** a park-like area in a city. **5.** an L-shaped or T-shaped instrument for determining or testing right angles. **6.** *Arith.*, *Alg.* Also, **square number.** the second power of a number or quantity. —*v.t.* **7.** to reduce to square, rectangular, or cubical form. **8.** to mark in squares. **9.** *Math.* a. to find the equivalent of in square measure. b. to multiply (a number or quantity) by itself. c. to find a square equivalent to. **10.** to bring to the form of a right angle. **11.** to make straight, level, or even. **12.** to adjust or settle. —*v.i.* **13.** to assume a posture of defense or offense. **14.** to accord or agree. —*adj.* **15.** of the form of a right angle. **16.** having four sides and four right angles, often cubical. **17.** perpendicular. **18.** designating a unit representing an area in the form of a square. **19.** pertaining to such units. **20.** of a specified length on each side of a square. **21.** straight, level, or even. **22.** having all accounts settled. **23.** just, fair, or honest. **24.** straightforward. **25.** *Colloq.* substantial or satisfying. —*adv.* **26.** so as to be square. **27.** *Colloq.* fairly; honestly. —**square'ly**, *adv.* —**square'ness**, *n.*

square dance, a dance, as a quadrille, by a set of couples arranged in a square or in some set form. —**square dancing.**

square-rigged (skwâr'rĭgd'), *adj.* *Naut.* having square sails as the principal sails.

square root, the quantity of which a given quantity is the square.

square shooter, *Colloq.* an honest, fair person.

squash[1] (skwŏsh), *v.t.* **1.** to press flat; crush. **2.** to suppress or quash. **3.** *Colloq.* to silence. —*n.* **4.** a game resembling tennis played in a walled court.

squash[2] (skwŏsh), *n.* **1.** the fruit of any of certain vinelike, tendril-bearing plants, used as a vegetable. **2.** any of these plants.

squash·y (skwŏsh'ĭ), *adj.*, **squashier, squashiest.** **1.** easily squashed; pulpy. **2.** soft and wet, as ground. —**squash'i·ness**, *n.*

squat (skwŏt), *v.*, **squatted** or **squat, squatting,** *adj.*, *n.* —*v.i.* **1.** to sit with the legs drawn up closely beneath the body. **2.** to crouch. **3.** to settle on land without title or right. **4.** to settle on public land under government regulation, as to acquire title. —*adj.* **5.** Also, **squat'ty.** short and thickset. —*n.* **6.** a squatting position. —**squat'ter**, *n.*

squaw (skwô), *n.* a North American Indian woman or wife.

squawk (skwôk), *v.i.*, *v.t.* **1.** to utter (with) a loud, harsh cry. **2.** *Slang.* to complain vehemently. —*n.* **3.** a loud, harsh cry or sound. **4.** *Slang.* a loud, vehement complaint. —**squawk'er**, *n.*

squeak (skwēk), *n.* **1.** a short, sharp, shrill sound. —*v.i.* **2.** to utter or emit a squeak. —**squeak'er**, *n.* —**squeak'y**, *adj.*

squeal (skwēl), *n.* **1.** a prolonged, sharp, shrill cry. —*v.i.* **2.** to utter or emit a squeal. **3.** *Slang.* to turn informer. —**squeal'er**, *n.*

squeam·ish (skwē'mĭsh), *adj.* **1.** easily shocked; prudish. **2.** excessively scrupulous. **3.** fastidious or dainty. **4.** easily nauseated. —**squeam'ish·ly**, *adv.* —**squeam'ish·ness**, *n.*

squee·gee (skwē'jē, skwē jē'), *n.*, *v.*, **-geed, -geeing.** —*n.* **1.** an implement edged with rub-

ber or the like, for removing water from surfaces. —*v.t.* **2.** to scrape with a squeegee.

squeeze (skwēz), *v.*, **squeezed, squeezing,** *n.* —*v.t.* **1.** to press together; compress, as to extract something. **2.** to thrust forcibly; cram. **3.** to force out; extract. **4.** to oppress (a person, etc.) by exactions, etc. —*v.i.* **5.** to exert a compressing force. —*n.* **6.** act of squeezing. **7.** fact of being squeezed. **8.** a hug or close embrace. **9.** *Colloq.* a situation from which extrication is difficult. —**squeez'er**, *n.*

squelch (skwĕlch), *v.t.* **1.** to crush; squash. **2.** *Colloq.* to suppress or silence. —*n.* **3.** a crushing retort. —**squelch'er**, *n.*

squib (skwĭb), *n.*, *v.*, **squibbed, squibbing.** —*n.* **1.** a short remark, notice, etc., often a witty one. **2.** a firecracker. —*v.i.* **3.** to write squibs.

squid (skwĭd), *n.*, *pl.* **squids,** (*esp. collectively*) **squid.** any of various decapod marine animals, esp., any of certain species much used for bait.

squint (skwĭnt), *v.i.* **1.** to look with the eyes partly closed. **2.** to be cross-eyed. —*v.t.* **3.** to close (the eyes) partly in looking. —*n.* **4.** act of squinting. **5.** *Pathol.* strabismus.

squire (skwīr), *n.*, *v.*, **squired, squiring.** —*n.* **1.** (in England) a country gentleman. **2.** *U.S.* a justice of the peace or other local dignitary. **3.** a young man who, as an aspirant to knighthood, attended upon a knight. **4.** a personal attendant or escort. —*v.t.* **5.** to attend as a squire.

squirm (skwûrm), *v.i.* **1.** to wriggle or writhe. —*n.* **2.** a squirming movement. —**squirm'y**, *adj.*

squir·rel (skwûr'əl), *n.* any of certain arboreal bushy-tailed rodents.

squirt (skwûrt), *v.i.*, *v.t.* **1.** to cause (liquid) to issue in a jet from a narrow orifice. —*n.* **2.** a jet, as of water. **3.** *Colloq.* an insignificant, self-assertive fellow. —**squirt'er**, *n.*

Sr, *Chem.* strontium.

Sr., **1.** Senior. **2.** Sir.

S.R.O., standing room only.

S.S., **1.** steamship. **2.** Sunday School.

St., **1.** Saint. **2.** Strait. **3.** Street.

stab (stăb), *v.*, **stabbed, stabbing,** *n.* —*v.t.* **1.** to pierce or wound with a pointed weapon. **2.** to thrust or plunge (a knife, etc.). —*n.* **3.** a thrust with a pointed weapon. **4.** a wound made by stabbing. —**stab'ber**, *n.*

sta·bil·i·ty (stə bĭl'ə tĭ), *n.*, *pl.* **-ties.** **1.** firmness in position. **2.** permanence. **3.** steadfastness.

sta·bi·lize (stā'bə līz'), *v.t.*, **-lized, -lizing.** to make or keep stable. —**sta'bi·li·za'tion**, *n.*

sta·bi·liz·er (stā'bə lī'zər), *n.* **1.** one that stabilizes. **2.** *Aeron.* a device for stabilizing an aircraft, as a tail surface. **3.** any compound which, when included with an explosive, decreases its ability to decompose spontaneously.

sta·ble[1] (stā'bəl), *n.*, *v.*, **-bled, -bling.** —*n.* **1.** a building for horses, cattle, etc. **2.** *Racing.* an establishment where race horses are kept and trained. —*v.t.*, *v.i.* **3.** to put or live in a stable.

sta·ble[2] (stā'bəl), *adj.* **1.** firm; steady. **2.** permanent. **3.** steadfast. **4.** *Chem.* not readily decomposing.

stac·ca·to (stə kä'tō), *adj.* *Music.* **1.** detached, disconnected, or abrupt. **2.** with breaks between the successive tones.

stack (stăk), *n.* **1.** a large orderly pile or heap. **2.** (*often pl.*) a set of bookshelves, as in a library. **3.** a chimney or funnel for smoke. **4.** *Colloq.* a great quantity. **5.** a number of rifles standing in a conical group. —*v.t.* **6.** to pile or arrange in a stack. **7.** to arrange unfairly. —**stack'er**, *n.*

sta·di·um (stā'dĭ əm), *n.*, *pl.* **-diums, -dia** (-dĭə). a building for athletic events, usually open and circular, with tiers of seats for spectators.

staff (stăf, stäf), *n.*, *pl.* **staves** (stāvz) *or* **staffs** for 1–4; **staffs** for 5, 6; *v.* —*n.* **1.** a stick or rod for aid in walking, for use as a weapon, etc. **2.** a pole on which a flag is hung. **3.** something which serves to support. **4.** a body of assistants to a manager, superintendent, or executive head. **5.** a body of persons charged with carrying out certain work, as a group of administrative army officers. **6.** *Music.* a set of five horizontal lines, music being written on them and the intervening spaces. —*v.t.* **7.** to provide with a staff.

staff sergeant, *U.S. Army.* a noncommissioned officer below a technical sergeant and above a sergeant.

stag (stăg), *n.* **1.** an adult male deer. **2.** *Colloq.* a man unaccompanied by a woman at a social gathering. —*adj.* **3.** for men only.

stage (stāj), *n.*, *v.*, **staged, staging.** —*n.* **1.** a single step or degree in a process. **2.** a raised platform, as for speakers or theater performers. **3.** the theater, the drama, or the dramatic profession. **4.** the scene of any action or career. **5.** a stagecoach. **6.** a portion or period of a course. —*v.t.* **7.** to put, represent, or exhibit on a stage.

stage-coach (stāj'kōch'), *n.* a coach that runs regularly over a fixed route with passengers, parcels, etc.

stag-ger (stăg'ər), *v.i.* **1.** to walk or stand unsteadily; sway. **2.** to begin to give way, as troops. **3.** to waver; hesitate. —*v.t.* **4.** to cause to reel or totter. **5.** to arrange in a zigzag order. **6.** to arrange at such intervals that there is a continuous overlapping. —*n.* **7.** a reeling or tottering movement. **8.** a staggered arrangement. **9.** (*pl. construed as sing.*) a disease in horses, cattle, etc., characterized by blindness, staggering, etc. —**stag'ger-ing-ly,** *adv.*

stag-ing (stā'jĭng), *n.* scaffolding.

stag-nant (stăg'nənt), *adj.* **1.** not running or flowing, as water, air, etc. **2.** foul from standing, as a pool of water. **3.** inactive, sluggish, or dull. —**stag'nan-cy,** *n.*

stag-nate (stăg'nāt), *v.i.*, **-nated, -nating.** to become stagnant. —**stag-na'tion,** *n.*

stag-y (stā'jĭ), *adj.*, **stagier, stagiest.** theatrical. —**stag'i-ness,** *n.*

staid (stād), *adj.* settled or sedate. —**staid'ly,** *adv.* —**staid'ness,** *n.*

stain (stān), *n.* **1.** a discoloration or spot. **2.** a blemish. **3.** coloration produced by staining. **4.** a dye used to color woods, textiles, etc. —*v.t.* **5.** to discolor with spots. **6.** to blemish. **7.** to corrupt. **8.** to color in a particular way. —*v.i.* **9.** to produce a stain. **10.** to become stained. —**stain'a-ble,** *adj.* —**stain'er,** *n.* —**stain'less,** *adj.*

stair (stâr), *n.* **1.** a series of steps from one floor or level to another. **2.** a single step of such a series.

stair-case (stâr'kās'), *n.* a flight of stairs with its framework, balusters, etc. Also, **stair'way'.**

stake[1] (stāk), *n.*, *v.*, **staked, staking.** —*n.* **1.** a pointed stick or post driven into the ground as a boundary mark, a part of a fence, etc. **2.** a post to which a person is bound for execution by burning. —*v.t.* **3.** to mark, protect, separate, etc., by stakes.

stake[2] (stāk), *n.*, *v.*, **staked, staking.** —*n.* **1.** that which is wagered. **2.** an interest held in something. **3.** (*often pl.*) a prize in a contest. **4.** state of being at hazard. —*v.t.* **5.** to wager or hazard. **6.** *Slang.* to furnish with necessaries or resources.

sta-lac-tite (stə lăk'tīt, stăl'ək tīt'), *n.* a deposit, usually of calcium carbonate, shaped like an icicle, hanging from the roof of a cave or the like.

sta-lag-mite (stə lăg'mīt, stăl'əg mīt'), *n.* a deposit, usually of calcium carbonate, resembling an inverted stalactite, formed on the floor of a cave or the like.

stale (stāl), *adj.*, **staler, stalest,** *v.*, **staled, staling.** —*adj.* **1.** not fresh; flat, dry, or hardened. **2.** hackneyed; trite. **3.** having lost fresh vigor, intelligence, or the like, as from overstrain. —*v.t.*, *v.i.* **4.** to make or become stale. —**stale'ly,** *adv.* —**stale'ness,** *n.*

stale-mate (stāl'māt'), *n.*, *v.*, **-mated, -mating.** —*n.* **1.** *Chess.* a position of the pieces when no move can be made by a player without putting his own king in check, the result being a draw. **2.** any standstill or deadlock. —*v.t.* **3.** to subject to a stalemate. **4.** to bring to a standstill.

Sta-lin (stä'lĭn, -lēn), *n.* **Joseph V.,** born 1879, Soviet statesman and political leader.

Sta-lin-grad (stä'lĭn grăd'), *n.* a city in the SE Soviet Union in Europe. 445,476.

stalk[1] (stôk), *n.* **1.** the stem or main axis of a plant. **2.** any slender supporting or connecting part.

stalk[2] (stôk), *v.i.*, *v.t.* **1.** to pursue or approach (game, etc.), stealthily. **2.** to walk with slow, stiff, or haughty strides. —*n.* **3.** a slow, stiff stride. —**stalk'er,** *n.*

stalk-ing-horse (stô'kĭng hôrs'), *n.* anything put forward to mask plans or efforts; pretext.

stall[1] (stôl), *n.* **1.** a compartment in a stable or shed, for one animal. **2.** *Chiefly Brit.* a booth in which business is carried on. **3.** *Chiefly Brit.* an enclosed seat in the choir or chancel of a church for a clergyman. **4.** *Aeron.* the condition of a plane losing the air speed necessary to sustain itself. —*v.t.* **5.** to put or keep in a stall. **6.** to bring to a standstill. —*v.i.* **7.** to come to a standstill. **8.** *Aeron.* **a.** (of an airplane) to go into a stall. **b.** (of an aviator) to put an airplane into a stall.

stall[2] (stôl), *Slang.* —*n.* **1.** anything used as a pretext, pretense, or means of delay. —*v.i.* **2.** to act evasively or deceptively. **3.** to delay. —*v.t.* **4.** to put off, evade, or delay.

stal-lion (stăl'yən), *n.* a male horse not castrated.

stal-wart (stôl'wərt), *adj.* **1.** strongly built; robust. **2.** brave; valiant. **3.** steadfast. —*n.* **4.** a stalwart person.

sta-men (stā'mən), *n.* *Bot.* the pollen-bearing organ of a flower, consisting of the filament and anther.

Stam-ford (stăm'fərd), *n.* a city in SW Connecticut. 47,938.

stam-i-na (stăm'ə nə), *n.* strength of physical constitution; vigor.

stam-mer (stăm'ər), *v.i.*, *v.t.* **1.** to speak with involuntary breaks or with spasmodic repetitions of sounds. —*n.* **2.** a stammering mode of utterance. —**stam'mer-er,** *n.*

stamp (stămp), *v.t.* **1.** to strike, trample, etc., with a forcible downward thrust of the foot. **2.** to crush or pound. **3.** to impress with a particular mark. **4.** to impress (a design, words, etc.). **5.** to affix an adhesive paper stamp to (a letter, etc.). **6.** to characterize; distinguish. —*v.i.* **7.** to bring the foot down forcibly. —*n.* **8.** act of stamping. **9.** a device for impressing a mark. **10.** a mark made with a stamp. **11.** a mark indicating genuineness, payment of a duty, etc. **12.** a small adhesive piece of paper printed with a distinctive design, esp. one issued by a government for a fixed sum, for attaching to documents, letters, etc., to show that a charge has been paid. —**stamp'er,** *n.*

stam-pede (stăm pēd'), *n.*, *v.*, **-peded, -peding.** —*n.* **1.** a sudden scattering or headlong flight, esp. of a body of cattle or horses in fright. —*v.i.*, *v.t.* **2.** to scatter or flee in a stampede.

stance (stăns), *n.* *Golf, etc.* the position of a player's feet when making a stroke.

stanch[1] (stänch, stănch), *v.t.* **1.** to stop the flow of (a liquid, esp. blood). **2.** to stop the flow of blood from (a wound).

stanch[2] (stänch, stănch), *adj.* **1.** firm or steadfast. **2.** strong; substantial. **3.** impervious to water or liquids. —**stanch'ly,** *adv.* —**stanch'ness,** *n.*

stan-chion (stăn'shən), *n.* an upright bar, beam, post, or support.

stand (stănd), *v.*, **stood, standing,** *n.* —*v.i.* **1.** to take or keep an upright position on the feet. **2.** to halt; stop. **3.** to take a specified position, attitude, or course. **4.** to remain firm or steadfast. **5.** to be in an upright position. **6.** to be located. **7.** (of a score, etc.) to show a specified position of the parties concerned. **8.** to remain erect and unchanged. **9.** to continue in force. **10.** to be or become stagnant, as water. **11.** *Chiefly Brit.* to be a candidate. —*v.t.* **12.** to cause to stand. **13.** to endure; undergo. **14.** to tolerate. **15.** *Colloq.* to pay for. **16. stand by, a.** to aid, uphold, or sustain. **b.** to adhere to. **17. stand for, a.** to represent or mean. **b.** to uphold. **c.** to tolerate. **18. stand out, a.** to project. **b.** to be prominent. —*n.* **19.** act of standing. **20.** a halt or stop. **21.** an attitude; a determined effort against or for something. **22.** the place where a person or thing stands. **23.** the place where a witness sits or stands to testify in court. **24.** a raised platform. **25.** a framework or table on or in which articles are placed for support, exhibition, etc. **26.** a shop, booth, or the like where business is carried on. **27.** a station for vehicles which ply for hire. **28.** the trees on a given area. **29.** a halt of a theatrical company on tour, to give a performance.

stand-ard (stăn'dərd), *n.* **1.** an approved model or criterion. **2.** a certain commodity in which the basic monetary unit is stated, usually gold or silver. **3.** a grade or level of excellence. **4.** a flag, ensign, emblematic figure, etc. **5.** an upright support. —*adj.* **6.** serving as a basis of weight, measure, value, comparison, or judgment. **7.** of recognized excellence. **8.** characterized by preferred pronunciations, expressions, grammatical constructions, etc., the use of which is considered essential to social or other prestige.

stand-ard-ize (stăn'dər dīz'), *v.t.*, **-ized, -izing.**

to make of an established standard size, quality, strength, or the like. **—stand′ard·i·za′tion,** *n.*

stand-by (stănd′bī′), *n., pl.* **-bys.** **1.** a stanch adherent. **2.** a chief support.

stand-ing (stăn′dĭng), *n.* **1.** status, as to rank, reputation, etc. **2.** length of existence, membership, etc. **—adj. 3.** erect or upright. **4.** performed in or from an erect position. **5.** still; stagnant. **6.** lasting or permanent. **7.** established; fixed.

stand-pipe (stănd′pīp′), *n.* a vertical pipe or tower into which water is pumped.

stand-point (stănd′point′), *n.* **1.** the point from which one views something. **2.** the mental position from which one views things.

stand-still (stănd′stĭl′), *n.* a cessation of movement or action; stop.

Stan-ley (stăn′lĭ), *n.* **Sir Henry Morton,** 1841–1904, British explorer in Africa.

stan-num (stăn′əm), *n.* *Chem.* tin.

stan-za (stăn′zə), *n.* **1.** *Pros.* a group of lines of verse, arranged according to a fixed plan and forming a poem. **2.** a regularly repeated metrical division of a poem. **—stan·za·ic** (stăn zā′ĭk), *adj.*

sta-ple[1] (stā′pəl), *n., v.,* **-pled, -pling. —n. 1.** a bent piece of wire put through papers, etc., to bind them together. **2.** a loop of metal with pointed ends. **—v.t. 3.** to fasten by a staple.

sta-ple[2] (stā′pəl), *n.* **1.** a principal commodity, feature, etc. **2.** the fiber of wool, cotton, flax, rayon, etc. **3.** raw material. **—adj. 4.** chief or principal. **5.** principally used.

sta-pler (stā′plər), *n.* a wire-stitching machine, esp. one used in bookbinding.

star (stär), *n., adj., v.,* **starred, starring. —n. 1.** any of the heavenly bodies appearing as apparently fixed luminous points in the sky at night. **2.** *Astron.* any of the self-luminous bodies outside the solar system. **3.** a figure having (usually) five or six points. **4.** *Print., etc.* an asterisk. **5.** a prominent actor, singer, athlete, etc. **—adj. 6.** prominent; chief; leading. **—v.t. 7.** to set with stars; spangle. **8.** to present (an actor, etc.) as a star. **9.** to mark with a star. **—v.i. 10.** (of an actor, etc.) to appear as a star. **—star′dom,** *n.*

star-board (stär′bōrd′, -bərd), *Naut.* **—n. 1.** the side of a ship to the right of a person facing forward. **—adj. 2.** of or on the right side. **—adv. 3.** toward the right side.

starch (stärch), *n.* **1.** a white, tasteless solid, chemically a carbohydrate, forming an important constituent of rice, corn, wheat, beans, potatoes, etc. **2.** a preparation of this substance used (in water) to stiffen linen, etc., in laundering. **3.** formality. **—v.t. 4.** to stiffen with starch. **—starch′y,** *adj.*

stare (stâr), *v.,* **stared, staring,** *n.* **—v.i. 1.** to gaze fixedly. **2.** to stand out boldly. **—v.t. 3.** to put, bring, etc., by staring. **—n. 4.** a fixed look.

star-fish (stär′fĭsh′), *n., pl.* **-fishes,** (*esp. collectively*) **-fish.** a marine animal having a star-shaped body.

stark (stärk), *adj.* **1.** sheer; utter; downright. **2.** stiff or rigid. **3.** desolate. **—adv. 4.** utterly; absolutely. **—stark′ly,** *adv.*

star-ling (stär′lĭng), *n.* **1.** any of certain black Old World passerine birds which have been introduced into North America. **2.** any of various not closely related passerine birds, esp. the **American starlings.**

star-ry (stär′ĭ), *adj.,* **-rier, -riest. 1.** full of stars. **2.** of, like, or pertaining to the stars.

Stars and Stripes, the national flag of the United States.

Star-Spangled Banner, The, the American national anthem, composed in 1814 by Francis Scott Key.

start (stärt), *v.i., v.t.* **1.** to begin. **2.** to come, rise, or issue suddenly. **3.** to spring or move suddenly. **—n. 4.** a beginning or outset. **5.** a sudden, springing movement. **6.** a lead or advance over competitors or pursuers. **7.** a spurt of activity. **—start′er,** *n.*

star-tle (stär′təl), *v.,* **-tled, -tling,** *n.* **—v.t. 1.** to disturb suddenly by a surprise, alarm, or the like. **—n. 2.** a sudden shock of surprise, alarm, or the like. **—star′tling,** *adj.* **—star′tling·ly,** *adv.*

star-va-tion (stär vā′shən), *n.* **1.** the condition of being starved. **2.** the process of starving.

starve (stärv), *v.,* **starved, starving. —v.i. 1.** to die from hunger. **2.** to suffer severely from hunger or other need. **—v.t. 3.** to weaken, kill, subdue, etc., by hunger.

starve-ling (stärv′lĭng), *adj.* **1.** starving. **—n. 2.** a person, animal, or plant that is starving.

stash (stăsh), *v.t., v.i.* *U.S. Slang.* to put away, as for safekeeping or in a prepared place.

state (stāt), *n., adj., v.,* **stated, stating. —n. 1.** condition, structure, phase, or the like. **2.** a person's station or rank. **3.** pomp. **4.** a body of people occupying a definite territory and organized under one government. **5.** (*usually cap.*) any of the commonwealths, each more or less independent as regards internal affairs, which together make up a federal union, as in the United States of America. **6.** the civil government. **—adj. 7.** of or pertaining to civil government. **8.** characterized by ceremony. **9.** used on occasions of ceremony. **—v.t. 10.** to declare or say. **—state′hood,** *n.*

stat-ed (stā′tĭd), *adj.* fixed or settled.

State-house (stāt′hous′), *n.* *U.S.* the building in which the legislature of a State sits.

state-ly (stāt′lĭ), *adj., v.,* **-lier, -liest.** dignified or majestic. **—state′li·ness,** *n.*

state-ment (stāt′mənt), *n.* **1.** something stated. **2.** a communication or declaration. **3.** *Com.* an abstract of an account, as one rendered to show the balance due. **4.** act of stating something.

Stat-en Island (stăt′ən), an island in New York Bay, comprising Richmond borough of New York City. 174,441 pop.; 64¹⁄₂ sq. mi.

state-room (stāt′rōōm′, -rŏŏm′), *n.* a private room or compartment on a ship, train, etc.

states-man (stāts′mən), *n., pl.* **-men.** a man of outstanding ability in directing the affairs of a government. **—states′man·like′, states′man·ly,** *adj.* **—states′man·ship′,** *n.*

stat-ic (stăt′ĭk), *adj.* Also, **stat′i·cal. 1.** fixed; stationary. **2.** *Elect.* denoting or pertaining to electricity at rest, as that produced by friction. **3.** denoting or pertaining to atmospheric electricity, interfering with radio reception, etc. **—n. 4.** static or atmospheric electricity. **5.** interference due to such electricity. **—stat′i·cal·ly,** *adv.*

stat-ics (stăt′ĭks), *n. pl. construed as sing.* that branch of mechanics which deals with bodies at rest or forces in equilibrium.

sta-tion (stā′shən), *n.* **1.** a position, esp. one assigned for duty, service, etc. **2.** a regular stopping place, as on a railroad. **3.** a railroad depot. **4.** a place equipped for some particular kind of work, research, or the like. **5.** standing, in terms of estimation, rank, or dignity. **6.** a place that transmits or receives radio broadcasts, etc. **—v.t. 7.** to assign a place or post to.

sta-tion·ar·y (stā′shə nĕr′ĭ), *adj.* **1.** standing still. **2.** not movable. **3.** not changing.

sta-tion·er (stā′shən ər), *n.* one who sells the materials used in writing, as paper, pens, pencils, ink, etc.

sta-tion·er·y (stā′shə nĕr′ĭ), *n.* writing materials, as paper, pens, pencils, etc.

station wagon, an automobile having an enclosed, paneled body with several rows of folding or removable seats behind the driver.

stat-is-ti-cian (stăt′əs tĭsh′ən), *n.* one versed in statistics.

sta-tis-tics (stə tĭs′tĭks), *n.* **1.** (*construed as sing.*) the science which deals with the collection, classification, and use of numerical facts. **2.** (*construed as pl.*) the numerical facts themselves. **—sta·tis′ti·cal,** *adj.* **—sta·tis′ti·cal·ly,** *adv.*

stat-u·ar·y (stăch′ŏŏ ĕr′ĭ), *n., pl.* **-aries,** *adj.* **—n. 1.** statues collectively. **—adj. 2.** of, pertaining to, or suitable for statues.

stat-ue (stăch′ōō), *n.* a representation of a person or an animal carved, molded, or cast.

stat-u·esque (stăch′ŏŏ ĕsk′), *adj.* like a statue, as in grace or beauty.

stat-u·ette (stăch′ŏŏ ĕt′), *n.* a small statue.

stat-ure (stăch′ər), *n.* **1.** height. **2.** development attained.

sta-tus (stā′təs, stăt′əs), *n.* **1.** condition of affairs. **2.** position or standing socially, professionally, or otherwise.

status quo (kwō), *Latin.* the state in which anything was or is. Also, **status in quo.**

stat-ute (stăch′ŏŏt), *n.* an enactment by a legislature.

statute law, law established by legislative enactments.

stat-u·to·ry (stăch′ŏŏ tōr′ĭ), *adj.* **1.** of or prescribed by statute. **2.** (of an offense) legally punishable.

staunch (stônch, stänch), v.t., adj. stanch.

stave (stāv), n., v., **staved** or **stove, staving.**
—n. 1. one of the thin, narrow pieces of wood which form the sides of a cask, tub, or similar vessel. 2. a stick, rod, pole, or the like. 3. *Music.* a staff. —v.t. 4. to break a hole in. 5. to furnish with a stave or staves. 6. to put, ward, or keep (fol. by *off*), as by force or evasion. —v.i. 7. to break in or up.

stay[1] (stā), v., **stayed** or **staid, staying,** n.
—v.i. 1. to remain, dwell, or reside. 2. to continue to be. 3. to stop or halt. 4. to linger or tarry. 5. to endure. —v.t. 6. to stop or halt. 7. to restrain. 8. to suspend or delay. 9. to remain through or during (a period of time). —n. 10. act of stopping. 11. a stop, halt, or pause. 12. a sojourn. 13. *Law.* a suspension of a judicial proceeding.

stay[2] (stā), n., v., **stayed, staying.** —n. 1. a support, prop, brace, etc. —v.t. 2. to support or prop.

stay[3] (stā), n., v., **stayed, staying.** *Chiefly Naut.* —n. 1. a strong rope, now commonly of wire, used to support a mast. 2. any rope similarly used. —v.t. 3. to support with stays.

Ste., (F *Sainte*) Saint (female).

stead (stĕd), n. 1. the place of a person or thing as occupied by a successor or substitute. 2. service; advantage.

stead·fast (stĕd'fäst', -fäst', -fəst), adj. 1. fixed. 2. firm, resolute, loyal, or unwavering. —stead'fast'ly, adv. —stead'fast'ness, n.

stead·y (stĕd'ĭ), adj., **steadier, steadiest,** n., pl. **steadies,** v., **steadied, steadying.** —adj. 1. firmly fixed; stable. 2. uniform; continuous. 3. constant, regular, or habitual. 4. free from excitement. 5. steadfast. 6. settled; staid. —n. 7. *Slang.* a person's regular sweetheart. —v.t., v.i. 8. to make or become steady. —stead'i·ly, adv. —stead'i·ness, n.

steak (stāk), n. a slice (or patty) of meat, usually beef or fish, for broiling, frying, etc.

steal (stēl), v., **stole, stolen, stealing,** n. —v.t., v.i. 1. to take (something) wrongfully, esp. secretly. 2. to take, get, or win by insidious, surreptitious, or subtle means. 3. to move, bring, convey, or put secretly or quietly. —n. 4. *Colloq.* a theft. 5. the thing stolen. 6. something acquired at very little cost. —steal'er, n.

stealth (stĕlth), n. secret, clandestine, or surreptitious procedure. —stealth'y, adj. —stealth'i·ly, adv. —stealth'i·ness, n.

steam (stēm), n. 1. water in the form of gas or vapor. 2. the mist formed when the gas or vapor from boiling water condenses in the air. 3. *Colloq.* power or energy. —v.i. 4. to give off steam or vapor. 5. to rise or pass off in the form of steam. 6. to become covered with condensed steam. 7. to produce steam, as in a boiler. 8. to move by the agency of steam. —v.t. 9. to expose to or treat with steam. 10. to emit (steam or vapor). —adj. 11. heated by, or heating with, steam. 12. propelled by or propelling with a steam engine. 13. operated by steam. 14. conducting steam. —steam'y, adj.

steam·er (stē'mər), n. 1. something operated by steam, as a steamship. 2. one that steams. 3. a container in which something is steamed.

steam fitter, one who installs and repairs steam pipes and their accessories.

steam roller, a steam-locomotive engine having a heavy roller for crushing, compacting, or leveling materials in road making.

steam·ship (stēm'shĭp'), n. a commercial ship propelled by steam power. Also, **steam'boat'.**

steam shovel, a machine for excavating, operated by its own engine and boiler.

ste·a·rin (stē'ə rĭn, stĭr'ĭn), n. *Chem.* a soft, white, odorless solid found in many natural fats. —ste·ar·ic (stĭ ăr'ĭk, stĭr'ĭk), adj.

steed (stēd), n. 1. a horse, esp. one for riding. 2. *Archaic.* a high-spirited horse.

steel (stēl), n. 1. iron in a modified form, artificially produced, containing a certain amount of carbon and other constituents: used in making tools, girders, etc. 2. a sword. —adj. 3. pertaining to or made of steel. 4. like steel in color, hardness, or strength. —v.t. 5. to fit with steel, as by pointing, edging, or overlaying. 6. to render inflexible, determined, etc. —steel'y, adj.

steel·yard (stēl'yärd', stĭl'yərd), n. a portable type of scale.

steen·bok (stēn'bŏk', stän'-), n. a small South African antelope.

steep[1] (stēp), adj. 1. having an almost perpendicular slope or pitch. 2. *Colloq.* unduly high; exorbitant. —n. 3. a steep place. —steep'ly, adv. —steep'ness, n.

steep[2] (stēp), v.t., v.i. 1. to soak, drench, saturate, or imbue. 2. to absorb deeply. —n. 3. a liquid in which something is steeped. —steep'er, n.

stee·ple (stē'pəl), n. 1. a lofty tower attached to a church, temple, or the like, and often containing bells. 2. such a tower with a spire surmounting it. 3. a spire on the top of the tower or roof of a church or the like.

stee·ple·chase (stē'pəl chās'), n. 1. a race, esp. of horses, over a course furnished with artificial ditches, hedges, and other obstacles. 2. a horse race across country. —stee'ple·chas'er, n.

stee·ple·jack (stē'pəl jăk'), n. a man who climbs steeples, tall chimneys, or the like, to make repairs, etc.

steer[1] (stĭr), v.t., v.i. 1. to guide or direct the course (of). —n. 2. *U.S. Slang.* a piece of advice. —steer'a·ble, adj. —steer'er, n.

steer[2] (stĭr), n. a castrated male bovine, esp. one raised for beef; ox.

steer·age (stĭr'ĭj), n. (in a ship) the part allotted to the passengers who travel at the cheapest rate.

steers·man (stĭrz'mən), n., pl. **-men.** one who steers a ship; helmsman.

stein (stīn), n. an earthenware mug, esp. for beer.

Stein (stīn), n. Gertrude, 1874–1946, U.S. author, in France.

Stein·beck (stīn'bĕk), n. John Ernst, born 1902, U.S. novelist.

stein·bok (stīn'bŏk'), n. the steenbok.

stel·lar (stĕl'ər), adj. 1. of or pertaining to the stars. 2. starlike.

stel·late (stĕl'ĭt, -āt), adj. star-shaped.

stem[1] (stĕm), n., v., **stemmed, stemming.** —n. 1. the ascending axis of a plant. 2. the stalk which supports a leaf, flower, or fruit. 3. the trunk of a tree, shrub, or other plant. 4. a long, slender part. 5. ancestry or pedigree. 6. *Gram.* the element common to all the forms of an inflectional paradigm, or to some subset thereof, usually more than a root. —v.t. 7. to remove the stem from. —v.i. 8. to arise or originate. —stem'less, adj.

stem[2] (stĕm), v.t., **stemmed, stemming. 1.** to stop or check. 2. to dam up.

stem[3] (stĕm), v.t., **stemmed, stemming.** to make headway against (a tide, gale, etc.).

stem[4] (stĕm), n. *Naut.* the forward part of a ship.

stench (stĕnch), n. an offensive odor.

sten·cil (stĕn'səl), n., v., **-ciled, -ciling** or (*esp. Brit.*) **-cilled, -cilling.** —n. 1. a thin sheet cut through in such a way as to reproduce a design when color is rubbed through it. —v.t. 2. to produce (letters, etc.) by means of a stencil.

ste·nog·ra·pher (stə nŏg'rə fər), n. a person who specializes in taking dictation, or in reporting, stenographically.

ste·nog·ra·phy (stə nŏg'rə fĭ), n. the art of writing in shorthand. —sten·o·graph·ic (stĕn'ə grăf'ĭk), sten'o·graph'i·cal, adj. —sten'o·graph'i·cal·ly, adv.

Sten·o·type (stĕn'ə tīp'), n. *Trademark.* a keyboard instrument resembling a typewriter, used in a system of shorthand. —sten'o·typ'y, n.

sten·to·ri·an (stĕn tōr'ĭ ən), adj. very loud or powerful in sound.

step (stĕp), n., v., **stepped, stepping.** —n. 1. a movement made by lifting the foot and setting it down again in a new position, as in walking. 2. the space passed over by one movement of the foot in stepping. 3. the sound made by the foot in stepping. 4. a footprint. 5. the manner of stepping; gait. 6. pace in marching. 7. pace uniform with that of another or others, or in time with music. 8. (pl.) movements or course in stepping or walking. 9. a proceeding, as toward some end. 10. a stage in a process. 11. a support for the foot in ascending or descending. 12. a very short distance. 13. a pattern of movement in a dance. —v.i. 14. to move, go, etc., by one or more steps. 15. to go briskly or fast. 16. to tread (*on* or *upon*), by intention or accident. 17. to press with the foot. —v.t. 18. to take (a step, pace, stride, etc.). 19. to make or arrange in the manner of a series of steps. 20. *Naut.* to fix (a mast) in its place. —step'per, n.

step-, a prefix indicating connection between members of a family by the remarriage of a parent, and not by blood.

step·broth·er (stĕp′brŭth′ər), n. one's stepfather's or stepmother's son by a former marriage. —**step′sis′ter**, n.fem.

step·child (stĕp′chīld′), n., pl. **-children.** a child of one's husband or wife by a former marriage. —**step′son′**, n. —**step′daugh′ter**, n.fem.

step·fa·ther (stĕp′fä′thər), n. a man who occupies one's father's place by marriage to one's mother. —**step′moth′er**, n.fem.

step-in (stĕp′ĭn′), adj. 1. (of garments, shoes, etc.) put on by being stepped into. —n. 2. Also, **step′-ins′**. a step-in garment, etc.

step·lad·der (stĕp′lăd′ər), n. a ladder having flat steps or treads in place of rungs.

steppe (stĕp), n. 1. an extensive plain, esp. one without trees. 2. **The Steppes.** the vast Russian grasslands, esp. those in the S and E European and W and SW Asiatic parts of the Soviet Union.

stepping stone, 1. a stone in shallow water, a marshy place, or the like, used for stepping on in crossing. 2. anything serving as a means of advancing or rising.

stere (stîr), n. a cubic meter, equivalent to 35.314 cu. ft., used to measure cordwood.

ster·e·op·ti·con (stĕr′ĭ ŏp′tĭ kən, stîr′-), n. a type of lantern-slide projector.

ster·e·o·scope (stĕr′ĭ ə skōp′, stîr′-), n. an optical instrument through which two pictures of the same object, taken from slightly different points of view, are viewed, one by each eye, producing the effect of a single picture of the object, with the appearance of depth or relief.

ster·e·o·type (stĕr′ĭ ə tīp′, stîr′-), n., v., **-typed, -typing.** —n. 1. a process of making metal printing plates by taking a mold of composed type or the like in papier-mâché or other material and then taking from this mold a cast (plate) in type metal. 2. a plate of type metal made by this process. 3. a set form. —v.t. 4. to make a stereotype of. 5. to give a fixed form to. —**ster′e·o·typ′er**, n.

ster·e·o·typed (stĕr′ĭ ə tīpt′, stîr′-), adj. 1. reproduced in stereotype plates. 2. fixed in form; hackneyed; conventional.

ster·ile (stĕr′ĭl), adj. 1. free from living germs or microörganisms. 2. incapable of producing offspring. 3. barren. 4. unproductive of results. —**ster′ile·ly**, adv. —**ste·ril·i·ty** (stə rĭl′ə tĭ), n.

ster·i·lize (stĕr′ə līz′), v.t., **-lized, -lizing.** 1. to destroy microörganisms in, usually by bringing to a high temperature with steam, dry heat, or boiling liquid. 2. to destroy the ability of to reproduce. —**ster′i·li·za′tion**, n. —**ster′i·liz′er**, n.

ster·ling (stûr′lĭng), adj. 1. consisting of or pertaining to British money. 2. (of silver) being of standard quality, 92¹/₂% pure silver. 3. made of sterling silver. 4. thoroughly excellent. —n. 5. manufactured goods of sterling silver.

stern¹ (stûrn), adj. 1. firm, strict, or uncompromising. 2. hard, harsh, or severe. 3. grim. —**stern′ly**, adv. —**stern′ness**, n.

stern² (stûrn), n. the hinder part, esp. of a ship.

Sterne (stûrn), n. **Laurence,** 1713–68, British clergyman and novelist.

ster·num (stûr′nəm), n., pl. **-na** (-nə), **-nums.** Anat. a flat, narrow bone connected with the clavicles and the true ribs; breastbone.

stet (stĕt), v., **stetted, stetting.** —v.i. 1. let it stand: a direction on a printer's proof or the like to retain canceled matter. —v.t. 2. to mark with the word "stet."

steth·o·scope (stĕth′ə skōp′), n. Med. an instrument used in auscultation, to convey sounds in the chest or other parts of the body to the ear of the examiner.

Steu·ben·ville (stū′bən vĭl′, stoō′-), n. a city in E Ohio. 37,651.

ste·ve·dore (stē′və dōr′), n., v., **-dored, -doring.** —n. 1. a firm or individual engaged in the loading or unloading of a vessel. —v.t., v.i. 2. to load or unload the cargo of (a ship).

Ste·ven·son (stē′vən sən), n. 1. **Adlai,** born 1900, U. S. political leader. 2. **Robert Louis** (Balfour), 1850–94, Scottish author.

stew (stū, stoō), v.t., v.i. 1. to cook (food) by simmering or slow boiling. 2. Colloq. to fret. —n. 3. a preparation of meat, fish, or other food cooked by stewing. 4. Colloq. a state of agitation or worry.

stew·ard (stū′ərd, stoō′-), n. 1. one who manages another's property, household, or financial affairs. 2. an employee who has charge of the table, the servants, etc., in a club, on a ship, etc. 3. a ship's officer who keeps the stores and arranges for the table. —**stew·ard·ess** (stū′ər dĭs, stoō′-), n. fem. —**stew′ard·ship′**, n.

stewed (stūd, stoōd), adj. 1. cooked by stewing. 2. Slang. intoxicated or drunk.

St. He·le·na (hə lē′nə), a British island in the S Atlantic: Napoleon's place of exile, 1815–21. 4748 pop.; 47 sq. mi.

stib·i·um (stĭb′ĭ əm), n. Chem. antimony.

stick¹ (stĭk), n. 1. a branch or shoot of a tree or shrub cut or broken off. 2. a long and slender piece of wood. 3. an elongated, sticklike piece of some material. 4. Sports. the bat used in hockey or lacrosse. 5. Aeron. a lever by which the longitudinal and lateral motions of an airplane are controlled. 6. (pl.) U.S. Colloq. the backwoods.

stick² (stĭk), v., **stuck, sticking.** —v.t. 1. to pierce, puncture or stab. 2. to thrust (something pointed) in, into, through, etc. 3. to fasten in position by thrusting the point into something. 4. to fix or impale upon something pointed. 5. to thrust or put into a place or position indicated. 6. to fasten or attach by causing to adhere. 7. to render unable to proceed or go back. 8. Slang. to impose upon or cheat. —v.i. 9. to remain attached by adhesion. 10. to hold, cleave, or cling. 11. to remain persistently. 12. to remain firm in resolution, opinion, etc. 13. to keep steadily at a task. 14. to become fastened, hindered, checked, or stationary. 15. to extend. —n. 16. a stab.

stick·er (stĭk′ər), n. 1. one that sticks. 2. an adhesive label. 3. a persistent, diligent person. 4. Colloq. something that nonpluses or puzzles one. 5. a bur, thorn, or the like.

stick·le (stĭk′əl), v.i., **-led, -ling.** 1. to haggle insistently. 2. to scruple; demur. —**stick·ler** (stĭk′lər), n.

stick·le·back (stĭk′əl băk′), n. any of certain small, pugnacious, spiny-backed fishes.

stick-up (stĭk′ŭp′), n. Slang. a holdup or robbery.

stick·y (stĭk′ĭ), adj., **stickier, stickiest.** 1. adhering; adhesive. 2. covered with adhesive matter. 3. (of the weather, etc.) humid. —**stick′i·ly**, adv. —**stick′i·ness**, n.

stiff (stĭf), adj. 1. rigid; not flexible, pliant, or easily bent. 2. not moving or working easily. 3. (of a person, etc.) moving only with difficulty, as from cold, age, exhaustion, etc. 4. blowing strongly. 5. strong, as liquors. 6. stubborn. 7. rigidly formal. 8. awkward. 9. Colloq. hard to deal with, accomplish, endure, pay, believe, etc. 10. laborious or difficult. 11. severe, as a penalty. 12. firm from tension; taut. —n. Slang. 13. a corpse. 14. a formal person. —**stiff′ly**, adv. —**stiff′ness**, n.

stiff·en (stĭf′ən), v.t., v.i. to make or become stiff. —**stiff′en·er**, n.

sti·fle¹ (stī′fəl), v., **-fled, -fling.** —v.t. 1. to smother. 2. to repress. 3. to suppress; crush; stop. —v.i. 4. to become stifled or suffocated.

sti·fle² (stī′fəl), n. the joint of the hind leg of a horse, dog, etc., between the femur and the tibia. Also, **stifle joint.**

sti·fling (stī′flĭng), adj. suffocating; oppressively close. —**sti′fling·ly**, adv.

stig·ma (stĭg′mə), n., pl. **stigmata** (stĭg′mə tə), **stigmas.** 1. a mark of disgrace or infamy. 2. Pathol. a spot or mark on the skin. 3. Zool. a small mark, spot, pore, or the like, on an animal or organ. 4. Bot. that part of a pistil which receives the pollen. —**stig·mat·ic** (stĭg măt′ĭk), adj.

stig·ma·tize (stĭg′mə tīz′), v.t., **-tized, -tizing.** 1. to mark with a stigma or brand. 2. to set some mark of disgrace or infamy upon. —**stig′ma·ti·za′tion**, n.

stile (stīl), n. 1. a series of steps or the like for getting over a fence or wall. 2. a turnstile.

sti·let·to (stĭ lĕt′ō), n., pl. **-tos, -toes, -toed, -toing.** —n. 1. a dagger having a narrow blade, thick in proportion to its width. —v.t. 2. to stab with a stiletto.

still¹ (stĭl), adj. 1. motionless; stationary. 2. free from sound or noise; silent. 3. hushed. 4. quiet; tranquil; calm. 5. without waves or perceptible current. 6. not effervescent. —n. 7. Poetic. silence. 8. a single photographic picture of a subject. —adv. 9. as previously. 10. up to this or that time. 11. in the future as in the past. **12.** even or yet. **13.** yet; nevertheless. —*conj.* **14.** and yet; nevertheless. —*v.t.* **15.** to silence or hush. **16.** to calm, appease, or allay. **17.** to quiet (waves, winds, passion, etc.). —*v.i.* **18.** to become still or quiet. —**still/ness,** *n.*

still[2] (stĭl), *n.* a distilling apparatus, consisting of a vessel in which the substance is heated and vaporized and a cooling device or coil for condensing the vapor.

still·born (stĭl/bôrn/), *adj.* dead when born.

still life, a picture represénting inanimate objects such as fruit, flowers, etc.

stil·ly (*adv.* stĭl/lĭ/; *adj.* stĭl/ĭ), *adv.* **1.** quietly; silently. —*adj.* **2.** *Poetic.* still; quiet.

stilt (stĭlt), *n.* **1.** one of two poles, each with a support for the foot at some distance above the ground. **2.** one of several high posts underneath any structure built above land or over water. **3.** any of certain birds with very long legs, long neck, and slender bill, living esp. in marshes. —*v.t.* **4.** to raise on stilts.

stilt·ed (stĭl/tĭd), *adj.* stiffly dignified or formal; pompous.

Stim·son (stĭm/sən), *n.* Henry Lewis, 1867–1950, U.S. statesman.

stim·u·lant (stĭm/yə lənt), *n.* **1.** *Physiol., Med.* something that temporarily quickens some process or activity. **2.** an alcoholic liquor. —*adj.* **3.** stimulating.

stim·u·late (stĭm/yə lāt/), *v.t., v.i.,* -lated, -lating. **1.** to rouse to action or effort; spur on; incite. **2.** *Physiol., Med., etc.* to excite (an organ, etc.) to its functional activity. —**stim/u·lat/er, stim/u·la/tor,** *n.* —**stim/u·la/tion,** *n.* —**stim/-u·la/tive,** *adj.*

stim·u·lus (stĭm/yə ləs), *n., pl.* **-li** (-lī/). **1.** something that incites one or quickens action, thought, etc. **2.** *Physiol., etc.* something that excites an organ or part to functional activity.

sting (stĭng), *v.,* **stung** or (*Archaic or Obs.*) **stang, stung,** stinging, *n.* —*v.t.* **1.** to prick or wound with the sharp-pointed organ with which certain animals are furnished. **2.** to pain sharply, hurt, or wound. **3.** to goad. **4.** *Slang.* to impose upon, charge exorbitantly, or the like. —*v.i.* **5.** to use or have a sting. **6.** to cause or feel a sharp, smarting pain. —*n.* **7.** act of stinging. **8.** a wound, pain, or smart caused by stinging. **9.** a stimulus or incitement. **10.** a sharp-pointed organ of insects and other animals, capable of inflicting wounds. —**sting/er,** *n.*

sting·ray (stĭng/rā/), *n.* any of the rays, having a long, flexible tail with which they can inflict severe wounds.

stin·gy (stĭn/jĭ), *adj.,* -gier, -giest. **1.** reluctant to give or spend; miserly. **2.** scanty or meager. —**stin/gi·ly,** *adv.* —**stin/gi·ness,** *n.*

stink (stĭngk), *v.,* **stank** or **stunk, stunk,** stinking, *n.* —*v.i.* **1.** to emit a strong offensive smell. —*v.t.* **2.** to cause to stink. —*n.* **3.** a strong offensive smell; stench. —**stink/er,** *n.* —**stink/-ing·ly,** *adv.*

stink·bug (stĭngk/bŭg/), *n.* any of certain broad, flat bugs, many species of which feed on plant juices.

stink·weed (stĭngk/wēd/), *n.* any of various ill-smelling plants, as the jimson weed.

stint (stĭnt), *v.t.* **1.** to limit or restrict. —*v.i.* **2.** to stint oneself. —*n.* **3.** limitation or restriction. **4.** an allotted amount or piece of work. —**stint/er,** *n.*

stipe (stīp), *n. Bot.* a stalk.

sti·pend (stī/pĕnd), *n.* **1.** regular pay; salary. **2.** any periodic payment.

sti·pen·di·ar·y (stī pĕn/dĭ ĕr/ĭ), *adj., n., pl.* -aries. —*adj.* **1.** receiving a stipend. —*n.* **2.** one who receives a stipend.

stip·ple (stĭp/əl), *v.,* -pled, -pling, *n.* —*v.t.* **1.** to paint, engrave, or draw by means of dots. —*n.* **2.** Also, **stip/pling.** the method of painting, engraving, etc. by stippling. —**stip/pler,** *n.*

stip·u·late (stĭp/yə lāt/), *v.i., v.t.,* -lated, -lating. to make an express demand or arrangement (for), as a condition of agreement.

stip·u·la·tion (stĭp/yə lā/shən), *n.* **1.** act of stipulating. **2.** a condition in an agreement.

stip·ule (stĭp/ūl), *n. Bot.* one of a pair of lateral appendages, often leaflike, at the base of a leaf petiole in many plants. —**stip/u·lar,** *adj.*

stir[1] (stûr), *v.,* **stirred, stirring,** —*v.t., v.i.* **1.** to move or agitate (a liquid, or any matter in separate particles or pieces). **2.** to move. **3.** to rouse from inactivity, indifference, etc. **4.** to incite. **5.** to excite. **6.** to be in circulation, cur-

rent, or afoot. —*n.* **7.** movement. **8.** general excitement; commotion.

stir[2] (stûr), *n. Slang.* a prison.

stir·ring (stûr/ĭng), *adj.* **1.** moving, active, or lively. **2.** exciting; thrilling. —**stir/ring·ly,** *adv.*

stir·rup (stûr/əp, stĭr/əp), *n.* **1.** a loop, ring, or other contrivance of metal, wood, leather, etc., suspended from the saddle of a horse to support the rider's foot. **2.** any of various similar supports.

stitch (stĭch), *n.* **1.** one complete movement of a threaded needle through a fabric or material, as in sewing, embroidery, etc. **2.** a portion of thread disposed in place by one movement in sewing. **3.** one complete movement of the needle or other implement used in knitting, crocheting, etc. **4.** a sudden, sharp pain. —*v.t., v.i.* **5.** to sew. —**stitch/er,** *n.*

sti·ver (stī/vər), *n.* **1.** a minor Dutch coin. **2.** a worthless thing.

St. John, 1. a seaport in SE Canada, 51,741. **2.** a river forming a part of the boundary between Maine and Canada. ab. 450 mi.

St. John's, a seaport in SE Canada. With suburbs, 62,823.

St. Joseph, a city in NW Missouri, on the Missouri river. 75,711.

St. Lawrence, a river in SE Canada, flowing NE from Lake Ontario into the **Gulf of St. Lawrence** (an arm of the Atlantic). 760 mi.

St. Lou·is (lōō/ĭs, lōō/ĭ), a city in E Missouri. 816,048.

St. Mo·ritz (mōr/ĭts), a resort town in SE Switzerland. 3968.

stoat (stōt), *n.* the ermine, esp. when in brown summer fur.

stock (stŏk), *n.* **1.** an aggregate of goods kept on hand by a merchant. **2. in stock,** on hand, as for sale. **3. out of stock,** lacking, esp. temporarily, from a stock. **4.** a quantity of something accumulated. **5.** livestock. **6.** *Hort.* a stem, tree, or plant that furnishes cuttings. **7.** a line of descent; a tribe, race, or ethnic group. **8.** the wooden or metal piece to which the barrel and mechanism of a rifle or like firearm are attached. **9.** the stump of a tree left standing. **10.** (*pl.*) an old instrument of punishment consisting of a framework with holes for the ankles and (sometimes) the wrists of an offender exposed to public derision. **11.** (*pl.*) the frame on which a boat rests while under construction. **12.** the raw material from which anything is made. **13.** *Cookery.* the broth prepared by boiling meat, etc., and used as a foundation for soups, sauces, etc. **14.** *Finance.* **a.** the outstanding capital of a company or corporation. **b.** the shares of a particular company or corporation. —*adj.* **15.** staple; standard. **16.** common or ordinary. **17.** commonplace. **18.** designating or pertaining to livestock raising. **19.** of or pertaining to stock. —*v.t., v.i.* **20.** to furnish with a supply. **21.** to furnish with livestock. **22.** to store (something), as for future use.

Stocks (def. 10)

stock·ade (stŏ kād/), *n., v.,* -aded, -ading. —*n.* **1.** a barrier of strong posts fixed upright in the ground, as for defense. —*v.t.* **2.** to protect, fortify, or encompass with a stockade.

stock·bro·ker (stŏk/brō/kər), *n.* a broker who, for a commission, buys and sells stocks and other securities for customers.

stock company, *Theat.* a company acting a repertoire of plays, more or less permanently together, usually at their own theater.

stock exchange, 1. Also, **stock market. a.** place where stocks and other securities are bought and sold. **2.** an association of dealers in stocks and bonds.

stock·hold·er (stŏk/hōl/dər), *n. Chiefly U.S.* an owner of stock or shares.

Stock·holm (stŏk/hōm, -hōlm), *n.* the capital of Sweden, in the SE part. 671,601.

stock·ing (stŏk/ĭng), *n.* a close-fitting covering, usually knitted of wool, cotton, nylon, silk, etc., for the foot and l g. —**stock/ing·less,** *adj.*

stock-still (stŏk/stĭl/), *adj.* motionless.

Stock·ton (stŏk/tən), *n.* a city in central California. 55,865.

stock·y (stŏk′ĭ), *adj.*, **stockier, stockiest.** of solid and sturdy build. —**stock′i·ly,** *adv.* —**stock′i·ness,** *n.*

stock·yard (stŏk′yärd′), *n.* an enclosure for livestock, connected with a slaughterhouse, railroad, market, etc.

stodg·y (stŏj′ĭ), *adj.*, **stodgier, stodgiest.** dull; uninteresting. —**stodg/i·ly,** *adv.* —**stodg/i·ness,** *n.*

sto·gy (stō′gĭ), *n., pl.* **-gies.** a long, slender, inexpensive cigar. Also, **sto/gie.**

Sto·ic (stō′ĭk), *adj.* **1.** of or pertaining to the school of ancient Greek philosophy which held that men should be unmoved by joy or grief and submit to unavoidable necessity. **2.** (*l.c.*) stoical. —*n.* **3.** a member of the Stoic school. **4.** (*l.c.*) one who maintains the attitude required by the Stoics.

sto·i·cal (stō′ə kəl), *adj.* impassive; characterized by calm or austere fortitude. —**sto/i·cal·ly,** *adv.*

Sto·i·cism (stō′ə sĭz′əm), *n.* **1.** the philosophy of the Stoics. **2.** (*l.c.*) repression of emotion.

stoke (stōk), *v.t., v.i.*, **stoked, stoking. 1.** to poke, stir up, and feed (a fire). **2.** to tend the fire of (a furnace). —**stok/er,** *n.*

stoke·hole (stōk′hōl′), *n.* **1.** a compartment where furnace fires are tended. **2.** a hole through which a furnace is stoked.

Stoke-on-Trent (stōk′ŏn trĕnt′), *n.* a city in W England. 265,590.

Sto·kow·ski (stə kou′skĭ), *n.* **Leopold Antoni Stanislaw,** born 1882, U.S. orchestra conductor.

stole (stōl), *n.* **1.** an ecclesiastical vestment, a narrow strip of material worn over the shoulders. **2.** a long scarf of fur or fabric, extending downward in front, worn by women.

stol·id (stŏl′ĭd), *adj.* not easily stirred mentally; impassive. —**sto·lid·i·ty** (stə lĭd′ə tĭ), **stol′id·ness,** *n.* —**stol′id·ly,** *adv.*

sto·ma (stō′mə), *n., pl.* **stomata** (stō′mə tə, stŏm′ə tə). **1.** *Bot.* any of various small apertures, esp. one of the minute slits in the epidermis of leaves, etc. **2.** *Zool.* a mouth.

stom·ach (stŭm′ək), *n.* **1.** (in man and other vertebrates) a saclike enlargement of the alimentary canal, forming an organ of storage, dilution, and digestion. **2.** any analogous digestive cavity or tract in invertebrates. **3.** the part of the body containing the stomach. **4.** appetite for food. **5.** desire; liking. —*v.t.* **6.** to take into the stomach. **7.** to tolerate. —**sto·mach·ic** (stō-măk′ĭk), *adj.*

stom·ach·er (stŭm′ək ər), *n.* an article of women's dress for covering the stomach and chest.

stone (stōn), *n., pl.* **stones** (*except* **stone** *for def. 4*), *adj., v.*, **stoned, stoning,** *adv.* —*n.* **1.** the hard substance of which rocks consist. **2.** a small rock. **3.** precious stone. **4.** *Brit.* a unit of weight equal to 14 pounds. **5.** any hard, stone-like seed or pit. **6.** *Med.* a concretion in the body, as in the kidney, gall bladder, or urinary bladder. **7.** a tombstone. —*adj.* **8.** made of or pertaining to stone. —*v.t.* **9.** to throw stones at. **10.** to put to death by pelting with stones. **11.** to free from stones, as fruit. —*adv.* **12.** (usually in compounds) entirely.

stone·cut·ter (stōn′kŭt′ər), *n.* one who carves stone. —**stone/cut/ting,** *n.*

stone·ware (stōn′wâr′), *n.* a more or less vitrified pottery ware.

stone·work (stōn′wûrk′), *n.* work in stone.

ston·y (stō′nĭ), *adj.*, **stonier, stoniest. 1.** full of stones or rock. **2.** pertaining to or characteristic of stone. **3.** resembling stone. **4.** unfeeling; merciless. **5.** petrifying. —**ston/i·ly,** *adv.* —**ston/i·ness,** *n.*

stooge (stōōj), *n., v.*, **stooged, stooging.** *U.S.* —*n.* **1.** *Colloq.* a person who feeds lines to a comedian and is the object of his ridicule. **2.** *Slang.* one who acts on behalf of another, esp. in obsequious fashion. —*v.i.* **3.** to act as a stooge.

stool (stōōl), *n.* **1.** a wooden seat without arms or a back. **2.** the stump of a tree or other plant which has been cut down, from which shoots are produced. **3.** a privy. **4.** a bowel movement. —*v.i.* **5.** *Slang.* to act as a stool pigeon.

stool pigeon, *Chiefly U.S. Slang.* a spy for the police, employer, etc.

stoop[1] (stōōp), *v.i., v.t.* **1.** to bend (the head and shoulders) forward and downward. **2.** to carry the head and shoulders habitually forward. **3.** to condescend; deign. —*n.* **4.** a stooping. **5.**

a stooping posture. **6.** a descent from dignity; condescension.

stoop[2] (stōōp), *n.* *U.S.* a raised entrance platform with steps leading up to it.

stop (stŏp), *v.*, **stopped** or (*Poetic*) **stopt; stopping;** *n.* —*v.t., v.i.* **1.** to cease. **2.** to put an end to. **3.** to interrupt, halt, or check. **4.** to prevent. **5.** to block, obstruct, or close. **6.** to fill or close with a cork, plug, or the like. **7.** to halt for a brief visit or rest. —*n.* **8.** a cessation or end. **9.** a stay or sojourn. **10.** a place where trains or other vehicles halt. **11.** an obstacle, impediment, or hindrance. **12.** *Music.* **a.** a device for closing a fingerhole, etc., or pressing down a string in order to produce a particular note. **b.** a knob or handle which controls some part of an organ. **13.** *Photog.* the diaphragm opening of a lens. **14.** *Chiefly Brit.* a punctuation mark.

stop·gap (stŏp′găp′), *n.* **1.** a temporary substitute; makeshift. —*adj.* **2.** makeshift.

stop·page (stŏp′ĭj), *n.* **1.** cessation of activity, etc. **2.** state of being stopped.

stop·per (stŏp′ər), *n.* **1.** one that stops. **2.** a plug for closing a bottle, tube, or the like. —*v.t.* **3.** to close with a stopper.

stop·ple (stŏp′əl), *n., v.*, **-pled, -pling.** —*n.* **1.** a stopper for a bottle or the like. —*v.t.* **2.** to close or fit with a stopple.

stor·age (stōr′ĭj), *n.* **1.** act of storing. **2.** state or fact of being stored. **3.** space for storing. **4.** a place where something is stored. **5.** the price charged for storing goods.

storage battery, a voltaic battery whose energy is renewed by passing a current through the cells in a direction opposed to the electromotive force.

store (stōr), *n., v.*, **stored, storing.** —*n.* **1.** *Chiefly U.S.* a place where goods are kept for sale. **2.** a supply or stock. **3.** *Chiefly Brit.* a storehouse. **4.** esteem or regard. —*v.t.* **5.** to supply or stock. **6.** to lay up for future use. **7.** to deposit in a warehouse, etc., for keeping.

store·house (stōr′hous′), *n.* a house or building in which things are stored.

store·keep·er (stōr′kē′pər), *n.* *Chiefly U.S.* one who has charge of a store or stores.

store·room (stōr′rōōm′, -rŏŏm′), *n.* a room in which stores are kept.

sto·rey (stōr′ĭ), *n., pl.* **-reys.** *Brit.* story[2].

sto·ried[1] (stōr′ĭd), *adj.* recorded or celebrated in history or story.

sto·ried[2] (stōr′ĭd), *adj.* having floors.

stork (stôrk), *n.* any of certain long-legged, long-necked, long-billed wading birds, allied to the ibises and herons.

storm (stôrm), *n.* **1.** a heavy fall of rain, snow, or hail, or a violent outbreak of thunder and lightning, usually accompanied by strong wind. **2.** a wind of 64–75 miles per hour. **3.** a violent assault on a fortified place, strong position, or the like. **4.** a violent disturbance of affairs. —*v.i.* **5.** to blow, rain, snow, hail, etc., strongly. **6.** to rage with fury. **7.** to assault or attack. —**storm/y,** *adj.* —**storm/i·ly,** *adv.* —**storm/i·ness,** *n.*

sto·ry[1] (stōr′ĭ), *n., pl.* **-ries. 1.** a narrative in prose or verse; tale. **2.** a very short fictitious tale. **3.** the plot of a novel, poem, drama, etc. **4.** a report or account of a matter, esp. in a newspaper. **5.** *Colloq.* a lie.

sto·ry[2] (stōr′ĭ), *n., pl.* **-ries.** one of the floors or levels of a building.

sto·ry·tell·er (stōr′ĭ tĕl′ər), *n.* one who tells stories. —**sto/ry·tell/ing,** *adj., n.*

stoup (stōōp), *n.* a basin for holy water, as at the entrance of a church.

stout (stout), *adj.* **1.** solidly built; corpulent; fat. **2.** bold; dauntless. **3.** firm; stubborn. **4.** strong of body. —*n.* **5.** strong ale, beer, or porter. **6.** a stout person. **7.** (*often pl.*) a garment for such a person. —**stout/ly,** *adv.* —**stout/ness,** *n.*

stout-heart·ed (stout′här′tĭd), *adj.* brave and resolute; dauntless.

stove (stōv), *n.* an apparatus for furnishing heat, as for comfort, cooking, or mechanical purposes, commonly using coal, oil, gas, or electricity.

stow (stō), *v.t.* **1.** *Naut.* to place (cargo, etc.) in a ship. **2.** to put in a place or receptacle as for storage or reserve. —*v.i.* **3.** **stow away,** to conceal oneself aboard a ship or other conveyance in order to get a free trip. —**stow·age** (stō′ĭj), *n.* —**stow·a·way** (stō′ə wā′), *n.*

Stowe (stō), *n.* Harriet Elizabeth Beecher, 1811–96, U.S. writer.

St. Paul, the capital of Minnesota, in the SE part. 287,736.

St. Pe·ters·burg (pē′tərz bûrg′), **1.** a seaport in W Florida. 60,812. **2.** the capital of Russia under the czars: renamed Petrograd in 1914, and Leningrad in 1924.

St. Pierre and Miq·ue·lon (pyâr; mĭk′ə-lŏn′), two small islands off the S coast of Newfoundland: France's only colony in North America. 4354; 93 sq. mi. *Cap.:* St. Pierre.

stra·bis·mus (strə bĭz′məs), *n. Pathol.* a disorder of vision due to the nonparallel direction of one or both eyes; cross-eye.

strad·dle (străd′əl), *v.,* -dled, -dling, *n.* —*v.i., v.t.* **1.** to walk, stand, or sit with one leg on each side of (something). **2.** *Colloq.* to take an equivocal position. —*n.* **3.** act of straddling. —**strad′dler,** *n.*

strafe (strāf, sträf), *v.t.,* strafed, strafing. **1.** to attack (ground troops, etc.) from airplanes with machine-gun fire. **2.** to bombard heavily. —**straf′er,** *n.*

strag·gle (străg′əl), *v.i.,* -gled, -gling. **1.** to stray from the road, course, or line of march. **2.** to ramble. **3.** to go, come, or spread in a scattered, irregular fashion. —**strag′gler,** *n.* —**strag′gly,** *adj.*

straight (strāt), *adj.* **1.** not curved; direct. **2.** evenly formed or set. **3.** candid. **4.** honest, honorable, or upright. **5.** *Colloq.* reliable. **6.** right or correct. **7.** in the proper condition. **8.** continuous. **9.** *U.S.* thoroughgoing. **10.** *U.S.* undiluted. —*adv.* **11.** in a straight line. **12.** in an even form or position. **13.** directly. **14.** honestly, honorably, or virtuously. **15.** without discount for quantity purchased. —*n.* **16.** *Poker.* a sequence of five cards of various suits. —**straight′ness,** *n.*

straight·en (strā′tən), *v.t., v.i.* to make or become straight. —**straight′en·er,** *n.*

straight·for·ward (strāt′fôr′wərd), *adj.* **1.** going straight ahead. **2.** direct. **3.** honest; frank. —*adv.* **4.** straight ahead. —**straight′-for′ward·ly,** *adv.* —**straight′for′ward·ness,** *n.*

straight·way (strāt′wā′), *adv.* at once.

strain[1] (strān), *v.t.* **1.** to stretch or exert to the utmost. **2.** to injure by overexertion, as a muscle. **3.** to stretch beyond the proper limit. **4.** to make excessive demands upon. **5.** to pass (liquid matter) through a filter, sieve, or the like, in order to hold back the denser or solid constituents. **6.** to squeeze; hug. —*v.i.* **7.** to pull forcibly. **8.** to stretch one's muscles, etc., to the utmost. **9.** to strive hard. **10.** to undergo tension or stress. **11.** to filter, percolate, or ooze. —*n.* **12.** any force or pressure tending to alter shape, cause fracture, etc. **13.** great or excessive effort, esp. physical. **14.** an injury to a muscle, etc., due to excessive tension or use. **15.** severe or wearing pressure. **16.** (*sing. or pl., often collective pl.*) a passage of music or song. **17.** tone, style, or spirit in expression.

strain[2] (strān), *n.* **1.** the descendants of a common ancestor. **2.** a variety. **3.** ancestry or descent. **4.** hereditary character, tendency, or trait. **5.** a streak or trace.

strain·er (strā′nər), *n.* **1.** one that strains. **2.** a filter, sieve, or the like.

strait (strāt), *n.* **1.** (*often pl. with sing. sense*) a narrow passage of water connecting two large bodies of water. **2.** (*often pl.*) a position of difficulty, distress, or need. —**strait′ly,** *adv.* —**strait′ness,** *n.*

strait·en (strā′tən), *v.t.* **1.** to put into difficulties, esp. financial ones. **2.** to restrict in range, amount, etc.

strait jacket, a coat for confining the arms of violently insane persons, etc.

strait-laced (strāt′lāst′), *adj.* excessively strict in morality; puritanic; prudish.

Straits Settlements, a former British crown colony in SE Asia which included Singapore.

strand[1] (strănd), *v.t., v.i.* **1.** to drive or run aground on a shore. **2.** to bring or come into a helpless position. —*n.* **3.** *Poetic.* the shore.

strand[2] (strănd), *n.* **1.** one of the parts twisted together to form a rope, cord, or the like. **2.** a tress of hair. **3.** a string of beads, etc.

strange (strānj), *adj.,* **stranger, strangest,** *adv.* —*adj.* **1.** unusual, extraordinary, or odd. **2.** out of one's natural environment. **3.** hitherto unknown; unfamiliar. **4.** unacquainted. —*adv.*

5. *Colloq.* in a strange manner. —**strange′ly,** *adv.* —**strange′ness,** *n.*

stran·ger (strān′jər), *n.* **1.** a person with whom one has no personal acquaintance. **2.** an outsider. **3.** a newcomer in a place.

stran·gle (străng′gəl), *v.,* -gled, -gling. —*v.t.* **1.** to kill by compression of the windpipe; choke. **2.** to suppress. —*v.i.* **3.** to be choked, stifled, or suffocated. —**stran′gler,** *n.*

strangle hold, 1. *Wrestling.* a hold by which the adversary's breathing is stopped. **2.** anything which prevents motion.

stran·gu·late (străng′gyə lāt′), *v.t.,* -lated, -lating. **1.** *Pathol., Surg.* to compress (a duct, intestine, etc.) so as to impede its function. **2.** to strangle. —**stran′gu·la′tion,** *n.*

strap (străp), *n., v.,* strapped, strapping. —*n.* **1.** a narrow strip of flexible material, esp. leather, for fastening or holding things together, etc. **2.** any strip or band. —*v.t.* **3.** to fasten with a strap or straps.

strap·ping (străp′ĭng), *adj. Colloq.* **1.** tall, robust, and strongly built. **2.** whopping.

strat·a·gem (străt′ə jəm), *n.* a plan, scheme, or trick.

stra·te·gic (strə tē′jĭk), *adj.* **1.** of or pertaining to strategy. **2.** important in strategy. Also, **stra·te′gi·cal.** —**stra·te′gi·cal·ly,** *adv.*

strat·e·gist (străt′ə jĭst), *n.* one versed in strategy.

strat·e·gy (străt′ə jĭ), *n., pl.* -gies. **1.** the science of planning and directing large military operations. **2.** skillful management, operation, or planning. —**strat′e·gist,** *n.*

Strat·ford-on-A·von (străt′fərd ŏn ā′vən), *n.* a town in central England: Shakespeare's birthplace. 13,503.

strat·i·fy (străt′ə fī′), *v.,* -fied, -fying. —*v.t.* **1.** to form or place in layers. —*v.i.* **2.** to form or lie in layers. —**strat′i·fi·ca′tion,** *n.*

strat·o·sphere (străt′ə sfîr′, strā′tə-), *n. Meteorol.* the region of the atmosphere outside the troposphere but within the ionosphere, characterized by relatively uniform temperature over considerable differences in altitude. —**strat′o-spher′ic,** *adj.*

strat·o·vi·sion (străt′ə vĭzh′ən), *n.* the transmission of television and FM programs from airplanes flying in the stratosphere, which extends the area over which broadcasts may be received.

stra·tum (strā′təm, străt′əm), *n., pl.* **strata** (strā′tə, străt′ə), **stratums. 1.** a layer of material, often one of a number of parallel layers placed one upon another. **2.** a level of a people with reference to social position or education.

Straus (strous), *n.* Oscar, born 1870, Austrian composer.

Strauss (strous), *n.* **1. Johann,** 1804–49, Austrian composer. **2.** his son, **Johann,** 1825–99, Austrian composer, esp. of waltzes. **3. Richard,** born 1864, German composer and conductor.

Stra·vin·ski (strə vĭn′skĭ), *n.* **Igor Fëdorovich,** born 1882, Russian composer, now in U.S.

straw (strô), *n.* **1.** a single stalk or stem, esp. of wheat, rye, oats, or barley. **2.** a mass of such stalks, esp. after drying and threshing, used as fodder, as material for hats, etc. **3.** a hollow tube used in drinking some beverages, etc. —*adj.* **4.** of straw. **5.** sham; fictitious.

straw·ber·ry (strô′bĕr′ĭ), *n., pl.* -ries. **1.** the fruit of any of certain stemless herbs of the rose family, consisting of an enlarged fleshy receptacle bearing achenes on its exterior. **2.** the plant bearing it.

stray (strā), *v.i.* **1.** to go from the proper course or place; ramble or wander. —*n.* **2.** a person, animal, or thing that has strayed. —*adj.* **3.** straying. **4.** isolated or occasional.

streak (strēk), *n.* **1.** a long, narrow mark, smear, band of color, or the like. **2.** a vein, stratum, or admixture. **3.** *U.S. Colloq.* a run (of luck). —*v.t.* **4.** to mark with, or arrange as, a streak or streaks. —*v.i.* **5.** to become streaked. **6.** to flash or go rapidly. —**streak′y,** *adj.*

stream (strēm), *n.* **1.** a body of water in a channel, as a river or brook. **2.** a steady current, flow, or beam. —*v.i.* **3.** to flow, pass, or issue in a stream. **4.** to move or proceed continuously. **5.** to wave or float outward. **6.** to hang in a loose, flowing manner. —*v.t.* **7.** to send forth in a stream.

stream·er (strē′mər), *n.* **1.** a long, narrow flag, ribbon, or the like. **2.** a stream of light. **3.** a headline which extends across the width of the newspaper.

stream·line (strēm/līn/), *adj.*, *n.*, *v.*, **-lined**, **-lining.** —*adj.* **1.** having a shape offering the least possible resistance in passing through the air, etc. —*n.* **2.** a teardrop line of contour belonging to a streamline airfoil shape. —*v.t.* **3.** to shape with a streamline. **4.** to plan efficiently.

street (strēt), *n.* **1.** a public road, as in a city. **2.** the roadway as distinguished from the sidewalk.

street·car (strēt/kär/), *n.* *U.S.* a public passenger car running regularly along certain streets, usually on rails.

street·walk·er (strēt/wô/kər), *n.* a soliciting prostitute.

strength (strĕngkth, strĕngth), *n.* **1.** bodily or muscular power. **2.** mental power, force, or vigor. **3.** moral power or firmness. **4.** power by reason of influence, authority, etc. **5.** number, as of ships. **6.** effective force. **7.** power of resisting strain, wear, etc. **8.** vigor of action, language, feeling, etc. **9.** the proportion of essential properties of a beverage, chemical, or the like; intensity.

strength·en (strĕngk/thən, strĕng/-), *v.t.*, *v.i.* to make or grow stronger. —**strength/en·er,** *n.*

stren·u·ous (strĕn/yŏŏ əs), *adj.* vigorous; energetic; active. —**stren/u·ous·ly,** *adv.*

strep·to·coc·cus (strĕp/tə kŏk/əs), *n.*, *pl.* **-coc·ci** (-kŏk/sī). *Bacteriol.* one of a group of organisms which cause such diseases as scarlet fever, erysipelas, etc.

strep·to·my·cin (strĕp/tō mī/sĭn), *n.* a potent medicinal substance similar to penicillin.

stress (strĕs), *v.t.* **1.** to lay emphasis on; emphasize. **2.** *Phonet.* to pronounce strongly. —*n.* **3.** emphasis. **4.** *Phonet.* relative loudness resulting from special emphasis. **5.** accent or emphasis on syllables, as in a metrical pattern. **6.** physical pressure, pull, or other force; strain.

stretch (strĕch), *v.t.*, *v.i.* **1.** to extend (oneself, the body, limbs, wings, etc.) to the full length. **2.** to hold out (the hand or something held, the head, etc.). **3.** to extend or spread. **4.** to draw tight or taut. **5.** to lengthen, widen, distend, or enlarge. **6.** to become stretched to greater length, width, etc. —*n.* **7.** act of stretching. **8.** state of being stretched. **9.** a continuous length, tract, expanse, or period.

stretch·er (strĕch/ər), *n.* **1.** a litter, usually of canvas stretched on a frame, for carrying the sick, wounded, or dead. **2.** any of various instruments for extending, widening, distending, etc.

strew (strōō), *v.t.*, **strewed, strewed** or **strewn**, **strewing. 1.** to scatter or sprinkle. **2.** to cover with something scattered or sprinkled.

stri·ate (*v.* strī/āt; *adj.* strī/ĭt, -āt), *v.*, **-ated**, **-ating**, *adj.* —*v.t.* **1.** to furrow, stripe, or streak. —*adj.* **2.** Also, **stri/at·ed.** furrowed, striped, or streaked. —**stri·a/tion,** *n.*

strick·en (strĭk/ən), *adj.* **1.** struck. **2.** afflicted, as with disease, trouble, or sorrow. **3.** deeply affected, as with horror or other emotion.

strict (strĭkt), *adj.* **1.** conforming closely to requirements or principles. **2.** stringent or exacting. **3.** rigorously enforced or maintained. **4.** exact or precise. **5.** careful; minute. **6.** complete. —**strict/ly,** *adv.* —**strict/ness,** *n.*

stric·ture (strĭk/chər), *n.* **1.** an adverse criticism. **2.** a morbid contraction of any passage of the body.

stride (strīd), *v.*, **strode, stridden, striding**, *n.* —*v.i.*, *v.t.* **1.** to walk with long steps (along, on, over, etc.). **2.** to straddle. —*n.* **3.** a long step in walking. **4.** a regular or steady course, pace, etc. **5.** a step forward in progress. —**strid/er,** *n.*

stri·dent (strī/dənt), *adj.* harsh in sound; grating. —**stri/dence, stri/den·cy,** *n.* —**stri/dent·ly,** *adv.*

strife (strīf), *n.* **1.** conflict, discord, or variance. **2.** a quarrel, struggle, or clash.

strike (strīk), *v.*, **struck, struck** or **stricken**, **striking**, *n.* —*v.t.* **1.** to deliver a blow with. **2.** to deal a blow to (a person or thing). **3.** to inflict (a blow, stroke, etc.). **4.** to drive or thrust forcibly. **5.** to produce (fire, light, etc.) by friction, etc.; cause to ignite. **6.** to come into contact or collision with. **7.** to enter the mind of. **8.** to impress, esp. strongly. **9.** to encounter unexpectedly. **10.** to find (ore, oil, etc.) in prospecting, boring, or the like. **11.** to lower or take down (a sail, flag, etc.). **12.** to efface or cancel, as with the stroke of a pen. **13.** to stamp (a coin, medal, etc.). **14.** to indicate (the hour of day) by a stroke or strokes. **15.** to afflict suddenly or

affect deeply. **16.** to render (blind, dumb, etc.) suddenly. **17.** to cause (a feeling) to enter suddenly. **18.** to assume (an attitude or posture). **19.** to make, conclude, or ratify. **20.** to begin or form. **21.** *Baseball.* (of the pitcher) to cause (a batter) to strike out. —*v.i.* **22.** to deal a blow. **23.** to knock, rap, or tap. **24.** to come into forcible contact. **25.** to fall, as light does (fol. by *on* or *upon*). **26.** to make an impression. **27.** to come unexpectedly. **28.** to sound by percussion. **29.** to be indicated by such sounding. **30.** to be ignited. **31.** to go, proceed, or advance. **32.** (of an employee or employees) to engage in a strike. **33. strike out,** *Baseball.* (of a batter) to make three strikes and be declared "out." —*n.* **34.** an act of striking. **35.** a concerted stopping of work in order to compel an employer to accede to workers' demands. **36.** *Baseball.* an unsuccessful attempt on the part of the batter to hit a pitched ball, or anything ruled equivalent to this. **37.** *U.S. Bowling.* the knocking down of all the pins with the first bowl. **38.** the discovery of a rich vein of ore in mining, of petroleum in boring, etc. —**strik/er,** *n.*

strike·break·er (strīk/brā/kər), *n.* one who takes part in breaking a strike of workers.

strik·ing (strī/kĭng), *adj.* **1.** attractive; impressive. **3.** being on strike, as workmen. —**strik/ing·ly,** *adv.*

string (strĭng), *n.*, *v.*, **strung, stringing.** —*n.* **1.** a line, cord, or thread, used for tying parcels, etc. **2.** a number of objects, as beads, threaded on a cord. **3.** any closely connected series of things. **4.** a set or number. **5.** (in musical instruments) a tightly stretched cord or wire which produces a tone when caused to vibrate. **6.** (*pl.*) stringed musical instruments. **7.** a cord or fiber in a plant. **8.** *Colloq.* a limitation on any proposal. —*v.t.* **9.** to furnish with a string or strings. **10.** to extend (a cord, etc.) from one point to another. **11.** to thread on a string. **12.** to arrange in a series or succession. **13.** to tighten the strings of (a musical instrument) to the required pitch. **14.** to provide or adorn with something suspended. **15.** to remove strings from. **16.** to kill by hanging. **17.** *Slang.* to fool or hoax. —*v.i.* **18.** to form into or move in a string. —**string/er,** *n.* —**stringed,** *adj.*

string bean, 1. any of certain kinds of bean (plant), the unripe pods of which are used as food. **2.** the pod itself.

strin·gent (strĭn/jənt), *adj.* **1.** rigorously strict; severe. **2.** urgent. **3.** convincing. —**strin/gent·ly,** *adv.* —**strin/gen·cy,** *n.*

string·y (strĭng/ĭ), *adj.*, **stringier, stringiest.** **1.** of or like string. **2.** toughly fibrous. **3.** sinewy or wiry. **4.** ropy. —**string/i·ness,** *n.*

strip[1] (strĭp), *v.*, **stripped, stripping.** —*v.t.* **1.** to deprive of covering or clothing. **2.** to remove. **3.** to rob or deprive. **4.** to empty. **5.** to dismantle. **6.** to tear off the thread of (a screw, etc.) or the teeth of (a gear, etc.). —*v.i.* **7.** to strip oneself of clothes. —**strip/per,** *n.*

strip[2] (strĭp), *n.*, *v.*, **stripped, stripping.** —*n.* **1.** a long narrow piece, usually flat. —*v.t.* **2.** to cut into strips.

stripe[1] (strīp), *n.*, *v.*, **striped, striping.** —*n.* **1.** a long, narrow band different from the rest of a surface. **2.** a striped fabric. **3.** a strip of braid or the like. **4.** (*pl.*) a number of such strips, worn on a uniform as a badge of rank, service, etc. **5.** style, variety, sort, or kind. —*v.t.* **6.** to mark with a stripe or stripes.

stripe[2] (strīp), *n.* a stroke with a whip, rod, etc., as in punishment.

strip·ling (strĭp/lĭng), *n.* a youth just passing from boyhood to manhood.

strip tease, a burlesque act in which a woman disrobes garment by garment to the accompaniment of music.

strive (strīv), *v.i.*, **strove, striven, striving.** **1.** to try or work hard. **2.** to battle or struggle vigorously.

stroke[1] (strōk), *n.*, *v.*, **stroked, stroking.** —*n.* **1.** an act of striking; blow. **2.** something causing pain, injury, or death, as an attack of paralysis. **3.** a piece of luck, etc., befalling one. **4.** a single complete movement, esp. one continuously repeated in some process. **5.** each of the succession of movements of the arms and legs in swimming. **6.** a method of swimming. **7.** a vigorous attempt to attain some object. **8.** a feat or achievement. **9.** an act, piece, or amount of work, etc. **10.** a movement or mark of a pen, pencil, brush, or the like. **11.** *Rowing.* a pull of the oar. —*v.t.* **12.** to mark with a stroke or strokes.

stroke² (strōk), v., **stroked, stroking,** n. —v.t. **1.** to rub gently, as in soothing or caressing. —n. **2.** act of stroking.

stroll (strōl), v.i., v.t. **1.** to ramble or saunter (along or through). **2.** to roam. —n. **3.** a ramble or saunter.

stroll·er (strō′lər), n. **1.** one who strolls. **2.** an itinerant performer. **3.** a light baby carriage, often collapsible.

strong (strông, strŏng), adj. **1.** physically powerful, vigorous, or robust. **2.** powerful, able, or competent. **3.** of great moral power. **4.** powerful in influence, authority, resources, etc. **5.** clear and firm; loud. **6.** well supplied. **7.** of great effectiveness. **8.** able to resist strain, wear, etc. **9.** firm or unfaltering. **10.** moving or acting with force or vigor. **11.** containing alcohol, or much alcohol. **12.** intense, as light. **13.** distinct; marked. **14.** strenuous or forceful. **15.** fervent; thoroughgoing. **16.** having a large proportion of the essential properties. **17.** having a high degree of flavor or odor, sometimes unpleasant. **18.** Com. characterized by steady or advancing prices. **19.** Gram. indicating differentiation in tense by internal vowel change. —adv. **20.** powerfully; forcibly; vigorously. —**strong′ly,** adv.

strong-arm (strông′ärm′, strŏng′-), Colloq. —adj. **1.** involving physical force. —v.t. **2.** to employ violent methods upon.

strong·hold (strông′hōld′, strŏng′-), n. a strong or well-fortified place; fortress.

stron·ti·um (strŏn′shǐ əm, -tǐ əm), n. Chem. a bivalent metallic element. Symbol: Sr; at. wt.: 87.63; at. no.: 38; sp. gr.: 2.6.

strop (strŏp), n., v., **stropped, stropping.** —n. **1.** a strip of leather or other flexible material used for sharpening razors. —v.t. **2.** to sharpen on a strop.

stro·phe (strō′fǐ), n. **1.** the first of two metrically corresponding series of lines forming divisions of a lyric poem (the second being the **antistrophe**). **2.** any separate section or extended movement in a poem.

struck (strŭk), adj. shut down or otherwise affected by a strike of workers.

struc·ture (strŭk′chər), n. **1.** mode of building or of arrangement of parts. **2.** something constructed. **3.** a complex system. **4.** the manner by which atoms in a molecule are joined to each other. —**struc′tur·al,** adj. —**struc′tur·al·ly,** adv.

stru·del (strōō′dəl), Ger. shtrōō′dəl), n. any of a variety of pastries, usually with fruits, cheeses, etc., in a paper-thin dough.

strug·gle (strŭg′əl), v., **-gled, -gling,** n. —v.i. **1.** to contend with an adversary, task, problem, etc. —n. **2.** act or process of struggling. **3.** a strong effort against any adverse forces or conditions. —**strug′gler,** n.

strum (strŭm), v., **strummed, strumming,** n. —v.t., v.i. **1.** to play on (a stringed musical instrument) unskillfully or carelessly. —n. **2.** act of strumming. —**strum′mer,** n.

strum·pet (strŭm′pǐt), n. a prostitute.

strut¹ (strŭt), v., **strutted, strutting,** n. —v.i. **1.** to walk with a vain, pompous bearing. —n. **2.** a strutting walk.

strut² (strŭt), n., v., **strutted, strutting.** —n. **1.** a member of a structure, designed for the reception of pressure or weight in the direction of its length. —v.t. **2.** to brace by a strut or struts.

strych·nine (strǐk′nǐn, -nēn, -nǐn), n. a colorless crystalline poison. Also, **strych·nin** (strǐk′nǐn).

St. Thomas, one of the Virgin Islands, in the U.S. part. 11,265 pop.; 32 sq. mi.

Stu·art (stū′ərt, stōō′-), n. **1.** the royal house which reigned in Scotland from 1371 to 1603 and in England and Scotland from 1603 to 1714. **2.** Gilbert, 1755–1828, American portrait painter.

stub (stŭb), n., v., **stubbed, stubbing.** —n. **1.** a stump, as of a tree. **2.** a short remaining piece, as of a pencil, cigar, etc. **3.** something unusually short. **4.** (in a checkbook) the leaf on which a record is kept. —v.t. **5.** Chiefly U.S. to strike, as one's toe, against something.

stub·ble (stŭb′əl), n. **1.** (usually pl.) the stump of a grain stalk or the like. **2.** any short, rough growth, as of beard. —**stub′bly,** adj.

stub·born (stŭb′ərn), adj. **1.** unreasonably obstinate. **2.** resolute. **3.** persistent. **4.** hard to deal with. —**stub′born·ly,** adv. —**stub′born·ness,** n.

stub·by (stŭb′ǐ), adj., **-bier, -biest. 1.** of or resembling a stub. **2.** short and thick or broad.

3. full of stubs. **4.** bristly, as the beard. —**stub′bi·ness,** n.

stuc·co (stŭk′ō), n., pl. **-coes, -cos,** v., **-coed, -coing.** —n. **1.** a plaster or cement for coating exterior walls of houses, etc. —v.t. **2.** to cover with stucco.

stuck-up (stŭk′ŭp′), adj. Colloq. conceited.

stud¹ (stŭd), n., v., **studded, studding.** —n. **1.** a knob or other protuberance, esp. as an ornament. **2.** a post or upright prop. **3.** any of various projecting pins, lugs, or the like, on machines, etc. **4.** a small detachable button used on shirts, etc. —v.t. **5.** to set with studs, knobs, or the like. **6.** to scatter over with things set at intervals. **7.** (of things) to be scattered over the surface of. **8.** to support by studs.

stud² (stŭd), n. **1.** a number of horses, as for racing or hunting, belonging to one owner. **2.** a stallion.

stu·dent (stū′dənt, stōō′-), n. one who is engaged in study, as at a college.

stud·ied (stŭd′ǐd), adj. **1.** deliberate; planned. **2.** carefully considered.

stu·di·o (stū′dǐ ō′, stōō′-), n., pl. **-dios. 1.** the workroom of an artist, etc. **2.** a room or set of rooms specially equipped for broadcasting radio programs.

stu·di·ous (stū′dǐ əs, stōō′-), adj. **1.** fond of study. **2.** painstaking. —**stu′di·ous·ly,** adv. —**stu′di·ous·ness,** n.

stud·y (stŭd′ǐ), n., pl. **studies,** v., **studied, studying.** —n. **1.** application of the mind to the acquisition of knowledge. **2.** a particular course of effort to acquire knowledge. **3.** something studied or to be studied. **4.** deep thought. **5.** a room for private study, reading, writing, or the like. **6.** something intended as an exercise or experiment. —v.t., v.i. **7.** to apply oneself to acquiring a knowledge of (a subject). **8.** to examine or investigate carefully.

stuff (stŭf), n. **1.** material, esp. raw material. **2.** Brit. fabric. **3.** inward character or qualities. **4.** worthless matter or things. —v.t. **5.** to pack or cram full. **6.** to fill (an aperture, cavity, etc.). **7.** to fill (a chicken, etc.), esp. with seasoned bread crumbs. **8.** to fill the skin of (a dead animal) with material, preserving the natural form and appearance. **9.** U.S. to put fraudulent votes into (a ballot box). —v.i. **10.** to eat gluttonously.

stuff·ing (stŭf′ǐng), n. **1.** act of one that stuffs. **2.** that with which anything is stuffed. **3.** seasoned bread crumbs or other filling used to stuff a chicken, turkey, etc., before cooking.

stuff·y (stŭf′ǐ), adj., **stuffier, stuffiest. 1.** ill-ventilated; lacking fresh air. **2.** affected with a sensation of obstruction in the respiratory passages. **3.** dull or self-important. —**stuff′i·ly,** adv. —**stuff′i·ness,** n.

stul·ti·fy (stŭl′tə fī′), v.t., **-fied, -fying.** to make, or cause to appear, foolish.

stum·ble (stŭm′bəl), v., **-bled, -bling,** n. —v.i. **1.** to trip by striking the foot against something in walking, running, etc. **2.** to walk unsteadily. **3.** to blunder. **4.** to proceed in a hesitating or blundering manner. **5.** to come unexpectedly. —v.t. **6.** to trip. —n. **7.** act of stumbling. —**stum′bler,** n. —**stum′bling·ly,** adv.

stumbling block, an obstacle or hindrance, esp. to progress, belief, etc.

stump (stŭmp), n. **1.** the lower end of a tree or plant left after the main part falls or is cut off. **2.** the part of a limb of the body remaining after the rest has been cut off. **3.** a short remnant of a pencil, candle, cigar, etc. **4.** a wooden leg. **5.** Colloq. a leg. **6.** a platform or place for political speechmaking. —v.t. **7.** to nonplus; embarrass. **8.** Colloq. to make political speeches in or to. —v.i. **9.** to walk heavily or clumsily. **10.** Colloq. to make political speeches. —**stump′y,** adj.

stun (stŭn), v., **stunned, stunning,** n. —v.t. **1.** to deprive of consciousness or strength by a blow, fall, etc. **2.** to astound; amaze. —n. **3.** act of stunning. **4.** the condition of being stunned. —**stun′ner,** n.

stun·ning (stŭn′ǐng), adj. **1.** that stuns. **2.** Colloq. of striking excellence, beauty, etc. —**stun′ning·ly,** adv.

stunt¹ (stŭnt), v.t. **1.** to check the growth or development of. **2.** to check (growth, etc.). —n. **3.** a check in growth or development.

stunt² (stŭnt), Colloq. —n. **1.** a performance serving as a display of strength, activity, skill, or the like. —v.i. **2.** to do a stunt or stunts. —v.t. **3.** to use in doing stunts.

stu·pe·fy (stū′pə fī′, stōō′-), v.t., **-fied, -fying.**

1. to put into a state of stupor. **2.** to stun as with a narcotic, a shock, strong emotion, etc. **3.** to overwhelm with amazement; astound. —**stu-pe-fac-tion** (stū′pə făk′shən, stōō′-), *n.*

stu-pen-dous (stū pĕn′dəs, stōō-), *adj.* **1.** amazing; astounding; marvelous. **2.** amazingly large or great; immense. —**stu-pen′dous-ly,** *adv.*

stu-pid (stū′pĭd, stōō′-), *adj.* **1.** lacking or not showing ordinary activity and keenness of mind. **2.** tediously uninteresting. **3.** stupefied. —*n.* 4. *Colloq.* a stupid person. —**stu′pid-ly,** *adv.* —**stu′pid-ness, stu-pid-i-ty** (stū pĭd′ə tĭ, stōō-), *n.*

stu-por (stū′pər, stōō′-), *n.* suspension or great diminution of sensibility.

stur-dy (stûr′dĭ), *adj.,* **-dier, -diest. 1.** strongly built; stout. **2.** indomitable. —**stur′di-ly,** *adv.* —**stur′di-ness,** *n.*

stur-geon (stûr′jən), *n.* any of certain large fishes found in fresh and salt waters of the North Temperate Zone, and valued for their flesh and as a source of caviar and isinglass.

stut-ter (stŭt′ər), *v.t., v.i.* **1.** to utter (sounds) in which the rhythm is interrupted by blocks or spasms, repetitions, or prolongation of sounds. —*n.* 2. such speech. —**stut′ter-er,** *n.* —**stut′-ter-ing-ly,** *adv.*

Stutt-gart (stŭt′gärt), *n.* a city in SW Germany. 458,429.

Stuy-ve-sant (stī′və sənt), *n.* Peter, 1592–1672, last governor of the Dutch colony of New Netherlands (1646–64).

St. Vi-tus's dance (vī′təs ĭz), *Pathol.* chorea. Also, **St. Vitus dance.**

sty[1] (stī), *n., pl.* **sties,** *v.,* **stied, stying.** —*n.* 1. *Chiefly Brit.* a pen for swine. **2.** any filthy abode. —*v.t., v.i.* 3. to lodge in a sty.

sty[2] (stī), *n., pl.* **sties.** *Pathol.* an inflammatory swelling on the eyelid.

styg-i-an (stĭj′ĭ ən), *adj.* **1.** of or pertaining to the river Styx or the lower world. **2.** dark or gloomy. **3.** infernal; hellish.

style (stīl), *n., v.,* **styled, styling.** —*n.* 1. a particular kind, sort, or type. **2.** elegant or fashionable mode of living. **3.** a mode of fashion, as in dress, esp. good or approved fashion. **4.** characteristic mode of writing or speaking. **5.** a pointed instrument for drawing, etching, or writing. **6.** *Bot.* a narrow, usually cylindrical, extension of the ovary, which, when present, bears the stigma at its apex. —*v.t.* 7. to name; call. **8.** to design in accordance with a given or new style. —**sty-lis′tic,** *adj.* —**sty-lis′ti-cal-ly,** *adv.*

styl-ish (stī′lĭsh), *adj.* fashionably elegant; smart. —**styl′ish-ly,** *adv.* —**styl′ish-ness,** *n.*

styl-ist (stī′lĭst), *n.* **1.** a writer or speaker skilled in literary style. **2.** one who designs clothing, interior decorations, etc.

styl-ize (stī′līz), *v.t.,* **-ized, -izing.** to conform to a conventional style. —**styl′i-za′tion,** *n.*

sty-lus (stī′ləs), *n.* **1.** a pointed instrument for writing on wax, etc. **2.** a cutting tool used to make phonograph records.

sty-mie (stī′mĭ), *n., v.,* **-mied, -mieing.** —*n.* 1. *Golf.* an opponent's ball on a putting green when it is directly between the player's ball and the hole for which he is playing. —*v.t.* 2. to hinder or block with, or as with, a stymie.

styp-tic (stĭp′tĭk), *adj.* Also, **styp′ti-cal. 1.** contracting organic tissue; astringent. **2.** checking bleeding. —*n.* 3. a styptic agent or substance.

Styx (stĭks), *n. Gk. Myth.* a river of the lower world, over which the souls of the dead were ferried.

sua-sion (swā′zhən), *n.* **1.** act of advising, urging, or persuading. **2.** a persuasive effort. —**sua-sive** (swā′sĭv), *adj.*

suave (swäv, swăv), *adj.* smoothly agreeable or polite. —**suave′ly,** *adv.* —**suav′i-ty, suave′-ness,** *n.*

sub-, a prefix meaning "under," freely used like *under* as an attribute (*subarctic*), also attached to stems not used as words with extended meanings (*subvert*).

sub-ac-id (sŭb ăs′ĭd), *adj.* slightly acid.

sub-al-tern (sŭb ôl′tərn or, esp. 4, sŭb′əl-tûrn′), *adj.* **1.** having a subordinate rank. **2.** *Brit. Mil.* of or pertaining to a lieutenant. —*n.* 3. a subordinate. **4.** *Brit. Mil.* a subaltern officer.

sub-com-mit-tee (sŭb′kə mĭt′ĭ), *n.* a secon-

dary committee appointed out of a main committee.

sub-con-scious (sŭb kŏn′shəs), *adj.* **1.** existing or operating beneath or beyond consciousness. —*n.* 2. the totality of mental processes of which the individual is not aware. —**sub-con′scious-ly,** *adv.* —**sub-con′scious-ness,** *n.*

sub-cu-ta-ne-ous (sŭb′kū tā′nĭ əs), *adj.* situated or introduced under the skin. —**sub′cu-ta′ne-ous-ly,** *adv.*

sub-di-vide (sŭb′dĭ vīd′), *v.t., v.i.,* **-vided, -viding. 1.** to divide (a part) into smaller parts. **2.** to divide into parts. —**sub-di-vi-sion** (sŭb′-dĭ vĭzh′ən), *n.*

sub-due (səb dū′, -dōō′), *v.t.,* **-dued, -duing. 1.** to conquer and bring into subjection. **2.** to overpower. **3.** to reduce the intensity, force, or vividness of; soften.

sub-head (sŭb′hĕd′), *n.* a subordinate division or title.

subj., 1. subject. **2.** subjunctive.

sub-ja-cent (sŭb jā′sənt), *adj.* underlying.

sub-ject (*n., adj.* sŭb′jĭkt; *v.* səb jĕkt′), *n.* **1.** something that forms a matter of thought, investigation, etc. **2.** a melodic phrase on which a musical work is based. **3.** an object, scene, incident, or the like, as represented in art. **4.** one who owes allegiance to a government and lives under its protection. **5.** *Gram.* the word or words of a sentence which represent the person or object performing the action expressed in the predicate. **6.** one that undergoes some action, influence, etc. —*adj.* 7. being under control or influence. **8.** owing allegiance (to). **9.** exposed. **10.** dependent or conditional upon. **11.** liable. —*v.t.* 12. to bring under control or influence. **13.** to cause to undergo or experience. **14.** to make liable or expose. —**sub-jec-tion** (səb jĕk′shən), *n.*

sub-jec-tive (səb jĕk′tĭv), *adj.* **1.** existing in the mind (opposed to *objective*). **2.** personal; individual. **3.** *Psychol.* belonging to the thinking subject. **4.** introspective. **5.** *Gram.* pertaining to or constituting the subject of a sentence. —**sub-jec′tive-ly,** *adv.* —**sub-jec-tiv-i-ty** (sŭb′-jĕk tĭv′ə tĭ), **sub-jec′tive-ness,** *n.*

sub-join (səb join′), *v.t.* to append.

sub-ju-gate (sŭb′jə gāt′), *v.t.,* **-gated, -gating.** to subdue; bring under complete control. —**sub′ju-ga′tion,** *n.* —**sub′ju-ga′tor,** *n.*

sub-junc-tive (səb jŭngk′tĭv), *Gram.* —*adj.* 1. designating a verb mode having among its functions use in various subordinate clauses. —*n.* 2. the subjunctive mode. **3.** a verb in it.

sub-lease (*n.* sŭb′lēs′; *v.* sŭb lēs′), *n., v.,* **-leased, -leasing.** —*n.* 1. a lease granted by one who is himself a lessee of the property. —*v.t.* 2. to sublet. **3.** to take a sublease of. —**sub-les-see** (sŭb′lĕ sē′), *n.* —**sub-les-sor** (sŭb lĕs′ôr, sŭb′lĕ sôr′), *n.*

sub-let (sŭb lĕt′), *v.t.,* **-let, -letting.** to let to another person, the party letting being himself lessee.

sub-li-mate (*v.* sŭb′lə māt′; *n., adj.* sŭb′lə mĭt, -māt′), *v.,* **-mated, -mating.** —*v.t.* 1. *Psychol.* to deflect (sexual or other biological energies) into socially constructive or creative channels. **2.** *Chem., etc.* to sublime. —*v.i.* 3. to become sublimated. —*n.* 4. *Chem.* the crystals, deposit, or other material obtained when a substance is sublimed. —*adj.* 5. sublimated. —**sub′-li-ma′tion,** *n.*

sub-lime (sə blīm′), *adj., n., v.,* **-limed, -liming.** —*adj.* 1. lofty in thought, language, etc. **2.** inspiring awe, veneration, etc. **3.** supreme or perfect. —*n.* 4. that which is sublime. **5.** the highest degree or example. —*v.t., v.i.* 6. to make higher, nobler, or purer. **7.** *Chem., etc.* to convert (a solid substance) by heat into a vapor, which on cooling condenses again to solid form, without apparent liquefaction. **8.** *Chem., etc.* to cause to be given off by this or some analogous process. —**sub-lime′ly,** *adj.* —**sub-lime′ness, sub-lim-i-ty** (sə blĭm′ə tĭ), *n.*

sub-ma-chine gun (sŭb′mə shēn′), a lightweight automatic or semiautomatic gun, fired from the shoulder or hip.

sub-mar-gin-al (sŭb mär′jə nəl), *adj.* not worth cultivating, as land.

sub-ma-rine (*n.* sŭb′mə rēn′; *adj.* sŭb′mə-rēn′), *n.* **1.** a vessel that can be submerged and navigated under water, esp. one used in warfare for the discharge of torpedoes, etc. —*adj.* 2. situated, occurring, operating, or living under the surface of the sea. **3.** of, pertaining to, or carried on by submarine boats.

sub·max·il·lar·y (sŭb′măk′sə lĕr′Y), *adj.* of the lower jaw or jawbone.

sub·merge (səb mûrj′), *v.t., v.i.,* **-merged, -merging.** 1. to sink or plunge under water, etc. 2. to cover completely. **—sub·mer′gence,** *n.*

sub·merse (səb mûrs′), *v.t.,* **-mersed, -mersing.** to submerge. **—sub·mer·sion** (səb mûr′shən, -zhən), *n.*

sub·mit (səb mYt′), *v.t., v.i.,* **-mitted, -mitting.** 1. to yield in surrender, compliance, or obedience. 2. to refer to the judgment of another. 3. to state or urge with deference. **—sub·mis′sion,** *n.* **—sub·mis′sive,** *adj.* **—sub·mis′sive·ly,** *adv.* **—sub·mis′sive·ness,** *n.* **—sub·mit′ter,** *n.*

sub·nor·mal (sŭb nôr′məl), *adj.* below the normal. **—sub/nor·mal/i·ty,** *n.*

sub·or·di·nate (*adj., n.* sə bôr′də nYt; *v.* sə-bôr′də nāt′), *adj., n., v.,* **-nated, -nating.** —*adj.* 1. in a lower order or rank. 2. of inferior importance; secondary. 3. under the authority of a superior. —*n.* 4. a subordinate person or thing. —*v.t.* 5. to place in a lower order or rank. 6. to make secondary. 7. to make subject. **—sub·or/di·na/tion,** *n.*

sub·orn (sə bôrn′), *v.t.* to bribe (a person) unlawfully to commit some act of wickedness, usually perjury.

sub·poe·na (sə pē′nə, səb-), *n., v.,* **-naed, -naing.** *Law.* —*n.* 1. the usual writ process for the summoning of witnesses. —*v.t.* 2. to serve with a subpoena. Also, **sub·pe/na.**

sub·scribe (səb skrīb′), *v.t., v.i.,* **-scribed, -scribing.** 1. to promise to give (a sum of money) as a contribution, payment, etc. 2. to express assent to (a contract, etc.) by signing one's name. 3. to sign (one's name) to a document, etc. 4. to obtain a subscription to a magazine, newspaper, etc. 5. to give consent or sanction. **—sub·scrib′er,** *n.*

sub·script (sŭb′skrYpt), *adj.* 1. written below. 2. placed low on the line. —*n.* 3. something written below.

sub·scrip·tion (səb skrYp′shən), *n.* 1. a contribution, payment, etc. 2. the right to receive a periodical for a sum subscribed. 3. a fund raised through sums of money subscribed. 4. act of subscribing. 5. agreement expressed by signing one's name.

sub·se·quent (sŭb′sə kwənt), *adj.* 1. coming later or after. 2. following in order. **—sub/se·quent·ly,** *adv.*

sub·serve (səb sûrv′), *v.t.,* **-served, -serving.** to be useful or instrumental in promoting (a purpose, action, etc.).

sub·ser·vi·ent (səb sûr′vY ənt), *adj.* 1. servile; excessively submissive; obsequious. 2. subordinate. 3. of use as a means to promote a purpose or end. **—sub·ser/vi·ence, sub·ser/vi·en·cy,** *n.* **—sub·ser/vi·ent·ly,** *adv.*

sub·side (səb sīd′), *v.i.,* **-sided, -siding.** 1. to sink to a lower level. 2. to become less active; abate. 3. to settle. **—sub·sid·ence** (səb sī′dəns, sŭb′sə dəns), *n.*

sub·sid·i·ar·y (səb sYd′Y ĕr′Y), *adj., n., pl.* **-aries.** —*adj.* 1. auxiliary; supplementary. 2. subordinate. —*n.* 3. a subsidiary thing or person.

sub·si·dy (sŭb′sə dY), *n., pl.* **-dies.** 1. a direct pecuniary aid furnished by a government to a private industrial undertaking, a charity organization, or the like. 2. any grant or contribution of money. **—sub/si·dize/,** *v.t.*

sub·sist (səb sYst′), *v.i.* 1. to exist. 2. to live, as on food, resources, etc. **—sub·sist/ence,** *n.*

sub·soil (sŭb/soil′), *n.* the stratum of earth immediately under the surface soil.

sub·son·ic (sŭb sŏn′Yk), *n.* less than the speed of propagation of sound; moving slower than about 700 miles per hour.

sub·stance (sŭb′stəns), *n.* 1. matter or material. 2. the subject matter of thought, discourse, study, or the like. 3. the actual matter of a thing; the reality. 4. solid quality. 5. body. 6. the meaning or gist.

sub·stand·ard (sŭb stăn′dərd), *adj.* below standard.

sub·stan·tial (səb stăn′shəl), *adj.* 1. real or actual. 2. of considerable amount, quantity, size, etc. 3. solid, firm, or strong. 4. essential; basic. 5. wealthy or influential. 6. pertaining to the substance of a thing. **—sub·stan/ti·al/i·ty,** *n.* **—sub·stan/tial·ly,** *adv.*

sub·stan·ti·ate (səb stăn′shY āt′), *v.t.,* **-ated, -ating.** 1. to establish by proof or evidence. 2. to give substantial existence to. **—sub·stan/ti·a/tion,** *n.*

sub·stan·tive (sŭb′stən tYv), *n.* 1. *Gram.* a noun, pronoun, or other word or phrase having the function or inflections of a noun. —*adj.* 2. *Gram.* a. pertaining to substantives. b. used in a sentence like a noun. 3. having independent existence. 4. essential. **—sub·stan·ti·val** (sŭb/stən tī′vəl), *adj.*

sub·sti·tute (sŭb/stə tūt′, -tōōt′), *n., v.,* **-tuted, -tuting.** —*n.* 1. a person or thing acting in place of another. —*v.t., v.i.* 2. to put (one person or thing) in the place of another. 3. to replace. **—sub/sti·tu/tion,** *n.*

sub·stra·tum (sŭb strā′təm, -străt′əm), *n., pl.* **-strata** (-strā′tə, -străt′ə). a stratum or layer lying under another.

sub·struc·ture (sŭb strŭk′chər, sŭb/strŭk/-), *n.* a structure forming the foundation of a building or the like.

sub·tend (səb tĕnd′), *v.t. Geom., etc.* to extend under; be opposite to.

sub·ter·fuge (sŭb/tər fūj′), *n.* an excuse or expedient employed to escape or conceal something.

sub·ter·ra·ne·an (sŭb/tə rā′nY ən), *adj.* 1. underground. 2. hidden or secret.

sub·tile (sŭt′əl, sŭb/tYl), *adj.* subtle.

sub·ti·tle (sŭb/tī′təl), *n.* a subordinate title of a literary work.

sub·tle (sŭt′əl), *adj.* 1. fine or delicate, often when likely to elude understanding. 2. faint and mysterious. 3. characterized by mental acuteness. 4. cunning, wily, or crafty. 5. thin, tenuous. or rarefied. **—sub/tle·ness, sub·tle·ty** (sŭt′əl tY), *n.* **—sub·tly** (sŭt′lY), *adv.*

sub·tract (səb trăkt′), *v.t., v.i.* to withdraw or take (one number or quantity) from another; deduct. **—sub·tract/er,** *n.* **—sub·trac/tion,** *n.* **—sub·trac/tive,** *adj.*

sub·tra·hend (sŭb/trə hĕnd′), *n.* the quantity taken from another in subtraction.

sub·trop·i·cal (sŭb trŏp′ə kəl), *adj.* 1. bordering on the tropics. 2. of or occurring in a region between tropical and temperate. **—sub·trop/-ics,** *n.pl.*

sub·urb (sŭb/ûrb), *n.* (*often pl.*) a district lying immediately outside a city, esp. a residential section. **—sub·ur·ban** (sə bûr/bən), *adj.*

sub·ven·tion (səb vĕn′shən), *n.* a grant of pecuniary aid, esp. by a government.

sub·vert (səb vûrt′), *v.t.* 1. to overthrow (something established or existing). 2. to cause the downfall, ruin, or destruction of. **—sub·vert/er,** *n.* **—sub·ver/sion,** *n.* **—sub·ver/sive,** *adj.*

sub·way (sŭb/wā′), *n.* 1. *U.S.* an electric railroad beneath the streets in a city. 2. *Chiefly Brit.* an underground passageway.

suc·ceed (sək sēd′), *v.i.* 1. to turn out or end, esp. successfully. 2. to accomplish what is intended. 3. to follow or replace another, as by descent, election, etc. —*v.t.* 4. to come after and take the place of. 5. to follow.

suc·cess (sək sĕs′), *n.* 1. the favorable termination of endeavors. 2. the gaining of wealth, position, or the like. 3. a successful achievement. 4. a thing or a person that is successful.

suc·cess·ful (sək sĕs′fəl), *adj.* 1. achieving or having success. 2. resulting in or attended with success. **—suc·cess/ful·ly,** *adv.*

suc·ces·sion (sək sĕsh′ən), *n.* 1. the coming of one after another in sequence. 2. a number of persons or things following one another in sequence. 3. the right, act, or process by which one person succeeds to the office, rank, estate, or the like, of another. 4. the order or line of those entitled to succeed.

suc·ces·sive (sək sĕs′Yv), *adj.* following in order. **—suc·ces/sive·ly,** *adv.*

suc·ces·sor (sək sĕs′ər), *n.* 1. one that follows. 2. one who succeeds another in an office, position, or the like.

suc·cinct (sək sYngkt′), *adj.* concise; terse. **—suc·cinct/ly,** *adv.* **—suc·cinct/ness,** *n.*

suc·cor (sŭk/ər), *n.* 1. help; assistance. 2. an aid. —*v.t.* 3. to help in need. Also, *esp. Brit.,* **suc/cour.**

suc·co·tash (sŭk/ə tăsh′), *n.* a dish of corn (removed from the cob) and beans.

suc·cu·lent (sŭk/yə lənt), *adj.* juicy. **—suc/cu·lence, suc/cu·len·cy,** *n.* **—suc/cu·lent·ly,** *adv.*

suc·cumb (sə kŭm′), *v.i.* to yield, esp. to disease, wounds, old age, etc.

such (sŭch), *adj.* 1. of that kind, character, degree, extent, etc. **2.** like or similar. **3.** so great, good, bad, etc. **4.** being as stated or indicated. **5.** being definite but not specified. —*pron.* **6.** such a person or thing, or such persons or things.

suck (sŭk), *v.t., v.i.* **1.** to draw (something) into the mouth by action of the lips and tongue which produces a partial vacuum. **2.** to draw (water, moisture, air, etc.) by any process resembling this. **3.** to take into the mouth. —*n.* **4.** act of sucking. **5.** that which is sucked.

suck·er (sŭk′ər), *n.* **1.** one that sucks. **2.** a part of an animal adapted for sucking nourishment. **3.** any of certain fresh-water fishes, mostly North American, esteemed as food. **4.** a pipe or tube through which anything is drawn. **5.** *Colloq.* a lollypop. **6.** *U.S. Slang.* a person easily imposed upon. **7.** *Bot.* a shoot rising from a subterranean stem or a root.

suck·le (sŭk′əl), *v.t., v.i.,* **-led, -ling. 1.** to nurse at the breast. **2.** to nourish.

suck·ling (sŭk′lĭng), *n.* an infant or a young animal that is not yet weaned.

Su·cre (soo′krě), *n.* **1.** a city in S Bolivia: the nominal capital. 30,000. **2.** (*l.c.*) an Ecuadorian monetary unit and silver coin worth 7 U.S. cents.

suc·tion (sŭk′shən), *n.* **1.** act, process, or condition of sucking. **2.** the tendency to suck a substance into an interior space when the atmospheric pressure is reduced in the space.

Su·dan (soo dăn′), *n.* a vast region in N Africa, S of the Sahara and Libyan deserts, from the Atlantic to the Red Sea.

sud·den (sŭd′ən), *adj.* **1.** happening, coming, made, or done quickly or unexpectedly. —*n.* **2.** all of a sudden, quite unexpectedly. —**sud′den·ly,** *adv.* —**sud′den·ness,** *n.*

suds (sŭdz), *n.pl.* **1.** soapy water. **2.** foam or lather. —**suds′y,** *adj.*

sue (soo), *v.t., v.i.,* **sued, suing. 1.** to institute process in law (against). **2.** to make petition or appeal (to). **3.** to woo or court. —**su·er** (soo′ər), *n.*

suède (swād), *n.* leather finished with a soft, napped surface.

su·et (soo′ĭt), *n.* the hard fatty tissue about the loins and kidneys of the ox, sheep, etc., used in cookery, etc. —**su′et·y,** *adj.*

Suez (soo′ĕz′, soo′ĕz), *n.* **1.** a seaport in NE Egypt. 49,000. **2. Isthmus of,** an isthmus in NE Egypt, joining Africa and Asia. 72 mi. wide.

Suez Canal, a canal across the Isthmus of Suez, connecting the Mediterranean and the Red Sea. ab. 100 mi. long.

MEDITERRANEAN SEA

suf·fer (sŭf′ər), *v.i., v.t.* **1.** to undergo (pain, distress, injury, loss, or anything unpleasant). **2.** to undergo (any action, process, etc., not necessarily unpleasant. **3.** to tolerate. **4.** to allow or permit. —**suf′fer·a·ble,** *adj.* —**suf′fer·a·bly,** *adv.* —**suf′fer·er,** *n.* —**suf′fer·ing,** *n.*

suf·fer·ance (sŭf′ər əns, sŭf′rəns), *n.* **1.** tolerance. **2.** capacity to endure pain, etc.

suf·fice (sə fīs′, -fīz′), *v.t., v.i.,* **-ficed, -ficing.** to be enough or adequate (for).

suf·fi·cient (sə fĭsh′ənt), *adj.* enough or adequate. —**suf·fi′cient·ly,** *adv.* —**suf·fi′cien·cy,** *n.*

suf·fix (sŭf′ĭks), *n. Gram.* an affix which follows the element to which it is added, as *-ly* in *kindly.* —**suf·fix·al** (sŭf′ĭk səl), *adj.*

suf·fo·cate (sŭf′ə kāt′), *v.t., v.i.,* **-cated, -cating.** to kill by preventing the access of air to the lungs or analogous organs; stifle; smother. —**suf′fo·cat′ing·ly,** *adv.* —**suf·fo·ca′tion,** *n.*

suf·fra·gan (sŭf′rə gən), *adj.* **1.** assisting. —*n.* **2.** a bishop assisting an archbishop or bishop who is his superior.

suf·frage (sŭf′rĭj), *n.* the right of voting.

suf·fuse (sə fūz′), *v.t.,* **-fused, -fusing.** to overspread with a liquid, color, etc.

sug·ar (shoog′ər), *n.* **1.** a sweet crystalline substance obtained chiefly from the juice of the sugar cane or sugar beet: extensively used for food purposes. **2.** a member of the same class of carbohydrates. —*v.t.* **3.** to cover or sweeten with sugar. —**sug′ar·y,** *adj.*

sugar cane, a tall grass of warm regions, hav-

ing a stout, jointed stalk, and constituting the chief source of sugar.

sug·ar-coat (shoog′ər kōt′), *v.t.* **1.** to cover with sugar. **2.** to make more acceptable or less distasteful.

sug·ar-plum (shoog′ər plŭm′), *n.* a small candy made largely of sugar.

sug·gest (səg jĕst′), *v.t.* **1.** to place (an idea, etc.) before a person's mind for consideration or action. **2.** to show indirectly or without plain expression.

sug·gest·i·ble (səg jĕs′tə bəl), *adj.* capable of being influenced by suggestion.

sug·ges·tion (səg jĕs′chən), *n.* **1.** act of suggesting. **2.** state of being suggested. **3.** the idea or thing suggested. **4.** a slight trace.

sug·ges·tive (səg jĕs′tĭv), *adj.* **1.** that suggests ideas, etc. **2.** suggesting something improper or indecent. —**sug·ges′tive·ly,** *adv.* —**sug·ges′tive·ness,** *n.*

su·i·cide[1] (soo′ə sīd′), *n.* the intentional destruction of one's own life, interests, or prospects. —**su′i·cid′al,** *adj.*

su·i·cide[2] (soo′ə sīd′), *n.* one who intentionally takes his own life.

suit (soot), *n.* **1.** a set of outer garments. **2.** legal prosecution. **3.** *Cards.* one of the four sets (spades, clubs, hearts, and diamonds) into which playing cards are divided. **4.** the courting of a woman. **5.** a petition. —*v.t., v.i.* **6.** to clothe; array. **7.** to make appropriate, adapt, or accommodate. **8.** to be appropriate, satisfactory, or agreeable.

suit·a·ble (soo′tə bəl), *adj.* appropriate; fitting; becoming. —**suit′a·bil′i·ty,** *n.* —**suit′a·bly,** *adv.*

suit·case (soot′kās′), *n.* an oblong valise.

suite (swēt), *n.* **1.** a connected series of rooms. **2.** a series or set. **3.** a set of furniture. **4.** *Music.* an ordered series of instrumental dances. **5.** a retinue.

suit·ing (soo′tĭng), *n.* a fabric for suits.

suit·or (soo′tər), *n.* **1.** one who courts a woman. **2.** *Law.* a petitioner.

sul·fa drugs (sŭl′fə), a group of compounds containing the radical SO_2NH_2, used as antibacterials in treatment of various diseases, wounds, burns, etc., including **sul·fa·nil·a·mide** (sŭl′fə nĭl′ə mīd′, -mĭd), **sul·fa·pyr·i·dine** (sŭl′fə pĭr′ə dēn′, -dĭn), and **sul·fa·thi·a·zole** (sŭl′fə thī′ə zōl′).

sul·fate (sŭl′fāt), *n., v.,* **-fated, -fating.** —*n.* **1.** *Chem.* a salt of sulfuric acid. —*v.t.* **2.** to combine or treat with sulfuric acid.

sul·fide (sŭl′fīd), *n. Chem.* a compound of sulfur with a more electropositive element or a radical. Also, **sul·fid** (sŭl′fĭd).

sul·fur (sŭl′fər), *n. Chem.* a nonmetallic element used in making gunpowder and matches, in medicine, etc. *Symbol:* S; *at. wt.:* 32.06; *at. no.:* 16; *sp. gr.:* 2.07 at 20°C. Also, **sulphur.**

sul·fu·ric (sŭl fyoor′ĭk), *adj.* of, pertaining to, or containing sulfur.

sulfuric acid, *Chem.* the dibasic acid of sulfur, a colorless oily liquid derived from sulfur dioxide: used in many industrial processes.

sul·fur·ous (sŭl′fər əs, sŭl fyoor′əs), *adj.* relating to or containing sulfur.

sulk (sŭlk), *v.i.* **1.** to hold aloof in a sullenly ill-humored or offended mood. —*n.* **2.** a state or fit of sulking. **3.** (*pl.*) ill humor shown by sulking.

sulk·y (sŭl′kĭ), *adj.,* **sulkier, sulkiest,** *n., pl.* **sulkies.** —*adj.* **1.** sullenly ill-humored or resentful. —*n.* **2.** a light two-wheeled one-horse carriage for one person. —**sulk′i·ly,** *adv.* —**sulk′i·ness,** *n.*

sul·len (sŭl′ən), *adj.* **1.** silently and persistently ill-humored; morose. **2.** gloomy or dismal. —**sul′len·ly,** *adv.* —**sul′len·ness,** *n.*

Sul·li·van (sŭl′ə vən), *n.* **Sir Arthur Seymour,** 1842–1900, British composer.

sul·ly (sŭl′ĭ), *v.t., v.i.,* **-lied, -lying. 1.** to soil, stain, or tarnish. **2.** to defile.

sul·phate (sŭl′fāt), *v.t., n.,* **-phated, -phating,** *n.* sulfate.

sul·phide (sŭl′fīd), *n.* sulfide.

sul·phur (sŭl′fər), *n.* sulfur.

sul·phu·ric (sŭl fyoor′ĭk), *adj.* sulfuric.

sul·phur·ous (sŭl′fər əs, sŭl fyoor′əs), *adj.* **1.** sulfurous. **2.** hellish or satanic. **3.** fiery or heated.

sul·tan (sŭl′tən), *n.* the sovereign of a Mohammedan country, as (*cap.*) of Turkey.

sul·tan·a (sŭl tăn'ə, -tä'nə), *n.* a wife or a concubine of a sultan.

sul·tan·ate (sŭl'tə nāt'), *n.* the office or territory of a sultan.

sul·try (sŭl'trĭ), *adj.*, **-trier, -triest. 1.** oppressively hot and close; sweltering. **2.** passionate. **—sul'tri·ness,** *n.*

sum (sŭm), *n., v.,* **summed, summing. —n. 1.** the aggregate of two or more numbers, quantities, etc. **2.** a quantity, esp. of money. **3.** the total amount. **4.** the substance or gist of a matter. **—v.t. 5.** to total. **6.** to summarize.

su·mac (shōō'măk, sōō'-), *n.* any of certain shrubs or small trees with long pinnate leaves and pyramidal panicles of crimson drupes. Also, **su'mach.**

Su·ma·tra (sŏō mä'trə), *n.* a large island in the W part of the Dutch East Indies. 7,677,826 pop.; 164,147 sq. mi.

sum·ma·rize (sŭm'ə rīz'), *v.t.,* **-rized, -rizing.** to make or be a summary of. **—sum'ma·ri·za'tion,** *n.*

sum·ma·ry (sŭm'ə rĭ), *n., pl.* **-ries,** *adj.* **—n. 1.** a brief and comprehensive presentation of facts or statements. **—adj. 2.** brief and comprehensive; concise. **3.** prompt; unceremoniously fast. **—sum·ma·ri·ly** (sŭm'ə rə lĭ; *emphatic* sə mĕr'ə lĭ), *adv.* **—sum'ma·ri·ness,** *n.*

sum·ma·tion (sŭm ā'shən), *n.* **1.** the process of summing. **2.** an aggregate. **3.** *Law.* the final arguments of opposing counsel.

sum·mer (sŭm'ər), *n.* **1.** the warmest season of the year, between spring and autumn. **—adj. 2.** of, pertaining to, or characteristic of summer. **—v.i. 3.** to spend or pass the summer. **—sum'mer·y,** *adj.*

sum·mer·house (sŭm'ər hous'), *n.* a simple, shaded structure in a park or garden.

sum·mit (sŭm'ĭt), *n.* the highest point or part; apex.

sum·mon (sŭm'ən), *v.t.* **1.** to call as with authority to some duty, task, or performance. **2.** to call for the presence of. **3.** to rouse; call forth.

sum·mons (sŭm'ənz), *n.* an authoritative command, message, or signal by which one is summoned.

sump (sŭmp), *n.* a pit, well, or the like, in which water or other liquid is collected.

sump·tu·ous (sŭmp'chŏō əs), *adj.* **1.** expensive; costly. **2.** luxuriously fine. **—sump'tu·ous·ly,** *adv.* **—sump'tu·ous·ness,** *n.*

sun (sŭn), *n., v.,* **sunned, sunning. —n. 1.** the star which is the central body of the solar system and around which the planets revolve, and from which they receive light and heat. **2.** the sunshine. **—v.t., v.i. 3.** to expose (oneself) to the sun's rays. **4.** to warm, dry, etc., in the sunshine. **—sun'less,** *adj.*

Sun., Sunday. Also, **Sund.**

sun·bon·net (sŭn'bŏn'ĭt), *n.* a large bonnet shading the face and neck.

sun·burn (sŭn'bûrn'), *n., v.,* **-burned** or **-burnt, -burning. —n. 1.** superficial inflammation of the skin, caused by exposure to the sun's rays. **2.** the color tan so produced. **—v.t., v.i. 3.** to affect or be affected with sunburn.

sun·dae (sŭn'dĭ), *n.* a portion of ice cream with fruit or other syrup poured over it.

Sun·day (sŭn'dĭ), *n.* **1.** the Christian Sabbath, observed in commemoration of the resurrection of Christ. **2.** the first day of the week.

sun·der (sŭn'dər), *v.t., v.i.* to separate.

sun·di·al (sŭn'dī'əl), *n.* an instrument for indicating the time of day by the position of a shadow cast by the sun on a marked surface.

sun·down (sŭn'doun'), *n.* sunset; the time of sunset.

sun·dry (sŭn'drĭ), *adj.* **1.** various. **2. all and sundry,** everyone.

sun·fish (sŭn'fĭsh'), *n., pl.* **-fishes,** (*esp. collectively*) **-fish. 1.** a huge fish with a deep body, seeming to consist of little more than the head. **2.** any of certain fresh-water fishes of the perch family.

sun·flow·er (sŭn'flou'ər), *n.* a tall plant of the aster family with yellow-rayed flowers, its seeds being valued as food for poultry and as the source of an oil.

sunk·en (sŭngk'ən), *adj.* **1.** submerged. **2.** having settled down to a lower level. **3.** lying below the general level, as a garden. **4.** hollow.

sun·light (sŭn'līt'), *n.* the light of the sun.

sun·lit (sŭn'lĭt'), *adj.* lighted by the sun.

sun·ny (sŭn'ĭ), *adj.,* **-nier, -niest. 1.** abounding in sunshine. **2.** exposed to the direct rays of the sun. **3.** solar. **4.** cheery.

sun·rise (sŭn'rīz'), *n.* the ascent of the sun above the horizon in the morning. Also, **sun'up'.**

sun·set (sŭn'sĕt'), *n.* the descent of the sun below the horizon in the evening.

sun·shade (sŭn'shād'), *n.* something used as a protection from the rays of the sun.

sun·shine (sŭn'shīn'), *n.* **1.** the direct light of the sun. **2.** radiance; cheerfulness.

sun·spot (sŭn'spŏt'), *n.* one of the dark patches appearing periodically on the surface of the sun.

sun·stroke (sŭn'strōk'), *n. Pathol.* an illness caused suddenly by excessive exposure to the sun's rays or to heat.

sun·up (sŭn'ŭp'), *n.* sunrise.

Sun Yat-sen (sŏōn'yät'sĕn'), 1867–1925, Chinese political leader.

sup (sŭp), *v.i.,* **supped, supping.** to eat supper.

sup., 1. superior. **2.** superlative.

su·per (sōō'pər), *n.* **1.** *Colloq.* a shortened form of *superintendent,* etc. **—adj. 2.** *Slang.* excellent.

super-, a prefix of superiority applied variously, as of quality (*superman*), size (*superdreadnought*), degree (*superheat, supersensitive*), space (*superstructure*), and other meanings (*supersede, supernatural*).

su·per·a·bun·dant (sōō'pər ə bŭn'dənt), *adj.* exceedingly or excessively abundant. **—su'per·a·bun'dance,** *n.* **—su'per·a·bun'dant·ly,** *adv.*

su·per·add (sōō'pər ăd'), *v.t.* to add as a further addition.

su·per·an·nu·at·ed (sōō'pər ăn'yŏō ā'tĭd), *adj.* **1.** retired on account of age or infirmity. **2.** too old for use, work, service, etc.

su·perb (sŏō pûrb', sə-), *adj.* **1.** stately; majestic. **2.** admirably excellent. **—su·perb'ly,** *adv.*

su·per·car·go (sōō'pər kär'gō), *n., pl.* **-goes, -gos.** an officer on a merchant ship who is in charge of the cargo, etc.

su·per·charg·er (sōō'pər chär'jər), *n.* a mechanism attached to an internal-combustion engine to deliver to the cylinders a volume of air greater than that from the suction of the pistons alone, used to increase power.

su·per·cil·i·ous (sōō'pər sĭl'ĭ əs), *adj.* haughtily disdainful. **—su'per·cil'i·ous·ly,** *adv.* **—su'per·cil'i·ous·ness,** *n.*

su·per·e·go (sōō'pər ē'gō, -ĕg'ō), *n. Psychoanal.* that part of the psychic apparatus which mediates between ego drives and social ideals, acting as a conscience.

su·per·e·rog·a·to·ry (sōō'pər ə rŏg'ə tōr'ĭ), *adj.* **1.** going beyond the requirements of duty. **2.** superfluous. **—su·per·e·ro·ga·tion** (sōō'pər·ĕr'ə gā'shən), *n.*

su·per·fi·cial (sōō'pər fĭsh'əl), *adj.* **1.** of, at, on, or near the surface. **2.** external or outward. **3.** not profound or thorough. **4.** apparent, rather than real. **—su·per·fi·ci·al·i·ty** (sōō'pər fĭsh'ĭ·ăl'ə tĭ), *n.* **—su'per·fi·cial·ly,** *adv.*

su·per·flu·i·ty (sōō'pər flōō'ə tĭ), *n., pl.* **-ties. 1.** superabundant amount. **2.** something superfluous.

su·per·flu·ous (sŏō pûr'flŏō əs), *adj.* **1.** being over and above what is sufficient or required. **2.** unnecessary. **—su·per'flu·ous·ly,** *adv.* **—su·per'flu·ous·ness,** *n.*

Su·per·for·tress (sōō'pər fôr'trĭs), *n. Trademark.* a heavy four-engine bomber, bearing the U.S. Army designation B-29.

su·per·het·er·o·dyne (sōō'pər hĕt'ər ə dīn'), *adj. Radio.* denoting or pertaining to a method of receiving radio signals by which the incoming modulated wave is changed to a lower frequency and then submitted to stages of radio-frequency and audio-frequency amplification.

su·per·hu·man (sōō'pər hū'mən), *adj.* **1.** above or beyond what is human. **2.** exceeding ordinary human power, etc.

su·per·im·pose (sōō'pər ĭm pōz'), *v.t.,* **-posed, -posing.** to impose, place, or set on something else.

su·per·in·tend (sōō'pər ĭn tĕnd', sōō'prĭn-), *v.t.* to oversee and direct (work, an institution, etc.). **—su'per·in·tend'ence, su'per·in·tend'en·cy,** *n.*

su·per·in·tend·ent (sōō'pər ĭn tĕn'dənt, sōō'prĭn-), *n.* **1.** one who directs some work, enterprise, institution, etc. **—adj. 2.** superintending.

su·pe·ri·or (sə pĭr′ĭ ər, sōō-), adj. 1. higher in rank, degree, or grade. 2. above the average in excellence, merit, etc. 3. greater in amount. 4. arrogant; condescending. 5. not susceptible. —n. 6. one superior to another or others. 7. the head of a monastery, convent, or the like. —su·pe·ri·or·i·ty (sə pĭr′ĭ ŏr′ə tĭ, -ŏr′-, sōō-), n.

Su·pe·ri·or (sə pĭr′ĭ ər, sōō-), n. 1. Lake, the northernmost of the Great Lakes, between the United States and Canada. ab. 31,810 sq. mi. 2. a city in NW Wisconsin. 35,136.

superl., superlative.

su·per·la·tive (sə pûr′lə tĭv, sōō-), adj. 1. of the highest kind; surpassing all other or others. 2. Gram. denoting the highest degree of the comparison of adjectives and adverbs, as English smoothest in contrast to smooth and smoother. —n. 3. something superlative. 4. Gram. the superlative degree, or a form therein. —su·per′·la·tive·ly, adv.

su·per·man (sōō′pər măn′), n., pl. -men. a man of more than human powers.

su·per·nal (sōō pûr′nəl), adj. 1. heavenly; divine. 2. lofty. —su·per′nal·ly, adv.

su·per·nat·u·ral (sōō′pər năch′ə rəl), adj. 1. being above or beyond what is natural. —n. 2. that which is supernatural. 3. the action of the supernatural as it intervenes in the natural order. —su′per·nat′u·ral·ly, adv. —su′per·nat′u·ral·ism′, n.

su·per·nu·mer·ar·y (sōō′pər nū′mə rĕr′ĭ, -nōō′-), adj., n., pl. -aries. —adj. 1. additional; extra. —n. 2. an extra person or thing. 3. Theat. one not belonging to the regular company, who appears on the stage but has no lines to speak.

su·per·pose (sōō′pər pōz′), v.t., -posed, -posing. to place above or upon something else.

su·per·scribe (sōō′pər skrīb′), v.t., -scribed, -scribing. to write (words, letters, one's name, etc.) above or on (something). —su′per·scrip′tion, n.

su·per·sede (sōō′pər sēd′), v.t., -seded, -seding. to replace in power, use, etc.; supplant.

su·per·son·ic (sōō′pər sŏn′ĭk), adj. 1. referring to periodic disturbances in a medium above the audible limit (above 20,000 cycles per second). 2. greater than the speed of propagation of sound.

su·per·sti·tion (sōō′pər stĭsh′ən), n. a belief, regardless of reason or knowledge, of the ominous significance of a particular thing, circumstance, occurrence, etc. —su′per·sti′tious, adj. —su′per·sti′tious·ly, adv.

su·per·struc·ture (sōō′pər strŭk′chər), n. 1. all of an edifice above the foundation. 2. any structure built on something else. 3. Naut. the parts of a vessel above the main deck.

su·per·tax (sōō′pər tăks′), n. U.S. a surtax.

su·per·vene (sōō′pər vēn′), v.i., -vened, -vening. 1. to come as something additional or extraneous. 2. to ensue. —su·per·ven·tion (sōō′pər vĕn′shən), n.

su·per·vise (sōō′pər vīz′), v.t., -vised, -vising. to oversee (work, workers, etc.); superintend. —su′per·vi′sion, n. —su′per·vi′sor, n. —su′per·vi′so·ry, adj.

su·pine (sōō pīn′), adj. 1. lying on the back. 2. inactive; passive; inert. —su·pine′ly, adv. —su·pine′ness, n.

supp., supplement. Also, suppl.

sup·per (sŭp′ər), n. the evening meal.

sup·plant (sə plănt′, -plänt′), v.t. 1. to displace or supersede. 2. to replace. —sup·plant′er, n.

sup·ple (sŭp′əl), adj., -pler, -plest. 1. pliant; flexible. 2. limber; lithe. 3. adaptable. —sup′ple·ly, adv. —sup′ple·ness, n.

sup·ple·ment (n. sŭp′lə mənt; v. sŭp′lə mĕnt′), n. 1. something added to complete a thing, supply a deficiency, etc. 2. Math. the quantity by which an angle or an arc falls short of 180° or a semicircle. —v.t. 3. to complete, add to, or extend by a supplement. —sup·ple·men·ta·ry (sŭp′lə mĕn′tə rĭ), sup′ple·men′tal, adj.

sup·pli·ant (sŭp′lĭ ənt), n. 1. a humble petitioner. —adj. 2. supplicating. —sup′pli·ant·ly, adv. —sup′pli·ance, n.

sup·pli·cant (sŭp′lə kənt), adj. 1. supplicating. —n. 2. a suppliant.

sup·pli·cate (sŭp′lə kāt′), v.i., v.t., -cated, -cating. to beg humbly. —sup′pli·ca′tion, n. —sup·pli·ca·to·ry (sŭp′lə kə tôr′ĭ), adj.

sup·ply¹ (sə plī′), v., -plied, -plying, n., pl. -plies. —v.t. 1. to furnish or provide. 2. to

make up for (a loss, lack, etc.). —n. 3. act of supplying. 4. that which is supplied. 5. a stock or store. —sup·pli′er, n.

sup·ply² (sŭp′lĭ), adv. supplely.

sup·port (sə pōrt′), v.t. 1. to hold up (a load, part, etc.). 2. to withstand (weight, etc.) without giving way. 3. to undergo or endure. 4. to provide food, shelter, etc., for. 5. to uphold (a person, cause, policy, etc.) by aid. 6. to advocate (a theory, etc.). 7. to corroborate. 8. to act with (a leading actor). —n. 9. act of supporting. 10. state of being supported. 11. maintenance, as of a person, family, etc. 12. a thing or a person that supports. —sup·port′a·ble, adj. —sup·port′er, n.

sup·pose (sə pōz′), v.t., v.i., -posed, -posing. 1. to assume (something), without reference to its being true or false. 2. to consider as a possibility. 3. to assume as true. 4. to take for granted; presume. 5. to think. 6. to require logically; presuppose. —sup·pos′a·ble, adj.

sup·posed (sə pōzd′), adj. assumed as true; hypothetical. —sup·pos·ed·ly (sə pō′zĭd lĭ), adv.

sup·po·si·tion (sŭp′ə zĭsh′ən), n. 1. act of supposing. 2. an assumption. —sup′po·si′tion·al, adj.

sup·press (sə prĕs′), v.t. 1. to put an end to the activities of (a person, etc.). 2. to abolish; stop. 3. to repress (a feeling, smile, etc.). 4. to withhold from disclosure or publication (truth, a book, etc.). 5. to quell; subdue. —sup·pres′sor, sup·press′er, n. —sup·press′i·ble, adj. —sup·pres·sion (sə prĕsh′ən), n.

sup·pu·rate (sŭp′yə rāt′), v.i., -rated, -rating. to produce or discharge pus. —sup′pu·ra′tion, n. —sup′pu·ra′tive, adj.

su·pra·re·nal (sōō′prə rē′nəl), Anat. —adj. 1. situated above or on the kidney. 2. pertaining to or connected with a suprarenal. —n. 3. a suprarenal body, capsule, or gland.

su·preme (sə prēm′, sōō-), adj. 1. highest in rank or authority; chief. 2. of the highest quality, importance, etc. 3. greatest, utmost, or extreme. 4. last. —su·preme′ly, adv. —su·preme′ness, su·prem·a·cy (sə prĕm′ə sĭ, sōō-), n.

Supreme Being, God.

Supreme Court, U.S. the highest court of the U.S. or of a State.

Supt., superintendent. Also, supt.

Su·ra·ba·ya (sōō′rä bä′yä), n. a seaport in NE Java. 341,675.

sur·cease (sûr sēs′), n. Archaic. end.

sur·charge (sûr′chärj′, sûr chärj′; v. sûr·chärj′), n., v., -charged, -charging. —n. 1. an additional or excessive charge, load, burden, etc. —v.t. 2. to overcharge. 3. to put an additional or excessive burden upon.

sur·cin·gle (sûr′sĭng′gəl), n. a girth for a horse or other animal, passing over and keeping in place a blanket, pack, or the like.

sure (shŏōr), adj., surer, surest, adv. —adj. 1. free from doubt; certain. 2. confident. 3. convinced; positive. 4. reliable. 5. firm or stable. 6. unfailing. 7. never missing, slipping, etc. 8. for sure, as a certainty. 9. to be sure, certainly. —adv. 10. Colloq. certainly. —sure′ly, adv. —sure′ness, n.

sure-foot·ed (shŏōr′fŏōt′ĭd), adj. 1. not liable to stumble, slip, or fall. 2. unerring.

sure·ty (shŏōr′tĭ, shŏōr′ə tĭ), n., pl. -ties. 1. security against loss or damage. 2. one who has made himself responsible for another. 3. Archaic. certainty. —sure′ty·ship′, n.

surf (sûrf), n. the swell of the sea which breaks upon a shore or upon shoals.

sur·face (sûr′fĭs), n., adj.; v., -faced, -facing. —n. 1. the outer face, or outside, of a thing. 2. any face of a body or thing. 3. extent or area of outer face. 4. the outward appearance. —adj. 5. superficial. —v.t. 6. to make even or smooth. —v.i. 7. to come to the surface. —sur′fac·er, n.

surf·board (sûrf′bōrd′), n. a narrow board used in a sport consisting of riding the crest of a wave towards shore.

sur·feit (sûr′fĭt), n. 1. excess, esp. in eating or drinking. 2. general disgust caused by excess. —v.t., v.i. 3. to overeat; satiate.

surg., 1. surgeon. 2. surgery. 3. surgical.

surge (sûrj), n., v., surged, surging. —n. 1. a swelling or rolling movement, rush, or sweep. 2. a wavelike volume or body. 3. the rolling swell of the sea. 4. a swelling wave. 5. Elect. a sudden rush of current, etc. —*v.i.* **6.** to rise and fall, or move along, on the waves, as a ship. **7.** to increase or rush suddenly.

sur·geon (sûr′jən), *n.* one who practices surgery.

sur·ger·y (sûr′jə rY), *n., pl.* **-geries. 1.** the treatment of diseases, injuries, or deformities by manual operation or instrumental appliances. **2.** a room for surgical operations. **—sur·gi·cal** (sûr′jə kəl), *adj.* **—sur′gi·cal·ly,** *adv.*

Su·ri·nam (sŏŏr′ə năm′), *n.* a Dutch colony on the NE coast of South America. 189,000 pop.; 60,230 sq. mi. *Cap.:* Paramaribo.

sur·ly (sûr′lY), *adj.,* **-lier, -liest. 1.** churlishly rude or ill-humored. **2.** ill-tempered and unfriendly. **—sur′li·ly,** *adv.* **—sur′li·ness,** *n.*

sur·mise (*v.* sər mīz′; *n.* sər mīz′, sûr′mīz), *v.,* **-mised, -mising,** *n.* **—v.t., v.i. 1.** to conjecture; guess. **—n. 2.** a matter of conjecture.

sur·mount (sər mount′), *v.t.* **1.** to get or be on the top of. **2.** to get over (obstacles, etc.). **—sur·mount′a·ble,** *adj.*

sur·name (*n.* sûr′nām′; *v.* sûr′nām′, sûr nām′), *n., v.,* **-named, -naming. —n. 1.** the family name. **—v.t. 2.** to give a surname to.

sur·pass (sər păs′, -päs′), *v.t.* **1.** to be greater than; exceed. **2.** to be superior to; excel. **3.** to transcend. **—sur·pass′ing·ly,** *adv.*

sur·plice (sûr′plYs), *n.* a loose-fitting, broad-sleeved white vestment worn by clergymen and choristers.

sur·plus (sûr′plŭs, -pləs), *n.* **1.** an amount of assets in excess of what is requisite to meet liabilities. **2.** that which remains above what is used or needed. **—adj. 3.** being a surplus.

sur·prise (sər prīz′), *v.,* **-prised, -prising,** *n.* **—v.t. 1.** to come upon suddenly and unexpectedly. **2.** to strike with a feeling of wonder, as at something unexpected. **—n. 3.** act of surprising. **4.** state or feeling of being surprised. **5.** something that excites this feeling. **—sur·pris′ing,** *adj.* **—sur·pris′ing·ly,** *adv.*

Anglican surplice

sur·re·al·ism (sə rē′ə lYz′əm), *n.* a recent movement in literature and art (influenced by psychoanalysis) seeking to suggest the activities of the subconscious mind. **—sur·re′al·ist,** *n., adj.* **—sur·re′al·is′tic,** *adj.* **—sur·re′al·is′ti·cal·ly,** *adv.*

sur·ren·der (sə rěn′dər), *v.t., v.i.* **1.** to yield; give up. **—n. 2.** act of surrendering.

sur·rep·ti·tious (sûr′əp tYsh′əs), *adj.* stealthy; secret and unauthorized; clandestine. **—sur′rep·ti′tious·ly,** *adv.* **—sur′rep·ti′tious·ness,** *n.*

sur·rey (sûr′Y), *n., pl.* **-reys.** a light, four-wheeled, two-seated carriage for four persons.

sur·ro·gate (*n.* sûr′ə gāt′, -gĭt; *v.* sûr′ə gāt′), *n., v.,* **-gated, -gating. —n. 1.** a deputy. **2.** *U.S.* a judicial officer having jurisdiction over the probate of wills, the administration of estates, etc. **—v.t. 3.** to substitute.

sur·round (sə round′), *v.t.* **1.** to enclose on all sides; encompass. **2.** to encircle.

sur·round·ing (sə roun′dYng), *n.* **1.** that which surrounds. **2.** (*pl.*) environing circumstances, conditions, etc. **—adj. 3.** that encloses, encircles, or environs.

sur·tax (sûr′tăks), *n.* **1.** an additional tax on something already taxed. **2.** one of a graded series of additional taxes on incomes exceeding a certain amount.

sur·veil·lance (sər vā′ləns, -vāl′yəns), *n.* **1.** watch kept over a person, etc., esp. over a suspect or the like. **2.** supervision.

sur·vey (*v.* sər vā′; *n.* sûr′vā, sər vā′), *v., n., pl.* **-veys. —v.t., v.i. 1.** to take a general view (of). **2.** to view in detail. **3.** to determine the form, boundaries, etc., of (a part of the earth's surface, etc.), by linear and angular measurements. **—n. 4.** act of surveying. **5.** a formal examination of something. **6.** a description embodying the result of this. **7.** a determining of form, boundaries, etc., by linear and angular measurements. **—sur·vey′ing,** *n.* **—sur·vey′or,** *n.*

sur·viv·al (sər vī′vəl), *n.* **1.** act of surviving. **2.** one that survives, esp. a surviving custom, belief, or the like.

sur·vive (sər vīv′), *v.t., v.i.,* **-vived, -viving. 1.** to remain alive (after); outlive. **2.** to continue to exist (after). **—sur·vi′vor,** *n.*

sus·cep·ti·ble (sə sěp′tə bəl), *adj.* **1.** capable

of recei... [o...]tting, undergoing, or being affected b... ...hing. **2.** especially liable. **3.** impressiona... **—sus·cep′ti·ble·ness, sus·cep′ti·bil′i·ty,** *n.* **—sus·cep′ti·bly,** *adv.*

sus·pect (*v.* sə spěkt′; *n., adj.* sŭs′pěkt, sə spěkt′), *v.t.* **1.** to imagine to be guilty, false, bad, etc., without proof. **2.** to imagine to be the case. **—n. 3.** a person suspected of a crime, offense, or the like. **—adj. 4.** open to suspicion.

sus·pend (sə spěnd′), *v.t., v.i.* **1.** to hang by attachment to something above. **2.** to stay in place as if by hanging. **3.** to refrain from forming. **4.** to postpone. **5.** to stop, usually for a time. **6.** to debar, usually for a time.

sus·pend·er (sə spěn′dər), *n.* **1.** (*pl.*) *Chiefly U.S.* straps worn over the shoulders for holding up the trousers. **2.** *Brit.* a garter.

sus·pense (sə spěns′), *n.* tense mental uncertainty, as in awaiting a decision.

sus·pen·sion (sə spěn′shən), *n.* **1.** act of suspending. **2.** state of being suspended. **3.** temporary abrogation, as of a law. **4.** stoppage of payment of debts or claims. **5.** *Physics.* the state in which particles of a solid are mixed with a fluid but are undissolved. **6.** a substance in such a state. **7.** *Phys. Chem.* a system consisting of small particles kept dispersed by agitation or by the molecular motion in the surrounding medium. **8.** something by which something else is suspended. **9.** *Music.* the prolongation of a tone in one chord into the following chord, usually producing a temporary dissonance.

suspension bridge, a bridge in which the roadway is suspended from cables, usually hung between towers of masonry or steel, and fastened at the extremities.

sus·pen·so·ry (sə spěn′sə rY), *adj., n., pl.* **-ries. —adj. 1.** serving or fitted to suspend. **—n. 2.** a suspensory bandage, ligament, etc.

sus·pi·cion (sə spYsh′ən), *n.* **1.** act of suspecting of guilt, falsity, defect, or the like, without evidence. **2.** an instance of suspecting something. **3.** a vague notion. **4.** a slight trace.

sus·pi·cious (sə spYsh′əs), *adj.* **1.** liable to cause suspicion. **2.** inclined to suspect; distrustful. **—sus·pi′cious·ly,** *adv.* **—sus·pi′cious·ness,** *n.*

Sus·que·han·na (sŭs′kwə hăn′ə), *n.* a river flowing from central New York through E Pennsylvania and NE Maryland into Chesapeake Bay. 444 mi.

sus·tain (sə stān′), *v.t.* **1.** to hold up; bear the weight of. **2.** to bear (a burden, charge, etc.). **3.** to undergo, suffer, or endure. **4.** to keep (a person, the mind, etc.) from giving way, as under affliction. **5.** to keep going, as an action. **6.** to supply with food and drink, etc. **7.** to uphold as valid, just, or correct. **8.** to corroborate. **—sus·tain′a·ble,** *adj.* **—sus·tain′er,** *n.*

sustaining program, a radio program without a commercial sponsor.

sus·te·nance (sŭs′tə nəns), *n.* **1.** nourishment. **2.** means of livelihood.

su·ture (sōō′chər), *n., v.,* **-tured, -turing. —n. 1.** *Surg.* **a.** a joining of the edges of a wound or the like by stitching. **b.** a particular method of doing this. **c.** one of the stitches employed. **2.** *Anat.* the line of junction of two bones, esp. of the skull, in an immovable articulation. **—v.t. 3.** to unite by a suture.

su·ze·rain (sōō′zə rYn, -rān′), *n.* **1.** a state exercising political control over another. **2.** a feudal overlord.

su·ze·rain·ty (sōō′zə rYn tY, -rān′-), *n., pl.* **-ties.** the position or authority of a suzerain.

svelte (svělt), *adj.* slender; lithe.

SW, 1. southwest. **2.** southwestern. Also, **S.W.**

swab (swŏb), *n., v.,* **swabbed, swabbing. —n. 1.** a large mop. **2.** a bit of cloth or the like for applying medicaments, etc. **—v.t. 3.** to clean with a swab.

swad·dle (swŏd′əl), *v.t.,* **-dled, -dling.** to bind (an infant, esp. a newborn infant) with long, narrow strips of cloth (**swaddling clothes**) to prevent free movement.

swag (swăg), *n. Slang.* plundered property; booty.

swag·ger (swăg′ər), *v.i.* **1.** to walk or strut with a defiant or insolent air. **—n. 2.** swaggering gait, bearing, or air. **—swag′ger·er,** *n.* **—swag′ger·ing·ly,** *adv.*

swain (swān), *n. Chiefly Poetic.* **1.** a country lad. **2.** a country gallant. **3.** a lover.

swale (swāl), *n.* a low place in a tract of land, usually having a rank vegetation.

swal·low[1] (swŏl'ō), *v.t.* **1.** to take (food, etc.) into the stomach through the throat. **2.** to assimilate; consume. **3.** *Colloq.* to accept without question, suspicion, or opposition. **4.** to suppress (a sob, etc.). **5.** to retract (one's words, etc.). —*n.* **6.** a quantity swallowed at one time. —**swal'low·er**, *n.*

swal·low[2] (swŏl'ō), *n.* any of certain small, long-winged passerine birds notable for their swift, graceful flight and for the extent and regularity of their migrations.

swa·mi (swä'mĭ), *n.*, *pl.* **-mis.** a title for a Hindu religious teacher.

swamp (swŏmp), *n.* **1.** a tract of wet, spongy land; marshy ground. —*v.t.*, *v.i.* **2.** to flood or drench with water or the like. **3.** *Naut.* to fill (a boat) with water. **4.** to overwhelm or be overwhelmed. —**swamp'y,** *adj.*

swamp·land (swŏmp'lănd'), *n.* land covered with swamps.

swan (swŏn), *n.* **1.** any of certain large, stately swimming birds which have a long, slender neck, and in most species a pure-white plumage in the adult. **2.** *Astron.* (*cap.*) a northern constellation.

swank (swăngk), *n.* **1.** *Slang.* dashing smartness; style. **2.** swagger. —*adj.* Also, **swank'y.** **3.** *Slang.* pretentiously stylish.

swan's-down (swŏnz'doun'), *n.* **1.** the down of a swan, used for trimming, powder puffs, etc. **2.** a fine, soft, thick woolen cloth. Also, **swans'-down'.**

swap (swŏp), *v.*, **swapped, swapping,** *n.* —*v.t.*, *v.i.* **1.** to exchange, barter, or trade. —*n.* **2.** an exchange.

sward (swôrd), *n.* **1.** the grassy surface of land; turf. —*v.t.* **2.** to cover with turf.

swarm (swôrm), *n.* **1.** a group of honeybees which emigrate from a hive and fly off together to start a new colony. **2.** a group of bees settled together, as in a hive. **3.** a great number of things or persons, esp. in motion. —*v.i.* **4.** to fly off together to start a new colony. **5.** to move about, along, forth, etc., in great numbers. **6.** to be exceedingly numerous, as in a place. **7.** to be thronged or overrun. —**swarm'er,** *n.*

swart (swôrt), *adj. Dial.* swarthy.

swarth·y (swôr'thĭ, -thĭ), *adj.*, **swarthier, swarthiest.** dark-colored, esp. the skin. —**swarth'i·ness,** *n.*

swash·buck·ler (swŏsh'bŭk'lər), *n.* a swaggering swordsman or bully. Also, **swash'er.** —**swash'buck'ling,** *adj.*, *n.*

swas·ti·ka (swŏs'tĭ kə, swăs'-), *n.* **1.** a prehistoric symbol or ornament consisting of a cross with arms of equal length, each arm having a continuation at right angles, and all four continuations turning the same way. **2.** this figure with clockwise arms as the official emblem of the Nazi party and the Third Reich.

swat (swŏt), *v.*, **swatted, swatting,** *n. Colloq.* —*v.t.* **1.** to hit with a sharp or violent blow. —*n.* **2.** a sharp or violent blow. —**swat'ter,** *n.*

swatch (swŏch), *n.* a sample of cloth.

swath (swŏth, swôth), *n.* **1.** the space covered by the stroke of a scythe or the cut of a mowing machine. **2.** a strip so cut.

swathe (swāth), *v.*, **swathed, swathing,** *n.* —*v.t.* **1.** to wrap closely or fully. **2.** to enfold or envelop. —*n.* **3.** a band of linen or the like in which something is wrapped; bandage.

sway (swā), *v.i.*, *v.t.* **1.** to move or swing to and fro. **2.** to incline in opinion, sympathy, etc. **3.** to vacillate or cause to vacillate. **4.** to influence, rule, or control. —*n.* **5.** act of swaying. **6.** rule; dominion. **7.** dominating power or influence.

sway-backed (swā'băkt'), *adj.* having the back sagged to an unusual degree.

swear (swâr), *v.*, **swore** or (*Archaic*) **sware; sworn; swearing.** —*v.i.* **1.** to make a solemn declaration with an appeal to God or some superhuman being in confirmation of what is declared. **2.** to promise on oath or in a solemn manner; vow. **3.** to use profane language. —*v.t.* **4.** to affirm by swearing. **5.** to vow. **6.** to take (an oath). **7.** to bring, get, take, etc., by swearing. **8.** to bind by an oath. **9.** to admit to office or service by administering an oath. —**swear'er,** *n.*

sweat (swĕt), *v.*, **sweat** or **sweated, sweating,** *n.* —*v.i.*, *v.t.* **1.** to excrete (watery fluid) through the pores of the skin, as from heat, exertion, etc.; perspire. **2.** to gather (moisture) from the surrounding air by condensation. **3.** *Colloq.* to work

hard. **4.** *Colloq.* to suffer severely. **5.** *Slang.* to question (a person) severely in order to extract information, as for police purposes. —*n.* **6.** the process of perspiring, as from heat, exertion, etc. **7.** the secretions of sweat glands. **8.** *Colloq.* a state of perturbation, anxiety, or impatience. —**sweat'y,** *adj.* —**sweat'i·ly,** *adv.* —**sweat'i·ness,** *n.*

sweat·er (swĕt'ər), *n.* a knitted jacket, usually of wool.

sweat·shop (swĕt'shŏp'), *n.* a shop employing workers at low wages, during overlong hours, under unfavorable conditions.

Swe·den (swē'dən), *n.* a kingdom in N Europe, in the E part of the Scandinavian peninsula. 6,719,000 pop.; 173,394 sq. mi. *Cap.:* Stockholm. —**Swede** (swēd), *n.* —**Swed'ish,** *adj.*, *n.*

sweep (swēp), *v.*, **swept, sweeping,** *n.* —*v.t.* **1.** to move, drive, or bring by passing a broom, brush, or the like, over the surface occupied. **2.** to clear or clean (a floor, room, etc.) of dirt, etc., by means of a broom or the like. **3.** to clear (a surface, place, etc.) of something on or in it. **4.** to pass over (a region, etc.) with a steady, driving movement, as winds. —*v.i.* **5.** to sweep a floor, room, etc., as with a broom. **6.** to move steadily and strongly or swiftly. **7.** to move in a continuous course. —*n.* **8.** act of sweeping. **9.** reach, range, or compass. **10.** a continuous extent or stretch. **11.** *Chiefly Brit.* a chimney sweeper. —**sweep'er,** *n.*

sweep·ing (swē'pĭng), *adj.* **1.** of wide range or scope. **2.** moving over a wide area. —*n.* **3.** (*pl.*) matter swept out or up, as dust, refuse, etc. —**sweep'ing·ly,** *adv.*

sweep·stakes (swēp'stāks'), *n. sing. and pl.* **1.** a prize in a race or other contest, consisting of the stakes contributed by the various competitors, and taken by the winner. **2.** the race or contest itself.

sweet (swēt), *adj.* **1.** having the pleasant taste of sugar, honey, etc. **2.** fresh. **3.** pleasing to the ear. **4.** fragrant; perfumed. **5.** pleasing or agreeable; delightful. **6.** amiable; kind or gracious. **7.** dear; beloved. **8.** easily managed. **9.** (of wine) sweet-tasting. **10.** *Jazz.* in a straight or sentimental style. —*adv.* **11.** in a sweet manner. —*n.* **12.** sweet taste, flavor, or smell. **13.** that which is sweet. **14.** *Chiefly Brit.* candy. **15.** a beloved person. —**sweet'ish,** *adj.* —**sweet'ly,** *adv.* —**sweet'ness,** *n.*

sweet·bread (swēt'brĕd'), *n.* the pancreas of an animal, esp. a calf or a lamb, used for food.

sweet·bri·er (swēt'brī'ər), *n.* a rose with a tall stem, stout prickles, and single pink flowers. Also, **sweet'bri'ar.**

sweet corn, any maize of a sweetish flavor and suitable for eating.

sweet·en (swē'tən), *v.t.*, *v.i.* to make or become sweet. —**sweet'en·er,** *n.*

sweet·en·ing (swē'tən ĭng, swēt'nĭng), *n.* something that sweetens food, etc.

sweet·heart (swēt'härt'), *n.* a beloved person.

sweet·meat (swēt'mēt'), *n.* a sweet confection, as sugar-covered nuts, bonbons, etc.

sweet pea, an annual climbing plant bearing sweet-scented flowers.

sweet potato, 1. a plant of the morning-glory family, grown for its sweet, edible roots. **2.** the root.

sweet william, a kind of pink bearing small flowers of various colors in dense clusters.

swell (swĕl), *v.*, **swelled, swelled** or **swollen, swelling,** *n.*, *adj.* —*v.i.* **1.** to grow in bulk, as by inflation, distention, growth, or the like. **2.** to rise in waves, as the sea. **3.** to bulge out, as a sail. **4.** to grow in amount, degree, force, or the like. **5.** to behave or talk arrogantly or pretentiously. —*v.t.* **6.** to cause to swell. —*n.* **7.** increase in bulk. **8.** a bulging part. **9.** a wave. **10.** increase in amount, degree, force, etc. **11.** *Slang.* a fashionable person of high social standing. —*adj. Slang.* **12.** stylish. **13.** first-rate; excellent. —**swell'ing,** *n.*, *adj.*

swel·ter (swĕl'tər), *v.i.* **1.** to perspire profusely from oppressive heat. —*n.* **2.** a sweltering condition. —**swel'ter·ing,** *adj.* —**swel'ter·ing·ly,** *adv.*

swerve (swûrv), *v.*, **swerved, swerving,** *n.* —*v.i.*, *v.t.* **1.** to turn aside. —*n.* **2.** act of swerving.

swift (swĭft), *adj.* **1.** moving with great speed; fleet; rapid. **2.** coming, happening, or performed quickly. **3.** quick or prompt to act, etc. —*adv.* **4.** swiftly. —*n.* **5.** any of certain small, long-winged birds notable for their rapid flight. —**swift′ly**, *adv.* —**swift′ness**, *n.*

Swift (swĭft), *n.* Jonathan, 1667–1745, British satirist.

swig (swĭg), *n.*, *v.*, **swigged**, **swigging**. *Colloq.* —*n.* **1.** a large or deep drink. —*v.t.*, *v.i.* **2.** to drink heartily. —**swig′ger**, *n.*

swill (swĭl), *n.* **1.** liquid or partly liquid kitchen refuse given to swine. **2.** garbage. **3.** any liquid matter. **4.** a deep draft of liquor. —*v.i.*, *v.t.* **5.** to drink greedily or to excess; guzzle. —**swill′er**, *n.*

swim (swĭm), *v.*, **swam**, **swum**, **swimming**, *n.* —*v.i.* **1.** to move along or in water by movements of the limbs, fins, tail, etc. **2.** to float. **3.** to be immersed in or flooded with a liquid. **4.** to be dizzy or giddy. —*v.t.* **5.** to cross by swimming. —*n.* **6.** an act or period of swimming. **7.** *Colloq.* the current of affairs. —**swim′mer**, *n.*

swim·ming·ly (swĭm′ĭng lĭ), *adv.* without difficulty; with great success.

Swin·burne (swĭn′bərn), *n.* Algernon Charles, 1837–1909, British poet and critic.

swin·dle (swĭn′dəl), *v.*, **-dled**, **-dling**, *n.* —*v.t.*, *v.i.* **1.** to cheat (a person), as out of money; defraud. —*n.* **2.** act of swindling. —**swin′dler**, *n.*

swine (swĭn), *n.*, *pl.* **swine**. **1.** the domestic hog. **2.** *Chiefly Brit.* a coarse, gross, or brutishly sensual person. —**swin′ish**, *adj.* —**swin′ish·ly**, *adv.* —**swin′ish·ness**, *n.*

swing[1] (swĭng), *v.*, **swung** or (*Archaic and Dial.*) **swang**; **swung**; **swinging**; *n.* —*v.t.*, *v.i.* **1.** to move to and fro; sway; oscillate. **2.** to move (something held) in a curve; brandish. **3.** to suspend, or be suspended, so as to hang freely. **4.** *U.S. Colloq.* to influence or manage. —*n.* **5.** act, manner, or extent of swinging. **6.** *Colloq.* a shift or period of work. **7.** freedom of action. **8.** active operation. **9.** a seat suspended from above, as between ropes. in which one may sit and swing to and fro for sport. —**swing′er**, *n.*

swing[2] (swĭng), *n.*, *adj.*, *v.*, **swung**, **swinging**. —*n.* **1.** dance music characterized by ingenious modern interpretations and played in a stimulating rhythm, tempo, etc. —*adj.* **2.** pertaining to swing. —*v.t.*, *v.i.* **3.** to play (music) in such a manner.

swing shift, *U.S. Colloq.* a work shift in industry, from mid-afternoon until midnight.

swipe (swīp), *n.*, *v.*, **swiped**, **swiping**. —*n.* **1.** *Colloq.* a sweeping stroke. —*v.t.* **2.** *Colloq.* to strike with a sweeping blow. **3.** *Slang.* to steal.

swirl (swûrl), *v.i.*, *v.t.* **1.** to move with a whirling motion; whirl; eddy. —*n.* **2.** a swirling movement; whirl; eddy.

swish (swĭsh), *v.i.* **1.** to move with a sibilant or rustling sound. —*n.* **2.** a swishing movement or sound.

Swiss (swĭs), *adj.* **1.** of or pertaining to Switzerland or its people. —*n.* **2.** a native or inhabitant of Switzerland.

Swiss cheese, a firm, pale-yellow cheese containing many holes.

switch (swĭch), *n.* **1.** a slender, flexible rod, etc., used esp. in whipping, etc. **2.** act of switching. **3.** a slender growing shoot. **4.** a separate bunch or tress of long hair worn by women to supplement their own hair. **5.** a device for turning on or off or directing an electric current. **6.** *Railroads.* a device for shifting moving trains, cars, etc., from one track to another. **7.** a turning, shifting, or changing. —*v.t.*, *v.i.* **8.** to whip with a switch or the like. **9.** to turn, shift, or divert. **10.** *Elect.* to connect, disconnect, or redirect an electric circuit. —**switch′er**, *n.*

switch·board (swĭch′bôrd′), *n.* a panel of switches, instruments, etc., for the control of electric energy.

switch·man (swĭch′mən), *n.*, *pl.* **-men.** one who has charge of switches on a railroad.

Switz·er·land (swĭt′sər lənd), *n.* a republic in central Europe. 4,466,000 pop.; 15,944 sq. mi. *Cap.*: Bern.

swiv·el (swĭv′əl), *n.*, *v.*, **-eled**, **-eling** or (*esp. Brit.*) **-elled**, **-elling.** —*n.* **1.** a device which allows the thing fastened to turn round freely upon it. **2.** a pivoted support for allowing something to turn round in a horizontal plane. —*v.t.*, *v.i.* **3.** to turn on a swivel.

swol·len (swō′lən), *adj.* **1.** swelled; enlarged; puffed up; tumid. **2.** turgid or bombastic.

swoon (swoōn), *v.i.*, *n.* faint.

swoop (swoōp), *v.i.* **1.** to sweep through the air, esp. down upon prey. **2.** to come down in a sud-

den, s ——*v.t.* **3.** to take at one stroke. —*n.* **4.** swift descent.

swop (sw t., *v.i.*, **swopped**, **swopping**, *n.* swap.

sword (sôrd), *n.* a weapon consisting typically of a long sharp-edged blade fixed in a hilt or handle.

sword·fish (sôrd′fĭsh′), *n.*, *pl.* **-fishes**, (*esp. collectively*) **-fish.** a large edible marine fish with the upper jaw elongated into a swordlike form.

sword·play (sôrd′plā′), *n.* the action, practice, or art of wielding a sword.

swords·man (sôrdz′mən), *n.*, *pl.* **-men.** **1.** one who uses a sword. **2.** a fencer. **3.** a soldier.

sworn (sôrn), *adj.* bound by an oath.

syb·a·rite (sĭb′ə rīt′), *n.* one devoted to luxury and pleasure. —**syb·a·rit·ic** (sĭb′ə rĭt′ĭk), *adj.*

syc·a·more (sĭk′ə môr′), *n.* **1.** *U.S.* a plane tree, the buttonwood. **2.** *Eng.* a maple tree. **3.** a tree of the Near East, allied to the common fig.

syc·o·phant (sĭk′ə fənt), *n.* a self-seeking flatterer. —**syc·o·phan·cy**, *n.* —**syc·o·phan·tic** (sĭk′ə făn′tĭk), *adj.*

Syd·ney (sĭd′nĭ), *n.* a seaport in SE Australia. With suburbs, 1,398,000.

syl·lab·ic (sĭ lăb′ĭk), *adj.* of, pertaining to, or consisting of a syllable or syllables. —**syl·lab·i·cal·ly**, *adv.*

syl·lab·i·cate (sĭ lăb′ə kāt′), *v.t.*, **-cated**, **-cating.** to form or divide into syllables. —**syl·lab·i·ca′tion**, *n.*

syl·lab·i·fy (sĭ lăb′ə fī′), *v.t.*, **-fied**, **-fying.** to syllabicate. —**syl·lab·i·fi·ca′tion**, *n.*

syl·la·ble (sĭl′ə bəl), *n.*, *v.*, **-bled**, **-bling.** —*n.* **1.** a segment of speech uttered with a single impulse of air pressure from the lungs. **2.** the least mention. —*v.t.*, *v.i.* **3.** to utter (in) syllables.

syl·la·bus (sĭl′ə bəs), *n.*, *pl.* **-buses**, **-bi** (-bī′). a tabular or brief statement of a course of study, etc.

syl·lo·gism (sĭl′ə jĭz′əm), *n.* *Logic.* an argument with two premises and a conclusion. —**syl·lo·gis′tic**, *adj.*

sylph (sĭlf), *n.* a slender, graceful woman or girl.

syl·van (sĭl′vən), *adj.* **1.** of, pertaining to, or inhabiting the woods. **2.** wooded. —*n.* **3.** a person dwelling in a woodland region.

sym., **1.** symbol. **2.** symptom.

sym·bol (sĭm′bəl), *n.* **1.** an emblem, token, or sign. **2.** a letter, figure, or other character or mark, or a combination of letters or the like, used to represent something.

sym·bol·ic (sĭm bŏl′ĭk), *adj.* **1.** serving as a symbol. **2.** of, pertaining to, or expressed by a symbol. **3.** involving the use of symbols. Also, **sym·bol′i·cal.** —**sym·bol′i·cal·ly**, *adv.*

sym·bol·ism (sĭm′bə lĭz′əm), *n.* **1.** the practice of representing things by symbols. **2.** a set or system of symbols. **3.** symbolic meaning.

sym·bol·ist (sĭm′bəl ĭst), *n.* one who uses symbols or symbolism. —**sym·bol·is′tic**, *adj.*

sym·bol·ize (sĭm′bə līz′), *v.t.*, **-ized**, **-izing.** **1.** to be a symbol of. **2.** to represent by a symbol. —**sym·bol·i·za′tion**, *n.*

sym·me·try (sĭm′ə trĭ), *n.*, *pl.* **-tries.** **1.** the correspondence, in size, form, and arrangement, of parts on opposite sides of a plane, line, or point. **2.** the proper or excellent proportion of the parts of a body or whole to one another with regard to size and form. —**sym·met·ri·cal** (sĭ met′rə kəl), **sym·met′ric**, *adj.* —**sym·met′ri·cal·ly**, *adv.*

sym·pa·thet·ic (sĭm′pə thĕt′ĭk), *adj.* **1.** sympathizing; compassionate. **2.** congenial. **3.** *Colloq.* looking with favor or liking upon. —**sym′pa·thet′i·cal·ly**, *adv.*

sym·pa·thize (sĭm′pə thīz′), *v.i.*, **-thized**, **-thizing.** **1.** to be in sympathy or agreement of feeling. **2.** to feel a compassionate sympathy. **3.** to express sympathy. **4.** to be in approving accord. **5.** to agree, correspond, or accord. —**sym′pa·thiz′er**, *n.*

sym·pa·thy (sĭm′pə thĭ), *n.*, *pl.* **-thies.** **1.** community of feeling. **2.** compassion; commiseration. **3.** favor or approval. **4.** agreement, consonance, or accord. **5.** *Physiol.*, *Pathol.* the relation between parts whereby a condition of one part induces some effect in another.

sym·pho·ny (sĭm′fə nĭ), *n.*, *pl.* **-nies.** **1.** *Music.* an elaborate instrumental composition in three or more movements, written for an orchestra. **2.** anything characterized by a harmonious combination of elements. —**sym·phon·ic** (sĭm-fŏn′ĭk), *adj.*

sym·po·si·um (sĭm pō′zĭ əm), *n., pl.* **-siums, -sia** (-zĭ ə). **1.** a meeting for discussion of some subject. **2.** a collection of opinions or articles contributed on a given topic.

symp·tom (sĭmp′təm), *n.* **1.** a sign or indication of something. **2.** *Pathol.* a phenomenon which arises from and indicates a particular disease or disorder. —**symp′to·mat′ic, symp′to·mat′i·cal,** *adj.*

syn., synonym.

syn·a·gogue (sĭn′ə gŏg′, -gŏg′), *n.* **1.** an assembly of Jews for religious instruction and worship. **2.** the building for such assembly.

syn·chro·nism (sĭng′krə nĭz′əm), *n.* coincidence in time; contemporaneousness.

syn·chro·nize (sĭng′krə nīz′), *v.,* **-nized, -nizing.** —*v.i.* **1.** to occur at the same time. **2.** to go on at the same rate and exactly together. —*v.t.* **3.** to cause to indicate the same time, as one timepiece with another. —**syn′chro·ni·za′tion,** *n.* —**syn′chro·niz′er,** *n.*

syn·chro·nous (sĭng′krə nəs), *adj.* **1.** occurring at the same time; contemporaneous. **2.** going on at the same rate and exactly together. **3.** *Physics, Elect., etc.* having the same frequency and no phase difference. —**syn′chro·nous·ly,** *adv.*

syn·co·pate (sĭng′kə pāt′, sĭn′-), *v.t.,* **-pated, -pating. 1.** *Music.* **a.** to place (the accents) on beats which are normally unaccented. **b.** to employ tones so affected in (a passage, piece, etc.). **2.** *Gram.* to contract (a word) by omitting one or more sounds from the middle. —**syn′co·pa′tion,** *n.*

syn·di·cal·ism (sĭn′də kə lĭz′əm), *n.* a form of trade unionism which aims ultimately at the control of society by the federated bodies of industrial workers. —**syn′di·cal·ist,** *adj., n.*

syn·di·cate (*n.* sĭn′də kĭt; *v.* sĭn′dĭ kāt′), *n., v.,* **-cated, -cating.** —*n.* **1.** a combination of persons or companies for carrying out some project requiring large resources of capital. **2.** any agency which buys and supplies articles, stories, etc., for simultaneous publication in newspapers, etc. —*v.t.* **3.** to publish simultaneously, as a syndicate does. —**syn′di·ca′tion,** *n.*

Synge (sĭng), *n.* **John Millington,** 1871–1909, Irish dramatist.

syn·od (sĭn′əd), *n.* **1.** an assembly of ecclesiastics or church delegates for the discussion and decision of ecclesiastical affairs. **2.** any council. —**syn′od·al,** *adj.*

syn·od·ic (sĭ nŏd′ĭk), *adj. Astron.* pertaining to a conjunction, or to two successive conjunctions of the same bodies. Also, **syn·od′i·cal.**

syn·o·nym (sĭn′ə nĭm), *n.* a word having the same, or nearly the same, meaning as another in the language.

syn·on·y·mous (sĭ nŏn′ə məs), *adj.* equivalent in meaning; expressing the same idea. —**syn·on′y·mous·ly,** *adv.*

syn·op·sis (sĭ nŏp′sĭs), *n., pl.* **-ses** (-sēz). a brief or condensed statement giving a general view of some subject.

syn·tax (sĭn′tăks), *n. Gram.* the patterns of formation of sentences and phrases from words in a particular language.

syn·the·sis (sĭn′thə sĭs), *n., pl.* **-ses** (-sēz′). **1.** the combination of parts into a complex whole. **2.** a complex whole made up of parts or elements combined.

syn·the·size (sĭn′thə sīz′), *v.t.,* **-sized, -sizing. 1.** to make up by combining parts. **2.** to combine into a complex whole. **3.** to treat synthetically.

syn·thet·ic (sĭn thĕt′ĭk), *adj.* **1.** of, pertaining to, proceeding by, or involving synthesis. **2.** *Chem.* noting or pertaining to compounds formed by chemical reaction in a laboratory, as opposed to those of natural origin. Also, **syn·thet′i·cal.** —**syn·thet′i·cal·ly,** *adv.*

syph·i·lis (sĭf′ə lĭs), *n. Pathol.* a chronic, infectious venereal disease communicated by contact or heredity. —**syph·i·lit·ic** (sĭf′ə lĭt′ĭk), *adj., n.*

Syr·a·cuse (sĭr′ə kūs′; *for 1 also* sĕr′-), *n.* **1.** a city in central New York. 205,967. **2.** a seaport in SE Sicily. 62,699.

Syr·i·a (sĭr′ĭ ə), *n.* a republic in W Asia at the E end of the Mediterranean. 2,883,600 pop.; ab. 66,000 sq. mi. *Cap.:* Damascus. —**Syr′i·an,** *adj., n.*

sy·rin·ga (sə rĭng′gə), *n.* **1.** any of certain shrubs cultivated for their fragrant white flowers. **2.** a lilac.

sy·ringe (sĭr′ĭnj, sĭ rĭnj′), *n., v.,* **-inged, -inging.** —*n.* **1.** a small device fitted with a piston or rubber bulb for drawing in a quantity of fluid and ejecting it in a stream: used for cleaning wounds, etc. —*v.t.* **2.** to cleanse, inject, etc., by means of a syringe.

syr·inx (sĭr′ĭngks), *n., pl.* **syringes** (sə rĭn′jēz), **syrinxes. 1.** *Anat.* the Eustachian tube. **2.** *Ornith.* the vocal organ of birds. **3.** a Panpipe.

syr·up (sĭr′əp, sûr′-), *n.* any of various sweet, viscid liquids, as preparations of water or fruit juices boiled with sugar. —**syr′up·y,** *adj.*

sys·tem (sĭs′təm), *n.* **1.** an assemblage of parts forming a complex whole. **2.** an ordered and comprehensive assemblage of facts, principles, etc., in a particular field of knowledge. **3.** a coördinated body of methods. **4.** any plan or procedure. **5.** orderliness. **6.** a number of heavenly bodies associated and acting together according to certain natural laws. **7.** the universe.

sys·tem·at·ic (sĭs′tə măt′ĭk), *adj.* **1.** having, showing, or involving a system. **2.** methodical. **3.** arranged in an ordered system. **4.** concerned with classification. Also, **sys′tem·at′i·cal.** —**sys′tem·at′i·cal·ly,** *adv.*

sys·tem·a·tize (sĭs′təm ə tīz′), *v.t.,* **-tized, -tizing.** to arrange in or according to a system. —**sys′tem·a·ti·za′tion,** *n.*

sys·tem·ic (sĭs tĕm′ĭk), *adj.* **1.** of or pertaining to a system. **2.** *Physiol., Pathol.* pertaining to or affecting the entire bodily system.

sys·to·le (sĭs′tə lē′, -lĭ′), *n. Physiol., etc.* the normal rhythmical contraction of the heart, esp. that of the ventricles, which drives the blood into the aorta and the pulmonary artery. —**sys·tol·ic** (sĭs tŏl′ĭk), *adj.*

T

T, t (tē), *n., pl.* **T's** or **Ts, t's** or **ts. 1.** a consonant, the 20th letter of the English alphabet. **2.** to a T, exactly.

T., **1.** Territory. **2.** Tuesday.

t., **1.** teaspoon. **2.** ton. **3.** transitive.

Ta, *Chem.* tantalum.

tab (tăb), *n., v.,* **tabbed, tabbing.** —*n.* **1.** a small flap. **2.** a tag or label. **3.** **keep tab on,** *Colloq.* to keep account of or a check on. —*v.t.* **4.** to furnish with a tab or tabs.

Ta·bas·co (tə băs′kō), *n. Trademark.* a pungent condiment sauce prepared from the fruit of a variety of capsicum.

tab·by (tăb′ĭ), *n., pl.* **-bies,** *adj.* —*n.* **1.** a cat

with a striped or brindled coat. **2.** a watered-silk fabric. —*adj.* **3.** striped or brindled.

tab·er·nac·le (tăb′ər năk′əl), *n.* **1.** a temporary habitation. **2.** a dwelling place. **3.** the Jewish temple. **4.** any place or house of worship.

ta·ble (tā′bəl), *n., v.,* **-bled, -bling.** —*n.* **1.** an article of furniture consisting of a flat top resting on legs. **2.** the food placed on a table to be eaten. **3.** a company of persons at a table. **4.** a level area. **5.** an arrangement of words, numbers, or signs, or combinations of them, as in parallel columns, to exhibit a set of facts or relations in a definite, compact, and comprehensive form. **6. on the table,** *Parl. Proc.* postponed. —*v.t.* **7.** to place (a card, etc.) on a table. **8.** to enter

tableau 478 **take**

in or form into a list. **9.** *U.S. Parl. Proc.* to place (a proposal, etc.) on the table of an assembly for future discussion.

tab·leau (tăb/lō, tă·blō/), *n.*, *pl.* **-leaux,** **-leaus. 1.** a picture, as of a scene. **2.** a picturesque grouping or scene.

ta·ble·cloth (tā/bəl klôth/, -klŏth/), *n.* a cloth for the top of a table during a meal.

ta·ble d'hôte (tăb/əl dōt/, tä/bəl), a restaurant meal of prearranged courses served at a fixed time and price.

ta·ble·land (tā/bəl lănd/), *n.* an elevated and level region of considerable extent.

ta·ble·spoon (tā/bəl spōōn/, -spōōn/), *n.* **1. a** spoon larger than a teaspoon, used in the service of the table and as a standard measuring unit in recipes. **2.** a unit of capacity, equal to 1/2 fluid ounce or 3 household teaspoons. **3.** a tablespoonful.

ta·ble·spoon·ful (tā/bəl spōōn fōōl/, -spōōn-), *n.*, *pl.* **-fuls.** the quantity a tablespoon holds, about half a fluid ounce.

tab·let (tăb/lĭt), *n.* **1.** a pad of sheets of writing paper or the like. **2.** a small, flat slab, esp. one bearing an inscription, carving, or the like. **3.** a small, flat cake of some solid substance, as a drug, chemical, or the like.

tab·loid (tăb/loid), *n.* **1.** a newspaper, about one half the ordinary page size, emphasizing pictures and concise writing. **2.** a compressed portion of various drugs, chemicals, etc. —*adj.* **3.** compressed in or as in a tabloid.

ta·boo (tə bōō/, tă-), *adj.*, *n.*, *pl.* **-boos,** *v.*, **-booed, -booing.** —*adj.* **1.** separated as sacred or unclean; forbidden. —*n.* **2.** a prohibition or interdiction of anything. **3.** the system or practice whereby things are set apart as sacred, forbidden to general use, or placed under a prohibition or interdiction. —*v.t.* **4.** to prohibit or forbid. Also, **ta·bu/.**

ta·bor (tā/bər), *n.* a small drum formerly in use, esp. as an accompaniment to a fife.

tab·u·lar (tăb/yə lər), *adj.* **1.** pertaining to or of the nature of a tabulated arrangement. **2.** computed by the use of tables. **3.** flat and expansive.

tab·u·late (tăb/yə lāt/), *v.t.*, **-lated, -lating.** to put or form into a table, scheme, or synopsis. —**tab/u·la/tion,** *n.* —**tab/u·la/tor,** *n.*

ta·chom·e·ter (tə kŏm/ə tər), *n.* an instrument for measuring velocity or speed, as of a machine, a river, the blood, etc.

tac·it (tăs/ĭt), *adj.* **1.** silent; saying nothing. **2.** implied, understood, or inferred. **3.** unspoken. —**tac/it·ly,** *adv.*

tac·i·turn (tăs/ə tûrn/), *adj.* inclined to silence, or reserved in speech. —**tac/i·tur/ni·ty,** *n.* —**tac/i·turn/ly,** *adv.*

tack (tăk), *n.* **1.** a short, sharp-pointed nail, usually with a large, flat head. **2.** a temporary stitch. **3.** *Naut.* one of the series of straight runs which make up the zigzag course of a ship proceeding to windward. **4.** a course of action or conduct. —*v.t.*, *v.i.* **5.** to fasten by a tack or tacks. **6.** *Naut.* to navigate (a ship) by a series of tacks.

tack·le (tăk/əl), *n.*, *v.*, **-led, -ling.** —*n.* **1.** equipment, esp. for fishing. **2.** an apparatus, as a rope and block, for hoisting, lowering, and shifting objects. **3.** *Football.* **a.** an act of tackling. **b.** either of two players stationed next to the ends in the forward line. —*v.t.* **4.** to undertake to deal with, solve, etc. **5.** *Football.* to seize and stop (an opponent having the ball). —**tack/ler,** *n.*

tack·y (tăk/ĭ), *adj.*, **tackier, tackiest.** *U.S. Colloq.* shabby; dowdy.

Ta·co·ma (tə kō/mə), *n.* **1.** a seaport in W Washington. 109,408. **2. Mount,** Mount Rainier.

tact (tăkt), *n.* skill in dealing with delicate situations. —**tact/ful,** *adj.* —**tact/ful·ly,** *adv.* —**tact/ful·ness,** *n.* —**tact/less,** *adj.* —**tact/less·ly,** *adv.* —**tact/less·ness,** *n.*

tac·ti·cian (tăk tĭsh/ən), *n.* one versed in tactics.

tac·tics (tăk/tĭks), *n.* **1.** the art or science of disposing military or naval forces for battle and maneuvering them in battle. **2.** (*construed as pl.*) mode of procedure for achieving something. —**tac/ti·cal,** *adj.* —**tac/ti·cal·ly,** *adv.*

tac·tile (tăk/tĭl), *adj.* **1.** of or pertaining to the organs or sense of touch. **2.** tangible. —**tac·til/i·ty,** *n.*

tad·pole (tăd/pōl/), *n.* the aquatic larva or immature form of frogs, toads, etc.

taf·fe·ta (tăf/ə tə), *n.* a lightweight, lustrous, silk or rayon fabric of plain weave.

taff·rail (tăf/rāl/), *n.* *Naut.* the rail across the stern.

taf·fy (tăf/ĭ), *n.* **1.** a candy made of sugar or molasses boiled down, often with butter, nuts, etc. **2.** *Colloq.* flattery.

Taft (tăft), *n.* **William Howard,** 1857–1930, 27th president of United States (1909–13).

tag[1] (tăg), *n.*, *v.*, **tagged, tagging.** —*n.* **1.** a piece of strong paper, or the like, for attaching by one end to something as a mark or label. **2.** the last words of a speech in a play, etc. —*v.t.*, *v.i.* **3.** to furnish with a tag or tags. **4.** *Colloq.* to follow closely.

tag[2] (tăg), *n.*, *v.*, **tagged, tagging.** —*n.* **1.** a children's game in which one player chases the others till he touches one of them, who then takes his place as pursuer. —*v.t.* **2.** to touch in tag.

Ta·hi·ti (tä hē/tē, tī/tē), *n.* the principal island of the Society Islands, in the S Pacific. 19,029 pop.; 402 sq. mi. *Cap.:* Papeete. —**Ta·hi·ti·an** (tä hē/tĭ ən, tə hē/shən), *adj.*, *n.*

Tai·ho·ku (tī hō/kōō), *n.* the capital of Formosa, in the N part. 340,114.

tail (tāl), *n.* **1.** the hindmost part of an animal, esp. when forming a distinct flexible appendage to the trunk. **2.** something resembling this. **3.** the hinder, bottom, or concluding part; rear. **4.** *Astron.* the luminous train extending from the head of a comet. **5.** (*pl.*) *Colloq.* the reverse of a coin. **6.** the after portion of an aircraft. **7.** (*pl.*) *Colloq.* full-dress attire. —*adj.* **8.** coming from behind. **9.** being in the back or rear. —*v.t.*, *v.i.* **10.** *Slang.* to follow (a suspect, etc.) close behind.

tail·light (tāl/līt/), *n.* a light, usually red, at the rear of an automobile, train, etc.

tai·lor (tā/lər), *n.* **1.** one whose business it is to make or mend outer garments. —*v.i.* **2.** to do the work of a tailor. —*v.t.* **3.** to make by tailor's work. **4.** to fit or furnish with clothing.

tail·piece (tāl/pēs/), *n.* **1.** a piece added at the end. **2.** *Print.* a small decorative design, as at the end of a chapter. **3.** a relatively short beam inserted in a wall.

tail spin, *Aeron.* a descent of an airplane in a steep spiral course.

taint (tānt), *n.* **1.** a touch or trace of something deleterious, as infection, contamination, dishonor, etc. —*v.t.* **2.** to modify as by a taint; contaminate. —*v.i.* **3.** to become tainted.

take (tāk), *v.*, **took, taken, taking,** *n.* —*v.t.* **1.** to get into one's hold, possession, control, etc., by one's own action. **2.** to seize, catch, or capture. **3.** to grasp, grip, or embrace. **4.** to receive or accept willingly. **5.** to receive by way of payment or charge. **6.** to get or obtain. **7.** to receive into the body or system. **8.** to contract (disease, etc.). **9.** to select. **10.** to carry off or remove. **11.** to subtract or deduct. **12.** to carry. **13.** to conduct or lead. **14.** to get over, through, round, etc. **15.** to attack, as a disease does. **16.** to become affected by. **17.** *Chess, Tennis, etc.* to gain or capture (a piece, point, etc.). **18.** to subscribe to. **19.** to adopt and enter upon (a way, course, etc.). **20.** to use (a vehicle, etc.) as a means of travel. **21.** to proceed to occupy. **22.** to receive in a specified manner. **23.** to avail oneself of (an opportunity, etc.). **24.** to obtain (satisfaction or reparation). **25.** to receive or win. **26.** to occupy or consume (space, material, time, etc.). **27.** to attract and hold. **28.** to captivate. **29.** to adopt (a symbol, badge, or the like). **30.** to make, put forth, etc. **31.** to write down (notes, a copy, etc.). **32.** to enter. **33.** to make a picture, esp. a photograph, of. **34.** to make or perform (a measurement, observation, etc.). **35.** to ascertain by inquiry, measurement, etc. **36.** to experience or feel (delight, pride, etc.). **37.** to have effect; act. **38.** to assume as a fact. **39.** to regard or consider. **40.** to undertake (a function, duty, etc.). **41.** to assume, adopt, or appropriate. **42.** to do, perform, execute, etc. **43.** to enter into the enjoyment of (a holiday, etc.). **44.** to require. **45.** to deceive, trick, or cheat. **46.** *Gram.* to have by usage, either as part of itself or with it in construction (a particular form, accent, etc., or a case, mode, etc.). —*v.i.* **47.** to catch or engage. **48.** to strike root. **49.** to have the intended result. **50.** to detract. **51.** to become (sick or ill). **52. take after, a.** to follow the example of. **b.** to resemble. **53. take down, a.** to pull down. **b.** to remove by taking apart. **c.** to write down. **d.** to lower in power, pride, etc. **54. take off, a.** to remove. **b.** to lead off or away. **c.** to depart. **d.** to leave the ground, as an airplane. **e.** *Colloq.* to mimic. **55. take on, a.** to hire. **b.** to undertake to handle. **56. take to, a.** to apply or devote oneself to. **b.** to be disposed (kindly, etc.) to. **c.** to take oneself to. —*n.* **57.** act of taking. **58.** that which is taken. **59.** the quantity of fish, etc., taken at one time. **60.** *Slang.* the profit. **61.** *Motion Pictures.* a portion photographed at one time without break. —tak′er, *n.*

take-off (tāk′ôf′, -ŏf′), *n.* **1.** the leaving of the ground in leaping or (of an aircraft) in beginning a flight. **2.** the place at which one takes off. **3.** *Colloq.* a mimicking.

talc (tălk), *n.*, *v.*, **talcked, talcking** or **talced** (tălkt), **talcing** (tăl′kĭng). —*n.* **1.** Also, **tal·cum** (tăl′kəm). a soft, green-to-gray mineral, hydrous magnesium silicate: used in making lubricants, talcum powder, etc. —*v.t.* **2.** to treat with talc.

talcum powder, powdered talc.

tale (tāl), *n.* **1.** a narrative about some event; story. **2.** a falsehood; lie. **3.** a rumor or piece of gossip.

tale·bear·er (tāl′bâr′ər), *n.* one who spreads gossip. Also, **tale′tell′er.** —**tale′bear′ing, tale′tell′ing,** *adj.*, *n.*

tal·ent (tăl′ənt), *n.* **1.** a special natural ability or aptitude. **2.** persons of ability. **3.** an ancient unit of weight, varying with time and place. **4.** this weight as a monetary unit. —**tal′ent·ed,** *adj.*

tales·man (tālz′mən, tā′lēz mən), *n.*, *pl.* **-men.** a person summoned for jury duty.

tal·is·man (tăl′ĭs mən, -ĭz-), *n.*, *pl.* **-mans.** a stone, ring, or other object supposed to possess occult powers and worn as an amulet or charm.

talk (tôk), *v.i.* **1.** to speak or converse. **2.** to consult. **3.** to gossip. —*v.t.* **4.** to utter. **5.** to discuss. **6.** to bring, put, drive, etc., by talk. —*n.* **7.** speech; conversation. **8.** a conference. **9.** rumor; gossip. **10.** a subject or occasion of talking, esp. of gossip. **11.** mere empty speech. **12.** a way of talking. —**talk′er,** *n.*

talk·a·tive (tô′kə tĭv), *adj.* inclined to talk a great deal. —**talk′a·tive·ly,** *adv.* —**talk′a-tive·ness,** *n.*

talk·ie (tô′kĭ), *n.* *Colloq.* a motion picture with accompanying synchronized speech, singing, etc.

talk·ing-to (tô′kĭng tōō′), *n.*, *pl.* **-tos.** *Colloq.* a scolding.

tall (tôl), *adj.* **1.** of more than average height. **2.** having height as specified. **3.** *Colloq.* high or large in amount. **4.** *Colloq.* difficult to believe. **5.** *Colloq.* grandiloquent.

Tal·la·has·see (tăl′ə hăs′ĭ), *n.* the capital of Florida, in the N part. 16,240.

tal·low (tăl′ō), *n.* **1.** suet. **2.** the hard fat of sheep, cattle, etc., separated by melting from the fibrous and membranous matter naturally mixed with it: used to make candles, soap, etc.

tal·ly (tăl′ĭ), *n.*, *pl.* **-lies,** *v.*, **-lied, -lying.** —*n.* **1.** a stick of wood with notches cut to indicate the amount of a debt or payment. **2.** anything on which a score or account is kept. **3.** a mark made on or in a tally. **4.** an account or record of debit and credit. —*v.t.* **5.** to mark on a tally; record. **6.** to count up. —*v.i.* **7.** to correspond; accord or agree. —**tal′li·er,** *n.*

tal·ly·ho (*n.* tăl′ĭ hō′; *interj.* tăl′ĭ hō′), *n.*, *pl.* **-hos,** *interj.* *Chiefly Brit.* —*n.* **1.** a mail coach or a pleasure coach. —*interj.* **2.** a huntsman's cry on catching sight of the fox.

Tal·mud (tăl′mŭd), *n.* a collection of non-Biblical Jewish laws. —**Tal·mud′ic, Tal·mud′-i·cal,** *adj.*

tal·on (tăl′ən), *n.* a claw, esp. of a bird of prey.

tam (tăm), *n.* tam-o′-shanter.

ta·ma·le (tə mä′lĭ), *n.* a Mexican dish of corn, meat, red peppers, etc.

tam·a·rind (tăm′ə rĭnd), *n.* **1.** the fruit of a large tropical tree, a pod whose juicy acid pulp is used in beverages and food. **2.** the tree, cultivated esp. for its fruit and timber.

tam·bou·rine (tăm′bə rēn′), *n.* a small drum with metal disks in the frame, played by striking with the knuckles, shaking, etc.

tame (tām), *adj.*, **tamer, tamest,** *v.*, **tamed, taming.** —*adj.* **1.** not wild or savage; domesticated. **2.** lacking in animation; dull; insipid. —*v.t.* **3.** to domesticate; subdue. —**tam′a·ble, tame′a·ble,** *adj.* —**tame′ly,** *adv.* —**tame′ness,** *n.* —**tam′er,** *n.*

tam-o′-shan·ter (tăm′ə shăn′tər), *n.* a cap, of Scottish origin, with a flat crown.

tamp (tămp), *v.t.* to force in or down by repeated, light strokes. —**tamp′er,** *n.*

Tam·pa (tăm′pə), *n.* a seaport in W Florida. 108,391.

tam·per (tăm′pər), *v.i.* to meddle, esp. for the purpose of altering, damaging, misusing, etc. —**tam′per·er,** *n.*

tan (tăn), *v.*, **tanned, tanning,** *n.*, *adj.* —*v.t.* **1.** to convert (a hide) into leather. **2.** to make brown by exposure to the sun. **3.** *Colloq.* to thrash. —*v.i.* **4.** to become tanned. —*n.* **5.** the brown color imparted to the skin by exposure to the sun. **6.** light brown. **7.** the bark of the oak, hemlock, etc., bruised and broken by a mill, and used for tanning hides. —*adj.* **8.** yellowish-brown.

tan·a·ger (tăn′ə jər), *n.* any of numerous small, usually brightly colored oscine birds, most of which inhabit the warmer parts of South America.

tan·dem (tăn′dəm), *adv.* **1.** one behind another. —*adj.* **2.** having animals, seats, parts, etc., one behind another. —*n.* **3.** a team of horses so harnessed. **4.** a two-wheeled carriage drawn by horses in tandem. **5.** a tandem bicycle or the like.

tang (tăng), *n.* **1.** a taste or flavor, esp. a strong or distinctive one. **2.** a trace or suggestion of something.

Tan·gan·yi·ka (tăn′gən yē′kə, tăng′-), *n.* Lake, a lake in central Africa: longest freshwater lake in world. ab. 12,700 sq. mi.

tan·gent (tăn′jənt), *adj.* **1.** touching. **2.** *Geom.* touching, as a straight line in relation to a curve or surface. —*n.* **3.** *Geom.* a tangent line or plane. **4.** *Trigon.* (of an angle) a trigonometric function equal to the ratio of the ordinate of the end point of the arc to the abscissa of this end point, the origin being at the center of the circle on which the arc lies and the initial point of the arc being on the x-axis. **5.** a sudden divergence from one course, thought, etc., to another. —**tan′gen·cy,** *n.* —**tan·gen·tial** (tăn jĕn′shəl), *adj.* —**tan·gen′-tial·ly,** *adv.*

tan·ge·rine (tăn′jə rēn′), *n.* a small, loose-skinned variety of mandarin orange.

tan·gi·ble (tăn′jə bəl), *adj.* **1.** discernible by the touch; material. **2.** real or actual. **3.** definite; not vague. —**tan·gi·bil′i·ty, tan′gi·ble·ness,** *n.* —**tan′gi·bly,** *adv.*

Tan·gier (tăn jĭr′), *n.* a seaport in NW Africa, near the Strait of Gibraltar. 79,886.

tan·gle (tăng′gəl), *v.*, **-gled, -gling,** *n.* —*v.t.*, *v.i.* **1.** to bring or come together into a mass of confusedly intertwisted parts; snarl. **2.** to involve in something that hampers or overgrows. **3.** to catch and hold in a net or snare. —*n.* **4.** a tangled condition or mass.

tan·go (tăng′gō), *n.*, *pl.* **-gos,** *v.*, **-goed, -going.** —*n.* **1.** a ballroom dance of Spanish-American origin. —*v.i.* **2.** to dance the tango.

tank (tăngk), *n.* **1.** a large receptacle for water or other liquid or a gas. **2.** a swimming pool. **3.** *Mil.* an armored, self-propelled combat vehicle moving on a caterpillar tread. —*v.t.* **4.** to put or store in a tank.

tank·ard (tăngk′ərd), *n.* a large drinking cup with a handle and hinged cover.

tank·er (tăngk′ər), *n.* a ship having its hold arranged to carry oil or other liquid in bulk.

tan·ner (tăn′ər), *n.* one whose occupation it is to tan hides.

tan·ner·y (tăn′ə rĭ), *n.*, *pl.* **-neries.** a place where tanning is carried on.

tan·nic (tăn′ĭk), *adj.* *Chem.* of, derived from, or related to tan (def. 7).

tan·nin (tăn′ĭn), *n.* *Chem.* any of a group of astringent vegetable compounds, as the whitish compound (**tannic acid**) which occurs in large quantities in nutgalls.

tan·ta·lize (tăn′tə līz′), *v.t.*, **-lized, -lizing.** to torment with the sight of something desired but out of reach. —**tan′ta·li·za′tion,** *n.* —**tan′ta·liz′er,** *n.* —**tan′ta·liz′ing·ly,** *adv.*

tan·ta·lum (tăn′tə ləm), *n.* *Chem.* a rare acid-resistant element. *Symbol:* Ta; *at. wt.:* 180.88; *at. no.:* 73; *sp. gr.:* 16.6.

tan·ta·mount (tăn′tə mount′), *adj.* equivalent, as in value, effect, or signification.

tan·trum (tăn′trəm), *n.* *Colloq.* a burst of ill humor; a fit of ill temper.

tap¹ (tăp), *v.*, **tapped, tapping,** *n.* —*v.t.*, *v.i.* **1.** to strike lightly. —*n.* **2.** a light but audible blow. **3.** (*pl.*) a signal on a drum, bugle, or trumpet, at which all lights in the soldiers′ or sailors′ quarters must be extinguished.

tap² (tăp), *n.*, *v.*, **tapped, tapping.** —*n.* **1.** a cylindrical plug for an opening through which liquid is drawn, as in a cask. **2.** *Chiefly Brit.* a faucet. **3. on tap,** ready. **4.** an instrument for cutting the thread of an internal screw. —*v.t.* **5.** to draw off (liquid) by opening a tap; draw liquid from (any vessel). **6.** to penetrate, reach, etc., for the purpose of drawing something off. **7.** to open outlets from (power lines, highways, pipes, etc.).

tap dance, a dance in which a rhythm is audibly tapped out by the toe or heel. —**tap'-dance,** *v.i.*

tape (tāp), *n.*, *v.*, **taped, taping.** —*n.* **1.** a long narrow strip of linen, cotton, paper, metal, etc. **2.** a tapeline. **3.** a string across the finishing line in a race. —*v.t.* **4.** to furnish with a tape or tapes. **5.** to tie up or wind with tape.

tape·line (tāp'lĭn'), *n.* a long strip, as of linen or steel, marked in inches, feet, etc., for measuring. Also, **tape measure.**

ta·per (tā'pẽr), *v.i.*, *v.t.* **1.** to become or make slenderer toward one end. **2.** to reduce gradually. —*n.* **3.** gradual decrease of size, force, capacity, etc. **4.** a candle, esp. a very slender one. —**ta'per·ing·ly,** *adv.*

tap·es·try (tăp'ĭs trĭ), *n.*, *pl.* **-tries,** *v.*, **-tried, -trying.** —*n.* **1.** a fabric woven with a design, often pictorial, and used for wall hangings, furniture coverings, etc. —*v.t.* **2.** to furnish with tapestry.

tape·worm (tāp'wûrm'), *n.* any of certain flat worms parasitic when adult in the alimentary canal of man and other vertebrates.

tap·i·o·ca (tăp'ĭ ō'kə), *n.* a granular farinaceous food substance prepared from cassava starch, used in puddings, etc.

ta·pir (tā'pẽr), *n.* any of certain slate-colored, swinelike animals, mostly of tropical America, having a flexible proboscis.

tap·room (tăp'rōōm', -rŏŏm'), *n.* *Brit.* a place in which liquor is sold; saloon.

tap·root (tăp'rŏŏt', -rŏŏt'), *n.* *Bot.* a main root descending downward from the radicle and giving off small lateral roots.

tar¹ (tär), *n.*, *v.*, **tarred, tarring.** —*n.* **1.** any of various dark-colored viscid products obtained by the destructive distillation of certain organic substances, such as coal, wood, etc. —*v.t.* **2.** to cover with tar.

tar² (tär), *n.* *Colloq.* a sailor.

tar·an·tel·la (tăr'ən těl'ə), *n.* a rapid, whirling southern Italian dance.

ta·ran·tu·la (tə răn'chə lə), *n.*, *pl.* **-las, -lae** (-lē'). any of certain large, hairy spiders whose bite is painful but not dangerous.

Ta·ra·wa (tä rä'wä), *n.* one of the Gilbert Islands, in the central Pacific: taken by U.S. Marines after severe fighting, Nov., 1943. 2530 pop.; 14 sq. mi.

tar·dy (tär'dĭ), *adj.*, **-dier, -diest. 1.** late. **2.** slow; sluggish. —**tar'di·ly,** *adv.* —**tar'di·ness,** *n.*

tare¹ (târ), *n.* any of various weeds.

tare² (târ), *n.* the weight of the wrapping, receptacle, or conveyance containing goods.

tar·get (tär'gĭt), *n.* **1.** a device, usually marked with concentric circles, aimed at in shooting practice or contests. **2.** anything aimed at. **3.** an object of abuse, scorn, etc.; butt.

tar·iff (tăr'ĭf), *n.* **1.** an official list of duties imposed on exports or imports. **2.** the system of duties so imposed. **3.** any duty in such a list.

tarn (tärn), *n.* *N. Eng.*; *Literary in U.S.* a small mountain lake or pool.

tar·nish (tär'nĭsh), *v.t.* **1.** to dull or alter the luster of; discolor. **2.** to sully. —*v.i.* **3.** to lose luster. **4.** to become sullied. —*n.* **5.** a tarnished coating. **6.** tarnished condition.

tar·pau·lin (tär pô'lĭn), *n.* a protective covering of canvas or other waterproofed material.

tar·pon (tär'pŏn), *n.* a large silvery fish of the warmer waters of the Atlantic, highly prized by anglers.

tar·ry (tăr'ĭ), *v.i.*, **-ried, -rying. 1.** to remain or stay. **2.** to linger or delay.

tart¹ (tärt), *adj.* **1.** sour or acid. **2.** cutting; caustic. —**tart'ly,** *adv.* —**tart'ness,** *n.*

tart² (tärt), *n.* **1.** *U.S.* a small shell of pastry, filled with cooked fruit, etc., and having no top crust. **2.** *Brit.* a covered pie containing fruit. **3.** *Slang.* a prostitute.

tar·tan (tär'tən), *n.* a plaid woolen or worsted cloth, worn chiefly by the Scottish Highlanders, each clan having its distinctive pattern.

tar·tar (tär'tẽr), *n.* **1.** a hard substance deposited on the teeth by the saliva. **2.** the deposit from wines, potassium bitartrate. **3.** the partially purified form of potassium bitartrate, used in baking powder, etc.

Tar·tar (tär'tẽr), *n.* **1.** a member of any of a mingled host of Mongolian, Turkish, and other tribes, now inhabiting large parts of the Soviet Union. **2.** (*also l.c.*) a savage, intractable person. **3.** one who proves unexpectedly troublesome or powerful.

tar·tar·ic (tär tăr'ĭk, -tär'ĭk), *adj.* pertaining to or derived from tartar.

task (tăsk, täsk), *n.* **1.** a definite piece of work assigned or falling to a person. **2. take to task,** to blame or censure. —*v.t.* **3.** to put a strain upon.

task force, *Naval, Mil.* a temporary group of units for carrying out a specific mission.

task·mas·ter (tăsk'mäs'tẽr, täsk'mäs'-), *n.* one who assigns tasks to others.

Tas·ma·ni·a (tăz mā'nĭ ə), *n.* an island S of Australia: one of the states of Australia. 251,063 pop.; 26,215 sq. mi. *Cap.*: Hobart.

tas·sel (tăs'əl), *n.*, *v.*, **-seled, -seling** or (*esp. Brit.*) **-selled, -selling.** —*n.* **1.** an ornamental bunch of threads, small cords, or strands hanging from a roundish knob. —*v.t.* **2.** to furnish with tassels.

taste (tāst), *v.*, **tasted, tasting,** *n.* —*v.t.* **1.** to try the flavor of (something) by taking some into the mouth. **2.** to eat or drink a little (of). **3.** to perceive the flavor of (something). **4.** to experience (something). **5.** to have a particular flavor. —*n.* **6.** act of tasting. **7.** the sense by which the flavor of things is perceived when they are brought into contact with special organs of the mouth. **8.** flavor as perceived by these organs. **9.** a small quantity tasted. **10.** a liking. **11.** the sense of what is fitting, harmonious, or beautiful. **12.** a slight experience or a sample of something. —**taste'ful,** *adj.* —**taste'ful·ly,** *adv.* —**taste'ful·ness,** *n.* —**taste'less,** *adj.* —**taste'less·ly,** *adv.* —**taste'less·ness,** *n.* —**tast'er,** *n.*

tast·y (tās'tĭ), *adj.*, **tastier, tastiest.** *Colloq.* **1.** pleasing to the taste; savory. **2.** having or showing good taste. —**tast'i·ly,** *adv.* —**tast'i·ness,** *n.*

tat (tăt), *v.i.*, *v.t.*, **tatted, tatting.** to do, or make by, tatting.

tat·ter (tăt'ẽr), *n.* **1.** a torn piece hanging loose or separately. **2.** (*pl.*) ragged clothing. —*v.t.* **3.** to tear or wear to tatters. —*v.i.* **4.** to become ragged. —**tat'tered,** *adj.*

tat·ting (tăt'ĭng), *n.* **1.** the making of a kind of knotted lace with a shuttle. **2.** such lace.

tat·tle (tăt'əl), *v.*, **-tled, -tling,** *n.* —*v.i.*, *v.t.* **1.** to let out (secrets). **2.** to chatter or gossip. —*n.* **3.** act of tattling. **4.** idle talk; gossip. —**tat'tler,** *n.*

tat·too¹ (tă tōō'), *n.*, *pl.* **-toos.** a signal on a drum, bugle, or trumpet at night, for soldiers or sailors to repair to their quarters.

tat·too² (tă tōō'), *n.*, *pl.* **-toos,** *v.*, **-tooed, -tooing.** —*n.* **1.** act of marking the skin with indelible pictures, etc., by making punctures in it and inserting pigments. **2.** a picture, etc., so made. —*v.t.* **3.** to mark with tattoos. —**tat·too'er,** *n.*

tau (tô, tou), *n.* the nineteenth letter (T, τ) of the Greek alphabet.

taunt (tônt, tänt), *v.t.* **1.** to reproach in a sarcastic or insulting manner. **2.** to twit. —*n.* **3.** an insulting gibe or sarcasm.

Taun·ton (tän'tən), *n.* a city in SE Massachusetts. 37,395.

taupe (tōp), *n.* dark gray usually tinged with brown, purple, yellow, or green.

Tau·rus (tôr'əs), *n.*, *gen.* **Tauri** (tôr'ī). **1.** the Bull, a zodiacal constellation. **2.** the second sign of the zodiac.

taut (tôt), *adj.* **1.** tightly drawn; tense. **2.** in good order; tidy; neat. —**taut'ly,** *adv.* —**taut'ness,** *n.*

tau·tol·o·gy (tô tŏl'ə jĭ), *n.*, *pl.* **-gies.** needless repetition of an idea, esp. in other words. —**tau·to·log·i·cal** (tô'tə lŏj'ə kəl), *adj.* —**tau'to·log'-i·cal·ly,** *adv.*

tav·ern (tăv'ẽrn), *n.* **1.** a place where liquors are sold to be drunk on the premises. **2.** an inn.

taw (tô), *n.* **1.** a choice playing marble with which to shoot. **2.** a game of marbles.

taw·dry (tô'drĭ), *adj.*, **-drier, -driest.** gaudy; showy and cheap. —**taw'dri·ly,** *adv.* —**taw'dri·ness,** *n.*

taw·ny (tô′nĭ), *adj.*, **-nier, -niest,** *n.* —*adj.* **1.** of a dark yellowish color. —*n.* **2.** dull yellowish brown.

tax (tăks), *n.* **1.** a payment of money for the use of the government. **2.** a burdensome charge, obligation, duty, or demand. —*v.t.* **3.** to impose a tax on. **4.** to lay a burden on. **5.** to censure; reprove. —**tax′a·ble,** *adj.* —**tax′a·bil′i·ty, tax′a·ble·ness,** *n.* —**tax′er,** *n.*

tax·a·tion (tăks ā′shən), *n.* **1.** act of taxing. **2.** fact of being taxed. **3.** a tax imposed. **4.** the revenue raised by taxes.

tax·i (tăk′sĭ), *n.*, *pl.* **taxis,** *v.*, **taxied, taxiing** or **taxying.** —*n.* **1.** taxicab. —*v.i.* **2.** to ride in a taxicab. **3.** (of an airplane) to move over the surface of the ground or water under its own power. —*v.t.* **4.** to cause (an airplane) to taxi.

tax·i·cab (tăk′sĭ kăb′), *n.* an automobile that carries passengers at a certain price.

tax·i·der·my (tăk′sə dûr′mĭ), *n.* the art of preserving the skins of animals and mounting them in lifelike form. —**tax′i·der′mist,** *n.*

tax·on·o·my (tăks ŏn′ə mĭ), *n.* classification, esp. in relation to its principles or laws.

tax·pay·er (tăks′pā′ər), *n.* one who pays a tax or is subject to taxation.

Tay·lor (tā′lər), *n.* **Zachary,** 1784–1850, 12th president of the U.S., 1849–50.

Tb, *Chem.* terbium.

t.b., **1.** trial balance. **2.** tuberculosis.

tbs., tablespoon; tablespoons. Also, **tbsp.**

Tchai·kov·sky (chī kôf′skĭ), *n.* See **Tschaikovsky.**

Te, *Chem.* tellurium.

tea (tē), *n.* **1.** the dried and prepared leaves of a certain Oriental shrub, from which a bitter, aromatic beverage is prepared by infusion in hot water. **2.** the shrub itself. **3.** the beverage so prepared. **4.** *Brit.* a meal (other than dinner) in the late afternoon or the evening. **5.** an afternoon reception at which tea is served.

teach (tēch), *v.t.*, *v.i.*, **taught, teaching.** to impart knowledge of or skill (in or to). —**teach′a·ble,** *adj.* —**teach′er,** *n.* —**teach′ing,** *n.*

tea·cup (tē′kŭp′), *n.* a cup in which tea is served, usually of moderate size.

teak (tēk), *n.* **1.** a large East Indian tree with a hard, durable wood for shipbuilding, etc. **2.** the wood.

tea·ket·tle (tē′kĕt′əl), *n.* a small kettle in which to boil water.

teal (tēl), *n.*, *pl.* **teals,** (*esp. collectively*) **teal.** any of certain small fresh-water ducks.

team (tēm), *n.* **1.** a number of persons associated in some joint action, esp. one side in a match. **2.** two or more horses, oxen, or other animals harnessed together to draw a vehicle, plow, or the like. —*v.t.* **3.** to join together in a team.

team·ster (tēm′stər), *n.* one who drives a team or a truck for hauling.

team·work (tēm′wûrk′), *n.* the work of a team with reference to coördination of effort and to collective efficiency.

tea·pot (tē′pŏt′), *n.* a container in which tea is made and from which it is poured.

tear[1] (tĭr), *n.* a drop of the limpid fluid secreted by the lachrymal gland, appearing in or flowing from the eye. Also, **tear′drop′.**

tear[2] (târ), *v.*, **tore, torn, tearing,** *n.* —*v.t.* **1.** to pull apart by force. **2.** to pull violently or with force. **3.** to distress greatly. **4.** to divide. **5.** to lacerate. **6.** to produce by rending. **7.** to remove by force. —*v.i.* **8.** to become torn. **9.** to make a tear. **10.** *Colloq.* to go with great haste. —*n.* **11.** act of tearing. **12.** a rent or fissure. **13.** a rage or passion. **14.** *Slang.* a spree.

tear·ful (tĭr′fəl), *adj.* **1.** weeping. **2.** causing tears. —**tear′ful·ly,** *adv.*

tear gas (tĭr), a gas used esp. in riots, which makes the eyes smart and water.

tease (tēz), *v.*, **teased, teasing,** *n.* —*v.t.*, *v.i.* **1.** to annoy (a person, etc.) by persistent raillery, etc., usually in sport. —*n.* **2.** act of teasing. **3.** state of being teased. **4.** *Colloq.* one who teases or annoys. —**teas′er,** *n.* —**teas′ing·ly,** *adv.*

tea·spoon (tē′spoon′, -spoon′), *n.* **1.** the small spoon commonly used to stir tea, coffee, etc. **2.** a unit of capacity for household purposes, equal to 1⅓ fluid drams. —**tea′spoon·ful′,** *n.*

teat (tēt), *n.* the protuberance on the breast or udder in most female mammals where the milk ducts discharge; nipple.

tech., technical.

tech·nic (tĕk′nĭk), *n.* **1.** technique. —*adj.* **2.** technical.

tech·ni·cal (tĕk′nə kəl), *adj.* **1.** peculiar to or characteristic of a particular art, science, profession, trade, etc. **2.** using technical terms; treating a subject technically. **3.** skilled in a particular art, trade, etc. **4.** pertaining to or connected with the mechanical or industrial arts and the applied sciences. **5.** so considered from a technical point of view. —**tech′ni·cal·ly,** *adv.* —**tech′ni·cal·ness, tech·ni·cal·i·ty** (tĕk′nə kăl′ə tĭ), *n.*

tech·ni·cian (tĕk nĭsh′ən), *n.* one versed in the technicalities of a subject.

Tech·ni·col·or (tĕk′nə kŭl′ər), *n.* *Trademark.* a system of making color motion pictures by means of superimposing the three primary colors to produce a final colored print.

tech·nique (tĕk nēk′), *n.* method or technical skill, esp. in artistic work.

tech·noc·ra·cy (tĕk nŏk′rə sĭ), *n.* a theory advocating control of industrial resources and reorganization of the social system, based on the findings of technologists and engineers.

tech·nol·o·gy (tĕk nŏl′ə jĭ), *n.* **1.** the branch of knowledge that deals with the industrial arts. **2.** technical nomenclature. —**tech·nol′o·gist,** *n.* —**tech·no·log·i·cal** (tĕk′nə lŏj′ə kəl), **tech′no·log′ic,** *adj.* —**tech′no·log′i·cal·ly,** *adv.*

Te De·um (tē dē′əm), an ancient hymn of praise and thanksgiving.

te·di·ous (tē′dĭ əs, tē′jəs), *adj.* long and tiresome. —**te′di·ous·ly,** *adv.* —**te′di·ous·ness,** *n.*

te·di·um (tē′dĭ əm), *n.* state of being wearisome; tediousness.

tee (tē), *n.*, *v.*, **teed, teeing.** *Golf.* —*n.* **1.** a hard mound of earth at the beginning of play for each hole. **2.** a rubber, plastic, or wood object from which the ball is driven at the beginning of a hole. —*v.t.*, *v.i.* **3.** to place (the ball) on a tee. **4.** to strike (the ball) from a tee.

teem (tēm), *v.i.* to abound or swarm.

teens (tēnz), *n.pl.* the years of one's age (13–19) of which the numbers end in *-teen.* —**teen′-ag′er,** *n.*

tee·pee (tē′pē), *n.* tepee.

tee·ter (tē′tər), *Chiefly U.S. Colloq.* —*v.i.*, *v.t.* **1.** to seesaw. **2.** to move unsteadily. —*n.* **3.** a seesaw.

teethe (tēth), *v.i.*, **teethed, teething.** *Dentistry.* to grow teeth; cut one's teeth.

tee·to·tal (tē tō′təl), *adj.* **1.** of, advocating, or pledged to total abstinence from intoxicating drink. **2.** *Colloq.* complete. —**tee·to′tal·er,** *n.* —**tee·to′tal·ly,** *adv.*

Te·gu·ci·gal·pa (tĕ goo′sĕ gäl′pä), *n.* the capital of Honduras, in the S part. 47,223.

Te·he·ran (tĕ′ə răn′, -răn′), *n.* the capital of Iran, in the N part. 540,087. Also, **Te·hran′.**

tel., **1.** telegram. **2.** telegraph. **3.** telephone.

Tel-A·viv (tĕl′ə vēv′), *n.* a city in W Israel. 166,660.

tel·e·cast (tĕl′ə kăst′, -käst′), *v.*, **-cast** or **-casted, -casting,** *n.* —*v.i.*, *v.t.* **1.** to broadcast by television. —*n.* **2.** a television broadcast.

tel·e·gram (tĕl′ə grăm′), *n.* a communication sent by telegraph.

tel·e·graph (tĕl′ə grăf′, -gräf′), *n.* **1.** an apparatus, system, or process for transmitting messages to a distance, esp. over connecting electric wires. —*v.t.*, *v.i.* **2.** to transmit (a message) by telegraph. —**te·leg·ra·pher** (tə lĕg′rə fər); *Brit.,* **te·leg′ra·phist,** —**tel·e·graph′ic, tel′e·graph′i·cal,** *adj.* —**tel′e·graph′i·cal·ly,** *adv.*

te·leg·ra·phy (tə lĕg′rə fĭ), *n.* the art or practice of operating telegraphs.

te·lep·a·thy (tə lĕp′ə thĭ), *n.* communication of one mind with another by some means beyond what is ordinary or normal. —**te·lep′a·thist,** *n.* —**tel·e·path·ic** (tĕl′ə păth′ĭk), *adj.* —**tel′e·path′i·cal·ly,** *adv.*

tel·e·phone (tĕl′ə fōn′), *n.*, *v.*, **-phoned, -phoning.** —*n.* **1.** an apparatus, system, or process for transmission of sound or speech to a distant point, esp. by an electrical device. —*v.t.*, *v.i.* **2.** to speak to (a person) by telephone. **3.** to send (a message) by telephone. —**tel′e·phon′er,** *n.* —**tel·e·phon·ic** (tĕl′ə fŏn′ĭk), *adj.* —**tel′e·phon′i·cal·ly,** *adv.*

te·leph·o·ny (tə lĕf′ə nĭ), *n.* the art or practice of operating telephones.

tel·e·pho·to (tĕl′ə fō′tō), *adj.* noting or pertaining to telephotography or to a telephotographic lens.

tel·e·pho·tog·ra·phy (tĕl'ə fə tŏg'rə fĭ), n. 1. the art of photographing objects with a lens that produces a large image from a given distance. 2. the art of electrically reproducing facsimiles over a communications channel. —**tel·e·pho·to·graph·ic** (tĕl'ə fō'tə grăf'ĭk), adj.

tel·e·ran (tĕl'ə răn'), n. a system of aircraft navigation using radar to map the sky above an airfield, which, together with other pertinent data, is transmitted by television to the airplane approaching the field.

tel·e·scope (tĕl'ə skōp'), n., adj., v., -scoped, -scoping. —n. 1. an optical instrument for making distant objects appear nearer and larger. —adj. 2. consisting of parts which fit and slide one within another. —v.t., v.i. 3. to force or slide together, one into another. —**tel·e·scop·ic** (tĕl'ə skŏp'ĭk), **tel'e·scop'i·cal**, adj. —**tel'e·scop'i·cal·ly**, adv.

Tel·e·type (tĕl'ə tīp'), n. Trademark. teletypewriter.

tel·e·type·writ·er (tĕl'ə tīp'rī'tər), n. a telegraphic apparatus by which signals are sent and received on instruments resembling typewriters.

tel·e·view (tĕl'ə vū'), v.t., v.i. to view with a television receiver. —**tel'e·view'er**, n.

tel·e·vise (tĕl'ə vīz'), v.t., -vised, -vising. to send or receive by television.

tel·e·vi·sion (tĕl'ə vĭzh'ən), n. a system of transmitting scenes to great distances by first changing light waves into electrical waves, and then, at the receiving set, changing the electrical waves into light waves again.

tell (tĕl), v., told, telling. —v.t. 1. to narrate; relate. 2. to make known; communicate. 3. to announce or proclaim. 4. to utter (the truth, etc.). 5. to divulge (something secret). 6. to say positively. 7. to discern so as to identify. 8. to distinguish. 9. to inform (a person, etc.) of something. 10. to assure emphatically. 11. to bid, order, or command. 12. to mention one after another, as in enumerating. 13. tell off, to scold or rebuke severely. —v.i. 14. to give an account. 15. to disclose something secret. 16. to operate effectively. 17. to produce a marked effect.

tell·er (tĕl'ər), n. 1. a narrator. 2. one employed in a bank to receive or pay out money over the counter. 3. one who counts votes in a legislative body.

tell·ing (tĕl'ĭng), adj. effective; striking. —**tell'ing·ly**, adv.

tell·tale (tĕl'tāl'), n. 1. one who reveals private or confidential matters. 2. a thing serving to reveal or disclose something. —adj. 3. that reveals what is not intended to be known.

tel·lu·ri·um (tĕ lŏŏr'ĭ əm), n. Chem. a rare poisonous silver-white element. Symbol: Te; at. wt.: 127.61; at. no.: 52.

te·mer·i·ty (tə mĕr'ə tĭ), n. reckless boldness; rashness.

temp., 1. temperature. 2. temporary.

tem·per (tĕm'pər), n. 1. the particular state or habit of mind, esp. with respect to irritability. 2. heat of mind or passion, shown in outbursts of anger, etc. 3. calm disposition. 4. the particular degree of hardness and elasticity imparted to steel, etc., by tempering. —v.t. 5. to moderate or mitigate. 6. to soften or tone down. 7. to heat and cool or quench (metal) to bring the proper degree of hardness, elasticity, etc. 8. to tune (a keyboard instrument, as a piano, etc.) so as to make the tones available in different keys. —v.i. 9. to be or become tempered. —**tem'pered**, adj.

tem·per·a·ment (tĕm'pər ə mənt, -prə mənt), n. natural disposition.

tem·per·a·men·tal (tĕm'pər ə mĕn'təl, -prə mĕn'-), adj. 1. having a strongly marked individual temperament. 2. moody, irritable, or sensitive. 3. constitutional. —**tem'per·a·men'tal·ly**, adv.

tem·per·ance (tĕm'pər əns), n. moderation or self-control, esp. in the use of alcoholic liquors.

tem·per·ate (tĕm'pər ĭt), adj. 1. moderate or self-restrained, esp. in the use of alcoholic liquors. 2. moderate in temperature. —**tem'per·ate·ly**, adv. —**tem'per·ate·ness**, n.

Temperate Zone, Geog. the parts of the earth's surface lying between each of the tropics and the polar circles nearest to it.

tem·per·a·ture (tĕm'pər ə chər, -prə chər), n. 1. the property of a body that determines the sensation of warmth or coldness received from it.

2. Physiol., Pathol. a. the degree of heat of a living body. b. the excess of this above the normal.

tem·pest (tĕm'pĭst), n. 1. a violent wind, usually attended with rain, hail, or snow. 2. a violent commotion, disturbance, or tumult. —**tem·pes·tu·ous** (tĕm pĕs'chŏŏ əs), adj. —**tem·pes'tu·ous·ly**, adv. —**tem·pes'tu·ous·ness**, n.

tem·ple[1] (tĕm'pəl), n. 1. a place dedicated to the worship of a deity or deities. 2. (also cap.) any of the three successive buildings in ancient Jerusalem devoted to the worship of Jehovah. 3. any large building.

tem·ple[2] (tĕm'pəl), n. the flat region on either side of the human forehead.

tem·po (tĕm'pō), n., pl. -pos, -pi (-pē). 1. Music. relative rapidity or rate of movement. 2. characteristic rate, rhythm, or pattern of work or activity.

tem·po·ral[1] (tĕm'pə rəl), adj. 1. of or pertaining to time. 2. secular or worldly. 3. temporary; transitory. —**tem'po·ral·ly**, adv.

tem·po·ral[2] (tĕm'pə rəl), adj. Anat. noting or pertaining to the temple.

tem·po·rar·y (tĕm'pə rĕr'ĭ), adj. existing or effective for a time only; not permanent. —**tem'po·rar·i·ly**, adv.

tem·po·rize (tĕm'pə rīz'), v.i., -rized, -rizing. 1. to act indecisively or evasively to delay matters. 2. to yield temporarily or ostensibly to current opinion or circumstances. 3. to effect a compromise. —**tem'po·ri·za'tion**, n. —**tem'po·riz'er**, n.

tempt (tĕmpt), v.t. 1. to induce by enticement. 2. to appeal strongly to. 3. to incite, esp. to evil. 4. to provoke. —**tempt'er**, n. —**tempt'ress**, n. fem. —**tempt'ing**, adj. —**tempt'ing·ly**, adv.

temp·ta·tion (tĕmp tā'shən), n. 1. act of tempting. 2. something that tempts. 3. fact or state of being tempted. 4. an instance of it.

ten (tĕn), n. 1. a cardinal number, nine plus one. 2. a symbol for this number, as 10 or X. —adj. 3. amounting to ten in number.

ten·a·ble (tĕn'ə bəl), adj. capable of being defended, as against attack. —**ten'a·bly**, adv.

te·na·cious (tĭ nā'shəs), adj. 1. holding fast. 2. highly retentive. 3. persistent or obstinate. 4. adhesive or sticky. 5. cohesive; tough. —**te·na'cious·ly**, adv. —**te·na'cious·ness**, **te·nac·i·ty** (tĭ năs'ə tĭ), n.

ten·an·cy (tĕn'ən sĭ), n., pl. -cies. 1. holding, as of lands, by any kind of title; tenure. 2. the period of a tenant's occupancy. 3. a holding, or piece of land held by a tenant.

ten·ant (tĕn'ənt), n. 1. one who holds land, a house, or the like, of another (the landlord) for a period of time. 2. an occupant of any place. —v.t. 3. to hold or occupy as a tenant. —**ten'ant·less**, adj.

Ten Commandments, the precepts spoken by God to Israel (Exodus 20, Deut. 10) or delivered to Moses (Exodus 24:12, 34) on Mount Sinai.

tend[1] (tĕnd), v.i. 1. to incline, or be inclined, in action or effect. 2. to lead, as a road, etc.

tend[2] (tĕnd), v.t. 1. to attend to by work, care, etc. 2. to watch over and care for. —v.i. 3. to attend or wait with service. 4. to attend by action, care, etc.

tend·en·cy (tĕn'dən sĭ), n., pl. -cies. 1. natural or prevailing disposition to move, proceed, or act toward some point, end, or result. 2. an inclination, bent, or predisposition.

ten·der[1] (tĕn'dər), adj. 1. soft or delicate. 2. not strong or hardy. 3. young or immature. 4. soft-hearted; sympathetic. 5. kind; compassionate. 6. affectionate or loving. 7. acutely or painfully sensitive. 8. easily broken; fragile. 9. requiring careful or tactful handling. —v.t. 10. to make tender. —**ten'der·ly**, adv. —**ten'der·ness**, n.

ten·der[2] (tĕn'dər), v.t. 1. to present formally for acceptance. 2. to offer. —n. 3. an offer of something for acceptance. 4. that which is offered. 5. Law. an offer, as of money, in payment of a debt or other obligation. —**ten'der·er**, n.

tend·er[3] (tĕn'dər), n. 1. one who tends. 2. an auxiliary vessel employed to attend one or more other vessels, as for supplying provisions. 3. a car attached to a steam locomotive, for carrying coal, water, etc.

ten·der·foot (tĕn'dər fŏŏt'), n., pl. -foots, -feet (-fēt'). Colloq. 1. an inexperienced person; novice. 2. Western U.S. a newcomer to the ranching and mining regions.

ten·der-heart·ed (tĕn'dər här'tĭd), *adj.* soft-hearted; sympathetic. —**ten'der-heart'ed·ness,** *n.*

ten·der·loin (tĕn'dər loin'), *n.* **1.** a strip of tender meat forming part of the loin of beef, pork, etc. **2.** (*cap.*) a district in a city noted for vice and police corruption.

ten·don (tĕn'dən), *n.* *Anat.* a band of dense, tough, inelastic, white fibrous tissue, serving to connect a muscle with a bone or part; sinew.

ten·dril (tĕn'drĭl), *n.* *Bot.* a threadlike organ of climbing plants which attaches itself to some other body so as to support the plant.

ten·e·ment (tĕn'ə mənt), *n.* **1.** a dwelling house. **2.** a tenement house.

tenement house, a crowded, dilapidated apartment house in the poorer part of a large city.

ten·et (tĕn'ĭt, tē'nĭt), *n.* any opinion, principle, doctrine, dogma, or the like.

ten·fold (*adj.* tĕn'fōld'; *adv.* tĕn'fōld'), *adj.,* *adv.* ten times as great or as much.

Ten·nes·see (tĕn'ə sē'), *n.* **1.** a State in the SE United States. 2,997,826 pop.; 42,246 sq. mi. *Cap.*: Nashville. *Abbr.*: **Tenn.** **2.** a river flowing from E Tennessee through N Alabama, W Tennessee, and SW Kentucky into the Ohio near Paducah. 652 mi. —**Ten'nes·se'an,** *adj., n.*

ten·nis (tĕn'ĭs), *n.* a game in which a ball is driven with a racket (**tennis racket**) back and forth over a net, usually by two players, in a specially constructed, enclosed, oblong court (**tennis court**).

Ten·ny·son (tĕn'ə sən), *n.* **Alfred, 1st Baron,** 1809–1892, British poet.

ten·on (tĕn'ən), *n.* a projection at the end of a piece of wood, etc., for insertion in a corresponding cavity (mortise) in another piece, so as to form a joint.

ten·or (tĕn'ər), *n.* **1.** continuous course, progress, or movement. **2.** the purport; drift. **3.** *Music.* **a.** the adult male voice intermediate between the bass and the alto. **b.** a singer with such a voice. —*adj.* **4.** *Music.* of, pertaining to, or having the compass of, a tenor.

ten·pins (tĕn'pĭnz'), *n.* **1.** (*construed as sing.*) a game played with ten wooden pins at which a ball is bowled to knock them down. **2.** (*construed as pl.*) the pins used in such a game.

tense¹ (tĕns), *adj.,* **tenser, tensest,** *v.,* **tensed, tensing.** —*adj.* **1.** stretched tight; taut; rigid. **2.** in a state of mental or nervous strain. **3.** characterized by a strain upon the feelings. —*v.t., v.i.* **4.** to make or become tense. —**tense'·ly,** *adv.* —**tense'ness, ten'si·ty,** *n.*

tense² (tĕns), *n.* *Gram.* a category of verb inflection denoting the location of the action or state in past, present, or future time.

ten·sile (tĕn'sĭl), *adj.* **1.** of or pertaining to tension. **2.** ductile. —**ten·sil'i·ty,** *n.*

ten·sion (tĕn'shən), *n.* **1.** act of stretching or straining. **2.** state of being stretched or strained. **3.** mental or emotional strain. **4.** a strained state of mutual relations. **5.** *Physics.* pressure.

tent (tĕnt), *n.* **1.** a portable shelter, usually of canvas, supported by one or more poles and extended by ropes fastened to pegs in the ground. —*v.i.* **2.** to live in a tent.

ten·ta·cle (tĕn'tə kəl), *n.* **1.** *Zool.* any of various slender, flexible processes or appendages which serve as organs of touch, etc. **2.** *Bot.* a sensitive filament. —**ten·tac·u·lar** (tĕn tăk'yə·lər), *adj.*

ten·ta·tive (tĕn'tə tĭv), *adj.* made or done as a trial; experimental. —**ten'ta·tive·ly,** *adv.* —**ten'ta·tive·ness,** *n.*

ten·ter·hook (tĕn'tər hŏŏk'), *n.* **1.** one of the hooks which hold cloth stretched on a frame. **2. on tenterhooks,** in suspense.

tenth (tĕnth), *adj.* **1.** next after the ninth. **2.** being one of ten equal parts. —*n.* **3.** a tenth part, esp. of one (¹/₁₀). **4.** the tenth member of a series. —**tenth'ly,** *adv.*

ten·u·ous (tĕn'yŏŏ əs), *adj.* **1.** thin or slender in form. **2.** rare or rarefied. **3.** of slight importance or significance. —**ten'u·ous·ly,** *adv.* —**ten'u·ous·ness, ten·u·i·ty** (tĕn ū'ə tĭ, tĭ nōō'-), *n.*

ten·ure (tĕn'yər), *n.* **1.** the holding or possessing of anything, esp. real property. **2.** the period or terms of holding something.

te·pee (tē'pē), *n.* a wigwam.

tep·id (tĕp'ĭd), *adj.* lukewarm. —**te·pid'i·ty, tep'id·ness,** *n.* —**tep'id·ly,** *adv.*

ter·bi·um (tûr'bĭ əm), *n.* *Chem.* a rare-earth metallic element. *Symbol:* **Tb;** *at. no.:* **65;** *at. wt.:* 159.2.

term (tûrm), *n.* **1.** any word, or group of linguistic forms, naming something, esp. as used in some particular field of knowledge. **2.** the period through which something lasts. **3.** each of certain stated periods into which instruction is regularly organized for students in schools. **4.** a set time or date, as for the payment of rent. **5.** (*pl.*) conditions with regard to payment, price, wages, etc. **6.** (*pl.*) stipulations limiting what is proposed to be granted or done. **7.** (*pl.*) footing or standing. **8.** (*pl.*) an agreement. **9.** *Alg., Arith., etc.* each of the members of which an expression or the like is composed. —*v.t.* **10.** to name; call; designate.

ter·ma·gant (tûr'mə gənt), *n.* a violent, turbulent, or brawling woman; shrew. —**ter'ma·gan·cy,** *n.*

ter·mi·na·ble (tûr'mə nə bəl), *adj.* that may be terminated. —**ter'mi·na·bly,** *adv.*

ter·mi·nal (tûr'mə nəl), *adj.* **1.** situated at or forming the end; concluding. —*n.* **2.** a terminal part or structure; end or extremity. **3.** an originating and terminating point for trains, airlines, buses, etc., often including yards, shop facilities, etc. **4.** *Elect.* the mechanical device by means of which an electrical connection to an apparatus is established. —**ter'mi·nal·ly,** *adv.*

ter·mi·nate (tûr'mə nāt'), *v.,* **-nated, -nating.** —*v.t.* **1.** to bring to an end. **2.** to occur at the conclusion of. —*v.i.* **3.** to end, conclude, or cease.

ter·mi·na·tion (tûr'mə nā'shən), *n.* **1.** act of terminating. **2.** fact of being terminated. **3.** a bound or limit. **4.** an end or extremity. **5.** *Gram.* a suffix or ending.

ter·mi·nol·o·gy (tûr'mə nŏl'ə jĭ), *n., pl.* **-gies.** the system of terms belonging to a science, art, or subject.

ter·mi·nus (tûr'mə nəs), *n., pl.* **-ni** (-nī'), **-nuses.** **1.** the end or extremity of anything. **2.** either end of a railroad line, bus line, etc. **3.** a goal or end. **4.** a boundary or limit.

ter·mite (tûr'mīt), *n.* any of certain pale-colored, soft-bodied, social insects which are very destructive to buildings, furniture, etc.

tern (tûrn), *n.* any of certain aquatic birds allied to the gulls but usually having a slenderer body and bill, smaller feet, a long and deeply forked tail, and a more graceful flight.

Terp·sich·o·re (tûrp sĭk'ə rĭ), *n.* *Gk. Myth.* the Muse of dancing and choral song.

Worker termite (³⁄₄ in. long)

terp·si·cho·re·an (tûrp'sə kə rē'ən), *adj.* **1.** pertaining to dancing. **2.** (*cap.*) of or pertaining to Terpsichore. —*n.* **3.** *Colloq.* a dancer.

ter·race (tĕr'əs), *n., v.,* **-raced, -racing.** —*n.* **1.** a raised level with a sloping front, esp. one of a series of such levels. **2.** the flat roof on a house. **3.** an open (usually paved) area connected with a house and serving as an outdoor living area. **4.** a row of houses running along the face or top of a slope. —*v.t.* **5.** to form into or furnish with a terrace.

ter·ra cot·ta (tĕr'ə kŏt'ə), **1.** a hard, usually unglazed earthenware of fine quality, used for statuettes, vases, etc. **2.** something made of this. **3.** a brownish-orange color. —**ter'ra-cot'ta,** *adj.*

ter·ra fir·ma (tĕr'ə fûr'mə), solid earth.

ter·rain (tĕ rān', tĕr'ān), *n.* a tract of land, esp. with reference to its natural features, military advantages, etc.

ter·ra·pin (tĕr'ə pĭn), *n.* any of certain edible North American fresh-water or tide-water turtles.

Ter·re Haute (tĕr'ə hōt'), a city in W Indiana. 62,693.

ter·res·tri·al (tə rĕs'trĭ əl), *adj.* **1.** pertaining to, consisting of, or representing the earth. **2.** growing or living on land or in the ground. **3.** worldly; mundane.

ter·ri·ble (tĕr'ə bəl), *adj.* **1.** causing terror; dreadful. **2.** distressing; severe. **3.** *Colloq.* extremely unpleasant or bad. —**ter'ri·ble·ness,** *n.* —**ter'ri·bly,** *adv.*

ter·ri·er (tĕr'ĭ ər), *n.* a variety of dog with a propensity to pursue prey, as the fox, badger, etc., into its burrow. Among its breeds are the fox terrier, schnauzer, and Scotch terrier.

ter·rif·ic (tə rĭf'ĭk), *adj.* **1.** terrifying. **2.** *Colloq.* extraordinarily great, intense, etc. —**ter·rif'i·cal·ly,** *adv.*

ter·ri·fy (tĕr′ə fī′), *v.t.*, **-fied, -fying.** to fill with terror. —**ter′ri·fi′er,** *n.*

ter·ri·to·ry (tĕr′ə tōr′Y), *n., pl.* **-ries.** **1.** a region or district. **2.** the land and waters under the jurisdiction of a state, sovereign, etc. **3.** (*cap.*) **a.** *U.S.* a region not admitted to the Union as a State but having its own legislature, with a governor and other officers appointed by the President and confirmed by the Senate. **b.** some similar district elsewhere, as in Canada. **4.** the district assigned to a sales representative, agent, or the like. —**ter′ri·to′ri·al,** *adj.* —**ter′ri·to′ri·al·ly,** *adv.*

ter·ror (tĕr′ər), *n.* **1.** intense, sharp, overmastering fear. **2.** a feeling, instance, or cause of intense fear.

ter·ror·ism (tĕr′ə rĭz′əm), *n.* **1.** the use of terrorizing methods. **2.** state of fear and submission so produced. —**ter′ror·ist,** *n.* —**ter′ror·is′tic,** *adj.*

ter·ror·ize (tĕr′ə rīz′), *v.t.,* **-ized, -izing. 1.** to fill with terror. **2.** to dominate by intimidation. —**ter′ror·i·za′tion,** *n.*

ter·ry (tĕr′Y), *n., pl.* **-ries.** a pile fabric with loops on both sides. Also, **terry cloth.**

terse (tûrs), *adj.,* **terser, tersest.** concise; brief and pithy. —**terse′ly,** *adv.* —**terse′ness,** *n.*

ter·ti·ar·y (tûr′shY ĕr′Y, tûr′shə rY), *adj.* of the third order, rank, formation, etc.

test (tĕst), *n.* **1.** that by which the presence, quality, or genuineness of anything is determined; trial. **2.** a trial of the quality of something. **3.** *Educ.* a form of examination for evaluating the performance and capabilities of a student or class. —*v.t.* **4.** to subject to a test. —**test′a·ble,** *adj.* —**test′er,** *n.*

Test., Testament.

tes·ta·ment (tĕs′tə mənt),· *n.* **1.** *Law.* a formal declaration, usually in writing, of a person's wishes as to the disposition of his property after his death. **2.** See **Old Testament** and **New Testament.** —**tes′ta·men′ta·ry,** *adj.*

tes·ti·cle (tĕs′tə kəl), *n. Anat., Zool.* the male sex gland, either of two oval glands located in the scrotal sac.

tes·ti·fy (tĕs′tə fī′), *v.i., v.t.,* **-fied, -fying. 1.** to give or afford evidence (of). **2.** *Law.* to give (testimony) under oath or solemn affirmation. **3.** to declare, profess, or acknowledge openly. —**tes′ti·fi′er,** *n.*

tes·ti·mo·ni·al (tĕs′tə mō′nY əl), *n.* **1.** a writing certifying to a person's character or qualifications, or to a thing's value, excellence, etc. —*adj.* **2.** pertaining to or serving as testimony.

tes·ti·mo·ny (tĕs′tə mō′nY), *n., pl.* **-nies. 1.** *Law.* the statement of a witness under oath or affirmation. **2.** proof. **3.** open declaration or profession, as of faith.

tes·tis (tĕs′tYs), *n., pl.* **-tes** (-tēz). testicle.

test tube, *Chem.* a hollow cylinder of thin glass with one end closed.

tes·ty (tĕs′tY), *adj.,* **-tier, -tiest.** irritably impatient; touchy. —**tes′ti·ly,** *adv.* —**tes′ti·ness,** *n.*

tet·a·nus (tĕt′ə nəs), *n. Pathol.* an infectious, often fatal disease, due to a bacillus which enters the body through wounds, characterized by violent spasms and rigidity of many or all the voluntary muscles.

tête-à-tête (tāt′ə tāt′), *adj.* **1.** of, between, or for two persons together, without others. —*n.* **2.** a private conversation. —*adv.* **3.** together in private.

teth·er (tĕth′ər), *n.* **1.** a rope, chain, or the like, by which an animal is fastened, as to a stake. —*v.t.* **2.** to fasten or confine with or as with a tether.

tet·ra·he·dron (tĕt′rə hē′drən), *n., pl.* **-drons, -dra** (-drə). *Geom.* a solid contained by four plane faces; a triangular pyramid. —**tet′ra·he′dral,** *adj.*

te·tram·e·ter (tĕ trăm′ə tər), *Pros.* —*adj.* **1.** having four measures. —*n.* **2.** a tetrameter line.

tet·ra·va·lent (tĕt′rə vā′lənt, tĕ trăv′ə lənt), *adj. Chem.* having a valence of 4.

Teu·ton (tū′tən, tōō′tən), *n.* **1.** a native of Germany or a person of German origin. —*adj.* **2.** Teutonic.

Teu·ton·ic (tū tŏn′Yk, tōō-), *adj.* **1.** of or pertaining to the ancient Germanic people. **2.** German. **3.** denoting or pertaining to the northern European stock which includes the German, Dutch, Scandinavian, British, and related peoples. **4.** (of languages) Germanic.

Tex·as (tĕk′səs), *n.* a State in the S United States. 6,959,481 pop.; 267,339 sq. mi. *Cap.:* Austin. *Abbr.:* **Tex.** —**Tex′an,** *adj., n.*

text (tĕkst), *n.* **1.** the main body of matter in a book or manuscript. **2.** the original words of an author in distinction from a translation, paraphrase, or the like. **3.** any of the various forms in which a writing exists. **4.** a textbook. **5.** a short passage of Scripture, esp. as the subject of a sermon, etc.

text·book (tĕkst′bŏŏk′), *n.* a book used by students as a standard work for a particular branch of study.

tex·tile (tĕks′tYl, -tīl), *n.* **1.** any woven material. —*adj.* **2.** woven or capable of being woven. **3.** of or pertaining to weaving.

tex·tu·al (tĕks′chŏŏ əl), *adj.* of or pertaining to the text. —**tex′tu·al·ly,** *adv.*

tex·ture (tĕks′chər), *n.* the characteristic surface structure or disposition of the constituent parts of a body. —**tex′tur·al,** *adj.*

-th, the suffix of ordinal numerals (*fourth, tenth, twentieth*), the form *-th* being added in one or two cases to altered stems of the cardinal.

Th, *Chem.* thorium.

T.H., Territory of Hawaii.

Thack·er·ay (thăk′ə rY), *n.* **William Makepeace,** 1811–63, British novelist.

Thai·land (tī′land), *n.* Official name of **Siam.** —**Thai** (tä′ē, tī), *adj., n.*

thal·li·um (thăl′Y əm), *n. Chem.* a soft, malleable, rare, metallic element. *Symbol:* Tl; *at. wt.:* 204.39; *at. no.:* 81; *sp. gr.:* 11.85 at 20°C.

Thames (tĕmz), *n.* a river flowing from SW England E through London to the North Sea. 209 mi.

than (thăn; *unstressed* thən),· *conj.* a particle used after comparative adjectives and adverbs and certain other words, such as *other, otherwise, else,* etc., to introduce the second member of a comparison.

than·a·top·sis (thăn′ə tŏp′sYs), *n.* a view or contemplation of death.

thane (thān), *n. Early Eng. Hist.* a person ranking between an earl and an ordinary freeman, holding lands of the king or lord by military service.

thank (thăngk), *v.t.* **1.** to express gratitude to. **2.** to be responsible or at fault for. —*n.* **3.** (*usually pl.*) the expression of grateful feeling by words or otherwise. **4.** (*pl.*) a common elliptical expression used in acknowledging a favor, service, courtesy, or the like. **5. thanks to,** a. thanks be given to. b. as a result of. —**thank′ful,** *adj.* —**thank′ful·ly,** *adv.* —**thank′ful·ness,** *n.* —**thank′less,** *adj.* —**thank′less·ly,** *adv.* —**thank′less·ness,** *n.*

thanks·giv·ing (thăngks′gYv′Yng), *n.* **1.** grateful acknowledgment of benefits or favors, esp. to God. **2.** (*cap.*) *U.S.* Thanksgiving Day.

Thanksgiving Day, *U.S.* an annual festival in acknowledgment of Divine favor, usually the last Thursday of November.

that (thăt; *unstressed* thət), *pron., pl.* **those,** and *adj.; adv.; conj.* —*pron. and adj.* **1.** a demonstrative pronoun and adjective indicating: **a.** a person, thing, idea, etc., as pointed out, present, mentioned, etc. **b.** one of two persons, things, etc., already mentioned (opposed to *this*). **2.** a relative pronoun used: **a.** as the subject or object of a relative clause (sometimes replaceable by *who, whom,* or *which*). **b.** as the object of a preposition, the preposition standing at the end of the relative clause. **c.** in various special or elliptical constructions. —*adv.* **3.** to that extent; —*conj.* **4.** a conjunction used: **a.** to introduce a clause as the subject or object of the principal verb or as the necessary complement to a statement made, or a clause expressing reason, aim, result, etc. **b.** elliptically, to introduce a sentence or clause expressing desire, surprise, or indignation.

thatch (thăch), *n.* **1.** a material, as straw, rushes, leaves, or the like, used to cover roofs, etc. —*v.t.* **2.** to cover with thatch. —**thatch′er,** *n.* —**thatch′y,** *adj.*

thaw (thô), *v.i.* **1.** to melt. **2.** to become less formal or reserved. —*v.t.* **3.** to cause to thaw. —*n.* **4.** act or process of thawing. **5.** a condition of the weather caused by the rise of the temperature above the freezing point.

the[1] (*stressed* thē; *unstressed before a consonant* thə; *unstressed before a vowel* thY), *def. art.* a word used, esp. before nouns, with a specifying or particularizing effect, as opposed to the indefinite or generalizing force of the indefinite article *a* or *an*.

the² (t͟hə, t͟hĭ), *adv.* a word used to modify an adjective or adverb in the comparative degree, signifying "in or by that," "on that account," "in or by so much," or "in some or any degree."

theat., theater.

the·a·ter (thē′ə tər), *n.* **1.** a building designed to house dramatic presentations, etc. **2.** the drama. **3.** a place of action; field of operations. Also, *esp. Brit.,* **the′a·tre.**

the·at·ri·cal (thĭ ăt′rə kəl), *adj.* Also, **the·at′·ric. 1.** of or pertaining to the theater. **2.** artificial, pompous, spectacular, or extravagantly histrionic. —*n.* **3.** (*pl.*) dramatic performances. —**the·at′ri·cal·ly,** *adv.*

Thebes (thēbz), *n.* an ancient ruined city in Upper Egypt, on the Nile: a former capital of Egypt. —**The·ban** (thē′bən), *adj., n.*

thee (t͟hē), *pron. Archaic.* you.

theft (thĕft), *n.* **1.** act of stealing. **2.** an instance of this.

their (t͟hâr; *unstressed* t͟hər), *pron.* **1.** the possessive form of **they** used before a noun. **2.** (*pl.*) the form of **their** used predicatively or without a noun following.

the·ism (thē′ĭz əm), *n.* the belief in one God as the creator and ruler of the universe. —**the′ist,** *n., adj.* —**the·is′tic,** *adj.*

Thebes (c1450 B.C.)

them (t͟hĕm; *unstressed* t͟həm), *pron.* objective case of **they.**

theme (thēm), *n.* **1.** a subject of discourse, discussion, meditation, or composition; topic. **2.** a short, informal essay. **3.** *Music.* **a.** a principal subject in a composition. **b.** a short subject from which variations are developed. —**the·mat·ic** (thē măt′ĭk), *adj.*

them·selves (t͟həm sĕlvz′), *pron.* **1.** an emphatic form of **them** or **they. 2.** a reflexive form of **them.**

then (t͟hĕn), *adv.* **1.** at that time. **2.** soon afterward. **3.** next in order of time. **4.** at another time. **5.** in addition; besides. **6.** in that case. **7.** therefore. —*adj.* **8.** being; being such. —*n.* **9.** that time.

thence (t͟hĕns), *adv.* **1.** from that place. **2.** from that time. **3.** therefore.

thence·forth (t͟hĕns′fôrth′, t͟hĕns′fôrth′), *adv.* from that time or place onward. Also, **thence·for·ward** (t͟hĕns′fôr′wərd).

the·oc·ra·cy (thē ŏk′rə sĭ), *n., pl.* **-cies.** a form of government in which God or a deity is recognized as the supreme civil ruler, His laws being interpreted by the ecclesiastical authorities.

theol., theology.

the·o·lo·gian (thē′ə lō′jən, -jĭ ən), *n.* one versed in theology.

the·ol·o·gy (thē ŏl′ə jĭ), *n., pl.* **-gies.** the science which treats of God, His attributes, and His relations to the universe. —**the·o·log′i·cal** (thē′ə lŏj′ə kəl), *adj.* —**the′o·log′i·cal·ly,** *adv.*

the·o·rem (thē′ə rəm, thĭr′əm), *n.* **1.** *Math.* a statement embodying something to be proved. **2.** a rule or law, esp. one expressed by an equation or formula.

the·o·ret·i·cal (thē′ə rĕt′ə kəl), *adj.* **1.** of or in theory; not practical. **2.** hypothetical. **3.** speculative. Also, **the′o·ret′ic.** —**the′o·ret′i·cal·ly,** *adv.*

the·o·rist (thē′ə rĭst), *n.* one who deals mainly with the theory of a subject.

the·o·rize (thē′ə rīz′), *v.i.,* **-rized, -rizing.** to form a theory. —**the′o·riz′er,** *n.*

the·o·ry (thē′ə rĭ, thĭr′ĭ), *n., pl.* **-ries. 1.** a coherent group of general propositions used as principles of explanation for a class of phenomena. **2.** a proposed explanation whose status is still conjectural. **3.** a body of principles or the like belonging to one subject. **4.** that department of a science or art which deals with its principles.

the·os·o·phy (thē ŏs′ə fĭ), *n.* any of various forms of thought in which claim is made to a special insight into the divine nature or to a special divine revelation.

ther·a·peu·tic (thĕr′ə pū′tĭk), *adj.* pertaining to the treating or curing of disease. Also, **ther′a·peu′ti·cal.**

ther·a·peu·tics (thĕr′ə pū′tĭks), *n.* the branch of medicine concerned with the remedial treatment of disease.

ther·a·py (thĕr′ə pĭ), *n., pl.* **-pies.** the treatment of disease. —**ther′a·pist,** *n.*

there (t͟hâr), *adv.* **1.** in or at that place. **2.** at that point in an action, speech, etc. **3.** in that matter, particular, or respect. **4.** into or to that place. —*n.* **5.** that place.

there·a·bout (t͟hâr′ə bout′), *adv.* **1.** near that place or time. **2.** about that number, amount, etc. Also, **there′a·bouts′.**

there·af·ter (t͟hâr ăf′tər, -äf′-), *adv.* after that in time or sequence; afterward.

there·at (t͟hâr ăt′), *adv. Archaic.* **1.** at that place, time, etc.; there. **2.** by reason of that.

there·by (t͟hâr bī′), *adv.* **1.** by means of that. **2.** in that connection.

there·for (t͟hâr fôr′), *adv.* for that or this.

there·fore (t͟hâr′fôr′), *adv.* as a result; consequently.

there·from (t͟hâr frŏm′, -frŭm′), *adv.* from that place, thing, etc.

there·in (t͟hâr ĭn′), *adv.* **1.** in that place or thing. **2.** in that matter, etc.

there·in·to (t͟hâr ĭn′tōō, t͟hâr′ĭn tōō′), *adv.* into that place, thing, matter, etc.

there·of (t͟hâr ŏv′, -ŭv′), *adv.* **1.** of that or it. **2.** from that as a source of origin.

there·on (t͟hâr ŏn′, -ôn′), *adv.* **1.** on or upon that or it. **2.** immediately after that.

there·to (t͟hâr tōō′), *adv.* to that place, thing, matter, etc.

there·un·der (t͟hâr ŭn′dər), *adv.* **1.** under that. **2.** under the authority of that.

there·up·on (t͟hâr′ə pŏn′, -pôn′), *adv.* **1.** immediately following that. **2.** in consequence of that. **3.** upon that or it. **4.** with reference to that.

there·with (t͟hâr wĭth′, -wĭth′), *adv.* **1.** with that. **2.** in addition to that. **3.** following upon that; thereupon.

there·with·al (t͟hâr′wĭth ôl′, -wĭth-), *adv.* **1.** together with that. **2.** following upon that.

ther·mal (thûr′məl), *adj.* of or pertaining to heat or temperature.

ther·mo·dy·nam·ics (thûr′mō dī năm′ĭks, -dĭ-), *n.* the science concerned with the relations between heat and mechanical energy or work. —**ther′mo·dy·nam′ic,** **ther′mo·dy·nam′i·cal,** *adj.*

ther·mo·e·lec·tric·i·ty (thûr′mō ĭ lĕk′trĭs′ə tĭ, -ē′lĕk-), *n.* electricity produced directly from heat, as that generated (in the form of a current) when the ends of two dissimilar metallic conductors are joined to form a closed circuit and one of the junctions is heated. —**ther′mo·e·lec′tric,** **ther′mo·e·lec′tri·cal,** *adj.*

ther·mom·e·ter (thər mŏm′ə tər), *n.* an instrument for measuring temperature, as by means of the expansion and contraction of mercury or alcohol in a capillary tube and bulb.

ther·mo·plas·tic (thûr′mə plăs′tĭk), *adj.* **1.** soft and pliable whenever heated, as some plastics, without any change of the inherent properties. —*n.* **2.** such a plastic.

Ther·mop·y·lae (thər mŏp′ə lē′), *n.* a narrow pass in E Greece: heroic defense by the Spartans against the Persians, 480 B.C.

Ther·mos (thûr′məs), *n. Trademark.* a bottle or the like so made that the interior container is protected by a vacuum which keeps the contents hot or cold.

ther·mo·set·ting (thûr′mō sĕt′ĭng), *adj.* pertaining to a type of plastic which becomes hard and unmoldable when it is heated and which is resistant to additional applications of heat once it is set, as the urea resins.

ther·mo·stat (thûr′mə stăt′), *n.* a device which regulates the temperature of a heating system, etc., or signals a change in temperature for manual adjustment. —**ther′mo·stat′ic,** *adj.* —**ther′mo·stat′i·cal·ly,** *adv.*

the·sau·rus (thĭ sôr′əs), *n., pl.* **-sauri** (-sôr′ī). **1.** a storehouse of words or knowledge; dictionary. **2.** a treasury.

these (t͟hēz), *pron.* pl. of **this.**

The·seus (thē′sōōs, -sĭ əs), *n. Gk. Legend.* the chief hero of Attica (region around Athens).

the·sis (thē′sĭs), *n., pl.* **-ses** (-sēz). **1.** a proposition to be discussed and proved or to be maintained against objections. **2.** a subject for a composition. **3.** a dissertation, as one presented by a candidate for a degree. **4.** *Music.* (in conducting) the downward stroke in a measure.

Thes·pi·an (thĕs'pĭ ən), *adj.* **1.** of or pertaining to the dramatic art; tragic; dramatic. —*n.* **2.** an actor or actress.

the·ta (thā'tə, thē'tə), *n.* the eighth letter (Θ, θ) of the Greek alphabet.

they (thā), *pron.* **1.** nominative plural of **he, she,** and **it.** **2.** people in general.

thi·a·mine (thī'ə mēn', -mĭn), *n. Biochem.* a complex organic compound whose chloride, vitamin B₁, is important in the prevention of beriberi. Also, **thi·a·min** (thī'ə mĭn).

thick (thĭk), *adj.* **1.** having relatively great extent from one surface or side to its opposite; not thin. **2.** measuring in depth. **3.** compact; dense. **4.** numerous; abundant. **5.** filled; covered. **6.** having relatively great consistency. **7.** (of darkness, etc.) dense; deep. **8.** husky; hoarse; muffled. **9.** containing much solid matter in suspension or solution. **10.** *Colloq.* intimate. **11.** slow of mental apprehension. —*adv.* **12.** in a thick manner. —*n.* **13.** that which is thick. **14.** the thickest, densest, or most crowded part. **15. through thick and thin,** under all circumstances; unwaveringly. —**thick'ly,** *adv.* —**thick'ness,** *n.*

thick·en (thĭk'ən), *v.t., v.i.* to make or become thicker. —**thick'en·er,** *n.* —**thick'en·ing,** *n.*

thick·et (thĭk'ĭt), *n.* a thick growth of shrubs, bushes, or small trees.

thick-set (thĭk'sĕt'), *adj.* **1.** set thickly; dense. **2.** heavily or solidly built.

thick-skinned (thĭk'skĭnd'), *adj.* **1.** having a thick skin. **2.** not sensitive to criticism, reproach, rebuff, etc.

thief (thēf), *n., pl.* **thieves.** one who steals, esp. secretly or without open force.

thieve (thēv), *v.t., v.i.* **thieved, thieving.** to steal. —**thiev'ish,** *adj.* —**thiev'ish·ly,** *adv.* —**thiev'ish·ness,** *n.*

thiev·er·y (thē'və rĭ), *n., pl.* **-eries.** stealing; theft.

thigh (thī), *n.* that part of the leg between the hip and the knee in man.

thim·ble (thĭm'bəl), *n.* a small cap, usually of metal or plastic, worn on the finger to push the needle in sewing.

thin (thĭn), *adj.,* **thinner, thinnest,** *adv., v.,* **thinned, thinning.** —*adj.* **1.** having relatively little extent from one surface or side to its opposite; not thick. **2.** slender. **3.** having little flesh; lean. **4.** not dense; sparse; scanty. **5.** having relatively slight consistency, as a liquid; fluid; rare or rarefied, as air, etc. **6.** unsubstantial. **7.** flimsy. **8.** weak and shrill. **9.** lacking body, richness, or strength. —*adv.* **10.** in a thin manner. —*v.t., v.i.* **11.** to make or become thinner. —**thin'ly,** *adv.* —**thin'ner,** *n.* —**thin'ness,** *n.*

thine (thīn), *pron., adj. Archaic.* the possessive form of *thou* used predicatively or without a noun following, or before a noun beginning with a vowel or *h.* Cf. **thy.**

thing (thĭng), *n.* **1.** an inanimate object. **2.** some entity, object, or creature. **3.** a matter or affair. **4.** a fact or circumstance. **5.** an action, deed, or performance. **6.** a particular or respect. **7.** clothes or apparel. **8.** *(pl.) Colloq.* personal belongings. **9. the thing, a.** that which is proper, correct, or fashionable. **b.** that which is important or necessary.

think (thĭngk), *v.,* **thought, thinking.** —*v.t.* **1.** to form or conceive (a thought, etc.) in the mind. **2.** to meditate; ponder. **3.** to recollect or remember. **4.** to have in mind, intent, or purpose. **5.** to hold as an opinion; believe. **6.** to give continued thought to, as in order to reach a decision. —*v.i.* **7.** to use the mind. **8.** to form or have an idea. **9.** to reflect upon the matter in question. **10.** to remember. **11.** to have consideration or regard. **12.** to form or have a plan. **13.** to have a (high, low, or other) opinion. **14. think better of, a.** to think more favorably of. **b.** to think more sensibly of. —**think'a·ble,** *adj.* —**think'er,** *n.*

think·ing (thĭngk'ĭng), *adj.* **1.** reasoning. **2.** thoughtful. —*n.* **3.** thought.

thin-skinned (thĭn'skĭnd'), *adj.* **1.** having a thin skin. **2.** sensitive to criticism, etc.

third (thûrd), *adj.* **1.** next after the second. **2.** being one of three equal parts. —*n.* **3.** a third part, esp. of one (1/3). **4.** the third member of a series. **5.** *Music.* **a.** a tone on the third degree from a given tone. **b.** the interval between such tones. —**third'ly,** *adv.*

third degree, *Chiefly U.S.* the use of brutal

measures by the police (or others) in extorting information or a confession.

thirst (thûrst), *n.* **1.** a sensation of dryness in the mouth and throat caused by need of drink. **2.** strong or eager desire; craving. —*v.i.* **3.** to be thirsty. **4.** to have a strong desire.

thirst·y (thûrs'tĭ), *adj.,* **thirstier, thirstiest. 1.** craving drink. **2.** dry or arid. **3.** eagerly desirous; eager. —**thirst'i·ly,** *adv.* —**thirst'i·ness,** *n.*

thir·teen (thûr'tēn'), *n.* **1.** a cardinal number, ten plus three. **2.** a symbol for this number, as 13 or XIII. —*adj.* **3.** amounting to thirteen in number. —**thir'teenth',** *adj., n.*

thir·ty (thûr'tĭ), *n., pl.* **-ties,** *adj.* —*n.* **1.** a cardinal number, ten times three. **2.** a symbol for this number, as 30 or XXX. —*adj.* **3.** amounting to thirty in number. —**thir'ti·eth,** *adj., n.*

thir·ty-sec·ond note (thûr'tĭ sĕk'ənd), *Music.* a note or rest having 1/32 of the time value of a whole note or rest.

this (thĭs), *pron., pl.* **these** (thēz), *and adj.; adv.* —*pron. and adj.* **1.** a demonstrative term indicating a person, thing, idea, etc., as pointed out, present, or near, etc. —*adv.* **2.** to the present or indicated extent.

this·tle (thĭs'əl), *n.* **1.** any of certain prickly composite plants, one species of which has handsome purple flower heads. **2.** any of various other prickly plants. —**this'tly,** *adj.*

thith·er (thĭth'ər, thĭth'ər), *adv.* to or toward that place or point.

tho (thō), *conj., adv.* though.

thole (thōl), *n.* a pin inserted in a boat's gunwale or the like, to act as a fulcrum for the oar, or either of two such pins between which the oar works. Also, **thole·pin** (thōl'pĭn').

Thom·as (tŏm'əs), *n.* **1.** *Bible.* an apostle who demanded proof of Christ's resurrection. **2. Norman Mattoon,** born 1884, U.S. socialist leader.

thong (thông), *n.* **1.** a narrow strip of hide or leather, used as a fastening, as the lash of a whip, etc. **2.** a similar strip of some other material.

Thor (thôr), *n. Scand. Myth.* the ancient god of thunder.

tho·rac·ic (thō răs'ĭk), *adj.* of or pertaining to the thorax.

tho·rax (thôr'ăks), *n., pl.* **thoraxes, thoraces** (thôr'ə sēz'). **1.** the part of the trunk between the neck and the abdomen, containing the cavity in which the heart, lungs, etc., are situated. **2.** (in insects) the portion of the body between the head and the abdomen.

Tho·reau (thôr'ō, thə rō'), *n.* **Henry David,** 1817–62, U.S. naturalist and author.

tho·ri·um (thôr'ĭ əm), *n. Chem.* a radioactive metallic element. *Symbol:* Th; *at. wt.:* 232.12; *at. no.:* 90; *sp. gr.:* 11.2.

thorn (thôrn), *n.* **1.** a sharp excrescence on a plant; prickle. **2.** any of certain thorny shrubs or trees. **3.** something that wounds or causes annoyance. —**thorn'y,** *adj.*

tho·ron (thôr'ŏn), *n. Chem.* a radioactive isotope of radon, produced by the disintegration of thorium. *Symbol:* Tn; *at. wt.:* 220; *at. no.:* 86.

thor·ough (thûr'ō), *adj.* **1.** complete or perfect. **2.** thoroughgoing; leaving nothing undone. Also, **thor'o.** —**thor'ough·ly,** *adv.* —**thor'ough·ness,** *n.*

thor·ough·bred (thûr'ō brĕd', thûr'ə-), *adj.* **1.** of pure breed, stock, or race, as a horse. **2.** well-bred. —*n.* **3.** a thoroughbred animal. **4.** a well-bred person.

thor·ough·fare (thûr'ō fâr', thûr'ə-), *n.* a road, street, or the like, open at both ends.

thor·ough·go·ing (thûr'ō gō'ĭng, thûr'ə-), *adj.* **1.** doing things thoroughly. **2.** complete; unqualified.

those (thōz), *pron., adj. pl.* of **that.**

thou (thou), *pron.* you (now little used except provincially, archaically, in poetry or elevated prose, in addressing the Deity, and by Quakers).

though (thō), *conj.* **1.** notwithstanding that. **2.** even if. **3.** yet, still, or nevertheless. **4.** if (usually in *as though*). —*adv.* **5.** however.

thought (thôt), *n.* **1.** the product of mental action. **2.** an idea or notion. **3.** mental activity. **4.** intention; purpose. **5.** expectation. **6.** attention; regard.

thought·ful (thôt'fəl), *adj.* **1.** contemplative; meditative. **2.** full of thought. **3.** careful, heedful, or mindful. **4.** considerate. —**thought'ful·ly,** *adv.* —**thought'ful·ness,** *n.*

thought·less (thôt/lĭs), *adj.* **1.** unthinking, careless, or heedless. **2.** showing lack of thought. **3.** inconsiderate. —**thought/less·ly,** *adv.* —**thought/less·ness,** *n.*

thou·sand (thou/zənd), *n.* **1.** a cardinal number, ten times one hundred. **2.** a symbol for this number, as 1000 or M. —*adj.* **3.** amounting to one thousand in number. —**thou/sand·fold/,** *adj., adv.* —**thou/sandth,** *adj., n.*

thrall (thrôl), *n.* **1.** a bondman or slave. **2.** Also, **thrall/dom.** bondage; slavery.

thrash (thrăsh), *v.t.* **1.** to beat or defeat thoroughly. **2.** to thresh (wheat, etc.). —*v.i.* **3.** to beat, toss, or plunge wildly. —*n.* **4.** act of thrashing.

thrash·er (thrăsh/ər), *n.* **1.** one that thrashes. **2.** any of certain long-tailed thrushlike birds allied to the mockingbird.

thread (thrĕd), *n.* **1.** a fine cord of flax, cotton, or other fibrous material spun out to considerable length. **2.** a filament of glass or other ductile substance. **3.** something having the fineness of a thread, as a fine line of color or a thin seam of ore. **4.** the helical ridge of a screw. **5.** that which runs through the whole course of something, connecting successive parts, as the sequence of events in a narrative. —*v.t., v.i.* **6.** to pass the end of a thread through the eye in (a needle). **7.** to fix (beads, etc.) upon a thread that is passed through. **8.** to make (one's way) through (a forest, a crowd, etc.).

thread·bare (thrĕd/bâr/), *adj.* **1.** shabby. **2.** hackneyed or trite. **3.** meager, scanty, or poor.

threat (thrĕt), *n.* **1.** a declaration of an intention to inflict punishment, pain, or loss on someone in retaliation for some action; menace. **2.** an indication of probable evil to come.

threat·en (thrĕt/ən), *v.t., v.i.* **1.** to utter a threat (against); menace. **2.** to endanger. **3.** to offer (a punishment, etc.) by way of a threat. **4.** to give an ominous indication (of). —**threat/en·ing·ly,** *adv.*

three (thrē), *n.* **1.** a cardinal number, two plus one. **2.** a symbol for this number, as 3 or III. —*adj.* **3.** amounting to three in number. —**three/fold/,** *adj., adv.*

three·pence (thrĭp/əns, thrĕp/əns), *n.* **1.** a sum of three English pennies. **2.** a British silver coin worth three pennies.

three·ply (thrē/plī/), *adj.* consisting of three thicknesses, layers, or the like.

thren·o·dy (thrĕn/ə dĭ), *n., pl.* **-dies.** a song of lamentation, esp. for the dead.

thresh (thrĕsh), *v.t., v.i.* **1.** to separate the grain or seeds from (a cereal plant, etc.), as by beating with a flail. **2.** to discuss (a matter) exhaustively. —**thresh/er,** *n.*

thresh·old (thrĕsh/ōld, thrĕsh/hōld), *n.* **1.** the sill of a doorway. **2.** the entrance to a building. **3.** *Psychol., Physiol.* the limit below which a given stimulus, or the difference between two stimuli, ceases to be perceptible.

thrice (thrīs), *adv.* three times.

thrift (thrĭft), *n.* economical management; frugality. —**thrift/less,** *adj.*

thrift·y (thrĭf/tĭ), *adj.,* **thriftier, thriftiest.** frugal; provident. —**thrift/i·ly,** *adv.* —**thrift/i·ness,** *n.*

thrill (thrĭl), *v.t., v.i.* **1.** to affect (one) with a sudden wave of keen emotion. **2.** to vibrate or quiver. —*n.* **3.** a tremor or tingling sensation passing through the body as the result of sudden keen emotion. **4.** thrilling quality, as of a story. **5.** a vibration or quivering. —**thrill/ing·ly,** *adv.*

thrill·er (thrĭl/ər), *n.* **1.** one that thrills. **2.** *Colloq.* a sensational play or story.

thrive (thrīv), *v.i.,* **throve** or **thrived, thrived** or **thriven, thriving. 1.** to grow vigorously; flourish. **2.** to prosper.

throat (thrōt), *n.* the passage from the mouth to the stomach or to the lungs.

throat·y (thrō/tĭ), *adj.,* **throatier, throatiest.** produced or modified in the throat.

throb (thrŏb), *v.,* **throbbed, throbbing,** *n.* —*v.i.* **1.** to beat with increased force or rapidity; palpitate. **2.** to vibrate. —*n.* **3.** act of throbbing.

throe (thrō), *n.* **1.** a violent spasm or pang. **2.** (*pl.*) the pains of childbirth. **3.** (*pl.*) the agony of death.

throm·bo·sis (thrŏm bō/sĭs), *n. Pathol.* coagulation of the blood in any part of the circulatory system.

throne (thrōn), *n., v.,* **throned, throning.** —*n.* **1.** the official chair occupied by a sovereign,

bishop, or other exalted personage. **2.** sovereign power or authority. —*v.t., v.i.* **3.** to set or sit on a throne.

throng (thrông, thrŏng), *n.* **1.** a multitude of people; crowd. —*v.i., v.t.* **2.** to crowd.

throt·tle (thrŏt/əl), *n., v.,* **-tled, -tling.** —*n.* **1.** a lever, pedal, or other device to control the amount of fuel being fed to an engine. —*v.t.* **2.** to strangle, choke, or suffocate. **3.** to silence or check. **4.** *Mach.* to obstruct the flow of (steam, etc.) by means of a throttle.

through (thrōō), *prep.* **1.** in at one end or side of and out at the other. **2.** during the whole period of. **3.** having reached the end of. **4.** having finished successfully. **5.** by means of. **6.** by reason of. —*adv.* **7.** in at one end, side, or surface and out at the other. **8.** all the way. **9.** throughout. **10.** to the end. **11.** to a favorable or successful conclusion. —*adj.* **12.** passing from one end to the other. **13.** that goes with little or no interruption.

through·out (thrōō out/), *prep.* **1.** in or to every part of. **2.** from the beginning to the end of. —*adv.* **3.** in every part. **4.** at every moment or point.

throw (thrō), *v.,* **threw, thrown, throwing,** *n.* —*v.t.* **1.** to propel or cast. **2.** to project (a shadow, etc.). **3.** to put hastily. **4.** *Mach.* to move (a lever, etc.) in order to connect or disconnect parts of an apparatus. **5.** to cause to fall to the ground. **6.** *U.S. Colloq.* to permit an opponent to win (a race, contest, or the like). **7.** (of a horse, etc.) to cause to fall off. —*v.i.* **8.** to cast, fling, or hurl a missile, etc. —*n.* **9.** a cast or fling. **10.** the distance to which anything is thrown. —**throw/er,** *n.*

throw·back (thrō/băk/), *n.* **1.** a setback or check. **2.** reversion to an ancestral type.

thru (thrōō), *prep., adv., adj.* through.

thrum (thrŭm), *v.,* **thrummed, thrumming,** *n.* —*v.i., v.t.* **1.** to play on (a stringed instrument, as a guitar), by plucking the strings. **2.** to tap with the fingers. —*n.* **3.** act or sound of thrumming. —**thrum/mer,** *n.*

thrush (thrŭsh), *n.* any of certain passerine birds, most of which are moderate in size, migratory, gifted as songsters, and not brightly colored.

thrust (thrŭst), *v.,* **thrust, thrusting,** *n.* —*v.t., v.i.* **1.** to push forcibly; shove. **2.** to put (one, oneself, etc.) forcibly into some condition, etc. **3.** to stab or pierce. —*n.* **4.** a forcible push or drive; lunge or stab. **5.** the linear force generated by an engine-driven propeller or by exciting gases (as in jet propulsion). **6.** *Mech., Archit., etc.* a pushing force or pressure exerted by a thing or a part against a contiguous one.

thud (thŭd), *n., v.,* **thudded, thudding.** —*n.* **1.** a dull sound, as of a heavy fall. —*v.i., v.t.* **2.** to beat or strike with a dull sound of heavy impact.

thug (thŭg), *n.* a gangster or killer.

thu·li·um (thōō/lĭ əm), *n. Chem.* a rare-earth metallic element. *Symbol:* Tm; *at. wt.:* 169.4; *at. no.:* 69.

thumb (thŭm), *n.* **1.** the short, thick inner finger of the human hand, next to the forefinger. **2.** under the thumb of, under the power or influence of. —*v.t.* **3.** to soil or wear with the thumbs in handling. **4.** to run through (the pages of a book, etc.) quickly. **5.** to solicit or get (a ride) by pointing the thumb in the direction of one's travel.

thumb·screw (thŭm/skrōō/), *n.* **1.** an old instrument of torture by which one or both thumbs were compressed. **2.** a screw whose head may be turned easily with the thumb and a finger.

thumb·tack (thŭm/tăk/), *n.* a tack with a large, flat head, pushed by the thumb.

thump (thŭmp), *n.* **1.** a dull-sounding blow with something thick and heavy. **2.** the sound made by such a blow. —*v.t., v.i.* **3.** to pound. **4.** to beat violently, as the heart.

thun·der (thŭn/dər), *n.* **1.** the loud noise which accompanies a flash of lightning, due to violent disturbance of the air by a discharge of electricity. **2.** any loud, resounding noise. —*v.i.* **3.** to give forth thunder. **4.** to speak in a very loud tone. —**thun/der·er,** *n.* —**thun/der·ous,** *adj.*

thun·der·bolt (thŭn/dər bōlt/), *n.* **1.** a flash of lightning with the accompanying thunder. **2.** something very destructive, terrible, severe, sudden, or startling.

thun·der·clap (thŭn/dər klăp/), *n.* a crash of thunder.

thun·der·cloud (thŭn/dər kloud/), *n.* an electrically charged cloud producing lightning and thunder.

thun·der·head (thŭn′dər hĕd′), *n.* one of the round swelling masses of cumulous clouds appearing above the horizon when conditions are right for thunderstorms.

thun·der·show·er (thŭn′dər shou′ər), *n.* a shower accompanied by thunder and lightning.

thun·der·storm (thŭn′dər stôrm′), *n.* a storm of thunder and lightning, and usually rain.

thun·der·struck (thŭn′dər strŭk′), *adj.* overcome with consternation; confounded or astounded.

Thurs., Thursday. Also, **Thur.**

Thurs·day (thûrz′dĭ), *n.* the fifth day of the week, following Wednesday.

thus (thŭs), *adv.* 1. in this way. 2. accordingly; consequently. 3. to this extent.

thwack (thwăk), *v.t.* 1. to strike or beat vigorously with something flat. —*n.* 2. a sharp blow with something flat.

thwart (thwôrt), *v.t.* 1. to oppose successfully; frustrate; prevent. —*n.* 2. a seat across a boat, esp. one used by an oarsman. —*adj.* 3. cross; transverse. —*prep.*, *adv.* 4. across.

thy (thī), *pron.*, *adj.* the possessive form corresponding to **thou** and **thee**, used before a noun. Cf. **thine.**

thyme (tīm), *n.* any of certain plants of the mint family, esp. one with aromatic leaves used for seasoning.

thy·mus (thī′məs), *n. Anat.* a glandular body of uncertain function near the base of the neck. An animal thymus used as food is called *sweetbread.*

thy·roid (thī′roid), *adj.* 1. noting or pertaining to the thyroid gland. 2. noting or pertaining to the principal cartilage of the larynx, known in men as "Adam's apple." —*n.* 3. the thyroid gland. 4. the thyroid cartilage.

thyroid gland, a ductless gland on either side of the windpipe. Its internal secretion is important in regulating the rate of metabolism and, consequently, body growth.

thy·self (thī sĕlf′), *pron.* 1. an emphatic appositive to **thou** or **thee.** 2. a substitute for reflexive **thee.**

ti (tē), *n. Music.* the seventh note of the diatonic scale; si.

Ti, *Chem.* titanium.

ti·ar·a (tī âr′ə, tī är′ə), *n.* 1. a jeweled ornamental coronet worn by women. 2. a diadem worn by the Pope.

Ti·ber (tī′bər), *n.* a river in central Italy, flowing through Rome into the Mediterranean. 244 mi.

Ti·bet (tǐ bĕt′), *n.* a country in S Asia, N of the Himalayas: nominally a dependency of China. 3,700,000 pop.; ab. 469,400 sq. mi. *Cap.:* Lhasa. —**Ti·bet′an,** *adj.*, *n.*

tib·i·a (tǐb′ĭ ə), *n.*, *pl.* **tibiae** (tǐb′ĭ ē′), **tibias.** the inner of the two bones of the lower leg, extending from the knee to the ankle. —**tib′i·al,** *adj.*

tic (tǐk), *n. Pathol.* a sudden, painless, purposeless muscular twitch.

tick[1] (tǐk), *n.* 1. a slight, sharp, recurring click, as of a clock. 2. a small mark serving as a check or the like. —*v.i.* 3. to produce a tick, as a clock. —*v.t.* 4. to mark with a tick.

tick[2] (tǐk), *n.* any of certain bloodsucking, mitelike animals.

tick[3] (tǐk), *n.* 1. the cloth case of a mattress, pillow, etc., containing hair, feathers, or the like. 2. *Colloq.* ticking.

tick·er (tǐk′ər), *n.* 1. one that ticks. 2. a telegraphic instrument which automatically prints stock prices and market reports, etc., on a tape (**ticker tape**). 3. *Slang.* the heart.

tick·et (tǐk′ĭt), *n.* 1. a slip, usually of cardboard, serving as evidence of the holder's title to some service, right, or the like. 2. a label or tag. 3. *U.S.* a list of candidates named by a political party, faction, etc. —*v.t.* 4. to attach a ticket to.

tick·ing (tǐk′ĭng), *n.* a strong cotton fabric, usually twilled, used esp. for ticks.

tick·le (tǐk′əl), *v.*, **-led, -ling,** *n.* —*v.t.*, *v.i.* 1. to touch (a person, etc.) lightly with the fingers, a feather, etc., so as to excite a tingling or itching sensation in; titillate. 2. to gratify. 3. to amuse. —*n.* 4. act of tickling. 5. a tickling sensation. —**tick′ler,** *n.*

tick·lish (tǐk′lǐsh), *adj.* 1. sensitive to tickling.

2. risky; difficult. —**tick′lish·ly,** *adv.* —**tick′lish·ness,** *n.*

Ti·con·der·o·ga (tī′kŏn də rō′gə), *n.* a village in NE New York: captured by Americans under Ethan Allen (1775). 3402.

tid·al (tī′dəl), *adj.* 1. of, pertaining to, or characterized by tides. 2. dependent on the state of the tide as to time of departure.

tidal wave, a large, destructive, ocean wave produced by an earthquake or the like.

tid·bit (tǐd′bǐt′), *n.* 1. a delicate bit of food. 2. a choice bit of anything, as news.

tid·dly·winks (tǐd′lǐ wǐngks′), *n.* a game, the object of which is to snap small disks into a cup.

tide (tīd), *n.*, *v.*, **tided, tiding.** —*n.* 1. the periodic rise and fall of the waters of the ocean and its inlets, due to the attraction of the moon and sun. 2. a stream or current. —*v.t.* 3. to get (a person, etc.) over a difficulty, a period of distress, or the like.

tide·wa·ter (tīd′wô′tər, -wŏt′ər), *n.* 1. water affected by the tide. 2. seacoast.

ti·dings (tī′dǐngz), *n.pl.* (*sometimes construed as sing.*) news; information.

ti·dy (tī′dǐ), *adj.*, **-dier, -diest,** *v.*, **-died, -dying,** *n.*, *pl.* **-dies.** —*adj.* 1. neat; orderly. 2. *Colloq.* moderately satisfactory. 3. *Colloq.* considerable. —*v.t.*, *v.i.* 4. to make tidy. —*n.* 5. *Chiefly U.S.* an ornamental covering for protecting the back of a chair, etc. —**ti′di·ly,** *adv.* —**ti′di·ness,** *n.*

tie (tī), *v.*, **tied, tying,** *n.* —*v.t.*, *v.i.* 1. to bind or fasten with a cord, string, or the like. 2. to confine, restrict, or limit. 3. to oblige, as to do something. 4. to equal, or be equal, in a contest. —*n.* 5. that with which anything is tied. 6. a necktie. 7. a state of equality in points, votes, etc., as among competitors. 8. a match or contest in which this occurs. 9. anything, as a beam, rod, etc., joining two or more things or parts. 10. *Music.* a curved line connecting two notes on the same line or space to indicate that the sound is to be sustained for their joint value, not repeated. 11. *Railroads.* one of the transverse beams, commonly of wood, to which the rails that form a track are fastened. —**ti′er,** *n.*

Tien·tsin (tǐn′tsǐn′), *n.* a city and port in NE China. 1,218,000.

tier (tǐr), *n.* 1. a row, range, or rank. 2. one of a series of rows rising one behind or above another. —*v.t.* 3. to arrange in tiers. —*v.i.* 4. to rise in tiers.

tie-up (tī′ŭp′), *n.* a stoppage of business, transportation, etc., on account of a strike, storm, accident, etc.

tiff (tǐf), *n.* 1. a petty quarrel. —*v.i.* 2. to have a petty quarrel.

ti·ger (tī′gər), *n.* a large, carnivorous feline of Asia, tawny-colored, striped with black, ranging from India and the Malay Peninsula to Siberia. —**ti·gress** (tī′grǐs), *n. fem.*

tiger lily, a lily with flowers of a dull-orange color spotted with black.

tight (tīt), *adj.* 1. firmly or closely fixed in place. 2. drawn tense; taut. 3. fitting closely. 4. difficult to deal with. 5. of such close or compacted texture as to be impervious to water, air, etc. 6. *Colloq.* nearly even. 7. *Colloq.* stingy. 8. *Slang.* drunk. 9. (of a commodity) difficult to obtain. —*adv.* 10. closely; firmly; securely; tensely. —**tight′ly,** *adv.* —**tight′ness,** *n.*

tight·en (tī′tən), *v.t.*, *v.i.* to make or become tight or tighter. —**tight′en·er,** *n.*

tight-fist·ed (tīt′fǐs′tǐd), *adj.* stingy.

tight·rope (tīt′rōp′), *n.* a rope stretched tight, on which acrobats perform feats of balancing.

tights (tīts), *n.pl.* a close-fitting garment worn esp. by dancers, acrobats, etc.

tight·wad (tīt′wŏd′), *n. U.S. Slang.* a stingy person.

Ti·gris (tī′grǐs), *n.* a river flowing from SE Turkey SE through Iraq, joining the Euphrates to empty into the Persian Gulf. ab. 1150 mi.

til·de (tǐl′də), *n.* a diacritical mark (~) placed over a letter.

tile (tīl), *n.*, *v.*, **tiled, tiling.** —*n.* 1. a thin piece of baked clay used for covering roofs, lining walls, etc. 2. a pottery tube or pipe used for draining land. —*v.t.* 3. to cover with tiles. —**til′er,** *n.*

til·ing (tī′lǐng), *n.* 1. the operation of covering with tiles. 2. tiles collectively.

till[1] (tǐl), *prep.*, *conj.* 1. until. 2. (with a negative) before. 3. near (a specified time).

till[2] (tĭl), v.t., v.i. **1.** to labor, as by plowing, etc., upon (land) for the raising of crops. **2.** to plow. —**till'a·ble**, adj. —**till'er**, n.

till[3] (tĭl), n. a drawer or the like under the back of a counter, as in a shop, in which money is kept.

till·age (tĭl'ĭj), n. **1.** the operation, practice, or art of tilling land. **2.** tilled land.

till·er (tĭl'ər), n. Naut. a handle fitted to the head of a rudder. —**till'er·less**, adj.

tilt (tĭlt), v.t., v.i. **1.** to lean, incline, or slant. **2.** to charge, as in a joust. **3.** to hold poised for attack, as a lance. **4.** to engage in a joust, tournament, or similar contest. —n. **5.** act of tilting. **6.** a sloping position. **7.** a joust or any other contest. **8.** a dispute.

tim·bale (tĭm'bəl), n. **1.** a preparation of minced meat, etc., cooked in a mold. **2.** the mold, usually of paste, sometimes fried.

tim·ber (tĭm'bər), n. **1.** Chiefly U.S. the wood of growing trees suitable for structural uses. **2.** Chiefly U.S. growing trees themselves. **3.** wood, esp. when suitable for building houses, ships, etc. **4.** a single beam forming part of a structure. —v.t. **5.** to furnish with timber. **6.** to support with timber. —**tim'bered**, adj.

timber line, the altitude or latitude at which timber ceases to grow.

timber wolf, a large brindled wolf of forested Canada and the northern United States.

tim·bre (tĭm'bər), n. **1.** the characteristic quality of a sound, independent of pitch and loudness. **2.** Music. the characteristic quality of sound produced by a particular instrument or voice.

Timber wolf
(Total length 4½ to 5½ ft.)

tim·brel (tĭm'brəl), n. a tambourine.

Tim·buk·tu (tĭm bŭk'tōō, tĭm'bŭk tōō'), n. a town in French West Africa. 5300.

time (tīm), n., adj., v., timed, timing. —n. **1.** indefinite continuous duration regarded as that in which events succeed one another. **2.** a system of measuring the passage of time. **3.** a limited extent of time, as between two successive events. **4.** a particular period, esp. one considered as distinct from other periods. **5.** a prescribed or allotted period, as of one's life, for payment of a debt, etc. **6.** occasion or experience. **7.** Colloq. a term of imprisonment. **8.** leisure or spare time. **9.** a particular or definite point in time. **10.** a particular part of a year, day, etc. **11.** an appointed, fit, due, or proper time. **12.** each occasion of a recurring action or event. **13.** (pl.) multiplied by. **14.** Music, etc. **a.** relative rapidity of movement. **b.** the metrical duration of a note or rest. **15.** Mil. rate of marching. **16.** at times, occasionally. **17.** in time, **a.** soon enough. **b.** eventually. **c.** following the correct tempo. **18.** on time, **a.** punctually. **b.** for a designated period of time. **c.** involving the extension of credit. **19.** time and (time) again, repeatedly. —adj. **20.** of, pertaining to, or showing the passage of time. **21.** containing a device so that it will detonate at the desired moment. **22.** Com. payable a stated period of time after presentment. **23.** of or pertaining to purchases with payment postponed. —v.t. **24.** to ascertain or record the duration or rate of. **25.** to regulate as to time, as a train. **26.** to choose the occasion for. —**tim'er**, n.

time·keep·er (tīm'kē'pər), n. **1.** one that keeps time. **2.** a timepiece.

time·less (tīm'lĭs), adj. **1.** eternal. **2.** referring to no particular time.

time·ly (tīm'lĭ), adj., -lier, -liest, adv. —adj. **1.** occurring at a suitable time; opportune. —adv. **2.** opportunely. —**time'li·ness**, n.

time·piece (tīm'pēs'), n. a chronometer, clock, or watch.

time·ta·ble (tīm'tā'bəl), n. a schedule showing the times at which trains, airplanes, etc., arrive and depart.

tim·id (tĭm'ĭd), adj. easily alarmed; shy. —**ti·mid'i·ty**, **tim'id·ness**, n. —**tim'id·ly**, adv.

tim·ing (tī'mĭng), n. the control of the speed or occasion of an action, event, etc., so that it occurs at the proper moment.

tim·or·ous (tĭm'ər əs), adj. **1.** full of fear; fearful. **2.** timid. —**tim'or·ous·ly**, adv. —**tim'or·ous·ness**, n.

Tim·o·thy (tĭm'ə thĭ), n. **1.** a disciple of the apostle Paul, to whom Paul addressed the two New Testament epistles bearing his name. **2.** either of these epistles.

tim·o·thy (tĭm'ə thĭ), n. a coarse grass with cylindrical spikes, valuable as fodder.

tim·pa·ni (tĭm'pə nē'), n. pl., sing. -no (-nō'). kettledrums. —**tim'pa·nist**, n.

tin (tĭn), n., adj., v., tinned, tinning. —n. **1.** Chem. a low-melting, metallic element. Symbol: Sn; at. wt.: 118.70; at. no.: 50; sp. gr.: 7.31 at 20°C. **2.** Chiefly Brit. a pot, pan, can, or box made of tin. —adj. **3.** of tin or tin plate. —v.t. **4.** to cover with tin. **5.** Chiefly Brit. to can.

tinc·ture (tĭngk'chər), n., v., -tured, -turing. —n. **1.** Pharm. a solution of a medicinal substance in alcohol. **2.** a trace. —v.t. **3.** to tinge.

tin·der (tĭn'dər), n. **1.** a material formerly used for catching the spark from a flint and steel struck together for fire. **2.** any highly inflammable substance.

tin·der·box (tĭn'dər bŏks'), n. **1.** a box for holding tinder. **2.** a highly excitable person or thing.

tine (tīn), n. a prong, as of a fork.

ting (tĭng), v.i., v.t. **1.** to make, or cause to make, a high, clear, ringing sound. —n. **2.** a tinging sound.

tinge (tĭnj), v., tinged, tingeing or tinging, n. —v.t. **1.** to impart a trace of color, taste, etc., to. —n. **2.** a slight admixture.

tin·gle (tĭng'gəl), v., -gled, -gling, n. —v.i. **1.** to have or cause a sensation of slight stings, as from cold. —n. **2.** a tingling sensation. **3.** the tingling action of cold, etc.

tink·er (tĭngk'ər), n. **1.** Chiefly Brit. a mender of pots, kettles, pans, etc. —v.i., v.t. **2.** to do the work of a tinker. **3.** to work or repair unskillfully or clumsily.

tin·kle (tĭng'kəl), v., -kled, -kling, n. —v.i., v.t. **1.** to make, or cause to make, short, light, ringing sounds. —n. **2.** a tinkling sound. **3.** act of tinkling. —**tin'kling**, n., adj.

tin·ny (tĭn'ĭ), adj., -nier, -niest. of, like, or containing tin.

tin·sel (tĭn'səl), n., adj., v., -seled, -seling or (esp. Brit.) -selled, -selling. —n. **1.** a glittering metallic substance, as copper, etc., in thin pieces, strips, etc. **2.** a metallic yarn usually wrapped around a core yarn. **3.** anything showy with little or no real worth. —adj. **4.** of or containing tinsel. **5.** showy; gaudy; tawdry. —v.t. **6.** to adorn with tinsel.

tint (tĭnt), n. **1.** a color or hue, esp. a delicate or pale one. —v.t. **2.** to apply a tint or tints to; tinge.

tin·tin·nab·u·la·tion (tĭn'tĭ năb'yə lā'shən), n. the ringing or sound of bells.

ti·ny (tī'nĭ), adj., -nier, -niest. very small.

-tion, a suffix used to form abstract nouns from verbs or stems not identical with verbs, whether as expressing action (revolution, commendation), or a state (contrition, starvation), or associated meanings (relation, temptation).

tip[1] (tĭp), n., v., tipped, tipping. —n. **1.** a slender or pointed extremity. **2.** the top. **3.** a small part, as of metal, forming an extremity. —v.t. **4.** to furnish with a tip.

tip[2] (tĭp), v.t., v.i., tipped, tipping. **1.** to tilt. **2.** to overturn or upset. **3.** to take off (the hat) in salutation.

tip[3] (tĭp), n., v., tipped, tipping. —n. **1.** a small present of money. **2.** a piece of private information, as for use in betting, etc. **3.** a useful hint. —v.t., v.i. **4.** to give a tip or tips (to). —**tip'per**, n.

tip[4] (tĭp), n., v., tipped, tipping. —n. **1.** a light, smart blow; tap. —v.t. **2.** to hit with a light, smart blow; tap.

tip-off (tĭp'ŏf', -ŏf'), n. a hint or warning.

tip·pet (tĭp'ĭt), n. a scarf of fur or wool for covering the neck and shoulders.

tip·ple (tĭp'əl), v., -pled, -pling, n. —v.t., v.i. **1.** to drink (intoxicating liquor), esp. repeatedly, in small quantities. —n. **2.** intoxicating liquor. —**tip'pler**, n.

tip·sy (tĭp'sĭ), adj., -sier, -siest. slightly intoxicated. —**tip'si·ly**, adv. —**tip'si·ness**, n.

tip·toe (tĭp'tō'), n., v., -toed, -toeing. —n. **1.** the tip of a toe. **2.** on tiptoe, **a.** on the tips of the toes. **b.** eagerly expectant. **c.** stealthy. —v.i. **3.** to move on tiptoe.

tip·top (tĭp'tŏp'), n. **1.** the extreme top.

—*adj.* **2.** situated at the very top. **3.** *Colloq.* of the highest excellence.

ti·rade (tī/rād, tə rād/), *n.* **1.** a prolonged denunciation. **2.** a long, vehement speech.

Ti·ra·na (tē rä/nə), *n.* the capital of Albania, in the central part. 59,887.

tire[1] (tīr), *v.*, **tired, tiring.** —*v.t.* **1.** to exhaust the strength, interest, patience, etc., of. —*v.i.* **2.** to have the strength, interest, patience, etc., exhausted.

tire[2] (tīr), *n., v.*, **tired, tiring.** —*n.* **1.** a hoop or band of metal, rubber, air-filled rubber tube, or the like, placed around a wheel of a vehicle to form the tread. —*v.t.* **2.** to furnish with a tire or tires.

tired (tīrd), *adj.* **1.** exhausted; fatigued. **2.** weary. —**tired/ly,** *adv.* —**tired/ness,** *n.*

tire·less (tīr/lĭs), *adj.* untiring; indefatigable. —**tire/less·ly,** *adv.* —**tire/less·ness,** *n.*

tire·some (tīr/səm), *adj.* wearisome; annoying or vexatious. —**tire/some·ly,** *adv.* —**tire/some·ness,** *n.*

tis·sue (tĭsh/ōō), *n.* **1.** *Biol.* **a.** the substance of which an organism or part is composed. **b.** an aggregate of cells and cell products forming a definite kind of structural material in an animal or plant. **2.** a woven fabric, esp. one of light or gauzy texture. **3.** an interconnected series. **4.** tissue paper.

tissue paper, a very thin paper used for wrapping delicate articles, etc.

tit[1] (tĭt), *n.* a titmouse.

tit[2] (tĭt), *n.* teat.

Ti·tan (tī/tən), *n.* **1.** *Gk. Myth.* **a.** any of a family of lawless deities of enormous size and strength who were overthrown by Zeus. **b.** the sun god, Helios (Sol). **2.** a person or thing of enormous size, strength, etc. —*adj.* **3.** titanic; gigantic. Also, **titan** for 2, 3.

Ti·tan·ic (tī tăn/ĭk), *adj.* **1.** of, pertaining to, or characteristic of the Titans. **2.** Also, **titanic.** of enormous size, strength, etc..

ti·ta·ni·um (tī tā/nĭ əm, tĭ-), *n.* *Chem.* a metallic element isolated as a dark-gray powder. *Symbol:* Ti; *at. wt.:* 47.90; *at. no.:* 22; *sp. gr.:* 4.5 at 20°C.

tit for tat, an equivalent given in retaliation, repartee, etc.

tithe (tīth), *n., v.*, **tithed, tithing.** —*n.* **1.** (*often pl.*) the tenth part of the annual produce of agriculture, etc., due as a tax for the support of the priesthood, etc. **2.** a tenth part. —*v.t., v.i.* **3.** to pay a tithe (of).

ti·tian (tĭsh/ən), *n.* a yellowish- or golden-brown color made famous by Titian.

Ti·tian (tĭsh/ən), *n.* (*Tiziano Vecellio*) c1477–1576, Italian painter.

tit·il·late (tĭt/ə lāt/), *v.t.*, **-lated, -lating.** **1.** to tickle. **2.** to excite agreeably. —**tit/il·la/tion,** *n.*

tit·i·vate (tĭt/ə vāt/), *v.t., v.i.*, **-vated, -vating.** *Colloq.* to make (oneself, etc.) smart or spruce. —**tit/i·va/tion,** *n.*

ti·tle (tī/təl), *n., v.*, **-tled, -tling.** —*n.* **1.** the distinguishing name of a book, picture, piece of music, or the like. **2.** a descriptive caption. **3.** a distinctive appellation, esp. one belonging to a person by right of rank, office, attainment, etc. **4.** *Sports.* the championship. **5.** established or recognized right to something. **6.** *Law.* **a.** legal right to the possession of property. **b.** the instrument constituting evidence of such right. —*v.t.* **7.** to furnish with a title; entitle. —**ti/tled,** *adj.*

tit·mouse (tĭt/mous/), *n., pl.* **-mice** (-mīs/). any of certain small birds of the New and Old Worlds, including the chickadee.

Ti·to (tē/tō), *n.* **Marshal,** (*Josip Broz*) born 1891, premier of Yugoslavia since 1945.

tit·ter (tĭt/ər), *v.i.* **1.** to laugh in a low, half-restrained way. —*n.* **2.** a tittering laugh.

tit·tle (tĭt/əl), *n.* a jot or whit.

tit·tle-tat·tle (tĭt/əl tăt/əl), *n., v.*, **-tled, -tling.** gossip. —**tit/tle-tat/tler,** *n.*

tit·u·lar (tĭch/ə lər, tĭt/yə-), *adj.* **1.** of or pertaining to a title. **2.** having a title, esp. of rank. **3.** existing or being such in title only. —*n.* **4.** one who bears a title. —**tit/u·lar·ly,** *adv.*

tiz·zy (tĭz/ĭ), *n., pl.* **-zies.** *Slang.* dither.

Tl, *Chem.* thallium.

Tm, *Chem.* thulium.

Tn, *Chem.* thoron.

tn., ton.

TNT, trinitrotoluene. Also, **T.N.T.**

to (tōō; *unstressed* tŏŏ, tə), *prep.* **1.** a particle serving to specify a point approached and reached. **2.** *To* is used to supply the place of the dative in other languages, connecting transitive verbs with their indirect objects, etc. **3.** *To* is used as the ordinary sign of the infinitive. —*adv.* **4.** toward a person, thing, or point implied or understood. **5.** to action or work. **6.** to consciousness. **7.** **to and fro,** to and from some place or thing.

toad (tōd), *n.* any of certain tailless (i.e., froglike) amphibians.

toad·stool (tōd/stōōl/), *n.* any of certain fleshy fungi having a stalk with an umbrellalike cap.

toad·y (tō/dĭ), *n., pl.* **toadies,** *v.*, **toadied, toadying.** —*n.* **1.** a fawning flatterer. —*v.t., v.i.* **2.** to be a toady (to).

toast[1] (tōst), *n.* **1.** bread in slices superficially browned by heat. —*v.t., v.i.* **2.** to brown by exposure to heat. —**toast/er,** *n.*

toast[2] (tōst), *n.* **1.** a person whose health is proposed and drunk. **2.** a proposal to drink to some person or thing. **3.** act of thus drinking. —*v.t.* **4.** to propose as a toast. **5.** to drink to the health of. —**toast/er,** *n.*

toast·mas·ter (tōst/măs/tər, -mäs/-), *n.* one who introduces after-dinner speakers or who proposes toasts.

to·bac·co (tə băk/ō), *n., pl.* **-cos, -coes.** **1.** any of certain plants of the nightshade family whose leaves are prepared for smoking or chewing or as snuff. **2.** the leaves so prepared.

to·bac·co·nist (tə băk/ə nĭst), *n.* *Chiefly Brit.* a dealer in or manufacturer of tobacco.

to·bog·gan (tə bŏg/ən), *n.* **1.** a long, narrow, flat-bottomed sled made of a thin board curved upward and backward at the front end. —*v.i.* **2.** to use, or coast on, a toboggan. **3.** to fall rapidly, as prices. —**to·bog/gan·er, to·bog/gan·ist,** *n.*

toc·ca·ta (tə kä/tə), *n.* *Music.* a composition in the style of an improvisation, for the piano, organ, or other keyboard instrument, intended to exhibit the player's technique.

toc·sin (tŏk/sĭn), *n.* **1.** a signal, esp. of alarm. **2.** a bell used to sound an alarm.

to·day (tə dā/), *n.* **1.** this present day. **2.** this present time or age. —*adv.* **3.** on this present day. **4.** at the present time. Also, **to-day/.**

tod·dle (tŏd/əl), *v.*, **-dled, -dling,** *n.* —*v.i.* **1.** to go with short, unsteady steps, as a child. —*n.* **2.** act of toddling. **3.** an unsteady gait. —**tod/dler,** *n.*

tod·dy (tŏd/ĭ), *n., pl.* **-dies.** a drink made of alcoholic liquor and hot water, sweetened and sometimes spiced.

to-do (tə dōō/), *n., pl.* **-dos.** *Colloq.* fuss.

toe (tō), *n., v.*, **toed, toeing.** —*n.* **1.** one of the terminal digits of the foot. **2.** a part, as of a stocking or shoe, to cover the toes. —*v.t.* **3.** to touch or reach with the toes. —*v.i.* **4.** to place or move the toes in a manner specified.

toe·nail (tō/nāl/), *n.* the nail growing on each of the toes of the human foot.

tof·fee (tŏf/ĭ, tôf/ĭ), *n.* taffy. Also, **tof/fy.**

tog (tŏg), *n., v.*, **togged, togging.** *Colloq.* —*n.* **1.** a garment. **2.** (*usually pl.*) clothes. —*v.t.* **3.** to clothe; dress.

to·ga (tō/gə), *n., pl.* **-gas, -gae** (-jē). the loose outer garment of the citizens of ancient Rome. —**to·gaed** (tō/gəd), *adj.*

to·geth·er (tōō gĕth/ər), *adv.* **1.** into or in one group or mass. **2.** into or in union, proximity, contact, or collision. **3.** into or in association, etc. **4.** considered collectively. **5.** at the same time. **6.** continuously; uninterruptedly. **7.** in coöperation. **8.** mutually; reciprocally.

tog·ger·y (tŏg/ə rĭ), *n.* *Colloq.* clothes.

toil (toil), *n.* **1.** hard and exhausting work. —*v.i.* **2.** to work hard or arduously. **3.** to move or travel with difficulty. —**toil/er,** *n.*

toi·let (toi/lĭt), *n.* **1.** *U.S.* a bathroom. **2.** *U.S.* a water closet. **3.** the act or process of dressing, including bathing, arranging the hair, etc. Also, **toi·lette** (toi lĕt/) for 3.

toilet water, a scented liquid used as a light perfume.

toil·some (toil/səm), *adj.* laborious or fatiguing. —**toil/some·ly,** *adv.* —**toil/some·ness,** *n.*

To·kay (tō kā/), *n.* **1.** a rich, sweet, aromatic wine. **2.** the variety of grape from which it is made.

to·ken (tō/kən), *n.* **1.** something serving to represent or indicate some fact, event, feeling,

etc.; sign or symbol. **2.** a memento; keepsake.
3. a stamped piece of metal, etc., issued as a
limited medium of exchange, as for bus fares.

To·ky·o (tō′kĭ ō′), *n.* a seaport in and the
capital of Japan. 3,442,106. Also, **To′ki·o′**.

To·le·do (tə lē′dō), *n.* **1.** a city in NW Ohio.
282,349. **2.** a city in central Spain. 34,592.

tol·er·a·ble (tŏl′ər ə bəl), *adj.* **1.** endurable.
2. fairly good. **3.** *Colloq.* in fair health. **—tol′er·a·bly,** *adv.*

tol·er·ance (tŏl′ər əns), *n.* **1.** the disposition
to be patient and fair toward those whose
opinions or practices differ from one's own.
2. *Med.* the power of enduring or resisting the
action of a drug, poison, etc. **3.** *Mach.* an allowable variation in the dimensions of a machine or
part.

tol·er·ant (tŏl′ər ənt), *adj.* **1.** showing tolerance; forbearing. **2.** *Med.* able to endure or
resist the action of a drug, poison, etc. **—tol′er·ant·ly,** *adv.*

tol·er·ate (tŏl′ə rāt′), *v.t.,* **-ated, -ating. 1.** to
allow or permit. **2.** to put up with. **3.** *Med.* to
endure or resist the action of (a drug, poison, etc.).
—tol′er·a′tion, *n.*

toll¹ (tōl), *v.t.* **1.** to cause (a large bell) to sound
with single strokes slowly and regularly repeated,
esp. for announcing a death. **2.** to announce (a
death, the hour, etc.) by such strokes. **—***v.i.*
3. *U.S.* to sound with single strokes slowly and
regularly repeated, as a bell. **—***n.* **4.** act or sound
of tolling a bell.

toll² (tōl), *n.* **1.** a payment exacted by the state,
etc., for some right or privilege, as for passage
over a bridge. **2.** a payment made for a long-
distance telephone call.

Tol·stoy (tŏl′stoi), *n.* **Lev** (*Eng.* **Leo**) **Nikolae-
vich,** 1828–1910, Russian novelist.

tom·a·hawk (tŏm′ə hôk′), *n.* **1.** a light ax
used by the North American Indians as a weapon
and tool. **—***v.t.* **2.** to strike, cut, or kill with a
tomahawk.

Tom and Jerry, a hot drink of rum, milk,
and beaten eggs.

to·ma·to (tə mā′tō, -mä′-), *n., pl.* **-toes. 1.** a
widely cultivated plant of the nightshade family
bearing a pulpy fruit, commonly red, used as a
vegetable. **2.** the fruit itself.

tomb (tōōm), *n.* **1.** an excavation for the reception of a dead body. **2.** a grave or mausoleum.
—*v.t.* **3.** to bury.

tom·boy (tŏm′boi′), *n.* a boisterous, romping
girl. **—tom′boy·ish,** *adj.*

tomb·stone (tōōm′stōn′), *n.* a stone, usually
bearing an inscription, set to mark a tomb.

tom·cat (tŏm′kăt′), *n.* a male cat.

Tom Col·lins (kŏl′ĭnz), a tall iced drink containing gin, lemon or lime juice, and carbonated
water.

tome (tōm), *n.* **1.** a volume forming a part of a
larger work. **2.** a heavy volume.

tom·fool·er·y (tŏm′fōō′lə rĭ), *n., pl.* **-eries.**
foolish or silly behavior.

Tom·my At·kins (tŏm′ĭ ăt′kĭnz), a private
in the British army. Also, **tom′my.**

Tommy gun, *Slang.* a type of submachine gun.

tom·my·rot (tŏm′ĭ rŏt′), *n. Slang.* nonsense.

to·mor·row (tə môr′ō, -mŏr′ō), *n.* **1.** the day
after this day. **—***adv.* **2.** on the day after this
day. Also, **to·mor′row.**

tom-tom (tŏm′tŏm′), *n.* **1.** a native drum of
indefinite pitch. **2.** a dully repetitious drumbeat
or similar sound.

ton (tŭn), *n.* a unit of weight, commonly equivalent to 2000 pounds avoirdupois (**short ton**) in
the U.S. and 2240 pounds avoirdupois (**long ton**)
in Great Britain.

ton·al (tō′nəl), *adj. Music.* pertaining to tonality. **—ton′al·ly,** *adv.*

to·nal·i·ty (tō năl′ə tĭ), *n., pl.* **-ties.** *Music.*
1. the sum of relations, melodic and harmonic,
existing between the tones of a scale or musical
system. **2.** a particular scale or system of tones.

tone (tōn), *n., v.,* **toned, toning. —***n.* **1.** any
sound considered with reference to its quality,
pitch, strength, source, etc. **2.** quality of sound.
3. vocal sound. **4.** a particular quality, modulation, etc., of the voice as expressive of some feeling, etc. **5.** *Music.* **a.** a musical sound of definite
pitch. **b.** a whole tone or step. **6.** a variety of
color; tint. **7.** *Art.* the prevailing effect of
harmony of color and values. **8.** *Physiol.* the
state of firmness proper to the organs or tissues

of the body. **9.** spirit, character, or tenor.
10. prevailing character or style. **11.** style, distinction, or elegance. **—***v.t., v.i.* **12.** to give the
proper or desired tone (to). **13. tone down,** to
soften; moderate. **14.** to harmonize in tone or
color.

tong¹ (tông, tŏng), *n.* (*pl.,* sometimes *construed
as sing.*) an implement consisting of two arms
fastened together, for seizing, holding, or lifting
something.

tong² (tông, tŏng), *n.* (in the U.S.) a Chinese
society, usually exclusive but not secret.

tongue (tŭng), *n., v.,* **tongued, tonguing. —***n.*
1. an organ occupying the floor of the mouth,
being the principal organ of taste, and, in man,
of articulate speech. **2.** the tongue of an animal,
as an ox, as used for food. **3.** the language of a
particular people, country, or locality. **4.** something resembling a tongue in shape, position, or
function. **5.** a strip of leather under the lacing
or fastening of a shoe. **6.** a suspended piece
inside a bell that produces a sound on striking
against the side. **—***v.t., v.i.* **7.** to modify (the
tones of a flute, cornet, etc.) by strokes of the
tongue. **8.** to touch with the tongue.

tongue-tie (tŭng′tī′), *n., v.,* **-tied, -tying. —***n.*
1. impeded motion of the tongue. **—***v.t.* **2.** to
make tongue-tied.

tongue-tied (tŭng′tīd′), *adj.* **1.** unable to
speak, as from shyness. **2.** affected with tongue-
tie.

ton·ic (tŏn′ĭk), *n.* **1.** a medicine that invigorates
or strengthens. **2.** *Music.* the first degree of the
scale; keynote. **—***adj.* **3.** invigorating physically,
mentally, or morally. **4.** characterized by distinctions of tone or accent. **5.** *Music.* **a.** of or
pertaining to a tone or tones. **b.** pertaining to
or founded on the keynote of a musical scale.

to·nic·i·ty (tō nĭs′ə tĭ), *n.* **1.** tonic quality or
condition. **2.** the state of bodily tone.

to·night (tə nīt′), *n.* **1.** this present or coming
night. **—***adv.* **2.** on this present night. Also, **to-
night′.**

ton·nage (tŭn′ĭj), *n.* **1.** the carrying capacity
of a vessel. **2.** ships collectively. **3.** a duty on
ships at so much per ton of cargo or according to
the capacity in tons.

ton·neau (tŭ nō′), *n., pl.* **-neaus, -neaux** (-nōz′).
a rear compartment of an automobile, with seats
for passengers.

ton·sil (tŏn′səl), *n. Anat.* either of two oval
masses of lymphoid tissue situated one on each
side of the fauces. **—ton′sil·lar,** *adj.*

ton·sil·lec·to·my (tŏn′sə lĕk′tə mĭ), *n., pl.*
-mies. *Surg.* the operation of excising or removing one or both tonsils.

ton·sil·li·tis (tŏn′sə lī′tĭs), *n. Pathol.* inflammation of a tonsil or the tonsils.

ton·so·ri·al (tŏn sōr′ĭ əl), *adj.* (often in humorous use) of or pertaining to a barber.

ton·sure (tŏn′shər), *n.* **1.** the shaving of the
head, or of some part of it, as a religious practice
or rite, as before entering the priesthood, etc.
2. the part of a cleric's head left bare by shaving
the hair. **—ton′sured,** *adj.*

too (tōō), *adv.* **1.** in addition; also. **2.** to an
excessive extent. **3.** more (as specified) than
should be. **4.** extremely.

tool (tōōl), *n.* **1.** an instrument for performing
mechanical operations, as a hammer, saw, file,
etc. **2.** a person used by another for his own
ends. **—***v.t., v.i.* **3.** to work or shape with a tool.
4. to work decoratively with a hand tool. **5.** *Brit.
Colloq.* to drive (a coach, etc.).

toot (tōōt), *v.i.* **1.** (of a horn) to give forth its
characteristic sound. **—***v.t.* **2.** to cause (a horn,
etc.) to sound by blowing it. **—***n.* **3.** an act or
sound of tooting. **—toot′er,** *n.*

tooth (tōōth), *n., pl.* **teeth** (tēth), *v.* **—***n.* **1.** (in
most vertebrates) one of the hard bodies usually
attached in a row to each jaw, serving for the
mastication of food, as weapons of attack or
defense, etc. **2.** a projection, as of a comb, rake,
saw, etc. **3.** taste, relish, or liking. **—***v.t.* **4.** to
furnish with teeth. **5.** to cut teeth upon.
—toothed (tōōtht, tōōthd), *adj.* **—tooth′less,**
adj.

tooth·ache (tōōth′āk′), *n.* a pain in a tooth or
teeth or in the jawbone.

tooth·brush (tōōth′brŭsh′), *n.* a small brush
with a long handle, for cleaning the teeth.

tooth·pick (tōōth′pĭk′), *n.* a small pointed
piece of wood, etc., for removing substances between the teeth.

tooth·some (tōōth′səm), *adj.* pleasing to the taste. —**tooth′some·ness**, *n.*

top[1] (tŏp), *n., adj., v.,* **topped, topping.** —*n.* 1. the highest point or part. 2. the uppermost or upper part, surface, etc. 3. the highest or leading place, rank, etc. 4. the highest point, pitch, or degree. 5. one that occupies the highest or leading position. 6. the best or choicest part. 7. a covering or lid, as of a box. 8. the head. 9. the crown of the head. —*adj.* 10. pertaining to, situated at, or forming the top. 11. highest in degree; greatest. 12. foremost; chief. —*v.t.* 13. to put a top on. 14. to be at or constitute the top of. 15. to reach the top of. 16. to rise above. 17. to exceed in height, amount, etc. 18. to surpass.

top[2] (tŏp), *n.* a child's toy, often conical, with a point on which it is made to spin.

to·paz (tō′păz), *n.* a mineral, usually occurring in prismatic crystals of various colors, used as a gem.

top·coat (tŏp′kōt′), *n.* a light overcoat.

To·pe·ka (tə pē′kə), *n.* the capital of Kansas, in the NE part. 67,833.

top·er (tō′pər), *n.* a chronic drunkard.

top·gal·lant (tŏp′găl′ənt; *Naut.* tə găl′ənt), *Naut. n.* the spars and rigging of the third section of the mast above the deck in a square-rigged vessel.

top hat, a man's tall silk hat.

top-heav·y (tŏp′hěv′ĭ), *adj.* having the top disproportionately heavy.

top·ic (tŏp′ĭk), *n.* a subject of conversation, discussion, or writing.

top·i·cal (tŏp′ə kəl), *adj.* 1. pertaining to or dealing with matters of current or local interest. 2. pertaining to the subject of a discourse, composition, etc. 3. local. —**top′i·cal·ly,** *adv.*

top kick, *Mil. Slang.* a first sergeant.

top·knot (tŏp′nŏt′), *n.* a tuft or knot of hair on the top of the head.

top·most (tŏp′mōst, -məst), *adj.* highest.

top·notch (tŏp′nŏch′), *adj. Colloq.* first-rate.

to·pog·ra·phy (tə pŏg′rə fĭ), *n., pl.* **-phies.** 1. the detailed description of the features of a relatively small area, district, or locality. 2. the relief features or surface configuration of an area. —**to·pog′ra·pher,** *n.* —**top·o·graph·ic** (tŏp′ə-grăf′ĭk), **top′o·graph′i·cal,** *adj.*

top·per (tŏp′ər), *n.* 1. one that tops. 2. *Slang.* a top hat. 3. a short coat worn by women.

top·ple (tŏp′əl), *v., -pled, -pling.* —*v.i.* 1. to fall forward as having too heavy a top. —*v.t.* 2. to cause to topple.

top·sail (tŏp′sāl′; *Naut.* -səl), *n. Naut.* a square sail next above the lowest or chief sail.

top secret, *Chiefly Mil.* extremely secret.

top·side (tŏp′sīd′), *n.* the upper side.

top·soil (tŏp′soil′), *n.* the surface or upper part of the soil.

top·sy-tur·vy (tŏp′sĭ′ tûr′vĭ), *adv., adj., n., pl.* **-vies.** —*adv.* 1. upside down. 2. in confusion or disorder. —*adj.* 3. turned upside down; inverted; reversed. 4. confused or disorderly. —*n.* 5. inversion of the natural order. 6. confusion.

toque (tōk), *n.* a hat with little or no brim.

To·rah (tōr′ə), *n.* 1. the five books of Moses; Pentateuch. 2. (*also l.c.*) the whole Scripture. Also, **To′ra.**

torch (tôrch), *n.* 1. a light to be carried in the hand, consisting of some combustible substance. 2. a source of illumination, guidance, etc. 3. any of various lamplike devices which produce a hot flame and are used for soldering, etc. 4. *Brit.* a flashlight. —**torch·bear·er** (tôrch′bâr′ər), *n.*

tor·e·a·dor (tôr′ĭ ə dôr′), *n.* a bullfighter, esp. one who fights on horseback.

tor·ment (*v.* tôr mĕnt′; *n.* tôr′mĕnt), *v.t.* 1. to afflict with great bodily or mental suffering; pain. 2. to annoy excessively. 3. to disturb. —*n.* 4. suffering; agony; misery. 5. something that causes great pain or suffering. —**tor·men′tor, tor·ment′er,** *n.*

tor·na·do (tôr nā′dō), *n., pl.* **-does, -dos.** a destructive storm of the middle United States, usually appearing as a whirling, advancing funnel under a mass of black cloud. —**tor·nad·ic** (tôr-năd′ĭk), *adj.*

To·ron·to (tə rŏn′tō), *n.* a city in SE Canada: the capital of Ontario. With suburbs, 900,491.

tor·pe·do (tôr pē′dō), *n., pl.* **-does,** *v.,* **-doed, -doing.** —*n.* 1. a long, self-propelled explosive missile launched from a submarine, torpedo boat,

or the like, to explode on impact with the ship fired at. 2. a device fastened to the top of a rail and exploded by the pressure of the locomotive or car, to give an audible signal to members of the train crew. 3. any of various other explosive devices, as a firework. —*v.t., v.i.* 4. to attack, hit, damage, or destroy (a ship) with a torpedo or torpedoes.

torpedo boat, a small, speedy warship used primarily for torpedo attacks.

tor·pid (tôr′pĭd), *adj.* 1. inactive, sluggish. 2. dull; apathetic; lethargic. —**tor·pid′i·ty,** *n.* —**tor′pid·ly,** *adv.*

tor·por (tôr′pər), *n.* 1. a state of suspended physical powers and activities. 2. sluggish inactivity or inertia. 3. apathy.

torque (tôrk), *n.* 1. *Mech.* that which produces rotation. 2. *Mach.* the turning power of a shaft.

tor·rent (tôr′ənt, tŏr′-), *n.* 1. a stream of water flowing with great rapidity and violence. 2. a rushing, violent, or abundant stream of anything. —**tor·ren·tial** (tô rĕn′shəl, tŏ-), *adj.* —**tor·ren′tial·ly,** *adv.*

tor·rid (tôr′ĭd, tŏr′-), *adj.* 1. subject to parching heat, esp. of the sun. 2. oppressively hot, as climate. 3. passionate.

Torrid Zone, the part of the earth's surface between the tropics of Cancer and Capricorn.

tor·sion (tôr′shən), *n.* 1. act of twisting. 2. *Mech.* a. the twisting of a body by two equal and opposite torques. b. the internal torque so produced. —**tor′sion·al,** *adj.*

tor·so (tôr′sō), *n., pl.* **-sos, -si** (-sē). the trunk of the human body.

tort (tôrt), *n. Law.* a civil wrong (other than a breach of contract or trust) such as the law requires compensation for in damages.

tor·til·la (tôr tē′yä), *n.* (in Mexico, etc.) a thin, round, unleavened corn-meal cake.

tor·toise (tôr′təs), *n.* 1. a turtle, esp. a terrestrial turtle. 2. a very slow person or thing.

tor·tu·ous (tôr′chŏŏ əs), *adj.* 1. twisting, winding, or crooked. 2. not direct or straightforward. 3. deceitfully indirect or morally crooked. —**tor′tu·ous·ly,** *adv.* —**tor′tu·ous·ness,** *n.*

tor·ture (tôr′chər), *n., v., -tured, -turing.* —*n.* 1. act of inflicting excruciating pain, esp. from sheer cruelty. 2. (*often pl.*) excruciating pain or agony. —*v.t.* 3. to subject to torture. 4. to twist or force into some unnatural position or form. 5. to distort (language, etc.). —**tor′tur·er,** *n.*

To·ry (tôr′ĭ), *n., pl.* **-ries,** *adj.* —*n.* 1. a member of the Conservative party in Great Britain. 2. a conservative. 3. *Amer. Hist.* a member of the British party during the Revolutionary period. —*adj.* 4. of or pertaining to the Tories. 5. conservative. Also, **tory** for 2, 5. —**To′ry·ism,** *n.*

Tos·ca·ni·ni (tŏs′kə nē′nĭ), *n.* Arturo, born 1867, U.S. orchestra conductor.

toss (tôs, tŏs), *v.,* **tossed** or (*Poetic*) **tost; tossing;** *n.* —*v.t., v.i.* 1. to throw, pitch, or fling. 2. to throw or pitch about. 3. to throw, raise, or jerk upward suddenly. 4. to fling oneself restlessly about, esp. in sleep. 5. to throw (a coin or other object) into the air in order to decide something by the way it falls. —*n.* 6. a throw or pitch. 7. a tossing of a coin to decide something. 8. a sudden fling of the body, esp. a quick upward movement of the head or body.

toss·up (tôs′ŭp′, tŏs′-), *n.* 1. the tossing of a coin to decide something by its fall. 2. *Colloq.* an even chance.

tot[1] (tŏt), *n.* a small child.

tot[2] (tŏt), *v.,* **totted, totting,** *n. Chiefly Brit. Colloq.* —*v.t.* 1. to add. —*n.* 2. a total.

to·tal (tō′tal), *adj., n., v., -taled, -taling* or (*esp. Brit.*) **-talled, -talling.** —*adj.* 1. entire; whole. 2. complete; utter. —*n.* 3. the total amount; sum. —*v.t., v.i.* 4. to add up. 5. to amount (to). —**to·tal·i·ty** (tō tăl′ə tĭ), *n.* —**to′tal·ly,** *adv.*

to·tal·i·tar·i·an (tō tăl′ə târ′ĭ ən), *adj.* 1. pertaining to a centralized form of government in which those in control grant neither recognition nor tolerance to parties of differing opinion. —*n.* 2. an adherent of totalitarian principles. —**to·tal′i·tar′i·an·ism,** *n.*

tote (tōt), *v.,* **toted, toting,** *n. U.S. Colloq.* —*v.t.* 1. to carry or bear, as a burden. —*n.* 2. act or course of toting. 3. that which is toted.

to·tem (tō′təm), *n.* an object in nature, often an animal, assumed as the emblem of a clan, family, or related group. —**to·tem·ic** (tō tĕm′-ĭk), *adj.*

totem pole, a pole carved and painted with totemic figures, erected by Indians of the northwest coast of North America, esp. in front of their houses.

tot·ter (tŏt/ər), *v.i.* **1.** to go with faltering steps. **2.** to sway or rock as if about to fall. **3.** to shake or tremble. —*n.* **4.** an unsteady movement or gait. —**tot/ter·y,** *adj.*

tou·can (tōō/kăn, tōō kän/), *n.* any of certain fruit-eating birds of tropical America, with an enormous beak.

touch (tŭch), *v.t.* **1.** to put the hand, finger, etc., in contact with (something) to feel it. **2.** to come into contact with and perceive (something). **3.** to bring (the hand, finger, etc., or something held) into contact with something. **4.** to tap gently or lightly. **5.** to come into or be in contact with. **6.** *Geom.* (of a line or surface) to be tangent to. **7.** to be adjacent to. **8.** to reach; attain. **9.** to attain equality with. **10.** to modify (a picture, etc.) by adding a stroke here and there. **11.** to mark slightly, as with color. **12.** to stop at (a place), as a ship. **13.** to affect with some emotion, esp. tenderness, pity, etc. **14.** to handle, use, or have to do with (something) in any way. **15.** to refer or allude to. **16.** *Slang.* to ask for or get a loan from. —*v.i.* **17.** to place the hand, finger, etc., on or in contact with something. **18.** to come into or be in contact. **19.** to make a stop at a place, as a ship. **20.** to mention briefly. —*n.* **21.** act of touching. **22.** state or fact of being touched. **23.** that sense by which anything material **is** perceived by means of the contact with it **of some** part of the body. **24.** the sensation caused by touching something. **25.** a coming into or **being in contact. 26.** a close relation of communication, sympathy, or the like. **27. a** slight blow. **28.** a slight attack, as of illness. **29.** a slight added action or effort in doing any piece of work. **30.** manner of execution in artistic work. **31.** a slight amount of some quality, attribute, etc. **32.** a slight quantity or degree. **33.** *Slang.* the act of asking for or getting a loan. —**touch/a·ble,** *adj.* —**touch/er,** *n.*

touch·back (tŭch/băk/), *n.* *Football.* act of a player in touching the ball to the ground on or behind his own goal line when it has been driven there by the opposing side.

touch·down (tŭch/doun/), *n.* *Football.* act of a player in touching the ball down to the ground behind the opponent's goal line.

touched (tŭcht), *adj.* **1.** moved; stirred. **2.** slightly crazy; unbalanced.

touch·ing (tŭch/Ĭng), *adj.* **1.** affecting; moving. —*prep.* **2.** concerning; about. —**touch/-ing·ly,** *adv.*

touch-me-not (tŭch/mĭ nŏt/), *n.* a yellow-flowered plant whose ripe seed vessels burst open when touched.

touch·stone (tŭch/stōn/), *n.* **1.** a black stone used to test the purity of gold and silver by the color of the streak produced on it by rubbing it with the metals. **2.** any criterion.

touch·y (tŭch/Ĭ), *adj.,* **touchier, touchiest. 1.** apt to take offense easily; irritable. **2.** delicate or ticklish, as a subject. —**touch/i·ly,** *adv.* —**touch/i·ness,** *n.*

tough (tŭf), *adj.* **1.** not easily broken or cut. **2.** not brittle or tender. **3.** difficult to chew. **4.** sturdy; hardy. **5.** hardened; incorrigible. **6.** hard, trying, or troublesome. **7.** hard to endure. —*n.* **8.** *U.S.* a ruffian; rowdy. —**tough/ly,** *adv.* —**tough/ness,** *n.*

tough·en (tŭf/ən), *v.i., v.t.* to make or become tough. —**tough/en·er,** *n.*

tou·pee (tōō pā/, -pē/), *n.* a wig or patch of false hair worn to cover a bald spot.

tour (tŏŏr), *v.i.* **1.** to travel from place to place. —*v.t.* **2.** to travel through (a place). —*n.* **3.** a traveling around from place to place, as of a theatrical company. **4.** *Chiefly Mil.* a period of duty at one place.

tour·ist (tŏŏr/Ĭst), *n.* one who makes a tour, esp. for pleasure.

tour·na·ment (tŭr/nə mənt, tŏŏr/-), *n.* **1.** a meeting for contests, esp. in athletic sports. **2.** *Hist.* a contest between two opposing parties of mounted and armored knights.

tour·ney (tŭr/nĭ, tŏŏr/nĭ), *n., pl.* **-neys, *v.,* -neyed, -neying.** —*n.* **1.** a tournament. —*v.i.* **2.** to contend in a tournament.

tour·ni·quet (tŏŏr/nə kĕt/, -kā/, tŭr/-), *n.* any of various devices for arresting bleeding by compressing a blood vessel.

tou·sle (tou/zəl), *v.,* **-sled, -sling,** *n.* —*v.t.* **1.** to disorder or dishevel. —*n.* **2.** a tousled mass of hair.

tout (tout), *Colloq.* —*v.i., v.t.* **1.** to solicit (business, votes, etc.) importunately. **2.** to proclaim. **3.** to give a tip on (a race horse, etc.). —*n.* **4.** one who touts. —**tout/er,** *n.*

tow[1] (tō), *v.t.* **1.** to drag (a boat, car, etc.) by a rope or chain. —*n.* **2.** act of towing. **3.** the thing being towed. **4.** a rope or chain for towing. —**tow/age,** *n.*

tow[2] (tō), *n.* the fiber of flax, hemp, or jute prepared for spinning.

to·ward (*prep.* tōrd, tə wôrd/; *adj.* tōrd), *prep.* Also, **to·wards/. 1.** in the direction of. **2.** with respect to. **3.** nearly. **4.** as a help to. —*adj.* **5.** promising. **6.** imminent.

tow·boat (tō/bōt/), *n.* a tugboat.

tow·el (tou/əl), *n., v.,* **-eled, -eling** or (*esp. Brit.*) **-elled, -elling.** —*n.* **1.** a cloth or paper for wiping and drying something wet. —*v.t.* **2.** to wipe or dry with a towel.

tow·el·ing (tou/əl Ĭng), *n.* a fabric of cotton or linen used for hand or dish towels.

tow·er (tou/ər), *n.* **1.** a tall structure, either isolated or forming part of a building. **2.** such a structure used as a fortress, prison, etc. —*v.i.* **3.** to rise or extend far upward.

tow·er·ing (tou/ər Ĭng), *adj.* **1.** very lofty. **2.** very great. **3.** very violent or intense.

tow·head (tō/hĕd/), *n.* **1.** a head of light-colored hair. **2.** a person with such hair.

tow·line (tō/līn/), *n.* a line, hawser, or the like, by which anything is towed.

town (toun), *n.* **1.** a community (usually) somewhat smaller than a city. **2.** a township. **3.** the townspeople. **4.** the shopping area. **5.** **go to town,** *Slang.* to be successful.

town·ship (toun/shĭp), *n.* **1.** (in the U.S. and Canada) an administrative division of a county. **2.** (in U.S. surveys of public land) a district 6 miles square.

towns·man (tounz/mən), *n., pl.* **-men. 1.** an inhabitant, or fellow inhabitant, of a town. **2.** (in New England) a selectman.

towns·peo·ple (tounz/pē/pəl), *n.pl.* the inhabitants collectively of a town. Also, **towns·folk** (tounz/fōk/).

tox·ic (tŏk/sĭk), *adj.* **1.** of or caused by a toxin or poison. **2.** poisonous. —**tox·ic·i·ty** (tŏks Ĭs/-ə tĬ), *n.*

tox·i·col·o·gy (tŏk/sə kŏl/ə jĭ), *n.* the science of poisons, their effects, antidotes, detection, etc. —**tox/i·col/o·gist,** *n.*

tox·in (tŏk/sĬn), *n.* any of the specific poisonous products constituting the causative agents in various diseases, as tetanus, diphtheria, etc.

toy (toi), *n.* **1.** an object for children to play with; plaything. **2.** a trifle. **3.** something diminutive. —*adj.* **4.** of or like a toy. **5.** made as a toy. —*v.i.* **6.** to play; sport. **7.** to trifle.

tp., township.

Tr, *Chem.* terbium.

tr., **1.** transitive. **2.** transpose.

trace[1] (trās), *n., v.,* **traced, tracing.** —*n.* **1.** a mark or evidence of the former presence, existence, or action of something; vestige. **2.** the track made by the passage of a person, animal, or thing. **3.** a very small amount. —*v.t.* **4.** to follow the footprints, course, etc., of. **5.** to find out; discover. **6.** to draw (a line, outline, figure, etc.). **7.** to copy (a drawing, plan, etc.) on a superimposed transparent sheet. —**trace/a·ble,** *adj.* —**trace/a·bly,** *adv.* —**trac/ing,** *n.*

trace[2] (trās), *n.* each of the two straps, ropes, or chains by which a wagon or the like is drawn by a harnessed animal.

trac·er (trā/sər), *n.* **1.** one that traces. **2.** an inquiry form sent to trace a missing shipment, parcel, or the like. **3.** a bullet, shell, etc., containing a burning composition, fired to show the path of the projectile.

trac·er·y (trā/sə rĬ), *n., pl.* **-eries. 1.** ornamental work consisting of ramified ribs, bars, or the like. **2.** any delicate interlacing work of lines, threads, etc.

tra·che·a (trā/kĬ ə), *n., pl.* **tracheae** (trā/kĬ ē/). **1.** (in air-breathing vertebrates) the tube from the larynx to the bronchi for conveying air to and from the lungs; windpipe. **2.** (in insects and other arthropods) one of the air-conveying tubes of the respiratory system. —**tra/che·al,** *adj.*

track (trăk), *n.* **1.** a pair of parallel lines of rails to provide a road for railroad trains. **2.** a wheel rut. **3.** a footprint or other mark left. **4.** a path, as for races. **5.** a course of travel, action, or motion. **6.** sight or knowledge. —*v.t.* **7.** to follow up or pursue. **8.** *U.S.* to make footprints upon (a floor, etc.). **9.** *U.S.* to make a track with (dirt, snow, etc.) carried on the feet in walking. —**track/age,** *n.* —**track/less,** *adj.*

tract[1] (trăkt), *n.* **1.** a stretch of land, water, etc.; region. **2.** *Anat.* a definite region or group of related parts.

tract[2] (trăkt), *n.* a brief treatise.

trac·ta·ble (trăk/tə bəl), *adj.* **1.** easily managed; docile. **2.** malleable. —**trac/ta·bil/i·ty, trac/ta·ble·ness,** *n.* —**trac/ta·bly,** *adv.*

trac·tion (trăk/shən), *n.* **1.** act of drawing or pulling. **2.** the drawing of a vehicle, train, or the like, along a road, track, etc. **3.** the adhesive friction of a body, as of a wheel on a rail. —**trac/tion·al,** *adj.*

trac·tor (trăk/tər), *n.* **1.** something used for drawing or pulling. **2.** a self-propelled vehicle for pulling farm machinery or the like.

trade (trād), *n., v.,* **traded, trading.** —*n.* **1.** the buying, selling, or exchanging of commodities; commerce. **2.** a purchase, sale, or exchange. **3.** an occupation pursued as a business, esp. one involving skilled mechanical work. **4.** people engaged in a particular line of business. **5.** customers. **6.** (*pl.*) the trade winds. —*v.t.* **7.** to buy and sell; barter. **8.** to exchange. —*v.i.* **9.** to carry on trade. **10.** to make an exchange. —**trad/er,** *n.*

trade·mark (trād/märk/), *n.* **1.** the name, symbol, etc., adopted and used by a manufacturer or merchant to distinguish his goods from those manufactured or sold by others. —*v.t.* **2.** to place a trademark upon. **3.** to register the trademark of.

trade name, a word or phrase whereby a particular class of goods is designated.

trades·man (trādz/mən), *n., pl.* **-men.** a man engaged in trade.

trade union, **1.** a labor union. **2.** a union of workers in related crafts. Also, *Brit.,* **trades union.** —**trade unionism.** —**trade unionist.**

trade wind, one of the winds prevailing over the oceans from about 30° north latitude to about 30° south latitude, and blowing toward the equator.

tra·di·tion (trə dĭsh/ən), *n.* **1.** the handing down of beliefs, legends, customs, etc., from generation to generation. **2.** that which is so handed down. —**tra·di/tion·al,** *adj.* —**tra·di/tion·al·ly,** *adv.*

tra·duce (trə dūs/, -dōōs/), *v.t.,* **-duced, -ducing.** to slander or malign. —**tra·duc/er,** *n.*

Tra·fal·gar (trə făl/gər), *n.* Cape, a cape on the SW coast of Spain, W of Gibraltar: British naval victory under Nelson over the French and Spanish fleets, 1805.

traf·fic (trăf/ĭk), *n., v.,* **-ficked, -ficking.** —*n.* **1.** the movement of persons, vehicles, ships, etc., along a way of travel. **2.** the persons, vehicles, etc., going along such a way. **3.** the transportation of goods for the purpose of trade. **4.** trade; commerce. —*v.i.* **5.** to carry on trade. —**traf/fick·er,** *n.*

tra·ge·di·an (trə jē/dĭ ən), *n.* **1.** an actor of tragedy. **2.** a writer of tragedy.

trag·e·dy (trăj/ə dĭ), *n., pl.* **-dies.** **1.** a dramatic composition of serious or somber character, with an unhappy ending. **2.** a lamentable, dreadful, or fatal event or affair.

trag·ic (trăj/ĭk), *adj.* **1.** sad or pathetic. **2.** dreadful, calamitous, disastrous, or fatal. **3.** pertaining to tragedy. Also, **trag/i·cal.** —**trag/i·cal·ly,** *adv.*

trail (trāl), *v.t.* **1.** to draw or drag along behind. **2.** to track. —*v.i.* **3.** to be drawn or dragged along the ground. **4.** to pass by gradual change, as into silence. —*n.* **5.** a path. **6.** the track, scent, or the like, left by an animal, person, or thing. —**trail/less,** *adj.*

trail·er (trā/lər), *n.* **1.** one that trails. **2.** a vehicle, esp. one used as a mobile house, drawn by another vehicle. **3.** a plant growing along the ground.

train (trān), *n.* **1.** a railroad locomotive and a connected series of cars moving together. **2.** a line of persons, vehicles, animals, etc., traveling together. **3.** a series of objects, parts, events, ideas, etc. **4.** a trailing part. **5.** a retinue.

—*v.t.* **6.** to instruct; educate. **7.** to make (a person, etc.) fit by proper exercise, diet, etc., as for some athletic feat. **8.** to point, aim, or direct, as a firearm, a camera, etc. —*v.i.* **9.** to give or undergo instruction, drill, practice, etc. —**train/er,** *n.* —**train/ing,** *n.*

train·ee (trā nē/), *n.* one receiving vocational or military training.

train·man (trān/mən), *n., pl.* **-men.** a member of the crew of a railroad train.

trait (trāt), *n.* a distinguishing feature or quality; characteristic.

trai·tor (trā/tər), *n.* **1.** one who betrays a person, a cause, or any trust. **2.** one guilty of treason. —**trai/tress,** *n. fem.* —**trai/tor·ous,** *adj.* —**trai/tor·ous·ly,** *adv.*

tra·jec·to·ry (trə jĕk/tə rĭ), *n., pl.* **-ries.** the curve described by a projectile in its flight through the air.

tram (trăm), *n. Brit.* a streetcar.

tram·mel (trăm/əl), *n., v.,* **-meled, -meling** or (*esp. Brit.*) **-melled, -melling.** —*n.* **1.** (*usually pl.*) anything that impedes free action. **2.** an instrument for describing ellipses. **3.** a fine-meshed net for catching fish, birds, etc. —*v.t.* **4.** to hamper; restrain. **5.** to catch in a net. —**tram/mel·er;** *esp. Brit.,* **tram/mel·ler,** *n.*

tramp (trămp), *v.i., v.t.* **1.** to tread or walk with a firm, heavy, resounding step. **2.** to walk steadily; march. **3.** to traverse on foot. —*n.* **4.** a firm, heavy, resounding tread. **5.** a long walk; hike. **6.** a vagabond. **7.** a freight vessel which does not run regularly between fixed ports. —**tramp/er,** *n.*

tram·ple (trăm/pəl), *v.i., v.t.,* **-pled, -pling.** **1.** to step heavily or roughly (upon). **2.** to domineer (over).

trance (trăns, träns), *n.* a half-conscious, dazed, or hypnotic state.

tran·quil (trăng/kwĭl), *adj.,* **-quiler, -quilest.** peaceful; quiet; calm. —**tran/quil·ly,** *adv.* —**tran/quil·ness, tran·quil/li·ty,** *n.* —**tran/quil·ize/,** *v.t., v.i.*

trans-, a prefix meaning "across," "beyond," freely applied in geographical terms (*transcontinental, trans-Siberian*).

trans., **1.** transitive. **2.** translation.

trans·act (trăns äkt/, trănz-), *v.t., v.i.* to carry through (affairs, business, etc.) to a conclusion or settlement. —**trans·ac/tor,** *n.*

trans·ac·tion (trăns äk/shən, trănz-), *n.* **1.** act of transacting. **2.** fact of being transacted. **3.** a piece of business. **4.** (*pl.*) records or reports of a learned society or the like.

trans·at·lan·tic (trăns/ət lăn/tĭk, trănz/-), *adj.* **1.** passing across the Atlantic. **2.** on the other side of the Atlantic.

trans·cend (trăn sĕnd/), *v.t., v.i.* **1.** to go or be beyond. **2.** to surpass; excel.

trans·cend·ent (trăn sĕn/dənt), *adj.* **1.** extraordinary. **2.** superior or supreme. **3.** *Theol.* (of God) transcending the material universe.

trans·cen·den·tal (trăn/sĕn dĕn/təl), *adj.* **1.** transcendent. **2.** supernatural. —**tran/scen·den/tal·ly,** *adv.*

trans·cen·den·tal·ism (trăn/sĕn dĕn/tə lĭz/əm), *n.* **1.** transcendental character. **2.** any philosophy based upon the doctrine that the principles of reality are to be discovered by the study of the processes of thought. —**tran/scen·den/tal·ist,** *n., adj.*

trans·con·ti·nen·tal (trăns/kŏn tə nĕn/təl), *adj.* **1.** passing across a continent. **2.** on the other side of a continent.

tran·scribe (trăn skrīb/), *v.t.,* **-scribed, -scribing.** **1.** to make a copy of, often in special symbols. **2.** to make a recording of (a radio program, etc.) for broadcasting. —**tran·scrib/er,** *n.*

tran·script (trăn/skrĭpt), *n.* a copy.

tran·scrip·tion (trăn skrĭp/shən), *n.* **1.** act of transcribing. **2.** a copy. **3.** *Chiefly Radio.* a phonograph record, etc., for broadcasting.

tran·sept (trăn/sĕpt), *n. Archit.* the transverse portion (or portions) of a cross-shaped church.

trans·fer (*v.* trăns fûr/; *n.* trăns/fər), *v.,* **-ferred, -ferring,** *n.* —*v.t.* **1.** to convey, hand over, or remove from one place, person, etc., to another. —*v.i.* **2.** to transfer oneself. **3.** to be transferred. **4.** to change from one streetcar, train, or the like, to another, as on a transfer (def. 8). —*n.* **5.** means or system of transferring. **6.** act of transferring. **7.** fact of being transferred. **8.** a ticket entitling a passenger to continue his journey on another streetcar, train, or the like. —**trans·fer/a·ble,**

adj. —**trans'fer·a·bil'i·ty,** *n.* —**trans·fer'-ence,** *n.*

trans·fig·u·ra·tion (trăns'fĭg yə rā'shən), *n.* 1. act of transfiguring. 2. state of being transfigured. 3. (*cap.*) the change in the appearance of Christ on the mountain.

trans·fig·ure (trăns fĭg'yər), *v.t.*, **-ured, -uring.** 1. to change in appearance; transform. 2. to glorify.

trans·fix (trăns fĭks'), *v.t.* 1. to pierce through. 2. to fix fast with or on something sharp. 3. to paralyze with terror, etc.

trans·form (trăns fôrm'), *v.t.*, *v.i.* to change in form, appearance, condition, nature, or character. —**trans·for·ma·tion** (trăns'fər mā'shən), *n.*

trans·form·er (trăns fôr'mər), *n.* 1. one that transforms. 2. *Elect.* a device for transforming a comparatively small alternating current into a larger current of lower voltage, or the reverse.

trans·fuse (trăns fūz'), *v.t.*, **-fused, -fusing.** 1. to transfer or transmit, as by pouring. 2. *Med.* to transfer (blood) from the veins or arteries of one person or animal into those of another. —**trans·fu'sion,** *n.*

trans·gress (trăns grĕs', trănz-), *v.t.*, *v.i.* 1. to go beyond (a limit, etc.). 2. to violate (a law, etc.); infringe. —**trans·gres'sion,** *n.* —**trans·gres'sor,** *n.*

tran·sient (trăn'shənt), *adj.* 1. not enduring; transitory. 2. temporary. —*n.* 3. a temporary guest, boarder, or the like. —**tran'sient·ly,** *adv.*

trans·it (trăn'sĭt, -zĭt), *n.*, *v.*, **-ited, -iting.** —*n.* 1. passage or conveyance from one place to another. 2. *Survey.* an instrument for measuring angles. —*v.t.* 3. to pass across or through.

tran·si·tion (trăn zĭsh'ən), *n.* passage from one position, state, stage, etc., to another. —**tran·si'tion·al,** *adj.* —**tran·si'tion·al·ly,** *adv.*

tran·si·tive (trăn'sə tĭv), *Gram.* —*adj.* 1. (of a verb) regularly accompanied by a direct object. —*n.* 2. a transitive verb. —**tran'si·tive·ly,** *adv.*

tran·si·to·ry (trăn'sə tōr'ĭ), *adj.* 1. not enduring or eternal. 2. brief; transient. —**tran'si·to'ri·ly,** *adv.* —**tran'si·to'ri·ness,** *n.*

Trans-Jor·dan (trăns jôr'dən, trănz-), *n.* a kingdom in SW Asia, E of Palestine. ab. 300,000 pop.; 34,750 sq. mi. *Cap.:* Amman.

trans·late (trăns lāt', trănz-), *v.t.*, *v.i.*, **-lated, -lating.** 1. to turn (something written or spoken) from one language into another. 2. to transform or convert. 3. to transfer. —**trans·lat'a·ble,** *adj.* —**trans·la'tion,** *n.* —**trans·la'tor,** *n.*

trans·lit·er·ate (trăns lĭt'ə rāt', trănz-), *v.t.*, **-ated, -ating.** to change (letters, words, etc.) into corresponding characters of another alphabet or language. —**trans'lit·er·a'tion,** *n.*

trans·lu·cent (trăns loo'sənt, trănz-), *adj.* transmitting light diffusely or imperfectly. —**trans·lu'cence,** **trans·lu'cen·cy,** *n.* —**trans·lu'cent·ly,** *adv.*

trans·mi·gra·tion (trăns'mī grā'shən, trănz'-), *n.* 1. act of migrating. 2. the passage of a soul at death into another body.

trans·mis·sion (trăns mĭsh'ən, trănz-), *n.* 1. act of transmitting. 2. fact of being transmitted. 3. that which is transmitted. 4. *Auto.* the mechanism for transmitting power from the revolutions of the engine shaft to the driving wheels. 5. *Radio.* the broadcasting of electromagnetic waves from the transmitting station to the receiving station.

trans·mit (trăns mĭt', trănz-), *v.t.*, **-mitted, -mitting.** 1. to send over or along; forward, dispatch, or convey. 2. to communicate, as news. 3. to hand down, as to heirs. 4. *Physics.* a. to cause or permit (light, heat, sound, etc.) to pass through a medium. b. to convey (an impulse, force, etc.). 5. *Radio.* to emit (electromagnetic waves). —**trans·mit'tal, trans·mit'-tance,** *n.*

trans·mit·ter (trăns mĭt'ər, trănz-), *n.* 1. one that transmits. 2. *Radio.* a device for sending electromagnetic waves. 3. that part of a telephonic or telegraphic apparatus which converts sound waves into corresponding electrical waves.

trans·mute (trăns mūt', trănz-), *v.t.*, **-muted, -muting.** to change from one nature, substance, or form into another. —**trans·mut'a·ble,** *adj.* —**trans·mut'er,** *n.*

trans·o·ce·an·ic (trăns'ō shĭ ăn'ĭk, trănz'-), *adj.* across or beyond the ocean.

tran·som (trăn'səm), *n.* 1. a crosspiece between a door and a window above it. 2. a window above such a crosspiece.

trans·pa·cif·ic (trăns'pə sĭf'ĭk), *adj.* 1. passing across the Pacific. 2. on the other side of the Pacific.

trans·par·en·cy (trăns pâr'ən sĭ, -păr'-), *n.*, *pl.* **-cies.** 1. the property of being transparent. 2. a picture, design, or the like, on glass or some translucent substance, made visible by light shining through from behind.

trans·par·ent (trăns pâr'ənt, -păr'-), *adj.* 1. having the property of allowing objects to be seen clearly through it. 2. frank; candid. 3. manifest or obvious. —**trans·par'ent·ly,** *adv.*

tran·spire (trăn spīr'), *v.i.*, *v.t.*, **-spired, -spir-ing.** 1. (*regarded as incorrect or vulgar by many*) to occur; happen. 2. to emit or give off (waste matter, watery vapor, an odor, etc.) through the surface. —**tran·spi·ra·tion** (trăn'spə rā'shən), *n.*

trans·plant (trăns plănt', -plänt'), *v.t.* 1. to remove from one place to another. 2. to bring (a colony, etc.) from one country to another for settlement. —**trans'plan·ta'tion,** *n.* —**trans·plant'er,** *n.*

trans·port (*v.* trăns pōrt'; *n.* trăns'pōrt), *v.t.* 1. to convey from one place to another. 2. to carry away by strong emotion. 3. to carry into penal banishment. —*n.* 4. a ship employed for transporting soldiers, military stores, etc. 5. an airplane carrying freight or passengers as part of a transportation system. 6. *Chiefly Brit.* conveyance. —**trans·port'a·ble,** *adj.* —**trans·port'er,** *n.*

trans·por·ta·tion (trăns'pər tā'shən), *n.* 1. act of transporting. 2. state of being transported. 3. means of conveyance. 4. cost of transport or travel.

trans·pose (trăns pōz'), *v.t.*, **-posed, -posing.** 1. to alter the relative position or order of. 2. *Alg.* to bring (a term) from one side of an equation to the other, with change of the plus or minus sign. 3. *Music.* to reproduce in a different key. —**trans'po·si'tion,** *n.*

trans·son·ic (trăns sŏn'ĭk), *adj.* *Chiefly Aeron.* close to the speed of propagation of sound; moving at 700–780 miles per hour.

tran·sub·stan·ti·a·tion (trăn'səb stăn'shĭ ā'-shən), *n.* 1. the changing of one substance into another. 2. *Rom. Cath. Theol.* the conversion, in the Eucharist, of the whole substance of the bread into the body, and of the whole substance of the wine into the blood, of Christ, only the appearance of bread and wine remaining.

Trans·vaal (trăns väl', trănz-), *n.* a NE province in the Union of South Africa. 4,183,800 pop.; ab. 110,450 sq. mi. *Cap.:* Pretoria.

trans·verse (trăns vûrs', trănz-), *adj.* 1. lying or being across; athwart. —*n.* 2. something which is transverse. —**trans·verse'ly,** *adv.*

trap (trăp), *n.*, *v.*, **trapped, trapping.** —*n.* 1. a contrivance used for taking game or other animals, as a snare. 2. any device, stratagem, or the like, for catching one unawares. 3. any of various mechanical contrivances for preventing the passage of steam, water, etc. 4. (*usually pl.*) *Chiefly Jazz.* a percussion instrument, as a bass drum with a cymbal attached to it. —*v.t.* 5. to catch in a trap. 6. to set traps for game. 7. to engage in catching animals in traps for their furs. —**trap'per,** *n.*

tra·peze (tră pēz'), *n.* a gymnasium apparatus consisting of a short horizontal bar at the ends of two suspended ropes.

tra·pe·zi·um (trə pē'zĭ əm), *n.*, *pl.* **-ziums, -zia** (-zĭ ə). *Geom.* a quadrilateral plane figure of which no two sides are parallel.

trap·e·zoid (trăp'ə zoid'), *n.* *Geom.* a quadrilateral plane figure having only two parallel sides.

trap·pings (trăp'ĭngz), *n.pl.* articles of equipment or dress, esp. of an ornamental character.

Trap·pist (trăp'ĭst), *n.* 1. a member of a monastic body observing an extremely austere rule. —*adj.* 2. of or pertaining to the Trappists.

trash (trăsh), *n.* 1. anything useless; rubbish. 2. nonsense. 3. a disreputable person. 4. such persons collectively. —**trash'y,** *adj.*

trau·ma (trô'mə, trou'-), *n.*, *pl.* **-mata** (-mə tə), **-mas.** *Pathol.* a bodily injury produced by violence, or any thermal, chemical, etc., extrinsic agent. —**trau·mat·ic** (trô mât'ĭk), *adj.*

trav·ail (trăv'āl, trăv'əl), *n.* 1. toil or exertion. 2. the labor and pain of childbirth. —*v.i.* 3. to suffer the pangs of childbirth.

trav·el (trăv'əl), *v.*, **-eled, -eling** or (*esp. Brit.*) **-elled, -elling,** *n.* —*v.i.* 1. to go from one place to another; make a journey. 2. to move in a fixed course, as a piece of mechanism. 3. to pass, or be transmitted, as light, sound, etc. —*n.* 4. act of traveling; journeying. 5. (*pl.*) journeys. —**trav′-el·er;** *esp. Brit.*, **trav′el·ler,** *n.*

trav·eled (trăv′əld), *adj.* 1. having traveled much. 2. used by travelers.

trav·e·logue (trăv′ə lôg′, -lŏg′), *n.* a lecture describing travel, usually illustrated, as with moving pictures. Also, **trav′e·log′.**

trav·erse (trăv′ərs, trə vûrs′), *v.*, **-ersed, -ers·ing,** *n., adj.* —*v.t.* 1. to pass across, over, or through. 2. to obstruct or thwart. 3. to contradict or deny. —*n.* 4. act of traversing. 5. something that crosses, obstructs, or thwarts. —*adj.* 6. cross; transverse. —**trav′ers·a·ble,** *adj.* —**trav′ers·er,** *n.*

trav·es·ty (trăv′ĭs tĭ), *n., pl.* **-ties,** *v.,* **-tied, -tying.** 1. a literary composition characterized by burlesque or ludicrous treatment of a serious work or subject. 2. any grotesque or debased likeness. —*v.t.* 3. to make a travesty on.

trawl (trôl), *n.* 1. a strong fishing net dragged along the sea bottom. 2. a buoyed fishing line having numerous short lines with baited hooks attached at intervals. —*v.i.* 3. to fish with a trawl.

trawl·er (trô′lər), *n.* 1. one who trawls. 2. a vessel used in trawling.

tray (trā), *n.* a flat, shallow container or receptacle of wood, metal, etc.

treach·er·ous (trĕch′ər əs), *adj.* 1. disloyal; traitorous. 2. untrustworthy. —**treach′er·ous·ly,** *adv.* —**treach′er·ous·ness,** *n.*

treach·er·y (trĕch′ə rĭ), *n., pl.* **-eries.** 1. betrayal of trust; treason. 2. an act of perfidy.

trea·cle (trē′kəl), *n. Brit.* molasses.

tread (trĕd), *v.,* trod or (*Archaic*) trode; trodden or trod; treading; *n.* —*v.t., v.i.* 1. to step, walk, or trample (on, about, in, or along). 2. to domineer harshly (over); crush. 3. to execute by walking or dancing. —*n.* 4. a stepping or walking, or the sound of this. 5. manner of walking. 6. a single step as in walking. 7. the sole of the foot or of a shoe. 8. the horizontal upper surface of a step in a stair, on which the foot is placed. 9. the part of a wheel, tire, or runner which bears on the road, rail, etc. —**tread′er,** *n.*

trea·dle (trĕd′əl), *n., v.,* **-dled, -dling.** —*n.* 1. a lever or the like worked by the foot to impart motion to a machine. —*v.i.* 2. to work a treadle.

tread·mill (trĕd′mĭl′), *n.* an apparatus for producing rotary motion by the weight of men or animals treading on moving steps around a horizontal cylinder.

treas., 1. treasurer. 2. treasury.

trea·son (trē′zən), *n.* violation by a subject of his allegiance to his sovereign or to the state.

trea·son·a·ble (trē′zən ə bəl), *adj.* 1. of the nature of treason. 2. traitorous. Also, **trea′son·ous.** —**trea′son·a·ble·ness,** *n.* —**trea′son·a·bly,** *adv.*

treas·ure (trĕzh′ər), *n., v.,* **-ured, -uring.** —*n.* 1. wealth or riches accumulated. 2. any thing or person greatly valued. —*v.t.* 3. to put away for future use. 4. to prize; cherish.

treas·ur·er (trĕzh′ər ər), *n.* one who is in charge of a treasury, as of a corporation, private society, state, city, etc.

treas·ur·y (trĕzh′ə rĭ), *n., pl.* **-uries.** 1. a place where public revenues, the funds of a corporation, etc., are deposited, kept, and disbursed. 2. the funds or revenue of a state, corporation, etc. 3. the department of government which has control over the collection, management, and disbursement of the public revenue.

treat (trēt), *v.t.* 1. to act toward in some specified way. 2. to regard and deal with. 3. to deal with (a disease, patient, etc.) in order to relieve or cure. 4. to discuss. 5. to deal with, develop, or represent artistically. 6. to subject to some agent or action. 7. to entertain with food, drink, amusement, etc. —*v.i.* 8. to deal with. 9. to bear the expense of a treat. 10. to negotiate. —*n.* 11. an entertainment of food, drink, amusement, etc., given as an expression of friendly regard. 12. one's turn to treat. —**treat′er,** *n.*

trea·tise (trē′tĭs), *n.* a book or writing treating of some particular subject.

treat·ment (trēt′mənt), *n.* 1. act or manner of treating. 2. behavior toward a person, etc. 3. management in the application of medicines, surgery, etc.

trea·ty (trē′tĭ), *n., pl.* **-ties.** a formal agreement between two or more states in reference to international relations.

tre·ble (trĕb′əl), *adj., n., v.,* **-bled, -bling.** —*adj.*

1. threefold; triple. 2. *Music.* **a.** of or pertaining to the highest part in harmonized music. **b.** of the highest pitch or range. **c.** high in pitch; shrill. —*n.* 3. *Music.* **a.** the treble part. **b.** a treble voice, singer, or instrument. 4. a high or shrill voice or sound. —*v.t., v.i.* 5. to triple. —**tre·bly** (trĕb′lĭ), *adv.*

treble clef, *Music.* a sign which locates the G above middle C, placed on the second line of the staff, counting up.

tree (trē), *n., v.,* **treed, treeing.** —*n.* 1. a perennial plant having a permanent, woody trunk, usually developing branches at some distance from the ground. 2. any of various similar shrubs, bushes, and herbaceous plants. 3. a diagram in the outline form of a tree, indicating the source, main stem, and branches of a family. —*v.t.* 4. to drive up a tree. —**tree′less,** *adj.*

tre·foil (trē′foil), *n.* 1. any of certain herbs having leaves of three leaflets, including the common clovers. 2. an ornamental figure or structure resembling a three-leaf clover.

trek (trĕk), *v.,* **trekked, trekking,** *n.* —*v.i.* 1. to travel; migrate. —*n.* 2. act of trekking.

trel·lis (trĕl′ĭs), *n.* 1. a lattice, esp. one used for the support of growing vines, etc. —*v.t.* 2. to furnish with or support on a trellis.

trem·ble (trĕm′bəl), *v.,* **-bled, -bling,** *n.* —*v.i.* 1. to quiver, as from fear, cold, etc. —*n.* 2. act of trembling. —**trem′bling·ly,** *adv.*

trem·bly (trĕm′blĭ), *adj.* trembling; tremulous.

tre·men·dous (trĭ mĕn′dəs), *adj. Colloq.* 1. extraordinarily great in size, amount, degree, etc. 2. unusual. —**tre·men′dous·ly,** *adv.*

trem·o·lo (trĕm′ə lō′), *n., pl.* **-los.** *Music.* a tremulous effect produced on certain instruments and in the human voice.

trem·or (trĕm′ər, trē′mər), *n.* 1. involuntary shaking of the body or limbs, as from fear, weakness, etc. 2. a vibration.

trem·u·lous (trĕm′yə ləs), *adj.* 1. trembling, as from fear, nervousness, etc. 2. fearful; timorous. 3. vibratory. —**trem′u·lous·ly,** *adv.* —**trem′u·lous·ness,** *n.*

trench (trĕnch), *n.* 1. *Fort.* a long, narrow, defensive excavation. 2. a deep furrow, ditch, or cut. —*v.t., v.i.* 3. to dig a trench or trenches (in).

trench·ant (trĕn′chənt), *adj.* 1. incisive or keen. 2. vigorous; effective. —**trench′ant·ly,** *adv.*

trend (trĕnd), *n.* 1. the general course, drift, or tendency. —*v.i.* 2. to have a general tendency.

Tren·ton (trĕn′tən), *n.* the capital of New Jersey, in the W part. 124,697.

trep·i·da·tion (trĕp′ə dā′shən), *n.* 1. tremulous alarm or agitation. 2. vibration.

tres·pass (trĕs′pəs), *v.i.* 1. to make an improper inroad on a person's presence, property, time, etc. 2. to transgress; sin. —*n.* 3. act of trespassing. —**tres′pass·er,** *n.*

tress (trĕs), *n.* a braid, lock, or curl of hair.

tres·tle (trĕs′əl), *n.* 1. a frame used as a support, consisting typically of a horizontal beam fixed at each end to a pair of spreading legs. 2. a supporting framework, as for carrying railroad tracks across a gap.

trey (trā), *n. Cards or Dice.* three.

tri-, a word element meaning "three," as in *triangle.*

tri·ad (trī′ăd), *n.* 1. a group of three. 2. *Chem.* an element, atom, or radical having a valence of three. 3. *Music.* a chord of three tones, esp. one consisting of a given tone with its major or minor third and its perfect, augmented, or diminished fifth.

tri·al (trī′əl), *n., pl.* **-als.** 1. *Law.* the examination before a judicial tribunal of the facts put in issue in a cause. 2. test; proof. 3. an attempt or effort to do something. 4. an experiment. 5. state of a person or thing being tested. 6. suffering or affliction. —*adj.* 7. done or used by way of trial, test, proof, or experiment.

tri·an·gle (trī′ăng′gəl), *n.* 1. a geometrical plane figure formed by three straight lines and three angles. 2. *Music.* an instrument of percussion, made of a steel rod bent into the form of a triangle. 3. a group of three people involved in a love entanglement. —**tri·an′gu·lar,** *adj.*

tri·an·gu·late (*adj.* trī ăng′gyə lĭt, -lāt′; *v.* trī ăng′gyə lāt′), *adj., v.,* **-lated, -lating.** —*adj.* 1. triangular. —*v.t.* 2. to make triangular. 3. to divide into triangles. 4. *Survey.* **a.** to survey (a region, etc.) by establishing dividing points into triangles and measuring the angles of these triangles. **b.** to determine trigonometrically. —tri'an·gu·la'tion, *n.*

tribe (trīb), *n.* **1.** any large group of people united by descent from a common ancestor, community of traditions, adherence to the same leaders, etc. **2.** a class, kind, or sort. **3.** any of the twelve divisions of ancient Israel, claiming descent from the twelve sons of Jacob. —trib'al, *adj.*

tribes·man (trībz'mən), *n., pl.* **-men.** a man belonging to a tribe; a member of a tribe.

trib·u·la·tion (trĭb'yə lā'shən), *n.* **1.** grievous trouble. **2.** an affliction, trouble, or trial.

tri·bu·nal (trī bū'nəl, trĭ-), *n.* **1.** a court of justice. **2.** a place of judgment.

trib·une[1] (trĭb'ūn), *n.* **1.** a person who defends popular rights. **2.** *Rom. Hist.* any of ten officers elected to protect the interests and rights of the plebeians from the patricians.

trib·une[2] (trĭb'ūn), *n.* a raised platform, rostrum, or pulpit.

trib·u·tar·y (trĭb'yə tĕr'ĭ), *n., pl.* **-taries,** *adj.* —*n.* **1.** a stream flowing into a larger stream or other body of water. **2.** one who pays tribute. —*adj.* **3.** (of a stream) flowing into a larger stream or other body of water. **4.** paying tribute.

trib·ute (trĭb'ūt), *n.* **1.** a personal offering, compliment, or the like, given in gratitude, esteem, or regard. **2.** a stated sum paid by one sovereign or state to another as the price of peace, security, protection, or the like. **3.** a rent, tax, or the like.

trice[1] (trīs), *n.* a very short time; instant.

trice[2] (trīs), *v.t.,* **triced, tricing.** *Naut.* to haul up and fasten with a rope.

tri·ceps (trī'sĕps), *n. Anat.* the extensor muscle at the back of the upper arm.

tri·chi·na (trĭ kī'nə), *n., pl.* **-nae** (-nē). a worm, the adults of which live in the intestines, esp. of pigs, rats, and man.

trich·i·no·sis (trĭk'ə nō'sĭs), *n. Pathol.* a disease due to the presence of trichinae in the intestines and muscular tissues. —trich'i·nous, *adj.*

trick (trĭk), *n.* **1.** an artifice, stratagem, ruse, or wile. **2.** a deceptive appearance. **3.** a roguish or mischievous prank. **4.** an ingenious shift; dodge. **5.** the art or knack of doing something. **6.** *Cards.* the cards collectively which are played and won in one round. **7.** *U.S. Colloq.* a child or young girl. **8.** a turn of duty. —*adj.* **9.** pertaining to or having the nature of tricks. **10.** made for tricks. —*v.t., v.i.* **11.** to deceive by trickery. **12.** to cheat or swindle. **13.** to beguile by trickery. —trick'er·y, *n.*

trick·le (trĭk'əl), *v.,* **-led, -ling,** *n.* —*v.t., v.i.* **1.** to flow by drops or in a small stream. —*n.* **2.** a trickling flow or stream.

trick·y (trĭk'ĭ), *adj.,* **trickier, trickiest. 1.** crafty; wily. **2.** skilled in clever tricks. **3.** deceptive; ticklish to handle. —trick'i·ly, *adv.* —trick'i·ness, *n.*

tri·col·or (trī'kŭl'ər), *adj.* **1.** having three colors. —*n.* **2.** a tricolor flag. **3.** the national flag of France.

tri·cus·pid (trī kŭs'pĭd), *adj.* having three cusps or points, as a tooth.

tri·cy·cle (trī'sĭk əl), *n.* a velocipede with three wheels.

tri·dent (trī'dənt), *n.* **1.** *Class. Myth.* the three-pronged spear carried by Neptune. **2.** a fish spear having three prongs. —*adj.* **3.** having three prongs or tines.

tried (trīd), *adj.* tested; proved.

tri·en·ni·al (trī ĕn'ĭ əl), *adj.* **1.** lasting three years. **2.** occurring every three years. —*n.* **3.** a period of three years. **4.** a third anniversary.

Tri·este (trī ĕst'), *n.* a seaport at the N end of the Adriatic: formerly in NE Italy; included in the internationalized **Free Territory of Trieste** (503 sq. mi.), placed under United Nations control, 1947. 257,956.

tri·fle (trī'fəl), *n., v.,* **-fled, -fling.** —*n.* **1.** an article of small value. **2.** a trivial matter, sum, or amount. —*v.i., v.t.* **3.** to deal without due seriousness or respect. **4.** to act or talk in an idle or frivolous way. **5.** to pass (time) idly or frivolously. —tri'fler, *n.*

tri·fling (trī'flĭng), *adj.* **1.** trivial; insignificant. **2.** of small value, cost, or amount. **3.** frivolous; light. —tri'fling·ly, *adv.*

tri·fo·li·ate (trī fō'lĭ ĭt, -āt'), *adj.* having three leaves, leaflike parts, or foils.

tri·fo·ri·um (trī fōr'ĭ əm), *n., pl.* **-foria** (-fōr'-

Y ə). *Archit.* (in a church) the wall at the side of the nave, choir, or transept.

trig., trigonometry.

trig·ger (trĭg'ər), *n.* **1.** (in firearms) a small projecting tongue which when pressed by the finger liberates the mechanism and discharges the weapon. **2.** a device, as a lever, the pulling or pressing of which releases a spring.

trig·o·nom·e·try (trĭg'ə nŏm'ə trĭ), *n.* the branch of mathematics that deals with the relations between the sides and angles of triangles (plane or spherical), and the calculations, etc., based on these. —trig·o·no·met·ric (trĭg'ə nə-mĕt'rĭk), trig'o·no·met'ri·cal, *adj.* —trig'o·no·met'ri·cal·ly, *adv.*

tri·lat·er·al (trī lăt'ər əl), *adj.* having three sides. —tri·lat'er·al·ly, *adv.*

trill (trĭl), *v.t., v.i.* **1** to sing or play with a vibratory effect. **2.** *Phonet.* to pronounce with vibrating articulation. **3.** (of birds, etc.) to sing. —*n.* **4.** act or sound of trilling.

tril·lion (trĭl'yən), *n.* **1.** a cardinal number represented by 1 followed (in the U.S. and France) by 12 zeros and (in Gt. Britain and Germany) by 18 zeros. —*adj.* **2.** amounting to one trillion in number.

tril·li·um (trĭl'ĭ əm), *n.* any of certain herbs of the lily family characterized by a whorl of three leaves from the center of which rises a solitary flower.

tril·o·gy (trĭl'ə jĭ), *n., pl.* **-gies.** a group of three related dramas, operas, novels, etc.

trim (trĭm), *v.,* **trimmed, trimming,** *n., adj.,* **trimmer, trimmest,** *adv.* —*v.t.* **1.** to put into a neat or orderly state by clipping, paring, etc. **2.** to remove by clipping, paring, or the like. **3.** *Naut.* to adjust (the sails or yards). **4.** to dress or array. **5.** to deck with ornaments, etc. **6.** *Colloq.* to defeat. —*n.* **7.** proper condition or order. **8.** condition or order of any kind. **9.** *Naut.* **a.** the set of a ship in the water. **b.** the adjustment of the sails, etc. **10.** dress, array, or equipment. **11.** decorative trimming. **12.** *Carp.* the visible woodwork of the interior of a building. —*adj.* **13.** pleasingly neat. **14.** in good condition or order. —*adv.* **15.** Also, **trim'ly.** in a trim manner. —trim'ness, *n.* —trim'mer, *n.*

trim·e·ter (trĭm'ə tər), *Pros.* —*n.* **1.** a verse of three measures or feet. —*adj.* **2.** consisting of three measures or feet.

trim·ming (trĭm'ĭng), *n.* **1.** anything serving to trim or decorate. **2.** a garnish. **3.** *(pl.)* pieces trimmed off. **4.** *Colloq.* a defeat.

Trin·i·dad (trĭn'ə dăd'), *n.* an island in the West Indies, off the NE coast of Venezuela: part of the British colony of **Trinidad and Tobago.** 427,995 pop.; 1864 sq. mi.

Trin·i·tar·i·an (trĭn'ə târ'ĭ ən), *adj.* believing in the doctrine of the Trinity.

tri·ni·tro·tol·u·ene (trī nī'trō tŏl'yŏŏ ēn'), *n. Chem.* a high explosive used in modern warfare, etc.: commonly known as TNT.

Trin·i·ty (trĭn'ə tĭ), *n., pl.* **-ties. 1.** the union of three persons (Father, Son, and Holy Ghost) in one Godhead. **2.** *(l.c.)* a group of three.

trin·ket (trĭng'kĭt), *n.* **1.** a small bit of jewelry or the like. **2.** anything trifling.

tri·no·mi·al (trī nō'mĭ əl), *Alg.* —*adj.* **1.** consisting of or pertaining to three terms connected by the sign +, the sign −, or both of these. —*n.* **2.** a trinomial expression.

tri·o (trē'ō), *n., pl.* **trios. 1.** a musical composition for three voices or instruments. **2.** a company of three singers or players. **3.** any group of three persons or things.

tri·ox·ide (trī ŏk'sīd, -sĭd), *n. Chem.* an oxide containing three oxygen atoms.

trip (trĭp), *n., v.,* **tripped, tripping.** —*n.* **1.** a journey or voyage. **2.** a stumble. **3.** a sudden impeding or catching of a person's foot so as to throw him down, esp. in wrestling. **4.** a slip, mistake, or blunder. —*v.i.* **5.** to stumble. **6.** to make a slip or mistake. **7.** to dance. **8.** to go with a light, quick tread. —*v.t.* **9.** to cause to stumble. **10.** to overthrow. **11.** to cause to make a slip or error. **12.** to perform with a light or tripping step, as a dance. **13.** *Mach.* to release or operate suddenly (a catch, etc.).

tri·par·tite (trī pär'tīt, trĭp'ər tīt'), *adj.* **1.** divided into or consisting of three parts. **2.** participated in by three parties, as a treaty.

tripe (trīp), *n.* **1.** the first and second divisions of the stomach of a ruminant, esp. of the ox kind, prepared for use as food. **2.** *Slang.* anything worthless.

tri·ple (trĭp/əl), adj., n., v., **-pled, -pling.** —adj.
1. consisting of three parts. 2. three times as
great. —n. 3. an amount, number, etc., three
times as great as another. 4. Baseball. a three-
base hit. —v.t. 5. to make triple. —v.i. 6. to
become triple. 7. Baseball. to hit a three-base
hit. —**tri·ply** (trĭp/lĭ), adv.

tri·plet (trĭp/lĭt), n. 1. one of three children
(**triplets**) born at one birth. 2. Music. a group
of three notes to be performed in the time of two
ordinary notes of the same kind.

trip·li·cate (v. trĭp/lə kāt/; adj., n. trĭp/lə kĭt,
-kāt/), v., **-cated, -cating,** adj., n. —v.t. 1. to
triple. —adj. 2. threefold; triple. —n. 3. one of
three things.

tri·pod (trī/pŏd), n. a stool, pedestal, stand, or
the like, with three legs, as one for supporting a
camera.

Trip·o·li (trĭp/ə lĭ), n. 1. one of the former
Barbary States of N Africa: now a part of Libya.
2. a seaport in and the capital of Libya, in the
NW part. 96,412.

trip·per (trĭp/ər), n. 1. one that trips. 2.
Mach. a tripping device.

trip·tych (trĭp/tĭk), n. 1. Art. a set of three
panels side by side, bearing pictures, carvings, or
the like. 2. a hinged three-leaved writing tablet.

tri·reme (trī/rēm), n. Class. Hist. a galley with
three rows of oars on each side, one above another.

Tris·tram (trĭs/trəm), n. one of the knights of
the Round Table. Also, **Tris·tan** (trĭs/tən).

tri·syl·la·ble (trī sĭl/ə bəl, trī-), n. a word of
three syllables.

trite (trīt), adj., **triter, tritest.** hackneyed;
commonplace. —**trite/ly,** adv. —**trite/ness,** n.

Tri·ton (trī/tən), n. Class. Myth. a sea god having the head and trunk of a man and the tail of
a fish, and bearing a conch-shell trumpet.

trit·u·rate (trĭch/ə rāt/), v., **-rated, -rating,** n.
—v.t. 1. to reduce to fine particles or powder;
pulverize. —n. 2. a triturated substance.
—**trit/u·ra/tion,** n.

tri·umph (trī/əmf), n. 1. victory; conquest. 2.
joy over success or victory. —v.i. 3. to be victorious. 4. to prevail. 5. to achieve success.
6. to rejoice over success. —**tri·um·phal** (trī-
ŭm/fəl), adj. —**tri·um/phant,** adj. —**tri·um/-
phant·ly,** adv.

tri·um·vir (trī ŭm/vər), n., pl. **-virs, -viri** (-və-
rī/). Rom. Hist. one of three magistrates exercising the same public function. —**tri·um/vi·
ral,** adj.

tri·um·vi·rate (trī ŭm/və rĭt, -rāt/), n. **.** 1.
Rom. Hist. the office of a triumvir. 2. the government of three joint magistrates. 3. any association of three in office. 4. any group of three.

tri·va·lent (trī vā/lənt, trĭv/ə lənt), adj. Chem.
having a valence of three.

triv·et (trĭv/ĭt), n. 1. a small metal plate with
short legs put under a hot dish at the table. 2.
any three-legged stand.

triv·i·a (trĭv/ĭ ə), n. pl. trifles.

triv·i·al (trĭv/ĭ əl), adj. trifling; insignificant.
—**triv/i·al·ly,** adv. —**triv·i·al·i·ty** (trĭv/ĭ ăl/ə-
tĭ), n.

tro·che (trō/kĭ), n. Pharm. a small tablet of
some medicinal substance.

tro·chee (trō/kē), n. Pros. a foot of two syllables, a long followed by a short. —**tro·cha·ic**
(trō kā/ĭk), adj.

trog·lo·dyte (trŏg/lə dīt/), n. 1. a cave dweller. 2. a person living in seclusion. 3. one unacquainted with affairs of the world.

Troi·lus (troi/ləs, trō/ĭ ləs), n. Class. and Med.
Legend. the warrior son of King Priam of Troy:
lover of Cressida.

Tro·jan (trō/jən), adj. 1. of ancient Troy.
—n. 2. a native or inhabitant of Troy. 3. Colloq.
one who shows pluck or energy.

Trojan War, Class. Legend. a ten-years' war
waged by the confederated Greeks against the
Trojans to avenge the abduction of Helen, wife of
a Greek king, by Paris, son of the Trojan king
Priam, and ending in the sack and burning of
Troy.

troll[1] (trōl), v.t., v.i. 1. to sing in a full, rolling
voice. 2. to sing as a round. 3. to fish with (a
moving line), as one trailed behind a boat. —n.
4. a song whose parts are sung in succession;
round. —**troll/er,** n.

troll[2] (trōl), n. (in Scandinavian folklore) a supernatural giant or dwarf inhabiting caves.

trol·ley (trŏl/ĭ), n., pl. **-leys.** 1. a trolley car.

2. a pulley on an overhead track, serving to support and move a suspended object. 3. a pulley
carried on the end of a pole (**trolley pole**) by an
electric car, and held in contact with an overhead
wire from which it receives current.

trolley car, a streetcar propelled electrically
by current taken from a conductor by means of
a trolley.

trol·lop (trŏl/əp), n. 1. an untidy or slovenly
woman; slattern. 2. prostitute.

Trol·lope (trŏl/əp), n. **Anthony,** 1815–82, British novelist.

trom·bone (trŏm/bōn, trŏm bōn/), n. a musical wind instrument consisting of a cylindrical
metal tube expanding into a bell and bent twice
in U shape, usually equipped with a slide (in
which case, called **slide trombone**). —**trom/bon-
ist,** n.

troop (trōōp), n. 1. an assemblage of persons or
things. 2. a multitude. 3. Mil. an armored
cavalry unit. 4. (pl.) a body of soldiers, police,
etc. 5. a unit of 32 Boy Scouts. —v.i. 6. to
gather together. 7. to go or come in great numbers. 8. to walk, go, or pass away.

troop·er (trōō/pər), n. 1. a horse-cavalry soldier. 2. a mounted policeman.

troop·ship (trōōp/shĭp/), n. a ship for the conveyance of military troops; transport.

trope (trōp), n. Rhet. a figure of speech.

tro·phy (trō/fĭ), n., pl. **-phies.** 1. anything
taken in war, hunting, etc., as a memento. 2.
anything serving as a token of victory, valor, etc.

trop·ic (trŏp/ĭk), n. 1. Geog. either of two corresponding parallels of latitude on the terrestrial
globe, one (**tropic of Cancer**) about 23¹/₂° north,
and the other (**tropic of Capricorn**) about 23¹/₂°
south, of the equator, being the boundaries of the
torrid zone. 2. **the tropics,** the regions lying between and near these parallels of latitude. —adj.
3. tropical.

trop·i·cal (trŏp/ə kəl), adj. of, occurring in, or
inhabiting the tropics. —**trop/i·cal·ly,** adv.

tro·pism (trō/pĭz əm), n. Biol. the response of
a plant or animal, as in growth, to the influence of
external stimuli. —**tro·pis/tic,** adj.

trop·o·sphere (trŏp/ə sfĭr/), n. Meteorol. the
inner layer of the atmosphere, varying in height
between about 6 miles and 12 miles, within which
nearly all cloud formations occur.

trot (trŏt), v., **trotted, trotting,** n. —v.i. 1. (of a
horse, etc.) to go at a gait between a walk and a
run, in which the legs move in diagonal pairs but
not quite simultaneously. 2. to go briskly,
bustle, or hurry. —v.t. 3. to cause to trot. 4. to
ride at a trot. 5. Colloq. to show for inspection.
—n. 6. the gait of a horse, etc., when trotting.
7. a jogging gait between a walk and a run.
—**trot/ter,** n.

troth (trŏth, trōth), n. Archaic. 1. fidelity or
loyalty. 2. truth. 3. a promise.

Trot·sky (trŏt/skĭ), n. **Leon,** 1879–1940, Russian revolutionary leader.

trou·ba·dour (trōō/bə dōr/, -dōōr/), n. one of
the lyric poets who flourished in S France, E
Spain, and N Italy from the 11th to the 13th
century, and wrote chiefly on chivalric love and
gallantry.

trou·ble (trŭb/əl), v., **-bled, -bling,** n. —v.t. 1.
to distress; worry. 2. to put to inconvenience,
exertion, or the like. 3. to cause bodily pain or
inconvenience to. 4. to bother. 5. to disturb or
agitate. —v.i. 6. to put oneself to inconvenience.
7. to worry. —n. 8. harassment, annoyance, or
difficulty. 9. unfortunate circumstances. 10. disturbance or disorder. 11. inconvenience endured.
12. something that troubles. —**trou/bler,** n.

trou·ble-shoot·er (trŭb/əl shōō/tər), n. an
expert in discovering and eliminating the cause of
some trouble.

trou·ble·some (trŭb/əl səm), adj. 1. causing
trouble; vexatious. 2. difficult. —**trou/ble-
some·ly,** adv. —**trou/ble·some·ness,** n.

trou·blous (trŭb/ləs), adj. Archaic. 1. disturbed. 2. restless. 3. troublesome.

trough (trôf, trŏf), n. 1. an open, boxlike receptacle, as for food for animals. 2. a channel for
rainwater, as under the eaves of a building. 3.
any long hollow.

trounce (trouns), v.t., **trounced, trouncing.** 1.
to beat severely. 2. Colloq. to defeat.

troupe (trōōp), n. a company, esp. of players,
singers, or the like.

troup·er (trōō/pər), n. 1. an actor in a theatrical company. 2. a veteran actor.

trou·sers (trou′zərz), *n. pl.* a loose-fitting outer garment for men and boys, covering the lower part of the trunk and each leg separately.

trous·seau (trōō sō′, trōō′sō), *n., pl.* **-seaux, -seaus.** a bride's outfit of clothes, etc.

trout (trout), *n., pl.* **trouts,** (*esp. collectively*) **trout.** any of certain fishes of the salmon family, many species of which are noted for their gameness and prized as food.

trow (trō), *v.i. Archaic.* to believe.

trow·el (trou′əl), *n., v.,* **-eled, -eling** or (*esp. Brit.*) **-elled, -elling.** —*n.* 1. any of various flat-bladed tools used for spreading or smoothing plaster or the like. 2. a similar tool with a scoop-like blade, used in gardening. —*v.t.* 3. to apply or smooth with a trowel.

Troy (troi), *n.* 1. an ancient ruined city in NW Asia Minor. 2. a city in E New York. 70,304.

troy weight (troi), a system of weights in use for precious metals and gems.

tru·ant (trōō′ənt), *n.* 1. a student who stays away from school without leave. 2. one who shirks his duty. —*adj.* 3. staying away from school without leave. 4. of a truant. —**tru′an·cy,** *n.*

truce (trōōs), *n.* 1. *Mil.* a suspension of hostilities, by agreement, for a specified period; armistice. 2. respite.

truck[1] (trŭk), *n.* 1. an automotive vehicle designed for carrying heavy loads. 2. any of various wheeled frames, esp. for moving heavy articles. —*v.t., v.i.* 3. to transport (goods, etc.) by a truck or trucks. 4. to drive a truck. —**truck′age,** *n.* —**truck′er,** *n.*

truck[2] (trŭk), *n.* 1. *U.S.* vegetables, etc., raised for the market. 2. miscellaneous articles. 3. *Colloq.* rubbish. 4. *Colloq.* dealings. 5. barter. 6. a deal. —*v.t., v.i.* 7. to exchange; trade.

truck·le (trŭk′əl), *v.i.,* **-led, -ling.** to submit or yield obsequiously. —**truck′ler,** *n.* —**truck′ling·ly,** *adv.*

truckle bed, a low bed on casters, usually pushed under another when not in use.

truc·u·lent (trŭk′yə lənt, trōō′kyə-), *adj.* fierce and cruel; bullying. —**truc′u·lence, truc′u·len·cy,** *n.* —**truc′u·lent·ly,** *adv.*

trudge (trŭj), *v.,* **trudged, trudging,** *n.* —*v.i.* 1. to walk, esp. wearily. —*n.* 2. a laborious walk. —**trudg′er,** *n.*

true (trōō), *adj.,* **truer, truest,** *adv., v.,* **trued, truing** or **trueing.** —*adj.* 1. conforming to fact; not false. 2. real or genuine. 3. sincere. 4. loyal; faithful. 5. exact; correct. 6. properly so called. —*adv.* 7. in a true manner. 8. exactly or accurately. —*v.t.* 9. to shape, adjust, place, etc., exactly or accurately. —**true′ness,** *n.*

true-blue (trōō′blōō′), *adj.* stanch; true.

truf·fle (trŭf′əl, trōō′fəl), *n.* any of certain subterranean edible fungi.

tru·ism (trōō′iz əm), *n.* an obvious truth.

trull (trŭl), *n.* a prostitute; strumpet.

tru·ly (trōō′lĭ), *adv.* 1. faithfully. 2. in accordance with fact or truth. 3. exactly or accurately. 4. rightly. 5. really or genuinely.

Tru·man (trōō′mən), *n.* **Harry S.,** born 1884, 33rd president of the U.S., 1945–1953 (from death of F. D. Roosevelt; elected to full term in 1948).

trump[1] (trŭmp), *Cards.* —*n.* 1. any playing card of a suit that for the time outranks the other suits. 2. the suit itself. —*v.t.* 3. to take with a trump. —*v.i.* 4. to play a trump.

trump[2] (trŭmp), *v.t.* to devise deceitfully or unfairly; fabricate.

trum·pet (trŭm′pĭt), *n.* 1. *Music.* any of a family of musical wind instruments with a penetrating, powerful tone, consisting of a tube with a flaring bell at one end. —*v.i.* 2. to blow a trumpet. 3. to emit a loud sound, as an elephant. —*v.t.* 4. to proclaim.

Piston trumpet

trum·pet·er (trŭm′pĭt ər), *n.* 1. one who plays a trumpet. 2. one who proclaims something with a trumpet.

trun·cate (trŭng′kāt), *v.,* **-cated, -cating,** *adj.* —*v.t.* 1. to shorten by cutting off a part. 2. *Geom.* to cut off the apex, vertex, or end of by a plane. —*adj.* 3. truncated. —**trun·ca′tion,** *n.*

trun·cheon (trŭn′chən), *n.* 1. *Chiefly Brit.* a club carried by a policeman. 2. a baton, or staff of authority. —*v.t.* 3. to beat with a club.

trun·dle (trŭn′dəl), *v.,* **-dled, -dling,** *n.* —*v.t.,*

v.i. 1. to roll along; roll, as on wheels. —*n.* 2. a small wheel, roller, or the like.

trunk (trŭngk), *n.* 1. the main stem of a tree. 2. a box for holding clothes and other articles. 3. the body of a human being or of an animal, without the head and limbs. 4. the main body of anything. 5. the main line of a river, railroad, canal, or the like. 6. a telephone line or channel between two central offices. 7. (*pl.*) short trousers, worn by athletes, etc. 8. the long, flexible, cylindrical nasal appendage of the elephant.

truss (trŭs), *v.t.* 1. to tie, bind, or fasten. 2. *Bldg. Trades, etc.* to furnish or support with a truss or trusses. —*n.* 3. *Bldg. Trades, etc.* a combination of beams, bars, or the like, arranged to form a rigid framework: used in bridges, roofs, etc. 4. *Med.* an apparatus for maintaining a hernia in a reduced state. 5. a bundle; pack.

trust (trŭst), *n.* 1. reliance on the integrity, justice, etc., of a person. 2. confident hope. 3. confidence in the ability or intention of a person to pay at some future time for goods, etc.; credit. 4. obligation or responsibility. 5. care or custody. 6. something entrusted to one, as an office, duty, etc. 7. *Law.* a fiduciary relationship in which one person holds the title to property for the benefit of another. 8. *Com.* a. a combination of companies having a central board of trustees, controlling each of the constituent companies. b. a monopolistic organization. —*adj.* 9. *Law.* of or pertaining to trusts or a trust. —*v.i.* 10. to have or place reliance or confidence. 11. to hope. 12. to sell goods on credit. 13. **trust to,** to depend on. —*v.t.* 14. to rely on. 15. to believe. 16. to hope. 17. to permit to be in some place, position, etc., or to do something, without fear of consequences. 18. to give credit to (a person) for goods, etc., supplied. —**trust′er,** *n.*

trus·tee (trŭs tē′), *n. Law.* 1. a person appointed to administer the affairs of a company, etc. 2. a person who holds the title to property for the benefit of another.

trus·tee·ship (trŭs tē′shĭp), *n.* 1. the office of a trustee. 2. the administrative control of a territory granted to a country by the United Nations. 3. a territory so controlled.

trust·ful (trŭst′fəl), *adj.* trusting; confiding. —**trust′ful·ly,** *adv.* —**trust′ful·ness,** *n.*

trust·ing (trŭs′tĭng), *adj.* that trusts. —**trust′ing·ly,** *adv.* —**trust′ing·ness,** *n.*

trust·wor·thy (trŭst′wûr′thĭ), *adj.* worthy of trust; reliable. —**trust′wor′thi·ly,** *adv.* —**trust′wor′thi·ness,** *n.*

trust·y (trŭs′tĭ), *adj.,* **trustier, trustiest,** *n., pl.* **trusties.** —*adj.* 1. trustworthy; reliable. —*n.* 2. one that is trusted. 3. a trustworthy convict given special privileges. —**trust′i·ly,** *adv.* —**trust′i·ness,** *n.*

truth (trōōth), *n.* 1. the true or actual facts of a case. 2. conformity with fact or reality. 3. a verified or indisputable fact, principle, or the like. 4. the state or character of being true.

truth·ful (trōōth′fəl), *adj.* 1. telling the truth. 2. conforming to truth. —**truth′ful·ly,** *adv.* —**truth′ful·ness,** *n.*

try (trī), *v.,* **tried, trying,** *n., pl.* **tries.** —*v.t.* 1. to attempt to do or accomplish. 2. to test or experiment with. 3. *Law.* to examine and determine judicially. 4. to strain the endurance, patience, etc., of. —*v.i.* 5. to make an attempt or effort. —*n.* 6. *Colloq.* an attempt.

try·ing (trī′ĭng), *adj.* annoying; distressing.

try·out (trī′out′), *n. U.S. Colloq.* a trial or test to ascertain fitness for some purpose.

tryst (trĭst, trīst), *n.* 1. an appointment to meet. 2. an appointed meeting. 3. an appointed place of meeting. —*v.t., v.i.* 4. to meet. —**tryst′er,** *n.*

tsar (tsär), *n.* czar.

Tschai·kov·sky (chī kôf′skĭ), *n.* **Pëtr Ilich** (Eng. *Peter Ilych*), 1840–93, Russian composer.

tset·se fly (tsĕt′sĭ), any of the blood-sucking flies of Africa, some of which transmit parasites which cause sleeping sickness.

Tsing·tao (tsĭng′tou′), *n.* a seaport in E China. 590,000.

tsp., teaspoon.

T square, a T-shaped ruler used in mechanical drawing for making straight lines, etc.

Tu, *Chem.* thulium.

tub (tŭb), *n., v.,* **tubbed, tubbing.** —*n.* 1. a bathtub. 2. *Colloq.* a bath in a tub. 3. a keglike container, as for butter. 4. as much as a tub will hold. 5. *Colloq.* a slow, clumsy ship or boat.

—*v.t., v.i.* **6.** to put in a tub. **7.** *Colloq.* to wash (oneself) in a tub.

tu·ba (tū′bə, tōō′bə), *n., pl.,* **-bas, -bae** (-bē). a brass wind instrument of low pitch equipped with valves.

tub·by (tŭb′ĭ), *adj.,* **-bier, -biest.** short and fat. —**tub′bi·ness,** *n.*

tube (tūb, tōōb), *n.* **1.** a hollow pipe of metal, glass, rubber, or other material, for conveying fluids, etc. **2.** a small, compressible container for paint, toothpaste, etc. **3.** *Biol.* any hollow, cylindrical vessel or organ. **4.** the tunnel in which an underground railroad runs. **5.** *Colloq.* the railroad itself. **6.** *Electronics.* an electron tube.

tu·ber (tū′bər, tōō′-), *n.* *Bot.* a fleshy thickening or outgrowth of a subterranean stem or shoot.

tu·ber·cle (tū′bər kəl, tōō′-), *n.* **1.** a small rounded projection or excrescence. **2.** *Pathol.* **a.** a small, firm, rounded nodule or swelling. **b.** such a swelling as the characteristic lesion of tuberculosis.

tu·ber·cu·lar (tū bûr′kyə lər, tōō-), *adj.* **1.** pertaining to tuberculosis. **2.** pertaining to or having a tubercle or tubercles.

tu·ber·cu·lo·sis (tū bûr′kyə lō′sĭs, tōō-), *n.* *Pathol.* an infectious disease affecting any of various tissues of the body, characterized by the production of tubercles. —**tu·ber′cu·lous,** *adj.*

tube·rose (tūb′rōz′, tōōb′-), *n.* a bulbous plant cultivated for its spike of fragrant, creamy-white lilylike flowers.

tu·ber·ous (tū′bər əs, tōō′-), *adj.* **1.** covered with or characterized by tubers. **2.** bearing tubers.

tub·ing (tū′bĭng, tōō′-), *n.* **1.** material in the form of a tube. **2.** tubes collectively.

tu·bu·lar (tū′byə lər, tōō′-), *adj.* **1.** of or pertaining to a tube or tubes. **2.** tube-shaped.

tuck (tŭk), *v.t.* **1.** to thrust into some narrow space. **2.** to thrust the edge or end of (a napkin, etc.) between retaining parts. **3.** to cover snugly. **4.** to draw up in folds. —*n.* **5.** a tucked piece or part. **6.** *Needlework.* a fold made by doubling cloth upon itself.

tuck·er (tŭk′ər), *n.* **1.** a piece of linen, muslin, or the like, worn by women about the neck and shoulders. —*v.t.* **2.** *U.S. Colloq.* to tire; exhaust.

Tuc·son (tōō sŏn′, tōō′sŏn), *n.* a city in S Arizona: health resort. 36,818.

Tu·dor (tū′dər, tōō′-), *n.* the royal house which reigned in England from 1485 to 1603.

Tues., Tuesday.

Tues·day (tūz′dĭ, tōōz′-), *n.* the third day of the week, following Monday.

tuft (tŭft), *n.* **1.** a bunch of feathers, hairs, etc., fixed at the base. **2.** a small clump of bushes, trees, etc. **3.** a cluster of flowers, leaves, etc. —*v.t.* **4.** to arrange in a tuft or tufts. **5.** *Upholstery.* to draw together (a cushion, etc.) by passing a thread through at regular intervals. —*v.i.* **6.** to form a tuft or tufts. —**tuft′ed,** *adj.*

tug (tŭg), *v.,* **tugged, tugging,** *n.* —*v.t., v.i.* **1.** to pull with force or effort; drag; haul. —*n.* **2.** act of tugging. **3.** a tugboat.

tug·boat (tŭg′bōt′), *n.* a heavily powered vessel for towing other vessels.

tu·i·tion (tū ĭsh′ən, tōō-), *n.* **1.** the charge for instruction. **2.** instruction.

tu·lip (tū′lĭp, tōō′-), *n.* any of certain plants of the lily family having large, showy, cup-shaped flowers.

tulle (tōōl), *n.* a thin silk or rayon net.

Tul·sa (tŭl′sə), *n.* a city in NE Oklahoma. 142,157.

tum·ble (tŭm′bəl), *v.,* **-bled, -bling,** *n.* —*v.i.* **1.** to fall over or down, as by losing footing. **2.** to fall rapidly in price. **3.** to perform leaps, somersaults, or other gymnastic feats. **4.** to roll about; toss. —*v.t.* **5.** to send tumbling. **6.** to disorder. —*n.* **7.** an act of tumbling; fall. **8.** disorder or confusion.

tum·ble-down (tŭm′bəl doun′), *adj.* dilapidated; ruinous.

tum·bler (tŭm′blər), *n.* **1.** a drinking glass. **2.** one who performs leaps, somersaults, etc. **3.** (in a lock) any part which locks the bolt.

tum·ble·weed (tŭm′bəl wēd′), *n.* *U.S.* any of certain plants whose upper part becomes detached in autumn and is driven about by the wind.

tu·mid (tū′mĭd, tōō′-), *adj.* **1.** swollen. **2.** pompous, turgid, or bombastic. —**tu·mid′i·ty,** **tu′mid·ness,** *n.* —**tu′mid·ly,** *adv.*

tu·mor (tū′mər, tōō′-), *n.* **1.** a swollen part. **2.** *Pathol.* an abnormal swelling, esp. a morbid overgrowth of new tissue. —**tu′mor·ous,** *adj.*

tu·mult (tū′mŭlt, tōō′-), *n.* **1.** commotion or uproar. **2.** a mental or emotional disturbance.

tu·mul·tu·ous (tū mŭl′chŏŏ əs, tōō-), *adj.* **1.** full of or marked by tumult or uproar. **2.** disorderly or noisy. **3.** disturbed or agitated. —**tu·mul′tu·ous·ly,** *adv.* —**tu·mul′tu·ous·ness,** *n.*

tun (tŭn), *n.* a large cask for liquids, etc., esp. wine, ale, or beer.

tu·na (tōō′nə), *n.* **1.** any of certain large oceanic fishes closely related to the tunny. **2.** the tunny. Also, **tuna fish.**

tun·dra (tŭn′drə, tōōn′-), *n.* a vast, level, treeless plain of arctic regions.

tune (tūn, tōōn), *n., v.,* **tuned, tuning.** —*n.* **1.** a succession of musical sounds forming a melody. **2.** state of being in the proper pitch. **3.** harmony. **4.** due agreement, as of radio instruments, with respect to frequency. **5.** mood. **6.** accord. **7.** due or good condition. —*v.t., v.i.* **8.** to adjust (a musical instrument) to a correct pitch. **9.** to adjust a radio apparatus so as to receive (the signals of a sending station). **10.** to adjust. —**tun′a·ble, tune′a·ble,** *adj.* —**tune′ful,** *adj.* —**tune′less,** *adj.* —**tun′er,** *n.*

tung·sten (tŭng′stən), *n.* *Chem.* a rare metallic element used for making electric-lamp filaments, etc. *Symbol:* W; *at. wt.:* 183.92; *at. no.:* 74; *sp. gr.:* 19.3.

tu·nic (tū′nĭk, tōō′-), *n.* **1.** *Chiefly Brit.* a coat worn as part of a military or other uniform. **2.** a gownlike garment worn by both sexes among the ancient Greeks and Romans. **3.** a woman's garment, extending below the waist and over the skirt.

tuning fork, a small two-pronged steel instrument designed to produce, when struck, a pure musical tone of a definite, constant pitch.

Tu·nis (tū′nĭs, tōō′-), *n.* the capital of Tunisia, in the NE part. 219,578.

Tu·ni·sia (tū nĭsh′ə, tōō′-), *n.* a French protectorate in N Africa. 2,608,313 pop.; 60,166 sq. mi. *Cap.:* Tunis.

tun·nel (tŭn′əl), *n., v.,* **-neled, -neling,** or (*esp. Brit.*) **-nelled, -nelling.** —*n.* **1.** an underground passage. —*v.i.* **2.** to make a tunnel.

tun·ny (tŭn′ĭ), *n., pl.* **-nies,** (*esp. collectively*) **-ny.** any of certain widely distributed, edible fishes of the mackerel family.

tur·ban (tûr′bən), *n.* **1.** a headdress worn by men of Eastern nations, consisting of a scarf wound around the head or around a cap. **2.** some headdress resembling this.

tur·bid (tûr′bĭd), *adj.* **1.** opaque or muddy. **2.** dense. **3.** confused; muddled. —**tur·bid′i·ty,** **tur′bid·ness,** *n.* —**tur′bid·ly,** *adv.*

tur·bine (tûr′bĭn, -bīn), *n.* a motor in which a vaned wheel is made to revolve by the pressure of water, steam, gas, air, etc.

tur·bo·jet (tûr′bō jĕt′), *n.* a jet-propulsion engine in which air is compressed by a turbine-driven compressor.

tur·bu·lent (tûr′byə lənt), *adj.* **1.** given to or marked by disorder or insubordination. **2.** disturbed; tumultuous. —**tur′bu·lent·ly,** *adv.* —**tur′bu·lence,** *n.*

tu·reen (tōō rēn′, tyŏŏ-), *n.* a large deep dish with a cover, for soup, etc., at table.

turf (tûrf), *n.* **1.** the covering of grass and roots forming the surface of grassland. **2.** the turf, **a.** a track for horse races. **b.** horse racing. **3.** peat as a fuel. —*v.t.* **4.** to cover with turf. —**turf′y,** *adj.*

Tur·ge·nev (tŏŏr gĕ′nyĕf), *n.* **Ivan Sergee-vich,** 1818–83, Russian novelist.

tur·gid (tûr′jĭd), *adj.* **1.** swollen. **2.** pompous or bombastic. —**tur·gid′i·ty,** **tur′gid·ness,** *n.* —**tur′gid·ly,** *adv.*

Tu·rin (tyŏŏr′ĭn, tyŏŏ rĭn′), *n.* a city in NW Italy. 703,765.

Turk (tûrk), *n.* a native or inhabitant of Turkey, esp. a Mohammedan.

Tur·ke·stan (tûr′kĭ stăn′, -stän′), *n.* a vast region in W and central Asia, E of the Caspian Sea.

tur·key (tûr′kĭ), *n., pl.* **-keys.** either of two large American domesticated birds esteemed for eating.

Tur·key (tûr′kĭ), *n.* a republic in W Asia and SE Europe. 17,820,079 pop.; 296,184 sq. mi. *Cap.:* Ankara. —**Turk′ish,** *adj., n.*

tur·moil (tûr′moil), *n.* commotion or disturbance; tumult.

turn (tûrn), *v.t.* **1.** to cause to move round; rotate. **2.** to reverse or change the position of. **3.** to divert; deflect. **4.** to change. **5.** to cause to become sour, fermented, or the like. **6.** to cause (the stomach) to reject food. **7.** to put to some use. **8.** to go round. **9.** to pass (a certain age, time, etc.). **10.** to direct or aim. **11.** to avert (the eyes, face, etc.). **12.** to shape on a lathe. **13.** to send; drive. **14.** to curve, bend, or twist. —*v.i.* **15.** to move round; rotate. **16.** to direct one's thought, desire, etc. **17.** to hinge or depend. **18.** to change the course or position. **19.** to curve; bend. **20.** to be affected with nausea. **21.** to change or alter. **22.** to become sour, fermented, or the like. **23.** to become of a different color, as leaves. **24.** to become. **25. turn down,** *Slang.* to refuse or reject. **26. turn in,** *Colloq.* to go to bed. **27. turn up,** to make one's or its appearance. —*n.* **28.** a movement of rotation. **29.** act of changing position or course. **30.** the time for action which comes in due order to each of a number of persons, etc. **31.** a point at which a change occurs. **32.** direction, drift, or trend. **33.** a short walk, ride, or the like. **34.** natural inclination or aptitude. **35.** an act of service or disservice. **36. to a turn,** to just the proper degree.

turn·buck·le (tûrn′bŭk′əl), *n.* a link with a swivel at one end and an internal screw thread at the other, or with an internal screw thread at each end, used as a means of coupling two parts.

turn·coat (tûrn′kōt′), *n.* a renegade.

tur·nip (tûr′nəp), *n.* **1.** the thick, fleshy edible root of certain plants of the cabbage family, including the common **white turnip** and the **Swedish turnip** (or rutabaga). **2.** the plant itself.

turn·key (tûrn′kē), *n., pl.* **-keys.** one who has charge of the keys of a prison.

turn·out (tûrn′out′), *n.* **1.** the body of persons who come to an assemblage, spectacle, or the like. **2.** output. **3.** act of turning out. **4.** equipment or outfit.

turn·o·ver (tûrn′ō′vər), *n.* **1.** upset. **2.** the aggregate of worker replacements in a given period in a given business. **3.** the number of times that capital is invested and reinvested in a line of merchandise during a specified period of time. **4.** the total amount of business done in a given time. **5.** a small semicircular pie.

turn·pike (tûrn′pīk′), *n.* a barrier set across a road (**turnpike road**) to stop passage until toll is paid.

turn·stile (tûrn′stīl′), *n.* a structure of two horizontal crossed bars on a post, set in a gateway.

turn·ta·ble (tûrn′tā′bəl), *n.* **1.** *Railroads.* a rotating, track-bearing platform. **2.** the rotating disk bearing the record in a phonograph.

tur·pen·tine (tûr′pən tīn′), *n.* **1.** any of certain oleoresins derived from coniferous trees, yielding a volatile oil and a resin when distilled. **2.** this oil.

tur·pi·tude (tûr′pə tūd′, -tōōd′), *n.* shameful depravity.

tur·quoise (tûr′koiz, -kwoiz), *n.* **1.** a greenish-blue compact opaque mineral, much used in jewelry. **2.** bluish green.

tur·ret (tûr′ĭt), *n.* **1.** a small tower. **2.** *Naval, Mil.* a low, towerlike, heavily armored structure, usually revolving horizontally, within which guns are mounted.

tur·tle (tûr′təl), *n.* any of certain marine reptiles having the body enclosed in a shell from which the head, tail, and four legs protrude.

tur·tle·dove (tûr′təl dŭv′), *n.* a small, slender Old World dove.

tusk (tŭsk), *n.* **1.** a tooth developed to great length, usually as one of a pair, as in the elephant, walrus, wild boar, etc. **2.** a long, pointed, or protruding tooth. —**tusked** (tŭskt), *adj.*

tus·sle (tŭs′əl), *v.i.,* **-sled, -sling,** *n.* struggle, fight, or scuffle.

tu·te·lage (tū′tə lĭj, tōō′-), *n.* **1.** guardianship. **2.** instruction. —**tu·te·lar·y** (tū′tə lĕr′ĭ, tōō′-), **tu·te·lar** (tū′tə lər, tōō′-), *adj.*

tu·tor (tū′tər, tōō′-), *n.* **1.** a private instructor. **2.** (in some U.S. colleges) a teacher of academic rank lower than instructor. —*v.t.* **3.** to instruct, esp. privately. **4.** to train or discipline. —*v.i.* **5.** to act as a tutor. —**tu′tor·ship′,** *n.* —**tu·to·ri·al** (tū tōr′ĭ əl, tōō-), *adj.*

tux·e·do (tŭk sē′dō), *n., pl.* **-dos.** *U.S.* a tail-

less coat, usually dark, for semiformal wear by men.

TVA, Tennessee Valley Authority.

twad·dle (twŏd′əl), *v.,* **-dled, -dling,** *n.* —*v.i.* **1.** to prate. —*n.* **2.** trivial, feeble, silly, or tedious talk or writing. —**twad′dler,** *n.*

twain (twān), *adj., n.* *Archaic.* two.

Twain (twān), *n.* **Mark,** (*Samuel Langhorne Clemens*) 1835–1910, U.S. writer.

twang (twăng), *v.i.* **1.** to give out a sharp, ringing sound. **2.** to have a sharp, nasal tone. —*n.* **3.** a sharp, ringing sound. **4.** a sharp, nasal tone.

tweak (twēk), *v.t.* **1.** to seize and pull with a sharp jerk and twist. —*n.* **2.** a sharp pull and twist.

tweed (twēd), *n.* a coarse wool cloth in a variety of weaves and colors.

tweez·ers (twē′zərz), *n.pl.* small pincers for taking up small objects, etc.

twelve (twĕlv), *n.* **1.** a cardinal number, ten plus two. **2.** a symbol for this number, as 12 or XII. **3.** a set of this many persons or things. —*adj.* **4.** amounting to twelve in number. —**twelfth** (twĕlfth), *adj., n.*

twen·ty (twĕn′tĭ), *n., pl.* **-ties,** *adj.* —*n.* **1.** a cardinal number, ten times two. **2.** a symbol for this number, as 20 or XX. **3.** a score of persons or things. —*adj.* **4.** amounting to twenty in number. —**twen′ti·eth,** *adj., n.*

twice (twīs), *adv.* **1.** two times. **2.** doubly.

twid·dle (twĭd′əl), *v.t.,* **-dled, -dling.** **1.** to turn round and round, esp. with the fingers. **2.** to twirl (one's fingers) about each other.

twig (twĭg), *n.* a slender shoot of a tree or from a branch.

twi·light (twī′līt′), *n.* **1.** the light from the sky when the sun is below the horizon, esp. in the evening. **2.** the time during which this light prevails. —*adj.* **3.** of or like twilight.

twilight sleep, *Med.* a state of semiconsciousness usually produced by hypodermic injections, esp. to effect relatively painless childbirth.

twill (twĭl), *n.* **1.** a fabric woven with an effect of parallel diagonal lines. **2.** this weave. —*v.t.* **3.** to weave in twill construction.

twin (twĭn), *n.* **1.** one of two children or animals (**twins**) brought forth at a birth. **2. Twins,** *Astron.* the zodiacal constellation or sign Gemini. —*adj.* **3.** born at the same birth. **4.** forming a pair or couple.

twine (twīn), *n., v.,* **twined, twining.** —*n.* **1.** a strong thread composed of strands twisted together. **2.** a twist or turn. —*v.t.* **3.** to twist together. **4.** to encircle or enfold. —*v.i.* **5.** to become twisted together. **6.** to wind.

twinge (twĭnj), *n., v.,* **twinged, twinging.** —*n.* **1.** a sudden, sharp pain. —*v.t., v.i.* **2.** to give or have a twinge or twinges.

twin·kle (twĭng′kəl), *v.,* **-kled, -kling,** *n.* —*v.i.* **1.** to shine with slight, quick gleams o light. —*n.* **2.** a twinkling.

twin·kling (twĭng′klĭng), *n.* **1.** act of shining with little gleams of light. **2.** an instant.

twirl (twûrl), *v.t., v.i.* **1.** to rotate rapidly; spin; whirl. **2.** to twiddle. —*n.* **3.** a twirling; spin; whirl; twist.

twist (twĭst), *v.t., v.i.* **1.** to combine, as two or more strands, by winding together. **2.** to contort or distort. **3.** to wrest from the proper meaning. **4.** to form into a coil, knot, or the like. **5.** to bend tortuously. **6.** to wind or twine about (something). **7.** to writhe or squirm. **8.** to wind, curve, or bend. **9.** to turn or rotate. —*n.* **10.** a curve, bend, or turn. **11.** rotation; spin. **12.** a wrench. **13.** spiral arrangement or form. **14.** a peculiar turn, as in the mind. **15.** a loaf of dough twisted and baked.

twist·er (twĭs′tər), *n.* **1.** one that twists. **2.** a ball pitched with a spinning motion. **3.** *U.S.* a whirlwind or tornado.

twit (twĭt), *v.t.,* **twitted, twitting,** *n.* taunt or reproach.

twitch (twĭch), *v.t., v.i.* **1.** to give a short, sudden pull (at); jerk. **2.** to move (a part of the body) with a jerk. —*n.* **3.** a quick, jerky movement of the body, or of some part of it. **4.** a short, sudden pull; jerk.

twit·ter (twĭt′ər), *v.i.* **1.** to utter small, tremulous sounds, as a bird. **2.** to tremble with excitement. —*n.* **3.** a twittering sound. **4.** a state of tremulous excitement.

two (tōō), *n.* **1.** a cardinal number, one plus one. **2.** a symbol for this number, as 2 or II. **3.** a set of this many persons or things. —*adj.* **4.** amounting to two in number. —**two'fold'**, *adj.*, *adv.*

two-some (tōō'səm), *n.* two together, esp. in a golf match.

two-step (tōō'stĕp'), *n.* **1.** a round dance in duple rhythm. **2.** a piece of music for this dance.

ty·coon (tī kōōn'), *n.* *U.S. Colloq.* a businessman having great wealth and power.

tyke (tīk), *n.* **1.** a cur. **2.** a small child.

Ty·ler (tī'lər), *n.* **John,** 1790–1862, 10th president of the United States, 1841–45.

tympanic membrane, *Anat.*, *Zool.* a membrane separating the middle ear from the passage of the external ear.

tym·pa·nist (tĭm'pə nĭst), *n.* one who plays the percussion instruments in an orchestra.

tym·pa·num (tĭm'pə nəm), *n.*, *pl.* **-nums, -na** (-nə). *Anat.*, *Zool.* the middle ear, comprising that part of the ear just inside the tympanic membrane. **2.** the tympanic membrane. —**tympan·ic** (tĭm păn'ĭk), *adj.*

type (tīp), *n.*, *v.*, **typed, typing.** —*n.* **1.** a kind, class, or distinctive group. **2.** a representative specimen. **3.** *Print.* **a.** a rectangular piece, usually of metal, having on its upper surface a letter in relief. **b.** such pieces or blocks collectively. **c.** a printed character or printed characters. —*v.t.*, *v.i.* **4.** to typewrite.

type·write (tīp'rīt'), *v.t.*, *v.i.*, **-wrote, -written, -writing.** to write with a typewriter.

type·writ·er (tīp'rī'tər), *n.* a machine for writing mechanically in letters like those produced by printers' types.

ty·phoid fever (tī'foid), *Pathol.* an infectious, often fatal, febrile disease, characterized by

intestinal inflammation and ulceration. Also, **typhoid.**

ty·phoon (tī fōōn'), *n.* a tropical cyclone or hurricane of the western Pacific area.

ty·phus (tī'fəs), *n.* *Pathol.* an acute infectious disease caused by a specific microörganism transmitted by lice and fleas.

typ·i·cal (tĭp'ə kəl), *adj.* **1.** serving as a type or representative specimen. **2.** conforming to the type. **3.** characteristic or distinctive. —**typ'i·cal·ly,** *adv.*

typ·i·fy (tĭp'ə fī'), *v.t.*, **-fied, -fying. 1.** to serve as the typical specimen of. **2.** to symbolize.

typ·ist (tī'pĭst), *n.* one who operates a typewriter.

ty·pog·ra·phy (tī pŏg'rə fī), *n.* **1.** the art or process of printing with types. **2.** the general character or appearance of printed matter. —**ty·pog'ra·pher,** *n.* —**ty/po·graph'i·cal,** *adj.*

ty·ran·ni·cal (tĭ răn'ə kəl, tī-), *adj.* despotic; severely oppressive. Also, **tyr·an·nous** (tĭr'ə nəs). —**ty·ran'ni·cal·ly,** *adv.*

tyr·an·nize (tĭr'ə nīz'), *v.i.*, *v.t.*, **-nized, -nizing.** to rule despotically or cruelly.

tyr·an·ny (tĭr'ə nī), *n.*, *pl.* **-nies. 1.** despotic abuse of authority. **2.** the rule of a tyrant. **3.** a state ruled by a tyrant.

ty·rant (tī'rənt), *n.* **1.** a ruler who uses his power oppressively or unjustly. **2.** an absolute ruler.

Tyre (tīr), *n.* an ancient seaport of Phoenicia, famous for its navigators and traders.

ty·ro (tī'rō), *n.*, *pl.* **-ros.** a novice.

Tyr·ol (tĭr'ŏl), *n.* an alpine region in W Austria and N Italy.

tzar (tsär), *n.* czar.

U

U, u (ū), *n.*, *pl.* **U's** or **Us, u's** or **us.** a consonant, the 21st letter of the English alphabet.

U, *Chem.* uranium.

UAW, United Automobile Workers.

u·biq·ui·ty (ū bĭk'wə tī), *n.* state or capacity of being everywhere at the same time; omnipresence. —**u·biq'ui·tous,** *adj.*

U-boat (ū'bōt'), *n.* a German submarine.

ud·der (ŭd'ər), *n.* a mammary gland, esp. of a cow.

ug·ly (ŭg'lī), *adj.*, **-lier, -liest. 1.** repulsive or displeasing in appearance. **2.** morally revolting. **3.** disagreeable or vicious. **4.** threatening disadvantage or danger. —**ug'li·ness,** *n.*

U.K., United Kingdom.

u·kase (ū'kās, ū kāz'), *n.* **1.** an edict of a Czar. **2.** any official proclamation.

U·kraine (ū'krān, ū krān', ū krīn'), *n.* a constituent republic of the Soviet Union, in the SW part. 30,960,221 pop.; ab. 223,000 sq. mi. *Cap.:* Kiev. —**U·krain'i·an,** *adj.*, *n.*

u·ku·le·le (ū'kə lā'lī), *n.* a small guitar with four strings.

ul·cer (ŭl'sər), *n.* *Pathol.* an open sore accompanied by the disintegration of tissue and the formation of pus, etc. —**ul'cer·ous,** *adj.*

ul·cer·ate (ŭl'sə rāt'), *v.t.*, *v.i.*, **-ated, -ating.** to make or become ulcerous. —**ul'cer·a'tion,** *n.*

ul·na (ŭl'nə), *n.*, *pl.* **-nae** (-nē) **-nas.** that one of the two bones of the forearm which is on the side opposite to the thumb. —**ul'nar,** *adj.*

Ul·ster (ŭl'stər), *n.* **1.** a province in the N part of the Republic of Ireland. 265,654 pop.; 3123 sq. mi. **2.** (*l.c.*) a long, loose, heavy overcoat.

ul·te·ri·or (ŭl tĭr'ĭ ər), *adj.* **1.** intentionally kept concealed. **2.** coming at a subsequent time or stage. **3.** being beyond.

ul·ti·mate (ŭl'tə mĭt), *adj.* **1.** final or highest. **2.** fundamental; elemental. —*n.* **3.** the final result. **4.** a fundamental fact or principle. —**ul'ti·mate·ly,** *adv.*

ul·ti·ma·tum (ŭl'tə mā'təm), *n.*, *pl.* **-tums, -ta**

(-tə). a final proposal or statement of conditions.

ul·ti·mo (ŭl'tə mō'), *adv.* in or of the month preceding the present. *Abbr.:* **ult.**

ul·tra (ŭl'trə), *adj.* excessive; extreme.

ultra-, a prefix meaning: **1.** beyond (in space or time), as in *ultraplanetary.* **2.** excessive; excessively, as in *ultraconservative.*

ul·tra·ma·rine (ŭl'trə mə rēn'), *n.* **1.** a blue pigment consisting of powdered lapis lazuli. **2.** a similar artificial blue pigment. **3.** a deep-blue color.

ul·tra·vi·o·let (ŭl'trə vī'ə lĭt), *adj.* of or denoting the invisible rays of the spectrum outside the violet end of the visible spectrum.

ul·u·late (ŭl'yə lāt', ŭl'-), *v.i.*, **-lated, -lating.** to howl, as a wolf. —**ul'u·la'tion,** *n.*

U·lys·ses (ū lĭs'ēz), *n.* Latin name for **Odysseus.**

um·bel (ŭm'bəl), *n.* *Bot.* an inflorescence in which a number of flower stalks spread from a common center. —**um'bel·late,** *adj.*

um·ber (ŭm'bər), *n.* **1.** an earth consisting chiefly of a hydrated oxide of iron, used in its natural state (**raw umber**) as a brown pigment, or after heating (**burnt umber**) as a reddish-brown pigment. **2.** dark brown or reddish brown.

umbilical cord, *Anat.* a cord connecting the embryo with the placenta of the mother, and transmitting nourishment from the mother.

um·bil·i·cus (ŭm bĭl'ə kəs, ŭm'bə lī'kəs), *n.* *Anat.* the navel, or depression on the middle of the abdomen indicating the point of attachment of the umbilical cord. —**um·bil'i·cal,** *adj.*

um·bra (ŭm'brə), *n.*, *pl.* **-brae** (-brē). **1.** shade; shadow. **2.** *Astron.* the complete shadow of an opaque body, such as a planet.

um·brage (ŭm'brĭj), *n.* offense given or taken; resentful displeasure.

um·brel·la (ŭm brĕl'ə), *n.* a portable, cloth-covered, circular framework used for protection from rain, sunlight, etc.

um·laut (ŏŏm'lout), *n.* *Gram.* two dots as a diacritic over a vowel to indicate a different vowel sound than that of the letter without the diacritic, esp. as so used in German.

um·pire (ŭm′pīr), *n., v.,* **-pired, -piring.** —*n.* **1.** a person selected to rule on the plays in a game. **2.** a person to whose decision a controversy between parties is referred; arbiter. —*v.t., v.i.* **3.** to act as umpire (in). —**um′pire·ship′,** *n.*

UMW, United Mine Workers.

un-¹, a prefix meaning "not," freely used as an English formative, giving a negative or opposite force, in adjectives (including participial adjectives) and their derivative adverbs and nouns, as in *unfair, unfairly, unfairness, unfelt, unseen, unfitting, unformed, unheard-of, un-get-at-able;* and less freely in certain other nouns, as in *unfaith, unrest, unemployment.*

Note: Of the words in **un-¹,** only a selected number are separately entered below, since in most formations of this class, the meaning, spelling, and pronunciation may readily be determined by reference to the simple word from which each is formed.

un-², a prefix freely used in English to form verbs expressing a reversal of some action or state, or removal, deprivation, release, etc., as in *unbend, uncork, unfasten,* etc., or to intensify the force of a verb already having such a meaning, as in *unloose.*

U.N., United Nations.

un·a·ble (ŭn ā′bəl), *adj.* not able; lacking ability or power (to).

un·ac·count·a·ble (ŭn′ə koun′tə bəl), *adj.* **1.** not answerable. **2.** not to be explained. —**un′·ac·count′a·bly,** *adv.*

un·ad·vised (ŭn′əd vīzd′), *adj.* **1.** without advice. **2.** indiscreet; rash. —**un′ad·vis·ed·ly** (ŭn′əd vī′zĭd lĭ), *adv.* —**un′ad·vis′ed·ness,** *n.*

un·af·fect·ed¹ (ŭn′ə fĕk′tĭd), *adj.* free from affectation; sincere; genuine. —**un′af·fect′ed·ly,** *adv.*

un·af·fect·ed² (ŭn′ə fĕk′tĭd), *adj.* not affected, acted upon, or influenced.

u·nan·i·mous (ū năn′ə məs), *adj.* **1.** in complete accord; agreed. **2.** showing complete accord. —**u·nan′i·mous·ly,** *adv.* —**u·na·nim′i·ty** (ū′nə nĭm′ə tĭ), *n.*

un·arm (ŭn ärm′), *v.t.* **1.** to deprive of weapons. —*v.i.* **2.** to lay down one's arms. —**un·armed′,** *adj.*

un·as·sum·ing (ŭn′ə sōō′mĭng), *adj.* modest. —**un′as·sum′ing·ly,** *adv.*

un·a·vail·ing (ŭn′ə vā′lĭng), *adj.* futile.

un·a·void·a·ble (ŭn′ə voi′də bəl), *adj.* not to be avoided; inevitable.

un·a·ware (ŭn′ə wâr′), *adj.* **1.** not aware; unconscious. —*adv.* **2.** unawares.

un·a·wares (ŭn′ə wârz′), *adv.* **1.** unknowingly or inadvertently. **2.** unexpectedly.

un·bal·anced (ŭn băl′ənst), *adj.* **1.** not balanced. **2.** mentally disordered.

un·bar (ŭn bär′), *v.t., v.i.,* **-barred, -barring. 1.** to remove a bar (from). **2.** to unlock.

un·be·known (ŭn′bĭ nōn′), *adj. Colloq.* unknown; without a person's knowledge.

un·be·lief (ŭn′bĭ lēf′), *n.* lack of belief. —**un′·be·liev′er,** *n.* —**un′be·liev′ing,** *adj.*

un·bend (ŭn bĕnd′), *v.t., v.i.,* **-bent** or **-bended, -bending. 1.** to relax by laying aside formality. **2.** to straighten.

un·bend·ing (ŭn bĕn′dĭng), *adj.* rigid; inflexible. —**un·bend′ing·ly,** *adv.*

un·bind (ŭn bīnd′), *v.t.,* **-bound, -binding. 1.** to release from bands or restraint; free. **2.** to unfasten, as a band.

un·blush·ing (ŭn blŭsh′ĭng), *adj.* shameless.

un·bolt (ŭn bōlt′), *v.t.* to open the bolt of (a door, etc.).

un·born (ŭn bôrn′), *adj.* not yet born.

un·bos·om (ŭn bŏŏz′əm, -bōō′zəm), *v.t., v.i.* to disclose (one's thoughts, etc.) esp. in confidence.

un·bound·ed (ŭn boun′dĭd), *adj.* **1.** unlimited: boundless. **2.** unrestrained.

un·bri·dled (ŭn brī′dəld), *adj.* **1.** not having a bridle on. **2.** unrestrained.

un·bro·ken (ŭn brō′kən), *adj.* **1.** whole; intact. **2.** uninterrupted; continuous. **3.** not tamed.

un·buck·le (ŭn bŭk′əl), *v.t.,* **-led, -ling.** to unfasten the buckle or buckles of.

un·bur·den (ŭn bûr′dən), *v.t.* **1.** to free from a burden. **2.** to relieve (one's mind, etc., or oneself) by confession of something.

un·but·ton (ŭn bŭt′ən), *v.t.* to unfasten the button or buttons of (a garment, etc.).

un·called-for (ŭn kôld′fôr′), *adj.* unnecessary and improper; unwarranted.

un·can·ny (ŭn kăn′ĭ), *adj.* **1.** preternaturally good. **2.** unnaturally strange.

un·cer·tain (ŭn sûr′tən), *adj.* **1.** not surely known; doubtful. **2.** not confident, assured, or decided. **3.** not fixed. **4.** vague; indistinct. **5.** not to be depended on. **6.** variable; capricious. **7.** unsteady or fitful, as light. —**un·cer′tain·ly,** *adv.* —**un·cer′tain·ness, un·cer′tain·ty,** *n.*

un·chain (ŭn chān′), *v.t.* to free from chains.

un·civ·il (ŭn sĭv′əl), *adj.* **1.** without good manners; rude; impolite. **2.** uncivilized. —**un·civ′·il·ly,** *adv.*

un·civ·i·lized (ŭn sĭv′ə līzd′), *adj.* barbarous; unenlightened.

un·clasp (ŭn klăsp′, -kläsp′), *v.t.* **1.** to unfasten. **2.** to release from the grasp.

un·cle (ŭng′kəl), *n.* **1.** a brother of one's father or mother. **2.** an aunt's husband.

un·clean (ŭn klēn′), *adj.* **1.** not clean; dirty. **2.** morally or ceremonially impure.

Uncle Sam (săm), the government or people of the United States.

un·cloak (ŭn klōk′), *v.t.* **1.** to remove the cloak from. **2.** to reveal; expose.

un·close (ŭn klōz′), *v.t., v.i.,* **-closed, -closing.** to open.

un·clothe (ŭn klōth′), *v.t.,* **-clothed** or **-clad, -clothing. 1.** to strip of clothes. **2.** to uncover.

un·coil (ŭn koil′), *v.t., v.i.* to unwind.

un·com·mon (ŭn kŏm′ən), *adj.* **1.** unusual or rare. **2.** unusual in amount or degree. **3.** exceptional. —**un·com′mon·ly,** *adv.*

un·con·cern (ŭn′kən sûrn′), *n.* lack of concern; indifference. —**un′con·cerned′,** *adj.* —**un′·con·cern′ed·ly,** *adv.*

un·con·scion·a·ble (ŭn kŏn′shən ə bəl), *adj.* **1.** unscrupulous. **2.** not just or reasonable. **3.** unreasonably excessive. —**un·con′scion·a·bly,** *adv.*

un·con·scious (ŭn kŏn′shəs), *adj.* **1.** not conscious. **2.** unintentional. —**un·con′scious·ly,** *adv.* —**un·con′scious·ness,** *n.*

un·cork (ŭn kôrk'), v.t. to draw the cork from.

un·count·ed (ŭn koun'tĭd), adj. **1.** not counted. **2.** innumerable.

un·cou·ple (ŭn kŭp'əl), v.t., -pled, -pling. to undo the coupling of; disconnect.

un·couth (ŭn kōōth'), adj. awkward or unmannerly. —un·couth'ly, adv. —un·couth'ness, n.

un·cov·er (ŭn kŭv'ər), v.t., v.i. **1.** to disclose; reveal. **2.** to remove the covering (from).

unc·tion (ŭngk'shən), n. **1.** act of anointing. **2.** the oil used in certain r ligious rites. **3.** something soothing or comforting. **4.** earnestness or fervor.

unc·tu·ous (ŭngk'chŏŏ əs), adj. **1.** oily; greasy. **2.** excessively smooth, suave, or bland. —unc·tu·os·i·ty (ŭngk'chŏŏ ŏs'ə tĭ), unc'tu·ous·ness, n.

un·curl (ŭn kûrl'), v.t., v.i. to straighten out.

un·de·ceive (ŭn'dĭ sēv'), v.t., -ceived, -ceiv·ing. to free from deception or mistake.

un·de·ni·a·ble (ŭn'dĭ nī'ə bəl), adj. **1.** not to be refuted. **2.** that cannot be refused. **3.** unquestionably good. —un'de·ni'a·bly, adv.

un·der (ŭn'dər), prep. **1.** beneath; below. **2.** as designated by. **3.** less than. **4.** subject to. **5.** with the authority or aid of. **6.** in accordance with. —adv. **7.** under or beneath. **8.** in a lower place, rank, amount, etc. —adj. **9.** beneath. **10.** lower in rank, place, amount, etc.

under-, a prefixal attributive use of under, as to indicate place or situation below or beneath, lower in grade or dignity, of lesser degree, extent, or amount, or insufficiency.

un·der·brush (ŭn'dər brŭsh'), n. shrubs, small trees, etc., growing under large trees in a wood or forest.

un·der·charge (ŭn'dər chärj'), v.t., -charged, -charging. to charge (a person, etc.) less than the proper price.

un·der·clothes (ŭn'dər klōz', -klōᵺz'), n.pl. clothes worn under outer clothes.

un·der·cov·er (ŭn'dər kŭv'ər), adj. working or done out of public sight; secret.

un·der·cur·rent (ŭn'dər kûr'ənt), n. a current below the surface.

un·der·cut (ŭn'dər kŭt'), v.t., -cut, -cutting. **1.** to cut under or beneath. **2.** to sell or work at a lower price than.

un·der·dog (ŭn'dər dôg', -dŏg'), n. Colloq. the weaker person in a fight, contest, etc.

un·der·es·ti·mate (v. ŭn'dər ĕs'tə māt'; n. ŭn'dər ĕs'tə mĭt, -māt'), v., -mated, -mating, n. —v.t. **1.** to estimate at too low a value, rate, or the like. —n. **2.** an estimate that is too low.

un·der·foot (ŭn'dər fŏŏt'), adv. **1.** under the feet. **2.** in the way.

un·der·go (ŭn'dər gō'), v.t., -went, -gone, -going. **1.** to experience. **2.** to suffer.

un·der·grad·u·ate (ŭn'dər grăj'ŏŏ ĭt), n. a student in a college who has not taken his first degree.

un·der·ground (adv., adj. ŭn'dər ground'; n. ŭn'dər ground'), adv. **1.** beneath the ground. **2.** in concealment or secrecy. —adj. **3.** existing, operating, or taking place beneath the ground. **4.** hidden or secret. —n. **5.** a secret organization fighting the occupation forces, esp. one in the fascist-overrun nations of Europe before and during World War II. **6.** Chiefly Brit. a subway train.

un·der·growth (ŭn'dər grōth'), n. shrubs or small trees growing beneath large trees.

un·der·hand (ŭn'dər hănd'), adj. Also, **un'der·hand'ed.** **1.** secret or sly. **2.** done with the hand below the shoulder, as in pitching a ball. —adv. **3.** in an underhand manner.

un·der·lie (ŭn'dər lī'), v.t., -lay, -lain, -lying. **1.** to lie beneath. **2.** to be at the basis of.

un·der·line (ŭn'dər lĭn', ŭn'dər lĭn'), v.t., -lined, -lining. to mark with a line or lines underneath.

un·der·ling (ŭn'dər lĭng), n. a subordinate (esp. in disparagement); inferior.

un·der·mine (ŭn'dər mĭn', ŭn'dər mĭn'), v.t., -mined, -mining. **1.** to make an excavation under. **2.** to wear away the foundations of. **3.** to weaken by secret means. **4.** to destroy gradually.

un·der·neath (ŭn'dər nēth', -nēᵺ'), prep., adv. under; beneath; below.

un·der·pass (ŭn'dər păs', -päs'), n. a passageway under a railway, road, etc.

un·der·priv·i·leged (ŭn'dər prĭv'ə lĭjd), adj. denied the enjoyment of the normal privileges or rights of a society because of low economic and social status.

un·der·score (ŭn'dər skôr'), v.t., -scored, -scoring. to underline.

un·der·sea (ŭn'dər sē'), adj. submarine.

un·der·sell (ŭn'dər sĕl'), v.t., -sold, -selling. to sell at a lower price than (a competitor).

un·der·shirt (ŭn'dər shûrt'), n. an inner shirt, worn next to the skin.

un·der·side (ŭn'dər sīd'), n. the under or lower side.

un·der·sign (ŭn'dər sīn', ŭn'dər sīn'), v.t. to affix one's signature to.

un·der·stand (ŭn'dər stănd'), v.t., v.i., -stood, -standing. **1.** to perceive the meaning (of); comprehend. **2.** to be thoroughly familiar with (something). **3.** to realize. **4.** to learn. —un'der·stand'a·ble, adj.

un·der·stand·ing (ŭn'dər stăn'dĭng), n. **1.** comprehension. **2.** intelligence. **3.** a mutual comprehension, agreement, or friendly relationship. —adj. **4.** that understands. —un'der·stand'ing·ly, adv.

un·der·state (ŭn'dər stāt'), v.t., -stated, -stating. to state less strongly than truth allows. —un'der·state'ment, n.

un·der·stood (ŭn'dər stŏŏd'), adj. **1.** agreed upon by all concerned. **2.** implied; assumed.

un·der·stud·y (ŭn'dər stŭd'ĭ), n., pl. -studies, v., -studied, -studying. —n. **1.** a person trained to substitute for an actor or actress. —v.t. **2.** to act as understudy to.

un·der·take (ŭn'dər tāk'), v.t., v.i., -took, -taken, -taking. **1.** to attempt. **2.** to oblige oneself by formal promise. **3.** to act as a funeral director. —un'der·tak'ing, n.

un·der·tak·er (ŭn'dər tā'kər for 1; ŭn'dər tā'kər for 2), n. **1.** one who undertakes something. **2.** one whose business it is to prepare the dead for burial and to take charge of funerals.

un·der·tone (ŭn'dər tōn'), n. **1.** a low tone, as of utterance. **2.** an undercurrent. **3.** a subdued color.

un·der·tow (ŭn'dər tō'), n. a strong current below the surface of a body of water, moving in a direction different from that of the surface current.

un·der·wa·ter (ŭn'dər wô'tər, -wŏt'ər), adj. **1.** being or occurring under water. **2.** designed to be used under water.

un·der·wear (ŭn'dər wâr'), n. underclothes.

un·der·weight (ŭn'dər wāt'), adj. lacking usual or required weight.

un·der·wood (ŭn'dər wŏŏd'), n. underbrush.

un·der·world (ŭn'dər wûrld'), n. **1.** the criminal part of human society. **2.** the lower world; Hades.

un·der·write (ŭn'dər rīt'), v.t., v.i., -wrote, -written, -writing. **1.** to agree to meet the expense of. **2.** to guarantee the sale of. **3.** to insure. —un'der·writ'er, n.

un·do (ŭn dŏŏ'), v.t., -did, -done, -doing. **1.** to cause to be as if never done. **2.** to remove. **3.** to

un'con·soled'	un·dam'aged	un·des'ig·nat'ed	un·dis'ci·plined'
un'con·sti·tu'tion·al	un·dat'ed	un'de·sir'a·ble	un'dis·closed'
un'con·strained'	un·daunt'ed	un'de·sired'	un'dis·cour'aged
un'con·strict'ed	un'de·cid'ed	un'de·spair'ing	un'dis·cov'ered
un'con·test'ed	un'de·ci'phered	un'de·stroyed'	un'dis·crim'i·nat'ing
un'con·trol'la·ble	un'de·clared'	un'de·tect'ed	
un'con·ven'tion·al	un·dec'o·rat'ed	un'de·ter'mined	un'dis·guised'
un'con·vinced'	un'de·feat'ed	un'de·vel'oped	un'dis·mayed'
un·cooked'	un'de·fend'ed	un·de'vi·at'ing	un'dis·posed'
un·crit'i·cal	un'de·fin'a·ble	un'di·gest'ed	un'dis·put'ed
un·crowd'ed	un'de·fined'	un·dig'ni·fied'	un'dis·tin'guished
un·crowned'	un'de·liv'ered	un·di·lut'ed	un'dis·tract'ed
un·cul'ti·vat'ed	un'dem·o·crat'ic	un'di·min'ished	un'dis·trib'ut·ed
un·cured'	un'de·mon'stra·tive	un'dip·lo·mat'ic	un'dis·turbed'
un·curled'	un'de·served'	un'di·rect'ed	un'di·vid'ed

ruin or destroy. 4. to unfasten, untie or open. —un·do'ing, n.

un·doubt·ed (ŭn dout'ĭd), adj. accepted as beyond doubt; undisputed. —un·doubt'ed·ly, adv.

un·dress (ŭn drĕs'), v.t., v.i. 1. to take off the clothes (of); disrobe. —n. 2. ordinary or informal dress. —adj. 3. informal as to dress.

Und·set (ŏŏn'sĕt), n. **Sigrid,** 1882–1949, Norwegian novelist.

un·due (ŭn dū', -dŏŏ'), adj. 1. excessive. 2. not proper. 3. not yet owing or payable. —un·du'ly, adv.

un·du·late (ŭn'dyə lĭt, -lāt', -də-), v., -lated, -lating, adj. —v.i. 1. to have a wavy motion, form, or surface. —adj. 2. wavy. —un·du·la'tion, n. —un·du·la·to·ry (ŭn'dyə lə tōr'Ĭ, -də-), adj. —un·du·lant (ŭn'dyə lənt, -də-), adj.

un·dy·ing (ŭn dī'Ĭng), adj. immortal.

un·earth (ŭn ûrth'), v.t. 1. to dig up. 2. to uncover or discover.

un·earth·ly (ŭn ûrth'lĭ), adj. 1. not of this earth or world. 2. supernatural; weird. 3. Colloq. extraordinary. —un·earth'li·ness, n.

un·eas·y (ŭn ē'zĭ), adj., -easier, -easiest. 1. uncomfortable or disturbed. 2. constrained. —un·eas'i·ly, adv. —un·eas'i·ness, n.

un·e·qual (ŭn ē'kwəl), adj. 1. not equal. 2. not adequate. 3. not evenly proportioned or balanced. 4. not even or regular. 5. unfair; unjust. —un·e'qual·ly, adv.

un·e·qualed (ŭn ē'kwəld), adj. matchless.

un·err·ing (ŭn ûr'Ĭng, -ĕr'-), adj. 1. not erring. 2. unfailingly right, exact, or sure. —un·err'ing·ly, adv.

un·e·ven (ŭn ē'vən), adj. 1. not level; rough. 2. irregular; varying. 3. not fair. 4. not equal. 5. (of a number) odd. —un·e'ven·ly, adv. —un·e'ven·ness, n.

un·ex·am·pled (ŭn'Ĭg zăm'pəld, -zăm'-), adj. having no similar case; unprecedented.

un·ex·cep·tion·a·ble (ŭn'Ĭk sĕp'shən ə bəl), adj. beyond criticism.

un·ex·pect·ed (ŭn'Ĭk spĕk'tĭd), adj. unforeseen; sudden. —un'ex·pect'ed·ly, adv. —un'ex·pect'ed·ness, n.

un·fail·ing (ŭn fā'lĭng), adj. 1. incapable of being exhausted. 2. reliable; steadfast. —un·fail'ing·ly, adv.

un·fair (ŭn fâr'), adj. 1. biased or unjust. 2. using unethical business practices. —un·fair'ly, adv. —un·fair'ness, n.

un·faith·ful (ŭn fāth'fəl), adj. 1. false to duty or promises; disloyal. 2. dishonest. 3. not faithfully accurate or exact. 4. guilty of adultery. —un·faith'ful·ly, adv. —un·faith'ful·ness, n.

un·fas·ten (ŭn făs'ən, -fäs'-), v.t., v.i. to loosen, undo, or open (a fastening).

un·feel·ing (ŭn fē'lĭng), adj. 1. devoid of feeling. 2. unsympathetic. —un·feel'ing·ly, adv.

un·fit (ŭn fĭt'), adj. 1. not fit or suitable. 2. unqualified or incompetent. —un·fit'ness, n.

un·fix (ŭn fĭks'), v.t. to detach; loosen.

un·fold (ŭn fōld'), v.t., v.i. 1. to spread or open out. 2. to develop. 3. to reveal or display.

un·for·get·ta·ble (ŭn'fər gĕt'ə bəl), adj. never to be forgotten.

un·for·tu·nate (ŭn fôr'chə nĭt), adj. 1. not

fortunate; unlucky. —n. 2. an unfortunate person. —un·for'tu·nate·ly, adv.

un·found·ed (ŭn foun'dĭd), adj. baseless.

un·friend·ly (ŭn frĕnd'lĭ), adj. hostile; inimical; unkindly.

un·frock (ŭn frŏk'), v.t. to deprive of the priestly or clerical robe.

un·furl (ŭn fûrl'), v.t., v.i. to spread or shake out from a furled state, as a sail or a flag.

un·gain·ly (ŭn gān'lĭ), adj. awkward.

un·god·ly (ŭn gŏd'lĭ), adj. 1. irreligious; wicked. 2. Colloq. outrageous.

un·guent (ŭng'gwənt), n. any salve or ointment.

un·gu·late (ŭng'gyə lĭt, -lāt'), adj. 1. having hoofs, as the horse. —n. 2. a hoofed mammal.

un·hand (ŭn hănd'), v.t. to take the hand or hands from; release from a grasp.

un·hap·py (ŭn hăp'Ĭ), adj., -pier, -piest. 1. sad or wretched. 2. unfortunate. 3. inauspicious. 4. infelicitous. —un·hap'pi·ly, adv. —un·hap'pi·ness, n.

un·heard-of (ŭn hûrd'ŏv', -ŭv'), adj. 1. unknown. 2. unprecedented.

un·hinge (ŭn hĭnj'), v.t., -hinged, -hinging. 1. to take (a door, etc.) off the hinges. 2. to remove the hinges from. 3. to unbalance (the mind, etc.).

un·ho·ly (ŭn hō'lĭ), adj., -lier, -liest. 1. not holy. 2. wicked. 3. Colloq. unseemly. —un·ho'li·ness, n.

un·hook (ŭn hŏŏk'), v.t. 1. to loose from a hook. 2. to open by loosening a hook or hooks.

un·horse (ŭn hôrs'), v.t., -horsed, -horsing. to throw from a horse, as in battle.

u·ni·corn (ū'nə kôrn'), n. a fabulous animal with a single long horn, said to elude every captor save a virgin, and seldom caught.

u·ni·form (ū'nə fôrm'), adj. 1. having but one form; unvarying or alike. 2. without diversity. 3. regular; even. —n. 4. a distinctive dress of uniform style, materials, and color worn by all the members of a military, naval, or other body. —v.t. 5. to clothe with a uniform. —u'ni·form'ly, adv. —u'ni·form'i·ty, n.

Unicorn

u·ni·fy (ū'nə fī'), v.t., -fied, -fying. to form into one. —u'ni·fi·ca'tion, n.

u·ni·lat·er·al (ū'nə lăt'ər əl), adj. 1. one-sided. 2. undertaken or performed by one side only. 3. Law. affecting one party only.

un·ion (ūn'yən), n. 1. act of uniting; junction; combination. 2. a number of persons, societies, states, or the like, joined together for some common purpose. 3. a marriage. 4. a labor union. —un'ion·ism', n. —un'ion·ist, n.

Union City, a city in NE New Jersey. 56,173.

un·ion·ize (ūn'yən īz'), v.t., v.i., -ized, -izing. to organize into a trade or labor union. —un'ion·i·za'tion, n.

Union Jack, the British national flag.

Union of South Africa, a dominion in the British Commonwealth of Nations, in S Africa. 11,258,858 pop.; 472,550 sq. mi. Capitals: Pretoria and Cape Town.

---

un'dra·mat'ic	un'ex·cit'ing	un·gen'tle·man·ly	un'im·pas'sioned
un·dreamed'	un'ex·pired'	un·gov'ern·a·ble	un'im·peach'a·ble
un·earned'	un'ex·plained'	un·grace'ful	un'im·por'tance
un·eat'en	un'ex·plored'	un·gra'cious	un'im·por'tant
un·ed'i·fy'ing	un·ex'pur·gat'ed	un'gram·mat'i·cal	un'im·pos'ing
un·ed'u·cat'ed	un'ex·tin'guished	un·grate'ful	un'im·pressed'
un·e'man·ci·pat'ed	un·fad'ing	un·grat'i·fied'	un'im·proved'
un·em·bar'rassed	un·fal'ter·ing	un·grudg'ing	un'in·cum'bered
un·em·bel'lished	un·fa·mil'iar	un·guard'ed	un·in'flu·enced
un·e·mo'tion·al	un·fash'ion·a·ble	un·hal'lowed	un'in·formed'
un·em·ployed'	un·fa'vor·a·ble	un·hand'y	un'in·hab'it·ed
un·em·ploy'ment	un·fear'ing	un·ham'pered	un·in·hib'it·ed
un·en·cum'bered	un·fed'	un·harmed'	un'i·ni'ti·at'ed
un·end'ing	un·fet'tered	un·health'y	un·in'jured
un·en·joy'a·ble	un·fin'ished	un·heard'	un'in·spired'
un·en·light'ened	un·flag'ging	un·heed'ed	un'in·struct'ed
un·en·thu'si·as'tic	un·flat'ter·ing	un·her'ald·ed	un·in·tel'li·gent
un·en'vi·a·ble	un'fore·seen'	un·hes'i·tat'ing	un·in·tel'li·gi·ble
un·e'quipped'	un'for·giv'ing	un·hin'dered	un·in·tend'ed
un·e·quiv'o·cal	un·formed'	un·hurt'	un'in·ten'tion·al
un·es'ti·mat'ed	un'fre·quent'ed	un·hy·gi·en'ic	un·in'ter·est·ed
un·eth'i·cal	un·fruit'ful	un'i·den'ti·fied'	un'in·ter·est·ing
un·e'vent'ful	un·ful·filled'	un·il'lu·mi·nat'ed	un'in·ter·rupt'ed
un·ex·celled'	un·fur'nished	un·im·ag'i·na'tive	un'in·tim'i·dat'ed
un'ex·cep'tion·a·ble	un·gen'er·ous	un'im·paired'	un'in·vit'ed

Union of Soviet Socialist Republics, official name of the **Soviet Union.**

u·nique (ū nēk′), *adj.* **1.** sole; only. **2.** having no like or equal. **3.** rare or unusual. **—u·nique′ly,** *adv.* **—u·nique′ness,** *n.*

u·ni·son (ū′nə sən, -zən), *n.* **1.** coincidence in pitch of two or more tones, voices, etc. **2.** accord or agreement.

un·is·sued (ŭn ĭsh′ōōd), *adj.* not issued.

u·nit (ū′nĭt), *n.* **1.** a single thing, person, or group. **2.** a specified amount used as a standard of weight, measure, etc.

U·ni·tar·i·an (ū′nə târ′Y ən), *n.* **1.** a member of a Christian denomination founded upon the doctrine that God is one being. **—adj. 2.** pertaining to the Unitarians or their doctrines. **—U′ni·tar′i·an·ism,** *n.*

u·nite (ū nīt′), *v.t., v.i.,* **united, uniting.** to join, combine, or incorporate in one.

United Kingdom, a kingdom in NW Europe, consisting of Great Britain and Northern Ireland. 47,217,200 pop.; 93,377 sq. mi. *Cap.:* London. Official name, **United Kingdom of Great Britain and Northern Ireland.**

United Nations, 1. the fifty nations (with subsequent additions) who, in 1945, established an international organization for the preservation of world peace and the promotion of human welfare. **2.** the organization itself. **3.** the nations that signed the joint declaration in Washington, D.C., Jan. 2, 1942, pledging to employ full resources against the Axis powers, etc.

United Provinces, a province in N India. 55,021,000 pop.; 106,247 sq. mi. *Cap.:* Allahabad.

United States, a republic in North America, consisting of 48 States, the District of Columbia, the territories of Alaska and Hawaii, and other possessions. Continental United States, 144,239,-000 pop.; 3,022,387 sq. mi. *Cap.:* Washington, D.C. Also, **United States of America.**

u·ni·ty (ū′nə tY), *n., pl.* **-ties. 1.** state or fact of being one or united. **2.** a whole as combining all its parts into one. **3.** freedom from or absence of diversity or variety. **4.** concord, harmony, or agreement.

univ., **1.** universal. **2.** university.

u·ni·va·lent (ū′nə vā′lənt, ū nĭv′ə-), *adj. Chem:* having a valence of one.

u·ni·ver·sal (ū′nə vûr′səl), *adj.* **1.** of, pertaining to, used by, or characteristic of all. **2.** general. **3.** existing everywhere. **4.** of or pertaining to the universe. **5.** *Logic.* relating or applicable to all the members of a class or genus. **6.** *Mach., etc.* adapted or adaptable for all or various uses, angles, sizes, etc. **—n. 7.** that which may be applied throughout the universe to many things. **8.** *Logic.* a universal proposition. **—u·ni·ver·sal·i·ty** (ū′nə vûr săl′ə tY), *n.* **—u′ni·ver′sal·ly,** *adv.*

u·ni·verse (ū′nə vûrs′), *n.* the totality of existing things, including the earth, the heavenly bodies, and all else throughout space

u·ni·ver·si·ty (ū′nə vûr′sə tY), *n., pl.* **-ties.** an institution of higher learning having a college of liberal arts, a graduate school, and several professional schools.

University City, a city in E Missouri. 33,023.

un·kempt (ŭn kĕmpt′), *adj.* **1.** not combed. **2.** untidy. **—un·kempt′ness,** *n.*

un·lace (ŭn lās′), *v.t.,* **-laced, -lacing.** to undo the lacing of (a garment, etc.).

un·latch (ŭn lăch′), *v.t.* to unfasten or open (a door, etc.) by lifting the latch.

un·learn (ŭn lûrn′), *v.t.* to discard or lose knowledge of; forget.

un·leash (ŭn lēsh′), *v.t.* to release from a leash; set free.

un·less (ŭn lĕs′), *conj.* **1.** if it be (or were) not that, or if . . . not. **—prep. 2.** except.

un·like (ŭn līk′), *adj.* **1.** not like; different. **—prep. 2.** differently from. **—un·like′ness,** *n.*

un·load (ŭn lōd′), *v.t., v.i.* **1.** to remove the burden, cargo, or freight (from). **2.** *Colloq.* to get rid of.

un·lock (ŭn lŏk′), *v.t.* **1.** to open the lock of. **2.** to disclose.

un·looked-for (ŭn lŏŏkt′fôr′), *adj.* not looked for; unexpected; unforeseen.

un·loose (ŭn lōōs′), *v.t.,* **-loosed, -loosing.** to let loose; release. Also, **un·loos′en.**

un·man (ŭn măn′), *v.t.,* **-manned, -manning.** to deprive of virility.

un·mask (ŭn măsk′, -mäsk′), *v.t.* **1.** to strip of a mask. **2.** to expose. **—v.i. 3.** to put off a mask or disguise.

un·mor·al (ŭn môr′əl, -mŏr′-), *adj.* having no moral aspect.

un·nat·u·ral (ŭn năch′ə rəl), *adj.* not natural or usual. **—un·nat′u·ral·ly,** *adv.* **—un·nat′u·ral·ness,** *n.*

un·nerve (ŭn nûrv′), *v.t.,* **-nerved, -nerving.** to deprive of self-control or courage.

un·num·bered (ŭn nŭm′bərd), *adj.* **1.** not numbered. **2.** countless; innumerable.

un·pack (ŭn păk′), *v.t., v.i.* **1.** to take out (something packed). **2.** to remove the contents packed in (a box, trunk, etc.).

un·pin (ŭn pĭn′), *v.t.,* **-pinned, -pinning.** to remove the pin or pins from.

un·prec·e·dent·ed (ŭn prĕs′ə dĕn′tYd), *adj.* having no precedent.

un·prin·ci·pled (ŭn prĭn′sə pəld), *adj.* lacking sound moral principles; unethical.

un·quote (ŭn kwōt′), *v.t.,* **-quoted, -quoting.** to close a quotation.

un·rav·el (ŭn răv′əl), *v.,* **-eled, -eling** or (*esp. Brit.*) **-elled, -elling. —v.t. 1.** to disentangle the threads of (a fabric, rope, etc.). **2.** to solve. **—v.i. 3.** to become unraveled.

un·reel (ŭn rēl′), *v.t., v.i.* to unwind from a reel.

un·rest (ŭn rĕst′), *n.* **1.** restless state. **2.** strong, almost rebellious, dissatisfaction.

---

un·just′	un·men′tion·a·bly	un·par′don·a·ble	un·ques′tion·ing
un·jus′ti·fi′a·ble	un·mer′ci·ful	un·pa·tri·ot′ic	un·qui′et
un·kind′	un·mer′it·ed	un·per·turbed′	un·rav′aged
un·know′a·ble	un·mind′ful	un·pit′y·ing	un·read′
un·know′ing	un·mis·tak′a·ble	un·placed′	un·read′a·ble
un·known′	un·mis·tak′en	un·planned′	un·read′y
un·la′beled	un·mit′i·gat′ed	un·pleas′ant	un·re′al
un·la′dy·like′	un·mixed′	un·ploughed′	un·re·al′i·ty
un·law′ful	un·mo·lest′ed	un·pol′ished	un·re′al·ized′
un·learned′	un·mount′ed	un·pop′u·lar	un·rea′son·a·ble
un·leav′ened	un·mu′si·cal	un·prac′ti·cal	un·rea′son·ing
un·let′tered	un·muz′zled	un·prac′ticed	un·re·claimed′
un·li′censed	un·named′	un·pre·dict′a·ble	un·rec′og·niz′a·ble
un·light′ed	un·nat′u·ral·ized′	un·prej′u·diced	un·re·cord′ed
un·like′ly	un·nec′es·sar′y	un·pre·med′i·tat′ed	un·re·deemed′
un·lim′it·ed	un·no′ticed	un·pre·pared′	un·re·fined′
un·lined′	un·ob·jec′tion·a·ble	un·pressed′	un·re·gen′er·ate
un·lit′	un·ob·scured′	un·pre·tend′ing	un·reg′is·tered
un·lo′cat·ed	un·ob·serv′ant	un·pre·ten′tious	un·re·hearsed′
un·loved′	un·ob·struct′ed	un·print′a·ble	un·re·laxed′
un·love′ly	un·ob·tain′a·ble	un·pro·duc′tive	un·re·lent′ing
un·luck′y	un·ob·tru′sive	un·pro·fes′sion·al	un·re·li′a·ble
un·man′age·a·ble	un·oc′cu·pied′	un·prof′it·a·ble	un·re·lieved′
un·man′ly	un·of·fend′ing	un·prom′is·ing	un·re·li′gious
un·manned′	un·of·fi′cial	un·pro·nounce′a·ble	un·re·mit′ting
un·man′ner·ly	un·o′pen	un·pro·tect′ed	un·rent′ed
un·marred′	un·op·posed′	un·prov′en	un·re·pent′ing
un·marked′	un·or·gan·ized′	un·pro·vid′ed	un·re·port′ed
un·mar′ried	un·o·rig′i·nal	un·pub′lished	un·re·pressed′
un·matched′	un·or′tho·dox′	un·qual′i·fied′	un·re·quit′ed
un·meas′ured	un·paid′	un·ques′tion·a·ble	un·re·served′
un·men′tion·a·ble	un·pal′at·a·ble	un·ques′tioned	un·re·spon′sive

un·roll (ŭn rōl/), *v.t.* **1.** to open (something rolled). **2.** to reveal. —*v.i.* **3.** to become unrolled.

UNRRA (ŭn/rə), United Nations Relief and Rehabilitation Administration.

un·ru·ly (ŭn rōō/lĭ), *adj.* ungovernable; turbulent; lawless. —**un·ru/li·ness,** *n.*

un·sa·vor·y (ŭn sā/və rĭ), *adj.* **1.** not savory; tasteless. **2.** unpleasant. **3.** morally offensive.

un·say (ŭn sā/), *v.t.,* **-said, -saying.** to retract (something said).

un·scram·ble (ŭn skrăm/bəl), *v.t.,* **-bled, -bling.** *Colloq.* to put into order.

un·screw (ŭn skrōō/), *v.t.* **1.** to draw the screw or screws from. **2.** to unfasten by withdrawing screws.

un·seal (ŭn sēl/), *v.t.* to open the seal of.

un·seat (ŭn sēt/), *v.t.* **1.** to displace from a seat. **2.** to throw from a saddle. **3.** to depose from office.

un·set·tle (ŭn sĕt/əl), *v.t.,* **-tled, -tling. 1.** to render unstable; disturb. **2.** to weaken (beliefs, feelings, etc.) or derange.

un·sex (ŭn sĕks,) *v.t.* to change from the actual sex (esp. of women).

un·shack·le (ŭn shăk/əl), *v.t.* to free from shackles; unfetter.

un·sheathe (ŭn shēth/), *v.t.,* **-sheathed, -sheathing.** to draw from a sheath, as a sword.

un·ship (ŭn shĭp/), *v.t.,* **-shipped, -shipping.** to put or take off from a ship, as goods.

un·sight·ly (ŭn sīt/lĭ), *adj.* not pleasing to the sight. —**un·sight/li·ness,** *n.*

un·strung (ŭn strŭng/), *adj.* nervous; jittery.

un·tan·gle (ŭn tăng/gəl), *v.t.,* **-gled, -gling. 1.** to bring out of a tangled state. **2.** to clear up (anything confused or perplexing).

un·think·ing (ŭn thĭngk/ĭng), *adj.* thoughtless; heedless. —**un·think/ing·ly,** *adv.*

un·tie (ŭn tī/), *v.t.,* **-tied, -tying.** to loose or unfasten (anything tied).

un·til (ŭn tĭl/), *conj.* **1.** up to the time that or when. **2.** (with negatives) before. —*prep.* **3.** up to the time of. **4.** (with negatives) before.

un·to (ŭn/tōō; *unstressed* ŭn/tə or, *before consonant,* ŭn/tə), *prep. Archaic.* **1.** to. **2.** until; till.

un·told (ŭn tōld/), *adj.* **1.** not related or revealed. **2.** not numbered. **3.** countless.

un·touch·a·ble (ŭn tŭch/ə bəl), *adj.* **1.** intangible. **2.** too distant to be touched. **3.** loathsome to the touch. —*n.* **4.** a member of the lower classes in India whose touch is believed to defile a high-caste Hindu.

un·to·ward (ŭn tōrd/), *adj.* unfavorable or unfortunate. —**un·to/ward·ly,** *adv.*

un·truth (ŭn trōōth/), *n.* **1.** lack of truth. **2.** a falsehood or lie.

un·twine (ŭn twīn/), *v.t., v.i.,* **-twined, -twin-**

ing. to bring or come out of a twined condition.

un·twist (ŭn twĭst/), *v.t., v.i.* to bring or come out of a twisted condition.

un·u·su·al (ŭn ū/zhōō əl), *adj.* not usual, common, or ordinary; uncommon. —**un·u/su·al·ly,** *adv.* —**un·u/su·al·ness,** *n.*

un·var·nished (ŭn vär/nĭsht), *adj.* **1.** not varnished. **2.** not embellished; plain.

un·veil (ŭn vāl/), *v.t.* to reveal.

un·weave (ŭn wēv/), *v.t.,* **-wove, -woven, -weaving.** to undo (something woven).

un·wept (ŭn wĕpt/), *adj.* **1.** unmourned. **2.** not shed, as tears.

un·wield·y (ŭn wēl/dĭ), *adj.* not readily handled or managed in use or action, as from size, shape, or weight. —**un·wield/i·ness,** *n.*

un·wind (ŭn wīnd/), *v.,* **-wound, -winding.** —*v.t.* **1.** to undo (something wound). —*v.i.* **2.** to become unwound.

un·wit·ting (ŭn wĭt/ĭng), *adj.* unaware; unconscious. —**un·wit/ting·ly,** *adv.*

un·wont·ed (ŭn wŭn/tĭd, -wŏn/-), *adj.* not customary, habitual, or usual. —**un·wont/ed·ly,** *adv.*

un·wrap (ŭn răp/), *v.,* **-wrapped, -wrapping.** —*v.t.* **1.** to bring out of a wrapped condition. —*v.i.* **2.** to become unwrapped.

unwritten law, law which rests for its authority on custom, judicial decision, etc., as distinguished from law originating in written command, statute, or decree.

un·yoke (ŭn yōk/), *v.t.,* **-yoked, -yoking.** to free from or as from a yoke.

up (ŭp), *adv., prep., adj., n., v.,* **upped, upping.** —*adv.* **1.** to, toward, or in a more elevated position. **2.** to or in an erect position. **3.** out of bed. **4.** above the horizon. **5.** to or at a higher point in a scale, as of rank, size, etc. **6.** to or at a point of equal advance, extent, etc. **7.** equal. **8.** well versed. **9.** into or in activity, operation, etc. **10.** in process of happening. **11.** into view. **12.** into or in a place of safekeeping, etc. **13.** into or in a state of union, contraction, etc. **14.** to the required or final point. **15.** to or at an end. **16.** *Baseball.* at bat. **17.** *Colloq.* confronting. **18.** *Colloq.* engaged in. **19.** *Golf.* ahead of an opponent a specified number of holes. **20.** *Colloq.* (in tennis, handball, etc.) each, apiece. —*prep.* **21.** to, toward, or at a higher place on or in. **22.** to, toward, near, or at the top of. **23.** toward the source, origin, etc., of. —*adj.* **24.** going or directed up. —*n.* **25.** an ascent. **26.** a rise of fortune. —*v.t. Colloq.* **27.** to put or take up. **28.** to make larger. **29.** to raise. —*v.i.* **30.** *Colloq.* to get or start up.

up·braid (ŭp brād/), *v.t., v.i.* to reproach for some fault or offense; chide.

up·bring·ing (ŭp/brĭng/ĭng), *n.* the care and training of a person from childhood.

un/re·strained/	un·shad/ed	un/sub·stan/tial	un·trust/wor/thy
un/re·straint/	un·shake/a·ble	un/suc·cess/ful	un·truth/ful
un/re·strict/ed	un·shaped/	un/suit·a·ble	un·tu/tored
un/re·tard/ed	un·shav/en	un/suit/ed	un·typ/i·cal
un/re·turned/	un·shel/tered	un·sung/	un·used/
un/re·vised/	un·shod/	un/sup·port/ed	un·ut/ter·a·ble
un/re·ward/ed	un·shrink/ing	un/sup·pressed/	un·ut/tered
un·rhymed/	un·signed/	un·sure/	un·van/quished
un·right/eous	un·skilled/	un/sur·mount/a·ble	un·var/ied
un·ripe/	un·skill/ful	un/sus·pect/ed	un·veiled/
un·ri/valed	un·smil/ing	un/sus·pect/ing	un·ven/ti·lat/ed
un/ro·man/tic	un·so/cia·ble	un·swayed/	un·ver/i·fied/
un·ruf/fled	un·soiled/	un·sweet/ened	un·vis/it·ed
un·safe/	un·sold/	un·swept/	un·voiced/
un·said/	un/so·lic/it·ed	un·swerv/ing	un·want/ed
un·sal/a·ried	un·solved/	un/sym·pa·thet/ic	un·war/rant·ed
un·san/i·tar/y	un/so·phis/ti·cat/ed	un·tamed/	un·war/y
un/sat·is·fac/to·ry	un·sort/ed	un·tapped/	un·washed/
un·sat/is·fied/	un·sound/	un·tar/nished	un·watched/
un·scathed/	un·spar/ing	un·taught/	un/wa/ver·ing
un·schooled/	un·speak/a·ble	un·taxed/	un·weak/ened
un/sci·en·tif/ic	un·spe/cial·ized/	un·ten/ant·ed	un·wea/ried
un·scratched/	un·spec/i·fied/	un·thank/ful	un·wea/ry
un·scru/pu·lous	un·spo/ken	un·think/a·ble	un·wed/
un·sealed/	un·sports/man·like/	un·ti/dy	un·wel/come
un·sea/son·a·ble	un·sta/ble	un·time/ly	un·well/
un·sea/soned	un·stained/	un·tir/ing	un·whole/some
un·seat/ed	un·stamped/	un·ti/tled	un·wife/ly
un·sea/wor/thy	un·starched/	un·touched/	un·will/ing
un/se·cured/	un·stat/ed	un·trained/	un·wise/
un·seem/ly	un·states/man·like/	un·tram/meled	un·wom/an·ly
un·seen/	un·stead/y	un/trans·lat/a·ble	un·work/a·ble
un·seized/	un·ster/i·lized/	un·trav/eled	un·world/ly
un/se·lect/ed/	un·stitched/	un·tried/	un·worn/
un·self/ish	un·stressed/	un·trimmed/	un·wor/thy
un/sen·ti·men/tal	un·stud/ied	un·trou/bled	un·writ/ten
un·set/tled	un/sub·dued/	un·true/	un·yield/ing

up·coun·try (ŭp'kŭn'trĭ), *adj.* **1.** interior. —*n.* **2.** the interior of the country.

up·grade (ŭp'grād'), *n.* an upward incline or direction.

up·heave (ŭp hēv'), *v.t.,* **-heaved** or **-hove, -heaving.** to heave or lift up. —**up·heav'al,** *n.*

up·hill (ŭp'hĭl'), *adv.* **1.** up the slope of a hill. —*adj.* **2.** going upward on a hill. **3.** difficult.

up·hold (ŭp hōld'), *v.t.,* **-held, -holding. 1.** to raise or support. **2.** to sustain. —**up·hold'er,** *n.*

up·hol·ster (ŭp hōl'stər), *v.t.* to provide (chairs, etc.) with coverings, stuffing, etc. —**up·hol'ster·er,** *n.* —**up·hol'ster·y,** *n.*

up·keep (ŭp'kēp'), *n.* **1.** the maintenance, operation, and repair of an establishment, a machine, etc. **2.** the cost of this.

up·land (ŭp'lənd, -lănd'), *n.* **1.** an elevated region. —*adj.* **2.** of or pertaining to uplands.

up·lift (*v.* ŭp lĭft'; *n.* ŭp'lĭft'), *v.t.* **1.** to raise. **2.** to reform or improve. —*n.* **3.** elevation. **4.** reform or improvement.

up·on (ə pŏn', ə pôn'), *prep.* on.

up·per (ŭp'ər), *adj.* **1.** higher. **2.** superior. —*n.* **3.** the part of a shoe above the sole.

up·per·most (ŭp'ər mōst'), *adj.* **1.** highest. **2.** predominant.

up·pish (ŭp'ĭsh), *adj. Colloq.* arrogant. Also, **up·pi·ty** (ŭp'ə tĭ). —**up'pish·ly,** *adv.*

up·right (ŭp'rīt', ŭp rīt'), *adj.* **1.** erect or vertical. **2.** righteous; honest. —*n.* **3.** something standing erect or vertical. —*adv.* **4.** vertically. —**up'right'ness,** *n.*

up·ris·ing (ŭp'rī'zĭng, ŭp rī'zĭng), *n.* **1.** an insurrection or revolt. **2.** an ascent.

up·roar (ŭp'rōr'), *n.* **1.** violent and noisy disturbance. **2.** confused noise or din. —**up·roar'i·ous,** *adj.* —**up·roar'i·ous·ly,** *adv.*

up·root (ŭp rōot', -rŏot'), *v.t.* **1.** to tear up by the roots. **2.** to eradicate.

up·set (*v., adj.* ŭp sĕt'; *n.* ŭp'sĕt'), *v.,* **-set, -setting,** *n., adj.* —*v.t.* **1.** to overturn. **2.** to defeat. **3.** to disturb or derange mentally. —*v.i.* **4.** to become upset. —*n.* **5.** an overturn or overthrow. **6.** *Colloq.* a defeat of a contestant favored to win. —*adj.* **7.** overturned. **8.** put in disorder. **9.** worried. —**up·set'ter,** *n.*

up·shot (ŭp'shŏt'), *n.* the final result.

up·side (ŭp'sīd'), *n.* the upper side or part.

up·si·lon (ŭp'sə lŏn'), *n.* the twentieth letter (Υ, υ) of the Greek alphabet.

up·stage (ŭp'stāj'), *adv.* **1.** on or to the back of the stage. —*adj.* **2.** of the back of the stage. **3.** *Slang.* haughty.

up·stairs (ŭp'stârz'), *adv.* **1.** to or on an upper floor. —*adj.* **2.** on an upper floor. —*n.* **3.** an upper story.

up·stand·ing (ŭp stăn'dĭng), *adj.* **1.** standing erect. **2.** upright; honorable.

up·start (ŭp'stärt'), *n.* one who has risen suddenly to wealth or power.

up·stream (ŭp'strēm'), *adv.* against the current.

up-to-date (ŭp'tə dāt'), *adj.* **1.** extending to the present time. **2.** modern. **3.** keeping up with the times, as in information.

up·town (ŭp'toun'), *adv., adj.* to or in the upper part of a town.

up·turn (*v.* ŭp tûrn'; *n.* ŭp'tûrn'), *v.t., v.i.* **1.** to turn up. —*n.* **2.** an upward turn.

up·ward (ŭp'wərd), *adv.* Also, **up'wards. 1.** toward a higher place, rank, etc. **2.** more. —*adj.* **3.** moving or directed upward. —**up'ward·ly,** *adv.*

U·ral (yŏor'əl), *n.* a mountain system in the Soviet Union, forming a natural boundary between Europe and Asia.

u·ra·ni·um (yŏo rā'nĭ əm), *n. Chem.* a white, lustrous, radioactive metallic element. The isotope U-235 is capable of continuous fission and is used in the atomic bomb. *Symbol:* U; *at. wt.:* 238.07; *at. no.:* 92; *sp. gr.:* 18.7.

U·ra·nus (yŏor'ə nəs), *n.* **1.** *Astron.* the seventh major planet in order from the sun. **2.** *Gk. Myth.* the personification of Heaven.

ur·ban (ûr'bən), *adj.* of or living in a city or town.

ur·bane (ûr bān'), *adj.* **1.** polite. **2.** suave. —**ur·ban·i·ty** (ûr băn'ə tĭ), *n.*

ur·chin (ûr'chĭn), *n.* **1.** a mischievous youngster. **2.** a ragged or untidy child.

u·re·a (yŏo rē'ə, yŏor'ĭ ə), *n.* a colorless, crystalline substance used in fertilizers and in making plastics and adhesives.

u·re·mi·a (yŏo rē'mĭ ə), *n. Pathol.* the morbid condition resulting from the retention of urinary constituents. —**u·re'mic,** *adj.*

u·re·ter (yŏo rē'tər), *n. Anat.* a muscular duct conveying the urine from a kidney to the bladder.

u·re·thra (yŏo rē'thrə), *n., pl.* **-thrae** (-thrē), **-thras.** *Anat.* the membranous tube which extends from the bladder to the exterior. In the male it conveys semen as well as urine. —**u·re'thral,** *adj.*

urge (ûrj), *v.,* **urged, urging,** *n.* —*v.t., v.i.* **1.** to push or force along. **2.** to impel or incite. **3.** to entreat or exhort. **4.** to advocate. —*n.* **5.** act of urging, or an impulse.

ur·gent (ûr'jənt), *adj.* pressing; requiring immediate action or attention. —**ur'gent·ly,** *adv.* —**ur'gen·cy,** *n.*

u·ric (yŏor'ĭk), *adj.* pertaining to or obtained from urine.

u·ri·nal (yŏor'ə nəl), *n.* **1.** a receptacle for urine. **2.** a place for urinating.

u·ri·nal·y·sis (yŏor'ə năl'ə sĭs), *n., pl.* **-ses** (-sēz'). urine analysis.

u·ri·nate (yŏor'ə nāt'), *v.i.,* **-nated, -nating.** to pass urine. —**u·ri·na'tion,** *n.*

u·rine (yŏor'ĭn), *n.* the secretion of the kidneys (in mammals, a fluid). —**u'ri·nar'y,** *adj.*

u·ri·nous (yŏor'ə nəs), *adj.* pertaining to, resembling, or containing urine. Also, **u·ri·nose** (yŏor'ə nōs').

urn (ûrn), *n.* **1.** a vase, esp. one for holding the ashes of the dead after cremation. **2.** a vessel used at table for making tea, coffee, etc.

u·rog·e·nous (yŏo rŏj'ə nəs), *adj. Physiol.* **1.** secreting or producing urine. **2.** contained in urine.

u·ros·co·py (yŏo rŏs'kə pĭ), *n. Med.* inspection of the urine as a means of diagnosis, etc. —**u·ro·scop·ic** (yŏor'ə skŏp'ĭk), *adj.* —**u·ros'co·pist,** *n.*

Ur·quhart (ûr'kərt), *n.* **Sir Thomas,** 1611–60, Scottish author and translator.

Ur·sa Ma·jor (ûr'sə mā'jər), *Astron.* the Great Bear, the most prominent constellation in the northern heavens, containing the seven stars that form the Dipper.

Ur·sa Mi·nor (ûr'sə mī'nər), *Astron.* the Little Bear, a northern constellation containing the stars forming the Little Dipper.

ur·sine (ûr'sīn, -sĭn), *adj.* **1.** of or pertaining to a bear or bears. **2.** bearlike.

Ur·spra·che (ōōr'shprä'кнə), *n.* a hypothetically reconstructed parent language, e.g., the primitive Germanic (reconstructed by comparative linguistics) from which the Germanic languages have developed.

Ur·su·la (ûr'syŏo lə, -sə lə), *n.* **Saint,** a legendary British Christian princess said to have been put to death, with 11,000 attendant virgins, by the Huns, at Cologne, in the 3rd (or 5th) century.

ur·ti·car·i·a (ûr'tə kâr'ĭ ə), *n. Pathol.* a skin disease characterized by transient eruptions of itching wheals caused chiefly by gastric derangement; hives. —**ur'ti·car'i·al,** *adj.*

U·ru·guay (yŏor'ə gwā'), *n.* a republic in SE South America. 2,500,000 pop.; 72,172 sq. mi. *Cap.:* Montevideo. —**U'ru·guay'an,** *adj., n.*

us (ŭs), *pron.* objective case of **we.**

U.S., United States.

U.S.A., 1. United States of America. **2.** Also, **USA.** United States Army.

USAF, United States Air Force. Also, **U.S.A.F.**

us·age (ū'sĭj, ū'zĭj), *n.* **1.** a custom or practice. **2.** customary manner of using a language. **3.** treatment.

us·ance (ū'zəns), *n.* **1.** *Com.* the length of time, exclusive of days of grace, allowed by custom or usage for the payment of foreign bills of exchange (it varies between different places). **2.** *Econ.* the income of benefits of every kind derived from the ownership of wealth.

U.S.C.G., United States Coast Guard.

use (*v.* ūz; *n.* ūs), *v.,* **used, using,** *n.* —*v.t.* **1.** to employ or apply to one's purposes. **2.** to expend. **3.** to make a practice of. **4.** to treat. **5.** to accustom. —*v.i.* **6.** to be accustomed. —*n.* **7.** act of using. **8.** state of being used. **9.** a way of being used. **10.** service or utility. **11.** help; profit. **12.** occasion or need. **13.** custom. **14.** treatment. —**us'a·ble, use'a·ble,** *adj.* —**use'ful,** *adj.* —**use'ful·ly,** *adv.* —**use'ful·ness,** *n.* —**use'less,** *adj.* —**use'less·ly,** *adv.* —**use'less·ness,** *n.* —**us'er,** *n.*

USES, United States Employment Service.

U-shaped (ū/shăpt/), *adj.* being in the form of a U.

ush·er (ŭsh/ər), *n.* 1. one who escorts persons to seats in a church, theater, etc. —*v.t.* 2. to act as an usher to.

Usk (ŭsk), *n.* a river in SE Wales and SW England, flowing into the Severn estuary. ab. 70 mi.

U.S.M., 1. United States Mail. 2. United States Marine(s). 3. United States Mint.

U.S.M.A., United States Military Academy.

U.S.M.C., United States Marine Corps.

USN, United States Navy. Also, **U.S.N.**

U.S.N.A., 1. United States National Army. 2. United States Naval Academy.

U.S.N.G., United States National Guard.

U.S.N.R., United States Naval Reserve.

U.S.P., United States Pharmacopoeia.

Us·pal·la·ta Pass (ōōs/pä yä/tä), a mountain pass in the Andes, linking Mendoza, Argentina, and Santiago, Chile: "Christ of the Andes" statue nearby. ab. 12,800 ft. high.

U.S.P.H.S., United States Public Health Service.

us·que·baugh (ŭs/kwĭ bô/, -bä/), *n.* (in Scotland and Ireland) whiskey.

U.S.S., 1. United States Senate. 2. United States Service. 3. United States Ship. 4. United States Steamer. 5. United States Steamship.

U.S.S.R., Union of Soviet Socialist Republics. Also, **USSR.**

usu., 1. usual. 2. usually.

u·su·al (ū/zhōō əl), *adj.* 1. habitual or customary. 2. ordinary. 3. common. —**u/su·al·ly,** *adv.* —**u/su·al·ness,** *n.*

u·surp (ū zûrp/, -sûrp/), *v.t.* to seize and hold (a position, power, etc.) by force or without right. —**u·surp/er,** *n.* —**u·sur·pa·tion** (ū/zər pā/shən, ū/sər-), *n.*

u·su·ry (ū/zhə rĭ), *n., pl.* **-ries.** 1. an exorbitant rate of interest. 2. the lending of money at an exorbitant rate of interest. —**u/su·rer,** *n.* —**u·su·ri·ous** (ū zhōōr/ĭ əs), *adj.*

usw, *German.* und so weiter (and so forth). Also, **u.s.w.**

ut (ŭt, ōōt), *n. Music.* the syllable once generally used for the first tone or keynote of a scale and sometimes for the tone C: now commonly superseded by *do.*

U·tah (ū/tô, ū/tä), *n.* a State in the W United States. 636,821 pop.; 84,916 sq. mi. *Cap.:* Salt Lake City. *Abbr.:* Ut. —**U/tah·an,** *adj., n.*

u·ten·sil (ū těn/səl), *n.* an instrument or implement, esp. one for kitchen use.

u·ter·us (ū/tər əs), *n., pl.* **uteri** (ū/tə rī/). *Anat., Zool.* that portion of the oviduct in which the fertilized ovum develops before birth. —**u/ter·ine,** *adj.*

U·ther (ū/thər), *n. Arthurian Romance.* king of Britain and father of Arthur. Also, **Uther Pendragon.**

U·ti·ca (ū/tə kə), *n.* a city in central New York. 100,518.

u·ti·lise (ū/tə līz/), *v.t.,* **-lised, -lising.** *Chiefly Brit.* utilize.

u·til·i·tar·i·an (ū tĭl/ə târ/ĭ ən), *adj.* 1. pertaining to utility. 2. concerned with usefulness rather than beauty, etc. —*n.* 3. an adherent of utilitarianism.

u·til·i·tar·i·an·ism (ū tĭl/ə târ/ĭ ə nĭz/əm), *n.* the ethical doctrine that conduct should be directed toward promoting the greatest happiness of the greatest number of persons.

u·til·i·ty (ū tĭl/ə tĭ), *n., pl.* **-ties.** 1. usefulness. 2. something useful. 3. a public service, as a streetcar line.

utility man, 1. a worker expected to serve in any capacity when called on. 2. an actor of miscellaneous small parts.

u·ti·lize (ū/tə līz/), *v.t.,* **-lized, -lizing.** to put to use. —**u/ti·li·za/tion,** *n.*

ut·most (ŭt/mōst/, -məst), *adj.* 1. greatest or highest. 2. furthest. —*n.* 3. the greatest amount.

U·to·pi·a (ū tō/pĭ ə), *n.* a place or state of ideal perfection. —**U·to/pi·an,** *adj., n.*

U·trecht (ū/trĕkt), *n.* a city in central Netherlands. 176,394.

ut·ter[1] (ŭt/ər), *v.t.* 1. to speak or pronounce. 2. to give forth (cries, etc.). 3. to express.

ut·ter[2] (ŭt/ər), *adj.* complete. —**ut/ter·ly,** *adv.*

ut·ter·ance[1] (ŭt/ər əns), *n.* 1. act of uttering; vocal expression. 2. manner of speaking; power of speaking. 3. something uttered; a word or words uttered; a cry, animal's call, or the like. 4. a putting into circulation.

ut·ter·ance[2] (ŭt/ər əns), *n. Obs.* the utmost extremity; death.

U-235, the uranium isotope with an atomic weight of 235.

U-238, the uranium isotope with an atomic weight of 238; it comprises about 99 percent of natural uranium.

U-239, the uranium isotope with an atomic weight of 239. It is artificially produced by the neutron bombardment of U-238, and undergoes radioactive decay.

u·vu·la (ū/vyə lə), *n., pl.* **-las, -lae** (-lē/). *Anat.* the small, fleshy, conical body projecting downward from the middle of the soft palate. —**u/vu·lar,** *adj.*

ux·o·ri·al (ŭk sōr/ĭ əl, ŭg zōr/-), *adj.* of or pertaining to a wife; typical of or befitting a wife.

ux·o·ri·cide[1] (ŭk sōr/ə sīd/, ŭg zōr/-), *n.* one who kills his wife. —**ux·o/ri·cid/al,** *adj.*

ux·o·ri·cide[2] (ŭk sōr/ə sīd/, ŭg zōr/-), *n.* act of killing one's wife.

ux·o·ri·ous (ŭk sōr/ĭ əs, ŭg zōr/-), *adj.* excessively or foolishly fond of one's wife; doting on a wife. —**ux·o/ri·ous·ly,** *adv.* —**ux·o/ri·ous·ness,** *n.*

V

V, v (vē), *n., pl.* **V's** or **Vs, v's** or **vs.** 1. a consonant, the 22nd letter of the English alphabet. 2. See **Roman numerals.**

V, 1. *Chem.* vanadium. 2. (*l.c.*) volt.

V., 1. Venerable. 2. Viscount.

v., 1. verb. 2. versus. 3. volume.

Va., Virginia.

VA, Veterans' Administration. Also, **V.A.**

v.a., verb active.

va·can·cy (vā/kən sĭ), *n., pl.* **-cies.** 1. state of being vacant. 2. vacant space. 3. an unoccupied position.

va·cant (vā/kənt), *adj.* 1. empty. 2. devoid. 3. unoccupied. 4. free from work, etc. 5. unintelligent. —**va/cant·ly,** *adv.*

va·cate (vā/kāt), *v.t., v.i.,* **-cated, -cating.** 1. to make vacant. 2. to quit. 3. to annul.

va·ca·tion (vā kā/shən), *n.* 1. freedom or release from duty, business, or activity. 2. a holiday period. —*v.i.* 3. to take or have a vacation. —**va·ca/tion·ist,** *n.*

vac·ci·nal (văk/sə nəl), *adj. Med.* pertaining or due to vaccine or vaccination.

vac·ci·nate (văk/sə nāt/), *v.t.,* **-nated, -nating.** *Med.* 1. to inoculate with the vaccine of cowpox, so as to render the subject immune to smallpox. 2. to inoculate with the modified virus of any of various other diseases. —**vac/ci·na/tion,** *n.*

vac·cine (văk/sēn, -sĭn), *n.* 1. the virus of cowpox, used in vaccination. 2. the modified virus of any of various other diseases.

vaccine point, *Med.* a thin, pointed, vaccine-coated piece of bone or the like, for use in vaccinating.

vac·ci·ni·za·tion (văk/sə nə zā/shən), *n. Med.* a vaccination produced by a series of virus inoculations.

vac·il·late (văs/ə lāt/), *v.i.,* **-lated, -lating.** 1.

to waver; stagger. 2. to fluctuate. 3. to be irresolute or hesitant. —vac'il·la'tion, *n.*

va·cu·i·ty (va kū'ə tY), *n.*, *pl.* **-ties.** 1. emptiness. 2. a vacuum. 3. lack of intelligence.

vac·u·o·late (văk'yŏŏ ə lYt, -lāt'), *adj.* provided with or containing a vacuole or vacuoles. Also, **vac'u·o·lat'ed.**

vac·u·o·la·tion (văk'yŏŏ ə lā'shən), *n.* 1. the formation of vacuoles. 2. state of being vacuolate. 3. a system of vacuoles.

vac·u·ole (văk'yŏŏ ōl'), *n.* 1. a cavity within a cell, often containing a watery liquid or secretion. 2. a minute cavity or vesicle in organic tissue.

vac·u·ous (văk'yŏŏ əs), *adj.* 1. empty. 2. lacking intelligence. —vac'u·ous·ly, *adv.*

vac·u·um (văk'yŏŏ əm), *n.*, *pl.* **vacuums, vacua** (văk'yŏŏ ə), *adj.*, *v.* —*n.* 1. a space entirely void of matter. 2. an enclosed space from which air (or other gas) has been removed. —*adj.* 3. of, using, or producing a vacuum. —*v.t.* 4. *Colloq.* to clean with a vacuum cleaner.

vacuum bottle, a bottle or flask protected by a vacuum jacket which prevents the escape of heat from hot contents or the entrance of heat to cold contents.

vacuum cleaner, an apparatus for cleaning carpets, floors, etc., by suction.

vacuum fan, a fan which ventilates a room or the like by drawing out the vitiated air by suction.

vacuum gauge, a device for measuring pressures below atmospheric pressure in the receiver of an air pump, in steam condensers, and the like.

vacuum pump, a pump or device by which a partial vacuum can be produced.

vacuum tube, a sealed glass bulb used in radio and electronics to detect or rectify alternating currents, to generate electric oscillations, etc.

va·de me·cum (vā'dY mē'kəm), *Latin.* 1. anything that a person carries about with him as being of service. 2. a book for ready reference; a manual or handbook.

vag·a·bond (văg'ə bŏnd'), *adj.* 1. wandering; homeless; nomadic. 2. worthless. —*n.* 3. a wanderer or vagrant. 4. a rascal.

va·gar·y (və gâr'Y), *n.*, *pl.* **-garies.** a capricious or fantastic action or idea.

va·gi·na (və jī'nə), *n.*, *pl.* **-nas, -nae** (-nē). 1. *Anat.* the passage leading from the uterus to the vulva in a female mammal. 2. *Bot.* a sheathlike part. —**vag·i·nal** (văj'ə nəl, və jī'nəl), *adj.* —vag·i·nate (văj'ə nYt, -nāt'), *adj.*

va·grant (vā'grənt), *n.* 1. an idle wanderer; vagabond; tramp. —*adj.* 2. wandering; nomadic. —va'gran·cy, *n.*

vague (vāg), *adj.*, **vaguer, vaguest.** 1. not definite or precise. 2. indistinct. —**vague'ly,** *adv.* —vague'ness, *n.*

vain (vān), *adj.* 1. worthless or futile. 2. **in vain,** without effect. 3. conceited. —**vain'ly,** *adv.* —vain'ness, *n.*

vain·glo·ry (vān glôr'Y), *n.* inordinate pride over one's achievements, abilities, etc. —**vain-glo'ri·ous,** *adj.*

val·ance (văl'əns), *n.* a short piece of drapery across the top of a window.

vale[1] (vāl), *n.* *Chiefly Poetic.* a valley.

va·le[2] (vā'lY), *interj.*, *n.* *Latin.* good-by; farewell.

val·e·dic·tion (văl'ə dYk'shən), *n.* a bidding farewell; a leave-taking.

val·e·dic·to·ri·an (văl'ə dYk tôr'Y ən), *n.* the student (usually the one who ranks highest in scholarship) who gives the farewell oration at the graduating exercises.

val·e·dic·to·ry (văl'ə dYk'tə rY), *adj.*, *n.*, *pl.* **-ries.** —*adj.* 1. bidding farewell. —*n.* 2. a valedictory address.

va·lence (vā'ləns), *n.* *Chem.* 1. the quality which determines the number of atoms or radicals with which any single atom or radical will unite chemically. 2. the relative combining capacity of an atom or radical compared with the standard hydrogen atom. Also, **va'len·cy.**

Va·len·ci·a (və lĕn'shY ə, -chə), *n.* a seaport in E Spain. 508,000.

val·en·tine (văl'ən tīn'), *n.* 1. an amatory or sentimental card or some gift, sent by one person to another on Saint Valentine's Day. 2. a sweetheart chosen on Saint Valentine's Day.

Val·en·tine (văl'ən tīn'), *n.* Saint, died A.D. c270, Christian martyr at Rome.

Va·lé·ry (vȧ lĕ rē'), *n.* Paul, 1871–1945, French poet and philosopher.

val·et (văl'Yt, văl'ā), *n.* 1. a personal manservant. 2. an attendant for patrons of a hotel, etc., who serves as a personal manservant.

Val·hal·la (văl hăl'ə), *n.* *Scand. Myth.* the hall of immortality for heroes slain in battle.

val·ian·cy (văl'yən sY), *n.* quality of being valiant; valor; bravery; courage. Also, **val'iance.**

val·iant (văl'yənt), *adj.* brave; courageous. —val'iant·ly, *adv.*

val·id (văl'Yd), *adj.* 1. sound; logical. 2. authoritative. 3. legally sound or binding. —**val'id·ly,** *adv.*

val·i·date (văl'ə dāt'), *v.t.*, **-dated, -dating.** 1. to make valid. 2. to legalize. —va·lid'i·ty, *n.*

va·lise (və lēs'), *n.* a traveling bag for clothes, toilet articles, etc.

Val·kyr·ie (văl kĭr'Y, -kī'rY, văl'kĭr Y), *n.* *Scand. Myth.* one of the handmaidens of Odin who ride through the air to battle and choose the heroes who are to be slain and taken to Valhalla.

Val·la·do·lid (vä'lyä dō lēd'), *n.* a city in N Spain: Columbus died here, 1506. 116,024.

val·la·tion (və lā'shən), *n.* *Fort.* 1. a rampart or intrenchment. 2. the process or technique of constructing ramparts.

val·ley (văl'Y), *n.*, *pl.* **-leys.** an elongated depression between uplands, hills, or mountains.

Valley Forge, a village in SE Pennsylvania: winter quarters of George Washington and his army, 1777–78.

Valley of Ten Thousand Smokes, a volcanic area in SW Alaska, in the Katmai National Monument, including numerous small smoke and steam vents.

val·or (văl'ər), *n.* boldness or firmness in braving danger; bravery or heroic courage, esp. in battle. Also, *Brit.,* **val'our.** —**val'or·ous,** *adj.* —val'or·ous·ly, *adv.*

val·or·ize (văl'ə rīz'), *v.t.*, **-ized, -izing.** 1. to assign a value to. 2. (of a government) to fix the value or price of (a commercial commodity), and provide for maintaining it against a decline (as to a price below the cost of production), by purchase of the commodity at the fixed price or by other means (used esp. with reference to the action of Brazil in fixing the price of coffee). —**val'or·i·za'tion,** *n.*

Val·pa·rai·so (văl'pə rī'sō, -zō), *n.* a seaport in central Chile. 209,945.

valse (văls), *n.* *French.* waltz.

val·u·a·ble (văl'yŏŏ ə bəl, văl'yə bəl), *adj.* 1. of monetary worth, esp. much worth. 2. of considerable use or importance. —*n.* 3. (*usually pl.*) a valuable article. —**val'u·a·ble·ness,** *n.* —val'-u·a·bly, *adv.*

val·u·a·tion (văl'yŏŏ ā'shən), *n.* 1. an estimation of the value of a thing. 2. estimated worth.

val·u·a·tor (văl'yŏŏ ā'tər), *n.* one who estimates value; an appraiser.

val·ue (văl'ū). *n.*, *v.*, **-ued, -uing.** —*n.* 1. worth, merit, or importance. 2. equivalent worth or return. 3. estimated worth. 4. force, import or significance. 5. (*pl.*) the cherished ideals in life. 6. *Painting.* degree of lightness or darkness in a color. 7. *Music.* the relative length or duration of a tone signified by a note. —*v.t.* 8. to estimate the worth of. 9. to regard or esteem highly.

val·ued (văl'ūd), *adj.* 1. highly regarded or esteemed. 2. estimated or appraised. 3. having the value specified.

val·ue·less (văl'yŏŏ lYs), *adj.* without value; worthless. —**val'ue·less·ness,** *n.*

val·u·er (văl'yŏŏ ər), *n.* 1. one who values. 2. *Brit.* an appraiser.

valve (vălv), *n.* 1. any device for controlling the flow of liquids, gases, etc. 2. *Anat.* a membranous structure which controls the flow of a fluid. 3. *Music.* a device for changing the length of the air column to alter the pitch of a tone, as on a trumpet. 4. *Zool.* one of the two or more separable pieces composing certain shells. —**val·vu·lar** (văl'vyə lər), *adj.*

valve-in-head engine (vălv'Yn hĕd'), an internal-combustion engine in which the cylinder head contains the inlet and exhaust valves.

va·moose (vă mŏŏs'), *v.i.*, *v.t.*, **-moosed, -moosing.** *U.S. Slang.* to leave hurriedly.

vamp[1] (vămp), *n.* 1. the upper front part of a shoe or boot. 2. *Music.* a simple improvised accompaniment. —*v.t.*, *v.i.* 3. to repair. 4. *Music.* to improvise.

vamp² (vămp), *Slang.* —*n.* **1.** a flirt. —*v.t.* **2.** to flirt with.

vam·pire (văm′pīr), *n.* **1.** a reanimated corpse supposed to suck the blood of sleeping persons. **2.** an extortionist. **3.** a self-seeking or unscrupulous flirt. **4.** Also, **vampire bat.** any of various South and Central American bats, including the **true vampires,** which actually suck the blood of animals including man.

van¹ (văn), *n.* the foremost part of an army, fleet, or any body of advancing individuals.

van² (văn), *n.* **1.** a covered truck for moving furniture, etc. **2.** *Brit.* a railroad car for baggage, etc.

van³ (văn; *Du.* vän; *Ger.* fän), *prep.* (in personal names) of, from; written with a small or capital *v* according to the preference of the person owning the name. (In foreign languages it is commonly written with a small *v*.)

va·na·di·um (və nā′dĭ əm), *n.* *Chem.* a rare element used as an ingredient of steel (**vanadium steel**) to toughen it and increase its elasticity. *Symbol:* V; *at. wt.*: 50.95; *at. no.*: 23; *sp.gr.*: 5.96.

Van·brugh (văn brōō′ or, *esp. Brit.*, văn′brə), *n.* **John,** 1664–1726, British dramatist and architect.

Van Bu·ren (văn byŏŏr′ən), **Martin,** 1782–1862, 8th president of the U.S., 1837–41.

Van·cou·ver (văn kōō′vər), *n.* **1.** a large island in SW Canada. 147,262 pop.; 12,408 sq. mi. **2.** a seaport in SW British Columbia. With suburbs, 351,491.

van·dal (văn′dəl), *n.* **1.** one who damages or destroys works of art, valuable property, etc. **2.** (*cap.*) a member of a Germanic people which in A.D. 455 sacked Rome. —**van′dal·ism′,** *n.*

Van·den·berg (văn′dən bûrg′), *n.* **Arthur Hendrick,** 1884–1951, U.S. statesman.

Van·der·bilt (văn′dər bĭlt), *n.* **Cornelius,** 1794–1877, U.S. capitalist.

Van Do·ren (văn dōr′ən), **1. Carl,** 1885–1950, U.S. writer. **2.** his brother, **Mark,** born 1894, U.S. writer.

Van Dyck (văn dīk′), **Sir Anthony,** 1599–1641, Flemish painter. Also, **Van·dyke′.**

van·dyke (văn dīk′), *n.* a short, pointed beard.

Vandyke collar, a wide collar of lace or the like with the edge formed into deep points.

vane (văn), *n.* **1.** a device, fixed upon an elevated object in such a way as to move with the wind and indicate its direction. **2.** any plate, blade, or the like, attached to an axis and moved by or in air or a liquid.

Van Gogh (văn gō′, gŏкн′; *Du.* vän кнŏкн′), **Vincent** (vĭn sĕnt′). See **Gogh.**

van·guard (văn′gärd′), *n.* **1.** the foremost part of an army, etc.; van. **2.** the leaders of a movement. **3.** the leading position in any field.

va·nil·la (və nĭl′ə), *n.* **1.** any of certain tropical climbing orchids, esp. one whose podlike fruit (**vanilla bean**) yields an extract used in flavoring food, etc. **2.** the bean. **3.** the extract.

va·nil·lic (və nĭl′ĭk), *adj.* pertaining to, derived from, or resembling vanilla or vanillin.

van·il·lin (văn′ə lĭn, və nĭl′ĭn), *n.* a white crystalline compound, $C_8H_8O_3$, the active principle of vanilla, now prepared artificially and used as a flavoring agent and a substitute for vanilla. Also, **van·il·line** (văn′ə lĭn, -lēn′, və nĭl′ĭn, -ēn).

van·ish (văn′ĭsh), *v.i.* **1.** to disappear, esp. quickly. **2.** to cease. —**van′ish·er,** *n.*

vanishing point, **1.** a point of disappearance. **2.** *Perspective.* that point toward which receding parallel lines appear to converge.

van·i·ty (văn′ə tĭ), *n.*, *pl.* **-ties.** **1.** excessive pride in one's appearance, achievements, etc. **2.** worthlessness. **3.** a vanity case. **4.** a dressing table.

vanity case, a small case with a mirror, a powder puff, etc., carried by a woman.

van·quish (văng′kwĭsh, văn′-), *v.t.* **1.** to conquer or defeat. **2.** to overcome. —**van′quish·a·ble,** *adj.* —**van′quish·er,** *n.*

van·tage (văn′tĭj, vän′-), *n.* position or situation affording superiority.

vantage ground, a position which gives one an advantage, as for action or defense; favorable position.

van·ward (văn′wərd), *adj., adv.* toward or in the van or front.

vap·id (văp′ĭd), *adj.* **1.** insipid; flat. **2.** dull, uninteresting, or tedious. —**va·pid′i·ty, vap′id·ness,** *n.* —**vap′id·ly,** *adv.*

va·por (vā′pər), *n.* **1.** a visible or invisible ex-

halation, as fog, mist, condensed steam, etc. **2.** a substance in the gaseous state. **3.** something unsubstantial or transitory. —*v.t., v.i.* **4.** to pass off in, or as in, vapor. Also, *Brit.*, **va′pour.** —**va′-por·ous,** *adj.*

va·por·if·ic (vā′pə rĭf′ĭk), *adj.* **1.** producing vapor, or connected with the production of vapor; tending toward vapor. **2.** pertaining to or of the nature of vapor.

va·por·im·e·ter (vā′pə rĭm′ə tər), *n.* an instrument for measuring vapor pressure or volume.

va·por·ize (vā′pə rīz′), *v.t., v.i.,* **-ized, -izing.** to change into vapor. —**va′por·iz′a·ble,** *adj.* —**va′por·i·za′tion,** *n.*

va·por·iz·er (vā′pə rī′zər), *n.* **1.** one who or that which vaporizes. **2.** a form of atomizer.

va·que·ro (vä kĕ′rō), *n., pl.* **-ros** (-rōs). *Sp. America and S.W. U.S.* a cowboy.

var., **1.** variant. **2.** various.

Var·gas (vär′gəs), *n.* **Getulio Dornelles,** born 1883, Brazilian statesman.

var·i·a·ble (vâr′Y ə bəl), *adj.* **1.** changeable or alterable. **2.** inconstant or fickle. **3.** *Biol.* deviating from the usual type. —*n.* **4.** something variable. **5.** *Math.* a symbol which may represent any one of a given set of objects. **6.** a shifting wind. —**var′i·a·bil′i·ty, var′i·a·ble·ness,** *n.* —**var′i·a·bly,** *adv.*

var·i·ance (vâr′Y əns), *n.* **1.** divergence or discrepancy. **2.** degree of variation. **3.** a disagreement or dispute.

var·i·ant (vâr′Y ənt), *adj.* **1.** exhibiting diversity; varying. **2.** being an altered or different form. —*n.* **3.** a variant form, spelling, etc.

var·i·a·tion (vâr′Y ā′shən), *n.* **1.** change in condition, character, degree, etc. **2.** amount or rate of change. **3.** a variant. **4.** *Music.* **a.** the transformation of a melody or theme with changes or elaborations in harmony, rhythm, and melody. **b.** a varied form of a melody or theme. —**var′i·a′tion·al,** *adj.*

var·i·col·ored (vâr′Y kŭl′ərd), *adj.* **1.** having various colors. **2.** varied.

var·i·cose (vâr′ə kōs′, vâr′-), *adj.* **1.** enlarged and swollen, as a vein. **2.** of or affected with varicose veins.

var·ied (vâr′Yd), *adj.* **1.** diversified; characterized by variety. **2.** changed.

var·i·e·gate (vâr′Y ə gāt′, -Y gāt′), *v.t.,* **-gated, -gating.** **1.** to mark with different colors, etc. **2.** to give variety to. —**var′i·e·ga′tion,** *n.*

var·i·e·gat·ed (vâr′Y ə gā′tĭd, -Y gā′tĭd), *adj.* **1.** varied in appearance or color; marked with patches or spots of different colors. **2.** varied; diversified; diverse.

va·ri·e·tal (və rī′ə təl), *adj.* **1.** of, pertaining to, or characteristic of a variety. **2.** constituting a variety. —**va·ri′e·tal·ly,** *adv.*

va·ri·e·ty (və rī′ə tĭ), *n., pl.* **-ties.** **1.** diversity; absence of uniformity. **2.** difference. **3.** a number of different things. **4.** a kind or sort. **5.** a different form, condition, or phase of something. **6.** a category within a species. **7.** *Chiefly Brit. Theat.* vaudeville.

va·ri·o·la (və rī′ə lə), *n.* *Pathol.* smallpox.

var·i·o·rum (vâr′Y ōr′əm), *adj.* **1.** (of an edition, etc.) characterized by various versions of the text or commentaries by various editors. —*n.* **2.** a variorum edition, etc.

var·i·ous (vâr′Y əs), *adj.* **1.** different or diverse. **2.** several or many. **3.** changeable. —**var′i·ous·ly,** *adv.*

var·let (vär′lĭt), *n.* *Archaic.* a scoundrel.

var·mint (vär′mənt), *n.* *Dial.* vermin. Also, **var′ment.**

var·nish (vär′nĭsh), *n.* **1.** a solution containing resinous matter, which, when applied to a surface, dries into a hard, glossy coating. **2.** something resembling a coating of varnish; a gloss. **3.** a merely external show. —*v.t.* **4.** to lay varnish on. **5.** to give an improved or deceptive appearance to. —**var′nish·er,** *n.*

var·si·ty (vär′sə tĭ), *n., pl.* **-ties.** the first-string team which represents a school, college, or the like.

var·y (vâr′Y), *v.,* **varied, varying.** —*v.t.* **1.** to change, as in form, appearance, degree, etc. **2.** to cause to be different. **3.** to diversify. —*v.i.* **4.** to be different or show diversity. **5.** to undergo or be subject to change. —**var′y·ing·ly,** *adv.*

vas (văs), *n., pl.* **vasa** (vā′sə). *Anat., Zool., Bot.* a vessel or duct.

Va·sa·ri (vä zä′rē), *n.* **Giorgio,** 1511–74, Italian painter, architect, and art historian.

vas·cu·lar (văs′kyə lər), *adj. Zool., Bot.* of or provided with vessels or ducts which convey fluids.

vascular tissue, *Bot.* plant tissue consisting of ducts or vessels which, in highly developed plants, form the system by which sap is conveyed through the plant.

vase (vās, vāz *or, esp. Brit.,* väz), *n.* a container used chiefly for flowers.

Vas·e·line (văs′ə lēn′, -lĭn), *n. Trademark.* a semisolid petroleum product used esp. as an ointment.

vas·o·con·stric·tor (văs′ō kən strĭk′tər), *adj. Physiol.* serving to constrict blood vessels, as certain nerves or chemical substances.

vas·o·di·la·tor (văs′ō dĭ lā′tər, -dī-), *adj. Physiol.* serving to dilate or relax blood vessels, as certain nerves or chemical substances.

vas·o·mo·tor (văs′ō mō′tər), *adj. Physiol.* serving to regulate the caliber of blood vessels, as certain nerves.

vas·sal (văs′əl), *n.* **1.** (in the feudal system) a person holding lands by the obligation to render military service or its equivalent to his superior. **2.** a subject, follower, servant, or slave. —*adj.* **3.** of or characteristic of a vassal. —**vas′sal·age,** *n.*

vast (văst, väst), *adj.* of very great extent, size, intensity, etc.; immense; enormous. —**vast′ly,** *adv.* —**vast′ness,** *n.*

vast·y (văs′tĭ, väs′tĭ), *adj. Poetic.* vast; immense.

vat (văt), *n., v.,* **vatted, vatting.** —*n.* **1.** a large container for liquids. —*v.t.* **2.** to put into or treat in a vat.

Vat·i·can (văt′ə kən), *n.* **1.** the palace of the popes in Rome. **2.** the papal power or government.

Vatican City, an independent state within Rome, including the Vatican: established in 1929, ruled by the pope. 1000 pop.; 109 acres.

Vau·ban (vō bäN′), *n.* **Sébastien le Prestre de,** 1633–1707, French military engineer and marshal.

vaude·ville (vōd′vĭl, vō′də vĭl), *n. Chiefly U.S.* theatrical entertainment consisting of a number of individual acts, as of singing, dancing, gymnastic exhibitions, etc.

Vaughan (vôn), *n.* **Henry,** 1622–95, British poet and mystic.

Vaughan Wil·liams (vôn wĭl′yəmz), **Ralph,** born 1872, British composer.

vault[1] (vôlt), *n.* **1.** an arched ceiling or roof. **2.** an arched space, chamber, or passage, esp. one underground. —*v.t.* **3.** to construct or cover with a vault. —**vault′ed,** *adj.*

vault[2] (vôlt), *v.i., v.t., n.* leap.

vault·ing[1] (vôl′tĭng), *n.* **1.** act or process of constructing vaults. **2.** the structure forming a vault or vaults. **3.** a vault, vaulted ceiling, or the like, or such structures collectively.

vault·ing[2] (vôl′tĭng), *adj.* **1.** that vaults. **2.** used in vaulting. **3.** exaggerated.

vaunt (vônt, vänt), *v.t., v.i.* **1.** to speak boastfully (of). —*n.* **2.** boastful utterance. —**vaunt′ing·ly,** *adv.*

vb., **1.** verb. **2.** verbal.

V.C., **1.** Veterinary Corps. **2.** Vice-Chairman. **3.** Vice-Chamberlain. **4.** Vice-Chancellor. **5.** Vice-Consul. **6.** Victoria Cross.

Vd, *Chem.* vanadium.

V.D., venereal disease. Also, **VD**

V-Day (vē′dā′), *n.* the day proclaimed as marking the final victory for the Allies in World War II (Dec. 31, 1946).

veal (vēl), *n.* the flesh of the calf as used for food.

Veb·len (věb′lən), *n.* **Thorstein,** 1857–1929, U.S. economist.

vec·tor (věk′tər), *n. Math.* a complex quantity possessing both magnitude and direction and represented by any of a system of equal and parallel line segments.

Ve·da (vā′də, vē′də), *n.* (*sometimes pl.*) the entire sacred scriptures of Hinduism. —**Ve·dic** (vā′dĭk, vē′dĭk), *adj.*

Ve·dan·ta (vĭ dän′tə, -dän′-), *n.* the chief philosophy among the Hindus, a system of idealistic monism, chiefly as expounded by the philosopher S(h)ankara about A.D. 800 with some varieties occurring later. —**Ve·dan′tic,** *adj.* —**Ve·dan′tism,** *n.* —**Ve·dan′tist,** *n.*

V-E Day, the day of victory in Europe for the Allies in World War II (May 8, 1945).

veer (vĭr), *v.i.* **1.** to change direction; shift, change, or vary. —*n.* **2.** a change of direction. —**veer′ing·ly,** *adv.*

Ve·ga (vē′gə), *n. Astron.* a brilliant white star of the first magnitude in the constellation Lyra.

veg·e·ta·ble (věj′tə bəl, věj′ə-), *n.* **1.** any herbaceous plant whose parts are used as food, as the bean, beet, potato, cabbage, etc. **2.** any plant. —*adj.* **3.** of, consisting of, or made from (edible) vegetables.

vegetable butter, any of various concrete, fixed, vegetable fats which are solid at ordinary temperatures, but usually melt at or below body temperature.

vegetable tallow, any of several tallowlike substances of vegetable origin, used in making candles, soap, etc., and as lubricants.

veg·e·tal (věj′ə tal), *adj.* vegetable.

veg·e·tar·i·an (věj′ə târ′Y ən), *n.* **1.** one who on principle (**vegetarianism**) lives on vegetable food (refusing meat, etc.). —*adj.* **2.** of, devoted to, or advocating vegetarianism. **3.** consisting of vegetables.

veg·e·tate (věj′ə tāt′), *v.i.,* **-tated, -tating. 1.** to grow in the manner of plants. **2.** to live in an inactive, unthinking way.

veg·e·ta·tion (věj′ə tā′shən), *n.* **1.** plants collectively. **2.** act or process of vegetating.

veg·e·ta·tive (věj′ə tā′tĭv), *adj.* **1.** growing, like plants. **2.** pertaining to vegetation. **3.** inactive; quiescent. —**veg′e·ta′tive·ly,** *adv.* —**veg′e·ta′tive·ness,** *n.*

ve·he·ment (vē′ə mənt), *adj.* **1.** eager, impetuous, or impassioned. **2.** violent in feeling or endeavor. **3.** passionate. —**ve′he·ment·ly,** *adv.* —**ve′he·mence, ve′he·men·cy,** *n.*

ve·hi·cle (vē′ə kəl), *n.* **1.** any means of transport, conveyance, transmission, or communication. **2.** *Painting.* a liquid, as oil, in which a pigment is mixed. —**ve·hic·u·lar** (vē hĭk′yə lər), *adj.*

Ve·ii (vē′yī), *n.* an ancient Etruscan city in central Italy, near Rome: often at war with ancient Rome.

veil (vāl), *n.* **1.** a piece of material, usually light and transparent, worn over the head or face, as to conceal the face. **2.** a part of the headdress of a nun. **3.** something that covers, screens, or conceals. **4.** a mask, disguise, or pretense. —*v.t.* **5.** to cover with a veil. —**veiled,** *adj.*

veil·ing (vā′lĭng), *n.* **1.** a veil. **2.** a thin net for veils.

vein (vān), *n.* **1.** one of the system of branching vessels conveying blood from various parts of the body to the heart. **2.** one of the tubular riblike thickenings that ramify in an insect's wing. **3.** one of the strands or bundles of vascular tissue forming the principal framework of a leaf. **4.** any body or stratum of ore, coal, etc. **5.** spirit; mood. —*v.t.* **6.** to furnish or mark with veins. —**veined,** *adj.*

vein·ing (vā′nĭng), *n.* a process, of forming or arrangement of veins or veinlike markings.

vein·let (vān′lĭt), *n.* a small vein.

ve·lar (vē′lər), *adj.* **1.** of or pertaining to a velum or veil, esp. that of the palate. **2.** *Phonet.* with the back of the tongue held close to or touching the soft palate. —*n.* **3.** a velar sound.

Ve·láz·quez (vě läth′kěth), *n.* **Diego Rodríguez de Silva y,** 1599–1660, Spanish painter. Also, **Ve·lás·quez** (vě läs′kěth).

veld (vělt, fělt), *n.* the open, relatively treeless parts of southern Africa. Also, **veldt.**

vel·le·i·ty (və lē′ə tĭ), *n., pl.* **-ties. 1.** volition in its weakest form. **2.** a mere wish, unaccompanied by an effort to obtain it.

vel·lum (věl′əm), *n.* **1.** a sheet of calfskin prepared as parchment. **2.** a texture of paper or cloth resembling such parchment.

ve·loc·i·pede (və lŏs′ə pēd′), *n.* a bicyclelike vehicle with two or three wheels.

ve·loc·i·ty (və lŏs′ə tĭ), *n., pl.* **-ties. 1.** rapidity; swiftness. **2.** *Physics.* a time rate of change of displacement.

ve·lours (və lŏŏr′), *n. sing. and pl.* velvet. Also, **ve·lour′.**

ve·lum (vē′ləm), *n., pl.* **-la** (-lə). **1.** *Biol.* any of various veillike or curtainlike membranous partitions. **2.** *Anat.* the soft palate.

ve·lure (və lŏŏr′), *n., v.,* **-lured, -luring.** —*n.* **1.** velvet or a substance resembling it. **2.** a hatters' pad of velvet, plush, or the like, for smoothing or dressing silk hats. —*v.t.* **3.** to smooth or dress (a hat) with a velure.

vel·vet (vĕl′vĭt), *n.* **1.** a fabric of silk, silk and cotton, cotton, etc., with a thick, soft pile. **2.** *Slang.* clear gain or profit. —*adj.* **3.** made of or resembling velvet. —**vel′vet·y,** *adj.*

velvet carpet, a carpet or rug of pile weave resembling Wilton.

vel·vet·een (vĕl′və tēn′), *n.* a cotton pile fabric with short pile.

ve·na ca·va (vē′nə kā′və), *pl.* **venae cavae** (vē′nē kā′vē). *Anat.* either of two large veins discharging into the right auricle of the heart.

ve·nal (vē′nəl), *adj.* **1.** open to bribery; corrupt. **2.** influenced by bribery. —**ve′nal·ly,** *adv.* —**ve·nal·i·ty** (vē nǎl′ə tĭ′), *n.*

ve·na·tion (vē nā′shən), *n.* **1.** the arrangement of veins, as in a leaf or an insect's wing. **2.** these veins collectively. —**ve·na′tion·al,** *adj.*

vend (vĕnd), *v.t., v.i.* to sell. —**vend′er, ven′dor,** *n.*

vend·ee (vĕn dē′), *n.* the buyer.

ven·det·ta (vĕn dĕt′ə), *n.* a feud in which a murdered man's relatives execute vengeance on the slayer or his relatives.

vending machine, a coin-operated machine for selling small articles.

ve·neer (və nĭr′), *v.t.* **1.** to overlay with thin sheets of fine wood, etc. **2.** to give a superficially fair appearance to. —*n.* **3.** a thin layer of fine wood, etc., used in veneering. **4.** a superficially fair appearance.

ven·er·a·ble (vĕn′ər ə bəl), *adj.* worthy of reverence. —**ven′er·a·bil′i·ty, ven′er·a·ble·ness,** *n.* —**ven′er·a·bly,** *adv.*

ven·er·ate (vĕn′ə rāt′), *v.t.,* **-ated, -ating.** to regard with reverence. —**ven′er·a′tion,** *n.*

ve·ne·re·al (və nĭr′Ĭ əl), *adj.* arising from or connected with sexual intercourse, esp. with an infected person.

ven·er·y[1] (vĕn′ə rĭ), *n. Archaic.* the gratification of sexual desire.

ven·er·y[2] (vĕn′ə rĭ), *n. Archaic.* the practice or sport of hunting; the chase.

Venetian blind, a window blind with horizontal slats that may be opened or closed.

Ven·e·zue·la (vĕn′ə zwē′lə), *n.* a republic in N South America. 4,300,000 pop.; 352,143 sq. mi. *Cap.:* Caracas. —**Ven′e·zue′lan,** *adj., n.*

venge·ance (vĕn′jəns), *n.* **1.** the avenging of wrong, injury, or the like; revenge. **2. with a vengeance, a.** with force or violence. **b.** extremely. **c.** with unexpected force, thoroughness, etc.

venge·ful (vĕnj′fəl), *adj.* seeking vengeance; vindictive. —**venge′ful·ly,** *adv.* —**venge′ful·ness,** *n.*

ve·ni·al (vē′nĬ əl), *adj.* **1.** that may be forgiven or pardoned. **2.** excusable.

venial sin, *Rom. Cath. Ch.* a voluntary transgression of God's law, which without destroying charity or union with God retards man in attaining final union with Him.

Ven·ice (vĕn′Ĭs), *n.* a seaport in NE Italy. 301,376. —**Ve·ne·tian** (və nē′shən), *adj., n.*

ve·ni·re fa·ci·as (vĭ nī′rē fā′shĬ ǎs′), *Law.* a writ or precept directed to the sheriff, requiring him to summon qualified citizens to act as jurors in the trial of cases. Also, **ve·ni′re.**

ve·ni·re·man (vĭ nī′rē mən), *n., pl.* **-men.** *Law.* a man summoned under a venire facias.

ven·i·son (vĕn′ə zən), *n.* the flesh of a deer or similar animal.

ve·ni, vi·di, vi·ci (vē′nī, vī′dī, vī′sī; wā′nē, wē′dē, wē′kē), *Latin.* I came, I saw, I conquered (words used by Julius Caesar in reporting one of his victories).

Ve·ni·ze·los (vĕ′nē zĕ′lôs), *n.* **Eleutherios,** 1864–1936, prime minister of Greece for many years.

ven·om (vĕn′əm), *n.* **1.** the poisonous fluid which some snakes, spiders, etc., secrete and inject by biting, stinging, etc. **2.** spite or malice. —**ven′om·ous,** *adj.*

vent[1] (vĕnt), *n.* **1.** an opening serving for outlet, as of a fluid. **2.** an outlet, as from confinement.

vent[2] (vĕnt), *n.* **1.** expression or utterance. —*v.t.* **2.** to give free course or expression to (an emotion, etc.).

vent[3] (vĕnt), *n.* the slit in the back of a coat.

vent·age (vĕn′tĬj), *n.* a small hole or vent, as one of the fingerholes of a flute.

ven·ti·late (vĕn′tə lāt′), *v.t.,* **-lated, -lating. 1.** to provide (a room, etc.) with fresh air. **2.** to introduce fresh air into. **3.** to submit (a question, etc.) to discussion. —**ven′ti·la′tion,** *n.*

ven·ti·la·tor (vĕn′tə lā′tər), *n.* **1.** one who or that which ventilates. **2.** any contrivance for replacing foul or stagnant air by fresh air.

ven·tral (vĕn′trəl), *adj.* of, pertaining to, or on the belly; abdominal. —**ven′tral·ly,** *adv.*

ventral fin, (in fishes) either of a pair of fins on the lower surface of the body, and corresponding to the hind limbs of higher vertebrates.

ven·tri·cle (vĕn′trə kəl), *n.* one of the two main cavities of the heart which receive the blood from the auricles and propel it into the arteries. —**ven·tric·u·lar** (vĕn trĭk′yə lər), *adj.*

ven·tril·o·quism (vĕn trĭl′ə kwĭz′əm), *n.* the art of speaking in such a manner that the voice appears to come not from the speaker but from some other source. Also, **ven·tril′o·quy.** —**ven·tril′o·quist,** *n.*

ven·ture (vĕn′chər), *n., v.,* **-tured, -turing.** —*n.* **1.** a hazardous or daring undertaking. **2.** a business enterprise. —*v.t.* **3.** to risk. **4.** to undertake to express, as if with a sense of daring. —*v.i.* **5.** to risk oneself. **6.** to take a risk; dare. —**ven′ture·some, ven′tur·ous,** *adj.*

ven·ue (vĕn′ū, vĕn′ōō), *n. Law.* **1.** the place of a crime or cause of action. **2.** the county or place where the jury is gathered and the trial held.

Ve·nus (vē′nəs), *n.* **1.** the Roman goddess of love and beauty. **2.** a beautiful woman. **3.** *Astron.* the most brilliant planet, having an orbit second from the sun.

Venus of Mi·lo (mē′lō), the most famous extant Greek statue of antiquity, found (1820) in Milo or Melos, and now in the Louvre, Paris. It represents Venus naked above the thighs; the arms are missing. Also, **Venus of Melos.**

Ve·nus's-fly·trap (vē′nəs Ĭz flī′trăp′), *n.* a plant, native of North and South Carolina, whose leaves have two lobes which close like a trap when certain delicate hairs on them are irritated, as by a fly.

ver., **1.** a verse; verses. **2.** version.

ve·ra·cious (və rā′shəs), *adj.* **1.** truthful. **2.** true. —**ve·ra′cious·ly,** *adv.*

ve·rac·i·ty (və rǎs′ə tĬ), *n., pl.* **-ties. 1.** truthfulness. **2.** correctness or accuracy. **3.** a truth.

Ver·a·cruz (vĕr′ə krōōz′), *n.* a seaport in E Mexico: the chief port of Mexico. 70,882.

ve·ran·da (və răn′də), *n.* an open, usually roofed, porch. Also, **ve·ran′dah.**

verb (vûrb), *n. Gram.* **1.** one of the major form classes, or parts of speech, comprising words which express the occurrence of an action, existence of a state, and the like, and such other words as show similar grammatical behavior. **2.** any such word. —**verb′less,** *adj.*

ver·bal (vûr′bəl), *adj.* **1.** of or pertaining to words. **2.** consisting of or in the form of words. **3.** oral. **4.** concerned with words only, rather than ideas. **5.** corresponding word for word. **6.** *Gram.* of, pertaining to, derived from, or like a verb. —*n.* **7.** *Gram.* a word derived from a verb. —**ver′bal·ly,** *adv.*

ver·bal·ism (vûr′bə lĬz′əm), *n.* **1.** a verbal expression; a word or phrase. **2.** a formal phrase or sentence, with little or no meaning. **3.** predominance of mere words, as over ideas or realities.

ver·bal·ist (vûr′bə lĬst), *n.* **1.** one skilled in words. **2.** one who deals with words merely, rather than ideas or realities.

ver·bal·ize (vûr′bə līz′), *v.,* **-ized, -izing.** —*v.t.* **1.** to express in words. **2.** *Gram.* to convert into a verb. —*v.i.* **3.** to use many words; be verbose. —**ver′bal·i·za′tion,** *n.* —**ver′bal·iz′er,** *n.*

verbal noun, *Gram.* a noun derived from a verb, esp. in a language where nouns are derived by the same or similar means from all or nearly all verbs.

ver·ba·tim (vər bā′tĬm), *adv.* word for word; in exactly the same words.

ver·ba·tim et lit·te·ra·tim (vər bā′tĬm ĕt lĭt′ə rā′tĬm), *Latin.* word for word and letter for letter; in exactly the same words.

ver·be·na (vər bē′nə), *n.* any of certain plants characterized by elongated or flattened spikes of flowers.

ver·bi·age (vûr′bĬ Ĭj), *n.* wordiness.

ver·bose (vər bōs′), *adj.* wordy. —**ver·bose′ly,** *adv.* —**ver·bose′ness, ver·bos·i·ty** (vər bŏs′ə tĬ), *n.*

ver·bo·ten (fĕr bō'tən), *adj.* forbidden, as by law; prohibited.

Ver·cin·get·o·rix (vûr'sĭn jĕt'ə rĭks, -gĕt'-), *n.* died 45? B.C., Gallic chieftain conquered by Caesar.

ver·dant (vûr'dənt), *adj.* **1.** green. **2.** inexperienced. —**ver'dan·cy,** *n.* —**ver'dant·ly,** *adv.*

Ver·di (vĕr'dē), *n.* Giuseppe, 1813–1901, Italian composer.

ver·dict (vûr'dĭkt), *n.* a judgment or decision, esp. by a jury.

ver·di·gris (vûr'də grēs', -grĭs), *n.* a green or bluish patina formed on copper, brass, or bronze surfaces exposed to the atmosphere for long periods of time, consisting principally of basic copper sulfate.

Ver·dun (vâr dün'), *n.* a fortress city in NE France. 14,609.

ver·dure (vûr'jər), *n.* **1.** greenness. **2.** green vegetation.

Ver·ein (fĕr īn'), *n.* German. a union, association, or society.

verge¹ (vûrj), *n., v.,* verged, verging. —*n.* **1.** the edge, rim, or margin. —*v.i.* **2.** to be on the verge; border.

verge² (vûrj), *v.i.,* verged, verging. to incline or tend.

Ver·gil (vûr'jĭl), *n.* 70–19 B.C., Roman poet. Also, Virgil.

ver·i·fy (vĕr'ə fī'), *v.t.,* -fied, -fying. **1.** to prove (something) to be true; confirm. **2.** to ascertain the truth or correctness of. **3.** to state to be true. —**ver'i·fi'a·ble,** *adj.* —**ver'i·fi'er,** *n.* —**ver'i·fi·ca'tion,** *n.*

ver·i·ly (vĕr'ə lĭ), *adv. Archaic.* truly.

ver·i·si·mil·i·tude (vĕr'ə sĭ mĭl'ə tūd', -tōōd'), *n.* appearance of truth; probability.

ver·i·ta·ble (vĕr'ə tə bəl), *adj.* genuine; real. —**ver'i·ta·ble·ness,** *n.* —**ver'i·ta·bly,** *adv.*

ver·i·ty (vĕr'ə tĭ), *n., pl.* -ties. **1.** truth. **2.** a true statement, idea, or the like.

ver·juice (vûr'jōōs'), *n.* **1.** an acid liquor made from the sour juice of crab apples, unripe grapes, etc., formerly much used for culinary and other purposes. **2.** sourness, as of temper or expression. —*adj.* Also, **ver'juiced'. 3.** of or pertaining to verjuice. **4.** sour in temper, expression, etc.

Ver·laine (vĕr lĕn'), *n.* Paul, 1844–96, French symbolist poet.

Ver·meer (vər mȳr'; *Du.* -mār'), *n.* Jan (*Jan van der Meer of Delft*) 1632–75, Dutch painter.

ver·mi·cel·li (vûr'mə sĕl'ĭ, -chĕl'ĭ), *n.* a food paste in long, slender, solid threads.

ver·mi·cide (vûr'mə sīd'), *n.* any agent that kills worms; esp. a drug used to kill parasitic intestinal worms. —**ver'mi·cid'al,** *adj.*

ver·mi·form (vûr'mə fôrm'), *adj.* like a worm in form; long and slender.

vermiform appendix, *Anat.* a narrow blind tube protruding from the caecum.

ver·mi·fuge (vûr'mə fūj'), *adj.* **1.** serving to expel worms or other animal parasites from the intestines, as a medicine. —*n.* **2.** a vermifuge medicine or agent.

ver·mil·ion (vər mĭl'yən), *n.* **1.** brilliant red. **2.** a bright-red pigment consisting of mercuric sulfide. —*adj.* **3.** of the color of vermilion.

ver·min (vûr'mĭn), *n. pl. or sing.* **1.** noxious, troublesome, or objectionable animals collectively. **2.** objectionable or obnoxious persons collectively. —**ver'min·ous,** *adj.*

ver·mi·na·tion (vûr'mə nā'shən), *n.* **1.** the breeding of vermin. **2.** the fact of being infested with vermin, esp. parasitic vermin.

Ver·mont (vər mŏnt'), *n.* a State in the NE United States. 352,999 pop.; 9609 sq. mi. *Cap.:* Montpelier. *Abbr.:* Vt.

Ver·mont·er (vər mŏn'tər), *n.* a native or inhabitant of Vermont.

ver·mouth (vûr'mōōth, vər mōōth'), *n.* an aromatic white wine in which flavorings have been steeped.

ver·nac·u·lar (vər năk'yə lər), *adj.* **1.** native in the place of its use; indigenous. —*n.* **2.** the native speech or language of a place. **3.** the language or phraseology peculiar to a class or profession.

ver·nac·u·lar·ism (vər năk'yə lə rĭz'əm), *n.* **1.** a vernacular word or expression. **2.** the use of the vernacular.

ver·nal (vûr'nəl), *adj.* **1.** of or pertaining to

spring. **2.** belonging to youth. —**ver'nal·ly,** *adv.*

Verne (vûrn), *n.* Jules, 1828–1905, French novelist.

ver·ni·er (vûr'nĭ ər), *n.* a small, movable, graduated scale running parallel with a fixed, graduated scale on an instrument, and used for measuring a fractional part of one of the divisions of the fixed scale.

Ver·o·nal (vĕr'ə nəl), *n. Trademark.* barbital.

Ver·ra·za·no (vĕr'rä tsä'nô), *n.* Giovanni da, c1480–1527?, Italian navigator who explored along the coast of North America for France. Also, **Ver'raz·za'no** or **Ver·ra·za·ni** (vĕr'rä tsä'-nē).

Ver·sailles (vər sālz'), *n.* a city in N France, ab. 12 mi. SW of Paris; palace of Louis XIV; treaty of peace between the Allies and Germany (1919). 70,141.

ver·sa·tile (vûr'sə tĭl), *adj.* capable of or adapted for turning with ease from one to another of various tasks, subjects, etc. —**ver'sa·tile·ly,** *adv.* —**ver'sa·til·i·ty,** *n.*

vers de so·ci·é·té (vĕr də sô syĕ tĕ'), *French.* humorous light verse dealing with fashions and foibles of the time.

verse (vûrs), *n.* **1.** one of the lines of a poem. **2.** a particular type of metrical line or composition. **3.** a poem. **4.** poetry. **5.** a short division of a chapter in the Bible, usually one sentence.

versed (vûrst), *adj.* expert; skilled.

ver·si·cle (vûr'sə kəl), *n.* **1.** a little verse. **2.** *Eccles.* one of a series of short sentences, or parts of sentences, usually from the Psalms, said or sung by the officiant, as distinguished from the response of the choir or congregation.

ver·si·fy (vûr'sə fī'), *v.,* -fied, -fying. —*v.t.* **1.** to treat in verse. **2.** to turn into verse. —*v.i.* **3.** to compose verses. —**ver'si·fi'er,** *n.* —**ver'si·fi·ca'tion,** *n.*

ver·sion (vûr'zhən, -shən), *n.* **1.** a translation. **2.** one of several accounts of some matter.

vers li·bre (vĕr lē'br), *French.* free verse.

ver·so (vûr'sō), *n., pl.* -sos. **1.** *Print.* the left-hand page of a book or manuscript. **2.** the reverse, back, or other side of some object.

ver·sus (vûr'səs), *prep.* against.

ver·te·bra (vûr'tə brə), *n., pl.* -brae (-brē'), -bras. *Anat., Zool.* any of the bones or segments composing the spinal column. —**ver'te·bral,** *adj.*

vertebral column, the spinal column.

ver·te·brate (vûr'tə brāt', -brĭt), *adj.* **1.** having vertebrae; having a spinal column. —*n.* **2.** a vertebrate animal.

ver·tex (vûr'tĕks), *n., pl.* -texes, -tices (-tə-sēz'). **1.** the highest point; apex; top. **2.** *Math.* the point farthest from the base.

ver·ti·cal (vûr'tə kəl), *adj.* **1.** perpendicular to the plane of the horizon; upright. **2.** of, pertaining to, or situated at the vertex. —*n.* **3.** a vertical line, plane, position, or the like. —**ver'ti·cal·ly,** *adv.*

vertical union, a labor union which attempts to organize workers according to industry rather than skill or craft.

ver·ti·go (vûr'tə gō'), *n., pl.* vertigoes, vertigines (vər tĭj'ə nēz'). *Pathol.* dizziness.

Ver·tum·nus (vər tüm'nəs), *n.* the Roman divinity of gardens and orchards, worshiped as the god of the changing seasons. Also, **Vortumnus.**

verve (vûrv), *n.* enthusiasm, liveliness, or vigor.

ver·y (vĕr'ĭ), *adv., adj.,* verier, veriest. —*adv.* **1.** extremely; exceedingly. —*adj.* **2.** identical. **3.** mere. **4.** sheer. **5.** actual. **6.** true.

ves·i·cant (vĕs'ə kənt), *adj.* **1.** producing a blister or blisters. —*n.* **2.** a vesicant agent or substance.

ves·i·cate (vĕs'ə kāt'), *v.t.,* -cated, -cating. to raise vesicles or blisters on; blister. —**ves'i·ca'tion,** *n.*

ves·i·ca·to·ry (vĕs'ə kə tōr'ĭ, və sĭk'ə tōr'ĭ), *adj., n., pl.* -ries. vesicant.

ves·i·cle (vĕs'ə kəl), *n.* **1.** a little sac or cyst. **2.** *Biol.* a small cavity, esp. one filled with fluid. **3.** *Pathol.* a blister. —**ve·sic·u·lar** (və sĭk'yə-lər), **ve·sic·u·late** (və sĭk'yə lĭt, -lāt'), *adj.*

Ves·pa·si·an (vĕs pā′zhǐ ən, -zhən), n. (*Titus Flavius Sabinus Vespasianus*) A.D. 9–79, Roman emperor from A.D. 70 to 79.

ves·per (vĕs′pər), n. 1. evening. 2. (*cap.*) the evening star, esp. Venus. 3. an evening prayer, service, song, etc.

ves·per·tine (vĕs′pər tǐn, -tīn′), adj. 1. of, pertaining to, or occurring in the evening. 2. *Bot.* opening or expanding in the evening, as certain flowers. 3. *Zool.* appearing or flying in the early evening; crepuscular. Also, **ves·per·ti·nal** (vĕs′-pər tī′nəl).

Ves·puc·ci (vĕs pōōt′chē), n. **Amerigo,** (*Americus Vespucius*) 1451–1512, Italian merchant, adventurer, and explorer.

ves·sel (vĕs′əl), n. 1. a ship or boat. 2. an airship. 3. a hollow or concave container, as a cup, bowl, pot, pitcher, vase, bottle, etc. 4. *Anat., Zool.* a tube or duct, as an artery, vein, or the like, containing or conveying blood or some other body fluid.

vest (vĕst), n. 1. a short, sleeveless garment worn by men under a coat. 2. an undershirt. —*v.t.* 3. to clothe, dress, or robe. 4. to put in the possession or control of. 5. to endow (a person, etc.) with powers, functions, etc.

Ves·ta (vĕs′tə), n. *Rom. Myth.* the goddess of the hearth and hearth fire.

ves·tal (vĕs′təl), adj. 1. of, pertaining to, or like a vestal virgin; virgin; chaste. —*n.* 2. a vestal virgin. 3. any virgin. 4. a nun.

vestal virgin, (in ancient Rome) one of the virgins consecrated to Vesta and to the service of watching the sacred fire kept burning perpetually on her altar.

vest·ed (vĕs′tĭd), adj. 1. placed completely and firmly in the possession of a person or persons. 2. clothed or robed.

vest·ee (vĕs tē′), n. a front piece worn under a woman's jacket or blouse.

ves·ti·bule (vĕs′tə būl′), n. a passage, hall, or antechamber between the outer door and the interior parts of a house, building, etc. —**ves·tib·u·lar** (vĕs tǐb′yə lər), adj.

vestibule school, a department of an industrial establishment in which new employees are trained for the work they are to perform.

ves·tige (vĕs′tǐj), n. 1. a mark or trace of something no longer present or in existence. 2. *Biol.* a degenerate or imperfectly developed structure having little or no utility, but which in an earlier stage of the individual or in preceding organisms performed a useful function. —**ves·tig′i·al,** adj.

vest·ment (vĕst′mənt), n. 1. a garment, robe, or gown. 2. an official or ceremonial robe, as one worn by a clergyman.

vest-pock·et (vĕst′pŏk′ǐt), adj. miniature; designed to be carried in a pocket of the vest.

ves·try (vĕs′trǐ), n., pl. **-tries.** 1. a room in a church, in which the vestments, etc., are kept. 2. (in some churches) a room used for prayer meetings, for the Sunday school, etc. 3. (in the Protestant Episcopal Church in the U.S.) a committee that helps to manage the temporal affairs of a church. —**ves′try·man,** n.

Ve·su·vi·us (və sōō′vǐ əs), n. **Mount,** an active volcano in SW Italy. ab. 4000 ft.

vet[1] (vĕt), n. *Colloq.* veterinarian.

vet[2] (vĕt), n. *Colloq.* a veteran.

vet., 1. veteran. 2. veterinarian; veterinary.

vetch (vĕch), n. any of certain leguminous plants, mostly climbing herbs, cultivated for forage and soil improvement.

vet·er·an (vĕt′ər ən, vĕt′rən), n. 1. one who has seen long service in some field, esp. a soldier. —*adj.* 2. experienced through long service.

vet·er·i·nar·i·an (vĕt′ər ə nâr′ĭ ən, vĕt′rə-), n. one who practices veterinary medicine or surgery.

vet·er·i·nar·y (vĕt′ər ə nĕr′ĭ, vĕt′rə-), n., pl. **-naries,** adj. —*n.* 1. a veterinarian. —*adj.* 2. of or pertaining to the medical and surgical treatment of domesticated animals.

veterinary medicine, that branch of medicine that concerns itself with the study, prevention, and treatment of animal diseases.

ve·to (vē′tō), n., pl. **-toes,** v., **-toed, -toing.** —*n.* 1. the power or right of a chief executive, as a president or governor, to reject bills passed by the legislature. 2. a prohibition directed against some proposed or intended act. 3. the power or right of preventing action by a prohibition. —*v.t.* 4. to reject by veto. —**ve′to·er,** n.

vet. sci., veterinary science.

vex (vĕks), v.t. 1. to irritate; annoy; make angry. 2. to torment; worry. 3. to agitate or discuss with vigor. —**vex·a′tion,** n. —**vex·a′tious,** adj.

vexed (vĕkst), adj. 1. disturbed; troubled; annoyed. 2. much discussed or disputed, as a question. 3. tossed about, as waves. —**vex·ed·ly** (vĕk′sĭd lǐ), adv. —**vex′ed·ness,** n.

V.F.W., Veterans of Foreign Wars.

Vi, *Chem.* virginium.

v.i., verb intransitive.

vi·a (vī′ə), prep. by way of.

vi·a·ble (vī′ə bəl), adj. capable of living.

vi·a·duct (vī′ə dŭkt′), n. a bridge for carrying a road, railroad, etc., over a valley, ravine, or the like.

vi·al (vī′əl, vīl), n. a small vessel, as of glass, for liquids.

vi·a me·di·a (vī′ə mē′dǐ ə), *Latin.* a middle way; a mean between two extremes.

Viaduct

vi·and (vī′ənd), n. an article of food.

vi·at·i·cum (vī ăt′ə kəm), n., pl. **-ca** (-kə), **-cums.** *Eccles.* the Eucharist or Communion as given to a person dying or in danger of death.

vi·brant (vī′brənt), adj. 1. vibrating. 2. (of sounds) resonant. 3. full of vigor; energetic. —**vi′bran·cy,** n.

vi·brate (vī′brāt), v.i., v.t., **-brated; -brating.** 1. to move to and fro, as a pendulum does; oscillate. 2. to quiver; tremble. 3. (of sounds) to resound. 4. to thrill.

vi·bra·tile (vī′brə tǐl, -tīl′), adj. 1. capable of vibrating, or susceptible of being vibrated. 2. having a vibratory motion. 3. pertaining to or of the nature of vibration. —**vi·bra·til·i·ty** (vī′brə tǐl′ə tǐ), n.

vi·bra·tion (vī brā′shən), n. 1. act of vibrating; oscillation. 2. state of vibrating. 3. *Physics.* **a.** the oscillating, reciprocating, or other periodic motion of a rigid or elastic body forced from a position or state of equilibrium. **b.** the analogous motion of the particles of a mass of air, etc., whose state of equilibrium has been disturbed, as in transmitting sound, etc. **c.** the vibratory motion of a string or other sonorous body, producing musical sound. 4. a single vibrating motion; oscillation; quiver or tremor. —**vi·bra′tion·al,** adj. —**vi·bra′tion·less,** adj.

vi·bra·tor (vī′brā tər), n. 1. one that vibrates. 2. any of various instruments or devices causing a vibratory motion or action. 3. an appliance with a rubber or other tip of variable shape, made to oscillate very rapidly, used in vibratory massage. 4. *Elect.* a device in which, by continually repeated impulse, an appropriately designed component is set in continuous vibration. 5. a device for producing electrical oscillations.

vi·bra·to·ry (vī′brə tōr′ĭ), adj. 1. producing vibration. 2. vibrating, or admitting of vibration. 3. of the nature of or consisting in vibration. 4. pertaining to vibration.

vic·ar (vǐk′ər), n. 1. *Ch. of Eng.* a person acting as priest of a parish in place of the rector. 2. *Prot. Episc. Ch.* a clergyman whose sole or chief charge is a chapel dependent on the church of a parish. 3. *Rom. Cath. Ch.* **a.** an ecclesiastic representing the Pope or a bishop. **b.** the Pope as the representative on earth of God or Christ. 4. a substitute or deputy. —**vic′ar·ship′,** n.

vic·ar·age (vǐk′ər ǐj), n. 1. the residence of a vicar. 2. the benefice of a vicar.

vic·ar-gen·er·al (vǐk′ər gĕn′ər əl), n., pl. **vic·ars-general.** 1. *Rom. Cath. Ch.* a priest deputized by a bishop to assist him in the administration of a diocese. 2. *Ch. of Eng.* an ecclesiastical officer, usually a layman, who assists a bishop or an archbishop in the discharge of his judicial or administrative duties.

vi·car·i·al (vī kâr′ĭ əl, vǐ-), adj. 1. of or pertaining to a vicar or vicars. 2. acting as or holding the office of a vicar. 3. delegated or vicarious, as powers.

vi·car·i·ate (vī kâr′ĭ ǐt, -āt′, vǐ-), n. 1. the office or authority of a vicar. 2. a district under a vicar. Also, **vic·ar·ate** (vǐk′ər ǐt, -rāt′).

vi·car·i·ous (vī kâr′ĭ əs, vǐ-), adj. 1. performed, exercised, received, or suffered in place of another. 2. serving as a substitute. —**vi·car′i·ous·ly,** adv.

Vicar of (Jesus) Christ, *Rom. Cath. Ch.* the pope, with reference to his claim to stand in the place of Jesus Christ and possess His authority in the church.

vice[1] (vīs), *n.* **1.** an immoral or evil habit or fault. **2.** immoral conduct. **3.** a particular form of depravity. **4.** a fault or defect.

vice[2] (vīs), *n., v.t.,* **viced, vicing. vise.**

vi·ce[3] (vī'sĭ), *prep.* instead of.

vice-, a prefix denoting a substitute, deputy, or subordinate: *vice-chairman.*

vice-ad·mi·ral (vīs'ăd'mə rəl), *n.* a naval officer next in rank below an admiral.

vice-con·sul (vīs'kŏn'səl), *n.* a consular officer of a grade below that of consul.

vice·ge·ren·cy (vīs jĭr'ən sĭ), *n., pl.* **-cies. 1.** the position, government, or office of a vicegerent. **2.** the territory or district under a vicegerent.

vice·ge·rent (vīs jĭr'ənt), *n.* **1.** an officer deputed by a ruler or supreme head to exercise the powers of the ruler or head. **2.** any deputy. —*adj.* **3.** exercising delegated powers. **4.** characterized by delegation of powers.

vice-pres·i·dent (vīs'prĕz'ə dənt), *n.* an officer next in rank to a president and taking his place under certain conditions. —**vice'-pres'i-den·cy,** *n.* —**vice'-pres·i·den'tial,** *adj.*

vice·re·gal (vīs rē'gəl), *adj.* of or pertaining to a viceroy. —**vice·re'gal·ly,** *adv.*

vice-re·gent (vīs'rē'jənt), *n.* **1.** a deputy regent; one who acts in the place of a ruler, governor, or sovereign. —*adj.* **2.** of, pertaining to, or occupying the position of a vice-regent. —**vice'-re'gen·cy,** *n.*

vice·roy (vīs'roi), *n.* one appointed to rule a country or province as the deputy of the sovereign.

vi·ce ver·sa (vī'sĭ vûr'sə), conversely.

Vi·chy (vĭsh'Y), *n.* a city in central France: capital of unoccupied France, 1940–44. 29,391.

vi·chy water (vĭsh'Y). **1.** a natural mineral water from springs at Vichy, containing sodium bicarbonate, other alkaline salts, etc., used in the treatment of digestive disturbances, gout, etc. **2.** some water of similar composition, natural or artificial. Also, **Vi'chy, vichy.**

vi·cin·i·ty (vĭ sĭn'ə tĭ), *n., pl.* **-ties. 1.** the neighborhood. **2.** proximity; propinquity.

vi·cious (vĭsh'əs), *adj.* **1.** immoral; depraved; profligate. **2.** evil or bad. **3.** reprehensible, blameworthy, or wrong. **4.** spiteful or malignant. **5.** *Colloq.* unpleasantly severe. **6.** faulty; defective. **7.** having an ugly disposition. —**vi'cious·ly,** *adv.* —**vi'cious·ness,** *n.*

vicious circle, 1. a situation in which solution of one problem creates problems whose solution is incompatible with the original circumstances. **2.** *Logic.* the use of one proposition to establish a second, when the second proposition is in turn used to establish the first.

vi·cis·si·tude (vĭ sĭs'ə tūd', -tōōd'), *n.* a change or variation occurring in the course of anything.

Vicks·burg (vĭks'bûrg), *n.* a city in W Mississippi. 24,460.

vic·tim (vĭk'tĭm), *n.* **1.** a sufferer from any destructive, injurious, or adverse action. **2.** a dupe. **3.** a person or animal sacrificed. —**vic'tim·ize',** *v.t.*

vic·tor (vĭk'tər), *n.* a conqueror or winner.

Victor Emmanuel III, born 1869, king of Italy, 1900–46. In June, 1944 his royal powers were given to Crown Prince Humbert but he kept his title of king and his position as head of the House of Savoy until the dissolution of the monarchy.

Vic·to·ri·a (vĭk tōr'Y ə), *n.* **1.** 1819–1901, queen of Great Britain and Ireland (1837–1901), and empress of India (1876–1901). **2.** a seaport in SW Canada, on Vancouver Island. **3.** Lake, a lake in E Africa: principal headwaters of the Nile. 26,828 sq. mi. **4.** (*l.c.*) a low, light, four-wheeled carriage with a folding top, a seat for two passengers, and a perch in front for the driver.

Victoria Cross, a British decoration awarded to soldiers and sailors for acts of conspicuous bravery in the presence of the enemy.

Victoria Falls, falls of the Zambezi river in S Africa. ab. 400 ft. high; over a mile wide.

Vic·to·ri·an (vĭk tōr'Y ən), *adj.* **1.** of or pertaining to Queen Victoria or her reign. **2.** having the characteristics usually attributed to the Victorians, as bigotry and prudishness. —*n.* **3.** a person belonging to the Victorian period. —**Vic·to'ri·an·ism',** *n.*

vic·to·ri·ous (vĭk tōr'Y əs), *adj.* **1.** having achieved a victory. **2.** characterized by or pertaining to victory. **3.** conquering; triumphant. —**vic·to'ri·ous·ly,** *adv.* —**vic·to'ri·ous·ness,** *n.*

vic·to·ry (vĭk'tə rY), *n., pl.* **-ries.** success or triumph in a battle or any contest.

Victory Medal, a round bronze medal awarded to all men who served in the armed forces of the United States during World War I.

victory ribbon, a service ribbon worn on the left breast by men entitled to wear the Victory Medal

Vic·tro·la (vĭk trō'lə), *n. Trademark.* a phonograph.

vict·ual (vĭt'əl), *n., v.,* **-ualed, -ualing** or (*esp. Brit.*) **-ualled, -ualling.** —*n.* **1.** (*pl.*) *Chiefly Dial. or Colloq.* articles of food prepared for use. —*v.t.* **2.** to supply with victuals. —**vict'ual·er,** *n.*

vi·cu·ña (vĭ kōōn'yə, vĭ kū'nə), *n.* a wild South American ruminant of the Andes having a soft, delicate wool.

vi·de in·fra (vī'dĭ Yn'frə), *Latin.* see below.

vi·de·li·cet (vĭ dĕl'ə sĭt), *adv.* namely.

vid·e·o (vĭd'Y ō'), *adj.* **1.** pertaining to or employed in the transmission or reception of a televised image. —*n.* **2.** television.

vi·de su·pra (vī'dĭ sōō'prə), *Latin.* see above.

vie (vī), *v.i.,* **vied, vying.** to contend for superiority.

Vi·en·na (vĭ ĕn'ə), *n.* the capital of Austria, in the NE part. 1,611,448. —**Vi·en·nese** (vē'ə-nēz', -nēs'), *adj., n.*

Vi·et Nam (vē ĕt năm'), a republic within French Indo-China, constituted in 1945 (recognized by the French, 1946).

view (vū), *n.* **1.** a seeing or beholding; an examination by the eye. **2.** sight or vision. **3.** range of sight or vision. **4.** a sight or picture of some landscape, scene, etc. **5.** the aspect of something. **6.** a mental survey. **7.** contemplation or consideration. **8.** aim, intention, or purpose. **9.** prospect or expectation. **10.** a conception, notion, opinion, or theory. —*v.t.* **11.** to see or behold. **12.** to look at, survey, or inspect. **13.** to consider or regard.

view halloa, the shout uttered by a huntsman on seeing a fox break cover.

view·less (vū'lYs), *adj.* **1.** that cannot be viewed or seen; invisible. **2.** without views or opinions. —**view'less·ly,** *adv.*

view·point (vū'point'), *n.* **1.** a place affording a view of something. **2.** an attitude of mind.

vig·il (vĭj'əl), *n.* **1.** a keeping awake during the natural hours of sleep, esp. as a watch. **2.** *Eccles.* **a.** a devotional watch during the customary hours of sleep. **b.** (*often pl.*) a nocturnal devotional service, esp. on the eve before a church festival.

vigilance committee, *U.S.* **1.** an unauthorized committee of citizens organized for the maintenance of order and the summary punishment of crime in the absence of regular or efficient courts. **2.** *Hist.* (in the South) an organization of citizens using extralegal means to control or intimidate Negroes and abolitionists, and, during the Civil War, to suppress loyalty to the Union.

vig·i·lant (vĭj'ə lənt), *adj.* **1.** keenly attentive to detect danger; wary. **2.** alert; sleeplessly watchful. —**vig'i·lant·ly,** *adv.* —**vig'i·lance,** *n.*

vig·i·lan·te (vĭj'ə lăn'tY), *n. U.S.* a member of an unauthorized committee organized to maintain order and enforce law.

vi·gnette (vĭn yĕt'), *n., v.,* **-gnetted, -gnetting.** —*n.* **1.** a decorative design or small illustration used esp. on the title page of a book. **2.** a photograph or the like shading off gradually at the edges. **3.** a small, graceful literary sketch. —*v.t.* **4.** to finish (a picture, etc.) in the manner of a vignette. —**vi·gnett'ist,** *n.*

Vi·gny (vē nyē'), *n.* **Alfred Victor de,** 1797–1863, French poet, novelist, and dramatist.

vig·or (vĭg'ər), *n.* **1.** active strength or force. **2.** energy. Also, *esp. Brit.,* **vig'our.** —**vig'or·ous,** *adj.* —**vig'or·ous·ly,** *adv.*

Vi·king (vī'kĭng), *n.* a Scandinavian sea robber of the type that infested the seas about northwestern Europe during the 8th, 9th, and 10th centuries, making raids upon the coasts. Also, **viking.**

vile (vīl), *adj.,* **viler, vilest. 1.** wretchedly bad. **2.** highly offensive, objectionable, or disgusting. **3.** morally base. **4.** foul as language. **5.** poor or wretched, as in quality or state. —vile′ly, adv. —vile′ness, n.

vil·i·fy (vĭl′ə fī′), v.t., -fied, -fying. to speak evil of; defame. —vil′i·fi·ca′tion, n. —vil′i·fi′er, n.

vil·la (vĭl′ə), n. a residence, usually of some size and pretensions, in the suburbs, in the country, or at the seashore.

Vil·la (vē′yä), n. Francisco, (Doroteo Arango, "Pancho Villa") 1872?-1923, Mexican general and revolutionist.

vil·lage (vĭl′ĭj), n. 1. a small assemblage of houses, generally smaller than a town. 2. the inhabitants collectively. —vil′lag·er, n.

vil·lain (vĭl′ən), n. a wicked person; scoundrel. —vil′lain·ous, adj. —vil′lain·ous·ly, adv.

vil·lain·y (vĭl′ən ĭ), n., pl. -lainies. 1. the conduct of a villain. 2. a villainous act.

Vil·la-Lo·bos (vē′lyä lô′bŏŏsh, -bŏŏs), n. Heitor, born 1881, Brazilian composer.

Vil·lard (vĭ lärd′, vĭ′lärd′), n. Oswald Garrison, born 1872, U.S. journalist and author.

vil·lein (vĭl′ən), n. a member of a class of half-free persons under the feudal system who were serfs with respect to their lord but had the rights and privileges of freemen with respect to others.

Vil·lon (vē yôN′), n. François, 1431–after 1463, French poet.

Vil·na (vĭl′nə), n. a city in the W Soviet Union: capital of the Lithuanian Republic; formerly in Poland. 195,100.

vim (vĭm), n. force; energy; vigor.

Vi·my (vē mē′), n. a town in N France: battle of Vimy Ridge (1917). 2508.

vin·ai·grette (vĭn′ə grĕt′), n. a small ornamental bottle or box for holding aromatic vinegar, smelling salts, or the like.

vinaigrette sauce, a cold, tart sauce of oil, vinegar, chopped pickle, seasonings, and herbs.

Vin·ci (vēn′chē), n. Leonardo da, 1452–1519, Italian painter, sculptor, architect, musician, engineer, and scientist.

vin·ci·ble (vĭn′sə bəl), adj. capable of being conquered or overcome. —vin′ci·bil′i·ty, vin′ci·ble·ness, n.

vin·di·ca·ble (vĭn′də kə bəl), adj. that may be vindicated.

vin·di·cate (vĭn′də kāt′), v.t., -cated, -cating. 1. to clear, as from suspicion. 2. to uphold or justify. —vin′di·ca′tion, n. —vin′di·ca′tor, n.

vin·dic·tive (vĭn dĭk′tĭv), adj. inclined to hold a grudge; revengeful. —vin·dic′tive·ly, adv. —vin·dic′tive·ness, n.

vine (vīn), n. any plant with a long, slender stem that trails or creeps on the ground or climbs by winding itself about a support or holding fast with tendrils or claspers.

vin·e·gar (vĭn′ə gər), n. a sour liquid consisting of dilute and impure acetic acid, obtained by fermentation from wine, cider, beer, ale, or the like, and used as a condiment, preservative, etc.

vin·er·y (vī′nə rĭ), n., pl. -eries. 1. a grapery; vineyard. 2. vines collectively.

vine·yard (vĭn′yərd), n. a plantation of grapevines, for producing grapes for winemaking, etc.

vin·i·cul·ture (vĭn′ə kŭl′chər), n. the study or science of winemaking.

vin or·di·naire väN ôr dē nĕr′), French. a cheap wine of popular consumption.

Vin·son (vĭn′sən), n. Frederick Moore, born 1890, chief justice of the U.S. Supreme Court since 1946.

vin·tage (vĭn′tĭj), n. 1. the wine from a particular harvest. 2. the annual produce of the grape harvest. 3. an exceptionally fine wine from the crop of a good year. 4. Colloq. the crop or output of anything.

vint·ner (vĭnt′nər), n. Brit., Archaic in U.S. a dealer in wine; wine merchant.

vi·nyl (vī′nĭl, vĭn′ĭl), n. Chem. the univalent radical CH_2:CH, derived from ethylene, compounds of which undergo polymerization to form plastics and resins of high molecular weight.

vi·ol (vī′əl), n. a bowed musical instrument, roughly resembling the violin.

vi·o·la (vĭ ō′lə, vī-), n. a four-stringed musical instrument of the violin class, slightly larger than the violin.

vi·o·la·ble (vī′ə lə bəl), adj. that may be violated. —vi′o·la·bly, adv.

vi·o·late (vī′ə lāt′), v.t., -lated, -lating. 1. to break, infringe, or transgress (a law, promise, etc.). 2. to disturb rudely. 3. to break through or pass by force or without right. 4. to desecrate or profane. 5. to rape. —vi′o·la′tion, n. —vi′o·la′tor, n.

vi·o·lence (vī′ə ləns), n. 1. rough force. 2. injurious action or treatment. 3. any injury, wrong, or outrage.

vi·o·lent (vī′ə lənt), adj. 1. acting with or characterized by uncontrolled, strong, rough force. 2. acting with, characterized by, or due to injurious or destructive force. 3. intense; severe; extreme. 4. immoderately vehement or ardent. —vi′o·lent·ly, adv.

vi·o·les·cent (vī′ə lĕs′ənt), adj. tending to a violet color.

vi·o·let (vī′ə lĭt), n. 1. any of certain low, stemless or leafy-stemmed herbs with purple, blue, yellow, white, or variegated flowers. 2. a bluish purple color. —adj. 3. bluish-purple.

violet ray, the visible light of shortest wave length.

vi·o·lin (vī′ə lĭn′), n. 1. the treble of the family of modern bowed musical instruments, which is held nearly horizontal by the player's arm, with the lower part supported against the collarbone or shoulder. 2. any modern instrument of the same general class, as a viola or a cello. —vi′o·lin′ist, n.

vi·o·lon·cel·lo (vē′ə lən chĕl′ō), n., pl. -los. a cello. —vi′o·lon·cel′list, n.

vi·per (vī′pər), n. 1. any of certain Old World venomous snakes. 2. a malicious or treacherous person.

vi·per·ine (vī′pər ĭn, -pə rīn′), adj. of, pertaining to, or resembling a viper.

vi·per·ous (vī′pər əs), adj. 1. of the nature of a viper or vipers; viperlike. 2. pertaining to vipers. 3. characteristic of vipers. 4. venomous or malignant. —vi′per·ous·ly, adv.

vi·ra·go (vĭ rä′gō, vī-), n., pl. -goes, -gos. a shrew.

vir·e·o (vĭr′ĭ ō′), n., pl. vireos. any of certain small American insectivorous birds.

vi·res·cent (vĭ rĕs′ənt), adj. 1. turning green. 2. tending to a green color; slightly greenish.

Vir·gil (vûr′jĭl), n. Vergil.

vir·gin (vûr′jĭn), n. 1. a woman, esp. a young woman, who has had no sexual intercourse. 2. the Virgin, Mary, the mother of Christ. 3. (cap.) the zodiacal constellation or sign Virgo. —adj. 4. being a virgin. 5. of or like a virgin; pure. 6. untouched, untried, or unused. —vir′gin·al, adj. —vir·gin′i·ty, n.

virgin birth, Theol. the doctrine or dogma that the birth of Christ did not, by the miraculous agency of God, impair or prejudice the virginity of Mary. Cf. Immaculate Conception.

Vir·gin·ia (vər jĭn′yə), n. a State in the E United States. 2,985,851 pop.; 40,815 sq. mi. Cap.: Richmond. Abbr.: Va. —Vir·gin′ian, adj., n.

Virginia City, a mining town in W Nevada: famous for the discovery of the rich Comstock silver lode, 1859.

Virginia reel, an American dance in which the partners face each other in two lines.

Virgin Islands, a group of islands in the West Indies, E of Puerto Rico, divided into the Virgin Islands of the United States, including the islands of St. Thomas, St. John, and St. Croix (27,160 pop.; 133 sq. mi.; Cap.: Charlotte Amalie), and the British Virgin Islands (6813 pop.; 67 sq. mi.; Cap.: Road Town).

vir·gin·i·um (vər jĭn′ĭ əm), n. Chem. a rare metallic element. Symbol: Vi; at. no.: 87.

Virgin Mary, Mary, the mother of Jesus.

Virgin Queen, Queen Elizabeth of England.

virgin wool, wool which has never gone through the manufacturing process.

Vir·go (vûr′gō), n. 1. Astron. an equatorial constellation south of Ursa Major, containing the bright star Spica; Virgin. 2. the sixth sign of the zodiac.

vir·gule vûr′gūl), n. Print. a short oblique stroke (/) between two words designating that the interpretation may be made in either sense. Example: and/or.

vir·i·des·cent (vĭr′ə dĕs′ənt), adj. slightly green or greenish. —vir′i·des′cence, n.

vir·ile (vĭr′əl, vī′rəl), adj. 1. masculine or manly. 2. strong, vigorous, or forceful. 3. pertaining to or capable of procreation. —vi·ril·i·ty (və rĭl′ə tĭ), n.

vir·tu (vər tōō', vûr'tōō), *n.* **1.** excellence or merit in objects of art, curios, and the like. **2.** (*construed as pl.*) such objects or articles collectively. **3.** a taste for or knowledge of such objects.

vir·tu·al (vûr'chŏŏ əl), *adj.* being such in power, force, or effect, although not actually or expressly such. —**vir'tu·al·ly,** *adv.*

vir·tue (vûr'chōō), *n.* **1.** moral excellence or goodness. **2.** uprightness; rectitude. **3.** chastity. **4.** an excellence, merit, or good quality. **5.** potency or efficacy.

vir·tu·os·i·ty (vûr'chŏŏ ŏs'ə tĭ), *n., pl.* **-ties.** the character or skill of a virtuoso.

vir·tu·o·so (vûr'chŏŏ ō'sō), *n., pl.* **-sos, -si** (-sē). **1.** one who has special skill in any field, esp. in music. **2.** a connoisseur of art.

vir·tu·ous (vûr'chŏŏ əs), *adj.* **1.** morally excellent or good; conforming or conformed to moral laws; upright; righteous; moral; chaste. **2.** *Archaic.* having effective virtue, potent, or efficacious. —**vir'tu·ous·ly,** *adv.* —**vir'tu·ous·ness,** *n.*

vir·u·lent (vĭr'yə lənt, vĭr'ə-), *adj.* **1.** actively poisonous, malignant, or deadly. **2.** violently hostile. —**vir'u·lent·ly,** *adv.* —**vir'u·lence, vir'u·len·cy,** *n.*

vi·rus (vī'rəs), *n.* **1.** an infective agent, often one smaller than a common microörganism and requiring living cells for multiplication. **2.** a corrupting influence.

Vis., **1.** Viscount. **2.** Viscountess.

vi·sa (vē'zə), *n., v.,* **-saed, saing.** —*n.* **1.** an endorsement made upon a passport of one country for passage to the country granting the visa. —*v.t.* **2.** to put a visa on.

vis·age (vĭz'ĭj), *n.* **1.** the face, esp. of a human being. **2.** aspect; appearance.

vis-à-vis (vē'zə vē'), *adv., adj.* face to face.

Visc., **1.** Viscount. **2.** Viscountess.

vis·cer·a (vĭs'ər ə), *n.pl., sing.* **viscus** (vĭs'kəs). **1.** the soft interior organs of the body, including the brain, lungs, heart, stomach, intestines, etc. **2.** the intestines or bowels. —**vis'cer·al,** *adj.*

vis·cid (vĭs'ĭd), *adj.* sticky, adhesive, or gluelike. Also, **vis·cous** (vĭs'kəs). —**vis·cos·i·ty** (vĭs kŏs'ə tĭ), *n.*

vis·cose (vĭs'kōs), *n.* **1.** a viscous solution prepared by treating cellulose with caustic soda and carbon bisulfide: used in manufacturing regenerated cellulose fibers, sheets, or tubes, as rayon or cellophane. —*adj.* **2.** relating to, or made from, viscose.

vis·co·sim·e·ter (vĭs'kō sĭm'ə tər), *n.* apparatus for determining the viscosity of liquids, either through rate of flow through an orifice or resistance to movement of a submerged object.

vis·count (vī'kount), *n.* a nobleman next below an earl or count and next above a baron: —**vis'count·ess,** *n.fem.*

vise (vīs), *n., v.,* **vised, vising.** —*n.* **1.** any of various devices, usually having two jaws, used to hold an object firmly while work is being done upon it. —*v.t.* **2.** to hold, press, or squeeze with a vise.

vi·sé (vē'zā, vē zā'), *n., v.t.,* **viséed, viséing.** visa.

Vish·nu (vĭsh'nōō), *n. Hinduism.* "the Preserver": the second member of an important trinity, along with Brahma the Creator and Siva the Destroyer.

vis·i·bil·i·ty (vĭz'ə bĭl'ə tĭ), *n., pl.* **-ties.** **1.** state or fact of being visible; capability of being seen. **2.** the relative capability of being seen under given conditions of distance, light, atmosphere, etc. **3.** something visible; a visible thing.

vis·i·ble (vĭz'ə bəl), *adj.* **1.** capable of being seen; open to view. **2.** perceptible by the mind. **3.** apparent; manifest. —**vis'i·ble·ness,** *n.* —**vis'i·bly,** *adv.*

Vis·i·goth (vĭz'ĭ gŏth'), *n.* a member of the westerly division of the Goths, which formed a monarchy about A.D. 418, maintaining it in southern France until A.D. 507 and in Spain until A.D. 711. —**Vis'i·goth'ic,** *adj.*

vi·sion (vĭzh'ən), *n.* **1.** the power, faculty, or sense of sight. **2.** act or power of perceiving by some supernatural endowment or by intellectual acuteness. **3.** a mental view or image, whether of supernatural origin or merely imaginative, of what is not actually present in place or time.

vi·sion·al (vĭzh'ən əl), *adj.* **1.** of or pertaining to visions. **2.** belonging to or seen in a vision. —**vi'sion·al·ly,** *adv.*

vi·sion·ar·y (vĭzh'ə nĕr'ĭ), *adj., n., pl.* **-aries.** —*adj.* **1.** fanciful or unpractical. **2.** seen in a vision. **3.** unreal or imaginary. —*n.* **4.** one who sees visions. **5.** one given to unpractical ideas or schemes.

vis·it (vĭz'ĭt), *v.t., v.i.* **1.** to go to see (a person, place, etc.) in the way of friendship, business, curiosity, or the like. **2.** to come upon or assail. **3.** to afflict with suffering, trouble, etc. —*n.* **4.** an act of visiting. **5.** a call paid to a person, family, etc. **6.** a stay or sojourn as a guest. —**vis'i·tor,** *n.*

vis·it·a·ble (vĭz'ĭt ə bəl), *adj.* **1.** capable of or suitable for being visited. **2.** liable or subject to official visitation.

vis·it·ant (vĭz'ə tənt), *n.* **1.** a visitor; a guest; a temporary resident. **2.** a migratory bird or other animal, at a temporary feeding place, etc., or on its nesting-ground (**summer visitant**) or wintering ground (**winter visitant**). —*adj.* **3.** visiting; paying a visit.

vis·it·a·tion (vĭz'ə tā'shən), *n.* **1.** a visit. **2.** (*cap. or l.c.*) the visit of the Virgin Mary to her cousin Elizabeth. **3.** (*cap.*) a church festival, July 2, in commemoration of this visit. **4.** a visiting with comfort or aid, or with affliction or punishment, as by God.

visiting card, a calling card.

vi·sor (vī'zər, vĭz'ər), *n.* **1.** the movable front elements of a helmet, covering the face. **2.** the projecting forepiece of a cap, for protecting the eyes from the sun, etc.

vis·ta (vĭs'tə), *n.* **1.** a view, esp. one seen through a long, narrow avenue or passage. **2.** a mental view of a far-reaching kind.

Vis·tu·la (vĭs'chŏŏ lə), *n.* a river in Poland, flowing from the Carpathian Mountains past Warsaw into the Baltic near Danzig. ab. 650 mi.

vis·u·al (vĭzh'ŏŏ əl), *adj.* **1.** of or pertaining to sight. **2.** used in sight. **3.** visible. —**vis'u·al·ly,** *adv.*

visual aid, *Educ.* a device, technique, or the like, which uses the student's sense of sight in carrying on or assisting the learning process.

vis·u·al·ize (vĭzh'ŏŏ ə lĭz'), *v.t., v.i.,* **-ized, -izing.** **1.** to make visual or visible. **2.** to form a mental image (of). —**vis/u·al·i·za'tion,** *n.*

vi·tal (vī'təl), *adj.* **1.** of or pertaining to life. **2.** having life; living. **3.** being the source of life. **4.** necessary to life. **5.** indispensable; essential. **6.** of critical importance. **7.** vitalizing; invigorating. —**vi'tal·ly,** *adv.*

vital force, the animating force in animals and plants. Also, **vital principle.**

vi·tal·ism (vī'tə lĭz'əm), *n.* **1.** the doctrine that phenomena are only partly controlled by mechanical forces and that they are in some measure self-determining (opposed to *mechanism*). **2.** *Biol.* the doctrine that ascribes the functions of a living organism to a vital principle distinct from chemical and other forces. —**vi'tal·ist,** *n., adj.* —**vi'tal·is'tic,** *adj.*

vi·tal·i·ty (vī tăl'ə tĭ), *n., pl.* **-ties.** **1.** vital force. **2.** the principle of life. **3.** power to live, or physical strength as a condition of life. **4.** exuberant physical vigor. **5.** power of continued existence, as of an institution, a book, etc. **6.** something having vital force. **7.** (*pl.*) vital powers or energies.

vi·tal·ize (vī'tə līz'), *v.t.,* **-ized, -izing.** **1.** to give life to. **2.** to give vigor to; animate. —**vi'tal·i·za'tion,** *n.*

vital statistics, statistics concerning human life or the conditions affecting human life and the maintenance of population.

vi·ta·min (vī'tə mĭn), *n.* any of a group of food factors essential in small quantities to maintain life but not themselves supplying energy. The absence of any one of them results in a characteristic deficiency disease. —**vi'ta·min·ic,** *adj.*

vi·tel·line (vī tĕl'ĭn, vī-), *adj.* **1.** pertaining to the egg yolk. **2.** having a yellow color.

vitelline membrane, the membrane surrounding the egg yolk.

vi·tel·lus (vī tĕl'əs, vī-), *n.* the yolk of an egg.

vi·ti·ate (vĭsh'ĭ āt'), *v.t.,* **-ated, -ating.** **1.** to impair; mar. **2.** to corrupt; spoil. **3.** to invalidate. —**vi'ti·a'tion,** *n.*

vi·ti·at·ed (vĭsh'ĭ ā'tĭd), *adj.* spoiled; corrupted; rendered invalid.

vit·i·cul·ture (vĭt'ə kŭl'chər, vī'tə-), *n.* **1.** the culture or cultivation of the grapevine; grape growing. **2.** the study or science of grapes and their culture.

vit·i·li·go (vĭt′ə lī′gō), *n. Pathol.* a disease in which smooth white patches are formed on various parts of the body, owing to loss of the natural pigment.

vit·re·ous (vĭt′rĭ əs), *adj.* of or resembling glass; glassy.

vitreous humor, *Anat.* the transparent gelatinous substance filling the eyeball behind the crystalline lens.

vi·tres·cent (vĭ trĕs′ənt), *adj.* 1. turning into glass. 2. tending to become glass. 3. capable of being formed into glass. —**vi·tres′cence,** *n.*

vit·ri·form (vĭt′rə fôrm′), *adj.* having the form or appearance of glass.

vit·ri·fy (vĭt′rə fī′), *v.t., v.i.,* **-fied, -fying.** to convert or be converted into glass. —**vit′ri·fi·ca′tion,** *n.*

vit·ri·ol (vĭt′rĭ əl), *n.* 1. *Chem.* any of certain metallic sulfates of glassy appearance, as of copper (**blue vitriol**), of iron (**green vitriol**), of zinc (**white vitriol**), etc. 2. sulfuric acid. 3. something highly caustic, as criticism.

vit·ri·ol·ic (vĭt′rĭ ŏl′ĭk), *adj.* 1. of or pertaining to vitriol. 2. obtained from vitriol; resembling vitriol. 3. severely caustic or scathing.

vit·ri·ol·ize (vĭt′rĭ ə līz′), *v.t.,* **-ized, -izing.** 1. to treat with or change into vitriol. 2. to injure or burn with vitriol or sulfuric acid, as by throwing it on one's face. —**vit′ri·ol·i·za′tion,** *n.*

vi·tu·per·ate (vī tū′pə rāt′, -tōō′-, vī-), *v.t.,* **-ated, -ating.** 1. to find fault with abusively. 2. to revile. —**vi·tu′per·a′tion,** *n.* —**vi·tu′per·a′tive,** *adj.*

vi·va (vē′vä), *interj.* 1. *Italian.* "(long) live (the person named)!"—used in phrases of acclamation. —*n.* 2. a shout of "viva!"

vi·va·ce (vē vä′chě), *adj. Music.* vivacious; lively.

vi·va·cious (vī vā′shəs, vĭ-), *adj.* lively; animated. —**vi·va′cious·ly,** *adv.* —**vi·va′cious·ness, vi·vac·i·ty** (vĭ văs′ə tĭ, vī-), *n.*

vi·van·dière (vē vän dyěr′), *n.* a woman accompanying a French or other Continental regiment to sell provisions and liquor to the soldiers.

vi·var·i·um (vī vâr′ĭ əm), *n., pl.* **-variums, -varia** (-vâr′ĭ ə). a place, such as a laboratory, where animals are kept alive in conditions simulating their natural state.

vi·va vo·ce (vī′və vō′sī), orally.

vive (vēv), *interj. French.* "(long) live (the person named)!" —used in phrases of acclamation.

vive le roi (vēv lə rwä′), *French.* long live the king!

viv·id (vĭv′ĭd), *adj.* 1. strikingly bright, as color, light, objects, etc. 2. full of life. 3. intense, as feelings. 4. clearly perceptible to the eye or mind. —**viv′id·ly,** *adv.* —**viv′id·ness,** *n.*

viv·i·fy (vĭv′ə fī′), *v.t.,* **-fied, -fying.** 1. to give life to. 2. to enliven.

vi·vip·a·rous (vī vĭp′ə rəs), *adj. Zool.* bringing forth living young (rather than eggs), as most mammals and some reptiles and fishes.

viv·i·sect (vĭv′ə sĕkt′, vĭv′ə sĕkt′), *v.t.* 1. to dissect the living body of. —*v.i.* 2. to practice vivisection.

viv·i·sec·tion (vĭv′ə sĕk′shən), *n.* the practice of subjecting living animals to cutting operations, esp. in order to advance physiological and pathological knowledge. —**viv′i·sec′tion·ist,** *n.*

vix·en (vĭk′sən), *n.* 1. an ill-tempered or quarrelsome woman. 2. a female fox.

viz., videlicet.

vi·zier (vĭ zîr′, vĭz′yər), *n.* a principal helper of a Mohammedan sovereign.

vi·zor (vī′zər, vĭz′zər), *n.* visor.

V-J Day, the day of victory in Japan for the Allies in World War II (Sept. 2, 1945).

Vla·di·vos·tok (vlăd′ə vŏs′tŏk), *n.* a seaport in the SE Soviet Union in Asia, on the Sea of Japan. 206,432.

V-mail (vē′māl′), *n.* a service during World War II, for despatching letters to U.S. armed forces outside the continental U.S., esp. by miniature films.

voc., vocative.

vocab., vocabulary.

vo·cab·u·lar·y (vō kăb′yə lĕr′ĭ), *n., pl.* **laries.** 1. the stock of words used by a people, or by a particular class or person. 2. a collection of the words of a language, author, branch of science, or the like, usually in alphabetical order and defined.

vocabulary entry, 1. a word entered in a vocabulary. 2. (in dictionaries) a word or phrase listed with its definition, etc., in alphabetical order or listed for identification after the word from which it is derived or to which it is related.

vo·cal (vō′kəl), *adj.* 1. of or pertaining to the voice; oral. 2. rendered by or intended for singing. 3. articulate, talkative, or clamorous. —**vo′cal·ize,** *v.t., v.i.* —**vo′cal·i·za′tion,** *n.* —**vo′cal·ly,** *adv.*

vocal cords, *Anat.* folds of mucous membrane projecting into the cavity of the larynx, the edges of which can be drawn tense and made to vibrate by the passage of air from the lungs, thus producing vocal sound.

vo·cal·ic (vō kăl′ĭk), *adj.* 1. of or pertaining to a vowel or vowels; vowellike. 2. containing many vowels.

vo·cal·ist (vō′kəl ĭst), *n.* a singer.

vo·cal·ize (vō′kə līz′), *v.,* **-ized, -izing.** —*v.t.* 1. to make vocal; form into voice; utter or articulate; sing. 2. to endow with voice or utterance. 3. *Phonet.* a. to use as a vowel, as the *l* of *bottle*. b. to change into a vowel. c. to voice. —*v.i.* 4. to use the voice, as in speech or song. 5. *Phonet.* to become changed into a vowel. —**vo′cal·i·za′tion,** *n.* —**vo′cal·iz′er,** *n.*

vocat., vocative.

vo·ca·tion (vō kā′shən), *n.* 1. a particular occupation, business, or profession. 2. a summons, as to the priesthood. —**vo·ca′tion·al,** *adj.*

voc·a·tive (vŏk′ə tĭv), *Gram.* —*adj.* 1. designating a case that indicates the person or thing addressed. —*n.* 2. the vocative case.

vo·cif·er·ant (vō sĭf′ər ənt), *adj.* 1. vociferating. —*n.* 2. one who vociferates.

vo·cif·er·ate (vō sĭf′ə rāt′), *v.i., v.t.,* **-ated, -ating.** to cry out loudly or noisily; shout; bawl. —**vo·cif′er·a′tion,** *n.*

vo·cif·er·ous (vō sĭf′ər əs), *adj.* clamorous; shouting. —**vo·cif′er·ous·ly,** *adv.* —**vo·cif′er·ous·ness,** *n.*

vod·ka (vŏd′kə), *n.* a Russian alcoholic liquor, distilled from corn or other cereals, and potatoes.

vogue (vōg), *n.* 1. the fashion, as at a particular time. 2. popular currency or favor.

voice (vois), *n., v.,* **voiced, voicing.** —*n.* 1. the sound or sounds uttered through the mouth. 2. such sounds considered with reference to their quality. 3. the condition of the voice for speaking or singing. 4. any sound likened to vocal utterance. 5. expression in spoken or written words, or by other means. 6. choice. 7. the right to express an opinion or choice; vote. 8. *Gram.* a category of verb inflection denoting the relation between the action expressed by the verb and the subject of the sentence (e.g., as acting or as acted upon). —*v.t.* 9. to give, express, declare, or proclaim.

voiced (voist), *adj.* 1. having a voice. 2. *Phonet.* uttered with tonal vibration of the vocal cords.

voice·less (vois′lĭs), *adj.* 1. having no voice. 2. silent. 3. *Phonet.* uttered without tonal vibration of the vocal cords.

voice part, *Music.* the melody or succession of tones for one of the voices or instruments in a harmonic or concerted composition.

void (void), *adj.* 1. without legal force. 2. useless; vain. 3. empty; devoid; destitute. 4. without contents. —*n.* 5. an empty space. —*v.t.* 6. to invalidate; nullify. 7. to empty. —**void′a·ble,** *adj.*

void·ance (voi′dəns), *n.* 1. act of voiding. 2. annulment, as of a contract. 3. ejection from a benefice. 4. vacancy, as of a benefice.

voile (voil), *n.* a thin cotton fabric.

voi·ture (vwä tyr′), *n. French.* a carriage, wagon, or wheeled vehicle.

vol., volume.

Vo·la·pük (vō′lə pyk′), *n.* one of the earliest of the artificially constructed international auxiliary languages, invented about 1879. Also, **Vol·a·puk** (vŏl′ə pŏŏk′).

vol·a·tile (vŏl′ə tĭl), *adj.* 1. evaporating rapidly. 2. changeable of mind; flighty. 3. transient. —**vol·a·til′i·ty,** *n.* —**vol′a·til·ize′,** *v.i., v.t.*

volatile oil, a distilled oil, esp. an essential oil distilled from plant tissue.

vol·can·ic (vŏl kăn′ĭk), *adj.* 1. of or pertaining to a volcano or volcanoes. 2. discharged from or produced by volcanoes. 3. characterized by the presence of volcanoes. 4. suggestive of a volcano, or its latent force, eruptive violence, etc. —**vol·can′i·cal·ly,** *adv.* —**vol·can·ic·i·ty** (vŏl′kə nĭs′ə tĭ), *n.*

vol·can·ism (võl'kə nĭz'əm), n. the phenomena connected with volcanoes and volcanic activity.

vol·ca·no (võl kā'nō), n., pl. **-noes, -nos. 1.** a vent in the earth's crust through which molten rock (lava), steam, ashes, etc., are expelled from within. **2.** a mountain having such a vent.

Vol·ga (võl'gə), n. a river flowing from the W Soviet Union E and then S to the Caspian Sea. 2325 mi.

vo·li·tion (vō lĭsh'ən), n. **1.** act of willing. **2.** the power of willing. **—vo·li'tion·al,** adj.

Volks·lied (fôlks'lēt'), n., pl. **-lieder** (-lē'dər). German. a folksong.

vol·ley (võl'Y), n., pl. **-leys,** v., **-leyed, -leying. —n. 1.** the flight or discharge of a number of missiles together. **2.** Tennis. **a.** a flight of a ball in play before striking the ground. **b.** a return of the ball by the racket before it touches the ground. **—v.t. 3.** to discharge in a volley. **4.** Tennis. to return (the ball) before it strikes the ground. **—v.i. 5.** to fire a volley or sound together, as firearms.

vol·ley·ball (võl'Y bôl'), n. a game the object of which is to keep a large ball in motion, from side to side over a high net, by striking it with the hands before it touches the ground.

vo·lost (vō'lŏst), n. **1.** (formerly) a small administrative peasant division in Russia. **2.** a rural soviet.

vol·plane (võl'plān), v.i., **-planed, -planing.** to glide toward the earth in an airplane. with no motor power or with the power shut off.

Vol·stead (võl'stĕd), n. **Andrew Joseph,** 1860–1946, U.S. legislator.

Vol·stead·ism (võl'stĕd Yz'əm), n. **1.** the policy of prohibiting the sale of liquor to be used as or for a beverage. **2.** the enforcement of this policy, so called after Congressman A. J. Volstead, author of such a prohibition bill passed in 1919 and repealed in 1933.

Vol·sun·ga Sa·ga (võl'sŏŏng gə sä'gə), (in Icelandic literature) the mythical history of the Volsungs and Nibelungs. Its central hero is Sigurd (the Siegfried of the Nibelungenlied). It is the principal source of Wagner's "Ring des Nibelungen."

volt (võlt), n. Elect. the unit of electromotive force: that electromotive force which will cause a current of one ampere to flow through a resistance of one ohm. **—volt'age,** n.

vol·ta·ic (võl tā'Yk), adj. denoting or pertaining to the electricity produced by chemical action; galvanic.

Vol·taire (võl târ'), n. **François Marie Arouet de,** 1694–1778, French philosopher and author.

vol·tam·e·ter (võl tăm'ə tər), n. a device for measuring the quantity of electricity passing through a conductor by the amount of electrolytic decomposition it produces, or for measuring the strength of a current by the amount of such decomposition in a given time. **—vol·ta·met·ric** (võl'tə mĕt'rYk), adj.

volt·me·ter (võlt'mē'tər), n. an instrument for measuring the voltage between two points.

vol·u·ble (võl'yə bəl), adj. glibly fluent. **—vol'u·bil'i·ty,** n. **—vol'u·bly,** adv.

vol·ume (võl'ūm, -yəm), n. **1.** a collection of sheets bound together into a book. **2.** a book forming one of a set. **3.** the size, measure, or amount of anything in three dimensions. **4.** a mass or quantity, esp. a large quantity, of anything. **5.** amount. **6.** loudness or softness. **7.** fullness of tone or sound.

vo·lu·mi·nous (və lōō'mə nəs), adj. **1.** forming or filling many volumes. **2.** of great or ample size or extent. **—vo·lu'mi·nous·ly,** adv.

vol·un·tar·y (võl'ən tĕr'Y), adj., n., pl. **-taries. —adj. 1.** done, made, undertaken, etc., of one's own free choice. **2.** acting of one's own will. **3.** Physiol. subject to or controlled by the will. **—n. 4.** a piece of music performed as a prelude to a larger work. **—vol'un·tar'i·ly,** adv.

vol·un·teer (võl'ən tYr'), n. **1.** one who offers himself for any service or undertaking, esp. military duty. **—adj. 2.** entering voluntarily into any service. **3.** consisting of volunteers. **—v.i., v.t. 4.** to offer (one's services, etc., or oneself) for some duty or purpose. **5.** to tell or say voluntarily.

Volunteers of America, a religious reform and relief organization, similar to the Salvation Army, founded in New York City in 1896, by Ballington Booth, son of William Booth, founder of the Salvation Army.

vo·lup·tu·ar·y (və lŭp'chŏŏ ĕr'Y), n. one given up to luxurious or sensuous pleasures.

vo·lup·tu·ous (və lŭp'chŏŏ əs), adj. **1.** luxurious or sensuous. **2.** sensuously pleasing or delightful. **—vo·lup'tu·ous·ly,** adv. **—vo·lup'·tu·ous·ness,** n.

vom·it (võm'Yt), v.i. **1.** to eject the contents of the stomach by the mouth. **2.** to be ejected with violence. **—v.t. 3.** to eject from the stomach through the mouth. **4.** to eject with force or copiously. **—n. 5.** matter ejected in vomiting.

vom·i·to·ry (võm'ə tōr'Y), adj., n., pl. **-ries. —adj. 1.** inducing vomiting; emetic. **2.** pertaining to vomiting. **—n. 3.** an emetic. **4.** an opening through which something is ejected or discharged.

von (võn; Ger. fôn, unstressed fən), prep. German. from; of; much used in German personal names, orig. before names of places or estates, and later before family names as an indication of nobility or rank.

voo·doo (vōō'dōō), n., pl. **-doos,** adj. **—n. 1.** a class of mysterious rites or practices, of the nature of sorcery, witchcraft, or conjuration, prevalent among the Negroes of the West Indies and the southern U.S., and probably of African origin. **2.** one who practices such rites. **—adj. 3.** pertaining to or practicing voodoo. **—voo'doo·ism',** n.

vo·ra·cious (võ rā'shəs), adj. greedy in eating; ravenous. **—vo·ra'cious·ly,** adv. **—vo·rac'i·ty** (võ răs'ə tY), n.

Vo·ro·nezh (võ rô'nĕsh), n. a city in the central Soviet Union in Europe. 326,836.

Vo·ro·shi·lov (võ rô shē'lôf), n. **Kliment Efremovich,** born 1881. Soviet general.

vor·tex (vôr'tĕks), n., pl. **-texes, -tices** (-tə-sēz'). **1.** a whirling movement or mass of water, as a whirlpool. **2.** a whirling movement or mass of air, as a whirlwind.

Vosges (vōzh), n. a range of low mountains in NE France. Highest peak, 4668 ft.

vo·ta·ry (vō'tə rY), n., pl. **-ries. 1.** one who is bound by a vow; a monk or a nun. **2.** a devotee.

vote (vōt), n., v., **voted, voting. —n. 1.** a formal expression of will, wish, or choice in some matter, as by ballot, etc. **2.** the right to such expression. **3.** a number of votes collectively. **—v.i. 4.** to express the will or choice in a matter undergoing decision, as by a ballot. **—v.t. 5.** to enact, establish, or grant by vote. **6.** to support by one's vote. **—vot'er,** n.

voting machine, a mechanical substitute for the paper ballot, which automatically registers and counts votes.

voting paper, Brit. a ballot.

vo·tive (vō'tYv), adj. offered, given, dedicated, etc., in accordance with a vow.

vouch (vouch), v.i. **1.** to answer (for) as being true, certain, reliable, etc. **2.** to give one's own assurance, as surety or sponsor (fol. by for).

vouch·er (vou'chər), n. **1.** one that vouches. **2.** a document, receipt, stamp, or the like, which proves the truth of a claimed expenditure.

vouch·safe (vouch sāf'), v.t., **-safed, -safing.** to grant, allow, or permit.

vow (vou), n. **1.** a solemn promise, pledge, or personal engagement. **—v.t., v.i. 2.** to make a vow (of). **3.** to declare earnestly.

vow·el (vou'əl), n. **1.** Phonet. a speech sound articulated so that there is a clear channel for the voice through the middle of the mouth. **2.** Gram. a letter which usually represents a vowel. **—adj. 3.** pertaining to a vowel.

vox (võks), n., pl. **voces** (vō'sēz). voice; sound; word; expression.

vox pop., vox populi.

vox po·pu·li (põp'yŏŏ lī'), Latin. the voice or opinion of the people.

voy·age (voi'Yj), n., v., **-aged, -aging. —n. 1.** a passage or journey, esp. to a distant place. **—v.i. 2.** to make or take a voyage. **—voy'ag·er,** n.

vo·ya·geur (vwà yà zhœr'), n., pl. **-geurs** (-zhœr). French. a French Canadian or half-breed who is an expert woodsman and boatman, esp. one hired as a guide by a fur company whose stations are in remote and unsettled regions.

vo·yeur (vwà yœr'), n. a pervert who attains sexual gratification by looking at sexual objects or situations.

vo·yeur·ism (vwà yœr'Yz əm), n. a perversion in which sexual gratification is obtained by looking at nude or partly nude bodies.

V.P., Vice-President. Also, **V. Pres.**

v.p., verb passive.

vs., 1. verse. 2. versus.

V-shaped (vē'shāpt'), *adj.* in the shape of the letter V.

Vt., Vermont.

v.t., verb transitive.

Vul., Vulgate.

Vul·can (vŭl'kən), *n.* the Roman god of fire and metalworking.

Vul·ca·ni·an (vəl kā'nĭ ən), *adj.* **1.** pertaining to or associated with Vulcan. **2.** (*l.c.*) volcanic. **3.** (*l.c.*) of or pertaining to metalworking.

vul·can·ite (vŭl'kə nīt'), *n.* a hard rubber obtained by vulcanizing India rubber with a large amount of sulfur.

vul·can·ize (vŭl'kə nīz'), *v.t.,* **-ized, -izing.** to treat (India rubber) with sulfur and moderate heat in order to render it nonplastic and give greater elasticity, durability, etc. —**vul'can·i·za'tion,** *n.* —**vul'can·iz'er,** *n.*

Vulg., Vulgate.

vulg., 1. vulgar. 2. vulgarly.

vul·gar (vŭl'gər), *adj.* **1.** marked by lack of good breeding or taste, as manners, language, dress, etc. **2.** crudely unrefined, as persons. **3.** of or current among the general mass of the people. **4.** vernacular. **5.** common or ordinary. —**vul'gar·ly,** *adv.* —**vul'gar·ness, vul·gar·i·ty** (vəl gâr'ə tĭ), *n.*

vul·gar·i·an (vəl gâr'ĭ ən), *n.* a vulgar person, esp. one whose vulgarity is the more conspicuous for his wealth, prominence, or pretensions to good breeding.

vul·gar·ism (vŭl'gə rĭz'əm), *n.* **1.** vulgar character or action. **2.** a word or phrase used only in common colloquial, and esp. in coarse, speech.

Vulgar Latin, popular Latin, as opposed to literary or standard Latin; esp. those forms of popular Latin speech from which sprang the Romance languages of later times.

Vul·gate (vŭl'gāt, -gĭt), *n.* the Latin version of the Scriptures, accepted as the authorized version of the Roman Catholic Church. It was prepared near the end of the 4th century A.D.

vul·ner·a·ble (vŭl'nər ə-bəl), *adj.* **1.** liable to physical hurt. **2.** not proof against criticism, temptation, etc. **3.** (of a fortress, etc.) open to attack or assault. **4.** *Contract Bridge.* exposed to greater than usual penalties. —**vul'ner·a·bil'i·ty,** *n.* —**vul'ner·a·bly,** *adv.*

Vulture (3 ft. long)

vul·pine (vŭl'pīn, -pĭn), *adj.* **1.** pertaining to or characteristic of a fox. **2.** resembling a fox.

vul·ture (vŭl'chər), *n.* any of certain large, carrion-eating birds related to the eagles, kites, hawks, falcons, etc., but having less powerful toes and straighter claws.

vul·va (vŭl'və), *n., pl.* **-vae** (-vē), **-vas.** *Anat.* the external female genitals.

vv., 1. verses. 2. violins.

v.v., vice versa.

vy·ing (vī'ĭng), *adj.* that vies; competing.

W

W, w (dŭb'əl yōō), *n., pl.* **W's** or **Ws, w's** or **ws.** the 23rd letter of the English alphabet.

W, 1. watt. 2. west. 3. western.

W., 1. Wednesday. 2. west.

w., 1. watt. 2. west. 3. wide.

W.A.A.C., 1. *Brit.* Women's Army Auxiliary Corps. 2. *U.S.* former name of the WAC.

Wa·bash (wô'băsh), *n.* a river flowing from W Ohio through Indiana and S along part of the boundary between Indiana and Illinois into the Ohio river. 475 mi.

wab·ble (wŏb'əl), *v.i., v.t.,* **-bled, -bling,** *n.* wobble. —**wab'bler,** *n.* —**wab'bling,** *adj.* —**wab'bling·ly,** *adv.* —**wab'bly,** *adj., adv.*

WAC (wăk), *U.S.* **1.** Women's Army Corps. **2.** a member of the WAC.

wack (wăk), *n. Slang.* an erratic, irrational, or unconventional person.

wack·y (wăk'ĭ), *adj. Slang.* erratic, irrational, or unconventional.

Wa·co (wā'kō), *n.* a city in central Texas. 55,982.

wad (wŏd), *n., v.,* **wadded, wadding.** —*n.* **1.** a small mass of cotton, wool, or other soft material, used for stuffing, padding, packing, etc. **2.** a roll, as of paper money. —*v.t.* **3.** to form into a wad. **4.** to stuff; pad. —**wad'ding,** *n.*

wad·dle (wŏd'əl), *v.,* **-dled, -dling,** *n.* —*v.i.* **1.** to walk with short steps and swaying from side to side, as a duck. —*n.* **2.** a waddling gait.

wade (wād), *v.,* **waded, wading,** *n.* —*v.i.* **1.** to walk through any substance, as water, snow, sand, etc., that impedes free motion. **2.** to make one's way with difficulty. **3.** *Colloq.* to make a sharp attack or energetic beginning. —*v.t.* **4.** to pass through by wading. —*n.* **5.** act of wading. —**wad'er,** *n.*

wa·di (wä'dĭ), *n., pl.* **-dis.** (in Arabia, Syria, northern Africa, etc.) **1.** the channel of a watercourse which is dry except during periods of rainfall. **2.** the stream or watercourse itself.

WAF (wăf), *U.S.* **1.** Women's Air Force. **2.** a member of the WAF.

wa·fer (wā'fər), *n.* **1.** a thin cake or biscuit, often sweetened and flavored. **2.** a thin disk of unleavened bread, used in the Eucharist. **3.** a thin disk of dried paste, gelatin, adhesive paper, or the like, used for sealing letters, etc.

waf·fle (wŏf'əl), *n.* a batter cake indented by the special griddle (**waffle iron**) in which it is baked.

waft (wăft, wäft), *v.t., v.i.* **1.** to carry, or be carried, through the air or over water. —*n.* **2.** a sound, odor, etc., carried through the air. **3.** act of wafting. —**waft'er,** *n.*

waf·ture (wăf'chər, wäf'-), *n.* **1.** act of wafting. **2.** something wafted.

wag (wăg), *v.,* **wagged, wagging,** *n.* —*v.t., v.i.* **1.** to move back and forth, esp. rapidly and repeatedly. —*n.* **2.** act of wagging. **3.** a humorous person; joker. —**wag'gish,** *adj.*

wage (wāj), *n., v.,* **waged, waging.** —*n.* (*usually pl., sometimes construed as sing.*). **1.** that which is paid for work; pay. **2.** recompense or return. —*v.t.* **3.** to carry on (a battle, war, conflict, etc.).

wage earner, one who works for wages (sometimes distinguished from salaried employees).

wa·ger (wā'jər), *n., v.t., v.i.* bet. —**wa'ger·er,** *n.*

wage scale, **1.** a schedule of wages paid workers performing connected operations in an industry or shop. **2.** a particular employer's wage schedule.

wage·work·er (wāj'wûr'kər), *n.* a member of the laboring class; a worker for wages; wage earner.

wag·gish (wăg'ĭsh), *adj.* **1.** like a wag; roguish in merriment and good humor; jocular. **2.** characteristic of or befitting a wag. —**wag'gish·ly,** *adv.* —**wag'gish·ness,** *n.*

wag·gle (wăg'əl), *v.,* **-gled, -gling,** *n.* —*v.t., v.i.* **1.** to wag with short, quick movements. —*n.* **2.** a waggling motion.

wag·gon (wăg'ən), *n. Brit.* wagon.

Wag·ner (väg'nər), *n.* Richard, 1813–83, German composer.

wag·on (wăg'ən), *n.* **1.** any of various kinds of

four-wheeled vehicles, esp. one for heavy loads, etc. **2.** *Brit.* a railroad freight car. —*v.t.* **3.** to transport by wagon. Also, *Brit.*, **waggon.** —**wag'on-er,** *n.*

wa·gon-lit (và gôN lē'), *n.* (in French and other Continental use) a sleeping car.

wag·on·load (wăg'ən lōd'), *n.* the load carried by a wagon.

waif (wāf), *n.* **1.** a person without home or friends, esp. a child. **2.** a stray article.

Wai·ki·ki (wī'kē kē', wī'kē kē'), *n.* a famous bathing beach in the Hawaiian Islands, in Honolulu harbor.

wail (wāl), *v.i.* **1.** to utter a long, mournful cry, as in grief. —*v.t.* **2.** to lament. —*n.* **3.** act of wailing. **4.** a wailing cry. —**wail'er,** *n.*

Wailing Wall of the Jews, an enclosure in Jerusalem where, traditionally, Jews hold prayers and lamentation each Friday. One wall reputedly is built of stones from the temple of Solomon. Also, **Wailing Wall.**

wain·scot (wān'skət, -skŏt), *n., v.,* **-scoted,** **-scoting** or (*esp. Brit.*) **-scotted, -scotting.** —*n.* **1.** wood, usually in panels, serving to line the walls of a room, etc. —*v.t.* **2.** to line with wainscot. —**wain'scot·ing,** *n.*

wain·wright (wān'rīt'), *n.* a wagon maker.

Wain·wright (wān'rīt'), *n.* **Jonathan Mayhew,** born 1883, U.S. general.

waist (wāst), *n.* **1.** the part of the human body between the ribs and the hips. **2.** a garment, or a part of a garment, covering the body from the shoulders to the waistline, esp. in women's or children's dress. **3.** a central or middle part.

waist·band (wāst'bănd', -bənd), *n.* a band encircling the waist, esp. as a part of a skirt, trousers, etc.

waist·coat (wāst'kōt', wĕs'kət), *n.* *Chiefly Brit.* a man's vest.

waist·line (wāst'līn'), *n.* the line of the waist, between the chest and hips.

wait (wāt), *v.i.* **1.** to stay or rest in expectation. **2.** to be in readiness. **3.** to remain neglected for a time. **4. wait on** or **upon, a.** to serve, esp. at the table. **b.** to attend. —*v.t.* **5.** to await. —*n.* **6.** act of waiting; delay. **7.** ambush.

wait·er (wā'tər), *n.* **1.** a man who waits on table, esp. in a restaurant. **2.** a tray on which dishes, etc., are carried. —**wait'ress,** *n. fem.*

wait·ing (wā'tĭng), *n.* attendance, as upon a king, queen, etc.

waiting room, a room for persons waiting, as in a railroad station, a physician's office, etc.

waive (wāv), *v.t.,* **waived, waiving. 1.** to forbear to insist on; relinquish; forgo. **2.** to defer.

waiv·er (wā'vər), *n.* *Law.* **1.** an intentional relinquishment of some right, interest, or the like. **2.** an express or written statement of such relinquishment.

wake¹ (wāk), *v.,* **waked** or **woke; waked** or (*Archaic and Dial.*) **woken; waking;** *n.* —*v.i.* **1.** to stop sleeping. **2.** to be or continue awake. **3.** to become active. —*v.t.* **4.** to rouse from sleep. **5.** to rouse from inactivity, etc. —*n.* **6.** a watching; vigil. **7.** an all-night watch beside the body of a dead person before burial. —**wake'ful,** *adj.* —**wake'ful·ly,** *adv.* —**wake'ful·ness,** *n.*

wake² (wāk), *n.* **1.** the track left by a ship moving in the water. **2.** the path of anything that has passed.

Wake Island, a small island in the N Pacific, belonging to the U.S. 3 sq. mi.

wak·en (wā'kən), *v.t., v.i.* to wake.

Wald (wôld), *n.* **Lillian,** 1867–1940, U.S. social worker.

Wal·den·ses (wŏl dĕn'sēz), *n.pl.* a Christian sect which arose after 1170 in southern France under the leadership of Pierre Waldo, a merchant of Lyons, and in the 16th century joined the Reformation movement. —**Wal·den·si·an** (wŏl-dĕn'sĭ ən, -shən), *adj., n.*

Wal·dorf salad (wôl'dôrf), a salad of celery, diced apples, nuts, and mayonnaise dressing.

wale¹ (wāl), *n., v.,* **waled, waling.** —*n.* **1.** a streak, stripe, or ridge produced on the skin by the stroke of a rod or whip; welt. **2.** a ridge or raised line formed in the weave of cloth. **3.** the texture of a fabric; the kind of weave. —*v.t.* **4.** to mark with wales. **5.** to weave with wales.

wale² (wāl), *n., v.,* **waled, waling.** *Scot. and N. Eng.* —*n.* **1.** the choicest or best specimen, part, etc. —*v.t.* **2.** to choose, select; pick out.

Wales (wālz), *n.* a division of the United Kingdom: the SW part of Great Britain. 2,489,000 pop.; 8016 sq. mi.

Wal·hal·la (wăl hăl'ə, wäl hä'lə), *n.* *Scand. Myth.* Valhalla.

walk (wôk), *v.i.* **1.** to go or travel on foot at a moderate pace. **2.** to go about on the earth, or appear to living persons, as a ghost. **3.** *Baseball.* to take first base as a base on balls. —*v.t.* **4.** to proceed through, over, or upon by walking. **5.** to make, put, drive, etc., by walking. **6.** to cause to walk. **7.** *Baseball.* to pitch a base on balls to. —*n.* **8.** act or course of walking. **9.** a spell of walking for exercise or pleasure. **10.** a distance walked or to be walked. **11.** gait or pace. **12.** manner of walking. **13.** branch of activity, etc. **14.** *Baseball.* a base achieved by having four balls pitched to the batter. **15.** a sidewalk or path. —**walk'er,** *n.*

walk·a·way (wôk'ə wā'), *n.* an easy victory or conquest.

walk·ie-talk·ie (wô'kĭ tô'kĭ), *n.* *Radio.* a combined transmitter and receiver light enough to be carried by one man; developed for military use in World War II.

walking delegate, (formerly) an official appointed by a trade union to go from place to place in the interests of the union.

walking stick, *Chiefly Brit.* a stick used in walking; a cane.

walk·out (wôk'out'), *n.* *Colloq.* a strike of laborers or workers.

walk·o·ver (wôk'ō'vər), *n.* *Colloq.* an unopposed or easy victory.

walk·up (wôk'ŭp'), *U.S. Colloq.* —*n.* **1.** a building, esp. an apartment, that has no elevator. —*adj.* **2.** having no elevator.

wall (wôl), *n.* **1.** an upright structure of stone, brick, or similar material, serving for enclosure, division, support, protection, etc. **2.** (*usually pl.*) a rampart. **3.** anything which resembles a wall. —*v.t.* **4.** to enclose, shut off, divide, protect, etc., with a wall.

wal·la·by (wŏl'ə bĭ), *n., pl.* **-bies,** (*esp. collectively*) **-by.** any of certain small kangaroos, some of which are no larger than rabbits.

Wal·lace (wŏl'ĭs, wô'lĭs), *n.* **1. Henry Agard,** born 1888, U.S. statesman and political leader. **2. Sir William,** c1272–1305, Scottish military hero.

wall·board (wôl'bōrd'), *n.* an artificial sheet material for use in making or covering walls, ceilings, etc., as a substitute for wooden boards or plaster.

Wal·ler (wŏl'ər, wô'lər), *n.* **Edmund,** 1607–87, British poet.

wal·let (wŏl'ĭt, wô'lĭt), *n.* a small leather case for papers, paper money laid flat, etc., usually carried in a pocket or purse.

wall·eye (wôl'ī'), *n.* any of certain fishes with large, staring eyes.

wall·eyed (wôl'īd'), *adj.* **1.** having eyes in which there is an abnormal amount of the white showing, because of divergent strabismus. **2.** having large, staring eyes, as some fishes.

wall·flow·er (wôl'flou'ər), *n.* **1.** *Colloq.* a person, esp. a woman, who looks on at a dance, esp. from failure to obtain a partner. **2.** a European perennial, growing wild on old walls, cliffs, etc., with sweet-scented flowers.

Wal·loon (wŏ lōōn'), *n.* **1.** one of a people inhabiting chiefly the southern and southeastern parts of Belgium and adjacent regions in France. **2.** the French dialect of Belgium, esp. of the southeast. —*adj.* **3.** of or pertaining to the Walloons or their language.

wal·lop (wŏl'əp), *v.t.* *Colloq.* **1.** to beat soundly; thrash. **2.** to defeat thoroughly. —*n.* **3.** *Colloq.* a vigorous blow.

wal·lop·er (wŏl'əp ər), *n.* *Colloq.* **1.** one who or that which wallops. **2.** something big, huge, or inordinately exaggerated.

wal·lop·ing (wŏl'əp ĭng), *Colloq.* —*n.* **1.** a sound beating or thrashing. **2.** a thorough defeat. —*adj.* **3.** big.

wal·low (wŏl'ō), *v.i.* **1.** to roll the body about, or lie, in water, mud, or the like. **2.** to live contentedly or luxuriously. —*n.* **3.** act of wallowing. **4.** a place to which animals resort to wallow.

wall·pa·per (wôl'pā'pər), *n.* paper, commonly with printed decorative patterns in color, for pasting on and covering the walls or ceilings of rooms, etc.

Wall Street, 1. a street in New York City

famous as the chief financial center of the U.S.
2. the money market or the financiers of the U.S.

wal·nut (wôl'nŭt', -nət), n. 1. the edible nut of certain trees of the north temperate zone. 2. a tree bearing this nut, which also yields a valuable timber. 3. the wood of such a tree.

Wal·pole (wôl'pōl, wŏl'-), n. 1. Horace, (4th Earl of Orford) 1717–97, British author. 2. Sir Robert, (1st Earl of Orford) 1676–1745, prime minister of England, 1721–42.

Wal·pur·gis Night (väl pŏŏr'gĭs), the eve of (before) May 1, the feast day of St. Walpurgis (an English missionary and abbess in Germany, who died about A.D. 780), on which, according to German popular superstition, witches ride to some appointed rendezvous, esp. the Brocken, the highest of the Harz Mountains.

wal·rus (wôl'rəs, wŏl'-), n., pl. -ruses, (esp. collectively) -rus. either of two large marine mammals of arctic seas, related to the seals, and having flippers, a pair of large tusks, and a thick, tough skin.

Wal·sing·ham (wôl'sĭng əm), n. Sir Francis, 1530?–1590, British statesman; secretary of state to Elizabeth, 1573–90.

Wal·tham (wôl'thəm), n. a city in E Massachusetts. 40,020.

Wal·ton (wôl'tən), n. Izaak, 1593–1683, British writer and famous fisherman.

waltz (wôlts), n. 1. a round dance in triple rhythm, danced by couples. 2. a piece of music for this dance. —v.i., v.t. 3. to dance a waltz (with). —waltz'er, n.

wam·pum (wŏm'pəm, wôm'-), n. 1. cylindrical beads made from shells, pierced and strung, used by North American Indians as money and for ornament. 2. Slang. money.

wan (wŏn), adj. 1. pale or pallid. 2. showing ill health, worn condition, unhappiness, etc. —wan'ly, adv.

Wan·a·ma·ker (wŏn'ə mā'kər), n. John, 1838–1922, U.S. merchant.

wand (wŏnd), n. 1. a slender stick, esp. one used by a conjurer. 2. a rod borne as a symbol of authority. 3. a slender shoot, stem, or branch.

wan·der (wŏn'dər), v.i. 1. to ramble without any definite course. 2. to go aimlessly or casually. 3. (of the mind, etc.) to take one direction or another without intention or control. 4. to stray from a path, companions, etc. 5. to deviate in conduct, belief, etc. —wan'der·er, n. —wan'der·ing·ly, adv.

Wandering Jew, a legendary character condemned to roam without rest because he struck Christ on the day of crucifixion.

wan·der·lust (wŏn'dər lŭst'), n. instinctive impulse to travel about.

wane (wān), v., waned, waning, n. —v.i. 1. (of the moon) to decrease periodically in the extent of its illuminated portion after the full moon. 2. to decline in power, prosperity, etc. 3. to decrease in strength, intensity, etc. 4. to approach an end. —n. 5. gradual decrease or decline.

wan·gle (wăng'gəl), v.t., v.i., -gled, -gling. Colloq. to accomplish or obtain (something) by scheming or insidious methods.

wan·nish (wŏn'ĭsh), adj. somewhat wan.

want (wŏnt, wônt), v.t. 1. to feel a need or desire for. 2. to wish or desire. 3. to be without or be deficient in. 4. to fall short by. 5. Chiefly Brit. to require. —v.i. 6. to be lacking or absent. 7. to be deficient by the absence of some part or thing. 8. to have need. —n. 9. something lacking, but desired or needed; necessity. 10. need. 11. absence, deficiency, or lack. 12. destitution; poverty.

want ad, Colloq. a one-column-wide notice, usually of a few lines, to advertise opportunities for employment, real estate, etc., needed or for sale.

want·age (wŏn'tĭj, wôn'-), n. that which is wanting or lacking; an amount lacking.

want·ing (wŏn'tĭng, wôn'-), adj. 1. lacking or absent. 2. deficient. —prep. 3. lacking; without. 4. less; minus.

wan·ton (wŏn'tən), adj. 1. done, shown, used, etc., maliciously or unjustifiably. 2. loose, lascivious, or lewd. 3. Now Poetic. frolicsome, as children. 4. Chiefly Poetic. having free play. —n. 5. a lascivious person, esp. a woman. —v.i. 6. to act, grow, etc., in a wanton manner. —wan'ton·ly, adv. —wan'ton·ness, n.

wap·i·ti (wŏp'ə tĭ), n., pl. -tis, (esp. collectively)

-ti. a North American species of deer with long, slender antlers, usually called elk.

war (wôr), n., v., warred, warring, adj. —n. 1. conflict carried on by force of arms, as between nations. 2. active hostility; conflict. —v.i. 3. to carry on war; fight. —adj. 4. of, belonging to, used in, or due to war.

War between the States, Amer. Hist. the Civil War (used esp. in the former Confederate States).

war·ble (wôr'bəl), v., -bled, -bling, n. —v.i., v.t. 1. to sing with trills, quavers, or melodic embellishments. —n. 2. a warbled tone.

war·bler (wôr'blər), n. 1. one that warbles. 2. any of certain small, insectivorous New World birds.

war cry, 1. a cry or a word or phrase shouted in charging or in rallying to attack; a battle cry. 2. a party cry in any contest.

ward (wôrd), n. 1. a division of a city or town, as for administrative or representative purposes. 2. a division of a hospital or the like. 3. Law. a person, esp. a minor, who has been legally placed under the care of a guardian or a court. 4. custody. —v.t. 5. to avert, repel, or turn aside, as danger, an attack, etc. —ward'ship, n.

Ward (wôrd), n. 1. Artemas (är'tə məs), 1727–1800, American general in the Revolutionary War. 2. Artemus, (Charles Farrar Browne) 1834–67, U.S. humorist. 3. Mrs. Humphrey, (Mary Augusta Arnold) 1851–1920, British novelist.

war dance, a dance among primitive people preliminary to a warlike excursion or in celebration of a victory.

ward·en (wôr'dən), n. 1. one charged with the care or custody of something; keeper. 2. the chief administrative officer in charge of a prison.

ward·er (wôr'dər), n. a guard.

ward heeler, U.S. a minor hanger-on of a political machine who canvasses voters and does party chores.

ward·robe (wôrd'rōb'), n. 1. a stock of clothes or costumes. 2. a piece of furniture for holding clothes.

ward·room (wôrd'rōōm', -rŏŏm'), n. (in a warship) 1. the apartment constituting the living quarters of commissioned officers other than the commanding officer. 2. the dining saloon and lounge for these officers. 3. these officers collectively.

ware (wâr), n. 1. (usually pl.) articles of merchandise; goods. 2. pottery.

ware·house (n. wâr'hous'; v. wâr'houz', -hous'), n., v., -housed, -housing. —n. 1. a storehouse for wares or goods. —v.t. 2. to store in a warehouse. —ware'house'man, n.

ware·room (wâr'rōōm', -rŏŏm'), n. a room in which goods are stored or are displayed for sale.

war·fare (wôr'fâr'), n. operations against an enemy; war.

war game, Mil. a training exercise that imitates war, in which commanders, staffs, and assistants perform war duties, but no troops are used.

war head, the forward, explosive-containing section of a self-propelled torpedo.

war horse, 1. a horse used in war. 2. Colloq. a person who has taken part in many conflicts, controversies, etc.

war·i·ly (wâr'ə lĭ), adv. in a wary manner.

war·i·ness (wâr'ĭ nĭs), n. quality of being wary.

war·like (wôr'līk'), adj. 1. fit, qualified, or ready for war; martial. 2. threatening war. 3. of war.

warm (wôrm), adj. 1. having, giving, or feeling a moderate degree of sensible heat. 2. of or characterized by comparatively high temperature. 3. (of color, etc.) inclining toward red, orange, or yellow (rather than green or blue). 4. having or showing lively feelings, emotions, sympathies, etc. 5. intimate. 6. cordial. 7. lively or vigorous. 8. Colloq. relatively close to something sought. —v.t., v.i. 9. to make or become warm. 10. to make or become ardent, enthusiastic, friendly, etc. 11. to prepare for play by practice and calisthenics. —warm'er, n. —warm'ish, adj. —warm'ly, adv. —warm'ness, warmth, n.

warm-blood·ed (wôrm'blŭd'ĭd), adj. denoting or pertaining to animals, as mammals and birds, whose blood ranges in temperature from about 98° to 112° F.

warm front, Meteorol. 1. the contact surface

between two air masses where the warmer mass is advancing against and over the cooler mass. **2.** the line of intersection of this surface with the surface of the earth.

warm-heart·ed (wôrm/här/tĭd), *adj.* having or showing sympathy, cordiality, etc. —**warm/-heart/ed·ly,** *adv.* —**warm/-heart/ed·ness,** *n.*

warming pan, a long-handled, covered flat vessel, as of brass, for holding hot coals or the like, formerly in common use for warming beds before being occupied.

war·mong·er (wôr/mŭng/gər), *n.* one who advocates war or seeks to bring it about.

Warm Springs, a city in W Georgia: site of foundation for treatment of poliomyelitis. 608.

warn (wôrn), *v.t.* **1.** to give notice to (a person, etc.) of danger, impending evil, or the like. **2.** to caution or admonish. **3.** to notify. —**warn/er,** *n.* —**warn/ing,** *n., adj.* —**warn/ing·ly,** *adv.*

War of American Independence, *Brit.* American Revolution.

War of 1812, a war between the United States and Great Britain, 1812–15.

War of Secession, *Amer. Hist.* the Civil War.

War of the Spanish Succession, a war (1701–1714) fought by Austria, England, the Netherlands, and Prussia, against France and Spain, arising out of disputes about the succession in Spain after the death of Charles II.

warp (wôrp), *v.t., v.i.* **1.** to bend or twist out of shape. **2.** to distort from the truth, fact, etc.; bias. **3.** *Naut.* to move (a ship, etc.) into some desired position by hauling on a rope fastened to a buoy, anchor, or the like. —*n.* **4.** a bend or twist, as in wood that has dried unevenly. **5.** yarns placed lengthwise in the loom, across the weft or woof, and interlaced. **6.** *Naut.* a rope for hauling a ship or the like along or into a position.

war paint, 1. paint applied to the face and body by savages upon going to war. **2.** *Colloq.* full dress; finery.

war·path (wôr/păth/, -päth/), *n.* **1.** the path taken by American Indians on a warlike expedition. **2. on the warpath, a.** to engage in, seek, or be prepared for war. **b.** wrathful.

war·plane (wôr/plān/), *n.* an airplane for warfare.

war·rant (wôr/ənt, wŏr/-), *n.* **1.** authorization; sanction, or justification. **2.** a guarantee. **3.** a document certifying or authorizing something. —*v.t.* **4.** to authorize, sanction, or justify. **5.** to vouch for or guarantee. —**war/rant·a·ble,** *adj.* —**war/rant·a·bly,** *adv.* —**war/ran·tee/,** *n.* —**war/ran·ter, war/ran·tor,** *n.*

warrant officer, a military officer of either of two grades ranking above enlisted men and below commissioned officers.

war·ran·ty (wôr/ən tĭ, wŏr/-), *n., pl.* -**ties.** **1.** act of warranting. **2.** a guarantee or assurance.

war·ren (wôr/ən, wŏr/ən), *n.* a place where rabbits breed or abound.

War·ren (wôr/ən, wŏr/-), *n.* a city in NE Ohio, NW of Youngstown. 42,837.

war·ren·er (wôr/ən ər, wŏr/-), *n.* the keeper of a warren.

war·ri·or (wôr/ĭ ər, wŏr/-, -yər), *n.* a man engaged or experienced in warfare; soldier.

war risk insurance, government insurance for members of the armed forces of the U.S.

War·saw (wôr/sô), *n.* the capital of Poland, in the E central part. 476,538.

war·ship (wôr/shĭp/), *n.* a ship built or armed for combat purposes.

wart (wôrt), *n.* a small, usually hard, abnormal elevation on the skin, caused by a filtrable virus. —**wart/y,** *adj.*

wart hog, an African wild swine having large tusks and warty excrescences on the face.

war·time (wôr/tīm/), *n.* a time of war.

war whoop, a whoop or yell uttered by American Indians, or others, in attacking, etc.

war·y (wâr/ĭ), *adj.,* **warier, wariest.** watchful; cautious; careful. —**war/i·ly,** *adv.* —**war/i·ness,** *n.*

was (wŏz, wŭz; *unstressed* wəz), *v.* first and third pers. sing., pt. indicative of **be.**

Wa·satch Range (wô/săch), a mountain range in N Utah and SE Idaho. Highest peak, Mt. Timpanogos, 11,957 ft.

wash (wŏsh, wôsh), *v.t.* **1.** to cleanse by dipping, rubbing, or scrubbing in water, etc. **2.** to remove (dirt, stains, paint, or any matter) with or as with

water. **3.** to wet with water or other liquid. **4.** to flow over or against. **5.** to carry (along, up, down, etc.) with water or any liquid. **6.** *Mining, etc.* **a.** to subject (earth, etc.) to the action of water in order to separate valuable material. **b.** to separate (valuable material, as gold) thus. **7.** to cover with a thin coat of color. —*v.i.* **8.** to wash oneself. **9.** to wash clothes. **10.** to cleanse anything with or in water or the like. **11.** to undergo washing, esp. without injury. **12.** *Colloq.* to stand being put to the proof. **13.** to be carried (along, ashore, etc.) by water. —*n.* **14.** act of washing. **15.** a quantity of clothes, etc., washed, or to be washed at one time. **16.** a liquid with which something is washed, over-spread, etc. **17.** the flow, dash, or breaking of water. **18.** the rough water left behind a moving ship, etc. **19.** *Aeron.* the disturbance in the air left behind by a moving airplane or any of its parts. **20.** a fen, marsh, or a bog. **21.** a shallow arm of the sea. **22.** alluvial matter transferred and deposited by flowing water. **23.** *Art.* a broad, thin layer of color applied by a continuous movement of the brush. **24.** refuse food, etc., from the kitchen, as for hogs. —*adj.* **25.** washable. —**wash/ing,** *n.*

Wash (wŏsh, wôsh), *n.* **The,** a shallow bay of the North Sea, on the E coast of England. ab. 22 mi. long; ab. 15 mi. wide.

wash·a·ble (wŏsh/ə bəl, wôsh/-), *adj.* capable of being washed, esp. without injury.

wash·board (wŏsh/bôrd/, wôsh/-), *n.* a board with a corrugated surface, on which clothes are rubbed in the process of washing.

wash·bowl (wŏsh/bōl/, wôsh/-), *n.* a bowl or basin for use in washing the person. Also, *esp. Brit.,* **wash·ba·sin** (wŏsh/bā/sən, wôsh/-).

wash·cloth (wŏsh/klôth/, -klŏth/, wôsh/-), *n.* a small cloth for washing the body.

wash·day (wŏsh/dā, wôsh/-), *n.* the day set apart in a household for washing clothes.

washed-out (wŏsht/out/, wôsht/-), *adj.* **1.** faded. **2.** *Colloq.* utterly fatigued.

washed-up (wŏsht/ŭp/, wôsht/-), *adj.* **1.** *Colloq.* utterly fatigued. **2.** *Slang.* having failed, esp. abjectly.

wash·er (wŏsh/ər, wôsh/-), *n.* **1.** one that washes. **2.** a machine for washing something. **3.** a flat ring of leather, rubber, metal, etc., used to give tightness to a joint, to prevent leakage, etc.

wash·er·wom·an (wŏsh/ər wŏŏm/ən, wôsh/-), *n., pl.* -**women.** a woman who washes clothes, etc. for hire.

wash goods, textiles not faded or weakened by washing.

washing machine, an apparatus for washing clothing or other material.

Wash·ing·ton (wŏsh/ĭng tən, wôsh/-), *n.* **1.** **Booker Taliaferro,** 1859?–1915, U.S. writer and educator. **2. George,** 1732–99, American general and 1st president of U.S. 1789–97. **3.** the capital of the United States, on the Potomac between Maryland and Virginia: coextensive with the District of Columbia. 663,091. **4.** a State in the NW United States, on the Pacific coast. 2,254,-098 pop.; 68,192 sq. mi. *Cap.:* Olympia. *Abbr.:* Wash. —**Wash·ing·to·ni·an** (wŏsh/ĭng tō/nĭ ən, wôsh/-), *adj., n.*

Washington pie, a layer cake with a cream, chocolate, jelly, or other filling.

wash·out (wŏsh/out/, wôsh/-), *n.* **1.** a washing out of earth, etc., by water, as from a roadway by heavy rain. **2.** the hole produced. **3.** *Slang.* a failure or fiasco.

wash·rag (wŏsh/răg/, wôsh/-), *n.* washcloth.

wash·room (wŏsh/rŏŏm/, -rŏŏm/, wôsh/-), *n.* a room having toilet facilities.

wash·stand (wŏsh/stănd/, wôsh/-), *n.* **1.** a piece of furniture for holding a basin, a pitcher, etc., for use in washing the person. **2.** a stationary fixture having faucets with running water, for the same purpose.

wash·tub (wŏsh/tŭb/, wôsh/-), *n.* a tub for use in washing something, esp. clothes, etc. Also, *Brit.,* **washing tub.**

wash·wom·an (wŏsh/wŏŏm/ən, wôsh/-), *n., pl.* -**women.** washerwoman.

wash·y (wŏsh/ĭ, wôsh/ĭ), *adj.,* **washier, washiest.** too diluted; weak.

wasp (wŏsp), *n.* any of certain hymenopterous, stinging insects.

wasp·ish (wŏs/pĭsh), *adj.* **1.** easily irritated; irascible. **2.** having a slender waist.

wasp waist, a slender, or tightly laced, waist. —**wasp′-waist′ed,** *adj.*

was·sail (wŏs′əl, wăs′-), *n.* **1.** a salutation wishing health to a person; toast. **2.** a drinking party or revel. **3.** spiced ale.

Was·ser·mann reaction (wäs′ər mən), a diagnostic test for syphilis using the fixation of a complement by the serum of a syphilitic individual. Also, **Wassermann test.**

wast (wŏst: *unstressed* wəst), *v.* 2nd pers. sing. pt. indic. of **be** (now only in solemn or poetic use).

waste (wāst), *v.,* **wasted, wasting,** *n., adj.* —*v.t.* **1.** to consume, spend, or employ uselessly or without adequate return; squander. **2.** to fail or neglect to use. **3.** to destroy or consume gradually. **4.** to wear down in health or strength. **5.** to devastate or ruin. —*v.i.* **6.** to be or become wasted. —*n.* **7.** useless consumption or expenditure. **8.** neglect. **9.** gradual destruction, impairment, or decay. **10.** devastation or ruin. **11.** an uncultivated tract of land. **12.** anything left over or superfluous. —*adj.* **13.** not used or in use. **14.** (of land, etc.) wild, desolate, or barren. **15.** left over or superfluous. **16.** useless or worthless. —**wast′age,** *n.* —**waste′ful,** *adj.* —**waste′ful·ly,** *adv.* —**waste′ful·ness,** *n.* —**wast′er,** *n.*

waste·bas·ket (wāst′băs′kĭt, -bäs′-), *n.* a basket for wastepaper, or papers, scraps of paper, etc., to be disposed of as refuse. Also, **wastepaper basket.**

waste·pa·per (wāst′pā′pər), *n.* paper thrown away as useless.

waste pipe, 1. a pipe for conveying away water, etc. **2.** *Plumbing.* a pipe carrying liquid wastes from all fixtures except water closets.

wast·ing (wās′tĭng), *adj.* **1.** gradually reducing the fullness and strength of the body. **2.** laying waste; devastating; despoiling.

wast·rel (wās′trəl), *n.* **1.** a wasteful person; spendthrift. **2.** *Chiefly Eng.* an idler.

watch (wŏch), *v.i.* **1.** to look attentively, as to see what comes, is done, happens, etc. **2.** to be careful or cautious. **3.** to keep a vigilant watch (*over*), as for protection. **4.** to keep guard. —*v.t.* **5.** to keep under attentive view or observation. **6.** to look or wait attentively and expectantly for. **7.** to watch over or guard for protection or safekeeping. —*n.* **8.** close, constant observation for the purpose of seeing or discovering something. **9.** a lookout, as for something expected. **10.** vigilant guard. **11.** a keeping awake for some special purpose. **12.** a period of time for watching or keeping guard. **13.** *Naut.* a period of time (usually four hours) during which one part of a ship's crew is on duty. **14.** a small, portable timepiece with a spring-driven mechanism. —**watch′er,** *n.*

watch·case (wŏch′kās′), *n.* the case or outer covering for the works of a watch.

watch·dog (wŏch′dôg′, -dŏg′), *n.* a dog kept to guard property.

watch fire, a fire maintained during the night as a signal and for a watching party.

watch·ful (wŏch′fəl), *adj.* vigilant or alert. —**watch′ful·ly,** *adv.* —**watch′ful·ness,** *n.*

watch guard, a chain, cord, or ribbon for securing a watch when worn on the person.

watch·mak·er (wŏch′mā′kər), *n.* one whose occupation it is to make and repair watches. —**watch′mak′ing,** *n.*

watch·man (wŏch′mən), *n., pl.* **-men.** one who keeps guard over a building at night to protect it from fire or thieves.

watch meeting, a religious meeting or service held at night, usually on the last night of the year, and terminated on the arrival of the new year.

watch night, 1. the last night of the year, observed in a watch meeting. **2.** a watch meeting.

watch·tow·er (wŏch′tou′ər), *n.* a tower on which a sentinel watches for enemies, etc.

watch·word (wŏch′wûrd′), *n.* **1.** a password or countersign. **2.** a rallying cry; slogan.

wa·ter (wô′tər, wŏt′ər), *n.* **1.** the liquid which in a pure state is a transparent, odorless, tasteless liquid, a compound of hydrogen and oxygen, H_2O. **2.** a special form or variety of this liquid, as rain. **3.** the water of a river, etc., with reference to its relative height. **4.** the surface of water. **5.** a liquid solution or preparation. **6.** any of various solutions of volatile or gaseous substances in water. **7.** any liquid or aqueous organic secretion or the like, as tears, perspira-

tion, etc. —*v.t.* **8.** to sprinkle, moisten, or drench with water. **9.** to supply with water. **10.** to dilute with water. **11.** *Finance.* to issue (shares of stock) without receiving a corresponding amount of cash or property. **12.** to produce a wavy lustrous pattern on (fabrics, metals, etc.). —*v.i.* **13.** to discharge, fill with, or secrete water or liquid. —*adj.* **14.** of or pertaining to water. **15.** holding water. **16.** worked or powered by, or treating, water.

water back, a reservoir, set of pipes, or the like, at the back of a stove or fireplace, providing a supply of hot water.

water bird, an aquatic bird, or bird that frequents the water; a swimming or wading bird.

water biscuit, a crackerlike biscuit prepared from flour and water.

water blister, a blister which contains a clear, serous fluid, as distinguished from a blood blister.

wa·ter·borne (wô′tər bôrn′, wŏt′ər-), *adj.* **1.** supported by the water; carried by the water. **2.** conveyed by ship or boat.

water buffalo, the common flat-horned buffalo of the Old World tropics.

Wa·ter·bur·y (wô′tər bĕr′Y), *n.* a city in W Connecticut. 99,314.

water clock, a device for measuring time by the flow of water.

water closet, a privy having some contrivance for carrying off the discharges through a waste pipe by water.

water color, *Painting.* **1.** a pigment for which water is used as a vehicle. **2.** the art or method of painting with such pigments. **3.** a painting or design executed by this method. —**wa′ter·col′or,** *adj.*

wa·ter·cool (wô′tər kōōl′, wŏt′ər-), *v.t.* to cool by means of water, esp. by water circulating in pipes or a jacket. —**wa′ter-cooled′,** *adj.*

water cooler, a vessel for holding drinking water which is cooled and drawn off for use by a faucet.

wa·ter·course (wô′tər kôrs′, wŏt′ər-), *n.* **1.** a stream of water, as a river or brook. **2.** the bed of such a stream. **3.** a natural channel conveying water. **4.** a channel or canal made for the conveyance of water.

wa·ter·craft (wô′tər krăft′, -kräft′, wŏt′ər-), *n.* **1.** skill in boating and water sports. **2.** any boat or ship. **3.** boats and ships collectively.

water cress, a perennial plant, usually growing in clear, running water, and bearing pungent leaves that are used for salads, soups, and as a garnish.

water dog, 1. a dog accustomed to or delighting in the water, or trained to go into the water to retrieve game. **2.** *Colloq.* a person who is at home on or in the water.

wa·ter·fall (wô′tər fôl′, wŏt′ər-), *n.* a steep fall of water from a height; cascade.

wa·ter·find·er (wô′tər fīn′dər, wŏt′ər-), *n.* one who uses a divining rod to discover water in the ground.

wa·ter·fowl (wô′tər foul′, wŏt′ər-), *n.* **1.** a water bird, esp. a swimming bird. **2.** such birds collectively, esp. swimming game birds.

water front, a part of a city or town beside a harbor, lake, etc.

water gap, a transverse gap in a mountain ridge, cut by and giving passage to a stream.

water gas, a poisonous gas used for illuminating purposes, etc., made by passing steam over incandescent coal or other carbon fuel, and consisting of a mixture of various gases, chiefly carbon monoxide and hydrogen.

water glass, 1. a glass or goblet for drinking. **2.** a vessel of glass to hold water. **3.** a glass tube used to indicate water level, as in a boiler. **4.** a device for observing objects beneath the surface of the water, consisting essentially of an open tube or box with a glass bottom. **5.** sodium silicate, esp. a solution of it in water, or a similar preparation of potassium silicate, used to produce a transparent coating on objects in order to protect, preserve, or fireproof them; soluble glass; liquid glass. Also, **wa′ter-glass′.**

water ice, 1. ice formed by direct freezing of fresh or salt water, and not by compacting of snow. **2.** *Chiefly Brit.* sherbet.

wa·ter·i·ness (wô′tər Y nYs, wŏt′ər-), *n.* watery state.

wa·ter·ing (wô′tər Yng, wŏt′ər-), *n.* **1.** act of one who or that which waters. **2.** a watered appearance on silk, etc. —*adj.* **3.** that waters.

4. pertaining to medicinal springs or a sea-bathing resort.

watering place, 1. *Chiefly Brit.* a place of resort for its mineral waters. **2.** *Chiefly Brit.* a resort for bathing, boating, etc. **3.** a place where water may be obtained.

watering pot, a vessel, esp. with a spout having a perforated nozzle, for watering or sprinkling plants, etc.

water jacket, a casing or compartment containing water, placed about something to keep it cool or otherwise regulate its temperature, as around the cylinder or cylinders of an internal-combustion engine.

wa·ter-jack·et (wô'tər jăk'ĭt, wŏt'ər-), *v.t.* to surround or fit with a water jacket.

water jump, any small body of water which a horse must jump over, as in a steeplechase.

water level, 1. the surface level of any body of water. **2.** *Naut.* water line.

water lily, any of certain aquatic plants which have large, disklike, floating leaves and showy, fragrant flowers.

water line, *Naut.* **1. a.** that part of the outside of the hull of a ship that is just at the water level. **b.** any of several lines marked on the hull of a ship, showing the depth to which it sinks when unloaded and when partially or fully loaded. **2.** water level. **3.** the line in which water at its surface borders upon a floating body. Also, **wa'-ter-line'.**

wa·ter-logged (wô'tər lôgd', -lŏgd', wŏt'ər-), *adj.* **1.** so filled with water, by leakage or overflow, as to be heavy or unmanageable, as a ship, etc. **2.** excessively saturated with water.

Wa·ter·loo (wô'tər lōō', wô'tər lōō'), *n.* **1.** a village in central Belgium, S of Brussels: scene of Napoleon's decisive defeat, June 18, 1815. **2.** a decisive or crushing defeat. **3.** a city in E Iowa. 51,743.

water main, a main or principal pipe or conduit in a system for conveying water.

wa·ter·man (wô'tər-mən, wŏt'ər-), *n.*, *pl.* **-men. 1.** a man who manages, or works on, a boat; boat-man. **2.** a person with reference to his skill in rowing, etc.

wa·ter·mark (wô'tər märk', wŏt'ər-), *n.* **1.** a mark indicating the height to which water rises or has risen, as in a river, etc. **2.** a figure or design impressed in the fabric in the manufacture of paper and visible when held to the light. —*v.t.* **3.** to mark (paper) with a watermark.

wa·ter·mel·on (wô'tər mĕl'ən, wŏt'ər-), *n.* **1.** the large, roundish fruit of a trailing vine, having a hard, green rind and a (usually) pink pulp which abounds in a sweet, watery juice. **2.** the plant or vine.

water meter, a device for measuring and registering the quantity of water that passes through a pipe, etc.

water mill, a mill with machinery driven by water.

water motor, any form of prime mover, or motor, that is operated by the kinetic energy, pressure, or weight of water, esp. a small turbine or water wheel fitted to a pipe supplying water.

water of crystallization, *Chem.* water of hydration: formerly thought necessary to crystallization, but now usually regarded as affecting crystallization only as it forms new molecular combinations.

water of hydration, *Chem.* that portion of a hydrate which is represented as, or can be driven off as, water: now usually regarded as being in true molecular combination with the other atoms of the compound, and not existing in the compound as water.

water ou·zel (ōō'zəl), any of several plump, thick-plumaged aquatic birds allied to the thrushes.

water ox, water buffalo.

water polo, a water game played by two teams, each having six swimmers, with a semi-inflated ball, in which the object is to carry or pass the ball over the goal line.

water power, the power of water used to drive machinery, etc.

wa·ter·proof (wô'tər prōōf', wŏt'ər-), *adj.* **1.** impervious to water. —*n.* **2.** any of several coated fabrics which will hold water. **3.** *Chiefly Brit.* an outer garment of waterproof material. —*v.t.* **4.** to make waterproof.

wa·ter-re·pel·lent (wô'tər rĭ pĕl'ənt, wŏt'-ər-), *adj.* finished to decrease the absorption of water (contrasted with *waterproof*).

water right, the right to make use of the water from a particular stream, lake, or irrigation canal.

wa·ter·scape (wô'tər skăp', wŏt'ər-), *n.* a picture or view of the sea or other body of water.

wa·ter·shed (wô'tər shĕd', wŏt'ər-), *n.* **1.** *Chiefly Brit.* the ridge dividing two drainage areas. **2.** the region or area drained by a river, etc.

wa·ter-sick (wô'tər sĭk', wŏt'ər-), *adj. Agric.* excessively watered, esp. by irrigation, so that tilling and planting cannot be done.

wa·ter·side (wô'tər sīd', wŏt'ər-), *n.* **1.** the margin, bank, or shore of the sea, a river, a lake, etc. —*adj.* **2.** of, relating to, or situated at the waterside. **3.** working by the waterside.

wa·ter·soak (wô'tər sōk', wŏt'ər-), *v.t.* to soak with water.

wa·ter·sol·u·ble (wô'tər sŏl'yə bəl, wŏt'ər-), *adj. Biochem.* (of certain vitamins) able to dissolve in water.

water spaniel, a curly-haired spaniel of either of two varieties, taking to water and readily trained for hunting.

wa·ter·spout (wô'tər spout', wŏt'ər-), *n.* **1. a.** pipe running down the side of a house to take away water from the gutter of the roof. **2. a** spout from which water is discharged. **3.** a tornadolike storm over the ocean or other body of water.

water sprite, a sprite or spirit inhabiting the water.

water system, 1. a river and all its branches. **2.** a system of supplying water.

water table, 1. *Civ. Eng., etc.* the depth below which the ground is saturated with water. **2.** *Archit.* a projecting stringcourse or similar member placed to throw off water.

wa·ter·tight (wô'tər tīt', wŏt'ər-), *adj.* **1.** impervious to water. **2.** without fault.

water tower, 1. a vertical pipe or tower into which water is pumped to obtain a required head. **2.** a fire-extinguishing apparatus throwing a stream of water on the upper parts of a tall burning building.

Wa·ter·town (wô'tər toun'), *n.* **1.** a town in E Massachusetts. 35,427. **2.** a city in N New York. 33,385.

water vapor, gaseous water, esp. when diffused and below the boiling point: distinguished from steam.

water wave, 1. a wave of water. **2.** a wave set into lotioned hair with combs and then allowed to dry by the application of the heat from a drier.

wa·ter-wave (wô'tər wāv', wŏt'ər-), *v.t.*, **-waved, -waving.** to set (hair) in a water wave.

wa·ter·way (wô'tər wā', wŏt'ər-), *n.* **1. a** river, canal, or other body of water as a route of travel or transport. **2.** a channel for vessels.

water wheel, 1. a wheel turned by water and used to perform mechanical work; a water turbine. **2.** a wheel with buckets for raising water.

water wings, a fabric contrivance shaped like a pair of wings and inflated with air, usually worn under the arms to keep the body afloat while one learns to swim.

water witching, the supposed discovering of subterranean streams by means of a divining rod. Also, **water witch.**

wa·ter·works (wô'tər wûrks', wŏt'ər-), *n.pl.* (*often construed as sing.*) an aggregate of apparatus and structures by which water is collected, preserved, and distributed for domestic and other purposes, as for a city.

wa·ter·worn (wô'tər wôrn', wŏt'ər-), *adj.* worn by the action of water; smoothed by water in motion.

wa·ter·y (wô'tə rĭ, wŏt'ə rĭ), *adj.* **1.** pertaining to or full of water. **2.** tearful, as the eyes. **3.** of the nature of water. **4.** resembling water in appearance, color, or consistency.

watt (wŏt), *n.* a unit of power equal to one joule per second. —**watt'age,** *n.*

Watt (wŏt), *n.* **James,** 1736–1819, British engineer and inventor (of the steam engine).

Wat·teau (wŏ tō/), *n.* **Jean Antoine,** 1684–1721, French painter.

watt-hour (wŏt/our/), *n. Elect.* the product of average power in watts and the time in hours during which such power is maintained: the commonly used unit of electrical energy.

wat·tle (wŏt/əl), *n., v.,* **-tled, -tling. —*n.* 1.** a fleshy appendage hanging down from the throat or chin of certain birds, as the turkey, etc. **2.** (*pl. or sing.*) *Chiefly Brit.* rods interwoven with twigs for making fences, walls, etc. —*v.t.* **3.** to bind, fence, roof, etc., with wattles. —**wat/tled,** *adj.*

watt·less (wŏt/lĭs), *adj. Elect.* without watts or power: *a wattless alternating current* (one differing in phase by 90 degrees from the associated emf); *a wattless electromotive force* (one differing in phase by 90 degrees from the current).

watt·me·ter (wŏt/mē/tər), *n. Elect.* an instrument for measuring electric power in watts.

Watts (wŏts), *n.* **1. George Frederick,** 1817–1904, British painter and sculptor. **2. Isaac,** 1674–1748, British theologian and hymnist.

Watts-Dun·ton (wŏts/dŭn/tən), *n.* **Walter Theodore,** 1832–1914, British critic, poet, and novelist.

Waugh (wô), *n.* **Evelyn Arthur St. John,** born 1903, British novelist.

Wau·ke·gan (wô kē/gən), *n.* a city in NE Illinois. 34,241.

wave (wāv), *n., v.,* **waved, waving. —*n.* 1.** a ridgelike disturbance of the surface of a liquid body, as the sea. **2.** a swell, surge, or rush, as of feeling, prosperity, etc. **3.** a curve or series of curves, as in the hair. **4.** *Physics.* a progressive vibrational disturbance propagated through a medium, as air, without corresponding progress of the parts or particles themselves, as in the transmission of sound, light, etc. **5.** act of waving. **6.** a sign made with a wave of the hand, a flag, etc. —*v.i., v.t.* **7.** to move with waves, as the sea, a flag, etc. **8.** to curve alternately in opposite directions. **9.** to bend or sway. **10.** to signal by a wave. —**wav/er,** *n.*

Wave (wāv), *n.* an enlisted member of the Waves.

wave front, *Physics.* an imaginary surface that is the locus of all adjacent points at which the phase of vibration is the same.

wave length, *Physics.* the distance, measured in the direction of propagation of a wave, between two successive points characterized by the same phase of vibration.

wave·let (wāv/lĭt), *n.* a small wave; ripple.

wa·ver (wā/vər), *v.i.* **1.** to sway to and fro; flutter. **2.** to flicker. **3.** to become unsteady; shake or tremble. **4.** to vacillate. **5.** to fluctuate or vary. —**wa/ver·er,** *n.* —**wa/ver·ing·ly,** *adv.*

Waves (wāvz), *n. pl.* Women's Reserve, U.S. Naval Reserve.

wave train, *Physics.* a group or series of successive waves sent out along the same path or course by a vibrating body, a wireless antenna, or the like.

wav·y (wā/vĭ), *adj.,* **wavier, waviest.** having, or full of, waves. —**wav/i·ly,** *adv.* —**wav/i·ness,** *n.*

wax[1] (wăks), *n.* **1.** a solid yellowish substance secreted by bees for use in constructing their honeycomb. **2.** any of various similar substances. —*v.t.* **3.** to rub, smear, stiffen, polish, etc., with wax. —**wax/en,** *adj.* —**wax/er,** *n.*

wax[2] (wăks), *v.i.* **waxed; waxed** or (*Poetic*) **waxen; waxing. 1.** to increase in extent, quantity, intensity, power, etc. **2.** (of the moon) to increase in the extent of its illuminated portion before the full moon. **3.** to become.

wax bean, any variety of snap bean with a yellowish color and waxy appearance.

wax paper, paper made moistureproof by coating with paraffin.

wax·wing (wăks/wĭng/), *n.* any of certain passerine birds having a showy crest and small red appendages at the tips of some feathers.

wax·work (wăks/wûrk/), *n.* **1.** figures, ornaments, etc., made of wax, or one such figure. **2.** (*pl. construed as sing.*) an exhibition of wax figures, ornaments, etc.

wax·y (wăk/sĭ), *adj.,* **waxier, waxiest. 1.** resembling wax. **2.** abounding in, covered with, or made of wax. **3.** pliable; yielding. —**wax/i·ness,** *n.*

way (wā), *n.* **1.** manner, mode, or fashion. **2.** characteristic or habitual manner. **3.** a course, plan, or means for attaining an end. **4.** respect

or particular. **5.** direction. **6.** passage or progress on a course. **7.** distance. **8.** a road, route, passage, or channel. **9.** (*often pl.*) a habit or custom. **10.** one's preferred mode of procedure. **11.** *Colloq.* condition, as to health, prosperity, etc. **12.** course of life, action, or experience. **13.** (*pl.*) (in shipbuilding) the timbers on which a ship is launched. **14. by the way, a.** incidentally. **b.** on the way.

way·bill (wā/bĭl/), *n.* a list of goods sent by a common carrier, as a railroad, with shipping directions.

way·far·ing (wā/fâr/ĭng), *adj., n.* traveling, esp. on foot. —**way/far/er,** *n.*

way·lay (wā/lā/), *v.t.,* **-laid, -laying.** to assail from ambush, as in order to rob. —**way/lay/er,** *n.*

way·leave (wā/lēv/), *n. Brit.* right of way.

Wayne (wān), *n.* **Anthony,** 1745–1796, American Revolutionary general.

-ways, a suffix of manner creating adverbs, as in *sideways, lengthways.*

ways and means, 1. legislation, methods, and means of raising revenue for the use of the government. **2.** methods and means of accomplishing something.

way·side (wā/sīd/), *n.* the edge of the road or highway.

way station, *U.S.* a station intermediate between principal stations, as on a railroad.

way train, a local train.

way·ward (wā/wərd), *adj.* **1.** turning away from what is right or proper. **2.** capricious. **3.** irregular. —**way/ward·ly,** *adv.* —**way/ward·ness,** *n.*

way·worn (wā/wôrn/), *adj.* worn or wearied by travel.

W/B, waybill. Also, **W.B.**

W.C., *Chiefly Brit.* water closet.

W.C.T.U., Woman's Christian Temperance Union.

wd., 1. ward. **2.** word.

we (wē; *unstressed* wĭ), *pron.* nominative pl. of **I.**

weak (wēk), *adj.* **1.** liable to yield, break, or collapse under strain; fragile; not strong. **2.** feeble; infirm. **3.** deficient in power or authority. **4.** impotent, ineffectual, or inadequate. **5.** lacking in logical or legal force. **6.** deficient in mental power, intelligence, or judgment. **7.** deficient in moral character. **8.** deficient in amount, loudness, intensity, etc.; faint. **9.** deficient in the essential or desirable properties. **10.** unstressed. **11.** inflected with suffixes, without inherited change of the root vowel. —**weak/ness,** *n.*

weak·en (wē/kən), *v.t., v.i.* to become or make weak or weaker. —**weak/en·er,** *n.*

weak ending, *Pros.* a verse ending in which the metrical stress falls on a word or syllable which would not be stressed in natural utterance, as a preposition whose object is carried over to the next line.

weak·fish (wēk/fĭsh/), *n., pl.* **-fishes,** (*esp. collectively*) **-fish.** any of certain common food fishes.

weak-kneed (wēk/nēd/), *adj.* yielding readily to opposition, intimidation, etc.

weak·ling (wēk/lĭng), *n.* a weak creature.

weak·ly (wēk/lĭ), *adj.,* **-lier, -liest,** *adv.* —*adj.* **1.** feeble; sickly. —*adv.* **2.** in a weak manner. —**weak/li·ness,** *n.*

weak-mind·ed (wēk/mīn/dĭd), *adj.* **1.** having or showing a want of firmness of mind. **2.** having or showing a weak or feeble mind. —**weak/-mind/ed·ness,** *n.*

weal (wēl), *n. Archaic.* well-being, prosperity, or happiness.

weald (wēld), *n. Poetic.* an open country.

wealth (wĕlth), *n.* **1.** a great store of valuable possessions, property, or riches. **2.** *Econ.* **a.** all things having a value in money, in exchange, or in use. **b.** anything having utility and capable of being appropriated or exchanged. **3.** affluence.

wealth·y (wĕl/thĭ), *adj.,* **wealthier, wealthiest. 1.** rich. **2.** abundant or ample. —**wealth/i·ly,** *adv.* —**wealth/i·ness,** *n.*

wean (wēn), *v.t.* **1.** to accustom (a child or animal) to food other than its mother's milk. **2.** to withdraw or detach.

wean·ling (wēn/lĭng), *n.* **1.** a child or animal newly weaned. —*adj.* **2.** newly weaned.

weap·on (wĕp/ən), *n.* any instrument for use in combat, as a sword, rifle, cannon, etc.

wear (wâr), *v.,* **wore, worn, wearing,** *n.* —*v.t.*

1. to carry or have on the body or about the person as a covering, ornament, or the like. **2.** to impair, deteriorate, or consume gradually, as by use. **3.** to diminish gradually by rubbing, scraping, washing, etc. **4.** to make (a hole, channel, etc.) by such action. **5.** to bring, reduce, make, take, etc. (as specified), by wear or any gradual change. **6.** to weary or exhaust. —*v.i.* **7.** to undergo gradual impairment, diminution, reduction, etc., from wear, use, or other causes. **8.** to last under use or continued strain. **9.** to become. **10.** to pass, as time, etc., esp. slowly or tediously. —*n.* **11.** act of wearing; use, as of a garment. **12.** clothing, garments, or other articles for wearing. **13.** style of dress, adornment, etc. **14.** gradual impairment, wasting, diminution, etc., as from use. —**wear'a·ble,** *adj.* —**wear'er,** *n.*

wear and tear, diminution, decay, or injury sustained by ordinary use.

wea·ri·ful (wĭr'Ĭ fəl), *adj.* wearisome; tedious. —**wea'ri·ful·ly,** *adv.* —**wea'ri·ful·ness,** *n.*

wea·ri·less (wĭr'Ĭ lĭs), *adj.* unwearying; tireless.

wearing apparel, dress in general; garments.

wea·ri·some (wĭr'Ĭ səm), *adj.* **1.** causing weariness. **2.** tedious. —**wea'ri·some·ly,** *adv.* —**wea'ri·some·ness,** *n.*

wea·ry (wĭr'Ĭ), *adj.,* **-rier, -riest,** *v.,* **-ried, -rying.** —*adj.* **1.** exhausted physically or mentally; fatigued; tired. **2.** tedious; irksome. —*v.t., v.i.* **3.** to make or become weary. —**wea'ri·ly,** *adv.* —**wea'ri·ness,** *n.*

wea·sand (wē'zənd), *n.* *Archaic.* the windpipe or trachea.

wea·sel (wē'zəl), *n.* **1.** any of certain small carnivorous animals having a long, slender body, and feeding largely on small rodents. **2.** a cunning, sneaking fellow.

weasel words, intentionally ambiguous statements.

weath·er (wĕth'ər), *n.* **1.** state of the atmosphere with respect to wind, temperature, cloudiness, moisture, pressure, etc. **2.** windy or stormy weather. **3. under the weather,** *Colloq.* **a.** ill; ailing. **b.** drunk. —*v.t., v.i.* **4.** to expose to the weather. **5.** to come safely through (a storm, danger, trouble, etc.). **6.** *Naut.* (of a ship, mariner, etc.) to pass or sail to the windward of. —*adj.* **7.** *Naut.* of or pertaining to the windward side or part.

weath·er-beat·en (wĕth'ər bē'tən), *adj.* seasoned or hardened by exposure to weather.

weath·er·board (wĕth'ər bôrd'), *n.* **1.** *Chiefly Brit.* one of a series of thin boards, usually thicker along one edge than along the other, nailed on an outside wall or a roof in overlapping fashion to form a protective covering which will shed water. **2.** *Naut.* the side of a vessel toward the wind. —*v.t.* **3.** *Chiefly Brit.* to cover or furnish with weatherboards.

weath·er·board·ing (wĕth'ər bôr'dĭng), *n.* *Chiefly Brit.* **1.** a covering or facing of weatherboards or the like. **2.** weatherboards collectively.

weath·er-bound (wĕth'ər bound'), *adj.* delayed by bad weather.

Weather Bureau, a bureau of the U.S. Department of Agriculture, having charge of the gathering of the meteorological reports in order to forecast the weather, issue warnings of storms, floods, etc.

weath·er·cock (wĕth'ər kŏk'), *n.* a weather vane, esp. one in the shape of a cock.

weath·ered (wĕth'ərd), *adj.* **1.** seasoned or otherwise affected by exposure to the weather or elements. **2.** (of wood) discolored or stained by the action of air, rain, etc., or by artificial means. **3.** (of rocks) worn, disintegrated, or changed in color or composition, by the action of the elements. **4.** *Archit.* made sloping or inclined, as a window sill, to prevent the lodgment of water.

weather gauge, 1. the (advantageous) position of a ship when it is to windward of another ship. **2.** the position of advantage; the upper hand.

weath·er·glass (wĕth'ər glăs', -gläs'), *n.* any of various instruments, as a barometer, indicating the state of the atmosphere.

weath·er·man (wĕth'ər măn'), *n., pl.* **-men.** *Colloq.* one who foretells weather.

weather map, a map or chart showing weather conditions over a wide area at a particular time, compiled from simultaneous observations at different places.

weath·er·proof (wĕth'ər prōōf'), *adj.* able to withstand exposure to any weather.

weather station, an installation equipped and used for the making of meteorological observations.

weather strip, a narrow strip, as of India rubber, covering the joint between a door, window sash, or the like, and the jamb, casing, etc., to exclude wind, rain, etc.

weath·er-strip (wĕth'ər strĭp'), *v.t.,* **-stripped, -stripping.** to fit with weather strips.

weather stripping, 1. weather strip. **2.** weather strips collectively.

weather vane, a vane for indicating the direction of the wind.

weath·er-wise (wĕth'ər wīz'), *adj.* **1.** skillful in predicting weather. **2.** skillful in predicting reactions, opinions, etc.

weave (wēv), *v.,* **wove; woven** or **wove; weaving;** *n.* —*v.t., v.i.* **1.** to interlace (threads, yarns, strips, etc.) so as to form a fabric. **2.** to form by interlacing threads, strips, etc. **3.** to form by combining various elements into a connected whole. **4.** to introduce as an element into a connected whole. **5.** to follow in a winding course. —*n.* **6.** a manner of interlacing yarns. —**weav'er,** *n.*

web (wĕb), *n., v.,* **webbed, webbing.** —*n.* **1.** something formed as by weaving. **2.** a thin silken fabric spun by spiders and by the larvae of some insects; cobweb. **3.** a woven fabric. **4.** *Zool.* a membrane which connects the toes or digits of an animal. —*v.t.* **5.** to cover with a web; envelop. —**webbed,** *adj.* —**web'bing,** *n.* —**web'by,** *adj.*

Webb (wĕb), *n.* **1. Beatrice Potter,** 1858–1943, British writer on economic and social problems. **2.** her husband, **Sidney James,** (*Lord Passfield*) 1859–1947, British economist, sociologist, and statesman.

We·ber (vā'bər), *n.* **Baron Karl Maria von,** 1786–1826, German composer.

web·foot (wĕb'fŏŏt'), *n., pl.* **-feet.** a foot with the toes joined by a web. —**web'-foot'ed** or **web'-toed',** *adj.*

Web·ster (wĕb'stər), *n.* **1. Daniel,** 1782–1852, U.S. statesman. **2. Noah,** 1758–1843, U.S. lexicographer and writer.

web·ster (wĕb'stər), *n.* *Obs.* or *Dial.* a weaver.

wed (wĕd), *v.t., v.i.,* **wedded, wedded** or **wed, wedding. 1.** to bind oneself to (a person) in marriage. **2.** to unite (a couple) in marriage. **3.** to attach firmly.

Wed., Wednesday.

wed·ded (wĕd'Ĭd), *adj.* **1.** united in matrimony; married. **2.** joined. **3.** joined by devotion.

Wed·dell Sea (wĕd'əl), a wide arm of the S Atlantic, in Antarctica.

wed·ding (wĕd'Ĭng), *n.* act or ceremony of marrying; marriage; nuptials.

wedge (wĕj), *n., v.,* **wedged, wedging.** —*n.* **1.** a piece of material with two principal faces meeting in a sharply acute angle. **2.** something that serves to part, divide, etc. —*v.t.* **3.** to split with a wedge. **4.** to pack tightly by driving in a wedge or wedges. **5.** to thrust, drive, or fix (in, between, etc.) like a wedge. —*v.i.* **6.** to force a way (in, etc.) like a wedge.

Wedg·wood (wĕj'wŏŏd'), *n.* **1. Josiah,** 1730–95, British potter. **2.** Wedgwood ware. —*adj.* **3.** pertaining to, or made or originated by Josiah Wedgwood.

Wedgwood ware, a type of artistic pottery with tinted ground and white decoration in relief in designs patterned after Greek and Roman models.

wed·lock (wĕd'lŏk), *n.* state of marriage.

Wednes·day (wĕnz'dĬ), *n.* the fourth day of the week, following Tuesday.

wee (wē), *adj.* **1.** little; very small. —*n.* **2.** *Scot. and Prov. Eng.* a short time.

weed[1] (wēd), *n.* **1.** a plant occurring obtrusively in cultivated ground to the exclusion or injury of the desired crop. **2. the weed,** *Colloq.* tobacco. **3.** *Colloq.* a cigar or cigarette. **4.** a thin, ungainly person or animal. —*v.t.* **5.** to free from weeds. **6.** to remove as being undesirable or superfluous. —*v.i.* **7.** to remove weeds or the like. —**weed'er,** *n.* —**weed'like',** *adj.* —**weed'y,** *adj.*

weed[2] (wēd), *n.* (*pl.*) mourning garments.

week (wēk), *n.* **1.** a period of seven successive days, commonly beginning with Sunday. **2.** the working portion of the seven-day period.

week·day (wēk′dā′), *n.* **1.** any day except Sunday. —*adj.* **2.** of a weekday.

week end, the period from Friday night or Saturday to Monday, as a time for recreation, visiting, etc. —**week′-end′,** *adj., v.i.*

week·ly (wēk′lĭ), *adj., adv., n., pl.* **-lies.** —*adj.* **1.** pertaining to a week, or to each week. **2.** done, happening, appearing, etc., once a week, or every week. **3.** continuing for a week. —*adv.* **4.** once a week. **5.** by the week. —*n.* **6.** a periodical appearing once a week.

Weems (wēmz), *n.* **Mason Locke,** 1759–1825, U.S. clergyman and biographer.

ween (wēn), *v.i., v.t. Archaic.* to think.

weep (wēp), *v., wept, weeping, n.* —*v.i., v.t.* **1.** to shed (tears), as from sorrow, unhappiness, etc.; cry. **2.** to drip or exude. **3.** to mourn. —*n.* **4.** *Colloq.* weeping. —**weep′er,** *n.*

weep·ing (wē′pĭng), *adj.* **1.** that weeps. **2.** (of trees, etc.) having slender, drooping branches.

wee·vil (wē′vəl), *n.* any of certain beetles, many of which are destructive to nuts, grain, fruit, the stems of leaves, the pith of trees, etc. —**wee′vil·y,** *adj.*

weft (wĕft), *n.* **1.** woof or filling yarns which interlace with warp running from selvage to selvage. **2.** a woven piece.

weigh (wā), *v.t.* **1.** to ascertain the heaviness of by a scale or other mechanical device. **2.** to measure (a certain quantity of something) according to weight. **3.** to bear (down) by heaviness, oppression, etc. **4.** to consider carefully. **5.** to raise or lift. —*v.i.* **6.** to have weight or heaviness. **7.** to have importance. **8.** to bear down as a burden. **9.** to consider carefully. —**weigh′er,** *n.*

weight (wāt), *n.* **1.** amount of heaviness. **2.** the force which gravitation exerts upon a material body. **3.** a system of units for expressing weight or mass. **4.** a unit of weight or mass. **5.** a body of determinate mass, as of metal, for using on a balance or scale. **6.** any heavy mass or object. **7.** pressure or oppressive force. **8.** a burden, as of care. **9.** importance or effective influence. —*v.t.* **10.** to add weight to. **11.** to burden with weight.

weight·y (wā′tĭ), *adj.,* **weightier, weightiest.** **1.** heavy; ponderous. **2.** burdensome. **3.** important. **4.** influential. —**weight′i·ly,** *adv.* —**weight′i·ness,** *n.*

weir (wĭr), *n.* **1.** *Chiefly Brit.* a dam to stop and raise the water, as for irrigation, etc. **2.** a fence or a net set in a stream, channel, etc., for catching fish.

weird (wĭrd), *adj.* **1.** supernatural; unearthly or uncanny. **2.** *Colloq.* queer. —**weird′ly,** *adv.* —**weird′ness,** *n.*

weird sisters, the Fates.

Weis·mann (vīs′män), *n.* **August,** 1834–1914, German biologist.

Weis·mann·ism (vīs′män ĭz′əm), *n.* the theories and teachings of the German biologist August Weismann, esp. his theory respecting the continuity of the germ plasm and its isolation from the body plasm, with the accompanying doctrine that acquired characters in the latter are not and cannot be inherited.

weiss beer (vīs), a light-colored, highly effervescent beer prepared largely from malted wheat.

Welch (wĕlch, wĕlsh), *adj., n.* Welsh.

welch (wĕlch, wĕlsh), *v.t., v.i. Slang.* welsh. —**welch′er,** *n.*

Welch·man (wĕlch′mən, wĕlsh′-), *n., pl.* **-men.** Welshman.

wel·come (wĕl′kəm), *interj., n., v.* **-comed, -coming,** *adj.* —*interj.* **1.** a word of kindly greeting as to one whose coming gives pleasure. —*n.* **2.** a kindly greeting or reception. —*v.t.* **3.** to greet the coming of (a person, etc.) with pleasure. **4.** to regard as welcome. —*adj.* **5.** gladly received. **6.** agreeable. **7.** given full right by the cordial consent of others. **8.** free to enjoy courtesies, etc., without being under obligation (used in conventional response to thanks). —**wel′com·er,** *n.*

weld (wĕld), *v.t.* **1.** to unite (pieces of metal, etc.) by hammering, compression, or the like, esp. after rendering soft by heat. **2.** to bring into intimate union. —*n.* **3.** a welded junction or joint. **4.** act of welding. —**weld′a·ble,** *adj.* —**weld′er,** *n.*

wel·fare (wĕl′fâr′), *n.* well-being.

Welfare Island, an island in the East river, in New York City: city prison, hospitals, and other municipal institutions. Formerly, **Blackwells Island.**

welfare work, work devoted to the welfare of persons in a community, employees of an industrial or business establishment, or the like.

wel·kin (wĕl′kĭn), *n. Archaic.* the sky.

well[1] (wĕl), *adv., compar.* **better,** *super.* **best,** *adj., interj.* —*adv.* **1.** in a satisfactory, favorable, or advantageous manner. **2.** in a good manner. **3.** commendably; excellently. **4.** with propriety or reason. **5.** adequately or sufficiently. **6.** thoroughly. **7.** to a considerable extent. **8.** personally; intimately. —*adj.* **9.** in good health. **10.** satisfactory or good. **11.** proper or fitting. **12.** well-off. —*interj.* **13.** (used to express surprise, agreement, or merely as a preliminary to further speech).

well[2] (wĕl), *n.* **1.** a hole drilled into the earth to reach water, petroleum, etc. **2.** a spring. **3.** a source. **4.** a container. **5.** a deep vertical space, as for air, light, stairs, etc. —*v.i.* **6.** to rise, spring, or gush.

Wel·land Canal (wĕl′ənd), a ship canal in S Canada, in Ontario, connecting lakes Erie and Ontario: 8 locks raise or lower ships 325 ft. 25 mi. long; 25 ft. deep.

well·a·way (wĕl′ə wā′), *interj. Archaic.* an exclamation of sorrow. Also, **well·a·day** (wĕl′ə-dā′).

well-bal·anced (wĕl′băl′ənst), *adj.* **1.** rightly balanced, adjusted, or regulated. **2.** sensible; sane.

well-be·haved (wĕl′bĭ hāvd′), *adj.* characterized by good behavior or conduct.

well-be·ing (wĕl′bē′ĭng), *n.* good or satisfactory condition of existence; welfare.

well·born (wĕl′bôrn′), *adj.* of good family.

well-bred (wĕl′brĕd′), *adj.* having or showing good behavior, manners, etc.

well-con·tent (wĕl′kən tĕnt′), *adj.* satisfied; finding no displeasure.

well-dis·posed (wĕl′dĭs pōzd′), *adj.* **1.** rightly or properly disposed; well-meaning. **2.** favorably or kindly disposed.

well-do·er (wĕl′dōō′ər), *n.* **1.** one who does well or acts rightly. **2.** a doer of good deeds.

well-do·ing (wĕl′dō′ĭng), *n.* good conduct or action.

Welles (wĕlz), *n.* **Sumner** (sŭm′nər), born 1892, U.S. diplomat.

well-fa·vored (wĕl′fā′vərd), *adj.* of pleasing appearance; good-looking; handsome. Also, *Brit.,* **well′-fa′voured.**

well-fed (wĕl′fĕd′), *adj.* fat; plump.

well-found (wĕl′found′), *adj.* well furnished with supplies, necessaries, etc.

well-found·ed (wĕl′foun′dĭd), *adj.* rightly or justly founded, as on good grounds.

well-groomed (wĕl′grōōmd′), *adj.* well cared for, as in personal appearance.

well-ground·ed (wĕl′groun′dĭd), *adj.* **1.** based on good grounds or reasons; well-founded. **2.** well or thoroughly instructed in the first principles of a subject.

well-in·formed (wĕl′ĭn fôrmd′), *adj.* **1.** having full information on a subject. **2.** having information on a variety of subjects.

Wel·ling·ton (wĕl′ĭng tən), *n.* **1. Arthur Wellesley, 1st Duke of,** 1769–1852, British general and statesman. **2.** a seaport in and the capital of New Zealand, in the S part of North Island. Including suburbs, 160,500.

well-known (wĕl′nōn′), *adj.* **1.** clearly or fully known. **2.** familiarly known; familiar. **3.** generally or widely known.

well-man·nered (wĕl′măn′ərd), *adj.* polite; courteous.

well-mean·ing (wĕl′mē′nĭng), *adj.* **1.** meaning or intending well. **2.** Also, **well-meant** (wĕl′mĕnt′). proceeding from good intentions.

well-nigh (wĕl′nī′), *adv.* very nearly.

well-off (wĕl′ôf′, -ŏf′), *adj.* **1.** in a satisfactory, favorable, or good position or condition. **2.** moderately rich.

well-pre·served (wĕl′prĭ zûrvd′), *adj.* preserving a young or new appearance.

well-read (wĕl′rĕd′), *adj.* **1.** having read much. **2.** having an extensive and intelligent knowledge of books or literature.

Wells (wĕlz), *n.* **Herbert George,** 1866–1946, British novelist and writer.

well-spo·ken (wĕl′spō′kən), *adj.* **1.** speaking well, fittingly, or pleasingly. **2.** polite in speech. **3.** spoken well.

well·spring (wĕl/sprĭng/), *n.* **1.** a fountain-head. **2.** a source of anything.

well-thought-of (wĕl/thôt/ŏv/, -ŭv/), *adj.* having a high reputation.

well-timed (wĕl/tīmd/), *adj.* fittingly timed; opportune; timely.

well-to-do (wĕl/tə dōō/), *adj.* well-off; prosperous.

well-wish·er (wĕl/wĭsh/ər), *n.* one who wishes well to a person, a cause, etc. —**well/-wish/ing,** *adj., n.*

well-worn (wĕl/wôrn/), *adj.* **1.** much worn or affected by use. **2.** trite, hackneyed, or stale. **3.** fittingly or becomingly worn or borne.

Welsh (wĕlsh, wĕlch), *adj.* **1.** of or pertaining to Wales, its people, or their language. —*n.* **2.** the people of Wales. **3.** the Celtic language of Wales. —**Welsh/man,** *n.*

welsh (wĕlsh, wĕlch), *v.t., v.i.* *Slang.* to cheat by evading payment. —**welsh/er,** *n.*

Welsh Cor·gi (kôr/gĭ), a dog of either of two ancient Welsh breeds, resembling the dachshund, but having erect ears, the **Cardigan** variety having a long tail and the **Pembroke** a short tail.

Welsh rabbit, melted cheese, usually mixed with ale or beer, milk, etc., eaten on toast. Also, **Welsh rarebit.**

Welsh terrier, a black-and-tan terrier of a breed developed in Wales as a hunting dog.

welt (wĕlt), *n.* **1.** *Colloq.* a ridge on the body, as from a whip. **2.** a strip of leather between the edges of the inner sole and upper and the outer sole of a shoe. **3.** a finish along a seam, the edge of a garment, etc. —*v.t.* **4.** *Colloq.* to beat soundly, as with a whip. **5.** to furnish with a welt or welts.

Welt·an·schau·ung (vĕlt/än/shou/ŏŏng), *n.* *German.* the philosophy of an individual or a group (esp. a race) with an interpretation of world history or civilization.

Welt·an·sicht (vĕlt/än/zĭkнt), *n.* *German.* a world view; an attitude toward, or interpretation of, reality.

wel·ter (wĕl/tər), *v.i.* **1.** to roll, toss, or heave, as waves. **2.** to wallow. —*n.* **3.** commotion or turmoil.

wel·ter·weight (wĕl/tər wāt/), *n.* a boxer or wrestler with a maximum weight of 147 pounds, intermediate in weight between a middleweight and lightweight.

Welt·schmerz (vĕlt/shmĕrts/), *n.* *German.* sorrow felt and accepted as the necessary portion of the world; sentimental pessimism.

wen (wĕn), *n.* *Pathol.* a sebaceous cyst.

wench (wĕnch), *n.* **1.** a girl. **2.** a strumpet. —*v.i.* **3.** to consort with strumpets. —**wench/-er,** *n.*

Wen·chow (wĕn/chou/), *n.* a seaport in E China. 631,276.

wend (wĕnd), *v.,* wended or (*Archaic*) went; wending. —*v.t.* **1.** *Poetic or Literary.* to direct (one's way, etc.). —*v.i.* **2.** *Archaic.* to go.

went (wĕnt), *v.* **1.** pt. of **go.** **2.** archaic pt. and pp. of **wend.**

were (wûr; *unstressed* wər), *v.* pt. ind. pl. and subj. sing. and pl. of **be.**

were·wolf (wĭr/wŏŏlf/, wûr/-), *n., pl.* **-wolves** (-wŏŏlvz/). (in old superstition) a human being turned preternaturally into a wolf but retaining human intelligence.

Wer·fel (vĕr/fəl), *n.* Franz, 1890–1945, German novelist, dramatist, and poet, born in Prague.

wert (wûrt; *unstressed* wərt), *v.* 2nd pers. sing. pt. indic. and subj. of **be** (now only in solemn or poetic use).

We·ser (vā/zər), *n.* a river flowing through NW Germany into the North Sea. ab. 300 mi.

Wes·ley (wĕs/lĭ), *n.* **1.** Charles, 1707–88, British Methodist preacher and hymn writer. **2.** his brother, John, 1703–91, British preacher, founder of Methodism.

Wes·ley·an (wĕs/lĭ ən or, *esp. Brit.,* wĕz/-), *adj.* **1.** of or pertaining to John Wesley, the founder of Methodism. **2.** pertaining to Methodism. —*n.* **3.** a follower of John Wesley. **4.** *Chiefly Brit.* a member of the denomination founded by him; a Methodist. —**Wes/ley·an·ism,** *n.*

Wes·sex (wĕs/ĭks), *n.* (in the Middle Ages) a kingdom in S England.

west (wĕst), *n.* **1.** a cardinal point of the compass, 90° to the left of north. **2.** the direction in which this point lies. **3.** (*l.c. or cap.*) an area situated in this direction. **4.** (*cap.*) the western

part of the world, as distinguished from the Orient. —*adj.* **5.** directed or proceeding toward the west. **6.** coming from the west, as wind. **7.** lying toward or situated in the west. —*adv.* **8.** toward or in the west. **9.** from the west (as of wind.)

West (wĕst), *n.* **1.** Benjamin, 1738–1820, American painter in England. **2.** Rebecca, (*Cecily Fairfield*) born 1892, British novelist and critic.

West Al·lis (ăl/ĭs), a city in SE Wisconsin. 36,364.

west·er (wĕs/tər), *v.i.* to move or tend toward the west.

west·er·ly (wĕs/tər lĭ), *adj., adv., n., pl.* **-lies.** —*adj.* **1.** moving, directed, or situated toward the west. **2.** coming from the west. —*adv.* **3.** toward the west. **4.** from the west. —*n.* **5.** a westerly wind.

Wes·ter·marck (wĕs/tər märk/; *Fin.* vĕs/tər-), *n.* Edward Alexander, 1862–1939, Finnish sociologist.

west·ern (wĕs/tərn), *adj.* **1.** lying toward or situated in the west. **2.** directed or proceeding toward the west. **3.** coming from the west, as a wind. **4.** (*l.c. or cap.*) of or pertaining to the west. —*n.* **5.** *Colloq.* a story or motion picture dealing with the West of the U.S. —**west/ern·most/,** *adj.*

Western Church, the Roman Catholic Church, sometimes with the Anglican Church, or, more broadly, the Christian churches of western Europe and those churches elsewhere which are connected with or derived from them.

west·ern·er (wĕs/tər nər), *n.* a person of or from the western U.S.

Western Hemisphere, 1. a hemisphere of the earth cut along a meridian so chosen as to include all of North and South America, but no part of any other continent. **2.** that half of the earth traversed in passing westward from the prime meridian to 180° longitude.

west·ern·ism (wĕs/tər nĭz/əm), *n.* a word, idiom, or practice peculiar to western people, esp. those of the western U. S.

west·ern·ize (wĕs/tər nīz/), *v.t.,* **-ized, -izing.** to make western in ideas, character, ways, etc.

West Hartford, a town in central Connecticut. 33,776.

West Haven, a town in S Connecticut. 30,021.

West Indies, an archipelago in the N Atlantic between North and South America, enclosing the Caribbean Sea and the Gulf of Mexico: divided into the Greater Antilles, the Lesser Antilles, and the Bahama Islands. —**West Indian.**

west·ing (wĕs/tĭng), *n.* the distance due west made by a ship on any course tending westward; westerly departure; distance westward.

West·ing·house (wĕs/tĭng hous/), *n.* George, 1846–1914, U.S. inventor.

West·min·ster Abbey (wĕst/mĭn/stər), a large Gothic church in London, England: burial place of many distinguished Englishmen.

West New York, a town in NE New Jersey, across from New York City. 39,439.

West Palm Beach, a city in SE Florida: winter resort. 33,693.

West Point, a military reservation in SE New York, on the Hudson: seat of the U.S. Military Academy.

West Virginia, a State in the E United States. 1,807,091 pop.; 24,181 sq. mi. *Cap.:* Charleston. *Abbr.:* W.Va. —**West Virginian.**

west·ward (wĕst/wərd), *adj.* **1.** moving, bearing, facing, or situated toward the west. —*adv.* **2.** Also, **west/wards.** toward the 'west; west. —*n.* **3.** the westward part, direction, or point. —**west/ward·ly,** *adj., adv.*

wet (wĕt), *adj.,* **wetter, wettest,** *n., v.,* **wet** or **wetted, wetting.** —*adj.* **1.** covered or soaked with water or some other liquid. **2.** moist; damp. **3.** rainy. **4.** *U.S.* characterized by or favoring allowance of the manufacture and sale of alcoholic liquors for use as beverages. —*n.* **5.** moisture. —*v.t., v.i.* **6.** to make or become wet. —**wet/ness,** *n.*

wet blanket, a person or thing that dampens ardor or has a depressing effect.

wet-blan·ket (wĕt/blăng/kĭt), *v.t.* to dampen the ardor of.

wet cell, *Elect.* a cell whose electrolyte is in liquid form and free to flow.

weth·er (wĕth/ər), *n.* a castrated male sheep.

wet nurse, a woman employed to suckle the infant of another. —**wet/-nurse/,** *v.t.*

wet pack, *Med.* a type of bath in which wet sheets are applied to the patient.

wf, *Print.* wrong font. Also, **w.f.**

wh., watt-hour.

whack (hwăk), *v.t., v.i.* **1.** *Colloq.* to strike (with) a smart, resounding blow or blows. —*n.* **2.** *Colloq.* a smart, resounding blow. **3.** *Slang.* a trial or attempt. **4.** *Slang.* a portion or share. —**whack′er,** *n.*

whack·ing (hwăk′ĭng), *adj. Chiefly Brit. Colloq.* large; whopping.

whale[1] (hwāl), *n., pl.* **whales,** (*esp. collectively*) **whale,** *v.,* **whaled, whaling.** —*n.* **1.** any of certain large marine mammals with fishlike bodies, modified foreflippers, and a horizontally flattened tail. **2.** *Slang.* something extraordinarily big, great, or fine. —*v.i.* **3.** to carry on the work of taking whales.

whale[2] (hwāl), *v.t.,* **whaled, whaling.** *Colloq.* to whip, thrash, or beat soundly.

whale·back (hwāl′băk′), *n.* a vessel having a rounded deck which meets the sides in a continuous curve, sometimes with upper works, much used on the Great Lakes.

whale·boat (hwāl′bōt′), *n.* a type of boat designed for use in rough sea.

whale·bone (hwāl′bōn′), *n.* **1.** an elastic horny substance growing in place of teeth in the upper jaw of certain whales, and forming a series of thin, parallel plates on each side of the palate. **2.** a thin strip of this material, used for stiffening corsets.

whale·man (hwāl′mən), *n., pl.* **-men.** a man engaged in whaling.

whal·er (hwā′lər), *n.* a person or vessel engaged in whaling.

Whales (hwālz), *n.* **Bay of,** an inlet of the Ross Sea, in Antarctica: Little America is located here.

whal·ing (hwā′lĭng), *n.* the work or industry of taking whales; whale fishing.

wharf (hwôrf), *n., pl.* **wharves** (hwôrvz, hwôrfs). a structure built at the shore of a harbor, etc., so that vessels may be moored alongside.

wharf·age (hwôr′fĭj), *n.* **1.** the use of a wharf. **2.** storage of goods at a wharf. **3.** the charge for the use of a wharf. **4.** wharves collectively.

wharf·in·ger (hwôr′fĭn jər), *n.* one who owns, or has charge of, a wharf.

Whar·ton (hwôr′tən), *n.* **Edith,** 1862–1937, U.S. novelist.

what (hwŏt, hwŭt; *unstressed* hwət), *pron., pl.* **what,** *adv., conj.* —*pron.* **1.** (as an interrogative pronoun) which one from among a number of choices. **2.** (as a relative pronoun): **a.** that which. **b.** the kind of thing or person that; such. **c.** anything that; whatever. **d.** (in parenthetic clauses) something that. **e.** that, which, or who. —*adv.* **3.** how much? **4.** partly. —*conj.* **5.** *Prov.* or *Colloq.* to the extent that.

what·ev·er (hwŏt ĕv′ər), *pron.* **1.** (as a relative pronoun): **a.** anything that. **b.** any amount that. **c.** no matter what. **2.** (as an interrogative pronoun): *Brit. Colloq.* what? (used emphatically). —*adj.* **3.** any . . . that. **4.** no matter what. **5.** being what or who it may be.

what·not (hwŏt′nŏt′), *n.* **1.** a stand with shelves for bric-a-brac, books, etc. **2.** *Colloq.* anything.

what·so·ev·er (hwŏt′sō ĕv′ər), *pron., adj.* intensive form of **whatever.**

wheal (hwēl), *n.* a small, burning or itching swelling on the skin.

wheat (hwēt), *n.* **1.** the grain of a widely distributed cereal grass, used extensively in the form of flour for white bread, cakes, pastry, etc. **2.** the plant, which bears the edible grain in dense spikes. —**wheat′en,** *adj.*

whee·dle (hwē′dəl), *v.t., v.i.,* **-dled, -dling. 1.** to endeavor to influence (a person) by smooth, flattering, or beguiling words. **2.** to get by artful persuasions. —**whee′dler,** *n.* —**whee′dling·ly,** *adv.*

wheel (hwēl), *n.* **1.** a circular frame or disk arranged to turn on an axis, as in vehicles, machinery, etc. **2.** any instrument, machine, etc., shaped like a wheel or using a wheel. **3.** *Colloq.* a bicycle or a tricycle. **4.** anything resembling or suggesting a wheel in shape, movement, etc. **5.** (*pl.*) moving, propelling, or animating agencies. —*v.t.* **6.** to cause to turn, rotate, or revolve, as on an axis. **7.** to move, roll, or convey on wheels, casters, etc. —*v.i.* **8.** to turn, rotate, or revolve. **9.** to move in a circular or curving course. **10.** to roll or move along on wheels. —**wheeled** (hwēld), *adj.*

wheel and axle, a device (one of the so-called simple machines) consisting, in its typical form, of a cylindrical drum to which a wheel, concentric with the drum, is firmly fastened. Ropes are so applied that as one unwinds from the wheel, the other is wound on to the drum.

wheel·bar·row (hwēl′băr′ō), *n.* a frame or box for conveying a load, usually supported at one end by a wheel and at the other by two vertical legs.

wheel·base (hwēl′bās′), *n. Auto.* the distance measured in inches from the center of the front-wheel spindle to the center of the rear-wheel axle.

wheel chair, a chair mounted on large wheels, and used by invalids.

wheel·er (hwē′lər), *n.* **1.** one who or that which wheels. **2.** something provided with a wheel or wheels. **3.** a wheel horse (def. 1).

wheel horse, 1. a horse, or one of the horses, harnessed behind others and next to the fore wheels of a vehicle. **2.** a plodding, steady, and obedient worker.

Wheel·ing (hwē′lĭng), *n.* a city in N West Virginia. 61,099.

wheel lock, an old type of gunlock in which sparks are produced by the friction of a small steel wheel against a piece of iron pyrites.

wheel·man (hwēl′mən), *n., pl.* **-men. 1.** the man at the steering wheel of a vessel; a steersman. **2.** a rider of a bicycle, tricycle, or the like.

wheel·work (hwēl′wûrk′), *n. Mach.* an apparatus consisting of a train of gears.

wheel·wright (hwēl′rīt′), *n.* one who makes or repairs wheeled carriages, etc.

wheeze (hwēz), *v.,* **wheezed, wheezing,** *n.* —*v.i.* **1.** to breathe with difficulty and with a whistling sound. —*n.* **2.** a wheezing breath or sound. **3.** a theatrical gag. **4.** a trite saying, story, etc. —**wheez′y,** *adj.*

whelm (hwĕlm), *v.t.* **1.** to submerge; engulf. **2.** to overcome utterly; overwhelm.

whelp (hwĕlp), *n.* **1.** the young of the dog, or of the wolf, bear, lion, tiger, seal, etc. **2.** (in contemptuous use) a youth. —*v.t., v.i.* **3.** (of a dog, lioness, etc.) to bring forth (young).

when (hwĕn), *adv.* **1.** at what time. —*conj.* **2.** at what time. **3.** at the time that. **4.** at any time. **5.** and then. **6.** while on the contrary. —*n.* **7.** what time. **8.** which time. **9.** the time of anything.

when·as (hwĕn ăz′), *conj. Archaic.* when; while; whereas.

whence (hwĕns), *adv.* **1.** from what place? **2.** from what source, origin, or cause? —*conj.* **3.** from what place, source, cause, etc.

whence·so·ev·er (hwĕns′sō ĕv′ər), *adv., conj.* from whatsoever place, source, or cause.

when·ev·er (hwĕn ĕv′ər), *conj.* **1.** at whatever time. —*adv.* **2.** *Colloq.* when? (used emphatically).

when·so·ev·er (hwĕn′sō ĕv′ər), *adv., conj.* at whatsoever time.

where (hwâr), *adv.* **1.** in or at what place? **2.** in what position or circumstances? **3.** in what particular, respect, way, etc.? **4.** to what place, point, or end, or whither? **5.** from what source? —*conj.* **6.** in or at what place, part, point, etc. **7.** in or at the place, part, point, etc., in or at which. **8.** in a position, case, etc., in which. **9.** in any place, position, case, etc., in which. **10.** to what or whatever place. **11.** and there. —*n.* **12.** what place. **13.** a place.

where·a·bouts (hwâr′ə bouts′), *adv.* **1.** where? —*conj.* **2.** near or in what place. —*n.* **3.** the place where a person or thing is.

where·as (hwâr ăz′), *conj., n., pl.* **whereases.** —*conj.* **1.** while on the contrary. **2.** considering that. —*n.* **3.** a statement having "whereas" as the first word.

where·at (hwâr ăt′), *adv., conj.* at what or at which.

where·by (hwâr bī′), *adv., conj.* **1.** by what or by which. **2.** by what? how?

where·e'er (hwâr âr′), *Poetic.* wherever.

where·fore (hwâr′fōr′), *adv.* **1.** for what? why? —*conj.* **2.** for what or which cause or reason. —*n.* **3.** the cause or reason.

where·from (hwâr frŏm′), *adv.* from which; whence.

where·in (hwâr ĭn′), *adv.* in what or in which.

where·in·to (hwâr ĭn′tōō, hwâr′ĭn tōō′), *adv., conj.* into what or into which.

where·of (hwâr ŏv′, -ŭv′), *adv., conj.* of what, which, or whom.

where·on (hwâr ŏn′, -ôn′), *adv., conj.* on what or on which.

where·so·ev·er (hwâr′sō ĕv′ər), *adv., conj.* wherever.

where·up·on (hwâr′ə pŏn′, -pôn′), *adv.* 1. upon what? —*conj.* 2. upon what or upon which. 3. at or after which.

wher·ev·er (hwâr ĕv′ər), *conj.* 1. in, at, or to whatever place. 2. in any case or condition. —*adv.* 3. *Colloq.* where? (used emphatically).

where·with (hwâr wĭth′, -wĭth′), *adv.* 1. with what? —*conj.* 2. with what or which. 3. (by ellipsis) that with which. —*n.* 4. wherewithal.

where·with·al (hwâr′wĭth ôl′), *n.* that with which to do something.

wher·ry (hwĕr′ĭ), *n., pl.* -ries. 1. a light row-boat for one person. 2. any of certain larger boats (fishing vessels, barges, etc.).

whet (hwĕt), *v.t.*, **whetted, whetting.** 1. to sharpen (a knife, tool, etc.), as by grinding. 2. to make keen or eager.

wheth·er (hwĕth′ər), *conj.* a word introducing, in dependent clauses or the like, the first of two or more alternatives, and sometimes repeated before the second or later alternative (used in correlation with *or*).

whet·stone (hwĕt′stōn′), *n.* a stone for sharpening cutlery or tools by friction.

whew (hwū), *interj.* 1. a whistling exclamation or sound expressing astonishment, dismay, etc. —*n.* 2. an utterance of "whew."

whey (hwā), *n.* milk serum, separating as a watery liquid from the curd after coagulation, as in cheesemaking.

whey·ey (hwā′ĭ), *adj.* of, like, or containing whey.

whey·face (hwā′fās′), *n.* a face or a person that is pallid, as from fear. —**whey′faced′,** *adj.*

which (hwĭch), *pron.* 1. (as an interrogative pronoun): what one (of a certain number mentioned or implied)? 2. (as a relative pronoun): a. in clauses conveying an additional idea. b. in clauses defining or restricting the antecedent. 3. (as a compound relative pronoun) what particular one; the or any one that. 4. (in parenthetic clauses) a thing that. —*adj.* 5. what one of (a certain number mentioned or implied). 6. no matter what; any that. 7. being previously mentioned.

which·ev·er (hwĭch ĕv′ər), *pron.* 1. any one (of those in question) that. 2. no matter which.

whid (hwĭd), *v.i.*, **whidded, whidding.** *Scot.* to move briskly and quietly.

whiff (hwĭf), *n.* 1. a slight blast or puff of wind, air, odor, smoke, etc. —*v.i., v.t.* 2. to blow in whiffs or puffs.

whif·fet (hwĭf′ĭt), *n.* 1. a small dog. 2. *U.S. Colloq.* an insignificant person; whippersnapper. 3. a little whiff.

whif·fle (hwĭf′əl), *v.*, **-fled, -fling.** —*v.i.* 1. to blow in light or shifting gusts or puffs, as the wind; veer irregularly (about). 2. to shift about in; vacillate. —*v.t.* 3. to blow with light, shifting gusts. —**whif′fler,** *n.*

whif·fle·tree (hwĭf′əl trē′, -trĭ′), *n.* a crossbar, pivoted at the middle, to which the traces of the harness are fastened in a cart, carriage, plow, etc.

Whig (hwĭg), *n.* 1. *Amer. Hist.* a. a member of the party favoring the Revolution against England. b. a member of a political party (c1834–1855) which was formed in opposition to the Democratic party. 2. *Brit. Hist.* a member of a political party, in general holding liberal principles and more recently known as the "Liberal party." —*adj.* 3. being a Whig. 4. of, pertaining to, or characteristic of the Whigs.

Whig·ger·y (hwĭg′ə rĭ), *n., pl.* -geries. the principles or practices of Whigs.

Whig·gish (hwĭg′ĭsh), *adj.* 1. of, pertaining to, or characteristic of Whigs. 2. inclined to Whiggism. —**Whig′gish·ly,** *adv.* —**Whig′gish·ness,** *n.*

Whig·gism (hwĭg′ĭz əm), *n.* the principles of Whigs.

while (hwīl), *n., conj., v.*, **whiled, whiling.** —*n.* 1. a space of time. 2. **the while,** during this time. 3. **worth one's while,** worth time, pains, or expense. —*conj.* 4. during or in the time that. 5. as long as. 6. at the same time that. —*v.t.* 7. to cause (time) to pass, esp. in some pleasant manner.

whiles (hwīlz), *Archaic or Dial.* —*adv.* 1. at times. 2. in the meantime. —*conj.* 3. while.

whi·lom (hwī′ləm), *Archaic.* —*adv.* 1. at one time; formerly. —*adj.* 2. former.

whilst (hwīlst), *conj.* *Chiefly Brit.* while.

whim (hwĭm), *n.* 1. an odd or fanciful notion or desire. 2. capricious humor.

whim·per (hwĭm′pər), *v.i., v.t.* 1. to cry with low, plaintive, broken sounds, as a child or a dog. —*n.* 2. a whimpering cry or sound. —**whim′-per·er,** *n.* —**whim′per·ing·ly,** *adv.*

whim·sey (hwĭm′zĭ), *n., pl.* -seys. whimsy.

whim·si·cal (hwĭm′zə kəl), *adj.* 1. given to whims; capricious. 2. odd, quaint, or comical. —**whim′si·cal·ly,** *adv.* —**whim′si·cal·ness, whim′si·cal·i·ty,** *n.*

whim·sy (hwĭm′zĭ), *n., pl.* -sies. an odd or fanciful notion or thing.

whim-wham (hwĭm′hwăm′), *n.* any odd or fanciful object or thing; a gimcrack.

whine (hwīn), *v.*, **whined, whining.** —*v.i.* 1. to utter a low, complaining cry or sound. —*n.* 2. a whining utterance, sound, or tone. —**whin′er,** *n.* —**whin′ing·ly,** *adv.*

whin·ny (hwĭn′ĭ), *v.i., v.t.*, **-nied, -nying,** *n., pl.* -nies. neigh.

whip (hwĭp), *v.*, **whipped** or **whipt, whipping,** *n.* —*v.t.* 1. to strike with quick, repeated strokes, as with a rod; flog; thrash. 2. *Colloq.* to beat, outdo, or defeat. 3. to move, pull, jerk, snatch, seize, put, etc., with a sudden movement. 4. to fish (a stream, etc.) with a rod and line. 5. to cover (cord, etc.) with cord, thread, or the like wound about it. 6. to gather by overcasting the turned edge with small stitches and then drawing up the thread. 7. to beat (eggs, cream, etc.) to a froth with a fork or other implement. —*v.i.* 8. to move or go quickly and suddenly; dart; whisk. 9. to beat or lash about. —*n.* 10. an instrument to strike with, as in driving animals or in punishing, typically consisting of a lash or other flexible part with a more rigid handle. 11. a lashing stroke or motion. 12. *Pol.* a party manager in a legislative body. 13. a dish made of cream or egg whites whipped to a froth with flavoring, etc., often with fruit pulp or the like. —**whip′-per,** *n.*

whip·cord (hwĭp′kôrd′), *n.* a worsted fabric with a diagonally ribbed surface.

whip graft, a graft prepared by cutting both the scion and the stock in a sloping direction and inserting a tongue in the scion into a slit in the stock.

whip hand, control or advantage.

whip·lash (hwĭp′lăsh′), *n.* the lash of a whip.

whip·per·snap·per (hwĭp′ər snăp′ər), *n.* an insignificant, presumptuous person.

whip·pet (hwĭp′ĭt), *n.* a small, swift dog, used especially in racing.

whip·ping (hwĭp′ĭng), *n.* 1. a beating administered with a whip or the like, as for punishment; a flogging. 2. an arrangement of cord, twine, or the like whipped or wound about a thing, as to bind parts together.

whipping boy, 1. a scapegoat. 2. (formerly) a boy educated along with and taking punishment in place of a young prince or nobleman.

whipping post, a post to which persons are fastened to undergo whipping as a legal penalty.

whip·ple·tree (hwĭp′əl trē′, -trĭ′), *n.* whiffletree.

whip·poor·will (hwĭp′ər wĭl′), *n.* a nocturnal North American bird with a variegated plumage of gray, black, white, and tawny.

whip·stitch (hwĭp′stĭch′), *v.t.* 1. to sew with stitches passing over an edge, in joining, finishing, or gathering. —*n.* 2. one such stitch. 3. *U.S. Colloq.* an instant.

whip·stock (hwĭp′stŏk′), *n.* the handle of a whip.

whir (hwûr), *v.*, **whirred, whirring,** *n.* —*v.i., v.t.* 1. to go, fly, dart, revolve, or move quickly with a buzzing sound. —*n.* 2. act or sound of whirring.

whirl (hwûrl), *v.i., v.t.* 1. to turn round, spin, or rotate rapidly. 2. to turn about or aside quickly. 3. to move, travel, or be carried rapidly along on wheels or otherwise. —*n.* 4. act of whirling; rapid rotation or gyration. 5. a whirling movement. 6. a short drive, run, walk, or the like. 7. something that whirls, as a current or mass. 8. a rapid round of events, affairs, etc. 9. a state marked by a dizzying succession or mingling of feelings, thoughts, etc. —**whirl′er,** *n.*

whirl·i·gig (hwûr′lĭ gĭg′), *n.* 1. something

that whirls, revolves, or goes round. **2.** a merry-go-round. **3.** a toy for whirling or spinning.

whirl·pool (hwûrl′pōōl′), *n.* a whirling eddy or current, as in a river or the sea.

whirl·wind (hwûrl′wĭnd′), *n.* a rapidly rotating mass of air moving over the surface of the land or sea.

whirr (hwûr), *v.i., v.t., n.* whir.

whish (hwĭsh), *v.i.* **1.** to make, or move with, a whiz or swish. —*n.* **2.** a whishing sound.

whisk (hwĭsk), *v.t., v.i.* **1.** to sweep (dust, crumbs, etc., or a surface) with a whisk broom, brush, or the like. **2.** to move with a rapid, sweeping stroke. **3.** to draw, snatch, carry, etc., lightly and rapidly. —*n.* **4.** act of whisking.

whisk broom, a small broom for brushing clothes, etc.

whisk·er (hwĭs′kər), *n.* **1.** (*usually pl.*) the hair growing on the side of a man's face, esp. when worn long. **2.** (*pl.*) the beard generally. **3.** a single hair of the beard. **4.** one of the long, stiff, bristly hairs growing about the mouth of certain animals, as the cat, rat, etc. —**whisk′ered,** *adj.*

whis·key (hwĭs′kĭ), *n., pl.* **-keys.** a distilled alcoholic liquor made from grain, as barley, rye, maize, etc.

whis·ky (hwĭs′kĭ), *n., pl.* **-kies.** whiskey.

whis·per (hwĭs′pər), *v.i., v.t.* **1.** to speak or utter with soft, low sounds, using the breath, lips, etc., without vibration of the vocal cords. **2.** to talk or tell softly and privately. —*n.* **3.** the mode of utterance, or the voice, of one who whispers. **4.** a sound, word, remark, or the like, uttered by whispering. —**whis′per·er,** *n.*

whis·per·ing (hwĭs′pər ĭng), *n.* **1.** whispered talk or conversation; a whisper or whispers. —*adj.* **2.** that whispers; making a sound like a whisper. **3.** like a whisper. —**whis′per·ing·ly,** *adv.*

whist (hwĭst), *n.* a card game played by four players, two against two, with 52 cards.

whis·tle (hwĭs′əl), *v.,* **-tled, -tling,** *n.* —*v.i.* **1.** to make a clear, shrill sound, as by the forcible expulsion of the breath through a small orifice formed by contracting the lips. —*v.t.* **2.** to produce by whistling. —*n.* **3.** an instrument for producing whistling sounds, as by the breath, steam, etc. **4.** a sound produced by or as by whistling. —**whis′tler,** *n.*

Whis·tler (hwĭs′lər), *n.* **James Abbott Mc-Neill,** 1834–1903, U.S. artist.

whis·tling (hwĭs′lĭng), *n.* **1.** act of one who or that which whistles. **2.** the sound produced. **3.** *Vet. Sci.* a form of roaring characterized by a peculiarly shrill sound.

whit (hwĭt), *n.* a particle; bit; jot.

Whit·by (hwĭt′bĭ), *n.* a seaport in NE England: ruins of an abbey; church council, A.D. 664. 12,698.

white (hwĭt), *adj.,* **whiter, whitest,** *n.* —*adj.* **1.** of the color of pure snow; reflecting light without absorbing any of the rays composing it. **2.** having a light-colored skin. **3.** noting or pertaining to the Caucasian race. **4.** dominated by or including only members of the white race. **5.** pallid or pale, as from fear. **6.** gray, as hair. **7.** royalist or reactionary. **8.** *Colloq.* honorable, trustworthy, or square. **9.** (of wines) light-colored or yellowish. —*n.* **10.** a color without hue at one extreme end of the scale of grays, opposite to black. **11.** a member of the Caucasian race. **12.** *Biol.* the albumen. **13.** the white part of the eyeball. **14.** *Chess, Checkers.* the men or pieces which are light-colored. —**white′ness,** *n.*

White (hwĭt), *n.* **1. Edward Douglass,** 1845–1921, U.S. jurist, chief justice of the Supreme Court, 1910–21. **2. Gilbert,** 1720–1793, British clergyman and writer on natural history. **3. Stanford,** 1853–1906, U.S. architect. **4. William Allen,** 1868–1944, U.S. journalist.

white ant, a termite.

white·bait (hwĭt′bāt′), *n., pl.* **-bait.** any small delicate fish cooked whole without being cleaned. In Europe, the sprat constitutes much of the whitebait.

white bear, the polar bear.

white·beard (hwĭt′bĭrd′), *n.* a man having a white or gray beard; old man.

white book, an official document, bound in white.

white·cap (hwĭt′kăp′), *n.* a wave with a broken white crest.

white clover, a clover with white flowers, common in pastures and meadows.

white coal, water, as of a stream, used for power.

white-col·lar (hwĭt′kŏl′ər), *adj.* *U.S.* belonging or pertaining to workers, professional men, etc., who may wear conventional dress at work.

white damp, carbon monoxide.

white elephant, 1. an abnormally whitish or pale elephant, found usually in Siam. **2.** a possession of great value but entailing even greater expense. **3.** an annoyingly useless possession.

white-faced (hwĭt′fāst′), *adj.* **1.** having a white or pale face. **2.** marked with white on the front of the head, as a horse. **3.** having a white front or surface.

white feather, a symbol of cowardice.

White·field (hwĭt′fēld′), *n.* **George,** 1714–70, British Methodist preacher.

white·fish (hwĭt′fĭsh′), *n., pl.* **-fishes,** (*esp. collectively*) **-fish.** any of certain fishes similar to the trout but with smaller mouths and larger scales, some species being highly desirable food fishes.

white flag, an all-white flag, used as a symbol of surrender, etc.

White·fri·ars (hwĭt′frī′ərz), *n.* a district (a sanctuary until 1697) in central London, England: named from a former Carmelite monastery in Fleet Street, founded in 1241.

white gold, any of several gold alloys possessing a white color due to the presence of nickel or platinum. Commercial alloys contain gold, nickel, copper, and zinc in varying proportions.

White·hall (hwĭt′hôl′), *n.* **1.** the main London thoroughfare between Trafalgar Square and the Houses of Parliament, flanked by government offices. **2.** the government or the policies of the British Empire.

White·head (hwĭt′hĕd′), *n.* **Alfred North,** 1861–1947, British mathematician and philosopher, in the U.S.

white-head·ed (hwĭt′hĕd′ĭd), *adj.* **1.** having the head entirely or partly covered with white hair, etc. **2.** having fair or flaxen hair. **3.** *Colloq.* favorite.

white heat, a stage of intense activity, excitement, feeling, etc.

white-hot (hwĭt′hŏt′), *adj.* **1.** very hot. **2.** showing white heat.

White House, The, 1. the official residence ("Executive Mansion") of the president of the United States, at Washington, D.C. **2.** *Colloq.* the executive branch of the Federal government.

white lead, a white, heavy powder used as a pigment, in putty, and in medicinal ointments for burns.

white lie, a pardonable lie.

white-liv·ered (hwĭt′lĭv′ərd), *adj.* **1.** pale or unhealthy. **2.** cowardly.

white man's burden, the alleged duty of the white race to care for and educate ignorant or uncivilized peoples, esp. subject peoples, of other races.

white matter, *Anat.* nervous tissue, esp. of the brain and spinal cord containing fibers only, and nearly white in color.

white meat, any light-colored flesh meat, as veal, the breast of chicken, etc.

White Mountains, a mountain range in N New Hampshire. Highest peak, 6293 ft.

whit·en (hwī′tən), *v.t., v.i.* to make or become white. —**whit′en·er,** *n.*

White Pass, a mountain pass in SE Alaska, near Skagway. ab. 2800 ft. high.

white pepper, a condiment prepared from the husked dried berries of the pepper plant, used either whole or ground.

white pine, 1. a pine of eastern North America, yielding a light-colored, soft, light wood of great commercial importance. **2.** the wood itself. **3.** any of various other similar species of pine.

white plague, tuberculosis, esp. pulmonary tuberculosis.

White Plains, a city in SE New York, near New York City. 40,327.

white poplar, an Old World poplar widely cultivated in the U.S., having the under side of the leaves covered with a dense silvery-white down.

white potato, Irish potato.

white primary, *U.S.* a direct primary of the Democratic party in southern states in which only white persons may vote.

White River, a river flowing from NW Arkansas generally SE to the Mississippi river. ab. 690 mi.

White Russia, 1. Official name, **White Russian Soviet Socialist Republic.** a constituent republic of the Soviet Union, in the W part. 5,567,976 pop.; 87,100 sq. mi. *Cap.*: Minsk. **2.** a region in the W part of czarist Russia, inhabited by the White Russians.

White Russian, a member of a division of the Russian people dwelling in White Russia and in adjoining regions.

white sauce, a sauce made of butter, flour, seasonings, and milk or sometimes chicken or veal stock.

White Sea, an arm of the Arctic Ocean, in the NW Soviet Union. ab. 36,000 sq. mi.

white slave, a white woman who is sold or forced to serve as a prostitute.

white slaver, a person engaged in the traffic in white slaves.

white slavery, the condition of or the traffic in white slaves.

white·slav·ing (hwīt/slā/vĭng), *n.* traffic in white slaves.

white squall, *Naut.* a whirlwind or violent disturbance of small radius, which is not accompanied by the usual clouds, but is indicated merely by the whitecaps and turbulent water beneath it.

white·wash (hwīt/wŏsh/, -wôsh/), *n.* **1.** a composition, as of lime and water, used for whitening walls, etc. **2.** anything used to cover up defects, faults, etc. —*v.t.* **3.** to whiten with whitewash. **4.** to cover up the defects, faults, errors, etc., of. **5.** *Colloq.* (in various games) to defeat utterly. —**white/wash/er,** *n.*

white wax, *Brit.* paraffin.

whith·er (hwĭth/ər), *Archaic and Literary; now replaced by* where. —*adv.* **1.** to what place? **2.** to what point, end, course, etc., or to what? —*conj.* **3.** to what, whatever, or which place, point, end, etc.

whith·er·so·ev·er (hwĭth/ər sō ĕv/ər), *adv.* to whatsoever place.

whith·er·ward (hwĭth/ər wərd), *adv.* Archaic. toward what place; in what direction. Also, **whith/er·wards.**

whit·ing[1] (hwī/tĭng), *n.* a slender Atlantic shore fish.

whit·ing[2] (hwī/tĭng), *n.* pure white chalk (calcium carbonate) which has been ground and washed, used in making putty, whitewash, etc., and for cleaning silver, etc.

whit·ish (hwī/tĭsh), *adj.* somewhat white.

whit·low (hwĭt/lō), *n.* *Pathol.* an inflammation of the deeper tissues of a finger or toe, esp. of the terminal phalanx, usually terminating in suppuration.

Whit·man (hwĭt/mən), *n.* **Walt,** 1819–1892, U.S. poet.

Whit·ney (hwĭt/nĭ), *n.* **1.** Eli, 1765–1825, American inventor (of the cotton gin). **2.** William Dwight, 1827–1894, U.S. philologist and lexicographer. **3.** Mount, a mountain in E California: highest peak in the U.S. proper. 14,495 ft.

Whit·sun (hwĭt/sən), *adj.* of or pertaining to Whitsunday or Whitsuntide.

Whit·sun·day (hwĭt/sŭn/dĭ, hwĭt/sən dā/), *n.* the seventh Sunday after Easter, celebrated as a festival in commemoration of the descent of the Holy Spirit on the day of Pentecost.

Whit·sun·tide (hwĭt/sən tīd/), *n.* the week beginning with Whitsunday, esp. the first three days of this week.

Whit·ti·er (hwĭt/ĭ ər), *n.* **John Greenleaf,** 1807–92, U.S. poet.

Whit·ting·ton (hwĭt/ĭng tən), *n.* **Dick,** died 1423, lord mayor of London about whom many legends survive.

whit·tle (hwĭt/əl), *v.t.*, *v.i.*, -tled, -tling. **1.** to cut, trim, or shape (a stick, piece of wood, etc.) by taking off bits with a knife. **2.** to reduce. —**whit/tler,** *n.*

whit·tling (hwĭt/lĭng), *n.* **1.** act of one who whittles. **2.** (*usually pl.*) a bit or chip whittled off.

whit·y (hwī/tĭ), *adj.* whitish.

whiz (hwĭz), *v.*, **whizzed, whizzing,** *n.* —*v.i.* **1.** to make a humming or hissing sound, as an object passing rapidly through the air. **2.** to move with such a sound. —*n.* **3.** the sound of a whizzing object. Also, **whizz.**

whiz-bang (hwĭz/băng/), *n.* **1.** *Mil.* a small,

high-speed shell whose sound as it flies through the air arrives almost at the same instant as its explosion. **2.** a firecracker with a similar effect. Also, **whizz/-bang/.**

whiz·zer (hwĭz/ər), *n.* **1.** something that whizzes. **2.** a centrifugal machine for drying sugar, grain, clothes, etc.

who (hōō), *pron.* —*interrog. pron.* **1.** what person? **2.** (of a person) what as to character, origin, position, importance, etc. —*rel. pron.* **3.** the or any person that. **4.** in clauses conveying an additional idea or in clauses defining or restricting the antecedent.

whoa (hwō), *interj.* Stop! (used esp. to horses).

who·dun·it (hōō dŭn/ĭt), *n.* *Slang.* a short novel dealing with a murder or a series of murders and the detection of the criminal.

who·ev·er (hōō ĕv/ər), *pron.* —*indef. rel. pron.* **1.** whatever person, or anyone that. **2.** no matter who. —*interrog. pron.* **3.** *Colloq.* who? (used emphatically).

whole (hōl), *adj.* **1.** entire, full, total; complete. **2.** undivided. **3.** *Math.* integral; not fractional. **4.** uninjured, undamaged, or unbroken. **5.** being fully or entirely such. —*n.* **6.** the entire quantity, account, extent, or number. **7.** a thing complete in itself. —**whole/ness,** *n.*

whole-heart·ed (hōl/här/tĭd), *adj.* **1.** hearty; sincere. **2.** singlehearted. —**whole/-heart/ed·ly,** *adv.* —**whole/-heart/ed·ness,** *n.*

whole hog, *Slang.* **1.** entireness; completeness. **2.** to go (the) whole hog, to involve oneself to the fullest extent.

whole-life insurance (hōl/lĭf/), life insurance for the whole of life, the face of the policy being paid upon death at any time, or upon the attainment of specified age.

whole milk, milk containing all its constituents as received from the cow, or other milkgiving animal.

whole note, *Music.* the longest note in common use.

whole number, an integer: 0, 1, 2, 3, 4, 5 ∷∷

whole·sale (hōl/sāl/), *n.*, *adj.*, *adv.*, *v.*, -saled, -saling. —*n.* **1.** the sale of commodities in large quantities, as to retailers rather than to consumers directly (opposed to *retail*). —*adj.* **2.** of, pertaining to, or engaged in sale by wholesale. **3.** extensive and indiscriminate. —*adv.* **4.** in a wholesale way. —*v.t.*, *v.i.* **5.** to sell by wholesale. —**whole/sal/er,** *n.*

whole-seas (hōl/sēz/), *adj.* completely under the influence of liquor. Also, **whole-seas over.**

whole·some (hōl/səm), *adj.* **1.** conducive to well-being; salutary; beneficial. **2.** healthful; salubrious. —**whole/some·ly,** *adv.* —**whole/some·ness,** *n.*

whole-souled (hōl/sōld/), *adj.* wholehearted; hearty.

whole step, *Music.* an interval of two semitones, as A–B or B–C♯; a major second. Also, **whole tone.**

whole-wheat (hōl/hwēt/), *adj.* prepared with the complete wheat kernel.

whol·ly (hō/lĭ, hōl/lĭ), *adv.* **1.** entirely; totally; altogether; quite. **2.** to the whole amount, extent, etc. **3.** so as to comprise or involve all.

whom (hōōm), *pron.* objective case of **who.**

whoop (hōōp, hwōōp), *n.* **1.** the cry or shout uttered by one who whoops. **2.** the whooping sound characteristic of whooping cough. **3.** not worth a whoop, *Colloq.* not worth a thing. —*v.i.* **4.** to utter a loud cry or shout, as a call, or in enthusiasm, frenzy, etc. **5.** to make the characteristic sound accompanying the deep inhalation after a series of coughs in whooping cough. —*v.t.* **6.** to utter with a whoop or whoops.

whoop·ee (hwōō/pē, hwōōp/ē), *U.S. Slang.* —*n.* **1.** uproarious festivity. —*interj.* **2.** a shout of "whoopee."

whoop·er (hōō/pər, hwōō/-), *n.* **1.** one who or that which whoops. **2.** a common Old World swan notable for its whooping cry.

whoop·ing cough (hōō/pĭng, hōōp/ĭng), an infectious disease of the respiratory mucous membrane, esp. of children, characterized by a series of short, convulsive coughs followed by a deep inhalation accompanied by a whooping sound.

whop·per (hwŏp/ər), *n.* *Colloq.* **1.** something uncommonly large. **2.** a big lie.

whop·ping (hwŏp/ĭng), *adj.* *Colloq.* very large of its kind; thumping; huge.

whore (hōr), *n.*, *v.*, **whored, whoring.** —*n.*
1. a prostitute. —*v.i.* **2.** to act as a whore. **3.** to consort with whores. —*v.t.* **4.** to make a whore of; debauch.

whore·dom (hōr′dəm), *n. Rare.* **1.** prostitution. **2.** (in Biblical use) idolatry.

whore·mon·ger (hōr′mŭng′gər), *n. Rare.* one who consorts with whores. Also, *Rare,* **whore·mas·ter** (hōr′măs′tər, -mäs′-).

whore·son (hōr′sən), *Obs.* —*n.* **1.** a bastard. **2.** (in contemptuous or abusive use) a person. —*adj.* **3.** being a bastard. **4.** mean; scurvy.

whorl (hwûrl, hwôrl), *n.* **1.** a circular arrangement of like parts, as leaves, flowers, etc., round a point on an axis. **2.** one of the turns or volutions of a spiral shell. **3.** *Anat.* one of the turns in the cochlea of the ear. **4.** anything shaped like a coil. —**whorled,** *adj.*

whose (hōōz), *pron.* possessive case of *who,* and historically also of *what.*

who·so (hōō′sō), *pron.* whoever.

who·so·ev·er (hōō′sō ĕv′ər), *pron.* whoever; whatever person.

whr., watt-hour.

why (hwī), *adv.*, *n.*, *pl.* **whys,** *interj.* —*adv.*
1. for what cause, reason, or purpose? **2.** for what cause or reason. **3.** for which, or on account of which (after *reason,* etc.). **4.** the reason for which. —*n.* **5.** the cause or reason. —*interj.* **6.** an expression of surprise, hesitation, etc.

w.i., when issued; denoting a transaction to be completed when the security is to be issued at a later date.

W.I., **1.** West Indian. **2.** West Indies.

Wich·i·ta (wĭch′ə tô′), *n.* a city in S Kansas. 114,966.

Wichita Falls, a city in N Texas. 45,112.

wick (wĭk), *n.* a twist or braid of soft threads which in a candle, lamp, oil stove, or the like serves to draw up the melted tallow or wax or the oil or other inflammable liquid to be burned gradually at its own top or end.

wick·ed (wĭk′ĭd), *adj.* **1.** evil; morally bad; sinful. **2.** mischievous. **3.** *Colloq.* distressingly severe. **4.** *Colloq. or Dial.* savage; vicious. **5.** *Colloq.* extremely trying, unpleasant, or troublesome. —**wick′ed·ly,** *adv.* —**wick′ed·ness,** *n.*

wick·er (wĭk′ər), *n.* **1.** a slender, pliant twig. **2.** wickerwork. —*adj.* **3.** consisting or made of wicker.

wick·er·work (wĭk′ər wûrk′), *n.* work consisting of plaited or woven twigs or osiers.

wick·et (wĭk′ĭt), *n.* **1.** a small door or gate. **2.** a window or opening, often closed by a grating or the like. **3.** a gate by which a flow of water is regulated, as to a water wheel. **4.** *Cricket.* **a.** either of the two frameworks, each consisting of three stumps with two bails in grooves across their tops, at which the bowler aims the ball. **b.** the area between the wickets. **5.** *Croquet.* a hoop or arch. **6.** a turnstile in an entrance.

wick·et·keep·er (wĭk′ĭt kē′pər), *n. Cricket.* the player on the fielding side who stands immediately behind the wicket to stop balls that pass it.

wick·ing (wĭk′ĭng), *n.* material for wicks.

wick·i·up (wĭk′ĭ ŭp′), *n.* **1.** (in Nevada, Arizona, etc.) an American Indian hut made of brushwood or covered with mats. **2.** *Western U.S.* any rude hut.

Wick·liffe (wĭk′lĭf), *n.* **John.** See **Wycliffe.** Also, **Wic′lif.**

wide (wīd), *adj.*, **wider, widest,** *adv.*, *n.* —*adj.* **1.** having great extent from side to side; broad. **2.** having a certain or specified extent from side to side. **3.** extensive; vast; spacious. **4.** of great range or scope. **5.** expanded; distended. **6.** full, ample, or roomy. **7.** apart or remote from a specified point or object. —*adv.* **8.** to a great, or relatively great, extent from side to side. **9.** over an extensive space or region, or far abroad. **10.** to the full extent of opening. **11.** to the utmost. **12.** away from a point, mark, purpose, or the like; astray. —*n.* **13.** that which goes wide. —**wide′ly,** *adv.* —**wide′ness,** *n.*

wide-an·gle (wīd′ăng′gəl), *adj.* noting or pertaining to lenses taking pictures including a wider angle, i.e., including more of the subject from a given position.

wide-a·wake (wīd′ə wāk′), *adj.* **1.** fully awake. **2.** alert; keen.

wid·en (wī′dən), *v.t.*, *v.i.* to make or become wider; broaden. —**wid′en·er,** *n.*

wide-o·pen (wīd′ō′pən), *adj.* **1.** opened to the

full extent. **2.** denoting the loose or irregular enforcement or the nonenforcement of laws concerning liquor, vice, gambling, etc.

wide·spread (wīd′sprĕd′), *adj.* **1.** occupying a wide space. **2.** occurring in many places or among many individuals. Also, **wide′-spread′-ing.**

widg·eon (wĭj′ən), *n.* any of several freshwater ducks between the mallard and teal in size.

wid·ow (wĭd′ō), *n.* **1.** a woman who has lost her husband by death and has not married again. **2.** *Cards.* an additional hand or part of a hand, as one dealt to the table. —*v.t.* **3.** to make (one) a widow. —**wid′ow·er,** *n.masc.* —**wid′ow·hood′,** *n.*

widow's mite, a small gift of money given in good spirit by one who can ill afford it.

widow's peak, *Colloq.* a point formed by the hair growing down in the middle of the forehead.

width (wĭdth), *n.* **1.** extent from side to side; breadth. **2.** a piece of the full wideness.

width·wise (wĭdth′wīz′), *adv.* in the direction of the width. Also, **width·ways** (wĭdth′wāz′).

wie geht's? (vē gāts′), *German.* how goes it with you? how do you do? (short for *wie geht es Ihnen*).

wield (wēld), *v.t.* **1.** to exercise (power, authority, influence, etc.), as in ruling. **2.** to manage (a weapon, instrument, etc.) in use. —**wield′a·ble,** *adj.* —**wield′er,** *n.*

wield·y (wēl′dĭ), *adj.* readily managed.

wie·ner (wē′nər), *n. U.S.* a variety of sausage. Also, **wie·ner·wurst** (wē′nər wûrst′).

Wie·ner schnit·zel (vē′nər shnĭt′səl), a breaded veal cutlet, variously seasoned or garnished.

Wies·ba·den (vēs′bä′dən), *n.* a city in W Germany: health resort; mineral springs. 170,354.

wife (wīf), *n.*, *pl.* **wives** (wīvz). a woman joined in marriage to a man as husband. —**wife′ly,** *adj.* —**wife′hood,** *n.* —**wife′dom,** *n.* —**wife′-less,** *adj.* —**wife′less·ness,** *n.*

wig (wĭg), *n.*, *v.*, **wigged, wigging.** —*n.* **1.** an artificial covering of hair for the head, worn to conceal baldness, for disguise, etc. —*v.t.*, *v.i.* **2.** to furnish with a wig or wigs. **3.** *Brit. Colloq.* to scold. —**wigged,** *adj.* —**wig′less,** *adj.* —**wig′-like′,** *adj.*

wig·eon (wĭj′ən), *n.* widgeon.

Wig·gin (wĭg′ĭn), *n.* **Kate Douglas,** 1856–1923, U.S. author of children's books.

wig·ging (wĭg′ĭng), *n. Brit. Colloq.* a scolding or reproof.

wig·gle (wĭg′əl), *v.*, **-gled, -gling,** *n.* —*v.i.* **1.** to move or go with short, quick, irregular movements from side to side; wriggle. —*v.t.* **2.** to cause to wiggle. —*n.* **3.** a wiggling movement or course. **4.** a wiggly line. —**wig′gler,** *n.* —**wig′gly,** *adj.*

Wig·gles·worth (wĭg′əlz wûrth′), *n.* **Michael,** 1631–1705, American theologian and author, born in England.

wight (wīt), *n. Archaic or Dial.* a person.

Wight (wīt), *n.* **Isle of,** an island off the S coast of England. 88,000 pop.; 147 sq. mi.

wig·wag (wĭg′wăg′), *v.*, **-wagged, -wagging,** *n.* —*v.t.*, *v.i.* **1.** to signal by flags or the like waved according to a code. —*n.* **2.** signaling by flags or the like. **3.** a message so signaled. —**wig′wag′ger,** *n.*

wig·wam (wĭg′wŏm, -wôm), *n.* an American Indian hut or lodge, of poles overlaid with bark, etc.

wik·i·up (wĭk′ĭ ŭp′), *n.* wickiup.

Wil·ber·force (wĭl′bər fōrs′), *n.* **William,** 1759–1833, British statesman, philanthropist, and religious writer.

Wil·cox (wĭl′kŏks), *n.* **Ella Wheeler,** 1850–1919, U.S. poet.

wild (wīld), *adj.* **1.** living or growing in a state of nature or without cultivation. **2.** uninhabited, or waste, as land. **3.** uncivilized or barbarous, as savages. **4.** violent; furious. **5.** frantic; violently excited; unrestrained. **6.** extravagant or fantastic. **7.** disorderly or disheveled. **8.** wide of the mark. **9.** *Cards.* (of a card) having its value decided by the wishes of the player. —*adv.* **10.** wildly. —*n.* **11.** an uncultivated, uninhabited, or desolate region or tract. —**wild′ly,** *adv.* —**wild′ness,** *n.*

wild boar, a wild Old World swine, the supposed original of most of the domestic hogs.

wild·cat (wīld′kăt′), *n.*, *adj.*, *v.*, **-catted, -cat·ting.** —*n.* **1.** any of several North American felines of the genus *Lynx.* **2.** any of certain other felines. **3.** *U.S. Colloq.* a single locomotive, with its tender, operating alone. **4.** an exploratory well drilled in an effort to discover deposits of oil or gas. **5.** a reckless or unsound enterprise. —*adj.* **6.** characterized by or proceeding from reckless or unsafe business methods. **7.** running apart from the regular schedule, as a train. —*v.i.*, *v.t.* **8.** to search for oil, ore, or the like, independently. —wild′cat′ting, *n.*, *adj.*

wildcat bank, *U.S. Colloq.* a bank which issued notes without adequate security, in the period before the establishment of the national banking system in 1864.

wildcat strike, a labor strike not sanctioned by the union.

wild·cat·ter (wīld′kăt′ər), *n.* *U.S. Colloq.* one who prospects for oil or ores or takes other ventures; a prospector.

Wilde (wīld), *n.* **Oscar Fingal O'Flahertie Wills,** 1856–1900, British writer.

wil·de·beest (wīl′də bēst′), *n.* gnu.

wil·der (wīl′dər), *Archaic or Poetic.* —*v.t.* **1.** to cause to lose one's way. **2.** to bewilder. —*v.i.* **3.** to lose one's way. **4.** to be bewildered. —wil′der·ment, *n.*

Wil·der (wīl′dər), *n.* **Thornton (Niven),** born 1897, U.S. novelist and playwright.

wil·der·ness (wīl′dər nĭs), *n.* **1.** a wild or desolate region, as of forest or desert; a waste. **2.** a bewildering mass or collection.

Wil·der·ness (wīl′dər nĭs), *n.* a wooded area in NE Virginia: battle between Grant and Lee, 1864.

wild-eyed (wīld′īd′), *adj.* glaring in an angry or wild manner.

wild·fire (wīld′fīr′), *n.* **1.** a highly inflammable composition, formerly used in warfare. **2.** anything that runs or spreads with extraordinary rapidity. **3.** sheet lightning. **4.** the will-o'-the-wisp.

wild flower, 1. the flower of a plant not anywhere in cultivation. **2.** such a plant. Also, **wild′flow′er.**

wild fowl, the birds ordinarily sought as game, esp. ducks, geese, and the like. Also, **wild′fowl′.** —wild′-fowl′er, *n.* —wild′-fowl′ing, *n.*, *adj.*

wild-goose chase, 1. a wild or absurd chase, as after something as erratic in its course as a wild goose. **2.** any senseless pursuit of an object or end.

wild oat, 1. any uncultivated species of a common grass resembling the cultivated oat. **2. sow one's wild oats,** to live a hectic, dissolute youth.

wild pansy, the common pansy in a wild state, varying between an inconspicuous field weed and showy varieties.

wild rose, any native species of rose, usually having a single flower with the corolla consisting of one circle of roundish spreading petals.

wild West, the western frontier region of the U.S., before the establishment of stable government.

wild·wood (wīld′wŏŏd′), *n.* a forest.

wile (wīl), *n.*, *v.*, **wiled, wiling.** —*n.* **1.** artifice, stratagem, or cunning. —*v.t.* **2.** to pass (time). **3.** to entice.

wil·ful (wĭl′fəl), *adj.* willful.

Wil·hel·mi·na I (wĭl′ə mē′nə), born 1880, queen of The Netherlands, 1890 until abdication in 1948.

Wil·helms·ha·ven (vĭl′hĕlms hä′fən), *n.* a seaport on the North Sea in NW Germany. 118,193.

Wilkes (wĭlks), *n.* **1. Charles,** 1798–1877, U.S. rear admiral and explorer. **2. John,** 1727–97, British politician, journalist, and writer.

Wilkes-Bar·re (wĭlks′băr′ĭ), *n.* a city in E Pennsylvania. 86,236.

Wil·kins (wĭl′kĭnz), *n.* **Sir George Hubert,** born 1888, Australian antarctic explorer, aviator, and aerial navigator.

will[1] (wĭl), *auxiliary.* **1.** am about or going to. **2.** am (is, are, etc.) disposed or willing to. **3.** am expected or required to. **4.** may be expected or supposed to. **5.** am determined or sure to (used emphatically). **6.** am accustomed to, or do usually or often. —*v.t.*, *v.i.* **7.** to wish; desire; like.

will[2] (wĭl), *n.*, *v.*, **willed, willing.** —*n.* **1.** the

faculty of conscious and esp. of deliberate action. **2.** power of choosing or determining one's own actions. **3.** the process of willing, or volition. **4.** wish, desire, or pleasure. **5.** disposition (good or ill) toward another. **6.** *Law.* **a.** a legal declaration of a person's wishes as to the disposition of his (real) property, etc., after his death. **b.** the document containing such a declaration. —*v.t.* **7.** to decide, determine on, or elect by act of will. **8.** to give by will or testament. **9.** to influence by exerting will power. —*v.i.* **10.** to exercise the will. **11.** to determine, as by act of will. —willed, *adj.* —will′er, *n.*

will·a·ble (wĭl′ə bəl), *adj.* capable of being willed, or fixed by will.

Wil·lam·ette (wĭ lăm′ĭt), *n.* a river flowing N through NW Oregon into the Columbia river at Portland. ab. 250 mi.

Wil·lard (wĭl′ərd), *n.* **1. Emma,** 1787–1870, U.S. educator. **2. Frances Elizabeth,** 1839–98, U.S. educator, writer, and temperance advocator.

Wil·lem·stad (wĭl′əm stät′), *n.* a seaport in and the capital of Curaçao colony in the Dutch West Indies, on the island of Curaçao. 37,200.

will·ful (wĭl′fəl), *adj.* **1.** voluntary or intentional. **2.** headstrong; perversely obstinate. —will′ful·ly, *adv.* —will′ful·ness, *n.*

Wil·liam I (wĭl′yəm), (*William the Conqueror*) king of England, 1066–87: first king of Norman line.

William II, (*William Rufus, William the Red*) 1056?–1100, king of England, 1087–1100 (son of William I).

William III, (*Prince of Orange*) 1650–1702, king of Great Britain and Ireland, 1689–1702 (successor and nephew of James II, and husband of Mary II). Also, **William of Orange.**

William IV, 1765–1837, king of Great Britain and Ireland, 1830–37 (brother of George IV).

Wil·liams (wĭl′yəmz), *n.* **Roger,** c1603–83, British clergyman and colonist in Rhode Island.

Wil·liams·burg (wĭl′yəmz bûrg′), *n.* a city in SE Virginia: its colonial capital; now restored as it was in pre-Revolutionary times. 3942.

Wil·liams·port (wĭl′yəmz pōrt′), *n.* a city in central Pennsylvania. 44,355.

William Tell (tĕl), a legendary Swiss patriot.

will·ing (wĭl′ĭng), *adj.* **1.** disposed or consenting. **2.** done, given, used, etc., with cheerful readiness. —will′ing·ly, *adv.* —will′ing·ness, *n.*

Will·kie (wĭl′kĭ), *n.* **Wendell Lewis** (wĕn′dəl), 1892–1944, U.S. political leader.

will-o'-the-wisp (wĭl′ə ŧ͟hə wĭsp′), *n.* **1.** a flitting phosphorescent light seen at night, chiefly over marshy ground. **2.** anything that deludes or misleads by luring on.

wil·low (wĭl′ō), *n.* **1.** any of certain trees or shrubs, many species of which have tough, pliable twigs or branches used for wickerwork, etc. **2.** the wood. —wil′low·like′, *adj.*

willow pattern, a pattern used in china, employing the design of the willow tree, and originated in approximately 1780 by Thomas Turner in England.

wil·low·ware (wĭl′ō wâr′), *n.* china using the willow pattern.

wil·low·y (wĭl′ō ĭ), *adj.* **1.** gracefully slender and supple. **2.** abounding with willows.

will power, control of one's impulses and actions.

wil·ly-nil·ly (wĭl′ĭ nĭl′ĭ), *adv.* **1.** willingly or unwillingly. —*adj.* **2.** vacillating.

Wil·ming·ton (wĭl′mĭng tən), *n.* **1.** a seaport in N Delaware. 112,504. **2.** a seaport in SE North Carolina. 33,407.

Wil·son (wĭl′sən), *n.* **(Thomas) Woodrow,** 1856–1924, 28th president of the U.S., 1913–21.

Wilson Dam, a power dam on the Tennessee river, in NW Alabama, at Muscle Shoals: a part of the Tennessee Valley Authority. ab. 4600 ft. long; 137 ft. high.

wilt (wĭlt), *v.i.*, *v.t.* **1.** to become or make limp and drooping; wither. —*n.* **2.** act of wilting. **3.** state of being wilted.

Wil·ton carpet (wĭl′tən), a kind of carpet, woven on a Jacquard loom like Brussels carpet, but having the loops cut to form a velvet pile. Also, **Wilton.**

wil·y (wī′lĭ), *adj.*, **wilier, wiliest.** full of, marked by, or proceeding from wiles; crafty; cunning. —wil′i·ly, *adv.* —wil′i·ness, *n.*

Wim·ble·don (wĭm′bəl dən), *n.* a city in SE

England, near London: international tennis meets. 56,160.

wim·ple (wĭm′pəl), *n., v.,* **-pled, -pling.** —*n.* **1.** a woman's headcloth drawn in folds about the chin, worn by nuns. —*v.t.,* *v.i.* **2.** to muffle with a wimple. **3.** to ripple, as water.

win (wĭn), *v.,* **won** or (*Obs.*) **wan; won; winning;** *n.* —*v.i.* **1.** to succeed by striving or effort. **2.** to gain the victory. —*v.t.* **3.** to get by effort, as through labor, competition, or conquest. **4.** to gain (a prize, fame, victory, etc.). **5.** to persuade. **6.** to persuade to love or marriage. —*n.* **7.** *Colloq.* an act of winning; a success; a victory.

wince (wĭns), *v.,* **winced, wincing,** *n.* —*v.i.* **1.** to shrink, as in pain or from a blow; flinch. —*n.* **2.** a wincing movement. —**winc′er,** *n.*

winch (wĭnch), *n.* **1.** the crank or handle of a revolving machine. **2.** a windlass turned by a crank.

Win·ches·ter (wĭn′chĕs′tər, wĭn′chĭs tər), *n.* a city in S England: cathedral; capital of the early Wessex kingdom and of medieval England. 25,-500.

Winchester rifle, a type of magazine rifle, first made in about 1866.

wind[1] (*n.* wĭnd, *Poetic* wīnd; *v.* wĭnd), *n.* **1.** air in motion. **2.** a gale or storm. **3.** gas generated in the stomach and bowels. **4.** a wind instrument or wind instruments collectively. **5.** animal odor. **6.** breath or breathing. **7.** a hint or intimation. **8.** empty talk. —*v.t.* **9.** to expose to wind. **10.** to follow by the scent. **11.** to make short of breath. **12.** to let recover breath, as by resting. —**wind′less,** *adj.*

wind[2] (wīnd), *v.,* **wound** or (*Rare*) **winded; winding;** *n.* —*v.i.* **1.** to change direction; take or have a frequently bending course. **2.** to proceed circuitously or indirectly. —*v.t.* **3.** to encircle or wreathe. **4.** to roll or coil (thread, etc.) into a ball or the like. **5.** to twine or wrap about something. **6.** to adjust for operation by some turning process. **7.** to make (one's or its way) in a winding course or by indirect or insidious procedure. —*n.* **8.** a winding; a bend or turn. —**wind′er,** *n.*

wind[3] (wīnd, wĭnd), *v.t.,* **winded** or **wound, winding.** to blow (a horn, etc.); signal by blowing.

wind·a·ble (wīn′də bəl), *adj.* that can be wound.

wind·age (wĭn′dĭj), *n.* **1.** the influence of the wind in deflecting a missile. **2.** the amount of such deflection.

wind·bag (wĭnd′băg′), *n.* *Slang.* an empty, voluble, pretentious talker.

wind-blown (wĭnd′blōn′), *adj.* **1.** blown by the wind. **2.** (of trees) growing in a certain shape because of strong prevailing winds. **3.** bobbed short, with the ends of the hair combed toward the forehead.

wind-borne (wĭnd′bôrn′), *adj.* carried by the wind, as pollen or seed.

wind·break (wĭnd′brāk′), *n.* anything serving as a shelter from the wind.

wind·break·er (wĭnd′brā′kər), *n.* **1.** a kind of short jacket of suede or chamois leather or the like, with close-fitting elastic hip band, cuffs, and (often) collar, for sports or other outdoor wear. **2.** (*cap.*) a trade name for such a jacket.

wind-bro·ken (wĭnd′brō′kən), *adj.* (of horses, etc.) having the breathing impaired; affected with heaves.

wind·ed (wĭn′dĭd), *adj.* **1.** having wind or breath. **2.** out of breath. —**wind′ed·ness,** *n.*

wind·fall (wĭnd′fôl′), *n.* **1.** something blown down by the wind. **2.** unexpected good fortune.

wind gap, a cut that indents only the upper part of a mountain ridge.

wind·ing (wĭn′dĭng), *n.* **1.** act of one that winds. **2.** a bend or turn. **3.** something wound or coiled. **4.** *Elect.* a symmetrically laid, electrically conducting current path in any device. —*adj.* **5.** bending, turning, or spiral. —**wind′ing·ly,** *adv.*

winding sheet, a sheet in which a corpse is wrapped for burial.

wind instrument (wĭnd), a musical instrument sounded by the player's breath or by artificial wind.

wind·jam·mer (wĭnd′jăm′ər), *n.* *Colloq.* any vessel propelled wholly by sails.

wind·lass (wĭnd′ləs), *n.* a device for raising weights, etc., usually consisting of a horizontal cylinder turned by a crank, lever, or the like,

upon which a cable or the like winds, the outer end of the cable being attached to the thing to be moved.

wind·mill (wĭnd′mĭl′, wĭn′-), *n.* **1.** a mill or machine, as for grinding or pumping, operated by the wind acting on a set of arms, vanes, sails, or slats attached to a horizontal axis so as to form a vertical revolving wheel. **2.** the wheel itself.

win·dow (wĭn′dō), *n.* an opening in the wall or roof of a building, etc., for the admission of air or light, or both, commonly fitted with a frame containing panes of glass. —**win′dow·less,** *adj.*

window box, 1. one of the vertical hollows at the sides of the frame of a window, for the weights counterbalancing a sliding sash. **2.** a box for growing plants, placed at or in a window.

window dresser, a person employed to dress the windows of a store, or arrange in them attractive displays of goods for sale.

window dressing, the action or work of a window dresser.

win·dow·pane (wĭn′dō pān′), *n.* a plate of glass used in a window.

window sash, the frame holding the pane or panes of a window.

window seat, a seat built beneath the sill of a recessed or other window.

window shade, a shade or blind for a window.

win·dow-shop (wĭn′dō shŏp′), *v.i.,* **-shopped, -shopping.** to look at instead of buying. —**win′dow-shop′per,** *n.* —**win′dow-shop′-ping,** *adj., n.*

wind·pipe (wĭnd′pīp′), *n.* the trachea.

wind-pol·li·nat·ed (wĭnd′pŏl′ə nā′tĭd), *adj.* *Bot.* pollinated by air-borne pollen. —**wind′-pol′li·na′tion,** *n.*

Wind River Range, a range of the Rocky Mountains in W Wyoming. Highest peak, Gannett Peak, 13,785 ft.

wind rose, *Meteorol.* a diagram which shows for a given locality or area the frequency and strength of the wind from various directions.

wind·row (wĭnd′rō′, wĭn′-), *n.* a row or line, as of hay or leaves raked together to dry or swept together by the wind.

wind scale, a numerical scale, like the Beaufort scale, for designating relative wind intensities.

wind shake, 1. a flaw in wood supposed to be caused by the action of strong winds upon the trunk of the tree. **2.** such flaws collectively.

wind-shak·en (wĭnd′shā′kən), *adj.* **1.** affected by wind shake. **2.** shaken by the wind.

wind·shield (wĭnd′shēld′), *n.* *Auto.* a framed shield of glass above and across the dashboard.

Wind·sor (wĭn′zər), *n.* **1.** the royal house of England since 1917. It comprises the Kings George V, Edward VIII and George VI. **2.** Duke of. See **Edward VIII. 3.** Also, **New Windsor.** a city in S England, in Berkshire, on the Thames: the site of **Windsor Castle,** a residence of English sovereigns since William the Conqueror. **4.** a city in SE Canada, in Ontario, opposite Detroit, Michigan. With suburbs, 121,112.

Windsor chair, a wooden chair of many varieties, having a spindle back and legs slanting outward; common in eighteenth century England and American colonies.

Windsor tie, a wide, soft silk necktie in a loose bow.

wind·storm (wĭnd′stôrm′), *n.* a storm with heavy wind, but little or no precipitation.

wind-swept (wĭnd′swĕpt′), *adj.* open or exposed to the wind.

wind·tight (wĭnd′tīt′), *adj.* so tight as to prevent passage of wind or air.

wind-up (wīnd′ŭp′), *n.* **1.** the end or close. **2.** *Baseball.* the preparatory movements of the arm before delivering a pitched ball.

wind vane, a device using a pivoted arm with a vertical vane to indicate the direction of the wind.

wind·ward (wĭnd′wərd; *Naut.* wĭn′dərd), *adj.* **1.** pertaining to, situated in, or moving toward the quarter from which the wind blows. —*n.* **2.** the point or quarter from which the wind blows. —*adv.* **3.** toward the wind.

Windward Islands, 1. an island group in the West Indies, comprising the S part of the Lesser Antilles. **2.** a British possession in this island group, comprising the colonies of Dominica, Grenada, St. Lucia, and St. Vincent. 272,000 pop.; 821 sq. mi. *Cap.:* St. George's.

wind·y (wĭn′dĭ), *adj.*, **windier, windiest. 1.** characterized by wind. **2.** swept by the wind. **3.** consisting of or resembling wind. **4.** windward. **5.** voluble. —**wind′i·ly**, *adv.* —**wind′i·ness**, *n.*

wine (wīn), *n.*, *v.*, **wined, wining. —*n.* 1.** the fermented juice of the grape, used as a beverage and in cookery, religious rites, etc. **2.** the juice, fermented or unfermented, of various other fruits or plants. **3.** a dark-reddish color. **4.** something that invigorates, cheers, or intoxicates like wine. —*v.t.* **5.** to entertain with wine.

wine cellar, 1. a cellar for the storage of wine. **2.** the wine stored there; a store or stock of wines.

wine color, color of (red) wine; dark purplish red; deep carmine. —**wine′-col′ored**, *adj.*

wine gallon, *Brit.* a former gallon of 231 cu. in., equal to the present U.S. standard gallon.

wine·glass (wīn′glăs′, -gläs′), *n.* a small drinking glass for wine.

wine·glass·ful (wīn′glăs fŏŏl′, -gläs-), *n.*, *pl.* -fuls. the capacity of a wineglass, commonly considered as equal to 2 fluid ounces or ¹/₄ cup.

wine·grow·er (wīn′grō′ər), *n.* one who owns or works in a vineyard and winery.

wine·grow·ing (wīn′grō′ĭng), *n.* act or business of a winegrower.

wine press, a machine in which the juice is pressed from grapes for wine. Also, **wine presser.**

win·er·y (wī′nə rĭ′), *n.*, *pl.* -eries. an establishment for making wine.

Wine·sap (wīn′săp′), *n.* a long-keeping, red, winter apple of the U.S.

wine·shop (wīn′shŏp′), *n.* a shop where wine is sold.

wing (wĭng), *n.* **1.** either of the two anterior extremities of most birds and of bats, adapted for flight or aerial locomotion. **2.** either of two corresponding but functionless parts in certain other birds, as ostriches. **3.** any winglike structure. **4.** one of the thin, flat, movable, lateral extensions by means of which the insects fly. **5.** a similar structure with which gods, angels, demons, etc., are conceived to be provided for the purpose of flying. **6.** a means or instrument of flight, travel, or progress. **7.** protection or care. **8.** act or manner of flying. **9.** flight; departure. **10.** *Aeron.* **a.** that portion of a main supporting surface confined to one side of an airplane. **b.** a winglike structure; plane. **11.** *Archit.* a projecting or subordinate part of a building. **12.** *U.S.* an administrative and tactical Air Force unit. **13.** (*pl.*) *Mil.*, *Colloq.* the insignia or emblem worn by a flier. **14.** *Theat.* the platform or space on the right or left of the stage. **15.** a group within a political party. —*v.t.* **16.** to equip with wings or with a winglike part. **17.** to transport on wings. **18.** to traverse in flight. **19.** to wound or disable in the wing or (*Colloq.*, of a person) in a nonvital part. —*v.i.* **20.** to fly. —**wing′like′**, *adj.* —**wing′less**, *adj.*

wing and wing, *Naut.* with a sail extended on each side by a boom, as a schooner sailing with the foresail out on one side and the mainsail out on the other.

wing back formation, *Am. Football.* **1.** **single wing back formation**, an offensive arrangement in which one of the backfield is put outside of and behind the end. **2.** **double wing back formation**, two backs so arranged behind each end.

wing chair, a large upholstered chair, with winglike parts projecting from the back above the arms.

winged (wĭngd *or, esp. Poetic.*, wĭng′ĭd), *adj.* **1.** having wings or winglike parts. **2.** moving or passing on or as if on wings. **3.** disabled in the wing or in a nonvital part.

wing-foot·ed (wĭng′fŏŏt′ĭd), *adj. Poetic.* having winged feet; rapid; swift.

wing·spread (wĭng′sprĕd′), *n.* the distance between the most outward tips of the wings.

wink (wĭngk), *v.i.*, *v.t.* **1.** to close and open (the eyes) quickly; blink. **2.** to close and open (one eye) quickly as a hint or signal. **3.** to be purposely blind to a thing. **4.** to twinkle. —*n.* **5.** act of winking. **6.** a winking movement, esp. of one eye. **7.** an instant. **8.** **forty winks**, a short nap. **9.** twinkle. —**wink′er**, *n.*

Win·ne·pe·sau·kee (wĭn′ə pə sô′kĭ′), *n.* Lake, a lake in central New Hampshire: summer resort. 25 mi. long.

win·ner (wĭn′ər), *n.* one who or that which wins.

win·ning (wĭn′ĭng), *n.* **1.** act of one that wins. **2.** (*usually pl.*) that which is won. —*adj.* **3.** that wins. **4.** taking, engaging, or charming. —**win′ning·ly**, *adv.*

winning gallery, *Court Tennis.* the opening that is farthest from the spectator's gallery (so named because any ball struck into it is called a winning ball).

winning post, a post on a racecourse, forming the goal of a race.

Win·ni·peg (wĭn′ə pĕg′), *n.* a city in S Canada: the capital of Manitoba. With suburbs, 290,-540.

win·now (wĭn′ō), *v.t.*, *v.i.* **1.** to free (grain, etc.) from chaff, refuse particles, etc., by means of wind or driven air; fan. **2.** to separate or distinguish. **3.** to flutter. —*n.* **4.** a device for winnowing grain, etc. **5.** act of winnowing. —**win′now·er**, *n.*

Wins·low (wĭnz′lō), *n.* Edward, 1595–1655, British colonist and governor of the Plymouth colony.

win·some (wĭn′səm), *adj.* engaging or charming. —**win′some·ly**, *adv.* —**win′some·ness**, *n.*

Win·ston-Sa·lem (wĭn′stən sā′ləm), *n.* a city in N North Carolina. 79,815.

win·ter (wĭn′tər), *n.* **1.** the last and the coldest season of the year. **2.** a period of decline, decay, adversity, etc. —*adj.* **3.** of, pertaining to, or characteristic of winter. —*v.i.* **4.** to spend or pass the winter. **5.** to keep during the winter, as plants or cattle. —**win′ter·er**, *n.* —**win′ter·less**, *adj.*

win·ter·ber·ry (wĭn′tər bĕr′ĭ), *n.*, *pl.* -ries. any of several North American species of holly with red berries that are persistent through the winter.

win·ter·bourne (wĭn′tər bôrn′, -bŏŏrn′), *n.* a channel filled only at a time of excessive rainfall.

win·ter·green (wĭn′tər grēn′), *n.* **1.** a small, creeping evergreen shrub of eastern North America, with aromatic leaves which yield oil of wintergreen. **2.** something flavored with this oil.

win·ter·kill (wĭn′tər kĭl′), *v.t.*, *v.i.* *U.S.* to kill by or die from exposure to the cold of winter, as wheat. —**win′ter·kill′ing**, *adj.*, *n.*

winter lambs, well-fed lambs born in the fall or early winter and sold prior to May 20.

win·ter·time (wĭn′tər tīm′), *n.* the season of winter. Also, *Poetic*, **win·ter·tide** (wĭn′tər tīd′).

Win·throp (wĭn′thrŏp), *n.* **1.** John, 1588–1649, governor of the colony of Massachusetts. **2.** his son, John, 1606–76, governor of the colony of Connecticut.

win·try (wĭn′trĭ), *adj.*, **-trier, -triest. 1.** of, pertaining to, or characteristic of winter. **2.** having the season or cold of winter. Also, **win·ter·y** (wĭn′tə rĭ′, -trĭ). —**win′tri·ness**, *n.*

win·y (wī′nĭ), *adj.* **1.** of the nature of or resembling wine. **2.** pertaining to or characteristic of wine. **3.** affected by wine.

wipe (wīp), *v.*, **wiped, wiping.** —*v.t.* **1.** to rub lightly with or on a cloth, paper, etc., in order to clean or dry. **2.** to remove as if by rubbing; blot (out). **3.** to rub or draw over a surface, as in cleaning or drying. —*n.* **4.** act of wiping. **5.** a rub, as of one thing over another. **6.** *Colloq. or Dial.* a sweeping blow. —**wip′er**, *n.*

wire (wīr), *n.*, *adj.*, *v.*, **wired, wiring.** —*n.* **1.** a piece of slender, flexible metal of varying thickness. **2.** such pieces as a material. **3.** a long wire or cable used in a telegraph, telephone, or cable system. **4.** *Colloq.* a telegram. **5.** *Colloq.* the telegraphic system. **6.** *Pol.* secret means of directing the action of others. **7.** a metallic string of a musical instrument. —*adj.* **8.** made of, consisting of, or constructed with wires. —*v.t.* **9.** to furnish or bind with wire. **10.** to install an electric system of wiring, as for lighting, etc. **11.** *Colloq.* to send (a telegraphic message) (to). **12.** to snare by means of a wire or wires. —*v.i.* **13.** *Colloq.* to telegraph. —**wire′like′**, *adj.*

wire cloth, a texture of wires of moderate fineness, used for strainers, or in the manufacture of paper, etc.

wire·danc·er (wīr′dăn′sər, -dän′-), *n.* one who dances or performs other feats upon a high wire. —**wire′danc′ing**, *n.*

wire·draw (wīr′drô′), *v.t.*, **-drew, -drawn, -drawing. 1.** to draw (metal) out into wire, esp. by pulling forcibly through a series of holes gradually decreasing in diameter. **2.** to draw out to great length, in quantity or time; stretch out to excess. **3.** to strain unwarrantably, as in meaning. —**wire′draw′er,** *n.* —**wire′draw′ing,** *n.*

wire gauge, a gauge calibrated for standard wire diameters.

wire gauze, a gauzelike texture woven of very fine wires.

wire glass, glass having wire netting embedded within it, as to increase its strength.

wire-hair (wīr′hâr′), *n.* a fox terrier having a wiry coat. Also, **wire′-haired′ terrier.**

wire-less (wīr′lĭs), *adj.* **1.** having no wire. **2.** denoting or pertaining to any of various devices which are operated with or set in action by electromagnetic waves. **3.** *Chiefly Brit.* radio. —*n.* **4.** wireless telegraphy or telephony. **5.** a wireless telegraph or telephone or the like. **6.** a wireless message. **7.** *Chiefly Brit.* radio. —*v.t., v.i.* **8.** to telegraph or telephone by wireless.

wireless telegraphy, telegraphy in which there are no connecting wires, the signals being transmitted by the radiated energy of electromagnetic waves.

wireless telephone, a telephone in which the signal is transmitted by wireless telegraphy.

wireless telephony, a system of transmitting and exchanging voice messages by means of radio.

wire-pho-to (wīr′fō′tō), *n.* *Trademark.* a method of sending photographs by wire.

wire-pull-ing (wīr′pŏŏl′ĭng), *n.* **1.** act of pulling the wires, as of puppets. **2.** *Colloq.* the guiding and controlling of any body of persons, esp. a political party, by underhand influence or management. —**wire′pull′er,** *n.*

wire recorder, *Electronics.* a device to record sound on a steel wire by magnetizing it as it passes an electromagnet, the sound being reproduced by the motion of the wire past a receiver.

wire rope, a rope with strands of wire.

wire tapper, one who illicitly taps wires to learn the nature of messages passing over them. —**wire tapping.**

wir-ing (wīr′ĭng), *n.* *Elect.* the aggregate of wires in a lighting system, switchboard, radio, etc.

wir-ra (wĭr′ə), *interj.* *Irish.* an exclamation of sorrow or lament.

wir-y (wīr′ĭ), *adj.,* **wirier, wiriest. 1.** of, resembling, or produced by wire. **2.** lean and sinewy. —**wir′i-ly,** *adv.* —**wir′i-ness,** *n.*

wis (wĭs), *v.t.* *Archaic.* to know.

Wis-con-sin (wĭs kŏn′sən), *n.* a State in the N central U.S. 3,168,158 pop.; 56,154 sq. mi. *Cap.:* Madison. *Abbr.:* **Wis.** or **Wisc.**

wis-dom (wĭz′dəm), *n.* **1.** knowledge of what is true or right coupled with just judgment as to action; sagacity. **2.** scholarly knowledge. **3.** wise sayings or teachings. **4.** a wise act or saying.

Wisdom of Solomon, a book of the Apocrypha, on wisdom and its relation to righteousness.

wisdom tooth, the third molar tooth: the last tooth to erupt.

wise[1] (wīz), *adj.,* **wiser, wisest. 1.** having the power of discerning and judging properly as to what is true or right. **2.** judicious or prudent. **3.** learned. **4.** having information as to facts, circumstances, etc. **5.** *Slang.* aware or cognizant. —**wise′ly,** *adv.*

wise[2] (wīz), *n.* **1.** way of proceeding. **2.** respect; degree.

-wise, a suffixal use of **wise**[2] in adverbs denoting manner, direction, position, etc., as in *anywise, edgewise, sidewise.*

wise-a-cre (wĭz′ā′kər, wĭ′zə kər), *n.* one who affects to possess great wisdom.

wise-crack (wīz′krăk′), *Slang.* —*n.* **1.** a smart or facetious remark. —*v.i.* **2.** to make wisecracks. —**wise′crack′er,** *n.*

wish (wĭsh), *v.t., v.i.* **1.** to want; desire; long for. **2.** to desire (a person or thing) to be (as specified). **3.** to entertain wishes, favorably or otherwise (for). **4.** to bid, as in greeting or leave-taking. **5.** to command, force, impose. —*n.* **6.** a desire, felt or expressed. **7.** an expression of a wish. **8.** that which is wished. —**wish′er,** *n.* —**wish′-ful,** *adj.* —**wish′ful-ly,** *adv.* —**wish′ful-ness,** *n.*

wish-bone (wĭsh′bōn′), *n.* the forked bone in front of the breastbone in most birds.

wish-y-wash-y (wĭsh′ĭ wŏsh′ĭ, -wôsh′ĭ), *adj.* thin and weak.

wisp (wĭsp), *n.* **1.** a handful or small tuft, etc.

2. a will-o′-the-wisp. —*v.t.* **3.** to twist into a wisp. —**wisp′like′,** *adj.* —**wisp′y,** *adj.*

Wiss-ler (wĭs′lər), *n.* **Clark,** born 1870, U.S. anthropologist.

Wis-ter (wĭs′tər), *n.* **Owen,** 1860–1938, U.S. author.

wis-te-ri-a (wĭs tēr′ĭ ə), *n.* any of certain leguminous climbing shrubs, with pendent racemes of purple flowers. Also, **wis-tar-i-a** (wĭs târ′ĭ ə).

wist-ful (wĭst′fəl), *adj.* **1.** pensive or melancholy. **2.** showing longing tinged with melancholy. —**wist′ful-ly,** *adv.* —**wist′ful-ness,** *n.*

wit[1] (wĭt), *n.* **1.** the perception and expression of those connections between ideas which awaken pleasure and amusement. **2.** a person endowed with such wit. **3.** understanding, intelligence, or sagacity. **4.** (*pl.*) mental abilities, faculties, or senses.

wit[2] (wĭt), *v.t., v.i.* **1.** *Archaic.* to know. **2.** to wit, namely.

witch (wĭch), *n.* **1.** a person, now esp. a woman, who is supposed to practice magic; a sorceress. **2.** an ugly old woman. —*v.t.* **3.** to affect by or as by witchcraft. —**witch′like′,** *adj.*

witch-craft (wĭch′krăft′, -kräft′), *n.* **1.** sorcery; magic. **2.** magical influence; witchery.

witch doctor, a medicine man, esp. among the Kaffirs and other African peoples.

witch-er-y (wĭch′ə rĭ), *n., pl.* **-eries. 1.** witchcraft; magic. **2.** fascination; charm.

witch hazel, 1. a shrub of eastern North America, whose bark and leaves afford a preparation used for inflammation, bruises, etc. **2.** this preparation.

witch-ing (wĭch′ĭng), *n.* **1.** the use of witchcraft. **2.** fascination. —*adj.* **3.** magical. **4.** enchanting. —**witch′ing-ly,** *adv.*

wit-e-na-ge-mot (wĭt′ə nə gə mōt′), *n.* *Early English Hist.* the national council attended by the king, aldermen, bishops, and nobles.

with (wĭth̸, wĭth), *prep.* **1.** accompanied by. **2.** in some particular relation to. **3.** having. **4.** by the use of. **5.** using or showing. **6.** in proportion to. **7.** in regard to. **8.** owing to. **9.** in the region, sphere, or view of. **10.** from. **11.** against, as in opposition or competition. **12.** in the keeping or service of.

with-al (wĭth̸ ôl′, wĭth-), *adv., prep.* *Archaic.* besides.

with-draw (wĭth̸ drô′, wĭth-), *v.t., v.i.,* **-drew, -drawn, -drawing. 1.** to draw back; remove. **2.** to retract. —**with-draw′al, with-draw′ment,** *n.*

withe (wĭth, wĭth̸, wĭth), *n., v.,* **withed, withing.** —*n.* **1.** any tough, flexible twig or stem for binding things together. **2.** an elastic handle for a tool. —*v.t.* **3.** to bind with withes.

with-er (wĭth̸′ər), *v.i.* **1.** to shrivel; fade; decay. —*v.t.* **2.** to cause to lose freshness, vigor, etc. **3.** to abash. —**with′er-ing-ly,** *adv.*

With-er (wĭth̸′ər), *n.* **George,** 1588–1667, British poet. Also, **With-ers** (wĭth̸′ərz).

with-ers (wĭth̸′ərz), *n.pl.* the highest part of a horse′s or other animal′s back, behind the neck.

With-er-spoon (wĭth̸′ər spōōn′), *n.* **John,** 1723–94, American theologian: signer of the Declaration of Independence, born in Scotland.

with-hold (wĭth hōld′, wĭth̸-), *v.t., v.i.,* **-held, -holding. 1.** to hold back. **2.** to refrain from giving or granting. —**with-hold′er,** *n.*

with-in (wĭth̸ ĭn′, wĭth-), *adv.* **1.** in or into the interior or inner part; inside or indoors. **2.** internally. **3.** inwardly. —*prep.* **4.** in or into the interior of. **5.** inside of. **6.** in the compass or limits of. **7.** at some point not beyond. **8.** at or to some amount or degree not exceeding. **9.** in the course or period of. **10.** not transgressing.

with-in-doors (wĭth̸ ĭn′dôrz′, wĭth-), *adv.* into or inside the house.

with-in-named (wĭth̸ ĭn′nāmd′, wĭth̸-), *adj.* that is named herein.

with-out (wĭth̸ out′, wĭth-), *prep.* **1.** not with; lacking. **2.** excluding. **3.** outside of. **4.** beyond the compass, limits, range, or scope of. —*adv.* **5.** in or into space outside. **6.** without, or lacking, something implied or understood. **7.** as regards the outside; outwardly. **8.** *Colloq.* unless.

with-stand (wĭth stănd′, wĭth̸-), *v.t., v.i.,* **-stood, -standing.** to stand or hold out (against).

wit-less (wĭt′lĭs), *adj.* stupid; foolish. —**wit′-less-ly,** *adv.* —**wit′less-ness,** *n.*

wit-ling (wĭt′lĭng), *n.* a petty or would-be wit.

wit-ness (wĭt′nĭs), *v.t., v.i.* **1.** to see or know by personal presence and perception. 2. to testify (to). 3. to attest by one's signature. —*n.* 4. one who personally sees or perceives a thing. 5. one who gives testimony. 6. one who signs a document in attestation of its genuineness. 7. testimony. —**wit′ness·er,** *n.*

witness stand, the place occupied by one giving testimony in a court.

Wit·ten·berg (wĭt′ən bûrg′), *n.* a city in E Germany: Luther taught in the university here; beginnings of the Reformation, 1517. 37,082.

wit·ti·cism (wĭt′ə sĭz′əm), *n.* a witty remark.

wit·ting (wĭt′ĭng), *adj.* knowing; aware; conscious. —**wit′ting·ly,** *adv.*

wit·ty (wĭt′ĭ), *adj.* **-tier, -tiest.** 1. possessing or characterized by wit. 2. *Scot. and Brit. Dial.* wise; intelligent. —**wit′ti·ly,** *adv.* —**wit′ti·ness,** *n.*

Wit·wa·ters·rand (wĭt wä′tərs ränt′, -ränd′), *n.* a rocky ridge in the Union of South Africa, near Johannesburg: the richest gold fields in the world. Also, **The Rand.**

wive (wīv), *v.i., v.t.,* **wived, wiving.** to marry.

wiz·ard (wĭz′ərd), *n.* 1. a magician or sorcerer. 2. a conjurer or juggler. 3. *Colloq.* a clever person. —*adj.* 4. of or pertaining to a wizard. 5. magic. —**wiz′ard·like′,** *adj.* —**wiz′ard·ry,** *n.*

wiz·en (wĭz′ən; *Dial.* wē′zən), *Scot. and Brit. Dial.* —*v.i., v.t.* 1. to wither; shrivel; dry up. —*adj.* 2. wizened.

wiz·ened (wĭz′ənd; *Dial.* wē′zənd), *adj.* withered; shriveled.

wk., *pl.* **wks.** 1. week. 2. work.

wkly., weekly.

WNW, west-northwest. Also, **W.N.W.**

wo (wō), *n., interj.* woe.

W.O., warrant officer.

wob·ble (wŏb′əl), *v.,* **-bled, -bling,** *n.* —*v.i., v.t.* 1. to incline or move to one side and to the other alternately or unsteadily. 2. to tremble. 3. *Colloq.* to vacillate. —*n.* 4. *Colloq.* a wobbling motion. —**wob′bler,** *n.* —**wob′bly,** *adj.*

Wode·house (wŏŏd′hous), *n.* **Pelham Grenville,** born 1881, British novelist.

Wo·den (wō′dən), *n.* the chief English heathen god, identical with the Scandinavian Odin. Also, **Wo′dan.**

woe (wō), *n.* 1. grievous distress or affliction. —*interj.* 2. an exclamation of grief.

woe·be·gone (wō′bĭ gôn′, -gŏn′), *adj.* affected by woe, esp. in appearance. Also, **wo′be·gone′.**

woe·ful (wō′fəl), *adj.* 1. full of woe; wretched; unhappy. 2. affected with, characterized by, or indicating woe. 3. of wretched quality; sorry; poor. Also, **wo′ful.** —**woe′ful·ly,** *adv.* —**woe′ful·ness,** *n.*

Wof·fing·ton (wŏf′ĭng tən), *n.* **Margaret,** ("*Peg Woffington*") 1714–60, Irish actress in England.

wold (wōld), *n.* an open, elevated tract of country.

wolf (wŏŏlf), *n., pl.* **wolves** (wŏŏlvz), *v.* —*n.* 1. a large, wild carnivore of Europe, Asia, and North America, belonging to the dog family: a swift-footed, crafty, rapacious animal, destructive to game, sheep, etc. 2. the fur of such an animal. 3. a cruelly rapacious person. —*v.t.* 4. *Colloq.* to devour or swallow ravenously. —*v.i.* 5. to hunt for wolves. —**wolf′like′,** *adj.* —**wolf′ish,** *adj.* —**wolf′ish·ly,** *adv.*

wolf cub, *Brit.* a member of the junior division (8–11) of the Boy Scouts.

Wolfe (wŏŏlf), *n.* **Thomas,** 1900–1938, U.S. novelist.

Wolf-Fer·ra·ri (vôlf′fĕr rä′rē), *n.* **Ermanno,** born 1876, Italian composer.

wolf·hound (wŏŏlf′hound′), *n.* a hound of any of various breeds.

wolf·ram·ite (wŏŏl′frə mīt′, vôl′-), *n.* a heavy mineral, an important ore of tungsten. Also, **wolf·ram** (wŏŏl′frəm).

Wol·fram von Esch·en·bach (vôl′främ fən ĕsh′ən bäKH′), died 1220?, German epic poet.

wolf's-bane (wŏŏlfs′bān′), *n.* a plant of the genus *Aconitum,* esp. a yellow-flowered species. Also, **wolfs′bane′.**

Wol·sey (wŏŏl′zĭ), *n.* **Thomas,** 1475?–1530, British cardinal and statesman.

wol·ver·ine (wŏŏl′və rēn′), *n.* glutton². Also, **wol′ver·ene′.**

wom·an (wŏŏm′ən), *n., pl.* **women** (wĭm′ĭn), *adj.* —*n.* 1. the female human being (distinguished from *man*). 2. a wife. 3. feminine

nature, characteristics, or feelings. 4. a female servant. —*adj.* 5. of or pertaining to women. —**wom′an·less,** *adj.* —**wom′an·ish,** *adj.* —**wom′an·ish·ly,** *adv.* —**wom′an·ish·ness,** *n.* —**wom′an·like′,** *adj.* —**wom′an·ly,** *adj., adv.* —**wom′an·li·ness,** *n.*

wom·an·hood (wŏŏm′ən hŏŏd′), *n.* 1. womanly character. 2. women collectively.

wom·an·kind (wŏŏm′ən kīnd′), *n.* women, as distinguished from men; the female sex.

woman of the world, a woman versed in the ways and usages of the world, esp. the world of society.

woman's rights, the rights claimed for woman, equal to those of man, with respect to suffrage, property, the professional fields, etc.

woman suffrage, the right of woman to vote; female suffrage. —**wom′an-suf′frage** *adj.* —**wom′an-suf′fra·gist,** *n.*

womb (wŏŏm), *n.* 1. the uterus of the human female and some of the higher mammalian quadrupeds. 2. the place in which anything is formed or produced. 3. the interior of anything.

wom·bat (wŏm′băt), *n.* any of certain burrowing marsupials of Australia.

wom·en·folk (wĭm′ĭn fōk′), *n.pl.* 1. women in general. 2. a particular group of women. Also, **wom′en·folks′.**

won·der (wŭn′dər), *v.i., v.t.* 1. to think or speculate curiously (about). 2. to marvel (at). —*n.* 3. something strange and surprising. 4. the emotion excited by what is strange and surprising. 5. a miracle. —**won′der·er,** *n.*

won·der·ful (wŭn′dər fəl), *adj.* of a kind to excite wonder; extraordinary. —**won′der·ful·ly,** *adv.* —**won′der·ful·ness,** *n.*

won·der·ing (wŭn′dər ĭng), *adj.* expressing admiration or amazement. —**won′der·ing·ly,** *adv.*

won·der·land (wŭn′dər lănd′), *n.* 1. a land of wonders. 2. a wonderful region.

won·der·ment (wŭn′dər mənt), *n.* 1. wonder. 2. a cause or occasion of wonder.

won·der-strick·en (wŭn′dər strĭk′ən), *adj.* struck or affected with wonder. Also, **won·der-struck** (wŭn′dər strŭk′).

won·der·work·er (wŭn′dər wûr′kər), *n.* a worker or performer of wonders or marvels.

won·drous (wŭn′drəs), *Literary.* —*adj.* 1. wonderful. —*adv.* 2. remarkably. —**won′drous·ly,** *adv.* —**won′drous·ness,** *n.*

wont (wŭnt, wŏnt), *adj.* 1. accustomed; used. —*n.* 2. custom or habit.

won't (wōnt, wŭnt), contraction of *will not.*

wont·ed (wŭn′tĭd, wōn′-), *adj.* habitual. —**wont′ed·ly,** *adv.* —**wont′ed·ness,** *n.*

woo (wŏŏ), *v.t.* 1. to seek the favor of, esp. with a view to marriage. 2. to seek to win or persuade. 3. to invite (consequences) by one's own action. —**woo′er,** *n.*

wood (wŏŏd), *n.* 1. the hard, fibrous substance composing most of the stem and branches of a tree or shrub, beneath the bark; xylem. 2. timber or lumber. 3. firewood. 4. a cask, barrel, or keg. 5. *Music.* **a.** a wooden wind instrument. **b.** such instruments collectively. 6. (*often pl.*) a grove or forest. 7. made of wood. 8. used for wood. 9. dwelling or growing in woods. —*v.t., v.i.* 10. to cover or plant with trees. 11. to get supplies of wood (for). —**wood′ed,** *adj.* —**wood′less,** *adj.*

Wood (wŏŏd), *n.* 1. **Grant,** 1892–1942, U.S. painter. 2. **Leonard,** 1860–1927, U.S. military doctor and political administrator.

wood alcohol, methyl alcohol.

wood·bin (wŏŏd′bĭn′), *n.* a box for wood fuel. Also, **wood′box.**

wood·bine (wŏŏd′bīn′), *n.* any of certain vines of Europe and America.

wood block, 1. a block of wood engraved in relief, for printing from; a woodcut. 2. a print or impression from such a block.

wood·chuck (wŏŏd′chŭk′), *n.* a common North American marmot of stout, heavy form; ground hog.

wood·cock (wŏŏd′kŏk′), *n., pl.* **-cocks,** (*esp. collectively*) **-cock.** a game bird of Europe and eastern North America.

wood·craft (wŏŏd′kraft′, -kräft′), *n.* 1. skill in anything which pertains to the woods or forest. 2. forestry. 3. the art of making wooden objects.

wood·cut (wŏŏd′kŭt′), *n.* 1. a carved or engraved block of wood for printing from. **2.** the print or impression. Also, **wood block.**

wood·cut·ter (wŏŏd′kŭt/ər), *n.* one who cuts wood. **—wood′cut′ting,** *n.*

wood·en (wŏŏd′ən), *adj.* **1.** consisting or made of wood. **2.** awkward, spiritless, or dull. **3.** indicating the fifth event of a series. **—wood′en·ly,** *adv.* **—wood′en·ness,** *n.*

wood·en·head (wŏŏd′ən hĕd′), *n. Colloq.* a blockhead; a dull or stupid person.

wood·en·head·ed (wŏŏd′ən hĕd′Ĭd), *adj. Colloq.* thick-headed; dull; stupid. **—wood′en·head′ed·ness,** *n.*

wooden horse, *Class. Legend.* the gigantic, hollow, wooden figure of a horse, filled with armed Greeks, and brought into Troy, thus insuring the destruction of the city.

wood·en·ware (wŏŏd′ən wâr′), *n.* vessels, utensils, etc., made of wood.

wood·house (wŏŏd′hous′), *n.* a house or shed in which wood is stored.

wood·land (*n.* wŏŏd′lănd′, -lənd; *adj.* wŏŏd′-lənd), *n.* **1.** land covered with trees. **—adj. 2.** sylvan.

wood·land·er (wŏŏd′lən dər), *n.* an inhabitant of the woods.

wood·lark (wŏŏd′lärk′), *n.* a small European songbird less famous than the skylark but equally gifted as an aerial songster.

wood·man (wŏŏd′mən), *n., pl.* **-men. 1.** one who dwells in the woods. **2.** one who fells timber.

wood note, a wild or natural musical tone, as that of a forest bird.

wood·peck·er (wŏŏd′pĕk/ər), *n.* any of certain birds having a hard, chisellike bill for boring into wood after insects.

wood·pile (wŏŏd′pīl′), *n.* a pile or stack of wood, esp. wood for fuel.

wood pulp, wood reduced to pulp through mechanical and chemical treatment and used in the manufacture of newsprint and book paper.

wood·shed (wŏŏd′shĕd′), *n.* a shed for keeping wood for fuel.

woods·man (wŏŏdz′mən), *n., pl.* **-men. 1.** one skilled in the arts of the woods. **2.** a lumberman.

woods·y (wŏŏd′zĭ), *adj. U.S.* of or suggestive of the woods.

wood tar, a dark viscid product obtained from wood by distillation or slow burning.

wood turning, the forming of wood articles upon a lathe. **—wood turner.**

wood wind (wĭnd), *Music.* **1.** (*pl.*) the group of wind instruments which comprises the flutes, clarinets, oboes, and bassoons. **2.** an instrument of this group.

wood·work (wŏŏd′wûrk′), *n.* the interior wooden fittings of a house or the like. **—wood′-work′er,** *n.* **—wood′work′ing,** *n.*

wood·worm (wŏŏd′wûrm′), *n.* a worm or larva that is bred in or bores in wood.

wood·y (wŏŏd′Ĭ), *adj.,* **woodier, woodiest. 1.** wooded. **2.** belonging or pertaining to the woods. **3.** of, containing, or resembling wood. **—wood′-i·ness,** *n.*

woof (wŏŏf), *n.* **1.** yarns which travel from selvage to selvage in a loom, interlacing with the warp weft; filling. **2.** texture; fabric.

wool (wŏŏl), *n.* **1.** the fine, soft, curly hair that forms the fleece of sheep and certain other animals, that of sheep constituting one of the most important materials of clothing. **2.** fabrics and garments made from sheep's wool. **3.** woolen yarn used for knitting, crocheting, etc. **4.** any of various substances used commercially as substitutes for the wool of sheep, etc. **5.** any finely fibrous or filamentous matter suggestive of the wool of sheep. **6.** any coating of short, fine hairs or hairlike processes. **7.** *Colloq.* the human hair. **8. pull the wool over one's eyes,** to deceive or delude one.

wool·en (wŏŏl′ən), *n.* **1.** (*pl.*) wool cloth or clothing. **—adj. 2.** made or consisting of wool. **3.** of or pertaining to wool. Also, *esp. Brit.,* **wool′len.**

Woolf (wŏŏlf), *n.* **Virginia,** (*Virginia Stephen, Mrs. Leonard Woolf*) 1882–1941, British novelist and critic.

wool·fell (wŏŏl′fĕl′), *n.* the skin of a wool-bearing animal with the fleece still on it.

wool·gath·er·ing (wŏŏl′găth/ər Ĭng), *n.* indulgence in desultory fancies. **—wool′gath′er·er,** *n.*

wool·grow·er (wŏŏl′grō/ər), *n.* one who

raises sheep or other wool-bearing animals for the production of wool. **—wool′grow/ing,** *n.*

Wooll·cott (wŏŏl′kət), *n.* **Alexander,** 1887–1943, U.S. author and journalist.

wool·ly (wŏŏl′Ĭ), *adj.,* **-lier, -liest,** *n., pl.* **-lies. —adj. 1.** consisting of, resembling, or covered with wool. **2.** *Bot.* covered with soft hairs resembling wool. **—n. 3.** *Western U.S.* a sheep. **4.** *Colloq.* an article of woolen clothing. **—wool′-li·ness,** *n.*

wool·sack (wŏŏl′săk′), *n.* **1.** a sack or bag of wool. **2.** (in the British House of Lords) one of a number of cloth-covered seats or divans stuffed with wool, for the use of judges, esp. one for the Lord Chancellor. **3.** the Lord Chancellor's office.

Wool·worth (wŏŏl′wûrth), *n.* **Frank Winfield,** 1852–1919, U.S. merchant.

Woon·sock·et (wŏŏn sŏk′Ĭt), *n.* a city in NE Rhode Island. 49,303.

wooz·y (wŏŏ′zĭ, wŏŏz′Ĭ), *adj. Slang.* muddled.

Worces·ter (wŏŏs′tər), *n.* **1.** a city in central Massachusetts. 193,694. **2. Joseph Emerson,** 1784–1855, U. S. lexicographer.

word (wûrd), *n.* **1.** a sound or a combination of sounds, or its written or printed representation, used in any language as the sign of a conception. **2.** *Gram.* an element which can stand alone as an utterance, not divisible into two or more parts similarly characterized. **3.** (*often pl.*) speech or talk. **4.** a short conversation. **5.** an expression or utterance. **6.** (*pl.*) the text of a song as distinguished from the music. **7.** (*pl.*) angry speech. **8.** warrant or promise. **9.** intelligence or tidings. **10.** a verbal signal. **11.** an authoritative utterance or command. **12.** (*cap.*) *Theol.* the Scriptures or Bible (often, **the Word of God). —v.t. 13.** to express in words. **—word′less,** *adj.*

word·age (wûr′dĬj), *n.* words collectively.

word·book (wûrd′bŏŏk′), *n.* **1.** a dictionary. **2.** the libretto of an opera.

word·ing (wûr′dĬng), *n.* act or manner of expressing in words; phrasing.

word order, the arrangement in a sequence of the words of a sentence or smaller construction, usually to show meaning, as *Jack ate the beef* vs. *the beef Jack ate.*

word square, a set of words such that when arranged one beneath another in the form of a square they read alike horizontally and vertically.

```
s a t e d
a t o n e
t o a s t
e n s u e
d e t e r
```

Words·worth (wûrdz′wûrth), *n.* **William,** 1770–1850, British poet.

word·y (wûr′dĬ), *adj.,* **wordier, wordiest. 1.** characterized by or given to the use of many, or too many, words; verbose. **2.** pertaining to or consisting of words; verbal. **—word′i·ly,** *adv.* **—word′i·ness,** *n.*

work (wûrk), *n., adj., v.,* **worked** or **wrought, working. —n. 1.** exertion directed to produce or accomplish something; labor. **2.** that on which exertion or labor is expended; task. **3.** productive activity. **4.** *Physics.* **a.** *Mech.* the product of the force acting upon a body and the distance through which the point of application of force moves. **b.** the transference of energy from one body or system to another. **5.** employment. **6.** materials on which one works. **7.** the result or product of exertion, labor, or activity. **8.** a building, bridge, dock, or the like. **9.** a fortified place. **10.** (*pl. often construed as sing.*) a factory. **11.** (*pl.*) the working parts of a mechanical contrivance. **12.** (*pl.*) *Theol.* acts performed in obedience to the law of God. **—adj. 13.** of, for, or concerning work. **—v.i. 14.** to do work, as a person. **15.** to be in operation, as a machine. **16.** to act or operate effectively. **17.** to have an effect or influence. **18.** to move in agitation. **19.** to make way. **20.** to give slightly, or move improperly. **21.** to ferment. **—v.t. 22.** to use or manage (an apparatus, etc.) in operation. **23.** to bring, put, get, etc., by work, effort, or action. **24.** to bring about (any result) by or as by work. **25.** to expend work on. **26.** to operate. **27.** to fashion or achieve by work. **28.** to keep (a person, a horse, etc.) at work. **29.** to solve. **30.** to influence or persuade, esp. insidiously. **31.** to move, stir, or excite in feeling, etc. **32.** to make or decorate by needlework or embroidery. **—work′a·ble,** *adj.* **—work′a·bil′i·ty, work′a·ble·ness,** *n.* **—work′er,** *n.* **—work′ing,** *adj., n.* **—work′-less,** *adj.*

work·a·day (wûr/kə dā/), *adj.* working; practical; everyday.

work·bench (wûrk/bĕnch/), *n.* a bench at which an artisan works.

work·book (wûrk/bŏŏk/), *n.* **1.** a manual of operating instructions. **2.** a book for a student containing instructional material, questions, etc. **3.** a book in which a record is kept of work completed or planned.

work·day (wûrk/dā/), *n.* **1.** working day. —*adj.* **2.** workaday.

worked (wûrkt), *adj.* that has undergone working.

work·house (wûrk/hous/), *n.* **1.** *U.S.* a house of correction. **2.** *Brit.* a poorhouse.

working assets, *Accounting.* invested capital which is comparatively liquid.

working capital, **1.** the amount of capital needed to carry on a business. **2.** *Accounting.* current assets minus current liabilities. **3.** *Finance.* liquid as distinguished from fixed capital assets.

working day, **1.** the amount of time that a worker must work for an agreed daily wage. **2.** a day ordinarily given to working (opposed to *holiday*). **3.** the daily period of hours for working.

work·ing·man (wûr/kĭng măn/), *n., pl.* -men. a man of the working class; a man (skilled or unskilled) who earns his living at some manual or industrial work.

working papers, legal papers giving information often required for employment.

work·man (wûrk/mən), *n., pl.* -men. **1.** a man employed or skilled in some form of manual, mechanical, or industrial work. **2.** a male worker. —**work/man·like/,** *adj.* —**work/man·ship/,** *n.*

workmen's compensation insurance, insurance required by law from employers for the protection of employees while engaged in the employer's business. The amount of the claim is stipulated by law (**workmen's compensation law**).

work of art, a piece of creative work in the arts, esp. a painting or a piece of sculpture.

work·out (wûrk/out/), *n. Colloq.* a trial at any sport, usually in preparation for a contest, exhibition, etc.

work·peo·ple (wûrk/pē/pəl), *n.pl. Chiefly Brit.* people employed at work or labor.

work·room (wûrk/rōōm/, -rŏŏm/), *n.* a room in which work is carried on.

works council, *Brit.* **1.** an elected body of employee representatives which deals with management regarding grievances, working conditions, wages, etc., and which is consulted by management in regard to labor matters. **2.** a joint council or committee representing employer and employees which discusses working conditions, wages, etc. within a plant or business.

work·shop (wûrk/shŏp/), *n.* a shop or building in which work, esp. mechanical work, is carried on.

work·ta·ble (wûrk/tā/bəl), *n.* a table for working at, often with drawers or receptacles for materials, etc., as for sewing.

work·wom·an (wûrk/wŏŏm/ən), *n., pl.* -women. **1.** a female worker. **2.** a woman employed or skilled in some manual, mechanical, or industrial work.

world (wûrld), *n.* **1.** the earth or globe. **2.** a particular division of the earth. **3.** the earth, with its inhabitants, affairs, etc., during a particular period. **4.** mankind. **5.** the class of persons devoted to the affairs or pursuits of this life. **6.** any sphere, realm, or domain, with all that pertains to it. **7.** the universe. **8.** one of the three general groupings of physical nature, as the animal world, mineral world, vegetable world. **9.** any period, state, or sphere of existence. **10.** a very great quantity or extent. **11.** any heavenly body.

World Court, officially, **Permanent Court of International Justice.** an international tribunal, sitting at The Hague, Netherlands, provided for in the Covenant of the League of Nations, and established in September 1921, by action of the assembly of that body, and empowered to render decisions or advisory opinions in disputes threatening future war.

world·ling (wûrld/lĭng), *n.* a worldly person.

world·ly (wûrld/lĭ), *adj.,* -lier, -liest, *adv.* —*adj.* **1.** secular (as opposed to *religious*, etc.). **2.** earthly (as opposed to *spiritual*, etc.). **3.** devoted to or connected with the affairs or interests of this world. **4.** of or pertaining to this world.

—*adv.* **5.** in a worldly manner. —**world/li·ness,** *n.*

world·ly-mind·ed (wûrld/lĭ mīn/dĭd), *adj.* having or showing a worldly mind, or devotion to the affairs and interests of this world. —**world/·ly-mind/ed·ly,** *adv.* —**world/ly-mind/ed·ness,** *n.*

world·ly-wise (wûrld/lĭ wīz/), *adj.* wise as to the affairs of this world.

world power, a nation, organization, or institution so powerful that it is capable of influencing or changing the course of world events.

World Series, *Baseball.* a group of games played each fall between the winning teams of the two major leagues to determine the professional champions of the U.S. Also, **World's Series.**

World War, 1. Also, **World War I.** the war in Europe and elsewhere, from July 28, 1914, to Nov. 11, 1918, between Great Britain, France, Russia, Belgium, Serbia, Japan, Italy, the United States, etc., on the one side, and Germany, Austria-Hungary, Turkey, and Bulgaria on the other side, which ended with the collapse of the latter group. **2.** Also, **World War II.** the worldwide conflict (1939–45), which arose from the undeclared wars of Japan and China (1931–41) and the threats to peace by Italy and Germany in Ethiopia, Spain, and central Europe (1935–39); began with the German attack on Poland, Sept. 1, 1939, when France and Great Britain declared war. The early German triumphs in Europe encouraged Italian entry in June, 1940, but the superiority of resources and industrial production, best visualized in air power and the atom bomb, esp. after the entry of the Soviet Union and the U.S. (1941), enabled the United Nations to defeat Italy in September, 1943, Germany in May, 1945, and Japan in August, 1945.

world-wea·ry (wûrld/wĭr/ĭ), *adj.* weary of the world or of existence.

world-wide (wûrld/wīd/), *adj.* extending or spread throughout the world.

worm (wûrm), *n.* **1.** *Zool.* any of certain long, slender, soft-bodied, bilateral, invertebrates. **2.** any of numerous small, creeping animals with slender, elongated bodies, and without limbs or with very short ones. **3.** something resembling or suggesting a worm in appearance, movement, etc., as a spiral or screw thread. **4.** an abject or miserable person. **5.** (*pl.*) *Pathol.* any disorder caused by parasitic worms in the intestines. —*v.i., v.t.* **6.** to move like a worm. **7.** to get by insidious procedure. **8.** to free from worms. —**worm/er,** *n.* —**worm/less,** *adj.* —**worm/·like/,** *adj.* —**worm/y,** *adj.*

worm-eat·en (wûrm/ē/tən), *adj.* **1.** eaten into or gnawed by worms. **2.** impaired by time; decayed or antiquated.

worm gear, *Mach.* **1.** a worm wheel. **2.** such a worm wheel together with the endless screw forming a device by which the rotary motion of one shaft can be transmitted to another shaft at right angles to it.

worm-hole (wûrm/hōl/), *n.* a hole made by a burrowing or gnawing worm, as in timber, nuts, etc.

Worms (wûrmz), *n.* **1.** a city in SW Germany, on the Rhine. 50,661. **2. Diet of,** an assemblage held here, 1521, at which Luther was condemned as a heretic.

worm wheel, *Mach.* a toothed wheel which engages with a revolving worm, or endless screw, in order to receive or impart motion. Cf. **worm gear.**

worm·wood (wûrm/wŏŏd/), *n.* **1.** a bitter, aromatic herb, now used chiefly in making absinthe. **2.** something bitter.

worn (wōrn), *adj.* **1.** impaired by wear or use. **2.** exhausted.

worn-out (wōrn/out/), *adj.* **1.** worn or used until no longer fit for use. **2.** exhausted.

wor·ri·ment (wûr/ĭ mənt), *n. Colloq.* **1.** harassing annoyance. **2.** worry; anxiety.

wor·ri·some (wûr/ĭ səm), *adj.* **1.** causing worry. **2.** inclined to worry. —**wor/ri·some·ly,** *adv.*

wor·ry (wûr/ĭ), *v.,* -ried, -rying, *n., pl.* -ries. —*v.i., v.t.* **1.** to feel, or cause to feel, uneasy or anxious; get (along or through) by constant effort. **2.** to worry (prey or the like) by seizing with the teeth and shaking. —*n.* **3.** uneasiness or anxiety. **4.** a cause of uneasiness. **5.** act of worrying. —**wor/ri·er,** *n.*

worse (wûrs), *adj., used as compar.* of **bad.** **1.** inferior in excellence, quality, or character.

2. more unfavorable. **3.** in less good condition. **—n. 4.** that which is worse. **—adv. 5.** in a worse manner. Also, *Dial.*, **wors/er** for 1–3, 5.

wors·en (wûr'sən), *v.t.*, *v.i.* to make or become worse.

wor·ship (wûr'shĭp), *n.*, *v.*, **-shiped, -shiping** or (*esp. Brit.*) **-shipped, -shipping. —n. 1.** reverent honor and homage paid to God or to any object or personage regarded as sacred. **2.** formal rendering of such honor and homage. **3.** adoring reverence or regard. **—v.t.**, *v.i.* **4.** to render religious reverence (to). **5.** to feel an adoring reverence (for). **—wor/ship·er,** *esp. Brit.*, **wor/-ship·per,** *n.* **—wor/ship·ful,** *adj.*

worst (wûrst), *adj.*, *used as superl. of* **bad. 1.** most faulty or unsatisfactory. **2.** most unfavorable. **3.** in the poorest condition. **—n. 4.** that which is worst. **—adv. 5.** in the worst manner. **—v.t. 6.** to defeat; beat.

wor·sted (wŏŏs'tĭd), *n.* **1.** firmly twisted yarn or thread spun from combed long-staple wool. **2.** wool cloth woven from such yarns. **—adj. 3.** made of worsted.

wort[1] (wûrt), *n.* the unfermented or fermenting infusion of malt which after fermentation becomes beer or mash.

wort[2] (wûrt), *n.* a plant; herb; vegetable; now chiefly in composition, as in *liverwort, figwort, colewort,* etc.

worth (wûrth), *adj.* **1.** good or important enough to justify (what is specified). **2.** having a value of. **3.** having property to the value of. **—n. 4.** excellence of character. **5.** usefulness, importance, or value. **6.** a quantity of something, of a specified value. **—worth/less,** *adj.* **—worth/less·ly,** *adv.* **—worth/less·ness,** *n.*

worth-while (wûrth'hwĭl'), *adj.* such as to repay one's time, attention, interest, etc.

wor·thy (wûr'thĭ), *adj.*, **-thier, -thiest,** *n.*, *pl.* **-thies. —adj. 1.** of adequate merit or character. **2.** deserving. **—n. 3.** a person of eminent merit. **—wor/thi·ly,** *adv.* **—wor/thi·ness,** *n.*

would (wŏŏd; *unstressed* wəd), *v.* pt. of **will**[1] used: **1.** in expressing a wish. **2.** often in place of *will,* to make a statement or question less direct or blunt.

would-be (wŏŏd'bē'), *adj.* **1.** wishing or pretending to be. **2.** intended to be.

wound (wŏŏnd), *n.* **1.** an injury to an organism, due to external violence rather than disease. **2.** an injury or hurt to the feelings, etc. **—v.t.**, *v.i.* **3.** to inflict a wound (upon).

wove paper, paper with plain surface, in contrast with the wire marks in laid paper.

wow (wou), *n. Slang.* something that proves an extraordinary success.

wow·ser (wou'zər), *n. Australia,* an excessively puritanical person.

WPA, Works Projects Administration.

wrack (răk), *n.* wreckage or ruin.

wraith (rāth), *n.* a visible spirit. **—wraith/-like/,** *adj.*

Wran·gel (răng'gəl), *n.* a Russian island in the Arctic Ocean, off the coast of the NE Soviet Union in Asia: meteorological station. ab. 2000 sq. mi.

Wran·gell (răng'gəl), *n.* **Mount,** a volcano in SE Alaska, in the Wrangell Mountains. 14,005 ft.

Wrangell Mountains, a mountain range in SE Alaska. Highest peak, Mt. Bona, 16,420 ft.

wran·gle (răng'gəl), *v.*, **-gled, -gling,** *n.* **—v.i.**, *v.t.* **1.** to argue or dispute. **2.** *Western U.S.* to tend (horses). **—n. 3.** an altercation. **—wran/-gler,** *n.*

wrap (răp), *v.*, **wrapped** or **wrapt, wrapping,** *n.* **—v.t. 1.** to enclose, envelop, or protect in something wound or folded about. **2.** to wind, fold, or bind (something) about as a covering. **—v.i. 3.** to wrap oneself (up). **4.** to fold. **—n. 5.** (*often pl.*) outdoor garments or coverings.

wrap·per (răp'ər), *n.* **1.** one that wraps. **2.** that in which something is wrapped. **3.** a long, loose garment.

wrap·ping (răp'ĭng), *n.* (*usually pl.*) that in which something is wrapped.

wrath (răth, räth; *Brit.* rôth), *n.* **1.** strong, stern, or fierce anger. **2.** vengeance or punishment. **—wrath/ful,** *adj.* **—wrath/ful·ly,** *adv.* **—wrath/ful·ness,** *n.* **—wrath/y,** *adj.*

wreak (rēk), *v.t.* to inflict. **—wreak/er,** *n.*

wreath (rēth), *n., pl.* **wreaths** (rēthz). something bent into a circular form, as a band of flowers, foliage, etc. **—wreath/less,** *adj.* **—wreath/like/,** *adj.*

wreathe (rēth), *v.*, **wreathed; wreathed** or (*Archaic*) **wreathen; wreathing. —v.t. 1.** to encircle or envelop with or as with a wreath. **2.** to form as a wreath. **—v.i. 3.** to take the form of a wreath.

wreck (rĕk), *n.* **1.** any building, structure, or thing reduced to a state of ruin. **2.** that which is cast ashore by the sea; shipwreck. **3.** the ruin or destruction of anything. **—v.t. 4.** to cause the wreck or destruction of. **—v.i. 5.** to suffer wreck. **6.** to act as a wrecker. **—wreck/age,** *n.* **—wreck/er,** *n.*

wren (rĕn), *n.* any of numerous small, active, passerine birds of England and America.

Wren (rĕn), *n.* **Christopher,** 1632–1723, British architect.

wrench (rĕnch), *v.t.*, *v.i.* **1.** to twist suddenly and forcibly. **2.** to injure by a sudden, violent twist. **3.** to affect distressingly. **4.** to wrest, as from the right use or meaning. **—n. 5.** a wrenching movement or twist. **6.** a sharp, distressing strain, as to the feelings. **7.** a tool for gripping and turning the head of a bolt, a nut, a pipe, or the like, commonly consisting of a bar of metal with fixed or adjustable jaws.

Wrens (rĕnz), *n. Brit. Colloq.* Women's Royal Naval Service.

wrest (rĕst), *v.t.* **1.** to twist or turn violently. **2.** to get by effort. **—n. 3.** a twist or wrench. **4.** a key or small wrench for tuning stringed musical instruments. **—wrest/er,** *n.*

Wrenches (def. 7)
A, Single end; B, S wrench

wres·tle (rĕs'əl), *v.*, **-tled, -tling,** *n.* **—v.i.**, *v.t.* **1.** to contend (with) in, or as in, wrestling. **—n. 2.** an act of or a bout at wrestling. **3.** a struggle. **—wres/tler,** *n.*

wres·tling (rĕs'lĭng), *n.* **1.** a sport in which two persons struggle, each striving to force the other to the ground. **2.** act of one who wrestles.

wretch (rĕch), *n.* **1.** a deplorably unfortunate person. **2.** a person of base character.

wretch·ed (rĕch'ĭd), *adj.* **1.** very unfortunate; pitiable. **2.** despicable. **3.** poor, sorry, or pitiful. **—wretch/ed·ly,** *adv.* **—wretch/ed·ness,** *n.*

wrick (rĭk), *v.t.* wrench or strain.

wrig·gle (rĭg'əl), *v.*, **-gled, -gling,** *n.* **—v.i.**, *v.t.* **1.** to twist to and fro, writhe, or squirm. **2.** to make (one's way) by shifts or expedients. **—n. 3.** a wriggling movement. **—wrig/gler,** *n.* **—wrig/gly,** *adj.*

wright (rīt), *n.* a workman, esp. a constructive workman; now chiefly in composition, as in *wheelwright, playwright,* etc.

Wright (rīt), *n.* **Orville,** 1871–1948, and **Wilbur,** 1867–1912, U.S. aeronautical inventors.

wring (rĭng), *v.*, **wrung** or (*Rare*) **wringed; wringing;** *n.* **—v.t. 1.** to twist forcibly, or compress without twisting, in order to force out water, etc. **2.** to expel by twisting or compression. **3.** to affect painfully. **4.** to clasp tightly. **—v.i. 5.** to perform the action of wringing something. **—n. 6.** a forcible twist or squeeze. **—wring/er,** *n.*

wrin·kle[1] (rĭng'kəl), *n.*, *v.*, **-kled, -kling. —n. 1.** a ridge or furrow on a surface, due to contraction, rumpling, or the like. **—v.t.**, *v.i.* **2.** to form a wrinkle or wrinkles (in); crease. **—wrin/kle·less,** *adj.* **—wrin/kly,** *adj.*

wrin·kle[2] (rĭng'kəl), *n. Colloq.* a novel or clever trick or device.

wrist (rĭst), *n.* **1.** the part of the arm between the forearm and the hand. **2.** the joint between the radius and the carpus (**wrist joint**).

wrist·band (rĭst'bănd/, rĭz'bənd), *n.* the band or part of a sleeve, as of a shirt, which covers the wrist.

wrist·let (rĭst'lĭt), *n.* **1.** a band worn around the wrist, esp. to protect it from cold. **2.** a bracelet.

wrist·lock (rĭst'lŏk/), *n. Wrestling.* a hold whereby the opponent is made defenseless by a wrenching grasp on the wrist.

wrist pin, *Mach.* a stud or pin projecting from the side of a crank, wheel, or the like, and attaching it to a connecting rod leading to some other part of the mechanism.

wrist watch, a watch (timepiece) attached to a strap or band worn about the wrist.

writ (rĭt), *n.* **1.** *Law.* a formal order enjoining the person to whom it is addressed to do or refrain from some specified act. **2.** something written.

write (rīt), *v.t.*, *v.i.*, **wrote** or (*Archaic*) **writ**; **written** or (*Archaic*) **writ**; **writing. 1.** to trace or form (characters, letters, words, etc.) on the surface of some material, as with a pen, pencil, or other instrument or means; inscribe. **2.** to express or communicate in writing. **3.** to execute or produce by setting down words, etc. **4.** to produce as author or composer. **5.** to impress the marks or indications of. —**writ′er**, *n.* —**writ′ing**, *n.*

writer's cramp, *Pathol.* spasmodic contractions of the muscles of the thumb and forefinger during writing, sometimes associated with pain.

write-up (rīt′ŭp′), *n. Colloq.* a written description or account of something.

writhe (rīth), *v.*, **writhed, writhing,** *n.* —*v.i.*, *v.t.* **1.** to twist (the body, oneself, etc.) about, as in pain, etc **2.** to shrink mentally. —*n.* **3.** a writhing movement. —**writh′er**, *n.*

writing desk, 1. a piece of furniture with a surface for writing upon, usually with drawers and pigeonholes to hold writing materials, etc. **2.** a portable case for holding writing materials and affording, when opened, a surface for writing upon.

writ of assistance, *Amer. Hist.* a writ issued by a superior colonial court authorizing officers of the crown to summon aid and enter and search any premises.

writ of prohibition, *Law.* a command by a higher court that a lower court shall not exercise jurisdiction in a particular case.

wrong (rông, rŏng), *adj.* **1.** not in accordance with what is morally right or good. **2.** deviating from truth or fact. **3.** not proper or suitable. **4.** out of order. **5.** that should be worn or kept inward or under. —*n.* **6.** that which is wrong; evil. **7.** state of being wrong. —*adv.* **8.** in a wrong manner. —*v.t.* **9.** to do wrong to. **10.** to impute evil to unjustly. —**wrong′ly,** *adv.* —**wrong′ness,** *n.* —**wrong′do′er,** *n.* —**wrong′do′ing,** *n.* —**wrong′ful,** *adj.* —**wrong′ful·ly,** *adv.*

wrong font, *Printing.* the improper font, or size and style, for its place. *Abbr.*: w.f.

wrong-head·ed (rông′hĕd′ĭd, rŏng′-), *adj.* misguided. —**wrong′-head′ed·ly,** *adv.* —**wrong′-head′ed·ness,** *n.*

wroth (rôth, rŏth or, *esp. Brit.*, rōth), *adj.* angry.

wrought (rôt), *adj.* **1.** worked. **2.** elaborated.

3. produced or shaped by beating with a hammer.

wrought iron, a comparatively pure form of iron which contains practically no carbon, and is easily forged, welded, etc.

wrought-up (rôt′ŭp′), *adj.* excited; perturbed.

wry (rī), *adj.*, **wrier, wriest. 1.** produced by the distortion of the facial features. **2.** abnormally bent or turned to one side. **3.** misdirected or distorted. —**wry′ly,** *adv.* —**wry′ness,** *n.*

WSW, west-southwest. Also, **W.S.W.**

wt., weight.

Wu-chang (woo′chäng′), *n.* a city in E China. 359,800.

Wundt (voont), *n.* **Wilhelm Max,** 1832–1920, German physiologist, psychologist, and philosopher.

W.Va., West Virginia.

Wy., Wyoming.

Wy·an·dot (wī′ən dŏt′), *n.* **1.** an Indian of the former Huron tribe or confederacy; a few mixed-blood survivors now live in Oklahoma but the Huron language is extinct. **2.** an Iroquoian language.

Wy·an·dotte (wī′ən dŏt′), *n.* a city in SE Michigan. 30,618.

Wy·att (wī′ət), *n.* **Thomas,** 1503?–42, British diplomatist and poet.

Wych·er·ley (wĭch′ər lǐ), *n.* **William,** c1640–1716, British dramatist.

Wyc·liffe (wĭk′lĭf), *n.* **John,** 1320?–1384, British religious reformer.

Wyc·lif·fite (wĭk′lĭf ĭt′), *adj.* **1.** of or pertaining to Wycliffe or the Wycliffites. —*n.* **2.** a follower of John Wycliffe; a Lollard. Also, **Wyc′lif·ite′.**

Wye (wī), *n.* a river flowing from central Wales through SW England into the Severn estuary, ab. 130 mi.

Wyld (wĭld), *n.* **Henry Cecil Kennedy,** 1870–1947, British lexicographer and linguist.

Wy·lie (wī′lǐ), *n.* **Elinor,** (*Mrs. William Rose Benét*) 1885–1928, U.S. poet and novelist.

Wy·o·ming (wī ō′mǐng), *n.* a State in the NW United States. 262,895 pop.; 97,914 sq. mi. *Cap.*: Cheyenne. *Abbr.*: **Wyo.** or **Wy.** —**Wy·o′ming·ite′,** *n.*

Wyoming Valley, a valley of the Susquehanna river, in NE Pennsylvania: Indian massacre, 1778.

X

X, x (ĕks), *n.*, *pl.* **X's** or **Xs, x's** or **xs. 1.** a consonant, the 24th letter of the English alphabet. **2.** a symbol for an unknown quantity, person, thing, etc.

X, 1. Christ. **2.** Christian.

x, abscissa.

xan·the·in (zăn′thǐ ĭn), *n.* that part of the yellow coloring matter in yellow flowers which is soluble in water. Cf. **xanthin** (def. 1).

xan·thin (zăn′thǐn), *n.* **1.** that part of the yellow coloring matter in yellow flowers which is insoluble. **2.** a yellow coloring matter in madder.

Xan·thip·pe (zăn tǐp′ǐ), *n.* **1.** the wife of Socrates, proverbial as a scold. **2.** a shrew. Also, **Xan·tip′pe.**

xan·thous (zăn′thəs), *adj.* **1.** yellow. **2.** denoting or pertaining to the peoples with a yellow complexion (the Mongolians).

Xa·vi·er (zā′vǐ ər, zăv′ǐ-), *n.* **St. Francis,** 1506–52, Spanish Jesuit missionary.

X chromosome, *Biol.* the sex chromosome having major control in sex determination.

Xe, *Chem.* xenon.

xe·bec (zē′bĕk), *n.* a small three-masted vessel of the Mediterranean.

xe·ni·a (zē′nǐ ə), *n. Bot.* the immediate influ-

ence or effect on the seed or fruit by the pollen other than on the embryo.

Xe·noc·ra·tes (zə nŏk′rə tēz′), *n.* 396–314 B.C., Greek philosopher.

xen·o·lith (zĕn′ə lĭth), *n. Petrog.* a rock fragment foreign to the igneous rock in which it is embedded.

xen·o·mor·phic (zĕn′ə môr′fĭk), *adj. Petrog.* denoting or pertaining to a mineral constituent of a rock, which does not have its characteristic crystalline form, but one forced upon it by other constituents of the rock. —**xen′o·mor′phi·cal·ly,** *adv.*

xe·non (zē′nŏn, zĕn′ŏn), *n. Chem.* a heavy, inactive, gaseous element present in the atmosphere. *Symbol*: Xe; *at. wt.*: 131.3; *at. no.*: 54.

Xe·noph·a·nes (zə nŏf′ə nēz′), *n.* c570–c480 B.C., Greek philosopher and poet.

xen·o·pho·bi·a (zĕn′ə fō′bǐ ə), *n.* fear or hatred of foreigners.

Xen·o·phon (zĕn′ə fən), *n.* c434–c355 B.C., Greek historian and writer.

xe·ro·der·ma (zǐr′ō dûr′mə), *n. Pathol.* a disease in which the skin becomes dry and hard, and usually scaly.

xe·roph·i·lous (zǐ rŏf′ə ləs), *adj.* **1.** *Bot.* growing in, or adapted to dry, esp. dry and hot, regions. **2.** *Zool.* living in dry situations. —**xe·roph/i·ly,** *n.*

xe·roph·thal·mi·a (zĭr/ŏf thăl/mĭ ə), *n.* *Pathol.* abnormal dryness of the eyeball, usually due to long-continued conjunctivitis.

xe·ro·phyte (zĭr/ə fīt/), *n.* a plant adapted for growth under dry conditions. —**xe·ro·phyt·ic** (zĭr/ə fĭt/ĭk), *adj.*

Xerx·es (zûrk/sēz), *n.* c519–465 B.C., king of Persia, 486–465 B.C.

xi (zī, sī), *n.* the fourteenth letter (Ξ, ξ) of the Greek alphabet.

Xin·gú (shĭng gōō/), *n.* a river flowing N through central Brazil into the Amazon. ab. 1300 mi.

-xion, a rare var. of *-tion,* as in *inflexion, flexion.*

Xmas, Christmas.

Xn., Christian. Also, **Xtian.**

Xnty., Christianity. Also, **Xty.**

XP (kī/rō/, kē/rō/), the Christian monogram made from the first two letters of the Greek word for Christ.

x-ray (ĕks/rā/), *n.* **1.** (*pl.*) electromagnetic radiation of extremely short wave length, approximately 1 angstrom, generated by sudden changes in the velocity of an electric charge, as in atomic transitions or when rapid cathode rays hit a target made of a heavy metal. These rays act on photographic plates, penetrate through solids, and ionize gases. **2.** one of the x-rays. **3.** a radiograph made by means of x-rays. —*v.t.* **4.** to examine by means of x-rays. **5.** to make an x-ray radiograph of. **6.** to treat with x-rays.

x-ray photograph, a radiograph made with x-rays.

x-ray therapy, *Med.* treatment of a disease, such as cancer, using controlled quantities of x-rays.

Xt., Christ.

xy·lem (zī/lĕm), *n.* *Bot.* the woody tissue of plants.

xy·lene (zī/lēn), *n.* *Chem.* any of three isomeric hydrocarbons, $C_6H_4(CH_3)_2$, of the benzene series, occurring as oily, colorless liquids obtained chiefly from coal tar, and used in making dyes, etc.

xy·lo·graph (zī/lə grăf/, -grăf/), *n.* an engraving on wood. —**xy·log·ra·pher** (zī lŏg/rə fər), *n.*

xy·log·ra·phy (zī lŏg/rə fĭ), *n.* the art of engraving on wood, or of printing from such engravings. —**xy·lo·graph·ic** (zī/lə grăf/ĭk), **xy·lo·graph/i·cal,** *adj.*

xy·loid (zī/loid), *adj.* resembling wood; ligneous.

xy·loph·a·gous (zī lŏf/ə gəs), *adj.* eating or destroying wood, as some larvae, mollusks, etc.

xy·lo·phone (zī/lə fōn/, zĭl/ə-), *n.* a musical instrument consisting of a graduated series of wooden bars, usually sounded by striking with small wooden hammers. —**xy·loph·o·nist** (zī/lə fō/nĭst, zī lŏf/ə nĭst, zĭl-), *n.*

xy·lot·o·mous (zī lŏt/ə məs), *adj.* boring into or cutting wood, as certain insects.

xys·ter (zĭs/tər), *n.* a surgical instrument for scraping bones.

Y

Y, y (wī), *n., pl.* **Y's** or **Ys, y's** or **ys.** the 25th letter of the English alphabet.

-y¹, a suffix of adjectives meaning "characterized by or inclined to" the substance or action of the word or stem to which the suffix is attached, as in *juicy, dreamy, chilly.*

-y², a diminutive suffix, often affectionate, common in names, as in *Billy, pussy, Whitey.*

-y³, a suffix forming action nouns from verbs, also found in other abstract nouns.

Y, *Chem.* yttrium.

y, *Math.* **1.** an ordinate. **2.** an unknown quantity.

Y., Young Men's Christian Association.

y., 1. yard; yards. 2. year; years.

yab·ber (yăb/ər), *n.* *Australia.* jabber.

Ya·blo·noi Mountains (yä/blŏ noi/), a mountain range in the SE Soviet Union in Asia, E of Lake Baikal. Also, **Ya·blo·no·voi** (yä/blŏ nŏ voi/).

yacht (yŏt), *n.* **1.** a noncommercial or pleasure vessel. —*v.i.* **2.** to sail, voyage, or race in a yacht. —**yacht/ing,** *n.* —**yachts/man,** *n.*

yah (yä, yà), *interj.* an exclamation of impatience or derision.

Ya·hoo (yä/hōō, yä/-, yä hōō/), *n.* **1.** (in Swift's *Gulliver's Travels*) one of a race of brutes having the form of man and all his degrading passions. **2.** (*l.c.*) a rough, coarse, or uncouth person.

Yah·weh (yä/wĕ), *n.* *Old Test.* a name of God.

Yah·wism (yä/wĭz əm), *n.* **1.** the religion of the ancient Hebrews, as based on the worship of Yahweh as the national deity. **2.** the use of Yahweh as the name of God. Also, **Yah·vism** (yä/vĭz əm).

yak (yăk), *n.* **1.** the long-haired wild ox of the Tibetan highlands. **2.** a domesticated variety of the same species.

Yale (yāl), *n.* Elihu (ĕl/ə hū/), 1648–1721, British colonial official and patron of Yale college.

Yal·ta (yäl/tä), *n.* a seaport in the SW Soviet Union. 28,838.

Yalta Conference, a meeting of Roosevelt, Churchill, and Stalin in Yalta (Feb. 4–12, 1945) to continue war and peace planning and esp. to agree upon voting procedure (**Yalta Formula**) in the proposed Security Council of the U.N.

Ya·lu (yä/lĭ/), *n.* a river forming part of the boundary between Manchuria and Korea, flowing SW to the Yellow Sea. ab. 300 mi.

yam (yăm), *n.* **1.** the starchy, tuberous root of any of various climbing vines of warm climates, used as food. **2.** any of these plants. **3.** *Southern U.S.* the sweet potato.

Ya·ma·shi·ta (yä/mä shē/tä), *n.* **Tomoyuki** (*"the Tiger of Malaya"*) 1885–1946, Japanese general.

ya·men (yä/mən), *n.* (in China, under the imperial system prior to 1912) the residence or office (often combined) of any official.

yam·mer (yăm/ər), *v.i., v.t.* *Colloq.* or *Dial.* to whine or chatter. —**yam/mer·er,** *n.*

Yang·tze (yăng/sē/), *n.* a river flowing from the Tibetan plateau E through central China to the East China Sea. ab. 3200 mi.

yank (yăngk), *Colloq. v.t., v.i., n.* jerk.

Yank (yăngk), *n., adj.* *Slang.* Yankee.

Yan·kee (yăng/kĭ), *n.* **1.** a native or inhabitant of New England. **2.** a native or inhabitant of a Northern State. **3.** a native or inhabitant of the U.S. **4.** a Federal soldier in the American Civil War. —*adj.* **5.** of, pertaining to, or characteristic of the Yankees.

Yan·kee·dom (yăng/kĭ dəm), *n.* **1.** the region inhabited by the Yankees. **2.** Yankees collectively.

Yankee Doo·dle (dōō/dəl), a British song (about 1755), taken over by the American troops during the Revolutionary War.

Yan·kee·ism (yăng/kĭ ĭz/əm), *n.* **1.** Yankee character or characteristics. **2.** a Yankee peculiarity, as of speech.

yap (yăp), *v.,* **yapped, yapping,** *n.* *Chiefly Slang or Dial.* —*v.i.* **1.** to yelp. **2.** to talk snappishly or foolishly. —*n.* **3.** a yelp. **4.** snappish or foolish talk.

Yap (yăp), *n.* one of the Caroline Islands, in the W Pacific: U.S. cable station. 4116 pop.; 83 sq. mi.

yapp (yăp), *adj.* **1.** designating or pertaining to a style of bookbinding in limp leather or the like with projecting flaps overlapping the edges of the pages, used esp. on Bibles. —*n.* **2.** yapp binding.

yar·bor·ough (yär/bûr/ō or, esp. Brit., -bə rə),

n. Whist, Bridge. a hand, none of the cards of which are higher than a nine.

yard[1] (yärd), *n.* **1.** a common unit of linear measure in English-speaking countries, equal to 3 ft. or 36 in., and equivalent to 0.9144 meter. **2.** *Naut.* a long cylindrical spar with a taper toward each end.

yard[2] (yärd), *n.* **1.** a piece of enclosed ground, usually near a house, used as a lawn, garden, for animals, etc. **2.** a place where work is carried on, esp. where railroad cars are kept, switched, etc. —*v.t.* **3.** to put into or enclose in a yard.

yard·age (yär/dĭj), *n.* measurement, or the amount measured, in yards.

yard·arm (yärd/ärm/), *n. Naut.* either end of a yard of a square sail.

yard grass, a coarse annual grass of the Old World, common in dooryards and fields.

yard·mas·ter (yärd/măs/tər, -mäs/-), *n.* a man employed to superintend a terminal yard of a railway.

yard·stick (yärd/stĭk/), *n.* **1.** a stick a yard long, used to measure with. **2.** any standard of measurement.

yare (yâr), *adj. Archaic or Dial.* **1.** ready or prepared. **2.** prompt; brisk or quick.

Yar·mouth (yär/məth), *n.* a seaport in southeastern Canada, in southwestern Nova Scotia: summer resort. 7790.

yarn (yärn), *n.* **1.** a thread made of twisted fibers, as cotton or wool, or of manufactured filaments, as nylon. **2.** *Colloq.* a tale of adventure. —*v.i.* **3.** *Colloq.* to spin a yarn; tell stories.

yarn-dyed (yärn/dīd/), *adj.* (of fabrics) woven from yarns previously dyed.

yar·row (yăr/ō), *n.* a plant of the aster family, used in medicine.

Yar·row (yăr/ō), *n.* a river in SE Scotland, flowing into the Tweed: eulogized in Wordsworth's poetry. 14 mi.

yash·mak (yăsh·mäk/ yäsh/mäk), *n.* the veil worn by Moslem women in public. Also, **yashmac/.**

ya-ta-ta (yä/tə tä/), *n. U.S. Slang.* empty conversation.

yau·pon (yô/pən), *n.* a shrub or small tree, a species of holly, of the southern U.S., with leaves which are sometimes used as a substitute for tea.

yaw (yô), *v.i., v.t.* **1.** to deviate, or cause to deviate temporarily from the straight course, as a vessel or an aircraft. —*n.* **2.** a movement of deviation from the direct course, as of a vessel.

yawl (yôl), *n.* **1.** a ship's small boat. **2.** a fore-and-aft-rigged vessel with a large mainmast forward and a much smaller mast set far aft.

yawn (yôn), *v.i.* **1.** to open the mouth involuntarily with a prolonged, deep inspiration, as from weariness. **2.** to extend or stretch wide. —*n.* **3.** act of yawning. **4.** an opening or chasm. —**yawn/er,** *n.* —**yawn/-ing·ly,** *adv.*

Yawl (def. 2)

yawp (yôp, yäp), *v.i., n. Colloq. or Dial.* bawl. —**yawp/er,** *n.*

Ya·zoo (yăz/ōō), *n.* a river flowing from N Mississippi into the Mississippi river at Vicksburg. ab. 300 mi.

Yb, *Chem.* ytterbium.

Y chromosome, *Biol.* the mate of the X chromosome.

y·clept (ĭ klĕpt/), *pp. Archaic.* named.

yd., yard; yards.

yds., yards.

ye[1] (yē; *unstressed* yĭ), *pron. Archaic.* plural of thou.

ye[2] (t͟hē), *pron.* an archaic spelling of **the**[1].

yea (yā), *adv.* **1.** yes indeed; truly. —*n.* **2.** an affirmative reply or vote. **3.** one who votes in the affirmative.

yean (yēn), *v.t., v.i.* (of a sheep or goat) to bring forth (young).

yean·ling (yēn/lĭng), *n.* **1.** the young of a sheep or a goat; a lamb or a kid. —*adj.* **2.** just born; infant.

year (yĭr), *n.* **1.** a period of 365 or 366 days, divided into 12 calendar months, now reckoned as beginning Jan. 1 and ending Dec. 31. **2.** a space of 12 calendar months reckoned from any

point. **3.** (in scientific use) the time interval between one vernal equinox and the next. **4.** the true period of the earth's revolution round the sun. **5.** the time in which any planet completes a revolution round the sun. **6.** a period out of every 12 months, devoted to a certain activity. **7.** (*pl.*) age, esp. old age. **8.** (*pl.*) a long time. —**year/ly,** *adj., adv., n.*

year·book (yĭr/bŏok/), *n.* a book published annually.

year·ling (yĭr/lĭng, yûr/-), *n.* **1.** an animal one year old or in the second year of its age. —*adj.* **2.** a year old. **3.** of a year's duration.

year·long (yĭr/lông/, -lŏng/), *adj.* lasting for a year.

yearn (yûrn), *v.i.* **1.** to have an earnest or strong desire; long. **2.** to be moved or attracted tenderly. —**yearn/ing,** *n.*

yeast (yēst), *n.* **1.** a yellowish semifluid substance consisting of the aggregated cells of certain minute fungi: employed to induce fermentation in the manufacture of alcoholic liquors and as a leaven to render bread, etc., light and spongy. **2.** a commercial substance of living yeast cells and some meallike material, used in raising dough for bread, etc. **3.** ferment or agitation. —*v.i.* **4.** to ferment. **5.** to be covered with froth. —**yeast/y,** *adj.*

yeast cake, living yeast cells compressed with a little starch into a small cake. In **dried yeast cake,** yeasts are inactive; in a **compressed yeast cake,** they are active and the product is perishable.

Yeats (yāts), *n.* **William Butler,** 1865–1939, Irish writer.

Yed·do (yĕd/dō/), *n.* former name of **Tokyo.** Also, **Ye/do/.**

yegg (yĕg), *n. U.S. Slang.* a criminal.

yegg·man (yĕg/mən), *n., pl.* **-men.** yegg.

yeld (yĕld), *adj. Scot.* (of a cow, etc.) **1.** barren. **2.** not giving milk.

yell (yĕl), *v.i., v.t.* **1.** to cry or scream loudly and clearly, as with pain, etc. —*n.* **2.** such a sound. —**yell/er,** *n.*

yel·low (yĕl/ō), *adj.* **1.** of a bright color like that of butter, lemons, etc. **2.** having the yellowish skin characteristic of Mongolians or mulattoes. **3.** of sallow complexion. **4.** *Slang.* cowardly. **5.** *Colloq.* morbidly sensational. **6.** jealous. —*n.* **7.** a hue between green and orange in the spectrum. **8.** the yolk of an egg. —*v.t., v.i.* **9.** to make or become yellow. —**yel/low·ish,** *adj.* —**yel/low·ness,** *n.*

yellow fever, *Pathol.* a dangerous, often fatal, infectious febrile disease of warm climates, due to a filterable virus transmitted by a mosquito.

yel·low-green (yĕl/ō grēn/), *n.* **1.** color about midway between green and yellow in the spectrum. —*adj.* **2.** of the color yellow-green.

yellow jack, 1. the (yellow) flag of quarantine. **2.** yellow fever.

yellow jacket, any of certain yellow-and-black social wasps.

yellow journalism, the use of sensational reporting and conspicuous displays as a means of attracting readers to a newspaper or journal. —**yellow journal.**

yellow metal, 1. a yellow alloy consisting of approximately three parts of copper and two of zinc. **2.** gold.

yellow peril, 1. the alleged danger of a predominance of the yellow race, with its enormous numbers, over the white race and Western civilization generally. **2.** the yellow race, regarded as presenting such a danger.

yellow pine, 1. any common American pine with a notably strong yellowish wood, usually with needles in clusters of three. **2.** the wood of any such tree.

yellow race, the Mongolian or Mongoloid race.

yel·lows (yĕl/ōz), *n.* **1.** *Bot.* one of various plant diseases such as peach **yellows,** cabbage **yellows,** and **aster yellows,** whose most prominent symptom is a loss of green pigment in the leaves. **2.** jaundice, esp. in animals. **3.** *Obs.* jealousy.

yellow sapphire, a transparent yellow variety of sapphire.

Yellow Sea, an arm of the Pacific between China and Korea.

yellow spot, *Anat.* a small, circular, yellowish area on the retina, opposite the pupil.

Yel·low·stone National Park (yĕl′ō stōn′), a park in NW Wyoming and parts of Montana and Idaho: geysers, hot springs. 3458 sq. mi.

yel·low·throat (yĕl′ō thrōt′), n. any of several American ground-inhabiting warblers having a yellow throat, esp. the so-called **Maryland yellowthroat.**

yellow warbler, a small American warbler, the male of which has a bright-yellow plumage streaked with brown on the under parts.

yel·low·weed (yĕl′ō wēd′), n. Local U.S. any of certain coarse species of goldenrod.

yelp (yĕlp), v.i., v.t. **1.** to give or express by a quick, sharp, shrill cry. —n. **2.** a quick, sharp bark or cry. —**yelp′er,** n.

Yem·en (yĕm′ən), n. a kingdom in SW Arabia. 3,500,000 pop.; ab. 75,000 sq. mi. Cap.: San′a.

yen[1] (yĕn), n., pl. **yen.** the gold monetary unit of Japan, worth about 49⁴/₅ U.S. cents.

yen[2] (yĕn), n., v.i., **yenned, yenning.** Colloq. desire.

Yen·an (yĕn′än′), ′n. a city in N China, in Shensi province: the capital of Communist China prior to the capture of the city by Nationalist forces, 1947.

yeo·man (yō′mən), n., pl. **-men. 1.** a petty officer in the navy. **2.** Archaic or Hist. an attendant in a great household. **3.** Brit. an independent farmer.

yeo·man·ly (yō′mən lĭ′), adj. **1.** of the condition or rank of a yeoman. **2.** pertaining to or befitting a yeoman. —adv. **3.** like or as befits a yeoman.

yeoman of the (royal) guard, a member of the bodyguard of the English sovereign, instituted in 1485, which now consists of 100 men (with their officers), having purely ceremonial duties.

yeo·man·ry (yō′mən rĭ′), n. **1.** a British volunteer cavalry force, orig. composed largely of yeomen, which became part of the British Territorial Army. **2.** yeomen collectively.

yeoman's service, good, useful, or substantial service.

Yer·ba Bue·na (yâr′bə bwā′nə), an island in San Francisco Bay between Oakland and San Francisco, California: a 500 ft. two-story tunnel across this island connects the two. spans of the San Francisco-Oakland bridge.

yes (yĕs), adv., n., pl. **yeses.** —adv. **1.** a word used to express affirmation or assent or to mark the addition of something emphasizing and amplifying a previous statement. —n. **2.** an affirmative reply.

yes man, Colloq. one who registers unequivocal agreement with his superior, without consideration.

yes·ter·day (yĕs′tər dĭ′, -dā′), adv. **1.** on the day preceding this day. **2.** a short time ago. —n. **3.** the day preceding this day. **4.** time in the immediate past. —adj. **5.** belonging or pertaining to the day before or to a time in the immediate past.

yes·ter·year (yĕs′tər yĭr′), adv., n. Chiefly Poetic. last year.

yet (yĕt), adv. **1.** as soon as the present time. **2.** up to a particular time, or thus far. , **3.** in the time still remaining, or before all is done. **4.** at this or that time, as previously. **5.** in addition, or again. **6.** moreover. **7.** even or still (with comparatives). **8.** though the case be such, or nevertheless. **9. as yet,** up to the present time. —conj. **10.** and yet, but yet, or nevertheless.

yew (ū), n. **1.** an evergreen coniferous tree having a thick, dark foliage and a fine-grained elastic wood, used in bows. **2.** the wood.

Yid·dish (yĭd′ĭsh), n. **1.** a group of closely similar High German dialects, with vocabulary admixture from Hebrew and Slavic. —adj. **2.** Jewish.

yield (yēld), v.t. **1.** to give forth or produce by a natural process. **2.** to give as due, or as payment, profit, or interest. **3.** to give up, surrender, relinquish, or resign. —v.i. **4.** to give a return, as for labor expended. **5.** to surrender, submit, or give way to. **6.** to give place or precedence. —n. **7.** the action of yielding. **8.** that which is yielded. —**yield′er,** n. —**yield′ing,** adj.

yill (yĭl), n. Scot. ale.

yin (yĭn), adj., n., pron. Scot. one.

yip (yĭp), v.i., **yipped, yipping.** Colloq.·to bark sharply, as a small dog.

Y.M.C.A., Young Men's Christian Association.

Y.M.H.A., Young Men's Hebrew Association.

Y·mir (ē′mĭr, y′mĭr), n. Scand. Myth. a giant, the first created being, progenitor of the race.

yo·del (yō′dəl), v., **-deled, -deling** or (esp. Brit.) **-delled, -delling,** n. —v.t., v.i. **1.** to sing with frequent changes from the ordinary voice to falsetto and back again. —n. **2.** a song, etc., so sung. —**yo′del·er;** esp. Brit., **yo′del·ler,** n.

yo·dle (yō′dəl), v.t., v.i., **-dled, -dling,** n. yodel. —**yo′dler,** n.

Yo·ga (yō′gə), n. Hinduism. ascetic practice aiming to effect union of the human soul with the Universal Spirit. Also, **yo′ga.**

yo·gi (yō′gē), n., pl. **-gis** (-gēz). **1.** one who practices the Yoga system. **2.** the doctrine or practice of the yogis.

yo·gurt (yō′gŏŏrt), n. **1.** a kind of thickened fermented liquor made from milk, used by the Turks and others. **2.** an artificially curdled milk product, used esp. medicinally.

yo·heave·ho (yō′hēv′hō′), interj. a chant formerly shouted by sailors when heaving together.

yo·ho (yō hō′), interj., v., **-hoed, -hoing.** —interj. **1.** a call or shout to attract attention, accompany effort, etc. —v.i. **2.** to shout "yo-ho!"

yoicks (yoiks), interj. Chiefly Brit. a cry used to urge on the hounds in fox hunting.

yoke (yōk), n., v., **yoked, yoking.** —n. **1.** a contrivance for joining together a pair of draft animals, esp. oxen, usually consisting of a crosspiece with two bow-shaped pieces, each bow enclosing the head of an animal. **2.** a pair of draft animals fastened together by a yoke (pl., after a numeral, **yokes** or **yoke**). **3.** something resembling a yoke or a bow of a yoke in form or use. **4.** an emblem or token of subjection, servitude, slavery, etc. **5.** something that couples or binds together; tie. —v.t., v.i. **6.** to join or couple by means of a yoke. **7.** to harness a draft animal to (a plow or vehicle).

yoke·fel·low (yōk′fĕl′ō), n. **1.** an intimate associate; a partner. **2.** a spouse. Also, **yoke·mate** (yōk′māt′).

yo·kel (yō′kəl), n. a rustic.

Yo·ko·ha·ma (yō′kə hä′mə), n. a seaport in central Japan. 706,557.

yolk (yōk, yōlk), n. the yellow and principal substance of an egg, as distinguished from the white. —**yolk′less,** adj. —**yolk′y,** adj.

Yom Kip·pur (yŏm kĭp′ər), the Day of Atonement, an annual Jewish fast day.

yon (yŏn), adj., adv. Archaic or Dial. yonder.

yon·der (yŏn′dər), adj., adv. over there.

Yon·kers (yŏng′kərz), n. a city in SE New York, on the Hudson. 142,598.

yore (yōr), adv., adj. Archaic. long ago.

York (yôrk), n. **1.** English royal house, 1461–85. **2.** a city in SE Pennsylvania. 56,712.

York·shire pudding (yôrk′shĭr, -shər), a pudding made of batter (unsweetened), baked under meat, so as to catch the drippings.

Yorkshire terrier, a short-legged, long-bodied terrier with silky hair, golden-tan on the head and bluish or silver on the body.

York·town (yôrk′toun′), n. a town in SE Virginia: surrender of Cornwallis, 1781.

Yo·sem·i·te (yō sĕm′ə tĭ′), n. a deep valley in E California.

Yosemite Falls, a series of falls in eastern California. Upper Fall, 1430 ft. high; Middle Fall, 626 ft. high; Lower Fall, 320 ft. high. Total height (including rapids) 2526 ft.

you (ū), pron. the ordinary pronoun of the second person, orig. the objective (plural) of ye, but now used regularly as either objective or nominative, and with either plural or singular meaning, but always, when used as subject, taking a plural verb.

young (yŭng), adj. **1.** being in the first or early stage of life, growth, progress, operation, etc.; not old. **2.** having the appearance or other qualities of youth. **3.** of or pertaining to youth. **4.** not far advanced in years in comparison with another or others. **5.** advocating progressive tendencies, policies, or the like. —n. **6.** young offspring. —**young′ish,** adj.

Young (yŭng), n. **Brigham,** 1801–77, U.S. Mormon leader.

young·ber·ry (yŭng′bĕr′ĭ), n., pl. **-ries.** Hort. the large, dark-purple, sweet fruit of a trailing blackberry in the southwest U.S., a cross between several blackberries.

young blood, youthful people, ideas, practices, etc.

young-eyed (yŭng´īd´), *adj.* **1.** clear-eyed; bright-eyed. **2.** having a youthful outlook; enthusiastic; fresh.

Young Pretender, Charles Edward Stuart, grandson of James II of England, and son of James, the Old Pretender, whose landing in Scotland precipitated the rebellion of 1745.

young·ster (yŭng´stər), *n.* a child.

Youngs·town (yŭngz´toun´), *n.* a city in NE Ohio. 167,720.

youn·ker (yŭng´kər), *n.* **1.** *Archaic.* a youngster. **2.** *Obs.* a young gentleman or knight.

your (yŏŏr), *pron., adj.* the possessive form of *you, ye,* used before a noun.

yours (yŏŏrz), *pron.* form of *your* used predicatively or without a noun following.

your·self (yŏŏr sĕlf´), *pron., pl.* **-selves** (-sĕlvz´). **1.** an emphatic appositive of *you* or *ye.* **2.** a substitute for reflexive *you.*

yours truly, 1. a conventional phrase used at the end of a letter. **2.** *Colloq.* I, myself, or me.

youth (ūth), *n., pl.* **youths** (ūths, ūt͡hz), (*collectively*) **youth. 1.** the condition of being young. **2.** the appearance, freshness, vigor, spirit, etc., characteristic of one that is young. **3.** early life. **4.** adolescence. **5.** young persons collectively. **6.** a young person. **—youth·less,** *adj.*

youth·ful (ūth´fəl), *adj.* **1.** characterized by, pertaining to, or befitting youth. **2.** having the appearance, vigor, etc., of youth. **3.** early in time. **—youth´ful·ly,** *adv.* **—youth´ful·ness,** *n.*

yow (you), *interj., n.* a shout of pain, dismay, etc.

yowl (youl), *v.i., n.* howl.

yo-yo (yō´yō), *n., pl.* **-yos.** a toy, consisting of a round, flat-sided block of wood with a groove around the edge, in which a string is wound. The yoyo is spun and reeled in by the string.

Y·pres (ē´pr), *n.* a town in W Belgium: the scene of many battles, 1914–18. 16,483.

Yp·si·lan·ti (ĭp´sə län´tĭ), *n.* **1. Prince Alexander,** 1792–1828, Greek patriot and revolutionary leader. **2.** his brother, **Demetrios,** 1793–1832, Greek patriot and revolutionary leader. Also, **Yp·si·lan·tis, Yp·se·lan·tes** (ē´psē län´dēs).

Y·quem (ē kĕm´), *n.* a fine, very rich, sweet white wine.

yr., **1.** year; years. **2.** your.

yrs., **1.** years. **2.** yours.

Y·ser (ē zĕr´), *n.* a river flowing from N France through NW Belgium into the North Sea: battles, 1914–18. 55 mi.

Y.T., Yukon Territory.

Yt, *Chem.* yttrium.

yt·ter·bi·um (ĭ tûr´bĭ əm), *n.* *Chem.* a rare metallic element. *Symbol:* Yb; *at. wt.:* 173.04; *at. no.:* 70.

yt·tri·um (ĭt´rĭ əm), *n.* *Chem.* a rare trivalent metallic element. *Symbol:* Y *or* Yt; *at. wt.:* 88.92; *at. no.:* 39; *sp. gr.:* 5.5.

yu·an (ū än´), *n., pl.* **-an.** **1.** the Chinese monetary unit, valued at $0.4611 in U.S. money. **2.** a silver coin having 23.9025 grams of silver, used in China. **3.** (in China) a department of government, or a council.

Yüan Shih-kai (yʏ än´ shē´kī´), *n.* 1859–1916, president of China, 1912–16.

Yu·ca·tán (ū´kə tän´), *n.* a peninsula comprising parts of SE Mexico, N Guatemala, and British Honduras.

yuc·ca (yŭk´ə), *n.* any of certain plants of warmer America, having pointed leaves and whitish flowers.

Yu·ga (yŏŏg´ə), *n.* (in Hindu use) **1.** an age of time. **2.** one of four ages distinguished in a period of the world's existence, the first being a golden age, with deterioration in those following.

Yu·go·sla·vi·a (ū´gō slä´vĭ ə), *n.* a republic in S Europe: formed in 1918. 16,261,125 pop.; 95,-558 sq. mi. *Cap.:* Belgrade. **—Yu´go·slav´, Yu´go·sla´vi·an,** *adj., n.* **—Yu´go·slav´ic,** *adj.*

Yu·kon (ū´kŏn), *n.* **1.** a river flowing from NW Canada generally W through central Alaska to the Bering Sea. ab. 2300 mi. **2.** a territory in NW Canada. 4914 pop.; 207,076 sq. mi. *Cap.:* Dawson.

yule (ūl), *n.* Christmas, or the Christmas season.

yule log, a large log of wood which in olden times formed the backlog of the fire at Christmas. Also, **yule block, yule clog.**

yule·tide (ūl´tīd´), *n.* the Christmas season.

Y.W.C.A., Young Women's Christian Association.

Y.W.H.A., Young Women's Hebrew Association.

Z

Z, z (zē *or, esp. Brit.,* zĕd; *old fash.* ʏz´ərd), *n., pl.* **Z's** *or* **Zs, z's** *or* **zs.** a consonant, the 26th letter of the English alphabet.

Z, *Chem.* atomic number.

z, an unknown quantity.

zaf·fer (zăf´ər), *n.* an artificial mixture containing cobalt oxide and usually silica, used to produce a blue color in glass and other ceramic products. Also, **zaf´fre.**

Za·greb (zä´grĕb), *n.* a city in NW Yugoslavia. 185,581.

zai·bat·su (zī´bät sōō´), *n., pl. or sing.* the great industrial families of Japan.

Za·ma (zā´mə, zä´mä), *n.* an ancient town in N Africa, SW of Carthage: the Romans defeated Hannibal near here in the final battle of the second Punic War, 202 B.C.

Zam·be·zi (zăm bē´zĭ), *n.* a river in S Africa. ab. 2200 mi.

Zam·bo·an·ga (säm´bō äng´gä), *n.* a seaport in the Philippine Islands. 131,455.

Zanes·ville (zānz´vĭl), *n.* a city in SE Ohio. 37,500.

Zang·will (zăng´wĭl), *n.* **Israel,** 1864–1926, British novelist and dramatist.

za·ny (zā´nĭ), *n., pl.* **-nies,** *adj.* **—n. 1.** a clown or buffoon. **—adj. 2.** silly.

Zan·zi·bar (zăn´zə bär´, zăn´zə bär´), *n.* **1.** an island off the E coast of Africa. 150,000 pop.; 640 sq. mi. **2.** a British protectorate comprising the islands of Zanzibar and Pemba and adjacent smaller islands. 250,000 pop.; 1020 sq. mi.

Za·pa·ta (sä pä´tä), *n.* **Emiliano,** 1877?–1919, Mexican political leader, and active revolutionist, 1911–16.

Za·po·rozh·e (zä´pŏ rôzh´yĕ), *n.* a city in the SW Soviet Union, on the Dnieper river. 289,188. Formerly, **Aleksandrovsk.**

Zar·a·thus·tra (zăr´ə thŏŏs´trə), *n.* Zoroaster. **—Zar·a·thus·tri·an** (zăr´ə thŏŏs´trĭ ən), *adj., n.*

zarf (zärf), *n.* a cuplike holder, usually of ornamental metal, for a coffee cup without a handle, as used in the Levant.

zeal (zēl), *n.* ardor for a person, cause, or object; eager desire or endeavor.

Zea·land (zē´lənd), *n.* the largest island of Denmark. 1,482,978 pop.; 2709 sq. mi.

zeal·ot (zĕl´ət), *n.* **1.** one who displays zeal. **2.** one carried away by excess of zeal.

zeal·ot·ry (zĕl´ət rĭ), *n.* undue or excessive zeal; fanaticism.

zeal·ous (zĕl´əs), *adj.* full of, characterized by, or due to zeal; ardently active, devoted, or diligent. **—zeal´ous·ly,** *adv.* **—zeal´ous·ness,** *n.*

ze·bec (zē´bĕk), *n.* xebec. Also, **ze´beck.**

Zeb·e·dee (zĕb′ə dē′), *n.* father of the apostles James and John (Matt. 4:21).

ze·bra (zē′brə), *n.* a wild, horselike animal, fully and regularly striped with dark bands on a light ground, or with alternating dark and light bands.

ze·bu (zē′bū), *n.* a bovine animal widely domesticated in India, China, eastern Africa, etc.

Zech., Zechariah.

Zech·a·ri·ah (zĕk′ə rī′ə), *n.* **1.** Hebrew prophet of the sixth century (fl. 520 B.C.), author of a book of the Old Testament. **2.** the book itself.

zed (zĕd), *n.* *Chiefly Brit.* a name for the letter z.

zee (zē), *n.* *Chiefly U.S.* a name for the letter z.

Zee·brug·ge (zē′brŏŏg′ə), *n.* a seaport in NW Belgium: German submarine base in World War I.

Zeit·geist (tsīt′gīst′), *n.* *German.* the spirit of the time; general drift of thought or feeling characteristic of a particular period of time.

Zem·strom (zĕm′strəm), *n.* *U.S.S.R.* an elective assembly of a local district or of a province, having the oversight and regulation of affairs within its territory.

ze·na·na (zĕ nä′nə), *n.* (in India) **1.** that part of the house in which the women and girls of a family are secluded. **2.** its occupants collectively.

Zeng·er (zĕng′ər), *n.* **John Peter,** 1697–1746, American journalist, born in Germany.

ze·nith (zē′nĭth *or, esp. Brit.,* zĕn′ĭth), *n.* **1.** the point of the celestial sphere vertically above any place or observer, and diametrically opposite to the nadir. **2.** highest point or state; culmination.

zenith tube, *Astron.* a telescope mounted to point only at the zenith, used at the U.S. Naval and other modern observatories for taking time from the stars.

Ze·no of Ci·ti·um (zē′nō; sĭsh′ĭ əm), c336–c264 B.C., Greek philosopher and founder of the Stoic school.

Zeno of Elea, fl. c475 B.C., Greek philosopher.

Zeph., Zephaniah.

Zeph·a·ni·ah (zĕf′ə nī′ə), *n.* **1.** Hebrew prophet of the seventh century B.C. and author of an Old Testament book. **2.** the book itself.

zeph·yr (zĕf′ər), *n.* **1.** a mild breeze. **2.** any of various things of fine, light quality, as a fabric, etc.

zephyr cloth, a light type of cassimere used for women's clothing.

Zeph·y·rus (zĕf′ə rəs), *n.* the west wind personified.

zephyr yarn, a soft worsted yarn used in embroidery and knitting. Also, **zephyr worsted.**

Zep·pe·lin (zĕp′ə lĭn), *n.* (*often l.c.*) a large dirigible balloon consisting of a long, cylindrical, covered framework containing compartments or cells filled with gas, and of various structures for holding the engines, passengers, etc.

Zep·pe·lin (tsĕp′ə lēn′), *n.* **Ferdinand von, Count,** 1838–1917, German general and airship builder.

ze·ro (zĭr′ō), *n., pl.* **-ros, -roes,** *v.,* **-roed, -roing.** —*n.* **1.** the figure or symbol 0, which stands for the absence of quantity in the Arabic notation for numbers; a cipher. **2.** the line or point from which all divisions of a scale are measured in either a positive or a negative direction. **3.** naught or nothing. **4.** the lowest point or degree. —*v.t.* **5.** to adjust (any apparatus) to an arbitrary reading from which all other readings are to be measured.

zero hour, *Colloq.* the time at which any contemplated move is to begin.

zest (zĕst), *n.* **1.** anything added to impart flavor or cause relish. **2.** piquancy or interest. **3.** hearty enjoyment. —*v.t.* **4.** to give zest to. —**zest′ful,** *adj.* —**zest′ful·ly,** *adv.* —**zest′ful·ness,** *n.* —**zest′less,** *adj.*

ze·ta (zā′tə, zē′tə), *n.* the sixth letter (Z, ζ) of the Greek alphabet.

zeug·ma (zōōg′mə), *n.* *Gram., Rhet.* a figure in which a verb is associated with two subjects or objects, or an adjective with two nouns, although appropriate to but one of the two, as in "to wage war and peace." —**zeug·mat·ic** (zōōg măt′ĭk), *adj.*

Zeus (zōōs), *n.* chief god of the ancient Greeks, identified by the Romans with Jupiter.

Zhu·kov (zhōō′kôf), *n.* **Grigori Konstantinovich,** born 1895?, Russian general.

zib·el·ine (zĭb′ə līn′, -lĭn), *adj.* **1.** of or pertaining to the sable. —*n.* **2.** the fur of the sable. **3.** a thick woolen cloth with a flattened hairy nap. Also, **zib′el·line′.**

Zieg·feld (zĭg′fĕld), *n.* **Florenz,** 1867–1932, U.S. theatrical producer.

zig·zag (zĭg′zăg′), *n., adj., adv., v.,* **-zagged, -zagging.** —*n.* **1.** a line characterized by sharp turns first to one side and then to the other. **2.** one of a series of such turns. —*adj., adv.* **3.** with frequent sharp turns from side to side. —*v.t.; v.i.* **4.** to move in a zigzag direction.

Zil·pah (zĭl′pə), *n.* *Bible.* mother of Gad and Asher by Jacob. Gen. 30:10–13.

Zim·ba·list (zĭm′bə lĭst), *n.* **Efrem,** born 1889, Russian violinist, in U.S.

zinc (zĭngk), *n., v.,* **zincked, zincking** or **zinced** (zĭngkt), **zincing** (zĭngk′ĭng). —*n.* **1.** *Chem.* a bluish-white metallic element: used in making galvanized iron and in alloys such as brass, as an element in voltaic cells, etc. *Symbol:* Zn; *at. wt.:* 65.38; *at. no.:* 30; *sp. gr.:* 7.14 at 20°C. —*v.t.* **2.** to coat or cover with zinc.

zinc·if·er·ous (zĭngk ĭf′ər əs, zĭn sĭf′-), *adj.* yielding or containing zinc.

zinc·i·fy (zĭngk′ə fī′), *v.t.,* **-fied, -fying.** to cover or impregnate with zinc. —**zinc′i·fi·ca′tion,** *n.*

zin·co·graph (zĭng′kə grăf′, -gräf′), *n.* **1.** a zinc plate produced by zincography. **2.** a print from such a plate.

zin·cog·ra·phy (zĭng kŏg′rə fĭ), *n.* the process of producing a printing surface on a zinc plate.

zinc ointment, *Pharm.* an ointment composed of paraffin, white petroleum, and 20 percent of zinc oxide, employed to treat skin conditions.

zinc·ous (zĭngk′əs), *adj.* pertaining to zinc.

zinc oxide, a compound of zinc and oxygen, used for the treatment of certain skin diseases.

zinc white, a white pigment consisting of zinc oxide, used in paints.

zing (zĭng), *n., v.i., interj.* a sharp singing sound.

zin·ni·a (zĭn′ĭ ə), *n.* any of certain composite plants bearing bright-colored flower heads.

Zi·nov·iev (zĭ nôf′yĕf), *n.* **Grigori Evseevich,** 1883–1936, Russian Communist leader.

Zins·ser (zĭn′sər), *n.* **Hans,** 1878–1940, U.S. bacteriologist.

Zi·on (zī′ən), *n.* **1.** a hill of Jerusalem, the site of the Temple. **2.** the Israelites. **3.** the theocracy, or church of God. **4.** heaven.

Zi·on·ism (zī′ə nĭz′əm), *n.* a modern plan or movement to colonize Hebrews in Palestine. —**Zi′on·ist,** *n., adj.* —**Zi′on·is′tic,** *adj.*

zip (zĭp), *n., v.,* **zipped, zipping.** *Colloq.* —*n.* **1.** a sudden, brief, hissing sound. **2.** energy. —*v.i.* **3.** to make, move, or proceed with a zip. —*v.t.* **4.** to fasten with a zipper.

Zip·per (zĭp′ər), *n.* **1.** *Trademark.* a fastener consisting of an interlocking device set along two edges to unite them (or separate them) when an attached piece sliding between them is pulled, and used on clothing, bags, etc. **2.** (*l.c.*) a kind of overshoe.

zip·py (zĭp′ĭ), *adj.,* **-pier, -piest.** *Colloq.* lively; smart.

zir·con (zûr′kŏn), *n.* a common mineral, zirconium silicate, occurring in crystals or grains of various colors.

zir·co·ni·um (zər kō′nĭ əm), *n.* *Chem.* a metallic element found combined in zircon, etc. *Symbol:* Zr; *at. wt.:* 91.22; *at. no.:* 40; *sp. gr.:* 6.4 at 20°C.

Zis·ka (zĭs′kə), *n.* **Jan,** c1370–1424, Bohemian general, and leader of the followers of John Huss.

zith·er (zĭth′ər), *n.* a musical folk instrument consisting of a flat sounding box with numerous strings stretched over it, played with a plectrum and the fingertips.

zith·ern (zĭth′ərn), *n.* zither.

zlo·ty (zlô′tĭ), *n., pl.* **-tys,** (*collectively*) **-ty.** the gold monetary unit and a nickel coin of Poland, equivalent at present to approx. 1 U.S. cent.

Zn, *Chem.* zinc.

zod., zodiac.

zo·di·ac (zō′dĭ ăk′), *n.* **1.** an imaginary belt of the heavens, within which are the apparent paths of the sun, moon, and principal planets. It contains twelve constellations and hence twelve divisions (called *signs*). **2.** a diagram representing this belt, and usually containing pictures of the animals, etc., associated with the constellations and signs. —**zo·di·a·cal** (zō dī′ə kəl), *adj.*

zodiacal light, a luminous tract in the sky,

seen in the west after sunset or in the east before sunrise and supposed to be the light reflected from a cloud of meteoric matter revolving round the sun.

Zo·la (zō′lə), *n.* Émile, 1840–1902, French novelist.

Zoll·ver·ein (tsôl′fĕr īn′), *n. German.* 1. a union of German states for the maintenance of a uniform tariff on imports from other countries, and of free trading among themselves. 2. any similar union or arrangement between a number of states; a customs union.

zom·bi (zŏm′bĭ), *n., pl.* -bis. a dead body brought to life by some supernatural force. Also, **zom′bie.**

zon·ate (zō′nāt), *adj.* 1. marked with a zone or zones, as of color, texture, or the like. 2. arranged in a zone or zones. Also, **zon′at·ed.**

zo·na·tion (zō nā′shən), *n.* 1. zonate state or condition. 2. arrangement or distribution in zones.

zone (zōn), *n., v.,* **zoned, zoning.** —*n.* 1. any continuous tract or area which differs or is distinguished in some respect from adjoining tracts or areas. 2. *Geog.* any of five great divisions of the earth's surface, bounded by lines parallel to the equator, and named according to the prevailing temperature. 3. a ringlike or surrounding area, or one of a series of such areas, about a particular place, to all points within which a uniform charge is made for transportation or some similar service. 4. an area or district in a city or town under special restrictions as to building. 5. *Chiefly Poetic.* a girdle. —*v.t.* 6. to encircle or mark with zones. 7. to divide into zones, tracts, or areas, as according to existing characteristics, or as distinguished for some purpose. —*v.i.* 8. to be formed into a zone or zones. —**zon′al,** *adj.* —**zoned,** *adj.*

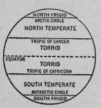

Terrestrial zones

zoo (zōō), *n.* a zoölogical garden.

zoo-, a word element meaning "living being," as in *zoöchemistry.* Also, **zoo-.**

zo·ö·chem·is·try (zō′ə kĕm′ĭs trĭ), *n.* the chemistry of the constituents of the animal body; animal chemistry. —**zo·ö·chem·i·cal** (zō′ə kĕm′ə kəl), *adj.*

zoögeog., zoögeography.

zo·ö·ge·og·ra·phy (zō′ə jĭ ŏg′rə fĭ), *n.* 1. the science treating of the geographical distribution of animals. 2. the study of the causes, effects, and other relations involved in such distributions. —**zo·ö·ge·og′ra·pher,** *n.* —**zo·ö·ge·o·graph·ic** (zō′ə jē′ə grăf′ĭk), **zo·ö·ge·o·graph·i·cal,** *adj.* —**zo·ö·ge·o·graph·i·cal·ly,** *adv.*

zo·ög·ra·phy (zō ŏg′rə fĭ), *n.* that branch of zoölogy which deals with the description of animals. —**zo·ög·raph·ic** (zō′ə grăf′ĭk), **zoö·graph′i·cal,** *adj.*

zo·öid (zō′oid), *n.* 1. any organic body or cell which is capable of spontaneous movement and of an existence more or less apart from or independent of the parent organism. —*adj.* 2. Also, **zo·öi′dal.** resembling, or of the nature of, an animal.

zool., 1. zoölogical. 2. zoölogist. 3. zoölogy.

zoölogical garden, a park in which live animals are kept for public exhibition.

zo·öl·o·gy (zō ŏl′ə jĭ), *n.* 1. the science that treats of animals or the animal kingdom. 2. the animals existing in a particular region. —**zo·ö·log′i·cal, zo·ö·log′ic,** *adj.* —**zo·öl′o·gist,** *n.*

zoom (zōōm), *v.i., v.t.* 1. to make a continuous humming sound. 2. to drive (an airplane) suddenly and sharply upward at great speed for a short distance. —*n.* 3. act of zooming.

zo·ö·mor·phic (zō′ə môr′fĭk), *adj.* 1. ascribing animal form or attributes to beings or things not animal; representing a deity under the form of an animal. 2. characterized by or involving such ascription or representation. 3. representing or using animal forms.

zo·ö·mor·phism (zō′ə môr′fĭz əm), *n.* 1. zoömorphic representation, as in ornament. 2. zoömorphic conception, as of a deity.

zo·öph·i·lous (zō ŏf′ə ləs), *adj.* 1. *Bot.* adapted to pollination by the agency of animals. 2. loving animals.

zo·ö·pho·bi·a (zō′ə fō′bĭ ə), *n.* a morbid fear of animals.

zo·ö·phyte (zō′ə fīt′), *n.* any of various animals resembling a plant, as a coral, a sea anemone, etc. —**zo·ö·phyt·ic** (zō′ə fĭt′ĭk), **zo·ö′phyt·i·cal,** *adj.*

zo·ö·plas·ty (zō′ə plăs′tĭ), *n. Surg.* the transplantation of living tissue from a lower animal to the human body. —**zo′ö·plas′tic,** *adj.*

zo·öt·o·my (zō ŏt′ə mĭ), *n.* the dissection of the anatomy of animals. —**zo·ö·tom·ic** (zō′ə tŏm′ĭk), **zo′ö·tom′i·cal,** *adj.* —**zo′ö·tom′i·cal·ly,** *adv.* —**zo·öt′o·mist,** *n.*

zoot suit (zōōt), *U.S. Slang.* a suit with baggy, tight-cuffed pants and an oversized coat.

Zorn (sôrn), *n.* Anders Leonhard, 1860–1920, Swedish painter, etcher, and sculptor.

Zo·ro·as·ter (zôr′ō ăs′tər), *n.* fl. c1000? B.C., Persian religious teacher.

Zo·ro·as·tri·an (zôr′ō ăs′trĭ ən), *adj.* 1. pertaining to Zoroaster, or to the ancient Persian religion founded by him. —*n.* 2. one of the followers of Zoroaster.

Zo·ro·as·tri·an·ism (zôr′ō ăs′trĭ ə nĭz′əm), *n.* the strongly ethical dualism, started in ancient Persia (Iran), which teaches a continuous struggle between the Good Spirit of the cosmos against the Evil Spirit. Also, **Zo′ro·as′trism.**

Zou·ave (zōō äv′, zwäv), *n.* 1. (*also l.c.*) one of a body of infantry in the French army, wearing a picturesque Oriental uniform. 2. a soldier wearing a similar dress.

zounds (zoundz), *interj. Archaic.* a minced oath.

Zr, *Chem.* zirconium.

zuc·chet·to (tsōōk kət′tô), *n., pl.* -tos. a small, round skullcap worn by Roman Catholic ecclesiastics, a priest's being black, a bishop's violet, a cardinal's red, and the Pope's white.

Zui·der Zee (zī′dər zē′), a former shallow inlet of the North Sea, in central Netherlands.

Zu·lu (zōō′lōō), *n., pl.* -lus, -lu, *adj.* —*n.* 1. a great Bantu nation of southeastern Africa. 2. a member of the Zulu nation. 3. their language. —*adj.* 4. of or pertaining to the Zulus or their language.

Zu·lu·land (zōō′lōō länd′), *n.* a territory in the Union of South Africa. 362,400 pop.; 10,427 sq. mi. *Cap.:* Eshowe.

Zu·ñi (zōō′nyē, sōō′-), *n., pl.* -ñis. a member of a tribe of North American Indians in western New Mexico. —**Zu′ñi·an,** *adj., n.*

Zu·rich (zōōr′ĭk), *n.* a city in N Switzerland. 347,600.

Zuy·der Zee (zī′dər zē′), Zuider Zee.

Zweig (tsvīкн), *n.* 1. Arnold, born 1887, German novelist, essayist, and dramatist. 2. Stefan, 1881–1942, German dramatist, critic, biographer, and novelist.

zwie·back (tswē′bäk′, swē′-, swī′bäk′), *n.* a kind of dried bread.

Zwing·li (tsvĭng′lē), *n.* Ulrich or Huldreich, 1484–1531, Swiss Protestant reformer.

Zwing·li·an (zwĭng′glĭ ən, tsvĭng′lĭ-), *adj.* 1. of or pertaining to Ulrich Zwingli or his doctrines, which were largely in agreement with those of Luther and offered a distinctive, spiritualist interpretation of the Lord's Supper. —*n.* 2. a follower of Zwingli. —**Zwing′li·an·ism,** *n.* —**Zwing′li·an·ist,** *n., adj.*

zwit·ter·i·on (tsvĭt′ər ī′ən), *n. Phys. Chem.* an ion carrying both a positive and a negative charge. Also, **zwit′ter·i′on.** —**zwit·ter·i·on·ic** (tsvĭt′ər ī ŏn′ĭk), *adj.*

zy·gote (zī′gōt, zĭg′ōt), *n. Biol.* 1. the cell produced by the union of two gametes. 2. the individual developing from such a cell.

zy·mase (zī′mās), *n. Biochem.* an enzyme in yeast which causes the decomposition of sugar into alcohol and carbon dioxide.

zy·mol·o·gy (zī mŏl′ə jĭ), *n.* the science that treats of fermentation and the action of enzymes. —**zy·mo·log·ic** (zī′mə lŏj′ĭk), *adj.* —**zy·mol′o·gist,** *n.*

zy·mol·y·sis (zī mŏl′ə sĭs), *n.* 1. *Biochem.* the digestive and fermentative action of enzymes. 2. fermentation or other hydrolytic reactions produced by an enzyme. —**zy·mo·lyt·ic** (zī′mə lĭt′ĭk), *adj.*

zy·mur·gy (zī′mûr jĭ), *n.* that branch of chemistry which deals with fermentation.

GUIDE TO CORRECT GRAMMAR: *Harrison Platt**

WHAT IS GOOD USAGE?

People who lack confidence in their knowledge of good English would like to have each spelling, pronunciation, meaning, and grammatical usage decided for them, once and for all, so that they could know that one is right and another wrong. They feel uncertain when choices are clearly permissible. Partly because they would like to have a fixed standard to settle all questions of usage, they come to believe that one exists and operates, and constantly repeat judgments and rules without examining the basis for them.

But if a fixed standard does exist, it must have a basis. Let us examine some of the possible bases for a rigid standard of good English.

The appeal to immemorial custom and history will not support a fixed standard. The whole history of the language has been one of change. No one would want to outlaw all innovations since *Beowulf*, and it is more than questionable that the language of Chaucer would suit today's needs as well as the speech we use. A word or a construction has no special virtue merely because it is old.

Only in a police state, rigidly controlled, could a fixed standard of correctness rest on a "supreme authority." In the United States we would want to know who is to pick the authority. Moreover, if the judgments of an authority ran counter to the speech habits of many people, its rulings would be ignored. This is indicated by the experience of some countries in which a single central authority to "reform" or control the language has been tried. When the French Academy was set up in the time of Cardinal Richelieu, one of its functions was supervision of the language. The Academy issued dictionaries and from time to time ruled on questions of grammar, spelling, and the like, which were submitted to its judgment. Although the Academy has no doubt had some influence on the French language, dialects have continued to flourish in the provinces, a rich and varied slang has never ceased being born in Paris and throughout the country, and even the literary language has evolved very largely without reference to the fiats of the Academy.

In spelling, pronunciation, meaning, and grammar, then, one looks in vain for a fixed standard or for an ultimate authority. Does this mean that there is no standard of good English and that one way of using the language is no better and no worse than any other? Not at all. There are two standards which can be safely followed.

(1) The purpose of language is communication—not communication in a void but communication between the writer or speaker and his audience. The personality and background of the writer or speaker must be taken into account. The way he expresses himself should be in keeping with his nature and background. It should be natural to him, to his habits of speech and thought. It should be as far as possible suitable to his audience. It should take into account their probable knowledge of what he is speaking about, their acquaintance with the concepts and vocabulary of his subject, their ability to follow abstract discussion, or their need for illustration, example, and explanation. Finally, the way he expresses himself should be adapted to his subject matter. An incident at a ball game requires a different sort of exposition from an explanation of atomic fission. A doctor discussing a problem of nutrition would properly use a different vocabulary, a different sentence structure, and a different approach to his subject if he were addressing, respectively, a convention of doctors, a parent-teacher association, and a class of fourth-grade pupils. That English is good English which communicates well the thought of a given speaker to a given audience. Change the thought, the speaker, or the audience, and the same mode of expression might be extremely bad. The measure of English is the effectiveness of its communication, and this in turn depends on its appropriateness to the subject, the speaker, and the audience.

(2) The second measure of language is social, not functional. People are accustomed to make judgments on the basis of language, just as they do on the basis of clothes and manners. A tuxedo is not better than slacks and sport shirt, it is simply more formal. One is suitable for certain occasions, the others for other occasions. In both formal and informal dress a reasonable degree of neatness and care is expected. It is the same with language.

Writing *thier* for *their* or *her's* for *hers* or saying *it ain't* for *it isn't* does not seriously interfere with communication, but it makes the writer or speaker look ignorant. Noticeably inappropriate mixtures of formal, polysyllabic vocabulary with slang or casual, informal phrases permit the same sort of adverse judgments that wearing a violently colored shirt with otherwise formal dress would. This principle is easy to apply to many language situations.

* *Harrison Platt is the coauthor (with Porter G. Perrin and others) of* Current Expressions of Fact and Opinion, Writing Good English, *and* Using Good English. *Formerly a member of the Department of English at Brown University, he is now associate editor at the Bobbs-Merrill Company.*

In sum, we may say that English usage is never just good. It is good in respect to a particular situation, speaker, and audience. If it is appropriate to all three, and if it is effective in communication, it is good.

What, in the light of these remarks, is the role of a dictionary in settling questions of pronunciation or meaning or grammar? It is *not* a legislating authority on good English. It attempts to record what usage at any time actually is. Insofar as possible, it points out divided usage. It indicates regional variations of pronunciation or meaning wherever practical. It points out meanings and uses peculiar to a trade, profession, or special activity. It suggests the levels on which certain words or usages are appropriate. A dictionary such as this, based on a realistic sampling of usage, furnishes the information necessary for a sound judgment of what is good English in a given situation. To this extent the dictionary is an authority, and beyond this authority should not go.

SECTION I. PUNCTUATION AND MECHANICS

Since English no longer uses more than a handful of inflectional endings (such as are still found in German nouns or French verbs), the relation between the words of a sentence is indicated by their order. Yet there is a great flexibility in word order. In spoken English the rise and fall of the voice and the natural pauses in speaking group the words in their proper relation to one another. In written English this grouping must be indicated by the various marks of punctuation.

In the nineteenth century, writers tended to write long, somewhat formal sentences. In order to guide the reader through the intricate patterns of these long sentences, they ordinarily used much more punctuation than is common today. Modern writers tend toward short sentences, approximating the informality of everyday speech.

The amount of punctuation should vary with the length and complexity of the writer's sentences. Excessive punctuation interferes with ready reading just as much as too little punctuation. Words and punctuation should combine to bring meaning. Any system of punctuation that calls for a particular mark of punctuation regardless of the length and difficulty of the sentence is mechanical and unlikely to produce in practice an easily read or "good" style. The proper punctuation is an integral part of writing a sentence just as the proper arrangement of the words is.

Here is the place for a useful bit of advice. If a sentence is very difficult to punctuate so as to make the meaning clear, the chances are that the arrangement of words and ideas is at fault. The writer will do better if he rearranges his word order instead of wrestling with his punctuation. A badly worded sentence cannot be made clear by any punctuation.

Grammars and handbooks of English give many rules of punctuation. These are useful for certain arbitrary customs, such as the use of apostrophes, quotation marks, and hyphens. For all the marks indicating pauses they are not very helpful. The difficulty is not so much in deciding what mark to use in a recognized and well understood situation (as the rule makers seem to think) but in recognizing a situation that will benefit by punctuation. In the great variety of English sentences, long and short, complicated or simple, these situations are not always clear-cut and require judgment on the writer's part.

On the other hand, there are only a few kinds of punctuation situations. To learn them and learn what to do with them is within the reach of anyone.

Ending Sentences

The sentence is the common unit of thought and language. At the end of a spoken sentence the voice usually drops and always makes a complete pause. In the written language this full stop has to be indicated by punctuation.

STATEMENTS. Most sentences are statements. They may be a single statement like the one just before this, or they may consist of two or more *very closely related in thought*, like this one. The full stop at the end of a statement is commonly indicated by a period (.). Any sentence in this paragraph will serve as an example.

QUESTIONS. If the sentence consists of a question instead of a statement, the full stop at the end is commonly indicated by a question mark (?):

Who owns this book?

Polite orders or requests are often put in question form. Sometimes no question is intended, as in the following:

Will you pass the bread, please.

The writer can use either a period or a question mark, depending on whether he feels there is a real question intended.

EXCLAMATIONS. An exclamation, whether long or short, even a single word, is closed by an exclamation point (!). Single words or characteristic phrasings offer no problem:

Gosh! What a beautiful day!

The degree of feeling or excitement will determine the proper close of sentences like the following:

Get out of here! (or) Get out of here.

An excessive number of exclamatory sentences often bothers readers. They should be used with caution for this reason.

INTERRUPTED THOUGHT. Especially in narrative, a writer sometimes has to deal with a sentence not entirely completed. A sentence broken off abruptly by an interruption may be closed off with a long (2-em) dash:

"Oh, the train doesn't leave for five——"
"All aboard," shouted the conductor.

If a thought is allowed to trail off unfinished, many writers close the sentence with an ellipsis (. . .).

If a writer knows when he has finished a sentence, the best choice of punctuation is not much of a problem. The knowledge that

552

he has finished it is sometimes less simple than it seems.

Punctuation to Separate

Within the sentence it is necessary to separate, with punctuation, groups of words which might otherwise run together and cause confusion.

MAIN CLAUSES. One of the major categories of sentence elements that should be kept distinct is that of main clauses in compound or in compound complex sentences. Main clauses are grammatically exactly like sentences. Where two or more are very closely related in thought, they are frequently joined together in a single sentence, sometimes with a conjunction between, sometimes with none. Although they are joined, they are not merged.

The old rule taught in most schools called for a semicolon between main clauses if there was no conjunction or if there was interior punctuation within either clause. If there was a conjunction between the clauses, it and a comma were sufficient to separate the clauses. To use a comma when a semicolon was called for, or no punctuation when the rule prescribed a comma, was regarded as a high crime against good English and branded the transgressor, to quote more than one textbook, as "deficient in sentence sense." The offense was called a comma fault, comma blunder, or, among the relatively charitable, a run-on sentence.

A close examination of the actual practice of publishers in current books and magazines will show that these rules are not observed with any regularity. In some magazines there will not be a single semicolon on a close-packed page. If a writer habitually uses a maximum of punctuation, if he writes long, involved clauses, he very frequently does use semicolons to separate them. But if he normally employs a minimum of punctuation and if his clauses are rather short and easily followed, he is likely to separate his clauses with a comma or, if a conjunction is present, by no punctuation at all.

The punctuation to be used depends on the writer's usual method of punctuation and on the length and difficulty of the particular sentence under consideration. Examples follow:

HEAVY OR FORMAL PUNCTUATION

With the abundance of the sea and the lush growth all around, poverty is no spur; and the native will work, if he will work at all, only at tasks which amuse him.

Battleships without air cover were proved fatally vulnerable; their preëminence was gone.

LIGHT OR INFORMAL PUNCTUATION

He could forgive, he could not forget. She stumbled against him and his arms went around her.

Compound verbs within the same clause are sometimes separated but need not be if the sentence is clearly written and easily followed:

He swung the car into the side road and gradually eased down the accelerator.

COÖRDINATE ELEMENTS. Many sentences contain series of coördinate (equal and similar) elements. They may be nouns, verbs, adjectives, adverbs, phrases, or clauses. If conjunctions (and, or, or the like) are used between them, no punctuation is ordinarily used to separate them. If, however, conjunctions are omitted entirely or used only between the last two elements, they are commonly separated by punctuation. If the elements in the series are simple and contain no internal punctuation, commas are ordinarily used. If commas lead to confusion because of internal punctuation, semicolons are used.

When a conjunction appears between the last two elements of a series, usage is divided on whether there should also be punctuation here. As in compound sentences, the answer is in the general system of punctuation being used. If heavy punctuation is the established system, the last two elements of a series should be separated by punctuation, regardless of the presence of the conjunction. If light punctuation is used elsewhere, the punctuation is omitted between the last two elements of a series:

The flag is red, white (,) and blue.

The group consisted of Charles White, the pianist; Willis Twyford, the trap drummer; Elmer Smith, on trumpet(;) and Bill Stone, guitar.

(In the last example, without the semicolons the quartet might be thought of as a sextet.)

Running, blocking, kicking (,) and passing with deadly precision, Young did as he pleased in the second half.

During the long, hot afternoons we splashed in the cool, green, sun-speckled water of the lake.

SUBORDINATE PHRASES OR CLAUSES. Usage is divided as to separating a phrase or a clause preceding a main clause. Again the question of heavy or light punctuation enters in. If the phrase or clause is short and closely related to the main clause, many writers prefer to omit a comma. If the phrase or clause is long or not very closely related to the main clause, as this one is, it is commonly separated from the main clause by a comma. This is a question of judgment, and the writer can decide whether punctuation would make his sentence clearer.

When words are brought together so as to form an apparent phrase not called for by the meaning, they should always be separated by punctuation, usually a comma:

Inside, Norah was weeping as she washed the dishes.

(A reader not guided by the comma might read: Inside Norah.)

To Frances, North seemed an old man.

(A reader not guided by the comma might read: To Frances North.)

QUOTATIONS. A quotation is separated from its introductory clause by a colon or a comma. If the quotation is long or formally introduced, most writers use a colon:

The President spoke as follows:

In informal quotation, such as dialogue in a story, a comma is the common mark:

Becky answered, "I'm staying right here."

Punctuation to Set Off

A child beginning to form sentences frequently succeeds in getting only a single, uncomplicated idea into each one. The result is the primer sentence: I see the dog. The dog is black. It has a curly tail. The next step is to join the three sentences together with *and's* between. The adult mind combines, producing a simple sentence: I see the black dog with a curly tail.

NONRESTRICTIVE PHRASES OR CLAUSES. Frequently a writer wants to add extra information not essential to the central meaning of the sentence. For example, the clause *who is six* does not affect the central meaning of the following sentence:

My niece, *who is six*, almost never cries.

Any word, phrase, or clause thus added to a sentence should be set off by a mark of punctuation *at beginning and end*. If the added information is very loosely related to the sentence, parentheses might be used to set it off. Obviously two marks are required, one at the beginning and one at the close of the added material:

Leningrad (*formerly called Petrograd*) was under siege for months.

Slightly more closely related information would be set off by paired dashes or commas, more commonly by commas. Again the punctuation requires two marks unless one would fall at the beginning or end of the sentence:

Lester Eaker—*a full-blooded Indian*—was the fastest man on the squad.

The radio, *which was playing softly*, filled in the pause.

RESTRICTIVE PHRASES OR CLAUSES. The sense is the best test of whether information is essential to the main meaning of the sentence. If a writer is in doubt, he can read the sentence with the questionable phrase or clause omitted:

People *who mutilate books* should not be allowed library privileges.

People . . . should not be allowed library privileges.

Obviously the writer of the original sentence did not mean that all people should be forbidden the use of the library, but only those few who mutilate books. The omission of the clause changes the main meaning of the sentence. It is therefore essential and should not be set off.

The third baseman, *who was left-handed*, came to bat.

The third baseman . . . came to bat.

The information that the batter was left-handed is not essential. Its omission does not change the main meaning. It should therefore be set off.

Look for additional, nonessential information in situations like the following:

Mary, I want you to clean your room. And you, *Tom*, should cut the grass.

Mr. Elkins, *the football coach*, was very popular with the boys.

The common automobile, *not the airplane*, is the most dangerous form of transportation.

Most of the climbers—*all but three*—turned back when the fog closed down.

It might be added, *incidentally*, that the rumor had no foundation.

Isak Dinesen's *Seven Gothic Tales* (*published by Random House*) is a remarkable book of short stories.

Although parentheses, paired dashes, or commas serve the same purpose and may be used to set off added but nonessential information, parentheses and dashes often make a break or pause too strong to suit the situation. Commas are by far the most widely used and the most satisfactory for this purpose. There is a prejudice against the use of many dashes held by publishers because they believe a page speckled with dashes is unsightly, and held by teachers because students unable to decide whether to use a comma or a semicolon compromise on a dash, again and again.

Styles of Punctuation

Throughout the whole discussion of punctuation, a conclusion has been emerging more and more clearly. Usage is almost everywhere divided, but this fact does not mean that there is no standard. In philosophical writing, thoughtful political or economic analysis, and the like, authors are aiming at fine distinctions, carefully weighed judgments. Their sentences are frequently long and much qualified. They tend, therefore, to punctuate heavily to help the reader through their complex thought. The norm in this sort of writing is rather heavy, rather formal punctuation. It should be consistently maintained.

On the other hand, the aim of the mystery story, the news magazine, the light novel is rapid, effortless reading. Sentences are usually rather simple in structure, short and informal. They need little punctuation and would merely be slowed down if more were put in. Publishers offering this sort of fare try to keep punctuation to its minimum essentials.

The aims of writers and publishers of all sorts are clarity and suitability to the general style. If these two aims are achieved consistently, the punctuation is good.

The use of the apostrophe, the hyphen, and quotation marks is to a great extent formalized, not subject to judgment, although divided usage will be found here too. The principal uses of these marks are discussed below.

The Apostrophe

POSSESSIVE FORMS. The most common use of the apostrophe is in spelling the possessive forms of nouns and some pronouns. If the word ends with any sound except that of *s* (or sometimes *sh* or *z*), the possessive is formed by the addition of *'s*. If the word ends with the sound of *s* (or sometimes *sh* or z), the possessive is formed by the addition of ' alone:

Ending not in s	Ending in s
girl's	companies'
nobody's	conscience'
men's	several horses'

Because most singulars do not end in s and form the possessive by adding 's, many writers feel uncomfortable when they form the possessive of a singular ending in s merely by the addition of '. There is a growing tendency to add an extra s to such words, especially when they consist of a single syllable. The extra s then provides an extra syllable and differentiates the sound of the possessive from the simple form:

Tom *Jones's* house instead of Tom *Jones'* house.

The *moss's* color instead of the *moss'* color.

Possessives of the personal pronouns do *not* take the apostrophe:

my, mine	our, ours
your, yours	your, yours
her, hers	their, theirs
his	whose
its

The possessive is used not only in its obvious function but in such phrases as: two *hours'* work, a *week's* trip.

OMISSION. The apostrophe is also used to show the omission of one or more letters in contractions: *he'll*, *I'm*, *it's* [*it is*], *can't*. In quoted dialogue or speech, an apostrophe indicates a speaker's omission of sounds represented by the conventional spelling of the word, for instance: the state of *No'th* Carolina.

PLURAL OF NUMBERS, ETC. An apostrophe is generally used in forming the plural of numbers, letters, or words thought of as words:

two *e's*	the *1890's*
four *6's*	the last two *the's*

PLURAL OF ABBREVIATIONS. Initials used as abbreviations are often treated the same way:

two GI's | no more IOU's

The Hyphen

The hyphen is regularly used when a word has to be broken at the end of a line to show that the remainder of the word is to follow on the next line. A word should be broken only between syllables: *port-able*, *run-ning*, *dis-pense*.

It is bad printing or typing practice to carry over a syllable of only two letters and virtually forbidden to carry over a single letter. It is equally forbidden to leave a single letter at the end of a line. Never break: *e-lapse*, *read-y*, *e-rase*. Avoid breaking: *real-ly*, *el-bow*, *du-ly*.

The hyphen is also used in a variety of compounds. Here usage is divided violently. A *half-finished* building stands beside a *half finished* building. *Slow-moving* traffic flows along with *slow moving* traffic. A *drug-store* clerk works in a *drug store* called The Evans *Drugstore*. Some publishers prefer to bring compounds into single words without space

or hyphen. A wag once said of *Time Magazine*, "*Time* abhors the hyphen." Other publishers simply follow the usage of a given dictionary. Others prefer wherever possible to break compounds into two words. Choose a system and try to be consistent.

The hyphen is sometimes used between a prefix ending with a vowel and a root beginning with the same vowel (*re-enter*, *co-operate*). Many writers prefer to write *re-ënter* and *coöperate* or *reenter* and *cooperate*. Again, usage is violently divided.

A hyphen is used when a prefix added would make confusion with another word:

Re-cover a chair but *recover* from an illness.

He decided to *re-turn* the bacon but *return* postage guaranteed.

A hyphen is used between a prefix and a proper name:

pro-Republican | anti-Russian

Compound numerals between twenty-one and ninety-nine and fractions are usually hyphenated:

one hundred and thirty-one
three-quarters

Some writers now omit this hyphen.

Quotations

In a piece of writing, words spoken by someone other than the author, directly quoted, are usually marked as quotation. Indirectly quoted words are not so marked:

DIRECT: President Coolidge said, "I do not choose to run."

INDIRECT: President Coolidge said that he did not choose to run.

Material is quoted or it is not; there can be no compromise between direct and indirect quotation.

The indication of quotation follows no logic but custom, and the system is arbitrary. Short quotations are usually marked off by quotation marks placed at the beginning and end of the actual quotation. If the quotation is interrupted (for example, by *he said*), the interruption makes a new end and beginning which should be marked off by quotation marks:

"Won't you come to dinner?" he asked.

"Come straight from the office."

In the United States quotations are usually indicated by double quotes (like those used above) and quotations within quotations are marked off by single quotes. ('These are single quotes.') In England the opposite system is used. Some publishers of American books and magazines use the English system. Either method is clear, and many book designers claim that the single quotes give a less speckled appearance.

The position of quotation marks in relation to other punctuation is ruled by a rather rigid custom in the United States, although the usage in England, equally fixed, is different. In the United States final quotes follow a period or a comma:

" . . . the greatest of these is charity."

The better class of pickers are "blanket

stiffs," men who own their own bedding.

Final quotes precede semicolons or colons:

"Divided we fall"; this truth illustrates itself day by day.

These two rules were built up in deference to the aesthetic feelings of a generation or two of typesetters.

The position of final quotes in relation to exclamation points, question marks, or dashes is determined by meaning. The test is the same for all three. If a question mark, for example, belongs with the quotation but not with the whole sentence, it goes inside final quotes:

The sentry called, "Who goes there?"

If it goes with the whole sentence, it should be placed outside the final quotes:

Who can say without vanity, "I am an honest man"?

Dashes usually come inside final quotes, but the meaning is the test.

Long quotations are often printed in a different type or with wider margins or with the lines closer together than the main text, to indicate quotation. If this method is followed, no quotation marks are used. It is much used where a number of rather long passages must be quoted, particularly in serious nonfiction.

If a quotation of two or more paragraphs is marked off by quotation marks, beginning quotes are usually placed at the beginning of each paragraph but no final quotes are written until the end of the quotation is reached.

Long or formal quotations are often marked off from their introductory sentences by colons. Short, informal quotations, such as the dialogue in a story, are usually marked off by a comma. Very short quotations, one or two words, require no punctuation:

FORMAL: The Secretary of State spoke as follows: ". . .

INFORMAL: "Hollywood," he said, "always reminds me of a stage set."

VERY SHORT: He said "No." (or) He said No (or) no.

Titles of songs, stories, poems, chapters of a book are usually written in quotes. Titles of books, plays, operas, motion pictures, symphonies, and the like are sometimes put in quotes although they are more commonly put in italics.

Capitalization

Although there is considerable variation in the use of capital letters in many situations, copyreaders and compositors have worked out rules for their own use, and for the most part capitalization follows well defined conventions. Some of the commoner conventions are as follows:

1. Capitalize the first word of each sentence; also the beginning of a word or phrase standing independently, like a sentence.

2. Capitalize the beginning of each line of poetry or conventional verse:

The steed bit his master;
How came this to pass?
He heard the good pastor
Cry, "All flesh is grass."
—ANON.

Exception: Some modern poetry is written without capitals or only with such capitals as prose would have.

3. Capitalize proper nouns and adjectives:

George Washington	French
the United States	Germanic
Elizabeth	New England

4. The German *von* and Dutch *van* in proper names are commonly not printed with a capital when part of a name, but usage varies:

Paul von Hindenburg
Vincent van Gogh

5. The French particles *de* and *du* and the Italian *di* and *da* are commonly written in lower case when they are preceded by a first name or title. Without title or first name, the particle is sometimes dropped, sometimes capitalized. One American newspaper's style book adds: "Except De Gaulle, which is always capped."

Marquis de Lafayette	Count de Mirabeau
[De] Lafayette	[De] Mirabeau

In English or American names these particles are commonly capitalized in all positions:

William De Morgan	Lee De Forest
De Morgan	De Forest

6. Do not capitalize words made from proper nouns now having a special meaning distinct from the proper name:

antimacassar	china
pasteurize	macadam

7. Capitalize recognized geographical names:

Ohio River	Strait of Juan de Fuca
Cascade Mountains	Gulf of Mexico

8. Capitalize the following when they follow a single proper name and are written in the singular:

Butte	Gap	Peninsula
Canyon	Glacier	Plateau
County (in U.S.)	Harbor	Range
Creek	Head	Mountain
Delta	Ocean	Valley

For example, the *Sacramento River*, but the *Tennessee and Cumberland rivers*.

9. Capitalize the following in the singular and plural when they follow a proper name:

Hill	Mountain
Island	Narrows

10. Capitalize in the singular whether placed before or after the name. Capitalize in the plural when they come before the name and sometimes following a single name:

Bay	Lake	Point
Cape	Military Camp	Shoal
Desert	Mount	Sea
Gulf	Peak	Strait
Isle	Plain	Zone

For example, *Lakes George and Champlain* but *Malheur and Goose lakes.* Contrast *Muscle Shoals.*

11. Capitalize compass directions when they designate particular regions, also the nicknames or special names for regions or districts:

East Tennessee   the South
Middle Atlantic States   the Near East
the Hub   Upper Michigan

Exceptions: Do not capitalize merely directional parts of states or countries:

eastern Washington   southern Indiana

12. Capitalize the names of streets, parks, buildings, etc.:

Forty-second Street   Central Park
Merchandise Mart   Palmolive Building

Exceptions: Do not capitalize such categories of buildings as *library, post office,* or *museum,* written without a proper name, unless local custom makes the classification equivalent to a proper name.

13. Capitalize the names of political parties, alliances, movements, classes, religious groups, etc.:

Democratic party   Royalist Spain
Labor party   Axis powers
Republicans   Soviet Russia
Protestants   Negroes

14. Capitalize divisions, departments, and offices of government when the official name is used. Do not capitalize incomplete or roundabout designations:

Department of Commerce
Circuit Court of Marion County
Bureau of Labor Statistics
Congress (United States)
Senate (United States)
House of Burgesses
United States Army (but army doctor)
Board of Aldermen
the council
the lower house (of Congress)
the bureau
the legislature

15. Capitalize the names of wars, battles, treaties, and important events:

Revolutionary War   Black Death
Congress of Vienna   War of 1812

Do not capitalize *war* or *treaty* when used without the distinguishing name.

16. Capitalize the numeral used with kings, dynasties, or organizations. Numerals preceding the name are ordinarily spelled out; those following the name are commonly put in Roman numerals:

Nineteenth Amendment   Third Army
Forty-eighth Congress   Henry IV

17. Capitalize titles of rank or honor, military or civil, academic degrees, decorations, etc., when written with the name, and all titles of honor or rank when used for specific persons in place of the name:

General Bradley
the Senator from Ohio (but a senator)
Nicholas Murray Butler, Doctor of Letters
the Earl of Rochester
King George
the Archbishop of Canterbury

18. Capitalization of the titles of books, plays, articles, pieces of music, and so forth is handled in two ways. The commoner method is to capitalize all main words (the nouns, verbs, adjectives, and adverbs) as well as the first word. The Library of Congress style, however, until recently called for the capitalization of only the first word and any proper nouns or adjectives appearing in the title.

The Gem of the Prairie
Mourning Becomes Electra

Titles of chapters in a book, and references to parts of a specific book, such as *Bibliography, Index,* or *Table of Contents,* are commonly capitalized.

In references to the names of newspapers and periodicals, an initial article need not be capitalized or treated as part of the title:

The story was reprinted in the *Reader's Digest.*

19. Capitalize the first word of a direct quotation:

An aide reported, "The left wing is being driven back in confusion."

20. Capitalize the first person singular pronoun in the nominative: I. None of the other pronouns are capitalized.

21. Capitalize personifications:

Darwin drew a picture of Nature red in tooth and claw.

The Senator talked grandly of Industry as a mother holding twin children, Labor and Capital, on her capacious lap.

22. Capitalize the various names of God or of the Christian Trinity, both nouns and adjectives, and also pronouns clearly referring to the Deity:

the Savior   the Word   Jehovah
the Messiah   the Son   Yahweh
the Almighty   the Virgin Mary   Holy Ghost

23. In expressions of time and date, A.M., P.M., B.C. and A.D. are usually set in small capitals without space between them:

9:40 A.M.   12:00 M. (noon)   6:10 P.M.
12:00 P.M.   A.D. 1491   42 B.C.

SECTION II. SPELLING

Many scholars have maintained that English spelling either should represent by a simple phonetic system the sounds of the words or by a careful preservation of ancient spellings indicate the etymology. Whatever value can be attached to these goals, it is certain that English spelling makes a poor compromise and achieves neither one.

Originally Germanic, the language received a strong coloring of French following the Norman Conquest, and from the Renaissance to the present it borrowed extensively from Latin and Greek. Other languages, such as Spanish, Hebrew, Persian, and the American Indian languages, have also been drawn on.

English speech has had sufficient vigor to anglicize the pronunciation to a considerable degree. But since the Norman Conquest the language has lacked an equally effective system of phonetic representation. Many of the anglicized foreign words still retain a good part of their original spelling.

Greek remains in such spellings as *paradigm, psychology,* and *pneumonia.* Germanic spellings linger in *gnaw, knight, knee,* and *sigh.* Latin plurals are still found in words like *data, alumnae,* and *radii.* French spellings are found in *façade, racquet, mortgage,* and *oblique.* Efforts to indicate French sounds have made three different words from the French *gentil: gentle, genteel,* and *jaunty.*

Long lists of such words, containing remnants of foreign or ancient spellings, and other lists of words modeled on them by analogy could easily be made up.

It is true that English spelling has gradually changed. Etymology has been obscured in many words, but still no simple phonetic system has been developed. Many proposals for reform of spelling have been put forward, good and bad, well based and badly based, but none of them has gone to the root of the problem and none of them has had sufficient popular support to overcome conservatism and inertia.

The result is that anyone who wants to spell with the precision of an educated man must devote a disproportionate amount of his study to mastering the unsystematic system of English spelling, with its myriads of exceptions.

A lesser result, but by no means an unimportant one, is a great amount of divided usage, not only between England and America, but among educated people in the same region.

It has already been said that English lacks an effective system of phonetic representation; that is, it has no single character to represent each English sound. Frequently as many as six or seven letters or combinations of letters can be used to indicate the same sound. Meantime, the same letters or combinations are also used to indicate other sounds.

Spelling Rules

No spelling rule should be followed blindly, for every rule has exceptions and words analogous in some forms may differ in others.

1. SILENT E DROPPED. Silent *e* at the end of a word is usually dropped before a suffix beginning with a vowel: *abide, abiding; recite, recital; balance, balancing; dose, dosage; plague, plaguing, plaguy; force, forcible; virile, virility.*

Exceptions: Words ending in *ce* or *ge* retain the *e* before a suffix beginning with *a* or *o* to keep the soft sound of the consonant: *charge, chargeable; notice, noticeable; courage, courageous. Mortgagor,* beside *mortgager* and pronounced the same, follows the main rule and is an exception to the exceptions. *Dye, hoe,* and *shoe* retain the *e* before *ing. Mileage* retains *e,* and variant forms of some words in *-able (saleable, useable)* keep the *e.*

2. SILENT E KEPT. A silent *e* following a consonant (or another *e*) is usually retained before a suffix beginning with a consonant: *late, lateness; agree, agreement; spite, spiteful;* but *argue, argument.*

Exceptions: *fledgling, acknowledgment, judgment, wholly,* and a few similar words.

3. FINAL CONSONANT DOUBLED. A final consonant following a single vowel in one-syllable words or in a syllable that will take the main accent when combined with a suffix is doubled before a suffix beginning with a vowel: *begin, beginning; occur, occurred; refer, referring* (but *reference,* since the accent shifts); *defer, deferred* (but *deference*); *quiz, quizzing; swim, swimming; bag, baggage; squat, squatter* (*u* = consonant *w*).

Exceptions: *h* and *x* (*ks*) in final position. *Transferable, gaseous,* and a few others.

4. FINAL CONSONANT SINGLE. A final consonant following another consonant or a double vowel or diphthong or not in a stressed syllable is not doubled before a suffix beginning with a vowel: *travel, traveler; part, parting; remark, remarkable; rival, rivaled; river, riverine.*

Exceptions: An unaccented syllable does not prevent doubling of the final consonant by many writers, especially in British usage: *traveller* beside *traveler,* etc.

5. DOUBLE CONSONANTS REMAIN. Double consonants are usually retained before a suffix except when a final *l* is to be followed by *ly* or *less.* To avoid a triple *lll,* one *l* is usually dropped: *full, fully; dull, dully.*

Exceptions: Usage is divided, with *skilful* beside *skillful, instalment* beside *installment,* etc.

6. FINAL Y. If the *y* follows a consonant, change *y* to *i* before all endings except *ing.* Do not change it before *ing* or if it follows a vowel: *bury, buried, burying; marry, marriage, marrying; apply, application; try, tries;* but *attorney, attorneys; employ, employed.*

Exceptions: *day, daily; gay, gaily; lay, laid; say, said.* Possessive case retains the *y* before '*s: country's.* There is also some divided usage as *dryly,* beside *drily.*

7. FINAL IE TO Y. Words ending in *ie* change to *y* before *ing: die, dying; lie, lying.*

8. DOUBLE AND TRIPLE E REDUCED. Words ending in double *e* drop one *e* before an ending beginning in *e,* to avoid a triple *e.* Words ending in silent *e* usually drop the *e* before endings beginning in *e* to avoid forming a syllable. Other words ending in a vowel sound commonly retain the letters indicating the sound. *Free-ed = freed; tree-ed = treed; cue-ed = cued; shoe-ed = shoed;* but *canoe-ing = canoeing; hoeing, shoeing,* etc.

9. EI OR IE. (1) Words having the sound of *ē* are commonly spelled *ie* following all letters but *c;* with a preceding *c,* the common spelling is *ei.* Examples: *believe, achieve, besiege* but *conceit, ceiling, receive, conceive.* When the sound is *ā* the common spelling is *ei* regardless of the preceding letter. Examples: *eight, weight, deign, inveigh.*

Exceptions: *either, neither, seize, financier;* some words in which *e* and *i* are pronounced separately, such as *notoriety;* a few words having the characteristic spelling but neither the *ē* nor the *ā* sound: *height, sleight.*

10. WORDS ENDING IN C. Before an ending beginning with *e, i,* or *y,* words ending in *c* commonly add *k* to keep the *c* hard: *panic, panicky; traffic, trafficked; picnic, picnicking.*

11. COMPOUNDS. Some compounds written

as a unit bring together unusual combinations of letters. They are seldom changed on this account. *Bookkeeper, roommate, untilled, upreach, tearoom, withhold.*

Exceptions: A few words are regularly clipped when compounded, such as *full* and *mass* as suffixes in *awful, cupful, plentiful, Christmas, Michaelmas,* etc. Also a few ancient compounds such as *welcome, welfare.* Also, in a sense, all cases of assimilation in compounds, as in *immature.*

SPELLING CAUTION. Beware of homonyms: *bear* and *bare; flare* and *flair; their* and *there,* etc.

SECTION III. PLURALS

1. SIMPLE PLURALS. The great majority of English words used as nouns form plurals by adding *s* to the singular form, the *s* becoming part of the syllable to which it is added: *state, states; stare, stares; trolley, trolleys.*

2. NEW SYLLABLES WITH S OR ES. Words ending, regardless of spelling, with the sound of *ch, j* (as in *bridge*), *s, sh, x,* or *z* would become unpronounceable with *s* added to the final syllable. A new syllable is formed by the addition of *es* or, if they end in a silent *e, s* alone: *lurch, lurches; ax, axes; judge, judges; pass, passes; flush, flushes.*

3. FINAL F. Some words ending in *f* form their plurals regularly in *s,* others change *f* to *v* and their plurals end *ves.* A few have plurals in either form. *Gulf, gulfs; handkerchief, handkerchiefs; proof, proofs; pontiff, pontiffs;* but *calf, calves; half, halves; knife, knives; leaf, leaves; self, selves;* and *hoof, hoofs, hooves; scarf, scarfs, scarves.*

4. FINAL O. Some words ending in *o* form their plurals regularly in *s,* others add *es* and some have both forms: *canto, cantos; folio, folios; dynamo, dynamos; piano, pianos; silo, silos;* but *echo, echoes; potato, potatoes; tomato, tomatoes;* and *cargo, cargos, cargoes; tornado, tornados, tornadoes,* etc.

5. FINAL S. Some words ending in *s* in the singular have the same form in the plural: *athletics, civics, headquarters, mathematics, means.*

6. FINAL Y. Nouns ending in *y* following a consonant usually change the *y* to *i* and end *ies* in the plural: *body, bodies; fly, flies; berry, berries.*

7. SINGULAR AND PLURAL ALIKE. The names of many, but not all, animals are the same in the singular and plural: *deer, elk, fowl, salmon, quail,* etc. Some also have plural forms, rarely used.

Some collectives have plurals in *s* and also plurals like their singulars: *five thousand, many thousands,* etc.

8. PLURALS WITH SINGULAR LACKING OR RARE. Some words like the following are virtually always plural: *barracks, quarters, gallows, calipers, means, chicken pox (pocks), measles, mumps, scissors, pliers, trousers, tactics, species.*

9. PLURALS BY CHANGE OF VOWEL. A few common words retain an old plural formed by change of the internal vowel: *man, men; foot, feet; mouse, mice; louse, lice; tooth, teeth;*

woman, women; and compounds of any of these.

10. OLD PLURALS IN EN. A few common words survive with an old plural in *en: child, children; brother, brethren* (beside *brothers*); *ox, oxen; eye,* rare *eyen* (beside *eyes*).

11. SPECIAL PLURALS. For special plurals, such as *radius, radii; dilettante, dilettanti; alumna, alumnae; datum, data; crisis, crises.* see the entries in the dictionary proper.

SECTION IV. CORRESPONDENCE

Every business letter performs a double function. The original carries a message to its recipient. The carbon copy, retained in the sender's files, serves as an automatic record. Since either the original or the carbon may be referred to long afterward, both must contain all the information that will then be required.

In addition to the material in the letter proper, the letter must contain the name and address of the recipient (necessary for the file copy) and the name and address of the sender (necessary for reply to the original) as well as the date of writing and often other information.

Certain more or less standardized forms have been worked out for furnishing this information briefly and with a minimum of typing effort, clearly and with an attractive appearance. Within these broad conventions each company or organization works out and employs its own preferred style for all correspondence. A newcomer can familiarize himself with an organization's house style by a few minutes' study of the correspondence files.

Most letters today are variations of the block style because it permits a stenographer to get out a maximum of work in a minimum of time. Brief descriptions of the principal variations will follow a discussion of the standard block style.

Heading

On plain paper the heading consists of the sender's address and the date of writing. It is commonly placed so as to align with the right margin of the body of the letter, at least two inches below the top of the sheet. Each line should be started directly below the line above so as to form a block:

19483 Hartwell Street
Detroit 21, Michigan
June 23, 1949

No punctuation is required at the end of a line.

On a letterhead the sender's address is printed and only the date need be typed in. It is placed so as to end in alignment with the right margin of the letter proper, usually about four spaces below the head but lower down if the letter is short. Sometimes the date is centered below the head.

Inside Address

The inside address should contain the recipient's name and full address. The state is commonly written on the same line as the city. Each line is aligned with the left margin of the letter proper. It is usually placed four spaces below the heading but a little lower if the letter is short.

In letters addressed to an individual some business organizations prefer to have the inside address appear at the end of the letter, two to four spaces below the signature. This position is also useful for personal typewritten correspondence of which a carbon is to be kept. It gets the formal information into the carbon but it avoids a formal look at the opening.

In addressing an individual with a long title the following forms are convenient:

Mr. John Jackson, Chairman
Committee on International
  Commerce
Mr. John Jackson
Chairman of the Committee on
  International Commerce

Frequently people are proud of a military rank, an honorary title, or a doctor's degree. They will appreciate the accurate use of rank or title. *Dr.* and *Mr.* are regular abbreviations. Abbreviations of other titles may be used, but it is more courteous to write them out in full. However, some college professors and nonmedical doctors prefer not to use the title. When the recipient's preference is known it should always be followed.

Salutation

Beginning at the left margin, usually two spaces below the inside address, in a letter to a single individual write *Dear Sir: Dear Madam: Dear Mr.* (or *Mrs.* or *Miss*)————:. A woman whose marital status is unknown to the writer should always be addressed as *Miss.* In a letter to an organization, corporation, company, or group of any kind begin *Gentlemen:* . . . . After any of these it is conventional to use a colon.

Some letters addressed to an organization or company may be directed to the attention of a particular individual or official. This may be done as follows:

Attention of the Sales Manager (or)
  Attention: Sales Manager
Attention of Mr. Wilbur M. Schwartz (or)
  Attention: Mr. Wilbur M. Schwartz

The line is usually placed between the inside address and the salutation, with two spaces above and below. It is sometimes written on the same line with the salutation placed so as to end in alignment with the right-hand margin. To bring it to the immediate notice of the recipient, it is sometimes underlined. Even though the letter is directed to the attention of a single person, since it is addressed to an organization the proper salutation remains *Gentlemen:*.

The proper arrangement of inside address, direction of attention, and salutation is as follows:

Stamford Brass Co., Inc.
516 Little Street
Stamford 4, Connecticut
Attention: Advertising Manager
Gentlemen:

Some companies and organizations regularly indicate the subject of the letter to follow. A special place for a brief statement of the subject is provided on some letterheads. On plain paper it is usually centered on the same line as the salutation or two spaces below it:

Nonpareil Woolens
Woonsocket 2, R. I.
Gentlemen: Subject: *Insurance*

The body of the letter follows, typed in single space with double space between paragraphs. Each line begins at the left margin without indentation.

Complimentary Close

In formal business correspondence the complimentary close is limited to *Yours truly*, or variations of it such as *Very truly yours*, or, if the letter is addressed to a person of high reputation or office, *Respectfully yours.* Any of these phrases is followed by a comma.

A few conservative writers cling to the old form, now rapidly dropping out of use, in which the final sentence of the body of the letter is run into the complimentary close in the following manner:

Hoping to hear from you soon, I remain

Very truly yours,

The complimentary close should be set two spaces below the body of the letter. It is usually begun at the center or very slightly to the right of center.

Signature

The signature of a letter is handled in a variety of ways. If the firm name is used, it should be typed in full, two spaces below the complimentary close. Below it, or below the complimentary close if no firm name is used, space is left for the longhand signature of the writer. Below the space is typed the writer's position, often preceded by his typewritten name. It may be arranged in block or in an oblique form as the writer prefers:

(1) Yours truly,
    ACME MANUFACTURING COMPANY
    Richard Smith
    Sales Manager
(2) Yours truly,
    ACME MANUFACTURING COMPANY
        Richard Smith
        Sales Manager
(3) Yours truly,
    Richard Smith
    Sales Manager
(4) Yours truly,
        Richard Smith
        Sales Manager

When the writer has a personal friendship with the recipient of the letter, he need not restrict himself to the formal phrase. He is free to avail himself of any of the closing phrases of personal correspondence.

In order to identify the writer of the letter and the stenographer, it is customary to put the initials of the writer, followed by those of the stenographer, in the lower left-hand corner: RLS/J or RLS/AJ. If any enclosures are to be made, *Encl.* or *Enclosures* is added directly below these initials as a reminder to the person who puts the letter in its envelope.

Address on Envelope

The address should start at or near the center. Double spacing is preferred. Arrangement may be either block or oblique. Where zone numbers are provided, they should be written after the name of the city. The Post Office prefers to have the State written on a separate line. If the address requires more than four lines, the least essential information, such as the room number in a building, should be written separately in the left-hand corner of the envelope.

Special Letters

Occasionally it is necessary to write to an official of the city, State, or national government, to a college president, a dignitary of the Roman Catholic Church, or the like. If the writer happens to be intimately acquainted with the recipient, he can write as he likes. If not, standard forms are used. Here is a list:

U. S. SENATOR

Name: The Hon. Horace Dana
Address: United States Senate, Washington, D. C.
Salutation: My dear Senator: (or, less formal)
Dear Mr. Dana:
Close: Yours very truly,

CONGRESSMAN

Name: The Hon. Horace Dana
Address: United States House of Representatives, Washington, D. C.
Salutation: Dear Sir: (or, less formal) Dear Mr. Dana:
Close: Yours very truly,

CABINET MEMBER

Name: The Secretary of the Interior
Address: Washington, D. C.
Salutation: Dear Mr. Secretary:
Close: Yours very truly,

PRESIDENT OF THE UNITED STATES

Name: The President
Address: Washington, D. C.
Salutation: Sir: (or, less formal) Dear Mr. President:
Close: Yours very truly,

GOVERNOR OF A STATE

Name: The Hon. Warren Dewey
Address: Governor's Office (or State House or Executive Mansion), State capital, State
Salutation: Dear Sir:
Close: Yours very truly,

MAYOR

Name: The Hon. E. E. Harper
Address: Mayor's Office, city, State
Salutation: Dear Sir: (or, less formal) Dear Mr. Mayor:
Close: Yours very truly,

JUDGE

Name: The Hon. Frank Murphy
Address: United States Supreme Court, Washington, D. C.
Salutation: Dear Sir:
Close: Yours very truly,

FOREIGN AMBASSADOR

Name: His Excellency the Brazilian Ambassador
Address: Washington, D. C.
Salutation: Dear Mr. Ambassador:
Close: Yours very truly,

FOREIGN CONSUL

Name: The British Consul
Address: street, city, State
Salutation: Dear Mr. Consul:
Close: Yours very truly,

BISHOP

Name: The Rt. Rev. James Trenton, D. D.
Address: Bishop of Portland, Portland, Oregon
Salutation: Sir: (or) Right Reverend Bishop:
Close: Yours sincerely, or Very truly yours, "Sincerely yours in Christ," should be used by a Catholic writer.

PARISH PRIEST

Name: The Rev. John Kelly
Address: Rector of St. ————'s Church, street and number, city, State.
Salutation: Dear Reverend Father: (or) Reverend and dear Father:
Close: Sincerely yours, (or) Very truly yours,

Variations in Style

There are many variations of style. Stenographers should remember that no single style has any special claim to correctness and that a style different from that which they were taught in business school or which they used in a preceding job is not therefore to be condemned. Within limits, each part of the letter may be arranged to suit the preference of the writer.

Block Indented is about as much used as block. It is the same as block except that the first line of each paragraph is indented five spaces or more.

Extreme Block is an ultra-modern arrangement. Heading, inside address, salutation, complimentary close, and signature are all aligned with the left margin of the letter proper. Because the carriage of the typewriter is always thrown clear over, it is quick and easy for the typist. The extreme block is, however, open to the objection that its balance is likely to be too heavy on the left.

Oblique is a legacy of the handwritten letter. In this style the heading, the inside address, and the signature are arranged with each successive line several spaces to the right of the line above. Because this style puts a heavy burden on the stenographer and mistakes in spacing are likely to occur, the use of it has almost disappeared.

SECTION V. PREPARATION OF COPY FOR THE TYPESETTER OR PUBLISHER

In the event that a piece of writing is to be printed, the writer wants his manuscript in proper form before he sends it in. To prepare a manuscript so as to cause a minimum of resetting and correction, the writer must begin at a point before the final typing of the manuscript is made.

If the manuscript is to go directly to the

typesetter, it will have no editing after it leaves the hands of the author. The writer should study similar publications and note details of punctuation, capitalization, the use of italics or quotes for titles, a useful arrangement of footnote material, if any, and so forth. Before the final draft is typed, he should put his manuscript in the form he has decided to adopt.

If the manuscript is to be published in a magazine or book put out by a regular publisher, he should study the publisher's preferred style and, as far as he can, make his own manuscript conform to it. He should also expect that the publisher will have his copy gone over and altered where it fails to conform to the publisher's regular style.

With the rough draft of the manuscript corrected, the final typing is the next step. *It is simple common sense always to make at least one carbon, usually two.* Many a manuscript has gone astray in the mail, or been lost or burned up in a fire. Frequently, too, the publisher or typesetter has a question that requires reference to the text, and if the writer has no text handy he is in an embarrassing position.

The final typing should be double-spaced on one side of regular 8½″ x 11″ typewriter paper. Margins should be ample, at least an inch and a half at the top and left, at least an inch at the right and bottom. A black typewriter ribbon and fresh carbon paper help to make both original and carbons easily read. Everyone who has to read and handle manuscript appreciates the use of opaque paper.

If corrections are necessary, they should be made neatly and clearly. If an addition is too long to be written clearly between the typed lines, it may be written in the margin and a guide line drawn to the point of insertion. If the corrections on any page destroy legibility, or even impair it, the page should be retyped.

Proofreader's Marks and Proofreading

The common marks used by proofreaders and typesetters are listed and illustrated here. If the writer feels the slightest doubt of his ability to make clear his intention with them, he can write on the margin a brief note to the typesetter, explaining precisely what he wants done.

After a piece of writing is set in type, proofs are pulled and sent to the author for correction or approval. Usually the proofs are galleys, long sheets equal to a little more than three pages of an ordinary book. Each galley represents a heavy tray of metal at the typesetter's, and any change in the proof must be duplicated in the type itself.

When the original manuscript was set in type, the typesetter read each line of the manuscript, word for word, and transcribed it. When the corrected galleys go back to the typesetter so that the type can be made to correspond with the amended galleys, the typesetter does not read them. He looks only at the margins. Any correction not clearly marked outside the type area will be ignored. All corrections should be made in the margins and leader lines drawn to the precise spot.

PROOFREADER'S MARKS

⩑	Insert comma	⌄	Superscript (number specified)
⩛	Insert apostrophe		
⩛	Insert quotation marks	⩘	Subscript (number specified)
⊙	Insert period		
⊙	Insert colon	⌗	Insert space
;/	Insert semicolon	hr⌗	Hair space between letters
?/	Insert question mark	↓	Push down space
=/	Insert hyphen	⊏	Move to left
⅟M	One-em dash	⊐	Move to right
2/M	Two-em dash	⊔	Lower
en	En dash	⊓	Elevate
|.|.|.|	Ellipsis (If preceded by a period there will be 4 dots.)	X	Broken letter
		⌢	Ligature (ÆEsop)
		ⓢⓟ	Spell out (U.S.)
ℐ	Delete	stet	Let it stand (some day)
⌒	Close up	wf	Wrong font
⌔	Delete and close up	bf	Set in boldface type
⩲	Reverse; upside-down	rom	Set in roman type
∧	Insert (caret)	ital	Set in italic type
ℛ	Paragraph	sc	Small capitals
noℛ	No paragraph; run in	caps	Capitals
tr	Transpose (this for only is)	lc	Set in lower case
=	Align	ld>	Insert lead between lines

RAPID VOCABULARY BUILDER: *S. Stephenson Smith*[*]

A good dictionary rightly used is an ideal first aid for increasing your command of words. When you look up a word, form the habit of acquiring all its meanings.

Take the word *sport*. Its more common senses are very familiar. To a scientist, however, a *sport* is not necessarily a jauntily dressed generous spender interested in anything he can bet on. In the biological sense, a *sport* is "a mutation." How did this odd sense develop? The Romans called a freak *lusus naturae*, "one of nature's jokes," and thought such a creature a proper object of laughter. So did the Elizabethans, who translated the Latin phrase as "a sport of nature." Dropping the qualifying phrase, the scientists took over the term, using *sport* as the general term for "a mutation—a plant or animal deviating sharply from type." The Elizabethans also used *sport* to mean "amorous dalliance," a sense now obsolete.

Thus, a good look through the telescope of history, as the dictionary focuses it, yields new meanings for many an ordinary word. This may seem like an attempt to progress while sitting still, since no new words are added to the total stock. Actually, since new meanings have been acquired, the vocabulary has been effectively stretched. You will, in fact, find you have greatly extended your effective vocabulary by gaining full mastery of words you only half knew.

If at the same time you learn the system of dictionary shorthand—the abbreviations by which the dictionary-maker indicates what part of speech a word is, and the labels showing possible limitations on its use—you can employ the word far more resourcefully in your own talk and writing. For you will know it in the round. You will also become more fully aware of words. A thoroughly awakened interest in words—even in familiar ones—is the best stimulus for enlarging vocabulary.

Systematic Memorizing

It is possible to collect new words as a magpie assembles a heap of shiny bits of glass and metal. Crossword puzzle addicts acquire such a collection. But anyone who intends to put new words to sensible use wants some order in the heap. He looks for a pattern into which new words will fit.

* *S. Stephenson Smith is the author of* The Command of Words, How To Double Your Vocabulary, *and the* Style Rule. *He is the managing editor of the* International Musician *and research director for The American Federation of Musicians, and teaches courses in editing and in vocabulary building at New York University.*

Occasionally a novel word may be remembered because of a random association. But if a number of words are to be added, and the vocabulary steadily expanded, ways must be found to insure that new words fall into place in the systematic memory, where they become permanent possessions.

Your Own Word Book

To achieve this end, you may well want to start a word book of your own—preferably a looseleaf notebook of pocket size. Here are some of the handy memory pegs and devices for organizing such a memory aid:

1. TIE SEVERAL WORDS TO ONE. Many of the words in a dictionary are defined by giving one or more of the closest synonyms for the key word. Group them together, and write sentences which show the different shades of meaning of these synonyms. Any of the words which are new to you will thus be fixed in your memory.

Readiness

2. TRY SUMMONING UP SEVERAL WORDS TO EXPRESS A GIVEN IDEA. By this means you will start to build working synonym lists of your own. You can then check them in the dictionary, to see which word will best serve your purpose.

In business writing, for example, the notion of decrease occurs often, particularly in a falling market. Business writers do not content themselves with the dictionary synonyms for *decrease:* they speak of a *drop*, a *dwindling*, a *shrinkage*, a *falling off*, a *sag*, a *lessening*, or a *lowering*. These are not all exact synonyms for *decrease*, but any of them will serve fairly well to keep from stacking up repetitions of *decrease* on a page. The exact learned synonym, *diminution*, would be pedantic on a business page.

You can try your hand at this game—say by giving equivalents for *increase*, many of which will be words of opposite meaning to those which serve to replace *decrease*. In this connection, it may be well to bear in mind the French view that the surest way to prove you know a word is by giving its antonym.

Sureness

3. LEARN NEW WORDS TWO WAYS, so that you not only know the dictionary definition, but can also summon up the word when you feel the need of it to express a certain meaning. When you learn a new word, do not be content with only a knowledge of its meaning; try it in a few sentences; use it when an appropriate occasion arises.

4. ALWAYS REMEMBER THE NEW KEY WORD IN A JOKE. When Fred Allen in one of his scripts speaks of "the legless invertebrate," and you find out a few lines later that he is talking about a worm, make a note of the fact that you can cash in even on a comedian's tricks with words as a way of improving your vocabulary. To be sure, they use long, hard words chiefly to make fun of them or to pun on them.

Since, however, a good part of the burden of extending word knowledge beyond the commonest ten thousand words (which make up the average American's reading vocabulary) consists in the effort required to master the long, hard words—the classical element in our language—you should not overlook any approach which will facilitate picking up these words.

The Case for Long, Hard Words

There is a serious case for long, hard words. One such word can take the place of ten. It can serve as a necessary synonym to prevent repetition. It is sometimes the only exact word to express a given technical meaning. On all these counts, it is worthwhile putting in work on long, hard words— even though you will use them only on rare occasions, and even though they make up less than two percent of the running words encountered in reading. When you need them, however, you need them badly. So it will not do to leave them to the comedians.

Word Histories

5. RUN DOWN THE HISTORY OF ANY INTERESTING NEW WORD WHICH YOU ENCOUNTER. Often you will find clues in the dictionary which invite you to engage in detective work on words. By so doing, you will learn a great deal about the history of other words, and you will also begin to see how words change meaning. Take, for example, the familiar colloquial word *gag*.

In mid-eighteenth century England, a *gag* was a pit prop, used to shore up sagging timbers in the roof of a mine tunnel. In the early 19th century, when a British music hall act was sagging badly, and needed propping up, the mining term *gag* was a natural for the impromptu jokes that the actors ran into the act, in desperation. This stage sense of the word—which is still with us—was reinforced by another and probably different word *gag*. This other *gag* is a bobtailed form of the word *gaggle*, a change rung on *gabble*, or "meaningless chatter." As a final touch, the commonest meaning of *gag* also bolstered the stage sense. If a gag is thrust between the jaws, the throat often twitches, and the victim goes "ga-ga." We speak of this twitching as "gagging at something." So our word *gag* has a long history. It's really four *gags* in one, a mine pit prop, first aid for a slipping show, a bobtailed gaggle, and, in the throat-choking sense, a glottal stop. In its radio and stage sense, *gag* as a verb (often with *up*) is slang; as a noun, meaning any contrived piece of wordplay or horseplay, it is now labeled *U.S. Colloquial*.

6. KEEP AN EAR OUT FOR EXPRESSIVE COLLOQUIAL OR SLANG WORDS, WHICH ARE LANGUAGE IN THE MAKING. Remember that the label *Colloquial* means "usable in informal speech or writing." It is dictionary shorthand for the halfway house between slang and standard language.

Slang: Its Use and Abuse

Slang, in the dictionary sense, consists of substandard words which have obtained sufficient national currency in journalistic writing, fiction, radio, or movie use to force their way into the list of dictionary entries. It is amusing to note that there are words (or phrases) which have been knocking around for several hundred years, which are still rightly labeled slang by dictionary-makers: *bones* (Chaucer, 1386) for dice; *chisel* (Jameson, 1808) for cheat. Most contemporary slang, however, is short-lived.

Slang definitely has its uses for the student of words. Just as the expert studies primitive societies in order to find out how they arrive at "the do's and don'ts" in their moral code and how they determine class and rank, so the student of language may find in slang easily detectible clues pointing up (1) the way in which "the do's and don'ts" of language develop, as well as (2) how words travel up or down the social scale. In this connection, it is entertaining to browse through a dictionary, noting the words labeled *Slang* or *Colloquial*, to see if you agree with the labels.

No one needs, however, to expand his slang vocabulary; most of us, rather, need some shrinkage in this direction. For slang, while it is a kind of wrong-way poetry, usually limits the range of intelligibility. Most slang is derogatory, and hence lowers the tone of talk or writing, though it undeniably has its uses for comic effect.

In rare instances, slang may express a shade of meaning for which traditional language has no exact equivalent, and such slang may eventually become standard. *Razz* is a case in point. It is still slang, though the late President Roosevelt used it in his political speeches. *Razz* is of British origin, from "Give him the raspberry," the last word being the predominantly British equivalent of the American "Bronx cheer." Americans shortened the saying to "Give him the razz," and the noun soon became a verb.

7. TIE INTO ONE PACKAGE NEW WORDS THAT BELONG TO A GIVEN SUBJECT. Anyone who has to break himself into a new line of work is well advised to pay close attention to the special vocabulary of the field. See how you would make out writing business definitions for these words: *margin, capacity, merger, potential output, liquidation, facilities, equipment, tools, subsidy, inventory, index, monopoly, depreciation, specifications, inflation, cartel, royalties, weighted average, bottleneck, allocation, reconversion, parity, durable, marginal, bullish, bearish, amortization.*

Try your hand also at giving both ordinary and scientific (or technical) definitions of the following terms: *antennae, solution, resonance, reflection, radiation, negative, insulate, dynamic, contraction, variation, conductor, solvent, aberration, accretion, abrasion, amalgamation, bromide, exponent, amplify, absorption, inertia, contact, conjunction, bugs, grid.*

A Caution

Many of the new technical terms are not so easy to sight-read, and they are so numerous that no one could possibly keep up with all of them. Nor should anyone try. These words are rightly left to specialists. The general reader need add only those which he wants in order to explore a particular field of interest to him. And he is better advised not to tackle such words unless he has a chance for first-hand contact with the objects or processes labeled by the terms. Leonardo da Vinci said of the Scholastics, "They mistake words for things." It is all too easy to fall into this trap.

8. Lastly, take the most effective short cut known: USE WORD-ANALYSIS TO SIGHT-READ THE BASIC MEANING OF NEW WORDS. Fundamentally, word-analysis consists of taking words apart, particularly words of Greek and Latin origin which have either been in the learned vocabulary for a long time, or which have recently made their way in through scientific or technical routes.

Anyone who knows the commoner Greek and Latin prefixes and suffixes, and the hundred or so commonest Greek and Latin stems, can sight-read about five thousand words in the highbrow part of the vocabulary—whether he has seen them before or not. At least he can get at their literal sense—which is not always the same thing as their current meaning. However, once a reader has the literal meaning in mind, he can usually get the drift of the passage in which such a word occurs.

This type of word-analysis should be frankly considered as a blend of sight-reading and playing by ear. It is best to try it first with a dictionary at hand, to check your guesses. After a while it becomes a good resource for deciphering word meanings when there is no dictionary handy. One thing is certain: a practiced word-analyzer can add words to his vocabulary by handfuls, rather than one at a time; and he will find word-analysis a game which is a constant challenge to the problem-solving motive. Also, the materials are always at hand, since anyone who reads widely is likely to encounter new words at any time.

The hitch about this particular short cut, for learning words by families rather than as individuals, has always been that such analysis involved turning over a great many pages to find the various constituent parts of the word under examination. By way of demonstrating that word-analysis can be a real short cut, instead of a wearisome search, the materials and methods for it are presented on the next two pages in a spread which is self-contained and self-explanatory.

General Purpose English

Whatever special or technical words a reader may decide to add to his working stock, he must arrive at an understanding of new words through definitions phrased in "general purpose" English. What words comprise it? Roughly speaking, the 20,000 commonest in the language, which, by actual count, make up 99½ percent of the running words in print. Of these, the 10,000 commonest constitute 98 percent; those in the range from 10,001 to 20,000 displace only 1½ percent of the total volume of printed words. At the 20,000 mark (where *prevaricate, Elysian, jowl, phlegmatic,* and *squalor* are found), a given word turns up on the average only once in a million running words. At the 30,000 level (where *apothegm, amino acid, excoriate, flagellation,* and *multilateral* are typical entries), one encounters a particular word only four times in 18,000,000 running words—the overall limit of the Thorndike-Lorge word-counts, on which all these figures are based.

This means that in reading 180 average-length books, in a wide diversity of fields, one would in all likelihood run into words of this level only four times each. (The average American, according to the American Booksellers' Association, reads three-and-a-half books a year.) Beyond the 30,000 level the rest of the half million or so words in the language are encountered so seldom that for practical purposes they are statistical "sports."

Vocabulary Range

It is possible to make a rough guess about anyone's probable vocabulary range if his reading habits are known. Here are the figures (based on sampling word-counts) of the vocabulary ranges required in reading typical national publications:

Medium	Vocabulary Range
Sunday N.Y. Times (entire)	40,000
New Yorker	35,000
Astounding Science-Fiction	30,000
N.Y. Herald Tribune, Washington Post, Atlantic Monthly, Harper's	25,000
Fortune, Time	20,000
Newsweek	16,000
Associated Press, United Press, International News Service	12,000
N.Y. Daily News, Daily Mirror (any other tabloid)	9,000

Some figures may be of interest on the size of the vocabularies of some contemporary men who work in words—writers, judges, and dictionary-makers. George Bernard Shaw probably has a reading vocabulary of around 80,000 words; Judge Learned Hand of about 70,000. A professional lexicographer, the late Henry Cecil Wyld, probably knew around 100,000. These are all reading vocabularies based on multiplying writing vocabularies by five—the latter being ascertained by count.

LATIN PREFIXES

ab-	away from
ad-	to
ambi-, an-	around
ante-	before
bene-	well
circum-	around
con-, cum-	with
contra-	against
de-	away, down
dis-	apart, not
ex-	out of
inter-	between
in-	not
in-	into, in
male-	evil, badly
non-	not
ob-	against
per-	through
post-	after
pre-	before
pro-	for
re-	again
retro-	back
se-	away from
sub-	under
super-	over
trans-	across

The 100 commonest Latin and Greek stems figure in more than 5000 English derivatives in the range just beyond the average American's vocabulary of 10,000 words. Learn to use the 100 classical stems to sight-read these 5000 words and you have a short cut that will put you a long way on the road toward doubling your vocabulary. Many of the 5000 are terms used in business, medicine, chemistry, and technology. If you know the 100 stems, and the most-used Latin and Greek affixes (prefixes and suffixes), you can analyze many words new to you, when you run into them in your reading. A break-down of the word will show you first the stem, and by the method of remainders, the prefix and suffix that make it up. You can thus get at its literal meaning. Since you have seen it also in context, you can guess at its present meaning, once you know the

inter-	POSIT	*-ion*	
between	placing	act of	"act of placing between"

LATIN STEM	MEANING	DERIVATIVES
AG, ACT	to do, drive	transaction, exigency
AM, AMAT	to love	amative, amicability
APT	fit or fitted	adaptability, readaptation
ART	art, skill, method	artifact, artificer
AUD, AUDIT	to hear	inaudible, audition
CAD, CAS	to fall	casualty, cadence
CAN, CANT	to sing	recantation, incantation
CAP, CAPT	to take, seize	capacity, exceptionable
CAPIT	head	decapitation, precipitate
CED, CESS	to yield, go	intercession, antecedent
CERN, CRET	to distinguish	discernible, indiscretion
CLAM, CLAMAT	to cry out	exclamatory, reclamation
CLUD, CLUS	to close	exclusive, occlusion
COR, CORD	heart	discordant, concordance
CRED, CREDIT	to believe	incredibility, accredited
CUR, CURAT	to care for	insecurity, procurator
CURR, CURS	to run	precursor, recurrent
DAT	to give	extradition, antedate
DIC, DICT	to speak, say	abdication, contradictory
DIGN	worthy	indignity, condign
DUC, DUCT	to lead	deduction, noninductive
EQU	equal	inequitable, inequivalent
FAC, FACT	to make, do	benefactor, unification
FER, LAT	to bear, carry	correlation, nontransferable
FORM	form	conformation, conformity
FRANG, FRACT	to break	irrefrangible, refraction
GER, GEST	to bear, perform	congestion, vicegerent
GRAT	pleasing	ingratitude, gratuity
HAB, HABIT	to have	rehabilitation, inhibition
JAC, JECT	to throw	trajectory, interjection
JUNG, JUNCT	to join, bind	disjunctive, conjuncture
LEG, LECT	to read, choose	predilection, lectern, dialectic
MAN	hand	manumission, manuscript
MITT, MISS	to send	intermittent, emissary
MOD	measure, manner	immoderate, accommodation
MOV, MOT	to move	motivation, demobilize
NOT	to know	connotation, denotation
PAND, PASS	to spread	expansive, surpassable
PAR, PARAT	to prepare	reparation, irreparable
PART	part	departmentalize, partisan
PET, PETIT	to seek	centripetal, repetitive
PLAC, PLACIT	to please	implacability, complacency
PLIC, PLICAT	to fold, bend	complicity, implication
PON, POSIT	to place	deposition, transposition
PORT, PORTAT	to carry	deportation, exportation
PREHEND	to seize	reprehensible, apprehension
QUER, QUISIT	to seek	inquisitorial, perquisite
RAP, RAPT	to seize, hurry away	surreptitious, rapturous
REG, RECT	to rule, direct	insurrection, rectitude
RUPT	to break, destroy	incorruptible, irruption

GREEK PREFIXES

a(an)- not	*amphi-* on both sides	*ana-* up	*anti-* against	*apo-* from	*cata-* down	*di(a)-* through	*ex(ec)-* from
hyper- over	*hypo-* under	*meta-* beyond	*para-* beside	*peri-* around	*pro-* before	*pseudo-* false	*syn-* with

literal sense. Below is the technique for sight-reading meanings: Pick out the stem involved, and locate it in the table. For the Latin verb stems, two forms are given: the stem from the present infinitive, e.g., AG ..."to do." ACT, the second form, is from the perfect passive participle, meaning "done." The English equivalents give only the present tense. You should supply the past participle, and where the derivative uses that form of the Latin stem, substitute the past participial equivalent in English. The prefix and/or suffix will stand out as separate. Locate them in the lists. Place the English equivalents under the prefix, stem, and suffix. Reshuffle the English equivalents to make sense. A word from the Latin is analyzed on the left hand page; a Greek word just below.

anti- against	PATH feeling	-y state of	means "state of feeling against"
SAL, SALT	to leap	salient, exultation	
SCRIB, SCRIPT	to write	indescribable, scriptorium	
SED, SESS	to sit	nonsedentary, residuary	
SENT, SENS	to feel, perceive	insensibility, presentiment	
SEQU, SECUT	to follow	obsequious, prosecutor	
SERV, SERVAT	to save, protect	conservatory, preservative	
SIGN	sign	assignation, designation	
SPIC, SPECT	to look at	inauspicious, perspicuity	
STA, STAT	to stand	static, circumstance	
SIST	to cause to stand	inconsistency, irresistible	
STRING, STRICT	to bind	astringent, constriction	
TANG, TACT	to touch	tangential, contingent	
TEN, TENT	to hold	untenable, sustenance	
TEND, TENS	to stretch	tensile, distension	
TRAH, TRACT	to draw	retraction, contractile	
UT, US	to use	usury, peruse	
VEN, VENT	to come	provenience, contravene	
VERT, VERS	to turn	irreversible, transverse	
VID, VIS	to see	provisional, improvident	
VOC	voice	provocation, vociferous	

GREEK STEM	MEANING	DERIVATIVES	
AGON	contest	protagonist, antagonize	
ALLO	other	allotropic, allomorph	
ARCH	chief, first, rule	anarchical, monarchical	
BIBLIO, BIBLO	book	bibliography, bibliophile	
DEMO	the people	antidemocratic, demotic	
DRA	to do, act	dramaturgy, dramatize	
DYNAMI	power	hydrodynamics, aerodynamic	
ELECTRO	amber (electric)	electronics, dielectric	
ERGO	work	allergy, ergometer	
GEO	earth	geological, geometrical	
GRAPH	to write	epigraphy, graphology	
HOMO	the same	homonym, homophone	
HYDRO	water	hydrostatic, dehydrate	
ISO	equal	isometric, isotope	
K(C)LINO	to bend, slant	declination, isoclinal	
K(C)RYPTO	hidden	cryptography, cryptic	
LOGO	word, reason, study	neologism, physiological	
METRO	measure	geometrical, photometer	
NEO	new	neophyte, neologist	
PATHO	feeling	psychopathology, empathy	
PHILO	loving, fond of	philology, zoöphile	
PHOB	fear	zoöphobia, photophobia	
PHONO	sound	phonology, gramophone	
PHOTO	light	photoelectric, photometric	
PHYS	nature	monophysite, physiography	
PROTO	first	protozoa, prototype	
PSYCHE	mind, soul	psychometric, psychology	
TECH	art, craft	technological, technical	
THEO	god	theological, theocentric	
ZOO	animal	zoöphyte, zoögraphy	

-ac pertaining to	-et one who	-ic, -ical pertaining to, made of, one who
-ic, -ice science of	-ise, -ize to make, give	-ist one who -y state of being

LATIN SUFFIXES

-able, -ible — able to be
-acy — state or quality of being
-al — pertaining to, act of
-an, -ant, -ent — one who or -ing
-ary — belonging to
-ate — having
-ency — state of being
-er, -or — one who
-ern — belonging to
-ic — pertaining to
-ice — state or quality of being
-ive — one who, that which is
-oon, -ion — one who, that which
-ory — relating to, thing which, place where
-ose, -ous — full of
-tion — state of that which
-tude — state of being
-ure — state or act of
-y — state of being

GREEK SUFFIXES

GRAMMAR AT A GLANCE

Grammar is a means of analyzing the ways in which words are grouped together to make sense. In informal conversation where we have the advantage of a direct exchange of remarks and the opportunity of observing gestures, facial expressions, voice tones, and pauses, we often get by with fragmentary word patterns or even single words. But such fragments would not make sense in writing and could not be relied upon exclusively in extended conversation.

Conventional writing and speech is based upon the sentence—a group of words expressing a complete thought.

SUBJECT AND PREDICATE

Every sentence has a subject and a predicate. The subject is the person or thing talked about; the predicate asserts something about the subject.

The radio program	was not entertaining.
SUBJECT	PREDICATE

Disease	kills thousands.
SUBJECT	PREDICATE

PARTS OF SPEECH

In order to understand the structure of a sentence we must be familiar with the terms used to identify the words or groups of words which compose it. These identifications are called parts of speech. Your dictionary indicates the part of speech of each word after its pronunciation. The part of speech of a word often varies according to its use in a sentence.

There are eight parts of speech: noun, pronoun, adjective, verb, adverb, preposition, conjunction, interjection.

1. Nouns

A noun is the name of a person, place, or thing: *man, James, city, England, train*. It may also be used to denote a quality, collection, or action: *intelligence, group, reading*.

2. Pronouns

A pronoun has the same function as a noun and is often used in place of it: *I, me, mine, he, him, who, what*, etc.

3. Adjectives and Articles

An adjective is used to modify a noun or pronoun.

a *large* theater

Used as adjectives, the words *a, an,* and *the* are called articles. *The* is a definite article because it specifies a particular thing: *I bought the house. A* and *an* are indefinite articles: *I bought a house. A* is used before words beginning with a consonant; *an* is used before words beginning with a vowel or vowel sound.

4. Verbs

A verb is a word which expresses action (*fly, write, think*) or a state of being (*seem, is, are*).

The batter *hit* the ball.

The patient *is* better.

A. FINITE VERBS

Every sentence must contain a finite verb. This is a verb that makes a meaningful statement about the subject of the sentence. It is distinguished from verbals (infinitives, gerunds, and participles) which cannot make sense when they stand alone.

Finite verbs: *works, sang, will play*

Verbals: *working, sung, playing*

B. PRINCIPAL PARTS

Every verb has three principal parts: (1) present infinitive, (2) past tense, (3) past participle. They are used in forming the various tenses of a verb.

In *regular* verbs, the past tense and past participle are formed by the addition of *d* or *ed* to the infinitive.

Present Infinitive	Past Tense	Past Participle
spell	spelled	spelled
wait	waited	waited
face	faced	faced

Irregular verbs have vowel changes in the past tense and past participle.

Present Infinitive	Past Tense	Past Participle
go	went	gone
be	was	been
write	wrote	written

If there is any doubt concerning the principal parts of irregular verbs, the dictionary should be consulted.

C. TENSE

Tense indicates the time of the action of a verb. There are six tenses. Each tense may have a progressive form which represents a continuing action or state of being during the time referred to. The progressive form consists of some part of the verb *be* followed by the present participle: *is going*. The present participle is formed by adding *ing* to the present infinitive.

The verb *take* is used below as an example of tense formation. Its principal parts are: *take, took, taken.*

Tense	Example
Present tense	*I take*
Progressive present	*I am taking*
Past tense	*I took*
Progressive past	*I was taking*
Future tense	*I shall take*
Progressive future	*I shall be taking*
Present perfect	*I have taken*
Progressive present perfect	*I have been taking*
Past perfect	*I had taken*
Progressive past perfect	*I had been taking*
Future perfect	*I shall have taken*
Progressive future perfect	*I shall have been taking*

D. TRANSITIVE AND INTRANSITIVE VERBS

A transitive verb is one which has a *direct object*—a noun or pronoun that is the receiver of the action.

He *read* the book.

We *saw* the city.

An intransitive verb has no direct object. Its meaning may even be complete in itself.

They *traveled* for days.

It rarely *appears.*

An intransitive verb may take a *predicate complement*—that is, a noun or an adjective to complete its meaning.

Miss Jones *is* a teacher (predicate noun).

They *seem* disturbed (predicate adjective).

In the above sentences *is* and *seem* are called *linking* or *copulative* verbs because they serve as a connecting link between the subject and the predicate of a sentence.

Many verbs may be used both transitively and intransitively.

She often *sings* (intransitive).

She often *sings* popular songs (transitive).

E. AUXILIARY VERBS

These are verbs which are often joined with other verbs or verbals to form a *verb phrase*. They may change the tense of another verb.

They *see* the papers (present tense—no auxiliary here).

They *will see* the papers (auxiliary *will* changes the verb to future tense).

They may also complete the meaning of the present infinitive or participial forms of another verb.

They *have seen* the papers (the past participle *seen* cannot stand alone; *have* is the auxiliary which completes its meaning).

An auxiliary may often make sense when used independently.

They *have* the papers.

Some of the principal auxiliary verbs are forms of the verbs *be* (*is, are, been,* etc.), *have, can, will, may, must, should.*

F. VOICE

The voice of a verb indicates whether the subject of the verb performs the action or receives the action.

Active Voice: the subject performs the action.

Several people *helped* her.

Passive Voice: the subject receives the action.

She *was helped* by several people.

The passive voice is formed by the combination as, in the sentence above, of a form of the auxiliary verb *be* with the past participle of the verb.

Normally, only transitive verbs are used in the passive voice.

5. Adverbs

An adverb is a word used to modify a verb, adjective, or other adverb. It serves to indicate when, where, how, or how much about the word it modifies.

The guests arrived *early* (modifies verb *arrived*).

It is a *remarkably* good play (modifies adjective *good*).

He drove *very* recklessly (modifies adverb *recklessly*).

6. Prepositions

A preposition precedes a noun or a pronoun (the object of the preposition) to show the relation of the noun or pronoun to another word in the sentence.

The leader *of* the group was pleased (*group* is the object of the preposition *of*).

The planes flew *over* the city (*city* is the object of the preposition *over*).

7. Conjunctions

A conjunction connects words or groups of words within a sentence and shows the relationship between them.

There are three general types of conjunctions:

1. Coördinating conjunctions: *and, but, or, nor, for, yet.*
These connect words or groups of words (phrases and clauses) of equal grammatical rank.

Fuel *and* food had to be rationed, *but* there were few people who complained. (Here *and* connects two words; *but* connects two independent clauses.)

2. Subordinating conjunctions: *because, for, since, as, although, if, unless,* etc.
These conjunctions introduce subordinate clauses and connect them with the independent or main clause in a sentence.

Since yesterday was a holiday, the stores were closed.

3. Correlative conjunctions: *either—or, neither—nor, both—and, not only—but also.* Used in pairs, these conjunctions connect words, phrases, or clauses that are equal in rank.

Either Jack *or* I will join you.

8. *Interjections*

An interjection is an exclamatory word used to express strong emotion or feeling.

Hurray! We won the game.

Oh, I'm surprised to see you.

VERBALS

Verbals include infinitives, participles, and gerunds. Although they are formed from verbs, they do not function as verbs. They cannot substitute for finite verbs unless they are accompanied by auxiliary verbs which help to complete their meaning.

1. *Infinitives*

An infinitive usually includes the word *to* joined with the present form of a verb: *to go, to make, to celebrate.* (Often *to* is omitted, but understood.)

An infinitive may function as a noun, an adjective, or an adverb.

To walk that distance is ridiculous (used as noun).

He had no desire *to walk* (used as adjective modifying *desire*).

He was too tired *to walk* (used as adverb modifying *tired*).

2. *Gerunds*

A gerund is a verbal which always ends in *ing* and is always used as a noun.

Fishing was his hobby (subject of *was*).

He was also fond of *hunting* (object of preposition *of*).

3. *Participles*

A participle is a verbal used as an adjective.

The present participle, like the gerund, ends in *ing*.

The past participle ends in *d* or *ed* if the verb is regular: *received, resisted.* Irregular verbs have a variety of past participial endings, the more common ones being *n, en, d,* or *t: known, shaken, heard, burst.*

A participle may be used as (1) an adjective to modify a noun:

The *damaged* plane was forced to land. or (2) part of a phrase which functions as an adjective:

The salesman (*demonstrating* the machine) was very effective.

CLAUSES

Every sentence is composed of one or more clauses. Clauses, like sentences, have a subject-predicate relationship. They may be classified into (1) Independent, Principal, or Main Clauses and (2) Dependent or Subordinate Clauses.

An independent (main or principal) clause can stand alone and express a complete thought. In itself it constitutes a sentence: *He founded the organization.*

The main clause may be connected with a subordinate clause. A subordinate clause cannot stand alone and express a complete thought. It must be combined with a main clause in order to convey a complete idea.

When you return, you will find me here.

SUBORDINATE   MAIN

PHRASES

A phrase consists of a preposition, a participle, a gerund, or an infinitive followed by a noun and its modifiers.

The chairman *of the meeting* rose (prepositional phrase).

The man, *driving a Model-T Ford* and *attired in an old-fashioned suit,* amused the crowd (participial phrases).

Note that this is a simple sentence. The phrases are descriptive but they do not change the basic structure of the sentence.

CLASSIFICATION OF SENTENCES

Sentences are classified into four groups, depending on the number and type of the clauses they contain.

1. A simple sentence consists of one independent clause.

He arrived in the big city.

2. A complex sentence contains one main clause and one or more subordinate clauses.

When she entertains or when she visits,

SUBORDINATE   SUBORDINATE

she likes to knit.

MAIN

3. A compound sentence contains two or more main or independent clauses. It makes two complete statements.

He completed his schooling, and

MAIN

now he is ready to work.

MAIN

4. A compound-complex sentence is a compound sentence which contains, in addition, one or more subordinate clauses.

After the building was completed,

SUBORDINATE

it was advertised

MAIN

and it was quickly occupied.

MAIN

Weights and Measures

LINEAR MEASURE

12 inches	= 1 foot
3 feet	= 1 yard
5½ yards	= 1 rod
40 rods	= 1 furlong
8 furlongs (5280 feet)	= 1 statute mile

MARINERS' MEASURE

6 feet	= 1 fathom
1000 fathoms (approx.)	= 1 nautical mile
3 nautical miles	= 1 league

SQUARE MEASURE

144 square inches	= 1 square foot
9 square feet	= 1 square yard
30¼ square yards	= 1 square rod
160 square rods	= 1 acre
640 acres	= 1 square mile

CUBIC MEASURE

1728 cubic inches	= 1 cubic foot
27 cubic feet	= 1 cubic yard

SURVEYORS' MEASURE

7.92 inches	= 1 link
100 links	= 1 chain

LIQUID MEASURE

4 gills	= 1 pint
2 pints	= 1 quart
4 quarts	= 1 gallon
31½ gallons	= 1 barrel
2 barrels	= 1 hogshead

APOTHECARIES' FLUID MEASURE

60 minims	= 1 fluid dram
8 fluid drams	= 1 fluid ounce
16 fluid ounces	= 1 pint
2 pints	= 1 quart
4 quarts	= 1 gallon

DRY MEASURE

2 pints	= 1 quart
8 quarts	= 1 peck
4 pecks	= 1 bushel

WOOD MEASURE

16 cubic feet	= 1 cord foot
8 cord feet	= 1 cord

TIME MEASURE

60 seconds	= 1 minute
60 minutes	= 1 hour
24 hours	= 1 day
7 days	= 1 week
4 weeks (28 to 31 days)	= 1 month
12 months (365 or 366 days)	= 1 year
100 years	= 1 century

ANGULAR AND CIRCULAR MEASURE

60 seconds	= 1 minute
60 minutes	= 1 degree
90 degrees	= 1 right angle
180 degrees	= 1 straight angle
360 degrees	= 1 circle

TROY WEIGHT

24 grains	= 1 pennyweight
20 pennyweights	= 1 ounce
12 ounces	= 1 pound

AVOIRDUPOIS WEIGHT

27$\frac{11}{32}$ grains	= 1 dram
16 drams	= 1 ounce
16 ounces	= 1 pound
100 pounds	= 1 short hundredweight
20 short hundredweight	= 1 short ton

APOTHECARIES' WEIGHT

20 grains	= 1 scruple
3 scruples	= 1 dram
8 drams	= 1 ounce
12 ounces	= 1 pound